27981

STATISTICAL ABSTRACT
of the United States

1978

D1319558

99th Annual Edition

U.S. Department of Commerce
Juanita M. Kreps, Secretary
Courtenay M. Slater, Chief Economist

BUREAU OF THE CENSUS
Manuel D. Plotkin, Director

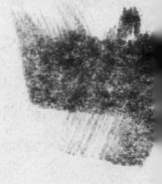

BUREAU OF THE CENSUS

Manuel D. Plotkin, Director
Robert L. Hagan, Deputy Director
James W. Turbitt, Associate Director for
Administration and Field Operations

Michael G. Garland, Chief
Data User Services Division

ACKNOWLEDGMENTS
99th Annual Edition

Prepared under the direction of
William Lerner
Assistant Division Chief
for Statistical Reports

Helen E. Teir, Chief, Statistical Compendia Staff, Data User Services Division, was responsible for general supervision and compilation. She was assisted in research and analytical phases of assigned sections and in the developmental aspects of new tables by **Glenn W. King, Elisabeth A. Busse, Lars B. Johanson,** and **Edward C. Jagers,** who was also responsible for content and preparation of graphic charts. **Minerva K. Moreland** was responsible for technical editorial supervision, assisted by **Mary A. Rahall** for editing and clerical operations.

The cooperation of the many contributors to this volume is gratefully acknowledged. The source note below each table credits the various government and private agencies which have collaborated in furnishing information for the *Statistical Abstract.*

In a few instances, contributors have requested that their data be designated as subject to copyright restrictions, as indicated in the source notes to the tables affected. Permission to use copyright material should be obtained directly from the copyright owner.

September 1978

SUGGESTED CITATION

U.S. Bureau of the Census, *Statistical Abstract of the United States: 1978.*
(99th edition.) Washington, D.C., 1978.

For sale by the Superintendent of Documents, U.S. Government Printing Office, Washington, D.C. 20402. Tel. (202) 783-3238, or any U.S. Department of Commerce district office.
Stock Number: 003-024-01648-6 (cloth); 003-024-01647-8 (paper).

PREFACE

The *Statistical Abstract of the United States,* published annually since 1878, is the standard summary of statistics on the social, political, and economic organization of the United States. It is designed to serve as a convenient volume for statistical reference and as a guide to other statistical publications and sources. The latter function is served by the introductory text to each section, the source note appearing below each table, and Appendix IV, which comprises Guide to Sources of Statistics and Guide to State Statistical Abstracts.

This volume includes a selection of data from many statistical publications, both governmental and private. Publications cited as sources usually contain additional statistical detail and more comprehensive discussions of definitions and concepts than can be presented here. Data not available in publications issued by the contributing agency but obtained from unpublished records are identified in the source notes as "unpublished data." More information on the subjects covered in tables so noted may generally be obtained from the source.

Except as otherwise indicated, figures are for the United States as presently constituted. Although emphasis in the *Statistical Abstract* is given primarily to national data, many tables present data for regions and individual States and a smaller number for metropolitan areas and cities. Appendix II, Metropolitan Area Concepts and Components, presents explanatory text and a complete current listing of official standard metropolitan statistical areas (SMSA's), standard consolidated statistical areas (SCSA's), and New England county metropolitan areas (NECMA's). Statistics for the Commonwealth of Puerto Rico and for outlying areas of the United States are included in many State tables and are supplemented by information in section 32. Additional information for cities, counties, metropolitan areas, congressional districts, and other small units, as well as more historical data, are available in various supplements to the Abstract (see inside back cover).

The "Recent Trends" section, beginning on p. xiii, is available separately in a reprint, *Recent Social and Economic Trends;* and *USA Statistics in Brief,* 1978, the pocket-size loose insert in front of the book, is also available separately. Price information can be obtained from, and orders sent to, the Superintendent of Documents, Washington, D.C. 20402, or any U.S. Department of Commerce district office located in certain large cities. A 25-percent discount will be allowed on orders of 100 copies or more sent to the same address.

Changes in the 1978 edition.— This year, Appendix III, Statistical Methodology and Reliability, first introduced in the 1976 *Abstract,* has undergone a major revision. The information about the censuses and surveys has been reorganized in columnar form into 7 major categories (e.g. universe, frequency, type of data, data collection and imputation procedures). This was done to achieve a more compact and uniform presentation. In addition, to facilitate reference, the description of each of the censuses and/or surveys now appears under the title of the section to which it is most relevant. This appendix attempts, in relatively nontechnical language, to provide the user of statistics in this book with an appreciation of some hazards to be kept in mind when using the data and, in specific cases, with a better understanding of how the data were collected, a measure of their validity, and references to further information.

Statistics in this edition, the 99th, are for the most recent year or period available by mid-September 1978. Each year the more than 1,500 tables and charts are reviewed and evaluated; new tables and charts of current interest are added, continuing series are updated, and less timely data are condensed or eliminated. Text notes and appendixes are revised as appropriate.

In all, there are 88 new tables, distributed among 30 of the 33 sections. In addition, graphic charts have been revised or updated and many sections have undergone tabular rearrangement and format changes designed to improve the organization of subject matter. Of the tables included in the 1977 edition, 33 were omitted from this issue. The omissions represent primarily tables for which comparable details appear in other tables or for which no recent data are available, or tables for which the subject matter shown was considered relatively less important in the light of the space required for presentation.

Preface

Many new tables reflect current public interest in the behavior and activities of people and the workings of government and industry.

Among new tables relating to people are those on:

Household characteristics, by race and Spanish origin, p. 44

Persons living alone, by age and sex, p. 50

Characteristics of widows, by age, p. 51

First births, at intervals from woman's first marriage, p. 64

Death rates from heart disease and cancer, p. 77

Fees for office visits, by medical specialty, p. 106

Medical malpractice insurance premiums, p. 107

Average weights and heights, p. 119

Children immunized against specific diseases, p. 121

Earned degrees below bachelor's, p. 170

Societal dependency ratios, p. 338

Characteristics of volunteer workers, p. 365

Unemployment, by industry of last job, p. 411

Nobel prize laureates, p. 627

Licensed drivers and traffic deaths, p. 648

Income of farm and nonfarm families, p. 687

New tables reflecting Government concerns include:

Alien deportation, p. 91

Public school employment, p. 153

Expenditures for environmental quality control, p. 213

Assessed property values and property tax revenue, p. 309

Effect of changes in social security contribution rates, p. 338

Military reserve costs, p. 384

Real growth rates of GNP, p. 442

Congressional campaign finances, p. 525

Business and industrial activities are covered in new tables on:

Major collective bargaining settlements, p. 425

Foreign lending by large U.S. banks, p. 544

Funds raised in credit markets by non-financial sectors, p. 545

Determinants of business fixed investment, p. 568

Energy consumption, by source and sector, p. 607

Motor vehicle safety defect recalls, p. 653

Interstate natural gas pipelines summary, p. 665

Characteristics of corporate farms, p. 689

Fish catch in new U.S. Fishery Conservation Zone, p. 744

Petroleum industry expenditures for new plant and equipment, p. 763

Sales prices of new one-family homes, p. 800

Total and per capita retail sales, p. 841

U.S. liabilities to foreigners, p. 863

Historical statistics.—Specific headnote references in this *Abstract* link many tables to earlier data shown in *Historical Statistics of the United States, Colonial Times to 1970.* (See pp. 932-934.)

Statistical reliability and responsibility.—The contents of this volume were taken from many sources. All data from either censuses and surveys or from administrative records are subject to error arising from a number of factors: Sampling variability (for statistics based on samples), reporting errors in the data for individual units, incomplete coverage, nonresponse, imputations, and processing error. (See also Appendix III, pp. 945-963.) The Bureau of the Census cannot accept the responsibility for the accuracy or limitations of the data presented here, other than for those which it collects. The responsibility for selection of the material and for proper presentation, however, rests with the Bureau.

For additional information on data presented.—Please consult the source publications available in local libraries or write to the agencies indicated in the source notes. Write to the Bureau of the Census only if it is cited as the source.

Suggestions and comments.—Users of the *Statistical Abstract* and its supplements (see inside back cover) are urged to make their data needs known for consideration in planning future editions. Suggestions and comments for improving coverage and presentation of data should be sent to the Director, Bureau of the Census, Washington, D.C. 20233.

CONTENTS

[Numbers following subjects are page numbers]

Page

vi # Contents

Page

CONTENTS

vii

viii CONTENTS

Page

CONTENTS

ix

Page

X CUSTOMARY AND METRIC WEIGHTS AND MEASURES

[For information regarding conversion, call or write the Metric Information Office,
National Bureau of Standards, Washington, D.C. 20234 (301-921-2401)]

APPROXIMATE CONVERSIONS

Customary			Metric	Metric			Customary
Inches (in)	X	25.4 =	millimeters	Millimeters (mm)	X	.04 =	inches
Feet (ft)	X	.3 =	meters	Meters (m)	X	3.3 =	feet
Yards (yd)	X	.9 =	meters	Meters (m)	X	1.1 =	yards
Miles (mi)	X	1.6 =	kilometers	Kilometers (km)	X	.6 =	miles
Square inches (in²)	X	6.5 =	sq centimeters	Sq centimeters (cm²)	X	.2 =	sq inches
Square feet (ft²)	X	.1 =	sq meters	Square meters (m²)	X	10.8 =	sq feet
Square yards (yd²)	X	.8 =	sq meters	Square meters (m²)	X	1.2 =	sq yards
Acres	X	.4 =	hectares	Hectares (ha)	X	2.5 =	acres
Cubic feet (ft³)	X	.03 =	cu meters	Cu meters (m³)	X	35.3 =	cu feet
Cord (cd)	X	3.6 =	cu meters	Liters (l)	X	1.1 =	quarts (lq)
Quarts (lq) (qt)	X	.9 =	liters	Cu meters (m³)	X	264.2 =	gallons
Gallons (gal)	X	.004 =	cu meters	Grams (g)	X	.04 =	ounces (avdp)
Ounces (avdp) (oz)	X	28.4 =	grams	Kilograms (kg)	X	2.2 =	pounds (avdp)
Pounds (avdp) (lb)	X	.5 =	kilograms	Kilowatts (kW)	X	1.3* =	horsepower
Horsepower (hp)	X	.7 =	kilowatts	Degrees Celsius	X	9/5 + 32 =	degrees
Degrees Fahrenheit (−32)	X	5/9 =	degrees Celsius				Fahrenheit

UNITS OF LENGTH AND AREA

Customary			Metric	Metric			Customary
Inch (in)		=	25.4 millimeters	Millimeter (mm)	=	.001 meter =	.039 inch
Foot (ft)	=	12 in =	.305 meter	Centimeter (cm)	=	.01 meter =	.394 inch
Yard (yd)	=	36 in = or 3 ft	.914 meter	Decimeter (dm)	=	.1 meter =	3.937 inches
				Meter (m)		=	3.281 feet
Mile (mi)	=	5,280 ft =	1.609 kilometers	Kilometer (km)	=	1,000 meters =	.621 mile
In² (sq in)		=	6.452 cm²	Sq millimeter (mm²)	=	.000001 m² =	.002 sq in
Ft² (sq ft)	=	144 sq in =	.093 m²	Sq centimeter (cm²)	=	.0001 m² =	.155 sq in
Yd² (sq yd)	=	1,296 sq in = or 9 sq ft	.836 m²	Sq decimeter (dm²)	=	.01 m² =	15.5 sq in
				Sq meter (m²)		=	10.764 sq ft
Acre	=	43,560 sq ft =	.405 ha	Hectare (ha)	=	10,000 m² =	2.471 acres
Mile² (sq mi)	=	640 acres =	2.59 km²	Sq kilometer (km²)	=	1,000,000 m² =	.386 sq mi

UNITS OF WEIGHT (OR MASS)

Customary			Metric	Metric			Customary
Avoirdupois Weight[1]							
Grain		=	.065 gram	Gram (g)		=	.035 oz avdp or .032 oz t
Ounce (oz avdp)	=	437.5 grains = or 16 drams	28.350 grams	Dekagram (dag)	=	10 g =	.353 oz avdp or .322 oz t
Pound (lb avdp)	=	7,000 grains = or 16 ounces	.454 kilogram	Hectogram (hg)	=	100 g =	3.527 oz avdp or 3.215 oz t
Hundredweight (cwt)	=	100 pounds =	45.359 kg				
Ton, short (tn)	=	2,000 pounds =	.907 metric ton	Kilogram (kg)	=	1,000 g =	2.205 lb avdp or 2.679 lb t
Ton, long	=	2,240 pounds =	1.016 metric tons				
Troy Weight[2]				Metric ton	=	1,000 kg =	1.102 short tons or .984 long ton
Ounce (oz t)[3]	=	480 grains =	31.104 grams				
Pound (lb t)	=	5,760 grains = or 12 ounces	.373 kilogram				

[1]For weighing ordinary commodities. [2]For weighing precious metals, jewels, etc. [3]Also known as fine ounces.

UNITS OF CAPACITY

Customary			Metric	Customary			Metric
Liquid				**Dry**			
Fluid ounce (fl oz)		=	29.573 ml	Pint (pt)		=	.551 dm³
Pint (pt)	=	16 fl oz =	.473 liter	Quart (qt)	=	2 pints =	1.101 dm³
Quart (qt)	=	32 fl oz or 2 pt =	.946 liter	Peck (pk)	=	8 quarts =	8.810 dm³
Gallon (gal)	=	8 pt or 4 qt =	3.785 liters	Bushel (bu)	=	32 quarts =	35.238 dm³

Metric			Customary		
Milliliter (ml)	=	.001 liter =	.034 fl oz (liquid) =	.002 pt (dry)	
Liter (l)		=	1.057 qt (liquid) =	.908 qt (dry)	
Hectoliter (hl)	=	100 liters =	26.418 gal (liquid) =	2.838 bu (dry)	

The following symbols, used in the tables throughout this book, are explained in condensed form in footnotes to the tables where they appear:

— Represents zero or rounds to less than half the unit of measurement shown.

B   Base figure too small to meet statistical standards for reliability of derived figure.

D   Figure withheld to avoid disclosure of information pertaining to a specific organization or individual.

NA Data not enumerated, tabulated, or otherwise available separately.

NS Percent change irrelevant or insignificant.

S   Figure does not meet publication standards for reasons other than that covered by symbol B, above.

X   Figure not applicable because column heading and stub line make an entry impossible, absurd, or meaningless.

Z   Entry would amount to less than half the unit of measure shown.

In many tables, details will not add to the totals shown because of rounding.

Example of table structure:

Table number and title

No. 215. Enrollment in Public and Private Schools: 1960 to 1977

Unit indicator

[**In millions of persons 3 to 34 years of age.** As of **October.** Elementary includes grades 1–8; high school, grades 9–12. College data represent degree-credit enrollment] — *Headnote*

Footnote indicator

LEVEL	1960 [1]			1970			1977		
	Total	Public	Private	Total	Public	Private	Total	Public	Private
Total	46.3	39.0	7.2	60.4	52.2	8.1	60.0	51.6	8.4
Nursery	(NA)	(NA)	(NA)	1.1	.3	.8	1.6	.6	1.1
Kindergarten	2.1	1.7	.4	3.2	2.6	.5	3.2	2.7	.5
Elementary	30.3	25.8	4.5	34.0	30.0	3.9	29.2	26.0	3.3
High school	10.2	9.2	1.0	14.7	13.5	1.2	15.8	14.5	1.2
College	3.6	2.3	1.3	7.4	5.7	1.7	10.2	7.9	2.3

Spanner / Column heads / Stub / Field / Heavy rule

Footnotes → NA Not available. [1] Data are for persons 5 to 34 years of age.

Parallel rule Source: U.S. Bureau of the Census, *Current Population Reports*, series P-20.

Headnotes immediately below table titles provide information important for correct interpretation or evaluation of the table as a whole or for a major segment of it.

Footnotes below the bottom rule of tables give information relating to specific items or figures within the table.

Unit indicators ("In thousands," "In millions of dollars," etc.) are usually given in boldface type as the first element of the headnote. In tables where several units are used, the unit indicators are generally given in the stub or in the column headings.

Parallel vertical rules are used to the right of a total column to indicate—

    (1) that the components which follow add to the total (e.g., tables 1, 5, 29, etc.);

    (2) in the case of derived figures, that the underlying data are additive to their total (e.g., table 28 for ratios, table 49 for percentages, table 81 for rates, and table 98 for averages).

Heavy vertical rules are used—

    (1) in tables where the stub is continued into one or more additional columns across the table to separate each segment of stub and its accompanying data columns from the continued segments (e.g., tables 2, 4, 26, etc.);

    (2) to set off independent sections of a table (e.g., tables 1, 3, 8, etc.).

Averages. An average is a single number or value that is often used to represent the "typical value" of a group of numbers. It is regarded as a measure of "location" or "central tendency" of a group of numbers.

The *arithmetic mean* is the type of average used most frequently. It is derived by summing the individual item values of a particular group and dividing the total by the number of items. The arithmetic mean is often referred to as simply the "mean" or "average."

The *median* of a group of numbers is the middle number or value when each item in the group is arranged according to size (lowest to highest or vice versa); it generally has the same number of items above it as below it. If there is an even number of items in the group, the median is taken to be the average of the two middle items.

Per capita (or per person) quantities. A per capita figure represents an average computed for every person in a specified group (or population). It is derived by taking the total for an item (such as income, taxes, or retail sales) and dividing it by the number of persons in the specified population.

Index numbers. An index number is a measure of difference or change, usually expressed as a percent, relating one quantity (the variable) of a specified kind to another quantity of the same kind. Index numbers are widely used to express changes in prices over periods of time but may also be used to express differences between related subjects for a single point in time.

To compute a price index, a base year or period is selected. The base year price (of the commodity or service) is then designated as the base or reference price to which the prices for other years or periods are related. Many price indexes use the year 1967 as the base year; in tables, this is shown as "1967 = 100." A method of expressing the price relationship is:

$$\frac{\text{Price of a set of one or more items for related year}}{\text{Price of the same set of items for base year}}$$

The result multiplied by 100 provides the index number. When 100 is subtracted from the index number, the result equals the percent change in price from the base year.

Average annual percent change. Unless otherwise stated in the *Abstract* (as in Section 1, Population), average annual percent change is computed by use of a *compound interest formula*. This formula assumes that the rate of change is constant throughout a specified compounding period (one year for average annual rates of change). The formula is similar to that used to compute the balance of a savings account which receives compound interest. According to this formula, at the end of a compounding period the amount of accrued change (e.g., school enrollment or bank interest) is added to the amount which existed at the beginning of the period. As a result, over time (e.g., with each year or quarter) the same rate of change is applied to a larger and larger figure.

The *exponential formula,* which is based on continuous compounding, is often used to measure population change. It is preferred by population experts because they view population and population-related subjects as changing without interruption, ever ongoing. Both exponential and compound interest formulas assume a constant rate of change. The former, however, applies the amount of change continuously to the base rather than at the end of each compounding period.

When the average annual rates are small (e.g., less than 5 percent) both formulas give virtually the same results. For an explanation of these two formulas as they relate to population, see U.S. Bureau of the Census, *The Methods and Materials of Demography,* Vol. 2, 3d printing (rev.), 1975, pp. 372-381.

Reference table	Subject	Unit of measure	1960	1965	1970	1975	1976	1977	Average annual percent change 1960–70	1970–75	1975–77[1]
	POPULATION[2]										
2	Total, incl. Armed Forces abroad	Millions	180.7	194.3	204.9	213.6	215.1	216.8	1.3	.8	.8
	Net annual increase over previous year	Millions	2.84	2.41	2.20	1.66	1.58	1.68	(ns)	(ns)	(ns)
5	Under 5 years old	Millions	20	20	17	16	15	15	−1.7	−1.5	−2.1
5	5–17 years old	Millions	44	50	53	50	50	49	1.7	−.8	−1.4
5	18–24 years old	Millions	16	20	25	28	28	29	4.4	2.3	1.8
5	18 years old and over	Millions	116	125	135	147	150	153	1.5	1.7	1.8
5	21 years old and over	Millions	109	115	124	135	137	140	1.3	1.7	1.8
5	65 years old and over	Millions	17	18	20	22	23	23	1.9	2.2	2.4
5	Male	Millions	89.3	95.6	100.3	104.2	104.9	105.7	1.2	.8	.7
5	Female	Millions	91.4	98.7	104.6	109.3	110.2	111.1	1.4	.9	.8
26	White	Millions	160.0	171.2	179.5	185.6	186.6	187.7	1.2	.7	.6
26	Black and other	Millions	20.6	23.1	25.4	28.0	28.5	29.1	2.1	2.0	1.9
	Black	Millions	19.0	21.1	22.8	24.5	24.9	25.2	1.8	1.5	1.4
	Percent of total population	Percent	11	11	11	11	12	12	(ns)	(ns)	(ns)
	Percent in the South	Percent	60	54	53	52	53	54	(ns)	(ns)	(ns)
34	Persons of Spanish origin[3]	Millions	(na)	(na)	(na)	11.2	11.1	11.3	(na)	(na)	.3
11	Resident population	Millions	180.0	193.5	203.8	213.0	214.7	216.3	1.3	.9	.8
	Per square mile	Persons	51	55	57	60	61	61	1.1	1.1	.8
	Northeast	Millions	44.8	47.5	49.2	49.5	49.4	49.3	.9	.1	−.2
	North Central	Millions	51.7	54.2	56.7	57.6	57.7	57.9	.9	.3	.3
	South	Millions	55.2	59.6	63.0	68.0	69.0	69.8	1.3	1.5	1.3
	West	Millions	28.3	32.2	34.9	37.9	38.6	39.3	2.1	1.6	1.8
19	Metropolitan area population[4]	Millions	128.2	(na)	149.8	155.5	156.8	(na)	1.6	.8	.8
	Percent of total resident	Percent	71.2	(na)	73.5	73.0	73.0	(na)	(ns)	(ns)	(ns)
19	Nonmetropolitan area population[4]	Millions	51.7	(na)	54.0	57.5	58.1	(na)	.4	1.3	1.0
51	Male, 18 years old and over[5]	Millions	[6]60.6	58.0	62.5	67.9	69.1	70.3	.3	1.7	1.8
	Single	Percent	25.3	17.7	18.9	20.8	21.2	21.9	(ns)	(ns)	(ns)
	Married	Percent	69.1	76.2	75.3	72.8	72.2	70.9	(ns)	(ns)	(ns)
	Divorced	Percent	1.9	2.5	2.5	3.7	4.0	4.5	(ns)	(ns)	(ns)
51	Female, 18 years old and over[5]	Millions	[6]64.9	63.8	70.0	75.3	76.7	77.9	.8	1.5	1.7
	Single	Percent	19.0	12.4	13.7	14.6	15.0	15.6	(ns)	(ns)	(ns)
	Married	Percent	65.6	70.5	68.5	66.7	66.2	65.3	(ns)	(ns)	(ns)
	Divorced	Percent	2.6	3.3	3.9	5.3	5.7	6.2	(ns)	(ns)	(ns)
56	Households	Millions	52.8	57.4	63.4	71.1	72.9	74.1	1.9	2.3	2.1
	Average size of households	Persons	3.33	3.29	3.14	2.94	2.89	2.86	(ns)	(ns)	(ns)
57	One-person households	Millions	6.9	8.6	10.9	13.9	15.0	15.5	4.6	5.1	5.6
57	Two-person households	Millions	14.7	16.1	18.3	21.8	22.3	22.8	2.3	3.5	2.3
56	Families	Millions	45.1	[7]48.0	[7]51.6	55.7	56.2	56.7	1.4	1.6	.9
	Female head	Millions	4.5	5.0	5.6	7.2	7.5	7.7	2.2	5.3	3.2
60	White	Millions	40.9	[7]43.1	[7]46.0	49.5	49.9	50.1	1.2	1.5	.6
	Female head	Percent	8.7	9.0	9.1	10.5	10.8	10.9	(ns)	(ns)	(ns)
56	Average size	Persons	3.61	3.64	3.54	3.36	3.32	3.31	(ns)	(ns)	(ns)
60	Black and other	Millions	4.2	[7]4.8	[7]5.2	6.3	6.4	6.6	2.1	3.7	2.9
	Female head	Percent	22.4	23.7	26.7	32.4	33.0	33.9	(ns)	(ns)	(ns)
56	Average size	Persons	4.39	4.37	4.32	3.89	3.92	3.81	(ns)	(ns)	(ns)
78	Births, live	Millions	4.26	3.76	3.73	3.14	3.17	3.31	−1.3	−3.4	2.7
79	Black and other	Percent	15.4	16.9	17.2	18.8	18.9	(na)	(ns)	(ns)	(ns)
78	Rate, all races, per 1,000 population	Rate	23.7	19.4	18.4	14.8	14.8	15.3	−2.5	−4.3	1.7
79	White	Rate	22.7	18.3	17.4	13.8	13.8	(na)	−2.6	−4.5	−
79	Black and other	Rate	32.1	27.6	25.1	21.2	21.1	(na)	−2.4	−3.3	−.5
91	Births to unwed mothers	1,000	224	291	399	448	468	(na)	5.9	2.4	4.5
78	Deaths	Millions	1.71	1.83	1.92	1.89	1.91	1.90	1.2	−.3	.1
	Rate, all races, per 1,000 population .	Rate	9.5	9.4	9.5	8.9	8.9	8.8	−	−1.3	−.6

See notes on p. xxiv.

Reference table	Subject	Unit of measure	1960	1965	1970	1975	1976	1977	1960 –70	1970 –75	1975 –77[1]
									Average annual percent change		

POPULATION[2] — Con.

106	Infant death rate, per 1,000 live births ...	Rate	26.0	24.7	20.0	16.1	15.2	14.0	-2.6	-4.3	-6.8
	White	Rate	22.9	21.5	17.8	14.2	13.3	(na)	-2.5	-4.4	-6.3
	Black and other	Rate	43.2	40.3	30.9	24.2	23.5	(na)	-3.3	-4.8	-2.9
108	Deaths per 100,000 population	Rate	952	943	945	889	890	878	-.1	-1.2	-.6
	Diseases of heart	Rate	369	367	362	336	337	(na)	-.2	-1.5	.3
	Malignancies	Rate	149	154	163	172	176	(na)	.9	1.1	2.4
	Cerebrovascular diseases	Rate	108	104	102	91	88	(na)	-.6	-2.2	-3.5
	Accidents	Rate	52	56	56	48	47	(na)	.8	-3.0	-3.1
114	Marriages	1,000	1,523	1,800	2,159	2,153	2,155	2,176	3.6	-.1	.5
	Per 1,000 population	Rate	8.5	9.3	10.6	10.1	10.0	10.1	2.2	-1.0	—
	Per 1,000 unmarried women, 15 yr. old and over	Rate	74	75	77	67	65	(na)	.4	-2.7	-2.5
114	Divorces	1,000	393	479	708	1,036	1,083	1,097	6.1	7.9	2.9
	Per 1,000 population	Rate	2.2	2.5	3.5	4.9	5.0	5.1	4.8	7.0	2.0
	Per 1,000 married women, 15 yr. old and over	Rate	9	11	15	20	21	(na)	4.9	6.4	3.9
120	Immigrants, total	1,000	265	297	373	386	399	462	3.5	.7	9.4

HEALTH

98	Life expectancy at birth, male	Years	66.6	66.8	67.1	68.7	69.0	(na)	.1	.5	.4
98	Life expectancy at birth, female	Years	73.1	73.7	74.8	76.5	76.7	(na)	.2	.5	.3
140	National health expenditures, total	Bil. dol.	25.9	38.9	69.2	123.7	141.0	162.6	10.4	12.3	14.7
	Expenditures per capita	Dollars	142	198	334	571	646	736	8.9	11.4	13.6
	Public	Percent	24.7	24.5	37.0	42.3	42.7	42.1	(ns)	(ns)	(ns)
146	Private consumer expenditures for health care	Bil. dol.	17.3	25.9	38.7	61.6	70.6	82.6	8.4	9.8	15.8
	Met by private insurance benefits	Percent	27.2	32.0	37.2	45.7	45.5	47.6	(ns)	(ns)	(ns)
141	Indexes of medical care prices, total	1967= 100	79.1	89.5	120.6	168.6	184.7	202.4	4.3	6.9	9.6
	Physicians' fees		77.0	88.3	121.4	169.4	188.5	206.0	4.7	6.9	10.3
	Semiprivate room rates		57.3	75.9	145.4	236.1	268.8	299.5	9.8	10.2	12.6
154	Physicians, active M.D.'s	1,000	247	278	311	366	379	(na)	2.3	3.3	3.3
	Patient care, general practice[8]	1,000	(na)	66	53	50	50	(na)	[9]-4.3	-1.2	—
152	Newly-licensed physicians	1,000	8	9	11	17	18	(na)	3.2	8.9	5.1
151	Dentists, active[8]	1,000	85	86	96	108	110	(na)	1.2	2.4	1.9
151	Nurses, registered, active	1,000	504	613	700	906	961	(na)	3.3	5.3	6.1
165	Hospitals	1,000	6.9	7.1	7.1	7.2	7.1	(na)	.4	.1	-1.0
	Beds	Millions	1.7	1.7	1.6	1.5	1.4	(na)	-.3	-1.9	-2.2
	Beds per 1,000 population	Rate	9.3	8.9	8.0	6.9	6.7	(na)	(ns)	(ns)	(ns)
169	Average in-patients treated daily	Millions	1.4	1.4	1.3	1.1	1.1	(na)	-.8	-2.8	-3.1
169	Occupancy rate[10]	Rate	84.6	82.3	80.3	76.7	76.0	(na)	-.5	-.9	-.9
165	Short-term hospitals[11]	1,000	5.4	5.7	5.9	6.0	6.0	(na)	.8	.4	-.4
	Beds	Millions	.6	.7	.8	.9	1.0	(na)	2.9	2.2	1.5
	Beds per 1,000 population	Rate	3.6	3.9	4.2	4.4	4.5	(na)	(ns)	(ns)	(ns)
169	Average in-patients treated daily	Millions	.5	.6	.7	.7	.7	(na)	3.3	1.4	1.0
169	Occupancy rate[10]	Rate	74.7	76.0	78.0	74.8	74.4	(na)	.4	-.8	-.5
166	Expense per patient day	Dollars	32	44	81	151	173	(na)	9.7	13.3	14.0
176	Patient-care episodes in mental health facilities	1,000	(na)	2,637[12]	4,038	6,409	(na)	(na)	[12]7.4	[12]12.2	(na)
179	Bed disability: Days per male	Days	5.3	5.3	5.2	5.4	6.1	(na)	(ns)	(ns)	(ns)
	Days per female	Days	6.7	7.0	6.9	7.6	8.1	(na)	(ns)	(ns)	(ns)
	Federal food programs:											
201	School lunches, pupil participants[1,3]	Millions	14.1	18.7	23.1	25.3	25.8	26.7	5.1	1.8	2.7
	Federal cost	Mil. dol.	94	130	300	1,289	1,489	1,668	12.3	33.9	13.8
204	Food stamps — monthly participation	Millions	(x)	.4	4.3	17.1	18.5	17.1	[9]59.2	31.5	.1
	Stamps issued, retail value	Mil. dol.	(x)	85	1,090	7,266	8,700	8,339	[9]66.6	46.1	7.1
	Paid for by participants	Percent	(x)	62.4	49.5	39.6	38.8	39.4	(ns)	(ns)	(ns)
	Federal contribution	Mil. dol.	(x)	32	550	4,386	5,327	5,056	[9]76.6	51.5	7.4
	Avg. monthly Federal cost per participant	Dollars	(x)	6	11	21	24	25	[9]10.6	15.2	7.4

See notes on p. xxiv.

Reference table	Subject	Unit of measure	1960	1965	1970	1975	1976	1977	1960 –70	1970 –75	1975 –77[1]
									Average annual percent change		
	EDUCATION										
212	School expenditures, total	Bil. dol.	24.7	40.2	70.4	111.1	121.8	131.0	11.0	9.6	8.6
	Elementary and secondary	Bil. dol.	18.0	27.3	45.7	72.2	79.1	85.5	9.8	9.6	8.8
	Higher education	Bil. dol.	6.7	12.9	24.7	38.9	42.7	45.5	13.9	9.5	8.2
	Public	Bil. dol.	19.7	31.0	56.8	91.3	100.2	107.6	11.2	10.0	8.6
	Nonpublic	Bil. dol.	5.0	9.2	13.6	19.8	21.6	23.4	10.5	7.8	8.7
215	School enrollment, total	Millions	46.3	53.8	60.4	61.0	60.5	60.0	2.7	.2	-.8
	Nursery	Millions	(na)	(na)	1.1	1.7	1.5	1.6	(na)	9.1	-3.0
	Elementary (kinderg. and grades 1-8) .	Millions	32.4	35.1	37.2	33.9	33.3	32.4	1.4	-1.8	-2.2
	High school (grades 9-12)	Millions	10.2	13.0	14.7	15.7	15.7	15.8	3.7	1.3	.3
	Nonpublic elementary and secondary .	Millions	6.0	6.8	5.7	5.0	4.8	5.0	-.5	-2.4	.2
	Higher education	Millions	3.6	5.7	7.4	9.7	10.0	10.2	7.5	5.6	2.5
215	Enrollment in public schools	Millions	39.0	45.1	52.2	52.8	52.4	51.6	3.0	.2	-1.1
	Elementary and secondary	Millions	36.7	41.3	46.1	44.6	44.2	43.2	2.3	-.7	-1.6
236	Current expenditures per pupil in a.d.a[14] .	Dollars	375	[15]537	816[16]	[16]1,207	1,509	(na)	8.1[16]	10.3[16]	11.8
215	Enrollment in nonpublic schools	Millions	7.2	8.7	8.1	8.2	8.1	8.4	1.2	.3	1.2
221	White pupils enrolled[17]	Millions	40.3	46.7	51.7	51.4	50.8	50.2	2.5	-.1	-1.3
	Elementary and secondary	Millions	37.0	41.4	44.1	41.5	40.9	40.0	1.8	-1.2	-1.8
	Higher education	Millions	3.3	5.3	6.8	8.5	8.6	8.8	7.3	4.7	1.7
221	Black and other pupils enrolled[17]	Millions	5.9	7.1	8.6	9.5	9.7	9.9	3.9	2.0	1.7
	Elementary and secondary	Millions	5.7	6.7	7.8	8.0	8.1	8.2	3.2	.7	.7
	Higher education	Millions	.2	.4	.7	1.2	1.3	1.4	11.2	12.6	9.0
225	Years of school completed, persons 25 years old and over:										
	Median for all persons	Years	10.6	11.8	12.2	12.3	12.4	12.4	(ns)	(ns)	(ns)
	Median for Black persons	Years	8.0	9.0	9.9	10.9	11.1	11.4	(ns)	(ns)	(ns)
245	Public school teachers, elem. and sec . . .	1,000	1,408	1,710	2,055	2,196	2,193	(na)	3.9	1.3	-.1
245	Pupil-teacher ratio: Public elementary . .	Ratio	28.4	27.6	24.4	21.7	21.7	(na)	(ns)	(ns)	(ns)
	Public secondary	Ratio	21.7	20.8	19.8	18.8	18.5	(na)	(ns)	(ns)	(ns)
247	Public school teachers, avg. annual salary .	$1,000	5.0	6.2	8.6	11.7	12.6	13.3	5.6	6.4	6.6
257	High school graduates	Millions	1.9	2.7	2.9	3.1	3.2	(na)	4.5	1.6	.4
257	College graduates	Millions	.4	.5	.8	.9	.9	(na)	7.3	3.1	.3
271	Higher education charges (academic yr.) per full-time resident student:										
	Public institutions	Dollars	820	950	1,204	1,617	1,725	1,874	3.9	6.1	7.7
	Private institutions	Dollars	1,513	1,907	2,531	3,386	3,691	4,058	5.3	6.0	9.5
	LAW ENFORCEMENT										
286	Number of crimes, total	1,000	3,384	4,739	8,098	11,257	11,305	10,936	9.1	6.8	-1.4
	Against persons	1,000	288	387	739	1,026	987	1,010	9.9	6.8	-.8
	Murders, nonnegl. manslaughters .	1,000	9.1	10.0	16.0	20.5	18.8	19.1	5.8	5.1	-3.5
	Robbery	1,000	108	139	350	465	420	405	12.5	5.9	-6.7
	Against property	1,000	3,096	4,352	7,359	10,230	10,318	9,926	9.0	6.8	-1.5
286	Crimes per 100,000 inhabitants	Rate	1,887	2,449	3,985	5,282	5,266	5,055	7.8	5.8	-2.2
	Against persons	Rate	161	200	364	482	460	467	8.5	5.8	-1.6
	Against property	Rate	1,726	2,249	3,621	4,800	4,807	4,588	7.7	5.8	-2.2
301	Law enforcement officers killed by felons .	Number	(na)	53	100	129	111	93	[9]13.5	5.2	-15.1
309	Public expenditures for law enforcement .	Bil. dol.	3.3	4.6	8.6	17.2	19.7	(na)	9.9	15.0	14.1
	Police protection	Bil. dol.	2.0	2.8	5.1	9.8	11.0	(na)	9.6	14.0	12.7
	Judicial	Bil. dol.	.6	.7	1.2	2.1	2.4	(na)	7.1	11.7	17.4
	Corrections	Bil. dol.	.7	1.0	1.7	3.8	4.4	(na)	9.0	17.6	14.1
	Federal	Bil. dol.	.3	.4	1.0	2.2	2.5	(na)	12.9	17.5	11.9
	State	Bil. dol.	.8	1.1	2.1	4.6	5.2	(na)	10.8	16.7	12.8
	Local	Bil. dol.	2.3	3.1	5.5	10.4	12.0	(na)	9.1	13.9	15.1
310	Federal outlays for crime reduction	Bil. dol.	.5	.6	.9	2.8	3.0	3.2	6.0	26.9	7.3
311	Police employees:										
	State and local government	1,000	303.8	348.6	449.7	555.8	557.0	(na)	4.0	4.3	.2
	Local government	1,000	271.6	308.5	393.8	463.4	466.6	(na)	3.8	3.3	.7
311	Corrections employees:										
	State and local government	1,000	(na)	110.7	142.3	213.8	227.6	(na)	[9]5.2	8.5	6.4
	Local government	1,000	(na)	41.2	52.0	86.9	93.2	(na)	[9]4.8	10.8	7.2
331	Prisoners in Federal and State institutions.	1,000	213	211	196	241	263	(na)	-.8	4.1	9.4

See notes on p. xxiv.

Reference table	Subject	Unit of measure	1960	1965	1970	1975	1976	1977	Average annual percent change		
									1960 –70	1970 –75	1975 –77[1]

ENVIRONMENT

Reference table	Subject	Unit of measure	1960	1965	1970	1975	1976	1977	1960 –70	1970 –75	1975 –77[1]
346	Water use, daily average[18]	Bil. gal.	323	270	378	361	(na)	(na)	1.6	–.9	(na)
354	Capital expenditures for pollution abatement by business, total	Bil. dol.	(na)	(na)	(na)	6.5	6.8	6.9	(na)	(na)	2.9
	Water	Bil. dol.	(na)	(na)	(na)	2.4	2.7	2.8	(na)	(na)	8.6
	Air	Bil. dol.	(na)	(na)	(na)	3.8	3.6	3.7	(na)	(na)	–1.3
351	Federal obligations for pollution control	Bil. dol.	(na)	(na)	1.1	6.1	7.5	10.0	(na)	41.6	28.2
	Water	Bil. dol.	(na)	(na)	.7	5.2	6.1	8.7	(na)	50.2	29.6
	Air	Bil. dol.	(na)	(na)	.2	.3	.4	.4	(na)	13.0	9.3
353	State government expenditures:										
	Water quality control	Mil. dol.	(na)	(na)	157	751	939	(na)	(na)	36.8	25.0
	Air quality control	Mil. dol.	(na)	(na)	23	95	157	(na)	(na)	32.8	65.3
358	Air pollutants emitted: Sulfur oxides	Mil. tons	(na)	(na)	32.1	28.3	29.6	(na)	(na)	–2.5	4.6
	Carbon monoxides	Mil. tons	(na)	(na)	110.0	94.7	96.1	(na)	(na)	–3.0	1.5
	Hydrocarbons	Mil. tons	(na)	(na)	32.7	28.9	30.7	(na)	(na)	–2.4	6.2
	Particulates[19]	Mil. tons	(na)	(na)	24.9	15.9	14.8	(na)	(na)	–8.6	–6.9
	Nitrogen oxides	Mil. tons	(na)	(na)	22.5	24.5	25.3	(na)	(na)	1.7	3.3

FEDERAL GOVERNMENT

Reference table	Subject	Unit of measure	1960	1965	1970	1975	1976	1977	1960 –70	1970 –75	1975 –77[1]
416	Budget receipts	Bil. dol.	93	117	194	281	299	357	7.7	7.7	12.7
420	Individual income tax receipts	Bil. dol.	41	49	90	122	132	157	8.3	6.3	13.2
	Percent of total	Percent	44.0	41.8	46.7	43.6	44.1	43.9	(ns)	(ns)	(ns)
437	Income tax per capita	Dollars	219	256	413	586	584	661	6.6	7.3	6.2
420	Social insurance taxes[20]	Bil. dol.	15	22	45	86	93	109	11.9	13.8	12.2
	Percent of total	Percent	15.9	19.1	23.4	30.7	31.0	30.5	(ns)	(ns)	(ns)
420	Corporation income tax receipts	Bil. dol.	22	26	33	41	41	55	4.3	4.4	16.3
	Percent of total	Percent	23.2	21.8	16.9	14.5	13.8	15.4	(ns)	(ns)	(ns)
416	Budget outlays	Bil. dol.	92	118	197	326	366	402	7.9	10.7	11.0
418	In constant (1972) dollars	Bil. dol.	151	173	221	253	266	272	3.9	2.8	3.6
422	National defense	Bil. dol.	45	48	79	86	89	98	5.7	1.7	6.8
	Percent of total	Percent	49.0	40.1	40.0	26.2	24.5	24.3	(ns)	(ns)	(ns)
422	Income security	Bil. dol.	18	26	43	109	127	137	8.9	20.3	12.3
	Percent of total	Percent	19.8	21.7	21.9	33.3	34.6	34.1	(ns)	(ns)	(ns)
422	Education, manpower, social services	Bil. dol.	1	2	9	16	19	21	24.0	12.9	15.3
422	Net interest	Bil. dol.	7	9	14	23	27	30	7.6	10.1	13.5
422	Health	Bil. dol.	1	2	13	28	33	39	32.3	16.2	18.4
416	Surplus (+) or deficit (–)	Bil. dol.	+.3	–1.6	–2.8	–45.1	–66.4	–45.0	(ns)	(ns)	(ns)
449	Gross public debt outstanding	Bil. dol.	284	314	370	533	620	699	2.7	7.6	14.5
449	Gross public debt per capita	Dollars	1,572	1,613	1,807	2,496	2,884	2,884	1.4	6.7	7.5
458	Federal civilian employment	Millions	2.4	2.5	2.9	2.9	2.9	2.8	2.0	–.2	–1.0
	Department of Defense	Percent	43.7	40.9	40.9	36.0	35.0	34.6	(ns)	(ns)	(ns)
454	Percent of total employment	Percent	3.7	3.6	3.7	3.1	3.0	2.9	(ns)	(ns)	(ns)
454	Federal civilian payrolls, total annual	Bil. dol.	13.2	18.0	28.6	40.7	42.3	45.9	8.0	7.3	6.2
	Percent of total Federal outlays	Percent	14.4	15.2	14.5	12.5	11.6	11.4	(ns)	(ns)	(ns)

STATE AND LOCAL GOVERNMENTS

Reference table	Subject	Unit of measure	1960	1965	1970	1975	1976	1977	1960 –70	1970 –75	1975 –77[1]
469	Revenue, all governments, incl. Federal	Bil. dol.	153	203	334	517	573	(na)	8.1	9.1	10.8
	State	Bil. dol.	26	39	69	117	140	(na)	10.3	11.1	19.7
	Local	Bil. dol.	27	38	60	98	109	(na)	8.3	10.3	11.2
469	Expenditures, all govts., incl. Federal	Bil. dol.	151	206	333	557	626	(na)	8.2	10.8	12.4
	State	Bil. dol.	22	31	56	104	124	(na)	9.8	13.2	19.2
	Local	Bil. dol.	39	55	92	161	180	(na)	9.0	11.8	11.8
469	Debt outstanding, all govts., incl. Federal	Bil. dol.	356	417	514	765	871	(na)	3.7	8.3	13.9
	State	Bil. dol.	19	27	42	72	84	(na)	8.3	11.4	16.7
	Local	Bil. dol.	51	72	102	149	156	(na)	7.2	7.9	4.7
478	Aid from Federal Government	Bil. dol.	7.0	10.9	24.0	49.7	59.0	68.4	13.1	15.7	17.3
	Revenue sharing	Bil. dol.	(x)	(x)	(x)	6.1	6.2	6.8	(x)	(x)	5.0
	Public assistance	Bil. dol.	2.1	2.8	4.1	5.1	5.8	6.4	7.2	4.3	11.4
	Medicaid	Bil. dol.	(x)	.3	2.7	6.8	8.6	9.9	9 58.6	20.2	20.2
	Highways	Bil. dol.	2.9	4.0	4.3	4.7	6.3	6.0	4.0	1.7	13.2
482	General revenue, total, State and local	Bil. dol.	51	74	131	228	256	(na)	10.0	11.8	12.3
	From Federal Government	Percent	13.8	14.9	16.7	20.6	21.7	(na)	(ns)	(ns)	(ns)
	From own taxes	Percent	71.5	69.2	66.4	62.0	61.2	(na)	(ns)	(ns)	(ns)
	Taxes per capita	Dollars	201	264	427	664	731	(na)	7.8	9.2	10.1

See notes on p. xxiv.

Reference table	Subject	Unit of measure	1960	1965	1970	1975	1976	1977	1960 -70	1970 -75	1975 -77[1]
									Average annual percent change		

STATE AND LOCAL GOVERNMENTS – Con.

Ref.	Subject	Unit	1960	1965	1970	1975	1976	1977	1960-70	1970-75	1975-77[1]
480	Direct expenditures, State and local	Bil. dol.	61	87	148	266	304	(na)	9.3	12.4	14.5
	Education	Percent	30.7	33.0	35.6	33.1	32.0	(na)	(ns)	(ns)	(ns)
	Highways	Percent	15.5	14.1	11.1	8.5	7.9	(na)	(ns)	(ns)	(ns)
	Public welfare	Percent	7.2	7.3	9.9	10.3	10.3	(na)	(ns)	(ns)	(ns)
482	Direct general expenditures per capita[21] .	Dollars	288	385	646	1,076	1,191	(na)	8.4	10.7	10.7
504	State and local govt. employment, Oct ...	Millions	6.4	8.0	10.1	12.1	12.2	12.6	4.7	3.6	1.9
	Education	Millions	2.9	4.0	5.3	6.3	6.3	6.5	6.1	3.4	1.8
505	Local	Millions	2.4	3.2	4.1	4.9	4.9	5.0	5.4	3.4	1.4
504	State and local govt. payroll, Oct.	Bil. dol.	2.2	3.4	5.9	9.6	10.4	11.3	10.3	10.3	8.2
	City government finances, all cities:										
498	Revenue	Bil. dol.	14.9	20.3	32.7	59.7	66.9	(na)	8.2	12.8	11.9
	From Federal and State govts	Bil. dol.	2.3	3.5	7.9	19.6	22.2	(na)	13.0	20.0	13.2
	Property taxes	Bil. dol.	5.2	6.5	9.1	13.0	14.2	(na)	5.8	7.4	8.6
498	General expenditure	Bil. dol.	11.8	16.0	27.7	48.9	54.4	(na)	8.9	12.1	11.2
499	Per capita	Dollars	102	138	210	359	398	(na)	7.5	11.3	10.9
498	Gross debt outstanding	Bil. dol.	23.2	31.9	43.8	65.2	68.8	(na)	6.6	8.3	5.5
499	Per capita	Dollars	200	274	332	481	503	(na)	5.2	7.7	4.6

WELFARE

Ref.	Subject	Unit	1960	1965	1970	1975	1976	1977	1960-70	1970-75	1975-77[1]
514	Private social welfare expenditures	Bil. dol.	27.8	42.7	67.4	109.4	121.6	(na)	9.3	10.2	11.2
517	Public social welfare expenditures, total .	Bil. dol.	52.3	77.2	145.9	286.5	331.4	(na)	10.8	14.5	15.7
515	Percent of GNP	Percent	10.5	11.7	15.2	19.7	20.6	(na)	(ns)	(ns)	(ns)
515	Percent of total govt. expenditures ..	Percent	38.4	42.2	48.2	57.9	59.7	(na)	(ns)	(ns)	(ns)
517	Percent from non-trust funds	Percent	29.9	33.4	38.3	46.5	48.6	(na)	(ns)	(ns)	(ns)
517	Federal	Bil. dol.	25.0	37.7	77.3	167.2	198.3	(na)	12.0	16.7	18.6
517	State and local	Bil. dol.	27.3	39.5	68.5	119.3	133.0	(na)	9.6	11.7	11.5
518	Per capita, current dollars	Dollars	285	391	701	1,320	1,514	(na)	9.4	13.5	14.7
	1976 dollars	Dollars	519	664	1,003	1,398	1,514	(na)	6.8	6.9	8.3
517	Social insurance	Bil. dol.	19.3	28.1	54.7	122.9	146.6	(na)	11.0	17.6	19.2
516	OASDHI[22] (Social Security)	Bil. dol.	11.0	17.0	36.8	78.4	90.4	(na)	12.8	16.3	15.3
	Medicare	Bil. dol.	(x)	(x)	7.1	14.8	17.8	(na)	(x)	15.6	20.3
516	Unemployment insurance	Bil. dol.	2.8	3.0	3.8	13.9	19.7	(na)	3.1	29.4	42.0
517	Education	Bil. dol.	17.6	28.1	50.8	77.9	86.4	(na)	11.2	8.9	10.9
517	Public aid	Bil. dol.	4.1	6.3	16.5	40.7	48.9	(na)	14.9	19.8	20.2
517	Health and medical[23]	Bil. dol.	4.5	6.2	9.9	17.4	19.2	(na)	8.3	12.0	10.1
517	Veterans	Bil. dol.	5.5	6.0	9.1	17.0	19.0	(na)	5.2	13.4	11.7
517	Housing	Bil. dol.	.2	.3	.7	3.0	3.1	(na)	14.8	33.5	5.4
522	Public income–maintenance payments ..	Bil. dol.	25.9	36.6	64.5	139.6	152.5	(na)	9.6	16.7	9.2
	Percent of personal income	Percent	6.5	6.8	8.0	11.2	11.1	(na)	(ns)	(ns)	(ns)
523	Employment covered by OASDHI[22] ...	Millions	59.4	65.6	72.1	77.8	80.7	(na)	2.0	1.5	3.7
	Percent of paid employment	Percent	88.0	89.1	89.5	90.2	90.7	(na)	(ns)	(ns)	(ns)
532	OASDHI[22] beneficiaries, end of year ...	Millions	14.8	20.9	26.2	32.1	33.0	34.1	5.9	4.1	3.1
	Retired workers	Millions	8.1	11.1	13.3	16.6	17.2	17.8	5.2	4.4	3.7
	Benefit payments during year (except lump-sum)	Bil. dol.	11.1	18.1	31.6	66.6	75.3	84.3	11.0	16.1	12.5
	Average monthly benefits paid to retired workers, 1977 dollars	Dollars	154	164	184	232	240	243	1.8	4.8	2.3
528	Social Security (old–age and survivors) trust fund assets, end of year	Bil. dol.	20.3	18.2	32.5	37.0	35.4	32.5	4.8	2.7	-6.3
550	Hospital insurance enrollment (Medicare)	Millions	(x)	[24]19.1	20.4	24.6	25.3	(na)	[24]2.1	3.9	2.7
	Benefit payments	Bil. dol.	(x)	[24]2.5	5.1	11.3	13.2	(na)	[24]26.6	17.2	16.8
550	Medical insurance enrollment (Medicare) .	Millions	(x)	[24]17.7	19.6	23.9	24.6	(na)	[24]3.4	4.1	3.0
	Benefit payments	Bil. dol.	(x)	[24].7	2.0	4.2	5.0	(na)	[24]43.4	16.4	19.3
562	Public aid recipients: Aged[25]	Millions	2.3	2.1	2.1	2.3	2.1	2.1	-1.0	2.1	-5.7
	Permanently, totally disabled[25]	Millions	.4	.6	.9	1.9	2.0	2.1	9.7	15.6	4.5
	Families with dependent children ...	Millions	.8	1.1	2.6	3.6	3.6	3.5	12.3	6.8	-.3
	Individual recipients	Millions	3.1	4.4	9.7	11.4	11.2	10.8	12.1	3.3	-2.8
563	Public aid payments, total	Bil. dol.	3.3	4.6	14.4	30.5	32.9	34.9	15.9	16.2	7.1
	Aged[25]	Bil. dol.	1.6	1.6	1.9	2.6	2.5	2.4	1.3	7.0	-3.1
	Permanently, totally disabled[25] ...	Bil. dol.	.2	.4	1.0	3.1	3.4	3.7	15.5	25.7	8.7
	Families with dependent children ...	Bil. dol.	1.0	1.7	4.9	9.2	10.0	10.2	17.1	13.7	5.2
	Medical assistance	Bil. dol.	(x)	(x)	5.9	14.2	15.5	17.1	(x)	19.1	10.0

See notes on p. xxiv.

Reference table	Subject	Unit of measure	1960	1965	1970	1975	1976	1977	Average annual percent change 1960–70	1970–75	1975–77[1]
	NATIONAL DEFENSE										
584	Federal outlays for national defense . . .	Bil. dol.	45.2	47.5	78.6	85.6	89.4	97.5	5.7	1.7	6.7
	In constant 1978 dollars	Bil. dol.	115.4	108.4	141.1	104.9	102.3	103.8	2.0	−5.8	−.5
	Percent of total Federal outlays	Percent	49.0	40.1	40.0	26.2	24.5	24.2	(ns)	(ns)	(ns)
	Percent of gross national product . . .	Percent	9.1	7.2	8.2	5.9	5.5.	5.3	(ns)	(ns)	(ns)
588	Worldwide military expenditures	Bil. dol.	(na)	[24]201	242	371	399	(na)	[24]6.4	8.9	7.6
	U.S. as percent of world total	Percent	(na)	[24]39	33	25	24	(na)	(ns)	(ns)	(ns)
591	Foreign military assistance programs[26] . .	Bil. dol.	2.1	1.1	2.7	1.2	.2	.3	2.3	−15.4	−47.7
591	Foreign military sales deliveries	Bil. dol.	.3	.7	1.4	3.3	4.0	6.9	15.4	19.5	44.0
599	Defense–related Federal employment[27] . .	1,000	3,571	3,776	4,399	3,216	3,152	3,127	2.1	−6.1	−1.4
605	Military personnel on active duty	1,000	2,476	2,653	3,066	2,127	2,081	2,074	2.2	−7.1	−1.3
609	U.S. military in foreign countries	1,000	633	853	888	454	449	460	3.4	−12.6	.7
619	Military reserves not on active duty	1,000	4,147	2,576	3,639	2,656	2,419	2,249	−1.3	−6.1	−8.0
584	Federal outlays for veterans benefits . . .	Bil. dol.	5.5	5.7	8.7	16.6	18.4	18.0	4.7	13.8	4.1
623	Veterans, total living	Millions	23.8	25.3	27.6	29.5	29.6	29.8	1.5	1.3	.7
631	Veterans receiving benefits[28]	Millions	4.0	4.5	4.7	4.9	4.9	4.9	1.8	.6	.6
	EMPLOYMENT AND EARNINGS										
645	Labor force, total	Millions	72.1	77.2	85.9	94.8	96.9	99.5	1.8	2.0	2.5
	Civilian labor force	Millions	69.6	74.5	82.7	92.6	94.8	97.4	1.7	2.3	2.6
	Percent female	Percent	32.3	34.0	36.7	39.1	39.7	40.3	(ns)	(ns)	(ns)
	Employed	Millions	65.8	71.1	78.6	84.8	87.5	90.5	1.8	1.5	3.3
679	Percent white-collar	Percent	43.4	44.8	48.3	49.8	50.0	49.9	(ns)	(ns)	(ns)
645	Unemployed, total	Millions	3.9	3.4	4.1	7.8	7.3	6.9	.6	13.9	−6.4
667	Teenagers (16–19 yr. old)	Millions	.7	.9	1.1	1.8	1.7	1.6	4.5	9.7	−3.2
667	Unemployment rate, total	Percent	5.5	4.5	4.9	8.5	7.7	7.0	(ns)	(ns)	(ns)
	White	Percent	4.9	4.1	4.5	7.8	7.0	6.2	(ns)	(ns)	(ns)
	Male	Percent	4.8	3.6	4.0	7.2	6.4	5.5	(ns)	(ns)	(ns)
	Female	Percent	5.3	5.0	5.4	8.6	7.9	7.3	(ns)	(ns)	(ns)
	Black and other	Percent	10.2	8.1	8.2	13.9	13.1	13.1	(ns)	(ns)	(ns)
	Male	Percent	10.7	7.4	7.3	13.7	12.7	12.4	(ns)	(ns)	(ns)
	Female	Percent	9.4	9.2	9.3	14.0	13.6	14.0	(ns)	(ns)	(ns)
	Teenagers (16–19 yr. old)	Percent	14.7	14.8	15.3	19.9	19.0	17.7	(ns)	(ns)	(ns)
	Married men, wife present	Percent	3.7	2.4	2.6	5.1	4.2	3.6	(ns)	(ns)	(ns)
667	Insured unemployed, average weekly . . .	Millions	1.9	1.3	1.8	4.0	3.0	2.6	−.6	17.2	−18.5
673	Nonfarm employment, total	Millions	54.2	60.8	70.9	77.1	79.4	82.1	2.7	1.7	3.3
	Manufacturing	Millions	16.8	18.1	19.3	18.3	19.0	19.6	1.4	−1.1	3.2
	Wholesale and retail trade	Millions	11.4	12.7	15.0	17.0	17.7	18.3	2.8	2.5	3.7
	Government	Millions	8.4	10.1	12.6	14.7	14.9	15.2	4.2	3.2	1.6
655	Female labor force, total	Millions	22.5	26.0	31.2	36.5	37.8	39.4	3.3	3.2	3.9
	Married, husband present	Percent	54.4	56.7	58.8	57.9	57.0	56.8	(ns)	(ns)	(ns)
657	Working women, husband present, with children under 18 years	Millions	6.6	8.0	10.2	11.4	11.7	12.1	4.5	2.3	3.0
	Labor force participation rate	Percent	27.6	32.2	39.7	44.9	46.1	48.2	(ns)	(ns)	(ns)
677	Indexes of private economy:[29] Productivity	1967=100	78	95	105	112	117	120	3.0	1.4	3.4
	Manufacturing		79	98	105	116	124	127	2.9	2.2	4.5
	Compensation per hour		71	88	123	180	197	214	5.6	7.9	9.0
	Manufacturing		77	91	122	179	195	212	4.7	8.1	8.7
684	Average weekly earnings (current dollars) .	Dollars	81	95	119	164	176	190	3.9	6.6	7.6
	Manufacturing	Dollars	90	108	134	190	208	227	4.1	7.2	9.3
	Contract construction	Dollars	113	138	195	265	285	297	5.6	6.3	5.9
	Retail trade	Dollars	58	67	82	108	114	121	3.5	5.7	5.9
684	Average weekly earnings (1977 dollars) . .	Dollars	165	182	186	185	188	190	1.2	−.1	1.3
	Manufacturing	Dollars	183	206	209	213	221	227	1.3	.4	3.2
	Contract construction	Dollars	231	266	305	299	303	297	2.8	−.4	−.3
	Retail trade	Dollars	118	128	129	122	121	121	.9	−1.1	−.4
689	Minimum hourly wage rate[30]	Dollars	1.00	1.25	1.60	2.10	2.30	2.30	(ns)	(ns)	(ns)
698	Labor union membership (U.S.)	Millions	17.0	17.3	19.4	[16]20.2	19.4	(na)	1.3	[16]1.0	[16]−1.9
	Percent of nonfarm employment . . .	Percent	31.4	28.4	27.5	[16]25.8	24.5	(na)	(ns)	(ns)	(ns)
702	Work stoppages	Number	3,333	3,963	5,716	5,031	5,648	(na)	5.5	−2.5	12.3
	Workers involved	Millions	1.3	1.6	3.3	1.7	2.4	(na)	9.6	−12.0	38.6

See notes on p. xxiv.

Refer-ence table	Subject	Unit of measure	1960	1965	1970	1975	1976	1977	Average annual percent change		
									1960 –70	1970 –75	1975 –77[1]
	INCOME AND PRICES										
708	Gross national product, current dollars . .	Bil. dol.	506	688	982	1,529	1,707	1,890	6.9	9.3	11.2
714	Per capita	Dollars	2,801	3,541	4,795	7,159	7,930	8,713	5.5	8.4	10.3
708	Personal consumption expenditures . .	Bil. dol.	325	430	619	980	1,094	1,211	6.7	9.6	11.2
708	Gross private domestic investment . .	Bil. dol.	76	112	141	189	243	294	6.3	6.1	24.7
708	Net exports of goods and services . . .	Bil. dol.	4	8	4	20	8	–11	(ns)	(ns)	(ns)
708	Govt. purchases of goods and services .	Bil. dol.	100	138	219	339	361	395	8.1	9.1	8.0
710	Gross national product, 1972 dollars . . .	Bil. dol.	737	926	1,075	1,202	1,275	1,337	3.9	2.3	5.5
714	Per capita	Dollars	4,078	4,765	5,248	5,629	5,923	6,167	2.6	1.4	4.7
716	National income	Bil. dol.	412	566	798	1,217	1,364	1,521	6.8	8.8	11.8
716	Personal income	Bil. dol.	400	537	801	1,253	1,383	1,537	7.2	9.4	10.7
716	Disposable personal income	Bil. dol.	349	472	686	1,084	1,186	1,309	7.0	9.6	9.9
714	Per capita, current dollars	Dollars	1,934	2,430	3,348	5,077	5,511	6,037	5.6	8.7	9.1
716	Personal saving	Bil. dol.	17	30	51	80	66	67	11.5	9.7	–8.4
729	Median money income:[31]										
	All families, current dollars	$1,000	5.6	7.0	9.9	13.7	15.0	16.0	5.8	6.8	8.0
	White families	$1,000	5.8	7.3	10.2	14.3	15.5	16.7	5.8	6.9	8.3
	Black and other families	$1,000	3.2	4.0	6.5	9.3	9.8	10.1	7.3	7.4	4.3
	All families, 1977 dollars	$1,000	11.5	13.4	15.4	15.4	15.9	16.0	3.0	.1	1.8
749	Median money income of persons:[31]										
	Male	$1,000	4.1	5.0	6.7	8.9	9.4	10.1	5.0	5.8	6.9
	Female	$1,000	1.3	1.5	2.2	3.4	3.6	3.9	5.9	8.6	7.9
756	Families below poverty level[31]	Millions	8.2	[15]5.8	5.3	5.5	5.3	5.3	–4.4	.7	–1.3
	Percent of all families	Percent	18.1	[15]11.8	10.1	9.7	9.4	9.3	(ns)	(ns)	(ns)
756	Persons below poverty level, total[31] . . .	Millions	39.9	[15]28.5	25.4	25.9	25.0	24.7	–4.4	.4	–2.3
	White	Millions	28.3	[15]19.3	17.5	17.8	16.7	16.4	–4.7	.3	–3.9
	Percent of total White	Percent	17.8	[15]11.3	9.9	9.7	9.1	8.9	(ns)	(ns)	(ns)
	Black	Millions	(na)	[32]8.9	7.5	7.5	7.6	7.7 [32]	–4.0	(–z)	1.2
	Percent of total Black	Percent	(na)	[15]41.8	33.5	31.3	31.1	31.3	(ns)	(ns)	(ns)
754	Persons below 125% of poverty level[31] . .	Millions	54.6	[15]41.3	35.6	37.2	35.5	35.7	–4.2	.9	–2.1
	Percent of total population	Percent	30.4	[15]21.3	17.6	17.6	16.7	16.7	(ns)	(ns)	(ns)
781	Purchasing power of the dollar:										
	Producer prices (1967=$1.00)	Dollars	1.05	1.04	.91	.57	.52	.52	–1.5	–8.8	–5.1
	Consumer prices (1967=$1.00)	Dollars	1.13	1.06	.86	.62	.59	.55	–2.7	–6.3	–5.8
787	Producer price index, all commodities . .	} 1967= 100	94.9	96.6	110.4	174.9	183.0	194.2	1.5	9.6	5.4
	Industrial commodities		95.3	96.4	110.0	171.5	182.4	195.1	1.4	9.3	6.7
	Farm products and food		93.7	97.1	111.7	184.2	183.1	188.8	1.8	10.5	1.2
	Fuels, related products, and power . .		96.1	95.5	106.2	245.1	265.6	302.2	1.0	18.2	11.0
793	Consumer price index, all items	} 1967= 100	88.7	94.5	116.3	161.2	170.5	181.5	2.8	6.8	6.1
	Food		88.0	94.4	114.9	175.4	180.8	192.2	2.7	8.8	4.7
	Homeownership cost[33]		86.3	92.7	128.5	181.7	191.7	204.9	4.1	7.2	6.2
	Rent		91.7	96.9	110.1	137.3	144.7	153.5	1.9	4.5	5.7
	Fuel and utilities		95.9	98.3	107.6	167.8	182.7	202.2	1.2	9.3	9.8
	Transportation		89.6	95.9	112.7	150.6	165.5	177.2	2.3	6.0	8.5
	Medical care		79.1	89.5	120.6	168.6	184.7	202.4	4.3	6.9	9.6
	All services		83.5	92.2	121.6	166.6	180.4	194.3	3.8	6.5	8.0
801	Average retail prices:										
	Bread, white, per lb	Cents	20.3	20.9	24.3	36.0	35.3	35.5	1.8	8.2	–.7
	Hamburger, per lb	Cents	52.4	50.8	66.2	87.8	87.6	85.4	2.4	5.8	–1.4
	Steak, sirloin, per lb	Cents	109	134	135	199	193	192	2.2	8.1	–1.8
	Milk, fresh (grocery, 1/2 gal.)	Cents	(na)	47.3	57.4	78.5	82.7	83.9	[9]4.0	6.5	3.4
	Potatoes, per lb	Cents	7.2	9.4	9.0	13.4	14.6	15.0	2.3	8.3	5.8
	BANKING AND FINANCE										
859	Number of banks	1,000	14.0	14.3	14.2	15.1	15.2	15.2	.1	1.3	.3
	Number of branches	1,000	11.1	16.6	23.0	32.1	33.5	33.5	7.5	6.9	5.1
866	Commercial banks, total assets	Bil. dol.	261	383	582	975	1,040	1,177	8.4	10.9	9.9
	Loans, gross	Bil. dol.	121	205	300	513	552	632	9.6	11.3	11.1
	Commercial and industrial loans . .	Bil. dol.	43	72	113	181	185	207	10.1	9.8	7.0
	Investment securities	Bil. dol.	82	105	143	226	244	253	5.7	9.6	5.9
866	Commercial banks, deposits	Bil. dol.	231	334	486	793	845	947	7.7	10.3	9.3
869	Savings and loan associations: Total assets	Bil. dol.	72	130	176	338	392	459	9.4	13.9	16.5
	Mortgage loans outstanding	Bil. dol.	60	110	150	279	323	381	9.6	13.1	17.0
	Savings capital	Bil. dol.	62	110	146	286	336	387	9.0	14.3	16.4
	Mortgage loans made	Bil. dol.	14	24	21	55	79	107	4.1	20.8	39.7

See notes on p. xxiv.

Reference table	Subject	Unit of measure	1960	1965	1970	1975	1976	1977	Average annual percent change		
									1960 –70	1970 –75	1975 –77[1]
	BANKING AND FINANCE – Con.										
873	Mortgage debt outstanding	Bil. dol.	207	333	474	802	889	1,020	8.6	11.1	12.8
	Residential nonfarm	Percent	78.3	77.5	75.5	73.8	74.4	74.7	(ns)	(ns)	(ns)
881	Net public and private debt . . . . [31]	Bil. dol.	874	1,253	1,882	3,029	3,355	(na)	8.0	10.0	10.8
885	Private liquid assets held by the public . .	Bil. dol.	387	559	770	1,290	1,423	1,596	7.1	10.9	11.2
	Demand deposits and currency	Bil. dol.	134	155	201	266	280	303	4.1	5.8	6.7
	Time deposits	Bil. dol.	172	296	432	789	915	1,027	9.7	12.8	14.1
	U.S. savings bonds and short-term securities	Bil. dol.	78	86	94	134	139	153	1.9	7.4	6.9
	Money market rates per year:										
890	Federal Reserve discount rate (high) .	Rate	4.00	4.50	6.00	7.25	6.00	6.00	(ns)	(ns)	(ns)
890	Prime commercial paper (4–6 mo.) . .	Rate	3.9	4.4	7.7	6.3	5.4	5.6	(ns)	(ns)	(ns)
893	Home mortgages, conventional, new .	Rate	[34]6.0	5.8	8.5	9.1	9.0	9.0	(ns)	(ns)	(ns)
893	Corporate bonds, Aaa	Rate	4.4	4.5	8.0	8.8	8.4	8.0	(ns)	(ns)	(ns)
890	Prime rate charged by banks	Rate	4.8	4.5	7.9	7.9	6.8	6.8	(ns)	(ns)	(ns)
876	Consumer credit outstanding	Bil. dol.	56	90	127	201	224	261	8.5	9.6	14.0
	Installment	Percent	76.6	78.9	80.3	82.2	82.7	83.1	(ns)	(ns)	(ns)
895	N.Y. Stock Exch. common stock index (Dec. 31, 1965 = 50)	Index	30.0	47.4	45.7	45.7	54.5	53.7	4.3	(z)	8.4
895	Dow-Jones industrial (30 stocks) mo. avg., dollars per share	Dollars	618.0	910.9	753.2	802.5	974.9	894.9	2.0	1.3	5.6
896	Sales of stocks	Bil. dol.	45	89	131	157	195	187	11.3	3.7	9.1
899	Mutual funds	Number	161	170	356	423	452	477	8.3	3.5	6.2
	Assets	Bil. dol.	17.0	35.2	47.6	45.8	51.3	48.9	10.8	–.8	3.3
	Sales	Bil. dol.	2.1	4.4	4.6	10.2	13.7	17.1	8.2	17.0	29.7
	Life insurance:										
902	Value of policies in force	Bil. dol.	586	901	1,402	2,140	2,343	2,583	9.1	8.8	9.9
903	Sales	Bil. dol.	78	150	207	317	352	393	10.6	8.9	11.4
903	Income	Bil. dol.	23	33	49	78	89	98	7.9	9.7	12.1
903	Payments to policy holders	Bil. dol.	11	17	26	38	41	44	8.4	8.3	8.0
905	Life insurance companies, assets	Bil. dol.	120	159	207	289	322	352	5.7	6.9	10.2
	Net interest earned on assets	Rate	4.1	4.6	5.3	6.4	6.6	6.9	(ns)	(ns)	(ns)
907	Health insurance: Premiums written[35] .	Bil. dol.	4.7	7.4	11.5	21.2	24.3	(na)	9.5	13.0	14.3
	Benefit payments[36]	Bil. dol.	3.1	5.2	9.1	15.1	18.2	(na)	11.5	10.8	20.2
	BUSINESS ENTERPRISE										
915	Proprietorships and partnerships:										
	Number	Millions	10.0	10.0	10.3	12.0	(na)	(na)	.3	3.0	(na)
	Receipts	Bil. dol.	245	274	331	485	(na)	(na)	3.1	7.9	(na)
915	Corporations, number	Millions	1.1	1.4	1.7	2.0	(na)	(na)	3.9	4.0	(na)
	Receipts	Tril. dol.	.8	1.2	1.8	3.2	(na)	(na)	7.5	12.8	(na)
914	New business incorporations	1,000	183	204	264	326	376	436	3.7	4.3	15.7
930	Business expenditures for new plant and equipment	Bil. dol.	36.8	54.4	79.7	112.8	120.5	135.8	8.1	7.2	9.7
	Manufacturing	Bil. dol.	15.1	23.4	32.0	48.0	52.5	60.2	7.8	8.5	12.0
	Public utilities	Bil. dol.	5.2	6.1	13.1	20.1	22.3	25.8	9.6	8.9	13.2
	Communications	Bil. dol.	3.2	5.3	10.1	12.7	13.3	15.5	12.0	4.8	10.1
935	Active corporations, number	1,000	1,141	1,424	1,666	2,024	(na)	(na)	3.9	4.0	(na)
	With assets of $100 million or more . .	1,000	1.4	1.9	2.6	4.0	(na)	(na)	6.4	9.0	(na)
	Percent of total	Percent	.1	.1	.2	.2	(na)	(na)	(ns)	(ns)	(ns)
935	Active corporations, assets	Bil. dol.	1,207	1,724	2,635	4,287	(na)	(na)	8.1	10.2	(na)
	With assets of $100 million or more . .	Bil. dol.	671	1,027	1,752	3,121	(na)	(na)	10.1	12.2	(na)
	Percent of total	Percent	55.6	59.6	66.5	72.8	(na)	(na)	(ns)	(ns)	(ns)
946	Share of assets held by 200 largest manufacturing corporations	Percent	56.3	56.7	60.4	57.5	58.0	58.4	(ns)	(ns)	(ns)
948	Corporate profits after taxes	Bil. dol.	25.8	44.3	37.0	73.4	92.1	102.5	3.7	14.7	18.2
948	Capital consumption allowances	Bil. dol.	25.3	37.4	56.6	89.5	97.2	104.7	8.4	9.6	8.2
954	Profit rates after taxes on stockholders' equity in manufacturing corporations[31] .	Rate	9.2	13.0	9.3	11.6	14.0	14.2	(ns)	(ns)	(ns)
955	Mergers of mfg. and mining concerns . . .	1,000	.8	1.0	1.4	.4	.6	.6	4.8	–20.1	15.9
958	Industrial and commercial failures	1,000	15.4	13.5	10.7	11.4	9.6	7.9	–3.6	1.2	–16.8
	Per 10,000 concerns in business	Rate	57	53	44	43	35	28	–2.6	–.5	–19.3
	Current liabilities	Bil. dol.	.9	1.3	1.9	4.4	3.0	3.1	7.2	18.3	–15.9

See notes on p. xxiv.

Reference table	Subject	Unit of measure	1960	1965	1970	1975	1976	1977	1960 –70	1970 –75	1975 –77[1]
									Average annual percent change		
	COMMUNICATIONS										
963	Postal service revenues	Bil. dol.	3.3	4.5	7.7	11.6	12.7	14.6	8.9	8.5	12.3
	Deficit	Mil. dol.	597	793	165	988	1,176	688	(ns)	(ns)	(ns)
967	Pieces of domestic mail	Billions	63.1	71.3	84.0	88.3	88.8	91.3	2.9	1.0	1.7
	Per capita	Number	352	369	411	415	414	423	1.6	.2	1.0
970	Telephone systems, operating revenues	Bil. dol.	8.4	11.8	18.2	31.3	35.6	(na)	8.0	11.5	13.7
	Net income	Bil. dol.	1.3	1.9	2.3	3.6	4.3	(na)	5.9	9.4	19.4
969	Bell system, operating revenues	Bil. dol.	8.1	11.3	17.4	29.6	33.5	37.3	7.9	11.2	12.2
	Net income	Bil. dol.	1.3	1.9	2.3	3.3	4.0	4.7	6.1	7.4	20.1
972	Households with telephones	Percent	79	85	91	95	95	96	(ns)	(ns)	(ns)
977	Commercial broadcast stations, total	Number	4,218	4,867	5,584	6,228	6,339	(na)	2.9	2.2	1.8
	TV stations	Number	530	588	686	693	701	(na)	2.6	.2	1.2
977	Commercial broadcast revenues, total	Bil. dol.	1.9	2.8	3.9	5.8	7.2	(na)	7.8	8.1	24.0
	TV revenues	Bil dol.	1.3	2.0	2.8	4.1	5.2	(na)	8.3	7.8	27.0
987	Households with TV sets	Percent	87	93	95	97	97	97	(ns)	(ns)	(ns)
991	Daily newspapers	Number	1,763	1,751	1,748	1,756	1,762	1,753	-.1	.1	-.1
	Net paid circulation	Millions	58.9	60.4	62.1	60.7	61.0	61.5	.5	-.5	.7
	ENERGY AND SCIENCE										
1000	Horsepower of all prime movers	Billions	11	15	20	25	26	26	6.4	4.2	2.7
1001	Production of energy (Btu)	Quadril.	41.8	49.6	62.6	60.2	60.0	60.2	4.1	-.8	(z)
	Crude petroleum [37]	Percent	36	33	33	30	29	29	(ns)	(ns)	(ns)
	Natural gas [38]	Percent	34	36	39	37	36	36	(ns)	(ns)	(ns)
1004	Consumption of energy (Btu)	Quadril.	44.5	53.3	67.1	70.6	74.4	75.8	4.2	1.0	3.6
	Per capita (Btu)	Millions	247	276	329	331	346	351	2.9	.1	3.0
1001	By source: Coal	Percent	23	22	19	18	19	19	(ns)	(ns)	(ns)
	Natural gas [37]	Percent	29	30	33	28	27	26	(ns)	(ns)	(ns)
	Crude petroleum [38]	Percent	45	44	44	46	47	49	(ns)	(ns)	(ns)
1014	Industrial and miscellaneous	Percent	33	32	30	26	26	25	(ns)	(ns)	(ns)
1014	Residential and commercial	Percent	23	22	21	20	20	20	(ns)	(ns)	(ns)
1010	Crude oil imports	Mil. bbl.	372	452	483	1,498	1,935	2,397	2.7	25.4	26.5
1010	Petroleum products imports	Mil. bbl.	293	449	765	712	741	794	10.1	-1.4	5.8
1010	Petroleum products exports	Mil. bbl.	71	67	90	74	79	70	2.4	-3.8	-2.7
1018	Electric energy production (kWh)	Billions	842	1,158	1,636	2,003	2,124	2,211	6.9	4.1	5.1
	Installed capacity	Mil. kW	186	255	361	527	550	576	6.9	7.9	4.6
	Per kW of installed capacity	kWh	4,529	4,548	4,438	3,801	3,862	3,839	-.2	-3.1	.5
1023	Electric utilities operating revenues	Bil. dol.	10	13	20	45	51	(na)	6.9	17.6	13.4
	Net income	Bil. dol.	1.8	2.6	3.4	6.1	7.2	(na)	6.7	12.5	17.4
1028	Gas utility and pipeline industry revenues	Bil. dol.	8.7	11.5	16.4	30.6	37.6	46.3	6.5	13.3	23.1
	Net income	Bil. dol.	.8	1.1	1.4	2.5	2.9	3.2	5.6	11.9	13.0
1033	Nuclear capacity, yearend (net mega W)	1,000	.4	.9	5.2	38.6	41.1	47.0	29.5	49.6	10.4
	Percent of total electric utility capacity	Percent	.2	.4	1.9	7.7	8.1	9.0	(ns)	(ns)	(ns)
1039	Research & development (R&D) funds	Bil. dol.	13.5	20.0	25.9	35.2	38.6	42.7	6.7	6.3	10.2
	Basic research funds	Percent	8.9	12.7	13.6	12.9	12.5	12.3	(ns)	(ns)	(ns)
	Federal funds	Percent	64.6	64.9	56.6	51.6	50.6	51.0	(ns)	(ns)	(ns)
	Industry funds	Percent	32.7	32.2	39.7	44.2	45.1	44.8	(ns)	(ns)	(ns)
1038	Defense-related outlays [39]	Percent	52	33	33	27	26	25	(ns)	(ns)	(ns)
1038	Space-related outlays [39]	Percent	3	21	10	8	8	8	(ns)	(ns)	(ns)
1041	Federal obligations for R&D	Bil. dol.	7.6	14.6	15.3	19.0	20.8	24.5	7.3	4.4	13.4
1047	Scientists and engineers employed [40]	1,000	[41]426	495	547	536	550	566	[41]2.5	-.4	2.8
	Industry [42]	1,000	[41]312	348	376	364	372	385	[41]1.9	-.6	2.9
1061	Science doctorates conferred	1,000	6.3	10.5	17.7	18.4	17.9	17.4	11.0	.7	-2.7
1063	Federal space program outlays	Bil. dol.	.9	6.9	5.5	4.9	5.3	5.5	19.9	-2.2	6.4
	NASA outlays	Bil. dol.	.3	5.0	3.6	3.0	3.3	3.4	26.9	-3.7	6.9
	TRANSPORTATION										
1069	Intercity freight traffic, ton-miles	Billions	1,330	1,651	1,936	2,066	2,188	(na)	3.8	1.3	5.9
	Moved by railroad	Percent	44.7	43.7	39.8	36.7	36.5	(na)	(ns)	(ns)	(ns)
1070	Intercity passenger traffic, passenger-miles	Billions	784	920	1,185	1,352	1,441	(na)	4.2	2.7	6.6
	Moved by private automobile	Percent	90.1	88.9	86.6	86.1	85.8	(na)	(ns)	(ns)	(ns)
1074	Total highway mileage	Millions	3.5	3.7	3.7	3.8	3.9	(na)	.5	.6	.5
1083	State and local highway long-term debt outstanding	Bil. dol.	13.2	15.3	19.1	23.8	24.6	25.1	3.8	4.5	2.6

See notes on p. xxiv.

Refer- ence table	Subject	Unit of measure	1960	1965	1970	1975	1976	1977	1960 -70	1970 -75	1975 -77[1]
									Average annual percent change		

TRANSPORTATION – Con.

Ref.	Subject	Unit	1960	1965	1970	1975	1976	1977	1960-70	1970-75	1975-77
1085	Motor vehicle travel, vehicle–miles	Billions	719	888	1,121	1,330	1,409	(na)	4.5	3.5	6.0
1092	Motor vehicle registrations	Millions	74	90	108	133	139	144	3.9	4.2	4.0
1093	New passenger car retail sales	Millions	6.6	9.3	8.4	8.6	10.1	11.2	2.4	.6	13.8
	Domestic	Millions	6.1	8.8	7.1	7.1	8.6	9.1	1.5	-.2	13.6
	Imports[43]	Millions	.5	.6	1.3	1.6	1.5	2.1	9.9	4.3	14.4
	Percent of total	Percent	8	6	15	18	15	19	(ns)	(ns)	(ns)
1101	Motor fuel consumption	Bil. gal.	58	71	92	109	116	120	4.8	3.4	4.9
1088	Deaths from motor vehicle accidents	1,000	38	49	55	46	47	(na)	3.7	-3.4	2.7
1109	Revenue passengers carried, local transit	Billions	7.5	6.8	5.9	5.6	5.7	5.7	-2.4	-1.0	.7
1068	Operating revenues: Railroads	Bil. dol.	10.0	10.7	12.5	17.4	19.9	(na)	2.3	6.8	14.4
	Motor carriers of property	Bil. dol.	7.2	10.1	14.6	22.0	26.0	(na)	7.3	8.6	18.2
1121	R.R. revenue freight net ton-mi. (Class I)	Billions	572	698	763	765	795	868	2.9	.1	6.5
1120	R.R. revenue passenger-miles (Class I)	Billions	21.3	17.4	10.8	9.9	10.6	10.3	-6.6	-1.7	2.0
1130	Scheduled air carriers, domestic revenue	Bil. dol.	2.1	3.6	7.1	11.9	13.8	15.7	12.9	10.8	14.7
1134	Revenue passengers carried	Millions	56	92	153	189	206	222	10.6	4.3	8.4
1134	Express and freight ton-miles flown	Billions	.4	.9	2.0	2.3	2.5	2.6	17.7	3.5	6.5
1145	Waterborne commerce, total cargo, sh. tons	Billions	1.1	1.3	1.5	1.7	1.8	(na)	3.4	2.0	8.3
	Domestic, short tons	Billions	.8	.8	1.0	.9	1.0	(na)	2.3	-.1	3.5

AGRICULTURE, FORESTRY, FISHERIES

Ref.	Subject	Unit	1960	1965	1970	1975	1976	1977	1960-70	1970-75	1975-77
1164	Farm population	Millions	15.6	12.4	9.7	8.9	8.3	7.8	-4.7	-1.8	-6.2
1166	Farms	Millions	4.0	3.4	2.9	2.8	2.7	2.7	-2.9	-1.3	-1.1
	Average land per farm	Acres	297	340	374	391	394	397	2.3	.9	.8
1164	Farm employment[44]	Millions	7.1	5.6	4.5	4.3	4.4	4.2	-4.4	-.8	-2.2
1191	Agricultural assets, total	Bil. dol.	203	238	315	516	579	655	4.5	4.5	12.7
1193	Farm income, gross	Bil. dol.	38	46	59	97	104	108	4.3	10.6	5.6
	Cash marketing receipts	Percent	89.0	86.5	86.3	91.0	90.8	88.9	(ns)	(ns)	(ns)
	Government payments	Percent	1.8	5.4	6.3	.8	.7	1.7	(ns)	(ns)	(ns)
1193	Average income per farm	$1,000	2.9	3.8	4.8	8.8	6.8	7.6	5.1	13.0	-7.4
1194	Personal income, farm population	Bil. dol.	18.4	22.6	27.5	44.5	41.2	43.0	4.1	10.2	-1.8
	Per capita	Dollars	1,174	1,828	2,829	5,026	4,994	5,503	9.2	12.2	4.6
1192	Value of farm products: Current dollars	Bil. dol.	38	44	55	99	101	104	3.7	12.6	2.5
	Constant (1972) dollars	Bil. dol.	52	57	63	66	67	70	1.9	.9	2.8
1214	Farm output index	1967=100	91	98	101	114	117	121	1.1	2.5	3.0
1213	Farm output per man-hour, index	1967=100	65	89	112	144	152	149	5.6	5.2	1.7
	Livestock and products		62	86	121	160	175	180	6.9	5.8	6.1
	Crops		66	90	110	130	133	131	5.2	3.4	.4
1216	Agricultural exports	Bil. dol.	4.8	6.2	7.3	21.9	23.0	23.7	4.2	24.7	4.0
	Percent of all exports	Percent	24	23	17	21	20	20	(ns)	(ns)	(ns)
1222	Harvested crops, total	Mil. acres	324	298	293	337	338	342	-1.0	2.8	.7
1221	Wheat production	Mil. bu.	1,355	1,316	1,352	2,122	2,142	2,026	(|-z)	9.4	-2.3
1221	Corn for grain, production	Mil. bu.	3,907	4,103	4,152	5,829	6,266	6,357	.6	7.0	4.4
1221	Wheat exports	Mil. bu.	653	852	741	1,173	950	1,100	1.3	9.6	-3.2
1221	Corn for grain, exports	Mil. bu.	292	687	517	1,711	1,684	1,750	5.9	27.0	1.1
1271	Lumber production, board feet	Billions	33	37	35	30	33	(na)	.5	-3.1	12.7
1274	Pulpwood production, total, cords	Millions	40	52	71	69	77	77	5.8	-.5	5.8
1275	Woodpulp production, total, short tons	Millions	25	34	44	43	49	50	5.6	-.2	7.5
1283	Fisheries, catch	Bil. lb.	4.9	4.8	4.9	4.8	5.4	5.2	.1	-.3	3.6
	Value	Mil. dol.	354	446	613	971	1,353	1,515	5.6	9.6	24.9
1299	Canned fishery products, value	Mil. dol.	388	495	742	1,071	1,430	1,558	6.7	7.6	20.6
1296	Imports of fishery products, value	Mil. dol.	363	601	1,037	1,637	2,332	2,621	11.1	9.6	26.5

· MINERAL PRODUCTION

Ref.	Subject	Unit	1960	1965	1970	1975	1976	1977	1960-70	1970-75	1975-77
1302	Mineral production:										
	Current dollars	Bil. dol.	18	22	30	62	69	(na)	5.2	15.9	11.1
	Fuels	Bil. dol.	12	14	20	48	53	(na)	5.3	18.7	10.3
	Nonmetals	Bil. dol.	4	5	6	10	11	(na)	3.9	10.8	11.6
	Metals	Bil. dol.	2	3	4	5	6	(na)	6.9	5.9	17.3
	Constant (1967) dollars	Bil. dol.	19	22	27	25	25	(na)	3.6	-1.6	.8
1302	Mineral imports	Bil. dol.	3	3	3	23	31	(na)	.3	46.2	34.4
1302	Mineral exports	Bil. dol.	2	1	2	5	4	(na)	-1.7	24.1	-8.5

See notes on p. xxiv.

Refer- ence table	Subject	Unit of measure	1960	1965	1970	1975	1976	1977	Average annual percent change		
									1960 –70	1970 –75	1975 –77[1]
	MINERAL PRODUCTION – Con.										
1304	Mining production, index	1967=	80	93	112	113	114	118	3.4	.2	2.2
	Oil and gas extraction	100	78	91	112	113	112	118	3.7	.2	2.2
1312	U.S. direct investment position abroad –										
	In mining and petroleum	Bil. dol.	14	19	25	33	36	38	6.2	5.2	8.1
	In petroleum	Bil. dol.	11	15	20	26	28	31	6.3	5.6	9.0
1318	Coal production, short tons	Millions	434	527	613	655	685	678	3.5	1.3	1.7
	Value	Bil. dol.	2.1	2.4	3.9	12.7	13.4	14.3	6.3	26.7	6.4
	Average employment	1,000	169	134	140	190	202	215	–1.9	6.3	6.4
1322	Crude petroleum production, domestic ..	Bil. bbl.	2.6	2.8	3.5	3.1	3.0	3.0	3.2	–2.8	–1.2
	Value (at wells)	Bil. dol.	7.4	8.2	11.2	23.1	24.2	25.6	4.2	15.7	5.2
1322	Crude petroleum, proved reserves	Bil. bbl.	31.6	31.4	39.0	32.7	30.9	29.5	2.1	–3.5	–5.0
1322	Refined petroleum products at refineries .	Bil. bbl.	3.0	3.3	4.0	4.5	4.9	5.3	3.0	2.7	8.5
1322	Crude petroleum production, world	Bil. bbl.	7.7	11.1	16.7	19.5	20.9	21.8	8.1	3.1	5.9
1328	Natural gas, marketed production, cu. ft. .	Trillions	13	16	22	20	20	20	5.6	–1.7	–.3
	Value	Bil. dol.	1.8	2.5	3.7	8.9	11.6	15.0	7.7	19.0	29.5
1328	Natural gas, proved reserves, cu. ft	Trillions	264	286	291	228	216	209	1.0	–4.8	–4.3
1339	Iron ore production, long tons	Millions	89	87	90	79	80	55	.1	–2.6	–16.5
	Value of shipments	Mil. dol.	724	801	942	1,621	1,871	1,411	2.7	11.5	–6.7
1342	Copper ore production, short tons	Millions	135	173	258	263	284	(na)	6.7	.4	8.0
	CONSTRUCTION AND HOUSING										
1353	Value of new construction	Bil. dol.	55	74	95	135	149	173	5.7	7.2	13.3
	Private	Bil. dol.	39	52	67	94	110	135	5.6	7.0	19.9
	Residential (including farm)	Bil. dol.	23	28	32	46	61	81	3.3	7.8	32.0
	Public	Bil. dol.	16	22	28	41	38	38	5.9	7.8	–3.8
1354	Value of new construction, 1972 dollars .	Bil. dol.	(na)	110	107	97	103	110	[9]–.5	–1.9	6.5
1357	Composite construction cost index		83	93	122	189	198	216	3.9	9.2	6.9
1357	New one-family homes, price index	1967=	(na)	93	117	174	191	216	[9]4.7	8.2	11.2
1358	Wholesale prices of construction materials .	100	96	96	113	174	188	205	1.7	9.2	8.5
1357	Union hourly wages, building trades ...		75	91	129	188	201	212	5.5	7.9	6.2
1373	Year-round housing units	Millions	56.6	(na)	67.7	77.8	79.3	(na)	1.8	2.8	2.0
	Occupied units	Millions	53.0	(na)	63.4	72.5	74.0	(na)	1.8	2.7	2.0
	Owner-occupied	Millions	32.8	(na)	39.9	46.9	47.9	(na)	2.0	3.3	2.2
	Renter-occupied	Millions	20.2	(na)	23.6	25.7	26.1	(na)	1.5	1.7	1.7
	Vacant units	Millions	3.6	(na)	4.3	5.0	5.3	(na)	1.8	3.4	5.6
1375	Units lacking some or all plumbing –										
	Owner-occupied units	Percent	10.6	(na)	4.5	1.8	1.5	(na)	(ns)	(ns)	(ns)
	Renter-occupied units	Percent	21.3	(na)	8.3	4.8	4.6	(na)	(ns)	(ns)	(ns)
1367	New housing units started	Millions	1.3	1.5	1.5	1.2	1.5	2.0	1.3	–4.4	30.4
	Structures with two or more units ...	Percent	22	36	45	24	25	27	(ns)	(ns)	(ns)
	New one-family houses sold:										
1368	Price index, 1972 = 100	Index	(na)	71	89	131	142	159	[9]4.6	8.0	10.3
1393	Median sales price	$1,000	(na)	20.0	23.4	39.3	44.2	48.8	[9]3.2	10.9	11.4
1389	Rental vacancy rate	Percent	8.1	8.3	5.3	6.0	5.6	5.2	(ns)	(ns)	(ns)
1387	Low-rent occupied public housing units .	1,000	478	605	894	1,180	1,182	1,188	6.5	5.7	.3
	For the elderly	1,000	1	36	143	288	293	295	62.7	15.0	1.2
1397	First mortgage loans, conventional, April:										
	New homes[45] contract interest rate ..	Percent	(na)	5.7	8.2	8.7	8.7	8.7	(ns)	(ns)	(ns)
	Existing homes[45] contract interest rate .	Percent	(na)	5.9	8.2	8.9	8.9	8.7	(ns)	(ns)	(ns)
	MANUFACTURES										
1403	Industrial production, index	1967=	66	90	108	118	130	137	5.1	1.8	7.8
	Manufacturing	100	65	90	106	116	130	137	5.0	1.8	8.7
1405	Manufacturing: Relation of output to capacity	Percent	80	90	79	74	80	82	(ns)	(ns)	(ns)
1401	Value added by manufacture	Bil. dol.	164	225	300	442	511	(na)	6.2	8.1	15.6
1401	Employment in manufactures, annual avg. .	Millions	17	18	19	18	19	(na)	1.1	–1.1	5.6
1408	Manufacturers' shipments	Bil. dol.	371	492	634	1,039	1,186	1,335	5.5	10.4	13.3
1408	Manufacturers' inventories	Bil. dol.	54	68	101	158	170	180	6.6	9.3	6.7
1408	Manufacturers' new orders	Bil. dol.	363	505	625	1,021	1,190	1,354	5.6	10.3	15.2
1414	Capital expenditures	Bil. dol.	10	17	22	37	41	(na)	8.2	11.0	8.8
1446	Raw steel production, short tons	Millions	99	131	132	117	128	125	2.9	–2.4	3.6
1443	Steel mill products, net shipments, short tons	Millions	71	93	91	80	89	91	2.5	–2.5	6.7

Recent Trends

Refer-ence table	Subject	Unit of measure	1960	1965	1970	1975	1976	1977	Average annual percent change 1960 –70	1970 –75	1975 –77[1]
DOMESTIC TRADE AND SERVICES											
1461	Retail store sales, all stores	Bil. dol.	220	284	371	580	643	708	5.4	9.4	10.5
	Constant (1972) dollars	Bil. dol.	287	354	400	450	479	500	3.4	2.4	5.5
	Per capita sales	Dollars	1,232	1,483	1,840	2,746	3,016	3,299	4.1	8.3	9.6
1464	Department store sales	Bil. dol.	[46]14	[46]23	38	57	63	72	10.7	8.4	11.7
932	Retail trade inventories	Bil. dol.	27	34·	44	71	78	87	5.0	10.0	10.7
	Inventory-sales ratio	Ratio	1.5	1.4	1.4	1.4	1.4	1.4	(ns)	(ns)	(ns)
1474	Merchant wholesaler sales	Bil. dol.	140	187	287	536	581	642	7.5	13.3	9.5
1478	Merchant wholesaler inventories	Bil. dol.	[46]14	[46]18	33	55	61	68	8.8	10.9	11.1
1478	Inventory-sales ratio [47]	Percent	[46]122	[46]113	133	121	120	119	(ns)	(ns)	(ns)
1487	Advertising expenditures	Bil. dol.	12	15	20	28	34	38	5.0	7.6	16.2
	National	Percent	61	61	58	55	55	55	(ns)	(ns)	(ns)
	Local	Percent	39	39	42	45	45	45	(ns)	(ns)	(ns)
FOREIGN COMMERCE AND AID											
1496	Balance on current account	Bil. dol.	2.8	5.4	2.4	18.4	4.3	-15.2	(ns)	(ns)	(ns)
1497	Exports of goods and services	Bil. dol.	29	41	66	156	171	183	8.6	18.8	8.5
1497	Imports of goods and services	Bil. dol.	-24	-33	-60	-133	-162	-194	9.7	17.2	20.9
1501	U.S. net international investment position	Bil. dol.	45	62	59	75	83	(na)	(ns)	(ns)	(ns)
	U.S. assets and investments abroad	Bil. dol.	86	120	166	296	347	(na)	6.8	12.3	17.5
	Foreign assets and investments in U.S	Bil. dol.	41	59	107	221	265	(na)	10.1	15.7	19.8
1499	U.S. reserve assets	Bil. dol.	19.4	15.5	14.5	16.2	18.7	19.3	-2.9	2.3	9.1
	Gold stock, U.S	Bil. dol.	17.8	13.8	11.1	11.6	11.6	11.7	-4.6	.9	.5
1506	U.S. foreign grants and credits	Bil. dol.	4.6	5.1	5.9	8.7	7.9	6.7	2.5	8.0	-12.0
1507	Economic and military aid	Bil. dol.	5.2	5.7	6.8	7.2	6.6	7.9	2.7	1.3	4.8
	Economic aid	Bil. dol.	3.4	2.0	3.7	4.9	3.9	5.6	.9	6.0	6.7
1516	Exports of merchandise	Bil. dol.	20.6	27.5	43.2	107.6	115.0	120.2	7.7	20.0	5.7
	To developed countries	Percent	64.4	66.7	69.1	60.2	61.4	61.4	(ns)	(ns)	(ns)
	To developing countries	Percent	34.7	32.8	30.1	36.4	35.1	36.0	(ns)	(ns)	(ns)
1516	General imports of merchandise	Bil. dol.	14.7	21.4	40.0	96.9	120.7	146.8	10.6	19.4	23.1
	From developed countries	Percent	58.7	65.8	73.2	58.5	55.5	53.3	(ns)	(ns)	(ns)
	From developing countries	Percent	40.7	33.4	26.1	40.6	43.6	46.0	(ns)	(ns)	(ns)
1511	Merchandise trade balance	Bil. dol.	5.0	5.3	2.7	10.2	-5.9	-26.7	(ns)	(ns)	(ns)

Note: Average annual percent changes were computed using the compound interest rate formula. Whenever possible, absolute values or values with less rounding than appear here were used in the computations.

The reference table cited for each item generally provides more complete information and notations concerning the item. In a number of instances, figures represent revisions and supersede figures shown elsewhere in this volume.

Symbols: — Represents zero or rounds to zero.   na Not available.   ns Percent change not relevant or significant.
x Not applicable.   z Less than .05 percent or half the unit of measure shown.
[1]Where na occurs in 1977 column, percent change calculated refers to 1975-1976 period.
[2]These data are as of different dates in the years shown. See reference tables for further information.
[3]Data not strictly comparable year to year because of changes in definition.
[4]Based on 277 standard metropolitan statistical areas (SMSA's) as defined in 1977.
[5]Excludes Armed Forces living in barracks in U.S.   [6]For 1960, 14 years old and over.
[7]Will not add to total families; estimates derived using different controls.   [8]Excludes Federal practitioners.   [9]1965-1970.
[10]Average daily census per 100 beds.   [11]Average patient stay of 30 days or less.
[12]1971 data. Percent changes are calculated for 1965-1971 and 1971-1975.   [13]Peak month for each year.
[14]In average daily attendance in public day schools.   [15]1966 data.
[16]1974 data. Percent changes are calculated for 1970-1974 and 1974-1976.   [17]Beginning 1970, includes nursery school.
[18]1965 not strictly comparable with other years; decline in water use in 1975 reflects the increasing use of recycled water.
[19]Particles of smoke, dust, fumes, droplets of viscous liquid, etc.
[20]Comprises employment taxes and contributions, unemployment insurance taxes, and other contributions.
[21]Excludes utilities, insurance trusts, and government liquor stores.   [22]Old-age, survivors, disability, and health insurance.
[23]Excludes care covered by social welfare programs; e.g. medical assistance under public aid, Medicare under social insurance, etc.
[24]1967 data. Percent change is calculated for 1967-1970.
[25]Beginning 1975, refers to federally financed Supplemental Security Income.
[26]Includes Military Assistance Service Funded Program and excess defense articles delivered.   [27]Includes Armed Forces.
[28]Includes deceased veterans whose dependents receive pensions and compensation benefits.   [29]Output per paid hour.
[30]For nonfarm workers as prescribed by Federal legislation. Represents rate in effect on Jan. 1 of year stated.
[31]Beginning 1975, not strictly comparable with earlier years due to revised procedures.
[32]1966 data. Percent change is calculated for 1966-1970.
[33]Includes home purchase, mortgage, interest, taxes, insurance, maintenance, and repairs.   [34]1961 data.
[35]Beginning 1975, refers to earned income.   [36]Excludes benefit payments resulting from accidents.
[37]Excludes natural gas liquids.   [38]Includes natural gas liquids.   [39]Federally funded.
[40]Full-time equivalent employees; excludes State and local government agencies.
[41]1961 data. Percent change is calculated for 1961-1970.
[42]Excludes social scientists.   [43]Excludes domestic models produced in Canada.
[44]Includes farm operators doing one or more hours of farmwork and unpaid family members doing 15 or more hours of farmwork in survey week.   [45]Single-family.
[46]Not strictly comparable with later years.   [47]Based on December-adjusted sales and yearend inventory estimates.

Section 1

Population

This section presents statistics on the growth, distribution, and characteristics of the U.S. population. The principal source of these data is the Bureau of the Census, which conducts a decennial census of population, a monthly population survey, a program of population estimates and projections, and a number of other periodic surveys relating to population characteristics. For a list of publications, see the Guide to Sources in Appendix IV.

Decennial censuses.—The U.S. Constitution provides for a census of the population every 10 years, primarily to establish a basis for apportionment of Members of the House of Representatives among the States. For over a century after the first census in 1790, the census organization was a temporary one, created only for each decennial census. In 1902, the Bureau of the Census was established as a permanent Federal agency, responsible for enumerating the population and also for compiling statistics on other subjects.

The census of population is a complete count. That is, an attempt is made to account for every person, for each person's residence, and for other characteristics (sex, age, family relationships, etc.). Since the 1940 census, however, some data have been obtained from representative samples of the population rather than from a complete count, as follows: 5 percent in 1940, 20 percent in 1950, 25 percent in 1960, and 5, 15, and 20 percent in 1970. Exact agreement is not to be expected among the various samples, nor between them and the complete census count. Sample data may be used with confidence where large numbers are involved and assumed to indicate patterns, trends, and relationships where small numbers are involved. For tables of sampling errors for sampled data, see *Census of Population: 1970*, PC(1)-C, *General Social and Economic Characteristics*, Appendix C.

Estimates based on evaluation studies of the 1970 census results indicate a total net underenumeration of about 5.3 million persons, compared with 5.1 million in 1960. Among the persons who were not counted in 1970, about 3.4 million were White and about 1.9 million were Black. The overall rate of net underenumeration in 1970 was about 2.5 percent, compared with 2.7 percent in 1960 and 3.3 percent in 1950. Data from the 1950, 1960, and 1970 censuses have not been adjusted for the estimated underenumeration. For details, see *Estimates of Coverage of Population by Sex, Race, and Age: Demographic Analysis*, PHC(E)-4, February 1974.

In an attempt to estimate the extent of underenumeration in the 1970 census for areas within the United States, such as States, the Bureau has developed several alternate sets of estimates for each State. These estimates suggest variations in the extent of coverage by a number of factors (e.g. region, sex, race). While the State data presented here are not adjusted for underenumeration, detail concerning the Bureau's estimates may be found in *Developmental Estimates of the Coverage of the Population of the United States in the 1970 Census: Demographic Analysis*, series P-23, No. 65.

Current Population Survey (CPS).—This is a monthly nationwide survey of a scientifically selected sample representing, in most cases, the noninstitutional civilian population 14 years old and over. The sample is drawn from about 600 areas comprising approximately 1,100 counties and independent cities with coverage in every State and the District of Columbia and is subject to sampling error. At the present time (1978), about 5,000 housing units or other living quarters are designated for the sample at any time, of which about 55,000 are occupied by households eligible for interview; of these, in turn, about 4 to 6 percent are, for various reasons, unavailable for interview.

1

While the primary purpose of CPS is to obtain monthly statistics on the labor force, it also serves as a vehicle for inquiries on other subjects. Using CPS data, the Bureau issues a series of publications under the general title of *Current Population Reports*, which cover population characteristics (series P–20), consumer·income (series P–60), special studies (series P–23), and other topics.

Population estimates and projections.—National population estimates are derived by use of decennial census data as benchmarks and of data available from various agencies as follows: Births and deaths (National Center for Health Statistics); immigrants (Immigration and Naturalization Service); Armed Forces (Department of Defense); net movement between Puerto Rico and the U.S. mainland (Puerto Rico Planning Board); and Federal employees abroad (Civil Service Commission and Department of Defense). State estimates are based on similar data and also on a variety of data series, including school statistics from State departments of education and parochial school systems.

National population projections indicate the approximate future level and characteristics of the population under given assumptions as to future fertility, mortality, and net immigration. The method used to develop the projections involves preparation of projections of each of the components of population change—births, deaths, and net immigration—and the combination of these with July 1 estimates of the current population. Projections for States and metropolitan areas incorporate further assumptions about the redistribution of population as a consequence of migration.

Population estimates and projections are published in the P–25 series of *Current Population Reports*. These estimates and projections are generally consistent with official decennial census figures and do not reflect the amount of estimated census underenumeration. For details on methodology, see the sources cited below the individual tables.

Standard Metropolitan Statistical Areas (SMSA) and Standard Consolidated Statistical Areas (SCSA).—The general concept of an SMSA is one of an integrated economic and social unit with a large population nucleus; SCSA's are large metropolitan agglomerations consisting of groups of adjacent SMSA's. SMSA's and SCSA's were defined by the Office of Management and Budget (OMB) for several years. However, this function was transferred to the Department of Commerce in October 1977. According to the criteria, the entire territory of the United States is classified as *metropolitan* (inside SMSA's) or *nonmetropolitan* (outside SMSA's). SMSA's and SCSA's are defined in terms of entire counties except in New England, where the definitions are in terms of cities and towns. To summarize data for New England that are available only by counties, New England County Metropolitan Areas (NECMA's) have been developed as a convenience for data users. Periodically, changes in SMSA definitions are made. New SMSA's may be created and the boundaries of others may change. As a result, data for SMSA's over time may not be comparable. For descriptive details, tables showing changes in SMSA definitions, and a listing of area titles and components of each SMSA, SCSA, and NECMA see Appendix II.

Urban and rural areas.—According to the 1970 census definition, the urban population comprises all persons in (a) places of 2,500 inhabitants or more incorporated as·cities, villages, boroughs (except Alaska), and towns (except in New England, New York, and Wisconsin), but excludes persons living in the rural portions of "extended cities" (places with relatively low population density in one or more large parts of their area), (b) unincorporated places of 2,500 inhabitants or more; and (c) other territory, incorporated or unincorporated, included in urbanized areas. An urbanized area consists of a central city, or twin cities, with a total of 50,000 inhabitants or more, together with contiguous closely settled territory (urban fringe).

In censuses prior to 1950, the urban population comprised all persons living in incorporated places of 2,500 inhabitants or more, and certain areas (usually minor civil divisions) classified as urban under special rules relating to population size and density. The previous urban definition was replaced in 1950 by the current definition except for minor modifications and the introduction of the "extended cities" concept in 1970. In all definitions, the population not classified as urban constitutes the rural population.

Residence.—In determining residence, the Bureau of the Census counts each person as an inhabitant of a usual place of residence (i.e. the place where one usually eats and sleeps). While this place is not necessarily a person's legal residence or voting residence, the use of these different bases of classification should produce the same results in the vast majority of cases.

Race.—For census purposes, the population is divided into three major groups on the basis of race: White, Black or Negro, and other. For the 1960 and 1970 censuses, data were obtained on race principally through self-enumeration; thus, the data represent essentially self-classification by people according to the race with which they identify themselves. Persons of Mexican or Puerto Rican birth or ancestry who did not identify themselves as of a race other than White were classified as White. In 1970, the father's race was used for persons of mixed parentage who were in doubt as to their classification. In 1960, persons who reported mixed parentage of White and any other race were classified according to the other race; mixtures of races other than White were classified according to the father's race.

In the Current Population Survey and other household sample surveys in which data are obtained through personal interview, race is determined by interviewer observation except for persons unrelated to the household head, in which case race is specifically asked for. Race of the father is reported for persons of mixed parentage where such mixture is given by the respondent.

Ethnic origin.—"Ethnic origin" is determined on the basis of a question in the Current Population Survey asking for self-identification of the person's origin or descent and is, therefore, a report on what persons perceive their origin to be. The answers to this question produce results somewhat different from those based on inferences from such characteristics as place of birth, country of origin, language spoken in the home, or surname. Persons of Spanish origin may be of any race.

Nativity.—The native population consists of all persons born in the U.S., the Commonwealth of Puerto Rico, or an outlying area of the U.S. It also includes persons born at sea or in a foreign country who have at least one parent born in the U.S. All others are classified as "foreign born."

Living arrangement.—Living arrangements may be in households or in group quarters. A "household" comprises all persons who occupy a "housing unit," that is, a house, an apartment or other group of rooms, or a room that constitutes "separate living quarters." A household includes the related family members and all the unrelated persons, if any, such as lodgers, foster children, wards, or employees who share the housing unit. A person living alone or a group of unrelated persons sharing the same housing unit as partners is also counted as a household. See text, section 28, Construction and Housing, for definition of "housing unit."

All persons not living in households are classified as living in *group quarters*. These individuals may be *institutionalized*, e.g. under care or custody in jails, correctional centers, hospitals, or rest homes; or they may be residents in college dormitories, military barracks, rooming houses, etc. (see table 72).

Mobility status.—The U.S. population is classified according to mobility status on the basis of a comparison between the place of residence of each individual at the time of the survey or census and the place of residence at a specified earlier date. *Nonmovers* are all persons who were living in the same housing unit at the end of the period as at the beginning of the period. *Movers* are all persons who were living in a different housing unit in the U.S. at the end of the period from that which they were living in at the beginning of the period. *Movers from abroad* include all persons, either citizens or aliens, whose place of residence was outside the U.S. at the beginning of the period, that is, in an outlying area under the jurisdiction of the U.S. or in a foreign country.

Family.—The term "family" refers to a group of two or more persons related by blood, marriage, or adoption and residing together in a household. A primary family consists of the head of a household and all other persons in the household related to the head. A secondary family comprises two or more persons such as guests, lodgers, or resident employees and their relatives, living in a household and related to each other but not to the household head.

Subfamily.—A "subfamily" consists of a married couple and their children, if any, or one parent with one or more unmarried children under 18 years old, living in a household and related to the head of the household (husband or wife). Members of a subfamily are also members the of primary family with whom they live. The number of subfamilies, therefore, is not included in the number of families.

Married couple.—A "married couple" is defined as a husband and wife living together in the same household, with or without children and other relatives.

Unrelated individuals.—"Unrelated individuals" refers to persons (other than inmates of institutions) who are not living with any relatives. A primary individual is a household head living alone or with nonrelatives only. A secondary individual in a household is a person such as a guest, lodger, or resident employee who is not related to any other persons in the household. Persons in group quarters, except inmates of institutions, are classified as secondary individuals.

Average annual change.—In this section, average annual percent change is computed by the exponential or continuous-compounding method; see p. xii.

Statistical reliability.—For a discussion of statistical collection and estimation, sampling procedures, and measures of statistical reliability applicable to Census Bureau data, see Appendix III.

Historical statistics.—Tabular headnotes provide cross-references, where applicable, to *Historical Statistics of the United States, Colonial Times to 1970*. See Appendix I.

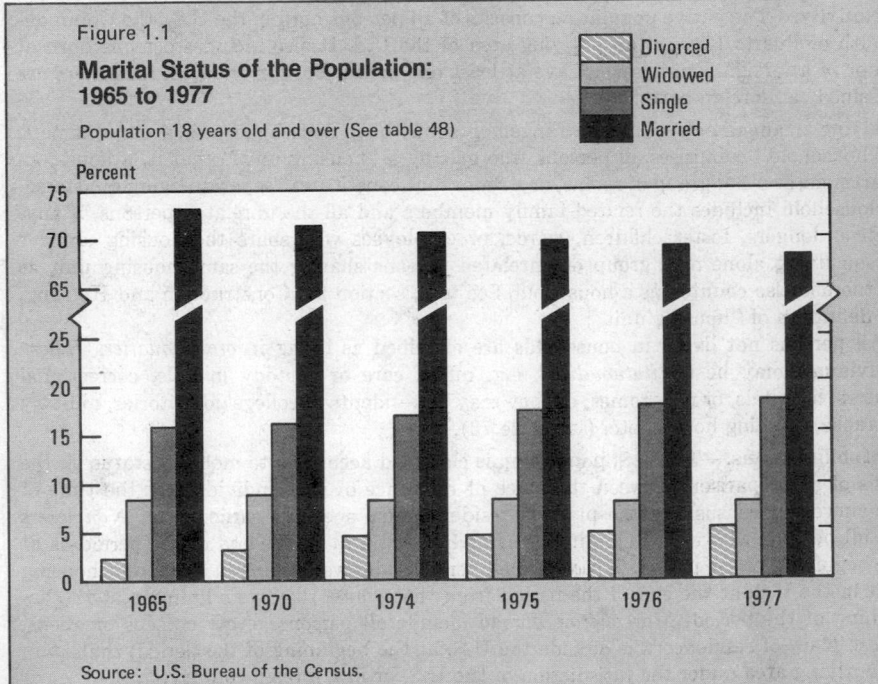

Figure 1.1

Marital Status of the Population: 1965 to 1977

Population 18 years old and over (See table 48)

Divorced
Widowed
Single
Married

Source: U.S. Bureau of the Census.

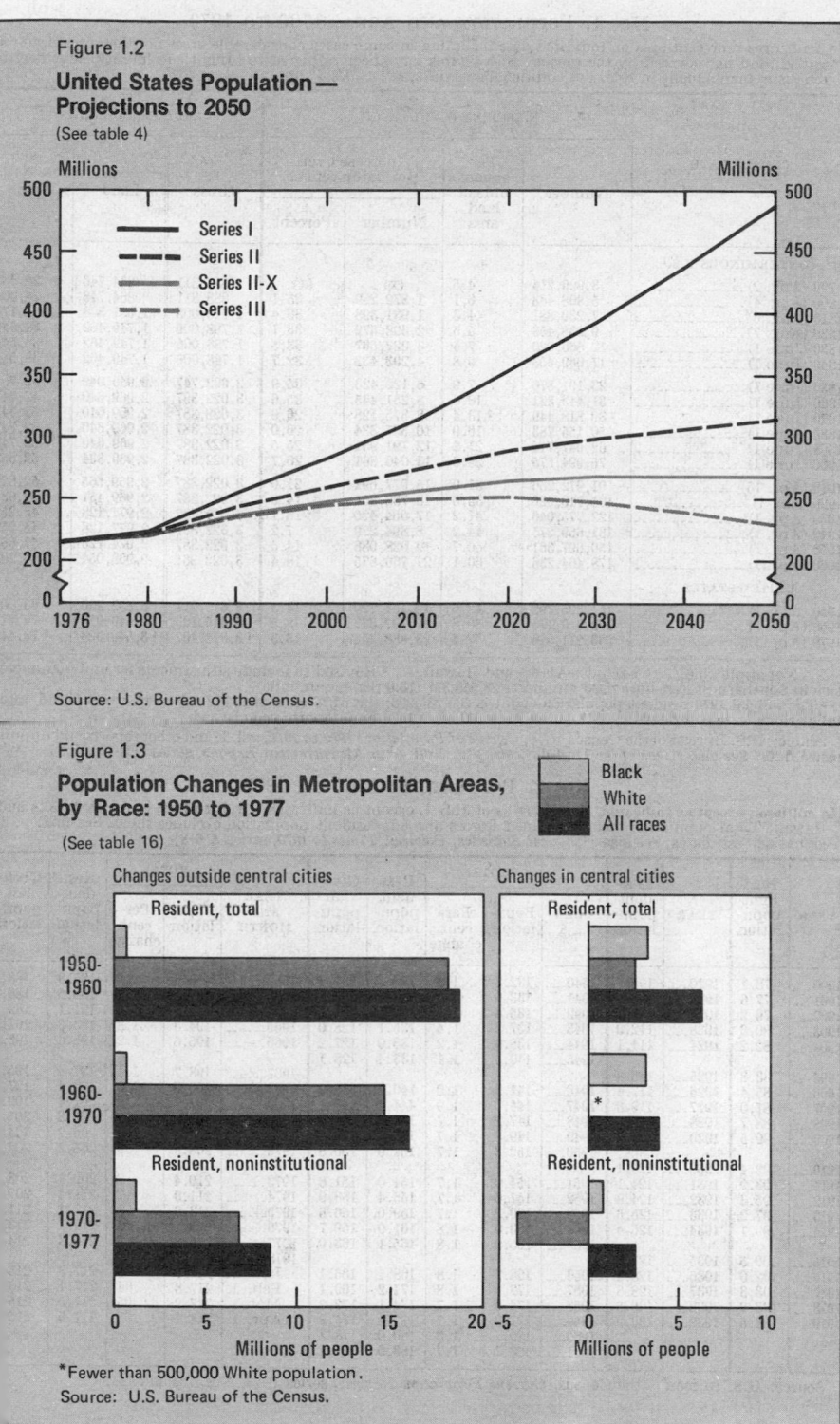

Figure 1.2

**United States Population—
Projections to 2050**

(See table 4)

Millions

Series I
Series II
Series II-X
Series III

Source: U.S. Bureau of the Census.

Figure 1.3

**Population Changes in Metropolitan Areas,
by Race: 1950 to 1977**

(See table 16)

Black
White
All races

Changes outside central cities

Resident, total

1950-1960

1960-1970

Resident, noninstitutional

1970-1977

Millions of people

Changes in central cities

Resident, total

Resident, noninstitutional

Millions of people

*Fewer than 500,000 White population.

Source: U.S. Bureau of the Census.

No. 1. POPULATION AND AREA: 1790 TO 1970

[Area figures represent area on indicated date including in some cases considerable areas not then organized or settled, and not covered by the census. Area figures have been adjusted to bring them into agreement with remeasurements made in 1940. For additional area data, see tables 4 and 339]

CENSUS DATE	RESIDENT POPULATION		Increase over preceding census		AREA (square miles)		
	Number	Per square mile of land area	Number	Percent	Gross	Land	Water
CONTERMINOUS U.S.[1]							
1790 (Aug. 2)	3,929,214	4.5	(X)	(X)	888,811	864,746	24,065
1800 (Aug. 4)	5,308,483	6.1	1,379,269	35.1	888,811	864,746	24,065
1810 (Aug. 6)	7,239,881	4.3	1,931,398	36.4	1,716,003	1,681,828	34,175
1820 (Aug. 7)	9,638,453	5.5	2,398,572	33.1	1,788,006	1,749,462	38,544
1830 (June 1)	12,866,020	7.4	3,227,567	33.5	1,788,006	1,749,462	38,544
1840 (June 1)	17,069,453	9.8	4,203,433	32.7	1,788,006	1,749,462	38,544
1850 (June 1)	23,191,876	7.9	6,122,423	35.9	2,992,747	2,940,042	52,705
1860 (June 1)	31,443,321	10.6	8,251,445	35.6	3,022,387	2,969,640	52,747
1870 (June 1)	[2] 39,818,449	[2] 13.4	8,375,128	26.6	3,022,387	2,969,640	52,747
1880 (June 1)	50,155,783	16.9	10,337,334	26.0	3,022,387	2,969,640	52,747
1890 (June 1)	62,947,714	21.2	12,791,931	25.5	3,022,387	2,969,640	52,747
1900 (June 1)	75,994,575	25.6	13,046,861	20.7	3,022,387	2,969,834	52,553
1910 (Apr. 15)	91,972,266	31.0	15,977,691	21.0	3,022,387	2,969,565	52,822
1920 (Jan. 1)	105,710,620	35.6	13,738,354	14.9	3,022,387	2,969,451	52,936
1930 (Apr. 1)	122,775,046	41.2	17,064,426	16.1	3,022,387	2,977,128	45,259
1940 (Apr. 1)	131,669,275	44.2	8,894,229	7.2	3,022,387	2,977,128	45,259
1950 (Apr. 1)	150,697,361	50.7	19,028,086	14.5	3,022,387	2,974,726	47,661
1960 (Apr. 1)	178,464,236	60.1	27,766,875	18.4	3,022,261	2,968,054	54,207
UNITED STATES							
1950 (Apr. 1)	151,325,798	42.6	19,161,229	14.5	3,615,211	3,552,206	63,005
1960 (Apr. 1)	179,323,175	50.6	27,997,377	18.5	3,615,123	3,540,911	74,212
1970 (Apr. 1)	[3] 203,211,926	57.4	23,888,751	13.3	[4] 3,618,467	[4] 3,540,023	[4] 78,444

X Not applicable. [1] Excludes Alaska and Hawaii. [2] Revised to include adjustments for underenumeration in Southern States; unrevised number is 38,558,371 (13.0 per square mile). [3] The official 1970 resident population count is 203,235,298; the difference of 23,372 is due to errors found after tabulations were completed. [4] Figures corrected after 1970 final reports were issued.

Source: U.S. Bureau of the Census, *U.S. Census of Population: 1920 to 1970*, vol. I; and other reports and unpublished data. See also *Areas of the United States, 1940*, and *Area Measurement Reports*, series GE-20, No. 1.

No. 2. POPULATION: 1900 TO 1978

[In millions, except as indicated. Estimates as of July 1, except as indicated. Prior to 1940, excludes Alaska and Hawaii. Total population includes Armed Forces abroad: resident population excludes them. See text, p. 2, for basis of estimates. See also *Historical Statistics, Colonial Times to 1970*, series A 6-8]

YEAR	Resident population	YEAR	Resident population	YEAR	TOTAL		Resident population	Civilian population	YEAR AND MONTH	TOTAL		Resident population	Civilian population
					Population	Percent change				Population	Percent change		
1900	76.1	1920	106.5	1940	132.6	1.3	132.5	132.1	1962	186.6	1.5	185.8	183.
1901	77.6	1921	108.5	1941	133.9	1.0	133.7	132.1	1963	189.2	1.4	188.5	186.
1902	79.2	1922	110.1	1942	135.4	1.1	134.6	131.4	1964	191.9	1.4	191.1	189.
1903	80.6	1923	112.0	1943	137.3	1.4	135.1	128.0	1965	194.3	1.3	193.5	191.
1904	82.2	1924	114.1	1944	138.9	1.2	133.9	127.2	1966	196.6	1.2	195.6	193.
				1945	140.5	1.1	133.4	128.1					
1905	83.8	1925	115.8						1967	198.7	1.1	197.5	195.
1906	85.4	1926	117.4	1946	141.9	1.0	140.7	138.9	1968	200.7	1.0	199.4	197.
1907	87.0	1927	119.0	1947	144.7	1.9	144.1	143.1	1969	202.7	1.0	201.4	199.
1908	88.7	1928	120.5	1948	147.2	1.7	146.7	145.7	1970	204.9	1.1	203.8	201.
1909	90.5	1929	121.8	1949	149.8	1.7	149.3	148.2	1971	207.1	1.1	206.2	204.
				1950	152.3	1.7	151.9	150.8	1972	208.8	.9	208.2	206.
1910	92.4	1930	123.1										
1911	93.9	1931	124.1	1951	154.9	1.7	154.0	151.6	1973	210.4	.7	209.9	208.
1912	95.3	1932	124.8	1952	157.6	1.7	156.4	153.9	1974	211.9	.7	211.4	209.
1913	97.2	1933	125.6	1953	160.2	1.7	159.0	156.6	1975	213.6	.8	213.1	211.
1914	99.1	1934	126.4	1954	163.0	1.8	161.9	159.7	1976	215.1	.7	214.7	213.
				1955	165.9	1.8	165.1	163.0	1977	216.8	.8	216.3	214.
1915	100.5	1935	127.3						1978:				
1916	102.0	1936	128.1	1956	168.9	1.8	168.1	166.1	Jan. 1	217.7	.43	217.3	215
1917	103.3	1937	128.8	1957	172.0	1.8	171.2	169.1	Feb. 1	217.8	.04	217.4	215
1918	103.2	1938	129.8	1958	174.9	1.7	174.1	172.2	Mar. 1	217.9	.05	217.5	215
1919	104.5	1939	130.9	1959	177.8	1.7	177.1	175.3	Apr. 1	218.1	.07	217.6	216
				1960	180.7	1.6	180.0	178.1					
				1961	183.7	1.7	183.0	181.1					

Source: U.S. Bureau of the Census, *Current Population Reports*, series P-25, Nos. 706 and 724.

No. 3. Population and Area—United States and Outlying Areas: 1950 to 1970

[For area of individual States, see table 340. Minus sign (−) denotes decrease. See also *Historical Statistics, Colonial Times to 1970*, series A 9–22 and J 1–2]

AREA	RESIDENT POPULATION				Gross area (land and water), 1970 (sq. mi.)
	1950 (April 1)	1960 (April 1)	1970 (April 1)	Percent change, 1960–70	
Total	154,233,234	183,285,009	207,976,452	13.5	[1] 3,631,407
United States	151,325,798	179,323,175	[2] 203,211,926	13.3	[1] 3,618,467
Puerto Rico [3]	2,210,703	2,349,544	2,712,033	15.4	3,435
Outlying areas	[4] 215,188	[4] 237,869	314,657	32.3	9,505
Territories	106,219	123,151	179,519	45.8	463
Guam	59,498	67,044	84,996	26.8	212
Virgin Islands of the U.S	26,665	32,099	62,468	94.6	133
American Samoa	18,937	20,051	27,159	35.4	76
Midway Islands	416	2,356	2,220	−5.8	2
Wake Island	349	1,097	1,647	50.1	3
Canton Island and Enderbury Island [6]	272	320	−	−100.0	27
Johnston Island and Sand Island	46	156	1,007	645.5	(z)
Swan Islands	36	28	22	−21.4	1
Other	−	−	−	(X)	[7] 9
Canal Zone [8]	52,822	42,122	44,198	4.9	553
Trust Territory of the Pacific Islands [9]	[10] 54,843	[11] 70,724	90,940	28.6	[12] 8,489
U.S. population abroad [13]	[14] 481,545	1,374,421	1,737,836	26.4	(X)
Federal employees	328,505	647,730	1,114,224	72.0	(X)
Armed Forces	301,595	609,720	[15] 1,057,776	73.5	(X)
Civilians	26,910	38,010	56,448	48.5	(X)
Dependents of Federal employees	107,350	506,393	371,366	−26.7	(X)
Crews of merchant vessels	45,690	32,464	15,910	−51.0	(X)
Other citizens	(NA)	[16] 187,834	[16] 236,336	25.8	(X)

− Represents zero. NA Not available. X Not applicable. Z Less than .5 square mile.
[1] Figures corrected after 1970 final reports were issued. [2] See footnote 3, table 1.
[3] Puerto Rico was ceded to the United States by Spain in 1898. On July 25, 1952, pursuant to acts of Congress, achieved the political status of the Commonwealth of Puerto Rico.
[4] Includes population of Corn Islands (1950, 1,304; 1960, 1,872) not shown separately. Lease of Corn Islands om Republic of Nicaragua was terminated in 1971. Area total excludes area of these islands (4 square miles).
[5] Enderbury Island uninhabited in 1950 and 1960; Canton and Enderbury uninhabited in 1970.
[6] Sand Island uninhabited at time of enumeration.
[7] Area is for Navassa (2 square miles), Baker, Howland, and Jarvis (3 square miles), and Palmyra (4 square iles); uninhabited at time of enumeration.
[8] Under jurisdiction of the United States in accordance with treaty of Nov. 18, 1903, with Republic of Panama.
[9] Administered by United States since July 18, 1947, under United Nations Trusteeship system.
[10] Estimated civilian population as of June 30, 1950.
[11] Census of 1958 conducted by the Office of the High Commissioner, Trust Territory of the Pacific Islands.
[12] Comprises 717 square miles of land area and 7,772 square miles of water area.
[13] Excludes U.S. citizens temporarily abroad on private business, travel, etc. Such persons were enumerated at eir usual place of residence in the United States as absent members of their own households.
[14] Based on 20-percent sample of reports received.
[15] Based partially on tabulations provided by Dept. of Defense.
[16] Represents U.S. citizens abroad for extended periods. Since this population was enumerated on a voluntary sis, its coverage is probably less complete than that of other categories of Americans abroad.

Source: U.S. Bureau of the Census, *Census of Population: 1970*, vol. I.

No. 4. Projections of Total Population: 1976 to 2050

[millions. As of July 1. Includes Armed Forces abroad. The base date for the projections is 1976. See p. 2 for derivation of projections. For projection assumptions, see headnote, table 5]

YEAR	SERIES				YEAR	SERIES			
	I	II	III	II-X		I	II	III	II-X
6	215				2015	335	283	253	262
					2020	354	290	253	265
0	224	222	221	220	2025	373	296	252	267
5	239	233	229	229	2030	393	300	249	269
0	255	244	236	237					
					2035	414	304	246	269
5	269	253	242	244	2040	438	308	241	269
0	283	260	246	248	2045	463	312	236	269
5	298	268	249	253	2050	488	316	231	269
0	315	275	251	257					

urce: U.S. Bureau of the Census, *Current Population Reports*, series P-25, No. 704.

No. 5. Estimated and Projected Population, by Age and Sex, 1950 to 2000, and Zero Growth Projections, 1980 to 2050

[In thousands, except percent. As of July 1. Includes Armed Forces abroad. The base date for the projections is 1976. These projections were prepared using the "cohort-component" method. Series I, II, and III assume a slight improvement in mortality, an annual net immigration of 400,000, and completed cohort fertility rates (i.e., average number of lifetime births per 1,000 women) that move toward the following levels: I—2,700; II—2,100; III—1,700. Series II—X differs from Series II only in that it assumes no net immigration. The Series II and Series II—X fertility assumption represents "replacement level" fertility (i.e., the level of fertility at which the population would exactly replace itself in the absence of net immigration). See p. 2 for derivation of estimates and projections. See also Historical Statistics, Colonial Times to 1970, series A 23–25 and A 29–41]

YEAR, SERIES, AND SEX	Total, all ages	Under 5 years	5-13 years	14-17 years	18-21 years	22-24 years	25-34 years	35-44 years	45-54 years	55-64 years	65 years and over	16 years and over	18 years and over	21 years and over	Median age (yr.)
TOTAL															
1950	152,271	16,410	22,423	8,444	8,947	7,129	24,036	21,637	17,463	13,396	12,397	109,141	104,994	98,341	30.2
1960	180,671	20,341	32,965	11,219	9,555	6,573	22,919	24,221	20,578	15,625	16,675	121,835	116,146	108,856	29.4
1970	204,878	17,148	36,636	15,910	14,707	9,980	25,294	23,142	23,310	18,664	20,087	142,956	135,184	124,031	27.9
1975	213,540	15,882	33,440	16,934	16,484	11,120	30,918	22,815	23,768	19,774	22,405	155,702	147,285	134,756	28.8
1976	215,142	15,343	32,962	16,893	16,767	11,396	32,049	23,080	23,641	20,065	22,947	158,340	149,945	137,207	29.0
1977	216,817	15,236	32,227	16,783	16,956	11,646	33,149	23,543	23,389	20,395	23,494	161,009	152,572	139,690	29.4
Percent of total:															
1950	100.0	10.8	14.7	5.5	5.9	4.7	15.8	14.2	11.5	8.8	8.1	71.7	69.0	64.6	(X)
1960	100.0	11.3	18.2	6.2	5.3	3.6	12.7	13.4	11.4	8.6	9.2	67.4	64.3	60.3	(X)
1970	100.0	8.4	17.9	7.8	7.2	4.9	12.3	11.3	11.4	9.1	9.8	69.4	66.0	60.5	(X)
1975	100.0	7.4	15.7	7.9	7.7	5.2	14.5	10.7	11.1	9.3	10.5	72.9	69.0	63.1	(X)
1976	100.0	7.1	15.3	7.9	7.8	5.3	14.9	10.7	11.0	9.3	10.7	73.6	69.7	63.8	(X)
1977	100.0	7.0	14.9	7.7	7.8	5.4	15.3	10.9	10.8	9.4	10.8	74.3	70.4	64.4	(X)
Projections:															
1980—I	224,066	17,027	30,197	15,763	17,117	12,346	36,172	25,721	22,698	21,198	24,927	168,335	160,179	147,290	29.9
1980—II	222,159	16,020													30.2
1980—III	220,732	14,593													30.4
1985—I	238,878	22,887	31,012	14,392	15,442	12,411	39,859	31,376	22,457	21,737	27,305	177,607	170,587	159,218	30.7
1985—II	232,880	18,803	29,098												31.5
1985—III	228,879	16,235	27,665												32.0
1990—I	254,715	24,616	38,591	12,771	14,507	10,642	41,086	36,592	25,311	20,776	29,824	185,082	178,737	167,787	31.4
1990—II	243,513	19,437	32,568												32.8
1990—III	236,264	16,211	28,546												33.7
2000—I	282,837	23,638	44,725	19,698	17,692	10,336	34,450	41,344	35,875	23,257	31,822	204,408	194,776	181,139	32.5
2000—II	260,378	17,852	35,080	16,045	14,990	9,663						199,324	191,400	179,893	35.5
2000—III	245,876	14,158	28,915	13,831	13,006	9,219						195,865	188,972	178,989	37.3
MALE															
1950	75,849	8,362	11,415	4,269	4,484	3,525	11,804	10,706	8,715	6,714	5,856	53,893	51,803	48,460	29.8
1960	89,320	10,339	16,762	5,682	4,810	3,284	11,327	11,327	10,142	7,559	7,542	59,413	56,536	52,859	28.5
1970	100,269	8,742	18,667	8,101	7,437	5,000	12,621	11,316	11,251	8,828	8,407	68,714	64,759	59,121	26.6
1975	104,202	8,115	17,047	8,624	8,343	5,567	15,348	11,149	11,490	9,344	9,176	74,698	70,415	64,077	27.6
1976	104,927	7,840	16,811	8,605	8,585	5,703	15,912	11,272	11,436	9,488	9,371	75,944	71,672	65,228	27.8
1977						5,826	16,464	11,496	11,326	9,650	9,569	77,215	72,916	66,400	28.2

	Total											21+	18+	16+	Median age
Projections:															
1980—I	109,200	9,178	15,418	8,036	8,662	6,176	17,993	12,560	11,028	10,041	10,108	80,727	76,568	70,049	28.8
II	108,223	8,201													29.0
III	107,491	7,469													29.2
1985—I	116,441	11,726	15,869	7,346	7,820	6,208	19,825	15,374	10,915	10,346	11,012	85,079	81,500	75,750	29.5
II	113,366	9,632	14,888												30.8
III	111,315	8,315	14,154												30.2
1990—I	124,232	12,618	19,772	6,533	7,358	5,320	20,424	17,964	12,299	9,945	11,999	88,553	85,310	79,758	31.6
II	118,490	9,963	16,685												32.5
III	114,775	8,309	14,624												30.8
2000—I	138,091	12,121	22,928	10,090	9,002	5,188	17,124	20,261	17,518	11,141	12,717	97,882	92,952	86,018	34.1
II	126,588	9,153	17,981	8,218	7,626	4,849						95,292	91,236	85,386	36.0
III	119,162	7,259	14,819	7,083	6,616	4,624						93,529	90,001	84,926	
FEMALE															
1950	76,422	8,048	11,008	4,175	4,463	3,603	12,233	10,931	8,738	6,682	6,541	55,248	53,191	49,881	30.5
1960	91,352	10,002	16,203	5,537	4,745	3,289	11,591	12,349	10,436	8,067	9,133	62,422	59,610	55,997	30.3
1970	104,609	8,406	17,968	7,809	7,270	4,980	12,772	11,826	12,059	9,838	11,681	74,243	70,425	64,910	29.3
1975	109,338	7,767	16,391	8,310	8,140	5,553	15,570	11,666	12,279	10,431	13,228	81,004	76,870	70,678	30.0
1976	110,215	7,503	16,151	8,288	8,277	5,693	16,138	11,808	12,204	10,576	13,576	82,396	78,273	71,979	30.2
1977	111,119	7,446	15,789	8,228	8,372	5,819	16,684	12,047	12,063	10,746	13,925	83,794	79,655	73,290	30.6
Projections:															
1980—I	114,865	8,749	14,780	7,727	8,455	6,170	18,179	13,160	11,669	11,158	14,819	87,607	83,610	77,241	31.2
II	113,936	7,819													31.5
III	113,241	7,124													31.7
1985—I	122,437	11,161	15,144	7,046	7,621	6,204	20,034	16,002	11,542	11,390	16,293	92,528	89,087	83,468	31.9
II	119,514	7,919	14,210												32.7
III	117,564	11,998	13,512												32.7
1990—I	130,483	9,474	18,820	6,238	7,148	5,321	20,663	18,626	13,012	10,831	17,824	96,530	93,427	88,029	33.9
II	125,023	7,902	15,883												34.8
III	121,489	11,517	13,923												34.1
2000—I	144,746	21,489	21,797	9,607	8,690	5,148	17,326	21,084	18,356	12,116	19,105	106,525	101,825	95,121	36.8
II	133,790	8,699	17,099	7,827	7,363	4,815						104,032	100,165	94,508	38.5
III	126,714	6,899	14,096	6,748	6,390	4,595						102,336	98,971	94,063	
SERIES II–X ILLUSTRATIVE PROJECTIONS [1]															
1980	220,497	15,782	29,951	15,645	16,978	12,222	35,720	25,545	22,604	21,140	24,910	167,215	159,119	146,333	30.3
1985	228,912	18,283	28,423	14,136	15,153	12,165	38,842	30,856	22,218	21,693	27,244	174,960	168,071	156,916	31.7
1990	237,028	18,680	31,353	12,361	14,076	10,288	39,636	35,556	24,861	20,826	29,690	180,780	174,634	164,005	33.0
2000	248,372	16,698	33,014	15,147	14,106	9,037	32,295	39,369	34,570	22,684	31,451	190,991	183,513	172,675	36.0
2025	267,418	17,207	32,525	14,530	13,977	9,777	33,405	35,535	29,773	32,067	48,621	210,317	203,156	192,561	38.4
2050	269,411	17,499	32,314	14,367	14,125	10,084	33,882	34,351	31,438	31,522	49,829	212,335	205,230	194,556	38.6
Percent distribution in ultimate stationary population	100.0	6.5	11.7	5.2	5.2	3.3	12.7	12.5	12.2	11.2	19.0	79.2	76.6	72.8	38.9

X Not applicable.   [1] Series II–X, which would reach zero growth around the middle of the twenty-first century, is one of many possible approaches to zero growth. Immediate cessation of net immigration, combined with replacement level fertility would not lead to immediate zero growth because the U.S. has a relatively young age structure (due to the post-World War II baby boom) which provides momentum for continued growth. Immediate zero growth in 1977 (assuming no dramatic change in mortality) would require an annual total fertility rate of about 900 with net immigration at the current level, or about 1,000 with no net immigration. Total fertility rate in 1977 was about 1,800.

Source: U.S. Bureau of the Census, *Current Population Reports*, series P-25, Nos. 310, 311, 519, 704, and 721.

No. 6. Center of Population: 1790 to 1970

["Center of population" is that point which may be considered as the center of population gravity of the United States, or that point upon which the United States would balance if it were a rigid plane without weight and the population distributed thereon with each individual being assumed to have equal weight and to exert an influence on a central point proportional to his distance from that point]

YEAR [1]	North latitude			West longitude			Approximate location
	°	′	″	°	′	″	
1790	39	16	30	76	11	12	23 miles east of Baltimore, Md.
1850	38	59	0	81	19	0	23 miles southeast of Parkersburg, W. Va.
1900	39	9	36	85	48	54	6 miles southeast of Columbus, Ind.
1950	38	50	21	88	9	33	8 miles north-northwest of Olney, Richland County, Ill.
1960	38	35	58	89	12	35	In Clinton Co. about 6½ miles northwest of Centralia, Ill.
1970	38	27	47	89	42	22	5.3 miles east-southeast of the Mascoutah City Hall in St. Clair County, Ill.

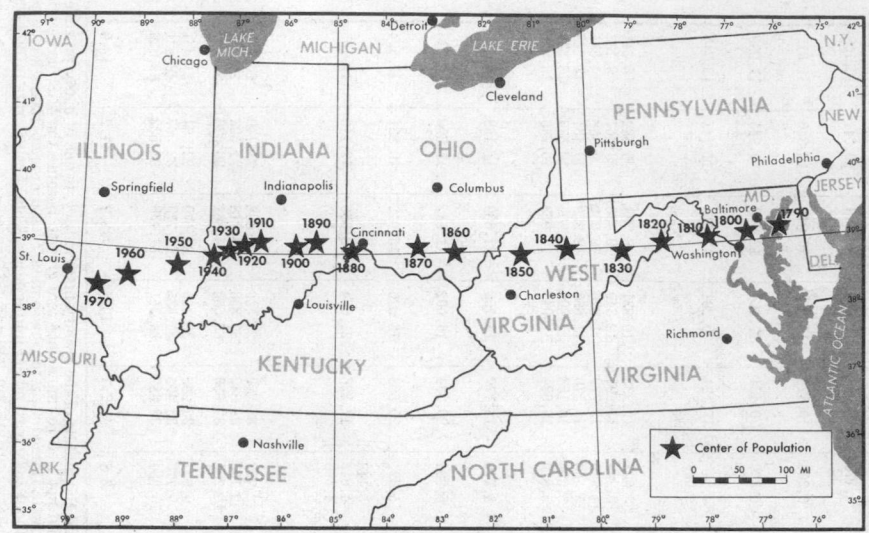

[1] For dates of admissions of the States and changes in areal definition, see "State Origins and Boundaries," *United States Summary, U.S. Census of Population: 1960*, vol. I. For year of admission to statehood, see table 340.

Source: U.S. Bureau of the Census, *Census of Population: 1970*, vol. I.

No. 7. Resident Population and Population Density in Counties Within 50 Miles of Coastal Shorelines: 1940 to 1976

[As of **April 1**. Excludes Alaska and Hawaii. Covers 611 counties and independent cities which are entirely or substantially within 50 miles of U.S. coastal shorelines. Great Lakes region includes St. Lawrence River]

YEAR	U.S. total	COUNTIES IN COASTAL REGIONS					Balance of U.S.
		Total	Atlantic	Pacific	Great Lakes	Gulf of Mexico	
Land area, 1970_____1,000 sq. mi__	2,964	468	122	118	134	94	2,496
POPULATION							
1940_____mil__	131.7	60.5	29.9	7.5	18.9	4.2	71.2
1950_____mil__	150.7	73.5	34.6	11.5	21.8	5.6	77.2
1960_____mil__	178.5	92.7	41.7	16.8	26.4	7.8	85.7
1970_____mil__	202.2	108.5	48.2	21.5	29.3	9.5	93.8
1976_____mil__	213.4	113.4	49.8	23.0	29.6	11.0	100.0
1940_____percent__	100	46	23	6	14	3	54
1950_____percent__	100	49	23	8	15	4	51
1960_____percent__	100	52	23	9	15	4	48
1970_____percent__	100	54	24	11	15	5	46
1976_____percent__	100	53	23	11	14	5	47
Population per square mile:							
1940	44.4	129.3	244.4	64.1	140.9	44.8	28.5
1950	50.8	157.2	283.3	97.6	162.9	59.8	30.9
1960	60.2	198.3	341.6	142.7	197.3	83.1	34.3
1970	68.2	232.0	394.4	182.5	219.1	101.1	37.6
1976	72.0	242.6	407.3	195.5	221.4	117.7	40.0

Source: U.S. Bureau of the Census, unpublished data.

No. 8. Components of Population Change: 1930 to 1986

[For 1930 and 1935, excludes Alaska, Hawaii, and Armed Forces abroad. Minus sign (−) denotes net outmigration. For explanation of series projections assumptions, see headnote, table 5]

| YEAR OR PERIOD | Population at start of period (1,000) | TOTAL (Jan. 1–Dec. 31)[1] | | | | | | RATE PER 1,000 MIDYEAR POPULATION | | | | |
| | | Net increase[2] | | Natural increase | | Net civilian immigration (1,000) | Net growth rate[2] | Natural increase | | | Net civilian immigration rate |
		Total (1,000)	Percent[3]	Births[4] (1,000)	Deaths[5] (1,000)			Total	Birth rate[4]	Death rate[5]	
1930	122,487	1,128	.9	2,618	1,419	113	9.2	9.7	21.3	11.5	.9
1935	126,874	853	.7	2,377	1,421	−2	6.7	7.5	18.7	11.2	(Z)
1940	132,054	1,221	.9	2,570	1,432	77	9.2	8.6	19.4	10.8	.6
1945	139,767	1,462	1.1	2,873	1,549	162	10.4	9.4	20.5	11.0	1.2
1950	151,135	2,486	1.7	3,645	1,468	299	16.3	14.3	23.9	9.6	2.0
1955	164,588	2,925	1.8	4,128	1,537	337	17.6	15.6	24.9	9.3	2.0
1960	179,386	2,901	1.6	4,307	1,708	327	16.1	14.4	23.8	9.5	1.8
1965	193,223	2,315	1.2	3,801	1,830	373	11.9	10.1	19.6	9.4	1.9
1968	199,808	1,952	1.0	3,535	1,948	398	9.7	7.9	17.6	9.7	2.0
1970	203,849	2,227	1.1	3,739	1,927	438	10.9	8.8	18.2	9.4	2.1
1971	206,076	2,012	1.0	3,556	1,930	387	9.7	7.9	17.2	9.3	1.9
1972	208,088	1,623	.8	3,258	1,965	325	7.8	6.2	15.6	9.4	1.6
1973	209,711	1,496	.7	3,137	1,974	331	7.1	5.5	14.9	9.4	1.6
1974	211,207	1,541	.7	3,160	1,935	316	7.3	5.8	14.9	9.1	1.5
1975	212,748	1,699	.8	3,144	1,894	449	8.0	5.9	14.7	8.9	2.1
1976	214,446	1,611	.8	3,168	1,910	353	7.5	5.8	14.7	8.9	1.6
1977	216,057	1,728	.8	3,313	1,901	315	8.0	6.5	15.3	8.8	1.5
ANNUAL AVERAGE											
1930–1934	(X)	877	.7	2,453	1,398	−1	7.0	8.5	19.7	11.2	.4
1935–1939	(X)	915	.7	2,421	1,447	29	7.1	7.5	18.8	11.2	.2
1940–1944	(X)	1,543	1.1	2,872	1,468	114	11.4	10.4	21.2	10.8	.8
1945–1949	(X)	2,274	1.6	3,491	1,464	231	15.7	14.0	24.1	10.1	1.6
1950–1954	(X)	2,690	1.7	3,902	1,500	285	17.1	15.2	24.8	9.5	1.8
1955–1959	(X)	2,960	1.7	4,259	1,614	316	17.2	15.4	24.8	9.4	1.8
1960–1964	(X)	2,767	1.5	4,210	1,757	346	14.9	13.2	22.6	9.4	1.9
1965–1969	(X)	2,125	1.1	3,628	1,888	419	10.7	8.7	18.3	9.5	2.1
1970–1974	(X)	1,780	.9	3,370	1,946	359	8.6	6.8	16.2	9.3	1.7
1970–1975	(X)	1,766	.8	3,333	1,940	374	8.4	6.7	15.9	9.2	1.8
1970–1976	(X)	1,744	.8	3,309	1,934	371	8.3	6.6	15.7	9.2	1.8
1976–1977	(X)	1,669	.8	3,240	1,905	334	7.8	6.2	15.0	8.8	1.6
PROJECTIONS (July 1–June 30)											
Series I:											
1980–1981	224,066	2,746	1.2	4,438	2,091	400	12.2	10.4	19.7	9.3	1.8
1985–1986	238,878	3,163	1.3	5,006	2,243	400	13.2	11.5	20.8	9.3	1.7
Series II:											
1980–1981	222,159	2,053	.9	3,733	2,080	400	9.2	7.4	16.7	9.3	1.8
1985–1986	232,880	2,181	.9	4,007	2,226	400	9.3	7.6	17.1	9.5	1.7
Series III:											
1980–1981	220,732	1,551	.7	3,223	2,072	400	7.0	5.2	14.6	9.4	1.8
1985–1986	228,879	1,581	.7	3,397	2,216	400	6.9	5.1	14.8	9.6	1.7

X Not applicable.   Z Less than .05 percent.   [1] Except as indicated.   [2] For 1940–1976, includes admissions into, less discharges from, Armed Forces abroad. Through 1970, includes "error of closure" (the amount necessary to make the components of change add to the net change between censuses), for which figures are not shown separately.   [3] Percent of population at beginning of period.   [4] Adjusted for underregistration prior to April 1, 1970.   [5] Prior to April 1, 1960, adjusted for underregistration of infant deaths.

Source: U.S. Bureau of the Census, *Current Population Reports*, series P-25, Nos. 704, 706, and forthcoming report.

No. 9. Population, by Size of States: 1960, 1970, and 1977

[As of April, except 1977 as of July. Includes District of Columbia. Gross area comprises land and water]

| POPULATION SIZE | Number of States | POPULATION, 1960 | | Number of States | POPULATION, 1970 | | GROSS AREA, 1970 | | Number of States | POPULATION, 1977, est. | |
		Total (1,000)	Percent of total		Total (1,000)	Percent of total	Total (1,000 sq. mi.)	Percent of total		Total (1,000)	Percent of total
Total	51	179,323	100.0	51	203,235	100.0	3,618	100.0	51	216,332	100.0
Over 10 million	4	53,900	30.1	6	82,951	40.8	619	17.1	6	86,381	39.9
5 million–10 million	5	38,325	21.4	6	38,798	19.1	222	6.1	8	51,731	23.9
3 million–5 million	13	49,995	27.9	12	46,733	23.0	576	15.9	10	39,700	18.4
2 million–3 million	7	17,214	9.6	7	16,739	8.2	488	13.5	9	22,716	10.5
1 million–2 million	6	9,883	5.5	6	8,999	4.4	475	13.1	5	6,964	3.2
Under 1 million	16	10,007	5.6	14	9,015	4.4	1,238	34.2	13	8,841	4.1

Source: U.S. Bureau of the Census, *Census of Population: 1970*, vol. I, part A, and *Current Population Reports*, series P-20, No. 324.

No. 10. POPULATION, RANK, PERCENT CHANGE, AND

[As of census date: **Jan. 1, 1920**, and **Apr. 1** thereafter, except as noted. Insofar as possible, population shown is that of regions, see fig. I, inside front cover. See *Historical Statistics, Colonial Times to 1970*,

STATE OR OTHER AREA	POPULATION (1,000)									
	1920	1930	1940	1950	1960			1970		
					Total	Male	Female	Total	Male	Female
U.S.	106,022	123,203	132,165	151,326	179,323	88,331	90,992	203,212	98,912	104,300
Regions:										
N. East	29,662	34,427	35,977	39,478	44,678	21,726	22,952	49,041	23,563	25,478
N. Cen	34,020	38,594	40,143	44,461	51,619	25,472	26,147	56,572	27,563	29,009
South	33,126	37,858	41,666	47,197	54,973	27,065	27,908	62,795	30,588	32,208
West	9,214	12,324	14,379	20,190	28,053	14,067	13,986	34,804	17,199	17,606
N.E.	7,401	8,166	8,437	9,314	10,509	5,121	5,388	11,842	5,715	6,127
Maine	768	797	847	914	969	479	490	992	483	509
N.H	443	465	492	533	607	298	309	738	361	377
Vt	352	360	359	378	390	192	198	444	217	227
Mass	3,852	4,250	4,317	4,691	5,149	2,486	2,662	5,689	2,719	2,970
R.I	604	687	713	792	859	422	438	947	464	482
Conn	1,381	1,607	1,709	2,007	2,535	1,244	1,291	3,032	1,470	1,561
M.A	22,261	26,261	27,539	30,164	34,168	16,605	17,563	37,199	17,848	19,351
N.Y	10,385	12,588	13,479	14,830	16,782	8,123	8,659	18,237	8,715	9,522
N.J	3,156	4,041	4,160	4,835	6,067	2,972	3,095	7,168	3,467	3,701
Pa	8,720	9,631	9,900	10,498	11,319	5,510	5,810	11,794	5,665	6,128
E.N.C	21,476	25,297	26,626	30,399	36,225	17,863	18,362	40,252	19,602	20,650
Ohio	5,759	6,647	6,908	7,947	9,706	4,764	4,942	10,652	5,163	5,489
Ind	2,930	3,239	3,428	3,934	4,662	2,299	2,364	5,194	2,531	2,662
Ill	6,485	7,631	7,897	8,712	10,081	4,953	5,128	11,114	5,392	5,722
Mich	3,668	4,842	5,256	6,372	7,823	3,883	3,940	8,875	4,349	4,526
Wis	2,632	2,939	3,138	3,435	3,952	1,965	1,987	4,418	2,167	2,250
W.N.C	12,544	13,297	13,517	14,061	15,394	7,609	7,785	16,319	7,960	8,359
Minn	2,387	2,564	2,792	2,982	3,414	1,693	1,721	3,805	1,864	1,941
Iowa	2,404	2,471	2,538	2,621	2,758	1,359	1,398	2,824	1,373	1,452
Mo	3,404	3,629	3,785	3,955	4,320	2,108	2,212	4,677	2,256	2,421
N. Dak	647	681	642	620	632	323	309	618	312	306
S. Dak	637	693	643	653	681	344	336	666	330	335
Nebr	1,296	1,378	1,316	1,326	1,411	700	711	1,483	724	759
Kans	1,769	1,881	1,801	1,905	2,179	1,081	1,097	2,247	1,102	1,145
S.A	13,990	15,794	17,823	21,182	25,972	12,792	13,179	30,671	14,944	15,728
Del	223	238	267	318	446	221	225	548	267	281
Md	1,450	1,632	1,821	2,343	3,101	1,533	1,567	3,922	1,916	2,006
D.C	438	487	663	802	764	358	406	757	351	405
Va	2,309	2,422	2,678	3,319	3,967	1,979	1,988	4,648	2,297	2,351
W. Va	1,464	1,729	1,902	2,006	1,860	915	945	1,744	845	900
N.C	2,559	3,170	3,572	4,062	4,556	2,247	2,309	5,082	2,488	2,594
S.C	1,684	1,739	1,900	2,117	2,383	1,176	1,207	2,591	1,272	1,318
Ga	2,896	2,909	3,124	3,445	3,943	1,926	2,017	4,590	2,231	2,359
Fla	968	1,468	1,897	2,771	4,952	2,437	2,515	6,789	3,276	3,514
E.S.C	8,893	9,887	10,778	11,477	12,050	5,909	6,141	12,803	6,213	6,591
Ky	2,417	2,615	2,846	2,945	3,038	1,508	1,530	3,219	1,579	1,640
Tenn	2,338	2,617	2,916	3,292	3,567	1,741	1,826	3,924	1,898	2,026
Ala	2,348	2,646	2,833	3,062	3,267	1,592	1,675	3,444	1,662	1,782
Miss	1,791	2,010	2,184	2,179	2,178	1,068	1,110	2,217	1,074	1,143
W.S.C	10,242	12,177	13,065	14,538	16,951	8,364	8,587	19,321	9,431	9,889
Ark	1,752	1,854	1,949	1,910	1,786	879	907	1,923	932	991
La	1,799	2,102	2,364	2,684	3,257	1,592	1,665	3,641	1,771	1,870
Okla	2,028	2,396	2,336	2,233	2,328	1,148	1,180	2,559	1,246	1,313
Texas	4,663	5,825	6,415	7,711	9,580	4,745	4,835	11,197	5,481	5,716
Mt	3,336	3,702	4,150	5,075	6,855	3,449	3,406	8,282	4,102	4,180
Mont	549	538	559	591	675	344	331	694	347	347
Idaho	432	445	525	589	667	338	329	713	356	357
Wyo	194	226	251	291	330	169	161	332	167	166
Colo	940	1,036	1,123	1,325	1,754	870	883	2,207	1,089	1,118
N. Mex	360	423	532	681	951	480	471	1,016	501	515
Ariz	334	436	499	750	1,302	655	647	1,771	871	900
Utah	449	508	550	689	891	445	446	1,059	523	536
Nev	77	91	110	160	285	148	138	489	248	241
Pac	5,878	8,622	10,229	15,115	21,198	10,619	10,579	26,523	13,097	13,426
Wash	1,357	1,563	1,736	2,379	2,853	1,435	1,418	3,409	1,694	1,715
Oreg	783	954	1,090	1,521	1,769	880	889	2,091	1,024	1,067
Calif	3,427	5,677	6,907	10,586	15,717	7,837	7,880	19,953	9,817	10,136
Alaska	55	³ 59	³ 73	129	226	129	97	300	163	137
Hawaii	256	368	423	500	633	338	295	769	399	369
P.R.	1,300	1,544	1,869	2,211	2,350	1,163	1,187	2,712	1,330	1,382

X Not applicable.   Z Less than .05 percent.   ¹ For U.S., population of U.S. has been divided by total land area. For each State and Puerto Rico, population at given census has been divided by land area as then constituted.

DENSITY—STATES AND PUERTO RICO: 1920 TO 1970

of present area of State; for area figures of States, see table 340. Minus sign (−) denotes decrease. For composition series A 172, for population by regions and A 195–196 for population and density by States]

RANK 1920	1940	1960	1970	PERCENT CHANGE 1920–1930	1930–1940	1940–1950	1950–1960	1960–1970	POPULATION PER SQ. MILE OF LAND AREA[1] 1920	1930	1940	1950	1960	1970	STATE OR OTHER AREA
(X)	(X)	(X)	(X)	16.2	7.3	14.5	18.5	13.3	29.9	34.7	37.2	42.6	50.6	[2]57.4	U.S.
															Regions:
(X)	(X)	(X)	(X)	16.1	4.5	9.7	13.2	9.8	183.1	210.3	219.8	241.2	273.4	300.4	N. East.
(X)	(X)	(X)	(X)	13.4	4.0	10.8	16.1	9.6	45.0	51.1	53.1	58.8	68.6	75.2	N. Cen.
(X)	(X)	(X)	(X)	14.3	10.1	13.3	16.5	14.2	37.7	43.0	47.4	53.7	62.8	71.9	South.
(X)	(X)	(X)	(X)	33.7	16.7	40.4	38.9	24.1	5.3	7.0	8.2	11.5	16.0	19.9	West.
(X)	(X)	(X)	(X)	10.3	3.3	10.4	12.8	12.7	119.4	129.2	133.5	147.5	166.8	188.1	N.E.
35	35	36	38	3.8	6.2	7.9	6.1	2.4	25.7	25.7	27.3	29.4	31.3	32.1	Maine.
41	44	45	41	5.0	5.6	8.5	13.8	21.5	49.1	51.6	54.5	59.1	67.2	81.7	N.H.
44	46	47	48	2.0	−.1	5.2	3.2	14.0	38.6	38.8	38.7	40.7	42.0	47.9	Vt.
6	8	9	10	10.3	1.6	8.7	9.8	10.5	479.2	537.4	545.9	396.2	657.3	727.0	Mass.
38	36	39	39	13.7	3.8	11.0	8.5	10.1	566.4	649.8	674.2	748.5	819.3	902.5	R.I.
29	31	25	24	16.4	6.4	17.4	26.3	19.6	286.4	328.0	348.9	409.7	520.6	623.6	Conn.
(X)	(X)	(X)	(X)	18.0	4.9	9.5	13.3	8.9	222.6	261.3	274.0	300.1	340.2	370.8	M.A.
1	1	1	2	21.2	7.1	10.0	13.2	8.7	217.9	262.6	281.2	309.3	350.6	381.3	N.Y.
10	9	8	8	28.1	2.9	16.2	25.5	18.2	420.0	537.3	553.1	642.8	805.5	953.1	N.J.
2	2	3	3	10.5	2.8	6.0	7.8	4.2	194.5	213.8	219.8	233.1	251.4	262.3	Pa.
(X)	(X)	(X)	(X)	17.8	5.3	14.2	19.2	11.1	87.5	103.2	108.7	124.1	148.2	164.9	E.N.C.
4	4	5	6	15.4	3.9	15.0	22.1	9.7	141.4	161.6	168.0	193.8	236.6	260.0	Ohio.
11	12	11	11	10.5	5.8	14.8	18.5	11.4	81.3	89.4	94.7	108.7	128.8	143.9	Ind.
3	3	4	5	17.7	3.5	10.3	15.7	10.2	115.7	136.4	141.2	155.8	180.4	199.4	Ill.
7	7	7	7	32.0	8.5	21.2	22.8	13.4	63.8	84.9	92.2	111.7	137.7	156.2	Mich.
13	13	15	16	11.7	6.8	9.5	15.1	11.8	47.6	53.7	57.3	62.8	72.6	81.1	Wis.
(X)	(X)	(X)	(X)	6.0	1.7	4.0	9.5	6.0	24.6	26.0	26.5	27.5	30.3	32.1	W.N.C.
17	18	18	19	7.4	8.9	6.8	14.5	11.5	29.5	32.0	34.9	37.3	43.1	48.0	Minn.
16	20	24	25	2.8	2.7	3.3	5.2	2.4	43.2	44.1	45.3	46.8	49.2	50.5	Iowa.
9	10	13	13	6.6	4.3	4.5	9.2	8.3	49.5	52.4	54.6	57.1	62.6	67.8	Mo.
36	38	44	45	5.3	−5.7	−3.5	2.1	−2.3	9.2	9.7	9.2	8.8	9.1	8.9	N. Dak.
37	37	40	44	8.8	−7.2	1.5	4.3	−2.2	8.3	9.1	8.4	8.5	9.0	8.8	S. Dak.
31	32	34	35	6.3	−4.5	.7	6.5	5.1	16.9	18.0	17.2	17.3	18.4	19.4	Nebr.
24	29	28	28	6.3	−4.3	5.8	14.3	3.1	21.6	22.9	21.9	23.2	26.6	27.5	Kans.
(X)	(X)	(X)	(X)	12.9	12.9	18.8	22.6	18.1	52.0	58.8	66.4	79.0	97.1	114.9	S.A.
47	47	46	46	6.9	11.8	19.4	40.3	22.8	113.5	120.5	134.7	160.8	225.2	276.5	Del.
28	28	21	18	12.5	11.6	28.6	32.3	26.5	145.8	165.0	184.2	237.1	313.5	396.6	Md.
(X)	(X)	(X)	(X)	11.3	36.2	21.0	−4.8	−1.0	7,293	7,982	10,870	13,151	12,524	12,402	D.C.
20	19	14	14	4.9	10.6	23.9	19.5	17.2	57.4	60.7	67.1	83.2	99.6	116.9	Va.
27	25	30	34	18.1	10.0	5.4	−7.2	−6.2	60.9	71.8	79.0	83.3	77.2	72.5	W. Va.
14	11	12	12	23.9	12.7	13.7	12.2	11.5	52.5	64.5	72.7	82.7	93.2	104.1	N.C.
26	26	26	26	3.3	9.3	11.4	12.5	8.7	55.2	56.8	62.1	69.9	78.7	85.7	S.C.
12	14	16	15	.4	7.4	10.3	14.5	16.4	49.3	49.7	53.4	58.9	67.8	79.0	Ga.
32	27	10	9	51.6	29.2	46.1	78.7	37.1	17.7	27.1	35.0	51.1	91.5	125.5	Fla.
(X)	(X)	(X)	(X)	11.2	9.0	6.5	5.0	6.3	49.5	54.8	59.7	63.8	67.2	71.5	E.S.C.
15	16	22	23	8.2	8.8	3.5	3.2	5.9	60.2	65.2	70.9	73.9	76.2	81.2	Ky.
19	15	17	17	11.9	11.4	12.9	8.4	10.0	56.1	62.4	69.5	78.8	86.2	94.9	Tenn.
18	17	19	21	12.7	7.1	8.1	6.7	5.4	45.8	51.8	55.5	59.9	64.2	67.9	Ala.
23	23	29	29	12.2	8.7	−.2	(z)	1.8	38.6	42.4	46.1	46.1	46.0	46.9	Miss.
(X)	(X)	(X)	(X)	18.9	7.3	11.3	16.6	14.0	23.8	28.3	30.3	33.8	39.5	45.2	W.S.C.
25	24	31	32	5.8	5.1	−2.0	−6.5	7.7	33.4	35.2	37.0	36.3	34.2	37.0	Ark.
22	21	20	20	16.9	12.5	13.5	21.4	11.8	39.6	46.5	52.3	59.4	72.2	81.0	La.
21	22	27	27	18.1	−2.5	−4.4	4.3	9.9	29.2	34.6	33.7	32.4	33.8	37.2	Okla.
5	6	6	4	24.9	10.1	20.2	24.2	16.9	17.8	22.1	24.3	29.3	36.4	42.7	Texas.
(X)	(X)	(X)	(X)	11.0	12.1	22.3	35.1	20.8	3.9	4.3	4.8	5.9	8.0	9.7	Mt.
39	39	41	43	−2.1	4.1	5.6	14.2	2.9	3.8	3.7	3.8	4.1	4.6	4.8	Mont.
42	42	42	42	3.0	17.9	12.1	13.3	6.8	5.2	5.4	6.3	7.1	8.1	8.6	Idaho.
48	48	48	49	16.0	11.2	15.9	13.6	.7	2.0	2.3	2.6	3.0	3.4	3.4	Wyo.
33	33	33	30	10.2	8.4	18.0	32.4	25.8	9.1	10.0	10.8	12.8	16.9	21.3	Colo.
43	41	37	37	17.5	25.6	28.1	39.6	6.8	2.9	3.5	4.4	5.6	7.8	8.4	N. Mex.
45	43	35	33	30.3	14.6	50.1	73.7	36.0	2.9	3.8	4.4	6.6	11.5	15.6	Ariz.
40	40	38	36	13.0	8.4	25.2	29.3	18.9	5.5	6.2	6.7	8.4	10.8	12.9	Utah.
49	49	49	47	17.6	21.1	45.2	78.2	71.3	.7	.8	1.0	1.5	2.6	4.4	Nev.
(X)	(X)	(X)	(X)	46.7	18.7	47.8	40.2	25.1	6.6	9.6	11.4	16.8	23.8	29.7	Pac.
30	30	23	22	15.2	11.1	37.0	19.9	19.5	20.3	23.3	25.9	35.6	42.8	51.2	Wash.
34	34	32	31	21.8	14.2	39.6	16.3	18.2	8.2	9.9	11.3	16.8	18.4	21.7	Oreg.
8	5	2	1	65.7	21.7	53.3	48.5	27.0	22.0	36.2	44.1	67.5	100.4	127.6	Calif.
50	50	50	50	7.7	22.3	77.4	75.8	32.8	.1	[3].1	[3].1	.2	.4	[2].5	Alaska.
46	45	43	40	43.9	14.8	18.2	26.2	21.5	39.9	57.5	66.0	78.0	98.5	119.6	Hawaii.
(X)	(X)	(X)	(X)	18.8	21.1	18.3	6.3	15.4	379.7	451.0	546.1	645.8	686.4	792.8	P.R.

[2] Figures for Alaska corrected after 1970 final reports were issued.   [3] 1930 as of Oct. 1, 1929; 1940 as of Oct. 1, 1939.

Source: U.S. Bureau of the Census, Census of Population: 1970, vol. I.

No. 11. POPULATION—STATES: 1960 TO 1977

[Estimates as of July 1. Includes Armed Forces stationed in area. See p. 2 for basis of estimates. For explanation of methodology, see source. For enumerated population, 1920 to 1970, see table 10. Minus sign (−) denotes decrease]

DIVISION AND STATE	1960 (1,000)	1965 (1,000)	1970 (1,000)	1974 (1,000)	1975 (1,000)	1976 (1,000)	1977 POPULATION, prel.			AVERAGE ANNUAL PERCENT CHANGE		
							Rank order	Total (1,000)	Per sq. mi. of land area [1]	1950–1960	1960–1970	1970–1977
U.S.	[2]179,979	[2]193,526	[2]203,806	211,389	213,032	214,669	(X)	216,332	61.2	1.7	1.3	.9
N.E.	10,532	11,329	11,883	12,147	12,187	12,205	(X)	12,242	194.5	1.2	1.2	.5
Maine	975	997	997	1,048	1,058	1,071	38	1,085	35.1	.6	.2	1.2
N.H.	609	676	742	805	812	827	42	849	94.0	1.4	2.0	1.9
Vt.	389	404	446	468	472	477	48	485	52.2	.3	1.4	1.1
Mass.	5,160	5,502	5,706	5,800	5,814	5,791	10	5,782	738.8	1.0	1.0	.2
R.I.	855	893	951	941	931	936	39	935	890.9	.8	1.1	−.2
Conn.	2,544	2,857	3,041	3,085	3,100	3,102	24	3,108	639.3	2.4	1.8	.3
M.A.	34,270	36,122	37,274	37,250	37,269	37,195	(X)	37,038	369.2	1.3	.8	−.1
N.Y.	16,838	17,734	18,268	18,094	18,076	18,053	2	17,924	374.7	1.3	.8	−.2
N.J.	6,103	6,767	7,193	7,329	7,333	7,339	9	7,329	974.5	2.3	1.7	.3
Pa.	11,329	11,620	11,813	11,827	11,860	11,802	4	11,785	262.1	.8	.4	(−Z)
E.N.C.	36,291	38,406	40,313	40,878	40,945	40,918	(X)	41,057	168.2	1.7	1.1	.3
Ohio	9,734	10,201	10,664	10,735	10,735	10,690	6	10,701	261.2	2.0	.9	.1
Ind.	4,674	4,922	5,202	5,312	5,313	5,313	12	5,330	147.7	1.7	1.1	.4
Ill.	10,086	10,693	11,128	11,178	11,197	11,193	5	11,245	201.7	1.4	1.0	.2
Mich.	7,834	8,357	8,890	9,094	9,111	9,113	7	9,129	160.7	2.0	1.3	.4
Wis.	3,962	4,232	4,429	4,559	4,589	4,610	16	4,651	85.4	1.4	1.1	.7
W.N.C.	15,424	15,819	16,360	16,650	16,690	16,797	(X)	16,884	33.3	.9	.6	.5
Minn.	3,425	3,592	3,815	3,901	3,921	3,954	19	3,975	50.1	1.3	1.1	.6
Iowa	2,756	2,742	2,832	2,853	2,861	2,874	25	2,879	51.5	.5	.3	.3
Mo.	4,326	4,467	4,688	4,772	4,767	4,787	15	4,801	69.6	.9	.8	.4
N. Dak.	634	649	620	634	637	645	45	653	9.4	.2	−.2	.8
S. Dak.	683	692	668	680	681	686	44	689	9.1	.4	−.2	.5
Nebr.	1,417	1,471	1,488	1,540	1,544	1,552	35	1,561	20.4	.7	.5	.7
Kans.	2,183	2,206	2,249	2,270	2,280	2,299	31	2,326	28.4	1.3	.3	.5
S.A.	26,091	28,743	30,805	33,263	33,658	33,934	(X)	34,305	128.5	2.1	1.7	1.5
Del.	449	507	551	576	579	582	47	582	293.4	3.4	2.1	.8
Md.	3,113	3,600	3,938	4,100	4,122	4,125	18	4,139	418.4	2.8	2.4	.7
D.C.	765	797	756	723	712	700	(X)	690	(3)	−.5	−.1	−1.3
Va.	3,986	4,411	4,659	4,927	4,981	5,052	13	5,135	129.1	1.9	1.6	1.4
W. Va.	1,853	1,786	1,751	1,783	1,799	1,832	34	1,859	77.2	−.8	−.6	.9
N.C.	4,573	4,863	5,098	5,381	5,441	5,462	11	5,525	113.2	1.2	1.1	1.1
S.C.	2,392	2,494	2,597	2,774	2,816	2,844	26	2,876	95.1	1.2	.8	1.4
Ga.	3,956	4,332	4,607	4,897	4,931	4,984	14	5,048	86.9	1.4	1.5	1.3
Fla.	5,004	5,954	6,848	8,102	8,277	8,353	8	8,452	156.3	5.9	3.2	3.0
E.S.C.	12,073	12,627	12,839	13,395	13,515	13,689	(X)	13,837	77.3	.5	.6	1.1
Ky.	3,041	3,140	3,231	3,353	3,387	3,436	23	3,458	87.2	.4	.6	1.0
Tenn.	3,575	3,798	3,937	4,137	4,173	4,234	17	4,299	104.0	.7	1.0	1.2
Ala.	3,274	3,443	3,451	3,575	3,615	3,653	21	3,690	72.8	.5	.5	.9
Miss.	2,182	2,246	2,220	2,330	2,341	2,365	29	2,389	50.7	(Z)	.2	1.0
W.S.C.	17,010	18,209	19,388	20,523	20,867	21,361	(X)	21,707	50.7	1.5	1.3	1.6
Ark.	1,789	1,894	1,932	2,062	2,110	2,117	33	2,144	41.3	−.6	.8	1.3
La.	3,260	3,496	3,652	3,761	3,806	3,875	20	3,921	87.3	1.9	1.1	1.0
Okla.	2,336	2,440	2,567	2,683	2,715	2,770	27	2,811	40.9	.5	.9	1.3
Tex.	9,624	10,378	11,236	12,017	12,237	12,599	3	12,830	48.9	2.2	1.6	1.9
Mt.	6,916	7,740	8,348	9,422	9,625	9,820	(X)	10,031	11.7	3.1	1.9	2.6
Mont.	679	706	698	735	746	755	43	761	5.2	1.4	.3	1.3
Idaho	671	686	718	794	813	833	41	857	10.4	1.3	.7	2.5
Wyo.	331	332	334	361	376	391	50	406	4.2	1.3	(Z)	2.8
Colo.	1,769	1,985	2,223	2,507	2,541	2,575	28	2,619	25.2	2.9	2.3	2.3
N. Mex.	954	1,012	1,023	1,119	1,144	1,172	37	1,190	9.8	3.3	.7	2.2
Ariz.	1,321	1,584	1,792	2,157	2,212	2,249	32	2,296	20.2	5.7	3.1	3.5
Utah	900	991	1,066	1,175	1,203	1,232	36	1,268	15.4	2.6	1.7	2.5
Nev.	291	444	493	574	590	613	46	633	5.8	6.0	5.4	3.6
Pac.	21,368	24,464	26,600	27,862	28,274	28,750	(X)	29,232	32.8	3.4	2.2	1.3
Wash.	2,855	2,967	3,413	3,505	3,559	3,611	22	3,658	54.9	1.8	1.8	1.0
Oreg.	1,772	1,937	2,101	2,251	2,284	2,326	30	2,376	24.7	1.5	1.7	1.8
Calif.	15,870	18,585	20,007	20,907	21,198	21,522	1	21,896	140.0	4.0	2.3	1.2
Alaska	229	271	304	344	365	408	49	407	.7	5.4	2.9	4.1
Hawaii	642	704	774	855	868	884	40	895	139.3	2.6	1.9	2.1

X Not applicable.　Z Less than .05 percent.　[1] For area figures used to derive these data, see table 340.
[2] U.S. total revised. State data revisions not available; therefore, detail will not add to total.　[3] 11,312.4.

Source: U.S. Bureau of the Census, *Current Population Reports*, series P-25, No. 460, and series P-20, No. 324.

No. 12. COMPONENTS OF POPULATION CHANGE—STATES: 1960–1970 AND 1970–1977

[In thousands, except percent. Total resident population. For explanation of methodology, see source. Minus sign
(−) denotes decrease or net outmigration. See also *Historical Statistics, Colonial Times to 1970,* series C 25–75]

| STATE | April 1, 1960, TO April 1, 1970 | | | | | April 1, 1970, TO July 1, 1977 | | | | |
| | Net change | | Births | Deaths | Net total migration [2] | Net change | | Births | Deaths | Net total migration [2] |
	Number	Percent [1]				Number	Percent [1]			
United States	23,912	13.3	39,033	18,192	3,070	13,027	6.4	23,870	13,982	3,140
New England	1,338	12.7	2,169	1,147	316	394	3.3	1,180	822	37
Maine	24	2.5	203	109	−69	91	9.2	117	78	52
New Hampshire	131	21.5	133	71	69	111	15.0	87	54	78
Vermont	55	14.1	85	45	15	39	8.7	52	32	18
Massachusetts	541	10.5	1,040	574	74	93	1.6	545	402	−51
Rhode Island	90	10.5	171	93	13	−15	−1.6	91	67	−39
Connecticut	497	19.6	537	255	214	76	2.5	288	190	−22
Middle Atlantic	3,034	8.9	6,725	3,749	59	−175	−.5	3,739	2,682	−1,232
New York	1,458	8.7	3,361	1,852	−51	−318	−1.7	1,850	1,295	−873
New Jersey	1,101	18.2	1,259	645	488	158	2.2	721	487	−76
Pennsylvania	475	4.2	2,105	1,252	−378	−16	−.1	1,168	901	−283
East North Central	4,028	11.1	7,832	3,652	−153	791	2.0	4,689	2,701	−1,197
Ohio	946	9.7	2,047	975	−126	44	.4	1,225	718	−464
Indiana	531	11.4	1,023	475	−16	135	2.6	630	349	−146
Illinois	1,033	10.2	2,153	1,077	−43	132	1.2	1,295	781	−382
Michigan	1,052	13.4	1,754	729	27	248	2.8	1,052	557	−247
Wisconsin	466	11.8	856	395	4	233	5.3	487	296	42
West North Central	930	6.0	3,133	1,604	−599	557	3.4	1,835	1,178	−100
Minnesota	391	11.5	744	327	−25	169	4.4	423	244	−11
Iowa	68	2.4	541	291	−183	54	1.9	306	209	−43
Missouri	358	8.3	857	502	2	123	2.6	523	367	−33
North Dakota	−15	−2.3	135	55	−94	36	5.8	75	41	1
South Dakota	−14	−2.1	146	65	−94	23	3.4	82	49	−11
Nebraska	72	5.1	291	146	−73	76	5.1	175	108	10
Kansas	70	3.2	419	218	−130	77	3.4	250	160	−13
South Atlantic	4,700	18.1	5,965	2,598	1,332	3,627	11.8	3,719	2,192	2,100
Delaware	102	22.8	109	45	38	34	6.1	64	35	5
Maryland	822	26.5	740	303	385	215	5.5	411	237	42
District of Columbia	−7	−1.0	182	89	−100	−67	−8.8	83	57	−92
Virginia	682	17.2	909	369	141	483	10.4	541	291	233
West Virginia	−116	−6.2	339	190	−265	115	6.6	210	144	49
North Carolina	526	11.5	1,032	412	−94	441	8.7	633	334	142
South Carolina	208	8.7	573	216	−149	285	11.0	359	172	98
Georgia	646	16.4	975	379	51	460	10.0	623	307	144
Florida	1,838	37.1	1,107	596	1,326	1,661	24.5	797	614	1,478
East South Central	754	6.3	2,665	1,213	−698	1,029	8.0	1,658	940	311
Kentucky	181	6.0	647	313	−153	238	7.4	408	242	72
Tennessee	357	10.0	755	353	−45	373	9.5	478	282	178
Alabama	177	5.4	729	319	−233	245	7.1	444	248	49
Mississippi	39	1.8	534	228	−267	172	7.8	329	169	13
West South Central	2,371	14.0	4,012	1,599	−42	2,380	12.3	2,655	1,314	1,040
Arkansas	137	7.7	401	193	−71	221	11.5	249	156	128
Louisiana	386	11.9	832	316	−130	277	7.6	504	247	19
Oklahoma	231	9.9	461	244	13	251	9.8	314	195	133
Texas	1,617	16.9	2,318	847	146	1,632	14.6	1,587	716	760
Mountain	1,429	20.8	1,724	602	307	1,741	21.0	1,265	509	985
Montana	20	2.9	144	66	−58	67	9.6	88	49	27
Idaho	46	6.9	146	58	−42	144	20.3	112	47	79
Wyoming	2	.7	70	28	−39	74	22.2	48	22	49
Colorado	453	25.8	401	163	215	409	18.5	290	130	249
New Mexico	65	6.8	263	68	−130	173	17.0	157	58	74
Arizona	470	36.1	365	122	228	520	29.3	282	119	358
Utah	169	18.9	245	65	−11	209	19.7	221	54	42
Nevada	203	71.3	91	31	144	145	29.6	67	31	108
Pacific	5,328	25.1	4,808	2,028	2,547	2,683	10.1	3,129	1,642	1,196
Washington	556	19.5	591	284	249	245	7.2	378	218	85
Oregon	323	18.2	346	182	159	285	13.6	241	147	191
California	4,236	27.0	3,634	1,511	2,113	1,925	9.6	2,342	1,235	817
Alaska	76	33.6	73	13	16	105	34.6	53	11	62
Hawaii	137	21.7	164	37	11	125	16.2	115	31	40

[1] 1960 to 1970 based on 1960 population; 1970 to 1977 based on 1970 population.
[2] Comprises both net immigration from abroad and net interdivisional or interstate migration according to
the area shown. Includes movements of persons in the Armed Forces.

Source: U.S. Bureau of the Census, *Current Population Reports,* series P–25, No. 460 and forthcoming report; .
and unpublished data.

No. 13. POPULATION PROJECTIONS—STATES: 1985 TO 2000

[In thousands. As of July 1. National population projections series II assumes that cohort fertility will approach 2.1 births per woman. Letters represent various interstate migration assumptions: A assumes that the 1965 to 1975 migration patterns will continue; B assumes that the 1970 to 1975 migration patterns will continue; and C assumes no interstate migration after 1975. For further description of series assumptions, see also table 3]

STATE	SERIES II-A			SERIES II-B			SERIES II-C		
	1985	1990	2000	1985	1990	2000	1985	1990	2000
United States	232,371	243,004	259,869	232,371	243,004	259,869	232,371	243,004	259,869
New England	13,141	13,703	14,615	13,070	13,600	14,449	13,246	13,867	14,855
Maine	1,143	1,192	1,273	1,196	1,273	1,405	1,140	1,191	1,274
New Hampshire	939	1,007	1,121	935	1,002	1,113	881	923	991
Vermont	528	560	614	517	543	586	513	538	578
Massachusetts	6,186	6,415	6,787	6,209	6,450	6,842	6,312	6,606	7,073
Rhode Island	1,000	1,040	1,107	1,003	1,045	1,117	1,014	1,061	1,141
Connecticut	3,345	3,489	3,713	3,210	3,287	3,386	3,386	3,548	3,798
Middle Atlantic	38,338	39,144	40,239	37,700	38,196	38,703	40,326	42,084	44,912
New York	18,288	18,528	18,816	17,927	17,995	17,961	19,902	20,938	22,727
New Jersey	7,964	8,344	8,958	7,741	8,010	8,425	7,962	8,326	8,901
Pennsylvania	12,086	12,272	12,465	12,032	12,191	12,317	12,462	12,820	13,284
East North Central	43,371	44,847	47,005	42,314	43,260	44,398	44,669	46,747	49,951
Ohio	11,251	11,570	11,999	10,861	10,988	11,051	11,644	12,144	12,895
Indiana	5,621	5,804	6,069	5,481	5,595	5,731	5,778	6,038	6,441
Illinois	11,688	12,015	12,491	11,454	11,665	11,923	12,246	12,833	13,777
Michigan	9,866	10,302	10,970	9,546	9,814	10,148	10,049	10,562	11,356
Wisconsin	4,945	5,156	5,476	4,972	5,198	5,545	4,952	5,170	5,482
West North Central	17,495	18,016	18,782	17,550	18,101	18,909	17,903	18,620	19,661
Minnesota	4,209	4,382	4,637	4,179	4,338	4,561	4,253	4,448	4,732
Iowa	2,930	2,988	3,058	2,957	3,031	3,131	3,047	3,165	3,329
Missouri	5,051	5,226	5,506	4,985	5,129	5,346	5,055	5,223	5,469
North Dakota	631	633	631	675	698	732	699	736	791
South Dakota	676	679	679	707	724	748	743	781	839
Nebraska	1,628	1,679	1,755	1,665	1,738	1,851	1,667	1,739	1,848
Kansas	2,370	2,429	2,516	2,380	2,443	2,540	2,439	2,528	2,653
South Atlantic	38,648	41,182	45,400	39,675	42,727	47,949	36,269	37,622	39,666
Delaware	648	684	742	626	651	689	630	658	697
Maryland	4,721	5,048	5,612	4,637	4,928	5,436	4,489	4,683	4,964
District of Columbia	694	693	697	667	651	627	781	812	861
Virginia	5,585	5,899	6,414	5,730	6,117	6,768	5,433	5,664	6,008
West Virginia	1,837	1,869	1,912	1,907	1,973	2,076	1,908	1,971	2,071
North Carolina	6,026	6,332	6,830	6,185	6,573	7,226	5,883	6,102	6,426
South Carolina	3,164	3,346	3,644	3,261	3,494	3,893	3,097	3,241	3,472
Georgia	5,638	6,006	6,625	5,721	6,133	6,840	5,412	5,654	6,047
Florida	10,335	11,305	12,924	10,941	12,207	14,394	8,636	8,837	9,120
East South Central	14,512	15,063	15,918	14,822	15,526	16,661	14,606	15,193	16,124
Kentucky	3,647	3,796	4,032	3,751	3,953	4,290	3,652	3,799	4,035
Tennessee	4,552	4,755	5,085	4,592	4,816	5,183	4,463	4,612	4,827
Alabama	3,842	3,967	4,148	3,958	4,140	4,425	3,912	4,069	4,314
Mississippi	2,471	2,545	2,653	2,521	2,617	2,763	2,579	2,713	2,948
West South Central	23,437	24,791	27,017	23,742	25,254	27,792	23,043	24,196	26,107
Arkansas	2,292	2,390	2,545	2,353	2,479	2,690	2,256	2,336	2,463
Louisiana	4,090	4,245	4,471	4,096	4,255	4,486	4,201	4,417	4,761
Oklahoma	2,976	3,116	3,347	3,016	3,178	3,449	2,906	3,007	3,163
Texas	14,079	15,040	16,654	14,277	15,342	17,167	13,680	14,436	15,714
Mountain	11,274	12,075	13,351	11,857	12,936	14,732	10,841	11,501	12,601
Montana	793	821	862	843	894	977	817	859	921
Idaho	926	982	1,069	979	1,061	1,195	913	968	1,061
Wyoming	408	425	450	442	474	527	415	437	471
Colorado	3,007	3,237	3,615	3,123	3,409	3,892	2,818	2,962	3,181
New Mexico	1,262	1,322	1,409	1,361	1,466	1,636	1,305	1,395	1,541
Arizona	2,771	3,031	3,452	2,926	3,261	3,822	2,490	2,643	2,911
Utah	1,398	1,493	1,643	1,449	1,571	1,775	1,435	1,557	1,781
Nevada	709	764	851	734	800	908	648	680	721
Pacific	32,157	34,184	37,539	31,641	33,405	36,277	31,467	33,172	35,991
Washington	4,047	4,312	4,759	3,792	3,936	4,161	3,869	4,042	4,311
Oregon	2,610	2,781	3,066	2,610	2,781	3,070	2,446	2,533	2,651
California	24,081	25,588	28,083	23,767	25,111	27,309	23,678	24,994	27,191
Alaska	419	441	474	455	491	544	433	470	531
Hawaii	1,000	1,062	1,157	1,017	1,086	1,193	1,041	1,133	1,301

Source: U.S. Bureau of the Census, *Current Population Reports*, series P-25, forthcoming report.

No. 14. Metropolitan and Nonmetropolitan Area Population, Current SMSA Definitions: 1940 to 1976

[Metropolitan area definition as of year shown, except as noted; see Appendix II. SMSA = standard metropolitan statistical area. See also text, p. 2. Data are for total resident population]

ITEM	1940 [1]	1950	1960	1970	1975	1976
Metropolitan areas: Number of SMSA's	168	168	209	243	272	277
Population_____1,000__	69,279	84,501	112,885	139,419	155,021	156,754
Percent change over previous year shown_____	(x)	22.0	33.6	23.5	11.2	1.1
Percent of total U.S. population_____	52.6	56.1	63.0	68.6	72.8	73.0
Land area, percent of U.S. land area_____	7.0	7.0	8.7	10.9	13.9	14.1
Nonmetropolitan areas, population_____1,000__	62,390	66,196	66,438	63,793	58,045	58,114

X Not applicable.   [1] 1950 metropolitan area definition.

Source: U.S. Bureau of the Census, *U.S. Census of Population: 1940; 1950; 1960;* and *1970;* and *Current Population Reports,* series P-25, No. 649, and forthcoming report.

No. 15. Number and Population of SMSA's, 1970 and 1976, and Change, 1960 to 1976

[SMSA = standard metropolitan statistical area. Data exclude Puerto Rico. For definitions, see Appendix II. Minus sign (−) denotes decrease. See also *Historical Statistics, Colonial Times to 1970,* series A 264-275]

POPULATION-SIZE CLASS OF SMSA'S	243 SMSA's [1]				277 SMSA's [3]				
	Number, 1970 [2]	Population, 1970			Number, 1976 [2]	Population, 1970 (mil.)	Population, 1976		
		Total (mil.)	Percent in each class	Percent change, 1960-1970			Total (mil.)	Percent in each class	Percent change, 1970-1976
Total SMSA's_____	243	139.4	100.0	16.6	277	149.5	156.8	100.0	4.9
3,000,000 or more_____	6	37.7	27.0	11.9	7	39.3	38.9	24.8	−.9
1,000,000-3,000,000_____	27	42.9	30.8	20.7	28	45.0	47.8	30.5	6.3
500,000-1,000,000_____	32	21.9	15.7	18.9	37	24.7	26.2	16.7	6.1
250,000-500,000_____	60	19.8	14.2	15.3	70	22.5	24.3	15.5	7.9
100,000-250,000_____	92	15.0	10.7	16.1	112	16.2	17.7	11.3	8.8
Less than 100,000_____	26	2.1	1.5	15.6	23	1.9	1.9	1.2	5.3

[1] As defined in 1970 census publications.   [2] Based on size class in 1970 and 1976, respectively.
[3] As defined by U.S. Office of Federal Statistical Policy and Standards in March 1977.

Source: U.S. Bureau of the Census, *Census of Population: 1970,* vol. I, parts A and B, and *Current Population Reports,* series P-25, Nos. 649-698.

No. 16. Population, by Metro.-Nonmetro. Residence and Race: 1950 to 1977

[In millions, except percent. Covers 243 standard metropolitan statistical areas (SMSA's) as defined in 1970 census publications. Data for 1950-1970 as of April. Data for 1977 are **five-quarter annual averages centered on April** from the Current Population Survey, which excluded inmates of institutions and members of the Armed Forces living in barracks and similar types of quarters; see text, pp. 1-3. Minus sign (−) denotes decrease. See also *Historical Statistics, Colonial Times to 1970,* series A 276-287]

RESIDENCE AND RACE	TOTAL RESIDENT POPULATION							NONINSTITUTIONAL POPULATION		
	1950	1960		1970		Average annual percent change [1]		1970, adjusted [2]	1977	Average annual percent change, [1] 1970-1977 [2]
		Total	Percent	Total	Percent	1950-1960	1960-1970			
All races_____	151.3	179.3	100.0	[3]203.2	100.0	1.7	1.3	199.8	211.8	.8
SMSA's, total_____	94.6	119.6	66.7	139.4	68.7	2.3	1.5	137.1	143.2	.6
Central cities_____	53.7	59.9	33.4	63.8	31.6	1.1	.6	62.9	60.3	−.6
Outside central cities_____	40.9	59.6	33.3	75.6	37.0	3.8	2.4	74.2	82.8	1.6
Nonmetropolitan areas_____	56.7	59.7	33.3	63.8	31.4	.5	.7	62.8	68.6	1.3
White_____	135.2	158.8	100.0	177.7	100.0	1.6	1.1	175.3	183.7	.7
SMSA's_____	85.1	105.8	66.7	120.6	67.8	2.1	1.3	118.9	121.8	.3
Central cities_____	46.8	49.4	31.1	49.4	27.8	.6	(z)	48.9	44.9	−1.2
Outside central cities_____	38.3	56.4	35.5	71.1	40.0	3.8	2.3	70.0	76.9	1.3
Nonmetropolitan areas_____	50.1	53.0	33.4	57.2	32.2	.7	.8	56.3	61.9	1.3
Black_____	15.0	18.9	100.0	22.6	100.0	2.3	1.8	22.1	24.5	1.5
SMSA's_____	8.9	12.7	67.5	16.8	74.3	3.6	2.7	16.3	18.4	1.7
Central cities_____	6.6	9.9	52.3	13.1	58.2	4.1	2.9	12.9	13.7	.9
Outside central cities_____	2.2	2.9	15.2	3.6	16.1	2.1	2.4	3.4	4.6	4.2
Nonmetropolitan areas_____	6.1	6.1	32.5	5.8	25.7	−.1	−.5	5.7	6.1	1.0

Z Less than .05 percent.   [1] Computed using the formula for continuous compounding; see p. xii.   [2] 1970 census data adjusted to exclude inmates of institutions and members of the Armed Forces living in barracks and similar types of quarters for comparability with 1977 data from Current Population Survey.   [3] See footnote 3, Table 1. Totals include corrections and some annexations that are not included in data by race.

Source: U.S. Bureau of the Census, *U.S. Census of Population: 1960* and *1970,* vol. I; *Current Population Reports,* series P-20, No. 324.

No. 17. POPULATION AND AVERAGE ANNUAL CHANGE IN REGIONS, BY METROPOLITAN AREA STATUS: 1960 TO 1975

[In thousands. Covers 246 standard metropolitan areas and 13 New England County Metropolitan areas as defined on Dec. 31, 1976. Large metropolitan areas defined as having 1.5 million or more inhabitants in 1970. For composition of regions, see fig. I, inside front cover]

REGION AND METROPOLITAN AREA STATUS	POPULATION			AVERAGE ANNUAL POPULATION CHANGE					
				Net change		Natural increase		Net migration	
	1960	1970	1975	1960– 1970	1970– 1975	1960– 1970	1970– 1975	1960– 1970	1970– 1975
United States_____	179,311	203,305	213,051	2,399	1,952	2,046	1,456	354	496
Large metropolitan_____	69,262	81,472.	82,899	1,221	285	804	539	417	−254
Other metropolitan_____	58,676	68,355	73,198	968	969	750	576	218	393
Nonmetropolitan_____	51,373	53,478	56,954	211	698	492	341	−281	357
Northeast_____	44,678	49,061	49,454	438	79	397	218	41	−139
Large metropolitan_____	26,309	28,933	28,569	262	−73	236	123	26	−196
Other metropolitan_____	12,300	13,548	13,842	125	59	112	63	13	−4
Nonmetropolitan_____	6,069	6,580	7,043	51	93	49	32	2	61
North Central_____	51,619	56,593	57,665	497	217	567	391	−68	−175
Large metropolitan_____	20,049	22,593	22,612	254	4	249	171	6	−167
Other metropolitan_____	14,810	16,815	17,290	201	95	188	140	13	−45
Nonmetropolitan_____	16,760	17,185	17,763	43	118	130	81	−87	37
South_____	54,961	62,812	68,101	785	1,079	700	554	86	525
Large metropolitan_____	10,232	13,702	15,000	347	260	152	124	195	136
Other metropolitan_____	22,347	26,117	28,546	377	506	312	267	65	239
Nonmetropolitan_____	22,382	22,993	24,555	61	312	236	163	−174	150
West_____	28,053	34,839	37,831	679	578	385	294	293	284
Large metropolitan_____	12,672	16,244	16,718	357	94	168	122	189	−28
Other metropolitan_____	9,219	11,875	13,520	266	309	139	106	126	203
Nonmetropolitan_____	6,162	6,720	7,593	56	175	78	66	−22	109

Source: U.S. Bureau of the Census, *Current Population Reports*, series P-25, No. 709.

No. 18. LAND AREA, POPULATION, AND DENSITY OF URBAN AND RURAL TERRITORY, BY METROPOLITAN AND NONMETROPOLITAN STATUS: 1960 AND 1970

[Areas as defined for the 1960 and 1970 censuses, respectively. Changes in land area between the censuses reflect (a) changes in the extent of urban territory and of standard metropolitan statistical areas (SMSA's) and (b) alterations resulting from remeasurement of land areas, including changes in the extent of inland water area See also *Historical Statistics, Colonial Times to 1970*, series A 73, for total, urban, and rural population]

RESIDENCE	1960 (212 SMSA's)					1970 (243 SMSA's)				
	Land area		Population			Land area		Population		
	Total (sq. mi.)	Percent of U.S.	Total (1,000)	Percent of U.S.	Per sq. mi.	Total (sq. mi.)	Percent of U.S.	Total (1,000)	Percent of U.S.	Per sq. mi.
Total_____	1 3,548,974	100.0	179,323	100.0	51	2 3,540,023	100.0	203,212	100.0	5
Urban_____	40,238	1.1	125,269	69.9	3,113	54,103	1.5	149,325	73.5	2,76
In urbanized areas_	1 25,544	.7	3 95,848	53.4	3,752	35,081	1.0	118,447	58.3	3,37
Other urban_____	14,694	.4	29,420	16.4	2,002	19,022	.5	30,878	15.2	1,62
Rural_____	3,508,736	98.9	54,054	30.1	15	2 3,485,920	98.5	53,887	26.5	)
Inside SMSA's_____	310,233	8.7	112,885	63.0	364	2 387,594	10.9	139,419	68.6	36
Urban_____	(NA)	(NA)	99,563	55.5	(NA)	(NA)	(NA)	123,007	60.5	(NA)
Rural_____	(NA)	(NA)	13,323	7.4	(NA)	(NA)	(NA)	16,412	8.1	(NA)
Outside SMSA's_____	3,238,741	91.3	66,438	37.0	21	2 3,152,429	89.1	63,793	31.4	2
Urban_____	(NA)	(NA)	25,706	14.3	(NA)	(NA)	(NA)	26,318	13.0	(NA)
Rural_____	(NA)	(NA)	40,732	22.7	(NA)	(NA)	(NA)	37,475	18.4	(NA)

NA Not available.   1 Revised since 1960 census as a result of area remeasurement to 3,540,911 for total U.S. and to 24,979 for total inside urbanized areas; revisions not reflected in other territorial categories.
2 Revised since publication of 1970 census reports.
3 Revised to 95,834,251 since publication of 1960 census; revisions not reflected in the total 1960 urban populatio

Source: U.S. Bureau of the Census, *Census of Population: 1970*, vol. I, parts A and B.

No. 19. Metropolitan and Nonmetropolitan Area Population—States: 1960 to 1976

[Excludes Armed Forces abroad. Refers to 277 SMSA's as defined in *Standard Metropolitan Statistical Areas, 1975, Revised Edition* (December 1975); see Appendix II. Minus sign (−) denotes decrease]

STATE	METROPOLITAN AREA POPULATION							NONMETROPOLITAN AREA POPULATION						
	Total (1,000)			Percent change		Percent of State or division		Total (1,000)			Percent change		Percent of State or division	
	1960 (Apr.)	1970 (Apr.)	1976 (July)	1960–1970	1970–1976	1970	1976	1960 (Apr.)	1970 (Apr.)	1976 (July)	1960–1970	1970–1976	1970	1976
U.S.	127,662	149,487	156,754	17.1	4.3	73.5	73.0	51,648	53,818	58,114	4.2	9.6	26.5	27.1
N.E.	8,041	9,048	9,147	12.5	1.1	76.4	74.9	2,468	2,799	3,068	13.3	9.5	23.6	25.1
Maine	233	243	250	4.1	2.9	24.4	23.3	736	751	823	2.0	9.6	75.6	76.7
N.H.	194	262	300	34.9	14.8	35.5	36.3	413	476	527	15.3	10.6	64.5	63.7
Vt.	−	−	−	(X)	(X)	(X)	(X)	390	445	481	14.1	8.0	100.0	100.0
Mass.	4,563	4,980	4,991	9.1	.2	87.5	86.2	586	709	802	21.1	13.1	12.5	13.9
R.I.	786	864	867	9.8	.3	91.3	92.3	73	83	73	13.1	−15.5	8.7	7.7
Conn.	2,265	2,697	2,740	19.1	1.6	89.0	88.3	270	335	363	24.1	8.2	11.0	11.7
M.A.	29,901	32,628	32,318	9.1	−1.0	87.7	86.7	4,266	4,585	4,947	7.5	7.9	12.3	13.3
N.Y.	14,968	16,290	16,001	8.8	−1.8	89.3	88.5	1,814	1,951	2,073	7.6	6.3	10.7	11.5
N.J.	5,807	6,756	6,807	16.3	.8	94.2	92.2	260	415	572	59.6	37.8	5.8	7.8
Pa.	9,127	9,582	9,510	5.0	−.8	81.2	80.5	2,193	2,219	2,302	1.2	3.7	18.8	19.5
E.N.C.	27,728	31,233	31,489	12.6	.8	77.6	76.9	8,497	9,033	9,487	6.3	5.0	22.4	23.2
Ohio	7,745	8,596	8,558	11.0	−.4	80.7	79.9	1,962	2,061	2,154	5.1	4.5	19.3	20.1
Ind.	3,119	3,534	3,603	13.3	2.0	68.0	67.8	1,543	1,662	1,710	7.7	2.9	32.0	32.2
Ill.	8,074	9,056	9,104	12.2	.5	81.5	81.3	2,007	2,057	2,091	2.5	1.6	18.5	18.7
Mich.	6,440	7,354	7,447	14.2	1.3	82.8	81.4	1,383	1,528	1,699	10.5	11.2	17.2	18.6
Wis.	2,350	2,693	2,776	14.6	3.1	61.0	60.2	1,601	1,725	1,834	7.7	6.3	39.0	39.8
W.N.C.	7,345	8,428	8,665	14.7	2.8	51.6	51.5	8,049	7,899	8,150	−1.9	3.2	48.4	48.5
Minn.	2,052	2,451	2,555	19.5	4.2	64.4	64.4	1,362	1,355	1,416	−.6	4.5	35.6	35.7
Iowa	937	1,033	1,074	10.3	4.0	36.6	37.4	1,822	1,792	1,800	−1.6	.4	63.4	62.6
Mo.	2,692	3,042	3,039	13.0	−.1	65.0	63.5	1,628	1,636	1,748	.5	6.9	35.0	36.5
N. Dak.	116	135	146	16.5	8.6	21.8	22.7	517	483	499	−6.5	3.3	78.2	77.3
S. Dak.	87	95	101	10.0	5.8	14.3	14.7	594	571	585	−3.9	2.5	85.7	85.3
Nebr.	542	637	694	17.4	9.0	42.9	44.7	869	849	858	−2.4	1.1	57.2	55.3
Kans.	920	1,035	1,055	12.5	2.0	46.0	45.9	1,259	1,215	1,245	−3.5	2.5	54.0	54.1
S.A.	15,945	20,223	22,469	26.8	11.1	65.9	66.2	10,014	10,456	11,493	4.4	9.9	34.1	33.8
Del.	307	386	401	25.5	3.9	70.4	68.9	139	162	181	16.9	11.5	29.6	31.1
Md.	2,583	3,357	3,509	29.9	4.5	85.6	85.1	518	567	616	9.6	8.6	14.4	14.9
D.C.	764	757	700	−1.0	−7.5	100.0	100.0	−	−	−	(X)	(X)	(X)	(X)
Va.	2,428	3,074	3,327	26.6	8.2	66.1	65.6	1,527	1,577	1,742	3.3	10.4	33.9	34.4
W. Va.	681	664	666	−2.6	.3	38.1	36.4	1,179	1,080	1,166	−8.4	7.9	61.9	63.7
N.C.	1,870	2,285	2,473	22.2	8.2	44.9	45.3	2,686	2,799	2,989	4.2	6.8	55.1	54.7
S.C.	1,033	1,223	1,374	18.4	12.3	47.2	48.3	1,349	1,367	1,470	1.4	7.5	52.8	51.7
Ga.	2,048	2,594	2,830	26.6	9.1	56.5	56.8	1,895	1,994	2,154	5.2	8.0	43.5	43.2
Fla.	4,230	5,884	7,189	39.1	22.2	86.6	86.0	722	908	1,174	25.9	29.4	15.9	14.0
E.S.C.	5,967	6,679	7,117	11.9	6.6	52.1	52.0	6,082	6,129	6,573	.8	7.2	47.9	48.0
Ky.	1,324	1,511	1,563	14.1	3.4	46.9	45.5	1,714	1,710	1,873	−.3	9.5	53.1	54.5
Tenn.	2,216	2,497	2,670	12.7	6.9	63.6	63.1	1,351	1,429	1,564	5.7	9.5	36.4	37.0
Ala.	1,987	2,129	2,259	7.2	6.1	61.8	61.8	1,280	1,316	1,396	2.8	6.1	38.2	38.2
Miss.	441	543	626	23.0	15.3	24.5	26.5	1,737	1,674	1,740	−3.6	3.9	75.5	73.5
W.S.C.	10,842	13,129	14,785	21.1	12.6	67.9	69.2	6,109	6,197	6,588	1.4	6.3	32.1	30.8
Ark.	622	734	813	18.1	10.7	38.2	38.4	1,164	1,189	1,304	2.1	9.6	61.8	61.6
La.	1,985	2,262	2,467	14.0	9.1	62.1	63.4	1,272	1,382	1,423	8.7	2.9	37.9	36.6
Okla.	1,179	1,412	1,537	19.7	8.9	55.2	55.6	1,149	1,148	1,230	−.1	7.2	44.9	44.5
Tex.	7,057	8,722	9,968	23.6	14.3	77.9	79.1	2,523	2,478	2,631	−1.8	6.2	22.1	20.9
Mt.	3,672	4,951	5,933	34.8	19.8	59.7	60.4	3,182	3,338	3,886	4.9	16.4	40.3	39.6
Mont.	152	169	184	11.0	8.8	24.4	24.4	522	525	571	.6	8.8	75.6	75.6
Idaho	93	112	140	20.1	24.6	15.7	16.8	574	601	693	4.7	15.4	84.3	83.2
Wyo.	−	−	−	(X)	(X)	(X)	(X)	330	332	391	.7	17.5	100.0	100.0
Colo.	1,326	1,776	2,076	34.0	16.9	80.4	80.6	428	433	500	1.1	15.5	19.6	19.4
N. Mex.	276	333	393	20.6	17.9	32.7	33.6	675	684	778	1.4	13.8	67.3	66.4
Ariz.	929	1,323	1,675	42.4	26.6	74.5	74.5	373	453	574	21.3	26.8	25.5	25.5
Utah	683	843	971	23.4	15.1	79.6	78.8	207	216	262	4.3	21.1	20.4	21.2
Nev.	212	394	495	86.2	25.6	80.7	80.9	74	94	117	28.4	24.2	19.2	19.2
Pac.	18,219	23,167	24,831	27.2	7.2	87.3	86.4	2,979	3,381	3,923	13.5	16.0	12.7	13.6
Wash.	2,031	2,491	2,576	22.6	3.4	73.0	71.4	822	922	1,035	12.2	12.2	27.0	28.7
Oreg.	1,038	1,281	1,392	23.3	8.7	61.2	59.9	730	811	934	11.0	15.1	38.8	40.1
Calif.	14,566	18,638	19,968	28.0	7.1	93.3	92.8	1,151	1,333	1,555	15.8	16.6	6.7	7.2
Alaska	83	126	179	52.6	42.0	41.7	43.7	143	176	231	22.8	31.2	58.2	56.3
Hawaii	500	631	715	26.0	13.3	81.9	80.9	132	139	169	5.3	21.2	18.1	19.1

− Represents zero or rounds to zero.   X Not applicable.

Source: U.S. Bureau of the Census, *Census of Population: 1970*, vol. I, part A; and *Current Population Reports*, Series P-25, forthcoming report.

No. 20. Large Metropolitan Areas—Population: 1960 to 1976

[In thousands, except as indicated. Covers 163 large SMSA's with estimated population of 200,000 or more as of July 1, 1976, and 13 standard consolidated statistical areas (SCSA's) as defined in *Standard Metropolitan Statistical Areas, 1975, Revised Edition* (Dec. 1975), issued by the Executive Office of the President, Office of Management and Budget. Figures for 1970 include corrections through December 1977. Change measured from April 1, 1960, to April 1, 1970, and from April 1, 1970, to July 1, 1976; minus sign (−) denotes decrease. Rank based on unrounded figures. For definitions and components of SMSA's, SCSA's, and New England County Metropolitan Areas (NECMA's), see Appendix II]

METROPOLITAN AREA	POPULATION Apr. 1, 1960	POPULATION Apr. 1, 1970	POPULATION July 1, 1976 Total	POPULATION July 1, 1976 Rank	POPULATION CHANGE 1960–1970 Number	POPULATION CHANGE 1960–1970 Percent	POPULATION CHANGE 1960–1970 Net migration	POPULATION CHANGE 1970–1976 Number	POPULATION CHANGE 1970–1976 Percent	POPULATION CHANGE 1970–1976 Net migration
Akron, Ohio	605	679	670	55	74	12.2	1	−10	−1.4	−34
Albany-Schenectady-Troy, N.Y	715	778	797	46	63	8.8	9	19	2.4	4
Albuquerque, N. Mex	276	333	393	93	57	20.6	17	60	17.9	38
Allentown-Bethlehem-Easton, Pa.-N.J.	545	594	623	59	49	9.0	16	29	4.9	21
Anaheim-Santa Ana-Garden Grove, Calif	704	1,421	1,756	19	717	101.9	553	334	23.5	256
Ann Arbor, Mich	172	234	248	143	62	35.8	32	14	6.1	1
Appleton-Oshkosh, Wis	232	277	286	124	45	19.4	9	9	3.2	−2
Atlanta, Ga	1,169	1,596	1,805	18	426	36.5	233	209	13.1	115
Augusta, Ga.-S.C	230	276	285	125	46	19.9	12	9	3.3	−6
Austin, Tex	267	360	461	78	93	34.9	51	101	27.9	77
Bakersfield, Calif	292	330	356	104	38	13.1	−5	25	7.7	9
Baltimore, Md	1,804	2,071	2,144	14	267	14.8	54	7.3	3.6	18
Baton Rouge, La	300	376	426	85	76	25.3	21	50	13.4	26
Beaumont, Port Arthur-Orange, Tex	331	348	357	103	17	5.1	−25	10	2.8	−3
Binghamton, N.Y.-Pa	284	303	306	114	19	6.7	−12	3	1.1	−5
Birmingham, Ala	747	767	800	45	21	2.8	−52	33	4.2	8
Boston, Mass	2,688	2,899	2,862	8	211	7.9	(NA)	−37	−1.3	(NA)
Boston-Lowell-Brockton-Lawrence-Haverhill, Mass.-N.H. NECMA	3,457	3,849	3,893	(X)	392	11.3	61	44	1.2	−37
Bridgeport, Conn	350	402	395	91	52	14.7	(NA)	−7	−1.6	(NA)
Bridgeport-Stamford-Norwalk-Danbury, Conn. NECMA	654	793	799	(X)	139	21.3	72	6	.8	−11
Buffalo, N.Y	1,307	1,349	1,328	27	42	3.2	−82	−21	−1.6	−49
Canton, Ohio	361	394	403	89	33	9.0	−3	9	2.4	−4
Charleston-North Charleston, S.C	279	336	378	95	57	20.5	−1	42	12.6	19
Charleston, W. Va	276	257	258	139	−19	−7.0	−46	−	.2	−7
Charlotte-Gastonia, N.C	444	558	593	62	114	25.7	45	35	6.3	6
Chattanooga, Tenn.-Ga	340	371	393	92	31	9.1	−7	23	6.1	7
Chicago, Ill	6,221	6,975	6,993	3	754	12.1	16	18	.3	−246
Cincinnati, Ohio-Ky.-Ind	1,268	1,387	1,364	26	119	9.4	−32	−23	−1.7	−72
Cleveland, Ohio	1,909	2,064	1,967	17	154	8.1	−44	−96	−4.7	−152
Colorado Springs, Colo	146	239	284	126	93	63.6	62	45	18.7	23
Columbia, S.C	261	323	372	98	62	23.8	24	49	15.3	30
Columbus, Ga.-Ala	218	239	230	150	21	9.5	−22	−9	−3.7	−23
Columbus, Ohio	845	1,018	1,072	35	173	20.4	52	54	5.3	8
Corpus Christi, Tex	267	285	303	117	18	6.8	−33	18	6.2	−5
Dallas-Ft. Worth, Tex	1,738	2,378	2,611	10	640	36.8	368	233	9.8	103
Davenport-Rock Island-Moline, Iowa-Ill	319	363	373	97	43	13.5	6	10	2.8	−3
Dayton, Ohio	727	853	837	43	125	17.2	27	−16	−1.8	−52
Daytona Beach, Fla	125	169	210	159	44	35.2	43	40	23.8	43
Denver-Boulder, Colo	935	1,240	1,438	22	305	32.6	165	199	16.0	136
Des Moines, Iowa	287	314	333	109	26	9.2	−8	20	6.3	7
Detroit, Mich	3,950	4,435	4,406	5	485	12.3	−17	−29	−.7	−209
Duluth-Superior, Minn.-Wis	277	265	265	137	−11	−4.1	−30	−1	−.3	−5
El Paso, Tex	314	359	431	83	45	14.4	−29	72	19.9	35
Erie, Pa	251	264	276	130	13	5.2	−13	13	4.8	3
Eugene-Springfield, Oreg	163	215	246	145	53	32.2	29	30	14.0	23
Evansville, Ind.-Ky	272	285	287	123	13	4.7	−9	2	.8	−
Fayetteville, N.C	148	212	230	149	64	42.9	21	18	8.4	−
Flint, Mich	428	509	524	71	81	18.9	6	15	2.9	−1
Fort Lauderdale-Hollywood, Fla	334	620	847	42	286	85.7	257	226	36.5	22
Fort Wayne, Ind	306	362	371	99	56	18.2	12	9	2.6	−
Fresno, Calif	366	413	464	77	47	12.9	−3	50	12.2	3
Gary-Hammond-East Chicago, Ind	574	633	644	57	60	10.4	−24	10	1.6	−2
Grand Rapids, Mich	462	539	569	67	77	16.7	11	30	5.5	
Greensboro-Winston-Salem-High Point, N.C	622	724	766	49	102	16.4	20	42	5.8	1
Greenville-Spartanburg, S.C	413	473	528	70	61	14.7	7	54	11.4	3
Hamilton-Middletown, Ohio	199	226	247	144	27	13.6	1	20	9.1	1
Harrisburg, Pa	372	411	426	84	39	10.5	7	15	3.8	
Hartford, Conn	588	721	730	52	132	22.5	(NA)	9	1.3	(NA)
Hartford-New Britain-Bristol, Conn. NECMA	847	1,035	1,056	(X)	188	22.2	83	21	2.0	−
Honolulu, Hawaii	500	631	715	53	130	26.0	18	84	13.3	3
Houston, Tex	1,430	1,999	2,423	11	569	39.8	317	423	21.2	28
Huntington-Ashland, W.Va.-Ky.-Ohio	284	287	293	118	3	1.0	−24	6	2.0	−
Huntsville, Ala	202	282	287	122	81	39.9	38	5	1.8	−
Indianapolis, Ind	944	1,111	1,141	32	167	17.7	38	29	2.7	−2
Jackson, Miss	221	259	292	119	38	17.0	(z)	33	12.6	1

See footnotes at end of table.

No. 20. LARGE METROPOLITAN AREAS—POPULATION: 1960 TO 1976—Continued

[In thousands, except as indicated. See headnote, p. 20]

METROPOLITAN AREA	POPULATION				POPULATION CHANGE					
	Apr. 1, 1960	Apr. 1, 1970	July 1, 1976		1960–1970			1970–1976		
			Total	Rank	Number	Percent	Net migration	Number	Percent	Net migration
Jacksonville, Fla	530	622	695	54	92	17.4	13	73	11.8	42
Jersey City, N.J	611	608	573	66	−3	−.5	−46	−35	−5.8	−46
Johnson City-Kingsport-Bristol, Tenn.-Va	347	374	403	90	26	7.6	−11	29	7.9	16
Johnstown, Pa	281	263	267	135	−18	−6.4	−33	4	1.7	–
Kalamazoo-Portage, Mich	218	258	265	138	40	18.2	12	7	2.8	−4
Kansas City, Mo.-Kans	1,109	1,274	1,281	28	165	14.9	31	7	.6	−44
Killeen-Temple, Tex	118	160	207	161	42	35.4	15	47	29.6	29
Knoxville, Tenn	377	409	443	82	33	8.7	−7	33	8.1	21
Lakeland-Winter Haven, Fla	195	229	277	128	33	17.1	12	48	21.2	40
Lancaster, Pa	278	320	344	108	42	15.0	11	24	7.5	12
Lansing-East Lansing, Mich	342	424	449	80	82	24.0	28	24	5.8	1
Las Vegas, Nev	127	273	346	107	146	115.2	110	72	26.5	54
Lawrence-Haverhill, Mass.-N.H	218	259	269	133	40	18.4	(NA)	11	4.2	(NA)
Lexington-Fayette, Ky	212	267	291	120	55	25.8	26	25	9.2	12
Lima, Ohio	197	210	212	157	13	6.6	−10	2	1.0	−7
Little Rock-North Little Rock, Ark	272	323	364	100	51	18.9	12	40	12.5	21
Long Branch-Asbury Park, N.J	334	462	494	73	127	38.1	89	32	7.0	20
Lorain-Elyria, Ohio	218	257	266	136	39	18.1	6	9	3.6	−5
Los Angeles-Long Beach, Calif	6,039	7,042	6,997	2	1,003	16.6	269	−45	−.6	−312
Louisville, Ky.-Ind	754	867	887	40	113	15.0	21	20	2.3	−15
Lowell, Mass	167	218	229	152	51	30.8	(NA)	11	5.0	(NA)
Lubbock, Tex	156	179	200	163	23	14.7	−11	21	11.7	8
Macon, Ga	197	227	240	146	30	15.2	(z)	13	5.9	2
Madison, Wis	222	290	310	112	68	30.7	29	19	6.6	6
McAllen-Pharr-Edinburg, Tex	181	182	232	148	1	.4	−43	50	27.8	26
Melbourne-Titusville-Cocoa, Fla	111	230	226	154	119	106.4	87	−4	−1.6	−12
Memphis, Tenn.-Ark.-Miss	727	834	877	41	107	14.7	−4	43	5.1	−1
Miami, Fla	935	1,268	1,450	21	333	35.6	255	182	14.4	161
Milwaukee, Wis	1,279	1,404	1,415	24	125	9.8	−37	11	.8	−36
Minneapolis-St. Paul, Minn.-Wis	1,598	1,965	2,048	15	368	23.0	118	83	4.2	−3
Mobile, Ala	363	377	416	87	13	3.7	42	39	10.4	19
Modesto, Calif	157	195	225	155	37	23.7	19	30	15.5	22
Montgomery, Ala	218	226	252	141	7	3.4	−18	26	11.6	16
Nashville-Davidson, Tenn	597	699	764	50	102	17.2	30	64	9.2	36
Nassau-Suffolk, N.Y	1,967	2,556	2,677	9	589	29.9	359	121	4.8	56
Newark, N.J	1,833	2,057	1,993	16	224	12.2	47	−65	−3.2	−113
New Bedford-Fall River, Mass. NECMA	398	444	464	(x)	46	11.5	15	19	4.4	9
New Brunswick-Perth Amboy-Sayreville, N.J	434	584	593	63	150	34.6	87	9	1.5	−11
New Haven-West Haven, Conn	359	411	413	88	52	14.4	(NA)	2	.4	(NA)
New Haven-West Haven-Waterbury-Meriden, Conn. NECMA	660	745	759	(x)	85	12.8	20	14	1.9	−3
New London-Norwich, Conn.-R.I	196	242	253	140	46	23.2	(NA)	11	4.5	(NA)
New London-Norwich, Conn. NECMA	186	231	243	(x)	45	24.2	15	13	5.5	4
New Orleans, La	907	1,046	1,137	33	139	15.4	11	90	8.6	41
Newport News-Hampton, Va	255	333	359	101	78	30.8	31	25	7.6	6
New York, N.Y.-N.J	9,540	9,974	9,509	1	434	4.5	−319	−465	−4.7	−663
Norfolk-Virginia Beach-Portsmouth, Va.-N.C	629	733	782	47	104	16.5	−2	50	6.8	11
Northeast Pa	621	622	632	58	1	.1	−13	11	1.7	12
Oklahoma City, Okla	566	699	762	51	133	23.5	54	63	9.0	27
Omaha, Nebr.-Iowa	458	543	581	65	85	18.5	9	39	7.2	10
Orlando, Fla	338	453	583	64	116	34.3	70	130	28.6	108
Oxnard-Simi Valley-Ventura, Calif	199	378	448	81	179	90.1	134	70	18.4	46
Paterson-Clifton-Passaic, N.J	407	461	470	75	54	13.3	13	9	1.9	−6
Pensacola, Fla	203	243	274	131	40	19.5	(z)	31	12.9	16
Peoria, Ill	313	342	358	102	29	9.1	−8	16	4.6	2
Philadelphia, Pa.-N.J	4,343	4,824	4,803	4	481	11.1	57	−21	−.4	−135
Phoenix, Ariz	664	969	1,224	30	306	46.1	190	253	26.0	195
Pittsburgh, Pa	2,405	2,401	2,303	13	−4	−.2	−166	−98	−4.1	−121
Portland, Maine NECMA	206	216	232	(x)	10	5.1	−9	16	7.2	9
Portland, Oreg.-Wash	822	1,007	1,096	34	185	22.5	117	89	8.9	60
Poughkeepsie, N.Y	176	222	234	147	46	26.3	26	11	5.1	5
Providence-Warwick-Pawtucket, R.I.-Mass	821	909	905	39	88	10.7	(NA)	−3	−.4	(NA)
Providence-Warwick-Pawtucket, R.I. NECMA	778	855	855	(x)	78	10.0	12	–	–	−16
Raleigh-Durham, N.C	324	419	478	74	95	29.4	49	59	14.1	41
Reading, Pa	275	296	305	115	21	7.6	6	8	2.8	5
Richmond, Va	462	548	594	61	86	18.6	35	47	8.5	30
Riverside-San Bernardino-Ontario, Calif	810	1,139	1,265	29	329	40.6	214	126	11.0	81

See footnotes at end of table.

No. 20. Large Metropolitan Areas—Population: 1960 to 1976—Continued

[In thousands, except as indicated. See headnote, p. 20]

METROPOLITAN AREA	POPULATION		July 1, 1976		POPULATION CHANGE					
	Apr. 1, 1960	Apr. 1, 1970			1960–1970			1970–1976		
			Total	Rank	Number	Percent	Net migration	Number	Percent	Net migration
Roanoke, Va	179	203	214	156	24	13.6	9	11	5.4	6
Rochester, N.Y	801	962	978	37	161	20.1	68	16	1.7	−15
Rockford, Ill	230	272	269	134	42	18.2	8	−3	−1.3	−17
Sacramento, Calif	626	804	908	38	178	28.5	89	104	13.0	73
Saginaw, Mich	191	220	229	151	29	15.2	2	9	4.0	−3
Salem, Oreg	147	187	209	160	39	26.6	26	23	12.2	17
Salinas-Seaside-Monterey, Calif	198	247	272	132	49	24.8	16	24	9.7	9
Salt Lake City, Utah	576	705	800	44	129	22.4	8	94	13.4	27
San Antonio, Tex	736	888	996	36	152	20.7	18	108	12.2	44
San Diego, Calif	1,033	1,358	1,624	20	325	31.4	169	266	19.6	204
San Francisco-Oakland, Calif	2,649	3,109	3,158	6	460	17.4	184	49	1.6	−26
San Jose, Calif	642	1,065	1,205	31	423	65.9	285	140	13.2	85
Santa Barbara-Santa Maria-Lompoc, Calif	169	264	290	121	95	56.4	65	25	9.6	16
Santa Rosa, Calif	147	205	250	142	58	39.0	45	45	22.2	40
Seattle-Everett, Wash	1,107	1,425	1,419	23	317	28.7	188	−6	−.4	−46
Shreveport, La	321	336	353	105	15	4.6	−32	17	5.1	−
South Bend, Ind	271	280	277	129	9	3.3	−18	−3	−1.2	−12
Spokane, Wash	278	287	309	113	9	3.3	−14	22	7.6	12
Springfield-Chicopee-Holyoke, Mass.-Conn	504	542	546	68	38	7.5	(NA)	4	.8	(NA)
Springfield-Chicopee-Holyoke, Mass. NECMA	533	583	597	(X)	50	9.4	(NA)	14	2.4	1
St. Louis, Mo.-Ill	2,144	2,411	2,384	12	266	12.4	24	−27	−1.1	−105
Stamford, Conn	178	206	203	162	28	15.7	(NA)	−4	−1.8	(NA)
Stockton, Calif	250	291	304	116	41	16.4	16	13	4.4	4
Syracuse, N. Y	564	637	651	56	73	12.9	2	15	2.3	−6
Tacoma, Wash	322	412	420	86	91	28.2	46	8	1.9	−10
Tampa-St. Petersburg, Fla	809	1,089	1,367	25	279	34.5	253	278	25.6	282
Toledo, Ohio-Mich	695	763	780	48	67	9.7	−8	18	2.3	−14
Trenton, N.J	266	304	318	111	38	14.2	12	14	4.6	6
Tucson, Ariz	266	352	451	79	86	32.3	48	99	28.3	80
Tulsa, Okla	475	549	598	60	74	15.5	25	49	9.0	27
Utica-Rome, N.Y	331	340	333	110	10	2.9	−21	−8	−2.3	−16
Vallejo-Fairfield-Napa, Calif	200	251	284	127	51	25.3	20	33	13.3	22
Washington, D.C.-Md.-Va	2,097	2,910	3,037	7	813	38.8	427	127	4.4	−11
Waterbury, Conn	191	217	228	153	26	13.7	(NA)	11	4.9	(NA)
West Palm Beach-Boca Raton, Fla	228	349	465	76	121	53.0	101	116	33.1	113
Wichita, Kans	382	389	391	94	8	2.0	−46	1	.3	−16
Wilmington, Del.-N.J.-Md	415	499	518	72	85	20.5	28	18	3.7	−
Worcester, Mass	354	372	377	96	18	5.1	(NA)	5	1.3	(NA)
Worcester-Fitchburg-Leominster, Mass. NECMA	583	637	646	(X)	54	9.2	4	9	1.5	−4
York, Pa	290	330	351	106	39	13.5	10	21	6.5	11
Youngstown-Warren, Ohio	509	537	544	69	28	5.5	−18	7	1.3	−9
STANDARD CONSOLIDATED STATISTICAL AREA (SCSA) [1]										
Boston-Lawrence-Lowell, Mass.-N.H	3,169	3,526	3,525	7	357	11.3	(NA)	−1	−	(NA)
Chicago-Gary, Ill.-Ind	6,794	7,608	7,637	3	814	12.0	−9	29	.4	−269
Cincinnati-Hamilton, Ohio-Ky.-Ind	1,468	1,613	1,611	12	146	9.9	−31	−2	−.2	−62
Cleveland-Akron-Lorain, Ohio	2,732	3,000	2,903	8	267	9.8	−36	−97	−3.2	−191
Detroit-Ann Arbor, Mich	4,122	4,669	4,654	5	547	13.3	14	−15	−.3	−209
Houston-Galveston, Tex.[2]	1,571	2,169	2,611	9	598	38.1	328	442	20.4	299
Los Angeles-Long Beach-Anaheim, Calif.[3]	7,752	9,983	10,466	2	2,231	28.8	1,172	485	4.9	71
Miami-Fort Lauderdale, Fla	1,269	1,888	2,296	10	619	48.8	512	408	21.6	383
Milwaukee-Racine, Wis	1,421	1,575	1,591	13	154	10.9	−29	16	1.0	−35
New York-Newark-Jersey City, N.Y.-N.J.-Conn.[4]	15,405	17,035	16,638	1	1,631	10.6	265	−397	−2.3	(NA)
Philadelphia-Wilmington-Trenton, Pa.-Del.-Md.-N.J	5,024	5,628	5,639	4	604	12.0	98	11	.2	−121
San Francisco-Oakland-San Jose, Calif.[5]	3,492	4,426	4,648	6	934	26.8	490	222	5.0	81
Savannah, Ga	205	208	212	158	3	1.6	47	4	−.6	−21
Seattle-Tacoma, Wash	1,429	1,837	1,839	11	408	28.6	235	2	.1	−51

− Represents zero or rounds to zero.   NA Not available.   X Not applicable.   Z Less than 500.
[1] See Appendix II for component parts.   [2] Includes Galveston-Texas City SMSA also.
[3] Includes Oxnard-Simi Valley-Ventura SMSA and Riverside-San Bernardino-Ontario SMSA also.
[4] Includes Nassau-Suffolk SMSA, Long Branch-Asbury Park SMSA, New Brunswick-Perth Amboy-Sayreville SMSA, Paterson-Clifton-Passaic SMSA, and Stamford and Norwalk SMSA's also.
[5] Includes Vallejo-Fairfield-Napa SMSA also.

Source: U.S. Bureau of the Census, *Census of Population and Housing, 1970*, PHC (2), *General Demographi* *Trends for Metropolitan Areas, 1960 to 1970, Characteristics of the Population*, Part 1, *United States Summary; an Current Population Reports*, series P-25, forthcoming report.

No. 21. URBAN AND RURAL POPULATION, BY RACE: 1960 AND 1970

[In thousands, except percent. An urbanized area comprises at least one city of 50,000 inhabitants (central city) plus contiguous, closely settled areas (urban fringe). For urban definitions, see text, pp. 2, 3. See also *Historical Statistics, Colonial Times to 1970*, series A 73–90]

YEAR AND AREA	Total	White	Black and other	PERCENT DISTRIBUTION		
				Total	White	Black and other
1960, total population	179,323	158,832	20,491	100.0	100.0	100.0
Urban	125,269	110,428	14,840	69.9	69.5	72.4
Inside urbanized areas	95,848	83,770	12,079	53.5	52.7	58.9
Central cities	57,975	47,627	10,348	32.3	30.0	50.5
Urban fringe	37,873	36,143	1,731	21.1	22.8	8.4
Outside urbanized areas	29,420	26,658	2,762	16.4	16.8	13.5
Rural	54,054	48,403	5,651	30.1	30.5	27.6
1970, total population	¹ 203,212	177,749	25,463	100.0	100.0	100.0
Urban	149,325	128,773	20,552	73.5	72.4	80.7
Inside urbanized areas	118,447	100,952	17,495	58.3	56.8	68.7
Central cities	63,922	49,547	14,375	31.5	27.9	56.5
Urban fringe	54,525	51,405	3,120	26.8	28.9	12.3
Outside urbanized areas	30,878	27,822	3,057	15.2	15.7	12.0
Rural	53,887	48,976	4,911	26.5	27.6	19.3

See footnote 3, table 1.

No. 22. URBAN AND RURAL POPULATION, BY SIZE OF PLACE: 1950 TO 1970

[Includes both incorporated and unincorporated places of 2,500 or more and unincorporated territory included in urbanized areas. See text, pp. 2, 3, and *Historical Statistics, Colonial Times to 1970*, series A 43–72]

CLASS AND SIZE	PLACES			POPULATION (1,000)			PERCENT OF TOTAL POPULATION		
	1950	1960	1970	1950	1960	1970	1950	1960	1970
United States	(X)	(X)	(X)	151,326	179,323	¹ 203,212	100.0	100.0	100.0
Urban	4,764	6,041	7,062	96,847	125,269	149,325	64.0	69.9	73.5
Places of 1,000,000 or more	5	5	6	17,404	17,484	18,769	11.5	9.8	9.2
Places of 500,000–1,000,000	13	16	20	9,187	11,111	12,967	6.1	6.2	6.4
Places of 250,000–500,000	23	30	30	8,242	10,766	10,442	5.4	6.0	5.1
Places of 100,000–250,000	66	81	100	9,727	11,652	14,286	6.4	6.5	7.0
Places of 50,000–100,000	126	201	240	8,931	13,836	16,724	5.9	7.7	8.2
Places of 25,000–50,000	253	432	520	8,835	14,951	17,848	5.8	8.3	8.8
Places of 10,000–25,000	779	1,134	1,385	11,878	17,568	21,415	7.8	9.8	10.5
Places of 5,000–10,000	1,184	1,394	1,839	8,193	9,780	12,924	5.4	5.5	6.4
Places of 2,500–5,000	1,858	2,152	2,295	6,529	7,580	8,038	4.3	4.2	4.0
Places under 2,500	457	596	627	578	690	727	.4	.4	.4
Unincorporated parts of urbanized areas	(X)	(X)	(X)	7,344	9,851	15,186	4.9	5.5	7.5
Rural	13,851	13,749	13,706	54,479	54,054	53,887	36.0	30.1	26.5
Places of 1,000–2,500	4,186	4,151	4,191	6,515	6,497	6,656	4.3	3.6	3.3
Places under 1,000	9,665	9,598	9,515	4,037	3,894	3,852	2.7	2.2	1.9
Other rural	(X)	(X)	(X)	43,927	43,664	43,379	29.0	24.3	21.3

X Not applicable.   ¹ See footnote 3, table 1.

Source of tables 21 and 22: U.S. Bureau of the Census, *U.S. Census of Population: 1960* and *1970*, vol. I.

No. 23. CITIES, BY POPULATION SIZE: 1960 TO 1975

[Covers incorporated places of 10,000 population or more]

POPULATION SIZE	NUMBER OF CITIES			POPULATION (mil.)			PERCENT OF TOTAL			CUMULATIVE PERCENT		
	1960	1970	1975	1960	1970	1975	1960	1970	1975	1960	1970	1975
Total	1,654	1,967	2,122	91.0	105.6	109.3	100.0	100.0	100.0	(X)	(X)	(X)
1,000,000 or more	5	6	6	17.5	18.8	17.8	19.2	17.8	16.3	19.2	17.8	16.3
500,000–1,000,000	16	20	17	11.1	13.0	11.3	12.2	12.3	10.3	31.4	30.1	26.6
250,000–500,000	30	30	35	10.8	10.5	12.2	11.8	9.9	11.1	43.2	40.0	37.8
100,000–250,000	79	97	105	11.4	13.9	14.9	12.5	13.1	13.6	55.7	53.1	51.4
50,000–100,000	180	232	230	12.5	16.2	16.1	13.7	15.3	14.7	69.5	68.5	66.1
25,000–50,000	366	455	514	12.7	15.7	17.9	14.0	14.9	16.4	83.5	83.3	82.6
10,000–25,000	978	1,127	1,215	15.1	17.6	19.1	16.5	16.7	17.4	100.0	100.0	100.0

X Not applicable.

Source: U.S. Bureau of the Census, *Census of Population: 1970*, vol. I, part A, and *Current Population Reports*, series P-25, Nos. 649–698.

No. 24. CITIES WITH 100,000 INHABITANTS OR MORE IN 1970—POPULATION, 1950 TO 1976, AND AREA, 1970

[1950-1970, as of April 1; 1976 as of July 1. Data for 1950, 1960, and 1970 refer to municipal limits as of each census. 1976 data include annexations since 1970]

CITY	1950 (1,000)	1960 Total (1,000)	1960 Percent Black	1970 Total (1,000)	1970 Black Number (1,000)	1970 Black Percent of total	1970 Other minority races (1,000)	1970 Land area (sq. mi.)[1]	1970 Population per square mile	1976, est. Total (1,000)	1976, est. Rank
Akron, Ohio	275	290	13.0	275	48	17.5	1	54.2	5,082	250	56
Albany, N.Y	135	130	8.3	116	14	12.2	1	20.9	5,540	109	138
Albuquerque, N. Mex	97	201	1.8	244	5	2.2	5	82.2	2,965	285	47
Alexandria, Va	62	91	11.4	111	16	14.1	1	14.7	7,547	108	141
Allentown, Pa	107	108	.7	110	2	1.8	(z)	17.8	6,153	105	149
Amarillo, Tex	74	138	5.6	127	7	5.3	1	60.7	2,092	141	102
Anaheim, Calif	15	104	(z)	167	(z)	(z)	3	33.3	5,006	199	64
Anchorage, Alaska [2]	11	44	5.1	48	3	5.9	3	16.2	2,965	179	77
Ann Arbor, Mich	48	67	4.7	100	7	6.7	2	21.8	4,578	105	146
Atlanta, Ga	331	487	38.3	497	255	51.3	1	131.5	3,779	426	29
Austin, Tex	132	187	13.1	252	30	11.8	2	72.1	3,492	313	45
Baltimore, Md	950	939	34.7	906	420	46.4	6	78.3	11,568	827	8
Baton Rouge, La.[3]	126	152	29.8	166	46	27.8	1	40.4	4,108	(NA)	(X)
Beaumont, Tex	94	119	29.3	116	36	30.7	(z)	71.6	1,619	117	129
Berkeley, Calif	114	111	19.6	117	27	23.5	10	10.6	11,011	110	137
Birmingham, Ala	326	341	39.6	301	126	42.0	1	79.5	3,785	281	50
Boston, Mass	801	697	9.1	641	105	16.3	12	46.0	13,936	618	18
Bridgeport, Conn	159	157	9.8	157	26	16.3	2	16.1	9,723	140	106
Buffalo, N.Y	580	533	13.3	463	94	20.4	4	41.3	11,205	400	31
Cambridge, Mass	121	108	2.5	100	7	6.8	2	6.2	16,187	101	161
Camden, N.J	125	117	23.4	103	40	39.1	1	9.0	11,395	91	183
Canton, Ohio	117	114	9.7	110	14	12.5	(z)	19.0	5,792	100	162
Cedar Rapids, Iowa	72	92	1.2	111	2	1.6	(z)	50.7	2,182	109	140
Charlotte, N.C	134	202	27.9	241	73	30.3	1	76.0	3,173	282	49
Chattanooga, Tenn	131	130	33.2	119	43	35.8	(z)	52.5	2,268	162	91
Chicago, Ill	3,621	3,550	22.9	3,367	1,103	32.7	57	222.6	15,126	3,074	2
Cincinnati, Ohio	504	503	21.6	453	125	27.6	2	78.1	5,794	410	30
Cleveland, Ohio	915	876	28.6	751	288	38.3	5	75.9	9,893	626	17
Colorado Springs, Colo	45	70	4.5	135	7	5.2	2	60.8	2,221	181	76
Columbia, S.C	87	97	30.3	114	34	29.9	1	106.2	1,069	113	132
Columbus, Ga.[4]	80	117	26.7	167	40	26.2	1	69.5	2,218	163	90
Columbus, Ohio	376	471	16.4	540	100	18.5	3	134.6	4,009	533	21
Corpus Christi, Tex	108	168	5.5	205	11	5.1	2	100.6	2,033	217	61
Dallas, Tex	434	680	19.0	844	210	24.9	8	265.6	3,179	849	7
Dayton, Ohio	244	262	21.8	244	74	30.5	1	38.3	6,360	201	63
Dearborn, Mich	95	112	(z)	104	(z)	(z)	(z)	24.5	4,253	95	176
Denver, Colo	416	494	6.1	515	47	9.1	9	95.2	5,406	480	25
Des Moines, Iowa	178	209	4.9	201	11	5.7	1	63.2	3,174	195	65
Detroit, Mich	1,850	1,670	28.9	1,511	660	43.7	12	138.0	10,953	1,314	6
Duluth, Minn	105	107	.5	101	1	.9	1	67.3	1,494	95	178
Elizabeth, N.J	113	108	10.9	113	17	15.5	1	11.7	9,629	103	152
El Paso, Tex	130	277	(z)	322	7	2.3	3	118.3	2,724	391	32
Erie, Pa	131	138	4.8	129	9	6.6	(z)	18.9	6,838	127	115
Evansville, Ind	129	142	6.6	139	10	7.3	(z)	36.0	3,855	134	111
Flint, Mich	163	197	17.5	193	54	28.1	1	32.8	5,894	170	81
Fort Lauderdale, Fla	36	84	23.3	140	20	14.6	(z)	29.6	4,716	153	98
Fort Wayne, Ind	134	162	7.2	178	19	10.6	1	51.5	3,450	183	73
Fort Worth, Tex	279	356	15.8	393	78	19.9	3	205.0	1,919	368	37
Fremont, Calif	(5)	44	(z)	101	(z)	(z)	3	84.3	1,197	119	123
Fresno, Calif	92	134	7.8	166	16	9.6	6	41.8	3,971	183	72
Garden Grove, Calif	(5)	84	(z)	123	(z)	(z)	2	17.4	7,042	118	128
Gary, Ind	134	178	38.8	175	93	52.8	1	42.0	4,177	164	89
Glendale, Calif	96	119	.1	133	(z)	(z)	2	29.4	4,515	134	116
Grand Rapids, Mich	177	177	8.0	198	22	11.3	1	44.9	4,402	186	77
Greensboro, N.C	74	120	25.8	144	41	28.2	1	54.4	2,648	157	92
Hammond, Ind	88	112	2.2	108	5	4.3	(z)	24.1	4,473	103	154
Hampton, Va.[6]	6	89	21.1	121	31	25.4	1	54.7	2,208	129	119
Hartford, Conn	177	162	15.3	158	44	27.9	2	17.4	9,081	135	107
Hialeah, Fla	20	67	1.3	102	1	1.1	(z)	20.0	5,115	122	122
Hollywood, Fla	14	35	6.3	107	4	3.7	1	25.1	4,258	117	133
Honolulu, Hawaii [7]	248	294	.4	325	2	.7	212	83.9	3,872	1,455	(X)
Houston, Tex	596	938	22.9	1,233	317	25.7	11	433.9	2,841	1,455	9
Huntington Beach, Calif	5	11	(z)	116	(z)	(z)	2	26.6	4,359	159	94

See footnotes at end of table.

No. 24. Cities With 100,000 Inhabitants or More in 1970—Population, 1950 to 1976, and Area, 1970—Continued

[See headnote, p. 24]

CITY	1950 (1,000)	1960 Total (1,000)	1960 Percent Black	1970 Total (1,000)	1970 Black Number (1,000)	1970 Black Percent of total	1970 Other minority races (1,000)	1970 Land area (sq. mi.)[1]	1970 Population per square mile	1976, est. Total (1,000)	1976, est. Rank
Huntsville, Ala	16	72	13.8	138	17	12.1	1	109.1	1,263	143	101
Independence, Mo	37	62	1.1	112	1	.6	(z)	47.8	2,336	111	135
Indianapolis, Ind.[8]	427	476	20.6	734	134	18.0	2	379.4	1,963	709	11
Jackson, Miss	98	144	35.7	154	61	39.7	(z)	50.2	3,067	188	68
Jacksonville, Fla.[9]	205	201	23.2	504	118	22.3	3	766.0	690	532	22
Jersey City, N.J	299	276	13.3	261	55	21.0	3	15.1	17,255	240	57
Kansas City, Kans	130	122	23.1	168	34	20.4	1	56.8	2,961	168	84
Kansas City, Mo	457	476	17.5	507	112	22.1	4	316.3	1,603	458	26
Knoxville, Tenn	125	112	18.5	175	22	12.7	1	77.0	2,267	186	70
Lansing, Mich	92	108	6.3	132	12	9.3	1	33.4	3,939	126	117
Las Vegas, Nev	25	64	15.0	126	14	11.2	2	51.6	2,438	154	97
Lexington, Ky.[10]	56	63	25.8	108	18	17.0	(z)	23.0	4,702	189	67
Lincoln, Nebr	99	129	1.5	150	2	1.5	1	49.3	3,033	164	88
Little Rock, Ark	102	108	23.5	132	33	25.0	(z)	52.8	2,509	152	99
Livonia, Mich	18	67	(z)	110	(z)	(z)	(z)	36.1	3,050	111	136
Long Beach, Calif	251	344	2.8	359	19	5.3	11	48.7	7,364	338	40
Los Angeles, Calif	1,970	2,479	13.5	2,816	504	17.9	139	463.7	6,073	2,744	3
Louisville, Ky	369	391	17.9	361	86	23.8	1	60.0	6,025	330	44
Lubbock, Tex	72	129	8.0	149	11	7.3	1	75.7	1,970	166	86
Macon, Ga	70	70	44.3	122	46	37.3	(z)	49.0	2,498	122	122
Madison, Wis	96	127	1.2	173	3	1.5	2	48.5	3,572	170	79
Memphis, Tenn	396	498	37.0	624	243	38.9	2	217.4	2,868	668	14
Miami, Fla	249	292	22.4	335	76	22.7	2	34.3	9,763	355	39
Milwaukee, Wis	637	741	8.4	717	105	14.7	7	95.0	7,548	661	16
Minneapolis, Minn	522	483	2.4	434	19	4.4	9	55.1	7,884	372	34
Mobile, Ala	129	195	32.4	190	67	35.4	(z)	116.6	1,630	202	62
Montgomery, Ala	107	134	35.1	133	45	33.4	(z)	46.4	2,875	156	94
Nashville-Davidson, Tenn.[11]	174	171	19.1	426	88	19.6	1	507.8	882	431	28
New Bedford, Mass	109	102	3.0	102	4	3.5	1	19.5	5,219	99	164
New Haven, Conn	164	152	14.5	138	36	26.3	2	18.4	7,484	125	118
New Orleans, La	570	628	37.2	593	267	45.0	3	197.1	3,011	581	19
New York, N.Y	7,892	7,782	14.0	7,895	1,668	21.1	178	299.7	26,343	7,423	1
Bronx Borough	1,451	1,425	11.5	1,472	358	24.3	33	41.2	35,721	1,331	(X)
Brooklyn Borough	2,738	2,627	14.1	2,602	656	25.2	40	70.3	37,013	2,387	(X)
Manhattan Borough	1,960	1,698	23.4	1,539	380	24.7	69	22.7	67,808	1,409	(X)
Queens Borough	1,551	1,810	8.1	1,986	258	13.0	33	108.0	18,393	1,969	(X)
Staten Island Borough	192	222	4.4	295	16	5.3	2	57.5	5,138	328	(X)
Newark, N.J	439	405	34.1	382	207	54.2	7	23.5	16,273	331	43
Newport News, Va.[12]	42	114	34.0	138	39	28.4	1	69.1	2,000	141	104
Norfolk, Va	214	305	25.8	308	87	28.3	6	52.6	5,855	284	48
Oakland, Calif	385	368	22.8	362	125	34.5	23	53.4	6,771	332	42
Oklahoma City, Okla	244	324	11.6	366	50	13.7	9	635.7	577	369	36
Omaha, Nebr	251	302	8.3	347	34	9.9	2	76.6	4,534	371	35
Orlando, Fla	52	88	23.3	99	29	29.5	(z)	27.5	3,600	112	133
Parma, Ohio	29	83	.2	100	(z)	(z)	(z)	20.8	4,818	99	166
Pasadena, Calif	105	116	12.5	113	18	16.1	5	22.7	4,992	107	143
Paterson, N.J	139	144	14.7	145	39	26.9	2	8.4	17,241	154	95
Peoria, Ill	112	103	9.3	127	15	11.5	1	37.4	3,395	126	116
Philadelphia, Pa	2,072	2,003	26.4	1,949	654	33.6	16	128.5	15,164	1,797	4
Phoenix, Ariz	107	439	4.8	582	28	4.8	11	247.9	2,346	680	13
Pittsburgh, Pa	677	604	16.7	520	105	20.2	3	55.2	9,422	449	27
Portland, Oreg	374	373	4.2	383	22	5.6	8	89.1	4,294	380	33
Portsmouth, Va	80	115	34.2	111	44	39.9	1	29.0	3,826	109	139
Providence, R.I	249	207	5.4	179	16	8.9	2	18.1	9,901	165	87
Raleigh, N.C	66	94	23.4	122	28	22.7	1	44.9	2,708	137	107
Richmond, Va	230	220	41.8	250	105	42.0	1	60.3	4,140	227	59
Riverside, Calif	47	84	4.7	140	7	5.2	3	71.5	1,959	152	100
Roanoke, Va	92	97	17.0	92	18	19.3	(z)	26.6	3,412	102	159
Rochester, N.Y	332	319	7.4	296	50	16.8	2	36.7	8,072	263	54
Rockford, Ill	93	127	4.2	147	12	8.3	(z)	34.2	4,309	141	103
Sacramento, Calif	138	192	6.3	254	27	10.7	20	93.8	2,712	262	55
St. Louis, Mo	857	750	28.6	622	254	40.9	3	61.2	10,167	519	23
St. Paul, Minn	311	313	2.6	310	11	3.5	3	52.2	5,938	272	51
St. Petersburg, Fla	97	181	13.3	216	32	14.8	1	55.4	3,903	238	58
Salt Lake City, Utah	182	189	.8	176	2	1.2	4	59.3	2,966	169	82
San Antonio, Tex	408	588	7.1	654	50	7.6	6	184.0	3,555	784	10
San Bernardino, Calif	63	92	8.8	104	15	14.0	1	44.4	2,348	103	157
San Diego, Calif	334	573	6.0	697	53	7.6	24	316.9	2,199	789	9
San Francisco, Calif	775	740	10.0	716	96	13.4	108	45.4	15,764	663	15

See footnotes at end of table.

No. 24. CITIES WITH 100,000 INHABITANTS OR MORE IN 1970—POPULATION, 19 50 TO 1976, AND AREA, 1970—Continued

[See headnote, p. 24]

CITY	1950 (1,000)	1960 Total (1,000)	1960 Per-cent Black	1970 Total (1,000)	Black Number (1,000)	Black Per-cent of total	Other minor-ity races (1,000)	Land area (sq. mi.)¹	Popu-lation per square mile	1976, est. Total (1,000)	Rank
San Jose, Calif	95	204	1.0	446	11	2.5	17	136.2	3,273	574	20
Santa Ana, Calif	46	100	1.8	157	7	4.3	4	27.0	5,800	181	74
Savannah, Ga	120	149	35.5	118	53	44.9	1	26.8	4,416	111	134
Scranton, Pa	126	111	.6	104	1	.8	(Z)	25.7	4,030	94	178
Seattle, Wash	468	557	4.8	531	38	7.1	29	83.6	6,350	491	24
Shreveport, La	127	164	34.4	182	62	34.1	(Z)	56.9	3,200	188	69
South Bend, Ind	116	132	9.8	126	18	14.1	1	29.2	4,301	114	131
Spokane, Wash	162	182	1.3	171	2	1.3	3	50.8	3,357	176	78
Springfield, Mass	162	174	7.5	164	21	12.6	1	31.7	5,171	168	85
Springfield, Mo	67	96	2.4	120	2	2.0	(Z)	61.5	1,953	131	112
Stamford, Conn	74	93	8.0	109	13	12.3	1	38.1	2,856	105	150
Stockton, Calif	71	86	8.5	108	12	11.0	10	29.9	3,600	119	126
Syracuse, N.Y	221	216	5.2	197	21	10.8	2	25.8	7,644	181	75
Tacoma, Wash	144	148	4.0	155	10	6.8	4	47.7	3,241	154	96
Tampa, Fla	125	275	16.8	278	55	19.7	1	84.5	3,287	271	52
Toledo, Ohio	304	318	12.6	384	53	13.8	2	81.2	4,727	367	38
Topeka, Kans	79	119	7.7	125	10	8.4	2	47.5	2,632	120	123
Torrance, Calif	22	101	(Z)	135	(Z)	(Z)	5	20.5	6,565	135	108
Trenton, N.J	128	114	22.5	105	40	37.9	1	7.5	13,952	100	163
Tucson, Ariz	45	213	3.3	263	9	3.5	4	80.0	3,287	302	46
Tulsa, Okla	183	262	8.6	332	35	10.6	9	171.9	1,929	334	41
Virginia Beach, Va.¹³	5	8	15.3	172	16	9.1	2	220.0	782	225	60
Warren, Mich	1	89	(Z)	179	(Z)	(Z)	1	34.2	5,242	170	80
Washington, D.C	802	764	53.9	757	538	71.1	10	61.4	12,321	700	12
Waterbury, Conn	104	107	6.6	108	11	10.1	(Z)	27.6	3,914	106	144
Wichita, Kans	168	255	7.8	277	27	9.7	3	86.5	3,197	267	53
Winston-Salem, N.C	88	111	37.1	133	46	34.3	(Z)	56.5	2,352	140	105
Worcester, Mass	203	187	1.1	177	3	1.9	1	37.4	4,721	169	83
Yonkers, N.Y	153	191	4.0	204	13	6.4	1	17.7	11,542	192	66
Youngstown, Ohio	168	167	19.0	140	35	25.2	1	33.6	4,160	130	113

NA Not available.   X Not applicable.   Z Less than 500 or .05 percent.   ¹ Land area information supplied by the individual cities.   ² Anchorage city merged with Greater Anchorage Area Borough in 1975. ³ For 1976, the only estimate available (302) is for Baton Rouge which includes all of East Baton Rouge Parish (except Baker City and Zachary Town).   ⁴ Columbus and the unincorporated balance of Muscogee County consolidated on Jan. 1, 1971.   ⁵ Not incorporated in 1950.   ⁶ Hampton and Elizabeth City County consolidated between 1950 and 1960.   ⁷ For 1976, the only estimate available (715) is for the entire county of Honolulu. ⁸ Indianapolis and the unincorporated balance of Marion County consolidated between 1960 and 1970. ⁹ Jacksonville and the unincorporated balance of Duval County consolidated between 1960 and 1970. ¹⁰ Lexington and Fayette County consolidated between 1970 and 1975.   ¹¹ Nashville and the unincorporated balance of Davidson County consolidated between 1960 and 1970.   ¹² Newport News and Warwick consolidated between 1950 and 1960.   ¹³ Virginia Beach and Princess Anne County consolidated between 1960 and 1970.

Source: U.S. Bureau of the Census, Census of Population: 1970, vol. I, parts A and B, and Current Population Reports, series P-25, forthcoming report.

No. 25. COMPONENTS OF POPULATION CHANGE, BY RACE, BETWEEN 1960 AND 1978

[In thousands, except as indicated. Resident population, excluding Armed Forces abroad. Growth, birth, and death rates per 1,000 population estimated as of July 1]

ITEM	Total¹	White	Black	ITEM	Total¹	White	Black
APR. 1, 1960, TO APR. 1, 1970				1960 (calendar year):			
Population, beg. of period	179,323	158,832	18,872	Net growth rate	16.1	15.1	22.1
Net change during period ²	23,912	19,266	3,709	Birth rate	23.9	22.7	32.9
Births ³	39,073	32,543	5,948	Death rate	9.5	9.4	10.3
Deaths	18,209	15,986	2,107	General fertility rate ⁴	118.0	113.2	152.7
Net civilian immigration	3,887	3,362	234	1970 (calendar year):			
Population, end of period	203,235	178,098	22,581	Net growth rate	12.0	10.6	18.0
APR. 1, 1970, TO JAN. 1, 1978				Birth rate	18.3	17.3	25.4
Population, beg. of period	203,235	178,098	22,581	Death rate	9.4	9.4	10.0
Net change during period ²	14,068	9,921	2,731	General fertility rate ⁴	87.5	83.5	114.7
Births	25,578	20,850	4,125	1977 (calendar year): ⁵			
Deaths	14,913	13,080	1,723	Net growth rate	7.9	6.2	14.3
Net civilian immigration	2,793	1,564	304	Birth rate	15.3	14.3	21.7
Population, end of period	217,303	188,019	25,312	Death rate	8.8	8.9	8.6
				General fertility rate ⁴	67.5	63.7	90.2

¹ Includes other races not shown separately.   ² Includes changes due to movement of Armed Forces to posts overseas and the "error of closure" (the amount necessary to make the components of change add to the net change between censuses).   ³ Adjusted for underregistration.   ⁴ Registered births per 1,000 resident females aged 15 to 44 as of July 1.   ⁵ Preliminary.

Source: U.S. Bureau of the Census, U.S. Census of Population: 1960 and 1970, vol. I; Current Population Reports, series P-25, forthcoming report; and unpublished data.

No. 26. Resident Population, Natural Increase, and Net Migration, by Race—
States: 1960 to 1970 and 1970 to 1975

[In thousands, except percent. For basis of estimates, see p. 2. Minus sign (−) denotes decrease or net outmigration. For composition of regions, see fig. I, inside front cover. See *Historical Statistics, Colonial Times to 1970*, series C 25–75, for net migration]

REGION, DIVISION, AND STATE	APRIL 1, 1960, TO APRIL 1, 1970						APRIL 1, 1970, TO JULY 1, 1975					
	White			Black			White			Black		
	Natural increase[1]	Net migration[2]		Natural increase[1]	Net migration[2]		Natural increase[1]	Net migration[2]		Natural increase[1]	Net migration[2]	
		Number	Percent[3]		Number	Percent[3]		Number	Percent[3]		Number	Percent[3]
U.S.	16,496	2,284	1.4	3,886	−85	−.5	5,360	1,623	.9	1,614	232	1.0
North	8,174	−1,792	−2.0	1,446	995	15.4	2,283	−1,883	−2.0	677	68	.8
South	5,045	1,806	4.2	2,132	−1,380	−12.2	1,816	2,395	4.7	797	44	.4
West	3,278	2,269	8.8	308	301	27.7	1,262	1,112	3.5	140	119	7.0
N. Eng.	941	205	2.0	73	72	29.5	237	40	.4	36	9	2.3
Maine	91	−69	−7.2	1	−2	(B)	28	36	3.6	−	(B)	(B)
N.H.	61	68	11.2	1	(Z)	(B)	24	48	6.6	−	(B)	(B)
Vt.	39	14	3.5	(Z)	(Z)	(B)	15	10	2.2	−	(B)	(B)
Mass.	432	23	.5	31	33	29.5	93	−13	−.2	16	19	10.9
R.I.	72	4	.5	5	2	12.2	17	−38	−4.2	2	−2	−.9
Conn.	245	166	6.8	35	38	35.4	59	−3	−.1	17	−10	−5.7
Mid. Atl.	2,323	−724	−2.3	628	540	19.4	512	−956	−2.9	267	78	2.0
N.Y.	1,141	−638	−4.2	353	396	27.9	244	−701	−4.4	153	60	2.8
N.J.	475	336	6.1	135	120	23.3	113	−85	−1.3	64	35	4.5
Pa.	707	−423	−4.0	139	25	2.9	155	−169	−1.6	50	−18	−1.8
E. No. Cent.	3,524	−617	−1.9	632	356	12.3	1,136	−852	−2.4	323	−15	−.4
Ohio	928	−191	−2.1	139	45	5.8	313	−313	−3.2	65	−6	−.6
Ind.	490	−58	−1.3	56	32	12.0	180	−97	−2.0	28	3	.7
Ill.	805	−215	−2.4	261	127	12.2	234	−308	−3.2	128	−14	−1.0
Mich.	872	−124	−1.7	149	124	17.3	289	−163	−2.1	85	3	.3
Wis.	429	−29	−.8	27	27	36.1	120	29	.6	16	−1	−.6
W. No. Cent.	1,386	−655	−4.4	112	26	4.6	397	−116	−.7	50	−3	−.5
Minn.	404	−39	−1.2	5	7	33.3	121	−17	−.5	4	1	3.6
Iowa	244	−189	−6.9	6	2	6.0	63	−34	−1.2	3	5	14.6
Mo.	279	−25	−.6	75	14	3.7	79	−26	−.6	33	−6	−1.2
N. Dak.	74	−94	−15.2	1	1	(B)	20	−5	−.8	−	(B)	−17.4
S. Dak.	69	−92	−14.0	1	(Z)	(B)	18	−10	−1.7	−	(B)	1.9
Nebr.	134	−76	−5.6	9	2	7.3	42	6	.5	4	3	6.4
Kans.	182	−139	−6.7	16	−1	−.9	53	−29	−1.4	6	−5	−5.1
So. Atl.	2,224	1,807	9.0	1,117	−538	−9.2	728	1,597	6.6	414	143	2.2
Del.	50	32	8.4	14	4	6.6	16	9	1.9	5	2	1.9
Md.	329	290	11.3	104	79	15.2	91	−39	−1.2	41	87	12.5
D.C.	1	−137	−39.7	90	36	8.7	−7	−14	−6.8	27	−53	−9.9
Va.	409	206	6.5	128	−79	−9.7	144	96	2.6	40	29	3.3
W. Va.	144	−247	−14.0	4	−20	−22.2	47	8	.5	−	−3	−4.5
N.C.	412	81	2.4	196	−175	−15.7	148	132	3.4	71	−4	−.4
S.C.	200	44	2.8	157	−197	−23.8	80	61	3.4	57	21	2.7
Ga.	372	198	7.0	223	−154	−13.7	151	83	2.4	86	16	1.3
Fla.	307	1,340	33.0	200	−32	−3.6	58	1,261	22.0	88	49	4.7
E. So. Cent.	991	−153	−1.6	458	−560	−20.8	357	247	2.4	170	−86	−3.3
Ky.	309	−158	−5.6	25	1	.5	107	42	1.4	10	4	1.5
Tenn.	305	1	(Z)	95	−51	−8.7	109	103	3.1	37	−7	−1.2
Ala.	251	−5	−.2	159	−231	−23.6	89	58	2.3	57	−41	−4.5
Miss.	126	10	.8	179	−279	−30.4	51	44	3.2	66	−42	−5.1
W. So. Cent.	1,830	152	1.1	557	−282	−10.2	730	551	2.4	213	−13	−.4
Ark.	128	38	2.7	81	−112	−28.7	45	111	7.1	23	−19	−5.4
La.	302	26	1.2	212	−163	−15.7	104	4	.2	80	−32	−3.0
Okla.	171	−4	−.2	28	−3	−2.1	60	65	2.8	11	9	−5.3
Tex.	1,229	92	1.1	237	−4	−.3	521	371	3.8	99	29	2.1
Mt.	988	295	4.5	42	16	12.6	462	761	9.8	19	25	13.6
Mont.	69	−57	−8.7	1	(Z)	(B)	23	24	3.6	−	(B)	(B)
Idaho	85	−44	−6.6	1	(Z)	(B)	43	56	8.0	−	(B)	(B)
Wyo.	40	−39	−12.2	1	(Z)	(B)	16	25	7.6	−	(B)	(B)
Colo.	224	187	11.0	10	16	40.9	103	199	9.4	6	14	21.2
N. Mex.	160	−120	−13.8	7	−4	−24.7	58	54	5.8	2	(B)	(B)
Ariz.	187	248	21.2	14	−4	−10.2	93	299	18.5	6	8	15.2
Utah	174	−16	−1.9	2	1	(B)	105	34	3.3	1	(B)	(B)
Nev.	49	136	51.5	8	6	48.0	21	71	15.9	4	4	14.1
Pac.	2,289	1,974	10.2	266	286	29.7	799	351	1.5	121	95	6.2
Wash.	280	220	8.0	13	10	20.0	97	21	.6	6	3	3.5
Oreg.	155	145	8.4	4	4	20.9	58	121	6.0	2	2	8.5
Calif.	1,777	1,528	10.6	244	272	30.7	606	183	1.0	110	87	6.2
Alaska	40	22	12.6	3	(Z)	(B)	21	27	11.1	1	(B)	(B)
Hawaii	38	58	28.8	2	1	(B)	17	−1	−.2	1	(B)	(B)

− Represents zero.   B Not shown; for 1960 to 1970, base less than 10,000; for 1970 to 1975, base less than 25,000.
Z Less than 500 or .05 percent.   [1] Births minus deaths.   [2] Comprises net immigration from abroad and net interdivisional or interstate migration according to the area shown. Includes Armed Forces.
[3] For 1960–1970, base is 1960 resident population; for 1970–1975, base is 1970 resident population.
Source: U.S. Bureau of the Census, *Current Population Reports*, series P-23, No. 67, and series P-25, No. 460.

No. 27. POPULATION, BY SEX, RACE, RESIDENCE, AND MEDIAN AGE: 1790 TO 1977

[In thousands, except as indicated. Total resident population excluding Armed Forces abroad. For definition of median, see p. xii. See also *Historical Statistics, Colonial Times to 1970*, series A 73–81 and A 143–149]

DATE	SEX		RACE				RESIDENCE [1]		MEDIAN AGE (years)		
	Male	Female	White	Black Number	Black Percent	Other	Urban	Rural	All races	White	Black
CONTERMINOUS U.S.[2]											
1790 (Aug. 2)	(NA)	(NA)	3,172	757	19.3	(NA)	202	3,728	(NA)	(NA)	(NA)
1800 (Aug. 4)	(NA)	(NA)	4,306	1,002	18.9	(NA)	322	4,986	(NA)	16.0	(NA)
1810 (Aug. 6)	(NA)	(NA)	5,862	1,378	19.0	(NA)	525	6,714	(NA)	16.0	(NA)
1820 (Aug. 7)	4,897	4,742	7,867	1,772	18.4	(NA)	693	8,945	16.7	16.5	17.2
1830 (June 1)	6,532	6,334	10,537	2,329	18.1	(NA)	1,127	11,739	17.2	17.2	16.9
1840 (June 1)	8,689	8,381	14,196	2,874	16.8	(NA)	1,845	15,224	17.8	17.9	17.3
1850 (June 1)	11,838	11,354	19,553	3,639	15.7	(NA)	3,544	19,648	18.9	19.2	17.3
1860 (June 1)	16,085	15,358	26,923	4,442	14.1	79	6,217	25,227	19.4	19.7	17.7
1870 (June 1)	19,494	19,065	33,589	4,880	12.7	89	9,902	28,656	20.2	20.4	18.5
1880 (June 1)	25,519	24,637	43,403	6,581	13.1	172	14,130	36,026	20.9	21.4	18.0
1890 (June 1)	32,237	30,711	55,101	7,489	11.9	358	22,106	40,841	22.0	22.5	17.8
1900 (June 1)	38,816	37,178	66,809	8,834	11.6	351	30,160	45,835	22.9	23.4	19.4
1910 (Apr. 15)	47,332	44,640	81,732	9,828	10.7	413	41,999	49,973	24.1	24.5	20.8
1920 (Jan. 1)	53,900	51,810	94,821	10,463	9.9	427	54,158	51,553	25.3	25.6	22.3
1930 (Apr. 1)	62,137	60,638	110,287	11,891	9.7	597	68,955	53,820	26.4	26.9	23.5
1940 (Apr. 1)	66,062	65,608	118,215	12,866	9.8	589	74,424	57,246	29.0	29.5	25.3
1950 (Apr. 1)	74,833	75,864	134,942	15,042	10.0	713	96,468	54,230	30.2	30.8	26.2
1960 (Apr. 1)	87,865	90,600	158,455	18,860	10.6	1,149	124,699	53,765	29.6	30.3	23.5
UNITED STATES											
1950 (Apr. 1)	75,187	76,139	135,150	15,045	9.9	1,131	96,847	54,479	30.2	30.7	26.2
1960 (Apr. 1)	88,331	90,992	158,832	18,872	10.5	1,620	125,269	54,054	29.5	30.3	23.5
1970 (Apr. 1)	98,926	104,309	178,098	22,581	11.1	2,557	149,325	53,887	28.0	28.9	22.4
1971 (July 1, est.)	100,445	105,775	180,411	23,084	11.2	2,725	(NA)	(NA)	28.0	28.8	22.5
1972 (July 1, est.)	101,477	106,757	181,894	23,465	11.3	2,875	(NA)	(NA)	28.2	29.0	22.7
1973 (July 1, est.)	102,240	107,619	183,032	23,796	11.3	3,031	(NA)	(NA)	28.4	29.3	22.9
1974 (July 1, est.)	102,954	108,435	184,083	24,113	11.4	3,193	(NA)	(NA)	28.7	29.5	23.2
1975 (July 1, est.)	103,723	109,328	185,158	24,436	11.5	3,457	(NA)	(NA)	28.8	29.6	23.5
1976 (July 1, est.)	104,477	110,192	186,227	24,772	11.5	3,670	(NA)	(NA)	29.0	29.8	23.8
1977 (July 1, est.)	105,240	111,092	187,365	25,112	11.6	3,856	(NA)	(NA)	29.4	30.3	24.1

NA Not available.   [1] Beginning 1950, current definition. For explanation of change, see text, p. 2.
[2] Excludes Alaska and Hawaii.

Source: U.S. Bureau of the Census, *U.S. Census of Population: 1930*, vol. II; *1940*, vol. II, part 1, and vol. IV, part 1; *1950*, vol. II, part 1; *1960*, vol. I; *1970*, vol. I, part B; and *Current Population Reports*, series P-25, Nos. 614 and 721.

No. 28. RATIO OF MALES TO FEMALES BY AGE GROUPS, 1910 TO 1977, AND BY RACE, 1977

[Represents number of males per 100 females. Total resident population]

AGE (years)	1910 (Apr. 15)	1920 (Jan. 1)	1930 (Apr. 1)	1940 (Apr. 1)	1950 (Apr. 1)	1960 (Apr. 1)	1970 (Apr. 1)	1975 (July 1)	1977 (July 1) Total	1977 (July 1) White	1977 (July 1) Black	1977 (July 1) Spanish origin [1]
All ages	106.0	[2]104.1	[2]102.5	100.7	98.6	97.1	94.8	94.9	94.7	95.3	90.8	94.9
Under 14	102.1	102.1	102.6	103.0	103.7	103.4	103.9	104.2	104.3	104.8	101.5	105.4
14–24	101.2	97.3	98.4	98.9	98.2	98.7	98.7	101.3	101.5	102.3	96.1	94.1
25–44	110.2	105.1	101.8	98.5	96.4	95.7	95.5	96.5	96.6	98.6	84.0	87.3
45–64	114.4	115.2	109.1	105.2	100.1	95.7	91.6	91.7	91.9	92.6	86.0	90.2
65 and over	101.1	101.3	100.5	95.5	89.6	82.8	72.1	69.4	68.7	68.1	71.8	83.4

[1] March data. Persons of Spanish origin may be of any race. Computed from *Current Population Reports*, series P-20, forthcoming report.   [2] Includes "age not reported."

Source: U.S. Bureau of the Census, based on *U.S. Census of Population: 1950; 1960;* and *1970*, part B; and *Current Population Reports*, series P-25, No. 721, and earlier issues.

No. 29. POPULATION, BY AGE, RACE, AND SEX: 1960 TO 1977

[In thousands, except percent. 1960 and 1970 data based on enumerated population as of April 1; 1977 data based on estimated population as of July 1. Excludes Armed Forces overseas. See also Historical Statistics, Colonial Times to 1970, series A 119–134]

YEAR, SEX, AND RACE	Total, all years	Under 5 years	5-13 years	14-17 years	18-21 years	22-24 years	25-34 years	35-44 years	45-54 years	55-64 years	65 years and over	16 years and over	18 years and over	21 years and over	Median age (yr.)
1960, total [1]	179,323	20,321	32,726	11,155	9,214	6,390	22,818	24,081	20,485	15,572	16,560	120,780	115,121	108,124	29.5
Male	88,331	10,330	16,640	5,646	4,526	3,123	11,179	11,755	10,093	7,537	7,503	58,575	55,716	52,273	28.7
Female	90,992	9,991	16,087	5,508	4,688	3,268	11,639	12,326	10,393	8,036	9,056	62,205	59,406	55,851	30.3
White	158,832	17,359	28,341	9,779	8,080	5,605	20,144	21,564	18,479	14,177	15,304	108,339	103,353	97,217	30.3
Male	78,367	8,849	14,446	4,961	3,982	2,753	9,940	10,564	9,114	6,850	6,908	52,635	50,111	47,084	29.4
Female	80,465	8,509	13,895	4,818	4,098	2,852	10,204	11,000	9,364	7,327	8,396	55,704	53,242	50,133	31.1
Black	18,872	2,731	4,051	1,271	1,045	718	2,420	2,315	1,864	1,281	1,176	11,443	10,820	10,025	23.4
Male	9,114	1,363	2,023	632	499	336	1,119	1,086	891	617	547	5,406	5,096	4,714	22.4
Female	9,758	1,368	2,027	639	546	382	1,301	1,229	973	663	629	6,037	5,724	5,311	24.4
1970, total [1]	203,235	17,163	36,675	15,851	14,155	9,559	24,923	23,101	23,235	18,602	19,972	141,268	133,546	122,722	28.0
Male	98,926	8,750	18,687	8,069	6,929	4,655	12,225	11,239	11,206	8,799	8,367	67,347	63,419	58,078	26.8
Female	104,309	8,413	17,988	7,783	7,227	4,904	12,697	11,863	12,028	9,803	11,605	73,920	70,127	64,644	29.3
White	178,098	14,464	31,171	13,578	12,240	8,415	21,850	20,382	20,887	16,839	18,272	125,520	118,884	109,540	28.9
Male	86,906	7,396	15,928	6,932	6,011	4,123	10,811	10,005	10,112	7,974	7,615	60,034	56,650	52,025	27.6
Female	91,192	7,068	15,242	6,647	6,229	4,292	11,038	10,377	10,776	8,865	10,657	65,486	62,234	57,515	30.1
Black	22,581	2,434	5,008	2,072	1,714	1,007	2,683	2,395	2,114	1,608	1,544	14,053	13,065	11,735	22.4
Male	10,749	1,220	2,509	1,039	816	466	1,226	1,085	979	740	669	6,476	5,981	5,341	21.0
Female	11,832	1,214	2,499	1,035	897	541	1,456	1,311	1,134	869	876	7,577	7,084	6,394	23.6
1977, total [1]	216,332	15,236	32,227	16,781	16,798	11,551	32,990	23,480	23,382	20,395	23,494	160,524	152,089	139,320	29.4
Male	105,240	7,790	16,438	8,553	8,436	5,740	16,312	11,433	11,319	9,650	9,569	76,756	72,460	66,050	28.2
Female	111,092	7,446	15,789	8,228	8,361	5,811	16,677	12,047	12,062	10,746	13,925	83,768	79,629	73,270	30.6
White	187,365	12,535	26,816	14,125	14,295	9,921	28,722	20,491	20,724	18,419	21,316	141,001	133,888	123,031	30.3
Male	91,429	6,424	13,716	7,213	7,207	4,972	14,354	10,085	10,085	8,738	8,635	67,706	64,076	58,608	29.0
Female	95,936	6,111	13,100	6,912	7,088	4,949	14,368	10,406	10,639	9,681	12,681	73,295	69,812	64,424	31.6
Black	25,112	2,316	4,750	2,363	2,193	1,397	3,552	2,556	2,286	1,764	1,934	16,856	15,682	14,002	24.1
Male	11,947	1,172	2,388	1,190	1,070	658	1,634	1,155	1,065	807	808	7,787	7,197	6,374	22.9
Female	13,164	1,144	2,362	1,173	1,123	740	1,918	1,401	1,221	957	1,125	9,068	8,485	7,627	25.2
PERCENT															
1960	100.0	11.3	18.2	6.2	5.1	3.6	12.7	13.4	11.4	8.7	9.2	67.4	64.2	60.3	(X)
1970	100.0	8.4	18.0	7.8	7.0	4.8	12.3	11.3	11.4	9.2	9.9	69.6	65.8	60.5	(X)
1977, total	100.0	7.0	14.9	7.8	7.8	5.3	15.2	10.9	10.8	9.4	10.9	74.2	70.3	64.4	(X)
Male	100.0	7.4	15.6	7.8	8.0	5.5	15.5	10.9	10.8	9.2	9.1	72.9	68.9	62.8	(X)
Female	100.0	6.7	14.2	7.4	7.5	5.2	15.0	10.8	10.9	9.7	12.5	75.4	71.7	66.0	(X)
White	100.0	6.7	14.3	7.5	7.6	5.3	15.3	10.9	11.1	9.8	11.4	75.3	71.5	65.7	(X)
Black	100.0	9.2	18.9	9.4	8.7	5.6	14.1	10.2	9.1	7.0	7.7	67.1	62.4	55.8	(X)

X Not applicable. [1] Includes other races, not shown separately.

Source: U.S. Bureau of the Census, *U.S. Census of Population: 1960 and 1970*, vol. I; and *Current Population Reports*, series P-25, Nos. 519 and 721.

No. 30. POPULATION, BY AGE—STATES: 1977

[In thousands. Preliminary. As of July 1. Resident population. See *Historical Statistics, Colonial Times to 1970*, series A 204–209, for decennial census data]

STATE	Total	Under 5 years	5–13 years	14–17 years	18–20 years	21–44 years	45–64 years	65 years and over	18 years and over	PERCENT		
										Under 5 years	5 to 17 years	65 years and over
U.S.	216,332	15,236	32,227	16,781	12,769	72,049	43,777	23,494	152,089	7.0	22.7	10.9
New Eng.	12,242	729	1,807	944	728	4,042	2,570	1,421	8,762	6.0	22.5	11.6
Maine	1,085	76	166	87	64	340	222	130	756	7.0	23.3	12.0
N.H.	849	57	130	67	48	287	165	93	594	6.7	23.3	11.0
Vt.	483	34	76	38	31	163	88	54	336	7.0	23.6	11.1
Mass.	5,782	331	842	444	355	1,914	1,209	687	4,166	5.7	22.2	11.9
R.I.	935	55	137	70	54	296	205	118	673	5.9	22.1	12.6
Conn.	3,108	176	456	238	176	1,042	681	340	2,238	5.7	22.3	10.9
Mid. Atl.	37,038	2,290	5,367	2,770	2,023	11,976	8,291	4,321	26,611	6.2	22.0	11.7
N.Y.	17,924	1,113	2,603	1,329	978	5,890	3,930	2,082	12,879	6.2	21.9	11.6
N.J.	7,329	455	1,088	563	386	2,372	1,658	808	5,224	6.2	22.5	11.0
Pa.	11,785	722	1,677	878	659	3,714	2,703	1,432	8,508	6.1	21.7	12.1
E. No. Cent.	41,057	2,904	6,319	3,259	2,474	13,662	8,199	4,240	28,575	7.1	23.3	10.3
Ohio	10,701	750	1,635	832	647	3,554	2,173	1,110	7,484	7.0	23.1	10.4
Ind.	5,330	391	828	421	320	1,774	1,041	554	3,690	7.3	23.4	10.4
Ill.	11,245	801	1,692	879	654	3,724	2,302	1,194	7,873	7.1	22.9	10.6
Mich.	9,129	652	1,456	738	567	3,094	1,774	850	6,284	7.1	24.0	9.3
Wis.	4,651	310	708	389	286	1,516	908	534	3,244	6.7	23.6	11.5
W. No. Cent.	16,884	1,163	2,469	1,360	1,022	5,461	3,303	2,107	11,893	6.9	22.7	12.5
Minn.	3,975	270	607	332	247	1,331	734	454	2,765	6.8	23.6	11.4
Iowa	2,879	193	426	236	165	906	580	374	2,025	6.7	23.0	13.0
Mo.	4,801	326	686	371	284	1,558	954	622	3,417	6.8	22.0	12.9
N. Dak.	653	49	97	57	42	202	129	77	450	7.5	23.6	11.7
S. Dak.	689	53	102	59	43	205	139	88	475	7.7	23.3	12.7
Nebr.	1,561	112	227	126	95	501	300	199	1,095	7.2	22.6	12.8
Kans.	2,326	160	324	178	145	759	466	293	1,664	6.9	21.6	12.6
S. Atl.	34,305	2,400	5,044	2,599	2,040	11,522	6,868	3,834	24,263	7.0	22.3	11.2
Del.	582	40	89	46	38	201	115	53	407	6.8	23.1	9.2
Md.	4,139	254	634	330	255	1,469	837	359	2,921	6.1	23.3	8.7
D.C.	690	44	96	46	46	254	134	71	505	6.3	20.6	10.3
Va.	5,135	344	760	400	333	1,826	1,019	454	3,631	6.7	22.6	8.8
W. Va.	1,859	138	272	137	98	584	412	219	1,313	7.4	22.0	11.8
N.C.	5,525	404	836	420	337	1,909	1,087	530	3,864	7.3	22.7	9.6
S.C.	2,876	233	458	232	183	990	532	247	1,953	8.1	24.0	8.6
Ga.	5,048	399	806	393	307	1,763	925	456	3,450	7.9	23.8	9.0
Fla.	8,452	546	1,093	594	443	2,525	1,807	1,444	6,219	6.5	20.0	17.1
E. So. Cent.	13,837	1,061	2,132	1,096	807	4,540	2,692	1,510	9,548	7.7	23.3	10.9
Ky.	3,458	262	524	271	204	1,140	676	382	2,402	7.6	23.0	11.0
Tenn.	4,299	308	636	328	243	1,455	865	465	3,028	7.2	22.4	10.8
Ala.	3,690	281	571	295	216	1,204	725	398	2,543	7.6	23.5	10.8
Miss.	2,389	211	401	202	143	740	426	266	1,575	8.8	25.3	11.1
W. So. Cent.	21,707	1,757	3,362	1,719	1,300	7,239	4,105	2,225	14,869	8.1	23.4	10.2
Ark.	2,144	165	318	167	115	670	424	285	1,494	7.7	22.6	13.3
La.	3,921	326	653	334	243	1,287	717	363	2,609	8.3	25.2	9.3
Okla.	2,811	209	397	211	163	919	563	349	1,994	7.5	21.6	12.4
Tex.	12,830	1,056	1,995	1,006	779	4,364	2,402	1,228	8,773	8.2	23.4	9.6
Mt.	10,031	878	1,547	822	630	3,365	1,871	918	6,784	8.8	23.6	9.1
Mont.	761	59	113	66	45	244	155	79	523	7.7	23.6	10.4
Idaho	857	79	133	71	52	274	165	84	574	9.2	23.8	9.7
Wyo.	406	35	61	33	25	134	84	35	278	8.5	23.1	8.6
Colo.	2,619	200	383	207	172	955	477	224	1,828	7.7	22.5	8.6
N. Mex.	1,190	105	195	107	77	390	218	98	783	8.8	25.4	8.2
Ariz.	2,296	201	349	184	135	740	437	250	1,562	8.7	23.2	10.9
Utah	1,268	152	216	102	87	410	201	98	797	12.0	25.1	7.7
Nev.	633	48	96	51	37	218	134	51	439	7.5	23.2	8.0
Pac.	29,232	2,055	4,181	2,213	1,745	10,243	5,877	2,919	20,784	7.0	21.9	10.0
Wash.	3,658	249	535	285	220	1,277	706	386	2,589	6.8	22.4	10.6
Oreg.	2,376	168	333	180	133	802	485	274	1,695	7.1	21.6	11.5
Calif.	21,896	1,522	3,104	1,642	1,298	7,687	4,457	2,185	15,627	7.0	21.7	10.0
Alaska	407	40	72	36	32	159	58	9	258	9.9	26.7	2.3
Hawaii	895	75	136	70	62	318	172	63	615	8.3	23.0	7.1

Source: U.S. Bureau of the Census, *Current Population Reports*, series P-25, forthcoming report.

No. 31. POPULATION—TOTAL AND PERSONS 14 TO 24 YEARS OLD, BY RACE AND SEX, 1930 TO 1977, AND PROJECTIONS, 1980 AND 1990

[As of July 1. Prior to 1950, excludes Alaska and Hawaii. Beginning 1940, includes Armed Forces abroad. Projections are consistent with series II]

AGE, SEX, AND RACE	1930	1940	1950	1960	1970	1975	1976	1977	1980	1990
Total_____1,000__	123,077	132,122	152,271	180,671	204,878	213,359	215,142	216,817	222,159	243,513
14-24 years old____1,000__	24,852	26,460	24,519	27,346	40,597	44,538	45,056	45,385	45,225	37,919
Percent of total_____	20.2	20.0	16.1	15.1	19.8	20.9	20.9	20.9	20.4	15.6
Male_____1,000__	12,325	13,209	12,277	13,777	20,537	22,534	22,798	22,966	22,873	19,212
Female_____1,000__	12,528	13,252	12,242	13,572	20,059	22,004	22,258	22,419	22,352	18,708
Percent of total_____	10.2	10.0	8.0	7.5	9.8	10.3	10.3	10.3	10.1	7.7
White_____1,000__	110,559	118,629	135,984	160,023	179,494	185,571	186,608	187,747	191,581	207,257
14-24 years old____1,000__	22,034	23,562	21,556	24,007	35,129	38,006	38,359	38,538	38,086	30,913
Percent of total_____	19.9	19.9	15.9	15.0	19.6	20.5	20.6	20.5	19.9	14.9
Male_____1,000__	10,980	11,825	10,851	12,142	17,841	19,308	19,486	19,574	19,333	15,712
Female_____1,000__	11,053	11,736	10,706	11,865	17,289	18,698	18,873	18,964	18,754	15,200
Percent of total_____	10.0	9.9	7.9	7.4	9.6	10.1	10.1	10.1	9.8	7.3
Black and other_____1,000__	12,518	13,494	16,288	20,648	25,385	27,988	28,533	29,070	30,578	36,256
14-24 years old____1,000__	2,820	2,898	2,963	3,339	5,467	6,533	6,696	6,846	7,140	7,007
Percent of total_____	22.5	21.5	18.2	16.2	21.5	23.3	23.5	23.6	23.4	19.3
Male_____1,000__	1,344	1,383	1,428	1,633	2,697	3,227	3,312	3,392	3,542	3,499
Female_____1,000__	1,475	1,515	1,536	1,706	2,771	3,306	3,385	3,455	3,598	3,507
Percent of total_____	11.8	11.2	9.4	8.3	10.9	11.8	11.9	11.9	11.8	9.7

Source: U.S. Bureau of the Census, *Current Population Reports*, series P-25, Nos. 311, 519, and 721.

No. 32. PERSONS 65 YEARS OLD AND OVER—CHARACTERISTICS, BY SEX: 1960 TO 1977

CHARACTERISTIC	1960		1965		1970		1975		1977	
	Male	Female	Male	Female	Male	Female	Male	Female	Male	Female
Total [1]_____mil__	7.5	9.0	7.9	10.2	8.3	11.5	8.7	12.4	9.1	13.0
Percent of total population__	8.6	9.9	8.4	10.3	8.5	11.1	8.6	11.5	8.9	11.8
White [1]_____mil__	6.9	8.4	7.3	9.4	7.6	10.6	7.9	11.3	8.2	11.8
Black [1]_____mil	.5	.6	.6	.8	.7	.9	.8	1.1	.8	1.1
Age: [2]										
65-69 years_____percent__	3.3	3.7	3.1	3.6	3.2	3.7	3.5	4.1	3.5	4.2
70-74 years_____percent__	2.5	2.8	2.5	3.0	2.3	3.0	2.4	3.0	2.5	3.2
75-79 years_____percent__	1.5	1.9	1.6	2.0	1.6	2.2	1.5	2.2	1.5	2.2
80 years and over_____percent__	1.2	1.6	1.3	1.9	1.4	2.3	1.5	2.7	1.6	2.9
Median income: [1][3]										
Families_____dol__	(NA)	(NA)	(NA)	(NA)	4,779	4,986	7,469	7,722	8,752	8,546
Unrelated individuals_____dol__	(NA)	(NA)	(NA)	(NA)	2,191	1,777	3,410	2,901	4,030	3,412
Percent below poverty level: [1][4]										
Family heads_____	29.7	31.5	22.4	27.0	16.6	23.5	7.9	12.3	8.0	14.4
Unrelated individuals_____	58.5	69.1	49.6	64.8	40.0	49.9	25.8	31.7	25.9	31.5
PERCENT DISTRIBUTION										
Marital status: [1]										
Single_____	7.3	8.5	6.6	7.7	7.5	7.7	4.7	5.8	5.9	6.4
Married_____	71.7	36.8	71.3	36.0	73.1	35.6	79.3	39.1	76.7	38.8
Spouse present_____	69.0	35.0	67.9	34.1	69.9	33.9	77.3	37.6	74.2	37.0
Spouse absent_____	2.7	1.8	3.4	1.9	3.2	1.7	2.0	1.5	2.5	1.8
Widowed_____	19.4	53.1	19.5	54.4	17.1	54.4	13.6	52.5	14.2	52.1
Divorced_____	1.7	1.5	2.6	1.9	2.3	2.3	2.5	2.6	3.2	2.8
Family status: [1]										
In families_____	82.3	67.7	80.3	62.9	79.2	58.5	83.3	59.3	83.0	57.8
Primary individuals_____	12.8	26.8	13.9	30.6	14.9	35.2	15.4	39.4	15.3	40.8
Secondary individuals_____	2.4	3.0	2.3	2.2	2.4	1.9	1.2	1.3	1.8	1.4
Residents of institutions [1]_____	2.5	2.4	3.5	4.3	3.6	4.4	(NA)	(NA)	(NA)	(NA)
Labor force participation: [5]										
Employed_____	30.9	9.9	26.8	10.2	26.2	10.0	21.1	7.8	18.0	8.1
Unemployed_____	1.7	.4	1.3	.4	1.0	.3	1.2	.4	1.3	.4
Not in labor force_____	67.3	89.7	71.9	89.5	72.8	89.7	77.7	91.8	80.6	91.6
Living arrangements: [1]										
Living in household_____	97.4	97.0	96.2	95.3	95.5	95.0	99.8	99.8	99.8	99.4
Living alone_____	(NA)	(NA)	13.1	28.6	14.1	33.8	14.8	38.0	14.7	39.6
Spouse present [6]_____	73.2	36.9	67.9	34.1	69.9	33.9	77.3	37.6	74.2	37.0
Living with someone else_____	(NA)	(NA)	15.2	32.6	11.5	27.4	7.7	24.2	10.8	22.7
Not in household [7]_____	2.6	3.0	3.8	4.7	4.5	5.0	.2	.2	.2	.6

NA Not available. [1] Resident population as of March. Beginning 1975, excludes institutional population. [2] Estimated total resident population as of July. [3] Income for preceding year. [4] Poverty status based on income in preceding year. [5] Source: U.S. Bureau of Labor Statistics, *Employment and Earnings*, monthly. [6] For 1960 and 1965, includes a small number of "spouse present" in group quarters. [7] In institutions and other group quarters.

Source: Except as noted, U.S. Bureau of the Census, *Current Population Reports*, series P-20, No. 323, and earlier reports; series P-23, Nos. 57 and 59; series P-25, No. 721; and series P-60, Nos. 105, 106, and forthcoming report.

No. 33. Population, by Ethnic Origin—Selected Characteristics: 1973

[Based on Current Population Survey; sample designed on basis of 1970 census. See text, pp. 1-3. Includes civilian noninstitutional population and members of Armed Forces living off post or with families on post. For definition of median, see p. xii]

ORIGIN	Total (1,000)	Males per 100 females	Median age (years)	PERCENT		Percent high school graduates [1]	Number of families (1,000)	Median family income in 1972
				Under 18 years old	65 years and over			
Total	206,295	94.0	28.1	33.1	9.8	59.9	54,398	$11,233
English [2]	25,993	90.2	39.0	20.8	15.2	70.4	8,338	12,278
French	3,939	92.6	36.7	19.2	13.3	53.7	1,305	10,877
German	20,517	103.1	35.5	21.3	13.3	63.9	7,064	12,217
Irish	12,240	87.4	38.1	19.9	14.6	60.1	3,962	11,518
Italian	7,101	103.5	38.4	18.2	11.2	54.1	2,479	12,520
Polish	3,686	92.8	41.8	15.0	12.5	54.9	1,223	13,069
Russian	1,747	96.5	45.5	12.8	17.7	75.1	601	14,627
Spanish [3]	10,577	96.5	20.1	46.1	3.8	35.0	2,312	8,183
Mexican	6,293	100.9	18.8	48.4	3.6	27.3	1,340	7,908
Puerto Rican	1,548	89.7	18.8	48.7	1.2	26.0	373	7,163
Other	97,593	92.6	21.5	43.1	7.0	59.7	20,466	10,856
Not reported	22,902	96.9	30.0	27.5	10.3	52.7	6,649	9,886

[1] Persons 25 years old and over. [2] Includes Scottish and Welsh.
[3] Includes persons of Central or South American, Cuban, and other Spanish origin, not shown separately.
Source: U.S. Bureau of the Census, *Current Population Reports*, series P-20, No. 264, and unpublished data.

No. 34. Persons of Spanish Origin—Selected Characteristics: 1977

[As of **March**. Persons of Spanish origin may be of any race. See headnote, table 33]

CHARACTERISTIC	Total	Mexican	Puerto Rican	Other [1]	CHARACTERISTIC	Total	Mexican	Puerto Rican	Other [1]
Total 1,000	11,269	6,545	1,742	2,981	Persons 16 yr. old and over 1,000	6,953	3,958	1,004	1,991
Male 1,000	5,486	3,223	809	1,455	In civilian labor force 1,000	4,158	2,420	486	1,252
Female 1,000	5,782	3,322	934	1,526	Percent of total	59.8	61.1	48.4	62.9
PERCENT DISTRIBUTION					Percent unemployed	11.4	10.9	14.4	11.3
Age (in years):					Male:				
Under 5	12.4	13.3	12.8	10.1	Employed 1,000	2,287	1,392	269	625
5-13	21.5	21.6	25.3	19.3	Percent dist	100.0	100.0	100.0	100.0
14-17	8.4	9.0	7.7	7.8	White-collar workers	23.4	16.8	28.1	36.2
18-21	8.3	8.5	7.3	8.4	Blue-collar workers	57.2	63.3	51.3	46.4
22-24	5.7	6.4	4.9	4.7	Service workers	14.8	12.9	19.4	17.3
25-34	15.1	15.1	16.2	14.6	Farm workers	4.6	7.1	1.2	.3
35-44	11.2	10.8	11.4	12.1	Female:				
45-54	8.2	7.2	7.6	10.6	Employed 1,000	1,397	766	146	485
55-64	5.0	4.5	4.1	6.4	Percent dist	100.0	100.0	100.0	100.0
65 and over	4.1	3.6	2.8	5.9	White-collar workers	44.4	40.9	50.7	48.0
					Blue-collar workers	28.9	26.0	33.8	32.2
Marital status: [2]					Service workers	25.2	30.5	15.4	19.8
Single	30.2	30.4	29.7	30.1	Farm workers	1.5	2.6	.2	–
Married	60.4	60.9	60.3	59.5	Families, total 1,000	2,583	1,455	443	686
Widowed	4.3	4.1	4.1	4.7	Percent headed by—				
Divorced	5.0	4.5	5.9	5.7	Husband and wife	76.6	80.1	60.5	79.4
					Female [5]	20.0	16.2	37.2	17.1
Years of school completed: [3]					Family money income, 1976:				
Male:					Percent with income of—				
Less than 5 yr	17.2	22.2	19.3	6.1	Under $3,000	7.1	6.8	9.7	6.0
High school, 4 or more yr	42.4	36.5	32.7	58.5	$3,000-$5,999	18.2	16.2	30.7	14.1
College, 4 or more yr	8.1	4.7	4.1	16.8	$6,000-$9,999	23.4	25.2	21.6	21.1
Female:					$10,000-$14,999	21.5	22.6	18.5	20.7
Less than 5 yr	18.7	24.4	18.3	9.3	$15,000-$19,999	15.4	15.5	8.6	19.1
High school, 4 or more yr	37.2	30.8	29.1	52.3	$20,000-$24,999	7.7	7.3	6.8	9.0
College, 4 or more yr	4.5	3.2	1.7	8.0	$25,000 and over	7.0	6.3	4.0	9.9
					Median income $1,000	10.3	10.3	7.7	12.1
Residence of families:									
Metro. areas (SMSA's) [4]	85.0	79.5	96.1	89.5	Percent below poverty level [6]	23.1	22.0	38.8	15.5
Central cities	51.3	44.4	77.2	49.4	Percent below 125% of poverty level [6]	33.5	34.5	48.4	22.5
Nonmetro. areas	15.0	20.5	3.9	10.5					

– Represents zero.   [1] See footnote 3, table 33.   [2] Persons 14 years old and over.   [3] Persons 25 years old and over.   [4] Standard metropolitan statistical areas as defined for the 1970 Census of Population. See Appendix II.   [5] No spouse present.   [6] For poverty levels, see table 754.

Source: U.S. Bureau of the Census, *Current Population Reports*, series P-20, No. 317, and unpublished data.

No. 35. Resident Population, by Race—States: 1960 to 1975

[In thousands, except percent. For composition of regions, see fig. I, inside front cover. See also *Historical Statistics, Colonial Times to 1970*, series A 199–201]

STATE	1960 (April 1) White	Black	Other	1970 [1] (April 1) White	Black	Other	1975 (July 1) White	Black	Other	PERCENT BLACK OF TOTAL 1960	1970	1975
U.S.	158,832	18,872	1,620	178,158	22,589	2,558	185,141	24,435	3,456	10.5	11.1	11.5
Regions:												
Northeast	41,522	3,028	127	44,416	4,346	299	44,249	4,736	472	6.8	8.9	9.6
No. Cent	48,002	3,446	171	51,717	4,570	306	52,283	4,926	427	6.7	8.1	8.5
South	43,477	11,312	185	50,492	11,973	348	54,702	12,815	524	20.6	19.1	18.8
West	25,830	1,085	1,138	31,533	1,699	1,606	33,907	1,959	2,034	3.9	4.9	5.2
N. Eng	10,242	243	24	11,406	389	53	11,683	434	71	2.3	3.3	3.6
Maine	963	3	2	987	3	4	1,051	[2]	[2]	.3	.3	[2]
N.H	604	2	1	733	3	2	806	[2]	[2]	.3	.3	[2]
Vt	389	1	(z)	443	1	1	469	[2]	[2]	.1	.2	[2]
Mass	5,023	112	14	5,483	176	30	5,564	211	39	2.2	3.1	3.6
R.I	839	18	2	919	25	6	897	28	[2]	2.1	2.7	3.0
Conn	2,424	107	4	2,840	181	11	2,896	188	[2]	4.2	6.0	6.1
Mid. Atl	31,280	2,785	103	33,010	3,957	246	32,566	4,302	401	8.2	10.6	11.5
N.Y	15,287	1,418	78	15,891	2,170	181	15,434	2,382	260	8.4	11.9	13.2
N.J	5,539	515	13	6,365	771	35	6,393	871	70	8.5	10.8	11.9
Pa	10,454	853	13	10,753	1,017	31	10,739	1,049	72	7.5	8.6	8.8
E. No. Cent	33,253	2,885	87	36,216	3,872	178	36,500	4,180	265	8.0	9.6	10.2
Ohio	8,910	786	11	9,656	974	27	9,656	1,034	46	8.1	9.1	9.6
Ind	4,389	269	5	4,825	358	13	4,908	389	[2]	5.8	6.9	7.3
Ill	9,010	1,038	33	9,623	1,420	70	9,549	1,534	114	10.3	12.8	13.7
Mich	7,086	718	20	7,849	992	40	7,976	1,080	55	9.2	11.2	11.9
Wis	3,859	75	18	4,262	128	28	4,411	144	34	1.9	2.9	3.1
W. No. Cent	14,749	561	84	15,501	699	128	15,783	746	162	3.6	4.3	4.5
Minn	3,372	22	20	3,739	35	32	3,843	40	39	.7	.9	1.0
Iowa	2,729	25	4	2,785	33	8	2,814	40	[2]	.9	1.2	1.4
Mo	3,923	391	6	4,182	480	16	4,235	507	25	9.0	10.3	10.6
N. Dak	620	1	12	600	2	15	616	[2]	[2]	.1	.4	[2]
S. Dak	653	1	26	631	2	33	639	[2]	40	.2	.3	[2]
Nebr	1,075	29	7	1,400	40	10	1,404	40	[2]	2.1	2.7	3.0
Kans	2,079	91	9	2,128	107	15	2,152	108	[2]	4.2	4.8	4.7
So. Atl	20,048	5,845	80	24,138	6,390	151	26,463	6,948	247	22.5	20.8	20.6
Del	384	61	1	467	78	3	491	85	[2]	13.6	14.3	14.7
Md	2,574	518	8	3,199	700	24	3,252	829	42	16.7	17.8	20.1
D.C	345	412	7	211	538	7	190	511	[2]	53.9	71.1	71.9
Va	3,142	816	8	3,767	862	23	4,008	931	42	20.6	18.5	18.7
W. Va	1,770	89	1	1,674	67	3	1,729	64	[2]	4.8	3.9	3.6
N.C	3,399	1,116	41	3,905	1,127	52	4,185	1,193	63	24.5	22.2	21.9
S.C	1,551	829	2	1,796	789	6	1,937	867	[2]	34.8	30.5	30.8
Ga	2,817	1,123	3	3,392	1,187	9	3,626	1,288	[2]	28.5	25.9	26.1
Fla	4,064	880	8	5,726	1,042	23	7,045	1,179	53	17.8	15.3	14.2
E. So. Cent	9,339	2,699	12	10,211	2,572	25	10,815	2,656	45	22.4	20.1	19.7
Ky	2,820	216	2	2,985	231	5	3,134	244	[2]	7.1	7.2	7.2
Tenn	2,978	587	3	3,297	621	7	3,509	651	[2]	16.5	15.8	15.6
Ala	2,284	980	3	2,535	904	6	2,682	920	[2]	30.0	26.2	25.4
Miss	1,258	916	5	1,394	816	7	1,490	841	[2]	42.0	36.8	35.9
W. So. Cent	14,090	2,768	93	16,143	3,011	172	17,424	3,211	232	16.3	15.6	15.4
Ark	1,396	389	2	1,567	352	4	1,723	356	31	21.8	18.3	16.9
La	2,212	1,039	6	2,547	1,087	11	2,656	1,134	[2]	31.9	29.8	29.8
Okla	2,108	153	67	2,284	171	104	2,409	191	115	6.6	6.7	7.1
Tex	8,375	1,187	18	9,745	1,401	53	10,637	1,530	70	12.4	12.5	12.5
Mt	6,514	123	218	7,826	180	284	9,049	224	352	1.8	2.2	2.3
Mont	651	2	23	664	2	29	711	[2]	34	.2	.3	[2]
Idaho	657	2	8	700	2	11	799	[2]	[2]	.2	.3	[2]
Wyo	323	2	5	324	3	6	364	[2]	[2]	.7	.8	[2]
Colo	1,701	40	13	2,120	66	23	2,422	87	33	2.3	3.0	3.4
N. Mex	876	17	58	920	20	77	1,032	[2]	91	1.8	1.9	[2]
Ariz	1,170	43	89	1,615	53	107	2,007	67	137	3.3	3.0	3.0
Utah	874	4	13	1,034	7	19	1,173	[2]	[2]	.5	.6	[2]
Nev	263	14	8	449	28	12	542	36	[2]	4.7	5.7	6.0
Pac	19,316	962	920	23,708	1,519	1,322	24,858	1,734	1,682	4.5	5.7	6.1
Wash	2,752	49	53	3,261	71	81	3,379	80	100	1.7	2.1	2.3
Oreg	1,732	18	19	2,035	26	30	2,215	31	39	1.0	1.3	1.3
Calif	14,455	884	378	17,871	1,404	695	18,660	1,601	937	5.6	7.0	7.6
Alaska	175	7	45	239	9	54	287	[2]	67	3.0	3.0	[2]
Hawaii	202	5	426	301	8	461	317	[2]	540	.8	1.0	[2]

Z   Fewer than 500.
[1] Includes corrections through November 1976.   [2] Not shown; estimated population less than 25,000.

Source: U.S. Bureau of the Census, *U.S. Census of Population: 1960*, vol. I, and *1970*, vol. I; and *Current Population Reports*, series P-23, No. 67.

No. 36. Population, by Sex and Race—States: 1960 and 1970

[In thousands. As of April 1. Resident population. See *Historical Statistics, Colonial Times to 1970*, series A 197–198, for sex by States]

STATE	1960 Male	1960 Female	1970 Male White	1970 Male Black	1970 Female White	1970 Female Black	STATE	1960 Male	1960 Female	1970 Male White	1970 Male Black	1970 Female White	1970 Female Black
U.S.	88,331	90,992	86,721	10,748	91,028	11,832	S.A.—Con.						
							W. Va.	915	945	811	32	862	36
N.E.	5,121	5,388	5,498	185	5,891	204	N.C.	2,247	2,309	1,921	541	1,981	586
Maine	479	490	479	2	506	1	S.C.	1,176	1,207	892	377	903	412
N.H.	298	309	358	1	375	1	Ga.	1,926	2,017	1,667	558	1,725	629
Vt.	192	198	216	(z)	226	(z)	Fla.	2,437	2,515	2,763	499	2,957	543
Mass.	2,486	2,662	2,619	83	2,859	93	E.S.C.	5,909	6,141	4,985	1,213	5,217	1,358
R.I.	422	438	448	13	467	13	Ky.	1,508	1,530	1,464	112	1,517	119
Conn.	1,244	1,291	1,377	86	1,458	96	Tenn.	1,741	1,826	1,602	292	1,692	330
M.A.	16,605	17,563	15,846	1,842	17,076	2,113	Ala.	1,592	1,675	1,235	423	1,298	480
N.Y.	8,123	8,659	7,596	1,002	8,238	1,167	Miss.	1,068	1,110	685	387	710	429
N.J.	2,972	3,095	3,080	364	3,270	407	W.S.C.	8,364	8,587	7,894	1,436	8,211	1,574
Pa.	5,510	5,810	5,169	477	5,568	540	Ark.	879	907	763	167	803	185
E.N.C.	17,863	18,362	17,647	1,848	18,513	2,025	La.	1,592	1,665	1,250	515	1,292	572
Ohio	4,764	4,942	4,686	461	4,961	509	Okla.	1,148	1,180	1,113	81	1,167	91
Ind.	2,299	2,364	2,352	172	2,469	186	Tex.	4,745	4,835	4,768	673	4,949	726
Ill.	4,953	5,128	4,675	673	4,925	753	Mt.	3,449	3,406	3,860	93	3,938	88
Mich.	3,883	3,940	3,845	479	3,989	512	Mont.	344	331	331	1	331	1
Wis.	1,965	1,987	2,090	62	2,169	66	Idaho	338	329	349	1	350	1
W.N.C.	7,609	7,785	7,557	335	7,924	364	Wyo.	169	161	162	1	161	1
Minn.	1,693	1,721	1,829	18	1,907	17	Colo.	870	883	1,041	34	1,071	32
Iowa	1,359	1,398	1,353	16	1,430	17	N. Mex.	480	471	453	10	464	10
Mo.	2,108	2,212	2,020	226	2,157	254	Ariz.	655	647	789	27	816	26
N. Dak.	323	309	302	2	297	1	Utah	445	446	509	4	523	3
S. Dak.	344	336	313	1	318	1	Nev.	148	138	228	14	221	14
Nebr.	700	711	700	19	733	21	Pac.	10,619	10,579	11,629	744	11,950	770
Kans.	1,081	1,097	1,040	53	1,082	54	Wash.	1,435	1,418	1,613	38	1,638	33
S.A.	12,792	13,179	11,806	3,053	12,307	3,336	Oreg.	880	889	995	13	1,038	13
Del.	221	225	228	38	238	41	Calif.	7,837	7,880	8,731	683	9,030	717
Md.	1,533	1,567	1,565	337	1,629	363	Alaska	129	97	130	5	107	4
D.C.	358	406	94	253	115	285	Hawaii	338	295	160	5	138	3
Va.	1,979	1,988	1,865	419	1,897	442							

Z Fewer than 500.

Source: U.S. Bureau of the Census, *U.S. Census of Population: 1960*, vol. I, and *1970*, vol. I.

No. 37. Black Population, by Age—States: 1970

[In thousands. As of April 1. Resident population. For State totals, see table 36]

STATE	Under 5 years	5–17 years	18–24 years	25–44 years	45–64 years	65 and over	STATE	Under 5 years	5–17 years	18–24 years	25–44 years	45–64 years	65 and over
U.S.	2,433	7,076	2,719	5,075	3,720	1,559	Mo.	50	151	55	104	80	40
							Mont.	(z)	1	1	(z)	(z)	(z)
Ala.	95	300	102	163	157	86	Nebr.	5	13	5	9	5	2
Alaska	1	2	2	3	1	(z)	Nev.	4	9	3	7	3	1
Ariz.	6	18	7	11	8	4	N.H.	(z)	(z)	(z)	1	(z)	(z)
Ark.	38	119	37	55	60	43	N.J.	89	235	89	199	118	41
Calif.	150	425	175	358	224	69	N. Mex.	2	7	3	4	2	1
Colo.	7	20	10	17	9	3	N.Y.	232	615	249	602	358	113
Conn.	23	56	22	47	25	7	N.C.	116	366	149	224	192	80
Del.	9	25	9	17	13	5	N. Dak.	(z)	1	1	1	(z)	(z)
D.C.	52	145	72	142	97	30	Ohio	98	297	113	228	170	65
Fla.	116	341	119	231	168	67	Okla.	18	55	21	32	28	18
Ga.	131	383	148	244	192	89	Oreg.	3	8	4	6	5	1
Hawaii	1	2	2	2	(z)	(z)	Pa.	102	298	114	238	190	76
Idaho	(z)	1	(z)	(z)	(z)	(z)	R.I.	3	7	4	6	3	1
Ill.	158	454	163	353	219	79	S.C.	87	272	101	149	126	53
Ind.	38	116	42	81	58	23	S. Dak.	(z)	(z)	(z)	(z)	(z)	(z)
Iowa	4	10	5	7	5	2	Tenn.	64	198	74	121	108	57
Kans.	11	33	15	22	17	9	Texas	152	433	172	304	226	112
Ky.	22	69	29	45	42	24	Utah	1	2	1	1	1	(z)
La.	124	362	130	211	171	89	Vt.	(z)	(z)	(z)	(z)	(z)	(z)
Maine	(z)	1	1	1	(z)	(z)	Va.	84	268	105	185	155	65
Md.	74	220	84	169	113	39	Wash.	8	21	11	17	11	3
Mass.	21	53	24	44	24	9	W. Va.	5	20	7	10	15	10
Mich.	111	299	125	231	169	56	Wis.	17	44	17	31	15	4
Minn.	4	10	5	8	5	2	Wyo.	(z)	1	(z)	1	(z)	(z)
Miss.	97	287	91	132	130	79							

Z Fewer than 500.

Source: U.S. Bureau of the Census, *Census of Population: 1970*, vol. I.

No. 38. POPULATION, BY RACE AND SEX, 1940 TO 1970, AND URBAN-RURAL RESIDENCE, 1960 AND 1970

[In thousands. As of April 1. Resident population. Prior to 1960, excludes Alaska and Hawaii. See also *Historical Statistics, Colonial Times to 1970*, series A 91–104]

RACE AND SEX	1940	1950	1960			1970		
			Total	Urban [1]	Rural [1]	Total	Urban [1]	Rural [1]
Total	131,669	150,697	179,323	125,268	54,054	[2] 203,212	149,325	53,887
White	118,215	134,942	158,832	110,428	48,403	177,749	128,773	48,976
Black	12,866	15,042	18,872	13,808	5,064	22,580	18,367	4,213
Indian	334	343	524	146	378	793	356	437
Japanese	127	142	464	381	83	591	524	68
Chinese	77	118	237	227	11	435	419	16
Filipino	46	62	176	130	47	343	293	50
Other [3]	5	49	218	150	68	721	593	127
Male	66,062	74,833	88,331	60,733	27,598	98,912	71,959	26,954
White	59,449	67,129	78,367	53,631	24,736	86,721	62,210	24,511
Black	6,269	7,299	9,113	6,557	2,556	10,748	8,657	2,091
Indian	171	179	263	72	191	389	172	217
Japanese	72	77	225	184	41	271	240	31
Chinese	57	77	136	129	6	229	220	8
Filipino	40	46	112	80	32	189	159	31
Other [3]	4	27	115	79	36	365	300	64
Female	65,608	75,864	90,992	64,536	26,456	104,300	77,366	26,933
White	58,766	67,813	80,465	56,797	23,667	91,028	66,563	24,465
Black	6,596	7,744	9,758	7,251	2,508	11,832	9,710	2,122
Indian	163	165	260	74	187	404	184	220
Japanese	55	65	240	197	43	320	283	37
Chinese	20	41	102	97	4	206	199	8
Filipino	6	16	64	50	14	154	134	19
Other [3]	1	22	103	71	33	356	293	63

[1] Based on 1960 urban definition; see text, p. 3.   [2] See footnote 3, table 1.   [3] Aleuts, Asian Indians, Eskimos, Hawaiians, Indonesians, Koreans, Polynesians, and other races not shown separately.

Source: U.S. Bureau of the Census, *U.S. Census of Population, 1950*, vol. II, part 1, and vol. IV, part 3; *1960* and *1970*, vol. I.

No. 39. POPULATION OF RACES OTHER THAN WHITE OR BLACK, BY STATES: 1970

[As of April 1. Resident population]

STATE	Indian	Japanese	Chinese	Filipino	All other [1]	STATE	Indian	Japanese	Chinese	Filipino	All other [1]
U.S.	792,730	591,290	435,062	343,060	720,520	Mo.	5,405	2,382	2,815	2,010	6,222
						Mont.	27,130	574	289	236	1,142
Ala.	2,443	1,079	626	540	2,179	Nebr.	6,624	1,314	551	324	1,902
Alaska	16,276	916	228	1,498	35,786	Nev.	7,933	1,087	955	817	2,007
Ariz.	95,812	2,394	3,878	1,253	9,271	N.H.	361	360	420	157	772
Ark.	2,014	587	743	289	1,302	N.J.	4,706	5,681	9,233	5,623	22,721
Calif.	91,018	213,280	170,131	138,859	178,671	N. Mex.	72,788	940	563	386	5,953
Colo.	8,836	7,831	1,489	1,068	9,272	N.Y.	28,355	20,351	81,378	14,279	89,565
Conn.	2,222	1,621	2,209	2,177	6,845	N.C.	44,406	2,104	1,255	905	5,144
Del.	656	359	392	392	1,403	N. Dak.	14,369	239	165	204	805
D.C.	956	651	2,582	1,662	3,675	Ohio	6,654	5,555	5,305	3,490	13,539
Fla.	6,677	4,090	3,133	5,092	9,457	Okla.	98,468	1,408	999	612	5,488
Ga.	2,347	1,836	1,584	1,253	4,164	Oreg.	13,510	6,843	4,814	1,633	6,198
Hawaii	1,126	217,307	52,039	93,915	98,441	Pa.	5,533	5,461	7,053	4,560	17,056
Idaho	6,687	2,255	498	206	1,989	R.I.	1,390	629	1,093	1,761	1,757
Ill.	11,413	17,299	14,474	12,654	32,081	S.C.	2,241	826	521	1,222	2,235
Ind.	3,887	2,279	2,115	1,365	6,235	S. Dak.	32,365	221	163	83	715
Iowa	2,992	1,009	993	614	3,410	Tenn.	2,276	1,160	1,610	846	2,604
Kans.	8,672	1,584	1,233	758	5,286	Texas	17,957	6,537	7,635	3,442	45,026
Ky.	1,531	1,095	558	612	2,351	Utah	11,273	4,713	1,281	392	3,071
La.	5,294	1,123	1,340	1,249	3,970	Vt.	229	134	173	53	427
Maine	2,195	348	206	453	770	Va.	4,853	3,500	2,805	7,496	6,958
Md.	4,239	3,733	6,520	5,170	8,370	Wash.	33,386	20,335	9,201	11,462	12,422
Mass.	4,475	4,393	14,012	2,361	10,488	W. Va.	751	368	373	722	1,201
Mich.	16,854	5,221	6,407	3,657	18,404	Wis.	18,924	2,648	2,700	1,209	5,067
Minn.	23,128	2,603	2,422	1,456	4,456	Wyo.	4,980	566	292	108	878
Miss.	4,113	461	1,441	475	1,369						

[1] Aleuts, Asian Indians, Eskimos, Hawaiians, Indonesians, Koreans, Polynesians, and other races not shown separately.

Source: U.S. Bureau of the Census, *Census of Population: 1970*, vol. I.

No. 40. POPULATION, BY RACE, NATIVITY, AND SEX, 1920 TO 1970, AND BY URBAN AND RURAL RESIDENCE, 1970

[In thousands, except percent. Prior to 1960, excludes Alaska and Hawaii. In some instances, breakdown does not add to total because data are derived from different tabulations. Parentage data, all data for 1960 and 1970, and all other data, as noted, based on sample. See *Historical Statistics, Colonial Times to 1970*, series A 105–118 for foreign born and A 135–142 for native born]

RACE, NATIVITY, AND SEX	1920	1930	1940	1950	1960	1970 Total	1970 Urban	1970 Rural
Total	105,711	122,775	131,669	150,697	179,326	203,210	149,332	53,878
Native	91,790	108,571	120,074	1 139,869	169,588	193,591	140,612	52,979
Percent of total	86.8	88.4	91.2	92.8	94.6	95.3	94.2	98.3
Foreign born	13,921	14,204	11,595	1 10,347	9,738	9,619	8,720	899
Percent of total	13.2	11.6	8.8	6.9	5.4	4.7	5.8	1.7
White	94,821	110,287	118,215	134,942	158,838	178,119	129,077	49,042
Native	81,108	96,303	106,796	124,781	149,544	169,385	121,187	48,198
Native parentage	58,422	70,401	84,125	100,805	125,759	146,231	101,687	44,545
Foreign parentage	15,695	17,408	15,184	14,816	23,784	23,154	19,500	3,654
Mixed parentage	6,992	8,495	7,974	8,763				
Foreign born	13,713	13,983	11,419	10,161	9,294	8,734	7,890	844
Other races 2	1 10,890	1 12,488	13,455	15,755	20,488	25,091	20,255	4,836
Male	53,900	62,137	66,062	74,833	88,303	98,882	71,939	26,942
Native	(NA)	(NA)	59,940	1 68,942	83,543	94,478	(NA)	(NA)
Foreign born	(NA)	(NA)	6,122	1 5,258	4,760	4,404	(NA)	(NA)
White	48,431	55,923	59,449	67,129	78,348	86,893	62,352	24,541
Native	40,902	48,420	53,438	61,953	73,840	82,910	58,769	24,141
Foreign born	7,528	7,502	6,011	5,176	4,508	3,983	3,583	399
Other races 2	1 5,470	1 6,215	6,613	7,704	9,956	11,989	9,587	2,401
Female	51,810	60,638	65,608	75,864	91,022	104,328	77,393	26,936
Native	(NA)	(NA)	60,134	1 70,927	86,045	99,113	(NA)	(NA)
Foreign born	(NA)	(NA)	5,473	1 5,089	4,978	5,216	(NA)	(NA)
White	46,390	54,364	58,766	67,813	80,490	91,226	66,725	24,501
Native	40,206	47,883	53,358	62,828	75,703	86,475	62,419	24,057
Foreign born	6,184	6,481	5,408	4,985	4,786	4,751	4,307	444
Other races 2	1 5,420	1 6,274	6,841	8,052	10,533	13,102	10,668	2,435

NA Not available.　　1 Based on sample.　　2 Blacks, Aleuts, Chinese, Eskimos, Filipinos, Hawaiians, Indians, Indonesians, Japanese, Koreans, Polynesians, and other races.

Source: U.S. Bureau of the Census, *U.S. Census of Population: 1930*, vol. II; *1950*, vol. II, part 1, and vol. IV, part 3; *1960*, vol. I and vol. II, part 1A; and *1970*, vol. I, part 1C.

No. 41. USUAL AND SECOND LANGUAGE SPOKEN IN HOUSEHOLDS: 1975

[As of July]

USUAL LANGUAGE OF HOUSEHOLD	HOUSEHOLDS Number (1,000)	HOUSEHOLDS Percent	PERSONS 4 YEARS OLD AND OVER 1 Number (1,000)	PERSONS 4 YEARS OLD AND OVER 1 Percent	SECOND LANGUAGE IN HOUSEHOLD	HOUSEHOLDS Number (1,000)	HOUSEHOLDS Percent	PERSONS 4 YEARS OLD AND OVER 1 Number (1,000)	PERSONS 4 YEARS OLD AND OVER 1 Percent
All languages	71,537	100.0	196,796	100.0	Total	71,537	100.0	196,796	100.0
English	67,308	94.1	185,545	94.3	With second language	8,369	11.7	24,810	12.6
Spanish	1,448	2.0	4,822	2.5	English	2,224	3.1	6,993	3.6
Chinese	111	.2	353	.2	Spanish	1,610	2.3	5,189	2.6
Filipino	43	.1	122	.1	Chinese	68	.1	196	.1
					Filipino	70	.1	255	.1
French	125	.2	285	.1	French	683	1.0	1,990	1.0
German	59	.1	157	.1	German	822	1.1	2,131	1.1
Greek	50	.1	161	.1	Greek	105	.1	327	.2
Italian	195	.3	522	.3					
					Italian	785	1.1	2,331	1.2
Japanese	43	.1	109	.1	Japanese	119	.2	418	.2
Korean	35	(z)	123	.1	Korean	40	.1	126	.1
Portuguese	43	.1	143	.1	Portuguese	87	.1	206	.1
					All other	1,756	2.5	4,648	2.4
Other	397	.6	966	.5	No second language	61,347	85.8	168,191	85.5
Not reported	1,680	2.3	3,487	1.8	Not reported	1,822	2.5	3,795	1.9

Z Less than .05 percent.　　1 Persons in households.

Source: U.S. Bureau of the Census, *Current Population Reports*, series P-23, No. 60.

No. 42. Nativity and Parentage of the Foreign Stock—States: 1960 and 1970

[In thousands, except percent. 1960 data based on 25-percent sample; 1970, on 15-percent sample. See source for sampling variability. U.K. = United Kingdom]

| STATE | 1960 | | FOREIGN STOCK, 1970 | | | | |
	Foreign stock	Percent of U.S. division or State	Total	Percent of U.S. division or State	Foreign born	Native of foreign or mixed parentage	Leading countries of origin and percent of division or State population
U.S.	34,050	19.0	33,575	16.5	9,619	23,956	Italy, 2.1; Germany, 1.8; Canada, 1.5.
N. Eng	3,870	36.8	3,617	30.5	929	2,688	**Canada, 7.9; Italy, 5.2; U.K., 2.5.**
Maine	226	23.3	193	19.4	43	150	Canada, 13.8; U.K., 1.2; Ireland, .7.
N.H	177	29.2	171	23.2	37	134	Canada, 13.1; U.K., 1.6; Ireland, 1.1.
Vt	86	22.1	81	18.2	18	63	Canada, 10.4; U.K., 1.6; Italy, 1.1.
Mass	2,058	40.0	1,892	33.3	495	1,397	Canada, 8.2; Italy, 5.2; Ireland, 3.8.
R.I	340	39.6	311	32.8	74	237	Italy, 7.7; Canada, 7.0; U.K., 3.6.
Conn	982	38.7	970	32.0	262	708	Italy, 7.5; Canada, 4.2; Poland, 3.4.
Mid. Atl	11,098	32.5	10,284	27.6	3,190	7,094	**Italy, 6.2; Poland, 2.7; Germany, 2.5.**
N.Y	6,487	38.7	5,995	32.9	2,110	3,885	Italy, 7.3; U.S.S.R., 3.1; Poland, 3.1.
N.J	2,109	34.8	2,156	30.1	635	1,521	Italy, 7.2; Germany, 3.1; Poland, 3.0.
Pa	2,502	22.1	2,133	18.1	446	1,687	Italy, 3.8; Poland, 2.1; Germany, 1.7.
E. No. Cent	7,129	19.7	6,297	15.6	1,584	4,713	**Germany, 2.4; Poland, 1.8; Italy, 1.4.**
Ohio	1,491	15.4	1,311	12.3	316	995	Germany, 1.8; Italy, 1.6; Poland 1.1.
Ind	377	8.1	351	6.8	83	268	Germany, 1.2; Poland, .7; U.K., .6.
Ill	2,449	24.3	2,202	19.8	629	1,573	Germany, 2.8; Poland, 2.7; Italy, 2.1.
Mich	1,899	24.3	1,684	19.0	424	1,260	Canada, 4.0; Poland, 2.4; Germany, 2.1.
Wis	914	23.1	748	16.9	131	617	Germany, 5.3; Poland, 1.6; Norway, 1.2.
W. No. Cent	2,425	15.8	1,951	12.0	290	1,661	**Germany, 2.9; Norway, 1.2; Sweden, 1.1.**
Minn	875	25.6	707	18.6	98	609	Germany, 3.6; Sweden, 3.0; Norway, 3.0.
Iowa	388	14.1	297	10.5	40	257	Germany, 3.6; Sweden, .7; Norway, .7.
Mo	367	8.5	312	6.7	66	246	Germany, 1.7; Italy, .6; U.K., .5.
N. Dak	190	30.1	146	23.6	18	128	Norway, 6.3; U.S.S.R., 5.4; Germany, 3.4.
S. Dak	142	20.9	109	16.4	11	98	Germany, 4.0; Norway, 2.8; U.S.S.R., 2.1.
Nebr	258	18.3	205	13.8	29	176	Germany, 4.2; Czech., 1.3; Sweden, 1.2.
Kans	206	9.5	175	7.8	28	147	Germany, 1.9; U.S.S.R., .8; U.K., .7.
So. Atl	1,714	6.6	2,409	7.9	879	1,530	**Germany, .9; Cuba, .9; U.K., .8.**
Del	59	13.2	65	11.9	16	49	Italy, 2.2; U.K., 1.5; Poland, 1.3.
Md	372	12.0	454	11.6	124	330	Germany, 1.5; Italy, 1.3; U.S.S.R., 1.2.
D.C	97	12.7	73	9.7	34	39	Germany, .7; U.K., .7; U.S.S.R., .7.
Va	178	4.5	252	5.4	72	180	Germany, .7; U.K., .7; Canada, .5.
W. Va	91	4.9	74	4.2	17	57	Italy, 1.0; U.K., .5; Germany, .4.
N.C	68	1.5	95	1.9	29	66	Germany, .3; U.K., .3; Canada, .2.
S.C	38	1.6	49	1.9	14	35	Germany, .4; U.K., .3; Canada, .2.
Ga	78	2.0	112	2.4	33	79	Germany, .5; U.K., .3; Canada, .2.
Fla	733	14.8	1,236	18.2	540	696	Cuba, 3.7; Germany, 1.8; U.K., 1.7.
E. So. Cent	218	1.8	236	1.8	60	176	**Germany, .4; U.K., .2; Italy, .2.**
Ky	75	2.5	73	2.3	17	56	Germany, .7; U.K., .2; Canada, .1.
Tenn	59	1.7	68	1.7	19	49	Germany, .3; U.K., .2; Canada, .2.
Ala	55	1.7	64	1.9	16	48	Germany, .4; U.K., .3; Italy, .2.
Miss	29	1.3	31	1.4	8	23	Germany, .2; Italy, .2; U.K., .2.
W. So. Cent	1,329	7.8	1,469	7.6	378	1,091	**Mexico, 3.7; Germany, .8; U.K., .4.**
Ark	34	1.9	37	1.9	8	29	Germany, .5; U.K., .2; Canada, .2.
La	124	3.8	140	3.8	40	100	Italy, .8; Germany, .4; U.K., .3.
Okla	89	3.8	93	3.6	20	73	Germany, .8; U.K., .4; Canada, .3.
Tex	1,082	11.3	1,199	10.7	310	889	Mexico, 6.4; Germany, .9; U.K., .4.
Mt	1,046	15.3	1,098	13.3	246	852	**Mexico, 2.4; Germany, 1.6; U.K., 1.4.**
Mont	150	22.2	122	17.6	20	102	Canada, 3.0; Germany, 2.2; Norway, 2.1.
Idaho	83	12.4	74	10.4	13	61	Canada, 1.5; U.K., 1.5; Germany, 1.4.
Wyo	48	14.5	38	11.4	7	31	Germany, 1.7; U.K., 1.6; Canada, .9.
Colo	261	14.9	280	12.7	60	220	Germany, 2.0; U.S.S.R., 1.2; U.K., 1.2.
N. Mex	79	8.3	89	8.8	23	66	Mexico, 3.7; Germany, .7; U.K., .6.
Ariz	236	18.1	297	16.8	77	220	Mexico, 6.4; Canada, 1.5; Germany, 1.4.
Utah	139	15.6	132	12.5	30	102	U.K., 2.7; Germany, 1.3; Canada, 1.1.
Nev	50	17.5	68	13.9	18	50	Italy, 1.6; Canada, 1.6; Germany, 1.4.
Pac	5,222	24.6	6,214	23.4	2,064	4,150	**Mexico, 4.3; Canada, 2.4; Germany, 1.8.**
Wash	654	22.9	638	18.7	156	482	Canada, 4.0; Germany, 2.1; U.K., 1.8.
Oreg	301	17.0	295	14.1	66	229	Canada, 2.5; Germany, 1.9; U.K., 1.4.
Calif	3,994	25.4	4,992	25.0	1,758	3,234	Mexico, 5.6; Canada, 2.2; U.K., 1.9.
Alaska	31	13.7	33	11.0	8	25	Canada, 2.2; Germany, 1.2; U.K., 1.0.
Hawaii	243	38.4	257	33.4	76	181	Japan, 13.7; China, 2.7; Canada, .8.

Source: U.S. Bureau of the Census, *U.S. Census of Population: 1960*, vol. I, and *1970*, vol. I.

No. 43. FOREIGN STOCK, BY COUNTRY OF ORIGIN: 1960 AND 1970

[In thousands, except as indicated. 1960 based on 25-percent sample; 1970 on 15-percent sample. See source for sampling variability. See also *Historical Statistics, Colonial Times to 1970*, series C 195–295]

COUNTRY OF ORIGIN	1960		1970						
	Total	Per-cent	Total	Per-cent	For-eign born	Native of for-eign or mixed parent-age	Per-cent high school grad-uates [1]	Num-ber of fami-lies	Median family income [2]
All countries	34,050	100.0	33,575	100.0	9,619	23,956	48.1	11,706	$10,719
United Kingdom	2,885	8.5	2,465	7.3	686	1,779	60.0	810	11,120
Ireland (Eire)	1,773	5.2	1,450	4.3	251	1,199	54.6	506	11,509
Norway	775	2.3	615	1.8	97	517	48.7	238	9,615
Sweden	1,047	3.1	806	2.4	127	679	52.4	326	10,038
Denmark	399	1.2	326	1.0	61	264	52.8	129	9,711
Netherlands	399	1.2	384	1.1	111	273	48.1	141	10,730
Switzerland	263	.8	219	.7	50	169	(NA)	(NA)	(NA)
France	352	1.0	343	1.0	105	238	55.6	95	10,389
Germany [3]	4,321	12.7	3,622	10.8	833	2,789	42.3	1,221	9,505
Poland	2,780	8.2	2,374	7.1	548	1,826	41.4	961	11,767
Czechoslovakia	918	2.7	760	2.3	161	599	42.6	300	10,676
Austria	1,099	3.2	975	2.9	214	761	49.0	389	11,733
Hungary	702	2.1	604	1.8	183	420	48.3	236	11,845
Yugoslavia	449	1.3	447	1.3	154	294	44.6	170	11,388
U.S.S.R.	2,290	6.7	1,943	5.8	463	1,480	60.0	817	13,165
Lithuania	403	1.2	331	1.0	76	255	52.0	133	12,317
Greece	379	1.1	435	1.3	177	257	53.6	154	11,132
Italy	4,544	13.3	4,241	12.6	1,009	3,232	40.1	1,740	11,115
Other Europe	1,173	3.4	1,214	3.6	405	809	(NA)	(NA)	(NA)
Asia [4]	1,142	3.4	1,745	5.2	825	920	(NA)	(NA)	(NA)
Western Asia [5]	335	1.0	399	1.2	174	225	(NA)	(NA)	(NA)
China (incl. Taiwan)	208	.6	339	1.0	172	167	57.5	84	10,683
Japan	322	.9	394	1.2	120	274	68.1	106	12,772
Other Asia	276	.8	613	1.8	358	255	(NA)	(NA)	(NA)
Canada	3,181	9.3	3,035	9.0	812	2,222	54.6	950	10,794
Mexico	1,736	5.1	2,339	7.0	760	1,579	24.1	637	7,263
Cuba	124	.4	561	1.7	439	122	44.6	143	8,728
Other America	456	1.3	963	2.9	605	358	(NA)	(NA)	(NA)
Other [4] and not reported	462	1.4	1,380	4.1	466	914	(NA)	(NA)	(NA)

NA Not available.   [1] Persons 25 years old and over.   [2] Income received during 1969; for definition of median, see p. xii.   [3] German Democratic Republic and Federal Republic of Germany.
[4] For 1960, United Arab Republic included in Asia; for 1970, in "Other."   [5] Includes Turkey in Europe.

Source: U.S. Bureau of the Census, *U.S. Census of Population: 1960*, vol.I, and *1970*, vol. I, and vol. II, PC(2)-1A.

No. 44. NATIVE POPULATION, BY PLACE OF BIRTH: 1900 TO 1970

[In thousands, except percent. 1950 based on 20-percent sample; 1960 on 25-percent sample; 1970 on 15-percent sample. See source for sampling variability. See also *Historical Statistics, Colonial Times to 1970*, series C 1–10]

YEAR	Total	Born in State of residence	BORN IN OTHER STATES		State of birth not reported	Born in outlying areas [1]	Born abroad or at sea of American parents
			Number	Percent			
1900	65,653	51,902	13,501	20.6	180	3	67
1910	78,456	61,185	16,910	21.6	286	7	68
1920	91,790	71,071	20,274	22.1	314	38	93
1930	108,571	82,678	25,388	23.4	238	136	131
1940	120,074	92,610	26,906	22.4	280	157	122
1950	139,869	102,788	35,284	25.2	1,370	330	96
1960	169,588	119,293	44,691	26.4	4,541	660	402
1970	193,591	131,718	50,639	26.2	8,973	891	1,370

[1] Through 1950, includes Alaska and Hawaii. Includes Puerto Rico, a U.S. possession from 1898 to 1952 and a commonwealth since 1952.

Source: U.S. Bureau of the Census, *U.S. Census of Population: 1960*, vol. II, part 2A, and *1970*, vol. I, parts C and D.

No. 45. MOBILITY STATUS OF THE POPULATION, BY RACE AND SPANISH ORIGIN: 1975–1977

[For persons 2 years old and over. Based on Current Population Survey; see source for sampling variability. Includes members of the Armed Forces living off post or with their families on post, but excludes all other members of the Armed Forces. See also text, p. 3. Persons of Spanish origin may be of any race. Refers to 243 SMSA's as defined in 1970 census publications; see Appendix II]

RESIDENCE IN 1977 COMPARED WITH RESIDENCE IN 1975	NUMBER (1,000)				PERCENT DISTRIBUTION			
	All races	White	Black	Spanish origin	All races	White	Black	Spanish origin
Total	206,419	179,253	23,559	10,673	100.0	100.0	100.0	100.0
Same housing units (nonmovers)	149,789	130,510	17,135	6,794	72.6	72.8	72.7	63.7
Central cities of SMSA's	40,919	30,700	9,326	3,340	19.8	17.1	39.6	31.3
Balance of SMSA's	59,008	55,426	2,900	2,317	28.6	30.9	12.3	21.7
Outside SMSA's	49,862	44,384	4,909	1,137	24.2	24.8	20.8	10.7
Different housing units in the U.S.	54,620	47,318	6,279	3,513	26.5	26.4	26.7	32.9
Within same SMSA	26,671	21,898	4,176	2,478	12.9	12.2	17.7	23.2
Between SMSA's	7,634	6,815	653	429	3.7	3.8	2.8	4.0
From outside SMSA's to SMSA's	3,202	2,975	194	132	1.6	1.7	.8	1.2
From SMSA's to outside SMSA's	3,815	3,578	197	94	1.8	2.0	.8	.9
Outside SMSA's at both dates	13,298	12,052	1,058	380	6.4	6.7	4.5	3.6
Movers from abroad	2,010	1,424	145	366	1.0	.8	.6	3.4

Source: U.S. Bureau of the Census, *Current Population Reports*, series P-20, No. 320.

No. 46. MOBILITY STATUS OF THE POPULATION, BY GEOGRAPHIC REGIONS: 1970–1975

[In thousands of persons 5 years old and over, except percent. For composition of regions, see fig. I, inside front cover. Based on Current Population Survey; see source for sampling variability. Includes members of Armed Forces living off post or with their families on post, but excludes other Armed Forces. See text, p. 3]

RESIDENCE IN 1970	RESIDENCE IN 1975									
	U.S.		Northeast		North Central		South		West	
	Number	Percent	Number	Percent	Number	Percent	Number	Percent	Number	Percent
Total, 5 years old and over	193,512	100.0	44,868	100.0	52,421	100.0	61,526	100.0	34,696	100.0
Same housing unit (nonmovers)	99,651	51.5	26,852	59.8	28,808	55.0	29,607	48.1	14,384	41.5
Different housing unit in U.S.	79,838	41.3	13,792	30.7	20,394	38.9	28,517	46.3	17,136	49.4
Same county	46,835	24.2	8,853	19.7	12,638	24.1	15,765	25.6	9,580	27.6
Different county	33,003	17.1	4,939	11.0	7,756	14.8	12,752	20.7	7,556	21.8
Same State	16,349	8.4	2,806	6.3	4,411	8.4	5,668	9.2	3,465	10.0
Different State	16,654	8.6	2,134	4.8	3,345	6.4	7,084	11.5	4,091	11.8
Abroad or not known	14,023	7.2	4,224	9.4	3,220	6.1	3,403	5.5	3,176	9.2

Source: U.S. Bureau of the Census, *Current Population Reports*, series P-20, No. 305.

No. 47. MOBILITY OF THE POPULATION, 5 YEARS OLD AND OVER—STATES: 1970

[In thousands, except percent. Based on a 15-percent sample. See source for sampling variability]

STATE	Population, 5 yr. and over, 1970	Percent movers, 1965–1970 [1]	STATE	Population, 5 yr. and over, 1970	Percent movers, 1965–1970 [1]	STATE	Population, 5 yr. and over, 1970	Percent movers, 1965–1970 [1]	STATE	Population, 5 yr. and over, 1970	Percent movers, 1965–1970 [1]
U.S.	186,094	41.8	E.N.C.—Con.			S.A.—Con.			Mt	7,536	48.3
			Mich	8,071	40.2	W.Va.	1,607	35.7	Mont	637	45.8
N.E.	10,858	36.8	Wis	4,036	37.7	N.C.	4,648	40.7	Idaho	649	46.2
Maine	909	38.3				S.C.	2,357	39.8	Wyo	304	47.4
N.H.	672	40.0	W.N.C.	14,982	40.9	Ga.	4,170	45.5	Colo	2,021	51.3
Vt	405	41.5	Minn	3,473	39.1	Fla	6,290	49.8	N. Mex.	919	44.5
Mass	5,220	36.0	Iowa	2,591	39.7				Ariz	1,612	51.6
R.I.	873	36.1	Mo	4,306	41.3	E.S.C.	11,702	40.9	Utah	948	40.5
Conn	2,779	36.7	N. Dak.	566	40.6	Ky	2,949	41.3	Nev	445	54.2
			S. Dak.	611	39.4	Tenn	3,600	41.4			
M.A.	34,199	34.8	Nebr	1,362	41.0	Ala	3,145	40.9	Pac	24,341	50.4
N.Y.	16,751	35.5	Kans	2,072	44.5	Miss	2,008	39.2	Wash	3,129	49.1
N.J.	6,581	37.7							Oreg	1,928	48.2
Pa	10,868	31.9	S.A.	28,105	43.7	W.S.C.	17,620	45.3	Calif	18,318	50.9
			Del	500	38.8	Ark	1,766	44.2	Alaska	268	60.4
E.N.C.	36,752	40.3	Md	3,579	42.3	La	3,295	37.8	Hawaii	698	48.0
Ohio	9,732	40.3	D.C.	697	39.7	Okla	2,362	47.0			
Ind	4,738	41.7	Va	4,258	44.0	Tex	10,197	47.5			
Ill	10,175	40.7									

[1] Excludes movers for whom place of residence in 1965 was not reported.

Source: U.S. Bureau of the Census, *Census of Population, 1970*, PC(2)-2B, *Mobility for States and the Nation*.

No. 48. Marital Status of the Population, by Sex: 1940 to 1977

[1940–1960, persons 14 years old and over; thereafter, 18 and over. As of **March**, except as noted. Prior to 1960, excludes Alaska and Hawaii. Beginning 1950, based on Current Population Survey and excludes Armed Forces except those living off post or with their families on post; see text, p. 1. See *Historical Statistics, Colonial Times to 1970*, series A 160–171, for decennial data]

SEX AND MARITAL STATUS	1940 [1]	1950	1960	1965	1970	1973	1974	1975	1976	1977
Total_____mil__	101.1	111.7	125.5	121.8	132.5	138.0	140.6	143.2	145.8	148.3
Single_____mil__	31.5	25.5	27.7	18.2	21.4	22.9	23.9	25.1	26.2	27.5
Married_____mil__	60.3	74.9	84.4	89.2	95.0	98.2	99.1	99.7	100.6	100.8
Widowed_____mil__	7.8	9.3	10.6	10.9	11.8	11.8	11.7	11.9	11.8	11.9
Divorced_____mil__	1.4	2.1	2.9	3.5	4.3	5.2	6.0	6.5	7.2	8.0
Percent of total___	100.0	100.0	100.0	100.0	100.0	100.0	100.0	100.0	100.0	100.0
Single_____	31.2	22.8	22.0	14.9	16.2	16.6	17.0	17.5	18.0	18.5
Married_____	59.6	67.0	67.3	73.2	71.7	71.1	70.5	69.6	69.0	68.0
Widowed_____	7.8	8.3	8.4	9.0	8.9	8.5	8.3	8.3	8.1	8.0
Divorced_____	1.4	1.9	2.3	2.9	3.2	3.8	4.2	4.6	4.9	5.4
Males, total_____mil__	50.6	54.8	60.6	58.0	62.5	65.2	66.6	67.9	69.1	70.3
Single_____mil__	17.6	14.3	15.4	10.3	11.8	12.7	13.4	14.1	14.7	15.4
Married_____mil__	30.2	37.2	41.8	44.2	47.1	48.6	49.0	49.4	49.8	49.9
Widowed_____mil__	2.1	2.3	2.3	2.1	2.1	1.9	1.9	1.8	1.8	1.9
Divorced_____mil__	.6	.9	1.1	1.4	1.6	2.0	2.3	2.5	2.8	3.2
Percent of total_____	100.0	100.0	100.0	100.0	100.0	100.0	100.0	100.0	100.0	100.0
Single_____	34.8	26.2	25.3	17.7	18.9	19.5	20.1	20.8	21.2	21.9
Married_____	59.7	68.0	69.1	76.2	75.3	74.5	73.7	72.8	72.2	70.9
Widowed_____	4.2	4.2	3.7	3.7	3.3	2.9	2.8	2.7	2.6	2.7
Divorced_____	1.2	1.7	1.9	2.5	2.5	3.0	3.5	3.7	4.0	4.5
Standardized for age: [2]										
Single_____	30.7	26.2	25.3	16.4	16.5	15.7	16.2	16.6	16.7	17.2
Married_____	62.6	67.4	69.1	77.5	77.6	78.0	77.1	76.6	76.2	75.1
Widowed_____	5.4	4.7	3.7	3.6	3.3	3.1	2.9	2.8	2.7	2.8
Divorced_____	1.3	1.7	1.9	2.5	2.6	3.2	3.7	4.0	4.3	4.8
Females, total___mil__	50.5	57.0	64.9	63.8	70.0	72.8	74.0	75.3	76.7	77.9
Single_____mil__	13.9	11.1	12.3	7.9	9.6	10.1	10.6	11.0	11.5	12.2
Married_____mil__	30.1	37.6	42.6	45.0	47.9	49.5	50.0	50.3	50.8	50.9
Widowed_____mil__	5.7	7.0	8.3	8.8	9.7	9.9	9.8	10.1	10.0	10.0
Divorced_____mil__	.8	1.2	1.7	2.1	2.7	3.3	3.6	4.0	4.4	4.9
Percent of total_____	100.0	100.0	100.0	100.0	100.0	100.0	100.0	100.0	100.0	100.0
Single_____	27.6	19.6	19.0	12.4	13.7	13.9	14.3	14.6	15.0	15.6
Married_____	59.5	66.1	65.6	70.5	68.5	68.1	67.6	66.7	66.2	65.3
Widowed_____	11.3	12.2	12.8	13.8	13.9	13.5	13.3	13.4	13.1	12.9
Divorced_____	1.6	2.2	2.6	3.3	3.9	4.5	4.9	5.3	5.7	6.2
Standardized for age: [2]										
Single_____	24.2	20.0	19.0	11.6	12.1	11.9	12.2	12.4	12.6	13.1
Married_____	59.3	63.9	65.6	71.8	70.8	70.4	70.0	69.2	68.9	68.0
Widowed_____	14.8	14.0	12.8	13.3	13.0	13.0	12.7	12.8	12.4	12.2
Divorced_____	1.6	2.1	2.6	3.3	4.1	4.8	5.2	5.6	6.1	6.7

[1] As of April.   [2] 1960 age distribution used as standard; standardization improves comparability over time by removing effects of changes in age distribution of population.

Source: U.S. Bureau of the Census, *U.S. Census of Population: 1950*, vol. II, part 1, and *Current Population Reports*, series P-20, Nos. 144, 255, 271, 306, and 323.

No. 49. Marital Status of the Black Population: 1960 to 1977

[1960 and 1965, persons 14 years old and over; thereafter, 18 and over. **1960** as of **April**; based on 25-percent sample; other years as of **March** and based on Current Population Survey; see headnote, table 50]

SEX AND YEAR	NUMBER OF PERSONS (1,000)					PERCENT DISTRIBUTION				
	Total	Single	Married	Widowed	Divorced	Total	Single	Married	Widowed	Divorced
MALE										
1960_____	5,713	1,692	3,619	264	139	100.0	29.6	63.3	4.6	2.4
1965_____	6,211	1,980	3,795	245	191	100.0	31.9	61.1	3.9	3.1
1970_____	5,898	1,435	3,944	307	212	100.0	24.3	66.9	5.2	3.6
1973_____	6,115	1,699	3,829	335	252	100.0	27.8	62.6	5.5	4.1
1974_____	6,284	1,712	3,959	308	305	100.0	27.2	63.0	4.9	4.9
1975_____	6,368	1,733	3,990	319	327	100.0	27.2	62.7	5.0	5.1
1976_____	6,560	1,861	4,042	271	386	100.0	28.4	61.6	4.1	5.9
1977_____	6,756	2,039	4,024	327	367	100.0	30.2	59.6	4.8	5.4
FEMALE										
1960_____	6,375	1,386	3,842	910	237	100.0	21.7	60.3	14.3	3.7
1965_____	7,062	1,621	4,201	949	291	100.0	23.0	59.5	13.4	4.1
1970_____	7,074	1,233	4,366	1,120	355	100.0	17.4	61.7	15.8	5.0
1973_____	7,514	1,522	4,295	1,210	486	100.0	20.3	57.2	16.1	6.5
1974_____	7,702	1,556	4,429	1,209	508	100.0	20.2	57.5	15.7	6.6
1975_____	7,894	1,716	4,383	1,202	593	100.0	21.7	55.5	15.2	7.5
1976_____	8,108	1,882	4,416	1,181	631	100.0	23.2	54.5	14.6	7.8
1977_____	8,320	1,963	4,452	1,170	734	100.0	23.6	53.5	14.1	8.8

Source: U.S. Bureau of the Census, *U.S. Census of Population, 1960*, PC(2)1C, *Nonwhite Population by Race*; and *Current Population Reports*, series P-20, Nos. 155, 255, 271, 306, and 323.

No. 50. MARITAL STATUS OF THE SPANISH-ORIGIN POPULATION: 1970 TO 1977

[Persons 14 years old and over. **1970** as of **April**; other years as of **March** and based on Current Population Survey, which includes members of Armed Forces living off post or with their families on post but excludes all other members of Armed Forces. See text, p. 1]

SEX AND YEAR	NUMBER OF PERSONS (1,000)					PERCENT DISTRIBUTION				
	Total	Single	Married	Widowed	Divorced	Total	Single	Married	Widowed	Divorced
Total: 1970	5,872	1,718	3,666	287	201	100.0	29.3	62.4	4.9	3.4
1971	5,606	1,614	3,599	230	163	100.0	28.8	64.2	4.1	2.9
1972	5,765	1,668	3,687	234	176	100.0	28.9	64.0	4.1	3.1
1973	6,631	1,952	4,217	280	184	100.0	29.4	63.6	4.2	2.8
1974	6,857	2,079	4,300	261	218	100.0	30.3	62.7	3.8	3.2
1975	7,264	2,293	4,378	298	296	100.0	31.6	60.3	4.1	4.1
1976	7,192	2,203	4,358	297	335	100.0	30.6	60.6	4.1	4.7
1977	7,448	2,252	4,502	318	376	100.0	30.2	60.4	4.3	5.0
Male: 1970	2,838	914	1,801	56	67	100.0	32.2	63.5	2.0	2.3
1971	2,679	841	1,748	47	44	100.0	31.4	65.2	1.7	1.6
1972	2,751	890	1,790	37	34	100.0	32.4	65.0	1.4	1.2
1973	3,171	1,056	2,040	43	33	100.0	33.3	64.3	1.4	1.0
1974	3,282	1,120	2,058	41	63	100.0	34.1	62.7	1.2	1.9
1975	3,520	1,277	2,103	42	98	100.0	36.3	59.7	1.2	2.8
1976	3,415	1,197	2,065	55	99	100.0	35.0	60.5	1.6	2.9
1977	3,526	1,182	2,151	66	126	100.0	33.5	61.0	1.9	3.6
Female: 1970	3,033	804	1,864	231	134	100.0	26.5	61.5	7.6	4.4
1971	2,927	773	1,851	183	119	100.0	26.4	63.3	6.3	4.1
1972	3,014	778	1,897	197	142	100.0	25.8	63.0	6.5	4.7
1973	3,460	896	2,177	237	151	100.0	25.9	62.9	6.8	4.4
1974	3,575	959	2,242	220	155	100.0	26.8	62.7	6.2	4.3
1975	3,744	1,016	2,275	256	198	100.0	27.1	60.8	6.8	5.3
1976	3,777	1,006	2,293	242	236	100.0	26.6	60.7	6.4	6.3
1977	3,922	1,070	2,350	252	250	100.0	27.3	59.9	6.4	6.4

Source: U.S. Bureau of the Census, *Census of Population, 1970*, PC(2)1C, *Persons of Spanish Origin*, and *Current Population Reports*, series P-20, No. 323, and earlier issues.

No. 51. MARITAL STATUS OF THE POPULATION, BY SEX AND AGE: 1977

[In thousands of persons 18 years old and over, except percent. As of **March**. Based on Current Population Survey, which includes members of Armed Forces living off post or with their families on post, but excludes all other members of the Armed Forces. See text, p. 1. See *Historical Statistics, Colonial Times to 1970*, series A 160–171, for decennial census data]

SEX AND AGE	Total	Single	Married	Widowed	Divorced	PERCENT DISTRIBUTION				
						Total	Single	Married	Widowed	Divorced
Male	70,328	15,380	49,889	1,887	3,172	100.0	21.9	70.9	2.7	4.5
18–19 years	3,984	3,742	236	–	6	100.0	93.9	5.9	–	.2
20–24 years	9,426	6,009	3,261	2	154	100.0	63.7	34.6	(Z)	1.6
25–29 years	8,592	2,240	5,888	5	458	100.0	26.1	68.5	.1	5.3
30–34 years	7,271	883	5,960	11	416	100.0	12.1	82.0	.2	5.7
35–44 years	11,191	793	9,643	44	712	100.0	7.1	86.2	.4	6.4
45–54 years	11,255	625	9,784	204	642	100.0	5.6	86.9	1.8	5.7
55–64 years	9,476	549	8,109	323	495	100.0	5.8	85.6	3.4	5.2
65–74 years	6,141	400	4,937	571	233	100.0	6.5	80.4	9.3	3.8
75 years and over	2,991	139	2,070	727	55	100.0	4.6	69.2	24.3	1.8
Female	77,947	12,152	50,912	10,023	4,859	100.0	15.6	65.3	12.9	6.2
18–19 years	4,190	3,322	831	2	35	100.0	79.3	19.8	(Z)	.8
20–24 years	9,804	4,438	5,029	21	316	100.0	45.3	51.3	.2	3.2
25–29 years	8,868	1,432	6,725	40	671	100.0	16.1	75.8	.5	7.6
30–34 years	7,553	528	6,256	74	696	100.0	7.0	82.8	1.0	9.2
35–44 years	11,917	599	9,908	278	1,132	100.0	5.0	83.1	2.3	9.5
45–54 years	12,047	512	9,700	837	999	100.0	4.3	80.5	6.9	8.3
55–64 years	10,600	492	7,434	2,023	652	100.0	4.6	70.1	19.1	6.2
55–74 years	8,000	504	3,959	3,287	250	100.0	6.3	49.5	41.1	3.1
75 years and over	4,968	327	1,070	3,463	108	100.0	6.6	21.5	69.7	2.2

– Represents zero. Z Less than .05 percent.

Source: U.S. Bureau of the Census, *Current Population Reports*, series P-20, No. 323.

No. 52. SINGLE (NEVER-MARRIED) PERSONS 18 YEARS OLD AND OVER AS PERCENT OF TOTAL POPULATION, BY AGE AND SEX: 1960 TO 1977

[1960, as of April; thereafter, based on Current Population Survey as of March. See headnote, table 50]

AGE	MALE					FEMALE				
	1960	1970	1975	1976	1977	1960	1970	1975	1976	1977
Total	17.3	18.9	20.8	21.2	21.9	11.9	13.7	14.6	15.0	15.6
18 years	94.6	95.1	96.8	95.6	97.5	75.6	82.0	83.7	84.0	84.8
19 years	87.1	89.9	89.3	87.9	90.2	59.7	68.8	71.4	72.1	73.8
20–24 years	53.1	54.7	59.9	62.1	63.7	28.4	35.8	40.3	42.6	45.3
20 years	75.8	78.3	80.1	80.9	82.6	46.0	56.9	59.1	60.9	63.3
21 years	63.4	66.2	67.2	72.7	71.8	34.6	43.9	49.2	51.2	53.1
22 years	51.6	52.3	61.9	61.6	64.5	25.6	33.5	38.1	41.4	45.6
23 years	40.5	42.1	46.5	52.2	54.1	19.4	22.4	31.0	31.2	34.5
24 years	33.4	33.2	40.2	39.8	44.0	15.7	17.9	21.1	26.4	27.6
25–29 years	20.8	19.1	22.3	24.9	26.1	10.5	10.5	13.8	14.8	16.1
30–34 years	11.9	9.4	11.1	12.3	12.2	6.9	6.2	7.5	7.0	7.0
35–39 years	8.8	7.2	8.6	7.9	7.3	6.1	5.4	5.0	5.2	5.4
40–44 years	7.3	6.3	7.2	6.6	6.9	6.1	4.9	4.8	4.2	4.7
45–54 years	7.4	7.5	6.3	5.6	5.6	7.0	4.9	4.6	4.4	4.2
55–64 years	8.0	7.8	6.5	5.6	5.8	8.0	6.8	5.1	4.9	4.6
65 years and over	7.7	7.5	4.7	4.4	5.9	8.5	7.7	5.8	5.9	6.4

Source: U.S. Bureau of the Census, Current Population Reports, series P-20, Nos. 287, 306, and 323.

No. 53. PRIMARY (UNRELATED) INDIVIDUALS, BY MARITAL STATUS, SEX, AND AGE: 1970 AND 1977

[In thousands. Persons 14 years old and over. "Married" represents spouse absent. Based on Current Population Survey as of March; see headnote, table 50. Minus sign (−) denotes decrease]

AGE AND MARITAL STATUS	1970		1977		INCREASE 1970–1977		AGE AND MARITAL STATUS	1970		1977		INCREASE 1970–1977	
	Male	Female	Male	Female	Male	Female		Male	Female	Male	Female	Male	Female
All ages	4,062	7,883	6,971	10,698	2,909	2,815	35–64 yr	1,730	2,971	2,415	3,381	685	410
							Single	664	590	768	625	104	35
Single	1,765	1,608	3,332	2,564	1,567	956	Married	319	307	447	333	128	26
Married	545	516	909	654	364	138	Widowed	240	1,476	232	1,497	−8	21
Widowed	996	4,915	1,082	5,992	86	1,077	Divorced	507	598	969	927	462	329
Divorced	756	844	1,649	1,488	893	644	65 yr. and over	1,238	4,057	1,395	5,292	157	1,235
Under 35 yr	1,093	857	3,162	2,025	2,069	1,168	Single	258	376	256	401	−2	25
Single	843	643	2,306	1,539	1,463	896	Married	108	92	133	143	25	51
Married	119	117	329	179	210	62	Widowed	749	3,436	843	4,478	94	1,042
Widowed	6	3	9	17	3	14	Divorced	124	152	164	270	40	118
Divorced	125	95	517	290	392	195							

No. 54. TWO-PERSON HOUSEHOLD-SHARING BY PRIMARY (UNRELATED) INDIVIDUALS: 1970 TO 1977

[A primary individual is a household head living alone or with nonrelatives only. See headnote, table 50]

ITEM	Total primary individuals	MALE INDIVIDUALS					FEMALE INDIVIDUALS				
		Total	Under 25 yr.	25–44 yr.	45–64 yr.	65 and over	Total	Under 25 yr.	25–44 yr.	45–64 yr.	65 and over
1970 (April), total 1,000	11,945	4,062	441	1,136	1,244	1,238	7,883	426	771	2,630	4,057
In 2-person households 1,000	991	488	144	163	104	77	504	126	94	127	157
Percent of total	8.3	12.0	32.7	14.3	8.4	6.2	6.4	29.6	12.2	4.8	3.9
Sharing with opposite sex 1 1,000	327	174	21	43	59	51	153	8	17	64	64
Percent of 2-person households	33.0	35.7	14.6	26.4	56.7	66.2	30.4	6.3	18.1	50.4	40.8
1976 (Mar.), total 1,000	16,811	6,548	1,076	2,467	1,607	1,398	10,263	831	1,371	2,807	5,254
In 2-person households 1,000	1,479	901	298	425	127	51	578	199	155	123	101
Percent of total	8.8	13.8	27.7	17.2	7.9	3.6	5.6	23.9	11.3	4.4	1.9
Sharing with opposite sex 1 1,000	660	460	108	222	85	45	200	47	48	68	38
Percent of 2-person households	44.6	51.1	36.2	52.2	66.9	88.2	34.6	23.6	31.0	55.3	37.6
1977 (Mar.), total 1,000	17,669	6,971	1,235	2,754	1,588	1,395	10,698	875	1,606	2,925	5,292
In 2-person households 1,000	1,739	1,039	378	494	125	42	700	251	181	131	138
Percent of total	9.8	14.9	30.6	17.9	7.9	3.0	6.5	28.7	11.3	4.5	2.6
Sharing with opposite sex 1 1,000	754	489	143	242	71	31	265	55	60	74	75
Percent of 2-person households	43.4	47.1	37.8	49.0	56.8	73.8	37.9	21.9	33.1	56.5	54.3

1 Sharing with unrelated person of opposite sex.

Source of tables 53 and 54: U.S. Bureau of the Census, Current Population Reports, series P-20, Nos. 306 and 323

No. 55. Households, by Race of Head, and Population Per Household: 1930 to 1977

[Prior to 1960, excludes Alaska and Hawaii. Data for 1930-1970 are for census dates. Thereafter, based on Current Population Survey, see headnote, table 56. For definition of household, see text, p. 3. See also *Historical Statistics, Colonial Times to 1970*, series A 288, A 304, and A 320-322]

ITEM	1930 (Apr.)	1940 (Apr.)	1950 (Apr.)	1960 (Apr.)	1970 (Apr.)	1974 (Mar.)	1975 (Mar.)	1976 (Mar.)	1977 (Mar.)
All households_____1,000__	29,905	34,949	42,857	53,021	63,450	69,859	71,120	72,867	74,142
Average annual change since prior year shown.1,000__	[1] 542	504	791	1,016	1,043	[2] 1,636	[2] 1,560	[2] 1,592	[2] 1,546
Percent [3]_____	2.02	1.56	2.06	2.15	1.80	[2] 2.46	[2] 2.32	[2] 2.34	[2] 2.25
Population per household [4]_____	4.11	3.77	3.52	3.38	3.20	3.02	2.99	2.94	2.91
White households_____1,000__	26,983	31,680	[5] 39,044	47,868	56,529	61,965	62,945	64,392	65,353
Percent of total_____	90.2	90.6	91.2	90.3	89.1	88.7	88.5	88.4	88.1
Black households_____1,000__	2,804	3,142	[5] 3,633	} 5,153	{ 6,180	7,040	7,262	7,489	7,776
Other-race households_____1,000__	118	127	[5] 149		{ 741	854	913	986	1,013

[1] Average change from 1920.   [2] Average annual change since 1970.
[3] Computed using the formula for continuous compounding; see p. xii.
[4] Obtained by dividing resident population by number of households; hence, not strictly average size of household because resident population includes members of group quarters. See table 1 for population 1930-1970; table 48 for population thereafter.   [5] Occupied housing units from U.S. Census of Housing reports.

Source: U.S. Bureau of the Census, *U.S. Census of Population: 1930, 1950,* and *1970;* and *Current Population Reports,* series P-20, forthcoming report, and earlier issues.

No. 56. Households, Families, Subfamilies, Married Couples, and Unrelated Individuals: 1950 to 1977

[In thousands, except as indicated. As of March, except as noted. Prior to 1960, excludes Alaska and Hawaii. Based on Current Population Survey; includes members of Armed Forces living off post or with their families on post, but excludes all other members of Armed Forces; see text, pp. 1, 2. Minus sign (−) denotes decrease. For definition of terms, see text, pp. 3, 4. See also *Historical Statistics, Colonial Times to 1970,* series A 288-319]

TYPE OF UNIT	1950	1955 [1]	1960	1965 [2]	1970 [2]	1975	1976	1977	PERCENT CHANGE 1960-1970	PERCENT CHANGE 1970-1977
Households_____	43,554	47,874	52,799	57,436	63,401	71,120	72,867	74,142	20.1	16.9
Primary families_____	38,838	41,732	44,905	47,838	51,456	55,563	56,056	56,472	14.6	9.7
Primary individuals___	4,716	6,142	7,895	9,598	11,945	15,557	16,811	17,669	51.3	47.9
Avg. size of household___	3.37	3.33	3.33	3.29	3.14	2.94	2.89	2.86	(X)	(X)
Families_____	39,303	41,951	45,111	47,956	51,586	55,712	56,245	56,710	14.4	9.9
Husband-wife_____	34,440	36,378	39,329	41,749	44,755	46,971	47,318	47,497	13.8	6.1
Other male head_____	1,184	1,339	1,275	1,181	1,239	1,499	1,444	1,500	−2.8	21.1
Female head_____	3,679	4,234	4,507	5,026	5,591	7,242	7,482	7,713	24.1	38.0
Primary families_____	38,838	41,732	44,905	47,838	51,456	55,563	56,056	56,472	14.6	9.7
Husband-wife_____	34,075	36,251	39,254	41,689	44,728	46,951	47,297	47,471	13.9	6.1
Other male head_____	1,169	1,328	1,228	1,167	1,228	1,485	1,424	1,461	−	19.0
Female head_____	3,594	4,153	4,422	4,982	5,500	7,127	7,335	7,540	24.4	37.1
Secondary families_____	465	219	207	118	130	149	189	238	−37.2	83.1
Husband-wife_____	365	127	75	60	27	20	22	26	−64.0	(B)
Other male head_____	15	11	47	14	11	14	20	39	(B)	(B)
Female head_____	85	81	85	44	91	115	147	173	7.1	90.1
Avg. size of family_____	3.54	3.59	3.67	3.70	3.58	3.42	3.39	3.37	(X)	(X)
Subfamilies_____	2,402	1,973	1,514	1,293	1,150	1,349	1,190	1,176	−24.0	2.3
Husband-wife_____	1,651	1,178	871	729	617	576	547	505	−29.2	−18.2
Other male head_____	113	69	115	72	48	69	52	52	−58.3	(B)
Female head_____	638	726	528	492	484	705	591	619	−8.3	27.9
Married couples_____	36,091	37,556	40,200	42,478	45,373	47,547	47,866	48,002	12.9	5.8
With own household___	34,075	36,251	39,254	41,689	44,728	46,951	47,297	47,471	13.9	6.1
Without own household	2,016	1,305	946	789	645	596	569	531	−31.8	−17.7
Percent without_____	5.6	3.5	2.4	1.9	1.4	1.3	1.2	1.1	(X)	(X)
Unrelated individuals____	9,136	9,891	11,092	12,333	14,988	19,100	20,509	21,722	35.1	44.9
Primary individuals___	4,716	6,142	7,895	9,598	11,945	15,557	16,811	17,669	51.3	47.9
Male_____	1,668	2,059	2,716	3,277	4,063	5,912	6,548	6,971	49.6	71.6
Female_____	3,048	4,083	5,179	6,321	7,882	9,645	10,263	10,698	52.2	35.7
Secondary individuals_	4,420	3,749	3,198	2,735	3,043	3,543	3,698	4,053	−4.8	33.2
Male_____	2,541	2,128	1,746	1,432	1,631	2,087	1,965	2,231	−6.6	36.8
Female_____	1,879	1,621	1,451	1,303	1,412	1,456	1,733	1,821	−2.7	29.0

− Represents zero.   B Percent not shown; base less than 75,000.   X Not applicable.
[1] As of April.   [2] Data revised using population controls based on the 1970 census; therefore, figures do not gree with tables 58 and 60. The latter use population controls based on the 1960 census. These data were not revised by race or other characteristics.

Source: U.S. Bureau of the Census, *Current Population Reports,* series P-20, No. 313, and earlier issues.

No. 57. HOUSEHOLD CHARACTERISTICS, BY RACE AND SPANISH ORIGIN: 1977

[As of **March** Based on Current Population Survey; see headnote, table 56. For composition of regions, see fig. I, inside front cover]

CHARACTERISTIC	ALL HOUSEHOLDS			BLACK HOUSEHOLDS			SPANISH-ORIGIN HOUSEHOLDS		
	Number (1,000)	Percent	Persons per household	Number (1,000)	Percent	Persons per household	Number (1,000)	Percent	Persons per household
Total	74,142	100.0	2.86	7,776	100.0	3.15	3,081	100.0	3.47
Northeast	16,855	22.7	2.87	1,438	18.5	2.90	716	23.2	3.17
North Central	19,628	26.5	2.91	1,589	20.4	3.16	216	7.0	3.83
South	23,669	31.9	2.88	3,967	51.0	3.31	898	29.2	3.63
West	13,990	18.9	2.74	783	10.1	2.78	1,250	40.6	3.46
Nonfarm	71,656	96.6	2.85	7,663	98.5	3.14	3,060	99.3	3.46
Farm	2,485	3.4	3.19	113	1.5	4.09	21	.7	(B)
In metropolitan areas	50,414	68.0	2.83	5,981	76.9	3.03	2,646	85.9	3.40
In central cities	22,741	30.7	2.63	4,566	58.7	2.95	1,640	53.2	3.28
Outside central cities	27,672	37.3	3.00	1,415	18.2	3.28	1,005	32.6	3.60
One million pop. or more	29,124	39.3	2.82	3,953	50.8	3.00	1,788	58.0	3.31
In central cities	12,246	16.5	2.60	3,025	38.9	2.94	1,074	34.9	3.18
Outside central cities	16,878	22.8	2.99	928	11.9	3.21	714	23.2	3.51
Under 1 million pop	21,290	28.7	-2.84	2,028	26.1	3.08	857	27.8	3.59
In central cities	10,495	14.2	2.66	1,541	19.8	2.98	566	18.4	3.46
Outside central cities	10,795	14.6	3.01	487	6.3	3.40	291	9.4	3.84
Outside metropolitan areas	23,728	32.0	2.92	1,795	23.1	3.56	435	14.1	3.87
Nonfarm	21,703	29.3	2.89	1,690	21.7	3.53	419	13.6	3.86
Farm	2,025	2.7	3.21	105	1.4	4.08	16	.5	(B)
Relationship to head:									
All members related	71,244	96.1	2.85	7,350	94.5	3.14	2,951	95.8	3.48
All members unrelated	2,138	2.9	2.36	279	3.6	2.45	83	2.7	2.46
Some members unrelated	761	1.0	4.68	147	1.9	5.04	47	1.5	(B)
Marital status:									
Male head	55,903	75.4	3.15	4,592	59.1	3.34	2,320	75.3	3.72
Married, wife present	47,471	64.0	3.43	3,405	43.8	3.93	1,975	64.1	4.06
Married, wife absent	1,152	1.6	1.55	320	4.1	1.55	69	2.2	(B)
Separated	864	1.2	1.52	280	3.6	1.59	38	1.2	(B)
Other	288	.4	1.65	40	.5	(B)	31	1.0	(B)
Widowed	1,473	2.0	1.64	205	2.6	1.97	51	1.7	(B)
Divorced	2,039	2.8	1.57	239	3.1	1.53	75	2.4	1.71
Single	3,768	5.1	1.50	422	5.4	1.55	149	4.8	1.80
Female head	18,238	24.6	1.97	3,184	40.9	2.89	761	24.7	2.71
Married, husband absent	2,351	3.2	2.89	870	11.2	3.38	219	7.1	3.28
Separated	1,887	2.5	2.98	784	10.1	3.39	185	6.0	3.17
Other	464	.6	2.54	86	1.1	3.31	34	1.1	(B)
Widowed	8,367	11.3	1.61	971	12.5	2.54	179	5.8	2.26
Divorced	3,964	5.3	2.45	626	8.1	3.10	190	6.2	2.89
Single	3,556	4.8	1.67	718	9.2	2.57	173	5.6	2.24
Age of head:									
14–24 years	5,991	8.1	2.28	755	9.7	2.57	368	11.9	2.70
25–34 years	16,167	21.8	3.06	1,788	23.0	3.21	879	28.5	3.54
35–44 years	12,482	16.8	4.03	1,532	19.7	4.05	686	22.3	4.37
45–54 years	12,905	17.4	3.37	1,342	17.3	3.54	535	17.4	3.69
55–64 years	11,780	15.9	2.42	1,121	14.4	2.77	328	10.6	3.03
65 years and over	14,816	20.0	1.78	1,239	15.9	2.24	285	9.2	2.14
Size of household:									
One person	15,532	20.9	1.00	1,744	22.4	1.00	428	13.9	1.00
Two persons	22,775	30.7	2.00	1,854	23.8	2.00	657	21.3	2.00
Three persons	12,794	17.3	3.00	1,390	17.9	3.00	616	20.0	3.00
Four persons	11,630	15.7	4.00	1,096	14.1	4.00	576	18.7	4.00
Five persons	6,285	8.5	5.00	698	9.0	5.00	371	12.0	5.00
Six persons	2,864	3.9	6.00	422	5.4	6.00	229	7.4	6.00
Seven persons or more	2,263	3.1	7.72	572	7.4	7.96	205	6.6	7.81
Employment status:									
In labor force	53,970	72.8	3.14	5,174	66.5	3.30	2,319	75.3	3.63
Civilian labor force	53,082	71.6	3.13	5,058	65.0	3.30	2,285	74.2	3.64
Employed	50,236	67.8	3.14	4,552	58.5	3.34	2,088	67.8	3.63
Unemployed	2,846	3.8	2.96	507	6.5	2.99	197	6.4	3.36
Not in labor force	20,172	27.2	2.11	2,602	33.5	2.86	762	24.7	2.96
Employed	50,236	67.8	3.14	4,552	58.5	3.34	2,088	67.8	3.63
White-collar	24,057	32.4	2.98	1,338	17.2	2.96	553	18.0	3.27
Blue-collar	19,708	26.6	3.41	2,042	26.3	3.70	1,149	37.3	3.83
Farm workers	1,662	2.2	3.35	120	1.5	3.93	76	2.5	4.6
Service workers	4,809	6.5	2.83	1,051	13.5	3.05	311	10.1	3.4

B Base less than 75,000.

Source: U.S. Bureau of the Census, *Current Population Reports*, series P-60, No. 109.

No. 58. Households, by Number of Persons: 1950 to 1977

[In millions, except percent. As of March. Based on Current Population Survey; see headnote, table 56. See also Historical Statistics, Colonial Times to 1970, series A 335–349]

SIZE OF HOUSEHOLD	1950 [1] [2]	1955 [2]	1960 [2]	1965 [2]	1970 [2]	1972	1973	1974	1975	1976	1977
Total	43.5	47.8	52.6	57.3	62.9	66.7	68.3	69.9	71.1	72.9	74.1
1 person	4.7	5.2	6.9	8.6	10.7	12.2	12.6	13.4	13.9	15.0	15.5
Male	1.8	1.7	2.3	2.9	3.5	4.1	4.4	4.7	4.9	5.4	5.6
Female	3.0	3.5	4.6	5.7	7.2	8.1	8.2	8.6	9.0	9.6	9.9
2 persons	12.5	13.6	14.6	16.1	18.1	19.5	20.6	21.5	21.8	22.3	22.8
3 persons	9.8	9.7	9.9	10.2	10.9	11.5	11.8	11.9	12.4	12.5	12.8
4 persons	7.7	9.1	9.3	9.2	9.9	10.7	10.7	10.9	11.1	11.4	11.6
5 persons	4.4	5.3	6.1	6.3	6.5	6.4	6.4	6.5	6.4	6.3	6.3
6 persons	2.2	2.6	3.0	3.3	3.5	3.4	3.2	3.1	3.1	3.0	2.9
7 or more	2.1	2.3	2.9	3.5	3.2	3.0	2.8	2.7	2.5	2.4	2.3
Percent of total:											
1 person	10.9	10.9	13.1	15.0	17.0	18.3	18.5	19.1	19.6	20.6	20.9
2 persons	28.8	28.5	27.8	28.1	28.8	29.2	30.2	30.8	30.6	30.6	30.7
3 persons	22.6	20.4	18.9	17.9	17.3	17.3	17.3	17.1	17.4	17.2	17.3
4 persons	17.8	18.9	17.6	16.1	15.8	16.0	15.7	15.6	15.6	15.7	15.7
5 persons	10.0	11.1	11.5	11.0	10.4	9.6	9.4	9.3	9.0	8.6	8.5
6 persons	5.1	5.4	5.7	5.8	5.6	5.1	4.8	4.4	4.3	4.1	3.9
7 or more	4.9	4.9	5.4	6.1	5.1	4.5	4.1	3.8	3.5	3.2	3.1

[1] Covers related persons only; therefore, not strictly comparable with later years.   [2] See footnote 2, table 56.
Source: U.S. Bureau of the Census, Current Population Reports, series P-20, forthcoming report, and earlier issues.

No. 59. Households, Families, and Individuals—Projections: 1978 to 1990

[In thousands. As of July 1. Includes members of the Armed Forces living off post or with their families on post, but excludes all other members of the Armed Forces. See text, pp. 3 and 4, for definitions of households and families. Series B assumes that the trends in marital status and household proportions observed over the period 1960 to 1974 will continue to 1990. Series A and Series C are based on weighted averages of the Series B proportions and the 1974 observed proportions. Series K assumes that the levels of proportions observed in 1974 will continue to 1990. For additional explanation, see source]

YEAR AND SERIES	HOUSEHOLDS							All families	Un-related individuals [1]
	Total	Primary families				Primary individuals			
		Total	Husband-wife	Other male head	Female head	Male	Female		
1978:									
Series A	76,597	59,160	50,191	1,517	7,452	6,742	10,694	59,250	20,652
Series B	76,223	59,108	50,201	1,514	7,393	6,583	10,533	59,201	20,423
Series C	75,474	59,002	50,220	1,507	7,275	6,264	10,208	59,105	19,970
Series K	75,099	58,948	50,229	1,503	7,216	6,104	10,046	59,057	19,744
1980:									
Series A	79,953	61,230	51,806	1,566	7,858	7,331	11,393	61,312	21,853
Series B	79,356	61,144	51,825	1,561	7,758	7,076	11,135	61,234	21,477
Series C	78,159	60,974	51,864	1,550	7,560	6,565	10,620	61,080	20,735
Series K	77,560	60,891	51,885	1,543	7,463	6,309	10,361	61,004	20,368
1985:									
Series A	88,456	66,380	55,715	1,723	8,942	8,932	13,144	66,440	24,877
Series B	87,188	66,181	55,757	1,713	8,711	8,395	12,612	66,255	24,054
Series C	84,655	65,791	55,845	1,686	8,260	7,320	11,545	65,894	22,437
Series K	83,391	65,599	55,891	1,668	8,040	6,783	11,010	65,718	21,645
1990:									
Series A	96,318	70,909	59,033	1,893	9,983	10,541	14,868	70,943	27,712
Series B	94,270	70,551	59,073	1,877	9,601	9,688	14,032	70,606	26,389
Series C	90,185	69,850	59,163	1,830	8,857	7,981	12,354	69,947	23,788
Series K	88,144	69,502	59,209	1,798	8,495	7,129	11,513	69,622	22,514

[1] Includes primary individuals, shown separately, and secondary individuals (14 years old and over), not shown separately; see text, p. 4.
Source: U.S. Bureau of the Census, Current Population Reports, series P-25, No. 607.

No. 60. Households and Families, by Type of Head: 1960 to 1977

[As of **March.** Based on Current Population Survey; see headnote, table 56. See also *Historical Statistics, Colonial Times to 1970*, series A 292–295 and A 320–334]

TYPE OF HEAD	NUMBER (1,000)					PERCENT				
	1960	1965 [1]	1970 [1]	1975	1977	1960	1965 [1]	1970 [1]	1975	1977
Households, total__	52,799	57,251	62,874	71,120	74,142	(X)	(X)	(X)	(X)	(X)
White_____	47,665	51,441	56,248	62,945	65,353	100.0	100.0	100.0	100.0	100.0
Husband-wife_____	36,175	38,132	40,781	42,951	43,372	76.2	74.1	72.5	68.2	66.4
Other male head_____	3,365	3,839	4,367	6,295	7,120	6.8	7.5	7.8	10.0	10.9
Female head_____	8,125	9,470	11,099	13,700	14,861	17.0	18.4	19.7	21.8	22.7
Black and other_____	5,134	5,808	6,626	8,175	8,789	100.0	100.0	100.0	100.0	100.0
Husband-wife_____	3,079	3,455	3,627	4,000	4,099	60.3	59.5	54.7	48.9	46.6
Other male head_____	579	599	813	1,103	1,313	11.0	10.3	12.3	13.5	14.9
Female head_____	1,476	1,754	2,187	3,073	3,378	28.7	30.2	33.0	37.6	38.4
Families, total_____	45,111	47,836	51,237	55,712	56,710	(X)	(X)	(X)	(X)	(X)
White_____	40,869	43,081	46,022	49,451	50,083	100.0	100.0	100.0	100.0	100.0
Husband-wife_____	36,212	38,171	40,802	42,969	43,397	88.7	88.6	88.7	86.9	86.7
Other male head_____	1,100	1,028	1,036	1,270	1,219	2.6	2.4	2.3	2.6	2.4
Female head_____	3,557	3,882	4,185	5,212	5,467	8.7	9.0	9.1	10.5	10.9
Black and other_____	4,242	4,752	5,215	6,262	6,627	100.0	100.0	100.0	100.0	100.0
Husband-wife_____	3,117	3,474	3,634	4,002	4,100	73.6	73.1	69.7	63.9	61.9
Other male head_____	175	153	185	230	280	4.0	3.2	3.5	3.7	4.2
Female head_____	950	1,125	1,395	2,030	2,246	22.4	23.7	26.7	32.4	33.9

X   Not applicable.   [1] See footnote 2, table 56.

Source: U.S. Bureau of the Census, *Current Population Reports*, series P-20, Nos. 153, 218, 276, 311, and forthcoming report.

No. 61. Percent Distribution of Families, by Number of Own Children Under 18 Years Old: 1950 to 1977

[As of **March,** except **1955** as of **April.** Prior to 1960, excludes Alaska and Hawaii. Based on Current Population Survey; see headnote, table 56. See also *Historical Statistics, Colonial Times to 1970*, series A 353–358]

NUMBER OF CHILDREN	1950	1955	1960	1965	1970	1973	1974	1975	1976	1977
Families_____1,000__	39,303	41,951	45,111	47,956	51,586	54,373	55,053	55,712	56,245	56,710
Percent distribution_____	100.0	100.0	100.0	100.0	100.0	100.0	100.0	100.0	100.0	100.0
No children_____	48.3	44.7	43.0	43.4	44.1	45.6	46.0	46.0	46.3	46.8
1 child_____	21.1	19.1	18.5	17.7	18.2	19.3	19.2	19.7	19.7	19.6
2 children_____	16.5	18.7	18.0	16.8	17.4	17.4	17.9	18.0	18.3	18.9
3 children_____	7.8	9.9	11.1	11.0	10.6	9.7	9.5	9.3	9.3	9.0
4 or more children_____	6.3	7.6	9.4	11.1	9.8	7.9	7.4	6.9	6.3	5.7

Source: U.S. Bureau of the Census, *Current Population Reports*, series P-20, No. 311, forthcoming report, and earlier issues.

No. 62. Households, by Selected Characteristics of Head: 1968 to 1977

[As of **March.** Based on Current Population Survey; see headnote table 56]

CHARACTERISTIC	1968	1969	1970	1972	1973	1974	1975	1976	1977
Total_____mil__	60.8	62.2	63.4	66.7	68.3	69.9	71.1	72.9	74.1
PERCENT DISTRIBUTION									
Male_____	79.6	79.2	78.9	77.8	77.4	77.1	76.4	75.8	75.4
Female_____	20.4	20.8	21.1	22.2	22.6	22.9	23.6	24.2	24.6
White_____	89.6	89.6	89.5	89.2	88.8	88.7	88.5	88.4	88.1
Black and other_____	10.4	10.4	10.5	10.8	11.2	11.3	11.5	11.6	11.9
Age of head:									
14–24 years_____	6.3	6.6	6.8	7.8	8.0	8.4	8.2	8.1	8.1
25–34 years_____	17.5	18.3	18.5	19.2	19.9	20.5	21.0	21.3	21.8
35–44 years_____	19.7	19.0	18.6	17.3	17.2	16.8	16.7	16.8	16.8
45–54 years_____	19.8	19.7	19.5	19.1	18.8	18.5	18.2	17.6	17.4
55–64 years_____	17.1	17.1	17.1	16.7	16.4	16.0	15.9	16.0	15.9
65 years and over_____	19.5	19.4	19.5	19.9	19.7	19.9	20.1	20.3	20.0
Educational attainment:									
Less than 8 years_____	16.1	15.5	14.6	13.5	12.9	12.4	12.1	11.5	11.1
8 years_____	14.1	13.5	13.2	12.2	11.6	11.0	10.3	9.7	9.5
1–3 years high school____	17.3	16.7	16.7	16.5	16.1	15.7	15.3	15.3	15.3
4 years high school_____	29.5	30.6	31.0	32.0	32.6	32.7	33.0	33.1	33.0
1–3 years college_____	10.5	10.9	11.4	11.9	12.4	13.1	13.6	14.0	14.2
4 years college or more___	12.5	12.7	13.1	13.9	14.3	15.1	15.7	16.4	16.9

Source: U.S. Bureau of the Census, *Current Population Reports*, series P-60, No. 107, and earlier issues.

No. 63. Households—States: 1950 to 1977

[1950 through 1970, as of April 1; 1976 and 1977 estimated as of July 1. For definition of household, see text, p. 3. For composition of regions, see fig. I, inside front cover]

STATE	TOTAL HOUSEHOLDS									HUSBAND-WIFE HOUSEHOLDS (1,000)			
	Number (1,000)				Percent change		Average annual percent change [1]						
	1960	1970	1976	1977	1960–1970	1970–1977	1950–1960	1960–1970	1970–1977	1960	1970	1976	1977
U.S.	53,021	63,450	73,297	74,601	19.7	17.6	2.1	1.8	2.2	39,210	44,062	47,556	47,758
Regions:													
Northeast	13,521	15,482	16,991	17,126	14.5	10.6	1.8	1.4	1.4	9,829	10,487	10,779	10,719
No. Cent	15,377	17,537	19,516	19,778	14.0	12.8	1.7	1.3	1.7	11,593	12,451	13,003	13,021
South	15,503	19,258	23,157	23,662	24.2	22.9	2.0	2.2	2.8	11,595	13,573	15,300	15,445
West	8,619	11,172	13,633	14,035	29.6	25.6	3.4	2.6	3.1	6,193	7,551	8,474	8,573
N. Eng	3,116	3,645	4,121	4,180	17.0	14.7	1.7	1.6	1.9	2,277	2,511	2,673	2,678
Maine	280	303	356	364	8.2	20.2	1.0	.8	2.5	209	215	240	243
N.H.	180	225	276	286	25.0	26.9	1.5	2.2	3.3	134	162	188	193
Vt	111	132	157	161	18.9	21.9	.7	1.8	2.7	82	93	105	107
Mass	1,535	1,760	1,964	1,984	14.7	12.7	1.6	1.4	1.7	1,096	1,176	1,231	1,227
R.I.	257	292	319	321	13.6	9.9	1.3	1.3	1.3	186	200	206	204
Conn	753	933	1,049	1,064	23.9	14.0	2.8	2.2	1.8	571	665	703	704
Mid. Atl	10,405	11,837	12,870	12,946	13.8	9.4	1.9	1.3	1.2	7,552	7,976	8,106	8,041
N.Y.	5,248	5,914	6,368	6,389	12.7	8.0	1.9	1.2	1.1	3,690	3,838	3,828	3,777
N.J	1,806	2,218	2,458	2,481	22.8	11.8	2.7	2.1	1.5	1,374	1,573	1,642	1,637
Pa	3,351	3,705	4,044	4,076	10.6	10.0	1.4	1.0	1.3	2,487	2,565	2,636	2,627
E. No. Cent	10,710	12,382	13,709	13,896	15.6	12.2	1.9	1.5	1.6	8,107	8,804	9,133	9,144
Ohio	2,852	3,289	3,594	3,633	15.3	10.4	2.1	1.4	1.4	2,178	2,354	2,416	2,414
Ind	1,388	1,609	1,787	1,808	15.9	12.3	1.7	1.5	1.6	1,068	1,174	1,228	1,229
Ill	3,085	3,502	3,814	3,867	13.5	10.4	1.8	1.3	1.4	2,254	2,405	2,437	2,436
Mich	2,239	2,653	2,985	3,029	18.5	14.2	2.2	1.7	1.8	1,730	1,915	2,016	2,020
Wis	1,146	1,329	1,529	1,559	16.0	17.3	1.7	1.5	2.2	877	956	1,036	1,045
W. No. Cent	4,668	5,155	5,807	5,882	10.4	14.1	1.2	1.0	1.8	3,486	3,647	3,870	3,877
Minn	992	1,154	1,327	1,348	16.3	16.8	1.6	1.5	2.1	742	821	886	890
Iowa	841	896	999	1,008	6.5	12.5	.7	.6	1.6	638	645	681	681
Mo	1,360	1,521	1,686	1,704	11.8	12.1	1.3	1.1	1.6	987	1,050	1,093	1,091
N. Dak	173	182	211	215	5.2	18.4	.7	.5	2.3	133	132	146	147
S. Dak	195	201	228	231	3.1	15.0	.6	.3	1.9	148	144	155	155
Nebr	433	474	540	546	9.5	15.3	.9	.9	2.0	327	335	359	359
Kans	673	727	816	830	8.0	14.1	1.4	.8	1.8	511	520	550	554
So. Atl	7,268	9,439	11,517	11,768	29.9	24.7	2.7	2.6	3.0	5,410	6,595	7,525	7,591
Del	129	165	192	195	27.9	18.3	3.5	2.5	2.3	98	118	128	128
Md	863	1,175	1,363	1,386	36.2	18.0	3.0	3.1	2.3	661	833	900	902
Dist. of Col	252	263	273	273	4.4	4.0	1.2	.4	.5	131	113	101	98
Va	1,074	1,391	1,665	1,714	29.5	23.3	2.4	2.6	2.9	814	997	1,115	1,131
W. Va	521	547	623	636	5.0	16.2	(Z)	.5	2.1	394	389	423	428
N.C	1,205	1,510	1,792	1,830	25.3	21.2	1.9	2.3	2.7	933	1,098	1,226	1,239
S.C	604	734	896	915	21.5	24.6	1.6	2.0	3.0	451	522	596	603
Ga	1,070	1,369	1,621	1,659	27.9	21.2	1.8	2.5	2.6	803	964	1,065	1,075
Fla	1,550	2,285	3,092	3,160	47.4	38.3	6.3	3.9	4.5	1,125	1,561	1,971	1,987
E. So. Cent	3,307	3,868	4,496	4,581	17.0	18.4	1.0	1.6	2.3	2,507	2,763	3,039	3,064
Ky	852	984	1,137	1,152	15.5	17.1	.9	1.4	2.2	651	710	782	784
Tenn	1,003	1,213	1,424	1,457	20.9	20.1	1.4	1.9	2.5	768	874	967	979
Ala	884	1,034	1,196	1,219	17.0	17.9	1.2	1.6	2.3	669	737	806	813
Miss	568	637	739	753	12.1	18.3	.2	1.1	2.3	419	442	484	488
W. So. Cent	4,928	5,952	7,144	7,313	20.8	22.9	1.8	1.9	2.8	3,679	4,215	4,736	4,790
Ark	524	615	729	742	17.4	20.6	(Z)	1.6	2.6	392	438	493	497
La	892	1,052	1,229	1,255	17.9	19.3	2.1	1.6	2.4	649	725	793	800
Okla	735	851	994	1,013	15.8	19.1	1.0	1.5	2.4	540	596	654	659
Tex	2,778	3,434	4,192	4,303	23.6	25.3	2.4	2.1	3.1	2,098	2,456	2,796	2,834
Mt	1,976	2,518	3,272	3,375	27.4	34.0	3.1	2.4	4.0	1,489	1,805	2,180	2,215
Mont	202	217	261	265	7.4	21.9	1.4	.7	2.7	147	152	172	172
Idaho	194	219	274	284	12.9	29.7	1.4	1.2	3.6	151	163	193	198
Wyo	99	105	133	139	6.1	32.9	1.6	.5	3.9	75	76	92	94
Colo	529	691	892	917	30.6	32.7	3.0	2.7	3.9	390	484	577	584
N. Mex	251	289	371	383	15.1	32.3	3.5	1.4	3.9	195	209	248	252
Ariz	367	539	753	777	46.9	44.1	5.6	3.9	5.0	276	386	501	509
Utah	242	298	370	381	23.1	27.9	2.5	2.1	3.4	190	226	263	268
Nev	92	160	218	229	73.9	43.1	6.0	5.6	4.9	65	109	134	138
Pac	6,644	8,654	10,361	10,660	30.3	23.2	3.5	2.6	2.9	4,704	5,746	6,294	6,358
Wash	894	1,106	1,293	1,324	23.7	19.8	1.9	2.1	2.5	648	768	830	837
Oreg	558	692	843	868	24.0	25.5	1.5	2.1	3.1	413	486	551	560
Calif	4,981	6,574	7,848	8,083	32.0	23.0	4.0	2.8	2.8	3,488	4,284	4,658	4,705
Alaska	57	79	117	118	38.6	49.3	6.1	3.2	5.5	43	60	82	81
Hawaii	153	203	260	267	32.7	31.5	3.1	2.8	3.8	112	148	173	175

Z Less than .05 percent. [1] Computed using the formula for continuous compounding; see p. xii.

Source: U.S. Bureau of the Census, *Current Population Reports*, series P-25, No. 725, and earlier issues.

No. 64. FAMILIES, BY CHARACTERISTICS: 1960 TO 1977

[As of **March**. Based on Current Population Survey; includes members of Armed Forces living off post or with families on post, but excludes other Armed Forces; see text, p. 1. For definition of families, see text, p. 4]

CHARACTERISTIC	ALL FAMILIES		MALE HEAD, MARRIED, WIFE PRESENT		MALE HEAD, OTHER MARITAL STATUS		FEMALE HEAD		FAMILIES OF OTHER THAN WHITE PERSONS	
	Number (1,000)	Percent	Number (1,000)	Percent	Number (1,000)	Percent	Number (1,000)	Percent	Number (1,000)	Percent
1960	45,111	100.0	39,329	100.0	1,275	100.0	4,507	100.0	(NA)	(NA)
1965	47,956	100.0	41,749	100.0	1,181	100.0	5,026	100.0	(NA)	(NA)
1970	51,586	100.0	44,755	100.0	1,239	100.0	5,591	100.0	5,324	100.0
1975	55,712	100.0	46,971	100.0	1,499	100.0	7,242	100.0	6,262	100.0
1976	56,245	100.0	47,318	100.0	1,444	100.0	7,482	100.0	6,372	100.0
1977, total	56,710	100.0	47,497	100.0	1,500	100.0	7,713	100.0	6,627	100.0
White	50,083	88.3	43,397	91.4	1,219	81.3	5,467	70.9	(X)	(X)
Black and other	6,627	11.7	4,100	8.6	281	18.7	2,246	29.1	6,627	100.0
Size of family:										
2 persons	21,530	38.0	17,186	36.2	923	61.5	3,421	44.4	1,909	28.8
3 persons	12,472	22.0	10,068	21.2	360	24.0	2,044	26.5	1,553	23.4
4 persons	11,483	20.2	10,243	21.6	119	7.9	1,121	14.5	1,254	18.9
5 persons	6,209	10.9	5,580	11.7	56	3.7	572	7.4	809	12.2
6 persons	2,800	4.9	2,513	5.3	18	1.2	269	3.5	470	7.1
7 or more persons	2,216	3.9	1,907	4.0	23	1.5	286	3.7	632	9.5
Own children under age 18:										
None	26,565	46.8	22,622	47.6	1,014	67.6	2,929	38.0	2,496	37.7
1	11,100	19.6	8,854	18.6	274	18.3	1,972	25.6	1,440	21.7
2	10,707	18.9	9,117	19.2	138	9.2	1,452	18.8	1,213	18.3
3	5,091	9.0	4,288	9.0	46	3.1	756	9.8	735	11.1
4 or more	3,247	5.7	2,617	5.5	27	1.8	604	7.8	743	11.2
Own children under age 6:										
None	43,796	77.2	36,369	76.6	1,413	94.2	6,014	78.0	4,761	71.8
1	9,048	16.0	7,739	16.3	75	5.0	1,234	16.0	1,279	19.3
2	3,280	5.8	2,917	6.1	8	.5	355	4.6	449	6.8
3 or more	586	1.0	471	1.0	5	.3	109	1.4	139	2.1

NA Not available.   X Not applicable.

Source: U.S. Bureau of the Census, *Current Population Reports*, series P-20, Nos. 276, 291, 296, and 311, and forthcoming report.

No. 65. FEMALE FAMILY HEADS—CHARACTERISTICS, BY RACE: 1960 TO 1977

[Covers persons 14 years old and over. **1960**, census data as of **April**; thereafter, based on Current Population Survey as of **March**. See headnote, table 64]

CHARACTERISTIC	1960	1970	1977	CHARACTERISTIC	1960	1970	1977
WHITE				**BLACK**			
Female heads _____1,000__	3,306	4,185	5,467	Female heads _____1,000__	890	1,349	2,151
Median age _____years__	52.2	50.4	44.7	Median age _____years__	43.8	41.3	38.6
Percent, by marital status:				Percent, by marital status:			
Single	11.8	9.2	9.7	Single	10.8	16.2	22.6
Married, spouse absent	17.6	18.5	18.4	Married, spouse absent	37.4	39.7	32.8
Separated	9.6	11.4	14.5	Separated	30.2	33.8	29.7
Other	7.9	7.2	3.9	Other	7.2	5.9	3.1
Widowed	52.5	47.0	33.8	Widowed	40.2	29.9	23.3
Divorced	18.1	25.3	38.0	Divorced	11.6	14.2	21.3
Percent, by presence of children under 18:				Percent, by presence of children under 18:			
No own children	57.8	52.0	41.8	No own children	44.4	33.5	28.5
With own children	42.2	48.0	58.2	With own children	55.6	66.6	71.5
1 child	19.2	18.8	25.9	1 child	16.9	19.1	24.5
2 children	12.0	15.0	18.8	2 children	12.8	14.4	19.0
3 children	6.1	7.8	8.3	3 children	9.4	12.5	13.5
4 or more children	5.0	6.4	5.1	4 or more children	16.5	20.6	14.6
Mean number of children	.85	1.00	1.85	Mean number of children	1.57	1.96	2.25
Children under 18 in all families _____mil__	54.5	58.5	53.1	Children under 18 in all families _____mil__	8.4	9.3	9.3
Percent living with—				Percent living with—			
Both parents	91.9	88.1	85.3	Both parents	69.2	58.7	47.3
Mother only	6.2	8.6	12.0	Mother only	20.6	30.8	42.2

Source: U.S. Bureau of the Census, *Current Population Reports*, series P-20, Nos. 306 and 323 and series P-23, No. 50.

No. 66. Families Not Headed by a Husband and Wife: 1960 to 1977

[In thousands, except percent. As of March. Persons 18 years old and over, except as noted. See headnote, table 64]

CHARACTERISTIC	Total, 1960 [1]	Total, 1970	Total, 1976	1977 Total	Age of head (in years) 18–24	25–34	35–44	45–54	55–64	65 or older
Number of family units	5,727	6,778	8,909	9,192	851	2,002	1,940	1,743	1,224	1,432
Percent distribution	(X)	(X)	(X)	100.0	9.3	21.8	21.1	19.0	13.3	15.6
Male head	1,233	1,211	1,441	1,491	138	195	260	359	254	285
Married, wife absent	166	200	232	248	16	50	52	69	41	20
Widowed	465	414	388	391	–	4	25	93	97	172
Divorced	115	180	386	402	10	59	127	125	57	24
Single	487	416	435	450	112	82	56	72	59	69
Female head	4,494	5,567	7,468	7,701	713	1,807	1,680	1,384	970	1,147
Married, husband absent	1,099	1,321	1,769	1,733	206	583	489	304	117	34
Widowed	2,325	2,389	2,375	2,380	12	84	218	491	627	948
Divorced	694	1,258	2,359	2,563	132	870	862	500	162	37
Single	376	599	965	1,025	363	270	111	89	64	128
PERCENT BY MARITAL STATUS										
Male head	100.0	100.0	100.0	100.0	100.0	100.0	100.0	100.0	100.0	100.0
Married, wife absent	13.5	16.5	16.1	16.6	11.6	25.6	20.0	19.2	16.1	7.0
Widowed	37.7	34.2	26.9	26.2	–	2.1	9.6	25.9	38.2	60.4
Divorced	9.3	14.9	26.8	27.0	7.2	30.3	48.8	34.8	22.4	8.4
Single	39.5	34.4	30.2	30.2	81.2	42.1	21.5	20.1	23.2	24.2
Female head	100.0	100.0	100.0	100.0	100.0	100.0	100.0	100.0	100.0	100.0
Married, husband absent	24.5	23.7	23.7	22.5	28.9	32.3	29.1	22.0	12.1	3.0
Widowed	51.7	42.9	31.8	30.9	1.7	4.6	13.0	35.5	64.6	82.7
Divorced	15.4	22.6	31.6	33.3	18.5	48.1	51.3	36.1	16.7	3.2
Single	8.4	10.8	12.9	13.3	50.9	14.9	6.6	6.4	6.6	11.2

– Represents zero.   X Not applicable.   [1] Persons 14 years old and over.

Source: U.S. Bureau of the Census, *Current Population Reports*, series P-20, No. 323, and earlier issues.

No. 67. Persons in Families and Unrelated Individuals, by Sex, Age, and Type of Family: 1960 to 1977

[In millions, except percent. Based on Current Population Survey as of March; see headnote, table 64]

YEAR AND AGE	PERSONS IN FAMILIES Total	Percent of all persons	Male	Female	Husband-wife families	Female-headed families [1] Number	Percent of total	Male-headed families [1]	UNRELATED INDIVIDUALS Total	Male	Female
1960: Total	165.4	92.7	81.9	83.5	148.3	14.2	8.6	3.5	11.1	4.5	6.6
Under 18 yr	63.5	99.2	32.2	31.3	(NA)	(NA)	(NA)	(NA)	.3	.2	.1
18–64 yr	89.8	91.8	43.6	46.2	(NA)	(NA)	(NA)	(NA)	7.0	3.2	3.8
65 yr. and over	12.1	73.3	6.1	6.0	(NA)	(NA)	(NA)	(NA)	3.8	1.1	2.6
1965: Total	177.6	92.5	87.8	89.8	157.8	16.3	9.2	3.4	12.3	4.7	7.6
Under 18 yr	69.6	99.2	35.4	34.2	(NA)	(NA)	(NA)	(NA)	.3	.1	.2
18–64 yr	95.3	91.9	46.1	49.2	(NA)	(NA)	(NA)	(NA)	7.3	3.3	4.1
65 yr. and over	12.7	70.5	6.4	6.4	(NA)	(NA)	(NA)	(NA)	4.6	1.3	3.3
1970: Total	184.9	91.4	91.0	93.9	163.3	18.0	9.7	3.6	15.0	5.7	9.3
Under 18 yr	68.9	98.9	35.0	33.8	60.2	7.8	11.3	.9	.4	.2	.2
18–64 yr	102.6	91.1	49.3	53.3	92.2	8.4	8.2	2.0	8.8	4.0	4.8
65 yr. and over	13.3	67.1	6.6	6.7	10.9	1.8	13.5	.7	5.7	1.4	4.3
1975: Total	190.5	90.9	93.7	96.8	162.9	23.2	12.2	4.4	19.1	8.0	11.1
Under 18 yr	66.0	99.4	33.6	32.4	54.4	10.5	15.9	1.1	.4	.2	.2
18–64 yr	109.9	90.0	52.8	57.1	96.2	11.0	10.0	2.6	12.3	6.4	5.9
65 yr. and over	14.6	69.2	7.3	7.4	12.3	1.8	12.3	.6	6.5	1.5	5.0
1977: Total	190.8	89.8	93.9	97.0	162.5	24.2	12.7	4.1	21.7	9.2	12.5
Under 18 yr	63.9	99.4	32.6	31.3	52.1	10.8	16.9	1.0	.4	.2	.2
18–64 yr	111.9	88.7	53.7	58.1	97.9	11.5	10.3	2.5	14.3	7.5	6.8
65 yr. and over	15.1	68.2	7.6	7.5	12.5	2.0	13.2	.6	7.0	1.6	5.5

NA Not available.   [1] No spouse present.

Source: U.S. Bureau of the Census, *Current Population Reports*, series P-20, Nos. 106, 140, 144, 212, 218, 287, 291, and forthcoming report.

No. 68. PERSONS UNDER 18 YEARS OLD, BY PRESENCE OF PARENTS AND WHETHER LIVING WITH MOTHER ONLY, BY MARITAL STATUS OF MOTHER: 1968 TO 1977

[As of **March**. Excludes persons under 18 years old who were heads and spouses of heads of families and subfamilies. Based on Current Population Survey; see headnote, table 64]

YEAR AND RACE	Persons under 18 years old (1,000)	Percent living with both parents	PERCENT LIVING WITH MOTHER ONLY WHO IS—				Percent living with father only	Percent living with neither parent
			Married, but separated [1]	Widowed	Divorced	Single		
1968: Total [2]	70,617	85.0	4.9	2.3	2.9	.7	1.1	3.2
White	59,953	89.4	3.1	1.8	2.7	.2	.9	2.0
Black	9,775	58.3	15.5	5.6	4.1	3.8	2.1	10.4
1970: Total [2]	69,458	84.9	4.7	2.0	3.3	.8	1.1	3.3
White	59,026	89.2	2.8	1.7	3.1	.2	.9	2.2
Black	9,483	58.1	16.2	4.2	4.6	4.4	2.2	10.4
1975: Total [2]	66,087	80.3	5.8	2.4	5.5	1.8	1.5	2.7
White	55,500	85.4	3.8	1.9	5.1	.5	1.5	1.7
Black	9,472	49.4	18.7	5.1	8.1	9.1	1.8	7.9
1977: Total [2]	64,062	79.2	5.6	2.0	6.6	2.1	1.4	3.1
White	53,394	84.8	3.7	1.5	6.1	.6	1.4	1.9
Black	9,374	46.8	17.1	4.4	9.6	10.5	1.4	10.1

[1] Includes married but husband absent.   [2] Includes races not shown separately.

Source: U.S. Bureau of the Census, *Current Population Reports*, series P-20, No. 323, and earlier issues.

No. 69. PERSONS LIVING ALONE, BY AGE AND SEX: 1960 TO 1977

[1960, census data as of **April**; thereafter, based on Current Population Survey as of **March**. See headnote, table 64]

SEX AND AGE	NUMBER OF PERSONS (1,000)					PERCENT				
	1960	1965	1970	1975	1977	1960	1965	1970	1975	1977
Both sexes	7,064	8,602	10,851	13,939	15,532	100.0	100.0	100.0	100.0	100.0
14–24 years	234	305	556	1,111	1,340	3.3	3.5	5.1	8.0	8.6
25–44 years	1,212	1,281	1,604	2,744	3,501	17.2	14.9	14.8	19.7	22.5
45–64 years	2,720	3,073	3,622	4,076	4,210	38.5	35.7	33.4	29.2	27.1
65 years and over	2,898	3,943	5,071	6,008	6,482	41.0	45.8	46.7	43.1	41.7
Male	2,628	2,923	3,532	4,918	5,639	37.2	34.0	32.5	35.3	36.3
14–24 years	124	141	274	610	752	1.8	1.6	2.5	4.4	4.8
25–44 years	686	737	933	1,689	2,114	9.7	8.6	8.6	12.1	13.6
45–64 years	965	1,013	1,152	1,329	1,431	13.7	11.8	10.6	9.5	9.2
65 years and over	853	1,033	1,174	1,290	1,343	12.1	12.0	10.8	9.3	8.6
Female	4,436	5,679	7,319	9,021	9,893	62.8	66.0	67.5	64.7	63.7
14–24 years	110	164	282	501	588	1.6	1.9	2.6	3.6	3.8
25–44 years	526	544	671	1,055	1,387	7.4	6.3	6.2	7.6	8.9
45–64 years	1,755	2,060	2,470	2,747	2,779	24.8	23.9	22.8	19.7	17.9
65 years and over	2,045	2,910	3,897	4,718	5,139	28.9	33.8	35.9	33.8	33.1

Source: U.S. Bureau of the Census, *U.S. Census of Population: 1960*, Subject Report, PC(2)-4B, and *Current Population Reports*, series P-20, Nos. 144, 287, and 313.

No. 70. LIVING ARRANGEMENTS OF ELDERLY WIDOWED PERSONS: 1968 TO 1977

[Persons 65 years and over. As of **March**. Noninstitutional population. Based on Current Population Survey; see headnote, table 64]

WIDOWED PERSONS	HOUSEHOLD HEAD				NOT A HOUSEHOLD HEAD		
	Total (1,000)	Percent primary family head	Percent primary individual		Total (1,000)	Percent in families	Percent secondary individuals
			Living alone	Living with non-relatives			
1968: Total	4,902	24.5	71.8	3.7	2,047	91.2	8.8
Widow	3,948	24.5	72.2	3.3	1,613	92.2	7.8
Widower	954	24.3	69.8	6.0	434	87.6	12.4
1970: Total	5,296	22.3	74.6	3.1	1,984	89.4	10.5
Widow	4,344	22.2	75.0	2.9	1,519	92.2	7.7
Widower	952	22.9	73.0	4.1	465	80.0	19.8
1975: Total	6,117	18.6	78.9	2.5	1,588	92.3	7.7
Widow	5,110	18.8	78.7	2.4	1,407	93.5	6.5
Widower	1,007	17.3	79.4	3.2	181	82.9	17.1
1977: Total	6,440	17.4	80.4	2.2	1,607	92.3	7.7
Widow	5,425	17.4	80.3	2.2	1,325	94.6	5.4
Widower	1,015	16.9	81.1	2.1	282	81.6	18.4

Source: U.S. Bureau of the Census, *Current Population Reports*, series P-20, No. 323, and earlier issues.

No. 71. CHARACTERISTICS OF WIDOWS, BY AGE GROUP: 1970 AND 1977

[In thousands, except as indicated. Persons 14 years old and over. Based on Current Population Survey as of March; see headnote, table 64]

CHARACTERISTIC	1970 [1]					1977				
	Total	Under 45 yr.	45–64 yr.	65–74 yr.	75 yr. and over	Total	Under 45 yr.	45–64 yr.	65–74 yr.	75 yr. and over
Total	9,734	392	3,063	3,065	3,214	10,024	414	2,860	3,287	3,463
Percent, by age	100.0	4.0	31.5	31.5	33.0	100.0	4.1	28.5	32.8	34.5
Per 100 widowers	475	478	564	501	395	531	668	543	576	476
In labor force [2]	2,542	223	1,732	587		2,251	271	1,442	538	
Employed	2,463	(NA)	(NA)	(NA)		2,108	248	1,349	511	
			PERCENT					PERCENT		
White	8,559	3.2	30.5	31.6	34.6	8,739	3.4	27.3	33.6	35.8
Black	1,120	10.4	38.1	30.4	21.2	1,171	9.7	37.0	27.6	25.7
Living arrangement:										
Head of household	7,308	4.7	34.9	32.8	27.6	8,367	4.5	30.7	34.5	30.4
Primary family	2,392	12.1	47.0	22.0	18.9	2,375	13.1	47.0	22.4	17.5
Primary individual	4,915	1.1	29.0	38.0	31.9	5,992	1.0	24.2	39.2	35.5
Not household head	2,426	2.0	21.1	27.6	49.3	1,657	2.5	17.5	24.4	55.6
In families	1,862	2.3	22.1	29.4	46.2	1,544	2.1	16.6	23.7	57.5
Inmates of institutions	362	–	8.0	18.2	73.8	(NA)	(NA)	(NA)	(NA)	(NA)
Family heads with own children under 18:										
No children	1,753	(NA)	(NA)	(NA)	(NA)	1,718	(NA)	(NA)	(NA)	(NA)
One child	295	(NA)	(NA)	(NA)	(NA)	332	(NA)	(NA)	(NA)	(NA)
2 or more children	349	(NA)	(NA)	(NA)	(NA)	329	(NA)	(NA)	(NA)	(NA)

– Represents zero. NA Not available. [1] Data revised using population controls from the 1970 census; therefore, figures will not agree with table 70.
[2] Covers widows 16 years old and over. Source: U.S. Bureau of Labor Statistics.

Source: Except as noted, U.S. Bureau of the Census, *Current Population Reports*, series P-20, No. 323, and unpublished data.

No. 72. POPULATION IN INSTITUTIONS AND OTHER GROUP QUARTERS, BY RACE, TYPE OF QUARTERS, AND SEX: 1960 AND 1970

[In thousands. 1960 based on 25-percent sample; 1970, on 20-percent sample. See *Historical Statistics, Colonial Times to 1970*, series A 359–371, for inmates of institutions]

RACE, AND TYPE OF QUARTERS	1960			1970		
	Total	Male	Female	Total	Male	Female
Total	4,902	3,122	1,780	5,786	3,438	2,349
White	4,253	2,664	1,589	5,037	2,909	2,129
Black and other	649	458	190	749	529	220
Institutional inmates	1,887	1,117	770	2,127	1,126	1,000
Correctional institutions [1]	346	330	16	328	314	15
Mental hospitals and residential treatment centers	630	336	294	434	245	189
Tuberculosis hospitals	65	46	19	17	12	5
Chronic disease hospitals (excl. TB and mental)	42	25	17	67	38	29
Homes for the aged and dependent	470	188	282	928	299	629
Homes and schools for the mentally handicapped [2]	175	95	80	202	114	88
Homes and schools for the physically handicapped [2]	24	13	11	23	16	6
Homes for dependent and neglected children [2]	73	41	32	48	28	19
Homes for unwed mothers [2]	3	1	3	4	(Z)	4
Training schools for juvenile delinquents	46	34	12	66	53	14
Detention homes	11	8	3	10	7	4
Diagnostic and reception centers	1	1	(Z)	(NA)	(NA)	(NA)
Military barracks	868	868	(NA)	1,025	1,005	20
College dormitories	829	455	374	1,765	891	874
Rooming and boarding houses	634	400	234	330	191	139
Other	684	282	402	539	224	315

NA Not available. Z Fewer than 500.
[1] See also table 326. [2] For similar but not strictly comparable data, see table 172.
Source: U.S. Bureau of the Census, *U.S. Census of Population: 1960*, vol. I, Chapter D, and vol. II; and *Census of Population: 1970*, vols. I and II.

No. 73. Inmates of Institutions, by Type of Institution: 1970

STATE	All inmates	Correc-tional insti-tutions	Mental hos-pitals [1]	TB and chronic disease hos-pitals [2]	HOMES AND/OR SCHOOLS FOR—				
					Aged and depend-ent	Men-tally handi-capped	Physi-cally handi-capped	Dependent and neglected children and unwed mothers	Training schools for juvenile delin-quents [3]
U.S.	2,126,719	328,020	433,890	84,032	927,514	201,992	22,739	51,803	76,729
Ala	31,060	5,651	8,397	1,786	10,848	2,510	675	608	585
Alaska	1,345	337	340	32	353	111	–	75	97
Ariz	11,143	3,331	1,376	255	3,606	1,237	282	112	944
Ark	20,291	2,121	2,853	463	11,696	1,009	640	799	710
Calif	214,068	49,858	27,941	6,787	101,065	13,685	979	2,072	11,681
Colo	21,987	3,041	3,265	548	11,720	1,781	404	399	829
Conn	34,055	3,626	6,376	2,294	15,707	4,472	831	391	358
Del	5,176	655	1,552	967	1,403	155	–	103	341
D.C	12,172	1,256	4,484	193	5,331	57	38	570	243
Fla	60,641	16,189	11,442	1,064	21,570	5,853	1,037	928	2,558
Ga	46,239	14,447	10,501	1,461	14,550	1,915	648	1,422	1,295
Hawaii	4,224	372	782	710	1,334	869	42	18	97
Idaho	6,063	617	554	238	3,692	548	77	56	281
Ill	111,874	12,181	23,478	3,962	54,300	10,603	748	3,549	3,053
Ind	51,332	8,232	8,353	469	22,889	7,126	811	1,702	1,750
Iowa	37,184	2,275	3,175	596	27,422	2,526	114	477	599
Kans	30,846	4,816	4,246	619	18,209	1,512	591	256	597
Ky	27,187	5,625	3,440	1,178	13,321	1,256	455	1,076	836
La	31,859	7,748	5,171	659	12,083	3,401	764	703	1,330
Maine	10,723	729	3,179	242	5,000	960	40	172	401
Md	39,448	8,923	9,116	2,428	11,497	4,803	368	537	1,776
Mass	77,242	5,478	15,244	4,010	41,866	8,170	664	640	1,170
Mich	86,437	12,898	17,623	2,919	36,281	12,167	568	1,145	2,836
Minn	50,389	3,228	6,137	687	33,326	5,098	566	301	1,046
Miss	16,036	2,622	7,070	52	4,329	1,221	17	430	295
Mo	47,523	6,848	6,975	2,001	25,001	3,691	644	847	1,516
Mont	7,577	612	1,295	154	3,861	990	43	163	459
Nebr	22,197	1,660	1,157	1,106	13,282	3,100	154	1,242	496
Nev	3,234	1,217	514	83	892	–	–	57	471
N.H	8,738	463	2,128	192	4,235	1,026	205	166	323
N.J	60,009	8,872	14,734	4,515	23,141	7,011	138	804	794
N. Mex	6,083	1,522	495	369	1,946	804	183	352	412
N.Y	217,582	23,628	74,235	13,549	68,024	22,320	1,177	6,002	8,647
N.C	47,589	10,850	9,873	992	14,418	5,231	942	2,596	2,687
N. Dak	9,033	255	1,071	326	5,742	1,257	123	123	136
Ohio	106,599	14,290	22,583	3,587	49,229	8,938	310	4,108	3,554
Okla	37,125	6,035	3,556	684	20,851	2,384	265	2,035	1,315
Oreg	24,268	2,636	3,594	1,382	13,082	2,214	349	329	682
Pa	123,780	12,715	34,043	5,244	47,726	14,632	1,538	3,923	3,959
R.I	10,502	520	2,004	1,688	4,917	976	–	235	162
S.C	22,802	5,087	8,774	261	5,994	1,054	–	985	647
S. Dak	10,761	469	1,808	413	5,901	1,143	304	34	689
Tenn	34,402	6,716	6,781	5,128	8,764	2,934	695	1,156	2,228
Texas	116,034	21,591	15,949	2,883	51,318	13,247	1,030	5,450	4,566
Utah	6,792	875	512	84	3,772	75	1,150	13	311
Vt	5,339	402	1,344	25	2,390	646	105	88	339
Va	46,102	11,324	13,266	1,620	12,491	3,697	667	936	2,101
Wash	38,180	5,894	3,577	403	21,259	4,646	519	313	1,569
W. Va	13,841	2,301	5,235	613	3,954	60	337	334	1,007
Wis	58,051	4,667	11,440	2,057	30,546	6,871	502	771	1,197
Wyo	3,555	315	852	54	1,380	–	–	200	754

– Represents zero.   [1] Includes residential treatment centers.   [2] Excludes mental hospitals.   [3] Includes detention homes.

Source: U.S. Bureau of the Census, *Census of Population: 1970*, vol. II, *Persons in Institutions and Other Group Quarters.*

No. 74. Religious Bodies—Selected Data

[Represents latest information available from religious bodies with memberships of 50,000 or more; excludes a few groups giving no data. Not all groups follow same calendar year nor count membership in same way; some groups give only approximate figures. Roman Catholics count all baptized persons, including infants; Jews regard as members all Jews in communities having congregations; Eastern Orthodox Churches include all persons in their nationality or cultural groups; most Protestant bodies count only persons who have attained full membership, and previous estimates have indicated that all but a small minority of these are over 13 years of age; however, many Lutheran bodies and The Episcopal Church now report all baptized persons, and not only those confirmed. Data which appear in italics are "noncurrent," i.e., they are reported for 1975 or earlier. All other data are "current" and were reported in 1976 or 1977]

RELIGIOUS BODY	Year	Churches reported	Member-ship (1,000)	Pastors serving parishes	Sunday school en-rollment [1] (1,000)
Total_____	(x)	333,063	131,898	271,473	34,255
Bodies with membership of 50,000 or more_____	(x)	318,806	130,448	260,377	33,907
Current data_____	(x)	238,391	107,415	189,572	33,907
Noncurrent data	(x)	*80,415*	*23,033*	*70,805*	(NA)
African Methodist Episcopal Church_____	*1951*	*5,878*	*1,166*	*5,878*	(NA)
African Methodist Episcopal Zion Church_____	*1973*	*5,994*	*1,025*	*6,700*	(NA)
American Baptist Association_____	*1975*	*3,570*	*1,071*	*4,000*	(NA)
American Baptist Churches in the U.S.A._____	1976	5,937	1,594	5,320	(NA)
American Carpatho-Russian Orthodox Greek Catholic Church_____	1976	70	100	61	4
American Lutheran Church, The_____	1976	4,814	2,402	4,250	607
Antiochian Orthodox Christian Archdiocese of North America, The_____	1977	110	152	120	(NA)
*Apostolic Overcoming Holy Church of God*_____	*1956*	*300*	*75*	*300*	(NA)
*Armenian Apostolic Church of America*_____	*1972*	*29*	*125*	*23*	(NA)
*Armenian Church of America, Diocese of the (incl. Diocese of California)*_____	*1972*	*58*	*372*	*62*	(NA)
Assemblies of God_____	1977	9,208	1,302	13,684	1,436
Baptist General Conference_____	1976	669	118	670	116
Baptist Missionary Association of America_____	1976	1,478	216	1,400	107
*Buddhist Churches of America*_____	*1975*	*60*	*60*	*80*	(NA)
*Bulgarian Eastern Orthodox Church (Diocese of N. und S. America and Australia)*_____	*1971*	*13*	*86*	(NA)	(NA)
Christian and Missionary Alliance_____	1976	1,236	150	942	151
Christian Church (Disciples of Christ)_____	1976	4,426	1,279	4,100	411
Christian Churches and Churches of Christ_____	1976	5,436	1,041	5,055	(NA)
Christian Congregation, Inc., The_____	1976	1,107	79	1,107	51
*Christian Methodist Episcopal Church*_____	*1965*	*2,598*	*467*	*2,214*	(NA)
Christian Reformed Church in North America_____	1976	538	211	483	53
*Church of God, The*_____	*1973*	*2,035*	*76*	*1,910*	(NA)
Church of God (Anderson, Ind.)_____	1976	2,270	170	1,761	245
Church of God (Cleveland, Tenn.)_____	1976	4,644	365	7,800	379
*Church of God in Christ, The*_____	*1965*	*4,500*	*425*	*4,000*	(NA)
*Church of God in Christ, International, The*_____	*1971*	*1,041*	*501*	(NA)	(NA)
*Church of God of Prophecy, The*_____	*1975*	*1,791*	*66*	(NA)	(NA)
Church of Jesus Christ of Latter-day Saints, The____	1976	5,739	2,392	17,217	2,777
Church of the Brethren_____	1976	1,041	178	824	78
Church of the Nazarene_____	1976	4,727	449	(NA)	950
Churches of Christ_____	1976	17,000	2,500	11,000	(NA)
Community Churches, National Council of_____	1977	185	125	(NA)	(NA)
Congregational Christian Churches, National Association of_____	1977	376	90	340	(NA)
Conservative Baptist Association of America_____	1976	1,117	300	(NA)	(NA)
Cumberland Presbyterian Church_____	1976	860	93	527	52
Episcopal Church, The_____	1976	7,116	2,882	6,364	598
Evangelical Covenant Church of America_____	1976	512	73	451	68
*Evangelical Free Church of America*_____	*1971*	*562*	*70*	(NA)	(NA)
Evangelical Lutheran Churches, The Association of__	1977	210	95	274	16
Free Methodist Church of North America_____	1976	1,059	68	(NA)	120
Free Will Baptists_____	1976	2,407	229	(NA)	228
Friends United Meeting_____	1976	519	66	346	29
General Association of Regular Baptist Churches_____	1977	1,542	240	(NA)	(NA)
*General Baptists (General Association of)*_____	*1974*	*800*	*70*	*1,000*	(NA)
Greek Orthodox Archdiocese of North and South America_____	1977	535	1,950	610	(NA)
*Independent Fundamental Churches of America*_____	*1975*	*614*	*88*	*633*	(NA)
*International Church of the Foursquare Gospel*_____	*1963*	*714*	*89*	*741*	(NA)
Jehovah's Witnesses_____	1976	7,341	577	(x)	(x)
*Jewish Congregations*_____	*1972*	*5,000*	*6,115*	*5,100*	(NA)
Lutheran Church in America_____	1976	5,771	2,975	4,803	731

See footnotes at end of table.

No. 74. RELIGIOUS BODIES—SELECTED DATA—Continued

[See headnote, p. 53]

RELIGIOUS BODY	Year	Churches reported	Membership (1,000)	Pastors serving parishes	Sunday school enrollment [1] (1,000)
Bodies with membership of 50,000 or more—Con.					
Lutheran Church—Missouri Synod, The	1976	5,832	2,757	4,725	683
Mennonite Church	1976	1,059	96	1,806	106
Moravian Church in America (Unitas Fratrum)	1976	145	54	142	18
National Baptist Convention of America	1956	11,398	2,669	7,598	(NA)
National Baptist Convention, U.S.A., Inc	1958	26,000	5,500	26,000	(NA)
National Baptist Evangelical Life and Soul Saving Assembly of U.S.A.	1951	264	58	128	(NA)
National Primitive Baptist Convention, Inc.	1975	606	250	460	(NA)
North American Old Roman Catholic Church	1975	121	60	85	(NA)
Orthodox Church in America	1975	410	1,000	443	(NA)
Pentecostal Church of God of America, Inc.	1975	1,300	135	1,200	(NA)
Pentecostal Holiness Church	1972	1,340	74	(NA)	(NA)
Plymouth Brethren	1976	745	74	(NA)	36
Polish National Catholic Church of America	1960	162	282	151	(NA)
Presbyterian Church in America	1976	405	69	457	37
Presbyterian Church in the U.S.	1976	4,036	878	2,773	444
Primitive Baptists	1950	1,000	72	(NA)	(NA)
Progressive National Baptist Convention, Inc.	1967	655	522	(NA)	(NA)
Reformed Church in America	1976	902	351	873	114
Reorganized Church of Jesus Christ of Latter Day Saints	1976	1,053	186	15,701	(NA)
Roman Catholic Church, The	1976	24,158	49,326	(NA)	8,752
Russian Orthodox Church in the U.S.A., Patriarchal Parishes of the	1975	41	52	55	(NA)
Russian Orthodox Church Outside Russia, The	1955	81	55	92	(NA)
Salvation Army, The	1976	1,178	381	2,302	100
Serbian Eastern Orthodox Church for the U.S.A. and Canada	1967	52	65	56	(NA)
Seventh-day Adventists	1976	3,446	510	1,779	412
Southern Baptist Convention	1976	35,031	12,918	31,300	7,454
Syrian Orthodox Church of Antioch (Archdiocese of the U.S.A. and Canada)	1972	10	50	14	(NA)
Triumph the Church and Kingdom of God in Christ (International)	1972	475	54	860	(NA)
Ukrainian Orthodox Church in the U.S.A	1966	107	88	107	(NA)
Unitarian Universalist Association	1976	942	185	(NA)	42
United Church of Christ	1976	6,528	1,801	5,146	553
United Free Will Baptist Church	1952	836	100	915	(NA)
United Methodist Church, The	1976	38,795	9,861	20,235	4,654
United Pentecostal Church, International	1977	2,701	405	2,722	(NA)
United Presbyterian Church in the U.S.A., The	1976	8,618	2,607	7,644	1,036
Wesleyan Church, The	1976	1,735	96	1,488	207
Wisconsin Evangelical Lutheran Synod	1976	1,082	399	880	52
Bodies with membership of less than 50,000	(X)	14,257	1,448	11,096	347

NA Not available.   X Not applicable.   [1] Includes pupils, officers, and teachers.

No. 75. RELIGIOUS BODIES—CHURCH MEMBERSHIP, 1950 TO 1976, AND NUMBER OF CHURCHES, 1976

[Membership in thousands, except as indicated. See headnote, table 74. See also *Historical Statistics, Colonial Times to 1970*, series H 793–799]

RELIGIOUS BODY	MEMBERSHIP						Number of churches, 1976
	1950	1960	1965	1970	1975	1976	
Total	86,830	114,449	124,682	131,046	131,012	131,898	333,063
Members as percent of population [1]	57	64	64	63	61	61	(X)
Average members per local church	304	359	382	399	393	396	(X)
Buddhist Churches of America	73	20	92	100	60	60	60
Eastern Churches	1,650	2,699	3,172	3,850	3,696	3,755	1,554
Jewish Congregations [2]	5,000	5,367	5,600	5,870	6,115	6,115	5,000
Old Catholic, Polish National Catholic, and Armenian Churches	250	590	484	848	846	846	422
The Roman Catholic Church	28,635	42,105	46,246	48,215	48,882	49,326	24,158
Protestants [3]	51,080	} 63,669	69,088	{ 71,713	71,043	71,587	300,670
Miscellaneous [4]	142			449	372	209	1,199

X Not applicable.   [1] Based on Bureau of the Census estimated total population as of July 1.   [2] Includes Orthodox, Conservative, and Reformed Congregations.   [3] Includes nonprotestant bodies such as "Latter-Day Saints" and "Jehovah's Witnesses."   [4] Includes nonchristian bodies such as "Spiritualists," "Ethical Culture Movement," and "Unitarian-Universalists."

Source of tables 74 and 75: National Council of the Churches of Christ in the United States of America, New York, N.Y., *Yearbook of American and Canadian Churches*, annual. (Copyright.)

No. 76. RELIGIOUS BODIES—CHURCH CONTRIBUTIONS

[Data are for 43 U.S. Communions reporting in 1976 or 1977. Data are incomplete as not all U.S. churches have current data available. For additional data, see source]

RELIGIOUS BODY	CONTRIBUTIONS			BENEVOLENCES	
	Total ($1,000)	Per capita inclusive member- ship [1]	Congre- gational finances ($1,000)	Total ($1,000)	Percent of total contri- butions
United States Communions	6,207,153	$137.18	4,917,208	1,289,945	20.8
American Baptist Churches in the U.S.A	188,926	118.56	163,134	25,792	13.7
American Lutheran Church, The	292,006	121.56	215,528	76,478	26.2
Associate Reformed Presbyterian Church (General Synod)	5,490	172.34	4,371	1,119	20.4
Baptist General Conference	34,067	288.77	27,720	6,347	18.6
Baptist Missionary Association of America	25,851	119.43	22,060	3,792	14.7
Brethren in Christ Church	5,127	450.72	4,088	1,038	20.3
Christian Church (Disciples of Christ)	158,821	124.20	135,008	23,812	15.0
Church of God (Anderson, Ind.)	56,046	329.13	47,191	8,854	15.8
Church of God, General Conference (Oregon, Ill.)	1,205	158.14	1,100	105	8.7
Church of the Brethren	30,166	169.33	22,134	8,032	26.6
Church of the Nazarene	148,495	330.57	128,294	20,200	13.6
Conservative Congregational Christian Conference	4,643	211.25	3,138	1,505	32.4
Cumberland Presbyterian Church	12,569	135.15	10,920	1,649	13.1
Episcopal Church, The	375,942	130.44	312,435	63,507	16.9
Evangelical Congregational Church	5,994	207.83	4,861	1,133	18.9
Evangelical Covenant Church of America	28,350	385.94	21,452	6,899	24.3
Evangelical Lutheran Churches, The Association of	11,662	122.52	10,273	1,389	11.9
Evangelical Lutheran Synod	2,571	131.37	2,115	456	17.7
Free Lutheran Congregations, The Association of	748	53.67	317	431	57.6
Free Methodist Church of North America	29,216	428.51	19,954	9,261	31.7
Friends United Meeting	8,440	128.69	6,749	1,691	20.0
General Conference of Mennonite Brethren Churches	4,696	276.93	3,335	1,361	29.0
Lutheran Church in America	302,210	101.59	243,449	58,761	19.4
Lutheran Church—Missouri Synod, The	343,930	124.73	287,098	56,832	16.5
Mennonite Church	29,475	306.74	17,215	12,260	41.6
Mennonite Church, The General Conference	9,839	270.33	4,981	4,858	49.4
Moravian Church in America, Northern Province	4,662	144.85	4,088	574	12.3
Moravian Church in America, Southern Province	2,824	132.66	1,973	851	30.1
North American Baptist Conference	12,205	288.69	8,903	3,302	27.1
Orthodox Presbyterian Church	4,181	273.13	3,288	893	21.4
Presbyterian Church in America	20,322	294.56	15,149	5,173	25.5
Presbyterian Church in the United States	207,983	236.97	166,125	41,858	20.1
Primitive Methodist Church, U.S.A	2,078	197.51	1,621	457	22.0
Reformed Church in America	62,465	178.09	49,252	13,214	21.2
Reformed Church in the United States	483	125.03	367	116	24.0
Reformed Presbyterian Church, Evangelical Synod	7,490	308.90	5,999	1,491	19.9
Seventh-day Adventists	266,226	522.22	81,577	184,648	69.4
Seventh-day Baptist General Conference	904	175.98	693	212	23.4
Southern Baptist Convention	1,644,939	127.33	1,382,794	262,145	15.9
United Church of Christ	241,349	133.99	207,486	33,863	14.0
United Methodist Church, The	1,081,080	109.63	831,974	249,106	23.0
United Presbyterian Church in the United States	480,158	184.16	396,981	83,177	17.3
Wisconsin Evangelical Lutheran Synod	51,318	128.58	40,018	11,300	22.0

[1] Inclusive membership refers to those who are full, communicant, or confirmed members, plus other members listed as baptized, or nonconfirmed, or noncommunicant.

Source: National Council of the Churches of Christ in the United States of America, New York, N.Y., *Year-book of American and Canadian Churches*, annual. (Copyright.)

No. 77. NATIONAL NON-PROFIT ASSOCIATIONS—NUMBER, BY TYPE: 1968 TO 1977

[Covers organizations of national scope]

TYPE	1968	1970	1977	TYPE	1968	1970	1977
Total	[1] 10,299	[1] 10,734	13,273	Public affairs	446	498	883
Trade, business, commercial	2,832	2,895	2,944	Fraternal, foreign interest, nationality, ethnic	640	610	444
Agriculture	491	508	631	Religious	794	806	750
Legal, governmental, pub- lic admin., military	301	346	461	Veteran, hereditary, patriotic	197	198	205
Scientific, engineering, tech	488	548	913	Hobby, avocational	423	444	721
Educational and cultural	1,286	1,383	2,151	Athletic, sports	318	336	469
Social welfare	389	475	807	Labor unions	237	226	234
Health, medical	791	830	1,236	Chambers of Commerce [2]	126	110	104
				Greek letter societies	351	334	321

[1] Includes associations not shown separately. [2] National, binational, and international.

Source: Gale Research Co., Detroit, Mich. Compiled from *Encyclopedia of Associations*. (Copyright.)

Figure 2.1

Birth and Death Rates 1955 to 1977

(See table 78)

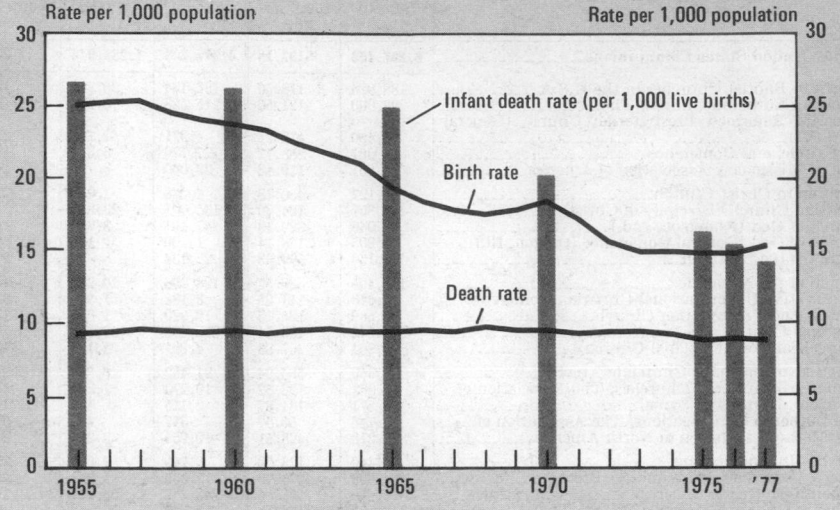

Rate per 1,000 population   Rate per 1,000 population

Infant death rate (per 1,000 live births)

Birth rate

Death rate

Source: Chart prepared by U.S. Bureau of the Census. Data from U.S. National Center for Health Statistics.

Figure 2.2

Marriages and Divorces: 1960 to 1977

(See table 114)

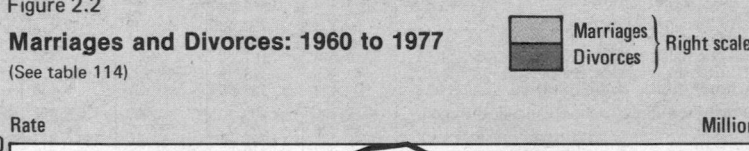

Marriages / Divorces } Right scale

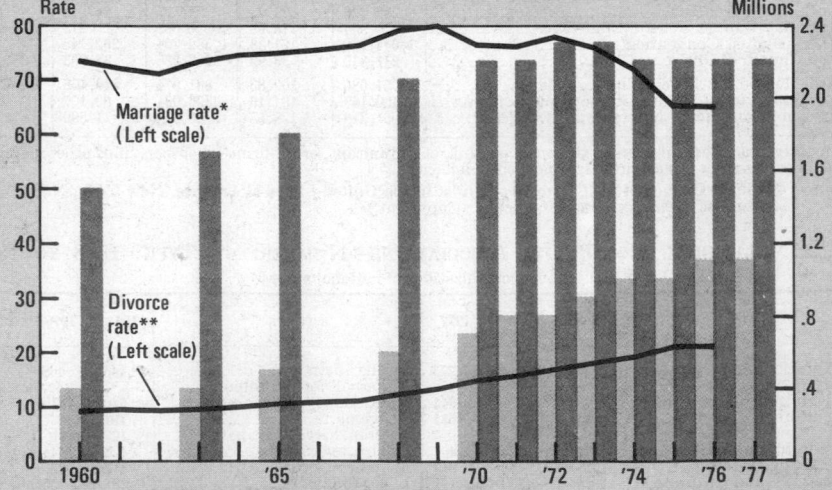

Rate   Millions

Marriage rate* (Left scale)

Divorce rate** (Left scale)

*Rate per 1,000 unmarried women, 15 years old and over.

**Rate per 1,000 married women, 15 years old and over.

Source: Chart prepared by U.S. Bureau of the Census. Data from U.S. National Center for Health Statistics.

Section 2

Vital Statistics

This section presents vital statistics—data on births; deaths; abortions; fetal deaths, including still-births; fertility; life expectancy; marriages; and divorces. Vital statistics are compiled for the country as a whole by the National Center for Health Statistics (NCHS) and published in its annual report, *Vital Statistics of the United States*, in certain reports of the *Vital and Health Statistics* series, and in the *Monthly Vital Statistics Report*. Reports in this field are also issued by the various State bureaus of vital statistics. Data on fertility, on age of persons at first marriage, and on marital status and marital history are compiled by the Bureau of the Census from its Current Population Survey (see text, p. 1) and published in *Current Population Reports*, series P-20.

Registration of vital events.—The registration of births, deaths, fetal deaths, and other vital events in the United States is primarily a State and local function. The civil laws of every State provide for a continuous and permanent birth and death registration system. Many States also provide for marriage- and divorce-registration systems.

Births and deaths.—The live-birth, death, and fetal-death statistics prepared by NCHS are based on copies of vital records received from registration offices of all States, of certain cities, and of the District of Columbia. The annual collection of death statistics on a national basis began in 1900 with a national death-registration area of 10 States and the District of Columbia; a similar annual collection of birth statistics for a national birth-registration area began in 1915, also with 10 reporting States and the District of Columbia. Since 1933, the birth- and death-registration areas have comprised the entire U.S., including Alaska (beginning 1959) and Hawaii (beginning 1960). National statistics on fetal deaths were first compiled for 1918 and annually since 1922.

Prior to 1951, birth statistics came from a complete count of records received in the Public Health Service (now received in NCHS). From 1951 through 1971, they were based on a 50-percent sample of all registered births (except for a complete count in 1955 and a 20- to 50-percent sample in 1967). Beginning in 1972, they have been based on a complete count for States in the Cooperative Health Statistics System (for details, see the technical appendix in *Vital Statistics of the United States*) and on a 50-percent sample of all other areas. Mortality data have been based on a complete count of records for each area (except for a 50-percent sample in 1972). Beginning in 1970, births to, and deaths of, U.S. nonresidents have been excluded from the data. Fetal deaths and deaths among Armed Forces abroad are excluded. Data based on samples are subject to sampling error; for details, see annual issues of *Vital Statistics of the United States*.

Mortality statistics by cause of death are compiled in accordance with World Health Organization (WHO) regulations, which specify that member nations classify causes of death according to the *International Classification of Diseases* (ICD). The current classification, the eighth revision of the ICD, has been in use since 1968.

Fertility and life expectancy.—Fertility rates, narrowly defined as the number of births that 1,000 women would have in their lifetime if, at each year of age, they experienced the birth rates occurring in the specified year, are compiled and published by NCHS. Other data relating to social and medical factors which affect fertility rates, such as contraceptive use and birth expectations, are collected and made available by both NCHS and the Bureau of the Census. NCHS figures are based on information in birth and fetal death certificates and on the 1973 and 1976 National Surveys of Family Growth; Bureau of the Census data are based on decennial censuses and periodic surveys.

Life expectancy rates are computed and published by NCHS. Age-at-time-of-death data are obtained by examination of death certificates sent to NCHS. The population data on which the rates are based are supplied by the Bureau of the Census and consist of decennial census figures and annual population estimates. For details, see the technical appendix in *Vital Statistics of the United States.*

Marriage and divorce.—The compilation of nationwide statistics on marriages and divorces in the U.S. began in 1887–1888 when the National Office of Vital Statistics prepared estimates for the years 1867–1886. Although periodic updates took place after 1888, marriage and divorce statistics were not collected and published annually until 1944 by that Office. In 1957 and 1958, respectively, the same Office established marriage- and divorce-registration areas. At the beginning of 1957, the marriage-registration area comprised 32 States, the Virgin Islands, and Puerto Rico; by 1977, it also included nine additional States and the District of Columbia. The divorce-registration area, starting with 16 States and the Virgin Islands in 1958, included a total of 29 States and the Virgin Islands by early 1977. Procedures for estimating the number of marriages and divorces in the registration States are discussed in *Vital Statistics of the United States*, vol. III— *Marriage and Divorce*. Data for nonregistration States are gathered mainly by collecting already summarized data on marriages and divorces reported by nonregistration State offices of vital statistics and by county offices of registration.

Another important source of data on marriage and divorce trends in the United States is the Current Population Survey carried out monthly by the Bureau of the Census. For further details, see text, p. 1.

Vital statistics rates.—Vital statistics rates computed by NCHS are based on decennial census population figures as of April 15, 1910; January 1, 1920; and April 1 for 1930, 1940, 1950, 1960, and 1970; and on midyear population figures for other years, as estimated by the Bureau of the Census (see text, p. 2).

Race.—Data by race for births, deaths, marriages, and divorces from NCHS are based on information contained in the certificates of registration. In NCHS's National Survey of Family Growth and the Census Bureau's Current Population Survey, race is determined by interviewer observation. The terms "Negro" and "Black" are interchangeable. With some exceptions, specific usage here is dependent on the source of the data.

Statistical reliability.—For discussion of statistical collection, estimation, and sampling procedures and measures of statistical reliability applicable to Census Bureau and NCHS data, see Appendix III.

Historical statistics.—Tabular headnotes provide cross-references, where applicable, to *Historical Statistics of the United States, Colonial Times to 1970*. See Appendix I.

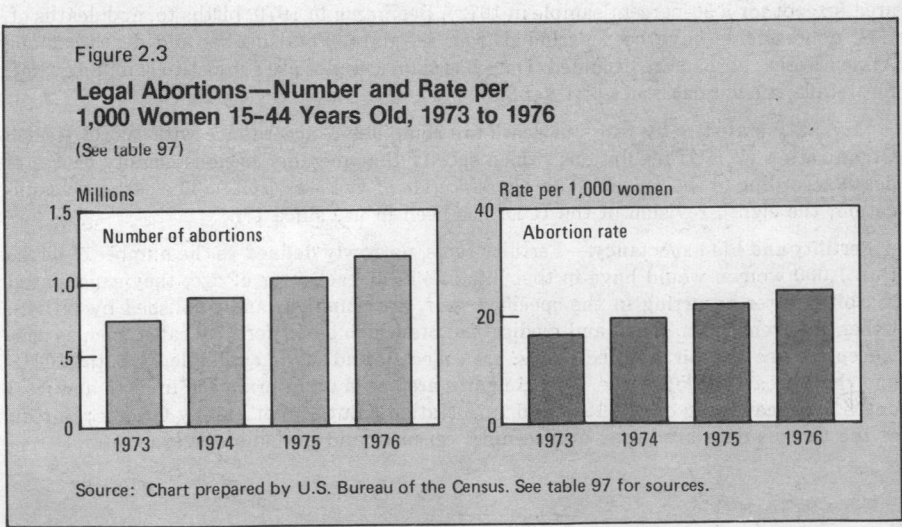

Figure 2.3

Legal Abortions—Number and Rate per 1,000 Women 15-44 Years Old, 1973 to 1976

(See table 97)

Source: Chart prepared by U.S. Bureau of the Census. See table 97 for sources.

No. 78. Live Births, Deaths, Marriages, and Divorces: 1910 to 1977

[Prior to 1960, excludes Alaska and Hawaii. Figures for deaths and death rates for 1910–1930 are for death-registration States only. Beginning 1970, excludes births to, and deaths of, nonresidents of the U.S. See also *Historical Statistics, Colonial Times to 1970*, series B 1–5, B 142, B 167, B 214, and B 216]

YEAR	NUMBER (1,000)					RATE PER 1,000 POPULATION				
	Births [1]	Deaths		Mar-riages [3]	Di-vorces [4]	Births [1]	Deaths		Mar-riages [3]	Di-vorces [4]
		Total	Infant [2]				Total	Infant [2]		
1910	2,777	697	(NA)	948	83	30.1	14.7	(NA)	10.3	.9
1915	2,965	816	78	1,008	104	29.5	13.2	99.9	10.0	1.0
1920	2,950	1,118	130	1,274	171	27.7	13.0	85.8	12.0	1.6
1925	2,909	1,192	135	1,188	175	25.1	11.7	71.7	10.3	1.5
1930	2,618	1,327	142	1,127	196	21.3	11.3	64.6	9.2	1.6
1935	2,377	1,393	120	1,327	218	18.7	10.9	55.7	10.4	1.7
1940	2,559	1,417	111	1,596	264	19.4	10.8	47.0	12.1	2.0
1945	2,858	1,402	105	1,613	485	20.4	10.6	38.3	12.2	3.5
1950	3,632	1,452	104	1,667	385	24.1	9.6	29.2	11.1	2.6
1955	4,097	1,529	107	1,531	377	25.0	9.3	26.4	9.3	2.3
1960	4,258	1,712	111	1,523	393	23.7	9.5	26.0	8.5	2.2
1962	4,167	1,757	105	1,577	413	22.4	9.5	25.3	8.5	2.2
1963	4,098	1,814	103	1,654	428	21.7	9.6	25.2	8.8	2.3
1964	4,027	1,798	100	1,725	450	21.0	9.4	24.8	9.0	2.4
1965	3,760	1,828	93	1,800	479	19.4	9.4	24.7	9.3	2.5
1966	3,606	1,863	86	1,857	499	18.4	9.5	23.7	9.5	2.5
1967	3,521	1,851	79	1,927	523	17.8	9.4	22.4	9.7	2.6
1968	3,502	1,930	76	2,069	584	17.5	9.7	21.8	10.4	2.9
1969	3,600	1,922	75	2,145	639	17.8	9.5	20.7	10.6	3.2
1970	3,731	1,921	75	2,159	708	18.4	9.5	20.0	10.6	3.5
1971	3,556	1,928	68	2,190	773	17.2	9.3	19.1	10.6	3.7
1972	3,258	1,964	60	2,282	845	15.6	9.4	18.5	11.0	4.1
1973	3,137	1,973	56	2,284	915	14.9	9.4	17.7	10.9	4.4
1974	3,160	1,934	53	2,230	977	14.9	9.2	16.7	10.5	4·6
1975	3,144	1,893	51	2,153	1,036	14.8	8.8	16.1	10.1	4.9
1976	3,168	1,909	48	2,155	1,083	14.8	8.9	15.2	10.0	5.0
1977 [5]	3,313	1,898	47	2,176	1,090	15.3	8.8	14.0	10.1	5.0

NA Not available.　[1] Through 1955, figures adjusted for underregistration.
[2] Infants under 1 year old, exclusive of fetal deaths; rates per 1,000 registered live births.
[3] Includes estimates and marriage licenses for some States for all years.
[4] Includes reported annulments and some estimated State figures for all years.　[5] Preliminary.

No. 79. Births and Birth Rates: 1940 to 1976

[Births in thousands and rates per 1,000 population, except as indicated. Prior to 1960, excludes Alaska and Hawaii. For 1940–1955, births adjusted for underregistration; thereafter, registered births. Beginning 1970, excludes births to nonresidents of U.S. Minus sign (−) denotes decrease. For population bases used to derive these data, see text, p. 57. See also *Historical Statistics, Colonial Times to 1970*, series B 1, B 5–7, and B 20]

ITEM	1940	1950	1955	1960	1965	1970	1971	1972	1973	1974	1975	1976
Live births	2,559	3,632	4,097	4,258	3,760	3,731	3,556	3,258	3,137	3,160	3,144	3,168
Average annual percent change from prior year shown	[1] −.2	3.6	2.4	.8	−2.5	−.2	−4.7	−8.4	−3.7	.7	−.5	.8
White	2,198	3,108	3,485	3,601	3,124	3,091	2,920	2,656	2,551	2,576	2,552	2,568
Black and other	360	524	613	657	636	640	636	603	586	584	592	600
Percent of total	14.1	14.4	14.0	15.4	16.9	17.2	17.9	18.5	18.7	18.5	18.8	18.9
Male	1,313	1,863	2,099	2,180	1,927	1,915	1,823	1,670	1,608	1,622	1,613	1,624
Female	1,246	1,768	1,998	2,078	1,833	1,816	1,733	1,588	1,529	1,538	1,531	1,543
Males per 100 females	105.4	105.4	105.1	104.9	105.1	105.5	105.2	105.1	105.2	105.5	105.4	105.3
Birth rate	19.4	24.1	25.0	23.7	19.4	18.4	17.2	15.6	14.9	14.9	13.8	14.8
White	18.6	23.0	23.8	22.7	18.3	17.4	16.2	14.6	13.9	14.0	13.8	13.8
Black and other	26.7	33.3	34.5	32.1	27.6	25.1	24.7	22.9	21.9	21.4	21.2	21.1
Male	23.6	24.9	25.8	24.7	20.3	19.4	18.1	16.5	15.7	15.8	15.6	15.5
Female	21.5	23.3	23.9	22.8	18.6	17.4	16.4	14.9	14.2	14.2	14.0	14.0
Fertility rate [2]	79.9	106.2	118.3	118.0	96.6	87.9	81.8	73.4	69.2	68.4	66.7	65.8
Plural birth rate [3]	20.8	20.9	21.1	20.4	20.1	(NA)	18.1	18.4	18.4	18.6	19.2	19.5

NA Not available.　[1] Change from 1930.　[2] Births per 1,000 women, 15–44 years old.
[3] Per 1,000 live births.

Source of tables 78 and 79: U.S. National Center for Health Statistics, *Vital Statistics of the United States*, annual.

No. 80. Total Fertility Rate and Intrinsic Rate of Natural Increase, by Race: 1940 to 1976

[Excludes Alaska prior to 1959 and Hawaii prior to 1960. Prior to 1960, based on births adjusted for underregistration; thereafter, registered births only. The *total fertility rate* is the number of births that 1,000 women would have in their lifetime if, at each year of age, they experienced the birth rates occurring in the specified year. A total fertility rate of 2,110 represents "replacement level" fertility for the total population under current mortality conditions (assuming no net immigration). The *intrinsic rate of natural increase* is the rate that would eventually prevail if a population were to experience, at each year of age, the birth rates and death rates occurring in the specified year and if these rates remained unchanged over a long period of time. Minus sign (−) denotes decrease. See also *Historical Statistics, Colonial Times to 1970*, series B 11]

ANNUAL AVERAGE AND YEAR	TOTAL FERTILITY RATE			INTRINSIC RATE OF NATURAL INCREASE			YEAR	TOTAL FERTILITY RATE			INTRINSIC RATE OF NATURAL INCREASE		
	Total	White	Black and other	Total	White	Black and other		Total	White	Black and other	Total	White	Black and other
1940–1944	2,523	2,460	3,010	4.6	3.9	9.8	1968	2,477	2,368	3,197	5.9	4.2	16.0
1945–1949	2,985	2,916	3,485	11.7	10.9	17.2	1969	2,465	2,360	3,148	5.7	4.1	15.4
1950–1954	3,337	3,221	4,185	16.8	15.4	25.7	1970	2,480	2,385	3,067	6.0	4.5	14.4
1955–1959	3,690	3,549	4,716	21.1	19.5	30.7							
							1971	2,275	2,168	2,933	2.8	1.0	12.8
1960–1964	3,459	3,331	4,375	18.6	17.1	27.7	1972	2,022	1,918	2,651	−1.7	−3.7	8.9
1965–1969	2,636	2,516	3,447	8.2	6.4	18.6	1973	1,896	1,798	2,474	−4.2	−6.1	6.1
1970–1974	2,106	2,007	2,700	−.4	−2.2	9.4	1974	1,857	1,768	2,377	−5.0	−6.8	4.6
1975–1976	1,784	1,694	2,299	−6.4	−8.4	3.4							
							1975	1,799	1,708	2,322	−6.1	−8.1	3.7
1965	2,928	2,790	3,891	12.1	10.3	23.1	1976	1,768	1,679	2,276	−6.7	−8.6	3.0
1967	2,573	2,453	3,385	7.4	5.6	18.2							

No. 81. Live Birth Rates, by Race and Age of Mother: 1950 to 1976

[Births per 1,000 women in each specified group. Prior to 1960, excludes Alaska and Hawaii. Data for 1950 and 1955 are adjusted for underregistration; thereafter, registered births only. Beginning 1970, excludes births to non-residents of U.S. For population bases used to derive these data, see text, p. 58. See also *Historical Statistics, Colonial Times to 1970*, series B 8–10 and B 12–19]

YEAR	WOMEN, 15–44 YEARS [1]			AGE OF MOTHER							
	Total	White	Black and other	10–14 years	15–19 years	20–24 years	25–29 years	30–34 years	35–39 years	40–44 years	45–49 years [2]
1950	106.2	102.3	137.3	1.0	81.6	196.6	166.1	103.7	52.9	15.1	1.2
1955	118.5	113.8	155.3	.9	90.5	242.0	190.5	116.2	58.7	16.1	1.0
1960	118.0	113.2	153.6	.8	89.1	258.1	197.4	112.7	56.2	15.5	.9
1965	96.6	91.4	133.9	.8	70.4	196.8	162.5	95.0	46.4	12.8	.8
1970	87.9	84.1	113.0	1.2	68.3	167.8	145.1	73.3	31.7	8.1	.5
1971	81.8	77.5	109.5	1.1	64.7	150.6	134.8	67.6	28.7	7.1	.4
1972	73.4	69.2	100.3	1.2	62.0	131.0	118.7	60.2	24.8	6.2	.4
1973	69.2	65.3	94.3	1.3	59.7	120.7	113.6	56.1	22.0	5.4	.3
1974	68.4	64.7	91.0	1.2	58.1	119.0	113.3	54.4	20.2	4.8	.3
1975	66.7	63.0	89.3	1.3	56.3	114.7	110.3	53.1	19.4	4.6	.3
1976	[3] 65.8	62.2	87.6	1.2	53.5	112.1	108.8	54.5	19.0	4.3	.2

[1] Rates computed by relating total births, regardless of age of mother, to women aged 15–44 years.
[2] Through 1960, rates computed by relating births to mothers aged 45 years and over to women aged 45–49 years.
[3] Live birth rate for 1977 was 67.4; detailed data not available.

No. 82. Birth Rates, All Women, by Live-Birth Order, by Race: 1950 to 1976

[Births per 1,000 women 15–44 years old. 1950 excludes Alaska and Hawaii. Live-birth order refers to number of children born alive. Figures for births of order not stated are distributed. See also headnote, table 81, and *Historical Statistics, Colonial Times to 1970*, series B 20–27]

LIVE BIRTH ORDER	1950		1960		1965		1970		1975		1976	
	White	Black and other	White	Black and other	White	Black and other	White	Black and other	White	Black and other	White	Black and other
Total	102.3	137.3	113.2	153.6	91.4	133.9	84.1	113.0	63.0	89.3	62.2	87.6
First birth	33.3	33.8	30.8	33.6	28.9	35.8	32.9	42.4	26.9	37.3	26.5	35.9
Second birth	32.3	30.3	29.2	29.3	23.0	26.6	23.7	26.9	20.5	25.1	20.4	25.3
Third birth	17.9	22.9	22.7	24.0	16.2	19.6	13.3	15.9	8.9	12.8	9.0	13.1
Fourth birth	8.4	15.3	14.1	18.6	10.2	14.6	6.8	9.7	3.6	6.2	3.4	6.2
Fifth birth	4.1	10.4	7.5	14.1	5.8	10.8	3.4	6.1	1.5	3.2	1.4	3.0
Sixth and seventh	3.7	12.6	6.1	18.4	5.0	13.8	2.7	6.7	1.1	2.8	1.0	2.5
Eighth and over	2.5	12.0	2.8	15.6	2.4	12.6	1.2	5.3	.5	1.8	.4	1.5

Source of tables 80–82: U.S. National Center for Health Statistics, *Vital Statistics of the United States*, annual.

No. 83. Live Births—Total and Rate, 1960 to 1976: States

:By place of residence. Represents registered births. Beginning 1970, excludes births to nonresidents of the U.S.:

STATE	NUMBER (1,000)							RATE PER 1,000 POPULATION [1]						
	1960	1965	1970	1973	1974	1975	1976	1960	1965	1970	1973	1974	1975	1976
U.S.	4,258	3,760	3,731	3,137	3,160	3,144	3,168	23.7	19.4	18.4	14.9	14.9	14.8	14.8
N.E.	237	213	200	156	152	148	145	22.5	19.1	16.9	12.8	12.5	12.1	11.9
Maine	23	20	18	16	15	15	14	24.0	19.9	17.9	15.2	14.4	14.4	14.0
N.H.	15	13	13	12	12	11	11	22.8	19.5	17.9	14.6	14.4	13.5	13.6
Vt.	9	8	8	7	7	7	7	24.1	20.5	18.8	14.6	14.7	14.3	14.2
Mass.	115	101	95	72	70	68	66	22.4	18.8	16.6	14.2	12.1	11.7	11.4
R.I.	18	17	16	12	11	11	11	21.4	19.4	16.5	12.6	12.2	11.6	11.7
Conn.	57	54	50	38	37	36	36	22.4	19.2	16.7	12.2	11.9	11.6	11.4
M.A.	733	665	630	488	486	477	475	21.5	18.3	16.9	13.0	13.0	12.8	12.7
N.Y.	359	336	318	239	240	236	236	21.4	18.6	17.4	13.1	13.2	13.0	13.0
N.J.	132	125	120	96	95	92	91	21.8	18.5	16.8	13.0	13.0	12.6	12.4
Pa.	241	205	193	153	151	149	148	21.3	17.8	16.3	12.9	12.8	12.6	12.5
E.N.C.	877	751	754	619	616	610	603	24.2	19.7	18.7	15.1	15.1	14.9	14.7
Ohio	231	195	200	161	161	159	155	23.8	19.1	18.7	15.0	15.0	14.8	14.5
Ind.	113	98	99	84	83	82	81	24.2	20.0	19.1	15.8	15.6	15.5	15.2
Ill.	239	208	205	169	169	169	170	23.7	19.6	18.5	15.1	15.2	15.2	15.2
Mich.	195	167	172	141	138	134	131	25.0	20.1	19.4	15.6	15.1	14.6	14.4
Wis.	100	83	78	63	65	65	65	25.2	20.0	17.6	13.7	14.3	14.1	14.1
W.N.C.	369	297	284	237	243	246	249	24.0	18.7	17.4	14.2	14.6	14.7	14.8
Minn.	88	71	68	54	56	56	57	25.7	19.9	18.0	13.8	14.2	14.4	14.3
Iowa	64	51	48	39	40	41	42	23.3	18.5	17.1	13.4	14.1	14.4	14.5
Mo.	98	81	81	69	70	69	69	22.7	18.1	17.3	14.5	14.6	14.4	14.4
N.Dak.	17	13	11	10	10	11	11	26.3	20.2	17.6	15.2	15.7	16.7	16.6
S.Dak.	18	14	12	11	11	11	12	25.9	19.7	17.0	15.6	16.4	16.5	17.0
Nebr.	34	28	26	23	24	24	24	24.3	18.8	17.3	14.8	15.4	15.3	15.3
Kans.	51	39	38	32	33	34	35	23.3	17.6	17.0	14.1	14.5	15.0	15.3
S.A.	629	575	574	500	497	482	481	24.2	20.0	18.7	15.4	15.0	14.3	14.2
Del.	12	11	11	8	8	8	8	25.9	21.2	19.2	14.3	14.4	14.2	13.9
Md.	77	74	69	54	53	53	53	24.9	21.0	17.6	13.2	13.1	12.9	12.7
D.C.	20	18	15	11	10	10	10	26.0	22.5	20.1	14.5	13.9	13.6	13.8
Va.	96	80	86	72	71	70	70	24.1	20.0	18.6	15.0	14.5	14.1	13.9
W.Va.	39	32	31	28	28	28	29	21.2	17.7	17.8	15.4	15.6	15.6	15.7
N.C.	110	98	98	86	84	81	81	24.1	19.9	19.3	16.3	15.7	14.8	14.7
S.C.	60	53	52	49	49	47	48	25.1	20.8	20.1	18.0	17.4	16.6	16.8
Ga.	100	94	97	85	83	80	79	25.3	21.7	21.1	17.8	17.1	16.2	15.9
Fla.	116	107	115	108	110	106	105	23.8	18.4	16.9	14.0	13.6	12.7	12.4
E.S.C.	294	258	248	222	221	219	219	24.4	20.1	19.4	16.7	16.5	16.2	16.0
Ky.	72	62	60	54	53	55	55	23.8	19.4	18.7	16.0	15.9	16.1	16.1
Tenn.	82	73	72	64	64	62	63	23.0	19.0	18.4	15.6	15.6	14.9	14.9
Ala.	81	71	67	60	59	58	58	24.7	20.4	19.4	16.8	16.6	16.1	15.8
Miss.	59	52	49	45	44	44	43	27.2	22.5	22.1	19.5	19.0	18.7	18.2
W.S.C.	431	375	386	351	354	361	366	25.4	20.2	20.0	17.3	17.2	17.3	17.3
Ark.	41	37	35	34	35	34	34	22.7	18.7	18.5	16.5	16.8	16.3	16.2
La.	90	80	74	66	66	68	70	27.7	22.5	20.4	17.6	17.5	17.9	18.2
Okla.	51	43	45	41	42	43	44	21.9	17.3	17.5	15.3	15.7	15.7	15.8
Tex.	249	216	231	210	211	216	219	26.0	20.4	20.6	17.8	17.5	17.6	17.5
Mt.	187	160	172	166	174	177	185	27.3	20.6	20.7	18.1	18.4	18.3	18.8
Mont.	17	14	13	11	12	12	13	25.9	19.3	18.2	15.8	16.7	16.1	16.7
Idaho	17	13	14	15	16	16	17	25.7	19.3	20.3	18.9	19.5	19.8	20.9
Wyo.	9	7	7	6	7	7	7	25.8	19.3	19.6	17.2	18.2	18.6	18.9
Colo.	43	37	42	39	39	40	41	24.5	18.7	18.8	15.8	15.6	15.9	15.9
N.Mex.	31	24	22	21	21	21	22	32.3	23.6	21.8	18.8	19.0	18.3	18.9
Ariz.	37	34	38	38	40	40	40	28.2	21.1	21.3	18.4	18.5	17.8	17.6
Utah	26	22	27	28	30	32	35	29.5	22.5	25.5	24.2	25.5	26.3	28.7
Nev.	7	9	10	9	9	9	10	25.5	21.5	19.6	15.7	15.6	15.3	15.8
Pac.	501	465	483	398	417	425	444	23.6	19.0	18.2	14.5	15.0	15.0	15.5
Wash.	65	53	61	48	50	51	53	22.9	17.7	17.8	13.9	14.4	14.3	14.7
Oreg.	38	33	35	31	33	33	35	21.7	17.4	16.8	13.9	14.4	14.6	15.0
Calif.	372	356	363	298	312	317	332	23.7	19.1	18.2	14.5	14.9	15.0	15.4
Alaska	8	7	8	7	7	7	8	33.4	27.9	25.1	20.0	20.9	21.2	20.8
Hawaii	17	16	16	15	16	16	16	27.2	23.0	21.4	18.5	18.3	18.2	18.5

[1] Based on population (excluding Armed Forces abroad) enumerated as of Apr. 1 for 1960 and 1970, and estimated as of July 1 for other years.

Source: U.S. National Center for Health Statistics, *Vital Statistics of the United States*, annual, and *Monthly Vital Statistics Report*.

No. 84. Live Births, by Race—States: 1970 to 1976

[In thousands. By place of residence. Represents registered births. Excludes births to nonresidents of the U.S.]

STATE	1970 White	1970 Black and other	1975 White	1975 Black and other	1976 White	1976 Black and other	STATE	1970 White	1970 Black and other	1975 White	1975 Black and other	1976 White	1976 Black and other
U.S.	3,091	640	2,552	592	2,568	600	S.A.— Con.						
N.E.	188	12	137	11	135	10	W.Va.	30	1	27	1	27	1
Maine	18	(Z)	15	(Z)	15	(Z)	N.C.	70	29	55	26	55	25
N.H.	13	(Z)	11	(Z)	11	(Z)	S.C.	33	19	28	19	29	19
Vt.	8	(Z)	7	(Z)	7	(Z)	Ga.	66	30	52	28	51	28
Mass.	90	5	63	5	61	5	Fla.	87	28	78	28	76	28
R.I.	15	1	10	1	10	1							
Conn.	45	6	31	4	31	4	E.S.C.	182	66	159	60	159	60
							Ky.	55	5	50	5	50	5
M.A.	523	108	386	91	381	92	Tenn.	57	15	49	14	49	14
N.Y.	257	61	184	52	182	53	Ala.	45	22	38	20	37	21
N.J.	98	22	73	18	72	18	Miss.	26	23	23	21	23	20
Pa.	168	25	129	20	127	21							
							W.S.C.	306	80	283	78	287	79
E.N.C.	645	109	510	99	505	98	Ark.	26	9	25	9	25	9
Ohio	175	25	137	22	134	21	La.	46	28	41	27	42	28
Ind.	90	9	73	9	72	9	Okla.	38	7	35	8	35	8
Ill.	163	43	130	39	131	39	Tex.	195	36	182	34	185	34
Mich.	144	28	110	24	108	24							
Wis.	73	4	60	5	60	5	Mt.	157	15	160	17	167	16
							Mont.	11	1	11	1	11	1
W.N.C.	262	22	224	21	226	22	Idaho	14	(Z)	16	(Z)	17	(Z)
Minn.	67	2	54	2	54	3	Wyo.	6	(Z)	7	(Z)	7	(Z)
Iowa	47	1	40	1	40	1	Colo.	39	2	38	3	38	3
Mo.	68	13	57	11	58	11	N. Mex.	19	3	18	3	18	4
N. Dak.	10	1	10	1	10	1	Ariz.	32	5	33	6	34	6
S. Dak.	10	1	10	2	10	2	Utah	26	1	31	1	34	1
Nebr.	24	1	22	1	22	1	Nev.	8	1	8	1	8	1
Kans.	35	3	31	3	32	3							
							Pac.	413	69	354	70	369	75
S.A.	416	159	338	145	335	144	Wash.	56	5	46	5	48	5
Del.	8	2	6	2	6	2	Oreg.	33	2	32	2	33	2
Md.	52	17	38	15	37	16	Calif.	313	50	267	50	278	54
D.C.	2	13	1	8	1	8	Alaska	6	2	5	2	6	2
Va.	67	19	53	17	53	17	Hawaii	5	12	4	11	4	12

Z Fewer than 500.

Source: U.S. National Center for Health Statistics, *Vital Statistics of the United States*, annual, and *Monthly Vital Statistics Report*.

No. 85. Attended Live Births, and Median and Low Birth Weight, by Race: 1950 to 1976

[Represents registered births. Prior to 1960, excludes Alaska and Hawaii. Beginning 1970, excludes births to nonresidents of the U.S. For number of births, see table 79]

YEAR	BIRTHS ATTENDED (1,000) By physician In hospital [1]	By physician Not in hospital	By midwife or other [2]	MEDIAN BIRTH WEIGHT Total	MEDIAN BIRTH WEIGHT White	MEDIAN BIRTH WEIGHT Black and other	PERCENT OF BIRTHS WITH LOW BIRTH WEIGHT [3] Total	PERCENT OF BIRTHS WITH LOW BIRTH WEIGHT [3] White	PERCENT OF BIRTHS WITH LOW BIRTH WEIGHT [3] Black and other
1950	3,126	252	177	7 lb.-5 oz.	7 lb.-5 oz.	7 lb.-3 oz.	7.6	7.2	10.4
1955	3,819	101	128	7 lb.-5 oz.	7 lb.-5 oz.	7 lb.-1 oz.	7.7	6.9	11.8
1960	4,114	49	94	7 lb.-5 oz.	7 lb.-6 oz.	6 lb.-15 oz.	7.7	6.8	12.8
1965	3,661	33	66	7 lb.-4 oz.	7 lb.-5 oz.	6 lb.-14 oz.	8.3	7.2	13.8
1970	3,708	5	18	7 lb.-4 oz.	7 lb.-5 oz.	6 lb.-14 oz.	7.9	6.8	13.3
1972	3,234	7	18	7 lb.-5 oz.	7 lb.-6 oz.	6 lb.-15 oz.	7.7	6.5	12.9
1973	3,115	7	16	7 lb.-5 oz.	7 lb.-6 oz.	6 lb.-15 oz.	7.6	6.4	12.5
1974	3,134	11	16	7 lb.-5 oz.	7 lb.-7 oz.	6 lb.-15 oz.	7.4	6.3	12.4
1975	3,105	11	28	7 lb.-5 oz.	7 lb.-7 oz.	6 lb.-15 oz.	7.4	6.3	12.2
1976	3,124	12	32	7 lb.-6 oz.	7 lb.-7 oz.	7 lb.-0 oz.	7.3	6.1	12.1

[1] Includes all births in hospitals or institutions and in clinics. [2] Includes births with attendant not specified.
[3] Less than 2,500 grams (5 lb.-5 oz.) at birth.

Source: U.S. National Center for Health Statistics, *Vital Statistics of the United States*, annual.

No. 86. PLURAL BIRTH RATIOS, BY RACE AND AGE OF MOTHER: 1965 TO 1976

[Ratios are all plural live births per 1,000 total live births in specified groups. Beginning 1971, excludes births to nonresidents of the U.S.]

AGE OF MOTHER (in years)	1965			1971			1975			1976		
	Total	White	Black and other	Total	White	Black and other	Total	White	Black and other	Total	White	Black and other
Total	20.1	19.0	25.8	18.7	17.8	20.8	19.2	18.5	22.1	19.5	18.8	22.3
Under 15	10.8	12.3	10.1	11.2	9.8	11.9	10.6	9.9	11.1	11.9	10.5	12.9
15–19	12.6	11.7	15.1	12.1	11.2	14.0	12.8	11.8	15.4	13.0	11.9	15.5
20–24	17.3	16.4	22.6	17.0	15.9	20.6	17.9	16.8	23.0	18.4	17.3	23.3
25–29	21.9	20.3	31.3	20.8	19.8	24.4	21.4	20.7	25.5	21.6	21.0	25.1
30–34	27.0	25.1	36.9	25.1	24.1	26.7	25.0	24.1	30.1	24.3	23.5	29.0
35–39	29.5	27.6	38.8	28.4	27.0	30.8	26.3	25.5	29.4	27.3	26.3	31.5
40–44	23.3	22.4	27.9	23.9	23.5	23.4	23.7	22.9	26.7	23.2	23.0	23.8
45–49	16.9	17.2	15.7	13.9	16.6	4.5	8.6	8.1	10.2	6.2	8.4	–

- Represents zero.

Source: U.S. National Center for Health Statistics, *Vital Statistics of the United States*, annual.

No. 87. LIFETIME BIRTHS EXPECTED PER 1,000 WIVES: 1967 TO 1977

[Refers to currently married women in the civilian noninstitutional population]

YEAR AND MONTH	BIRTHS TO ALL WIVES AGED—				BIRTHS TO WHITE WIVES AGED—				BIRTHS TO BLACK WIVES AGED—			
	18–24	25–29	30–34	35–39	18–24	25–29	30–34	35–39	18–24	25–29	30–34	35–39
1967 (Feb.–Mar.)	2,852	3,037	3,288	3,300	2,859	3,001	3,200	3,215	2,762	3,407	4,257	4,226
1971 (June)	2,375	2,619	2,989	3,257	2,353	2,577	2,936	3,189	2,623	3,112	3,714	4,223
1972 (June)	2,255	2,452	2,915	3,218	2,243	2,420	2,842	3,155	2,309	2,930	3,749	4,096
1973 (June)	2,262	2,387	2,804	3,234	2,262	2,352	2,762	3,180	2,256	2,799	3,332	3,933
1974 (June)	2,165	2,335	2,724	3,090	2,154	2,304	2,689	3,040	2,215	2,779	3,238	3,642
1975 (June)	2,173	2,200	2,610	3,058	2,147	2,233	2,564	2,989	2,489	2,587	3,212	3,962
1976 (June)	2,141	2,202	2,536	2,994	2,127	2,176	2,514	2,949	2,303	2,508	2,923	3,579
1977 (June)	2,137	2,197	2,468	2,948	2,140	2,183	2,424	2,876	2,092	2,304	2,990	3,867

No. 88. NUMBER OF BIRTHS EXPECTED BY WIVES, BY RACE—PERCENT DISTRIBUTION: 1967 TO 1977

[As of June, except 1967 as of Feb.–Mar. Refers to currently married women in the civilian noninstitutional population]

YEAR AND AGE OF WIVES	WHITE BIRTHS					BLACK BIRTHS				
	None	One	Two	Three	Four or more	None	One	Two	Three	Four or more
1967: 18–24 yr	1.3	5.7	37.5	29.6	25.9	.9	9.7	33.1	32.0	24.3
25–29 yr	2.1	4.8	30.0	34.3	28.9	2.4	9.1	22.1	27.7	38.7
30–34 yr	3.4	5.9	25.9	27.1	37.8	6.1	5.4	18.6	14.9	55.0
35–39 yr	4.9	7.3	25.8	26.6	35.3	6.9	13.1	14.7	15.3	50.0
1971: 18–24 yr	4.0	8.0	52.5	24.1	11.5	3.6	10.7	40.8	20.4	24.5
25–29 yr	3.3	6.8	45.1	27.8	16.9	2.1	6.7	31.0	25.8	34.3
30–34 yr	4.7	6.7	29.7	29.1	29.9	4.4	5.8	18.9	22.5	48.4
35–39 yr	4.7	7.5	24.7	26.1	36.9	6.6	11.1	14.4	15.5	52.4
1975: 18–24 yr	4.4	11.2	58.8	19.3	6.3	1.1	9.4	52.0	22.4	15.1
25–29 yr	4.9	11.5	51.5	23.1	8.9	4.3	12.2	37.2	27.0	19.3
30–34 yr	5.5	9.6	38.8	27.7	18.4	3.8	10.3	30.6	16.8	38.5
35–39 yr	4.1	9.1	27.1	28.4	31.4	5.6	10.0	14.4	20.4	49.6
1976: 18–24 yr	5.0	11.9	58.1	18.7	6.4	2.8	13.6	47.2	26.9	9.5
25–29 yr	6.7	11.0	52.3	21.7	8.3	3.6	12.7	40.8	25.9	17.0
30–34 yr	5.8	9.9	41.0	25.3	18.1	1.9	15.2	28.4	24.2	30.3
35–39 yr	4.6	9.3	29.2	26.7	30.2	6.3	9.9	21.5	16.2	46.2
1977: 18–24 yr	5.3	12.3	56.4	18.5	7.5	5.1	16.7	50.1	22.7	5.4
25–29 yr	6.6	11.2	51.0	22.7	8.5	3.5	17.3	43.4	22.8	13.0
30–34 yr	6.1	10.7	43.4	24.3	15.4	4.5	10.7	27.5	27.5	29.8
35–39 yr	5.3	8.9	30.2	27.2	28.4	4.6	9.6	18.0	17.0	50.7

Source of tables 87 and 88: U.S. Bureau of the Census, *Current Population Reports*, series P-20, Nos. 211, 263, 301, 308, and 316.

No. 89. CHILDLESS WOMEN AND CHILDREN BORN, BY AGE OF WOMEN: 1950 TO 1977

[Prior to 1960, excludes Alaska and Hawaii. 1950, 1960, and 1970 based on sample of decennial census, see source; all other years based on Current Population Survey, see text, p. 1. See also *Historical Statistics, Colonial Times to 1970*, series B 49–66]

AGE (in years)	1950 (Apr.)	1954 (Apr.)	1960 (Apr.)	1965 (June)	1970 (Apr.)	1975 (June)	1976 (June)	1977 (June)		
								Total	White	Black
PERCENT CHILDLESS AMONG WOMEN EVER MARRIED										
15–44	22.8	18.1	15.0	14.2	16.4	18.0	18.8	19.2	20.0	11.8
15–19	52.8	47.0	43.6	48.0	50.9	50.6	55.1	50.4	51.6	(B)
20–24	33.3	24.3	24.2	28.0	35.7	42.3	41.7	42.8	44.4	25.1
25–29	21.1	16.9	12.6	11.7	15.8	21.1	21.7	24.4	25.5	14.4
30–34	17.3	13.4	10.4	7.2	8.3	8.8	10.5	11.2	11.6	7.4
35–39	19.1	15.9	11.1	8.7	7.3	5.3	6.6	6.7	6.9	4.2
40–44	20.0	17.8	14.1	11.0	8.6	7.0	7.5	7.3	7.2	7.7
45–49	20.4	19.0	18.1	13.9	10.6	7.3	7.8	7.5	7.0	12.0
50–59	18.1	(NA)	20.7	19.3	15.6	11.5	11.4	(NA)	(NA)	(NA)
CHILDREN EVER BORN PER 1,000 WOMEN EVER MARRIED										
15–44	1,859	2,037	2,314	2,477	2,360	2,140	2,082	2,061	1,998	2,720
15–19	604	667	792	685	636	601	548	603	579	(B)
20–24	1,082	1,337	1,441	1,328	1,071	886	897	867	819	1,359
25–29	1,654	1,930	2,241	2,360	1,984	1,580	1,539	1,460	1,419	1,830
30–34	2,059	2,247	2,627	2,950	2,806	2,387	2,291	2,207	2,151	2,749
35–39	2,247	2,334	2,686	3,016	3,170	2,994	2,931	2,855	2,769	3,620
40–44	2,364	2,335	2,564	2,856	3,097	3,282	3,190	3,266	3,149	4,197
45–49	2,492	2,436	2,402	2,603	2,854	3,152	3,206	3,256	3,157	4,037
50–59	2,822	(NA)	2,420	2,350	2,520	2,759	2,824	(NA)	(NA)	(NA)

B Base less than 75,000. NA Not available.

Source: U.S. Bureau of the Census, *U.S. Census of Population: 1950*, Special Report, *Fertility*, part 5; *U.S. Census of Population: 1960* and *1970*, vol. I, *Characteristics of the Population*, part 1, *U.S. Summary; Current Population Reports*, series P-20, Nos. 65, 186, 301, 308, and forthcoming report; and unpublished data.

No. 90. FIRST BIRTHS TO WOMEN AT STATED INTERVALS FROM FIRST MARRIAGE, BY RACE: 1930 TO 1975

[As of **June**. Data limited to women born since 1900. Based on Current Population Survey; see text, p. 1]

RACE AND PERIOD OF FIRST MARRIAGE	Number of women (1,000)	CUMULATIVE PERCENT WITH FIRST CHILD BORN—				RACE AND PERIOD OF FIRST MARRIAGE	Number of women (1,000)	CUMULATIVE PERCENT WITH FIRST CHILD BORN—			
		Before first marriage	After first marriage—					Before first marriage	After first marriage—		
			7 mos.	12 mos.	24 mos.				7 mos.	12 mos.	24 mos.
All women: First married—						**White women:** First married— Con.—					
1930–1934	3,639	5.1	11.4	27.3	48.4	1955–1959	5,262	4.5	14.8	39.7	67.6
1935–1939	4,870	4.0	10.1	26.8	49.3	1960–1964	5,520	5.1	17.7	41.1	66.0
1940–1944	5,711	4.7	10.1	25.7	50.2	1965–1969	6,426	5.1	19.9	37.2	55.1
1945–1949	6,653	5.6	11.8	32.9	57.5	1970–1974	6,896	6.1	[1]18.6	[1]29.6	[1]45.4
1950–1954	6,031	6.5	14.5	35.0	60.6						
1955–1959	6,062	7.6	18.7	42.0	68.2	**Black women:** First married—					
1960–1964	6,268	8.2	21.6	43.8	67.3	1930–1934	} 759	17.9	30.4	43.7	57.4
1965–1969	7,337	8.3	22.9	39.6	57.2	1935–1939					
1970–1974	7,845	9.5	[1]22.1	[1]32.9	[1]48.4	1940–1944	}1,104	25.2	38.5	50.4	60.5
						1945–1949					
White women: First married—						1950–1954	}1,308	28.8	44.1	56.0	71.3
1930–1934	3,282	3.9	9.5	25.8	47.7	1955–1959					
1935–1939	4,393	2.7	8.2	25.0	48.1	1960–1964	645	34.1	54.8	67.2	79.1
1940–1944	5,180	2.9	7.6	23.6	49.5	1965–1969	754	35.1	50.0	62.1	75.0
1945–1949	5,968	3.4	8.8	30.8	56.9	1970–1974	758	37.5	[1]52.5	[1]62.0	[1]72.5
1950–1954	5,337	4.2	11.5	33.1	59.8						

[1] Data adjusted for the part of the cohort that has not completed the stated interval since first marriage.

Source: U.S. Bureau of the Census, *Current Population Reports*, series P-20, No. 315.

No. 91. Births to Unmarried Women, by Race and Age of Mother: 1950 to 1976

[Prior to 1960, excludes Alaska and Hawaii. Beginning 1970, excludes births to nonresidents of U.S. Includes estimates for States in which marital status data were not reported. No estimates included for misstatements on birth records or failures to register births. See also *Historical Statistics, Colonial Times to 1970*, series B 28-35]

RACE AND AGE	1950	1955	1960	1965	1970	1971	1972	1973	1974	1975	1976
Total live births____1,000__	141.6	183.3	224.3	291.2	398.7	401.4	403.2	407.3	418.1	447.9	468.1
Percent of all births [1]____	3.9	4.5	5.3	7.7	10.7	11.3	12.4	13.0	13.2	14.2	14.8
Rate [2]_____	14.1	19.3	21.6	23.5	26.4	25.6	24.9	24.5	24.1	24.8	24.7
White_____	6.1	7.9	9.2	11.6	13.8	12.5	12.0	11.9	11.8	12.6	12.7
Black and other_____	71.2	87.2	98.3	97.6	89.9	90.6	86.9	84.2	81.5	80.4	78.1
Births, by race of mother:											
White_____1,000__	53.5	64.2	82.5	123.7	175.1	163.8	160.5	163.0	168.5	186.4	197.1
Black and other____1,000__	88.1	119.2	141.8	167.5	223.6	237.5	242.7	244.3	249.6	261.6	271.0
Percent of total_____	62.2	65.0	63.2	57.5	56.1	59.2	60.2	60.0	59.7	58.4	57.9
Births, by age of mother:											
Under 15 years_____1,000__	3.2	3.9	4.6	6.1	9.5	9.5	9.9	10.9	10.6	11.0	10.3
15–19 years_____1,000__	56.0	68.9	87.1	123.1	190.4	194.1	202.3	204.9	210.8	222.5	225.0
20–24 years_____1,000__	43.1	55.7	68.0	90.7	126.7	125.2	119.6	119.1	122.7	134.0	145.4
25–29 years_____1,000__	20.9	28.0	32.1	36.8	40.6	40.9	41.2	43.1	44.9	50.2	55.4
30–34 years_____1,000__	10.8	16.1	18.9	19.6	19.1	19.3	19.0	18.5	18.6	19.8	21.0
35 and over_____1,000__	7.7	10.7	13.6	15.1	12.4	12.4	11.3	10.8	10.5	10.4	10.9
19 yr. and under__percent__	[3] 41.8	39.7	40.9	44.4	50.1	50.7	52.6	53.0	53.0	52.1	50.3

[1] Through 1955, based on data adjusted for underregistration; thereafter, registered births. For total birth figures used to derive these data, see table 78.
[2] Rate per 1,000 unmarried (never married, widowed, and divorced) women aged 15–44 years enumerated as of April 1 for 1950, 1960, and 1970, and estimated as of July 1 for all other years.   [3] Under 18 years.

Source: U.S. National Center for Health Statistics, *Vital Statistics of the United States*, annual.

No. 92. Children Ever Born to Single Women, by Age of Woman: 1970 to 1977

[Refers to never-married women only. 1970 as of April, based on the enumerated resident population. 1976 and 1977 as of June, based on the civilian noninstitutional population from Current Population Survey. See text, p. 1]

ITEM	ALL SINGLE WOMEN			WHITE SINGLE WOMEN			BLACK SINGLE WOMEN		
	Total, 18–49 years	18–29 years	30–49 years	Total, 18–49 years	18–29 years	30–49 years	Total, 18–49 years	18–29 years	30–49 years
1970									
Single women_____1,000__	8,107	6,664	1,443	6,788	5,615	1,173	1,177	933	244
Children ever born_____1,000__	1,755	1,024	731	693	407	286	1,021	592	429
Rate per 1,000 women_____	216	154	506	102	72	244	867	635	1,758
Percent distribution by number born:									
None_____	90.0	91.1	82.6	94.7	95.7	90.6	60.2	64.1	45.6
One_____	} 10.0	8.9	{ 6.6	3.1	3.0	4.5	19.5	20.3	15.8
Two or more_____			10.8	2.2	1.2	4.9	20.2	15.5	38.6
1976									
Single women_____1,000__	10,180	8,823	1,357	8,189	7,157	1,032	1,772	1,476	296
Children ever born_____1,000__	2,198	1,425	773	608	405	203	1,544	983	561
Rate per 1,000 women_____	216	162	570	74	57	197	871	666	1,895
Percent distribution by number born:									
None_____	88.1	89.5	79.3	95.1	95.7	90.4	56.1	59.3	40.1
One_____	6.8	6.9	6.8	3.4	3.3	4.2	22.7	24.0	16.2
Two or more_____	5.0	3.7	13.9	1.5	.9	5.4	21.2	16.7	43.8
1977									
Single women_____1,000__	10,866	9,329	1,537	8,672	7,536	1,136	1,978	1,607	371
Children ever born_____1,000__	2,455	1,495	960	594	411	183	1,828	1,060	768
Rate per 1,000 women_____	226	160	625	68	55	161	924	660	2,070
Percent distribution by number born:									
None_____	87.5	89.0	77.9	95.0	95.5	91.2	54.1	58.1	36.6
One_____	7.9	7.7	9.0	3.9	3.7	5.2	25.8	26.9	20.7
Two or more_____	4.7	3.3	13.1	1.2	.8	3.6	20.2	14.9	42.7

Source: U.S. Bureau of the Census, *Census of Population: 1970, Women by Number of Children Ever Born*, PC(2)-3A; and *Current Population Reports*, series P-20, No. 308 and forthcoming report.

No. 93. Unwanted Fertility of All Mothers, 15–44 Years Old: 1973 and 1976

[Data represent the birth experience to date of all mothers 15–44 years old who have been married or are single with children of their own in the household. From the 1973 and 1976 National Survey of Family Growth; based on a multi-stage area probability sample. Data are subject to sampling variability]

	1973				1976				Births per mother	
	Num- ber of moth- ers (1,000)	Births			Num- ber of moth- ers (1,000)	Births				
CHARACTERISTIC		Live births [1] (1,000)	Unwanted [2]			Live births [1] (1,000)	Unwanted [2]		All births	Un- want- ed [2]
			Num- ber (1,000)	Per- cent			Num- ber (1,000)	Per- cent		
Total mothers [3]	**25,803**	**68,184**	**8,910**	**13.1**	**27,055**	**67,849**	**8,125**	**12.0**	**2.51**	**.30**
Race: White	22,182	57,551	6,068	10.5	22,837	56,238	5,350	9.5	2.46	.23
Black	3,359	9,984	2,783	27.9	3,726	10,525	2,716	25.8	2.82	.73
Education: Less than high school	2,622	9,123	1,501	16.5	2,187	7,274	1,264	17.4	3.33	.58
High school: 1–3 years	5,697	16,884	3,024	17.9	5,478	15,543	2,405	15.5	2.84	.44
4 years	12,161	29,917	3,307	11.1	12,651	30,405	3,391	11.2	2.40	.27
College: 1–3 years	3,182	7,585	734	9.7	3,763	8,391	776	9.3	2.23	.21
4 years or more	2,140	4,675	344	7.4	2,925	6,114	286	4.7	2.09	.10
Currently married mothers [3]	**21,816**	**57,524**	**6,418**	**11.2**	**22,253**	**55,900**	**5,516**	**9.9**	**2.51**	**.25**
Race: White	19,764	51,391	5,055	9.8	19,921	49,453	4,299	8.7	2.48	.22
Black	1,822	5,561	1,331	23.9	1,927	5,533	1,177	21.3	2.87	.61
Education: Less than high school	1,948	6,846	838	12.2	1,663	5,584	832	14.9	3.36	.50
High school: 1–3 years	4,482	13,274	2,114	15.9	3,951	11,226	1,320	11.8	2.84	.33
4 years	10,646	26,494	2,586	9.8	10,741	26,120	2,547	9.8	2.43	.24
College: 1–3 years	2,816	6,722	602	9.0	3,244	7,381	597	8.1	2.28	.18
4 years or more	1,924	4,187	279	6.7	2,613	5,503	219	4.0	2.11	.08

[1] Multiple births counted only once.   [2] All births which mothers report as "not wanted" or "probably not wanted" at time of becoming pregnant.   [3] Includes races not shown separately.

Source: U.S. National Center for Health Statistics, *Wanted and Unwanted Births Reported by Mothers, 15–44 Years of Age: United States, 1973; Advance Data from Vital and Health Statistics,* HRA 77–1250; and unpublished data.

No. 94. Contraceptive Use by Currently Married Women 15–44 Years Old, by Method of Contraception, Race, and Age: 1965 to 1976

[Data from 1965 and 1970 National Fertility Survey and 1976 National Survey of Family Growth]

RACE AND AGE (in years)	Number of currently married women (1,000)	Percent using contra- ception	PERCENT USING SPECIFIED METHOD OF CONTRACEPTION								
			Sterilization		Pill	IUD [1]	Dia- phragm	Condom	Foam	Rhythm	All other
			Wife	Hus- band							
1965											
White, 15–44	22,382	64.9	4.1	3.5	15.6	.7	6.8	14.5	2.0	7.5	10.2
15–24	4,724	59.6	.6	1.0	30.7	.9	2.6	9.2	2.6	4.9	7.1
25–34	8,387	69.4	4.3	4.0	17.3	.8	6.5	16.3	2.8	7.4	10.0
35–44	9,271	63.2	5.6	4.4	6.3	.4	9.1	15.6	1.0	9.0	11.8
Black, 15–44	2,091	57.2	8.3	.3	12.4	1.7	2.9	9.7	3.5	1.4	17.0
15–24	555	61.5	1.9	.4	17.1	3.5	1.9	10.9	5.8	1.6	18.4
25–34	794	62.8	7.9	.3	17.1	1.9	2.7	12.8	3.5	2.2	14.4
35–44	742	47.9	13.4	.3	3.8	–	3.8	5.5	1.7	.6	18.8
1970											
White, 15–44	23,220	65.7	4.9	5.5	22.4	4.8	3.8	9.7	4.0	4.4	6.2
15–24	5,595	63.8	.4	.8	37.6	5.3	1.7	5.9	4.8	2.3	5.0
25–34	9,578	69.0	4.9	5.4	23.7	6.6	3.9	9.7	4.9	4.1	5.8
35–44	8,047	63.5	8.2	8.9	10.2	2.3	5.2	12.4	2.4	6.3	7.6
Black, 15–44	2,031	59.2	11.4	.6	22.1	4.5	3.1	4.0	3.6	1.0	8.8
15–24	506	60.5	1.0	–	35.9	6.2	1.5	4.1	4.1	.5	7.2
25–34	787	67.3	11.2	.7	26.4	5.6	3.6	3.6	4.3	1.3	10.6
35–44	738	49.4	18.7	1.1	8.1	2.1	3.5	4.2	2.5	1.1	8.1
1976											
White, 15–44	24,518	[2] 69.1	[2] 9.7	[2] 10.5	22.5	6.1	3.0	7.4	2.9	3.5	3.5
15–24	5,339	69.3	2.4	1.1	43.9	6.3	2.8	5.1	2.9	2.4	1.9
25–34	10,840	71.9	10.9	10.0	23.2	7.1	3.2	7.6	3.0	3.3	3.5
35–44	8,339	65.3	12.7	17.1	7.8	4.6	3.0	8.6	2.8	4.3	4.3
Black, 15–44	2,145	[2] 58.4	[2] 11.0	[2] 1.9	22.1	6.1	1.8	4.5	3.8	1.4	5.8
15–24	504	58.6	3.7	.3	35.8	5.8	.2	3.4	1.8	3.4	4.1
25–34	900	62.2	9.3	.4	26.1	7.1	1.7	5.5	4.3	.4	7.4
35–44	741	53.6	18.1	4.8	7.7	5.0	2.9	4.1	4.5	1.4	5.0

– Represents zero.   [1] Intra-uterine device.   [2] Due to changes in wording of the question on contraceptive intent of sterilization operations in the 1976 survey, estimates should be considered conservative.

Source: 1965–1970, Westoff, C. F., "Trends in Contraceptive Practice: 1965–1973." In Alan Guttmacher Institute, *Family Planning Perspectives,* vol. 8, No. 2, 1976; 1976, unpublished data from U.S. National Center for Health Statistics, 1976 National Survey of Family Growth.

No. 95. Legal Abortions—Estimated Number and Rate, by Woman's Race and Age: 1972–1974

[Covers women 15 to 44 years old at time of abortion. Based on age distribution in States reporting age data to U.S. Center for Disease Control. For details, see source]

AGE OF WOMAN	NUMBER OF WOMEN, ANNUAL AVERAGE (1,000)		NUMBER OF ABORTIONS, ANNUAL AVERAGE [1] (1,000)		PERCENT DISTRIBUTION		ABORTION RATE PER 1,000 WOMEN PER YEAR [2]			ABORTION RATIO PER 1,000 LIVE BIRTHS		
	White	Black and other races	White	Black and other races	White	Black and other races	White	Black and other races	Ratio: Black and other to White	White	Black and other races	Ratio: Black and other to White
Total	39,098	6,212	550	193	100.0	100.0	14.1	31.1	2.2	213	329	1.5
Under 20 yr	8,601	1,501	177	66	32.2	34.0	20.6	43.8	2.1	324	315	1.0
20–24 yr	7,847	1,288	179	59	32.5	30.6	22.8	45.9	2.0	193	313	1.6
25–29 yr	6,840	1,011	96	35	17.5	18.3	14.0	35.0	2.5	132	327	2.5
30–34 yr	5,673	885	54	20	9.8	10.2	9.5	22.4	2.4	192	378	2.0
35–39 yr	4,997	771	31	10	5.6	5.2	6.2	13.0	2.1	338	459	1.4
40–44 yr	5,140	756	13	3	2.4	1.7	2.5	4.3	1.7	569	535	.9

[1] Total abortions reported for 1972–1974 divided by 3.   [2] Per 1,000 women in specific age group.

Source: Tietze, C. "Legal Abortions in the United States: Rates and Ratios by Race and Age, 1972–1974." In Alan Guttmacher Institute, *Family Planning Perspectives*, vol. 9, No. 1.

No. 96. Characteristics of Women Obtaining Reported Legal Abortions— Selected States: 1974 to 1976

By State of occurrence. Based on available data from central health agencies with statewide reporting systems; therefore, figures may differ from those shown in table 97 which are based on surveys of hospitals and physicians]

STATE	NUMBER OF ABORTIONS			RATIO: ABORTIONS TO 1,000 LIVE BIRTHS			PERCENT DISTRIBUTION,[1] 1976						
							Weeks of gestation		Marital status		Number of living children		
	1974	1975	1976	1974	1975	1976	12 or less	13 or more	Married	Unmarried	None	1	2	3 or more
Alaska	1,025	1,248	1,213	146	169	153	94.6	2.8	27.0	71.3	61.3	17.8	12.1	8.2
Ariz	(NA)	(NA)	5,202	(NA)	(NA)	130	84.3	11.5	21.2	74.6	58.3	19.5	12.3	9.9
Ark	1,694	1,925	3,286	50	57	98	87.2	12.8	27.1	72.9	(NA)	(NA)	(NA)	(NA)
Calif	135,762	142,067	142,593	447	448	429	80.6	15.8	21.2	74.7	34.1	24.1	16.5	20.8
Colo	9,027	9,744	11,539	231	241	282	64.9	18.2	23.3	61.0	53.2	13.7	9.5	6.9
Conn	7,083	10,820	13,447	255	301	385	92.2	5.2	(NA)	(NA)	(NA)	(NA)	(NA)	(NA)
D.C	22,688	22,721	31,407	1,115	(2)	967	89.5	6.7	19.9	75.7	(NA)	(NA)	(NA)	(NA)
Ga	22,009	23,733	25,586	265	297	323	94.9	4.7	27.9	70.5	55.3	20.0	14.7	10.0
Hawaii	4,158	4,545	5,163	269	290	317	82.7	15.8	37.9	62.1	97.7	1.0	.8	.6
Ill	33,370	58,743	66,356	197	347	390	92.8	2.7	21.9	75.7	47.8	19.9	16.2	15.3
Ind	6,029	7,859	8,610	72	95	107	98.7	1.3	25.4	72.6	53.9	17.3	13.7	15.1
Kans	10,171	9,160	9,154	311	272	259	78.0	21.7	21.2	78.7	59.4	16.5	12.7	10.6
La	974	4,180	6,350	28	62	91	98.3	1.0	21.6	77.7	(NA)	(NA)	(NA)	(NA)
Md	15,975	18,865	20,641	301	358	392	88.9	11.0	20.1	78.9	58.0	20.4	13.2	8.3
Mass	(NA)	315	32,801	(NA)	(NA)	485	91.8	8.2	(NA)	(NA)	(NA)	(NA)	(NA)	(NA)
Minn	8,732	10,565	14,124	158	187	250	83.4	16.6	14.6	78.2	73.4	11.9	8.3	6.4
Miss	140	315	1,510	3	7	35	90.0	4.2	32.7	66.8	55.8	18.2	14.4	11.0
Mo	(NA)	10,244	12,881	(NA)	150	190	95.1	4.8	20.0	78.7	51.2	19.2	15.0	13.4
Mont	732	1,535	1,803	118	130	146	82.8	5.8	22.0	78.0	64.4	14.1	11.5	8.6
Nebr	3,094	3,406	3,977	131	144	167	80.4	18.1	18.7	81.1	64.6	13.6	11.6	10.1
Nev	1,614	1,807	2,382	185	204	240	93.3	5.0	24.4	72.3	58.4	18.6	13.4	9.6
N.H	668	1,396	1,958	58	126	175	96.3	1.0	20.2	77.6	12.0	12.1	10.7	7.3
N.Y	161,521	147,229	147,860	675	624	629	85.2	12.7	28.6	71.4	43.1	19.3	16.3	21.0
City	120,829	106,317	102,016	1,138	(2)	967	87.1	11.2	28.5	71.5	34.2	22.2	17.9	25.2
Upstate	40,692	40,912	45,844	306	313	354	81.0	15.8	28.9	71.1	62.9	12.9	12.7	11.5
N.C	16,463	19,960	23,561	195	247	293	81.8	13.3	27.3	71.3	51.7	20.3	13.6	9.3
Ohio	(NA)	(NA)	37,192	(NA)	(NA)	240	70.1	4.8	25.3	71.6	33.7	19.7	14.3	11.1
Oreg	8,794	10,641	12,590	271	319	361	90.5	8.7	20.8	78.4	(NA)	(NA)	(NA)	(NA)
Pa	38,110	43,319	52,261	258	291	353	89.0	9.2	(NA)	(NA)	(NA)	(NA)	(NA)	(NA)
R.I	2,867	3,253	3,863	245	303	358	86.9	13.1	31.3	67.7	50.6	19.5	14.5	12.1
S.C	3,760	4,511	5,702	80	97	120	81.3	7.9	21.3	76.4	53.1	19.4	13.0	11.5
S. Dak	1,601	1,475	1,561	143	131	134	70.1	29.3	19.3	75.6	54.5	14.0	10.3	9.1
Tenn	7,406	11,081	16,967	110	178	271	86.0	7.6	20.4	66.9	49.7	20.5	14.6	10.8
Utah	1,189	2,146	2,542	51	68	72	90.3	8.2	20.2	78.8	27.6	16.7	13.9	11.7
Vt	1,930	2,100	2,322	281	313	344	97.6	2.4	19.7	76.4	73.1	10.9	9.4	6.3
Va	14,372	17,999	22,635	210	257	323	89.7	9.5	25.1	74.7	53.6	18.2	13.2	9.7
Wash	18,185	20,963	22,790	381	412	456	92.7	7.0	24.8	74.4	(NA)	(NA)	(NA)	(NA)

NA Not available.   [1] "Unknown" categories not shown separately.   [2] More than 1,000.

Source: U.S. Center for Disease Control, Atlanta, Ga., *Abortion Surveillance Report—Legal Abortions*, annual ummary.

No. 97. Legal Abortions—Number, Rate per 1,000 Women 15–44 Years Old, and Ratio per 1,000 Live Births, by State of Occurrence: 1974 to 1976

[Numbers of legal abortions are from two surveys of hospitals, clinics, and physicians identified as providers of abortion services, conducted by the Alan Guttmacher Institute. Abortion rates are computed per 1,000 women 15–44 years of age on July 1 of specified year; abortion ratios are computed as the number of abortions per 1,000 live births from July 1, 1974, to June 30, 1975, from July 1, 1975, to June 30, 1976, and from July 1, 1976, to June 30, 1977, respectively, by State of occurrence]

STATE	NUMBER OF ABORTIONS (1,000)			RATE PER 1,000 WOMEN			RATIO TO 1,000 LIVE BIRTHS		
	1974	1975	1976	1974	1975	1976	1974	1975	1976
U.S.	899.9	1,034.2	1,179.3	19.6	22.1	24.5	282	331	361
N. Eng	44.6	54.1	65.8	17.0	20.1	24.0	297	372	443
Maine	1.9	2.0	2.6	9.1	9.5	11.5	129	136	176
N.H.	.8	1.8	2.5	5.0	10.8	13.6	71	178	230
Vt	1.9	2.2	2.8	18.7	22.1	25.0	303	350	405
Mass	27.8	33.3	38.3	22.0	25.7	29.2	394	488	559
R.I.	2.9	3.3	3.9	14.4	16.0	19.6	257	298	340
Conn	9.3	11.4	15.7	13.4	16.1	22.3	259	328	440
Mid. Atl	233.5	250.6	267.1	28.4	29.7	32.7	484	532	555
N.Y	169.2	170.7	170.9	41.3	40.7	42.6	698	727	711
N.J	22.7	32.4	39.9	13.9	19.4	24.9	251	369	447
Pa	41.6	47.4	56.4	16.6	18.5	22.0	278	320	372
E. No. Cent	136.0	166.6	199.7	14.9	17.8	21.4	220	280	322
Ohio	30.4	44.6	53.4	12.5	17.9	21.9	188	290	330
Ind	6.0	7.7	8.7	5.1	6.3	7.2	71	94	104
Ill	51.1	60.3	73.3	20.4	23.6	29.0	303	363	425
Mich	37.8	42.7	49.9	18.4	20.3	23.6	278	330	371
Wis	10.7	11.3	14.4	11.1	11.4	13.8	162	176	213
W. No. Cent	45.8	51.4	56.8	13.1	14.3	15.2	184	208	221
Minn	12.5	12.8	15.7	14.7	14.7	17.1	219	229	267
Iowa	6.0	6.2	6.8	10.3	10.4	10.8	145	150	157
Mo	8.4	11.0	13.6	8.2	10.5	12.8	116	156	190
N. Dak	.2	.9	1.6	1.2	7.1	11.9	14	80	135
S. Dak	1.6	1.6	1.6	12.3	11.5	11.0	148	138	137
Nebr	3.2	4.6	4.6	10.1	14.3	13.5	133	193	184
Kans	13.9	14.3	13.0	29.4	29.5	25.6	433	440	376
So. Atl	143.0	172.4	190.8	20.2	23.8	25.3	288.	362	383
Del	2.2	2.4	2.6	16.6	17.4	18.8	256	280	293
Md	17.2	21.8	23.6	17.8	22.2	24.2	365	485	509
D.C	33.0	31.4	32.2	169.7	158.0	192.1	1,602	1,619	1,574
Va	16.5	20.3	25.2	15.0	18.0	22.0	239	303	362
W. Va	(Z)	.1	1.0	.1	.3	2.5	1	4	32
N.C	16.8	20.0	23.7	14.4	16.7	19.1	199	252	285
S.C	5.1	6.2	5.8	8.7	10.3	9.0	109	137	119
Ga	21.7	23.8	25.8	20.0	21.4	22.4	259	294	313
Fla	30.4	46.5	51.1	20.4	30.5	30.3	279	449	468
E. So. Cent	27.4	32.5	43.2	9.7	11.2	14.2	121	146	187
Ky	7.8	8.5	10.2	11.1	12.0	13.4	142	148	176
Tenn	14.2	17.6	22.9	15.9	19.2	24.0	210	269	333
Ala	5.1	6.0	8.4	6.7	7.7	10.2	86	105	143
Miss	.4	.3	1.7	.8	.6	3.3	8	7	37
W. So. Cent	48.4	65.9	81.0	11.0	14.6	17.0	132	179	213
Ark	1.9	2.6	4.2	4.8	6.3	9.4	56	78	123
La	4.4	5.3	8.6	5.3	6.2	9.9	65	78	117
Okla	4.4	6.8	7.6	7.8	11.8	12.5	105	163	174
Tex	37.7	51.2	60.7	14.4	19.1	21.4	169	226	265
Mt	25.8	33.6	38.6	13.3	16.9	17.2	147	188	201
Mont	1.2	1.5	1.7	8.4	9.9	10.0	103	124	130
Idaho	.9	1.1	1.3	5.1	7.0	7.2	50	67	76
Wyo	.3	.5	.6	4.5	7.3	6.5	50	79	80
Colo	11.3	13.6	14.9	20.2	24.6	24.2	279	338	352
N. Mex	3.6	5.1	5.7	15.7	21.7	21.6	170	249	250
Ariz	5.6	6.7	7.9	13.5	15.8	15.9	138	170	193
Utah	1.5	2.0	2.6	5.9	7.8	9.1	47	60	69
Nev	1.5	3.0	3.8	11.6	23.2	27.7	174	322	393
Pac	195.5	207.3	236.2	30.9	32.0	35.8	463	490	512
Wash	19.9	20.9	22.9	25.2	25.8	27.7	398	435	425
Oreg	9.6	13.3	12.8	19.9	27.0	24.2	280	381	346
Calif	159.5	165.6	192.9	33.2	33.6	39.0	506	523	555
Alaska	1.2	1.6	1.7	15.9	21.7	18.2	158	202	208
Hawaii	5.3	5.9	5.9	28.9	31.6	31.0	344	363	351

Z Fewer than 50 legal abortions reported by providers.

Source: 1974, Weinstock, E., C. Tietze, F. Jaffe, and J. G. Dryfoos, "Abortion Need and Services in the United States, 1974–75." In Alan Guttmacher Institute, *Family Planning Perspectives*, vol. 8, No. 2. 1975, derived from Sullivan, E., C. Tietze, and J. Dryfoos, "Legal Abortion in the United States, 1975–1976." In Alan Guttmacher Institute, *Family Planning Perspectives*, vol. 9, No. 3. 1976, The Alan Guttmacher Institute, "Abortion Need and Services in the United States, 1976–77," forthcoming report.

No. 98. Expectation of Life at Birth: 1920 to 1976

[In years. Prior to 1960, excludes Alaska and Hawaii. Data prior to 1940 for death-registration States only; see text, p. 57. See also *Historical Statistics, Colonial Times to 1970*, series B 107–115]

YEAR	TOTAL			WHITE			NEGRO AND OTHER		
	Total	Male	Female	Total	Male	Female	Total	Male	Female
1920	54.1	53.6	54.6	54.9	54.4	55.6	45.3	45.5	45.2
1930	59.7	58.1	61.6	61.4	59.7	63.5	48.1	47.3	49.2
1940	62.9	60.8	65.2	64.2	62.1	66.6	53.1	51.5	54.9
1950	68.2	65.6	71.1	69.1	66.5	72.2	60.8	59.1	62.9
1955	69.6	66.7	72.8	70.5	67.4	73.7	63.7	61.4	66.1
1960	69.7	66.6	73.1	70.6	67.4	74.1	63.6	61.1	66.3
1965	70.2	66.8	73.7	71.0	67.6	74.7	64.1	61.1	67.4
1970	70.9	67.1	74.8	71.7	68.0	75.6	65.3	61.3	69.4
1971	71.1	67.4	75.0	72.0	68.3	75.8	65.6	61.6	69.7
1972	71.1	67.4	75.1	72.0	68.3	75.9	65.6	61.5	69.9
1973	71.3	67.6	75.3	72.2	68.4	76.1	65.9	61.9	70.1
1974	71.9	68.1	75.8	72.7	68.9	76.6	67.0	62.9	71.3
1975	72.5	68.7	76.5	73.2	69.4	77.2	67.9	63.6	72.3
1976	72.8	69.0	76.7	73.5	69.7	77.3	68.3	64.1	72.6

Source: U.S. National Center for Health Statistics, *Vital Statistics of the United States*, annual.

No. 99. Selected Life Table Values: 1939 to 1976

[Prior to 1960, excludes Alaska and Hawaii. See *Historical Statistics, Colonial Times to 1970*, series B 116–125]

AGE AND SEX	WHITE						NEGRO AND OTHER					
	1939–1941	1949–1951	1959–1961	1969–1971	1975	1976	1939–1941	1949–1951	1959–1961	1969–1971	1975	1976
Average expectation of life in years:												
At birth: Male	62.8	66.3	67.6	67.9	69.4	69.7	52.3	58.9	61.5	61.0	63.6	64.1
Female	67.3	72.0	74.2	75.5	77.2	77.3	55.5	62.7	66.5	69.1	72.3	72.6
Age 20: Male	47.8	49.5	50.3	50.2	51.4	51.6	39.7	43.7	45.8	44.4	46.3	46.8
Female	51.4	54.6	56.3	57.2	58.6	58.7	42.1	46.8	50.1	51.9	54.7	54.9
Age 40: Male	30.0	31.2	31.7	31.9	33.0	33.1	25.2	27.3	28.7	28.3	29.8	30.0
Female	33.3	35.6	37.1	38.1	39.4	39.5	27.3	29.8	32.2	33.9	36.2	36.4
Age 50: Male	22.0	22.8	23.2	23.3	24.3	24.4	19.2	20.3	21.3	21.2	22.4	22.5
Female	24.7	26.8	28.1	29.1	30.3	30.4	21.0	22.7	24.3	26.0	27.9	28.0
Age 65: Male	12.1	12.8	13.0	13.0	13.7	13.7	12.2	12.8	12.8	12.9	13.7	13.8
Female	13.6	15.0	15.9	16.9	18.1	18.1	14.0	14.5	15.1	16.0	17.5	17.6
Annual rate of mortality per 1,000 living at specified age:												
At birth: Male	48.1	30.7	25.9	20.1	15.9	14.9	83.0	50.9	47.0	34.1	26.3	25.9
Female	37.9	23.6	19.6	15.3	12.3	11.8	66.8	40.9	38.3	27.7	22.2	21.7
Age 20: Male	2.1	1.6	1.6	1.9	1.8	1.8	(NA)	3.1	2.4	3.6	2.8	2.5
Female	1.5	.7	.6	.6	.6	.6	(NA)	2.3	1.2	1.2	.9	.9
Age 40: Male	5.1	3.9	3.3	3.4	2.9	2.8	13.6	8.8	7.5	9.0	7.4	7.0
Female	3.7	2.4	1.9	1.9	1.7	1.6	11.8	7.7	5.6	5.1	3.7	3.5
Age 50: Male	11.6	10.1	9.6	8.9	8.0	7.7	25.4	19.1	15.7	16.8	14.5	14.4
Female	7.6	5.6	4.7	4.7	4.2	4.1	21.9	16.0	11.7	10.1	7.9	7.9
Age 65: Male	36.9	34.5	33.9	33.9	30.3	30.0	(NA)	45.8	43.7	41.7	35.5	35.6
Female	26.4	20.6	17.4	15.6	13.9	13.9	(NA)	37.0	30.7	27.4	19.8	19.3
Number surviving to specified age per 1,000 born live:												
Age 20: Male	923	951	959	964	970	972	868	919	931	941	956	958
Female	940	965	971	976	980	981	885	935	947	959	968	969
Age 40: Male	869	912	924	925	934	937	728	828	857	840	870	879
Female	898	941	953	957	964	965	759	861	897	910	933	936
Age 65: Male	583	635	658	652	694	701	359	452	514	486	543	550
Female	687	768	807	809	832	835	407	524	608	652	715	721

NA Not available.

Source: U.S. National Center for Health Statistics, *U.S. Life Tables and Actuarial Tables, 1939–41; 1949–51; 1959–61;* and *Vital Statistics of the United States*, annual.

No. 100. Expectation of Life and Mortality Rates, by Race, Age, and Sex: 1976

AGE IN 1976 (years)	EXPECTATION OF LIFE IN YEARS					MORTALITY RATE PER 1,000 LIVING AT SPECIFIED AGE				
	Total	White		Negro and other		Total	White		Negro and other	
		Male	Female	Male	Female		Male	Female	Male	Female
Under 1	72.8	69.7	77.3	64.1	72.6	15.36	14.91	11.79	25.86	21.74
1	72.9	69.8	77.2	64.9	73.3	.94	.99	.74	1.33	1.09
2	72.0	68.9	76.3	63.9	72.3	.74	.75	.59	1.11	.91
3	71.0	67.9	75.3	63.0	71.4	.60	.60	.48	.94	.75
4	70.1	67.0	74.4	62.1	70.5	.50	.50	.40	.81	.61
5	69.1	66.0	73.4	61.1	69.5	.43	.45	.34	.70	.50
6	68.1	65.0	72.4	60.2	68.5	.38	.42	.30	.62	.40
7	67.2	64.0	71.5	59.2	67.6	.35	.39	.26	.54	.34
8	66.2	63.1	70.5	58.2	66.6	.31	.35	.24	.47	.29
9	65.2	62.1	69.5	57.3	65.6	.27	.31	.21	.41	.26
10	64.2	61.1	68.5	56.3	64.6	.25	.27	.19	.37	.25
11	63.2	60.1	67.5	55.3	63.6	.25	.27	.19	.37	.26
12	62.3	59.1	66.5	54.3	62.6	.29	.35	.22	.43	.28
13	61.3	58.2	65.5	53.3	61.7	.40	.51	.27	.57	.31
14	60.3	57.2	64.6	52.4	60.7	.55	.74	.34	.77	.36
15	59.3	56.2	63.6	51.4	59.7	.72	1.00	.42	.98	.41
16	58.4	55.3	62.6	50.5	58.7	.87	1.24	.50	1.22	.48
17	57.4	54.4	61.6	49.5	57.8	1.01	1.44	.55	1.48	.56
18	56.5	53.4	60.7	48.6	56.8	1.11	1.58	.58	1.78	.65
19	55.5	52.5	59.7	47.7	55.8	1.17	1.68	.58	2.11	.76
20	54.6	51.6	58.7	46.8	54.9	1.24	1.76	.57	2.45	.88
21	53.7	50.7	57.8	45.9	53.9	1.30	1.84	.57	2.79	1.00
22	52.7	49.8	56.8	45.0	53.0	1.34	1.88	.57	3.08	1.10
23	51.8	48.9	55.8	44.2	52.0	1.35	1.85	.57	3.30	1.17
24	50.9	48.0	54.9	43.3	51.1	1.33	1.79	.58	3.47	1.23
25	50.0	47.1	53.9	42.5	50.2	1.31	1.70	.59	3.64	1.28
26	49.0	46.1	52.9	41.6	49.2	1.29	1.62	.59	3.81	1.33
27	48.1	45.2	52.0	40.8	48.3	1.28	1.56	.61	3.94	1.40
28	47.1	44.3	51.0	39.9	47.3	1.29	1.54	.63	4.02	1.46
29	46.2	43.3	50.0	39.1	46.4	1.31	1.54	.67	4.07	1.53
30	45.3	42.4	49.1	38.2	45.5	1.34	1.56	.71	4.11	1.61
31	44.3	41.5	48.1	37.4	44.6	1.38	1.58	.75	4.17	1.70
32	43.4	40.5	47.1	36.6	43.6	1.44	1.62	.81	4.29	1.80
33	42.4	39.6	46.2	35.7	42.7	1.50	1.68	.86	4.49	1.91
34	41.5	38.7	45.2	34.9	41.8	1.59	1.76	.92	4.77	2.04
35	40.6	37.7	44.2	34.0	40.9	1.69	1.86	.99	5.08	2.18
36	39.6	36.8	43.3	33.2	40.0	1.81	1.99	1.07	5.41	2.34
37	38.7	35.9	42.3	32.4	39.1	1.95	2.15	1.17	5.76	2.56
38	37.8	35.0	41.4	31.6	38.2	2.13	2.35	1.28	6.15	2.83
39	36.9	34.0	40.4	30.8	37.3	2.33	2.57	1.42	6.57	3.16
40	35.9	33.1	39.5	30.0	36.4	2.56	2.83	1.56	7.04	3.52
41	35.0	32.2	38.6	29.2	35.5	2.82	3.13	1.72	7.54	3.90
42	34.1	31.3	37.6	28.4	34.6	3.10	3.46	1.90	8.07	4.27
43	33.2	30.4	36.7	27.6	33.8	3.41	3.85	2.12	8.61	4.62
44	32.4	29.5	35.8	26.8	32.9	3.74	4.27	2.35	9.18	4.97
45	31.5	28.7	34.9	26.1	32.1	4.12	4.75	2.61	9.77	5.33
46	30.6	27.8	33.9	25.3	31.3	4.52	5.27	2.89	10.42	5.73
47	29.7	26.9	33.0	24.6	30.5	4.95	5.82	3.18	11.20	6.19
48	28.9	26.1	32.1	23.9	29.6	5.40	6.41	3.47	12.14	6.72
49	28.0	25.3	31.3	23.2	28.8	5.89	7.04	3.77	13.20	7.30
50	27.2	24.4	30.4	22.5	28.0	6.42	7.74	4.09	14.36	7.94
51	26.4	23.6	29.5	21.8	27.3	7.00	8.50	4.45	15.57	8.60
52	25.6	22.8	28.6	21.1	26.5	7.63	9.32	4.84	16.77	9.27
53	24.7	22.0	27.8	20.5	25.7	8.30	10.23	5.27	17.94	9.94
54	24.0	21.3	26.9	19.8	25.0	9.02	11.21	5.74	19.11	10.61
55	23.2	20.5	26.1	19.2	24.3	9.78	12.24	6.24	20.26	11.26
56	22.4	19.7	25.2	18.6	23.5	10.60	13.37	6.78	21.49	11.96
57	21.6	19.0	24.4	18.0	22.8	11.56	14.69	7.40	23.00	12.86
58	20.9	18.3	23.6	17.4	22.1	12.70	16.25	8.11	24.88	14.01
59	20.1	17.6	22.8	16.9	21.4	13.99	18.01	8.91	27.04	15.35
60	19.4	16.9	22.0	16.3	20.7	15.42	19.94	9.80	29.56	16.99
61	18.7	16.2	21.2	15.8	20.1	16.90	21.94	10.74	32.07	18.62
62	18.0	15.6	20.4	15.3	19.5	18.29	23.96	11.62	34.06	19.74
63	17.3	14.9	19.6	14.8	18.8	19.51	25.93	12.40	35.17	20.06
64	16.7	14.3	18.9	14.3	18.2	20.65	27.91	13.15	35.63	19.88
65	16.0	13.7	18.1	13.8	17.6	21.79	29.97	13.94	35.59	19.26
70	12.9	10.9	14.4	11.3	14.3	32.38	44.20	21.62	51.87	34.29
75	10.1	8.5	11.2	9.7	12.3	50.87	67.45	37.58	74.73	54.66
80	7.9	6.6	8.5	8.6	10.9	76.55	100.28	62.16	92.85	68.28
85 and over	6.1	5.1	6.4	7.2	9.1	1,000.00	1,000.00	1,000.00	1,000.00	1,000.00

Source: U.S. National Center for Health Statistics, *Vital Statistics of the United States*, annual.

No. 101. Average Lifetime in Years, by Sex—States: 1969-71

[States are ranked according to the average lifetime for the total population]

STATE	Both sexes	Male	Fe-male	STATE	Both sexes	Male	Fe-male	STATE	Both sexes	Male	Fe-male
U.S.	70.75	67.04	74.64	Wash	71.72	68.07	75.78	N. Mex	70.32	66.51	74.51
				Calif	71.71	68.19	75.37	Wyo	70.29	66.19	75.19
Hawaii	73.60	71.02	76.79	Vt	71.64	67.76	75.77	Md	70.22	66.47	74.17
Minn	72.96	69.38	76.80	Okla	71.42	67.40	75.70	Ill	70.14	66.48	73.96
Utah	72.90	69.49	76.55	N.H	71.23	67.48	75.19	Tenn	70.11	66.15	74.26
N. Dak	72.79	69.23	77.01	Maine	70.93	67.24	74.85	Ky	70.10	66.22	74.31
Nebr	72.60	68.85	76.61	N.J	70.93	67.52	74.38	Va	70.08	66.26	74.17
Kans	72.58	68.83	76.54	Tex	70.90	67.05	74.99	Del	70.06	66.29	74.07
Iowa	72.56	68.83	76.50	Ind	70.88	67.23	74.72	W. Va	69.48	65.56	73.74
Wis	72.48	69.15	76.04	Ohio	70.82	67.25	74.55	Alaska	69.31	66.05	74.03
Conn	72.48	69.04	75.94	Mo	70.69	66.88	74.66	N.C	69.21	64.94	73.78
Oreg	72.13	68.43	76.20	Ark	70.66	66.68	74.97	Ala	69.05	64.90	73.41
S. Dak	72.08	68.49	76.19	Fla	70.66	66.61	74.96	Nev	69.03	65.60	73.32
Colo	72.06	68.40	75.43	Mich	70.63	67.09	74.48	La	68.76	64.85	72.88
R.I	71.90	68.31	75.48	Mont	70.56	66.73	75.08	Ga	68.54	64.27	73.01
Idaho	71.87	68.20	76.10	Ariz	70.55	66.57	75.04	Miss	68.09	64.06	72.40
Mass	71.83	68.12	75.45	N.Y	70.55	66.95	74.15	S.C	67.96	63.85	72.29
				Pa	70.43	66.90	74.06				

Source: U.S. National Center for Health Statistics, *U.S. Decennial Life Tables, 1969-71*, vol. II, DHEW Publication No. (HRA) 75-1151.

No. 102. Deaths and Death Rates, by Sex, Race, and Age: 1940 to 1976

[Rates are per 1,000 population for specified groups. Prior to 1960, excludes Alaska and Hawaii. Beginning 1970, excludes deaths of nonresidents of the U.S. Excludes fetal deaths. 1972 figures based on 50-percent sample of deaths. Rates based on enumerated population as of Apr. 1 for 1940 to 1960 and 1970, and July 1 estimates for other years. See text, p. 57. See also *Historical Statistics, Colonial Times to 1970*, series B 167-173 and B 181-192]

ITEM	1940	1950	1960	1965	1970	1971	1972	1973	1974	1975	1976
Deaths_____1,000__	1,417	1,452	1,712	1,828	1,921	1,928	1,964	1,973	1,934	1,893	1,909
Male_____1,000__	791	828	976	1,035	1,078	1,077	1,096	1,097	1,072	1,051	1,052
Female_____1,000__	626	625	736	793	843	850	868	876	863	842	857
White_____1,000__	1,231	1,276	1,505	1,605	1,682	1,690	1,721	1,728	1,697	1,660	1,675
Male_____1,000__	691	731	861	911	942	942	958	958	937	918	919
Female_____1,000__	540	545	644	695	740	747	764	770	761	743	756
Black and other_____1,000__	186	176	207	223	239	238	242	245	237	233	234
Male_____1,000__	100	96	115	125	136	135	139	139	135	133	133
Female_____1,000__	86	80	92	98	103	103	104	106	102	99	101
Death rates_____	10.8	9.6	9.5	9.4	9.5	9.3	9.4	9.4	9.2	8.9	8.9
Male_____	12.0	11.1	11.0	10.9	10.9	10.7	10.8	10.7	10.4	10.1	10.0
Female_____	9.5	8.2	8.1	8.0	8.1	8.0	8.1	8.1	8.0	7.7	7.8
White_____	10.4	9.5	9.5	9.4	9.5	9.3	9.5	9.4	9.2	9.0	9.0
Male_____	11.6	10.9	11.0	10.8	10.9	10.7	10.8	10.7	10.4	10.2	10.1
Female_____	9.2	8.0	8.0	8.0	8.1	8.1	8.2	8.2	8.1	7.8	7.9
Black and other_____	13.8	11.2	10.1	9.6	9.4	9.2	9.2	9.1	8.7	8.3	8.2
Male_____	15.1	12.5	11.5	11.1	11.2	10.8	11.0	10.8	10.4	10.0	9.8
Female_____	12.6	9.9	8.7	8.2	7.8	7.7	7.6	7.6	7.2	6.8	6.8
Male, by age:											
Under 1 year_____	61.9	37.3	30.6	27.1	24.1	21.4	20.6	20.3	19.7	18.3	17.6
1-4 years_____	3.1	1.5	1.2	1.0	.9	.9	.9	.9	.8	.8	.8
5-14 years_____	1.2	.7	.6	.5	.5	.5	.5	.5	.5	.4	.4
15-24 years_____	2.3	1.7	1.5	1.6	1.9	1.9	1.9	1.9	1.8	1.8	1.7
25-34 years_____	3.4	2.2	1.9	2.0	2.2	2.1	2.1	2.1	2.1	2.0	1.9
35-44 years_____	5.9	4.3	3.7	3.9	4.0	3.9	3.9	3.8	3.6	3.5	3.3
45-54 years_____	12.5	10.7	9.9	9.7	9.6	9.3	9.4	9.2	8.9	8.6	8.3
55-64 years_____	[1]26.1	[1]24.0	23.1	23.1	22.8	22.3	22.5	22.1	21.1	20.3	20.0
65-74 years_____	[1]54.6	[1]49.3	49.1	50.5	48.7	47.6	48.2	47.3	45.8	44.1	43.4
75-84 years_____	121.3	104.3	101.8	98.2	100.1	99.2	101.2	101.1	97.9	95.2	95.1
85 years and over_____	246.4	216.4	211.9	212.8	178.2	197.5	196.0	198.1	188.8	175.7	179.8
Female, by age:											
Under 1 year_____	47.7	28.5	23.2	20.9	18.6	16.6	15.9	15.7	15.3	14.4	14.2
1-4 years_____	2.7	1.3	1.0	.8	.8	.7	.7	.7	.7	.6	.6
5-14 years_____	.9	.5	.4	.3	.3	.3	.3	.3	.3	.3	.3
15-24 years_____	1.8	.9	.6	.6	.7	.7	.7	.7	.6	.6	.6
25-34 years_____	2.7	1.4	1.1	1.1	1.0	1.0	1.0	.9	.9	.9	.8
35-44 years_____	4.5	2.9	2.3	2.3	2.3	2.3	2.2	2.2	2.0	1.9	1.8
45-54 years_____	8.6	6.4	5.3	5.2	5.2	5.0	5.0	4.9	4.7	4.6	4.5
55-64 years_____	[1]18.0	[1]14.0	12.0	11.3	11.0	10.8	10.8	10.8	10.5	10.1	10.1
65-74 years_____	[1]42.2	[1]33.3	28.7	27.7	25.8	25.0	25.3	24.5	23.6	22.5	22.0
75-84 years_____	103.7	84.0	76.3	70.0	66.8	65.3	65.8	65.6	63.3	60.3	60.0
85 years and over_____	227.6	191.9	190.1	195.3	155.2	162.2	162.0	162.3	153.9	140.3	143.1

[1] Based on population adjusted for age bias in the population for Black and other races, 55 to 69 years old.

Source: U.S. National Center for Health Statistics, *Vital Statistics of the United States*, annual.

No. 103. DEATH RATES, BY RACE, SEX, AND AGE: 1970 AND 1976

[Number of deaths per 100,000 population. Excludes deaths of nonresidents of the U.S.]

AGE (in years)	1970 All races	1970 White	1970 Other races	1976 All races Both sexes	1976 All races Male	1976 All races Female	1976 White Both sexes	1976 White Male	1976 White Female	1976 Other races Both sexes	1976 Other races Male	1976 Other races Female
All ages [1]	945	946	938	890	1,007	778	899	1,010	794	825	984	680
Under 1	2,142	1,870	3,597	1,595	1,763	1,419	1,356	1,512	1,192	2,782	3,012	2,542
1–4	85	75	134	70	78	61	64	72	56	97	108	86
5–9	42	40	54	35	41	28	33	38	27	45	55	35
10–14	41	38	53	35	44	25	34	43	24	40	50	29
15–19	110	103	154	97	140	53	96	138	53	103	150	57
20–24	148	131	268	131	198	64	120	182	57	200	300	107
25–29	144	121	311	129	187	72	111	160	62	255	390	139
30–34	173	141	392	145	197	95	122	164	81	298	437	181
35–39	247	205	544	198	262	139	168	219	119	405	581	262
40–44	377	324	785	313	406	225	272	352	194	601	811	426
45–49	584	524	1,093	498	648	356	450	587	319	864	1,138	626
50–54	889	820	1,519	768	1,017	537	707	941	488	1,280	1,683	929
55–59	1,361	1,283	2,093	1,175	1,578	807	1,108	1,496	751	1,797	2,353	1,313
60–64	2,004	1,917	2,834	1,823	2,496	1,231	1,744	2,408	1,158	2,579	3,371	1,917
65–69	2,969	2,870	3,869	2,542	3,587	1,713	2,489	3,543	1,652	2,990	3,963	2,229
70–74	4,371	4,274	5,434	3,948	5,434	2,856	3,824	5,341	2,722	5,335	6,394	4,452
75–79	6,722	6,703	6,960	6,187	8,263	4,851	6,103	8,247	4,745	7,131	8,429	6,133
80–84	10,158	10,290	8,458	9,034	11,521	7,633	9,183	11,774	7,743	7,395	9,010	6,334
85 and over	16,345	16,890	10,750	15,487	17,984	14,312	16,069	18,768	14,823	10,019	11,519	9,175

[1] Includes unknown age.

Source: U.S. National Center for Health Statistics, unpublished data.

No. 104. DEATHS, BY RACE—STATES: 1970 TO 1976

[In thousands. By place of residence. Excludes deaths of nonresidents of the U.S.]

STATE	1970 White	1970 Black and other	1975 White	1975 Black and other	1976 White	1976 Black and other
U.S.	1,682	239	1,660	233	1,675	234
N. Eng.	113	3	107	3	108	3
Maine	11	(Z)	10	(Z)	10	(Z)
N.H.	7	(Z)	7	(Z)	7	(Z)
Vt	4	(Z)	4	(Z)	4	(Z)
Mass	56	1	53	1	53	1
R.I.	9	(Z)	9	(Z)	9	(Z)
Conn.	25	1	24	1	25	1
Mid. Atl.	344	39	319	36	322	37
N.Y.	168	20	151	19	153	20
N.J.	61	7	59	7	59	7
Pa.	115	12	110	11	110	11
E. No. Cent.	340	37	325	37	326	37
Ohio	91	10	87	9	87	9
Ind.	45	3	43	3	44	3
Ill.	97	14	90	14	90	13
Mich.	67	9	65	9	67	9
Wis.	40	1	39	1	39	1
W. No. Cent.	156	8	150	8	150	8
Minn.	33	(Z)	32	(Z)	32	1
Iowa	29	(Z)	28	(Z)	27	(Z)
Mo.	46	5	44	5	44	5
N. Dak.	5	(Z)	5	(Z)	5	(Z)
S. Dak.	6	(Z)	6	(Z)	6	(Z)
Nebr.	15	(Z)	14	(Z)	14	(Z)
Kans.	21	1	21	1	21	1
So. Atl.	223	67	236	65	241	65
Del.	4	1	4	1	4	1
Md.	26	6	26	6	26	7
D.C.	3	5	2	5	2	5
Va.	30	9	31	9	31	9
So. Atl—Con.						
W. Va.	19	1	18	1	19	1
N.C.	33	12	34	12	34	12
S.C.	15	8	16	8	16	8
Ga.	29	13	30	12	30	12
Fla.	64	11	76	11	79	11
E. So. Cent.	98	31	99	29	100	29
Ky.	30	3	30	3	30	3
Tenn.	31	7	32	7	32	7
Ala.	23	11	24	10	24	10
Miss.	14	10	14	9	14	9
W. So. Cent.	143	33	149	32	152	32
Ark.	16	4	18	4	17	4
La.	22	12	23	11	23	11
Okla.	24	3	24	3	24	3
Tex.	80	14	85	14	87	14
Mt.	63	4	67	4	68	4
Mont.	6	(Z)	6	(Z)	6	(Z)
Idaho	6	(Z)	6	(Z)	7	(Z)
Wyo.	3	(Z)	3	(Z)	3	(Z)
Colo.	17	1	17	1	17	1
N. Mex.	7	1	7	1	7	1
Ariz.	13	1	16	1	16	2
Utah	7	(Z)	7	(Z)	7	(Z)
Nev.	4	(Z)	4	(Z)	4	(Z)
Pac.	203	18	207	20	208	20
Wash.	29	1	29	1	29	1
Oreg.	19	(Z)	20	(Z)	20	(Z)
Calif.	153	13	156	15	156	15
Alaska	1	(Z)	1	(Z)	1	1
Hawaii	1	3	1	3	1	3

Z   Fewer than 500.

Source: U.S. National Center for Health Statistics, *Vital Statistics of the United States*, annual.

No. 105. Deaths—Total and Rate, 1960 to 1976: States

[By place of residence. Beginning 1970, excludes deaths of nonresidents of the U.S.]

STATE	DEATHS (1,000)							RATE PER 1,000 POPULATION [1]						
	1960	1965	1970	1973	1974	1975	1976	1960	1965	1970	1973	1974	1975	1976
U.S.	1,712	1,828	1,921	1,973	1,934	1,893	1,909	9.5	9.4	9.5	9.4	9.2	8.9	8.9
N.E.	112	117	116	116	114	110	112	10.6	10.5	9.8	9.6	9.4	9.1	9.1
Maine	11	11	11	11	11	10	10	11.1	10.9	11.1	10.6	10.2	9.7	9.8
N.H.	7	7	7	8	8	7	7	11.0	10.9	10.0	9.6	9.6	8.8	9.0
Vt.	4	5	4	5	4	4	4	11.4	11.6	10.0	9.7	9.4	9.1	9.0
Mass.	57	59	57	57	56	54	54	11.0	11.0	10.1	9.9	9.7	9.3	9.3
R.I.	9	10	9	10	9	9	9	10.5	10.9	10.0	9.8	9.7	9.6	9.9
Conn.	24	26	26	27	26	26	26	9.4	9.1	8.6	8.7	8.5	8.3	8.4
M.A.	359	376	383	377	367	356	359	10.5	10.3	10.3	10.0	9:8	9.5	9.6
N.Y.	178	185	188	181	177	170	173	10.6	10.2	10.3	9.9	9.8	9.4	9.5
N.J.	59	65	68	69	67	65	65	9.8	9.6	9.5	9.3	9.2	9.0	8.9
Pa.	121	126	127	127	123	121	121	10.7	10.9	10.8	10.6	10.4	10.2	10.2
E.N.C.	348	368	377	381	373	361	363	9.6	9.7	9.4	9.3	9.1	8.8	8.9
Ohio	93	98	100	102	99	96	96	9.6	9.6	9.4	9.5	9.2	9.0	9.0
Ind.	45	48	49	50	48	47	47	9.7	9.8	9.3	9.3	9.1	8.8	8.8
Ill.	103	108	111	111	108	104	104	10.2	10.2	10.0	9.8	9.7	9.3	9.2
Mich.	68	74	76	78	76	75	76	8.7	9.0	8.6	8.7	8.4	8.1	8.3
Wis.	38	40	41	41	41	40	40	9.7	9.7	9.2	9.0	8.9	8.7	8.7
W.N.C.	156	161	164	165	163	158	158	10.1	10.1	10.1	9.9	9.7	9.5	9.4
Minn.	32	33	34	34	34	33	33	9.3	9.2	8.9	8.7	8.6	8.3	8.3
Iowa	29	29	29	29	29	28	28	10.4	10.7	10.4	10.1	10.1	9.8	9.7
Mo.	48	50	52	52	51	49	49	11.2	11.2	11.1	10.9	10.6	10.3	10.3
N. Dak.	5	6	6	6	6	5	6	8.6	8.5	9.1	9.0	9.1	8.7	8.6
S. Dak.	7	7	7	7	7	6	7	9.7	9.3	9.9	9.7	9.6	9.5	9.8
Nebr.	14	15	15	15	15	15	15	10.0	10.0	10.1	9.7	9.7	9.4	9.4
Kans.	21	22	22	23	22	22	22	9.7	9.7	9.7	10.0	9.8	9.6	9.5
S.A.	236	262	290	311	307	301	305	9.1	9.1	9.5	9.6	9.3	8.9	9.0
Del.	4	5	5	5	5	5	5	9.4	9.0	9.0	8.5	8.7	8.1	8.2
Md.	28	31	33	33	33	32	33	9.0	8.8	8.4	8.0	8.1	7.8	7.0
D.C.	0	9	9	8	8	7	7	11.5	11.3	11.7	10.8	10.9	10.4	10.4
Va.	34	37	39	41	40	40	40	8.7	8.3	8.4	8.6	8.2	8.0	8.0
W. Va.	18	19	20	20	20	20	20	0.7	10.6	11.5	11.1	10.9	10.8	10.8
N.C.	38	42	45	48	46	46	46	8.4	8.5	8.8	9.1	8.6	8.4	8.4
S.C.	21	22	23	25	24	23	24	8.7	8.5	8.8	9.1	8.7	8.3	8.3
Ga.	35	38	42	44	43	41	42	9.0	8.8	9.1	9.2	8.8	8.4	8.4
Fla.	48	59	75	88	88	87	90	9.7	10.2	11.0	11.5	10.9	10.4	10.6
E.S.C.	115	121	128	134	131	128	129	9.5	9.5	10.0	10.1	9.8	9.5	10.6
Ky.	30	31	33	34	34	33	32	9.9	9.8	10.3	10.3	10.0	9.8	9.4
Tenn.	33	35	38	40	39	39	39	9.2	9.1	9.7	9.6	9.5	9.2	9.2
Ala.	30	33	34	35	35	34	34	9.3	9.4	9.8	10.0	9.7	9.3	9.3
Miss.	22	23	23	24	23	23	23	10.0	9.8	10.5	10.5	10.0	9.7	9.8
W.S.C.	148	159	175	186	183	181	184	8.7	8.6	9.1	9.2	8.9	8.7	8.7
Ark.	18	19	21	22	22	22	21	10.0	9.8	10.7	10.9	10.8	10.3	10.1
La.	30	32	33	35	34	34	35	9.1	9.1	9.2	9.3	8.9	8.9	9.0
Okla.	23	24	27	27	27	27	27	9.8	9.6	10.5	10.3	10.1	10.0	9.8
Tex.	77	84	94	102	99	98	101	8.1	7.9	8.4	8.6	8.3	8.0	8.1
Mt.	55	60	66	72	71	71	72	8.1	7.8	8.0	7.9	7.5	7.3	7.3
Mont.	7	7	7	7	7	7	7	9.7	9.3	9.5	9.5	8.9	8.7	9.0
Idaho	5	6	6	6	6	7	7	8.1	8.6	8.6	8.4	8.1	7.9	8.0
Wyo.	3	3	3	3	3	3	3	8.5	8.3	8.8	8.7	8.8	8.2	8.1
Colo.	15	16	17	19	18	17	18	8.7	8.2	7.9	7.7	7.2	6.9	7.0
N. Mex.	7	7	7	8	8	8	8	6.9	6.6	7.3	7.3	7.2	7.0	7.0
Ariz.	10	12	15	17	17	17	17	7.8	7.5	8.4	8.2	7.9	7.6	7.6
Utah	6	7	7	8	7	8	7	6.8	6.7	6.7	6.6	6.3	6.2	6.1
Nev.	3	3	4	4	4	4	5	8.9	7.3	7.9	7.8	7.6	7.6	7.5
Pac.	184	204	221	230	226	227	228	8.7	8.3	8.3	8.4	8.1	8.0	7.9
Wash.	27	27	30	31	30	30	30	9.3	9.2	8.8	9.0	8.6	8.4	8.4
Oreg.	17	18	20	21	20	20	20	9.5	9.6	9.3	9.4	9.0	8.8	8.8
Calif.	136	153	166	173	170	171	171	8.6	8.2	8.3	8.4	8.2	8.1	7.9
Alaska	1	1	1	1	1	2	2	5.8	5.3	4.8	4.4	4.4	4.3	4.2
Hawaii	4	4	4	4	4	4	4	5.6	5.1	5.2	5.3	5.1	5.0	5.0

[1] Based on population (excluding Armed Forces abroad) enumerated as of Apr. 1 for 1960 and 1970, and estimated as of July 1 for other years.

Source: U.S. National Center for Health Statistics, *Vital Statistics of the United States,* annual.

No. 106. INFANT, MATERNAL, FETAL, AND NEONATAL DEATH RATES, BY RACE: 1940 TO 1976

[Deaths per 1,000 live births, except as noted. Prior to 1960, excludes Alaska and Hawaii. Beginning 1970, excludes deaths of nonresidents of U.S. See also *Historical Statistics, Colonial Times to 1970*, series B 136–147]

ITEM	1940	1950	1960	1965	1969	1970	1971	1972 [1]	1973	1974	1975	1976
Infant deaths [2]	47.0	29.2	26.0	24.7	20.7	20.0	19.1	18.5	17.7	16.7	16.1	15.2
White	43.2	26.8	22.9	21.5	18.4	17.8	17.1	16.4	15.8	14.8	14.2	13.3
Other races	73.8	44.5	43.2	40.3	32.9	30.9	28.5	27.7	26.2	24.9	24.2	23.5
Maternal deaths [3]	376.0	83.3	37.1	31.6	22.2	21.5	18.8	18.8	15.2	14.6	12.8	12.3
White	319.8	61.1	26.0	21.0	15.5	14.4	13.0	14.3	10.7	10.0	9.1	9.0
Other races	773.5	221.6	97.9	83.7	55.7	55.9	45.3	38.5	34.6	35.1	29.0	26.5
Fetal deaths [4]	(NA)	19.2	16.1	16.2	14.1	14.2	13.4	12.7	12.2	11.5	10.7	10.5
White	(NA)	17.1	14.1	13.9	12.4	12.4	11.8	11.2	10.8	10.2	9.5	9.3
Other races	(NA)	32.5	26.8	27.2	22.5	22.6	21.2	19.5	18.6	17.0	16.0	15.2
Neonatal deaths [5]	28.8	20.5	18.7	17.7	15.6	15.1	14.2	13.6	13.0	12.3	11.6	10.9
White	27.2	19.4	17.2	16.1	14.2	13.8	13.0	12.4	11.8	11.1	10.4	9.7
Other races	39.7	27.5	26.9	25.4	22.5	21.4	19.6	19.2	17.9	17.2	16.8	16.3

NA Not available.   [1] Based on a 50-percent sample of deaths.
[2] Represents deaths of infants under 1 year old, exclusive of fetal deaths.
[3] Per 100,000 live births from deliveries and complications of pregnancy, childbirth, and the puerperium. For 1969–1976, deaths are classified according to eighth revision of *International Classification of Diseases* (ICD); deaths n prior years classified according to ICD revision in use at the time.
[4] Includes only fetal deaths (stillbirths) for which period of gestation was at least 20 weeks (or 5 months) or was not stated.   [5] Represents deaths of infants under 28 days old, exclusive of fetal deaths.

Source: U.S. National Center for Health Statistics, *Vital Statistics of the United States*, annual.

No. 107. INFANT DEATH RATES—STATES: 1960 TO 1976

[Deaths per 1,000 live births, by place of residence. Represents deaths under 1 year old, exclusive of fetal deaths. See *Historical Statistics, Colonial Times to 1970*, series B 143–147, for U.S. total by race]

STATE	1960 White	1960 Other races	1970 [1] White	1970 [1] Other races	1976 [1] White	1976 [1] Other races	STATE	1960 White	1960 Other races	1970 [1] White	1970 [1] Other races	1976 [1] White	1976 [1] Other races
U.S.	22.9	43.2	17.8	30.9	13.3	23.5	So. Atl.—Con.						
							W. Va.	24.8	37.7	22.8	27.7	16.6	22.3
N. Eng.	21.7	35.2	16.8	30.3	12.0	21.4	N.C.	22.3	52.4	19.3	36.1	15.0	23.9
Maine	25.7	12.9	21.0	25.0	11.0	8.4	S.C.	23.9	48.5	18.2	31.1	14.0	27.8
N.H.	23.7	10.6	18.0	20.5	11.7	–	Ga.	24.6	48.1	17.2	32.9	12.2	22.5
Vt.	24.2	–	17.6	19.2	12.7	–	Fla.	23.6	46.1	17.8	33.2	12.2	22.9
Mass.	21.1	34.4	16.0	31.4	11.6	17.8							
R.I.	22.4	44.4	19.3	27.7	13.8	22.9	E. So. Cent.	25.6	48.4	18.7	35.2	14.3	27.1
Conn.	20.0	36.9	15.5	30.4	12.3	27.0	Ky.	26.0	48.3	18.8	27.8	14.1	20.9
							Tenn.	25.3	43.5	18.8	30.6	13.9	24.2
Mid. Atl.	22.0	41.4	17.3	31.7	13.4	24.8	Ala.	24.9	45.0	18.6	36.0	15.1	28.1
N.Y.	21.5	41.6	16.9	30.2	13.5	24.6	Miss.	26.6	54.3	18.7	39.2	14.5	29.5
N.J.	21.9	41.7	16.9	33.0	12.3	25.4							
Pa.	22.6	40.6	18.2	34.2	13.9	24.9	W. So. Cent.	24.9	44.3	19.6	31.4	14.2	24.3
							Ark.	22.5	38.7	18.3	31.1	13.4	21.3
E. No. Cent.	22.1	39.4	17.8	31.0	13.1	25.7	La.	22.6	46.9	19.8	32.3	12.9	25.3
Ohio	22.2	39.4	17.2	28.7	13.6	23.3	Okla.	22.7	42.8	20.3	26.3	15.9	19.8
Ind.	22.6	37.7	18.5	27.8	13.6	22.9	Tex.	26.3	43.9	19.6	31.8	14.3	25.3
Ill.	22.2	39.6	18.3	33.6	13.2	28.6							
Mich.	22.1	40.4	18.6	30.4	13.0	25.0	Mt.	25.7	51.7	18.1	27.0	13.5	18.4
Wis.	21.2	35.3	16.0	29.8	11.8	21.3	Mont.	24.2	34.5	21.2	24.7	16.4	17.0
							Idaho.	22.7	33.3	17.3	[2]11.6	13.1	10.3
W. No. Cent.	21.7	42.5	17.3	31.4	13.6	24.0	Wyo.	27.5	48.6	19.6	27.6	16.2	22.9
Minn.	21.6	22.6	17.3	24.0	13.6	20.5	Colo.	26.9	44.0	19.7	23.5	12.8	15.6
Iowa.	21.7	35.2	18.3	31.4	14.0	23.4	N. Mex.	30.9	52.8	19.5	28.9	15.3	16.4
Mo.	21.4	45.4	17.0	33.4	13.4	24.9	Ariz.	26.6	60.8	16.0	28.0	14.1	22.3
N. Dak.	24.1	43.3	14.3	[2]14.3	13.3	20.4	Utah.	18.8	54.0	14.9	[2]17.5	11.5	17.9
S. Dak.	24.2	76.0	16.7	37.3	15.0	29.9	Nev.	29.6	33.9	22.2	37.0	14.2	14.2
Nebr.	21.3	34.3	18.5	34.6	13.8	21.7							
Kans.	21.3	33.4	16.7	27.5	13.1	22.9	Pac.	22.6	30.5	16.7	21.9	12.3	14.9
							Wash.	22.7	36.7	18.1	26.4	14.6	13.6
So. Atl.	23.6	47.2	18.0	32.6	13.5	24.4	Oreg.	23.0	29.2	16.0	14.1	12.6	13.9
Del.	17.8	50.6	16.3	31.6	10.8	19.4	Calif.	22.5	29.7	16.5	22.1	11.8	15.5
Md.	22.3	44.6	16.4	29.0	13.9	25.4	Alaska.	27.9	68.2	20.3	29.0	11.9	28.2
D.C.	29.4	39.6	26.3	29.5	10.1	28.0	Hawaii.	21.5	24.0	17.8	18.9	12.1	10.4
Va.	24.6	45.5	17.0	33.3	13.3	25.4							

– Represents zero.   [1] Excludes deaths of nonresidents of U.S.   [2] Based on a frequency of less than 20.

Source: U.S. National Center for Health Statistics, *Vital Statistics of the United States*, annual.

No. 108. DEATH RATES, 1960 TO 1976, AND DEATHS, 1970 TO 1976, FROM SELECTED CAUSES

[Beginning 1970, excludes deaths of nonresidents of the U.S. Prior to 1970, causes of death classified according to seventh revision of *International Classification of Diseases;* thereafter, to eighth revision. See also *Historical Statistics, Colonial Times to 1970,* series B149–166]

CAUSE OF DEATH	DEATHS PER 100,000 POPULATION [1]							DEATHS (1,000)			
	1960	1965	1970	1973	1974	1975	1976	1970	1974	1975	1976
All causes	954.7	943.2	945.3	940.2	915.1	888.5	889.6	1,921.0	1,934.4	1,892.9	1,909.4
Major cardiovascular diseases	515.1	510.9	496.0	494.4	478.2	455.8	454.0	1,008.0	1,010.9	971.0	974.4
Diseases of heart	369.0	367.4	362.0	360.8	349.2	336.2	337.2	735.6	738.2	716.2	723.9
Percent of total	38.8	39.0	38.3	38.4	38.2	37.8	37.9	38.3	38.2	37.8	37.9
Active rheumatic fever and chronic rheumatic heart disease	10.3	8.0	7.3	6.5	6.3	6.1	6.1	14.9	13.3	12.9	13.1
Hypertensive heart disease [2]	37.0	28.4	7.4	6.1	5.7	5.2	5.0	15.0	12.1	11.0	10.7
Ischemic heart disease		309.4	328.1	326.0	314.5	301.7	301.0	666.7	664.9	642.7	646.1
Chronic disease of endocardium and other myocardial insufficiency	321.8	6.6	3.3	2.4	2.3	2.1	2.0	6.7	4.9	4.9	4.2
All other forms of heart disease		15.1	15.9	19.7	20.4	21.2	23.2	32.3	43.0	45.1	49.8
Hypertension	7.1	6.0	4.1	3.5	3.3	3.0	2.9	8.3	6.9	6.3	6.1
Cerebrovascular diseases	108.0	103.7	101.9	102.1	98.1	91.1	87.9	207.2	207.4	194.0	188.6
Arteriosclerosis	20.0	19.7	15.6	15.5	15.3	13.6	13.7	31.7	32.2	28.9	29.4
Other	11.0	14.1	12.5	12.4	12.4	12.0	12.3	25.3	26.2	25.6	26.4
Malignancies	149.2	153.5	162.8	167.3	170.5	171.7	175.8	330.7	360.5	365.7	377.3
Percent of total	15.7	16.3	17.2	17.8	18.6	19.3	19.8	17.2	18.6	19.3	19.8
Accidents	52.3	55.7	56.4	55.2	49.5	48.4	46.9	114.6	104.6	103.0	100.8
Motor vehicle	21.3	25.4	26.9	26.5	22.0	21.5	21.9	54.6	46.4	45.9	47.0
Falls	10.6	10.3	8.3	7.9	7.7	7.0	6.6	16.9	16.3	14.7	14.1
Drowning	2.9	2.8	3.1	3.4	3.1	3.1	2.6	6.4	6.5	6.6	5.6
All other	17.5	17.3	18.1	17.4	16.7	16.7	15.8	36.7	35.4	35.9	33.9
Influenza and pneumonia	[3] 37.3	31.0	30.0	29.0	25.9	26.1	28.8	62.7	54.8	55.7	61.9
Influenza	4.4	1.2	1.8	2.4	1.0	2.0	3.7	3.7	2.2	4.3	7.9
Pneumonia	[3] 32.9	29.8	28.2	26.5	24.9	24.1	25.2	59.0	52.6	51.4	54.0
Diabetes mellitus	16.7	17.1	18.9	18.2	17.7	16.5	16.1	38.3	37.3	35.2	34.5
Certain diseases of early infancy	37.4	28.6	21.3	14.5	13.6	12.5	11.6	43.2	28.8	26.6	24.8
Cirrhosis of liver	11.3	12.8	15.5	15.9	15.8	14.8	14.7	31.4	33.3	31.6	31.5
Bronchitis, emphysema, and asthma	(4)	14.4	15.2	14.2	12.7	12.0	11.4	30.9	26.9	25.5	24.4
Chronic and unqualified bronchitis	(4)	2.5	2.9	2.6	2.4	2.2	2.2	5.8	5.1	4.7	4.6
Emphysema	(4)	9.6	11.2	10.6	9.4	8.8	8.3	22.7	19.9	18.8	17.8
Asthma	3.0	2.3	1.1	.9	.9	.9	.9	2.3	1.9	2.0	2.0
Suicide	10.6	11.1	11.6	12.0	12.1	12.7	12.5	23.5	25.7	27.1	26.8
Homicide	4.7	5.5	8.3	9.8	10.2	10.0	9.1	16.8	21.5	21.3	19.6
Congenital anomalies	12.2	10.1	8.3	6.7	6.4	6.2	6.1	16.8	13.5	13.2	13.0
Peptic ulcer	6.3	5.4	4.2	3.7	3.3	3.2	3.0	8.6	7.1	6.7	6.4
Hernia and intestinal obstruction	5.1	5.2	3.6	3.2	3.1	2.9	2.8	7.2	6.5	6.2	5.9
Nephritis and nephrosis	7.6	6.2	4.4	4.0	3.8	3.8	4.0	8.9	8.1	8.1	8.5
Infections of kidney	4.3	5.1	4.0	2.9	2.6	2.1	1.9	8.2	5.5	4.5	4.0
Tuberculosis, all forms	6.1	4.1	2.6	1.8	1.7	1.6	1.5	5.2	3.5	3.3	3.1
Cholelithiasis, cholecystitis, and cholangitis	2.6	2.4	2.0	1.6	1.5	1.4	1.4	4.0	3.2	3.0	3.0
Enteritis and other	(4)	2.0	1.3	1.1	1.1	.9	.9	2.6	2.3	2.0	1.9
Hyperplasia of prostate	2.5	1.8	1.1	.8	.7	.6	.5	2.2	1.4	1.2	1.1
Meningitis	1.3	1.2	.8	.7	.7	.8	.7	1.7	1.5	1.6	1.6
Acute bronchitis and bronchiolitis	(4)	.5	.6	.4	.4	.3	.4	1.3	.8	.7	.9
Syphilis and its sequelae	1.6	1.3	.2	.2	.1	.1	.1	.5	.3	.3	.2
Infective hepatitis	.5	.4	.5	.3	.3	.3	.3	1.0	.6	.6	.6
Other infective and parasitic diseases	3.7	1.5	3.6	4.0	4.3	4.6	5.0	7.4	9.0	9.7	10.7
Ill-defined symptoms and conditions	11.4	12.1	12.7	14.5	14.7	14.9	14.3	25.8	31.1	31.8	30.8
All other causes	51.9	42.6	58.8	63.0	64.2	64.4	66.0	119.5	135.8	137.1	141.8

[1] Based on resident population enumerated as of Apr. 1 for 1960 and 1970, and estimated as of July 1 for other years. [2] With or without renal disease. [3] Excludes pneumonia of newborn. [4] Included in "All other causes." Comparable data not available separately.

Source: U.S. National Center for Health Statistics, *Vital Statistics of the United States,* annual.

No. 109. Death Rates, by Cause, Sex, and Age—States: 1976

[Rates per 100,000 estimated midyear population in each area. By place of residence. Excludes nonresidents of U.S. Causes of death classified according to eighth revision of the *International Classification of Diseases*]

STATE, SEX, AND AGE	Diseases of heart	Malignant neoplasms	Cerebrovascular diseases	Accidents	Pneumonia, flu	Diabetes mellitus	Cirrhosis of liver	Arteriosclerosis	Suicide	Early infancy diseases
U.S.	337.2	175.8	87.9	46.9	28.8	16.1	14.7	13.7	12.5	11.6
Male	383.5	196.6	77.1	67.3	31.1	13.4	19.8	11.3	18.7	13.6
15–24 yr	3.4	8.0	1.4	94.1	1.6	.4	.3	–	18.5	(X)
25–44 yr	40.3	27.5	6.8	65.7	4.4	3.1	12.4	.1	23.3	(X)
45–64 yr	554.9	338.7	63.1	65.0	24.7	18.3	56.9	3.9	27.8	(X)
65 yr. and over	2,906.9	1,324.0	694.7	133.8	259.6	99.0	56.6	117.1	37.3	(X)
Female	293.4	156.0	98.0	27.7	26.6	18.6	9.8	15.9	6.7	9.6
15–24 yr	1.9	5.1	1.1	25.3	1.4	.4	.3	–	4.8	(X)
25–44 yr	12.6	32.5	6.8	16.7	3.0	2.3	6.1	.1	9.1	(X)
45–64 yr	184.4	264.0	50.2	23.7	12.5	18.4	26.0	2.0	12.0	(X)
65 yr. and over	2,039.3	741.0	694.5	84.3	177.6	114.4	22.7	125.8	7.8	(X)
N. Eng.	357.2	195.6	82.2	36.8	38.1	17.3	15.5	16.0	10.3	7.9
Maine	385.4	202.7	97.0	45.4	33.0	15.0	13.9	19.0	12.6	7.2
N.H.	329.0	187.6	83.2	39.2	34.5	19.0	16.2	23.7	13.0	8.0
Vt	347.3	170.0	73.5	46.4	35.5	14.5	12.0	23.1	15.5	9.2
Mass	366.3	197.1	81.7	37.2	46.6	17.4	16.6	14.3	9.0	7.0
R.I.	416.1	227.7	80.5	33.0	23.3	22.9	16.1	14.6	12.0	8.7
Conn	322.1	186.8	79.6	32.1	29.7	16.1	14.2	15.6	10.0	9.1
Mid. Atl.	398.1	200.8	79.9	34.6	31.6	19.0	18.3	12.1	9.6	11.1
N.Y.	393.1	201.2	75.0	31.7	36.3	19.2	21.4	10.2	9.3	11.6
N.J.	376.1	197.2	75.7	32.5	24.8	17.5	17.0	9.9	7.5	10.6
Pa	419.3	202.5	89.9	40.3	28.6	19.5	14.4	16.4	11.5	10.7
E. No. Cent.	352.8	174.9	87.9	42.8	25.2	17.6	13.8	15.0	11.6	11.8
Ohio	354.8	180.6	88.1	39.4	24.8	18.9	13.2	16.1	12.6	11.7
Ind	335.3	170.4	102.3	48.3	23.7	18.1	9.8	20.6	10.7	11.9
Ill	385.1	182.7	85.7	43.1	26.6	16.0	15.3	12.4	9.4	13.4
Mich	321.5	163.6	80.9	42.8	23.2	18.9	16.3	13.3	13.0	11.3
Wis	350.9	170.4	90.5	43.3	28.5	15.1	11.5	15.8	13.0	8.7
W. No. Cent.	357.4	179.5	101.6	52.0	36.4	16.1	9.6	18.0	11.2	11.1
Minn	307.8	161.4	92.8	45.5	35.5	12.8	9.7	15.5	9.9	9.9
Iowa	378.0	192.4	108.4	52.1	38.3	16.7	9.1	18.3	11.0	11.6
Mo	385.7	195.7	107.8	52.8	31.5	19.0	10.3	18.2	13.0	11.4
N. Dak	322.4	152.4	90.2	61.3	41.2	14.6	9.8	17.0	10.9	10.4
S. Dak	366.8	181.2	105.1	65.7	44.0	14.9	12.0	15.9	11.1	14.7
Nebr	353.2	169.9	103.4	51.1	43.9	15.3	8.8	19.5	9.7	10.6
Kans	368.0	174.7	96.0	55.3	37.2	16.6	8.7	21.1	11.2	11.2
So. Atl.	333.0	175.0	91.2	50.2	25.8	15.9	15.5	12.1	13.9	12.5
Del	346.6	166.8	58.2	39.9	14.9	21.3	16.3	12.0	12.2	8.9
Md	305.6	174.5	58.0	37.8	20.0	16.5	14.7	10.5	11.5	12.6
D.C.	320.4	220.7	77.2	41.0	35.2	22.1	51.0	27.5	13.0	24.1
Va	296.4	150.1	78.8	48.3	27.8	12.3	12.5	11.6	15.9	11.6
W. Va	431.2	190.5	97.9	57.9	33.0	17.6	14.6	15.3	10.0	14.5
N.C.	307.5	150.9	92.0	57.3	24.9	16.0	12.3	10.6	12.4	13.4
S.C.	294.8	138.9	95.9	57.0	23.7	16.7	10.5	8.2	9.7	17.1
Ga	293.9	142.9	105.4	55.5	27.5	12.9	12.2	11.2	13.5	12.9
Fla	399.7	230.5	106.5	47.3	26.2	17.9	20.7	14.2	17.4	9.4
E. So. Cent.	334.2	167.0	113.2	58.7	27.6	15.8	9.4	12.9	11.6	14.2
Ky	364.1	172.1	104.1	56.6	30.3	17.3	9.9	13.6	12.6	12.0
Tenn	341.9	170.9	114.9	54.1	29.4	12.8	9.1	13.2	13.2	12.5
Ala	302.7	163.3	116.2	63.1	22.4	17.6	9.3	12.5	10.4	15.0
Miss	326.0	158.2	118.6	63.4	28.5	15.9	9.3	11.9	9.2	19.5
W. So. Cent.	303.7	162.4	92.8	54.9	29.1	16.3	11.1	14.2	11.9	14.3
Ark	369.7	186.8	121.3	58.4	27.7	17.6	8.5	14.5	11.7	12.0
La	328.4	167.6	89.2	59.9	25.7	22.3	10.8	15.2	11.3	17.8
Okla	359.9	184.5	108.5	61.1	35.6	14.8	12.9	16.0	12.7	12.6
Tex	272.4	151.8	85.6	51.5	28.9	14.6	11.3	13.5	11.9	14.0
Mt.	233.9	132.4	63.5	61.7	30.3	11.9	13.5	12.3	17.4	12.2
Mont	290.6	156.8	85.3	78.5	40.4	13.0	14.9	21.6	17.1	13.7
Idaho	263.2	141.2	82.7	68.2	36.2	14.1	9.4	16.5	16.4	12.0
Wyo	283.8	126.4	65.1	90.0	35.6	10.5	13.6	14.9	17.7	14.4
Colo	237.2	120.1	60.2	53.0	35.5	10.1	11.0	12.7	17.3	9.6
N. Mex	171.1	122.4	52.5	76.6	30.7	12.8	16.6	10.5	18.3	12.2
Ariz	237.9	153.9	62.1	59.4	26.6	12.8	15.5	10.4	17.1	12.4
Utah	205.1	100.2	54.4	46.8	20.5	12.1	7.6	9.7	13.0	16.0
Nev	241.6	149.7	68.9	60.8	17.5	11.0	26.1	7.0	26.7	12.6
Pac.	282.5	163.6	81.3	49.9	25.4	11.3	18.1	12.7	16.7	9.0
Wash	301.7	169.5	85.7	51.1	34.4	13.4	13.6	15.8	14.8	9.3
Oreg	313.1	171.5	96.7	55.9	34.3	12.4	14.6	19.7	15.0	7.6
Calif	284.5	165.9	81.6	48.6	23.4	10.7	19.7	12.0	17.5	9.0
Alaska	80.6	59.4	17.8	113.1	12.6	3.1	13.4	2.9	19.4	12.0
Hawaii	161.3	107.4	43.0	33.0	20.9	15.9	8.5	2.6	10.0	9.8

– Represents zero.   X   Not applicable.

Source: U.S. National Center for Health Statistics. *Vital Statistics of the United States,* annual.

No. 110. DEATH RATES FROM HEART DISEASE, BY SEX, AGE, AND SELECTED TYPE: 1950 TO 1976

[Deaths per 100,000 resident population in specified age groups. Beginning 1970, based on the "Eighth Revision International Classification of Diseases, Adapted for Use in the United States"]

AGE AT DEATH AND SELECTED TYPE OF HEART DISEASE	MALE					FEMALE				
	1950	1960	1970	1975	1976	1950	1960	1970	1975	1976
Total U.S. rate	424.7	439.5	422.5	385.2	383.5	289.7	300.6	304.5	289.7	293.4
25-44 years	70.2	67.6	57.3	42.4	40.3	36.2	25.2	19.5	13.9	12.6
45-54 years	441.2	420.4	376.4	326.7	317.7	177.8	127.5	109.9	91.3	89.5
55-64 years	1,100.5	1,066.9	987.2	860.2	840.6	507.0	429.4	351.6	300.0	293.9
65 years and over	3,269.3	3,314.7	3,258.0	3,933.0	2,906.9	2,496.3	2,415.6	2,268.2	2,036.7	2,039.3
Persons 45-54 years:										
Ischemic heart disease	316.6	347.1	338.0	292.3	281.3	76.0	72.4	84.0	70.9	68.8
Rheumatic heart dis	24.3	19.9	11.4	7.3	6.9	23.8	19.5	10.6	6.1	6.2
Hypertensive heart dis	48.0	23.9	4.6	2.9	3.1	48.7	21.5	3.9	2.2	2.1
Persons 55-64 years:										
Ischemic heart disease	792.9	885.2	904.6	779.1	756.1	275.0	295.6	299.1	252.9	245.9
Rheumatic heart dis	35.0	29.0	21.5	16.2	15.8	30.5	28.4	20.8	15.3	15.5
Hypertensive heart dis	128.2	71.2	11.7	8.1	8.0	119.0	63.9	9.1	6.1	5.7
Persons 65 years and over:										
Ischemic heart disease	2,041.1	2,586.4	3,022.5	2,684.3	2,646.5	1,334.0	1,691.2	2,071.5	1,841.3	1,834.8
Rheumatic heart dis	58.3	32.9	32.9	30.5	32.1	52.6	34.8	32.3	31.8	32.1
Hypertensive heart dis	442.4	268.5	54.9	36.2	34.6	487.9	321.2	60.0	41.2	38.5

Source: U.S. National Center for Health Statistics, *Vital Statistics of the United States*, and unpublished data.

No. 111. DEATH RATES FROM CANCER, BY SEX, AGE, AND TYPE OF CANCER: 1940 TO 1976

[Deaths per 100,000 resident population in the specified age groups]

AGE AT DEATH AND SELECTED TYPE OF CANCER	MALE						FEMALE					
	1940	1950	1960	1970	1975	1976	1940	1950	1960	1970	1975	1976
Total U.S. rate	114.1	142.9	162.5	182.1	192.3	196.6	126.4	136.8	136.4	144.4	152.1	156.0
25-44 years	24.6	31.0	34.2	33.9	28.7	27.5	50.3	49.1	45.8	40.3	33.4	32.5
45-54 years	135.3	156.2	170.8	183.5	187.4	187.9	204.1	194.0	183.0	181.5	176.6	176.5
55-64 years	352.2	413.1	459.9	511.8	512.3	520.4	384.1	368.2	337.7	343.2	357.7	364.9
65 years and over	896.2	968.9	1,066.2	1,221.2	1,301.1	1,324.0	792.3	755.7	709.1	708.3	725.2	741.0
Persons, 45-54 years old:												
Respiratory system	23.3	39.3	54.7	72.1	78.2	78.8	6.2	6.7	10.1	22.2	28.1	29.7
Digestive organs, peritoneum	70.7	59.9	53.2	45.9	44.8	44.8	58.6	47.0	38.9	32.5	29.7	29.4
Breast	.3	.4	.2	.4	.2	.2	47.5	46.9	51.4	52.6	50.4	51.1
Genital organs	5.6	4.8	4.0	3.4	3.3	3.6	69.2	59.0	44.8	34.4	29.9	28.5
Lymphatic and hematopoietic tissues, excl. leukemia	(NA)	9.7	11.6	12.8	11.0	10.8	(NA)	5.7	7.1	8.3	7.4	7.5
Urinary organs	9.1	8.7	8.3	8.0	8.1	8.3	4.5	3.8	3.5	3.5	3.3	3.4
Mouth, throat, and pharynx	6.0	6.3	7.9	7.9	8.2	7.9	1.6	1.8	2.8	2.8	3.0	2.6
Leukemia	5.6	6.5	7.2	6.6	5.9	6.4	4.6	5.1	5.3	4.9	4.4	3.9
Persons, 55-64 years old:												
Respiratory system	45.7	94.2	150.2	202.3	214.1	217.4	12.6	15.4	17.0	38.9	58.3	62.2
Digestive organs, peritoneum	195.3	174.8	153.7	139.0	129.5	130.0	149.1	125.1	102.2	86.0	83.5	82.5
Breast	.8	.8	1.0	.6	.8	.6	74.9	69.9	70.8	77.6	79.2	82.2
Genital organs	30.7	26.2	23.5	22.8	23.3	24.1	100.9	87.4	73.0	58.2	53.0	54.1
Lymphatic and hematopoietic tissues, excl. leukemia	(NA)	18.2	23.1	27.1	26.7	25.4	(NA)	11.5	15.7	17.7	17.5	18.2
Urinary organs	23.7	26.9	25.9	26.4	24.8	25.3	11.8	11.2	9.3	9.4	9.0	8.7
Mouth, throat, and pharynx	16.1	16.2	16.3	20.1	18.9	19.1	3.0	3.3	3.8	6.2	6.8	6.6
Leukemia	10.6	14.1	16.1	15.4	14.9	15.5	7.5	10.1	10.6	9.0	8.6	8.2

NA Not available.

Source: U.S. National Center for Health Statistics, *Vital Statistics of the United States*, and unpublished data.

No. 112. DEATHS AND DEATH RATES FROM ACCIDENTS: 1965 TO 1976

[For 1965, includes deaths of nonresidents of the U.S. See also *Historical Statistics, Colonial Times to 1970*, series B 163–165]

TYPE OF ACCIDENT	DEATHS					RATE				
	1965	1970	1974	1975	1976	1965	1970[1]	1974	1975	1976
All accidents	108,004	114,638	104,622	103,030	100,761	55.7	56.4	49.5	48.4	46.9
Motor-vehicle accidents	49,163	54,633	46,402	45,853	47,038	25.4	26.9	22.0	21.5	21.9
Traffic	48,050	53,493	45,314	44,820	46,012	24.8	26.3	21.4	21.0	21.4
Nontraffic	1,113	1,140	1,088	1,033	1,026	.6	.6	.5	.5	.5
Other road-vehicle accidents	319	257	275	255	238	.2	.1	.1	.1	.1
Water-transport accidents	1,493	1,651	1,579	1,570	1,371	.8	.8	.7	.7	.6
Air and space transport accidents	1,529	1,612	1,687	1,552	1,445	.8	.8	.8	.7	.7
Railway accidents	962	852	716	608	552	.5	.4	.3	.3	.3
Accidental falls	[2]19,984	16,926	16,339	14,896	14,136	[2]10.3	8.3	7.7	7.0	6.6
Fall from one level to another	5,802	4,798	4,218	4,005	3,818	3.0	2.4	2.0	1.9	1.8
Fall on the same level	5,738	828	622	532	504	3.0	.4	.3	.2	.2
Unspecified falls	8,444	11,300	11,499	10,359	9,814	4.4	5.6	5.4	4.9	4.6
Accidental drowning	5,485	6,391	6,463	6,640	5,645	2.8	3.1	3.1	3.1	2.6
Accidents caused by—										
Fire and flames	7,347	6,718	6,236	6,071	6,338	3.8	3.3	2.9	2.8	3.0
Firearms	2,344	2,406	2,513	2,380	2,059	1.2	1.2	1.2	1.1	1.0
Accidental poisoning by—										
Drugs and medicines	(NA)	2,505	2,742	3,132	2,839	(NA)	1.2	1.3	1.5	1.3
Solid and liquid substances	2,110	1,174	1,274	1,562	1,322	1.1	.6	.6	.7	.6
Gases and vapors	1,526	1,620	1,518	1,577	1,569	.8	.8	.7	.7	.7
Complications due to medical procedures	1,494	3,581	3,021	3,184	3,009	.8	1.8	1.4	1.5	1.4
Inhalation and ingestion of objects	1,836	2,753	2,991	3,106	3,033	.9	1.4	1.4	1.5	1.4
Industrial type accidents	(NA)	5,968	5,594	5,495	5,203	(NA)	2.9	2.6	2.6	2.4
Electric current	1,071	1,140	1,157	1,224	1,041	.6	.6	.5	.6	.5
Explosive material	(³)	530	459	389	442	(³)	.3	.2	.2	.2
Hot substances, etc	420	275	217	209	210	.2	.1	.1	.1	.1
Cutting or piercing instrument	(³)	152	112	140	135	(³)	.1	.1	.1	.1
Other	(³)	3,871	3,649	3,533	3,375	(³)	1.9	1.7	1.7	1.6
All other accidents	10,921	5,591	5,272	5,149	4,964	5.6	2.8	2.5	2.4	2.3

NA Not available. [1] Per 100,000 resident population as of Apr. 1; other years, per 100,000 population estimated as of July 1. [2] Data not comparable with later years due to change in classification.
[3] Not available separately because of change in classification; included in "all other accidents."
Source: U.S. National Center for Health Statistics, *Vital Statistics of the United States*, annual.

No. 113. CATASTROPHIC ACCIDENTS AND DEATHS, BY TYPE OF ACCIDENT: 1941 TO 1977

[Catastrophic accidents defined as those in which five or more persons were killed. In some instances data may be incomplete]

TYPE OF ACCIDENT	ACCIDENTS					DEATHS				
	1941–1950	1951–1960	1961–1970	1971–1976	1977, prel.	1941–1950	1951–1960	1961–1970	1971–1976	1977, prel.
All types [1]	1,050	1,483	1,340	612	91	13,213	13,790	12,513	6,482	1,097
Motor vehicle	292	666	561	175	10	1,985	4,037	3,553	1,178	66
Percent of total	27.8	44.9	41.9	28.6	11.0	15.0	29.3	28.4	18.2	6.0
Bus	59	32	31	15	–	539	264	313	164	–
Collision with railroad train	12	5	5	4	–	139	35	90	28	–
Motor vehicle other than bus	233	634	530	160	10	1,446	3,773	3,240	1,014	66
Collision with railroad train	69	94	55	12	1	431	574	346	76	10
Air transportation [2]	88	112	176	110	24	1,371	2,133	2,868	1,473	251
Water transportation	89	82	45	15	3	974	719	416	245	32
Railroad [3]	45	24	6	3	1	861	369	52	60	11
Fire and explosion	330	420	420	229	38	4,529	3,099	3,090	1,633	443
Percent of total	31.4	28.3	31.3	37.4	41.8	34.3	22.5	24.7	25.2	40.4
Dwellings, apartments	166	312	322	153	25	1,034	1,917	1,969	911	147
Hotels, boarding houses, rooming houses	36	24	25	20	6	515	175	243	174	53
Homes for aged convalescent, hospitals, etc	16	17	12	16	–	281	254	200	151	–
Places of amusement	5	2	3	–	2	679	26	99	–	170
Other	107	65	58	40	5	2,020	727	579	397	73
Tornadoes, floods, hurricanes, etc	111	98	80	49	11	2,292	2,682	2,010	1,456	235
Mines and quarries	53	22	15	5	1	870	339	298	137	9
All other	42	59	37	26	3	331	412	226	300	50

– Represents zero. [1] Excludes military aviation accidents. [2] Accidents occurring within U.S. only.
[3] Collisions of railroad trains with motor vehicles are classified as motor vehicle accidents.
Source: Metropolitan Life Insurance Company, New York, N.Y., *Statistical Bulletin*, March 1977, and unpublished data.

No. 114. Marriages and Divorces: 1950 to 1977

[Prior to 1960, excludes Alaska and Hawaii. For definition of median, see p. xii. See also *Historical Statistics, Colonial Times to 1970*, series A 158-159 and B 214-220]

MARRIAGE AND DIVORCE	1950	1955	1960	1965	1970	1972	1973	1974	1975	1976	1977
MARRIAGES											
Total_____1,000__	1,667	1,531	1,523	1,800	2,159	2,282	2,284	2,230	2,153	2,155	[1] 2,176
Rate per 1,000 population____	11.1	9.3	8.5	9.3	10.6	11.0	10.9	10.5	10.1	10.0	[1] 10.1
Rate per 1,000 unmarried women:											
15-44 years old_____	166.4	161.1	148.0	144.3	140.2	141.3	137.3	128.4	118.5	113.4	(NA)
15 years old and over_____	90.2	80.9	73.5	75.0	76.5	77.9	76.0	72.0	66.9	65.2	(NA)
First marriage of bride [2]_____1,000__	(NA)	(NA)	664	1,043	1,252	1,364	1,331	1,271	1,191	1,163	(NA)
Rate per 1,000 single women:											
14 years old and over____	(NA)	(NA)	87.5	84.4	82.9	84.5	81.0	74.8	68.1	64.8	(NA)
18-19 years_____	(NA)	(NA)	208.4	166.9	151.4	151.9	144.8	133.5	115.0	105.1	(NA)
20-24 years_____	(NA)	(NA)	263.9	237.3	220.1	192.9	177.1	159.5	143.8	133.4	(NA)
25-44 years_____	(NA)	(NA)	(NA)	96.4	82.5	94.2	94.8	85.7	81.7	81.8	(NA)
45-64 years_____	(NA)	(NA)	(NA)	9.0	8.8	10.8	11.3	9.6	9.2	9.3	(NA)
Median age at first marriage: [2]											
Male_____years__	[3] 22.8	[3] 22.6	[3] 22.8	22.5	22.5	22.4	22.5	22.5	22.7	22.9	(NA)
Female_____years__	[3] 20.3	[3] 20.2	[3] 20.3	20.4	20.6	20.5	20.6	20.6	20.8	21.0	(NA)
Remarriages of bride [2] 1,000__	(NA)	(NA)	197	305	393	457	488	494	510	518	(NA)
Rate per 1,000 widowed and divorced:											
14 years old and over____	(NA)	(NA)	32.7	33.7	36.6	39.3	40.6	40.0	40.1	39.7	(NA)
14-24 years_____	(NA)	(NA)	407.7	471.0	317.6	398.0	391.2	332.1	319.9	324.4	(NA)
25-44 years_____	(NA)	(NA)	(NA)	139.6	142.3	155.3	154.3	147.3	144.5	133.2	(NA)
45-64 years_____	(NA)	(NA)	22.0	24.5	24.8	25.4	25.7	24.4	23.5	23.5	(NA)
Median age at remarriage: [2]											
Male_____years__	(NA)	(NA)	(NA)	39.6	37.5	36.5	36.3	35.7	35.5	35.1	(NA)
Female_____years__	(NA)	(NA)	(NA)	35.5	33.3	32.8	32.3	32.1	32.0	31.7	(NA)
Percent married, of population 18 yr. old and over: [3]											
Male_____	71.8	76.1	76.4	76.2	75.0	74.8	74.5	73.7	72.8	72.2	72.9
White_____	(NA)	(NA)	77.3	76.9	76.1	76.0	75.9	74.9	73.9	73.4	70.3
Black and other_____	(NA)	(NA)	68.4	70.2	65.4	64.8	62.8	63.1	63.5	62.0	60.6
Female_____	70.9	71.9	71.6	70.5	68.5	68.5	68.1	67.6	66.7	66.2	65.3
White_____	(NA)	(NA)	72.2	70.9	69.3	69.6	69.3	68.8	68.0	67.6	66.7
Black and other_____	(NA)	(NA)	66.3	67.6	62.6	60.2	58.5	58.9	57.3	56.2	55.4
DIVORCES [4]											
Total_____1,000__	385	377	393	479	708	845	915	977	1,036	1,083	[1] 1,097
Rate per 1,000 population____	2.6	2.3	2.2	2.5	3.5	4.1	4.4	4.6	4.9	5.0	[1] 5.1
Rate per 1,000 married women, 15 yr. old and over____	10.3	9.3	9.2	10.6	14.9	17.0	18.2	19.3	20.3	21.1	(NA)
Percent divorced, 18 yr. old and over: [3]											
Male_____	1.8	1.9	2.0	2.5	2.5	2.8	3.0	3.5	4.0	4.0	4.5
White_____	(NA)	(NA)	2.0	2.4	2.4	2.7	2.9	3.3	3.6	3.8	4.4
Black and other_____	(NA)	(NA)	2.2	3.4	3.4	3.2	4.0	4.8	4.6	5.5	5.0
Female_____	2.3	2.4	2.9	3.3	3.9	4.3	4.5	4.9	5.3	5.7	6.2
White_____	(NA)	(NA)	2.7	3.1	3.8	4.1	4.3	4.7	5.0	5.5	6.0
Black and other_____	(NA)	(NA)	4.8	4.5	4.8	5.9	6.1	6.3	7.1	7.4	8.2
Rate per 1,000 married, spouse present [3]_____	29	31	35	41	47	52	56	63	69	75	84
Male_____	24	26	28	34	35	38	42	49	54	58	66
Female_____	34	36	42	49	60	66	70	77	84	92	101
Median duration of marriage [5]_____years__	5.3	6.2	7.1	7.2	[6] 6.7	6.7	6.6	6.5	6.5	6.5	(NA)
Median age at divorce after 1st marriage: [2]											
Male_____years__	(NA)	(NA)	(NA)	(NA)	(NA)	(NA)	30.6	30.3	30.2	30.3	(NA)
Female_____years__	(NA)	(NA)	(NA)	(NA)	(NA)	(NA)	28.2	28.1	28.1	28.2	(NA)
Children involved per divorce [7]_____	(NA)	.92	1.18	1.32	1.22	1.20	1.17	1.12	1.08	1.03	(NA)

NA Not available. [1] Preliminary. [2] Number of States reporting: 1960, 33, including New York but excluding New York City; 1965, 38; 1970, 39; and, beginning 1972, 41. Beginning 1965, includes D.C.
[3] Source: U.S. Bureau of the Census, *Current Population Reports*, series P-20, No. 323, and earlier issues.
[4] Includes annulments. [5] Based on sample. [6] 1969 data.
[7] Beginning 1970, based on divorce-registration area frequencies instead of 16 States as for prior years.

Source: Except as noted, U.S. National Center for Health Statistics, *Vital Statistics of the United States*, annual.

No. 115. MARITAL HISTORY—PERCENT DISTRIBUTION, BY SEX, RACE, AND YEAR OF BIRTH: 1975

[As of June]

ITEM	Total [1]	White [1]	Black [1]	YEAR OF BIRTH				
				1945–1954	1935–1944	1925–1934	1915–1924	1900–1914
Men, total	100.0	100.0	100.0	100.0	100.0	100.0	100.0	100.0
Single in 1975	26.1	25.2	33.3	38.0	8.3	5.1	5.3	4.9
Men ever married in 1975:								
Once	62.5	63.7	53.2	57.8	78.3	79.6	77.5	73.9
Twice or more	11.3	11.1	13.5	4.2	13.4	15.3	17.2	21.2
Women, total	100.0	100.0	100.0	100.0	100.0	100.0	100.0	100.0
Single in 1975	20.6	19.5	29.0	25.8	5.8	4.2	4.5	6.3
Women ever married in 1975:								
Once	67.0	68.1	57.7	67.8	79.8	78.8	77.6	73.9
Twice or more	12.4	12.4	13.3	6.4	14.4	17.1	17.9	19.7
Ever divorced, total	13.9	13.6	16.1	10.8	19.5	20.2	17.0	14.3
After first marriage only	12.6	12.4	15.0	10.3	17.9	18.0	15.1	12.8
Ever widowed	11.1	10.9	13.1	.7	2.7	7.7	17.6	41.2

[1] Persons born between 1900 and 1959.
Source: U.S. Bureau of the Census, *Current Population Reports*, series P-20, No. 297.

No. 116. PERCENT OF EVER-MARRIED PERSONS 25–54 YEARS OLD WHO WERE DIVORCED OR SEPARATED, BY AGE, RACE, AND SEX: 1970 AND 1977

[As of March]

AGE (in years) AND SEX	EVER MARRIED (1,000)			PERCENT DIVORCED			PERCENT SEPARATED		
	Total [1]	White	Black	Total [1]	White	Black	Total [1]	White	Black
1970									
Male, total	31,304	28,189	2,817	3.3	3.1	5.5	1.8	1.1	9.4
25–34	10,402	9,318	975	3.0	2.9	3.9	1.6	1.2	5.1
35–44	10,518	9,464	953	3.0	2.6	5.8	2.1	1.1	11.6
45–54	10,384	9,407	889	3.9	3.7	6.7	1.9	1.0	11.7
Female, total	34,299	30,401	3,505	5.2	5.0	7.7	3.3	1.8	16.3
25–34	11,590	10,220	1,236	5.0	4.7	6.6	3.8	2.1	17.6
35–44	11,264	9,917	1,188	5.6	5.3	8.8	3.1	1.6	16.3
45–54	11,445	10,264	1,081	5.1	4.9	7.6	3.1	1.9	14.9
1977									
Male, total	33,768	30,243	2,939	6.5	6.5	8.2	2.6	1.9	10.3
25–34	12,740	11,453	1,058	6.9	7.0	6.3	3.1	2.4	11.2
35–44	10,398	9,243	954	6.8	6.5	10.7	2.3	1.6	8.9
45–54	10,630	9,547	927	5.9	5.9	7.9	2.2	1.5	10.7
Female, total	37,314	32,731	3,862	9.4	8.8	14.9	4.3	2.7	18.2
25–34	14,461	12,659	1,482	9.5	9.0	13.6	5.0	3.4	19.8
35–44	11,318	9,854	1,250	10.0	9.2	17.0	4.4	2.6	19.2
45–54	11,535	10,218	1,130	8.7	8.1	14.1	3.2	1.9	15.0

[1] Includes races not shown separately.
Source: U.S. Bureau of the Census, *Current Population Reports*, series P-20, No. 323.

No. 117. DIVORCES AND ANNULMENTS—MEDIAN DURATION OF MARRIAGE FOR SELECTED STATES: 1960 TO 1975

[In years. By place of occurrence. Reporting States only. For definition of median, see p. xii]

STATE	1960	1965	1970	1973	1974	1975	STATE	1960	1965	1970	1973	1974	1975
Total	7.1	7.2	6.7	6.6	6.5	6.5	Mont	5.1	5.8	5.1	4.8	4.8	4.7
Ala	7.3	6.6	5.3	5.3	5.0	4.7	Nebr	6.3	6.3	6.0	5.7	5.9	5.9
Alaska	6.2	6.0	5.4	5.3	5.1	5.1	N.Y	(NA)	(NA)	9.3	8.7	8.0	8.0
Calif	(NA)	(NA)	6.8	6.9	6.7	6.8	Ohio	(NA)	7.8	6.3	6.2	6.3	6.0
Conn	(NA)	(NA)	8.6	8.4	8.1	8.2	Oreg	5.9	5.9	5.9	5.8	5.8	5.8
Ga	6.3	6.1	5.4	5.2	5.2	5.2	Pa	9.2	8.9	8.1	7.6	7.7	7.7
Hawaii	6.3	5.8	7.2	5.6	5.3	5.4	R.I	(NA)	9.1	9.2	8.4	8.0	7.8
Idaho	4.8	5.1	4.6	4.5	4.7	4.8	S.C	(NA)	(NA)	(NA)	6.9	6.8	6.6
							S. Dak	6.3	6.3	5.9	5.9	5.6	5.6
Ill	(NA)	(NA)	6.6	6.5	6.1	6.1	Tenn	6.3	6.1	5.6	5.2	5.2	5.3
Iowa	5.7	5.9	5.6	5.6	5.6	5.5							
Kans	5.8	5.9	5.1	5.2	5.2	5.2	Utah	4.7	5.2	5.3	4.8	4.9	4.9
Ky	(NA)	(NA)	5.7	5.5	5.5	5.9	Vt	(NA)	(NA)	8.3	7.9	7.9	7.5
Md	9.0	9.2	8.8	9.0	8.5	8.3	Va	8.3	9.0	7.7	7.9	7.8	7.7
Mich	(NA)	7.9	7.0	6.6	6.7	6.8	Wis	8.2	8.2	7.9	7.4	7.2	7.0
Mo	(NA)	5.8	5.4	5.4	5.4	5.6	Wyo	5.4	5.5	4.6	4.5	4.8	4.7

NA Not available.
Source: U.S. National Center for Health Statistics, *Vital Statistics of the United States*, annual.

No. 118. Marriages—Number and Rate, by States: 1965 to 1976

[By place of occurrence]

STATE	NUMBER (1,000)						RATE PER 1,000 POPULATION [1]					
	1965	1970	1973	1974	1975	1976	1965	1970	1973	1974	1975	1976
U.S.	1,800.2	2,159.0	2,284.1	2,229.7	2,152.7	2154.8	9.3	10.6	10.9	10.5	10.1	10.0
N.E.	86.5	105.4	106.4	101.4	96.8	94.5	7.8	8.9	8.8	8.3	7.9	7.7
Maine	8.7	11.0	11.9	11.5	11.2	11.3	8.8	11.0	11.6	11.0	10.6	10.6
N.H.	9.0	10.0	9.6	9.2	8.8	8.4	13.4	13.6	12.1	11.4	10.8	10.2
Vt	3.6	4.5	5.1	4.7	4.6	4.3	9.0	10.2	10.9	9.9	9.7	9.0
Mass	37.9	47.4	46.6	44.2	42.1	40.9	7.1	8.3	8.0	7.6	7.2	7.0
R.I.	6.3	7.5	7.7	7.3	6.7	6.9	7.1	7.9	7.9	7.7	7.2	7.5
Conn	21.0	25.0	25.5	24.5	23.4	22.6	7.4	8.2	8.3	7.9	7.6	7.3
M.A.	260.0	312.4	316.5	301.1	287.4	277.5	7.1	8.4	8.4	8.1	7.7	7.4
N.Y.	133.5	161.2	155.7	148.0	142.8	136.7	7.4	8.9	8.5	8.2	7.9	7.6
N.J.	46.3	56.6	59.7	56.4	53.0	52.3	6.8	7.9	8.1	7.7	7.2	7.1
Pa	80.2	94.5	101.1	96.7	91.7	88.6	6.9	8.0	8.5	8.2	7.8	7.5
E.N.C.	339.3	384.8	412.3	405.7	387.4	384.7	8.9	9.6	10.1	9.9	9.5	9.4
Ohio	79.0	90.1	99.5	102.5	101.1	97.9	7.7	8.5	9.3	9.5	9.4	9.2
Ind	49.7	55.2	58.4	60.5	56.1	56.4	10.2	10.6	11.0	11.4	10.6	10.6
Ill	101.0	115.5	119.8	116.4	111.5	111.3	9.5	10.4	10.7	10.5	10.0	9.9
Mich	81.2	89.7	94.5	88.0	82.9	83.2	9.8	10.1	10.4	9.7	9.0	9.1
Wis	28.4	34.4	40.0	38.2	35.9	36.0	6.9	7.8	8.8	8.4	7.8	7.8
W.N.C.	131.0	160.5	169.2	168.4	161.9	156.8	8.3	9.8	10.1	10.1	9.7	9.3
Minn	26.5	31.3	33.0	33.5	32.3	33.2	7.4	8.2	8.5	8.6	8.2	8.4
Iowa	20.2	24.6	27.5	27.2	25.6	25.6	7.3	8.7	9.5	9.5	8.9	8.9
Mo	40.2	50.1	52.0	51.4	50.1	44.8	8.9	10.7	10.9	10.8	10.5	9.4
N. Dak	4.9	5.3	5.9	5.9	6.0	5.6	7.6	8.6	9.2	9.3	9.4	8.8
S. Dak	8.3	11.0	12.3	11.9	11.1	10.8	12.1	16.6	17.9	17.5	16.2	15.7
Nebr	12.1	15.7	14.0	13.9	13.1	13.4	8.3	10.6	9.1	9.0	8.5	8.6
Kans	18.8	22.4	24.6	24.5	23.8	23.4	8.4	10.0	10.8	10.8	10.5	10.1
S.A.	311.7	371.0	398.5	385.5	366.6	366.1	10.8	12.1	12.3	11.6	10.9	10.8
Del	3.1	4.3	4.3	4.1	3.9	3.9	6.2	7.8	7.5	7.2	6.8	6.8
Md	47.2	59.0	40.2	47.0	44.8	44.9	13.4	13.3	11.8	11.5	10.9	10.8
D.C.	9.2	7.3	5.7	5.3	4.9	4.7	11.4	9.6	7.6	7.3	6.9	6.7
Va	46.0	52.0	58.4	56.6	54.7	56.5	10.4	11.2	12.1	11.5	11.0	11.2
W. Va	14.2	15.9	18.2	17.4	17.0	17.1	7.8	9.1	10.1	9.7	9.5	9.4
N.C.	40.7	48.3	47.0	45.0	42.3	42.5	8.2	9.5	8.9	8.4	7.8	7.8
S.C.	46.3	57.9	56.9	53.0	50.2	50.0	18.2	22.3	20.9	19.0	17.8	17.6
Ga	55.5	63.9	70.4	66.7	63.2	60.2	12.6	13.9	14.7	13.7	12.8	12.1
Fla	49.4	69.2	89.6	90.3	85.4	86.2	8.5	10.2	11.7	11.2	10.2	10.2
E.S.C.	132.1	154.9	167.2	161.8	155.2	162.3	10.3	12.1	12.6	12.1	11.5	11.9
Ky	[2]28.3	36.3	34.4	32.8	32.1	34.8	[2]8.9	11.3	10.3	9.8	9.4	10.2
Tenn	40.1	45.4	56.3	54.6	51.5	53.4	10.4	11.6	13.6	13.2	12.3	12.7
Ala	40.4	47.0	48.0	46.8	45.3	47.6	11.6	13.6	13.6	13.1	12.5	13.0
Miss	23.3	26.3	28.5	27.6	26.3	26.5	10.1	11.9	12.5	11.9	11.2	11.2
W.S.C.	192.2	237.2	258.2	[3]256.1	254.9	258.8	10.4	12.3	12.7	[3]12.4	12.2	12.2
Ark	19.2	23.3	25.2	[3]24.7	24.3	22.6	9.9	12.1	12.4	[3]12.0	11.5	10.7
La	29.0	35.4	39.5	38.2	37.3	39.1	8.1	9.7	10.5	10.1	9.8	10.2
Okla	32.6	39.0	41.4	40.2	40.1	40.7	13.3	15.2	15.5	14.8	14.8	14.7
Tex	111.5	139.5	152.2	153.0	153.2	156.5	10.5	12.5	12.9	12.7	12.5	12.5
Mt	[4]157.9	187.5	211.7	213.7	212.0	208.0	[4]20.5	22.6	23.1	22.7	22.0	21.2
Mont	4.7	6.9	7.8	7.7	7.3	7.3	6.7	10.0	10.8	10.5	9.8	9.7
Idaho	15.9	10.9	12.2	12.5	12.7	13.1	22.9	15.3	15.9	15.6	15.5	15.8
Wyo	3.6	4.5	5.5	6.0	5.6	5.8	10.9	13.5	15.6	16.8	15.1	14.8
Colo	[3]18.7	25.0	28.0	26.0	27.6	27.1	[2]9.6	11.3	11.5	10.4	10.9	10.5
N. Mex	[2,4]13.2	12.4	15.2	15.9	15.8	12.4	[2,4]13.0	12.2	13.7	14.2	13.8	10.6
Ariz	12.1	18.5	26.2	27.0	26.6	28.3	7.7	10.4	12.7	12.6	11.9	12.5
Utah	8.7	11.7	14.8	15.2	14.9	14.3	8.8	11.0	12.8	12.9	12.4	11.6
Nev	[2]81.0	97.6	102.1	103.3	101.6	99.7	[2]186.7	199.7	186.3	180.3	171.6	163.5
Pac	189.3	245.0	244.0	236.1	230.3	225.5	7.8	9.2	8.9	8.5	8.2	7.8
Wash	[2]31.5	41.3	41.4	41.6	41.8	40.7	[2]10.6	12.1	12.1	12.0	11.8	11.3
Oreg	13.3	17.3	19.7	20.0	19.3	19.5	6.8	8.3	8.8	8.8	8.4	8.4
Calif	136.1	172.4	169.3	160.9	154.8	150.7	7.4	8.6	8.2	7.7	7.3	7.0
Alaska	2.4	3.4	3.9	3.9	4.7	4.9	9.0	11.2	11.7	11.7	13.4	12.8
Hawaii	6.1	10.6	9.8	9.6	9.7	9.8	8.6	13.8	11.8	11.4	11.2	11.0

[1] Based on total population residing in area; population enumerated as of Apr. 1 for 1970, estimated as of July 1 for all other years.   [2] Marriage licenses.   [3] Incomplete.   [4] Estimated.

Source: U.S. National Center for Health Statistics, *Vital Statistics of the United States*, annual, and *Monthly Vital Statistics Report*.

No. 119. Divorces—Number and Rate, by States: 1965 to 1976

[By place of occurrence. Includes reported annulments]

STATE	NUMBER (1,000)						RATE PER 1,000 POPULATION [1]					
	1965	1970	1973	1974	1975	1976	1965	1970	1973	1974	1975	1976
U.S. [2]	479.0	708.0	915.0	977.0	1,036.0	1,083.0	2.5	3.5	4.4	4.6	4.9	5.0
N.E.	17.5	25.8	35.0	[3] 40.0	43.2	43.7	1.6	2.2	2.9	[3] 3.3	3.5	3.6
Maine	2.5	3.9	4.6	4.9	5.5	5.5	2.6	3.9	4.4	4.7	5.2	5.2
N.H.	1.6	2.4	3.9	4.1	4.2	4.3	2.3	3.3	4.9	5.0	5.2	5.3
Vt	.6	1.0	1.6	[3] 1.6	1.9	1.9	1.5	2.3	3.4	[3] 3.5	4.1	4.0
Mass	7.8	11.0	14.5	16.1	16.6	17.0	1.5	1.9	2.5	2.8	2.8	2.9
R.I.	1.2	1.7	2.4	2.5	2.7	3.3	1.3	1.8	2.5	2.7	2.9	3.5
Conn	3.7	5.8	8.1	10.8	12.2	11.7	1.3	1.9	2.6	3.5	4.0	3.8
M.A.	30.4	59.9	100.6	106.5	110.0	112.6	.8	1.6	2.7	2.9	3.0	3.0
N.Y.	8.2	26.4	47.9	54.0	55.6	54.2	.5	1.5	2.6	3.0	3.1	3.0
N.J.	5.6	10.8	21.8	19.9	19.4	21.8	.8	1.5	3.0	2.7	2.7	3.0
Pa	16.6	22.6	31.0	32.6	35.0	36.5	1.4	1.9	2.6	2.8	3.0	3.1
E.N.C.	[4] 94.5	129.8	[3] 166.5	[3] 185.7	[3] 186.2	[3] 199.9	[4] 2.5	3.2	(S)	[3] 4.5	(S)	[3] 4.9
Ohio	25.8	39.3	48.0	49.2	52.6	59.3	2.5	3.7	4.5	4.6	4.9	5.5
Ind	[4] 18.5	15.2	[3] 22.3	[3] 33.9	[3] 28.8	[3] 31.2	[4] 3.8	2.9	(S)	[3] 6.4	(S)	[3] 5.9
Ill	24.7	36.5	45.2	48.4	51.0	51.8	2.3	3.3	4.0	4.3	4.6	4.6
Mich	20.3	30.0	39.4	41.9	40.8	43.1	2.4	3.4	4.4	4.6	4.5	4.7
Wis	5.2	8.9	11.6	12.4	13.1	14.6	1.3	2.0	2.5	2.7	2.8	3.2
W.N.C.	33.4	48.2	60.7	64.1	70.1	73.0	2.1	3.0	3.6	3.8	4.2	4.3
Minn	4.9	8.3	11.2	12.2	13.2	[4] 13.8	1.4	2.2	2.9	3.1	3.4	[4] 3.5
Iowa	5.3	7.2	9.2	9.5	10.3	10.8	1.9	2.5	3.2	3.3	3.6	3.8
Mo	13.2	17.9	21.8	22.1	24.5	25.4	2.9	3.8	4.6	4.6	5.1	5.3
N. Dak	.7	1.0	1.4	1.6	1.7	1.9	1.1	1.6	2.2	2.5	2.7	2.9
S. Dak	1.0	1.4	1.8	2.0	2.2	2.4	1.5	2.0	2.6	3.0	3.3	3.4
Nebr	2.5	3.7	4.9	5.2	5.6	5.9	1.7	2.5	3.2	3.4	3.6	3.8
Kans	5.8	8.8	10.5	11.5	12.6	12.8	2.6	3.9	4.6	5.1	5.5	5.6
S.A.	[3] 73.3	106.1	150.2	159.9	174.8	182.0	[3] 2.6	3.5	4.6	4.8	5.2	5.4
Del	.7	1.7	2.2	2.4	2.8	3.2	1.5	3.2	3.8	4.1	4.8	5.6
Md	7.0	9.3	14.1	15.1	15.4	16.1	2.0	2.4	3.5	3.7	3.8	3.9
D.C	1.3	2.3	3.0	3.2	3.8	3.1	1.7	3.0	4.0	4.4	5.3	4.4
Va	8.9	11.9	16.1	16.7	19.5	21.4	2.0	2.6	3.3	3.4	3.9	4.2
W. Va	3.9	5.6	7.1	7.2	8.6	8.9	2.1	3.2	3.9	4.0	4.8	4.9
N.C	11.2	13.7	18.5	20.0	22.1	24.3	2.3	2.7	3.5	3.7	4.1	4.4
S.C	3.0	5.8	8.3	8.8	9.7	10.6	1.2	2.3	3.0	3.2	3.4	3.7
Ga	[3] 12.0	18.6	25.1	26.9	29.5	31.2	[3] 2.7	4.1	5.2	5.5	6.0	6.3
Fla	25.3	37.2	56.0	59.6	63.4	63.2	4.4	5.5	7.3	7.4	7.6	7.5
E.S.C.	36.2	50.6	66.3	70.5	74.4	79.3	2.8	4.0	5.0	5.3	5.5	5.8
Ky	8.3	10.7	13.0	13.8	14.5	16.0	2.6	3.3	3.9	4.1	4.3	4.7
Tenn	11.1	16.6	22.1	23.7	24.6	27.0	2.9	4.2	5.3	5.7	5.9	6.4
Ala	11.0	15.1	20.4	21.1	23.0	24.1	3.2	4.4	5.8	5.9	6.4	6.6
Miss	5.7	8.2	10.8	11.9	12.3	12.2	2.5	3.7	4.7	5.1	5.2	5.2
W.S.C.	[3] 64.4	82.7	[3] 106.6	[3] 115.9	[3] 122.8	[3] 132.3	(S)	4.3	(S)	(S)	(S)	[3] 6.2
Ark	6.6	9.3	[3] 15.2	[3] 15.8	[3] 16.7	[3] 18.4	3.4	4.8	[3] 7.5	[3] 7.7	[3] 7.9	[3] 8.7
La	[3] 4.6	5.1	[3] 7.3	[3] 7.8	[3] 8.7	[3] 12.6	(S)	1.4	(S)	(S)	(S)	[3] 3.3
Okla	11.9	16.8	19.9	22.5	20.6	21.5	4.8	6.6	7.5	8.3	7.6	7.8
Tex	41.3	51.5	64.2	69.8	76.7	79.9	3.9	4.6	5.4	5.8	6.3	6.4
Mt	[3][4] 38.1	49.0	[3] 59.4	66.9	70.7	75.5	[3][4] 5.0	5.9	(S)	7.1	7.3	7.7
Mont	2.0	3.0	3.8	3.9	4.3	4.9	2.8	4.4	5.2	5.4	5.7	6.4
Idaho	2.9	3.6	4.3	4.8	5.2	5.7	4.1	5.1	5.6	6.0	6.3	6.9
Wyo	1.4	1.8	2.3	2.5	2.8	2.9	4.3	5.4	6.4	7.0	7.6	7.3
Colo	[4] 6.7	10.4	14.4	15.1	15.7	17.5	[4] 3.4	4.7	5.9	6.0	6.2	6.8
N. Mex	[3] 3.7	4.4	[3] 5.4	7.9	8.4	9.1	[3] 3.6	4.3	(S)	7.0	7.3	7.8
Ariz	8.6	12.7	14.0	16.9	17.6	19.0	5.4	7.2	6.8	7.9	7.9	8.4
Utah	2.9	3.9	5.3	5.7	6.1	6.2	2.9	3.7	4.6	4.8	5.1	5.0
Nev	10.0	9.1	10.0	10.0	10.5	10.3	23.0	18.7	18.2	17.5	17.8	16.9
Pac	89.9	144.7	157.7	165.7	177.0	184.9	3.7	5.5	5.8	6.0	6.3	6.4
Wash	11.5	17.9	21.6	23.9	25.8	27.1	3.9	5.2	6.3	6.9	7.3	7.5
Oreg	6.2	9.6	12.4	13.5	15.6	16.1	3.2	4.6	5.6	6.0	6.8	6.9
Calif	69.9	112.9	117.5	121.7	128.5	133.8	3.8	5.7	5.7	5.8	6.1	6.2
Alaska	1.1	1.7	2.1	2.5	2.9	3.2	4.2	5.6	6.2	7.3	8.1	8.4
Hawaii	1.1	2.6	4.2	4.1	4.3	4.7	1.6	3.4	5.0	4.9	4.9	5.3

S   Does not meet publication standards because reporting less than 90 percent complete.
[1] Based on total population residing in area; population enumerated as of Apr. 1 for 1970, estimated as of July 1 for all other years.   [2] U.S. total and some States are estimated; therefore, State data do not add to total.
[3] Incomplete.   [4] Estimated.

Source: U.S. National Center for Health Statistics, *Vital Statistics of the United States*, annual, and *Monthly Vital Statistics Report*.

Section 3
Immigration and Naturalization

This section presents statistics related to immigration, naturalization, and alien registration. The principal source of these data is the *Annual Report of the Immigration and Naturalization Service*. Immigration statistics are prepared from entry visas and change of immigration status forms. Statistics for naturalization are compiled from periodic reports by Federal courts and specially designated State courts conducting such proceedings. Alien registration data are compiled from alien address report cards.

The continuous recording of U.S. immigration statistics began in 1819 with the collection of data on immigrants arriving in ports. Under the Act of 1819, the captain or master of a vessel arriving from abroad was required to deliver to the local officials of the U.S. collector of customs a list containing information such as age and sex of all passengers taken on board. Copies of these lists were transmitted to the U.S. Secretary of State, who reported the information periodically to Congress. Subsequently, the Act of 1855 prescribed quarterly reports to the Secretary of State and annual reports to Congress. Later acts were expanded to include gathering data on immigrants arriving at land borders. Beginning in 1906, those arriving were divided into two groups (immigrants and nonimmigrants) depending on how long they intended to remain in the United States (see below).

Immigration statistics were compiled by the Department of State for 1820–1870; by the Treasury Department for 1867–1895; and, since 1892, by a separate Office or Bureau of Immigration, presently a part of the Immigration and Naturalization Service (INS), a unit of the Department of Justice. For 1892–1932, the data appeared in annual reports of the Bureau of Immigration; for 1933–1940, in the *Annual Report of the Secretary of Labor;* for 1941, in the *Annual Report of the Attorney General;* and, since then, in the *Annual Report of the Immigration and Naturalization Service.*

Immigrants.—Immigrants are nonresident aliens admitted to the United States for permanent residence (one year or longer).

Nonimmigrants.—Nonimmigrants are nonresident aliens admitted to the United States for a temporary period. Included in this group are visitors for business and pleasure, students and their spouses and children, foreign and government officials, exchange visitors and their spouses and children, international representatives, treaty traders and investors, representatives of foreign information media, fiances(ees) of U.S. citizens and their children, officials of the North Atlantic Treaty Organization (NATO), aliens in transit, and, for statistical purposes, permanent resident aliens returning after short trips abroad. Excluded are border crossers, crewmen, and insular travelers. Certain temporary admissions such as of persons in possession of border-crossing identification cards are not included in the nonimmigrant totals.

Quota and nonquota immigrants.—Between May 1921, and July 1968, immigrants were required by Federal law to be classified as quota and nonquota immigrants. Quota immigrants were those subject to congressionally-mandated quotas for Eastern Hemisphere countries and their dependencies. Nonquota immigrants included natives of the Western Hemisphere and their spouses and children, immediate relatives of U.S. citizens, and certain groups of special immigrants.

Prior to 1921, Federal law prohibited from entry into the United States only particular categories of persons (convicts, the mentally defective and insane, children under age 16 unaccompanied by parents, persons likely to become public welfare dependents, etc.), usually without respect to country of origin. (The Chinese exclusion law of 1882 which was repealed in 1943 and the automatic exclusion sections of the 1917 Act which barred entry to certain peoples from the geographic regions of Asia and Pacific Islands are

83

important exceptions.) In 1921, Congress enacted the first numerical ceiling on immigration (357,000 per year) into the United States, although it applied only to Eastern Hemisphere countries and their dependencies. The 1921 Act also established a quota system whereby the total number of immigrants from any individual country was not to exceed 3 percent of that country's U.S. residents in 1910.

For 1925–1929, the congressionally-mandated annual quota of 164,667 was based on 2 percent of foreign-born U.S. residents as determined by the 1890 census. The "national origins" formula which determined quotas from 1929 until 1965, provided that the annual quota equal one-sixth of one percent of the number of White inhabitants in the continental United States in 1920, less Western Hemisphere immigrants and their descendants. The annual quota for each nationality was then determined by the same ratio to 150,000 as the number of inhabitants of each nationality living in the continental United States in 1920 to the total inhabitants, although a minimum quota for any nationality was 100.

The Act of Oct. 1965 abolished the quota system and in its place set up an annual numerical limitation of 170,000 immigrants from the Eastern Hemisphere, with no more than 20,000 immigrants to come from any one country. In July 1968, the new law and the system of numerical limitations went fully into effect. At that time a numerical limitation of 120,000 per year was imposed on Western Hemisphere immigration, which had previously been unrestricted. The 1965 Act thereby abolished the "national origins" system and gave persons from every country within each hemisphere an equal chance to immigrate to the United States. Since 1968, immigrants have been classified as those subject to numerical limitations of the Eastern Hemisphere and to numerical limitations of the Western Hemisphere, and those exempt from numerical limitations (see table 122). Those exempt include immediate relatives (parents, spouses, and children) of U.S. citizens and various classes of special immigrants.

Displaced persons and refugees.—The Displaced Persons Act of 1948 was the first of a number of special acts passed to provide for the admission of refugees from Communist-dominated countries, victims of natural calamities, and orphan children without regard to quotas or the numerical ceilings specified above.

Status of Cubans.—Effective November 2, 1966, Cubans admitted or paroled (i.e. admitted without an immigration visa) into the United States after January 1, 1959, and present in the United States for at least 2 years may obtain permanent resident status. The Act was last amended in 1976; for details, see Public Law 94–571, signed on October 20, 1976.

Alien registration.—The Immigration and Nationality Act of 1952 provides that each alien who is required to be registered under the Alien Registration Act of 1940, and who is in the United States on January 1, must report his current address each year to the U.S. Attorney General during the month of January.

Naturalization.—Prior to 1907 each Federal court and each specially designated State court which conducted naturalization proceedings kept records of naturalizations but no national data were compiled. The Act of June 29, 1906, provided for periodic returns by all courts conducting naturalization proceedings, and for the filing with a central Federal agency of a duplicate copy of each declaration of intention and petition for naturalization filed, and of each certificate of naturalization issued.

Most aliens acquire U.S. citizenship under the general provisions of the Immigration and Nationality Act of 1952, as amended. As specified by that Act, the requirements which must be met by a prospective citizen relate to residency, language proficiency, moral character, loyalty to the United States, attachment to the principles of the Constitution, etc. Spouses and children of U.S. citizens can be naturalized under less stringent conditions. In certain cases, an administrative, judicial, legislative, or executive waiver of the requirements may be obtained. Naturalization statistics are also maintained by INS.

Historical statistics.—Tabular headnotes provide cross-references, where applicable, to *Historical Statistics of the United States, Colonial Times to 1970.* See Appendix I.

Figure 3.1

Immigrants from Leading Countries, by Country of Birth: 1975, 1976, and 1977

(See table 124)

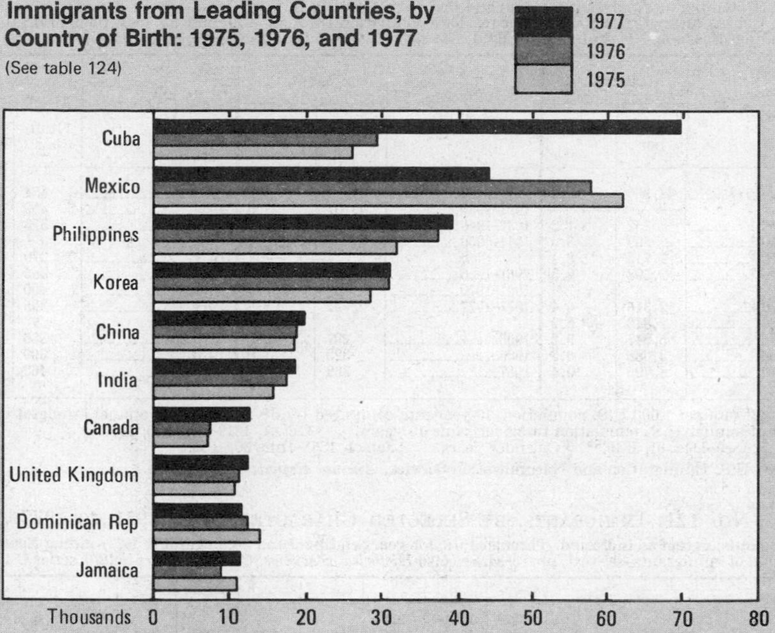

1977
1976
1975

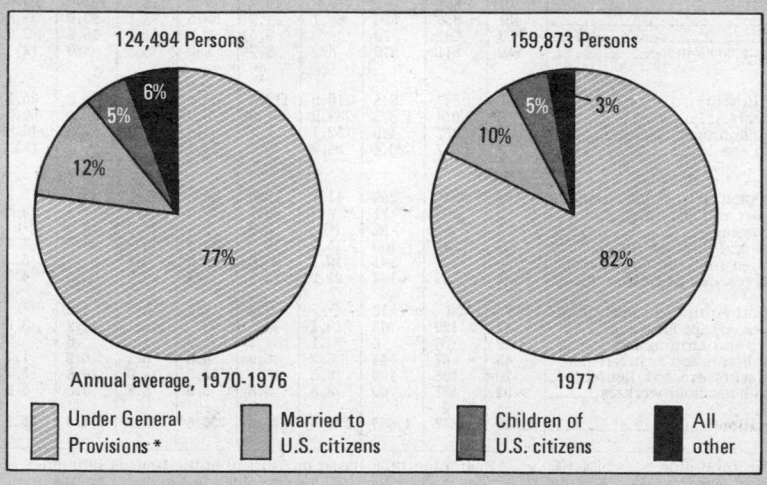

| | Thousands 0 | 10 | 20 | 30 | 40 | 50 | 60 | 70 | 80 |

Cuba
Mexico
Philippines
Korea
China
India
Canada
United Kingdom
Dominican Rep
Jamaica

Source: Chart prepared by U.S. Bureau of the Census. Data from U.S. Immigration and Naturalization Service.

Figure 3.2

Aliens Naturalized: 1970 to 1977

(See table 138)

124,494 Persons

6%
5%
12%
77%

159,873 Persons

5%
3%
10%
82%

Annual average, 1970-1976

1977

Under General Provisions *

Married to U.S. citizens

Children of U.S. citizens

All other

* See text for explanation

Source: Chart prepared by U.S. Bureau of the Census. Data from U.S. Immigration and Naturalization Service.

No. 120. Immigration: 1820 to 1977

[In thousands, except rate. Through 1976, for years ending June 30, except as noted; beginning 1977, ending Sept. 30 For definition of immigrants, see text, pp. 83–84. For 1820–1867, alien passengers arriving; 1868–1891 and 1895–1897, immigrants arriving; 1892–1894 and 1898 to the present, immigrants admitted. Rates based on Bureau of the Census estimates as of July 1 for resident population through 1929, and for total population thereafter (excluding Alaska and Hawaii prior to 1959). See also *Historical Statistics, Colonial Times to 1970*, series C 89]

PERIOD	TOTAL		PERIOD OR YEAR	TOTAL		YEAR	TOTAL	
	Number	Rate [1]		Number	Rate [1]		Number	Rate [1]
1820–1977	47,960	3.5	1911–1920	5,736	5.7	1968	454	2.3
			1921–1930	4,107	3.5	1969	359	1.8
1820–1830 [2]	152	1.2	1931–1940	528	.4	1970	373	1.8
1831–1840 [3]	599	3.9	1941–1950	1,035	.7			
1841–1850 [4]	1,713	8.4				1971	370	1.8
1851–1860 [4]	2,598	9.3	1951–1960	2,515	1.5	1972	385	1.8
			1961–1970	3,322	1.7	1973	400	1.9
1861–1870 [5]	2,315	6.4	1971–1977	2,797	1.9	1974	395	1.9
1871–1980	2,812	6.2						
1881–1890	5,247	9.2	1965	297	1.5	1975	386	1.8
1891–1900	3,688	5.3	1966	323	1.6	1976	399	1.9
1901–1910	8,795	10.4	1967	362	1.8	1977	462	2.1

[1] Annual rate per 1,000 U.S. population. 10-year rate computed by dividing sum of annual immigration totals by sum of annual U.S. population totals for same 10 years.   [2] Oct. 1, 1819–Sept. 30, 1830. [3] Oct. 1, 1830–Dec. 31, 1840.   [4] Calendar years.   [5] Jan. 1, 1861–June 30, 1870.

Source: U.S. Immigration and Naturalization Service, *Annual Report*.

No. 121. Immigrants, by Selected Characteristics: 1951 to 1977

[In thousands, except as indicated. Through 1976, for years ending June 30; beginning 1977, ending Sept. 30. For definition of immigrants, see text, pp. 83–84. See also *Historical Statistics, Colonial Times to 1970*, series C 120–142]

CHARACTERISTIC	1951–1960, total	1961–1970, total	1971–1977, total	1973	1974	1975	1976	1977	PERCENT	
									1961–1970	1971–1977
Total	2,515	3,322	2,797	400.1	394.9	386.2	398.6	462.3	100.0	100.0
Male	[1] 859	1,488	1,305	186.3	184.5	180.7	184.8	216.4	44.8	46.7
Married	368	651	647	92.8	89.9	88.7	92.8	112.2	19.6	23.1
Single	467	816	643	91.7	92.7	90.1	89.4	100.6	24.6	23.0
Other	24	21	16	1.8	1.9	1.9	2.6	3.6	.6	.6
Female	[1] 1,014	1,834	1,492	213.7	210.3	205.5	213.8	245.9	55.2	53.3
Married	501	883	825	119.0	116.9	112.2	118.8	135.6	26.6	29.4
Single	451	856	596	85.7	84.9	83.5	83.1	93.9	25.8	21.3
Other	63	95	72	9.0	8.5	9.8	11.9	16.4	2.9	2.6
Males per 1,000 females	850	811	876	872	877	880	865	880	(X)	(X)
Age:										
Under 16 years	576	847	848	110.8	110.8	105.4	102.2	108.2	25.5	23.4
16–44 years	1,596	2,018	1,873	237.2	234.0	226.0	234.0	266.9	60.7	57.7
45 years and over	343	457	449	52.1	50.1	54.8	62.3	87.2	13.8	18.9
Median age yr	[1] 24.8	25.7	26.4	24.0	23.7	24.4	24.9	26.5	(X)	(X)
Occupation: [2]										
Professional, tech., and kindred	184	337	299	41.1	35.5	38.5	41.1	45.0	10.1	10.7
Managers and administrators [3]	53	66	71	9.2	9.2	10.0	11.6	17.4	2.0	2.5
Sales workers	[4]	[4]	21	[4]	3.0	3.4	3.9	5.6	[4]	.8
Clerical and kindred workers	[4] 197	[4] 245	103	[4] 15.9	13.2	14.1	14.9	20.5	[4] 7.4	3.7
Craftsmen and kindred workers	196	207	141	19.1	20.0	20.6	18.8	21.3	6.2	5.0
Operatives, except transport	[5] 168	[5] 162	144	[5] 21.2	15.5	18.4	20.9	30.5	[5] 4.9	5.1
Transport equipment operatives	[5]	[5]	13	[5]	2.5	2.9	3.2	4.0	[5]	.5
Laborers, except farm	133	129	103	18.4	18.3	13.0	12.1	12.2	3.9	3.7
Farmers and farm managers	49	26	5	.1	.2	.9	1.4	.6	.7	.2
Farm laborers and farm foremen	43	57	44	6.2	6.9	6.3	6.2	6.9	1.7	1.6
Service wkrs. exc. pvt. household	70	108	109	16.5	18.1	15.5	14.0	16.8	3.3	3.9
Private household workers	94	127	60	8.8	8.8	5.9	6.8	8.5	3.8	2.1
No occupation [6]	1,329	1,857	1,685	243.6	243.6	236.6	243.9	273.0	55.9	60.2

X Not applicable.   [1] 1954–1960.   [2] Beginning 1974, based on Bureau of the Census 1970 index of occupations; prior years based on 1950 and 1960 indexes. The occupations contained in the major groups are, therefore, not necessarily identical to the groupings of prior years.   [3] Except farm.   [4] Sales workers included in "Clerical and kindred workers."   [5] Transport equipment operatives included in "Operatives, except transport."   [6] Includes dependent women and children, and other aliens without occupation or occupation not reported.

Source: U.S. Immigration and Naturalization Service, *Annual Report*, and releases.

No. 122. IMMIGRANTS ADMITTED, BY CLASSES: 1940 TO 1977

[For years ending **June 30** except, beginning **1977**, ending **September 30**. For definition of immigrants, see text, pp. 83–84. Excludes border crossers, crewmen, and aliens admitted on documentary waivers. See also *Historical Statistics, Colonial Times to 1970*, series C 143–157]

CLASS OF ADMISSION	1940	1950	1955	1960	1965	1967	1968	1969
Annual quota	153,774	154,206	154,657	154,887	158,561	158,261	(X)	(X)
Immigrants admitted	70,756	249,187	237,790	265,398	296,697	361,972	454,448	358,579
Natives of Eastern Hemisphere	51,997	197,460	82,232	101,373	99,381	152,079	156,212	157,306
Natives of Western Hemisphere	11,985	33,238	94,274	91,701	153,199	151,031	245,449	133,689
Immediate relatives of U.S. citizens	5,474	16,275	30,882	34,215	32,714	46,903	43,677	60,016
Other	1,300	2,214	30,402	38,109	11,403	10,956	9,110	7,568

CLASS OF ADMISSION	1970	1972	1973	1974	1975	1976	1977
Numerical limitation (1968 Act): [1]							
Natives of Eastern Hemisphere	170,000	170,000	170,000	170,000	170,000	170,000	170,000
Natives of Western Hemisphere	120,000	120,000	120,000	120,000	120,000	120,000	120,000
Immigrants, total	373,326	384,685	400,063	394,861	386,194	398,613	462,315
Percent of aliens admitted	7.8	6.9	6.3	5.4	5.2	5.0	5.4
Natives of Eastern Hemisphere	172,547	164,849	166,108	159,059	160,460	166,204	241,433
Natives of Western Hemisphere	114,736	118,817	116,803	115,072	121,101	118,569	102,073
Immediate relatives of U.S. citizens	79,213	86,332	100,953	104,844	91,504	102,019	105,957
Other	6,830	14,686	16,199	15,886	13,129	11,821	12,852
Subject to East. Hemisphere limitations	172,547	164,849	166,108	159,059	160,460	166,204	241,433
Relative preferences	92,432	83,165	92,054	94,915	95,945	102,007	130,784
Unmarried sons and daughters of U.S. citizens and their children (1st pref.)	1,089	858	936	932	871	931	1,473
Spouses, unmarried sons and daughters of resident aliens, and their children (2d preference)	30,714	36,484	38,680	43,920	43,077	44,439	54,914
Married sons and daughters of U.S. citizens (4th preference)	8,350	3,971	4,060	3,404	3,623	4,077	4,818
Brothers and sisters of U.S. citizens (5th preference)	52,279	41,852	48,378	46,659	48,374	52,660	69,579
Occupational preferences	34,016	33,714	26,767	28,482	29,334	26,361	23,585
Immigrants in professions (3d pref.)	10,142	10,385	8,521	7,763	8,363	8,318	6,554
Other workers (6th preference)	8,786	7,915	4,549	6,420	6,724	4,792	4,673
Their spouses and children	15,088	15,414	13,697	14,299	14,247	13,251	12,358
Conditional entrants (7th preference)	9,863	10,396	9,808	9,076	9,129	11,907	9,575
Nonpreference (incl. private bill cases)	36,058	37,387	37,363	26,475	25,961	25,775	77,358
Adjustments under Sec. 244 of the I & N Act	176	185	114	104	86	143	125
Foreign Govt. officials, Act of Sept. 1957	2	2	2	7	5	11	6
Subject to West. Hemisphere limitations	114,736	118,817	116,803	115,072	121,101	118,569	35,067
Natives of Western Hemisphere, their spouses and children	102,529	101,232	96,762	99,800	96,547	91,319	34,115
Immigrants, Act of November 1966 [2]	12,207	17,585	20,041	15,272	24,554	27,250	952
Exempt from numerical limitations	86,043	101,019	117,152	120,730	104,633	113,840	185,815
Immediate relatives	79,213	86,332	100,953	104,844	91,504	102,019	105,957
Wives of U.S. citizens	36,276	36,801	40,165	40,274	33,719	37,856	36,104
Husbands of U.S. citizens	15,619	21,496	27,123	27,284	21,901	22,234	26,105
Children of U.S. citizens	18,095	18,797	22,990	24,758	22,315	23,889	22,572
Parents of U.S. citizens	9,223	9,238	10,675	12,528	13,569	18,040	21,176
Immigrants, Act of Nov. 1966 [2]	–	–	–	–	–	–	67,958
Special immigrants	6,342	7,146	7,098	6,904	7,080	5,961	5,736
Ministers of religion, their spouses and children	1,497	1,505	1,549	1,416	1,231	1,368	1,301
Employees of the U.S. Government abroad, their spouses and children	290	368	508	1,176	1,622	449	224
Children born abroad to resident aliens or subsequent to issuance of visa	3,012	3,566	3,760	3,477	3,636	3,405	3,550
Aliens adjusted [3]	1,543	1,707	1,281	895	591	739	661
Immigrants, various Acts, 1957–1962	54	30	16	7	1	12	1
Refugee-escapees, Act of July 14, 1960	20	4	–	–	–	–	–
Spouses of U.S. citizens and their children, Act of April 7, 1970	9	6,828	8,276	7,885	5,057	5,014	5,598
Others not subj. to numerical limitation	405	678	809	1,030	991	834	565

– Represents zero.   X Not applicable.   [1] See text, p. 84.
[2] As of Jan. 1977, Act of Nov. 1966 not subject to numerical limitations.
[3] Under sections 244 and 249, Immigration and Naturalization Act.
Source: U.S. Immigration and Naturalization Service, *Annual Report*.

No. 123. Immigrants, by Country of Last Permanent Residence: 1820 to 1977

[In thousands, except percent. For years ending June 30 except, beginning 1977, ending September 30. For definition of immigrants, see text, pp. 83–84. Data prior to 1906 refer to country from which aliens came. Because of boundary changes and changes in list of countries separately reported, data for certain countries not comparable throughout. See also *Historical Statistics, Colonial Times to 1970*, series C 89–119]

COUNTRY	1820–1977, total	1951–1960, total	1961–1970, total	1972	1973	1974	1975	1976	1977	PERCENT 1820–1977	PERCENT 1961–1970	PERCENT 1971–1977
Total	47,960	2,515.5	3,321.7	384.7	400.1	394.9	386.2	398.6	462.3	100.0	100.0	100.0
Europe	36,108	1,325.6	1,123.4	86.3	91.2	80.4	72.8	73.0	74.0	75.3	33.8	20.4
Austria [1]	4,314	67.1	20.6	2.3	1.6	.7	.5	.5	.5	8.9	.6	.3
Hungary		36.6	5.4	.5	1.0	.9	.6	.6	.5		.2	.2
Belgium	202	18.6	9.2	.5	.4	.4	.4	.5	.5	.4	.3	.1
Czechoslovakia	137	.9	3.3	1.2	.9	.4	.3	.3	.3	.3	.1	.2
Denmark	364	11.0	9.2	.5	.4	.5	.3	.4	.4	.8	.3	.1
Finland	33	4.9	4.2	.3	.3	.2	.2	.2	.2	.1	.1	.1
France	747	51.1	45.2	2.9	2.6	2.2	1.8	2.0	2.7	1.6	1.4	.6
Germany [1]	6,968	477.8	190.8	7.8	7.6	7.2	5.9	6.6	7.4	14.5	5.7	1.8
Great Britain [2]	4,879	195.5	210.0	11.5	11.9	11.7	12.2	13.0	14.0	10.2	6.3	3.1
Greece	646	47.6	86.0	10.5	10.3	10.6	9.8	8.6	7.8	1.3	2.6	2.6
Ireland [3]	4,722	57.3	37.5	1.4	1.6	1.3	1.1	1.0	1.0	9.9	1.1	.3
Italy	5,285	185.5	214.1	22.4	22.3	15.0	11.0	8.0	7.4	11.0	6.4	3.9
Netherlands	358	52.3	30.6	1.0	1.0	1.0	.8	.9	1.0	.8	.9	.2
Norway	856	22.9	15.5	.4	.4	.4	.4	.3	.3	1.8	.5	.1
Poland [1]	510	10.0	53.5	3.8	4.1	3.5	3.5	3.2	3.3	1.1	1.6	.8
Portugal	432	19.6	76.1	9.5	10.0	10.7	11.3	11.0	10.0	.9	2.3	2.6
Spain	254	7.9	44.7	4.3	5.5	4.7	2.6	2.8	5.6	.5	1.3	1.0
Sweden	1,271	21.7	17.1	.7	.6	.6	.5	.6	.6	2.7	.5	.2
Switzerland	348	17.7	18.5	1.0	.7	.7	.7	.8	.8	.7	.6	.2
U.S.S.R. [1][4]	3,367	.6	2.3	.4	.9	.9	4.7	7.4	5.4	7.0	.1	.7
Yugoslavia	111	8.2	20.4	2.8	5.2	5.0	2.9	2.3	2.3	.2	.6	.9
Other Europe	304	10.8	9.2	.6	1.9	1.8	1.3	2.0	2.0	.6	.3	.4
Asia	2,573	153.3	427.8	116.0	120.0	127.0	129.2	146.7	150.8	5.4	12.9	31.7
China [5]	510	9.7	34.8	8.5	9.2	10.0	9.2	9.9	12.5	1.0	1.0	2.4
Hong Kong	[6] 169	15.5	75.0	10.9	10.3	10.7	12.5	13.7	12.3	.4	2.3	2.8
India	140	2.0	27.2	15.6	12.0	11.7	14.3	16.1	16.8	.3	.8	3.5
Iran	[6] 33	3.4	10.3	2.9	2.9	2.5	2.2	2.6	4.2	.1	.3	.7
Israel	[6] 80	25.5	29.6	3.0	2.9	2.9	3.5	5.2	4.4	.2	.9	.8
Japan	400	46.3	40.0	5.0	6.1	5.4	4.8	4.8	4.5	.8	1.2	1.3
Jordan	[6] 34	5.8	11.7	2.4	2.1	2.5	2.3	2.4	2.9	.1	.3	.6
Korea	[6] 211	6.2	34.5	18.1	22.3	27.5	28.1	30.6	30.7	.4	1.0	6.1
Lebanon	[6] 46	4.5	15.2	3.0	2.6	3.0	4.0	5.0	5.5	.1	.5	.9
Philippines	[7] 343	19.3	98.4	28.7	30.2	32.5	31.3	36.8	38.5	.7	3.0	8.1
Turkey	384	3.5	10.1	1.5	1.4	1.4	1.1	1.0	1.0	.8	.3	.3
Vietnam	[8] 26	2.7	4.2	3.4	4.5	3.1	2.7	2.4	3.4	.1	.1	.8
Other Asia	197	9.0	36.7	13.0	13.5	13.8	13.2	16.2	14.1	.4	1.2	3.4
America	8,740	996.9	1,716.4	173.2	179.6	178.8	174.7	169.2	223.2	18.2	51.7	45.4
Argentina	[9] 89	19.5	49.7	2.5	2.9	2.9	2.8	2.7	3.1	.2	1.5	.7
Brazil	[9] 55	13.8	29.3	1.8	1.8	1.6	1.4	1.4	1.9	.1	.9	.4
Canada	4,077	378.0	413.3	18.6	14.8	12.3	11.2	11.4	18.0	8.5	12.4	3.9
Colombia	[9] 133	18.0	72.0	5.2	5.3	5.9	6.4	5.7	8.2	.3	2.2	1.5
Cuba	[10] 490	78.9	208.5	19.9	22.5	17.4	25.6	28.4	66.1	1.0	6.3	7.2
Dominican Rep.	[9] 194	9.9	93.3	10.8	14.0	15.7	14.1	12.4	11.6	.4	2.8	3.2
Ecuador	[9] 80	9.8	36.8	4.4	4.2	4.8	4.7	4.5	5.2	.2	1.1	1.2
El Salvador	[9] 38	5.9	15.0	2.0	2.0	2.3	2.4	2.4	4.4	.1	.4	.6
Guatemala	[9] 36	4.7	15.9	1.7	1.8	1.6	1.9	2.0	3.7	.1	.5	.5
Haiti	[10] 76	4.4	34.5	5.5	4.6	3.8	5.0	5.3	5.2	.1	1.0	1.3
Honduras	[9] 31	6.0	15.7	1.0	1.4	1.4	1.4	1.3	1.6	.1	.5	.3
Mexico	2,015	299.8	453.9	64.2	70.4	71.9	62.6	58.4	44.6	4.2	13.7	15.1
Panama	[9] 43	11.7	19.4	1.6	1.7	1.7	1.7	1.8	2.5	.1	.6	.5
Peru	[9] 42	7.4	19.1	1.5	1.8	2.0	2.3	2.6	3.9	.1	.6	.6
West Indies	684	29.8	133.9	24.2	21.6	24.4	22.3	19.6	27.1	1.4	4.0	5.9
Other America	657	99.2	106.2	8.3	8.8	9.1	8.9	9.3	16.1	1.3	3.2	2.5
Africa	119	14.1	29.0	5.5	5.5	5.2	5.9	5.7	9.6	.3	.9	1.5
Australia and New Zealand	116	11.5	19.6	2.6	2.5	2.0	1.8	2.1	2.5	.2	.6	.6
All other	304	14.0	5.7	1.2	1.3	1.4	1.8	1.9	2.2	.6	.2	.4

[1] 1938–1945, Austria included with Germany; 1899–1919, Poland included with Austria-Hungary, Germany, and U.S.S.R.   [2] Beginning 1952, includes data for United Kingdom not specified, formerly included with "Other Europe."   [3] Comprises Eire and Northern Ireland.   [4] Europe and Asia.   [5] Beginning 1957, includes Taiwan.   [6] Prior to 1951, included with "Other Asia."   [7] Prior to 1951, Philippines included with "All other."   [8] Prior to 1953, data for Vietnam not available.   [9] Prior to 1951, included with "Other America."   [10] Prior to 1951, included with "West Indies."

Source: U.S. Immigration and Naturalization Service, *Annual Report*.

No. 124. IMMIGRANTS, BY COUNTRY OF BIRTH: 1951 TO 1977

[In thousands. For years ending June 30 except, beginning 1977, ending September 30. For definition of immigrants, see text, pp. 83–84]

COUNTRY OF BIRTH	1951–1960, total	1961–1970, total	1971–1975, total	1976	1977	COUNTRY OF BIRTH	1951–1960, total	1961–1970, total	1971–1975, total	1976	1977
All countries	2,515.5	3,321.7	1,936.3	398.6	462.3	Asia [1]	157.1	445.3	611.8	149.9	157.8
						China [2]	32.7	96.7	85.6	18.8	19.8
Europe [1]	1,492.2	1,238.6	434.6	72.4	70.0	Hong Kong	3.1	25.6	21.5	5.8	5.6
Austria	29.7	13.7	2.6	.3	.4	India	3.1	31.2	72.9	17.5	18.6
Belgium	12.9	8.5	1.9	.4	.4	Japan	44.7	38.5	23.8	4.3	4.2
Czechoslovakia	28.8	21.4	6.3	.6	.6	Jordan	5.1	14.0	13.2	2.6	2.5
Denmark	13.7	11.8	2.3	.4	.4	Korea	7.0	35.8	112.5	30.8	30.9
Finland	6.7	5.8	1.8	.3	.3	Philippines	18.1	101.6	153.3	37.3	39.1
						Vietnam	2.0	4.6	19.3	3.0	4.6
France	38.0	34.3	8.8	1.5	1.6	North America [1]	769.1	1,351.1	735.4	142.3	187.3
Germany	345.5	200.0	32.5	5.8	6.4	Canada	274.9	286.7	47.8	7.6	12.7
Greece	48.4	90.2	58.5	8.4	7.8	Mexico	319.3	443.3	318.1	57.9	44.0
Hungary	64.5	17.3	7.1	.9	.9	West Indies [1]	122.8	519.5	324.7	66.8	114.0
Ireland	64.4	42.4	8.3	1.2	1.2	Cuba	78.3	256.8	110.7	29.2	69.7
Italy	188.0	206.7	93.2	8.4	7.5	Dominican Republic	9.8	94.1	67.1	12.5	11.7
Netherlands	47.2	27.8	5.0	.9	1.0	Jamaica	8.7	71.0	61.5	9.0	11.5
Norway	24.7	16.4	2.1	.3	.3	Central America	44.6	97.7	44.5	9.9	16.5
Poland	128.0	73.3	20.5	3.8	4.0						
Portugal	20.4	79.3	55.9	10.5	9.7	South America [1]	72.2	228.3	105.7	22.7	32.9
Romania	17.4	14.9	7.3	2.2	2.0	Argentina	14.3	42.1	10.1	2.3	2.8
Spain	10.7	30.5	18.5	2.3	2.5	Brazil	8.9	20.5	5.9	1.0	1.5
Sweden	18.9	16.7	2.9	.5	.6	Colombia	17.6	70.3	29.1	5.7	8.3
						Ecuador	9.5	37.0	23.0	4.5	5.3
Switzerland	17.2	16.3	3.1	.6	.6	Africa	16.6	39.3	32.9	7.7	10.2
U. Kingdom	208.9	230.5	53.0	11.4	12.5	Australia	4.6	9.8	6.7	1.4	1.4
U.S.S.R	46.5	15.7	9.1	8.2	5.7	New Zealand	1.8	3.7	2.3	.4	.6
Yugoslavia	58.7	46.2	28.9	2.8	2.8	Other countries	1.9	5.7	6.9	1.8	2.1

[1] Includes countries not shown separately.   [2] Includes Taiwan.

Source: U.S. Immigration and Naturalization Service, Annual Report, and releases.

No. 125. IMMIGRANTS—REFUGEES ADMITTED, BY COUNTRY OF BIRTH: 1954 TO 1977

[For years ending June 30 except, beginning 1977, ending September 30. Comprises admissions of refugees under 1953 Refugee Relief Act and later acts; Hungarian parolees under July 1958 Act; refugee-escapee parolees under July 1960 Act; conditional entries by refugees under Oct. 1965 Act; and Cuban parolees under Nov. 1966 Act]

COUNTRY OF BIRTH	1954–1977	1974	1975	1976	1977	COUNTRY OF BIRTH	1954–1977	1974	1975	1976	1977
Total	732,551	25,650	34,665	39,228	78,485	Europe [1]—Con.					
Europe [1]	324,775	5,990	5,571	8,017	6,520	U.S.S.R	20,993	409	3,141	5,847	3,972
Austria	5,697	27	16	9	8	Yugoslavia	49,954	2,771	659	267	44
Belgium	592	–	3	6	3	Other	5,561	34	17	20	53
Bulgaria	3,403	126	73	117	70						
Czechoslovakia	11,282	165	118	119	138	Asia [1]	70,870	3,186	3,637	3,869	3,451
Denmark	41	–	–	–	–	China [2]	24,418	1,548	1,586	1,364	975
Estonia	690	–	–	–	–	India	119	3	5	9	7
Finland	56	–	–	–	–	Indonesia	15,956	1	23	11	21
France	1,394	17	14	9	13	Israel	830	6	5	36	10
						Japan	4,355	2	–	–	3
Germany	22,084	9	10	14	21	Korea	4,442	4	1	1	2
Greece	19,268	28	30	95	76	Palestine	918	9	2	13	6
Hungary	51,779	528	303	320	271	Philippines	358	1	–	–	3
Ireland	21	–	–	–	–	Vietnam	1,334	–	1	5	1,319
Italy	60,390	67	26	13	22	Other Asia	18,140	1,614	2,014	2,430	1,105
Latvia	1,704	–	–	–	–						
Lithuania	1,861	1	1	2	1	N. America	327,238	16,131	25,228	27,092	68,171
						Canada	97	2	14	2	3
Netherlands	17,428	1	5	–	–	Mexico	256	9	24	21	40
Norway	39	–	–	–	–	Cuba	325,486	16,087	25,136	26,996	67,985
Poland	19,430	580	425	389	504	Other West Indies	556	16	35	35	80
Portugal	5,006	2	2	1	–	Central America	251	17	19	37	63
Romania	16,066	602	453	617	722	Other North America	592	–	–	1	–
Spain	9,012	622	267	165	602						
Sweden	91	–	–	1	–	S. America	754	50	84	94	258
Switzerland	122	–	1	–	–	Africa	8,757	292	144	156	85
U. Kingdom	811	1	7	6	–	Other	157	1	1	–	–

– Represents zero.   [1] Through 1970, Turkey included in Europe; thereafter, included in Asia.
[2] Includes Taiwan.

Source: U.S. Immigration and Naturalization Service, Annual Report.

No. 126. INDOCHINA REFUGEES, 1975 TO 1977 AND BY CHARACTERISTICS, 1975

[As of Dec. 31, except as noted. Includes only refugees resettled in U.S.]

CHARACTERISTIC	Number (1,000)	Percent	CHARACTERISTIC	Number (1,000)	Percent
Refugees, total, 1977_____	[1]148.4	100.0	Occupation [3]—Continued		
Refugees, total, 1976_____	144.1	100.0	Service_____	2.3	7.6
Refugees, total, 1975_____	[2]123.3	100.0	Farming, fishing, and forestry_	1.5	4.9
Male_____	67.5	54.7	Agricultural processing_____	.1	.4
Female_____	55.8	45.3	Machine trades_____	2.7	8.7
Age:			Benchwork, assembly, repair__	1.2	4.1
Under 6 years_____	20.4	16.6			
6–17 years_____	36.1	29.3	Structural and construction___	2.0	6.6
18–24 years_____	22.7	18.4	Transportation, miscellaneous_	5.2	16.9
25–44 years_____	32.3	26.2	Unknown_____	2.4	7.9
45–62 years_____	9.3	7.5			
63 years and over_____	2.5	2.0	Educational level [4]_____	67.0	100.0
Occupation [3]_____	30.6	100.0	None_____	1.4	2.1
Medical professions_____	2.2	7.2	Elementary_____	12.0	17.9
Professional, technical, and			Secondary_____	25.4	37.9
managerial_____	7.4	24.0	University and above_____	13.1	19.5
Clerical and sales_____	3.6	11.7	Unknown_____	15.1	22.6

[1] As of Dec. 31, 1977, 54,794 were resettled in other countries.   [2] Covers period from April 18, 1975, to Dec. 10, 1975.   [3] For heads of households.   [4] For persons 18 years old and over.

Source: 1976 and 1977, U.S. Dept. of Health, Education, and Welfare, Task Force for Indochina, *Report to the Congress;* 1975, U.S. Dept. of State, Interagency Task Force for Indochina, *Report to the Congress.*

No. 127. CUBAN REFUGEE PROGRAM: 1961 TO 1977

[For years ending June 30, except as indicated]

ITEM	1961–1965, total	1966–1970, total	1969	1970	1971	1972	1973	1974	1975	1976	1977
Cuban Refugee Center, Miami, Fla.:											
Registrations_____1,000__	177.7	178.2	42.3	46.5	46.9	19.0	6.9	4.6	5.3	3.2	2.0
Resettlements to other areas__1,000__	89.7	139.4	31.6	30.2	32.4	12.5	2.7	.5	.4	.4	.3
Refugees receiving welfare assistance											
(in June)_____1,000__	(X)	(X)	52.7	66.2	77.7	90.7	86.8	[1]34.0	29.1	28.8	22.2
In Florida_____1,000__	(X)	(X)	27.7	32.6	32.4	35.6	39.6	14.9	12.9	12.5	11.2
In other States_____1,000__	(X)	(X)	25.0	33.6	45.3	55.1	47.2	19.1	16.2	16.3	11.0
Total cost of program_____mil. dol__	177.2	294.8	70.6	87.4	112.1	136.7	143.7	114.8	84.2	83.8	67.2

X   Not applicable.   [1] Through State and local public welfare agencies with 100 percent Federal reimbursement from the Cuban Refugee Program. For January through May 1974, includes only medical assistance; their basic maintenance payments were made from the Federal Supplemental Security Income program.

Source: U.S. Social Security Administration, unpublished data.

No. 128. FOREIGN LABORERS ADMITTED OR PAROLED, BY COUNTRY OF LAST PERMANENT RESIDENCE: 1960 TO 1977

[For years endnig June 30 except, beginning 1977, ending September 30. Mexican agricultural laborers were employed under the provisions of Public Law 78 from 1949 until December 31, 1964. After that date, Mexican agricultural laborers, like workers from other countries, entered the United States under the Immigration and Nationality Act, which provides for the importation of foreign workers if like workers are not available in the United States]

COUNTRY	1960	1965	1970	1971	1972	1973	1974	1975	1976	1977
Total_____	[1]447,207	155,761	47,483	42,142	38,752	37,294	33,908	25,434	22,124	21,671
Agricultural laborers:										
Mexico_____	427,240	[2]103,563	–	–	–	–	–	–	–	–
Canada_____	7,804	8,149	3,156	6,156	1,895	1,458	1,250	970	572	399
West Indies_____	10,874	15,397	15,895	11,390	12,171	11,712	11,625	11,245	11,568	11,661
Japan_____	969	31	–	–	–	–	–	–	–	–
Spain (Basque sheepherders)_____	213	453	463	551	321	381	322	211	185	206
Others:										
Canada woodsmen___	(NA)	13,281	8,238	7,178	7,373	8,310	5,685	3,671	2,696	2,303
U.S. Virgin Islands workers_____	(NA)	13,514	15,459	11,752	11,580	10,582	9,901	7,286	5,967	4,304
Workers paroled into Guam_____	–	1,373	4,272	5,115	5,412	4,851	5,125	2,051	1,136	2,798

–   Represents zero.   NA   Not available.   [1] Includes British Honduras, not shown separately.   [2] Includes 100,876 Mexican laborers admitted under Public Law 78 prior to Dec. 31, 1964.

Source: U.S. Immigration and Naturalization Service, *Annual Report.*

No. 129. Entries of Aliens and Citizens Over International Land Boundaries: 1950 to 1977

[In millions. For years ending June 30 except, beginning 1977, ending September 30. Each entry of same person counted separately. Partially estimated]

YEAR	ALL ENTRIES			VIA CANADIAN BORDER			VIA MEXICAN BORDER		
	Total	Aliens	Citizens	Total	Aliens	Citizens	Total	Aliens	Citizens
1950	87.5	41.3	46.2	38.8	16.6	22.1	48.7	24.7	24.1
1955	119.8	61.6	58.2	48.0	24.8	23.2	71.8	36.8	35.0
1960	154.0	89.0	65.0	55.5	29.8	25.7	98.5	59.2	39.3
1965	175.8	101.8	74.0	59.8	33.3	26.5	116.0	68.5	47.5
1970	216.0	126.5	89.6	71.6	39.8	31.8	144.4	86.7	57.7
1971	220.4	128.1	92.3	72.6	40.0	32.7	147.8	88.2	59.6
1972	227.2	132.0	95.2	74.6	40.7	33.9	152.6	91.3	61.3
1973	238.3	138.4	99.9	77.4	42.5	34.8	160.9	95.8	65.1
1974	245.3	143.7	101.6	75.7	42.1	33.7	169.6	101.7	67.9
1975	236.8	141.1	95.7	78.4	43.6	34.8	158.4	97.5	60.9
1976	249.8	152.2	97.6	81.7	46.5	35.2	168.1	105.7	62.4
1977	242.4	150.3	92.1	85.6	49.9	35.7	156.8	100.4	56.4

No. 130. Aliens Admitted and Expelled: 1941 to 1977

[In thousands. For years ending June 30 except, beginning 1977, ending September 30. See also *Historical Statistics, Colonial Times to 1970*, series C 144, C 149, and C 158–160]

STATUS	1941– 1950	1951– 1960	1961– 1970	1970	1972	1973	1974	1975	1976	1977
Aliens admitted	3,496	9,629	27,429	4,805	5,556	6,377	7,304	7,470	8,054	8,499
Immigrant	1,035	2,515	3,321	373	385	400	395	386	399	462
Nonimmigrant	2,461	7,113	24,107	4,432	5,171	5,977	6,909	7,084	7,655	8,037
Deportable aliens apprehended	1,377	3,584	1,608	345	500	656	788	767	876	1,042
Entry without inspection [1]	(NA)	(NA)	780	244	398	551	693	668	773	935
From Mexico	(NA)	(NA)	756	240	392	542	681	655	757	921
From other North American countries	(NA)	(NA)	28	4	4	5	5	5	4	11
Aliens departed	2,262	6,682	19,277	3,246	3,866	4,594	5,059	5,130	5,146	5,381
Aliens expelled	1,582	4,014	1,431	320	467	585	738	679	793	897
Deported	111	130	96	17	16	17	19	23	28	30
Required to depart	1,471	3,884	1,334	303	451	568	719	656	765	867

NA Not available. [1] Includes other countries not shown separately.

No. 131. Alien Deportation, by Selected Causes: 1951 to 1977

[For years ending June 30 except, beginning 1977, ending September 30]

CAUSE	1951– 1960	1961– 1970	1970	1971	1972	1973	1974	1975	1976	1977
Total	129,887	96,374	16,893	17,639	16,266	16,842	18,824	23,438	27,998	30,228
Entry without inspection or by false statements	54,457	43,561	8,035	9,483	8,486	9,342	11,839	16,529	21,777	25,012
Failure to maintain or comply with conditions of nonimmigrant status	25,260	31,334	4,436	4,140	3,966	3,989	3,839	3,649	3,782	3,150
Criminal	6,742	3,694	268	286	266	226	191	225	272	285
Violation of narcotic laws	947	1,462	202	232	307	395	396	583	464	372
Previously excluded or deported	4,002	3,601	393	476	487	594	440	526	481	315
Entry without proper documents	35,090	11,831	3,511	2,979	2,710	2,247	2,086	1,896	1,185	1,066
Other	3,389	891	48	43	44	49	33	30	37	28

Source of tables 129 to 131: U.S. Immigration and Naturalization Service, *Annual Report*.

No. 132. Immigration and Nationality Violations—Summary: 1960 to 197?

[For years ending June 30 except, beginning 1977, ending September 30]

ITEM	1960	1965	1970	1972	1973	1974	1975	1976	1977
Prosecutions disposed of	2,773	3,714	6,034	13,200	16,415	17,734	14,172	17,126	17,176
Immigration violations	2,589	3,288	5,510	12,799	16,201	17,608	13,947	16,928	16,797
Nationality violations	184	426	524	401	214	126	225	198	379
Convictions	2,557	3,442	5,497	12,189	15,458	16,634	12,811	15,772	15,388
Immigration violations	2,400	3,037	4,991	12,063	15,386	16,570	12,676	15,653	15,223
Percent of prosecutions	92.7	92.4	90.6	94.2	95.0	94.1	90.9	92.1	89.6
Nationality violations	157	405	506	126	72	64	135	119	165
Percent of prosecutions	85.3	95.1	96.6	31.4	33.6	50.8	60.0	60.1	41.2
Aggregate fines_____$1,000	39	126	250	687	1,008	927	755	1,050	879
Aggregate imprisonment___years	1,994	3,422	4,042	4,895	5,755	5,998	5,313	6,367	6,478

No. 133. Immigration Border Patrol Activities: 1965 to 1977

[In thousands, except as indicated. For years ending June 30 except, beginning 1977, ending September 30]

ITEM	1965	1970	1971	1972	1973	1974	1975	1976	1977
Persons apprehended [1]	53.3	233.9	305.9	373.9	503.9	640.9	602.2	701.6	820.4
Deportable aliens located [2]	52.4	231.1	302.5	369.5	498.1	634.8	596.8	696.0	812.5
Mexican	44.2	219.3	290.2	355.1	480.6	616.6	579.4	678.4	792.6
Canadian	5.8	7.8	7.5	8.2	8.7	7.4	7.3	5.9	5.8
Other	2.5	4.1	4.9	6.2	8.9	10.8	10.1	11.7	14.1
Aliens smuggled into U.S.	1.8	18.7	19.8	24.9	41.6	83.1	80.4	82.9	138.8
Aliens located (prev. expelled)	14.0	67.4	90.4	115.8	152.4	182.4	184.6	186.9	241.1
Aliens located (previous criminal records)	4.0	3.8	4.2	4.4	11.2	10.9	10.3	13.1	12.3
Conveyances examined	1,172	1,792	2,024	2,473	2,666	2,905	3,470	3,277	3,677
Automobiles	752	1,311	1,508	1,893	2,020	2,230	2,663	2,440	2,647
Persons questioned [3]	5,285	6,805	7,664	9,024	9,507	10,202	11,265	10,783	11,606
In automobiles	1,877	3,416	4,029	4,855	5,135	5,591	6,888	6,145	6,844
Pedestrians	2,065	1,661	1,752	1,982	2,145	2,243	2,056	2,293	2,333
Value of seizures_____$1,000	594	4,547	6,153	12,961	25,954	47,210	28,654	18,019	19,557
Narcotics_____$1,000	394	3,865	5,379	11,709	23,464	45,056	26,302	16,035	17,071

[1] Foreign nationals arrested because they entered U.S. illegally or were present in violation of terms of lawful admission.   [2] Foreign nationals who entered U.S. illegally at other than ports of entry or who were admitted at ports of entry but became deportable as result of violations of terms of their admission.
[3] Includes types not shown separately.

Source of tables 132 and 133: U.S. Immigration and Naturalization Service, *Annual Report.*

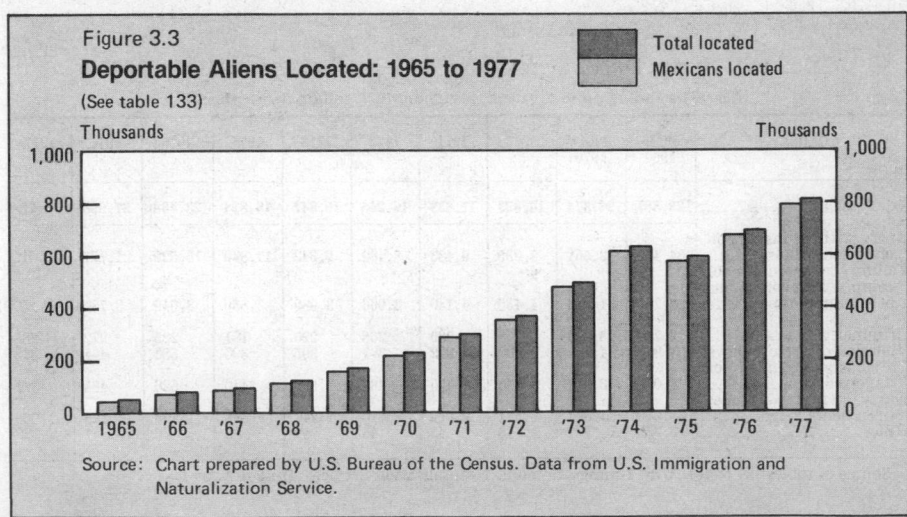

Figure 3.3
Deportable Aliens Located: 1965 to 1977

☐ Total located
☐ Mexicans located

(See table 133)

Source: Chart prepared by U.S. Bureau of the Census. Data from U.S. Immigration and Naturalization Service.

No. 134. NONIMMIGRANTS ADMITTED, BY CLASSES: 1965 TO 1977

[In thousands. For years ending June 30 except, beginning 1977, ending September 30. For definition of nonimmigrants, see text, p. 83. Excludes border crossers, crewmen, and insular travelers. See also *Historical Statistics, Colonial Times to 1970*, series C 149–157]

CLASS OF ADMISSION	1965–1969, avg.	1970	1971	1972	1973	1974	1975	1976	1977
Nonimmigrants	2,774.4	4,431.9	4,403.8	5,171.5	5,977.3	6,908.7	7,083.9	7,654.5	8,036.9
Temporary visitors, total	2,001.2	3,345.2	3,460.8	3,837.6	4,528.5	5,326.3	5,587.4	6,096.8	6,381.4
Percent of total	72.1	75.5	78.6	74.2	75.8	77.1	78.9	79.6	79.4
For pleasure	1,770.2	3,020.4	3,127.7	3,475.0	4,087.0	4,782.5	5,060.0	5,513.2	5,697.3
For business	231.0	324.8	333.1	362.6	441.5	543.8	527.4	583.6	684.1
Returning resident aliens [1]	308.0	493.5	363.5	682.6	789.4	842.3	800.0	844.3	897.7
Transit aliens	193.7	231.9	225.7	265.3	264.6	296.5	273.0	263.8	252.1
Foreign government officials	42.2	50.5	49.4	63.7	57.6	70.7	68.4	77.0	71.2
Treaty traders and investors	10.9	19.2	23.2	27.3	41.3	36.9	35.0	37.4	44.0
Students [2]	72.7	107.3	103.0	106.1	100.0	119.9	118.0	133.0	171.0
Representatives to international organizations	17.7	23.8	26.0	29.2	29.7	34.4	32.6	37.1	38.2
Temporary workers and industrial trainees	69.1	86.5	62.3	66.7	66.9	71.7	67.3	56.5	56.3
Workers of distinguished merit and ability	9.3	11.1	12.0	14.1	15.7	15.1	15.6	14.8	15.7
Other temporary workers	56.2	69.3	37.6	39.3	37.3	40.9	37.5	29.7	27.7
Industrial trainees	3.6	5.3	5.1	3.5	4.0	4.4	3.8	2.8	3.2
Their spouses and children	(x)	.8	7.7	9.7	9.9	11.4	10.6	9.2	9.7
Representatives of foreign information media	3.3	4.7	4.7	5.4	5.6	6.1	6.1	8.2	8.4
Exchange visitors [2]	53.3	66.6	69.8	64.6	63.6	69.2	63.4	62.8	71.5
NATO officials	2.3	2.3	2.5	3.2	3.3	4.1	4.0	5.1	5.1
Persons betrothed to U.S. citizens and their children	(x)	.1	5.7	8.6	9.5	9.4	6.4	6.2	7.2
Intracompany transferees [2]	(x)	.4	7.1	11.2	17.4	21.3	22.3	26.3	32.8

X Not applicable.
[1] Returning resident aliens who have once been counted as immigrants are included with nonimmigrants.
[2] Includes spouses and children.

No. 135. NONIMMIGRANTS ADMITTED, BY COUNTRY OF BIRTH: 1965 TO 1977

[In thousands. For years ending June 30 except, beginning 1977, ending September 30. For definition of nonimmigrants, see text, p. 83. Excludes border crossers, crewmen, and insular travelers. Students and others entering with multiple entry documents are only counted on the first admission. Includes returning resident aliens admitted with documents in addition to the Alien Registration Receipt Card]

COUNTRY	1965–1969, avg.	1970–1974, avg.	1975	1976	1977	COUNTRY	1965–1969, avg.	1970–1974, avg.	1975	1976	1977
Total	2,774	5,379	7,084	7,655	8,037	Asia [1]	232	763	1,260	1,310	1,461
						China [3]	20	47	63	74	80
Europe [1]	1,123	1,803	2,076	2,246	2,451	Hong Kong	6	18	28	34	30
Austria	19	28	32	32	38	India	21	49	69	77	80
Belgium	19	32	37	40	48	Iran	8	20	35	54	98
Czechoslovakia	9	14	12	13	12	Israel	15	32	46	49	57
Denmark	22	31	34	39	44	Japan	87	442	810	770	807
Finland	9	17	22	25	26	Korea	8	22	31	36	45
						Philippines	29	53	65	75	82
France	114	183	191	216	246	Turkey [2]	8	12	13	14	17
Germany	190	319	385	414	450						
Greece	29	49	52	54	60	America [1]	1,236	2,585	3,477	3,774	3,750
Hungary	10	13	14	14	16	Argentina	36	53	96	66	90
Ireland	27	49	48	50	53	Bahamas	47	89	71	72	87
						Brazil	31	61	93	119	68
Italy	115	171	171	186	183	Canada	118	183	223	249	275
Netherlands	56	83	98	108	126	Colombia	40	80	91	101	121
Norway	21	35	41	45	50						
Poland	20	28	42	41	39	Dominican Rep	77	112	149	156	155
Portugal	16	35	43	43	48	Jamaica	53	97	124	137	128
						Mexico	482	1,360	1,997	2,170	1,990
Spain	35	55	68	80	86	Trinidad and Tobago	19	41	43	47	52
Sweden	32	54	65	76	86	Venezuela	46	64	87	114	176
Switzerland	37	56	73	80	98	Cent. America	85	49	170	193	229
U.S.S.R. [2]	7	11	16	16	16						
Un. Kingdom	299	494	582	619	665	Africa	37	64	89	104	130
Yugoslavia	12	23	27	29	30	Australia and New Zealand	64	30	149	187	210
						Other countries	82	134	33	34	35

[1] Includes countries not shown separately. [2] Europe and Asia. [3] Includes Taiwan.
Source of tables 134 and 135: U.S. Immigration and Naturalization Service, *Annual Report*.

No. 136. ALIENS REPORTING UNDER ALIEN ADDRESS PROGRAM: 1960 TO 1977

[In thousands, except percent. All aliens in the United States on January 1 are required to report their addresses to the Department of Justice in January, except foreign government officials and their dependents, representatives to international organizations, and, for 1960, Mexican agricultural workers]

NATIONALITY	1960	1970	1976	1977 Number	1977 Percent	STATE OR AREA OF RESIDENCE	1960	1970	1976	1977 Number	1977 Percent
Total	2,949	4,247	4,776	4,964	100.0	Total	2,949	4,247	4,776	4,964	100.0
Canada	295	428	344	337	6.8	Ariz	35	49	61	64	1.3
China [1]	48	107	133	138	2.8	Calif	567	982	1,179	1,261	25.4
Colombia	12	59	68	68	1.4	Colo	20	23	32	33	.7
Cuba	63	433	399	374	7.5	Conn	75	109	93	95	2.0
Dominican Rep	(NA)	72	90	97	2.0	Fla	84	290	390	369	7.4
Ecuador	6	31	44	46	.9	Hawaii	51	53	68	69	1.4
France	35	47	37	38	.8	Ill	199	264	282	287	5.8
Germany	263	229	171	171	3.4	Ind	29	30	33	33	.7
Greece	49	73	77	73	1.5	Md	28	48	62	66	1.3
India	10	42	98	109	2.2	Mass	128	169	172	175	3.5
Ireland	68	52	32	31	.6						
Italy	257	247	210	203	4.1	Mich	142	146	135	139	2.8
Jamaica	(NA)	60	79	64	1.3	N.J	151	233	267	277	5.6
Japan	72	82	99	102	2.0	N.Y	554	821	764	801	16.1
Korea	10	31	121	143	2.9	Ohio	109	98	90	88	1.8
Mexico	510	734	910	963	19.4	Pa	126	110	111	110	2.2
Netherlands	40	48	37	38	.8	R.I	18	26	30	31	.6
Philippines	61	125	212	226	4.6	Texas	238	258	350	378	7.6
Poland	167	124	89	86	1.7	Va	19	31	46	52	1.0
Portugal	32	81	118	123	2.5	Wash	51	63	64	72	1.4
Trinidad and Tobago	(NA)	19	33	31	.6	Wis	35	35	32	33	.7
United Kingdom	227	330	307	319	6.4	P.R	6	52	45	45	.9
Vietnam	(NA)	4	120	125	2.5	V.I	3	19	21	21	.4
Yugoslavia	51	43	43	41	.8		281				
All other	673	746	905	1,018	20.5	All other		338	449	465	9.4

NA Not available.   [1] Includes Taiwan.

No. 137. ALIEN NATURALIZATION—DECLARATIONS, PETITIONS, AND CERTIFICATES: 1907 TO 1977

[In thousands. For years ending June 30 except, beginning 1977, ending September 30. No national data compiled prior to fiscal year 1907. Includes U.S. outlying areas. See also *Historical Statistics, Colonial Times to 1970*, series C 168 and C 180]

PERIOD OR YEAR	Declarations filed [1]	PETITIONS [2] Filed	PETITIONS [2] Denied	CERTIFICATES ISSUED Total	CERTIFICATES ISSUED Status Civilian	CERTIFICATES ISSUED Status Military	CERTIFICATES ISSUED Sex Male	CERTIFICATES ISSUED Sex Female
Total, 1907–1977	8,976.2	11,309.4	498.0	[3] 10,667.1	10,029.4	637.7	4,933.2	4,140.9
1907–1910	526.3	164.0	17.7	111.7	111.7	–	(NA)	(NA)
1911–1920	2,686.9	1,381.4	118.7	1,129.0	884.7	244.3	(NA)	(NA)
1921–1930	2,709.0	1,884.3	165.5	1,773.2	1,717.0	56.2	[4] 1,166.2	[4] 255.2
1931–1940	1,369.5	1,637.1	45.8	1,518.5	1,498.6	19.9	968.4	550.1
1941–1950	920.3	1,938.1	64.8	1,987.0	1,837.2	149.8	941.5	1,045.5
1951–1960	323.8	[5] 1,230.5	27.6	[5] 1,189.9	1,148.2	41.7	503.5	686.4
1961–1970	144.9	1,143.0	23.6	1,120.3	1,084.2	36.1	513.5	606.8
1950	93.5	66.0	2.3	66.4	64.3	2.1	25.7	40.6
1955	10.9	[5] 213.5	4.6	[5] 209.6	197.0	12.0	95.9	113.7
1960	16.3	127.5	2.3	119.4	117.8	1.6	50.9	68.5
1965	13.1	106.8	2.1	104.3	101.2	3.1	48.5	55.8
1967	12.5	108.4	2.0	104.9	102.2	2.7	46.0	58.9
1968	13.6	103.1	2.0	102.7	100.3	2.4	45.1	57.6
1969	14.1	102.3	2.0	98.8	93.3	5.5	45.2	53.5
1970	18.8	114.8	2.0	110.4	99.8	10.6	52.7	57.7
1971	19.7	109.9	2.0	108.4	98.9	9.5	51.1	57.3
1972	21.2	121.9	1.8	116.2	107.7	8.5	55.4	60.8
1973	17.4	126.9	1.7	120.7	112.9	7.8	56.9	63.8
1974	14.0	136.2	2.2	131.7	124.9	6.8	60.8	70.8
1975	12.2	149.4	2.3	141.5	135.3	6.2	66.6	75.0
1976	10.7	157.9	2.2	142.5	136.9	5.6	66.0	76.5
1977	7.5	186.4	2.8	160.0	154.7	5.3	73.3	86.4

– Represents zero.   NA Not available.   [1] Declaration of intention to become citizen.   [2] Petition for naturalization.   [3] Includes 1,592,449 not distributed by sex.
[4] 1923–1930 only.   [5] Includes aliens serving in U.S. Armed Forces who were naturalized abroad.
Source of tables 136 and 137: U.S. Immigration and Naturalization Service, *Annual Report*.

No. 138. Aliens Naturalized—Characteristics: 1960 to 1977

[For years ending June 30 except, beginning 1977, ending September 30. Includes U.S. outlying areas. For definition of median see p. xii. See also *Historical Statistics, Colonial Times to 1970*, series C 162–167 and C 170–171]

CHARACTERISTIC	1960	1965	1970	1971	1972	1973	1974	1975	1976	1977
Total naturalized	119,442	104,299	110,399	108,407	116,215	120,740	131,655	141,537	142,504	159,873
Under general naturalization provisions [1]	91,548	76,630	79,761	79,491	89,475	94,039	103,450	113,289	114,653	131,331
Under special provisions	27,894	27,669	30,638	28,916	26,740	26,701	28,205	28,248	27,851	28,542
Married to U.S. citizens	19,799	16,602	14,899	14,162	13,211	13,380	14,768	15,416	15,138	15,394
Children of U.S. citizens [2]	6,149	7,914	5,023	5,116	4,961	5,461	6,511	6,568	7,038	7,787
Filipinos [3]	88	3	–	5	1	–	1	–	–	–
Military	1,594	3,085	10,616	9,549	8,475	7,796	6,848	6,214	5,631	5,291
Other	264	65	100	84	92	64	77	50	44	70
By sex and marital status:										
Males [4]	50,896	48,495	52,666	51,164	55,416	56,901	60,823	66,587	66,007	73,377
Single	14,341	15,358	14,196	13,781	14,917	15,423	16,946	17,789	16,973	18,709
Married	34,517	31,766	36,979	35,724	38,794	39,752	41,982	46,723	46,898	52,342
Widowed	1,183	593	397	412	461	405	423	401	370	381
Divorced	852	773	1,088	1,208	1,244	1,321	1,472	1,674	1,766	1,945
Females [4]	68,546	55,804	57,733	57,243	60,799	63,839	70,832	74,950	76,497	86,496
Single	10,330	11,746	11,458	11,852	12,373	13,103	14,964	15,392	15,977	17,677
Married	52,252	40,483	42,128	41,169	43,907	46,271	50,880	54,487	55,308	62,887
Widowed	4,694	2,416	2,240	2,136	2,301	2,267	2,298	2,171	2,082	2,343
Divorced	1,262	1,156	1,901	2,059	2,215	2,198	2,690	2,900	3,130	3,589
Males per 1,000 females	743	869	912	894	911	891	859	888	863	848
Median age _____ years	38.0	34.1	34.1	33.9	34.4	34.4	34.1	33.9	33.2	34.4
Male _____ years	38.9	34.6	34.4	34.3	34.9	35.0	34.6	34.7	35.0	35.0
Female _____ years	37.3	33.7	33.8	33.7	33.9	33.8	33.6	33.3	31.4	33.7

- Represents zero. [1] See text, p. 84. [2] Includes adopted children.
[3] With U.S. residence beginning prior to May 1, 1934. [4] Includes unknown, not shown separately.

No. 139. Aliens Naturalized, by Country of Former Allegiance, and by State of Residence: 1970 to 1977

[For years ending June 30 except, beginning 1977, ending September 30. Includes U.S. outlying areas. See also *Historical Statistics, Colonial Times to 1970*, series C 169–179]

COUNTRY OF FORMER ALLEGIANCE	1970	1975	1977 Number	1977 Percent	STATE OR AREA OF RESIDENCE	1970	1975	1977 Number	1977 Percent
Total	110,399	141,537	159,873	100.0	Total	110,399	141,537	159,873	100.0
Canada	6,340	3,548	3,759	2.4	Arizona	1,007	1,088	1,120	.7
Central America [1]	2,480	2,773	3,094	1.9	California	20,054	26,834	27,835	17.4
China [2]	3,099	9,683	11,143	7.0	Colorado	716	878	1,438	.9
Colombia	970	1,699	2,029	1.3	Connecticut	2,444	3,509	3,099	2.0
Czechoslovakia	506	1,738	1,438	.9	Florida	11,556	10,576	17,478	10.9
Egypt	377	1,988	1,883	1.2	Georgia	873	853	1,131	.7
Germany	10,067	5,187	4,856	3.0	Hawaii	2,658	3,094	4,532	2.8
Greece	2,906	6,647	6,151	3.9	Illinois	6,823	9,707	8,999	5.6
India	325	2,720	5,574	3.5	Indiana	749	1,113	1,132	.7
Italy	7,892	8,798	7,891	4.9	Maryland	1,855	2,227	2,710	1.7
Israel	1,516	1,844	1,548	1.0	Massachusetts	3,813	5,448	5,532	3.5
Korea	1,687	6,007	11,987	7.5	Michigan	2,865	3,674	3,271	2.1
Mexico	6,195	5,781	6,301	3.9	Minnesota	515	1,011	1,321	.8
Philippines	5,469	15,330	16,145	10.1	Missouri	744	983	1,403	.9
Poland	3,426	3,069	2,768	1.7	New Jersey	6,633	8,207	11,749	7.4
Portugal	1,374	3,728	3,739	2.3	New York	21,684	31,700	32,599	20.4
United Kingdom [3]	7,549	8,532	9,345	5.9	Ohio	2,589	3,741	4,098	2.6
Vietnam	282	1,369	1,412	.9	Oregon	481	734	1,032	.7
West Indies [1]	22,675	22,692	29,931	18.7	Pennsylvania	3,169	3,499	4,046	2.5
Cuba	20,888	15,546	20,506	12.8	Texas	4,858	4,569	5,544	3.4
Dominican Rep	538	1,518	1,904	1.2	Virginia	1,509	2,207	2,230	1.4
Haiti	433	1,966	1,870	1.2	Washington	1,352	2,124	2,011	1.2
Jamaica	479	2,152	3,849	2.4	Wisconsin	913	992	1,246	.8
Other West Indies	337	1,510	1,802	1.1	Guam	556	1,130	683	.4
Yugoslavia	1,725	3,273	2,447	1.5	Puerto Rico	1,535	1,625	1,749	1.1
Other	23,539	25,131	26,432	16.5	Other	8,448	10,014	11,885	7.4

[1] Independent countries. [2] Includes Taiwan. [3] Includes colonies and dependencies.

Source of tables 138 and 139: U.S. Immigration and Naturalization Service, *Annual Report*, and releases.

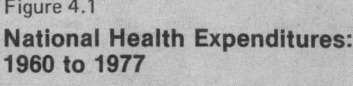

Figure 4.1

National Health Expenditures: 1960 to 1977

(See table 140)

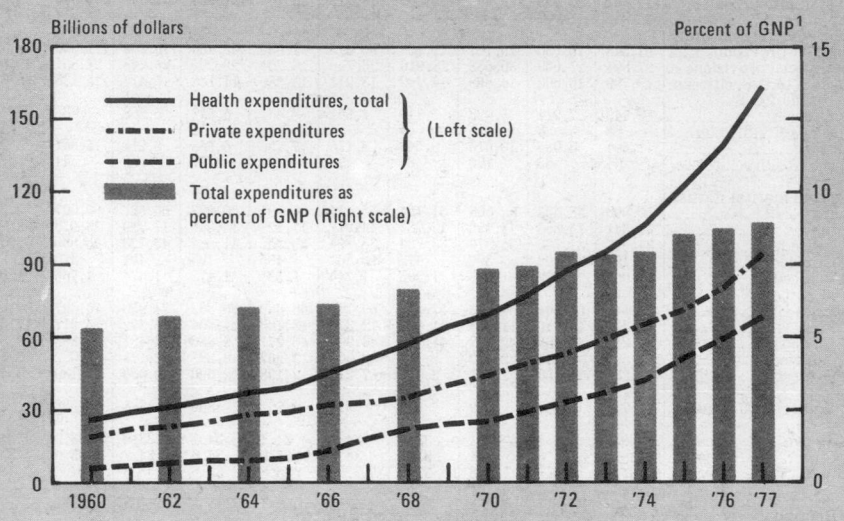

Billions of dollars   Percent of GNP[1]

——— Health expenditures, total

—··—··— Private expenditures   } (Left scale)

— — — Public expenditures

▮ Total expenditures as percent of GNP (Right scale)

[1] Gross national product.

Source: Chart prepared by U.S. Bureau of the Census. Data from U.S. Social Security Administration.

Figure 4.2

Indexes of Medical Care Prices: 1960 to 1977

(See table 141)

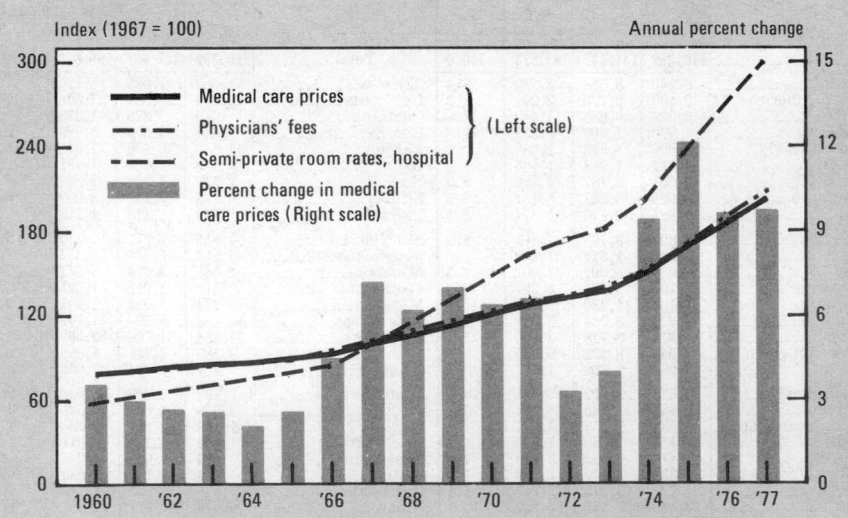

Index (1967 = 100)   Annual percent change

——— Medical care prices

—··—··— Physicians' fees   } (Left scale)

— — — Semi-private room rates, hospital

▮ Percent change in medical care prices (Right scale)

Source: Chart prepared by U.S. Bureau of the Census. Data from U.S. Bureau of Labor Statistics.

Section 4
Health and Nutrition

This section presents statistics on health expenditures and insurance coverage; medical personnel; hospitals; nursing homes and other care facilities; incidence of health handicaps and diseases; nutritional intake of the population; per capita food consumption; and Federal food programs. Data on national health expenditures, medical costs, insurance coverage, and hospital costs, which, prior to 1977, were collected by the Social Security Administration (SSA) are now collected by the Health Care Financing Administration (HCFA), and appear in the *Social Security Bulletin*, issued monthly. Statistics on health personnel and inpatient and outpatient facilities are published annually by the U.S. National Center for Health Statistics (NCHS) in *Health Resources Statistics*. Additional data on health personnel are collected by NCHS and are published in the annual *Vital and Health Statistics*. Statistics on hospitals are published annually by the American Hospital Association in *Hospital Statistics*. Primary sources for data on nutrition and Federal food programs are the quarterly *National Food Review* and the annual *Agricultural Statistics*, both issued by the U.S. Department of Agriculture. In addition, NCHS conducts periodic surveys of nutrient levels in the population and clinical signs of malnutrition.

National health expenditures.—Estimates of national health care expenditures prior to 1977 were compiled by type of expenditure and source of funds by the U.S. Social Security Administration. Beginning in 1977, the HCFA has derived these estimates. Estimates for total outlays are drawn from a number of sources of data such as the American Hospital Association; the Veterans Administration; the Department of Defense; the Internal Revenue Service; the Department of Commerce national income accounts in the *Survey of Current Business*; the National Center for Health Statistics; the Social Security Administration; the Bureau of the Census, *Government Finances*; the U.S. Office of Education; the Occupational Safety and Health Administration; the National Aeronautics and Space Administration; and the National Institutes of Health. For details, see the section on "Definitions, Methodology, and Sources of Data" in the annual report on national health expenditures published in the *Social Security Bulletin*.

The general method for arriving at national private health expenditures is to estimate the *total* national outlays (public and private) for each type of medical service or expenditure. From these outlays are then deducted the amounts paid to public and private hospitals, physicians in private practice, etc., under the various Federal, State, and local programs identified as components of total welfare expenditures.

Since 1974, data on public (Federal, State, and local governmental) expenditures have been organized and reported under 10 broad categories of health programs: Health insurance for the aged and disabled (Medicare); temporary disability insurance (medical benefits); workmen's compensation (medical benefits); public assistance (vendor medical payments); general hospital and medical care; Defense Department hospital and medical care (including military dependents); maternal and child health services; other public health activities; veterans' hospital and medical care; and medical vocational rehabilitation. For several Federal health programs, the data are taken from the Office of Management and Budget (OMB) special analysis of health programs. For the remainder, the data are supplied by various Federal, State, and local agencies.

Health resources.—Hospital statistics based on data from the American Hospital Association's yearly survey are published annually in *Hospital Statistics*, and cover all hospitals accepted for registration by the Association. To be accepted for registration, a hospital must meet certain requirements relating to number of beds, construction, equipment, medical and nursing staff, patient care, clinical records, surgical and obstetrical facilities, diagnostic and treatment facilities, laboratory services, etc. Data obtained from NCHS cover all U.S. hospitals which meet certain criteria for inclusion. They are published in the annual *Health Resources Statistics*, DHEW Publication No. (HRA) 1509, and in *Vital and Health Statistics* reports, series 14. In these reports, a hospital is defined as a facility with at least six inpatient beds that is licensed as a hospital by a State, or is operated as a hospital by a Federal or State agency.

These last two reports also present statistics on the number, geographic distribution, and characteristics of health resources including physicians, dentists, nurses, other health occupations, hospitals, nursing homes, and outpatient facilities. Statistics on the demographic characteristics of persons employed in the health occupations are based on data compiled by the U.S. Bureau of Labor Statistics and reported in *Employment and Earnings* (monthly). Data based on sample surveys of health personnel and utilization of health facilities providing long-term care, ambulatory care, hospital care, and family planning services are presented in NCHS series 13, *Health Resources Utilization Survey*. Statistics on patient visits to health care providers, as reported in health interviews, appear in NCHS series 10, *Health Interview Survey*.

The Social Security Administration's *Health Insurance Statistics* presents data for hospitals and nursing homes as well as extended care facilities and home health agencies. These data are based on records of the Federal Health Insurance for the Aged program (Medicare) begun in 1966 and differ from those of other sources because they are limited to facilities meeting Federal eligibility standards for participation in Medicare.

Data on patients in hospitals for the mentally ill and on mental health facilities are collected by the National Institute of Mental Health (NIMH) and appear in the *Mental Health Statistics* reports, Series A and B, and the Mental Health Statistical Note series.

Institutional population data based on the 1960 and 1970 censuses of the population include information on persons in hospitals, in homes for the aged and dependent, and other group quarters (see tables 72 and 73). Data concerning long-term institutional care are available from the Survey of Institutionalized Persons conducted by the Bureau of the Census for the U.S. Department of Health, Education, and Welfare.

Disability and illness.—General health statistics, including morbidity, disability, injuries, preventive care, and findings from physiological and psychological testing, are collected by NCHS in its Health Interview Survey and its Health and Nutrition Examination Surveys and appear in *Vital and Health Statistics*, series 10 and 11. Morbidity data for members of the Armed Services are prepared and published by the Departments of the Army, Navy, and Air Force. The Department of Labor compiles statistics on industrial injuries (see Section 13). Annual incidence data on notifiable diseases are compiled by the Public Health Service (PHS) at its Center for Disease Control in Atlanta, Georgia, and published as a supplement to its *Morbidity and Mortality Weekly Report*. The list of diseases is revised biennially and includes those which, by mutual agreement of the States and PHS, are communicable diseases of national importance.

Nutrition.—Statistics on annual per capita consumption of food and its nutrient value are estimated by the U.S. Department of Agriculture and published quarterly (nutrient value, annually) in *National Food Review*. Historical data can be found in *Food Consumption, Prices, and Expenditures*, issued annually. Data on the Federally Funded Food Distribution Program for Needy Families and Children, the National School Lunch Program, the Special Milk Program, and the Food Stamp Program are published annually in *Agricultural Statistics*.

Statistical reliability.—For discussion of statistical collection, estimation, and sampling procedures and measures of statistical reliability applicable to data from NCHS and the Health Care Financing Administration, see Appendix III.

Historical statistics.—Tabular headnotes provide cross-references, where applicable, to *Historical Statistics of the United States, Colonial Times to 1970*. See Appendix I.

No. 140. NATIONAL HEALTH EXPENDITURES: 1950 TO 1977

[In millions of dollars, except percent. For years ending June 30 except, beginning 1977, ending Sept. 30. Prior to 1960, private expenditures exclude Alaska and Hawaii. See *Historical Statistics, Colonial Times to 1970*, series B 248–261, for calendar year data]

TYPE OF EXPENDITURE	1950	1955	1960	1965	1970	1973	1974	1975	1976	1977 [1]
Total	12,027	17,330	25,856	38,892	69,201	95,383	106,321	123,716	141,013	162,627
Percent of GNP [2]	4.5	4.5	5.2	5.9	7.2	7.7	7.8	8.5	8.7	8.8
Avg. annual percent change [3]	[4] 8.8	7.6	8.3	8.5	15.5	11.3	11.5	16.4	14.0	15.3
Private expenditures	8,962	12,909	19,461	29,357	43,810	58,715	64,809	71,348	80,831	94,185
Health and medical services [5]	8,710	12,529	18,816	28,028	41,329	55,571	61,584	68,421	78,051	91,294
Direct payments	7,107	8,992	12,576	17,577	24,272	30,501	32,988	33,465	38,450	43,274
Insurance benefits	879	2,358	4,698	8,280	14,406	20,434	23,051	28,115	32,119	39,299
Other	724	1,179	1,542	2,166	2,805	4,637	5,545	6,841	7,482	8,721
Medical research	37	55	121	157	193	203	227	280	273	284
Medical facilities construction	215	325	524	1,172	2,288	2,941	2,998	2,647	2,507	2,607
Public expenditures	3,065	4,421	6,395	9,535	25,391	36,668	41,512	52,368	60,182	68,442
Percent of total	25.5	25.5	24.7	24.5	37.0	38.4	39.0	42.3	42.7	42.1
Health and medical services	2,470	3,862	5,346	7,641	22,661	33,261	37,746	47,690	54,321	62,594
OASDHI (Medicare) [6]	(X)	(X)	(X)	(X)	7,149	9,479	11,348	14,809	17,769	21,591
Temporary disability insurance [7]	2	20	40	51	63	70	71	73	87	103
Workers' comp. (med.) [7]	193	315	420	580	985	1,355	1,600	1,860	2,125	2,609
Public assistance med. paym'ts [8]	51	212	493	1,367	5,213	9,209	10,372	13,275	15,376	17,620
General hospital, medical care [9]	886	1,298	1,973	2,516	3,554	4,945	5,293	[10] 7,517	[10] 7,645	[10] 8,296
Defense Dept. hospital, medical	336	745	820	858	1,496	1,990	2,267	} 3,086	3,163	3,392
Military dependents' medical	(X)	(X)	60	78	264	478	474			
Maternal, child health programs	30	93	141	223	431	455	493	545	593	637
School health (educ. depts.)	31	66	101	142	247	300	325	(10)	(10)	(10)
Other public health activities	351	384	401	677	1,475	2,218	2,531	2,960	3,485	3,729
Veterans' hospital, medical care	583	721	879	1,115	1,651	2,587	2,787	3,302	3,802	4,334
Medical vocational rehabilitation	7	9	18	34	134	175	185	263	276	283
Medical research	73	139	471	1,229	1,727	2,203	2,300	2,692	3,341	3,400
Medical facilities construction	522	419	578	665	1,003	1,204	1,466	1,986	2,520	2,448
Veterans Administration	162	34	60	77	71	105	119	137	(NA)	(NA)
Other	361	385	518	588	932	1,099	1,347	1,849	(NA)	(NA)
Personal health care [11]	10,400	15,231	22,729	33,498	60,113	82,490	91,315	107,383	122,453	142,586
Private expenditures	8,298	11,762	17,799	26,540	39,568	52,428	57,259	63,940	73,195	85,465
Percent of total	79.8	77.2	78.3	79.2	65.8	63.6	62.7	59.5	59.8	59.9
Under 19 years old	(NA)	(NA)	(NA)	(NA)	7,292	9,507	10,875	11,934	13,406	(NA)
19–64 years old	(NA)	(NA)	(NA)	(NA)	25,902	33,927	38,132	42,431	48,357	(NA)
65 years and over	(NA)	(NA)	(NA)	(NA)	6,376	8,994	8,252	9,574	11,433	(NA)
Public expenditures	2,102	3,469	4,930	6,958	20,545	30,062	34,056	43,443	49,259	57,121
Under 19 years old	(NA)	(NA)	(NA)	(NA)	2,335	3,504	3,866	4,296	4,771	(NA)
19–64 years old	(NA)	(NA)	(NA)	(NA)	8,073	12,433	14,264	18,152	20,472	(NA)
65 years and over	(NA)	(NA)	(NA)	(NA)	10,138	14,126	15,927	20,995	24,016	(NA)

NA Not available.   X Not applicable.   [1] Preliminary.   [2] Gross national product; see section 14. [3] Change from prior year shown, except as noted.   [4] Change from 1945.   [5] Total revised for 1965 and 1970; detail unrevised and will not add to total.   [6] Federal hospital and medical insurance under old-age, survivors, disability, and health insurance programs; see text, p. 323.   [7] Includes medical benefits paid under public law by private insurance carriers and self-insurers.   [8] Payments to vendors of medical services.   [9] Primarily State and local psychiatric hospitals.   [10] Beginning 1975, school health included under general hospital, medical care. [11] See headnote, table 145.

Source: U.S. Social Security Administration. Periodically in *Social Security Bulletin*. Data from U.S. Health Care Financing Administration.

No. 141. INDEXES OF MEDICAL CARE PRICES: 1960 TO 1977

[1967=100. 1960 excludes Alaska and Hawaii. These indexes are components of consumer price index; for explanation, see text, pp. 481 and 482. See also *Historical Statistics, Colonial Times to 1970*, series B 262–272]

YEAR	Index, total	Average annual percent change	Hospital semi-private room	PROFESSIONAL SERVICES				Drugs and pre-scrip-tions	Optometric examina-tion, eye-glasses
				Physi-cians' fees	Obstet-rical cases	Tonsillec-tomy, ade-noidectomy	Den-tists' fees		
1960	79.1	[1] 3.5	57.3	77.0	79.4	80.3	82.1	104.5	85.1
1965	89.5	[2] 2.5	75.9	88.3	89.0	91.0	92.2	100.2	92.8
1968	106.1	[2] 5.8	113.6	105.6	105.2	104.9	105.5	100.2	103.2
1969	113.4	6.9	128.8	112.9	113.5	110.3	112.9	101.3	107.6
1970	120.6	6.3	145.4	121.4	121.8	117.1	119.4	103.6	113.5
1971	128.4	6.5	163.1	129.8	129.0	125.2	127.0	105.4	120.3
1972	132.5	3.2	173.9	133.8	133.8	129.9	132.3	105.6	124.9
1973	137.7	3.9	182.1	138.2	138.1	132.8	136.4	105.9	129.5
1974	150.5	9.3	201.5	150.9	149.0	144.1	146.8	109.6	138.6
1975	168.6	12.0	236.1	169.4	167.2	163.3	161.9	118.8	149.6
1976	184.7	9.5	268.8	188.5	192.1	179.2	172.2	126.0	158.9
1977	202.4	9.6	299.5	206.0	207.8	200.2	185.1	134.1	168.2

[1] Change from 1955.   [2] Change from preceding year shown.

Source: U.S. Bureau of Labor Statistics, *Consumer Price Indexes for Selected Items and Groups, Monthly and Annual Averages*.

No. 142. National Health Expenditures, by Object: 1950 to 1977

[For years ending June 30 except, beginning 1977, ending Sept. 30. See Historical Statistics, Colonial Times to 1970, series B 221-235, for calendar year data]

OBJECT OF EXPENDITURE	EXPENDITURE (bil. dol.)									PERCENT		
	1950	1955	1960	1965	1970	1974	1975	1976	1977	1960	1970	1977
Total	12.0	17.3	25.9	38.9	69.2	106.3	123.7	141.0	162.6	100.0	100.0	100.0
Spent by:												
Consumers	8.3	11.9	18.1	27.1	40.2	59.8	65.6	74.9	87.8	69.9	58.1	54.0
Government	3.1	4.4	6.4	9.5	25.4	41.5	52.4	60.2	68.4	24.7	36.7	42.1
Philanthropy and other	.7	1.0	1.4	2.3	3.8	5.0	5.8	5.9	6.4	5.4	5.5	3.9
Spent for:												
Health services and supplies	11.2	16.4	24.2	35.7	64.1	99.3	116.1	132.4	153.9	93.4	92.6	94.6
Personal health care expense	10.4	15.2	22.7	33.5	60.1	91.3	107.4	122.5	142.6	87.9	86.9	87.7
Hospital care	3.7	5.7	8.5	13.2	25.9	41.0	48.4	55.6	65.6	32.9	37.4	40.4
Physicians' services	2.7	3.6	5.6	8.4	13.4	19.7	23.8	27.5	32.2	21.6	19.4	19.8
Dentists' services	.9	1.5	1.9	2.7	4.5	6.9	7.9	8.7	10.0	7.5	6.5	6.2
Other professional services [1]	.4	.6	.8	1.0	1.4	1.9	2.4	2.4	3.2	3.3	2.0	2.0
Drugs and sundries	1.6	2.3	3.6	4.6	7.1	9.4	10.4	11.3	12.5	13.9	10.3	7.7
Eyeglasses and appliances [2]	.5	.6	.8	1.2	1.8	1.7	1.8	1.9	2.1	2.9	2.6	1.3
Nursing home care	.2	.3	.5	1.3	3.8	7.5	9.3	10.7	12.6	1.9	5.5	7.8
Other health services	.4	.8	1.0	1.2	2.2	3.2	3.5	4.0	4.3	4.0	3.2	2.7
Expense for prepayment and administration [3]	.4	.7	1.0	1.5	2.5	5.5	5.8	6.4	7.6	3.9	3.6	4.7
Gov't public health activities	.4	.4	.4	.7	1.4	2.5	3.0	3.5	3.7	1.6	2.1	2.3
Research	.1	.2	.6	1.4	1.8	2.5	3.0	3.6	3.7	2.3	2.7	2.3
Construction	.7	.7	1.1	1.8	3.3	4.5	4.6	5.0	5.1	4.3	4.8	3.1

[1] Includes services of registered and practical nurses in private duty, visiting nurses, podiatrists, physical therapists, clinical psychologists, chiropractors, naturopaths, and Christian Science practitioners.
[2] Includes fees of optometrists and expenditures for hearing aids, orthopedic appliances, artificial limbs, crutches, wheelchairs, etc.   [3] Net cost of insurance and administrative expenses of federally financed health programs.

Source: U.S. Social Security Administration, Social Security Bulletin, July 1978. Data from U.S. Health Care Financing Administration.

No. 143. Health Services and Supplies—Per Capita National and Private Consumer Expenditures, by Object: 1950 to 1977

[In dollars. For years ending June 30 except, beginning 1977, ending Sept. 30. Prior to 1960, private expenditures exclude Alaska and Hawaii. Based on Bureau of the Census data for total U.S. population as of January 1 through 1976, as of April 1 beginning 1977; including Armed Forces and Federal employees abroad and civilian population of outlying areas. Excludes research and construction. See also Historical Statistics, Colonial Times to 1970, series B 222-232]

OBJECT OF EXPENDITURE	1950	1955	1960	1965	1970	1975	1976	1977
Total, national	72.83	98.14	132.35	181.34	308.81	536.09	606.19	697.32
Hospital care	24.09	34.06	46.56	66.87	124.74	223.36	254.49	297.38
Physicians' services	17.52	21.75	30.57	42.74	64.80	110.07	125.87	145.84
Dentists' services	6.12	8.72	10.65	13.87	21.56	36.34	39.99	45.41
Other professional services	2.50	3.30	4.65	5.03	6.68	10.98	12.59	14.56
Drugs and drug sundries	10.70	13.66	19.67	23.63	34.29	47.82	51.63	56.72
Eyeglasses and appliances [1]	3.09	3.62	4.11	5.85	8.56	8.08	8.90	9.45
Nursing home care	1.16	1.74	2.63	6.46	18.40	43.13	48.82	57.18
Other health services	2.57	4.65	5.66	5.87	10.73	16.02	18.48	19.59
Expenses for prepayment and administration [2]	2.79	4.37	5.66	7.61	12.12	26.63	29.46	34.31
Government public health activities	2.29	2.30	2.19	3.41	6.93	13.66	15.96	16.90
Total, private consumer	53.81	71.52	98.96	137.64	193.74	302.72	342.92	397.88
Hospital care	12.21	17.39	25.78	40.28	59.56	89.28	105.86	126.37
Physicians' services	16.61	20.26	28.53	40.01	50.62	82.75	94.72	110.19
Dentists' services	6.12	8.72	10.63	13.70	20.56	34.36	37.80	43.14
Other professional services	2.33	3.12	4.44	4.74	5.05	8.26	8.98	9.86
Drugs and drug sundries	10.64	13.51	19.31	22.95	32.14	43.55	46.72	51.54
Eyeglasses and appliances [1]	3.04	3.51	4.03	5.71	8.28	7.58	8.36	8.86
Nursing home care	1.07	1.44	1.89	4.07	10.23	18.54	20.73	24.21
Expenses for prepayment	1.78	3.57	4.34	6.16	7.30	18.40	19.75	23.71

[1] Includes fees of optometrists and expenditures for hearing aids, orthopedic appliances, artificial limbs, etc.
[2] Includes the net cost of insurance and administrative expenses of federally financed health programs.

Source: U.S. Social Security Administration, Social Security Bulletin, July 1978. Data from U.S. Health Care Financing Administration.

Health and Medical Expenditures 101

No. 144. Government Expenditures for Health and Medical Services, by Type of Service: 1975 to 1977

[In millions of dollars, except percent. For years ending June 30 except, beginning 1977, ending Sept. 30]

YEAR AND TYPE OF SERVICE	Total [1]	FEDERAL			State and local	Medicare [2] (OAS-DHI)	Public assistance [3]	OTHER HEALTH AND MEDICAL CARE		
		Amount	Percent of total					General [4]	Defense Dept.[5]	Veterans
1975, total [6]	47,690	31,129	65.3		16,561	14,809	13,275	7,517	3,086	3,302
Hospital care	27,759	18,699	67.4		9,060	10,677	4,393	6,424	2,337	2,748
Percent of total	58.2	60.1	(X)		54.4	72.1	33.1	85.5	75.7	83.2
Physicians' services	5,880	4,205	71.5		1,675	2,981	1,783	15	75	34
Nursing home care	5,250	2,985	56.9		2,265	273	4,815	–	–	162
Public health activities	2,960	1,148	38.8		1,812	–	–	–	–	–
Drugs and sundries	925	483	52.2		442	–	855	2	10	8
Administration	1,288	1,056	82.0		231	676	548	1	22	37
1976, total [6]	54,321	36,496	67.2		17,825	17,769	15,376	7,645	3,163	3,802
Hospital care	31,032	21,735	70.0		9,297	12,577	5,197	6,280	2,294	3,167
Percent of total	57.1	59.6	(X)		52.2	70.8	33.8	82.1	72.5	83.3
Physicians' services	6,763	4,921	72.8		1,842	3,580	1,923	19	82	42
Nursing home care	6,049	3,474	57.4		2,575	314	5,547	–	–	189
Public health activities	3,485	1,320	37.9		2,165	–	–	–	–	–
Drugs and sundries	1,072	567	52.9		505	–	991	2	11	11
Administration	1,577	1,330	84.3		248	832	681	–	25	-35
1977, total [6]	62,594	42,542	68.0		20,051	21,591	17,620	8,296	3,392	4,334
Hospital care	36,199	25,715	71.0		10,484	15,520	6,154	6,877	2,459	3,589
Percent of total	57.8	60.4	(X)		52.3	71.9	34.9	82.9	72.5	82.8
Physicians' services	7,824	5,808	74.2		2,016	4,431	1,885	21	91	58
Nursing home care	7,184	4,204	58.5		2,980	362	6,583	–	–	238
Public health activities	3,729	1,289	34.6		2,440	–	–	–	–	–
Drugs and sundries	1,143	614	53.7		529	–	1,048	3	12	13
Administration	1,743	1,430	82.0		313	821	846	–	31	40

– Represents zero.   X Not applicable.   [1] Includes other programs not shown separately.   [2] Federal hospital and medical insurance payments under old-age, survivors, disability, and health insurance program. [3] Payments made directly to suppliers of medical care. Primarily Medicaid.   [4] Primarily State and local psychiatric hospitals. Includes school health expenditures.   [5] Includes dependents of military personnel. [6] Includes other types of expenditures, not shown separately.

Source: U.S. Social Security Administration, *Social Security Bulletin*, July 1978, and unpublished data. Data from U.S. Health Care Financing Administration.

No. 145. Personal Health Care Expenditures, by Type, Source of Payment, and Age Group: 1977

[In millions of dollars, except as indicated. Estimates for year ending September 30. Covers all expenditures for health services and supplies except expenses for prepayment and administration, government public health activities, and expenditures of philanthropic agencies for fund raising activities]

SOURCE AND AGE GROUP	Total	Total expenditures per capita [1] (dol.)	Hospital care	Physicians' services	Dentists' services	Other professional services	Drugs and drug sundries	Eyeglasses and appliances	Nursing home care	Other health services
Total	142,586	646.11	65,627	32,184	10,020	3,212	12,516	2,086	12,618	4,322
Direct payments	43,274	196.09	3,866	12,502	7,965	1,398	10,401	1,918	5,226	–
Third party payments	99,312	450.02	61,761	19,682	2,055	1,814	2,115	169	7,393	4,322
Private health ins	39,299	178.08	24,021	11,817	1,554	777	973	39	118	–
Government	57,121	258.84	36,199	7,823	501	924	1,142	130	7,184	3,217
Philanthropy and ind.	2,891	13.10	1,540	42	–	113	–	–	91	1,105
Private [2]	85,465	387.27	29,427	24,360	9,520	2,288	11,373	1,956	5,434	1,105
Total expend., 65 yr. old and over	41,095	1,738.37	18,375	7,156	842	715	3,110	453	10,056	388
Percent of total	28.8	(X)	28.0	22.2	8.4	22.3	24.8	21.7	79.7	9.0
Public, 65 and over	27,778	1,175.04	17,274	4,255	46	490	436	9	4,911	355
Percent of total public	48.6	(X)	47.7	54.4	9.2	53.0	38.2	6.9	68.4	11.0
Private, 65 and over [2]	13,317	563.33	1,101	2,901	795	224	2,674	444	5,145	33
Percent of total private	15.6	(X)	3.7	11.9	8.4	9.8	23.5	22.7	94.7	3.0

– Represents zero.   X Not applicable.   [1] For basis of per capita figures, see headnote, table 143. [2] Covers direct payments, private health insurance, and philanthropy and industry.

Source: U.S. Social Security Administration, *Social Security Bulletin*, July 1978, and unpublished data. Data from U.S. Health Care Financing Administration.

No. 146. Personal Health Care—Third Party Payments and Private Consumer Expenditures: 1950 to 1977

[In millions of dollars, except percent. For years ending June 30 except, beginning 1977, ending Sept. 30. Prior to 1960, excludes Alaska and Hawaii]

ITEM	1950	1955	1960	1965	1970	1975	1976	1977
Personal health care expenditures [1]	10,400	15,231	22,729	33,498	60,113	107,383	122,453	142,586
Third party payments, total	3,293	6,239	10,153	15,921	35,841	73,918	84,003	99,312
Percent of total health care	31.7	41.0	44.7	47.5	59.6	68.8	68.6	69.7
Private insurance payments	879	2,358	4,698	8,280	14,406	28,115	32,119	39,299
Government expenditures	2,102	3,469	4,930	6,958	20,545	43,443	49,259	57,121
Philanthropy and others	312	412	525	683	890	2,360	2,625	2,891
Private consumer expenditures, total [2]	7,986	11,350	17,274	25,857	38,678	61,580	70,569	82,573
Percent met by insurance [3]	11.0	20.8	27.2	32.0	37.2	45.7	45.5	47.6
Hospital care	1,875	2,904	4,707	7,922	12,356	19,336	23,117	27,887
Percent met by insurance [3]	32.5	53.7	66.4	69.3	74.3	88.6	85.2	86.1
Physicians' services	2,549	3,384	5,209	7,869	10,502	17,923	20,684	24,318
Percent met by insurance [3]	10.6	23.6	29.3	32.5	42.5	48.3	47.1	48.6

[1] See headnote, table 145.
[2] Includes other expenditures not shown separately. Excludes expenses for prepayment.   [3] Private insurance.

Source: U.S. Social Security Administration, *Social Security Bulletin*, April 1977 and unpublished data. Data from U.S. Health Care Financing Administration.

No. 147. Private Health Insurance—Persons Covered for Specified Benefits: 1960 to 1976

[In millions, except percent. For persons covered under Federal Government programs, see tables 548–550. HIAA = Health Insurance Association of America. See *Historical Statistics, Colonial Times to 1970*, series B 401–412, for persons covered]

BENEFIT AND TYPE OF PLAN	1960	1965	1970	1972	1973	1974	1975	1976
Hospital benefits, persons covered:								
Estimate, household survey (net) [1]	[2]129.8	[3]145.5	154.1	155.3	(NA)	163.4	162.4	164.2
Percent of population covered [4]	[2]70.0	[3]73.9	75.9	74.9	(NA)	77.6	76.4	76.8
Estimate by HIAA (net) [5]	122.5	138.7	158.8	164.1	168.5	173.1	178.0	176.6
Percent of population covered [4]	68.2	71.9	78.2	79.2	80.6	82.2	83.8	82.6
Blue Cross-Blue Shield plans	57.5	63.7	75.5	78.6	81.3	83.8	85.8	(NA)
Insurance companies	76.6	87.0	107.2	110.5	111.2	114.2	117.3	(NA)
Group policies	54.4	63.0	80.5	81.5	83.6	85.4	87.2	(NA)
Individual policies	22.2	24.0	26.7	29.0	27.5	28.8	30.1	(NA)
Other plans [6]	6.0	7.0	8.1	9.0	9.1	8.6	9.1	(NA)
Surgical benefits, persons covered:								
Estimate, household survey (net) [1]	[2]120.5	[3]142.1	150.0	152.7	(NA)	159.5	160.2	162.2
Percent of population covered [4]	[2]65.0	[3]72.2	73.9	73.6	(NA)	75.7	75.4	75.8
Estimate by HIAA (net) [5]	111.5	130.5	151.4	154.7	162.6	166.4	168.9	167.4
Percent of population covered [4]	62.0	67.7	74.6	74.6	77.8	79.0	79.5	78.3
Blue Cross-Blue Shield plans	48.3	56.3	69.1	72.4	75.1	76.9	77.8	(NA)
Insurance companies	71.5	83.2	99.5	101.2	103.1	105.1	106.4	(NA)
Group policies	55.5	65.5	81.5	82.7	84.5	86.6	88.0	(NA)
Individual policies	16.0	17.7	18.0	18.6	18.6	18.5	18.5	(NA)
Other plans [6]	7.3	8.7	10.5	11.5	10.8	11.2	11.4	(NA)
In-hospital medical visits:								
Estimate by Social Security Admin	(NA)	(NA)	145.6	149.7	153.5	157.3	151.6	155.5
Percent of population covered [4]	(NA)	(NA)	71.7	72.2	73.4	74.7	71.4	72.7
Estimate by HIAA (net) [5]	83.2	109.6	138.7	140.9	146.3	158.2	161.9	163.1
Percent of population covered [4]	46.3	56.8	68.3	68.0	70.0	75.1	76.2	76.3
X-ray and lab. exams (out-of-hospital) (net) [7]	(NA)	79.5	142.4	149.4	152.8	152.2	156.7	150.9
Percent of population covered [4]	(NA)	41.2	70.2	72.1	73.1	72.3	73.8	70.6
Office and home visits (net) [7]	(NA)	(NA)	67.8	67.7	(NA)	126.2	127.7	124.1
Percent of population covered [4]	(NA)	(NA)	33.4	32.7	(NA)	59.9	60.1	58.0
Dental care (net) [7]	(NA)	3.1	12.2	17.9	22.0	32.9	34.5	46.6
Percent of population covered [4]	(NA)	1.6	6.0	8.6	10.5	15.6	16.2	21.8
Prescribed drugs (out-of-hospital) (net) [7]	(NA)	53.2	101.0	111.4	125.0	142.2	149.3	150.2
Percent of population covered [4]	(NA)	27.6	49.7	53.7	59.8	67.5	70.3	70.2
Private duty nursing (net) [7]	(NA)	56.0	100.2	109.0	118.8	140.4	145.9	147.3
Percent of population covered [4]	(NA)	29.0	49.4	52.6	56.9	66.6	68.7	68.9
Visiting nurse service (net) [7]	(NA)	60.1	106.9	115.9	122.7	135.8	141.6	145.9
Percent of population covered [4]	(NA)	31.2	52.6	55.9	58.7	64.5	66.6	68.2
Nursing home care (net) [7]	(NA)	9.9	32.4	45.5	69.2	69.6	70.1	70.4
Percent of population covered [4]	(NA)	5.1	16.0	21.9	33.1	33.0	33.0	32.9

NA Not available.   [1] Periodic surveys conducted by U.S. National Center for Health Statistics. Number of persons covered by type of insurer represents gross enrollment.   [2] 1962 data.   [3] 1967 data. [4] Based on Bureau of the Census estimated civilian population as of end of year.   [5] Includes duplication which occurs when persons are members of an independent prepaid or self-insured plan with which an insurance company has an administrative service agreement and/or a minimum premium plan.   [6] All private plans other than Blue Cross-Blue Shield and insurance companies; based on estimates from Social Security Admin. [7] Estimates.

Source: U.S. Social Security Administration, *Social Security Bulletin*, June 1977.

No. 148. Persons Covered by Private Health Insurance: 1967 to 1976

TYPE OF CARE	PERCENT UNDER 65 YEARS						PERCENT 65 YEARS AND OVER					
	1967	1970	1972	1974	1975	1976	1967	1970	1972	1974	1975	1976
Hospital care	77.0	78.6	77.0	79.9	78.1	78.5	45.0	51.4	56.4	57.9	62.7	62.8
Physicians' services:												
Surgical services	75.2	76.9	76.0	78.3	77.9	78.3	44.1	46.7	52.9	54.0	55.0	55.6
In-hospital visits	65.6	75.1	76.1	78.7	79.6	76.3	31.1	41.1	38.5	40.1	42.8	43.4
X-ray and laboratory exams	50.0	73.8	76.1	77.0	78.2	75.0	18.7	37.4	36.6	32.0	37.1	34.2
Office and home visits	(NA)	35.2	34.2	63.5	63.9	62.2	(NA)	17.3	19.1	29.2	28.6	24.1
Dental care	2.6	6.6	9.5	17.1	17.8	24.0	.4	.6	1.4	3.0	2.8	3.3
Prescribed drugs (out-of-hospital)	39.0	53.5	58.0	73.4	76.1	76.3	9.7	15.9	16.6	17.3	21.8	20.6
Private duty nursing	41.5	53.1	56.7	72.5	74.3	74.8	11.7	15.8	16.3	16.9	21.7	20.0
Visiting nurse service	44.6	56.4	59.9	69.6	71.8	73.9	13.0	18.8	21.2	20.6	24.1	21.6
Nursing home care	8.9	15.4	21.5	35.0	34.6	34.4	15.2	24.7	25.8	16.2	19.6	20.9

NA Not available.
Source: U.S. Social Security Administration, *Social Security Bulletin*, June 1977.

No. 149. Major Medical Expense Insurance—Persons Covered: 1960 to 1976

[In millions. As of Dec. 31. Beginning 1975, includes Puerto Rico and outlying areas. Represents persons covered by insurance companies only. Coverage provides protection against especially heavy medical bills resulting from "catastrophic" or prolonged illness, and is used to supplement basic medical care insurance or as a comprehensive integrated program providing both basic and major medical protection, including charges for private duty nursing, drugs, and medical appliances]

TYPE OF COVERAGE	1960	1965	1970	1971	1972	1973	1974	1975	1976
Insurance companies, net total	25.4	53.0	77.1	80.3	83.7	87.8	91.0	92.2	93.2
Group policies, net total	24.4	49.7	73.7	77.0	79.0	82.7	86.0	87.0	88.5
Supplementary	18.0	42.5	61.7	63.4	64.4	66.2	67.9	67.3	66.8
Comprehensive	8.5	13.0	20.2	22.1	23.4	25.7	27.6	29.4	31.6
Individual and family policies	1.6	4.5	5.4	5.5	6.6	7.3	7.2	7.3	6.7

No. 150. Health Insurance Benefits Paid, 1970 to 1975, and Average Cost Per Patient to Community Hospitals, 1975 and 1976—States

[Cost data cover non-Federal short-term general or special hospitals (excluding psychiatric or tuberculosis). Cost per patient based on total hospital expenses (payroll, employee benefits, professional fees, supplies, etc.)]

STATE	HEALTH INSURANCE BENEFITS PAID (mil. dol.)			AVERAGE COST TO HOSPITAL (dol.)				STATE	HEALTH INSURANCE BENEFITS PAID (mil. dol.)			AVERAGE COST TO HOSPITAL (dol.)			
				Per stay		Per day						Per stay		Per day	
	1970	1974	1975	1975	1976	1975	1976		1970	1974	1975	1975	1976	1975	1976
U.S.	17,177	27,294	31,670	1,164	1,330	151	173	Mo	428	653	753	1,059	1,228	129	150
								Mont	44	66	79	711	834	111	132
Ala	249	352	414	831	963	114	134	Nebr	107	160	191	945	1,065	117	133
Alaska	20	26	30	1,128	1,382	225	276	Nev	30	58	69	1,186	1,392	182	208
Ariz	130	239	297	1,296	1,448	175	198	N.H	49	82	90	919	1,046	130	147
Ark	89	151	182	664	772	102	121	N.J	590	899	1,056	1,239	1,428	142	162
Calif	1,846	2,931	3,422	1,435	1,674	217	254	N. Mex	51	80	90	839	1,062	142	177
Colo	177	274	347	983	1,182	149	176	N.Y	1,834	3,386	3,284	1,875	1,938	189	196
Conn	305	468	542	1,415	1,628	189	217								
Del	57	95	117	1,350	1,552	163	185	N.C	288	480	548	872	985	115	131
D.C	211	355	429	1,640	1,921	208	240	N. Dak	49	68	94	818	997	98	122
Fla	416	752	939	1,118	1,275	151	172	Ohio	1,054	1,604	1,928	1,140	1,312	139	162
Ga	293	503	574	889	1,007	139	157	Okla	157	246	301	862	1,010	129	155
Hawaii	60	114	144	1,049	1,289	152	187	Oreg	170	280	334	1,000.	1,199	159	190
								Pa	1,085	1,616	1,916	1,214	1,386	143	165
Idaho	41	64	76	765	866	121	144	R.I	84	129	151	1,506	1,732	188	211
Ill	1,033	1,551	1,779	1,281	1,489	160	186	S.C	138	230	278	831	938	114	130
Ind	464	684	824	1,004	1,163	127	147								
Iowa	225	323	375	856	1,001	110	132	S. Dak	32	42	54	690	813	98	116
Kans	161	264	337	881	1,016	113	132	Tenn	287	456	521	854	988	114	134
Ky	184	302	362	779	909	110	128	Tex	811	1,280	1,595	876	1,012	129	151
La	250	340	400	889	987	137	152	Utah	72	113	136	830	937	148	170
Maine	65	98	116	1,018	1,181	137	157	Vt	33	50	56	1,023	1,198	131	144
Md	272	448	509	1,502	1,715	181	202	Va	279	461	535	979	1,144	122	145
Mass	575	891	1,061	1,745	2,009	205	236	Wash	255	436	527	961	1,130	172	202
Mich	1,171	1,735	2,102	1,362	1,577	166	195	W. Va	130	225	246	832	954	109	129
Minn	289	403	467	1,073	1,222	122	140	Wis	409	627	752	1,047	1,257	128	150
Miss	107	172	197	705	802	102	118	Wyo	21	32	44	643	782	117	135

Source of tables 149 and 150: Health Insurance Institute, Washington, D.C., *Source Book of Health Insurance Data*, annual. Data from Health Insurance Association of America, New York, N.Y.

No. 151. Physicians, Dentists, and Nurses: 1950 to 1976

[Physicians as of **end of year**; dentists as of **midyear**; nurses as of **Jan. 1** following year stated, except **April 1** for 1950. Prior to 1960, data for nurses exclude Alaska and Hawaii. Data for physicians include Puerto Rico and outlying areas. See also *Historical Statistics, Colonial Times to 1970*, series B 275–290]

ITEM	1950	1955	1960	1965	1970	1973	1974	1975	1976
Physicians, number_____1,000__	233	255	275	305	348	382	394	409	426
Rate per 100,000 population [1]_____	149	150	148	153	166	178	182	188	194
Doctors of medicine [2]_____1,000__	220	242	260	292	334	366	380	394	409
Active (exc. in Federal service)__1,000__	(NA)	(NA)	(NA)	255	282	312	324	338	351
Rate per 100,000 population [3]_____	(NA)	(NA)	(NA)	130	137	147	151	157	161
Doctors of osteopathy_____1,000__	13	14	14	13	14	[4]15	[4]15	[4]15	[4]16
Physicians admitted to U.S. as immigrants [5]_____1,000__	1.9	1.0	1.6	2.0	3.2	7.1	6.3	7.1	8.1
Medical and osteopathic schools, number___	85	87	91	93	107	114	121	123	123
Students_____1,000__	26.9	30.5	32.0	34.1	39.7	50.1	53.7	57.2	59.6
Graduates_____1,000__	5.9	7.4	7.5	7.8	8.8	11.0	12.2	14.1	14.3
Dentists ,number [6]_____1,000__	87	95	103	109	116	122	(NA)	(NA)	(NA)
Active (exc. in Federal service)____1,000__	75	76	85	86	96	101	(NA)	108	110
Rate per 100,000 population [3]_____	50	47	47	45	47	48	(NA)	50	52
Dental schools, number_____	41	43	47	49	53	56	58	59	59
Students_____1,000__	11.5	12.6	13.6	13.9	16.0	18.4	19.4	20.1	20.8
Graduates_____1,000__	2.6	3.1	3.3	3.2	3.7	4.2	4.5	5.0	5.3
Nurses, number (active registered)___1,000__	375	430	504	613	700	815	857	906	961
Rate per 100,000 population [1]_____	249	259	282	319	345	390	404	427	449
Nursing schools, number_____	1,203	1,139	1,119	1,153	1,328	1,363	1,359	1,360	1,349
Students_____1,000__	99	108	115	130	151	213	233	244	250
Graduates_____1,000__	26	29	30	35	44	59	68	75	78

NA Not available.   [1] Based on Bureau of the Census resident population estimates; see source for estimates used.   [2] Excludes non-Federal physicians with temporary foreign addresses.   [3] Based on Bureau of the Census civilian population estimates; see source for estimate used.   [4] Estimated.   [5] Source: U.S. Immigration and Naturalization Service, *Annual Report.*   [6] Beginning 1960, excludes graduates of year stated.

Source: Except as noted, U.S. National Center for Health Statistics, *Health Resources Statistics,* annual.

No. 152. Newly-Licensed Physicians, by Origin of Training: 1960 to 1976

ORIGIN OF TRAINING	1960	1965	1970	1972	1973	1974	1975	1976
Newly-licensed physicians, total_____	8,030	9,147	11,032	14,476	16,689	16,706	16,859	17,724
Percent of total active M.D.'s_____	(NA)	3.3	3.5	4.3	4.9	4.8	4.6	4.7
Graduates of—								
U.S. and Canadian medical schools_____	6,611	7,619	8,016	7,815	9,270	10,093	10,894	11,288
Foreign medical schools_____	1,419	1,528	3,016	6,661	7,419	6,613	5,965	6,436
Percent of total newly-licensed_____	17.7	16.7	27.3	46.0	44.5	39.6	35.4	36.3
United States citizens_____	386	411	198	240	299	(NA)	(NA)	(NA)

NA Not available.

Source: American Medical Association, Chicago, Ill., *Medical Licensure Statistics,* annual; beginning 1974, *Physician Distribution and Medical Licensure in the U.S.,* annual. (Copyright.)

No. 153. Employed Persons in Selected Health Occupations: 1972 to 1977

[**Persons 16 years old and over.** Annual averages]

OCCUPATION	1972 (1,000)	1975 (1,000)	1977 Number (1,000)	1977 Percent— Female	1977 Percent— Other than White	OCCUPATION	1972 (1,000)	1975 (1,000)	1977 Number (1,000)	1977 Percent— Female	1977 Percent— Other than White
Total_____	3,511	4,041	4,393	73.7	15.0	Health administrators_____	118	152	175	45.1	5.1
Physicians, dentists, and related_____	624	647	724	10.6	6.9	Health technologists and technicians___	315	397	462	71.4	12.1
Dentists_____	107	110	105	2.9	5.7	Clinical laboratory_	142	177	194	74.2	15.5
Pharmacists_____	126	119	138	17.4	4.3	Radiology_____	68	79	85	71.8	7.1
Physicians, medical and osteopathic__	328	354	403	11.2	9.2	Other_____	104	142	183	67.8	10.4
Other practitioners_	64	64	79	5.1	–	Health service_____	1,505	1,718	1,747	89.2	22.7
Nurses, therapists, and dietitians_____	949	1,126	1,285	92.8	11.5	Health aides and trainees, except nursing_____	148	219	245	84.5	18.0
Registered nurses___	801	935	1,063	96.7	11.3	Nursing aides [1]_____	912	1,001	1,008	86.3	26.5
Therapists and dietitians_____	148	192	222	73.4	12.6	Practical nurses_____	342	370	376	96.8	21.6
						Other_____	103	128	123	98.4	5.7

– Represents zero.   [1] Includes orderlies and attendants.

Source: U.S. Bureau of Labor Statistics, *Employment and Earnings,* Oct. 1973, Jan. 1976, and Jan. 1978.

No. 154. Physicians, by Type of Practice: 1965 to 1976

[As of December 31. Includes Puerto Rico and outlying areas. 1965 data for doctors of medicine not comparable with later years due to changes in classification]

TYPE OF PRACTICE	NUMBER (1,000)							PERCENT DISTRIBUTION			
	1965	1970	1972	1973	1974	1975	1976	1965	1970	1975	1976
All physicians	305.1	348.3	371.4	381.6	394.5	409.0	425.8	100	100	100	100
Doctors of medicine	292.1	1 334.0	1 356.5	1 366.4	1 379.7	1 393.7	1 409.4	96	96	96	96
Active M.D.'s	277.6	311.2	333.3	338.1	350.6	366.4	378.6	91	89	90	89
Non-Federal	268.1	2 301.3	2 325.8	2 334.0	2 345.6	2 359.7	2 373.1	88	87	88	88
Patient care	239.3	255.0	269.1	272.9	278.5	287.8	294.7	78	70	69
Office based 3	185.3	188.9	199.0	199.1	203.9	213.3	214.7	61	54	52	50
General practice 4	66.4	53.3	52.1	50.2	50.2	50.3	50.3	22	15	12	1:
Other specialty, full-time	119.0	135.7	146.9	148.9	153.7	163.0	164.4	39	39	40	39
Training programs	39.6	45.8	49.5	53.9	54.5	53.5	58.9	13	13	13	14
Full-time hospital staff	14.3	20.3	20.6	19.8	20.1	21.0	21.1	5	6	5	5
Other professional activity	15.5	26.3	24.2	24.7	25.1	24.3	26.1	5	8	6	6
Retired, not in practice	13.3	19.6	20.1	22.6	21.6	21.4	22.1	4	6	5	5
Federal	22.8	29.5	27.6	26.8	26.6	28.2	27.6	8	8	7	6
Patient care	20.2	5 23.5	5 24.4	5 22.4	5 22.7	5 24.1	5 23.7	7	7	6	6
Training programs	3.9	5.4	4.0	4.4	4.5	4.3	4.1	1	2	1	1
Full-time hospital staff	16.3	14.6	16.7	15.7	16.2	17.7	17.7	5	4	4	4
Other professional activity	2.7	6.0	4.5	4.4	3.9	4.1	3.9	1	2	1	1
Not reported	1.2	3.2	3.2	5.6	7.5	5.9	8.8	(Z)	1	1	2
Doctors of osteopathy 6	13.0	14.3	14.9	15.2	14.8	15.4	16.4	4	4	4	4

Z Less than .5 percent.   1 Excludes 4,148 non-Federal physicians with temporary foreign addresses in 1970, 4,807 in 1972, 5,118 in 1973, 5,277 in 1974, 5,559 in 1975, and 5,604 in 1976.
2 Includes physicians not classified: 358 for 1970, 12,356 for 1972, 13,744 for 1973, 20,343 for 1974, 26,145 for 1975, and 30,129 in 1976.
3 Includes all physicians rendering patient care (or patient services by pathologists) in solo, partnership, group practice, or other arrangement and those in industry, insurance companies, health departments, laboratories, etc.
4 Includes family practice and no specialty reported or listed.
5 Includes 3,515 Federal physicians in office-based practice for 1970, 2,328 for 1972, 2,301 for 1973, 2,012 for 1974, 2,095 for 1975, and 1,823 for 1976.   6 Source, beginning 1970: American Osteopathic Association, Chicago, Ill.

No. 155. Physicians and Dentists, 1976, and Nurses, 1972—States

[See headnote, table 151. Excludes doctors of osteopathy and dentists in Federal service. Rates based on U.S. Bureau of the Census population estimates; see source]

STATE OR OTHER AREA	ACTIVE PHYSICIANS, 1976		ACTIVE DENTISTS, 1976		ACTIVE REGISTERED NURSES, 1972		STATE OR OTHER AREA	ACTIVE PHYSICIANS, 1976		ACTIVE DENTISTS, 1976		ACTIVE REGISTERED NURSES, 1972	
	Total	Rate 1	Total	Rate 2	Total	Rate 1		Total	Rate 1	Total	Rate 2	Total	Rate 1
Total	3 373,557	4 174	110,000	52	794,979	380	Mont	952	126	414	55	3,261	451
Ala	4,071	111	1,168	32	7,847	223	Nebr	2,144	138	853	55	6,802	443
Alaska	472	116	184	52	1,399	422	Nev	786	128	307	51	1,732	323
Ariz	4,117	183	1,085	48	8,513	428	N.H.	1,319	159	428	52	4,445	572
Ark	2,303	109	668	32	3,776	190	N.J.	12,974	177	4,465	61	31,943	432
Calif	47,223	219	13,743	65	68,668	334	N. Mex	1,714	146	481	42	2,778	258
Colo	5,087	198	1,488	59	11,780	491	N.Y.	46,116	126	12,642	70	89,375	485
Conn	6,951	224	1,978	64	17,887	579	N.C.	7,591	139	1,867	35	16,649	318
Del	905	155	256	44	2,935	514	N. Dak	758	118	279	44	2,885	455
D.C.	4,147	592	644	93	5,020	673	Ohio	16,063	150	4,826	45	42,032	389
Fla	14,604	175	3,806	46	26,202	353	Okla	3,339	121	1,044	38	6,514	246
Ga	6,794	136	1,894	39	12,492	263	Oreg	4,017	173	1,547	67	8,790	399
Hawaii	1,534	174	530	64	3,110	380	Pa	20,394	173	6,093	51	61,927	519
Idaho	871	105	418	51	2,518	329	R.I.	1,823	195	462	50	4,712	485
Ill	19,241	172	5,716	51	44,783	397	S.C.	3,484	123	948	34	7,916	295
Ind	6,234	117	2,073	39	15,841	298	S. Dak	675	98	298	44	3,149	462
Iowa	3,292	115	1,293	45	11,959	413	Tenn	6,230	147	1,901	45	9,446	233
Kans	3,301	144	1,010	44	9,098	400	Tex	18,421	146	5,043	41	28,213	240
Ky	4,401	128	1,276	38	8,487	256	Utah	2,014	163	771	63	3,260	285
La	5,457	141	1,449	38	9,133	245	Vt	968	203	260	55	2,854	612
Maine	1,455	136	455	43	4,810	464	Va	8,169	162	2,238	46	16,647	348
Md	11,160	271	2,277	56	14,847	363	Wash	6,413	178	2,461	69	14,476	420
Mass	14,169	245	3,868	67	37,620	649	W. Va	2,409	131	623	34	6,255	350
Mich	13,220	145	4,578	50	30,546	335	Wis	6,491	141	2,526	55	18,887	416
Minn	7,010	177	2,334	59	19,169	486	Wyo	441	113	178	46	1,480	425
Miss	2,424	102	694	30	5,129	226	P.R.	3,263	(NA)	(NA)	(NA)	(NA)	(NA)
Mo	7,406	155	2,160	45	14,982	312	Outlying areas	1,752	(NA)	(NA)	(NA)	(NA)	(NA)

NA Not available.   1 Per 100,000 resident population as of July 1.   2 Per 100,000 civilian population as of July 1.   3 Excludes physicians with addresses unknown.   4 U.S. only.

Source of tables 154 and 155: Except as noted, U.S. National Center for Health Statistics, *Health Resources Statistics*, annual; American Nurses Association, Kansas City, Mo., *The Nation's Nurses: 1972 Inventory of Registered Nurses* (copyright), and unpublished data.

No. 156. PHYSICIANS, BY SEX, SPECIALTY, AND MAJOR PROFESSIONAL ACTIVITY: 1970 TO 1976

[In thousands. As of December 31. Includes Puerto Rico and outlying areas]

SPECIALTY	1970, total	1975, total	1976, total	PATIENT CARE, 1976				OTHER PROFESSIONAL, 1976		
				Total	Office-based	Hospital-based		Medical teaching	Administration	Research and other
						Full-time	Residents [1]			
Total_____	[2] 334.0	[2] 393.7	[2] 409.4	318.4	216.5	38.8	63.0	6.9	11.7	11.4
Male_____	(NA)	[3] 358.1	[3] 370.7	292.5	204.0	34.4	54.2	6.1	10.6	10.3
Female_____	(NA)	[3] 35.6	[3] 38.8	25.9	12.6	4.5	8.8	.8	1.1	1.1
General practice_____	57.9	54.6	55.5	54.3	46.6	3.3	4.4	.2	.6	.3
Medical [4]_____	77.2	95.1	99.4	89.2	54.4	10.4	24.4	2.6	2.9	4.7
Internal medicine____	41.9	54.3	57.9	52.3	28.2	5.9	18.3	1.2	1.6	2.8
Pediatrics_____	17.9	21.7	22.5	20.5	13.0	2.2	5.4	.6	.7	.7
Surgical [4]_____	86.0	96.0	98.7	95.1	68.7	7.4	19.1	1.3	1.1	1.2
General surgery_____	29.8	31.6	32.3	31.1	19.9	2.7	8.5	.4	.5	.3
Obstetrics, gynecol'y_	18.9	21.7	22.3	21.3	16.0	1.5	3.8	.3	.4	.3
Ophthalmology_____	9.9	11.1	11.5	11.1	8.9	.5	1.6	.1	.1	.2
Orthopedic_____	9.6	11.4	11.8	11.5	8.4	1.0	2.1	.2	.1	.1
Other [4]_____	89.6	94.6	94.9	79.8	46.9	17.8	15.1	2.9	7.0	5.3
Anesthesiology_____	10.1	12.9	13.2	12.3	9.1	1.5	1.7	.5	.2	.1
Psychiatry_____	21.1	23.9	24.4	21.5	12.4	5.1	4.0	.5	1.8	.6
Pathology_____	10.3	11.7	11.9	9.8	4.3	3.0	2.6	.4	.5	1.2
Radiology_____	10.5	11.5	11.7	11.0	7.0	2.1	1.8	.3	.1	.4

NA Not available. [1] Includes interns. [2] 1970, includes 19,621 inactive, 358 not classified, 3,204 address unknown; 1975, 21,449 inactive, 26,145 not classified, 5,868 address unknown; 1976, 22,117 inactive, 30,129 not classified, and 8,757 address unknown. [3] Includes inactive, not classified, and address unknown. [4] Includes specialists not shown separately.

Source: American Medical Association, Chicago, Ill., *Distribution of Physicians in the U.S., 1970*; and *Physician Distribution and Medical Licensure in the U.S.*, annual. (Copyright.)

No. 157. PHYSICIAN AND DENTAL VISITS: 1970 TO 1976

[Refers to the civilian noninstitutional population]

SEX AND AGE OF PATIENT	PHYSICIAN VISITS					DENTAL VISITS				
	1970	1973	1974	1975	1976	1970	1973	1974	1975	1976
Total visits_____mil__	927	1,031	1,025	1,056	1,041	304	333	342	341	336
By males_____mil__	396	430	427	435	435	133	142	150	153	147
By females_____mil__	531	601	598	621	606	171	190	192	188	189
Visits per person_____	4.6	5.0	4.9	5.1	4.9	1.5	1.6	1.7	1.6	1.6
By males_____	4.1	4.3	4.3	4.3	4.3	1.4	1.4	1.5	1.5	1.4
By females_____	5.1	5.6	5.6	5.7	5.6	1.7	1.8	1.8	1.7	1.7
Under 6 years_____	5.9	6.2	6.3	6.5	6.3	.5	.5	.5	.6	.5
6–16 years_____	2.9	3.3	3.2	3.2	3.0	1.9	2.1	2.1	2.0	1.9
17–24 years_____	4.6	4.9	4.5	4.8	4.4	1.8	1.7	1.7	1.8	1.8
25–44 years_____	4.6	5.1	5.0	5.1	4.9	1.7	1.7	1.7	1.7	1.7
45–64 years_____	5.2	5.5	5.5	5.6	5.7	1.5	1.7	1.8	1.8	1.8
65 years and over_____	6.3	6.5	6.7	6.6	6.9	1.1	1.1	1.2	1.2	1.2

Source: U.S. National Center for Health Statistics, *Vital and Health Statistics*, series 10, Nos. 72, 95, 100, 115, 119, and unpublished data.

No. 158. AVERAGE FEES FOR INITIAL AND FOLLOW-UP OFFICE VISITS, BY MEDICAL SPECIALTY: 1971 TO 1975

[Initial office visit covers new patients. Follow-up office visit covers established patients previously seen by the physician. Based on sample survey of physicians and subject to sampling variability]

MEDICAL SPECIALTY	INITIAL OFFICE VISIT				FOLLOW-UP OFFICE VISIT			
	1971	1973	1974	1975	1971	1973	1974	1975
All specialties [1]_____	$16.00	$16.98	$19.55	$21.16	(NA)	(NA)	$12.45	$13.08
General practice_____	9.65	10.73	12.02	13.10	$6.93	$7.52	8.75	9.29
Internal medicine_____	24.04	20.34	23.12	26.11	9.96	11.13	12.28	13.56
Surgery_____	17.09	17.59	18.88	20.81	9.18	10.34	11.27	12.22
Pediatrics_____	11.18	11.96	14.48	16.18	7.89	8.65	10.38	11.07
Obstetrics-gynecology_____	17.59	19.59	22.08	23.57	9.52	11.53	13.10	13.73
Psychiatry_____	35.58	37.51	41.39	(NA)	(NA)	(NA)	(NA)	(NA)

NA Not available. [1] Includes other specialties, not shown separately.

Source: American Medical Association, Chicago, Illinois, *Reference Data on Profile of Medical Practice*, annual. (Copyright.)

No. 159. MALPRACTICE INSURANCE PREMIUMS, BY SPECIALTY: 1974 TO 1976

[Covers office-based, fee-for-service doctors of medicine (M.D.). Based on random sampling of all M.D.'s in this category]

YEAR	All M.D.'s	General practitioners	Family practitioners	Internists	General surgeons	Obstetricians [1]	Pediatricians
MEDIAN[2] PREMIUM							
1974_____dol__	1,300	1,000	1,000	700	2,600	3,300	600
1975_____dol__	1,900	1,300	1,200	900	4,000	4,900	800
1976_____dol__	3,000	1,750	1,700	1,500	6,000	7,500	1,300
PERCENT CHANGE							
1974–1975_____	46	30	20	29	54	48	33
1975–1976_____	58	35	42	67	50	53	63
PERCENT OF DOCTORS WITH NO COVERAGE							
1974_____	2	4	1	(Z)	(Z)	(Z)	1
1975_____	2	6	1	(Z)	1	1	1
1976_____	7	13	6	3	7	8	3

Z Less than 1 percent.   [1] Includes gynecologists.   [2] For definition of median, see p. xii.

Source: Medical Economics Company, Oradell, N.J., *Medical Economics*, December 27, 1976. (Copyright (c) 1976 by Litton Industries, Inc. Published by Medical Economics Company, a Litton division, at Oradell, N.J. Reprinted by permission.)

No. 160. MALPRACTICE INSURANCE FOR PHYSICIANS AND SURGEONS: 1960 TO 1972

ITEM	1960	1962	1964	1966	1968	1970	1971	1972
Premium cost:								
Per physician [1]_____dol__	111	115	133	154	250	621	712	767
Per surgeon [2]_____dol__	229	279	378	439	571	1,881	2,094	2,307
Cost as percent of income: [3]								
Per physician [1]_____	(NA)	.5	.5	.6	.8	1.7	1.9	2.2
Per surgeon [2]_____	(NA)	(NA)	1.2	1.2	1.4	4.2	4.6	5.1
Index of cost (1966=100):								
Per physician [1]_____	72	75	86	100	162	403	462	498
Per surgeon [2]_____	52	64	86	100	130	429	478	526

NA Not available.   [1] Performing minor surgery or assisting in major surgery on their own patients. [2] General surgeons, cardiac surgeons, urologists, etc.   [3] Income data: copyright © 1976 by Litton Industries, Inc. Published by Medical Economics Company, a Litton division, at Oradell, N.J. Reprinted by permission.

Source: U.S. Dept. of Health, Education, and Welfare, *Medical Malpractice: Report*, Pub. No. (O.S.) 73–88.

No. 161. AVERAGE NET INCOME OF PHYSICIANS, BY GEOGRAPHIC DIVISION AND AREA OF RESIDENCE: 1970 TO 1974

[In thousands of dollars. Represents net income from practice after payment of tax-deductible professional expenses but before payment of income taxes. Relates to non-Federal, office-based, patient-care physicians. Based on periodic sample survey of physicians and subject to sampling variability. For composition of divisions, see fig. I, inside front cover]

GEOGRAPHIC DIVISION	METROPOLITAN AREAS (SMSA'S) WITH—							NONMETROPOLITAN AREAS			
	Under 1 million inhabitants [1]				1 million inhabitants or more [2]			1970	1972	1973	1974
	1970 [3]	1972	1973	1974	1972	1973	1974				
United States_____	42.0	49.3	50.9	54.5	46.5	47.5	51.5	40.4	45.1	47.2	48.8
New England_____	38.4	46.2	46.9	48.7	41.3	41.3	46.7	[4] 35.3	[4] 33.9	37.4	37.0
Middle Atlantic_____	37.5	45.3	43.2	49.8	42.6	44.0	47.6	[4] 40.4	42.0	44.0	41.6
East North Central_____	46.6	51.5	51.2	55.7	49.0	51.4	54.3	50.3	45.7	46.4	50.4
West North Central_____	41.5	49.3	62.0	58.3	45.2	49.9	53.2	40.2	44.4	45.4	50.7
South Atlantic_____	44.5	50.3	51.3	54.7	44.1	47.6	56.8	36.7	51.0	53.0	49.7
East South Central_____	41.0	56.4	55.0	61.7	(NA)	(NA)	(S)	43.9	49.8	50.3	52.7
West South Central_____	45.5	50.7	54.6	59.5	50.8	53.1	57.0	39.3	44.7	48.3	55.1
Mountain_____	39.5	45.1	50.4	49.0	46.6	45.4	53.5	38.7	37.2	46.3	43.9
Pacific_____	44.4	46.5	49.7	53.2	50.5	48.4	50.5	41.1	43.1	43.4	49.0

NA Not available.   S Estimate does not meet criteria for reliability.   [1] Includes all counties in standard metropolitan statistical areas (SMSA's) with 50,000 to 999,000 inhabitants and all counties considered potential SMSA's. For definition of SMSA, see Appendix II.   [2] Includes all counties in SMSA's with 1 million or more inhabitants.   [3] Areas with 1 million inhabitants or more included with areas with under 1 million inhabitants.   [4] Based on fewer than 30 observations.

Source: American Medical Association, Chicago, Ill., *Reference Data on Profile of Medical Practice*, annual. (Copyright.)

No. 162. SELF-EMPLOYED PHYSICIANS AND DENTISTS—MEDIAN NET EARNINGS FROM PRACTICE: 1959 TO 1976

[Represents net income from practice after payment of tax-deductible professional expenses but before payment of income taxes. For 1959-1970, data relate to self-employed physicians under age 65; 1971 and 1972, to office-based, patient care physicians under age 65; 1973-1976, to office-based, patient care physicians, all ages. Based on random sampling of all physicians in this category. For 1976 survey, number of usable questionnaires returned represented about 28 percent of the questionnaires mailed. Number of responses to specific questions may be fewer than questionnaires returned. Data for dentists cover gross income (total collected fees) minus professional expenses and include incorporated dentists. For definition of median, see p. xii. See *Historical Statistics, Colonial Times to 1970*, series D 918-919, for physicians and dentists]

FIELD OF PRACTICE	1959	1965	1970	1971	1972	1973	1974	1975	1976
All physicians	**$22,100**	**$28,960**	**$41,500**	**$42,700**	**$40,730**	**$42,140**	**$44,580**	**$47,520**	**$52,430**
General practitioners	20,000	25,090	37,400	37,450	34,290	37,890	37,600	38,560	43,660
Internists	22,300	27,730	41,250	42,900	41,780	43,100	43,990	53,670	53,550
General surgeons	27,900	32,510	45,000	45,900	45,340	47,290	51,180	53,700	61,410
Obstetricians-gynecologists	27,900	30,520	47,050	50,000	47,020	51,830	55,730	57,500	63,410
Pediatricians	20,700	25,240	35,900	38,350	37,500	38,330	41,030	43,460	45,880
Psychiatrists	(NA)	(NA)	(NA)	(NA)	37,200	37,440	39,460	(NA)	(NA)
Family practitioners	(NA)	(NA)	(NA)	(NA)	(NA)	40,630	44,210	48,160	50,660
Orthopedic surgeons	(NA)	(NA)	(NA)	(NA)	(NA)	62,240	62,410	(NA)	(NA)
All dentists [1]	[2] **13,366**	[3] **12,650**	28,100	(NA)	32,500	(NA)	30,200	(NA)	(NA)

NA Not available.
[1] Source: American Dental Association, Chicago, Ill., *Survey of Dental Practice* (copyright).   [2] 1958.   [3] 1964.

No. 163. INCORPORATED PHYSICIANS—MEDIAN EARNINGS FROM PRACTICE: 1973 TO 1976

[In thousands of dollars. Comprises physicians who are shareholders of a medical corporation. Based on samples of 1,622, 1,753, 1,458, and 1,236 physicians (incorporated, office-based, patient-care medical doctors of all ages) for 1973, 1974, 1975, and 1976, respectively. See headnote, table 162, for comment on survey response. Earnings include salary, bonuses (if any), and funds set aside for retirement. For discussion of sampling procedures, see source. For definition of median, see p. xii]

FIELD OF PRACTICE	1973	1974	1975	1976	FIELD OF PRACTICE	1973	1974	1975	1976
All fields	**67.5**	**72.5**	**76.3**	**75.6**	Obstetricians-gynecologists	72.5	77.5	83.4	89.2
					Pediatricians	55.0	55.5	58.6	56.6
General practitioners	55.5	55.0	59.2	58.7	Psychiatrists	50.0	56.1	(NA)	(NA)
Internists	58.8	62.5	71.1	66.9	Family practitioners	55.0	60.0	61.9	59.4
General surgeons	67.5	75.5	83.3	78.4	Orthopedic surgeons	82.5	87.5	(NA)	(NA)

NA Not available.

Source of tables 162 and 163: Except as noted, Medical Economics Company, Oradell, N.J., *Medical Economics*. Copyrighted © by Litton Industries. Further reproduction prohibited without the written permission of the copyright owner.

No. 164. INPATIENT HEALTH FACILITIES: 1968 TO 1976

YEAR AND TYPE OF FACILITY	Total	FACILITIES UNDER—			FACILITIES WITH—			Residents [1] (1,000)	Full-time employees (1,000)
		Govt. control	Profit control	Non-profit control	6-24 beds	25-74 beds	75 or more beds		
1968: All facilities	26,176	4,147	15,313	6,716	8,582	10,294	7,300	2,034	2,450
Hospitals	7,991	2,771	1,265	3,955	803	2,911	4,277	1,250	(NA)
Nursing homes	18,185	1,376	14,048	2,761	7,779	7,383	3,023	783	(NA)
1971: All facilities	29,682	4,178	18,091	7,413	8,902	10,959	9,821	2,262	3,007
Hospitals	7,678	2,810	1,042	3,826	636	2,700	4,342	1,186	2,439
Nursing homes	22,004	1,368	17,049	3,587	8,266	8,259	5,479	1,076	568
1973: All facilities	29,272	4,063	17,712	7,497	7,876	10,616	10,780	2,318	3,196
Hospitals	7,438	2,744	1,000	3,694	493	2,535	4,410	[2] 1,120	2,560
Nursing homes	21,834	1,319	16,712	3,803	7,383	8,081	6,370	1,198	636
1975: All hospitals	7,336	2,670	1,016	3,650	447	2,420	4,469	1,072	2,770
1976: All facilities	27,456	4,022	16,149	7,285	5,994	9,755	11,707	2,336	(NA)
Nursing homes [3]	20,185	1,369	15,153	3,663	5,558	7,418	7,209	1,286	(NA)
All hospitals [4]	7,271	2,653	996	3,622	436	2,337	4,498	1,050	2,845
General	6,361	2,220	800	3,341	376	2,086	3,899	795	2,485
Psychiatric	502	296	117	89	16	114	372	202	258
Chronic	63	40	4	19	–	12	51	18	23
Tuberculosis	21	19	–	2	–	4	17	2	5

– Represents zero.   NA Not available.   [1] Number of residents as of date of interview, except as noted.
[2] Average daily patients.   [3] See footnote 2, table 173.   [4] Includes types not shown below.

Source: U.S. National Center for Health Statistics, *Health Resources Statistics*, annual.

No. 165. HOSPITALS—TYPE OF SERVICE AND CONTROL: 1950 TO 1976

[1950, excludes Alaska and Hawaii. Covers hospitals accepted for registration by American Hospital Association; see text, pp. 97 and 98. Short-term hospitals have an average patient stay of less than 30 days; long-term, an average stay of longer duration. See also Historical Statistics, Colonial Times to 1970, series B 305-318 and B 331-344]

ITEM	1950	1960	1965	1970	1971	1972	1973	1974	1975	1976
Hospitals	6,788	6,876	7,123	7,123	7,097	7,061	7,123	7,174	7,156	7,082
With 100 beds or more	(NA)	2,903	3,153	3,488	3,479	3,509	3,566	3,665	3,691	3,723
Beds_____1,000	1,456	1,658	1,704	1,616	1,556	1,550	1,535	1,513	1,466	1,434
Rate per 1,000 population [1]	9.6	9.3	8.9	8.0	7.5	7.4	7.3	7.2	6.9	6.7
Beds per hospital	214	241	239	227	219	220	215	211	205	202
Occupancy rate [2]	86.0	84.6	82.3	80.3	79.5	78.0	77.5	77.2	76.7	76.0
TYPE OF SERVICE AND OWNERSHIP										
Federal hospitals, all types	414	435	443	408	407	401	397	387	382	380
Beds_____1,000	189	177	174	161	148	143	142	136	132	129
Occupancy rate [2]	80.4	87.2	86.1	79.6	83.2	80.0	79.0	80.7	80.7	79.3
Non-Federal hospitals	6,374	6,441	6,680	6,715	6,690	6,660	6,726	6,787	6,774	6,702
Beds_____1,000	1,266	1,481	1,530	1,455	1,408	1,407	1,392	1,377	1,334	1,305
Short-term general and special	5,031	5,407	5,736	5,859	5,865	5,843	5,891	5,977	5,979	5,956
Beds_____1,000	505	639	741	848	867	884	903	931	947	961
Rate per 1,000 population [1]	3.3	3.6	3.9	4.2	4.2	4.2	4.3	4.4	4.4	4.5
Occupancy rate [2]	73.7	74.7	76.0	78.0	76.7	75.2	75.4	75.3	74.8	74.4
Long-term general and special	412	308	283	236	218	216	229	221	215	197
Beds_____1,000	70	67	66	60	54	54	57	54	51	49
Occupancy rate [2]	85.7	86.9	85.3	82.0	83.4	83.0	82.1	82.5	82.1	82.7
Psychiatric	533	488	483	519	513	529	543	543	544	528
Beds_____1,000	620	722	685	527	469	457	422	383	330	291
Occupancy rate [2]	97.9	93.1	88.6	84.8	83.8	82.8	81.1	80.0	80.3	79.1
Tuberculosis	398	238	178	101	94	72	63	46	36	21
Beds_____1,000	72	52	37	20	18	13	10	8	6	4
Occupancy rate [2]	86.1	75.4	70.0	61.8	60.7	61.2	61.9	63.2	57.7	57.8
NON-FEDERAL OWNERSHIP OR CONTROL										
State hospitals	(3)	556	546	577	580	570	568	558	551	519
Beds_____1,000	(3)	752	708	558	498	482	449	409	358	317
Occupancy rate [2]	(3)	91.8	87.5	83.3	82.2	81.6	80.0	79.2	79.2	78.2
Local government hospitals	[3] 1,654	1,324	1,495	1,680	1,700	1,730	1,757	1,753	1,755	1,747
Beds_____1,000	[3] 844	201	216	219	219	219	218	215	211	208
Occupancy rate [2]	[3] 81.8	77.1	76.3	75.6	74.2	73.0	72.8	72.0	71.5	70.9
Nongov'tal nonprofit hospitals	3,250	3,579	3,670	3,600	3,565	3,515	3,518	3,576	3,562	3,551
Beds_____1,000	368	482	552	619	629	641	652	673	681	692
Occupancy rate [2]	74.8	77.3	78.2	80.2	79.1	77.6	78.0	78.0	77.6	77.3
For-profit hospitals	1,470	982	969	858	845	845	883	900	906	885
Beds_____1,000	55	46	54	59	61	65	73	80	84	87
Occupancy rate [3]	63.6	67.6	69.1	72.4	71.3	68.9	68.6	68.2	66.6	65.5

NA Not available.   [1] Based on Bureau of the Census estimated resident population as of July 1.
[2] Ratio of average daily census to every 100 beds.   [3] State hospitals included with "Local."

No. 166. HOSPITAL EXPENSE PER PATIENT DAY: 1950 TO 1976

[In dollars. Prior to 1960, excludes Alaska and Hawaii. For definitions, see headnote, table 165. See also Historical Statistics, Colonial Times to 1970, series B 389-400]

EXPENSE BY HOSPITAL TYPE	1950	1955	1960	1965	1970	1971	1972	1973	1974	1975	1976
Total expense	7.98	11.24	16.46	25.29	53.95	63.82	73.89	83.67	97.23	118.69	139.64
Avg. annual per-cent change	[1] 11.3	7.1	7.9	9.0	16.4	18.3	15.8	13.2	16.2	22.1	17.7
Non-Federal:											
Short-term, gen. and spec.	15.62	23.12	32.23	44.48	81.01	92.31	105.21	114.69	128.05	151.42	172.59
Long-term, gen. and spec.	5.39	8.06	12.82	19.79	36.17	38.44	43.91	47.40	53.44	63.01	66.59
Psychiatric (incl. short-term)	2.43	3.73	4.91	7.50	16.63	19.56	22.65	26.83	33.12	41.36	49.61
Tuberculosis	7.22	10.13	13.37	17.39	34.20	38.86	41.65	48.37	54.39	75.69	84.18
Federal	12.77	14.60	20.11	28.67	53.10	62.69	75.40	85.85	99.44	116.74	142.01
Payroll expense	4.79	7.20	10.92	16.70	33.16	39.07	44.17	49.18	55.93	66.12	75.71
Percent of total	60.0	64.1	66.3	66.0	61.5	61.2	59.8	58.8	57.5	55.7	54.2
Non-Federal:											
Short-term, gen. and spec.	8.86	14.26	20.08	27.44	47.30	53.80	59.79	63.86	69.83	80.34	88.81
Long-term, gen. and spec.	3.32	5.36	9.01	13.96	24.00	26.46	29.69	31.52	34.98	39.85	41.40
Psychiatric (incl. short-term)	1.38	2.17	3.45	5.60	12.24	14.49	16.71	19.74	23.84	28.84	34.31
Tuberculosis	4.06	6.48	8.92	12.20	23.94	26.88	28.74	33.08	36.59	47.55	54.48
Federal	9.35	11.63	16.34	23.12	37.44	43.60	51.06	58.08	66.37	75.31	91.29

[1] Change from 1946.

Source of tables 165 and 166: American Hospital Association, Chicago, Ill., Hospitals, Guide Issue, annual; beginning 1972, Hospital Statistics, annual. (Copyright.)

No. 167. Hospitals—Assets, Expenses, and Personnel, by Type of Control and Service: 1960 to 1976

[See also *Historical Statistics, Colonial Times to 1970*, series B 413–422]

SUBJECT AND YEAR	All hospitals	Federal hospitals	NON-FEDERAL HOSPITALS							
			Total	Psychiatric	Tuberculosis	Long-term [1]	Short-term [1]			
							Total	Voluntary nonprofit	For profit	State and local govt.
Assets (mil. dol.):										
1960	17,714	2,124	15,590	3,437	508	787	10,858	8,422	243	2,193
1965	24,502	2,552	21,950	4.167	421	998	16,364	12,476	414	3,474
1970	36,159	3,183	32,976	4,816	311	1,176	26,674	20,502	871	5,301
1972	43,157	3,255	39,902	4,927	253	1,093	33,629	25,686	1,365	6,577
1973	47,369	3,401	43,967	4,846	225	1,259	37,637	28,643	1,725	7,269
1974	51,706	3,528	48,178	4,776	166	1,396	41,840	31,482	2,288	8,070
1975	57,302	3,707	53,595	4,804	132	1,403	47,256	35,827	2,538	8,890
1976	64,029	4,135	59,894	4,761	91	1,351	53,691	40,857	3,031	9,802
Expenses [2] (mil. dol.):										
1960	8,421	1,134	7,287	1,205	192	273	5,617	4,139	275	1,203
1965	12,948	1,568	11,380	1,662	165	406	9,147	6,643	510	1,994
1970	25,556	2,483	23,073	2,712	152	649	19,560	14,163	1,068	4,328
1972	32,667	3,148	29,520	3,134	119	718	25,549	18,384	1,407	5,758
1973	36,290	3,524	32,766	3,351	114	805	28,496	20,418	1,689	6,389
1974	41,406	3,971	37,434	3,708	102	873	32,751	23,494	2,046	7,211
1975	48,706	4,540	44,166	3,997	93	966	39,110	27,965	2,561	8,584
1976	55,655	5,313	50,342	4,175	64	986	45,116	32,796	3,085	9,235
Personnel [3] (1,000):										
1960	1,598	186	1,412	238	39	55	1,080	792	48	241
1965	1,952	199	1,754	274	29	65	1,386	1,011	70	306
1970	2,537	216	2,321	305	18	69	1,929	1,387	97	444
1972	2,671	232	2,439	307	12	63	2,056	1,474	105	477
1973	2,769	238	2,530	303	11	67	2,149	1,535	117	497
1974	2,919	244	2,675	308	9	69	2,289	1,634	133	522
1975	3,023	256	2,766	292	7	68	2,399	1,714	139	546
1976	3,108	269	2,839	285	5	66	2,483	1,793	147	543
Personnel per 100 patients: [3]										
1960	114	120	113	35	99	95	226	232	196	215
1965	139	133	140	45	111	115	246	252	218	234
1970	196	169	198	68	146	140	292	292	256	298
1972	221	203	223	81	155	142	310	308	267	325
1973	233	212	235	88	168	145	315	314	272	333
1974	250	223	253	100	184	154	326	323	283	351
1975	269	240	272	110	216	162	339	336	288	365
1976	285	263	287	124	225	163	347	346	297	367

[1] For definition, see headnote, table 165. Comprises both general and special hospitals.
[2] Excludes cost of new construction. [3] Includes full-time equivalents of part-time personnel.

Source: American Hospital Association, Chicago, Ill., *Hospitals*, Guide Issue, annual; beginning 1972, *Hospital Statistics*, annual. (Copyright.)

No. 168. Hospital Use: 1950 to 1976

[Prior to 1960, excludes Alaska and Hawaii. See also *Historical Statistics, Colonial Times to 1970*, series B 381–388]

TYPE OF HOSPITAL	1950	1955	1960	1965	1970	1972	1973	1974	1975	1976
General and special: [1]										
Admissions per 1,000 population [2]	110	125	136	146	152	156	160	165	166	168
Days in hospital per 1,000 population [2]	1,165	1,238	1,265	1,329	1,440	1,395	1,414	1,425	1,425	1,424
Average length of stay [3] days	10.6	9.9	9.3	9.1	9.5	8.9	8.8	8.7	8.6	8.5
Occupancy rate [4] percent	[5] 73	74	77	77	78	76	76	76	75	75
Outpatient visits per 1,000 population [2]	(NA)	(NA)	(NA)	640	869	1,026	1,084	1,155	1,165	1,230
Psychiatric:										
Admissions per 1,000 population [2]	2.0	2.2	2.3	2.9	3.3	3.2	3.1	3.2	3.2	3.1
Days in hospital per 1,000 population [2]	1,659	1,645	1,491	1,261	862	714	641	574	495	429
Tuberculosis: [6]										
Admissions per 10,000 population [2]	7.0	7.0	3.8	2.7	1.8	1.4	1.2	1.0	.7	.5
Days in hospital per 10,000 population [2]	1,747	1,459	796	491	225	138	112	88	56	34

NA Not available.   [1] Long- and short-term; excludes psychiatric and tuberculosis.
[2] Based on Bureau of the Census estimated resident population as of July 1.   [3] Number of inpatient days divided by number of admissions.   [4] Ratio of average daily census to every 100 beds.   [5] Excludes Federal hospitals.   [6] Beginning 1960, excludes short-term.

Source: 1950–1965, U.S. National Center for Health Statistics, *Health, Education, and Welfare Trends.* (Based on data prepared by American Medical Association and American Hospital Association.) Beginning 1970, American Hospital Association, Chicago, Ill., *Hospital Statistics*, annual, (copyright).

No. 169. Hospital Facilities—Total, 1960 to 1976, and States and Puerto Rico, 1976

[For definition of short-term, see headnote, table 165. See also *Historical Statistics, Colonial Times to 1970*, series B 305–308 and B 359–362]

YEAR AND STATE OR OTHER AREA	HOSPITALS		BEDS (1,000)		Bassinets (1,000)	PATIENTS ADMITTED (millions)		AVERAGE DAILY CENSUS[2] (1,000)		OCCUPANCY RATE[3]		Personnel[4] (1,000)
	Total	Short-term[1]	Total	Short-term hospitals[1]		Total	Short-term hospitals[1]	Total	Short-term hospitals[1]	Total	Short-term hospitals[1]	
1960	6,876	5,407	1,658.0	639.1	102.8	25.0	23.0	1,401.9	477.4	84.6	74.7	1,598
1965	7,123	5,736	1,703.5	741.3	101.3	28.8	26.5	1,402.6	563.4	82.3	76.0	1,952
1968	7,137	5,820	1,663.2	805.9	97.3	29.8	27.3	1,378.4	630.4	82.9	78.2	2,309
1969	7,144	5,853	1,649.7	825.8	94.9	30.7	28.3	1,346.3	650.8	81.6	78.8	2,426
1970	7,123	5,859	1,615.8	848.2	97.1	31.8	29.3	1,297.7	661.5	80.3	78.0	2,537
1971	7,097	5,865	1,555.6	866.5	94.3	32.7	30.1	1,236.8	664.8	79.5	76.7	2,589
1972	7,061	5,843	1,549.7	883.7	93.0	33.3	30.8	1,208.9	664.1	78.0	75.2	2,671
1973	7,123	5,891	1,534.7	903.3	90.1	34.4	31.8	1,189.0	681.5	77.5	75.4	2,769
1974	7,174	5,977	1,512.7	931.2	88.3	35.5	32.9	1,167.4	701.3	77.2	75.3	2,919
1975	7,156	5,979	1,465.8	947.0	86.9	36.2	33.5	1,124.9	708.1	76.7	74.8	3,023
1976, U.S.	7,082	5,956	1,433.5	961.2	85.3	36.8	34.1	1,089.7	714.8	76.0	74.4	3,108
Ala.	146	131	25.0	17.6	1.8	.7	.7	18.8	12.9	75.3	73.4	51
Alaska	25	15	1.6	.8	.2	.1	(z)	1.0	.5	65.2	65.3	5
Ariz.	80	59	11.1	8.3	.9	.4	.3	8.1	6.1	73.5	73.2	29
Ark.	96	90	13.3	9.7	1.0	.4	.4	9.7	6.9	72.8	70.5	26
Calif.	631	542	119.4	82.8	6.7	3.3	3.0	81.1	54.2	68.0	65.4	277
Colo.	100	83	14.7	10.7	1.0	.5	.4	10.7	7.6	72.9	71.3	39
Conn.	67	40	19.5	11.0	1.0	.5	.4	15.6	8.6	79.6	78.5	45
Del.	15	8	4.6	2.0	.2	.1	.1	4.0	1.7	87.7	82.1	9
D.C.	20	13	10.6	5.0	.5	.2	.2	8.3	3.9	78.0	77.5	27
Fla.	243	208	53.4	40.4	2.6	1.5	1.4	38.8	28.3	72.7	70.1	117
Ga.	186	159	30.9	21.0	2.3	1.0	.8	22.8	14.5	73.7	69.3	69
Hawaii	27	20	3.9	2.6	.4	.1	.1	2.8	1.8	73.1	68.1	10
Idaho	52	47	3.7	3.2	.4	.1	.1	2.5	2.1	67.2	65.6	8
Ill.	287	247	77.3	55.1	4.3	2.0	1.9	60.1	41.9	77.9	76.0	182
Ind.	100	116	31.0	23.6	2.1	.9	.8	27.1	18.1	77.7	76.7	71
Iowa	143	133	21.7	16.8	1.5	.6	.6	15.3	11.4	70.4	67.9	41
Kans.	164	147	18.2	13.0	1.4	.5	.4	13.1	9.0	71.9	69.6	37
Ky.	125	107	19.4	14.6	1.4	.6	.6	15.2	11.3	78.0	77.9	41
La.	154	135	24.7	17.2	1.9	.7	.7	17.6	12.0	71.1	70.2	51
Maine	54	49	7.3	4.9	.5	.2	.2	5.4	3.6	74.4	72.4	16
Md.	81	50	25.1	13.3	1.1	.5	.5	20.5	10.9	81.5	82.4	58
Mass.	190	125	48.3	26.3	1.9	1.0	.9	39.0	20.7	80.6	78.7	119
Mich.	253	213	53.2	39.8	3.6	1.5	1.4	41.8	30.8	78.6	77.4	128
Minn.	189	173	31.4	23.6	2.1	.7	.7	23.0	16.8	73.2	71.2	59
Miss.	111	101	17.3	11.0	1.1	.5	.4	12.6	7.9	73.1	71.6	30
Mo.	171	150	35.1	26.0	2.0	1.0	.9	26.3	19.6	74.8	75.6	79
Mont.	65	58	4.4	3.8	.4	.1	.1	2.7	2.3	60.8	59.8	9
Nebr.	108	99	11.4	9.3	1.0	.3	.3	7.7	6.3	67.1	67.1	22
Nev.	23	18	3.2	2.5	.2	.1	.1	2.1	1.7	65.3	68.4	7
N.H.	33	29	5.1	3.4	.4	.1	.1	3.8	2.4	73.4	71.0	11
N.J.	144	111	47.6	30.0	2.4	1.1	1.0	38.3	24.5	80.5	81.7	93
N. Mex.	54	37	6.6	3.8	.6	.2	.2	4.6	2.5	69.1	66.5	15
N.Y.	394	315	152.0	84.9	6.4	2.8	2.7	128.3	72.4	84.4	85.2	325
N.C.	159	130	34.1	21.6	2.3	.9	.8	26.3	16.9	77.2	78.1	69
N. Dak.	60	53	5.7	4.2	.5	.1	.1	4.0	3.0	70.3	69.9	10
Ohio	248	211	70.4	49.5	4.3	1.9	1.8	56.0	39.9	79.6	80.5	155
Okla.	140	120	17.1	12.1	1.3	.5	.5	12.0	8.1	69.9	67.1	38
Oreg.	87	80	12.1	9.0	.8	.4	.3	8.3	6.0	69.0	66.3	26
Pa.	318	251	92.6	55.8	4.4	2.0	1.9	73.2	43.6	79.1	78.0	184
R.I.	21	14	7.3	3.5	.3	.1	.1	6.0	2.8	82.4	82.1	17
S.C.	88	74	17.6	10.8	1.2	.5	.4	13.4	8.0	76.0	74.4	34
S. Dak.	70	58	5.8	3.7	.5	.1	.1	4.1	2.4	69.8	63.2	10
Tenn.	154	136	30.5	22.0	1.9	.9	.8	23.7	16.3	77.5	74.2	62
Tex.	563	500	77.6	57.1	5.2	2.4	2.1	55.3	39.5	71.3	69.1	169
Utah	38	33	5.0	3.8	.6	.2	.2	3.6	2.7	73.0	72.2	13
Vt.	21	17	3.6	2.3	.2	.1	.1	2.5	1.7	71.1	73.8	8
Va.	129	99	32.2	19.6	1.8	.8	.7	24.9	15.1	77.4	77.0	65
Wash.	129	110	16.3	12.0	1.2	.6	.5	11.3	8.0	69.2	66.4	40
W. Va.	85	70	15.8	10.3	.8	.4	.4	12.2	7.8	76.8	75.6	29
Wis.	172	146	31.1	24.5	2.0	.8	.7	22.5	17.3	72.3	70.5	65
Wyo.	30	26	2.7	1.7	.2	.1	.1	1.7	1.0	64.2	57.1	5
P.R.	65	59	11.6	9.0	.9	.4	.3	8.8	6.6	76.4	73.4	23

Z Less than 50,000. [1] Non-Federal. [2] Average inpatients receiving treatment each day; excludes newborn. [3] Ratio of average daily census to every 100 beds. [4] Includes full-time equivalents of part-time personnel.

Source: American Hospital Association, Chicago, Ill., *Hospitals*, Guide Issue, annual; beginning 1972, *Hospital Statistics*, annual. (Copyright.)

No. 170. HOSPITAL UTILIZATION RATES: 1965 TO 1976

[Covers estimates of inpatients discharged from noninstitutional, short-stay hospitals, exclusive of Federal hospitals. Excludes newborn. Based on sample data collected from the Hospital Discharge Survey, a sample survey of hospital records of patients discharged in year shown; subject to sampling variability]

YEAR AND PATIENT'S AGE CLASS (in years)	Patients discharged (1,000)	PATIENTS DISCHARGED PER 1,000 PERSONS [1]			DAYS OF CARE PER 1,000 PERSONS [1]			AVERAGE STAY (days)			Beds used per day [2]
		Total	Male	Female	Total	Male	Female	Total	Male	Female	
1965	28,792	152	121	180	1,186	1,018	1,339	7.8	8.4	7.4	325
1970	29,185	146	119	171	1,173	1,033	1,297	8.0	8.7	7.6	321
1971	29,459	146	120	170	1,143	1,004	1,269	7.8	8.4	7.5	313
1972	31,627	155	128	180	1,200	1,056	1,330	7.7	8.3	7.4	328
1973	32,125	156	129	181	1,212	1,066	1,345	7.8	8.3	7.4	332
1974	33,018	159	131	185	1,233	1,089	1,365	7.7	8.3	7.4	338
1975	34,043	163	134	190	1,255	1,104	1,395	7.7	8.2	7.4	344
1976, total	34,372	163	135	189	1,236	1,093	1,369	7.6	8.1	7.2	339
Under 1	621	205	233	176	1,242	1,384	1,092	6.1	5.9	6.2	340
1–4	1,112	90	102	79	352	399	304	3.9	3.9	3.9	97
5–14	2,011	54	59	50	230	243	217	4.2	4.1	4.3	63
15–24	5,539	141	80	200	669	469	862	4.8	5.9	4.3	183
25–34	5,273	169	92	242	917	598	1,217	5.4	6.5	5.0	251
35–44	3,460	153	122	182	1,047	889	1,194	6.8	7.3	6.6	287
45–64	8,444	195	190	200	1,717	1,679	1,752	8.8	8.8	8.8	470
65 and over	7,912	363	388	345	4,164	4,401	3,998	11.5	11.3	11.6	1,141

[1] Total civilian noninstitutional population.
[2] Average daily number of beds occupied per 100,000 civilian noninstitutional population.

Source: U.S. National Center for Health Statistics, *Vital and Health Statistics*, series 13 publications.

No. 171. SURGICAL OPERATIONS IN SHORT-STAY HOSPITALS, 1965 TO 1976, AND BY TYPE OF OPERATION, 1973 AND 1976, BY SEX

[1965–1971 for ages 15 and over only; 1973–1976 for all ages. See headnote, table 170]

YEAR	NUMBER (mil.)			RATE [1]			TYPE OF OPERATION	MALE (1,000)		FEMALE (1,000)	
	Total	Male	Female	Total	Male	Female		1973	1976	1973	1976
1965	14.7	5.8	8.9	7,735	6,269	9,090	Abdominal	1,357	1,386	1,389	1,422
1968	14.6	5.9	8.7	7,487	6,229	8,628	Repair of inguinal				
1971	15.8	6.2	9.6	7,805	6,333	9,151	hernia	464	455	61	51
1973	18.4	6.9	11.5	8,952	6,985	10,777	Orthopedic	1,217	1,348	1,133	1,293
1974	19.3	7.2	12.1	9,291	7,154	11,273	Otorhinolaryngology	903	892	930	857
1975	20.0	7.4	12.7	9,584	7,315	11,700	Tonsillectomy [4]	398	292	486	337
1976	20.1	7.5	12.5	9,539	7,429	11,506	Urological	1,032	1,125	420	445
							Obstetrical procedures	(X)	(X)	1,077	1,282
							Plastic surgery	543	551	497	531
TYPE OF OPERATION	MALE (1,000)		FEMALE (1,000)				Biopsy	300	385	618	731
							Vascular and cardiac	410	585	308	380
	1973	1976	1973	1976			Ophthalmology	295	334	358	438
							Proctological	303	305	262	279
Total operations	6,936	7,548	11,480	12,538			Dental [5]	245	260	286	297
Gynecological [2]	(X)	(X)	3,565	3,834			Breast	19	23	317	359
Dilation and curettage of uterus [3]	(X)	(X)	934	983			Neurosurgery	157	176	152	198
Hysterectomy	(X)	(X)	690	678			Thoracic	138	162	102	118
							Thyroid, parathyroid, thymus, and adrenals	17	18	64	74

X Not applicable.   [1] Rate per 100,000 civilian noninstitutional population as of July.
[2] Includes other subcategories of surgery, not shown separately.
[3] Diagnostic.
[4] With or without adenoidectomy.
[5] Includes oral and maxillofacial surgery.

Source: U.S. National Center for Health Statistics, *Vital and Health Statistics*, series 13 publications.

No. 172. Long-Term Care Institutions—Summary: 1976

[Covers facilities which offer residential care to persons for an average stay of 30 days or more. Based on Survey of Institutionalized Persons (S.I.P.) which contained samples of institutions, of selected residents in sample institutions, and of families of sample residents. Data differ from tables 164 and 173–175, which list each facility with a separate license as a separate institution. In the S.I.P., a facility was counted as a separate institution for each type of care provided. Thus, a facility providing several types of care was counted as several separate institutions. Resident is any person who was on the patient roster and who was living at the institution or for whom a bed was being held. For definition of median, see p. xii]

INSTITUTIONS AND RESIDENTS	Total	Percent of total	Nursing homes	Physi- cally handi- capped	Psychi- atric [1]	Men- tally handi- capped [2]	Chil- dren's [3]	Other [4]
Total institutions	23,608	100.0	18,261	387	1,567	1,705	1,324	363
Facilities with—								
1–99 beds	18,778	79.5	14,254	227	1,439	1,433	1,200	224
100–349 beds	4,518	19.1	3,914	133	105	128	117	121
350 or more beds	312	1.3	93	27	23	144	7	18
By ownership:								
Government	1,889	8.0	872	165	243	274	206	129
Proprietary	12,429	52.6	11,213	86	130	788	117	96
Private nonprofit	9,290	39.4	6,177	136	1,194	643	1,001	138
Median charges [5] ____dol__	477	(X)	501	377	292	316	385	699
Median cost [5] _____dol__	481	(X)	482	431	640	378	528	934
Total residents [6] ____1,000__	1,550	100.0	1,183	38	65	189	44	31
Male_____1,000__	597	38.5	378	22	46	110	26	14
Female_____1,000__	948	61.1	803	15	18	78	17	17
White_____1,000__	1,410	91.0	1,101	31	49	169	31	29
Black and other_____1,000__	135	8.7	80	6	15	20	13	2
Under 18 years old_____1,000__	152	9.9	9	19	28	56	40	(Z)
18–64 years old_____1,000__	334	21.5	154	16	32	125	3	5
65 years old and over_____1,000__	1,028	66.3	989	2	5	6	(Z)	26
Length of stay:								
Less than 1 year_____1,000__	525	33.8	432	7	41	15	21	9
1 to 2 years_____1,000__	273	17.6	233	4	9	11	9	7
3 to 4 years_____1,000__	280	18.1	234	5	6	23	5	8
5 to 9 years_____1,000__	272	17.6	200	8	4	50	6	5
10 to 19 years_____1,000__	97	6.3	36	10	2	46	1	2
20 or more years_____1,000__	45	2.9	2	2	2	40	(Z)	(Z)

X Not applicable. Z Fewer than 500.
[1] Facilities for the emotionally disturbed and residential treatment or rehabilitation centers for alcoholics and drug abusers.
[2] Facilities for mentally retarded and other neurologically handicapped persons.
[3] Orphanages and homes for dependent children, homes for unwed mothers, and sheltered or custodial care homes.
[4] Institutions offering care for chronic diseases and extended-care facilities of short-term hospitals.
[5] Per resident per month calculated on basis of institutions which charge for their services.
[6] Includes not reported, not shown separately.
Source: U.S. Bureau of the Census, *Current Population Reports*, P-23, No. 69.

No. 173. Nursing and Related Care Facilities: 1963 to 1977

[Count of nursing and related care homes based on Master Facility Inventory, a complete census of inpatient health facilities compiled by the U.S. National Center for Health Statistics; see Appendix III]

ITEM	1963	1967	1969	1970	1971	1973	1975	1976	1977
Nursing and related care: [1]									
Facilities, number	16,701	19,141	18,910	(NA)	22,004	21,834	(NA)	[2] 20,185	(NA)
Beds_____1,000__	569	837	944	(NA)	1,202	1,328	(NA)	[2] 1,407	(NA)
Resident patients_____1,000__	491	756	850	(NA)	1,076	1,198	(NA)	[2] 1,286	(NA)
Personnel employed [3] ____1,000__	242	383	444	(NA)	568	636	(NA)	(NA)	(NA)
Per 1,000 patients	491	507	522	(NA)	528	531	(NA)	(NA)	(NA)
Skilled nursing facilities, no. [4]	(NA)	[5] 4,160	4,840	4,646	4,277	3,970	3,932	3,928	4,002
Beds_____1,000__	(NA)	[5] 291	341	333	307	287	287	310	350
Per 1,000 enrollees [6]	(NA)	15.2	17.3	16.8	15.3	13.7	11.8	12.4	15.4

NA Not available. [1] Places providing some form of nursing, personal, or domiciliary care; standards vary widely among States. Includes skilled nursing facilities. [2] Preliminary. Some changes in data beginning 1976 may be due to dependence on State collection; see Appendix III. [3] Full-time employees only. [4] Source: Prior to 1977, U.S. Social Security Administration, *Health Insurance Statistics*. 1977, U.S. Health Care Financing Administration, *Participating Health Facilities Under Medicare*, semiannual. As of June 30, except rate per enrollees. Covers facilities certified for participation under Medicare, which have transfer agreements with one or more participating hospitals, and are engaged primarily in providing skilled nursing care and related services for the rehabilitation of injured, disabled, or sick persons. [5] As of July. [6] Based on enrollees in Medicare hospital insurance program as of Jan. 1 of year stated, except 1973 based on July 1, 1972.

Source: Except as noted, U.S. National Center for Health Statistics, *Health Resources Statistics*, annual.

No. 174. NURSING HOMES—SELECTED CHARACTERISTICS OF HOMES AND RESIDENTS, RESIDENT CHARGES, AND PRIMARY SOURCES OF PAYMENT: 1964 TO 1977

[Count based on periodic surveys; for details, see Appendix III. Except as noted, covers only nursing homes and personal care homes with nursing]

NURSING HOMES	1964	1969	1973–1974	1977 [1][2]	RESIDENTS IN NURSING AND PERSONAL CARE HOMES	1964 [1]	1969 [1]	1973–1974	1977 [1][2]
Estimated number_1,000__	14.6	15.0	15.7	18.3	Total_____1,000__	554	815	1,076	1,287
Beds, total_____1,000__	576	879	1,175	1,384	White_____1,000__	(NA)	779	1,010	1,180
Average per home_____	39	59	75	76	Black and other____1,000__	(NA)	37	65	107
Per 1,000 persons 65					Under 65 years old__1,000__	66	93	114	190
years old and over____	32.2	45.2	55.2	58.9	65 yr. old and over__1,000__	488	722	962	1,098
Employment in					Percent of total_____	88.0	88.6	89.4	85.3
homes [3]_____1,000__	246	495	713	(NA)	Male_____1,000__	194	252	318	369
Per 100 residents_____	47.4	63.5	66.3	(NA)	Under 65 yr. old__1,000__	36	45	52	86
Average monthly resident					65 yr. old and over_____1,000__	158	207	266	283
charge_____dol__	186	328	479	670	Percent of male_____	81.3	82.2	83.5	76.7
Primary source of pay-					65–74_____1,000__	40	51	65	76
ment:					75–84_____1,000__	74	91	102	118
Percent, by type:					85 and over_____1,000__	43	64	98	90
Medicare_____	(X)	3.4	1.1	(NA)	Female_____1,000__	360	563	758	918
Medicaid_____	(X)	13.3	47.9	48.5	Under 65 yr. old__1,000__	30	48	62	103
Public assistance_____	47.0	36.5	11.4	6.0	65 yr. old and over_____1,000__	330	515	696	815
Other_____	54.0	46.9	39.7	43.9	Percent of female____	91.6	91.5	91.8	88.7
Residents, total___1,000__	519	778	1,076	1,287	65–74_____1,000__	64	86	98	126
					75–84_____1,000__	157	232	283	353
					85 and over_____1,000__	109	198	315	336

NA Not available.   X Not applicable.   [1] Includes personal care homes without nursing. [2] Preliminary.   [3] Full-time equivalent.

Source: U.S. National Center for Health Statistics, *Vital and Health Statistics,* series 12 and series 13; and unpublished data.

No. 175. NURSING AND RELATED CARE FACILITIES, BY STATES: 1971 AND 1976

[Data are for places providing some form of nursing, personal, or domiciliary care; standards vary widely among States. For detailed definitions, see source. See headnote, table 173]

STATE	FACILITIES		BEDS (1,000)		RESIDENT PATIENTS (1,000)		STATE	FACILITIES		BEDS (1,000)		RESIDENT PATIENTS (1,000)	
	1971	1976 [1]	1971	1976 [1]	1971	1976 [1]		1971	1976 [1]	1971	1976 [1]	1971	1976 [1]
U.S._____	22,004	20,185	1,202	1,407	1,076	1,286	Miss_____	134	144	7.1	8.9	6.2	8.4
							Mo.[2]_____	494	472	32.0	33.6	28.5	30.6
Ala._____	192	214	13.4	19.3	12.3	18.1	Mont_____	103	105	4.5	5.3	4.1	5.1
Alaska_____	8	11	.7	.8	.5	.7	Nebr.[2]_____	253	281	15.1	23.0	13.7	20.9
Ariz.[2]_____	82	71	5.2	5.9	4.6	5.6	Nev_____	43	35	1.4	1.6	1.2	1.4
Ark_____	218	213	15.1	18.7	13.8	17.5	N.H._____	140	114	5.5	6.3	5.0	5.8
Calif._____	4,277	3,440	146.0	139.1	121.5	125.3	N.J._____	548	468	30.8	34.5	27.7	32.7
Colo.[2]_____	212	241	16.4	22.7	14.9	19.1	N. Mex.____	60	66	3.3	3.0	2.6	2.7
							N.Y._____	1,096	996	81.1	102.6	76.3	95.5
Conn._____	380	350	21.9	24.4	20.6	23.5							
Del._____	34	29	1.9	2.2	1.7	2.0	N.C.[2]_____	843	711	19.2	24.4	17.5	22.5
D.C._____	73	71	2.8	2.9	2.5	2.5	N. Dak_____	109	102	6.2	6.8	5.9	6.5
Fla._____	373	331	35.9	32.9	29.6	29.5	Ohio_____	1,191	937	59.5	64.1	53.2	60.0
Ga._____	283	324	22.8	29.6	20.8	28.3	Okla_____	411	353	26.9	26.1	23.8	23.8
Hawaii_____	132	140	2.3	3.2	2.2	2.9	Oreg_____	311	279	17.2	15.9	16.0	14.7
							Pa.[2]_____	753	666	57.7	64.1	52.5	58.4
Idaho [2]_____	64	67	3.9	4.8	3.4	4.6	R.I.[2]_____	185	120	6.5	7.3	6.1	6.6
Ill._____	1,046	928	66.9	87.8	61.1	80.2	S.C._____	118	118	7.5	8.6	6.6	7.9
Ind_____	522	490	32.5	35.9	29.0	32.2	S. Dak_____	153	153	7.0	7.8	6.6	7.5
Iowa_____	747	537	33.8	32.9	30.4	30.7							
Kans_____	480	381	21.9	22.5	20.0	21.3	Tenn.[2]_____	234	289	14.3	20.1	12.2	19.3
Ky._____	344	313	18.6	20.5	16.5	18.7	Tex.[2]_____	937	1,099	70.8	101.4	60.8	83.6
							Utah_____	142	102	4.8	4.6	4.4	4.3
La._____	212	204	14.6	19.1	13.3	18.2	Vt.[2]_____	101	263	3.0	5.1	2.8	4.5
Maine_____	288	292	7.4	8.6	6.8	8.2	Va.[2]_____	335	341	15.7	28.5	14.1	26.4
Md._____	195	187	14.7	18.9	13.8	17.9	Wash_____	385	366	28.6	30.1	25.2	27.7
Mass.[2]_____	960	869	49.7	50.9	46.1	48.2	W. Va._____	124	127	3.9	5.6	3.5	5.0
Mich.[2]_____	562	699	43.3	66.4	40.2	58.5	Wis.[2]_____	490	530	37.6	52.6	34.0	48.0
Minn.[2]_____	593	517	41.1	43.0	38.0	41.1	Wyo_____	34	29	1.7	1.8	1.6	1.7

[1] Preliminary.   [2] See footnote 2, table 173.

Source: U.S. National Center for Health Statistics, *Health Resources Statistics,* annual.

No. 176. Patient Care Episodes in Mental Health Facilities, by Type of Treatment Facility: 1955 to 1975

["Patient care episodes" is defined as the number of residents in inpatient facilities or the number of persons on the rolls of outpatient facilities, plus the total additions to both types of facilities during the year. Excludes private psychiatric office practice, psychiatric service modes of all types in hospitals or outpatient clinics of Federal agencies other than Veterans Administration (VA), inpatient service modes of multiservice facilities not shown in this table, all partial care episodes, and outpatient episodes of VA hospitals]

ITEM AND YEAR	All facilities	INPATIENT SERVICES						OUTPATIENT PSYCHIATRIC SERVICES		
		Total	Mental hospitals		General [2]	VA	Community mental health centers [3]	Total	Community mental health centers [3]	Other
			State and county	Private[1]						
Patient care episodes (1,000):										
1955	1,675	1,296	819	123	266	88	(NA)	379	(NA)	379
1965	2,637	1,566	805	125	519	116	(NA)	1,071	(NA)	1,071
1971	4,038	1,721	745	127	543	177	130	2,317	623	1,694
1975	6,409	1,791	599	165	566	214	247	4,618	1,585	3,033
Percent distribution:										
1955	100.0	77.4	48.9	7.3	15.9	5.3	(NA)	22.6	(NA)	22.6
1965	100.0	59.4	30.5	4.8	19.7	4.4	(NA)	40.6	(NA)	40.6
1971	100.0	42.6	18.5	3.1	13.4	4.4	3.2	57.4	15.4	42.0
1975	100.0	27.9	9.3	2.6	8.8	3.3	3.9	72.1	24.7	47.4
Rate per 100,000 population:										
1955	1,028	795	502	76	163	54	(NA)	233	(NA)	233
1965	1,376	817	420	65	271	60	(NA)	559	(NA)	559
1971	1,977	843	365	62	266	87	64	1,134	305	829
1975	3,033	847	283	78	268	101	117	2,185	750	1,435

NA Not available.
[1] Includes estimates of episodes of care in residential treatment centers for emotionally disturbed children.
[2] Hospitals (non-VA) with psychiatric inpatient units.   [3] Federally funded.
Source: U.S. National Institute of Mental Health, *Statistical Note 139*, DHEW Publication, No. (ADM) 77-158, 1977.

No. 177. Public Facilities for the Mentally Retarded: 1950 to 1976

[For years ending June 30. Data as submitted by many State agencies; therefore, in many instances figures reflect estimates rather than substantiated figures. For example, resident patients at the end of a year do not equal the number at the beginning of a succeeding year. Includes estimates for underreporting wherever possible. See also *Historical Statistics, Colonial Times to 1970*, series B 428-443]

ITEM	1950	1960	1965	1970	1971	1975	1976
Number of institutions	96	108	143	190	190	210	244
Resident patients, beginning of year	103,377	158,682	181,549	189,956	185,855	166,689	(NA)
Admissions [1]	10,369	14,701	17,300	14,985	15,370	13,424	8,312
Patients under treatment	113,746	173,383	198,849	204,941	201,225	180,113	(NA)
Deaths in institutions	1,971	3,202	3,583	3,496	3,183	2,752	(NA)
Net live releases [2]	4,681	6,451	7,993	14,702	17,080	18,320	12,657
Resident patients, end of year	107,094	163,730	187,273	186,743	180,963	159,041	157,134
Rate per 100,000 population [3]	71.0	91.9	97.7	92.6	88.6	75.2	73.8
Average daily resident patients	127,830	163,282	189,172	187,897	181,058	161,061	153,584
Personnel, full-time, total [4]	25,744	54,277	79,056	117,327	118,909	(NA)	97,243
Rate per 100 avg. daily resident patients	20.1	33.2	41.8	62.4	65.7	(NA)	63.3
Maintenance expenditures [4][5] mil. dol.	92	266	442	871	1,003	1,837	(NA)
Per average daily resident patient:							
Per year dol.	746	1,650	2,335	4,635	5,537	11,315	13,052
Per day dol.	2	5	6	13	15	31	36

NA Not available.
[1] Through 1975, excludes transfers. 1976 includes transfers.
[2] Excess of patients released alive from hospital over those returning to hospital.
[3] Based on Bureau of the Census estimated civilian population as of July 1.
[4] Reporting facilities only.   [5] Includes salaries and wages, purchased provisions, fuel, light, water, etc.
Source: U.S. Office of Human Development Services, *Residents in Public Institutions for the Mentally Retarded*, annual, through 1971; thereafter, unpublished data.

Health and Nutrition

No. 178. Patients in Mental Care Facilities: 1975 and 1976

[Additions comprise admissions and readmissions]

STATE	MENTAL HOSPITALS,[1] 1975				Outpatient psychiatric services, additions,[1][2] 1975	General hospitals with psychiatric inpatient units, additions,[1][3] 1975	PUBLIC INSTITUTIONS FOR MENTALLY RETARDED[4]		
	State and county		Private				Resident patients, as of June 30, 1976	Total admissions, 1975	Net live releases,[5] 1975
	Resident patients, end of year	Total additions	Resident patients, end of year	Total additions					
Facilities, number	313		182		1,801	791	244	210	
United States	191,395	433,529	11,576	125,529	1,594,148	543,731	157,134	13,424	18,320
Alabama	2,534	3,214	114	2,902	10,846	7,433	1,799	84	65
Alaska	115	671	–	–	1,251	–	110	12	14
Arizona	673	1,503	41	694	18,579	5,182	1,011	159	102
Arkansas	421	2,867	–	–	3,306	3,938	1,541	361	289
California	9,373	28,708	1,448	18,793	171,428	54,192	5,358	806	496
Colorado	1,298	6,543	168	2,260	24,468	4,298	1,741	59	146
Connecticut	3,026	15,990	639	2,455	28,367	6,741	4,863	600	631
Delaware	845	2,054	45	580	5,597	–	555	163	153
Dist. of Columbia	2,825	5,344	170	1,234	9,761	2,321	–	8	206
Florida	6,392	8,019	365	6,880	48,342	26,730	5,340	245	369
Georgia	6,507	24,703	269	5,095	33,472	11,516	3,601	626	735
Hawaii	214	791	–	–	5,091	757	638	17	66
Idaho	216	910	–	–	48	1,081	472	96	100
Illinois	7,053	25,278	427	5,898	84,812	32,864	8,289	393	627
Indiana	4,581	8,698	29	342	22,425	11,086	3,388	171	447
Iowa	1,269	5,253	–	–	18,827	10,178	1,450	116	80
Kansas	1,475	4,327	218	652	15,105	14,685	1,517	143	290
Kentucky	686	1,263	344	4,496	8,793	9,170	602	56	51
Louisiana	2,577	9,520	354	3,638	15,355	4,840	3,038	417	328
Maine	786	1,321	–	–	2,057	–	597	165	236
Maryland	5,244	12,236	552	2,187	39,140	5,379	3,201	767	762
Massachusetts	5,272	13,383	659	7,209	63,572	7,928	5,913	228	403
Michigan	5,076	14,924	490	6,096	136,824	17,905	6,933	295	996
Minnesota	4,064	7,829	–	–	24,256	17,077	3,251	296	479
Mississippi	2,826	5,320	49	884	2,376	2,219	1,850	329	391
Missouri	3,817	18,124	144	1,710	41,077	14,321	2,191	832	939
Montana	904	1,962	–	–	229	2,355	353	13	158
Nebraska	746	3,691	–	–	7,373	4,533	1,054	24	115
Nevada	264	775	–	–	4,445	2,447	151	55	66
New Hampshire	1,184	1,197	11	22	5,625	1,105	818	19	46
New Jersey	9,467	13,829	365	3,864	41,413	15,495	7,832	231	136
New Mexico	337	1,296	48	760	2,910	1,585	615	88	123
New York	35,804	37,791	920	6,507	283,891	64,162	19,278	1,116	2,194
North Carolina	4,596	17,456	190	1,443	33,105	13,528	3,689	206	413
North Dakota	592	2,232	–	–	1,064	2,146	898	28	64
Ohio	9,903	19,939	427	4,888	84,598	30,680	9,181	135	392
Oklahoma	2,239	7,758	59	909	14,956	5,845	2,738	184	279
Oregon	1,183	5,265	26	130	21,045	7,447	1,857	129	274
Pennsylvania	14,002	8,027	927	10,840	74,354	26,417	9,347	733	782
Rhode Island	1,597	5,025	114	1,306	7,909	–	742	38	37
South Carolina	4,097	4,730	–	–	5,173	6,642	3,024	556	418
South Dakota	673	1,699	–	–	5,264	1,322	181	73	110
Tennessee	4,292	11,935	125	2,100	24,282	8,611	2,215	380	567
Texas	7,454	26,552	500	5,494	37,538	31,792	11,214	839	1,147
Utah	296	603	–	–	4,214	3,849	870	120	105
Vermont	489	1,021	165	501	3,422	482	453	19	44
Virginia	6,473	15,215	789	8,237	22,220	11,286	4,254	142	318
Washington	1,266	3,619	73	1,270	29,459	9,212	2,557	140	192
West Virginia	2,869	4,129	39	1,211	10,663	4,847	544	58	52
Wisconsin	1,227	8,229	273	2,042	29,823	16,102	2,464	630	863
Wyoming	276	761	–	–	3,998	–	556	24	24

– Represents zero. [1] Includes estimates for non-reporting facilities. [2] Excludes federally funded community mental health centers. [3] Non-federal. [4] Source: U.S. Office of Human Development Services, unpublished data. [5] Excess of patients released alive from hospital (direct discharges plus leave placements) over those returning to hospitals.

Source: Except as noted, U.S. National Institute of Mental Health, unpublished data.

No. 179. Days of Disability, by Type, and by Sex of Patient: 1965 to 1976

[1965, for year ending **June 30**; thereafter, calendar years. Refers to civilian noninstitutional population. Based on sample and subject to sampling variability; see source. For region components, see fig. I, inside front cover]

ITEM	TOTAL DAYS OF DISABILITY (millions)						DAYS PER PERSON					
	1965	1970	1973	1974	1975	1976	1965	1970	1973	1974	1975	1976
Restricted-activity days [1]	3,086	2,913	3,392	3,566	3,734	3,840	16.4	14.6	16.5	17.2	17.9	18.2
Male	1,339	1,273	1,458	1,564	1,574	1,666	14.7	13.2	14.7	15.6	15.6	16.4
Female	1,747	1,640	1,934	2,001	2,160	2,174	18.0	15.8	18.1	18.7	20.0	19.9
White	(NA)	2,526	2,904	3,042	3,179	3,280	(NA)	14.4	16.1	16.8	17.5	17.9
Black and other	(NA)	387	488	523	555	560	(NA)	15.6	18.8	19.7	20.4	20.2
Under 65 years old	2,420	2,331	2,714	2,778	2,916	2,969	14.1	12.9	14.6	14.9	15.5	15.7
65 years old and over	666	582	678	788	818	871	38.5	30.7	33.5	38.0	38.4	40.0
Northeast	(NA)	709	675	741	819	792	(NA)	14.5	13.9	15.2	16.7	16.3
North Central	(NA)	691	875	917	888	962	(NA)	12.4	15.5	16.2	15.9	17.1
South	(NA)	996	1,198	1,225	1,253	1,264	(NA)	15.9	18.4	18.8	18.7	18.7
West	(NA)	518	644	683	774	823	(NA)	15.6	18.1	18.1	20.8	21.5
Family income: [2]												
Under $5,000	(NA)	982	1,006	993	1,030	943	(NA)	23.3	28.8	30.5	32.4	32.5
$5,000-$9,999	(NA)	857	851	879	914	865	(NA)	12.8	16.5	18.4	20.2	20.3
$10,000-$14,999	(NA)	539	660	715	676	700	(NA)	11.5	13.0	13.9	14.4	15.7
$15,000 and over	(NA)	331	655	751	863	973	(NA)	10.9	12.2	11.9	12.4	12.8
Bed-disability days [3]	1,160	1,222	1,311	1,392	1,371	1,500	6.2	6.1	6.4	6.7	6.6	7.1
Male	484	503	528	584	546	619	5.3	5.2	5.3	5.8	5.4	6.1
Female	677	720	783	807	825	882	7.0	6.9	7.3	7.5	7.6	8.1
Under 65 years old	914	959	1,045	1,095	1,097	1,172	5.3	5.3	5.6	5.9	5.8	6.2
65 years old and over	246	263	265	297	274	328	14.2	13.8	13.1	14.3	12.9	15.1
Work-loss days [4]	400	417	451	414	433	465	5.7	5.4	5.4	4.9	5.2	5.3
Male	261	243	264	245	246	269	5.7	5.0	5.2	4.8	4.9	5.2
Female	139	175	187	169	187	196	5.6	5.9	5.8	5.1	5.7	5.6
School-loss days [5]	214	222	222	242	217	219	5.2	4.9	5.1	5.6	5.1	5.2
Male	103	108	103	126	103	105	4.9	4.7	4.7	5.7	4.8	4.9
Female	111	114	118	116	115	114	5.4	5.1	5.5	5.5	5.5	5.5

NA Not available.   [1] A day when a person cut down on his usual activities for the whole day because of illness or injury. Includes bed-disability, work-loss, and school-loss days.   [2] Excludes those with unknown income.
[3] A day when a person was kept in bed either all or most of the day because of illness or injury. Includes those work-loss and school-loss days actually spent in bed.

[4] A day when a person lost the entire work day because of illness or injury. Computed for persons 17 years of age and over in the currently employed population, defined as those who were working or had a job or business from which they were not on layoff during the 2-week period preceding the week of interview.

[5] Child's loss of entire school day because of illness or injury. Computed for children 6–16 years of age.

Source: U.S. National Center for Health Statistics, *Vital and Health Statistics*, series 10, Nos. 72, 95, 100, 115, and 119; and unpublished data.

No. 180. Civilians With Visual Impairment or Legally Blind, By Sex: 1972

[**In thousands.** Estimates less than 25,000 are subject to large relative sampling errors. Based on data from the Health Interview Survey, the 1973–74 Nursing Home Survey, National Society for the Prevention of Blindness, National Disease and Therapeutic Index, and Model Reporting Area for Blindness Statistics]

TYPE OF AFFECTION	ALL VISUAL IMPAIRMENT [1]			SEVERE VISUAL IMPAIRMENT [2]			LEGAL BLINDNESS [3]		
	Total	Male	Female	Total	Male	Female	Total	Male	Female
Total	10,659	5,315	5,344	1,483	557	926	468	224	244
Glaucoma	1,070	453	617	207	79	128	56	26	30
Cataract	1,711	702	1,008	217	72	144	64	28	36
Retinal disorder	815	340	473	392	134	257	118	53	65
Myopia	715	375	340	36	15	21	14	7	7
Cornea or sclera	294	179	115	67	25	42	22	10	12
Uveitis	285	148	137	67	27	40	23	11	12
Optic nerve disease	121	62	59	107	55	52	41	24	17
Multiple affections	90	24	66	90	24	66	23	8	15
Refractive errors with lesser disability	1,662	880	782	–	–	–	–	–	–
Other and unknown	3,896	2,151	1,745	301	125	176	108	56	52

– Represents zero.   [1] Impaired vision includes blindness in one or both eyes, cataract, glaucoma, color blindness, detached retina or other condition of the retina, or any other trouble seeing with one or both eyes even when wearing glasses.   [2] Severe visual impairment is defined as an inability to read ordinary newsprint with glasses using both eyes, or having no useful vision in either eye, or blindness in both eyes.
[3] Legal blindness is defined as visual acuity for distant vision of 20/200 or less in the better eye, with best correction, or widest diameter of visual field subtending an angle less than 20 degrees.

Source: U.S. National Eye Institute, unpublished data.

No. 181. Persons Wearing Corrective Lenses: 1971

[Data refer to civilian noninstitutional population 3 years old and over. Based on sample and subject to sampling variability; see source. Total wearing lenses includes group unknown as to type but excludes sunglasses worn only to filter light, safety glasses for protection, hand magnifiers, and other such devices]

ITEM	Total	SEX		AGE (in years)			
		Male	Female	3–16	17–24	25–44	45 and over
Population, 3 years old and over_____1,000__	191,602	92,121	99,481	55,786	27,275	47,428	61,113
Wearing lenses_____1,000__	94,284	40,757	53,527	9,249	11,114	19,978	53 944
Eyeglasses only_____1,000__	90,313	39,669	50,644	8,920	9,306	18,555	53,532
Contact lenses (with or without glasses)__1,000__	2,403	654	1,750	138	1,140	819	306
Percent wearing lenses_____	49.2	44.2	53.8	16.6	40.7	42.1	88.3
Eyeglasses only_____	47.1	43.1	50.9	16.0	34.1	39.1	87.6
Contact lenses (with or without glasses)_____	1.3	.7	1.8	.2	4.2	1.7	.5

Source: U.S. National Center for Health Statistics, *Vital and Health Statistics*, series 10, No. 79; and unpublished data.

No. 182. Selected Preventive Care Procedures: 1973

[Covers civilian noninstitutional population. Based on sample and subject to sampling variability; see source]

TYPE OF PROCEDURE AND AGE GROUP	BOTH SEXES			MALE			FEMALE		
	Population (1,000)	Percent with care		Population (1,000)	Percent with care		Population (1,000)	Percent with care	
		At any time	In past year		At any time	In past year		At any time	In past year
Electrocardiogram:									
Total, 40 years and over_____	73,949	60.4	24.5	33,917	64.6	27.1	40,032	56.8	22.3
40–44 years_____	11,162	48.0	18.5	5,367	55.1	22.3	5,795	41.6	14.9
45–64 years_____	42,534	60.4	24.0	20,164	64.6	27.0	22,370	56.6	21.4
65 years and over_____	20,253	67.2	28.9	8,386	70.7	30.5	11,867	64.8	27.8
Glaucoma test:									
Total, 40 years and over_____	73,949	53.7	23.4	33,917	50.1	21.9	40,032	56.7	24.8
40–44 years_____	11,162	40.0	18.8	5,367	38.0	18.5	5,795	41.9	19.0
45–64 years_____	42,534	56.4	23.9	20,164	53.0	22.4	22,370	59.3	25.3
65 years and over_____	20,253	55.7	25.0	8,386	50.9	22.7	11,867	59.0	26.6
Chest X-ray:									
Total, 17 years and over_____	141,802	80.1	31.2	66,641	80.3	31.9	75,161	80.0	30.7
17–24 years_____	29,063	65.6	26.6	14,000	66.1	26.5	15,062	65.2	26.6
25–44 years_____	49,953	84.6	31.0	24,091	83.9	31.2	25,862	85.3	30.8
45–64 years_____	42,534	85.3	34.5	20,164	85.1	35.7	22,370	85.6	33.3
65 years and over_____	20,253	78.9	31.7	8,386	82.4	33.5	11,867	76.5	30.5
Breast examination:									
Total, 17 years and over_____	(X)	(X)	(X)	(X)	(X)	(X)	75,161	76.3	48.0
17–24 years_____	(X)	(X)	(X)	(X)	(X)	(X)	15,062	65.2	51.4
25–44 years_____	(X)	(X)	(X)	(X)	(X)	(X)	25,862	88.8	59.7
45–64 years_____	(X)	(X)	(X)	(X)	(X)	(X)	22,370	78.6	42.5
65 years and over_____	(X)	(X)	(X)	(X)	(X)	(X)	11,867	59.1	28.5
Pap smear:									
Total, 17 years and over_____	(X)	(X)	(X)	(X)	(X)	(X)	75,161	75.2	45.9
17–24 years_____	(X)	(X)	(X)	(X)	(X)	(X)	15,062	61.4	50.2
25–44 years_____	(X)	(X)	(X)	(X)	(X)	(X)	25,862	90.0	60.0
45–64 years_____	(X)	(X)	(X)	(X)	(X)	(X)	22,370	78.9	39.3
65 years and over_____	(X)	(X)	(X)	(X)	(X)	(X)	11,867	53.7	22.0

X Not applicable.

Source: U.S. National Center for Health Statistics, *Vital and Health Statistics*, series 10, No. 95; *Monthly Vital Statistics Reports*, vol. 24, No. 6 and No. 7 supplements, Sept. and Oct. 1975; and unpublished data.

No. 183. Persons Injured, by Sex, 1970 to 1976, and by Circumstance, 1976

[Data refer to civilian noninstitutional population and comprise incidents leading to restricted activity and/or medical attention. Sum of estimates may be greater than total because circumstances are not mutually exclusive. Based on a sample and subject to sampling variability; see source for explanation. 1975 data not strictly comparable with other years]

YEAR	PERSONS INJURED (millions)			RATE PER 100 POPULATION			CIRCUMSTANCE	PERSONS INJURED (millions)			RATE PER 100 POPULATION		
	Both sexes	Male	Female	Both sexes	Male	Female		Both sexes	Male	Female	Both sexes	Male	Female
1970_____	56.0	31.8	24.2	28.0	33.0	23.3	**1976, total___**	65.4	37.1	28.3	31.1	36.5	26.0
1972_____	64.3	37.0	27.3	31.5	37.6	25.8	While at work___	9.3	7.5	1.8	4.4	7.4	1.6
1973_____	60.0	34.8	25.2	29.1	35.0	23.7	Home_____	26.0	13.5	12.5	12.3	13.3	11.4
1974_____	59.1	33.6	25.6	28.5	33.6	23.8	Motor vehicle___	4.6	2.2	2.5	2.2	2.1	2.3
1975_____	71.9	39.4	32.5	34.4	39.1	30.0	Other_____	27.6	15.4	12.2	13.1	15.2	11.1

Source: U.S. National Center for Health Statistics, *Vital and Health Statistics*, series 10, Nos. 72, 85, 95, 100, 115, and 119.

No. 184. Percent of Population Engaged in Physical Exercise, by Type of Exercise, Sex, and Age: 1975

[Based on a household sample of the civilian noninstitutional population, 20 years old and over]

SEX AND AGE	Total population (1,000)	Percent exercising regularly [1]	PERCENT, BY TYPE OF EXERCISE [2]						
			Ride bicycle	Calisthenics	Jog	Lift weights	Swim	Walk	All other
Total, 20 years and over___	135,655	48.6	10.9	13.5	4.8	3.4	11.8	33.8	6.8
20–44 years_____	71,084	53.7	16.1	17.3	7.3	5.4	16.9	33.8	6.9
45–64 years_____	43,145	43.4	6.5	10.8	2.7	1.5	8.0	32.9	6.5
65 years and over_____	21,426	42.3	2.9	6.1	1.2	(B)	2.8	35.7	6.9
Male, 20 years and over____	63,665	48.5	10.8	13.5	7.2	6.3	13.3	32.5	6.4
20–44 years_____	34,268	52.7	14.9	17.5	10.6	10.1	18.8	31.4	6.2
45–64 years_____	20,567	42.0	6.7	10.1	3.8	2.6	8.1	31.4	5.9
65 years and over_____	8,830	47.3	4.3	5.9	2.1	(B)	4.1	39.4	8.1
Female, 20 years and over__	71,990	48.7	11.1	13.5	2.7	.8	10.5	35.0	7.1
20–44 years_____	36,816	54.6	17.2	17.1	4.1	1.1	15.0	36.0	7.5
45–64 years_____	22,579	44.6	6.4	11.4	1.6	(B)	7.8	34.2	7.1
65 years and over_____	12,595	38.7	1.8	6.3	(B)	(B)	1.9	33.0	6.0

B Base less than minimum required for reliability.
[1] Regular exercise is any exercise done on a weekly basis.
[2] More than one type of exercise can be reported per person.

Source: U.S. National Center for Health Statistics, *Health, United States, 1976–1977.*

No. 185. Average Heights and Weights, by Age and Sex: 1960–1962 and 1971–1974

[Height was measured without shoes. For 1960–1962, two pounds are deducted to allow for weight of clothing; for 1971–1974 total weights of all clothing ranged from .2 to .6 pounds, which are not deducted from weights shown]

SEX, YEAR, AND HEIGHT (feet and inches)	18–24 years	25–34 years	35–44 years	45–54 years	55–64 years	65–74 years
MEN	HEIGHT (inches)					
1960–1962_____	68.7	69.1	68.5	68.2	67.4	66.9
1971–1974_____	69.7	69.6	69.1	68.9	68.3	67.3
WOMEN						
1960–1962_____	63.8	63.7	63.5	62.9	62.4	(1.5
1971–1974_____	64.3	64.1	64.1	63.6	62.8	62.3
MEN	WEIGHT (lb.)					
1960–1962, total_____	158	169	170	170	164	158
1971–1974, total_____	165	176	178	175	171	164
5'2"_____	130	141	143	147	143	143
5'3"_____	135	145	148	152	147	147
5'4"_____	140	150	153	156	153	151
5'5"_____	145	156	158	160	158	156
5'6"_____	150	160	163	164	163	160
5'7"_____	154	165	169	169	168	164
5'8"_____	159	170	174	173	173	169
5'9"_____	164	174	179	177	178	173
5'10"_____	168	179	184	182	183	177
5'11"_____	173	184	190	187	189	182
6'_____	178	189	194	191	193	186
6'1"_____	183	194	200	196	197	190
6'2"_____	188	199	205	200	203	194
WOMEN						
1960–1962, total_____	127	134	142	145	150	144
1971–1974, total_____	132	140	148	149	149	146
4'9"_____	114	118	125	129	132	130
4'10"_____	117	121	129	133	136	134
4'11"_____	120	125	133	136	140	137
5'_____	123	128	137	140	143	140
5'1"_____	126	132	141	143	147	144
5'2"_____	129	136	144	147	150	147
5'3"_____	132	139	148	150	153	151
5'4"_____	135	142	152	154	157	154
5'5"_____	138	146	156	158	160	158
5'6"_____	141	150	159	161	164	161
5'7"_____	144	153	163	165	167	165
5'8"_____	147	157	167	168	171	169

Source: U.S. National Center for Health Statistics, *Advance Data,* No. 3, Nov. 19, 1976.

No. 186. ACUTE CONDITIONS, BY TYPE, 1970 TO 1976, AND BY SELECTED CHARACTERISTICS, 1976

[Data refer to civilian noninstitutional population. Based on a sample and subject to sampling variability; see source for detailed explanation. Estimates include only acute conditions which were medically attended or caused at least one day of restricted activity. For composition of regions, see fig. I, inside front cover]

YEAR AND CHARACTERISTIC	NUMBER OF CONDITIONS (1,000)					RATE PER 100 POPULATION				
	Infective and parasitic	Respiratory		Digestive system	Injuries	Infective and parasitic	Respiratory		Digestive system	Injuries
		Upper	Other				Upper	Other		
1970, total	48,215	127,263	92,501	23,014	59,227	24.1	63.7	46.3	11.5	29.6
1971, total	55,099	140,763	95,092	22,510	66,152	27.2	69.6	47.0	11.1	32.7
1972, total	46,665	132,403	114,244	22,965	67,823	22.9	64.9	56.0	11.2	33.2
1973, total	40,003	100,578	88,240	17,205	63,233	19.4	48.9	42.9	8.4	30.7
1974, total	40,465	94,868	100,874	16,193	63,085	19.5	45.8	48.7	7.8	30.4
1975, total	47,608	123,991	108,969	21,618	76,192	22.8	59.3	52.1	10.3	36.4
1976, total	52,603	127,656	123,048	21,997	67,714	25.0	60.6	58.4	10.4	32.1
Male	24,608	59,303	56,387	10,314	38,388	24.2	58.4	55.5	10.1	37.8
Female	27,995	68,353	66,661	11,683	29,326	25.7	62.7	61.1	10.7	26.9
Northeast	14,178	30,829	19,058	5,186	14,883	29.2	63.4	39.2	10.7	30.6
North Central	8,696	34,049	41,253	5,739	18,999	15.5	60.5	73.4	10.2	33.8
South	23,300	38,901	28,440	7,405	19,870	34.5	57.6	42.1	11.0	29.4
West	6,430	23,876	34,297	3,667	13,962	16.8	62.5	89.7	9.6	36.5
Inside SMSA [1]	36,100	90,657	84,433	14,521	47,435	25.0	62.9	58.5	10.1	32.9
Outside SMSA: [1]										
Nonfarm	15,420	33,743	35,495	6,800	18,663	25.8	56.4	59.3	11.4	31.2
Farm	1,083	3,256	3,120	676	1,615	16.6	49.8	47.7	10.3	24.7
Under 6 yr	11,490	25,239	13,349	2,237	7,629	60.7	133.4	70.6	11.8	40.3
6–16 yr	16,179	34,573	30,225	6,929	14,900	38.5	82.4	72.0	16.5	35.5
17–44 yr	17,365	46,541	54,664	8,629	30,159	20.5	54.9	64.5	10.2	35.6
45 yr. and over	7,570	21,303	24,811	4,202	15,025	11.6	32.7	38.1	6.5	23.1

[1] For definition of standard metropolitan statistical area (SMSA), see Appendix II.

Source: U.S. National Center for Health Statistics, *Vital and Health Statistics*, series 10, Nos. 72, 85, 95, 100, 115, and 119; and unpublished data.

No. 187. PERSONS WITH ACTIVITY LIMITATION, BY SELECTED CHRONIC CONDITIONS: 1969–1970 AND 1976

[Based on household interviews of a sample of the civilian noninstitutional population and subject to sampling variability]

CONDITION	BOTH SEXES		MALE				FEMALE			
	All ages	65 yr. and over	All ages	Under 45 yr.	45–64 yr.	65 yr. and over	All ages	Under 45 yr.	45–64 yr.	65 yr. and over
1969–1970										
Persons with limitation___mil__	**23.2**	**8.0**	**11.7**	**3.9**	**4.1**	**3.7**	**11.5**	**3.4**	**3.9**	**4.3**
Percent limited by—										
Heart conditions	15.5	20.5	16.5	5.5	22.3	21.8	14.6	7.3	15.6	19.3
Arthritis and rheumatism	14.1	21.2	9.3	3.1	10.7	14.4	18.9	5.9	21.0	27.1
Visual impairments	4.8	7.0	5.3	4.8	4.3	7.0	4.3	2.1	3.2	7.0
Hypertension without heart involvement	4.6	6.4	3.0	1.3	3.7	4.0	6.2	2.4	6.8	8.5
Mental and nervous conditions	4.5	3.0	4.1	4.8	4.7	2.6	4.9	6.0	5.5	3.4
Percent of all persons with—										
No activity limitation	88.3	57.7	87.7	94.2	78.9	54.1	88.8	95.3	82.0	60.4
Activity limitation	11.7	42.3	12.3	5.8	21.1	45.8	11.2	4.7	18.0	39.6
In major activity	9.1	37.0	9.5	3.5	17.3	41.7	8.6	3.1	14.2	33.5
1976										
Persons with limitation___mil__	**30.2**	**9.9**	**14.6**	**5.1**	**5.2**	**4.3**	**15.6**	**4.7**	**5.3**	**5.6**
Percent limited by—										
Heart conditions	15.7	23.4	16.7	3.6	22.2	25.3	14.8	5.0	15.9	22.0
Arthritis and rheumatism	16.8	24.9	11.4	3.7	14.9	16.3	21.7	7.4	24.2	31.6
Visual impairments	5.4	8.2	5.7	5.2	4.7	7.6	5.0	2.8	3.2	8.6
Hypertension without heart involvement	6.9	8.9	4.8	1.9	6.8	6.1	8.9	3.6	11.1	11.1
Mental and nervous conditions	4.9	3.0	4.4	6.2	4.7	2.0	5.4	6.1	6.6	3.8
Percent of all persons with—										
No activity limitation	85.7	54.6	85.7	93.0	74.9	51.7	85.7	93.6	76.5	56.6
Activity limitation	14.3	45.4	14.3	7.0	25.1	48.3	14.3	6.4	23.5	43.4
In major activity	10.8	39.4	10.8	4.1	20.0	43.7	10.7	3.9	18.2	36.4

Source: U.S. National Center for Health Statistics, *Vital and Health Statistics*, series 10, No. 80, and unpublished data.

No. 188. Percent of Children 1 to 4 Years Old Immunized Against Specified Diseases: 1965 to 1977

[Covers civilian noninstitutional population]

ITEM	1965	1968	1970	1971	1972	1973	1974	1975	1976	1977, prel.
Children, 1–4 yr___1,000__	16,502	14,994	14,123	14,112	13,905	13,874	13,210	12,729	12,276	12,071
Percent immunized against—										
Diphtheria-tetanus-pertussis (3 or more doses)_____	73.9	76.5	76.1	78.7	75.6	72.6	73.9	75.2	71.4	69.5
Polio (3 or more oral doses)_____	[1] 73.9	68.3	65.9	67.3	62.9	60.4	63.1	64.8	61.6	60.1
Measles_____	33.2	58.8	57.2	61.0	62.2	61.2	64.5	65.5	65.9	63.1
Rubella_____	(NA)	(NA)	37.2	51.2	56.9	55.6	59.8	61.9	61.7	59.4
Mumps_____	(NA)	(NA)	(NA)	(NA)	(NA)	34.7	39.4	44.4	48.3	48.1

NA Not available.   [1] Inactivated doses or oral doses.

Source: U.S. Center for Disease Control, Atlanta, Ga., *United States Immunization Survey*, annual.

No. 189. Specified Reportable Diseases—Cases Reported: 1950 to 1976

[Prior to 1960, excludes Alaska and Hawaii, except for tuberculosis. Figures should be interpreted with caution. Although reporting of some of these diseases is incomplete, the figures are of value in indicating trends of disease incidence. See *Historical Statistics, Colonial Times to 1970*, series B 291–303, for related data]

DISEASE	1950	1955	1960	1965	1970	1972	1973	1974	1975	1976
Amebiasis_____	4,568	3,348	3,424	2,768	2,888	2,199	2,235	2,743	2,775	2,906
Aseptic meningitis_____	(NA)	(NA)	1,593	2,329	6,480	4,634	4,846	3,197	4,475	3,510
Botulism_____	20	16	12	19	12	22	34	28	17	37
Brucellosis (undulant fever)_____	3,510	1,444	751	262	213	196	202	240	310	296
Chickenpox_____1,000__	(NA)	(NA)	(NA)	(NA)	(NA)	164.1	182.9	141.5	154.2	184.0
Diphtheria_____	5,796	1,984	918	918	435	152	228	272	307	128
Encephalitis: Primary infectious____	}1,135	2,166	2,341	{1,722	1,580	1,059	1,618	1,066	3,815	1,551
Post infectious_____				981	370	243	349	316	486	255
Hepatitis: Serum_____1,000__	} 2.8	32.0	41.7	33.9	{ 8.3	9.4	8.5	10.6	13.1	15.0
Infectious_____1,000__					56.8	54.1	50.7	40.4	35.9	33.3
Unspecified_____1,000__	(NA)	(NA)	(NA)	(NA)	(NA)	(NA)	(NA)	8.4	7.2	7.5
Leprosy_____	44	75	54	96	129	130	146	118	162	145
Leptospirosis_____	30	24	53	84	47	41	57	68	93	73
Malaria_____	2,184	522	72	147	3,051	742	237	293	373	471
Measles_____1,000__	319.1	555.2	441.7	261.9	47.4	32.3	26.7	22.1	24.4	41.1
Meningococcal infections_____	3,788	3,455	2,259	3,040	2,505	1,323	1,378	1,346	1,478	1,605
Mumps_____1,000__	(NA)	(NA)	(NA)	(NA)	105.0	74.2	69.6	59.1	59.6	38.5
Pertussis (whooping cough)__1,000__	120.7	62.8	14.8	6.8	4.2	3.3	1.8	2.4	1.7	1.0
Poliomyelitis, acute_____	33,300	28,985	3,190	72	33	31	8	7	8	13
Psittacosis_____	26	334	113	60	35	52	33	164	49	78
Rabies in animals_____	7,901	5,799	3,567	4,574	3,224	4,369	3,640	3,151	2,627	3,090
Rheumatic fever, acute [1]_____	(NA)	(NA)	9,022	4,998	3,227	2,614	2,560	2,431	2,854	1,865
Rubella (German measles)___1,000__	(NA)	(NA)	(NA)	(NA)	56.6	25.5	27.8	11.9	16.7	12.5
Salmonellosis [2]_____1,000__	1.2	5.4	6.9	17.2	22.1	22.2	23.8	22.0	22.6	22.9
Shigellosis [3]_____1,000__	23.4	13.9	12.5	11.0	13.8	20.2	22.6	22.6	16.6	13.1
Streptococcal sore throat and scarlet fever_____1,000__	64.5	147.5	315.2	395.2	433.4	[4] 421.5	[4] 474.2	[4] 407.0	[4] 330.8	[4] 394.5
Tetanus_____	486	462	368	300	148	128	101	101	102	75
Trichinosis_____	327	264	160	199	109	89	102	120	252	115
Tuberculosis [5]_____1,000__	(NA)	76.2	55.5	49.0	37.1	32.9	31.0	30.1	34.0	32.1
Tularemia_____	927	584	390	264	172	152	171	144	129	157
Typhoid fever_____	2,484	1,704	816	454	346	398	680	437	375	419
Typhus fever:										
Flea-borne (endemic-murine)_____	685	135	68	28	27	18	32	26	44	69
Tick-borne (Rocky Mountain spotted fever)_____	464	295	204	281	380	523	668	754	844	937
Venereal diseases (civilian cases):										
Gonorrhea_____1,000__	286.7	236.2	258.9	324.9	600.1	767.2	842.6	898.9	999.9	1,002
Syphilis_____1,000__	217.6	122.4	122.0	112.8	91.4	91.1	87.5	83.8	80.4	71.8
Other_____1,000__	8.2	3.9	2.8	2.0	2.2	2.3	1.6	1.4	1.1	1.1

NA Not available.   [1] Based on reports from States: 37 in 1960, 36 in 1965 and 1973–1975, 38 in 1970, 35 in 1972, and 40 in 1976.   [2] Excludes typhoid fever.   [3] Bacillary dysentery.   [4] Based on reports from States: 46 in 1972 and 1973, 42 in 1974 and 1976, and 41 in 1975.   [5] Beginning 1960, newly reported active cases. New diagnostic standards introduced in 1975.

Source: U.S. National Center for Health Statistics, *Vital Statistics—Special Reports*, vol. 37, No. 9, and U.S. Center for Disease Control, Atlanta, Ga., *Morbidity and Mortality Weekly Report* (annual supplements).

No. 190. Drugs and Toiletries—Retail Sales: 1975 to 1977

[In millions of dollars. Excludes government and hospital use, except as noted]

PRODUCT	1975	1976	1977	PRODUCT	1975	1976	1977
Total sales	[1]21,625	24,461	26,625	Toiletries	7,963	8,534	9,396
Drugs and other health aids [2]	[1]13,662	15,927	16,869	Hair products	2,172	2,306	2,414
				Shampoos	632	694	732
Prescriptions	8,146	8,949	9,618	Shaving products	1,223	1,304	1,379
Packaged medications	[3]3,511	3,762	4,359				
Vitamin concentrates [4]	452	476	520	Oral hygiene	1,057	1,143	1,301
Cough and cold remedies	735	810	844	Dentifrices	494	545	575
Internal analgesics	719	782	[5]832	Hand products	329	372	447
Other	1,605	1,694	[5]2,163	Cosmetics	1,409	1,620	1,906
Sickroom and convalescent aids	371	388	400	Lipsticks	389	458	552
First aid products	336	361	386	Fragrances	608	612	621
Baby needs	1,074	1,143	1,245	Toilet water, cologne	429	427	427
Disposable diapers, liners	577	608	642	Personal hygiene [6]	1,165	1,178	1,329
Feminine needs	552	585	[5]595	Bath soaps [7]	558	578	722
Veterinary	413	467	(NA)	Deodorants	599	591	598

NA Not available.
[1] Adjusted for duplication.   [2] Includes items not shown separately.
[3] Includes prescription as well as proprietary items.   [4] Includes sales to hospitals.
[5] Effervescent compounds previously reported under internal analgesics and contraceptives previously reported under feminine needs now included in other packaged medications.
[6] Includes personal insect repellents.   [7] Medicated soaps included in packaged medications.

Source: Medical Economics Company, Oradell, N.J., *Drug Topics*, Marketing Guide, annual. Copyrighted © by Litton Industries. Further reproduction prohibited without the written permission of the copyright owner.

No. 191. Estimated Alcoholism, by Sex—Total, 1970 and 1975, and by States, 1970

[Population, 20 years old and over. An "alcoholic" is defined as one who is unable consistently to choose whether he shall drink or not, and who, if he drinks, is unable consistently to choose whether he shall stop or not. "Alcoholics with complications" are those who have developed bodily or mental disorders through prolonged excessive drinking. Data are rough approximations derived by the original Jellinek formula. In the early 1940's, E. M. Jellinek proposed a formula for estimating the number of "alcoholics-with-complications" from statistics on liver cirrhosis deaths. To arrive at the total number of alcoholics (those with and without complications) the results of the formula were multiplied by a factor, R, the value of which was thought to be 4. Subsequently it appeared that the value of R should have been 5. The formula was applicable to the years 1940–1945 but is thought not to have worked reliably after 1945. However, if the rate of the 1940–1945 period has remained substantially the same, then, with a further necessary correction of R to 5.3, applying the 1945 rates of alcoholism to the 1970 and 1975 population, yields the number of alcoholics. The formula may be less reliable with smaller populations. For Alaska and Hawaii, incomplete base data add uncertainty to the estimates]

STATE	ALCOHOLICS (1,000)			RATE PER 100,000 POPULATION				STATE	ALCOHOLICS (1,000)			RATE PER 100,000 POPULATION			
	Total	Male	Female	Total	Rank	Male	Female		Total	Male	Female	Total	Rank	Male	Female
1975	5,750	4,800	950	4,200	(X)	7,300	1,300	Miss	29.8	23.7	6.1	2,320	43	3,950	900
1970,								Mo	150.6	125.8	24.8	5,090	8	9,110	1,570
U.S.[1]	5,400	4,500	900	4,200	(X)	7,300	1,300	Mont	15.5	13.5	2.0	3,730	21	6,550	950
Ala	38.0	30.5	7.5	1,830	49	3,150	670	Nebr	28.4	21.8	6.6	3,087	31	4,970	1,370
Alaska	5.3	4.5	.8	3,110	29	4,690	1,130	Nev	20.6	18.0	2.6	6,770	1	11,650	1,730
Ariz	33.0	26.5	6.5	3,110	30	5,180	1,190	N.H.	16.7	12.9	3.8	3,660	22	5,950	1,600
Ark	34.7	29.8	4.9	2,890	34	5,280	780	N.J.	224.8	181.1	43.7	4,930	10	8,460	1,800
Calif	833.4	689.5	143.9	6,610	2	11,350	2,200	N. Mex	18.1	14.2	3.9	3,160	27	5,140	1,320
Colo	57.1	46.3	10.8	4,240	15	7,110	1,560	N.Y.	647.3	516.2	131.1	5,500	5	9,500	2,070
Conn	94.5	77.2	17.3	4,940	9	8,554	1,710	N.C.	63.7	55.8	7.9	2,050	47	3,770	490
Del	13.4	11.5	1.9	4,040	18	7,290	1,110	N. Dak	13.1	11.0	2.1	3,570	24	6,010	1,130
D.C.	27.3	23.3	4.0	5,430	(X)	10,290	1,440	Ohio	283.6	231.7	51.9	4,340	13	7,540	1,500
Fla	100.1	132.5	27.6	3,590	23	6,340	1,160	Okla	34.8	27.9	6.9	2,140	45	3,620	810
Ga	70.8	61.4	9.4	2,550	40	4,690	640	Oreg	34.4	28.6	5.8	2,610	39	4,530	840
Hawaii	8.3	7.2	1.1	1,780	50	2,930	500	Pa	329.1	274.0	55.1	4,360	12	7,810	1,370
								R.I.	37.1	32.2	4.9	6,070	3	11,020	1,520
Idaho	8.4	7.5	.9	1,990	48	3,600	410	S.C.	42.0	35.2	6.8	2,760	37	4,850	860
Ill	356.1	300.8	55.3	5,140	6	9,210	1,510	S. Dak.	10.5	8.4	2.1	2,640	38	4,320	1,010
Ind	124.5	102.8	21.7	3,940	20	6,870	1,300								
Iowa	48.9	41.4	7.5	2,800	36	5,030	810	Tenn	71.5	63.4	8.1	2,920	32	5,540	620
Kans	35.2	29.1	6.1	2,490	41	4,290	820	Tex	191.9	158.1	33.8	2,830	35	4,890	950
Ky	65.1	58.1	7.0	3,290	26	6,180	670	Utah	12.2	8.9	3.3	2,070	46	3,130	1,070
La	83.9	71.3	12.6	3,110	19	7,200	1,130	Vt	11.2	10.1	1.1	4,170	16	7,940	780
Maine	26.3	21.0	5.3	4,290	14	7,220	1,640	Va	68.2	57.0	11.2	2,370	42	4,080	760
Md	98.6	85.7	12.9	4,100	17	7,460	1,020	Wash	61.8	51.9	9.9	2,910	33	5,010	910
Mass	211.0	179.3	31.7	5,850	4	10,770	1,630	W.Va.	34.3	29.6	4.7	3,130	28	5,740	810
Mich	236.2	201.1	35.1	4,460	11	7,940	1,270	Wis	136.3	118.5	17.8	5,110	7	9,287	1,277
Minn	77.6	64.2	13.4	3,400	25	5,880	1,130	Wyo	4.6	3.3	1.3	2,390	44	3,360	1,310

X Not applicable.   [1] Jellinek formula applied to State and U.S. populations separately.

Source: Rutgers Center of Alcohol Studies, *Statistics on Consumption of Alcohol and on Alcoholism*, by Keller, M., and C. Gurioli, 1976. Copyright by Journal of Studies on Alcohol, Inc., New Brunswick, N.J.

No. 192. DRUG USE, BY TYPE OF DRUG AND BY AGE GROUP: 1977

[Current users are those who used drugs at least once within month prior to this study. Based on national samples of 1,272 youths, 1,500 young adults, and 1,822 older adults. Subject to sampling variability; see source]

TYPE OF DRUG	PERCENT OF YOUTHS (12–17 yr.)		PERCENT OF YOUNG ADULTS (18–25 yr.)		PERCENT OF OLDER ADULTS (26 yr. and older)	
	Ever used	Current user	Ever used	Current user	Ever used	Current user
Marihuana and/or hashish	28.2	16.1	60.1	27.7	15.4	3.2
Inhalants	9.0	.7	11.2	(Z)	1.8	(Z)
Hallucinogens	4.6	1.6	19.8	2.0	2.6	(Z)
Cocaine	4.0	1.0	19.1	3.7	2.6	(Z)
Heroin	1.1	(Z)	3.6	(Z)	.8	(Z)
Other opiates	6.1	.6	13.5	1.0	2.8	(Z)
Stimulants [1]	5.2	1.3	21.2	2.5	4.7	.6
Sedatives [1]	3.1	.8	18.4	2.8	2.8	(Z)
Tranquilizers [1]	3.8	.7	13.4	2.4	2.6	(Z)
Alcohol	52.6	31.2	84.2	70.0	77.9	54.9
Cigarettes	47.3	22.3	67.6	47.3	67.0	38.7

Z Less than .5 percent.   [1] Prescription drugs.

No. 193. MARIHUANA USE, BY CHARACTERISTICS AND RESIDENCE OF USER: 1974 AND 1977

[See headnote, table 192. For composition of regions, see fig. I, inside front cover]

CHARACTERISTIC	PERCENT EVER USED		PERCENT CURRENT USER		CHARACTERISTIC	PERCENT EVER USED		PERCENT CURRENT USER	
	1974	1977	1974	1977		1974	1977	1974	1977
Youths, 12–17 yr	23	28	12	16	Adults (18 yr. and over)	19	25	7	8
Male	24	33	12	19	Male	24	30	9	11
Female	21	23	11	13	Female	14	19	5	6
White	24	29	12	17	White	18	24	7	8
Black and other	17	26	9	12	Black and other	27	27	8	8
12–13 years	6	8	2	4	18–25 years	53	60	26	28
14–15 years	22	29	12	15	26–34 years	30	44	8	12
16–17 years	39	47	20	29	35 years and over	4	7	(Z)	1
Northeast	26	35	14	21	Northeast	22	29	7	11
North Central	21	29	11	19	North Central	17	24	7	8
South	17	19	6	7	South	13	17	5	4
West	30	36	19	22	West	29	32	11	11
Large metro. areas [1]	27	37	14	22	Large metro. areas [1]	24	30	9	11
Other SMSA's	22	28	11	16	Other SMSA's	20	26	8	9
Nonmetro. areas	18	18	10	10	Nonmetro. areas	12	16	4	4

Z Less than .5 percent.   [1] Comprises 25 largest standard metropolitan statistical areas (SMSA) as of 1970. For definition of SMSA, see Appendix II.

No. 194. MARIHUANA USE, BY AGE GROUP: 1971 TO 1977

[See headnote, table 192]

AGE GROUP	PERCENT EVER USED					PERCENT CURRENT USER				
	1971	1972	1974	1976	1977	1971 [1]	1972 [1]	1974	1976	1977
Youths	14	14	23	23	28	6	7	12	12	16
12–13 years	6	4	6	6	8	2	1	2	2	4
14–15 years	10	10	22	21	29	7	6	12	13	15
16–17 years	27	29	39	40	47	10	16	20	22	29
Young adults: 18–25 yr	39	48	53	53	60	17	28	26	25	28
Adults: 26–34 years	19	20	30	36	44	5	9	8	11	12
35 years and over	7	3	4	6	7	(Z)	(Z)	(Z)	1	1

Z Less than .5 percent.   [1] Person designated self as current user.

Source of tables 192–194: Abelson, Fishburne, and Cisin, *The National Survey on Drug Abuse: 1977*, vol. 1, *Main Findings*. Data from survey conducted for U.S. National Institute on Drug Abuse, 1977.

No. 195. CIGARETTE SMOKING AND HEALTH CHARACTERISTICS: 1970 AND 1976

[For 1970, population 17 years old and over; for 1976, 20 years old and over. Based on household interviews of a sample of the civilian, noninstitutional population. Smoking data were obtained from self-respondents only]

SEX, AGE, AND HEALTH CHARACTERISTIC	Total population [1]	Persons who never smoked	Persons who ever smoked	Former smokers	PRESENT SMOKERS				
					Total [2]	Cigarettes smoked per day (heaviest amount)			
						Under 15	15–24	25–34	35 or more
1970									
Male ____ 1,000__	62,310	19,144	42,773	15,861	26,912	7,163	11,458	3,160	3,959
17–24 years ____ 1,000__	12,034	5,844	6,016	1,131	4,885	1,822	2,053	442	277
25–44 years ____ 1,000__	22,542	5,779	16,641	5,235	11,406	2,516	5,124	1,505	1,895
45–64 years ____ 1,000__	19,644	4,513	15,065	6,302	8,763	2,047	3,603	1,081	1,625
65 years and over ____ 1,000__	8,090	3,007	5,051	3,193	1,858	778	678	131	162
Female ____ 1,000__	70,822	40,531	29,905	7,998	21,907	8,354	9,170	2,096	1,748
17–24 years ____ 1,000__	13,908	8,582	5,188	991	4,198	1,927	1,635	286	192
25–44 years ____ 1,000__	24,349	11,302	12,958	3,550	9,408	3,211	4,004	1,106	900
45–64 years ____ 1,000__	21,658	11,813	9,744	2,632	7,111	2,675	3,056	648	583
65 years and over ____ 1,000__	10,907	8,835	2,015	825	1,190	541	475	56	74
1976									
Male ____ 1,000__	64,556	16,563	40,121	16,379	23,741	5,685	10,517	3,467	3,821
20–24 years ____ 1,000__	8,997	3,200	4,443	935	3,508	1,095	1,732	384	259
25–44 years ____ 1,000__	25,966	6,657	15,652	4,909	10,743	2,447	4,656	1,795	1,701
45–64 years ____ 1,000__	20,632	3,946	14,337	6,785	7,551	1,388	3,305	1,130	1,668
65 years and over ____ 1,000__	8,961	2,761	5,689	3,750	1,939	754	823	158	193
Female ____ 1,000__	72,922	37,833	31,883	9,588	22,294	8,020	9,632	2,288	2,028
20–24 years ____ 1,000__	9,666	4,999	4,028	940	3,089	1,311	1,288	231	211
25–44 years ____ 1,000__	27,802	12,878	13,914	3,790	10,124	3,391	4,459	1,155	940
45–64 years ____ 1,000__	22,618	10,637	10,923	3,418	7,505	2,549	3,277	818	777
65 years and over ____ 1,000__	12,836	9,319	3,018	1,441	1,577	769	608	85	100
Restricted-activity days per person: [3]									
Male ____	19.8	15.8	22.6	25.7	20.4	24.4	18.4		20.2
Female ____	24.4	23.5	25.0	28.6	23.6	23.6	22.3		26.7
Bed-days per person: [3]									
Male ____	6.9	4.8	7.7	9.0	6.7	8.2	6.5		6.0
Female ____	9.4	8.3	9.8	10.9	9.4	10.1	8.6		9.9
Work-loss days per person: [3]									
Male ____	5.0	4.3	5.4	5.7	5.2	2.6	5.9		5.7
Female ____	5.8	5.1	6.5	6.3	6.6	6.2	5.7		9.3

[1] Includes persons for whom smoking status is unknown.   [2] Includes smokers for whom the number of cigarettes smoked per day is unknown.   [3] For definition of terms, see footnotes 1, 3, and 4 of table 179.

Source: U.S. National Center for Health Statistics, *Vital and Health Statistics*, vol. 21, No. 3 supplement, June 1972; and unpublished data.

No. 196. FOUR INDEXES OF CIVILIAN PER CAPITA FOOD CONSUMPTION: 1950 TO 1977

[1967= 100. Represents retail weight equivalent of products shown in table 200 along with other minor products. See also *Historical Statistics, Colonial Times to 1970*, series B 444–447]

INDEX	1950	1955	1960	1965	1970	1972	1973	1974	1975	1976	1977, prel.
Food consumption [1] ____	95	97	96	97	103	104	102	103	102	105	104
Food use [2] ____	96	98	96	97	102	104	100	102	101	104	104
Food consumed, pounds [3] __	106	104	101	99	101	102	101	100	100	102	102
Calories per capita [4] ____	102	99	98	98	103	104	103	102	101	105	105

[1] Retail weight equivalent, weighted by constant retail prices.
[2] Farm weight equivalent, weighted by constant prices received by farmers (or equivalent).
[3] Retail weight equivalent.   [4] Available for consumption at retail level.

Source: U.S. Dept. of Agriculture, Economic , Statistics, and Cooperatives Service, *Food Consumption, Prices, and Expenditures*, annual.

No. 197. Nutrition—Nutrients Available for Civilian Consumption per Capita per Day: 1950 to 1977

[For 1950, excludes Alaska and Hawaii. Based on Bureau of the Census estimated population as of July 1. Quantities of nutrients computed by Science and Education Administration, Consumer and Food Economics Institute, on the basis of estimates of per capita food consumption (retail weight), including estimates of produce of home gardens, prepared by the Economics, Statistics, and Cooperatives Service. No deduction made in nutrient estimates for loss or waste of food in the home, use for pet food, or for destruction or loss of nutrients during the preparation of food. Data include iron, thiamin, riboflavin, and niacin added to flour and cereal products; other nutrients added primarily as follows: Vitamin A value to margarine, milk of all types, milk extenders; vitamin B6 to cereals, meal replacements, infant formulas; vitamin B12 to cereals; ascorbic acid to fruit juices and drinks, flavored beverages and dessert powders, milk extenders, and cereals. Minus sign (−) denotes decrease. See *Historical Statistics, Colonial Times to 1970*, series G 851–856, for related data]

NUTRIENT AND UNIT	1950	1960	1965	1970	1974	1975	1976	1977, prel.	PERCENT CHANGE		
									1950–1960	1960–1970	1970–1977
Food energy_____calories__	3,260	3,140	3,150	3,300	3,280	3,250	3,380	3,380	−3.7	5.1	2.4
Protein_____grams__	95	95	96	100	100	99	103	103	−	5.3	3.0
Fat_____grams__	145	143	144	156	156	152	159	159	−1.4	9.1	1.9
Carbohydrate_____grams__	402	375	372	380	376	377	390	391	−6.7	1.3	2.9
Calcium_____grams__	.99	.97	.96	.94	.92	.92	.95	.94	−2.0	−3.1	−
Phosphorus_____grams__	1.55	1.53	1.52	1.55	1.53	1.53	1.57	1.57	−1.3	1.3	1.3
Iron_____milligrams__	16.6	16.4	16.7	18.0	18.2	18.2	18.7	18.6	−1.2	9.8	3.3
Magnesium____milligrams__	364	346	339	342	341	341	349	347	−4.9	−1.2	1.5
Vitamin A_____int'l units__	8,500	8,000	7,700	8,200	8,200	8,100	8,200	8,200	−5.9	2.5	−
Thiamin_____milligrams__	1.90	1.85	1.81	1.92	1.97	2.03	2.08	2.09	−2.6	3.8	8.9
Riboflavin_____milligrams__	2.31	2.30	2.30	2.37	2.36	2.44	2.52	2.50	−	3.0	5.5
Niacin_____milligrams__	20.5	21.2	21.9	23.6	23.8	24.8	25.5	25.6	3.4	11.3	8.5
Vitamin B6____milligrams__	1.97	2.00	2.02	2.22	2.21	2.21	2.28	2.29	1.5	11.0	3.2
Vitamin B12__micrograms__	8.8	8.9	9.1	9.9	9.7	9.6	9.7	9.7	1.1	11.2	−2.0
Ascorbic acid__milligrams__	106	106	97	110	113	118	118	116	−	3.8	5.5

− Represents zero.

No. 198. Nutrition—Index of Per Capita Civilian Food Consumption of Selected Nutrients: 1940 to 1977

[1967=100. See also *Historical Statistics, Colonial Times to 1970*, series B 448–450]

NUTRIENT	1940	1945	1950	1955	1960	1965	1970	1972	1973	1974	1975	1976	1977, prel.
Protein_____	94	104	96	97	96	97	101	102	100	101	100	104	104
Fat_____	95	92	97	97	95	96	104	106	103	104	101	106	106
Carbohydrate_____	115	112	107	101	100	99	102	102	102	101	101	104	105

Source of tables 197 and 198: U.S. Dept. of Agriculture, Science and Education Administration, *Food Consumption, Prices, and Expenditures*, annual, and *National Food Review*, quarterly.

No. 199. Daily Per Capita Intake of Selected Nutrients, by Race and Income Levels: 1971–74

[Covers persons 1–74 years old. For definition of median and mean, see p. xii. Based on unpublished findings of a sample survey in the first Health and Nutrition Examination Survey]

NUTRIENT	ALL PERSONS (1–74 years old)			PERSONS WITH INCOME [1]—					
				Below poverty level			Above poverty level		
	Total	White	Black	Total	White	Black	Total	White	Black
Calories, mean_____	1,994	2,017	1,825	1,817	1,858	1,742	2,021	2,032	1,886
Median_____	1,820	1,840	1,668	1,645	1,675	1,583	1,845	1,858	1,725
Protein (g), mean_____	77.83	78.92	69.65	68.76	70.42	65.65	79.11	79.67	72.50
Median_____	69.63	70.78	60.85	61.41	63.75	57.92	70.96	71.47	64.27
Calcium (mg), mean_____	867	897	654	782	849	658	882	903	652
As percent of standard_____	175	181	131	156	171	129	178	182	132
Median_____	727	755	553	653	722	558	740	760	549
Iron (mg), mean_____	11.95	12.10	10.80	10.70	10.90	10.26	12.13	12.21	11.21
As percent of standard_____	98	99	86	88	90	81	99	100	91
Median_____	10.58	10.69	9.55	9.38	9.58	8.79	10.77	10.81	9.97
Vitamin A (I.U.), mean_____	4,774	4,802	4,613	4,381	4,286	4,587	4,821	4,837	4,714
As percent of standard_____	150	150	150	145	142	152	151	151	151
Median_____	3,060	3,132	2,569	2,627	2,685	2,475	3,147	3,190	2,654
Vitamin C (mg), mean_____	86.32	86.99	80.01	72.05	69.33	75.97	88.53	88.83	83.31
As percent of standard_____	167	168	159	146	140	157	171	171	162
Median_____	59.23	60.42	49.09	41.37	39.89	46.61	61.97	62.92	50.92

[1] See text, p. 438, and tables 754 and 755.

Source: U.S. National Center for Health Statistics, unpublished data.

No. 200. Civilian Per Capita Consumption of Major Food Commodities: 1960 to 1977

[In pounds, except as indicated. Civilian consumption represents the residual after exports, nonfood use, military procurement, and ending stocks are subtracted from the sum of beginning stocks, domestic production, and imports. For estimating techniques, see Agriculture Handbook No. 365, vol. 5, April 1972. Based on Bureau of the Census estimates of the civilian population as of July 1. See also *Historical Statistics, Colonial Times to 1970*, series G 881–915]

COMMODITY	1960	1965	1970	1972	1973	1974	1975	1976	1977, prel.
Meats (carcass weight)	173.6	175.6	192.6	192.9	178.0	190.5	182.4	194.8	193.3
Beef	85.1	99.5	113.7	116.1	109.6	116.8	120.1	129.3	125.9
Veal	6.1	5.2	2.9	2.2	1.8	2.3	4.2	4.0	3.9
Lamb and mutton	4.8	3.7	3.3	3.3	2.7	2.3	2.0	1.9	1.7
Pork (including lard)	77.6	67.2	72.7	71.3	63.9	69.1	56.1	59.6	61.8
Fish (edible weight)	10.3	10.8	11.8	12.5	12.9	12.2	12.2	12.9	12.8
Fresh and frozen	5.7	6.0	6.9	7.2	7.4	7.0	7.5	8.1	8.0
Canned	4.0	4.3	4.5	4.9	5.1	4.8	4.3	4.3	4.3
Cured	.6	.5	.4	.4	.4	.4	.4	.5	.5
Poultry products:									
Eggs, farm basis____number	335	314	311	308	294	288	279	276	272
Chicken (ready-to-cook)	27.8	33.4	40.5	42.0	40.7	41.1	40.3	43.3	44.3
Turkey (ready-to-cook)	6.2	7.5	8.0	9.0	8.5	8.9	8.6	9.2	9.2
Dairy products:									
Total milk fat solids	24.5	22.9	20.6	20.6	20.3	20.0	20.1	20.1	20.2
Total nonfat milk solids	43.4	40.6	39.8	39.6	39.8	38.2	38.1	39.0	38.7
Cheese	8.3	9.5	11.5	13.2	13.7	14.6	14.5	15.9	16.3
Condensed and evaporated whole milk	13.7	10.6	7.1	6.4	6.0	5.6	5.3	5.1	4.8
Fluid milk and cream	322	302	264	263	257	246	245	245	238
Ice cream (product weight)	18.3	18.5	17.7	17.4	17.5	17.5	18.7	18.1	17.7
Fats and oils, total (fat content)	45.3	47.8	53.0	54.3	54.3	53.2	53.4	56.1	54.4
Butter (actual weight)	7.5	6.4	5.3	4.9	4.8	4.6	4.8	4.4	4.4
Margarine (actual weight)	9.4	9.9	11.0	11.3	11.3	11.3	11.2	12.2	11.6
Lard	7.6	6.4	4.7	3.8	3.4	3.2	3.0	2.7	2.3
Shortening	12.6	14.1	17.3	17.7	17.3	17.0	17.3	18.1	17.6
Other edible fats and oils	11.5	14.1	17.9	19.8	20.8	20.3	20.3	22.0	21.6
Fruits:									
Fresh, total (farm weight)	93.9	81.4	81.6	77.5	77.0	79.6	84.4	86.6	85.4
Citrus [1]	33.7	29.2	29.0	27.6	27.8	27.9	29.7	29.4	26.0
Apples (commercial)	18.3	16.3	18.3	17.4	14.7	16.1	17.9	18.8	17.8
Other (excluding melons)	41.9	35.9	34.3	32.5	34.5	35.6	36.8	38.4	41.6
Processed:									
Canned fruit	22.6	23.5	23.3	21.4	21.3	19.6	19.3	19.2	19.2
Canned juices (excl. frozen)	13.0	10.9	14.6	15.5	15.9	14.7	15.3	15.3	13.7
Frozen (including juices)	9.1	8.5	9.8	10.4	11.2	11.3	12.6	12.2	12.4
Dried [2]	3.1	3.0	2.7	2.0	2.6	2.5	3.0	2.7	2.6
Vegetables:									
Fresh [3]	105.7	98.3	98.5	98.3	100.2	101.1	101.6	102.5	101.2
Canned (excluding potatoes and sweet potatoes)	43.4	46.9	51.2	52.2	54.3	53.3	52.1	52.8	52.8
Frozen (excluding potatoes)	7.0	8.1	9.6	10.0	10.7	10.2	9.7	10.2	9.7
Potatoes and sweet potatoes:									
Potatoes (fresh equivalent) [4]	108	107	118	119	116	116	122	115	121
Frozen potatoes (product)	2.7	5.7	11.1	12.3	13.3	13.2	13.9	14.8	15.1
Sweet potatoes (fresh equiv.) [4]	7.1	6.2	5.6	5.1	5.1	5.6	5.5	5.9	5.4
Dry edible beans	7.3	6.6	5.9	6.3	6.4	6.7	6.5	6.3	6.0
Melons	25.8	23.6	23.3	21.9	21.7	19.0	19.3	20.6	21.0
Sugar (refined)	97.4	97.0	101.8	102.8	101.5	96.6	90.2	94.7	95.7
Grains:									
Cornmeal and other [5]	14.3	15.1	15.8	15.8	15.9	16.0	16.1	16.1	16.1
Corn sirup and sugar	13.8	18.2	20.8	23.5	26.9	30.3	34.0	37.5	39.5
Oat food products	3.6	3.4	3.2	3.2	3.2	3.2	3.2	3.2	3.2
Barley food products [6]	1.1	1.2	1.2	1.2	1.2	1.2	1.2	1.2	1.2
Wheat flour [7]	118	113	110	109	109	106	107	111	107
Wheat breakfast cereals	2.8	2.9	2.9	2.9	2.9	2.9	2.9	2.9	2.9
Rye flour	1.1	1.1	1.2	1.1	1.3	1.3	1.0	.9	.8
Rice, milled [1]	6.1	7.6	6.7	7.0	7.0	7.6	7.7	7.2	7.6
Other:									
Coffee (green beans)	15.8	14.8	13.7	13.8	13.7	13.0	12.4	12.8	9.4
Tea	.6	.7	.7	.8	.8	.8	.8	.8	.9
Cocoa beans	3.6	4.0	3.9	4.4	4.2	3.7	3.3	3.8	3.4
Peanuts (shelled) [8]	4.9	5.6	5.9	6.2	6.6	6.4	6.5	6.3	6.4

[1] For crop year beginning in previous year.　　[2] For pack year.
[3] Excludes produce from home gardens.　　[4] Includes quantities canned and frozen.
[5] Includes cornstarch, corn cereal, and hominy.　　[6] In terms of malt equivalent.
[7] Comprises white, whole wheat, and semolina flour.　　[8] For crop year beginning September of year shown.

Source: U.S. Dept. of Agriculture, Economics, Statistics, and Cooperatives Service. Published quarterly in *National Food Review*.

No. 201. FEDERAL FOOD PROGRAMS: 1950 TO 1977

[For years ending June 30 except, beginning 1977, ending Sept. 30. Includes institutions. Includes Puerto Rico, Guam, Trust Territory of the Pacific Islands, Virgin Islands, and, beginning 1965, American Samoa]

PROGRAM	1950	1955	1960	1965	1970	1973	1974	1975	1976	1977, prel.
Food distribution:										
Needy family programs and institutions: [1]										
Persons participating [2]__1,000__	1,125	4,624	5,753	7,148	6,876	6,075	5,369	3,661	2,255	2,196
Quantity_____mil. lb__	255	297	654	1,313	1,320	1,110	708	201	131	161
Federal cost [3]_____mil. dol__	24	97	75	257	312	282	229	76	53	65
Child feeding programs:										
Children participating [2]___mil__	10.1	10.2	15.6	20.4	24.2	28.3	28.5	29.7	31.2	32.6
Quantity_____mil. lb__	467	298	523	973	1,073	980	961	764	824	1,216
Federal cost [3]_____mil. dol__	55	83	132	272	266	260	319	418	424	536
National School Lunch program: [4]										
Children participating [2]____mil__	8.6	12.0	14.1	18.7	23.1	25.2	25.0	25.3	25.8	26.7
Percent of total enrolled_____	34.1	35.7	35.0	39.2	44.4	49.0	56.4	56.6	57.4	59.4
Schools participating_____1,000__	54	58	62	70	76	86	88	89	89	92
Federal cost [5]_____mil. dol__	65	69	94	130	300	882	1,085	1,289	1,489	1,668
Special milk program: [6]										
Quantity reimbursed_mil. ½ pt__	(X)	450	2,385	.2,967	2,902	2,561	1,426	2,139	2,305	2,247
Federal cost_____mil. dol__	(X)	17	80	97	101	91	49	123	144	153
Food stamp program:										
Participants, mo. avg_____mil__	(X)	(X)	(X)	.4	4.3	12.2	12.9	17.1	18.5	17.1
Federal cost_____mil. dol__	(X)	(X)	(X)	33	550	2,131	2,718	4,386	5,327	5,056

X Not applicable.   [1] Institutions include but not limited to: Homes for aged, orphanages, child-care centers. [2] Peak month for each year.   [3] Cost to Fed. Govt. of commodity as delivered to State distributing agency. [4] See headnote, table 205.   [5] Refers to subsidy payments by the Fed. Govt.; excludes administrative costs. [6] Initiated in September 1954 to increase the consumption of fluid milk in schools and child-care institutions.

No. 202. FEDERAL FOOD PROGRAM FOR NEEDY FAMILIES: 1950 TO 1977

[For years ending June 30 except, beginning 1977, ending September 30. Participation data for peak month. Prior to 1965, excludes Hawaii, and 1970, Alaska. Includes American Samoa, Guam, Puerto Rico, Trust Territory of Pacific Islands, and Virgin Islands]

YEAR	Distribu. tion points	RECIPIENTS (1,000)			COMMODITIES DONATED		
		Total	Public assistance	Other [1]	Quantity (mil. lb.)	Cost [2] (mil. dol.)	Avg. monthly cost per participant [2]
1950_____	(NA)	248	(NA)	(NA)	46	6	$5.38
1955_____	587	3,291	733	2,558	201	62	2.38
1960_____	1,182	4,309	2,043	2,266	526	59	1.18
1965_____	1,667	5,842	2,848	2,994	1,141	227	3.56
1970_____	1,351	4,129	2,453	1,676	1,155	280	6.13
1971_____	1,223	3,974	2,200	1,774	1,266	307	6.82
1972_____	1,089	3,616	2,056	1,560	1,169	298	7.22
1973_____	977	2,838	1,751	1,087	918	241	7.55
1974_____	388	2,393	1,519	874	549	189	7.96
1975_____	39	792	495	297	104	37	9.34
1976_____	42	89	42	47	33	12	11.86
1977, prel_____	45	89	34	55	39	12	11.73

NA Not available.   [1] Unemployed and low-income persons except those on regular public assistance rolls. [2] Total cost to Federal Government including commodity cost, warehousing, processing, transport, etc.

Source of tables 201 and 202: U.S. Dept. of Agriculture, Food and Nutrition Service. In *Agricultural Statistics*, annual; and unpublished data.

No. 203. COST PER MONTH OF U.S. DEPT. OF AGRICULTURE FOOD PLANS: 1978

[As of March. Cost represents U.S. average. For quantities of food used in plans, see winter 1975 and winter 1976 issues of source. The thrifty plan is the basis for the coupon allotment in the Food Stamp Program. The other three plans are the basis for the food component of three family budgets shown in table 797]

FAMILY	Thrifty plan	Low-cost plan	Moderate-cost plan	Liberal plan
Family of 2: 20–54 years_____	$107.50	$140.10	$175.50	$209.60
55 years and over_____	96.60	125.30	154.70	184.10
Family of 4:				
Couple, 20–54 years, and children—				
1–2 and 3–5 years_____	151.20	194.70	242.70	289.80
6–8 and 9–11 years_____	181.80	234.60	293.80	350.90
Family of 6:				
Couple, 20–54 years, and children—				
1–2, 3–5, 6–8, 9–11 years_____	223.50	286.80	358.20	427.70
6–8, 9–11, boy and girl 12–19 years___	.265.00	340.20	425.20	507.60

Source: U.S. Dept. of Agriculture, Science and Education Administration, *Family Economics Review*, quarterly.

No. 204. Federal Food Stamp Program: 1961 to 1977

[Beginning 1975, includes Puerto Rico, Guam, and Virgin Islands]

YEAR (ending June 30)	Number of participating areas	Participants (1,000)	Average monthly participation (1,000)	VALUE OF STAMPS ISSUED				
				Total retail value (mil. dol.)	Cost to participants (mil. dol.)	Federal Govt. contribution		
						Total (mil. dol.)	Percent of total retail value	Average monthly per participant
1961	6	50	50	1	(Z)	(Z)	46.1	$7.68
1962	8	141	143	35	22	13	37.4	7.67
1963	42	358	226	50	31	19	37.4	6.89
1964	43	360	367	73	44	29	39.0	6.51
1965	110	633	425	85	53	32	38.0	6.38
1966	324	1,218	864	174	109	65	37.2	6.25
1967	838	1,832	1,447	296	190	106	35.6	6.08
1968	1,027	2,402	2,210	452	279	173	38.3	6.52
1969	1,489	3,222	2,878	603	374	229	37.9	6.63
1970	1,747	6,457	4,340	1,090	540	550	50.4	10.55
1971	2,027	10,549	9,368	2,713	1,190	1,523	56.1	13.55
1972	2,126	11,594	11,109	3,309	1,512	1,797	54.3	13.48
1973	2,228	12,107	12,166	3,884	1,753	2,131	54.9	14.60
1974	2,818	13,524	12,862	4,727	2,009	2,718	57.5	17.61
1975	3,035	19,197	17,064	7,266	2,880	4,386	60.4	21.41
1976	3,035	17,982	18,549	8,700	3,373	5,327	61.2	23.93
1977, prel.[1]	3,035	16,050	17,104	8,339	3,283	5,056	60.6	24.70

Z Less than $500,000. [1] For year ending Sept. 30.

Source: U.S. Dept. of Agriculture, Food and Nutrition Service. In *Agricultural Statistics*, annual.

No. 205. School Lunch Program—States and Other Areas: 1977

[For year ending **September 30**. Preliminary. Comprises public and private elementary and secondary schools and residential child care institutions. Sponsors of school lunch programs are reimbursed by the Federal Government for local purchases of food on a basis of quality and quantity of meals served]

STATE OR OTHER AREA	Schools participating, year-end	PUPILS PARTICIPATING (Dec.) [1]		Federal cost (mil. dol.)	STATE OR OTHER AREA	Schools participating, year-end	PUPILS PARTICIPATING (Dec.) [1]		Federal cost (mil. dol.)
		Number (1,000)	Percent of NSLP [2] enrollment				Number (1,000)	Percent of NSLP [2] enrollment	
Total	91,563	26,748	59.4	1,667.9	Mont	612	95	58.4	4.6
					Nebr	1,234	204	64.6	8.9
U.S.	88,636	26,157	59.2	1,610.3	Nev	229	64	46.8	3.3
Ala	1,336	632	77.8	44.1	N.H.	430	94	56.7	5.2
Alaska	197	30	46.2	1.1	N.J.	2,098	691	48.8	52.1
Ariz	850	259	55.1	16.4	N. Mex	677	181	63.1	14.3
Ark	1,315	353	79.4	22.8	N.Y.	5,720	1,744	51.5	127.0
Calif	6,986	1,742	43.3	136.8	N.C.	2,073	954	78.5	66.8
Colo	1,259	301	58.2	15.2	N. Dak	507	94	66.9	4.1
Conn	1,122	288	51.4	15.7	Ohio	4,349	1,125	48.2	57.2
Del	222	75	59.6	4.1	Okla	1,913	399	63.0	22.2
D.C.	206	71	57.6	6.9	Oreg	1,208	254	58.4	12.6
Fla	2,081	1,025	67.4	72.5	Pa	4,397	1,303	52.2	71.7
Ga	1,849	901	81.9	62.0	R.I.	397	81	44.3	5.9
Hawaii	266	162	85.6	7.4	S.C.	1,198	498	77.2	38.8
Idaho	522	107	54.0	4.7	S. Dak	658	98	64.9	5.4
Ill	4,270	1,154	57.6	68.2	Tenn	1,736	664	75.9	41.0
Ind	2,292	787	66.3	26.5	Tex	5,340	1,560	54.8	113.8
Iowa	2,113	474	75.4	18.3	Utah	563	210	67.8	9.0
Kans	1,716	319	69.4	14.5	Vt	371	60	57.4	3.2
Ky	1,553	584	73.4	33.7	Va	1,875	726	65.3	40.7
La	1,748	781	84.4	53.2	Wash	1,591	352	48.9	19.8
Maine	797	143	62.0	9.6	W. Va	1,257	249	62.9	16.3
Md	1,459	410	46.8	25.3	Wis	2,404	535	55.3	23.6
Mass	2,473	718	60.5	39.7	Wyo	272	48	58.9	1.9
Mich	3,256	830	48.7	46.7	P. Rico	2,638	522	69.0	51.5
Minn	2,121	620	66.4	24.4	Am. Samoa	36	8	96.4	.7
Miss	941	443	84.5	37.8	Guam	49	18	58.3	1.1
Mo	2,577	665	64.7	33.3	Virgin I	58	21	72.9	1.9
					Trust Territory	146	22	81.2	2.4

[1] December was peak month for participation in most States. [2] National School Lunch Program.

Source: U.S. Dept. of Agriculture, Food and Nutrition Service, *National School Lunch Program*, annual.

No. 206. HOUSEHOLDS PARTICIPATING IN FEDERAL FOOD STAMP PROGRAM—SELECTED CHARACTERISTICS: 1973 TO 1975

[Based on Current Population Survey; see text, p. 1, and Appendix III. For composition of regions, see fig. I, inside front cover]

YEAR AND CHARACTERISTIC	TOTAL [1]			WHITE			BLACK		
	House-holds partici-pating (1,000)	Percent of all house-holds	Percent distri-bution	House-holds partici-pating (1,000)	Percent of all house-holds	Percent distri-bution	House-holds partici-pating (1,000)	Percent of all house-holds	Percent distri-bution
1973, May	3,110	(NA)	(X)	1,903	(NA)	(X)	1,182	(NA)	(X)
1974, July	3,519	5.0	(X)	2,115	3.4	(X)	1,362	18.9	(X)
1975, July, total	4,423	6.2	100.0	2,763	4.4	100.0	1,601	21.5	100.0
SIZE OF HOUSEHOLD									
1 person	962	6.8	21.7	648	5.2	23.5	307	19.4	19.2
2 persons	827	3.8	18.7	575	2.9	20.8	238	13.7	14.7
3 persons	780	6.5	17.6	462	4.4	16.7	304	23.0	19.0
4-5 persons	1,049	6.2	23.7	656	4.3	23.8	383	23.3	23.9
6 persons or more	740	13.7	16.8	386	9.1	14.0	345	32.3	21.5
Not reported	65	6.8	1.5	36	4.3	1.3	24	28.2	1.5
ANNUAL TOTAL MONEY INCOME [2]									
Under $2,000	915	27.7	20.7	529	21.7	19.1	375	44.3	23.4
$2,000-$2,999	972	23.2	22.0	573	17.3	20.7	386	45.4	24.1
$3,000-$3,999	767	17.6	17.3	497	14.1	18.0	260	32.9	16.2
$4,000-$5,999	888	11.4	20.1	515	8.0	18.6	360	28.3	22.4
$6,000-$9,999	508	4.0	11.6	362	3.2	13.1	141	9.5	8.8
$10,000 and over	239	.7	5.4	185	.6	6.7	49	2.8	3.1
Not reported	134	2.3	3.0	102	1.9	3.7	30	6.9	1.9
HEAD OF HOUSEHOLD									
Under 35 years	1,716	8.3	38.8	1,072	5.9	38.8	620	25.6	38.7
35 to 54 years	1,429	5.8	32.3	834	3.9	30.2	573	21.0	35.8
55 to 64 years	517	4.4	11.7	315	3.0	11.4	197	18.1	12.3
65 years and over	761	5.4	17.2	542	4.2	19.6	211	17.7	13.2
Employed [3]	1,275	2.6	28.8	851	1.9	30.8	400	9.1	25.0
Unemployed [3]	553	19.6	12.5	356	15.9	12.9	192	35.8	12.0
Not in labor force [3]	2,594	13.6	58.6	1,556	9.5	56.3	1,009	40.5	63.0
Male head	1,846	3.4	41.7	1,350	2.8	48.9	472	10.5	29.5
Married, wife present	1,563	3.3	35.3	1,176	2.8	42.6	365	10.8	22.8
Other marital status	283	3.7	6.4	174	2.7	6.3	107	9.6	6.7
Female head	2,576	15.0	58.2	1,414	10.1	51.2	1,129	38.4	70.5
Married, husband absent	778	37.0	17.6	362	28.5	13.1	404	50.2	25.2
Widowed or divorced	1,329	11.5	30.0	881	8.9	31.9	437	29.2	27.3
Never married	469	13.3	10.6	171	6.1	6.2	288	45.3	18.0
PUBLIC ASSISTANCE									
Received public assistance	2,671	54.0	60.4	1,522	49.5	55.1	1,113	61.6	69.5
Did not receive public assist-ance	1,752	2.6	39.6	1,241	2.1	44.9	488	8.7	30.5
RESIDENCE									
Metropolitan	2,862	6.0	64.7	1,650	4.0	59.7	1,171	20.4	73.1
In central cities	1,982	8.8	44.8	959	5.5	34.7	985	21.6	61.5
Outside central cities	880	3.4	19.9	691	2.9	25.0	186	15.8	11.6
Nonmetropolitan and farm	1,561	6.7	35.3	1,113	5.2	40.3	430	25.4	26.9
REGION									
Northeast	1,081	6.5	24.4	738	4.9	26.7	332	22.4	20.7
North Central	960	5.0	21.7	597	3.4	21.6	360	23.3	22.5
South	1,709	7.6	38.6	911	4.9	33.0	791	21.6	49.4
West	672	5.2	15.2	517	4.4	18.7	118	16.0	7.4

NA Not available.   X Not applicable.
[1] Includes other races, not shown separately.   [2] Income during previous 12-month period.
[3] Refers to employment status as of week prior to August 1975 Current Population Survey interview.

Source: U.S. Bureau of the Census, *Current Population Reports*, series P-23, No. 61, and unpublished data.

No. 207. FEDERAL FOOD STAMP PROGRAM—PARTICIPATION AND VALUE, BY STATES AND OTHER AREAS: 1974 TO 1977

[For years ending June 30 except, beginning 1977, ending September 30. Covers distribution of food stamps]

STATE OR OTHER AREA	PERSONS PARTICIPATING (1,000)				VALUE OF COUPONS ISSUED [1] (mil. dol.)							
					1974		1975		1976		1977, prel.	
	1974	1975	1976	1977, prel.	Total	Federal bonus	Total	Federal bonus	Total	Federal bonus	Total	Federal bonus
Total	13,524	19,197	17,982	16,050	4,727.5	2,718.3	7,265.6	4,385.5	8,700.2	5,326.5	8,339.3	5,056.3
Ala	291	393	344	301	85.2	57.5	155.8	102.8	170.6	112.6	151.6	98.8
Alaska	14	12	8	9	8.6	6.7	8.6	6.6	6.2	4.7	7.2	5.4
Ariz	99	166	159	123	31.4	21.4	57.7	40.8	71.9	50.1	63.4	44.6
Ark	240	267	226	196	87.4	56.3	115.2	74.9	116.8	75.5	104.2	66.0
Calif	1,250	1,517	1,432	1,259	469.2	252.9	615.6	360.8	696.3	392.8	648.8	332.9
Colo	124	162	153	137	45.1	28.1	65.8	44.2	77.0	52.4	72.7	48.4
Conn	139	189	184	169	48.8	23.2	68.0	34.5	89.2	47.7	86.3	44.7
Del	19	39	26	24	1.3	.8	12.6	7.7	17.4	10.8	14.2	8.3
D.C	109	111	109	95	42.1	22.0	49.3	25.7	53.5	28.7	48.6	25.5
Fla	490	767	768	688	183.7	127.3	281.9	206.6	378.3	281.5	356.8	261.0
Ga	347	569	508	418	116.4	69.9	205.9	129.3	247.8	161.2	217.8	142.5
Hawaii	65	84	105	105	28.4	14.8	42.1	23.6	59.8	32.9	65.0	34.6
Idaho	32	39	47	30	7.6	4.8	16.0	10.4	17.4	11.1	15.6	9.9
Ill	830	948	960	876	322.4	164.5	414.6	235.7	499.8	302.3	482.7	282.1
Ind	177	255	217	177	56.7	36.0	92.0	58.2	109.9	69.2	92.7	58.6
Iowa	107	118	111	99	40.2	24.0	49.2	28.1	54.2	30.0	51.6	29.0
Kans	40	63	64	58	11.8	6.0	24.5	12.3	29.9	15.0	29.9	15.0
Ky	391	449	406	365	139.5	97.3	191.4	128.4	208.1	135.7	195.4	128.3
La	508	502	469	402	191.6	133.1	216.8	148.0	228.5	151.6	205.4	134.4
Maine	58	151	117	90	10.0	5.9	50.8	31.0	58.6	36.3	47.3	28.5
Md	248	273	264	239	96.1	62.4	117.2	76.2	133.9	86.0	127.9	83.8
Mass	31	560	589	563	8.6	3.9	162.8	81.7	265.7	144.9	266.2	148.9
Mich	580	685	677	599	180.2	79.8	257.2	123.4	299.4	143.7	282.0	130.5
Minn	169	191	176	151	57.0	29.2	74.1	40.3	83.8	46.2	77.0	42.9
Miss	335	390	355	312	117.3	78.7	162.7	109.7	171.6	115.6	159.5	106.3
Mo	259	299	250	199	83.1	52.0	132.0	82.0	135.8	85.4	108.6	68.5
Mont	30	38	31	24	10.3	6.5	16.3	10.9	15.4	10.3	13.1	8.7
Nebr	45	50	44	37	16.5	9.1	20.1	11.3	21.4	11.9	19.0	10.7
Nev	17	34	23	16	3.8	2.7	14.0	10.5	14.2	10.3	9.2	6.5
N.H	–	66	49	39	–	–	19.3	11.3	25.9	15.5	21.3	12.9
N.J	403	565	536	483	140.0	72.2	222.5	125.2	276.5	164.0	265.2	157.4
N. Mex	152	154	129	105	56.4	38.8	67.1	46.4	66.3	45.7	57.7	39.7
N.Y	1,190	1,398	1,494	1,431	432.9	164.0	517.5	209.9	659.9	302.6	792.1	382.6
N.C	285	537	460	387	87.8	54.2	192.3	121.9	223.4	144.8	203.5	133.4
N. Dak	21	19	17	14	7.2	4.2	7.8	4.5	7.7	4.5	7.3	4.3
Ohio	737	924	877	730	269.5	174.4	374.7	253.4	432.5	292.3	392.4	260.5
Okla	138	184	172	145	34.1	18.4	72.0	37.7	81.9	42.2	75.4	37.2
Oreg	150	208	167	140	49.3	30.3	86.0	56.1	85.7	50.9	73.2	42.3
Pa	734	893	858	826	252.8	115.6	367.5	174.9	421.5	204.7	424.1	205.2
R.I	73	104	89	74	26.8	12.3	38.4	18.0	45.5	22.5	37.9	18.5
S.C	359	421	320	250	130.0	92.4	172.2	121.3	167.6	115.3	133.8	89.5
S. Dak	28	31	28	23	10.2	5.9	13.5	7.7	13.9	8.2	12.2	7.5
Tenn	329	435	400	372	121.5	80.4	170.8	115.4	199.5	137.5	191.4	133.6
Tex	1,043	1,085	903	744	308.8	207.6	469.3	315.2	451.1	298.7	383.9	255.1
Utah	40	50	43	33	15.9	8.7	19.9	11.0	22.3	12.4	17.2	8.9
Vt	38	46	46	36	12.7	6.2	18.2	9.3	21.6	11.6	19.7	10.6
Va	178	293	252	213	62.0	35.8	104.5	63.2	122.6	74.9	112.0	69.6
Wash	235	239	227	201	93.2	54.8	112.2	69.0	118.0	70.4	106.0	62.5
W. Va	214	204	180	226	70.7	44.4	88.4	56.1	90.1	55.8	91.4	60.7
Wis	123	163	177	162	41.9	18.9	60.0	29.3	78.6	37.8	81.5	37.7
Wyo	10	11	10	7	3.4	2.0	4.3	2.7	4.5	2.8	4.1	2.6
P. Rico	–	1,800	1,672	1,595	–	–	362.5	261.0	717.8	541.1	785.1	597.3
Guam	–	21	30	22	–	–	5.9	3.5	18.7	13.6	15.1	10.0
Virgin I	–	25	24	26	–	–	8.6	5.9	14.5	10.2	16.1	11.6

– Represents zero.   [1] Bonus coupons represent the difference between the value of coupons received by recipients and the purchase requirement (amount paid by recipients).

Source: U.S. Dept. of Agriculture, Food and Nutrition Service, unpublished data.

Section 5
Education

This section presents data primarily concerning formal education as a whole, at various levels, and for public and private schools. Data shown relate to the school-age population and school enrollment, educational attainment, education personnel, and financial aspects of education. In addition, data are shown for libraries, adult education, and vocational training. The chief sources are the decennial census of population and the Current Population Survey (CPS), both conducted by the Bureau of the Census (see text, page 1), and annual, biennial, and other periodic surveys conducted by the National Center for Education Statistics.

The census of population has included data on school enrollment since 1840 and on educational attainment since 1940. The CPS has reported on school enrollment annually since 1945 and on educational attainment and illiteracy periodically since 1947.

The National Center for Education Statistics (NCES), created in 1974 as part of the U.S. Department of Health, Education, and Welfare, is continuing the pattern of statistical studies and surveys conducted by the U.S. Office of Education since 1870. The annual *Digest of Education Statistics* provides summary data on pupils, staff, finances, and organization at elementary, secondary, and higher education levels and is also the primary source for detailed information on Federal funds for education and related activities. Projections of enrollment, graduates, teachers, and expenditures appear in the annual *Projections of Education Statistics. The Condition of Education*, also issued annually, presents a summary of educational information.

Other sources of data include special studies by NCES, publications of the National Education Association, and annual or biennial reports of education agencies in individual States. The census of governments, conducted by the Bureau of the Census every 5 years (for the years ending in "2" and "7"), provides data on school district finances. Reports published by the Bureau of Labor Statistics contain data relating employment experience to educational attainment. Data on vocational training are available in *Vocational and Technical Education*, issued annually by the U.S. Office of Education.

Types and sources of data.—The statistics in this section are of two general types. One type, exemplified by data from the Bureau of the Census, is based on direct interviews with individuals to obtain information about their own and their families' education. Data of this type relate to school enrollment and level of education attained, classified by age, sex, and other characteristics of the population. The school enrollment statistics reflect attendance or enrollment in any regular school within a given period; educational attainment statistics reflect the highest grade completed by an individual.

The second type, exemplified by data from NCES and the National Education Association, is based on reports from administrators of educational institutions and of local and State agencies having jurisdiction over education. Data of this type relate to enrollment, attendance, staff, and finances for the Nation, individual States, and local areas.

Unlike NCES, the Census Bureau does not regularly include specialized vocational, trade, business, or correspondence schools in its surveys. Both the Bureau of the Census and NCES include kindergartens in enrollment figures; the Census Bureau also includes all nursery schools, while NCES includes only publicly financed ones. At the higher education level, the statistics of both agencies are concerned with institutions granting degrees or offering work acceptable for degree-credit, such as junior colleges.

School attendance.—All States except Mississippi require that children attend school. While State laws vary as to the ages and circumstances of compulsory attendance, generally they require that formal schooling begin by age 7 and continue to age 16.

131

Schools.—NCES defines a *school* as "a division of the school system consisting of a group of pupils composed of one or more grade groups, organized as one unit with one or more teachers to give instruction of a defined type, and housed in a school plant of one or more buildings. More than one school may be housed in one school plant, as is the case when the elementary and secondary programs are housed in the same school plant."

Regular schools are those which advance a person toward a diploma or degree. They include public and private nursery schools, kindergartens, graded schools, colleges, universities, and professional schools. *Public* schools are schools controlled and supported by local, State, or Federal governmental agencies; *private* or *nonpublic* schools are those controlled and supported mainly by religious organizations or by private persons or organizations.

The Bureau of the Census defines *elementary* schools as including grades 1 through 8; *high* schools as including grades 9 through 12; and *colleges* as including junior or community colleges, regular 4-year colleges, and graduate or professional schools. Statistics reported by NCES and the National Education Association by type of organization, such as elementary level and secondary level, may not be strictly comparable with those from the Bureau of the Census because the grades included at the two levels vary, depending on the organization of junior high schools.

School year.—Except as otherwise indicated in the tables, data relating to enrollment and staff refer to the school year which generally begins in September of the preceding year and ends in June of the year stated. For the most part, statistics concerning school finances are for a 12-month period, usually July 1 to June 30.

Statistical reliability.—For a discussion of statistical collection, estimation, and sampling procedures and measures of statistical reliability applicable to Census Bureau and NCES data, see Appendix III.

Historical statistics.—Tabular headnotes provide cross-references, where applicable, to *Historical Statistics of the United States, Colonial Times to 1970.* See Appendix I.

No. 208. Public and Private Schools—Number, by Level: 1940 to 1977

[Prior to 1960, excludes Alaska and Hawaii. Schools classified by type of organization, rather than by grade-group; elementary excludes kindergarten and secondary includes junior high schools. See Appendix III and also *Historical Statistics, Colonial Times to 1970,* series H 413–417 and H 689]

TYPE OF SCHOOL	1940	1950	1960	1966	1970	1973	1974	1975	1976	1977
Elementary___1,000__	194.4	138.6	105.4	88.6	81.2	78.9	79.1	77.6	77.2	(NA)
Public [1]_____1,000__	[2] 183.1	128.2	91.9	73.2	66.8	64.9	65.1	[3] 63.6	[3] 63.2	(NA)
One-teacher____1,000__	[2] 107.7	59.7	20.2	6.5	2.1	1.5	1.4	1.2	1.2	(NA)
Nonpublic [4]_____1,000__	11.3	10.4	13.6	15.3	14.4	14.0	14.0	14.0	14.0	(NA)
Secondary____1,000__	28.7	27.9	29.8	31.2	30.5	29.6	29.5	29.4	29.0	(NA)
Public [1]_____1,000__	[2] 25.1	24.5	25.8	26.6	26.3	25.9	25.9	[3] 25.7	[3] 25.3	(NA)
Nonpublic [4]_____1,000__	3.6	3.3	4.1	4.6	4.2	3.7	3.6	3.7	3.7	(NA)
Higher education [5]___	1,708	1,851	2,008	2,230	2,525	2,665	2,720	2,747	2,765	2,785
Public_____	603	641	701	821	1,060	1,182	1,200	1,214	1,219	1,231
Private_____	1,105	1,210	1,307	1,409	1,465	1,483	1,520	1,533	1,546	1,554

NA Not available.   [1] Includes combined elementary-secondary schools.   [2] 1942 data.
[3] Excludes special education schools for the handicapped.   [4] Partially estimated.
[5] Universities, colleges, professional schools, teachers colleges, junior colleges, and U.S. service schools. Branch campuses not counted separately; considered part of parent institution.

Source: U.S. National Center for Education Statistics, 1940 and 1950, *Biennial Survey of Education in the United States,* chapter on Statistical Summary of Education; thereafter, *Digest of Education Statistics,* annual.

Figure 5.1

Percent of Adults Who Have Completed
Four Years of High School or More: 1950 to 1977
(See table 226)

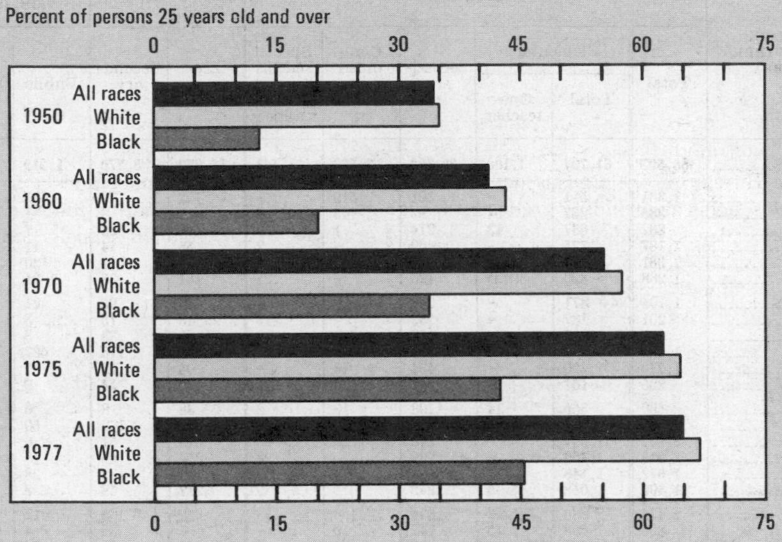

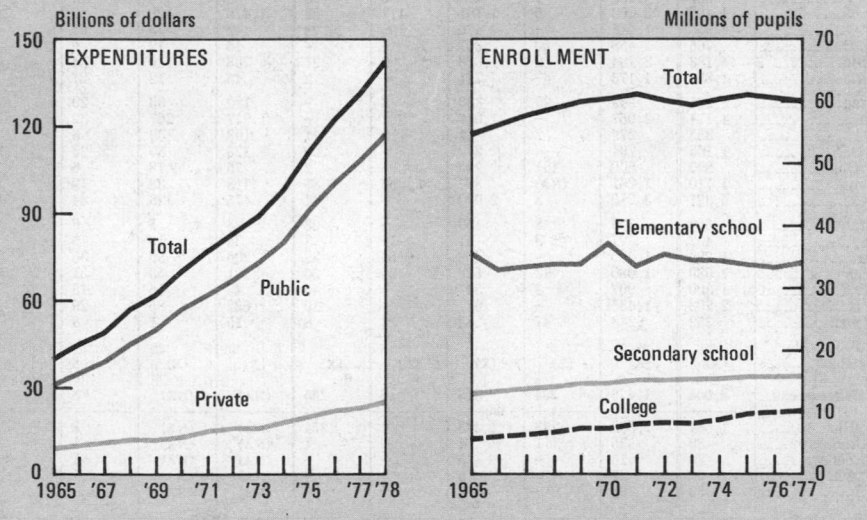

Percent of persons 25 years old and over

Source: U.S. Bureau of the Census.

Figure 5.2

School Expenditures—Public and Private, and School
Enrollment, by Level of Instruction: 1965 to 1978
(See tables 211 and 217. Includes nursery and kindergarten)

Source: Chart prepared by U.S. Bureau of the Census. Data from U.S. Bureau of the Census
and U.S. National Center for Education Statistics.

No. 209. PUBLIC AND PRIVATE SCHOOLS, BY LEVEL—STATES AND OTHER AREAS: 1971 AND 1976

[Schools classified by type of organization, rather than by grade-group; elementary excludes kindergarten and secondary includes junior high school. See Appendix III]

STATE OR OTHER AREA	PUBLIC, 1976						NONPUBLIC, 1971		HIGHER EDUCA-TION, 1976[1]	
	Total	Elementary		Secondary	Combined elem.-secondary	Special schools for the handicapped	Elementary	Secondary	Public	Private
		Total	One-teacher							
U.S.	88,597	61,704	1,166	23,792	1,538	1,563	14,372	3,770	1,219	1,546
Ala.	1,331	511	–	301	519	–	197	76	31	22
Alaska	385	237	54	97	45	6	13	8	1	2
Ariz.	862	637	13	214	1	10	100	28	17	5
Ark.	1,187	725	–	460	–	2	58	14	11	12
Calif.	7,381	5,515	58	1,529	5	332	1,234	333	120	111
Colo.	1,268	820	(NA)	426	–	22	151	38	21	12
Conn.	1,104	871	–	233	–	–	259	95	21	24
Del.	2 201	137	–	52	–	12	43	15	3	4
D.C.	197	132	–	53	–	12	49	33	3	15
Fla.	1,988	1,431	1	458	55	44	354	116	37	34
Ga.	1,770	1,290	–	434	46	–	94	49	32	31
Hawaii	225	161	–	51	8	5	60	14	9	3
Idaho	560	355	14	193	10	2	38	8	6	3
Ill.	4,621	3,232	–	1,274	7	108	1,053	172	50	86
Ind.	2,149	1,547	–	510	26	66	373	51	6	41
Iowa	1,903	1,166	–	709	–	28	254	46	18	39
Kans.	1,672	1,148	7	514	–	10	144	32	28	23
Ky.	1,409	1,058	5	342	–	9	217	48	8	29
La.	1,474	886	2	379	156	53	322	105	12	11
Maine	835	683	15	142	10	–	71	36	4	15
Md.	1,346	991	1	317	20	18	266	95	26	21
Mass.	2,576	1,899	(NA)	518	(NA)	159	477	193	32	84
Mich.	4,062	2,860	19	1,100	21	81	700	170	42	47
Minn.	1,751	1,123	2	620	8	–	401	61	26	34
Miss.	1,069	639	1	430	–	–	166	123	24	18
Mo.	2,288	1,539	1	749	–	–	432	89	22	53
Mont.	816	620	126	196	–	–	49	14	9	3
Nebr.	1,804	1,407	484	397	–	–	181	45	13	13
Nev.	263	158	10	80	16	9	16	3	5	1
N.H.	475	379	6	96	–	–	81	32	10	14
N.J.	2,477	1,973	4	436	–	68	604	163	28	31
N. Mex.	635	425	1	185	2	23	64	19	8	3
N.Y.	4,428	3,062	5	1,161	117	88	1,476	420	80	189
N.C.	2,055	1,445	–	476	106	28	142	53	57	42
N. Dak.	765	458	50	307	–	–	46	12	9	4
Ohio	4,183	3,134	2	1,026	2	21	703	149	34	68
Okla.	1,889	1,173	–	714	–	2	45	12	27	15
Oreg.	1,285	949	25	333	3	–	120	33	20	22
Pa.	4,174	2,957	–	1,016	201	–	1,217	267	32	113
R.I.	355	279	2	64	1	11	108	30	3	9
S.C.	1,165	794	–	342	–	29	128	30	23	24
S. Dak.	827	600	181	225	–	2	75	18	6	10
Tenn.	1,710	1,261	(NA)	307	56	86	118	38	19	44
Tex.	5,327	3,213	3	2,070	–	44	475	126	84	55
Utah	558	376	3	159	–	23	23	5	9	4
Vt.	402	327	8	61	11	3	38	19	6	16
Va.	1,786	1,245	–	458	50	33	206	80	36	34
Wash.	1,689	1,090	13	529	20	50	191	53	31	14
W. Va.	1,300	907	3	347	–	46	43	15	15	11
Wis.	2,263	1,636	–	617	–	10	682	85	29	28
Wyo.	352	243	47	85	16	8	15	1	8	–
U.S. service schools	(X)	(X)	(X)	(X)	(X)	(X)	(X)	(X)	8	–
Other areas	2,004	1,426	234	316	6	255	(NA)	(NA)	3 8	9
P. Rico	1,884	1,333	233	293	4	254	(NA)	(NA)	3	9
Am. Samoa	30	25	1	4	–	1	(NA)	(NA)	1	–
C. Zone	20	15	–	5	–	–	(NA)	(NA)	1	–
Guam	37	27	–	9	–	–	(NA)	(NA)	1	–
V.I.	33	26	–	5	2	–	(NA)	(NA)	1	–

– Represents zero.   NA Not available.   X Not applicable.   [1] Branch campuses not counted separately; considered part of parent institution.   [2] For 1977.   [3] Includes Trust Territory of the Pacific Islands.

Source: U.S. National Center for Education Statistics, *Digest of Education Statistics, 1977–78.*

No. 210. SCHOOL ENROLLMENT, BY TYPE OF SCHOOL: 1940 TO 1976

[In thousands. Prior to 1960, excludes Alaska and Hawaii. Through 1960, for school year; thereafter, as of fall of preceding year. See Historical Statistics, Colonial Times to 1970, series H 421-429, for kindergarten, elementary, and secondary. See also Appendix III]

TYPE OF SCHOOL	1940	1950	1960	1966	1970	1972	1973	1974	1975	1976
Total	29,751	31,319	45,228	54,306	58,566	59,394	59,318	59,080	59,677	59,817
Kindergarten [1]	661	1,175	2,293	2,493	2,821	2,683	2,710	2,838	3,002	3,164
Public	595	1,034	1,923	2,262	2,601	2,483	2,502	2,639	2,784	2,945
Nonpublic	57	[2]133	[2]354	212	[3]200	[3]180	[3]190	[3]180	[3]200	[3]200
Grades 1-8 [4]	20,466	21,032	30,119	33,266	34,190	33,697	33,034	32,297	32,019	31,118
Public	18,237	18,353	25,679	28,315	29,996	29,782	29,342	28,694	28,137	27,542
Nonpublic	2,096	[3]2,575	[3]4,286	4,763	[3]4,000	[3]3,720	[3]3,510	[3]3,420	[3]3,700	[3]3,400
Residential schools for exceptional children [5]	56	[6]49	[7]59	[3]85	[3]87	[3]87		[3]85	[3]85	[3]83
Federal schools:										
For Indians	17	20	25	32	34	34	[3][4]182	33	31	29
On Fed. installations	(NA)	(NA)	19	29	[3]33	[3]33		[3]25	25	23
Grades 9-12 [4]	7,130	6,453	9,600	13,021	14,418	15,214	15,309	15,427	15,633	15,804
Public high schools	6,601	5,725	8,485	11,597	13,022	13,816	13,909	14,076	14,132	14,304
Nonpublic high schools	458	[3]672	[3]1,035	1,329	[3]1,300	[3]1,300	[3]1,300	[3]1,250	[3]1,400	[3]1,400
Residential schools for exceptional children [5]	10	[6]10	[7]24	[3]35	[3]37	[3]39		[3]41	[3]41	[3]41
Federal schools:										
For Indians	7	8	12	14	12	[3]12	[3][4]100	11	11	11
On Fed. installations	(NA)	(NA)	1	[3]3	[3]3	[3]3		4	4	3
Higher education [8]	1,494	2,659	3,216	5,526	7,136	7,800	8,265	8,518	9,023	9,731
Publicly controlled	797	1,355	1,832	3,624	5,112	5,745	6,159	6,389	6,838	7,426
Privately controlled	698	1,304	1,384	1,902	2,024	2,055	2,106	2,130	2,185	2,306

NA Not available.   [1] Includes subcollegiate departments of institutions of higher education, residential schools for exceptional children, and Federal schools, not shown separately.   [2] Data from U.S. Bureau of the Census, Current Population Reports, series P-20.   [3] Estimated.   [4] Includes subcollegiate departments of institutions of higher education, not shown separately.   [5] Schools for blind, deaf, mentally deficient, epileptic, and delinquent.   [6] 1946 data.   [7] Estimate based on 1958 survey.   [8] Excludes subcollegiate departments of institutions of higher education. Degree-credit enrollment only.

Source: U.S. National Center for Education Statistics, Biennial Survey of Education in the United States, chapter on Statistical Summary of Education, and Digest of Education Statistics, annual.

No. 211. SCHOOL EXPENDITURES—PUBLIC AND NONPUBLIC, BY TYPE OF CONTROL AND LEVEL OF INSTRUCTION: 1940 TO 1978

[In billions of dollars, except percent. Prior to 1960, excludes Alaska and Hawaii. For school years ending in year shown. Includes nursery, kindergarten, and special programs when provided by school system. Nonpublic elementary and secondary school expenditures are estimates. Data for 1978 are projections. See Historical Statistics, Colonial Times to 1970, series H 494, 499, and 500 for related but not comparable data and H 513-519 for private schools. See also Appendix III]

CONTROL AND LEVEL	1940	1950	1960	1966	1970	1972	1973	1974	1975	1976	1977	1978, est.
Total [1]	[2]3.20	[2]8.80	[3]24.7	45.2	70.4	83.0	89.7	98.0	111.1	121.8	131.0	142.3
Percent of GNP [4]	3.2	3.3	5.0	6.3	7.3	7.5	7.2	7.2	7.6	7.5	7.3	(NA)
Current expenditures [5]	2.83	7.23	20.2	37.6	60.8	73.7	81.0	88.0	100.0	110.4	118.9	129.7
Capital outlay [6]	.37	1.57	4.5	7.6	9.6	9.3	8.7	10.0	11.1	11.4	12.1	12.6
Public	2.70	7.06	19.7	35.3	56.8	67.4	72.8	80.1	91.3	100.2	107.6	116.9
Percent of total	84.3	80.2	79.8	78.1	80.7	81.2	81.6	81.3	82.2	82.3	82.1	82.2
Current expenditures [5]	2.38	5.77	16.1	29.4	49.0	59.8	65.7	71.9	82.1	90.7	97.5	106.4
Elementary and secondary [7]	2.10	4.87	13.1	22.7	36.3	43.8	48.0	52.2	59.3	65.2	70.6	76.3
Higher education	.27	.90	3.0	6.7	12.7	16.0	17.7	19.7	22.8	25.5	26.9	30.1
Capital outlay [6]	.32	1.29	3.6	5.9	7.8	7.6	7.1	8.2	9.2	9.5	10.1	10.5
Elementary and secondary [7]	.26	1.01	2.8	3.8	4.7	4.5	4.1	5.0	5.7	5.9	6.2	6.4
Higher education	.06	.28	.8	2.1	3.1	3.1	3.0	3.2	3.5	3.6	3.9	4.1
Nonpublic	.50	1.74	5.0	9.9	13.6	15.6	16.9	17.9	19.8	21.6	23.4	25.4
Current expenditures [5]	.46	1.46	4.1	8.2	11.8	13.9	15.3	16.1	17.9	19.7	21.4	23.3
Elementary and secondary [7]	.21	.65	1.7	3.0	4.2	5.0	5.7	5.9	6.6	7.3	8.0	8.7
Higher education	.25	.81	2.4	5.2	7.6	8.9	9.6	10.2	11.3	12.4	13.4	14.6
Capital outlay [6]	.05	.28	.9	1.7	1.8	1.7	1.6	1.8	1.9	1.9	2.0	2.1
Elementary and secondary [7]	.03	.14	.4	.5	.5	.5	.5	.6	.6	.7	.7	.7
Higher education	.02	.14	.5	1.2	1.3	1.2	1.1	1.2	1.3	1.2	1.3	1.4

NA Not available.   [1] Excludes schools of nursing not affiliated with colleges and universities.   [2] Excludes higher education current expenditures for auxiliary enterprises and other noneducational current-fund expenditures.   [3] Excludes residential schools for exceptional children.   [4] GNP=Gross national product; see section 14. For 1940, GNP for calendar year; thereafter, for fiscal-years ending in years shown.   [5] Includes interest.   [6] Includes plant expansion.   [7] See footnote 1, table 212.

Source: U.S. National Center for Education Statistics, 1940 and 1950, Biennial Survey of Education in the United States, chapter on Statistical Summary of Education; thereafter, Digest of Education Statistics, annual; and Projections of Education Statistics to 1986-87.

No. 212. School Expenditures, by Source of Funds: 1960 to 1978

[Estimates for school years ending in years shown. See Appendix III]

TYPE OF SCHOOL AND SOURCE OF FUNDS	TOTAL (bil. dol.)										PERCENT			
	1960	1966	1970	1972	1973	1974	1975	1976	1977	1978	1960	1970	1975	1978
Total	24.7	45.2	70.4	83.0	89.7	98.0	111.1	121.8	131.0	142.3	100.0	100.0	100.0	100.0
Federal	1.7	5.0	7.5	9.2	9.8	10.2	12.1	13.0	14.4	15.4	6.9	10.7	10.9	10.8
State	7.2	13.1	22.2	25.8	29.4	33.3	38.7	43.9	47.5	52.2	29.1	31.5	34.8	36.7
Local	9.7	15.1	22.6	26.7	28.1	29.8	33.2	35.1	37.1	39.7	39.3	32.1	29.9	27.9
All other	6.1	12.0	18.1	21.3	22.4	24.7	27.1	29.8	32.0	35.0	24.7	25.7	24.4	24.6
Public	19.7	35.3	56.8	67.4	72.8	80.1	91.3	100.2	107.6	116.9	79.8	80.7	82.2	82.2
Federal	1.2	3.6	5.8	7.4	7.8	8.3	9.8	10.5	11.7	12.5	4.8	8.2	8.8	8.8
State	7.2	13.0	22.1	25.6	29.2	33.0	38.4	43.6	47.2	51.8	29.1	31.4	34.6	36.4
Local	9.7	15.1	22.5	26.6	28.0	29.7	33.1	35.0	37.0	39.6	39.3	32.0	29.8	27.8
All other	1.6	3.6	6.4	7.8	7.8	9.1	10.0	11.1	11.7	13.0	6.5	9.1	9.0	9.1
Nonpublic	5.0	9.9	13.6	15.6	16.9	17.9	19.8	21.6	23.4	25.4	20.2	19.3	17.8	17.8
Federal	.5	1.4	1.7	1.8	2.0	1.9	2.3	2.5	2.7	2.9	2.0	2.4	2.1	2.0
State and local	(z)	.1	.2	.3	.3	.4	.4	.4	.4	.5	(z)	.2	.4	.4
All other	4.5	8.4	11.7	13.5	14.6	15.6	17.1	18.7	20.3	22.0	18.2	16.6	15.4	15.5
Elementary and secondary [1]	18.0	30.0	45.7	53.8	58.3	63.7	72.2	79.1	85.5	92.1	100.0	100.0	100.0	100.0
Federal	.7	2.1	3.4	4.6	4.7	5.1	6.0	6.5	7.4	7.8	3.9	7.4	8.3	8.5
State	5.6	9.6	15.8	18.0	20.5	23.6	27.2	31.1	34.0	37.1	31.1	34.6	37.7	40.3
Local	9.5	14.7	21.7	25.6	26.8	28.4	31.7	33.4	35.3	37.7	52.8	47.5	43.9	40.9
Public	15.9	26.5	41.0	48.3	52.1	57.2	65.0	71.1	76.8	82.7	88.3	89.7	90.0	89.8
Federal	.7	2.1	3.4	4.6	4.7	5.1	6.0	6.5	7.4	7.8	3.9	7.4	8.3	8.5
State	5.6	9.6	15.8	18.0	20.5	23.6	27.2	31.1	34.0	37.1	31.1	34.6	37.7	40.3
Local	9.5	14.7	21.7	25.6	26.8	28.4	31.7	33.4	35.3	37.7	52.8	47.5	43.9	40.9
All other	.1	.1	.1	.1	.1	.1	.1	.1	.1	.1	.6	.2	.1	.1
Nonpublic	2.1	3.5	4.7	5.5	6.2	6.5	7.2	8.0	8.7	9.4	11.7	10.3	10.0	10.2
Institutions of higher education	6.7	15.2	24.7	29.2	31.4	34.3	38.9	42.7	45.5	50.2	100.0	100.0	100.0	100.0
Federal	1.0	2.9	4.1	4.6	5.1	5.1	6.1	6.5	7.0	7.6	14.9	16.6	15.7	15.1
State	1.6	3.5	6.4	7.8	8.9	9.7	11.5	12.8	13.5	15.1	23.9	25.9	29.6	30.1
Local	.2	.4	.9	1.1	1.3	1.4	1.5	1.7	1.8	2.0	3.0	3.6	3.9	4.0
All other	3.9	8.4	13.3	15.7	16.1	18.1	19.8	21.7	23.2	25.5	58.2	53.9	50.9	50.8
Public	3.8	8.8	15.8	19.1	20.7	22.9	26.3	29.1	30.8	34.2	56.7	64.0	67.6	68.1
Federal	.5	1.5	2.4	2.8	3.1	3.2	3.8	4.0	4.3	4.7	7.5	9.7	9.8	9.4
State	1.6	3.4	6.3	7.6	8.7	9.4	11.2	12.5	13.2	14.7	23.9	25.5	28.8	29.3
Local	.2	.4	.8	1.0	1.2	1.3	1.4	1.6	1.7	1.9	3.0	3.2	3.6	3.8
All other	1.5	3.5	6.3	7.7	7.7	9.0	9.9	11.0	11.6	12.9	22.4	25.5	25.4	25.7
Nonpublic	2.9	6.4	8.9	10.1	10.7	11.4	12.6	13.6	14.7	16.0	43.3	36.0	32.4	31.9
Federal	.5	1.4	1.7	1.8	2.0	1.9	2.3	2.5	2.7	2.9	7.5	6.9	5.9	5.8
State and local	(z)	.1	.2	.3	.3	.4	.4	.4	.4	.5	(z)	.8	1.0	1.0
All other	2.4	4.9	7.0	8.0	8.4	9.1	9.9	10.7	11.6	12.6	35.8	28.3	25.4	25.1

Z Less than $50 million or less than .05 percent.   [1] Includes residential schools for exceptional children, Federal schools for Indians, and federally operated elementary and secondary schools on military posts; includes items not shown separately.

Source: U.S. National Center for Education Statistics, *Projections of Education Statistics to 1986–87.*

No. 213. Federal Outlays for Education and Related Activities, by Type of Support: 1960 to 1978

[In millions of dollars. For years ending June 30 except, beginning 1977, ending September 30. See headnote, table 214]

TYPE OF SUPPORT AND LEVEL OF EDUCATION	1960	1966	1970	1972	1973	1974	1975	1976	1977	1978
Outlays supporting education in educational institutions	1,734	5,844	9,236	11,782	12,696	13,090	17,604	19,483	19,427	18,446
Grants	1,493	5,232	8,728	11,433	12,350	12,739	17,125	19,087	18,962	17,959
Elementary-secondary	490	2,037	3,212	3,857	4,085	4,207	4,998	4,819	5,282	5,579
Higher education	830	2,272	3,911	5,172	5,965	6,064	7,992	9,605	9,204	8,002
Vocational-technical and continuing education [1]	173	923	1,604	2,404	2,300	2,467	4,135	4,662	4,476	4,378
Loans, higher education	240	612	508	349	346	352	480	396	465	487
Other outlays for education and related activities	2,267	3,820	3,417	4,516	4,706	4,847	5,863	6,216	7,349	6,617

[1] Not classifiable by level.

Source: U.S. National Center for Education Statistics, *Digest of Education Statistics,* annual.

No. 214. FEDERAL OUTLAYS FOR EDUCATION AND RELATED ACTIVITIES: 1970 TO 1978

[In millions of dollars, except percent. For years ending June 30 except, beginning 1977, ending September 30. Beginning 1977, represents estimates. Includes Puerto Rico and outlying areas. Minus sign (−) denotes repayments exceeding new loans for data on loans and decrease for percent change]

TYPE OF SUPPORT, LEVEL, AND PROGRAM AREA	1970	1972	1973	1974	1975	1976	1977	1978
Federal outlays supporting education in educational institutions, total	9,236	11,782	12,696	13,090	17,604	19,483	19,427	18,446
Grants	8,728	11,433	12,350	12,739	17,125	19,087	18,962	17,959
Average annual percent change	[1]9.7	14.5	8.0	3.2	34.4	11.5	−.5	−5.3
Elementary-secondary education [2]	3,212	3,857	4,085	4,207	4,998	4,819	5,282	5,579
School assistance—Fed. affected areas	656	649	580	559	619	599	847	496
Assistance for educationally deprived [3]	1,208	1,614	1,560	1,534	2,765	2,647	2,897	3,351
Economic opportunity [4]	534	473	719	730				
Supporting services [5]	296	310	318	274	361	336	331	363
Teacher Corps	18	24	32	33	39	24	29	19
Vocational education	181	283	306	290	351	388	367	390
Dependents' schools abroad	137	169	191	218	235	237	264	322
Public lands revenue for schools	82	73	91	110	149	131	88	198
Assistance in special areas [6]	79	157	177	160	136	118	123	119
Veterans education	6	17	44	67	114	140	104	84
Emergency school assistance	−	69	43	185	197	172	201	200
Higher education [2]	3,911	5,172	5,965	6,064	7,992	9,605	9,204	[7]8,002
Basic research in U.S. educational institutions proper [8]	984	1,192	1,175	1,300	1,271	1,387	1,483	(NA)
Research facilities [8]	225	176	205	183	168	189	325	(NA)
Training grants, fellowships, traineeships	896	982	969	998	1,082	1,037	999	834
Facilities and equipment	513	400	452	263	336	296	178	157
Other institutional support	178	292	340	364	428	488	478	473
Other student assistance	1,102	2,130	2,824	2,956	4,708	6,209	5,740	4,730
Vocational-technical and continuing	1,604	2,404	2,300	2,467	4,135	4,662	4,476	4,378
Vocational, technical and work training [9]	1,269	1,829	1,475	1,495	3,037	3,405	3,490	3,501
Veterans education	245	429	658	800	899	984	728	606
General continuing education [10]	66	126	150	148	152	208	187	190
Training of Federal, State, and local personnel	25	20	17	24	47	65	72	82
Loans, higher education	508	349	346	352	480	396	465	487
Student loan program, NDEA [11]	197	287	325	363	449	420	409	382
College facilities loans [12]	311	62	21	−11	31	−24	56	105
Other Federal outlays for education and related activities, total	3,417	4,516	4,706	4,847	5,863	6,216	7,349	[13]6,617
Average annual percent change	[1]−1.8	15.0	4.2	3.0	21.0	6.0	14.3	−10.0
Applied research and development [8]	1,240	1,471	1,465	1,709	2,067	2,246	2,336	(NA)
School lunch and milk programs	676	1,213	1,298	1,267	1,832	1,890	3,023	2,172
Training of Federal military personnel	676	950	1,056	968	996	976	1,097	1,172
Professional training, military	492	718	780	720	727	694	784	839
U.S. military academies	184	232	276	247	270	282	314	333
Library services	170	165	167	207	228	250	289	307
International education	193	123	78	95	93	74	88	97
Educational exchange program	31	38	28	31	32	33	35	37
Agency for Int'l Development projects	111	56	23	47	45	33	44	54
ACTION [14] and other	51	29	27	17	16	7	6	5
Other [2]	460	594	642	602	646	780	516	532
Agricultural extension service	125	170	186	193	219	219	241	240
Educational television facilities [15]	19	8	29	22	65	79	113	120
Education in Fed. correct'l institutions	5	9	9	10	11	12	14	15
Surplus personal property transferred [16]	246	300	277	256	216	295	(NA)	(NA)
Surplus real property transferred [17]	12	12	25	18	37	22	(NA)	(NA)

− Represents zero. NA Not available. [1] Change from 1968. [2] Includes other outlays not shown separately. [3] Comprises Elementary and Secondary Education Act Title I, handicapped children, dropout prevention, bilingual education, Kendall School for the Deaf, and Model School for the Deaf. [4] Comprises Office of Economic Opportunity, Indian education, Appalachian Regional Development, Department of Labor, and Head Start preschool. [5] Comprises supplemental centers, school library materials, strengthening of State education agencies, captioned films for the deaf, dissemination of information, school counseling and testing, American Printing House for the Blind, planning and evaluation, and equipment and minor remodeling. [6] Comprises funds for District of Columbia, Canal Zone, territories and dependencies, Cuban refugees, and payments in lieu of taxes other than P.L. 81-874 and P.L. 81-815 for federally affected areas. [7] Includes 1977 amounts for basic research and research facilities. [8] Data from U.S. National Science Foundation, Federal Funds for Research, Development, and Other Scientific Activities. Higher education data include university operated research and development centers. [9] Comprises adult vocational education and manpower training programs. [10] Comprises Office of Education, ACTION (see footnote 14), Social and Rehabilitation Service, Dept. of Housing and Urban Development, Office of Economic Development, and additional programs for continuing education. [11] Comprises National Defense Education Act and insured student loans. [12] Comprises net amounts (loans minus loan repayments) for Dept. of Housing and Urban Development college housing loans, Office of Education college facilities loans, and Federal loans to the District of Columbia for school construction. [13] Includes 1977 outlay for applied research and development. [14] Previously Peace Corps. [15] Includes education broadcasting facilities. [16] Acquisition cost. [17] Fair value.

Source: U.S. National Center for Education Statistics, Digest of Education Statistics, annual.

No. 215. ENROLLMENT IN PUBLIC AND PRIVATE SCHOOLS: 1970 TO 1977

[In millions of persons 3 to 34 years of age. As of October. Elementary includes grades 1-8; high school, grades 9-12. College data represent degree-credit enrollment]

LEVEL	1970 Total	1970 Public	1970 Private	1975 Total	1975 Public	1975 Private	1976 Total	1976 Public	1976 Private	1977 Total	1977 Public	1977 Private
Total	60.4	52.2	8.1	61.0	52.8	8.2	60.5	52.4	8.1	60.0	51.6	8.4
Nursery	1.1	.3	.8	1.7	.6	1.2	1.5	.5	1.1	1.6	.6	1.1
Kindergarten	3.2	2.6	.5	3.4	2.9	.5	3.5	3.0	.5	3.2	2.7	.5
Elementary	34.0	30.0	3.9	30.5	27.2	3.3	29.8	26.7	3.1	29.2	26.0	3.3
High school	14.7	13.5	1.2	15.7	14.5	1.2	15.7	14.5	1.2	15.8	14.5	1.2
College	7.4	5.7	1.7	9.7	7.7	2.0	10.0	7.7	2.2	10.2	7.9	2.3

Source: U.S. Bureau of the Census, *Current Population Reports*, series P-20, Nos. 222, 303, 319, and 321.

No. 216. ENROLLMENT IN PUBLIC AND NONPUBLIC SCHOOLS, BY LEVEL: 1965 TO 1976

[In thousands. As of fall. Elementary school covers kindergarten through 8th grade; secondary, grades 9 through 12 and postgraduates in secondary schools. Both are for regular day schools. Data do not include independent nursery schools and kindergartens, residential schools for exceptional children, subcollegiate departments of colleges, Federal schools for Indians, and federally operated schools on Federal installations. College data include degree-credit and non-degree-credit enrollment]

YEAR	TOTAL ENROLLMENT Total	TOTAL ENROLLMENT Public	TOTAL ENROLLMENT Non-public	ELEMENTARY Public	ELEMENTARY Non-public	SECONDARY Public	SECONDARY Non-public	COLLEGE Public	COLLEGE Non-public
1965	54,394	46,143	8,251	30,563	4,900	11,610	1,400	3,970	1,951
1970	59,890	52,337	7,553	32,577	4,100	13,332	1,300	6,428	2,153
1971	60,129	52,885	7,244	32,265	3,800	13,816	1,300	6,804	2,144
1972	59,958	52,814	7,144	31,831	3,700	13,913	1,300	7,070	2,144
1973	59,933	52,850	7,083	31,353	3,600	14,077	1,300	7,420	2,183
1974	60,276	53,041	7,235	30,921	3,600	14,132	1,400	7,988	2,235
1975	60,976	53,626	7,350	30,487	3,600	14,304	1,400	8,835	2,350
1976	60,347	52,988	7,359	30,012	3,600	14,323	1,400	8,653	2,359

Source: U.S. National Center for Education Statistics, *Projections of Education Statistics to 1986-87*.

No. 217. SCHOOL ENROLLMENT, BY SEX AND BY LEVEL: 1950 TO 1977

[In millions, except percent. As of fall. 1950 excludes Alaska and Hawaii. For 1950 and 1960, covers civilian non-institutional population 5 to 34 years old; thereafter, 3 to 34 years old. Elementary includes kindergarten and grades 1-8; high school, grades 9-12; and college, 1-4 year colleges and graduate and professional schools. Data for college represent degree-credit enrollment. Minus sign (−) denotes decrease]

YEAR	TOTAL Total enrolled [1]	TOTAL Elementary	TOTAL High school	TOTAL College	MALE Total enrolled [1]	MALE Elementary	MALE High school	MALE College	FEMALE Total enrolled [1]	FEMALE Elementary	FEMALE High school	FEMALE College
1950	30.3	21.4	6.7	2.2	15.9	11.0	3.3	1.5	14.4	10.4	3.3	.7
1960	46.3	32.4	10.2	3.6	24.2	16.7	5.2	2.3	22.0	15.7	5.1	1.2
1965	54.7	35.5	13.0	5.7	28.5	18.2	6.5	3.5	26.2	17.3	6.5	2.2
1970	60.4	37.1	14.7	7.4	31.4	19.0	7.4	4.4	28.9	18.1	7.3	3.0
1972	60.1	35.4	15.2	8.3	31.3	18.1	7.7	4.9	28.8	17.3	7.5	3.5
1973	59.4	34.5	15.3	8.2	30.9	17.7	7.8	4.7	28.5	16.8	7.5	3.5
1974	60.3	34.4	15.4	8.8	31.2	17.6	7.8	4.9	29.1	16.8	7.6	3.9
1975	61.0	33.8	15.7	9.7	31.6	17.3	8.0	5.3	29.4	16.5	7.7	4.4
1976	60.5	33.3	15.7	10.0	31.2	17.0	8.1	5.3	29.3	16.2	7.7	4.7
1977	60.0	32.4	15.8	10.2	30.8	16.6	8.0	5.4	29.2	15.8	7.8	4.8
Percent change:												
1950-60	52.8	51.6	54.0	61.2	52.8	51.9	55.0	54.4	52.8	51.2	52.9	76.1
1960-70	30.5	14.5	43.6	107.6	29.6	13.8	43.2	88.2	31.4	15.1	44.0	144.8
1970-75	1.0	−8.9	6.6	30.8	.5	−8.9	7.5	21.4	1.6	−8.9	5.7	44.5
1975-77	−1.6	−4.1	1.0	5.2	−2.5	−4.0	.9	1.9	−.7	−4.2	1.1	9.1

[1] Beginning 1965, includes nursery schools, not shown separately.

Source: U.S. Bureau of the Census, *Current Population Reports*, series P-20, Nos. 34, 110, 162, 222, 260, 272, 286, 303, 319, and 321; and unpublished data.

No. 218. SCHOOL ENROLLMENT—ELEMENTARY, SECONDARY, AND INSTITUTIONS OF HIGHER EDUCATION, BY STATES AND OTHER AREAS: 1975 TO 1977

[In thousands. As of fall of year. For grade levels, see headnote, table 237. Data for nonpublic elementary and secondary schools not revised; for revised U.S. totals, see table 216. See also Appendix III]

STATE OR OTHER AREA	ELEMENTARY [1]				SECONDARY [1]				HIGHER EDUCATION [3]			
	Nonpublic		Public		Nonpublic		Public		Nonpublic		Public	
	1975	1976	1976	1977 [2]	1975	1976	1976	1977 [2]	1976	1977	1976	1977
United States	3,400	3,900	[4]30,012	29,453	1,200	1,400	[4]14,323	14,234	2,359	2,436	[5]8,653	[5]8,924
New England	239	228	915	1,669	126	127	421	800	320	337	353	360
Maine	10	10	171	167	8	7	78	78	10	10	29	30
New Hampshire	17	15	120	118	8	6	55	55	16	17	23	22
Vermont	6	5	73	71	6	5	32	32	12	12	17	17
Massachusetts	121	105	(NA)	772	59	70	(NA)	380	197	211	164	165
Rhode Island	24	25	117	115	9	8	55	55	29	30	31	34
Connecticut	61	68	434	426	37	31	201	200	56	57	89	92
Middle Atlantic	1,007	1,039	4,639	4,552	348	435	2,360	2,346	653	667	1,050	1,055
New York	497	436	[2]2,237	2,195	173	269	1,142	1,135	397	405	542	540
New Jersey	180	247	[2]961	943	55	54	466	463	70	71	220	230
Pennsylvania	330	356	1,441	1,414	120	112	752	748	186	191	288	285
East No. Central	898	906	5,784	5,677	293	302	2,847	2,829	386	396	1,591	1,661
Ohio	212	219	1,504	1,476	75	65	745	741	99	100	346	353
Indiana	75	65	784	770	21	37	379	376	54	54	166	168
Illinois	300	324	1,506	1,478	98	88	732	727	143	150	466	509
Michigan	174	135	1,386	1,361	65	85	649	645	60	61	410	421
Wisconsin	136	163	604	592	34	27	342	340	30	31	203	210
West No. Central	278	325	2,259	2,218	78	87	1,184	1,174	180	186	609	622
Minnesota	83	81	554	544	22	19	308	306	38	40	148	148
Iowa	46	51	399	392	18	15	206	204	37	40	84	87
Missouri	82	112	631	619	11	29	319	317	67	67	155	154
North Dakota	8	10	82	80	3	3	47	47	2	2	28	30
South Dakota	8	11	97	96	3	3	51	50	8	9	22	22
Nebraska	28	34	206	202	12	11	106	105	14	14	63	67
Kansas	24	26	290	285	8	7	147	145	14	14	109	114
South Atlantic	281	441	4,855	4,765	114	159	2,204	2,191	312	325	1,218	1,264
Delaware	12	14	80	78	5	5	42	42	5	5	20	20
Maryland	77	104	587	576	28	30	274	272	29	30	181	188
Dist. of Col	12	14	90	88	9	5	36	36	66	71	14	13
Virginia	40	67	752	739	20	23	348	346	30	32	214	224
West Virginia	7	10	285	280	4	3	120	119	11	11	69	70
North Carolina	20	47	825	810	5	10	366	364	53	54	196	202
South Carolina	22	37	425	417	5	13	196	195	26	26	96	98
Georgia	19	51	769	754	10	20	327	325	31	32	138	142
Florida	72	97	1,042	1,023	29	50	495	492	61	64	284	301
East So. Central	135	163	1,946	1,911	63	76	852	847	94	99	471	481
Kentucky	41	55	[2]476	468	15	17	218	216	22	24	107	108
Tennessee	20	33	604	593	11	11	238	237	41	43	140	146
Alabama	37	36	513	503	12	21	239	238	20	21	137	140
Mississippi	37	39	353	347	24	27	157	156	11	11	87	87
West So. Central	194	266	3,306	3,245	65	66	1,415	1,406	130	134	858	889
Arkansas	8	16	319	313	3	5	141	141	9	10	58	61
Louisiana	94	130	582	571	33	36	258	256	22	22	133	132
Oklahoma	8	7	406	399	3	3	192	190	21	22	124	128
Texas	84	113	[2]1,999	1,962	26	22	824	819	78	80	543	568
Mountain	71	114	1,554	1,526	25	25	721	716	65	67	517	534
Montana	7	7	113	111	3	2	58	57	3	3	27	28
Idaho	4	4	136	133	2	1	64	64	8	8	31	32
Wyoming	2	3	62	61	(z)	(z)	28	28	-	-	19	20
Colorado	24	33	[2]385	378	8	8	185	184	14	14	136	140
New Mexico	9	9	192	189	3	5	93	92	4	4	50	51
Arizona	20	50	[2]354	348	7	7	149	147	5	5	170	176
Utah	3	3	216	212	1	1	98	98	31	33	54	56
Nevada	2	5	96	94	1	1	46	46	(z)	(z)	30	31
Pacific	298	419	3,964	3,890	89	125	1,938	1,925	218	226	1,969	2,041
Washington	30	27	524	514	12	18	257	255	24	23	224	236
Oregon	17	19	317	311	6	6	158	157	16	16	130	125
California	237	351	[2]2,940	2,885	66	87	1,440	1,431	175	183	1,553	1,608
Alaska	(z)	2	65	64	(z)	(z)	26	26	(z)	(z)	18	29
Hawaii	14	20	118	116	6	14	57	56	3	4	44	43
Other areas [6]	46	79	586	575	19	33	176	176	50	67	59	61
Puerto Rico	38	67	530	520	16	28	159	158	50	67	51	51
Guam	3	4	21	21	1	2	7	7	-	-	4	4
Virgin Islands	3	5	20	19	1	2	5	6	-	-	2	2

- Represents zero.   NA Not available.   Z Less than 500.   [1] Excludes data for private residential schools for exceptional children and subcollegiate departments of higher education.   [2] Estimated.   [3] See headnote, table 264.   [4] Includes estimate for Massachusetts.   [5] Includes U.S. military academies, not shown separately.   [6] Includes American Samoa, Canal Zone, and Trust Territories of the Pacific Islands.

Source: U.S. National Center for Education Statistics, Digest of Education Statistics, annual, and unpublished data.

No. 219. School Enrollment, by Sex and Age: 1970 to 1977

[In thousands, except percent. As of October. Covers persons 3 to 34 years old enrolled in nursery school and above. Data relate to civilian noninstitutional population and are based on Current Population Survey; see text, p. 1. See *Historical Statistics, Colonial Times to 1970*, series H 442–476, for population 5 to 34 years old]

YEAR AND AGE	TOTAL			MALE			FEMALE		
	Popu-lation	Enrolled		Popu-lation	Enrolled		Popu-lation	Enrolled	
		Number	Per-cent		Number	Per-cent		Number	Per-cent
1970, total	106,996	60,357	56.4	52,627	31,413	59.7	54,369	28,944	53.2
3 and 4 years	7,135	1,461	20.5	3,641	771	21.2	3,494	691	19.8
5 and 6 years	7,820	7,000	89.5	3,988	3,545	88.9	3,832	3,455	90.2
7–9 years	12,550	12,462	99.3	6,400	6,355	99.3	6,149	6,107	99.3
10–13 years	16,618	16,481	99.2	8,432	8,333	98.8	8,186	8,148	99.5
14 and 15 years	8,019	7,869	98.1	4,065	3,992	98.2	3,954	3,877	98.0
16 and 17 years	7,699	6,927	90.0	3,875	3,539	91.3	3,824	3,388	88.6
18 and 19 years	6,958	3,322	47.7	3,349	1,821	54.4	3,609	1,501	41.6
20–24 years	15,594	3,359	21.5	7,036	2,062	29.3	8,558	1,297	15.2
25–34 years	24,603	1,477	6.0	11,840	996	8.4	12,763	480	3.8
1975, total	113,445	60,969	53.7	56,289	31,555	56.1	57,156	29,414	51.5
3 and 4 years	6,676	2,101	31.5	3,409	1,052	30.9	3,267	1,049	32.1
5 and 6 years	6,956	6,590	94.7	3,546	3,346	94.4	3,410	3,244	95.1
7–9 years	10,354	10,287	99.3	5,277	5,236	99.2	5,078	5,051	99.5
10–13 years	15,936	15,817	99.3	8,119	8,031	98.9	7,817	7,786	99.6
14 and 15 years	8,453	8,300	98.2	4,300	4,231	98.4	4,153	4,070	98.0
16 and 17 years	8,313	7,398	89.0	4,201	3,811	90.7	4,112	3,587	87.2
18 and 19 years	8,024	3,765	46.9	3,891	1,940	49.9	4,133	1,825	44.2
20–24 years	18,363	4,121	22.4	8,833	2,334	26.4	9,530	1,786	18.7
25–34 years	30,370	2,589	8.5	14,714	1,573	10.7	15,656	1,016	6.5
1976, total	113,983	60,482	53.1	56,577	31,194	55.1	57,405	29,288	51.0
3 and 4 years	6,239	1,950	31.3	3,184	984	30.9	3,054	967	31.6
5 and 6 years	7,013	6,701	95.5	3,579	3,422	95.6	3,434	3,279	95.5
7–9 years	10,256	10,173	99.2	5,227	5,171	98.9	5,029	5,001	99.4
10–13 years	15,410	15,282	99.2	7,852	7,780	99.1	7,558	7,502	99.3
14 and 15 years	8,399	8,248	98.2	4,275	4,214	98.6	4,124	4,033	97.8
16 and 17 years	8,303	7,401	89.1	4,198	3,800	90.5	4,105	3,601	87.7
18 and 19 years	8,148	3,768	46.2	3,957	1,907	48.2	4,191	1,861	44.4
20–24 years	18,771	4,379	23.2	9,055	2,358	26.0	9,716	2,021	20.8
25–34 years	31,444	2,581	8.2	15,251	1,557	10.2	16,193	1,025	6.3
1977, total	114,305	60,013	52.5	56,727	30,822	54.3	57,578	29,191	50.7
3 and 4 years	6,041	1,935	32.0	3,086	990	32.1	2,954	945	32.0
5 and 6 years	6,718	6,433	95.8	3,429	3,246	94.7	3,289	3,187	96.9
7–9 years	10,339	10,285	99.5	5,271	5,244	99.5	5,068	5,041	99.5
10–13 years	14,857	14,767	99.4	7,566	7,507	99.2	7,291	7,260	99.6
14 and 15 years	8,255	8,130	98.5	4,201	4,144	98.7	4,054	3,985	98.3
16 and 17 years	8,327	7,399	88.9	4,213	3,790	90.0	4,114	3,609	87.7
18 and 19 years	8,151	3,762	46.2	3,961	1,919	48.4	4,190	1,844	44.0
20–24 years	19,180	4,390	22.9	9,257	2,401	25.9	9,923	1,988	20.0
25–34 years	32,438	2,912	9.0	15,743	1,580	10.0	16,695	1,332	8.0

Source: U.S. Bureau of the Census, *Current Population Reports*, series P–20, Nos. 222, 303, 319, and 321.

No. 220. Percent Enrolled in School, by Age and Race: 1960 to 1977

[As of October. See headnote, table 219. Data based on sample and subject to sampling variability]

AGE (in years)	1960		1965		1970		1975		1976		1977	
	White	Black and other	White	Black and other	White	Black and other	White	Black and other	White	Black and other	White	Black and other
Total, 3–34	[1]56.4	[1]55.9	55.6	55.3	56.2	57.7	53.1	57.4	52.3	57.5	51.6	57.6
3 and 4	(NA)	(NA)	10.3	11.8	19.9	23.1	30.8	34.9	30.4	35.1	31.1	36.2
5 and 6	82.0	73.3	85.8	79.9	90.3	85.4	94.8	94.5	95.8	94.1	95.6	96.7
7–9	99.7	99.3	99.4	99.0	99.3	99.4	99.4	99.2	99.1	99.4	99.5	99.3
10–13	99.5	99.0	99.4	99.3	99.1	99.4	99.3	99.0	99.2	98.9	99.4	99.1
14 and 15	98.1	95.9	99.0	98.2	98.2	97.6	98.3	97.6	98.1	98.9	98.5	98.2
16 and 17	83.3	76.9	87.8	84.6	90.6	86.2	89.3	87.3	89.1	89.1	88.5	90.9
18 and 19	38.9	34.6	47.1	40.1	48.7	41.9	46.5	49.6	45.4	51.0	45.5	49.9
20–24	13.9	7.5	20.2	10.2	22.5	15.2	22.7	20.6	23.4	22.1	22.7	24.0
25–34	3.8	1.9	4.9	3.1	6.1	5.2	8.5	9.0	8.0	9.5	8.7	10.7

NA Not available.   [1] Data are for persons 5 to 34 years old.

Source: U.S. Bureau of the Census, *Current Population Reports*, series P–20, Nos. 110, 162, 222, 303, 319, and 321; and unpublished data.

No. 221. SCHOOL ENROLLMENT, BY RACE, LEVEL, AND AGE: 1960 TO 1977

[In thousands, except percent. As of October. For grade levels, see headnote, table 217. Minus sign (=) denotes decrease]

YEAR AND AGE	WHITE				BLACK AND OTHER			
	Total enrolled [1]	Elementary	High school	College	Total enrolled [1]	Elementary	High school	College
1960, total	40,348	27,884	9,122	3,342	5,910	4,556	1,127	227
5–13 years	27,723	27,149	574	–	4,336	4,285	51	–
14–17 years	9,028	731	8,084	214	1,213	268	937	8
18–24 years	2,854	4	431	2,420	312	2	132	178
25–34 years	743	1	33	709	49	1	7	41
1970, total	51,719	31,348	12,723	6,759	8,639	5,789	1,992	654
3 and 4 years	1,181	358	–	–	281	102	–	–
5–13 years	30,460	30,066	327	–	5,482	5,391	67	–
14–17 years	12,769	898	11,639	230	2,027	295	1,703	30
18–24 years	5,979	14	661	5,304	701	5	196	499
25–34 years	1,326	5	95	1,224	150	–	24	125
1974, total	50,992	28,802	13,073	7,781	9,267	5,580	2,374	1,046
3 and 4 years	1,658	386	–	–	349	104	–	–
5–13 years	27,961	27,551	345	–	5,293	5,206	61	–
14–17 years	13,198	855	12,071	271	2,331	265	2,025	38
18–24 years	6,199	4	606	5,589	992	–	266	727
25–34 years	1,976	2	53	1,921	302	2	20	282
1975, total	51,435	28,268	13,225	8,514	9,536	5,581	2,461	1,182
3 and 4 years	1,703	364	–	–	405	115	–	–
5–13 years	27,387	27,004	295	–	5,309	5,213	70	–
14–17 years	13,312	880	12,176	253	2,385	250	2,095	39
18–24 years	6,789	8	666	6,115	1,099	4	276	820
25–34 years	2,246	12	90	2,147	343	2	20	322
1976, total	50,761	27,662	13,214	8,644	9,720	5,613	2,528	1,305
3 and 4 years	1,559	388	–	–	391	130	–	–
5–13 years	26,856	26,518	266	–	5,300	5,223	64	–
14–17 years	13,200	730	12,232	237	2,447	255	2,151	43
18–24 years	6,942	19	649	6,277	1,206	2	298	904
25–34 years	2,204	7	68	2,133	376	–	18	358
1977, total	50,151	26,873	13,152	8,812	9,863	5,552	2,601	1,405
3 and 4 years	1,541	312	–	–	393	117	–	–
5–13 years	26,178	25,810	287	–	5,305	5,212	67	–
14–17 years	13,061	736	12,097	228	2,468	216	2,208	45
18–24 years	6,002	8	685	6,207	1,250	5	310	931
25–34 years	2,467	9	82	2,375	446	4	16	424
Percent change:								
1960–1970	28.1	12.4	39.5	102.2	46.2	27.1	76.8	188.1
1970–1975	−.5	−9.8	3.9	26.0	10.4	−3.6	23.5	80.7
1975–1977	−2.5	−4.9	−.6	3.5	3.4	−.5	5.7	18.9

– Represents zero. [1] Beginning 1970, includes nursery schools, not shown separately.

Source: U.S. Bureau of the Census, *Current Population Reports*, series P-20, Nos. 110, 222, 286, 303, 319, and 321; and unpublished data.

No. 222. PERCENT ENROLLED IN SCHOOL, BY LEVEL, BY SEX AND AGE: 1977

SEX AND AGE	Civilian [1] population (1,000)	PERCENT ENROLLED (October)						PERCENT NOT ENROLLED		
		Total	Nursery school	Kindergarten	Elementary, grades 1–8	Secondary, grades 9–12	College [2]	Total	High school graduate	Not high school graduate
Male	56,727	54.3	1.5	2.8	26.4	14.1	9.5	45.7	32.8	12.8
3 and 4 years	3,086	32.1	25.4	6.7	–	–	–	67.9	(X)	(X)
5 and 6 years	3,429	94.7	2.2	40.6	51.8	–	–	5.3	(X)	(X)
7–13 years	12,837	99.3	–	–	98.1	1.2	–	.7	(X)	(X)
14–17 years	8,414	94.3	–	–	7.1	85.8	1.3	5.7	.9	4.8
18–24 years	13,218	32.7	–	–	.1	4.5	28.1	67.3	50.9	16.4
25–29 years	8,377	12.6	–	–	–	.3	12.3	87.4	74.7	12.7
30–34 years	7,366	7.1	–	–	.1	.1	6.9	92.9	75.5	17.4
Female	57,578	50.7	1.3	2.8	24.8	13.4	8.4	49.3	36.1	13.2
3 and 4 years	2,954	32.0	24.5	7.5	–	–	–	68.0	(X)	(X)
5 and 6 years	3,289	96.9	1.0	41.6	54.2	–	–	3.1	(X)	(X)
7–13 years	12,359	99.5	–	–	98.0	1.6	–	.5	(X)	(X)
14–17 years	8,168	93.0	–	–	4.3	86.7	2.0	7.0	1.8	5.3
18–24 years	14,113	27.2	–	–	–	2.8	24.3	72.9	57.7	15.2
25–29 years	8,892	9.1	–	–	–	.4	8.7	90.9	75.1	15.8
30–34 years	7,803	6.7	–	–	.1	.4	6.2	93.3	74.4	19.0

– Represents zero. X Not applicable. [1] Noninstitutional only. [2] Degree-credit enrollment.

Source: U.S. Bureau of the Census, *Current Population Reports*, series P-20, No. 321; and unpublished data.

No. 223. Preprimary School Enrollment of Children 3 to 5 Years Old, by Race and Age, and by Labor Force Status of Mother: 1967 to 1977

[As of October. Civilian noninstitutional population. Includes public and nonpublic prekindergarten and kindergarten programs; excludes 5-year-olds enrolled in programs above kindergarten]

RACE, AGE, AND LABOR FORCE STATUS	NUMBER (1,000)							PERCENT ENROLLED OF POPULATION			
	1967	1970	1973	1974	1975	1976	1977	1967	1970	1975	1977
Population, 3–5 years old	12,234	10,877	10,344	10,391	10,183	9,726	9,249	(X)	(X)	(X)	(X)
Total enrollment [1][2]	3,864	4,075	4,234	4,699	4,954	4,790	4,577	31.6	37.5	48.6	49.5
White	3,265	3,414	3,521	3,941	4,105	3,933	3,717	31.8	37.8	48.7	49.0
Black	535	585	619	678	731	745	728	29.8	34.9	48.1	50.9
3 years old	273	454	515	685	683	603	645	6.8	13.0	21.5	21.7
4 years old	870	1,003	1,177	1,322	1,418	1,348	1,290	21.3	27.9	40.5	42.1
5 years old	2,721	2,617	2,542	2,693	2,852	2,839	2,642	65.4	69.2	81.3	82.3
ALL RACES [2]											
With mother in labor force [3]	1,353	1,345	1,586	1,921	2,168	2,136	2,092	34.2	38.8	54.0	53.8
3 and 4 years old	466	526	707	874	973	898	992	18.1	23.5	38.0	38.7
5 years old	887	818	879	1,047	1,195	1,237	1,100	63.8	66.6	82.5	82.9
Married, spouse present	1,140	1,131	1,271	1,528	1,733	1,708	1,649	34.1	39.5	53.6	53.3
Other marital status	213	214	314	393	435	428	444	34.6	36.0	56.0	55.8
Employed	1,249	1,246	1,478	1,755	1,948	1,960	1,881	34.5	39.3	55.1	55.0
Full-time	817	770	956	1,150	1,236	1,254	1,240	33.9	38.6	55.1	54.5
Part-time	432	476	522	605	712	706	641	35.7	40.4	55.1	56.0
With mother not in labor force	2,448	2,694	2,580	2,703	2,704	2,589	2,385	30.2	37.0	45.1	46.2
WHITE											
With mother in labor force [3]	1,053	1,031	1,222	1,513	1,723	1,668	1,592	34.7	39.1	54.0	52.3
3 and 4 years old	340	374	523	670	740	667	740	17.4	22.1	36.6	36.6
5 years old	713	657	699	844	983	1,001	852	66.2	69.2	84.1	83.4
Married, spouse present	932	913	1,042	1,261	1,449	1,399	1,334	34.7	39.1	53.3	52.0
Other marital status	120	119	181	253	273	269	258	34.6	38.9	57.8	54.1
Employed	982	959	1,157	1,405	1,566	1,561	1,458	35.2	39.3	55.0	53.1
Full-time	613	557	696	858	941	936	912	33.8	38.2	54.3	52.0
Part-time	369	402	461	547	625	625	546	37.7	41.0	56.2	55.2
With mother not in labor force	2,166	2,354	2,253	2,388	2,331	2,220	2,057	30.5	37.4	45.3	46.6
BLACK											
With mother in labor force [3]	286	281	319	370	372	414	429	32.3	36.8	52.6	59.4
3 and 4 years old	122	138	166	180	191	202	214	20.7	27.3	41.0	46.7
5 years old	163	143	154	189	181	211	215	55.3	55.6	75.2	81.3
Married, spouse present	193	192	188	230	221	255	246	31.3	39.4	53.6	59.8
Other marital status	93	89	131	140	151	158	183	34.7	32.2	51.2	58.8
Employed	252	256	277	311	313	348	362	32.3	37.9	53.5	63.7
Full-time	194	195	219	259	244	282	292	34.4	39.0	56.7	64.7
Part-time	58	61	58	52	69	66	70	26.8	34.8	44.7	59.7
With mother not in labor force	236	298	277	279	330	312	269	26.9	33.9	44.1	42.1

X Not applicable.   [1] Includes children with mothers whose labor force status is unknown and children with no mother present in household, not shown separately.   [2] Includes races not shown separately. [3] Includes children with mothers who are unemployed, not shown separately.

Source: U.S. Bureau of the Census, *Current Population Reports*, series P-20, No. 318; and unpublished data.

No. 224. School Enrollment of Persons 5 to 17 Years Old, by Race and Residence: 1960 to 1977

[In millions. As of October. Beginning 1970, includes nursery schools. For definition of standard metropolitan statistical area (SMSA), see Appendix II. 1960 to 1970 data refer to 212 SMSA's as defined in 1960 census reports; later data refer to 243 SMSA's as defined in 1970 census reports]

RESIDENCE	WHITE						BLACK AND OTHER					
	1960	1965	1970	1975	1976	1977	1960	1965	1970	1975	1976	1977
Total	36.8	40.9	43.2	40.7	40.1	39.2	5.5	6.6	7.5	7.7	7.7	7.8
Inside SMSA's	22.3	26.3	26.8	27.1	26.3	25.5	3.4	4.3	5.2	5.9	5.9	5.6
Inside central cities	9.6	9.8	9.2	9.4	8.8	8.1	2.6	3.4	3.9	4.3	4.3	4.0
Outside central cities	12.6	16.5	17.6	17.8	17.5	17.4	.8	.9	1.2	1.6	1.6	1.6
Outside SMSA's	14.5	14.6	16.4	13.6	13.8	13.7	2.2	2.2	2.3	1.8	1.8	2.1

Source: U.S. Bureau of the Census, *Current Population Reports*, series P-20, Nos. 110, 162, 222, 303, and 319; and unpublished data.

No. 225. Years of School Completed, by Age and Race: 1940 to 1977

[Through 1960, as of **April 1.** 1940 based on complete count; 1950, on 20-percent sample; and 1960, on 25-percent sample. Beginning **1970,** as of **March,** based on Current Population Survey; see text, p. 1. Includes members of Armed Forces living off post or with families on post, but excludes all other members of Armed Forces. Beginning 1975, excludes inmates of institutions. For definition of median, see p. xii]

	ALL PERSONS					BLACK PERSONS				
	Percent—				Median school years completed	Percent—				Median school years completed
AGE AND YEAR	Not high school graduates		With 4 years of high school or more			Not high school graduates		With 4 years of high school or more		
	Total	With less than 5 years of school	Total	College, 4 years or more		Total	With less than 5 years of school	Total	College, 4 years or more	
25 years and over:										
1940	75.5	13.7	24.5	4.6	8.6	92.7	42.0	7.3	1.3	5.7
1950	65.7	11.1	34.3	6.2	9.3	87.1	32.9	12.9	2.1	6.8
1960	58.9	8.3	41.1	7.7	10.6	79.9	23.8	20.1	3.1	8.0
1970	44.8	5.3	55.2	11.0	12.2	66.3	15.1	33.7	4.5	9.9
1975	37.5	4.2	62.5	13.9	12.3	57.5	12.3	42.5	6.4	10.9
1976	35.9	3.9	64.1	14.7	12.4	56.2	11.3	43.8	6.6	11.1
1977	35.1	3.7	64.9	15.4	12.4	54.5	9.8	45.5	7.2	11.4
25–29 years:										
1940	61.9	5.9	38.1	5.9	10.3	(NA)	27.7	11.6	1.6	7.0
1950	49.5	4.7	52.8	7.7	12.0	80.4	16.8	22.2	2.7	8.6
1960	39.3	2.8	60.7	11.1	12.3	62.3	7.0	37.7	4.8	9.9
1970	24.6	1.1	75.4	16.4	12.6	43.9	2.5	56.2	7.3	12.2
1975	16.9	1.0	83.1	21.9	12.8	29.0	.5	71.0	10.7	12.5
1976	15.3	.8	84.7	23.7	12.9	26.1	.9	73.8	13.0	12.5
1977	14.6	.8	85.4	24.0	12.9	25.6	.8	74.4	12.6	12.6

NA Not available.

No. 226. Years of School Completed, by Race and Sex: 1960 to 1977

[Persons 25 years old and over. See headnote, table 225. For definition of median, see p. xii. See also *Historical Statistics, Colonial Times to 1970,* series H 602–617]

YEAR, RACE, AND SEX	Persons 25 years old and over (1,000)	PERCENT OF POPULATION COMPLETING—							Median school years completed
		Elementary school			High school		College		
		0–4 years	5–7 years	8 years	1–3 years	4 years	1–3 years	4 years or more	
1960, all races	99,438	8.3	13.8	17.5	19.2	24.6	8.8	7.7	10.6
White	89,581	6.7	12.8	18.1	19.3	25.8	9.3	8.1	10.9
Male	43,259	7.4	13.7	18.7	18.9	22.2	9.1	10.3	10.7
Female	46,322	6.0	11.9	17.8	19.6	29.2	9.5	6.0	11.2
Black	9,054	23.8	24.2	12.9	19.0	12.9	4.1	3.1	8.0
Male	4,240	28.3	23.9	12.3	17.3	11.3	4.1	2.8	7.7
Female	4,814	19.8	24.5	13.4	20.5	14.3	4.1	3.3	8.6
1970, all races	109,310	5.3	9.1	13.4	17.1	34.0	10.2	11.0	12.2
White	98,112	4.2	8.3	13.6	16.5	35.2	10.7	11.6	12.2
Male	46,606	4.5	8.8	13.9	15.6	30.9	11.3	15.0	12.2
Female	51,506	3.9	7.8	13.4	17.3	39.0	10.1	8.6	12.2
Black	10,089	15.1	16.7	11.2	23.3	23.4	5.9	4.5	9.9
Male	4,619	18.6	16.0	11.1	21.9	22.2	5.7	4.6	9.6
Female	5,470	12.1	17.3	11.3	24.5	24.4	6.0	4.4	10.2
1975, all races	116,897	4.2	7.4	10.3	15.6	36.2	12.4	13.9	12.3
White	104,065	3.3	6.6	10.6	15.0	37.3	12.8	14.5	12.4
Male	49,259	3.6	6.8	10.5	14.0	33.1	13.6	18.4	12.5
Female	54,806	3.0	6.4	10.6	15.9	41.1	12.1	11.0	12.3
Black	11,096	12.3	14.3	8.5	22.3	27.1	9.0	6.4	10.9
Male	4,925	15.3	14.7	8.1	20.2	25.2	9.7	6.7	10.7
Female	6,171	9.8	14.0	8.9	24.0	28.6	8.5	6.2	11.1
1977, all races	120,870	3.7	6.9	9.3	15.2	36.1	13.4	15.4	12.4
White	107,216	3.0	6.2	9.4	14.4	37.0	13.8	16.1	12.5
Male	50,782	3.1	6.3	9.6	13.5	32.7	14.6	20.2	12.5
Female	56,434	2.8	6.1	9.3	15.3	40.9	13.2	12.4	12.4
Black	11,698	9.8	13.5	8.6	22.6	28.4	9.8	7.2	11.4
Male	5,205	12.0	14.1	8.3	20.1	27.6	11.0	7.0	11.3
Female	6,493	8.0	13.1	8.8	24.7	29.1	8.9	7.4	11.4

Source of tables 225 and 226: U.S. Bureau of the Census, *U.S. Census of Population: 1940, 1950,* and *1960,* vol. I, and *Current Population Reports,* series P-20, Nos. 207, 295, and 314.

No. 227. Years of School Completed, by Race, Sex, and Age: 1977

[Persons 25 years old and over as of **March** 1977. See headnote, table 225. For definition of median, see p. xii]

RACE, SEX, AND AGE	Population (1,000)	PERCENT OF POPULATION COMPLETING—							Median school years completed
		Elementary school			High school		College		
		0–4 years	5–7 years	8 years	1–3 years	4 years	1–3 years	4 years or more	
All races_____	120,870	3.7	6.9	9.3	15.2	36.1	13.4	15.4	12.4
Male_____	56,917	4.0	7.0	9.4	14.0	32.1	14.2	19.2	12.5
Female_____	63,953	3.5	6.8	9.2	16.2	39.6	12.7	12.0	12.4
25–29 years_____	17,460	.8	1.7	1.8	10.3	39.9	21.5	24.0	12.9
30–34 years_____	14,824	.8	2.5	2.7	12.9	39.6	17.9	23.5	12.8
35–44 years_____	23,108	1.9	4.0	4.8	15.7	41.9	14.2	17.5	12.6
45–54 years_____	23,301	3.3	6.3	8.3	17.8	39.0	11.8	13.5	12.4
55 years and over_____	42,176	7.2	12.5	17.7	16.2	28.4	9.1	8.9	11.8
Black_____	11,698	9.8	13.5	8.6	22.6	28.4	9.8	7.2	11.4
25–29 years_____	1,899	.8	3.4	2.5	18.9	43.3	18.4	12.6	12.6
30–34 years_____	1,501	1.0	3.5	1.5	26.7	41.6	15.7	10.0	12.4
35–44 years_____	2,461	2.4	7.9	6.0	28.0	36.1	10.7	8.9	12.2
45–54 years_____	2,256	8.7	15.4	12.2	28.2	23.2	6.9	5.4	10.5
55 years and over_____	3,583	24.1	25.7	14.3	15.7	13.0	4.0	3.2	8.0

Source: U.S. Bureau of the Census, *Current Population Reports*, series P-20, No. 314.

No. 228. Percent of Population With Less Than 5 Years of School and With 4 Years of High School or More, by Age, Race, and Spanish Origin: 1970 and 1977

[Persons 25 years old and over as of **March** 1970 and **March** 1977. All races include those not shown separately]

RACE	LESS THAN 5 YEARS OF SCHOOL					4 YEARS OF HIGH SCHOOL OR MORE				
	1970	1977				1970	1977			
		Total	25–34 years	35–64 years	65 years and over		Total	25–34 years	35–64 years	65 years and over
All races_____	5.3	3.7	.8	3.1	9.8	55.2	64.9	83.4	65.1	37.5
White_____	4.2	3.0	.8	2.5	7.6	57.4	67.0	84.9	67.8	39.7
Black_____	15.1	9.8	.9	8.1	32.1	33.7	45.5	71.2	40.6	14.7
Spanish origin [1]_____	19.5	18.0	7.4	19.3	49.5	32.1	39.6	53.9	34.8	16.2
Mexican_____	28.5	23.3	9.6	25.7	65.4	24.2	33.6	50.0	27.1	5.6
Puerto Rican_____	20.5	18.8	5.7	22.2	(B)	23.4	30.6	42.7	24.9	(B)
Cuban_____	8.2	10.6	(B)	9.6	20.6	43.9	48.5	(B)	45.7	38.0
Other Spanish [2]_____	8.8	7.0	3.5	5.7	25.0	44.9	57.9	69.4	55.5	29.0

B Not shown; base less than 75,000.   [1] Persons of Spanish origin may be of any race.
[2] Includes persons of Central or South American or other Spanish origin.
Source: U.S. Bureau of the Census, *Current Population Reports*, series P–20, Nos. 207, 314, and 317; and unpublished data.

No. 229. Lifetime and Mean Income of Males, by Years of School Completed: 1972

[Figures for lifetime income based on application of appropriate life tables to arithmetic mean income, by age, as obtained for a cross section of the population. See also *Historical Statistics, Colonial Times to 1970*, series H 648–661]

YEARS OF SCHOOL COMPLETED	LIFETIME INCOME ($1,000)				ANNUAL MEAN INCOME ($1,000)			
	From age 18 to death	From age 25 to death	From age 18 to 64	From age 25 to 64	18 yr. old and over	25 yr. old and over	18–64 yr. old	25–64 yr. old
Less than 8 years_____	280	260	251	231	5.2	5.2	6.2	6.4
8 years_____	344	323	305	284	6.6	6.8	7.7	7.9
High school, 1–3 years_____	389	371	343	324	7.5	8.4	7.7	9.0
High school, 4 years_____	479	452	421	393	9.2	10.4	9.4	10.7
College, 1–3 years_____	543	525	480	461	9.2	11.9	9.3	12.2
College, 4 yr. or more_____	758	731	655	627	15.2	16.2	15.5	16.6

Source: U.S. Bureau of the Census, *Current Population Reports*, series P–60, No. 92.

No. 230. Illiteracy—Age, Sex, and Race: 1959 and 1969

[Persons 14 years old and over. Relates to civilian noninstitutional population. 1959 excludes Alaska and Hawaii. Based on Current Population Survey; see text, p. 1. Persons unable to both read and write in any language classified as illiterate. Information on illiteracy was obtained only for persons completing less than 6 years of school. See also *Historical Statistics, Colonial Times to 1970*, series H 669–688]

AGE AND SEX	1959 (March)					1969 (November)				
	Population (1,000)		Percent illiterate			Population (1,000)		Percent illiterate		
	Total	Illit- erate	Total	White	Black	Total	Illit- erate	Total	White	Black
Total, 14 and over_____	121,373	2,619	2.2	1.6	7.5	143,137	1,433	1.0	.7	3.6
14–24 years_____	25,118	144	.6	.5	1.2	36,853	97	.3	.2	.5
25–44 years_____	46,143	575	1.2	.8	5.1	46,501	237	.5	.4	1.3
45–64 years_____	35,205	929	2.6	1.8	11.3	40,985	449	1.1	.7	5.5
65 years and over_____	14,907	971	6.5	5.1	25.5	18,798	650	3.5	2.3	16.7
Male, 14 and over_____	58,378	1,480	2.5	1.7	9.8	67,306	708	1.1	.7	4.3
14–24 years_____	12,063	100	.8	.7	1.7	17,484	61	.3	.3	.6
25–44 years_____	22,486	363	1.6	1.0	7.1	22,272	118	.5	.4	2.1
45–64 years_____	17,059	548	3.2	2.0	15.6	19,513	257	1.3	.8	7.4
65 years and over_____	6,770	469	6.9	5.3	28.3	8,037	272	3.4	2.1	17.2
Female, 14 and over_____	62,995	1,139	1.8	1.4	5.4	75,831	727	1.0	.7	2.9
14–24 years_____	13,055	44	.3	.3	.7	19,369	37	.2	.2	.3
25–44 years_____	23,657	212	.9	.6	3.4	24,229	121	.5	.5	.6
45–64 years_____	18,146	381	2.1	1.6	7.3	21,472	191	.9	.6	4.0
65 years and over_____	8,137	502	6.2	5.0	23.0	10,761	378	3.5	2.4	16.2

Source: U.S. Bureau of the Census, *Current Population Reports*, series P-20, Nos. 99 and 217.

No. 231. Percent Illiterate of Population—States: 1900 to 1970

[Relates to population 15 years old and over for 1900 to 1930 and 14 years old and over for 1950 to 1970. Beginning 1950, data are estimated. Persons unable to both read and write in any language classified as illiterate. See *Current Population Reports*, series P-23, No. 8, for method of estimating illiteracy by States]

STATE	1900	1920	1930	1950	1960	1970	STATE	1900	1920	1930	1950	1960	1970
United States___	11.3	6.5	4.8	3.3	2.4	1.2	So. Atl.—Con.						
							Virginia_____	24.3	12.2	9.7	4.9	3.4	1.4
New England:					·		West Virginia___	12.6	7.2	5.5	3.5	2.7	1.4
Maine_____	5.5	3.6	3.0	2.0	1.3	.7	No. Carolina____	30.1	15.0	11.5	5.5	4.0	1.8
New Hampshire__	6.7	4.9	3.0	2.0	1.4	.7	So. Carolina_____	37.4	20.9	16.7	7.9	5.5	2.3
Vermont_____	6.4	3.3	2.4	1.7	1.1	.6	Georgia_____	32.1	16.7	10.4	6.9	4.5	2.0
Massachusetts___	6.5	5.3	4.0	2.8	2.2	1.1	Florida_____	23.4	10.2	7.7	3.9	2.6	1.3
Rhode Island____	9.2	7.2	5.5	3.1	2.4	1.3							
Connecticut_____	6.5	6.9	5.1	3.1	2.2	1.1	East So. Central:						
							Kentucky_____	18.1	9.4	7.3	4.3	3.3	1.6
Middle Atlantic:							Tennessee_____	21.9	11.3	8.0	4.7	3.5	1.7
New York_____	6.1	5.6	4.1	3.5	2.9	1.4	Alabama_____	35.1	17.8	14.0	6.2	4.2	2.1
New Jersey_____	6.5	5.8	4.3	2.9	2.2	1.1	Mississippi_____	34.1	18.8	14.8	7.1	4.9	2.4
Pennsylvania____	6.9	5.7	3.5	2.7	2.0	1.0							
							West So. Central:						
East No. Central:							Arkansas_____	21.3	10.2	7.6	5.0	3.6	1.9
Ohio_____	4.5	3.2	2.5	1.9	1.5	.8	Louisiana_____	39.6	23.4	15.1	9.8	6.3	2.8
Indiana_____	5.2	2.5	1.8	1.7	1.2	.7	Oklahoma_____	11.7	4.1	3.1	2.5	1.9	1.1
Illinois_____	4.8	3.8	2.7	2.3	1.8	.9	Texas_____	15.6	8.9	7.3	5.4	4.1	2.2
Michigan_____	4.8	3.4	2.2	2.0	1.6	.9							
Wisconsin_____	5.4	2.8	2.1	1.7	1.2	.7	Mountain:						
							Montana_____	6.6	2.5	1.9	1.8	1.0	.6
West No. Central:							Idaho_____	5.1	1.7	1.2	1.3	.8	.6
Minnesota_____	4.6	2.1	1.4	1.5	1.0	.6	Wyoming_____	4.4	2.3	1.8	1.7	.9	.6
Iowa_____	2.7	1.2	.9	.9	.7	.5	Colorado_____	4.5	3.6	3.1	2.0	1.3	.7
Missouri_____	7.0	3.4	2.5	2.1	1.7	.8	New Mexico____	35.7	17.4	14.9	6.6	4.0	2.2
North Dakota____	6.1	2.5	1.7	2.3	1.4	.8	Arizona_____	30.0	15.9	11.0	6.2	3.8	1.8
South Dakota____	5.8	1.9	1.4	1.5	.9	.5	Utah_____	3.6	2.2	1.4	1.4	.9	.6
Nebraska_____	2.6	1.5	1.3	1.2	.9	.6	Nevada_____	13.8	6.4	4.8	2.2	1.1	.5
Kansas_____	3.3	1.8	1.4	1.3	.9	.6							
							Pacific:						
South Atlantic:							Washington_____	3.4	1.9	1.1	1.3	.9	.6
Delaware_____	13.2	6.6	4.4	2.7	1.9	.9	Oregon_____	3.7	1.6	1.1	1.2	.8	.6
Maryland_____	12.1	6.1	4.2	2.7	1.9	.9	California_____	5.3	3.6	2.8	2.2	1.8	1.1
District of Columbia_____	9.4	3.0	1.7	1.8	1.9	1.1	Alaska_____	40.6	24.6	20.5	6.3	3.0	1.5
							Hawaii_____	35.2	21.2	17.5	8.4	5.0	1.9

Source: U.S. Bureau of the Census, unpublished data.

No. 232. Years of School Completed, by States: 1976

[In thousands of persons 18 years old and over, except as indicated. See source for sampling variability. For definition of median, see p. xii]

STATE OR OTHER AREA	Persons 18 years old and over	YEARS OF SCHOOL COMPLETED						Median school years completed	PERCENT HIGH SCHOOL GRADUATES				
		Elementary school		High school		College			Total	18-24 years		25 years and over	
		0-4 years	5-8 years	1-3 years	4 years	1-3 years	4 yr. or more			Male	Female	Male	Female
U.S.	146,349	4,928	20,621	23,337	52,696	24,382	20,385	12.5	66.6	78.2	79.7	64.1	63.5
N.E.	8,461	184	1,075	1,251	3,076	1,469	1,406	12.6	70.3	81.3	81.6	68.1	67.7
Maine	727	9	104	122	282	112	99	12.5	67.8	80.7	79.0	64.1	65.9
N.H.	562	6	76	84	204	105	86	12.6	70.3	73.3	82.0	67.9	69.6
Vt.	320	3	50	43	117	56	50	12.5	69.7	83.0	83.3	64.6	69.6
Mass.	4,046	98	453	571	1,505	739	680	12.6	72.3	84.3	80.6	70.1	69.7
R.I.	645	22	106	118	212	90	96	12.4	61.7	75.3	78.2	61.4	56.1
Conn.	2,162	46	285	312	757	367	395	12.6	70.3	78.8	85.0	68.3	67.3
M.A.	26,004	704	3,789	4,401	9,558	3,786	3,767	12.4	65.8	81.4	81.3	63.1	62.0
N.Y.	12,713	380	1,746	2,166	4,328	2,062	2,030	12.5	66.2	81.3	78.5	64.4	62.6
N.J.	5,040	138	716	840	1,854	741	752	12.4	66.4	78.9	81.3	64.1	62.9
Pa.	8,250	186	1,326	1,395	3,376	983	985	12.4	64.8	83.0	85.3	60.5	60.5
E.N.C.	27,685	545	3,782	4,619	11,010	4,290	3,439	12.4	67.7	79.7	81.1	64.3	65.1
Ohio	7,261	123	960	1,263	3,120	961	834	12.4	67.7	79.9	80.1	64.0	65.7
Ind.	3,571	68	492	618	1,505	494	394	12.4	67.0	81.4	80.4	64.4	63.2
Ill.	7,566	199	1,147	1,216	2,651	1,316	1,037	12.5	66.1	78.5	80.3	63.9	62.4
Mich.	6,159	111	711	1,109	2,436	1,016	776	12.5	68.6	79.6	82.3	63.7	67.3
Wis.	3,129	44	473	413	1,299	502	398	12.5	70.3	80.6	83.6	66.5	58.3
W.N.C.	11,382	168	1,811	1,445	4,567	1,919	1,471	12.5	69.9	82.9	84.7	65.7	67.5
Minn.	2,637	30	386	311	1,104	456	350	12.5	72.4	82.6	87.6	67.6	70.9
Iowa	1,942	18	287	233	838	318	248	12.5	72.3	84.9	84.8	67.6	71.1
Mo.	3,314	82	616	493	1,258	474	391	12.4	64.1	77.2	77.4	61.7	60.8
N. Dak.	417	7	86	43	143	88	51	12.5	67.6	85.7	89.0	57.7	66.4
S. Dak.	457	5	90	47	171	92	52	12.5	68.9	87.1	90.1	60.3	67.8
Nebr.	1,046	10	141	118	420	207	150	12.6	74.3	87.0	90.0	70.1	71.7
Kans.	1,569	16	206	199	633	285	229	12.6	73.1	87.5	86.9	69.6	69.8
S.A.	23,484	1,163	3,742	4,077	7,649	3,589	3,263	12.4	61.7	72.4	76.0	59.6	58.6
Del.	394	7	46	66	143	70	61	12.5	69.5	78.7	82.8	67.0	66.9
Md.	2,776	59	356	436	976	433	516	12.6	69.3	77.2	79.0	68.4	66.4
D.C.	504	18	69	86	138	79	114	12.6	65.7	69.4	77.6	62.5	64.7
Va.	3,429	157	490	579	1,089	551	563	12.4	64.2	68.0	79.1	62.4	61.9
W. Va.	1,271	63	315	215	418	143	117	12.1	53.3	72.7	72.7	49.3	49.8
N.C.	3,748	240	705	732	1,099	528	444	12.2	55.3	66.8	73.7	50.2	53.4
S.C.	1,871	129	310	363	606	267	195	12.2	57.1	69.5	74.6	53.7	53.0
Ga.	3,319	264	534	573	1,074	466	409	12.3	58.7	76.0	71.5	57.3	53.7
Fla.	6,171	226	917	1,028	2,104	1,052	844	12.4	64.8	75.3	77.0	63.9	61.6
E.S.C.	9,198	607	1,900	1,701	2,854	1,172	964	12.1	54.3	67.2	71.6	50.6	51.3
Ky.	2,307	132	548	397	728	270	231	12.1	53.3	72.1	69.1	49.1	49.9
Tenn.	2,921	187	621	508	906	392	307	12.2	54.9	70.0	73.7	51.8	50.7
Ala.	2,442	167	431	489	802	303	251	12.2	55.5	60.8	73.2	52.9	50.5
Miss.	1,527	121	300	307	417	207	175	12.1	52.3	64.0	68.7	47.2	50.6
W.S.C.	14,099	852	2,044	2,364	4,783	2,287	1,768	12.4	62.7	74.7	76.3	61.1	57.9
Ark.	1,473	88	280	277	519	175	134	12.2	56.2	69.0	73.0	54.1	52.5
La.	2,459	214	418	395	806	344	283	12.3	58.3	72.9	76.1	55.0	53.0
Okla.	1,875	54	291	300	686	324	220	12.4	65.6	82.5	82.6	62.5	61.0
Tex.	8,292	497	1,055	1,393	2,771	1,444	1,132	12.4	64.5	74.5	75.6	63.8	59.7
Mt.	6,490	143	630	892	2,374	1,389	1,061	12.7	74.3	81.2	81.9	72.9	72.1
Mont.	506	6	66	67	195	100	72	12.6	72.5	83.1	84.5	67.5	71.8
Idaho	547	8	61	87	204	113	74	12.6	71.5	82.1	80.6	68.6	69.2
Wyo.	255	3	25	36	101	54	37	12.6	75.3	85.1	84.6	71.5	73.7
Colo.	1,735	23	150	208	638	381	336	12.8	78.1	82.2	83.8	77.0	76.5
N. Mex.	750	43	98	116	250	128	115	12.5	65.7	75.2	75.0	63.8	63.0
Ariz.	1,528	51	154	214	534	334	240	12.5	72.5	79.0	80.0	72.0	69.7
Utah	758	5	42	103	285	190	133	12.8	80.2	85.4	85.6	79.8	77.7
Nev.	411	5	34	61	167	90	54	12.6	75.7	80.9	82.4	75.6	73.0
Pac.	19,547	561	1,848	2,587	6,825	4,483	3,243	12.7	74.4	81.4	81.5	73.3	82.4
Wash.	2,417	25	228	320	944	512	388	12.7	76.3	82.0	84.0	73.8	75.6
Oreg.	1,607	17	160	215	616	350	248	12.7	75.5	85.1	83.2	72.4	74.6
Calif.	14,741	482	1,385	1,966	4,984	3,450	2,474	12.7	74.0	80.4	80.6	73.4	81.8
Alaska	216	6	14	24	86	48	38	12.7	79.6	81.4	83.6	79.4	88.1
Hawaii	566	31	61	61	196	122	95	12.7	73.0	90.4	86.0	70.7	66.5

Source: U.S. Bureau of the Census, unpublished data.

No. 233. Years of High School Completed, by Major Group of Employed Persons, by Sex and Race: 1970 and 1977

[Relates to civilian noninstitutional population 18 years old and over in 1970, and 16 years old and over in 1977. As of **March**. Service includes private household workers. Based on Current Population Survey; see text, p. 1]

SEX, RACE, AND YEARS OF HIGH SCHOOL COMPLETED	1970					1977				
	Total (mil.)	White collar	Blue collar	Service	Farm	Total (mil.)	White collar	Blue collar	Service	Farm
Male, White:										
Less than 4 years	14.7	18.5	64.8	7.5	9.1	12.2	16.1	64.1	12.3	7.5
4 years or more	27.7	58.0	34.6	4.6	2.9	34.8	53.3	37.3	6.6	2.8
Male, Black and other:										
Less than 4 years	2.6	8.8	71.6	12.6	7.0	[1] 1.9	6.5	66.6	20.6	6.3
4 years or more	2.0	42.1	47.3	9.2	1.4	[1] 2.4	34.0	47.6	17.2	1.1
Female, White:										
Less than 4 years	6.9	30.3	35.6	31.0	3.2	6.9	31.6	30.0	36.5	1.8
4 years or more	18.1	77.9	9.0	12.3	.8	24.7	75.3	9.2	14.7	.7
Female, Black and other:										
Less than 4 years	1.7	10.3	21.5	67.0	1.2	[1] 1.4	12.6	25.9	60.5	1.1
4 years or more	1.9	56.8	15.8	27.3	.2	[1] 2.4	61.6	14.5	23.5	.3

[1] Data are for Black only.

Source: U.S. Bureau of Labor Statistics, *Special Labor Force Report*, No. 125, and forthcoming report.

No. 234. High School Graduates Not Enrolled in College, and School Dropouts, 16 to 21 Years Old—Employment Status, by Sex and Race: 1965 to 1977

[In thousands, except percent. As of October. Data for high school graduates relate to those not enrolled in college and include those who attended college prior to survey date; data for dropouts relate to persons not in regular school and not high school graduates. Based on samples and subject to sampling variability]

EMPLOYMENT STATUS, SEX, AND RACE	GRADUATES					DROPOUTS				
	1965	1970	1975 [1]	1976 [1]	1977 [1]	1965	1970	1975 [1]	1976 [1]	1977 [1]
Civilian population [2]	4,898	5,823	7,179	7,271	7,440	2,986	2,757	3,271	3,323	3,326
Not in labor force	1,129	1,257	1,235	1,181	1,078	1,123	1,146	1,276	1,191	1,154
In labor force	3,769	4,566	5,944	6,090	6,362	1,863	1,611	1,996	2,132	2,172
Percent of population	76.9	78.4	82.8	83.8	85.5	62.4	58.4	61.0	64.2	65.3
Employed	3,451	4,038	5,055	5,328	5,608	1,585	1,264	1,426	1,547	1,675
Percent of labor force	91.6	88.4	85.0	87.5	88.1	85.1	78.5	71.4	72.6	77.1
Male	1,512	1,730	2,542	2,700	2,764	1,105	805	952	1,040	1,159
Female	1,939	2,308	2,513	2,628	2,844	480	459	474	507	516
White	3,116	3,636	4,616	4,863	5,104	1,266	1,011	1,200	1,345	1,491
Black and other	335	402	441	466	[3] 432	319	253	227	200	[3] 169
Unemployed	318	528	889	762	754	278	347	570	585	497
Percent of labor force	8.4	11.6	15.0	12.5	11.9	14.9	21.5	28.6	27.4	22.9
Male	105	236	446	360	326	160	219	330	339	290
Female	213	292	443	402	428	118	128	240	246	207
White	259	429	712	582	557	203	232	414	455	344
Black and other	59	99	178	180	[3] 192	75	115	157	130	[3] 145

[1] Based on population estimates consistent with 1970 census and not strictly comparable with 1965 and 1970 data, which are based on 1960 population.   [2] Noninstitutional.   [3] Data are for Black only.

Source: U.S. Bureau of Labor Statistics, *Special Labor Force Report*, Nos. 66, 131, 191, and 208; and forthcoming report.

No. 235. High School Dropouts 14 to 24 Years Old, by Race and Age: 1967 to 1977

[As of **October**. See headnote, table 234. Total dropouts include races not shown separately]

RACE AND AGE	NUMBER OF DROPOUTS (1,000)						PERCENT OF POPULATION					
	1967	1970	1974	1975	1976	1977	1967	1970	1974	1975	1976	1977
Total dropouts	4,716	4,670	5,019	4,974	5,129	5,148	13.6	12.2	11.8	11.5	11.8	11.7
14–17 years	749	762	949	864	853	835	5.1	4.8	5.7	5.2	5.1	5.0
18–21 years	2,205	2,138	2,487	2,557	2,618	2,607	18.1	16.4	16.3	16.3	16.4	16.2
22–24 years	1,762	1,770	1,583	1,553	1,658	1,706	22.5	18.7	15.3	14.5	15.1	15.2
White	3,734	3,577	3,998	3,861	4,128	4,161	12.4	10.8	11.0	10.5	11.1	11.1
14–17 years	593	603	786	712	721	716	4.7	4.5	5.5	5.0	5.1	5.1
18–21 years	1,762	1,618	1,969	1,980	2,115	2,094	16.6	14.3	15.0	14.7	15.5	15.2
22–24 years	1,379	1,356	1,243	1,169	1,292	1,351	20.0	16.3	13.8	12.6	13.6	14.0
Black	940	1,047	930	1,024	924	911	22.8	22.2	17.3	18.5	16.4	15.9
14–17 years	152	150	150	147	121	103	8.3	7.4	6.6	6.3	5.2	4.4
18–21 years	427	500	468	540	479	481	29.9	30.5	24.7	27.0	23.2	23.2
22–24 years	361	397	312	337	324	327	42.3	37.8	25.8	27.8	25.9	24.9

Source: U.S. Bureau of the Census, *Current Population Reports*, series P–20, Nos. 190, 222, 286, 303, 319, and 321.

No. 236.   Public Elementary and Secondary Schools—Summary: 1940 to 1976

[Revenue and expenditure data for years ending **June 30**. Prior to 1960, excludes Alaska and Hawaii. See also *Historical Statistics, Colonial Times to 1970*, series H 420, H 487–507, and H 520–530]

ITEM	1940	1950	1960	1968	1970	1972	1974	1976
ENROLLMENT (day schools only)								
Total population [1]_____mil__	130.9	148.7	179.3	197.5	203.2	206.2	209.9	213.1
Population 5–17 years [1]_____mil__	30.2	30.2	43.9	51.4	52.5	52.3	51.5	50.4
Percent of total population_____	23.0	20.3	24.5	26.0	25.8	25.4	24.5	23.6
Pupils enrolled_____mil__	25.4	25.1	36.1	[2] 43.9	[2] 45.6	[2] 46.1	[2] 45.4	[2] 44.8
Percent of total population_____	19.4	16.9	20.1	22.2	22.4	22.3	21.6	21.0
Percent of population 5–17 years_____	84.4	83.2	82.2	85.5	86.9	88.1	88.2	88.9
Average daily attendance_____mil__	22.0	22.3	32.5	40.8	41.9	42.3	41.4	[3] 41.3
Percent of pupils enrolled_____	86.7	88.7	90.0	93.0	91.9	91.7	91.2	[3] 92.2
Average length of term in days_____	175.0	177.9	178.0	178.8	178.9	179.3	178.7	(NA)
Average number of days attended per enrolled pupil_____	151.7	157.9	160.2	163.2	161.7	161.7	159.5	(NA)
INSTRUCTIONAL STAFF (day schools only)								
Total_____1,000__	912	962	1,464	2,071	2,253	2,322	2,425	(NA)
Classroom teachers [4]_____1,000__	875	914	1,387	1,957	2,131	2,187	2,287	(NA)
Male [5]_____1,000__	195	195	402	616	691	737	766	(NA)
Percent [5]_____	22.2	21.3	29.0	31.5	32.4	33.7	33.5	(NA)
Female [5]_____1,000__	681	719	985	1,341	1,440	1,450	1,521	(NA)
Principals_____1,000__	32	39	64	86	91	97	100	(NA)
Supervisors_____1,000__	5	9	14	29	32	37	38	(NA)
REVENUES								
Total_____mil. dol__	2,261	5,437	14,747	31,903	40,267	50,004	58,231	[3] 70,803
Federal_____mil. dol__	40	156	652	2,806	3,220	4,468	4,930	[3] 6,210
State_____mil. dol__	684	2,166	5,768	12,276	16,063	19,133	24,113	[3] 31,065
Local (incl. intermediate)_____mil. dol__	1,537	3,116	8,327	16,821	20,985	26,402	29,187	[3] 33,527
EXPENDITURES								
Total_____mil. dol__	2,344	5,838	15,613	32,977	40,683	48,050	56,970	[3] 70,829
Current expenditure for day schools [6]_____mil. dol__	1,942	4,687	12,329	26,877	34,218	41,818	50,025	[3] 62,263
Other current expenditure [7]_____mil. dol__	13	36	133	866	636	[8] 395	[8] 453	[3] 751
Capital outlay [9]_____mil. dol__	258	1,014	2,662	4,256	4,659	4,459	4,979	[3] 5,920
Interest_____mil. dol__	131	101	490	978	1,171	1,378	1,514	[3] 1,896
In current dollars:								
Total expenditure:								
Per capita of total population___dol__	18	39	87	167	200	233	271	332
Per pupil in average daily attendance in day schools [10]_____	106	259	472	786	955	1,128	1,364	1,699
Current expenditure per pupil in average daily attendance in day schools [11]_dol__	88	209	375	658	816	990	1,207	1,509
Salaries of total instructional staff_____mil. dol__	1,314	2,896	7,671	16,373	20,879	(NA)	(NA)	(NA)
Average annual salary per member_____dol__	1,441	3,010	5,174	7,630	8,840	10,100	11,185	[12] 12,070
In 1976 dollars:								
Total expenditure:								
Per capita of total population___dol__	71	91	164	272	294	314	322	332
Per pupil in average daily attendance in day schools [10]_____dol__	421	607	891	1,282	1,403	1,521	1,622	1,699
Current expenditure per pupil in average daily attendance in day schools [11]_dol__	349	490	708	1,073	1,198	1,335	1,435	1,509
Average annual salary per member of total instructional staff_____dol__	5,719	7,050	9,768	12,441	12,983	13,615	13,302	[12] 12,927

NA   Not available.   [1] For 1960 and 1970, enumerated population as of Apr. 1; for all other years, estimated population as of July 1 of preceding year (1939, 1949, etc.). Excludes Armed Forces abroad.
[2] As of fall of preceding year.   [3] Preliminary.
[4] Includes librarians and other nonsupervisory instructional staff.   [5] Beginning 1960, estimated.
[6] Through 1950, includes community services; therefore, not comparable with later years.
[7] Comprises summer schools, community colleges, adult education, and, beginning 1960, community services.
[8] Excludes adult education and community colleges.
[9] Through 1960, excludes capital outlay by State and local schoolhousing authorities.
[10] Based on current expenditures allocable to pupil costs, capital outlay, and interest.
[11] Excludes current expenditures not allocable to pupil costs.   [12] 1975 data.

Source: U.S. National Center for Education Statistics, *Statistics of State School Systems*, biennial; and unpublished data.

No. 237. PUBLIC ELEMENTARY AND SECONDARY SCHOOLS—ENROLLMENT, 1970 TO 1977, ATTENDANCE, 1977, AND LENGTH OF TERM, 1974, STATES AND OTHER AREAS

[In thousands, except as indicated. Enrollment as of fall of preceding year. Elementary refers to kindergarten through grade 8; secondary, to grades 9 through 12 and postgraduates]

STATE OR OTHER AREA	ENROLLMENT						ENROLLMENT AS PER-CENT OF PERSONS, 5–17 YEARS [1]			Average daily attend-ance, 1977	Average length of school year (days), 1974
	1970		1976		1977		1970	1976	1977		
	Ele-men-tary	Sec-ond-ary	Ele-men-tary	Sec-ond-ary	Ele-men-tary	Sec-ond-ary					
U.S	32,597	13,022	30,545	14,294	[2] 30,012	[2] 14,323	86.9	89.0	[2] 88.9	40,835	178.7
N. Eng	1,794	671	1,749	807	915	421	83.2	89.2	(NA)	2,300	179.0
Maine	175	65	172	79	171	78	92.7	98.0	97.3	225	169.0
N.H	109	43	120	54	120	55	80.4	88.8	88.8	161	177.2
Vt	73	27	73	31	73	32	85.5	89.7	91.3	100	176.0
Mass	828	319	813	385	(NA)	(NA) [*]	81.7	88.5	(NA)	1,054	181.0
R.I	130	50	121	55	117	55	80.0	82.6	81.5	164	180.0
Conn	479	167	450	203	434	201	84.1	89.3	88.7	596	180.0
Mid. Atl	5,177	2,110	4,760	2,345	4,639	2,360	80.2	83.4	83.6	6,319	181.0
N.Y	2,526	988	2,281	1,120	2,237	1,142	80.6	82.9	83.4	2,999	180.0
N.J	1,045	410	998	460	961	466	80.9	84.4	84.1	1,290	183.6
Pa	1,606	712	1,481	765	1,441	752	79.3	83.5	83.5	2,030	180.9
E. No. Cent	6,524	2,594	5,969	2,857	5,784	2,847	85.1	88.6	88.2	7,862	179.3
Ohio	1,715	709	1,535	757	1,504	745	86.0	88.8	89.1	2,069	178.7
Ind	876	348	851	375	784	379	88.4	99.8	91.4	1,075	180.9
Ill	1,668	656	1,539	731	1,506	732	81.3	85.3	85.5	1,956	178.0
Mich	1,594	572	1,419	654	1,386	649	88.5	90.6	90.6	1,917	[3] 180.0
Wis	671	309	625	339	604	342	81.5	84.3	84.3	845	180.0
W. No. Cent	2,700	1,117	2,315	1,188	2,259	1,184	88.8	88.0	87.8	3,175	176.7
Minn	629	285	573	307	554	308	87.0	89.6	89.1	811	177.1
Iowa	465	196	408	204	399	206	88.9	88.6	89.0	541	176.6
Mo	791	286	646	319	631	319	91.0	88.0	87.9	851	174.0
N. Dak	101	47	84	48	82	47	84.6	83.0	82.2	124	180.7
S. Dak	116	51	100	51	97	51	89.3	90.4	90.2	139	176.9
Nebr	234	97	210	105	206	106	85.3	86.3	86.7	294	177.4
Kans	364	155	294	154	290	147	90.6	86.5	85.5	415	180.0
So. Atl	5,060	1,944	4,900	2,201	4,855	2,204	89.0	90.8	91.2	6,438	179.9
Del	94	36	84	43	80	42	87.2	90.1	87.8	110	100.0
Md	650	242	607	274	587	274	85.9	87.1	87.0	776	180.0
D.C	117	32	94	36	90	36	90.9	88.4	86.9	114	181.0
Va	784	203	759	344	752	348	89.9	93.8	93.9	1,015	180.2
W. Va	282	119	283	121	285	120	90.7	99.0	91.4	366	178.9
N.C	837	349	818	367	825	366	89.6	92.7	94.1	1,094	180.0
S.C	471	177	443	186	425	196	90.0	89.9	89.2	564	180.0
Ga	813	300	751	340	769	327	90.9	90.2	90.9	1,003	180.0
Fla	1,012	396	1,061	490	1,042	495	87.5	88.7	89.4	1,394	179.4
E. So. Cent	2,155	841	1,977	863	1,946	852	87.8	87.0	85.9	2,657	175.9
Ky	505	199	475	217	476	218	83.4	85.6	86.1	636	174.7
Tenn	643	248	626	251	604	238	88.9	90.7	87.0	831	176.1
Ala	589	237	520	239	513	239	88.5	86.2	85.9	710	176.0
Miss	418	157	356	156	353	157	90.6	84.3	84.0	480	177.3
W. So. Cent	3,367	1,315	3,310	1,401	3,306	1,415	90.4	93.1	92.5	4,301	178.7
Ark	326	134	317	139	319	141	92.6	91.9	94.1	416	175.0
La	625	229	592	255	582	258	82.0	85.2	84.2	761	179.8
Okla	433	180	408	186	406	192	95.6	97.5	97.9	559	175.4
Tex	1,983	772	1,992	821	1,999	824	91.8	95.0	93.9	2,565	179.8
Mt	1,488	612	1,532	709	1,554	721	90.9	93.6	95.4	2,104	178.4
Mont	121	54	115	57	113	58	89.3	92.5	92.9	155	180.7
Idaho	123	57	133	63	136	64	90.0	96.6	98.5	189	178.8
Wyo	61	26	59	29	62	28	93.5	96.7	97.8	83	180.0
Colo	385	153	384	185	385	185	91.5	93.7	95.2	527	176.5
N. Mex	195	81	183	91	192	93	89.0	89.3	92.8	270	180.0
Ariz	299	119	350	143	354	149	86.0	91.1	93.7	457	177.1
Utah	213	89	212	97	216	98	96.8	98.4	99.4	294	180.0
Nev	91	33	96	44	96	46	98.4	97.2	97.3	129	180.0
Pac	4,334	1,819	4,030	1,919	3,964	1,938	91.8	91.5	91.1	5,677	176.6
Wash	578	242	530	255	524	257	93.2	93.6	93.5	724	180.0
Oreg	325	154	321	156	317	158	89.7	91.9	91.9	425	177.0
Calif	3,243	1,355	2,993	1,427	2,940	1,440	92.0	91.5	91.2	4,279	176.0
Alaska	59	18	65	25	65	26	87.7	88.2	80.5	86	176.3
Hawaii	129	50	121	56	118	57	87.3	85.1	84.1	163	175.4
Other areas:											
P. Rico	537	135	523	174	530	159	(NA)	(NA)	(NA)	646	[4] 174.0
Am. Samoa	7	2	8	2	8	2	(NA)	(NA)	(NA)	(NA)	[4] 184.5
Canal Zone	10	4	8	3	7	3	(NA)	(NA)	(NA)	10	175.0
Guam	16	5	21	7	21	7	(NA)	(NA)	(NA)	26	180.0
Virgin I	(NA)	(NA)	20	5	20	5	(NA)	(NA)	(NA)	23	180.0

NA Not available. [1] 1970 based on Bureau of the Census resident population as of April 1, 1970; 1976 and 1977 on estimated resident population as of July 1, 1975, and July 1, 1976. [2] Includes estimates for Mass. [3] Legal minimum. [4] 1973 data.

Source: U.S. National Center for Education Statistics, *Statistics of State School Systems*, biennial; and *Digest of Education Statistics*, annual.

No. 238. PUBLIC ELEMENTARY AND SECONDARY SCHOOLS—ENROLLMENT, BY GRADE: 1960 TO 1977

[For school year through 1970; thereafter, as of fall of year. Ungraded and special classes prorated among grades. Twelfth grade includes postgraduates. See also *Historical Statistics, Colonial Times to 1970*, series H 420–424]

GRADE	ENROLLMENT (1,000)								PERCENT DISTRIBUTION			
	1960	1965	1970	1973	1974	1975	1976	1977	1960	1970	1975	1977
Pupils enrolled [1] ____	36,087	42,280	46,531	45,408	45,056	44,838	44,334	43,736	100.0	100.0	100.0	100.0
Kindergarten and grades 1-8 [1] _____	27,602	30,652	33,249	31,333	30,931	30,544	30,012	29,433	76.5	71.5	68.1	67.3
Kindergarten [1] _____	1,923	2,250	2,653	2,715	2,862	3,058	3,000	2,852	5.3	5.7	6.8	6.5
First_____	3,733	4,014	4,026	3,331	3,290	3,365	3,460	3,416	10.3	8.7	7.5	7.8
Second_____	3,436	3,800	3,876	3,284	3,195	3,150	3,204	3,315	9.5	8.4	7.0	7.6
Third_____	3,302	3,662	3,883	3,430	3,263	3,163	3,104	3,176	9.2	8.3	7.1	7.3
Fourth_____	3,146	3,523	3,820	3,605	3,440	3,247	3,143	3,101	8.7	8.2	7.2	7.1
Fifth_____	3,118	3,465	3,777	3,640	3,606	3,415	3,239	3,142	8.6	8.1	7.6	7.2
Sixth_____	3,070	3,362	3,721	3,697	3,656	3,610	3,425	3,242	8.5	8.0	8.1	7.4
Seventh_____	3,173	3,363	3,825	3,849	3,814	3,760	3,716	3,522	8.8	8.2	8.4	8.1
Eighth_____	2,701	3,212	3,668	3,782	3,805	3,776	3,721	3,667	7.5	7.9	8.4	8.4
Grades 9-12_____	8,485	11,628	13,282	14,075	14,125	14,294	14,322	14,303	23.5	28.5	31.9	32.7
Ninth_____	2,412	3,198	3,708	3,907	3,927	3,971	3,919	3,888	6.7	8.0	8.9	8.9
Tenth_____	2,258	3,085	3,541	3,750	3,769	3,814	3,831	3,799	6.3	7.6	8.5	8.7
Eleventh_____	2,063	2,778	3,171	3,411	3,388	3,430	3,462	3,488	5.7	6.8	7.6	8.0
Twelfth_____	1,752	2,567	2,862	3,007	3,041	3,079	3,110	3,128	4.8	6.1	6.9	7.2

[1] Beginning 1973, includes nursery schools.

Source: U.S. National Center for Education Statistics, *Statistics of State School Systems*, biennial; beginning 1973, *Fall Statistics of Public Schools*, annual.

No. 239. SPANISH AMERICAN ENROLLMENT IN PUBLIC SCHOOLS: 1968 TO 1974

[As of fall. Covers American students having Spanish surnames. For 1974, data are estimated from results of a survey of public school districts with a substantial minority group enrollment. "Minority group" refers to Blacks, American Indians, Asian Americans, and Spanish-surnamed Americans]

ITEM	1968, total	1970, total	1972, total	1974				
				Total	Ariz., Calif., Colo., N. Mex., Texas	Conn., Ill., N.J., N.Y.	Fla.	Other U.S. (except Hawaii)
Total students enrolled____1,000__	43,354	44,910	44,647	45,988	(NA)	(NA)	(NA)	(NA)
Spanish American_____1,000__	2,003	2,275	2,414	2,577	(NA)	(NA)	(NA)	(NA)
Percent Spanish American:								
Of total students_____	4.6	5.1	5.4	5.6	21.1	12.9	6.5	1.1
By minority group enrollment:								
Schools under 50 percent_____	45.3	44.2	43.5	42.3	37.5	19.3	39.6	68.6
Schools 50–100 percent_____	54.7	55.8	56.5	57.8	62.5	80.7	60.4	31.4
Schools 80–100 percent_____	31.7	33.1	32.9	33.0	34.5	61.2	32.3	13.6
Schools 100 percent_____	1.9	1.8	1.0	1.2	1.2	2.3	.3	.3

NA Not available.

Source: U.S. Office for Civil Rights, *The Directory of Public Elementary and Secondary Schools in Selected Districts—Enrollment and Staff by Racial/Ethnic Group, Fall 1968* and *Fall 1970; Fall 1972 Racial and Ethnic Enrollment in Public Elementary and Secondary Schools;* and unpublished data.

No. 240. SCHOOL ENROLLMENT OF INDIAN CHILDREN: 1960 TO 1977

[In thousands, except percent. As of fall. Relates to children 6-18 years of age through 1965; 5-18 thereafter]

STATUS OF CHILDREN	1960	1965	1970	1971	1972	1973	1974	1975	1976	1977
Total_____	146	149	206	207	213	205	209	209	216	219
In school_____	133	134	186	190	197	188	190	190	202	206
Percent of total_____	91.3	89.7	90.3	91.8	92.5	91.7	90.9	90.9	93.5	94.1
Federal_____	37	43	48	49	49	48	48	47	46	46
Public_____	85	82	127	131	139	129	132	133	145	149
Other_____	11	9	11	11	10	11	10	10	11	11
Not in school_____	9	9	12	10	9	8	8	11	9	8
Unknown [1]_____	4	7	8	7	7	7	9	11	8	5

[1] Children recorded on census records but residing off the reservation.

Source: U.S. Bureau of Indian Affairs, *Statistics Concerning Indian Education*, annual.

No. 241. BLACK ENROLLMENT IN PUBLIC ELEMENTARY AND SECONDARY SCHOOLS, BY SPECIFIED AREAS: 1970 TO 1974

[As of fall. Excludes Hawaii. See headnote, table 239]

ITEM	1970, total	1972, total	1974		
			Total	32 Northern and Western States [1]	6 Border States and Dist. of Col. [2]	11 Southern States [3]
Total students_____1,000__	44,910	44,647	45,988	(NA)	(NA)	(NA)
Black_____1,000__	6,713	6,796	6,684	(NA)	(NA)	(NA)
Percent Black:						
Of total students_____	14.9	15.2	14.5	19.2	26.6	29.9
By minority group enrollment:						
Schools under 50 percent_____	33.1	36.3	37.1	22.7	30.6	44.7
Schools 50–100 percent_____	66.9	63.7	63.0	77.3	69.4	55.3
Schools 95–100 percent_____	38.2	34.8	33.6	49.6	52.2	19.9
Schools 100 percent_____	14.0	11.2	11.4	14.0	22.6	8.0

NA Not available.

[1] Alaska, Ariz., Calif., Colo., Conn., Idaho, Ill., Ind., Iowa, Kans., Maine, Mass., Mich., Minn., Mont., Nebr., Nev., N.H., N.J., N.Mex., N.Y., N.Dak., Ohio, Oreg., Pa., R.I., S.Dak., Utah, Vt., Wash., Wis., Wyo.
[2] Del., Ky., Md., Mo., Okla., W.Va.   [3] Ala., Ark., Fla., Ga., La., Miss., N.C., S.C., Tenn., Tex., Va.

Source: U.S. Office for Civil Rights, *The Directory of Public Elementary and Secondary Schools in Selected Districts—Enrollment and Staff by Racial/Ethnic Group, Fall 1970; Fall 1972 Racial and Ethnic Enrollment in Public Elementary and Secondary Schools;* and unpublished data.

No. 242. CATHOLIC ELEMENTARY AND SECONDARY SCHOOLS: 1960 TO 1977

[As of October 1. Regular sessions only. See also *Historical Statistics, Colonial Times to 1970,* series H 535–544]

ITEM	1960	1965	1970	1972	1973	1974	1975	1976	1977
Elementary schools_____number__	10,501	10,879	9,362	8,766	8,569	8,437	8,340	8,281	8,223
Pupils enrolled_____1,000__	4,373	4,492	3,355	2,874	2,714	2,602	2,525	2,483	2,421
Teachers, total_____1,000__	108	120	112	105	103	100	99	100	100
Religious_____1,000__	79	76	52	44	41	38	35	34	32
Lay_____1,000__	29	44	60	61	62	62	64	66	68
Secondary schools_____number__	2,392	2,413	1,981	1,790	1,728	1,690	1,653	1,623	1,599
Pupils enrolled_____1,000__	880	1,082	1,008	927	907	902	890	882	868
Teachers, total_____1,000__	44	57	54	51	51	50	50	51	51
Religious_____1,000__	33	38	28	23	23	21	20	19	18
Lay_____1,000__	11	19	26	27	29	29	30	32	33

Source: National Catholic Educational Association, Washington, D.C., *A Statistical Report on Catholic Elementary and Secondary Schools for the Years 1967–68 to 1969–70,* and *U.S. Catholic Schools, 1973–74;* and National Catholic Educational Association/Ganley's, *Catholic Schools in America,* annual. (Copyright.)

No. 243. NONPUBLIC SCHOOLS, PUPILS, AND TEACHERS, BY LEVEL: 1971 TO 1978

[In thousands]

ITEM	ALL NONPUBLIC SCHOOLS, 1971				ROMAN CATHOLIC			
	Total	Roman Catholic	Other affiliated [1]	Non-affiliated	1975	1976	1977	1978
Schools, total_____	18	11	4	3	10	10	10	10
Elementary_____	14	9	3	2	8	8	8	8
Secondary_____	4	2	1	1	2	2	2	2
Pupils, total_____	5,370	4,363	549	458	3,504	3,415	3,365	3,289
Elementary_____	4,056	3,355	429	273	2,602	2,525	2,483	2,421
Secondary_____	1,314	1,008	120	185	902	890	882	868
Teachers, total_____	[2] 226	[2][3] 158	[2] 31	[2] 36	150	149	151	151
Elementary_____	[2] 151	[2][3] 110	[2] 21	[2] 19	100	99	100	100
Secondary_____	[2] 75	[2][3] 48	[2] 9	[2] 17	50	50	51	51

[1] Includes unknown.   [2] Full-time equivalent.   [3] Estimated.

Source: U.S. National Center for Education Statistics, *Digest of Educational Statistics,* annual; and National Catholic Educational Association/Ganley's, *Catholic Schools in America,* annual (copyright).

No. 244. BLACK ENROLLMENT IN PUBLIC ELEMENTARY AND SECONDARY SCHOOLS, BY MINORITY-GROUP SCHOOL ENROLLMENT—STATES: 1974

[As of fall. Excludes Hawaii. "Minority group" refers to Blacks, American Indians, Asian Americans, and Spanish-surnamed Americans. Data are based on a survey of public school districts with a substantial minority-group enrollment. Extent of undercoverage (districts not included) will vary by State. As of fall 1974, there were a total of 7.1 million Black students enrolled in public elementary and secondary schools according to the U.S. Bureau of the Census (see Current Population Report, series P-23, No. 286]

| | | BY MINORITY-GROUP SCHOOL ENROLLMENT | | | | | | |
| | | Under 50 percent | | 50-100 percent | | 95-100 percent | | 100 percent | |
STATE	Total (1,000)	Number (1,000)	Percent	Number (1,000)	Percent	Number (1,000)	Percent	Number (1,000)	Percent
Total	6,273.9	2,151.3	34.3	4,122.5	65.7	2,210.1	35.2	743.6	11.9
Alabama	256.1	106.0	41.4	150.1	58.6	83.6	32.7	48.2	18.8
Alaska	2.2	2.1	95.3	.1	4.7	-	-	-	-
Arizona	14.7	4.7	31.7	10.1	68.3	3.3	22.0	.5	3.5
Arkansas	102.2	51.4	50.3	50.8	49.7	2.1	2.0	.9	.9
California	395.9	85.0	21.5	310.9	78.5	175.2	44.3	21.2	5.3
Colorado	20.1	12.7	63.3	7.4	36.7	2.7	13.2	-	-
Connecticut	50.3	16.9	33.7	33.3	66.3	13.7	27.3	.9	1.9
Delaware	18.9	5.2	27.3	13.7	72.7	5.5	29.3	.9	4.5
District of Columbia	125.1	.3	.2	124.8	99.8	117.2	93.7	51.7	41.3
Florida	344.7	226.6	65.7	118.1	34.3	35.0	10.2	11.5	3.3
Georgia	360.3	144.0	40.0	216.3	60.0	80.3	22.3	34.3	9.5
Idaho	.2	.2	100.0	-	-	-	-	-	-
Illinois	385.7	38.5	10.0	347.2	90.0	295.9	76.7	171.5	44.5
Indiana	102.0	38.8	38.0	63.2	62.0	39.6	38.8	9.8	9.6
Iowa	9.1	6.6	73.1	2.4	26.9	-	-	-	-
Kansas	27.8	18.3	65.7	9.5	34.3	6.4	23.1	.8	2.7
Kentucky	48.5	25.0	51.7	23.4	48.3	17.3	35.7	3.2	6.6
Louisiana	339.4	120.3	35.4	219.1	64.6	111.0	32.7	62.7	18.5
Maine	.1	.1	100.0	-	-	-	-	-	-
Maryland	229.7	94.0	40.9	135.6	59.1	87.3	38.0	34.7	15.1
Massachusetts	48.7	22.6	46.5	26.0	53.5	8.1	16.7	1.8	3.8
Michigan	273.5	45.8	16.7	227.8	83.3	147.3	53.9	34.8	12.7
Minnesota	11.1	10.8	96.8	.4	3.2	-	-	-	-
Mississippi	249.4	67.4	27.0	182.0	73.0	65.9	26.4	18.0	7.2
Missouri	125.6	17.2	13.7	108.3	86.3	86.3	68.7	45.8	36.5
Montana	.2	.2	100.0	-	-	-	-	-	-
Nebraska	12.8	5.7	44.3	7.1	55.7	2.6	20.5	-	-
Nevada	12.0	11.7	97.3	.3	2.7	-	-	-	-
New Hampshire	-	-	-	-	-	-	-	-	-
New Jersey	184.6	28.4	15.4	156.2	84.6	89.5	48.5	22.3	12.1
New Mexico	5.3	2.9	55.9	2.3	44.1	.4	6.8	.1	1.2
New York	451.4	93.4	20.7	358.0	79.3	226.2	50.1	34.6	7.7
North Carolina	338.1	211.7	62.6	126.4	37.4	8.1	2.4	3.0	.9
North Dakota	.3	.3	100.0	-	-	-	-	-	-
Ohio	244.4	58.2	23.8	186.3	76.2	110.1	45.0	34.1	13.9
Oklahoma	42.9	31.5	73.5	11.3	26.5	1.4	3.2	.4	.9
Oregon	8.2	5.8	70.8	2.4	29.2	.5	6.2	-	-
Pennsylvania	248.2	46.1	18.6	202.1	81.4	134.4	54.1	24.7	10.0
Rhode Island	5.4	4.7	87.7	.7	12.3	-	-	-	-
South Carolina	260.7	109.9	42.2	150.8	57.8	34.2	13.1	16.9	6.5
South Dakota	.1	.1	98.0	(z)	2.0	-	-	-	-
Tennessee	175.9	68.0	38.6	107.9	61.4	29.9	17.0	14.2	8.1
Texas	407.1	153.0	37.6	254.1	62.4	157.7	38.7	34.3	8.4
Utah	1.0	.9	92.4	.1	7.6	-	-	-	-
Vermont	(z)	(z)	100.0	-	-	-	-	-	-
Virginia	255.6	122.6	48.0	132.9	52.0	5.8	2.3	1.7	.7
Washington	19.0	12.2	64.4	6.8	35.6	.4	2.2	(z)	.2
West Virginia	12.8	11.4	89.0	1.4	11.0	-	-	-	-
Wisconsin	46.3	11.7	25.2	34.6	74.8	25.0	54.0	4.2	9.0
Wyoming	.5	.4	77.4	.1	22.6	-	-	-	-

- Represents zero.   Z Less than 50.

Source: U.S. Office for Civil Rights, unpublished data.

No. 245. ELEMENTARY AND SECONDARY SCHOOLS—ENROLLMENT AND TEACHERS, BY TYPE OF CONTROL: 1960 TO 1976

[In thousands, except ratio. As of fall of year. Enrollment data are not directly comparable with enrollment figures given for an entire school year in other tables. Schools are classified by type of organization, rather than by grade group; elementary includes kindergarten; secondary includes junior high schools. Data for nonpublic schools and, beginning 1971, for classroom teachers in public schools, are estimated, except as indicated]

ENROLLMENT AND TEACHERS	1960	1965	1970	1971	1972	1973	1974	1975	1976
PUPILS ENROLLED									
Total	42,181	48,473	51,309	51,181	50,744	50,329	50,053	49,791	49,335
Elementary	29,150	31,570	31,601	31,488	31,023	30,035	29,982	29,240	29,030
Secondary	13,031	16,904	19,708	19,693	19,721	20,295	20,071	20,551	20,305
Public	36,281	42,173	45,909	46,081	45,744	45,429	45,053	44,791	44,335
Elementary	24,350	26,670	27,501	27,688	27,323	26,435	26,382	25,640	25,430
Secondary	11,931	15,504	18,408	18,393	18,421	18,995	18,671	19,151	18,905
Nonpublic	5,900	6,300	5,400	5,100	5,000	4,900	5,000	5,000	5,000
Elementary	4,800	4,900	4,100	3,800	3,700	3,600	3,600	3,600	3,600
Secondary	1,100	1,400	1,300	1,300	1,300	1,300	1,400	1,400	1,400
CLASSROOM TEACHERS									
Total	1,600	1,933	2,288	2,294	2,338	2,376	2,404	2,441	2,440
Elementary	991	1,112	1,281	1,262	1,292	1,305	1,320	1,336	1,328
Secondary	609	822	1,007	1,032	1,046	1,071	1,084	1,105	1,112
Public	1,408	1,710	2,055	2,063	2,103	2,138	2,165	2,196	2,193
Elementary	858	965	1,128	1,111	1,140	1,152	1,167	1,180	1,170
Secondary	550	748	927	952	963	986	998	1,016	1,023
Nonpublic	192	223	233	231	235	238	239	245	247
Elementary	133	[1] 147	[1] 153	151	152	153	153	156	158
Secondary	59	[1] 76	[1] 80	80	83	85	86	89	89
PUPIL-TEACHER RATIO									
Public:									
Elementary	28.4	27.6	24.4	24.9	24.0	22.9	22.6	21.7	21.7
Secondary	21.7	20.8	19.8	19.3	19.1	19.3	18.7	18.8	18.5
Nonpublic:									
Elementary	38.1	33.5	26.5	25.2	24.3	23.5	23.5	23.1	22.8
Secondary	18.3	18.1	16.4	16.3	15.7	15.3	16.3	15.7	15.7

[1] Reported data from Office of Education surveys.

Source: U.S. National Center for Education Statistics, *Fall Statistics of Public Schools*, annual; *Digest of Education Statistics*, annual; and *Projections of Education Statistics to 1986-87*.

No. 246. PUBLIC SCHOOL EMPLOYMENT, BY SEX, RACE, AND OCCUPATION: 1974 AND 1975

[In thousands. Covers full-time employment. Excludes Hawaii and District of Columbia. Based on sample survey of school districts with 250 or more students; see source for sampling variability]

OCCUPATION	1974					1975				
	Total [1]	Male	Female	White [2]	Black [2]	Total [1]	Male	Female	White [2]	Black [2]
All occupations	3,452	1,231	2,221	2,906	433	3,590	1,273	2,317	3,001	461
Officials and administrators	39	33	6	36	2	43	37	7	40	2
Principals and asst. principals	107	91	16	95	11	112	94	18	98	12
Classroom teachers [3]	1,995	679	1,316	1,754	199	2,047	696	1,351	1,791	209
Elementary schools	987	165	822	854	111	1,005	168	836	865	114
Secondary schools	885	481	405	796	72	902	488	414	808	75
Other professional staff	226	75	151	196	24	237	78	159	205	26
Teacher aides [4]	220	16	204	149	49	240	19	221	161	54
Clerical, secretarial staff	215	5	210	192	16	230	5	225	203	18
Service workers [5]	649	331	319	485	131	681	344	337	504	141

[1] Includes other races and individuals of Spanish origin, not shown separately.
[2] Excludes individuals of Spanish origin.   [3] Includes other classroom teachers, not shown separately.
[4] Includes technicians.   [5] Includes craftworkers and laborers.

Source: U.S. Equal Employment Opportunity Commission, *Employment Opportunity in the Schools*, 1977.

No. 247. PUBLIC ELEMENTARY AND SECONDARY SCHOOLS—NUMBER AND AVERAGE SALARY OF CLASSROOM TEACHERS, 1960 TO 1978, AND BY STATES, 1978

[Estimates for school year ending in June. Schools classified by type of organization rather than by grade-group; elementary includes kindergarten and secondary includes junior high schools]

YEAR AND STATE	TEACHERS (1,000)			AVG. SALARY ($1,000)			STATE	TEACHERS (1,000)			AVG. SALARY ($1,000)		
	Total	Elementary school	Secondary school	All teachers	Elementary school	Secondary school		Total	Elementary school	Secondary school	All teachers	Elementary school	Secondary school
1960	1,355	834	521	5.0	4.8	5.3	Mass	65.2	30.7	34.5	15.2	15.0	15.3
1965	1,648	940	708	6.2	6.0	6.5	Mich	86.7	45.5	41.2	17.5	18.7	17.1
1970	2,013	1,107	907	8.6	8.4	8.9	Minn	44.6	20.1	24.5	14.9	14.3	15.4
							Miss	24.8	13.8	11.0	10.5	10.3	10.8
1974	2,155	1,176	979	10.8	10.5	11.1	Mo	48.3	24.4	23.9	12.1	11.9	12.4
1975	2,172	1,171	1,001	11.7	11.3	12.0	Mont	9.5	5.5	4.0	12.9	12.1	13.2
1976	2,188	1,169	1,019	12.6	12.3	13.0	Nebr	17.8	9.4	8.4	11.8	11.2	12.3
1977	2,187	1,167	1,020	13.3	13.0	13.7							
							Nev	6.1	3.0	3.0	14.1	14.1	14.2
1978,							N.H	9.2	4.8	4.4	11.1	11.0	11.7
U.S	2,177	1,169	1,007	14.2	13.9	14.7	N.J	76.5	47.5	29.0	15.4	15.2	15.8
							N. Mex	13.8	6.9	6.9	12.8	12.6	13.0
Ala	37.0	18.0	19.0	11.8	11.8	12.0	N.Y	164.3	77.2	87.1	[2]18.0	[2]17.8	[2]18.2
Alaska	4.9	2.6	2.4	[1]22.4	22.5	22.6	N.C	55.2	37.3	17.9	12.9	12.6	13.7
Ariz	24.2	16.9	7.3	14.4	13.4	14.9							
Ark	22.5	10.9	11.6	10.0	9.8	10.2	N. Dak	7.5	4.4	3.1	11.3	11.1	11.6
Calif	181.7	109.1	72.6	[2]17.4	[2]16.2	[2]18.8	Ohio	105.3	54.0	51.3	13.3	13.0	13.9
Colo	30.0	15.5	14.5	14.0	13.8	14.2	Okla	30.9	15.6	15.3	11.4	11.2	11.7
Conn	36.3	21.5	14.9	14.5	14.3	14.7	Oreg	23.8	13.1	10.7	14.0	13.7	14.2
Del	6.0	2.5	3.5	13.7	13.5	14.0	Pa	112.4	54.8	57.6	14.4	14.2	14.6
							R.I	9.1	5.0	4.1	15.1	14.0	15.2
D.C	6.0	3.6	2.4	(NA)	(NA)	(NA)							
Fla	74.5	38.1	36.4	11.2	11.1	11.4	S.C	29.3	17.5	11.8	11.3	11.0	11.8
Ga	53.5	33.1	20.4	12.2	12.0	12.5	S. Dak	8.3	5.3	3.0	11.0	10.8	11.0
Hawaii	7.9	4.4	3.5	17.5	18.2	17.1	Tenn	40.4	24.6	15.8	11.9	11.7	12.4
Idaho	9.6	4.9	4.7	11.7	11.5	11.9	Tex	151.5	79.4	72.1	12.8	12.6	13.1
Ill	107.3	54.9	52.4	15.2	14.7	16.2	Utah	13.0	6.6	6.4	13.1	12.8	13.3
Ind	53.4	26.2	27.1	13.6	13.2	13.9	Vt	6.2	3.3	2.9	11.3	10.9	11.6
Iowa	33.3	15.9	17.5	13.4	12.9	13.8	Va	58.8	33.8	25.0	12.9	12.4	13.5
Kans	25.8	13.8	11.9	12.1	11.4	13.1	Wash	33.7	17.9	15.8	16.2	15.8	16.7
Ky	32.5	20.5	12.0	11.7	11.4	12.3	W. Va	20.8	11.2	9.6	12.0	11.8	12.3
La	41.4	23.3	18.1	13.9	13.7	14.2	Wis	55.4	30.0	25.4	13.7	13.5	14.1
Maine	12.3	7.4	4.9	11.7	11.2	12.3	Wyo	5.4	2.7	2.7	13.3	13.0	13.6
Md	43.2	20.7	22.5	15.8	15.5	16.1							

NA Not available. [1] Includes special education teachers not classifiable by level. [2] Median salary; for definition of median, see p.xii.

Source: National Education Association, Research Division, Washington, D.C., *Estimates of School Statistics, 1977-78.* (Copyright © 1978 by the National Education Association. All rights reserved.)

No. 248. PUBLIC ELEMENTARY AND SECONDARY SCHOOLS—CLASSROOM TEACHERS, BY EXPERIENCE AND DEGREES HELD: 1966 TO 1976

[As of spring. Based on sample and subject to sampling variability. For definition of median, see p. xii]

EXPERIENCE AND DEGREE	1966		1971				1976			
	Elementary	Secondary	Elementary	Secondary	Men	Women	Elementary	Secondary	Men	Women
Percent with teaching experience of:										
1-2 years	16.2	21.0	15.2	18.5	16.5	17.0	10.1	12.5	10.7	11.7
3-4 years	12.2	16.7	16.4	14.7	15.7	15.5	15.9	15.9	15.4	16.3
5-9 years	19.8	23.9	21.4	27.7	26.0	23.0	28.6	29.0	27.2	29.7
10-14 years	14.1	14.3	14.3	17.2	20.1	13.3	15.6	19.0	20.0	16.0
15-19 years	11.0	8.5	10.4	8.9	9.8	9.6	12.1	12.9	15.1	11.1
20 years or more	26.7	15.7	22.5	13.7	12.1	21.6	17.5	10.6	11.5	15.2
Median years	10	7	8	7	8	8	8	8	9	8
Percent, highest degree held:										
No degree	} 12.9	} .6	{ 1.0	.4	.8	.7	.6	.6	.9	.4
2-year degree			{ 3.6	.7	1.3	2.7	.1	.4	.7	.1
Bachelor's degree	71.4	67.7	74.5	64.2	54.8	77.4	69.8	53.8	46.9	68.9
Master's degree	14.9	29.6	20.3	32.5	40.7	18.5	27.1	41.2	47.1	27.9
Professional degree, 6 years	.8	1.9	.6	1.4	1.9	.5	2.2	3.3	4.4	2.0
Doctor's degree	–	.3	–	.8	.6	.3	.1	.7	–	.7

– Represents zero.

Source: National Education Association, Research Division, Washington, D.C., *Status of the American Public School Teacher, 1965-66, 1970-71,* and *1975-76.* (Copyright © 1967, 1972, and 1977 by the National Education Association. All rights reserved.)

No. 249. PUBLIC ELEMENTARY AND SECONDARY SCHOOLS—PUPIL TRANSPORTATION:
1940 TO 1976

[Prior to 1960, excludes Alaska and Hawaii. See also *Historical Statistics, Colonial Times to 1970*, series H 531–534]

ITEM	1940	1950	1960	1966	1968	1970	1972	1974	1976
Pupils transported:									
At public expense [1]_____mil__	4.1	6.9	12.2	15.5	17.1	18.2	19.5	21.3	22.8
Percent of pupils in ADA [1]_____	16.3	27.7	37.6	39.7	42.0	43.4	46.1	51.5	55.1
Expenditure of public funds [2]____mil. dol__	83	215	486	787	981	1,219	1,508	1,858	2,372
Cost per pupil transported [1]_____dol__	20	31	40	51	57	67	77	87	104

[1] Prior to 1960 based on enrollment; thereafter, on pupils in average daily attendance (ADA).
[2] Excludes capital outlay.

Source: U.S. National Center for Education Statistics, *Digest of Education Statistics*, annual.

No. 250. SCHOOL DAYS LOST ASSOCIATED WITH ACUTE AILMENTS: 1975 AND 1976

[Children 6–16 years of age. Based on a sample of the civilian noninstitutional population; see Appendix III]

CONDITION	TOTAL DAYS LOST (mil.)						DAYS LOST PER 100 CHILDREN PER YEAR					
	1975			1976			1975			1976		
	Total	Male	Female	Total	Male	Female	Total	Male	Female	Total	Male	Female
All acute conditions_____	193	97	96	194	94	99	451	447	456	459	440	479
Infective and parasitic diseases__	35	19	16	35	17	17	81	86	77	82	80	84
Respiratory conditions_____	112	52	60	118	56	62	261	239	284	280	260	301
Upper respiratory_____	52	25	27	51	22	29	121	113	130	120	102	140
Influenza and other_____	60	27	32	67	34	33	140	126	154	160	158	161
Digestive system conditions____	9	4	4	8	4	5	21	20	21	20	17	23
Injuries_____	22	14	8	15	11	5	52	67	36	37	50	22
All other acute conditions_____	15	7	8	17	7	10	36	34	38	41	33	49

Source: U.S. National Center for Health Statistics, series 10, No. 114, *Acute Conditions, Incidence and Associated Disability*; and unpublished data.

No. 251. PUBLIC ELEMENTARY AND SECONDARY SCHOOLS—SUMMARY FOR SELECTED
CITIES: 1970 AND 1977

CITY	ENROLLMENT [1] (1,000)		TOTAL EXPENDITURES [2] (mil. dol.)		CURRENT EXPENDITURE PER PUPIL IN ADA [3]		PUPIL-TEACHER RATIO [1]		AVG. SALARY, CLASSROOM TEACHERS	
	1970	1977	1970	1977	1970	1977	1970	1977	1970	1977
Baltimore, Md_____	193	159	187	264	$862	$1,756	19.6	19.3	$8,998	$13,489
Boston, Mass_____	98	[2][4] 85	84	277	768	3,393	22.5	[4] 20.1	9,300	[2][5] 13,032
Chicago, Ill_____	562	524	538	1,219	972	2,333	24.4	[2] 22.7	10,400	[6] 17,302
Cleveland, Ohio_____	151	123	152	225	880	1,837	23.4	23.1	9,220	14,588
Dallas, Tex_____	160	141	111	214	570	1,451	27.0	21.2	7,800	13,600
Detroit, Mich_____	[7] 293	236	[8] 206	409	722	1,770	[7] 29.2	26.7	[9] 8,416	18,617
Houston, Tex_____	237	[4] 209	151	[10] 238	535	[2][10] 1,123	26.8	[4] 21.0	7,837	[2][10] 12,135
Indianapolis, Ind____	[11] 103	82	[12] 90	130	[12] 847	1,578	[11] 24.9	23.3	[12] 10,019	12,930
Los Angeles, Calif__	654	601	626	1,275	775	1,769	21.6	[2] 21.0	10,350	17,399
Memphis, Tenn_____	[11] 147	120	[12] 126	132	[12] 697	1,124	[11] 23.7	21.2	[12] 8,750	12,060
Milwaukee, Wis_____	132	109	122	227	940	2,352	26.2	20.3	9,394	19,296
New Orleans, La_____	112	93	81	135	676	1,530	27.0	21.3	7,700	[6] 11,399
New York, N.Y_____	1,123	[2] 1,097	1,595	2,616	1,300	2,607	18.5	[2] 21.1	9,800	[13] 19,000
Philadelphia, Pa_____	294	261	383	670	1,144	2,685	24.6	18.7	10,000	15,959
Phoenix, Ariz_____	[11] 174	[2] 177	[12] 148	275	[12] 846	1,360	[11] 23.2	[2] 22.2	[12] 10,136	13,510
St. Louis, Mo_____	113	82	89	132	936	1,832	28.5	26.9	9,878	13,000
San Antonio, Tex____	[11] 75	66	[12] 67	81	[12] 711	1,283	[11] 22.8	20.6	[12] 8,090	12,757
San Diego, Calif_____	[11] 129	121	[12] 126	235	[12] 918	1,554	[11] 23.2	[2] 22.3	[12] 12,300	16,767
San Francisco, Calif_	92	69	123	213	1,107	2,377	19.2	[2] 16.8	10,900	17,239
Washington, D.C____	149	126	196	246	[14] 920	2,060	20.1	20.8	10,660	16,460

[1] As of fall of preceding year. Includes nursery schools and kindergartens operated as part of the regular public school system.   [2] Estimated.   [3] ADA=Average daily attendance.
[4] Fall 1975 data.   [5] School year 1974–75 data.   [6] Includes nonteaching personnel.
[7] Fall 1968 data.   [8] School year 1967–68 data.   [9] School year 1966–67 data.
[10] School year 1975–76 data.   [11] Fall 1971 data.   [12] School year 1971–72 data.
[13] Median salary; for definition of median, see p. xii.   [14] School year 1968–69 data.

Source: U.S. National Center for Education Statistics, *Statistics of Public Elementary and Secondary Day Schools*, annual.

No. 252.   PUBLIC SCHOOL PUPIL TRANSPORTATION—SUMMARY, BY STATES: 1970 TO 1976

STATE	AVERAGE DAILY ATTENDANCE (ADA) OF PUPILS TRANSPORTED AT PUBLIC EXPENSE						EXPENDITURES FOR TRANSPORTING PUPILS					
	Pupils transported (1,000)			Percent of total ADA			Total (mil. dol.)				Average cost per pupil	
	1970	1972	1974	1970	1972	1974	1970	1972	1974	1976	1970	1974
U.S. [1]	18,198.6	19,474.4	21,347.0	43.4	46.1	51.5	1,218.6	1,507.8	1,858.1	2,371.8	$66.96	$87.04
Ala	396.5	410.3	425.1	51.0	55.0	58.8	13.6	15.7	19.6	25.1	34.39	46.06
Alaska	27.8	32.3	34.6	38.4	41.5	44.5	4.3	5.7	7.3	10.6	156.31	210.05
Ariz	139.8	159.1	183.5	35.7	37.2	40.7	6.3	7.8	10.4	17.0	45.11	56.95
Ark	210.5	231.1	249.5	50.8	56.0	59.6	11.3	13.9	15.6	20.6	53.46	62.66
Calif	920.4	929.0	1,500.0	20.8	20.9	34.4	74.9	89.0	110.5	90.6	81.39	73.66
Colo	161.0	178.2	212.5	32.2	33.9	39.9	11.3	13.8	19.0	24.6	69.96	89.24
Conn	359.8	393.5	388.8	58.1	63.3	63.2	22.2	27.1	32.5	40.1	61.84	83.68
Del	71.5	79.8	80.5	59.2	64.4	66.5	4.8	6.0	8.0	9.5	67.51	98.88
D.C.[2]	2.6	3.8	2.1	1.8	2.9	1.7	1.7	5.7	6.8	8.3	(2)	(2)
Fla	418.0	521.3	633.9	31.8	38.5	45.2	19.8	29.4	42.6	53.6	47.39	68.86
Ga	550.1	597.0	640.3	54.0	59.7	64.8	24.6	29.6	36.0	51.6	44.73	56.20
Hawaii	29.0	35.1	40.0	17.2	20.8	24.8	2.5	3.5	3.8	5.9	85.72	94.77
Idaho	87.6	92.9	93.4	51.2	52.9	53.7	5.2	6.0	6.7	9.3	59.34	71.62
Ill	662.1	723.9	745.5	31.8	34.4	36.8	50.8	70.3	90.5	112.7	76.67	121.43
Ind	585.5	642.6	651.6	52.7	57.8	60.4	36.9	43.8	49.2	63.6	63.10	75.45
Iowa	269.0	286.9	286.2	43.1	46.3	48.5	23.6	27.2	30.1	40.8	87.69	105.17
Kans	168.0	161.9	160.2	35.7	35.4	37.4	14.6	15.6	17.8	22.7	86.71	110.81
Ky	403.8	429.5	437.7	62.3	64.4	67.1	18.8	21.3	26.7	40.5	46.55	61.04
La	486.4	477.0	568.3	62.6	61.8	74.6	29.7	40.2	43.5	61.5	61.08	76.46
Maine	145.5	155.8	166.7	64.6	67.5	73.0	8.7	10.7	13.2	17.2	60.11	79.13
Md	451.3	497.1	528.8	57.4	59.4	65.8	29.0	36.9	44.9	57.2	64.29	84.92
Mass	468.1	493.8	628.0	44.3	45.9	58.9	31.4	45.3	65.5	81.6	67.11	104.31
Mich	748.8	860.0	913.9	37.6	42.8	46.0	56.2	71.3	92.8	122.4	75.07	101.57
Minn	429.9	536.2	489.4	49.7	60.5	60.0	40.9	48.9	57.2	78.1	95.21	101.22
Miss	293.3	296.1	293.5	55.9	59.9	60.7	14.6	16.2	18.8	24.8	49.74	64.08
Mo	581.4	604.2	628.3	64.2	65.7	70.5	30.2	36.1	42.9	53.4	51.91	68.33
Mont	[3] 50.1	(NA)	57.2	[3] 30.8	(NA)	35.6	6.8	7.8	9.0	10.9	(NA)	157.43
Nebr	56.0	60.4	65.8	17.8	19.2	21.7	7.3	9.0	10.7	14.4	131.04	161.82
Nev	45.3	50.6	44.4	39.9	42.0	36.1	2.9	3.5	4.4	6.9	63.63	99.28
N.H	75.6	86.1	87.4	53.9	56.0	55.8	4.9	6.2	7.8	9.6	65.34	89.30
N.J	[4] 540.8	[4] 584.6	[4] 612.7	[4] 40.9	[4] 43.0	[4] 46.1	45.2	57.9	73.3	91.9	83.68	119.60
N. Mex	117.5	126.0	127.8	45.2	48.4	52.1	8.5	8.8	10.8	15.9	72.29	84.60
N.Y	[4] 1,520.8	[4] 1,524.4	[4] 1,657.5	[4] 49.1	[4] 49.1	[4] 55.6	196.7	250.5	299.4	379.4	129.33	180.61
N.C	629.9	722.7	726.2	57.0	66.8	65.5	21.4	27.3	34.4	42.9	33.91	47.31
N. Dak	59.2	58.0	55.2	41.7	41.8	41.4	7.6	8.0	9.5	12.2	128.58	171.88
Ohio	1,042.2	1,119.8	1,208.9	46.4	49.9	55.9	44.5	52.2	68.0	88.5	42.71	56.21
Okla	187.6	244.3	268.9	33.4	42.3	48.1	12.5	15.5	19.9	25.5	66.58	73.89
Oreg	241.7	247.5	259.4	55.3	56.9	60.4	14.3	17.7	21.6	31.6	59.32	83.21
Pa	1,229.4	1,291.0	1,364.1	56.7	59.2	64.2	72.0	88.0	105.8	135.9	58.55	77.52
R.I	82.5	91.4	96.3	50.5	52.8	58.4	4.9	6.7	8.1	9.1	59.37	84.60
S.C	404.9	378.0	384.8	67.4	64.9	67.7	10.3	13.5	16.7	17.8	25.27	43.47
S. Dak	45.9	54.8	55.0	28.9	35.0	36.9	5.5	6.7	7.8	9.5	119.11	140.97
Tenn	411.0	444.1	496.5	49.2	52.5	60.7	18.0	21.3	28.4	37.0	43.69	57.21
Tex	535.0	611.7	694.7	22.0	24.5	27.6	29.4	33.3	42.8	64.7	55.01	61.67
Utah	90.4	92.4	93.3	31.4	33.3	33.7	4.0	4.9	6.4	9.2	44.49	68.66
Vt	56.7	67.6	71.6	58.0	65.5	72.0	3.9	5.0	5.8	7.3	67.99	81.47
Va	618.9	660.2	731.6	62.2	66.4	73.5	23.7	31.1	44.6	58.4	38.24	60.96
Wash	368.2	385.2	380.8	48.1	51.6	52.1	26.2	31.8	35.8	53.4	71.28	93.93
W. Va	257.4	272.4	282.0	69.2	72.3	75.3	15.1	18.2	21.8	30.0	58.76	77.16
Wis	436.0	446.1	512.8	49.5	49.6	58.5	41.2	41.9	49.3	58.8	94.49	96.13
Wyo	28.0	26.8	29.8	34.4	33.1	37.2	3.8	4.3	4.4	7.6	134.33	148.60

NA   Not available.   [1] Totals are for States reporting this information.   [2] Transportation program normally provides for handicapped children only; therefore, computations for cost not comparable to those of the States.   [3] 1967-68 school year.   [4] Includes private school pupils.

Source: U.S. National Center for Education Statistics, *Statistics of State School Systems*, biennial, and unpublished data.

No. 253. Public Elementary and Secondary Schools—Revenue and Expenditures: 1960 to 1976

[For years ending June 30. See also Appendix III and *Historical Statistics, Colonial Times to 1970*, series H 487–501]

TYPE OF REVENUE AND EXPENDITURE	TOTAL (bil. dol.)								PERCENT			
	1960	1966	1970	1972	1973	1974	1975	1976	1960	1966	1970	1976
Revenue, total	14.7	25.4	40.3	50.0	52.1	58.2	64.4	70.8	100.0	100.0	100.0	100.0
Federal sources	.7	2.0	3.2	4.5	4.5	4.9	5.8	6.2	4.4	7.9	8.0	8.8
State sources	5.8	9.9	16.1	19.1	20.8	24.1	27.2	31.1	39.1	39.1	39.9	43.9
Other sources [1]	8.3	13.4	21.0	26.4	26.7	29.2	31.4	33.5	56.5	53.0	52.1	47.4
Expenditures, total	15.6	26.2	40.7	48.1	51.9	57.0	64.8	70.8	100.0	100.0	100.0	100.0
Current	12.5	21.7	34.9	42.2	46.2	50.5	57.4	63.0	79.8	82.7	85.7	89.0
Day schools	12.3	21.1	34.2	41.8	45.4	50.0	56.7	62.3	79.0	80.2	84.1	87.9
Administration	.5	.9	1.6	1.9	2.0	2.3	2.7	3.2	3.4	3.6	3.9	4.5
Instruction [2]	8.4	14.4	23.3	28.1	30.1	32.6	36.5	39.6	53.5	55.0	57.2	55.9
Plant operation	1.1	1.8	2.5	3.1	[3] 4.7	3.8	[3] 6.1	[3] 6.6	6.9	6.7	6.2	[3] 9.3
Plant maintenance	.4	.6	1.0	1.2	(3)	1.5	(3)	(3)	2.7	2.4	2.4	(3)
Fixed charges	.9	1.7	3.3	4.1	4.8	5.6	6.3	7.3	5.8	6.5	8.0	10.3
Other services	1.0	1.6	2.6	3.4	3.8	4.2	5.1	5.6	6.6	6.0	6.3	7.9
Other current [4]	.1	.6	.6	[5] .4	.8	[5] .5	.7	.8	.9	2.5	1.6	1.1
Capital outlay	[6] 2.7	3.8	4.7	4.5	4.1	5.0	5.7	5.9	17.0	14.3	11.5	8.4
Interest	.5	.8	1.2	1.4	1.5	1.5	1.7	1.9	3.1	3.0	2.9	2.7

[1] Intermediate and local. Intermediate sources are administrative units or political subdivisions located between school districts and the State. Includes receipts from gifts and tuition, and transportation fees paid by patrons. [2] Includes salaries of clerical assistants, free textbooks, school library books, and supplies. [3] Plant maintenance included in plant operation. [4] Comprises current expenditures for summer schools, adult education, community colleges, and community services. [5] Excludes current expenditures for adult education and community colleges. [6] Excludes capital outlay by State and local schoolhousing authority.

Source: U.S. National Center for Education Statistics, *Digest of Education Statistics*, annual, and *Revenues and Expenditures for Public Elementary and Secondary Education*, annual.

No. 254. Public School Bonds—Elections and Sales: 1960 to 1976

[For years ending June 30, Covers bonds for financing construction of public elementary and secondary school facilities]

ITEM	1960	1966	1968	1970	1972	1973	1974	1975	1976
BOND ELECTIONS									
Number of bond issues:									
Proposed	(NA)	1,745	1,750	1,216	1,153	1,273	1,386	929	770
Approved	(NA)	1,265	1,183	647	542	719	779	430	391
Percent of proposed	(NA)	72.5	67.6	53.2	47.0	56.5	56.2	46.3	50.8
Par value of bond issues:									
Proposed mil. dol.	2,672	3,560	3,740	3,285	3,102	3,988	4,137	2,551	2,104
Approved mil. dol.	1,792	2,652	2,338	1,627	1,365	2,256	2,193	1,174	970
Percent of proposed	67.1	74.5	62.5	49.5	44.0	56.6	53.0	46.0	46.1
BOND SALES									
Number of sales, all agencies	2,674	1,941	1,722	1,309	1,547	1,336	1,234	1,060	1,093
State	24	12	6	14	8	6	7	10	8
County	66	61	60	85	71	71	56	53	61
City, town, township	228	151	135	112	235	127	100	70	71
School district	2,200	1,590	1,399	1,001	1,092	1,031	983	879	894
Authority	156	127	122	97	141	101	88	48	59
Sales, all agencies mil. dol.	2,195	2,883	2,917	2,813	3,368	2,905	2,959	3,579	3,688
State mil. dol.	182	241	167	188	216	103	164	715	465
County mil. dol.	66	140	170	220	161	113	171	209	199
City, town, township mil. dol.	257	368	381	287	565	383	317	361	340
School district mil. dol.	1,520	1,802	1,823	1,673	1,976	1,916	2,012	2,052	2,449
Authority mil. dol.	170	333	376	445	450	390	296	242	235
Average net interest cost, all agencies percent	3.91	3.67	4.57	6.39	5.01	4.91	5.35	6.27	6.25
State percent	3.70	3.50	4.25	6.22	4.50	4.64	4.88	5.59	5.64
County percent	3.71	3.63	4.43	6.43	5.03	5.03	5.33	6.00	6.34
City, town, township percent	3.70	3.62	4.45	6.38	4.94	4.84	5.26	6.43	6.76
School district percent	3.95	3.69	4.56	6.36	5.01	4.88	5.35	6.54	6.36
Authority percent	4.21	3.80	4.94	6.58	5.49	5.15	5.67	7.02	6.68

NA Not available.

Source: U.S. National Center for Education Statistics, *Bond Sales for Public School Purposes*, annual.

No. 255. Public School Expenditures, 1975 to 1978, and Personal Income, 1977, by States

[School data for years ending June 30]

STATE	Total expenditures, 1975 (mil. dol.)	Total expenditures, 1977 [1] (mil. dol.)	EXPENDITURES, 1978 [1]					PER CAPITA SCHOOL EXPENDITURES [4]			PER CAPITA PERSONAL INCOME, 1977 [5]	
			Total [2] (mil. dol.)	Current expenditures			Capital outlay (mil. dol.)	1975	1977	1978	Total	Rank
				Elem. and secondary (mil. dol.)	Average per pupil in ADA [3]							
					Total	Rank						
U.S. [6]	64,846	74,801	80,695	69,980	$1,740	(X)	6,404	$307	$348	$373	$7,019	(X)
Ala	753	912	(NA)	(NA)	(NA)	(X)	(NA)	211	249	(NA)	5,622	48
Alaska	220	309	339	277	3,341	1	42	640	809	833	10,586	1
Ariz	714	788	781	671	1,436	31	83	331	347	340	6,509	31
Ark	448	518	592	520	1,193	44	57	217	246	276	5,540	49
Calif	6,921	8,115	8,478	7,073	1,674	18	614	331	377	387	7,911	5
Colo	756	971	1,187	864	1,649	19	222	302	376	453	7,160	15
Conn	988	1,190	(NA)	(NA)	(NA)	(X)	(NA)	320	382	(NA)	8,061	2
Del	209	233	247	231	2,138	4	5	363	400	424	7,697	7
D.C	238	246	293	259	2,368	(X)	18	329	350	425	8,999	(X)
Fla	2,180	2,341	2,678	2,215	1,594	20	411	269	278	317	6,684	28
Ga	1,223	1,284	(NA)	(NA)	(NA)	(X)	(NA)	250	258	(NA)	6,014	35
Hawaii	256	311	359	310	1,963	11	38	299	351	401	7,677	8
Idaho	224	289	260	225	1,206	43	28	282	348	303	5,980	37
Ill	3,635	4,616	4,910	3,922	2,058	7	727	325	411	437	7,768	6
Ind	1,414	1,676	1,847	1,484	1,449	30	280	266	316	347	6,921	21
Iowa	827	1,054	1,245	1,115	2,002	9	107	290	367	432	6,878	23
Kans	609	708	824	696	1,682	17	71	268	306	354	7,134	16
Ky	649	810	900	827	1,294	40	43	194	236	260	5,945	39
La	963	1,064	1,242	1,130	1,481	27	79	256	277	317	5,913	42
Maine	272	338	(NA)	(NA)	(NA)	(X)	(NA)	260	316	(NA)	5,734	46
Md	1,506	1,486	1,546	1,373	1,810	16	129	367	359	374	7,572	10
Mass	1,968	2,313	2,468	2,240	2,137	5	125	339	398	427	7,258	14
Mich	3,333	3,859	4,263	3,685	1,975	10	320	367	424	467	7,619	9
Minn	1,494	1,793	1,898	1,565	1,962	12	167	383	452	477	7,129	17
Miss	458	549	618	575	1,220	41	35	197	233	259	5,030	50
Mo	1,146	1,247	1,323	1,184	1,425	32	90	240	261	276	6,654	29
Mont	243	301	332	296	(NA)	(X)	22	331	400	436	6,125	34
Nebr	404	477	457	435	1,526	[7]24	9	262	307	293	6,720	27
Nev	182	213	229	199	1,526	[7]24	19	317	349	362	7,988	4
N.H	228	223	237	218	1,366	35	13	283	271	279	6,536	30
N.J	2,660	2,957	3,102	2,900	2,333	3	70	363	403	423	7,994	3
N. Mex	346	449	464	395	1,476	28	54	309	384	390	5,857	43
N.Y	7,397	7,824	8,018	7,221	2,527	2	347	409	433	447	7,537	12
N.C	1,343	1,739	1,849	1,466	1,343	38	175	250	318	335	5,935	40
N. Dak	161	191	202	182	1,518	26	16	254	297	309	6,190	33
Ohio	2,942	3,363	3,446	3,161	1,581	21	180	274	315	322	7,084	18
Okla	647	792	901	815	1,461	29	66	241	286	321	6,346	32
Oreg	768	792	948	830	1,929	14	100	341	340	399	7,007	20
Pa	3,770	4,526	4,859	4,085	2,079	6	310	319	382	412	7,011	19
R.I	260	293	320	282	1,840	15	16	276	316	342	6,775	26
S.C	689	783	906	772	1,340	39	67	248	275	315	5,628	47
S. Dak	177	210	221	189	1,385	33	28	260	306	321	5,957	38
Tenn	958	1,149	1,150	993	1,209	42	98	232	273	268	5,785	45
Tex	3,219	3,502	4,039	3,492	1,352	37	380	268	280	315	6,803	25
Utah	362	485	530	404	1,363	36	99	308	395	418	5,923	41
Vt	148	166	170	153	1,550	23	8	316	349	352	5,823	44
Va	1,413	1,661	1,813	1,583	1,560	22	156	287	330	353	6,865	24
Wash	1,120	1,339	1,527	1,408	1,951	13	72	320	371	417	7,528	13
W. Va	448	562	593	501	1,374	34	73	251	309	319	5,986	36
Wis	1,410	1,601	(NA)	(NA)	(NA)	(X)	(NA)	309	347	(NA)	6,890	22
Wyo	147	190	203	173	2,007	8	23	407	487	500	7,562	11

NA Not available.   X Not applicable.   [1] Estimated.   [2] Includes interest on school debt and expenditures for summer schools, adult education, community services, and community colleges and technical institutes under the jurisdiction of local boards of education, not shown separately.   [3] Average daily attendance.   [4] Based on estimated resident population as of July 1, 1974, July 1, 1976, and July 1, 1977 from U.S. Bureau of the Census, Current Population Reports, series P-25, No. 642.   [5] Preliminary. Source: U.S. Bureau of Economic Analysis, Survey of Current Business, August 1978.   [6] Total includes estimates for nonreporting States.   [7] In order to have the lowest rank equal to the number of States presented, the number 25 is omitted. Nevada and Nebraska share the same rank, 24.

Source: Except as noted, U.S. National Center for Education Statistics, Revenues and Expenditures for Public Elementary and Secondary Education, annual, and Advance Statistics of Public Schools, annual.

No. 256. PUBLIC HIGH SCHOOL GRADUATES—STATES AND OTHER AREAS: 1974 TO 1977

[In thousands. Excludes graduates of subcollegiate departments of higher education, Federal schools for Indians, Federal schools on Federal installations, and residential schools for exceptional children. See Appendix III]

STATE	1974	1975	1976	1977	STATE OR OTHER AREA	1974	1975	1976	1977
U.S.[1]	2,763.3	2,822.6	2,836.0	2,840.0	Nebraska	22.3	22.2	22.2	[2] 23.1
					Nevada	7.0	7.2	7.6	8.0
Alabama	45.5	46.6	46.7	(NA)	New Hampshire	9.9	11.1	10.7	11.5
Alaska	4.2	4.2	4.2	4.5	New Jersey	93.9	[2] 96.0	[2] 98.0	97.5
Arizona	24.9	25.7	26.0	27.2	New Mexico	17.4	18.4	17.8	18.0
Arkansas	24.4	26.8	27.0	27.6	New York	207.4	210.8	[2] 213.1	[2] 215.1
California	268.5	273.4	[2] 272.5	[2] 266.1					
Colorado	34.4	35.0	35.6	36.6	North Carolina	69.1	70.1	70.5	71.1
Connecticut	39.2	[2] 42.8	40.6	(NA)	North Dakota	10.8	10.7	10.8	10.8
Delaware	8.2	8.2	8.2	8.2	Ohio	153.9	158.2	157.6	156.2
Dist. of Col	5.5	5.4	5.1	5.3	Oklahoma	36.8	37.8	37.7	38.6
Florida	74.8	86.5	[2] 89.4	88.1	Oregon	30.8	30.7	30.6	30.3
Georgia	58.0	59.8	61.1	(NA)	Pennsylvania	159.9	163.1	163.7	[2] 160.6
Hawaii	11.4	11.3	11.3	11.6	Rhode Island	11.1	11.0	10.8	10.8
Idaho	12.8	12.6	11.9	13.0	South Carolina	38.8	38.3	38.1	37.8
Illinois	139.1	[2] 141.3	146.6	142.0	South Dakota	11.9	11.7	11.3	11.3
Indiana	73.4	74.1	77.7	76.4	Tennessee	49.6	49.4	50.1	49.3
Iowa	43.5	43.0	[2] 42.3	43.7	Texas	157.0	159.5	159.9	163.6
Kansas	33.4	32.5	[2] 32.2	33.2	Utah	18.9	19.7	19.7	19.8
Kentucky	41.4	42.4	[2] 41.8	41.8	Vermont	6.3	6.5	6.6	6.7
Louisiana	46.8	47.7	47.4	[2] 48.2	Virginia	63.8	65.6	66.1	66.7
Maine	14.5	14.8	15.2	(NA)	Washington	51.9	51.0	51.0	50.9
Maryland	54.1	55.4	56.1	[2] 55.5	West Virginia	25.4	24.6	24.9	24.7
Massachusetts	78.0	[2] 79.0	81.3	75.4	Wisconsin	69.3	71.0	70.4	72.4
Michigan	134.3	135.5	130.9	135.2	Wyoming	5.8	5.6	5.8	5.9
Minnesota	64.0	66.5	66.4	68.2	Other areas:				
Mississippi	25.7	27.2	27.6	27.6	Puerto Rico	(NA)	27.1	25.8	(NA)
					Am. Samoa	.4	.4	.4	.4
Missouri	62.2	62.4	63.9	64.5	Canal Zone	.7	.7	.7	.6
Montana	12.1	12.3	12.1	(NA)	Guam	1.0	1.1	1.2	(NA)
					Virgin Islands	.6	.6	.7	.8

NA Not available.   [1] Includes estimates for nonreporting States.   [2] Estimated.

Source: U.S. National Center for Education Statistics, *Statistics of Public Elementary and Secondary Day Schools*, annual.

No. 257. HIGH SCHOOL AND COLLEGE GRADUATES, 1900 TO 1976, BY SEX, AND BY CONTROL OF HIGH SCHOOL

[In thousands, except percent. Prior to 1960, excludes Alaska and Hawaii. See also table 277; Appendix III; and *Historical Statistics, Colonial Times to 1970*, series H 598–601 and H 752–756]

YEAR OF GRADUATION	HIGH SCHOOL GRADUATES						COLLEGE GRADUATES [1]				
	Total		Sex		Control		Bachelor's degrees [2]				Master's and doctor's degrees [3]
	Number	Percent of persons 18 years old (Oct.)	Male	Female	Public	Private, est.	Total	Per 100 high school graduates 4 years earlier	Male	Female	
1900	95	6.3	38	57	(NA)	(NA)	27	36	22	5	2
1920	311	16.4	124	188	(NA)	(NA)	49	19	32	17	5
1940	1,221	49.3	579	643	(NA)	(NA)	187	18	110	77	30
1950	1,200	60.0	571	629	(NA)	(NA)	432	40	329	103	65
1955	1,351	62.5	648	703	1,208	143	286	24	183	103	67
1960	1,864	70.0	898	966	1,633	231	392	28	254	138	84
1965	2,665	73.9	1,314	1,351	2,366	[4] 298	501	25	289	213	162
1968	2,702	74.8	1,341	1,360	2,402	300	632	28	357	275	235
1969	2,829	75.9	1,402	1,427	2,529	300	728	27	410	318	256
1970	2,896	75.6	1,433	1,463	2,596	300	792	30	450	341	274
1971	2,944	75.0	1,457	1,487	2,644	300	840	31	476	364	301
1972	3,008	75.1	1,490	1,518	2,706	302	887	33	501	387	328
1973	3,043	74.6	1,503	1,540	2,737	306	922	33	518	404	348
1974	3,081	73.9	1,515	1,566	2,771	310	946	33	527	418	365
1975	3,140	74.4	1,545	1,595	2,830	310	923	31	505	418	382
1976	3,153	74.3	1,572	1,581	2,841	310	926	31	504	421	408

NA Not available.   [1] Data cover public and private institutions.   [2] Through 1960, bachelor's or first professional degree; thereafter, bachelor's degree only.   [3] Beginning 1965, includes first professional degrees.   [4] Reported data from U.S. Office of Education Surveys.

Source: U.S. National Center for Education Statistics, *Earned Degrees Conferred*, annual; *Digest of Education Statistics*, annual; *Projections of Education Statistics to 1986–87*; and unpublished data.

No. 258. SCHOOL RETENTION RATES—FIFTH GRADE THROUGH COLLEGE ENTRANCE: 1942–1950 TO 1968–1976

[Prior to 1962, excludes Alaska and Hawaii. Rates for the 5th grade through high school graduation are based on enrollments in successive grades in successive years in public elementary and secondary schools, and are adjusted to include estimates for nonpublic schools. See also *Historical Statistics, Colonial Times to 1970*, series H 587–597]

| YEAR OF ENTRANCE INTO 5TH GRADE | RETENTION PER 1,000 PUPILS WHO ENTERED 5TH GRADE | | | | | | | | High school graduates | Year of high school graduation | First-time college students |
	5th grade	6th grade	7th grade	8th grade	9th grade	10th grade	11th grade	12th grade			
1942	1,000	954	909	847	807	713	604	539	505	1950	205
1944	1,000	952	929	858	848	748	650	549	522	1952	234
1946	1,000	954	945	919	872	775	641	583	553	1954	283
1948	1,000	984	956	929	863	795	706	619	581	1956	301
1950	1,000	981	968	921	886	809	709	632	582	1958	308
1952	1,000	974	965	936	904	835	746	667	621	1960	328
1954	1,000	980	979	948	915	855	759	684	642	1962	343
1956	1,000	985	984	948	930	871	790	728	676	1964	362
1958	1,000	983	979	961	946	908	842	761	732	1966	384
1960	1,000	980	973	967	952	913	858	787	749	1968	452
1962	1,000	987	977	967	959	928	860	790	750	1970	461
1964	1,000	988	985	976	975	942	865	791	748	1972	433
1965	1,000	996	983	980	980	947	874	786	749	1973	433
1966	1,000	989	986	985	985	959	871	783	744	1974	448
1967	1,000	992	988	984	984	956	870	775	743	1975	452
1968	1,000	992	992	991	983	958	869	786	749	1976	(NA)

NA Not available.

Source: U.S. National Center for Education Statistics, *Digest of Education Statistics*, annual.

No. 259. HIGH SCHOOL GRADUATES AND COLLEGE ENROLLMENT OF PERSONS 20–24 YEARS OLD, BY SEX AND RACE: 1960 TO 1977

[In thousands, except percent. As of October. Covers civilian noninstitutional population]

| YEAR | ALL PERSONS | | | MALE | | | FEMALE | | |
	Total [1]	White	Black	Total [1]	White	Black	Total [1]	White	Black
High school graduates:									
1960	6,867	6,313	[2] 552	3,269	3,028	[2] 239	3,598	3,285	[2] 313
1970	12,663	11,359	1,159	5,750	5,181	503	6,913	6,176	657
1975	15,410	13,605	1,538	7,440	6,628	680	7,971	6,977	856
1976	15,715	13,806	1,624	7,555	6,723	686	8,160	7,082	938
1977	16,061	14,031	1,698	7,703	6,792	753	8,359	7,239	946
College enrollment:									
1960	1,233	1,153	[2] 80	823	780	[2] 42	410	373	[2] 37
1970	3,211	2,944	225	1,985	1,845	119	1,226	1,099	107
1975	3,992	3,503	405	2,267	2,043	183	1,726	1,460	222
1976	4,244	3,699	446	2,282	2,006	210	1,962	1,692	236
1977	4,229	3,630	452	2,316	2,014	219	1,914	1,616	234
As percent of high school grads.:									
1960	18.0	18.3	[2] 14.5	25.2	25.8	[2] 17.6	11.4	11.4	[2] 11.8
1970	25.4	25.9	19.4	34.5	35.6	23.7	17.7	17.8	16.3
1975	25.9	25.7	26.3	30.5	30.8	26.9	21.7	20.9	25.9
1976	27.0	26.8	27.5	30.2	29.8	30.6	24.0	23.9	25.2
1977	26.3	25.9	26.6	30.1	29.7	29.1	22.9	22.3	24.7

[1] Includes other races, not shown separately.   [2] Includes races other than White.

Source: U.S. Bureau of the Census, *U.S. Census of Population: 1960*, vol. I, *Characteristics of the Population*, part 1; *Current Population Reports*, series P–20, Nos. 222, 303, and 319; and unpublished data.

No. 260. COLLEGE ENROLLMENT OF PERSONS 14–34 YEARS OLD, BY SEX AND RACE: 1960 TO 1977

[In thousands. As of October. Covers civilian noninstitutional population. Degree-credit enrollment only]

SEX AND RACE	1960	1965	1967	1968	1969	1970	1971	1972	1973	1974	1975	1976	1977
Total [1]	3,570	5,675	6,401	6,801	7,435	7,413	8,087	8,313	8,179	8,827	9,697	9,950	10,217
Male	2,339	3,503	3,841	4,124	4,448	4,401	4,850	4,853	4,677	4,926	5,342	5,296	5,369
Female	1,231	2,172	2,560	2,677	2,987	3,013	3,236	3,460	3,502	3,901	4,355	4,654	4,848
White	3,342	5,317	5,905	6,255	6,827	6,759	7,273	7,458	7,324	7,781	8,516	8,644	8,812
Male	2,214	3,326	3,560	3,843	4,146	4,066	4,407	4,397	4,218	4,367	4,774	4,658	4,717
Female	1,128	1,991	2,345	2,412	2,681	2,693	2,867	3,061	3,105	3,413	3,743	3,986	4,095
Black	[2] 227	274	370	434	492	522	680	727	684	814	948	1,062	1,103
Male	[2] 125	126	199	221	236	253	363	384	358	422	442	489	490
Female	[2] 102	148	171	213	256	269	317	343	326	392	506	573	614

[1] Includes other races, not shown separately.   [2] Includes races other than White.

Source: U.S. Bureau of the Census, *Current Population Reports*, series P–20, Nos. 110, 294, and 321.

No. 261. Institutions of Higher Education—Faculty and Enrollment, by Characteristics: 1960 to 1976

[As of fall. Covers universities, colleges, professional schools, junior and teachers colleges, and normal schools, both publicly and privately controlled, regular session. Includes estimates for institutions not reporting. Except as noted, 2-year branch campuses are not counted separately and are included with 4-year institutions. See also Appendix III and *Historical Statistics, Colonial Times to 1970*, series H 680, H 699–705, and H 710]

ITEM	1960	1965	1970	1971	1972	1973	1974	1975	1976
Institutions	1,968	2,230	2,556	2,606	2,665	2,720	2,747	2,765	2,785
4-year	1,447	1,551	1,665	1,675	1,701	1,717	1,744	1,767	1,783
2-year	521	679	891	931	964	1,003	1,003	998	1,002
Resident instructional staff____1,000_	276	412	573	590	590	634	695	781	793
Instructor or above_____1,000_	236	340	474	492	500	527	567	628	633
Percent full-time_____	65.3	72.9	77.8	77.0	76.0	73.8	71.6	70.1	68.6
Junior instructional staff_____1,000_	40	72	101	97	90	107	128	153	160
Percent full-time_____	20.0	19.4	13.9	10.3	6.7	12.1	13.3	14.4	17.5
Total enrollment_____1,000_	**3,789**	**5,921**	**8,581**	**8,949**	**9,215**	**9,602**	**10,224**	**11,185**	**11,012**
Degree credit_____1,000_	3,583	5,526	7,920	8,116	8,265	8,518	9,023	9,731	(NA)
Male_____1,000_	2,257	3,375	4,637	4,717	4,701	4,771	4,969	5,321	[1] 5,811
Female_____1,000_	1,326	2,152	3,284	3,399	3,564	3,747	4,055	4,410	[1] 5,201
4-year institutions_____1,000_	3,131	4,685	6,290	6,391	6,473	6,597	6,825	7,223	[1] [2] 7,129
2-year institutions_____1,000_	451	841	1,630	1,725	1,792	1,921	2,198	2,508	[1] [2] 3,883
Full-time_____1,000_	2,466	3,910	5,489	5,676	5,647	5,683	5,817	6,147	[1] 6,717
Part-time_____1,000_	1,117	1,616	2,431	2,440	2,618	2,835	3,206	3,584	[1] 4,295
Public_____1,000_	2,116	3,624	5,800	6,014	6,159	6,389	6,838	7,426	[1] 8,653
Private_____1,000_	1,467	1,902	2,120	2,102	2,106	2,130	2,185	2,306	[1] 2,359
Graduate_____1,000_	[3] 356	697	1,031	1,012	1,066	1,123	1,190	1,263	[1] 1,085
Undergraduate [4]_____1,000_	3,227	4,829	6,889	7,104	7,199	7,395	7,833	8,468	[1] 9,927
Male_____1,000_	2,064	2,910	4,005	4,102	4,074	4,124	4,306	4,621	[1] 5,209
Female_____1,000_	1,223	1,919	2,884	3,002	3,125	3,271	3,527	3,847	[1] 4,719
4-year institutions_____1,000_	2,776	3,988	5,259	5,379	5,407	5,474	5,635	5,960	[1] 6,045
Full-time_____1,000_	2,077	3,159	4,234	4,358	4,350	4,350	4,429	4,619	[1] 4,622
Part-time_____1,000_	699	829	1,025	1,021	1,057	1,124	1,206	1,341	[1] 1,423
2-year institutions_____1,000_	451	841	1,630	1,725	1,792	1,921	2,198	2,508	[1] 3,883
Public_____1,000_	1,929	3,184	5,076	5,302	5,401	5,589	5,986	6,520	[1] 7,924
Private_____1,000_	1,298	1,645	1,813	1,802	1,799	1,806	1,847	1,948	[1] 2,003
1st time enrolled_____1,000_	923	1,442	1,780	1,766	1,740	1,757	1,851	1,910	[1] 2,347
Nondegree credit_____1,000_	206	395	661	830	950	1,084	1,200	1,453	(NA)

NA Not available. [1] Total enrollment, degree and nondegree credit. [2] Branch campuses classified according to actual status, e.g., 2-year branch included in 2-year category. [3] Includes resident only. [4] Includes first-professional enrollment and unclassified students.

Source: U.S. National Center for Education Statistics, *Digest of Education Statistics*, annual.

No. 262. Junior Colleges—Number and Enrollment: 1960 to 1977

[As of fall. Prior to 1972, excludes two-year branches of universities and other four-year institutions. 1960 covers degree-credit students only. See *Historical Statistics, Colonial Times to 1970*, series H 690–692 and H 705, for related but not comparable data. See also Appendix III]

ITEM	1960	1965	1970	1971	1972	1973	1974	1975	1976	1977
Institutions_____	**521**	**679**	**892**	**934**	**1,104**	**1,140**	**1,139**	**1,128**	**1,131**	**1,157**
Public_____	315	420	654	697	866	891	897	897	904	921
Private_____	206	259	238	237	238	249	242	231	227	236
Enrollment_____1,000_	**451**	**1,173**	**2,223**	**2,486**	**2,756**	**3,010**	**3,404**	**3,970**	**3,883**	**4,085**
Public_____1,000_	392	1,041	2,102	2,366	2,641	2,890	3,285	3,836	3,752	3,943
Private_____1,000_	59	132	121	120	115	120	119	134	132	141
Male_____1,000_	282	734	1,317	1,449	1,544	1,651	1,832	2,165	1,980	1,987
Female_____1,000_	169	439	906	1,037	1,212	1,359	1,572	1,805	1,903	2,098

Source: U.S. National Center for Education Statistics, *Digest of Education Statistics, 1977–78*.

No. 263. Black Institutions of Higher Education—Number and Enrollment, by Type: 1963 to 1976

[As of fall. Covers primarily traditional Black institutions, which were founded principally in the South after the Civil War for the education of Blacks. 1976 data include institutions reporting enrollments which had a Black majority. Number of institutions reporting may vary]

ENROLLMENT	1963 [1]	1968	1969	1970	1971	1972	1973	1974	1975	1976
Institutions, number_____	107	103	(NA)	111	115	114	114	120	113	149
Enrollment___1,000_	105.5	180.3	188.2	207.9	236.6	246.2	247.7	288.2	282.4	381.8
Public: 2-year____1,000_	4.3	23.1	24.3	33.0	49.8	53.7	53.2	88.7	59.0	130.6
4-year____1,000_	60.7	99.6	106.9	115.8	124.6	130.3	132.7	137.5	156.0	170.2
Private: 2-year___1,000_	1.9	2.3	2.3	2.6	2.6	2.6	2.4	2.2	1.9	11.5
4-year____1,000_	38.6	55.3	54.7	56.6	59.6	59.6	59.4	59.8	65.5	69.6

NA Not available. [1] Enrollment figures represent resident degree-credit students, regular session only.

Source: U.S. National Center for Education Statistics, *Report on Higher Education*, 1971; and *Digest of Education Statistics*, annual.

No. 264. Institutions of Higher Education—Number and Enrollment of Total and of First-Time Students, States and Other Areas: 1970 and 1976

[Number of institutions for academic year beginning 1976. Opening fall enrollment of resident and extension students attending full-time or part-time. Excludes students taking courses at home for credit, by mail, radio, or TV, and students in branches of U.S. institutions operated in foreign countries. See Appendix III]

STATE OR OTHER AREA	1970			1976							
	Total enrollment (1,000)	First-time students (1,000)	Number of institutions[1]	Total enrollment (1,000)					First-time students (1,000)		
				Total	Male	Female	Public	Private	Total	Male	Female
U.S.	8,580.9	2,063.4	2,785	11,012.1	5,810.8	5,201.3	8,653.5	2,358.6	2,347.0	1,170.3	1,176.7
N.E.	560.1	141.5	237	673.9	354.7	319.1	354.2	319.9	154.5	78.0	76.5
Maine	34.1	10.0	19	39.5	21.5	18.0	29.2	10.3	9.3	5.2	4.1
N.H.	29.4	7.6	24	39.4	22.1	17.3	23.0	16.4	10.6	6.0	4.6
Vt.	22.2	6.0	22	29.4	14.2	15.2	17.5	11.9	7.1	3.2	3.9
Mass.	303.8	76.1	116	360.9	189.2	171.6	164.1	196.8	80.9	39.4	41.5
R.I.	45.9	10.7	11	59.6	32.9	26.7	31.1	28.6	12.0	6.3	5.7
Conn.	124.7	31.1	45	145.1	74.8	70.3	89.3	55.9	34.6	17.9	16.7
N.A.	1,433.6	319.5	480	1,703.1	880.4	822.7	1,049.8	653.3	309.9	153.8	156.1
N.Y.	806.5	172.1	271	938.9	480.7	458.2	541.8	397.1	152.0	75.6	76.4
N.J.	216.1	56.9	60	290.6	146.9	143.7	220.3	70.3	57.8	27.6	30.2
Pa.	411.0	90.5	149	473.6	252.8	220.8	287.7	185.9	100.1	50.6	49.5
E.N.C.	1,615.9	388.7	437	1,976.5	1,044.0	932.7	1,590.3	386.1	470.9	234.3	236.6
Ohio	376.3	88.4	104	444.9	239.0	205.9	345.7	99.2	102.8	51.0	51.8
Ind.	192.7	43.3	47	220.2	120.2	100.0	166.0	54.2	44.7	24.4	20.3
Ill.	452.1	114.8	139	609.2	310.0	299.3	466.1	143.1	153.1	72.3	80.8
Mich.	392.7	90.8	90	469.5	249.6	219.9	409.8	59.6	107.9	54.5	53.4
Wis.	202.1	51.4	57	232.7	125.2	107.6	202.7	30.0	62.4	32.1	30.3
W.N.C.	685.1	165.8	299	788.6	423.3	365.4	608.9	179.9	182.0	90.7	91.3
Minn.	160.8	36.7	59	186.0	96.3	89.7	147.7	38.4	38.7	18.2	20.5
Iowa	108.9	29.3	57	121.0	65.9	55.1	84.2	36.8	31.3	15.9	15.4
Mo.	183.9	41.3	77	221.9	120.5	101.5	155.0	66.9	44.3	21.3	23.0
N. Dak.	31.5	9.4	13	30.2	16.6	13.6	28.2	2.0	9.1	4.8	4.3
S. Dak.	30.6	7.7	16	30.2	17.1	13.1	21.7	8.5	8.8	5.0	3.8
Nebr.	66.9	15.3	26	77.2	42.4	34.8	63.5	13.7	21.2	10.9	10.3
Kans.	102.5	26.1	51	122.1	64.5	57.6	108.6	13.6	28.6	14.6	14.0
S.A.	1,070.6	277.6	452	1,530.8	799.0	731.9	1,219.4	311.6	324.5	160.4	164.1
Del.	25.3	8.8	7	31.2	15.8	15.4	26.4	4.8	8.1	3.9	4.2
Md.	149.6	33.6	47	209.5	102.3	107.2	180.7	28.8	47.1	21.4	25.7
D.C.	77.2	10.4	19	80.3	43.5	36.8	13.9	66.4	10.2	4.7	5.5
Va.	151.9	43.4	69	244.3	120.0	124.3	214.4	29.9	38.9	17.8	21.1
W. Va.	63.2	15.9	26	80.2	41.8	38.4	69.4	10.8	15.8	7.7	8.1
N.C.	171.9	57.2	101	248.5	133.4	115.1	195.8	52.7	68.8	35.1	33.7
S.C.	69.5	23.8	47	121.5	66.5	55.0	95.9	25.6	30.8	16.3	14.5
Ga.	126.5	27.6	64	169.6	90.3	79.4	138.5	31.2	32.4	16.5	15.9
Fla.	235.5	56.9	72	345.7	185.4	160.3	284.4	61.4	72.4	37.0	35.4
E.S.C.	411.6	98.8	195	564.1	297.5	266.6	470.3	93.8	134.9	65.2	69.7
Ky.	98.6	21.3	37	128.9	66.9	61.9	106.8	22.1	26.2	12.5	13.7
Tenn.	135.1	29.1	63	181.3	96.9	84.5	139.9	41.5	40.6	20.3	20.3
Ala.	103.9	25.5	53	156.2	84.2	72.0	136.6	19.5	39.6	18.7	20.9
Miss.	74.0	22.9	42	97.7	49.5	48.2	87.0	10.7	28.5	13.7	14.8
W.S.C.	725.1	170.1	226	988.3	536.8	451.4	857.1	131.0	218.6	110.8	107.8
Ark.	52.0	13.5	22	67.5	35.0	32.5	58.0	9.4	16.0	7.9	8.1
La.	120.7	27.2	24	154.4	80.2	74.2	132.6	21.8	34.1	17.1	17.0
Okla.	110.2	27.4	42	145.2	80.5	64.7	123.8	21.4	32.1	16.3	15.8
Tex.	442.2	102.0	138	621.2	341.1	280.0	542.7	78.4	136.4	69.5	66.9
Mt.	452.8	107.9	114	581.6	318.9	262.6	516.8	64.8	154.6	80.1	74.5
Mont.	30.1	7.3	12	29.7	16.0	13.7	26.7	3.0	6.3	3.1	3.2
Idaho	34.6	11.6	9	38.4	20.0	18.4	30.8	7.7	11.4	5.2	6.2
Wyo.	15.2	4.8	8	19.2	10.2	8.9	19.2	–	4.7	2.3	2.4
Colo.	123.4	28.9	33	149.5	82.4	67.1	135.8	13.6	37.7	20.2	17.5
N. Mex.	44.5	9.4	11	54.4	29.1	25.4	50.2	4.3	10.4	5.4	5.0
Ariz.	109.6	25.9	22	174.7	94.3	80.3	169.8	4.8	59.4	30.4	29.0
Utah	81.7	16.6	13	85.7	49.3	36.4	54.5	31.2	21.6	11.9	9.7
Nev.	13.7	3.4	6	30.0	17.6	12.4	29.8	.2	3.1	1.6	1.5
Pac.	1,609.0	388.9	336	2,187.8	1,138.9	1,048.7	1,969.2	218.5	392.6	192.5	200.1
Wash.	183.5	53.3	46	248.4	131.3	117.1	224.1	24.3	27.1	12.1	15.0
Oreg.	122.2	37.7	42	146.1	76.2	69.8	130.3	15.8	34.6	17.6	17.0
Calif.	1,257.2	284.8	234	1,727.7	897.9	829.7	1,553.1	174.5	321.2	157.9	163.3
Alaska	9.5	2.2	3	18.5	8.2	10.3	18.0	.5	.7	.3	.4
Hawaii	36.6	10.9	11	47.1	25.3	21.8	43.7	3.4	9.0	4.6	4.4
U.S. military [2]	17.1	4.3	9	17.5	17.1	.4	17.5	–	4.5	4.2	.3
Other [3]	68.5	16.8	16	109.3	49.4	59.9	59.2	50.1	30.2	13.4	16.8
P. Rico	63.1	15.5	11	100.9	45.3	55.5	50.8	50.1	28.5	12.6	15.9
Canal Z.	1.2	.6	1	1.3	.7	.6	1.3	–	.2	.1	.1
Guam	2.7	.6	1	3.7	1.9	1.8	3.7	–	.9	.4	.5
V.I.	1.4	.2	1	2.1	.8	1.4	2.1	–	.1	(z)	.1

– Represents zero.   Z Less than 50.
[1] Branch campuses not counted separately; considered part of parent institution.
[2] Military academies.   [3] Includes American Samoa and Trust Territory.

Source: U.S. National Center for Education Statistics, Opening Fall Enrollment in Higher Education, annual.

No. 265. ENROLLMENT IN INSTITUTIONS OF HIGHER EDUCATION, BY SPECIFIED MINORITY GROUPS, 1968 TO 1976, AND BY GEOGRAPHIC DIVISION, 1976

[Enrollment in thousands. As of fall. Excludes Alaska and Hawaii. Covers full-time undergraduate students in 2-year and 4-year institutions taking credits equal to at least 75 percent of a normal load. Excludes federally controlled institutions. For composition of divisions, see fig. I, inside front cover]

YEAR AND GEOGRAPHIC DIVISION	Number of institutions	Total enrollment	BLACK ENROLLMENT		ENROLLMENT OF OTHER MINORITY GROUPS				
			Number	Percent	Total	Percent	American Indian	Asian American	Spanish-surnamed American
1968, total	2,054	4,820	287	6.0	169	3.5	29	48	91
1970, total	2,516	4,966	345	6.9	181	3.7	27	52	103
1972, total	2,665	5,531	459	8.3	219	4.0	32	57	130
1974, total	2,808	5,639	508	9.0	255	4.5	33	64	158
1976, total	2,805	5,726	604	10.6	309	5.4	38	81	190
New England	237	389	15	3.8	9	2.2	1	3	5
Middle Atlantic	479	935	88	9.4	51	5.4	3	12	35
East North Central	455	1,046	107	10.2	21	2.0	4	7	11
West North Central	294	479	19	4.0	10	2.1	4	3	3
South Atlantic	474	824	157	19.1	20	2.4	3	5	12
East South Central	198	358	73	20.4	2	.6	1	1	1
West South Central	238	571	80	14.0	51	8.9	6	3	42
Mountain	123	315	7	2.2	30	9.6	6	3	21
Pacific	307	812	59	7.3	116	14.3	11	45	60

Source: U.S. Office for Civil Rights, *Undergraduate Enrollment by Ethnic Group in Federally Funded Institutions of Higher Education, Fall 1968* and, beginning 1970, *Racial and Ethnic Enrollment Data From Institutions of Higher Education*, biennial.

No. 266. FOREIGN STUDENT ENROLLMENT IN INSTITUTIONS OF HIGHER EDUCATION, BY REGION OF ORIGIN, 1975 TO 1977, AND BY FIELD OF STUDY, 1976

[Covers nonimmigrant students only]

REGION OF ORIGIN	1975, total (1,000)	1976				1977, total (1,000)	REGION OF ORIGIN	1975, total (1,000)	1976				1977, total (1,000)
		Total (1,000)	Percent in—						Total (1,000)	Percent in—			
			Engineering	Science[1]	Business					Engineering	Science[1]	Business	
All regions	[2] 154.6	179.3	21	11	14	203.1	All regions—Con.						
Africa	18.4	25.3	14	14	18	25.9	Europe	13.7	14.4	12	12	13	16.7
Asia[3]	82.4	97.1	26	12	14	108.5	Latin Amer.[4]	26.3	29.8	18	11	13	37.2
Taiwan	10.3	11.3	26	27	8	12.1	No. America	8.6	9.7	6	7	9	11.4
Hong Kong	11.1	11.9	19	15	21	10.8	Canada	8.4	9.5	6	7	8	11.1
India	9.7	9.6	35	17	15	9.4	Oceania	[5] 5.2	2.7	4	9	10	3.1
Iran	13.8	19.9	40	8	10	23.3							

[1] Physical and life sciences.   [2] Distribution by region estimated for 30,416 students, origin unknown.
[3] Includes countries not shown separately.   [4] Includes Mexico, Central America, and Caribbean.
Source: Institute of International Education, New York, N.Y., *Open Doors*, annual. (Copyright.)

No. 267. HIGHER EDUCATION PRICE INDEXES: 1965 TO 1977

[1967=100. For years ending June 30. Reflects prices paid by colleges and universities]

YEAR	Index, total	Average annual percent change	PERSONNEL COMPENSATION					CONTRACTED SERVICES, SUPPLIES, AND EQUIPMENT				
			Total	Professional salaries	Nonprofessional salaries	Fringe benefits		Total	Services	Supplies and materials	Equipment	Books and periodicals	Utilities
1965	91	[1] 4.3	89	89	94	78		96	95	96	95	91	100
1970	121	5.9	124	121	118	146		111	113	106	111	121	104
1971	129	6.5	131	128	127	162		119	119	110	115	145	115
1972	136	5.6	138	133	136	180		126	126	113	119	164	122
1973	143	5.3	146	138	144	198		132	132	116	123	177	129
1974	153	7.1	155	145	153	222		145	138	132	131	195	158
1975	166	8.6	166	154	166	241		169	150	164	154	220	203
1976	177	6.6	176	162	179	267		180	157	172	163	252	219
1977	189	6.4	187	169	191	295		195	167	181	172	268	258

[1] Change from 1964.
Source: U.S. National Institute of Education, *Higher Education Prices and Price Indexes*, 1975, with annual supplements.

No. 268. College Enrollment of Dependent Family Members, 18 to 24 Years Old, by Family Income and Sex, in 1967 Dollars: 1967 to 1977

[As of October. Income in constant 1967 dollars. Covers civilian noninstitutional population. Degree credit enrollment. A dependent family member is a relative of the family head, excluding the head's spouse. Such persons are generally sons and daughters of the family head. Based on Current Population Survey; see text, p. 1]

FAMILY INCOME AND SEX	Approximate 1977 income intervals [1]	1967	1970	1971	1972	1973	1974	1975	1976	1977
ENROLLMENT (1,000)										
All dependent family members [2]	(X)	4,183	4,555	4,765	4,811	4,639	4,611	5,223	5,515	5,454
Less than $5,000	Less than $9,000	373	509	593	585	491	518	659	685	693
$5,000–$9,999	$9,000–$18,000	1,246	1,571	1,567	1,486	1,293	1,308	1,622	1,682	1,632
$10,000–$14,999	$18,000–$27,000	875	1,149	1,166	1,186	1,197	1,228	1,272	1,363	1,520
$15,000 and over	$27,000 and over	617	977	1,095	1,173	1,185	1,126	1,172	1,267	1,091
Male [2]	(X)	2,420	2,585	2,699	2,665	2,586	2,486	2,778	2,800	2,852
Less than $5,000	Less than $9,000	219	267	303	300	265	270	309	315	321
$5,000–$9,999	$9,000–$18,000	763	895	906	837	706	689	869	830	821
$10,000–$14,999	$18,000–$27,000	510	652	671	640	654	676	686	695	806
$15,000 and over	$27,000 and over	343	567	612	663	694	617	624	683	633
Female [2]	(X)	1,763	1,970	2,066	2,146	2,053	2,125	2,446	2,715	2,601
Less than $5,000	Less than $9,000	153	241	289	283	225	249	349	367	370
$5,000–$9,999	$9,000–$18,000	484	677	661	650	588	619	755	854	810
$10,000–$14,999	$18,000–$27,000	365	496	495	548	543	553	586	653	667
$15,000 and over	$27,000 and over	274	411	483	510	491	509	548	598	505
PERCENT OF POPULATION ENROLLED										
All dependent family members [2]	(X)	39.1	39.1	38.9	37.8	36.6	36.2	38.7	38.8	37.9
Less than $5,000	Less than $9,000	20.0	20.8	22.8	22.6	20.1	20.3	23.5	22.4	22.6
$5,000–$9,999	$9,000–$18,000	37.9	36.6	35.4	34.2	31.2	31.7	35.1	36.3	34.4
$10,000–$14,999	$18,000–$27,000	51.9	48.4	46.4	44.2	42.7	41.4	45.4	47.5	46.4
$15,000 and over	$27,000 and over	68.3	61.7	61.8	56.9	56.6	57.5	59.6	58.2	59.8
Male [2]	(X)	42.9	40.9	40.0	37.8	36.5	34.9	36.7	35.3	35.7
Less than $5,000	Less than $9,000	22.1	20.7	22.0	21.5	19.9	19.5	20.2	18.9	19.3
$5,000–$9,999	$9,000–$18,000	43.0	38.4	37.0	34.3	30.6	29.5	33.2	32.1	31.3
$10,000–$14,999	$18,000–$27,000	56.8	50.7	48.3	43.7	41.4	40.5	43.0	43.0	43.9
$15,000 and over	$27,000 and over	71.0	63.1	61.9	57.3	56.8	56.0	56.5	54.5	58.0
Female [2]	(X)	34.9	37.0	37.5	38.0	36.8	37.9	41.2	43.2	40.7
Less than $5,000	Less than $9,000	17.5	20.8	23.7	23.9	20.3	21.4	27.4	26.4	26.4
$5,000–$9,999	$9,000–$18,000	32.0	34.5	33.5	34.2	31.9	34.7	37.6	41.6	38.0
$10,000–$14,999	$18,000–$27,000	46.3	45.5	44.0	45.0	44.3	42.7	48.5	53.1	49.0
$15,000 and over	$27,000 and over	65.2	59.3	61.6	56.4	56.4	59.5	63.6	63.1	62.2

X Not applicable.   [1] Approximate comparable buying power of 1967 dollars in 1977.
[2] Includes persons with family income not reported, not shown separately.
Source: U.S. Bureau of the Census, *Current Population Reports*, series P-20, No. 319, and unpublished data.

No. 269. College Enrollment of the Population, 14 to 34 Years Old, by Major Field of Study and Sex: 1966 to 1974

[In thousands, except percent. As of October. Covers civilian noninstitutional population. Degree-credit enrollment only. Minus sign (−) denotes decrease. Based on Current Population Survey; see text, p. 1]

MAJOR FIELD OF STUDY	1966, total	1972			1974			Percent change, 1966–1974	Percent distribution	
		Total	Male	Female	Total	Male	Female		1966	1974
Total enrollment	5,999	8,313	4,853	3,459	8,827	4,926	3,901	47.1	100.0	100.0
Agriculture, forestry	73	97	87	11	104	90	14	42.5	1.2	1.2
Biological sciences	} 602	257	164	94	327	193	134	} 87.4	10.0	3.7
Health, medical profession		695	303	393	801	286	514			9.1
Business, commerce	888	1,157	890	268	1,376	940	436	55.0	14.8	15.6
Education	1,118	1,007	280	728	1,158	318	841	3.6	18.6	13.1
Engineering	534	357	350	7	410	382	28	−23.2	8.9	4.6
English, journalism	} 620	291	140	150	264	109	156	} 7.7	10.3	3.0
Other humanities		455	240	215	404	209	194			4.6
Law	(NA)	237	196	42	271	208	63	(NA)	(NA)	3.1
Mathematics, statistics [1]	236	239	156	82	243	153	90	3.0	3.9	2.8
Physical sciences	226	157	115	43	134	97	36	−40.7	3.8	1.5
Social sciences	642	954	501	453	771	429	342	20.1	10.7	8.7
Other	461	1,503	907	596	1,580	968	612	242.7	7.7	17.9
No major field [2]	600	906	525	380	984	544	440	64.0	10.0	11.1

NA Not available.   [1] Includes computer sciences.   [2] Includes not reported.
Source: U.S. Bureau of the Census, *Current Population Reports*, series P-20, Nos. 183, 260, and 289.

No. 270. Institutions of Higher Education—Median Annual Salaries of Instructional Staff and Administrative Officers: 1960 to 1976

[In dollars, except percent change. For fiscal years ending in year stated. For 4-year colleges and universities. Figures for instructional staff are for 9 months of full-time teaching; for others, usually for 11 or 12 months of service. For definition of median, see p. xii. See *Historical Statistics, Colonial Times to 1970*, series D 913]

POSITION	1960	1964	1968	1970	1972	1974	1976	PERCENT CHANGE	
								1960–1970	1970–1976
Instructional staff:									
All ranks	6,700	8,200	10,200	11,700	12,900	14,400	16,300	74.6	39.3
Professors	9,100	11,300	14,700	16,800	18,100	19,900	22,200	84.6	32.1
Associate professors	7,300	9,000	11,400	13,000	14,000	15,300	17,100	78.1	31.5
Assistant professors	6,200	7,500	9,500	10,700	11,500	12,600	14,100	72.6	31.8
Instructors	5,100	6,100	7,500	8,400	9,200	10,200	11,400	64.7	35.7
Administrative officers:									
President	13,800	17,300	22,300	26,000	29,800	31,300	(NA)	88.4	[1] 20.4
Vice-president	14,200	17,100	21,500	23,300	26,300	27,700	(NA)	64.1	[1] 18.9
Dean of the college	10,700	13,600	16,100	19,100	20,000	22,000	(NA)	78.5	[1] 15.2
Dean of students	8,800	10,700	14,100	16,100	17,800	19,100	(NA)	83.0	[1] 18.6
Dean of men	7,300	9,100	11,000	12,300	13,500	14,500	(NA)	68.5	[1] 17.9
Dean of women	6,600	8,200	10,300	11,400	12,400	13,200	(NA)	72.7	[1] 15.8
Dean of admissions	7,700	9,600	11,400	13,000	14,300	15,800	(NA)	68.8	[1] 21.5

NA Not available.   [1] Percent change, 1970–1974.

Source: National Education Association, Washington, D.C., Research Memo 1977-1, *Summary of Salaries Paid in Higher Education*, biennial. (Copyright © 1976 by the National Education Association. All rights reserved.)

No. 271. Institutions of Higher Education—Charges: 1965 to 1978

[In dollars. Estimated. Represents average charges per full-time resident degree-credit student]

ACADEMIC YEAR ENDING AND CONTROL	TUITION AND REQUIRED FEES				BOARD RATES				DORMITORY CHARGES			
	All institutions	2-yr. colleges	4-yr. universities	Other 4-yr. schools	All institutions	2-yr. colleges	4-yr. universities	Other 4-yr. schools	All institutions	2-yr. colleges	4-yr. universities	Other 4-yr. schools
1965: Public	243	99	298	224	436	361	462	402	271	178	291	241
Nonpublic	1,088	702	1,297	1,023	488	464	515	479	331	289	390	308
1970: Public	323	178	427	306	511	465	540	483	370	308	395	347
Nonpublic	1,533	1,034	1,809	1,469	562	547	608	543	436	413	500	409
1975: Public	470	316	597	473	642	640	674	612	505	425	526	494
Nonpublic	2,131	1,341	2,534	2,035	686	650	752	661	569	513	676	531
1977: Public	550	382	692	570	736	748	765	704	588	473	616	580
Nonpublic	2,564	1,620	3,139	2,381	813	770	888	777	681	614	822	617
1978: Public	575	407	741	598	781	807	810	746	626	490	659	615
Nonpublic	2,767	1,758	3,403	2,531	867	831	948	830	729	681	880	661

Source: U.S. National Center for Education Statistics, *Digest of Education Statistics*, annual, and *Projections of Education Statistics to 1986–87*.

No. 272. Monthly Salary Offers to Candidates for Degrees: 1970 to 1977

[In dollars. 1970, male only; thereafter, male and female. Data are average beginning salaries based on offers (not acceptances) made by business, industrial, and government employers to graduating students in selected curricula and graduate programs during Sept. to June. Data from representative colleges throughout U.S.]

FIELD OF STUDY	BACHELOR'S				MASTER'S [1]				DOCTOR'S			
	1970	1975	1976	1977	1970	1975	1976	1977	1970	1975	1976	1977
Accounting	836	981	1,018	1,062	(NA)	(NA)	1,201	1,247	(NA)	(NA)	(NA)	(NA)
Business, general [2]	721	843	872	927	1,044	1,250	1,323	1,410	(NA)	(NA)	(NA)	(NA)
Marketing [3]	702	801	840	896	(NA)	(NA)	(NA)	(NA)	(NA)	(NA)	(NA)	(NA)
Engineering: Civil	837	1,064	1,108	1,185	960	1,183	1,251	1,342	1,236	1,382	1,597	1,625
Chemical	902	1,196	1,279	1,389	1,036	1,310	1,407	1,509	1,375	1,645	1,793	1,882
Electrical	869	1,081	1,155	1,245	1,015	1,228	1,319	1,410	1,429	1,550	1,693	1,811
Mechanical	867	1,122	1,197	1,286	1,008	1,274	1,341	1,438	1,370	1,624	1,687	1,777
Chemistry	825	956	1,028	1,102	978	1,118	1,234	1,321	1,278	1,503	1,582	1,725
Mathematics	794	915	986	1,073	959	1,138	1,305	1,285	1,421	1,523	1,569	1,704
Physics	826	(NA)	(NA)	(NA)	985	1,216	1,209	(NA)	1,309	1,473	1,639	1,698
Humanities	} 700	723	775	810	(NA)	931	963	1,004	(NA)	(NA)	(NA)	(NA)
Social sciences		770	820	863	(NA)	953	1,009	1,036	(NA)	(NA)	(NA)	(NA)

NA Not available.   [1] Data are for candidates with 1 year or less of full-time nonmilitary employment.
[2] For master's degrees, offers are after nontechnical undergraduate degree.   [3] Includes distribution.

Source: College Placement Council, Inc., Bethlehem, Pa., *A Study of Beginning Offers*, annual. (Copyright.)

No. 273. Institutions of Higher Education—Finances: 1950 to 1976

[In millions of dollars. For years ending June 30. Prior to 1960, excludes Alaska and Hawaii. For coverage, see headnote, table 261. See also Appendix III and *Historical Statistics, Colonial Times to 1970*, series H 716–738 and H 747–749]

ITEM	1950	1960	1970	1972	1973	1974	1975	1976
Current income	2,375	5,786	21,515	26,234	28,606	31,712	35,687	39,703
Educational and general	1,833	4,688	16,486	20,200	22,127	24,628	(X)	(X)
Tuition and fees	395	1,157	4,420	5,594	6,011	6,500	7,233	8,172
Federal government	524	1,037	2,682	3,099	3,393	3,520	4,991	5,414
State government	492	1,374	5,788	7,121	7,918	9,182	10,857	12,261
Local government	62	152	775	991	1,144	1,263	1,424	1,617
Private gifts and grants [1]	119	383	1,001	1,208	1,300	1,431	1,745	1,917
Organized activities related to instruction	112	245	613	739	774	834	[2] 555	[2] 645
Miscellaneous	131	341	1,207	1,448	1,587	1,898	[3] 718	[3] 687
Auxiliary enterprises and activities [4]	541	1,097	5,029	6,034	6,479	7,085	[5] 8,163	[5] 8,990
Plant-fund receipts	529	1,309	(NA)	(NA)	(NA)	(NA)	6,336	7,286
Increase of endowment funds	(NA)	[6] 419	368	730	852	338	[6] 486	[6] 959
Current expenditures	2,246	5,601	21,043	25,560	27,956	30,713	35,058	38,903
Educational and general	1,706	4,513	15,789	19,201	21,078	23,257		
Administration and general expense	213	583	2,628	3,344	3,713	4,201		
Instruction and departmental research [7]	781	1,793	7,653	9,503	10,528	11,574		
Organized research	225	1,022	2,144	2,265	2,394	2,480		
Plant operation and maintenance	225	470	1,542	1,928	2,141	2,494	[8]）	[8]）
Organized activities related to instruction	119	303	648	780	791	838		
Libraries, extension, and public services	143	341	1,174	1,381	1,510	1,670		
Auxiliary enterprises and activities [4]	476	916	4,270	5,118	5,555	6,060		
Scholarships, fellowships, and prizes	63	172	985	1,241	1,322	1,396		
Gross addition to plant value [9]	417	1,192	4,233	4,163	3,967	4,312	4,761	4,702
Value of plant (grounds, bldgs., equip.)	4,800	13,449	42,094	50,153	53,815	58,004	62,183	66,348
Endowment (book value) [10]	2,601	5,445	10,854	11,983	13,000	13,303	13,403	13,952

NA Not available.   X Not applicable.   [1] Beginning 1970, private grants represent nongovernmental revenue for sponsored research and other sponsored programs. Beginning 1975, includes private contracts. [2] Represents sales and services of educational activities only.   [3] Endowment earnings only.   [4] Beginning 1970, includes "major public service programs" previously reported under "educational and general." [5] Excludes student-aid income and includes revenue from sales and services of auxiliary enterprises and hospitals, and other sources.   [6] Includes increase in student loan and annuity funds.   [7] Beginning 1970, includes "other sponsored programs." [8] Figures not available on comparable basis with earlier years because of revised reporting. For later data, see table 274.   [9] Includes expenditures from current funds for plant expansion. [10] Includes funds functioning as endowment, and prior to 1970, annuity funds.

Source: U.S. National Center for Education Statistics, 1950 and 1960, *Biennial Survey of Education in the United States*, chapter on Statistical Summary of Education; thereafter, *Digest of Education Statistics*, annual.

No. 274. Institutions of Higher Education—Expenditures, by Type of School: 1975 and 1976

[In millions of dollars, except percent. For years ending June 30]

PURPOSE	1975				1976			
	Total	Percent	Public	Private	Total	Percent	Public	Private
Current expenditures [1]	35,058	100.0	23,490	11,568	38,903	100.0	26,184	12,719
Educational and general	27,548	78.6	19,092	8,455	30,598	78.7	21,283	9,315
Instruction	11,798	33.7	8,574	3,224	13,095	33.7	9,516	3,579
Research	3,132	8.9	2,042	1,090	3,287	8.4	2,154	1,133
Institutional support	3,057	8.7	1,917	1,140	3,615	9.3	2,365	1,250
Plant operation [2]	2,787	7.9	1,935	852	3,083	7.9	2,158	925
Academic support	2,256	6.4	1,612	644	2,472	6.4	1,765	707
Libraries	1,002	2.9	680	322	1,224	3.1	825	399
Scholarships and fellowships	1,450	4.1	719	731	1,636	4.2	799	837
Unrestricted funds	632	1.8	267	365	687	1.8	277	410
Restricted funds	818	2.3	452	366	949	2.4	522	427
Student services	1,439	4.1	985	454	1,625	4.2	1,115	510
Public service	1,098	3.1	924	174	1,239	3.2	1,036	203
Mandatory transfers	532	1.5	386	147	546	1.4	375	171
Auxiliary enterprises [1]	4,074	11.6	2,537	1,537	4,477	11.5	2,828	1,649
Hospitals [1]	2,351	6.7	1,369	982	2,696	6.9	1,610	1,086
Independent operations [1]	1,087	3.1	492	594	1,132	2.9	463	669

[1] Includes mandatory transfers which are primarily current expenditures for plant.   [2] Includes maintenance.

Source: U.S. National Center for Education Statistics, *Digest of Education Statistics*, annual.

No. 275. VOLUNTARY FINANCIAL SUPPORT OF HIGHER EDUCATION, BY TYPE OF INSTITUTION, PURPOSE, AND SOURCE: 1965 TO 1977

[For school years ending in years shown; enrollment as of fall of preceding year. Voluntary support, as defined in *Gift Reporting Standards*, excludes income from endowment and other invested funds as well as all support received from Federal, State, and local governments and their agencies]

ITEM	1965	1970	1972	1973	1974	1975	1976	1977 Total	1977 Percent
Estimated support, total____mil. dol__	1,400	1,780	2,020	2,240	2,240	2,160	2,410	2,670	100
Foundations_____mil. dol__	402	434	523	524	535	497	549	558	21
Individuals_____mil. dol__	628	822	974	1,136	1,065	1,002	1,157	1,284	48
Alumni_____mil. dol__	280	381	481	536	509	486	588	638	24
Non-alumni_____mil. dol__	348	441	493	600	556	516	569	646	24
Business corporations_____mil. dol__	196	269	275	320	354	357	379	446	17
Religious denominations_____mil. dol__	101	102	101	99	116	112	130	136	5
Other_____mil. dol__	73	153	147	161	170	192	195	246	9
Current operations_____mil. dol__	603	951	1,077	1,230	1,300	1,370	1,470	1,620	61
Capital purposes_____mil. dol__	797	829	943	1,010	940	790	940	1,050	39
Enrollment, higher education_____1,000__	(NA)	8,005	8,949	9,215	9,602	10,224	11,291	11,121	(X)
Support per student_____dol__	(NA)	222	226	243	233	211	213	240	(X)
In 1967 dollars_____dol__	(NA)	196	183	188	166	137	128	136	(X)
Expenditures, higher education__bil. dol__	(NA)	24.7	29.2	31.4	34.3	38.9	42.7	45.5	(X)
Expenditures per student_____dol__	(NA)	3,090	3,260	3,410	3,570	3,800	3,780	4,090	(X)
In 1967 dollars_____dol__	(NA)	2,730	2,640	2,640	2,540	2,460	2,280	2,325	(X)
Institutions reporting support____number__	1,064	1,045	1,093	1,020	988	986	991	1,006	(X)
Total support reported_____mil. dol__	1,245	1,472	1,647	1,751	1,747	1,675	1,891	2,132	100
Percent of estimated support_____	89	83	82	78	78	78	78	80	(X)
Average per institution_____$1,000__	1,170	1,409	1,507	1,717	1,768	1,698	1,908	2,119	(X)
Private 4-yr. institutions_____mil. dol__	1,032	1,154	1,267	1,342	1,342	1,227	1,396	1,551	73
Public 4-yr. institutions_____mil. dol__	195	292	356	383	386	431	477	562	26
Junior colleges_____mil. dol__	18	26	23	25	19	17	18	18	1

NA Not available. X Not applicable.
Source: Council for Financial Aid to Education, New York, N.Y., *Voluntary Support of Education*, annual.

No. 276. INSTITUTIONS OF HIGHER EDUCATION—VALUE OF PLANT AND CURRENT OPERATIONS EXPENDITURE, STATES AND OTHER AREAS: 1975 AND 1976

[In millions of dollars For years ending June 30. Value of plant includes grounds, buildings, and equipment]

STATE	VALUE OF PLANT 1975	1976	GROSS ADDITION TO PLANT VALUE [1] 1975	1976	EXPENDITURE, CURRENT OPERATIONS 1975	1976	STATE OR OTHER AREA	VALUE OF PLANT 1975	1976	GROSS ADDITION TO PLANT VALUE [1] 1975	1976	EXPENDITURE, CURRENT OPERATIONS 1975	1976
U.S__	62,183	66,348	4,761	4,702	35,058	38,903	Mont_____	206	210	8	6	92	101
							Nebr_____	516	537	67	39	250	286
Ala_____	806	883	83	86	492	577	Nev_____	91	109	12	12	50	62
Alaska___	161	161	12	-	71	92	N.H_____	292	306	10	16	162	178
Ariz_____	586	602	44	28	354	378	N.J_____	1,643	1,771	190	133	765	854
Ark_____	384	434	41	57	206	235	N. Mex____	304	328	25	17	145	173
Calif____	5,444	5,760	463	424	4,393	4,971	N.Y_____	6,637	6,986	396	405	3,734	4,114
Colo_____	720	755	63	45	483	540	N.C_____	1,520	1,633	121	129	967	998
Conn_____	1,043	1,096	68	50	506	541	N. Dak___	220	234	9	17	101	120
Del_____	254	266	21	14	96	105	Ohio_____	2,814	3,015	172	216	1,382	1,502
D.C_____	671	670	57	56	460	519	Okla_____	709	749	75	52	329	369
Fla_____	1,360	1,470	121	169	911	977	Oreg_____	701	752	46	55	389	454
Ga_____	1,154	1,224	90	85	607	658	Pa_____	3,529	3,785	207	271	1,872	2,140
Hawaii___	224	245	28	24	140	151	R.I_____	415	426	20	19	192	210
Idaho____	225	241	15	27	104	121	S.C_____	761	792	93	90	390	423
Ill_____	3,279	3,457	275	218	1,990	2,213	S. Dak____	181	189	6	12	105	111
Ind_____	1,775	1,844	112	83	823	887	Tenn_____	1,172	1,274	141	129	620	686
Iowa_____	964	1,057	92	104	536	587	Texas_____	3,032	3,324	342	293	1,575	1,870
Kans_____	637	710	29	50	352	384	Utah_____	507	541	47	38	296	332
Ky_____	926	983	53	62	413	468	Vt_____	240	251	13	13	119	132
La_____	897	954	43	68	426	444	Va_____	1,213	1,264	124	63	655	760
Maine____	248	258	16	11	134	150	Wash_____	1,342	1,449	79	97	620	676
Md_____	1,144	1,244	134	127	726	808	W. Va_____	593	636	27	23	164	187
Mass_____	2,440	2,590	134	153	1,467	1,558	Wis_____	1,583	1,671	94	104	839	947
Mich_____	2,569	2,762	164	202	1,417	1,547	Wyo_____	119	122	6	3	60	71
Minn_____	1,434	1,629	137	94	749	747	U.S. schools [2]	664	741	20	70	322	361
Miss_____	495	533	37	45	304	351	Other areas_	241	244	12	14	243	248
Mo_____	1,339	1,425	80	98	706	777							

- Represents zero.
[1] Includes expenditures from current funds for plant expansion. [2] Military academies.
Source: U.S. National Center for Education Statistics, *Financial Statistics of Institutions of Higher Education*, annual.

No. 277. Earned Degrees Conferred, by Level of Degree: 1950 to 1976

[In thousands, except percent. Includes Puerto Rico; 1965, Guam; and 1970, Virgin Islands. See Appendix III]

YEAR	TOTAL Number	TOTAL Percent male	BACHELOR'S [1] Male	BACHELOR'S [1] Female	MASTER'S [2] Male	MASTER'S [2] Female	DOCTORATES Male	DOCTORATES Female	PERCENT OF TOTAL Bachelor's [1]	PERCENT OF TOTAL Master's [2]	PERCENT OF TOTAL Doctorates
1950	499	75.6	330	104	41	17	6.0	.6	87.0	11.7	1.3
1955	354	65.0	184	104	39	19	8.0	.8	81.1	16.4	2.5
1960	479	65.8	256	139	51	24	8.8	1.0	82.4	15.5	2.1
1965	668	61.5	320	219	76	36	14.7	1.8	80.7	16.8	2.5
1967	773	61.6	355	240	103	55	18.2	2.5	76.9	20.4	2.7
1968	872	60.4	393	279	114	63	20.2	2.9	77.0	20.3	2.6
1969	990	59.7	447	323	122	73	22.8	3.4	77.7	19.6	2.6
1970	1,073	59.6	487	346	126	83	25.9	4.0	77.7	19.5	2.8
1971	1,148	59.3	514	370	139	93	27.5	4.6	77.0	20.2	2.8
1972	1,224	59.1	545	393	150	103	28.1	5.3	76.6	20.7	2.7
1973	1,280	58.7	568	412	155	110	28.6	6.2	76.6	20.7	2.7
1974	1,321	58.0	580	429	158	120	27.4	6.5	76.4	21.1	2.6
1975	1,316	56.8	558	430	162	132	26.8	7.3	75.1	22.3	2.6
1976, prel	1,345	56.2	562	436	168	145	26.3	7.8	74.2	23.3	2.5

[1] Includes 1st professional degrees.   [2] Includes 2d level degrees.
Source: U.S. National Center for Education Statistics, *Earned Degrees Conferred*, annual.

No. 278. Degrees Conferred in Medicine, Dentistry, Law, and Engineering: 1950 to 1976

[First professional degrees for medicine, dentistry, and law. NA= Not available. See Appendix III]

TYPE OF DEGREE	1950	1955	1960	1965	1970	1973	1974	1975	1976
Medicine (M.D.):									
Institutions conferring degrees	72	72	79	81	86	97	99	104	107
Degrees conferred, total	5,612	7,014	7,032	7,304	8,314	10,307	11,356	12,447	13,426
Men	5,028	6,683	6,645	6,832	7,615	9,388	10,093	10,818	11,252
Women	584	331	387	472	699	919	1,263	1,629	2,174
Dentistry (D.D.S. or D.M.D.):									
Institutions conferring degrees	40	42	45	45	48	51	52	52	56
Degrees conferred, total	2,579	3,099	3,247	3,107	3,718	4,047	4,440	4,773	5,425
Men	2,561	3,071	3,221	3,085	3,684	3,992	4,355	4,627	5,187
Women	18	28	26	22	34	55	85	146	238
Law (L.L.B. or J.D.):									
Institutions conferring degrees	(NA)	128	134	134	145	152	151	154	166
Degrees conferred, total	(NA)	8,209	9,240	11,583	14,916	27,205	29,326	29,296	32,293
Men	(NA)	7,921	9,010	11,216	14,115	25,037	25,986	24,881	26,085
Women	(NA)	288	230	367	801	2,168	3,340	4,415	6,208
Engineering:									
Degrees conferred, total	58,066	27,527	45,624	50,664	63,753	71,376	68,977	65,308	65,494
Bachelor's	52,668	22,445	37,679	36,485	44,479	51,265	50,286	46,852	46,331
Master's	4,904	4,483	7,159	12,055	15,593	16,619	15,379	15,348	16,342
Doctorates	494	599	786	2,124	3,681	3,492	3,312	3,108	2,821

Source: U.S. National Center for Education Statistics, *Digest of Education Statistics, 1977-78.*

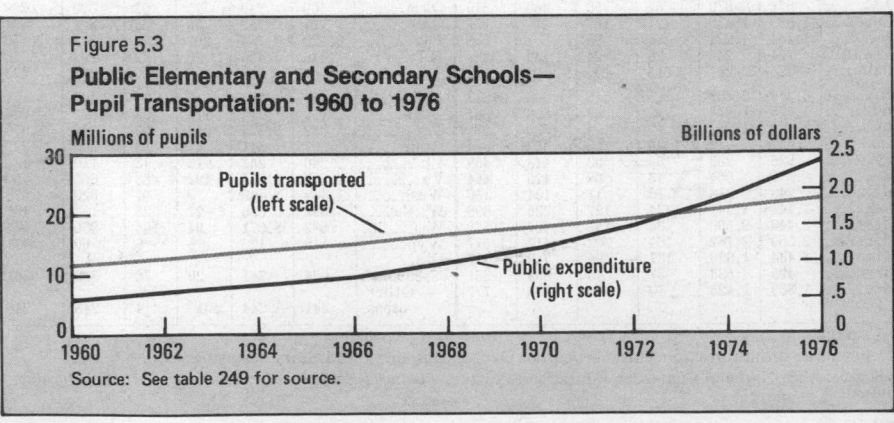

Figure 5.3

**Public Elementary and Secondary Schools—
Pupil Transportation: 1960 to 1976**

Source: See table 249 for source.

No. 279. EARNED DEGREES CONFERRED, BY FIELD OF STUDY, 1972 TO 1976, AND BY
LEVEL OF DEGREE AND SEX, 1976

[Includes Puerto Rico and outlying areas. See Appendix III]

MAJOR FIELD OF STUDY	BACHELOR'S [1] (1,000)				1976					
					Bachelor's [1] (1,000)		Master's		Doctorates	
	1972	1973	1974	1975	Total	Male	Total	Male	Total	Male
All fields	894.1	930.3	954.4	931.7	934.4	508.5	313,001	167,745	34,076	26,273
Agriculture	13.6	14.8	16.3	17.6	19.5	15.9	3,351	2,873	928	867
Animal science	2.7	2.9	3.1	3.4	3.9	2.8	443	376	135	125
Forestry	2.0	2.0	2.3	2.6	2.7	2.4	405	361	92	88
All other	8.9	9.9	10.9	11.5	12.9	10.6	2,503	2,136	701	654
Architecture	6.5	7.0	7.8	8.2	9.2	7.4	3,215	2,545	82	69
Area studies	2.8	3.1	3.2	3.1	3.1	1.4	945	517	182	124
Biological sciences	37.6	42.7	48.9	52.2	54.9	35.8	6,621	4,518	3,397	2,666
Biology, general	27.8	31.6	36.6	39.2	40.7	26.4	3,200	2,211	624	448
Zoology, general	5.2	5.4	5.8	5.7	5.6	4.0	529	380	276	234
All other	4.6	5.7	6.4	7.4	8.6	5.4	2,892	1,927	2,497	1,984
Business and management	123.3	128.2	133.9	135.5	145.0	116.3	42,728	37,754	956	904
Business management and administration	32.1	33.3	37.1	39.3	44.5	37.0	23,360	20,873	492	463
Business and commerce, general	31.7	30.3	33.0	31.5	30.4	24.3	8,455	7,463	129	121
Accounting	25.1	28.3	29.8	31.6	36.4	28.6	2,756	2,275	55	50
All other	34.4	36.4	34.1	33.0	33.7	26.4	8,157	7,143	280	270
Communications	12.3	14.3	17.1	19.2	21.3	12.5	3,128	1,820	204	154
Computer and information sciences	3.4	4.3	4.8	5.0	5.7	4.5	2,603	2,226	244	221
Education	192.4	195.6	186.6	168.7	156.5	42.5	128,410	45,819	7,769	5,176
Elementary, general	93.7	90.1	81.0	69.6	60.9	7.8	22,776	3,356	196	75
Physical	26.3	27.0	27.8	24.7	24.3	13.6	4,769	2,931	215	155
Music	7.1	7.5	7.8	8.1	7.9	3.2	1,382	681	80	55
Special education, general	4.1	5.5	6.7	7.8	8.2	1.0	7,692	1,459	208	119
Other education fields	61.2	65.6	63.3	58.6	55.2	16.9	91,791	37,392	7,070	4,772
Engineering	51.5	51.6	50.7	47.3	46.7	45.2	16,349	15,767	2,821	2,755
Fine and applied arts	33.9	36.1	40.0	41.1	42.4	16.6	8,820	4,507	620	447
Art [2]	13.5	15.3	16.4	16.2	16.6	5.7	2,654	1,337	84	38
Music [3]	6.3	6.8	7.9	8.7	9.1	4.3	3,217	1,684	368	298
Dramatic arts	4.5	4.8	5.4	5.5	5.7	2.4	1,394	714	112	82
All other	9.6	9.3	10.3	10.7	10.9	4.2	1,555	772	56	29
Foreign languages	19.4	19.5	19.5	18.2	15.6	3.7	3,541	1,179	864	450
Health professions	28.9	33.9	41.9	49.5	54.3	11.5	12,696	4,255	577	411
Nursing	13.2	15.5	19.4	23.8	26.8	1.4	3,058	90	16	–
Pharmacy	4.7	5.1	5.8	6.5	7.0	4.9	307	247	81	73
Medical lab. technology	3.4	3.8	4.8	5.1	5.4	1.1	266	129	–	–
All other	7.6	9.5	11.8	14.1	15.0	4.2	9,065	3,789	480	338
Home economics	12.2	13.6	15.4	16.9	17.5	1.0	2,187	186	178	51
Law (excl. first professional)	.5	.5	.5	.4	.5	.4	1,442	1,269	76	73
Letters	73.6	71.3	65.3	57.9	52.3	22.5	11,356	4,730	2,452	1,556
Library sciences	1.0	1.2	1.2	1.1	.8	.1	8,084	1,753	71	39
Mathematical subjects	23.8	23.2	21.8	18.3	16.1	9.5	3,863	2,550	856	762
Military sciences	.4	.3	.3	.4	1.2	1.2	–	–	–	–
Physical sciences	20.9	20.8	21.3	20.9	21.6	17.4	5,485	4,660	3,433	3,133
Chemistry, general	10.7	10.2	10.4	10.5	11.1	8.6	1,734	1,370	1,500	1,323
Physics	4.6	4.1	3.9	3.7	3.5	3.1	1,421	1,296	968	926
Geology	2.5	2.8	3.2	3.2	3.3	2.7	935	811	280	259
All other	3.1	3.6	3.8	3.5	3.8	3.1	1,395	1,183	685	625
Psychology	43.4	48.1	52.3	51.4	50.4	23.0	7,859	4,188	2,581	1,762
Public affairs and services	12.7	18.0	24.3	28.6	33.6	18.9	17,333	9,486	319	217
Social sciences	159.6	157.7	152.2	136.8	127.9	79.5	15,902	10,880	4,160	3,260
History	44.0	41.2	37.4	31.8	28.6	18.8	3,676	2,459	1,014	789
Sociology	35.6	36.0	35.9	31.8	28.0	11.4	2,010	1,166	729	511
Political science or government	28.3	30.2	30.9	29.3	28.5	21.3	2,192	1,719	723	602
Social sciences, general	21.4	18.3	17.1	14.0	12.5	7.1	2,272	1,445	85	66
Economics	15.3	14.9	14.4	14.1	14.9	11.9	2,093	1,759	763	682
All other	14.9	17.1	16.5	15.8	15.5	9.0	3,659	2,332	846	610
Theology	3.9	3.5	4.2	4.8	5.5	4.0	3,292	2,234	1,033	991
Theological professions, general	2.0	1.7	2.5	2.8	3.5	2.9	1,537	1,291	960	928
Religious education	1.1	1.0	1.3	1.4	1.5	.8	1,384	664	29	26
All other	.7	.8	.4	.7	.5	.4	371	279	44	37
Interdisciplinary studies [4]	16.7	20.8	24.9	28.5	32.8	18.0	3,791	2,029	273	185

– Represents zero. [1] Requiring 4 or 5 years. [2] Includes history and appreciation. [3] Includes performing and liberal arts, history, and appreciation. [4] Comprises general liberal arts and sciences, biological and physical sciences, humanities and social sciences, engineering, and other disciplines.

Source: U.S. National Center for Education Statistics, *Earned Degrees Conferred*, annual.

No. 280. EARNED DEGREES BELOW THE BACHELOR'S DEGREE, BY TYPE OF CURRICULUM: 1971 TO 1976

[In thousands. Includes Puerto Rico and outlying areas. Covers associate degrees and other awards based on post-secondary curriculums of less than 4 years in institutions of higher education. Arts and science include general programs]

TYPE OF CURRICULUM	1971	1972	1973	1974	1975	1976	PERCENT FEMALE	
							1971	1976
All degrees	303.4	351.9	389.0	429.7	448.5	487.7	44.5	48.1
Occupational	153.5	190.0	224.0	260.5	277.2	313.0	45.7	48.8
Science and engineering	87.7	107.9	129.9	147.3	159.0	174.8	42.0	48.2
Health service	34.5	45.4	58.9	70.3	76.7	83.5	91.6	86.4
Nursing, R.N	14.4	18.2	23.5	28.7	32.4	34.3	95.8	93.0
Mechanical and engineering	37.4	44.1	48.5	52.6	56.3	63.3	1.4	3.4
Natural science	7.0	9.4	14.0	16.4	18.0	19.5	22.8	32.8
Data processing	8.7	9.0	8.5	8.0	7.9	8.5	35.6	41.1
Business and commerce	51.0	61.1	66.7	80.5	83.0	96.8	54.0	55.0
Secretarial	16.5	20.3	22.0	27.3	27.5	29.0	98.3	98.9
Public service	14.8	21.0	27.3	32.8	35.2	41.4	38.8	37.0
Police and corrections	6.9	9.2	12.7	15.9	17.0	20.3	6.1	14.1
Arts and science	150.0	161.8	165.0	169.2	171.4	174.7	43.2	46.7

Source: U.S. National Center For Education Statistics, *Associate Degrees and Other Formal Awards Below the Baccalaureate*, annual.

No. 281. NON-COLLEGIATE POSTSECONDARY SCHOOLS—ENROLLMENT AND INSTRUCTIONAL STAFF, BY TYPE OF SCHOOL: 1976

[For school year ending in June. Includes Puerto Rico. Covers schools offering occupational programs]

ITEM	Total	Voca-tional and technical	Tech-nical insti-tute	Busi-ness and office	Cosme-tology and barber	Flight	Trade	Corre-spond-ence	Hos-pital	Other
Schools, number	8,605	1,218	211	1,221	2,347	1,406	733	106	1,112	251
Total enrollment..1,000	1,788	495	92	339	133	73	158	389	71	38
Percent female	51.2	48.6	21.2	61.5	84.4	6.7	28.6	(NA)	91.9	66.5
Full-time 1,000	1,024	350	67	264	112	13	121	–	70	27
Part-time 1,000	764	145	25	75	21	60	37	389	1	11
Public 1,000	469	367	41	1	1	6	35	–	10	8
Private 1,000	1,319	128	51	338	132	67	123	389	61	30
Instructional staff.1,000	51	15	3	7	7	5	4	1	8	1
Percent female	49.2	41.8	14.4	62.3	77.3	45.2	19.6	24.3	87.3	45.1

– Represents zero.   NA Not available.
Source: U.S. National Center for Education Statistics, *Directory of Postsecondary Schools with Occupational Programs, 1975–76*, and *Enrollments and Programs in Public and Private Noncollegiate Postsecondary Schools, 1976*.

No. 282. LIBRARIES—NUMBER, BY TYPE: 1970 TO 1976

[Covers listings in *American Library Directory*]

TYPE	1970	1972	1974	1976	TYPE	1970	1972	1974	1976
Total [1]	27,180	29,819	30,436	32,144	Special [4]	1,216	1,238	1,176	1,252
					Special [5]	274	500	450	85
United States	23,998	24,069	25,934	29,345	Law	477	482	656	806
					Law [4]	115	131	181	147
Public	7,190	7,109	7,652	8,504	Medical	1,315	1,406	1,645	1,955
Public, branch	4,855	4,881	5,538	5,477					
Public, military [2]	481	446	533	559	Medical [4]	181	156	156	157
					Religious	600	773	786	996
College and university	1,896	1,667	1,605	1,696	Religious [4]	49	24	26	19
Junior college	1,072	1,056	1,081	1,129					
Special [3]	4,277	4,200	4,449	6,563	Outlying areas	102	65	17	129

[1] Includes public libraries with annual incomes of less than $2,000 or book funds of less than $500, law libraries with less than 10,000 volumes each, Canadian libraries, and libraries in regions administered by the U.S., not shown separately.   [2] Military installations including veterans' hospitals.   [3] Includes science-technology, business and financial, advertising, newspaper and publishing, art and music libraries, and specialized colleges such as business and technical schools.   [4] Part of "college or university."
[5] Part of public systems or military installations; for 1976, part of military installation only.

Source: R. R. Bowker Co., New York, N.Y., *The Bowker Annual of Library and Book Trade Information* and *American Library Directory*, biennial. (Copyright by Xerox Corporation.)

No. 283. FEDERALLY AIDED VOCATIONAL PROGRAMS—ENROLLMENT AND EXPENDITURES, 1950 TO 1976, AND BY STATES AND OTHER AREAS, 1976

[For years ending **June 30.** Includes Puerto Rico for all years; Virgin Islands from 1955; Guam, from 1960; and American Samoa and Trust Territory of the Pacific Islands, from 1970. See also *Historical Statistics, Colonial Times to 1970,* series H 572–581]

YEAR AND STATE OR OTHER AREA	ENROLLMENT (1,000)					EXPENDITURES (mil. dol.)		
	Total [1]	Consumer and home-making [2]	Office occupations	Trades and industry	Agri-culture	Total	Federal	State and local
1950	3,365	1,430	–	805	765	128.7	26.6	102.1
1955	3,314	1,432	–	871	776	164.8	30.4	134.4
1960	3,768	1,588	–	938	796	238.8	45.3	193.5
1965	5,431	2,099	731	1,088	888	604.6	156.9	447.7
1970	8,794	2,570	2,111	1,906	853	1,866.2	300.7	1,565.5
1972	11,602	3,446	2,352	2,398	896	2,660.8	466.0	2,194.7
1973	12,072	3,517	2,499	2,702	928	3,033.7	482.4	2,551.3
1974	13,556	3,703	2,757	2,824	976	3,433.8	468.2	2,965.6
1975	15,340	3,746	2,951	3,017	1,013	4,037.3	536.1	3,501.1
1976, total	**15,133**	**3,515**	**3,115**	**3,110**	**1,060**	**5,150.2**	**543.2**	**4,607.0**
Alabama	265	76	28	68	58	59.0	7.6	51.4
Alaska	35	5	14	11	(Z)	13.3	1.0	12.3
Arizona	236	63	32	40	8	34.5	6.0	28.5
Arkansas	151	47	19	36	24	32.5	7.1	25.4
California	1,765	284	577	448	88	549.9	43.9	506.0
Colorado	144	31	38	30	7	52.3	6.6	45.7
Connecticut	239	88	58	30	2	45.1	6.2	38.9
Delaware	67	1	12	9	2	11.3	1.5	9.8
District of Columbia	17	11	1	4	(Z)	5.0	2.1	2.9
Florida	921	112	130	137	30	289.3	8.4	280.9
Georgia	487	109	120	71	55	73.7	13.9	59.8
Hawaii	61	22	15	15	3	11.7	2.0	9.7
Idaho	47	24	7	9	6	13.1	2.5	10.6
Illinois	721	33	242	229	34	234.7	19.3	215.4
Indiana	186	64	21	52	26	31.6	11.6	20.0
Iowa	319	84	22	41	42	56.8	8.3	48.5
Kansas	106	46	10	21	11	30.9	7.0	23.9
Kentucky	241	91	33	34	22	51.0	10.3	40.7
Louisiana	220	58	62	35	23	48.7	11.3	37.4
Maine	80	10	16	16	1	29.9	5.7	24.2
Maryland	257	97	66	34	5	122.2	13.5	108.7
Massachusetts	215	21	92	58	4	226.8	13.4	213.4
Michigan	410	81	70	100	15	161.9	26.2	135.7
Minnesota	388	91	48	97	48	113.5	13.0	100.5
Mississippi	187	40	14	46	23	42.3	7.7	34.6
Missouri	226	78	32	39	23	74.9	12.7	62.3
Montana	36	11	5	10	4	20.1	2.2	17.9
Nebraska	111	36	13	21	10	18.9	4.3	14.6
Nevada	29	2	9	11	1	(NA)	(NA)	(NA)
New Hampshire	77	22	13	10	2	12.1	2.5	9.5
New Jersey	489	147	138	79	5	123.9	13.9	110.0
New Mexico	52	16	7	7	6	20.3	3.7	16.6
New York	1,027	371	326	185	19	925.5	37.6	887.9
North Carolina	637	61	63	136	41	146.0	16.4	129.6
North Dakota	55	18	6	8	9	11.9	2.4	9.5
Ohio	715	158	74	110	41	209.3	34.5	174.8
Oklahoma	176	36	20	40	30	56.9	8.1	48.8
Oregon	217	55	36	37	7	55.6	6.0	49.6
Pennsylvania	420	78	98	121	21	253.0	27.0	226.0
Rhode Island	43	8	8	7	1	18.5	3.1	15.4
South Carolina	260	51	50	47	21	84.5	9.4	75.1
South Dakota	32	16	2	5	5	9.4	2.6	6.8
Tennessee	215	59	32	50	20	99.5	12.9	86.6
Texas	970	323	86	148	133	219.0	29.0	190.1
Utah	144	38	26	28	4	24.8	4.1	20.8
Vermont	24	8	4	5	2	9.4	1.5	7.9
Virginia	441	99	96	80	37	101.4	13.9	87.5
Washington	338	90	79	108	26	116.8	9.8	107.0
West Virginia	111	29	27	30	6	36.2	7.6	28.7
Wisconsin	329	47	95	97	36	124.8	13.0	111.8
Wyoming	22	5	7	4	2	6.0	1.1	4.9
Puerto Rico	180	66	19	19	5	30.1	8.1	22.0
American Samoa	2	(Z)	(Z)	.1	(Z)	.5	.1	.4

– Represents zero.   NA Not available.   Z Fewer than 500 persons.   [1] Includes programs not shown separately. Represents unduplicated enrollment.   [2] Prior to 1972, represents home economics.

Source: U.S. Office of Education, *Vocational and Technical Education,* annual.

No. 284. WORK AND TRAINING PROGRAMS—FIRST-TIME AND CURRENT ENROLLMENTS, AND OBLIGATIONS, BY PROGRAM: 1975 TO 1977

[First-time enrollments and obligations, for years ending June 30 except as noted. Current enrollment, as of June 30, except, beginning 1977, as of Sept. 30. Covers programs administered by the U.S. Dept. of Labor]

PROGRAM	FIRST-TIME ENROLLMENTS (1,000)			CURRENT ENROLLMENTS (1,000)			OBLIGATIONS (mil. dol.)		
	1975	1976	1977	1975	1976	1977	1975	1976	1977 [1]
Total	2,762	3,212	4,009	1,148	1,173	1,368	4,109	5,087	11,208
Comprehensive Employment and Training Act (CETA)	2,395	2,761	3,416	926	911	1,004	3,967	4,772	10,756
Training and Work Experience	1,126	1,250	1,423	573	505	367	1,585	1,528	2,266
Public Service Employment	384	488	814	279	300	524	1,541	2,290	7,297
Special Target Groups [2]	70	159	219	53	85	91	229	232	321
Job Corps	46	43	52	21	21	22	210	134	255
Summer Youth Program	716	821	907	(NA)	(NA)	(NA)	391	588	618
Emergency Employment Act [3]	53	(X)	(X)	(NA)	(X)	(X)	11	(X)	(X)
Older Americans Act	7	6	23	5	13	29	12	85	150
Work Incentive Program	360	445	571	217	249	335	130	230	302

NA Not available.   X Not applicable.   [1] For 15 months, July 1, 1976–Sept. 30, 1977.
[2] Includes Indian, Migrant, and Operation Mainstream programs.   [3] Funds made available to provide for the orderly transition of programs funded under legislation predating the Comprehensive Employment and Training Act. Program discontinued in 1976.

Source: U.S. Employment and Training Administration, Manpower Report of the President, annual.

No. 285. ADULT EDUCATION—PERCENT PARTICIPATION, BY SOURCE OF INSTRUCTION AND DESCRIPTION OF COURSE, 1969 TO 1975, AND BY SEX AND RACE, 1975

[For years ending in May. Covers persons 17 years old and over who were not full-time students in high school or college. 1969 and 1972 include all persons age 35 years old and over regardless of their enrollment status]

SOURCE OF INSTRUCTION AND COURSE	1969	1972	1975					
			Total	Sex		Race		
				Male	Female	White	Black	Other
Total participants 1,000	13,041	15,734	17,059	8,028	9,032	15,739	1,031	290
Percent of population participating	10.0	11.3	11.6	11.7	11.6	12.1	6.9	13.4
PERCENT DISTRIBUTION								
Source of instruction: [1]								
Grade schools and high schools	[2] 15.1	[2] 14.0	11.0	6.5	15.1	11.0	10.5	14.1
Two year colleges and tech. institutes	[2] 11.9	16.3	17.7	17.2	18.1	17.6	20.9	10.7
Four year colleges and universities	21.7	21.4	19.1	18.4	19.7	19.2	19.2	12.4
Community organizations	11.9	12.7	10.5	6.7	13.8	10.8	6.2	4.5
Trade, vocational, and business schools	[3] 11.5	[3] 11.3	8.6	9.6	7.7	8.2	14.5	12.4
Tutor or private instructor	(4)	(4)	6.9	4.3	9.2	7.2	.8	13.1
Employer	17.4	16.6	15.3	21.4	9.8	15.3	15.1	13.1
Labor unions and professional assns	(4)	(4)	6.1	8.4	4.0	6.3	2.2	8.3
Government agency	(4)	(4)	8.0	6.6	9.3	7.7	9.9	16.2
Other	20.0	22.0	11.7	14.2	9.5	11.9	9.5	11.0
Description of course: [1]								
Occupational training	44.6	46.5	48.7	62.1	36.8	48.7	48.2	50.7
General education	27.2	25.9	20.6	17.6	23.3	19.5	37.4	20.0
Personal and family living	12.1	14.0	14.8	10.3	18.9	15.2	9.4	13.4
Social life and recreation	11.9	12.0	15.9	8.1	22.8	16.6	3.6	20.0
Community issues	9.2	9.8	10.0	10.0	10.0	10.4	5.5	2.4
Other and not reported	4.4	3.4	3.2	3.0	3.4	3.2	2.9	4.5

[1] Percentages total more than 100 since some adults received instruction from more than one source or were enrolled in more than one course.   [2] Public schools only.
[3] Private schools only   [4] Included in other.

Source: U.S. National Center for Education Statistics, Participation in Adult Education, 1969, 1972, and 1975.

Section 6
Law Enforcement, Federal Courts, and Prisons

This section presents data on crimes committed and victims of crimes, arrests, law enforcement employment and expenditures, the legal profession, courts and judges, Federal court cases, Federal and State prisoners, juveniles in court custody, and use of the death penalty. A major source of data on these subjects is the Law Enforcement Assistance Administration (LEAA) which issues several reports including *Criminal Victimization in the United States, Prisoners in State and Federal Institutions, Children in Custody, National Survey of Court Organization,* and *Capital Punishment.* In addition, the annual *Expenditure and Employment Data for the Criminal Justice System* is issued jointly by LEAA and the Bureau of the Census. For other LEAA reports, see "Law Enforcement, Federal Courts, and Prisons" in Appendix IV.

Other major sources of these data include: *Uniform Crime Reports for the United States,* issued annually by the Federal Bureau of Investigation (FBI); the *Annual Report of the Director* and *Special Reports on Federal Offenders and Persons Under the Supervision of the Federal Probation System,* issued by the Administrative Office of the U.S. Courts; *Governmental Finances and Public Employment,* issued annually by the Bureau of the Census; the *Statistical Report,* issued annually by the Federal Bureau of Prisons; and the annual *Juvenile Court Statistics* issued by the U.S. Office of Human Development and the U.S. Office of Youth Development. Statistics on lawyers and law firms are compiled by the American Bar Foundation, Chicago, Illinois, and the Bureau of the Census, respectively.

Legal jurisdiction and law enforcement.—Law enforcement is, for the most part, a function of State and local officers and agencies. The U.S. Constitution reserves general police powers to the States. By act of Congress, Federal offenses include only offenses against the U.S. Government and against or by its employees while engaged in their official duties, and offenses which involve the crossing of State lines or an interference with interstate commerce. Consequently, criminal offenses such as murder, robbery, burglary, theft, assault, and rape are violations of State laws unless they involve Federal property or a Federal officer while engaged in his official duties, or unless they occur in Federal territories or reservations or on the high seas. Excluding the military, there are 52 separate criminal law jurisdictions in the United States: 1 in each of the 50 States, 1 in the District of Columbia, and the Federal jurisdiction. Each of these has its own criminal law and procedure and its own law enforcement agencies. While the systems of law enforcement are quite similar among the States, there are often substantial differences in the penalties for like offenses.

Law enforcement can be divided into three parts. The first, covering investigation of crimes and arrest of persons suspected of committing them, involves municipal, county, and State police; sheriffs, constables, marshals, and Federal agents; and many kinds of special officers. The second phase is prosecution of those charged with crime to judge whether they are legally guilty or innocent. The agencies concerned include courts; justices of the peace; municipal, State, and Federal juries; and prosecuting court officers. The third phase is concerned with the punishment or treatment of persons convicted of crime. While the courts usually determine the sentence after conviction, the penalty is enforced by the detention facility, or by probation or parole officials.

Crime.—There are two major approaches taken in determining the extent of crime. One perspective is provided by the FBI through its Uniform Crime Reporting Program. The FBI receives monthly and annual reports from law enforcement agencies throughout the country, currently representing 95 percent of the national population. Each month, city police, sheriffs, and State police file reports on the number of offenses that become known to them in the following seven crime categories—murder and nonnegligent manslaughter, forcible rape, robbery, aggravated assault, burglary, larceny-theft, and motor vehicle theft. These categories are the basis of the FBI Crime Index and are defined as follows: *Murder and nonnegligent manslaughter*, which is based on police investigations, as opposed to the determination of a medical examiner or judicial body, includes willful felonious homicides and excludes attempts and assaults to kill, suicides, accidental deaths, justifiable homicides, and deaths caused by negligence; *forcible rape* includes forcible rapes and attempts; *robbery* includes stealing or taking anything of value by force or violence or threat of force or violence and includes attempted robbery; *aggravated assault* includes assault with intent to kill; *burglary* includes any unlawful entry to commit a felony or a theft and includes attempted burglary and burglary followed by larceny; *larceny* includes theft of property or articles of value without use of force and violence or fraud and excludes embezzlement, "con games," forgery, etc.; *motor vehicle theft* includes all cases where vehicles are driven away and abandoned, but excludes vehicles taken for temporary use and returned by the taker.

The monthly Uniform Crime Reports also contain data on crimes cleared by arrest and on persons arrested for all criminal offenses, by age, sex, and race of the offender. Annual reports provide an accounting of the number of persons formally charged and their disposition. In summarizing and publishing crime data, the FBI does not vouch for the validity of the reports it receives, but presents the data as information useful to persons concerned with the problem of crime and criminal-law enforcement.

A second perspective on crime is provided by LEAA through the National Crime Survey conducted by the Bureau of the Census. This series of surveys, based on representative samples of households and commercial establishments, are designed to elicit information about experiences, if any, with selected crimes of violence and theft. The surveys, conducted nationally on a continuous basis and for selected cities periodically, focus on victims of crime. The results, published in a series of *Criminal Victimization* reports, present types of crime, frequency of victimization, characteristics of victims, victim-offender relationship (stranger-nonstranger), and whether or not police were notified about the incident.

Courts.—Court statistics on criminal offenses and the outcome of prosecutions are incomplete for the country as a whole, although data are available for many States individually. The only national compilations of such statistics were made by the Bureau of the Census for 1932 to 1945 covering a maximum of 32 States.

The bulk of civil and criminal litigation in the country is commenced and determined in the various State courts. Only when the U.S. Constitution and acts of Congress specifically confer jurisdiction upon the Federal courts may civil litigation be heard and decided by them. Generally, the Federal courts have jurisdiction over the following types of cases: Suits or proceedings by or against the United States; civil actions between private parties arising under the Constitution, laws, or treaties of the United States; civil actions between private litigants who are citizens of different States; civil cases involving admiralty, maritime, or prize jurisdiction; and all matters and proceedings in bankruptcy.

There are several types of courts with varying degrees of legal jurisdiction. These jurisdictions include original, appellate, general, and limited or special. A *court of original jurisdiction* is one having the authority initially to try a case and pass judgment on the law and the facts; a *court of appellate jurisdiction* is one with the legal authority to review cases and hear appeals; a *court of general jurisdiction* is a trial court of unlimited original jurisdiction in civil and/or criminal cases, also called a "major trial court"; a *court of limited or special jurisdiction* is a trial court with legal authority over only a particular class of cases, such as probate, juvenile, or traffic cases.

The 94 Federal courts of original jurisdiction are known as the U.S. district courts. One or more of these courts is established in every State and one each in the District of Columbia, Puerto Rico, the Virgin Islands, the Canal Zone, and Guam. Appeals from the district courts are taken to intermediate appellate courts of which there are 11, known as U.S. courts of appeals. The Supreme Court of the United States is the final and highest appellate court in the Federal system of courts.

Juvenile offenders.—For statistical purposes, the FBI and most States classify as juvenile offenders persons under the age of 18 years who have committed a crime or crimes.

Delinquency cases are all cases of youths referred to a juvenile court for violation of a law or ordinance or for seriously "antisocial" conduct. This broad definition includes conduct which violates the law only when committed by children (e.g. ungovernable behavior); such offenses are termed "juvenile offenses." Several types of facilities are available for those adjudicated delinquent, ranging from the short-term physically unrestricted environment (e.g. a shelter or halfway house) to the long-term very restrictive atmosphere (e.g., a training school).

Prisoners.—Statistics of prisoners have been collected and published for a longer period of time than have other criminal statistics. Data on prisoners in Federal and State prisons and reformatories were collected annually by the Bureau of the Census until 1950, transferred then to the Federal Bureau of Prisons and, in 1971, to LEAA. Adults convicted of criminal activity may be given a prison or jail sentence. A *prison* is a confinement facility having custodial authority over adults sentenced to confinement of more than one year. A *jail* is a facility, usually operated by a local law enforcement agency, holding persons detained pending adjudication and/or persons committed after adjudication to one year or less. Nearly every State publishes annual data either for its whole prison system or for each separate State institution.

Statistical reliability.—For discussion of statistical collection, estimation, and sampling procedures and measures of statistical reliability pertaining to the National Crime Survey, see Appendix III.

Historical statistics.—Tabular headnotes provide cross-references, where applicable, to *Historical Statistics of the United States, Colonial Times to 1970.* See Appendix I.

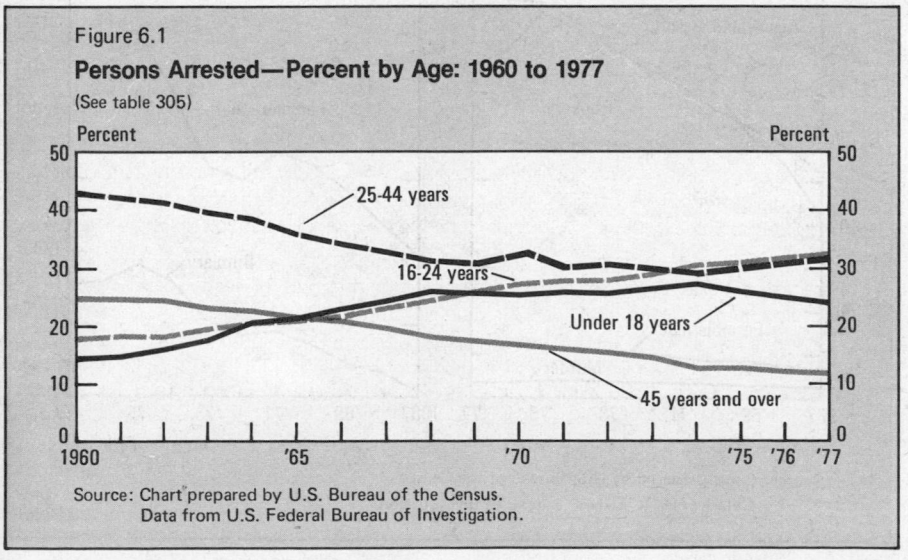

Figure 6.1

Persons Arrested—Percent by Age: 1960 to 1977

(See table 305)

Source: Chart prepared by U.S. Bureau of the Census.
Data from U.S. Federal Bureau of Investigation.

Figure 6.2

Homicide and Suicide Rates: 1965 to 1976

(See table 295. Rate per 100,000 resident
population 15 years old and over)

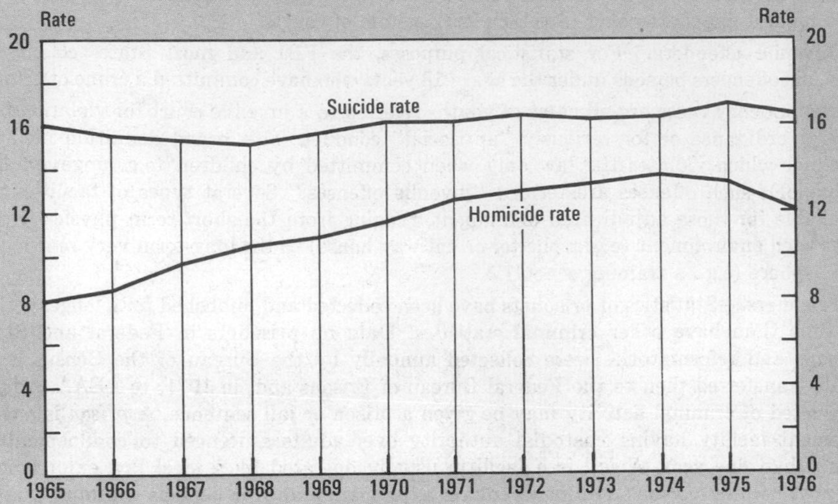

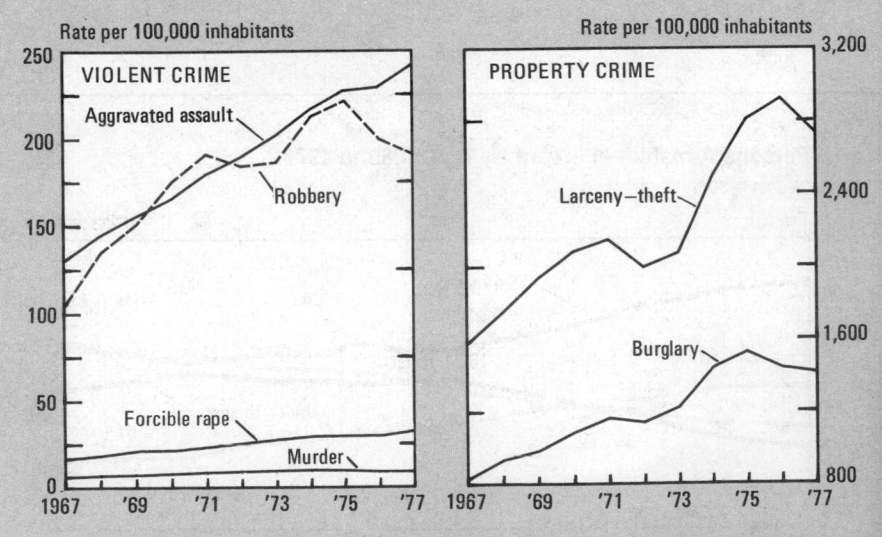

Source: Chart prepared by U.S. Bureau of the Census.
Data from U.S. National Center for Health Statistics.

Figure 6.3

Selected Crime Rates: 1967 to 1977

(See table 286)

Source: Chart prepared by U.S. Bureau of the Census.
Data from U.S. Federal Bureau of Investigation.

No. 286. CRIMES AND CRIME RATES, BY TYPE: 1967 TO 1977

[Data refer to offenses known to the police. Rates are based on Bureau of the Census population data, excluding Armed Forces abroad. For definitions of crimes, see text, p. 174. Minus sign (−) denotes decrease. See also *Historical Statistics, Colonial Times to 1970*, series H 952–961]

ITEM AND YEAR	Total	VIOLENT CRIME					PROPERTY CRIME			
		Total	Murder [1]	Forcible rape	Robbery	Aggravated assault	Total	Burglary	Larceny—theft	Motor vehicle theft
Number of offenses:										
1967----------------1,000--	5,903	500	12.2	27.6	203	257	5,404	1,632	3,112	660
1968----------------1,000--	6,720	595	13.8	31.7	263	287	6,125	1,859	3,483	784
1969----------------1,000--	7,410	662	14.8	37.2	299	311	6,749	1,982	3,889	879
1970----------------1,000--	8,098	739	16.0	38.0	350	335	7,359	2,205	4,226	928
1971----------------1,000--	8,588	817	17.8	42.3	388	369	7,772	2,399	4,424	948
1972----------------1,000--	8,249	835	18.7	46.9	376	393	7,414	2,376	4,151	887
1973----------------1,000--	8,718	876	19.6	51.4	384	421	7,842	2,566	4,348	929
1974----------------1,000--	10,253	975	20.7	55.4	442	456	9,279	3,039	5,263	977
1975----------------1,000--	11,257	1,026	20.5	56.1	465	485	10,230	3,252	5,978	1,001
1976----------------1,000--	11,305	987	18.8	56.7	420	491	10,318	3,090	6,271	958
1977----------------1,000--	10,936	1,010	19.1	63.0	405	523	9,926	3,052	5,906	968
Average annual percent change:										
1967–1977------------------	6.4	7.3	4.6	8.6	7.2	7.4	6.3	6.5	6.6	3.9
1970–1975------------------	6.8	6.8	5.1	8.1	5.9	7.7	6.8	8.1	7.2	1.5
1975–1977------------------	−1.4	−.8	−3.5	6.0	−6.7	3.8	−1.5	−3.1	−.6	−1.7
1976–1977------------------	−3.3	2.3	1.6	11.1	−3.6	6.5	−3.8	−1.2	−5.8	1.0
Rate per 100,000 inhabitants:										
1967----------------------	2,990	253	6.2	14.0	103	130	2,737	827	1,576	334
1968----------------------	3,370	298	6.9	15.9	132	144	3,072	932	1,747	393
1969----------------------	3,680	329	7.3	18.5	148	155	3,351	984	1,931	436
1970----------------------	3,985	364	7.9	18.7	172	165	3,621	1,085	2,079	457
1971----------------------	4,165	396	8.6	20.5	188	179	3,769	1,164	2,146	460
1972----------------------	3,961	401	9.0	22.5	181	189	3,560	1,141	1,994	426
1973----------------------	4,154	417	9.4	24.5	183	201	3,737	1,223	2,072	443
1974----------------------	4,850	461	9.8	26.2	209	216	4,389	1,438	2,490	462
1975----------------------	5,282	482	9.6	26.3	218	227	4,800	1,526	2,805	469
1976----------------------	5,266	460	8.8	26.4	196	229	4,807	1,439	2,921	446
1977----------------------	5,055	467	8.8	29.1	187	242	4,588	1,411	2,730	448
Average annual percent change:										
1967–1977------------------	5.4	6.3	3.6	7.6	6.2	6.4	5.3	5.5	5.7	3.0
1970–1975------------------	5.8	5.8	4.0	7.1	4.9	6.6	5.8	7.1	6.2	.5
1975–1977------------------	−2.2	−1.6	−4.3	5.2	−7.4	3.3	−2.2	−3.8	−1.4	−2.3
1976–1977------------------	−4.0	1.5	(Z)	10.2	−4.6	5.7	−4.6	−2.0	−6.5	.5

Z Less than .5 percent.   [1] Includes nonnegligent manslaughter.

No. 287. CRIMES KNOWN TO THE POLICE, BY TYPE AND AREA: 1976 AND 1977

[In thousands, except rate. Estimated totals based on reports from city and rural law enforcement agencies representing 95 percent of the national population. Covers crimes constituting "FBI Crime Index"; for definitions of crimes, see text, p. 174]

TYPE OF CRIME	1976						1977					
	SMSA's [1]		Other cities		Rural areas		SMSA's [1]		Other cities		Rural areas	
	Total	Rate [2]	Total	Rate [2]	Total	Rate [2]	Total	Rate [2]	Total	Rate [2]	Total	Rate [2]
Total--------	9,544	6,073	1,096	4,374	664	2,048	9,204	5,814	1,084	4,198	648	2,012
Violent crime-----------	865	550	67	266	55	170	885	559	69	267	56	173
Murder and nonnegligent manslaughter--	15	10	1	5	3	8	15	10	1	5	3	8
Forcible rape---------	49	31	3	13	4	13	55	35	4	14	5	14
Robbery------------	401	255	13	51	7	21	386	244	12	48	7	21
Aggravated assault----	400	255	49	196	41	128	429	271	52	200	42	130
Property crime-----------	8,679	5,523	1,030	4,108	609	1,878	8,319	5,255	1,015	3,931	592	1,840
Burglary-------------	2,586	1,646	254	1,014	249	768	2,548	1,609	257	997	247	767
Larceny—theft--------	5,222	3,323	724	2,889	325	1,002	4,897	3,093	702	2,718	307	954
Motor vehicle theft---	871	554	52	206	35	107	875	553	56	215	38	118

[1] For definition of standard metropolitan statistical areas, see text, Appendix II.   [2] Rate per 100,000 population based on Bureau of the Census estimated population as of July 1, excluding Armed Forces abroad.

Source of tables 286 and 287: U.S. Federal Bureau of Investigation, *Uniform Crime Reports for the United States*, annual.

No. 288. CRIME RATES, BY TYPE—STATES: 1976 AND 1977

[Offenses known to the police per 100,000 population. Based on Bureau of the Census estimated population as of July 1, excluding Armed Forces abroad. For definitions of crimes, see text, p. 174]

STATE	MURDER AND NON-NEGLIGENT MANSLAUGHTER		FORCIBLE RAPE		ROBBERY		AGGRAVATED ASSAULT		BURGLARY—BREAKING OR ENTERING		LARCENY—THEFT		MOTOR VEHICLE THEFT	
	1976	1977	1976	1977	1976	1977	1976	1977	1976	1977	1976	1977	1976	1977
U.S.1	8.8	8.8	26.4	29.1	195.8	187.1	229	242	1,439	1,411	2,921	2,730	446	448
N.E	3.2	3.3	14.8	17.5	129.6	126.0	164	183	1,468	1,416	2,539	2,432	878	802
Maine	2.7	2.4	9.9	13.5	37.9	38.7	169	170	1,313	1,253	2,337	2,351	214	247
N.H	3.3	3.2	9.7	10.7	24.8	23.2	48	76	937	1,042	2,335	2,344	252	293
Vt	5.5	1.4	14.9	15.9	17.9	30.8	80	101	1,023	1,348	1,853	2,201	198	265
Mass	3.3	3.1	17.7	20.8	180.2	169.9	198	232	1,662	1,532	2,447	2,311	1,313	1,140
R.I	2.4	3.6	8.5	10.5	91.0	86.5	198	201	1,414	1,490	3,051	2,844	886	791
Conn	3.1	4.2	14.4	16.8	122.9	129.5	133	132	1,384	1,346	2,786	2,621	562	593
M.A	8.2	8.1	22.2	24.4	340.1	305.9	223	232	1,440	1,400	2,543	2,412	569	568
N.Y	10.9	10.7	25.8	29.4	529.3	472.6	302	319	1,764	1,728	2,855	2,782	738	746
N.J	5.2	5.6	19.9	21.0	200.3	180.4	171	185	1,504	1,436	2,989	2,775	511	512
Pa	6.1	5.6	18.1	19.0	138.0	130.3	133	128	906	877	1,791	1,624	348	333
E.N.C	8.5	8.1	25.0	26.7	205.5	187.7	191	193	1,237	1,190	3,051	2,801	447	444
Ohio	7.4	7.8	25.8	27.3	183.8	190.5	172	181	1,203	1,216	2,978	2,697	378	400
Ind	7.1	7.4	23.2	26.5	128.8	123.2	156	153	1,216	1,086	2,770	2,499	372	377
Ill	10.3	9.9	21.5	21.8	219.5	211.3	218	209	1,090	1,085	2,992	2,828	505	529
Mich	11.1	9.3	36.1	38.9	332.6	261.9	266	275	1,669	1,523	3,551	3,159	613	546
Wis	3.0	2.8	11.8	12.9	59.3	52.2	64	64	844	847	2,696	2,614	223	221
W.N.C	4.6	5.1	19.6	20.0	103.2	102.1	136	145	1,094	1,066	2,684	2,482	293	294
Minn	2.3	2.7	18.3	19.5	80.4	85.9	88	86	1,122	1,135	2,673	2,559	347	343
Iowa	2.3	2.3	10.7	10.6	41.1	41.2	79	90	827	813	2,885	2,685	207	220
Mo	9.3	9.6	27.1	28.3	204.1	189.0	209	233	1,403	1,318	2,795	2,424	387	378
N. Dak	1.4	.9	5.6	9.0	16.2	13.3	49	44	479	446	1,805	1,843	159	145
S. Dak	1.7	2.0	15.3	13.5	23.2	17.9	146	156	620	571	1,684	1,704	150	147
Nebr	2.9	3.9	20.5	18.1	63.0	64.7	124	113	684	760	2,434	2,316	234	249
Kans	4.5	6.6	21.9	22.0	85.8	100.7	170	181	1,325	1,270	2,938	2,739	232	244
S.A.1	10.9	10.2	27.4	29.9	164.9	159.6	303	325	1,424	1,390	2,951	2,762	291	292
Del	6.2	6.0	17.7	24.9	128.7	157.0	169	194	1,543	1,683	3,916	3,678	484	467
Md	8.5	8.0	32.0	34.8	295.5	292.1	297	359	1,360	1,400	3,242	3,178	429	428
Va	9.5	9.0	22.2	23.3	108.2	92.1	168	166	1,019	986	2,650	2,521	226	227
W. Va	6.7	6.0	10.3	13.2	38.0	42.2	97	91	573	597	1,459	1,342	136	163
N.C	11.1	10.6	15.3	17.0	70.6	61.3	306	318	1,176	1,154	2,124	2,038	178	192
S.C	11.6	11.9	31.9	33.0	105.7	105.9	450	485	1,554	1,614	2,503	2,342	251	245
Ga	13.9	11.7	24.9	31.1	142.4	140.5	242	256	1,448	1,351	2,618	2,170	320	298
Fla	10.7	10.2	36.3	39.6	186.4	187.9	415	449	1,955	1,860	4,074	3,841	340	351
E.S.C	12.2	11.9	20.9	24.1	107.1	102.7	202	201	1,094	1,070	1,897	1,683	254	259
Ky	10.6	10.1	17.8	19.1	98.7	81.1	135	123	930	872	1,858	1,662	247	245
Tenn	11.0	10.1	25.4	29.7	147.5	145.8	209	204	1,321	1,260	2,219	1,776	326	314
Ala	15.1	14.2	21.7	25.2	96.0	96.8	256	278	1,170	1,136	1,987	1,882	262	281
Miss	12.5	14.3	16.3	19.6	64.1	65.7	203	189	811	916	1,239	1,240	122	144
W.S.C	11.4	12.6	28.1	32.1	121.2	133.7	202	230	1,383	1,421	2,869	2,685	316	356
Ark	10.1	8.8	24.2	27.6	76.7	83.2	193	203	937	973	2,014	1,862	151	183
La	13.2	15.5	26.8	30.9	124.3	142.9	309	335	1,141	1,166	2,447	2,470	301	338
Okla	6.4	8.6	27.0	29.2	70.3	73.8	183	205	1,317	1,288	2,570	2,228	306	327
Texas	12.2	13.3	29.4	33.8	139.0	152.4	175	208	1,548	1,603	3,209	2,989	351	398
Mt	7.1	7.4	29.7	32.9	115.7	126.3	240	263	1,713	1,697	3,841	3,589	376	389
Mont	5.0	5.4	13.5	16.7	35.6	39.2	126	157	841	805	2,933	2,773	308	309
Idaho	5.3	5.5	18.7	19.4	40.0	39.6	163	172	1,037	1,051	2,777	2,600	230	238
Wyo	6.9	5.4	24.9	21.9	29.2	39.7	157	174	765	812	2,750	2,772	242	282
Colo	6.8	6.3	33.8	42.0	139.7	170.7	237	293	1,880	1,935	4,043	3,903	442	477
N. Mex	9.7	8.8	41.0	39.1	124.7	109.6	379	343	1,680	1,419	3,652	3,009	330	259
Ariz	7.8	9.5	29.7	34.2	129.9	138.2	288	312	2,367	2,346	4,643	4,467	422	440
Utah	4.5	3.5	20.9	20.3	69.4	68.8	126	147	1,138	1,172	3,302	3,005	317	334
Nev	11.5	15.8	47.2	49.1	294.9	323.1	337	355	2,392	2,453	4,717	4,213	505	559
Pac	8.9	9.9	42.0	46.7	238.0	243.7	313	326	2,047	2,014	3,705	3,497	586	599
Wash	4.3	4.3	34.3	34.9	119.5	106.2	231	225	1,642	1,606	3,414	3,387	349	360
Oreg	4.2	4.9	35.6	39.9	132.7	124.1	285	287	1,700	1,636	3,807	3,506	395	389
Calif	10.3	11.5	44.7	49.4	275.6	287.0	339	358	2,175	2,139	3,746	3,500	644	663
Alaska	11.3	10.8	46.9	51.6	124.9	96.8	357	284	1,218	1,332	3,657	3,370	806	753
Hawaii	6.2	7.2	23.6	25.5	133.0	128.0	67	64	1,882	1,912	3,669	3,920	542	489

1 Includes District of Columbia, not shown separately.

Source: U.S. Federal Bureau of Investigation, *Uniform Crime Reports for the United States*, annual.

No. 289. Crime Rates for Violent Crimes in Cities, by Size Group and for Selected Cities: 1970 to 1977

[Offenses known to the police per 100,000 population. For types of violent crime, see table 290. Rates based on Bureau of the Census population estimates as of July 1 of each year. Minus sign (−) denotes decrease]

CITY-SIZE GROUP [1] AND CITY	1970	1971	1972	1973	1974	1975	1976	1977	ANNUAL PERCENT CHANGE		
									1970–1975	1975–1976	1976–1977
Cities with population of—											
250,000 or more	980	1,048	999	1,003	1,108	1,159	1,095	1,070	18.3	−5.5	−2.3
100,000–249,999	450	503	502	545	600	632	573	600	40.4	−9.3	4.7
50,000–99,999	274	300	322	372	406	451	416	444	64.6	−7.8	6.7
25,000–49,999	214	243	267	295	331	343	338	342	60.3	−1.5	1.2
10,000–24,999	159	188	200	221	250	268	254	264	68.6	−5.2	3.9
Under 10,000	141	171	204	199	218	232	216	230	64.5	−6.9	6.5
Selected cities:											
New York, N.Y	1,381	1,611	1,525	1,483	1,615	1,781	1,781	1,629	29.0	−	−8.5
Chicago, Ill	1,101	1,122	1,104	1,168	1,282	1,180	978	935	7.2	17.1	−4.4
Los Angeles, Calif	1,062	1,109	1,128	1,064	1,069	1,114	1,167	1,209	4.9	4.8	3.6
Philadelphia, Pa	571	754	785	755	871	867	684	635	51.8	−21.1	−7.2
Detroit, Mich	1,934	1,815	1,650	1,681	2,004	2,121	2,226	1,829	9.7	5.0	−17.8
Houston, Tex	799	715	627	686	732	650	545	577	−18.6	−16.2	5.9
Baltimore, Md	2,088	1,850	1,869	1,771	1,961	1,862	1,648	1,726	−10.8	−11.5	4.7
Dallas, Tex	966	1,051	905	998	866	885	815	1,019	−8.4	−7.9	25.0
Washington, D.C	2,227	2,171	1,685	1,558	1,603	1,774	1,481	1,427	−20.3	−16.5	−3.6
Cleveland, Ohio	1,060	1,170	1,129	1,008	1,358	1,576	1,323	1,475	48.7	−16.1	11.5
Indianapolis, Ind	704	659	483	505	709	925	838	744	31.4	−9.4	−11.2
Milwaukee, Wis	211	202	221	294	402	475	413	396	125.1	−13.1	−4.1
San Francisco, Calif	1,339	1,473	1,144	1,197	1,135	1,364	1,618	1,409	1.9	18.6	−12.9
San Diego, Calif	285	296	323	372	473	502	532	560	76.1	6.0	5.3
San Antonio, Tex	497	499	510	587	624	549	436	491	10.5	−20.6	12.6

− Represents zero.   [1] Population of cities as estimated by FBI.

No. 290. Crime Rates, by Type Population Groups and Selected Cities: 1977

[Offenses known to the police per 100,000 population. For definitions of crimes, see text, p. 174]

CITY-SIZE GROUP [1] AND CITY	Crime index total	VIOLENT CRIME					PROPERTY CRIME			
		Total	Murder	Forcible rape	Robbery	Aggravated assault	Total	Burglary—breaking or entering	Larceny—theft	Motor vehicle theft
Total, 9,783 agencies	5,240	492	9.3	31	202	250	4,747	1,460	2,816	471
Total, 7,298 cities	6,067	585	10.2	34	262	278	5,482	1,612	3,297	572
Cities with population of—										
250,000 or more	7,819	1,070	20.0	60	583	408	6,749	2,196	3,586	967
100,000–249,999	7,163	600	11.2	41	240	307	6,563	1,960	3,993	610
50,000–99,999	6,006	444	6.4	29	159	249	5,562	1,589	3,466	507
25,000–49,999	5,269	342	5.1	21	110	207	4,927	1,309	3,217	401
10,000–24,999	4,425	264	4.4	14	65	180	4,161	1,073	2,800	287
Less than 10,000	3,906	230	3.7	12	40	174	3,676	945	2,518	214
Suburbs, 4,140 agencies [2]	4,430	311	5.2	22	86	198	4,119	1,235	2,546	337
Rural areas, 1,910 agencies	2,085	176	7.9	14	21	132	1,909	789	999	121
Selected cities:										
New York, N.Y	8,154	1,629	20.8	52	994	562	6,525	2,391	2,872	1,262
Chicago, Ill	6,604	935	26.7	40	535	334	5,668	1,217	3,415	1,036
Los Angeles, Calif	7,821	1,209	20.7	84	547	557	6,612	2,295	3,139	1,177
Philadelphia, Pa	3,785	635	17.0	41	369	208	3,150	1,007	1,491	652
Detroit, Mich	9,401	1,829	36.5	97	1,203	492	7,572	2,715	3,188	1,669
Houston, Tex	7,270	577	23.3	60	381	112	6,693	2,071	3,771	851
Baltimore, Md	8,131	1,726	20.7	60	914	731	6,405	1,844	3,814	748
Dallas, Tex	9,821	1,019	25.6	73	416	504	8,802	2,795	5,355	653
Washington, D.C	7,220	1,427	27.8	58	964	376	5,794	1,680	3,717	397
Cleveland, Ohio	8,609	1,475	39.0	80	1,012	344	7,134	2,463	2,589	2,083
Indianapolis, Ind	6,734	744	15.7	68	420	240	5,990	1,702	3,546	741
Milwaukee, Wis	5,394	396	8.4	33	217	137	4,998	1,105	3,336	557
San Francisco, Calif	10,742	1,409	21.2	89	815	482	9,333	2,896	4,839	1,599
San Diego, Calif	8,298	560	6.3	38	315	201	7,738	2,385	4,551	802
San Antonio, Tex	7,225	491	19.1	36	191	245	6,734	2,499	3,718	517

[1] Population of cities as estimated by FBI.   [2] Agencies also included in other city groups.

Source of tables 289 and 290: U.S. Federal Bureau of Investigation, *Uniform Crime Reports for the United States,* annual.

No. 291. Victimization Rates of Crimes Against Persons, by Race and Sex of Victim, and Relationship of Victim and Offender: 1973 to 1976

[Rates per 1,000 persons, 12 years old and over. All figures include attempted crimes. Data are estimates subject to sampling errors. See Appendix III]

YEAR AND CRIME	Total¹	White	Black	MALE			FEMALE			VICTIM-OFFENDER RELATIONSHIP RATE	
				Total¹	White	Black	Total¹	White	Black	Stranger	Nonstranger
1973: Total²	32	31	41	44	43	53	22	20	32	21	11
Rape	1	1	1	(B)	(B)	(B)	2	2	3	1	(Z)
Robbery:											
With injury	2	2	5	3	3	7	1	1	3	2	(Z)
Without injury	4	4	8	7	6	12	2	2	5	4	1
Aggravated assault	10	9	16	15	14	23	5	5	10	6	4
Simple assault	15	15	11	19	20	11	11	11	12	9	6
Personal larceny	91	92	83	103	104	97	80	82	70	(NA)	(NA)
1975: Total²	33	31	43	44	42	53	23	21	34	21	11
Rape	1	1	1	(B)	(B)	(B)	2	2	2	1	(Z)
Robbery:											
With injury	2	2	5	3	3	8	1	1	3	2	(Z)
Without injury	5	4	9	7	6	14	3	2	5	4	1
Aggravated assault	10	9	14	14	14	19	5	5	11	6	3
Simple assault	16	16	13	20	21	12	12	12	14	9	7
Personal larceny	96	97	90	108	108	110	85	87	73	(NA)	(NA)
1976: Total²	33	31	44	43	42	55	23	21	36	21	12
Rape	1	1	2	(Z)	(Z)	(B)	1	1	3	1	(Z)
Robbery:											
With injury	2	2	4	3	2	6	2	1	3	2	(Z)
Without injury	4	4	10	7	6	15	2	2	6	4	1
Aggravated assault	10	9	16	14	14	19	6	5	13	6	4
Simple assault	15	16	13	19	20	15	12	12	12	9	7
Personal larceny	96	97	87	106	107	101	87	88	75	(NA)	(NA)

B   Rate not shown because estimated number of victimizations too small to be statistically reliable.
NA   Not available.   Z   Less than .5.
¹ Includes races not shown separately.   ² Excludes personal larceny.

Source: U.S. Law Enforcement Assistance Administration, *Criminal Victimization in the United States*, annual.

No. 292. Victimization Rates of Crimes Against Persons, Selected Cities: 1971–1972 and 1974–1975

[Rates per 1,000 persons, 12 years old and over. See headnote, table 291]

CITY	1971–1972						1974–1975					
	Total	Rape	Robbery	Assault		Personal larceny	Total	Rape	Robbery	Assault		Personal larceny
				Aggravated	Simple					Aggravated	Simple	
Atlanta, Ga.¹	48	2	16	15	15	100	44	2	17	12	11	93
Baltimore, Md.¹	56	1	26	13	15	79	78	2	35	21	20	105
Chicago, Ill.²	56	3	27	12	14	87	61	2	29	16	14	91
Cleveland, Ohio ¹	54	2	24	15	13	71	67	2	27	20	17	85
Dallas, Tex.¹	43	2	10	14	17	96	48	2	12	17	17	116
Denver, Colo.¹	67	3	18	20	27	134	71	3	19	23	27	134
Detroit, Mich.²	68	3	32	18	15	95	77	2	37	21	18	91
Los Angeles, Calif.²	53	2	16	15	19	105	59	2	18	17	22	119
New York, N.Y.²	36	1	24	4	6	51	43	1	24	9	10	65
Newark, N.J.¹	42	1	29	6	6	50	38	2	23	8	6	45
Philadelphia, Pa.²	63	1	28	17	17	95	49	1	21	13	13	85
Portland, Oreg.¹	59	3	17	16	24	123	71	4	16	22	30	143
St. Louis, Mo.¹	42	1	16	13	12	73	48	1	19	14	14	92

¹ For 12 months preceding surveys made in July–November 1972 and March–May 1975.
² For 12 months preceding surveys made in first quarter of 1973 and first quarter of 1975.

Source: U.S. Law Enforcement Assistance Administration, *Criminal Victimization Surveys in Eight American Cities: 1971–72 vs. 1974–75;* and *Criminal Victimization Surveys in Chicago, Detroit, Los Angeles, New York, Philadelphia: A Comparison of 1972 and 1974 Findings.*

No. 293. VICTIMIZATION RATES OF CRIMES AGAINST HOUSEHOLDS: 1974 TO 1976

[Rates per 1,000 households. Includes attempted offenses. Based on samples; for discussion of sampling error, see Appendix III; for further details, see source. For definitions of crimes, see text, p. 174]

HOUSEHOLD CHARACTERISTIC	BURGLARY			LARCENY			MOTOR VEHICLE THEFT		
	Total [1]	White	Black	Total [1]	White	Black	Total [1]	White	Black
1974									
All households	93	88	135	123	125	112	19	18	26
Homeowner	76	72	117	114	114	110	15	14	27
Renter	123	118	150	140	145	114	26	27	25
Households with income of—									
Under $7,500	98	90	136	107	107	104	15	15	15
$7,500–$14,999	86	82	142	139	141	121	20	19	38
$15,000 and over	100	99	139	137	136	157	23	21	67
1975									
All households	92	87	129	125	126	114	19	19	27
Homeowner	78	76	99	116	115	118	16	15	27
Renter	116	109	153	142	148	111	26	26	27
Households with income of—									
Under $7,500	102	94	134	112	113	98	15	14	15
$7,500–$14,999	84	80	129	137	137	135	22	20	42
$15,000 and over	91	90	113	136	136	151	23	22	48
1976									
All households	89	84	131	124	126	112	17	16	22
Homeowner	73	71	106	114	114	111	14	13	22
Renter	117	111	151	143	150	114	22	22	21
Households with income of—									
Under $7,500	101	94	135	107	108	98	12	12	13
$7,500–$14,999	81	77	126	137	137	138	19	18	36
$15,000 and over	87	85	133	140	141	137	20	19	34
Age of head:									
20–34 years	124	(NA)	(NA)	172	(NA)	(NA)	24	(NA)	(NA)
35–49 years	93	(NA)	(NA)	145	(NA)	(NA)	19	(NA)	(NA)
50–64 years	68	(NA)	(NA)	95	(NA)	(NA)	12	(NA)	(NA)
65 years and over	50	(NA)	(NA)	60	(NA)	(NA)	6	(NA)	(NA)

NA Not available.   [1] Includes other races not shown separately.

Source: U.S. Law Enforcement Assistance Administration, *Criminal Victimization in the United States,* annual.

No. 294. HOUSEHOLD AND COMMERCIAL CRIME VICTIMIZATION RATES, BY TYPE OF VICTIMIZATION, SELECTED CITIES: 1971–1972 AND 1974–1975

[Rates per 1,000 households and per 1,000 establishments. Data are estimates subject to sampling errors; see Appendix III]

CITY	HOUSEHOLD						COMMERCIAL			
	Burglary [1]		Household larceny [2]		Motor vehicle theft [2]		Burglary [1]		Robbery [2]	
	1971–1972	1974–1975	1971–1972	1974–1975	1971–1972	1974–1975	1971–1972	1974–1975	1971–1972	1974–1975
Atlanta, Ga.[3]	161	158	102	117	29	24	741	519	157	123
Baltimore, Md.[3]	116	118	100	124	35	42	578	465	135	123
Chicago, Ill.[4]	118	122	77	86	36	38	315	334	77	137
Cleveland, Ohio [3]	124	137	80	106	76	73	367	354	77	94
Dallas, Tex.[3]	147	161	147	178	24	23	355	424	48	55
Denver, Colo.[3]	158	166	168	187	44	40	443	435	54	79
Detroit, Mich.[4]	174	154	106	107	49	70	615	640	179	221
Los Angeles, Calif.[4]	148	149	131	145	42	39	311	306	47	64
New York, N.Y.[4]	68	77	33	46	26	28	328	291	103	101
Newark, N.J.[3]	123	98	44	49	37	40	631	506	98	106
Philadelphia, Pa.[4]	109	91	87	83	42	36	390	419	116	102
Portland, Ore.[3]	151	174	149	188	34	37	356	419	39	67
St. Louis, Mo.[3]	125	135	81	94	47	46	531	410	94	144

[1] Includes attempted forcible entry.   [2] Includes attempted offenses.
[3] See footnote 1, table 292.   [4] See footnote 2, table 292.

Source: U.S. Law Enforcement Assistance Administration, *Criminal Victimization Surveys in Eight American Cities: 1971–72 vs. 1974–75* and *Criminal Victimization Surveys in Chicago, Detroit, Los Angeles, New York, Philadelphia: A Comparison of 1972 and 1974 Findings.*

No. 295. Homicide Victims and Suicides, by Race and Sex: 1940 to 1976

[Rates per 100,000 resident population in specified group, 15 years old and over. See also *Historical Statistics, Colonial Times to 1970*, series H 971–986. Includes items not shown in FBI Crime Index]

YEAR	HOMICIDE VICTIMS					SUICIDES				
	Total	White		Black and other		Total	White		Black and other	
		Male	Female	Male	Female		Male	Female	Male	Female
NUMBER										
1940	8,329	2,977	796	3,670	886	18,907	13,990	4,294	476	147
1945	7,547	2,759	791	3,210	787	14,782	10,374	3,920	380	108
1950	7,942	2,586	952	3,503	901	17,145	12,755	3,713	542	135
1955	7,418	2,439	922	3,191	866	16,760	12,430	3,662	531	137
1960	8,464	2,832	1,154	3,437	1,041	19,041	13,825	4,296	714	206
1965	10,712	3,660	1,379	4,488	1,185	21,507	14,624	5,718	866	299
1968	14,686	5,106	1,700	6,417	1,463	21,372	14,520	5,692	859	301
1969	15,477	5,215	1,801	6,951	1,510	22,364	14,886	6,152	971	355
1970	16,848	5,865	1,938	7,413	1,632	23,480	15,591	6,468	1,038	383
1971	18,787	6,455	2,106	8,357	1,869	24,092	15,802	6,775	1,058	457
1972 [1]	19,638	6,820	2,156	8,822	1,840	25,004	16,476	6,788	1,292	448
1973	20,465	7,411	2,575	8,429	2,050	25,118	16,823	6,589	1,285	421
1974	21,465	7,992	2,656	8,755	2,062	25,683	17,263	6,660	1,332	428
1975	21,310	8,222	2,751	8,331	2,006	27,063	18,206	6,967	1,416	474
1976	19,554	7,568	2,547	7,574	1,865	26,832	17,996	6,858	1,497	481
RATE [2]										
1940	8.4	6.7	1.8	79.9	18.5	19.2	31.3	9.6	10.4	3.1
1945	7.7	6.8	1.7	71.4	15.2	15.1	25.6	8.2	8.5	2.1
1950	7.2	5.3	1.9	67.4	16.2	15.6	26.0	7.4	10.4	2.4
1955	6.4	4.8	1.7	57.8	14.4	14.5	24.5	6.9	9.6	2.3
1960	6.9	5.3	2.0	56.2	15.6	15.4	25.7	7.6	11.7	3.1
1965	8.0	6.3	2.2	66.6	15.9	16.1	25.3	9.2	12.9	4.0
1968	10.5	8.5	2.6	90.0	18.2	15.2	24.2	8.8	12.1	3.8
1969	10.9	8.6	2.7	95.1	18.3	15.7	24.4	9.3	13.3	4.3
1970	11.6	9.5	2.9	95.9	18.5	16.2	25.3	9.6	13.4	4.3
1971	12.6	10.2	3.1	105.9	20.7	16.2	25.0	9.9	13.4	4.8
1972 [1]	13.0	10.6	3.1	108.3	19.7	16.5	25.6	9.7	15.9	4.8
1973	13.3	11.3	3.6	100.7	21.4	16.3	25.7	9.3	15.4	4.4
1974	13.7	12.0	3.7	101.7	20.9	16.4	26.0	9.3	15.5	4.3
1975	13.4	12.2	3.8	93.9	19.7	17.0	27.0	9.6	16.0	4.6
1976	12.1	11.0	3.4	82.9	17.8	16.5	26.3	9.3	16.4	4.6

[1] Based on a 50-percent sample of deaths.   [2] Rate based on enumerated population figures of April 1 for 1940, 1950, 1960, and 1970; July 1 estimates for other years.

No. 296. Homicide Victims and Suicides: 1960 to 1976

[Excludes Armed Forces abroad. See also *Historical Statistics, Colonial Times to 1970*, series H 971–986]

ITEM	1960, total	1965, total	1970		1973		1974		1975		1976	
			Male	Female	Male	Female	Male	Female	Male	Female	Male	Female
Homicides	8,464	10,712	13,278	3,570	15,840	4,625	16,747	4,718	16,553	4,757	15,142	4,412
Assault by—												
Firearms	4,627	6,158	9,209	2,004	11,168	2,584	12,053	2,684	11,729	2,566	10,452	2,314
Percent of total	54.7	57.5	69.4	56.1	70.5	55.9	72.0	56.9	70.9	53.9	69.0	52.4
Cutting and piercing instruments	1,836	2,292	2,229	551	2,510	744	2,610	756	2,598	764	2,583	721
Other means	1,700	1,984	1,512	1,010	1,793	1,290	1,715	1,272	1,897	1,420	1,818	1,372
Intervention of police	245	271	328	5	369	7	369	6	329	7	289	5
Execution	56	7	–	–	–	–	–	–	–	–	–	–
Suicides	19,041	21,507	16,629	6,851	18,108	7,010	18,595	7,088	19,622	7,441	19,493	7,339
Firearms [1]	9,017	9,898	9,704	2,068	11,057	2,260	11,813	2,532	12,185	2,688	12,128	2,600
Percent of total	47.4	46.0	58.4	30.2	61.1	32.2	63.5	35.7	62.1	36.1	62.2	35.4
Poisoning [2]	4,330	5,995	3,299	3,285	3,149	3,107	2,944	3,049	3,297	3,129	3,076	3,068
Hanging and strangulation	3,366	3,197	2,422	831	2,671	877	2,661	816	2,815	846	2,834	855
Other	2,328	2,417	1,204	667	1,231	766	1,177	691	1,325	778	1,455	816
Infanticides [3]	199	213	80	70	81	80	78	88	102	76	88	82

– Represents zero.   [1] Includes explosives.
[2] Includes solids, liquids, and gases.   [3] Homicides under 1 year.

Source of tables 295 and 296: U.S. National Center for Health Statistics, *Vital Statistics of the United States*, annual.

No. 297. Homicide and Suicide Rates, Selected Countries: 1973 to 1975

[Crude rates per 100,000 population]

COUNTRY	HOMICIDES							SUICIDES						
	1973, total	1974			1975			1973, total	1974			1975		
		Total	Male	Female	Total	Male	Female		Total	Male	Female	Total	Male	Female
United States	9.8	10.2	16.3	4.4	10.0	16.0	4.4	12.0	12.1	18.1	6.5	12.7	18.9	6.8
Australia	1.9	1.8	2.4	1.3	(NA)	(NA)	(NA)	11.6	11.7	16.0	7.4	(NA)	(NA)	(NA)
Austria	1.4	1.5	1.9	1.3	1.6	2.1	1.3	22.1	23.7	34.0	14.5	24.1	35.5	13.9
Belgium	1.1	1.0	1.2	.9	.9	1.3	.5	14.9	15.6	21.4	10.1	16.2	21.1	11.5
Canada	2.4	2.5	3.1	1.8	2.6	3.4	1.7	12.6	12.9	18.7	7.1	11.8	17.2	6.4
Denmark	.9	.7	.5	.9	.6	.5	.7	23.8	26.0	33.7	18.5	24.1	29.9	18.4
Finland	2.7	2.6	4.2	1.0	(NA)	(NA)	(NA)	23.5	25.1	40.6	10.5	(NA)	(NA)	(NA)
France	.8	.9	1.2	.7	(NA)	(NA)	(NA)	15.5	15.6	22.7	8.8	(NA)	(NA)	(NA)
Germany, Fed. Rep	1.2	1.2	1.4	1.0	(NA)	(NA)	(NA)	20.8	21.0	27.9	14.7	(NA)	(NA)	(NA)
Greece	.8	.6	.9	.2	.8	1.2	.4	3.0	3.4	4.6	2.4	2.8	3.5	2.1
Ireland	.4	.7	1.0	.4	(NA)	(NA)	(NA)	3.4	3.8	5.9	1.7	(NA)	(NA)	(NA)
Israel [1]	.6	1.0	1.4	.6	(NA)	(NA)	(NA)	6.4	5.5	7.0	4.0	(NA)	(NA)	(NA)
Italy	1.2	1.1	1.7	.6	(NA)	(NA)	(NA)	5.7	5.4	7.3	3.5	(NA)	(NA)	(NA)
Japan	1.3	1.3	1.6	1.0	1.3	1.6	1.0	17.3	17.5	20.0	15.0	18.0	21.4	14.6
Mexico	13.0	22.1	40.1	3.9	(NA)	(NA)	(NA)	.7	2.1	3.4	.8	(NA)	(NA)	(NA)
Netherlands	.6	.8	1.1	.5	.7	1.0	.4	8.7	9.2	11.0	7.4	8.9	10.8	7.0
Norway	.8	.6	.7	.6	(NA)	(NA)	(NA)	8.6	10.4	16.3	4.5	(NA)	(NA)	(NA)
Philippines	2.3	1.3	2.4	.3	(NA)	(NA)	(NA)	1.4	1.2	1.3	1.0	(NA)	(NA)	(NA)
Poland	1.0	.9	1.2	.6	1.0	1.3	.8	11.7	11.3	18.7	4.2	11.3	19.3	3.7
Portugal	.8	1.3	2.2	.5	1.9	3.4	.5	8.6	8.5	13.2	4.4	8.5	13.4	4.2
Puerto Rico	14.5	17.7	32.3	3.7	16.4	29.6	3.6	9.1	7.7	12.5	3.0	7.7	13.3	2.4
Spain	.3	.4	.4	.3	(NA)	(NA)	(NA)	4.2	4.0	5.8	2.2	(NA)	(NA)	(NA)
Sweden	1.0	1.2	1.6	.9	1.1	1.5	.8	20.8	20.1	28.7	11.5	19.4	28.7	11.2
Switzerland	.7	1.0	1.2	.7	.9	1.0	.9	18.8	20.6	29.1	12.5	22.5	32.5	12.9
United Kingdom:														
England [2]	.9	1.0	1.1	.8	1.0	1.2	.8	7.8	7.9	9.5	6.4	7.5	9.1	6.0
Northern Ireland	10.1	13.6	25.3	2.2	(NA)	(NA)	(NA)	4.5	4.0	5.1	2.9	(NA)	(NA)	(NA)
Scotland	1.4	1.2	1.8	.7	1.5	2.1	.9	8.4	8.4	10.3	6.5	8.2	9.0	7.4

NA Not available.   [1] Jewish population.   [2] Includes Wales.
Source: United Nations World Health Organization, Geneva, Switzerland, unpublished data.

No. 298. U.S. Suicide Rates, by Sex, Race, and Age Groups: 1970 to 1976

[Rates per 100,000 population in specified group, 5 years old and over. Excludes deaths of nonresidents of the United States]

AGE	MALE								FEMALE							
	White				Black and other				White				Black and other			
	1970	1974	1975	1976	1970	1974	1975	1976	1970	1974	1975	1976	1970	1974	1975	1976
All ages	18.0	19.2	20.1	19.8	8.5	10.2	10.6	11.0	7.1	7.1	7.4	7.2	2.9	3.0	3.3	3.2
5–14 yr	.5	.8	.8	.7	.2	.4	.1	.3	.1	.2	.2	.2	.2	.2	.2	.4
15–24 yr	13.9	17.8	19.6	19.2	11.3	12.9	14.4	14.7	4.2	4.8	4.9	4.9	4.1	3.9	3.9	4.0
25–34 yr	19.9	23.3	24.4	23.7	19.8	22.9	24.6	22.8	9.0	8.7	8.9	8.6	5.8	6.3	6.5	6.5
35–44 yr	23.3	23.8	24.5	23.6	12.6	15.6	16.0	16.8	13.0	12.1	12.6	11.0	4.3	4.5	4.9	4.7
45–54 yr	29.5	28.3	29.7	27.7	14.1	11.9	12.8	13.5	13.5	14.1	13.8	13.8	4.5	4.0	4.5	4.3
55–64 yr	35.0	32.1	32.1	31.6	10.5	12.5	11.5	12.3	12.3	11.0	11.7	12.1	2.2	3.4	4.1	2.8
65 and over	41.1	38.9	39.4	39.7	10.8	15.3	11.8	14.5	8.5	7.7	8.5	8.3	3.6	2.3	3.0	3.2

Source: U.S. National Center for Health Statistics, Vital Statistics of the United States, annual.

No. 299. Political Assassinations and Assaults: 1835 to 1972

[Rates per 1 million population. Assault defined as any attack on persons holding political office or any individuals or groups of individuals for political reasons. For composition of regions, see fig. I, inside front cover]

REGION	Number	Rate	PERIOD	Number	Rate	PERIOD	Number	Rate
U.S., 1835–1968	81	(X)						
Northeast	7	.02	1835–1864	3	(Z)	1935–1944	4	.03
Southeast	28	.18	1865–1894	43	.03	1945–1954	[1] 11	.07
North Central	11	.03	1895–1924	12	(Z)	1955–1972	6	.03
South Central	25	.13	1925–1934	3	.02			
West	10	.10						

X Not applicable.   Z Less than .005 percent.   [1] Includes 5 Congressmen shot in 1954 in a single attack.
Source: National Commission on the Causes and Prevention of Violence, Task Force Report on Assassinations, 1969, and unpublished data.

No. 300. Murder Victims, by Weapons Used or Cause: 1965 to 1977

[Based solely on police investigation. See text, p. 174, for definition of murder]

YEAR	Murder victims, total	WEAPONS USED OR CAUSE OF DEATH				Blunt object [1]	Strangulations, beatings	Drownings, arson, etc.	All other [2]
		Guns		Cutting or stabbing					
		Total	Percent	Total	Percent				
1965	8,773	5,015	57.2	2,021	23.0	505	894	226	112
1967	11,114	6,998	63.0	2,200	19.8	589	957	211	159
1968	12,503	8,105	64.8	2,317	18.5	713	936	294	138
1969	13,575	8,876	65.4	2,534	18.7	613	1,039	322	191
1970	13,649	9,039	66.2	2,424	17.8	604	1,031	353	198
1972	15,832	10,379	65.6	2,974	18.8	672	1,291	331	185
1973	17,123	11,249	65.7	2,985	17.4	848	1,445	[3]173	423
1974	18,632	12,474	66.9	3,228	17.3	976	1,417	[3]153	384
1975	18,642	12,061	64.7	3,245	17.4	1,001	1,646	[3]193	496
1976	16,605	10,592	63.8	2,956	17.8	806	1,330	[3]227	694
1977	18,033	11,274	62.5	3,440	19.1	849	1,431	[3]252	787

[1] Refers to club, hammer, etc.　[2] Includes poison, explosives, unknown, and not stated; for 1973 to 1977, includes drowning.　[3] Arson only.

No. 301. Law Enforcement Officers Killed, by Geographic Divisions: 1960 to 1977

[Covers officers killed in line of duty; beginning 1972, includes Federal officers. For composition of divisions, see fig. I, inside front cover. See also *Historical Statistics, Colonial Times to 1970*, series H 987–998]

DIVISION	1960	1965	1969	1970	1971	1972	1973	1974	1975	1976	1977
Total killed	48	83	125	146	181	157	176	179	[1]185	[2]140	[3]123
By felons	(NA)	53	86	100	129	116	134	132	[1]129	[2]111	[3]93
In accidents	(NA)	30	39	46	52	41	42	47	56	29	[3]30
New England	3	3	3	2	5	2	7	2	4	4	2
Middle Atlantic	7	10	15	29	31	22	21	18	24	15	12
East North Central	9	10	31	38	32	23	21	43	32	19	10
West North Central	3	3	10	6	13	12	6	8	8	11	14
South Atlantic	13	15	15	23	28	38	37	42	31	34	31
East South Central	2	9	9	5	13	12	13	12	18	14	11
West South Central	6	14	19	15	23	27	30	23	22	21	21
Mountain	–	7	6	4	11	7	16	9	14	4	3
Pacific	5	12	17	24	22	12	21	18	22	13	15
Puerto Rico	(NA)	(NA)	(NA)	(NA)	3	2	4	4	8	4	1

– Represents zero.　NA Not available.
[1] Includes one officer each in Virgin Islands and Guam.　[2] Includes one officer killed at Bogota, Colombia.
[3] Includes one officer killed in U.S. Virgin Islands and 2 FBI agents accidentally killed.

Source of tables 300 and 301: U.S. Federal Bureau of Investigation, *Uniform Crime Reports for the United States*, annual.

No. 302. Percent of Firearms Usage in the Commission of Selected Crimes, by Region: 1974 to 1977

[For definitions of crimes, see text, p. 174. For composition of regions, see fig. I, inside front cover]

REGION	MURDER [1]				AGGRAVATED ASSAULT				ROBBERY			
	1974	1975	1976	1977	1974	1975	1976	1977	1974	1975	1976	1977
U.S., total	67.9	65.8	63.8	62.5	25.4	24.9	23.6	23.2	44.7	44.8	42.7	41.6
Northeast	51.7	51.3	49.2	50.8	18.9	17.6	15.9	15.1	34.0	32.7	31.4	30.9
North Central	72.6	70.7	66.4	65.7	27.4	28.5	26.8	25.6	51.4	52.7	50.9	48.6
South	75.5	72.7	71.2	69.3	30.0	29.2	27.6	26.9	55.5	53.4	49.5	48.0
West	60.8	59.0	55.4	56.0	23.7	22.3	22.1	22.5	42.5	44.4	44.3	43.0

[1] Includes nonnegligent manslaughter.

Source: U.S. Federal Bureau of Investigation, *Uniform Crime Reports for the United States*, annual.

No. 303. Selected Crimes, By Type: 1977

TYPE OF CRIME	Offenses (1,000)	PERCENT Change from 1976 [1]	PERCENT Incidence, 1977	Average value	TYPE OF CRIME	Offenses (1,000)	PERCENT Change from 1976 [1]	PERCENT Incidence, 1977	Average value
Robbery, total [2]	377	−7.2	100.0	377	Larceny—theft, total	5,525	−6.7	100.0	192
Highway	173	−9.0	45.8	261	Pocket picking	57	4.8	1.0	124
Commercial house	55	−10.2	14.6	428	Purse snatching	82	−8.8	1.5	98
Gas station	21	2.1	5.7	217	Shoplifting	616	−.4	11.1	42
Chain store	27	8.4	7.1	422					
Residence	44	−9.4	11.6	575	From motor vehicles	936	−21.4	16.9	231
Bank	4	2.1	1.1	4,858	Motor vehicle accessories	1,130	−13.7	20.5	128
Burglary, total	2,832	−5.7	100.0	475	Bicycles	618	.6	11.2	92
Residence, night	651	−3.1	23.0	460					
Residence, day	728	−2.3	25.7	503	From buildings	906	−.8	16.4	293
Residence [3]	462	−4.2	16.3	522	From coin-operated machines	55	−7.3	1.0	82
Nonresidence, night	581	−16.0	20.5	420	All other	1,124	5.2	20.3	295
Nonresidence, day	151	2.6	5.3	417					
Nonresidence [3]	259	−1.8	9.1	513					

[1] Minus sign (−) denotes decrease. [2] Includes types not shown separately. [3] Unknown.

No. 304. Offenses, Clearances, and Arrests, by Type of Crime: 1970 to 1977

[Covers crimes constituting "FBI Crime Index"; for definitions, see text, p. 174. Excludes pending cases]

ITEM	1970 Violent crime	1970 Property crime	1973 Violent crime	1973 Property crime	1974 Violent crime	1974 Property crime	1975 Violent crime	1975 Property crime	1976 Violent crime	1976 Property crime
Cities represented number	2,221		2,342		1,496		2,198		2,559	
FBI estimated population mil	60		50		32		33		35	
Offenses known 1,000	209	2,716	205	2,158	173	1,744	145	1,792	116	1,740
Offenses cleared 1,000	101	479	100	396	85	340	72	334	66	334
Percent cleared	48.2	17.6	48.8	18.3	48.9	19.5	49.8	18.6	56.6	19.2
Total arrests 1,000	89	472	83	370	58	314	50	325	50	315
Per 100 offenses	42.7	17.4	40.3	17.1	33.3	18.0	40.5	18.1	42.9	18.1
Persons charged 1,000	83	406	85	358	55	282	56	298	47	284
Per 100 offenses	39.7	15.0	41.4	16.6	31.5	16.2	38.4	16.6	40.7	16.3
Guilty as charged 1,000	20	119	20	103	13	83	14	92	15	95
Per 100 offenses	9.6	4.4	9.8	4.8	7.4	4.8	10.0	5.1	12.5	5.5
Guilty of lesser offenses 1,000	7	16	8	15	5	10	3	8	3	9
Per 100 offenses	3.4	.6	4.0	.7	2.7	.6	2.2	.4	2.7	.5
Acquitted or dismissed 1,000	18	47	21	45	12	34	12	33	10	34
Per 100 offenses	8.7	1.7	10.1	2.1	7.1	1.9	8.0	1.9	8.7	1.9
Referred to juvenile court 1,000	16	154	15	136	9	102	9	113	8	102
Per 100 offenses	7.5	5.7	7.3	6.3	5.1	5.8	6.4	6.3	6.6	5.9

ITEM	Total, serious crimes	Violent crime Total	Murder [1]	Forcible rape	Robbery	Aggravated assault	Property crime Total	Burglary [2]	Larceny-theft	Motor vehicle theft
Cities represented number					1,847					
FBI estimated population mil					30					
Offenses known 1,000	1,588	114	2.1	7.7	44	60	1,475	403	939	132
Offenses cleared 1,000	344	60	1.7	4.3	14	40	284	71	190	23
Percent cleared	21.7	52.9	82.2	56.2	31.6	66.9	19.3	17.5	20.3	17.5
Total arrests 1,000	317	45	2.0	3.5	14	26	272	64	189	20
Per 100 offenses	20.0	39.4	96.8	44.8	31.2	42.6	18.5	15.9	20.1	14.8
Persons charged 1,000	290	43	1.9	3.4	13	25	247	60	169	18
Per 100 offenses	18.3	37.6	91.0	43.4	29.4	40.9	16.8	14.9	18.0	13.6
Guilty as charged 1,000	94	13	.7	.9	4	8	81	13	65	3
Per 100 offenses	5.9	11.5	33.3	11.1	8.8	12.6	5.5	3.2	6.9	2.3
Guilty of lesser offenses 1,000	11	3	.2	.2	.6	2	8	3	5	.7
Per 100 offenses	.7	2.9	8.7	3.1	1.5	3.7	.5	.7	.5	.5
Acquitted or dismissed 1,000	34	9	.4	.7	2	6	25	7	18	2
Per 100 offenses	2.1	7.9	18.3	9.3	5.1	9.4	1.7	1.3	1.9	1.3
Referred to juvenile court 1,000	98	7	.1	.5	3	3	91	28	53	10
Per 100 offenses	6.2	6.3	6.0	7.0	7.4	5.4	6.2	7.0	5.7	7.3

[1] Includes nonnegligent manslaughter. [2] Breaking or entering.

Source of tables 303 and 304: U.S. Federal Bureau of Investigation, *Uniform Crime Reports for the United States*, annual; and unpublished data.

No. 305. Persons Arrested—Race, Sex, and Age: 1969 to 1977

[See also *Historical Statistics, Colonial Times to 1970*, series H 999–1011]

ITEM	1969	1970	1971	1972	1973	1974	1975	1976	1977
RACE									
Agencies reporting	4,627	5,208	5,610	6,114	5,914	5,222	7,993	10,058	10,864
Population represented____mil__	133	142	147	151	145	124	169	173	197
Persons arrested [1]_____1,000__	5,577	6,257	6,626	6,707	6,248	5,853	7,671	7,384	8,972
White_____1,000__	3,843	4,373	4,624	4,664	4,459	4,112	5,539	5,337	6,429
Percent of total_____	68.9	69.9	69.8	69.5	71.4	70.3	72.2	72.3	71.7
Black_____1,000__	1,559	1,688	1,791	1,848	1,636	1,562	1,935	1,870	2,308
Other_____1,000__	175	196	211	195	153	179	197	177	235
SEX AND AGE									
Agencies reporting	4,759	5,270	5,649	6,195	6,004	5,298	8,051	10,119	10,904
Population represented____mil__	144	152	155	160	155	134	179	175	198
Persons arrested [1]_____1,000__	5,862	6,570	6,967	7,013	6,500	6,179	8,014	7,912	9,029
Male_____1,000__	5,058	5,624	5,923	5,956	5,502	5,185	6,752	6,672	7,581
Percent of total_____	86.3	85.6	85.0	84.9	84.6	83.9	84.3	84.3	84.0
Percent under 18 yr. old_____	23.7	23.2	23.6	23.3	24.4	26.4	25.5	23.3	22.5
Female_____1,000__	804	947	1,044	1,057	998	994	1,262	1,240	1,448
Percent of total_____	13.7	14.4	15.0	15.1	15.4	16.1	15.7	15.7	16.0
Percent under 18 yr. old_____	37.6	37.5	38.4	38.4	37.6	36.1	35.5	33.5	32.2
Under 18 years_____1,000__	1,500	1,661	1,797	1,794	1,717	1,683	2,078	1,973	2,170
Percent of total_____	25.6	25.3	25.8	25.6	26.4	27.2	25.9	24.9	24.0
18–24 years_____1,000__	1,514	1,785	1,935	1,958	1,869	1,886	2,482	2,517	2,920
25–34 years_____1,000__	990	1,128	1,203	1,270	1,179	1,140	1,546	1,589	1,887
35–44 years_____1,000__	823	887	900	884	768	664	870	857	970
45–54 years_____1,000__	635	685	697	681	597	500	644	604	665
55 and over_____1,000__	398	425	430	413	360	299	386	367	409

[1] Represents each person arrested rather than number of charges filed against each. Includes persons for whom age was not known, not shown separately in breakdown by age.

No. 306. Arrests—Number, by Sex and Age: 1973 and 1977

[In thousands, except percent. Represents arrests reported by 4,170 agencies with a total 1977 population of 116,567,000 as estimated by FBI. Represents persons arrested, not charges]

OFFENSE CHARGED	MALE			FEMALE			PERCENT UNDER 18 YEARS OLD			
	1973	1977		1973	1977		Male		Female	
		Total	Under 18 yr.		Total	Under 18 yr.	1973	1977	1973	1977
Total persons arrested_____	4,379.7	4,455.1	1,091.8	780.6	915.8	314.5	24.2	24.5	39.0	34.3
Serious crimes_____	874.4	1,013.8	447.8	205.6	273.0	106.0	46.1	44.2	43.3	38.8
Murder [1]	9.3	9.3	1.0	1.7	1.6	.1	10.7	11.3	6.2	6.6
Manslaughter by negligence_____	2.4	1.5	.2	.8	.2	(Z)	21.7	11.4	64.4	12.9
Forcible rape_____	14.5	16.0	2.7	(X)	(X)	(X)	19.5	16.9	(X)	(X)
Robbery_____	69.0	70.6	22.0	4.8	5.8	1.7	32.5	31.2	31.3	30.0
Aggravated assault_____	99.2	111.7	20.1	14.9	16.9	3.6	17.5	18.0	20.6	21.4
Burglary—breaking or entering__	234.8	268.9	145.3	13.6	17.7	9.3	54.7	54.0	51.6	52.8
Larceny—theft_____	361.3	458.0	213.7	164.4	223.6	86.8	50.5	46.7	44.8	38.8
Motor vehicle theft_____	83.9	77.7	42.8	5.5	7.2	4.3	57.5	55.1	60.4	60.2
All other:										
Other assaults_____	192.6	219.7	43.8	30.7	36.4	11.8	19.6	19.9	32.0	32.4
Forgery and counterfeiting_____	21.2	27.3	3.9	8.1	12.2	1.6	11.9	14.1	11.7	12.9
Fraud_____	46.1	58.0	2.8	20.0	34.5	1.1	7.6	4.9	3.7	3.1
Embezzlement_____	2.9	3.0	.5	.9	.9	.1	10.3	15.6	7.6	13.8
Stolen property [2]_____	48.2	59.0	21.3	5.2	7.2	2.0	36.6	36.0	28.8	27.9
Weapons (carrying, possessing)__	83.8	82.3	14.5	7.1	7.5	1.0	16.4	17.6	10.3	13.2
Prostitution and commercial vice_	9.4	17.7	.8	31.1	39.2	1.7	3.8	4.6	3.5	4.4
Sex offenses [3]_____	34.9	37.2	6.9	3.2	4.4	.9	19.4	18.4	38.3	19.5
Drug abuse violations_____	334.2	310.4	73.1	57.4	52.9	14.5	25.7	23.6	33.3	27.5
Gambling_____	46.4	34.3	1.5	4.1	3.1	(Z)	3.8	4.5	2.3	2.3
Offenses against family and children_____	31.4	24.0	1.1	3.5	3.1	.7	2.9	4.8	14.8	22.6
Driving while intoxicated_____	483.0	520.7	11.3	38.5	49.6	1.2	1.4	2.2	1.3	2.4
Liquor laws_____	120.5	165.1	59.2	21.5	30.8	16.9	39.3	35.8	56.2	55.0
Drunkenness_____	868.0	675.6	26.9	66.3	53.1	4.4	2.9	4.0	6.1	8.3
Disorderly conduct_____	361.2	336.2	66.3	57.3	71.0	15.8	21.0	19.7	28.1	22.2
Vagrancy_____	26.8	17.8	3.1	4.3	5.1	.8	13.2	17.7	20.4	14.7
All other offenses, except traffic__	582.7	638.6	141.9	109.9	132.7	40.8	24.8	22.2	39.1	30.7

X Not applicable.   Z Fewer than 50.   [1] Includes nonnegligent manslaughter.
[2] Buying, receiving, possessing.   [3] Excludes rape and prostitution, shown separately.

Source, tables 305, 306: U.S. Federal Bureau of Investigation, *Uniform Crime Reports for the United States*, annual.

No. 307. Arrests—Selected Characteristics of Persons Charged: 1977

[Represents persons arrested (not charges) reported by 10,904 agencies with a total 1977 population of 198 million as estimated by FBI]

OFFENSE CHARGED	Total (1,000)	PERCENT							
		Male	Under 15 yr. old	Under 18 yr. old	18–24 yr. old	25–44 yr. old	45–54 yr. old	55–64 yr. old	65 and over
Total arrests	9,029	84.0	8.0	24.0	32.3	31.6	7.4	3.5	1.1
Serious crimes	1,986	79.9	15.9	41.2	31.8	21.8	3.1	1.4	.7
Murder and nonnegligent manslaughter	17	85.5	1.3	9.7	33.7	44.1	7.6	3.2	1.6
Manslaughter by negligence	3	88.8	1.4	11.1	40.2	37.3	6.5	3.3	1.5
Forcible rape	26	98.9	4.2	16.5	39.8	38.6	3.6	1.1	.4
Robbery	123	92.6	8.4	32.0	42.4	23.8	1.3	.3	.2
Aggravated assault	221	87.2	4.7	16.3	32.7	40.3	6.8	2.8	1.0
Burglary [1]	454	94.0	19.3	51.5	32.5	14.4	1.1	.3	.1
Larceny—theft	1,007	68.2	18.7	42.9	30.0	20.8	3.5	1.8	.9
Motor vehicle theft	135	91.9	13.9	53.0	30.4	14.8	1.3	.3	.1
All other:									
Other assaults	400	86.2	6.8	19.1	33.0	38.9	6.1	2.1	.7
Arson	17	88.7	30.6	49.8	23.2	21.2	3.8	1.4	.5
Forgery and counterfeiting	68	70.9	2.2	12.8	41.0	41.2	3.8	.9	.2
Fraud	217	64.4	4.7	10.3	30.3	50.8	6.2	1.8	.4
Embezzlement	7	77.3	1.8	11.8	33.3	45.6	6.8	1.8	.3
Stolen property [2]	104	89.2	9.6	32.9	38.3	24.7	2.8	.9	.3
Vandalism	197	91.6	32.5	60.3	23.2	13.8	1.7	.6	.2
Weapons (carrying, etc.)	136	92.0	3.8	16.0	35.2	38.0	6.8	2.8	1.1
Prostitution and commercialized vice	77	29.3	.5	4.3	60.2	31.3	2.6	1.1	.4
Sex offenses [3]	61	91.1	6.8	18.4	29.4	39.6	7.6	3.5	1.5
Drug abuse violations	569	86.1	3.3	23.2	50.7	24.3	1.3	.3	.1
Gambling	53	91.1	.6	4.2	16.6	44.7	19.0	10.6	4.8
Offenses against family and children	53	89.7	2.8	5.9	30.6	54.4	6.9	1.7	.4
Driving while intoxicated	1,104	91.7	(Z)	2.2	28.8	46.7	13.9	6.6	1.7
Liquor laws	322	85.2	3.0	37.3	44.0	13.0	3.4	1.7	.6
Drunkenness	1,209	92.8	.4	4.1	24.1	40.6	18.1	10.0	3.0
Disorderly conduct	625	82.8	5.9	19.4	39.0	32.0	6.0	2.6	.9
Vagrancy	44	65.4	3.1	12.7	43.8	32.8	6.3	3.3	1.2
Suspicion	23	85.7	8.3	26.5	43.2	25.9	2.8	1.0	.4
Curfew, loitering (juveniles)	86	78.1	28.1	100.0	(X)	(X)	(X)	(X)	(X)
Runaways (juveniles)	185	42.4	40.3	100.0	(X)	(X)	(X)	(X)	(X)
All other offenses, except traffic	1,487	84.6	7.2	20.8	35.0	34.5	6.4	2.5	.7

X Not applicable.   Z Less than .05 percent.   [1] Breaking or entering.
[2] Buying, receiving, possessing.   [3] Excludes forcible rape and prostitution, shown separately.
Source: U.S. Federal Bureau of Investigation, *Uniform Crime Reports for the United States*, 1977.

No. 308. Arrests—Number, by Race: 1977

[In thousands. Represents arrests reported by 10,864 agencies with a total 1977 population of 197 million as estimated by FBI. Represents persons arrested, not charges]

OFFENSE CHARGED	Total	White	Negro	Other	OFFENSE CHARGED	Total	White	Negro	Other
Total	8,972	6,429.0	2,308.4	234.7	All other—Con.:				
					Embezzlement, fraud	223	147.2	72.8	2.6
Serious crimes	1,974	1,267.6	662.0	44.0	Stolen property [2]	104	67.7	34.6	1.4
Murder and nonnegligent manslaughter	17	7.9	8.7	.5	Weapons (carrying, etc.)	136	78.7	53.4	3.6
Manslaughter by negligence	3	2.3	.6	.1	Prostitution and commercialized vice	77	34.1	41.2	1.5
Forcible rape	26	12.9	12.2	.6	Sex offenses [3]	61	46.3	12.8	1.4
Robbery	122	49.9	69.6	2.6	Drug abuse violations	565	434.5	122.6	8.3
Aggravated assault	221	130.4	85.6	4.5	Gambling	52	14.0	36.0	2.4
Burglary [1]	451	311.7	130.5	8.6					
Larceny—theft	1,000	657.0	319.8	23.3	Offenses against family and children	53	35.0	17.2	.8
Motor vehicle theft	134	95.5	35.0	3.8	Driving, intoxicated	1,096	924.0	142.5	29.2
All other:					Liquor laws	317	282.8	25.6	9.0
Other assaults	398	255.0	133.2	9.4	Drunkenness	1,204	946.8	215.4	41.6
Forgery and counterfeiting	68	45.3	21.5	.8	Disorderly conduct	621	406.7	191.0	23.4
					Vagrancy	44	26.5	16.5	1.1
					Other, except traffic	1,981	1,416.8	509.9	54.1

[1] Breaking or entering.   [2] Buying, receiving, possessing.   [3] See footnote 3, table 307.
Source: U.S. Federal Bureau of Investigation, *Uniform Crime Reports for the United States*, 1977.

No. 309. Criminal Justice System—Public Expenditures, 1965 to 1976, and Employment, 1970 to 1976, by Level of Government

[Expenditures are for fiscal years closing during the 12 months ending June 30. Employment as of October. Expenditures are direct expenditures only and on cash flow basis. See also Appendix III and Historical Statistics, Colonial Times to 1970, series H 1012–1027]

LEVEL OF GOVERNMENT AND ACTIVITY	EXPENDITURES (mil. dol.)						FULL-TIME EQUIVALENT EMPLOYMENT [1]					
							1970		1975		1976	
	1965	1970	1973	1974	1975	1976	Total (1,000)	Rate [2]	Total (1,000)	Rate [2]	Total (1,000)	Rate [2]
All governments	4,573	³8,571	³13,051	³14,954	³17,249	³19,681	775	38.0	³1,051	³49.3	³1,080	³50.3
Police	2,792	5,080	7,624	8,512	9,786	11,028	489	24.0	625	29.3	628	29.3
Judicial	748	1,190	1,579	1,798	2,068	2,428	96	4.7	132	6.2	137	6.4
Legal services	(⁴)	442	664	771	933	1,048	38	1.9	55	2.6	59	2.8
Public defense	(⁴)	102	207	245	280	331	3	.2	6	.3	7	.3
Corrections	1,033	1,706	2,740	3,240	3,843	4,386	148	7.3	225	10.5	239	11.1
Federal Government	377	³978	³1,695	³1,961	³2,189	³2,450	59	2.9	³96	³4.5	³99	³4.6
Police	243	589	1,089	1,222	1,461	1,612	40	1.9	69	3.2	71	3.3
Judicial	75	129	118	136	165	219	7	.3	7	.3	8	.4
Legal services	(⁴)	102	123	118	177	149	7	.3	7	.3	7	.3
Public defense	(⁴)	56	90	92	87	104	(Z)	(Z)	(Z)	(Z)	(Z)	(Z)
Corrections	59	83	171	215	217	256	6	.3	11	.5	12	.5
State governments	1,135	³2,134	³3,304	³3,900	³4,612	³5,204	172	8.5	³263	³12.4	³272	³12.7
Percent of total	24.8	24.9	25.3	26.1	26.7	26.4	22.2	(X)	25.0	(X)	25.2	(X)
Police	348	689	1,132	1,308	1,512	1,696	56	2.7	92	4.3	91	4.2
Judicial	155	282	386	439	498	585	18	.9	26	1.2	28	1.3
Legal services	(⁴)	83	143	178	216	248	7	.3	12	.6	13	.6
Public defense	(⁴)	9	37	52	65	70	1	(Z)	3	.1	3	.1
Corrections	632	1,051	1,534	1,813	2,193	2,475	90	4.4	127	6.0	134	6.3
Local governments	3,062	³5,454	³8,052	³9,092	³10,449	³12,027	543	26.7	³691	³32.4	³708	³33.0
Percent of total	67.0	63.6	61.7	60.8	60.6	61.1	70.1	(X)	65.7	(X)	65.6	(X)
Police	2,201	3,803	5,403	5,982	6,813	7,720	394	19.3	463	21.7	466	21.7
Judicial	518	779	1,075	1,223	1,405	1,624	70	3.4	99	4.7	102	4.8
Legal services	(⁴)	257	397	475	540	651	25	1.2	36	1.7	39	1.8
Public defense	(⁴)	37	79	101	· 128	157	3	.1	4	.2	4	.2
Corrections	343	572	1,035	1,213	1,434	1,654	52	2.6	87	4.1	93	4.3

X Not applicable. Z Less than 500 or .05. ¹ Derived by dividing total payroll by full-time payroll and multiplying result by full-time employees. ² Rate (total) per 10,000 estimated population as of July 1, excluding Armed Forces abroad. ³ Includes amounts not shown separately. ⁴ Not included prior to 1970.

Source: 1965, U.S. Bureau of the Census, Governmental Finances and Public Employment, both annual. Beginning 1970, U.S. Law Enforcement Assistance Administration and U.S. Bureau of the Census, Expenditure and Employment Data for the Criminal Justice System, annual.

No. 310. Federal Outlays for Crime Reduction, by Program: 1975 to 1978

[In millions of dollars. For years ending June 30 except, beginning 1977, ending September 30. Represents obligations. Includes intergovernmental (State and local) expenditures. Excludes U.S. Postal Service and Department of Defense military outlays for crime reduction]

PROGRAM	1975	1976	1977	1978, est.
Total	2,821	3,043	3,245	3,347
Criminal justice system support	195	184	185	180
Statistics	95	42	34	34
Research	12	13	13	10
Planning and coordination	84	127	136	134
Reform of criminal laws	4	2	2	2
Crime prevention services	420	303	307	363
Juvenile delinquency	111	82	94	96
Addict rehabilitation	259	174	173	196
Other programs	50	47	40	71
Law enforcement	872	1,042	1,146	1,216
Enforcement of Federal criminal law	821	939	1,039	1,111
Protection of individuals and facilities	51	76	75	78
Research and development	-	27	32	27

PROGRAM	1975	1976	1977	1978, est.
Law enforcement support	303	539	518	502
Adjudication	503	379	422	404
Preparation of Federal criminal cases	82	99	114	121
Operation of Federal court system	99	101	116	123
Assistance to States and localities	244	163	175	146
Research and development	78	17	17	14
Corrections	529	596	667	682
Operation of correctional institutions	183	193	227	261
Probation, parole, and community treatment	48	64	79	85
Inmate education	11	12	14	16
Improved correctional programs	264	288	302	273
Other programs	23	39	45	47

- Represents zero.

Source: U.S. Office of Management and Budget, Special Analyses, Budget of the United States Government, annual.

No. 311. STATE AND LOCAL GOVERNMENT POLICE AND CORRECTIONS EMPLOYMENT AND POLICE EXPENDITURES, 1960 TO 1976, AND BY STATES, 1976

[Employees as of October. Direct expenditures for police protection are for fiscal years ending June 30 in year stated. Local government data are estimates subject to sampling variation; see source]

YEAR AND STATE	EMPLOYEES (full-time equivalent)[1]							POLICE EXPENDITURES (mil. dol.)		
	Police protection				Corrections			Local		
	State and local	Rate[2]	Local		State and local	Rate[2]	Local		State and local	Local	
			Total	Per-cent			Total	Per-cent		Total	Per-cent
1960	303,771	1.7	271,634	89.4	(NA)	(NA)	(NA)	(NA)	1,857	1,612	87
1965	348,569	1.8	308,472	88.5	110,700	.6	41,163	37.2	2,549	2,201	86
1970	449,656	2.2	393,810	87.6	142,307	.7	51,973	36.5	4,491	3,803	85
1971	472,066	2.3	402,691	85.3	172,821	.8	66,776	38.6	5,361	4,489	84
1972	486,162	2.3	410,765	84.5	177,864	.9	70,079	39.4	5,941	4,950	83
1973	511,146	2.4	429,512	84.0	187,298	.9	75,122	40.1	6,535	5,405	83
1974	539,409	2.6	449,587	83.3	203,230	1.0	82,070	40.4	7,290	5,984	82
1975	555,849	2.6	463,404	83.4	213,813	1.0	86,880	40.6	8,326	6,813	82
1976	556,926	2.6	466,042	83.7	227,576	1.1	93,156	40.9	9,417	7,720	82
Ala	7,488	2.0	5,985	79.9	2,371	.6	889	37.5	100	76	76
Alaska	1,206	3.2	548	45.4	533	1.4	40	7.5	36	16	44
Ariz	6,730	3.0	5,229	77.7	2,629	1.2	1,429	54.4	136	103	76
Ark	3,796	1.8	2,984	78.6	1,279	.6	466	36.4	43	30	70
Calif	61,520	2.9	49,659	80.7	34,240	1.6	21,650	63.2	1,251	1,014	81
Colo	7,114	2.8	6,154	86.5	2,474	1.0	672	27.2	118	101	86
Conn	7,554	2.4	6,194	82.0	2,538	.8	5	.2	125	103	82
Del	1,493	2.6	845	56.6	831	1.4	–	–	24	14	58
D.C	4,968	7.1	4,968	100.0	2,932	4.2	2,932	100.0	95	95	100
Fla	24,323	2.9	21,335	87.7	13,023	1.5	3,211	24.7	382	332	87
Ga	12,359	2.5	10,094	81.7	6,164	1.2	2,215	35.9	159	127	80
Hawaii	2,503	2.8	2,409	96.2	637	.7	40	6.3	41	40	98
Idaho	1,983	2.4	1,661	83.8	602	.7	131	21.8	25	19	76
Ill	34,816	3.1	31,245	89.7	8,004	.8	3,624	41.2	633	526	83
Ind	10,700	2.0	8,722	80.8	3,621	.7	1,556	43.0	152	113	74
Iowa	5,235	1.8	4,137	79.0	2,145	.7	736	34.3	78	58	74
Kans	5,132	2.2	4,398	85.7	2,698	1.2	522	19.3	65	52	80
Ky	6,864	2.0	4,923	71.7	2,351	.7	838	35.6	104	72	69
La	11,941	3.1	9,133	76.5	4,224	1.1	1,203	28.5	161	121	75
Maine	2,158	2.0	1,594	73.9	760	.7	150	19.7	29	20	69
Md	12,111	2.9	9,558	78.9	6,028	1.5	1,068	17.7	209	164	78
Mass	16,982	2.9	14,652	86.3	5,714	1.0	2,352	41.2	308	271	88
Mich	22,100	2.4	18,652	84.4	7,883	.9	3,834	48.6	433	363	84
Minn	7,431	1.9	6,341	85.3	2,882	.7	1,358	47.1	132	109	83
Miss	4,428	1.9	3,338	75.4	1,277	.5	301	23.6	60	38	63
Mo	12,526	2.6	11,123	88.8	4,138	.9	1,736	42.0	181	155	86
Mont	1,718	2.3	1,432	83.4	700	.9	164	23.4	23	18	78
Nebr	3,131	2.0	2,486	79.4	1,233	.8	381	30.9	45	34	76
Nev	2,314	3.8	1,999	86.4	1,145	1.9	550	48.0	43	36	84
N.H	1,843	2.2	1,500	81.4	596	.7	225	37.8	25	19	76
N.J	24,051	3.3	20,759	86.3	8,734	1.2	5,007	57.3	416	360	87
N. Mex	3,154	2.7	2,306	73.1	1,011	.9	265	26.2	44	32	73
N.Y	65,870	3.6	59,426	90.2	23,102	1.3	10,632	46.0	1,315	1,204	92
N.C	11,232	2.1	8,849	78.8	6,872	1.3	872	12.7	155	111	72
N. Dak	1,079	1.7	916	84.9	368	.6	92	25.0	16	13	81
Ohio	23,038	2.2	20,314	88.2	10,166	1.0	3,764	37.0	378	331	88
Okla	6,253	2.3	4,671	74.7	2,607	.9	494	18.9	74	52	70
Oreg	5,390	2.3	4,067	75.5	2,638	1.1	961	36.4	92	70	76
Pa	28,372	2.4	22,801	80.4	9,638	.8	5,466	56.7	461	342	74
R.I	2,382	2.6	2,087	87.6	719	.8	–	–	35	29	83
S.C	6,156	2.2	4,585	74.5	3,401	1.2	650	19.1	78	54	69
S. Dak	1,222	1.8	985	80.6	403	.6	69	17.1	21	16	76
Tenn	8,943	2.1	7,749	86.6	4,136	1.0	1,381	33.4	117	100	85
Tex	27,781	2.2	22,956	82.6	8,865	.7	4,039	45.6	404	319	79
Utah	2,869	2.3	2,197	76.6	975	.8	195	20.0	40	28	70
Vt	993	2.1	583	58.7	449	.9	4	.9	14	7	50
Va	10,655	2.1	8,423	79.1	7,479	1.5	1,940	25.9	175	121	69
Wash	7,645	2.1	6,247	81.7	4,258	1.2	1,626	38.2	139	111	80
W. Va	2,954	1.6	2,037	69.0	1,134	.6	298	26.3	38	23	61
Wis	11,250	2.4	9,938	88.3	3,805	.8	1,053	27.7	175	153	87
Wyo	1,071	2.7	848	79.2	364	.9	70	19.2	14	9	64

– Represents zero.   NA Not available.
[1] See footnote 1, table 309.   [2] Rate per 1,000 estimated population, as of July 1.

Source: U.S. Law Enforcement Assistance Administration and U.S. Bureau of the Census, *Expenditure and Employment Data for the Criminal Justice System*, annual.

No. 312. AVERAGE ANNUAL SALARY SCALES OF POLICE AND FIREFIGHTERS, BY CITY-SIZE GROUPS: 1965 TO 1977

[Based on a study covering cities with a population of 100,000 or more. See also table 693]

EMPLOYEE GROUP AND YEAR	MINIMUM ANNUAL SCALES					MAXIMUM ANNUAL SCALES				
	Total	City population size				Total	City population size			
		100,000-249,999	250,000-499,999	500,000-999,999	1,000,000 or more		100,000-249,999	250,000-499,999	500,000-999,999	1,000,000 or more
POLICE										
1965	$5,763	$5,134	$5,404	$5,603	$6,193	$6,919	$6,007	$6,390	$6,659	$7,559
1970	8,448	7,357	7,926	7,888	9,300	10,017	8,648	9,385	9,616	10,927
1971	8,874	7,939	8,414	8,291	9,675	10,576	9,408	9,960	10,109	11,452
1972	9,449	8,350	8,754	8,749	10,465	11,334	9,992	10,423	10,667	12,496
1973	9,928	8,840	9,258	9,364	10,870	12,308	10,612	11,065	11,684	13,707
1974	10,537	9,394	9,891	9,790	11,595	13,079	11,303	11,907	12,239	14,611
1975	11,181	10,074	10,734	10,681	12,054	14,005	12,256	13,028	13,560	15,299
1976	11,913	10,653	11,362	11,249	13,078	14,931	13,041	13,826	14,333	16,556
1977	12,426	11,228	11,968	11,797	13,497	15,606	13,716	14,554	15,242	17,067
Percent change:										
1965-1970	47	43	47	41	50	45	44	47	44	45
1970-1975	32	37	35	35	30	40	42	39	41	40
1975-1977	11	11	11	10	12	11	12	12	12	12
FIREFIGHTERS										
1965	$5,633	$5,046	$5,310	$5,646	$6,293	$6,689	$5,892	$6,297	$6,607	$7,630
1970	8,041	7,103	7,685	7,786	9,253	9,482	8,349	9,089	9,293	10,828
1971	8,489	7,672	8,179	8,215	9,596	10,060	9,080	9,649	9,839	11,327
1972	9,019	8,101	8,459	8,743	10,410	10,725	9,642	10,080	10,485	12,284
1973	9,502	8,596	9,029	9,211	10,832	11,589	10,242	10,788	11,240	13,564
1974	10,047	9,087	9,708	9,571	11,541	12,309	10,874	11,680	11,808	14,450
1975	10,739	9,786	10,480	10,587	11,958	13,254	11,815	12,755	13,168	15,047
1976	11,403	10,301	11,167	11,074	13,044	14,085	12,511	13,614	13,835	16,325
1977	12,056	10,889	11,768	11,675	13,837	14,965	13,266	14,285	14,901	17,303
Percent change:										
1965-1970	43	41	45	38	47	42	42	44	41	42
1970-1975	34	38	36	36	29	40	42	40	42	39
1975-1977	12	11	12	10	16	13	12	12	13	15

Source: U.S. Bureau of Labor Statistics, *Current Wage Developments*, February 1978. Based on data from International City Management Assoc., Fraternal Order of Police, and International Assoc. of Firefighters.

No. 313. AUTHORIZED INTERCEPTS OF COMMUNICATION—SUMMARY: 1969 TO 1977

[Data for jurisdictions with statutes authorizing or approving interception of wire or oral communication]

ITEM	1969	1970	1971	1972	1973	1974	1975	1976	1977
Jurisdictions reporting interceptions [1]	9	12	14	18	20	19	18	21	19
Intercept applications authorized, total	301	596	816	855	864	728	701	686	626
Residence or apartment	202	366	553	569	556	419	455	435	410
Business or other	99	230	263	286	308	309	246	251	216
Installed	270	582	792	841	812	694	676	635	601
Average length _____days	23	22	22	22	24	23	22	23	25
Tap (telephone wiretap)	250	538	753	779	731	633	620	581	554
Bug (incl. unspecified) [2]	20	44	39	62	81	61	56	54	47
Federal	30	179	281	205	130	120	106	136	77
State	240	403	511	636	682	574	570	449	524
Avg. number of intercepted communications [3]	544	656	643	600	610	850	654	662	658
Incriminating	265	296	399	303	304	431	305	272	268
Persons arrested [4]	625	1,874	2,811	2,861	2,306	2,162	2,234	2,189	2,191
Convictions [4]	34	151	322	402	409	179	336	358	372
Major offense specified in application:									
Gambling	102	326	570	497	446	381	408	378	265
Drugs	89	127	126	230	229	199	178	190	237
Homicide and assault	22	20	18	35	47	21	16	10	22
Larceny and theft	10	31	31	22	36	22	5	9	20
Bribery	12	16	16	9	25	25	21	24	17
Other [5]	66	76	55	62	81	80	73	75	65
Racketeering	-	-	1	5	2	9	5	30	18
Loan sharking [6]	5	7	5	13	21	14	27	17	13
Stolen property [7]	5	5	2	13	28	18	13	10	10

- Represents zero.   [1] Jurisdictions include Federal Govt., States, and Dist of Col. as of Dec. 31, 1975.
[2] A listening device, e.g., a microphone. Includes use of a microphone and telephone wiretap simultaneously.   [3] Per authorized installation.   [4] Based on information received from intercepts installed in year shown.   [5] Includes other amounts not shown separately.   [6] Includes usury and extortion.   [7] Possession, transport, or receipt of.

Source: Administrative Office of the U.S. Courts, *Reports on Applications for Orders Authorizing or Approving the Interception of Wire or Oral Communications*, annual.

No. 314. LEGAL SERVICES—SELECTED DATA: 1972

[Money figures in millions of dollars]

ITEM	ALL ESTABLISHMENTS		ESTABLISHMENTS WITH PAYROLL			
	Number	Receipts	Number	Receipts	Annual payroll	Paid employees [1]
Total	144,452	10,938	77,282	9,724	2,318	267,656
By legal form of organization:						
Sole proprietorships	95,820	2,885	30,856	1,730	310	53,608
Partnerships	25,488	5,911	23,691	5,857	1,284	150,119
Corporations [2]	4,574	1,056	4,478	1,053	527	31,549
Other or legal form unknown [3]	18,570	1,086	18,257	1,084	197	32,380
By receipts size of establishment: [4]						
With annual receipts of:						
Less than $20,000	(NA)	(NA)	10,017	123	29	9,970
$20,000 to $99,999	(NA)	(NA)	42,087	2,080	360	67,236
$100,000 or more	(NA)	(NA)	20,620	6,867	1,777	173,248
Selected States:						
California	14,039	1,217	8,103	1,115	293	29,337
Illinois	8,865	718	4,166	628	148	15,529
New York	21,470	1,918	9,663	1,708	429	43,043
Pennsylvania	6,650	547	3,404	474	111	13,685
Texas	7,907	533	4,086	464	99	12,826

NA Not available. [1] For week including March 12. [2] Represents professional service organizations. [3] Includes estates, receiverships, and cooperatives. [4] Establishments operating entire year.

Source: U.S. Bureau of the Census, *1972 Census of Selected Service Industries, Legal Services Report*, SC 72-S-4.

No. 315. LAWYERS—SELECTED CHARACTERISTICS: 1954 TO 1970

[Data based on *Martindale-Hubbell Law Directory*. Represents all members of the bar, including those inactive or retired. See also *Historical Statistics, Colonial Times to 1970*, series H 1028-1062]

CHARACTERISTIC	1954	1957	1960	1963	1966	1970			
						Total	In cities with population—		
							Under 250,000	250,000– 499,999	Over 500,000
All lawyers [1]	241,514	262,320	285,933	296,069	316,856	355,242	172,030	41,075	142,137
Lawyers reporting [2]	221,600	235,783	252,385	268,782	289,404	324,818	159,291	37,411	128,116
In cities with population: [3]									
Less than 200,000	105,709	111,543	115,453	124,092	135,515	[4] 159,291	159,291	(X)	(X)
200,000–499,999	30,651	33,001	37,388	39,279	41,205	[5] 37,411	(X)	37,411	(X)
500,000 or more	85,240	91,239	99,544	105,411	112,684	128,116	(X)	(X)	128,116
Male	216,564	229,433	245,897	261,639	281,336	315,715	155,356	36,428	123,931
Female	5,036	6,350	6,488	7,143	8,068	9,103	3,935	983	4,185
Status in practice: [6]									
Government	21,279	24,245	25,621	29,314	31,280	35,803	16,116	3,613	16,074
Federal	9,040	12,458	13,045	15,113	16,284	18,710	5,234	1,591	11,885
State	3,561	4,000	4,316	6,486	7,416	9,293	5,444	1,332	2,517
City or county	8,678	7,787	8,260	7,715	7,580	7,800	5,438	690	1,672
Judicial	7,903	7,910	8,180	8,748	9,712	10,349	7,392	997	1,960
Federal	621	769	599	707	800	878	363	145	370
State or county	5,041	5,056	5,301	5,712	6,823	7,548	5,672	660	1,216
City	2,241	2,085	2,280	2,329	2,089	1,923	1,357	192	374
Private practice	189,423	188,955	192,353	200,586	212,662	236,085	119,507	27,166	89,412
Individual	127,389	122,389	116,911	113,127	113,273	118,963	62,377	12,529	44,057
Partner	51,668	54,966	60,709	70,064	78,544	92,442	48,697	11,285	32,460
Associate [7]	10,366	11,600	14,733	17,395	20,845	24,680	8,433	3,352	12,895
Salaried	16,648	21,054	25,198	29,510	33,222	40,486	15,453	5,562	19,471
Private industry	15,063	18,911	22,533	26,492	29,405	33,593	12,372	4,806	16,415
Educational instit	1,351	1,504	1,798	2,100	2,717	3,732	2,092	435	1,205
Other private employ	234	639	867	918	1,100	3,161	989	321	1,851
Inactive or retired	6,581	7,661	10,887	12,024	14,881	16,812	11,353	1,502	3,957

X Not applicable. [1] Includes lawyers not reporting and an adjustment (subtraction) for duplications. [2] Includes duplications: 1954, 4,440; 1957, 4,506; 1960, 4,504; 1963, 5,918; 1966, 6,787; 1970, 8,834. [3] 1954-1957, 1950 Census of Population; 1960, 1960 Census of Population; 1963 and 1966, unofficial estimates, *Editor & Publisher Yearbook;* and 1970, 1970 Census of Population. [4] Less than 250,000 population. [5] 250,000–499,000 population. [6] In some cases, if more than 1 subentry was applicable the individual was tabulated in each. [7] Lawyers employed by individual practitioners or partnerships.

Source: American Bar Foundation, Chicago, Ill., *The 1971 Lawyer Statistical Report, 1971.* (Copyright.)

No. 316. FEDERAL PROSECUTIONS OF PUBLIC OFFICIALS AND EMPLOYEES: 1970 TO 1977

[As of **December**. Prosecution of persons in violation of Federal Criminal Statutes. Detail will not always add to totals because some cases indicted in one year will carry over to the next and become convictions. Some cases carry over more than two years]

PROSECUTION STATUS	1970	1971	1972	1973	1974	1975	1976	1977
Total: Indicted	63	160	208	244	291	255	563	507
Convicted	44	108	142	181	217	179	380	440
Awaiting trial	–	–	5	18	5	27	199	210
Federal officials: Indicted	9	58	58	60	59	53	111	129
Convicted	9	40	42	48	51	43	101	94
Awaiting trial	–	–	4	2	1	5	1	32
State officials: Indicted	10	21	17	19	36	36	59	50
Convicted	7	16	10	17	23	18	35	38
Awaiting trial	–	–	–	–	–	5	30	33
Local officials: Indicted	26	46	106	85	130	139	194	157
Convicted	16	28	75	64	87	94	100	164
Awaiting trial	–	–	–	2	4	15	98	62
Others involved: [1] Indicted	18	35	27	80	66	27	199	171
Convicted	12	24	15	52	56	24	144	144
Awaiting trial	–	–	1	14	–	2	70	83

– Represents zero.   [1] Refers to individuals who are neither public officials nor employees but who were involved with public officials or employees in violating the law.

Source: U.S. Department of Justice, *Federal Prosecutions of Corrupt Public Officials, 1970–1977*, August 1978

No. 317. COURTS AND AUTHORIZED JUDGESHIPS, BY LEVEL OF JURISDICTION: 1972 AND 1977

[As of January]

STATE	NUMBER OF COURTS, BY JURISDICTION			AUTHORIZED JUDGESHIPS, BY JURISDICTION, 1972			STATE	NUMBER OF COURTS, BY JURISDICTION			AUTHORIZED JUDGESHIPS, BY JURISDICTION, 1972		
	General, 1977	Limited and special, 1972	Appellate, 1977	General	Limited and special	Appellate		General, 1977	Limited and special, 1972	Appellate, 1977	General	Limited and special	Appellate
U.S.	3,588	13,221	211	4,929	17,417	727	Mo.	117	410	4	104	427	16
							Mont.	56	66	1	28	79	5
Ala.	73	269	3	86	292	15	Nebr.	93	202	1	38	222	7
Alaska	4	66	1	16	78	5	Nev.	17	58	1	22	62	5
Ariz.	14	144	3	54	182	14	N.H.	10	76	1	10	122	5
Ark.	172	240	1	49	247	7							
Calif.	58	306	6	438	575	55	N.J.	42	586	2	168	655	22
							N. Mex.	19	121		26	194	9
Colo.	63	155	2	80	207	13	N.Y.	119	1,507	8	337	2,953	46
Conn.	14	158	1	35	210	6	N.C.	100	100	2	49	626	16
Del.	6	31	1	12	73	3	N. Dak.	53	158	1	19	170	5
D.C.	1	–	1	37	–	9							
Fla.	67	474	5	137	650	27	Ohio	88	417	89	291	487	45
							Okla.	77	169	6	180	192	18
Ga.	159	441	2	73	482	16	Oreg.	36	175	2	61	203	12
Hawaii	4	4	1	17	13	5	Pa.	67	589	3	234	623	21
Idaho	44	–	1	24	–	5	R.I.	4	51	1	13	60	5
Ill.	102	–	6	605	–	34							
Ind.	130	521	2	145	538	14	S.C.	46	484	1	16	521	5
							S. Dak.	64	85	1	21	46	5
Iowa	99	83	2	76	102	9	Tenn.	190	307	3	98	339	21
Kans.	105	509	2	61	539	7	Tex.	254	1,151	16	216	1,464	56
Ky.	120	473	2	76	519	7	Utah	29	90	1	22	98	5
La.	65	481	5	104	498	33							
Maine	16	47	1	11	53	6	Vt.	14	33	1	34	34	5
							Va.	122	284	1	100	374	7
Md.	24	47	2	79	145	17	Wash.	39	335	4	92	391	21
Mass.	14	91	2	46	202	7	W. Va.	58	463	1	40	466	5
Mich.	84	217	2	135	316	19	Wis.	142	133	1	176	135	7
Minn.	87	188	1	71	293	7	Wyo.	23	65	1	12	87	5
Miss.	184	161	1	55	173	9							

– Represents zero.

Source: U.S. Law Enforcement Assistance Administration, *National Survey of Court Organization*, 1973; and *1977 Supplement to State Judicial Systems*.

No 318. COURTS OF ORIGINAL CIVIL AND CRIMINAL JURISDICTION: 1972

[As of January]

STATE	Courts of original jurisdiction	COURTS OF ORIGINAL CIVIL JURISDICTION		COURTS OF ORIGINAL CRIMINAL JURISDICTION		STATE	Courts of original jurisdiction	COURTS OF ORIGINAL CIVIL JURISDICTION		COURTS OF ORIGINAL CRIMINAL JURISDICTION	
		Total	Percent hearing general civil cases	Total	Percent hearing felonies			Total	Percent hearing general civil cases	Total	Percent hearing felonies
U.S.	16,851	13,122	83	14,409	31	Mo	527	362	69	410	37
						Mont	122	102	99	122	45
Ala	342	219	65	271	26	Nebr	295	199	96	293	38
Alaska	70	70	100	70	7	Nev	75	62	98	75	43
Ariz	158	115	90	158	39	N.H	86	86	88	76	46
Ark	412	359	57	238	36						
Calif	364	364	100	364	17	N.J	628	105	59	570	13
Colo	218	130	97	215	29	N. Mex	153	125	72	121	26
						N.Y	1,626	1,575	91	1,459	12
Conn	170	170	24	30	100	N.C	200	200	100	200	50
Del	37	29	68	30	9	N. Dak	211	165	73	183	28
D.C	1	1	100	1	100	Ohio	505	273	99	505	25
Fla	541	256	76	453	19	Okla	246	77	100	246	31
Ga	600	468	57	485	32	Oreg	211	139	79	198	27
Hawaii	8	8	100	8	62	Pa	656	653	98	656	77
Idaho	44	44	100	44	100	R.I	55	54	20	12	91
Ill	102	102	100	102	100						
Ind	650	566	98	628	18	S.C	530	452	83	464	14
Iowa	182	125	99	182	54	S. Dak	149	131	96	148	43
						Tenn	503	392	68	306	36
Kans	614	430	51	404	36	Tex	1,405	1,067	88	1,364	29
Ky	593	493	78	560	21	Utah	119	113	94	114	36
La	546	536	99	118	54	Vt	47	47	61	28	100
Maine	63	63	74	47	34	Va	424	362	69	387	40
Md	71	71	69	48	70	Wash	374	177	94	372	12
Mass	105	105	83	89	89	W. Va	529	481	86	461	12
Mich	301	301	72	216	51	Wis	275	165	98	269	49
Minn	275	254	99	269	32	Wyo	88	70	88	88	36
Miss	345	209	70	252	36						

Source: U.S. Law Enforcement Assistance Administration, *National Survey of Court Organization.*

NO. 319. U.S. SUPREME COURT—CASES FILED AND DISPOSITION: 1970 TO 1977

[Statutory term of court begins first Monday in October; for statistical purposes, new term begins upon adjournment of the preceding term, usually in June. See *Historical Statistics, Colonial Times to 1970,* series H 1063–1078, for related but not comparable data]

ACTION	1970	1971	1972	1973	1974	1975	1976	1977
Total cases on docket	4,212	4,533	4,640	5,079	4,668	4,761	4,731	4,704
Appellate cases on docket	1,903	2,070	2,183	2,480	2,308	2,352	2,324	2,341
From prior term	325	362	442	412	540	431	452	472
Docketed during present term	1,578	1,708	1,741	2,068	1,768	1,921	1,872	1,869
Cases acted upon	1,613	1,752	1,834	1,948	1,967	1,900	2,019	1,979
Granted review	214	238	217	229	235	244	237	224
Denied, dismissed, or withdrawn	1,285	1,409	1,397	1,572	1,594	1,538	1,620	1,676
Summarily decided	114	105	220	147	138	118	162	79
Cases not acted upon	290	318	349	532	341	452	305	362
Pauper cases on docket	2,289	2,445	2,436	2,585	2,348	2,395	2,398	2,349
Cases acted upon	1,802	2,023	1,982	2,013	1,976	1,997	2,083	1,960
Granted review	41	61	35	30	28	28	30	24
Denied, dismissed, or withdrawn	1,683	1,781	1,902	1,942	1,914	1,903	2,013	1,899
Summarily decided	78	181	45	41	34	66	40	37
Cases not acted upon	487	422	454	572	372	398	315	389
Original cases on docket	20	18	21	14	12	14	8	14
Cases disposed of during term	7	8	8	4	4	7	2	3
Total cases available for argument	267	280	256	261	278	280	269	260
Cases disposed of	160	181	180	172	178	181	181	185
Cases argued	151	176	177	170	175	179	176	172
Cases dismissed or remanded without argument	9	5	3	2	3	2	5	13
Cases remaining	107	99	76	89	100	99	88	75
Cases decided by signed opinion	126	143	159	161	144	160	154	153
Cases decided by per curiam opinion	22	24	18	8	20	16	22	8
Number of signed opinions	109	129	140	140	123	138	126	129

Source: Office of the Clerk, Supreme Court of the United States, unpublished data.

No. 320. U.S. Courts of Appeals: 1950 to 1977

[For years ending June 30. See also *Historical Statistics, Colonial Times to 1970*, series H 1079–1096]

ITEM	1950	1955	1960	1965	1970	1972	1973	1974	1975	1976	1977
Cases commenced [1]	2,830	3,695	3,899	6,766	11,662	14,535	15,629	16,436	16,658	18,408	19,118
Criminal	308	677	623	1,223	2,660	3,980	4,453	4,067	4,187	4,650	4,738
U.S. civil	708	811	788	1,387	2,167	2,604	2,704	3,267	2,981	3,327	3,622
Private civil	1,114	1,363	1,534	2,677	4,834	5,795	6,172	6,157	6,511	7,077	7,358
Administrative appeals	485	576	737	1,106	1,522	1,509	1,616	2,205	2,290	2,515	2,564
Cases terminated [1]	3,064	3,654	3,713	5,771	10,699	13,828	15,112	15,422	16,000	16,426	17,784
Criminal	342	670	580	1,014	2,581	3,799	4,210	4,299	4,005	4,238	4,554
U.S. civil	783	893	750	1,229	1,912	2,512	2,722	2,791	3,094	2,853	3,198
Private civil	1,184	1,289	1,517	2,183	4,367	5,399	6,030	5,847	6,252	6,248	6,680
Administrative appeals	541	523	660	1,004	1,407	1,448	1,493	1,734	1,909	2,359	2,510
Cases disposed of [2]	2,355	2,809	2,681	3,546	6,139	8,537	9,618	8,451	9,077	9,351	11,400
Affirmed or granted	1,700	1,907	1,924	2,635	4,626	6,207	7,163	6,429	6,763	6,995	7,826
Reversed or denied	528	777	656	773	1,280	1,664	1,693	1,579	1,632	1,680	1,715
Other	127	125	101	138	233	666	762	443	682	676	1,859
Median months [3]	7.1	7.3	6.8	8.0	8.2	6.6	6.4	6.8	7.4	7.1	7.0

[1] Includes other types of cases not shown separately.　[2] After hearing or submission. Beginning 1974, data not comparable with earlier years due to changes in criteria.　[3] Median time interval from filing of complete record to final disposition.

No. 321. U.S. District Courts—Civil and Criminal Cases: 1960 to 1977

[For years ending June 30. See also *Historical Statistics, Colonial Times to 1970*, series H 1097–1111]

ITEM	1960	1965	1970	1972	1973	1974	1975	1976	1977
Civil cases: Commenced	[1]59,284	67,678	87,321	96,173	98,560	103,530	117,320	130,597	130,567
Cases terminated [2]	[1]48,847	63,137	79,466	94,256	97,402	96,701	103,787	108,298	115,484
No court action	(NA)	29,309	31,056	37,446	37,024	35,879	39,219	41,691	45,230
Court action, total	(NA)	33,828	48,410	56,810	60,378	60,822	64,568	66,607	70,254
Before pretrial	(NA)	17,089	29,429	35,590	36,873	38,576	40,271	41,593	43,505
Pretrial	(NA)	9,442	11,006	12,739	15,208	13,864	15,575	16,225	17,702
Trials	(NA)	7,297	7,975	8,481	8,297	8,382	8,722	8,789	9,047
Percent reaching trial	(NA)	11.6	10.0	9.0	8.5	8.7	8.4	8.1	7.8
Criminal cases: Commenced [3]	28,137	31,569	38,102	47,043	40,367	37,667	41,108	39,147	39,786
Defendants disposed of [1]	30,512	33,718	36,356	49,516	46,724	48,014	49,212	51,612	53,188
Not convicted	3,784	4,961	8,178	12,296	11,741	11,784	11,779	11,500	11,720
Dismissed	2,596	3,789	6,608	10,219	9,757	10,019	10,274	9,752	9,940
Acquitted	1,188	1,172	1,570	2,077	1,984	1,765	1,505	1,748	1,780
Convicted	26,728	28,757	28,178	37,220	34,983	36,230	37,433	40,112	41,468
By guilty plea [4]	24,245	25,923	24,111	31,714	29,009	30,660	31,816	34,041	35,336
By court or jury	2,483	2,834	4,067	5,506	5,974	5,570	5,617	6,071	6,132
Imprisonment	13,433	13,668	12,415	16,832	17,540	17,180	17,301	18,477	19,613
Probation	10,391	10,779	11,387	15,395	15,026	16,623	17,913	18,208	16,134
Fine and other	2,904	4,310	4,376	4,993	2,417	2,427	2,219	3,427	5,721

NA　Not available.　[1] Excludes D.C., Canal Zone, Guam, Virgin Islands, except, beginning 1973, defendants disposed of includes D.C.　[2] Excludes land condemnation cases.　[3] Excludes transfers.　[4] Includes nolo contendere.

No. 322. U.S. District Courts—Civil Cases Commenced and Terminated: 1977

[For year ending June 30]

NATURE OF SUIT	Cases commenced, total	Cases terminated, total	No court action	COURT ACTION				
				Total	Before pretrial	Pretrial	Trials, total	Percent reaching trial
Total	130,567	117,150	46,896	70,254	43,505	17,702	9,047	7.7
U.S. cases	40,210	34,450	15,002	19,448	15,860	2,260	1,328	3.9
Contract actions	3,842	3,407	2,218	1,189	867	237	85	2.5
Real property actions	6,757	5,110	3,996	1,114	909	127	78	1.5
Tort actions	2,296	2,079	844	1,235	578	374	283	13.6
Actions under statutes	27,130	20,866	6,691	14,175	12,218	1,255	702	3.4
Other actions	185	2,988	1,253	1,735	1,288	267	180	6.0
Private cases	90,357	82,700	31,894	50,806	27,645	15,442	7,719	9.3
Federal question	57,011	50,510	18,062	32,448	21,177	7,415	3,856	7.6
Contract actions	4,812	4,768	2,819	1,949	728	1,006	215	4.5
Tort actions	8,001	7,711	3,642	4,069	1,073	2,309	687	8.9
Actions under statutes	43,527	32,545	8,375	24,170	18,222	3,336	2,612	8.0
All other	671	5,486	3,226	2,260	1,154	764	342	6.2
Diversity of citizenship and only local jurisdiction	33,346	32,190	13,832	18,358	6,468	8,027	3,863	12.0

Source of tables 320–322: Administrative Office of the U.S. Courts. *Annual Report of the Director.*

No. 323. U.S. District Courts—Trials: 1950 to 1977

[For years ending June 30. Through 1960, trials commenced; thereafter, trials completed. Prior to 1965, excludes D.C., Alaska, Hawaii, and outlying areas. A trial is defined as a contested proceeding (other than a hearing on a motion) before either court or jury in which evidence is introduced and final judgment sought. See also *Historical Statistics, Colonial Times to 1970*, series H 1112–1118]

TYPE OF TRIAL	1950	1955	1960	1965	1970	1972	1973	1974	1975	1976	1977
Total	7,977	9,258	9,042	11,485	16,032	18,780	19,467	18,572	19,236	19,580	18,827
Civil trials	5,663	5,882	6,002	7,613	9,449	10,962	10,896	10,972	11,603	11,656	11,605
Nonjury	3,648	3,224	3,161	4,459	6,078	7,285	7,289	7,403	7,903	8,098	7,792
Jury	2,015	2,658	2,841	3,154	3,371	3,677	3,607	3,569	3,700	3,558	3,813
Criminal trials	2,314	3,376	3,040	3,872	6,583	7,818	8,571	7,600	7,633	7,924	7,222
Nonjury	825	1,151	943	1,143	2,357	2,968	2,927	2,753	2,726	2,773	2,661
Jury	1,489	2,225	2,097	2,729	4,226	4,850	5,644	4,847	4,907	5,151	4,561

No. 324. U.S. District Courts—Criminal Cases Commenced and Defendants Disposed of, by Nature of Offense: 1976 and 1977

[For years ending June 30. Excludes Canal Zone, Guam, and Virgin Islands]

NATURE OF OFFENSE	1976 Cases commenced (excl. transfers)	De fendants disposed of	1977, cases commenced (excl. transfers)	Not convicted Total	Not convicted Ac quitted	Convicted Total	Convicted By guilty plea	Convicted By court or jury	Sentenced Im prisonment	Sentenced Pro bation	Sentenced Fine and other
Total	38,278	51,550	39,055	¹11,700	1,780	41,468	35,336	6,132	19,613	16,134	5,721
General offenses:											
Homicide	134	161	111	36	16	117	69	48	99	18	–
Robbery	2,026	2,695	1,708	295	72	2,045	1,608	437	1,872	172	1
Assault	754	914	633	220	60	548	405	143	288	227	33
Burglary	277	314	293	117	10	400	362	38	236	162	2
Larceny—theft	3,896	5,230	4,657	926	190	4,741	4,231	510	1,911	2,313	517
Embezzlement and fraud	5,624	6,670	6,894	1,203	274	6,730	5,906	824	2,281	4,120	329
Auto theft	1,425	1,802	1,156	228	34	1,371	1,183	188	1,004	357	10
Forgery, counterfeiting	3,955	5,044	3,952	589	79	4,115	3,749	366	2,176	1,905	34
Sex offenses	107	161	119	62	24	138	86	52	86	44	8
Narcotics	5,989	10,762	4,721	2,106	352	7,635	5,970	1,665	5,223	2,324	88
Misc. general offenses	7,813	9,419	10,051	2,378	440	8,714	7,408	1,306	2,986	2,374	3,354
Special offenses:											
Immigration laws	2,027	2,246	1,399	214	29	1,396	1,295	101	857	506	33
Liquor, Internal Revenue	187	322	140	23	5	165	148	17	65	96	4
Selective Service Act	119	696	137	2,146	4	29	22	7	4	22	3
Other Federal statutes	3,945	5,114	3,084	1,157	191	3,324	2,894	430	525	1,494	1,305

– Represents zero. ¹ Excludes 20 defendants in civil rights cases whose cases were remanded to State courts.
Source of tables 323 and 324: Administrative Office of the U.S. Courts, *Annual Report of the Director*.

No. 325. U.S. District Courts—Defendants Charged With Violations of Drug Abuse Prevention and Control Act: 1974 to 1977

[For years ending June 30. Excludes Canal Zone, Guam, and Virgin Islands]

ITEM	MARIHUANA 1974	1975	1976	1977	NARCOTICS 1974	1975	1976	1977	CONTROLLED SUBSTANCES (prescribed drugs) 1974	1975	1976	1977
Defendants	3,938	3,741	3,234	2,744	5,370	5,217	5,832	5,553	1,352	1,666	1,475	1,296
Not convicted	896	911	800	607	1,346	1,292	1,469	1,127	308	348	323	285
Dismissed	810	828	700	524	1,160	1,114	1,275	906	275	315	301	242
Convicted	3,042	2,830	2,434	2,137	4,024	3,925	4,363	4,426	1,044	1,318	1,152	1,011
By guilty pleas	2,560	2,332	1,899	1,703	3,124	3,055	3,401	3,424	877	1,085	958	798
Sentenced to prison	1,732	1,529	1,323	1,285	2,765	2,626	3,063	3,300	551	683	591	598
Under 3 years	1,095	953	764	775	941	838	962	1,282	276	276	264	324
3–5 years	400	381	371	313	820	777	937	894	154	274	216	148
5 years and over	237	195	188	197	1,004	1,011	1,164	1,124	121	133	111	126
Avg. sentence mo	27.7	27.6	30.2	32.4	54.3	56.1	57.2	54.4	37.8	41.4	36.8	39.5
Probation	1,257	1,272	1,061	798	1,251	1,286	1,283	1,108	480	623	553	402
Fine and other	53	29	50	54	8	13	17	18	13	12	8	11

Source: Administrative Office of the U.S. Courts, *Federal Offenders in the U.S. District Courts*, annual.

No. 326. Juveniles Held in Custody, by Type of Facility—Summary: 1974 and 1975

[As of June 30, except expenditures for years ending June 30. Data based on private and State and local public juvenile detention and correctional facilities in operation when censuses were initiated (November 1974 and February 1976); also must have been in existence for at least a month before census reference date of June 30, and with a resident population at least 50 percent juvenile. However, a facility was included if it was considered a juvenile facility, even though the youthful offenders outnumbered juveniles at the time of the census. Further, at least 10 percent of a private facility's population had to have been adjudicated delinquent, in need of supervision, voluntarily admitted, awaiting court disposition, or awaiting transfer to another jurisdiction. Excludes juvenile detention centers operated as part of a jail and without a separate staff or budget, nonresidential facilities, facilities exclusively for drug abusers or for alcoholics, facilities exclusively for dependent and neglected children, foster homes, and Federal juvenile correctional facilities. For definition of terms, see source]

ITEM	PUBLIC		PRIVATE		ITEM	PUBLIC		PRIVATE	
	1974	1975	1974	1975		1974	1975	1974	1975
Facilities, total	829	874	1,337	1,277	**Juveniles held**	44,922	46,980	31,749	27,290
State-government administered	396	423	(X)	(X)	Male	34,783	37,926	22,104	19,152
					Female	10,139	9,054	9,645	8,138
Local-government administered	433	451	(X)	(X)	Type of facility:				
					Training schools	25,397	26,748	4,078	3,660
					Detention centers	11,010	11,089	} 163	161
Training schools	185	189	61	65	Reception centers [1]	1,376	1,436		
Detention centers	331	347	4	3	Ranches [2]	5,232	5,385	16,955	13,094
Reception centers [1]	19	17	5	5	Halfway houses [3]	1,727	2,122	9,919	9,706
Ranches [2]	107	103	395	295	Shelters	180	200	634	669
Halfway houses [3]	166	195	805	851	Detention status:				
Shelters	21	23	67	58	Adjudicated delinquent [6]	31,270	34,107	9,874	9,809
					Declared in need of supervision	4,644	4,494	4,969	4,316
Expenditures, mil. dol	508	594	294	274	Pending court disposition	7,373	7,011	481	} 529
Operating mil. dol	483	560	268	254	Awaiting transfer [7]	458	392	63	
Per person held [4] 1,000	10.3	11.5	8.5	9.5	Voluntary admission	679	516	7,635	5,879
Capital mil. dol	25	35	26	19	Dependent and neglected	498	451	7,104	4,844
Full-time staff [5] 1,000	39.4	41.2	20.6	} 27.7	Other [8]	–	9	1,623	1,913
Part-time staff [5] 1,000	6.9	11.4	8.0						

– Represents zero.   X Not applicable.   [1] Includes diagnostic centers.   [2] Includes forestry camps and farms.   [3] Includes group homes.   [4] Based on the average daily population of the facilities.   [5] Includes payroll and nonpayroll staff.   [6] See headnote, table 000.   [7] To another jurisdiction.   [8] The emotionally disturbed, the mentally retarded, and other.

Source: U.S. Law Enforcement Administration, *Children in Custody, Advance Report on the Juvenile Detention and Correctional Facility Census of 1974*, February 1977; and *1975*, October 1977; and unpublished data.

No. 327. Children's Cases Disposed of by Juvenile Courts: 1960 to 1975

[Excludes ordinary traffic cases handled by juvenile courts, except where traffic cases are adjudicated as "juvenile delinquency" cases. Dependency and neglect cases are all cases referred to the court for some form of neglect or inadequate care on the part of parents or guardians. For definition of delinquency cases, see text, p. 175. See also *Historical Statistics, Colonial Times to 1970*, series H 1119–1124]

ITEM	1960	1965	1970	1971	1972	1973	1974	1975
Population 10–17 years old [1] 1,000	25,368	29,536	32,614	32,969	33,120	33,377	33,365	33,045
Delinquency cases excluding traffic [2] 1,000	510	697	1,052	1,125	1,112	1,143	1,252	1,317
Per 1,000 population 10–17 years old	20.1	23.6	32.3	34.1	33.6	34.2	37.5	39.9
Male 1,000	415	555	800	846	828	845	927	1,002
Female 1,000	99	142	252	280	285	298	326	315
Percent of total cases	19.3	20.4	24.0	24.8	25.6	26.1	26.0	23.9
Population under 18 years old [1] 1,000	64,516	69,699	69,669	69,576	69,060	68,196	67,241	66,251
Dependency and neglect cases [2] 1,000	131	157	133	131	141	158	151	143
Per 1,000 population under 18 years old	2.0	2.3	1.9	1.9	2.0	2.3	2.2	2.2

[1] U.S. Bureau of the Census estimates of civilian population as of July 1, except 1960 and 1970, as of April 1.
[2] Delinquency cases based on data from a national sample of juvenile courts. Since 1970, based on all courts reporting, whose jurisdiction includes about two-thirds of the Nation's population; dependency and neglect cases based on reports from courts serving about one-half of the child population under 18 years of age.

Source: 1960–1973, U.S. Office of Human Development Services and U.S. Office of Youth Development, *Juvenile Court Statistics*, annual. Beginning 1974, The National Center for Juvenile Justice, Pittsburgh, Pa., unpublished data.

No. 328. FEDERAL AND STATE PRISONS—PRISONERS PRESENT AND PRISONERS RECEIVED: 1950 TO 1976

[Rate per 100,000 estimated civilian population. Prior to 1970, excludes State institutions in Alaska and, prior to 1960, those in Hawaii. See also *Historical Statistics, Colonial Times to 1970*, series H 1135–1140]

YEAR	PRESENT AT END OF YEAR						RECEIVED FROM COURTS					
	All institutions		Federal		State		All institutions		Federal		State	
	Number	Rate	Number	Rate	Number	Rate	Number	Rate	Number	Rate	Number	Rate
1950	166,123	110.3	17,134	11.4	148,989	98.9	69,473	46.1	14,237	9.5	55,236	36.7
1955	185,780	113.4	20,088	12.3	165,692	101.1	78,414	47.9	15,286	9.3	63,128	38.5
1960	212,953	118.6	23,218	12.9	189,735	105.7	88,575	49.3	13,723	7.6	74,852	41.7
1965	210,895	109.5	21,040	10.9	189,855	98.6	87,505	45.4	12,781	6.6	74,724	38.8
1970	196,429	96.7	20,038	9.8	176,391	86.8	79,351	39.1	12,047	5.9	67,304	33.1
1971	198,061	96.4	20,948	10.2	177,113	86.2	97,292	47.3	13,193	6.4	84,099	40.8
1972	196,183	94.6	21,713	10.5	174,470	84.2	¹ 119,316	57.6	16,104	7.8	103,212	49.9
1973	204,211	97.8	22,815	10.9	181,396	86.8	¹ 127,686	61.1	17,170	8.2	110,516	52.9
1974	218,466	103.6	22,361	10.6	196,105	93.2	103,754	49.3	14,511	6.9	89,243	42.4
1975	240,593	113.3	24,131	11.4	216,462	102.0	129,573	61.0	16,770	7.9	112,803	53.1
1976	263,291	123.1	26,799	12.5	236,492	110.6	129,482	60.5	17,437	8.2	112,045	52.4

¹ In addition to commitments from courts, includes parole, or conditional-release violators returned and escapees returned under old sentence.

Source: U.S. Law Enforcement Assistance Administration, 1950–1970, *National Prisoner Statistics*, Bulletin No. 47. Beginning 1971, *Prisoners in State and Federal Institutions on December 31*, annual.

No. 329. STATE PRISONS—SELECTED CHARACTERISTICS, BY TYPE OF INSTITUTION: 1974

[Based on data compiled in January 1974 by U.S. Bureau of the Census. Facility must have been an administratively separate institution and defined as a State correctional facility for adults or youthful offenders or a non-State-operated facility where majority of residents were State inmates. Excludes Massachusetts]

CHARACTERISTIC	All institutions ¹	Closed prisons	Prison camps ²	CHARACTERISTIC	All institutions ¹	Closed prisons	Prison camps ²
Inmates, number____1,000__	188.0	118.7	34.3	Institutions with—			
				Sick bay	350	139	83
Institutions, total	592	172	162	Library	481	167	131
				Athletic field	450	158	141
Year of initial construction:				Full-time staff:			
Before 1899 and unknown	75	48	4	Less than 20	250	7	87
1899–1923	61	25	8	20–99	136	41	42
1924–1948	186	47	46	100–299	86	50	19
1949–1969	237	44	98	300 or more	67	56	2
1970–1973	33	8	6	Unknown	53	18	12
Institutions with—				Annual operating expenditures—			
Group counseling	487	153	117	Less than $200,000	172		54
Individual counseling	540	167	131	$200,000–$1 million	202	37	82
Remedial education	526	170	137	$1 million–$3 million	81	41	16
Vocational training	477	163	112	$3 million or more	92	75	6
Alcoholic treatment	489	152	112	Unknown	45	11	4
Drug treatment	436	145	96				

¹ Includes types of institutions not shown separately.   ² Includes prison farms, road camps, and forest camps.

Source: U.S. Law Enforcement Assistance Administration; *Census of State Correctional Facilities, 1974, Advance Report*.

No. 330. JAILS—SUMMARY: 1972

[As of summer. Excludes Federal and State prisons or other correctional institutions; institutions exclusively for juveniles; State-operated jails in Conn., Del., and R.I.; and other facilities which retain persons for less than 2 days. For composition of regions, see fig. I, inside front cover]

CHARACTERISTIC	United States	North-east	North Central	South	West
Jails number	3,921	231	1,153	1,865	672
With less than 21 inmates number	2,901	91	970	1,356	484
With 21–249 inmates number	907	117	167	475	148
With 250 or more inmates number	113	23	16	34	40
With work–release programs number	1,665	127	559	603	376
With week–end sentence programs number	1,821	91	634	676	420
With medical facilities number	480	87	93	202	95
With recreational facilities number	2,422	214	769	997	439
Number of inmates 1,000	141.6	27.4	23.5	55.5	35.2
Per employee	3.2	2.5	2.4	3.7	4.1
Number of employees 1,000	44.3	10.9	9.9	14.9	8.6

Source: U.S. Law Enforcement Assistance Administration, *The Nation's Jails*, May 1975.

No. 331. FEDERAL AND STATE PRISONS—PRISONERS, BY STATES: 1960 TO 1976

[Data are as of Dec. 31, and represent inmates sentenced to maximum term of more than a year. See headnote, table 328]

STATE	1960	1965	1970	1972	1973	1974	1975	1976 Total	1976 Male	1976 Female
United States	212,953	210,895	196,429	196,183	204,211	218,466	240,593	263,291	253,308	9,983
Federal institutions [1]	23,218	21,040	20,038	21,713	22,815	22,361	24,131	26,799	25,429	1,370
State institutions	189,735	189,855	[2]176,391	174,470	181,396	196,105	216,462	236,492	227,879	8,613
Male	205,253	203,327	190,794	189,911	197,527	211,077	(NA)	253,308	253,308	(X)
Female	7,700	7,568	5,635	6,272	6,684	7,389	(NA)	9,983	(X)	9,983
New England	4,871	5,044	4,543	4,957	4,966	5,113	5,636	6,229	6,077	152
Maine	750	695	516	473	453	527	643	610	600	10
New Hampshire	180	205	244	240	277	219	250	248	248	–
Vermont	269	263	162	230	188	242	244	307	301	6
Massachusetts	1,920	1,929	2,053	1,856	1,981	2,226	2,242	2,651	2,573	78
Rhode Island	255	310	(NA)	340	404	435	408	490	481	9
Connecticut	1,497	1,642	1,568	1,818	1,663	1,464	1,849	1,923	1,874	49
Middle Atlantic	29,293	29,459	24,052	23,217	24,817	26,280	27,735	30,046	29,160	886
New York [3]	17,207	17,504	12,059	11,693	12,945	14,329	16,071	17,705	17,233	472
New Jersey	4,284	4,839	5,704	5,279	5,357	5,219	5,682	5,685	5,470	215
Pennsylvania	7,802	7,116	6,289	6,245	6,515	6,732	5,982	6,656	6,457	199
East North Central	37,938	34,338	31,755	28,260	26,695	30,261	37,023	42,228	40,753	1,475
Ohio	11,111	11,374	9,185	8,276	7,717	9,326	11,421	12,525	11,983	542
Indiana	5,429	4,486	4,137	3,847	3,357	3,051	3,897	4,203	4,051	152
Illinois	9,064	8,306	6,381	5,630	5,600	6,667	7,861	9,739	9,502	237
Michigan	9,550	7,342	9,079	8,471	7,874	8,630	10,852	12,462	12,057	405
Wisconsin	2,784	2,830	2,973	2,036	2,147	2,587	2,992	3,299	3,160	139
West North Central	12,317	12,188	10,186	9,294	9,322	9,452	11,289	12,668	12,243	425
Minnesota	2,059	1,772	1,585	1,337	1,402	1,372	1,685	1,624	1,561	63
Iowa	2,204	2,178	1,747	1,306	1,402	1,476	1,786	1,891	1,815	76
Missouri [4]	3,698	3,517	3,413	3,533	3,767	3,764	4,371	4,997	4,878	119
North Dakota	248	208	147	179	155	129	173	162	162	–
South Dakota	526	571	391	344	236	250	338	478	461	17
Nebraska	1,269	1,151	1,001	953	1,006	1,040	1,251	1,438	1,353	85
Kansas	2,313	2,791	1,902	1,642	1,354	1,421	1,685	2,078	2,013	65
South Atlantic	37,808	34,729	35,786	44,428	46,457	50,532	58,946	65,299	62,836	2,463
Delaware	226	315	596	279	325	436	582	684	665	19
Maryland	5,316	5,467	5,186	5,578	5,799	6,247	6,965	7,912	7,679	233
District of Columbia	1,958	1,604	1,423	2,500	2,331	2,072	2,302	2,299	2,220	79
Virginia	5,775	4,553	4,648	4,946	5,100	5,032	5,497	6,180	5,956	224
West Virginia	2,407	1,477	938	1,058	1,086	989	1,271	1,294	1,255	39
North Carolina	5,977	6,029	5,969	8,263	9,641	10,932	10,993	11,570	11,195	375
South Carolina	2,080	2,323	2,726	3,197	3,489	4,318	5,600	6,433	6,169	264
Georgia	6,985	5,966	5,113	8,225	8,310	9,289	10,421	11,134	10,689	445
Florida	7,084	6,995	9,187	10,382	10,376	11,217	15,315	17,793	17,008	785
East South Central	14,081	12,422	11,637	11,781	11,839	13,208	14,649	13,641	13,026	615
Kentucky	3,603	2,813	2,849	2,941	2,954	3,051	3,246	3,657	3,521	136
Tennessee	3,134	3,213	3,268	3,329	3,454	3,771	4,561	4,817	4,623	194
Alabama	5,369	4,377	3,790	3,632	3,693	4,259	4,420	3,032	2,823	209
Mississippi	1,975	2,019	1,730	1,879	1,738	2,127	2,422	2,135	2,059	76
West South Central	19,752	21,497	22,167	24,416	26,137	26,446	28,990	31,388	30,123	1,265
Arkansas	2,016	1,970	(NA)	1,619	1,679	1,938	2,162	2,431	2,323	108
Louisiana	3,749	3,844	4,196	3,421	4,033	4,779	4,758	4,591	4,403	188
Oklahoma	2,679	2,829	3,640	3,667	3,187	2,896	3,133	3,649	3,503	146
Texas	11,308	12,854	14,331	15,709	17,238	16,833	18,937	20,717	19,894	823
Mountain	7,292	8,188	6,351	6,200	6,598	7,450	8,506	9,583	9,238	345
Montana	602	586	260	283	316	336	429	551	551	–
Idaho	549	481	411	377	426	525	580	682	671	11
Wyoming	338	336	231	262	278	269	307	340	340	–
Colorado	2,078	2,766	2,066	1,925	1,894	1,968	2,039	2,239	2,162	77
New Mexico	1,243	1,002	742	597	726	902	999	1,220	1,167	53
Arizona	1,516	1,694	1,460	1,529	1,691	2,101	2,047	2,850	2,725	125
Utah	553	701	491	581	519	548	657	748	723	25
Nevada	413	622	690	646	748	801	848	953	899	54
Pacific	26,383	31,990	29,925	21,917	24,565	27,363	23,688	25,410	24,423	987
Washington	2,455	3,202	2,864	2,608	2,632	2,989	3,369	3,881	3,672	209
Oregon	1,710	2,000	1,800	1,856	1,670	1,993	2,480	2,859	2,749	110
California	21,660	26,325	25,033	16,970	19,794	21,897	17,296	18,113	17,459	654
Alaska	(NA)	(NA)	(NA)	183	174	175	207	230	226	4
Hawaii	558	463	228	300	295	309	336	327	317	10

– Represents zero.   NA Not available.   X Not applicable.   [1] Not included in State figures.
[2] Total excludes, and individual State figures include, transfers.
[3] Figures for 1960, 1965, and 1970 include prisoners out of institution on temporary absences.
[4] Data for 1972, 1973, and 1974 are for fiscal year.

Source: U.S. Law Enforcement Assistance Administration, 1960–70, *National Prisoner Statistics*, Bulletin No. 47
Beginning 1972, *Prisoners in State and Federal Institutions on December 31*, annual.

No. 332. AVERAGE TIME SERVED BY PRISONERS RELEASED FROM FEDERAL INSTITUTIONS FOR FIRST TIME: 1965 TO 1977

[For years ending June 30. For 1977, excludes 993 first releases (deaths, escapes, pardons, etc.) other than by parole, expiration of sentence, and mandatory release; also excludes 400 second or subsequent releases. In computing averages, sentences to life and more than 45 years were counted as 45 years; minority sentences of juvenile delinquents were counted from date of sentence to 21st birthday]

| YEAR AND OFFENSE | RELEASES, EXCLUDING PRISONERS SENTENCED UNDER THE YOUTH CORRECTIONS ACT [1] | | | | | | | | | | | | YOUTH CORRECTIONS ACT RELEASES | |
| | All first releases | | | | Parole | | | | Expiration of sentence and mandatory release | | | | | |
	Number	Average sentence (months)	Average time served Months	Percent of sentence	Number	Average sentence (months)	Average time served Months	Percent of sentence	Number	Average sentence (months)	Average time served Months	Percent of sentence	Number	Average time served (months)
1965, all offenses	12,100	32.6	19.9	61.0	3,394	42.6	18.3	43.0	8,706	28.7	20.5	71.4	1,226	21.6
1970, all offenses	8,487	38.6	19.7	51.0	2,754	55.0	20.0	36.3	5,733	30.7	19.6	63.7	947	21.7
1975, all offenses	11,313	39.8	18.5	46.4	4,367	73.7	27.8	37.8	6,946	18.5	12.6	67.8	1,136	21.6
1976, all offenses	10,463	32.3	15.1	46.8	3,111	74.3	26.9	36.2	7,349	14.4	10.1	69.8	958	19.7
1977, all offenses [2]	10,903	31.1	15.8	50.7	2,652	72.3	27.1	37.5	8,251	17.8	12.1	68.0	1,056	21.9
Counterfeiting	270	34.1	16.0	46.8	104	57.5	20.5	35.7	166	19.5	13.1	67.3	13	14.2
Drug laws	2,412	39.5	19.5	49.5	812	70.8	27.8	39.2	1,600	23.6	15.4	65.2	339	20.1
Embezzlement	193	20.1	11.0	54.8	60	40.9	18.0	44.0	133	10.7	7.8	73.5	14	13.4
Escape, flight, or harboring a fugitive	89	36.4	19.6	53.7	24	72.1	30.4	42.2	65	23.2	15.5	66.9	10	22.0
Firearms	666	27.2	16.1	59.2	136	53.2	22.4	42.1	530	20.5	14.5	70.6	48	19.9
Forgery	443	29.5	16.2	54.9	135	49.4	20.6	41.6	305	20.5	14.2	69.5	69	17.9
Fraud	435	18.8	10.6	56.3	94	41.0	16.2	39.6	341	12.7	9.0	71.3	9	21.9
Immigration	2,500	6.1	4.9	81.6	40	46.7	19.4	41.5	2,460	5.4	4.7	87.3	8	29.6
Income tax	193	13.7	8.3	60.5	25	39.4	19.9	50.4	168	9.8	6.5	66.6	-	-
Juvenile delinquency	138	31.5	17.7	56.1	42	41.0	16.3	39.7	96	27.4	18.3	66.8	-	-
Kidnaping	14	148.4	57.1	38.5	8	196.5	60.1	30.6	6	84.3	53.2	63.0	9	35.2
Larceny-theft	1,716	28.8	16.8	58.4	421	47.0	20.4	43.5	1,295	22.9	15.7	68.3	220	20.9
Motor vehicle, interstate	569	35.2	20.7	59.3	139	49.3	17.7	42.0	430	30.7	20.9	68.3	87	24.6
Liquor laws	63	24.1	13.7	57.0	29	35.2	17.7	50.1	34	14.6	10.4	71.1	-	-
Robbery	530	123.1	45.1	36.7	355	147.9	48.1	32.5	175	72.8	39.2	53.8	181	27.1
Securities, transporting false or forged	251	43.9	22.5	51.2	111	59.0	23.1	39.1	140	31.8	22.0	69.1	22	18.0
White slave traffic	24	59.7	26.0	43.5	14	83.2	31.1	37.3	10	26.8	18.9	70.5	1	20.0
Govt. reservation, high seas, territorial, and District of Columbia	255	50.5	22.1	43.8	71	109.2	32.7	29.9	184	27.9	18.0	64.6	69	25.6
Military court-martial cases	13	197.9	78.4	39.6	10	189.9	68.3	37.3	3	248.0	112.0	45.2	1	26.0

- Represents zero.   [1] Represents 81 percent of all first releases.   [2] Includes other offenses not shown separately. Includes releases from Bureau of Prisons and contract facilities.

Source: U.S. Bureau of Prisons, *Statistical Report*, annual.

No. 333. Federal Prisoners Under Sentence, by Offense and Race: 1977

[These data pertain only to the Federal offender population housed in Federal institutions during or on the last day of the fiscal year ending Sept. 30. Represents more than 90 percent of the Federal prisoner population]

OFFENSE	Total	WHITE		OTHER RACES		OFFENSE	Total	WHITE		OTHER RACES	
		Number	Average sentence (mo.)	Number	Average sentence (mo.)			Number	Average sentence (mo.)	Number	Average sentence (mo.)
Total [1]	26,193	15,884	92.0	10,309	114.7	Securities violations [3]	653	442	71.1	211	63.8
Drug laws	6,887	4,896	77.0	1,991	92.6	Counterfeiting	463	369	66.9	94	50.9
Robbery	5,484	2,573	171.2	2,911	164.4	Fraud	564	417	50.0	147	36.3
Larceny/theft	4,045	2,416	57.6	1,629	49.7	Kidnaping	442	325	327.1	117	346.4
Government [2]	1,949	492	247.3	1,457	182.7	Juvenile delin-					
Firearms	1,352	882	54.4	470	51.0	quency	20	13	34.4	7	69.1
Immigration	1,084	1,074	15.3	10	16.3	Burglary	145	84	82.8	61	74.3
Forgery	1,162	438	52.0	724	49.7						

[1] Includes offenses not shown separately.　[2] Includes offenses committed on government reservations, the high seas, territorial, and the District of Columbia.　[3] Transporting false or forged securities.

Source: U.S. Law Enforcement Assistance Administration, *Prisoners in State and Federal Institutions*, 1977.

No. 334. Jail Inmates—Reason for Retention and Selected Socioeconomic Characteristics, by Race: 1972

[As of summer. Jail: A locally administered institution with authority to retain adults for 48 hours or longer]

CHARACTERISTIC	Total [1]	White	Black	CHARACTERISTIC	Total [1]	White	Black
Total inmates	141,600	79,900	58,900	Marital status:			
				Never married	70,500	34,400	34,400
Serving sentence	60,200	35,400	23,200	Separated, divorced, or			
Awaiting trial	50,800	26,300	23,800	widowed	37,100	25,200	11,400
Other adjudication status	30,500	18,200	11,900	Married	33,900	20,300	13,100
Educational attainment: [2]				Prearrest annual income:			
8 years or less	32,200	20,300	11,000	Less than $2,000	61,800	33,500	26,800
9–12 years	94,500	49,200	43,500	$2,000–$2,999	16,100	8,600	7,000
Over 12 years	14,300	10,100	4,100	$3,000–$7,499	44,400	24,800	19,000
				$7,500 and over	15,100	10,800	4,300
Age: [3]				Unknown	4,300	2,200	2,000
14–17 years	5,200	2,900	2,200				
18–24 years	61,500	33,000	27,300				
25 years and over	74,700	43,900	29,400				

[1] Includes races not shown separately.　[2] Excludes 600 inmates for whom data were not available.　[3] Data by age include a small number of persons for whom information was not available, not shown separately.

Source: U.S. Law Enforcement Assistance Administration, *Survey of Inmates of Local Jails: Advance Report*, and unpublished data.

No. 335. Prisoners Under Sentence of Death: 1973 to 1977

[As of December 31. Excludes prisoners under sentence of death who remained within local correctional systems pending exhaustion of appellate process or who had not been committed to prison]

CHARACTERISTIC	1973	1974	1975	1976	1977	CHARACTERISTIC	1973	1974	1975	1976	1977
Total	162	254	479	444	443	Marital status:					
						Never married	57	107	217	206	192
White	79	116	214	243	244	Married	68	90	167	146	143
Black and other	83	138	265	201	199	Divorced [1]	37	57	95	92	108
Under 20 years	2	15	43	20	16	Time elapsed since					
20–24 years	35	80	139	133	135	sentencing:					
25–34 years	68	94	204	206	199	6 months or less	38	101	166	85	} 123
35–54 years	49	58	83	79	88	7–12 months	4	59	130	99	
55 years and over	8	7	10	6	5	1–3 years	38	39	155	256	314
						4–8 years	45	30	13	4	6
Completed school:						More than 8 years	37	25	15	–	–
7 years or less	29	48	71	49	49						
8 years	23	33	50	47	46	Legal status at arrest:					
9–11 years	41	88	167	145	137	Not under sentence	104	163	293	274	253
12 years	28	49	93	95	88	Parole or probation	19	32	51	50	60
More than 12 yr	7	11	21	26	25	Prison or escaped	7	19	27	22	20
Unknown	34	25	77	82	98	Unknown	32	40	108	98	110

– Represents zero.　[1] Includes persons married but separated, widows, widowers, and unknown.

Source: U.S. Law Enforcement Assistance Administration, *Capital Punishment, 1974, 1975, 1976*, and *1977* (Advance Report), SD–NPS–CP 3, 4, 5, and 6.

No. 336. Movement of Prisoners Under Sentence of Death: 1970 to 1977

[Prisoners reported under sentence of death by civil authorities. The term "under sentence of death" begins when the court pronounces the first sentence of death for a capital offense. For definition of median, see p. xii]

STATUS	1970	1971	1972	1973	1974	1975	1976 Total	1976 Murder [1]	1977 Total	1977 Murder [1]
Under sentence of death, Jan. 1 [2]	557	618	620	359	158	261	473	433	463	438
Rec'd death sentence during year	127	104	75	42	151	285	233	224	133	132
Other disposition [3]	76	102	365	239	55	67	262	236	153	130
Median elapsed time [4] _____ mo.	54.4	52.2	46.6	44.4	55	37	13	(NA)	21	(NA)
Under sentence of death, Dec. 31	608	620	330	162	254	479	444	421	443	440
Median elapsed time [5] _____ mo.	36.7	39.7	37.0	37.6	10	9	14	(NA)	20	(NA)

NA Not available. [1] Prisoners found guilty of murder or of murder and some other crime(s). [2] Differences in figures for Jan. 1 and Dec. 31 of following year result from revisions. [3] Includes commutations, resentencings, reversals of judgment, grants for new trial, deaths, etc. [4] Period between first imposition of death sentence and date of other disposition. [5] Period between first imposition of death sentence and Dec. 31 of year stated.

No. 337. Prisoners Executed Under Civil Authority: 1930 to 1977

[Excludes executions by military authorities. The Army (including the Air Force) carried out 160 (148 between 1942 and 1950, 3 each in 1954, 1955, and 1957, and 1 each in 1958, 1959, and 1961). Of the total, 106 were executed for murder (including 21 involving rape), 53 for rape, and 1 for desertion. The Navy carried out no executions during the period. See also *Historical Statistics, Colonial Times to 1970*, series H 1155–1167]

YEARS	Total [1]	White	Black	EXECUTED FOR MURDER Total [1]	White	Black	EXECUTED FOR RAPE Total [1]	White	Black	OTHER OFFENSES [2] Total [1]	White	Black
All years	3,860	1,752	2,066	3,335	1,665	1,630	455	48	405	70	39	31
1930–1939	1,667	827	816	1,514	803	687	125	10	115	28	14	14
1940–1949	1,284	490	781	1,064	458	595	200	19	179	20	13	7
1950–1959	717	336	376	601	316	280	102	13	89	14	7	7
1960–1964	181	90	91	145	79	66	28	0	22	8	5	3
1965–1967	10	8	2	10	8	2	–	–	–	–	–	–
1968–1976	–	–	–	–	–	–	–	–	–	–	–	–
1977	1	1	–	1	1	–	–	–	–	–	–	–

– Represents zero. [1] Includes races other than White or Black.
[2] 25 armed robbery, 20 kidnapping, 11 burglary, 8 espionage (6 in 1942, and 2 in 1953), and 6 aggravated assault.

No. 338. Prisoners Executed Under Civil Authority—States: 1940 to 1977

[No executions took place in Alaska, Hawaii, Maine, Michigan, Minnesota, New Hampshire, North Dakota, Rhode Island, and Wisconsin from 1940 to 1977. At no time during this period was the death penalty authorized in Alaska, Hawaii, Maine, Minnesota, and Wisconsin; it was abolished in Michigan in 1963 and lapsed in North Dakota in 1975 through statutory expiration; in the remaining two States, New Hampshire and Rhode Island, the death penalty was authorized the entire period]

STATE	1940–1949	1950–1959	1960–1967	1968–1976	1977	STATE	1940–1949	1950–1959	1960–1967	1968–1976	1977	STATE	1940–1949	1950–1959	1960–1967	1968–1976	1977
Total [1]	1,284	717	191	–	1	Iowa [3]	7	1	2	–	–	N.C	112	19	1	–	–
						Kans	5	5	5	–	–	Ohio	51	32	7	–	–
Ala	50	20	5	–	–	Ky	34	16	1	–	–	Okla	13	7	6	–	–
Ariz	9	8	4	–	–	La	47	27	1	–	–	Oreg [4]	12	4	1	–	–
Ark	38	18	9	–	–	Md	45	6	1	–	–	Pa	36	31	3	–	–
Calif	80	74	30	–	–												
Colo	13	3	6	–	–	Mass	9	–	–	–	–	S.C	61	26	8	–	–
						Miss	60	36	10	–	–	S.Dak [5]	1	–	–	–	–
Conn	10	5	1	–	–	Mo	15	7	4	–	–	Tenn	37	8	1	–	–
Del [2]	4	–	–	–	–	Mont	1	–	–	–	–	Tex	74	74	29	–	–
D.C	16	4	–	–	–	Nebr	2	–	–	–	–	Utah	4	6	1	–	1
Fla	65	49	12	–	–												
Ga	130	85	14	–	–	Nev	10	9	2	–	–	Vt	1	2	–	–	–
						N.J	14	17	3	–	–	Va	35	23	6	–	–
Idaho	–	3	–	–	–	N.Mex	2	3	1	–	–	Wash	16	6	2	–	–
Ill	18	9	2	–	–	N.Y	114	52	10	–	–	W.Va [3]	11	9	–	–	–
Ind	7	2	1	–	–							Wyo	2	–	1	–	–

– Represents zero. [1] Includes 23 Federal executions not shown by State (1940–1949, 13; 1950–1959, 9; and 1960–1967, 1). [2] Death penalty abolished from Apr. 2, 1958, to Dec. 18, 1961. [3] Death penalty abolished in 1965. [4] Death penalty abolished in 1964. [5] Death penalty abolished in 1977.

Source of tables 336–338: U.S. Law Enforcement Assistance Administration, *National Prisoner Statistics, Capital Punishment*, annual.

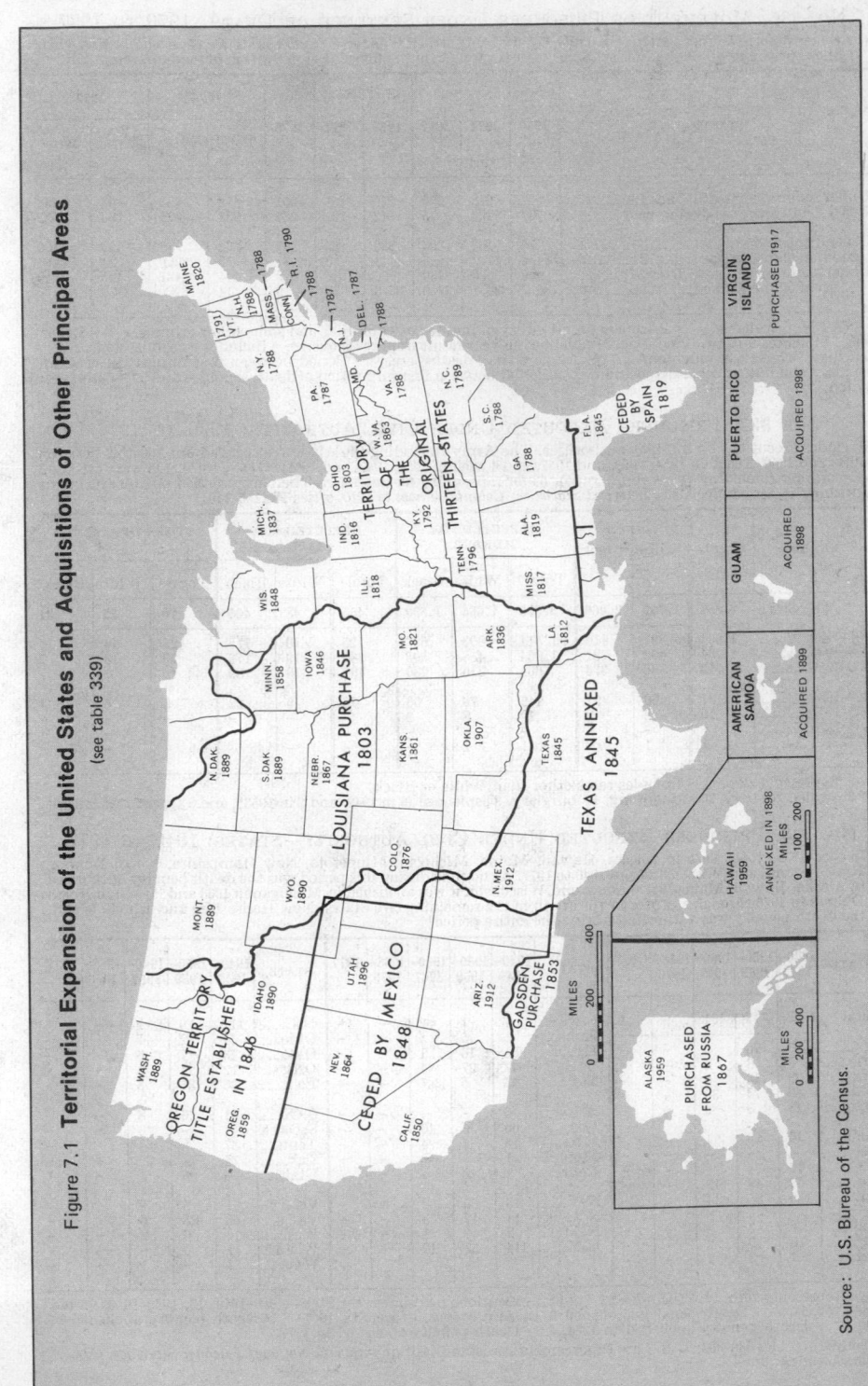

Figure 7.1 **Territorial Expansion of the United States and Acquisitions of Other Principal Areas**
(see table 339)

Source: U.S. Bureau of the Census.

Section 7

Geography and Environment

This section presents data on land and water areas, physical geography, and climate of the United States. Statistics on the quality of air and water, on environmental pollutants, and on expenditures for pollution abatement and control are also shown.

There are few publications other than those showing area measurements (issued irregularly by the Bureau of the Census) which present area and geography statistics of a national scope. However, many data are compiled for particular regions or for internal administrative purposes by such Federal agencies as the Geological Survey and National Oceanic and Atmospheric Administration (NOAA). Data on air and water quality and on types and sources of pollutants are compiled by various agencies under the general direction of the U.S. Council on Environmental Quality (CEQ); for details, see the annual report of CEQ, *Environmental Quality*.

Area.—Area measurements were first conducted for the United States as a whole, and gradually were extended to the individual States. The annual report of the U.S. General Land Office for 1850 contained the first reference to measurements of areas of the States and Territories. In 1881, as part of the 1880 Census of Population, the Bureau of the Census laid the foundation for accurate and detailed area measurement in the United States. For the first time an account was given of the methods and maps employed, the water bodies included, and the outer limits of the United States used as a basis for measurement. As part of the 1940 census, the Bureau published *Areas of the United States: 1940*, in which data were presented on the total land and inland water areas of the States, counties, places, and minor civil divisions. In the 1950 and 1960 census reports, adjustments in selected area figures were made because changes in boundaries, development of water reservoirs, or improvements in the maps from which measurements are made had taken place. In 1964, the Bureau undertook a new measurement of the areas of places with at least 1,000 inhabitants, minor civil divisions, and census county divisions of the 1960 census. The results are published in *Area Measurement Reports, Series GE-20*. The series consists of one report for each State and a U.S. summary. These reports include the same kinds of data as the 1940 report. Land areas of places with populations of 2,500 and over as of 1970 are shown in *Census of Population, 1970*, vol. 1, chapter A; data for counties are shown in the separate State reports.

Geography.—The Geological Survey, cooperating with State and local agencies, is responsible for topographic, geologic, and hydrologic maps; basic data on the quantity, quality, and movement of surface and ground water; and classification of Federal lands for mineral and waterpower potential. Data on water usage are published every five years in *Estimated Use of Water in the United States* (the most recent for 1975).

The National Ocean Survey, a division of NOAA, is responsible for coastal and geodetic surveys and measurement of certain physical phenomena. Currently, its primary functions are to provide charts for marine and air navigation, to maintain a basic network of geodetic control, and to compile other basic data for engineering, scientific, commercial, industrial, and defense needs.

Maps prepared by the Bureau of the Census show boundaries of various types of political and statistical areas, such as unincorporated places, the urbanized areas around large cities, county subdivisions, and census tracts.

Environment.—The CEQ is responsible for coordinating all environmental quality programs and for reviewing all other Federal programs affecting the environment. It

203

reports on its activities in its annual publication, *Environmental Quality*. The principal Federal agency responsible for research and enforcement activities related to pollution abatement and control is the Environmental Protection Agency (EPA). It is also responsible for establishing and monitoring national air quality standards.

Air sampling, conducted by the Public Health Service, began in 17 communities in 1953; in 1957 the National Air Surveillance Network was established and, by the late 1960's, covered approximately 260 urban and 30 rural stations. The operation of the stations was decentralized in 1972 to the 10 regional EPA offices and many of the stations were in turn assimilated into State and locally operated air monitoring networks. The Network determines the extent and nature of air pollution and studies trends in levels of atmospheric contaminants.

National Ambient Air Quality Standards for suspended particulate matter, sulfur dioxide, oxidants, carbon monoxide, and nitrogen dioxide were set by EPA in April 1971. Responsibility for demonstrating compliance with or progress toward achieving these standards lies with the State agencies. Non-Federal sampling stations for suspended particulates increased from approximately 800 in 1969 to over 4,000 in 1975. Data from these State networks are periodically submitted to EPA's National Aerometric Data Bank for summarization in quarterly reports on the nationwide status of, and trends in, air quality; for details, see *National Air Quality Emission Trends*.

Pollution abatement and control expenditures.—Data on expenditures for pollution abatement and control are compiled and published by the Office of Management and Budget (OMB), the U.S. Bureau of Economic Analysis (BEA), the U.S. Bureau of the Census, and the CEQ as part of ongoing programs. OMB collects and publishes figures annually on Federal funds spent for pollution abatement and control in *Special Analyses: Budget of the United States Government*. BEA conducts surveys on national expenditures for pollution abatement and control and presents the data in its *Survey of Current Business*. The U.S. Bureau of the Census collects data on State and local government and industry expenditures for water and air quality control. Data on government expenditures are reported in the annual *Environmental Quality Control: Government Finances*. Industry data are reported periodically in *Current Industrial Reports*. CEQ publishes data in *Environmental Quality*.

Climate.—NOAA, through the National Weather Service and the Environmental Data Service, is responsible for data on climate. NOAA maintains about 11,500 weather stations, of which over 3,000 produce autographic precipitation records, about 600 take automatic or hourly readings of a series of weather elements, and the remainder record data once a day. These data are reported on monthly, with an annual summary, in *Climatological Data: National Summary* and *Local Climatological Data*.

Nearly all weather stations have been moved several times in their history. Consequently, NOAA uses "normal" values of temperature and precipitation for comparative purposes rather than the daily, monthly, and yearly averages which have been derived from records accumulated at the different locations the stations may have had over the years. "Normal" values are obtained by adding the high and the low values recorded for a specified period of time and dividing by 2.

The base period for the normal values of temperature and precipitation is the 30-year period, 1941 through 1970. For stations having records for the entire 30 years from the same instrument site, monthly precipitation and temperature normals are the arithmetic averages of the monthly values for the 30 years. The annual normal temperature is obtained by dividing the sum of the monthly normals by 12.

For stations that did not have continuous records from the same instrument site for the entire 30 years, 1941 through 1970, the means have been adjusted to the record at the present site. In these adjustments, a "difference factor" was used for temperature and a "ratio factor" for precipitation. These factors were determined by parallel comparison with other nearby stations that have a continuous record for the 30-year period to obtain the resultant adjustment factors. Normals were thereafter obtained by the method described above.

The heating degree-day normals are derived from the monthly mean temperatures, and computed to base 65°F. The heating degree day has been defined as follows: "A unit, based upon temperature difference and time, used in estimating fuel consumption and specifying nominal heating load in winter. For any one day, when the mean temperature is less than 65°F., there exist as many degree days as there are Fahrenheit degree differences in the temperature between the average temperature for the day and 65°F."

Conversion factors.—For information concerning factors for converting figures to the metric system, see page x.

Historical statistics.—Tabular headnotes provide cross-references, where applicable, to *Historical Statistics of the United States, Colonial Times to 1970*. See Appendix I.

No. 339. TERRITORIAL EXPANSION OF THE UNITED STATES AND ACQUISITIONS OF OTHER AREAS

[One square mile = 2.59 square kilometers. Boundaries of all territories listed under "United States" were indefinite, at least in part, at time of acquisition. Area figures shown here represent precise determinations of specific territories which have been marked upon maps, based upon interpretations of the several treaties of cession, which are necessarily debatable. These determinations were made by a committee consisting of representatives of various governmental agencies in 1912. Subsequently these figures were adjusted to bring them into agreement with remeasurements made in 1960. See also *Historical Statistics, Colonial Times to 1970*, series J 1-2]

ACCESSION	Date	GROSS AREA (land and water)		ACCESSION	Date	GROSS AREA (land and water)	
		Sq. mi.	Sq. km.			Sq. mi.	Sq. km.
Total [1]	1970	3,631,410	9,405,352	Other:			
				The Philippines [3]	1898	115,600	299,404
United States [1]	(X)	3,618,467	9,371,829	Puerto Rico	[4] 1899	3,435	8,897
Territory in 1790 [2]	(X)	888,685	2,301,694	Guam	[5] 1899	212	549
Louisiana Purchase	1803	827,192	2,142,427				
By treaty with Spain:				American Samoa	[6] 1900	76	197
Florida	1819	58,560	151,670	Canal Zone [7]	1904	553	1,432
Other areas	1819	13,443	34,817	Corn Islands [8]	1914	4	10
Texas	1845	390,143	1,010,470				
Oregon	1846	285,580	739,652	Virgin Islands of the			
Mexican Cession	1848	529,017	1,370,154	U.S.	1917	133	344
Gadsden Purchase	1853	29,640	76,768	Trust Territory of the			
Alaska [1]	1867	589,757	1,527,470	Pacific Islands [9]	1947	8,489	21,987
Hawaii	1898	6,450	16,706	All other [10]	(X)	41	106

X Not applicable.
[1] Figure for Alaska corrected after 1970 Census of Population final reports were issued.
[2] Includes that part of drainage basin of Red River of the North, south of 49th parallel, sometimes considered part of Louisiana Purchase.
[3] Not included in total.   Ceded by Spain in 1898, the Philippines constituted a territorial possession of the United States from 1898 to 1946. Granted independence as of July 4, 1946, they then became the Republic of the Philippines.
[4] Ceded by Spain in 1898, ratified in 1899, and became Commonwealth of Puerto Rico by Act of Congress on July 25, 1952.   [5] Acquired 1898; ratified 1899.   [6] Acquired 1899; ratified 1900.
[7] Under jurisdiction of United States in accordance with treaty of Nov. 18, 1903, with Republic of Panama.
[8] Included in total for 1970. Leased (1914) from Republic of Nicaragua for 99 years but returned April 1971.
[9] Under trusteeship. See table 3, footnotes 9 and 12.
[10] Comprises following islands with gross areas as indicated, in sq. mi.: Midway (2), Wake (3), Palmyra (4), Canton and Enderbury (combined area, 27), Swan (1), Navassa (2), Baker, Howland, and Jarvis (combined area, 3), Johnston and Sand (combined area, less than .5), Kingman Reef (less than .5), and other islands for which area figures are not available.

Source: U.S. Bureau of the Census, unpublished data.

No. 340. Area of States and Other Areas: 1970

[One square mile = 2.59 square kilometers. See also *Historical Statistics, Colonial Times to 1970*, series A 210–263, for land area]

STATE OR OTHER AREA	Year admitted to statehood	Rank	TOTAL AREA Sq. mi.	TOTAL AREA Sq. km.	LAND AREA [1] Sq. mi.	LAND AREA [1] Sq. km.	WATER AREA [2] Sq. mi.	WATER AREA [2] Sq. km.
United States [3]	(X)	(X)	3,618,467	9,371,829	3,540,023	9,168,659	78,444	203,170
New England	(X)	(X)	66,608	172,515	62,951	163,043	3,657	9,472
Maine	1820	39	33,215	86,027	30,920	80,083	2,295	5,944
New Hampshire	[4] 1788	44	9,304	24,097	9,027	23,380	277	717
Vermont	1791	43	9,609	24,887	9,267	24,002	342	886
Massachusetts	[4] 1788	45	8,257	21,386	7,826	20,269	431	1,116
Rhode Island	[4] 1790	50	1,214	3,144	1,049	2,717	165	427
Connecticut	[4] 1788	48	5,009	12,973	4,862	12,593	147	381
Middle Atlantic	(X)	(X)	102,745	266,110	100,318	259,824	2,427	6,286
New York	[4] 1788	30	49,576	128,402	47,831	123,882	1,745	4,520
New Jersey	[4] 1787	46	7,836	20,295	7,521	19,479	315	816
Pennsylvania	[4] 1787	33	45,333	117,412	44,966	116,462	367	951
East North Central	(X)	(X)	248,283	643,053	244,101	632,222	4,182	10,831
Ohio	1803	35	41,222	106,765	40,975	106,125	247	640
Indiana	1816	38	36,291	93,994	36,097	93,491	194	502
Illinois	1818	24	56,400	146,076	55,748	144,387	652	1,689
Michigan	1837	23	58,216	150,779	56,817	147,156	1,399	3,623
Wisconsin	1848	26	56,154	145,439	54,464	141,062	1,690	4,377
West North Central	(X)	(X)	517,247	1,339,670	507,723	1,315,003	9,524	24,667
Minnesota	1858	12	84,068	217,736	79,289	205,359	4,779	12,378
Iowa	1846	25	56,290	145,791	55,941	144,887	349	904
Missouri	1821	19	69,686	180,487	68,995	178,697	691	1,790
North Dakota	1889	17	70,665	183,022	69,273	179,417	1,392	3,605
South Dakota	1889	16	77,047	199,552	75,955	196,723	1,092	2,828
Nebraska	1867	15	77,227	200,018	76,483	198,091	744	1,927
Kansas	1861	14	82,264	213,064	81,787	211,828	477	1,235
South Atlantic	(X)	(X)	278,776	722,030	266,970	691,452	11,806	30,578
Delaware	[4] 1787	49	2,057	5,328	1,982	5,133	75	194
Maryland	[4] 1788	42	10,577	27,394	9,891	25,618	686	1,777
District of Columbia	(X)	(X)	67	174	61	158	6	16
Virginia	[4] 1788	36	40,817	105,716	39,780	103,030	1,037	2,686
West Virginia	1863	41	24,181	62,629	24,070	62,341	111	287
North Carolina	[4] 1789	28	52,586	136,198	48,798	126,387	3,788	9,811
South Carolina	[4] 1788	40	31,055	80,432	30,225	78,283	830	2,150
Georgia	[4] 1788	21	58,876	152,489	58,073	150,409	803	2,080
Florida	1845	22	58,560	151,670	54,090	140,093	4,470	11,577
East South Central	(X)	(X)	181,964	471,287	178,982	463,563	2,982	7,723
Kentucky	1792	37	40,395	104,623	39,650	102,694	745	1,930
Tennessee	1796	34	42,244	109,412	41,328	107,040	916	2,372
Alabama	1819	29	51,609	133,667	50,708	131,334	901	2,334
Mississippi	1817	32	47,716	123,584	47,296	122,497	420	1,088
West South Central	(X)	(X)	438,884	1,136,710	427,791	1,107,979	11,093	28,731
Arkansas	1836	27	53,104	137,539	51,945	134,538	1,159	3,002
Louisiana	1812	31	48,523	125,675	44,930	116,369	3,593	9,306
Oklahoma	1907	18	69,919	181,090	68,782	178,145	1,137	2,945
Texas	1845	2	267,338	692,405	262,134	678,927	5,204	13,478
Mountain	(X)	(X)	863,887	2,237,467	856,047	2,217,162	7,840	20,306
Montana	1889	4	147,138	381,087	145,587	377,070	1,551	4,017
Idaho	1890	13	83,557	216,413	82,677	214,133	880	2,279
Wyoming	1890	9	97,914	253,597	97,203	251,756	711	1,841
Colorado	1876	8	104,247	270,000	103,766	268,754	481	1,246
New Mexico	1912	5	121,666	315,115	121,412	314,457	254	658
Arizona	1912	6	113,909	295,024	113,417	293,750	492	1,274
Utah	1896	11	84,916	219,932	82,096	212,629	2,820	7,304
Nevada	1864	7	110,540	286,299	109,889	284,613	651	1,686
Pacific [3]	(X)	(X)	920,073	2,382,989	895,140	2,318,413	24,933	64,576
Washington	1889	20	68,192	176,617	66,570	172,416	1,622	4,201
Oregon	1859	10	96,981	251,181	96,184	249,117	797	2,064
California	1850	3	158,693	411,015	156,361	404,975	2,332	6,040
Alaska [3]	1959	1	589,757	1,527,470	569,600	1,475,264	20,157	52,206
Hawaii	1959	47	6,450	16,706	6,425	16,641	25	65
Other areas:								
Puerto Rico	(X)	(X)	3,435	8,897	3,421	8,860	14	36
American Samoa	(X)	(X)	76	197	76	197	–	–
Canal Zone [5]	(X)	(X)	553	1,432	362	938	191	495
Guam	(X)	(X)	212	549	209	541	3	8
Trust Ter. of Pacific Is. [6]	(X)	(X)	8,489	21,987	717	1,857	7,772	20,129
Virgin Islands of U.S.	(X)	(X)	133	344	132	342	1	3

– Represents zero.   X Not applicable.   [1] Dry land and land temporarily or partially covered by water, as marshland, swamps, etc.; streams and canals under one-eighth statute mile wide; and lakes, reservoirs, and ponds under 40 acres of area.   [2] Permanent inland water surface, such as lakes, reservoirs, and ponds having 40 acres or more of area; streams, sloughs, estuaries, and canals one-eighth statute mile or more in width; deeply indented embayments and sounds, and other coastal waters behind or sheltered by headlands or islands separated by less than 1 nautical mile of water, and islands having less than 40 acres of area. Excludes areas of oceans, bays, sounds, etc., lying within U.S. jurisdiction but not defined as inland water.   [3] Figures for Alaska corrected after 1970 Census of Population final reports were issued.   [4] Year of ratification of Constitution; one of the original 13 States.   [5] See table 3, footnote 8.   [6] See table 3, footnotes 9 and 12.

Source: U.S. Bureau of the Census, *Census of Population: 1970*, vol. I, and *Area Measurement Reports*, series GE-20, No. 1.

No. 341. Coastline of the United States, by States

[One mile = 1.609 kilometers]

STATE	GENERAL COASTLINE [1] Statute miles	GENERAL COASTLINE [1] Kilo-meters	TIDAL SHORELINE [2] Statute miles	TIDAL SHORELINE [2] Kilo-meters	STATE	GENERAL COASTLINE [1] Statute miles	GENERAL COASTLINE [1] Kilo-meters	TIDAL SHORELINE [2] Statute miles	TIDAL SHORELINE [2] Kilo-meters
U.S	12,383	19,924	88,633	142,610	Gulf coast	1,631	2,624	17,141	27,580
					Ala	53	85	607	977
Atlantic coast	2,069	3,329	28,673	46,135	Fla	770	1,239	5,095	8,198
Conn	–	–	618	994					
Del	28	45	381	613	La	397	639	7,721	12,423
Fla	580	933	3,331	5,360	Miss	44	71	359	578
Ga	100	161	2,344	3,771	Tex	367	591	3,359	5,405
Maine	228	367	3,478	5,596					
Md	31	50	3,190	5,133	Pacific coast	7,623	12,265	40,298	64,839
Mass	192	309	1,519	2,444	Alaska	5,580	8,978	31,383	50,495
					Calif	840	1,352	3,427	5,514
N.H	13	21	131	211					
N.J	130	209	1,792	2,883	Hawaii	750	1,207	1,052	1,693
N.Y	127	204	1,850	2,977	Oreg	296	476	1,410	2,269
N.C	301	484	3,375	5,430	Wash	157	253	3,026	4,869
Pa	–	–	89	143					
R.I	40	64	384	618	Arctic coast, Alaska	1,060	1,706	2,521	4,056
S.C	187	301	2,876	4,627					
Va	112	180	3,315	5,334					

– Represents zero.
[1] Figures are lengths of general outline of seacoast. Measurements were made with a unit measure of 30 minutes of latitude on charts as near the scale of 1:1,200,000 as possible. Coastline of sounds and bays is included to a point where they narrow to width of unit measure, and includes the distance across at such point.
[2] Figures obtained in 1939–1940 with a recording instrument on the largest-scale charts and maps then available. Shoreline of outer coast, offshore islands, sounds, bays, rivers, and creeks is included to the head of tidewater or to a point where tidal waters narrow to a width of 100 feet.
Source: U.S. National Oceanic and Atmospheric Administration, *The Coastline of the United States*, 1975.

No. 342. Water Area, Other Than Inland Water—States

[Includes only that portion of body of water under the jurisdiction of the United States, excluding Alaska and Hawaii. Excludes inland waters; see footnote 2, table 340. One square mile = 2.59 square kilometers]

BODY OF WATER	AREA Sq. mi.	AREA Sq. km.	BODY OF WATER	AREA Sq. mi.	AREA Sq. km.
Total	74,364	192,603	Gulf of Mexico coastal water	3,837	9,938
			Alabama	560	1,450
			Florida	1,698	4,398
Atlantic coastal water	2,298	5,952	Louisiana	1,016	2,631
Florida	37	96	Mississippi	556	1,440
Georgia	48	124	Texas	7	18
Maine	1,102	2,854			
Massachusetts	959	2,484	Lake Michigan	22,178	57,441
Rhode Island	14	36	Illinois	1,526	3,952
South Carolina	138	357	Indiana	228	591
			Michigan	13,037	33,766
Chesapeake Bay	3,237	8,384	Wisconsin	7,387	19,132
Maryland	1,726	4,470			
Virginia	1,511	3,913	New York Harbor	92	238
			New Jersey	69	179
Delaware Bay	665	1,722	New York	23	60
Delaware	350	907	Lake Ontario: New York	3,033	7,855
New Jersey	315	816			
			Pacific coastal water	343	888
Lake Erie	5,002	12,955	California	69	179
Michigan	216	559	Oregon	48	124
New York	594	1,538	Washington	226	585
Ohio	3,457	8,954			
Pennsylvania	735	1,904	Puget Sound: Washington	561	1,453
			Lake St. Clair: Michigan	116	300
Straits of Georgia and Juan de Fuca:					
Washington	1,610	4,170	Lake Superior	21,118	54,696
Lake Huron: Michigan	8,975	23,245	Michigan	16,231	42,038
Long Island Sound	1,299	3,364	Minnesota	2,212	5,729
Connecticut	573	1,484	Wisconsin	2,675	6,928
New York	726	1,880			

Source: U.S. Bureau of the Census, *Areas of the United States: 1940*.

No. 343. Extreme and Mean Elevations—States and Other Areas

[One foot = .305 meter]

STATE OR OTHER AREA	HIGHEST POINT Name	Elevation Feet	Meters	LOWEST POINT Name	Elevation Feet	Meters	APPROXIMATE MEAN ELEVATION Feet	Meters
U.S___	Mt. McKinley (Alaska)____	20,320	6,198	Death Valley (Calif.)___	−282	−86	2,500	763
Ala____	Cheaha Mountain_____	2,407	734	Gulf of Mexico_____	(1)	(1)	500	153
Alaska___	Mount McKinley_____	20,320	6,198	Pacific Ocean_____	(1)	(1)	1,900	580
Ariz_____	Humphreys Peak_____	12,633	3,853	Colorado River_____	70	21	4,100	1,251
Ark_____	Magazine Mountain_____	2,753	840	Ouachita River_____	55	17	650	198
Calif.____	Mount Whitney_____	14,494	4,421	Death Valley_____	−282	−86	2,900	885
Colo____	Mount Elbert_____	14,433	4,402	Arkansas River_____	3,350	1,022	6,800	2,074
Conn_____	Mt. Frissell, on South slope_____	2,380	726	Long Island Sound____	(1)	(1)	500	753
Del_____	Ebright Road, New Castle Co._____	442	135	Atlantic Ocean_____	(1)	(1)	60	18
D.C_____	Tenleytown_____	410	125	Potomac River_____	1	(z)	150	46
Fla_____	Sec. 30, T6N, R20W, Walton County [2]_____	345	105	Atlantic Ocean_____	(1)	(1)	100	31
Ga_____	Brasstown Bald_____	4,784	1,459	Atlantic Ocean_____	(1)	(1)	600	183
Hawaii___	Mauna Kea_____	13,796	4,208	Pacific Ocean_____	(1)	(1)	3,030	924
Idaho____	Borah Peak_____	12,662	3,862	Snake River_____	710	217	5,000	1,525
Ill_____	Charles Mound_____	1,235	377	Mississippi River_____	279	85	600	183
Ind_____	Franklin Twp., Wayne Co.	1,257	383	Ohio River_____	320	98	700	214
Iowa_____	Sec. 29, T100N, R41W, Osceola County [2]_____	1,670	509	Mississippi River_____	480	146	1,100	336
Kans____	Mount Sunflower_____	4,039	1,232	Verdigris River_____	680	207	2,000	610
Ky_____	Black Mountain_____	4,145	1,264	Mississippi River_____	257	78	750	229
La_____	Driskill Mountain_____	535	163	New Orleans_____	−5	−2	100	31
Maine____	Mount Katahdin_____	5,268	1,607	Atlantic Ocean_____	(1)	(1)	600	183
Md_____	Backbone Mountain, near Kempton, W.Va_____	3,360	1,025	Atlantic Ocean_____	(1)	(1)	350	107
Mass____	Mount Greylock_____	3,491	1,065	Atlantic Ocean_____	(1)	(1)	500	153
Mich____	Mount Curwood_____	1,980	604	Lake Erie_____	572	174	900	275
Minn____	Eagle Mountain, Cook Co.	2,301	702	Lake Superior_____	602	184	1,200	366
Miss_____	Woodall Mountain, near Iuka_____	806	246	Gulf of Mexico_____	(1)	(1)	300	92
Mo_____	Taum Sauk Mountain____	1,772	540	St. Francis River_____	230	70	800	244
Mont____	Granite Peak_____	12,799	3,904	Kootenai River_____	1,800	549	3,400	1,037
Nebr_____	Johnson Twp., Kimball Co., T12N, R59W [2]____	5,426	1,665	Southeast corner of State_____	840	256	2,600	793
Nev_____	Boundary Peak_____	13,143	4,008	Colorado River_____	470	143	5,500	1,678
N.H_____	Mount Washington_____	6,288	1,918	Atlantic Ocean_____	(1)	(1)	1,000	305
N.J_____	High Point_____	1,803	550	Atlantic Ocean_____	(1)	(1)	250	76
N.Mex___	Wheeler Peak_____	13,161	4,014	Red Bluff Reservoir___	2,817	859	5,700	1,739
N.Y_____	Mount Marcy_____	5,344	1,630	Atlantic Ocean_____	(1)	(1)	1,000	305
N.C_____	Mount Mitchell_____	6,684	2,039	Atlantic Ocean_____	(1)	(1)	700	214
N.Dak____	White Butte, Slope Co.___	3,506	1,069	Red River_____	750	229	1,900	580
Ohio_____	Campbell Hill_____	1,550	473	Ohio River_____	433	132	850	259
Okla____	Black Mesa_____	4,973	1,517	Little River_____	287	88	1,300	397
Oreg____	Mount Hood_____	11,235	3,427	Pacific Ocean_____	(1)	(1)	3,300	1,007
Pa_____	Mount Davis_____	3,213	980	Delaware River_____	(1)	(1)	1,100	336
R.I_____	Jerimoth Hill_____	812	248	Atlantic Ocean_____	(1)	(1)	200	61
S.C_____	Sassafras Mountain_____	3,560	1,086	Atlantic Ocean_____	(1)	(1)	350	107
S.Dak____	Harney Peak_____	7,242	2,209	Big Stone Lake_____	962	293	2,200	671
Tenn____	Clingmans Dome_____	6,643	2,026	Mississippi River_____	182	56	900	275
Tex_____	Guadalupe Peak_____	8,751	2,669	Gulf of Mexico_____	(1)	(1)	1,700	519
Utah____	Kings Peak_____	13,528	4,126	Beaverdam Creek_____	2,000	610	6,100	1,861
Vt_____	Mount Mansfield_____	4,393	1,340	Lake Champlain_____	95	29	1,000	305
Va_____	Mount Rogers_____	5,729	1,747	Atlantic Ocean_____	(1)	(1)	950	290
Wash____	Mount Rainier_____	14,410	4,395	Pacific Ocean_____	(1)	(1)	1,700	519
W.Va____	Spruce Knob_____	4,863	1,483	Potomac River_____	240	73	1,500	458
Wis_____	Timms Hill_____	1,952	595	Lake Michigan_____	581	177	1,050	314
Wyo_____	Gannett Peak_____	13,804	4,210	Belle Fourche River___	3,100	946	6,700	2,044
Other areas: P.Rico__	Cerro de Punta_____	4,389	1,339	Atlantic Ocean_____	(1)	(1)	1,800	549
Am. Samoa_	Lata Mountain_____	3,160	964	Pacific Ocean_____	(1)	(1)	1,300	397
C.Zone__	Cerro Galera_____	1,205	368	Atlantic Ocean_____	(1)	(1)	280	85
Guam___	Mount Lamlam_____	1,329	405	Pacific Ocean_____	(1)	(1)	330	101
V.Is____	Crown Mountain_____	1,556	475	Atlantic Ocean_____	(1)	(1)	750	229

Z Less than .5 meter.
[1] Sea level.   [2] "Sec." denotes section; "T," township; "R," range; "N," north; "W," west.
Source: U.S. Geological Survey, *Elevations and Distances in the United States*, 1973.

No. 344. Lengths of Principal Rivers

[Comprises rivers 600 miles or more in length. Length represents distance to designated outflow from (a) original headwater of named river where name applies to entire length of channel, or (b) upper limit of channel so named, usually the junction of 2 tributaries or headwater streams. One mile = 1.609 kilometers]

RIVER/OUTFLOW	LENGTH		RIVER/OUTFLOW	LENGTH	
	Miles	Kilo-meters		Miles	Kilo-meters
Arkansas/Mississippi River	1,450	2,333	Missouri-Red Rock/Mississippi River	2,564	4,125
Brazos/Gulf of Mexico	1,309	2,106			
Canadian/Arkansas River	906	1,458	Mobile-Alabama-Coosa/Mobile Bay	639	1,028
Cimarron/Arkansas River	698	1,123	North Canadian/Canadian River	784	1,261
Colorado (U.S.-Mex.)/Gulf of Calif	1,450	2,333	North Platte/Platte River	680	1,094
Colorado (Texas)/Matagorda Bay	894	1,438	Ohio/Mississippi River	981	1,578
Columbia/Pacific Ocean	1,214	1,953	Ohio-Allegheny/Mississippi River	1,306	2,101
Columbia, Upper/to mouth of Snake River	890	1,432	Ouachita/Red River	605	973
			Pecos/Rio Grande	926	1,490
Cumberland/Ohio River	687	1,105	Red (Okla.-Tex.-La.)/Mississippi River	1,222	1,966
Gila/Colorado River	630	1,014			
Green (Utah-Wyo.)/Colorado River	730	1,175	Rio Grande/Gulf of Mexico	1,885	3,033
James (N.Dak.-S.Dak.)/Missouri River	710	1,142	St. Lawrence/Lake Ontario	800	1,287
			Snake/Columbia River	1,000	1,609
Kuskokwim/Kuskokwim Bay	800	1,287	Tanana/Yukon River	800	1,287
Milk/Missouri River	625	1,006	Tennessee/Ohio River	652	1,049
Mississippi/Mouth of SW Pass	2,348	3,778	Tennessee-French Broad/Ohio River	869	1,398
Mississippi, Upper/to mouth of Missouri River	1,171	1,884	Trinity/Trinity Bay	715	1,150
			Washita/Red River	626	1,007
Mississippi-Missouri-Red Rock/mouth of SW Pass	3,741	6,019	White (Ark.-Mo.)/Mississippi River	685	1,102
			Yellowstone/Missouri River	671	1,080
Missouri/Mississippi River	2,315	3,725	Yukon/Bering Sea	1,875	3,017

Source: U.S. Corps of Engineers, unpublished data.

No. 345. Areas of Selected Natural Lakes

[Comprises lakes with surface area of 150 square miles or more. One square mile = 2.59 square kilometers]

LAKE AND LOCATION	AREA		LAKE AND LOCATION	AREA	
	Sq. mi.	Sq. km.		Sq. mi.	Sq. km.
Becharof (Alaska)	458	1,186	Lake of the Woods (Minn. and Canada)	1,485	3,846
Champlain (N.Y., Vt., and Canada)	490	1,269			
Flathead (Montana)	197	510	Leech (Minn.)	176	456
Great Salt [1] (Utah)	[2] 1,685	[2] 4,365	Mille Lacs (Minn.)	207	536
			Naknek (Alaska)	242	627
Iliamna (Alaska)	1,000	2,590	Okeechobee (Fla.)	700	1,813
Lake Erie (Mich., N.Y., Ohio, Pa., and Canada)	9,940	25,745	Pontchartrain [1] (La.)	625	1,619
			Pyramid [1] (Nev.)	[2] 172	[2] 445
Lake Huron (Mich. and Canada)	23,010	59,596	Rainy (Minn. and Canada)	345	894
Lake Michigan (Ill., Ind., Mich., and Wis.)	22,400	58,016	Red Lake, Upper and Lower (Minn.)	451	1,168
			St. Clair (Mich. and Canada)	460	1,191
Lake Ontario (N.Y. and Canada)	7,540	19,529	Salton Sea [1] (Calif.)	[2] 374	[2] 969
Lake Superior (Mich., Minn., Wis., and Canada)	31,820	82,414	Tahoe (Calif. and Nev.)	193	500
			Teshekpuk (Alaska)	315	816
			Winnebago (Wis.)	215	557

[1] Salty. [2] Variable. Estimated from elevation of water surface as of December 1976.

Source: U.S. Geological Survey, *Principal Lakes of the United States*, Circular 476.

No. 346. ESTIMATED DAILY WATER USE: 1940 TO 1975, AND PROJECTIONS TO 2000

[Daily average. 1940–1960 not strictly comparable to later years due to differences in estimation procedures. Prior to 1960, excludes Alaska and Hawaii. One gallon=3.785 liters. See also *Historical Statistics, Colonial Times to 1970*, series J 92–103]

YEAR	TOTAL WATER USE [1]		IRRIGATION [2]		PUBLIC WATER UTILITIES [3]		SELF-SUPPLIED USES					
							Rural domestic [4]		Industrial and miscellaneous [5]		Steam electric utilities [1]	
	Total	Ground	Total	Ground	Total	Ground	Total	Ground	Total	Ground	Total	Ground
GALLONS (bil.)												
1940	136.43	22.56	71.03	11.22	10.10	2.82	3.10	2.64	29.00	5.86	23.20	.02
1950	202.70	35.19	100.00	19.80	14.10	3.78	4.60	4.09	38.10	7.47	45.90	.05
1960	322.90	58.17	135.00	35.24	22.00	5.68	6.00	5.58	61.20	11.57	98.70	.10
1965	269.62	48.57	110.85	30.04	23.74	5.96	4.08	3.86	46.41	8.63	84.54	.08
1970	377.50	63.18	130.00	46.80	27.03	6.65	4.50	3.61	46.00	6.00	170.00	.12
1975	337.55	82.14	158.23	56.30	26.36	10.70	3.98	3.90	60.08	9.77	88.90	1.47
1985	329.35	80.14	165.76	54.93	29.63	10.44	4.52	3.81	34.58	9.53	94.86	1.43
2000	306.03	74.47	153.54	51.04	34.17	9.70	4.91	3.54	33.36	8.86	80.05	1.33
LITERS (bil.)												
1940	516.39	85.39	268.85	42.47	38.23	10.67	11.73	9.99	109.77	22.18	87.81	.08
1950	767.22	133.19	378.50	74.94	53.37	14.31	17.41	15.48	144.21	28.27	173.73	.19
1960	1,222.18	220.17	510.98	133.38	83.27	21.50	22.71	21.12	231.64	43.79	373.58	.38
1965	1,020.51	183.84	419.57	113.70	89.86	22.56	15.44	14.61	175.66	32.66	319.98	.30
1970	1,428.95	239.14	492.05	177.14	102.31	25.17	17.03	13.66	174.11	22.71	643.45	.45
1975	1,277.63	310.90	598.90	213.10	99.77	40.50	15.06	14.76	227.41	36.98	336.49	5.56
1985	1,246.59	303.33	627.40	207.91	112.15	39.52	17.11	14.42	130.88	36.07	359.05	5.41
2000	1,158.32	281.87	581.15	193.19	129.33	36.71	18.58	13.40	126.27	33.54	302.99	5.03

[1] Beginning 1975, decline in water use reflects the increasing use of recycled treated effluents and cooling water by industrial water users and steam electric utilities.
[2] Total take, including delivery losses but not including reservoir evaporation.
[3] Includes domestic central and commercial water withdrawals.
[4] Rural farm and nonfarm household and garden use, and water for farm stock and dairies.
[5] For 1940–1960, includes manufacturing and mineral industries, rural commercial industries, air-conditioning, resorts, hotels, motels, military and other State and Federal agencies, and other miscellaneous uses; thereafter, includes manufacturing, mining and mineral processing, ordnance, construction, and other miscellaneous uses.

Source: U.S. Bureau of Domestic Business Development, 1940–1960 based principally on committee prints, *Water Resources Activities in the United States*, for the Senate Committee on National Water Resources, U.S. Senate, 1960; 1965, *National Assessment of the Water Resources Council*, 1968; 1970, U.S. Geological Survey Circular 676, *Estimated Use of Water in the United States in 1970*: thereafter U.S. Water Resources Council preliminary reports of the second *National Assessment by the Water Resources Council*.

No. 347. STATUS OF AUTHORIZED FEDERAL WATER PROJECTS OF THE CORPS OF ENGINEERS AND BUREAU OF RECLAMATION: 1979

[In millions of dollars, except number of projects. For year ending Sept. 30]

STATUS	Number of projects	Estimated Federal cost [1]	Allocation through 1978	1979 budget allocations	Balance to complete
CORPS OF ENGINEERS					
Total	4,377	55,257	27,490	1,296	19,659
Construction not started	251	10,810	147	21	10,642
Active underway	235	21,235	11,244	1,212	8,779
Completed projects	3,454	15,858	15,858	–	–
Deferred projects	123	1,679	40	–	–
Inactive projects	278	5,256	83	–	–
Other	36	419	118	63	238
BUREAU OF RECLAMATION					
Total	256	17,072	7,577	479	9,016
Construction not started	17	1,147	26	5	1,116
Active underway	69	13,277	5,628	462	7,187
Completed projects	158	1,831	1,831	–	–
Inactive projects	10	627	44	–	583
Other	2	190	48	12	130

– Represents zero.   [1] Gross cost, excluding reimbursements, revenues, and contributions by other parties.

Source: U.S. Corps of Engineers, *Civil Works Summary—Active Authorized Backlog, Fiscal Year 1979*, and U.S. Bureau of Reclamation, unpublished data.

No. 348. WATER WITHDRAWN PER DAY—STATES AND PUERTO RICO: 1970 AND 1975

[Quantities are given to two significant figures; therefore, figures do not add to totals. Withdrawal signifies water physically withdrawn from a source. Includes fresh and saline water; excludes water used for hydroelectric power]

STATE	WATER WITHDRAWN					Fresh water consumed,[2] 1975	STATE OR OTHER AREA	WATER WITHDRAWN					Fresh water consumed,[2] 1975
	1970		1975					1970		1975			
	Per capita[1]	Total	Per capita[1]	Total	Surface			Per capita[1]	Total	Per capita[1]	Total	Surface	
	Gal.	Bil. gal.	Gal.	Bil. gal.	Bil. gal.	Mil. gal.		Gal.	Bil. gal.	Gal.	Bil. gal.	Bil. gal.	Mil. gal.
Total	1,800	370.0	1,900	420.0	330	96,000	Mont	12,000	8.0	17,000	12.0	11	2,800
							Nebr	4,100	6.0	5,700	8.7	3	6,000
Ala	1,900	6.7	2,600	9.1	9	260	Nev	6,700	3.3	5,800	3.5	3	1,600
Alaska	830	.3	500	.2	(z)	6	N.H	940	.7	1,200	1.0	1	21
Ariz	3,900	6.8	3,500	7.8	3	5,900	N.J	870	6.3	890	6.6	6	440
Ark	1,600	3.0	2,400	5.1	3	2,200	N. Mex	3,100	3.2	2,800	3.2	2	1,600
Calif	2,400	48.0	2,400	51.0	31	23,000							
Colo	6,000	13.0	4,000	10.0	7	5,300	N.Y	970	18.0	1,200	24.0	23	740
Conn	1,200	3.5	850	2.7	3	160	N.C	1,200	5.9	1,100	6.0	6	490
Del	2,200	1.2	3,600	2.1	2	39	N. Dak	1,000	.7	1,400	.9	1	240
							Ohio	1,700	18.0	1,500	16.0	15	510
D.C	1,700	1.3	400	.3	(z)	18	Okla	590	1.5	690	2.3	1	1,200
Fla	2,300	15.0	2,200	18.0	15	2,300	Oreg	2,800	5.9	3,300	6.9	6	3,200
Ga	1,200	5.3	1,200	5.9	5	390							
Hawaii	3,500	2.7	3,100	2.5	2	560	Pa	1,700	20.0	1,500	18.0	17	830
Idaho	22,000	16.0	21,000	17.0	12	4,900	R.I	490	.5	520	.5	(z)	14
Ill	1,400	16.0	1,200	13.0	12	200	S.C	1,300	3.4	2,100	5.8	6	280
Ind	1,700	8.6	2,100	11.0	11	370	S.D	910	.6	800	.6	(z)	300
Iowa	750	2.1	1,200	3.5	3	220	Tenn	1,600	6.4	1,800	7.6	7	270
Kans	1,700	3.8	2,500	5.8	1	4,100	Tex	2,400	27.0	2,300	29.0	18	13,000
Ky	1,400	4.5	860	2.9	3	180	Utah	4,000	4.2	3,400	4.1	3	2,400
La	2,500	9.1	3,100	12.0	10	3,200	Vt	250	.1	700	.3	(z)	110
Maine	760	.8	1,100	1.2	1	41	Va	1,200	5.5	1,500	7.5	7	71
Md	1,300	5.2	1,800	7.4	7	110	Wash	2,100	7.2	2,100	7.2	7	2,500
Mass	740	4.2	1,500	8.8	8	110	W.Va	3,300	5.8	3,400	6.2	6	66
Mich	1,500	13.0	1,600	15.0	14	310	Wis	1,400	6.3	710	3.2	3	240
Minn	900	3.4	1,000	4.0	3	270	Wyo	17,000	5.8	17,000	7.2	7	2,100
Miss	950	2.1	910	2.1	1	530							
Mo	750	3.5	860	4.1	4	400	P.R.[3]	1,100	3.0	1,300	4.2	4	250

Z Less than 500 million.   [1] Based on population as of July 1.   [2] Evaporated, transpired, or incorporated into products; excludes irrigation conveyance losses by evapotranspiration.   [3] Includes Virgin Islands.

Source: U.S. Geological Survey, *Estimated Use of Water in the United States in 1975*, Circular 765.

No. 349. PERCENT OF POPULATION USING FLUORIDATED WATER—STATES AND PUERTO RICO: 1975

[Fluoridation status as of December 31, 1975; population estimates as of July 1, 1973. Includes both natural and adjusted fluoridation. Based on information supplied by State health departments]

STATE	Population, 1973, (1,000)	Percent using fluoridated water, 1975	STATE	Population, 1973, (1,000)	Percent using fluoridated water, 1975	STATE	Population, 1973, (1,000)	Percent using fluoridated water, 1975	STATE OR OTHER AREA	Population, 1973, (1,000)	Percent using fluoridated water, 1975
U.S	209,819	49.4	Idaho	775	33.5	Mont	729	26.6	S.C	2,723	53.4
			Ill	11,176	86.2	Nebr	1,532	46.1	S. Dak	681	61.5
Ala	3,545	31.5	Ind	5,304	61.1	Nev	551	2.7	Tenn	4,094	67.0
Alaska	330	47.2	Iowa	2,862	61.9	N.H	794	13.2	Tex	11,828	52.8
Ariz	2,073	31.2	Kans	2,264	95.7	N.J	7,325	21.4	Utah	1,150	2.3
Ark	2,034	38.3									
Calif	20,651	22.0	Ky	3,328	51.4	N. Mex	1,099	63.8	Vt	465	36.9
			La	3,745	23.2	N.Y	18,213	66.1	Va	4,843	51.3
Colo	2,467	83.8	Maine	1,038	40.6	N.C	5,302	45.4	Wash	3,431	39.8
Conn	3,079	79.4	Md	4,073	68.1	N. Dak	635	50.7	W. Va	1,788	50.7
Del	572	39.5	Mass	5,799	21.6	Ohio	10,743	41.4	Wis	4,539	62.2
D.C	733	98.4									
Fla	7,745	35.8	Mich	9,061	76.1	Okla	2,668	63.3	Wyo	352	21.0
			Minn	3,890	71.5	Oreg	2,219	10.7			
Ga	4,818	41.5	Miss	2,317	24.6	Pa	11,861	46.2	P.R	2,950	81.4
Hawaii	841	6.4	Mo	4,767	40.4	R.I	967	66.8			

Source: U.S. Center for Disease Control, Atlanta, Ga., *Fluoridation Census, 1975.*

No. 350. FEDERAL OUTLAYS FOR THE ENVIRONMENT, BY ACTIVITY: 1973 TO 1978

[In millions of dollars. Through 1976, for years ending June 30, except as noted; thereafter, for years ending Sept. 30]

ACTIVITY	1973	1974	1975	1976	1976, TQ [1]	1977	1978
Total	3,701	4,909	5,995	7,481	2,298	9,212	11,024
Annual percent change	28.9	32.6	22.1	24.8	(X)	23.1	19.7
Protection and enhancement	820	870	1,128	1,294	405	1,498	2,106
Aid to State and local governments	248	333	403	392	122	426	650
City recreation	69	93	110	98	49	205	306
Preservation and protection [2]	19	25	(Z)	2	1	–	(Z)
Noncity general recreation	84	121	151	142	35	145	182
Sport fish and wildlife	66	68	90	85	23	7	8
Historic preservation and rehabilitation	9	11	11	14	5	47	75
Other	1	15	41	50	10	22	79
Direct Federal activities	571	537	725	902	283	1,073	1,456
City recreation	46	108	145	139	36	113	172
Preservation and protection [2]	155	151	164	245	85	303	417
Noncity general recreation	172	128	189	264	94	325	380
Sport fish and wildlife	110	62	128	160	41	163	219
Historic preservation and rehabilitation	53	41	60	39	14	73	102
Other	36	48	39	55	14	95	166
Understanding, describing, and predicting	956	1,065	1,296	1,651	459	1,885	2,170
Observe and predict weather, ocean conditions, and disturbances [3]	452	484	595	661	187	709	712
Locate and describe natural resources	250	260	351	423	104	490	706
Physical environment surveys	103	115	146	155	37	199	209
Weather modification activities	17	22	24	17	8	20	17
Research on environmental impact on people	66	96	57	227	75	261	291
Ecological and other basic environmental research	66	89	125	169	49	206	234
Pollution abatement and control	1,925	2,974	3,571	4,536	1,434	5,829	6,748

– Represents zero.   X Not applicable.   Z Less than $500,000.
[1] Transition quarter, July–Sept.   [2] Unique natural areas and endangered species.   [3] Includes earthquakes.

Source: U.S. Office of Management and Budget, *Special Analyses, Budget of the United States Government*, annual.

No. 351. FEDERAL FUNDS FOR POLLUTION ABATEMENT AND CONTROL—SUMMARY: 1974 TO 1978

[In millions of dollars. Through 1975, for years ending June 30; thereafter, for years ending Sept. 30, except as noted. Obligations refer to liabilities, contracts, and other commitments entered into requiring payment of money by the Government. Outlays refer to the issuance of checks or disbursements of cash by the Government to liquidate obligations. Outlays during any fiscal year may be payments of obligations incurred in prior years or in same year:

MEDIA OR POLLUTANT	OBLIGATIONS					AGENCY	OUTLAYS				
	1974	1975	1976 [1]	1977	1978, est.		1974	1975	1976 [1]	1977	1978, est.
Total	4,333	6,103	7,536	10,029	6,432	Total	2,974	3,571	5,970	5,829	6,748
Water	3,465	5,179	6,128	8,693	5,044	EPA [4]	2,032	2,530	4,226	4,365	5,115
Air	490	348	419	416	409	Dept. of Energy [5]	(X)	(X)	(X)	242	281
Land	40	57	150	94	114	Dept. of Defense	240	355	580	482	425
Other [2]	338	519	840	825	864	Dept. of Agriculture [6]	123	143	223	193	200
Selected pollutants: [3]						Dept. of Interior	41	53	89	87	116
						Dept. of Commerce [6]	58	52	77	107	182
Radiation	121	160	144	97	110	Dept. of Transportation	59	80	92	120	141
Noise	61	50	56	60	69	National Aeronautics and Space Admin	23	75	87	79	79
Pesticides	64	59	79	75	88	Other [5]	398	283	596	154	209
Solid wastes	109	174	123	108	143						

X Not applicable.   [1] Covers 15 months ending Sept. 30.   [2] Includes more than one of media shown above and funds not assigned to specific media for: Pollution abatement and control in living things; research into pollution sources and effects; radiation research and control; standards-setting and development; technical support; personnel, contruction, and administrative costs.   [3] Funds for "Selected pollutants" included in "media" breakdown above.   [4] Environmental Protection Agency.   [5] Dept. of Energy succeeded the Federal Energy Administration (FEA), the Energy Research and Development Admin. (ERDA), and parts of several other agencies beginning in 1977. Funds for predecessor agencies are included in "Other."   [6] Includes expenditures for water and sewer programs.

Source: U.S. Office of Management and Budget, *Special Analyses, Budget of the United States Government*, annual.

No. 352. NATIONAL EXPENDITURES FOR POLLUTION ABATEMENT AND CONTROL, 1972 TO 1976, AND BY MEDIA, 1975 AND 1976

[In millions of dollars. Excludes agricultural business, real estate operators, private medical, legal, educational, and cultural services, and nonprofit organizations. Minus sign (−) denotes deductions for costs recovered which represent the value of reclaimed materials or engergy reused in production, or revenues received from the sale of these items]

TYPE	1972	1973	1974	1975, prel.				1976, prel.			
				Total [1]	Air	Water	Solid waste	Total [1]	Air	Water	Solid waste
Total expenditures	18,699	22,412	26,214	30,942	13,059	13,306	4,800	34,679	14,536	15,104	5,318
Percent Government of total	29.4	27.9	28.7	28.6	4.1	46.9	34.3	28.2	4.2	45.5	33.1
Pollution abatement	17,511	21,021	24,628	29,192	12,272	12,863	4,726	32,769	13,710	14,603	5,253
Personal consumption	1,604	2,158	2,746	3,675	3,675	−	−	4,430	4,430	−	−
Durable goods	473	669	685	1,349	1,349	−	−	1,815	1,815	−	−
Nondurable goods and services	1,131	1,489	2,061	2,326	2,326	−	−	2,615	2,615	−	−
Business	11,075	13,434	15,346	17,823	8,380	7,002	3,135	19,867	9,024	8,157	3,540
On capital account	5,709	7,024	7,345	8,416	4,575	3,422	420	9,004	4,571	3,981	452
On current account	5,365	6,410	8,001	9,407	3,805	3,580	2,715	10,863	4,452	4,177	3,088
Private	4,634	5,537	6,906	8,177	3,727	1,735	2,715	9,549	4,375	2,087	3,088
Govt. enterprise	1,147	1,343	1,633	1,923	78	1,845	−	2,168	78	2,090	−
Costs recovered	−415	−470	−538	−694	−	−	−	−855	−	−	−
Government	4,832	5,429	6,536	7,694	217	5,861	1,591	8,472	256	6,446	1,713
Federal	143	207	298	435	88	273	50	473	105	260	52
State and local	1,335	1,456	1,613	1,822	1	280	1,541	1,979	1	315	1,661
Govt. enterprise fixed capital	3,355	3,767	4,624	5,437	128	5,309	−	6,021	150	5,871	−
Regulation and monitoring	367	490	598	646	204	279	33	716	214	324	27
Federal	200	278	349	375	66	153	26	387	69	151	21
State and local	167	212	249	271	138	126	6	328	145	173	6
Research and development	822	902	988	1,104	583	164	42	1,194	612	177	39
Private	518	568	606	607	466	67	21	618	475	74	20
Federal	205	269	344	450	109	78	15	531	131	85	14
State and local	99	65	39	47	8	19	6	45	6	18	4

− Represents zero. [1] Includes expenditures for abatement and control of noise, radiation, and pesticide pollution, and unallocated business expenditures, not shown separately.

Source: U.S. Bureau of Economic Analysis, *Survey of Current Business*, February 1978.

No. 353. GOVERNMENTAL EXPENDITURES FOR WATER, LAND, AND AIR QUALITY CONTROL ACTIVITIES: 1974 TO 1976

[In millions of dollars. For fiscal years ending in year stated. Covers regulatory, administrative, operational, and other activities directly related to the prevention, control and abatement of water pollution, land pollution caused by improper disposal of solid and hazardous wastes, and air pollution]

LEVEL OF GOVERNMENT	WATER QUALITY CONTROL			LAND QUALITY CONTROL [1]			AIR QUALITY CONTROL		
	1974	1975	1976	1974	1975	1976	1974	1975	1976
Federal expenditures	2,106	2,552	3,139	50	62	98	231	213	242
Direct	246	377	456	45	55	94	195	179	189
Intergovernmental	1,860	2,175	2,682	5	7	4	36	34	53
State expenditures	636	751	939	81	105	108	72	95	157
Direct	212	316	326	66	89	87	64	86	148
Current operation	117	158	173	61	70	79	59	73	83
Capital outlay	95	157	153	5	19	8	5	14	65
Intergovernmental	424	436	613	16	16	21	7	9	10
Local expenditures, direct [1]	4,099	5,323	6,008	1,932	2,127	2,321	38	41	39
Current operation	1,446	1,695	1,988	1,181	1,845	2,086	33	38	38
Capital outlay	2,653	3,628	4,020	251	282	235	5	3	1

[1] Includes collection, disposal, and recycling of trash, garbage, and other solid or hazardous waste, street cleaning, State government highway litter program, licensing and inspection, enforcement, etc. See footnote 2.
[2] Local data for water quality control represents sewerage; for land quality control, "sanitation other than sewerage" activities; and for air quality control, represents expenditures only for the 48 largest cities and the 58 largest counties.

Source: U.S. Bureau of the Census, *Environmental Quality Control, Governmental Finances and Employment: Fiscal Year 1973–74* (GSS No. 76) and *Environmental Quality Control, Governmental Finances: Fiscal Year 1975–76* (GSS No. 86).

No. 354. Capital Expenditures by Business for Pollution Abatement, by Industry: 1974 to 1977

[Covers expenditures for new plant and equipment. See table 930 for final total capital outlays by business. Excludes expenditures of agricultural business and outlays charged to current account]

INDUSTRY	POLLUTION ABATEMENT EXPENDITURES (mil. dol.)							PERCENT OF TOTAL CAPITAL OUTLAYS BY BUSINESS [1]				
	1974	1975	1976	1977				1974	1975	1976	1977	
				Total	Air	Water	Solid waste				Total	Air
All industries	5,617	6,549	6,762	6,939	3,693	2,785	461	5.0	5.8	5.6	5.1	2.7
Manufacturing	3,656	4,475	4,382	4,282	2,032	1,993	258	8.0	9.3	8.3	7.0	3.3
Durable goods	1,648	1,775	1,560	1,668	941	636	91	7.3	8.1	6.6	5.9	3.3
Primary metals	798	1,012	923	927	607	295	26	16.6	17.2	15.7	15.7	10.3
Electrical machinery	207	136	148	111	30	65	15	6.8	5.8	5.6	3.4	.9
Machinery, except electrical	77	83	80	104	51	49	5	1.8	1.8	1.6	1.8	.9
Transportation equip.	140	116	125	163	58	74	31	3.7	3.4	3.4	3.1	1.1
Stone, clay, and glass	191	198	103	149	107	39	4	12.9	14.3	6.1	7.3	5.2
Other	235	229	181	213	88	116	10	4.5	5.3	3.9	3.6	1.5
Nondurable goods	2,008	2,700	2,821	2,615	1,091	1,357	167	8.7	10.3	9.6	8.0	3.3
Food, incl. beverages	150	175	175	176	71	96	8	4.7	5.2	4.5	4.2	1.7
Textiles	28	31	37	35	11	23	1	3.3	4.6	4.4	3.8	1.2
Paper	491	489	511	468	188	256	23	19.3	16.8	14.7	13.8	5.5
Chemicals	469	684	765	701	249	414	38	8.3	10.9	11.4	10.2	3.6
Petroleum	796	1,239	1,275	1,167	531	546	90	10.1	11.8	10.9	8.2	3.7
Rubber	47	41	37	47	31	12	4	3.2	4.0	3.4	3.3	2.1
Other	28	41	23	21	9	9	2	1.8	2.8	1.4	1.2	.5
Nonmanufacturing	1,961	2,074	2,381	2,657	1,661	792	204	3.0	3.2	3.5	3.5	2.2
Mining	57	73	86	97	38	32	27	1.8	1.9	2.2	2.2	.9
Railroad	29	35	27	28	4	23	2	1.2	1.4	1.1	1.0	.1
Air transportation	7	11	16	14	12	1	1	.4	.6	1.2	.8	.7
Other transportation	46	41	38	23	11	10	2	2.3	1.4	1.1	1.0	.5
Public utilities	1,622	1,700	2,032	2,300	1,525	654	121	7.9	8.4	9.1	8.8	5.8
Communication, commercial, and other [2]	201	214	182	195	73	72	51	.6	.6	.5	.5	.2

[1] Based on industry totals (pollution abatement and total new plant and equipment expenditures) reported in source.
[2] Includes trade, service, construction, finance, and insurance.

Source: U.S. Bureau of Economic Analysis, *Survey of Current Business*, June 1978.

No. 355. Solid Waste Generation, Resource Recovery, and Disposal by Type of Material: 1971 to 1976

[In millions of tons, except as indicated. Covers post-consumer residential and commercial solid wastes which comprise the major portion of typical municipal collections. Excludes mining, agricultural and industrial processing, demolition and construction wastes, sewage sludge, and junked autos and obsolete equipment wastes. Based on material-flows estimating procedure and wet weight as generated]

ITEM AND MATERIAL	1971	1972	1973	1974	1975	1976
Gross waste generated	132.9	139.3	144.2	144.1	136.1	144.7
Per person per day lb.	3.52	3.65	3.75	3.70	3.40	3.68
Resources recovered	8.1	8.8	9.6	9.4	8.0	9.2
Per person per day lb.	.21	.23	.23	.23	.20	.23
Net waste disposed of	124.8	130.5	134.6	134.8	128.2	135.5
Per person per day lb.	3.31	3.42	3.52	3.48	3.20	3.45
Paper	39.1	42.5	44.2	43.4	37.2	42.3
Glass	12.0	12.7	13.2	12.9	13.3	13.5
Metal	11.8	12.1	12.4	13.0	12.2	12.2
Plastics	4.2	4.7	5.0	4.5	4.4	5.1
Food waste	22.0	22.2	22.4	22.6	22.8	23.0
Yard waste	24.1	24.5	25.0	25.5	26.0	26.6
Other [1]	11.5	11.7	12.3	12.9	12.2	12.8

[1] Includes rubber and leather, wood, textiles, and miscellaneous organics.

Source: U.S. Environmental Protection Agency, *Resource Recovery and Source Reduction*, annual.

No. 356. NATIONAL AMBIENT AIR QUALITY STATIONS—TOTAL STATIONS REPORTING, AND NUMBER EXCEEDING AIR QUALITY STANDARDS, BY POLLUTANT: 1970 TO 1976

["Exceeding" refers to the number of times when volume of pollution measured in air samples was greater than the standard. Minimal data consist of at least three 24-hour samples or 400 hourly values. Valid annual data records must contain at least five of the scheduled 24-hour samples or 75 percent of possible hourly values in all four quarters. See text, p. 204. $\mu g/m^3$=micrograms of pollutant per cubic meter of air; mg/m^3=milligrams of pollutant per cubic meter of air]

ITEM	1970	1972	1973	1974	1975	1976 Total	1976 Exceeding by 50 percent
Suspended particulates:							
Stations reporting at least minimal data	1,283	2,972	3,762	4,270	4,177	4,205	(X)
Exceeding 24-hour secondary standard (150 $\mu g/m^3$)	668	1,275	1,458	1,421	1,269	1,360	520
Exceeding 24-hour primary standard (260 $\mu g/m^3$)	212	311	355	319	276	347	89
Stations with valid annual data	763	1,889	2,024	2,571	2,464	2,691	(X)
Exceeding annual secondary guide (60 $\mu g/m^3$)	550	1,060	996	1,060	984	1,206	267
Exceeding annual primary standard (75 $\mu g/m^3$)	385	626	521	537	453	595	106
Sulfur dioxide:							
Stations reporting at least minimal data	403	1,311	2,008	2,465	2,449	2,500	(X)
Exceeding 24-hour primary standard (365 $\mu g/m^3$)	33	42	103	113	88	74	41
Exceeding 3-hour secondary standard (1,300 $\mu g/m^3$)	13	26	52	76	54	44	25
Stations with valid annual data	184	588	716	1,398	1,374	1,552	(X)
Exceeding annual primary standard (80 $\mu g/m^3$)	29	20	24	40	35	34	4
Carbon monoxide:							
Stations reporting at least minimal data	73	191	299	407	431	432	(X)
Exceeding 1-hour standard (40 mg/m^3)	14	16	33	28	25	8	–
Exceeding 8-hour standard (10 mg/m^3)	60	114	192	233	237	216	76
Total oxidants or ozone:							
Stations reporting at least minimal data	51	162	265	368	492	549	(X)
Exceeding 1-hour standard (160 $\mu g/m^3$)	45	115	217	302	412	472	320
Nitrogen dioxide:							
Stations reporting valid annual data	28	47	67	773	892	1,123	(X)
Exceeding annual standard (100 $\mu g/m^3$)	9	8	10	19	20	21	–

– Represents zero. X Not applicable.

No. 357. AIR POLLUTANT EMISSIONS, BY SOURCE: 1970 TO 1976

[Estimates]

YEAR AND POLLUTANT	Total emissions (mil. tons)	CONTROLLABLE EMISSIONS (mil. tons)						Misc. uncontrollable (mil. tons)	PERCENT OF TOTAL		
		Transportation		Fuel combustion [1]		Industrial processes	Solid waste disposal		Transportation	Fuel combustion [1]	Industrial
		Total	Road vehicles	Total	Electric utilities						
1970:											
Carbon monoxide	110.0	87.3	76.8	1.3	.2	8.8	6.7	5.8	79.4	1.2	8.0
Sulfur oxides	32.1	.8	.3	24.6	17.3	6.5	.1	.1	2.4	76.6	20.3
Hydrocarbons	32.7	13.9	12.2	1.7	.1	9.4	1.9	6.0	42.4	5.1	28.6
Particulates [2]	24.9	1.2	.8	7.8	4.5	13.7	1.2	1.0	4.9	31.4	54.9
Nitrogen oxides	22.5	9.3	6.9	12.0	5.6	.7	.3	.2	41.3	53.3	3.1
1974:											
Carbon monoxide	100.8	81.5	72.3	1.4	.3	9.0	3.5	5.3	80.9	1.4	9.0
Sulfur oxides	31.1	.9	.4	24.1	18.7	5.8	.1	.1	2.8	77.7	18.8
Hydrocarbons	31.5	12.5	10.8	1.7	.1	10.1	1.0	6.3	39.5	5.2	32.2
Particulates [2]	19.3	1.3	.3	6.2	4.2	10.4	.6	.9	6.9	32.0	53.7
Nitrogen oxides	24.9	10.6	8.0	13.1	6.8	.8	.2	.2	42.5	52.7	3.1
1975:											
Carbon monoxide	94.7	78.8	69.8	1.3	.3	7.8	3.2	3.5	83.2	1.4	8.3
Sulfur oxides	28.3	.9	.4	22.7	18.4	4.6	–	.1	3.1	80.2	16.3
Hydrocarbons	28.9	12.0	10.4	1.5	.1	9.4	.9	5.1	41.6	5.3	32.4
Particulates [2]	15.9	1.3	.9	5.8	4.3	7.6	.4	.7	8.3	36.8	47.9
Nitrogen oxides	24.5	10.9	8.4	12.3	6.7	.8	.2	.2	44.6	50.5	3.2
1976:											
Carbon monoxide	96.1	76.8	67.7	1.3	.3	8.6	3.1	6.3	80.0	1.4	8.9
Sulfur oxides	29.6	.9	.4	24.1	19.4	4.5	–	.1	3.0	81.4	15.2
Hydrocarbons	30.7	11.9	10.2	1.5	.1	10.4	.9	6.1	38.7	5.0	33.7
Particulates [2]	14.8	1.3	.9	5.1	3.5	6.9	.4	1.0	9.0	34.3	47.0
Nitrogen oxides	25.3	11.1	8.6	13.0	7.3	.8	.1	.3	43.9	51.3	3.0

– Represents zero. [1] Stationary. [2] See footnote 1, table 358.

Source of tables 356 and 357: U.S. Environmental Protection Agency, *National Air Quality and Emission Trends Report*, 1976.

No. 358. Air Pollutants—National Emission Estimates: 1970 to 1976

[One short ton=.907 metric ton]

YEAR	SHORT TONS (mil.)					METRIC TONS (mil.)				
	Particulates [1]	Sulfur oxides	Nitrogen oxides	Hydrocarbons	Carbon monoxide	Particulates [1]	Sulfur oxides	Nitrogen oxides	Hydrocarbons	Carbon monoxide
1970	24.9	32.1	22.5	32.7	110.0	22.6	29.1	20.4	29.7	99.8
1971	23.6	30.7	23.5	32.3	110.4	21.4	27.9	21.3	29.3	100.2
1972	22.4	31.7	24.5	32.7	112.4	20.3	28.8	22.2	29.7	102.0
1973	21.9	32.7	25.2	32.8	108.3	19.9	29.7	22.9	29.8	98.3
1974	19.3	31.1	24.9	31.5	100.8	17.5	28.2	22.6	28.6	91.5
1975	15.9	28.3	24.5	28.9	94.7	14.4	25.7	22.2	26.2	85.9
1976	14.8	29.6	25.3	30.7	96.1	13.4	26.9	23.0	27.9	87.2

[1] Suspended particulate matter: Particles of smoke, dust, and fumes and droplets of viscous liquid remaining in the air for varying periods of time and ranging from less than 1 micron (1/25,000 inch) to 100 microns.

Source: U.S. Environmental Protection Agency, *National Air Quality and Emissions Trends Report*, 1976.

No. 359. Motor Vehicle Pollutant Emissions per Vehicle-Mile Traveled: 1970 to 1979

[In grams per mile. Estimated]

POLLUTANT AND SOURCE	1970	1971	1972	1973	1974	1975	1976	1977	1978	1979
All vehicles:										
Carbon monoxide	86.9	83.9	81.6	80.0	79.0	77.0	74.3	71.4	68.3	65.2
Hydrocarbons	12.1	11.4	10.8	10.3	9.9	9.4	8.9	8.4	7.9	7.3
Nitrogen oxides	4.7	4.7	4.9	4.8	4.7	4.6	4.4	4.1	3.9	3.8
Automobiles:										
Carbon monoxide	76.7	73.9	71.9	70.5	69.7	67.7	64.8	61.5	58.0	54.5
Hydrocarbons	10.8	10.2	9.6	9.1	8.7	8.3	7.7	7.2	6.6	6.0
Nitrogen oxides	3.8	3.9	4.0	3.9	3.8	3.6	3.4	3.1	2.9	2.7

Source: U.S. Environmental Protection Agency, *Mobile Source Emission Factors*, Final Document, March 1978.

No. 360. Automobile Pollutant Emissions, 1957-1967, and Federal Emission Standards, 1970-1981

[In grams per mile]

PERIOD	Hydrocarbons	Carbon monoxide	Nitrogen oxides	PERIOD	Hydrocarbons	Carbon monoxide	Nitrogen oxides
1957-1967 average	8.7	87	(NA)	1975-79 standards	1.5	15.0	[2] 2
1970-1971 standards	4.1	34	(X)	1980 standards	.41	7.0	2
1972-1974 standards	3.0	28	[1] 3	1981 standards	.41	3.4	1

NA Not available.   X Not applicable.   [1] Effective with 1973 model cars.
[2] Effective with 1977 model cars.
Source: U.S. Environmental Protection Agency, unpublished data.

No. 361. Major Oil Spills from Tankers and Barges in U.S. Waters: 1972 to 1977

[Covers spills larger than 50,000 gallons, within 200 miles of U.S. coastline. Summer=April through September; winter=October through March]

ITEM	1972-73	1973-74	1974-75	1975-76	1976-77
Number of spills, total	12	23	22	16	15
Summer	2	8	7	4	5
Winter	10	15	15	12	10
Oil spilled _____1,000 gal	5,294	5,182	7,331	9,251	11,516
Summer	1,998	1,614	1,909	1,259	972
Winter	3,296	3,568	5,422	7,992	10,544

Source: U.S. Council on Environmental Quality, *Major Oil Spills from Tankers, Barges, and Other Vessels in U.S. Waters—Analysis of Recent Trends and Patterns*, 1977.

No. 362. POLLUTING DISCHARGES REPORTED IN U.S. WATERS: 1970 TO 1976

[One gallon = 3.785 liters]

ITEM	Number of incidents	VOLUME		ITEM	Number of incidents	VOLUME	
		Gallons (1,000)	Liters (1,000)			Gallons (1,000)	Liters (1,000)
1970, total discharges	3,711	15,253	57,733	1976—Continued			
1971, total discharges	8,736	8,840	33,459	Marine facilities	560	377	1,426
1972, total discharges	9,931	18,806	71,181	Onshore/offshore	432	371	1,404
1973, total discharges	13,328	24,315	92,032	Land vehicles	464	614	2,323
1974, total discharges	13,966	16,916	64,027	Land facilities	182	443	1,676
1975, total discharges	12,057	14,967	56,653	Other and unknown	4,379	227	860
1976, total discharges	12,655	33,852	128,129	Type of pollutant:			
Vessel	3,296	11,192	42,362	Crude oil	2,667	4,991	18,890
Tank ship	623	8,930	33,800	Diesel oil	2,063	1,100	4,164
Tank barge	976	1,953	7,394	Other oil	5,930	17,035	64,477
Other	1,697	309	1,168	Other and unknown	1,995	10,726	40,598
Nontransportation facilities	3,121	16,469	62,336	Location:			
Onshore	708	6,435	24,355	Atlantic Coast	2,627	8,876	33,596
Offshore	1,358	275	1,040	Gulf Coast	4,482	7,640	28,916
Other	1,055	9,760	36,941	Pacific Coast	2,237	1,443	5,462
Pipelines	653	4,530	17,146	Great Lakes	973	8,757	33,145
				Inland	2,336	7,136	27,010

Source: U.S. Coast Guard, *Polluting Incidents In and Around U.S. Waters*, 1976.

No. 363. SYNTHETIC ORGANIC PESTICIDES—PRODUCTION AND SALES: 1960 TO 1976

[Includes a small quantity of soil conditioners. Minus sign (−) denotes decrease]

ITEM	1960	1965	1970	1972	1973	1974	1975	1976 [1]
Production, total ____mil. lb__	648	877	1,034	1,158	1,289	1,417	1,609	1,364
Average annual change [2] ____percent__	(NA)	6.2	3.3	5.8	11.3	9.9	13.5	−15.2
Value [3] ____mil. dol__	307	577	1,058	1,315	1,493	1,985	2,918	2,880
Average annual change [2] ___percent__	(NA)	13.5	12.9	12.8	11.0	33.0	47.0	−1.3
Sales, total [4] ____mil. lb__	570	764	881	1,022	1,199	1,365	1,317	1,193
Average annual change [2] ____percent__	(NA)	6.0	2.9	7.7	17.3	13.9	−3.5	−9.5
Value [3] ____mil. dol__	262	497	870	1,092	1,344	1,815	2,359	2,410
Average annual change [2] ___percent__	(NA)	13.7	11.9	12.0	23.1	35.1	29.9	2.2

NA Not available.   [1] Preliminary.   [2] From previous year shown.   [3] Unit value at manufacturers' level multiplied by quantity produced.   [4] As reported by U.S. International Trade Commission.

Source: U.S. Dept. of Agriculture, Agricultural Stabilization and Conservation Service, *The Pesticide Review*, 1977.

No. 364. TORNADOES, FLOODS, AND TROPICAL CYCLONES: 1946 TO 1976

[See also *Historical Statistics, Colonial Times to 1970*, series J 268–278]

ITEM	1946–1955	1956–1965	1966–1975	1970	1971	1972	1973	1974	1975	1976
Tornadoes, number [1]	2,969	6,572	8,030	653	888	741	1,102	947	920	835
Lives lost, total	1,751	924	1,172	72	156	27	87	361	60	44
Most in a single tornado	169	44	58	26	58	6	7	34	9	5
With property loss of $500,000 and over	130	191	428	30	35	29	76	107	42	47
Floods:										
Lives lost	808	557	1,528	135	74	540	105	121	114	187
Property loss ____mil. dol__	3,350	2,721	10,225	225	288	3,449	859	576	1,051	[2] 1,000
North Atlantic tropical cyclones and hurricanes: [3]										
Number reaching U.S. coast	40	33	25	4	5	3	1	1	1	2
Hurricanes only	21	14	13	1	3	1	−	1	1	1
Lives lost in U.S	495	692	504	11	8	121	5	1	21	9

− Represents zero.   [1] A violent, rotating column of air descending from a cumulonimbus cloud in the form of a tubular- or funnel-shaped cloud, characterized usually by movements along a narrow path and wind speeds from 100 to over 300 miles per hour. Also known as a "twister" or "waterspout."   [2] Preliminary estimate.
[3] Tropical cyclones have maximum winds of 39 to 73 miles per hour; hurricanes have maximum winds of 74 miles per hour or higher.

Source: U.S. National Oceanic and Atmospheric Administration, *Climatological Data: National Summary*. Monthly with annual summary.

No. 365. GROUND ELEVATION OF WEATHER STATIONS AND OCCURRENCE OF FREEZE—
SELECTED CITIES

[Date of freeze based on 30-year period, 1931–1960, except as indicated]

STATE AND STATION		Ground eleva-tion (feet)	OCCURRENCE OF FREEZE, 32° F. (0° C.)				Mean num-ber of days minimum temperature 32° F. or less	Length of record (yr.) [1]
			Spring date		Fall date			
			Mean	Latest	Mean	Earliest		
Ala.	Mobile [2]	211	Feb. 17	Mar. 20	Dec. 12	Nov. 14	20	10
Alaska	Juneau	12	May 13	June 7	Sept. 25	Aug. 24	152	29
Ariz.	Phoenix	1,117	Feb. 2	Mar. 14	Dec. 6	Nov. 5	15	12
Ark.	Little Rock	257	Mar. 17	Apr. 14	Nov. 10	Oct. 22	65	12
Calif.	Los Angeles	97	Jan. 1	Jan. 21	Dec. 30	Dec. 9	–	32
	Sacramento	17	Feb. 2	Apr. 8	Dec. 7	Nov. 4	20	12
	San Francisco	8	Jan. 17	Mar. 3	Dec. 22	Nov. 25	–	36
Colo.	Denver [2]	5,283	May 2	May 28	Oct. 14	Sept. 18	166	12
Conn.	Hartford [2]	169	Apr. 22	May 10	Oct. 19	Sept. 27	139	13
Del.	Wilmington [2]	74	Apr. 18	May 9	Oct. 26	Sept. 27	103	25
D.C.	Washington [2]	10	Apr. 10	May 12	Oct. 28	Oct. 2	80	12
Fla.	Jacksonville [2]	24	Feb. 6	Mar. 14	Dec. 16	Nov. 9	11	31
	Miami [2]	7	[3]	Feb. 6	[3]	[3]	–	8
Ga.	Atlanta	1,010	Mar. 19	Mar. 29	Nov. 10	Oct. 28	60	12
Hawaii	Honolulu [2]	7	[4]	[4]	[4]	[4]	[4]	15
Idaho	Boise [2]	2,838	Apr. 29	May 23	Oct. 16	Sept. 20	126	33
Ill.	Chicago	607	Apr. 19	May 4	Oct. 28	Oct. 7	120	9
	Peoria	652	Apr. 22	May 13	Oct. 20	Sept. 25	134	13
Ind.	Indianapolis [2]	792	Apr. 17	May 11	Oct. 27	Oct. 1	122	13
Iowa	Des Moines	938	Apr. 19	May 11	Oct. 22	Sept. 28	140	11
Kans.	Wichita [2]	1,321	Apr. 5	Apr. 21	Nov. 1	Sept. 27	114	19
Ky.	Louisville [2]	477	Apr. 1	Apr. 19	Nov. 7	Oct. 15	95	12
La.	New Orleans [2]	4	Feb. 15	Mar. 20	Dec. 3	Nov. 13	12	26
Maine	Portland [2]	43	Apr. 29	May 30	Oct. 15	Sept. 17	161	32
Md.	Baltimore [2]	148	Mar. 28	Apr. 16	Nov. 17	Oct. 20	101	22
Mass.	Boston	15	Apr. 5	Apr. 25	Nov. 8	Oct. 22	103	8
Mich.	Detroit	619	Apr. 24	May 12	Oct. 22	Sept. 29	125	39
	Sault Ste. Marie	721	May 19	June 21	Sept. 28	Aug. 22	179	31
Minn.	Duluth [2]	1,428	May 13	June 1	Oct. 3	Sept. 13	188	11
	Minneapolis [2]	834	Apr. 30	May 24	Oct. 13	Sept. 18	160	13
Miss.	Jackson [2]	310	Mar. 10	Apr. 13	Nov. 13	Oct. 17	50	9
Mo.	Kansas City	742	Apr. 6	Apr. 20	Oct. 30	Oct. 6	99	11
	St. Louis	535	Apr. 9	Apr. 25	Nov. 1	Oct. 7	108	12
Mont.	Great Falls [2]	3,662	May 14	June 8	Sept. 26	Sept. 7	155	11
Nebr.	Omaha [2]	977	Apr. 14	May 11	Oct. 19	Sept. 24	139	9
Nev.	Reno [2]	4,404	May 14	June 25	Oct. 2	Aug. 30	188	9
N.H.	Concord [2]	342	May 11	May 26	Sept. 30	Sept. 13	174	7
N.J.	Atlantic City	64	Mar. 31	Apr. 13	Nov. 11	Oct. 22	115	8
N. Mex.	Albuquerque [2]	5,311	Apr. 16	May 18	Oct. 29	Oct. 11	120	12
N.Y.	Albany [2]	275	Apr. 27	May 20	Oct. 13	Sept. 23	159	7
	Buffalo [2]	705	Apr. 30	May 24	Oct. 25	Sept. 23	138	12
	New York [2]	132	Apr. 7	Apr. 24	Nov. 12	Oct. 19	82	59
N.C.	Charlotte [2]	736	Mar. 21	Apr. 16	Nov. 15	Oct. 15	74	12
	Raleigh [2]	434	Mar. 24	Apr. 25	Nov. 16	Oct. 24	85	8
N. Dak.	Bismarck [2]	1,647	May 11	June 2	Sept. 24	Sept. 6	186	13
Ohio	Cincinnati [2]	761	Apr. 15	May 25	Oct. 25	Sept. 28	99	57
	Cleveland [2]	777	Apr. 21	May 14	Nov. 2	Sept. 29	127	12
	Columbus [2]	812	Apr. 17	May 9	Oct. 30	Oct. 7	124	13
Okla.	Oklahoma City [2]	1,285	Mar. 28	Apr. 17	Nov. 7	Oct. 14	82	7
Oreg.	Portland	21	Feb. 22	May 2	Dec. 3	Oct. 14	44	32
Pa.	Philadelphia [2]	5	Mar. 30	Apr. 20	Nov. 17	Oct. 19	104	13
	Pittsburgh [2]	1,137	Apr. 16	May 4	Nov. 3	Oct. 10	126	13
R.I.	Providence [2]	51	Apr. 13	Apr. 24	Oct. 27	Oct. 3	127	9
S.C.	Columbia [2]	213	Mar. 14	Apr. 13	Nov. 21	Nov. 1	65	6
S. Dak.	Sioux Falls [2]	1,418	May 5	May 29	Oct. 3	Sept. 12	172	9
Tenn.	Memphis [2]	258	Mar. 20	Apr. 15	Nov. 12	Oct. 17	60	31
	Nashville [2]	590	Mar. 28	Apr. 19	Nov. 7	Oct. 17	81	7
Tex.	Dallas	481	Mar. 18	Apr. 13	Nov. 12	Oct. 27	35	13
	El Paso	3,918	Mar. 14	Mar. 29	Nov. 12	Nov. 1	61	12
	Houston	96	Feb. 12	Mar. 27	Dec. 4	Nov. 3	22	3
Utah	Salt Lake City [2]	4,220	Apr. 12	Apr. 30	Nov. 1	Sept. 25	137	13
Vt.	Burlington [2]	332	May 8	May 27	Oct. 3	Sept. 13	168	8
Va.	Norfolk [2]	22	Mar. 18	Apr. 14	Nov. 27	Nov. 7	55	24
	Richmond [2]	164	Apr. 2	Apr. 20	Nov. 8	Oct. 21	85	43
Wash.	Seattle	400	Feb. 23	Apr. 2	Nov. 30	Oct. 19	32	13
	Spokane	2,536	Apr. 21	May 14	Oct. 8	Sept. 19	140	13
W. Va.	Charleston [2]	939	Apr. 18	May 11	Oct. 28	Sept. 29	100	25
Wis.	Milwaukee [2]	672	Apr. 20	May 9	Oct. 25	Sept. 24	149	12
Wyo.	Cheyenne [2]	6,126	May 20	June 18	Sept. 27	Sept. 5	173	8
P.R.	San Juan [2]	13	[4]	[4]	[4]	[4]	[4]	17

- Represents zero.   [1] Period ending in 1972.   [2] Period of record 1921–1950.   [3] When frequency of occurrence in either spring or fall is 1 year in 10, or less, mean dates are not given.   [4] 32° F. never recorded.

Source: U.S. National Oceanic and Atmospheric Administration, *Climates of the States*.

No. 366. NORMAL DAILY MEAN TEMPERATURE—SELECTED CITIES

[In Fahrenheit degrees. Airport data except as noted. Based on standard 30-year period, 1941 through 1970. See *Historical Statistics, Colonial Times to 1970*, series J 110–136 and J 164–267, for related data]

STATE AND STATION	Jan.	Feb.	Mar.	Apr.	May	June	July	Aug.	Sept.	Oct.	Nov.	Dec.	Annual avg.
Ala___ Mobile_____	51.2	54.0	59.4	67.9	74.8	80.3	81.6	81.5	77.5	68.9	58.5	52.9	67.4
Alaska_ Juneau_____	23.5	28.0	31.9	38.9	46.8	53.2	55.7	54.3	49.2	41.8	32.5	27.3	40.3
Ariz___ Phoenix_____	51.2	55.1	59.7	67.7	76.3	84.6	91.2	89.1	83.8	72.2	59.8	52.5	70.3
Ark___ Little Rock____	39.5	42.9	50.3	61.7	69.8	78.1	81.4	80.6	73.3	62.4	50.3	41.6	61.0
Calif__ Los Angeles___	54.5	55.6	56.5	58.8	61.9	64.5	68.5	69.5	68.7	65.2	60.5	56.9	61.7
Sacramento___	45.1	49.8	53.0	58.3	64.3	70.5	75.2	74.1	71.5	63.3	53.0	45.8	60.3
San Francisco__	48.3	51.2	53.0	55.3	58.3	61.6	62.5	63.0	64.1	61.0	55.3	49.7	56.9
Colo___ Denver_____	29.9	32.8	37.0	47.5	57.0	66.0	73.0	71.6	62.8	52.0	39.4	32.6	50.1
Conn__ Hartford_____	24.8	26.8	35.6	47.7	58.3	67.8	72.7	70.4	62.8	52.6	41.3	28.2	49.1
Del___ Wilmington____	32.0	33.6	41.6	52.3	62.4	71.4	75.8	74.1	67.9	57.2	45.7	34.7	54.0
D.C___ Washington____	35.6	37.3	45.1	56.4	66.2	74.6	78.7	77.1	70.6	59.8	48.0	37.4	57.3
Fla____ Jacksonville___	54.6	56.3	61.2	68.1	74.3	79.2	81.0	81.0	78.2	70.5	61.2	55.4	68.4
Miami_____	67.2	67.8	71.3	75.0	78.0	81.0	82.3	82.9	81.7	77.8	72.2	68.3	75.5
Ga_____ Atlanta_____	42.4	45.0	51.1	61.1	69.1	75.6	78.0	77.5	72.3	62.4	51.4	43.5	60.8
Hawaii_ Honolulu_____	72.3	72.3	73.0	74.8	76.9	78.9	80.1	80.7	80.4	78.9	76.5	73.7	76.6
Idaho__ Boise_____	29.0	35.5	41.1	49.0	57.4	64.8	74.5	72.2	63.1	52.1	39.8	32.1	50.9
Ill_____ Chicago_____	22.9	26.1	35.7	48.8	58.4	68.1	71.9	71.1	63.7	53.8	39.2	27.1	48.9
Peoria_____	23.8	27.7	37.3	51.3	61.5	71.3	75.1	73.5	65.5	55.0	39.9	28.0	50.8
Ind____ Indianapolis___	27.9	30.7	39.7	52.3	62.2	71.7	75.0	73.2	66.3	55.7	41.7	30.9	52.3
Iowa__ Des Moines___	19.4	24.2	33.9	49.5	60.9	70.5	75.1	73.3	64.3	54.3	37.8	25.0	49.0
Kans__ Wichita_____	31.3	36.3	43.6	56.6	66.1	75.8	80.7	79.7	70.6	59.6	44.8	34.5	56.6
Ky_____ Louisville_____	33.3	35.8	44.0	55.9	64.8	73.3	76.9	75.9	69.1	58.1	45.0	35.6	55.6
La_____ New Orleans___	52.9	55.6	60.7	68.6	75.1	80.4	81.9	81.9	78.2	69.8	60.1	54.8	68.3
Maine__ Portland_____	21.5	22.9	31.8	42.7	52.7	62.2	68.0	66.4	58.7	49.1	38.6	25.7	45.0
Md____ Baltimore_____	33.4	34.8	42.8	53.8	63.7	72.4	76.6	74.9	68.5	57.4	46.1	35.3	55.0
Mass__ Boston_____	29.2	30.4	38.1	48.6	58.6	68.0	73.3	71.3	64.5	55.4	45.2	33.0	51.3
Mich__ Detroit_____	25.5	26.9	35.4	48.1	58.4	69.1	73.3	71.9	64.5	54.3	41.1	29.6	49.9
Sault Ste. Marie_	14.2	15.2	24.0	38.2	49.0	58.7	63.8	63.2	55.3	46.2	32.8	20.1	40.0
Minn__ Duluth_____	8.5	12.1	23.5	38.6	49.4	59.0	65.6	64.1	54.4	45.3	28.4	14.4	38.6
Minneapolis-St. Paul____	12.2	16.5	28.3	45.1	57.1	66.9	71.9	70.2	60.0	50.0	32.4	18.6	44.1
Miss___ Jackson_____	47.1	49.8	56.1	65.7	72.7	79.4	81.7	81.2	76.0	65.8	55.3	48.9	65.0
Mo_____ Kansas City____	27.8	33.1	41.2	55.0	65.0	73.9	78.8	77.4	68.8	58.6	43.6	32.3	54.5
St. Louis_____	31.3	35.1	43.3	56.5	65.8	74.9	78.6	77.2	69.6	59.1	45.0	34.6	55.9
Mont__ Great Falls_____	20.5	26.6	30.5	43.4	53.3	60.8	69.3	67.4	57.3	48.3	34.6	26.5	44.9
Nebr___ Omaha_____	22.6	28.0	37.1	52.3	63.0	72.2	77.2	75.6	66.3	55.9	40.0	28.0	51.5
Nev____ Reno_____	31.9	37.1	40.3	46.8	54.6	61.5	69.3	66.9	60.2	50.3	40.1	33.0	49.4
N.H___ Concord_____	20.6	22.6	32.3	44.2	55.1	64.7	69.7	67.2	59.5	49.3	38.0	24.8	45.6
N.J____ Atlantic City___	32.7	33.9	41.1	51.7	61.6	70.3	75.1	73.4	67.1	56.7	46.0	35.1	53.7
N. Mex_ Albuquerque___	35.2	40.0	45.8	55.8	65.3	74.6	78.7	76.6	70.1	58.2	44.5	36.2	56.8
N.Y____ Albany_____	21.5	23.5	33.4	46.9	57.7	67.5	72.0	69.6	61.9	51.4	39.6	25.9	47.6
Buffalo_____	23.7	24.4	32.1	44.9	55.1	65.7	70.1	68.4	61.6	51.5	39.8	27.9	47.1
New York [1]	32.2	33.4	41.1	52.1	62.3	71.6	76.6	74.9	68.4	58.7	47.4	35.5	54.5
N.C____ Charlotte_____	42.1	44.0	50.6	60.8	68.8	75.9	78.5	77.7	72.0	61.7	51.0	42.5	60.5
Raleigh_____	40.5	42.2	49.2	59.5	67.4	74.4	77.5	76.5	70.6	60.2	50.0	41.2	59.1
N. Dak_ Bismarck_____	8.2	13.5	25.1	43.0	54.4	63.8	70.8	69.2	57.5	46.8	28.9	15.6	41.4
Ohio___ Cincinnati_____	31.1	33.3	41.7	53.9	63.2	72.1	75.6	74.4	67.8	56.8	43.8	33.7	54.0
Cleveland_____	26.9	27.9	36.1	48.3	58.3	67.9	71.4	70.0	63.9	53.8	41.6	30.3	49.7
Columbus_____	28.4	30.3	39.2	51.2	61.1	70.4	73.6	71.9	65.2	54.2	41.7	30.7	51.5
Okla___ Oklahoma City_	36.8	41.3	48.2	60.4	68.3	76.8	81.5	81.1	73.0	62.4	49.2	40.0	59.9
Oreg___ Portland_____	38.1	42.8	45.7	50.6	56.7	62.0	67.1	66.6	62.2	53.8	45.3	40.7	52.6
Pa_____ Philadelphia____	32.3	33.9	41.9	52.9	63.2	72.3	76.8	74.8	68.1	57.4	46.2	35.2	54.6
Pittsburgh_____	28.1	29.3	38.1	50.2	59.8	68.6	71.9	70.2	63.8	53.2	41.3	30.5	50.4
R.I_____ Providence_____	28.4	29.4	36.9	47.3	56.9	66.4	72.1	70.4	63.4	53.7	43.3	31.5	50.0
S.C____ Columbia_____	45.4	47.6	54.2	64.1	72.1	78.8	81.2	80.2	74.5	64.2	53.8	46.0	63.5
S. Dak_ Sioux Falls_____	14.2	19.4	30.0	46.1	57.7	67.6	73.3	71.8	60.9	50.2	33.1	20.0	45.4
Tenn___ Memphis_____	40.5	43.8	51.0	62.5	70.9	78.6	81.6	80.4	73.6	63.0	50.9	42.7	61.6
Nashville_____	38.3	41.0	48.7	60.1	68.5	76.6	79.6	78.5	72.0	60.9	48.4	40.4	59.4
Tex_____ Dallas-Fort Worth_____	44.8	48.7	55.0	65.2	72.5	80.6	84.8	84.9	77.7	67.6	55.8	47.9	65.5
El Paso_____	43.6	48.4	54.6	63.9	72.2	80.3	82.3	80.5	74.2	64.0	51.6	44.4	63.4
Houston_____	52.1	55.3	60.8	69.4	75.8	81.1	83.3	83.4	79.2	70.9	61.1	54.6	68.9
Utah___ Salt Lake City__	28.0	33.4	39.6	49.2	58.3	66.2	76.7	74.5	64.8	52.4	39.1	30.3	51.0
Vt_____ Burlington_____	16.8	18.6	29.1	43.0	54.8	65.2	69.8	67.4	59.3	48.8	37.0	22.6	44.4
Va_____ Norfolk_____	40.5	41.4	48.1	57.8	66.7	74.5	78.3	76.9	71.8	61.7	51.6	42.3	59.3
Richmond_____	37.5	39.4	46.9	57.8	66.5	74.2	77.9	76.3	70.0	59.3	49.0	39.0	57.8
Wash___ Seattle-Tacoma_	38.2	42.3	44.1	48.7	54.9	59.8	64.5	63.8	59.6	52.2	44.6	40.5	51.1
Spokane_____	25.4	32.2	37.5	46.1	54.7	61.5	69.7	68.0	59.6	47.8	35.5	29.0	47.3
W.Va___ Charleston_____	34.5	36.5	44.5	55.9	64.5	72.0	75.0	73.6	67.5	57.0	45.4	36.2	55.2
Wis____ Milwaukee_____	19.4	22.5	31.4	44.7	54.2	64.5	69.9	69.2	61.1	51.0	36.5	24.2	45.7
Wyo___ Cheyenne_____	26.6	29.0	31.6	42.7	52.4	61.3	69.1	67.6	58.2	47.9	35.5	29.2	45.9
P.R_____ San Juan_____	75.4	75.3	76.3	77.5	79.2	80.5	80.9	81.3	81.1	80.6	78.7	76.8	78.6

[1] City office data.

Source: U.S. National Oceanic and Atmospheric Administration, *Climatography of the United States*, No. 81.

220   Geography and Environment

No. 367. Normal Daily Maximum Temperature—Selected Cities

[In Fahrenheit degrees. Airport data except as noted. Based on standard 30-year period, 1941 through 1970]

STATE AND STATION	Jan.	Feb.	Mar.	Apr.	May	June	July	Aug.	Sept.	Oct.	Nov.	Dec.	Annual avg.
Ala_____ Mobile_____	61.1	64.1	69.5	78.0	85.0	89.8	90.5	90.6	86.5	79.7	69.5	63.0	77.3
Alaska_ Juneau_____	29.1	33.9	38.2	46.5	55.4	62.0	63.6	62.3	56.1	47.2	37.3	32.0	47.0
Ariz.___ Phoenix_____	64.8	69.3	74.5	83.6	92.9	101.5	104.8	102.2	98.4	87.6	74.7	66.4	85.1
Ark____ Little Rock_____	50.1	53.8	61.8	73.5	81.4	89.3	92.6	92.6	85.8	76.0	62.4	52.1	72.6
Calif.___ Los Angeles____	63.5	64.1	64.3	65.9	68.4	70.3	74.8	75.8	75.7	72.9	69.6	66.5	69.2
Sacramento_____	53.0	59.1	64.1	71.3	78.8	86.4	92.9	91.3	87.7	77.1	63.6	53.3	73.2
San Francisco___	55.3	58.6	61.0	63.5	66.6	70.2	70.9	71.6	73.6	70.3	63.3	56.5	65.1
Colo.___ Denver_____	43.5	46.2	50.1	61.0	70.3	80.1	87.4	85.8	77.7	66.8	53.3	46.2	64.0
Conn.___ Hartford_____	33.4	35.7	44.6	58.9	70.3	79.5	84.1	81.9	74.5	64.3	50.6	36.8	59.6
Del_____ Wilmington_____	40.2	42.2	51.1	63.0	73.1	81.6	85.5	83.9	78.2	67.8	55.2	43.0	63.7
D.C.___ Washington_____	43.5	46.0	55.0	67.1	76.6	84.6	88.2	86.6	80.2	69.8	57.2	45.2	66.7
Fla_____ Jacksonville____	64.6	66.9	72.2	79.0	84.6	88.3	90.0	89.7	86.0	79.2	71.4	65.6	78.1
Miami_____	75.6	76.6	79.5	82.7	85.3	88.0	89.1	89.9	88.3	84.6	79.9	76.6	83.0
Ga_____ Atlanta_____	51.4	54.5	61.1	71.4	79.0	84.6	86.5	86.4	81.2	72.5	61.9	52.7	70.3
Hawaii_ Honolulu_____	79.3	79.2	79.7	81.4	83.6	85.6	86.8	87.4	87.4	85.8	83.2	80.3	83.3
Idaho__ Boise_____	36.5	43.8	51.6	61.4	70.6	78.3	90.5	87.6	77.6	64.7	48.9	39.1	62.6
Ill_____ Chicago_____	31.1	34.3	44.6	59.4	69.7	79.1	83.1	82.3	75.4	65.5	48.3	35.0	59.0
Peoria_____	31.9	36.0	46.5	61.7	72.3	81.7	85.5	84.0	76.4	65.9	48.7	35.7	60.5
Ind_____ Indianapolis____	36.0	39.3	49.0	62.8	72.9	82.3	85.4	84.0	77.0	67.0	50.5	38.7	62.2
Iowa___ Des Moines_____	27.5	32.5	42.5	59.7	70.9	79.8	84.9	83.2	74.6	64.9	46.4	32.8	58.3
Kans___ Wichita_____	41.4	47.1	55.0	68.1	77.1	86.5	91.7	91.0	81.9	71.3	55.8	44.3	67.6
Ky_____ Louisville_____	42.0	45.0	54.0	66.9	75.6	83.7	87.3	86.8	80.5	70.3	54.9	44.1	65.9
La_____ New Orleans____	62.3	65.1	70.4	78.4	84.9	89.6	90.4	90.6	86.6	79.9	70.3	64.2	77.7
Maine__ Portland_____	31.2	33.3	40.8	52.8	63.6	73.2	79.1	77.6	69.9	60.2	47.5	34.9	55.3
Md_____ Baltimore_____	41.9	43.9	53.0	65.2	74.8	83.2	86.7	85.1	79.0	68.3	56.1	43.9	65.1
Mass___ Boston_____	35.9	37.5	44.6	56.3	67.1	76.6	81.4	79.3	72.2	63.2	51.7	39.3	58.7
Mich___ Detroit_____	31.7	33.7	43.1	57.6	68.5	79.1	83.1	81.6	74.2	63.4	47.7	35.4	58.3
Sault Ste. Marie_	22.0	23.7	32.5	47.2	59.4	70.0	75.1	73.4	64.5	54.8	39.0	26.8	49.0
Minn___ Duluth_____	17.6	22.1	32.6	47.8	60.0	69.7	76.4	74.4	64.0	54.3	35.3	22.5	48.1
Minneapolis-St. Paul_____	21.2	25.9	36.9	55.5	67.9	77.1	82.4	80.8	70.7	60.7	40.6	26.6	53.8
Miss___ Jackson_____	58.4	61.7	68.7	78.2	85.0	91.0	92.7	92.6	88.0	80.1	68.5	60.5	77.1
Mo_____ Kansas City____	36.2	41.9	50.5	64.8	74.3	82.6	88.0	86.7	78.8	68.9	52.7	40.4	63.7
St. Louis_____	39.9	44.2	53.0	67.0	76.0	84.9	88.4	87.2	80.1	69.8	54.1	42.7	65.6
Mont___ Great Falls_____	29.3	35.9	40.4	54.5	65.0	72.1	83.7	81.8	70.0	59.4	43.4	34.7	55.9
Nebr___ Omaha_____	32.7	38.5	47.7	64.4	74.4	83.1	88.6	87.2	78.6	69.1	50.9	37.8	62.8
Nev____ Reno_____	45.4	51.1	56.0	64.0	72.2	80.4	91.1	89.0	81.8	70.0	56.3	46.4	67.0
N.H.___ Concord_____	31.3	33.8	42.4	56.7	68.6	77.7	82.6	80.1	72.4	62.3	47.9	34.6	57.5
N.J.____ Atlantic City___	41.4	42.9	50.7	62.3	72.4	80.8	84.7	83.0	77.3	67.5	55.9	44.2	63.6
N. Mex. Albuquerque___	46.9	52.6	59.2	70.1	79.9	89.5	92.2	89.7	83.4	71.7	57.1	47.5	70.0
N.Y.___ Albany_____	30.4	32.7	42.6	58.0	69.7	79.4	83.9	81.4	73.7	62.8	48.1	34.1	58.1
Buffalo_____	29.8	31.0	39.0	53.3	64.3	75.1	79.5	77.6	70.8	60.2	46.1	33.6	55.0
New York [1]_____	38.5	40.2	48.4	60.7	71.4	80.5	85.2	83.4	76.8	66.8	54.0	41.4	62.3
N.C.___ Charlotte_____	52.1	54.9	62.2	72.7	80.2	86.4	88.3	87.4	82.0	73.1	62.4	52.5	71.2
Raleigh_____	51.0	53.2	61.0	72.2	79.4	85.6	87.7	86.8	81.5	72.4	62.1	51.9	70.4
N. Dak_ Bismarck_____	19.1	24.5	35.4	54.8	67.1	75.8	84.3	83.5	71.3	60.3	39.4	26.0	53.5
Ohio___ Cincinnati_____	39.7	42.7	51.8	65.0	74.4	83.2	86.5	85.8	79.7	68.5	53.2	42.0	64.4
Cleveland_____	33.4	35.0	44.1	58.0	68.4	78.2	81.6	80.4	74.2	63.8	48.8	36.4	58.5
Columbus_____	36.4	39.2	49.3	62.8	72.9	81.9	84.8	83.7	77.6	66.4	50.9	38.7	62.1
Okla___ Oklahoma City_	47.6	52.6	59.8	71.6	78.7	87.0	92.6	92.5	84.7	74.2	60.9	50.0	71.1
Oreg___ Portland_____	43.6	50.1	54.3	60.3	67.0	72.1	79.0	78.1	73.9	62.9	52.1	46.0	61.6
Pa_____ Philadelphia____	40.1	42.2	51.2	63.5	74.1	83.0	86.8	84.8	78.4	67.9	55.5	43.2	64.2
Pittsburgh_____	35.3	37.3	47.2	60.9	70.8	79.5	82.5	80.9	74.9	63.9	49.3	37.3	60.0
R.I.____ Providence_____	36.2	37.6	44.7	56.7	66.8	76.3	81.1	79.8	73.1	63.9	52.0	39.6	59.0
S.C.___ Columbia_____	56.9	59.7	66.5	76.9	84.5	90.3	92.0	91.0	85.4	77.1	66.9	57.9	75.4
S. Dak_ Sioux Falls_____	24.6	29.7	39.7	57.8	69.7	78.9	85.1	83.8	73.0	62.7	43.5	29.6	56.5
Tenn___ Memphis_____	49.4	53.1	60.8	72.7	81.2	88.7	91.6	90.6	84.3	74.9	61.5	51.7	71.7
Nashville_____	47.6	50.9	59.2	71.3	79.8	87.5	90.2	89.2	83.5	73.2	59.0	49.6	70.1
Tex____ Dallas-Fort Worth_____	55.7	59.8	66.6	76.3	82.8	90.8	95.5	96.1	88.5	79.2	67.5	58.7	76.5
El Paso_____	57.0	62.5	68.9	78.5	87.2	94.9	94.6	92.8	87.4	78.5	66.1	57.8	77.2
Houston_____	62.6	66.0	71.8	79.4	85.9	91.3	93.8	94.3	90.1	83.5	73.0	65.8	79.8
Utah___ Salt Lake City__	37.4	43.4	50.8	61.8	72.4	81.3	92.8	90.2	80.3	66.4	50.0	39.0	63.8
Vt_____ Burlington_____	25.9	28.2	38.0	53.3	66.1	76.5	81.0	78.3	70.0	58.7	44.3	30.3	54.2
Va_____ Norfolk_____	48.8	50.0	57.3	67.7	76.2	83.5	86.6	84.9	79.6	70.1	60.5	50.6	68.0
Richmond_____	47.4	49.9	58.2	70.3	78.4	85.4	88.2	86.6	80.9	71.2	60.6	49.1	68.8
Wash__ Seattle-Tacoma_	43.4	48.5	51.5	57.0	64.1	69.0	75.1	73.8	68.7	59.4	50.4	45.4	58.8
Spokane_____	31.1	39.0	46.2	57.0	66.5	73.6	84.3	81.9	72.5	58.1	41.8	33.9	57.2
W.Va.__ Charleston_____	43.6	46.2	55.2	67.9	76.6	83.4	85.6	84.4	79.0	69.1	55.8	45.2	66.0
Wis____ Milwaukee_____	27.3	30.3	39.4	54.6	65.0	75.3	80.4	79.7	71.5	61.4	44.4	31.5	55.1
Wyo___ Cheyenne_____	38.2	40.7	43.5	55.4	65.1	74.4	83.7	81.9	72.8	61.8	47.5	40.3	58.8
P.R.____ San Juan_____	81.9	82.1	83.6	84.4	85.6	87.0	87.0	87.5	87.6	87.4	85.0	83.1	85.2

[1] City office data.

Source: U.S. National Oceanic and Atmospheric Administration, *Climatography of the United States*, No. 81.

No. 368. NORMAL DAILY MINIMUM TEMPERATURE—SELECTED CITIES

[In Fahrenheit degrees. Airport data except as noted. Based on standard 30-year period, 1941 through 1970]

STATE AND STATION		Jan.	Feb.	Mar.	Apr.	May	June	July	Aug.	Sept.	Oct.	Nov.	Dec.	Annual avg.
Ala	Mobile	41.3	43.9	49.2	57.7	64.5	70.7	72.6	72.3	68.4	58.0	47.5	42.8	57.4
Alaska	Juneau	17.8	22.1	25.6	31.3	38.2	44.4	47.7	46.2	42.3	36.4	27.6	22.5	33.5
Ariz	Phoenix	37.6	40.8	44.8	51.8	59.6	67.7	77.5	76.0	69.1	56.8	44.8	38.5	55.4
Ark	Little Rock	28.9	31.9	38.7	49.9	58.1	66.8	70.1	68.6	60.8	48.7	38.1	31.1	49.3
Calif	Los Angeles	45.4	47.0	48.6	51.7	55.3	58.6	62.1	63.2	61.6	57.5	51.3	47.3	54.1
	Sacramento	37.1	40.4	41.9	45.3	49.8	54.6	57.5	56.9	55.3	49.5	42.4	38.3	47.4
	San Francisco	41.2	43.8	44.9	47.0	49.9	53.0	54.0	54.3	54.5	51.6	47.2	42.9	48.7
Colo	Denver	16.2	19.4	23.8	33.9	43.6	51.9	58.6	57.4	47.8	37.2	25.4	18.9	36.2
Conn	Hartford	16.1	17.9	26.6	36.5	46.2	56.0	61.2	58.9	51.0	40.8	31.9	19.6	38.6
Del	Wilmington	23.8	24.9	32.0	41.5	51.6	61.1	66.1	64.3	57.6	46.5	36.2	26.3	44.3
D.C	Washington	27.7	28.6	35.2	45.7	55.7	64.6	69.1	67.6	61.0	49.7	38.8	29.5	47.8
Fla	Jacksonville	44.5	45.7	50.1	57.1	63.9	70.0	72.0	72.3	70.4	61.7	51.0	45.1	58.7
	Miami	58.7	59.0	63.0	67.3	70.7	73.9	75.5	75.8	75.0	71.0	64.5	60.0	67.9
Ga	Atlanta	33.4	35.5	41.1	50.7	59.2	66.6	69.4	68.6	63.4	52.3	40.8	34.3	51.3
Hawaii	Honolulu	65.3	65.3	66.3	68.1	70.2	72.2	73.4	74.0	73.4	72.0	69.8	67.1	69.8
Idaho	Boise	21.4	27.2	30.5	36.5	44.1	51.2	58.5	56.7	48.5	39.4	30.7	25.0	39.1
Ill	Chicago	14.7	17.8	26.7	38.2	47.0	57.0	60.7	59.9	52.0	42.0	30.1	19.2	38.8
	Peoria	15.7	19.3	28.1	40.8	50.7	60.9	64.6	62.9	54.6	44.0	31.1	20.3	41.1
Ind	Indianapolis	19.7	22.1	30.3	41.8	51.5	61.1	64.6	62.4	54.9	44.3	32.8	23.1	42.4
Iowa	Des Moines	11.3	15.8	25.2	39.2	50.9	61.1	65.3	63.4	54.0	43.6	29.2	17.2	39.7
Kans	Wichita	21.2	25.4	32.1	45.1	55.0	65.0	69.6	68.3	59.2	47.9	33.8	24.6	45.6
Ky	Louisville	24.5	26.5	34.0	44.8	53.9	62.9	66.4	64.9	57.7	45.9	35.1	27.1	45.3
La	New Orleans	43.5	46.0	50.9	58.8	65.3	71.2	73.3	73.1	69.7	59.6	49.8	45.3	58.9
Maine	Portland	11.7	12.5	22.8	32.5	41.7	51.1	56.9	55.2	47.4	38.0	29.7	16.4	34.7
Md	Baltimore	24.9	25.7	32.5	42.4	52.5	61.6	66.5	64.7	57.9	46.4	36.0	26.6	44.8
Mass	Boston	22.5	23.3	31.5	40.8	50.1	59.3	65.1	63.3	56.7	47.5	38.7	26.6	43.8
Mich	Detroit	19.2	20.1	27.6	38.6	48.3	59.1	63.4	62.1	54.8	45.2	34.4	23.8	41.4
	Sault Ste. Marie	6.4	6.7	15.5	29.2	38.5	47.3	52.5	52.9	46.1	37.6	26.5	13.3	31.0
Minn	Duluth	−.6	2.0	14.4	29.3	38.8	48.3	54.7	53.7	44.8	36.2	21.4	6.3	29.1
	Minneapolis-St. Paul	3.2	7.1	19.6	34.7	46.3	56.7	61.4	59.6	49.3	39.2	24.2	10.6	34.3
Miss	Jackson	35.8	37.8	43.4	53.1	60.4	67.7	70.6	69.8	64.0	51.5	42.0	37.3	52.8
Mo	Kansas City	19.3	24.2	31.8	45.1	55.7	65.2	69.6	68.1	58.8	48.3	34.5	24.1	45.3
	St. Louis	22.6	26.0	33.5	46.0	55.5	64.8	68.8	67.1	59.1	48.4	35.9	26.5	46.2
Mont	Great Falls	11.6	17.2	20.6	32.3	41.5	49.5	54.9	53.0	44.6	37.1	25.7	18.2	33.8
Nebr	Omaha	12.4	17.4	26.4	40.1	51.5	61.3	65.8	64.0	54.0	42.6	29.1	18.1	40.2
Nev	Reno	18.3	23.0	24.6	29.6	37.0	42.5	47.4	44.8	38.6	30.5	23.9	19.6	31.7
N.H	Concord	9.9	11.3	22.1	31.7	41.5	51.6	56.7	54.2	46.5	36.3	28.1	14.9	33.7
N.J	Atlantic City	24.0	24.9	31.5	41.0	50.7	59.7	65.4	63.8	56.8	45.9	36.1	26.0	43.8
N. Mex	Albuquerque	23.5	27.4	32.3	41.4	50.7	59.7	65.2	63.4	56.7	44.7	31.8	24.9	43.5
N.Y	Albany	12.5	14.3	24.2	35.7	45.7	55.6	60.1	57.8	50.1	40.0	31.1	17.7	37.1
	Buffalo	17.6	17.7	25.2	36.4	45.9	56.3	60.7	59.1	52.3	42.7	33.5	22.2	39.1
	New York [1]	25.9	26.5	33.7	43.5	53.1	62.6	68.0	66.4	59.9	50.6	40.8	29.5	46.7
N.C	Charlotte	32.1	33.1	39.0	48.9	57.4	65.3	68.7	67.9	61.9	50.3	39.6	32.4	49.7
	Raleigh	30.0	31.1	37.4	46.7	55.4	63.1	67.2	66.2	59.7	48.0	37.8	30.5	47.8
N. Dak	Bismarck	−2.8	2.4	14.7	31.1	41.7	51.8	57.3	54.9	43.7	33.2	18.3	5.2	29.3
Ohio	Cincinnati	22.4	23.8	31.6	42.7	51.9	61.0	64.6	63.0	55.9	45.0	34.3	23.4	43.5
	Cleveland	20.3	20.8	28.1	38.5	48.1	57.5	61.2	59.6	53.5	43.9	34.4	24.1	40.8
	Columbus	20.4	21.4	29.1	39.5	49.3	58.9	62.4	60.1	52.7	42.0	32.4	22.7	40.9
Okla	Oklahoma City	26.0	30.0	36.5	49.1	57.9	66.6	70.4	69.6	61.3	50.6	37.4	29.2	48.7
Oreg	Portland	32.5	35.5	37.0	40.8	46.3	51.8	55.2	55.0	50.5	44.7	38.5	35.3	43.6
Pa	Philadelphia	24.4	25.5	32.5	42.3	52.3	61.6	66.7	64.7	57.8	46.9	36.9	27.2	44.9
	Pittsburgh	20.8	21.3	29.0	39.4	48.7	57.7	61.3	59.4	52.7	42.4	33.3	23.6	40.8
R.I	Providence	20.6	21.2	29.0	37.8	46.9	56.5	63.0	61.0	53.6	43.4	34.6	23.4	40.9
S.C	Columbia	33.9	35.5	41.9	51.3	59.6	67.2	70.3	69.4	63.5	51.3	40.6	34.1	51.5
S. Dak	Sioux Falls	3.7	9.0	20.2	34.4	45.7	56.3	61.5	59.8	48.7	37.6	22.7	10.4	34.2
Tenn	Memphis	31.6	34.4	41.1	52.3	60.6	68.5	71.5	70.1	62.8	51.1	40.3	33.7	51.5
	Nashville	29.0	31.0	38.1	48.8	57.3	65.7	69.0	67.7	60.5	48.6	37.7	31.1	48.7
Tex	Dallas-Fort Worth	33.9	37.6	43.3	54.1	62.1	70.3	74.0	73.7	66.8	56.0	44.1	37.0	54.4
	El Paso	30.2	34.3	40.3	49.3	57.2	65.7	69.9	68.2	61.0	49.5	37.0	30.9	49.5
	Houston	41.5	44.6	49.8	59.3	65.6	70.9	72.8	72.4	68.2	58.3	49.1	43.4	58.0
Utah	Salt Lake City	18.5	23.3	28.3	36.6	44.2	51.1	60.5	58.7	49.3	38.4	28.1	21.5	38.2
Vt	Burlington	7.6	8.9	20.1	32.6	43.5	53.9	58.5	56.4	48.6	38.8	29.7	14.8	34.5
Va	Norfolk	32.2	32.7	38.9	47.9	57.2	65.5	69.9	68.9	63.3	53.3	42.6	34.0	50.6
	Richmond	27.6	28.8	35.5	45.2	54.5	62.9	67.5	65.9	59.0	47.4	37.3	28.8	46.7
Wash	Seattle-Tacoma	33.0	36.0	36.6	40.3	45.6	50.6	53.8	53.7	50.4	44.9	38.8	35.5	43.3
	Spokane	19.6	25.3	28.8	35.2	42.8	49.4	55.1	54.0	46.7	37.5	29.2	24.0	37.3
W. Va	Charleston	25.3	26.8	33.8	43.8	52.3	60.6	64.3	62.8	55.9	44.8	35.0	27.2	44.4
Wis	Milwaukee	11.4	14.6	23.4	34.7	43.3	53.6	59.3	58.7	50.7	40.6	28.5	16.8	36.3
Wyo	Cheyenne	14.9	17.3	19.6	30.0	39.7	48.1	54.5	53.2	43.5	33.9	23.5	18.1	33.0
P.R	San Juan	68.8	68.4	68.9	70.6	72.8	74.0	74.8	75.1	74.6	73.7	72.3	70.5	72.0

[1] City office data.

Source: U.S. National Oceanic and Atmospheric Administration, *Climatography of the United States*, No. 81.

No. 369. HIGHEST TEMPERATURE OF RECORD—SELECTED CITIES

[In Fahrenheit degrees. Airport data unless otherwise noted. For period of record through 1977]

STATE AND STATION	Length of record (yr.)	Jan.	Feb.	Mar.	Apr.	May	June	July	Aug.	Sept.	Oct.	Nov.	Dec.	Annual
Ala — Mobile	36	84	82	90	92	100	102	104	102	98	93	87	81	104
Alaska — Juneau	34	57	55	55	71	82	86	90	83	72	61	56	54	90
Ariz — Phoenix	40	88	89	95	104	113	117	118	116	118	104	93	88	118
Ark — Little Rock	36	83	83	91	92	98	104	107	108	106	97	86	80	108
Calif — Los Angeles	42	88	92	88	95	97	100	97	98	110	106	101	94	110
Sacramento	27	70	76	86	92	104	115	114	108	108	101	87	72	115
San Francisco	50	72	78	85	88	96	106	104	98	103	95	85	75	106
Colo — Denver	43	72	76	84	85	96	104	104	101	97	88	79	74	104
Conn — Hartford	23	65	70	87	96	96	100	102	101	96	91	81	65	102
Del — Wilmington	30	75	74	86	91	95	99	102	101	100	91	85	72	102
D.C — Washington	36	79	82	89	95	97	101	103	100	100	94	86	75	103
Fla — Jacksonville	36	85	88	91	95	100	103	105	102	100	96	88	84	105
Miami	35	87	89	92	96	94	98	96	98	95	92	89	86	98
Ga — Atlanta	29	79	79	85	88	95	101	103	102	98	95	84	77	103
Hawaii — Honolulu	8	85	87	87	87	88	90	90	92	92	91	89	89	92
Idaho — Boise	38	63	69	78	92	98	109	111	110	102	91	73	65	111
Ill — Chicago	19	61	71	80	87	93	97	98	96	99	91	77	67	99
Peoria	38	68	72	81	89	92	100	103	101	100	90	81	71	103
Ind — Indianapolis	38	71	74	81	89	93	102	104	100	100	90	81	70	104
Iowa — Des Moines	38	62	73	83	90	98	101	105	102	101	95	76	69	105
Kans — Wichita	25	75	84	89	96	100	106	113	110	103	95	80	83	113
Ky — Louisville	30	77	77	85	91	95	102	105	101	104	92	84	73	105
La — New Orleans	31	83	85	87	91	96	100	99	100	97	92	86	84	100
Maine — Portland	37	64	64	86	85	92	97	99	103	95	88	74	62	103
Md — Baltimore	27	75	76	85	94	98	100	102	102	99	92	83	74	102
Mass — Boston	26	63	68	81	94	93	100	102	102	100	90	77	70	102
Mich — Detroit	43	67	68	82	87	93	104	105	101	100	92	81	66	105
Sault Ste. Marie	37	45	45	75	83	89	92	97	98	95	80	66	59	98
Minn — Duluth	36	52	55	78	88	90	93	97	97	95	86	69	55	97
Minneapolis-St. Paul	39	58	59	83	92	95	100	104	102	98	89	75	67	104
Miss — Jackson	14	82	84	88	92	99	103	102	99	98	91	88	81	103
Mo — Kansas City	5	61	74	82	85	91	98	107	104	98	92	78	67	107
St. Louis	20	76	85	88	92	92	98	106	105	100	94	81	76	106
Mont — Great Falls	40	62	67	72	87	90	99	105	106	98	91	76	69	106
Nebr — Omaha	42	69	78	89	93	99	105	114	110	104	96	80	72	114
Nev — Reno	36	70	74	83	88	95	101	104	103	101	91	77	70	104
N.H — Concord	36	68	66	85	95	97	98	102	101	98	90	80	63	102
N.J — Atlantic City	34	78	73	87	94	99	106	104	102	97	90	84	72	106
N. Mex — Albuquerque	38	69	75	85	89	95	105	104	100	98	87	77	72	105
N.Y — Albany	31	62	67	85	92	94	99	100	99	100	89	82	65	100
Buffalo	34	72	64	81	87	90	95	94	99	98	87	80	66	99
New York [1]	109	72	75	86	96	99	101	106	104	102	94	84	70	106
N.C — Charlotte	38	78	81	90	93	100	103	103	102	104	98	85	77	104
Raleigh	33	79	84	92	93	97	104	105	101	104	98	88	78	105
N. Dak — Bismarck	38	54	68	81	92	98	100	109	109	105	95	75	62	109
Ohio — Cincinnati	16	69	73	82	89	93	97	100	102	98	88	80	70	102
Cleveland	36	73	69	83	88	92	101	103	102	101	90	82	69	103
Columbus	38	74	73	85	89	94	102	100	100	100	90	80	72	102
Okla — Oklahoma City	24	79	84	93	100	96	102	108	107	102	96	84	86	108
Oreg — Portland	37	62	70	80	87	92	100	107	105	101	90	73	64	107
Pa — Philadelphia	36	74	74	87	94	96	100	104	101	100	96	81	72	104
Pittsburgh	25	68	69	80	87	91	96	99	97	97	87	82	72	99
R.I — Providence	24	66	69	78	98	94	95	100	104	93	85	78	69	104
S.C — Columbia	30	84	84	91	94	101	107	107	106	101	101	90	83	108
S. Dak — Sioux Falls	32	59	70	87	94	100	101	108	108	104	94	76	61	108
Tenn — Memphis	36	78	81	85	91	99	104	106	105	103	95	85	79	106
Nashville	38	78	84	86	90	97	106	107	104	105	94	84	76	107
Tex — Dallas-Fort Worth	24	88	88	96	95	96	105	109	108	105	98	89	88	109
El Paso	38	80	83	88	98	104	109	109	105	103	96	84	80	109
Houston	8	84	84	90	89	94	99	101	101	97	93	88	83	101
Utah — Salt Lake City	49	61	69	78	85	93	104	107	103	98	89	75	67	107
Vt — Burlington	34	63	60	84	91	93	96	99	101	94	85	75	62	101
Va — Norfolk	29	78	81	85	97	97	101	103	102	98	95	86	79	103
Richmond	48	80	83	93	96	100	104	105	102	103	99	88	80	105
Wash — Seattle-Tacoma	33	61	70	72	85	93	96	97	99	93	81	74	61	99
Spokane	30	59	61	71	90	92	100	103	108	96	85	67	54	108
W. Va — Charleston	30	79	78	87	91	93	98	102	100	102	92	85	80	102
Wis — Milwaukee	37	62	65	81	85	92	99	101	100	96	89	77	63	101
Wyo — Cheyenne	42	63	71	73	82	90	100	100	96	93	83	73	69	100
P.R — San Juan	23	90	92	93	94	94	96	93	96	94	95	92	90	96

[1] City office data.

Source: U.S. National Oceanic and Atmospheric Administration, *Comparative Climatic Data*, annual.

No. 370. Lowest Temperature of Record—Selected Cities

[In Fahrenheit degrees. Airport data unless otherwise noted. For period of record through 1977]

STATE AND STATION	Length of record (yr.)	Jan.	Feb.	Mar.	Apr.	May	June	July	Aug.	Sept.	Oct.	Nov.	Dec.	Annual
Ala_____ Mobile_____	36	8	11	11	36	43	56	60	59	42	32	22	10	8
Alaska____ Juneau_____	34	−22	−22	−15	6	25	31	36	27	23	12	−5	−21	−22
Ariz_____ Phoenix_____	40	17	22	25	32	40	50	61	60	47	34	25	22	17
Ark_____ Little Rock_____	36	−4	−5	11	28	40	46	54	52	37	31	17	−1	−5
Calif_____ Los Angeles_____	42	23	32	34	39	43	48	49	51	47	41	34	32	23
Sacramento_____	27	23	26	26	32	36	41	49	49	43	36	26	20	20
San Francisco_____	50	24	25	30	31	36	41	43	42	38	34	25	20	20
Colo_____ Denver_____	43	−25	−30	−11	−2	22	30	43	41	20	3	−8	−18	−30
Conn_____ Hartford_____	23	−26	−21	−6	9	28	37	44	36	30	18	12	−9	−26
Del_____ Wilmington_____	30	−4	−4	9	22	32	41	50	46	36	24	14	3	−4
D.C_____ Washington_____	36	2	4	11	24	34	47	55	51	39	29	16	1	1
Fla_____ Jacksonville____	36	19	19	25	35	45	56	61	64	50	36	21	12	12
Miami_____	35	31	32	37	46	53	65	69	68	69	51	39	34	31
Ga_____ Atlanta_____	29	−3	5	10	26	37	46	53	56	36	28	3	1	−3
Hawaii____ Honolulu_____	8	53	53	55	59	63	65	67	67	66	64	58	54	53
Idaho_____ Boise_____	38	−17	−10	6	19	26	33	41	37	23	11	−3	−23	−23
Ill_____ Chicago_____	19	−20	−17	−8	13	24	36	40	41	28	19	1	−17	−20
Peoria_____	38	−25	−16	−10	17	25	39	47	43	26	19	−2	−18	−25
Ind_____ Indianapolis____	38	−20	−19	−6	16	28	39	44	41	28	17	−2	−15	−20
Iowa_____ Des Moines_____	38	−24	−20	−22	9	30	38	47	40	26	14	−3	−16	−24
Kans_____ Wichita_____	25	−12	−6	−2	15	31	43	51	48	35	21	1	−5	−12
Ky_____ Louisville_____	30	−20	−19	−1	24	31	42	50	49	33	23	−1	−9	−20
La_____ New Orleans_____	31	14	19	26	32	41	55	60	60	42	35	24	17	14
Maine_____ Portland_____	37	−26	−39	−21	8	23	33	40	33	23	15	5	−21	−39
Md_____ Baltimore_____	27	−7	−1	6	20	32	40	52	48	35	25	13	0	−7
Mass_____ Boston_____	26	−12	−4	6	17	34	46	54	47	38	28	17	−4	−12
Mich_____ Detroit_____	43	−13	−16	−1	14	30	38	42	43	32	24	5	−5	−16
Sault Ste. Marie__	37	−30	−28	−24	1	18	28	36	32	25	16	−10	−24	−30
Minn_____ Duluth_____	36	−39	−32	−28	−5	17	27	36	33	22	8	−23	−33	−39
Minneapolis-St. Paul	39	−34	−28	−32	2	18	34	43	39	26	15	17	24	04
Miss_____ Jackson_____	14	6	11	18	30	38	49	51	55	35	30	17	14	6
Mo_____ Kansas City_____	5	−13	−2	8	12	30	49	52	50	39	21	1	−11	−13
St. Louis_____	20	−14	−5	−5	22	31	43	51	47	36	23	1	−10	−14
Mont_____ Great Falls_____	40	−37	−35	−29	−6	15	31	40	35	23	−3	−23	−43	−43
Nebr_____ Omaha_____	42	−22	−19	−16	5	27	39	44	43	30	13	−9	−15	−22
Nev_____ Reno_____	36	−16	−12	−2	13	18	25	33	24	20	8	1	−16	−16
N.H_____ Concord_____	36	−30	−37	−16	8	21	30	35	29	21	10	−1	−22	−37
N.J_____ Atlantic City___	34	−10	−7	7	12	25	37	46	40	32	23	11	−7	−10
N. Mex___ Albuquerque_____	38	−17	−5	8	19	28	42	54	52	37	25	−7	3	−17
N.Y_____ Albany_____	31	−28	−21	−21	10	26	36	41	37	24	16	5	−22	−28
Buffalo_____	34	−12	−20	−4	12	26	35	43	38	32	20	9	−4	−20
New York [1]_____	109	−6	−15	3	12	32	44	52	50	39	28	5	−13	−15
N.C_____ Charlotte_____	38	−3	5	10	24	32	45	53	53	39	24	11	2	−3
Raleigh_____	33	−1	5	11	23	31	38	48	46	39	19	11	4	−1
N. Dak___ Bismarck_____	38	−44	−37	−31	−12	15	30	35	33	11	5	−29	−43	−44
Ohio_____ Cincinnati_____	16	−25	−10	7	17	27	39	47	43	33	16	1	−11	−25
Cleveland_____	36	−19	−15	−5	10	25	31	41	41	32	22	3	−11	−19
Columbus_____	38	−19	−13	−2	18	25	35	43	39	31	20	5	−10	−19
Okla_____ Oklahoma City___	24	−4	3	3	20	39	47	53	51	37	22	11	1	−4
Oreg_____ Portland_____	37	−2	−3	19	29	29	39	43	44	34	26	13	6	−3
Pa_____ Philadelphia____	36	−5	−4	7	24	28	44	51	45	35	25	15	1	−5
Pittsburgh_____	25	−18	−9	−1	15	26	34	42	40	31	16	−1	−7	−18
R.I_____ Providence_____	24	−13	−6	1	14	29	41	49	40	34	20	14	−5	−13
S.C_____ Columbia_____	30	5	5	18	29	34	45	54	53	40	23	12	4	4
S. Dak___ Sioux Falls_____	32	−36	−31	−23	5	17	33	38	34	22	9	−17	−26	−36
Tenn_____ Memphis_____	36	−4	−11	12	29	38	48	52	48	36	25	9	−13	−13
Nashville_____	38	−15	−13	5	24	34	42	51	47	36	26	−1	−7	−15
Tex_____ Dallas-Ft. Worth_	24	4	12	17	30	41	51	59	56	46	29	20	10	4
El Paso_____	38	−8	8	14	24	31	50	59	56-	41	25	1	5	−8
Houston_____	8	18	22	25	31	45	52	62	62	48	33	19	21	18
Utah_____ Salt Lake City___	49	−22	−30	2	14	25	35	40	37	27	16	−14	−21	−30
Vt_____ Burlington_____	34	−30	−26	−20	2	24	33	39	35	25	15	−2	−23	−30
Va_____ Norfolk_____	29	5	8	20	28	36	45	56	52	45	27	20	14	5
Richmond_____	48	−12	−10	11	25	31	40	51	46	35	21	10	−1	−12
Wash_____ Seattle-Tacoma___	33	0	1	11	29	28	38	43	44	35	28	6	6	0
Spokane_____	30	−19	−12	−3	17	24	34	38	35	25	13	−11	−25	−25
W. Va____ Charleston_____	30	−12	−6	7	19	26	33	46	41	34	17	6	−2	−12
Wis_____ Milwaukee_____	37	−24	−19	−10	13	21	33	40	44	28	21	−5	−15	−24
Wyo_____ Cheyenne_____	42	−27	−34	−21	−8	16	25	38	36	18	2	−13	−24	−34
P.R_____ San Juan_____	23	61	62	60	64	66	69	69	70	69	67	66	63	60

[1] City office data.

Source: U.S. National Oceanic and Atmospheric Administration, *Comparative Climatic Data,* annual.

No. 371. NORMAL MONTHLY AND ANNUAL PRECIPITATION—SELECTED CITIES

[In inches. Airport data except as noted. Based on standard 30-year period, 1941 through 1970. See *Historical Statistics, Colonial Times to 1970*, series J 164–267, for related data]

STATE AND STATION	Jan.	Feb.	Mar.	Apr.	May	June	July	Aug.	Sept.	Oct.	Nov.	Dec.	Annual
Ala — Mobile	4.71	4.76	7.07	5.59	4.52	6.09	8.86	6.93	6.59	2.55	3.39	5.92	66.98
Alaska — Juneau	3.94	3.44	3.57	2.99	3.31	2.93	4.69	5.00	6.90	7.85	5.53	4.52	54.67
Ariz — Phoenix	.71	.60	.76	.32	.14	.12	.75	1.22	.69	.46	.46	.82	7.05
Ark — Little Rock	4.24	4.42	4.93	5.25	5.30	3.50	3.38	3.01	3.55	2.99	3.86	4.09	48.52
Calif — Los Angeles	2.52	2.32	1.71	1.10	.08	.03	.01	.02	.07	.22	1.76	2.39	12.23
Sacramento	3.73	2.68	2.17	1.54	.51	.10	.01	.05	.19	.99	2.13	3.12	17.22
San Francisco	4.37	3.04	2.54	1.59	.41	.13	.01	.03	.16	.98	2.29	3.98	19.53
Colo — Denver	.61	.67	1.21	1.93	2.64	1.93	1.78	1.29	1.13	1.13	.76	.43	15.51
Conn — Hartford	3.28	3.17	3.82	3.75	3.50	3.53	3.41	3.94	3.55	3.03	4.33	4.06	43.37
Del — Wilmington	2.85	2.75	3.74	3.20	3.35	3.24	4.31	3.98	3.42	2.60	3.49	3.32	40.25
D.C — Washington	2.62	2.45	3.33	2.86	3.68	3.48	4.12	4.67	3.08	2.66	2.90	3.04	38.89
Fla — Jacksonville	2.78	3.58	3.56	3.07	3.22	6.27	7.35	7.89	7.83	4.54	1.79	2.59	54.47
Miami	2.15	1.95	2.07	3.60	6.12	9.00	6.91	6.72	8.74	8.18	2.72	1.64	59.80
Ga — Atlanta	4.34	4.41	5.84	4.61	3.71	3.67	4.90	3.54	3.15	2.50	3.43	4.24	48.34
Hawaii — Honolulu	4.40	2.46	3.18	1.36	.96	.32	.60	.76	.67	1.51	2.99	3.69	22.90
Idaho — Boise	1.47	1.16	1.01	1.14	1.32	1.06	.15	.30	.41	.80	1.32	1.36	11.50
Ill — Chicago	1.70	1.30	2.52	3.38	3.41	4.15	3.46	2.73	3.01	2.32	2.10	1.64	31.72
Peoria	1.82	1.50	2.80	4.36	3.87	3.91	3.76	3.07	3.55	2.51	2.02	1.89	35.06
Ind — Indianapolis	2.86	2.36	3.75	3.87	4.08	4.16	3.67	2.80	2.87	2.51	3.10	2.71	38.74
Iowa — Des Moines	1.14	1.05	2.31	2.94	4.21	4.90	3.28	3.30	3.07	2.14	1.42	1.09	30.85
Kans — Wichita	.85	.98	1.78	2.95	3.60	4.49	4.35	3.10	3.69	2.50	1.17	1.12	30.58
Ky — Louisville	3.53	3.47	5.05	4.10	4.20	4.05	3.76	2.99	2.94	2.35	3.33	3.34	43.11
La — New Orleans	4.53	4.82	5.49	4.15	4.20	4.74	6.72	5.27	5.58	2.26	3.88	5.13	56.77
Maine — Portland	3.38	3.52	3.60	3.34	3.33	3.10	2.61	2.60	3.09	3.31	4.86	4.06	40.80
Md — Baltimore	2.91	2.81	3.69	3.07	3.61	3.77	4.07	4.21	3.12	2.81	3.13	3.26	40.46
Mass — Boston	3.69	3.54	4.01	3.49	3.47	3.19	2.74	3.46	3.16	3.02	4.51	4.24	42.52
Mich — Detroit	1.93	1.80	2.33	3.08	3.43	3.04	2.99	3.04	2.30	2.52	2.31	2.19	30.96
Sault Ste. Marie	1.92	1.48	1.74	2.22	3.01	3.31	2.60	3.10	3.85	2.85	3.26	2.36	31.70
Minn — Duluth	1.16	.85	1.76	2.55	3.41	4.44	3.73	3.79	3.06	2.30	1.73	1.40	30.18
Minneapolis-St. Paul	.73	.84	1.68	2.04	3.37	3.94	3.69	3.05	2.73	1.78	1.20	.89	25.94
Miss — Jackson	4.53	4.62	5.63	4.65	4.38	3.40	4.27	3.59	2.99	2.22	3.87	5.04	49.19
Mo — Kansas City	1.25	1.25	2.55	3.50	4.28	5.55	4.37	3.81	4.21	3.24	1.47	1.52	37.00
St. Louis	1.85	2.06	3.03	3.92	3.86	4.42	3.69	2.87	2.89	2.79	2.47	2.04	35.89
Mont — Great Falls	.88	.75	.97	1.18	2.37	3.11	1.27	1.09	1.17	.68	.81	.71	14.99
Nebr — Omaha	.76	.98	1.59	2.97	4.11	4.94	3.71	3.97	3.27	1.93	1.11	.84	30.18
Nev — Reno	1.21	.86	.70	.47	.66	.40	.26	.22	.23	.42	.68	1.09	7.20
N.H — Concord	2.67	2.45	2.77	2.92	3.02	3.35	3.14	2.89	3.06	2.68	3.96	3.26	36.17
N.J — Atlantic City	3.56	3.37	4.31	3.37	3.54	3.38	4.36	4.90	2.99	3.46	4.21	4.01	45.46
N. Mex — Albuquerque	.30	.39	.47	.48	.53	.50	1.39	1.34	.77	.79	.29	.52	7.77
N.Y — Albany	2.20	2.11	2.58	2.70	3.26	3.00	3.12	2.87	3.12	2.63	2.84	2.93	33.36
Buffalo	2.90	2.55	2.85	3.15	2.97	2.23	2.93	3.53	3.25	3.01	3.74	3.00	36.11
New York [1]	2.71	2.92	3.73	3.30	3.47	2.96	3.68	4.01	3.27	2.85	3.76	3.53	40.19
N.C — Charlotte	3.51	3.83	4.52	3.40	2.90	3.70	4.57	3.96	3.46	2.69	2.74	3.44	42.72
Raleigh	3.22	3.32	3.44	3.07	3.32	3.67	5.08	4.93	3.78	2.81	2.82	3.08	42.54
N. Dak — Bismarck	.51	.44	.73	1.44	2.17	3.58	2.20	1.96	1.32	.80	.56	.45	16.16
Ohio — Cincinnati	3.34	3.04	4.09	3.64	3.74	3.81	4.12	2.62	2.55	2.15	3.08	2.86	39.04
Cleveland	2.56	2.18	3.05	3.49	3.49	3.28	3.45	3.00	2.80	2.57	2.76	2.36	34.99
Columbus	2.87	2.32	3.44	3.71	4.10	4.13	4.21	2.86	2.41	1.89	2.68	2.39	37.01
Okla — Oklahoma City	1.11	1.32	2.05	3.47	5.20	4.22	2.66	2.56	3.55	2.57	1.40	1.26	31.37
Oreg — Portland	5.88	4.06	3.64	2.22	2.09	1.59	.47	.82	1.60	3.59	5.61	6.04	37.61
Pa — Philadelphia	2.81	2.62	3.69	3.29	3.35	3.70	4.09	4.11	3.03	2.53	3.39	3.32	39.93
Pittsburgh	2.79	2.35	3.60	3.40	3.63	3.84	3.15	2.85	2.52	2.52	2.47	2.48	36.23
R.I — Providence	3.52	3.45	3.99	3.72	3.49	2.65	2.85	3.90	3.26	3.27	4.52	4.13	42.75
S.C — Columbia	3.44	3.67	4.67	3.51	3.35	3.82	5.65	5.63	4.32	2.58	2.34	3.38	46.36
S. Dak — Sioux Falls	.57	1.04	1.40	2.30	3.37	4.32	2.94	2.84	2.85	1.50	.85	.74	24.72
Tenn — Memphis	4.93	4.73	5.10	5.42	4.39	3.46	3.53	3.33	3.01	2.58	3.92	4.70	49.10
Nashville	4.75	4.43	5.00	4.11	4.10	3.38	3.83	3.24	3.09	2.16	3.46	4.45	46.00
Tex — Dallas-Fort Worth	1.80	2.36	2.54	4.30	4.47	3.05	1.84	2.26	3.15	2.68	2.03	1.82	32.30
El Paso	.39	.42	.39	.24	.32	.60	1.53	1.12	1.16	.78	.32	.50	7.77
Houston	3.57	3.54	2.68	3.54	5.10	4.52	4.12	4.35	4.65	4.05	4.03	4.04	48.19
Utah — Salt Lake City	1.27	1.19	1.63	2.12	1.49	1.30	.70	.92	.68	1.16	1.31	1.39	15.17
Vt — Burlington	1.74	1.68	1.93	2.62	3.01	3.46	3.54	3.72	3.05	2.74	2.86	2.19	32.54
Va — Norfolk	3.35	3.31	3.42	2.71	3.34	3.62	5.70	5.92	4.20	3.06	2.94	3.11	44.68
Richmond	2.86	3.01	3.38	2.77	3.42	3.52	5.63	5.06	3.58	2.94	3.20	3.22	42.59
Wash — Seattle-Tacoma	5.79	4.19	3.61	2.46	1.70	1.53	.71	1.08	1.99	3.91	5.88	5.94	38.79
Spokane	2.47	1.68	1.53	1.12	1.46	1.36	.40	.58	.83	1.42	2.20	2.37	17.42
W. Va — Charleston	3.39	3.11	4.03	3.33	3.48	3.31	5.04	3.68	2.94	2.45	2.81	3.18	40.75
Wis — Milwaukee	1.63	1.13	2.24	2.76	2.88	3.58	3.41	2.68	3.02	1.98	2.01	1.75	29.07
Wyo — Cheyenne	.46	.46	1.05	1.57	2.52	2.41	1.82	1.45	1.03	.95	.58	.35	14.65
P.R — San Juan	3.73	2.50	2.04	3.40	6.54	5.64	6.41	6.98	6.07	5.64	5.49	4.71	59.15

[1] City office data.

Source: U.S. National Oceanic and Atmospheric Administration, *Climatography of the United States*. No. 81.

No. 372. Average Number of Days With Precipitation of .01 Inch or More—
Selected Cities

[Airport data, except as noted. For period of record through 1977]

STATE AND STATION		Length of record (yr.)	Jan.	Feb.	Mar.	Apr.	May	June	July	Aug.	Sept.	Oct.	Nov.	Dec.	Annual
Ala	Mobile	36	11	10	11	7	8	11	17	14	11	6	8	11	125
Alaska	Juneau	34	18	18	18	17	17	16	17	18	20	23	20	21	223
Ariz	Phoenix	38	3	4	3	2	1	1	4	5	3	3	2	4	35
Ark	Little Rock	35	10	9	11	10	10	8	9	7	7	6	8	9	104
Calif	Los Angeles	42	6	6	5	3	1	1	1	(z)	1	2	3	5	34
	Sacramento	38	10	9	8	6	3	1	(z)	(z)	1	3	7	9	57
	San Francisco	50	11	10	9	6	3	1	(z)	1	1	4	7	10	63
Colo	Denver	43	6	6	8	9	10	9	9	9	8	6	5	5	86
Conn	Hartford	23	11	11	11	11	12	12	10	10	10	8	11	13	130
Del	Wilmington	30	11	10	11	11	11	9	9	9	8	7	10	10	116
D.C.	Washington	36	10	9	11	10	11	9	10	9	8	7	8	9	111
Fla	Jacksonville	36	8	8	8	6	8	12	15	15	13	9	6	8	116
	Miami	35	7	6	6	6	11	15	16	17	17	15	8	7	131
Ga	Atlanta	43	11	10	12	9	9	10	12	9	7	6	8	10	113
Hawaii	Honolulu	28	10	10	9	9	7	6	8	7	7	9	10	10	102
Idaho	Boise	38	12	10	9	8	8	7	2	3	4	6	10	12	91
Ill	Chicago	19	11	10	13	12	11	10	10	8	10	9	10	11	125
	Peoria	38	9	8	11	12	12	10	9	8	9	7	9	10	114
Ind	Indianapolis	38	11	10	13	12	12	10	9	8	8	8	10	12	123
Iowa	Des Moines	38	7	7	10	10	11	11	9	9	9	7	6	7	103
Kans	Wichita	24	5	5	7	8	11	9	8	7	8	6	5	6	85
Ky	Louisville	30	12	11	13	12	11	10	11	8	8	7	10	11	124
La	New Orleans	29	10	9	9	7	7	10	15	13	10	6	7	10	113
Maine	Portland	37	11	10	11	12	13	11	9	9	8	9	12	12	127
Md	Baltimore	27	10	9	11	11	11	9	9	10	7	7	9	9	112
Mass	Boston	26	12	11	12	11	11	11	9	10	9	9	11	12	128
Mich	Detroit	35	13	12	13	12	12	11	9	9	9	9	11	13	133
	Sault Ste. Marie	36	19	15	13	11	11	11	10	11	14	13	18	19	165
Minn	Duluth	36	12	10	11	10	13	13	11	11	11	9	11	12	134
	Minneapolis-St. Paul	39	9	7	10	10	12	12	10	10	9	8	8	9	114
Miss	Jackson	14	11	9	11	9	9	8	11	10	9	6	9	10	112
Mo	Kansas City	5	9	6	11	10	11	9	5	8	10	8	7	8	102
	St. Louis	20	8	8	11	11	11	9	9	7	9	8	8	10	109
Mont	Great Falls	40	9	8	9	9	11	12	7	7	7	6	7	8	100
Nebr	Omaha	42	7	7	9	9	12	11	9	9	8	6	5	6	98
Nev	Reno	35	6	5	6	4	5	3	3	2	2	3	5	6	50
N.H.	Concord	36	11	10	11	11	12	11	10	10	9	8	11	11	125
N.J.	Atlantic City	34	11	10	11	11	10	9	9	9	8	7	9	10	114
N. Mex	Albuquerque	38	3	4	4	3	4	4	9	10	6	5	3	4	59
N.Y.	Albany	31	12	11	12	12	13	11	11	10	10	9	12	13	136
	Buffalo	34	20	17	16	14	13	10	10	11	11	11	16	20	169
	New York [1]	109	11	10	12	11	11	10	11	10	8	8	9	10	121
N.C.	Charlotte	38	10	10	12	9	9	10	12	9	7	7	7	10	112
	Raleigh	33	10	10	10	9	10	9	11	10	8	7	8	9	111
N. Dak	Bismarck	38	8	7	8	8	10	12	9	8	7	5	6	8	96
Ohio	Cincinnati	30	12	11	13	12	12	11	10	9	8	8	11	12	129
	Cleveland	36	16	15	16	14	13	11	10	9	10	11	15	16	156
	Columbus	38	13	12	14	13	13	11	11	9	9	8	11	13	137
Okla	Oklahoma City	38	5	6	7	8	10	9	7	6	7	6	5	5	81
Oreg	Portland	37	19	16	17	14	12	9	4	5	7	13	18	19	153
Pa	Philadelphia	37	11	9	11	11	11	10	9	9	8	7	9	10	115
	Pittsburgh	25	16	14	16	13	12	11	11	9	9	10	13	17	151
R.I.	Providence	24	11	11	12	11	11	11	9	10	9	8	11	12	126
S.C.	Columbia	30	10	10	11	8	9	10	12	11	8	6	7	9	111
S. Dak	Sioux Falls	32	6	6	8	8	10	11	9	9	8	6	6	6	93
Tenn	Memphis	27	10	10	11	10	9	8	9	8	7	6	8	10	106
	Nashville	36	11	11	12	11	11	10	10	9	8	7	9	11	120
Tex	Dallas-Fort Worth	24	7	6	7	9	8	6	5	5	7	6	6	6	78
	El Paso	38	4	3	2	2	2	3	8	7	5	4	2	4	46
	Houston	8	11	6	10	7	8	7	10	11	10	8	8	9	105
Utah	Salt Lake City	49	10	9	10	10	8	6	4	5	5	6	7	9	89
Vt	Burlington	34	14	12	13	12	13	12	12	12	12	11	14	15	152
Va	Norfolk	29	10	10	11	10	10	9	11	11	8	8	8	9	115
	Richmond	40	10	9	11	9	11	10	11	10	8	7	8	9	113
Wash	Seattle-Tacoma	33	19	16	18	14	10	9	5	7	9	14	18	20	159
	Spokane	30	15	11	11	8	9	8	4	5	6	8	12	16	113
W. Va	Charleston	30	15	14	15	14	13	11	13	11	9	9	12	14	150
Wis	Milwaukee	37	11	9	12	12	12	11	10	9	9	9	10	11	125
Wyo	Cheyenne	42	6	6	9	10	11	11	11	9	7	5	6	5	96
P.R.	San Juan	22	17	13	12	13	17	16	19	19	18	17	18	19	198

Z Less than ½ day.   [1] City office data.

Source: U.S. National Oceanic and Atmospheric Administration, *Comparative Climatic Data*, annual.

No. 373. Average Total Snow and Ice Pellets—Selected Cities

[In inches. Airport data, except as noted. For period of record through 1977. T denotes trace]

STATE AND STATION	Length of record (yr.)	Jan.	Feb.	Mar.	Apr.	May	June	July	Aug.	Sept.	Oct.	Nov.	Dec.	Annual
Ala — Mobile	36	.2	.2	T	–	–	–	–	–	–	–	T	.1	.5
Alaska — Juneau	34	25.6	21.2	19.0	4.8	.1	T	–	–	T	1.3	12.1	24.1	108.2
Ariz — Phoenix	40	T	T	T	T	–	–	–	–	–	–	–	T	T
Ark — Little Rock	35	2.2	1.2	.6	T	–	–	–	–	–	–	.2	.9	5.1
Calif — Los Angeles	42	T	T	–	–	–	–	–	–	–	–	–	T	T
Sacramento	29	T	.1	–	–	–	–	–	–	–	–	–	T	.1
San Francisco	50	T	T	T	–	–	–	–	–	–	–	–	T	T
Colo — Denver	43	8.0	7.8	12.7	9.5	1.5	T	–	–	1.8	3.8	7.7	6.2	59.0
Conn — Hartford	23	11.9	12.7	12.2	1.6	.1	–	–	–	–	T	1.7	12.8	53.0
Del — Wilmington	30	5.7	5.5	3.7	.1	T	–	–	–	–	T	1.0	3.9	19.9
D.C — Washington	34	4.7	4.9	2.3	T	T	–	–	–	–	T	.7	3.7	16.3
Fla — Jacksonville	36	T	T	T	–	–	–	–	–	–	–	–	T	T
Miami	35	–	–	–	–	–	–	–	–	–	–	–	–	–
Ga — Atlanta	43	.7	.4	.2	T	–	–	–	–	–	–	T	.2	1.5
Hawaii — Honolulu	31	–	–	–	–	–	–	–	–	–	–	–	–	–
Idaho — Boise	38	7.5	3.8	2.0	.8	.1	T	T	–	–	.1	1.8	5.4	21.5
Ill — Chicago	19	9.5	7.5	7.6	1.8	.1	–	–	–	T	.5	1.8	8.6	37.4
Peoria	34	6.0	4.7	4.6	.6	T	–	–	–	–	.1	2.4	5.9	24.3
Ind — Indianapolis	46	5.2	5.0	3.7	.5	T	–	–	–	–	T	2.2	5.0	21.6
Iowa — Des Moines	38	8.5	7.0	6.8	1.6	T	–	–	–	T	.1	2.7	6.4	33.1
Kans — Wichita	24	4.2	3.8	3.0	.2	–	–	–	–	–	T	1.0	2.9	15.1
Ky — Louisville	30	5.4	4.2	3.8	.2	–	–	–	–	–	T	1.6	2.4	17.6
La — New Orleans	31	T	.1	T	–	–	–	–	–	–	–	T	.1	.2
Maine — Portland	37	18.1	19.6	13.9	3.1	0.2	–	–	–	T	.3	3.3	16.0	74.5
Md — Baltimore	27	5.1	5.9	4.6	.1	T	–	–	–	–	T	1.1	4.4	21.2
Mass — Boston	42	12.2	11.8	8.1	.7	T	–	–	–	–	T	1.2	8.1	42.1
Mich — Detroit	38	7.9	7.7	5.4	1.1	T	–	–	–	–	T	2.5	7.1	31.7
Sault Ste. Marie	36	26.7	19.6	15.1	4.8	.7	T	–	–	.2	2.3	15.1	26.3	110.8
Duluth	34	17.1	11.8	14.1	6.8	.9	T	–	T	T	1.2	10.2	15.7	77.8
Minn — Minneapolis-St. Paul	39	9.2	8.3	10.7	2.5	.2	–	–	–	T	.4	5.8	9.0	46.1
Miss — Jackson	14	.5	.3	.4	T	–	–	–	–	–	–	T		1.2
Mo — Kansas City	43	5.9	3.8	3.7	.7	T	–	–	–	–	T	1.1	4.3	19.5
St. Louis	41	4.6	4.1	4.4	.2	T	–	–	–	–	T	1.5	3.7	18.5
Mont — Great Falls	40	10.0	8.3	9.8	7.5	1.4	.4	T	–	1.3	3.0	7.3	8.8	57.8
Nebr — Omaha	42	8.5	7.2	6.7	.9	.1	–	–	–	T	.3	2.5	5.8	32.0
Nev — Reno	35	6.3	5.4	5.3	1.6	1.1	T	–	–	T	.3	1.6	4.9	26.5
N.H — Concord	36	17.2	15.3	11.6	2.2	.2	–	–	–	–	.1	3.9	14.3	64.8
N.J — Atlantic City	33	4.9	4.8	3.1	.2	T	–	–	–	–	T	1.2	2.6	15.8
N. Mex — Albuquerque	38	2.3	1.8	2.1	.5	T	–	–	–	T	T	1.2	2.3	10.5
N.Y — Albany	31	15.0	15.3	12.0	2.5	.1	–	–	–	–	.1	4.5	16.2	65.7
Buffalo	34	23.0	18.1	12.2	3.2	.1	–	–	–	T	.3	13.2	22.8	92.9
New York [1]	109	7.6	8.6	5.2	.9	T	–	–	–	–	T	.9	5.8	29.0
N.C — Charlotte	38	2.1	1.3	1.0	T	–	–	–	–	–	–	.1	.7	5.3
Raleigh	33	2.6	1.8	1.3	T	–	–	–	–	–	–	.2	.9	6.8
N. Dak — Bismarck	38	7.0	5.9	7.9	3.7	1.0	T	–	–	.2	1.3	5.0	6.7	38.7
Ohio — Cincinnati	30	6.8	5.0	4.8	.5	T	–	–	–	–	.1	2.9	3.8	23.9
Cleveland	36	10.8	11.0	10.0	2.1	.1	–	–	–	T	.8	5.8	11.6	52.2
Columbus	30	7.5	5.8	4.9	.7	T	–	–	–	T	.1	2.8	5.9	27.7
Okla — Oklahoma City	38	2.8	2.2	1.7	T	–	–	–	–	–	T	.5	1.6	8.8
Oreg — Portland	37	4.2	.7	.6	T	T	–	–	–	T	T	.4	1.5	7.4
Pa — Philadelphia	35	5.7	5.9	3.7	.2	T	–	–	–	–	T	.7	4.0	20.2
Pittsburgh	25	11.2	10.3	9.1	1.5	.2	–	–	–	–	.2	4.0	8.8	45.3
R.I — Providence	24	9.6	10.2	9.0	.7	.3	–	–	–	–	.1	.5	7.6	38.0
S.C — Columbia	30	.4	.8	.2	–	–	–	–	–	–	–	T	.3	1.7
S. Dak — Sioux Falls	32	6.1	9.2	10.2	1.6	–	–	–	–	T	4.5	4.0	7.5	39.1
Tenn — Memphis	27	2.1	1.2	1.2	T	–	–	–	–	–	–	.1	.9	5.5
Nashville	36	4.0	2.5	1.7	.1	–	–	–	–	–	–	.6	2.0	10.9
Tex — Dallas	24	1.5	.7	.3	–	–	–	–	–	–	–	.2	.2	2.9
El Paso	38	1.4	.8	.4	T	–	–	–	–	–	T	1.1	1.0	4.7
Houston	43	.2	.2	T	–	–	–	–	–	–	–	T	T	.4
Utah — Salt Lake City	49	13.2	9.7	10.4	5.0	.6	T	–	–	.1	1.1	6.2	12.0	58.3
Vt — Burlington	34	17.9	18.0	12.4	3.6	.2	–	–	–	T	.2	7.4	19.6	79.3
Va — Norfolk	29	3.1	1.8	.9	T	–	–	–	–	–	–	T	1.2	7.0
Richmond	40	5.2	3.3	2.8	.1	–	–	–	–	–	T	.4	2.1	13.9
Wash — Seattle-Tacoma	33	6.8	1.6	1.7	.1	.1	–	–	–	T	.1	1.1	3.2	14.6
Spokane	30	18.3	7.6	4.8	.6	.1	T	–	–	–	.6	5.8	15.5	53.3
W. Va — Charleston	30	8.9	7.7	4.3	.4	T	–	–	–	–	.2	2.9	5.2	29.6
Wis — Milwaukee	37	12.2	9.0	9.5	1.8	T	–	–	–	–	T	3.1	10.2	45.9
Wyo — Cheyenne	42	5.8	5.5	11.9	9.3	3.1	.3	–	–	.7	3.4	6.0	5.2	51.2
P.R — San Juan	22	–	–	–	–	–	–	–	–	–	–	–	–	–

– Represents zero.   [1] City office data.

Source: U.S. National Oceanic and Atmospheric Administration, *Comparative Climatic Data*, annual.

No. 374. Average Percentage of Possible Sunshine—Selected Cities

[Airport data, except as noted. For period of record through 1977, except as noted]

STATE AND STATION		Length of record (yr.)	Jan.	Feb.	Mar.	Apr.	May	June	July	Aug.	Sept.	Oct.	Nov.	Dec.	Annual
Ala	Montgomery [1]	25	47	53	58	64	66	65	63	65	63	66	57	50	59
Alaska	Juneau	32	32	32	37	38	39	33	31	32	26	20	23	20	31
Ariz	Phoenix	82	78	80	83	88	93	94	85	85	89	88	84	77	86
Ark	Little Rock	32	46	54	57	61	68	73	71	73	68	69	56	48	63
Calif	Los Angeles [1]	32	69	72	73	70	66	65	82	83	79	73	74	71	73
	Sacramento	29	47	62	71	80	87	92	97	96	93	84	63	46	79
	San Francisco [1]	38	56	62	69	73	72	73	66	65	72	70	62	53	67
Colo	Denver	28	72	71	70	66	65	71	71	72	74	73	66	68	70
Conn	Hartford	23	58	57	57	57	58	58	62	63	59	58	46	48	57
Del	Wilmington [2]	25	50	54	57	57	59	64	63	61	60	60	54	51	53
D.C	Washington	29	49	52	56	58	59	64	63	63	62	59	52	47	58
Fla	Jacksonville	27	57	61	66	71	69	62	60	58	54	57	60	56	61
	Key West [1]	17	72	76	81	84	80	71	75	76	69	68	72	74	75
Ga	Atlanta	42	48	54	57	66	68	67	62	65	63	67	59	50	61
Hawaii	Honolulu	25	63	65	68	66	69	70	73	75	74	67	60	59	67
Idaho	Boise	36	41	52	63	68	72	75	88	85	82	67	45	40	67
Ill	Chicago [1]	33	44	47	51	53	61	67	70	68	63	62	41	38	57
	Peoria	34	46	50	52	55	59	66	69	67	64	62	45	40	58
Ind	Indianapolis	34	42	51	52	56	62	67	70	71	66	64	43	40	58
Iowa	Des Moines	27	51	54	54	56	60	67	72	69	64	63	50	45	60
Kans	Wichita	24	60	61	61	62	65	70	74	74	65	66	60	58	65
Ky	Louisville	30	42	47	51	55	62	66	66	68	64	62	47	40	57
La	New Orleans	4	47	65	53	69	58	69	58	55	63	68	53	53	60
Maine	Portland	37	56	59	56	57	56	59	64	65	61	59	47	53	58
Md	Baltimore	27	52	55	55	56	57	62	65	62	60	59	51	48	57
Mass	Boston	42	54	56	57	57	59	63	66	67	63	61	51	52	60
Mich	Detroit	32	32	43	49	52	59	65	70	65	61	56	35	32	54
	Sault Ste. Marie	36	35	46	54	55	57	58	63	58	45	41	23	28	48
Minn	Duluth	27	49	54	55	54	56	58	67	62	52	48	34	39	54
	Minneapolis-St. Paul	39	50	57	54	56	59	63	71	67	61	57	39	40	58
Miss	Jackson	13	49	57	59	62	62	69	62	62	58	64	53	47	59
Mo	Kansas City	5	62	61	65	72	74	76	82	68	57	64	53	59	67
	St. Louis	18	54	53	56	57	62	68	72	65	63	63	49	43	59
Mont	Great Falls	35	48	57	67	62	64	65	80	77	68	61	46	45	63
Nebr	Omaha [1]	40	55	55	55	59	62	68	76	72	67	67	52	48	62
Nev	Reno	35	66	68	75	80	81	85	92	93	92	84	71	64	81
N.H	Concord	36	52	54	52	53	55	57	62	61	55	54	42	47	54
N.J	Atlantic City	17	50	51	53	55	55	58	60	63	58	56	49	43	55
N. Mex	Albuquerque	38	73	73	74	76	80	83	76	76	80	79	78	72	77
N.Y	Albany	39	46	51	52	53	55	59	63	61	56	52	36	38	53
	Buffalo	34	33	39	46	53	58	66	69	66	59	53	29	27	52
	New York [3]	100	50	55	56	59	61	64	65	64	63	61	52	49	59
N.C	Charlotte	27	55	60	63	70	69	70	69	70	68	69	63	58	66
	Raleigh	23	55	59	63	65	59	60	61	60	60	62	62	56	60
N. Dak	Bismarck	38	54	55	60	59	63	64	76	73	65	59	45	47	62
Ohio	Cincinnati [1]	60	41	45	51	55	61	67	68	67	66	59	44	38	57
	Cleveland	34	32	37	44	53	59	65	68	64	60	55	31	26	52
	Columbus	26	37	42	44	52	58	61	63	63	61	57	38	31	52
Okla	Oklahoma City	23	59	61	63	63	65	73	75	77	69	68	60	59	67
Oreg	Portland	28	25	36	43	50	55	52	69	63	59	41	29	20	48
Pa	Philadelphia	35	51	54	56	57	57	62	63	63	59	59	52	49	58
	Pittsburgh	25	35	39	46	49	53	58	60	59	59	54	39	30	50
R.I	Providence	24	57	56	55	56	57	57	60	59	58	59	49	51	56
S.C	Columbia	24	57	61	63	68	65	64	64	66	64	66	64	60	64
S. Dak	Rapid City [1]	33	54	59	61	59	57	60	71	73	67	65	56	54	62
Tenn	Memphis	27	49	55	57	64	70	74	73	76	69	71	58	50	65
	Nashville	35	41	48	53	60	63	67	65	66	63	63	50	41	58
Tex	Amarillo [1]	34	69	68	71	73	73	77	77	78	74	75	73	67	73
	El Paso	35	78	82	85	87	89	89	79	80	82	84	83	78	83
	Houston	8	45	56	45	52	59	65	67	62	60	61	55	65	57
Utah	Salt Lake City	40	48	56	64	67	73	79	84	83	84	73	54	45	70
Vt	Burlington	34	42	48	51	51	56	60	65	62	54	50	30	33	51
Va	Norfolk	19	57	58	63	66	67	68	65	65	64	60	60	57	63
	Richmond	27	51	56	59	63	63	66	65	64	63	59	56	51	60
Wash	Seattle-Tacoma	11	21	43	49	52	59	55	67	62	61	41	28	17	49
	Spokane	29	26	40	53	60	63	65	80	77	70	51	29	20	57
W. Va	Parkersburg [1]	78	32	36	43	49	56	59	62	60	59	54	37	29	48
Wis	Milwaukee	37	45	47	51	54	59	64	71	67	60	56	41	38	56
Wyo	Cheyenne	42	61	65	65	60	58	64	68	67	69	68	60	59	64
P.R	San Juan	22	65	70	74	68	61	59	65	65	59	59	57	58	63

[1] For period of record through 1975
[2] Data not available; figures are for a nearby station.
[3] City office data.

Source: U.S. National Oceanic and Atmospheric Administration, *Comparative Climatic Data*, annual.

No. 375. AVERAGE WIND SPEED—SELECTED CITIES

[In miles per hour. Airport data, except as noted. For period of record through 1977]

STATE AND STATION	Length of record (yr.)	Jan.	Feb.	Mar.	Apr.	May	June	July	Aug.	Sept.	Oct.	Nov.	Dec.	Annual
Ala_____ Mobile_____	29	10.7	10.9	11.2	10.5	9.0	7.8	7.0	6.9	8.1	8.3	9.5	10.2	9.2
Alaska____ Juneau_____	34	8.5	8.8	8.8	8.9	8.5	7.9	7.6	7.5	8.0	9.7	8.7	9.3	8.5
Ariz_____ Phoenix_____	32	5.1	5.8	6.6	6.9	7.0	6.9	7.2	6.6	6.3	5.8	5.3	5.1	6.2
Ark_____ Little Rock_____	35	8.8	9.3	10.1	9.5	8.0	7.6	6.9	6.6	7.0	7.0	8.3	8.6	8.1
Calif_____ Los Angeles_____	29	6.6	7.3	8.0	8.4	8.2	7.9	7.7	7.6	7.2	6.8	6.5	6.4	7.4
Sacramento_____	29	7.7	7.9	9.1	9.1	9.4	10.0	9.2	8.7	7.8	6.8	6.3	7.1	8.3
San Francisco_____	50	7.1	8.5	10.4	12.1	13.2	13.9	13.5	12.8	11.0	9.3	7.2	6.8	10.5
Colo_____ Denver_____	29	9.2	9.4	10.1	10.4	9.6	9.2	8.5	8.2	8.2	8.2	8.7	9.0	9.1
Conn_____ Hartford_____	23	9.4	9.8	10.4	10.6	9.3	8.4	7.8	7.6	7.6	8.1	8.7	8.9	8.9
Del_____ Wilmington_____	29	9.8	10.5	11.2	10.4	9.0	8.4	7.7	7.4	7.9	8.2	9.2	9.4	9.1
D.C_____ Washington_____	29	10.0	10.5	10.9	10.5	9.2	8.8	8.1	8.0	8.2	8.6	9.3	9.4	9.3
Fla_____ Jacksonville_____	28	8.4	9.5	9.4	9.1	8.6	8.4	7.5	7.3	8.2	8.7	8.2	8.2	8.5
Miami_____	28	9.4	10.1	10.4	10.7	9.5	8.1	7.8	7.8	8.1	9.3	9.5	9.1	9.1
Ga_____ Atlanta_____	39	10.5	11.0	10.9	10.1	8.6	7.9	7.4	7.0	8.0	8.4	9.1	9.8	9.1
Hawaii____ Honolulu_____	28	9.9	10.8	11.6	12.2	12.3	12.9	13.7	13.5	11.7	10.9	11.1	11.0	11.8
Idaho_____ Boise_____	38	8.5	9.3	10.4	10.4	9.6	9.2	8.5	8.3	8.3	8.6	8.6	8.4	9.0
Ill_____ Chicago_____	19	11.6	11.6	11.8	12.1	10.5	9.1	8.0	8.1	8.7	9.8	11.0	10.9	10.3
Peoria_____	34	11.2	11.6	12.3	12.2	10.3	9.2	8.0	7.8	8.7	9.5	11.2	11.0	10.3
Ind_____ Indianapolis_____	29	11.1	11.2	11.9	11.4	9.6	8.6	7.5	7.2	8.1	8.9	10.6	10.5	9.7
Iowa_____ Des Moines_____	28	11.8	11.8	13.1	13.3	11.5	10.5	9.0	8.8	9.5	10.5	11.7	11.5	11.1
Kans_____ Wichita_____	24	12.4	13.0	14.5	14.5	12.9	12.5	11.2	11.3	11.6	12.2	12.3	12.2	12.5
Ky_____ Louisville_____	30	9.7	9.9	10.5	10.0	8.1	7.4	6.7	6.4	6.8	7.2	9.0	9.3	8.4
La_____ New Orleans_____	29	9.5	10.0	10.2	9.6	8.2	6.9	6.2	6.1	7.4	7.6	8.8	9.2	8.3
Maine_____ Portland_____	37	9.2	9.6	10.1	10.0	9.2	8.2	7.6	7.5	7.8	8.5	8.8	9.1	8.8
Md_____ Baltimore_____	27	9.9	10.7	11.2	10.9	9.5	8.7	8.1	8.1	8.3	8.9	9.5	9.4	9.4
Mass_____ Boston_____	20	14.2	14.1	14.0	13.4	12.2	11.3	10.8	10.8	11.2	12.1	13.0	13.8	12.6
Mich_____ Detroit_____	43	11.7	11.6	11.5	11.1	9.9	9.1	8.4	8.1	8.9	9.6	11.4	11.4	10.2
Sault Ste. Marie___	36	10.1	10.0	10.4	10.7	10.2	8.8	8.2	8.1	8.9	9.5	10.1	10.0	9.6
Minn_____ Duluth_____	28	12.0	11.8	12.1	13.1	12.3	10.8	9.8	9.7	10.5	11.4	12.1	11.4	11.4
Minneapolis-St. Paul	39	10.4	10.6	11.3	12.3	11.3	10.5	9.3	9.1	9.8	10.4	11.0	10.4	10.5
Miss_____ Jackson_____	14	9.0	8.9	9.6	8.8	7.2	6.3	6.0	5.7	6.5	6.5	7.8	8.6	7.6
Mo_____ Kansas City_____	5	10.9	11.9	12.4	11.9	9.5	9.5	8.4	8.9	8.6	9.7	11.0	10.9	10.3
St. Louis_____	28	10.3	10.9	11.8	11.3	9.3	8.6	7.7	7.4	7.9	8.5	9.9	10.3	9.5
Mont_____ Great Falls_____	36	15.8	14.9	13.6	13.1	11.6	11.4	10.2	10.5	11.5	13.6	14.9	16.0	13.1
Nebr_____ Omaha_____	42	11.1	11.4	12.7	13.1	11.4	10.4	9.1	9.1	9.6	10.0	11.1	10.8	10.8
Nev_____ Reno_____	35	5.8	6.1	7.6	8.0	7.7	7.3	6.6	6.2	5.5	5.3	5.2	5.0	6.4
N.H_____ Concord_____	36	7.3	7.9	8.3	7.9	7.1	6.3	5.6	5.3	5.5	5.9	6.5	7.0	6.7
N.J_____ Atlantic City_____	19	11.7	12.2	12.5	12.1	10.7	9.7	9.0	8.6	9.1	9.7	11.1	11.3	10.6
N. Mex____ Albuquerque_____	38	8.0	8.8	10.1	11.0	10.5	10.0	9.1	8.2	8.6	8.3	7.9	7.7	9.0
N.Y_____ Albany_____	39	9.8	10.4	10.7	10.5	9.1	8.2	7.4	7.0	7.3	8.0	8.9	9.2	8.9
Buffalo_____	38	14.5	14.1	13.8	13.0	11.8	11.2	10.6	10.0	10.6	11.4	13.0	13.5	12.3
New York [1]_____	58	10.7	10.8	11.0	10.4	8.8	8.1	7.7	7.6	8.1	9.0	9.9	10.4	9.4
N.C_____ Charlotte_____	28	8.0	8.5	8.9	9.0	7.6	6.9	6.6	6.6	6.8	7.1	7.3	7.4	7.6
Raleigh_____	28	8.6	9.2	9.5	9.2	7.8	7.0	6.7	6.5	6.9	7.3	7.9	8.1	7.9
N. Dak____ Bismarck_____	38	10.1	10.1	11.2	12.4	12.1	10.9	9.5	9.7	10.2	10.1	10.3	9.6	10.5
Ohio_____ Cincinnati_____	30	10.7	10.7	11.2	10.8	8.8	7.9	7.1	6.7	7.4	8.0	9.6	10.2	9.1
Cleveland_____	36	12.5	12.4	12.5	11.8	10.3	9.4	8.7	8.3	9.1	10.0	12.1	12.3	10.8
Columbus_____	28	10.3	10.5	10.8	10.1	8.6	7.5	6.7	6.4	6.8	7.7	9.6	9.9	8.7
Okla_____ Oklahoma City___	29	13.2	13.6	15.0	15.0	13.2	12.7	11.2	10.8	11.4	12.1	12.6	12.7	12.8
Oreg_____ Portland_____	29	10.0	8.9	8.4	7.2	6.9	7.0	7.5	7.1	6.4	6.4	8.4	9.6	7.8
Pa_____ Philadelphia_____	37	10.4	11.1	11.5	11.0	9.7	8.8	8.1	7.9	8.3	8.9	9.7	10.1	9.6
Pittsburgh_____	25	10.8	11.1	11.1	10.7	9.3	8.2	7.5	7.2	7.7	8.5	10.1	10.6	9.4
R.I_____ Providence_____	24	11.5	11.8	12.3	12.4	11.0	10.0	9.5	9.4	9.5	9.8	10.5	11.1	10.7
S.C_____ Columbia_____	29	7.0	7.6	8.3	8.4	7.0	6.7	6.5	6.0	6.1	6.2	6.4	6.6	6.9
S. Dak____ Sioux Falls_____	29	11.0	11.1	12.6	13.4	12.1	10.8	9.8	9.8	10.3	10.8	11.6	10.8	11.2
Tenn_____ Memphis_____	29	10.6	10.6	11.4	10.7	8.9	8.1	7.5	7.1	7.6	7.8	9.4	10.1	9.1
Nashville_____	36	9.2	9.5	10.0	9.5	7.6	7.0	6.3	6.1	6.3	6.6	8.4	8.9	8.0
Tex_____ Dallas_____	24	11.3	12.1	13.2	12.8	11.2	10.9	9.5	9.1	9.5	9.7	10.8	11.1	10.9
El Paso_____	35	9.0	9.9	11.8	11.8	11.0	10.0	8.9	8.4	8.3	8.1	8.5	8.5	9.5
Houston_____	8	8.1	8.7	9.5	9.2	7.9	7.4	6.4	5.3	6.5	6.4	7.7	7.7	7.6
Utah_____ Salt Lake City____	48	7.7	8.2	9.3	9.5	9.4	9.3	9.4	9.6	9.1	8.5	7.8	7.5	8.7
Vt_____ Burlington_____	34	9.6	9.4	9.4	9.3	8.8	8.2	7.8	7.5	8.0	8.6	9.5	9.7	8.8
Va_____ Norfolk_____	29	11.6	12.1	12.4	11.8	10.3	9.6	8.8	8.8	9.6	10.4	10.7	11.0	10.6
Richmond_____	29	7.9	8.6	8.9	8.8	7.7	7.2	6.7	6.3	6.6	6.8	7.4	7.5	7.5
Wash_____ Seattle-Tacoma____	29	10.2	9.9	10.2	9.7	9.2	8.9	8.4	8.0	8.2	8.8	9.3	10.0	9.2
Spokane_____	30	8.9	9.2	9.6	9.7	8.9	8.9	8.3	8.1	8.0	8.1	8.3	8.8	8.7
W. Va____ Charleston_____	30	7.6	8.0	8.5	7.7	6.3	5.6	5.0	4.4	4.8	5.3	6.9	7.3	6.5
Wis_____ Milwaukee_____	37	12.9	12.8	13.3	13.1	11.9	10.5	9.7	9.6	10.7	11.5	12.7	12.5	11.8
Wyo_____ Cheyenne_____	20	15.7	15.3	14.9	14.7	13.0	11.7	10.5	10.7	11.4	12.5	13.8	15.0	13.3
P.R_____ San Juan_____	22	9.2	9.3	9.7	9.4	8.8	9.2	10.0	9.3	7.7	7.0	7.7	8.8	8.8

[1] City office data.

Source: U.S. National Oceanic and Atmospheric Administration, *Comparative Climatic Data*, annual.

No. 376. Normal Monthly and Seasonal Heating Degree Days, 65° Base—Selected Cities

[Airport data, except as noted. Based on standard 30-year period, 1941 through 1970. For definition of "degree day," see text, p. 205]

STATION	Jan.	Feb.	Mar.	Apr.	May	June	July	Aug.	Sept.	Oct.	Nov.	Dec.	Seasonal
Ala.... Mobile	451	337	221	40	–	–	–	–	–	39	211	385	1,684
Alaska. Juneau	1,287	1,036	1,026	783	564	354	288	332	474	719	975	1,169	9,007
Ariz... Phoenix	428	292	185	60	–	–	–	–	–	17	182	388	1,552
Ark... Little Rock	791	619	470	139	21	–	–	–	5	143	441	725	3,354
Calif... Los Angeles	331	270	267	195	114	71	19	15	23	77	158	267	1,819
Sacramento	617	426	372	227	120	20	–	–	5	101	360	595	2,843
San Francisco	518	386	372	291	210	120	93	84	66	137	291	474	3,042
Colo... Denver	1,088	902	868	525	253	80	–	–	120	408	768	1,004	6,016
Conn... Hartford	1,246	1,070	911	519	226	24	–	12	106	384	711	1,141	6,350
Del... Wilmington	1,023	879	725	381	128	–	–	–	32	254	579	939	4,940
D.C... Washington	911	776	617	265	72	–	–	–	14	190	510	856	4,211
Fla.... Jacksonville	348	282	176	24	–	–	–	–	–	19	161	317	1,327
Miami	53	67	17	–	–	–	–	–	–	–	13	56	206
Ga.... Atlanta	701	560	443	144	27	–	–	–	8	137	408	667	3,095
Hawaii. Honolulu	–	–	–	–	–	–	–	–	–	–	–	–	–
Idaho... Boise	1,116	826	741	480	252	97	–	12	127	406	756	1,020	5,833
Ill... Chicago	1,305	1,089	908	486	240	45	7	18	90	360	774	1,175	6,497
Peoria	1,277	1,044	859	416	180	17	–	8	70	327	753	1,147	6,098
Ind.... Indianapolis	1,150	960	784	387	159	11	–	5	63	302	699	1,057	5,577
Iowa... Des Moines	1,414	1,142	964	465	186	26	–	13	94	350	816	1,240	6,710
Kans... Wichita	1,045	804	671	275	90	7	–	–	32	211	606	946	4,687
Ky.... Louisville	983	818	661	286	105	5	–	–	35	241	600	911	4,645
La.... New Orleans	403	299	188	29	–	–	–	–	–	40	179	327	1,465
Maine. Portland	1,349	1,179	1,029	669	381	106	27	55	200	493	792	1,218	7,498
Md.... Baltimore	980	846	688	340	110	–	–	–	27	250	567	921	4,729
Mass... Boston	1,110	969	834	492	218	27	–	8	76	301	594	992	5,621
Mich... Detroit	1,225	1,067	918	507	238	26	–	11	80	342	717	1,097	6,228
Sault Ste. Marie	1,575	1,394	1,271	804	496	200	96	125	291	583	966	1,392	9,193
Minn... Duluth	1,751	1,481	1,287	792	484	194	67	104	318	611	1,098	1,569	9,756
Minneapolis-St. Paul	1,637	1,358	1,138	597	271	65	11	21	173	472	978	1,438	8,150
Miss... Jackson	569	442	313	74	6	–	–	–	–	91	301	504	2,300
Mo.... Kansas City	1,153	893	745	314	111	12	–	–	42	235	642	1,014	5,161
St. Louis	1,045	837	682	272	103	10	–	–	35	224	600	942	4,750
Mont... Great Falls	1,380	1,075	1,070	648	367	162	18	42	260	524	912	1,194	7,652
Nebr... Omaha	1,314	1,036	865	391	148	20	–	6	71	301	750	1,147	6,049
Nev.... Reno	1,026	781	766	546	328	145	17	50	168	456	747	992	6,022
N.H... Concord	1,376	1,187	1,014	624	315	58	16	45	182	487	810	1,246	7,360
N.J.... Atlantic City	1,001	871	741	399	131	9	–	–	35	262	570	927	4,946
N.Mex. Albuquerque	924	700	595	282	58	–	–	–	7	218	615	893	4,292
N.Y.... Albany	1,349	1,162	980	543	253	39	9	22	135	422	762	1,212	6,888
Buffalo	1,280	1,137	1,020	603	321	58	12	33	138	419	756	1,150	6,927
New York [1]	1,017	885	741	387	137	–	–	–	29	209	528	915	4,848
N.C... Charlotte	710	588	461	145	34	–	–	–	10	152	420	698	3,218
Raleigh	760	638	502	180	48	–	–	–	12	186	450	738	3,514
N.Dak. Bismarck	1,761	1,442	1,237	660	339	122	18	35	252	564	1,083	1,531	9,044
Ohio... Cincinnati	1,051	888	722	341	138	9	–	–	44	271	636	970	5,070
Cleveland	1,181	1,039	896	501	244	40	9	17	95	354	702	1,076	6,154
Columbus	1,135	972	800	418	176	13	–	8	76	342	699	1,063	5,702
Okla... Oklahoma City	874	664	532	180	36	–	–	–	12	148	474	775	3,695
Oreg... Portland	834	622	598	432	264	128	48	56	119	347	591	753	4,792
Pa.... Philadelphia	1,014	871	716	367	122	–	–	–	38	249	564	924	4,865
Pittsburgh	1,144	1,000	834	444	208	26	7	16	98	372	711	1,070	5,930
R.I.... Providence	1,135	997	871	531	259	36	–	10	93	350	651	1,039	5,972
S.C... Columbia	608	493	360	83	12	–	–	–	–	112	341	589	2,598
S. Dak. Sioux Falls	1,575	1,277	1,085	567	259	65	10	18	165	465	957	1,395	7,838
Tenn... Memphis	760	594	457	131	22	–	–	–	7	142	423	691	3,227
Nashville	828	672	524	176	45	–	–	–	10	180	498	763	3,696
Tex.... Dallas-Fort Worth	626	456	335	88	–	–	–	–	–	60	287	530	2,382
El Paso	663	465	328	89	–	–	–	–	–	92	402	639	2,678
Houston	416	294	189	23	–	–	–	–	–	24	155	333	1,434
Utah... Salt Lake City	1,147	885	787	474	237	88	–	5	105	402	777	1,076	5,983
Vt..... Burlington	1,494	1,299	1,113	660	331	63	20	49	191	502	840	1,314	7,876
Va.... Norfolk	760	661	532	226	53	–	–	–	9	141	402	704	3,488
Richmond	853	717	569	226	64	–	–	–	21	203	480	806	3,939
Wash... Seattle-Tacoma	831	636	648	489	313	167	80	82	170	397	612	760	5,185
Spokane	1,228	918	853	567	327	144	21	47	196	533	885	1,116	6,835
W. Va. Charleston	946	798	642	287	113	10	–	–	46	267	588	893	4,590
Wis... Milwaukee	1,414	1,190	1,042	609	348	90	15	36	140	440	855	1,265	7,444
Wyo... Cheyenne	1,190	1,008	1,035	669	394	156	22	31	225	530	885	1,110	7,255
P.R.... San Juan	–	–	–	–	–	–	–	–	–	–	–	–	–

– Represents zero. [1] City office data.

Source: U.S. National Oceanic and Atmospheric Administration, *Climatography of the United States*, No. 81.

No. 377. Average Relative Humidity,

[Airport data, except as noted. Eastern standard time. For period of record through 1977. Hours selected to give, observations were made on

STATE AND STATION	Length of record (yr.)	JAN. 7:00 a.m.	1:00 p.m.	FEB. 7:00 a.m.	1:00 p.m.	MAR. 7:00 a.m.	1:00 p.m.	APR. 7:00 a.m.	1:00 p.m.	MAY 7:00 a.m.	1:00 p.m.	JUNE 7:00 a.m.	1:00 p.m.
Ala — Mobile	15	82	63	80	54	83	56	87	54	86	53	87	54
Alaska — Juneau	34	79	76	81	75	79	70	75	65	74	62	76	65
Ariz — Phoenix	17	43	30	37	25	32	22	23	15	18	13	17	12
Ark — Little Rock	17	81	61	79	57	78	56	82	56	86	56	86	54
Calif — Los Angeles	18	54	59	58	62	60	65	60	63	66	66	70	68
Sacramento	17	85	69	79	60	67	51	57	42	51	36	47	31
San Francisco	18	78	66	75	65	69	62	65	60	64	60	64	59
Colo — Denver	17	44	47	43	42	41	40	38	35	38	36	37	36
Conn — Hartford	18	71	57	73	56	72	53	69	44	73	47	78	52
Del — Wilmington	30	75	60	74	58	74	53	73	50	76	53	79	54
D.C — Washington	17	68	54	68	51	68	49	68	47	72	51	75	52
Fla — Jacksonville	41	87	57	85	52	85	49	85	48	84	50	86	56
Miami	13	84	60	83	57	82	57	79	54	83	61	87	67
Ga — Atlanta	17	79	60	75	54	78	52	80	51	83	55	86	58
Hawaii — Honolulu	8	81	63	76	59	73	59	70	58	66	54	65	53
Idaho — Boise	38	74	71	68	61	55	44	47	36	45	34	42	31
Ill — Chicago	19	76	68	76	65	78	61	76	55	76	54	78	55
Peoria	18	78	68	79	66	81	63	78	56	81	57	81	56
Ind — Indianapolis	18	81	69	80	66	80	63	78	55	82	56	83	58
Iowa — Des Moines	16	76	69	79	67	79	63	78	57	78	56	80	56
Kans — Wichita	24	79	63	78	59	76	53	77	52	83	55	82	53
Ky — Louisville	17	77	64	76	62	76	58	75	53	83	55	84	58
La — New Orleans	29	86	67	85	63	85	61	88	60	89	60	89	62
Maine — Portland	37	77	62	77	60	75	59	73	55	75	58	79	61
Md — Baltimore	24	72	58	71	55	71	51	72	49	77	52	80	53
Mass — Boston	13	66	57	67	57	68	57	66	53	70	57	74	60
Mich — Detroit	44	78	68	78	65	77	60	73	52	71	51	73	53
Sault Ste. Marie	36	82	76	82	73	83	68	80	61	79	56	85	62
Minn — Duluth	16	75	69	75	64	78	63	77	57	76	54	81	60
Minneapolis-St. Paul	18	73	67	74	65	77	64	76	54	76	53	79	54
Miss — Jackson	14	87	65	86	58	87	57	90	56	91	56	90	55
Mo — Kansas City	5	74	64	75	62	77	61	75	56	83	58	83	57
St. Louis	17	82	65	80	61	81	58	79	54	83	56	84	57
Mont — Great Falls	16	62	61	58	54	53	46	49	42	45	40	45	40
Nebr — Omaha	14	76	65	77	61	76	57	76	53	79	54	81	55
Nev — Reno	14	67	50	57	39	46	32	38	28	34	25	33	24
N.H — Concord	12	74	59	75	59	79	57	76	46	79	49	87	56
N.J — Atlantic City	13	75	57	77	56	77	55	75	50	78	56	83	58
N. Mex — Albuquerque	17	49	38	43	31	32	23	25	18	23	16	23	16
N.Y — Albany	12	79	63	76	58	73	54	69	46	75	52	79	56
Buffalo	17	78	73	79	70	80	67	76	58	76	56	78	57
New York [1]	56	68	60	68	58	67	55	67	51	71	53	74	55
N.C — Charlotte	17	78	57	75	51	79	50	79	47	84	53	86	57
Raleigh	13	78	55	74	48	79	48	80	44	87	55	88	57
N. Dak — Bismarck	18	73	67	76	68	78	62	79	53	79	49	84	53
Ohio — Cincinnati	15	78	67	76	62	77	60	76	53	79	53	82	55
Cleveland	17	76	69	77	68	77	65	75	57	77	58	80	59
Columbus	18	76	67	75	64	74	58	75	52	79	54	81	55
Okla — Oklahoma City	12	79	60	77	54	75	52	78	52	83	57	84	56
Oreg — Portland	37	82	76	79	67	72	60	68	54	66	53	64	49
Pa — Philadelphia	18	73	59	71	56	71	53	69	48	75	52	78	55
Pittsburgh	18	76	66	73	62	74	58	72	50	75	51	79	52
R.I — Providence	14	71	56	70	55	70	54	68	47	71	51	76	57
S.C — Columbia	11	83	56	81	47	83	48	83	43	88	50	88	53
S. Dak — Sioux Falls	14	75	67	78	66	81	62	80	55	80	52	83	55
Tenn — Memphis	38	79	64	78	59	77	56	78	53	82	55	83	56
Nashville	12	80	65	78	58	78	53	81	52	87	56	88	56
Tex — Dallas-Fort Worth	14	80	60	78	56	79	57	85	59	88	61	86	56
El Paso	17	42	33	34	25	28	20	22	15	22	15	24	17
Houston	8	88	64	87	55	88	61	91	60	94	61	92	59
Utah — Salt Lake City	18	69	67	63	57	51	44	44	39	37	31	31	26
Vt — Burlington	12	69	63	72	63	72	59	74	52	74	51	80	58
Va — Norfolk	29	75	59	74	56	73	54	73	50	78	56	79	57
Richmond	43	81	57	79	52	78	48	75	45	79	50	82	53
Wash — Seattle-Tacoma	18	79	75	76	66	75	63	71	58	68	54	67	53
Spokane	18	82	77	78	68	67	54	56	43	51	40	48	35
W. Va — Charleston	30	77	63	76	59	74	53	75	47	82	50	86	54
Wis — Milwaukee	17	75	68	76	67	79	66	79	62	78	61	82	62
Wyo — Cheyenne	18	44	48	43	45	45	45	41	39	39	40	39	40
P.R — San Juan	22	80	64	79	62	77	60	74	61	77	64	78	65

[1] City office data.

PERCENT—SELECTED CITIES

for most of country, approximation of average highest and average lowest humidity values. Relative humidity the half-hour prior to 1957]

JULY 7:00 a.m.	1:00 p.m.	AUG. 7:00 a.m.	1:00 p.m.	SEPT. 7:00 a.m.	1:00 p.m.	OCT. 7:00 a.m.	1:00 p.m.	NOV. 7:00 a.m.	1:00 p.m.	DEC. 7:00 a.m.	1:00 p.m.	ANNUAL 7:00 a.m.	1:00 p.m.	STATE AND STATION
89	60	89	61	88	61	85	52	85	56	84	62	85	57	Ala.___ Mobile.
81	70	84	74	87	78	87	81	85	82	82	81	81	73	Alaska_ Juneau.
28	20	33	23	32	23	30	22	37	27	46	34	31	22	Ariz.___ Phoenix.
87	58	88	56	89	60	85	51	82	57	80	62	84	57	Ark.___ Little Rock.
68	68	69	69	67	68	60	65	57	63	55	61	62	65	Calif.___ Los Angeles.
47	28	49	29	51	31	57	39	75	59	85	71	63	46	Sacramento.
66	60	67	62	65	59	67	59	74	64	78	69	69	62	San Francisco.
36	36	36	35	39	36	35	35	44	49	44	50	40	40	Colo.___ Denver.
79	51	84	53	87	56	84	52	79	57	78	62	77	53	Conn.__ Hartford.
80	54	83	56	85	55	84	54	80	56	77	60	78	55	Del.___ Wilmington.
75	52	79	54	80	55	78	51	73	52	71	57	73	52	D.C.___ Washington.
87	58	90	60	91	62	90	58	89	55	88	58	87	55	Fla.___ Jacksonville.
86	65	87	66	89	68	87	65	84	61	83	59	84	62	Miami.
90	63	91	62	90	61	84	53	81	54	80	59	83	57	Ga.___ Atlanta.
65	51	66	53	65	52	67	54	73	58	76	60	70	56	Hawaii_ Honolulu.
33	22	34	23	39	30	49	41	65	61	74	72	52	44	Idaho__ Boise.
81	57	84	57	84	58	81	55	81	64	80	71	79	60	Ill.___ Chicago.
86	58	87	60	87	59	84	58	83	66	83	72	82	61	Peoria.
87	60	90	61	90	60	88	57	85	67	83	73	84	62	Ind.___ Indianapolis.
81	56	84	58	84	60	78	55	79	63	80	70	80	61	Iowa__ Des Moines.
78	49	79	50	82	56	81	53	79	56	79	61	79	55	Kans.___ Wichita.
86	58	88	58	89	60	86	55	79	61	77	65	81	59	Ky.___ Louisville.
91	66	91	66	90	66	88	59	86	61	86	67	88	63	La.___ New Orleans.
80	60	84	59	86	61	85	59	84	63	80	62	80	60	Maine__ Portland.
81	53	84	55	85	56	82	54	77	54	74	59	77	54	Md.___ Baltimore.
73	56	75	57	79	61	76	57	74	61	72	61	72	58	Mass.___ Boston.
74	51	80	53	82	55	81	55	79	64	79	69	77	58	Mich.___ Detroit.
88	62	92	63	92	67	89	67	87	76	84	78	85	67	Sault Ste. Marie.
84	58	87	62	87	63	81	62	81	70	79	74	80	63	Minn.__ Duluth.
81	54	84	55	86	60	82	58	81	66	78	70	79	60	Minneapolis-St. Paul.
93	59	94	60	94	61	93	54	90	58	88	65	90	59	Miss.___ Jackson.
80	52	86	58	87	64	81	59	79	62	77	65	80	60	Mo.___ Kansas City.
86	57	89	57	91	61	85	55	84	62	85	69	84	59	St. Louis.
37	28	38	30	46	37	46	41	55	54	61	61	50	44	Mont.___ Great Falls.
83	56	86	59	87	61	82	56	80	62	80	67	80	59	Nebr.___ Omaha.
28	19	32	21	34	21	40	26	56	40	65	51	44	31	Nev.___ Reno.
88	53	90	54	92	58	88	54	85	62	81	66	83	56	N.H.___ Concord.
84	58	86	57	87	58	86	56	81	57	76	59	81	56	N.J.___ Atlantic City.
36	28	39	29	40	31	37	29	42	34	50	42	36	28	N.Mex._ Albuquerque.
80	55	84	56	88	59	85	56	82	63	81	67	79	57	N.Y.___ Albany.
79	55	83	58	83	60	82	61	82	71	82	75	80	63	Buffalo.
75	55	78	57	79	57	76	55	73	59	70	61	72	56	New York.[1]
88	58	89	59	90	57	88	53	83	52	80	57	83	54	N.C.___ Charlotte.
90	59	93	61	93	59	90	54	83	49	80	56	84	54	Raleigh.
82	46	81	43	82	49	78	50	79	62	76	69	79	56	N.Dak_ Bismarck.
85	57	88	57	88	59	83	55	79	63	79	69	81	59	Ohio___ Cincinnati.
82	58	85	60	84	61	80	60	79	67	77	71	79	63	Cleveland.
84	56	87	58	88	58	82	55	81	64	78	69	80	59	Columbus.
81	50	82	51	85	57	80	52	78	54	77	57	80	54	Okla.___ Oklahoma City.
61	45	65	46	67	49	79	64	82	74	84	79	72	60	Oreg.___ Portland.
79	54	81	55	83	56	82	53	77	55	74	60	76	55	Pa.___ Philadelphia.
83	53	86	55	86	57	81	54	79	62	76	67	78	57	Pittsburgh.
78	57	79	55	82	57	80	54	77	58	76	60	75	55	R.I.___ Providence.
90	56	93	59	94	57	91	52	88	49	85	55	87	52	S.C.___ Columbia.
81	51	83	51	86	57	80	55	85	64	79	70	81	59	S. Dak_ Sioux Falls.
85	57	86	56	86	56	83	51	80	55	79	62	81	57	Tenn.__ Memphis.
91	59	92	60	91	61	87	56	80	59	80	64	84	58	Nashville.
81	50	83	52	88	60	84	56	81	56	79	58	83	57	Tex.___ Dallas-Fort Worth.
39	30	40	31	44	34	36	28	37	31	43	35	34	26	El Paso.
93	58	94	61	94	65	93	59	90	60	88	62	91	60	Houston.
26	20	29	22	34	27	43	40	57	58	70	71	46	42	Utah___ Salt Lake City.
81	55	85	59	88	65	85	63	81	70	77	72	78	61	Vt.___ Burlington.
82	60	85	62	84	62	83	61	78	55	75	59	78	58	Va.___ Norfolk.
85	56	88	57	89	56	89	53	84	50	81	55	83	53	Richmond.
65	49	70	53	74	58	80	68	80	74	81	77	74	62	Wash.__ Seattle-Tacoma.
38	25	43	28	50	34	66	49	81	74	84	81	62	51	Spokane.
90	60	92	58	91	55	88	53	80	56	77	62	82	56	W.Va.__ Charleston.
82	60	87	62	87	63	82	63	81	67	80	73	81	64	Wis.___ Milwaukee.
34	37	34	35	36	37	36	39	41	47	43	49	40	42	Wyo.___ Cheyenne.
78	66	79	65	79	66	80	66	81	66	80	65	78	64	P.R.___ San Juan.

Source: U.S. National Oceanic and Atmospheric Administration, *Comparative Climatic Data*, annual.

Figure 8.1

Land Owned by the Federal Government: 1977

(See table 384)

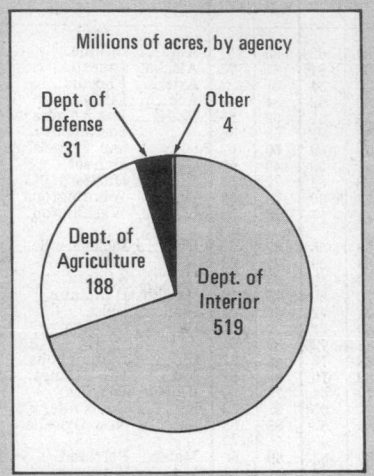

Millions of acres, by agency

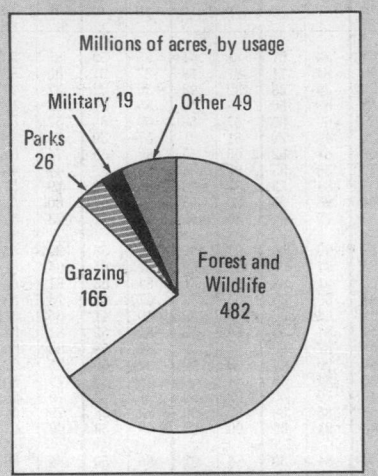

Millions of acres, by usage

Source: Chart prepared by U.S. Bureau of the Census.
         Data from U.S. General Services Administration.

Figure 8.2

**Overseas Travelers to and from
the United States: 1960 to 1977**

(See tables 412 and 415)

☐ Travelers to U.S.
▨ Travelers from U.S.

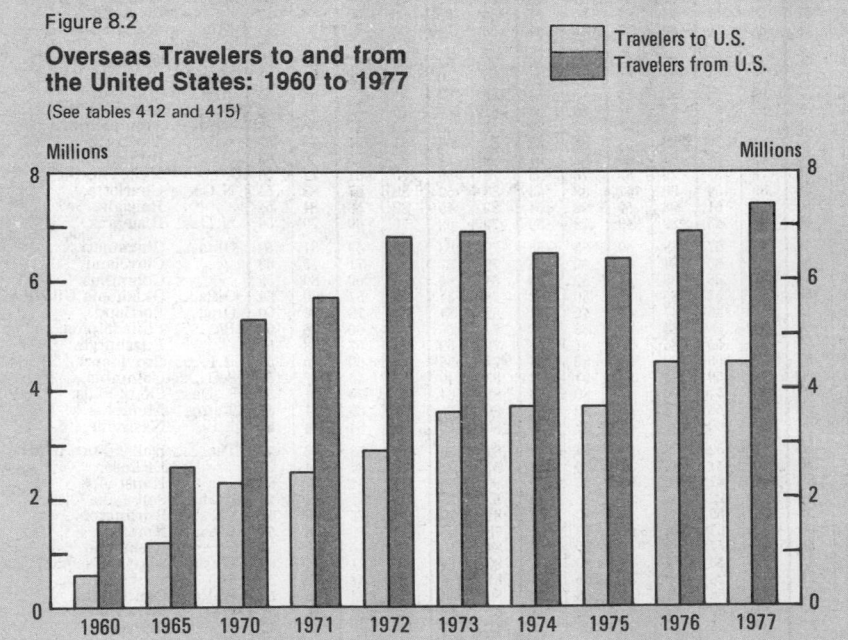

Source: Chart prepared by U.S. Bureau of the Census.
         Data from U.S. Bureau of Economic Analysis.

Section 8

Public Lands, Parks, Recreation, and Travel

This section presents statistics on the Federal public domain and federally owned and leased real property, Indian lands, public outdoor recreation acreage, national parks and forests, State and municipal parks, recreational activities, the performing arts, and domestic and foreign travel.

The primary source for data on public lands is *Public Land Statistics*, published annually by the Department of the Interior, Bureau of Land Management. Data on federally owned land and real property are collected by the General Services Administration and presented in its annual *Inventory Report on Real Property Owned by the United States Throughout the World*. The Economics, Statistics, and Cooperatives Service of the Department of Agriculture also issues statistics on land use and land ownership.

Public domain and acquired lands.—"Original public-domain land" refers to land which was untitled at the time the U.S. Government acquired sovereignty over it; that is, no claim of legal ownership had been established over it by a private individual, or by any State or political subdivision. Title to this land passed directly to the U.S. Government at the time sovereignty was acquired. (Federally owned land within the District of Columbia is not considered to be original public-domain land).

Any original public-domain land which the government has not disposed of under the public-land laws are "public domain lands," as are those lands declared by the Congress to be public lands. Acquired lands are lands the U.S. Government has gained by purchase, condemnation, and gift, for various public purposes, such as sites for public buildings, defense installations, and natural resources conservation activities. Such lands are referred to as "acquired lands."

Indian lands.—Indian lands are the private landholdings of individual Indians or Indian tribes that are subject to special restrictive provisions of Federal law administered by the Bureau of Indian Affairs. They have been set aside for Indian use by treaties, congressional acts, and executive orders. Although most of these lands are in reservations for specific tribes, there are groups of scattered off-reservation allotments in individual ownership and other small tracts of land occupied by Indian groups.

Entries, selections, patents, and certifications.—The data on entries, selections, patents, and certifications refer to transactions which involve the disposal, under the public land laws (including the homestead laws), of Federal public lands to non-Federal owners. In general, original entries and selections are applications to secure title to public lands which have been accepted as properly filed. Some types of applications, however, are not reported until issuance of the final certificate, which passes equitable title to the land to the applicant. Applications become final entries (perfected entries) upon issuance of a final certificate to the applicant after he has complied fully with the requirements of the laws relating to his application. Patents are instruments which pass legal title to the land to the applicant. Certifications are issued in lieu of patents in connection with certain State selections.

Parks and recreation.—The Department of the Interior has responsibility for administering the national parks. As part of this function, it compiles data on and issues various reports relating to the usage of public parks for recreation purposes. The National Park Service publishes information on visits to national parks in its monthly report (also issued cumulatively), *Public Use of the National Parks*; its semiannual report, *Areas Administered by the National Park Service*, presents data on acreage in public

233

parks; and its *National Parks and Landmarks* gives brief descriptions of each area administered by the Service and also covers sites eligible for registry as natural or national historic landmarks and non-federally owned national historic sites.

The Heritage Conservation and Recreation Service (formerly Bureau of Outdoor Recreation) in the Department of the Interior administers a land and water conservation fund which provides grants to States, counties, and cities for outdoor recreation purposes and to designated Federal agencies for acquisition of new recreational lands and waters. It also issues statistics on the fund and on other aspects of outdoor recreation. The Fish and Wildlife Service compiles and releases data on sport fishing and hunting and on the number and acreage of national wildlife refuges in its annual *Federal Aid in Fish and Wildlife Restoration*, and its *National Survey of Fishing and Hunting*, published every 5 years.

Statistics for State and municipal parks and playgrounds, as well as for other outdoor recreational activities, are compiled by the National Recreation and Park Association, Arlington, Va., which issues its *Recreation and Park Yearbook* at 5-year intervals, and its *Parks & Recreation* monthly. The Department of Agriculture's Forest Service, in its *Annual Report of the Chief*, issues data on recreational uses of the national forests.

Statistics on recreation other than usage of public lands have not generally been compiled and published in a systematic way. In general, many more data are available in the files of public and private bodies than have been published; and much of the publication is in forms not physically permanent nor likely to be preserved in libraries and other reference sources. The series presented here represent only the more readily available data.

Domestic and foreign travel.—Data on the volume and characteristics of domestic travel are collected and published by the Bureau of the Census as part of its Census of Transportation carried out every five years. The most recent data now available are from the 1977 census. Comparable data appear in the Bureau's 1963 *Passenger Transportation Survey*, vol. I, and its 1967 and 1972 *National Travel Survey*, vol. I.

Information on foreign travel and personal expenditures abroad, as well as expenditures by foreign citizens traveling in the United States, is compiled by the U.S. Bureau of Economic Analysis and published in the monthly *Survey of Current Business*. Data on the number of passports issued annually to U.S. citizens are to be found in the annual *Summary of Passport Statistics* issued by the U.S. Passport Office. Statistics on arrivals to and departures from the United States by air are reported by the Department of Transportation in cooperation with the U.S. Immigration and Naturalization Service in *International Air Travel Statistics*. Prior to 1976, data on sea travel were published by the U.S. Immigration and Naturalization Service in its *Annual Report*.

Statistical Reliability.—For a discussion of statistical collection and estimation, sampling procedures, and measures of statistical reliability pertaining to the Census of Transportation, see Appendix III.

Historical statistics.—Tabular headnotes provide cross-references, where applicable, to *Historical Statistics of the United States, Colonial Times to 1970*. See Appendix I.

No. 378. Area and Acquisition of the Federal Public Domain: 1781 to 1977

One acre=.4 hectare. Areas of acquisitions are as computed in 1912, and do not agree with figures in square miles shown in table 339 which include later adjustments and reflect subsequent remeasurement. Excludes outlying areas of the United States amounting to 647,655 acres (262,102 hectares) in 1977. See also *Historical Statistics, Colonial Times to 1970*, series J 3–6:

YEAR	LAND AREA [1]		YEAR AND ACQUISITION	ACRES (mil.)			HECTARES (mil.)		
	Acres (mil.)	Hec- tares (mil.)		Total	Land	Inland water	Total	Land	Inland water
1802	200	81	Aggregate	1,838	1,805	33	744	731	13
1850	1,200	486							
1880	900	365	1781-1802 (State Cessions)	237	233	3	96	94	1
1912	600	243	1803, Louisiana Purchase [2]	530	523	6	215	212	2
1946	413	167							
1950	412	167	1819, Cession from Spain	46	43	[3] 3	19	17	[3] 1
1955	408	165	Red River Basin [4]	30	29	1	12	12	(Z)
1959	769	311							
1960	772	313	1846, Oregon Compromise	183	181	3	74	73	1
1965	766	310	1848, Mexican Cession [2]	339	334	4	137	135	2
1970	761	308	1850, Purchase from Texas	79	79	(Z)	32	32	(Z)
1974	761	308	1853, Gadsden Purchase	19	19	(Z)	8	8	(Z)
1975	760	308	1867, Alaska Purchase	375	363	13	152	147	5
1976	762	308							
1977	742	300							

Z Less than 500,000.
[1] Owned by Federal Government. Comprises original public domain plus acquired lands. Estimated from imperfect data available for indicated years. Prior to 1959, excludes Alaska, and 1960, Hawaii. Source: Beginning 1955, U.S. General Services Administration, *Inventory Report on Real Property Owned by the United States Throughout the World*, annual.
[2] Data for Louisiana Purchase exclude areas eliminated by Treaty of 1819 with Spain. Such areas are included in figures for Mexican Cession.
[3] Includes 33,920 acres (13,738 hectares) subsequently part of Texas, which is not a public-domain State.
[4] Represents drainage basin of Red River of the North, south of 49th parallel. Authorities differ as to method and date of its acquisition. Some hold it as part of Louisiana Purchase; others, as acquired from Great Britain.

Source: Except as noted, U.S. Dept. of the Interior. Estimated area, Bureau of Land Management; all other data, Office of the Secretary, *Areas of Acquisitions to the Territory of the U.S.*, 1922.

No. 379. Ownership of Land, by Class: 1959 to 1974

[One acre=.4 hectare. See also *Historical Statistics, Colonial Times to 1970*, series J 66, J 71, and J 76]

CLASS	1959			1969			1974		
	Land		Per- cent	Land		Per- cent	Land		Per- cent
	Acres (mil- lions)	Hec- tares (mil- lions)		Acres (mil- lions)	Hec- tares (mil- lions)		Acres (mil- lions)	Hec- tares (mil- lions)	
Total [1]	2,271	919.8	100.0	2,264	916.9	100.0	2,264	916.9	100.0
Private land [2]	1,332	539.5	58.7	1,317	533.4	58.2	1,317	533.4	58.2
Indian land [3]	53	21.5	2.3	50	20.3	2.2	50	20.3	2.2
Public land	886	358.8	39.0	897	363.3	39.6	897	363.2	39.6
Federal land [4]	765	309.8	33.7	763	309.0	33.7	761	308.1	33.6
State land [5]	103	41.7	4.5	114	46.2	5.0	116	47.0	5.1
County and municipal land	18	7.3	.8	20	8.1	.9	20	8.1	.9

[1] Changes in total land area are due to variable methods and materials used in periodic remeasurements, and to the construction of artificial reservoirs.
[2] Land owned by individuals, partnerships, and corporations.
[3] Trust land held by tribes and individual owners exclusive of federally owned land used by Indians.
[4] Gross acreage of Federal holdings including highway and road rights-of-way in Federal areas.
[5] Includes the major part of highway and road rights-of-way through predominantly private land areas.

Source: U.S. Dept. of Agriculture, Economics, Statistics, and Cooperatives Service, *Major Uses of Land in the United States*, December 1973, and unpublished data.

No. 380. UNITED STATES SHORELINE—OWNERSHIP AND USE: 1971

REGION [1]	Total shore-line [2]	OWNERSHIP			SHORE USE			
		Federal	State and local	Private	Recreation		Non-recreational development	Unde-veloped
					Public	Private		
Total_____miles [3]__	84,240	45,290	10,080	26,310	3,390	5,820	6,230	68,800
North Atlantic_____	8,620	580	840	7,200	1,020	2,600	2,430	2,570
South Atlantic-Gulf_____	14,620	1,870	1,960	8,250	690	1,500	2,440	9,990
Lower Mississippi_____	1,940	240	330	1,370	20	30	50	1,840
Texas Gulf_____	2,500	390	50	2,060	400	160	110	1,830
Great Lakes_____	3,680	130	520	3,030	370	1,220	250	1,840
California_____	1,810	380	350	1,080	440	190	230	950
North Pacific_____	2,840	240	270	2,310	350	120	190	2,180
Alaska_____	47,300	41,350	5,500	450	10	-	330	46,960
Hawaii_____	930	110	260	560	90	-	200	640
Total____kilometers [3]__	135,567	72,885	16,221	42,340	5,455	9,366	10,025	110,719
North Atlantic_____	13,872	933	1,351	11,586	1,641	4,184	3,910	4,135
South Atlantic-Gulf_____	23,527	3,009	3,154	13,276	1,110	2,413	3,926	16,076
Lower Mississippi_____	3,122	386	531	2,204	32	48	80	2,961
Texas Gulf_____	4,023	627	80	3,315	643	257	177	2,945
Great Lakes_____	5,922	209	836	4,876	595	1,963	402	2,961
California_____	2,912	611	563	1,738	708	305	370	1,528
North Pacific_____	4,570	386	434	3,717	563	193	305	3,508
Alaska_____	76,119	66,544	8,851	724	16	-	531	75,572
Hawaii_____	1,496	177	418	901	144	-	321	1,029

- Represents zero.   [1] For definition of regions, see source.
[2] Includes "uncertain" ownership, not shown separately.   [3] One mile=1.609 kilometers.

Source: U.S. Corps of Engineers, *Report on the National Shoreline Study,* 1971.

No. 381. FEDERAL LAND AND BUILDINGS OWNED AND LEASED: 1955 TO 1977

[As of June 30 except, beginning 1976, as of Sept. 30. Covers Federal real property throughout the world, except as noted. Totals include data not shown separately]

ITEM AND AGENCY	1955	1960	1965	1970	1974	1975	1976	1977
Federally owned:								
Land, total_____mil. acres__	754	772	766	762	761	760	763	742
Dept. of Agriculture_____mil. acres__	189	186	187	187	188	188	190	188
Dept. of Defense_____mil. acres__	31	30	30	31	31	31	31	31
Dept. of the Interior_____mil. acres__	530	553	546	540	539	538	538	519
Buildings, number [1]_____1,000__	397	405	427	411	408	399	405	410
Dept. of Defense [1]_____1,000__	259	320	335	319	310	312	317	314
Dept. of the Interior_____1,000__	31	30	34	34	35	30	31	32
Buildings, floor area [1]_____mil. sq. ft__	2,231	2,415	2,458	2,507	2,513	2,466	2,515	2,579
Dept. of Defense [1]_____mil. sq. ft__	1,646	1,929	1,874	1,857	1,818	1,802	1,824	1,824
General Services Admin___mil. sq. ft__	123	121	172	205	191	194	196	201
Dept. of the Interior_____mil. sq. ft__	50	41	47	61	57	57	60	61
Veterans Administration__mil. sq. ft__	101	115	114	110	111	110	112	114
Cost of land, buildings, etc_____bil. dol__	38	53	66	79	87	91	96	101
Dept. of Defense_____bil. dol__	24	31	39	44	54	56	58	60
Dept. of the Interior_____bil. dol__	4	5	6	8	9	10	10	11
Federally leased:								
Land_____mil. acres__	(NA)	1.8	1.8	1.6	1.7	1.2	1.2	1.4
Dept. of Defense_____mil. acres__	(NA)	1.7	1.7	1.4	1.6	1.0	1.0	1.2
Buildings, floor area [1]_____mil. sq. ft__	(NA)	97	132	182	215	210	230	228
Dept. of Defense [1]_____mil. sq. ft__	(NA)	11	7	7	8	13	19	17
Rental property, cost_____mil. dol__	(NA)	174	282	451	633	664	742	796
Dept. of Defense_____mil. dol__	(NA)	35	35	63	58	65	65	75

NA Not available.   [1] Excludes data for Dept. of Defense military functions outside United States.

Source: U.S. General Services Administration, *Inventory Report on Real Property Owned by the United States Throughout the World,* annual, and *Inventory Report on Real Property Leased to the United States Throughout the World,* annual.

No. 382. Total Land, and Federally Owned Land and Buildings, 1955 to 1977, and by States, 1977

[As of **June 30**, except as noted]

YEAR AND STATE	LAND (1,000 acres)						Cost [2] of land owned by Federal Govt. (cumulative) (mil. dol.)	FEDERALLY OWNED BUILDINGS	
	Total	Not owned by Federal Government	Owned by Federal Government					Number	Cost (cumulative) (mil. dol.)
			Total [1]		Public domain	Acquired by other methods			
			Acres	Percent					
1955 [3]	1,903,825	1,495,929	407,896	21.4	357,210	50,686	2,369	384,916	14,475
1960	2,273,407	1,501,894	771,512	33.9	720,004	51,508	2,956	405,443	19,916
1965	2,271,343	1,505,546	765,797	33.7	712,525	53,272	4,128	426,863	24,368
1970	2,271,343	1,510,042	761,301	33.5	706,436	54,865	5,476	410,587	28,705
1971	2,271,343	1,511,140	760,204	33.5	704,794	55,410	5,778	406,528	29,339
1972	2,271,343	1,510,667	760,676	33.5	704,750	55,926	6,010	403,323	30,053
1973	2,271,343	1,510,344	760,999	33.5	704,751	56,248	6,198	403,409	30,987
1974	2,271,343	1,510,811	760,532	33.5	703,813	56,719	6,464	401,335	32,759
1975	2,271,343	1,510,929	760,414	33.5	702,866	57,548	6,872	398,737	34,345
1976	2,271,343	1,509,151	762,192	33.5	702,793	59,399	7,428	405,043	37,350
1977, total [4]	**2,271,343**	**1,529,834**	**741,509**	**32.6**	**683,286**	**58,223**	**7,860**	**403,105**	**39,951**
Ala	32,678	31,549	1,129	3.5	30	1,099	92	7,336	670
Alaska	365,482	34,635	330,847	90.5	330,829	18	15	7,708	1,262
Ariz	72,688	40,570	32,118	44.2	31,795	323	59	12,008	742
Ark	33,599	30,275	3,324	9.9	1,073	2,251	256	4,539	262
Calif	100,207	53,979	46,228	46.1	43,762	2,466	709	58,007	4,678
Colo	66,486	42,837	23,649	35.6	22,555	1,094	149	6,981	1,055
Conn	3,135	3,126	9	.3	–	9	43	2,101	225
Del	1,266	1,225	41	3.2	–	41	10	1,146	135
D.C	39	27	12	32.0	–	12	161	1,902	1,238
Fla	34,721	31,109	3,612	10.4	370	3,242	232	14,772	1,657
Ga	37,295	35,064	2,231	5.9	–	2,231	158	13,152	1,048
Hawaii	4,106	3,698	408	9.9	37	371	52	14,512	772
Idaho	52,933	19,211	33,722	63.7	32,912	810	52	4,217	298
Ill	35,795	35,230	565	1.6	–	565	133	6,998	1,309
Ind	23,158	22,664	494	2.1	24	470	139	5,392	412
Iowa	35,861	35,636	225	.6	–	225	57	1,603	205
Kans	52,511	51,783	728	1.4	26	702	276	7,042	534
Ky	25,512	24,124	1,388	5.4	–	1,388	342	6,706	656
La	28,868	27,793	1,075	3.7	25	1,050	92	4,542	636
Maine	19,848	19,714	134	.7	–	134	11	3,189	284
Md	6,319	6,114	205	3.2	–	205	103	11,962	1,765
Mass	5,035	4,952	83	1.7	–	83	108	5,774	756
Mich	36,492	33,056	3,436	9.4	297	3,139	86	6,409	521
Minn	51,206	47,803	3,403	6.6	1,166	2,237	67	2,369	254
Miss	30,223	28,542	1,681	5.6	3	1,678	114	5,537	431
Mo	44,248	42,066	2,182	4.9	3	2,179	353	6,112	817
Mont	93,271	65,643	27,628	29.6	25,226	2,402	89	6,110	250
Nebr	49,032	48,332	700	1.4	249	451	90	2,485	224
Nev	70,264	8,704	61,560	87.6	61,357	203	26	4,930	279
N.H	5,769	5,058	711	12.3	–	711	26	808	103
N.J	4,813	4,683	130	2.7	–	130	103	7,498	854
N. Mex	77,766	51,728	26,038	33.5	24,187	1,851	35	11,710	863
N.Y	30,681	30,434	247	.8	–	247	172	9,494	1,659
N.C	31,403	29,369	2,034	6.5	–	2,034	130	15,142	830
N. Dak	44,453	42,079	2,374	5.3	209	2,165	148	4,637	470
Ohio	26,222	25,881	341	1.3	–	341	233	5,329	1,360
Okla	44,088	42,518	1,570	3.6	150	1,420	466	7,182	540
Oreg	61,599	29,283	32,316	52.5	30,943	1,373	373	4,444	173
Pa	28,804	28,127	677	2.4	–	677	323	6,282	992
R.I	677	669	8	1.2	–	8	9	2,711	239
S.C	19,374	18,242	1,132	5.8	–	1,132	85	8,244	819
S. Dak	48,882	45,517	3,365	6.9	1,601	1,764	157	2,993	219
Tenn	26,728	24,924	1,804	6.7	–	1,804	371	5,858	1,155
Tex	168,218	164,925	3,293	2.0	–	3,293	373	26,455	2,398
Utah	52,697	18,381	34,316	65.1	33,762	554	24	4,863	375
Vt	5,936	5,648	288	4.8	–	288	18	324	40
Va	25,496	23,139	2,357	9.2	–	2,357	174	18,141	1,960
Wash	42,694	30,273	12,421	29.1	11,033	1,388	274	16,728	1,024
W. Va	15,411	14,327	1,084	7.0	–	1,084	197	1,208	153
Wis	35,011	33,152	1,859	5.3	10	1,849	42	4,342	253
Wyo	62,343	32,016	30,327	48.6	29,652	675	53	3,171	97

– Represents zero. [1] Excludes trust properties. [2] Excludes value of public-domain lands for which there are no costs. [3] Excludes Alaska and Hawaii. [4] As of Sept. 30.

Source: U.S. General Services Administration, *Inventory Report on Real Property Owned by the United States Throughout the World*, annual.

No. 383. Federally Owned Land, by Predominant Usage: 1960 to 1977

[As of **June 30** except, beginning **1977**, as of **Sept. 30**. Covers land in United States only (50 States and D.C.). Cost of land figures represent total cost to date and exclude unreserved public domain; public domain reserved for national parks, national forests, military installations and other purposes; and historical sites acquired by methods other than by purchase]

TYPE OF LAND	LAND (mil. acres)					COST OF LAND (mil. dol.)				
	1960	1965	1970	1975	1977	1960	1965	1970	1975	1977
Total	771.5	765.8	761.3	760.4	741.5	2,956	4,128	5,475	6,872	7,860
Forest and wildlife	513.5	508.4	503.2	502.3	482.2	130	237	350	589	693
Grazing	166.7	165.2	163.5	164.0	164.8	22	18	26	26	26
Military (except airfields)	18.3	15.7	17.7	18.1	18.7	348	298	331	334	377
Parks and historic sites	22.4	22.8	24.6	25.3	26.5	142	180	373	618	932
Reclamation and irrigation	8.0	7.8	7.5	7.0	6.1	170	224	312	313	335
Flood control and navigation	5.5	6.7	7.4	8.0	8.1	1,063	1,915	2,591	3,381	3,735
Power development and distribution	1.9	1.9	2.1	1.5	1.5	219	204	251	273	269
Airfields	2.0	2.0	1.5	2.3	1.5	195	203	162	199	135
Other	33.2	35.3	33.8	32.0	32.1	667	849	1,079	1,139	1,358

No. 384. Federally Owned Land, by Agency and Predominant Usage: 1977

[**In thousands of acres, except as indicated.** As of Sept. 30. Covers land in United States only]

AGENCY	Forest and wildlife	Grazing	Military exc. airfields	Parks and historic sites	Reclamation, irrigation	Flood control, navigation	Power development [1]	Airfields	Other
Total cost of land mil. dol	693	26	377	932	335	3,735	269	135	1,358
Total acreage	482,230	164,759	18,740	26,495	6,101	8,115	1,513	1,497	32,059
Agriculture	167,486	19,677	–	(z)	–	–	–	–	759
Energy Research and Development Administration	–	–	–	–	–	–	–	–	2,107
Defense	100	–	18,738	(z)	18	7,162	703	1,481	2,597
Army	–	–	9,851	–	–	–	–	61	1,114
Air Force	–	–	6,852	–	–	–	–	1,420	14
Navy	–	–	2,035	–	–	–	–	–	1,440
Corps of Engineers [2]	100	–	–	(z)	18	7,162	703	–	29
Interior	314,643	145,082	–	26,332	6,083	29	768	3	26,193
Tennessee Valley Authority	1	–	–	155	–	716	42	–	30
Other	–	–	2	8	–	208	–	13	373

– Represents zero.   Z Less than 500 acres.   [1] Includes distribution.   [2] Civil functions only.

Source of tables 383 and 384: U.S. General Services Administration, *Inventory Report on Real Property Owned by the United States Throughout the World*, annual.

No. 385. Public Lands—Disposal Transactions and Cash Receipts: 1951 to 1977

[For years ending **June 30**. For explanation of terms, see text, p. 233. Period figures are totals, not annual averages. See also *Historical Statistics, Colonial Times to 1970*, series J 10–15 and J 26–32]

ITEM	1951-1960	1961-1965	1966-1970	1971-1975	1973	1974	1975	1976	1977
Original entries and selections [1] 1,000 acres	3,176	13,643	3,875	13,078	132	1,092	11,762	102,810	10,518
Final entries [1] 1,000 acres	2,382	2,054	2,123	4,704	430	3,287	728	8,206	1,161
Patents and certifications [1] 1,000 acres	5,628	4,186	7,338	5,584	566	3,584	807	8,302	1,163
Homestead entries: [2]									
Original entries: Number	6,158	2,145	238	211	32	92	13	6	13
Acres 1,000	790	259	33	24	3	10	2	(z)	2
Final entries [3] 1,000 acres	442	118	54	42	6	5	4	4	5
Cash receipts [4] mil. dol	1,399	1,297	3,473	16,141	4,230	7,178	2,920	3,192	3,008
Mineral leases [5] mil. dol	1,050	967	3,045	15,415	4,088	7,001	2,731	2,983	2,688
Sales of timber mil. dol	209	193	286	496	105	128	108	131	235

Z Less than 500 acres.   [1] Includes homesteads.   [2] Excludes ceded Indian lands.   [3] Excludes commuted homesteads.   [4] Comprises Bureau of Land Management receipts from such sources as: Sales of public and ceded Indian lands; fees and commissions; mineral rentals, royalties, and bonuses; sales of timber; grazing fees and rentals; and land rentals.   [5] Act of Feb. 25, 1920. For 1977, includes oil and gas receipts of $296 million.

Source: U.S. Bureau of Land Management, *Public Land Statistics*, annual.

No. 386. PUBLIC DOMAIN LANDS—HOMESTEAD ENTRIES, 1951 TO 1977, AND VACANT LANDS, 1950 TO 1977, BY STATES

[In thousands of acres. Homestead entries for years ending June 30 through 1976, Sept. 30 thereafter; vacant lands as of June 30 through 1976, Sept. 30 thereafter. Excludes States with less than 500 acres in years specified. Vacant public lands are those which are unappropriated and unreserved. The former represent lands not covered by an entry; the latter, lands not reserved for some public purpose, i.e., available for entry or selection under appropriate laws. Data cover vacant public lands other than Alaska, withdrawn for classification in furtherance of Taylor Grazing Act and for conservation and development of natural resources. See text, p. 233. See *Historical Statistics, Colonial Times to 1970*, series J 8 for vacant lands excluding Alaska and J 14 for homestead entries]

STATE	HOMESTEAD ENTRIES [1]					VACANT LANDS [2]					
	1951–1960, total	1961–1970, total	1971–1975, total	1976	1977	1950	1960	1970	1975	1976	1977
Total	[3]790.0	291.9	23.9	.5	1.8	440,408	437,879	[4]159,139	[4]158,778	[4]158,337	159,204
Ala	–	–	–	–	–	27	3	1	3	3	3
Alaska	572.0	279.9	21.8	–	–	270,000	270,200	[5]257,133	[5]257,065	[5]250,974	[5]246,197
Ariz	9.4	1.3	–	–	–	12,545	12,442	11,597	11,592	11,589	11,575
Calif	3.9	–	.1	–	–	16,306	15,673	14,587	14,570	14,576	14,538
Colo	14.5	.2	–	–	–	8,070	8,090	6,485	6,440	6,418	6,107
Idaho	96.0	3.0	–	–	–	10,858	11,652	11,597	11,520	11,497	11,498
Minn	–	–	–	–	–	93	58	23	26	26	26
Mont	1.6	–	1.1	.5	1.8	6,773	6,385	6,143	6,140	6,139	6,141
Nebr	–	–	–	–	–	25	6	8	4	4	9
Nev	25.8	5.2	.2	–	–	47,158	46,027	47,310	47,367	46,801	48,450
N. Mex	3.9	1.5	.1	–	–	14,503	13,129	12,576	12,400	12,398	12,266
N. Dak	–	–	.2	–	–	96	79	69	68	68	68
Oreg	1.3	–	–	–	–	13,298	13,153	13,342	13,136	13,032	13,034
S. Dak	–	–	.5	–	–	290	272	276	276	276	276
Utah	53.6	.3	–	–	–	23,033	24,097	20,877	20,798	21,066	20,754
Wash	.8	.3	–	–	–	487	365	292	304	304	306
Wyo	2.5	.1	–	–	–	16,615	16,198	13,944	14,118	14,122	14,133
Other States	.5	.1	–	–	–	231	50	11	16	18	19

– Represents zero. [1] Original homestead entries. [2] Includes acreage of public lands within grazing districts, as follows (in thousands): 1950, 134,875; 1960, 141,645; 1970, 132,669; 1975, 132,203, 1976, 132,517 and 1977, 133,555. [3] Includes 4,200 acres for Bureau of Land Management. [4] Excludes Alaska; see footnote 5. [5] Effective Jan. 17, 1969, all unreserved lands in Alaska were withdrawn from all forms of appropriations or disposition under the Public Land Laws; land and resources were reserved until Dec. 31, 1970, for determination and protection of rights of native Aleuts, Eskimos, and Indians of Alaska. The Alaskan Native Claims Act of Dec. 18, 1971, and Public Land Order No. 5418 dated Mar. 25, 1974, withdraws all unreserved lands in Alaska.

No. 387. PUBLIC DOMAIN LAND—ENTRIES UNDER ALL ACTS, BY STATES: 1951 TO 1977

[In thousands of acres. For years ending June 30 except, beginning 1977, Sept. 30. Covers homestead, desert land, and mineral entries, public auction sales, Indian and State selections, and other disposal transactions. See text, p. 233. See also *Historical Statistics, Colonial Times to 1970*, series J 10–12]

STATE	ORIGINAL ENTRIES						FINAL ENTRIES			PATENTS AND CERTIFICATIONS		
	1951–1960, total	1961–1970, total	1971–1975, total	1975	1976	1977	1961–1970, total	1971–1975, total	1977	1961–1970, total	1971–1975, total	1977
Total	3,176	17,518	13,078	11,762	[1]102,810	10,518	4,178	4,704	1,161	[2]10,855	5,584	1,163
Alaska	1,535	15,019	12,898	11,752	[1]102,800	10,469	2,537	4,270	1,145	6,050	4,470	990
Ariz	240	1,286	32	(Z)	6	3	65	86	1	603	227	2
Calif	152	32	50	3	(Z)	38	139	50	(Z)	312	101	51
Idaho	402	258	57	4	3	4	276	98	6	312	129	13
Nev	462	425	12	2	(Z)	(Z)	339	74	1	823	110	1
Wyo	51	58	7	–	(Z)	(Z)	149	66	(Z)	189	68	4
Other	334	440	23	1	1	4	673	60	8	2,566	479	101

– Represents zero. Z Less than 500 acres. [1] Includes entries under the Alaska Native Claims Act of Dec. 18, 1971. [2] Excludes acreage for patents reissued.

Source of tables 386 and 387: U.S. Bureau of Land Management, *Public Land Statistics*, annual.

No. 388. Lands Under Jurisdiction of Bureau of Indian Affairs—Acreage, by States: 1920 to 1977

[In thousands of acres. Excludes States with less than 500 acres in years specified. Beginning 1960, taxable lands generally included. See also *Historical Statistics, Colonial Times to 1970*, series J 16-19]

STATE	1920	1940	1960	1970	1975	1976	1977 Total	1977 Indian Trust allotted	1977 Indian Tribal [1]	1977 Government owned
Total	[2] 71,399	55,406	[3] 58,076	55,408	[1] 52,316	[1] 52,390	52,670	9,954	42,222	494
Ala	(NA)	(NA)	4,168	4,170	117	116	118	31	87	–
Ariz	18,653	19,225	21,515	19,714	20,034	20,035	20,037	253	19,694	90
Calif	517	667	558	536	546	547	547	74	473	(Z)
Colo	469	667	752	755	782	782	782	4	778	(Z)
Fla	24	61	79	79	79	79	79	–	79	(Z)
Idaho	683	818	835	828	827	829	828	336	459	33
Iowa	3	3	4	4	4	4	4	–	4	(Z)
Kans	273	36	29	27	26	26	27	23	4	(Z)
Mich	153	27	22	21	21	21	21	9	12	–
Minn	1,509	653	756	763	764	764	764	51	713	(Z)
Miss	(X)	9	16	18	17	18	18	(Z)	18	(Z)
Mont	6,054	6,455	5,457	5,274	5,282	5,285	5,280	3,104	2,173	3
Nebr	360	76	68	62	61	65	65	43	22	(Z)
Nev	741	1,127	1,152	1,148	1,153	1,153	1,153	79	1,066	8
N. Mex	4,697	7,153	6,542	7,209	7,537	7,611	7,843	680	6,855	308
N.C	63	57	56	57	56	56	56	–	56	(Z)
N. Dak	2,105	1,036	879	850	850	851	851	656	194	1
Okla	19,552	2,844	1,855	1,424	1,306	1,282	1,269	1,175	85	9
Oreg	1,718	1,737	1,238	687	761	761	761	143	618	(Z)
S. Dak	6,686	5,865	5,064	4,975	5,020	5,030	5,085	2,562	2,485	38
Utah	1,641	1,693	2,125	2,271	2,276	2,276	2,277	36	2,241	(Z)
Wash	2,719	2,740	2,591	2,460	2,504	2,504	2,508	518	1,987	3
Wis	590	445	422	188	407	408	409	81	328	(Z)
Wyo	2,102	2,013	1,890	1,887	1,886	1,887	1,888	96	1,791	1

– Represents zero.   NA Not available.   X Not applicable.   Z Fewer than 500 acres.
[1] Includes tribal fee lands.   [2] Includes 88,000 acres in New York; partial jurisdiction over Indian lands resides with New York State and acreage not shown for later years.
[3] Includes 3,000 acres in South Carolina, not shown separately.
Source: U.S. Bureau of Indian Affairs, *Annual Report of Indian Land*, and unpublished data.

No. 389. Public Lands—Leases, Permits, and Licenses, by Class: 1960 to 1977

[As of June 30, through 1976; thereafter, as of Sept. 30 except as noted. Excludes leases on acquired, submerged, and military lands. See *Historical Statistics, Colonial Times to 1970*, series J 41-42, for oil and gas leases]

YEAR	Total	MINERAL CLASS Leases Total	MINERAL CLASS Leases Oil and gas [1]	MINERAL CLASS Leases Coal	MINERAL CLASS Leases Other	MINERAL CLASS Permits	MINERAL CLASS Licenses	OTHER CLASSES Leases Total	OTHER CLASSES Leases Grazing [2]	OTHER CLASSES Permits [3]
Number:										
1960	142,114	140,057	139,534	294	229	2,035	22	19,010	9,911	(NA)
1965	101,863	101,086	100,339	379	368	763	14	10,246	8,912	(NA)
1970	100,598	100,010	99,038	525	447	583	5	10,103	8,559	1,111
1973	95,639	95,315	94,362	526	427	322	2	9,658	8,134	1,260
1974	99,042	98,732	97,795	526	411	307	3	9,368	7,953	1,418
1975	104,075	103,762	102,815	529	418	309	4	9,253	7,785	1,354
1976	103,800	103,487	101,796	529	1,162	309	4	9,110	7,721	1,267
1977	104,377	104,079	102,130	523	1,426	294		9,349	7,981	1,286
Acreage (1,000):										
1960	118,157	114,136	113,667	199	270	4,020	1	18,615	18,532	914
1965	66,267	64,955	64,148	374	433	1,311	1	18,221	18,057	870
1970	65,374	64,323	63,030	764	529	1,051	(Z)	18,461	18,262	1,378
1973	69,682	68,928	67,664	778	486	754	(Z)	17,601	17,477	6,439
1974	74,520	73,800	72,537	781	483	720	(Z)	17,199	17,073	2,391
1975	82,618	81,885	80,621	780	485	733	(Z)	17,315	17,144	1,838
1976	83,543	82,791	80,226	795	1,770	752	(Z)	17,189	17,014	1,468
1977	86,902	86,274	83,319	791	2,164	626	2	17,242	17,122	1,453

NA Not available.   Z Less than 500 acres.   [1] Includes naval petroleum reserve: 17 leases, 9,227 acres.
[2] As of Dec. 31.   [3] Excludes grazing licenses and permits within grazing districts.
Source: U.S. Bureau of Land Management, *Public Land Statistics*, annual.

No. 390. Federal Acquisitions and Fund Grants for Outdoor Recreation: 1967 to 1977

[For years ending **June 30** except, beginning 1976, ending **Sept. 30.** Covers obligations only for projects financed by Land and Water Conservation Fund. Other Federal agencies also provide financial support. Federal acquisitions cost data and figures for Federal matching grants to States frequently include adjustments in prior years, e.g., refunds or deficiency judgments for condemnations, cost overruns, etc.]

ITEM	1967	1969	1970	1971	1972	1973	1974	1975	1976	1977
Federal real property acquisitions: [1]										
Acres purchased, total _____1,000__	130.7	255.3	215.0	105.8	150.5	175.1	123.3	95.4	212.8	314.3
National Park Service _____1,000__	52.6	124.5	60.4	52.1	57.5	37.6	63.2	62.4	149.2	218.3
Forest Service _____1,000__	78.1	129.9	139.6	49.0	81.0	133.4	55.8	29.4	37.3	67.3
Other [2] _____1,000__	(z)	.9	15.0	4.7	12.0	4.1	4.3	3.6	26.3	28.7
Cost, total _____mil. dol__	47.2	142.3	80.3	88.2	91.7	85.8	105.7	105.2	170.2	264.1
National Park Service _____mil. dol__	29.9	44.9	57.4	68.3	55.0	53.2	76.8	74.0	115.0	197.6
Forest Service _____mil. dol__	17.4	16.0	18.1	14.6	30.3	27.6	26.7	27.8	38.7	46.8
Other [2] _____mil. dol__	(z)	81.4	4.8	5.3	6.4	5.0	2.2	3.4	16.5	19.7
Federal matching grants to States [3]__mil. dol__	111.7	69.2	46.8	111.2	192.9	202.7	174.1	159.0	186.0	152.2
State recreation resources _____mil. dol__	79.1	34.4	26.0	50.1	85.1	68.8	84.8	55.9	60.7	40.7
County recreation resources _____mil. dol__	6.2	11.9	6.0	17.5	27.0	29.5	13.9	23.5	24.5	25.5
Local recreation resources _____mil. dol__	26.4	22.9	14.8	43.6	80.3	104.4	75.4	79.6	100.8	86.0
For acquisition _____mil. dol__	45.7	29.2	17.3	42.5	71.5	73.9	73.4	65.0	69.9	58.0
For develop. and/or planning ____mil. dol__	66.0	40.0	29.5	68.7	121.4	128.8	100.7	94.0	116.1	94.2
Total acres acquired by grants _____1,000__	227.3	173.1	53.0	109.7	187.5	143.1	149.6	101.4	139.1	266.2

Z Less than 50 acres or $50,000. [1] Covers land, waters, and improvements. [2] Fish and Wildlife Service and Bureau of Land Management. Cost figures also include administrative and acquisition expenses for Redwoods acquisition. [3] Includes grants to D.C., P.R., Guam, V.I., and American Samoa.

No. 391. Outdoor Recreation Acreage, by Area and Jurisdiction: 1972

[In thousands of acres. "Other" jurisdictions include park and recreation districts and regional councils]

AREA	Total	Federal	State	County	City	Township	Other
Total _____	319,243	266,720	41,795	8,132	1,629	631	336
Regional, community, and neighborhood parks and recreation _____	25,756	19,107	4,412	1,299	697	74	167
Forest _____	184,160	160,165	19,058	4,048	383	496	10
Fish and game _____	50,261	32,790	15,771	1,407	210	38	45
Historic and cultural _____	1,382	1,311	49	11	8	1	2
Wilderness, primitive, and natural _____	31,213	28,095	1,432	1,338	232	22	94
Other _____	26,471	25,253	1,071	29	99	1	18

No. 392. Participation in Selected Outdoor Recreation Activities: 1977

[Persons 12 years old and over. Participation from **June 1976 to June 1977.** Based on a home telephone survey of 4,029 persons drawn from noninstitutional population of conterminous U.S.]

ACTIVITY	PARTICIPANTS Number (mil.)	PARTICIPANTS Percent of population	PARTICIPATION 5 or more times (mil.)	PARTICIPATION For the first time (mil.)	ACTIVITY	PARTICIPANTS Number (mil.)	PARTICIPANTS Percent of population	PARTICIPATION 5 or more times (mil.)	PARTICIPATION For the first time (mil.)
Camping:					Golf _____	27.1	15	18.9	2.4
Developed areas _____	51.8	30	21.0	1.9	Tennis, outdoors _____	55.7	32	40.9	7.0
Undev. areas _____	36.0	21	15.0	.7	Other games or sports _____	94.8	55	73.1	2.6
Hunting _____	32.6	19	24.5	.3	Going to outdoor				
Fishing _____	91.0	53	61.9	1.9	sports events _____	104.3	61	75.5	.9
Riding off-road veh ____	43.6	25	33.8	2.0	Visiting zoos, parks,				
Hiking, backpack _____	48.1	28	28.1	1.9	fairs _____	123.6	72	66.1	.9
Other walking,					Sightseeing [2] _____	106.5	62	61.7	1.2
jogging _____	116.1	68	96.7	4.1	Picnicking _____	123.8	72	84.0	.3
Bicycling _____	79.4	46	66.1	1.5	Pleasure driving ____	118.3	69	97.9	.7
Horseback riding _____	25.2	14	13.5	1.0	Skiing, downhill ____	11.9	7	7.3	2.0
Water skiing _____	26.8	15	13.1	2.7	Ice skating, outdoor__	27.8	16	15.7	.9
Sailing _____	19.1	11	7.8	2.0	Sledding _____	35.5	20	20.8	.5
Canoeing, kayaking,					Snowmobiling _____	13.8	8	7.8	1.5
etc _____	26.9	15	9.0	2.6	Parachute jumping ____	.2	(z)	.2	.2
Other boating _____	57.3	33	34.3	1.5	Rock climbing _____	.2	(z)	–	–
Swimming:[1] Pool ____	107.4	63	83.5	.9	Gardening _____	3.4	2	2.7	.2
Other _____	77.9	45	59.5	.3	Exercising _____	.2	(z)	–	.2
Scuba diving _____	.2	(z)	.2	–	Skate boarding _____	.2	(z)	.2	.3

– Represents zero. Z Less than one percent. [1] Includes sunbathing. [2] Historic or national sites.
Source of tables 390–392: U.S. Heritage Conservation and Recreation Service, unpublished data.

No. 393. National Park System—Summary: 1950 to 1977

[For years ending **June 30** except, beginning 1977, ending **Sept. 30**, except as noted. Includes data for 5 areas in Puerto Rico and Virgin Islands. See also *Historical Statistics, Colonial Times to 1970*, series H 806–828]

ITEM	1950	1960	1965	1970	1972	1973	1974	1975	1976	1977
Finances (mil. dol.):										
Expenditures reported [1]	24.1	74.2	131.6	138.8	186.7	208.9	250.5	341.8	394.2	427.0
Salaries and wages	11.8	29.9	48.6	82.5	98.4	120.2	128.8	152.1	175.2	211.9
Improvements, maintenance	2.9	4.7	8.3	15.5	18.7	24.4	26.0	40.4	44.0	48.7
Construction	7.3	33.2	55.3	23.9	39.0	28.0	36.6	85.5	105.9	82.4
Other	2.0	6.5	19.5	17.0	30.5	36.3	59.1	63.8	69.0	84.0
Funds available	37.4	115.7	183.1	174.6	297.2	348.1	437.5	428.0	459.6	599.6
Appropriations	30.1	79.6	128.4	129.4	241.7	236.1	295.8	345.6	364.5	492.8
Other	7.3	36.2	54.7	45.2	55.5	112.1	141.7	82.4	95.1	106.8
Revenue from operations [2]	3.5	5.7	7.4	8.8	15.1	16.2	13.9	17.2	19.6	21.3
Visits (millions): [3]										
All areas	[4] 33.3	79.2	121.3	172.0	211.6	215.6	217.4	238.8	267.7	262.6
National parks [5]	13.9	26.6	36.6	45.9	54.4	54.7	53.1	58.8	60.6	62.0
National monuments	5.3	10.7	12.3	17.3	16.3	16.3	15.2	17.3	19.3	18.5
National historical, archeological, and military areas	9.5	21.8	40.7	47.0	72.6	71.6	72.9	75.7	82.8	85.5
National parkways	2.0	9.0	13.0	27.8	30.9	33.4	34.5	36.0	38.3	36.8
National recreation areas [5]	2.6	3.7	6.2	11.5	12.2	13.0	18.1	23.9	30.9	36.2
National seashores	(X)	.5	3.4	9.1	11.1	12.2	11.5	13.3	15.2	16.5
National Capital Parks	(NA)	6.9	9.2	10.3	9.7	10.9	8.7	11.2	12.0	2.9
Miscellaneous other areas	(X)	(X)	(X)	3	5	3	3	2.6	8.5	4.2
Overnight stays reported	[6] 4.5	9.4	13.0	16.2	14.6	15.3	15.4	16.7	17.4	17.5
Camper days	[4] 2.2	4.8	8.1	9.0	8.4	8.7	8.4	8.8	9.3	9.3
In commercial lodgings	2.3	2.8	3.3	4.9	3.4	3.5	3.7	4.0	3.1	4.0
Other	(NA)	1.8	1.6	2.2	2.8	3.2	3.3	3.9	5.0	4.2
Land (1,000 acres):										
Total [7]	23,836	25,704	26,549	28,543	28,878	29,117	29,031	29,091	29,389	29,571
Parks	12,222	13,208	13,619	14,307	14,730	14,740	14,777	15,344	15,365	15,374
Recreation areas	2,010	3,214	3,497	3,628	3,639	3,648	4,242	3,052	3,276	3,266
Other	9,605	9,283	9,432	10,608	10,509	10,729	10,012	9,795	10,748	10,931
Acquisition, gross	860	21	319	83	490	476	75	110	163	224
By purchase	2	6	42	74	420	456	59	70	107	218
By gift	785	10	13	1	47	13	10	(Z)	49	5
By transfer or exchange	73	5	264	10	23	6	6	40	7	(Z)
Exclusion	(Z)	(Z)	[8] (Z)	2	1	1	(Z)	(Z)	7	(Z)
Acquisition, net	860	21	318	82	490	476	75	110	156	224

NA Not available.   X Not applicable.   Z Less than 500 acres.   [1] Excludes transfers and allocations from appropriations to other agencies (e.g., Land and Water Conservation Fund, etc.).   [2] Receipts deposited in Treasury; beginning 1974, receipts from annual admission permit (Golden Eagle Passport) and special recreation use fees are available for NPS expenditure. They totaled $11.1 million in 1974 and in 1975, $15.2 million in 1976, and $21.3 million in 1977.   [3] For calendar year; 1950 data not adjusted for comparability with counting system as modified in 1960. Prior to 1965, excludes visits to White House.   [4] Excludes National Capital Parks.   [5] Beginning 1970, combined data for North Cascades National Park and two adjacent National Recreation Areas are included in National Parks total.   [6] Excludes "other" overnight stays.   [7] Federal land only, as of Dec. 31.   [8] Represents U.S. lands alienated by exchange of U.S. and private lands.

Source: U.S. National Park Service, *Campground Use in the National Park Service; Camper Days in Areas Administered by the National Park Service; Public Use of the National Parks*, monthly, and *Public Use of the National Park System*, semiannual; *Areas Administered by the National Park Service*, semiannual; and unpublished data.

No. 394. National Park System—Types of Areas: 1977

[As of **December 31**. Includes data for 5 areas in Puerto Rico and Virgin Islands. See also *Historical Statistics, Colonial Times to 1970*, series H 806–828]

TYPE OF AREA	Number of areas	Federal acreage	TYPE OF AREA	Number of areas	Federal acreage
National Park System	294	29,571,379	National seashores	10	450,616
			Parkways	4	154,896
National parks	37	15,374,137	National lakeshores	4	113,906
National historical parks	18	64,075	National wild and scenic rivers	6	162,196
National monuments	82	9,618,013	National Capital Parks	1	6,471
National military parks	11	33,247	White House	1	18
National Memorial Park	1	69,676			
			Parks, other	10	30,521
National battlefields	8	5,798	National recreation areas	16	3,265,952
National battlefield parks	3	6,655	National Scenic Trail	1	15,100
National battlefield sites	2	1,311	National preserves	2	179,123
National historic sites	53	13,618	National Visitor Center	1	–
National memorials	22	5,903	National Mall	1	146

– Represents zero.
Source: U.S. National Park Service, *Areas Administered by the National Park Service*, semiannual.

No. 395. OVERNIGHT STAYS IN SELECTED NATIONAL PARK SERVICE AREAS: 1976

[In thousands. An overnight stay is the passing of one night by a visitor within a park, and occurs each night a visitor remains in the park. Area selection based on minimum of 250,000 overnight stays during the year]

AREA	Total over-night stays	CONCESSIONERS		Camp grounds oper-ated by NPS	Back-country camp-ing	Mis-cel-lane-ous [3]
		Lodg-ing [1]	Camp-ing [2]			
Total, all areas [4]	17,545	3,157	883	9,306	2,570	1,629
Blue Ridge Parkway, Ga., N.C., Va	292	54	–	226	4	8
Cape Hatteras National Seashore, N.C	335	–	–	307	–	28
Death Valley National Monument, Calif	301	–	–	294	1	7
Glacier National Park, Mont	461	152	–	279	30	–
Glen Canyon Nat'l Recreation Area, Ariz., Utah	1,239	117	71	396	644	12
Grand Canyon National Park, Ariz	1,028	477	46	361	126	19
Grand Teton National Park, Wyo	606	179	57	312	26	33
Great Smokey Mountains Nat'l Park, N.C., Tenn	577	7	.–	446	102	21
Kings Canyon National Park, Calif	241	15	–	165	61	–
Lake Mead National Recreation Area, Ariz., Nev	1,503	69	397	490	475	73
Olympic National Park, Wash	536	73	18	304	140	2
Rocky Mountain National Park, Colo	333	–	–	258	63	13
Sequoia National Park, Calif	358	87	–	176	94	–
Shenandoah National Park, Va	591	127	–	355	91	18
Yellowstone National Park, Idaho, Mont., Wyo	1,473	518	114	776	54	11
Yosemite National Park, Calif	1,770	800	–	691	194	85

– Represents zero.
[1] Includes rooms and cabins.
[2] Includes campgrounds and trailer villages.
[3] Includes organized groups' camping, nights spent aboard boats, nonrecreational overnights, and stays not elsewhere classified.
[4] Includes 100 areas not shown separately.

Source: U.S. National Park Service, *Overnight Stays, 1977.*

No. 396. NATIONAL FOREST RECREATION USE—SUMMARY: 1977

[Estimated. Represents recreational use of National Forest land and water which aggregates 12 person-hours; may entail 1 person for 12 hours, 12 persons for 1 hour, or any equivalent combination of individual or group use, either continuous or intermittent. See also *Historical Statistics, Colonial Times to 1970,* series H 829–835]

PLACE WHERE USE OCCURRED	Visitor-days (1,000)	Percent	ACTIVITY	Visitor-days (1,000)	Percent
Sites and areas	204,797	100.0	Total	204,797	100.0
Developed sites	73,776	36.0	Camping	52,672	25.7
			Picnicking	8,317	4.1
Observation sites	1,142	.6	Recreation travel (mechanized)	49,325	24.1
Boating sites	1,948	1.0	Boating	5,940	2.9
Swimming sites, playgrounds	2,162	1.1	Swimming and scuba diving	4,422	2.2
Campgrounds	37,554	18.3	Winter sports	8,116	4.0
Picnic grounds	5,748	2.8			
			Fishing	16,029	7.8
Hotels, lodges, resorts	4,185	2.0	Hunting	14,517	7.1
Organization sites	5,153	2.5			
Recreation residence sites	6,858	3.3	Hiking and mountain climbing	10,258	5.0
Winter sports sites	6,970	3.4	Horseback riding	2,884	1.4
Visitor centers and concessions	2,056	1.0	Resort use	4,187	2.0
			Organization camp use	3,855	1.9
Dispersed areas	131,021	64.0			
			Recreation residence use	6,826	3.3
Roads (recreation)	49,606	24.2	Gathering forest products	2,813	1.4
Trails (recreation)	10,576	5.2	Nature study and other	3,071	1.5
Waters	24,367	11.9	Viewing scenery, sports	7,974	3.9
General undeveloped country	46,472	22.7	Visitor information (exhibits, etc.)	3,591	1.7

Source: U.S. Forest Service, unpublished data.

No. 397. State Park Systems—Summary: 1960 to 1975

[For years ending **June 30**, in most cases. Number of agencies which reported varies from year to year. Covers parks, historic sites, and parkways reported by State park and State historical agencies. See also *Historical Statistics, Colonial Times to 1970*, series H 836–848]

ITEM	1960	1967	1970	1975	ITEM	1960	1967	1970	1975
Areas [1]_____number__	2,664	3,202	3,425	3,804	Attendance_____mil__	259	391	483	[2] 566
Acreage [1]_____1,000__	5,602	7,352	8,555	9,838	Day visits_____mil__	238	355	432	465
					Overnight visits_____mil__	[2] 21	36	51	[2] 51
Expenditures_____mil. dol__	87	[2] 280	[2] 387	[2] 649	Cabins and hotels__mil__	2	2	3	3
Salaries and wages_mil. dol__	37	77	122	218	Organized camps___mil__	2	2	2	6
Supplies and equip.mil. dol__	19	37	65	99	Tent and trailer				
Lands_____mil. dol__	12	57	72	150	camps_____mil__	16	32	46	40
Improvements_____mil. dol__	19	108	126	167					
Funds available for					Personnel_____1,000__	17.5	29.3	34.3	44.9
expenditures_____mil. dol__	131	472	619	1,467	Professional_____1,000__	.7	(NA)	3.4	6.2
Appropriations____mil. dol__	69	174	260	483	Year-round_____1,000__	7.4	11.5	13.3	18.1
Other_____mil. dol__	62	298	359	984	Seasonal_____1,000__	10.1	17.8	21.0	26.8
Revenue from opera-tions_____mil. dol__	23	50	71	115					

NA Not available.
[1] Excludes State forests, wildlife refuges, and waysides not administered by State park agencies.
[2] Includes data for which the detailed breakdown is not available. 1975 attendance data exclude Texas.
Source: 1960, U.S. Heritage Conservation and Recreation Service (formerly U.S. Bureau of Outdoor Recreation), *State Outdoor Recreation Statistics—1962*. Later data, National Recreation and Park Association, Arlington, Va., *State Park Statistics, 1970* and *1975* (copyright).

No. 398. State Park and Recreation Areas—States: 1975

STATE	AREAS [1]		Expend-itures (mil. dol.)	STATE	AREAS [1]		Expend-itures (mil. dol.)	STATE	AREAS [1]		Expend-itures (mil. dol.)
	Number	Acres (1,000)			Number	Acres (1,000)			Number	Acres (1,000)	
U.S._____	3,804	9,838	649	Iowa_____	82	47	6	N.C_____	34	69	9
				Kans_____	35	24	3	N. Dak_____	18	14	(Z)
Ala_____	21	45	18	Ky_____	45	41	31	Ohio_____	[3] 124	[3] 204	21
Alaska_____	65	1,394	2	La_____	37	24	3	Okla_____	74	90	7
Ariz_____	15	25	2	Maine_____	(NA)	(NA)	3	Oreg_____	242	90	13
Ark_____	42	28	13	Md_____	45	62	25	Pa_____	119	296	30
Calif_____	230	843	91	Mass_____	126	235	15	R.I_____	85	12	4
Colo_____	44	159	4	Mich_____	93	224	11	S.C_____	48	63	8
Conn_____	234	191	4	Minn_____	92	175	7	S. Dak_____	45	90	3
Del_____	9	7	2	Miss_____	24	17	4	Tenn_____	83	116	21
Fla_____	115	283	43	Mo_____	58	79	8	Tex_____	87	102	31
				Mont_____	130	35	2	Utah_____	43	56	6
Ga_____	55	47	10	Nebr_____	92	113	3	Vt_____	41	35	3
Hawaii_____	53	18	15	Nev_____	16	144	2	Va_____	37	48	7
Idaho_____	22	29	9	N.H_____	65	105	3	Wash_____	171	79	17
Ill_____	186	287	13	N.J_____	106	253	20	W. Va_____	33	66	10
Ind_____	20	[2] 66	11	N. Mex_____	33	164	4	Wis_____	73	108	7
				N.Y_____	209	2,978	68	Wyo_____	48	157	1

NA Not available.　Z Less than $500,000.
[1] Covers 58 agencies in the 50 States, including all major ones that administer parks, recreation areas, historic sites, parkways, and related types of areas.
[2] Includes 11,000 acres leased from U.S. Army Corps of Engineers.　[3] Partially 1967 data.
Source: National Recreation and Park Association, Arlington, Va., *State Park Statistics, 1975*. (Copyright.)

No. 399. Municipal and County Park and Recreation Areas—Number, Acreage, Professional Personnel, and Selected Facilities: 1950 to 1970

[Represents only park and recreation systems which returned questionnaires (in 1965, 2,784 municipal and 358 county agencies and, in 1970, 1,119 local agencies). See also *Historical Statistics, Colonial Times to 1970*, series H 849–861]

ITEM	1950	1960	1965	1970	ITEM	1950	1960	1965	1970
Park and other recreation areas:					Selected facilities—Con: Golf courses, 9 and 18 hole__	454	585	1,005	518
Number_____	17,142	24,710	30,509	31,235	Outdoor swimming pools_____	1,289	2,513	4,277	4,435
Acreage_____1,000__	644	1,015	1,496	966	Tennis courts_____	13,085	15,676	19,926	12,343
Professional personnel__	58,029	99,696	119,515	87,717	Recreation bldgs_____	2,987	3,828	6,486	9,212
Full time, year-round__	6,784	9,216	19,208	17,287	Indoor recreation centers_____	6,630	13,142	16,041	14,237
Playground under leadership_____	14,747	20,107	24,298	11,691	Softball diamonds, 60 foot_____	12,266	14,832	17,467	14,808
Selected facilities:									
Ball diamonds, 90 ft__	5,502	7,044	9,335	4,486					
Bathing beaches_____	780	951	1,261	760					

Source: National Recreation and Park Association, Arlington, Va. For 1950–1965, *Recreation and Park Yearbook*; for 1970, *Parks & Recreation*, August 1971. (Copyright.)

No. 400. Personal Consumption Expenditures for Recreation: 1960 to 1976

[In millions of dollars. Represents market value of purchases of goods and services by individuals and nonprofit institutions. See *Historical Statistics, Colonial Times to 1970*, series H 878–893, for single-year figures prior to minor revisions issued in 1976:

TYPE OF PRODUCT OR SERVICE	1960	1965	1970	1972	1973	1974	1975	1976
Total recreation expenditures	17,855	25,907	40,999	49,100	55,199	60,892	66,171	72,587
Books and maps	1,139	1,648	2,356	2,530	2,769	3,034	3,397	3,590
Magazines, newspapers, sheet music	2,164	2,662	3,900	4,685	5,845	7,045	7,502	8,092
Nondurable toys and sport supplies	2,477	3,585	5,477	6,542	7,302	8,005	8,624	9,437
Wheel goods, durable toys, sports equip., boats, pleasure aircraft	1,976	2,888	5,511	7,315	8,167	8,644	9,508	10,530
Radio and television receivers, records, musical instruments	3,003	5,041	8,885	10,964	12,288	13,266	14,576	16,065
Radio and television repair	774	933	1,079	1,222	1,334	1,240	1,415	1,474
Flowers, seed, and potted plants	703	1,272	2,134	2,655	2,871	3,250	3,401	3,860
Admissions to specified amusements	1,652	2,123	3,141	3,487	3,870	4,621	4,899	5,598
Motion picture theaters	956	1,067	1,521	1,644	1,965	2,495	2,538	2,987
Legitimate theaters and opera, and entertainments of nonprofit institutions [1]	342	388	556	632	670	733	789	907
Spectator sports	354	668	1,064	1,211	1,235	1,393	1,572	1,704
Clubs and fraternal organizations [2]	728	859	1,197	1,266	1,331	1,434	1,564	1,654
Comm'l participant amusements [3]	1,200	1,695	2,317	2,650	2,931	3,227	3,557	3,901
Parimutuel net receipts	539	814	1,144	1,359	1,502	1,614	1,740	1,876
Other [4]	1,500	2,387	3,858	4,425	4,989	5,512	5,988	6,510

[1] Except athletic.   [2] Consists of dues and fees excluding insurance premiums.
[3] Consists of billiard parlors; bowling alleys; dancing, riding, shooting, skating, and swimming places; amusement devices and parks; golf courses; sightseeing buses and guides; and private flying operations.
[4] Consists of net receipts of lotteries and expenditures for purchase of pets and pet care services, cable TV, film processing, photographic studios, sporting and recreation camps, and recreational services, not elsewhere classified.
Source: U.S. Bureau of Economic Analysis, *The National Income and Product Accounts of the United States, 1929–1974*, and *Survey of Current Business, July 1977*.

No. 401. Selected Recreational Activities: 1960 to 1977

[See also *Historical Statistics, Colonial Times to 1970*, series H 862–864, H 871, H 874, and H 877]

ACTIVITY	Unit	1960	1965	1970	1973	1974	1975	1976	1977
Softball, amateur: [1]									
Adult participants [2]	Mil	(NA)	(NA)	16	21	24	26	28	28
Youth participants [2]	1,000	(NA)	(NA)	255	390	420	450	475	495
Adult teams [3]	1,000	(NA)	(NA)	36	56	64	66	72	80
Youth teams [3]	1,000	(NA)	(NA)	2	7	8	10	11	13
Golf: [4]									
Golfers (15 rounds or more)	1,000	4,400	7,750	9,700	11,000	11,660	12,036	12,328	12,451
Courses [5]	Number	6,385	8,323	10,188	11,956	12,299	12,306	12,305	12,511
9-hole	Number	3,660	4,554	5,343	6,051	6,080	6,024	5,938	5,960
18-hole and larger	Number	2,725	3,769	4,845	5,905	6,219	6,282	6,367	6,551
Classification:									
Private	Number	3,236	3,887	4,619	5,074	5,075	5,085	5,069	5,136
Daily fee	Number	2,254	3,368	4,248	5,212	5,477	5,473	5,445	5,538
Municipal	Number	895	1,068	1,321	1,670	1,747	1,748	1,791	1,837
Tennis: [6]									
Players	1,000	5,000	(NA)	10,655	20,158	33,949	(NA)	29,201	(NA)
Indoor	1,000	(NA)	(NA)	(NA)	1,567	3,463	(NA)	4,072	(NA)
Courts	1,000	(NA)	(NA)	(NA)	112.0	(NA)	130.0	141.0	(NA)
Indoor	1,000	(NA)	(NA)	(NA)	6.5	(NA)	7.8	9.0	(NA)
Tenpin bowling: [7][8]									
Establishments	Number	8,997	10,752	9,140	8,674	8,592	8,577	8,607	8,640
Lane [5]	1,000	108	159	141	139	139	141	143	147
Membership, total [9]	1,000	5,538	8,010	7,733	8,213	8,482	8,751	9,196	9,453
American Bowling Congress	1,000	3,665	4,944	4,210	4,150	4,200	4,300	4,500	4,583
Women's Bowling Congress	1,000	1,543	2,736	2,988	3,343	3,531	3,692	3,870	4,044
Duckpin bowling: [10][11][12]									
Establishments	Number	653	641	486	246	210	205	206	200
Lanes	Number	8,707	8,714	6,648	3,879	3,713	3,643	3,618	3,517
Teams	1,000	62.1	80.8	75.3	30.8	26.1	25.9	25.6	27.7
Motion picture theaters [13][14]	1,000	[11][15] 16	13	14	15	15	16	17	(NA)
Four-wall	1,000	[11][15] 12	9	10	11	11	12	13	(NA)
Drive-in	1,000	[11][15] 4	4	4	4	4	4	4	(NA)
Receipts, box office	Mil. dol	[11] 951	927	1,225	1,500	1,908	2,115.	2,036	2,372
Admission, average price	Dollars	[11][15] .65	[16] .85	1.55	1.76	1.89	2.05	2.13	2.23

See footnotes at end of table.

No. 401. SELECTED RECREATIONAL ACTIVITIES: 1960 TO 1977—Continued

[See also *Historical Statistics, Colonial Times to 1970*, series H 877, for outboard motors sold]

ACTIVITY	Unit	1960	1965	1970	1973	1974	1975	1976	1977
Outboard motors and boats: [17]									
Motors in use	1,000	5,800	6,645	7,215	7,510	7,595	7,649	7,700	7,760
Motors sold	1,000	468	393	430	585	545	435	468	462
Value, retail	Mil. dol	221	183	281	503	463	411	515	607
Horsepower, average	(X)	27.4	28.2	31.0	40.8	40.5	40.3	42.1	44.4
Outboard boats sold	1,000	[18] 294	250	276	448	425	328	341	336
Value, retail	Mil. dol	(NA)	133	177	325	310	263	358	391
Length, average	Feet	(NA)	15.3	15.4	15.4	14.2	14.4	14.8	14.9
Inboard/outdrive boats sold	1,000	([18])	17	43	78	70	70	80	84
Value, retail	Mil. dol	(NA)	64	182	410	387	420	576	672
Boat trailers sold	1,000	206	130	213	330	325	255	285	276
Value, retail	Mil. dol	(NA)	29	51	94	98	88	121	125

NA Not available. X Not applicable. [1] Source: Amateur Softball Association, Oklahoma City, Okla. [2] Represents participants on Amateur Softball Association teams and other amateur softball teams. [3] Amateur Softball Association teams only. [4] Source: National Golf Foundation, Chicago, Ill. [5] Prior to 1973, figures represent facilities. [6] Source: U.S. Tennis Association, New York, N.Y. Survey by A. C. Nielsen Company. [7] Source: American Bowling Congress, Greendale, Wis. [8] Season ending in year shown. [9] Includes American Jr. Bowling Congress. [10] Source: National Duckpin Bowling Congress, Washington, D.C. [11] Excludes Alaska and Hawaii. [12] Season beginning in year shown. [13] Source: Motion Picture Association of America, Inc., New York, N.Y. [14] Prior to 1973, figures represent theaters; thereafter, screens. [15] 1958 data. [16] 1963 data. [17] Source: Marex, Inc., Chicago, Ill. [18] Inboard/outdrive boats sold included with outboard boats sold.

Source: Compiled from sources listed in footnotes.

No. 402. SELECTED SPECTATOR SPORTS: 1960 TO 1977

[See also *Historical Statistics, Colonial Times to 1970*, series H 865–870 and H 872]

ACTIVITY	Unit	1960	1965	1970	1973	1974	1975	1976	1977
Baseball, major leagues: [1][2]									
Attendance	1,000	20,261	22,806	29,191	30,905	30,571	30,373	31,974	39,523
Regular season	1,000	19,911	22,442	28,747	30,109	29,994	29,789	31,318	38,710
National League	1,000	10,685	13,581	16,662	16,675	16,978	16,600	16,661	19,070
American League	1,000	9,227	8,861	12,085	13,434	13,016	13,189	14,658	19,640
Playoffs	1,000	(X)	(X)	191	438	317	276	432	475
World Series	1,000	350	364	253	358	260	308	223	338
Basketball, attendance: [1][3]									
National Basketball Assn [4]	1,000	1,986	2,750	5,147	6,834	6,885	7,863	8,494	10,706
American Basketball Assn. [4]									
Regular season	1,000	(X)	(X)	1,753	2,400	2,319	2,703	(NA)	(X)
Playoffs	1,000	(X)	(X)	213	364	265	388	(NA)	(X)
Football: [5]									
College:									
Teams	Number	620	616	617	630	634	634	637	638
Attendance	1,000	20,403	24,683	29,466	31,283	31,235	31,688	32,012	32,905
Professional, attendance	1,000	[6] 4,154	[6] 6,547	9,992	11,256	10,675	10,689	11,563	10,800
Regular season	1,000	[6] 4,054	[6] 6,416	9,533	10,731	10,236	10,213	11,071	10,327
Postseason games [7]	1,000	[6] 100	[6] 131	458	525	439	476	493	473
Hockey, attendance: [8][9]									
National Hockey League:									
Regular season	1,000	2,387	2,823	5,992	8,576	8,641	9,522	9,104	8,564
Playoffs	1,000	187	304	462	625	600	784	727	646
World Hockey Association:									
Regular season	1,000	(X)	(X)	(X)	2,480	2,765	4,096	4,123	3,625
Playoffs	1,000	(X)	(X)	(X)	236	289	336	446	401
Boxing, professional matches: [10]									
Boxers [11]	Number	[12] 2,920	2,202	5,071	7,384	8,469	7,647	8,327	8,964
Receipts, gross [13]	$1,000	[12] 5,902	8,264	10,642	12,634	14,250	13,179	[14] 18,000	[14] 19,036
Racing: [15]									
Horseracing: [16] Racing days	Number	6,099	8,051	9,962	11,805	12,211	13,110	13,570	14,312
Attendance	1,000	46,879	62,887	69,704	75,016	74,948	78,662	79,307	83,914
Parimutuel turnover	Mil. dol	3,358	4,615	5,977	7,027	7,513	7,862	9,421	9,694
Revenue to States	Mil. dol	258	370	486	537	567	582	616	[17] 750
Greyhound: Racing days	Number	2,478	3,443	3,023	3,630	3,842	3,960	4,589	6,688
Attendance	1,000	7,924	10,865	12,660	15,114	16,282	17,458	18,978	20,040
Parimutuel turnover	Mil. dol	322	460	730	1,016	1,164	1,261	1,429	1,604
Revenue to States	Mil. dol	22	33	53	72	84	91	107	117

NA Not available. X Not applicable. [1] Excludes Alaska and Hawaii. [2] Source: The National League of Professional Baseball Clubs, New York, N.Y.; and The American League of Professional Baseball Clubs, New York, N.Y., *American League Red Book*. [3] Season ending in year shown. Beginning 1977, the American Basketball Association ceased operation. [4] Location: New York, N.Y. [5] Source: National Collegiate Athletic Association, Shawnee Mission, Kans., and, for professional, National Football League, New York, N.Y. [6] Includes American Football League. Beginning 1970, American Football League merged with National Football League. [7] Beginning 1970, includes Pro Bowl, a non-championship game. [8] Source: National Hockey League, Montreal, Quebec, and The World Hockey League, Toronto, Ontario. [9] Season ending in year shown. [10] Source: The Ring, Inc., New York, N.Y., *The Ring Magazine* (copyright). [11] Boxers listed for one or more bouts. [12] Excludes Alaska. [13] Excludes closed circuit TV receipts. [14] Unpublished unofficial estimate. [15] Source: National Association of State Racing Commissioners, Lexington, Ky. [16] Includes thoroughbred, harness, quarter horse, and fairs. [17] Estimate.

Source: Compiled from sources listed in footnotes.

No. 403. SPORT FISHING AND HUNTING LICENSES—NUMBER AND COST: 1950 TO 1976

[For years ending June 30 except, beginning 1976, ending Sept. 30. Prior to 1960, fishing and hunting licenses exclude Alaska and Hawaii. See also *Historical Statistics, Colonial Times to 1970*, series H 875–876]

ITEM	1950	1955	1960	1965	1970	1973	1974	1975	1976
Fishing licenses: Sales [1]_millions__	15.3	18.9	23.3	25.0	31.1	33.5	34.3	34.7	34.9
Resident_____millions__	13.3	16.2	20.2	21.6	26.8	28.5	29.5	30.0	29.8
Nonresident_____millions__	2.0	2.6	3.1	3.4	4.3	5.0	4.8	4.7	5.1
Cost to anglers_____mil. dol__	34	40	52	63	91	118	128	142	155
Hunting licenses: Sales [1]_millions__	12.6	14.2	18.4	19.4	22.2	23.3	25.1	25.9	25.3
Resident_____millions__	12.4	13.9	17.8	18.5	21.0	22.1	23.8	24.7	24.0
Nonresident_____millions__	.2	.3	.6	.9	1.2	1.2	1.3	1.3	1.3
Cost to hunters_____mil. dol__	38	43	61	75	102	123	143	155	164
Federal duck stamps sold___1,000__	1,955	2,185	1,629	1,566	2,072	2,180	2,046	2,222	2,170

[1] Prior to 1960, paid license holders; for definition, see footnote 1, table 404.

No. 404. SPORT FISHING AND HUNTING LICENSES—NUMBER AND COST, BY STATES: 1976

[For year ending Sept. 30. Excludes Migratory Waterfowl Stamps (Duck Stamps)]

STATE	PAID LICENSE HOLDERS [1] (1,000)		COST OF LICENSES [2] ($1,000)		STATE	PAID LICENSE HOLDERS [1] (1,000)		COST OF LICENSES [2] ($1,000)	
	Fishing	Hunting	Fishing	Hunting		Fishing	Hunting	Fishing	Hunting
United States____	27,818	16,300	154,581	163,599	Missouri_____	887	475	6,066	5,257
					Montana_____	294	223	3,550	3,423
Alabama_____	593	332	1,985	1,990	Nebraska_____	260	182	1,242	1,813
Alaska_____	159	71	1,284	1,299	Nevada_____	159	60	1,261	1,161
Arizona_____	421	182	2,829	2,705	New Hampshire___	117	73	963	959
Arkansas_____	761	355	3,866	2,562					
California_____	2,347	612	18,202	6,732	New Jersey_____	190	187	1,709	2,064
					New Mexico_____	229	135	1,601	1,729
Colorado_____	679	317	4,887	8,355	New York_____	876	769	5,568	8,224
Connecticut_____	200	87	742	383	North Carolina____	487	384	2,884	3,504
Delaware_____	13	29	64	197	North Dakota_____	142	98	396	966
Florida_____	870	263	2,588	1,600					
Georgia_____	655	364	2,212	2,581	Ohio_____	948	584	3,865	3,669
					Oklahoma_____	591	251	7,110	1,002
Hawaii_____	8	12	27	04	Oregon_____	704	326	5,069	3,894
Idaho_____	392	218	2,343	3,588	Pennsylvania_____	966	1,281	7,023	14,796
Illinois_____	1,035	517	2,426	1,830	Rhode Island_____	30	16	93	67
Indiana_____	712	453	2,499	1,915					
Iowa_____	541	355	2,237	3,101	South Carolina_____	415	212	1,998	1,687
					South Dakota_____	165	148	570	1,811
Kansas_____	336	222	1,767	1,534	Tennessee_____	729	484	4,866	5,128
Kentucky_____	599	318	2,969	1,695	Texas_____	1,564	856	6,271	4,953
Louisiana_____	473	337	1,041	2,572	Utah_____	472	217	2,518	2,595
Maine_____	259	227	1,867	2,708					
Maryland_____	122	184	589	2,135	Vermont_____	141	132	749	1,733
					Virginia_____	420	416	2,466	4,235
Massachusetts_____	218	116	1,695	1,007	Washington_____	521	323	4,473	5,265
Michigan_____	1,255	946	8,608	8,814	West Virginia_____	259	301	1,640	2,349
Minnesota_____	1,491	449	5,888	4,698	Wisconsin_____	1,416	707	8,942	7,595
Mississippi_____	435	331	1,550	2,088	Wyoming_____	262	163	1,523	6,707

[1] Resident and nonresident. U.S. total includes multiple counting of license holders who bought nonresident licenses as well as a home State license. [2] Total cost to holders for all licenses, permits, tags, stamps, etc.

Source of tables 403 and 404: U.S. Fish and Wildlife Service, *Federal Aid in Fish and Wildlife Restoration*, annual.

No. 405. SPORT FISHERMEN AND HUNTERS: 1960 TO 1975

[In thousands. Persons 12 yr. old and over, except 1975, 9 yr. old and over. 1960 and 1975, persons who fished and hunted; 1965, persons who spent $5 or more; 1970, persons who spent $7.50 or more; also for 1965 and 1970, persons who reported 3 or more fishing and hunting days in year. 1960–1970 based on samples of approximately 18,000 households; for 1975, on 20,200 individuals]

ITEM	Fishermen and hunters, 1960	Fishermen and hunters, 1965	1970, PERSONS WHO—			1975, PERSONS WHO—		
			Fished and/or hunted	Fished	Hunted	Fished and/or hunted	Fished	Hunted
Total_____	30,435	32,881	36,277	33,158	14,336	59,530	53,929	20,591
Male_____	23,171	25,216	26,928	24,073	13,467	(NA)	37,265	18,964
Female_____	7,264	7,665	9,349	9,085	869	(NA)	16,664	1,627
Metropolitan areas_____	8,741	14,811	15,354	14,417	4,606	(NA)	36,672	11,531
Nonmetropolitan areas____	21,693	18,070	20,923	18,741	9,731	(NA)	17,257	9,060

NA Not available.

Source: U.S. Fish and Wildlife Service, *National Survey of Fishing and Hunting, 1960, 1965, 1970, and 1975*.

No. 406. GAMBLING OUTLAYS, BY TYPE, AND PERCENT OF ADULTS PARTICIPATING: 1974

[Covers gambling by persons 18 years old and over for types listed. The standard errors of the estimated total volume of legal and illegal betting are about 17 percent and 25 percent, respectively, of the mean values shown. Therefore, the chances are about 68 out of 100 that the true total lies within a range of $17.3 billion ± $3.0 billion for legal betting and $5.1 billion ± $1.3 billion for illegal. See also headnote, table 407]

| TYPE | Total outlays ventured (mil. dol.) | Net outlays[1] (mil. dol.) | ADULTS WHO GAMBLE | | TYPE | Total outlays ventured (mil. dol.) | Net outlays[1] (mil. dol.) | ADULTS WHO GAMBLE | |
			Percent of all adults	Average annual outlay (dol.)				Percent of all adults	Average annual outlay (dol.)
All types	22,421	4,385	48.0	387	Illegal	5,074	1,039	11.2	318
					Sports books	2,341	105	1.9	623
Legal	17,347	3,347	[2] 44.3	273	Horse books	1,368	227	2.4	416
Horses at track	7,930	1,247	13.7	448					
OTB[3], New York	967	171	13.5	1,118	Numbers	1,064	575	3.0	273
Legal casinos	6,076	1,004	9.4	448	Sports cards	191	115	3.0	44
Bingo	1,735	551	18.7	74	Casino games	110	19	(NA)	(NA)
Lotteries	639	374	24.0	25					

NA Not available.   [1] Represents the number of dollars lost by bettors or the amount taken out by commercial operators before the remainder is paid back as winnings to bettors.
[2] Includes dog tracks, jai alai, and other games not shown separately.   [3] Off-track betting.
Source: Institute for Social Research, University of Michigan, Ann Arbor, Michigan, *Gambling in the United States*, 1976.

No. 407. PERCENT OF ADULTS WHO GAMBLE, BY SELECTED CHARACTERISTICS AND BETTING STATUS: 1974

[**In percent, except as indicated.** Persons 18 years old and over living in housing units, except those living on military reservations. Based on a national sample of 1,736 respondents (usable interviews)]

| CHARACTERISTIC | All non-bettors | Never have bet | BETTORS | | | CHARACTERISTIC | All non-bettors | Never have bet | BETTORS | | |
			All[1]	Legal commercial[2]	Illegal				All[1]	Legal commercial[2]	Illegal
Total	39	32	61	44	11	Widowed	82	72	18	16	2
Population						Never married	30	27	70	53	15
equivalent mil	56.2	46.1	87.9	63.4	15.9						
						Not high school graduate	59	49	41	30	8
Male	32	25	68	47	17	High school graduate	34	29	66	48	12
Female	45	39	55	42	5	Some college	28	22	72	52	13
						College graduate	21	18	79	56	11
White	38	31	62	45	10						
Black and other	48	39	52	38	17	Catholic	20	17	80	65	16
						Protestant	46	38	54	36	9
18–24 years old	27	25	73	48	15	Baptist	55	47	45	30	10
25–44 years old	31	26	69	52	14	Methodist	37	30	63	41	11
45–64 years old	40	33	60	42	8	Bible-oriented sects	67	57	33	19	8
65 and over	77	65	23	17	2	Other[3]	26	20	74	51	10
						Jewish	23	23	77	66	19
Employed	29	23	71	50	15	Atheist, no preference	60	44	40	33	5
Unemployed	31	25	69	54	15						
						Northeast	20	17	80	67	19
Annual income of—						North Central	34	28	66	48	12
Under $5,000	76	66	24	17	3	South	60	52	40	23	6
$5,000–$10,000	49	42	51	39	8	West	35	24	65	47	7
$10,000–$15,000	31	24	69	46	10						
$15,000 and over	26	21	74	54	15	City, 100,000 or more	34	28	66	46	15
						Suburb of city over					
Married	38	31	62	44	11	500,000	28	23	72	56	14
Divorced or separated	29	23	71	57	16	Small cities, rural	47	39	53	38	7

[1] Bettors are persons who gambled at any time during the year. Includes betting only with friends, not shown separately.   [2] Covers bettors who made legal commercial bets and bets with friends and bettors who made only legal commercial bets.   [3] Presbyterian, Lutheran, Congregational, and Episcopal.

Source: Institute for Social Research, University of Michigan, Ann Arbor, Michigan, *Gambling in the United States*, 1976.

No. 408. Performing Arts—Selected Data: 1960 to 1977

[Receipts and expenditures in millions of dollars. For season ending in year shown, except as indicated]

ITEM	1960	1965	1970	1971	1972	1973	1974	1975	1976	1977
Legitimate theater: [1]										
Broadway shows:										
New productions	58	67	62	46	56	58	50	59	62	63
Playing weeks [2][3]	1,156	1,250	1,047	1,107	1,157	889	907	1,101	1,136	1,347
Gross box office receipts mil. dol	45.7	50.5	53.3	55.3	52.3	45.3	46.3	57.4	70.8	93.4
Road shows:										
Playing weeks [3]	728	643	1,024	898	909	1,056	899	799	814	987
Gross box office receipts mil. dol	27.3	25.9	48.0	49.8	49.7	55.9	45.7	50.9	52.6	82.6
Opera companies [4]	754	732	648	685	715	817	902	807	913	914
Major	(NA)	27	35	40	43	48	53	54	65	68
Expenditures mil. dol	(NA)	(NA)	36.0	41.2	(NA)	(NA)	(NA)	(NA)	71.8	79.7
Community	403	296	266	269	278	356	400	335	412	424
Workshops	351	409	347	376	394	413	449	418	436	422
Performances	4,232	4,176	4,779	5,246	5,723	5,993	6,676	6,428	7,109	7,389
Operas performed	287	331	341	324	364	425	403	387	427	427
World premiere	(NA)	(NA)	17	35	34	43	32	16	45	33
Attendance mil	(NA)	(NA)	4.6	(NA)	(NA)	(NA)	8.0	7.9	8.9	9.2
Symphony orchestras [5]	1,226	1,385	1,441	1,450	1,463	1,463	1,463	1,463	1,410	1,453
College	250	290	298	300	300	300	300	300	356	356
Community	933	1,032	1,021	1,023	1,023	1,017	1,003	1,003	872	888
Urban	(6)	(6)	24	22	31	36	43	41	56	69
Metropolitan	18	38	72	76	81	82	88	90	95	109
Major	25	25	28	28	28	28	29	29	31	31
Musicians	(NA)	2,216	2,513	2,539	2,521	2,454	2,614	2,635	2,782	2,772
Concerts played	(NA)	2,987	4,349	4,508	4,487	4,531	4,723	4,909	5,314	5,904
Attendance mil	(NA)	6.8	9.0	10.6	10.7	10.8	11.8	12.0	13.4	13.7
Ensemble concerts	(NA)	(NA)	(NA)	(NA)	899	812	1,208	1,191	946	1,002
Attendance 1,000	(NA)	(NA)	(NA)	(NA)	574	520	544	650	605	353
Gross expenditures	(NA)	27.7	58.8	66.3	70.7	75.6	85.6	96.6	108.4	121.5

NA Not available.   [1] Source: *Variety*, New York, N.Y., June 8, 1977 issue (copyright).   [2] All shows (new productions and holdovers from previous seasons).   [3] Eight performances are normally given in a playing week.   [4] Source: Central Opera Service, New York, N.Y., *Directory of American Opera Producing Organizations*. Major companies have annual budgets of $100,000 or more and issue American Guild of Musical Artists (AGMA) contracts to all soloists. Community companies have annual budgets of less than $100,000, issue AGMA contracts to some soloists, and give regularly scheduled performances. Workshops are primarily college and university opera companies.   [5] Source: American Symphony Orchestra League, Inc., Vienna, Va. For years ending Aug. 31. Orchestras other than college are principally defined by their annual budgets: Community, $100,000 or under prior to 1967, $50,000 or under thereafter; urban $50,000–$99,999; metropolitan, $100,000–$499,999; and major, $500,000 and over prior to 1976, $1,500,000 and over, thereafter. Prior to 1976, metropolitan included a few orchestras over $500,000. For 1976 and 1977 metropolitan includes 16 and 24 regional orchestras, respectively, with budgets between $500,000 and $1,499,999.   [6] Classification began in 1967.

Source: Compiled from sources listed in footnotes.

No. 409. Museums—Selected Data, by Major Museum Interest and Governing Authority: 1972

[For year ending June 30. Based on representative sample of 728 museums. See source for methodology]

ITEM	Total	MAJOR INTEREST					GOVERNING AUTHORITY		
		Art	History	Science	Art and history	Other combined [1]	Private nonprofit	Government	Educational body
Museums	1,821	340	683	284	186	328	1,018	623	180
Percent by annual budget size:									
Under $50,000	44	33	62	18	55	43	47	45	43
$50,000–$99,999	19	22	17	20	15	20	19	18	17
$100,000–$499,999	27	29	19	42	23	30	24	29	34
$500,000–$999,999	5	8	1	10	5	2	5	4	4
$1,000,000 and over	5	8	1	10	2	5	5	4	2
Museum visits mil	308	43	75	117	18	56	127	171	10
Full-time paid personnel 1,000	30	8	5	9	3	5	18	10	2
Part-time paid personnel 1,000	19	4	4	5	2	4	12	5	2
Volunteers 1,000	64	24	18	10	4	9	48	13	3
Total income mil. dol	513	158	69	153	53	80	333	152	28
Percent by source of income:									
Operating revenues	29	24	30	30	61	18	37	15	9
Private support	21	32	14	18	18	14	26	5	58
Non-operating revenues	13	23	8	8	10	9	18	2	15
Municipal and county govt	18	13	10	24	3	30	12	31	3
State government	7	2	24	3	4	12	4	15	8
Federal government	12	6	14	17	4	17	3	32	7

[1] Composed of art and science museums, history and science museums, and art, history, and science museums.
Source: U.S. National Endowment for the Arts, *Museums USA*, 1974.

No. 410. Volume and Characteristics of Travel: 1972 and 1977

[A trip is counted each time a person goes at least 100 miles away from home. Based on a nationwide probability sample of households concerning trips during 1972 and 1977; see Appendix III]

CHARACTERISTIC	1972				1977 (Jan.–Mar.)					
	Person-trips		Person-miles [1]		Household trips		Person-trips		Person-miles [1]	
	Number (mil.)	Percent	Number (bil.)	Percent	Number (mil.)	Percent	Number (mil.)	Percent	Number (bil.)	Percent
Total	458	100.0	362	100.0	79.9	100.0	127	100.0	88	100.0
Means of transport:										
Auto/truck, no camping equip	356	77.7	229	63.3	57.3	71.7	97	76.5	46	51.7
Auto/truck with camping equip	34	7.4	28	7.7	2.3	2.9	5	3.6	3	3.7
Bus	8	1.8	6	1.6	3.4	4.3	4	3.2	2	2.7
Train	2	.4	2	.5	.9	1.1	1	.8	1	1.0
Airplane	54	11.8	94	25.9	14.1	17.6	18	13.9	33	37.7
Other [2]	4	.8	4	1.2	1.9	2.4	3	2.0	2	3.1
Purpose of trip:										
Visiting	176	38.4	140	38.7	24.8	31.0	46	36.3	29	33.1
Business/convention	93	20.2	80	22.0	26.4	33.0	32	24.8	25	28.0
Outdoor recreation	57	12.4	33	9.0	7.5	9.4	13	10.4	7	8.3
Entertainment, sightseeing	61	13.3	56	15.3	7.7	9.6	13	10.6	11	13.0
Personal, shopping, medical	} 72	15.7	54	14.9	9.5	11.9	17	13.2	11	12.8
Other					3.9	4.9	6	4.6	4	4.9
Round-trip distance:										
200–399 miles	189	41.2	55	15.1	41.8	52.3	69	53.8	19	21.1
400–599 miles	92	20.0	44	12.1	13.4	16.8	22	16.9	10	11.8
600–799 miles	45	9.9	31	8.5	5.5	6.9	8	6.6	6	6.6
800–999 miles	25	5.5	22	6.1	3.1	3.9	5	3.6	4	4.5
1,000–1,999 miles	48	10.4	66	18.1	6.5	8.1	10	7.6	14	15.4
2,000 miles and over	41	8.9	145	40.0	7.4	9.3	11	8.5	36	40.6
Outside United States	18	4.0	(X)	(X)	2.1	2.6	4	2.9	–	–
Duration of trip:										
No nights out of town	83	18.0	31	8.6	18.2	22.8	27	21.3	8	9.6
1 night	(NA)	(NA)	(NA)	(NA)	13.8	17.3	23	17.9	9	10.7
2–3 nights	(NA)	(NA)	(NA)	(NA)	29.1	36.4	48	27.5	3	29.1
4–9 nights	(NA)	(NA)	(NA)	(NA)	13.1	16.4	20	15.9	26	29.5
10–15 nights	(NA)	(NA)	(NA)	(NA)	3.0	3.8	5	4.1	9	10.6
16 nights or more	16	3.4	35	9.7	2.7	3.4	4	3.3	9	10.5
Number on trip:										
1 person	120	26.2	106	29.3	51.7	64.7	52	40.7	39	44.6
2 persons	131	28.5	109	30.3	18.5	23.2	38	30.1	28	32.1
3–4 persons	(NA)	(NA)	(NA)	(NA)	7.9	9.9	28	21.8	15	17.5
5 persons or more	(NA)	(NA)	(NA)	(NA)	1.7	2.1	9	7.1	5	5.7

– Represents zero.   NA Not available.   X Not applicable.   [1] Miles of travelers adjusted for circuity based on type of transport.   [2] Includes different means of going and coming.

No. 411. U.S. Travel, by Selected Characteristics of Travelers: 1977

[For Jan.–Mar. 1977. See headnote, table 410]

CHARACTERISTIC	TRAVELERS						HOUSEHOLDS			
	Total		Person-trips		Person-miles		Traveling		Non-traveling	
	Number (mil.)	Percent	Number (mil.)	Percent	Number (bil.)	Percent	Number (mil.)	Percent	Number (mil.)	Percent
Total	58.7	100.0	127.3	100.0	88.1	100.0	27.9	100.0	46.6	100.0
Male	30.4	51.8	74.1	58.2	52.0	59.0	22.8	81.7	32.5	69.8
Female	28.3	48.2	53.2	41.8	36.1	41.0	5.1	18.3	14.1	30.2
White	54.2	92.4	118.5	93.1	82.1	93.2	25.7	92.2	39.9	85.8
Black and other	4.5	7.6	8.8	6.9	6.0	6.8	2.2	7.8	6.6	14.2
Under 18 years	13.0	22.0	22.2	17.5	12.6	14.4	(Z)	(Z)	(Z)	(Z)
18–24 years	8.8	15.0	19.2	15.1	11.9	13.5	3.2	11.4	3.8	8.3
25–44 years	19.4	33.1	47.8	37.6	32.9	37.4	12.0	43.3	16.3	34.9
45–64 years	13.6	23.2	31.3	24.6	24.3	27.5	9.6	34.5	14.8	31.8
65 and over	3.9	6.6	6.8	5.3	6.3	7.2	3.0	10.6	11.6	25.0
Owned dwelling	41.9	71.4	88.4	69.5	62.0	70.4	18.6	66.5	28.8	61.8
Rented dwelling [2]	16.8	28.7	38.8	30.5	26.1	29.7	9.3	33.5	17.8	38.2
Family income:										
Under $5,000	5.5	9.3	10.8	8.5	7.1	8.1	3.4	12.2	12.4	26.6
$5,000–$7,499	4.1	7.0	8.2	6.4	5.5	6.3	2.4	8.4	6.8	14.7
$7,500–$9,999	4.3	7.4	8.7	6.9	5.8	6.6	2.3	8.2	4.9	10.6
$10,000–$14,999	13.0	22.1	26.3	20.6	16.3	18.5	6.2	22.1	10.0	21.5
$15,000–$19,999	9.7	16.6	21.1	16.6	13.2	15.0	4.5	16.0	5.7	12.3
$20,000–$24,999	8.6	14.6	20.1	15.8	13.7	15.6	3.7	13.1	3.6	7.7
$25,000 and over	13.5	23.0	32.1	25.2	26.4	20.0	5.6	20.0	3.1	6.6

Z Less than 50 thousand or .05 percent.   [1] For sex, race, and age, refers to household head.
[2] Includes occupied without cash payment.

Source of tables 410 and 411: U.S. Bureau of the Census, *Census of Transportation, 1977, National Travel Survey.*

No. 412. U.S. Travel to Foreign Countries—Travelers and Expenditures: 1960 to 1977

[Travelers in thousands; expenditures in millions of dollars, except as indicated. Covers residents of United States and Puerto Rico. See also *Historical Statistics, Colonial Times to 1970*, series H 921–940]

ITEM AND COUNTRY	1960	1965	1970	1971	1972	1973	1974	1975	1976	1977 [1]
Total overseas travelers [2]	1,634	2,623	5,260	5,667	6,790	6,933	6,467	6,354	6,897	7,390
Means of transport from U.S.:										
Sea	317	237	120	95	73	57	47	36	55	(NA)
Air	1,317	2,386	5,140	5,572	6,717	6,876	6,420	6,318	6,842	(NA)
Region of destination:										
Europe and Mediterranean	832	1,405	2,898	3,202	3,843	3,915	3,325	3,185	3,523	3,920
Average length of stay____days	(NA)	39	27	26	27	24	24	24	24	19
Caribbean and Central America	641	891	1,663	1,736	1,992	2,032	2,147	2,065	2,201	2,203
South America	71	127	249	254	338	383	423	447	436	483
Other	90	200	450	475	617	603	572	657	737	784
Total expenditures [3]	2,623	3,768	6,180	6,728	7,902	8,472	9,406	10,143	10,868	11,924
Transportation: [4]										
Foreign flag carriers	513	720	1,215	1,290	1,596	1,790	2,095	2,263	2,568	2,843
United States flag carriers	360	610	985	1,065	1,264	1,156	1,331	1,463	1,444	1,630
Expenditures abroad	1,750	2,438	3,980	4,373	5,042	5,526	5,980	6,417	6,856	7,451
Canada	380	600	1,018	1,079	1,037	1,158	1,359	1,306	1,371	1,433
Mexico	383	540	778	959	1,135	1,264	1,475	1,637	1,723	1,918
Total overseas areas	987	1,298	2,184	2,335	2,870	3,104	3,146	3,474	3,762	4,100
Europe and Mediterranean	692	864	1,425	1,540	1,853	1,993	1,802	1,918	2,150	2,398
Average per trip [5]____dollars	830	611	490	481	482	509	542	602	610	612
Average per day____dollars	(NA)	15.67	18.15	18.50	17.85	21.21	22.58	25.19	25.42	32.21
Caribbean and Central America	166	220	390	408	504	570	685	787	784	790
South America	45	68	90	92	113	132	209	242	232	254
Japan	36	60	97	88	121	123	102	131	145	149
Other	48	86	182	207	279	286	348	396	451	509

NA Not available.   [1] Preliminary.   [2] Excludes the following: Travel to Canada and Mexico; travel between conterminous United States and Alaska, Hawaii, Puerto Rico, and Virgin Islands; cruise travelers; military personnel and other Government employees and their dependents stationed abroad, and U.S. citizens residing abroad.   [3] Includes shore expenditures of cruise travelers; excludes travel expenditures of military personnel and other Government employees and their dependents stationed abroad, and U.S. citizens residing abroad.   [4] Excludes passenger fares of emigrant aliens.   [5] Excludes transatlantic passenger fares.

Source: U.S. Bureau of Economic Analysis, *Survey of Current Business*, monthly.

No. 413. Passengers Arriving From and Departing to Foreign Places, by Citizenship, Area, Flag of Carrier, and Mode of Travel: 1965 to 1977

[In thousands. For years ending June 30 except, beginning 1976, ending Dec. 31. Compiled from passenger manifests or lists. Excludes travelers between United States and its outlying areas, border crossers, crewmen, and military personnel. See also *Historical Statistics, Colonial Times to 1970*, series C 296–331]

AREA, FLAG, ETC.	1965	1970	1975	1976	1977	AREA, FLAG, ETC.	1965	1970	1975	1976	1977
Arrivals	5,059	10,039	14,240	13,403	14,701	Arrivals—Con.					
Aliens	1,960	3,831	6,094	5,970	6,499	Mode of travel:					
Citizens	3,100	6,208	8,146	7,433	8,201	By sea	840	867	923	(NA)	(NA)
						By air	4,220	9,172	13,317	13,403	14,701
Embarkation:											
Europe [1] [2]	2,212	4,087	5,251	5,423	6,256	Departures	4,820	9,354	13,099	12,679	13,804
Asia [1] [3]	351	893	1,765	1,738	1,895						
Africa	15	30	56	94	116	Aliens	1,735	3,247	5,130	5,146	5,474
Oceania	96	225	402	435	446	Citizens	3,085	6,107	7,969	7,533	8,330
Canada and Greenland [2]	54	79	393	(NA)	(NA)	Debarkation:					
Mexico	441	880	1,613	1,707	1,647	Europe [1] [2]	2,111	3,907	4,827	5,060	5,826
West Indies	1,118	2,481	2,718	2,700	2,827	Asia [1] [3]	357	808	1,592	1,736	1,821
Cent. America	148	264	411	450	525	Africa	19	33	58	99	104
So. America	277	531	847	856	989	Oceania	105	221	389	390	432
Cruise	347	569	784	(NA)	(NA)	Canada and Greenland [2]	32	55	248	(NA)	(NA)
Arrivals:						Mexico	427	846	1,522	1,622	1,570
Boston	89	302	528	492	554	West Indies	1,030	2,157	2,463	2,487	2,572
Chicago	162	203	672	700	792	Cent. America	145	243	389	415	483
Honolulu	197	506	1,324	1,061	1,063	So. America	252	490	829	870	997
Houston	46	85	284	329	259	Cruise	343	594	782	(NA)	(NA)
Los Angeles	[4] 238	516	918	1,067	1,168						
Miami	772	1,515	1,963	1,716	1,996	Flag of carrier:					
New York	2,431	4,182	4,735	4,622	5,332	United States	2,089	4,612	6,226	6,244	6,889
Philadelphia	19	102	219	169	143	Foreign	2,731	4,742	6,874	6,435	6,915
San Francisco	115	192	340	238	322	Mode of travel:					
Flag of carrier:						By sea	813	859	864	(NA)	(NA)
United States	2,246	5,106	6,972	6,922	7,487	By air	4,007	8,495	12,236	12,679	13,804
Foreign	2,813	4,933	7,268	6,481	7,214						

NA Not available.   [1] Turkey included with Europe through 1970, with Asia thereafter.   [2] Beginning 1976, Greenland included with Europe.   [3] Includes Philippines.   [4] Includes San Pedro, California.

Source: 1965–1975, U.S. Immigration and Naturalization Service, *Annual Report*, and releases; thereafter, U.S. Transportation Systems Center, Cambridge, Mass., *U.S. International Air Travel Statistics*, annual.

No. 414. Passports, by Characteristics of Travelers and Travel: 1960 to 1977

[In thousands. Total passports are actual count; all other data based on a sample and prorated to total passports. Data subject to error since sample size varied through 1972; beginning 1973, based on a sample size of approximately 10 percent of total volume of passports. Data refer to number of passports issued, not travelers. Prior to 1970, covers new and renewed passports; thereafter, renewals eliminated. A single passport may cover more than one trip and more than one person. See also Historical Statistics, Colonial Times to 1970, series H 899–920]

CHARACTERISTIC	1960	1965	1970	1971	1972	1973	1974	1975	1976	1977
Total passports	853	1,330	2,219	2,399	2,728	2,729	2,415	2,334	2,817	3,107
Male	420	699	1,124	1,267	1,359	1,321	1,155	1,128	1,354	1,496
Female	433	631	1,095	1,132	1,369	1,408	1,260	1,206	1,463	1,611
Under 20 years	83	198	362	392	470	497	448	405	460	511
20–29 years	148	264	507	554	585	564	491	458	530	566
30–39 years	143	206	293	305	369	376	348	345	432	499
40–49 years	136	217	356	378	434	431	371	347	423	452
50–59 years	156	203	341	378	437	434	383	384	484	527
60 years and over	187	242	360	392	433	427	374	395	488	552
Independent business or profession	173	426	715	811	819	702	519	543	718	826
Student	90	222	446	506	548	559	459	406	478	533
Housewife	203	272	380	390	467	450	385	361	429	463
Skilled, technical or sales worker	139	47	66	48	143	279	367	322	365	371
Retired	54	75	121	135	157	160	150	161	207	239
Clerk-secretary	38	53	106	116	127	139	111	103	126	148
Teacher	44	57	128	136	147	139	111	112	128	129
Other and not stated	112	178	257	257	320	301	313	326	366	398
Object of travel: [1]										
Government	116	191	146	99	137	146	206	210	288	718
Personal reasons	322	487	1,791	2,157	2,043	1,246	385	377	603	1,006
Pleasure	351	535	217	109	441	1,077	1,382	1,316	1,511	1,102
Business	24	76	40	16	68	155	268	273	273	191
Education	31	31	20	16	33	95	153	132	126	79
Religion, health, other	9	10	5	2	6	10	21	28	16	11
First area destination:										
Africa	8	19	19	15	30	26	32	33	35	34
Australia and Oceania	35	51	51	48	79	81	101	96	107	108
Europe	670	993	1,910	2,140	2,244	2,181	1,715	1,611	1,991	2,292
Far East	56	111	117	73	135	140	162	155	180	187
North, Central, and So. America	59	100	72	69	136	189	287	318	347	317
Middle East	25	56	49	54	104	111	117	121	157	169

[1] Data not entirely comparable because of changes in classifications.

Source: U.S. Passport Office, Summary of Passport Statistics, annual.

No. 415. Foreign Travel to the United States—Travelers and Expenditures: 1960 to 1977

[Includes travelers for business and pleasure, foreigners in transit through the United States, and students; excludes travel by foreign government personnel and foreign businessmen employed in the United States. See also Historical Statistics, Colonial Times to 1970, series H 946–951]

ITEM	Total	Canada	Mexico	OVERSEAS					Fares to U.S. carriers [1]
				Europe	Carib.; Centr. Amer.	So. America	Japan	Other	
Travelers (1,000):									
1960	(NA)	(NA)	(NA)	274	(NA)	(NA)	20	308	(X)
1965	(NA)	(NA)	(NA)	564	(NA)	(NA)	44	596	(X)
1970	(NA)	(NA)	(NA)	984	484	318	207	295	(X)
1973	(NA)	(NA)	(NA)	1,623	497	358	639	437	(X)
1974	(NA)	(NA)	(NA)	1,544	508	401	764	483	(X)
1975	(NA)	(NA)	(NA)	1,500	478	438	747	511	(X)
1976	(NA)	(NA)	(NA)	1,892	573	510	766	715	(X)
1977	(NA)	(NA)	(NA)	1,885	578	573	750	723	(X)
Expenditures (mil. dol.):									
1960	1,025	469	226	90	(NA)	(NA)	12	122	106
1965	1,545	490	390	200	(NA)	(NA)	27	273	165
1970	2,708	859	583	318	170	164	101	136	377
1973	4,130	1,072	830	559	205	198	334	214	718
1974	4,845	1,225	1,142	570	216	237	402	240	813
1975	5,606	1,561	1,453	611	206	303	410	295	767
1976	6,743	1,983	1,428	852	289	360	439	455	937
1977	7,189	2,150	1,414	988	270	444	436	462	1,025

NA Not available.   X Not applicable.   [1] Includes fares paid to and from the United States only.

Source: U.S. Bureau of Economic Analysis, Survey of Current Business, monthly.

Section 9

Federal Government Finances and Employment

This section presents statistics relating to the financial structure and the civilian employment of the Federal Government. The fiscal data cover taxes, other receipts, outlays, and debt. The principal sources of fiscal data are *The Budget of the United States Government* and related documents, published annually by the Office of Management and Budget (OMB), and the Department of the Treasury's annual *Combined Statement of Receipts, Expenditures and Balances of the United States Government*, the official report relating to the receipts, appropriations, outlays, and fund accounts. The *Statistical Appendix* to the *Annual Report of the Secretary of the Treasury* is a convenient summary of yearly data relating to somewhat broader fields. Detailed data on tax returns and collections are published annually by the Internal Revenue Service. The personnel data relate to staffing and payrolls for the various public functions and agencies, to employee characteristics, and to civil service status; they are published by the Civil Service Commission and the Bureau of Labor Statistics (see p. 254).

Budget concept.—Under the unified budget concept, introduced in the 1969 budget, all Federal monies are included in one comprehensive budget. These monies comprise both Federal funds and trust funds. Federal funds are derived mainly from taxes and borrowing and are not restricted by law to any specific government purpose. Trust funds collect certain taxes and other receipts for specified purposes such as unemployment insurance. In recent years, however, the budget totals, under provisions of law, have excluded some Federal activities—including the Federal Financing Bank, the Postal Service, and the lending activities of the Rural Electrification Administration. For fiscal year 1978, these activities (i.e. off-budget Federal entities) are estimated to equal 2.5 percent of the unified budget. In addition, several privately owned, Government-sponsored activities which primarily perform lending functions are excluded (e.g. the Student Loan Marketing Association). These activities are estimated to equal 3.6 percent of the unified budget in 1978. Data showing unified budget totals of budget receipts and outlays are presented in the 1979 *Budget* for the years 1940 to 1978; more detailed tables generally show data since 1969.

Receipts arising from the Government's compulsory powers are reported as governmental receipts; all other receipts, e.g., from business-type or market-oriented activities, are offset against outlays. Outlays are reported on a checks-issued (net) basis.

Debt concept.—For most of U.S. history, the total debt consisted of debt borrowed by the Treasury (i.e. public debt); it did not include monies which agencies were authorized to borrow without going through the Treasury (e.g. the Postal Service). The new debt series, also introduced in 1969, includes both public debt and agency debt. The *gross Federal debt* includes money borrowed by the Treasury and by various Federal agencies; it is the broadest generally used measure of the Federal debt. *Total public debt* is restricted to borrowing by the Treasury and the value of savings bonds at current redemption value.

Treasury receipts and outlays.—All receipts of the Government, with a few exceptions, are deposited to the credit of the U.S. Treasury regardless of ultimate disposition or availability for expenditure. Under the Constitution, no money may be withdrawn from the Treasury unless appropriated by the Congress.

The day-to-day cash operations of the Federal Government clearing through the accounts of the U.S. Treasury are reported in the *Daily Treasury Statement*. Extensive detail on the public debt is published in the *Monthly Statement of the Public Debt of the United States*.

Budget receipts and outlays of the Government and other transactions appear in the *Monthly Treasury Statement of Receipts and Outlays of the United States Government.* The monthly *Treasury Bulletin* contains analytical material on fiscal operations and related Treasury activities, including financial statements of Government corporations and other business-type activities.

Receipts such as taxes, customs duties, and miscellaneous budget receipts, which are collected by Government agencies, and outlays represented by checks issued and cash payments made by disbursing officers are reported in the *Monthly Treasury Statement* cited above and in the annual *Combined Statement of Receipts, Expenditures and Balances.* These monthly and annual reports include deposits and collections in, and payments from, accounts of Government agencies held outside the Treasury as well as those of the general account of the United States Treasury and are on the same basis as the unified budget.

Income tax returns and tax collections.—Tax data are compiled by the Internal Revenue Service of the Treasury Department. The *Annual Report of the Commissioner of Internal Revenue* gives a detailed account of tax collections by kind of tax and by regions, districts, and States. The agency's three annual *Statistics of Income* reports present detailed data from individual income tax returns, corporation income tax returns, and business tax returns, respectively. The report on business tax returns presents financial data for sole proprietorships and partnerships. Periodic *Statistics of Income* publications present local area data for individuals as well as data from fiduciary income tax and estate tax returns, and data on sales of capital assets by individuals, foreign income and tax reported by corporations, and estate tax wealth.

Relation to national income accounts and GNP.—The Federal sector of the *national income and product accounts* focuses upon Federal transactions (comprising both Federal and trust funds) entering into national income, the gross national product, and other parts of the national economic accounts (see table 419). These accounts, however, include only receipts and outlays which directly affect the current flow of income and output, and therefore exclude such transactions as loans. Also, the Federal sector account records many taxes as they accrue, instead of as they are collected, and records most purchases at the time of delivery.

Employment and payrolls.—The Civil Service Commission collects employment and payroll data from all departments and agencies of the Federal Government, except the Central Intelligence Agency and the National Security Agency. Employment figures represent the number of persons who occupied civilian positions on the last day of the calendar month shown and who are paid for personal services rendered for the Federal Government, regardless of the nature of appointment or method of payment. Intermittent workers are counted if they performed any service during the reporting month.

Federal payrolls include all payments for personal services rendered during the calendar month and payments for accumulated annual leave of employees who separate from the service. Since most Federal employees are paid on a biweekly basis, the calendar month earnings are partially estimated on the basis of the number of work days in each month where payroll periods overlap consecutive months.

Federal employment and payroll figures are published by the Civil Service Commission in its *Annual Report* and its *Monthly Release, Federal Civilian Workforce Statistics.* It also publishes semiannual employment data for minority groups; annual reports on salary and wages; geographic distribution; and data on occupations of white- and blue-collar workers as well as data on women Federal employees. Data on Federal employment are also issued by the Bureau of Labor Statistics in its *Monthly Labor Review* and in *Employment and Earnings.*

Historical statistics.—Tabular headnotes provide cross-references, where applicable, to *Historical Statistics of the United States, Colonial Times to 1970.* See Appendix I.

Figure 9.1

The Government of the United States

(As of June 1, 1978. Only the major agencies are shown. See table 458)

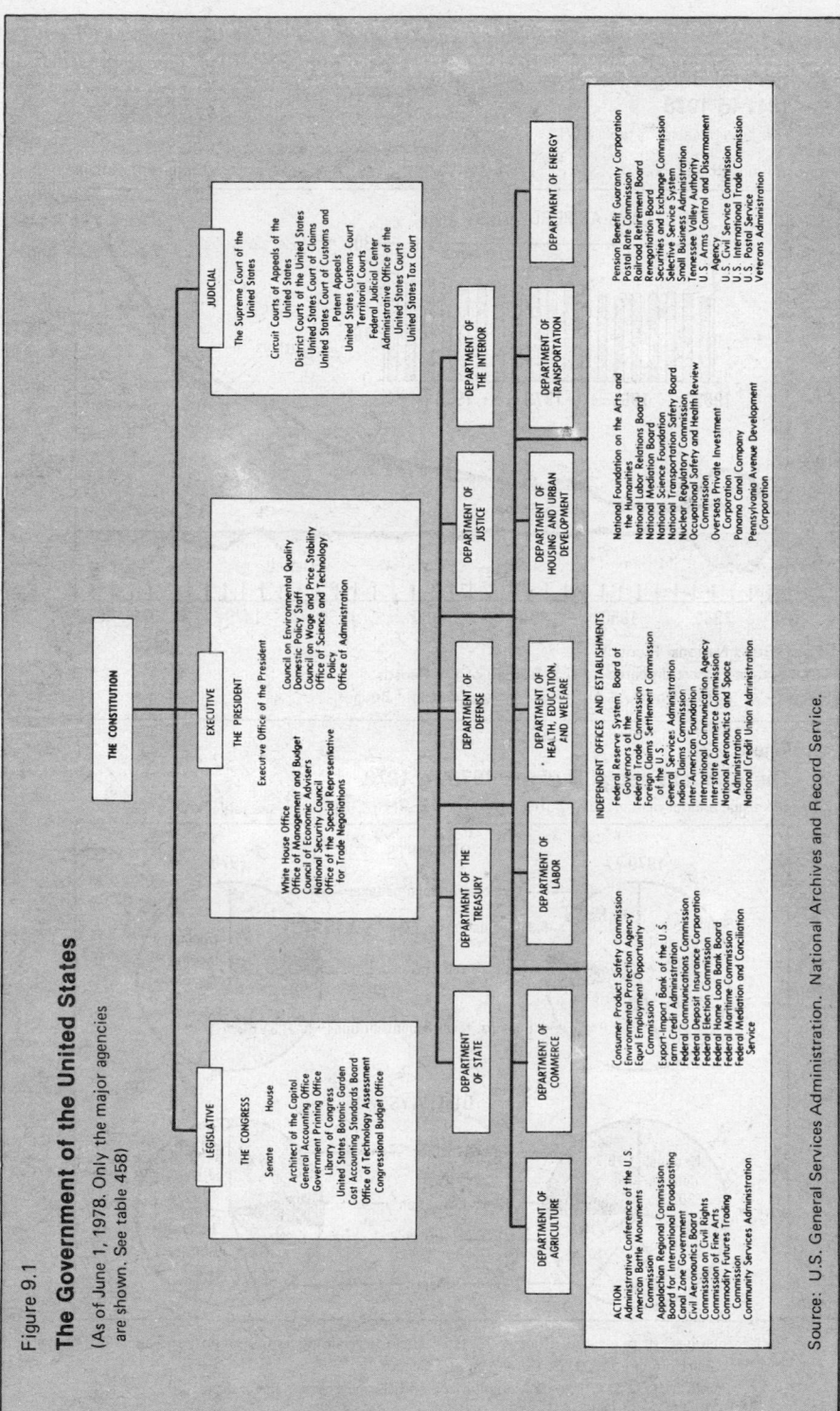

Source: U.S. General Services Administration. National Archives and Record Service.

Figure 9.2
Federal Budget Receipts and Outlays:
1941 to 1978
(For fiscal years; see table 417)

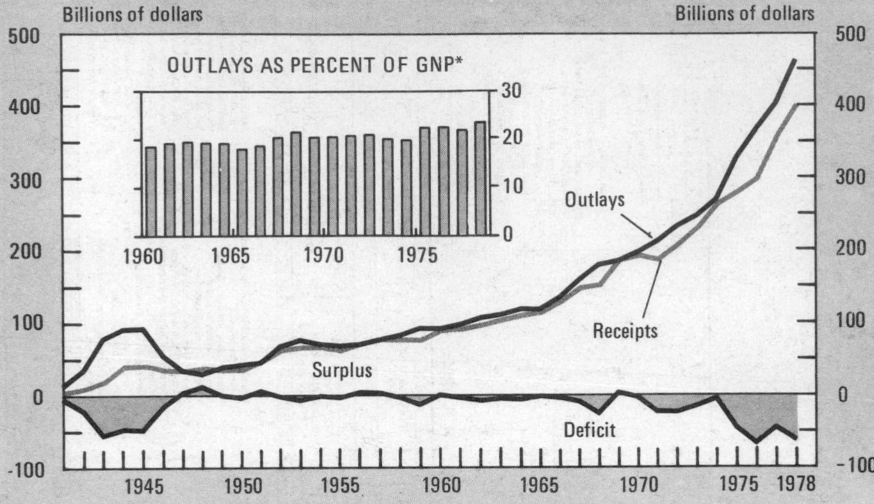

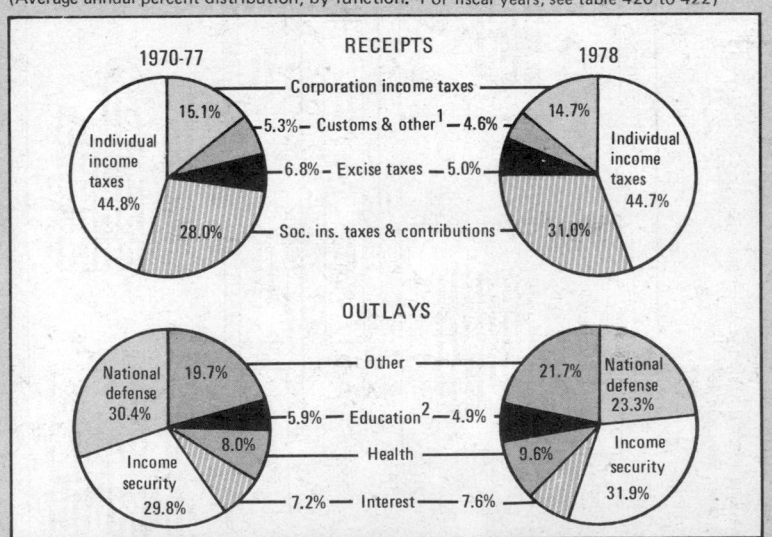

*Gross National Product.
Source: Chart prepared by U.S. Bureau of the Census.
        Data from U.S. Office of Management and Budget.

Figure 9.3
The Annual Federal Budget: 1970 to 1978
(Average annual percent distribution, by function. For fiscal years; see table 420 to 422)

[1] Other includes gift taxes and other receipts.   [2] Includes training, employment, and social services.
Source: Chart prepared by U.S. Bureau of the Census.
        Data from U.S. Office of Management and Budget.

No. 416. FEDERAL BUDGET RECEIPTS, OUTLAYS, AND DEBT: 1940 TO 1978

[In billions of dollars, except percent. Through 1976, for years ending **June 30**, except as noted; beginning **1977,** ending **Sept. 30**. See also *Historical Statistics, Colonial Times to 1970*, series Y 339–342]

YEAR	Receipts	Outlays	Surplus or deficit (−)	Out-standing debt [1]	ANNUAL PERCENT CHANGE			PERCENT OF GNP [2]	
					Receipts	Outlays	Out-standing debt	Outlays	Out-standing debt
1940	6.4	9.5	−3.1	50.7	(NA)	(NA)	[3] 5.1	10.0	97.7
1945	45.2	92.7	−47.5	260.1	48.0	60.0	39.0	42.7	119.5
1950	39.5	42.6	−3.1	256.9	−2.7	−14.4	−.3	16.1	51.1
1955	65.5	68.5	−3.0	274.4	10.6	10.0	1.3	18.0	72.2
1960	92.5	92.2	.3	290.9	7.2	6.1	1.2	18.5	58.5
1961	94.4	97.8	−3.4	292.9	2.1	6.0	.7	19.2	57.6
1962	99.7	106.8	−7.1	303.3	5.6	9.2	3.6	19.5	55.5
1963	106.6	111.3	−4.8	310.8	6.9	4.2	2.5	19.3	53.9
1964	112.7	118.6	−5.9	316.8	5.7	6.5	1.9	19.2	51.4
1965	116.8	118.4	−1.6	323.2	3.7	−.1	2.0	18.0	49.2
1966	130.9	134.7	−3.8	329.5	12.0	13.7	1.9	18.7	45.7
1967	149.6	158.3	−8.7	341.3	14.3	17.5	3.6	20.4	44.1
1968	153.7	178.8	−25.2	369.8	2.8	13.0	8.4	21.5	44.6
1969	187.8	184.5	3.2	367.1	22.0	3.2	−.7	20.4	40.6
1970	193.7	196.6	−2.8	382.6	3.2	6.5	4.2	20.5	39.9
1971	188.4	211.4	−23.0	409.5	−2.8	7.5	7.0	20.7	40.2
1972	208.6	232.0	−23.4	437.3	10.8	9.7	6.8	20.9	39.4
1973	232.2	247.1	−14.8	468.4	11.3	6.5	7.1	20.0	37.9
1974	264.9	269.6	−4.7	486.2	14.1	9.1	3.8	19.8	35.8
1975	281.0	326.1	−45.1	544.1	6.1	21.0	11.9	22.4	37.4
1976	299.2	365.6	−66.4	631.9	6.8	12.4	16.1	22.5	38.9
1976, TQ [4]	81.7	94.7	−13.0	646.4	(X)	(X)	(X)	(X)	(X)
1977	356.9	401.9	−45.0	709.1	18.9	9.7	12.2	21.9	38.6
1978, est	400.4	462.2	−61.8	785.6	12.2	15.0	10.6	22.6	38.4

NA Not available. X Not applicable. [1] End of fiscal year. [2] Gross national product as of fiscal year; for calendar year GNP, see p. 440. [3] Change from 1939. [4] Transition quarter, July–Sept.

No. 417. FEDERAL BUDGET RECEIPTS, OUTLAYS, AND DEBT: 1960 TO 1978

[In billions of dollars, except percent For years ending **June 30** except, beginning **1977**, ending **Sept. 30**; transition quarter, July–Sept. 1976, omitted. Beginning **1972**, budget totals include transactions of the Export-Import Bank. See also *Historical Statistics, Colonial Times to 1970*, series Y 339–342]

DESCRIPTION	1960	1965	1970	1971	1972	1973	1974	1975	1976	1977	1978, est.
Receipts	92.5	116.8	193.7	188.4	208.6	232.2	264.9	281.0	299.2	356.9	400.4
Federal funds	75.6	90.9	143.2	133.8	148.8	161.4	181.2	187.5	200.3	240.4	267.9
Trust funds	19.2	29.2	59.4	66.2	73.0	92.2	104.8	118.6	133.7	152.8	168.5
Interfund transactions	−2.4	−3.3	−8.8	−11.6	−13.2	−21.3	−21.1	−25.1	−34.8	−36.3	−36.0
Outlays	92.2	118.4	196.6	211.4	232.0	247.1	269.6	326.1	365.6	401.9	462.2
Federal funds	74.9	94.8	156.3	163.7	178.1	187.0	199.9	240.0	269.1	294.9	340.0
Trust funds	19.7	27.0	49.1	59.4	67.1	81.4	90.8	111.2	131.3	143.3	158.2
Interfund transactions	−2.4	−3.3	−8.8	−11.6	−13.2	−21.3	−21.1	−25.1	−34.8	−36.3	−36.0
Surplus or deficit (−)	.3	−1.6	−2.8	−23.0	−23.4	−14.8	−4.7	−45.1	−66.5	−45.0	−61.8
Federal funds	.8	−3.9	−13.1	−29.9	−29.3	−25.6	−18.7	−52.5	−68.9	−54.5	−72.1
Trust funds	−.5	2.3	10.3	6.8	5.9	10.7	14.0	7.4	2.4	9.5	10.3
Outstanding debt [1]	290.9	323.2	382.6	409.5	437.3	468.4	486.2	544.1	631.9	709.1	785.6
Gross Federal debt held by:											
Government agencies	53.7	61.5	97.7	105.1	113.6	125.4	140.2	147.2	151.6	157.3	167.7
The public	237.2	261.6	284.9	304.3	323.8	343.0	346.0	396.9	480.3	551.8	617.9
Federal Reserve System	26.5	39.1	57.7	65.5	71.4	75.2	80.6	85.0	94.7	105.0	(NA)
Others	210.7	222.5	227.2	238.8	252.3	267.9	265.4	311.9	385.6	446.8	(NA)
Outlays as percent of GNP [2]	18.5	18.0	20.5	20.7	20.9	20.0	19.8	22.4	22.5	21.9	22.6
National defense	9.3	7.6	8.3	7.5	6.9	6.1	5.8	5.9	5.5	5.3	5.3
Human resources [3]	5.1	5.4	7.6	8.7	9.4	9.3	9.7	11.7	12.3	11.7	11.7
All other	4.2	5.1	4.6	4.5	4.6	4.5	4.3	4.9	4.9	4.9	5.6

NA Not available. [1] End of fiscal year.
[2] Gross national product as of fiscal year; for calendar year GNP, see page 440.
[3] Education, training, employment, social services, health, income security, and veterans benefits and services.

Source of tables 416 and 417: U.S. Office of Management and Budget, *The Budget of the United States Government*, annual.

No. 418. **FEDERAL BUDGET OUTLAYS IN CURRENT AND CONSTANT (1972) DOLLARS: 1960 TO 1978**

[Through 1976, for years ending June 30, except as noted; beginning 1977, ending Sept. 30. Given the inherent imprecision in deflating outlays, the data shown in constant dollars present a reasonable perspective—not precision. The deflators and the categories that are deflated are as comparable over time as is feasible]

YEAR	OUTLAYS (bil. dol.)						PERCENT OF TOTAL OUTLAYS					Avg. annual percent change, total outlays
	Total	National defense	Total nondefense [1]	Payments for individuals	Net interest [2]	Aid to State and local govt.[3]	National defense	Total nondefense [1]	Payments for individuals	Net interest [2]	Aid to State and local govt.[3]	
CURRENT DOLLARS												
1960	92.2	45.2	47.0	22.9	6.9	7.0	49.0	51.0	24.8	7.5	7.6	[4]4.1
1965	118.4	47.5	71.0	30.4	8.6	10.9	40.1	60.0	25.7	7.3	9.2	5.1
1968	178.8	78.8	100.1	46.0	11.1	18.6	44.1	56.0	25.7	6.2	10.4	14.7
1969	184.5	79.4	105.1	52.8	12.7	20.3	43.0	57.0	28.6	6.9	11.0	3.2
1970	196.6	78.6	118.0	59.8	14.4	24.0	40.0	60.0	30.4	7.3	12.2	6.6
1971	211.4	75.8	135.6	74.5	14.8	28.1	35.9	64.1	35.2	7.0	13.3	7.5
1972	232.0	76.6	155.5	85.3	15.5	34.4	33.0	67.0	36.8	6.7	14.8	9.7
1973	247.1	74.5	172.5	95.9	17.4	41.8	30.1	69.8	38.8	7.0	16.9	6.5
1974	269.6	77.7	191.9	111.1	21.5	43.3	28.8	71.2	41.2	8.0	16.1	9.1
1975	326.1	85.6	240.5	142.7	23.3	49.7	26.2	73.7	43.8	7.1	15.2	21.0
1976	365.6	89.4	276.2	166.6	26.8	59.0	24.5	75.5	45.6	7.3	16.1	12.1
1976, TQ [5]	94.7	22.3	72.4	42.7	7.0	15.9	23.5	76.4	45.1	7.4	16.8	(X)
1977	401.9	97.5	304.4	181.7	30.0	68.4	24.3	75.7	45.2	7.5	17.0	9.9
1978, est	462.2	107.6	354.6	196.9	35.2	80.3	23.3	76.7	42.6	7.6	17.4	15.0
CONSTANT (1972) DOLLARS												
1960	150.8	73.8	77.0	32.1	16.3	11.2	48.9	51.1	21.3	10.8	7.4	[4]−2.0
1965	173.3	69.3	104.0	40.1	16.7	15.7	40.0	60.0	23.1	9.6	9.1	2.8
1968	229.5	101.4	128.1	55.6	16.9	23.5	44.2	55.8	24.2	7.4	10.2	9.8
1969	223.1	97.9	125.3	60.9	15.5	24.2	43.9	56.2	27.3	6.9	10.8	−2.8
1970	220.8	90.3	130.5	65.1	15.0	27.0	40.9	59.1	29.5	6.8	12.2	−1.0
1971	223.0	81.2	141.8	77.2	15.2	29.5	36.4	63.6	34.6	6.8	13.2	1.0
1972	232.0	76.5	155.5	85.3	15.5	34.3	33.0	67.0	36.8	6.7	14.8	4.0
1973	233.2	70.0	163.2	92.2	15.4	39.5	30.0	70.0	39.5	6.6	16.9	.5
1974	231.9	67.9	164.0	98.0	14.4	37.7	29.3	70.7	42.3	6.2	16.3	−.6
1975	253.4	67.1	186.2	113.3	14.6	38.9	26.5	73.5	44.7	5.8	15.4	9.3
1976	265.8	65.5	200.3	123.6	16.4	43.1	24.6	75.3	46.5	6.2	16.2	4.9
1976, TQ [5]	66.7	15.9	50.8	30.6	4.1	11.2	23.8	76.2	45.9	6.1	16.8	(X)
1977	272.0	66.5	205.5	125.4	17.4	46.3	24.4	75.6	46.1	6.4	17.0	2.3
1978, est	293.0	68.9	224.1	128.2	18.2	51.0	23.5	76.5	43.8	6.2	17.4	7.7

X Not applicable.   [1] Includes other items, not shown separately.   [2] Total interest less interest received by trust funds.   [3] Includes small grants for national defense function, less than $100 million in any year.   [4] Percent change from 1959; from previous year shown for all other years. Minus sign (−) denotes decrease.   [5] Transition quarter, July–Sept.

No. 419. **FEDERAL RECEIPTS AND EXPENDITURES IN THE NATIONAL INCOME ACCOUNTS: 1960 TO 1978**

[In billions of dollars. For years ending June 30 except, beginning 1977, ending Sept. 30; transition quarter July–Sept. 1976, omitted. Includes transactions of trust accounts]

RECEIPTS AND EXPENDITURES	1960	1965	1970	1972	1973	1974	1975	1976	1977	1978,[1]
Receipts, total	94.8	120.0	194.9	213.5	240.4	271.9	283.2	314.1	364.0	410.8
Personal tax and nontax receipts	42.5	51.4	93.6	100.3	107.3	122.6	127.3	137.2	165.5	185.5
Corporate profits tax accruals	22.3	27.1	33.0	34.2	41.0	43.8	41.6	52.2	57.4	63.1
Indirect business tax and nontax accruals	13.2	16.9	19.2	19.9	20.7	21.4	22.1	24.2	24.6	28.5
Contributions for social insurance	16.7	24.5	49.2	59.1	71.5	84.1	92.2	100.5	116.5	133.7
Expenditures, total [2]	91.3	118.5	195.6	232.9	256.2	278.9	328.7	372.3	411.8	463.6
Purchases of goods and services	52.9	64.6	97.0	100.9	101.7	104.6	117.9	126.5	140.7	158.4
National defense	44.5	47.9	75.3	72.5	73.3	74.1	80.3	85.8	92.0	99.8
Nondefense	8.4	16.6	21.7	28.4	28.4	30.5	37.6	40.7	48.7	58.6
Transfer payments	22.5	30.6	57.0	78.9	89.7	104.7	134.2	156.8	169.7	184.2
Domestic (to persons)	20.6	28.4	55.0	76.1	87.1	101.7	131.1	153.9	166.5	180.7
Foreign	1.8	2.2	2.0	2.8	2.7	3.0	3.1	3.0	3.2	3.5
Grants-in-aid to State and local governments	6.9	10.9	22.6	32.6	40.4	41.6	48.4	57.5	66.0	77.0
Net interest paid	6.8	8.2	13.6	14.1	15.9	19.8	21.9	25.4	29.3	34.5
Subsidies less current surplus of government enterprises	2.4	4.3	5.4	6.4	9.1	8.0	5.7	6.1	6.1	9.5
Surplus (+) or deficit (−)	+3.5	+1.5	−.6	−19.5	−15.7	−7.0	−45.0	−58.2	−47.8	−52.8

[1] Estimated.   [2] For some years, includes wage disbursements less accruals, not shown separately.

Source of tables 418 and 419: U.S. Office of Management and Budget, *The Budget of the United States Government*, annual.

No. 420. FEDERAL BUDGET RECEIPTS, BY MAJOR SOURCE: 1960 TO 1978

[In billions of dollars, except percent. For years ending June 30 except, beginning 1977, ending Sept. 30; transition quarter, July-Sept. 1976, omitted. For basic data and explanation of terms, see table 424. See also *Historical Statistics, Colonial Times to 1970*, series Y 343-351]

MAJOR SOURCE	1960	1965	1970	1971	1972	1973	1974	1975	1976	1977	1978, est.
Total receipts, by source	92.5	116.8	193.7	188.4	208.6	232.2	264.9	281.0	299.2	356.9	400.4
Individual income taxes	40.7	48.8	90.4	86.2	94.7	103.2	119.0	122.4	130.8	156.7	178.8
Corporation income taxes	21.5	25.5	32.8	26.8	32.2	36.2	38.6	40.6	41.4	54.9	58.9
Social insurance taxes and contributions	14.7	22.3	45.3	48.6	53.9	64.5	76.8	86.4	92.7	108.7	124.1
Employment taxes and contributions	11.2	17.4	39.1	41.7	46.1	54.9	65.9	75.2	79.9	92.2	104.0
Unemployment insurance	2.7	3.8	3.5	3.7	4.4	6.1	6.8	6.8	8.1	11.3	14.4
Other contributions	.8	1.1	2.7	3.2	3.4	3.6	4.1	4.5	4.8	5.2	5.7
Excise taxes	11.6	14.6	15.8	16.6	15.5	16.3	16.8	16.5	17.0	17.5	20.2
Estate and gift taxes	1.6	2.7	3.6	3.7	5.4	4.9	5.0	4.6	5.2	7.3	5.6
Customs duties	1.1	1.4	2.4	2.6	3.3	3.2	3.3	3.7	4.1	5.2	5.8
Miscellaneous receipts	1.2	1.6	3.4	3.9	3.6	3.9	5.4	6.7	8.0	6.5	6.9

PERCENT DISTRIBUTION

MAJOR SOURCE	1960	1965	1970	1971	1972	1973	1974	1975	1976	1977	1978, est.
Total receipts, by source	100.0	100.0	100.0	100.0	100.0	100.0	100.0	100.0	100.0	100.0	100.0
Individual income taxes	44.0	41.8	46.7	45.8	45.4	44.4	44.9	43.6	43.7	43.9	44.7
Corporation income taxes	23.2	21.8	16.9	14.2	15.4	15.6	14.6	14.5	13.8	15.4	14.7
Social insurance taxes and contributions	15.9	19.1	23.4	25.8	25.8	27.8	28.9	30.7	31.0	30.5	31.0
Employment taxes and contributions	12.1	14.9	20.1	22.1	22.1	23.6	24.9	26.8	26.7	25.8	26.0
Excise taxes	12.6	12.5	8.1	8.8	7.4	7.0	6.4	5.9	5.7	4.9	5.0
Customs, estate, and gift taxes	2.9	3.6	3.1	3.4	4.2	3.5	3.2	2.9	3.1	3.5	2.8
Miscellaneous receipts	1.3	1.4	1.8	2.0	1.7	1.7	2.0	2.4	2.7	1.8	1.7

No. 421. EXECUTIVE/LEGISLATIVE CONTROLLABILITY OF FEDERAL BUDGET OUTLAYS: 1070 TO 1978

[In billions of dollars, except percent. For years ending June 30 except, beginning 1977, ending Sept. 30; transition quarter, July-Sept. 1976, omitted. Outlays considered relatively uncontrollable are those which can neither be increased nor decreased by Presidential decisions without a change in existing Federal laws or are beyond administrative control, such as benefit payments that beneficiaries are entitled to by law or contractual agreement or other existing legally binding commitments]

OUTLAYS	1970	1971	1972	1973	1974	1975	1976	1977	1978, est.
Total outlays	196.6	211.4	232.0	247.1	269.6	326.1	365.6	401.9	462.2
Relatively uncontrollable outlays	125.8	140.4	153.5	173.1	194.6	237.6	267.1	293.6	344.7
Percent of total outlays	64.0	66.4	66.2	70.0	72.2	72.9	73.1	73.1	74.6
Open-ended programs and fixed costs	84.3	100.2	114.3	133.5	150.8	186.9	216.2	238.3	265.3
Payments for individuals	62.3	77.3	88.5	99.6	115.4	148.9	173.7	189.5	205.5
Social security and railroad retirement	31.3	37.2	41.5	50.7	57.6	68.4	76.2	87.7	97.2
Federal employees' retirement and insurance [1]	5.6	6.6	7.7	9.0	10.8	13.3	15.6	17.8	20.1
Unemployment assistance	3.7	6.6	7.5	5.7	6.5	14.0	19.8	15.8	13.0
Veterans' benefits	6.6	7.6	8.3	9.3	10.0	12.4	13.9	12.9	12.9
Medicare and Medicaid	9.9	11.2	13.4	14.1	17.2	21.6	26.3	31.4	36.5
Housing payments	.5	.7	1.1	1.6	1.8	2.1	2.5	2.9	3.7
Public assistance and related programs	4.7	7.4	8.9	9.1	11.5	17.1	19.4	20.9	22.2
Net interest	14.4	14.8	15.5	17.4	21.5	23.3	26.8	30.0	35.2
General revenue sharing	(X)	(X)	(X)	6.6	6.1	6.1	6.2	6.8	6.8
Farm price supports [2]	3.8	2.8	4.0	3.6	1.0	.6	.6	3.5	7.4
Other	3.8	5.2	6.4	6.3	6.8	8.0	8.8	8.6	10.3
Prior-year contracts and obligations [3]	41.5	40.2	39.2	39.6	43.8	50.7	50.9	55.3	79.3
National defense	24.1	21.1	19.4	17.7	20.4	22.3	17.9	18.5	29.9
Civilian programs	17.4	19.1	19.9	21.9	23.4	28.4	33.0	36.8	49.4
Relatively controllable outlays	73.3	73.7	81.2	76.9	78.4	92.5	102.8	112.9	122.6
National defense	51.6	51.3	53.2	52.5	52.2	57.0	64.2	70.8	68.4
Civilian programs	21.7	22.4	28.0	24.5	26.2	35.5	38.7	42.1	54.2
Undistributed employer share, employee retirement	-2.4	-2.6	-2.8	-2.9	-3.3	-4.0	-4.2	-4.5	-5.0

X Not applicable.   [1] Includes military retirement pay.   [2] Prices from Commodity Credit Corp.
[3] Excludes prior year contracts and obligations for items under open-ended programs and fixed costs.

Source of tables 420 and 421: U.S. Office of Management and Budget, *The Budget of the United States Government*, annual.

No. 422. Federal Budget Outlays, by Function: 1960 to 1978

[In billions of dollars, except percent. For years ending June 30 except, beginning 1977, ending Sept. 30; transition quarter, July–Sept. 1976, omitted. See table 424 for detailed functions. See also *Historical Statistics, Colonial Times to 1970*, series Y 466–487]

FUNCTION	1960	1965	1970	1971	1972	1973	1974	1975	1976	1977	1978, est.
Total budget outlays	92.2	118.4	196.6	211.4	232.0	247.1	269.6	326.1	365.6	401.9	462.2
National defense	45.2	47.5	78.6	75.8	76.6	74.5	77.8	85.5	89.4	97.5	107.6
Human resources	25.5	35.4	73.4	89.8	104.6	116.5	132.2	168.7	197.2	214.8	238.3
Income security	18.3	25.7	43.1	55.4	63.9	73.0	84.4	108.6	126.6	137.0	147.6
Health	.8	1.8	13.1	14.7	17.5	18.8	22.1	27.6	33.4	38.8	44.3
Veterans benefits and services	5.4	5.7	8.7	9.8	10.7	12.0	13.4	16.6	18.4	18.0	18.9
Education, training, employment [1]	1.0	2.1	8.6	9.8	12.5	12.7	12.3	15.8	18.7	21.0	27.5
Other nondefense	21.4	35.5	44.8	45.6	51.0	56.2	59.5	71.9	79.0	89.7	116.2
Commerce and housing credit	1.6	1.1	2.1	2.3	2.2	.9	3.9	5.6	3.8	(Z)	3.5
Transportation	4.1	5.8	7.0	8.1	8.4	9.1	9.2	10.4	13.4	14.6	16.3
Natural resources and environment	1.6	2.5	3.0	3.9	4.2	4.7	5.7	7.3	8.1	10.0	12.1
Energy	.5	.7	1.0	1.0	1.3	1.2	.8	2.2	3.1	4.2	7.8
Community and regional development	.2	1.1	2.4	2.8	3.4	4.6	4.1	3.7	4.7	6.3	9.7
Agriculture	2.6	3.9	5.2	4.3	5.3	4.9	2.2	1.7	2.5	5.5	9.1
Net interest	6.9	8.6	14.4	14.8	15.5	17.4	21.5	23.3	26.8	30.0	35.2
Revenue sharing [2]	.2	.2	.5	.5	.7	7.4	6.9	7.2	7.2	9.5	9.9
International affairs	3.0	5.2	4.3	4.1	4.7	4.0	5.6	6.9	5.6	4.8	6.7
General science, space, technology	.6	5.8	4.5	4.2	4.2	4.0	4.0	4.0	4.4	4.7	4.8
General government	1.0	1.5	1.9	2.2	2.5	2.7	3.3	3.1	3.0	3.4	4.1
Administration of justice	.4	.5	1.0	1.3	1.7	2.1	2.5	2.9	3.3	3.6	4.0
Undistributed offsetting receipts	−1.2	−1.4	−2.6	−3.7	−3.0	−6.9	−10.1	−6.4	−6.9	−6.9	−7.0

PERCENT DISTRIBUTION

	1960	1965	1970	1971	1972	1973	1974	1975	1976	1977	1978, est.
Total outlays	100.0	100.0	100.0	100.0	100.0	100.0	100.0	100.0	100.0	100.0	100.0
National defense	49.0	40.1	40.0	35.9	33.0	30.1	28.9	26.2	24.5	24.3	23.3
Income security	19.8	21.7	21.9	26.2	27.5	29.5	31.3	33.3	34.6	34.1	31.9
Health	.9	1.5	6.7	7.0	7.5	7.6	8.2	8.5	9.1	9.7	9.6
Veterans benefits and services	5.9	4.8	4.4	4.6	4.6	4.9	5.0	5.1	5.0	4.5	4.1
Education, training, employment [1]	1.1	1.8	4.4	4.6	5.4	5.1	4.6	4.8	5.1	5.2	5.9
Commerce and housing credit	1.7	.9	1.1	1.1	.9	.4	1.4	1.7	1.0	(Z)	.8
Transportation	4.4	4.9	3.6	3.8	3.6	3.7	3.4	3.2	3.7	3.6	3.5
Natural resources and environment	1.7	2.1	1.5	1.8	1.8	1.9	2.1	2.2	2.2	2.5	2.6
Energy	.5	.6	.5	.5	.6	.5	.3	.7	.8	1.0	1.7
Community and regional development	.2	.9	1.2	1.3	1.5	1.9	1.5	1.1	1.3	1.6	2.1
Agriculture	2.8	3.3	2.6	2.0	2.3	2.0	.8	.5	.7	1.4	2.0
Net interest	7.5	7.3	7.3	7.0	6.7	7.0	8.0	7.1	7.3	7.5	7.6
Revenue sharing [2]	.2	.2	.3	.2	.3	3.0	2.6	2.2	2.0	2.4	2.1
International affairs	3.3	4.4	2.2	1.9	2.0	1.6	2.1	2.1	1.5	1.2	1.4
General science, space, and technology	.7	4.9	2.3	2.0	1.8	1.6	1.5	1.2	1.2	1.2	1.0
General government	1.1	1.3	1.0	1.0	1.1	1.1	1.2	1.0	.8	.8	.9
Administration of justice	.4	.4	.5	.6	.7	.8	.9	.9	.9	.9	.9
Undistributed offsetting receipts	−1.3	−1.2	−1.3	−1.8	−1.3	−2.8	−3.7	−2.0	−1.9	−1.7	−1.5

Z Less than $50 million and .05 percent.   [1] Includes social services.   [2] Includes general purpose fiscal assistance.

Source: U.S. Office of Management and Budget, *The Budget of the United States Government*, annual.

No. 423. Government Sector Receipts and Expenditures in the National Income Accounts: 1960 to 1978

[In billions of dollars. Minus sign (−) denotes deficit]

ITEM	1960	1965	1970	1971	1972	1973	1974	1975	1976	1977	1978, est.
Total government: [1]											
Receipts	139.5	188.3	302.6	322.2	367.4	411.2	455.1	468.0	535.9	600.8	(NA)
Expenditures	136.4	187.8	311.9	340.5	370.9	404.9	458.2	532.3	571.5	621.1	(NA)
Surplus or deficit	3.1	.5	−9.4	−18.3	−3.5	6.3	−3.2	−64.3	−35.6	−20.3	(NA)
Federal Government: [1]											
Receipts	96.1	124.3	192.1	198.6	227.5	258.3	288.6	286.9	332.3	373.9	421.5
Expenditures	93.1	123.8	204.2	220.6	244.7	265.0	299.3	357.1	386.3	423.4	476.4
Surplus or deficit	3.0	.5	−12.1	−22.0	−17.3	−6.7	−10.7	−70.2	−54.0	−49.5	−54.9
State and local govt.: [1] [2]											
Receipts	49.9	75.1	134.9	152.6	177.4	193.5	210.4	235.7	264.7	294.4	(NA)
Expenditures	49.8	75.1	132.2	148.9	163.7	180.5	202.8	229.8	246.2	265.2	(NA)
Surplus or deficit	.1	(−Z)	2.8	3.7	13.7	13.0	7.6	5.9	18.4	29.2	(NA)

NA Not available.   Z Less than $50 million.   [1] Federal grants-in-aid to State and local government are included in Federal expenditures and State and local receipts. Total government data have been adjusted to eliminate this duplication.   [2] See table 481 for more detail.

Source: U.S. Bureau of Economic Analysis, *The National Income and Product Accounts of the United States, 1929–74*, and *Survey of Current Business*, July 1977 and February 1978.

No. 424. FEDERAL BUDGET—RECEIPTS, BY SOURCE, AND OUTLAYS, BY DETAILED
FUNCTION: 1975 TO 1978

[In billions of dollars. For years ending June 30 except, beginning 1977, ending Sept. 30; transition quarter, July–Sept. 1976, omitted. Receipts reflect collections; outlays stated in terms of checks issued or cash payments. Covers all Federal agencies and programs and both Federal funds and trust funds (see p. 253). Excludes government-sponsored but privately-owned corporations, Federal Reserve System, District of Columbia government, and money held in suspense as deposit funds. See *Historical Statistics, Colonial Times to 1970*, series Y 335–338, Y 343–351, and Y 472–487 for related data]

SOURCE OR FUNCTION	1975	1976	1977 [1]	1978, est.	FUNCTION	1975	1976	1977 [1]	1978, est.
Surplus or deficit (−)	−45.1	−66.4	−45.0	−61.8	**Total outlays [2]—Con.**				
					Transportation	10.4	13.4	14.6	16.3
BY SOURCE					Ground transportation	6.5	9.3	10.0	11.1
Total receipts [2]	281.0	299.2	356.9	400.4	Air transportation	2.4	2.6	2.8	3.3
					Water transportation	1.5	1.6	1.7	1.9
Individual income taxes	122.4	130.8	156.7	178.8	**Natural resources and**				
Corporation income taxes	40.6	41.4	54.9	58.9	**environment [2]**	7.3	8.1	10.0	12.1
Social insurance taxes and contributions	86.4	92.7	108.7	124.1	Water resources	2.7	2.8	3.2	3.7
Employment taxes and contributions	75.2	79.9	92.2	104.0	Conservation and land management	1.3	1.2	1.3	2.1
Unemployment insurance	6.8	8.1	11.3	14.4	Recreational resources	.8	.9	1.0	1.3
Contributions for other insur. and retirement	4.5	4.8	5.2	5.7	Pollution control and abatement	2.5	3.1	4.3	4.9
Excise taxes	16.6	17.0	17.5	20.2	Other natural resources	.8	.9	1.0	1.2
Estate and gift taxes	4.6	5.2	7.3	5.6	**Energy [2]**	2.2	3.1	4.2	7.8
Customs duties	3.7	4.1	5.2	5.8	**Community and re-**				
Miscellaneous receipts	6.7	8.0	6.5	6.9	**gional development [2]**	4.4	5.3	6.3	9.7
					Community develop	3.1	3.5	3.5	4.0
BY FUNCTION					Area and regional dev	.9	1.3	2.1	4.0
Total outlays [2]	326.1	365.6	401.9	462.2	Disaster relief and insurance	.4	.5	.6	1.7
National defense [2]	85.6	89.4	97.5	107.6	**Agriculture**	1.7	2.5	5.5	9.1
Dept. of Defense, military	85.0	88.0	95.7	105.3	Farm income stabilization	.8	1.6	4.5	7.9
Atomic energy defense activities	1.5	1.6	1.9	2.3	Research and services	.9	.9	1.1	1.2
Defense related activ	−.9	−.1	−.1	(Z)	**Interest**	31.0	34.6	38.1	43.8
Income security	108.6	126.6	137.0	147.6	On the public debt	32.7	37.1	41.9	48.6
General retirement and disability insurance	69.4	77.2	88.6	98.2	Other	−1.7	−2.5	−3.8	−4.8
Federal employee retirement and disability	7.0	8.2	9.5	10.8	**General revenue sharing**	6.1	6.2	6.8	6.8
Unemployment insurance	13.5	19.5	15.3	12.4	**Other general purpose fiscal assistance**	1.1	1.0	2.7	3.0
Public assist. and other income supplements	18.8	21.8	23.6	26.3	**International affairs [2]**	6.9	5.6	4.8	6.7
Health [2]	27.6	33.4	38.8	44.3	Foreign economic and financial assistance	3.7	3.6	4.2	5.3
Health care services	23.4	28.7	34.5	39.9	Military assistance	1.9	1.1	.5	.5
Health research and ed	2.7	3.1	2.5	2.7	Conduct of foreign affairs	.7	.7	1.0	1.1
Education and training of health care workforce	.9	1.0	1.0	.8	Foreign information and exchange	.3	.4	.4	.4
Consumer and occupational health and safety	.6	.7	.7	.8	**General science, space, and technology [2]**	4.0	4.4	4.7	4.8
Veterans benefits and services [2]	16.6	18.4	18.0	18.9	General science and basic research [3]	1.0	1.0	1.1	1.2
Income security	7.9	8.4	9.2	9.7	Space flight	1.7	2.0	2.3	2.2
Education, training, and rehabilitation	4.6	5.5	3.7	3.1	Space science, applications and technology	1.0	1.0	1.0	1.0
Hospital and med. care	3.7	4.0	4.7	5.4	**General government [2]**	3.1	2.9	3.4	4.1
Housing	(Z)	−.1	−.1	(−Z)	Legislative functions	.6	.7	.8	.9
Educ., training, employ., and social services [2]	15.9	18.7	21.0	27.5	Management, direction	.1	.1	.1	.1
Elementary, secondary, and vocational educ	4.6	4.7	5.1	5.7	Central fiscal operations	1.8	1.8	1.9	2.2
Higher education	2.1	2.7	3.1	3.8	Gen. property and records management	.4	.1	.1	.4
Research and general education aids	.9	.8	.9	1.2	**Administration of justice**	2.9	3.3	3.6	4.0
Training, employment	4.1	6.3	6.9	10.5	Fed. law enforcement	1.6	1.9	1.7	1.9
Social services	3.9	4.0	4.6	5.5	Fed. judicial activities	.3	.3	.8	1.0
Commerce and housing credit	5.6	3.8	(Z)	3.5	Federal correctional activities	.2	.2	.2	.3
Mortgage credit and thrift insurance	2.8	1.2	−3.3	.5	Criminal justice assistance	.9	.9	.8	.8
Payment to Postal Serv	1.9	1.7	2.3	1.8	**Undistributed offsetting receipts**	−14.1	−14.7	−15.1	−15.6
Other commerce	.9	.9	1.1	1.3	Employer share, employee retirement	−4.0	−4.2	−4.5	−5.0
					Interest received by trust funds	−7.7	−7.8	−8.1	−8.6
					Rents and royalties [4]	−2.4	−2.7	−2.4	−2.0

Z Less than $50 million. [1] For summaries of missing transition quarter (July–Sept. 1976) data, see tables 416 and 418. [2] Totals reflect interfund and intragovernmental transactions and applicable receipts, and other functions, not shown separately. [3] Includes Earth sciences. [4] On Outer Continental Shelf.

Source: U.S. Office of Management and Budget, *The Budget of the United States Government*, annual.

No. 425. FEDERAL TRUST FUND RECEIPTS AND OUTLAYS: 1965 TO 1978

[In billions of dollars. For years ending June 30 except, beginning 1977, ending Sept. 30; transition quarter July–Sept. 1976, omitted. Receipts based on collections received and deposited. Outlays stated on a checks issued basis, less refunds collected. See p. 253 for a definition of trust funds]

DESCRIPTION	1965	1970	1971	1972	1973	1974	1975	1976	1977	1978, est.
Total receipts [1]	29.2	59.4	66.2	73.0	92.2	104.8	118.6	133.7	152.8	168.5
OASDI [2] trust funds	17.6	36.1	38.9	43.2	49.6	57.7	66.7	70.7	81.2	89.8
Health insurance trust funds	(X)	7.5	8.5	8.8	11.3	15.4	16.9	18.5	22.8	27.5
State and local govt. fiscal assistance trust funds, deposits for gen. revenue sharing	(X)	(X)	(X)	(X)	8.3	6.1	6.2	6.4	6.7	6.9
Unemployment insurance funds	4.1	4.1	4.3	5.4	6.7	7.5	8.2	16.2	15.0	15.4
Railroad employees retirement funds	1.3	1.7	1.9	2.0	2.3	2.6	2.8	3.3	3.6	4.0
Federal employees retirement funds	2.7	4.7	5.9	6.8	7.6	9.0	11.5	13.2	16.7	17.9
Airport and airway trust funds	(X)	(X)	1.2	1.6	.8	.9	1.1	1.1	1.4	1.5
Highway trust funds	3.7	5.5	5.7	5.5	5.9	6.7	6.8	6.0	7.3	7.7
Foreign military sales trust funds	.8	.8	1.0	1.1	1.7	3.2	4.4	7.3	9.4	8.7
Veterans life insurance funds	.7	.8	.8	.8	.8	.9	.9	.9	1.0	1.0
Total outlays [3]	27.0	49.1	59.4	67.1	81.4	90.8	111.2	131.3	143.3	158.2
OASDI [2] trust funds	17.5	30.3	35.9	40.2	49.1	55.9	64.7	73.9	85.1	94.7
Health insurance trust funds	(X)	7.1	7.9	8.8	9.5	11.3	14.8	17.8	21.5	25.6
State and local govt. fiscal assistance trust funds, payments for general revenue sharing	(X)	(X)	(X)	(X)	6.6	6.1	6.1	6.2	6.8	6.8
Unemployment insurance funds	3.0	3.6	6.1	6.9	5.4	6.2	13.2	17.9	14.1	11.8
Railroad employees retirement funds	1.1	1.6	1.9	2.1	2.4	2.7	3.1	3.5	3.8	4.1
Federal employees retirement funds	1.4	2.8	3.3	3.8	4.6	5.7	7.1	8.4	9.7	11.0
Airport and airway trust funds	(X)	(X)	.3	1.4	.7	.5	.6	.5	.9	1.1
Highway trust funds	4.0	4.4	4.7	4.7	4.8	4.6	4.8	6.5	6.1	6.8
Foreign military sales trust funds	.7	1.0	1.0	1.2	1.4	2.7	3.5	6.7	8.2	8.5
Veterans life insurance funds	.6	.8	.7	.8	.6	.7	.8	.7	.8	.8

X Not applicable.
[1] Includes deductions for intrafund transactions, proprietary receipts from public, receipts from off-budget Federal agencies, and receipts and outlays from trust funds, not shown separately.
[2] Old-age, survivors, and disability insurance.
[3] Includes deductions for intrafund transactions and proprietary receipts from public, receipts from off-budget Federal agencies, and trust revolving funds on net basis (outlays less receipts).

Source: U.S. Office of Management and Budget, *Special Analyses, Budget of the United States Government*, annual.

No. 426. FEDERAL GOVERNMENT TRUST FUND BALANCES: 1970 TO 1978

[In billions of dollars. As of June 30 except, beginning 1977, as of Sept. 30. Balances are that portion of funds authorized for use which have not been spent. Amounts include both open-book balances with Treasury and investments in U.S. securities. Part of the balances is obligated, part unobligated. The balances on an authorization basis exceed the cash balances because, for a few accounts, budget authority is not the same as receipts. See text, p. 253, for discussion of the budget concept and of trust funds.

TRUST FUND	1970	1972	1973	1974	1975	1976	1977	1978, est.
Total	97.2	110.0	121.1	135.2	142.6	145.0	152.5	162.8
Federal old-age, survivors, and disability insurance trust funds	37.7	40.8	44.3	46.1	48.2	44.9	39.6	34.6
Health insurance trust funds	2.7	3.3	5.1	9.2	11.3	12.0	13.4	15.3
State and local govt. fiscal assistance trust funds	–	–	1.7	1.7	1.7	1.8	1.8	1.8
Unemployment trust fund	13.1	9.8	11.1	12.4	7.4	5.7	6.5	10.1
Railroad retirement accounts	4.8	4.8	4.6	4.6	4.3	4.0	3.2	3.1
Federal employees retirement funds	22.5	28.1	31.2	34.5	38.8	43.7	49.9	56.8
Airport and airway trust fund	–	1.1	1.2	1.5	2.0	2.6	3.3	3.7
Highway trust funds	2.6	4.5	5.6	7.7	9.6	9.1	10.2	11.1
Foreign military sales trust fund	.5	.4	.7	1.2	2.1	2.7	4.6	4.8
Veterans life insurance funds	7.1	7.2	7.4	7.6	7.7	7.8	8.0	8.3
Other trust funds (nonrevolving)	.6	.6	.7	.7	.7	.8	.9	1.1
Trust revolving funds	5.5	6.5	7.6	8.1	8.9	9.9	11.2	12.2

– Represents zero.
Source: U.S. Office of Management and Budget, *Special Analyses, Budget of the United States Government*, annual.

No. 427. BUDGET OUTLAYS, BY AGENCY: 1970 TO 1978

[In millions of dollars. For years ending June 30 except, beginning 1977, ending Sept. 30; transition quarter, July–Sept. 1976, omitted]

DEPARTMENT OR OTHER UNIT	1970	1972	1973	1974	1975	1976	1977	1978, est.
Total	196,588	232,021	247,074	269,620	326,092	365,643	401,902	462,234
Legislative branch	343	487	540	625	726	775	976	1,057
The Judiciary	128	173	183	205	284	325	392	458
Executive Office of the President	36	54	49	66	93	79	73	78
Funds appropriated to President	2,904	3,235	2,864	3,484	3,988	3,525	2,487	4,916
Departments:								
Agriculture	8,301	10,935	10,028	9,767	9,722	12,796	16,738	22,625
Commerce	1,079	1,250	1,368	1,455	1,583	2,020	2,606	4,524
Defense—Military	77,150	75,151	73,297	77,625	85,020	88,036	95,650	105,300
Defense—Civil	1,210	1,530	1,703	1,682	2,051	2,124	2,280	2,536
Energy [1]	(NA)	(NA)	(NA)	(NA)	(NA)	(NA)	5,217	8,152
Health, Education, and Welfare	52,670	72,352	82,340	93,744	112,411	128,785	147,455	164,595
Housing and Urban Develop	2,603	3,642	3,592	4,786	7,475	7,064	5,838	8,411
Interior	992	1,518	1,668	1,779	2,139	2,293	3,194	3,904
Justice	640	1,180	1,531	1,797	2,067	2,242	2,350	2,527
Labor	5,194	10,065	8,668	8,966	17,649	25,727	22,374	23,742
State	448	536	591	735	829	1,062	1,076	1,247
Transportation	6,412	7,524	8,176	8,104	9,247	11,936	12,514	14,395
Treasury	19,509	22,124	30,960	35,993	41,177	43,527	49,560	56,688
Independent agencies:								
ERDA [1]	2,459	2,384	2,386	2,308	3,165	3,759	(1)	(1)
Environmental Protection Agcy	384	763	1,114	2,030	2,530	3,118	4,365	5,063
General Services Admin	431	577	536	−433	−624	−92	−31	289
National Aero. and Space Admin	3,749	3,422	3,311	3,252	3,267	3,670	3,944	3,982
Veterans Administration	8,653	10,710	11,968	13,337	16,575	18,415	18,019	18,898
Other independent agencies	7,860	10,546	12,519	14,964	18,795	19,160	19,878	24,467
Undistributed offsetting receipts	−6,567	−8,137	−12,318	−16,651	−14,075	−14,704	−15,053	−15,619

NA Not available.   [1] Energy Research and Develop. Admin. was succeeded by Dept. of Energy.
Source: U.S. Office of Management and Budget, *The Budget of the United States Government*, annual.

No. 428. FEDERAL PARTICIPATION IN DOMESTIC CREDIT MARKETS: 1965 TO 1976

[In billions of dollars, except percent. For years ending June 30 except, beginning 1977, ending Sept. 30; transition quarter, July–Sept. 1976, omitted]

TYPE OF PARTICIPATION	1965	1970	1971	1972	1973	1974	1975	1976	1977
Total funds advanced in U.S. credit markets, including equities [1]	69.3	93.6	124.9	164.3	205.4	193.1	180.9	242.6	317.5
Advanced under Federal auspices [2]	8.9	17.4	16.5	22.8	26.7	26.6	26.9	26.9	36.6
Federal participation rate (percent)	13.0	18.6	13.2	13.9	13.0	13.8	14.9	11.0	11.5
Direct loans: On-budget	2.7	4.5	3.0	2.7	.3	2.2	4.3	4.2	2.6
Off-budget	–	–	–	.2	.7	2.2	8.5	6.7	9.0
Guaranteed loans	4.9	2.3	12.2	15.6	14.0	6.2	5.7	10.3	14.1
Sponsored agency loans [3]	1.3	10.6	1.3	4.3	11.6	16.3	8.5	5.4	11.0
Total funds raised in U.S. credit markets [1]	69.3	93.6	124.9	164.3	205.4	193.1	180.9	242.6	317.5
Raised under Federal auspices [2]	10.2	16.4	32.3	39.7	46.4	24.1	64.7	97.5	78.9
Federal participation rate (percent)	15.0	17.5	25.9	24.2	22.6	12.5	35.8	40.2	24.9
Federal borrowing from public	4.1	3.8	19.4	19.4	19.3	3.0	50.9	82.9	53.5
Guaranteed borrowing	4.9	2.3	12.2	15.6	14.0	6.2	5.7	10.3	14.1
Sponsored agency borrowing [3]	1.2	10.3	.6	4.7	13.2	14.8	8.2	4.3	11.4

– Represents zero.   [1] Nonfinancial sectors.   [2] Estimated.   [3] See table 872.

No. 429. FEDERAL DIRECT AND GUARANTEED LOANS: 1970 TO 1978

[In billions of dollars. As of June 30 except, beginning 1977, as of Sept. 30. Government guaranteed loans (loans for which the Government guarantees payment of principal or interest in whole or part) are not included in Federal budget outlays; they constitute contingent liabilities not resulting in outlays, except in event of default. Government direct loans are made by both on-budget and off-budget Federal agencies]

LOAN STATUS	1970	1971	1972	1973	1974	1975	1976	1977	1978, est.
Direct loans: [1]									
Net loan outlays	3.6	2.0	2.9	1.0	4.4	12.8	10.9	11.5	19.1
Gross (new) loans disbursed	12.4	12.1	13.8	15.7	15.8	28.8	34.5	35.4	46.2
Direct loans outstanding	51.1	53.2	56.1	57.1	61.5	74.3	85.9	100.9	120.0
Guaranteed loans: [2]									
Net loans guaranteed	9.4	15.2	18.8	16.6	10.3	8.6	11.1	13.5	16.4
Gross loans guaranteed	(NA)	(NA)	(NA)	(NA)	31.8	31.1	31.8	43.3	47.5
Guaranteed loans outstanding	119.5	134.7	153.5	170.1	180.4	189.0	200.7	214.1	230.5

NA Not available.   [1] Includes loans from "off-budget" Government accounts. One of these is the Federal Financing Bank which buys or originates loans guaranteed by other Federal agencies.   [2] Excludes guaranteed loans held by both on-budget and off-budget Government accounts but includes those held by Government-sponsored enterprises. See table 872 for sponsored enterprises.

Source of tables 428 and 429: U.S. Office of Management and Budget, *Special Analyses, Budget of the United States Government*, annual; and unpublished data.

No. 430. Federal Domestic Transfer Payments, by Function: 1965 to 1978

[In billions of dollars. For years ending June 30 except, beginning 1977, ending Sept, 30; transition quarter, July-Sept. 1976, omitted. Federal domestic transfer payments consist generally of monetary income received by individuals or nonprofit institutions in the United States for which no current services are rendered. Payments for retirees out of the social security trust fund are transfer payments]

PROGRAM FUNCTION	1965	1968	1969	1970	1971	1972	1973	1974	1975	1976	1977	1978, est.
Total	28.3	42.7	48.7	55.0	67.7	76.1	87.1	101.7	131.1	153.9	166.5	180.7
Percent of total outlays	23.9	23.9	26.4	28.0	32.0	32.8	35.2	37.7	40.2	42.1	41.4	39.1
Income security	21.5	28.5	32.3	36.7	46.7	52.8	61.7	72.8	95.2	112.2	120.4	129.1
Social security (OASDI)	16.4	22.5	25.8	28.6	34.0	38.0	46.6	53.2	61.5	70.3	81.2	90.3
Railroad retirement	1.1	1.4	1.5	1.6	1.9	2.1	2.4	2.6	3.0	3.4	3.7	4.0
Civil service retirement	1.4	2.1	2.4	2.7	3.2	3.7	4.5	5.6	7.0	8.2	9.4	10.8
Unemployment benefits	2.5	2.2	2.2	3.0	5.6	6.5	4.8	5.5	12.2	18.2	14.1	11.3
Benefits for coal miners	(X)	(X)	(X)	(Z)	.3	.4	.9	1.0	.9	1.0	.9	1.0
Supplemental security income	(X)	(X)	(X)	(X)	(X)	(X)	(X)	1.9	4.2	4.6	4.7	4.8
Food and nutrition	(Z)	.2	.2	.6	1.5	1.8	2.2	2.7	4.2	4.8	4.6	4.8
Special payments, Treasury	(X)	(X)	(X)	(X)	(X)	(X)	(X)	(X)	[1] 1.7	[1] .9	.9	1.2
Other	.1	.1	.2	.2	.3	.3	.3	.4	.5	.7	.8	.9
Health	.3	5.4	6.6	7.2	7.9	8.8	9.4	11.4	14.5	17.4	21.3	25.1
Medicare	(X)	5.0	6.2	6.7	7.5	8.3	9.0	10.9	14.0	16.8	20.6	24.4
Other	.3	.3	.3	.4	.4	.4	.4	.4	.5	.6	.7	.7
Education, training, employment, and social services	.2	1.0	1.0	1.3	1.5	1.7	1.7	1.7	1.9	2.4	3.0	3.6
Education	.1	.4	.4	.5	.7	.9	1.0	1.0	1.5	2.1	2.7	3.2
Training, employment, and social services	.1	.6	.7	.7	.9	.9	.7	.7	.4	.3	.3	.4
Veterans benefits	4.7	5.6	6.2	6.9	8.0	8.8	9.7	10.4	12.8	14.3	13.3	13.2
Retired pay for military	1.2	2.1	2.4	2.8	3.3	3.8	4.3	5.1	6.2	7.2	8.1	9.1
All other	.4	.1	.2	.2	.2	.2	.2	.4	.5	.6	.5	.6

X Not applicable.   Z Less than $50 million.   [1] Includes the $50 tax rebate and the earned income credit to the extent that tax credits exceed tax liabilities otherwise owed.

Source: U.S. Office of Management and Budget, *Special Analyses, Budget of the United States Government,* annual.

No. 431. Property of the Federal Government: 1960 to 1972

[In billions of dollars. As of June 30. Figures are acquisition costs]

PROPERTY AND FUNCTION	1960	1962	1964	1966	1968	1970	1972
Total	276.0	299.4	323.9	347.0	399.7	435.6	454.5
Personal property	200.1	213.3	230.1	244.4	286.9	305.4	313.2
Cash	8.9	11.2	11.7	13.6	10.1	11.8	14.9
Investments (other than public debt)	5.4	5.7	5.9	7.6	4.6	6.2	4.5
Accounts and notes receivable	5.1	4.5	5.2	6.2	5.9	7.0	7.5
Materials and supplies and work in process	9.6	9.9	9.9	9.2	9.1	8.7	8.1
Loans receivable	22.8	26.9	30.3	31.7	59.2	56.9	61.7
Machinery and equipment	11.4	12.2	13.5	14.6	15.5	16.7	16.9
Other assets	16.6	15.0	18.4	17.4	19.9	25.2	22.6
Department of Defense and Corps of Engineers [1]	120.4	127.9	135.2	144.0	162.5	172.9	177.0
Real property	75.8	86.1	93.8	102.6	112.9	130.2	141.3
Land and improvements	60.2	68.4	74.8	81.2	85.7	90.8	98.5
Department of Defense	36.8	41.5	43.6	46.1	47.6	50.6	52.4
Other	23.4	26.9	31.2	35.2	38.1	40.1	46.0
Public domain	15.6	17.7	19.0	21.3	27.1	39.4	42.7
MAJOR FUNCTION							
National defense	174.8	186.2	196.9	208.5	231.1	245.1	248.0
International affairs and finance	21.0	20.6	23.0	26.4	32.0	36.7	36.4
Space research and technology	.5	1.0	2.0	3.8	4.8	6.5	7.8
Agriculture and rural development	13.8	12.2	15.0	12.8	17.1	16.5	17.0
Natural resources	33.0	37.9	42.2	46.8	56.1	71.5	80.0
Commerce and transportation	10.3	9.5	10.6	11.2	12.2	13.7	14.0
Community development and housing	4.5	5.2	4.9	4.6	13.6	8.4	9.5
Education and manpower	.9	3.9	4.7	6.1	7.8	8.6	9.8
Veterans benefits and services	1.6	3.8	3.9	3.4	5.8	6.3	6.2
Health, income security, and general government	15.5	19.1	20.6	23.4	19.2	22.5	26.0

[1] Includes equipment, supplies, stock, inventories, etc.

Source: U.S. Congress, House Committee on Government Operations, *Federal Real and Personal Property Inventory Report,* biennial. (Discontinued in 1972.)

No. 432. Revenue Losses (Tax Expenditures) Due to Federal Tax Laws: 1975 to 1977

[In millions of dollars. For years ending June 30 except, beginning 1977, ending Sept. 30. Tax expenditures are the estimated revenue losses attributable to provisions of the Federal tax laws which allow a special exclusion, exemption, or deduction from gross income or which provide a special credit, a preferential rate of tax, or a deferral of tax liability. Estimates of each tax expenditure are made independently of any other tax provision. If 2 or more items were eliminated simultaneously, resulting revenue change might be larger or smaller than the sum' of estimates shown for individual items. Change in tax rates or other basic tax provisions would affect estimates for individual items. Therefore, totals give only estimated orders of magnitude. Year-to-year differences in estimates of particular items may be due to changes in tax law or revised estimating techniques]

BUDGET FUNCTION AND ITEM	1975	1976			1977 [1]		
		Total	Corpora-tions	Indi-viduals	Total	Corpora-tions	Indi-viduals
National defense:							
Exclusion of benefits and allowances to Armed Forces personnel	650	1,020	(X)	1,020	1,095	(X)	1,095
Exclusion of military disability pensions	70	90	(X)	90	105	(X)	105
International affairs:							
Exclusion of income earned abroad by U.S. citizens	130	145	(X)	145	545	(X)	545
Deferral of income of domestic international sales corporations (DISC)	1,130	1,220	1,220	(X)	945	945	(X)
Deferral of income of controlled foreign corporations	590	525	525	(X)	570	570	(X)
Special rate for Western Hemisphere trade corp	50	50	50	(X)	35	35	(X)
General science, space, and technology:							
Expensing of R and D expenditures	635	1,350	1,325	25	1,425	1,395	30
Energy:							
Expensing of exploration and development costs	620	800	640	160	1,030	820	210
Excess of percentage over cost depletion	2,475	1,295	1,010	285	1,395	1,090	305
Capital gain treatment of royalties on coal	(NA)	(NA)	(NA)	(NA)	55	10	45
Natural resources and environment:							
Exclusion of interest on State and local government pollution control bonds	110	160	110	50	255	170	85
Exclusion of payments in aid of construction of water and sewage utilities	(X)	(X)	(X)	(X)	15	15	(X)
Pollution control facilities: 5-year amortization	30	10	10	(X)	−80	−80	(X)
Capital gain treatment of certain timber income	205	385	290	95	240	185	55
Capital gain treatment of iron ore	(NA)	(NA)	(NA)	(NA)	10	5	5
Agriculture:							
Expensing of certain capital outlays	610	540	85	455	455	80	375
Capital gain treatment of certain ordinary income	485	325	10	315	340	10	330
Deductibility of noncash patronage dividends and certain other items of cooperatives	(NA)	255	410	−155	290	455	−165
Commerce and housing credit:							
Dividend exclusion	315	430	(X)	430	450	(X)	450
Exclusion of interest on State and local industrial development bonds	175	225	150	75	290	195	95
Exemption of credit union income	115	145	145	(X)	70	70	(X)
Financial institutions: Excess bad debt reserves	880	485	485	(X)	535	535	(X)
Deductibility of—							
Mortgage interest on owner-occupied homes	5,405	4,870	(X)	4,870	4,490	(X)	4,490
Property tax on owner-occupied homes	4,510	4,030	(X)	4,030	4,205	(X)	4,205
Interest on consumer credit	1,185	2,105	(X)	2,105	1,785	(X)	1,785
Expensing of construction period interest and taxes	1,510	630	415	215	625	475	150
Excess first-year depreciation	275	180	40	140	185	45	140
Depreciation on rental housing in excess of straight line	520	505	100	405	400	80	320
Depreciation on buildings (other than rental housing) in excess of straight line	440	425	225	200	300	160	140
Asset depreciation range	1,405	1,590	1,435	155	2,055	1,955	100
Capital gains (other than farming, timber, iron ore, and coal)	5,785	7,865	545	7,320	7,430	520	6,910
Deferral of capital gains on home sales	805	845	(X)	845	890	(X)	890
Capital gains at death	6,450	6,720	(X)	6,720	7,280	(X)	7,280
Corporate surtax exemption	3,345	4,170	4,170	(X)	3,875	3,875	(X)
Investment credit	5,810	9,495	7,685	1,810	10,955	8,880	2,075
Credit for purchase of new home	(X)	650	(X)	650	100	(X)	100
Transportation:							
Deductibility of nonbusiness State gasoline taxes	820	710	(X)	710	685	(X)	685
Railroad rolling stock: 5-year amortization	55	−25	−25	(X)	−35	−35	(X)
Deferral of tax on shipping companies	70	110	110	(X)	130	130	(X)
Community and regional development:							
Housing rehabilitation: 5-year amortization	115	40	15	25	25	10	15
Education, training, employment, and social services:							
Exclusion of scholarships and fellowship income	200	195	(X)	195	245	(X)	245
Parental personal exemptions for students age 19 and over	670	720	(X)	720	750	(X)	750

See footnotes at end of table.

No. 432. Revenue Losses (Tax Expenditures) Due to Federal Tax Laws: 1975 to 1977—Continued

[In millions of dollars. See headnote, p. 265]

BUDGET FUNCTION AND ITEM	1975	1976			1977 [1]		
		Total	Corporations	Individuals	Total	Corporations	Individuals
Education, training, employment, and social services:—Continued							
Exclusion of employee meals and lodging (other than military)	265	310	(X)	310	280	(X)	280
Exclusion of contributions to prepaid legal services plans	(X)	(X)	(X)	(X)	5	(X)	5
Investment credit for employee stock ownership plans (ESOP)	(X)	25	25	(X)	245	245	(X)
Deductibility of charitable contributions to—							
Education	645	700	190	510	760	235	525
Other than education and health	3,725	3,285	265	3,020	4,225	290	3,935
Maximum tax on personal service income	400	480	(X)	480	555	(X)	555
Credit for child and dependent care expenses	295	290	(X)	290	475	(X)	475
Credit for employment of public assistance recipients under work-incentive programs	10	10	10	(X)	15	15	(X)
Jobs credit	(X)	(X)	(X)	(X)	690	565	125
Health:							
Exclusion of employer contributions to medical insurance premiums and medical care	3,275	4,490	(X)	4,490	5,560	(X)	5,560
Deductibility of medical expenses	2,315	2,315	(X)	2,315	2,230	(X)	2,230
Expensing of removal of architectural and transportation barriers to the handicapped	(X)	(X)	(X)	(X)	5	5	(X)
Deductibility of charitable contributions (health)	1,045	930	130	800	935	145	790
Income security:							
Exclusion of social security benefits for—							
Disability insurance	275	330	(X)	330	470	(X)	470
OASI benefits for retired workers	2,740	2,725	(X)	2,725	3,790	(X)	3,790
Dependents and survivors	450	645	(X)	645	860	(X)	860
Exclusion of benefits from or for—							
Railroad retirement system benefits	170	190	(X)	190	250	(X)	250
Workmen's compensation	505	590	(X)	590	720	(X)	720
Disabled coal miners	50	50	(X)	50	50	(X)	50
Unemployment insurance	2,300	3,335	(X)	3,335	1,500	(X)	1,500
Public assistance	105	95	(X)	95	330	(X)	330
Sick pay	315	195	(X)	195	110	(X)	110
Net exclusion of pension contributions and earnings:							
Employer plans	5,225	7,290	(X)	7,290	8,715	(X)	8,715
Plans for self-employed and others	390	1,060	(X)	1,060	1,390	(X)	1,390
Exclusion of other employee benefits:							
Premiums on group term life insurance	740	765	(X)	765	860	(X)	860
Premiums on accident and disability insurance	50	65	(X)	65	70	(X)	70
Income of trusts to finance supplementary unemployment benefits	5	10	(X)	10	10	(X)	10
Exclusion of interest on life insurance savings	1,545	1,655	(X)	1,655	1,850	(X)	1,850
Exclusion of capital gains on home sales for persons age 65 and over	40	40	(X)	40	40	(X)	40
Additional exemption for elderly	1,100	1,145	(X)	1,145	1,140	(X)	1,140
Additional exemption for the blind	20	20	(X)	20	20	(X)	20
Excess of percentage standard deduction over minimum standard deduction	1,385	1,140	(X)	1,140	530	(X)	530
Deductibility of casualty losses	280	310	(X)	310	320	(X)	320
Tax credit for the elderly	130	110	(X)	110	230	(X)	230
Earned income credit:							
Nonrefundable portion	(X)	220	(X)	220	365	(X)	365
Refundable portion	(X)	810	(X)	810	900	(X)	900
Veterans benefits and services:							
Exclusion of veterans disability compensation	540	595	(X)	595	745	(X)	745
Exclusion of veterans pensions	25	30	(X)	30	35	(X)	35
Exclusion of GI bill benefits	255	305	(X)	305	260	(X)	260
General government: Credits and deductions for political contributions	40	35	(X)	35	85	(X)	85
General purpose fiscal assistance:							
Exclusion of interest on general-purpose State and local debt	3,805	4,365	2,845	1,520	4,830	3,105	1,725
Deductibility of nonbusiness State and local taxes (other than on owner-occupied homes and gasoline)	8,490	7,255	(X)	7,255	7,660	(X)	7,660
Tax credit for corporations doing business in U.S. possessions	245	240	240	(X)	450	450	(X)
Interest: Deferral of interest on savings bonds	525	550	(X)	550	585	(X)	585

NA Not available.   X Not applicable.   [1] All estimates are based on the tax code as of Dec. 31, 1977.

Source: U.S. Office of Management and Budget, *Special Analyses, Budget of the United States Government*, annual; and unpublished data.

No. 433. FEDERAL EXPENDITURES AND TAXES—NET FLOW AND PER CAPITA, BY MAJOR PROGRAM AREA AND BY STATES: 1975 AND 1976

[For years ending June 30. Minus sign (−) denotes an outflow. Data measure the flow of Federal dollars into and out of each State or region. Federal expenditures exclude interest payments]

REGION AND STATE	SPENDING-TAXES RATIO		NET FLOW [1] (mil. dol.)		1976			Per capita expenditures (dollars)					
	1975	1976	1975	1976	Taxes [2] (mil. dol.)	Expenditures (mil. dol.)	Per capita taxes [2] (dol.)	Total [3]	DOD [4] Contracts [5]	DOD [4] Salaries	Highways and sewers [6]	Welfare programs [7]	Retirement programs
U.S.	1.00	1.00	−	−	326,293	326,293	1,524	1,524	210	136	41	119	449
N.Eng	.96	.95	−762	−939	20,458	19,519	1,676	1,599	380	74	46	136	472
Maine	1.12	1.29	139	375	1,305	1,680	1,227	1,579	270	93	94	157	497
N.H	1.00	.99	1	−10	1,207	1,197	1,477	1,466	200	211	76	83	497
Vt	1.17	1.15	91	92	620	712	1,308	1,503	275	40	65	162	447
Mass	.95	.98	−462	−207	9,658	9,451	1,662	1,626	348	58	23	162	456
R.I	.92	.95	−107	−80	1,468	1,388	1,580	1,494	114	162	50	153	522
Conn	.92	.82	−425	−1,109	6,199	5,090	1,995	1,638	620	39	60	86	410
Mid.Atl	.83	.82	−10,013	−11,677	64,051	52,374	1,718	1,405	170	56	36	139	455
N.Y	.89	.85	−3,392	−4,710	32,009	27,299	1,770	1,510	186	32	20	167	443
N.J	.66	.67	−4,436	−4,514	13,835	9,321	1,886	1,271	146	85	77	115	438
Pa	.87	.87	−2,185	−2,453	18,207	15,754	1,535	1,328	159	76	36	111	482
E.No.Cent	.70	.70	−18,618	−20,094	66,858	46,764	1,633	1,142	98	53	36	101	407
Ohio	.70	.72	−4,634	−4,777	16,902	12,125	1,578	1,132	115	67	42	82	412
Ind	.73	.73	−2,036	−2,061	7,700	5,639	1,451	1,062	161	62	26	69	412
Ill	.72	.71	−5,290	−5,979	20,426	14,447	1,822	1,288	56	63	41	115	404
Mich	.65	.64	−4,971	−5,389	15,140	9,751	1,662	1,071	112	36	31	119	392
Wis	.73	.72	−1,686	−1,886	6,689	4,803	1,454	1,044	58	19	31	115	425
W.No.Cent	.94	1.03	−1,456	619	23,460	24,079	1,401	1,438	242	97	52	91	451
Minn	.83	.89	−934	−635	5,645	5,010	1,432	1,271	178	28	53	104	409
Iowa	.69	.79	−1,249	−858	4,013	3,155	1,400	1,101	89	18	63	84	446
Mo	1.10	1.33	657	2,191	6,624	8,815	1,388	1,847	511	125	54	102	484
N. Dak	1.35	1.34	283	281	816	1,097	1,275	1,714	293	268	67	73	396
S. Dak	1.29	1.28	215	218	783	1,001	1,145	1,161	49	143	70	81	432
Nebr	.84	.80	−351	−370	2,219	1,849	1,433	1,194	46	133	38	68	455
Kans	.98	.94	−78	−210	3,361	3,151	1,464	1,373	160	168	34	76	481
So.Atl	1.12	1.11	4,986	4,992	47,248	52,240	1,427	1,577	170	235	45	106	491
Del	.66	.63	−347	−411	1,109	698	1,912	1,204	65	167	65	89	413
Md	1.20	1.15	1,299	1,104	7,211	8,315	1,745	2,012	278	282	35	103	430
Va	1.34	1.40	2,257	2,922	7,341	10,263	1,466	2,050	382	458	85	79	517
W. Va	1.21	1.14	410	295	2,088	2,383	1,154	1,317	61	21	56	115	517
N.C	.98	1.00	−115	29	6,787	6,816	1,244	1,249	80	206	29	113	385
S.C	1.19	1.20	561	649	3,296	3,945	1,164	1,393	83	291	45	129	393
Ga	1.16	1.10	912	658	6,428	7,086	1,299	1,432	129	212	37	132	408
Fla	1.00	.98	9	−252	12,986	12,734	1,554	1,524	133	140	37	94	659
So.Cent	1.17	1.18	6,536	7,622	42,484	50,106	1,227	1,447	167	166	38	127	429
Ky	1.21	1.29	790	1,140	3,915	5,055	1,149	1,483	86	195	38	158	427
Tenn	1.13	1.22	627	1,188	5,318	6,506	1,268	1,551	91	61	37	135	414
Ala	1.34	1.33	1,255	1,342	4,046	5,388	1,112	1,480	152	172	40	131	440
Miss	1.76	1.79	1,621	1,749	2,219	3,968	945	1,690	438	156	29	158	407
La	1.16	1.08	652	361	4,438	4,799	1,161	1,255	132	104	64	161	361
Ark	1.24	1.26	492	582	2,251	2,833	1,067	1,342	76	95	57	158	501
Okla	1.22	1.28	711	937	3,361	4,298	1,227	1,569	154	258	35	118	494
Tex	1.03	1.02	388	325	16,934	17,259	1,370	1,396	196	204	30	96	430
Mt	1.30	1.24	3,631	3,208	13,345	16,553	1,372	1,701	173	211	58	83	443
Mont	1.28	1.22	246	212	979	1,191	1,305	1,588	103	131	129	84	450
Idaho	1.25	1.11	223	113	1,044	1,157	1,270	1,407	59	107	43	77	428
Wyo	1.21	1.00	102	−1	587	586	1,533	1,530	83	167	93	46	407
Colo	1.20	1.16	704	605	3,850	4,455	1,503	1,739	170	272	46	92	420
N. Mex	1.93	1.91	1,090	1,156	1,273	2,429	1,101	2,101	144	283	48	133	430
Ariz	1.31	1.23	853	701	3,100	3,801	1,383	1,696	302	187	34	61	515
Utah	1.35	1.32	455	461	1,436	1,897	1,181	1,560	171	304	57	72	388
Nev	.96	.96	−40	−40	1,077	1,037	1,795	1,729	60	223	127	80	439
Pac	1.17	1.15	7,008	7,238	47,019	54,257	1,650	1,904	410	218	40	142	453
Wash	1.40	1.26	2,008	1,511	5,743	7,254	1,602	2,023	412	236	41	117	510
Oreg	.94	.92	−202	−291	3,426	3,135	1,486	1,360	48	34	48	86	502
Calif	1.11	1.13	3,684	4,724	35,664	40,388	1,670	1,891	443	199	35	153	445
Alaska	2.44	1.89	776	636	718	1,354	1,920	3,620	553	822	234	93	210
Hawaii	1.58	1.45	741	658	1,468	2,126	1,672	2,421	487	838	67	146	388
D.C	7.67	7.59	8,690	9,032	1,370	10,402	1,938	14,713	1,579	861	110	261	1,004

− Represents zero. [1] Represents the total amount of money that flowed into or out of each State or region. [2] Represents the Federal tax burden with the Federal deficit distributed as an added tax. [3] Includes categories not shown separately. [4] Department of Defense. [5] Allocated to the location of the prime contractor. [6] Construction of highways and sewage treatment plants. [7] Covers medicaid, aid to families with dependent children, food stamps, supplemental security income, grants to States for social service programs, and unemployment compensation.

Source: Government Research Corporation, Washington, D.C., National Journal, June 26, 1976, and July 2, 1977, (copyright), and unpublished data.

No. **434.** Internal Revenue Collections, by Selected Sources: 1960 to 1977

[For years ending **June 30** except, beginning **1977**, ending **Sept. 30**. See also *Historical Statistics, Colonial Times to 1970*, series Y 358–373]

SOURCE OF REVENUE	COLLECTIONS (bil. dol.)							PERCENT OF TOTAL				
	1960	1965	1970	1974	1975	1976	1977	1960	1965	1970	1975	1977
All taxes	91.8	114.4	195.7	269.0	293.8	302.5	358.1	100.0	100.0	100.0	100.0	100.0
Individual income taxes	44.9	53.7	103.7	142.9	156.4	159.0	186.8	49.0	46.9	53.0	53.2	52.2
Withheld by employers	31.7	36.8	77.4	112.1	122.1	123.4	144.7	34.5	32.2	39.6	41.6	40.4
Employment taxes [1]	11.2	17.1	37.4	62.1	70.1	74.2	86.1	12.2	14.9	19.1	23.9	24.0
Old-age and disability insurance	10.2	15.8	35.7	59.1	67.1	71.0	82.3	11.1	13.8	18.2	22.8	23.0
Unemployment insurance	.3	.6	.8	1.5	1.4	1.6	1.9	.4	.5	.4	.5	.5
Corporation income taxes	22.2	26.1	35.0	41.7	45.7	46.8	60.0	24.2	22.8	17.9	15.6	16.8
Estate and gift taxes	1.6	2.7	3.7	5.1	4.7	5.3	7.4	1.8	2.4	1.9	1.6	2.1
Excise taxes [2]	11.9	14.8	15.9	17.1	16.8	17.3	17.8	12.9	12.9	8.1	5.7	5.0
Alcohol	3.2	3.8	4.7	5.4	5.4	5.4	5.4	3.5	3.3	2.4	1.8	1.5
Tobacco	1.9	2.1	2.1	2.4	2.3	2.5	2.4	2.1	1.9	1.1	.8	.7
Manufacturers [2]	4.7	6.4	6.7	5.7	5.5	5.5	6.1	5.2	5.6	3.4	1.9	1.7
Gasoline and lubricating oils	2.1	2.8	3.5	4.2	4.1	4.2	4.4	2.3	2.4	1.8	1.4	1.2
Motor vehicles and parts [3]	2.1	3.0	3.1	1.5	1.4	1.2	1.6	2.3	2.6	1.6	.5	.4
Retailers	.5	.7	.3	.4	.4	.4	.5	.5	.6	.1	.1	.1
Miscellaneous [2]	1.3	1.6	2.1	3.2	3.3	3.1	3.2	1.4	1.4	1.1	1.1	.9
General and toll telephones [4]	.7	1.1	1.5	1.9	2.0	1.8	1.7	.8	.9	.8	.7	.5
Transportation of persons	.3	.1	.3	.7	.8	.8	1.0	.3	.1	.1	.3	.3

[1] Includes railroad retirement, not shown separately.   [2] Includes other taxes, not shown separately.
[3] Includes tires, tubes, and tread rubber.   [4] Includes telegraph, radio, and cable services.
Source: U.S. Dept. of the Treasury, *Statistical Appendix* to the *Annual Report of the Secretary of the Treasury on the State of the Finances.*

No. **435.** Number of Tax Returns Filed, by Type: 1960 to 1977

[**In thousands.** For years ending **June 30** except, beginning **1977**, ending **Sept. 30**. Includes Puerto Rico and Virgin Islands]

TYPE OF RETURN	1960	1965	1970	1973	1974	1975	1976	1977
Total	94,399	102,492	113,079	117,242	121,914	126,049	127,348	133,685
Income tax [1]	70,151	76,113	89,225	91,311	95,313	96,311	95,497	98,807
Individual and fiduciary	61,260	66,965	78,370	79,545	83,029	85,518	84,366	87,274
Estimated tax declarations	6,309	6,197	7,375	6,995	7,437	7,543	7,844	8,088
Partnership	1,016	977	937	1,043	1,118	1,138	1,143	1,197
Corporation	1,072	1,420	1,726	1,946	1,981	2,112	2,144	2,247
Estate tax	62	94	132	202	212	216	236	248
Gift tax	91	122	148	244	253	260	302	387
Employment tax	20,227	22,266	21,994	23,998	24,794	24,757	24,677	25,023
Exempt organization	(NA)	(NA)	(NA)	(NA)	(NA)	374	474	554
Employee plan	(NA)	(NA)	(NA)	(NA)	(NA)	1,104	782	1,321
Excise tax [2]	3,868	3,898	1,580	1,488	1,342	1,427	1,392	1,468
Other	(NA)	(NA)	(NA)	(NA)	(NA)	1,600	3,987	5,877

NA Not available.   [1] Includes other returns, not shown separately.
[2] Includes alcohol, tobacco, and firearms tax returns.
Source: U.S. Internal Revenue Service, *Annual Report of the Commissioner.*

No. **436.** Number of Individual Income Tax Returns, by Marital Status and Size of Adjusted Gross Income: 1965 to 1976

[**In thousands.** Returns of single persons include those of surviving spouses]

ITEM	NUMBER OF RETURNS						PERCENT		
	1965	1970	1973	1974	1975	1976, prel.	1965	1970	1976, prel.
Total tax returns	67,596	74,280	80,693	83,340	82,229	84,536	100.0	100.0	100.0
Joint returns, husbands and wives	39,304	42,376	43,645	44,227	44,140	44,385	58.1	57.0	52.5
Separate returns, husbands and wives	2,851	2,370	2,339	2,355	1,939	1,874	4.2	3.2	2.2
Returns of heads of households	1,888	3,573	4,532	4,688	4,983	5,289	2.8	4.8	6.3
Returns of single persons	23,553	25,961	30,177	32,071	31,167	32,988	34.8	35.0	39.0
Returns with income under $10,000	56,491	50,611	47,620	47,353	44,855	43,743	100.0	100.0	100.0
Joint returns, husbands and wives	28,978	21,036	15,270	14,170	13,785	12,111	51.3	41.6	27.7
Separate returns, husbands and wives	2,786	2,184	1,989	1,900	1,504	1,367	4.9	4.3	3.1
Returns of heads of households	1,762	3,138	3,630	3,618	3,579	3,626	3.1	6.2	8.3
Returns of single persons	22,965	24,252	26,731	27,664	25,987	26,640	40.7	47.9	60.9
Returns with income over $10,000	11,105	23,669	33,073	35,987	37,375	40,793	100.0	100.0	100.0
Joint returns, husbands and wives	10,326	21,340	28,376	30,056	30,356	32,274	93.0	90.2	79.1
Separate returns, husbands and wives	65	185	350	455	435	507	.6	.8	1.2
Returns of heads of households	125	435	902	1,069	1,404	1,663	1.1	1.8	4.1
Returns of single persons	589	1,709	3,446	4,406	5,180	6,349	5.3	7.2	15.6

Source: U.S. Internal Revenue Service, *Statistics of Income, Individual Income Tax Returns*, annual.

No. 437. Federal Individual Income Tax Returns with Adjusted Gross Income—Summary: 1950 to 1976

[Includes Puerto Rico and Virgin Islands. Includes returns of resident aliens; based on a sample of unaudited returns as filed. Taxability or nontaxability is determined by presence or absence of income tax *after credits* (exemptions, deductions, etc.). Classification as "nontaxable" generally based on each return as originally filed and does not reflect subsequent changes (amended returns, audits, etc.). Adjusted gross income is gross income from all sources subject to tax reduced by legally permitted subtractions such as: Expenses of operating a business or trade, losses from sales of capital assets, etc. See *Historical Statistics, Colonial Times to 1970*, series Y 393–411, for related data]

NATURE OF RETURNS	1950	1955	1960	1965	1970	1973	1974	1975	1976, prel.
Total individual returns_____1,000__	52,656	57,818	60,593	67,199	73,863	80,693	83,340	82,229	84,536
With adjusted gross income of—									
Under $3,000_____1,000__	45,567	41,225	35,443	33,017	18,074	17,274	16,881	15,793	15,015
$3,000–$4,999_____1,000__					10,234	9,763	9,885	9,109	8,837
$5,000–$9,999_____1,000__			20,266	23,474	22,303	20,582	20,587	19,953	19,891
$10,000–$14,999_____1,000__					14,106	15,804	15,670	14,964	14,534
$15,000–$19,999_____1,000__					5,538	9,091	10,071	10,354	11,182
$20,000–$24,999_____1,000__					1,909	3,944	4,945	5,598	6,662
$25,000–$29,999_____1,000__	7,493	17,025	5,319	10,105	768	1,742	2,260	2,744	3,611
$30,000–$49,999_____1,000__					918	1,760	2,174	2,748	3,632
$50,000–$99,999_____1,000__					351	597	701	781	945
$100,000–$499,999_____1,000__					75	132	162	182	221
$500,000–$999,999_____1,000__					2	3	3	3	4
$1,000,000 and over_____1,000__					1	1	1	1	1
Returns with tax due_____1,000__	14,287	18,665	18,150	20,027	16,479	14,235	15,434	15,842	16,957
Returns with overpayments_____1,000__	31,965	35,420	39,372	42,766	55,273	64,225	65,764	63,825	64,805
Taxable_____1,000__	38,187	44,689	48,061	53,701	59,317	64,267	67,335	61,491	64,431
Percent of all returns_____	72.5	77.3	79.3	79.9	80.3	79.6	80.8	74.8	76.2
Nontaxable_____1,000__	14,469	13,129	12,532	13,499	14,546	16,425	16,005	20,739	20,105
Percent of all returns_____	27.5	22.7	20.7	20.1	19.7	20.4	19.2	25.2	23.8
Number of—									
Taxpayers_____mil__	84.6	93.9	98.7	107.6	117.0	124.3	127.6	126.6	126.6
Personal exemptions_____mil__	138.7	160.8	175.3	190.7	204.1	209.8	215.1	212.2	215.3
Adjusted gross income [1]_____bil. dol__	179.9	249.4	316.6	430.7	634.3	827.1	905.5	947.8	1,053.6
Taxable returns:									
Adjusted gross income [1]_____bil. dol__	158.5	229.6	297.2	400.3	610.3	799.7	880.4	898.3	1,003.9
Personal exemptions [2]_____bil. dol__	35.2	71.2	81.2	91.9	107.0	132.4	136.8	123.8	128.0
Income tax withheld_____bil. dol__	(NA)	22.1	31.9	38.5	74.2	101.1	115.3	114.8	128.8
Taxable income_____bil. dol__	(NA)	128.0	171.6	255.1	401.2	511.9	573.6	595.5	674.4
Percent of adjusted gross income_____	(NA)	51.3	54.2	59.2	63.2	61.9	63.4	62.8	64.0
Total income tax [3]_____bil. dol__	18.4	29.6	39.5	49.5	83.9	108.1	123.6	124.5	141.9
Percent of adjusted gross income_____	11.6	12.9	13.3	12.1	13.7	13.5	14.0	13.1	13.5
Percent of taxable income_____	(NA)	23.1	23.0	19.4	20.9	21.1	20.8	20.9	21.0
Average income per return_____dol__	4,152	5,138	6,183	7,623	10,288	12,447	13,075	14,608	15,581
Average income tax per return_____dol__	481	663	821	922	1,415	1,682	1,836	2,025	2,202
Income tax per capita of total									
population_____dol__	121	179	219	256	413	515	585	584	661
Percent of total population									
filing returns [4]_____	55.3	56.4	54.4	54.8	57.2	59.0	60.3	59.3	60.0
Returns with—									
Standard deductions_____1,000__	42,740	11,359	36,945	39,327	38,432	52,202	53,230	55,511	58,119
Itemized deductions_____1,000__	10,320	16,891	24,083	27,872	35,430	28,047	29,564	26,074	25,898
Adjusted gross income_____bil. dol__	55.1	108.5	181.1	267.3	448.7	486.3	544.3	532.6	580.3
Deductions, total_____bil. dol__	9.9	20.0	35.3	50.7	88.2	107.0	119.4	122.3	133.2
SOURCES OF INCOME (total returns)									
Salaries and wages, gross_____bil. dol__	139.0	[5]200.6	[5]257.7	346.8	531.3	686.3	758.6	795.4	879.8
Percent of adjusted gross income_____	77.3	80.4	81.4	80.5	83.8	82.6	83.8	83.9	83.5
Dividends_____bil. dol__	[6]6.1	[7]7.8	[7]9.5	12.9	15.7	18.5	20.9	21.9	24.5
Interest_____bil. dol__	1.6	2.6	5.0	11.2	21.8	31.9	39.5	43.4	48.4
Rents and royalties :_____bil. dol__	2.9	3.2	3.3	3.1	3.4	5.1	5.4	5.2	5.9
Business or profession [8]___bil. dol__	[9]16.0	[9]19.3	[9]22.1	25.2	31.0	39.1	39.0	39.4	44.4
Farm [8]_____bil. dol__	(9)	(9)	(9)	3.9	3.4	8.3	5.0	3.6	3.5
Partnerships [8]_____bil. dol__	8.4	9.2	9.2	11.1	11.7	12.5	11.0	10.8	12.1
Sales of capital assets [8]___bil. dol__	2.9	4.6	5.1	10.0	8.7	16.1	13.5	14.1	18.3
Sales of property [8][10]____bil. dol__	–	.7	.7	.7	.2	.5	.4	.1	.1
Pensions and annuities [11]__bil. dol__	.4	.9	1.6	3.6	7.9	13.0	16.7	20.9	24.5
Estates and trusts_____bil. dol__	1.7	.6	.7	3.0	1.4	2.0	2.3	2.6	2.8
Other sources_____bil. dol__	1.0	.8	2.4		-2.4	-2.6	6.9	-9.5	-10.7

– Represents zero.   NA Not available.   [1] 1950–1970, returns with adjusted gross income only. Beginning 1972, adjusted gross income less deficit.   [2] Exemptions: 1950–1965, $600; 1970, $625; 1973–1976, $750.   [3] Income tax after credits. Beginning 1970, includes additional tax for tax preferences.   [4] Joint returns counted twice in computing percent.   [5] Salaries after sick pay exclusion.   [6] Domestic and foreign.   [7] After exclusions.   [8] Figures represent net income.   [9] Farm included with business or profession.   [10] Other than capital assets.   [11] Taxable portion.

Source: U.S. Internal Revenue Service, *Statistics of Income, Individual Income Tax Returns*, annual.

No. 438. Individual Income Tax Returns, By Adjusted Gross Income Classes: 1965 to 1976

[Includes Puerto Rico and Virgin Islands. Based on sample of unaudited returns as filed]

ADJUSTED GROSS INCOME CLASS	TOTAL (bil. dol.)						PERCENT DISTRIBUTION					
	1965	1970	1973	1974	1975	1976 [1]	1965	1970	1973	1974	1975	1976 [1]
ADJUSTED GROSS INCOME [2]												
Total	430.7	634.2	827.1	905.5	947.8	1,053.6	100.0	100.0	100.0	100.0	100.0	100.0
Taxable returns	409.4	610.3	799.7	880.4	898.3	1,003.9	95.0	96.2	96.7	97.2	94.8	95.3
Under $5,000	59.5	47.2	40.7	41.7	26.9	25.5	13.8	7.4	4.9	4.6	2.8	2.4
$5,000–$9,999	167.4	162.9	146.6	146.8	129.9	128.6	38.9	25.7	17.7	16.2	13.7	12.2
$10,000–$14,999	91.6	171.6	194.5	193.0	182.8	177.9	21.3	27.1	23.5	21.3	19.3	16.9
$15,000–$19,999	69.4	94.4	155.7	173.2	177.4	192.9	16.1	14.9	18.8	19.1	18.7	18.3
$20,000–$24,999		42.1	87.1	109.4	123.7	147.5		6.6	10.5	12.1	13.1	14.0
$25,000–$49,999		54.8	111.9	140.9	174.0	229.7		8.6	13.5	15.6	18.4	21.8
$50,000–$99,999	12.4	23.0	39.2	46.1	51.2	62.0	2.9	3.6	4.7	5.1	5.4	5.9
$100,000–$499,999	7.1	11.7	20.4	25.1	27.9	34.2	1.7	1.9	2.5	2.8	2.9	3.3
$500,000–$999,999	.9	1.2	1.8	2.1	2.2	2.8	.2	.2	.2	.2	.2	.3
$1,000,000 and over	1.4	1.4	1.8	2.1	2.3	2.9	.3	.2	.2	.2	.2	.3
Nontaxable returns	21.3	23.9	27.4	25.1	49.5	49.7	5.0	3.8	3.3	2.8	5.2	4.7
TAXABLE INCOME												
Total	255.1	401.2	511.9	573.6	595.5	674.4	100.0	100.0	100.0	100.0	100.0	100.0
Taxable returns	254.3	400.9	510.6	572.4	590.4	669.2	99.7	99.8	99.7	99.8	99.1	99.2
Under $5,000	28.3	22.9	14.2	14.7	9.4	8.7	11.1	5.7	2.8	2.6	1.6	1.3
$5,000–$9,999	94.7	96.6	79.4	80.9	70.3	69.4	37.1	24.1	15.5	14.1	11.8	10.3
$10,000–$14,999	60.8	112.2	119.1	119.4	113.0	111.4	23.8	28.0	23.3	20.8	19.0	16.5
$15,000–$19,999	52.6	66.6	103.6	115.6	116.8	127.3	20.6	16.6	20.2	20.2	19.6	18.9
$20,000–$24,999		31.0	61.4	77.3	86.7	102.8		7.7	12.0	13.5	14.6	15.2
$25,000–$49,999		42.1	83.5	104.8	128.5	169.6		10.5	16.3	18.3	21.6	25.2
$50,000–$99,999	10.2	18.4	30.9	36.4	40.1	48.4	4.0	4.6	6.0	6.3	6.7	7.2
$100,000–$499,999	5.8	9.1	16.0	20.0	22.3	27.3	2.3	2.3	3.1	3.5	3.7	4.1
$500,000–$999,999	.8	.8	1.3	1.6	1.6	2.1	.3	.2	.3	.3	.3	.3
$1,000,000 and over	1.1	1.0	1.3	1.6	1.7	2.2	.4	.2	.3	.3	.3	.3
Nontaxable returns	.7	.3	1.3	1.2	5.1	5.3	.3	.1	.3	.2	.9	.8
INCOME TAX [3]												
Total	49.5	83.9	108.1	123.6	124.5	141.9	(X)	(X)	(X)	(X)	(X)	(X)
Taxable returns	49.5	83.9	108.1	123.6	124.5	141.9	100.0	100.0	100.0	100.0	100.0	100.0
Under $5,000	4.4	3.6	2.2	2.2	1.2	1.3	8.9	4.3	2.0	1.8	1.0	.9
$5,000–$9,999	15.4	16.7	13.3	13.7	10.7	9.9	31.2	19.9	12.3	11.1	8.6	7.0
$10,000–$14,999	10.7	20.6	21.2	21.5	19.2	18.0	21.6	24.6	19.6	17.4	15.4	12.7
$15,000–$19,999	11.5	13.2	19.7	22.1	21.2	22.4	23.2	15.7	18.2	17.9	17.0	15.8
$20,000–$24,999		6.7	12.5	15.8	17.0	19.8		8.0	11.6	12.8	13.7	14.0
$25,000–$49,999		10.8	19.8	24.8	29.6	38.9		12.8	18.3	20.1	23.8	27.4
$50,000–$99,999	3.7	6.6	10.4	12.2	13.4	16.2	7.5	7.9	9.6	9.9	10.8	11.4
$100,000–$499,999	2.8	4.5	7.4	9.2	10.2	12.8	5.7	5.4	6.8	7.4	8.2	9.0
$500,000–$999,999	.4	.5	.8	.9	1.0	1.3	.8	.6	.7	.7	.8	.9
$1,000,000 and over	.6	.6	.8	1.1	1.1	1.5	1.2	.8	.8	.9	.9	1.1

X Not applicable.   [1] Preliminary.
[2] Beginning 1973, adjusted gross income less deficit.
[3] Represents income tax after credits. Beginning 1970, includes additional tax for tax preferences.

No. 439. Nontaxable Individual Income Tax Returns—Number of Returns and Amount of Adjusted Gross Income: 1970 to 1976

ADJUSTED GROSS INCOME [1] CLASS	NUMBER OF RETURNS (1,000)					ADJUSTED GROSS INCOME (mil. dol.)				
	1970	1973	1974	1975	1976	1970	1973	1974	1975	1976
Total [2]	14,962	16,425	16,005	20,739	20,105	21,421	27,440	25,139	49,470	49,736
Under $5,000	14,077	15,050	14,503	17,735	17,047	20,421	23,191	22,119	26,433	26,748
$5,000–$9,999	430	798	798	2,615	2,701	2,717	5,177	5,267	16,680	17,176
$10,000–$14,999	25	77	105	239	220	295	911	1,241	2,867	2,610
$15,000–$24,999	9	43	38	120	99	171	777	692	2,177	1,833
$25,000–$49,999	4	12	15	23	35	121	409	503	776	1,129
$50,000–$99,999	1	2	3	5	3	63	164	177	324	164
$100,000–$199,999	.29	.46	.72	.73	.44	39	63	96	98	58
$200,000 or more	.11	.16	.24	.26	.06	47	70	110	117	19

[1] Adjusted gross income less deficit.   [2] Includes deficit returns, not shown separately.

Source of tables 438 and 439: U.S. Internal Revenue Service, *Statistics of Income, Individual Income Tax Returns,* annual.

No. 440. AVERAGE TAX OF TAXABLE INDIVIDUAL INCOME TAX RETURNS AND PERCENT TOTAL TAX OF TAXABLE INCOME, BY ADJUSTED GROSS INCOME CLASSES: 1960 TO 1976

ADJUSTED GROSS INCOME CLASS	1960	1965	1970	1971	1972	1973	1974	1975	1976, prel.
	AVERAGE TAX								
Total_____dol__	821	922	1,415	1,425	1,537	1,682	1,836	2,025	2,202
Under $3,000_____dol__	154	118	117	80	66	68	67	49	59
$3,000-$4,999_____dol__	381	316	344	261	236	242	246	196	179
$5,000-$9,999_____dol__	768	671	762	694	657	674	693	618	577
$10,000-$14,999_____$1,000__	1.7	1.4	1.5	1.4	1.3	1.4	1.4	1.3	1.3
$15,000-$24,999_____$1,000__	3.3	} 3.7 {	2.7	2.5	2.4	2.5	2.5	2.4	2.4
$25,000-$49,999_____$1,000__	8.2		6.4	6.0	5.7	5.7	5.6	5.4	5.4
$50,000-$99,999_____$1,000__	22.5	19.4	19.0	18.1	17.7	17.4	17.5	17.2	17.2
$100,000-$499,999_____$1,000__	68.9	63.0	60.6	59.3	57.3	56.3	57.2	56.3	58.0
$500,000-$999,999_____$1,000__	312.0	293.6	304.0	314.8	305.1	305.6	300.7	297.9	315.9
$1,000,000 and over_____$1,000__	950.7	966.8	992.0	960.4	1,021.8	934.9	969.2	987.1	1,089.3
	PERCENT TOTAL TAX [1] OF TAXABLE INCOME								
Total_____	23.0	19.5	20.9	20.7	21.0	21.2	21.6	21.1	21.2
Under $3,000_____	19.8	14.6	14.7	14.4	15.1	15.3	15.3	10.1	12.6
$3,000-$4,999_____	20.1	15.5	16.0	15.4	15.3	15.3	15.4	13.0	12.4
$5,000-$9,999_____	20.4	16.3	17.2	16.7	16.7	16.8	16.9	15.3	14.3
$10,000-$14,999_____	21.4	17.6	18.4	17.8	17.7	17.8	18.0	17.0	16.1
$15,000-$24,999_____	24.2	} 22.1 {	20.4	19.6	19.5	19.5	19.6	18.8	18.4
$25,000-$49,999_____	30.8		25.6	24.3	24.3	23.7	23.7	23.1	22.9
$50,000-$99,999_____	42.0	35.8	36.1	34.6	34.9	33.6	33.6	33.3	33.6
$100,000-$499,999_____	53.7	47.7	49.8	48.3	47.9	46.2	46.1	45.7	46.8
$500,000-$999,999_____	59.0	53.7	62.5	62.4	63.1	61.2	60.0	59.1	62.2
$1,000,000 and over_____	61.6	54.4	61.2	61.9	65.1	64.7	65.0	64.9	67.9

[1] Total tax represents income tax after credits. Beginning 1970, includes additional tax for tax preferences.
Source: U.S. Internal Revenue Service, Statistics of Income, Individual Income Tax Returns, annual

No. 441. FEDERAL INDIVIDUAL INCOME TAX RETURNS—SOURCES OF INCOME, BY ADJUSTED GROSS INCOME CLASSES: 1976

[In millions of dollars, except percent. See headnote, table 438]

SOURCE OF INCOME	Total income [1]	ADJUSTED GROSS INCOME CLASSES FOR TAXABLE RETURNS						
		Total [2]	Under $5,000 [3]	$5,000-$9,999	$10,000-$14,999	$15,000-$49,999	$50,000-$499,999	$500,000 and over
Adjusted gross income_____	1,059,434	1,003,857	25,471	128,618	177,866	570,002	96,208	5,693
Salaries, gross_____	878,438	835,939	22,395	108,581	157,611	494,506	51,887	959
Percent of gross income__	82.9	83.2	87.9	84.4	88.6	86.8	53.9	16.9
Dividends_____	24,266	23,366	348	1,646	1,664	8,398	9,595	1,714
Interest_____	48,039	43,724	1,791	7,848	6,911	20,608	6,219	346
Rents and royalties, net___	5,333	5,518	90	754	780	1,688	1,982	223
Business profession,[4] net___	42,301	42,752	399	3,068	4,787	23,007	11,169	323
Farm,[5] net_____	8,592	4,804	−54	26	329	3,563	978	−38
Partnership, net_____	13,786	13,196	−310	460	949	5,902	6,060	135
Sales of capital assets, net___	17,602	16,717	379	883	1,487	6,644	5,777	1,546
Sales of property,[5] net_____	−254	504	−7	8	77	282	127	16
Pensions and annuities [6]___	24,488	21,763	766	6,072	4,654	9,440	822	9
Other sources_____	−3,157	−4,425	−326	−729	−1,382	−4,038	1,591	458

[1] Excludes returns with no adjusted gross income.
[2] Income from sources subject to tax, less certain exclusions.
[3] Includes a small number of taxable returns with no adjusted gross income.
[4] Business profit and loss without deduction for net operating loss.
[5] Other than capital assets.
[6] Taxable portion.
Source: U.S. Internal Revenue Service, Preliminary Report, Statistics of Income, 1976, Individual Income Tax Returns.

No. 442. Federal Individual Income Tax Liability and Effective Rates, for Selected Income Groups: 1954 to 1978

[Refers to income after exclusions. Computations assume the low income allowance, standard deduction, or itemized deductions equal to 10 percent of adjusted gross income, whichever is greatest. Excludes self-employment tax. See *Historical Statistics, Colonial Times to 1970*, series Y 412–439, for similar data based on net income]

ADJUSTED GROSS INCOME [1]	TAX LIABILITY (dollars)						EFFECTIVE RATE [4] (percent)					
	1954-1963	1964	1970 [2]	1972-1973	1975	1977-1978 [3]	1954-1963	1964	1970 [2]	1972-1973	1975	1977-1978 [3]
Single person, no dependent:												
$2,000	240	180	58	–	–	–	12.0	9.0	2.9	–	–	–
$3,000	422	360	302	138	63	–	14.1	12.0	10.1	4.6	2.1	–
$5,000	818	720	683	491	404	274	16.4	14.4	13.7	9.8	8.1	5.5
$10,000	2,096	1,872	1,778	1,530	1,476	1,216	21.0	18.7	17.8	15.3	14.8	12.2
$15,000	3,787	3,378	3,224	2,703	2,587	2,457	25.2	22.5	21.5	18.0	17.2	16.4
$20,000	5,900	5,233	5,031	4,255	4,123	3,999	29.5	26.2	25.2	21.3	20.6	20.0
$25,000	8,324	7,410	7,144	5,895	5,865	5,715	33.3	29.6	28.6	23.6	23.5	22.9
$35,000	13,778	12,344	11,904	9,728	9,698	9,548	39.4	35.3	34.0	27.8	27.7	27.3
$50,000	22,788	20,384	19,695	16,740	16,710	16,560	45.6	40.8	39.4	33.5	33.4	33.1
$75,000	39,702	35,267	34,020	30,710	30,680	30,530	52.9	47.0	45.4	40.9	40.9	40.7
Married couple, no dependent:												
$2,000	120	64	–	–	–	–	6.0	3.2	–	–	–	–
$3,000	300	226	137	28	–	–	10.0	7.5	4.6	.9	–	–
$5,000	660	554	503	322	170	–	13.2	11.1	10.1	6.4	3.4	–
$10,000	1,636	1,440	1,366	1,190	1,054	757	16.4	14.4	13.7	11.9	10.5	7.6
$15,000	2,810	2,501	2,381	2,150	2,002	1,701	18.7	16.7	15.9	14.3	13.3	11.3
$20,000	4,192	3,744	3,557	3,400	3,175	2,899	21.0	18.7	17.8	17.0	15.9	14.5
$25,000	5,774	5,162	4,900	4,700	4,608	4,288	23.1	20.6	19.6	18.8	18.4	17.2
$35,000	9,601	8,523	8,177	7,880	7,820	7,700	27.4	24.4	23.4	22.5	22.3	22.0
$50,000	16,648	14,819	14,289	13,820	13,760	13,640	33.3	29.6	28.6	27.6	27.5	27.3
$75,000	30,415	27,266	26,299	25,520	25,460	25,340	40.6	36.4	35.1	34.0	33.9	33.8
Married couple, 2 dependents:												
$3,000	60	–	–	–	[5]–300	[5]–300	2.0	–	–	–	–10.0	–10.0
$5,000	420	325	275	98	[5]–300	[5]–300	8.4	6.5	5.5	2.0	–6.0	–6.0
$10,000	1,372	1,200	1,122	905	709	442	13.7	12.0	11.2	9.0	7.1	4.4
$15,000	2,486	2,209	2,091	1,820	1,612	1,375	16.6	14.7	13.9	12.1	10.7	9.2
$20,000	3,800	3,392	3,213	3,010	2,740	2,524	19.0	17.0	16.1	15.0	13.7	12.6
$25,000	5,318	4,754	4,490	4,240	4,092	3,857	21.3	19.0	18.0	17.0	16.4	15.4
$35,000	9,037	8,031	7,677	7,295	7,175	7,115	25.8	22.9	21.9	20.8	20.5	20.3
$50,000	15,976	14,213	13,674	13,100	12,980	12,920	32.0	28.4	27.3	26.2	26.0	25.8
$75,000	29,635	26,564	25,594	24,695	24,575	24,515	39.5	35.4	34.1	32.9	32.8	32.7

– Represents zero.   [1] Income from sources subject to tax, less certain exclusions.
[2] Includes income tax surcharge.   [3] Reflects current law as of March 4, 1978.
[4] Tax liability divided by stated income.   [5] Refundable earned income credit.
Source: U.S. Dept. of the Treasury, unpublished data.

No. 443. Individual Income Tax Returns with Itemized Deductions, by Adjusted Gross Income Classes: 1976

[Includes returns of resident aliens. Based on a sample of returns as filed, unaudited except to insure proper execution. Itemized deductions may be claimed when a taxpayer's specified personal expenses exceed the allowable standard deduction]

ADJUSTED GROSS INCOME CLASS	Returns with itemized deductions (1,000)	Adjusted gross income (mil. dol.)	Taxable income (mil. dol.)	ITEMIZED DEDUCTIONS (mil. dol.)						
				Total	Percent of— Adjusted gross income	Percent of— Taxable income	Taxes	Interest	Contributions	Medical and dental expenses	Other
Total	25,898	580,308	383,059	133,218	23.0	34.8	49,505	43,058	16,711	12,155	11,789
Taxable returns	24,567	570,228	381,636	126,167	22.1	33.1	47,998	40,986	16,048	10,089	11,046
Under $2,999	40	79	40	14	17.7	35.0	6	5	1	2	2
$3,000-$3,999	46	168	37	84	50.0	227.0	24	14	15	23	8
$4,000-$4,999	87	396	107	195	49.2	182.2	49	50	33	51	12
$5,000-$9,999	2,253	18,279	7,542	6,647	36.4	88.1	1,897	1,868	820	1,537	525
$10,000-$14,999	4,989	63,171	33,981	17,356	27.5	51.1	5,574	6,048	1,870	2,373	1,491
$15,000-$24,999	10,011	196,233	123,887	45,529	23.2	36.8	16,629	16,546	4,773	3,666	3,915
$25,000-$49,999	6,031	194,166	139,904	37,856	19.5	27.1	16,127	11,922	4,658	1,912	3,237
$50,000 and over	1,110	97,736	76,139	18,486	18.9	24.3	7,693	4,534	3,878	525	1,856
Nontaxable returns	1,331	10,080	1,423	7,051	70.0	495.5	1,507	2,072	663	2,066	743

Source: U.S. Internal Revenue Service, Preliminary Report, *Statistics of Income, 1976, Individual Income Tax Returns*.

No. 444. Federal Income and Payroll Taxes for a Four-Person Family With One Earner, by Selected Earnings Levels: 1963 to 1977

[Tax rate is percent of earnings, or tax liability divided by earnings. Data represent "effective" tax rates and were calculated from statutory individual income and payroll tax rates. Payroll taxes include both employee and employer taxes. For the $5,000, $10,000, and $15,000 categories, it is assumed that the standard deduction was taken. For the $25,000, $35,000, and $50,000 categories, itemized deductions are assumed. Income tax surcharge is included for 1968 and 1970]

YEAR AND ITEM	TAX (dol.) FOR EARNINGS LEVEL OF—						TAX RATE (percent) FOR EARNINGS LEVEL OF—					
	$5,000	$10,000	$15,000	$25,000	$35,000	$50,000	$5,000	$10,000	$15,000	$25,000	$35,000	$50,000
1963: Total	768	1,720	2,964	5,237	8,589	14,924	15.4	17.2	19.8	20.9	24.5	29.8
Income	420	1,372	2,616	4,889	8,241	14,576	8.4	13.7	17.4	19.6	23.5	29.2
Payroll	348	348	348	348	348	348	7.0	3.5	2.3	1.4	1.0	.7
1968: Total	748	1,884	3,075	5,048	8,067	13,788	15.0	18.8	20.5	20.2	23.0	27.6
Income	308	1,198	2,389	4,362	7,381	13,102	6.2	12.0	15.9	17.4	21.1	26.2
Payroll	440	686	686	686	686	686	8.8	6.9	4.6	2.7	2.0	1.4
1970: Total	759	1,871	2,953	4,880	7,750	13,193	15.2	18.7	19.7	19.5	22.1	26.4
Income	279	1,122	2,204	4,131	7,001	12,444	5.6	11.2	14.7	16.5	20.0	24.9
Payroll	480	749	749	749	749	749	9.6	7.5	5.0	3.0	2.1	1.5
1975: Total	285	1,879	3,262	5,350	8,054	13,220	5.7	18.8	21.7	21.4	23.0	26.4
Income	−300	709	1,612	3,700	6,404	11,570	−6.7	7.1	10.7	14.8	18.3	23.1
Payroll	585	1,170	1,650	1,650	1,650	1,650	11.7	11.7	11.0	6.6	4.7	3.3
1977: Total	285	1,616	3,135	5,571	8,275	13,441	5.7	16.2	20.9	22.3	23.6	26.9
Income	−300	446	1,380	3,640	6,344	11,510	−6.0	4.5	9.2	14.6	18.1	23.0
Payroll	585	1,170	1,755	1,931	1,931	1,931	11.7	11.7	11.7	7.7	5.5	3.9

Source: Brookings Institution, Washington, D.C., Setting National Priorities, the 1974 Budget, by Edward R. Fried, Alice M. Rivlin, Charles L. Schultze, and Nancy H. Teeters (copyright © 1973 by the Brookings Institution); and unpublished data.

No. 445. Federal Individual Income and Employment Tax Receipts—States: 1975 to 1977

[Through 1976, for years ending June 30 except, beginning 1977, ending Sept. 30. A State's receipts do not necessarily indicate its tax burden since, in many instances, taxes are collected in one State from residents of another]

STATE	TAX RECEIPTS (mil. dol.)			PERCENT OF PERSONAL INCOME [1]			STATE	TAX RECEIPTS (mil. dol.)			PERCENT OF PERSONAL INCOME [1]		
	1975	1976	1977	1975	1976	1977		1975	1976	1977	1975	1976	1977
Total [2]	226,540	233,172	272,832	18.1	17.0	18.0	S.A.—Con.						
							W. Va	931	994	1,190	10.4	9.9	10.7
N.E.	13,027	12,821	17,089	17.7	16.0	19.4	N.C.	3,723	3,752	4,457	13.8	12.5	13.6
Maine	626	630	756	12.4	11.0	12.2	S.C.	1,551	1,557	1,818	11.8	10.5	11.2
N.H.	589	579	719	13.4	11.7	13.0	Ga	3,786	3,563	4,003	15.3	12.9	13.2
Vt	276	273	333	11.9	10.6	11.8	Fla	6,446	6,284	8,922	13.8	12.3	15.8
Mass	6,143	6,053	6,950	17.4	15.8	16.6	E.S.C.	7,968	8,136	13,922	12.7	11.5	17.8
R.I	1,000	978	1,023	18.8	16.9	16.2	Ky	2,086	2,119	2,426	12.6	11.4	11.8
Conn	4,393	4,308	7,308	20.8	19.0	29.2	Tenn	2,814	2,880	7,877	14.0	12.8	31.7
M.A.	51,306	50,629	57,931	21.7	19.9	21.0	Ala	2,126	2,188	2,504	12.7	11.7	12.1
N.Y	28,874	28,354	26,821	24.5	22.7	19.9	Miss	942	949	1,115	10.0	8.8	9.3
N.J	8,406	8,377	16,996	16.9	15.6	29.0	W.S.C.	17,242	17,852	23,129	15.6	14.3	16.5
Pa	14,026	13,898	14,114	20.2	18.4	17.1	Ark	1,019	1,038	1,248	10.7	10.0	10.5
E.N.C.	51,777	52,001	62,494	20.9	19.0	20.7	La	2,586	2,698	3,075	14.1	13.0	13.3
Ohio	13,169	13,129	15,523	21.2	19.2	20.5	Okla	2,124	2,207	2,487	14.8	14.0	13.9
Ind	5,690	5,762	4,932	19.1	17.3	13.4	Tex	11,513	11,909	16,319	16.8	15.3	18.7
Ill	16,699	16,780	26,269	22.1	20.4	30.1	Mt	9,064	8,774	8,660	17.1	14.8	13.1
Mich	12,066	12,216	10,994	22.1	19.8	15.8	Mont	447	455	559	11.1	10.6	12.0
Wis	4,153	4,114	4,776	16.1	14.5	14.9	Idaho	710	744	799	16.9	15.7	15.6
W.N.C.	17,276	17,743	19,536	18.1	17.3	16.9	Wyo	270	289	348	11.7	10.9	11.3
Minn	4,794	5,003	5,911	21.2	20.3	20.9	Colo	4,041	3,715	2,683	26.6	22.1	14.3
Iowa	2,268	2,248	2,618	13.5	12.7	13.2	N. Mex	624	652	740	11.3	10.5	10.6
Mo	5,744	5,978	6,270	22.0	20.9	19.6	Ariz	1,583	1,547	1,787	13.3	11.6	12.0
N. Dak	465	492	538	12.4	13.2	13.3	Utah	800	793	960	13.6	11.9	12.8
S. Dak	404	397	464	11.8	11.4	11.3	Nev	589	579	784	15.1	13.1	15.5
Nebr	1,607	1,620	1,676	17.7	17.1	16.0	Pac	29,493	29,695	39,625	16.0	14.5	17.3
Kans	1,994	2,005	2,059	14.7	13.4	12.4	Wash	3,418	3,455	4,120	15.2	13.9	15.0
S.A.	27,759	27,765	33,861	15.0	13.6	15.1	Oreg	2,128	2,085	3,883	16.1	14.1	23.3
Del	1,055	998	1,154	27.8	24.1	25.8	Calif	22,641	22,690	29,956	16.2	14.6	17.3
Md. and D.C.	6,608	6,928	8,109	25.0	20.1	21.6	Alaska	489	678	735	13.9	16.4	17.0
Va	3,659	3,689	4,208	12.7	11.6	11.9	Hawaii	817	787	931	14.2	12.6	13.7

[1] See table 724 for base data.
[2] Includes Puerto Rico, International operations, and unallocated receipts and credits.

Source: U.S. Internal Revenue Service, Annual Report of the Commissioner.

No. 446. FEDERAL INDIVIDUAL INCOME RETURNS AND TAXES—STATES AND OTHER AREAS: 1970 TO 1976

[Aggregates in this table differ somewhat from those in other tables for individual returns with income because of a distinct weighting system for State data and the inclusion of returns with no adjusted gross income]

STATE OR OTHER AREA	1970				1975				1976, prel.			
	Number of returns (1,000)	Adjusted gross income[1] (mil. dol.)	Total income tax (mil. dol.)	Income tax per capita (dol.)	Number of returns (1,000)	Adjusted gross income[1] (mil. dol.)	Total income tax (mil. dol.)	Income tax per capita (dol.)	Number of returns (1,000)	Adjusted gross income[1] (mil. dol.)	Total income tax (mil. dol.)	Income tax per capita (dol.)
Total_	74,278	631,626	83,880	412	82,229	947,785	124,526	585	84,536	1,053,593	141,886	661
N.E._____	4,675	40,895	5,661	476	4,860	55,748	7,465	613	5,007	61,449	8,338	682
Maine__	359	2,523	292	293	407	3,843	440	416	415	4,270	504	471
N.H.___	299	2,362	303	409	338	3,529	436	537	354	4,081	523	636
Vt._____	160	1,240	149	335	179	1,776	204	432	189	1,895	213	448
Mass___	2,283	19,803	2,700	473	2,321	26,518	3,472	597	2,331	28,287	3,753	646
R.I.____	362	2,868	373	393	371	3,908	505	524	385	4,398	565	610
Conn___	1,212	12,099	1,844	606	1,244	16,174	2,408	777	1,333	18,518	2,780	892
M.A.____	14,308	131,545	18,326	492	14,368	177,156	23,913	642	14,406	189,990	25,981	697
N.Y.___	7,054	66,804	9,334	508	6,876	87,315	11,557	639	6,837	92,068	12,310	681
N.J.____	2,829	27,018	3,863	537	2,919	37,754	5,381	734	2,957	41,181	5,925	808
Pa.____	4,425	37,723	5,129	434	4,573	52,087	6,975	588	4,612	56,741	7,746	653
E.N.C.___	14,901	132,711	18,185	451	15,823	189,139	25,659	627	16,191	211,832	29,751	727
Ohio___	3,910	34,186	4,711	442	4,181	48,101	6,479	604	4,226	53,126	7,347	687
Ind_____	1,879	15,669	2,061	396	2,023	23,231	3,055	575	2,083	26,192	3,615	682
Ill._____	4,309	40,247	5,761	518	4,477	57,066	8,214	734	4,599	63,885	9,493	845
Mich___	3,155	29,268	4,008	451	3,353	41,102	5,526	607	3,461	46,834	6,554	720
Wis____	1,648	13,341	1,644	371	1,789	19,639	2,385	520	1,822	21,795	2,742	595
W.N.C.___	5,908	45,877	5,767	349	6,416	71,154	9,116	546	6,574	78,985	10,240	609
Minn___	1,389	11,172	1,382	362	1,527	17,392	2,124	542	1,568	19,447	2,433	614
Iowa___	1,029	7,880	969	342	1,106	12,650	1,608	562	1,135	14,024	1,830	638
Mo.____	1,681	13,643	1,798	384	1,784	19,261	2,537	532	1,832	21,975	2,939	615
N. Dak.	215	1,340	149	240	244	2,720	337	529	260	2,787	347	540
S. Dak.	229	1,414	156	233	253	2,390	279	410	260	2,625	316	461
Nebr___	552	4,031	510	243	615	6,646	867	562	626	7,106	902	581
Kans___	813	6,397	803	357	887	10,095	1,364	598	893	11,021	1,473	638
S.A.____	10,784	86,736	11,371	369	12,725	140,426	18,047	536	13,108	155,267	20,383	600
Del.____	207	1,989	299	543	236	2,938	405	700	234	3,179	474	814
Md.____	1,474	14,204	1,961	498	1,680	21,892	2,995	727	1,665	22,972	3,211	775
D.C.___	320	2,462	386	510	310	3,691	550	773	304	4,103	638	909
Va._____	1,659	14,024	1,863	400	1,919	22,635	3,000	602	1,977	25,170	3,384	673
W. Va__	556	4,208	539	308	610	6,707	890	495	640	7,601	1,030	566
N.C.___	1,743	12,523	1,518	298	2,004	19,973	2,285	420	2,078	22,044	2,615	478
S.C.___	840	5,732	644	248	1,009	9,866	1,093	388	1,044	11,110	1,280	449
Ga.____	1,542	11,802	1,481	321	1,776	18,484	2,187	444	1,842	20,682	2,502	503
Fla.____	2,443	19,792	2,680	582	3,181	34,240	4,642	561	3,324	38,406	5,249	623
E.S.C.___	3,970	28,800	3,453	269	4,599	46,466	5,711	423	4,819	52,832	6,561	480
Ky._____	1,034	7,553	920	285	1,159	11,799	1,520	449	1,203	13,378	1,686	492
Tenn___	1,316	9,819	1,232	313	1,529	15,660	1,949	467	1,607	17,544	2,232	530
Ala.___	1,030	7,462	856	248	1,190	12,275	1,498	414	1,262	14,259	1,751	478
Miss___	590	3,966	445	201	721	6,732	744	318	747	7,651	892	379
W.S.C.___	6,336	48,874	6,350	328	7,615	82,918	11,164	535	7,925	94,881	13,371	631
Ark____	596	4,001	466	241	698	6,479	757	359	740	7,737	924	438
La._____	1,062	7,871	987	270	1,277	13,758	1,785	469	1,327	15,961	2,178	567
Okla___	861	6,463	799	311	1,012	10,480	1,309	482	1,025	11,610	1,519	549
Tex____	3,817	30,539	4,098	365	4,628	52,201	7,313	598	4,833	59,573	8,750	701
Mt.____	3,006	23,648	2,927	351	3,779	40,736	5,073	527	3,974	46,365	5,845	594
Mont__	250	1,768	213	304	297	2,979	360	483	308	3,359	410	545
Idaho__	251	1,605	197	274	308	3,190	371	456	324	3,591	415	499
Wyo___	126	958	124	371	156	1,814	257	684	167	2,142	304	780
Colo___	826	6,802	852	383	1,041	12,051	1,572	619	1,086	13,496	1,783	690
N. Mex.	342	2,437	296	290	419	4,033	484	423	457	4,789	573	491
Ariz___	645	5,362	669	373	845	8,893	1,085	491	879	9,894	1,214	535
Utah___	358	2,694	307	288	440	4,690	521	433	466	5,459	625	509
Nev____	208	1,932	269	545	273	3,086	423	717	287	3,635	521	854
Pac____	9,989	89,822	11,544	434	11,543	139,264	17,939	635	12,043	157,192	20,909	728
Wash___	1,228	10,594	1,380	404	1,443	17,557	2,408	677	1,508	19,499	2,750	761
Oreg___	771	6,215	791	376	925	10,166	1,267	555	986	11,804	1,505	646
Calif.___	7,588	69,155	8,844	442	8,661	104,481	13,240	625	9,018	117,909	15,454	718
Alaska.	100	1,056	150	494	155	2,791	473	1,296	167	3,332	585	1,531
Hawaii_	302	2,802	379	490	359	4,269	551	635	364	4,648	615	693
Other[2]___	401	2,718	296	183	502	4,781	439	(Z)	490	-4,797	511	(Z)

Z Less than $.50.   [1] Less deficit occurring when deductions allowed for computation of adjusted gross income (for definition, see footnote 1, table 442) exceeded gross income.
[2] Returns with addresses outside the United States.

Source: U.S. Internal Revenue Service, *Statistics of Income, Individual Income Tax Returns*, annual.

No. 447. Corporation Income Tax Returns—Summary: 1950 to 1975

[In billions of dollars, except as indicated. Beginning 1955, estimates based on samples. All data based on returns for periods ending between July 1 of year shown and of following year, as filed. All corporations are required to file returns except those specifically exempt, such as fraternal, civic, and charitable organizations not operating for profit. Excludes returns of inactive corporations. See source for changes in law affecting comparability of historical data. Corporate data based on income tax returns appear on pp. 561–563 and 570–573. See also *Historical Statistics, Colonial Times to 1970*, series Y 381–392]

ITEM	1950	1955	1960	1965	1970	1971	1972	1973	1974	1975
All returns:										
Number of returns_____1,000__	629	807	1,141	1,424	1,665	1,733	1,813	1,905	1,966	2,024
Total receipts [1]_____	458	642	849	1,195	1,751	1,906	2,171	2,558	3,090	3,199
Net income less deficit [2]_____	43	47	44	74	66	80	97	120	146	143
Returns with net income:										
Number of returns_____1,000__	426	513	670	915	1,008	1,064	1,140	1,203	1,207	1,226
Total receipts [1]_____	431	585	724	1,080	1,453	1,621	1,895	2,266	2,647	2,703
Net income [2]_____	44	50	50	81	84	97	113	138	171	169
Total tax liability [3]_____	17	22	22	30	32	36	40	49	62	60
Distributions to stockholders [4]___	11	13	17	25	30	31	34	40	46	43
Returns without net income:										
Number of returns_____1,000__	203	294	470	509	657	669	673	702	759	797
Total receipts [1]_____	27	57	125	115	298	285	276	292	443	496
Deficit [2]_____	2	3	7	7	18	17	16	18	25	27
Inactive corporations, number of returns_____1,000__	37	35	47	66	82	71	74	76	77	76

[1] Consists of business receipts, taxable and nontaxable interest, rents, royalties, net gain from capital assets (as defined by law) and other property, dividends, and other taxable income. Includes nontaxable interest.

[2] Net income (less deficit) is a tax concept and therefore excludes wholly tax-exempt interest; beginning 1965, includes constructive taxable income from related foreign corporations.

[3] Tax liability is before deduction for foreign tax credit. Beginning 1965, data are after investment credit, and beginning 1972, after work incentive (WIN) credit. Beginning 1965, includes tax from recomputing prior year investment credit; 1970 and 1971, includes tax surcharge; 1970–1975, includes additional tax for tax preferences; beginning 1973, includes tax from recomputing prior year work incentive (WIN) credit.   [4] Other than own stock.

Source: U.S. Internal Revenue Service, *Statistics of Income, Corporation Income Tax Returns*, annual.

No. 448. Corporation Income Tax Returns—Selected Items, by Asset-Size Class: 1965 to 1975

[See headnote, table 447. See also *Historical Statistics, Colonial Times to 1970*, series V 108, 129, 136, 137, and 182–196]

YEAR AND ITEM	Total	ASSET-SIZE CLASS							
		Under $100 thous.	$100–$499.9 thous.	$500–$999.9 thous.	$1–$4.9 mil.	$5–$9.9 mil.	$10–$49.9 mil.	$50–$99.9 mil.	$100 mil. and over
1965:									
Number of returns_____1,000__	1,424	846	418	73	63	11	10	2	2
Total receipts_____bil. dol__	1,194.6	76.4	172.6	86.7	166.5	57.6	119.6	54.9	460.4
Income subject to tax____bil. dol__	70.8	1.7	3.7	2.4	7.4	3.5	8.5	4.2	39.6
Tax before credits [1]_____bil. dol__	31.7	.6	1.5	1.1	3.0	1.4	3.3	1.7	19.2
Tax after credits [1]_____bil. dol__	27.3	.5	1.4	1.0	2.8	1.3	3.1	1.5	15.7
Percent distribution:									
Number of returns_____	100	59	29	5	4	1	1	(Z)	(Z)
Total receipts_____	100	6	14	7	14	5	10	5	39
Tax after credits_____	100	2	5	4	10	5	11	5	58
1970:									
Number of returns_____1,000__	1,665	961	506	93	74	13	14	2	3
Total receipts_____bil. dol__	1,750.7	100.3	221.5	117.8	214.2	77.8	158.6	73.4	787.2
Income subject to tax____bil. dol__	72.4	2.1	5.6	3.0	7.0	2.9	6.7	3.1	42.0
Tax before credits [1]_____bil. dol__	33.3	.6	1.8	1.2	3.2	1.4	3.2	1.5	20.5
Tax after credits [1]_____bil. dol__	27.9	.6	1.7	1.2	3.1	1.4	3.0	1.4	15.4
Percent distribution:									
Number of returns_____	100	58	30	6	4	1	1	(Z)	(Z)
Total receipts_____	100	6	13	7	12	4	9	4	45
Tax after credits_____	100	2	6	4	11	5	11	5	55
1975:									
Number of returns_____1,000__	2,024	1,882		101	15	18	3	4	
Total receipts_____bil. dol__	3,198.6	616.2		384.6	131.5	277.3	131.4	1,657.6	
Income subject to tax [2]__bil. dol__	146.6	14.8		12.0	5.1	11.7	5.2	97.8	
Tax before credits [1]_____bil. dol__	66.1	4.3		5.1	2.3	5.4	2.4	46.5	
Tax after credits [1]_____bil. dol__	39.7	3.8		4.7	2.2	4.9	2.2	21.9	
Percent distribution:									
Number of returns_____	100	93		5	1	1	(Z)	(Z)	
Total receipts_____	100	19.3		12.0	4.1	8.7	4.1	51.8	
Tax after credits_____	100	9.6		11.8	5.5	12.3	5.5	55.2	

Z Less than .5 percent.   [1] Before (after) deduction for foreign tax credit, investment credit, and, for 1975, work incentive (WIN) credit. Includes tax from recomputing prior year investment credit and, for 1970 and 1975, additional tax for tax preferences. For 1975, includes tax from recomputing prior year work incentive (WIN) credit.   [2] Excludes tax preference items upon which additional tax for tax preferences is based.

Source: U.S. Internal Revenue Service, *Statistics of Income, Corporation Income Tax Returns, 1965, 1970*, and *975*.

No. 449. Public Debt of the Federal Government: 1900 to 1977

[As of **June 30** except, beginning **1977**, as of **Sept. 30**, except as noted. See also *Historical Statistics, Colonial Times to 1970*, series Y 461, 493, and 494]

YEAR	GROSS DEBT			INTEREST PAID		YEAR	GROSS DEBT			INTEREST PAID	
	Total [1] (bil. dol.)	Average annual per- cent change [2]	Per capita [3] (dol.)	Total (bil. dol.)	Per- cent of Fed- eral outlays [4]		Total [1] (bil. dol.)	Average annual per- cent change [2]	Per capita [3] (dol.)	Total (bil. dol.)	Per- cent of Fed- eral outlays [4]
1900	1.3	2.9	$17	(Z)	7.7	1964	308.1	1.8	1,604	10.7	9.0
1905	1.1	−2.2	14	(Z)	4.3	1965	313.8	1.9	1,613	11.3	9.5
1910	1.1	.3	12	(Z)	3.1	1966	316.1	.7	1,605	12.0	8.9
1915	1.2	.8	12	(Z)	3.0	1967	322.9	2.2	1,622	13.4	8.5
1920	24.3	80.0	228	1.0	15.9	1968	345.4	7.0	1,717	14.6	8.2
1925	20.5	−3.3	177	.9	28.8	1969	352.9	2.2	1,737	16.6	9.0
1930	16.2	−4.6	132	.7	19.2	1970	370.1	4.9	1,807	19.3	9.8
1935	28.7	12.1	226	.8	12.6	1971	397.3	7.4	1,919	21.0	9.9
1940	43.0	8.4	325	1.0	11.5	1972	426.4	7.3	2,042	21.8	9.4
1945	258.7	43.0	1,849	3.6	3.7	1973	457.3	7.2	2,174	24.2	9.8
1950	256.1	−.1	1,688	5.7	14.5	1974	474.2	3.7	2,238	29.3	10.9
1955	272.8	1.3	1,651	6.4	9.3	1975	533.2	12.4	2,496	32.7	10.1
1960	284.1	.9	1,572	9.2	10.0	1976	620.4	16.4	2,884	37.1	10.1
1961	286.4	.9	1,559	9.0	9.2	1976, [5]	634.7	(X)	2,951	8.1	8.6
1962	295.4	3.1	1,582	9.1	8.5	1977	698.8	10.1	2,884	41.9	10.4
1963	302.7	2.5	1,598	9.9	8.9						

X Not applicable.   Z Less than $50 million.   [1] Adjusted to exclude nonmarketable issues to the International Monetary Fund and other international institutions for each year as follows (in billions of dollars): 1950, .9; 1955, 1.6; 1960, 2.2; 1962, 2.8; 1963, 3.2; 1964, 3.6; 1965, 3.5; 1966, 3.8; 1967, 3.3; 1968, 2.2; and, 1969 through 1976, .8. [2] From preceding year shown; for 1900, from 1895. Minus sign (−) denotes decrease.   [3] Based on estimated July 1 population; prior to 1960, excludes Alaska and Hawaii.   [4] Calculated on total expenditures not reduced by interfund transactions representing interest and certain other payments to Treasury through 1950. Beginning 1955, outlays, net of applicable receipts.   [5] For 15 months ending Sept. 30.

Source: U.S. Dept. of the Treasury, *Statistical Appendix* to the *Annual Report of the Secretary of the Treasury on the State of the Finances* and *Final Monthly Treasury Statement of Receipts and Outlays of the U.S. Government.*

No. 450. Federal Government Interest-Bearing Public Debt: 1960 to 1977

[In billions of dollars. As of **June 30** except, beginning **1977**, as of **Sept. 30**. See also *Historical Statistics, Colonial Times to 1970*, series Y 497 and Y 500–504]

DEBT INSTRUMENT	1960	1965	1970	1974	1975	1976	1977	PERCENT OF TOTAL					
								1960	1965	1970	1975	1976	1977
Total	283.2	313.1	369.0	473.2	532.1	619.3	697.6	100.0	100.0	100.0	100.0	100.0	100.0
Computed inter- est rate	3.30	3.68	5.56	6.56	6.35	6.44	6.42	(X)	(X)	(X)	(X)	(X)	(X)
Marketable [1]	183.8	208.7	232.6	266.6	315.6	392.6	443.5	64.9	66.7	63.0	59.3	63.4	63.6
Bills	33.4	53.7	76.2	105.0	128.6	161.2	156.1	11.8	17.1	20.6	24.2	26.0	22.4
Notes	51.5	52.5	93.5	128.4	150.2	191.8	241.7	18.2	16.8	25.3	28.2	31.0	34.6
Treasury bonds [2]	81.2	102.5	63.0	33.1	36.8	39.6	45.7	28.7	32.7	17.1	6.9	6.4	6.6
Nonmarketable	99.4	104.5	136.4	206.7	216.5	226.7	254.1	35.1	33.4	37.0	40.7	36.6	36.4
U.S. savings bonds	47.5	50.0	51.3	61.9	65.4	69.7	75.4	16.8	16.0	13.9	12.3	11.3	10.8
Treasury bonds, other [3]	7.0	5.8	8.8	29.3	26.9	26.4	38.6	2.5	1.8	2.3	5.1	4.3	5.5
Govt. account series [4]	44.9	48.7	76.3	115.4	124.2	130.6	140.1	15.9	15.5	20.7	23.3	21.1	20.1
Marketable debt, by maturity:													
Within 1 year	70.5	87.6	105.5	139.9	163.9	204.2	217.9	24.9	28.0	28.6	30.8	33.0	31.2
1–5 years	72.8	56.2	89.6	77.2	101.9	127.0	148.4	25.7	17.9	24.3	19.2	20.5	21.3
5–10 years	20.2	39.2	15.9	27.0	26.8	35.6	45.9	7.1	12.5	4.3	5.0	5.7	6.6
10–20 years	12.6	8.5	10.5	17.4	14.5	14.0	13.0	4.4	2.7	2.8	2.7	2.3	1.9
20 years and over	7.7	17.2	11.0	5.1	8.4	11.9	18.3	2.7	5.5	3.0	1.6	1.9	2.6
Avg. length, yr.-mo	4–4	5–4	3–8	3–0	3–0	2–11	2–11	(X)	(X)	(X)	(X)	(X)	(X)

X Not applicable.   [1] For 1960, includes postal savings, certificates, and Panama Canal bonds, not shown separately.   [2] Bank eligible bonds.   [3] Comprises Treasury bonds, investment series (all years); Treasury bonds (various); certificates of indebtedness (various); certificates and notes; depositary bonds; U.S. retirement plan bonds, beginning 1965; and U.S. savings notes, beginning 1970.   [4] Prior to July 1974, known as U.S. Treasury special issues.

Source: U.S. Dept. of the Treasury, *Daily Statement of the U.S. Treasury* and *Monthly Statement of the Public Debt of the United States*. In *Statistical Appendix* to the *Annual Report of the Secretary of the Treasury on the State of the Finances* and in *Treasury Bulletin*, monthly.

No. 451. INTEREST-BEARING GOVERNMENT SECURITIES OUTSTANDING: 1950 TO 1977

[In billions of dollars. As of June 30 except, beginning 1977, as of Sept. 30. Par values, except U.S. savings bonds series E, F, J, and U.S. savings notes, which are included at current redemption values. Data for 1950–1960 not strictly comparable with later years]

TYPE OF SECURITY	1950	1955	1960	1965	1970	1971	1972	1973	1974	1975	1976	1977
Total	281	317	360	420	521	562	605	651	686	759	859	968
Tax exempt [1]	37	46	70	97	139	154	169	183	201	215	229	260
Percent of total	13.2	14.5	19.4	23.1	26.7	27.4	27.9	28.1	29.3	28.5	26.7	26.9
Taxable [2]	211	228	245	274	306	325	346	366	370	419	499	568
Government account series [3]	32	43	45	49	76	83	90	102	115	124	131	140
By issuer:												
U.S. Treasury	255	272	283	313	369	396	425	456	473	532	619	698
Government agencies [4]	1	3	8	9	13	12	11	11	12	11	11	10
State and local govts [1][5]	24	43	68	97	139	154	169	183	201	215	229	260

[1] Source: Board of Governors, Federal Reserve System. [2] Interest is subject to both normal and surtax rates of Federal income tax. [3] Prior to July 1, 1974, known as U.S. Treasury special issues.
[4] Excludes securities issued by Federal home loan banks and Federal land banks. Beginning 1970, also excludes securities issued by Federal National Mortgage Association, Federal intermediate credit banks, and banks for cooperatives. [5] Wholly tax-exempt. Includes Industrial Pollution Control Bonds.

No. 452. ESTIMATED OWNERSHIP OF FEDERAL SECURITIES: 1960 TO 1977

[In billions of dollars, except percent. As of June 30 except, beginning 1977, as of Sept. 30. Data refer to securities that are classified as debt under the unified budget concept. See also headnote, table 451]

OWNERSHIP	1960	1965	1970	1972	1973	1974	1975	1976	1977
Total outstanding [1]	290.9	323.1	382.6	437.3	468.4	486.2	544.1	631.4	708.7
Commercial banks [2]	56.1	60.7	54.8	62.7	60.7	55.6	70.9	94.4	102.3
Federal Reserve banks	26.5	39.1	57.7	71.4	75.2	80.7	84.9	94.7	105.0
U.S. Government accounts	53.7	61.6	97.8	113.7	125.4	140.2	147.3	151.6	157.3
Private nonbank investors	154.6	161.8	172.4	189.6	207.2	209.8	241.0	290.7	344.1
Individuals [3]	71.5	72.6	83.2	74.2	76.8	81.7	88.1	97.2	104.3
Insurance companies	12.3	11.1	8.0	7.2	6.9	6.3	7.5	11.0	15.0
Mutual savings banks	7.1	6.2	3.7	4.0	4.0	3.0	4.0	5.8	6.5
Corporations [4]	20.9	15.9	8.9	9.4	10.0	11.3	13.6	24.7	24.5
State and local governments	19.9	26.4	32.8	30.0	32.0	32.1	35.2	43.0	56.5
Other [1][5]	22.9	29.6	36.0	64.7	77.5	75.4	92.7	109.0	137.4
Percent distribution	100.0	100.0	100.0	100.0	100.0	100.0	100.0	100.0	100.0
Commercial banks [2]	19.3	18.8	14.3	14.3	13.0	11.4	13.1	15.0	14.4
Federal Reserve banks	9.1	12.1	15.0	16.3	16.0	16.6	15.6	15.0	14.8
U.S. Government accounts	18.5	19.1	25.6	26.0	26.8	28.8	27.1	24.0	22.2
Private nonbank investors	53.1	50.0	45.1	43.4	44.2	43.2	44.2	46.0	48.5
Individuals [3]	24.6	22.5	21.7	17.0	16.4	16.8	16.1	15.4	14.7
Insurance companies	4.2	3.4	2.1	1.6	1.5	1.3	1.4	1.7	2.1
Mutual savings banks	2.4	1.9	1.0	.9	.9	.6	.7	.9	.9
Corporations [4]	7.2	4.9	2.3	2.2	2.1	2.3	2.5	3.9	3.5
State and local governments	6.8	8.1	8.6	6.9	6.8	6.6	6.1	6.8	8.0
Other [1][5]	7.9	9.2	9.4	14.8	16.5	15.7	17.4	17.3	19.4

[1] Adjusted to exclude nonmarketable issues to the International Monetary Fund and other international institutions.
[2] Consists of commercial banks, trust companies, and stock savings banks in the U.S. and outlying areas.
[3] Includes partnerships and personal trust accounts. [4] Excludes banks and insurance companies.
[5] Consists of savings and loan associations, nonprofit associations, corporate pension trust funds, dealers and brokers, and investments of foreign balances and international accounts in this country. Also included are certain Government deposit accounts and Government-sponsored agencies.

Source of tables 451 and 452: Except as noted, U.S. Dept. of the Treasury, *Treasury Bulletin*, monthly, and *Statistical Appendix* to the *Annual Report of the Secretary of the Treasury on the State of the Finances*.

No. 453. U.S. SAVINGS BONDS: 1935 TO 1977

[In billions of dollars. See *Historical Statistics, Colonial Times to 1970*, series Y 500, for similar but not exactly comparable data]

BOND BALANCE	1935–1950	1955	1960	1965	1970	1971	1972	1973	1974	1975	1976	1977
Amounts outstanding [1]	58.0	57.9	47.2	50.3	51.8	54.3	57.6	60.3	63.3	67.5	71.9	76.6
Funds from sales	91.7	6.3	4.4	4.5	4.7	5.5	6.2	6.3	6.9	7.0	7.6	8.0
Accrued discounts	5.6	1.2	1.3	1.5	1.0	2.2	2.4	2.7	3.0	3.4	3.6	4.0
Redemptions [2]	39.0	7.3	6.7	5.4	6.3	5.2	5.4	6.2	6.8	6.3	6.8	7.1

[1] Interest-bearing debt only for amounts end of period or end of year.
[2] Comprises both matured and unmatured bonds.
Source: U.S. Dept. of the Treasury. Monthly data published currently in *Treasury Bulletin*.

No. 454. Federal Civilian Employment and Annual Payrolls, by Branch: 1955 to 1977

[Includes employees in U.S. territories (Commonwealth, Trust Territory, Condominium, Outlying Areas, and Disputed Island) and in foreign countries. Figures represent employees in active-duty status, including intermittent employees. Annual employment figures are for fiscal year and are averages of monthly (as of last day) figures. Excludes Central Intelligence Agency and National Security Agency. See *Historical Statistics, Colonial Times to 1970*, series Y 308-317, for employment as of June 30]

BRANCH OF GOVERNMENT	1955	1960	1965	1970	1973	1974	1975	1976	1977
Employment, total [1]___1,000__	2,402	[2]2,430	2,539	[2]2,928	2,788	2,866	2,882	2,879	2,855
Percent of all U.S. employed [3]___	3.9	3.7	3.6	3.7	3.3	3.1	3.1	3.0	2.9
Executive [1]_____1,000__	2,376	[2]2,403	2,507	[2]2,891	2,745	2,820	2,834	2,831	2,804
Rate per 1,000 population_____	14.3	13.1	12.8	14.1	13.1	13.3	13.3	13.2	12.8
Legislative_____1,000__	22	23	25	30	34	36	37	38	39
Judicial_____1,000__	4	5	6	7	9	9	10	11	12
Payrolls, total [1]____mil. dol__	10,295	[2]13,243	18,020	[2]28,562	34,474	37,590	40,699	42,259	45,895
Percent of total Federal outlays__	15.0	14.4	15.2	14.5	14.0	14.0	12.6	11.5	15.6
Executive [1]_____mil. dol__	10,146	[2]13,052	17,746	[2]28,117	33,869	36,935	39,944	41,450	44,976
Legislative_____mil. dol__	122	154	216	353	474	519	589	631	700
Judicial_____mil. dol__	26	36	58	92	131	137	166	179	219

[1] Includes Postal Service Christmas help.   [2] Includes 36,417 temporary census workers in 1960; 33,000 in 1970.
[3] Civilian only. See table 645.

No. 455. Federal Civilian Employment—Summary: 1960 to 1977

[In thousands. Partially estimated. As of Dec. 31. Excludes U.S. Territories and foreign countries, Central Intelligence Agency, Christmas help of the U.S. Postal Service, and National Security Agency]

CHARACTERISTIC OF EMPLOYMENT	UNITED STATES								WASHINGTON, D.C., SMSA [1]			
	1960	1965	1970	1973	1974	1975	1976	1977	1965	1970	1975	1977
Paid employment___	2,213	2,403	2,645	2,667	2,724	2,741	2,725	2,724	275	316	349	353
Male_____	1,668	1,813	1,931	1,875	1,896	1,896	1,867	1,846	165	180	206	203
Female_____	545	590	714	793	828	845	858	878	110	136	143	150
Full-time_____	2,084	2,267	2,516	2,422	2,480	2,496	2,464	2,463	268	308	333	335
Other_____	129	136	129	245	244	245	261	261	7	8	16	18
Competitive service [2]___	2,041	2,201	2,393	1,643	1,704	1,714	1,715	1,706	231	262	257	261
Career_____	1,676	1,788	1,991	1,281	1,284	1,300	1,322	1,361	173	198	191	205
Career-conditional____	251	298	290	296	358	354	335	289	49	53	55	47
Temporary [3]_____	114	115	112	66	62	60	58	56	9	11	11	9
Excepted service [2][4]____	172	202	252	1,000	1,020	1,027	1,010	1,018	44	54	91	92
Permanent_____	100	112	164	846	864	863	858	846	32	38	71	72
Other_____	72	90	88	154	156	164	152	172	12	16	20	20
White-collar_____	1,639	1,850	2,113	2,182	2,231	2,255	2,254	2,256	237	278	314	320
Blue-collar_____	574	553	532	486	493	486	471	468	38	38	35	33

[1] See footnote 2, table 457.   [2] In 1971, under Postal Reorganization Act of 1970, U.S. Postal Service employees were changed from competitive service to excepted service.   [3] Includes "indefinite."
[4] Excepted from competitive requirements of Civil Service Act.

No. 456. Federal Civilian Employees, Characteristics: 1963 to 1973

[As of June 30]

CHARACTERISTIC	1963				1970				1973			
	Total	Male	Female		Total	Male	Female		Total	Male	Female	
			Number	Percent			Number	Percent			Number	Percent
Employees, total_____1,000__	2,300	1,739	561	24.4	2,824	1,967	856	30.3	2,685	1,883	801	29.8
Under 30 years of age__1,000__	293	179	114	38.9	637	354	283	44.4	535	298	236	44.3
30-49 years_____1,000__	1,343	1,067	277	20.6	1,346	988	358	26.6	1,176	858	318	27.0
50 years and over_____1,000__	664	494	170	25.6	841	625	216	25.7	974	727	246	25.3
Average age_____years__	43.1	43.5	42.0	(X)	41.4	42.5	39.0	(X)	42.9	44.1	40.3	(X)
Employed: [1]												
Less than 5 years_____1,000__	313	167	146	46.7	730	353	378	51.7	408	198	209	51.2
5-9 years_____1,000__	441	324	116	26.3	549	385	163	29.8	572	340	232	40.6
10-19 years_____1,000__	889	693	196	22.0	770	584	186	24.2	774	588	185	23.9
20 years or more_____1,000__	657	555	103	15.9	775	646	129	16.6	837	698	139	16.6
Avg. length of service____years__	14.2	15.1	11.2	(X)	13.1	14.7	9.4	(X)	15.1	16.7	11.1	(X)

X Not applicable.   [1] 1973 figures exclude 95,001 employees whose length of service was unspecified.

Source of tables 454-456: U.S. Civil Service Commission, *Annual Report; Monthly Release of Federal Civilian Workforce Statistics;* and unpublished data.

No. 457. PAID CIVILIAN EMPLOYMENT IN THE FEDERAL GOVERNMENT—STATES AND OTHER AREAS: 1960 TO 1977

[As of December 31. Excludes Central Intelligence Agency, temporary Christmas help of the U.S. Postal Service, and National Security Agency]

STATE OR OTHER AREA	TOTAL EMPLOYMENT (1,000)						PERCENT OF U.S.			EMPLOYMENT IN SELECTED AGENCIES, 1977 [1] (1,000)			
	1960	1965	1970	1975	1976	1977	1970	1975	1977	Dept. of Defense	Postal Service	Veterans Admin.	Dept. of HEW
Total____	2,373	2,570	2,875	2,870	2,844	2,823	(X)	(X)	(X)	972.4	687.0	223.6	157.8
U.S._____	2,213	2,403	2,665	2,738	2,717	2,697	100.0	100.0	100.0	899.6	684.2	221.3	157.0
D.C.area²	236	275	318	335	338	329	11.9	12.2	12.2	79.7	17.8	6.4	37.6
50 States ²_	1,977	2,128	2,348	2,403	2,379	2,368	88.1	87.8	87.8	819.9	666.4	214.9	119.4
Ala._____	60.9	59.5	54.3	58.5	59.2	50.4	2.0	2.1	1.9	24.9	8.1	4.6	2.9
Alaska_____	12.6	13.5	14.5	15.1	15.8	16.5	.6	.6	.6	4.6	1.4	.1	1.7
Ariz_____	19.8	22.7	27.5	33.6	34.5	35.2	1.1	1.2	1.3	10.1	5.9	2.7	3.1
Ark_____	13.1	15.1	16.6	18.7	18.3	18.7	.6	.7	.7	4.5	5.4	3.5	.9
Calif_____	239.5	265.1	303.5	297.8	291.6	294.8	11.4	10.9	10.4	130.7	69.6	22.1	11.7
Colo_____	33.9	37.7	42.3	48.7	48.6	48.7	1.6	1.8	1.8	14.4	8.8	2.6	1.5
Conn_____	14.6	16.4	20.4	21.0	20.8	20.7	.8	.8	.8	3.1	10.1	2.5	.5
Del_____	3.4	3.7	4.7	5.2	5.2	5.1	.2	.2	.2	1.9	1.6	.7	.1
Fla_____	48.0	57.2	69.3	78.4	78.3	79.9	2.6	2.9	3.0	28.7	21.9	8.5	2.2
Ga_____	55.5	64.9	73.8	75.0	75.7	77.1	2.8	2.7	2.9	35.0	13.5	4.5	5.0
Hawaii_____	22.1	23.5	26.3	25.3	24.9	25.1	1.0	.9	.9	19.0	2.0	.2	.2
Idaho_____	6.2	7.4	8.2	9.8	10.3	11.0	.3	.4	.4	1.2	2.2	.5	.2
Ill_____	98.9	104.3	110.7	106.6	103.0	102.9	4.2	3.9	3.8	20.1	43.4	11.8	6.4
Ind_____	31.7	35.1	44.4	40.8	39.1	39.4	1.7	1.5	1.5	13.3	14.5	3.6	.9
Iowa_____	15.8	16.7	18.1	19.2	19.1	19.4	.7	.7	.7	1.5	9.7	3.2	.5
Kans_____	21.1	19.7	22.3	23.1	22.9	23.0	.8	.8	.9	6.4	8.1	3.2	.4
Ky_____	27.6	29.5	34.7	35.9	35.4	32.8	1.3	1.3	1.2	13.3	9.0	3.3	.8
La_____	22.9	25.2	27.6	30.6	31.2	31.7	1.1	1.1	1.2	8.7	9.0	3.5	2.2
Maine_____	17.3	15.1	15.1	12.1	9.3	9.3	.6	.4	.4	2.1	3.8	1.3	.2
Md. ²_____	45.3	51.8	62.0	64.7	64.4	62.7	2.3	2.4	2.3	21.7	9.4	2.9	23.8
Mass_____	62.2	60.0	63.5	58.4	57.0	58.5	2.4	2.1	2.2	11.7	22.1	7.4	2.7
Mich_____	42.4	47.3	53.4	54.6	53.9	53.9	2.0	2.0	2.0	12.2	24.4	5.5	1.9
Minn_____	24.6	26.9	29.3	30.3	29.6	29.9	1.1	1.1	1.1	3.1	13.7	4.8	1.0
Miss_____	15.7	17.6	20.3	24.1	24.5	25.4	.8	.9	.9	10.9	5.0	2.8	.7
Mo_____	50.0	56.2	65.0	66.4	66.1	66.3	2.4	2.4	2.5	20.7	18.3	5.7	4.9
Mont_____	8.4	9.8	10.3	12.2	12.3	12.8	.4	.4	.5	1.5	2.6	.6	.9
Nebr_____	15.4	14.9	15.1	16.1	15.7	15.7	.6	.6	.6	3.7	5.6	2.0	.3
Nev_____	5.8	7.4	8.1	8.9	9.1	9.3	.3	.3	.4	2.5	1.8	.6	.3
N.H_____	3.6	4.4	5.5	10.2	13.3	14.3	.2	.4	.5	8.9	2.6	.7	.2
N.J_____	53.8	58.3	65.9	71.0	69.2	68.8	2.5	2.6	2.6	27.5	28.7	4.7	1.6
N. Mex_____	22.8	24.3	25.1	26.9	27.2	27.4	.9	1.0	1.0	9.3	2.8	1.4	2.4
N.Y_____	179.8	173.1	177.8	172.3	166.5	166.2	6.7	6.3	6.2	19.4	76.3	20.3	10.5
N.C_____	28.5	31.4	37.3	42.3	41.6	42.1	1.4	1.5	1.6	13.9	12.6	4.8	1.8
N. Dak_____	5.9	6.9	8.1	9.1	8.9	8.9	.3	.3	.3	2.0	2.6	.6	.4
Ohio_____	88.8	93.5	96.9	93.6	92.4	92.3	3.6	3.4	3.4	33.3	32.3	8.3	2.8
Okla_____	42.1	46.9	52.8	47.7	47.5	47.4	2.0	1.7	1.8	24.1	8.2	2.3	1.7
Oreg_____	20.0	22.0	24.1	25.6	25.9	27.0	.9	.9	1.0	3.2	6.3	2.5	.7
Pa_____	129.1	133.3	137.7	132.3	127.8	127.3	5.2	4.8	4.7	49.6	39.1	11.1	6.9
R.I_____	12.3	13.2	14.6	10.1	9.7	10.6	.6	.4	.4	5.6	2.9	1.1	.2
S.C_____	22.5	25.8	29.3	30.7	31.1	31.6	1.1	1.1	1.2	18.8	6.0	2.2	.7
S. Dak_____	9.0	9.1	9.3	10.8	10.8	10.6	.3	.4	.4	1.4	2.6	1.8	.9
Tenn_____	34.1	40.7	44.8	55.4	57.5	37.1	1.7	2.0	1.4	8.3	12.3	5.9	.7
Tex_____	112.6	126.7	144.7	149.6	149.9	151.5	5.4	5.5	5.6	60.1	35.0	13.4	4.2
Utah_____	26.4	32.5	38.3	35.3	35.1	36.3	1.4	1.3	1.4	21.1	3.1	1.5	.2
Vt_____	3.1	3.2	3.7	4.4	4.3	4.5	.2	.2	.2	.5	1.9	.7	.1
Va. ²_____	66.9	70.7	74.0	78.0	78.1	79.0	2.8	2.9	2.9	51.0	10.3	5.0	1.3
Wash_____	45.6	48.3	52.6	57.8	57.7	59.7	2.0	2.1	2.2	24.9	10.3	3.9	2.5
W. Va_____	10.5	11.6	13.3	15.6	15.5	15.7	.5	.6	.6	1.6	5.7	2.7	.7
Wis_____	20.4	22.3	25.5	26.8	26.3	26.6	1.0	1.0	1.0	3.0	12.6	4.8	.9
Wyo_____	4.7	5.0	5.2	6.1	6.3	6.5	.2	.2	.3	.9	1.2	.5	.1
Outside U.S.	159.7	167.1	209.9	131.8	126.8	126.7	(X)	(X)	(X)	72.8	2.8	2.3	.8
Territories	32.2	33.8	36.9	33.0	33.3	33.7	(X)	(X)	(X)	10.2	2.8	2.0	.7
Foreign___	127.5	133.3	173.0	98.8	93.5	93.0	(X)	(X)	(X)	62.6	–	.3	.1

- Represents zero. X Not applicable. [1] Partially estimated.
² Washington, D.C., Standard Metropolitan Statistical Area includes District of Columbia, Alexandria and Falls Church cities, Arlington and Fairfax Counties, Va.; and Montgomery and Prince Georges Counties, Md.; beginning 1965, Fairfax City, Va.; beginning July 1967, Loudoun and Prince William Counties, Va.; beginning July 1973, Charles County, Md.; and beginning July 1975, Manassas and Manassas Park, Va. These areas are excluded from data for the 50 States.

Source: U.S. Civil Service Commission, *Monthly Release of Federal Civilian Workforce Statistics* and *Federal Civilian Employment in the United States by Geographic Area*, annual.

No. 458. Paid Civilian Employment in the Federal Government, by Agency, All Areas: 1960 to 1978

[As of June 30 through 1976; thereafter, as of Sept. 30 except as noted. See headnote, table 454. See also *Historical Statistics, Colonial Times to 1970*, series Y 308-317]

AGENCY	1960	1965	1970	1975	1976	1977	1978 [1]
All agencies	2,398,373	[2]2,527,492	2,921,909	2,896,944	2,883,134	2,841,152	2,838,806
Percent Dept. of Defense	43.7	40.9	40.9	36.0	35.0	34.6	34.6
Percent Postal Service	23.5	23.6	24.9	24.1	23.5	23.2	22.8
Legislative branch	22,886	25,947	30,715	38,531	39,234	39,429	39,148
Congress	7,091	9,296	11,815	17,317	18,019	18,329	18,069
United States Senate	2,817	3,474	4,362	6,144	6,733	6,591	6,512
U.S. House of Representatives	4,274	5,822	7,453	11,173	11,286	11,738	11,544
Comm. on Security and Cooperation in Europe [3]	(X)	(X)	(X)	(X)	(X)	14	13
Architect of the Capitol	1,363	1,519	1,631	2,061	2,103	2,249	2,214
General Accounting Office	5,066	4,274	4,631	5,513	5,417	5,355	5,382
Government Printing Office	6,540	7,416	8,557	8,549	8,260	7,788	7,672
Library of Congress	2,779	3,386	3,848	4,649	4,930	5,069	5,181
Judicial branch	4,992	5,904	6,887	10,399	11,259	12,625	12,785
United States Courts	(NA)	(NA)	6,664	10,122	10,956	12,311	12,459
Supreme Court	(NA)	(NA)	223	277	303	314	326
Executive branch	2,370,495	2,495,641	2,884,307	2,848,014	2,832,641	2,789,098	2,786,873
Executive Office of the President:							
White House Office	446	333	311	625	541	464	379
Office of Management and Budget	434	524	633	673	724	709	621
Council of Economic Advisers	32	46	59	40	39	38	34
Council on Environ. Quality [4]	(X)	(X)	32	69	59	49	51
Executive Mansion and Grounds	70	71	73	81	83	80	87
National Security Council	65	38	75	89	95	73	65
Office of Telecomm. Policy [5]	(X)	(X)	(X)	76	96	56	70
All other	1,872	1,837	3,559	265	252	247	409
Executive departments:							
Agriculture	98,694	113,017	116,012	120,999	128,052	127,497	114,099
Commerce	[6]49,300	33,668	[6]57,674	36,228	37,569	37,761	38,645
Defense	1,047,120	1,033,775	1,193,784	1,041,829	1,010,261	981,747	982,198
Office of the Secretary [7]	1,865	2,297	2,375	2,189	4,815	2,734	(X)
Department of the Army	390,046	366,726	443,369	378,937	368,219	350,549	350,130
Department of the Navy	347,760	333,271	376,340	319,719	315,885	310,119	311,108
Department of the Air Force	307,449	291,500	306,323	268,466	252,687	243,810	243,643
Other defense activities [7]	–	39,981	65,377	72,518	68,655	74,535	77,317
Energy [8]	(X)	(X)	(X)	(X)	(X)	(X)	19,743
Health, Education, and Welfare	61,641	87,316	108,044	147,125	155,096	155,886	158,364
Housing and Urban Development [9]	11,105	13,777	15,190	17,161	16,579	17,770	17,575
Interior	56,111	70,711	73,361	80,198	81,844	83,419	75,937
Justice	30,942	33,222	39,257	51,541	53,982	53,081	52,962
Labor	7,096	9,527	10,991	14,834	16,730	16,752	17,271
State	37,983	39,552	39,753	30,376	30,457	29,991	30,092
Agency for Int'l Development	[10]14,443	15,098	14,974	6,591	6,198	6,092	5,977
Transportation [11]	38,291	45,421	65,985	75,035	77,287	75,163	74,445
Treasury	76,179	88,761	92,521	121,546	325,600	123,615	132,393
Independent agencies:							
ACTION [12]	(X)	1,104	1,317	1,864	1,932	1,921	2,031
Amer. Battle Monuments Comm	461	439	404	399	399	386	385
Arms Control and Disarmament Agency	(X)	175	177	190	198	201	218
Atomic Energy Commission [13]	6,907	7,329	7,347	(X)	(X)	(X)	(X)
Board of Governors, Federal Reserve System	598	667	1,016	1,460	1,481	1,483	1,462
Canal Zone Government	2,625	3,028	3,318	3,299	3,215	3,280	3,292
Civil Aeronautics Board	755	846	682	728	758	784	797
Civil Service Commission	3,579	3,789	5,508	8,157	8,131	8,440	8,794
Commission on Civil Rights	82	109	153	275	301	331	320
Community Services Admin. [14]	(X)	(X)	(X)	1,112	1,099	1,057	1,065
Consumer Prod. Safety Comm. [15]	(X)	(X)	(X)	959	962	952	991
ERDA [8][13]	(X)	(X)	(X)	8,262	9,038	9,536	(X)
Environmental Protection Agency	(X)	(X)	(X)	10,772	11,089	11,339	12,423
Equal Empl. Opportunity Comm	(X)	19	850	2,183	2,399	2,373	2,368
Export-Import Bank, U.S.	237	308	358	444	451	426	432
Farm Credit Administration	245	235	235	223	239	254	259
Federal Communications Comm	1,403	1,541	1,537	2,137	2,094	2,136	2,118
Federal Deposit Insurance Corp	1,249	1,544	2,478	3,103	3,441	3,511	3,578
Federal Energy Administration [8][16]	(X)	(X)	(X)	3,245	3,478	3,807	(X)
Federal Home Loan Bank Board	1,000	1,300	1,273	1,452	1,454	1,450	1,467
Federal Maritime Commission [17]	(X)	251	233	314	309	307	302
Federal Mediation and Conciliation Service	347	422	450	523	541	547	575
Federal Power Commission [8]	859	1,163	1,132	1,322	1,365	1,363	(X)
Federal Trade Commission	782	1,157	1,330	1,661	1,739	1,719	1,777

See footnotes at end of table.

No. 458. PAID CIVILIAN EMPLOYMENT IN THE FEDERAL GOVERNMENT, BY AGENCY, ALL AREAS: 1960 TO 1978—Continued

[See headnote page 280]

AGENCY	1960	1965	1970	1975	1976	1977	1978 [1]
Independent agencies: —Continued							
General Services Administration___	28,211	36,524	37,945	39,561	38,857	36,625	37,624
International Communications Agency [18]_____	10,915	11,628	10,262	8,809	8,732	8,497	8,348
International Trade Commission [19]_	271	298	242	427	436	360	386
Interstate Commerce Commission__	2,381	2,427	1,755	2,115	2,178	2,145	2,115
Nat'l Aero. and Space Admin_____	10,232	34,049	32,548	26,447	26,244	24,435	24,191
Nat'l Credit Union Admin.[5]_____	(X)	(X)	419	570	594	582	584
National Foundation on the Arts and the Humanities [20]_____	(X)	(X)	103	503	513	557	893
National Labor Relations Board___	1,750	2,252	2,144	2,485	2,642	2,818	2,906
National Mediation Board_____	129	135	126	103	105	101	101
National Science Foundation_____	734	1,116	1,211	1,424	1,456	1,420	1,360
Nuclear Regulatory Commission [13]_	(X)	(X)	(X)	2,247	2,639	2,822	2,902
Panama Canal Company_____	11,436	11,936	12,571	11,689	10,597	10,898	11,409
Railroad Retirement Board_____	2,234	1,767	1,734	1,961	1,990	1,907	1,939
Renegotiation Board_____	284	184	236	198	183	178	176
Securities and Exchange Comm____	980	1,420	1,454	2,002	1,943	1,976	1,967
Selective Service System_____	6,230	7,587	8,395	2,257	208	70	70
Small Business Administration____	2,244	3,751	4,269	4,796	4,741	5,230	5,700
Smithsonian Institution_____	1,555	2,334	2,641	3,746	4,024	3,834	3,961
Soldiers' and Airmen's Home_____	1,041	1,134	1,126	1,041	1,049	1,027	1,030
Tennessee Valley Authority_____	14,993	16,797	22,244	28,423	31,302	37,657	40,121
U.S. Postal Service [21]_____	562,868	595,512	726,472	699,174	675,653	657,832	648,419
Veterans Administration_____	172,338	167,059	168,719	213,143	222,313	223,398	227,903
All other_____	1,159	709	579	2,019	2,783	2,728	2,665

– Represents zero. NA Not available. X Not applicable. [1] As of Jan. 31. Includes 25,359 employees exempted from personnel ceilings in Youth Program and Worker Trainee Opportunities Program. [2] Includes 33,480 appointments under Youth Opportunity Campaign. [3] Established in April 1977. [4] Agency established in 1969. [5] Agency established in 1970. [6] 1960 includes 15,574 temporary piece-rate workers on 1960 census; 1970 includes 24,278 enumerators on 1970 census. [7] Beginning 1978, data on Office of the Secretary are not available separately; included in Other defense activities. [8] Dept. of Energy established Oct. 1, 1977; comprises ERDA, Federal Energy Admin., Federal Power Comm., and the fuel elements of the Dept. of Interior. [9] Includes Housing and Home Finance Agency, transferred in 1965. [10] International Cooperation Administration, predecessor of AID. [11] 1960 and 1965 data represent Federal Aviation Admin. and St. Lawrence Seaway Development Corp., both of which were transferred to Dept. of Transportation in April 1967. [12] Formerly Peace Corps; became an independent agency in 1971. [13] In Jan. 1975, Atomic Energy Commission was divided into Energy Research and Development Admin. and Nuclear Regulatory Commission. [14] Established in 1974 as successor to Office of Economic Opportunity. [15] Established Oct. 1972. [16] Established June 28, 1974. [17] Became an independent agency in 1961. [18] In March 1978 United States Information Agency became International Communications Agency. [19] Formerly Tariff Commission. [20] Established in 1965. [21] Post Office, an executive department through 1970, reorganized and became U.S. Postal Service, an independent agency, as of July 1, 1971.

Source: U.S. Civil Service Commission, Annual Report and Monthly Release of Federal Civilian Workforce Statistics.

No. 459. ACCESSIONS TO AND SEPARATIONS FROM PAID CIVILIAN EMPLOYMENT IN THE FEDERAL GOVERNMENT: 1965 TO 1977

[For years ending June 30. Includes accessions and separations of part-time and intermittent employees]

ITEM	UNITED STATES					WASHINGTON, D.C., SMSA [1]				
	1965	1970	1975	1976	1977 [2]	1965	1970	1975	1976	1977 [2]
Accessions, total_____1,000__	480.4	560.7	601.2	572.5	67.3	59.5	64.5	74.5	71.1	67.3
Monthly rate [3]_____	1.7	1.7	1.9	1.8	1.6	1.9	1.8	1.9	1.8	1.6
Separations, total_____1,000__	445.5	641.1	588.9	590.4	67.4	51.0	69.5	69.3	67.4	67.4
Monthly rate [3]_____	1.6	2.0	1.8	1.8	1.6	1.6	1.9	1.8	1.7	1.6
Quit [4]_____1,000__	192.1	[5]311.5	213.2	198.8	28.4	31.8	[5]38.8	29.6	28.9	28.4
Reduction in force_____1,000__	16.1	[5]17.5	[5]10.4	47.8	[5].8	.2	[5].6	[5]1.1	2.5	[5].8
Discharge [6]_____1,000__	8.9	[5]19.7	[5]17.2	18.4	[5]12.1	.8	[5]2.0	[5]1.8	1.7	[5]12.1
Other [7]_____1,000__	228.4	[5]292.3	[5]348.1	325.4	[5]36.1	18.2	[5]28.1	[5]36.8	34.3	[5]36.1

[1] Standard Metropolitan Statistical Area. For areas included, see footnote 2, table 457. [2] Year ending Sept. 30. [3] Per 100 employees. [4] Represents resignation, transfer to other Federal agency, and abandonment of position. [5] Partially estimated.

[6] Represents separation required by an agency for disqualification or inefficiency, and removal for misconduct, delinquency, or other serious cause. [7] Represents termination of appointment, and separation for extended leave without pay, military leave, retirement, death, legal incompetency, and disability not entitled to retirement and displacement.

Source: U.S. Civil Service Commission, Monthly Release of Federal Civilian Workforce Statistics, and unpublished data.

No. 460. PAID CIVILIAN EMPLOYMENT IN FULL-TIME POSITIONS IN THE FEDERAL GOVERNMENT, ALL AREAS: 1960 TO 1977

[As of June 30 through 1970; as of March 31 thereafter. Excludes employees of Congress and Federal courts, maritime seamen of Department of Commerce, and small number for whom rates were not reported. See also *Historical Statistics, Colonial Times to 1970*, series Y 318–331]

COMPENSATION AUTHORITY	1960		1965		1970		1975		1976		1977	
	Employees (1,000)	Average pay (dol.)	Employees (1,000)	Average pay (dol.)	Employees (1,000)	Average pay (dol.)	Employees (1,000)	Average pay (dol.)	Employees (1,000)	Average pay (dol.)	Employees (1,000)	Average pay (dol.)
Total	2,237	5,273	2,398	6,868	2,806	9,234	2,582	13,529	2,557	14,576	2,502	15,874
General Schedule	973	5,705	1,112	7,707	1,287	11,065	1,349	14,483	1,358	15,343	1,390	16,230
Wage System	667	4,935	621	5,887	674	6,976	528	11,197	515	12,489	470	14,517
Postal Pay System	483	4,854	534	6,219	673	8,120	566	13,329	548	14,360	528	15,322
Other	114	5,344	131	7,032	172	8,741	139	13,951	136	15,687	113	19,704

Source: U.S. Civil Service Commission, *Pay Structure of the Federal Civil Service*, annual.

No. 461. FULL-TIME WHITE-COLLAR CIVILIAN EMPLOYMENT IN THE FEDERAL GOVERNMENT—TOTAL AND WOMEN, BY GRADE LEVELS: 1969 TO 1976

[As of October 31]

SEX AND GRADE [1]	1969	1970	1972	1973	1974	1975	1976
Total employment _____1,000__	1,990	1,982	1,992	1,894	1,957	1,976	1,981
Women _____1,000__	665	657	671	644	697	697	711
Percent of total	33.4	33.2	33.7	34.0	34.9	35.3	35.9
General Schedule Pay System _____1,000__	1,267	1,259	1,303	1,295	1,332	1,428	1,456
Women _____1,000__	518	507	522	526	553	601	621
Percent of total	40.9	40.3	40.1	40.6	41.5	42.1	42.6
Grades 1–6 ($5,800–$13,500) _____1,000__	546	531	555	554	574	585	587
Women _____1,000__	399	384	393	395	410	419	423
Percent of total	73.1	72.3	70.8	71.4	71.5	71.6	72.1
Grades 7–12 ($11,500–$26,600) ____1,000__	443	563	574	567	579	641	661
Women _____1,000__	113	117	122	123	134	172	186
Percent of total	25.6	20.8	21.1	21.7	23.2	26.8	28.1
Grades 13 and above ($24,300+) ____1,000__	278	165	174	174	179	203	208
Women _____1,000__	6	6	7	7	8	10	11
Percent of total	2.0	3.6	4.0	4.3	4.6	5.1	5.5
Postal Pay System _____1,000__	621	618	589	502	527	519	498
Women _____1,000__	101	102	105	75	86	86	81
Percent of total	16.2	16.4	17.7	15.0	16.3	16.5	16.2
Other pay systems _____1,000__	101	105	100	97	98	28	27
Women _____1,000__	46	48	44	43	44	10	9
Percent of total	45.8	45.8	44.4	43.9	44.4	35.4	34.0

[1] Pay ranges shown for General Schedule grades are as of Oct. 1, 1976, and apply only to the 1976 data.

Source: U.S. Civil Service Commission, *Occupations of Federal White-Collar Workers*, 1976.

No. 462. SALARIES OF SELECTED EXECUTIVE AND LEGISLATIVE OFFICIALS IN THE FEDERAL GOVERNMENT: 1907 TO 1978

YEAR [1]	President	Vice President	Cabinet officers	Congressmen	YEAR [1]	President	Vice President	Cabinet officers	Congressmen
1907	[2] $50,000	$12,000	$12,000	$7,500	1964	[3]	$43,000	35,000	[3]
1909	75,000	[3]	[3]	[3]	1965	[3]	[3]	[3]	30,000
1925	[3]	15,000	[4] 15,000	[4] 10,000	1969	[6] $200,000	[7] 62,500	60,000	42,500
1946	[3]	20,000	[3]	[5] 15,000	1975	[3]	[7] 65,600	63,000	44,600
1949	[6] 100,000	30,000	22,500	[3]	1976	[3]	[7] [8] 68,800	[8] 66,000	[8] 46,800
1955	[3]	35,000	[3]	22,500	1977	[3]	[7] 75,000	66,000	57,500
1956	[3]	[3]	$25,000	[3]	1978	[3]	[3]	[3]	[3]

[1] When salary change became effective.   [2] Compensation enacted in 1873.   [3] No change from prior year shown.   [4] Legislation reduced amounts by 15, 10, and 5 percent, successively, during 1932–35. Full salary restored Apr. 1, 1935.   [5] Includes $2,500 expense allowance that was tax free until 1953. Allowance discontinued Mar. 1, 1955. For income tax, members may deduct up to $3,000 a year for living expenses.   [6] Plus $50,000 for official expenses.   [7] Plus $10,000 expense allowance.   [8] Pursuant to Legislative Branch Appropriation Act, 1977, funds were not available to pay a salary at a rate which exceeded the rate in effect on Sept. 30, 1976; therefore, these officials were paid at the rate in effect on that date.

Source: U.S. Civil Service Commission, *Annual Report*.

No. 463. Minority Group Employment in the Federal Government, all Agencies, by Pay System: 1972 and 1977

[Covers full-time employment excluding Hawaii, Guam, Puerto Rico, and foreign nationals abroad]

PAY SYSTEM	Total employ- ees (1,000)	MAY 31, 1972				Total employ- ees (1,000)	MAY 31, 1977			
		Minority groups					Minority groups			
		Total [1] (1,000)	Per- cent of total	Negroes (1,000)	Spanish sur- named (1,000)		Total [1] (1,000)	Per- cent of total	Negroes (1,000)	Spanish sur- named (1,000)
All pay systems, total____	2,575	505.4	19.6	387.7	76.6	2,442	518.2	21.2	386.5	82.9
General schedule and similar [2]__	1,331	206.1	15.5	153.4	28.1	1,433	252.5	17.6	182.5	37.8
GS 1–4 ($6,219–$11,575)_____	306	85.3	27.9	66.3	10.2	305	85.7	28.1	63.1	11.8
GS 5–8 ($9,959–$17,757)_____	394	75.4	19.1	59.0	9.5	437	96.8	22.2	75.1	13.1
GS 9–11 ($15,090–$23,739)_____	319	29.4	9.2	18.8	5.4	335	43.7	13.0	28.5	8.1
GS 12–18 ($21,883–$58,245) [3]___	312	16.0	5.1	9.3	2.9	356	26.3	7.4	15.8	4.8
Wage systems_____	505	143.3	28.4	102.9	29.7	456	129.3	28.3	91.2	27.5
WG—Regular nonsupervisory_	385	119.4	31.0	85.3	25.9	342	106.3	31.1	74.1	23.7
WL—Regular leader_____	15	3.7	25.6	2.8	.7	13	3.7	28.8	2.7	.7
WS—Regular supervisory____	41	7.0	17.0	4.7	1.6	39	8.2	20.8	5.6	1.8
Other wage systems_____	64	13.1	20.6	10.1	1.6	62	11.1	18.0	8.8	1.3
U.S. Postal Service_____	687	151.1	22.0	127.9	18.1	520	130.0	25.0	108.8	16.3
Level 1–5 [4]_____	571	131.8	23.1	111.8	15.8	379	96.5	25.4	80.9	12.2
Level 6–12_____	110	18.8	17.1	15.7	2.2	78	24.7	31.8	20.9	2.9
Level 13 and above_____	6	.5	7.8	.4	(Z)	63	8.8	14.1	7.0	1.2
Other pay systems_____	52	4.9	9.4	3.6	.7	33	6.4	19.3	3.9	1.3

Z Less than 50. [1] Includes American Indians and Orientals. [2] Pay rates as of Sept. 1977, for general schedule. Each grade (except GS—18) includes several salary steps. Range is from lowest to highest step of grades shown. [3] Rates of basic pay for GS—16, steps 5–9; and all steps of GS—17 and GS—18 are limited by section 5308 of title 5 of the U.S. Code to the rate for level V of the Executive Schedule (as of Sept. 1977, the effective date of this salary adjustment, $47,500). [4] Includes 4th class postmasters and rural carriers

Source: U.S. Civil Service Commission, *Equal Employment Opportunity Statistics.*

No. 464. Federal Civilian Employment—Armed Forces and Other Uniformed Retirees Employed, by Agency and Selected Characteristic: 1975

[As of June 30. Includes uniformed retirees of the Air Force, Army, Coast Guard, National Oceanic and Atmospheric Administration, Marine Corps, Navy, and Public Health Service. Excludes employees of the Central Intelligence Agency, National Security Agency, Tennessee Valley Authority, Board of Governors of the Federal Reserve System, and the White House]

AGENCY	Total Federal employ- ment (1,000)	UNIFORMED RETIREES		AGENCY AND PAY SYSTEM	Total Federal employ- ment (1,000)	UNIFORMED RETIREES	
		Total (1,000)	Percent of total [1]			Total (1,000)	Percent of total [1]
All agencies [2]_____	2,809.5	141.8	5.1	Officer retiree_____	(X)	27.7	[3] 1.0
				Enlisted retiree_____	(X)	111.8	[3] 4.0
In competitive service_____	1,716.3	97.3	5.7	Unspecified_____	(X)	2.3	[3] .1
In excepted service_____	1,090.0	44.4	4.1				
				Pay system [4]:			
Executive branch_____	2,075.0	106.8	5.2	Under $6,000_____	122.0	1.5	1.2
Defense_____	1,002.3	78.1	7.8	$6,000–$9,999_____	600.8	24.6	4.1
Army_____	363.5	25.5	7.0	$10,000–$17,999_____	1,613.6	93.3	5.8
Navy_____	289.0	26.3	9.1	$18,000–$28,999_____	395.3	19.2	4.9
Marine Corps_____	17.7	2.0	11.4	$29,000–$35,999_____	53.6	2.2	4.0
Air Force_____	257.3	20.6	8.0	$36,000 and over_____	17.8	.8	4.5
Other Defense_____	74.8	3.7	5.0	Unspecified_____	6.5	.2	2.8
Veterans Administration__	217.7	7.3	3.4				
Other executive agencies___	855.0	21.4	2.5				
U.S. Postal Service_____	719.3	34.7	4.8				

X Not applicable.
[1] Percent of total Federal employment in specified category.
[2] Includes other categories not shown separately.
[3] Percent of total Federal employment.
[4] Represents retiree's compensation under various Federal civilian pay systems.

Source: U.S. Civil Service Commission, *Study of Retired Uniform Services Personnel in the Federal Civilian Service—December 1976,* February 28, 1977.

No. 465. FEDERAL FULL-TIME PERMANENT CIVILIAN EMPLOYMENT—EDUCATIONAL ATTAINMENT, BY MINORITY GROUP: 1974

[As of August 31. Covers only full-time permanent General Schedule and similar employees who comprise 74 percent of all Federal civilian nonpostal white-collar employees of all tenures and work schedules. See source for additional information on coverage and minority group designation]

EDUCATIONAL LEVEL	Total employees (1,000)	MINORITY GROUP EMPLOYEES (1,000)					Nonminority group (1,000)	PERCENT	
		Total	Male	Female	Black	Other[1]		Minority	Nonminority
Total	1,163	197	81	115	148	49	966	100.0	100.0
High school or less	373	79	29	50	61	18	294	40.1	30.4
Beyond high school, no college	152	31	8	23	25	7	121	15.7	12.5
College	638	87	44	43	63	24	551	44.2	57.0
One year or less	173	35	13	23	27	8	138	17.8	14.3
2 to 4 years, no degree	119	21	10	11	16	6	98	10.7	10.1
Bachelor's degree	156	15	9	6	10	5	142	7.6	14.7
Graduate study	189	15	12	4	10	6	174	7.6	18.0

[1] Comprises Spanish-surnamed, American Indian, and Asian American.

Source: U.S. Civil Service Commission, *Educational Attainment of General Schedule Employees, by Minority Group and Sex.*

No. 466. WHITE-COLLAR FULL-TIME CIVILIAN WORKERS IN THE FEDERAL GOVERNMENT, BY MAJOR OCCUPATION GROUP AND SEX: 1970 AND 1976

[As of October 31. Includes U.S. outlying areas and foreign countries, but excludes foreign nationals overseas]

MAJOR OCCUPATION GROUP	1970 Total (1,000)	1970 Percent male	1976 Total (1,000)	1976 Percent male	MAJOR OCCUPATION GROUP	1970 Total (1,000)	1970 Percent male	1976 Total (1,000)	1976 Percent male
Total	1,981.7	66.8	1,981.2	64.1	Physical sciences	43.0	90.8	41.7	90.4
					Biological sciences	41.5	93.6	46.2	90.5
Postal	594.8	83.5	469.6	84.5	Investigation	38.9	96.9	46.5	93.5
General admin., clerical, and office services	449.1	31.1	471.7	31.8	Social science, psychology, and welfare	34.2	73.0	53.1	65.4
Engineering and architecture	148.8	98.8	151.3	98.4	Transportation	42.6	84.5	43.7	83.8
Accounting and budget	113.2	52.9	121.6	51.8	Education	29.3	64.4	28.7	58.6
Medical, hospital, dental, and public health	93.7	44.6	120.5	40.3	Quality assurance inspection and grading	21.4	97.1	18.7	96.5
Supply	72.1	58.2	60.0	56.2	Information and arts	19.6	70.1	20.5	66.9
Business and industry	64.5	78.3	69.0	71.0	Equipment, facilities, and service	18.2	98.0	14.0	97.1
Legal and kindred	47.8	52.5	64.3	45.4	Math. and statistics	14.0	58.4	14.6	65.3
Personnel mgmt. and industrial relations	40.4	46.8	44.4	43.6	Library and archives	8.5	35.8	9.7	37.3
					Other	46.3	95.8	71.3	88.0

Source: U.S. Civil Service Commission, *Occupations of Federal White-Collar Workers,* annual.

No. 467. BLUE-COLLAR WORKERS IN THE FEDERAL GOVERNMENT: 1970 AND 1976

[As of October 31. Covers full-time Federal civilian workers; includes U.S. citizens working abroad]

MAJOR OCCUPATION GROUP	1970 Total (1,000)	1970 Percent Dept. of Defense	1976 Total (1,000)	1976 Percent Dept. of Defense	MAJOR OCCUPATION GROUP	1970 Total (1,000)	1970 Percent Dept. of Defense	1976 Total (1,000)	1976 Percent Dept. of Defense
Total	574.9	72.5	506.4	69.1	Electronic equip. install. and opr.[1]	30.1	96.6	26.1	97.1
					Machine tool work	21.8	89.0	21.3	86.2
Mobile industrial equip. operation[1]	74.7	73.3	65.2	70.6	Marine operations[1]	20.6	90.2	9.7	85.6
Manual labor	60.7	32.1	54.0	27.7	Ammunition and armament work	16.9	99.9	8.3	99.8
Warehousing	46.6	87.6	36.6	84.0	Woodworking	17.9	78.3	13.7	70.8
Fixed industrial equip. operation[1]	47.5	62.3	44.6	59.1	General maintenance and constr. opr.	16.7	40.7	18.3	39.3
Services	45.5	56.9	37.6	51.5	Pipefitting	15.9	79.8	16.9	74.7
Metal work and processing	32.7	87.3	30.2	84.6	Printing and reproduction	14.1	44.0	11.3	43.3
Aircraft repair, propeller work[2]	31.6	97.9	28.4	98.0	Painting and paperhanging	11.2	77.9	10.2	81.0
Electrical installation[1]	28.7	76.6	25.3	71.3	Other	42.1	77.1	48.6	79.4

[1] Includes maintenance.   [2] Includes engine overhaul.

Source: U.S. Civil Service Commission, *Occupations of Federal Blue-Collar Workers,* annual.

Section 10

State and Local Government Finances and Employment

This section presents data on revenues, expenditures, debt and government employment within State and local governments. Nationwide statistics relating to State and local governments, their numbers, finances, and employment, are compiled primarily by the Bureau of the Census through a program of censuses and surveys. Every fifth year (for years ending in "2" and "7") the Bureau conducts a Census of Governments involving collection of data for all governmental units in the United States. In addition, the Bureau conducts annual surveys which cover all the State governments and a sample of local governments.

Publications issued annually by the Bureau of the Census include a report on governmental finances which presents figures for the Federal Government, nationwide totals for State and local governments, by type, and State-local data by States. Also issued annually are a series of publications on State, city, and county finances, and on city, county, and other public employment. Financial data are published in the GF publication series; employment data in the GE series. There are also a series of quarterly reports covering tax revenue, and finances of major public employee retirement systems, as well as a series of special studies. *Recurrent Publications on Governments* describes the publication program.

Basic information for Census Bureau statistics on governments is obtained mainly by mail canvass from State and local officials; however, financial data for each of the State governments and for many of the large local governments are compiled from their official records and reports by Census Bureau personnel. Financial data on the Federal Government are obtained by the Bureau from the Office of Management and Budget and are published in the *Budget* (see page 253).

Governmental units.—The governmental structure of the United States includes, in addition to the Federal Government and the States, thousands of local governments—counties, municipalities, townships, school districts, and numerous kinds of "special districts." As shown by table 493, more than 79,800 local governments were identified by the 1977 Census of Governments. As defined by the census, governmental units include all agencies or bodies having an organized existence, governmental character, and substantial autonomy. While most of these governments can impose taxes, many of the special districts—such as independent public housing authorities, the New York Port Authority, and numerous local irrigation, power, and other types of districts—are financed from rentals, charges for services, benefit assessments, grants from other governments, toll charges, and other nontax sources. The count of governments excludes semi-autonomous agencies through which States, cities, and counties sometimes provide for certain functions—for example, "dependent" school systems, State institutions of higher education, and certain other "authorities" and special agencies which are under the administrative or fiscal control of an established governmental unit.

Finances.—Unless otherwise stated, financial data relate to fiscal years. Most States end their fiscal year June 30. This was also the practice of the Federal Government until 1976 when its fiscal year, by an act of Congress, began to extend from Oct. 1 to Sept. 30. A three month quarter (July 1 to Sept. 30, 1976) facilitated the transition. Beginning 1963, local government figures are for fiscal years which closed at various dates during the 12 months ended June 30 of the year specified; figures for 1962 and earlier years are for fiscal years ended during the calendar year.

Nationwide government finance statistics must be classified and presented in terms of uniform concepts and categories, rather than according to the highly diverse terminology,

285

organization, and fund structure utilized by individual governments. Accordingly, financial statistics which appear here for the Federal Government and for individual States have been standardized and may not agree directly with figures appearing in the original sources.

Statistics on governmental finances distinguish among general government, utilities, liquor stores, and insurance trusts. General government comprises all activities except utilities, liquor stores, and insurance trusts. Utilities include local government water supply, electric light and power, gas supply, and transit systems. Liquor stores are operated by 17 States and by local governments in four States. Insurance trusts relate to employee retirement, unemployment compensation, and other social insurance systems administered by State and local governments.

Employment and payrolls.—These data are mainly based on mail canvassing of State and local governments. Payroll includes all salaries, wages, and individual fee payments for the month specified, and employment relates to all persons on governmental payrolls during a pay period of the month covered—including paid officials, temporary help, and (unless otherwise specified) part-time as well as full-time personnel. Figures shown for individual governments cover major dependent agencies such as institutions of higher education, as well as the basic central departments and agencies of the government.

Statistical reliability.—For a discussion of statistical collection and estimation, sampling procedures, and measures of statistical reliability applicable to Census Bureau data, see Appendix III.

Historical statistics.—Tabular headnotes provide cross-references, where applicable, to *Historical Statistics of the United States, Colonial Times to 1970.* See Appendix I.

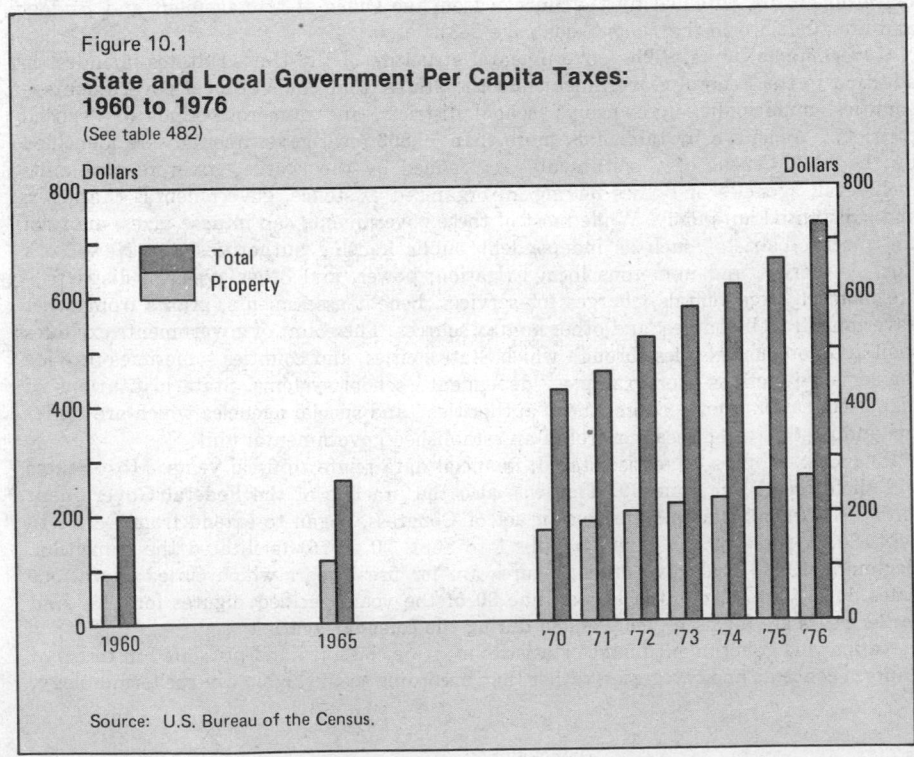

Figure 10.1

State and Local Government Per Capita Taxes: 1960 to 1976

(See table 482)

Source: U.S. Bureau of the Census.

No. 468. Number of Governmental Units, by Level of Government: 1942 to 1977

[See text, p. 285]

LEVEL OF GOVERNMENT	1942	1952	1957	1962	1967	1972	1977
Total	155,116	116,743	102,328	91,237	81,299	78,269	79,913
U.S. Government	1	1	1	1	1	1	1
States	48	48	48	50	50	50	50
Local governments	155,067	116,694	102,279	91,186	81,248	78,218	79,862
Counties	3,050	3,049	3,047	3,043	3,049	3,044	3,042
Municipalities	16,220	16,778	17,183	18,000	18,048	18,517	18,862
Townships and towns	18,919	17,202	17,198	17,142	17,105	16,991	16,822
School districts	108,579	67,346	50,446	34,678	21,782	15,781	15,174
Special districts	8,299	12,319	14,405	18,323	21,264	23,885	25,962

Source: U.S. Bureau of the Census, *Census of Governments: 1967, 1972,* and *1977,* vol. 1, *Governmental Organization.*

No. 469. All Governments—Revenue, Expenditure, and Debt: 1950 to 1976

[Prior to 1960, excludes Alaska and Hawaii. Excludes intergovernmental revenue and expenditure. Local government amounts are estimates subject to sampling variation; see source. See also *Historical Statistics, Colonial Times to 1970,* series Y 505–637 and Y 655–848]

ITEM AND YEAR	All governments, total (bil. dol.)	FEDERAL [1] (bil. dol.)		STATE AND LOCAL (bil. dol.)			ANNUAL PERCENT CHANGE [2]		PER CAPITA [3] (dollars)		
		Total	Percent of total	Total	State	Local	Federal	State and local	Total	Federal	State and local
Revenue:											
1950	67	44	65.3	23	11	12	−3.3	7.3	440	287	153
1955	106	72	67.6	34	17	18	12.9	9.3	644	435	209
1960	153	100	65.2	53	26	27	6.8	7.8	851	554	296
1965	203	126	62.1	77	39	38	4.8	8.5	1,045	649	396
1970	334	206	61.6	128	60	60	3.0	13.3	1,642	1,011	631
1971	345	205	59.4	140	73	67	−.5	9.4	1,670	992	678
1972	384	226	58.7	158	84	74	10.2	12.9	1,845	1,083	761
1973	432	254	58.8	178	97	81	12.7	12.6	2,059	1,211	850
1974	484	289	59.7	196	108	88	13.7	9.9	2,289	1,367	927
1975	517	302	58.5	215	117	98	5.1	9.5	2,425	1,418	1,007
1976	573	324	56.5	249	140	109	7.0	16.1	2,668	1,507	1,160
Expenditure:											
1950	70	42	60.3	28	11	17	11.1	15.5	464	280	184
1955	111	70	63.5	40	14	26	10.8	7.4	670	426	244
1960	151	90	59.7	61	22	39	5.2	8.8	841	502	339
1965	206	119	57.9	87	31	55	5.7	7.4	1,061	614	447
1970	333	185	55.5	148	56	92	4.5	12.1	1,638	910	728
1971	372	201	54.0	171	66	105	8.6	15.5	1,804	976	828
1972	400	212	52.8	189	72	116	5.5	10.5	1,923	1,016	907
1973	437	231	53.0	205	78	127	9.4	8.7	2,081	1,103	978
1974	478	253	52.8	226	86	139	9.2	10.1	2,263	1,195	1,069
1975	557	292	52.4	265	104	161	15.5	17.9	2,615	1,370	1,246
1976	626	322	51.4	304	124	180	10.3	14.6	2,917	1,500	1,417
Debt outstanding: [4]											
1950	281	257	91.4	24	5	19	.6	12.4	1,856	1,697	159
1955	319	274	86.1	44	11	33	1.3	12.9	1,928	1,660	268
1960	356	286	80.4	70	19	51	.9	9.7	1,979	1,591	389
1965	417	317	76.1	100	27	72	2.1	7.4	2,150	1,637	513
1970	514	371	72.1	144	42	102	4.8	7.5	2,531	1,825	706
1971	568	409	72.1	159	48	111	10.2	10.4	2,755	1,985	770
1972	612	437	71.5	175	54	120	6.8	10.1	2,938	2,100	838
1973	657	468	71.3	188	59	129	7.1	7.4	3,130	2,232	898
1974	693	486	70.2	207	65	142	3.8	9.6	3,278	2,300	977
1975	765	544	71.1	221	72	149	11.9	6.4	3,591	2,553	1,032
1976	871	631	72.4	240	84	156	16.0	9.2	4,059	2,941	1,118

[1] Data adjusted to system for reporting State and local data and therefore differ from figures in section 9 tables.
[2] Represents average for period of intervals shown; for 1950, change from 1948. Minus sign (−) denotes decrease.
[3] All years except 1970 based on estimated population as of July 1; 1970 based on resident population enumerated as of Apr. 1. Includes Armed Forces abroad through 1955; thereafter, resident population. Excludes intergovernmental amounts.
[4] As of end of fiscal year.

Source: U.S. Bureau of the Census, *Census of Governments: 1972,* vol. 4, No. 5, *Compendium of Government Finances,* and vol. 6, No. 4, *Historical Statistics on Governmental Finances and Employment;* and *Governmental Finances,* series GF No. 5, annual.

No. 470. ALL GOVERNMENTS—SUMMARY OF FINANCES: 1950 TO 1976

[In billions of dollars, except as indicated. Prior to 1960, excludes Alaska and Hawaii. Federal data adjusted to system for reporting State and local data. Local government amounts are estimates subject to sampling variation; see source. See also *Historical Statistics, Colonial Times to 1970*, series Y 522–530 and Y 534–566]

ITEM	1950	1955	1960	1965	1970	1973	1974	1975	1976
Revenue, total [1]	**66.7**	**106.4**	**153.1**	**202.6**	**333.8**	**432.1**	**484.0**	**517.1**	**572.6**
Revenue from own sources:									
Federal	43.5	71.9	99.8	125.8	205.6	254.2	288.5	302.5	323.5
Percent of total	65.2	67.6	65.2	62.1	61.6	58.9	59.6	58.5	56.5
State and local	23.2	34.5	53.3	76.7	128.2	178.4	196.0	214.6	249.1
State	11.5	16.7	26.1	38.5	68.7	97.1	107.6	116.8	140.5
Local	11.7	17.8	27.2	38.2	59.6	81.3	88.4	97.8	108.6
General revenue [1]	58.5	93.3	130.6	169.7	272.5	344.4	383.1	402.9	438.3
Taxes	51.1	81.1	113.1	145.0	232.9	286.1	314.8	331.4	358.2
Individual income	16.5	30.0	43.2	52.9	101.2	121.2	138.4	143.8	156.2
Corporation income	11.1	18.6	22.7	27.4	48.6	41.6	44.6	47.3	48.7
Sales and gross receipts	13.0	17.2	24.5	32.9	48.6	61.8	66.6	70.9	76.3
Property	7.3	10.7	16.4	22.6	34.1	45.3	47.7	51.5	57.0
Other	3.1	4.5	6.4	9.2	12.4	16.3	17.4	17.9	20.1
Charges and miscellaneous	7.4	12.2	17.5	24.7	39.6	58.3	68.3	71.4	80.1
Utilities and liquor stores	2.7	3.7	4.9	6.4	8.6	10.9	11.7	13.3	15.1
Insurance trusts	5.5	9.5	17.6	26.5	52.7	76.7	89.1	100.6	119.2
Old-age, survivors, disability, and health insurance (Federal Social Security)	2.1	5.1	10.7	16.7	38.5	56.1	66.1	75.6	80.3
Employee retirement	1.0	1.6	2.9	4.5	8.2	12.2	13.2	14.9	17.3
Unemployment compensation	1.2	1.3	2.5	3.4	3.2	5.1	5.8	5.8	17.0
Other	1.2	1.4	1.6	1.9	2.8	3.4	4.0	4.3	4.6
Expenditures, total [1]	**70.3**	**110.7**	**151.3**	**205.6**	**333.0**	**436.8**	**478.3**	**557.4**	**626.1**
Direct expenditure:									
Federal	42.4	70.3	90.3	119.0	184.9	231.4	252.6	291.9	322.0
Percent of total	60.3	63.5	59.7	57.9	55.5	53.0	52.8	52.3	51.4
State and local	27.9	40.4	61.0	86.7	148.1	205.3	225.7	265.2	304.1
State	10.9	14.4	22.2	31.5	56.2	67.3	74.0	104.2	124.1
Local	17.0	26.0	38.8	55.2	91.9	138.0	151.7	161.3	180.0
Current operation	51.6	58.1	81.7	122.6	197.0	249.2	269.8	305.2	335.3
Capital outlay	(NA)	28.7	31.9	33.7	47.5	55.4	57.3	66.6	71.6
Construction	6.8	12.6	15.8	20.9	28.4	32.9	35.7	43.0	45.2
Equipment	(NA)	} 16.1	{ 14.4	9.6	15.9	17.7	16.6	18.8	22.0
Land and existing buildings	(NA)		{ 1.7	3.3	3.2	4.7	5.0	4.8	4.4
Assistance and subsidies	(NA)	8.9	10.4	12.5	20.8	30.7	33.2	44.0	47.7
Interest on debt	5.0	5.9	9.7	12.0	19.2	26.2	31.3	35.1	41.0
Insurance benefits and repayments	6.9	9.0	17.6	24.9	48.5	75.3	86.7	106.5	130.4
Exhibit: Personal services	20.5	34.9	47.1	65.7	110.5	142.6	154.2	172.2	186.8
General expenditure [1]	60.7	97.8	128.6	173.7	275.0	348.4	377.2	433.6	476.1
Nat'l defense and internat'l relations	18.4	43.5	48.9	55.8	84.3	83.0	87.0	95.8	100.4
Military services only	12.1	35.8	41.3	48.4	76.6	72.1	79.1	86.6	91.0
Postal service	2.3	2.7	3.7	5.3	7.7	9.6	11.2	12.7	13.7
Education	9.6	12.7	19.4	29.6	55.8	74.9	81.7	95.0	106.3
State institutions of higher education	1.1	1.5	2.9	5.3	11.0	14.2	15.4	17.7	24.3
Local schools	5.9	10.1	15.2	22.0	37.5	48.8	53.1	61.5	67.7
Other education	2.6	1.1	1.3	2.3	7.3	11.9	13.2	15.8	14.3
Highways	3.9	6.5	9.6	12.3	16.7	18.9	20.2	22.8	24.2
Public welfare	3.0	3.2	4.5	6.4	17.5	27.0	31.0	39.4	45.1
Categorical public assistance [2]	2.0	2.3	3.0	3.7	6.9	10.4	11.6	14.1	15.6
Other public assistance [3]	.5	.3	.3	.3	.6	.8	.7	1.8	2.1
Other public welfare [4]	.4	.6	1.1	2.5	10.0	15.8	18.7	23.5	27.4
Hospitals	2.1	2.7	4.2	5.9	9.7	13.7	15.3	17.4	18.9
Health	.7	.7	1.0	1.8	3.9	5.0	6.4	7.5	8.6
Police	.9	1.4	2.0	2.8	4.9	7.7	8.3	9.6	10.7
Local fire protection	.5	.7	1.0	1.3	2.0	2.8	3.0	3.5	3.9
Local sanitation	.8	1.1	1.7	2.4	3.4	5.3	6.0	7.5	8.2
Natural resources	5.0	6.3	7.1	11.0	11.5	16.7	15.8	16.2	17.0
Stabilization of farm prices and income	2.7	3.9	3.4	5.8	4.3	6.0	4.1	2.4	1.3
Local parks and recreation	.3	.5	.8	1.1	1.9	2.6	3.0	3.5	3.9
Housing and urban renewal	.6	.6	1.1	2.2	3.2	6.9	5.9	5.9	5.4
Veterans services n.e.c.[5]	3.3	3.1	3.8	4.2	5.5	7.4	7.5	8.6	9.3
Financial administration and general control	1.6	2.1	2.9	3.8	6.3	9.2	10.0	11.9	13.4
Interest on general debt	4.9	5.7	9.3	11.4	18.4	25.1	30.1	33.8	39.6
Air and water transport and terminals	.6	1.1	2.0	2.7	4.0	4.9	4.8	5.2	5.4
Other and unallocable	2.2	3.2	5.6	13.7	18.2	27.7	29.9	37.0	42.1
Utility and liquor stores	2.7	3.9	5.1	7.1	9.4	13.0	14.4	17.3	19.5
Insurance trusts	6.9	9.0	17.6	24.9	48.5	75.3	86.7	106.5	130.4
Old-age, survivors, disability, and health insurance (Federal Social Security)	.7	4.3	10.8	16.6	35.8	56.4	64.7	76.6	88.3
Employee retirement	.6	1.2	2.2	3.5	6.4	10.4	12.3	14.6	16.8
Unemployment compensation	2.0	2.0	2.6	2.4	2.8	4.2	4.8	9.6	19.2
Other	3.6	1.5	2.0	2.4	3.5	4.4	5.0	5.7	6.2

NA Not available. [1] Excludes duplicative transactions between levels of government. [2] Old age assistance, aid to families with dependent children, aid to the blind, and aid to the disabled. [3] Cash assistance for general relief wholly financed from State and local sources. [4] Vendor payments under various public welfare programs, including the Medicaid program. [5] Not elsewhere classified.

Source: U.S. Bureau of the Census, *Governmental Finances*, series GF No. 5, annual.

No. 471. ALL GOVERNMENTS—PERCENT AND PER CAPITA DISTRIBUTION OF FINANCES: 1960 TO 1976

[See headnote, table 470. OASDHI=Old-age, survivors, disability, and health insurance]

ITEM	PERCENT DISTRIBUTION					PER CAPITA [1] (dol.)				
	1960	1965	1970	1975	1976	1960	1965	1970	1975	1976
Revenue, total [2]	100.0	100.0	100.0	100.0	100.0	851	1,045	1,642	2,425	2,668
Revenue from own sources:										
Federal	65.2	62.1	61.6	58.5	56.5	554	649	1,012	1,418	1,507
State and local	34.8	37.9	38.4	41.5	43.5	296	396	631	1,007	1,160
State	17.2	19.0	20.6	22.6	24.5	145	199	338	548	655
Local	17.5	18.9	17.9	18.9	19.0	151	197	293	459	506
General revenue [2]	87.7	83.8	81.6	78.0	76.5	726	876	1,341	1,892	2,042
Taxes	76.6	71.6	69.8	64.1	62.6	628	748	1,146	1,556	1,669
Individual income	24.7	26.1	30.3	27.8	27.3	240	273	498	675	728
Corporation income	16.6	13.5	11.0	9.1	8.5	126	141	180	222	227
Sales and gross receipts	19.5	16.2	14.6	13.7	13.3	136	170	239	333	355
Property	10.9	11.2	10.2	10.0	10.0	91	117	168	242	266
Other	4.6	4.5	3.7	3.5	3.5	36	47	61	85	94
Charges and miscellaneous	11.1	12.2	11.9	13.8	14.0	97	127	195	335	373
Utilities and liquor stores	4.0	3.2	2.6	2.6	2.6	27	33	42	63	70
Insurance trusts	8.2	13.1	15.8	19.5	20.8	98	137	259	472	555
OASDHI (Federal Social Security)	3.1	8.2	11.5	14.6	14.0	59	86	189	355	374
Employee retirement	1.5	2.2	2.5	2.9	3.0	16	23	40	70	81
Unemployment compensation	1.8	1.7	1.0	1.1	3.0	14	18	16	27	79
Other	1.8	.9	.8	.8	.8	9	10	14	20	21
Expenditures, total [2]	100.0	100.0	100.0	100.0	100.0	841	1,061	1,638	2,615	2,917
Direct expenditure:										
Federal	59.7	57.9	55.5	52.3	51.4	502	614	910	1,370	1,500
State and local	40.3	42.2	44.5	47.7	48.6	339	447	729	1,246	1,417
State	14.7	15.3	16.9	18.7	19.8	123	163	277	489	578
Local	25.6	26.8	27.6	28.9	28.7	216	285	452	757	838
Current operation	54.0	59.6	59.2	54.8	53.6	454	633	969	1,432	1,562
Capital outlay	21.1	16.4	14.3	12.0	11.4	177	174	234	313	334
Construction	10.4	10.2	8.5	7.7	7.2	88	108	140	202	211
Equipment	9.5	4.7	4.8	3.4	3.5	80	50	70	88	100
Land and existing buildings	1.1	1.6	1.0	.9	.7	.9	17	16	23	21
Assistance and subsidies	6.9	6.1	6.2	7.9	7.6	58	64	102	206	222
Interest on debt	6.4	5.8	5.8	6.2	6.5	54	62	94	165	191
Insurance benefits and repayments	11.6	12.1	14.6	19.1	20.8	98	128	239	500	608
Exhibit: Personal services	31.1	32.0	33.2	30.8	29.8	262	339	544	808	870
General expenditure [2]	85.0	84.5	82.6	77.8	76.0	714	896	1,353	2,035	2,219
Nat'l defense and int'l relations	32.3	27.1	25.3	17.2	16.0	272	288	415	449	468
Military services only	27.3	23.5	23.0	15.6	14.5	229	250	377	406	424
Postal service	2.4	2.6	2.3	2.3	2.2	21	27	38	59	64
Education	12.8	14.4	16.8	17.1	17.0	108	153	275	446	495
State institutions of higher educ	1.9	2.6	3.3	3.2	3.9	16	27	54	83	113
Local schools	10.0	10.7	11.3	11.1	10.8	84	114	185	289	315
Other education	.9	1.1	2.2	2.8	2.3	7	12	36	74	67
Highways	6.3	6.0	5.0	4.1	3.9	53	63	82	107	113
Public welfare [3]	3.0	3.1	5.3	7.1	7.2	25	33	86	185	210
Categorical public assistance	2.0	1.8	2.1	2.5	2.5	17	19	34	66	73
Other public assistance	.2	.1	.2	.3	.3	2	2	3	8	10
Other public welfare	.7	1.2	3.0	4.2	4.4	6	13	49	110	128
Hospitals	2.8	2.9	2.9	3.1	3.0	23	30	48	82	88
Health	.7	.9	1.2	1.3	1.4	6	9	19	35	40
Police	1.3	1.4	1.5	1.7	1.7	11	14	24	45	50
Local fire protection	.7	.6	.6	.6	.6	6	7	10	16	18
Local sanitation	1.1	1.2	1.0	1.3	1.3	9	12	17	35	38
Natural resources	4.7	5.4	3.5	2.9	2.7	39	57	57	76	79
Farm prices and income stabiliz.	2.2	2.8	1.3	.4	.2	19	30	21	11	6
Local parks and recreation	.5	.5	.6	.6	.6	4	6	9	16	18
Housing and urban renewal	.7	1.1	1.0	1.0	.9	6	11	16	27	25
Veterans services, n.e.c.[4]	2.5	2.0	1.7	1.6	1.5	21	22	27	42	44
Financial administration and general control	1.9	1.8	1.9	2.1	2.1	16	20	31	56	62
Interest on general debt	6.1	5.5	5.5	5.9	6.3	52	59	91	159	159
Air, water transport and terminals.	1.3	1.3	1.2	.9	.9	11	14	20	25	25
Other and unallocable	3.7	6.7	5.5	6.7	6.7	31	71	90	175	223
Utility and liquor stores	3.4	3.5	2.8	3.1	3.1	28	37	46	81	91
Insurance trusts	11.6	12.1	14.6	19.1	20.8	98	128	239	500	608
OASDHI (Federal Social Security)	7.1	8.1	10.8	13.8	14.1	60	86	176	359	411
Employee retirement	1.5	1.7	1.9	2.6	2.7	12	18	31	68	78
Unemployment compensation	1.7	1.2	.8	1.7	3.1	14	12	14	45	89
Other	1.3	1.2	1.1	1.0	1.0	11	12	17	27	29

[1] See footnote 3, table 469.   [2] See footnote 1, table 470.   [3] See footnotes 2, 3, and 4, table 470.
[4] Not elsewhere classified.

Source: U.S. Bureau of the Census, *Governmental Finances*, series GF No. 5, annual; and unpublished data.

No. 472. All Governments—Revenues, by Source and Level: 1970 to 1976

[In billions of dollars. Local government amounts are estimates subject to sampling variation; see source. See also *Historical Statistics, Colonial Times to 1970*, series Y 567–584, and Y 652–665]

SOURCE OF REVENUE	1970 Federal	1970 State and local	1973 Federal	1973 State and local	1974 Federal	1974 State and local	1975 Federal	1975 State and local	1976 Federal	1976 State and local
Total revenue	205.6	[1]150.1	254.2	[1]217.6	288.4	[1]237.9	303.5	[1]261.6	324.9	[1]304.7
General revenue	163.6	[1]130.8	193.5	[1]190.2	217.8	[1]207.7	223.0	[1]228.2	239.0	[1]256.2
Intergovernmental	(X)	21.9	(X)	39.3	.5	41.8	1.2	47.1	1.3	55.6
From Federal government	(X)	21.9	(X)	39.3	(X)	41.8	(X)	47.1	(X)	55.6
From State governments	(X)	(1)	(X)	(1)	.5	(1)	1.2	(1)	1.3	(1)
From local governments	(X)	(1)	(X)	(1)	(X)	(1)	(X)	(1)	(X)	(1)
From own sources	163.6	108.9	193.5	151.0	217.3	165.9	221.7	181.1	237.7	200.6
Taxes [2]	146.1	86.8	165.0	121.1	184.1	130.7	190.0	141.5	201.4	156.8
Property	(X)	34.1	(X)	45.3	(X)	47.7	(X)	51.5	(X)	57.0
Individual income	90.4	10.8	103.2	18.0	119.0	19.5	122.4	21.5	131.6	24.6
Corporation income	32.8	3.7	36.2	5.4	38.6	6.0	40.6	6.6	41.4	7.3
Sales and gross receipts [2]	18.3	30.3	19.7	42.0	20.5	46.1	21.1	49.8	21.7	54.5
Motor fuel	3.8	6.3	4.4	8.1	4.6	8.3	4.5	8.3	4.6	8.7
Alcoholic beverages	4.7	1.5	5.1	1.9	5.3	2.0	5.3	2.1	5.4	2.2
Tobacco products	2.1	2.4	2.3	3.3	2.4	3.4	2.3	3.4	2.5	3.6
Public utilities	1.7	1.5	2.5	2.4	2.7	2.6	2.9	3.1	2.7	3.6
Death and gift tax	3.6	1.0	4.9	1.4	5.0	1.4	4.6	1.4	5.2	1.5
Charges and miscellaneous [2]	17.5	22.1	28.4	29.8	33.2	35.2	31.8	39.7	36.3	43.8
Education	(Z)	5.8	(Z)	7.6	(Z)	8.4	(Z)	9.1	.1	10.4
Postal service	6.2	(X)	7.9	(X)	8.6	(X)	9.6	(X)	10.7	(X)
Hospitals	(Z)	3.1	(Z)	4.7	(Z)	5.4	(Z)	6.0	(Z)	7.2
Natural resources [3]	2.3	.6	3.3	.7	3.1	.8	3.0	.8	3.2	1.0
Sewerage and sanitation	(X)	1.2	(X)	2.0	(X)	2.2	(X)	2.5	(X)	2.9
Utility and liquor stores	(X)	8.6	(X)	10.9	(X)	11.7	(X)	13.3	(X)	15.1
Insurance trusts	42.0	10.7	60.2	16.5	70.6	18.4	80.5	20.1	85.8	33.4

X Not applicable.   Z Less than $50 million.
[1] Aggregates exclude duplicative transactions between State and local governments; see source.
[2] Includes other amounts not shown separately.   [3] Includes local parks and recreation.

No. 473. All Governments—General Expenditure, by Function and Level: 1970 to 1976

[In billions of dollars. Local government amounts are estimates subject to sampling variation; see source. Aggregates exclude duplicative transactions between levels of government. See also *Historical Statistics, Colonial Times to 1970*, series Y 605–631 and Y 682–704]

FUNCTION	1970 Federal	1970 State and local	1973 Federal	1973 State and local	1974 Federal	1974 State and local	1975 Federal	1975 State and local	1976 Federal	1976 State and local
All functions	166.9	[1]131.3	208.5	[1]181.2	221.4	[1]199.0	[1]253.5	[1]230.7	289.7	[1]256.8
Direct	143.7	131.3	167.2	181.2	178.6	198.7	203.9	229.7	220.6	255.6
Intergovernmental	23.3	(2)	41.3	(2)	42.9	[2].3	49.6	[2]1.0	69.1	[2]1.2
National defense and int'l relations	84.3	(X)	83.0	(X)	87.0	(X)	95.8	(X)	100.4	(X)
Postal service	7.7	(X)	9.6	(X)	11.2	(X)	12.7	(X)	13.7	(X)
Education	8.9	52.7	12.0	69.7	13.3	75.8	16.1	87.9	18.3	97.2
Highways	4.9	16.4	5.1	18.6	4.8	19.9	5.1	22.5	6.5	23.9
Public welfare	10.4	14.7	15.5	23.6	19.1	25.1	26.6	28.2	30.9	31.4
Health and hospitals	4.9	9.7	6.4	13.8	6.9	15.9	8.0	18.8	9.1	20.7
Natural resources	9.0	2.7	14.1	3.3	12.8	3.7	12.8	4.2	13.3	4.7
Housing and urban renewal	2.7	2.1	5.9	3.2	4.8	3.5	5.1	3.5	5.1	3.2
Space research and technology	3.7	(X)	3.3	(X)	3.3	(X)	3.3	(X)	3.7	(X)
Air transportation	1.2	1.0	2.0	1.4	1.9	1.3	2.0	1.4	2.2	1.5
Social insurance administration	1.7	.8	2.0	1.3	2.2	1.3	2.7	1.5	3.1	1.6
Interest on general debt	14.0	4.4	18.3	6.8	22.5	7.7	25.0	8.8	29.3	10.3
Other and combined	13.6	26.8	31.3	39.5	31.6	44.8	38.3	53.9	54.1	62.3

X Not applicable.   [1] Excludes duplicative transactions between State and local governments.
[2] State contributions to Federal government.

Source of tables 472 and 473: U.S. Bureau of the Census, *Governmental Finances*, series GF No. 5, annual.

No. 474. ALL GOVERNMENTS—TAX REVENUE, BY SOURCE AND LEVEL: 1950 TO 1976

[Prior to 1960, excludes Alaska and Hawaii. Local government amounts are estimates subject to sampling variation; see source. See also *Historical Statistics, Colonial Times to 1970,* series Y 507–512, Y 569–579, Y 657–662, Y 716–727, and Y 802–806]

SOURCE AND YEAR	ALL GOVERNMENT		FEDERAL		STATE AND LOCAL		ANNUAL PERCENT CHANGE [1]			PER CAPITA [2] (dollars)	
	Total (mil. dol.)	Percent of total	Total (mil. dol.)	Percent of all govt.	State (mil. dol.)	Local (mil. dol.)	Federal	State	Local	Federal	State and local
Total: [3]											
1950	51,100	100.0	35,186	68.9	7,930	7,984	3.6	8.5	10.0	232	105
1955	81,072	100.0	57,589	71.0	11,597	11,886	10.4	7.9	8.3	348	142
1960	113,120	100.0	77,003	68.1	18,036	18,081	6.0	9.2	8.8	428	201
1965	144,953	100.0	93,710	64.6	26,126	25,116	4.0	7.7	6.8	483	264
1970	232,877	100.0	146,082	62.7	47,962	38,833	9.3	12.9	9.1	719	427
1972	262,534	100.0	153,733	58.6	59,870	48,930	2.6	11.7	12.3	738	522
1973	286,132	100.0	165,030	57.7	68,069	53,032	7.3	13.7	8.4	786	577
1974	314,785	100.0	184,112	58.5	74,207	56,467	11.6	9.0	6.6	871	618
1975	331,435	100.0	189,970	57.3	80,155	61,310	3.2	8.0	8.5	892	664
1976	358,227	100.0	201,414	56.2	89,256	67,557	6.0	11.4	10.2	938	731
Individual income:											
1950	16,533	32.4	15,745	95.2	724	64	9.7	20.5	20.6	104	5
1955	29,984	37.0	28,747	95.9	1,094	143	12.8	8.6	17.4	174	7
1960	43,178	38.2	40,715	94.3	2,209	[4] 254	7.2	15.1	12.2	226	14
1965	52,882	36.5	48,792	92.3	3,657	[4] 433	3.7	10.6	11.3	252	21
1970	101,224	43.5	90,412	89.3	9,183	[4] 1,630	13.1	20.2	30.4	445	53
1972	109,974	41.9	94,737	86.1	12,996	[4] 2,241	2.4	19.0	17.3	455	73
1973	121,240	42.3	103,246	85.2	15,587	[4] 2,406	9.0	19.9	7.4	492	86
1974	138,443	43.9	118,952	85.9	17,078	[4] 2,413	15.2	9.6	.3	563	92
1975	143,840	43.4	122,386	85.1	18,819	[4] 2,635	2.9	10.2	9.2	574	101
1976	156,178	43.6	131,603	84.3	21,448	[4] 3,127	7.5	14.0	18.7	613	114
Corporation income: [3]											
1950	11,081	21.7	10,488	94.6	586	7	4.1	.1	(NA)	69	4
1955	18,604	22.9	17,861	96.0	737	7	11.2	4.7	–	108	5
1960	22,674	20.0	21,494	94.8	1,180	[4]	3.8	9.9	[4]	119	7
1965	27,390	18.9	25,461	93.0	1,929	[4]	3.4	10.3	[4]	131	10
1970	36,567	15.7	32,829	89.8	3,738	[4]	5.2	14.2	[4]	162	18
1972	36,582	13.9	32,166	87.9	4,416	[4]	–1.0	8.7	[4]	154	21
1973	41,578	14.5	36,153	87.0	5,425	[4]	12.4	22.8	[4]	172	26
1974	44,635	14.1	38,620	86.5	6,015	[4]	6.8	10.9	[4]	183	28
1975	47,263	14.3	40,621	85.9	6,642	[4]	5.2	10.4	[4]	191	31
1976	48,682	13.6	41,409	85.1	7,273	[4]	1.9	9.5	[4]	193	34
Sales, gross receipts: [5]											
1950	12,997	25.4	7,843	60.3	4,670	484	1.3	7.5	10.0	52	34
1955	17,221	21.2	9,578	55.6	6,864	779	4.1	8.0	10.0	58	46
1960	24,452	21.6	12,603	51.5	10,510	1,339	5.6	8.9	11.4	70	66
1965	32,904	22.7	15,786	48.0	15,059	2,059	4.6	7.5	9.0	81	88
1970	48,619	20.9	18,297	37.6	27,254	3,068	3.0	12.6	7.9	90	149
1972	57,589	21.9	20,101	34.9	33,250	4,238	4.8	10.5	18.7	97	180
1973	61,769	21.6	19,722	31.9	37,123	4,924	–1.9	11.6	16.2	94	200
1974	66,632	21.1	20,534	30.8	40,556	5,542	4.1	9.2	12.6	97	218
1975	70,905	21.4	21,090	29.7	43,346	6,468	2.7	6.9	16.7	99	234
1976	76,265	21.3	21,718	28.5	47,391	7,156	3.0	9.3	10.6	101	254
Property:											
1950	7,349	14.4	(X)	(X)	307	7,042	(X)	5.5	9.7	(X)	48
1955	10,735	13.2	(X)	(X)	412	10,323	(X)	6.1	8.0	(X)	65
1960	16,405	14.5	(X)	(X)	607	15,798	(X)	8.1	8.9	(X)	91
1965	22,583	15.6	(X)	(X)	766	21,817	(X)	4.8	6.7	(X)	117
1970	34,054	14.6	(X)	(X)	1,092	32,963	(X)	7.4	8.6	(X)	168
1972	42,133	16.0	(X)	(X)	1,257	40,876	(X)	7.3	11.4	(X)	202
1973	45,283	15.8	(X)	(X)	1,312	43,970	(X)	4.4	7.6	(X)	216
1974	47,705	15.1	(X)	(X)	1,301	46,404	(X)	–.8	5.6	(X)	226
1975	51,491	15.5	(X)	(X)	1,451	50,040	(X)	11.5	7.7	(X)	242
1976	57,001	15.9	(X)	(X)	2,118	54,884	(X)	46.0	9.7	(X)	266
Other taxes: [6]											
1950	3,140	6.1	1,110	35.4	1,643	387	5.5	10.7	(NA)	7	13
1955	4,527	5.6	1,402	31.0	2,490	634	4.8	8.7	10.4	8	19
1960	6,411	5.7	2,191	34.2	3,540	692	9.3	7.2	1.8	12	23
1965	9,191	6.3	3,670	39.9	4,715	807	10.9	6.0	3.1	19	28
1970	12,413	5.3	4,544	36.6	6,695	1,173	4.4	7.3	7.8	22	39
1972	16,256	6.2	6,729	41.4	7,951	1,575	21.7	9.0	15.9	32	46
1973	16,265	5.7	5,909	36.3	8,622	1,731	–12.2	8.4	9.9	28	49
1974	17,370	5.5	6,006	34.6	9,257	2,108	1.6	7.4	21.8	28	54
1975	17,936	5.4	5,873	32.7	9,897	2,166	–2.2	6.9	2.8	28	57
1976	20,101	5.6	6,684	33.3	11,026	2,390	13.8	11.4	10.3	31	63

- Represents zero.   NA Not available.
X Not applicable.
[1] Represents average for period of intervals shown here; for 1950, change from 1948. Minus sign (−) denotes decrease.
[2] See footnote 3, table 469.   [3] Federal includes excess profits tax, normal tax, and surtax.
[4] Corporation included with individual income.   [5] Federal taxes include customs.   [6] Includes licenses.

Source: U.S. Bureau of the Census, *Census of Governments: 1972,* vol. 4, No. 5, *Compendium of Government Finances,* and vol. 6, No. 4, *Historical Statistics on Governmental Finances and Employment;* and *Governmental Finances,* series GF No. 5, annual.

No. 475. All Governments—Expenditure for Capital Outlay: 1960 to 1976

[In millions of dollars. Local government amounts are estimates subject to sampling variation; see source. See also *Historical Statistics, Colonial Times to 1970*, series Y 523–524, Y 593–594, Y 673–674, Y 740–741, and Y 787–788]

YEAR AND FUNCTION	TOTAL CAPITAL OUTLAY					CONSTRUCTION EXPENDITURE ONLY				
	All governments	Federal	State and local			All governments	Federal	State and local		
			Total	State	Local			Total	State	Local
1960	31,946	16,842	15,104	6,607	8,497	15,832	3,480	12,352	5,509	6,843
1965	33,744	13,209	20,535	9,175	11,360	20,885	4,472	16,413	7,508	8,905
1970	47,519	17,869	29,650	13,295	16,355	28,402	4,150	24,252	11,185	13,067
1971	48,823	15,686	33,137	14,736	18,402	31,051	4,081	26,970	12,446	14,524
1972	55,053	20,816	34,237	15,283	18,953	32,908	4,801	28,107	13,022	15,085
1973	55,363	20,091	35,272	14,677	20,595	32,883	4,632	28,251	12,327	15,924
1974	57,250	19,166	38,084	15,417	22,667	35,651	5,109	30,542	12,655	17,887
1975	66,622	21,798	44,824	17,307	27,517	42,961	6,605	36,356	14,443	21,913
1976, total	71,631	25,100	46,531	18,009	28,522	45,223	6,924	38,299	15,285	23,014
National defense and international relations	18,158	18,158	(X)	(X)	(X)	2,810	2,810	(X)	(X)	(X)
Space research [1]	184	184	(X)	(X)	(X)	121	121	(X)	(X)	(X)
Education	10,114	3	10,111	3,164	6,947	7,484	(X)	7,484	2,249	5,235
Higher education	3,007	(X)	3,007	2,417	590	1,964	(X)	1,964	1,575	389
Local schools	6,547	(X)	6,547	190	6,357	5,019	(X)	5,019	174	4,845
Other	559	3	556	556	(X)	501	(X)	501	501	(X)
Highways	14,275	66	14,209	10,907	3,302	12,897	62	12,835	10,021	2,814
Natural resources	5,004	3,932	1,072	736	336	3,667	2,913	754	469	285
Health and hospitals	2,210	367	1,843	813	1,031	1,837	311	1,526	675	851
Sewerage	3,955	(X)	3,955	(X)	3,955	3,779	(X)	3,779	(X)	3,779
Local parks, recreation	1,314	(X)	1,314	(X)	1,314	940	(X)	940	(X)	940
Housing, urban renewal	2,208	810	1,398	217	1,180	1,070	(X)	1,070	217	853
Air transportation	1,090	288	802	208	594	850	201	649	186	462
Water transport [2]	633	283	350	105	245	580	276	304	89	215
Local utilities	5,355	(X)	5,355	(X)	5,355	4,441	(X)	4,441	(X)	4,441
All other	7,131	1,009	6,122	1,859	4,263	4,746	230	4,516	1,377	3,139

X Not applicable.   [1] Includes technology.   [2] Includes terminals.

Source: U.S. Bureau of the Census, *Census of Governments: 1972*, vol. 4, No. 5, *Compendium of Government Finances;* and *Governmental Finances*, series GF No. 5, annual.

No. 476. All Governments—Gross Fixed Capital Formation in Current and Constant (1972) Dollars: 1960 to 1976

[In billions of dollars, except percent. Minus sign (−) denotes decrease]

ITEM	1960	1965	1970	1971	1972	1973	1974	1975	1976
CURRENT DOLLARS									
Total	16.6	26.4	33.2	35.1	35.9	38.6	45.8	47.8	45.6
Average annual percent change [1]	.8	9.7	4.7	5.8	2.4	7.6	18.4	4.6	−4.8
Federal [2]	2.3	5.0	3.3	3.6	3.8	3.9	4.5	5.3	5.8
Structures	2.3	3.2	2.6	3.1	3.3	3.7	4.4	5.1	5.3
Durable equipment	(Z)	1.8	.8	.5	.4	.2	.1	.3	.5
Addendum: Military equipment and facilities	11.0	9.9	13.9	12.2	13.5	11.8	9.6	12.8	14.4
State and local	14.3	21.4	29.8	31.5	32.2	34.7	41.2	42.5	39.8
Structures [3]	12.7	19.0	25.8	27.0	27.2	29.1	34.7	35.5	32.5
Highways	5.6	7.9	10.3	11.0	10.7	10.7	12.3	10.9	9.8
Education	2.8	4.3	5.7	5.7	5.8	6.7	7.4	7.7	6.3
Sewer and water	1.5	2.5	2.7	2.8	3.1	3.5	4.8	6.6	6.9
Health care	.4	.4	.8	1.2	1.1	1.1	1.4	1.4	1.4
Airports and water terminals	.3	.4	.9	.7	.8	.8	1.0	1.0	.6
Durable equipment [3]	1.6	2.5	4.0	4.5	5.0	5.6	6.5	7.0	7.3
Education	.8	1.4	2.3	2.5	2.6	2.9	3.3	3.6	3.7
Highways	.2	.3	.4	.5	.5	.6	.6	.6	.6
Addendum: Government enterprises	3.4	5.0	7.0	7.1	7.7	8.5	10.6	12.1	11.3
CONSTANT (1972) DOLLARS									
Total	26.4	38.6	37.5	36.9	35.9	36.2	36.8	34.6	32.1
Average annual percent change [1]	1.6	7.9	−.5	−1.6	−2.7	.7	1.6	−5.9	−7.3
Federal	3.6	7.0	3.7	3.8	3.8	3.8	3.8	3.9	4.1
State and local	22.9	31.6	33.8	33.2	32.2	32.4	33.0	30.7	28.0

Z Less than $50 million.   [1] Represents average for period of intervals shown; for 1960, change from 1959.   [2] Excludes military facilities, military equipment, and net purchases of used structures by defense agencies.   [3] Includes other items not shown separately.

Source: U.S. Bureau of Economic Analysis, *The National Income and Product Accounts of the United States 1929–74; Survey of Current Business*, July 1977; and unpublished data.

No. 477. ALL GOVERNMENTS—REVENUE AND EXPENDITURE, BY LEVEL OF GOVERNMENT: 1976

[Local government amounts are estimates subject to sampling variation; see source. See also *Historical Statistics, Colonial Times to 1970*, series Y 505–637 and Y 652–848]

SOURCE OF REVENUE AND TYPE OF EXPENDITURE	All governments (mil. dol.)	Federal (mil. dol.)	State (mil. dol.)	Local (mil. dol.)	PERCENT		PER CAPITA [1] (dol.)	
					Federal	State and local	Federal	State and local
Revenue	[2]572,615	324,858	185,213	178,338	100.0	100.0	1,513	[2]1,417
Intergovernmental revenue	(2)	1,331	44,717	69,746	.4	18.2	6	259
Revenue from own sources	572,615	323,527	140,496	108,592	99.6	81.8	1,507	1,160
General revenue from own sources	438,299	237,713	107,401	93,186	73.2	65.8	1,107	934
Percent of total revenue	76.5	73.2	58.0	52.3	(X)	(X)	73.2	65.9
Taxes [3]	358,227	201,414	89,256	67,557	62.0	51.5	938	731
Property	57,001	(X)	2,118	54,884	(X)	18.7	(X)	266
Individual income	156,178	131,603	21,448	3,127	40.5	8.1	613	114
Corporation income	48,682	41,409	7,273	(4)	12.7	2.4	193	34
Sales and gross receipts	76,265	21,718	47,391	7,156	6.7	17.9	101	254
Customs duties	4,496	4,496	(X)	(X)	1.4	(X)	21	(X)
General sales and gross receipts	32,044	(X)	27,333	4,711	(X)	10.5	(X)	149
Selective sales and gross receipts [3]	39,724	17,222	20,058	2,445	5.3	7.4	80	105
Motor fuel	13,364	4,636	8,660	68	1.4	2.9	22	41
Alcoholic beverages	7,582	5,413	2,057	112	1.7	.7	25	10
Tobacco products	6,069	2,488	3,462	119	.8	1.2	12	17
Public utilities	6,354	2,729	2,060	1,564	.8	1.2	13	17
Motor vehicle and operators' licenses	4,677	(X)	4,356	320	(X)	1.5	(X)	22
Death and gift	6,729	5,216	1,513	(NA)	1.6	.5	24	7
Charges and misc. general revenue [3]	80,073	36,299	18,145	25,628	11.2	14.4	169	204
Current charges [3]	51,852	22,532	11,652	17,668	6.9	9.6	105	137
National defense and international relations	6,008	6,008	(X)	(X)	1.8	(X)	28	(X)
Postal service	10,656	10,656	(X)	(X)	3.3	(X)	50	(X)
Education [3]	10,479	53	6,347	4,079	(Z)	3.4	(Z)	49
School lunch sales	1,616	(X)	(X)	1,616	(X)	.5	(X)	8
Higher education	7,009	(X)	6,212	887	(X)	2.3	(X)	33
Natural resources	3,597	3,211	359	28	1.0	.1	15	2
Hospitals	7,206	40	2,116	5,051	(Z)	2.4	(Z)	33
Sewerage and sanitation	2,902	(X)	(X)	2,902	(X)	1.0	(X)	14
Local parks and recreation	568	(X)	(X)	568	(X)	.2	(X)	3
Housing and urban renewal	1,401	531	28	842	.2	.3	2	4
Air transportation	1,124	12	109	1,002	(Z)	.4	(Z)	5
Water transport and terminals	773	269	144	360	.1	.2	1	2
Special assessments	879	(X)	23	856	(X)	.3	(X)	4
Sale of property	1,022	696	73	253	.2	.1	3	2
Interest earnings	10,753	3,780	3,387	3,587	1.2	2.3	18	32
Utility revenue	12,573	(X)	(X)	12,573	(X)	4.1	(X)	59
Liquor stores revenue	2,553	(X)	2,196	357	(X)	.8	(X)	12
Insurance trust revenue	119,190	85,814	30,900	2,477	26.4	11.0	400	155
Expenditure	[2]626,116	391,085	181,966	[2]181,802	100.0	100.0	1,822	[2]1,422
Intergovernmental expenditure	(2)	69,057	57,858	1,822	17.7	.4	322	6
General revenue sharing	6,238	6,238	(X)	1,822	1.6	(X)	29	(X)
Direct expenditure	626,116	322,028	124,108	179,980	82.3	99.6	1,500	1,417
General expenditure	476,146	220,595	95,832	159,720	56.4	83.7	1,028	1,191
Percent of total expenditure	76.0	56.4	52.7	87.9	(X)	(X)	56.4	83.8
Utility expenditure	17,451	(X)	(X)	17,451	(X)	5.7	(X)	81
Liquor stores expenditure	2,091	(X)	1,781	310	(X)	.7	(X)	10
Insurance trust expenditure	130,427	101,433	26,495	2,499	25.9	9.5	473	135
By character and object:								
Current operation	335,331	130,944	68,175	136,212	33.5	67.0	610	952
Capital outlay	71,631	25,100	18,009	28,522	6.4	15.2	117	217
Construction	45,223	6,924	15,285	23,014	1.8	12.5	32	178
Equipment	22,004	16,629	1,450	3,925	4.3	1.8	77	25
Land and existing structures	4,404	1,547	1,274	1,583	.4	.9	7	13
Assistance and subsidies	47,739	35,245	7,290	5,205	9.0	4.1	164	58
Interest on debt	40,987	29,306	4,140	7,542	7.5	3.8	137	54
Insurance benefits and repayments	130,427	101,433	26,495	2,499	25.9	9.5	473	135
Expenditure for personal services	186,826	[5]70,360	32,856	83,610	18.0	38.2	328	543

NA Not available.   X Not applicable.   Z Less than $.50 or .05 percent.
[1] Based on estimated resident population as of July 1, 1976.
[2] Aggregates exclude duplicative transactions between levels of government; see source.
[3] Includes amounts not shown separately.   [4] Minor amount included in individual income tax.
[5] Includes pay and allowances of military personnel.

Source: U.S. Bureau of the Census, *Governmental Finances in 1975–76*, series GF 76, No. 5.

No. 478. Federal Aid to State and Local Governments: 1965 to 1978

[In millions of dollars, except percent. For years ending June 30 except, beginning 1977, ending Sept. 30. Comprises Federal funds and trust funds. See *Historical Statistics, Colonial Times to 1970*, series Y 638–651, for related data]

TYPE OF AID, FUNCTION, AND MAJOR PROGRAM	1965	1970	1972	1973	1974	1975	1976	1977	1978, est.
Grant-in-aid shared revenue	10,904	24,018	34,372	41,832	43,308	49,723	59,037	68,396	80,288
National defense	33	37	45	56	64	74	89	96	90
International affairs and finance	4	5	5	6	7	(1)	(1)	(1)	(1)
Natural resources and environment	182	429	758	1,066	1,994	2,436	3,026	4,189	4,895
Environmental Protection Agency	75	194	460	745	1,623	2,025	2,563	3,724	4,379
Other	107	235	298	321	371	411	463	465	516
Energy	9	25	30	32	36	43	56	74	270
Agriculture	517	603	494	484	480	404	425	371	391
Transportation	4,100	4,539	5,065	5,350	5,279	5,864	7,981	8,299	9,561
Airports	71	83	106	232	243	292	269	335	540
Highways	4,008	4,332	4,678	4,731	4,479	4,702	6,272	6,027	6,830
Railroads	–	–	–	–	–	(z)	2	22	69
Urban mass transit	11	105	179	291	348	688	1,262	1,615	1,909
Other	10	19	102	96	209	182	176	300	213
Commerce and housing credit	(z)	6	2	8	9	8	10	18	34
Community and regional development	689	2,428	3,181	3,218	3,222	2,842	3,445	4,496	6,700
Appalachian development	–	184	235	260	286	306	315	246	303
Community development block grants	(X)	(X)	(X)	(X)	(X)	38	983	2,089	2,584
Urban renewal	281	1,054	1,218	1,010	1,205	1,374	1,166	899	650
Other	408	1,190	1,728	1,948	1,731	1,124	981	1,262	3,163
Education, employment, training, and social services	981	5,745	8,775	8,828	8,721	12,131	14,141	15,753	20,812
Elementary and secondary education	81	1,470	1,883	1,819	1,665	2,276	2,159	2,340	2,556
School assistance in federally affected areas	341	622	602	519	530	577	558	719	744
Occupational, vocational, adult education	132	285	501	592	569	653	748	692	739
Library resources	26	105	68	85	137	210	137	160	192
Work incentives	–	81	163	266	323	304	299	348	352
Human development	2 102	2 441	807	1,038	1,240	1,596	1,594	1,820	1,973
Comprehensive manpower assistance	22	421	1,156	987	1,137	2,504	2,853	2,940	4,151
Temporary employment assistance	(X)	(X)	(X)	(X)	(X)	319	1,887	2,340	4,765
Social services	–	574	1,930	1,613	1,471	2,047	2,251	2,534	3,246
Other	277	1,746	1,665	1,909	1,649	1,675	1,655	1,860	2,094
Health	624	3,850	5,980	6,002	7,322	8,810	10,914	12,104	12,875
Alcohol, drug abuse, and mental health	(3)	(3)	(3)	319	302	590	535	471	564
Medicaid	272	2,727	4,601	4,600	5,818	6,840	8,568	9,876	10,846
Other	352	1,123	1,379	1,083	1,202	1,380	1,811	1,757	1,465
Income security	3,530	5,813	9,113	8,947	8,682	9,279	10,875	12,613	13,985
Public assistance	2,787	4,142	6,559	5,923	5,423	5,121	5,849	6,351	6,711
Food stamps—Administration 4	32	559	27	31	48	136	267	271	296
Child nutrition and special milk programs	263	379	708	685	793	1,565	1,878	2,775	2,794
Housing assistance	206	436	750	1,053	1,116	1,326	1,588	1,815	2,469
Other	242	297	1,069	1,255	1,302	1,131	1,293	1,401	1,715
Veterans benefits and services	8	18	19	20	26	32	52	79	85
Administration of justice	–	42	322	527	639	725	795	713	649
General government	13	49	92	76	95	103	128	154	197
General purpose fiscal assistance	214	430	490	7,211	6,730	6,971	7,102	9,438	9,743
General revenue sharing	(X)	(X)	(X)	6,636	6,106	6,130	6,243	6,758	6,827
Other	214	430	490	575	624	841	859	2,680	2,916
PERCENT DISTRIBUTION									
Total	100.0	100.0	100.0	100.0	100.0	100.0	100.0	100.0	100.0
Natural resources and environment	1.7	1.8	2.2	2.5	4.6	4.9	5.1	6.1	6.1
Energy	–	.1	.1	.1	.1	.1	.1	.1	.3
Agriculture	4.7	2.5	1.4	1.2	1.1	.8	.7	.5	.5
Transportation	37.6	18.9	14.7	12.8	12.2	11.8	13.5	12.1	11.9
Community and regional development	6.3	10.1	9.2	7.7	7.4	5.7	5.8	6.6	8.3
Education, employment, training, and social services	9.0	23.9	25.5	21.1	20.1	24.4	23.9	23.0	25.9
Health	5.7	16.0	17.4	14.3	16.9	17.7	18.5	17.7	16.0
Income security	32.4	24.2	26.5	21.4	20.0	18.7	18.4	18.4	17.4
Administration of justice	–	.2	.9	1.3	1.5	1.5	1.3	1.0	.8
General purpose fiscal assistance	2.0	1.8	1.4	17.2	15.5	14.0	12.0	13.8	12.1
Other	.6	.5	.7	.4	.6	.4	.7	.7	.7

– Represents zero.　　X Not applicable.　　Z Less than $500,000.　　1 Funds for this function now provided to a private institution.　　2 Excludes Office of Child Development.　　3 Prior to 1973 included in "Other" health grants.　　4 Beginning 1972, this program treated as a direct Federal program in President's Budget. Represents administration grants only.

Source: U.S. Office of Management and Budget, *Special Analyses, Budget of the United States Government*, annual.

No. 479. FEDERAL AID TO STATE AND LOCAL GOVERNMENTS—SELECTED PROGRAMS, TOTAL, 1970 TO 1977, AND BY STATES AND OTHER AREAS, 1977

[In millions of dollars, except per capita. Through 1976, for years ending June 30, except as noted; beginning 1977, ending Sept. 30]

YEAR, AND STATE OR OTHER AREA	Total, Federal aid [1]	Federal aid, per capita [2] (dol.)	SOCIAL AND REHABILITATION SERVICE		DEPARTMENT OF—		OE [4] elementary and secondary education	EPA [5] waste treatment facilities construction	HUD [6]		ETA [7] comprehensive manpower act
			Public assistance, total [3]	Medicaid	Treasury, general revenue sharing	Transportation, highway fund			Low rent public housing	Community development block grants	
1970, total	24,194	(NA)	7,445	(X)	(X)	4,300	1,469.5	(NA)	434.5	(X)	420.1
1972, total	35,941	(NA)	13,090	(X)	(X)	4,562	1,882.9	413.4	749.1	(X)	1,152.8
1973, total	43,964	(NA)	11,937	4,596	6,636	4,605	1,819.1	684.3	1,049.0	(X)	972.0
1974, total	46,040	(NA)	12,714	5,818	6,106	4,361	1,674.8	1,552.5	1,127.3	(X)	1,146.4
1975, total	49,723	(NA)	14,008	6,840	6,130	4,573	2,276.2	1,937.6	1,326.4	38.1	2,504.2
1976, total	59,112	(NA)	16,659	8,568	6,238	6,482	2,130.2	2,428.5	1,559.2	982.8	2,874.1
TQ [8]	16,444	(NA)	4,400	2,454	1,588	1,716	699.6	919.4	646.1	439.0	974.7
1977, total	68,437	(NA)	18,750	9,860	6,758	6,005	2,339.1	3,529.6	1,984.3	2,088.8	2,939.7
U.S.	66,083	305	18,687	9,828	6,758	5,941	2,302.1	3,509.7	1,877.3	2,036.2	2,861.4
Ala.	1,121	304	254	147	107	155	48.5	32.4	43.0	40.5	43.5
Alaska	382	939	32	11	13	120	6.4	16.9	8.5	4.8	6.1
Ariz.	648	282	47	–	64	107	50.3	16.9	20.0	14.8	35.0
Ark.	639	298	171	112	70	72	30.3	19.7	18.0	24.2	28.0
Calif.	6,814	311	2,477	1,190	709	349	162.1	256.6	147.7	159.5	341.5
Colo.	715	273	147	68	73	127	21.7	20.7	13.4	18.7	24.9
Conn.	895	288	225	105	84	51	24.8	71.6	34.3	51.3	50.2
Del.	187	321	34	12	21	18	6.3	21.2	5.5	4.0	8.8
D.C.	942	1,365	120	63	28	26	35.2	15.1	24.7	27.6	18.4
Fla.	1,988	235	356	148	202	255	82.6	162.4	63.1	51.5	128.4
Ga.	1,861	369	474	291	141	127	180.5	41.9	61.3	48.2	67.1
Hawaii	400	447	87	36	31	57	7.7	39.1	7.4	3.9	12.4
Idaho	287	335	51	25	25	69	6.4	6.5	2.1	5.8	10.7
Ill.	3,202	285	959	491	454	280	111.7	182.8	115.8	66.6	127.9
Ind.	1,095	205	245	151	141	82	31.9	75.2	33.2	45.8	67.0
Iowa	714	248	189	95	81	101	28.1	45.1	6.8	25.0	20.3
Kans.	549	236	158	85	59	70	19.8	22.3	11.1	21.7	14.0
Ky.	1,018	294	292	140	111	97	35.0	25.1	29.6	28.6	43.8
La.	1,237	315	327	200	147	180	53.6	44.0	39.9	23.8	46.9
Maine	412	380	116	69	41	34	9.5	50.8	8.6	11.6	16.3
Md.	1,245	301	284	148	133	139	44.7	83.6	35.6	45.9	45.2
Mass.	2,080	360	663	363	210	173	44.8	86.6	91.3	83.7	101.7
Mich.	2,915	319	970	457	273	217	90.9	201.7	32.2	89.8	155.1
Minn.	1,224	308	374	220	133	123	35.1	78.7	37.8	46.6	45.6
Miss.	801	335	165	114	101	84	45.8	23.1	13.8	33.1	29.2
Mo.	1,142	238	264	114	125	149	36.5	68.2	35.9	48.7	50.8
Mont.	348	457	50	29	24	96	8.3	7.3	2.5	6.6	11.0
Nebr.	368	236	69	48	42	58	22.6	19.7	10.0	10.9	12.2
Nev.	206	325	21	10	16	53	3.5	5.1	6.3	1.7	10.4
N.H.	234	276	53	30	22	38	6.1	22.9	7.8	4.3	9.0
N.J.	2,200	300	585	252	208	92	64.9	214.9	94.5	68.6	120.3
N. Mex.	449	377	72	39	43	48	22.5	7.8	11.8	18.7	17.0
N.Y.	7,447	415	2,919	1,716	750	260	181.9	554.2	234.4	202.7	275.9
N.C.	1,512	274	349	183	166	165	61.3	34.9	49.1	51.9	65.6
N. Dak.	224	343	38	21	18	46	8.1	2.7	6.8	6.9	5.5
Ohio	2,510	235	650	295	268	180	69.5	188.9	83.7	101.6	146.5
Okla.	782	278	228	150	73	65	24.0	27.3	31.5	32.7	27.4
Oreg.	836	352	211	89	72	86	23.6	45.7	16.6	13.8	39.4
Pa.	3,628	308	1,138	535	350	247	95.4	179.5	118.3	162.6	156.2
R.I.	358	383	115	67	29	16	10.8	27.7	14.5	16.4	17.4
S.C.	803	279	185	110	93	57	39.6	31.2	12.1	23.1	41.5
S. Dak.	240	348	49	23	21	45	8.9	5.0	6.8	9.7	3.9
Tenn.	1,189	277	278	164	123	138	42.6	41.1	42.1	38.2	49.8
Tex.	2,885	225	766	487	332	272	156.2	108.0	96.4	107.0	107.2
Utah	388	306	80	36	37	79	8.2	17.1	3.8	6.4	13.8
Vt.	223	462	59	33	19	30	5.5	9.3	4.3	3.5	7.1
Va.	1,311	255	293	148	143	206	45.9	98.3	27.7	45.8	49.5
Wash.	1,119	306	271	132	100	143	30.9	42.5	21.3	25.2	57.7
W. Va.	631	339	114	50	61	117	18.7	17.9	10.2	19.2	24.5
Wis.	1,493	321	604	321	161	94	90.4	88.8	22.9	27.0	50.9
Wyo.	186	458	13	5	11	50	3.5	2.9	1.1	2.8	2.2
Puerto Rico	939	(NA)	59	30	–	13	32.4	12.3	48.2	49.0	71.7
Virgin Islands	235	(NA)	4	2	–	–	.8	2.2	7.8	–	2.7
Other areas [9]	180	(NA)	4	–	–	–	3.8	5.4	1.8	3.3	3.9

- Represents zero. NA Not available. X Not applicable. [1] Includes amounts not shown separately. [2] Based on Bureau of the Census estimated resident population as of July 1, 1977, including Armed Forces stationed in area. [3] Includes child welfare services, maintenance assistance, social services, and State and local training not shown separately. [4] Office of Education. [5] Environmental Protection Agency. [6] Department of Housing and Urban Development. [7] Employment and Training Administration. [8] Transition quarter, July–Sept. [9] American Samoa, Guam, and Trust Territory of the Pacific Islands.

Source: U.S. Dept. of the Treasury, Federal Aid to States, annual.

No. 480. STATE AND LOCAL GOVERNMENTS—SUMMARY OF FINANCES: 1960 TO 1976

[In millions of dollars, except percent. Local government amounts are estimates subject to sampling variations; see source. See also *Historical Statistics, Colonial Times to 1970*, series Y 652–709]

SOURCE OF REVENUE AND TYPE OF EXPENDITURE	1960	1965	1970	1972	1973	1974	1975	1976 Total	1976 Percent
Revenue	60,277	87,777	150,106	189,724	217,616	237,856	261,592	304,678	100.0
From Federal Government [1]	6,974	11,029	21,857	31,253	39,256	41,320	47,034	55,589	18.2
Public welfare	2,070	3,098	7,574	12,358	13,771	13,432	14,357	17,000	5.6
Highways	2,905	3,997	4,608	4,918	4,705	4,552	5,320	6,339	2.1
Education	950	1,677	5,844	7,044	7,571	7,867	9,078	9,871	3.2
Employment security adminis..	325	413	664	1,152	1,281	1,299	1,525	1,664	.5
Other and unallocable	724	1,844	3,167	5,781	11,927	14,670	16,754	20,715	6.8
From State and local sources	53,302	76,748	128,248	158,471	178,360	196,036	214,558	249,089	81.8
General, net intergovernmental	43,530	62,971	108,898	135,100	150,958	165,850	181,137	200,586	65.8
Taxes	36,117	51,243	86,795	108,801	121,102	130,673	141,465	156,813	51.5
Property	16,405	22,583	34,054	42,133	45,283	47,705	51,491	57,001	18.7
Sales and gross receipts	11,849	17,118	30,322	37,488	42,047	46,098	49,815	54,547	17.9
Individual income	2,463	4,090	10,812	15,237	17,994	19,491	21,454	24,575	8.1
Corporation income	1,180	1,929	3,738	4,416	5,425	6,015	6,642	7,273	2.4
Other	4,220	5,521	7,868	9,527	10,354	11,364	12,063	13,417	4.4
Charges and miscellaneous	7,414	11,729	22,103	26,299	29,856	35,177	39,672	43,774	14.4
Utility and liquor stores	4,877	6,355	8,614	9,775	10,898	11,747	13,335	15,126	5.0
Water supply system	1,529	2,004	2,687	3,165	3,463	3,712	4,142	4,463	1.5
Electric power system	1,307	1,833	2,385	2,912	3,355	3,763	4,689	5,819	1.9
Transit system	581	776	1,135	1,235	1,267	1,366	1,411	1,566	.5
Gas supply system	196	295	401	475	536	551	625	725	.2
Liquor stores	1,264	1,447	2,006	2,188	2,276	2,355	2,468	2,553	.8
Insurance trust revenue [2]	4,896	7,422	10,736	13,398	16,504	18,439	20,086	33,376	11.0
Employee retirement	2,099	3,423	6,493	8,438	10,064	10,900	12,354	14,533	4.8
Unemployment compensation	2,323	3,244	3,101	3,601	4,964	5,729	5,734	16,575	5.4
Direct expenditure	60,999	86,554	148,052	188,825	205,336	225,691	265,508	304,088	100.0
By function:									
Direct general expenditure [2]	51,876	74,546	131,332	166,873	181,227	198,618	229,747	255,551	84.0
Education [2]	18,719	28,563	52,718	64,886	69,714	75,833	87,858	97,216	32.0
Higher education [3]	3,202	5,863	12,924	15,946	17,370	18,884	21,702	24,304	8.0
Local schools	15,166	21,966	37,461	45,658	48,789	53,059	61,485	67,674	22.3
Highways	9,428	12,221	16,427	19,010	18,615	19,946	22,528	23,907	7.9
Public welfare	4,404	6,315	14,679	21,070	23,582	24,745	27,191	31,435	10.3
Health	559	836	1,806	2,574	2,732	3,452	4,414	4,960	1.6
Hospitals	3,235	4,525	7,863	10,293	11,112	12,493	14,432	15,726	5.2
Police protection	1,857	2,549	4,494	5,976	6,710	7,289	8,526	9,531	3.1
Local fire protection	995	1,306	2,024	2,577	2,770	3,037	3,522	3,898	1.3
Natural resources	1,189	1,730	2,732	3,110	3,278	3,661	4,223	4,662	1.5
Sanitation and sewerage	1,727	2,360	3,413	4,729	5,322	5,995	7,438	8,239	2.7
Housing and urban renewal	858	1,250	2,138	2,781	3,165	3,461	3,460	3,151	1.0
Local parks and recreation	770	1,104	1,888	2,323	2,561	2,951	3,462	3,864	1.2
Financial administration	} 2,113	{ 1,267	2,030	2,480	2,811	3,165	3,594	3,960	1.3
General control		1,506	2,652	3,407	3,841	4,371	5,046	5,711	1.9
Interest on general debt [4]	1,670	2,490	4,374	5,963	6,785	7,666	8,782	10,269	3.4
Utility and liquor stores [4]	5,088	7,058	9,447	11,414	13,035	14,406	17,285	19,542	6.4
Water supply system	1,881	2,505	3,211	3,732	4,084	4,669	5,440	5,929	1.9
Electric power system	1,244	1,983	2,486	3,346	3,761	4,152	5,280	6,429	2.1
Transit system	750	1,127	1,753	2,186	2,865	3,161	3,977	4,432	1.5
Gas supply system	191	272	370	433	493	505	580	661	.2
Liquor stores	1,022	1,172	1,627	1,717	1,831	1,919	2,009	2,091	.7
Insurance trust expenditure [2]	4,031	4,950	7,273	10,538	11,074	12,667	18,475	28,994	9.5
Employee retirement	1,265	2,298	3,629	4,757	5,824	6,639	7,443	8,422	2.8
Unemployment compensation	2,364	2,008	2,723	4,741	4,081	4,703	9,577	18,942	6.2
By character and object:									
Current operation	36,318	53,929	97,915	125,630	138,974	154,810	180,976	204,387	67.0
Capital outlay	15,104	20,535	29,650	34,237	35,272	38,084	44,824	46,531	15.2
Construction	12,352	16,413	24,252	28,107	28,251	30,542	36,356	38,299	12.5
Land and existing structures..	1,560	2,471	2,631	3,012	3,279	3,350	3,367	2,857	.9
Equipment	1,192	1,652	2,768	3,118	3,741	4,192	5,101	5,375	1.8
Assistance and subsidies	3,518	4,127	8,090	11,527	12,187	11,290	11,146	12,494	4.1
Interest on debt (gen. and util.)	2,028	3,012	5,123	6,893	7,828	8,840	10,087	11,681	3.8
Insur. benefits and repayments.	4,031	4,950	7,273	10,538	11,074	12,667	18,475	28,994	9.5
Expenditure for personal services	*24,445*	*36,095*	*62,998*	*78,679*	*86,042*	*94,054*	*106,168*	*116,466*	*38.1*
Debt outstanding, end of year	69,955	99,512	143,570	174,502	188,485	206,616	221,256	240,086	100.0
Long-term	66,801	94,204	131,415	158,781	172,605	189,953	201,470	221,309	92.2
Short-term	3,154	5,309	12,155	15,722	15,879	16,663	19,786	18,777	7.8
Net change, end of year	*5,845*	*7,290*	*10,022*	*15,675*	*13,983*	*18,131*	*14,608*	*18,862*	(X)

X Not applicable. [1] Beginning 1972, based on estimates; prior years based on Federal expenditures. [2] Includes amounts not shown separately. [3] State institutions. [4] Interest on utility debt included in "utility expenditure." For total expenditure for interest on debt, see "Interest on debt (general and utility)," below.

Source: U.S. Bureau of the Census, *Census of Governments: 1972*, vol. 6, No. 4, *Historical Statistics on Governmental Finances and Employment;* and *Governmental Finances*, series GF No. 5, annual.

No. 481. STATE AND LOCAL GOVERNMENT RECEIPTS AND EXPENDITURES IN THE NATIONAL INCOME ACCOUNTS: 1960 TO 1977

[In billions of dollars. Includes transactions of trust accounts. For explanation of national income, see text, p. 437]

ITEM	1960	1965	1970	1971	1972	1973	1974	1975	1976	1977
Receipts	49.9	75.1	134.9	152.6	177.4	193.5	210.4	235.7	264.7	294.5
Personal tax and nontax receipts	6.7	10.9	23.1	26.4	33.0	36.1	39.2	43.4	49.6	56.8
Income taxes	2.5	4.4	11.1	12.7	17.5	19.1	20.6	22.8	26.8	31.7
Nontaxes	2.0	3.5	7.7	9.1	10.5	11.5	12.8	14.4	16.0	17.5
Other	2.3	3.0	4.3	4.6	5.1	5.5	5.8	6.2	6.8	7.6
Corporate profits tax accruals	1.2	2.0	3.7	4.2	5.0	5.7	6.5	7.1	8.9	9.7
Indirect business tax and nontax accruals	32.0	46.1	74.7	83.1	91.0	99.0	106.9	114.7	127.1	140.3
Sales taxes	12.2	18.2	31.5	35.3	39.6	44.0	48.0	51.4	57.3	63.8
Property taxes	16.2	23.2	36.5	40.3	43.0	46.0	48.7	52.3	57.6	62.8
Other	3.6	4.7	6.7	7.5	8.5	9.0	10.1	11.0	12.3	13.7
Contributions for social insurance	3.4	5.0	9.0	9.9	10.8	12.1	13.9	15.9	18.1	20.1
Federal grants-in-aid	6.5	11.1	24.4	29.0	37.5	40.6	43.9	54.6	61.0	67.6
Expenditures [1]	49.8	75.1	132.2	148.9	163.7	180.5	202.8	229.8	246.2	265.3
Purchases of goods and services	46.5	71.1	123.2	137.5	151.0	167.3	191.5	215.6	231.2	249.5
Compensation of employees	25.5	39.3	70.0	78.5	87.3	97.1	106.5	119.2	129.2	139.4
Other	21.1	31.8	53.3	59.0	63.7	70.2	85.1	96.4	102.0	110.2
Transfer payments to persons	5.4	7.3	14.6	17.2	18.9	20.3	20.5	23.8	25.9	28.0
Net interest and subsidies [2]	−2.1	−3.3	−5.6	−5.6	−6.3	−7.3	−9.1	−9.7	−10.9	−12.3
Surplus or deficit (−)	.1	-	2.8	3.7	13.7	13.0	7.6	5.9	18.4	29.2

- Represents zero.
[1] Includes wage accruals less disbursements of $170 million in 1971, −$150 million in 1972, and −$20 million in 1973, not shown separately. [2] Less current surplus of government enterprises.

Source: U.S. Bureau of Economic Analysis, *The National Income and Product Accounts of the United States, 1929–74*, and *Survey of Current Business*, July 1977 and February 1978.

No. 482. STATE AND LOCAL GOVERNMENTS—GENERAL REVENUES AND DIRECT GENERAL EXPENDITURES: 1960 TO 1976

[See *Historical Statistics, Colonial Times to 1970*, series Y 652–709, for totals]

ITEM	1960	1965	1970	1971	1972	1973	1974	1975	1976
General revenue _____ bil. dol	50.5	74.0	130.8	144.9	166.4	190.2	207.7	228.2	256.2
Percent of total:									
From Federal Government	13.8	14.9	16.7	18.0	18.8	20.6	20.1	20.6	21.7
Taxes	71.5	69.2	66.4	65.5	65.4	63.7	62.9	62.0	61.2
Property	32.5	30.5	26.0	26.1	25.3	23.8	23.0	22.6	22.3
Sales and gross receipts	23.5	23.1	23.2	22.9	22.5	22.1	22.2	21.8	21.3
Individual income	4.9	5.5	8.3	8.2	9.2	9.5	9.4	9.4	9.6
Other	10.7	10.1	8.9	8.3	8.4	8.3	8.4	8.2	8.1
Charges and miscellaneous	14.7	15.9	16.9	16.4	15.8	15.7	16.9	17.4	17.1
Per capita, total [1]	$281	$382	$643	$703	$799	$906	$983	$1,071	$1,194
From Federal Government	39	57	108	127	150	187	198	221	259
Taxes	201	264	427	460	522	577	618	664	731
Property tax	91	117	168	184	202	216	226	242	266
Charges and miscellaneous	41	61	109	115	126	142	166	186	204
Direct gen'l expenditure __ bil. dol	51.9	74.5	131.3	150.7	166.9	181.2	198.6	229.7	255.6
Percent of total:									
Education	36.1	38.3	40.1	39.4	38.9	38.5	38.2	38.2	38.0
Highways	18.2	16.4	12.5	12.0	11.4	10.3	10.0	9.8	9.4
Public welfare	8.5	8.5	11.2	12.1	12.6	13.0	12.5	11.8	12.3
Health and hospitals	7.5	7.2	7.4	7.4	7.7	7.6	8.0	8.2	8.1
Police protection and correction	3.6	4.7	4.7	4.7	4.8	5.0	5.1	5.2	5.2
Natural resources	2.3	2.3	2.1	2.0	1.9	1.8	1.8	1.8	1.8
Sanitation and sewerage	3.3	3.2	2.6	2.7	2.8	2.9	3.0	3.2	3.2
Housing and urban renewal	1.7	1.7	1.6	1.7	1.7	1.7	1.7	1.5	1.2
Interest on general debt	3.2	3.3	3.3	3.4	3.6	3.7	3.9	3.8	4.0
All other [2]	15.8	14.4	14.5	14.5	14.6	15.4	15.8	16.5	16.8
Per capita, total [1]	$288	$385	$646	$731	$801	$864	$940	$1,087	$1,191
Education	104	147	259	288	312	332	359	416	453
Highways	52	63	81	88	91	89	94	107	111
Public welfare	24	33	72	88	101	112	117	129	146
Health and hospitals	21	28	48	54	62	66	75	89	96
Police protection and correction	10	18	30	34	39	43	48	56	62
Natural resources	7	9	13	15	15	16	17	20	22
Sanitation and sewerage	10	12	17	20	23	25	28	35	38
Housing and urban renewal	5	6	11	12	13	15	16	16	15
Interest on general debt	9	13	22	25	29	32	36	42	48
All other [2]	45	56	94	106	117	133	148	177	199

[1] See footnote 3, table 469.
[2] Includes fire protection, financial administration, and general control, as well as miscellaneous lesser functions.

Source: U.S. Bureau of the Census, *Census of Governments: 1972*, vol. 6, No. 4, *Historical Statistics on Government Finances and Employment;* and *Governmental Finances*, series GF No. 5, annual.

No. 483. State and Local Governments—General Revenue, Origin and Allocation, by States: 1976

[Local government amounts are estimates subject to sampling variation; see source]

STATE	Total general revenue (mil. dol.)	ORIGINATING LEVEL OF GOVERNMENT [1]						FINAL RECIPIENT LEVEL [2]			
		Revenue (mil. dol.)			Percent			Revenue (mil. dol.)		Percent	
		Federal	State	Local	Federal	State	Local	State	Local	State	Local
U.S.	256,176	55,589	107,401	93,186	21.7	41.9	36.4	95,949	160,227	37.5	62.5
Ala	3,359	943	1,554	862	28.1	46.3	25.7	1,705	1,654	50.8	49.2
Alaska	1,279	308	762	210	24.1	59.5	16.4	849	430	66.4	33.6
Ariz	2,591	489	1,203	899	18.9	46.4	34.7	922	1,670	35.6	64.4
Ark	1,876	581	842	453	31.0	44.9	24.2	956	920	51.0	49.0
Calif	31,801	6,227	12,310	13,264	19.6	38.7	41.7	9,448	22,354	29.7	70.3
Colo	3,270	727	1,288	1,255	22.2	39.4	38.4	1,237	2,034	37.8	62.2
Conn	3,492	636	1,527	1,329	18.2	43.7	38.1	1,591	1,901	45.6	54.4
Del	799	173	472	154	21.7	59.0	19.3	443	355	55.5	44.5
D.C	1,602	812	(X)	790	50.2	(X)	49.8	(X)	1,602	(X)	100.0
Fla	8,116	1,491	3,347	3,278	18.4	41.2	40.4	2,501	5,615	30.8	69.2
Ga	5,031	1,244	1,947	1,840	24.7	38.7	36.6	2,181	2,850	43.3	56.7
Hawaii	1,428	393	802	233	27.5	56.2	16.3	1,077	351	75.4	24.6
Idaho	894	236	401	257	26.4	44.8	28.8	428	466	47.8	52.2
Ill	13,032	2,594	5,493	4,945	19.9	42.2	37.9	5,282	7,750	40.5	59.5
Ind	5,010	913	2,382	1,715	18.2	47.5	34.2	1,949	3,061	38.9	61.1
Iowa	3,318	678	1,446	1,194	20.4	43.6	36.0	1,233	2,085	37.2	62.8
Kans	2,478	494	1,051	934	19.9	42.4	37.7	1,081	1,397	43.6	56.4
Ky	3,367	898	1,705	763	26.7	50.7	22.7	1,911	1,455	56.8	43.2
La	4,408	1,053	2,264	1,092	23.9	51.4	24.8	2,186	2,222	49.6	50.4
Maine	1,171	300	629	242	25.6	53.7	20.7	655	516	55.9	44.1
Md	5,360	1,092	2,379	1,889	20.4	44.4	35.2	1,790	3,570	33.4	66.6
Mass	7,816	1,711	3,161	2,944	21.9	40.4	37.7	3,409	4,407	43.6	56.4
Mich	11,594	2,667	4,607	4,320	23.0	39.7	37.3	4,327	7,267	37.3	62.7
Minn	5,401	1,115	2,635	1,651	20.6	48.8	30.6	2,082	3,319	38.5	61.5
Miss	2,257	651	1,048	558	28.8	46.4	24.7	1,058	1,200	46.9	53.1
Mo	4,459	1,026	1,658	1,776	23.0	37.2	39.8	1,751	2,709	39.3	60.7
Mont	973	268	358	347	27.6	36.8	35.7	437	536	44.9	55.1
Nebr	1,737	369	623	744	21.3	35.9	42.9	708	1,029	40.8	59.2
Nev	859	169	341	349	19.7	39.7	40.7	328	531	38.2	61.8
N.H	782	183	263	336	23.4	33.6	43.0	335	447	42.9	57.1
N.J	8,617	1,568	2,904	4,145	18.2	33.7	48.1	2,608	6,009	30.3	69.7
N. Mex	1,422	373	824	226	26.2	57.9	15.9	757	665	53.2	46.8
N.Y	31,263	6,064	11,599	13,600	19.4	37.1	43.5	6,559	24,704	21.0	79.0
N.C	4,877	1,180	2,443	1,254	24.2	50.1	25.7	1,936	2,941	39.7	60.3
N. Dak	833	179	438	216	21.5	52.6	25.9	466	367	56.0	44.0
Ohio	10,347	1,988	4,068	4,291	19.2	39.3	41.5	3,494	6,852	33.8	66.2
Okla	2,743	681	1,315	746	24.8	48.0	27.2	1,390	1,353	50.7	49.3
Oreg	3,064	789	1,148	1,127	25.8	37.5	36.8	1,317	1,746	43.0	57.0
Pa	12,735	2,975	5,781	3,979	23.4	45.4	31.2	5,634	7,101	44.2	55.8
R.I	1,121	311	511	299	27.7	45.6	26.7	619	502	55.2	44.8
S.C	2,642	671	1,333	638	25.4	50.5	24.1	1,401	1,241	53.0	47.0
S. Dak	763	215	275	273	28.2	36.0	35.8	395	368	51.8	48.2
Tenn	3,815	1,016	1,516	1,283	26.6	39.7	33.6	1,626	2,189	42.6	57.4
Texas	12,376	2,559	5,303	4,515	20.7	42.8	36.5	5,204	7,172	42.0	58.0
Utah	1,361	381	604	375	28.0	44.4	27.6	691	670	50.8	49.2
Vt	630	190	270	170	30.2	42.8	26.9	385	245	61.1	38.9
Va	5,071	1,116	2,327	1,628	22.0	45.9	32.1	2,203	2,868	43.4	56.6
Wash	4,537	959	2,190	1,388	21.1	48.3	30.6	1,919	2,619	42.3	57.7
W. Va	1,919	553	973	394	28.8	50.7	20.5	1,110	810	57.8	42.2
Wis	5,821	1,189	2,832	1,800	20.4	48.7	30.9	2,037	3,784	35.0	65.0
Wyo	657	188	251	218	28.6	38.2	33.2	330	327	50.2	49.8

X Not applicable.
[1] Before intergovernmental transfers.
[2] After intergovernmental transfers.

Source: U.S. Bureau of the Census, *Governmental Finances in 1975-76*, series GF76, No. 5.

No. 484. STATE AND LOCAL GOVERNMENTS—GENERAL REVENUE, BY SOURCE, BY STATES: 1976

[Estimates subject to sampling variation; see source]

STATE	REVENUE (mil. dol.)						REVENUE PER CAPITA [1] (dollars)					
		From Federal Government	From own sources					From Federal Government	From own sources			
			Taxes			Charges and miscellaneous			Taxes			Charges and miscellaneous
	Total		All taxes	Property tax	Other		Total		All taxes	Property tax	Other	
U.S.	256,176	55,589	156,813	57,002	99,811	43,774	1,193	259	731	266	465	204
Ala.	3,359	943	1,669	210	1,459	748	916	257	455	57	398	204
Alaska	1,279	308	724	400	324	247	3,349	806	1,896	1,048	848	647
Ariz.	2,591	489	1,660	641	1,019	442	1,141	215	731	282	449	195
Ark.	1,876	581	957	213	744	339	890	275	454	101	353	161
Calif.	31,801	6,227	20,750	8,936	11,814	4,824	1,478	289	964	415	549	224
Colo.	3,270	727	1,880	701	1,179	663	1,266	281	728	271	457	257
Conn.	3,492	636	2,425	1,150	1,275	432	1,120	204	778	369	409	138
Del.	799	173	447	76	371	179	1,372	297	768	130	638	307
D.C.	1,602	813	649	147	502	141	2,283	1,157	924	210	715	201
Fla.	8,116	1,491	4,765	1,611	3,154	1,860	964	177	566	191	374	221
Ga.	5,031	1,244	2,727	884	1,843	1,060	1,012	250	549	178	371	213
Hawaii	1,428	393	829	154	675	206	1,610	443	935	174	761	232
Idaho	894	236	491	158	333	167	1,076	284	590	190	400	202
Ill.	13,032	2,594	8,640	3,189	5,451	1,798	1,161	231	769	284	485	160
Ind.	5,010	913	3,118	1,198	1,920	978	945	172	588	226	362	184
Iowa	3,318	678	2,011	797	1,214	629	1,156	236	701	278	423	219
Kans.	2,478	494	1,504	633	871	480	1,073	214	651	274	377	208
Ky.	3,366	898	1,881	359	1,522	587	982	262	549	105	445	171
La.	4,408	1,053	2,342	347	1,995	1,013	1,148	274	610	90	520	264
Maine	1,171	300	718	318	400	152	1,094	291	671	207	374	142
Md.	5,360	1,092	3,374	992	2,382	894	1,293	264	814	239	575	216
Mass.	7,816	1,711	5,244	2,501	2,743	861	1,345	295	903	431	472	148
Mich.	11,594	2,667	6,819	2,952	3,867	2,108	1,274	293	749	324	425	231
Minn.	5,401	1,115	3,262	1,008	2,254	1,024	1,362	281	823	254	568	258
Miss.	2,257	651	1,145	258	887	462	959	277	486	110	377	196
Mo.	4,459	1,026	2,724	931	1,793	709	933	215	570	195	375	148
Mont.	973	268	534	264	270	171	1,292	356	709	350	359	227
Nebr.	1,737	369	1,021	495	526	346	1,118	238	658	319	339	223
Nev.	859	169	500	166	334	189	1,408	277	820	272	548	311
N.H.	782	183	470	286	184	130	952	222	571	348	224	158
N.J.	8,617	1,568	5,816	3,275	2,541	1,233	1,175	214	793	446	346	168
N. Mex.	1,422	373	699	120	579	351	1,218	319	598	103	496	300
N.Y.	31,263	6,064	20,615	7,447	13,168	4,584	1,729	335	1,140	412	728	253
N.C.	4,877	1,180	2,884	712	2,172	814	892	216	527	130	397	149
N. Dak.	833	179	429	137	292	226	1,296	278	667	212	455	351
Ohio	10,347	1,988	6,262	2,391	3,871	2,096	968	186	586	224	362	196
Okla.	2,743	681	1,465	343	1,122	596	992	246	530	124	406	216
Oreg.	3,064	789	1,638	775	863	636	1,315	339	703	333	370	273
Pa.	12,735	2,975	8,113	2,083	6,030	1,647	1,074	251	684	176	508	139
R.I.	1,121	311	659	273	386	151	1,209	335	711	294	416	163
S.C.	2,642	671	1,393	330	1,063	578	928	236	489	116	373	203
S. Dak.	764	215	409	198	211	139	1,113	313	596	288	308	203
Tenn.	3,815	1,016	2,078	546	1,532	721	905	241	493	129	364	171
Texas	12,376	2,559	7,259	2,662	4,597	2,559	991	205	581	213	368	205
Utah	1,361	381	728	211	517	252	1,108	310	593	172	421	205
Vt.	630	190	353	147	206	86	1,324	400	742	308	434	182
Va.	5,071	1,116	3,066	869	2,197	889	1,008	222	609	173	437	177
Wash.	4,537	959	2,630	852	1,778	948	1,256	266	728	236	492	263
W. Va.	1,919	553	1,064	193	871	303	1,054	304	584	106	478	166
Wis.	5,821	1,189	3,644	1,330	2,314	988	1,263	258	791	289	502	214
Wyo.	657	188	330	137	193	139	1,689	482	847	352	495	356

[1] Based on estimated population as of July 1, 1976.

Source: U.S. Bureau of the Census, *Governmental Finances in 1975–76*, series GF76, No. 5.

No. 485. State and Local Governments—Direct General Expenditure, by States: 1976

STATE	EXPENDITURE (mil. dol.)						EXPENDITURE PER CAPITA [2] (dollars)					
	Total	Education	Highways	Public welfare	Health and hospitals	All other [1]	Total	Education	Highways	Public welfare	Health and hospitals	All other [1]
U.S.	255,551	97,216	23,907	31,435	20,686	82,307	1,191	453	111	146	96	383
Ala.	3,402	1,356	415	328	432	872	928	370	113	89	118	238
Alaska	1,176	372	190	49	42	523	3,079	974	498	128	110	1,368
Ariz.	2,611	1,190	267	105	184	865	1,150	524	118	46	81	381
Ark.	1,817	726	271	217	139	465	862	344	128	103	66	220
Calif.	30,734	11,442	1,672	4,604	2,305	10,712	1,428	532	78	214	107	498
Colo.	3,266	1,427	330	305	234	972	1,264	552	128	118	90	376
Conn.	3,403	1,249	262	409	193	1,291	1,092	401	84	131	62	414
Del.	800	330	82	69	38	281	1,375	566	140	119	66	484
D.C.	1,462	330	73	274	121	665	2,083	471	104	390	172	947
Fla.	8,475	3,163	749	486	920	3,157	1,006	376	89	58	109	375
Ga.	4,825	1,763	499	492	715	1,357	971	355	100	99	144	273
Hawaii	1,567	427	154	164	104	717	1,767	482	173	185	118	809
Idaho	913	342	148	75	69	278	1,099	412	178	90	84	335
Ill.	13,201	5,221	1,426	1,847	816	3,891	1,176	465	127	165	73	346
Ind.	4,805	2,192	554	429	466	1,165	906	413	104	81	88	220
Iowa	3,295	1,369	556	346	244	781	1,148	477	194	120	85	272
Kans.	2,516	998	360	254	239	665	1,089	432	156	110	103	288
Ky.	3,213	1,268	459	412	185	890	937	370	134	120	54	260
La.	4,277	1,479	642	407	375	1,374	1,113	385	167	106	98	358
Maine	1,083	405	139	153	49	337	1,012	379	130	143	46	314
Md.	5,580	2,142	510	513	376	2,040	1,346	517	123	124	91	492
Mass.	7,310	2,523	489	1,208	533	2,557	1,258	434	84	208	92	440
Mich.	11,904	4,791	907	1,892	942	3,372	1,308	526	100	208	103	370
Minn.	5,402	2,177	612	725	368	1,520	1,362	549	154	183	93	383
Miss.	2,264	855	385	208	245	571	962	363	163	89	104	243
Mo.	4,323	1,761	533	420	397	1,212	905	369	112	88	83	254
Mont.	949	407	154	65	54	269	1,260	540	204	87	71	357
Nebr.	1,643	676	252	131	145	439	1,058	436	162	84	93	282
Nev.	868	281	100	52	82	354	1,423	460	164	85	134	580
N.H.	855	321	133	102	48	253	1,041	390	162	124	58	307
N.J.	8,801	3,235	625	1,109	459	3,373	1,200	441	85	151	63	460
N. Mex.	1,304	579	170	96	104	354	1,116	496	146	83	89	303
N.Y.	31,383	9,340	1,512	5,083	3,215	12,234	1,735	516	84	281	178	677
N.C.	5,062	2,244	568	414	467	1,370	926	410	104	76	85	251
N. Dak.	758	305	140	50	27	236	1,179	475	217	78	42	367
Ohio	11,030	4,445	989	1,290	895	3,411	1,032	416	93	121	84	319
Okla.	2,631	1,054	296	337	226	717	951	381	107	122	82	259
Oreg.	3,155	1,279	312	310	166	1,089	1,355	549	134	133	71	468
Pa.	13,205	4,834	1,356	2,040	831	4,144	1,113	408	114	172	70	349
R.I.	1,113	402	59	194	81	377	1,201	434	64	209	87	407
S.C.	2,750	1,135	213	209	348	846	966	398	75	73	122	297
S. Dak.	778	310	144	69	38	217	1,134	452	211	101	55	316
Tenn.	3,940	1,486	540	383	413	1,119	935	353	128	91	98	265
Texas	11,983	5,338	1,180	1,082	1,067	3,315	960	427	95	87	85	265
Utah	1,373	700	157	103	86	328	1,118	570	127	84	70	267
Vt.	594	237	80	82	32	164	1,249	497	168	172	68	343
Va.	5,146	2,101	644	460	366	1,576	1,022	417	128	91	73	314
Wash.	4,379	1,861	424	401	238	1,456	1,212	515	117	111	66	403
W. Va.	1,902	687	398	172	125	520	1,044	377	218	94	69	286
Wis.	5,697	2,422	625	793	401	1,456	1,236	526	136	172	87	316
Wyo.	632	243	156	23	47	163	1,621	624	400	59	120	418

[1] Includes police protection, fire protection, natural resources, sanitation, local parks and recreation, financial administration, general control, and interest on general debt as well as miscellaneous lesser functions.
[2] Based on estimated resident population as of July 1, 1976.

Source: U.S. Bureau of the Census, *Governmental Finances in 1975–76*, series GF76, No. 5.

No. 486. State and Local Governments—Indebtedness and Debt Transactions: 1970 to 1976

[In billions of dollars, except per capita. Local government amounts are estimates subject to sampling variation; see source. See *Historical Statistics, Colonial Times to 1970*, series Y 680, Y 747, and Y 794, for debt outstanding]

ITEM	1970			1975			1976		
	Total	State	Local	Total	State	Local	Total	State	Local
Debt outstanding	143.6	42.0	101.6	221.3	72.1	149.1	240.1	84.4	155.7
Per capita [1] ____dol.	704	206	498	1,038	338	700	1,118	394	725
Long-term	131.4	38.9	92.5	201.5	67.5	133.9	221.3	78.4	142.9
Local schools	31.5	3.0	28.6	40.5	3.9	36.6	41.1	4.0	37.0
Local utilities	19.6	(X)	19.6	30.0	(X)	30.0	30.8	(X)	30.8
All other	80.3	35.9	44.4	131.0	63.7	67.3	149.5	74.3	75.1
Short-term	12.2	3.1	9.1	19.8	4.6	15.2	18.8	6.0	12.8
Net long-term debt outstanding	121.7	34.5	87.3	183.4	58.4	125.0	195.3	62.5	132.8
Long-term debt issued	12.8	3.9	8.9	21.1	8.4	12.7	31.7	13.9	17.8
Long-term debt retired	7.0	1.9	5.1	10.9	2.9	8.0	11.3	3.0	8.4

X Not applicable.　　[1] Based on estimated resident population as of July 1.

No. 487. State and Local Governments—Debt Outstanding, by States: 1970 and 1976

[As of end of fiscal year]

STATE	TOTAL DEBT (mil. dol.)		PER CAPITA [1] (dol.)		STATE	TOTAL DEBT (mil. dol.)		PER CAPITA [1] (dol.)		STATE	TOTAL DEBT (mil. dol.)		PER CAPITA [1] (dol.)	
	1970	1976	1970	1976		1970	1976	1970	1976		1970	1976	1970	1976
U.S.	[2] 143,570	240,086	704	1,118	Kans	1,162	2,110	517	913	N. Dak	224	353	362	549
					Ky	2,630	4,089	817	1,193	Ohio	5,852	8,533	549	798
Ala	2,529	3,000	734	819	La	3,087	4,342	847	1,130	Okla	1,621	2,297	633	830
Alaska	422	1,382	1,395	3,618	Maine	443	964	446	901	Oreg	1,343	3,351	642	1,439
Ariz	944	2,370	533	1,044	Md	3,321	5,822	847	1,405	Pa	9,065	15,624	760	1,317
Ark	1,005	1,115	523	529	Mass	4,158	8,760	731	1,508	R.I.	758	1,005	798	1,084
Calif	15,850	20,384	794	947										
					Mich	5,163	8,708	582	963	S.C.	861	2,167	333	761
Colo	1,178	2,094	533	811	Minn	2,618	4,784	688	1,207	S. Dak	136	225	203	327
Conn	3,427	4,991	1,130	1,601	Miss	1,234	1,757	557	747	Tenn	2,589	4,053	660	962
Del	727	1,137	1,326	1,954	Mo	2,269	2,806	485	587	Texas	7,025	12,096	627	969
D.C.	597	2,403	789	3,423	Mont	237	465	342	617	Utah	597	654	564	532
Fla	3,743	7,141	551	848	Nebr	1,347	2,553	908	1,644					
Ga	2,600	4,020	567	809						Vt	312	582	701	1,223
					Nev	362	673	740	1,103	Va	2,239	3,924	482	780
Hawaii	783	1,639	1,017	1,848	N.H	358	674	485	820	Wash	4,321	6,008	1,268	1,663
Idaho	200	261	281	314	N.J	5,016	9,005	700	1,228	W. Va	851	1,763	488	968
Ill	6,706	10,455	603	931	N. Mex	424	779	417	667	Wis	2,365	3,536	535	767
Ind	[2] 2,077	2,803	400	529	N.Y	23,805	46,037	1,305	2,546	Wyo	229	460	688	1,179
Iowa	1,047	1,315	371	458	N.C	1,741	2,559	342	468					

[1] Based on Bureau of the Census estimated resident population as of July 1, excluding Armed Forces abroad.
[2] Indiana figure includes adjustments not carried to U.S. total; therefore, breakdown will not add to total.
Source of tables 486 and 487: U.S. Bureau of the Census, *Governmental Finances*, series GF No. 5, annual.

No. 488. New Issues of State and Local Government Securities: 1970 to 1977

[In millions of dollars]

ITEM	1970	1971	1972	1973	1974	1975	1976	1977
All issues, total [1]	18,166	24,963	23,653	23,969	24,315	30,607	35,313	46,769
General obligations	11,850	15,220	13,305	12,257	13,563	16,020	18,040	18,042
Revenue	6,082	8,681	9,332	10,632	10,212	14,511	17,140	28,655
U.S. Housing Assistance Admin.[2]	131	1,000	959	1,022	461	–	–	–
U.S. Government loans	103	62	57	58	79	76	133	72
Type of issuer:								
State	4,167	5,993	4,991	4,212	4,784	7,438	7,054	6,354
Special district and statutory authority	5,553	8,690	9,482	9,493	8,638	12,441	15,304	21,717
Municipalities, counties, townships, school districts	8,347	10,219	9,125	10,205	10,817	10,660	12,845	18,623
Issues for new capital, total	18,015	24,434	22,023	22,342	23,508	29,495	32,108	36,189

– Represents zero.　　[1] New capital and refunding.　　[2] Only bonds sold pursuant to 1949 Housing Act, which are secured by contract requiring the HAA to make annual contributions to the local authority.
Source: Board of Governors of the Federal Reserve System, *Annual Statistical Digest: 1972-1976*, and *Federal Reserve Bulletin*, monthly.

No. 489. STATE GOVERNMENTS—REVENUE,

[In millions of dollars, except as indicated. For years ending June 30,

STATE	REVENUE								DEBT OUTSTANDING	
	Total¹	General								
		Total			Intergovernmental revenue		Taxes³	Charges and miscellaneous	Total	Per capita² (dol.)
		Amount	Rank	Per capita² (dol.)	From Federal Government	From local governments				
U.S.	185,213	152,118	(X)	711	42,013	2,704	89,256	18,145	84,379	394
Ala	2,827	2,343	22	639	775	14	1,243	311	979	267
Alaska	1,188	1,043	37	2,730	281	(Z)	599	163	828	2,167
Ariz	1,864	1,559	31	687	352	4	1,018	185	92	40
Ark	1,492	1,321	34	627	475	4	725	117	130	61
Calif	22,125	17,685	1	822	4,814	561	10,761	1,549	6,466	300
Colo	2,168	1,871	27	724	573	9	964	324	126	49
Conn	2,679	2,009	24	645	481	2	1,264	263	3,069	985
Del	662	598	44	1,027	124	2	359	113	738	1,267
Fla	5,179	4,405	9	523	1,030	28	2,936	412	1,740	207
Ga	3,358	2,923	19	588	965	11	1,676	271	1,290	260
Hawaii	1,330	1,106	36	1,246	297	6	639	163	1,304	1,471
Idaho	711	599	43	721	195	4	329	72	39	47
Ill	9,148	7,627	4	679	2,080	54	4,783	710	3,357	299
Ind	3,494	3,117	16	588	726	10	1,916	466	600	113
Iowa	2,314	1,990	25	693	514	30	1,200	247	126	44
Kans	1,645	1,459	33	632	398	11	854	197	408	177
Ky	2,747	2,448	20	714	738	4	1,404	301	1,997	582
La	3,498	3,092	17	805	816	12	1,656	608	1,458	380
Maine	1,051	891	40	833	255	8	531	98	535	500
Md	3,590	3,169	15	765	756	35	1,960	419	2,517	607
Mass	5,728	4,581	8	789	1,247	173	2,728	433	4,961	854
Mich	8,804	6,581	6	723	1,920	54	3,769	838	1,883	207
Minn	4,090	3,580	12	903	869	77	2,219	416	1,020	257
Miss	1,837	1,593	30	677	535	10	874	174	775	329
Mo	2,895	2,410	21	504	747	5	1,444	214	337	70
Mont	737	595	45	790	231	6	278	80	85	113
Nebr	1,007	931	39	600	288	19	489	134	64	41
Nev	689	482	46	790	136	6	294	47	53	87
N.H.	589	416	50	507	145	9	184	79	304	370
N.J.	5,739	4,117	10	561	1,140	73	2,292	612	4,013	547
N. Mex	1,245	1,119	35	958	280	15	575	248	187	160
N.Y	21,022	17,254	2	954	4,563	1,092	9,780	1,819	20,451	1,131
N.C	3,875	3,362	13	615	899	20	2,060	383	709	130
N. Dak	650	601	42	935	152	11	287	151	70	109
Ohio	8,086	5,628	7	527	1,510	50	3,311	757	3,030	283
Okla	2,032	1,864	28	674	533	16	1,000	315	948	343
Oreg	2,323	1,765	29	758	614	3	826	322	2,002	859
Pa	10,597	8,030	3	678	2,168	81	5,127	654	5,888	496
R.I	1,007	747	41	806	234	2	389	122	509	549
S.C	2,163	1,907	26	670	554	20	1,042	290	1,045	367
S. Dak	496	457	47	666	177	4	192	83	92	134
Tenn	2,643	2,301	23	546	770	15	1,273	243	951	226
Texas	7,943	7,284	5	583	1,954	27	4,214	1,088	2,082	167
Utah	1,118	945	38	770	330	11	475	130	152	124
Vt	538	444	48	932	172	2	205	65	421	885
Va	3,649	3,182	14	632	825	31	1,822	504	711	141
Wash	3,976	2,959	18	819	730	15	1,848	342	1,227	340
W. Va	1,772	1,460	32	802	487	(Z)	829	144	1,175	645
Wis	4,400	3,838	11	833	982	24	2,421	411	1,362	296
Wyo	494	429	49	1,100	174	4	193	58	75	193

X Not applicable.   Z Less than $500,000.
1 Includes liquor stores and insurance trust activities, not shown separately.

DEBT, AND EXPENDITURES BY STATES: 1976

except as follows: Alabama, Sept. 30; New York, Mar. 31; and Texas, Aug. 31]

Total [1]	Total			General						STATE
	Amount	Rank	Per capita [2] (dol.)	Education	Highways	Public welfare	Health and hospitals	Natural resources	All other	
181,966	153,690	(X)	718	59,630	18,100	29,633	11,111	3,863	31,352	U.S.
2,845	2,395	22	653	1,157	346	320	210	62	300	Ala.
1,033	957	37	2,506	319	169	49	31	46	343	Alaska.
1,839	1,601	31	705	789	248	87	85	38	354	Ariz.
1,483	1,335	34	633	543	261	217	83	51	180	Ark.
20,534	17,063	2	793	6,402	1,159	4,490	867	540	3,605	Calif.
1,997	1,811	27	701	858	245	302	120	47	238	Colo.
2,651	2,003	26	643	634	191	394	168	20	597	Conn.
702	629	42	1,081	291	71	70	38	13	146	Del.
5,158	4,485	9	533	1,971	613	434	359	188	920	Fla.
3,324	2,858	18	575	1,229	384	481	247	99	417	Ga.
1,382	1,223	35	1,378	427	104	168	101	55	369	Hawaii.
708	622	43	749	232	117	71	31	44	129	Idaho.
9,477	7,934	4	707	2,925	1,142	2,012	524	153	1,179	Ill.
3,522	3,096	16	584	1,346	498	361	197	58	636	Ind.
2,346	2,076	24	723	900	409	316	129	60	263	Iowa.
1,570	1,441	33	624	613	240	245	113	47	183	Kans.
2,641	2,356	23	687	962	421	405	122	107	340	Ky.
3,413	3,088	17	804	1,158	555	405	244	86	640	La.
1,036	868	40	811	381	94	154	42	40	156	Maine.
3,861	3,448	14	832	1,265	416	531	301	75	858	Md.
5,532	4,437	10	764	1,262	343	1,293	325	35	1,179	Mass.
8,711	6,819	6	749	2,533	739	1,892	474	124	1,058	Mich.
3,840	3,481	13	878	1,674	381	549	199	88	590	Minn.
1,826	1,643	30	698	689	301	204	103	69	277	Miss.
2,850	2,401	21	502	977	424	424	191	64	320	Mo.
688	579	44	770	221	124	58	38	32	106	Mont.
983	904	39	582	312	166	121	81	41	183	Nebr.
590	471	47	772	194	78	46	23	16	115	Nev.
632	488	46	594	138	93	75	45	13	124	N.H.
5,853	4,510	8	615	1,360	357	1,059	301	136	1,296	N.J.
1,071	990	36	848	468	148	94	69	34	178	N. Mex.
21,027	17,719	1	980	5,343	781	4,256	1,626	166	5,548	N.Y.
4,166	3,719	12	680	1,832	504	389	306	104	583	N.C.
576	537	45	835	218	100	48	26	24	122	N. Dak.
7,738	5,887	7	551	2,306	696	1,110	419	96	1,261	Ohio.
1,969	1,768	29	639	755	257	334	124	48	248	Okla.
2,161	1,782	28	765	613	273	305	116	75	401	Oreg.
11,134	8,697	3	733	3,137	1,150	1,982	700	166	1,562	Pa.
980	762	41	822	243	40	202	80	11	187	R.I.
2,266	2,033	25	714	847	211	202	197	62	514	S.C.
492	470	48	686	153	102	67	31	25	92	S. Dak.
2,808	2,433	20	577	1,013	473	365	192	68	322	Tenn.
7,386	6,831	5	547	3,577	754	1,058	550	160	732	Texas.
1,072	950	38	774	492	134	97	56	38	128	Utah.
531	445	49	935	147	57	86	31	13	110	Vt.
3,552	3,150	15	626	1,320	570	425	299	74	462	Va.
3,639	2,852	19	790	1,434	301	419	157	118	423	Wash.
1,726	1,450	32	796	507	381	171	84	49	257	W. Va.
4,190	3,777	11	819	1,339	327	770	241	64	1,035	Wis.
454	415	50	1,064	122	152	21	17	21	82	Wyo.

[2] Based on estimated resident population as of July 1.   [3] For details, see table 490.

Source: U.S. Bureau of the Census, *State Government Finances in 1976*, series GF76, No. 3.

No. 490. State Governments—Summary of Finances: 1960 to 1976

[In millions of dollars, except per capita. See also *Historical Statistics, Colonial Times to 1970*, series Y 710–782]

ITEM	1960	1965	1970	1973	1974	1975	1976 Total	1976 Per capita [1]
Borrowing and revenue	35,149	51,784	93,463	137,212	148,774	164,295	201,018	$940
Borrowing	2,312	2,957	4,524	7,404	7,959	9,663	15,805	74
Revenue	32,838	48,827	88,939	129,808	140,815	154,632	185,213	866
General revenue	27,363	40,930	77,755	113,132	122,327	134,611	152,118	711
Taxes	18,036	26,126	47,961	68,069	74,207	80,155	89,256	417
Sales and gross receipts	10,510	15,059	27,254	37,123	40,556	43,346	47,391	222
General	4,302	6,711	14,177	19,793	22,612	24,780	27,333	128
Motor fuels	3,335	4,300	6,283	8,058	8,207	8,255	8,660	40
Alcoholic beverages	650	917	1,420	1,817	1,909	1,963	2,057	10
Tobacco products	923	1,284	2,308	3,112	3,250	3,286	3,462	16
Other	1,300	1,847	3,065	4,342	4,578	5,061	5,878	28
Licenses	2,495	3,218	4,615	5,753	6,055	6,289	6,899	32
Motor vehicles	1,468	1,869	2,728	3,386	3,477	3,655	4,046	19
Corporations in general	426	528	764	970	1,052	1,041	1,135	5
Other	602	819	1,123	1,396	1,522	1,597	1,719	8
Individual income	2,209	3,657	9,183	15,587	17,078	18,819	21,448	100
Corporation net income	1,180	1,929	3,738	5,425	6,015	6,642	7,273	34
Property	607	766	1,092	1,312	1,301	1,451	2,118	10
Other	1,034	1,496	2,081	2,868	3,202	3,607	4,127	19
Intergovernmental revenue	6,745	10,320	20,248	32,700	33,170	37,827	44,717	209
From Federal Government	6,382	9,874	19,252	31,361	31,632	36,148	42,013	196
Public welfare	2,048	3,133	7,818	13,653	13,320	14,247	16,867	79
Education	727	1,393	4,554	6,430	6,720	7,879	8,661	40
Highways	2,883	3,987	4,431	4,648	4,503	5,260	6,262	29
Other	725	1,359	2,450	6,628	7,089	8,761	10,222	48
From local governments	363	447	995	1,339	1,538	1,680	2,704	13
Charges and misc. general revenue	2,583	4,483	9,545	12,363	14,950	16,629	18,145	85
Liquor stores revenue	1,128	1,270	1,748	1,985	2,049	2,129	2,196	10
Insurance trust revenue	4,347	6,627	9,437	14,690	16,439	17,892	30,900	144
Debt outstanding, fiscal year end	18,543	27,034	42,008	59,071	65,296	72,127	84,379	394
Long-term	18,128	26,235	38,903	55,397	61,697	67,548	78,368	366
Full faith and credit	8,912	11,819	17,736	28,139	30,855	33,736	38,421	180
Nonguaranteed	9,216	14,415	21,167	27,258	30,842	33,812	39,947	187
Short-term	415	800	3,104	3,674	3,599	4,579	6,011	28
Net long-term	15,595	22,504	34,478	49,021	53,847	58,388	62,488	292
Full faith and credit only	6,711	9,094	14,832	24,737	26,967	29,503	33,708	158
Expenditure and debt redemption	32,496	46,769	87,151	121,930	134,948	159,093	185,551	867
Debt redemption	900	1,130	2,096	3,094	2,814	2,922	3,585	17
Expenditure	31,596	45,639	85,055	118,836	132,134	156,171	181,966	850
General expenditure [2]	27,228	40,446	77,642	108,086	119,891	138,304	153,690	718
Public welfare	3,704	5,434	13,206	21,678	22,538	25,559	29,633	139
Education	8,857	14,532	30,865	41,599	46,860	54,012	59,630	279
Highways	7,317	9,844	13,483	15,025	15,847	17,483	18,100	85
Health and hospitals	2,072	2,943	5,355	7,350	8,443	10,158	11,110	52
State hospitals	1,618	2,254	3,941	5,274	5,957	6,891	7,572	35
Other hospitals and health	454	689	1,415	2,076	2,485	3,267	3,538	17
Housing and urban renewal	33	80	120	430	545	632	465	2
Natural resources	862	1,381	2,223	2,725	3,053	3,554	3,863	18
Correction	433	652	1,104	1,553	1,812	2,203	2,480	12
Police protection	251	352	741	1,118	1,262	1,423	1,569	7
Social insurance administration	313	457	767	1,277	1,304	1,509	1,570	7
Financial administration	447	609	1,032	1,393	1,594	1,792	1,955	9
General control	216	350	717	1,112	1,273	1,496	1,688	8
Miscellaneous and unallocable	2,722	3,810	8,029	12,828	15,361	18,483	21,626	100
Liquor stores expenditure	907	1,022	1,404	1,583	1,653	1,719	1,781	8
Insurance trust expenditure	3,461	4,170	6,010	9,167	10,590	16,149	26,495	124
Expenditure by character and object:								
Intergovernmental expenditure	9,433	14,174	28,892	40,822	45,941	51,978	57,858	270
Direct expenditure	22,152	31,465	56,163	78,013	86,193	104,193	124,108	580
Current operation	9,534	14,930	30,971	44,838	50,803	60,793	68,175	319
Capital outlay	6,607	9,307	13,295	14,677	15,417	17,307	18,009	84
Construction	5,509	7,600	11,185	12,327	12,655	14,443	15,285	71
Land and existing structures	802	1,176	1,240	1,322	1,540	1,475	1,274	6
Equipment	296	531	870	1,028	1,222	1,389	1,450	7
Assistance and subsidies	2,015	2,236	4,387	6,897	6,521	6,673	7,290	34
Interest on debt	536	822	1,499	2,434	2,863	3,272	4,140	19
Insurance benefits and repayments	3,461	4,170	6,010	9,167	10,590	16,149	26,495	124

[1] Based on estimated resident population as of July 1, 1976.   [2] Intergovernmental and direct.

Source: U.S. Bureau of the Census, *Census of Governments: 1972*, vol. 6, No. 4, *Historical Statistics on Governmental Finances and Employment;* and *State Government Finances*, series GF No. 3, annual.

No. 491. State Government Tax Collections and Excise Taxes, by Type of Tax—States: 1977

[Collections include local shares of State-imposed taxes. Excise taxes as of September 1]

STATE	STATE TAX COLLECTIONS [1] (mil. dol.)							EXCISE TAXES		
	Total [2]	Sales and gross receipts			Individual income	Corporation net income	Motor vehicle and operators' licenses	General sales and gross receipts (percent)	Cigarettes (cents per package)	Motor fuels (cents per gal., gasoline)
		Total [2]	General sales or gross receipts	Motor fuels	Alcoholic beverages and tobacco products					
U.S.[3]	101,026	52,351	30,870	9,087	5,635	25,453	9,187	4,582	(X)	(X)	(X)
Percent of total	100.0	51.8	30.6	9.0	5.6	25.2	9.1	4.5	(X)	(X)	(X)
Ala	1,404	909	455	165	121	262	76	40	[4] 4	12	7
Alaska	774	66	(X)	21	13	210	36	12	(X)	8	8
Ariz	1,160	711	503	112	53	191	52	52	[4] 4	13	8
Ark	803	491	274	119	64	164	67	45	[4] 3	17.75	8.5
Calif	12,589	6,005	4,314	811	399	3,621	1,642	359	[4] 4.75	10	7
Colo	1,077	550	360	102	53	339	81	44	[4] 3	15	7
Conn	1,457	1,053	583	159	99	59	202	73	7	21	11
D.C.	739	260	141	23	23	201	56	22	5	13	10
Del	391	69	(X)	30	17	168	29	21	(X)	14	11
Fla	3,275	2,415	1,399	384	373	(X)	194	295	4	21	8
Ga	1,907	1,135	687	245	151	496	171	50	[4] 3	12	7.5
Hawaii	686	445	341	33	27	203	28	[5] (Z)	4	([6])	[7] 8.5
Idaho	368	176	104	45	15	112	31	26	3	9.1	9.5
Ill	5,320	3,015	1,842	406	253	1,413	384	353	[4] 4	12	7.5
Ind	2,163	1,432	1,046	263	80	479	86	91	4	10.5	8
Iowa	1,293	572	347	133	61	447	92	122	3	13	7
Kans	969	521	327	119	49	209	123	62	[4] 3	11	8
Ky	1,560	838	464	184	37	338	131	46	[4] 5	3	9
La	1,715	851	482	173	102	134	95	40	3	11	8
Maine	468	296	170	55	49	75	35	24	5	16	9
Md	2,128	989	466	189	83	807	115	82	5	10	9
Mass	2,934	1,175	442	214	220	1,192	397	65	5	21	8.5
Mich	4,791	2,147	1,389	430	220	1,426	803	195	4	11	9
Minn	2,486	983	467	197	134	957	258	111	4	18	9
Miss	969	701	475	139	59	132	46	24	5	11	9
Mo	1,598	929	596	205	83	390	106	100	[4] 3.125	9	7
Mont	312	83	(X)	44	21	112	25	14	(X)	12	8
Nebr	610	343	199	88	33	171	42	36	[4] 3	13	9.5
Nev	329	257	116	30	22	(X)	(X)	18	[4,8] 3	10	6
N.H.	200	114	(X)	40	31	7	33	21	(X)	12	10
N.J.	3,104	1,577	913	293	223	710	333	206	5	19	8
N. Mex	598	376	257	65	20	26	29	31	[4] 4	12	7
N.Y.	10,743	3,963	2,218	512	484	4,527	1,295	304	[4] 4	15	8
N.C.	2,385	1,129	512	290	107	782	204	111	[4] 3	2	9
N. Dak	296	165	110	30	15	55	22	25	3	11	8
Ohio	3,571	2,133	1,135	393	269	615	315	192	[4] 4	15	7
Okla	1,139	493	205	124	86	217	71	104	[4] 2	13	6.58
Oreg	973	159	(X)	91	38	562	91	87	(X)	9	7
Pa	5,591	2,805	1,525	499	354	1,178	666	304	6	18	9
R.I.	439	255	142	41	32	104	41	19	6	18	10
S.C.	1,188	711	415	140	98	290	107	32	4	7	9
S. Dak	200	174	101	36	16	(X)	3	12	[4] 4	12	8
Tenn	1,530	1,130	734	193	110	22	156	95	[4] 4.5	13	7
Tex	4,749	3,181	1,696	444	439	(X)	(X)	266	[4] 4	18.5	5
Utah	531	307	227	55	13	158	25	17	[4] 4	8	7
Vt	230	113	32	23	22	70	17	18	3	12	9
Va	2,055	979	427	265	82	714	159	96	[4] 3	2.5	9
Wash	2,100	1,590	1,173	180	128	(X)	(X)	78	[4] 4.6	16	11
W. Va	904	654	439	79	49	165	23	37	3	12	8.5
Wis	2,733	1,053	668	171	123	1,144	252	99	[4] 4	16	7
Wyo	233	133	95	27	6	(X)	(X)	31	[4] 3	8	8

X Not applicable. 　 Z Less than $500,000. 　 [1] Preliminary. 　 [2] Includes amounts for types of taxes not shown separately. 　 [3] Excludes District of Columbia. 　 [4] Excludes State-collected supplemental local sales taxes imposed by local governments under State enabling legislation, as well as locally administered taxes. [5] Motor vehicle licenses only. 　 [6] 40 percent of wholesale price. 　 [7] State rate per gallon in Hawaii County, 11.5 cents. Combined State and local rates per gallon, in cents: Honolulu, 12; Kauai, 12.5; and Maui, 13.5. [8] Includes a mandatory State-imposed 1 percent county sales tax.

Source: U.S. Bureau of the Census, *State Government Tax Collections in 1977*, series GF77, No. 1.

No. 492. State Government Individual Income Taxes: 1977

[As of January 1. Only basic rates, brackets, and exemptions are shown. Taxable income rates and brackets apply to single individuals only; other schedules are used for married taxpayers filing separately or jointly or for heads of households in Alaska, California, Georgia, Hawaii, New Mexico, Oklahoma, Utah, and West Virginia. No income tax is levied in Florida, Nevada, South Dakota, Texas, Washington, and Wyoming]

| STATE | Taxable income rates (range in percent) | TAXABLE INCOME BRACKETS | | PERSONAL EXEMPTIONS [1] | | | SIZE OF STANDARD DEDUCTIONS | | | Federal income tax deductible |
		Lowest: amount under—	Highest: amount over—	Single	Married— joint return	Dependents	Percent	Single	Married— joint return	
Ala	1.5–5.0	$1,000	$5,000	$1,500	$3,000	$300	10	$1,000	$1,000	Yes
Alaska	3.0–14.5	2,000	200,000	750	1,500	750	(X)	2,200	3,200	No
Ariz	2.0–8.0	1,000	6,000	1,000	2,000	600	10	500	1,000	Yes
Ark	1.0–7.0	3,000	25,000	[2] 17.50	[2] 35	[2] 6	10	1,000	1,000	No
Calif	1.0–11.0	2,000	15,500	[2] 25	[2] 50	[2] 8	(X)	1,000	2,000	No
Colo	[3] 3.0–8.0	1,000	10,000	750	1,500	750	10	1,000	1,000	Yes
Conn	[4] 1.0–9.0	(5)	100,000	100	200	(X)	(X)	(X)	(X)	No
D.C	2.0–11.0	1,000	25,000	750	1,500	750	10	1,000	1,000	No
Del	1.6–19.8	1,000	100,000	600	1,200	600	10	1,000	1,000	[6] Yes
Ga	1.0–6.0	750	7,000	1,500	3,000	700	15	2,000	2,000	No
Hawaii	2.25–11.0	500	30,000	750	1,500	750	10	1,000	1,000	No
Idaho	2.0–7.5	1,000	5,000	750	1,500	750	(X)	2,200	3,200	No
Ill	2.5	Flat rate		1,000	2,000	1,000	(X)	(X)	(X)	No
Ind	2.0	Flat rate		1,000	(7)	500	(X)	(X)	(X)	No
Iowa	.5–13.0	1,000	75,000	[2] 15	[2] 30	[2] 10	10	1,000	1,000	Yes
Kans	2.0–9.0	2,000	25,000	750	1,500	750	16	2,400	2,800	[6] Yes
Ky	2.0–6.0	3,000	8,000	[2] 20	[2] 40	[2] 20	(X)	650	650	[6] Yes
La	2.0–6.0	10,000	50,000	[8] 2,500	[8] 5,000	[8] 400	(8)	(8)	(8)	Yes
Maine	1.0–10.0	2,000	25,000	1,000	2,000	1,000	16	2,400	2,800	No
Md	2.0–5.0	1,000	3,000	800	1,600	800	10	500	[9] 1,000	No
Mass	[10] 5.0	Flat rate		2,000	2,600	600	(X)	(X)	(X)	No
Mich	4.6	Flat rate		1,500	3,000	1,500	(X)	(X)	(X)	No
Minn	[11] 1.6–15.0	500	20,000	[2] 21	[2] 42	[2] 21	10	1,000	1,000	Yes
Miss	3.0–4.0	5,000	5,000	4,500	6,500	750	15	750	[12] 1,500	No
Mo	1.5–6.0	1,000	9,000	1,200	2,400	400	(X)	2,200	3,200	Yes
Mont	[13] 2.0–11.0	1,000	35,000	650	1,300	650	10	500	1,000	Yes
Nebr	(14)	Flat rate		(14)	(14)	(14)	(14)	(14)	(14)	No
N.H	[15] 5.0	Flat rate		600	(16)	(X)	(X)	(X)	(X)	No
N.J. [17]	2.0–2.5	20,000	20,000	1,000	2,000	1,000	(X)	(X)	(X)	No
N. Mex	.9–9.0	500	100,000	750	1,500	750	(X)	2,200	3,200	No
N.Y	[18] 2.0–15.0	1,000	25,000	650	1,300	650	15	2,000	2,000	No
N.C	3.0–7.0	2,000	10,000	1,000	(19)	600	10	500	(19)	No
N. Dak	[20] 1.0–10.0	1,000	8,000	750	1,800	750	16	2,400	2,800	Yes
Ohio	.5–3.5	5,000	40,000	650	1,300	650	(X)	(X)	(X)	No
Okla	.5–6.0	1,000	7,500	750	1,500	750	15	2,000	2,000	[6] Yes
Oreg	4.0–10.0	500	5,000	750	1,500	750	13	1,500	1,500	[6] Yes
Pa	[21] 2.0	Flat rate		(X)	(X)	(X)	(X)	(X)	(X)	No
R.I	(14)	Flat rate		(14)	(14)	(14)	(14)	(14)	(14)	No
S.C	2.0–7.0	2,000	10,000	800	1,600	800	10	500	1,000	[6] Yes
Tenn	[15] 6.0	Flat rate		(X)	(X)	(X)	(X)	(X)	(X)	No
Utah	2.25–7.75	750	4,500	750	1,500	750	15	2,000	2,000	Yes
Vt	(14)	Flat rate		(14)	(14)	(14)	(14)	(14)	(14)	No
Va	2.0–5.75	3,000	12,000	600	1,200	600	15	2,000	2,000	No
W. Va	2.1–9.6	2,000	200,000	600	1,200	600	10	1,000	1,000	No
Wis	3.1–11.4	1,000	14,000	[2] 20	[2] 40	[2] 20	15	2,000	2,000	No

X Not applicable.　[1] Many States also commonly allow other types of exemptions, such as physical or mental disability exemptions, and tax credits for items such as specified contributions or taxes paid to other jurisdictions.　[2] Tax credit.　[3] Effective minimum rate is 2.5% due to application of a tax reduction credit.　[4] Tax on capital gains and dividends applicable to taxpayers (individual or joint) with a Federal adjusted gross income in excess of $20,000.　[5] $20,000 to $21,999.　[6] Subject to specified limitations.　[7] Minimum exemption is $1,000; maximum exemption is $2,000.　[8] All exemptions and deductions are incorporated into tax tables which must be used when filing State tax returns.　[9] Incomes of husbands and wives filing joint returns are treated separately for purposes of taking the standard deduction; therefore, minimum deduction is $500 and maximum deduction is $1,000.　[10] Data apply to earned income and annuities; 10% (flat rate) imposed on net capital gains, interest, and dividends. Only income in excess of $3,000 for single taxpayers and $5,000 for married taxpayers filing jointly is taxable. A 7.5% surtax on tax liability is additional.　[11] No tax is due at specified minimum levels of income because an allowance is made for a tax credit equal to tax liability.　[12] Incomes of husbands and wives filing joint returns are treated separately for purposes of taking the standard deduction; therefore, minimum deduction is $750 and maximum deduction is $1,500.　[13] 10% surtax on tax liability is additional.　[14] Based on Federal income tax liability as follows: Nebraska, 18%; Rhode Island, 17%; Vermont, 25% plus 9% surtax. Since State tax is computed as a percentage of the Federal tax liability, in effect the Federal standard deduction and exemptions are adopted. As of January 1, 1977, the Federal standards comparable to the ones presented in this table were: Personal exemptions, single-$750, married filing joint return-$1,500, dependents-$750; standard deduction, percent-zero, single $2,200, married filing joint return-$3,200.　[15] Tax on interest and dividends.　[16] Each spouse having taxable income is eligible for $600 deduction; maximum exemption is, therefore, $1,200.　[17] Data apply to recently adopted personal income tax applicable July 1, 1976. Provisions vary for New York, Pennsylvania, and Delaware commuter taxes.　[18] No tax is due if adjusted gross income is below $2,500 for single taxpayers and $5,000 for married taxpayers filing jointly.　[19] Joint returns are inapplicable; however, a husband and wife may elect to file separate returns on a combined form.　[20] Plus a 1% tax on net income in excess of $2,000 of taxpayers who derive income from the operation of a business, trade, or profession other than as an employee. A 2% surtax on tax liability is additional.　[21] Refunds or forgiveness of tax due are based on specified poverty income levels.

Source: U.S. Bureau of the Census, State Government Tax Collections in 1977, series GF77, No. 1.

No. 493. NUMBER OF LOCAL GOVERNMENTS, BY TAXING POWER AND TYPE, AND PUBLIC SCHOOL SYSTEMS—STATES: 1972 AND 1977

[Limited to governments actually in existence. Excludes, therefore, a few counties and numerous townships and "incorporated places" existing as areas for which statistics can be presented as to population and other subjects, but lacking any separate organized county, township, or municipal government]

STATE	1972			1977								
	ALL TYPES OF LOCAL GOVERNMENTS			ALL TYPES OF LOCAL GOVERNMENTS		LOCAL GOVERNMENTS OTHER THAN SCHOOL DISTRICTS					School districts	Public school systems [2]
	Total	With property-taxing power	Excluding school districts	Total	With property-taxing power	Total	Counties [1]	Municipalities	Townships	Special districts		
U.S._	78,218	65,914	62,437	79,862	67,780	64,688	3,042	18,862	16,822	25,962	15,174	16,548
Ala._____	875	589	749	949	613	822	67	419	–	336	127	127
Alaska___	120	120	120	150	150	150	8	142	–	–	–	32
Ariz._____	406	377	169	420	418	190	14	70	–	106	230	237
Ark._____	1,283	917	895	1,346	923	966	75	467	–	424	380	380
Calif._____	3,819	3,498	2,687	3,806	3,595	2,697	57	413	–	2,227	1,109	1,110
Colo._____	1,319	1,168	1,132	1,459	1,394	1,274	62	262	–	950	185	185
Conn.____	428	340	414	434	359	418	–	33	149	236	16	165
Del._____	158	82	133	210	85	185	3	55	–	127	25	26
D.C._____	3	1	3	2	1	2	–	1	–	1	–	2
Fla._____	865	674	771	911	686	816	66	389	–	361	95	95
Ga._____	1,243	884	1,054	1,263	876	1,075	158	530	–	387	188	188
Hawaii__	19	4	19	19	4	19	3	1	–	15	–	1
Idaho____	901	730	784	972	792	855	44	199	–	612	117	117
Ill._____	6,385	5,337	5,208	6,620	5,522	5,557	102	1,274	1,436	2,745	1,063	1,063
Ind._____	2,792	2,206	2,477	2,854	2,216	2,547	91	563	1,008	885	307	307
Iowa_____	1,818	1,605	1,355	1,852	1,738	1,388	99	955	–	334	464	464
Kans.____	3,715	3,355	3,384	3,725	3,365	3,398	105	625	1,449	1,219	327	327
Ky._____	1,135	806	944	1,183	975	1,002	119	405	–	478	181	181
La._____	834	710	768	458	456	392	62	300	–	30	66	66
Maine___	714	601	636	779	610	693	16	24	475	178	86	256
Md._____	403	196	403	426	194	426	23	151	–	252	–	40
Mass.____	682	482	631	766	512	691	12	39	312	328	75	389
Mich.____	2,649	2,523	2,002	2,633	2,489	2,027	83	531	1,245	168	606	606
Minn.____	3,395	3,262	2,950	3,437	3,431	2,997	87	855	1,792	263	440	440
Miss.____	796	605	634	835	681	669	82	283	–	304	166	166
Mo._____	2,807	2,145	2,171	2,937	2,317	2,363	114	916	326	1,007	574	574
Mont.____	992	858	440	958	818	493	56	126	–	311	465	465
Nebr.____	3,561	3,265	2,187	3,485	3,248	2,290	93	534	471	1,192	1,195	1,195
Nev._____	184	102	167	182	117	165	16	17	–	132	17	17
N.H.____	499	461	341	506	478	347	10	13	221	103	159	168
N.J._____	1,456	1,238	929	1,517	1,254	968	21	335	232	380	549	615
N. Mex._	309	243	220	313	285	225	32	93	–	100	88	88
N.Y._____	3,306	3,297	2,560	3,309	3,296	2,569	57	618	930	964	740	773
N.C._____	802	590	802	874	644	874	100	472	–	302	–	200
N. Dak..	2,726	2,617	2,340	2,707	2,608	2,361	53	361	1,360	587	346	346
Ohio_____	3,259	3,098	2,619	3,285	3,116	2,654	88	935	1,319	312	631	632
Okla._____	1,683	1,287	1,026	1,675	1,284	1,050	77	567	–	406	625	625
Oreg._____	1,446	1,136	1,093	1,447	1,200	1,072	36	239	–	797	375	375
Pa._____	4,935	3,159	4,407	5,246	3,282	4,665	66	1,015	1,549	2,035	581	581
R.I._____	115	90	112	120	90	117	–	8	31	78	3	40
S.C._____	583	477	490	585	507	492	46	264	–	182	93	93
S. Dak...	1,770	1,667	1,542	1,727	1,632	1,533	64	311	1,010	148	194	194
Tenn.____	881	432	867	905	447	891	94	326	–	471	14	147
Tex._____	3,624	3,005	2,450	3,883	3,248	2,745	254	1,066	–	1,425	1,138	1,138
Utah____	459	389	419	492	422	452	29	216	–	207	40	40
Vt._____	658	632	386	647	623	375	14	57	237	67	272	272
Va._____	385	328	385	389	324	389	95	229	–	65	–	136
Wash.____	1,682	1,390	1,365	1,666	1,453	1,364	39	265	–	1,060	302	302
W. Va.__	508	337	453	595	338	540	55	227	–	258	55	55
Wis._____	2,448	2,331	2,031	2,518	2,379	2,108	72	576	1,270	190	410	452
Wyo._____	383	268	313	385	285	330	23	90	–	217	55	55

- Represents zero.

[1] Excluding areas corresponding to counties but having no organized county government.

[2] Includes 1,374 other local public school systems operated as part of a State, county, municipal, or township government and excluded from independent school-district figure and from "All types of local governments."

Source: U.S. Bureau of the Census, Census of Governments: 1977, vol. 1, No. 1, Governmental Organization.

No. 494. COUNTY, MUNICIPAL, AND TOWNSHIP GOVERNMENTS, 1977, AND THEIR ESTIMATED POPULATION, 1975, BY POPULATION–SIZE GROUPS

[Number of governments as of January 1977; population estimates as of July 1, 1975. Township governments include "towns" in the 6 New England States, New York, and Wisconsin]

POPULATION–SIZE GROUP	COUNTIES			MUNICIPALITIES			TOWNSHIPS		
	Number, 1977	Population, 1975		Number, 1977	Population, 1975		Number, 1977	Population, 1975	
		Number (1,000)	Percent		Number (1,000)	Percent		Number (1,000)	Percent
Total	3,042	189,691	100.0	18,862	136,761	100.0	16,822	48,344	100.0
250,000 or more	137	92,392	48.7	58	41,638	30.4	} 31	5,740	11.9
100,000–249,999	206	32,085	16.9	105	14,896	10.9			
50,000–99,999	336	23,503	12.4	230	16,091	11.8	72	4,799	9.9
25,000–49,999	596	20,976	11.0	514	17,939	13.1	190	6,479	13.4
10,000–24,999	980	16,079	8.5	1,212	19,002	13.9	660	10,185	21.1
5,000–9,999	496	3,758	2.0	1,461	10,299	7.5	870	6,081	12.6
2,500–4,999	} 291	897	.4	2,004	7,040	5.1	1,595	5,505	11.4
1,000–2,499				3,664	5,872	4.3	3,657	5,808	12.0
Less than 1,000				9,614	3,985	2.9	9,747	3,747	7.8

Source: U.S. Bureau of the Census, *Census of Governments: 1977*, vol. 1, No. 1, *Governmental Organization*.

No. 495. COUNTY GOVERNMENTS—SUMMARY OF FINANCES, 1973 TO 1976, AND PER CAPITA, BY POPULATION–SIZE GROUP: 1976

[Based on population estimates as of July 1, 1975. Covers fiscal years ending between July 1 of preceding year and June 30 of year stated]

ITEM	ALL COUNTIES (mil. dol.)				PER CAPITA (dollars), 1976					
					All counties		Counties [1] with 1975 population (1,000) of—			
	1973	1974	1975	1976	Total	Percent distribution	Less than 100 (2,700)[1]	100– 199.9 (163)[1]	200– 299.9 (72)[1]	300 or more (109)[1]
General revenue	26,880	30,246	32,893	36,942	188.14	100.0	153.41	165.73	183.75	224.34
Intergovernmental revenue [2]	11,736	13,799	14,755	16,677	84.93	45.1	71.85	76.71	86.81	97.77
From State govt	9,910	11,023	11,842	13,156	67.00	35.6	(NA)	(NA)	(NA)	(NA)
General rev. sharing	1,053	1,722	1,595	1,612	8.21	4.4	9.14	6.90	7.43	7.93
Tax rev. from own sources	11,066	11,662	12,660	14,130	71.96	38.2	50.78	60.17	65.66	94.31
Property	9,287	9,573	10,316	11,582	58.99	31.4	43.10	47.91	54.63	76.26
Charges and misc	4,079	4,784	5,478	6,135	31.24	16.6	30.78	28.85	31.28	32.26
General expenditure	26,141	28,879	32,744	37,478	190.87	100.0	153.23	165.28	192.30	229.14
Capital outlay	3,217	3,862	4,850	5,236	26.67	14.0	24.50	27.67	22.50	29.11
Other	22,924	25,017	27,894	32,241	164.20	86.0	128.67	137.69	169.80	200.05
Public welfare	6,232	6,342	6,169	7,079	36.05	18.9	16.08	28.71	44.84	53.04
Education	4,242	4,757	5,643	5,996	30.54	16.0	35.22	31.05	32.01	26.13
Highways	2,766	3,118	3,458	3,733	19.01	10.0	27.74	18.52	14.01	12.80
Hospitals	2,755	2,899	3,337	3,860	19.66	10.3	17.10	11.00	14.12	25.23
General control	1,518	1,706	1,986	2,282	11.62	6.1	7.89	10.95	12.04	14.87
Police protection	1,067	1,210	1,450	1,721	8.76	4.6	6.08	7.80	7.43	11.57
Financial administration	703	765	883	980	4.99	2.6	4.42	5.09	5.29	5.38
General public buildings	583	650	824	960	4.89	2.6	4.37	4.37	5.12	5.42
Health	904	1,128	1,428	1,684	8.58	4.5	4.71	8.92	11.03	11.24
Correction	698	818	980	1,110	5.65	3.0	2.29	3.56	5.40	9.10
Natural resources	387	429	510	664	3.38	1.8	2.05	1.89	1.74	5.24
Parks and recreation	516	609	741	820	4.10	2.1	1.28	2.93	3.43	7.11
Interest on general debt	613	695	795	896	4.56	2.4	2.93	4.69	5.51	5.72
Other and unallocable	3,157	3,752	4,541	5,692	28.99	15.2	16.60	30.51	32.29	38.39
Debt outstanding, end of year	15,635	17,486	18,935	20,372	103.75	100.0	62.40	116.06	118.60	132.00
Long-term	14,549	16,353	17,617	19,028	96.91	93.4	(NA)	(NA)	(NA)	(NA)
Short-term	1,086	1,133	1,318	1,343	6.84	6.6	(NA)	(NA)	(NA)	(NA)

NA Not available. [1] Figures in parentheses represent number of counties.
[2] Includes other Federal intergovernmental revenue not shown separately.
Source: U.S. Bureau of the Census, *County Government Finances in 1975–76*, series GF76, No. 8.

No. 496. STATE AND LOCAL GOVERNMENTS—ASSESSED VALUE OF PROPERTY AND REVENUE FROM PROPERTY TAXES: 1966 TO 1976

ITEM	1966	1971	1972	1973	1974	1975	1976
Gross assessed property_____bil. dol__	499.0	717.8	(NA)	872.6	(NA)	1,096.3	1,230.0
State assessed_____bil. dol__	41.6	53.5	(NA)	59.4	(NA)	74.8	84.8
Locally assessed_____bil. dol__	457.4	664.2	(NA)	813.2	(NA)	1,021.5	1,145.3
Real property_____bil. dol__	393.2	573.9	(NA)	704.6	(NA)	881.6	992.5
Percent of locally assessed_____	86.0	86.4	(NA)	86.6	(NA)	86.3	86.7
Net assessed value of locally taxable property [1]_____bil. dol__	484.1	694.6	(NA)	845.0	(NA)	1,062.9	1,189.4
Percent of gross assessed_____	97.0	96.8	(NA)	96.8	(NA)	97.0	96.8
REVENUE FROM PROPERTY TAXES							
Total revenue, State and local_____bil. dol__	24.7	37.9	42.1	45.3	47.8	51.5	57.0
Percent of general revenue_____	29.7	26.1	25.3	23.8	23.0	22.6	22.3
Percent of tax revenue_____	43.6	39.9	38.7	37.4	36.5	36.4	36.3
Revenue, State governments_____bil. dol__	.8	1.1	1.3	1.3	1.3	1.5	2.1
Annual average percent change from prior year shown_____	[2] 8.9	6.2	11.6	4.5	(−z)	11.4	46.0
Percent of all revenue_____	1.5	1.1	1.1	1.0	.9	.9	1.1
Percent of tax revenue_____	2.8	2.2	2.1	1.9	1.8	1.8	2.4
Revenue, local governments_____bil. dol__	23.8	36.7	40.9	44.0	46.5	50.0	54.9
Annual average percent change from prior year shown_____	[2] 9.3	9.0	11.3	7.6	5.6	7.7	9.7
Percent of all revenue_____	40.2	36.4	36.1	34.1	32.4	32.2	30.8
Percent of tax revenue_____	87.1	84.6	83.5	82.9	82.2	81.6	81.2

NA Not available. Z Less than .05 percent. [1] Assessed value subject to local general property taxation, including State-assessed property, after deduction of partial exemptions. [2] Change from 1965.

Source: U.S. Bureau of the Census, Census of Governments: 1967, 1972, and 1977, vol. 2; Property Values Subject to Local General Property Taxation in the United States: 1973 and 1975, series GSS Nos. 69 and 80; and Governmental Finances, series GF 76, No. 5, annual.

No. 497. GROSS ASSESSED VALUE OF PROPERTY SUBJECT TO LOCAL GENERAL PROPERTY TAXATION—STATES: 1976

[In billions of dollars, except percent. Excludes value of totally exempt property. U.S. figures excluding partially exempt property amounted to a net value of $1,190 million in 1976. Excluded from property tax base were: (1) Property owned by nonprofit and other qualifying groups or institutions (used for government, religion, nonprofit medical care, and education); (2) new industrial plants exempt for stated periods of time as inducement to new industry; and (3) property exempted by specific legislative action]

STATE	Total gross assessed property	Total locally assessed	STATE AND LOCAL GOVERNMENT REVENUE FROM PROPERTY TAX			STATE	Total gross assessed property	Total locally assessed	STATE AND LOCAL GOVERNMENT REVENUE FROM PROPERTY TAX		
			Total	Percent of—					Total	Percent of—	
				General revenue	Tax revenue					General revenue	Tax revenue
U.S.__	1,230.0	1,145.3	57.0	22.3	36.4	Mo_____	14.3	12.7	.9	20.9	34.2
						Mont.[2]___	1.4	1.0	.3	27.1	49.4
Ala_____	6.1	4.9	.2	6.3	12.6	Nebr_____	7.0	6.9	.5	28.5	48.5
Alaska___	9.2	6.4	.4	31.3	55.2	Nev_____	3.6	3.0	.2	19.3	33.2
Ariz_____	6.7	4.3	.6	24.7	38.6	N.H_____	7.4	7.4	.3	36.6	60.9
Ark_____	3.4	2.8	.2	11.4	22.3	N.J_____	79.5	79.5	3.3	38.0	56.3
Calif_____	93.8	88.2	8.9	28.1	43.1	N. Mex__	3.6	2.5	.1	8.4	17.2
Colo_____	10.1	9.2	.7	21.4	37.3	N.Y_____	82.9	79.4	7.4	23.8	36.1
Conn_____	26.4	26.4	1.2	32.9	47.4	N.C_____	64.8	57.8	.7	14.6	24.7
Del_____	3.3	3.3	.1	9.5	17.0	N. Dak.[2]_	.7	.7	.1	16.4	31.9
D.C_____	8.7	8.7	.1	9.2	22.7	Ohio_____	60.3	43.5	2.4	23.1	38.2
Fla_____	110.9	110.5	1.6	19.9	33.8	Okla_____	5.7	4.5	.3	12.5	23.4
Ga_____	27.5	24.8	.9	17.6	32.4	Oreg_____	37.6	34.4	.8	25.3	47.3
Hawaii [1]_	11.6	11.6	.2	10.8	18.6	Pa_____	25.2	25.2	2.1	16.4	25.7
Idaho____	1.7	1.4	.2	17.7	32.2	R.I_____	6.3	6.3	.3	24.3	41.4
Ill.[2]_____	58.1	56.7	3.2	24.5	36.9	S.C_____	2.0	1.5	.3	12.5	23.7
Ind_____	15.3	13.9	1.2	23.9	38.4	S. Dak___	3.9	3.7	.2	25.9	48.4
Iowa_____	45.0	41.2	.8	24.0	39.6	Tenn_____	11.4	9.8	.5	14.3	26.3
Kans_____	8.2	6.9	.6	25.5	42.1	Tex_____	41.5	41.4	2.7	21.5	36.7
Ky_____	33.8	30.0	.4	10.7	19.1	Utah_____	3.2	2.3	.2	15.5	29.0
La_____	7.4	5.8	.3	7.9	14.8	Vt_____	2.5	2.5	.1	23.3	41.6
Maine____	8.6	8.6	.3	27.1	44.3	Va_____	29.6	27.6	.9	17.1	28.3
Md_____	28.7	23.5	1.0	18.5	29.4	Wash____	51.6	48.6	.9	18.8	32.4
Mass_____	35.1	34.5	2.5	32.0	47.7	W. Va___	9.2	7.4	.2	10.1	18.1
Mich.[3]__	55.5	55.5	3.0	25.5	43.3	Wis_____	39.6	39.6	1.3	22.9	36.5
Minn_____	14.0	13.3	1.0	18.7	30.9	Wyo_____	2.5	.9	.1	20.9	41.5
Miss_____	3.6	2.8	.3	11.4	22.5						

[1] All assessment is performed by a State agency but assessed values are shown here as "locally assessed" for comparability with data presented for other States. [2] Two sets of values are locally recorded for taxable property. For comparability with data for other States, the assessed values shown here pertain to the final values against which tax rates are applied, rather than to the preliminary "full and true," "true and full," and "market," or (in Illinois) local unadjusted values. [3] Assessed values are State equalized values, which are the legal values for the levy of the authorized tax rates within the State.

Source: U.S. Bureau of the Census, Census of Governments: 1977, preliminary report No. 2, Assessed Valuations for Local General Property Taxation, and Governmental Finances in 1975-76, series GF 76, No. 5.

State and Local Finances and Employment

No. 498. City Governments—Summary of Finances: 1960 to 1976

[In millions of dollars, except percent. Represents all municipalities (see table 493) and their dependent agencies; excludes other local governments overlying city areas. Includes sample-based estimates for cities of less than 25,000 for 1960, and less than 50,000 beginning 1965; thus subject to sampling variation]

ITEM	1960	1965	1970	1973	1974	1975	1976	PERCENT OF TOTAL 1970	PERCENT OF TOTAL 1976
Revenue	14,915	20,318	32,704	48,461	52,822	59,744	66,856	100.0	100.0
General revenue	11,647	15,881	26,621	40,378	44,158	49,853	55,341	81.4	82.8
Intergovernmental revenue	2,321	3,534	7,906	14,697	16,624	19,648	22,234	24.2	33.3
From State governments only	1,868	2,745	6,173	9,694	10,464	13,053	13,772	18.9	20.6
Taxes	7,109	9,289	13,647	18,477	19,434	21,135	23,336	41.7	34.9
Property	5,197	6,537	9,127	11,879	12,244	13,046	14,165	27.9	21.2
Percent of total taxes	73.1	70.4	66.9	64.3	63.0	61.7	60.7	(X)	(X)
Sales and gross receipts	1,217	1,795	2,422	3,567	3,931	4,555	5,109	7.4	7.6
General	797	1,184	1,479	2,126	2,381	2,769	3,083	4.5	4.6
Selective	420	611	943	1,441	1,550	1,786	2,026	2.9	3.0
Licenses and other	695	957	2,098	3,031	3,259	3,534	4,063	6.4	6.1
Charges and miscellaneous	2,217	3,061	5,068	7,204	8,100	9,071	9,771	15.5	14.6
Current charges only	1,342	1,951	3,113	4,533	4,927	5,443	6,161	9.5	9.2
Utility and liquor store revenue	2,861	3,852	5,168	6,783	7,210	8,109	9,708	15.8	14.5
Water system	1,253	1,651	2,201	2,813	2,911	3,266	3,454	6.7	5.2
Electric power system	1,006	1,441	1,883	2,654	2,947	3,682	4,598	5.8	6.9
Gas supply system	162	215	292	388	401	448	522	.9	.8
Transit system	370	453	671	764	807	821	929	2.1	1.4
Liquor stores	71	92	121	164	173	192	204	.4	.3
Insurance trust revenue	407	582	915	1,300	1,424	1,482	1,807	2.8	2.7
Expenditure	15,251	20,680	34,173	48,151	52,535	60,703	67,460	100.0	100.0
General expenditure [1]	11,818	16,012	27,682	39,134	42,786	48,935	54,425	81.0	80.7
Police protection	1,275	1,739	2,994	4,434	4,797	5,420	6,015	8.8	8.9
Fire protection	885	1,146	1,762	2,407	2,643	2,968	3,257	5.2	4.8
Highways	1,573	1,807	2,499	2,925	3,327	3,861	4,245	7.3	6.3
Sewerage and other sanitation	1,332	1,774	2,553	3,826	4,218	5,229	5,557	7.5	8.2
Public welfare	608	927	2,215	3,413	3,490	3,846	4,544	6.5	6.7
Education	1,801	2,489	4,548	6,050	6,472	7,164	7,610	13.3	11.3
Libraries	185	267	407	500	556	632	684	1.2	1.0
Health and hospitals	799	1,115	1,944	2,834	3,220	3,641	3,462	5.7	5.1
Parks and recreation	551	775	1,306	1,723	1,998	2,274	2,558	3.8	3.8
Housing and urban renewal	464	686	1,154	1,676	1,734	1,752	1,525	3.4	2.3
Airports	189	182	435	539	498	615	671	1.3	1.0
Financial administration	} 598	{ 291	457	636	719	819	912	1.3	1.4
General control		468	776	1,096	1,275	1,440	1,611	2.3	2.4
General public buildings	182	329	430	608	680	845	934	1.3	1.4
Interest on general debt	431	603	1,098	1,736	1,918	2,294	2,683	3.2	4.0
Other and unallocable	946	1,414	3,104	4,731	5,241	6,135	8,157	9.1	12.1
Utility and liquor store expend	2,975	4,044	5,489	7,457	8,073	9,896	11,036	16.1	16.4
Water system	1,424	1,820	2,337	2,987	3,188	3,776	3,958	6.8	5.9
Electric power system	859	1,291	1,811	2,709	2,981	3,779	4,560	5.3	6.8
Gas supply system	143	193	260	349	357	407	463	.8	.7
Transit system	489	662	974	1,273	1,397	1,765	1,875	2.9	2.8
Liquor stores	60	78	107	139	150	169	179	.3	.3
Insurance trust expenditure	458	624	1,002	1,559	1,674	1,872	2,000	2.9	3.0
By character and object:									
Direct expenditure	15,093	20,425	33,792	47,555	51,931	59,989	65,890	98.9	97.7
Current operation	9,874	13,564	22,895	32,665	36,192	41,451	46,705	67.0	69.2
Capital outlay	3,691	4,750	7,103	9,182	9,904	12,054	11,923	20.8	17.7
Construction and equip	3,256	4,197	6,371	8,106	8,979	11,216	11,204	18.6	16.6
Land and existing structures	436	553	733	1,077	925	838	718	2.1	1.1
Assistance payments	386	530	1,245	1,799	1,575	1,594	1,787	3.6	2.6
Interest on debt	684	957	1,547	2,350	2,586	3,018	3,475	4.5	5.2
Insurance benefits, repayments	458	624	1,002	1,559	1,674	1,872	2,000	2.9	3.0
Intergovernmental expenditure	158	255	381	596	604	714	1,570	1.1	2.3
Total personal services [2]	*6,772*	*9,075*	*14,784*	*20,595*	*22,947*	*24,635*	*26,367*	*43.4*	*39.1*
Debt outstanding, year end	**23,178**	**31,862**	**43,773**	**56,041**	**61,187**	**65,239**	**68,797**	**100.0**	**100.0**
Long-term	21,904	29,280	38,870	49,286	53,390	55,789	62,119	88.8	90.3
Full faith and credit	14,473	18,477	22,005	28,912	30,733	31,886	36,839	50.3	53.5
Nonguaranteed	7,430	10,803	16,863	20,375	22,658	23,903	25,280	38.5	36.7
Short-term	1,274	2,582	4,903	6,755	7,796	9,450	6,677	11.2	9.7
Net long-term debt outstanding	20,103	26,774	36,087	45,517	49,394	51,437	57,322	82.4	83.3
Long-term debt issued	2,420	3,347	3,810	6,140	6,827	5,754	9,684	(X)	(X)
Long-term debt retired	1,318	1,776	2,310	3,079	3,258	3,656	3,868	(X)	(X)

X Not applicable.   [1] Includes intergovernmental expenditure.   [2] Included in items shown above.

Source: U.S. Bureau of the Census, *City Government Finances*, series GF No. 4, annual.

No. 499. CITY GOVERNMENTS—FINANCES, BY POPULATION-SIZE GROUPS: 1976

ITEM	All cities	CITIES HAVING A 1975 POPULATION OF—						
		Less than 50,000	50,000 to 99,999	100,000 to 199,999	200,000 to 299,999	300,000 to 499,999	500,000 to 999,999	1,000,000 or more
Number of cities, 1972	18,517	18,125	230	98	18	22	18	6
Population, 1975mil	136.7	64.2	16.1	13.4	4.7	8.5	12.0	17.8
General revenue [1]mil. dol	55,341	13,839	4,955	5,271	2,019	4,031	7,111	18,115
Intergovernmentalmil. dol	22,234	4,635	1,623	1,998	821	1,571	3,239	8,347
From State governmentsmil. dol	13,772	2,595	947	1,118	439	757	1,430	6,486
From Federal governmentmil. dol	7,442	1,656	595	760	331	687	1,651	1,762
Revenue sharingmil. dol	2,185	782	227	239	94	175	256	412
Taxes [1]mil. dol	23,336	5,850	2,296	2,280	845	1,539	2,831	7,695
Propertymil. dol	14,165	3,912	1,679	1,662	486	849	1,585	3,992
Percent of total taxes	60.7	66.9	73.1	72.9	57.5	55.2	56.0	51.9
Sales and gross receiptsmil. dol	3,083	796	291	250	109	221	342	1,073
Current chargesmil. dol	6,161	2,086	666	651	201	583	653	1,322
Water supply and other utilitymil. dol	9,504	3,950	866	1,070	197	593	1,053	1,775
General expenditure [1]mil. dol	54,425	13,465	5,052	5,434	2,104	4,124	7,260	16,986
Educationmil. dol	7,610	1,246	668	1,032	327	533	1,029	2,775
Highwaysmil. dol	4,245	1,886	497	438	170	251	549	454
Public welfaremil. dol	4,544	69	31	103	77	82	596	3,586
Health and hospitalsmil. dol	3,462	690	217	239	44	231	556	1,486
Police and fire protectionmil. dol	9,272	2,780	1,021	984	366	786	1,169	2,166
Sewerage and sanitationmil. dol	5,557	2,009	589	579	233	507	710	931
Housing and urban renewalmil. dol	1,525	160	172	188	77	135	191	602
Interest on general debtmil. dol	2,683	573	193	222	115	201	310	1,070
Water supply and other utilitymil. dol	10,856	4,140	969	1,145	251	647	1,247	2,457
Gross debt outstandingmil. dol	68,797	18,421	5,725	6,227	3,084	5,477	7,602	22,261
Long-termmil. dol	62,119	17,396	5,239	5,636	2,643	5,068	6,827	19,310
Short-termmil. dol	6,677	1,025	486	592	441	408	775	2,950
PERCENT DISTRIBUTION								
General revenue [1]	100.0	100.0	100.0	100.0	100.0	100.0	100.0	100.0
Intergovernmental	40.2	33.5	32.8	37.9	40.7	39.0	45.5	46.1
Taxes [1]	42.2	42.3	46.3	43.3	41.9	38.2	39.8	42.5
Property	25.6	28.3	33.9	31.5	24.1	21.1	22.3	22.0
Sales and gross receipts	5.6	5.8	5.9	4.7	5.4	5.5	4.8	5.9
Current charges	11.1	15.1	13.4	12.4	10.0	14.5	9.2	7.3
Water supply and other utility	17.2	28.5	17.5	20.3	9.8	14.7	14.8	9.8
General expenditure [1]	100.0	100.0	100.0	100.0	100.0	100.0	100.0	100.0
Education	14.0	9.3	13.2	19.0	15.5	12.9	14.2	16.3
Highways	7.8	14.0	9.8	8.1	8.1	6.1	7.6	2.7
Public welfare	8.3	.5	.6	1.9	3.7	2.0	8.2	21.1
Health and hospitals	6.4	5.1	4.3	4.4	2.1	5.6	7.7	8.7
Police and fire protection	17.0	20.6	20.2	18.1	17.4	19.1	16.1	12.8
Sewerage and sanitation	10.2	14.9	11.7	10.7	11.1	12.3	9.8	5.5
Housing and urban renewal	2.8	1.2	3.4	3.5	3.7	3.3	2.6	3.5
Interest on general debt	4.9	4.3	3.8	4.1	5.5	4.9	4.3	6.3
PER CAPITA [2]								
General revenue [1]dol	405	216	308	392	433	474	593	1,018
Intergovernmentaldol	163	72	101	149	176	185	270	469
From State governmentsdol	101	40	59	83	94	89	119	365
From Federal governmentdol	54	26	37	57	71	81	138	99
Revenue sharingdol	16	12	14	18	20	21	21	23
Taxes [1]dol	171	91	143	170	181	181	236	433
Propertydol	103	61	104	124	104	100	132	224
Sales and gross receiptsdol	23	12	18	19	23	26	29	60
Current chargesdol	45	33	41	48	43	69	54	74
Water supply and other utilitydol	70	62	54	80	42	70	88	100
General expenditure [1]dol	398	210	314	404	451	485	606	955
Educationdol	56	19	41	77	70	63	86	156
Highwaysdol	31	29	31	33	37	30	46	26
Public welfaredol	33	1	2	8	16	10	50	202
Health and hospitalsdol	25	11	13	18	9	27	46	84
Police and fire protectiondol	68	43	64	73	79	92	98	122
Sewerage and sanitationdol	41	31	37	43	50	60	59	52
Housing and urban renewaldol	11	2	11	14	16	16	16	34
Interest on general debtdol	20	9	12	16	25	24	26	60
Water supply and other utilitydol	79	65	60	85	54	76	104	138
Gross debt outstandingdol	503	287	355	463	661	644	634	1,252
Long-termdol	454	271	325	419	567	596	570	1,086
Short-termdol	49	16	30	44	94	48	65	166

[1] Includes items not shown separately.   [2] Based on population as of July 1, 1975.

Source: U.S. Bureau of the Census, *City Government Finances in 1975-76*, series GF76, No. 4.

No. 500. CITY GOVERNMENTS—FINANCES,

[In millions of dollars. For fiscal year closed in the 12 months ending June 30, 1976.

CITIES RANKED BY POPULATION SIZE	REVENUE								Gross debt outstanding
	Total [1]	General revenue							
		Total	Intergovernmental revenue		Taxes			Charges and miscellaneous	
			From State and local govts.	From Federal Government	Total [1]	Property	Sales and gross receipts		
Total, 59 cities	35,912	30,765	9,424.4	4,360.0	12,675.7	6,789.0	2,948.2	4,303.8	37,795
New York, N.Y.	15,473	13,846	5,990.9	961.2	5,555.1	3,002.4	1,245.0	1,338.7	15,566
Chicago, Ill.	1,284	1,069	164.5	145.9	624.2	317.9	223.6	134.1	1,393
Los Angeles, Calif.	1,739	1,038	124.0	147.9	535.9	267.3	177.3	230.0	2,370
Philadelphia, Pa.	1,081	1,011	156.3	234.1	466.6	110.1	3.2	154.1	1,465
Detroit, Mich.	934	782	139.4	214.7	303.3	163.1	24.8	124.6	753
Houston, Tex.	440	370	10.2	58.4	209.7	131.4	73.9	91.2	713
Baltimore, Md.	1,113	1,051	544.2	142.0	268.6	182.1	26.4	96.6	560
Dallas, Tex.	321	256	6.5	41.5	155.4	105.1	47.5	52.6	482
San Diego, Calif.	272	220	44.6	40.0	87.8	44.5	37.5	47.5	137
San Antonio, Tex.	393	132	6.5	33.9	55.5	34.3	20.0	35.9	438
Indianapolis, Ind.	274	267	73.5	54.0	86.3	83.5	.8	53.7	282
Washington, D.C.	1,561	1,414	37.2	655.4	648.7	147.1	225.1	72.4	1,380
Honolulu, Hawaii	288	268	12.5	81.7	145.0	117.2	12.6	28.9	254
Milwaukee, Wis.	295	248	93.6	33.6	78.7	76.1	.4	42.0	256
Phoenix, Ariz.	228	194	47.0	38.0	73.5	30.8	39.9	35.0	341
San Francisco, Calif.	881	760	195.7	133.5	305.0	201.8	63.3	125.4	578
Memphis, Tenn.	565	318	172.0	27.7	76.2	52.9	12.3	42.3	553
Cleveland, Ohio	297	249	25.4	41.6	95.4	39.5	.8	86.7	385
Boston, Mass.	762	713	171.6	129.6	328.6	325.9	–	83.5	565
New Orleans, La.	272	256	39.1	69.7	90.3	32.6	51.1	57.2	249
San Jose, Calif.	159	149	27.3	21.6	64.4	29.4	27.2	36.3	136
Columbus, Ohio	173	148	20.2	25.5	66.0	9.8	.7	36.5	294
Jacksonville, Fla.	393	200	40.2	36.2	57.8	37.6	16.1	65.8	547
St. Louis, Mo.	295	267	31.2	45.0	147.7	34.6	60.5	43.1	163
Seattle, Wash.	311	208	38.0	26.6	81.0	33.5	30.4	61.9	473
Denver, Colo.	373	335	62.2	47.7	126.3	52.0	60.3	98.3	405
Kansas City, Mo.	248	222	11.0	45.4	115.2	22.4	45.1	50.8	334
Pittsburgh, Pa.	142	127	17.6	35.5	63.5	43.3	6.4	10.9	135
Atlanta, Ga.	238	204	30.9	22.7	82.4	53.3	19.9	67.9	578
Nashville-Davidson, Tenn.	424	265	56.8	30.8	132.8	86.5	35.3	44.6	401
Cincinnati, Ohio	475	442	127.3	63.7	93.4	25.2	1.4	157.2	278
Buffalo, N.Y.	365	353	167.3	66.5	95.0	91.3	2.3	24.5	286
El Paso, Tex.	81	69	1.8	14.6	31.8	19.9	10.9	21.0	66
Minneapolis, Minn.	173	153	38.8	21.7	64.9	56.2	5.7	27.9	198
Omaha, Nebr.	110	107	13.0	32.4	47.0	27.8	16.1	14.5	117
Toledo, Ohio	110	102	12.1	22.3	40.6	6.2	.2	27.5	127
Oklahoma City, Okla.	119	103	6.5	25.1	42.2	20.6	20.3	29.0	393
Miami, Fla.	112	102	20.8	8.9	54.0	33.1	17.2	18.4	118
Fort Worth, Tex.	122	99	2.6	29.5	44.9	29.3	14.3	22.2	171
Portland, Oreg.	146	131	16.3	31.9	53.7	41.4	6.3	29.2	38
Newark, N.J.	361	350	192.7	16.1	130.9	100.1	18.4	10.7	171
Louisville, Ky.	183	160	22.6	42.6	52.1	16.9	1.9	42.2	306
Long Beach, Calif.	187	146	19.6	15.0	52.6	24.8	20.6	58.4	122
Tulsa, Okla.	131	117	5.8	38.4	43.1	9.7	32.2	29.8	253
Oakland, Calif.	152	144	18.5	25.1	59.7	34.7	20.3	40.7	168
Austin, Tex.	191	92	2.2	24.6	32.1	21.4	9.6	32.6	339
Tucson, Ariz.	113	94	20.4	18.4	40.0	8.6	29.9	15.1	164
Baton Rouge, La.	99	98	12.5	18.1	47.2	11.5	29.2	20.6	259
Norfolk, Va.	224	206	69.4	34.6	73.5	36.7	28.3	28.9	223
Charlotte, N.C.	111	101	19.4	24.0	40.9	39.4	–	16.5	177
Tampa, Fla.	128	112	14.9	37.4	34.0	16.2	15.1	25.9	116
St. Paul, Minn.	121	110	26.6	14.7	43.8	34.1	7.9	25.1	227
Albuquerque, N. Mex.	109	100	28.7	28.2	23.1	16.7	3.6	19.6	126
Birmingham, Ala.	122	100	9.0	19.0	47.7	10.0	14.8	24.0	260
Rochester, N.Y.[2]	194	184	81.2	7.9	80.9	76.4	2.4	13.5	267
Wichita, Kans.	98	86	11.5	17.4	27.0	22.2	3.7	30.3	245
Sacramento, Calif.	96	82	15.5	6.1	40.1	21.2	16.1	20.4	115
Akron, Ohio	92	83	7.0	17.8	34.3	8.8	.1	23.8	148
Jersey City, N.J.	158	151	50.6	16.3	78.4	60.6	12.1	5.8	129

– Represents zero.   Z Less than $50,000.   [1] Includes categories not shown separately.   [2] Data for 1975.

LARGEST CITIES: 1976

Cities ranked by size of population as of **July 1, 1975**]

	EXPENDITURE								
	General expenditure								
Total¹	Total¹	Education	Highways	Public welfare	Health and hospitals	Police protection	Fire protection	Housing and urban renewal	CITIES RANKED BY POPULATION SIZE
36,221	29,929	4,541.1	1,384.6	4,295.4	2,303.9	2,980.2	1,429.5	985.4	Total, 59 cities.
15,197	12,842	2,704.4	167.6	3,516.2	1,234.3	691.0	302.2	494.8	New York, N.Y.
1,241	1,078	26.2	93.9	17.0	50.9	287.4	93.1	15.0	Chicago, Ill.
1,681	944	17.5	95.8	.8	2.7	223.7	89.2	15.9	Los Angeles, Calif.
1,181	1,088	9.7	39.7	51.1	109.5	155.5	53.2	36.3	Philadelphia, Pa.
845	655	16.2	30.4	.6	74.3	129.6	40.0	39.7	Detroit, Mich.
467	378	.9	26.5	(z)	13.8	59.1	42.4	–	Houston, Tex.
1,108	1,053	288.9	150.9	129.3	61.8	74.0	34.7	44.1	Baltimore, Md.
316	230	–	28.1	–	4.8	39.0	24.6	–	Dallas, Tex.
261	205	8.7	11.8	(z)	.1	28.9	15.3	2.7	San Diego, Calif.
510	169	–	22.1	.9	6.1	24.7	16.1	4.8	San Antonio, Tex.
290	267	1.2	36.3	37.1	48.0	25.7	12.9	5.0	Indianapolis, Ind.
1,757	1,541	330.4	73.0	273.9	120.5	102.1	29.6	24.2	Washington, D.C.
308	287	–	39.2	–	3.3	33.8	16.1	9.6	Honolulu, Hawaii.
240	211	(z)	23.1	–	7.6	43.6	19.7	15.3	Milwaukee, Wis.
247	212	1.1	22.8	.3	.3	38.0	15.4	3.7	Phoenix, Ariz.
801	635	1.7	13.6	135.2	111.7	46.8	37.3	20.6	San Francisco, Calif.
579	335	140.6	18.0	.7	.7	29.3	25.7	1.5	Memphis, Tenn.
340	286	–	22.6	1.8	7.8	73.7	25.8	11.1	Cleveland, Ohio.
846	779	253.7	19.9	3.4	79.4	69.4	43.4	32.8	Boston, Mass.
270	247	2.1	15.0	6.1	7.9	32.6	19.4	.8	New Orleans, La.
140	141	=	19.8	–	–	20.8	12.0	2.7	San Jose, Calif.
188	158	–	13.2	–	6.0	27.8	17.2	1.1	Columbus, Ohio.
457	251	.4	11.3	4.2	30.5	23.3	12.3	9.6	Jacksonville, Fla.
271	251	.5	8.5	3.5	58.9	44.0	13.0	.1	St. Louis, Mo.
307	208	1.9	20.5	–	9.4	34.4	19.5	10.9	Seattle, Wash.
400	350	1.0	15.1	51.2	45.6	36.1	22.0	7.5	Denver, Colo.
240	219	9.8	17.9	.4	13.0	30.1	14.7	4.1	Kansas City, Mo.
159	139	.1	13.7	(z)	.2	22.6	13.9	9.5	Pittsburgh, Pa.
265	221	4.2	12.5	1.5	–	29.7	13.1	.6	Atlanta, Ga.
433	264	105.6	17.4	3.1	21.2	17.2	10.9	1.0	Nashville–Davidson, Tenn.
446	418	135.6	11.7	–	65.8	31.3	19.0	13.0	Cincinnati, Ohio.
360	351	126.0	8.7	(z)	.9	23.5	17.3	21.4	Buffalo, N.Y.
71	59	–	4.5	(z)	1.6	9.2	5.7	–	El Paso, Tex.
195	167	(z)	26.6	–	5.3	18.8	11.0	11.4	Minneapolis, Minn.
95	93	.1	13.4	.1	1.7	12.2	8.9	.2	Omaha, Nebr.
138	129	–	11.8	–	5.5	17.7	13.7	9.0	Toledo, Ohio.
122	100	(z)	5.0	–	–	11.5	10.3	8.9	Oklahoma City, Okla.
113	104	(z)	8.6	–	.2	24.3	12.8	–	Miami, Fla.
112	92	(z)	10.7	–	1.9	13.2	8.4	–	Fort Worth, Tex.
149	127	–	11.0	–	.6	21.2	15.1	5.8	Portland, Oreg.
352	338	147.2	1.2	25.2	8.2	45.6	22.3	1.2	Newark, N.J.
183	148	.1	3.6	–	5.4	21.4	12.6	11.0	Louisville, Ky.
215	178	.9	6.6	–	3.6	27.0	16.1	1.3	Long Beach, Calif.
143	126	–	7.1	–	15.1	9.4	9.1	5.3	Tulsa, Okla.
177	162	.5	12.3	–	–	21.3	15.7	10.4	Oakland, Calif.
248	130	–	11.3	–	26.0	10.8	6.0	2.7	Austin, Tex.
126	99	–	5.9	–	▼	14.7	9.9	2.4	Tucson, Ariz.
100	97	.2	10.9	.1	1.9	11.3	5.5	.1	Baton Rouge, La.
211	193	60.2	8.0	30.0	9.8	9.7	6.3	15.5	Norfolk, Va.
120	103	–	20.2	–	.1	10.8	8.7	5.5	Charlotte, N.C.
139	122	–	7.2	–	–	15.6	11.9	2.8	Tampa, Fla.
120	108	1.9	12.5	.2	3.0	12.2	8.8	4.5	St. Paul, Minn.
115	97	–	7.1	–	1.6	14.5	8.6	10.9	Albuquerque, N. Mex.
119	100	.5	7.3	–	3.2	13.3	9.1	–	Birmingham, Ala.
197	190	81.1	6.0	–	(z)	14.5	14.1	4.6	Rochester, N.Y.²
135	121	–	19.7	–	2.4	6.2	5.7	3.7	Wichita, Kans.
91	81	–	3.7	–	–	15.8	10.2	3.0	Sacramento, Calif.
94	85	–	19.2	–	2.6	11.0	7.5	3.1	Akron, Ohio.
185	167	60.1	2.4	1.4	7.4	18.3	13.5	1.8	Jersey City, N.J.

Source: U.S. Bureau of the Census, *City Government Finances in 1975–76*, series GF76, No. 4.

No. 501. CITY GOVERNMENTS—SELECTED FINANCIAL ITEMS PER CAPITA FOR LARGEST CITIES: 1970 TO 1976

[Cities ranked by size of population estimated as of **July 1, 1975**, except Honolulu ranked by county population. General expenditures, taxes, and indebtedness data reflect inclusion of fiscal activity of dependent school systems where applicable. 1970 data based on resident population enumerated as of **April 1, 1970**; later data based on resident population estimated as of **July 1, 1975**]

CITIES RANKED BY POPULATION SIZE	Population, 1975 (1,000)	GENERAL EXPENDITURES			TAXES			GROSS DEBT OUTSTANDING		
		1970	1975	1976	1970	1975	1976	1970	1975	1976
New York, N.Y	7,482	$838	$1,522	$1,717	$383	$635	$743	$1,101	$1,935	$2,081
Chicago, Ill	3,099	205	310	348	113	188	201	326	411	450
Los Angeles, Calif	2,727	169	306	346	110	175	196	483	837	869
Philadelphia, Pa	1,816	299	499	599	183	242	257	556	701	807
Detroit, Mich	1,335	234	449	491	148	208	227	438	550	564
Houston, Tex	1,327	112	224	285	82	137	158	365	495	537
Baltimore, Md	852	639	1,045	1,236	222	303	315	649	644	658
Dallas, Tex	813	159	301	283	106	176	191	348	587	593
San Diego, Calif	774	137	233	265	63	100	113	176	188	177
San Antonio, Tex	773	88	167	219	50	67	72	290	485	567
Indianapolis, Ind	715	127	325	374	67	121	121	205	368	395
Washington, D.C	712	1,011	1,960	2,166	517	741	912	621	1,571	1,940
Honolulu, Hawaii	705	204	322	407	134	178	206	367	304	360
Milwaukee, Wis	666	219	289	317	93	116	118	344	364	385
Phoenix, Ariz	665	130	312	319	72	106	111	295	497	513
San Francisco, Calif	665	603	853	955	300	388	459	575	732	870
Memphis, Tenn	661	294	483	506	75	110	115	588	829	836
Cleveland, Ohio	639	198	362	448	127	134	149	454	597	602
Boston, Mass	637	554	1,088	1,223	349	532	516	465	846	887
New Orleans, La	560	182	344	442	102	145	161	387	456	445
San Jose, Calif	556	156	229	253	66	105	116	235	269	245
Columbus, Ohio	536	192	261	295	58	116	123	451	549	550
Jacksonville, Fla	535	135	381	469	74	99	108	456	1,027	1,022
St. Louis, Mo	525	225	382	478	162	251	281	254	304	310
Seattle, Wash	487	209	390	426	75	155	166	537	943	971
Denver, Colo	485	306	581	721	136	230	261	532	720	835
Kansas City, Mo	473	245	396	464	111	210	244	570	695	707
Pittsburgh, Pa	459	192	251	302	119	132	138	278	287	295
Atlanta, Ga	436	236	422	507	92	162	189	538	1,237	1,326
Nashville-Davidson, Tenn	423	360	606	623	171	290	314	718	940	948
Cincinnati, Ohio	413	502	856	1,012	114	208	226	606	647	674
Buffalo, N.Y	407	367	726	863	143	224	233	519	711	703
El Paso, Tex	386	92	144	154	59	82	82	218	197	171
Minneapolis, Minn	378	178	407	441	92	144	172	183	424	523
Omaha, Nebr	371	116	359	249	65	119	187	145	310	315
Toledo, Ohio	368	171	291	351	77	104	110	193	305	346
Oklahoma City, Okla	366	154	257	275	70	102	115	705	1,009	1,075
Miami, Fla	365	135	231	286	105	143	148	268	300	323
Fort Worth, Tex	358	123	212	256	72	116	125	296	492	477
Portland, Oreg	357	196	292	356	95	124	151	162	120	106
Newark, N.J	340	451	854	996	281	314	385	317	422	504
Louisville, Ky	336	331	429	442	95	139	155	667	932	910
Long Beach, Calif	336	260	412	531	81	142	157	82	357	363
Tulsa, Okla	332	125	309	380	54	118	115	453	784	1,075
Oakland, Calif	331	232	364	490	122	164	181	251	438	507
Austin, Tex	301	169	324	433	61	97	107	661	899	1,126
Tucson, Ariz	296	149	329	335	66	115	135	271	647	552
Baton Rouge, La	294	146	264	329	87	148	160	413	833	881
Norfolk, Va	287	411	672	672	140	252	256	537	739	779
Charlotte, N.C	281	156	318	365	78	133	145	336	546	630
Tampa, Fla	280	139	313	433	91	114	121	341	438	415
St. Paul, Minn	280	214	345	388	83	127	157	449	718	811
Albuquerque, N. Mex	279	181	287	346	85	64	83	399	371	453
Birmingham, Ala	276	136	336	361	69	150	173	397	871	940
Rochester, N.Y	267	531	688	713	169	292	303	425	964	998
Wichita, Kans	265	222	377	455	71	93	102	679	833	924
Sacramento, Calif	261	208	272	309	101	132	154	379	401	440
Akron, Ohio	252	200	267	337	77	130	136	280	552	587
Jersey City, N.J	244	339	602	684	182	270	322	325	505	528

Source: U.S. Bureau of the Census, *City Government Finances*, series GF No. 4, annual.

No. 502. ESTIMATED STATE AND LOCAL TAXES PAID BY A FAMILY OF FOUR IN SELECTED LARGE CITIES, BY INCOME LEVEL: 1975

[Data based on average family of four (wage earner, wife or husband, and two children) which owns its own home and lives in city where taxes apply. Comprises State and local sales, income, auto, and real estate taxes]

CITY	$5,000 INCOME		$10,000 INCOME		$15,000 INCOME		$20,000 INCOME		$30,000 INCOME	
	Total tax paid	Percent of income	Total tax paid	Percent of income	Total tax paid	Percent of income	Total tax paid	Percent of income	Total tax paid	Percent of income
Atlanta	$393	7.9	$768	7.7	$1,245	8.3	$1,730	8.7	$2,670	8.9
Baltimore	420	8.4	959	9.6	1,442	9.6	1,930	9.7	2,862	9.5
Boston	811	16.2	1,618	16.2	2,420	16.1	3,169	15.8	4,499	15.0
Buffalo	719	14.4	1,326	13.3	2,026	13.5	2,739	13.7	4,314	14.4
Chicago	651	13.0	1,110	11.1	1,609	10.7	2,010	10.0	2,758	9.2
Cincinnati	441	8.8	759	7.6	1,144	7.6	1,510	7.6	2,248	7.5
Cleveland	397	7.9	669	6.7	1,007	6.7	1,326	6.3	1,968	6.6
Columbus	366	7.3	632	6.3	960	6.4	1,274	6.4	1,919	6.4
Dallas	455	9.1	720	7.2	1,009	6.7	1,252	6.3	1,653	5.5
Denver	459	9.2	853	8.5	1,251	8.3	1,679	8.4	2,505	8.3
Detroit	433	8.7	947	9.5	1,534	10.2	2,070	10.3	3,115	10.4
Houston	391	7.8	621	6.2	868	5.8	1,074	5.4	1,414	4.7
Indianapolis	537	10.7	917	9.2	1,326	8.8	1,667	8.3	2,312	7.7
Jacksonville	173	3.5	324	3.2	485	3.2	603	3.0	804	2.7
Kansas City	405	8.1	768	7.7	1,172	7.8	1,518	7.6	2,265	7.5
Los Angeles	584	11.7	1,116	11.2	1,820	12.1	2,484	12.4	3,826	12.8
Memphis	434	8.7	646	6.5	896	6.0	1,067	5.3	1,350	4.5
Milwaukee	429	8.6	1,333	13.3	2,135	14.2	2,936	14.7	4,424	14.7
Nashville	405	8.1	602	6.0	834	5.6	988	4.9	1,245	4.1
New Orleans	339	6.8	643	6.4	1,029	6.9	1,337	6.7	1,877	6.3
New York City	1,005	20.1	1,811	18.1	2,755	18.4	3,698	18.5	5,716	19.1
Philadelphia	473	9.5	1,015	10.2	1,487	9.9	1,901	9.5	2,674	8.9
Phoenix	441	8.8	788	7.9	1,131	7.5	1,514	7.6	2,310	7.7
Pittsburgh	552	11.0	1,083	10.8	1,566	10.4	1,976	9.9	2,698	9.0
San Antonio	537	10.7	856	8.6	1,200	8.0	1,493	7.5	1,984	6.6
San Diego	395	7.9	784	7.8	1,312	8.7	1,823	9.1	2,918	9.7
San Francisco	553	11.1	1,043	10.4	1,694	11.3	2,311	11.6	3,576	11.9
Seattle	510	10.2	785	7.9	1,072	7.1	1,298	6.5	1,687	5.6
St. Louis	475	9.5	871	8.7	1,316	8.8	1,696	8.5	2,503	8.3
Washington, D.C.	441	8.8	891	8.9	1,396	9.3	1,915	9.6	2,963	9.9
30-city average	487	9.7	909	9.1	1,371	9.1	1,800	9.0	2,635	8.8

No. 503. RESIDENTIAL PROPERTY TAX RATES IN SELECTED LARGE CITIES: 1975

CITY	EFFECTIVE TAX RATE PER $100		Assessment level (percent)	Nominal rate per $100	CITY	EFFECTIVE TAX RATE PER $100		Assessment level (percent)	Nominal rate per $100
	Rank	Rate				Rank	Rate		
Buffalo	1	$4.92	47.0	$10.47	Atlanta	16	$2.37	40.0	$5.93
Boston	2	4.52	23.0	19.67	San Diego	17	2.33	23.7	9.83
New York City	3	4.04	55.0	7.35	Seattle	18	1.90	89.1	2.13
Pittsburgh	4	3.78	50.0	7.56	St. Louis	19	1.89	33.3	5.69
San Antonio	5	3.75	47.6	7.88	Memphis	20	1.77	25.0	7.06
Milwaukee	6	3.74	99.1	3.77	Washington, D.C.	21	1.71	93.4	1.83
Los Angeles	7	3.62	25.3	14.29	New Orleans	22	1.69	20.6	8.19
Indianapolis	8	3.29	26.5	12.40	Denver	23	1.62	20.0	8.08
Detroit	9	3.18	48.4	6.58	Phoenix	24	1.60	12.8	12.52
Chicago	10	2.73	31.9	8.56	Cleveland	25	1.60	25.0	7.12
San Francisco	11	2.68	23.3	11.50	Cincinnati	26	1.51	35.0	4.78
Dallas	12	2.60	42.9	6.06	Kansas City	27	1.44	18.6	7.76
Baltimore	13	2.59	41.5	6.23	Jacksonville	28	1.42	80.0	1.78
Philadelphia	14	2.39	50.0	4.78	Nashville	29	1.28	21.3	6.00
Houston	15	2.38	41.0	5.81	Columbus	30	1.25	35.0	3.96

Source of tables 502 and 503: Government of the District of Columbia, Department of Finance and Revenue, *Tax Burden in Washington, D.C. Compared With Major State and Local Tax Burdens in the Nation's Thirty Largest Cities, 1975.*

No. 504. Governmental Employment and Payrolls: 1950 to 1977

[For October. 1950 excludes Alaska and Hawaii. Covers both full-time and part-time employees. See also *Historical Statistics, Colonial Times to 1970*, series Y 272–307]

LEVEL OF GOVERNMENT	1950	1955	1960	1965	1970	1972	1973	1974	1975	1976	1977
EMPLOYEES											
Total_____1,000__	6,402	7,432	8,808	10,589	13,028	13,759	14,139	14,628	14,973	15,012	15,406
Federal (civilian)____1,000__	2,117	2,378	2,421	2,588	2,881	2,795	2,786	2,874	2,890	2,843	2,848
State and local_____1,000__	4,285	5,054	6,387	8,001	10,147	10,964	11,353	11,754	12,084	12,169	12,558
Percent of total_____	66.9	68.0	72.5	75.6	77.9	79.7	80.3	80.4	80.7	81.1	81.5
State_____1,000__	1,057	1,250	1,527	2,028	2,755	2,957	3,013	3,155	3,271	3,343	3,467
Local_____1,000__	3,228	3,804	4,860	5,973	7,392	8,007	8,339	8,599	8,813	8,826	9,091
PAYROLL, OCT.											
Total_____mil. dol__	1,528	2,265	3,333	4,884	8,334	9,950	11,027	12,086	13,224	13,924	15,197
Federal (civilian)_mil. dol__	613	846	1,118	1,484	2,428	2,710	3,012	3,294	3,584	3,565	3,918
State and local__mil. dol__	915	1,419	2,215	3,400	5,906	7,240	8,015	8,792	9,640	10,359	11,279
Percent of total_____	59.9	62.6	66.5	69.6	70.9	72.8	72.7	72.7	72.9	74.4	74.2
State_____mil. dol__	218	340	524	849	1,612	1,937	2,158	2,410	2,653	2,894	3,200
Local_____mil. dol__	696	1,078	1,691	2,551	4,294	5,303	5,857	6,382	6,987	7,465	8,079
AVERAGE ANNUAL PERCENT CHANGE [1]											
Employees, total_____	−.5	3.0	3.5	3.8	4.2	2.8	2.8	3.5	2.4	.3	2.6
Federal_____	−8.9	2.4	.4	1.3	2.2	−1.5	−.3	3.2	.6	−1.6	.2
State and local_____	6.1	3.4	4.8	4.6	4.9	4.0	3.5	3.5	2.9	.7	3.2
Payrolls, total_____	6.6	8.2	8.0	7.9	11.3	9.3	10.8	9.6	9.6	5.3	9.2
Federal_____	−.9	6.7	5.7	5.8	10.3	5.7	11.1	9.4	8.8	−.5	9.9
State and local_____	14.3	9.2	9.3	8.9	11.7	10.7	10.7	9.7	9.9	7.6	8.9

[1] Represents average for period of interval shown; for 1950, change from 1945. Minus sign (−) denotes decrease.

No. 505. Governmental Employment and Payrolls, by Level of Government and by Function: 1976 and 1977

[For October. Comprises both full-time and part-time employees]

FUNCTION	EMPLOYEES (1,000)					OCTOBER PAYROLL (mil. dol.)				
	Total	Federal (civilian) [1]	State and local			Total	Federal (civilian) [1]	State and local		
			Total	State	Local			Total	State	Local
1976, total_____	15,012	2,843	12,169	3,343	8,826	13,924	3,565	10,359	2,894	7,465
National defense [2]_____	1,014	1,014	(X)	(X)	(X)	1,244	1,244	(X)	(X)	(X)
Postal service_____	661	661	(X)	(X)	(X)	820	820	(X)	(X)	(X)
Education_____	6,330	22	6,308	1,434	4,875	5,338	28	5,310	1,112	4,199
Teachers_____	3,567	(X)	3,567	425	3,143	3,822	(X)	3,822	532	3,290
Highways_____	587	5	582	262	320	513	8	505	256	249
Health and hospitals_____	1,466	246	1,219	614	606	1,259	277	981	517	465
Public welfare_____	353	(X)	353	161	192	298	(X)	298	144	154
Police protection_____	670	57	613	69	545	712	84	628	82	546
Fire protection_____	292	(X)	292	(X)	292	264	(X)	264	(X)	264
Sanitation and sewerage_____	214	(X)	214	(X)	214	183	(X)	183	(X)	183
Parks and recreation_____	208	(X)	208	(X)	208	130	(X)	130	(X)	130
Natural resources_____	467	263	204	169	35	510	335	175	150	25
Financial administration_____	399	106	293	117	177	371	129	241	113	129
All other_____	2,351	470	1,882	518	1,363	2,282	639	1,642	519	1,123
1977, total_____	15,406	2,848	12,558	3,467	9,091	15,198	3,918	11,279	3,200	8,079
National defense [2]_____	989	989	(X)	(X)	(X)	1,327	1,327	(X)	(X)	(X)
Postal service_____	652	652	(X)	(X)	(X)	890	890	(X)	(X)	(X)
Education_____	6,515	22	6,493	1,483	5,010	5,782	29	5,753	1,237	4,516
Teachers_____	3,642	(X)	3,642	444	3,198	5,012	(X)	5,012	589	4,423
Highways_____	592	5	587	260	327	550	9	541	275	266
Health and hospitals_____	1,509	254	1,254	638	616	1,391	318	1,073	573	498
Public welfare_____	386	(X)	368	167	200	330	(X)	330	161	169
Police protection_____	684	56	628	70	558	785	89	696	88	607
Fire protection_____	301	(X)	301	(X)	301	292	(X)	292	(X)	292
Sanitation and sewerage_____	223	(X)	223	(X)	223	199	(X)	199	(X)	199
Parks and recreation_____	221	(X)	221	(X)	221	142	(X)	142	(X)	142
Natural resources_____	483	273	210	176	34	557	372	185	159	26
Financial administration_____	415	108	307	119	189	409	140	269	123	146
All other_____	2,453	488	1,965	553	1,412	2,544	743	1,801	584	1,218

X Not applicable.   [1] Includes employees outside United States.   [2] Includes international relations.

Source of tables 504 and 505: U.S. Bureau of the Census, *Public Employment*, series GE No. 1, annual.

No. 506. GOVERNMENTAL EMPLOYMENT AND PAYROLLS—STATES: 1977

[For **October**, except as noted]

STATE	ALL EMPLOYEES (1,000)				FULL-TIME EQUIVALENT EMPLOYMENT OF STATE AND LOCAL GOVERNMENTS						OCTOBER PAYROLL [4] (mil. dol.)	
	All governments	Federal (civilian) [1]	State	Local [2]	Number (1,000)			Per 10,000 population [3]			State	Local
					Total	State	Local [2]	Total	State	Local [2]		
U.S.	15,275	2,717	3,467	9,091	10,498	2,902	7,596	485	134	351	3,200	8,079
Ala	262	59	69	133	177	59	118	480	160	320	61	95
Alaska	46	16	16	14	28	15	12	678	374	304	26	22
Ariz	185	35	41	110	127	34	93	552	146	405	36	103
Ark	132	18	38	76	96	32	64	447	149	298	29	46
Calif	1,670	292	289	1,089	1,088	232	856	497	106	391	325	1,152
Colo	225	49	56	120	142	42	100	541	159	382	49	104
Conn	178	21	51	106	132	43	89	426	138	288	44	99
Del	41	5	17	19	31	14	16	530	248	282	15	18
D.C	260	205	(X)	55	52	(X)	52	760	(X)	760	(X)	76
Fla	561	78	110	373	430	97	332	508	115	393	103	318
Ga	384	76	89	219	274	77	196	543	153	389	74	154
Hawaii	82	25	43	14	47	34	13	530	380	149	42	16
Idaho	66	10	20	36	44	15	29	513	176	337	16	25
Ill	725	103	142	480	494	116	378	439	103	336	134	460
Ind	328	39	83	206	236	61	175	443	115	328	72	156
Iowa	201	19	50	131	144	42	102	499	144	355	52	99
Kans	181	23	50	109	124	38	86	532	163	368	39	74
Ky	208	35	64	108	146	55	90	422	160	262	54	75
La	253	31	80	142	199	68	131	508	173	335	62	110
Maine	71	9	21	41	49	17	32	455	159	296	16	27
Md	377	133	77	167	217	72	145	524	174	350	76	168
Mass	390	58	80	252	280	70	210	484	122	363	74	236
Mich	607	54	145	408	428	117	311	468	128	340	153	384
Minn	273	30	68	176	194	52	142	488	130	358	66	156
Miss	102	25	42	95	118	90	82	494	151	940	91	59
Mo	320	66	75	179	213	61	152	444	128	316	59	140
Mont	66	12	20	34	43	15	27	559	200	359	17	27
Nebr	125	16	31	78	89	27	62	569	171	398	24	57
Nev	51	9	13	29	37	11	26	577	167	410	13	27
N.H	64	13	17	33	38	14	24	446	159	287	14	21
N.J	480	69	88	323	349	75	274	477	103	374	88	315
N. Mex	106	27	33	46	68	28	41	575	234	341	27	36
N.Y	1,220	167	210	844	918	194	724	512	108	404	218	930
N.C	354	42	99	213	279	87	192	504	157	347	85	166
N. Dak	60	9	16	35	31	11	20	478	176	302	12	20
Ohio	654	92	136	425	454	109	345	424	102	322	120	351
Okla	212	47	60	105	140	50	90	498	177	322	46	73
Oreg	187	25	53	108	127	41	86	537	173	363	50	95
Pa	680	128	149	402	474	133	341	402	113	290	154	348
R.I	61	10	23	28	44	19	25	474	204	270	20	28
S.C	203	31	63	109	146	56	90	506	194	313	52	70
S. Dak	60	11	16	33	33	12	21	485	176	309	12	17
Tenn	293	57	74	162	212	64	148	494	150	345	56	122
Tex	869	150	193	526	631	163	468	491	127	364	164	424
Utah	117	35	33	48	64	26	37	501	208	293	27	36
Vt	36	4	13	19	24	11	13	492	223	269	11	11
Va	441	142	105	194	262	89	173	510	174	336	88	155
Wash	287	58	85	145	189	66	123	516	180	336	81	146
W. Va	118	16	44	59	91	37	54	489	201	288	34	47
Wis	310	26	69	214	222	55	168	478	117	361	68	172
Wyo	35	6	9	19	24	8	16	586	202	384	9	14

X Not applicable.
[1] Federal civilian employment in United States as of December 1977. Total accordingly differs from Federal employment reported in table 504 which pertains to October of each year and includes employees working outside United States.
[2] Subject to sampling variation.
[3] Based on population estimated as of July 1, 1977.   [4] For all employees.

Source: U.S. Bureau of the Census, *Public Employment in 1977*, series G E 77, No. 1.

No. 507. State and Local Government Employment, Payrolls, and Monthly Earnings, by Level of Government: 1960 to 1977.

[See also Historical Statistics, Colonial Times to 1970, series Y 274-289 and Y 292-307]

LEVEL OF GOVERNMENT AND ITEM	1960	1965	1970	1972	1973	1974	1975	1976	1977
	EMPLOYEES, OCTOBER (1,000)								
Total	6,387	8,001	10,147	10,964	11,353	11,754	12,084	12,169	12,558
Full-time	5,320	6,595	8,024	8,578	8,838	9,177	9,397	9,514	9,775
Part-time	1,067	1,406	2,123	2,385	2,515	2,577	2,687	2,655	2,783
Full-time equivalent:									
State and local	5,570	6,937	8,528	9,237	9,578	9,852	10,098	10,206	10,498
Education	2,525	3,337	4,258	4,585	4,751	4,901	4,952	5,003	5,106
Health and hospitals	654	789	950	1,053	1,088	1,115	1,133	1,149	1,183
Police protection	304	349	450	487	516	532	544	546	561
Other	2,087	2,462	2,871	3,112	3,223	3,303	3,469	3,509	3,648
State, total [1]	1,353	1,751	2,302	2,487	2,547	2,653	2,744	2,799	2,902
Education	390	508	803	867	887	929	952	973	1,005
Health and hospitals	331	392	482	520	534	553	570	589	614
Highways	240	284	297	286	284	277	271	259	258
Local, total [1]	4,217	5,186	6,226	6,750	7,031	7,198	7,354	7,407	7,596
Education	2,136	2,829	3,455	3,718	3,863	3,973	4,000	4,030	4,102
Health and hospitals	324	397	469	532	555	562	562	559	569
Highways	259	266	271	275	282	284	298	292	299
Counties [1]	738	893	1,098	1,242	1,318	1,343	1,408	1,448	1,543
Education	(NA)	(NA)	228	262	285	282	279	294	321
Health and hospitals	(NA)	(NA)	227	252	266	277	281	282	297
Public welfare	(NA)	(NA)	111	132	130	128	139	142	148
Municipalities [1]	1,447	1,638	1,922	2,029	2,109	2,127	2,142	2,107	2,141
Education	(NA)	(NA)	359	378	402	405	376	360	353
Health and hospitals	(NA)	(NA)	158	167	173	169	165	158	157
Police protection	(NA)	(NA)	299	319	337	344	349	347	355
Fire protection	(NA)	(NA)	169	181	184	183	184	183	187
School districts	1,729	2,287	2,786	2,981	3,074	3,183	3,243	3,272	3,325
Townships	302 {	177	192	215	232	233	237	245	249
Special districts		191	228	283	298	312	324	335	338
	PAYROLL, OCTOBER (mil. dol.)								
Total	2,215	3,400	5,906	7,240	8,015	8,792	9,640	10,359	11,279
Full-time	(NA)	3,251	5,598	6,786	7,498	8,244	9,018	9,709	10,542
Part-time	(NA)	150	309	454	517	548	622	650	738
Education	1,095	1,778	3,170	3,814	4,185	4,580	4,960	5,310	5,753
Health and hospitals	198	292	529	672	758	832	907	981	1,073
Police protection	129	184	339	438	480	531	585	628	696
Other	795	1,147	1,802	2,317	2,593	2,849	3,206	3,439	3,757
State, total [1]	545	849	1,612	1,937	2,158	2,410	2,653	2,894	3,200
Education	172	290	630	747	822	933	1,022	1,112	1,237
Health and hospitals	104	150	283	343	391	432	472	517	573
Highways	90	129	193	213	232	238	251	256	275
Local, total [1]	1,670	2,551	4,294	5,303	5,857	6,382	6,987	7,474	8,079
Education	923	1,488	2,539	3,067	3,363	3,647	3,939	4,208	4,516
Health and hospitals	93	141	246	328	367	400	437	464	498
Highways	88	110	149	179	200	212	238	249	266
Counties [1]	229	377	639	857	952	1,057	1,183	1,295	1,441
Education	(NA)	89	149	205	233	241	252	285	321
Health and hospitals	(NA)	66	117	158	174	199	217	233	260
Public welfare	(NA)	30	61	83	85	92	106	114	127
Municipalities [1]	583	818	1,361	1,654	1,855	1,985	2,129	2,235	2,386
Education	(NA)	170	299	352	415	425	425	431	442
Health and hospitals	(NA)	56	90	112	127	132	143	145	149
Police protection	(NA)	130	231	298	323	349	384	407	453
Fire protection	(NA)	84	137	167	184	196	217	226	249
School districts	735	1,189	2,032	2,428	2,623	2,882	3,160	3,380	3,637
Townships	} 118 {	80	122	166	192	200	215	237	255
Special districts		87	140	198	234	258	300	326	361
	AVERAGE OCTOBER EARNINGS (dol.)								
Full-time employees, State and local	399	493	697	790	847	899	961	1,020	1,078
Education	437	538	756	848	904	949	1,013	1,073	1,135
Other	368	452	642	737	796	853	912	972	1,027

NA Not available. [1] Includes other categories not shown separately.

Source: U.S. Bureau of the Census, Public Employment, series GE No. 1, annual, and unpublished data.

No. 508. STATE AND LOCAL GOVERNMENT EMPLOYMENT (FULL-TIME EQUIVALENT) AND PAYROLLS, BY SELECTED FUNCTION—STATES: 1977

[For October]

STATE	EMPLOYMENT (1,000)					OCTOBER PAYROLL (mil. dol.)				
	Education		Health and hospitals	Highways	Police and local fire protection	Public welfare	Education		Health and hospitals	Highways	Police and local fire protection	Public welfare
	Total	Local schools only					Total	Local schools only				
U.S.	5,106.2	3,929.2	1,183.4	557.0	781.1	355.7	5,753.0	4,281.3	1,072.4	541.0	987.3	329.8
Ala	83.4	58.9	28.1	14.3	11.0	4.2	78.1	50.3	23.0	9.2	10.5	3.9
Alaska	11.7	9.0	1.2	1.8	1.4	.7	21.4	15.5	1.8	3.2	2.7	.9
Ariz	68.6	48.4	8.0	6.6	9.4	2.3	77.0	53.1	7.4	7.1	11.8	2.2
Ark	50.4	38.1	12.1	7.7	5.2	2.0	42.0	29.3	8.0	5.5	4.2	1.6
Calif	490.8	361.2	114.4	34.8	90.7	37.3	696.6	496.9	130.9	45.9	144.7	42.1
Colo	76.4	53.8	12.2	7.7	9.4	3.9	82.6	55.9	12.4	8.5	11.2	3.8
Conn	68.5	56.8	12.2	7.2	11.8	3.1	79.2	65.2	10.6	6.6	14.8	3.2
Del	16.0	11.3	2.5	1.6	1.8	1.1	18.6	12.5	2.1	1.7	2.2	.9
D.C	14.3	12.4	6.2	1.1	6.4	2.6	18.6	15.8	8.7	1.6	10.9	3.7
Fla	189.0	150.8	58.1	20.1	35.9	9.5	194.9	145.5	49.1	18.0	41.6	8.0
Ga	124.8	97.1	53.7	14.3	17.4	5.1	108.5	79.0	39.7	11.1	16.0	4.5
Hawaii	19.6	14.0	4.6	1.9	3.8	.9	26.5	18.3	4.8	2.1	5.1	.8
Idaho	22.3	16.6	3.8	3.1	2.8	1.3	20.9	14.8	3.1	3.1	2.6	1.3
Ill	246.3	190.2	45.9	21.3	44.4	15.8	316.5	237.3	45.5	23.8	61.7	13.6
Ind	127.2	96.2	27.4	12.0	16.3	6.9	138.9	97.0	22.0	9.4	15.7	5.0
Iowa	81.1	61.9	15.6	9.4	7.0	5.1	89.0	61.6	13.6	9.5	7.7	4.5
Kans	65.2	46.2	12.6	9.6	7.5	3.0	63.8	41.9	9.4	8.0	7.0	2.7
Ky	76.3	56.1	13.3	8.8	10.0	5.5	70.8	49.2	9.9	7.6	9.1	4.9
La	100.8	80.3	23.4	12.0	13.1	5.6	94.7	73.2	16.8	9.6	11.6	4.6
Maine	26.9	21.5	2.7	5.0	3.3	1.1	24.1	18.9	2.3	4.2	3.0	1.0
Md	107.9	78.6	23.6	9.9	17.5	5.7	131.6	98.9	22.3	9.4	20.9	5.9
Mass	127.2	110.4	30.1	13.0	29.9	7.7	151.5	130.2	28.1	12.8	37.0	7.9
Mich	234.1	177.9	44.5	16.6	30.8	15.3	305.1	225.0	47.2	19.2	46.1	17.6
Minn	101.4	78.3	20.3	12.4	9.8	7.9	118.2	85.9	20.8	14.8	12.9	7.8
Miss	58.8	42.9	18.7	9.0	6.5	3.2	49.1	32.8	11.5	5.7	5.4	2.2
Mo	104.6	84.2	29.5	12.6	17.1	6.7	103.2	80.0	24.2	10.9	18.8	5.2
Mont	21.2	17.0	3.1	3.6	2.4	1.4	23.9	18.1	2.7	3.9	2.4	1.2
Nebr	43.1	31.8	9.8	5.7	4.4	3.0	39.5	28.4	7.5	4.9	4.8	2.4
Nev	15.2	11.8	4.2	2.0	3.7	.8	15.7	11.4	4.4	2.4	4.8	.9
N.H	18.6	14.3	2.9	3.6	2.9	2.7	17.1	13.0	2.3	4.5	2.9	1.9
N.J	165.0	139.6	30.0	19.5	34.2	12.8	214.3	180.3	28.4	20.9	42.6	11.5
N. Mex	38.0	26.5	5.6	4.0	4.3	1.5	35.7	24.0	4.5	3.7	4.2	1.1
N.Y	353.1	293.6	145.8	47.0	77.7	48.7	492.6	416.3	149.7	48.5	132.8	45.6
N.C	149.4	110.7	31.0	15.0	16.8	8.2	139.4	100.1	25.7	13.1	16.2	6.8
N. Dak	17.1	12.5	2.2	2.5	1.4	1.0	19.1	13.4	1.8	2.3	1.5	.8
Ohio	225.1	177.1	44.8	23.1	33.6	17.2	246.4	186.8	39.5	22.8	40.7	13.6
Okla	70.4	50.8	16.7	9.0	9.4	5.5	64.4	43.4	11.7	6.2	8.5	4.6
Oreg	65.0	46.1	10.0	6.9	8.7	4.8	74.3	50.0	9.7	8.0	11.7	4.8
Pa	216.2	187.5	38.4	30.7	36.6	30.6	228.3	190.0	39.8	31.0	46.5	27.8
R.I	20.9	15.0	4.6	2.0	4.4	1.6	25.6	18.7	4.0	1.8	4.7	1.7
S.C	72.3	53.0	24.3	7.2	8.3	4.8	64.3	43.3	18.9	5.2	7.0	3.7
S. Dak	17.6	13.4	2.5	2.9	1.8	1.0	15.8	11.4	1.8	2.6	1.6	.8
Tenn	93.7	70.9	29.0	13.3	14.8	6.5	83.7	61.5	20.4	9.1	13.6	4.8
Tex	348.2	267.9	68.7	30.2	42.6	14.5	337.6	249.1	52.9	27.1	44.5	13.2
Utah	37.4	23.4	4.6	3.3	3.8	2.0	36.7	23.4	3.9	3.6	4.1	2.0
Vt	12.9	9.4	1.5	2.1	1.3	.6	11.8	8.3	1.4	2.0	1.3	.6
Va	140.2	108.7	26.2	16.0	15.8	6.2	136.7	99.1	21.2	13.1	16.1	5.2
Wash	92.0	65.1	14.4	10.7	12.3	5.5	114.1	76.9	14.0	14.1	16.3	5.3
W. Va	48.8	38.0	10.1	8.1	3.9	3.6	48.5	35.3	7.0	6.7	3.6	2.8
Wis	120.0	83.7	22.7	12.6	15.0	7.0	134.2	87.6	21.3	12.9	18.3	6.4
Wyo	11.3	8.1	3.2	2.0	1.4	.5	11.6	7.9	2.5	2.1	1.4	.4

Source: U.S. Bureau of the Census, *Public Employment in 1977*, series GE 77, No. 1.

No. 509. STATE AND LOCAL GOVERNMENT—EMPLOYMENT (FULL-TIME) AND SALARY, BY SEX AND RACE/ETHNIC GROUP: 1973 TO 1976

[As of **June 30.** Excludes school systems and educational institutions. Based on reports from State governments (44 in 1973, 46 in 1974, and 48 in 1975 and 1976) and a sample of county, municipal, township, and special district jurisdictions employing 15 or more nonelected, nonappointed full-time employees. For definition of median, see p. xii]

SEX AND RACE/ ETHNIC GROUP	NUMBER EMPLOYED (1,000)				PERCENT DISTRIBUTION				MEDIAN ANNUAL SALARY (dol.)			
	1973	1974	1975	1976	1973	1974	1975	1976	1973	1974	1975	1976
Total	3,809	3,984	3,899	4,369	100.0	100.0	100.0	100.0	8,568	9,146	9,827	10,367
Male	2,486	2,571	2,436	2,724	65.3	64.5	62.5	62.3	9,603	10,269	11,295	11,802
Female	1,322	1,412	1,464	1,645	34.7	35.5	37.5	37.7	7,030	7,523	8,178	8,649
White	3,115	3,209	3,102	3,490	81.8	80.5	79.6	79.9	8,844	9,408	10,167	10,718
Minority group, total [1]	693	775	797	880	18.2	19.5	20.4	20.1	7,464	8,051	8,788	9,248
Black	523	590	602	664	13.7	14.8	15.4	15.2	7,361	7,938	8,629	9,054
Hispanic [2]	125	138	147	165	3.3	3.5	3.8	3.8	7,429	7,985	8,872	9,429

[1] Includes other minority groups, not shown separately.
[2] Prior to 1976, this ethnic group was classified as "Spanish-surnamed American."

Source: U.S. Equal Employment Opportunity Commission, *Minorities and Women in State and Local Government*, annual.

No. 510. STATE AND LOCAL GOVERNMENT—EMPLOYMENT (FULL-TIME) AND SALARY, BY OCCUPATION, SEX, AND RACE/ETHNIC GROUP: 1976

[As of **June 30.** See headnote, table 509]

SEX AND ETHNIC/GROUP	Total	Officials/ administrators	Professionals	Technicians	Protective service	Paraprofessionals	Office/ clerical	Skilled craft	Service/ maintenance
NUMBER EMPLOYED (1,000)									
Total	4,369	220	770	424	603	366	831	368	787
Male	2,724	177	455	283	565	119	126	351	647
Female	1,645	43	314	141	38	247	704	18	139
White	3,490	203	669	361	529	244	672	309	503
Minority group, total [1]	880	18	101	63	74	123	159	59	283
Black	664	12	65	47	55	104	114	40	228
Hispanic	165	4	17	12	16	15	34	16	49
PERCENT DISTRIBUTION									
Total	100.0	100.0	100.0	100.0	100.0	100.0	100.0	100.0	100.0
Male	62.3	80.5	59.2	66.7	93.7	32.5	15.2	95.2	82.3
Female	37.7	19.5	40.8	33.3	6.3	67.5	84.8	4.8	17.7
White	79.9	92.0	86.9	85.0	87.8	66.5	80.9	84.0	64.0
Minority group, total [1]	20.1	8.0	13.1	15.0	12.2	33.5	19.1	16.0	36.0
Black	15.2	5.4	8.5	11.0	9.0	28.4	13.7	10.8	29.0
Hispanic	3.8	1.8	2.3	2.9	2.7	4.2	4.1	4.4	6.3
MEDIAN ANNUAL SALARY (dol.)									
Total	10,367	16,739	13,611	11,118	12,687	7,731	8,186	10,959	8,710
Male	11,802	16,847	14,990	12,244	12,915	8,673	9,382	11,142	9,140
Female	8,649	13,354	12,057	9,108	9,275	7,392	7,985	8,003	7,047
White	10,718	16,784	13,678	11,314	12,779	7,737	8,126	11,058	8,894
Minority group, total [1]	9,248	16,227	13,192	10,015	11,946	7,721	8,418	10,235	8,323
Black	9,054	16,212	12,666	9,740	11,730	7,649	8,438	9,940	8,216
Hispanic	9,429	15,303	13,433	10,537	12,528	8,167	8,057	10,517	8,621

[1] Includes other minority groups, not shown separately.

Source: U.S. Equal Employment Opportunity Commission, *Minorities and Women in State and Local Government*, annual.

No. 511. City Government Employment and Payrolls: 1950 to 1977

[For **October**. 1967 and 1972 based on complete count of all cities; other years based on sample and subject to sampling variation. Minus sign (−) denotes decrease]

YEAR	ALL EMPLOYEES, FULL-TIME AND PART-TIME (1,000)		OCTOBER PAYROLL (mil. dol.)		AVERAGE ANNUAL PERCENT CHANGE [2]		FULL-TIME EQUIVALENT EMPLOYMENT (1,000)			AVERAGE EARNINGS IN OCTOBER, FULL-TIME EMPLOYEES	
	Total	Excl. education	Total [1]	Excl. education [1]	All employees	Monthly payroll	Total [1]	Education	Other	Education	Other
1950	1,311	1,106	290	230	3.2	8.9	(NA)	(NA)	(NA)	(NA)	(NA)
1955	1,436	1,238	414	337	1.8	7.4	1,262	182	1,080	$422	$315
1960	1,692	1,439	583	471	3.3	7.1	1,447	225	1,222	502	387
1965	1,884	1,560	818	649	2.2	7.0	1,638	282	1,356	603	480
1967	1,993	1,633	972	769	2.9	9.0	1,715	306	1,410	664	546
1970	2,244	1,815	1,361	1,062	4.0	11.9	1,922	359	1,563	838	681
1971	2,273	1,838	1,482	1,167	1.3	8.9	1,960	366	1,594	876	735
1972	2,375	1,918	1,654	1,302	4.5	11.6	2,029	378	1,650	951	792
1973	2,471	1,992	1,855	1,441	4.0	12.2	2,109	402	1,707	1,045	846
1974	2,491	2,009	1,985	1,560	.8	7.0	2,127	405	1,722	1,060	909
1975	2,506	2,074	2,129	1,725	.6	8.3	2,142	376	1,782	1,130	972
1976	2,443	2,021	2,235	1,804	−2.5	5.0	2,107	360	1,747	1,207	1,035
1977	2,487	2,066	2,386	1,944	1.8	6.7	2,141	353	1,788	1,255	1,090

NA Not available.　[1] Includes only those school systems operated as part of the general city government.
[2] Represents average for period of intervals shown; for 1950, change from 1946.

No. 512. City Government Employment and Payrolls—All Cities and Cities with 50,000 Population or More: 1975 to 1977

[As of **October**]

TYPE OF EMPLOYMENT	EMPLOYEES (1,000)						OCTOBER PAYROLL (mil. dol.)					
	All cities			Cities with 50,000 population or more			All cities			Cities with 50,000 population or more		
	1975	1976	1977	1975	1976	1977	1975	1976	1977	1975	1976	1977
Total	2,506	2,443	2,487	1,630	1,572	1,605	2,130	2,235	2,386	1,612	1,668	1,770
Full-time	2,038	2,012	2,047	1,450	1,407	1,428	2,031	2,141	2,285	1,551	1,610	1,710
Part-time	468	431	440	180	165	177	98	95	100	60	57	60
Full-time equivalent	2,143	2,107	2,141	1,508	1,461	1,487	(X)	(X)	(X)	(X)	(X)	(X)
Education [1]	376	360	353	312	290	288	425	431	442	363	358	375
Percent of total	18	17	16	21	20	19	20	19	19	23	21	21
Teachers	277	266	261	226	212	211	346	352	362	295	297	308
Others	99	94	93	86	78	78	78	79	80	68	67	68
Highways	129	124	128	65	61	63	109	113	122	62	62	67
Public welfare	42	40	41	41	38	39	36	39	41	34	37	39
Hospitals	128	123	122	94	90	86	108	109	112	87	86	85
Health	38	35	35	35	32	32	35	36	37	33	33	34
Police protection	349	347	355	224	217	224	384	407	453	272	282	314
Fire protection	184	183	187	126	124	126	217	226	249	162	166	179
Sewerage	55	55	57	28	28	29	46	51	55	27	29	31
Sanitation	108	107	110	66	64	67	88	92	96	62	63	65
Parks and recreation	104	102	109	73	73	79	84	88	97	61	65	72
Housing and urban renewal	35	36	39	31	32	35	35	40	43	32	36	39
Correction	16	17	18	15	16	17	18	20	22	17	20	21
Libraries	38	38	36	28	27	26	30	32	33	23	24	25
Financial administration	61	62	65	34	34	36	54	58	64	33	35	39
General control	105	103	100	62	63	59	101	110	108	66	73	69
Local utilities [2]	200	197	195	136	132	130	206	216	220	155	161	160
Water supply	92	92	94	51	51	52	81	87	93	50	53	56
Electric power	46	45	42	27	26	23	49	51	51	32	34	32
Transit	56	54	52	54	52	50	71	72	70	70	71	68
All other functions	175	178	190	139	141	150	155	168	190	125	135	154

X Not applicable.　[1] City operated schools and colleges only.　[2] Includes gas supply, not shown below.
Source of tables 511 and 512: U.S. Bureau of the Census, *City Employment*, series GE, No. 2, annual.

No. 513. CITY GOVERNMENT EMPLOYMENT AND PAYROLL—SELECTED LARGE CITIES: 1970 TO 1977

[For October. Cities ranked by size of population as of July 1, 1975]

| CITY | FULL-TIME EQUIVALENT EMPLOYMENT | | | | | | OCTOBER PAYROLL (mil. dol.) | | | AVERAGE EARNINGS IN OCTOBER, FULL-TIME EMPLOYEES (dol.) | |
| | Total (1,000) | | | Per 10,000 population | | | | | | | |
	1970	1975	1977	1970 [1]	1975 [2]	1977 [2]	1970	1975	1977	1970	1977
New York, N.Y.[3][4]	375	348	311	476	464	415	326	435	429	869	1,396
Chicago, Ill	44	49	45	131	157	147	40	20	63	902	1,390
Los Angeles, Calif	42	47	45	150	172	167	42	64	66	990	1,464
Philadelphia, Pa	34	38	38	177	209	208	30	5	49	866	1,303
Detroit, Mich	26	21	24	172	153	179	21	26	34	802	1,405
Houston, Tex	10	14	16	81	107	97	7	13	17	679	1,057
Baltimore, Md.[3][4]	37	41	37	412	475	430	26	37	37	704	1,049
Dallas, Tex	11	13	13	134	163	165	8	13	15	693	1,088
San Diego, Calif	5	7	7	78	89	92	5	9	10	868	1,387
San Antonio, Tex	8	11	11	128	143	148	5	10	11	648	1,001
Indianapolis, Ind. [5]	6	11	11	78	160	160	3	8	9	500	799
Washington, D.C.[3][4]	49	46	45	642	643	633	39	57	65	804	1,463
Honolulu, Hawaii	7	9	10	110	126	145	6	9	12	811	1,186
Milwaukee, Wis	10	10	9	138	145	140	8	11	12	798	1,297
Phoenix, Ariz	5	7	9	94	110	130	4	7	10	718	1,177
San Francisco, Calif	20	22	22	285	324	326	19	27	29	945	1,333
Memphis, Tenn.[3]	24	22	25	387	328	373	15	20	25	618	984
Cleveland, Ohio	16	13	11	210	197	169	10	13	13	621	1,190
Boston, Mass	25	25	25	382	390	391	18	27	34	753	1,345
New Orleans, La	10	11	13	169	188	224	5	7	11	465	906
San Jose, Calif	3	4	4	59	66	77	3	5	6	970	1,504
Columbus, Ohio	5	7	7	94	124	132	4	7	8	734	1,150
Jacksonville, Fla. [5]	6	10	11	115	194	204	4	9	11	716	986
St. Louis, Mo	13	14	14	215	257	276	9	12	14	642	983
Seattle, Wash	10	9	8	188	180	174	8	10	12	820	1,390
Denver, Colo	9	12	12	173	252	252	6	13	15	710	1,205
Kansas City, Mo	6	7	7	113	137	147	4	7	8	686	1,146
Pittsburgh, Pa	7	6	6	135	121	125	5	5	6	679	1,116
Atlanta, Ga	7	9	10	147	204	234	4	7	9	612	872
Nashville-Davidson, Tenn.[3]	14	18	18	319	425	420	9	15	17	632	954
Cincinnati, Ohio	[4]13	[4]17	8	297	421	184	[4]9	[4]17	6	[4]648	1,137
Buffalo, N.Y. [3]	13	13	13	290	325	309	11	14	17	829	1,342
El Paso, Tex	3	4	4	85	90	106	2	3	4	562	1,087
Minneapolis, Minn	5	6	5	117	146	141	4	7	8	825	1,414
Omaha, Nebr	3	4	3	75	98	86	2	3	4	662	1,112
Toledo, Ohio	4	4	4	98	105	104	3	4	5	823	1,331
Oklahoma City, Okla	4	4	4	97	104	120	2	3	4	559	1,001
Miami, Fla	4	4	4	126	100	121	3	5	5	804	1,164
Fort Worth, Tex	4	4	5	100	122	134	3	4	4	647	933
Portland, Oreg	5	5	4	121	132	122	4	6	6	790	1,467
Newark, N.J. [3]	16	18	18	407	542	515	12	17	18	814	1,053
Louisville, Ky	[5]6	6	6	161	166	181	[5]4	5	5	[5]672	878
Long Beach, Calif	5	5	5	127	152	148	4	7	7	913	1,467
Tulsa, Okla	3	3	4	83	98	106	2	3	3	621	930
Oakland, Calif	4	4	5	102	132	147	4	6	7	953	1,522
Austin, Tex	4	6	6	166	204	210	3	6	6	602	1,024
Tucson, Ariz	2	4	4	94	150	145	2	4	5	697	1,088
Baton Rouge, La	3	3	4	89	104	124	1	2	3	528	907
Norfolk, Va. [3]	10	12	11	309	401	381	6	9	7	590	892
Charlotte, N.C	3	4	4	113	137	154	2	4	4	667	1,001
Tampa, Fla	4	4	5	146	152	191	2	4	5	453	967
St. Paul, Minn	3	3	3	89	120	120	2	3	5	874	1,391
Albuquerque, N. Mex	3	4	4	107	137	145	2	3	4	654	1,054
Birmingham, Ala	4	4	4	120	134	144	2	3	4	573	997
Rochester, N.Y. [3]	11	10	9	356	372	320	8	11	11	739	963
Wichita, Kans	3	3	3	95	115	119	2	3	3	607	1,018
Sacramento, Calif	3	3	3	112	131	127	2	4	4	824	1,343
Akron, Ohio	3	3	3	103	124	126	2	3	4	716	1,231
Jersey City, N.J. [3]	7	9	8	284	356	332	6	8	10	790	1,177

[1] Based on 1970 population.
[2] Based on 1975 population estimates.   [3] Includes city operated elementary and secondary schools.
[4] Includes city operated university or college.   [5] Represents city and county consolidated government.

Source: U.S. Bureau of the Census, *City Employment*, series GE, No. 2, annual.

Section 11

Social Insurance and Welfare Services

This section presents data related to governmental expenditures on social welfare; governmental programs for old-age, survivors, disability, and health insurance (OASDHI); governmental and railroad employee retirement; private pension and employee benefit plans; government unemployment and temporary disability insurance; Federal supplemental security income payments and aid to the needy; and maternal, child, and other welfare services. Also included here are selected data on workmen's compensation, including black lung benefits; vocational rehabilitation; the American Red Cross; United Way campaign; and philanthropic trusts and foundations.

The principal source for these data is the Department of Health, Education, and Welfare's (HEW) monthly *Social Security Bulletin*, which presents current data on many of the programs and summary data in annual statistical supplements. Current data on employment security are published monthly in the Department of Labor's *Unemployment Insurance Statistics*. Data on benefits for railroad workers appear in the Railroad Retirement Board's *RRB Quarterly Review* and *Annual Report*. Statistics on aid to families with dependent children (AFDC) are presented in the U.S. Social Security Administration's monthly publication, *Public Assistance Statistics*.

Social insurance under the Social Security Act.—Programs established by the Social Security Act provide protection against wage loss resulting from retirement, prolonged disability, death, or unemployment, and protection against the cost of medical care during old age and disability. The Federal OASDHI program provides monthly cash benefits to retired or disabled insured workers and their dependents and to qualified survivors of insured workers. To be eligible, a worker must have had a specified period of employment in which OASDHI taxes were paid. A worker becomes eligible for full benefits at age 65, although reduced benefits may be obtained up to 3 years earlier; the worker's spouse is under the same limitations. Special benefits are also provided to those persons 72 and over who do not meet insured status requirements. Under certain conditions, survivor benefits are payable to dependents of an insured worker, including aged parents and other qualifying dependents (widow or widower in place of spouse) who are eligible for retirement benefits. Disability benefits are payable to an insured worker under age 65 with a prolonged disability and to the worker's dependents on the same basis as dependents of retired workers. A lump sum benefit is also payable on the death of an insured worker.

Beginning in July 1966, a Federal health insurance program (medicare) has provided two coordinated plans for nearly all people age 65 and over: (1) A hospital insurance plan which covers hospital and related services and (2) a voluntary supplementary medical insurance plan, financed partially by monthly premiums paid by participants, which covers a portion of physicians' services and related medical services. Beginning July 1973, such insurance was extended to disabled beneficiaries of any age under certain circumstances and to persons with chronic kidney disease.

Retirement, survivors, disability, and hospital insurance benefits are paid for by a payroll tax on annual earnings (up to a maximum of earnings set by law) of workers, employers, and the self-employed. These taxes are adjusted periodically through Federal legislation to reflect increasing income levels (see table 527). Tax receipts and benefit payments are administered by Federal trust funds. The special benefits for uninsured persons, age 72 and over, and hospital benefits for persons 65 and over with specified amounts of social security coverage less than that required for cash benefit eligibility, are financed from Federal general revenues.

Both unemployment insurance and the public employment (placement) service are presently administered by the U.S. Employment and Training Administration and each State's employment security agency. By agreement with the U.S. Secretary of Labor, State agencies also administer unemployment compensation for eligible ex-servicemen and Federal employees, unemployment assistance under the Disaster Relief Act of 1970 to individuals unemployed because of major disasters, workers assistance and relocation allowances under the Trade Expansion Act, and direct aid (training and related cash allowances) under Federal manpower and adjustment acts.

State unemployment insurance laws pay benefits, related to the individual's past earnings, to unemployed eligible workers. State laws vary concerning the length of time one may collect benefits and their amount. In most States, benefits are payable for 26 weeks and, with Congressional approval during periods of high unemployment, extended benefits are payable under a Federal-State program to those who have exhausted their regular State benefits. The amount of the basic benefit can vary among States by over 100 percent. In addition, some States may adjust the basic benefit upward with allowances for dependents.

Funds for the payment of unemployment insurance are derived by a Federal unemployment tax levied on the taxable payrolls of most employers. Taxable payroll under the Federal Act and most State laws is the first $8,000 in wages paid each worker during a year. Employers are allowed a percentage credit of taxable payroll for contributions paid to States under State unemployment insurance laws. The remaining percent of the Federal tax finances administrative costs, the Federal share of extended benefits, and advances to States.

Excluded from Federal tax coverage are the railroad industry (see below), agricultural and domestic service, nonprofit organizations, and government employment although they may be covered by State law. Through temporary legislation, enacted in 1974, workers lacking sufficient covered employment to qualify for regular unemployment insurance benefits are eligible for special unemployment assistance if they had worked in an area with a high unemployment rate.

Social insurance for railroad workers. The Railroad Retirement Act, administered by the U.S. Railroad Retirement Board, covers railroad employees and companies and provides retirement annuities for aged and disabled workers and for spouses of retired employees, and benefits to survivors of deceased workers. Wage credits of railroad workers are combined with social security covered employment at the time of computation of benefits. These annuities and benefits, including medicare hospital insurance, are financed primarily through an employer-employee tax on earnings up to a monthly maximum of one-twelfth of the annual social security tax base. The 1978 tax rates are 15.55 percent for employers and 6.05 percent for employees. Supplemental annuities, which are financed by a special variable quarterly tax on railroad employers for each employee-hour compensated, have been provided for career employees since 1966. Also, medicare health insurance is available to railroad workers on the same basis as to workers covered by social security. The Railroad Unemployment Insurance Act provides benefits for unemployment and sickness financed by contributions from covered employers on earnings not over $400 a month. Contribution rates vary from year to year according to a graduated schedule based on account balances; the 8 percent maximum rate is applicable in 1978.

Social insurance for Government employees.—The civil service retirement program is the major system providing age and service, disability, and survivor annuities for Federal civilian employees. The employee contribution rate is 7 percent of total base pay; the Federal Government contributes the remainder of the cost. In addition, there are separate retirement systems for the uniformed services (supplementing OASDHI and for a few special groups of Federal civilian employees.

State and local government employees are covered for the most part by State and local retirement systems similar to the Federal civil service retirement system. In many jurisdictions these benefits supplement OASDHI coverage.

Workmen's compensation.—All States provide protection against work-connected injuries and deaths although some States exclude certain workers (e.g. domestic help). Federal laws cover Federal employees, private employees in the District of Columbia, and longshoremen and harbor workers. In addition, the Social Security Administration and the Department of Labor administer a "black lung" benefits program for coal miners disabled by pneumoconiosis and for specified dependents and survivors. Specified occupational diseases are compensable under most laws. In most States, benefits are related to the worker's salary. The benefits may or may not be augmented by dependents' allowances or automatically adjusted to prevailing wage levels.

Public aid.—Individuals who qualify are assisted through public assistance programs administered by the States and the supplemental security income (SSI) program administered by the Social Security Administration. Prior to 1974, States, assisted by Federal funds in the form of grants, provided social services and money payments to those eligible (e.g. the aged, blind, disabled, and families with dependent children). The Emergency Assistance program and general assistance were also available.

Beginning 1974, the SSI program replaced Federal grants for aid to the aged, blind, and disabled in the 50 States and the District of Columbia. Federal grants continue for the AFDC program, Emergency Assistance Program, social services, and Medicaid, and for all programs in Guam, Puerto Rico, and the Virgin Islands. The SSI program provides a minimum income for the aged, blind, and disabled and establishes uniform national basic eligibility requirements and payment standards. States are permitted to supplement the basic Federal payment to the extent they choose.

Health and welfare services.—Programs providing health and welfare services are aided through Federal grants to States for child welfare services, vocational rehabilitation, activities for the aged, maternal and child health services, maternity and infant care projects, comprehensive health services, and a variety of public health activities.

Statistical reliability.—For discussion of statistical collection, estimation, and sampling procedures and measures of statistical reliability applicable to HEW and Census Bureau data, see Appendix III.

Historical statistics.—Tabular headnotes provide cross-references, where applicable, to *Historical Statistics of the United States, Colonial Times to 1970.* See Appendix I.

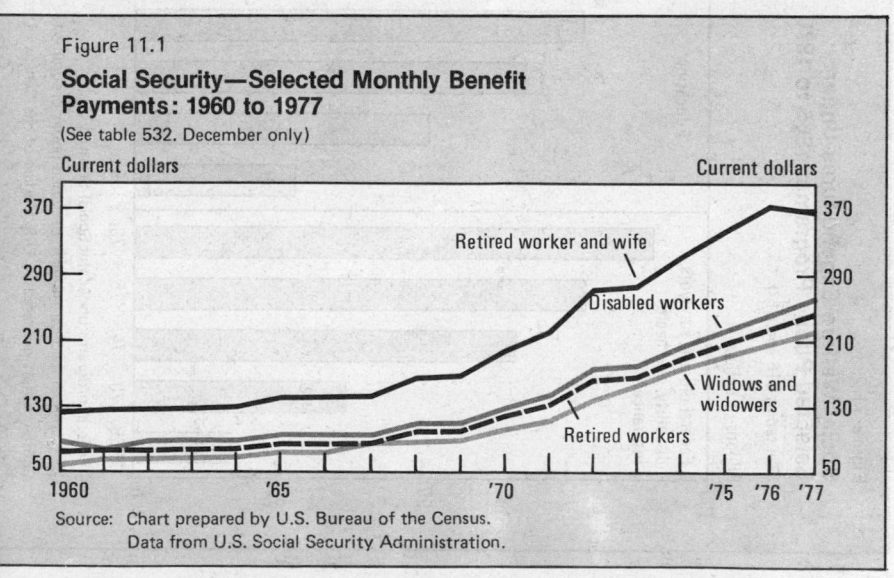

Figure 11.1

Social Security—Selected Monthly Benefit Payments: 1960 to 1977

(See table 532. December only)

Source: Chart prepared by U.S. Bureau of the Census.
Data from U.S. Social Security Administration.

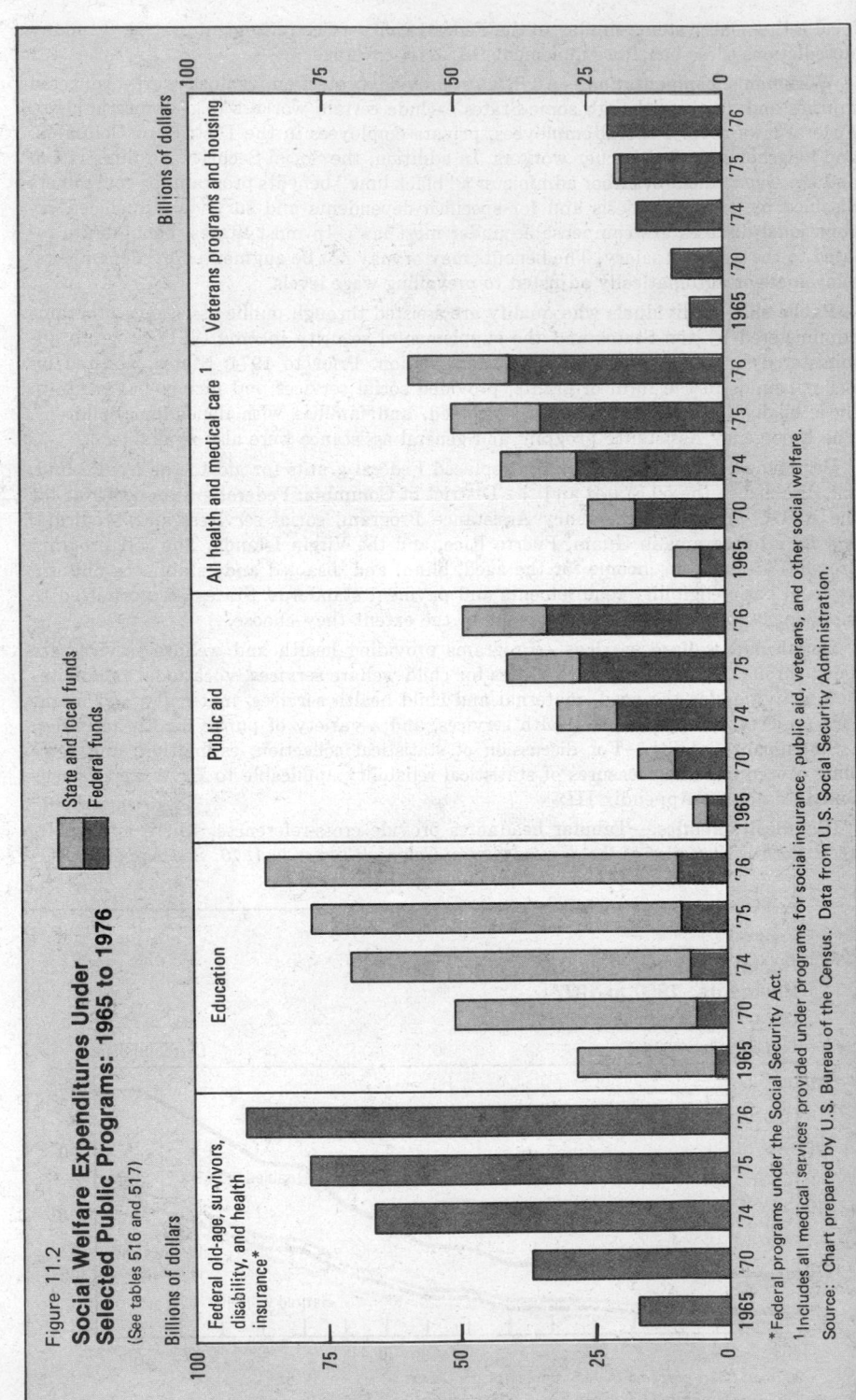

Figure 11.2

Social Welfare Expenditures Under Selected Public Programs: 1965 to 1976

(See tables 516 and 517)

Billions of dollars

State and local funds
Federal funds

*Federal programs under the Social Security Act.

1 Includes all medical services provided under programs for social insurance, public aid, veterans, and other social welfare.

Source: Chart prepared by U.S. Bureau of the Census. Data from U.S. Social Security Administration.

No. 514. PUBLIC AND PRIVATE EXPENDITURES FOR SOCIAL WELFARE: 1950 TO 1976

[In billions of dollars, except percent. For years ending June 30. "Public" refers to Federal, State, and local governments; "private" to nongovernmental agencies]

TYPE OF EXPENDITURE	1950	1960	1965	1970	1971	1972	1973	1974	1975	1976, prel.
Total, net [1]	35.4	78.7	117.8	209.3	241.6	268.2	298.5	338.9	395.9	453.0
Public	23.5	52.3	77.2	145.9	171.9	191.4	213.9	239.3	286.5	331.4
Private	12.2	27.8	42.7	67.4	74.4	82.1	90.6	99.6	109.4	121.6
Income maintenance	10.7	29.8	42.6	72.5	87.6	98.7	112.3	126.4	152.5	179.5
Public [2]	9.8	26.3	36.6	60.8	74.5	83.8	95.7	107.6	131.7	156.7
Private	1.0	3.5	6.0	11.7	13.1	14.8	16.6	18.7	20.9	22.8
Health	12.0	25.9	38.9	69.2	77.2	86.7	95.4	106.0	122.2	139.3
Public	3.1	6.4	9.5	25.4	28.8	33.5	36.7	41.5	50.9	58.8
Private	9.0	19.5	29.4	43.8	48.4	53.2	58.7	64.5	71.4	80.5
Education	11.0	21.8	34.1	61.7	69.1	73.1	80.0	87.1	96.5	106.8
Public	9.4	18.0	28.1	51.9	58.3	61.3	67.4	73.7	82.3	91.8
Private	1.6	3.7	6.0	9.9	10.8	11.8	12.7	13.4	14.2	15.0
Welfare and other services	2.0	2.7	4.3	9.8	12.4	15.0	16.8	19.3	24.6	27.5
Public [3]	1.3	1.6	2.9	7.8	10.3	12.7	14.2	16.4	21.6	24.1
Private	.7	1.1	1.4	2.0	2.1	2.3	2.6	2.9	3.0	3.4
PERCENT PUBLIC										
Total [4]	65.8	65.3	64.4	68.4	69.8	70.0	70.2	70.6	72.4	73.1
Income maintenance	91.0	88.1	86.0	83.9	85.0	85.0	85.2	85.2	86.3	87.3
Health	25.5	24.7	24.5	36.7	37.3	38.6	38.4	39.1	41.6	42.2
Education	85.3	82.8	82.5	84.0	84.4	83.9	84.2	84.6	85.3	86.0
Welfare and other services	65.8	59.1	68.0	79.6	83.1	84.7	84.5	85.0	87.8	87.6
PERCENT OF GNP [5]										
Total, net [1]	13.4	15.8	17.9	21.8	23.7	24.1	24.1	24.4	26.7	27.5
Income maintenance	4.0	6.0	6.5	7.5	8.6	8.9	9.1	9.3	10.5	11.1
Health	4.5	5.2	5.9	7.2	7.6	7.8	7.7	7.8	8.4	8.6
Education	4.1	4.4	5.2	6.4	6.8	6.6	6.5	6.4	6.6	6.6
Welfare and other services	.8	.5	.7	1.0	1.2	1.4	1.5	1.4	1.7	1.7

[1] Total expenditures adjusted to eliminate duplication resulting from use of cash payments received under social welfare programs to purchase medical care and educational services.
[2] Includes cash benefits and administrative costs under social insurance, public assistance, supplemental security income, and veterans' and emergency employment programs. Excludes cost of medical services provided in conjunction with those programs and for other welfare programs. See table 522.
[3] Includes food stamps, surplus food for the needy and for institutions, child nutrition, institutional care, child welfare, economic opportunity and manpower programs, veterans' welfare services, vocational rehabilitation, and housing.   [4] Before adjustment for elimination of duplication.   [5] Gross national product.

No. 515. SOCIAL WELFARE EXPENDITURES UNDER PUBLIC PROGRAMS AS PERCENT OF GNP AND TOTAL GOVERNMENT OUTLAYS: 1950 TO 1976

[See headnote, table 517]

	TOTAL EXPENDITURES				FEDERAL EXPENDITURES				STATE AND LOCAL GOVERNMENT EXPENDITURES			
			Percent of—				Percent of—				Percent of—	
YEAR	Total (bil. dol.)	Average annual percent change	Total GNP [1]	Total gov't outlays	Total (bil. dol.)	Average annual percent change	Total GNP [1]	Total Federal outlays	Total (bil. dol.)	Average annual percent change	Total GNP [1]	Total State and local gov't outlays
1950	23.5	[2] 20.6	8.9	37.4	10.5	[2] 19.4	4.0	26.2	13.0	[2] 21.7	4.9	59.2
1960	52.3	8.3	10.5	38.4	25.0	9.0	5.0	28.1	27.3	7.7	5.5	60.1
1965	77.2	8.1	11.7	42.2	37.7	8.6	5.7	32.6	39.5	7.6	6.0	60.4
1970	145.9	13.6	15.2	48.2	77.3	15.4	8.1	40.1	68.5	11.6	7.1	64.0
1971	171.9	17.9	16.9	51.7	92.6	19.7	9.1	44.9	79.3	15.8	7.8	64.0
1972	191.4	11.3	17.2	53.2	106.3	14.8	9.6	47.4	85.0	7.2	7.6	63.8
1973	213.9	11.8	17.3	55.5	122.6	15.3	9.9	50.5	91.4	7.5	7.4	64.9
1974	239.3	11.9	17.6	56.5	137.2	11.9	10.1	52.3	102.2	11.8	7.5	64.1
1975	286.5	19.7	19.7	57.9	167.2	21.9	11.5	54.0	119.3	16.8	8.2	65.0
1976, prel	331.4	15.7	20.6	59.7	198.3	18.6	12.3	56.0	133.0	11.5	8.3	66.9

[1] Gross national product.   [2] Change from 1945.
Source of tables 514 and 515: U.S. Social Security Administration, *Social Security Bulletin*, January 1977.

No. 516. SOCIAL WELFARE EXPENDITURES, BY SOURCE

[In millions of dollars. See headnote, table 517, and *Historical Statistics*,

PROGRAM	1960 Federal	1960 State and local	1970 Federal	1970 State and local	1971 Federal	1971 State and local	1972 Federal	1972 State and local
Total	24,957	27,337	77,337	68,519	92,587	79,320	106,327	85,031
Social insurance	14,307	4,999	45,246	9,446	53,903	12,466	61,248	13,561
Old-age, survivors, disability, health	11,032	(X)	36,835	(X)	43,123	(X)	48,229	(X)
Health insurance (Medicare)	(X)	(X)	7,149	(X)	7,875	(X)	8,819	(X)
Public employee retirement [1]	1,520	1,050	5,517	3,142	6,582	3,644	7,648	4,273
Railroad employee retirement	935	(X)	1,610	(X)	1,929	(X)	2,141	(X)
Unemployment insurance and employment services [2]	474	2,356	1,036	2,783	1,678	4,988	2,487	5,164
Other railroad employee insurance [3]	284	(X)	100	(X)	103	(X)	128	(X)
State temporary disability insurance [4]	(X)	348	(X)	718	(X)	773	(X)	784
Workmen's compensation [5]	63	1,245	148	2,803	488	3,062	616	3,340
Hospital and medical benefits	9	411	21	964	25	1,065	27	1,158
Public aid	2,117	1,984	9,649	6,839	12,990	8,272	16,291	9,787
Public assistance [6]	2,058	1,984	7,594	6,839	9,803	8,272	12,108	9,787
Vendor medical payments (Medicaid) [7]	200	293	2,607	2,606	3,374	2,904	4,166	3,585
Social services	(X)	(X)	522	191	692	258	1,598	562
Supplemental security income	(X)	(X)	(X)	(X)	(X)	(X)	(X)	(X)
Food stamps	(X)	(X)	577	(X)	1,576	(X)	1,867	(X)
Other [8]	59	(X)	1,477	(X)	1,611	(X)	2,316	(X)
Health and medical programs	1,737	2,727	4,775	5,132	5,148	5,939	6,322	6,544
Hospital and medical care	984	1,870	2,045	3,268	2,370	3,566	2,960	3,831
Civilian programs	103	1,870	286	3,268	414	3,566	619	3,831
Defense Department [9]	880	(X)	1,760	(X)	1,957	(X)	2,341	(X)
Maternal and child health programs	35	106	196	235	148	255	259	236
Medical research	426	23	1,485	150	1,497	163	1,693	179
Medical facilities construction	235	283	458	474	456	782	442	982
Defense Department	40	(X)	53	(X)	74	(X)	100	(X)
Other	57	445	590	1,004	678	1,173	968	1,316
Veterans programs	5,367	112	8,952	126	10,331	125	11,405	117
Pensions and compensation	3,403	(X)	5,394	(X)	5,878	(X)	6,209	(X)
Health and medical programs	954	(X)	1,784	(X)	2,027	(X)	2,431	(X)
Hospital and medical care	879	(X)	1,651	(X)	1,874	(X)	2,256	(X)
Hospital construction	60	(X)	71	(X)	85	(X)	110	(X)
Medical and prosthetic research	15	(X)	62	(X)	68	(X)	66	(X)
Education	410	(X)	1,018	(X)	1,622	(X)	1,925	(X)
Life insurance [10]	494	(X)	502	(X)	527	(X)	524	(X)
Welfare and other	107	112	253	126	278	125	316	117
Education [11]	868	16,758	5,876	44,970	6,597	50,107	6,721	52,664
Elementary and secondary	442	14,667	2,957	35,676	3,387	39,524	3,418	41,106
Construction [12]	71	2,591	36	4,623	20	4,532	20	4,439
Higher	293	1,898	2,155	7,752	2,202	8,633	2,220	9,363
Construction	1	357	466	1,101	438	1,128	351	1,131
Vocational and adult [12]	105	194	603	1,542	767	1,951	826	2,195
Housing	144	33	582	120	872	175	1,183	149
Other social welfare	417	723	2,259	1,886	2,746	2,237	3,155	2,209
Vocational rehabilitation	64	32	567	136	642	159	720	156
Medical services and research	18	7	137	27	130	33	160	36
Institutional care [13]	21	400	22	179	25	200	26	225
Child nutrition	306	93	711	185	988	216	1,232	270
Child welfare [14]	13	198	45	541	45	552	45	487
Special OEO and ACTION programs [15]	(X)	(X)	753	(X)	785	(X)	783	(X)
Welfare, not elsewhere classified [16]	12	[13]	161	845	261	1,110	350	1,070

X Not applicable.   [1] Excludes refunds to those leaving service. Federal data include military retirement
[2] Includes compensation for Federal employees and ex-servicemen, trade adjustment and cash training allow
ance, and payments under extended, emergency, disaster, and special unemployment insurance programs.
[3] Unemployment and temporary disability insurance.   [4] Cash and medical benefits in 5 areas.   [5] Benefit
by private insurance carriers, State funds, and self-insurers. Beginning 1970, Federal includes Black Lung benefi
programs.   [6] Includes payments under State general assistance programs and, beginning 1970, work incentiv
activities, not shown separately.   [7] Medical vendor payments are those made directly to suppliers of medica
care.   [8] Refugee assistance, surplus food for the needy, and work-experience training programs under the Eco
nomic Opportunity Act and the Comprehensive Employment and Training Act.   [9] Includes medical car
for military dependent families.   [10] Excludes servicemen's group life insurance.   [11] Federal expenditures fo
administrative costs (Office of Education) and research not shown separately, but included in total.

OF FUNDS AND PUBLIC PROGRAM: 1960 TO 1976

Colonial Times to 1970, series H 1-47, for related but not comparable data]

1973		1974		1975		1976, prel.		PROGRAM
Federal	State and local	Federal	State and local	Federal	State and local	Federal	State and local	
122,566	91,376	137,155	102,159	167,237	119,285	198,328	133,038	**Total.**
72,249	13,917	82,830	16,123	99,748	23,199	120,809	25,783	**Social insurance.**
57,767	(X)	66,287	(X)	78,430	(X)	90,441	(X)	Old-age, survivors, disability, health.
9,479	(X)	11,348	(X)	14,781	(X)	17,777	(X)	Health insurance (Medicare).
8,878	5,133	10,785	5,892	13,339	6,780	16,635	7,790	Public employee retirement.[1]
2,478	(X)	2,693	(X)	3,085	(X)	3,500	(X)	Railroad employee retirement.
								Unemployment insurance and employ-
1,869	4,197	1,722	4,940	3,465	10,407	8,491	11,209	ment services.[2]
80	(X)	57	(X)	75	(X)	227	(X)	Other railroad employee insurance.[3]
(X)	848	(X)	915	(X)	990	(X)	1,049	State temporary disability insurance.[4]
1,177	3,739	1,287	4,375	1,355	5,024	1,516	5,735	Workmen's compensation.[5]
32	1,323	36	1,564	50	1,810	66	2,059	Hospital and medical benefits.
18,061	10,630	20,388	11,133	27,208	13,502	33,245	15,701	**Public aid.**
13,372	10,630	13,307	10,520	14,547	12,212	16,968	14,204	Public assistance.[6]
4,997	4,211	5,833	4,539	7,056	5,928	8,381	6,939	Vendor medical payments (Medicaid).[7]
1,719	588	1,563	592	1,963	660	2,226	742	Social services.
46	(X)	2,219	613	4,802	1,290	5,051	1,497	Supplemental security income.
2,213	(X)	2,839	(X)	4,694	(X)	5,692	(X)	Food stamps.
2,430	(X)	2,023	(X)	3,166	(X)	5,534	(X)	Other.[8]
6,698	6,749	7,145	7,808	8,547	8,890	9,353	9,839	**Health and medical programs.**
3,273	4,140	3,577	4,457	4,280	5,210	4,497	5,636	Hospital and medical care.
805	4,140	836	4,457	1,195	5,210	1,265	5,636	Civilian programs.
2,468	(X)	2,741	(X)	3,085	(X)	3,232	(X)	Defense Department.[9]
221	234	235	259	277	269	307	287	Maternal and child health programs.
1,913	201	2,000	222	2,360	239	2,721	251	Medical research.
380	719	374	973	489	1,360	586	1,653	Medical facilities construction.
76	(X)	86	(X)	96	(X)	171	(X)	Defense Department.
911	1,455	959	1,898	1,141	1,812	1,243	2,012	Other.
12,903	123	13,874	230	16,570	445	18,791	215	**Veterans programs.**
6,606	(X)	6,777	(X)	7,579	(X)	8,269	(X)	Pensions and compensation.
2,766	(X)	2,984	(X)	3,517	(X)	4,102	(X)	Health and medical programs.
2,587	(X)	2,787	(X)	3,287	(X)	3,793	(X)	Hospital and medical care.
105	(X)	119	(X)	137	(X)	212	(X)	Hospital construction.
74	(X)	78	(X)	93	(X)	97	(X)	Medical and prosthetic research.
2,648	(X)	3,207	(X)	4,434	(X)	5,336	(X)	Education.
532	(X)	539	(X)	556	(X)	564	(X)	Life insurance.[10]
351	123	368	239	485	449	519	215	Welfare and other.
7,360	57,374	7,007	63,492	8,567	69,344	9,168	77,257	**Education.**[11]
3,548	44,529	3,675	48,749	4,500	52,322	4,544	57,857	Elementary and secondary.
20	4,988	22	4,957	21	5,471	26	5,957	Construction.[12]
2,646	10,294	2,178	11,778	2,864	13,521	3,394	15,400	Higher.
394	1,090	214	1,173	274	1,239	215	1,400	Construction.
903	2,551	915	2,966	940	3,501	956	4,000	Vocational and adult.[12]
1,750	430	2,009	545	2,335	632	2,428	700	**Housing.**
3,546	2,152	3,902	2,819	4,264	3,269	4,534	3,542	**Other social welfare.**
753	157	793	175	814	222	853	235	Vocational rehabilitation.
155	35	154	31	174	44	183	46	Medical services and research.
27	236	25	260	20	276	10	290	Institutional care.[13]
1,409	298	1,614	412	2,064	454	2,336	490	Child nutrition.
46	480	47	463	50	547	53	588	Child welfare.[14]
895	(X)	767	(X)	638	(X)	622	(X)	Special OEO and ACTION programs.[15]
415	980	657	1,510	677	1,770	661	1,940	Welfare, not elsewhere classified.[16]

[12] Construction costs of vocational and adult education programs included under elementary-secondary expenditures. [13] Federal expenditures represent primarily surplus foods for nonprofit institutions. 1960 State and local expenditures for welfare, n.e.c., included in Institutional care. [14] Represents primarily child welfare services under title V of the Social Security Act. [15] Includes domestic programs consolidated in 1972 under ACTION (former VISTA, Foster Grandparents, and other domestic volunteer programs) and OEO programs such as community action and migrant workers. [16] Federal expenditures include administrative expenses of the Secretary of Health, Education, and Welfare and of the Social and Rehabilitation Service; Indian welfare; and aging and juvenile delinquency activities. State and local include antipoverty and manpower programs, child care and adoption services, legal assistance, and other unspecified welfare services.

Source: U.S. Social Security Administration, *Social Security Bulletin*, January 1977.

No. 517. SOCIAL WELFARE EXPENDITURES UNDER PUBLIC PROGRAMS: 1950 TO 1976

[In millions of dollars, except percent. For Federal Government, most States, and some localities, years ending June 30. Represents outlays from trust funds (mostly social insurance funds built up by earmarked contributions from insured persons, their employers, or both) and budgetary outlays from general revenues. Includes administrative expenditures, capital outlay, and some expenditures and payments outside U.S. See table 516 for program detail. See *Historical Statistics, Colonial Times to 1970*, series H 1–47, for related but not comparable data]

YEAR AND SOURCE OF FUNDS	SOCIAL WELFARE OUTLAYS			Social insurance	Public aid	Health and medical programs [1]	Veterans programs	Education	Housing	Other social welfare	All health and medical care [2]
	Total	Average annual percent change	Percent from non-trust funds								
TOTAL											
1950	23,508	[3] 20.6	34.8	4,947	2,496	2,064	6,866	6,674	15	448	3,065
1960	52,293	8.3	29.9	19,307	4,101	4,464	5,479	17,626	177	1,139	6,395
1965	77,175	8.1	33.4	28,123	6,283	6,246	6,031	28,108	318	2,066	9,535
1968	113,840	13.8	33.6	42,740	11,092	8,459	7,247	40,590	428	3,285	20,038
1969	127,149	11.7	34.6	48,772	13,439	9,006	7,934	43,673	532	3,792	22,936
1970	145,856	14.7	38.3	54,691	16,488	9,907	9,078	50,845	701	4,145	25,391
1971	171,908	17.9	41.5	66,369	21,262	11,087	10,456	56,705	1,047	4,983	28,775
1972	191,357	11.3	43.1	74,809	26,078	12,866	11,522	59,385	1,332	5,364	33,473
1973	213,942	11.8	45.7	86,166	28,691	13,447	13,026	64,734	2,180	5,698	36,668
1974	239,314	11.9	45.9	98,953	31,520	14,953	14,112	70,499	2,554	6,722	41,512
1975	286,522	19.7	46.5	122,947	40,709	17,437	17,019	77,910	2,967	7,533	50,870
1976, prel	331,366	15.7	48.6	146,592	48,946	19,193	19,006	86,426	3,128	8,077	58,820
FEDERAL											
1950	10,541	[3] 19.4	24.7	2,103	1,103	604	6,386	157	15	174	1,362
1960	24,957	9.0	15.9	14,307	2,117	1,737	5,367	868	144	417	2,918
1965	37,712	8.6	18.9	21,807	3,594	2,781	6,011	2,470	238	812	4,625
1968	60,314	16.9	20.0	35,390	6,455	4,233	7,214	5,000	325	1,697	13,069
1969	68,355	13.3	21.4	40,847	7,829	4,543	7,883	4,923	426	1,905	15,229
1970	77,337	13.1	23.9	45,246	9,649	4,775	8,952	5,876	582	2,259	16,600
1971	92,587	19.7	28.3	53,903	12,990	5,148	10,331	6,597	872	2,746	18,766
1972	106,327	14.8	31.2	61,248	16,291	6,322	11,405	6,721	1,183	3,155	22,082
1973	122,566	15.3	34.1	72,249	18,061	6,698	12,903	7,360	1,750	3,546	24,280
1974	137,155	11.9	34.6	82,830	20,388	7,145	13,874	7,007	2,009	3,902	27,499
1975	167,237	21.9	36.6	99,748	27,208	8,547	16,570	8,567	2,335	4,264	34,126
1976, prel	198,328	18.6	39.2	120,809	33,245	9,353	18,791	9,168	2,428	4,534	39,863
STATE AND LOCAL											
1950	12,967	[3] 21.7	54.1	2,844	1,393	1,460	480	6,517	–	274	1,704
1960	27,337	7.7	56.2	4,999	1,984	2,727	112	16,758	33	723	3,478
1965	39,464	7.6	57.1	6,316	2,690	3,466	20	25,638	80	1,254	4,911
1968	53,526	10.7	57.2	7,350	4,636	4,226	33	35,589	103	1,589	6,970
1969	58,794	9.8	56.1	7,925	5,610	4,464	51	38,750	107	1,888	7,707
1970	68,519	16.5	61.2	9,446	6,839	5,132	126	44,970	120	1,886	8,791
1971	79,320	15.8	60.6	12,466	8,272	5,939	125	50,107	175	2,237	10,008
1972	85,031	7.2	60.4	13,561	9,787	6,544	117	52,664	149	2,209	11,391
1973	91,376	7.5	61.8	13,917	10,630	6,749	123	57,374	430	2,152	12,388
1974	102,159	11.8	60.8	16,123	11,133	7,808	239	63,492	545	2,819	14,013
1975	119,285	16.8	60.5	23,199	13,502	8,890	449	69,344	632	3,269	16,744
1976, prel	133,038	11.5	62.6	25,783	15,701	9,839	215	77,257	700	3,542	18,957
PERCENT OF TOTAL EXPENDITURES, BY TYPE											
1950	100.0	(X)	(X)	21.0	10.6	8.8	29.2	28.4	.1	1.9	13.0
1960	100.0	(X)	(X)	36.9	7.8	8.5	10.5	33.7	.3	2.2	12.2
1965	100.0	(X)	(X)	36.4	8.1	8.1	7.8	36.4	.4	2.7	12.4
1970	100.0	(X)	(X)	37.5	11.3	6.8	6.2	34.9	.5	2.8	17.4
1975	100.0	(X)	(X)	42.9	14.2	6.1	5.9	27.2	1.0	2.6	17.8
1976, prel	100.0	(X)	(X)	44.2	14.8	5.8	5.7	26.1	.9	2.4	17.8
PERCENT FEDERAL OF TOTAL											
1950	44.8	(X)	(X)	42.5	44.2	29.2	93.0	2.3	100.0	38.9	44.4
1960	47.7	(X)	(X)	74.1	51.6	38.9	98.0	4.9	81.2	36.6	45.6
1965	48.9	(X)	(X)	77.5	57.2	44.5	99.7	8.8	74.9	39.3	48.5
1970	53.0	(X)	(X)	82.7	58.5	48.2	98.6	11.6	82.9	54.5	65.4
1975	58.4	(X)	(X)	81.1	66.8	49.0	97.4	11.0	78.7	56.6	67.1
1976, prel	59.9	(X)	(X)	82.4	67.9	48.7	98.9	10.6	77.6	67.1	67.8

– Represents zero.   X Not applicable.
[1] Excludes programs which are part of social insurance, public aid, veterans, and other social welfare.
[2] Combines "Health and medical programs" with medical services provided in connection with social insurance, public aid, veterans, and other social welfare programs.   [3] Change from 1945.

Source: U.S. Social Security Administration, *Social Security Bulletin*, January 1977, and earlier issues.

No. 518. Social Welfare Expenditures Under Public Programs, Total and Per Capita, in Actual and 1976 Dollars: 1950 to 1976

[For years ending June 30. Per capita figures based on U.S. Bureau of the Census estimates of total U.S. population as of Jan. 1, including outlying areas, and Armed Forces and Federal civilian employees and dependents abroad. See headnote, table 517]

| YEAR | IN ACTUAL DOLLARS | | | | | | | | IN 1976 DOLLARS | | | | |
| | Total [1] (billions) | Per capita | | | | | | | Total [1] (billions) | Per capita | | | |
		Total [1] [2]	Social insurance	Education	Public aid	Health and medical	Veterans	All health and medical care [3]		Total [1] [2]	Social insurance	Education	Public aid
1950____	23.4	153	32	43	16	13	44	20	54.5	355	75	101	37
1955____	32.5	195	59	67	18	19	28	26	66.1	396	120	136	37
1960____	52.1	285	105	96	22	24	30	35	94.9	519	192	176	40
1965____	76.9	391	142	143	32	32	30	48	130.6	664	242	242	54
1968____	113.5	558	209	199	55	42	35	99	177.3	872	327	311	86
1969____	126.8	617	236	212	65	44	38	112	190.1	925	354	318	97
1970____	145.5	701	262	245	79	48	43	122	208.1	1,003	375	350	113
1971____	171.5	818	315	270	101	53	49	137	235.2	1,122	432	371	139
1972____	190.9	902	352	280	123	61	54	158	251.5	1,188	464	370	162
1973____	213.3	1,001	402	303	135	63	60	172	270.7	1,270	510	385	171
1974____	238.7	1,111	458	328	147	70	65	193	279.8	1,303	537	385	172
1975____	285.8	1,320	565	360	188	81	78	235	302.8	1,398	599	381	199
1976 [4]__	330.6	1,514	669	396	224	88	86	269	330.6	1,514	669	396	224

[1] Excludes expenditures within foreign countries for education, veterans payments, and OASDHI and civil service retirement benefits. [2] Includes data for programs not shown separately. [3] Combines health and medical programs with medical services provided in connection with social insurance, public aid, veterans, vocational rehabilitation, and antipoverty programs. [4] Preliminary.

Source: U.S. Social Security Administration, *Social Security Bulletin*, January 1977; and unpublished data.

No. 519. Federal Grants to State and Local Governments: 1960 to 1976

[In millions of dollars, except as indicated. Includes Puerto Rico, Guam, and Virgin Islands; see table 520. On basis of checks issued for years ending June 30, except as noted. See also *Historical Statistics, Colonial Times to 1970*, series Y 638-651]

| YEAR | ALL GRANTS | | SOCIAL WELFARE | | | | | | | | General revenue sharing | All other |
	Total	Per capita [1] (dol.)	Total	Percent of all grants	Public assistance [2]	Health [3]	Education [4]	Economic opportunity, manpower [5]	Miscellaneous [6]	Transportation [7]		
1960_____	6,838	37	3,610	52.8	2,059	214	441	(X)	896	2,999	(X)	229
1965_____	10,630	54	5,669	53.3	3,059	346	702	527	1,033	4,088	(X)	873
1967_____	14,820	74	9,845	66.4	4,175	436	2,370	1,610	1,254	4,086	(X)	889
1968_____	18,168	90	12,449	68.5	5,319	823	2,719	2,050	1,538	4,284	(X)	1,435
1969_____	19,771	97	13,802	69.8	6,280	866	2,666	2,087	1,904	4,265	(X)	1,698
1970_____	23,575	114	16,545	70.2	7,445	1,043	3,016	2,565	2,476	4,475	(X)	2,556
1971_____	27,691	132	19,544	70.6	9,640	914	3,540	2,989	2,462	4,720	(X)	3,426
1972_____	33,361	158	24,572	73.7	13,090	991	4,283	3,482	2,725	4,786	(X)	4,003
1973_____	40,986	192	24,446	59.6	11,891	1,073	4,348	3,635	3,499	4,961	6,636	4,943
1974_____	42,174	196	25,427	60.3	12,666	1,239	4,059	3,594	3,869	4,765	6,106	5,876
1975_____	48,510	224	30,216	62.3	13,959	1,892	4,671	4,815	4,879	4,995	6,130	7,169
1976_____	57,838	265	35,891	62.1	16,621	2,026	4,038	7,204	6,002	6,895	6,238	8,814
TQ [8]___	15,946	(NA)	9,970	62.5	4,386	682	1,012	2,258	1,631	1,833	1,588	2,555

NA Not available.   X Not applicable.   [1] Based on Bureau of the Census July 1 population estimates, excl. Armed Forces abroad.   [2] Old-age assistance, medical assistance for the aged, aid to families with dependent children, aid to the blind, aid to the permanently and totally disabled, the combined adult assistance program, and medical assistance through Dec. 31, 1973; thereafter, excludes adult cash assistance programs of old-age assistance, aid to the blind, aid to the disabled, and combined adult assistance in the 50 States and D.C.

[3] Health services delivery, mental health research and services, construction, preventive health services, health services planning and development, and others.   [4] Colleges of agriculture and mechanic arts; agricultural extension; agricultural experiment stations through 1968; vocational education; education of handicapped; maintenance and operation of schools; school construction; defense educational activities; elementary, secondary, and higher education activities; human development; and others.   [5] Manpower development and training, economic opportunity activities, employment services, public employment, and others.   [6] Vocational rehabilitation, State soldiers' homes, child welfare services, child nutrition and food stamp programs, public housing contributions, and others.   [7] Largely highway construction, beautification, and safety; includes relatively small amounts for other types of transport and safety programs.   [8] Transition quarter, July-Sept.

Source: U.S. Social Security Administration, *Social Security Bulletin*, October 1977, and earlier issues. Based on data from U.S. Dept. of the Treasury.

No. 520. Federal Grants to State and Local Governments, by Purpose—States and Other Areas: 1976

[For year ending **June 30**, except as noted. Per capita figures based on U.S. Bureau of the Census estimates of total population, excluding Armed Forces abroad, as of July 1, 1976. See headnote and footnotes, table 519]

STATE OR OTHER AREA	GRANTS (mil. dol.)					Total grants as percent of—		GRANTS PER CAPITA (dollars)				State rank for total grants[6]
	Total[1]	Public assistance[2]	Revenue sharing	Transportation	Economic opportunity and manpower[3]	Government revenues[4]	Personal income[5]	Total[1]	Public assistance[2]	Revenue sharing	Economic opportunity and manpower[3]	
Total	57,838	16,621	6,238	6,895	7,204	(X)	(X)	265	76	(X)	33	(X)
U.S.[7]	57,112	16,549	6,238	6,865	7,010	31.5	4.5	266	77	29	33	(X)
Ala	975	215	102	140	113	44.7	5.8	267	59	28	31	28
Alaska	307	24	9	135	32	56.0	9.0	752	59	22	78	1
Ariz	524	35	66	122	84	28.2	4.4	233	16	29	37	41
Ark	608	154	66	77	76	53.3	6.2	287	73	31	36	20
Calif	5,766	2,095	657	436	796	25.4	4.1	268	97	31	37	27
Colo	633	140	68	128	64	28.6	4.2	246	54	26	25	38
Conn	720	197	84	54	102	28.3	3.3	232	64	27	33	43
Del	159	31	19	25	20	28.1	4.1	273	53	33	34	25
D.C	516	135	27	34	65	75.7	9.2	737	193	39	93	(X)
Fla	1,520	285	198	169	243	25.3	3.2	182	34	24	29	50
Ga	1,414	382	133	192	150	40.7	5.7	284	77	27	30	23
Hawaii	306	65	28	61	34	32.2	5.4	346	74	32	38	6
Idaho	257	47	25	64	33	44.5	6.1	309	56	30	40	16
Ill	2,784	942	244	396	298	28.3	3.7	249	84	22	27	35
Ind	989	214	129	136	150	24.2	3.3	186	40	24	28	49
Iowa	654	168	84	121	61	27.7	3.8	228	58	29	21	44
Kans	514	123	58	93	48	29.0	3.8	224	54	25	21	45
Ky	1,007	256	102	155	102	44.6	6.1	293	75	30	30	18
La	1,128	309	137	169	132	38.7	6.1	291	80	35	34	19
Maine	365	100	40	34	39	49.8	7.2	341	93	37	36	7
Md	1,116	273	125	164	103	29.4	4.2	271	66	30	25	26
Mass	1,815	658	204	105	230	32.8	5.1	313	114	35	40	13
Mich	2,608	950	265	259	392	31.7	4.6	286	104	29	43	21
Minn	1,084	326	130	145	121	27.7	4.8	274	82	33	31	24
Miss	774	137	95	92	80	54.0	8.1	327	58	40	34	11
Mo	1,031	199	121	152	133	32.6	4.0	215	42	25	28	46
Mont	279	48	24	84	35	45.0	6.8	370	64	32	46	3
Nebr	394	83	42	76	43	32.1	4.2	254	53	27	28	32
Nev	192	24	14	51	32	30.6	4.8	313	39	23	52	14
N.H	210	44	20	31	21	38.7	4.8	254	53	24	25	31
N.J	1,855	549	197	96	284	28.5	3.8	253	75	27	39	33
N. Mex	399	67	40	66	47	43.3	7.3	340	57	34	40	8
N.Y	6,407	2,690	710	263	670	28.0	5.4	355	149	39	37	5
N.C	1,268	288	156	164	174	37.5	4.7	232	53	29	32	42
N. Dak	200	30	20	50	23	33.9	5.4	310	47	31	36	15
Ohio	2,128	580	256	208	293	28.0	3.4	199	54	24	27	48
Okla	683	196	70	73	74	37.3	4.8	247	71	25	27	37
Oreg	706	168	66	165	98	35.3	5.3	304	72	28	42	17
Pa	3,110	934	334	357	356	34.0	4.4	264	79	28	30	30
R.I	310	99	27	25	51	42.4	5.6	331	106	29	54	9
S.C	691	147	88	87	102	39.2	5.3	243	52	31	36	39
S. Dak	224	39	26	55	25	45.0	6.6	327	57	38	36	12
Tenn	1,047	234	118	165	127	40.7	5.1	247	55	28	30	36
Tex	2,593	691	305	359	299	30.8	3.8	206	55	24	24	47
Utah	350	70	37	82	44	41.8	5.8	284	57	30	36	22
Vt	175	51	19	36	23	42.3	7.6	367	107	40	48	4
Va	1,183	246	134	188	113	32.7	4.1	234	49	27	22	40
Wash	959	249	91	145	165	29.5	4.3	266	69	25	46	29
W. Va	687	105	58	190	66	57.9	7.7	375	57	32	36	2
Wis	1,160	448	159	123	126	27.9	4.4	252	97	34	27	34
Wyo	128	12	10	61	10	34.0	5.6	327	31	26	26	10
P.R	615	68	(X)	23	169	(X)	(X)	191	21	(X)	53	(X)
V.I	49	2	(X)	2	6	(X)	(X)	516	21	(X)	63	(X)
Other	62	2	(X)	6	19	(X)	(X)	-215	7	(X)	66	(X)

X Not applicable.   [1] Includes data for grants not shown separately.   [2] See footnote 2, table 519.   [3] See footnote 5, table 519.   [4] Total grants as percent of State and local government direct general revenues. Revenues (except trust fund revenues) from own sources for fiscal year 1974–75.   [5] Personal income for calendar year 1975.   [6] Based on unrounded figures.   [7] Includes small amounts undistributed by State.

Source: U.S. Social Security Administration, *Social Security Bulletin*, October 1977. Based on data from U.S. Dept. of the Treasury. Percents computed by U.S. Bureau of the Census.

No. 521. FEDERAL OUTLAYS FOR INCOME SECURITY BENEFITS: 1970 TO 1977

[For years ending **June 30** except, beginning **1977**, ending **September 30**]

CATEGORY AND PROGRAM	BENEFITS (mil. dol.)							PERCENT	
	1970	1972	1973	1974	1975	1976	1977	1970	1977
Total benefits	60,209	84,951	95,949	111,167	139,638	164,639	179,656	100.0	100.0
Cash benefits	48,567	67,319	76,703	88,255	109,585	128,763	138,299	80.7	77.0
In-kind benefits	11,641	17,632	19,246	22,912	30,053	35,875	41,357	19.3	23.0
Cash benefits	48,567	67,319	76,703	88,255	109,585	128,763	138,299	100.0	100.0
Social security	29,045	38,587	47,332	54,007	62,469	71,362	82,406	59.8	59.6
Old-age and survivors insurance	26,267	34,541	42,170	47,849	54,839	62,140	71,271	54.1	51.5
Disability insurance	2,778	4,046	5,162	6,159	7,630	9,222	11,135	5.7	8.1
Federal employee benefits	5,768	8,284	9,402	11,322	13,986	16,703	18,426	11.9	13.3
Unemployment compensation [1]	183	543	375	350	553	911	424	.4	.3
Worker's compensation	132	190	220	272	186	227	277	.3	.2
Military retirement	2,849	3,885	4,390	5,128	6,242	7,296	8,216	5.9	5.9
Civil service retirement	2,518	3,555	4,295	5,429	6,825	8,055	9,257	5.2	6.7
Other retirement	86	111	121	143	181	214	252	.2	.2
Veterans benefits	5,340	6,141	6,536	7,167	8,140	8,734	9,562	11.0	6.9
Disability dependency and indemnity compensation	2,974	3,485	3,836	3,985	4,680	5,154	5,722	6.1	4.1
Veterans and survivors pensions	2,255	2,531	2,565	2,530	2,739	2,859	3,113	4.6	2.2
Life insurance	18	22	21	518	527	529	535	(z)	.4
Other veterans benefits	93	103	114	135	193	191	192	.2	.1
Public assistance	3,868	5,567	5,490	6,832	8,672	9,803	10,059	8.0	7.3
Supplemental security income	(X)	(X)	(X)	1,815	4,081	4,440	4,618	(X)	3.3
Maintenance payments [2]	3,868	5,567	5,490	5,017	4,592	5,363	5,442	8.0	3.9
Unemployment insurance	2,886	6,098	4,494	5,208	12,221	17,612	12,928	5.9	9.3
Unemployment insurance, State programs	2,793	5,978	4,405	5,139	11,958	16,413	12,339	5.8	8.9
Other	93	120	89	69	263	1,199	589	.2	.4
Railroad retirement	1,586	2,108	2,388	2,621	3,034	3,445	3,768	3.3	2.7
Other programs	74	534	1,063	1,097	1,063	1,105	1,149	.2	.8
Special benefits for disabled coal miners	7	397	915	967	945	988	964	(z)	.7
Assistance to refugees	50	100	106	86	70	67	134	.1	.1
General assistance to Indians	16	37	42	45	48	50	50	(z)	(z)
In-kind benefits	11,641	17,632	19,246	22,912	30,053	35,875	41,357	100.0	100.0
Food and nutrition	[3] 1,590	3,422	3,842	4,466	6,468	7,714	8,278	[3] 13.7	20.0
Food stamps	551	1,842	2,136	2,728	4,357	5,266	5,028	4.7	12.2
Child nutrition	379	1,146	1,342	1,506	1,832	2,308	3,013	3.3	7.3
Special milk	102	93	90	49	124	88	163	.9	.4
Removal of surplus commodities	519	341	274	183	155	53	[4] 73	4.5	[4] .2
Health care [5]	9,576	13,093	13,806	16,673	21,518	25,896	30,674	82.3	74.2
Hospital insurance	4,804	6,108	6,648	7,806	10,355	12,267	14,906	41.3	36.0
Supplementary medical insurance	1,979	2,255	2,391	2,874	3,765	4,671	5,865	17.0	14.2
Medicaid	2,612	4,426	4,402	5,552	6,840	8,325	9,181	22.4	22.2
Medical care for military retirees	181	303	357	433	548	633	721	1.6	1.7
Housing	475	1,117	1,602	1,776	2,072	2,264	2,405	4.1	5.8
Public housing	(NA)	744	1,043	1,116	1,312	1,392	1,271	(NA)	3.1
Rent and mortgage interest supplements	(NA)	373	560	660	761	873	1,134	(NA)	2.7

NA Not available. X Not applicable. Z Less than .05 percent.
[1] Includes payments to ex-servicemen.
[2] Basically, aid to families with dependent children.
[3] Includes emergency food program, not shown separately.
[4] Reflects "Other Food Programs".
[5] Includes medical care for retired Public Health Service officers.

Source: U.S. Office of Management and Budget, *Special Analyses, Budget of the United States Government*, annual.

No. 522. PUBLIC INCOME–MAINTENANCE PROGRAMS—CASH BENEFIT PAYMENTS: 1960 TO 1976

[Includes payments outside the United States and benefits to dependents, where applicable]

PROGRAM	PAYMENTS (bil. dol.)								PERCENT	
	1960	1965	1970	1972	1973	1974	1975	1976	1970	1976
Total [1]	25.9	36.6	64.5	84.0	96.1	112.8	139.6	152.5	100.0	100.0
Percent of personal income [2]	6.5	6.8	8.0	8.9	9.1	9.8	11.2	11.1	(X)	(X)
Federal	20.7	30.7	50.3	66.0	77.6	91.4	109.2	123.5	78.0	81.0
State and local	4.9	5.4	13.6	17.3	17.8	20.7	29.6	28.3	21.1	18.6
OASDHI [3]	11.1	18.1	31.6	41.3	51.1	58.2	66.6	75.3	49.0	49.4
Public employee retirement [4]	2.6	4.6	9.2	12.6	14.7	17.9	21.3	24.5	14.3	16.1
Railroad retirement	.9	1.1	1.8	2.2	2.6	2.8	3.3	3.6	2.8	2.4
Veterans' pensions and compensation	3.4	4.2	5.5	6.3	6.4	7.1	7.7	8.4	8.5	5.5
Unemployment benefits	3.0	2.5	4.4	6.2	4.7	7.1	18.1	16.4	6.8	10.8
Temporary disability benefits	.4	.5	.7	.7	.8	.9	.9	1.0	1.1	.6
Workmen's compensation [5]	.9	1.2	2.0	2.8	3.6	4.0	4.5	5.2	3.1	3.4
Public assistance [6]	3.3	4.0	8.9	11.2	11.4	8.9	10.6	11.2	13.8	7.3
Supplemental security income [6]	(X)	(X)	(X)	(X)	(X)	5.2	5.9	6.1	(X)	4.0

X Not applicable.   [1] Includes lump sum death benefits, not shown separately.
[2] For base data, see table 722.   [3] Old-age, survivors, disability, and health insurance under Federal Social Security Act; see text, p. 323.   [4] Excludes refunds of contributions to employees who leave service.
[5] Includes black lung benefits.   [6] Beginning 1974, Federal grants to States for aid to aged, blind, and disabled replaced by supplemental security income programs; see text, p. 325.

Source: U.S. Social Security Administration, *Social Security Bulletin*, June 1977.

No. 523. SELECTED SOCIAL INSURANCE PROGRAMS—PAID EMPLOYMENT AND COVERAGE STATUS: 1950 TO 1976

[In millions, except percent. Prior to 1960, excludes Alaska and Hawaii. OASDHI=Old-age, survivors, disability, and health insurance. Represents civilian noninstitutional population aged 14 and over through 1965, 16 and over thereafter; and Armed Forces. Average employment data based on calendar week in March, June, September, and December for which Current Population Survey was taken, except as noted; see text, p. 1. Coverage status generally determined on basis of job with greatest number of hours worked during survey week. See also *Historical Statistics, Colonial Times to 1970*, series H 51–56 and H 186–196]

COVERAGE STATUS	1950	1955	1960	1965	1970	1971	1972	1973	1974	1975	1976
Paid average employment	60.0	64.5	67.5	73.6	80.6	81.5	83.5	85.9	87.1	86.2	89.0
Covered by OASDHI [1]	38.7	55.0	59.4	65.6	72.1	72.9	74.9	77.3	78.4	77.8	80.7
Percent of paid employment	64.5	85.3	88.0	89.1	89.5	89.4	89.6	90.0	90.0	90.2	90.7
Wage and salary	38.7	48.3	52.6	59.4	66.3	66.9	68.9	71.1	72.1	71.7	74.4
Self-employed [2]	(X)	6.7	6.8	6.2	5.9	6.0	6.0	6.2	6.3	6.1	6.3
Not covered by OASDHI	21.3	9.5	8.1	8.0	8.5	8.6	8.6	8.6	8.7	8.4	8.3
Excluded by Federal law	21.3	5.8	5.5	5.6	5.1	5.1	4.9	4.5	4.7	4.3	4.3
Federal civilian	1.7	1.8	2.0	2.2	2.5	2.5	2.3	2.3	2.5	2.3	2.3
Nonfarm self-employed	6.2	1.5	1.3	1.1	.9	.9	.9	.8	.7	.7	.6
Domestic service	2.0	.8	.9	.9	.5	.5	.5	.4	.4	.4	.4
Other [3]	11.4	1.7	1.3	1.4	1.2	1.2	1.2	1.0	1.1	.9	1.0
Permitted by Federal law [4]	(X)	3.7	2.6	2.4	3.4	3.5	3.7	4.1	4.0	4.1	4.0
Civilian workers covered by [5]—											
Retirement systems	43.1	57.8	60.5	67.7	74.8	75.6	78.4	81.5	81.3	81.7	85.7
OASDHI [6]	37.1	51.8	55.7	62.8	69.2	69.8	72.6	75.6	75.2	75.7	79.7
Railroad retirement	1.6	1.3	.9	.8	.6	.6	.6	.6	.6	.5	.5
Public employment [7]	4.4	4.7	3.9	4.1	5.0	5.2	5.2	5.3	5.5	5.5	5.5
Workmen's compensation	38.7	42.9	44.6	52.5	59.0	60.5	63.7	67.3	67.6	68.1	70.4
Unemployment insurance [8]	36.0	41.7	43.7	50.3	55.8	57.1	66.0	69.0	69.5	69.7	72.1
Temporary disability insurance [9]	10.3	11.2	11.3	13.3	14.6	14.8	16.0	16.0	15.7	15.7	16.2

X Not applicable.   [1] Includes railroad employees and all persons covered by Federal law except those on a group-elective or individual voluntary basis for whom coverage has not been arranged.
[2] Estimates based on number expected to report earnings at end of year.
[3] Farm workers, self-employed farmers, State and local government employees, employees of nonprofit organizations, and some additional small groups.
[4] Persons whose coverage was authorized but not arranged on a group-elective or individual voluntary basis, such as employees of State and local governments and self-employed farmers who were eligible to report a percentage of gross earnings rather than net earnings.   [5] As of December.
[6] Excludes railroad employees and Armed Forces.
[7] Excludes persons covered under both a government retirement system and OASDHI.
[8] State, railroad, and Federal employee programs.
[9] State and railroad programs. Excludes government employees covered by sick-leave provisions.

Source: U.S. Social Security Administration, *Annual Statistical Supplement* to the *Social Security Bulletin*.

No. 524. Social Insurance and Related Programs—Cash Beneficiaries and Benefits, by Program: 1965 to 1976

[OASDHI= Old-age, survivors, disability, and health insurance, Federal programs under Social Security Act; see p. 323. Partly estimated. Includes some beneficiaries and benefit payments for some programs in outlying areas. See also *Historical Statistics, Colonial Times to 1970*, series H 125–171]

PROGRAM	BENEFICIARIES [1] (1,000)					AMOUNT OF BENEFITS (mil. dol.)				
	1965	1970	1974	1975	1976	1965	1970	1974	1975	1976
Total	(X)	(X)	(X)	(X)	(X)	32,571	55,609	98,559	123,135	134,938
Percent of personal income	(X)	(X)	(X)	(X)	(X)	6.1	6.9	8.5	9.8	9.8
Retirement [2]	(X)	(X)	(X)	(X)	(X)	16,787	29,401	53,470	61,757	69,662
OASDHI	13,918	16,870	19,409	20,015	20,624	12,542	21,075	37,452	42,645	48,069
Public employee retirement	1,472	2,204	2,951	3,124	3,307	3,520	7,209	14,337	17,145	19,446
Federal civil service	359	477	700	732	759	897	1,849	4,279	5,229	5,884
Other Federal employee	388	642	856	912	968	1,233	2,700	4,988	6,071	6,876
State and local government	725	1,085	1,395	1,480	1,580	1,390	2,660	5,070	5,845	6,685
Railroad retirement	498	553	554	579	587	705	1,113	1,680	1,966	2,147
Veterans programs	14	3	1	1	(Z)	20	4	1	1	1
Disability [2][3]	(X)	(X)	(X)	(X)	(X)	7,041	11,001	18,901	21,847	25,065
OASDHI	1,654	2,573	3,712	4,142	4,524	1,573	3,067	6,903	8,414	9,966
Public employee retirement	326	419	502	526	551	751	1,312	2,236	2,702	3,101
Federal civil service	149	185	238	258	279	279	518	997	1,307	1,564
Other Federal employee	108	148	163	163	162	318	538	813	905	972
State and local government	69	86	100	105	110	155	255	425	490	565
Railroad retirement	102	95	102	102	101	149	219	404	403	421
Veterans programs	3,203	3,178	3,240	3,226	3,235	3,026	3,931	5,141	5,583	6,147
Workmen's compensation	(NA)	(NA)	(NA)	(NA)	(NA)	1,074	1,674	2,745	3,205	3,735
Black lung benefit program	(X)	25	336	333	321	(X)	77	600	595	593
Temporary disability:										
State insurance [4]	149	181	182	176	177	426	665	842	897	1,017
Railroad insurance	24	25	14	14	18	41	56	30	48	84
Survivor monthly benefits	(X)	(X)	(X)	(X)	(X)	5,872	10,272	18,349	20,694	23,043
OASDHI	4,681	6,369	7,197	7,302	7,416	3,979	7,428	13,839	15,596	17,207
Public employee retirement [5]	319	427	532	560	583	324	645	1,181	1,449	1,676
Federal civil service	220	297	368	382	394	191	429	785	975	1,115
Other Federal employee	7	10	25	32	39	9	16	56	84	112
State and local government	92	120	140	145	150	125	200	340	390	450
Railroad retirement	288	324	336	338	338	278	424	724	914	1,002
Veterans programs	1,900	2,284	2,295	2,258	2,221	1,150	1,545	1,935	2,084	2,261
Workmen's compensation	(NA)	(NA)	(NA)	(NA)	(NA)	140	197	315	360	420
Black lung benefit program	(X)	2	146	152	156	(X)	33	355	360	385
Lump-sum payments	(X)	(X)	(X)	(X)	(X)	421	582	779	808	864
OASDHI	(X)	(X)	(X)	(X)	(X)	217	294	327	337	332
Public employee retirement	(X)	(X)	(X)	(X)	(X)	125	189	298	321	373
Federal civil service	(X)	(X)	(X)	(X)	(X)	18	23	22	20	21
Other Federal employee	(X)	(X)	(X)	(X)	(X)	1	1	1	1	1
State and local government	(X)	(X)	(X)	(X)	(X)	105	165	275	300	350
Railroad retirement	(X)	(X)	(X)	(X)	(X)	22	26	28	25	24
Veterans programs [6]	(X)	(X)	(X)	(X)	(X)	57	73	125	124	135
Unemployment	(X)	(X)	(X)	(X)	(X)	2,452	4,353	7,061	18,030	16,305
State unemploy. insurance [7]	1,188	1,620	1,984	3,515	2,595	2,283	4,184	6,929	17,934	16,170
Railroad unemployment insurance	31	18	10	26	28	60	39	22	89	135
Training allowances [8]	75	60	19	(X)	(X)	108	131	110	7	(X)

NA Not available.   X Not applicable.   Z Fewer than 500.
[1] For old-age, survivors, disability, and health insurance (OASDHI), average monthly number; for railroad retirement program, public employee retirement systems, veterans programs, and the black lung benefit program, number on rolls June 30; for State unemployment and temporary disability insurance, average weekly number; for railroad unemployment and temporary disability insurance, average number during 14-day registration period; Area Redevelopment Act and Manpower Development and Training Act programs, number on rolls Dec. 31.   [2] Includes benefits to dependents where applicable.
[3] Excludes payments for medical care.   [4] Payable in Calif., N.J., N.Y., R.I., and Puerto Rico under public and private plans. Data for beneficiaries in N.J. not available.
[5] Number represents families for Federal programs under the Uniformed Services Contingency Option Act of 1953 and for State and local government retirement systems.   [6] Lump sums are for burial of deceased veterans.
[7] Includes payments made by the States as agents of the Federal Government under the Federal employees' unemployment compensation program and under the Ex-Servicemen's Compensation Act of 1958, and payment under the extended unemployment insurance programs, the Trade Expansion Act of 1962, and the Disaster Relief Act of 1970. Beneficiaries relate to regular State unemployment insurance, Federal employee, and ex-servicemen programs only. Includes Puerto Rico.
[8] Area Redevelopment Act of 1961 (Nov. 1961–June 1966) and Manpower Development Training Act of 1962 (Aug. 1962–June 1975).

Source: U.S. Social Security Administration, *Annual Statistical Supplement* to the *Social Security Bulletin*.

No. 525. Selected Social Insurance Programs—Estimated Payrolls of Covered Employment in Relation to Wages and Salaries: 1950 to 1976

[In billions of dollars, except percent. OASDHI: Old-age, survivors, disability, and health insurance, Federal programs under Social Security Act; see text, p. 323. Prior to 1960 excludes Alaska and Hawaii except that small amount of taxable wages included in railroad payrolls; data for Federal civilian and military personnel cover all areas. Gross amount before deduction of social insurance contributions. See also *Historical Statistics, Colonial Times to 1970*, series H 57-69]

PROGRAM	1950	1955	1960	1965	1970	1972	1973	1974	1975	1976
Total earnings [1]	185	254	319	419	612	710	794	851	892	980
All wages and salaries [1]	147	212	272	362	546	634	701	765	806	892
Civilian	142	201	262	349	526	612	679	742	783	868
Payrolls covered by retirement programs [2]	129	193	261	343	528	616	682	745	783	(NA)
OASDHI [3][4]	109	169	234	309	480	559	620	678	714	795
Railroad retirement [3]	5	6	6	6	6	7	8	8	8	9
Federal civil service retirement	6	8	12	16	26	30	32	34	37	39
State and local government	8	12	20	31	53	66	74	81	91	(NA)
Net earnings in self-employment covered by OASDHI [5]	(X)	24	29	40	48	54	63	66	69	80
Payrolls covered by:										
Unemployment insurance [3]	108	164	215	283	421	527	589	652	688	765
Workmen's compensation programs [6]	114	168	220	292	437	514	563	626	672	731
Percent of civilian payrolls covered by—										
OASDHI [3][7]	77.2	84.1	89.6	88.4	91.3	91.4	91.3	91.4	91.2	91.5
Railroad retirement [3]	3.8	2.9	2.2	1.6	1.2	1.2	1.2	1.1	1.1	1.1
Federal civil service retirement	4.3	4.1	4.6	4.7	5.0	4.9	4.7	4.6	4.7	4.4
State and local government retirement	5.6	6.2	7.8	9.0	10.1	10.8	10.9	10.9	11.6	(NA)
Unemployment insurance [3]	76.3	81.5	82.3	81.0	80.0	86.1	86.8	87.9	87.9	88.1
Workmen's compensation programs [6]	80.1	83.4	84.1	83.6	83.1	84.0	82.9	84.3	85.9	84.2

NA Not available.   x Not applicable.   [1] Data from U.S. Bureau of Economic Analysis. Earnings include self-employed; wages and salaries represent civilian and military pay in cash and in kind.   [2] Beginning 1953 adjusted for duplication in coverage by both OASDHI and State and local retirement systems.   [3] Taxable plus estimated nontaxable wages and salaries.   [4] Beginning 1957, includes Armed Forces in all areas.   [5] Effective 1951.   [6] Payrolls of employers insured with private carriers, State funds, or self-insured, and pay covered by Federal programs in all areas.   [7] Percent computed after excluding Armed Forces payroll covered by OASDHI.

Source: U.S. Social Security Administration, *Annual Statistical Supplement* to the *Social Security Bulletin*.

No. 526. Social Security (OASDHI)—Covered Employment and Earnings: 1950 to 1976

[Beginning 1955, includes Puerto Rico and Virgin Islands; and, beginning 1965, American Samoa and Guam. OASDHI: Old-age, survivors, disability, and health insurance. Represents all reported employment. See also *Historical Statistics, Colonial Times to 1970*, series H 172-185]

ITEM	1950	1955	1960	1965	1970	1972	1973	1974	1975	1976
Living covered workers [1]____mil__	80.8	94.7	107.4	118.1	133.5	138.2	140.6	142.9	145.2	148.3
With insured status [2]_____mil__	45.7	70.6	79.7	93.6	106.9	112.2	114.8	118.0	121.4	124.4
With uninsured status_____mil__	35.1	24.1	27.7	24.5	26.7	26.0	25.8	24.9	23.8	23.9
New entrants into covered employment_____mil__	2.5	4.8	3.1	4.6	4.4	5.2	5.7	4.9	4.1	4.8
Workers reported with—										
Taxable earnings [3]_____mil__	48	65	73	81	93	96	100	101	100	103
Maximum earnings_____mil__	14	17	20	29	24	24	20	15	15	15
Earnings in covered employment_____bil. dol__	110	196	265	352	532	618	687	748	788	880
Reported taxable [3]____bil. dol__	88	158	207	251	416	484	562	638	666	740
Percent of total_____	79.7	80.3	78.1	71.3	78.2	78.3	81.8	85.3	84.6	84.1
Average per worker:										
Total earnings_____dol__	2,274	3,008	3,656	4,359	5,711	6,420	6,879	7,378	7,844	8,532
Taxable earnings [3]_____dol__	1,812	2,416	2,854	3,108	4,464	5,030	5,628	6,293	6,636	7,176
Employers reporting taxable wages_____1,000__	3,350	4,910	5,670	6,090	5,690	5,710	5,760	5,750	5,720	5,850

[1] Estimated number of persons who had covered employment at any time during the period 1937 to year shown; not adjusted to reflect effect of (a) provisions that coordinate the OASDHI and railroad retirement programs and (b) wage credits for military service. Only partially adjusted to eliminate duplicate count of persons with taxable earnings reported on more than 1 account number; effect of such duplication is substantially less significant for the insured than for the uninsured.   [2] Fully or currently insured for retirement and/or survivor benefits.   [3] Beginning 1955, includes self-employment. See table 527 for maximum taxable earnings.

Source: U.S. Social Security Administration, *Annual Statistical Supplement* to the *Social Security Bulletin*.

No. 527. SOCIAL SECURITY (OASDHI)—EFFECTIVE AND SCHEDULED CONTRIBUTION RATES: 1950 TO 1982

[OASDI=Old-age, survivors, and disability insurance; HI=Hospital insurance]

YEAR	Annual maximum taxable earnings (dol.)	CONTRIBUTION RATES (percent)						Supplementary medical insurance, monthly rate[4] (dol.)
		Each employer and employee			Self-employed [3]			
		Total	OASDI [1]	HI [2]	Total	OASDI [1]	HI [2]	
In effect: 1950	3,000	1.50	1.50	(X)	[5] 2.25	[5] 2.25	(X)	(X)
1955	4,200	2.00	2.00	(X)	3.00	3.00	(X)	(X)
1960	4,800	3.00	3.00	(X)	4.50	4.50	(X)	(X)
1965	4,800	3.625	3.625	(X)	5.40	5.40	(X)	(X)
1970	7,800	4.80	4.20	.60	6.90	6.30	.60	[6] 5.30
1971	7,800	5.20	4.60	.60	7.50	6.90	.60	[6] 5.60
1972	9,000	5.20	4.60	.60	7.50	6.90	.60	[6] 5.80
1973	10,800	5.85	4.85	1.00	8.00	7.00	1.00	[7] 6.30
1974	13,200	5.85	4.95	.90	7.90	7.00	.90	[6] 6.70
1975	14,100	5.85	4.95	.90	7.90	7.00	.90	6.70
1976	15,300	5.85	4.95	.90	7.90	7.00	.90	[6] 7.20
1977	16,500	5.85	4.95	.90	7.90	7.00	.90	7.70
1978	17,700	6.05	5.05	1.00	8.10	7.10	1.00	[6] 8.20
Future schedule:								
1979	22,900	6.13	5.08	1.05	8.10	7.05	1.05	[6] 8.70
1980	25,900	6.13	5.08	1.05	8.10	7.05	1.05	[6] 9.20
1981	29,700	6.65	5.35	1.30	9.30	8.00	1.30	[6] 9.70
1982	31,800	6.70	5.40	1.30	9.35	8.05	1.30	[6] 10.20

X Not applicable. [1] Cash benefits for old-age, survivors, and disability insurance. [2] Hospital insurance for the aged, first effective in 1966; for the disabled, in 1973. [3] Self-employed persons brought under program for first time in 1951. [4] Program began July 1966. Voluntary program financed by equal contributions from participants 65 and older, and Federal Government. Beginning 1973, Federal Government finances cost of program not met by disabled and aged participants. [5] 1951 data. [6] Effective July 1. [7] Effective Aug. 13.

Source: U.S. Social Security Administration, *Annual Statistical Supplement* to the *Social Security Bulletin*.

No. 528. SOCIAL SECURITY (OASDHI) TRUST FUNDS: 1960 TO 1977

[In millions of dollars, except percent. OASDHI=Old-age, survivors, disability, and health insurance. See also *Historical Statistics, Colonial Times to 1970*, series H 238–242]

TYPE OF TRUST FUND	1960	1965	1967	1970	1973	1974	1975	1976	1977
Old-age and survivors:									
Net contribution income [1]	10,866	16,017	23,138	30,256	45,975	52,081	56,816	63,362	69,572
Transfers from general revenue [2]	(X)	(X)	78	449	442	447	425	614	613
Interest received	516	593	818	1,515	1,928	2,159	2,364	2,301	2,227
Benefit payments	10,677	16,737	19,468	28,796	45,741	51,618	58,509	65,699	73,113
Administrative expenses	203	328	406	471	647	865	896	959	981
Percent of benefit payments	1.9	2.0	2.1	1.6	1.4	1.7	1.5	1.5	1.3
Assets, end of year	20,324	18,235	24,222	32,454	36,487	37,777	36,987	35,388	32,491
Disability:									
Net contribution income [1]	1,010	1,188	2,286	4,481	5,932	6,826	7,444	8,233	9,138
Transfers from general revenue [2]	(X)	(X)	16	16	52	52	90	103	128
Interest received	53	59	78	277	458	500	502	422	304
Benefit payments	568	1,573	1,939	3,067	5,718	6,903	8,414	9,966	11,463
Administrative expenses	36	90	109	164	190	217	256	285	399
Percent of benefit payments	6.4	5.7	5.6	5.3	3.3	3.1	3.0	2.9	3.5
Assets, end of year	2,289	1,606	2,029	5,614	7,927	8,109	7,354	5,745	3,370
Hospital: [3]									
Net contribution income [1]	(X)	(X)	3,152	4,881	9,945	10,850	11,509	12,736	14,126
Transfers from general revenue [2]	(X)	(X)	312	874	499	519	669	141	946
Interest received	(X)	(X)	51	161	281	528	671	753	784
Benefit payments	(X)	(X)	3,353	5,124	7,057	9,101	11,318	13,343	15,743
Administrative expenses	(X)	(X)	77	157	232	271	263	336	276
Percent of benefit payments	(X)	(X)	2.3	3.1	3.3	3.0	2.3	2.5	2.5
Assets, end of year	(X)	(X)	1,073	3,202	6,467	9,119	10,517	10,605	10,442
Supplementary medical care: [4]									
Net contribution income [1]	(X)	(X)	640	1,096	1,550	1,804	1,918	2,060	2,247
Transfers from general revenue [2]	(X)	(X)	933	1,093	1,705	2,225	2,648	3,810	5,386
Interest received	(X)	(X)	24	12	57	95	106	106	172
Benefit payments	(X)	(X)	1,197	1,975	2,526	3,318	4,273	5,080	6,038
Administrative expenses	(X)	(X)	110	238	318	410	462	542	467
Percent of benefit payments	(X)	(X)	9.2	12.0	12.6	12.4	10.8	10.7	7.7
Assets, end of year	(X)	(X)	412	188	1,111	1,506	1,444	1,799	3,099

X Not applicable. [1] Includes deposits by States and deductions for refund of estimated employee-tax overpayment. For supplementary medical insurance represents voluntary premium payments from and in behalf of insured persons. [2] Transfers for military wage credits and for cost of hospital benefits for persons not insured for OASDHI or railroad retirement cash benefits. [3] See footnote 2, table 527. [4] See footnote 4, table 527.

Source: U.S. Social Security Administration, *Social Security Bulletin*, May 1978. Based on data from U.S. Dept. of the Treasury.

No. 529. SOCIAL SECURITY (OASDHI)—EFFECT OF CHANGES IN CONTRIBUTION RATES: 1958 TO 1979

[OASDHI= Old-age, survivors, disability, and health insurance programs. Effect of changes represents first full-year effect of changes in taxable wage base and combined tax rate]

YEAR	Workers taxable wage base (dol.)	Combined [1] tax rate (percent)	EFFECT OF CHANGES (bil. dol.)			YEAR	Workers taxable wage base (dol.)	Combined [1] tax rate (percent)	EFFECT OF CHANGES (bil. dol.)		
			Total	Wage base	Tax rate				Total	Wage base	Tax rate
1958	4,200	4.50	(2)	(2)	(2)	1971	(2)	10.40	3.2	(2)	3.2
1959	4,800	5.00	1.5	.6	.9	1972	9,000	(2)	2.9	2.9	(2)
1960	(2)	6.00	1.9	(2)	1.9	1973	10,800	11.70	10.8	4.6	6.2
1962	(2)	6.25	.5	(2)	.5	1974	13,200	(2)	3.9	3.9	(2)
1963	(2)	7.25	2.1	(2)	2.1	1975	14,100	(2)	1.4	1.4	(2)
1966	6,600	8.40	6.2	3.4	2.8	1976	15,300	(2)	2.1	2.1	(2)
1967	(2)	8.80	1.2	(2)	1.2	1977	16,500	(2)	2.1	2.1	(2)
1968	7,800	(2)	2.1	2.1	(2)	1978	17,700	12.10	5.6	2.1	3.5
1969	(2)	9.60	3.0	(2)	3.0	1979	22,900	12.26	9.5	7.9	1.7

[1] Employee and employer.
[2] No increase occurred.

Source: U.S. Bureau of Economic Analysis, Survey of Current Business, February 1978. Data from U.S. Social Security Administration.

No. 530. POPULATION 65 YEARS OLD AND OVER, 1960 TO 1977, AND PROJECTIONS TO 2000

[As of July 1. See headnote, table 5. Based on Current Population Survey; see text, pp. 1 and 2. Projected numbers in this table are the same for series I, II, and III; projected percents of total population are for series II. See also tables 30, 31, and 767]

AGE GROUP	NUMBER (1,000)							PERCENT DISTRIBUTION			
	1960	1970	1975	1977	1980	1990	2000	1960	1970	1977	2000
65 years and over	16,675	20,087	22,420	23,494	24,927	29,824	31,822	100.0	100.0	100.0	100.0
Percent, all ages	9.2	9.8	10.5	10.8	11.2	12.2	12.2	(X)	(X)	(X)	(X)
65–69 years	6,280	7,023	8,101	8,446	8,700	10,022	9,192	37.7	35.0	35.9	28.9
70–74 years	4,773	5,465	5,781	6,137	6,793	7,782	8,244	28.6	27.2	26.1	25.9
75–79 years	3,080	3,859	4,006	4,068	4,324	5,501	6,394	18.5	19.2	17.3	20.1
80–84 years	1,601	2,309	2,652	2,763	2,816	3,639	4,236	9.6	11.5	11.8	13.3
85 years and over	940	1,432	1,881	2,079	2,294	2,881	3,756	5.6	7.1	8.8	11.8

X Not applicable.

Source: U.S. Bureau of the Census, Current Population Reports, series P-25, Nos. 519, 704, and 721.

No. 531. SOCIETAL DEPENDENCY RATIOS, 1940 TO 1975, AND PROJECTIONS TO 2030

[As of July, except as noted. Includes Armed Forces overseas. Societal dependency ratios represent essentially the relative burden of older "dependents," defined either by age or economic status, on "productive" persons, also defined either by age or economic status. Projected numbers are for Series II; see headnote, table 5]

DEPENDENCY RATIO	1940	1950	1960	1970	1975	1980	1990	2000	2010	2020	2030
Persons, 65 years old and over, per 100 persons, 18 to 64 years old	11	13	17	17	18	18	19	19	19	24	29
Persons, 60 years old and over, per 100 persons, 20 to 59 years old	19	23	27	29	29	29	30	28	32	40	44
Nonworkers, 60 years old and over, per 100 workers, 20 to 59 years old	[1] 21	[1] 25	[2] 28	[2] 29	[2] 29	[2] 29	[2] 30	(NA)	(NA)	(NA)	(NA)

NA Not available.
[1] As of April.
[2] Labor force data are monthly averages based on or consistent with the Current Population Survey; see text, p. 1.

Source: U.S. Bureau of the Census, Current Population Reports, series P-23, No. 59.

No. 532. SOCIAL SECURITY (OASDHI)—BENEFITS, BY TYPE OF BENEFICIARY: 1960 TO 1977

[OASDHI= Old-age, survivors, disability, and health insurance. A person eligible to receive more than one type of benefit is generally classified or counted only once as a retired-worker beneficiary. See also headnote, table 526; and *Historical Statistics, Colonial Times to 1970*, series H 197-229]

TYPE OF BENEFICIARY	1960	1965	1970	1972	1973	1974	1975	1976	1977
BENEFITS IN CURRENT-PAYMENT STATUS [1] (END OF YEAR)									
Number of benefits_____1,000__	14,845	20,867	26,229	28,476	29,868	30,853	32,085	33,021	34,083
Retired workers [2]_____1,000__	8,061	11,101	13,349	14,555	15,365	15,959	16,588	17,164	17,832
Disabled workers [3]_____1,000__	455	988	1,493	1,833	2,017	2,237	2,489	2,670	2,834
Wives and husbands [2][4]_____1,000__	2,346	2,807	2,952	3,085	3,189	3,238	3,320	3,370	3,459
Children [5]_____1,000__	2,000	3,093	4,122	4,516	4,687	4,776	4,972	5,035	5,078
Widowed mothers [6]_____1,000__	401	472	523	541	572	574	582	578	582
Widows and widowers [2][7]___1,000__	1,544	2,371	3,227	3,510	3,656	3,770	3,889	3,994	4,119
Parents [2]_____1,000__	36	35	29	26	25	23	21	20	18
Special benefits [8]_____1,000__	(X)	(X)	534	410	358	278	224	188	159
Average monthly benefit, current dollars:									
Retired workers [2]_____	74	84	118	162	166	188	207	225	243
Retired worker and wife [2]_____	124	142	199	273	277	312	344	374	(NA)
Disabled workers [3]_____	89	98	131	179	183	206	226	245	265
Wives and husbands [2][4]_____	39	43	59	81	81	91	100	108	117
Widowed mothers [6]_____	59	65	87	115	118	134	147	160	174
Widows and widowers [2][7]_____	58	74	102	138	156	176	192	207	222
Parents [2]_____	60	76	103	139	141	158	172	185	198
Special benefits [8]_____	(X)	(X)	45	57	57	64	69	73	78
Average monthly benefit, 1977 dollars:									
Retired workers [2]_____	154	164	184	237	223	225	232	240	243
Retired worker and wife [2]_____	258	277	311	399	372	374	385	399	(NA)
Disabled workers [3]_____	185	191	205	262	246	247	253	262	265
Wives and husbands [2][4]_____	81	84	92	118	109	109	112	115	117
Widowed mothers [6]_____	123	127	136	168	159	160	165	171	174
Widows and widowers [2][7]_____	121	144	159	202	210	211	215	221	222
BENEFITS AWARDED DURING YEAR									
Number of benefits_____1,000__	2,336	3,072	3,722	4,203	4,221	4,101	4,427	4,341	4,611
Retired workers [2]_____1,000__	982	1,183	1,338	1,461	1,493	1,413	1,506	1,464	1,593
Full benefits payable_____1,000__	634	296	114	117	135	109	117	110	114
Reduced benefits [9]_____1,000__	207	579	745	843	912	903	964	972	1,075
Other [10]_____1,000__	141	308	479	501	446	401	425	382	404
Disabled workers [3]_____1,000__	208	253	350	455	492	536	592	552	569
Wives and husbands [2][4]____1,000__	394	390	436	478	478	451	499	494	543
Children [5]_____1,000__	416	783	1,091	1,265	1,250	1,220	1,332	1,327	1,366
Widowed mothers [6]_____1,000__	93	100	112	118	119	109	116	114	119
Widows and widowers [2][7]__1,000__	239	359	363	403	372	364	377	386	417
Parents [2]_____1,000__	5	3	2	2	2	1	1	1	1
Special benefits [8]_____1,000__	(X)	(X)	30	20	15	7	4	3	3
BENEFIT PAYMENTS DURING YEAR									
Total amount [11]_____mil. dol__	11,245	18,311	31,863	41,595	51,459	58,521	66,923	75,665	84,576
Monthly benefits [12]_____mil. dol__	11,081	18,094	31,570	41,275	51,130	58,194	66,586	75,332	84,264
Retired workers [2]_____mil. dol__	7,053	10,984	18,437	24,142	29,352	33,376	38,078	43,057	48,134
Disabled workers [3]____mil. dol__	489	1,246	2,448	3,626	4,676	5,662	6,908	8,190	9,456
Wives and husbands [2][4] mil. dol__	1,083	1,478	2,194	2,756	3,293	3,628	4,104	4,562	5,057
Children [5]_____mil. dol__	1,085	1,922	3,517	4,438	5,204	5,852	6,643	7,434	8,163
Widowed mothers [6]____mil. dol__	286	388	574	679	801	898	1,009	1,113	1,189
Widows and widowers [2][7]__mil. dol__	1,057	2,041	4,055	5,326	7,491	8,490	9,596	10,750	12,055
Parents [2]_____mil. dol__	28	35	39	43	48	49	50	51	52
Special benefits [8]_____mil. dol__	(X)	(X)	306	264	266	238	198	174	157
Lump sum_____mil. dol__	164	217	294	320	329	327	337	332	312

NA Not available.   X Not applicable.   [1] Benefit payment actually being made at a specified time with no deductions or with deductions amounting to less than a month's benefits, i.e., the benefits actually being received.   [2] 62 years and over, except 1960 for men, 65 years and over.   [3] Disabled workers under age 65. [4] Includes wife beneficiaries under age 65 with entitled children in their care and, beginning Sept. 1965, entitled divorced wives.   [5] Includes disabled persons aged 18 and over whose disability began before age 18 (22, beginning Jan. 1973) and, beginning Sept. 1965, entitled full-time students aged 18-21. [6] Includes surviving divorced mothers with entitled children in their care and, beginning June 1975, widowed fathers with entitled children in their care.   [7] Beginning Sept. 1965, includes widows aged 60-61 and surviving divorced wives aged 60 and over; beginning March 1968, disabled widows and widowers aged 50 and over; and beginning Jan. 1973, widowers aged 60-61.   [8] Benefits for persons aged 72 and over not insured under regular or transitional provisions of Social Security Act.   [9] Benefits payable with reduction for early retirement, at ages 62-64.   [10] Includes awards suspended chiefly because of earnings of the retired worker and awards converted from disability awards to retirement awards on attainment of age 65. Also includes awards to transitionally insured persons aged 72 and over.   [11] Represents total disbursements of benefit checks by the U.S. Dept. of the Treasury during the years specified.   [12] Distribution by type estimated.

Source: U.S. Social Security Administration, *Annual Statistical Supplement* to the *Social Security Bulletin*.

No. 533. Social Security (OASDI)—Benefits in Current-Payment Status and Benefit Payments, 1970 to 1977, and by States and Other Areas, 1977

[OASI—Old-age and survivors insurance. Number of benefits and average monthly amount for retired workers as of **June 30** except, beginning 1977, as of **Sept. 30**. Payments for year ending **June 30** except, beginning 1977, ending **Sept. 30**. By beneficiary's State of residence. See also headnote, table 532]

| YEAR AND STATE OR OTHER AREA | NUMBER OF BENEFITS (1,000) | | | BENEFIT PAYMENTS (mil. dol.) | | | | Average monthly benefits for retired workers [5] (dollars) |
| | OASI [1] | | Disability insurance [3] | Total [2] | OASI [1] | | Disability insurance [3] | |
	Retired workers and dependents [2]	Survivors			Retired workers and dependents [2]	Survivors [4]		
1970	16,815.8	6,369.6	2,567.5	29,045.5	19,201.0	7,066.3	2,778.1	117.10
1973	18,609.4	7,044.3	3,415.4	47,331.6	30,782.2	11,387.6	5,161.8	164.80
1974	19,339.2	7,209.5	3,690.1	54,007.4	34,623.3	13,225.6	6,158.6	186.47
1975	19,911.2	7,324.9	4,124.8	62,468.6	39,875.4	14,963.4	7,629.8	205.18
1976	20,496.1	7,446.3	4,532.8	71,362.7	45,324.6	16,815.8	9,222.2	222.37
1977, total	21.123.3	7,477.3	4.732.1	82.405.6	52.235.9	19.034.5	11.135.2	240.17
Ala	339.2	159.3	102.9	1,288.0	717.9	349.9	220.2	212.31
Alaska	9.2	6.1	2.6	41.3	21.9	13.5	5.9	238.86
Ariz	231.4	70.5	51.2	887.7	586.4	176.8	124.5	246.16
Ark	252.7	88.1	77.1	866.7	516.0	192.2	158.4	205.24
Calif	1,936.9	602.8	456.4	7,685.9	4,921.9	1,590.9	1,173.2	244.22
Colo	196.6	69.8	38.4	745.2	472.3	180.0	92.9	233.45
Conn	305.9	92.6	47.0	1,250.1	863.5	262.4	124.2	266.91
Del	49.1	19.3	10.7	207.2	129.8	50.9	26.6	251.59
D.C	54.3	22.5	11.6	198.0	123.4	47.4	27.1	213.34
Fla	1,240.9	314.7	206.8	4,468.8	3,130.6	824.9	513.3	241.86
Ga	387.7	182.5	143.5	1,545.0	842.0	397.8	305.2	211.28
Hawaii	67.9	19.2	10.7	230.5	159.4	45.6	25.5	242.10
Idaho	79.9	24.6	15.3	291.2	191.5	63.4	36.3	233.18
Ill	1,029.6	372.8	175.8	4,187.6	2,730.6	1,005.3	451.7	254.23
Ind	501.3	178.8	104.1	2,055.7	1,310.0	486.0	259.7	251.43
Iowa	330.9	102.0	45.3	1,193.7	808.0	275.6	110.2	238.95
Kans	253.4	76.9	32.4	903.6	619.8	205.1	78.8	237.88
Ky	331.5	138.0	105.0	1,246.5	705.5	321.8	219.3	213.70
La	290.4	151.8	115.5	1,188.2	615.8	339.4	232.9	214.33
Maine	122.3	38.8	26.0	442.1	288.8	97.2	56.1	225.83
Md	305.5	124.0	58.3	1,243.0	775.2	318.3	149.5	242.26
Mass	595.8	187.0	97.0	2,316.8	1,572.1	504.7	239.9	248.59
Mich	797.3	310.4	196.7	3,498.6	2,135.3	855.9	507.4	259.76
Minn	412.4	124.2	53.9	1,439.1	983.3	325.9	129.8	233.21
Miss	229.1	102.4	80.8	790.2	434.3	201.0	154.9	192.75
Mo	544.5	178.1	108.4	2,014.5	1,306.1	455.5	252.9	232.41
Mont	72.2	25.2	14.3	273.0	174.1	65.1	33.8	235.27
Nebr	173.4	51.7	20.7	598.1	415.0	134.9	48.3	233.29
Nev	47.1	16.0	11.6	190.9	119.5	41.2	30.3	239.67
N.H	90.4	25.5	13.9	337.8	235.3	68.5	34.0	244.99
N.J	707.1	241.5	144.8	3,015.2	1,967.7	669.6	377.8	263.44
N. Mex	90.7	37.8	29.7	343.7	201.7	83.1	58.9	224.50
N.Y	1,841.2	593.6	372.2	7,645.0	5,067.7	1,623.6	953.7	261.33
N.C	479.8	204.4	140.2	1,812.3	1,059.9	445.7	306.7	214.57
N. Dak	69.2	21.9	8.5	226.8	154.0	54.7	18.1	222.32
Ohio	954.5	379.2	226.8	4,045.9	2,446.1	1,034.5	565.3	248.92
Okla	293.4	99.8	68.9	1,066.5	666.4	245.6	154.5	223.05
Oreg	259.5	70.8	49.8	984.5	666.1	193.0	125.4	245.49
Pa	1,247.6	454.8	244.3	5,184.8	3,290.4	1,255.3	639.1	253.40
R.I	107.3	31.3	20.4	415.5	281.8	83.7	50.0	241.82
S.C	219.9	110.1	78.5	885.8	485.7	231.1	169.0	213.99
S. Dak	79.0	25.4	10.6	261.5	176.1	62.2	23.2	220.75
Tenn	406.8	161.5	120.7	1,498.9	874.5	366.2	258.3	212.61
Tex	1,041.2	418.2	232.5	3,823.3	2,323.7	994.0	505.6	221.42
Utah	88.6	30.1	15.4	338.6	222.4	78.6	37.6	243.81
Vt	49.9	16.2	10.0	187.2	122.7	41.7	22.8	236.79
Va	392.0	163.8	102.6	1,513.1	895.8	386.7	230.6	222.34
Wash	357.9	106.6	68.6	1,397.9	930.1	290.1	177.7	249.10
W. Va	189.2	87.5	75.2	829.2	437.4	220.2	171.6	234.15
Wis	498.2	152.5	79.5	1,885.1	1,272.3	416.6	196.1	247.33
Wyo	31.4	10.8	4.5	115.5	76.5	28.2	10.8	235.36
Puerto Rico	243.6	90.8	174.1	682.1	322.9	137.3	222.0	152.41
Outlying areas	5.6	3.7	1.6	17.7	10.0	5.4	2.3	207.90
Foreign countries	191.1	89.2	18.7	604.7	379.1	190.5	35.1	212.51

[1] Benefits payable from the old-age and survivor insurance trust fund to retired worker beneficiaries and their dependents and to survivors of deceased workers.   [2] Includes special benefits; see footnote 8, table 532.
[3] Benefits payable from the disability insurance trust fund to disabled-worker beneficiaries and their dependents.   [4] Includes lump-sum payments to survivors of deceased workers.   [5] Excludes persons with special benefits.

Source: U.S. Social Security Administration. Periodically in *Social Security Bulletin*.

No. 534. SOCIAL SECURITY (OASDHI)—RETIREMENT BENEFITS, BY SEX: 1960 TO 1977

[As of **end of year**. Benefits in current-payment status. OASDHI= Old-age, survivors, disability, and health insurance. Full benefits begin at age 65; reduced benefits at age 62. The latter began in 1956 for women and in 1961 for men. See also *Historical Statistics, Colonial Times to 1970*, series H 245–259]

ITEM	1960	1965	1970	1972	1973	1974	1975	1976	1977
MALE									
Number receiving benefits [1]_____1,000__	5,217	6,825	7,688	8,231	8,610	8,832	9,164	9,420	9,724
Full benefits_____1,000__	5,217	5,389	4,930	4,833	4,817	4,737	4,699	4,633	4,592
Reduced benefits_____1,000__	(X)	1,436	2,758	3,398	3,793	4,095	4,465	4,787	5,132
Average age_____years__	73.2	72.9	72.6	72.4	72.3	72.3	71.2	70.2	(NA)
Percent aged: 62–64 years_____	(X)	6.9	7.5	8.4	8.7	8.9	9.3	9.4	9.5
65–69 years_____	33.8	29.7	30.1	31.2	31.9	32.2	32.2	32.3	32.3
70–74 years_____	33.1	29.5	26.9	26.0	25.7	25.9	25.6	25.8	25.8
75 years and over_____	33.2	33.9	35.5	34.4	33.7	33.0	32.9	32.5	32.4
Average monthly benefits, total_____dol__	82	93	131	179	183	207	228	248	268
Full_____dol__	82	96	139	192	197	224	247	270	293
Reduced: Before reduction_____dol__	(X)	90	129	177	181	206	228	250	272
After reduction_____dol__	(X)	79	115	161	164	187	207	226	246
Minimum monthly benefits: [2]									
Full_____dol__	33	44	64	70	85	85	94	101	108
Reduced_____dol__	(X)	35	51	56	68	68	75	81	86
Maximum monthly benefits: [2]									
Full_____dol__	119	132	190	216	266	275	316	364	413
Reduced_____dol__	(X)	103	147	167	208	217	253	291	330
FEMALE									
Number receiving benefits [1]_____1,000__	2,845	4,276	5,661	6,324	6,754	7,126	7,424	7,744	8,109
Full benefits_____1,000__	1,896	2,192	2,352	2,402	2,527	2,526	2,521	2,670	2,673
Reduced benefits_____1,000__	949	2,083	3,309	3,922	4,227	4,601	4,903	5,074	5,436
Average age_____years__	71.0	71.8	72.0	72.0	72.0	72.1	71.2	70.3	(NA)
Percent aged: 62–64 years_____	12.6	12.2	11.5	11.9	11.9	11.8	11.8	11.6	11.6
65–69 years_____	36.3	31.6	30.1	30.3	30.7	30.6	30.4	30.2	30.0
70–74 years_____	29.0	28.1	25.4	24.5	24.2	24.2	24.2	24.4	24.3
75 years and over_____	22.2	28.1	33.1	33.4	33.1	33.4	33.6	33.8	34.1
Average monthly benefits, total_____dol__	60	70	101	140	146	165	182	197	213
Full_____dol__	62	75	112	156	164	186	206	224	242
Reduced: Before reduction_____dol__	64	74	106	145	144	163	180	(NA)	(NA)
After reduction_____dol__	56	65	94	130	135	154	169	183	198
Minimum monthly benefits: [2]									
Full_____dol__	33	44	64	70	85	85	94	101	108
Reduced_____dol__	26	35	51	56	68	68	75	81	86
Maximum monthly benefits: [2]									
Full_____dol__	119	136	196	225	276	285	334	379	422
Reduced_____dol__	95	105	152	173	213	220	253	303	338

NA Not available.   X Not applicable.
[1] Includes disability beneficiaries who attained age 65.   [2] Assumes retirement at beginning of year.

Source: U.S. Social Security Administration, *Social Security Bulletin*, monthly, and *Annual Statistical Supplement*.

No. 535. INDEXES OF PENSIONS, AVERAGE WEEKLY EARNINGS, AND CONSUMER PRICES, SELECTED COUNTRIES: 1965 TO 1974

[1960=100. Relates to national social security systems. Pensions and wages data refer to average worker in manufacturing; price trend based on annual changes in consumer price index]

COUNTRY AND INDEX	1965	1970	1972	1973	1974	COUNTRY AND INDEX	1965	1970	1972	1973	1974
United States:						**Netherlands:**					
Pensions_____	107	139	184	184	205	Pensions_____	232	381	473	547	645
Wages_____	120	149	172	185	197	Wages_____	148	229	287	325	370
Prices_____	107	131	141	150	167	Prices_____	118	149	173	187	204
Austria:						**Sweden:**					
Pensions_____	109	141	162	178	203	Pensions_____	154	209	245	259	295
Wages [1]_____	143	213	270	304	390	Wages [1]_____	148	212	249	264	321
Prices_____	121	142	158	170	187	Prices_____	120	149	169	181	198
France:						**Switzerland:**					
Pensions_____	173	254	310	344	379	Pensions_____	173	260	285	519	649
Wages_____	143	219	268	322	347	Wages_____	140	196	246	276	310
Prices_____	120	149	166	179	203	Prices_____	117	139	158	172	189
Germany, Fed. Rep.:						**United Kingdom:**					
Pensions_____	143	203	237	264	293	Pensions_____	160	208	270	310	400
Wages_____	153	219	260	297	311	Wages_____	127	182	228	261	309
Prices_____	115	131	145	155	162	Prices_____	119	149	174	191	221

[1] Average monthly wage.

Source: U.S. Social Security Administration, *Social Security Bulletin*, November 1976.

No. 536. FEDERAL CIVIL SERVICE RETIREMENT: 1950 TO 1977

[As of **June 30** or for years ending **June 30** except, beginning 1977, as of **Sept. 30** or for year ending **Sept. 30**. See text, p. 325. See also *Historical Statistics, Colonial Times to 1970*, series H 262-270]

ITEM	1950	1955	1960	1965	1970	1973	1974	1975	1976	1977
Annuities in force, total____1,000__	172	297	515	729	958	1,192	1,306	1,372	1,432	1,502
Disability_____1,000__	43	61	102	149	185	220	239	258	279	306
Annual value_____mil. dol__	182	358	792	1,354	2,660	4,412	5,729	7,234	8,513	9,919
Lump-sum payments:										
Separated employees_____1,000__	239	101	153	121	215	162	150	195	118	128
Refunds_____mil. dol__	88	73	114	112	197	192	212	201	187	265
Deceased and annuitants_1,000__	12	12	13	20	24	26	29	27	26	24
Refunds_____mil. dol__	8	9	11	17	23	20	21	20	23	19

Source: U.S. Civil Service Commission, *Report on Civil Service Retirement, Federal Employees Group Life Insurance, Federal Employees Health Benefits, Retired Federal Employees Health Benefits*, annual.

No. 537. STATE AND LOCAL GOVERNMENT RETIREMENT SYSTEMS: 1962 TO 1977

[Last month or end of fiscal year]

YEAR AND COVERAGE CLASS	Number of systems	Membership (1,000)	RECURRENT MONTHLY BENEFITS			CASH AND SECURITY HOLDINGS	
			Beneficiaries (1,000)	Benefits (mil. dol.)	Avg. per beneficiary	Total (mil. dol.)	Average per member
1962_____	2,346	5,367	739	101.4	$137	23,294	$4,340
1967_____	2,165	7,068	1,030	166.7	162	39,265	5,555
1972_____	2,304	9,089	1,463	326.4	223	68,760	7,565
1977, total_____	3,075	10,951	2,271	677.7	298	123,481	11,276
General coverage systems_____	600	6,787	1,366	323.4	237	66,415	9,786
State-administered_____	62	5,761	986	228.2	231	50,179	8,711
Locally administered_____	538	1,026	380	95.2	251	16,236	15,828
Limited coverage systems_____	2,475	4,165	905	354.3	391	57,066	13,701
School employees and teachers____	68	3,046	689	265.7	386	45,842	12,573
State-administered_____	44	3,473	635	235.3	371	41,692	12,005
Locally administered_____	24	173	54	30.4	563	4,150	23,988
Covering police and firemen_____	2,196	348	158	69.7	441	8,508	24,448
State-administered_____	35	134	31	10.8	348	2,430	18,134
Locally administered_____	2,161	214	127	58.9	464	6,078	28,402
Other limited coverage systems__	211	171	58	18.9	326	2,717	15,889

No. 538. STATE AND LOCAL GOVERNMENT RETIREMENT—FINANCES: 1967 TO 1977

[In millions of dollars. For fiscal years closed during the 12 months ending June 30]

YEAR AND LEVEL OF GOVERNMENT	RECEIPTS					BENEFITS AND WITHDRAWALS			Cash and security holdings
	Total	Employee contributions	Government contributions		Earnings on investments	Total	Benefits	Withdrawals	
			State	Local					
1967: All systems_____	6,580	1,960	1,353	1,702	1,565	2,609	2,103	506	39,265
State-administered_____	4,656	1,494	1,305	747	1,110	1,606	1,280	326	27,666
Locally administered_____	1,924	466	49	955	455	1,002	822	180	11,598
1970: All systems_____	9,848	2,788	2,046	2,554	2,460	3,638	3,037	601	54,918
State-administered_____	7,184	2,149	1,978	1,237	1,821	2,382	1,913	469	39,966
Locally administered_____	2,664	639	67	1,318	639	1,256	1,124	132	14,952
1975: All systems_____	18,898	4,488	4,093	5,023	5,294	7,490	6,540	950	98,064
State-administered_____	14,208	3,552	3,974	2,623	4,059	5,207	4,480	727	74,703
Locally administered_____	4,690	936	119	2,400	1,236	2,283	2,060	223	23,361
1976: All systems_____	21,848	4,869	4,523	6,129	6,327	8,422	7,507	915	111,322
State-administered_____	16,625	3,915	4,447	3,344	4,920	6,045	5,327	718	85,801
Locally administered_____	5,222	954	76	2,785	1,407	2,377	2,180	197	25,522
1977: All systems_____	25,347	5,233	4,960	7,410	7,744	9,559	8,455	1,104	123,481
State-administered_____	19,287	4,223	4,847	4,051	6,167	6,930	6,048	882	94,913
Locally administered_____	6,059	1,011	113	3,359	1,577	2,629	2,407	222	28,569

Source of tables 537 and 538: U.S. Bureau of the Census, *Census of Governments: 1977*, vol. 6, No. 1, *Employee-Retirement Systems of State and Local Governments*, and *Finances of Employee-Retirement Systems of State and Local Governments*, annual.

No. 539. Private Pension and Deferred Profit-Sharing Plans: 1950 to 1975

[Includes pay-as-you-go, multiemployer, union-administered, and nonprofit organization plans, and railroad plans supplementing the Federal railroad retirement program. Plans are classified as insured and noninsured, the former underwritten by insurance companies and the latter generally funded through trustees. See also *Historical Statistics, Colonial Times to 1970*, series H 287–304]

ITEM AND TYPE OF PLAN	1950	1955	1960	1965	1970	1972	1973	1974	1975
Coverage, net [1][2]_____1,000__	**9,800**	**14,200**	**18,700**	**21,800**	**26,300**	**27,500**	**29,200**	**29,800**	**30,300**
Insured plans, gross_____1,000__	2,600	3,800	4,900	6,200	8,900	9,500	10,200	10,800	11,600
Noninsured plans, gross__1,000__	7,200	11,600	16,300	19,100	22,000	24,000	25,600	26,200	26,800
Contributions:									
Employer_____mil. dol__	1,750	3,280	4,710	7,370	12,580	16,940	19,390	23,020	27,560
Insured plans_____mil. dol__	720	1,100	1,190	1,770	2,860	4,200	5,020	6,050	7,730
Noninsured plans____mil. dol__	1,030	2,180	3,520	5,600	9,720	12,740	14,370	16,970	19,830
Employee_____mil. dol__	330	560	780	990	1,420	1,600	1,710	2,000	2,290
Insured plans_____mil. dol__	200	280	300	320	350	400	440	540	690
Noninsured plans____mil. dol__	130	280	480	670	1,070	1,200	1,270	1,460	1,600
Monthly beneficiaries [1]_____1,000__	**450**	**980**	**1,780**	**2,750**	**4,740**	**5,550**	**6,080**	**6,390**	**7,050**
Insured plans_____1,000__	150	290	540	790	1,220	1,350	1,480	1,550	1,690
Noninsured plans_____1,000__	300	690	1,240	1,960	3,520	4,200	4,600	4,840	5,360
Benefit payments [3]_____mil. dol__	**370**	**850**	**1,720**	**3,520**	**7,360**	**10,000**	**11,220**	**12,930**	**14,810**
Insured plans_____mil. dol__	80	180	390	720	1,330	1,700	1,910	2,190	2,480
Noninsured plans [3]____mil. dol__	290	670	1,330	2,800	6,030	8,300	9,310	10,740	12,330
Reserves [1]_____bil. dol__	**12.1**	**27.5**	**52.0**	**86.5**	**137.1**	**167.8**	**180.2**	**191.7**	**212.6**
Insured plans_____bil. dol__	5.6	11.3	18.8	27.3	40.1	50.3	53.4	58.0	67.4
Noninsured plans_____bil. dol__	6.5	16.1	33.1	59.2	97.0	117.5	126.5	133.7	145.2

[1] As of end of year. [2] Excludes beneficiaries. [3] Includes refunds and lump sums.

Source: U.S. Social Security Administration, *Social Security Bulletin*, November 1977.

No. 540. Private Noninsured Pension Funds: 1960 to 1977

[In millions of dollars. Covers all pension funds of corporations, nonprofit organizations, unions, and multi-employer groups, except those managed by insurance companies. Also includes deferred profit-sharing plans; excludes health, welfare, and bonus plans. Minus sign (−) denotes loss]

ASSETS, RECEIPTS, AND DISBURSEMENTS	1960	1965	1970	1972	1973	1974	1975	1976	1977, prel.
Total assets [1][2]_____	**33,140**	**59,180**	**97,010**	**117,530**	**126,530**	**133,731**	**145,166**	**160,414**	**181,509**
Cash and deposits_____	550	940	1,800	1,860	2,340	4,286	2,962	2,199	3,721
U.S. Government securities_____	2,680	2,990	3,030	3,690	4,400	5,533	10,764	14,713	20,138
Corporate bonds_____	15,700	23,130	29,670	28,210	30,330	35,029	37,809	39,070	45,580
Preferred and common stock____	11,510	25,870	53,480	76,060	81,850	80,448	84,842	94,609	98,152
Mortgages_____	1,300	3,380	4,170	2,730	2,380	2,372	2,393	2,369	2,497
Receipts [2]_____	**5,410**	**9,280**	**13,200**	**20,070**	**19,670**	**21,060**	**26,583**	**(NA)**	**(NA)**
Employer contributions_____	3,520	5,600	9,720	12,740	14,370	16,970	19,828	(NA)	(NA)
Employee contributions_____	480	670	1,070	1,200	1,270	1,460	1,604	(NA)	(NA)
Investment income_____	1,260	2,390	3,870	4,300	4,840	5,980	6,703	(NA)	(NA)
Net profit on sale of assets_____	110	570	−1,590	1,720	−920	−3,480	−1,659	(NA)	(NA)
Disbursements_____	**1,370**	**2,880**	**6,180**	**8,490**	**9,540**	**11,030**	**12,597**	**(NA)**	**(NA)**
Benefits paid out_____	1,330	2,800	6,030	8,300	9,310	10,740	12,334	(NA)	(NA)
Expenses and other_____	50	90	150	200	230	290	263	(NA)	(NA)
Net receipts_____	4,040	6,400	7,020	11,580	10,130	10,030	13,986	(NA)	(NA)

NA Not available. [1] Book value, end of year. [2] Includes other items, not shown separately.

Source: U.S. Securities and Exchange Commission, *Statistical Bulletin*, monthly.

No. 541. Railroad Retirement Benefits: 1950 to 1977

[For years ending June 30 except, beginning 1977, ending Sept. 30. See also *Historical Statistics, Colonial Times to 1970*, series H 271–286]

ITEM	1950	1960	1965	1970	1974	1975	1976	1977
Average number of railroad employees_____1,000__	1,360	930	762	650	588	575	537	547
Retirement and survivor benefits:								
Monthly benefits awarded_____1,000__	65	115	85	99	95	137	107	96
Recipients_____1,000__	461	873	980	1,051	1,073	1,094	1,100	1,108
Monthly benefits in current payment status (end of year)_____1,000__	387	790	889	1,036	1,108	1,161	1,183	1,201
Lump-sum death benefits awarded [1]_____1,000__	33	22	23	19	18	16	14	15
Amount of benefit payments_____mil. dol__	302	926	1,118	1,594	2,671	3,060	3,470	3,787

[1] Excludes deferred insurance lump-sum benefits.

Source: U.S. Railroad Retirement Board, *Annual Report*. Current data in *RRB Quarterly Review*.

No. 542. Employee-Benefit Plans—Summary: 1960 to 1975

[Coverage data refer to civilian wage and salary workers at end of year; contributions, to amounts subscribed by employers and employees, in total. An "employee-benefit plan" is any type of plan sponsored or initiated unilaterally or jointly by employers or employees and providing benefits that stem from the employment relationship and that are not underwritten or paid directly by government (Federal, State, or local). In general, the intent is to include plans that provide in an orderly predetermined fashion for (1) income maintenance during periods when regular earnings are cut off because of death, accident, sickness, retirement, or unemployment and (2) benefits to meet medical expenses. Excludes workmen's compensation required by statute and employer's liability. See also *Historical Statistics, Colonial Times to 1970*, series H 70–114]

ITEM AND TYPE OF PLAN	1960	1965	1970	1972	1973	1974	1975
Covered employees:							
Life insurance and death [1]_____mil__	34.2	41.9	51.8	55.2	57.8	60.6	62.4
Accidental death and dismemberment_____mil__	20.9	28.4	38.7	40.7	42.7	44.3	46.5
Health benefits:							
Hospitalization [2][3]_____mil__	39.3	45.7	53.1	54.2	56.8	57.6	58.2
Surgical [2]_____mil__	37.4	43.4	51.5	52.9	55.4	56.1	56.6
Regular medical [2]_____mil__	28.2	38.2	48.0	49.4	53.7	54.9	56.1
Major medical [4]_____mil__	8.8	16.6	24.6	26.4	27.6	28.2	29.6
Coverage, private employees:							
Temporary disability [5]_____mil__	[6] 24.5	24.5	29.7	31.3	32.0	31.7	31.1
Long-term disability_____mil__	(6)	1.9	7.0	9.5	10.6	11.1	11.5
Retirement [7]_____mil__	18.7	21.8	26.1	27.5	29.2	29.8	30.3
Contributions:							
All employees, total [8]_____bil. dol__	12.5	19.9	34.9	45.4	50.5	57.7	67.3
Life insurance and death [1]_____bil. dol__	1.4	2.2	3.6	4.3	4.4	4.7	5.1
Accidental death and dismemberment.bil. dol__	.1	.1	.2	.3	.3	.3	.3
Health benefits:							
Hospitalization [3]_____bil. dol__	2.5	4.3	7.6	9.5	10.5	11.4	13.3
Surgical and regular medical_____bil. dol__	1.3	2.1	4.0	5.2	5.9	7.0	8.2
Major medical [4]_____bil. dol__	.5	1.1	2.3	3.6	4.1	4.6	5.7
Private employees:							
Temporary disability [5][9]_____bil. dol__	1.2	1.6	3.1	3.7	3.9	4.4	4.7
Retirement [7]_____bil. dol__	5.5	8.4	14.0	18.5	21.1	25.0	29.9
Benefits paid:							
All employees, total [8]_____bil. dol__	7.8	13.6	26.1	32.9	36.2	42.0	47.9
Life insurance and death [1]_____bil. dol__	1.0	1.6	2.5	2.9	3.2	3.4	3.6
Accidental death and dismemberment.bil. dol__	(Z)	.1	.2	.2	.2	.3	.3
Health benefits:							
Hospitalization [3]_____bil. dol__	2.4	4.2	7.3	8.9	9.6	11.1	13.1
Surgical and regular medical_____bil. dol__	1.1	1.8	3.6	4.5	5.2	6.3	7.4
Major medical [4]_____bil. dol__	.4	1.0	2.4	3.2	3.4	4.0	4.5
Private employees:							
Temporary disability [5][9]_____bil. dol__	1.0	1.3	2.5	3.0	3.2	3.7	3.8
Retirement [7]_____bil. dol__	1.7	3.5	7.4	10.0	11.2	12.9	14.8
PERCENT OF WORKERS COVERED [10]							
All employees:							
Life insurance and death_____	57.8	63.7	69.0	71.1	71.2	73.5	77.3
Accidental death and dismemberment_____	35.3	43.1	51.5	52.4	52.7	53.7	57.6
Health benefits:							
Hospitalization_____	66.5	69.4	70.7	69.8	70.0	69.9	72.2
Surgical_____	63.3	65.9	68.6	68.1	68.3	68.1	70.1
Regular medical_____	47.7	58.0	63.9	63.6	66.2	66.5	69.5
Major medical_____	14.8	25.2	32.7	34.0	34.0	34.2	36.7
Private employees:							
Temporary disability_____	[6] 48.7	44.3	47.9	49.1	47.9	46.8	47.5
Long-term disability_____	(6)	3.4	11.2	14.8	15.8	16.4	17.6
Retirement_____	37.2	39.5	42.1	43.1	43.7	44.0	46.2
PERCENT CONTRIBUTIONS OF TOTAL WAGES AND SALARIES [10]							
All employees:							
Life insurance and death_____	.54	.64	.68	.71	.65	.63	.65
Accidental death and dismemberment_____	.03	.03	.04	.05	.04	.04	.04
Health benefits_____	1.63	2.15	2.64	2.98	3.02	3.11	3.45
Private employees:							
Temporary disability_____	.53	.54	.71	.76	.71	.73	.75
Retirement_____	2.46	2.86	3.25	3.74	3.82	4.14	4.73

Z Less than $50 million.
[1] Includes group and wholesale life insurance but excludes Servicemen's Group Life Insurance program.
[2] Includes persons covered by group comprehensive major-medical insurance as well as those with basic benefits.
[3] Includes private hospital plans written in compliance with State temporary disability insurance law in California.
[4] Group supplementary and comprehensive major-medical insurance written by commercial insurance companies.
[5] Includes private plans written in compliance with State temporary disability insurance laws in California, Hawaii, New Jersey, and New York; and formal sick-leave plans. Excludes credit accident and health insurance.
[6] Long-term disability policies included in temporary disability.
[7] Includes pay-as-you-go and deferred profit-sharing plans, plans for non-profit organizations, union pension plans, and railroad plans supplementing the Federal railroad retirement program. Excludes plans for the self-employed and tax-sheltered annuities. Retirement coverage estimates exclude annuitants.
[8] Includes data for supplemental unemployment insurance benefits, not shown separately.
[9] Includes data under long-term disability policies.
[10] For all employees, coverage and contributions relate to private and government full-time and part-time civilian employees and payroll; for private employees, to wage and salary full-time and part-time labor force and payroll in private industry.

Source: U.S. Social Security Administration, *Social Security Bulletin*, November 1977.

No. 543. HEALTH BENEFITS IN PRIVATE INDUSTRY—PERCENT DISTRIBUTION OF PLANS AND WORKERS: 1974

[As of December. Covers wage and salary workers in private industry health plans, excluding most plans in nonprofit firms and plans with fewer than 26 participants. Data from sample survey of plans on file at U.S. Department of Labor and subject to sampling variability. Includes only plans that provided at least hospital benefits]

CHARACTERISTIC	Plans	Workers	CHARACTERISTIC	Plans	Workers
Plans_____1,000__	51.6	(X)	PERCENT—Con.		
Workers_____mil__	(X)	28.4	Basic benefits: [3]		
			Hospital daily room and board:		
PERCENT			Less than $40.00_____	16	9
Industry:			$40.00–$59.99_____	13	8
Manufacturing_____	45	53	$60.00 or more_____	5	6
Retail and wholesale trade_____	20	12	Service benefit_____	57	67
Construction_____	4	7	No basic benefit [4]_____	9	10
Transportation_____	4	6	Duration of hospital benefit (days):		
Other_____	28	23	Less than 32_____	17	9
Size of plan (number of workers):			32–70_____	17	17
26–99_____	54	5	71–120_____	23	24
100–999_____	37	21	121–365_____	9	24
1,000–4,999_____	7	26	366 or more_____	4	5
5,000–9,999_____	1	14	Dollar maximum_____	18	9
10,000–24,999_____	1	14	·No basic benefit [4]_____	13	11
25,000–49,999_____	(Z)	6	Surgical benefit for most expensive		
50,000 or more_____	(Z)	14	operation:		
Employer administered_____	93	76	Less than $400_____	16	13
Negotiated_____	18	32	$400–$599_____	18	20
Nonnegotiated_____	75	45	$600–$999_____	13	11
Worker-employer administered_____	6	23	$1,000 or more_____	12	11
Financing method: [1]			Service benefit_____	1	2
Employer_____	51	68	Reasonable and customary cost____	16	26
Worker and employer_____	37	28	No basic benefit [4]_____	23	17
Worker_____	3	1	Medical benefit per treatment in		
Insurer of hospital benefits:			hospital:		
Commercial insurance_____	65	62	$1–$4_____	8	8
Blue Cross_____	32	30	$5_____	23	16
Other_____	2	8	$6–$9_____	15	15
			$10 or more_____	10	10
Benefits during layoff: [2]			Service benefit_____	1	2
Covered_____	21	39	Reasonable and customary cost____	12	19
Not covered_____	79	61	No basic benefit [4]_____	31	29

X Not applicable.   Z Less than .5 percent.   [1] Excludes data for "information not available."
[2] Benefits continued at least one month.   [3] Benefits with no prior deductible or coinsurance payment.
[4] Includes workers for whom information was not available.

Source: U.S. Social Security Administration, *Social Security Bulletin*, February 1976 and March 1977; and unpublished data.

No. 544. SELECTED CHARACTERISTICS OF DISABLED AND NONDISABLED ADULTS: 1972

[Covers persons 20–64 years old. As of summer. Disability defined as a limitation in kind or amount of work an individual could perform as a result of a chronic health condition or impairment lasting 3 months or more. Based on a sample; subject to response and reporting errors and to sampling variability. For definition of median, see p. xii]

CHARACTERISTIC	DISABLED				Non-disabled
	Total	Severe [1]	Occupational [2]	Secondary work limitations [3]	
Persons, age 20–64_____mil__	15.6	7.7	3.5	4.4	90.7
Percent (except as indicated): [4]					
Male_____	45.2	38.5	55.3	49.2	47.8
Female_____	54.8	61.5	44.7	50.8	52.2
White_____	85.2	82.8	86.3	88.7	89.5
Black_____	13.6	15.9	12.9	10.1	8.9
Other_____	.8	1.0	.7	.4	1.2
20–34 years_____	19.2	12.0	19.7	31.9	42.8
35–49 years_____	30.0	26.3	34.7	32.8	32.1
50–59 years_____	31.2	34.2	31.7	25.6	18.9
60–64 years_____	19.5	27.6	13.9	9.7	6.3
Median age_____years__	50	53	48	44	38
Not in labor force_____	51.9	81.8	22.2	22.7	22.5
In labor force_____	47.5	17.4	77.8	76.7	77.2
Employed_____	42.9	14.0	71.4	71.5	73.7
Median weekly pay rates_____dol__	115	65	106	132	147

[1] Defined as unable to work altogether or unable to work regularly.   [2] Defined as able to work regularly but unable to do same work as before onset of disability or unable to work full time.   [3] Defined as able to work full time, regularly, and at same work, but with limitations in kind or amount of work performed.
[4] Percents may not add to 100 due to exclusion of persons not reporting.

Source: U.S. Social Security Administration, *Social Security Bulletin*, October 1976. Data from 1972 Survey of the Disabled.

No. 545. Protection Against Short-Term Sickness Income Loss: 1960 to 1976

[In millions of dollars, except percent. "Short-term sickness" refers to short-term or temporary nonwork-connected disability (lasting not more than 6 months) and the first 6 months of long-term disability. See also *Historical Statistics, Colonial Times to 1970*, series H 115–124]

ITEM	1960	1965	1970	1972	1973	1974	1975	1976
Short-term sickness: Income loss	8,591	11,333	16,757	19,507	21,059	21,804	23,565	26,468
Total protection provided [1]	2,430	3,349	5,872	6,807	[2] 7.369	[2] 8.135	[2] 8.830	[2] 9,674
Protection as percent of loss	28.3	29.6	35.0	34.9	35.0	37.3	37.5	36.5
Benefits provided by protection:								
Individual insurance	393	483	694	772	795	851	973	881
Group benefits to workers in private employment	1,211	1,602	2,952	3,390	3,650	4,144	4,329	4,953
Private cash insurance [3]	638	767	1,476	1,614	1,736	2,024	2,010	2,314
Publicly operated cash sickness funds [4]	172	269	411	412	446	485	538	581
Sick leave	400	566	1,066	1,364	1,469	1,634	1,781	2,059
Sick leave for govt. employees	826	1,264	2,225	2,645	2,714	3,010	3,368	3,670

[1] Provided by individual insurance, group benefits to workers in private employment, and sick leave for government employees.   [2] Includes benefits for the sixth month of disability payable under old-age, survivors, disability, and health insurance program, not shown separately.   [3] Group accident and sickness insurance and self-insurance privately written either on a voluntary basis or in compliance with State temporary disability insurance laws in Calif., N.J., and N.Y. Includes a small but undetermined amount of group disability insurance benefits paid to government workers and to self-employed persons through farm, trade, or professional associations.   [4] Includes State-operated plans in Rhode Island, California, and New Jersey; State Insurance Fund and special fund for disabled unemployed in New York; and provisions of Railroad Unemployment Insurance Act.

Source: U.S. Social Security Administration, *Social Security Bulletin*, May 1977, and unpublished data.

No. 546. Medical Insurance (Medicare) Under Social Security—Enrollees and Charges for Covered Services: 1969 to 1974

[Covers supplementary medical insurance under the old-age, survivors, disability, and health insurance program; see text, p. 323. For 1969–1972, "Deductible met" refers to enrollees whose charges equaled or exceeded $50 after which insurance makes partial payments; beginning 1973, it refers to enrollee charges over $60. "Deductible not met" refers to enrollees with expenditures less than these amounts]

ITEM	ENROLLEES AND CHARGES					PERCENT				
	1969	1970	1972	1973	1974	1969	1970	1972	1973	1974
Enrollees [1] _____1,000	20,299	20,684	21,559	22,117	22,606	100.0	100.0	100.0	100.0	100.0
Not using services	4,338	4,317	4,472	3,981	4,311	21.4	20.9	20.7	18.0	19.1
Using covered services [2]	15,961	16,367	17,087	18,136	18,296	78.6	79.1	79.3	82.0	80.9
Deductible not met	5,780	5,773	5,532	6,657	5,915	28.5	27.9	25.7	30.1	26.2
Deductible met	9,861	10,360	11,346	11,480	12,381	48.6	50.1	52.6	51.9	54.8
Total charges _____mil. dol	2,939	3,220	3,404	3,814	4,534	100.0	100.0	100.0	100.0	100.0
Deductible met	2,818	3,093	3,278	3,641	4,378	95.9	96.1	96.3	95.5	96.6
Potentially reimbursable	1,896	2,104	2,216	2,409	2,959	64.5	65.4	65.1	63.2	65.3
Average charges [3] _____dol	188	200	202	210	248	(X)	(X)	(X)	(X)	(X)
Deductible not met	21	22	22	26	26	(X)	(X)	(X)	(X)	(X)
Deductible met	286	299	289	317	354	(X)	(X)	(X)	(X)	(X)
Potentially reimbursable	192	203	195	210	239	(X)	(X)	(X)	(X)	(X)
Percent reimbursable [4]	67.3	68.0	67.6	66.2	67.6	(X)	(X)	(X)	(X)	(X)

X Not applicable.   [1] As of July 1. Includes newly-qualified persons and deaths and terminations.   [2] Includes persons using services for which a bill is not expected.   [3] Based on enrollees using covered services.   [4] Represents amount reimbursable as a percent of total charges for persons who met the deductible.

Source: U.S. Social Security Administration, *Current Medicare Survey*.

No. 547. Black Lung Benefit Program—Beneficiaries and Benefit Payments, 1970 to 1977, and by Selected States, 1977

[Benefits currently payable by the Social Security Administration to miners totally disabled because of pneumoconiosis and to their dependents and survivors under the "Black Lung" program established by the Federal Coal Mine Health and Safety Act of 1969]

BENEFICIARIES AND PAYMENTS	1970	1973	1974	1975	1976	1977							
						Total	Selected States						
							Pa.	W. Va.	Ky.	Ohio	Ill.	Va.	Ala.
Beneficiaries [1] ____1,000	112	461	487	482	470	457	138.0	80.6	55.8	26.8	25.6	25.9	20.0
Miners _____1,000	44	160	169	165	158	149	44.0	27.0	18.2	8.6	8.2	8.7	6.6
Widows _____1,000	25	124	135	139	143	145	47.9	21.2	12.8	9.1	10.4	6.4	6.5
Dependents [2] __1,000	43	178	183	177	169	164	46.2	32.3	24.8	9.1	6.9	10.8	6.9
Payments _____mil. dol	110	1,045	952	948	963	942	287	160	103	56	58	52	43
Avg. mo. payment: [2]													
Miner's family	$200	$253	$267	$282	$294	$317	$310	$319	$318	$311	$316	$334	$322
Widow's family	$150	$188	$197	$207	$216	$231	$227	$237	$239	$232	$226	$239	$234

[1] As of end of year.   [2] Dependent wife or child or surviving child, parent, brother, or sister.

Source: U.S. Social Security Administration. Quarterly in *Social Security Bulletin*.

No. 548. Health Insurance (Medicare) Under Social Security: 1970 to 1976

[Data reflect date claims approved for payment and cover only claims approved and recorded in the Social Security Administration central records for hospital and supplementary medical insurance before Dec. 31, 1977]

ITEM	65 YEARS OLD AND OVER						DISABLED		
	1970	1972	1973	1974	1975	1976	1974	1975	1976
HOSPITAL INSURANCE									
Claims approved_____1,000__	7,501	7,661	8,048	8,762	9,348	10,019	750	925	1,076
Reimbursements [1]____mil. dol__	4,844	5,915	6,507	7,659	9,381	11,401	690	980	1,289
Inpatients:									
Claims approved_____1,000__	6,306	6,728	6,957	7,481	7,817	8,227	689	839	968
Admissions_____1,000__	6,139	6,610	6,860	7,160	7,421	7,801	724	852	964
Annual rate [2]_____	304	316	321	328	333	343	377	394	405
Covered days of care_____mil__	80	79	80	83	84	88	8	9	10
Annual rate [2]_____	3,943	3,771	3,743	3,800	3,770	3,851	3,944	4,115	4,220
Per admission_____	13.0	11.9	11.7	11.6	11.3	11.2	10.5	10.4	10.4
Hospital charges_____mil. dol__	5,931	7,527	8,301	9,741	11,970	14,665	918	1,313	1,745
Per day_____dol__	74	95	104	118	142	168	121	148	174
Reimbursements [1]_____mil. dol__	4,569	5,710	6,260	7,351	8,999	10,935	677	960	1,264
Percent of charges_____	77.0	75.9	75.4	75.5	75.2	74.6	73.7	73.1	72.4
Per claim_____dol__	725	849	900	983	1,151	1,329	982	1,145	1,305
Home health:									
Claims approved_____1,000__	571	533	624	781	1,005	1,228	46	70	90
Reimbursements [1]_____mil. dol__	47	49	61	88	135	184	6	9	14
Per claim_____dol__	82	92	97	113	134	150	124	142	159
Skilled nursing facility:									
Claims approved_____1,000__	624	400	468	500	526	563	15	17	19
Reimbursements [1]_____mil. dol__	229	156	187	220	247	282	7	9	11
Per claim_____dol__	366	390	400	440	469	501	495	556	574
MEDICAL INSURANCE									
Total bills_____1,000__	[3]39,695	50,992	53,089	61,411	73,232	82,343	4,430	6,658	8,544
Physicians:									
Bills approved_____1,000__	32,850	41,674	42,764	49,181	57,206	63,987	3,118	4,597	5,843
Total charges_____mil. dol__	2,157	2,669	2,836	3,324	3,907	4,452	234	344	438
Per bill_____dol__	66	64	66	68	68	70	75	75	75
Percent reimbursed_____	72.9	72.6	72.4	73.0	74.1	75.5	74.5	75.6	76.9
Surgical_____	75.5	74.9	74.6	75.0	75.8	77.2	75.9	76.5	77.0
Medical_____	71.5	71.2	70.9	71.5	72.8	74.4	73.4	75.0	76.4
Outpatient hospital:									
Bills approved_____1,000__	4,031	5,562	5,839	6,949	8,985	10,442	861	1,344	1,752
Reimbursements [1]_____mil. dol__	85	136	153	210	315	420	88	143	196
Per bill_____dol__	21	25	26	30	35	40	102	106	112
Home health:									
Bills approved_____1,000__	430	270	312	417	544	644	32	44	55
Reimbursements [1]_____mil. dol__	23	15	22	35	55	74	3	5	7
Per bill_____dol__	53	54	69	85	101	114	100	116	129
Other:									
Bills approved_____1,000__	2,380	3,485	4,173	4,864	6,498	7,271	420	673	893
Reimbursements [1]_____mil. dol__	70	93	126	156	212	257	57	100	144
Per bill_____dol__	30	27	30	32	33	33	136	148	161

[1] Amounts paid to providers for covered services; excludes deductibles, coinsurance amounts, and noncovered services as specified by law.   [2] Per 1,000 enrollees; enrollment as of July 1.   [3] Data reflect date paid claims were recorded in Social Security Administration records and include bills for which type of service is unknown.

Source: U.S. Social Security Administration, *Social Security Bulletin*, monthly; *Health Insurance Statistics* (through 1975); and unpublished data. Data from U.S. Health Care Financing Administration.

No. 549. Medical Assistance (Medicaid) Under Social Security—Average Monthly Recipients and Payments: 1970 to 1977

[See text, p. 325]

BASIS OF ELIGIBILITY	RECIPIENTS (1,000)					PAYMENTS (mil. dol.)				
	1970	1974	1975	1976	1977	1970	1974	1975	1976	1977
Total_____	5,376	8,070	8,884	9,180	9,048	422	913	1,124	1,253	1,385
Age 65 and over_____	1,554	1,969	2,040	2,087	2,046	159	344	420	451	505
Blindness_____	42	52	46	45	45	3	7	7	8	8
Permanently and totally disabled__	608	1,076	1,217	1,348	1,392	87	210	271	326	378
AFDC [1] program, total_____	2,824	4,369	4,972	5,078	4,996	140	298	357	388	416
Children_____	(NA)	2,699	3,020	3,105	3,037	(NA)	146	176	194	207
Adults_____	(NA)	1,670	1,952	1,973	1,959	(NA)	152	181	194	208
Other_____	347	604	608	621	569	32	54	69	79	79

NA Not available.   [1] Aid to families with dependent children.

Source: U.S. Health Care Financing Administration, *Medical Assistance (Medicaid) Financed Under Title XIX of the Social Security Act*, Report B-1, annual.

No. 550. Hospital and Medical Insurance (Medicare) Under Social Security—Enrollment and Payments, 1970 to 1976, and by States, 1976

[Enrollment as of July 1; payments for calendar year. Payments reflect locations of hospitals and physicians. Effective July 1, 1973, coverage was extended to disability beneficiaries and persons with chronic renal disease]

YEAR AND STATE	HOSPITAL Enrollment[1] (1,000)	HOSPITAL Benefit payments[2] (mil. dol.)	MEDICAL Enrollment (1,000)	MEDICAL Benefit payments[2] (mil. dol.)	STATE	HOSPITAL Enrollment[1] (1,000)	HOSPITAL Benefit payments[2] (mil. dol.)	MEDICAL Enrollment (1,000)	MEDICAL Benefit payments[2] (mil. dol.)
1970	20,361	5,124	19,584	1,974	Minn	475	276	470	86
1972	21,115	6,416	20,351	2,349	Miss	290	108	287	56
1973	23,301	7,047	22,491	2,522	Mo	657	344	645	109
1974	23,924	9,063	23,167	3,358	Mont	85	31	83	13
1975	24,640	11,335	23,905	4,225	Nebr	207	90	203	30
1976, total	[3]25,313	13,240	[3]24,614	5.042	Nev	52	52	51	14
U.S.	[3]24,825	13,202	[3]24,436	5,024	N.H.	100	39	97	15
Ala	429	178	427	63	N.J.	845	431	836	178
Alaska	10	5	8	2	N. Mex	106	36	103	17
Ariz	252	128	245	59	N.Y	2,218	1,594	2,184	623
Ark	308	110	304	42	N.C	573	228	566	84
Calif	2,295	1,484	2,279	657	N. Dak	81	46	79	15
Colo	233	147	228	51	Ohio	1,185	630	1,158	229
Conn	351	226	346	77	Okla	365	144	359	59
Del	58	30	56	11	Oreg	291	135	280	57
D.C	73	75	71	33	Pa	1,524	611	1,493	275
Fla	1,385	780	1,383	363	R.I	126	74	123	30
Ga	497	189	493	84	S.C	275	88	270	33
Hawaii	64	30	64	21	S. Dak	92	40	90	12
Idaho	90	33	87	12	Tenn	505	238	500	78
Ill	1,255	758	1,234	174	Tex	1,270	601	1,262	268
Ind	589	273	575	85	Utah	101	41	97	17
Iowa	395	164	388	50	Vt	59	32	58	10
Kans	305	132	300	49	Va	481	208	469	83
Ky	420	161	416	51	Wash	407	180	398	79
La	397	162	372	61	W. Va	254	94	250	34
Maine	144	64	142	23	Wis	564	266	557	96
Md	368	206	359	78	Wyo	37	12	36	4
Mass	720	614	711	179	Puerto Rico	281	37	142	18
Mich	935	585	918	199	Other	6	1	5	(Z)

Z Less than $500,000. [1] Mailing address of beneficiary. [2] Estimates based on payment vouchers drawn by intermediaries and carriers, some of whom serve more than one State; amounts represent obligations rather than trust fund outlays. [3] Includes enrollees with residence unknown.

Source: Through 1975, U.S. Social Security Administration, *Health Insurance Statistics*; thereafter, U.S. Health Care Financing Administration, unpublished data.

No. 551. Recipients of Medicaid and Payments to Medical Vendors, 1970 to 1977, and by States and Other Areas, 1977

[Medical vendor payments are those made directly to suppliers of medical care]

STATE AND YEAR	Recipients (1,000)	PAYMENTS Total (mil. dol.)	PAYMENTS Per recipient (dol.)	STATE	Recipients (1,000)	PAYMENTS Total (mil. dol.)	PAYMENTS Per recipient (dol.)	STATE	Recipients (1,000)	PAYMENTS Total (mil. dol.)	PAYMENTS Per recipient (dol.)
1970, Nov	5,701	455.5	80	Ill	719	86.8	121	N.C	157	19.0	121
1972, Nov	7,015	628.6	90	Ind	99	19.5	197	N. Dak	13	2.8	215
1973, Nov	7,300	785.6	108	Iowa	80	14.1	176	Ohio	332	45.1	136
1974, Dec	8,215	948.4	115	Kans	82	13.9	170	Okla	64	15.2	238
1975, Dec	9,042	1,198.8	133	Ky	173	15.1	87	Oreg	74	14.0	189
1976, Dec	9,009	1,332.1	148	La	177	21.9	124	Pa	428	107.8	252
1977, Dec. total	9,006	1,444.2	160	Maine	55	7.7	140	R.I	52	9.5	183
Ala	132	13.8	105	Md	112	16.9	151	S.C	114	12.2	107
Alaska	2	2.7	1,350	Mass	431	68.1	158	S. Dak	14	2.9	207
Ariz	(1)	(1)	(1)	Mich	383	65.1	170	Tenn	156	17.5	112
Ark	101	14.3	142	Minn	117	32.0	274	Tex	340	54.1	159
Calif	1,299	182.2	140	Miss	121	10.4	86	Utah	22	4.6	209
Colo	79	15.0	190	Mo	153	15.3	100	Vt	24	4.2	175
Conn	124	20.6	166	Mont	17	3.8	224	Va	140	22.3	159
Del	21	3.4	162	Nebr	34	6.2	182	Wash	123	20.6	167
D.C	57	9.8	172	Nev	9	1.9	211	W. Va	58	4.4	76
Fla	181	20.8	115	N.H	23	4.2	183	Wis	174	41.9	241
Ga	222	30.1	136	N.J	287	38.0	132	Wyo	3	.7	233
Hawaii	42	6.2	148	N. Mex	34	4.5	132	P.R	310	7.3	24
Idaho	38	4.4	116	N.Y	1,001	269.3	269	V.I	3	.2	67

[1] Arizona had no Title XIX Medicaid program.

Source: U.S. Health Care Financing Administration, *Medical Assistance (Medicaid) Financed Under Title XIX of the Social Security Act*, Report B-1, annual.

No. 552. MEDICAL VENDOR PAYMENTS (MEDICAID)—BY TYPE OF SERVICE: 1970 TO 1977

[In millions of dollars. Medical vendor payments are those made directly to suppliers of medical care. Excludes Arizona, which has no Title XIX (Medicaid) program. Excludes payments for screening of children and payments to health insurance organizations, health maintenance organizations, and U.S. Social Security Administration. Medicaid program is federally aided but State administered and operated]

YEAR	Total	Inpatient hospital	Skilled nursing facility	Intermediate care facility	Physicians	Dental[1]	Outpatient hospital[2]	Laboratory[3]	Home health	Prescribed drugs	Family planning	Other care
1970	[4] 5,355	2,046	1,465	–	641	174	265	14	–	425	–	248
1971	[4] 6,634	2,748	1,768	–	756	176	358	34	–	495	–	278
1972	[4] 8,095	2,556	1,593	933	678	178	388	36	[5] 10	504	–	227
1973	9,503	3,372	1,893	1,320	1,042	326	544	79	28	664	19	215
1974	10,979	3,511	2,190	1,931	1,135	405	623	92	41	749	62	240
1975	13,525	4,295	2,628	2,459	1,338	506	829	118	112	901	81	257
1976	15,098	4,764	2,666	3,101	1,422	528	974	141	151	1,011	101	239
1977	16,654	5,246	2,861	3,764	1,516	540	1,010	157	189	1,026	122	223

- Represents zero. [1] Includes other practitioners' services except for 1971 and 1972. [2] Includes clinic services except for 1971 and 1972. [3] Includes radiological services. [4] Includes payments for which type of service was not reported, not shown separately. [5] 6 months only.

Source: U.S. Health Care Financing Administration, *Medical Assistance (Medicaid) Financed Under Title XIX of the Social Security Act*, Report B-1, annual.

No. 553. VOCATIONAL REHABILITATION—SUMMARY: 1950 TO 1977

[In thousands, except as indicated. For years ending June 30 except 1977, for year ending Sept. 30. Vocational rehabilitation of the disabled defined as restoration, preservation, or development of the ability to function in productive activity. Rehabilitation services provided by State agencies with matching State and Federal funds include medical restoration, training, guidance, and placement services. See also *Historical Statistics, Colonial Times to 1970*, series H 393-397]

ITEM	1950	1960	1965	1970	1973	1974	1975	1976	1977
Referred and extended evaluation cases processed [1]	158	258	396	765	1,020	1,047	1,164	1,088	998
Percent accepted into program	58	49	50	54	49	49	46	42	44
Federal and State expenditures..mil. dol..	29	79	154	558	730	810	867	898	956
Federal expenditures..........mil. dol..	20	48	94	432	572	636	673	700	733
Percent of total expenditures	69	61	61	77	78	79	78	78	77
Total persons rehabilitated [2]	**59.6**	**88.3**	**134.9**	**267.0**	**360.7**	**361.1**	**324.0**	**303.3**	**291.2**
Rehabilitation rate [3]....percent..	70	75	76	77	74	73	70	63	64
Disability:									
Amputation or missing members	7.6	8.6	9.0	9.5	8.8	8.5	7.7	7.4	7.0
Orthopedic impairments	18.2	27.0	36.9	45.7	56.3	56.6	52.7	51.6	52.7
Blindness and other visual	7.1	9.4	13.1	22.4	28.8	28.3	27.4	27.4	26.2
Deafness and other hearing	5.3	5.4	8.1	14.3	16.9	16.7	15.9	16.0	16.2
Mental illness	2.3	5.7	18.3	63.3	102.1	104.2	92.8	85.8	78.0
Mental retardation	.5	2.9	10.2	30.4	40.2	41.9	38.3	36.0	34.2
Digestive system disorders	(NA)	(NA)	(NA)	23.0	24.0	21.5	21.7	20.9	16.8
Genito-urinary system disorders	(NA)	(NA)	(NA)	7.8	8.7	8.2	9.3	9.2	8.8
Other disabilities	18.6	29.2	39.2	40.2	46.1	46.2	44.1	41.3	39.5
Not reported	(Z)	–	.1	10.4	29.0	29.1	14.1	7.6	11.7
Type of job placement:									
Professional, technical, managerial [4]	6.0	7.5	11.6	24.5	33.8	35.4	36.4	36.8	34.4
Clerical and sales [4]	11.2	15.2	20.9	40.0	48.9	50.5	46.3	43.0	41.2
Service	9.1	17.0	27.9	57.8	69.7	68.0	64.6	59.9	54.8
Agriculture, fishing, etc	5.7	7.0	7.6	9.2	10.5	9.8	9.5	9.2	7.9
Industrial: Skilled	9.3	10.9	15.2	22.1	31.9	31.6	28.4	27.1	25.8
Semiskilled and unskilled	12.1	18.5	26.0	55.9	80.4	81.1	66.8	60.6	58.4
Homemakers [5]	6.1	12.1	21.6	42.5	52.0	50.1	53.7	53.3	46.2
Other and not reported	(Z)	(Z)	4.1	14.9	33.5	34.5	18.2	13.5	22.4
Persons served, total [6]	**226**	**298**	**441**	**876**	**1,176**	**1,202**	**1,244**	**1,238**	**1,205**

- Represents zero.   NA Not available.   Z Less than 50.
[1] Referred cases only for 1950-1965.   [2] Persons rehabilitated and gainfully employed.
[3] Persons rehabilitated as a percent of all active case closures (whether rehabilitated or not).
[4] Includes vending stand personnel.   [5] Includes unpaid family workers.
[6] Includes active cases accepted during year plus active cases on hand at beginning of year.

Source: U.S. Office of Human Development Services, *Characteristics of Clients Rehabilitated, Caseload Statistics of State Vocational Rehabilitation Agencies in Fiscal Years*, and *State Vocational Rehabilitation Agency Program Data in Fiscal Years*, all annual.

No. 554. Vocational Rehabilitation—Cases and Expenditures, States and Other Areas: 1977

[For year ending Sept. 30. See headnote, table 553. See also *Historical Statistics, Colonial Times to 1970*, series H 392–395]

STATE OR OTHER AREA	REFERRED AND EXTENDED EVALUATION CASES		ACTIVE CASES		Expenditures, total [2] (mil. dol.)	STATE OR OTHER AREA	REFERRED AND EXTENDED EVALUATION CASES		ACTIVE CASES		Expenditures, total [2] (mil. dol.)
	Processed (1,000)	Percent accepted	Served [1] (1,000)	Rehabilitated (1,000)			Processed (1,000)	Percent accepted	Served [1] (1,000)	Rehabilitated (1,000)	
Total___	[3] 997.8	44	1,204.5	291.2	955.6	Nev_____	4.1	38	3.0	1.1	3.1
						N.H_____	3.1	46	5.1	1.1	3.7
Ala_____	24.0	58	36.7	9.1	24.6	N.J_____	34.1	32	27.3	7.5	20.9
Alaska___	2.3	40	2.0	.5	2.8	N. Mex___	5.9	34	5.4	1.3	7.2
Ariz_____	6.5	48	6.8	1.7	10.3	N.Y_____	60.5	37	75.0	10.5	57.9
Ark_____	13.6	45	17.5	5.2	16.4	N.C_____	42.8	42	52.1	13.3	34.8
Calif____	70.6	34	62.9	12.6	70.9						
Colo_____	8.7	50	10.8	2.5	10.5	N. Dak___	3.8	50	5.6	1.1	3.3
Conn_____	8.4	49	10.6	2.6	8.4	Ohio_____	39.4	33	35.7	9.5	43.6
Del_____	2.7	47	2.9	1.0	2.9	Okla_____	20.8	58	35.5	8.5	17.6
D.C_____	6.8	40	6.6	1.7	7.5	Oreg_____	17.1	38	14.0	3.8	14.5
						Pa_____	75.3	45	83.4	23.3	49.4
Fla_____	40.4	36	41.1	8.9	35.8	R.I_____	3.5	46	6.9	1.4	3.8
Ga_____	29.7	47	35.8	10.2	23.4						
Hawaii___	5.5	31	4.8	.6	3.2	S.C_____	33.6	41	44.4	12.9	20.8
Idaho____	4.0	47	4.9	1.4	4.7	S. Dak___	2.8	39	3.7	.9	3.7
Ill_____	30.2	43	35.9	9.0	33.8	Tenn_____	17.3	54	25.7	6.7	22.9
Ind_____	11.2	38	15.9	3.1	14.7	Tex_____	73.5	42	82.3	19.1	64.2
Iowa_____	9.7	45	13.7	3.4	13.0	Utah_____	5.7	57	12.2	3.0	7.0
Kans_____	9.8	45	9.3	3.2	9.4	Vt_____	2.7	48	2.9	.7	2.8
Ky_____	24.8	42	25.0	9.0	21.1	Va_____	26.4	40	27.2	6.7	22.5
La_____	16.2	59	34.3	6.9	23.5	Wash_____	13.3	50	19.3	5.0	14.0
Maine____	4.8	31	4.3	1.0	5.0	W. Va____	16.0	32	15.7	4.9	14.5
Md_____	23.8	53	28.4	7.1	14.4	Wis_____	16.0	48	23.0	4.7	21.3
Mass_____	21.9	53	31.1	7.0	22.6	Wyo_____	1.6	55	2.1	.5	2.6
Mich_____	28.2	65	42.8	9.8	31.2	P.R_____	9.8	52	25.6	4.1	21.3
Minn_____	20.8	47	30.5	6.0	18.3	Guam_____	.2	48	.3	.1	.8
Miss_____	14.8	48	18.3	6.0	16.9	V.I_____	.3	39	.3	.1	.7
Mo_____	19.0	51	22.6	7.2	21.4	T.T. of					
Mont_____	3.6	48	6.3	1.4	3.6	P.I.[4]___	.1	6	.2	.1	.4
Nebr_____	6.1	50	8.5	1.4	6.3						

[1] Persons served includes active cases accepted during year plus active cases on hand at beginning of year.
[2] Total Federal and State expenditures for basic support under Section 110 of the Rehabilitation Act of 1973. Excludes Federal grants of $92 million for the Federal Disability Insurance Trust Fund and $17 million for expansion projects.   [3] Includes 413,983 referrals certified for rehabilitation services; 542,960 referrals not accepted; 21,161 extended evaluation cases certified for services; and 19,672 extended evaluation cases not accepted.
[4] Trust Territory of the Pacific Islands.

Source: U.S. Office of Human Development Services, *Caseload Statistics of State Vocational Rehabilitation Agencies, 1977,* and *State Vocational Rehabilitation Agency Program Data, 1977.*

No. 555. Railroad Unemployment and Sickness Insurance—Benefits: 1960 to 1977

[For years ending June 30 except, beginning 1977, ending Sept. 30. See also *Historical Statistics, Colonial Times to 1970*, series H 318–331]

ITEM	1960	1965	1970	1973	1974	1975	1976	1977
Unemployment benefits:								
First-time applications_____1,000__	254	153	98	128	61	109	133	99
Claims received_____1,000__	2,026	979	438	506	274	443	875	608
Beneficiaries_____1,000__	221	127	79	105	48	78	105	86
Benefit payments, number_____1,000__	(NA)	927	407	476	254	412	826	611
Total benefit payments_____mil. dol__	209	71	35	41	22	38	143	102
Average benefit payment [1]_____dol__	[2] 79	79	92	91	95	94	176	191
Sickness benefits: [3]								
Applications received [4]_____1,000__	190	142	121	98	95	90	103	107
Claims received_____1,000__	880	688	707	527	487	453	512	539
Beneficiaries_____1,000__	142	106	91	74	71	67	77	83
Benefit payments, number_____1,000__	847	648	674	492	450	418	473	544
Total benefit payments_____mil. dol__	66	44	58	32	28	30	75	78
Average benefit payment [1]_____dol__	[2] 90	91	113	112	111	111	205	231

NA Not available.   [1] Per 2-week claim period. Based on sample data through 1975.
[2] Excludes retroactive payments under 1959 amendments and, for unemployment, extended benefits.
[3] Prior to 1970, includes maternity benefits; thereafter, regular sickness benefits paid for pregnancy and child birth.   [4] Beginning of each period of sickness.
Source: U.S. Railroad Retirement Board, *Annual Report.* Current data in *RRB Quarterly Review.*

No. 556. Unemployment Insurance—All Programs and Federal Programs, Summary, 1960 to 1977, and by States and Other Areas, 1977

YEAR AND STATE OR OTHER AREA	ALL REGULAR PROGRAMS [1]				UCFE (Federal employee) PROGRAM				UCX PROGRAM [5]	
	Initial claims (1,000)	Weeks compensated (1,000)	Average weekly beneficiaries (1,000)	Benefits paid [2] (mil. dol.)	Covered employment [3]		Beneficiaries, first payments [4] (1,000)	Benefits paid [2] ($1,000)	Beneficiaries, first payments [4] (1,000)	Benefits paid [2] ($1,000)
					Average monthly (1,000)	Annual wages (mil. dol.)				
1960	17,718	89,941	1,723	2,867	2,188	13,074	94	55,733	207	84,262
1965	12,441	61,804	1,189	2,283	2,609	17,877	73	49,951	153	67,478
1970	16,160	84,319	1,621	4,171	2,881	28,141	94	79,704	352	203,210
1973	13,362	76,229	1,466	4,487	2,832	33,878	106	128,301	230	209,377
1974	19,436	103,178	1,984	6,912	2,893	36,872	105	148,733	249	249,220
1975	25,479	182,835	3,516	19,628	2,900	39,968	120	277,298	304	528,468
1976	20,705	135,000	2,596	16,157	2,895	42,852	144	305,385	282	593,003
1977, total	20,070	119,526	2,299	12,922	[6] 2,878	[7] 45,746	125	275,372	234	470,660
Ala	322	1,764	34	167	63	1,028	4	4,712	4	9,135
Alaska	92	1,016	20	109	[8] 19	[8] 340	2	5,098	1	3,073
Ariz	150	749	14	67	36	536	2	2,624	3	4,643
Ark	204	903	17	75	19	276	1	1,674	3	4,887
Calif	2,670	15,495	298	1,634	316	4,995	18	41,630	37	69,850
Colo	175	842	16	92	50	783	2	2,413	3	4,798
Conn	371	2,591	50	307	21	332	1	1,765	3	7,328
Del	72	401	8	48	5	82	(z)	642	1	1,724
D.C	51	793	15	83	224	4,194	6	16,608	1	2,413
Fla	487	2,836	55	251	83	1,329	2	3,040	9	16,444
Ga	426	1,928	37	173	81	1,262	3	5,375	7	13,448
Hawaii	68	623	12	72	30	485	1	4,730	2	4,643
Idaho	89	390	8	35	12	172	2	2,155	1	2,165
Ill	871	7,441	143	975	[9] 104	[9]1,412	4	23,161	8	23,126
Ind	433	1,522	29	132	[8] 40	[8] 643	1	1,040	4	4,570
Iowa	154	1,056	20	116	19	288	(z)	723	4	7,717
Kans	99	753	14	76	25	367	1	1,784	3	4,599
Ky	304	1,461	28	140	39	563	3	4,456	3	6,942
La	236	1,942	37	197	33	496	2	3,462	5	12,390
Maine	198	834	16	80	10	136	1	1,789	2	2,587
Md	318	1,788	34	170	[8] 131	[8] 2,058	2	3,987	3	5,572
Mass	548	4,104	79	465	57	946	4	10,311	5	12,292
Mich	1,107	5,181	100	755	55	860	3	10,528	9	28,288
Minn	228	2,009	39	206	31	469	1	2,494	4	8,822
Miss	138	677	13	55	26	371	1	1,786	1	1,980
Mo	492	2,112	41	199	68	1,071	3	4,430	5	8,790
Mont	74	401	8	38	13	188	1	2,262	1	1,423
Nebr	71	362	7	30	16	238	(z)	466	(z)	463
Nev	96	469	9	52	9	145	1	1,441	1	1,805
N.H	61	263	5	19	14	223	(z)	190	1	849
N.J	763	6,554	126	895	73	1,247	4	12,220	6	18,883
N. Mex	70	423	8	33	28	424	2	2,435	2	3,069
N.Y	1,893	13,472	259	1,552	162	2,612	5	16,255	11	30,101
N.C	610	2,341	45	204	47	666	1	2,562	5	9,390
N. Dak	47	288	6	30	10	131	1	871	1	1,295
Ohio	891	4,465	86	465	91	1,533	3	5,616	11	21,047
Okla	129	851	16	75	48	736	2	4,607	3	4,439
Oreg	319	1,586	30	142	28	434	3	3,776	4	7,180
Pa	1,639	10,117	195	1,171	128	2,007	7	18,722	11	29,379
R.I	155	904	17	103	9	155	1	2,664	1	2,691
S.C	329	1,108	21	96	35	507	1	1,760	4	7,461
S. Dak	32	164	3	14	11	153	1	749	1	754
Tenn	355	1,958	38	179	64	1,026	7	8,331	5	12,127
Tex	430	2,554	49	188	161	2,501	5	7,189	11	11,781
Utah	75	540	10	46	37	518	3	3,623	2	1,415
Vt	47	323	6	33	4	62	(z)	519	1	1,050
Va	270	1,339	26	120	152	2,495	2	2,862	5	5,875
Wash	532	2,516	48	268	[8] 62	[8] 1,003	4	9,512	7	13,685
W. Va	169	935	18	71	15	223	(z)	438	2	2,213
Wis	431	2,348	45	224	[10] 26	[10] 400	1	1,806	5	6,682
Wyo	18	87	2	9	[8] 7	[8] 102	1	577	(z)	226
P.R	258	1,948	37	187	10	141	1	1,433	2	3,015
V.I	(X)	(X)	(X)	1	1	9	(z)	74	(z)	132

X Not applicable. Z Less than 500. [1] Includes State programs shown in table 557 and UCFE and UCX programs. Represents unduplicated counts. 1960 includes temporary unemployment programs and UCV (Korea Veterans) program which terminated Jan. 31, 1960. [2] Includes extended benefits payments made under regular State and Federal unemployment insurance and the temporary "Federal Supplemental Benefits Program," and the "Special Unemployment Assistance Program." [3] Source: U.S. Bureau of Labor Statistics, *Employment and Wages*, quarterly. [4] Excludes first payments filed jointly with State unemployment insurance programs. [5] Unemployment compensation for ex-servicemen. [6] Distribution by States excludes FBI employment for security reasons. [7] Includes wages not distributed by States. [8] Data for one quarter. [9] Data for four quarters. [10] Data for three quarters.

Source: Except as noted, U.S. Employment and Training Administration, *Unemployment Insurance Statistics*, monthly.

No. 557. STATE UNEMPLOYMENT INSURANCE—SUMMARY,

[Beginning 1965, includes Puerto Rico. Includes unemployment compensation for State and local government and for ex-servicemen, except as noted. See also table 556 and

| YEAR AND STATE OR OTHER AREA | Statutory coverage provisions¹ (effective January 1977) | COVERED EMPLOYMENT² | | | AVERAGE WEEKLY— | | | | Weeks compensated for all unemployment (1,000) |
| | | Average monthly number of workers³ (1,000) | Wages (mil. dol.) | | Insured unemployment | | Unemployment benefits | | |
			Total	Taxable⁴	Number (1,000)	Percent⁵	Current dollars	Percent of weekly wage	
1960	(X)	40,523	196,634	119,289	1,906	4.8	32.87	35.2	85,630
1965	(X)	45,495	260,210	143,977	1,328	3.0	37.19	33.8	58,813
1970	(X)	52,814	387,980	182,320	1,805	3.4	50.34	35.6	78,858
1972	(X)	60,807	490,688	237,105	1,848	3.5	56.76	36.6	81,261
1973	(X)	64,645	549,971	253,746	1,632	2.7	59.00	36.1	71,223
1974	(X)	66,696	609,894	265,375	2,262	3.5	64.25	36.5	97,803
1975	(X)	65,411	642,711	265,229	3,986	6.0	70.23	37.2	175,305
1976	(X)	67,890	716,066	303,222	2,991	4.6	75.16	37.1	127,425
1977	(X)	70,830	794,567	323,821	2,647	3.9	78.77	38.8	113,244
Ala	20 weeks	1,006	10,041	4,750	39	4.0	68.26	38.0	1,645
Alaska	At any time	11 121	11 2,735	11 1,465	13	10.3	86.69	17.9	952
Ariz	20 weeks	672	7,068	3,428	20	3.2	72.74	38.3	675
Ark	10 days	586	5,308	2,849	23	4.1	67.46	41.6	844
Calif	Over $100 in any quarter	7,543	89,194	44,375	321	4.5	72.58	34.2	14,545
Colo	20 weeks	863	9,437	3,569	22	2.7	87.25	44.2	760
Conn	20 weeks	1,242	14,447	5,862	54	4.5	83.20	39.4	2,531
Del	20 weeks	214	2,584	797	8	3.6	86.88	40.2	382
D.C	At any time	352	4,536	1,255	11	3.3	105.09	45.5	644
Fla	20 weeks	2,753	27,560	10,617	78	3.0	63.34	34.7	2,645
Ga	20 weeks	1,538	15,638	8,432	42	2.9	71.29	39.3	1,759
Hawaii	At any time 12	338	3,515	1,912	13	3.9	91.46	48.1	559
Idaho	20 wks. or $300 in qtr	248	2,897	1,507	10	4.2	77.37	42.3	349
Ill	20 weeks	13 3,822	13 45,177	13 15,787	165	4.4	93.59	40.9	7,198
Ind	20 weeks	11 1,761	11 20,526	11 7,427	35	2.1	70.05	33.6	1,459
Iowa	20 weeks	893	9,192	4,359	22	2.6	94.66	51.0	992
Kans	20 weeks	682	6,861	2,814	16	2.5	78.82	43.4	699
Ky	20 weeks	926	9,674	3,850	31	3.6	71.30	38.1	1,354
La	20 weeks	1,145	12,556	4,902	41	3.7	85.22	43.8	1,807
Maine	20 weeks	309	2,796	1,252	18	5.9	69.50	41.9	798
Md	At any time	11 1,177	11 12,655	11 4,683	40	3.5	74.07	39.4	1,689
Mass	13 weeks	2,004	21,689	7,630	87	4.5	79.78	40.7	3,928
Mich	20 wks. or $1,000 a yr	3,164	42,759	14,690	139	4.6	89.56	37.3	4,938
Minn	20 weeks	1,500	16,237	7,214	42	3.0	87.09	44.2	1,913
Miss	20 weeks	595	5,266	2,600	18	3.1	58.65	36.8	636
Mo	20 weeks	1,531	16,554	6,499	54	3.7	74.05	37.9	1,983
Mont	Over $500 in year	229	2,264	850	10	4.4	75.88	43.5	365
Nebr	20 weeks	474	4,517	1,784	10	2.1	72.19	41.5	352
Nev	$225 in quarter	260	2,866	1,677	10	4.3	77.32	39.0	447
N.H	20 weeks	289	2,719	1,167	6	2.2	67.19	40.0	252
N.J	$1,000 a year	2,306	28,011	12,484	126	5.6	83.16	37.8	6,362
N. Mex	20 wks. or $450 in qtr	305	2,954	1,597	11	3.7	58.08	33.7	361
N.Y	$300 in quarter	5,758	72,069	23,269	280	4.9	75.90	33.4	13,105
N.C	20 weeks	1,812	16,855	7,738	50	2.9	66.68	39.5	2,233
N. Dak	20 weeks	164	1,534	621	6	4.0	82.13	48.2	267
Ohio	20 weeks	3,899	47,075	14,674	102	2.7	91.77	42.5	4,225
Okla	20 weeks	796	8,220	3,286	19	2.5	65.23	35.9	767
Oreg	18 wks. or $225 in qtr	861	9,701	4,893	39	4.9	74.66	36.8	1,486
Pa	At any time	3,878	44,433	15,403	216	5.7	92.34	44.7	9,718
R.I	At any time	341	3,248	1,385	19	5.8	75.13	42.9	872
S.C	20 weeks	869	8,070	3,667	24	2.9	70.25	42.2	1,022
S. Dak	20 weeks	174	1,480	618	4	2.3	73.69	47.9	148
Tenn	20 weeks	1,344	13,058	5,577	45	3.5	62.81	35.9	1,777
Tex	20 weeks	4,128	45,198	18,310	58	1.5	57.23	29.4	2,316
Utah	$140 in quarter	386	3,948	2,311	12	3.2	80.14	43.9	485
Vt	20 weeks	142	1,319	723	7	5.2	73.00	43.2	310
Va	20 weeks	1,519	15,262	6,203	28	2.0	75.33	41.6	1,255
Wash	At any time	11 1,133	11 13,766	11 7,268	64	6.1	82.01	37.7	2,320
W. Va	20 weeks	500	5,818	2,273	21	4.4	64.91	31.0	901
Wis	20 weeks	14 1,688	14 18,887	14 7,812	54	3.5	87.90	44.3	2,236
Wyo	$500 in year	11 131	11 1,490	11 634	2	1.7	78.66	39.2	78
P.R	At any time	458	3,312	3,072	64	13.9	46.11	36.1	1,901

X   Not applicable.   ¹ Employer subject to State unemployment insurance law when he has employed at least one worker on at least 1 day in each of specified number of weeks within current or preceding calendar year and or specified wages as indicated.   ² Source: U.S. Bureau of Labor Statistics, *Employment and Wages*, quarterly.   ³ For pay period including the 12th of the month.   ⁴ Wages subject to unemployment insurance tax. Includes State and local government coverage as well as private industry coverage; see text, p. 324.
⁵ Percent of workers covered by insurance.   ⁶ Weeks compensated divided by first payments.
⁷ Based on first payments for 12-month period ending June 30.
⁸ Contributions from employers; also employees in States which tax workers.

1960 TO 1977, AND STATES AND PUERTO RICO, 1977

employees where covered by State law; excludes unemployment compensation for Federal employees
Historical Statistics, Colonial Times to 1970, series H 305–317]

Beneficiaries, first payments (1,000)	Average actual duration of benefits[6] (weeks)	CLAIMANTS EXHAUSTING BENEFITS		Contributions collected[8] (mil. dol.)	Benefits paid[9] (mil. dol.)	Funds available for benefits, end of year[10] (mil. dol.)	Average employer contribution rate (percent)	Ratio of benefits to contributions (percent)	YEAR AND STATE OR OTHER AREA
		Number (1,000)	As percent of first payment[7]						
6,753	12.7	1,603	26.1	2,289	2,727	6,643	1.9	119.1	1960
4,813	12.2	1,086	21.5	3,053	2,166	8,357	2.1	70.9	1965
6,402	12.3	1,295	24.4	2,507	3,848	11,896	1.3	153.5	1970
5,704	14.2	1,809	29.2	3,899	4,471	9,423	1.7	114.7	1972
5,329	13.4	1,495	27.7	5,000	4,008	10,934	2.0	80.2	1973
7,730	12.7	1,926	31.0	5,228	5,975	10,599	2.0	114.3	1974
11,160	15.7	4,195	37.8	5,227	11,755	4,523	1.9	224.9	1975
8,560	14.9	3,270	37.8	7,532	8,975	3,362	2.6	119.2	1976
7,985	14.2	2,850	33.4	9,170	8,357	4,387	2.8	91.1	1977
159	10.4	41	25.2	119	107	28	2.6	90.0	Ala.
50	18.9	15	28.9	66	85	75	4.4	130.0	Alaska.
53	12.8	17	30.9	78	46	66	2.4	58.1	Ariz.
70	12.1	20	24.7	62	51	26	2.3	81.5	Ark.
1,016	14.3	396	37.7	1,533	1,018	1,088	3.5	66.4	Calif.
71	10.8	29	38.9	91	65	57	2.6	71.9	Colo.
166	15.2	53	28.7	178	193	27	3.0	108.7	Conn.
28	13.5	8	26.2	22	32	4	2.9	141.9	Del.
31	20.5	14	43.4	37	55	7	2.7	149.1	D.C.
194	13.6	101	47.1	264	166	111	2.7	63.0	Fla.
197	8.9	60	28.0	143	117	250	1.8	81.6	Ga.
34	16.2	12	34.1	63	45	1	3.4	71.0	Hawaii.
32	10.8	9	26.7	31	24	62	2.1	78.6	Idaho.
415	17.4	172	39.3	484	648	−717	2.5	133.9	Ill.
153	9.5	44	30.6	142	98	261	2.0	69.0	Ind.
77	12.0	20	24.8	102	80	67	2.0	66.7	Iowa.
49	14.3	17	29.4	64	56	155	2.3	87.4	Kans.
124	10.9	32	23.9	110	90	146	2.9	82.0	Ky.
113	16.0	42	36.7	111	144	125	2.1	130.0	La.
69	11.6	22	31.8	44	52	3	3.6	116.4	Maine.
128	13.2	32	23.9	158	124	3	3.3	78.5	Md.
238	16.5	96	38.7	321	281	106	4.4	87.7	Mass.
406	12.2	155	34.4	592	407	351	4.1	68.7	Mich.
127	15.0	57	40.9	165	143	83	2.4	86.7	Minn.
55	11.6	14	24.4	59	37	124	2.4	62.7	Miss.
167	11.9	55	31.3	171	135	121	2.7	78.6	Mo.
28	13.1	9	32.0	27	26	7	3.1	97.1	Mont.
32	11.0	9	26.9	39	24	53	2.0	61.1	Nebr.
34	13.2	13	35.4	52	34	25	3.2	64.9	Nev.
32	8.0	2	4.4	22	17	41	1.9	76.4	N.H.
371	17.1	179	43.6	516	517	69	3.7	100.1	N.J.
21	17.1	7	29.6	27	21	38	1.9	76.8	N. Mex.
646	20.3	268	39.1	797	918	−29	3.5	122.9	N.Y.
203	11.0	56	20.1	148	140	274	2.0	94.7	N.C.
20	13.6	5	26.0	19	22	17	3.0	117.5	N. Dak.
316	13.4	78	22.4	417	368	221	2.9	88.2	Ohio.
51	14.9	26	41.9	77	47	44	2.4	61.2	Okla.
102	13.7	28	26.3	168	96	91	3.3	57.6	Oreg.
672	14.5	145	20.9	490	804	24	3.1	164.1	Pa.
57	15.2	22	65.5	55	61	−66	3.9	110.5	R.I.
101	10.1	24	37.6	78	68	90	2.2	87.3	S.C.
13	11.4	3	21.5	6	10	13	1.1	153.2	S. Dak.
159	11.2	44	24.2	103	107	168	1.9	104.3	Tenn.
181	12.8	70	24.8	172	129	249	.6	74.8	Tex.
37	13.0	11	36.6	41	33	32	1.9	80.1	Utah.
20	15.7	5	27.4	20	21	8	3.0	101.6	Vt.
104	12.0	32	26.1	92	91	90	1.5	99.6	Va.
154	15.1	57	28.7	204	166	−41	3.0	81.3	Wash.
97	9.3	13	34.7	47	56	64	2.1	120.1	W. Va.
178	12.6	116	13.6	239	177	231	2.7	74.2	Wis.
7	11.0	2	67.1	15	7	45	2.4	49.7	Wyo.
126	15.1	92	21.5	90	90	11	3.0	100.4	P.R.

[9] Includes payments under State (not Federal) temporary extended unemployment insurance provisions.
[10] Sum of balances in State clearing accounts, benefit-payment accounts, and State accounts in Federal unemployment trust funds. Minus sign (−) denotes deficit. [11] For one quarter. [12] Also covers employers of 20 or more agricultural workers in 20 weeks. [13] For four quarters. [14] For three quarters.

Source: Except as noted, U.S. Employment and Training Administration, Unemployment Insurance Statistics, monthly, and Annual Report of the Secretary of Labor.

No. 558. WORKMEN'S COMPENSATION PAYMENTS, BY STATES: 1950 TO 1976

[In millions of dollars. Payments represent cash and medical benefits and include insurance losses paid by private insurance carriers (compiled from the *Spectator (Insurance by States . . . of Casualty Lines)*, from reports of State Insurance commissions, and from A. M. Best Co.); net disbursements of State funds (from the *Spectator*, from *Argus Casualty and Surety Chart*, and from State reports), estimated for some States; and self-insurance payments, estimated from available State data. Calendar-year data, except fiscal-year data for Federal civilian and other programs and for a few States with State funds. Includes benefit payments under Longshoremen's and Harbor Workers' Compensation Act and Defense Bases Compensation Act for States in which such payments are made]

STATE	1950	1955	1960	1965	1970	1972	1973	1974	1975	1976
Total	614.7	915.7	1,294.9	1,813.8	3,030.6	4,038.8	5,092.2	5,765.0	6,518.3	7,462.2
Alabama	2.1	4.5	10.1	16.6	25.2	30.8	35.1	44.8	48.7	58.8
Alaska	(X)	(X)	2.9	3.8	6.9	9.2	10.5	13.2	18.5	34.3
Arizona	5.5	7.0	12.1	20.4	39.3	50.7	56.2	64.7	69.8	74.8
Arkansas	3.6	5.2	5.4	11.6	20.9	21.7	28.8	35.8	37.9	42.5
California	58.5	89.4	156.1	270.0	420.7	469.4	548.6	623.4	723.1	841.8
Colorado	3.4	6.5	10.5	15.3	23.8	27.1	30.0	37.0	44.2	51.7
Connecticut	9.5	15.9	19.9	19.4	39.5	47.3	52.2	58.1	64.0	68.2
Delaware	.7	1.2	2.0	2.7	5.2	7.4	7.9	9.4	10.3	11.9
District of Columbia	2.4	2.6	4.1	6.4	8.5	9.9	12.9	18.5	26.7	36.8
Florida	7.4	18.0	34.4	54.7	94.9	126.6	160.9	210.4	254.1	278.3
Georgia	4.8	7.6	11.3	19.8	34.8	43.7	51.0	65.1	77.5	93.7
Hawaii	(X)	(X)	4.6	7.0	13.7	16.3	19.5	22.1	27.1	28.6
Idaho	2.2	3.6	4.9	5.7	7.3	10.5	14.4	17.6	20.2	23.5
Illinois	31.1	45.7	67.4	87.0	144.1	155.3	178.8	219.7	238.7	305.6
Indiana	8.9	13.1	18.1	24.0	43.9	47.8	48.5	55.6	59.7	65.1
Iowa	5.0	6.7	9.3	12.0	18.6	21.4	24.6	31.5	37.4	46.2
Kansas	4.3	8.2	13.0	14.6	18.2	20.8	23.3	27.3	33.7	39.4
Kentucky	7.0	9.3	12.1	15.3	26.1	34.3	40.0	49.7	60.5	75.6
Louisiana	11.4	19.6	26.5	35.1	63.9	77.6	83.2	103.5	114.6	138.0
Maine	1.6	2.4	3.5	4.1	7.9	11.1	13.7	16.3	19.7	25.1
Maryland	6.9	12.1	20.1	26.6	38.8	49.6	58.7	65.8	73.4	86.4
Massachusetts	23.7	33.4	45.4	64.7	90.4	104.4	122.3	132.6	146.0	153.7
Michigan	23.1	31.0	48.9	77.8	197.9	242.8	273.5	311.8	333.7	384.4
Minnesota	9.7	14.9	22.0	27.9	46.5	57.6	62.8	76.4	86.0	108.0
Mississippi	2.3	4.7	8.4	11.8	16.2	17.8	21.5	23.8	26.7	29.5
Missouri	10.6	16.6	22.3	25.9	41.3	48.1	51.5	56.9	63.6	71.8
Montana	2.5	4.2	5.4	7.2	9.6	11.3	13.4	13.4	16.3	18.6
Nebraska	2.4	3.5	4.5	6.1	9.9	11.6	13.6	17.9	17.9	21.8
Nevada	1.7	3.6	4.4	6.8	11.4	15.8	18.0	21.6	25.2	31.6
New Hampshire	1.7	2.4	3.7	4.5	7.0	9.3	11.5	14.1	16.6	20.0
New Jersey	29.2	44.2	59.9	83.9	135.0	149.3	156.7	177.6	194.8	216.2
New Mexico	2.3	4.8	8.1	8.8	11.1	13.1	15.5	18.0	21.1	24.6
New York	115.7	143.9	164.5	196.7	273.9	321.3	342.4	369.9	406.8	447.2
North Carolina	6.4	10.0	14.9	20.6	29.6	35.6	40.6	48.9	50.8	62.0
North Dakota	1.1	1.9	2.4	3.6	4.8	5.2	5.7	5.8	7.6	9.5
Ohio	40.4	69.3	99.1	139.0	197.0	232.1	316.2	384.3	444.7	476.2
Oklahoma	8.1	13.2	15.4	19.9	29.1	34.4	40.7	52.1	59.7	72.3
Oregon	9.0	15.7	25.5	29.2	50.6	61.3	78.5	105.2	137.4	160.6
Pennsylvania	30.8	37.8	50.2	89.2	123.5	147.3	173.9	198.6	205.4	278.2
Rhode Island	3.8	5.9	6.7	7.5	11.1	13.1	14.8	16.2	18.6	23.1
South Carolina	4.1	5.2	8.1	10.8	17.6	18.6	21.8	25.8	31.1	36.1
South Dakota	1.0	1.1	2.0	2.2	3.0	3.6	4.4	5.3	5.5	6.4
Tennessee	5.3	9.5	14.3	20.7	35.3	42.8	48.4	56.3	61.6	73.5
Texas	33.4	50.0	69.7	89.1	159.1	188.4	227.1	290.4	360.3	400.1
Utah	1.9	2.5	3.5	5.0	7.2	10.1	11.0	13.1	16.3	17.8
Vermont	.9	1.2	1.7	2.5	3.8	4.0	4.7	5.8	6.4	4.0
Virginia	5.6	8.2	12.7	18.0	30.2	37.5	45.1	54.5	65.9	80.4
Washington	14.6	19.4	25.2	38.9	62.8	76.6	87.1	127.5	157.6	179.2
West Virginia	9.6	12.4	14.3	17.9	25.5	40.7	48.5	58.0	75.9	81.4
Wisconsin	13.4	16.7	22.1	30.4	44.1	49.6	56.5	64.4	70.0	83.0
Wyoming	1.0	1.4	1.6	2.0	2.2	2.5	3.0	3.6	4.3	4.5
Federal programs:										
Civilian employees	22.2	33.4	42.3	58.7	119.5	179.8	207.9	261.8	358.8	466.0
Black lung benefits [1]	(X)	(X)	(X)	(X)	110.0	554.4	1,045.2	955.1	957.2	980.8
Other [2]	1.1	15.0	17.6	14.7	12.0	10.1	9.8	8.8	8.7	11.2

X Not applicable. [1] Includes payments by Department of Labor.
[2] Primarily payments made to dependents of reservists who died while on active duty in the Armed Forces.

Source: U.S. Social Security Administration. Periodically in *Social Security Bulletin*.

No. 559. WORKMEN'S COMPENSATION PAYMENTS: 1950 TO 1976

[Prior to 1960, excludes Alaska and Hawaii. See headnote, table 558. See also *Historical Statistics, Colonial Times to 1970*, series H 332–345]

ITEM	1950	1960	1965	1970	1972	1973	1974	1975	1976
Workers covered [1]_____mil__	37	45	51	59	62	66	68	67	69
Annual benefits paid_____mil. dol__	**615**	**1,295**	**1,814**	**3,031**	**4,039**	**5,092**	**5,765**	**6,520**	**7,463**
By private carriers [2]_____mil. dol__	381	810	1,124	1,843	2,179	2,514	2,971	3,412	3,976
From State funds [3]_____mil. dol__	149	325	445	755	1,358	1,987	2,081	2,324	2,589
Employers' self-insurance [4]_____mil. dol__	85	160	244	432	502	592	713	784	898
Type of benefit:									
Medical/hospitalization_____mil. dol__	200	435	600	1,050	1,240	1,470	1,750	2,000	2,330
Compensation payments_____mil. dol__	415	860	1,214	1,981	2,799	3,622	4,015	4,520	5,133
Disability_____mil. dol__	360	755	1,074	1,751	2,339	2,962	3,345	3,800	4,328
Survivor_____mil. dol__	55	105	140	230	460	660	670	720	805
Percent of covered payroll:									
Workmen's compensation costs [5]_____	.89	.93	1.00	1.20	1.13	1.19	1.25	1.32	1.48
Benefits [6]_____	.54	.59	.61	.66	.67	.71	.76	.82	.88

[1] Estimated per month.   [2] Net cash and medical benefits paid under standard workmen's compensation policies.   [3] Net cash and medical benefits paid by competitive and exclusive State funds and by Federal workmen's compensation programs, including black lung benefit program beginning 1970.   [4] Cash and medical benefits paid by self-insurers, plus value of medical benefits paid by employers carrying workmen's compensation policies that exclude standard medical coverage.   [5] Premiums written by private carriers and State funds, and benefits paid by self-insurers increased by 5–10 percent to allow for administrative costs. Also includes benefits paid and administrative costs of Federal system for government employees.   [6] Excludes programs financed from general revenue—black lung benefits and supplemental pensions in some States.

Source: U.S. Social Security Administration, *Annual Statistical Supplement* to the *Social Security Bulletin*.

No. 560. U.S. EMPLOYMENT SERVICE—SELECTED ACTIVITIES: 1960 TO 1977

[In thousands. Beginning 1970, for years ending June 30. 1960 and 1965 include Puerto Rico, Virgin Islands, and Guam]

ITEM	1960	1965	1970	1972	1973	1974	1975	1976	1977
New applications_____	10,117	10,900	9,957	9,366	11,485	11,905	13,350	13,200	13,208
Counseling interviews_____	1,778	2,192	2,523	2,471	2,565	1,924	1,644	1,562	1,654
Placement transactions_____	15,267	11,174	9,154	6,133	6,617	6,671	5,872	5,234	5,932
Nonagricultural_____	5,818	6,473	4,604	3,610	4,517	4,913	4,374	4,641	5,544
Individuals placed [1]_____	(NA)	(NA)	(NA)	2,220	2,817	3,172	2,967	3,200	3,960
Men_____	(NA)	(NA)	(NA)	1,420	1,698	1,872	1,743	1,844	2,299
Veterans_____	(NA)	(NA)	(NA)	474	587	587	572	580	721
Handicapped_____	(NA)	(NA)	(NA)	224	205	204	186	167	202

NA Not available.   [1] Nonagricultural jobs.
Source: U.S. Employment and Training Administration, *Employment Service Statistics*, monthly, and *Key Facts, Employment Security Operations* (discontinued, Aug. 1968).

No. 561. ERRORS IN GOVERNMENT PAYMENTS FOR SELECTED PUBLIC AND HEALTH CARE PROGRAMS: 1976

For October 1975 to March 1976. Errors represent dollars misspent by government agencies due to ineligibility of recipients. Based on sample surveys and subject to sampling variability; for details, consult source]

PROGRAM	Total payments (mil. dol.)	RECIPIENTS			CLAIMS PAID			
		Total (1,000)	Ineligible		Ineligible		Recipient liability	
			Total (1,000)	Percent	Total (mil. dol.)	Percent	Over-stated (mil. dol.)	Under-stated (mil. dol.)
Total_____	**6,989**	**11,947**	**702**	**5.9**	**412**	**5.9**	**23**	**61**
Federal_____	3,946	(X)	(X)	(X)	231	5.9	13	34
Percent of total_____	56	(X)	(X)	(X)	56	(X)	56	56
State_____	3,043	(X)	(X)	(X)	181	5.9	10	27
AFDC [1]-Health care_____	1,817	5,974	247	4.1	75	4.1	(X)	(X)
SSI [2]-Health care_____	1,957	3,106	254	8.2	112	5.8	(X)	(X)
Medically needy [3]_____	3,215	2,867	201	7.0	225	7.0	23	61

X Not applicable.   [1] Aid to families with dependent children program.
[2] Supplemental security income program.   [3] Medicaid-eligible group not qualified for AFDC or SSI.
Source: U.S. Health Care Financing Administration, unpublished data.

No. 562. Public Aid—Recipients and Average Monthly Payments Under Public Assistance and Supplemental Security Income: 1950 to 1977

[Recipients in thousands, except as indicated. As of December, except rates as of June. SSI: supplemental security income; see text, p. 325. Excludes vendor payments for medical care (i.e. payments made directly to suppliers of medical care). SSI data exclude and public assistance data include Puerto Rico, Guam, and Virgin Islands. See also *Historical Statistics, Colonial Times to 1970*, series H 355–367]

PROGRAM	1950	1955	1960	1965	1970	1973	1974	1975	1976	1977
Recipients of cash payments:										
Old-age assistance	2,786	2,538	2,305	2,087	2,082	1,820	(1)	(1)	(1)	(1)
SSI for the aged	(X)	(X)	(X)	(X)	(X)	(X)	2,286	2,307	2,148	2,051
Aid to the blind	97	104	107	85	81	78	(1)	(1)	(1)	(1)
SSI for the blind	(X)	(X)	(X)	(X)	(X)	(X)	75	75	76	77
Aid to permanently, totally disabled	69	241	369	557	935	1,275	(1)	(1)	(1)	(1)
SSI for the disabled	(X)	(X)	(X)	(X)	(X)	(X)	1,636	1,933	2,012	2,109
Aid to dependent children:										
Families	651	602	803	1,054	2,552	3,156	3,312	3,553	3,571	3,533
Recipients [2]	2,233	2,192	3,073	4,396	9,659	10,815	11,006	11,383	11,184	10,761
Children	1,661	1,661	2,370	3,316	7,033	7,813	7,885	8,086	7,884	7,552
General assistance cases	413	314	431	310	547	469	585	692	685	653
Per 1,000 children under 18:										
AFDC [3] number	34	30	35	45	87	113	113	119	119	118
Average monthly cash payment (dol.):										
Old-age assistance	43	50	59	63	78	76	(1)	(1)	(1)	(1)
SSI for the aged	(X)	(X)	(X)	(X)	(X)	(X)	91	91	94	97
Aid to the blind	46	56	67	81	104	112	(1)	(1)	(1)	(1)
SSI for the blind	(X)	(X)	(X)	(X)	(X)	(X)	141	147	153	159
Aid to permanently, totally disabled	44	49	56	67	98	110	(1)	(1)	(1)	(1)
SSI for the disabled	(X)	(X)	(X)	(X)	(X)	(X)	142	141	146	150
Aid to dependent children:										
Families	71	85	108	137	190	195	216	230	236	242
Recipients	21	23	28	33	50	57	65	72	75	79
General assistance cases	47	55	72	69	112	122	140	144	154	157

X Not applicable.   [1] See footnote 2, table 563.   [2] Includes the children and one or both parents or one caretaker other than a parent in families where the needs of such adults were considered in determining the amount of assistance.   [3] Aid to families with dependent children program.

Source: U.S. Social Security Administration, *Annual Statistical Supplement* to the *Social Security Bulletin*, and *Public Assistance Statistics*, monthly.

No. 563. Public Aid Payments: 1960 to 1977

[In millions of dollars. Includes vendor payments for medical care (i.e. payments made directly to suppliers of medical care). Supplemental security income data exclude and public assistance data include Puerto Rico, Guam, and Virgin Islands. See also *Historical Statistics, Colonial Times to 1970*, series H 346–354]

PROGRAM	1960	1965	1970	1972	1973	1974	1975	1976	1977
Payments for year	3,282	4,611	14,365	19,775	21,205	25,536	30,490	32,904	34,949
Supplemental security income	(X)	(X)	(X)	(X)	(X)	5,246	5,878	6,068	6,304
Aged	(X)	(X)	(X)	(X)	(X)	2,503	2,605	2,508	2,448
Blind	(X)	(X)	(X)	(X)	(X)	130	131	138	146
Disabled	(X)	(X)	(X)	(X)	(X)	2,602	3,142	3,422	3,709
Public assistance	3,282	4,611	14,365	19,775	21,205	[1]20,290	[1]24,612	[1]26,836	[1]28,646
Old-age	1,630	1,601	1,862	1,877	1,744	(2)	(2)	(2)	(2)
Blind	86	85	98	106	104	(2)	(2)	(2)	(2)
Permanently, totally disabled	237	418	1,000	1,391	1,610	(2)	(2)	(2)	(2)
Families with dependent children	1,001	1,660	4,853	6,909	7,212	7,917	9,211	10,000	10,193
Medical assistance [3]	6	588	5,923	8,708	9,807	11,476	14,177	15,544	17,140
Emergency assistance [4]	(X)	(X)	11	44	39	64	78	56	66
General assistance	322	259	618	740	689	825	1,138	1,228	1,239

X Not applicable.   [1] Includes data for Puerto Rico, Guam, and Virgin Islands, not shown separately by program.   [2] Beginning 1974, program replaced by supplemental security income program in 50 States and the District of Columbia. See text, p. 325.   [3] Medical assistance for the aged program initiated in November 1960; terminated in 1969. Medical assistance program initiated in Jan. 1966. Intermediate care facilities program initiated in 1968; transferred to medical assistance program in 1972.   [4] Emergency assistance initiated in 1968.

Source: U.S. Social Security Administration, *Social Security Bulletin*, monthly; and *Public Assistance Statistics*, monthly.

No. 564. PUBLIC AID—RECIPIENTS OF AID TO FAMILIES WITH DEPENDENT CHILDREN AND SUPPLEMENTAL SECURITY INCOME, STATES AND OTHER AREAS: 1976 AND 1977

[In thousands]

STATE	1976 (Dec.) Aid to families with dependent children		1976 (Dec.) Supplemental security income [2]				1977 (Dec.) Aid to families with dependent children		1977 (Dec.) Supplemental security income [2]			
	Recipients, total [1]	Children	Total	Aged	Blind	Disabled	Recipients, total [1]	Children	Total	Aged	Blind	Disabled
Total	11,183.6	7,883.9	4,235.9	2,147.7	76.4	2,011.9	10,760.5	7,551.9	4,237.7	2,050.9	77.4	2,109.4
Ala	166.8	122.8	[3]143.3	[3]94.0	[3]1.9	[3]47.4	170.8	124.9	[3]141.0	[3]88.9	[3]1.9	[3]50.2
Alaska	10.5	7.7	[3]3.1	[3]1.3	[3].1	[3]1.7	12.5	9.0	[3]3.1	[3]1.3	[3].1	[3]1.8
Ariz	59.0	43.9	[3]28.4	[3]13.4	[3].5	[3]14.5	53.6	40.0	[3]28.7	[3]12.9	[3].5	[3]15.3
Ark	94.5	70.5	85.7	53.9	1.7	30.2	90.6	67.2	84.3	50.7	1.6	32.0
Calif	1,433.6	979.3	673.7	323.9	16.1	333.7	1,433.7	974.4	692.6	325.6	17.2	349.9
Colo	92.0	64.7	[3]33.7	[3]18.1	[3].3	[3]15.3	88.0	61.7	[3]33.6	[3]16.7	[3].3	[3]16.5
Conn	134.7	95.9	[3]22.6	[3]8.6	[3].3	[3]13.7	135.8	96.0	[3]22.7	[3]8.2	[3].3	[3]14.2
Del	30.4	21.9	6.8	3.1	.2	3.5	31.5	22.4	7.1	2.9	.2	4.0
D.C	94.1	67.2	14.8	4.8	.2	9.8	95.2	67.2	14.8	4.6	.2	10.0
Fla	241.1	178.5	160.8	90.6	2.5	67.6	246.3	181.2	164.5	88.4	2.6	73.5
Ga	255.1	189.9	161.1	86.6	3.0	71.6	225.6	167.4	160.6	82.2	3.0	75.5
Hawaii	55.2	37.6	9.3	5.2	.1	4.0	58.4	39.4	9.9	5.3	.1	4.6
Idaho	19.5	13.7	[3]8.3	[3]3.6	[3].1	[3]4.6	19.7	13.6	[3]7.9	[3]3.2	[3].1	[3]4.5
Ill	776.7	558.1	[3]131.5	[3]44.0	[3]1.6	[3]85.9	733.6	522.6	[3]127.8	[3]41.1	[3]1.6	[3]85.1
Ind	167.8	122.0	[3]41.7	[3]19.9	[3]1.0	[3]20.8	157.2	113.5	[3]41.1	[3]18.2	[3]1.1	[3]21.9
Iowa	95.7	64.9	27.9	14.6	1.1	12.1	94.5	63.5	27.0	13.3	1.1	12.5
Kans	75.4	55.2	23.1	11.3	.4	11.5	72.3	52.1	22.5	10.3	.3	11.9
Ky	208.7	144.3	[3]96.0	[3]52.4	[3]2.0	[3]41.6	172.9	123.1	[3]94.4	[3]48.6	[3]2.0	[3]43.8
La	223.1	166.8	149.2	85.9	2.2	61.1	210.6	157.4	148.1	80.0	2.2	65.9
Maine	60.0	42.0	23.5	12.4	.3	10.8	59.9	41.0	22.9	11.5	.3	11.1
Md	213.7	150.5	47.8	18.2	.6	29.0	208.8	145.7	48.1	17.6	.5	30.0
Mass	370.6	255.2	130.2	77.7	4.3	48.2	367.8	249.0	129.7	74.2	4.7	50.7
Mich	653.0	453.9	117.2	47.3	1.6	68.3	622.6	432.0	117.4	44.7	1.7	71.1
Minn	131.3	91.0	[3]36.4	[3]17.1	[3].6	[3]18.7	131.9	90.6	[3]35.5	[3]15.8	[3].7	[3]19.1
Miss	176.0	134.8	120.8	75.5	1.9	43.4	168.2	127.9	118.2	71.2	1.9	45.2
Mo	272.6	194.3	[3]96.5	[3]57.2	[3]1.8	[3]37.4	217.1	155.4	[3]92.3	[3]51.5	[3]1.6	[3]39.2
Mont	17.9	12.8	7.9	3.3	.1	4.5	17.8	12.6	7.5	2.9	.1	4.5
Nebr	34.5	24.6	[3]15.0	[3]7.5	[3].2	[3]7.2	35.3	25.0	[3]14.4	[3]6.8	[3].2	[3]7.4
Nev	12.8	9.2	5.8	3.5	.3	2.0	10.8	7.7	6.0	3.5	.4	2.2
N.H	25.2	17.4	[3]5.4	[3]2.8	[3].2	[3]2.4	22.6	15.4	[3]5.5	[3]2.5	[3].1	[3]2.8
N.J	447.8	318.1	79.8	35.8	1.0	43.0	464.3	324.9	80.6	34.3	1.0	45.3
N. Mex	56.0	40.2	[3]26.2	[3]12.0	[3].4	[3]13.8	51.9	36.9	[3]25.8	[3]11.4	[3].4	[3]14.0
N.Y	1,242.0	859.6	388.4	163.8	4.1	220.5	1,172.8	808.5	383.6	154.5	4.0	225.2
N.C	200.4	147.7	[3]146.3	[3]75.0	[3]3.6	[3]67.7	197.8	144.1	[3]144.5	[3]71.3	[3]3.5	[3]69.7
N. Dak	13.8	9.9	[3]7.5	[3]4.4	[3].1	[3]3.0	13.6	9.6	[3]7.2	[3]4.0	[3].1	[3]3.1
Ohio	571.5	390.2	127.3	48.1	2.4	76.8	524.1	360.9	125.8	44.3	2.3	79.1
Okla	89.3	66.8	[3]80.4	[3]47.0	[3]1.1	[3]32.3	87.7	65.0	[3]77.1	[3]43.2	[3]1.1	[3]32.8
Oreg	122.1	80.8	[3]24.4	[3]9.6	[3].6	[3]14.3	122.5	81.2	[3]23.6	[3]8.7	[3].6	[3]14.3
Pa	647.7	440.7	157.8	64.8	4.3	88.7	644.5	437.7	167.8	66.2	3.9	97.8
R.I	52.7	36.7	15.7	6.7	.2	8.8	51.5	35.9	15.6	6.5	.2	8.9
S.C	138.6	101.2	[3]82.5	[3]44.7	[3]1.9	[3]35.9	142.2	103.0	[3]83.2	[3]42.6	[3]1.9	[3]38.7
S. Dak	24.3	17.9	8.3	4.8	.1	3.4	22.2	16.2	8.3	4.4	.1	3.7
Tenn	202.9	148.1	134.5	73.5	1.8	59.2	167.9	122.5	134.1	69.7	1.8	62.6
Tex	321.0	239.0	[4]273.9	[4]178.1	[4]4.0	[4]91.8	307.0	228.6	[4]273.3	[4]169.1	[4]4.1	[4]100.2
Utah	36.6	26.8	[3]8.9	[3]3.3	[3].2	[3]5.4	38.0	27.7	[3]8.4	[3]2.9	[3].1	[3]5.4
Vt	22.8	14.9	8.7	4.3	.1	4.3	19.3	12.8	9.0	4.1	.1	4.7
Va	174.1	124.8	[3]77.5	[3]41.2	[3]1.4	[3]34.9	166.3	118.8	[3]79.1	[3]39.1	[3]1.4	[3]38.5
Wash	142.8	93.1	50.1	19.3	.5	30.3	143.0	93.0	49.1	18.3	.5	30.4
W. Va	64.7	44.7	[3]43.0	[3]18.7	[3].6	[3]23.6	63.0	45.4	[3]42.9	[3]17.2	[3].6	[3]25.1
Wis	200.7	139.6	65.1	33.9	.9	30.3	196.8	137.0	67.0	33.6	.9	32.5
Wyo	6.6	4.8	[3]2.4	[3]1.2	[3](Z)	[3]1.1	6.3	4.6	[3]2.2	[3]1.1	[3](Z)	[3]1.1
P.R	195.9	142.1	(X)	(X)	(X)	(X)	183.2	132.0	(X)	(X)	(X)	(X)
Guam	4.2	3.1	(X)	(X)	(X)	(X)	5.0	3.7	(X)	(X)	(X)	(X)
V.I	3.7	3.1	(X)	(X)	(X)	(X)	3.7	3.0	(X)	(X)	(X)	(X)
Unknown	(X)	(X)	.1	(Z)	(Z)	(Z)	(X)	(X)	(Z)	(Z)	-	(Z)

- Represents zero.   X Not applicable.   Z Less than 50.   [1] Includes the children and one or both parents, or one caretaker relative other than a parent, in families where the needs of such adults were considered in determining the amount of assistance.   [2] Includes persons with Federal supplemental security income (SSI) payments and/or federally-administered State supplementation, except as noted. See text, p. 325.   [3] Data for persons with Federal SSI payments only; State has State-administered supplementation.   [4] Data for persons with Federal SSI payments only; State supplementary payments not made.

Source: U.S. Social Security Administration, *Social Security Bulletin*, April and June 1977 and 1978.

No. 565. Public Aid—Federally Administered Supplemental Security Income Payments: 1974 to 1977

[Covers Federal supplemental security income (SSI) payments and/or federally administered State supplementation, except as noted. See text, p. 325]

STATE	PAYMENTS FOR YEAR (mil. dol.)								AVERAGE MONTHLY PAYMENT (Dec.)			
	1974	1975	1976			1977			Aged		Disabled	
			Total[1]	Aged	Disabled	Total[1]	Aged	Disabled	1976	1977	1976	1977
Total	5,096.8	5,716.1	5,900.2	2,420.4	3,345.8	[2]6,134.1	[2]2,363.9	[2]3,628.1	$94	$97	$146	$150
Ala.[3]	139.6	152.9	156.8	91.0	63.1	160.4	88.0	69.5	(NA)	(NA)	(NA)	(NA)
Alaska[3]	3.6	4.3	4.2	1.6	2.5	4.5	1.6	2.8	(NA)	(NA)	(NA)	(NA)
Ariz.[3]	30.0	34.9	37.5	14.5	22.2	39.9	14.4	24.6	(NA)	(NA)	(NA)	(NA)
Ark	82.3	89.9	89.8	50.6	36.9	90.9	48.2	40.4	77	79	107	111
Calif	1,105.6	1,256.3	1,340.2	525.2	776.8	1,432.1	538.0	850.7	137	142	203	213
Colo.[3]	38.8	39.0	39.4	17.2	21.8	40.5	16.3	23.8	(NA)	(NA)	(NA)	(NA
Conn.[3]	23.2	26.9	28.3	7.9	20.0	29.8	7.9	21.5	(NA)	(NA)	(NA)	(NA)
Del	7.0	8.0	8.2	2.8	5.1	8.6	2.6	5.7	73	74	128	126
D.C	21.3	22.4	21.9	5.3	16.2	22.8	5.0	17.4	88	92	139	146
Fla	156.3	185.8	202.5	103.0	95.7	214.7	102.8	108.0	96	98	125	130
Ga	159.6	177.6	184.1	86.2	93.5	190.3	82.8	103.1	82	84	115	120
Hawaii	13.0	14.4	14.3	6.8	7.2	15.4	7.1	8.0	112	116	161	158
Idaho[3]	8.0	9.0	8.9	3.0	5.7	9.0	2.8	6.0	(NA)	(NA)	(NA)	(NA)
Ill	[4]167.7	[3]165.8	[3]170.1	[3]40.9	[3]126.9	[3]172.2	[3]39.9	[3]129.8	(NA)	(NA)	(NA)	(NA)
Ind	36.3	41.7	[4]43.1	[4]16.2	[4]25.5	[3]45.1	[3]15.2	[3]28.4	(NA)	(NA)	(NA)	(NA)
Iowa	24.4	28.6	27.7	12.1	14.0	28.1	11.0	15.5	67	68	104	109
Kans	21.3	23.1	23.6	9.8	13.3	23.9	9.0	14.4	71	73	102	109
Ky.[3]	105.6	114.1	116.9	54.7	58.8	120.4	51.8	65.0	(NA)	(NA)	(NA)	(NA)
La	157.1	172.6	179.4	92.5	83.7	186.0	87.3	95.3	88	90	124	128
Maine	24.8	26.4	24.4	9.5	14.5	23.7	8.4	14.9	61	59	111	117
Md	59.9	64.1	64.2	17.2	46.2	65.4	16.6	47.9	79	79	135	140
Mass	208.6	234.8	217.6	107.2	100.8	217.1	101.5	104.7	112	114	176	179
Mich	151.1	173.3	182.0	57.8	121.4	187.7	55.5	129.2	101	107	154	161
Minn	39.2	[4]38.2	[3]36.0	[3]14.0	[3]21.2	[3]36.7	[3]13.1	[3]22.7	(NA)	(NA)	(NA)	(NA)
Miss	[4]128.5	137.4	139.5	75.9	60.8	143.2	73.5	66.8	83	85	123	128
Mo.[3]	106.0	110.4	109.7	56.2	51.1	110.5	52.0	56.3	(NA)	(NA)	(NA)	(NA)
Mont	8.4	8.9	9.4	2.8	6.4	9.4	2.5	6.7	69	70	127	131
Nebr.[3]	15.3	16.6	16.0	6.2	9.4	15.6	5.7	9.6	(NA)	(NA)	(NA)	(NA)
Nev	5.4	7.3	7.7	4.3	2.8	7.8	3.9	3.2	92	99	130	128
N.H.[3]	4.4	5.1	5.5	2.1	3.2	6.0	2.0	3.7	(NA)	(NA)	(NA)	(NA)
N.J	86.4	106.1	111.5	40.1	69.8	116.7	39.5	75.6	98	97	142	146
N. Mex.[3]	27.2	30.9	32.1	11.7	19.9	33.2	11.4	21.2	(NA)	(NA)	(NA)	(NA)
N.Y	648.0	687.7	667.5	214.1	445.3	672.4	205.3	459.3	108	111	173	175
N.C.[3]	131.4	157.5	163.6	67.0	91.3	169.4	66.0	98.2	(NA)	(NA)	(NA)	(NA)
N. Dak.[3]	7.4	8.2	8.1	3.9	4.1	8.2	3.7	4.5	(NA)	(NA)	(NA)	(NA)
Ohio	138.4	156.0	160.2	44.7	112.1	164.5	41.9	119.1	76	79	127	131
Okla.[3]	88.5	92.5	91.7	47.3	42.7	92.0	45.1	45.2	(NA)	(NA)	(NA)	(NA)
Oreg.[3]	25.8	28.5	29.0	8.3	20.0	29.4	7.8	20.9	(NA)	(NA)	(NA)	(NA)
Pa	166.2	203.7	239.4	78.8	153.5	258.3	77.2	174.4	102	98	155	157
R.I	17.0	19.6	19.6	6.0	13.3	20.0	5.9	13.8	74	77	128	134
S.C	68.0	[4]84.6	[3]91.6	[3]41.2	[3]47.6	[3]96.2	[3]39.9	[3]53.3	(NA)	(NA)	(NA)	(NA)
S. Dak	7.9	8.7	8.5	4.2	4.2	8.9	4.0	4.7	67	69	107	108
Tenn	128.1	147.3	152.8	68.9	81.2	158.8	66.7	89.3	77	79	121	126
Tex.[5]	238.8	274.5	285.7	165.6	114.4	296.5	160.3	130.3	(NA)	(NA)	(NA)	(NA)
Utah	10.4	[4]10.6	[3]10.6	[3]3.2	[3]7.2	[3]10.4	[3]3.0	[3]7.2	(NA)	(NA)	(NA)	(NA)
Vt	[4]9.5	12.7	12.1	4.8	7.1	12.4	4.5	7.7	92	94	141	149
Va.[3]	57.2	76.6	83.5	35.6	45.9	89.2	34.9	52.1	(NA)	(NA)	(NA)	(NA)
Wash	75.0	75.7	75.0	20.8	53.3	75.2	19.9	54.3	88	95	148	166
W. Va.[3]	43.0	51.8	55.4	19.0	35.4	58.1	17.8	39.3	(NA)	(NA)	(NA)	(NA)
Wis	66.8	89.1	89.5	39.4	48.5	95.3	38.3	55.3	137	94	175	150
Wyo	2.5	2.5	[4]2.6	[4]1.0	[4]1.5	[3]2.5	[3]1.0	[3]1.5	(NA)	(NA)	(NA)	(NA)
Unknown	1.4	1.1	1.2	.3	.8	3.5	(NA)	(NA)	(NA)	(NA)	(NA)	(NA)

- Represents zero. NA Not available. [1] Includes payment to the blind, not shown separately.
[2] Total includes payments to Indochina refugees (U.S. total, 5.7 million). In addition, the total was reduced to reflect returned checks and overpayment refunds in some States. [3] Federal SSI payments only; State has State-administered supplementation. [4] Includes federally administered State supplementation as follows: for Ill., months prior to Oct. 1974; for Miss. and Vt., for July–Dec. 1974; for S.C. and Utah, for months prior to July 1975; for Minn., prior to October 1975; for Ind. and Wyo., prior to October 1976.
[5] Federal SSI payments only; State supplementary payments not made.

Source: U.S. Social Security Administration, Annual Statistical Supplement to the Social Security Bulletin; Social Security Bulletin, April 1977 and 1978; and unpublished data.

No. 566. PUBLIC ASSISTANCE PAYMENTS TO FAMILIES WITH DEPENDENT CHILDREN (AFDC) AND FOR MEDICAL ASSISTANCE: 1970 TO 1977

STATE	PAYMENTS FOR YEAR (mil. dol.)								AVERAGE MONTHLY PAYMENTS PER FAMILY TO FAMILIES WITH DEPENDENT CHILDREN (dol.)			
	Aid to families with dependent children				Medical assistance [1]							
	1970	1975	1976	1977	1970	1975	1976	1977	1970	1975	1976	1977
Total__	4,853	9,211	10,000	10,193	[2] 5,923	14,177	15,544	17,140	183	220	234	238
Ala._____	26	59	66	76	75	164	177	193	62	96	103	113
Alaska___	6	13	13	16	(X)	10	17	22	191	271	287	296
Ariz._____	22	32	32	32	(X)	(X)	(X)	(X)	128	131	140	141
Ark._____	15	50	49	50	28	106	144	155	90	125	122	136
Calif._____	853	1,349	1,540	1,725	1,094	1,967	1,815	2,215	192	248	274	302
Colo._____	44	75	78	75	55	110	114	127	168	200	203	196
Conn._____	68	130	137	149	83	180	198	227	237	268	269	282
Del._____	9	22	24	27	6	17	20	27	131	178	200	207
D.C._____	32	92	89	91	34	106	111	120	212	239	239	238
Fla._____	64	118	119	139	66	198	206	245	89	122	127	140
Ga._____	78	136	109	102	104	283	270	345	103	100	96	100
Hawaii__	21	60	70	77	20	44	64	76	241	325	349	365
Idaho___	11	18	20	21	9	31	32	35	179	227	247	252
Ill._____	275	773	744	723	263	782	865	972	232	284	270	266
Ind._____	40	105	118	113	72	194	223	249	144	161	169	173
Iowa_____	43	95	97	96	24	101	145	164	190	278	260	251
Kans_____	38	61	72	75	54	121	147	166	194	215	226	227
Ky._____	49	119	137	133	59	134	176	194	113	177	174	169
La._____	55	98	97	94	57	177	223	244	84	121	121	120
Maine___	22	48	44	46	23	71	82	93	153	170	183	194
Md._____	74	144	152	156	102	262	248	253	161	175	175	176
Mass._____	212	415	415	442	307	596	682	721	276	309	297	300
Mich._____	206	655	718	711	249	705	751	876	210	273	288	292
Minn._____	74	134	141	150	120	278	329	396	234	256	264	267
Miss._____	18	32	31	30	21	[3] 54	124	142	47	49	48	47
Mo._____	57	130	149	151	65	125	149	195	114	126	140	148
Mont._____	8	13	13	14	11	30	35	44	147	155	171	177
Nebr._____	16	27	28	30	34	57	67	77	152	191	204	219
Nev._____	5	9	10	8	8	22	22	21	105	151	160	162
N.H._____	8	24	23	21	6	31	39	46	209	232	222	213
N.J._____	265	437	442	448	127	413	422	481	251	274	270	267
N. Mex._	22	32	32	31	18	33	43	48	122	142	144	150
N.Y._____	947	1,448	1,738	1,666	1,279	3,159	3,430	3,223	266	336	388	371
N.C._____	50	121	128	133	69	192	258	266	117	158	155	154
N. Dak._	8	12	13	13	12	26	28	35	205	226	238	232
Ohio_____	152	405	452	432	148	423	527	566	163	190	198	197
Okla_____	45	67	67	71	96	155	181	199	138	188	200	205
Oreg_____	50	97	123	135	35	101	111	143	175	224	253	261
Pa._____	361	610	678	703	321	760	866	1,072	241	268	285	283
R.I._____	29	47	55	55	39	78	98	110	220	241	269	263
S.C._____	15	46	46	48	30	96	123	153	78	88	86	84
S. Dak._	11	20	20	18	13	25	27	34	183	204	203	196
Tenn_____	53	85	85	78	41	167	198	236	110	106	104	103
Tex._____	92	146	129	122	239	570	640	723	119	108	105	104
Utah_____	20	34	36	38	20	37	45	54	159	227	237	247
Vt._____	9	21	22	20	15	34	40	43	200	261	259	256
Va._____	55	135	136	135	49	180	223	252	174	192	192	190
Wash_____	91	138	149	154	94	199	197	219	205	241	252	261
W. Va._	34	44	46	47	19	46	67	65	118	171	175	184
Wis._____	61	193	232	240	151	416	446	474	213	278	300	292
Wyo._____	3	5	5	6	3	6	7	9	150	163	190	195
P.R._____	28	25	24	25	56	102	92	93	47	46	45	49
Guam___	1	2	2	3	(Z)	1	(NA)	(NA)	182	191	198	193
V.I._____	1	2	2	2	1	2	3	2	125	129	129	128

NA Not available.   X Not applicable.   Z Less than $500,000.   [1] Source: U.S. Health Care Financing Administration, *Medical Assistance (Medicaid) Financed Under Title XIX of the Social Security Act*, Research Report B-1, annual.   [2] Includes intermediate care facilities program.   [3] Expenditures for Jan.-June.

Source: Except as noted, U.S. Social Security Administration, *Public Assistance Statistics*, monthly.

No. 567. Outlays for the Five Largest Welfare Programs—Total, Federal, and Per Recipient: 1976

[Covers outlays by Federal, State, and local governments for, in most cases, year ending June 30. AFDC: Aid to families with dependent children; SSI: Supplemental security income]

REGION AND STATE	ALL OUTLAYS		FEDERAL		MONTHLY BENEFITS PER RECIPIENT, BY PROGRAM (dollars)						
	Total (mil. dol.)	Per poor resident [1] (dol.)	Total (mil. dol.)	Percent of total outlays	Medicaid Total	Medicaid Federal	AFDC Total	AFDC Federal	SSI	Food stamps	General assistance [2]
U.S.	35,937	1,389	22,261	61.9	134	73	73	40	116	24	103
Northeast	11,990	2,428	6,441	53.7	185	95	96	49	134	21	108
Maine	195	1,711	148	75.9	119	84	55	39	88	23	22
N.H.	83	1,317	56	67.5	141	85	74	44	111	23	35
Vt.	89	2,244	66	74.2	139	97	78	55	115	20	–
Mass.	1,430	2,924	735	51.4	114	57	95	48	139	20	115
R.I.	193	2,075	116	60.1	139	79	76	43	102	19	79
Conn	431	1,850	238	55.2	155	77	83	42	135	22	70
N.Y.	6,314	2,859	3,234	51.2	224	112	111	56	144	17	117
N.J.	1,181	1,965	678	57.4	120	60	83	41	113	25	83
Pa.	2,073	1,886	1,172	56.5	234	130	85	47	128	20	122
Midwest	8,468	1,589	5,095	60.2	123	66	75	40	106	23	103
Ohio	1,396	1,474	927	66.4	130	71	65	35	102	26	74
Ind	435	1,087	297	68.3	154	88	55	31	82	24	–
Ill	2,185	1,970	1,254	57.4	85	43	79	39	118	26	114
Mich	1,860	2,601	973	52.3	138	69	88	44	131	18	134
Wis	765	1,947	456	59.6	176	106	98	59	111	18	82
Minn	569	1,745	345	60.6	239	136	90	51	88	21	103
Iowa	284	1,131	183	64.4	153	87	86	49	84	21	34
Mo	495	855	355	71.7	60	35	44	26	97	25	62
Kans	244	953	143	58.6	132	71	75	41	83	19	94
Nebr	121	738	79	65.3	150	84	65	37	95	21	–
S. Dak	63	578	47	74.6	149	100	67	45	86	23	18
N. Dak	50	625	34	68.0	201	116	79	46	88	22	25
South	8,750	784	6,985	79.8	105	66	42	28	95	26	71
Del	62	1,088	39	62.9	92	46	63	31	99	25	33
Md	552	1,643	339	61.4	123	61	58	29	111	26	102
D.C.	258	2,016	148	57.4	130	65	73	37	119	21	144
Va	495	924	347	70.1	126	73	64	37	89	23	78
W. Va	218	604	187	85.8	85	61	53	38	104	22	17
N.C	654	855	532	81.3	118	80	55	37	99	25	20
S.C	357	732	308	86.3	83	54	28	21	91	26	50
Ga	725	962	594	81.9	108	67	32	24	93	25	30
Fla	776	701	647	83.4	88	50	40	23	104	30	–
Ky	545	840	454	83.3	76	55	56	40	105	25	–
Tenn	552	779	465	84.2	94	61	34	24	92	27	–
Ala	501	651	419	83.6	84	54	30	22	92	25	13
Miss	400	530	353	88.3	62	41	14	11	94	26	12
La	642	693	551	85.8	95	68	36	26	100	26	53
Ark	334	705	291	87.1	79	59	39	30	86	26	1
Okla	386	869	288	74.6	217	146	60	41	111	20	11
Tex	1,293	681	1,023	79.1	135	81	32	23	85	24	–
West	6,729	1,512	3,740	55.6	115	60	82	42	152	23	101
Mont	64	653	47	73.4	157	99	55	35	95	26	32
Idaho	72	673	55	76.4	134	91	83	56	103	22	–
Wyo	17	370	13	76.5	(NA)	(NA)	63	39	87	24	37
Colo	292	1,659	194	66.4	123	67	67	37	101	27	71
Utah	102	713	76	74.5	151	106	81	57	97	21	101
Nev	51	962	32	62.7	190	95	55	27	107	29	–
Ariz	122	419	101	82.8	–	–	41	22	102	25	84
N. Mex	146	521	128	87.7	91	67	45	33	100	27	73
Calif	4,852	1,925	2,460	50.7	112	56	85	43	167	22	103
Oreg	299	1,068	203	67.9	111	66	85	50	102	23	83
Wash	491	1,379	308	62.7	119	64	84	45	124	24	103
Alaska	37	974	22	59.5	397	198	103	52	158	38	55
Hawaii	185	3,033	103	55.7	100	50	104	52	128	28	119

– Represents zero.   NA Not available.
[1] Based on U.S. Bureau of the Census estimates of poverty population in 1970 extrapolated to 1976 so that State total was equal to Bureau of the Census' 1976 national poverty population.
[2] Covers benefits paid by State and local governments to persons not covered by Federal programs.

Source: Havemann, Joel and Linda Demkovich, "Making Some Sense Out of the Welfare 'Mess,'" *National Journal*, Vol. 9, Number 2, January 1977. (Copyright.)

No. 568. State-Administered Supplemental Security Income (SSI)—Recipients and Payments, by States: 1975 to 1977

[1977 preliminary. Recipients comprise those receiving Federal SSI payments and State-administered supplementation and, in addition, those who receive only State-administered supplementary payments. See text, p. 325]

STATE	RECIPIENTS, DEC. (1,000)			PAYMENTS FOR YEAR (mil. dol.)			STATE	RECIPIENTS, DEC. (1,000)			PAYMENTS FOR YEAR (mil. dol.)		
	1975	1976	1977	1975	1976	1977		1975	1976	1977	1975	1976	1977
Total	303.4	274.4	264.2	162	166	170	Mo	53.1	45.6	39.2	25	20	17
							Nebr	5.4	5.7	6.7	3	3	4
Ala	23.2	20.8	19.9	12	10	12	N.H	3.3	3.4	3.6	2	2	3
Alaska	3.3	3.1	2.8	3	3	4	N. Mex. [1]	(Z)	(Z)	.3	(Z)	(Z)	(Z)
Ariz	1.5	1.2	1.0	2	1	1	N.C	10.3	9.7	9.9	14	17	18
Colo	31.1	30.7	29.8	15	17	18	N. Dak. [2]	.5	.3	.2	(Z)	(Z)	(Z)
Conn	9.7	10.4	10.8	9	9	11	Okla	72.6	65.1	63.0	21	24	24
Fla	2.1	2.2	2.3	1	1	1	Oreg	20.4	14.3	14.1	6	5	5
Idaho	3.0	2.9	3.3	1	2	2	S.C. [1]	1.2	1.2	1.3	1	1	1
Ill	45.2	40.2	38.6	34	32	31	S. Dak. [3]	.2	.3	.3	(Z)	(Z)	(Z)
Ky	9.0	9.1	8.9	9	10	11	Utah [4]	.2	–	(NA)	(Z)	(Z)	(NA)
Md	(NA)	.4	.3	(NA)	(Z)	(Z)	Va	2.1	2.0	2.0	1	1	1
Minn	5.9	5.6	5.6	3	5	4	W. Va	(NA)	(NA)	.1	(NA)	(NA)	(Z)

- Represents zero.   NA Not available.   Z Less than 50 recipients or $500,000.
[1] Optional supplementation program became effective July 1976.
[2] Excludes recipient data for optional supplementation program.
[3] Optional supplementation program became effective February 1975.
[4] Supplementation program State-administered effective July 1975; prior to July, these payments were federally administered.

Source: U.S. Social Security Administration, *Social Security Bulletin*, June 1976, 1977, and 1978.

No. 569. Aid to Families with Dependent Children (AFDC)—Percent Distribution of Characteristics of Recipient Families and Children: 1973 and 1975

[Refers to federally-aided State programs providing aid to needy children deprived of parental care or support. Based on a sample and subject to sampling variability; for details, see source]

CHARACTERISTIC	1973	1975	CHARACTERISTIC	1973	1975
Families receiving aid _____1,000	2,990	3,420	Children receiving aid _____1,000	7,725	8,121
PERCENT DISTRIBUTION			PERCENT DISTRIBUTION		
Metropolitan areas [1]	77.9	74.9	Basis for eligibility:		
Nonmetropolitan areas [2]	22.1	25.2	Father is—		
			Deceased	4.0	3.7
White	46.9	50.3	Incapacitated	10.2	7.7
Black	45.8	44.3	Unemployed	4.1	3.7
American Indian	1.1	1.1	Absent from home:		
Other [2]	6.2	4.3	Divorced	17.7	19.4
Number of children:			Separated [5]	28.8	28.6
1	33.8	37.9	Not married to mother	31.5	31.0
2	25.5	26.0	Other	2.4	4.3
3	16.3	16.1	Mother is absent, not father	1.2	1.6
4 or 5	17.2	15.0	Age:		
6 or more	7.2	5.0	Under 6, including unborn	34.8	34.6
Number of years as recipient: [3] [4]			6–11	34.7	33.7
Under 1 year	30.2	27.7	12–17	28.1	28.5
1–3 years	34.5	27.3	18–20	2.4	2.4
4–5 years	16.9	18.8	Unknown	–	.8
6–10 years	12.8	19.3			
11–15 years	3.5	4.3			
Over 15 years	1.5	2.0			

- Represents zero.
[1] For definition, see Appendix II.   [2] Includes unknown or not reported.
[3] Excludes unknown or not reported.   [4] Since recent opening of case.
[5] Includes legally and non-legally separated.

Source: U.S. Social and Rehabilitation Service, *Findings of the 1973 AFDC Study*, June 1974 (Part I), and U.S. Social Security Administration, *1975 Recipient Characteristic Study* (Part 1), September 1977.

No. 570. Supplemental Security Income—Percent Distribution of Recipients, by Characteristics: 1976 and 1977

[As of **December**. Covers persons receiving federally administered payments. See text, p. 325]

SEX AND RACE	1976					1977				
	Total recipients (1,000)	PERCENT DISTRIBUTION				Total recipients (1,000)	PERCENT DISTRIBUTION			
		Total	Aged	Blind	Disabled		Total	Aged	Blind	Disabled
Total	4,236	100.0	100.0	100.0	100.0	4,238	100.0	100.0	100.0	100.0
Male	1,483	35.0	29.0	45.6	41.1	1,472	34.7	28.5	43.9	40.5
Female	2,745	64.8	70.9	54.1	58.6	2,759	65.1	71.4	55.9	59.3
Sex not reported	8	.2	.1	.3	.3	7	.2	.1	.2	.2
White	2,673	63.1	64.7	60.4	61.6	2,758	65.1	65.4	63.6	64.8
Black	1,101	26.0	24.2	28.9	27.9	1,156	27.3	24.6	28.8	29.8
Other	110	2.6	2.7	2.6	2.5	128	3.0	3.2	3.1	2.8
Race not reported	352	8.3	8.5	8.1	8.0	196	4.6	6.8	4.5	2.6

Source: U.S. Social Security Administration, *Social Security Bulletin*, June 1978.

No. 571. Social Security—Child Beneficiaries and Benefits: 1960 to 1977

[Benefits in current-payment status at end of year]

ITEM	1960	1965	1970	1972	1973	1974	1975	1976	1977
Beneficiaries (1,000):									
Children	2,000	3,093	4,122	4,516	4,687	4,776	4,972	5,035	5,078
Under age 18	1,896	2,689	3,315	3,576	3,716	3,755	3,835	3,819	3,805
Disabled children [1]	104	198	271	305	320	341	362	382	404
Students [2]	(X)	206	537	634	652	679	774	835	869
Of retired workers	268	461	546	580	614	619	643	653	678
Of deceased workers	1,577	2,074	2,688	2,847	2,912	2,894	2,919	2,903	2,875
Of disabled workers	155	558	889	1,088	1,161	1,263	1,411	1,480	1,525
Of male workers [3]	1,904	2,910	3,706	4,011	4,131	4,199	4,357	4,398	4,425
Of female workers [3]	96	183	416	504	557	576	615	637	653
Annual benefits (mil. dol.):									
Children	1,085	1,922	3,517	4,438	5,219	5,852	6,643	7,434	8,163
Under age 18	1,038	1,632	2,701	3,337	3,930	4,353	4,823	5,296	5,758
Disabled children [1]	47	121	250	330	397	463	537	634	710
Students [2]	(X)	169	566	771	892	1,036	1,283	1,504	1,695
Of retired workers	92	175	303	382	457	533	634	722	746
Of deceased workers	945	1,515	2,760	3,433	4,002	4,399	4,888	5,384	5,914
Of disabled workers	48	232	454	623	760	920	1,121	1,328	1,503
Average monthly benefits, Dec. (dollars):									
Children of retired workers	28.25	31.98	44.85	59.90	61.10	69.63	77.42	85.64	94.85
Children of deceased workers	51.37	61.26	82.23	110.36	111.70	126.48	139.40	151.94	165.68
Children of disabled workers	30.21	31.61	38.63	49.38	50.30	56.38	61.95	68.26	75.23

X Not applicable.   [1] 18 years old and over. Disability began before age 18 and , beginning 1973, before age 22. [2] Students 18–21 years old.   [3] Household heads.

Source: U.S. Social Security Administration, *Annual Statistical Supplement* to the *Social Security Bulletin*.

No. 572. Orphans, by Type: 1960 to 1977

[Includes Puerto Rico and Virgin Islands; beginning 1972, also includes American Samoa, Guam, and citizens (including Armed Forces) overseas. Covers children under age 18 who have been orphaned at any time. Paternal orphan refers to loss of father, maternal orphan to loss of mother, full orphan to loss of both parents. Percent of child population based on U.S. Bureau of the Census estimated population of children under 18, as of July 1. Data not exactly comparable for all years because of changes in methodology]

YEAR	NUMBER (1,000)				PERCENT OF CHILD POPULATION			
	Total	Paternal	Maternal	Full	Total	Paternal	Maternal	Full
1960, January	2,955	2,055	840	60	4.5	3.1	1.3	.1
1965, January	3,290	2,330	890	70	4.7	3.3	1.3	.1
1970, July	3,260	2,300	890	70	4.6	3.2	1.3	.1
1972, July	3,074	2,166	838	70	4.4	3.1	1.2	.1
1976, July	3,507	2,445	1,008	54	5.2	3.6	1.5	.1
1977, July	3,363	2,354	957	52	5.1	3.6	1.4	.1

Source: U.S. Social Security Administration. Irregularly in *Social Security Bulletin*.

No. 573. CHILD ADOPTIONS—SELECTED STATES AND PUERTO RICO: 1970 AND 1975

[Represents voluntary reports by State welfare departments covering children under age 21 for whom adoption petitions were granted. States shown are those which filed complete data on total adoptions in 1975 or as noted. For additional details for individual States with varying degrees of coverage, see source. U.S. estimated total, 1970=175,000]

STATE	1970, total	1975		STATE	1970, total	1975		STATE	1970, total	1975	
		Total	By relatives [1] (percent)			Total	By relatives [1] (percent)			Total	By relatives [1] (percent)
Ala	1,414	2,675	81	La	2,921	2,847	74	Pa	7,621	5,983	62
Ark	924	769	68	Maine	1,431	1,042	72	S. Dak	575	517	61
Conn	1,875	[2] 722	[2] 31	Mass	(NA)	1,034	3	Tenn	2,154	[4] 2,107	[4] 73
Del	382	314	71	Mich	8,879	8,912	53	Tex	12,378	6,316	66
D.C	[3] 800	293	30	Minn	3,944	[2] 3,135	[2] 50	Vt	477	502	69
Fla	7,271	6,523	67	Nev	787	388	71	Va	3,742	3,866	69
Ga	2,803	2,047	68	N.H	677	648	67	Wash	4,382	2,885	65
Hawaii	1,124	742	81	N.J	3,923	2,626	52	W. Va	1,429	1,219	83
Ind	4,800	5,379	70	N. Mex	1,173	997	70	Wis	3,721	2,573	53
Iowa	3,087	2,521	68	N.C	3,116	3,701	71	Wyo	585	543	(NA)
Ky	1,870	1,560	47	Ohio	9,373	7,588	63	P.R	271	224	65

NA Not available.   [1] Relationship not reported for 24 percent in Kentucky, 11 percent in Michigan, 7 percent in Florida, and 0-4 percent in other States.   [2] For fiscal year 1976.   [3] For 1969.   [4] For fiscal year 1975.

Source: U.S. National Center for Social Statistics, *Adoptions in 1970* and *Adoptions in 1975*, NCSS Report E-10.

No. 574. CHILD ADOPTIONS, BY TYPE: 1952 TO 1971

[In thousands. Includes Puerto Rico and Virgin Islands. Based on reports from State departments of public welfare with estimates added for nonreporting States, number of which varied from year to year. Prior to 1960, represents number of adoption petitions filed; thereafter, number of petitions granted]

TYPE OF ADOPTION	1952	1955	1960	1965	1966	1967	1968	1969	1970	1971
Total	85	93	107	142	152	158	166	171	175	169
By relatives	43	45	49	65	71	74	80	82	86	86
By nonrelatives	42	48	58	77	81	84	86	89	89	83
Placed by social agencies	24	27	33	53	57	62	64	67	69	66

Source: U.S. Social and Rehabilitation Service, 1952-1960, *Child Welfare Statistics*; thereafter, *Supplement to Child Welfare Statistics*.

No. 575. HANDICAPPED CHILDREN, BY TYPE: 1975 AND 1977

[For school year ending in year shown. 1975 covers children, birth to 19 years old; 1977, 3 to 21 years old]

TYPE	1975				Handicapped children served, [3] 1977 (1,000)
	Total [1] (1,000)	Served		Unserved, number (1,000)	
		Number [2] (1,000)	Percent of total		
Total	7,886	3,947	50	3,939	3,722
Speech impaired	2,293	1,850	81	443	1,309
Learning disabilities	1,966	235	12	1,731	800
Mentally retarded	1,507	1,250	83	257	972
Emotionally disturbed	1,310	230	18	1,080	284
Deaf and hard of hearing	377	95	25	282	90
Visually handicapped	66	39	59	27	38
Crippled and other health impairments	328	235	72	93	87
Multi-handicapped	40	13	33	27	([4])

[1] Based on estimates from national agencies and organizations, plus State and local directors of special education.   [2] Estimated total obtained from State education agencies. Information by type of handicap projected from data provided by State education agencies for school year 1972-73.   [3] Average of two censuses reported by State education agencies.   [4] Reported under the condition for which they received the most special education and services.

Source: 1975, U.S. National Center for Education Statistics, unpublished data. 1977, U.S. Bureau of Education for the Handicapped, *BEH Data Notes*, September 1977.

No 576. Day Care Arrangements of Children 3 to 13 Years Old, by Selected Characteristics: 1974-1975

[Data for children 3 to 6 years old as of **February 1975** and for children 7 to 13 years old as of **October 1974.** Civilian noninstitutional population. Includes children with no mother present, not shown separately. Based on Current Population Survey; see text, p. 1]

CHARACTERISTIC	Total	CARE IN OWN HOME			CARE IN OTHER'S HOME		Day care center	Other and not reported
		Child's parent	Child's self-care	Other	Relative	Nonrelative		
CHILDREN AGES 3-13 YEARS (1,000)								
Total	13,758	11,136	20	666	695	838	219	184
Children, ages 3 to 6	27,007	21,674	1,808	1,978	479	438	107	523
Children, ages 7 to 13	40,765	32,810	1,828	2,644	1,174	1,276	326	707
Mother in labor force	17,555	11,168	1,620	1,994	965	1,187	284	336
Employed	16,046	9,797	1,595	1,962	932	1,165	279	319
Full-time	10,323	5,168	1,331	1,642	756	940	247	239
Mother not in labor force	22,498	21,214	159	522	171	53	26	350
Marital status of mother:								
Married, husband present	33,467	27,909	1,315	1,735	835	948	211	515
Separated, divorced, widowed	5,960	4,036	441	702	253	277	103	148
Never married	625	435	24	78	49	16	8	13
		PERCENT DISTRIBUTION						
Children, ages 3 to 13	100.0	80.5	4.5	6.5	2.9	3.1	.8	1.7
Mother in labor force	100.0	63.6	9.2	11.4	5.5	6.8	1.6	1.9
Employed	100.0	61.1	9.9	12.3	5.8	7.3	1.7	1.9
Full-time	100.0	50.1	12.9	15.9	7.3	9.1	2.4	2.3
Mother not in labor force	100.0	94.3	.7	2.3	.8	.2	.1	1.5
Marital status of mother:								
Married, husband present	100.0	83.4	3.9	5.2	2.5	2.8	.6	1.6
Separated, divorced, widowed	100.0	67.7	7.4	11.8	4.2	4.6	1.7	2.5
Never married	100.0	69.6	3.8	12.5	7.8	2.6	1.3	2.1
Children, ages 3 to 6	100.0	80.9	.1	4.8	5.1	6.1	1.6	1.3
White	100.0	82.5	.1	4.1	4.2	6.3	1.6	1.2
Enrolled in school	100.0	84.1	.2	4.5	3.4	5.0	2.1	.7
Mother in labor force	100.0	59.0	.3	9.2	9.7	16.2	3.9	1.8
Employed full-time	100.0	40.3	.6	13.2	13.5	23.3	6.6	2.5
Employed part-time	100.0	76.9	–	5.4	6.2	9.7	.7	1.1
Unemployed	100.0	89.6	–	2.2	3.1	3.7	1.0	.4
Mother not in labor force	100.0	96.9	–	.9	.8	.4	.2	.8
Black	100.0	72.4	.1	8.8	9.7	5.3	1.4	2.4
Enrolled in school	100.0	76.4	.3	8.5	8.8	3.5	1.5	1.1
Mother in labor force	100.0	54.0	.3	11.5	17.2	10.9	2.6	3.6
Employed full-time	100.0	44.5	.5	12.7	20.3	15.2	2.8	4.0
Employed part-time	100.0	63.2	–	13.2	15.0	5.9	2.7	–
Unemployed	100.0	78.7	–	4.5	7.7	1.3	.6	8.4
Mother not in labor force	100.0	90.4	–	5.8	2.6	.2	.3	1.2
Children, ages 7 to 13	100.0	80.3	6.7	7.4	1.8	1.6	.4	2.0
White	100.0	81.4	6.3	6.6	1.7	1.7	.4	2.0
Mother in labor force	100.0	67.6	12.5	10.9	2.8	3.5	.8	1.9
Employed	100.0	65.7	13.2	11.6	3.0	3.7	.8	2.0
Unemployed	100.0	95.7	2.4	1.2	.2	.3	–	.2
Mother not in labor force	100.0	93.6	1.0	2.5	.6	.2	.1	2.0
Black	100.0	74.5	7.9	11.8	2.6	1.0	.3	1.9
Mother in labor force	100.0	59.4	13.7	18.0	4.3	2.0	.5	2.0
Employed	100.0	55.9	14.9	19.9	4.6	2.2	.6	2.0
Unemployed	100.0	88.8	4.4	2.5	2.1	–	–	2.2
Mother not in labor force	100.0	91.1	1.7	4.8	.6	.1	.1	1.7
By family income:								
Less than $5,000	100.0	80.4	4.5	9.3	2.6	1.0	.2	2.0
$5,000–$6,999	100.0	76.7	7.5	8.4	1.9	2.7	.5	2.2
$7,000–$9,999	100.0	81.5	6.1	7.0	2.1	1.4	.3	1.7
$10,000–$14,999	100.0	82.0	6.5	5.9	1.9	2.0	.3	1.5
$15,000–$19,999	100.0	80.0	7.6	7.3	1.1	1.7	.6	1.7
$20,000 and more	100.0	81.0	7.3	6.6	.8	1.2	.8	2.3

– Represents zero.

Source: U.S. Bureau of the Census, *Current Population Reports*, series P-20, No. 298, and unpublished data.

No. 577. BOY SCOUTS AND GIRL SCOUTS—MEMBERSHIP AND UNITS: 1960 TO 1977

[In thousands. Boy Scout data as of Dec. 31; Girl Scout data as of Sept. 30. Includes Puerto Rico and outlying areas]

ITEM	1960	1965	1970	1974	1975	1976	1977
BOY SCOUTS OF AMERICA							
Membership	5,165	5,733	6,287	5,804	5,318	4,884	4,718
Boys	3,783	4,231	4,683	4,328	3,933	3,600	3,466
Cub Scouts (8-10 yr. old)	1,865	2,064	2,438	2,178	1,997	1,874	1,843
Boy Scouts (11-18 yr. old)	1,647	1,850	1,916	1,678	1,503	1,339	1,225
Explorers (14 yr. and over)	271	317	329	471	434	387	398
Adults	1,382	1,502	1,604	1,476	1,385	1,284	1,252
Total units (packs, troops, posts)	130	145	157	162	150	141	137
GIRL SCOUTS OF THE U.S.A.							
Membership	3,419	3,647	3,922	3,291	3,234	3,160	3,140
Girls	2,646	3,030	3,248	2,755	2,723	¹ 2,623	¹ 2,583
Brownies (7 and 8 yr. old)	(²)	1,072	1,259	1,115	1,160	1,156	1,199
Juniors (9-11 yr. old)	(²)	1,416	1,509	1,237	1,188	1,114	1,054
Cadettes (12-14 yr. old)	(²)	443	395	326	301	275	252
Seniors (15-17 yr. old)	(²)	99	85	77	74	68	64
Adults	773	617	674	536	511	537	557
Total units (troops)	164	153	164	158	159	157	159

¹ Includes girls registered as "Other" or "Associates."
² Comparable figures not available because of change in program.
Source: Boy Scouts of America, National Council, North Brunswick, N.J., *Annual Report;* and Girl Scouts of the United States of America, New York, N.Y., *Annual Report.*

No. 578. VOLUNTEER WORKERS—SELECTED CHARACTERISTICS: 1974

[For year ending in April. Covers civilian noninstitutional population, 14 years old and over. Volunteer work refers to *unpaid* volunteer activities for such groups as religious, educational, hospital, civic and community, social and welfare, etc. Based on Current Population Survey; see text, p. 1. Subject to sampling variability; see source]

CHARACTERISTIC	Number doing volunteer work (1,000)	Percent of population	Percent distribution	CHARACTERISTIC	Number doing volunteer work (1,000)	Percent of population	Percent distribution
Total volunteers	36,812	23.5	100.0	Married, spouse present	25,520	26.9	69.3
				Never married	7,956	19.9	21.6
Male	15,100	20.4	41.0	Other marital status	3,337	15.3	9.1
Female	21,712	26.4	59.0				
				Volunteer work ¹—			
White	34,380	24.9	93.4	Once a week	13,125	(X)	35.7
Other races	2,433	13.2	6.6	Once every 2 weeks	3,714	(X)	10.1
				Once a month	5,230	(X)	14.2
14-17 years old	3,747	22.5	10.2	Only a few times	7,979	(X)	21.7
18-24 years old	4,641	18.3	12.6	Once only	2,758	(X)	7.5
25-44 years old	15,540	30.5	42.2	Other	3,884	(X)	10.6
45-64 years old	9,929	23.2	27.0				
65 years and over	2,955	14.3	8.0	Volunteer work per year ¹—			
				Less than 25 hours	13,638	(X)	37.0
Employed	21,842	24.8	59.3	25-99 hours	12,578	(X)	34.2
Unemployed	853	17.0	2.3	100-299 hours	7,700	(X)	20.9
Not in labor force	14,117	22.2	38.3	300 hours or more	2,737	(X)	7.4
Family income:				Type of organization, April 7-13 ²—			
Under $4,000	2,189	12.3	5.9	Religious ³	7,711	(X)	49.9
$4,000-$7,499	3,837	16.4	10.4	Health	2,244	(X)	14.5
$7,500-$9,999	3,378	22.2	9.2	Education	2,271	(X)	14.7
$10,000-$14,999	9,072	27.0	24.6	Civic/community ⁴	4,058	(X)	26.3
$15,000-$19,999	5,337	30.6	14.5	Recreation	1,700	(X)	11.0
$20,000 and over	6,649	37.1	18.1	Social welfare	1,152	(X)	7.5
Not reported	6,349	20.5	17.2				

X Not applicable.   ¹ Excludes not reported.   ² During this week, there were 15.5 million volunteers. The single-week period was selected to get a higher rate of recall from volunteers. Some persons volunteered in more than one type of organization and responded to two or more types listed.   ³ Figures may overstate what is "typical" because of Apr. 7 Passover and April 14 Easter holidays.   ⁴ Includes citizenship activity.

Source: U.S. ACTION, *Americans Volunteer, 1974.*

No. 579. Private Philanthropy Funds, by Source and Allocation: 1960 to 1977

[In billions of dollars. Estimates for sources of funds based largely on reports of the Internal Revenue Service for itemized deductions, corporate profits, and bequests. Data adjusted for nonitemized IRS deductions and after comparison with levels of gross national product, personal income, population, and publicly reported large bequests. For bases of allocation of funds, see source. See *Historical Statistics, Colonial Times to 1970*, series H 398-411, for similar but not comparable data]

SOURCE AND ALLOCATION	1960	1965	1970	1972	1973	1974	1975	1976	1977
Sources, total	8.9	12.2	19.2	22.7	23.4	25.3	26.9	29.4	35.2
Individuals	7.2	9.3	14.4	16.9	18.4	19.8	21.5	23.6	29.5
Foundations	.7	1.1	1.9	2.2	2.0	2.1	2.0	2.1	2.0
Business corporations	.5	.8	.8	.8	1.1	1.3	1.2	1.4	1.6
Charitable bequests	.6	1.0	2.1	2.7	2.0	2.1	2.2	2.4	2.1
By allocation:									
Religion	4.5	6.0	8.3	9.8	10.1	10.9	11.7	12.8	16.5
Education	1.4	2.1	3.1	3.6	3.7	3.7	3.6	4.1	4.7
Human resources (welfare) [1]	1.3	.9	1.4	1.6	2.1	2.3	2.5	2.7	3.5
Health [1]	1.1	2.1	3.1	3.7	3.8	3.9	4.0	4.4	4.8
Civic and cultural activities	.5	.5	1.2	1.5	1.9	2.0	2.8	3.1	3.3
Foundations, int'l, and other		.7	2.2	2.5	1.9	2.4	2.4	2.4	2.5

[1] For 1960, contributions for health to welfare agencies are included with welfare; thereafter, with health.

Source: American Association of Fund-Raising Counsel, Inc., New York, N.Y., *Giving USA*, annual. (Copyright.)

No. 580. American National Red Cross—Summary: 1960 to 1977

[For years ending June 30]

ITEM	1960	1965	1970	1973	1974	1975	1976	1977
Membership (contributors of $1 or more) [1] __1,000	23,900	28,222	33,587	36,465	30,868	30,945	30,044	33,065
Red Cross chapters __number	3,665	3,448	3,240	3,177	3,150	3,142	3,135	3,128
Community volunteers [1] __1,000	2,000	2,000	2,310	1,594	1,476	1,371	1,387	1,441
Students participating in R.C. school programs __1,000	(NA)	(NA)	6,820	6,153	6,456	6,191	6,395	6,109
Blood donors—R.C. and community programs [1] __1,000	(NA)	(NA)	(NA)	3,115	3,825	4,262	3,800	3,752
Income, total __mil. dol	96.0	105.0	147.1	210.9	219.6	248.7	285.1	347.3
Fund campaign contributions	83.3	90.5	124.4	135.8	128.0	125.6	129.3	135.4
Blood program, U.S. Govt. research grants [2]	(3)	(3)	(3)	48.2	63.9	88.7	118.9	168.7
Other [4]	12.7	14.6	22.7	26.9	27.8	34.5	36.9	43.2
Expenditures, total __mil. dol	86.7	108.1	149.4	202.5	205.6	237.3	276.4	312.0
Services to Armed Forces, veterans, and families	33.6	39.1	56.8	50.0	50.2	52.7	51.0	46.4
Disaster services	6.5	15.8	32.6	37.7	18.9	22.0	42.3	29.2
Blood program	[3] 12.6	[3] 15.9	[3] 15.3	59.9	76.8	100.3	114.8	159.6
Community health and safety programs	7.2	8.8	10.0	13.8	15.2	16.9	17.3	19.9
Service and program assistance to chapters	5.1	4.7	5.4	(5)	(5)	(5)	8.8	8.7
Youth service activities	3.5	4.6	5.0	5.1	5.2	5.3	5.1	5.1
Community volunteer programs	.6	.7	1.2	9.9	11.0	11.1	11.1	13.0
International relations [6]	2.5	3.4	4.1	.9	1.0	1.3	1.3	1.7
Membership and fund raising	3.1	3.0	2.8	3.8	4.2	4.5	4.6	5.8
Management and general	12.0	12.1	12.8	16.3	16.8	18.2	20.1	22.6
Land, bldgs., acquisition, capital improvements	(NA)	(NA)	3.3	5.2	6.4	4.9	(NA)	(NA)
Major activities:								
Loans and grants to servicemen, veterans, and their families (most loans are repaid) __mil. dol	11.2	11.7	13.5	10.8	11.4	11.2	10.9	10.3
Disaster services:								
Disaster relief operations __number	325	435	688	626	963	1,023	1,005	963
Disaster incidents [7] __1,000	(NA)	11.9	20.4	24.6	28.9	31.0	31.0	35.9
Persons given emergency care __1,000	108	654	398	228	330	278	321	321
Families assisted, disaster situations __1,000	14.9	47.2	74.6	30.1	34.3	22.3	64.6	35.8
Red Cross blood program:								
Blood voluntarily donated __1,000 units	2,422	2,775	3,175	3,806	3,829	4,291	4,690	4,946
Hospitals and blood banks served __number	4,000	4,300	4,100	4,277	4,059	4,117	4,092	4,136
Certificates issued: Nursing and health __1,000	212	308	404	484	505	547	528	537
First aid, small craft, water safety __1,000	2,738	3,605	3,955	4,563	4,395	4,399	4,532	4,664

NA Not available.   [1] Estimated.   [2] Includes civilian and Federal hospital participation fees and other. [3] Expenditures reported net of income.   [4] Primarily income from endowment and other invested funds, legacies, and restricted contributions.   [5] Allocated to program cost.   [6] 1960-1970 includes public relations costs which were allocated to program costs beginning 1973.   [7] Mainly involving a small number of families.

Source: The American National Red Cross, Washington, D.C., *Annual Report*.

No. 581. Foundations—Number and Finances, States and Other Areas

[Figures are for latest year reported by foundations, usually 1975 or 1976. A foundation may be defined as a nongovernmental, nonprofit organization, with funds and programs managed by its own trustees or directors, and established to maintain or aid social, educational, charitable, religious, or other activities serving the common welfare, primarily by making grants. Excludes organizations which make general appeals to the public for funds, act as trade associations for industrial or other special groups, are restricted by charter solely to aiding one or several named institutions, or which are captive trusts, within colleges, churches, or other organizations, or are small—defined as having neither assets of $1,000,000 nor making grants of at least $100,000 in the latest year of record. There were approximately 23,500 small foundations]

STATE	Number	Assets (mil. dol.)	Expenditures (mil. dol.)	Grants (mil. dol.)	STATE	Number	Assets (mil. dol.)	Expenditures (mil. dol.)	Grants (mil. dol.)
Total	2,823	29,649	2,150	1,825	Minn	82	761	68	53
					Mo	68	388	31	26
Ala	14	50	3	3	Nebr	11	34	4	3
Ariz	12	35	3	2	Nev	1	115	7	6
Ark	7	13	1	1	N.H	11	23	2	1
Calif	218	1,732	136	121	N.J	70	1,412	83	74
Colo	30	293	15	13	N.Y	617	10,089	740	609
Conn	68	570	49	46	N.C	50	384	25	22
Del	31	305	19	14					
D.C	33	220	26	17	Ohio	191	1,059	91	83
					Okla	34	377	30	22
Fla	48	276	22	19	Oreg	22	72	5	4
Ga	59	413	25	21	Pa	191	2,452	155	134
Hawaii	14	99	6	6	R.I	11	63	5	4
Ill	197	942	104	96	S.C	16	74	6	6
Ind	47	951	75	68	Tenn	25	152	11	10
Iowa	21	71	6	5					
Kans	17	48	5	4	Tex	159	1,724	122	97
					Vt	2	22	1	1
Ky	8	97	9	7	Va	34	95	8	6
La	21	92	7	4	Wash	32	205	13	12
Md	30	119	13	10	Wis	68	312	36	31
Mass	115	512	38	34	Other States and				
Mich	110	2,946	141	127	P. Rico	28	55	5	4

Source: The Foundation Center, New York, N.Y., unpublished data.

No. 582. Foundations Grants Reported, by Subject Field: 1973 to 1977

[Based on reports of about 400 foundations reporting their grants by subject field which in any given year accounts for about 35 percent of all dollars given by all foundations and about 65 percent of all grants of $5,000 or more in size. Covers grants of $5,000 or more. See headnote, table 581, for definition of foundation]

SUBJECT FIELD	AMOUNT (mil. dol.)					PERCENT				
	1973	1974	1975	1976	1977	1973	1974	1975	1976	1977
Total	716	701	677	752	770	100	100	100	100	100
Education	258	199	177	217	200	36	28	26	29	26
Welfare	67	109	80	104	100	9	16	12	14	13
Health	172	138	162	141	167	24	20	24	19	22
Sciences	87	87	105	126	135	12	12	15	17	17
International activities	66	76	75	72	85	9	11	11	9	11
Humanities	57	78	65	81	66	8	11	10	11	9
Religion	9	14	13	12	17	2	2	2	1	2

Source: The Foundation Center, New York, N.Y., Foundation Grants Index, 1977, and unpublished data.

No. 583. United Way Campaign Funds Raised, by Major Donor Groups: 1960 to 1977

[In millions of dollars. "Campaign" defined as a series of operations or systematic effort to bring about a desired result or "goal"]

MAJOR DONOR GROUP	1960	1965	1970	1973	1974	1975	1976	1977
Total	457	598	788	916	979	1,023	1,104	[1] 1,204
Corporations	159	194	225	260	271	281	293	(NA)
Individuals:								
At workplace	231	349	478	560	601	643	700	(NA)
Residential	} 67	{ 22	37	36	36	40	34	(NA)
Other		{ 33	48	60	71	59	77	(NA)

NA Not available.   [1] Estimated.
Source: United Way of America, Alexandria, Va., United Way Annual Report, and unpublished data.

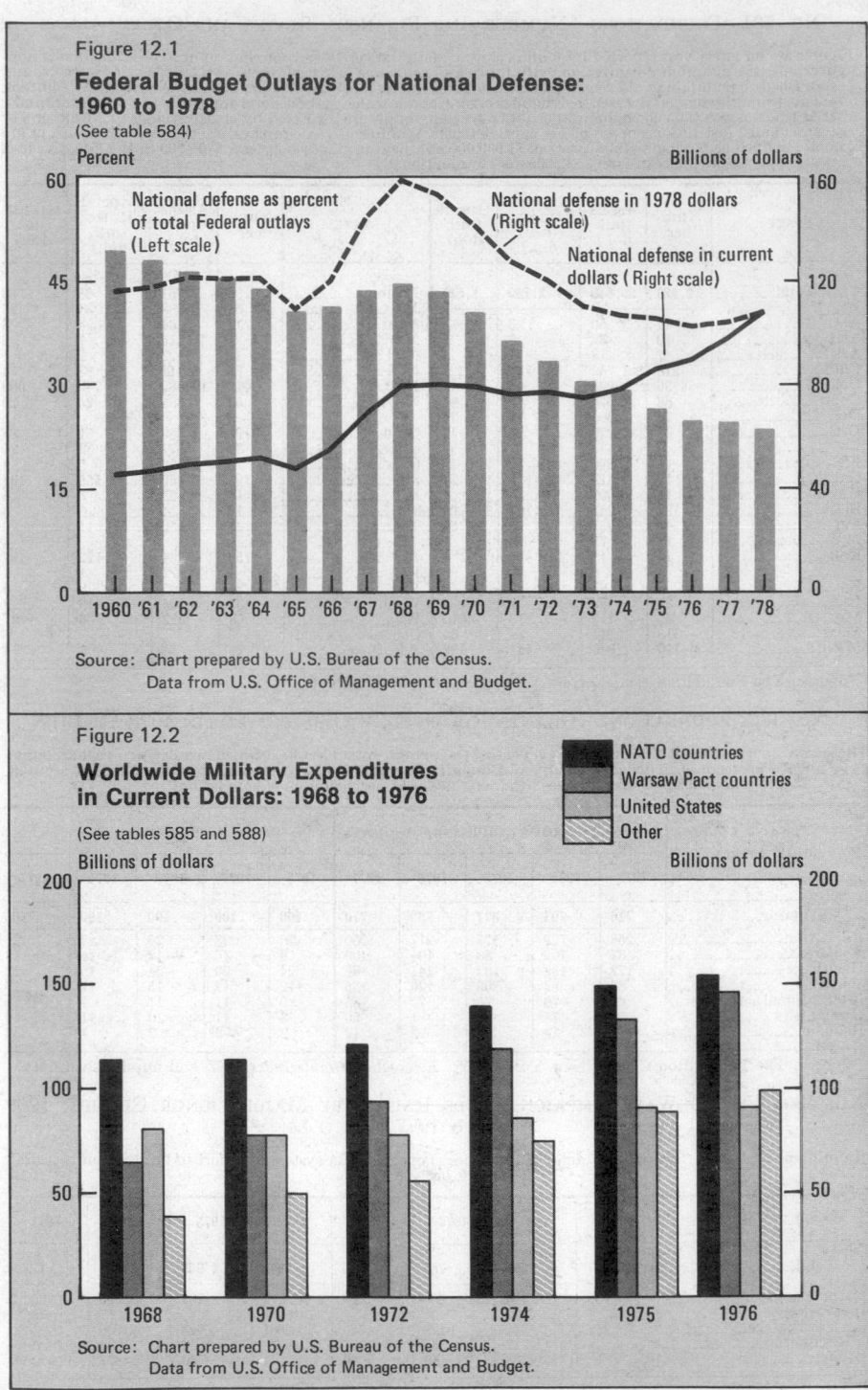

Figure 12.1

Federal Budget Outlays for National Defense: 1960 to 1978

(See table 584)

Source: Chart prepared by U.S. Bureau of the Census.
Data from U.S. Office of Management and Budget.

Figure 12.2

Worldwide Military Expenditures in Current Dollars: 1968 to 1976

(See tables 585 and 588)

Source: Chart prepared by U.S. Bureau of the Census.
Data from U.S. Office of Management and Budget.

Section 12

National Defense and Veterans Affairs

This section presents statistics on national defense and its human and financial costs; active and reserve military personnel, ships, and aircraft; Selective Service operations; and various federally sponsored programs and benefits for veterans. The principal sources of these data are the annual *Selected Manpower Statistics* and other reports issued by the Office of the Secretary of Defense; annual reports of the Departments of the Army, Navy, and Air Force, the Defense Civil Preparedness Agency, and the National Guard Bureau; the Selective Service System; *Annual Report of Administrator of Veterans Affairs*, Veterans Administration; and *The Budget of the United States Government*, Office of Management and Budget.

Department of Defense (DOD).—The Department of Defense is responsible for providing the military forces of the United States. It includes the Office of the Secretary of Defense, the Organization of the Joint Chiefs of Staff, the military departments (Army, Navy, Air Force), and the defense agencies (e.g. Defense Logistics Agency). The Secretary of Defense is appointed from civil life by the President with the approval of the U.S. Senate. The President serves as Commander in Chief of the Armed Forces; from him, the authority flows to the Secretary of Defense and through the Joint Chiefs of Staff to the commanders of unified (e.g. the overseas commands in Europe and the Pacific where Army, Navy, and Air Force activities are unified under command of a single person) and specified commands (e.g. Strategic Air Command).

The Joint Chiefs of Staff are the principal military advisers to the Secretary of Defense, the President, and the National Security Council. Members who are the senior military officers of their respective services are responsible for keeping the Secretary of their respective military departments fully informed on matters considered or acted upon by the Joint Chiefs of Staff. The chairman is the highest ranking U.S. military officer.

Each military department is separately organized under its own Secretary who is responsible to the Secretary of Defense for the operation of that department. Commanders of unified and specified commands are responsible to the President and the Secretary of Defense for missions assigned to them.

Selective Service.—The Selective Service System (SSS) is responsible for the registration, classification, selection, forwarding for examination, and transporting of men for induction into the Armed Forces whenever inductions are authorized by law. It is also authorized to determine availability of members of the Standby Reserve of the Armed Forces for order to active duty in time of war or national emergency. In addition, the SSS is responsible for determining whether a person's legal obligation may be fulfilled by alternative service (e.g. hospital work). The termination of examinations and inductions on July 1, 1973, was followed by a suspension of registration on April 1, 1975. All classification actions were terminated on January 27, 1976. Currently, the SSS is in a standby status.

Reserve Components.—Reserve personnel of the Armed Forces consist of the Army National Guard, Army Reserve, Naval Reserve, Marine Corps Reserve, Air National Guard, Air Force Reserve, and Coast Guard Reserve. They provide trained personnel available for active duty in the Armed Forces in time of war or national emergency and at such other times as authorized by law.

The National Guard has dual Federal-State responsibilities and uses jointly provided equipment, facilities, and budget support. In peacetime, the National Guard is State-administered, under the authority of the State Governors. The President is also empowered to mobilize the National Guard and to use such of the Armed Forces as he considers necessary to enforce Federal or State authority in any State.

Veterans Administration.—The Veterans Administration (VA) administers laws authorizing benefits for eligible former and present members of the Armed Forces, and for the beneficiaries of deceased members. Veterans benefits available under various acts of Congress include: Compensation for service-connected disability or death; pensions for nonservice-connected disability or death; vocational rehabilitation, education, and training; home loan insurance; life insurance; health care; special housing and automobiles or other conveyances for certain disabled veterans; burial and plot allowances; and educational assistance to families of deceased or totally disabled veterans, servicemen missing in action, or prisoners of war. Since these benefits are legislated by Congress, the dates they were enacted and the dates they apply to veterans may be different from the actual dates the conflicts occurred.

VA estimates of veterans cover all persons with service during periods of war or armed conflict and include those living outside the United States. Veterans whose active duty service was during periods of peacetime are eligible for some veterans benefits and, where appropriate, are included in VA estimates.

Historical statistics.—Tabular headnotes provide cross-references, where applicable, to *Historical Statistics of the United States, Colonial Times to 1970.* See Appendix I.

No. 584. FEDERAL BUDGET OUTLAYS FOR NATIONAL DEFENSE AND VETERANS BENEFITS AND SERVICES: 1950 TO 1978

[In billions of dollars, except percent. Through 1976, for years ending June 30, except as noted; beginning 1977, ending Sept. 30. Includes outlays of Department of Defense, Veterans Administration, and other agencies for activities primarily related to national defense and veterans programs. See *Historical Statistics, Colonial Times to 1970,* series Y 472–473 and Y 476, for related data]

			NATIONAL DEFENSE OUTLAYS						VETERANS BENEFITS AND SERVICES	
YEAR	Total Federal outlays, all functions	Total national defense and veterans outlays	Total		Current dollars as percent of—		Southeast Asia		Total outlays	Percent of total Federal outlays
			Current dollars	1978 dollars	Total Federal outlays	GNP [1]	Full costs [2]	Incremental costs [3]		
1950	42.6	21.2	12.4	45.9	29.1	4.7	(X)	(X)	8.8	20.7
1955	68.5	44.6	39.9	118.6	58.2	10.5	(X)	(X)	4.7	6.9
1960	92.2	50.6	45.2	115.4	49.0	9.1	(X)	(X)	5.4	5.9
1962	106.8	54.6	49.0	120.7	45.8	9.0	(X)	(X)	5.6	5.3
1963	111.3	55.6	50.1	120.2	45.0	8.7	(X)	(X)	5.5	5.0
1964	118.6	57.2	51.5	120.4	43.4	8.4	(X)	(X)	5.7	4.8
1965	118.4	53.2	47.5	108.4	40.1	7.2	.1	.1	5.7	4.8
1966	134.7	60.8	54.9	119.3	40.8	7.6	5.8	5.8	5.9	4.4
1967	158.3	75.1	68.2	143.8	43.1	8.8	20.1	18.4	6.9	4.4
1968	178.8	85.7	78.8	158.5	44.1	9.5	26.5	20.0	6.9	3.8
1969	184.5	87.0	79.4	153.0	43.0	8.8	28.8	21.5	7.6	4.1
1970	196.6	87.3	78.6	141.1	40.0	8.2	23.1	17.4	8.7	4.4
1971	211.4	85.6	75.8	126.9	35.9	7.4	14.7	11.5	9.8	4.6
1972	232.0	87.3	76.6	119.6	33.0	6.9	9.4	7.2	10.7	4.6
1973	247.1	86.5	74.5	109.4	30.1	6.0	6.3	5.3	12.0	4.9
1974	269.6	91.2	77.8	106.1	28.9	5.7	3.1	2.7	13.4	5.0
1975	326.1	102.2	85.6	104.9	26.2	5.9	1.4	1.1	16.6	5.1
1976	365.6	107.8	89.4	102.3	24.5	5.5	.3	.3	18.4	5.0
1976, TQ[4]	94.7	26.3	22.3	24.9	23.5	(NA)	.3	.1	4.0	4.2
1977	401.9	115.5	97.5	103.8	24.2	5.3	(X)	(X)	18.0	4.5
1978, est.	462.2	126.5	107.6	107.6	23.3	5.3	(X)	(X)	18.9	4.1

NA Not available. X Not applicable. [1] Gross national product; for definition, see text, p. 437.
[2] Included in national defense total. [3] Incremental war cost figures reflect estimated costs being incurred over and above normal peacetime operating costs of base line force. [4] Transition quarter, July–Sept.

Source: U.S. Office of Management and Budget, *The Budget of the United States Government,* annual, and unpublished data; U.S. Dept. of Defense, Office of the Comptroller, *The Economics of Defense Spending, A Look at the Realities,* July 1972, and unpublished data.

No. 585. BUDGET OUTLAYS FOR NATIONAL DEFENSE FUNCTIONS: 1965 TO 1978

[In billions of dollars, except as indicated. For years ending June 30 except, beginning 1977, ending Sept. 30. 1978 data are estimates. See *Historical Statistics, Colonial Times to 1970*, series Y 473, for total]

DEFENSE FUNCTION	1965	1967	1968	1969	1970	1971	1972	1973	1974	1975	1976	1977	1978
Total	47.5	68.2	78.7	79.4	78.6	75.8	76.6	74.5	77.8	85.5	89.4	97.5	107.6
Percent change [1]	1.0	19.8	15.4	.9	−1.0	−3.6	1.1	−2.7	4.4	9.9	4.6	9.1	10.4
Defense Dept., military	46.0	67.5	77.4	77.9	77.2	74.5	75.2	73.3	77.6	85.0	88.0	95.7	105.3
Military personnel	13.4	18.0	19.9	21.4	23.0	22.6	23.0	23.2	23.7	25.0	25.1	25.7	26.8
Percent of military	29.1	26.6	25.7	27.4	29.9	30.4	30.7	31.7	30.6	29.4	28.5	26.9	25.5
Active forces	12.7	17.1	19.0	20.5	22.0	21.4	21.6	21.7	22.1	23.2	23.3	23.9	24.9
Reserve forces	.7	.9	.9	.9	1.1	1.2	1.4	1.5	1.6	1.7	1.8	1.9	2.0
Military retirees	1.4	1.8	2.1	2.4	2.8	3.4	3.9	4.4	5.1	6.2	7.3	8.2	9.2
Operation, maintenance	12.3	19.0	20.6	22.2	21.6	20.9	21.7	21.1	22.5	26.3	27.8	30.6	33.5
Procurement [2]	11.8	19.0	23.3	24.0	21.6	18.9	17.1	15.7	15.2	16.0	16.0	18.2	21.6
Army	1.8	4.4	5.8	6.1	5.2	4.4	3.9	2.8	2.6	2.5	1.4	2.6	3.6
Navy [3]	4.9	6.5	8.0	8.5	7.9	7.3	7.1	7.0	7.3	8.1	8.0	8.5	9.3
Air Force	5.1	8.1	9.4	9.3	8.4	7.1	6.0	5.8	5.4	5.3	6.5	6.9	8.5
Research & developm't	6.2	7.2	7.7	7.5	7.2	7.3	7.9	8.2	8.6	8.9	8.9	9.8	10.7
Military construction	1.0	1.5	1.3	1.4	1.2	1.1	1.1	1.1	1.4	1.5	2.0	1.9	1.9
Family housing	.6	.5	.5	.6	.6	.6	.7	.7	.9	1.1	1.2	1.4	1.5
Civil defense	.1	.1	.1	.1	.1	.1	.1	.1	.1	.1	.1	.1	.1
Other [4]	−.9	.4	1.9	−1.7	−1.0	−.3	−.3	−1.1	−.2	−.1	−.4	−.2	(Z)
Atomic energy activities [5]	1.6	1.3	1.3	1.4	1.4	1.4	1.4	1.4	1.5	1.5	1.6	1.9	2.3
Defense-related activities	−.1	−.5	.1	.2	−	−.1	−	−.2	−1.3	−.9	−.1	−.1	(Z)

− Represents zero.   Z Less than $50 million.   [1] Average annual percent change. For 1965, change from 1960.   [2] Includes other defense agencies not shown separately.   [3] Includes Marine Corps.   [4] Revolving and management funds, trust funds, special foreign currency program, allowances, and offsetting receipts.   [5] Defense activities only.

No. 586. DEPARTMENT OF DEFENSE—FUNDS AVAILABLE AND OUTLAYS: 1965 TO 1978

[In billions of dollars, except as indicated. For years ending June 30 except, beginning 1977, ending Sept. 30. 1978 data are estimates. See *Historical Statistics, Colonial Times to 1970*, series Y 458–460 for outlays]

ITEM	1965	1967	1968	1969	1970	1971	1972	1973	1974	1975	1976	1977	1978
Funds available	64.2	89.0	92.9	93.5	90.5	85.8	88.8	92.7	95.9	102.9	114.8	131.0	136.4
New oblig. authority	50.5	73.6	77.8	78.3	75.4	72.6	76.8	79.6	82.9	87.6	97.9	110.7	115.5
Military	49.2	72.3	76.4	77.0	74.2	71.2	75.1	77.6	81.1	85.8	95.7	108.4	113.0
Civil	1.3	1.4	1.4	1.3	1.2	1.3	1.6	2.0	1.8	1.8	2.2	2.3	2.5
Unobligated balance	13.8	15.4	15.1	15.2	15.1	13.2	12.1	13.1	13.0	15.3	16.9	20.3	20.9
Military	13.6	15.1	14.8	14.9	14.8	13.0	11.9	12.7	12.6	15.1	16.7	20.0	20.7
Civil	.1	.2	.2	.3	.3	.2	.2	.4	.4	.2	.2	.3	.2
Outlays	47.2	68.8	78.7	79.1	78.4	75.9	76.7	75.0	79.3	87.1	90.2	98.0	107.8
Military	46.0	67.5	77.4	77.9	77.2	74.5	75.2	73.3	77.6	85.0	88.0	95.7	105.3
Civil	1.2	1.3	1.3	1.3	1.2	1.4	1.5	1.7	1.7	2.1	2.1	2.3	2.5
Ratio of outlays to—													
Funds available	.7	.8	.8	.8	.9	.9	.9	.8	.8	.8	.8	.7	.8
Unobligated balance	3.4	4.5	5.2	5.2	5.2	5.8	6.3	5.7	6.1	5.7	5.3	.8	5.2

Source of tables 585 and 586: U.S. Office of Management and Budget, *The Budget of the United States Government*, annual.

No. 587. DEPARTMENT OF DEFENSE OUTLAYS, BY BRANCH OF SERVICE: 1965 TO 1977

[For years ending June 30 except, beginning 1977, ending Sept. 30. Excludes civil functions. Includes military assistance to foreign countries. See also *Historical Statistics, Colonial Times to 1970*, series Y 458–460]

YEAR	OUTLAYS (mil. dol.)					PERCENT DISTRIBUTION			
	Total	Army	Navy	Air Force	Other	Army	Navy	Air Force	Other
1965	47,098	11,552	13,339	18,146	4,061	24.5	28.3	38.5	8.6
1970	78,349	25,147	22,656	25,233	5,313	32.1	28.9	32.2	6.8
1971	76,005	23,909	22,374	24,749	4,973	31.5	29.4	32.6	6.5
1972	76,674	23,473	22,736	24,845	5,620	30.6	29.7	32.4	7.3
1973	74,473	21,140	22,985	24,538	5,811	28.4	30.9	32.9	7.8
1974	77,651	22,371	24,616	25,736	4,927	28.8	31.7	33.1	6.4
1975	84,988	23,678	28,299	26,709	6,303	27.9	33.3	31.4	7.4
1976	87,950	25,025	30,404	28,248	4,272	28.5	34.6	32.1	4.9
1977	94,810	24,231	31,287	28,356	10,936	25.6	33.0	29.9	11.5

Source: U.S. Dept. of the Treasury, Office of the Secretary, *Combined Statement of Receipts, Expenditures, and Balances of the United States Government*, annual.

No. 588. WORLDWIDE MILITARY EXPENDITURES: 1967 TO 1976

[For military expenditures and armed forces by country, see tables 1574 and 1575]

COUNTRY GROUP	MILITARY EXPENDITURES (bil. dol.)										PER CAPITA (dol.)		
	1967	1968	1969	1970	1971	1972	1973	1974	1975	1976	1967	1970	1976
IN CURRENT DOLLARS													
Worldwide, total	201	218	231	242	255	271	293	333	371	399	57	64	95
Percent U.S. of total	39	38	36	33	30	30	28	27	25	24	(X)	(X)	(X)
Developed countries 1	171	184	191	197	205	221	236	265	290	308	176	198	294
Developing countries 1	31	34	39	45	50	51	57	67	81	91	12	16	29
NATO countries 2	108	114	116	114	114	121	125	139	149	154	209	214	274
Warsaw Pact countries	58	65	71	78	85	94	104	119	133	146	172	224	400
Other	35	39	44	50	56	56	64	75	89	99	13	17	31
IN CONSTANT 1975 DOLLARS													
Worldwide, total	319	330	334	332	333	345	351	361	371	380	90	88	90
Percent U.S. of total	39	38	36	33	30	29	27	27	25	24	(X)	(X)	(X)
Developed countries 1	270	278	277	271	268	278	280	288	290	294	279	272	279
Developing countries 1	49	52	57	62	65	67	71	73	81	87	19	22	26
NATO countries 2	171	173	167	157	150	152	149	150	149	147	331	295	261
Warsaw Pact countries	92	99	102	107	111	118	124	129	133	139	273	308	381
Other	56	58	65	68	72	75	78	82	89	94	21	24	29
AS PERCENT OF GNP 3													
Worldwide, total	7.1	6.9	6.7	6.3	6.1	6.0	5.7	5.8	5.9	5.8	(X)	(X)	(X)
United States	8.9	8.7	8.1	7.4	6.6	6.2	5.6	5.7	5.6	5.1	(X)	(X)	(X)
Developed countries 1	7.2	7.1	6.7	6.3	6.0	6.1	5.7	5.8	5.8	5.6	(X)	(X)	(X)
Developing countries 1	6.3	6.3	6.4	6.3	6.4	5.9	5.8	5.8	6.1	6.3	(X)	(X)	(X)
NATO countries 2	7.1	6.8	6.3	5.8	5.4	5.2	4.8	4.9	4.9	4.6	(X)	(X)	(X)
Warsaw Pact countries	10.7	10.9	11.0	10.7	10.7	11.8	11.0	10.9	10.9	11.0	(X)	(X)	(X)

X Not applicable.
1 Twenty-eight developed countries include all those in North America, in Oceania, in European NATO (except Greece and Turkey), in the Warsaw Pact (except Bulgaria), and also Austria, Finland, Ireland, Japan, South Africa, Sweden, and Switzerland; 114 developing countries include all those in Latin America, in the Near East, in South Asia, in East Asia (except Japan), in Africa (except South Africa), and also Albania, Bulgaria, Greece, Malta, Spain, Turkey, and Yugoslavia. 2 North Atlantic Treaty Organization.
3 Gross national product.

No. 589. VALUE OF ARMS EXPORTS AND IMPORTS, SUPPLIER AND RECIPIENT COUNTRIES, IN CONSTANT DOLLARS: 1967 TO 1976

[In millions of constant 1975 dollars. Countries ranked on basis of totals for 10-year period, 1967–1976]

COUNTRY	1967–1970	1971–1973	1974	1975	1976	COUNTRY	1967–1970	1971–1973	1974	1975	1976
World, total	32,565	36,340	12,280	12,000	12,780	RECIPIENTS—Con.					
SUPPLIERS						**Developing countries**	22,130	26,975	8,813	8,529	9,354
United States	16,960	15,580	4,510	4,850	4,960	Vietnam, South	4,518	4,060	720	906	(X)
U.S.S.R.	9,090	11,690	4,520	3,780	3,570	Iran	911	1,781	974	1,210	1,380
France	995	2,147	753	654	800	Israel	674	2,640	693	720	902
United Kingdom	794	1,522	589	501	608	Vietnam, Socialist Rep.	2,844	1,779	428	89	7
China, People's Rep.	971	1,265	381	136	108	Egypt	1,549	2,032	170	357	131
Germany, Fed. Rep.	647	751	216	393	625	Syria	306	2,019	1,110	313	354
Czechoslovakia	742	479	242	321	336	Iraq	512	972	694	525	729
Canada	817	662	117	76	111	Korea, Rep. of	1,660	1,116	123	185	312
Poland	888	477	146	106	138	Turkey	1,342	1,081	251	238	277
Other	661	1,767	806	1,183	1,524	China, Rep. of	1,054	763	136	165	154
RECIPIENTS						India	757	783	144	171	254
Developed countries	10,423	9,296	3,460	3,365	3,359	Libya	120	522	255	448	706
Germany, Fed. Rep.	1,025	1,874	598	525	441	Greece	607	675	184	197	367
German Dem. Rep.	779	1,175	445	504	414	Saudi Arabia	351	272	395	272	406
Poland	750	938	389	338	281	Korea, North	334	763	159	124	31
U.S.S.R.	1,203	508	206	220	230	Spain	231	430	101	166	221
Czechoslovakia	508	710	312	273	212	Pakistan	363	385	106	72	142
United Kingdom	1,421	187	87	116	182	Laos	422	396	72	22	11
United States	1,022	602	126	144	93	Brazil	223	295	78	88	161
Italy	356	521	203	80	135	Cambodia	104	270	327	128	(NA)
Australia	626	354	60	42	78	Jordan	235	208	66	137	128
Hungary	235	369	218	201	131	Peru	129	258	81	117	168
Romania	232	317	162	124	119	Algeria	138	93	22	85	225
Japan	326	251	100	53	171	Cuba	212	105	56	67	83
Canada	235	119	123	182	181	Nigeria	119	52	17	67	46
Other	1,705	1,371	431	563	691	Indonesia	48	88	38	23	72
						Other	2,358	3,137	1,413	1,637	2,087

NA Not available.   X Not applicable.
Source of tables 588 and 589: U.S. Arms Control and Disarmament Agency, *World Military Expenditures and Arms Transfers, 1967–1976,* July 1978.

No. 590. Estimates of Total Dollar Costs of American Wars, by Rank

[In millions of dollars, except percent. Service-connected veterans' benefits estimated at 40 percent of total veterans' benefits except as noted]

WAR	ORIGINAL INCREMENTAL COSTS [1]		SERVICE-CONNECTED VETERANS' BENEFITS		INTEREST PAYMENTS ON WAR LOANS		Estimated current cost to 1977
	Constant dollars (1967)	Current dollars	Total cost under present programs	Cost to July 1, 1976 [2]	Total cost to 1977 [3]	Percent of original incremental costs	
World War II	546,490	288,000	(⁴)	47,463	200,000	69	535,463
Vietnam conflict	106,526	111,000	(⁴)	4,835	3,000	3	118,835
Korean conflict	67,925	54,000	(⁴)	7,222	7,500	14	68,722
World War I	57,650	26,000	(⁴)	12,630	11,000	43	49,630
Civil War (Union only)	6,957	⁵ 3,200	3,300	3,288	1,200	60	7,688
Spanish-American War	1,600	400	2,500	2,067	60	15	2,527
American Revolution	(⁴)	100	28	28	20	20	148
War of 1812	182	93	20	20	14	15	127
Mexican War	270	73	26	26	10	14	109

[1] Except for Korean and Vietnam conflicts, original incremental costs are outlays for national security during war years minus average annual outlay for preceding five years. Vietnam conflict estimate is from Dept. of Defense and represents incremental costs from 1965–1977. Korean conflict estimate uses running average of national security outlays from 1948–1950 as a base, and then includes additional outlays over this base for 1951–1952 and one-half increase for 1953. This 50 percent figure for 1953 is used because outlays for the Cold War increased at same time outlays for Korean conflict declined.   [2] For World War I and later wars, benefits are actual service-connected figures from 1976 *Annual Report* of Veterans Administration. For earlier wars, service-connected veterans' benefits are estimated at 40 percent of total, the approximate ratio of service-connected to total benefits since World War I.   [3] Interest costs use same formula as in footnote 1.   [4] Unknown.   [5] Data from Goldin and Lewis, *The Economic Cost of the American Civil War, Journal of Economic History*, June 1975. Expenditures by Confederate Government are estimated by this study at $1 billion.

Source: Originally presented in U.S. Congress, Joint Economic Committee, *The Military Budget and National Economic Priorities*, Part 1, 91st Congress, 1st session (statement of James L. Clayton); subsequently revised and updated by James L. Clayton, University of Utah, Salt Lake City, Utah.

No. 591. U.S. Military Sales and Assistance to Foreign Governments: 1950 to 1977

[In millions of dollars, except as indicated. For years ending June 30 except, beginning 1977, ending Sept. 30. Department of Defense (DOD) sales deliveries covers deliveries against DOD sales orders authorized under the Arms Export Control Act, as well as earlier and applicable legislation. Commercial exports covers deliveries against orders placed directly by foreign governments to private firms. Military Assistance Program (MAP) and Excess Defense Articles (EDA) program are authorized by the Foreign Assistance Act of 1961, as amended. MAP grant aid deliveries represent military equipment and supplies delivered and expenditures for services. EDA deliveries represent deliveries of defense articles (costs at original acquisition) no longer needed by U.S. Armed Forces. Military Assistance Service Funded Program (MASF) aid, for 1966–1975, was used for providing military equipment and related services and training to countries engaged in hostilities in Southeast Asia. International Military Education and Training (IMET) program data, pursuant to new legislation under Foreign Assistance Act, as amended, show grant aid training of foreign military personnel as an independent program as of fiscal year 1976; training data, formerly provided under MAP and MASF, have been removed from MAP/MASF programs and included as an integral part of IMET]

ITEM	1950–1959	1960–1969	1970–1977 [1]	1970	1971	1972	1973	1974	1975	1976	1977
Military sales agreements	1,689	12,019	57,314	1,012	1,528	3,089	4,477	10,545	12,306	11,992	11,190
Credit program	173	1,588	10,326	70	742	547	531	2,889	850	2,192	1,911
Military sales deliveries	1,209	6,651	23,982	1,364	1,451	1,361	1,365	2,956	3,328	3,982	6,898
Commercial exports	(NA)	2,053	5,341	438	397	424	362	502	547	1,124	1,248
Military assistance program [2]	22,207	15,073	15,756	2,176	2,965	3,288	4,210	1,528	1,062	204	254
Excess defense items delivered [2]	1,307	2,792	2,509	511	560	548	375	306	100	37	64
International military education and training [2]	631	866	399	85	72	61	47	48	33	23	25
Students trained____1,000	94	223	171	22	26	52	37	12	9	6	5

NA Not available.   [1] Includes transition quarter, July–Sept. 1976.
[2] Includes Military Assistance Service Funded Program; 1977 estimated.

Source: U.S. Defense Security Assistance Agency, *Foreign Military Sales and Military Assistance Facts*, December 1977.

No. 592. U.S. MILITARY SALES DELIVERIES AND MILITARY ASSISTANCE DELIVERIES TO FOREIGN GOVERNMENTS, BY COUNTRY: 1960 TO 1977

[In millions of dollars. For years ending June 30 except, beginning 1977, ending Sept. 30. Represents Department of Defense military sales deliveries. Includes deliveries made under Military Assistance Program (MAP) and Military Assistance Service Funded Program (MASF); excludes training. For explanation of MAP and MASF programs, see headnote, table 591]

COUNTRY	MILITARY SALES DELIVERIES						MILITARY ASSISTANCE DELIVERIES					
	1960–1969	1970–1977 [1]	1974	1975	1976	1977	1960–1969	1970–1977 [1]	1974	1975	1976	1977
Argentina	57.7	76.3	11.9	8.0	7.5	6.1	31.0	3.0	(z)	(z)	–	–
Australia	487.5	516.6	196.0	19.9	13.7	28.9	–	–	–	–	–	–
Austria	42.1	50.2	1.8	2.0	2.3	28.6	39.0	(z)	–	–	–	–
Belgium	76.4	57.2	4.6	5.6	6.1	6.5	99.2	–	–	–	–	–
Bolivia	.5	.9	.1	.4	.3	(z)	12.3	12.8	2.4	1.9	1.3	1.1
Brazil	61.9	152.5	20.8	38.8	31.1	9.9	120.8	8.1	1.5	(z)	–	–
Canada	243.3	456.2	52.1	77.2	76.1	66.8	–	–	–	–	–	–
Chile	18.6	129.9	4.7	12.3	24.0	57.4	48.4	4.0	(z)	.5	–	–
China (Taiwan)	29.1	659.1	93.3	115.0	124.6	142.4	856.4	159.3	51.2	7.5	4.8	8.3
Colombia	2.6	11.4	3.9	.8	1.0	1.0	58.9	6.3	.1	(z)	–	–
Denmark	52.0	106.3	10.1	20.6	9.2	22.0	174.4	–	–	–	–	–
Dominican Rep	.9	.5	(z)	(z)	(z)	(z)	9.3	6.4	.6	.7	.3	.2
Ecuador	2.7	15.0	(z)	1.4	3.9	9.1	17.9	2.7	–	–	–	–
Egypt	1.6	10.5	–	–	–	10.5	–	–	–	–	–	–
Ethiopia	.2	88.6	–	9.8	15.6	59.2	86.6	68.3	7.5	8.1	10.0	3.6
France	258.9	67.0	3.5	3.7	10.0	3.4	116.8	–	–	–	–	–
Germany	2,471.1	2,754.1	406.5	394.1	358.7	342.6	104.4	–	–	–	–	–
Greece	22.7	767.1	101.1	131.8	133.6	242.9	619.9	137.2	2.6	2.7	.4	.2
Guatemala	2.0	20.1	1.5	3.4	1.4	2.3	9.6	6.0	1.5	.3	.3	.1
Honduras	.2	6.7	.8	.6	4.7	.4	3.3	1.4	.1	.1	.1	.2
India	19.3	10.8	.1	2.4	2.7	1.6	86.7	3.2	.2	.2	.3	.1
Indonesia	.6	35.3	.1	8.0	4.1	19.4	47.6	79.2	14.2	12.6	10.2	7.7
Iran	237.8	5,796.0	510.3	913.3	1,067.9	2,245.9	437.4	76.2	.2	(z)	–	–
Iraq	18.3	.3	–	–	–	–	–	–	–	–	–	–
Ireland	(z)	.5	(z)	.2	.1	(z)	–	–	–	–	–	–
Israel	156.2	4,139.9	977.9	656.5	609.9	875.3	–	–	–	–	–	–
Italy	322.8	335.1	20.4	52.2	33.9	41.1	496.2	–	–	–	–	–
Japan	179.6	212.8	25.5	24.8	13.8	24.2	313.0	–	–	–	–	–
Jordan	74.7	313.9	14.6	16.6	57.5	116.4	39.5	180.5	30.2	14.2	47.0	9.4
Korea [2]	2.2	421.9	13.3	57.5	137.3	184.8	1,997.1	1,776.0	91.6	136.6	93.8	16.7
Kuwait	–	116.6	(z)	7.6	15.8	88.5	–	–	–	–	–	–
Lebanon	1.7	12.1	.8	.9	2.1	1.0	1.4	5.2	.2	.2	(z)	–
Liberia	.4	2.5	.3	.4	.8	.5	4.2	.8	.1	.1	(z)	(z)
Libya	17.3	12.3	.3	(z)	–	–	11.2	.1	–	–	–	–
Luxembourg	1.6	1.1	.3	.3	(z)	(z)	(z)	–	–	–	–	–
Malaysia	3.9	49.4	2.1	29.0	12.4	2.3	–	–	–	–	–	–
Mexico	7.9	8.3	.9	.2	.7	4.2	–	–	–	–	–	–
Netherlands	74.3	133.7	25.0	24.6	15.5	24.6	163.1	–	–	–	–	–
New Zealand	53.0	63.4	12.4	2.9	1.3	3.3	–	–	–	–	–	–
Nicaragua	.6	2.3	.1	.2	.6	.4	3.1	3.2	.6	.2	.2	.1
Nigeria	.4	11.3	1.4	3.3	2.1	2.0	–	–	–	–	–	–
Norway	101.9	184.2	12.4	21.5	18.0	33.2	269.8	5.6	–	–	–	–
Oman	–	1.8	–	1.6	.2	(z)	–	–	–	–	–	–
Pakistan	40.3	110.1	11.7	13.0	13.1	38.6	301.1	–	–	–	–	–
Panama	(z)	4.4	.9	1.6	.9	.3	1.6	2.5	.2	.2	.2	.1
Paraguay	(z)	.1	(z)	(z)	(z)	(z)	4.2	4.5	.6	.5	.6	.4
Peru	16.4	75.5	4.4	8.2	29.3	26.0	50.3	1.6	–	–	–	–
Philippines [2]	3.5	63.0	1.7	5.1	13.1	33.9	200.4	106.1	14.8	12.5	12.3	7.0
Portugal	5.9	5.6	.5	.8	.5	.3	44.2	6.8	.6	1.0	.5	1.3
Saudi Arabia	126.6	3,584.1	255.0	342.2	685.7	1,617.4	13.4	–	–	–	–	–
Singapore	.8	36.2	3.7	4.2	6.1	15.2	–	–	–	–	–	–
South Vietnam	(z)	1.2	1.2	(z)	–	–	3,634.1	10,792.2	961.7	1,062.5	–	–
Sri Lanka	(z)	(z)	–	–	–	(z)	–	3.2	.1	–	–	–
Sweden	29.7	32.7	1.6	1.5	.4	19.3	–	–	–	–	–	–
Switzerland	50.5	142.3	4.8	7.3	5.3	51.9	–	–	–	–	–	–
Thailand [2]	.5	88.4	5.4	9.7	17.7	17.7	435.6	425.6	31.0	39.1	18.9	11.0
Tunisia	1.6	4.4	.2	.2	.6	3.3	20.6	19.1	4.7	1.6	1.6	.3
Turkey	1.5	263.5	17.1	89.3	103.6	38.2	1,110.1	490.5	63.2	62.9	–	–
Un. Kingdom	948.4	860.7	51.2	56.3	123.8	108.8	165.9	–	–	–	–	–
Uruguay	1.5	13.1	1.6	2.0	1.0	5.6	17.3	5.8	.8	.4	.5	.2
Venezuela	71.9	103.4	10.9	34.5	8.7	27.4	–	–	–	–	–	–
Yemen	–	27.0	–	1.8	.3	24.9	–	–	–	–	–	–
Yugoslavia	8.9	2.3	(z)	(z)	.2	1.5	–	–	–	–	–	–
Zaire	1.4	30.1	1.3	.8	2.8	8.2	20.0	3.3	–	–	–	–
International organizations	166.5	238.5	22.1	30.2	26.5	51.7	1,420.8	271.8	26.5	33.0	34.7	64.0

– Represents zero. Z Less than $50,000. [1] Includes transactions for the transition quarter, July–Sept. 1976. [2] Includes MAP and MASF Programs for military assistance deliveries.

Source: U.S. Defense Security Assistance Agency, *Foreign Military Sales and Military Assistance Facts*, December 1977.

No. 593. U.S. Assistance to Indochina and Thailand: 1950 to 1977

[In millions of dollars. For years ending June 30 except, beginning 1977, ending Sept. 30]

REGION, COUNTRY, AND TYPE OF ASSISTANCE	1950–1977 [1]	1950–1961	1962–1969	1970	1971	1972	1973	1974	1975	1976	1977
Indochina and Thailand [2]	30,314	5,000	10,106	2,401	3,178	3,814	4,658	2,460	1,368	84	65
Military assistance	20,931	1,829	6,246	1,841	2,452	3,215	3,973	1,475	944	65	47
Percent of total	69.0	36.6	61.8	76.7	77.2	84.3	85.3	60.0	69.0	77.4	72.3
Economic assistance	9,383	3,174	3,860	560	727	599	685	985	424	19	18
Indochina [3]	28,088	4,390	9,227	2,262	3,053	3,657	4,555	2,408	1,318	3	–
Military assistance [4]	19,389	1,489	5,669	1,731	2,352	3,092	3,909	1,438	901	–	–
MAP [5] grants	1,474	1,218	965	–	–	–	–	–	–	–	–
Service-funded grants	13,633	–	3,414	1,469	1,900	2,332	3,275	938	621	–	–
Economic assistance	8,699	2,901	3,558	531	703	565	646	970	417	3	–
Vietnam	23,395	3,717	8,255	2,054	2,521	3,058	3,851	1,596	866	6 3	–
Military assistance [4]	16,447	1,303	5,149	1,577	1,946	2,603	3,349	942	625	–	–
Economic assistance	6,948	2,414	3,106	477	576	455	502	654	241	6 3	–
Cambodia (Khmer Rep.)	2,187	293	84	9	278	256	269	696	405	–	–
Military assistance	1,335	73	26	9	201	198	176	420	256	–	–
Economic assistance	852	220	58	(z)	77	58	93	276	149	–	–
Laos	2,506	380	888	199	254	343	435	116	46	–	–
Military assistance	1,607	113	494	145	205	291	384	76	20	–	–
Economic assistance	899	267	394	54	50	52	51	40	27	–	–
Thailand	2,226	610	879	139	125	157	103	52	49	81	65
Military assistance [4]	1,542	337	577	110	100	123	64	37	43	65	47
MAP [5] grants	725	303	284	–	–	–	43	33	30	17	17
Service-funded grants	499	–	232	92	79	100	–	–	–	–	–
Economic assistance	7 684	273	302	29	24	34	39	15	7	16	18

– Represents zero. Z Less than $500,000. [1] Includes transition quarter, July–Sept. 1976. [2] For some programs, principally Agency for International Development (AID), includes obligations by year on a gross basis, that is, total new obligations entered into during each year, not adjusted for deobligations of prior year funds. The cumulative totals shown, however, are on a net basis, reflecting total deobligations during the entire span of years. [3] Indochina comprises Vietnam, Cambodia, Laos, and Indochina, undistributed. [4] Includes data not shown separately. [5] Military Assistance Program. [6] Program termination costs. [7] Includes $6 million obligated in fiscal year 1946.

Source: U.S. Agency for International Development, *U.S. Overseas Loans and Grants and Assistance from International Organizations*, annual.

No. 594. Summary of Major Military Forces: 1960 to 1977

[As of June 30 except, beginning 1977, as of Sept. 30]

DESCRIPTION	1960	1965	1970	1972	1973	1974	1975	1976	1977
Department of the Army:									
Divisions	14	16	16	13	13	13	14	16	16
Maneuver battalions	(NA)	176	191	138	138	140	148	160	163
Air defense battalions/batteries	288	227	195	185	182	184	147	156	150
Special forces groups	–	7	6	4	4	4	3	3	3
Total aircraft	5,564	7,142	12,166	10,480	9,923	9,708	9,517	9,298	8,789
Department of the Navy:									
Active fleet ships	812	936	769	654	584	512	496	476	464
Combatant ships	615	674	575	501	436	377	373	360	358
Auxiliary ships	197	262	194	153	148	135	123	116	106
Inactive fleet ships [1]	1,325	990	738	723	609	426	353	251	219
Tactical air squadrons [2]	104	113	88	80	79	79	79	74	69
Antisubmarine air squadrons	29	31	20	20	18	15	18	19	22
Marine divisions	3	3	3	3	3	3	3	3	3
Marine aircraft combat squad.:									
Fixed-wing squadrons	37	36	32	31	31	32	31	30	30
Rotary-wing squadrons	12	16	21	18	19	19	19	19	19
Total aircraft	11,272	9,725	8,646	7,836	7,448	7,423	7,035	6,839	6,593
Department of the Air Force:									
Intercontinental ballistic missile launchers	5	854	1,054	1,054	1,054	1,054	1,054	1,054	1,054
Selected aircraft squadrons	280	219	181	144	137	132	126	124	125
Strategic	142	65	33	31	31	29	28	27	26
Air defense	65	39	17	11	9	8	7	6	6
Tactical (excluding air-lift)	73	115	131	102	97	95	91	91	93
Total aircraft	21,283	16,487	14,983	13,295	12,044	11,376	10,736	10,276	10,140
Active	18,351	14,668	13,545	11,517	10,801	10,156	9,336	9,286	9,256

– Represents zero. NA Not available.
[1] Includes Navy retention ships, plus ships in disposal process. [2] Includes Special Mission.

Source: U.S. Dept. of Defense, Office of the Secretary, releases and unpublished data.

No. 595. Department of Defense Military Procurement: 1960 to 1977

[In billions of dollars. Net values; for years ending June 30 except, beginning 1977, ending Sept. 30. Includes all new prime contracts; debit or credit changes in contracts are included only if they involve over 10,000. Actions cover official awards, amendments, or other changes in prime contracts to obtain military supplies, services, or construction. Excludes term contracts and contracts which do not obligate a firm total dollar amount or fixed quantity, but includes job orders, task orders, and delivery orders against such contracts]

ITEM	1960	1965	1970	1971	1972	1973	1974	1975	1976	1977
Total military procurement [1]	**23.7**	**28.0**	**36.0**	**34.5**	**38.3**	**36.9**	**40.1**	**45.8**	**46.9**	**55.6**
Department of the Army [1][2]	5.9	6.3	10.3	9.1	10.0	10.3	10.6	11.5	10.5	12.0
Department of the Navy	7.4	9.0	10.9	11.8	13.5	11.9	13.3	15.6	15.4	17.6
Department of the Air Force	10.4	9.7	10.7	10.0	11.3	10.7	11.1	12.9	15.1	18.0
Defense Logistics Agency	(X)	3.0	4.1	3.5	3.8	3.9	5.1	5.7	5.9	6.8
With business firms for work in U.S. [1][3]	21.3	25.3	31.2	30.2	33.0	30.6	33.2	37.1	37.6	45.6
Department of the Army [2]	4.9	5.5	8.6	7.5	8.1	7.6	7.6	8.5	8.4	9.6
Department of the Navy	6.7	8.3	9.5	10.8	11.7	10.7	11.9	13.4	12.9	15.2
Department of the Air Force	9.6	8.8	9.6	8.9	10.0	9.0	9.4	10.4	11.4	14.2
Defense Logistics Agency	(X)	2.7	3.5	3.0	3.3	3.3	4.3	4.8	4.9	5.6
Advertised contract	3.0	4.7	3.9	3.5	3.6	3.5	3.0	3.4	3.2	3.9
Negotiated contract	18.3	20.6	27.3	26.7	29.4	27.1	30.2	33.7	34.4	41.7
Percent of total	86.0	81.6	87.6	88.5	89.0	88.5	91.0	90.9	91.6	91.5
With small business firms [4]	3.4	4.9	5.3	4.9	5.8	6.0	6.5	7.4	7.5	8.9
Advertised	1.2	1.1	1.0	1.0	1.2	1.1	1.2	1.1	1.1	1.3
Negotiated	2.3	3.9	4.2	4.0	4.6	4.9	5.3	6.3	6.4	7.6
Intragovernmental [5]	.8	.6	1.6	1.5	2.5	3.0	3.3	5.0	6.2	6.2
Educational and nonprofit inst	.4	.7	.7	.7	.8	.7	.8	.8	.9	.9
For work outside U.S.	1.2	1.4	2.4	2.1	2.0	2.2	2.4	2.4	2.3	2.8

X   Not applicable.   [1] Beginning 1973, includes Civilian Health and Medical Program of the Uniformed Services (CHAMPUS). Beginning 1977, includes other agencies not shown separately.   [2] Beginning 1965, includes defense agencies except Defense Logistics Agency (formerly Defense Supply Agency).   [3] Includes contracts awarded for work in U.S. possessions, Commonwealth of Puerto Rico, Trust Territories of the Pacific, and other areas subject to complete sovereignty of U.S.; contracts in a classified location; and any intragovernmental contracts entered into overseas.   [4] Covers firms not dominant in their fields of operation and employing fewer than 1,000, 750, or 500 persons, depending on industry classifications. For certain types of firms, other criteria are used, such as yearly gross sales.   [5] 1960 includes interservice purchases; thereafter, covers only purchases from other Federal agencies and reimbursable purchases on behalf of foreign governments.

Source: U.S. Dept. of Defense, Office of the Secretary, *Military Prime Contract Awards*, annual.

No. 596. Department of Defense Property: 1960 to 1977

[In billions of dollars. As of June 30, except, beginning 1977, as of Sept. 30. Excludes Civil Works Division, Chief of Engineers, Dept. of the Army]

DEPARTMENT AND TYPE OF PROPERTY	1960	1965	1970	1972	1973	1974	1975	1976	1977
Department of Defense	**154.6**	**176.2**	**214.6**	**219.4**	**220.3**	**227.9**	**237.3**	**249.5**	**263.4**
U.S. and possessions [1]	123.5	136.1	160.2	165.0	167.8	177.9	197.1	201.1	209.4
Foreign countries and afloat [2]	31.2	40.1	54.4	54.5	52.5	50.0	40.2	48.4	54.0
Real property inventory	32.0	37.6	40.3	41.0	41.3	41.7	43.0	44.3	46.0
Construction in progress	2.4	1.4	1.8	1.8	2.4	2.9	4.2	3.9	4.1
Personal property inventory	120.2	137.2	172.5	176.6	176.6	183.3	190.1	201.3	213.3
Army	38.3	36.4	50.4	49.1	47.9	49.4	51.6	58.1	60.5
Real property	9.8	10.7	12.3	12.2	12.1	12.3	12.8	13.2	14.1
Construction in progress	.3	.3	.4	.9	1.0	1.0	1.2	1.4	1.8
Personal property inventory	28.3	25.4	37.7	35.9	34.7	36.1	37.6	43.5	44.6
Navy (including Marine Corps)	57.4	69.7	85.4	87.9	87.6	90.8	100.9	99.1	100.1
Real property inventory	9.3	10.2	11.5	11.9	12.1	12.5	13.0	13.5	13.9
Construction in progress	.6	.5	1.1	.6	1.2	1.5	2.7	2.1	1.9
Personal property inventory	47.5	59.0	72.9	75.4	74.2	76.8	85.2	83.5	92.3
Air Force	58.8	67.3	74.9	79.0	78.8	79.8	77.4	83.5	87.0
Real property inventory	12.9	16.6	16.6	16.9	17.0	16.9	17.2	17.6	18.0
Construction in progress	1.5	.6	.2	.3	.2	.3	.4	.4	.4
Personal property inventory	44.4	50.1	58.1	61.8	61.6	62.5	59.9	65.5	68.6
DLA, personal property inventory [3]	(X)	2.5	3.4	2.9	5.3	5.9	6.2	8.2	7.1
OSD and other, personal property inventory [4]	(NA)	.3	.5	.6	.7	1.9	1.2	.6	.7

NA   Not available.   X   Not applicable.   [1] Includes Reserve Naval Fleet.   [2] Includes active-fleet, supplies afloat, and organic property of Fleet Marine Force.   [3] Formerly Defense Supply Agency.   [4] Office of the Secretary of Defense and other defense agencies.

Source: U.S. Dept. of Defense, Office of the Secretary, *Real and Personal Property of the Department of Defense*, annual.

No. 597. DEFENSE CONTRACT AWARDS AND PAYROLLS—STATES: 1975 TO 1977

[In millions of dollars. For years ending June 30 except, beginning 1977, ending Sept. 30. Contracts refer to awards made in year specified; expenditures relating to awards may extend over several years. Payroll estimates cover active duty military and direct hire civilian personnel, including Army Corps of Engineers]

STATE	CONTRACT AWARDS [1]			PAYROLL			STATE	CONTRACT AWARDS [1]			PAYROLL		
	1975	1976	1977	1975	1976	1977		1975	1976	1977	1975	1976	1977
Total	43,355	44,679	52,752	26,620	27,550	28,668	Mo	1,361	2,295	2,361	503	559	645
							Mont	[2]−5	23	174	81	84	96
Ala	417	418	421	530	565	609	Nebr	49	44	80	182	192	218
Alaska	132	145	123	294	300	296	Nev	45	19	28	115	128	138
Ariz	668	614	540	388	404	434	N.H	189	147	153	151	165	170
Ark	48	77	71	154	171	183	N.J	991	975	1,217	516	565	662
Calif	7,908	8,949	10,078	3,922	4,109	4,197	N. Mex	93	125	160	281	293	325
Colo	294	311	379	642	683	729	N.Y	3,744	3,304	4,300	478	497	523
Conn	2,349	1,913	1,974	91	101	107	N.C	399	347	374	1,050	1,083	1,131
Del	50	37	51	80	85	87	N. Dak	176	155	44	156	161	165
D.C	529	412	698	615	601	605	Ohio	1,014	921	1,164	631	654	686
Fla	1,030	972	1,061	1,051	1,118	1,142	Okla	215	255	293	631	663	740
Ga	630	477	518	930	1,000	1,157	Oreg	59	52	78	51	56	58
Hawaii	298	363	224	695	712	638							
							Pa	1,067	1,252	1,654	827	815	883
Idaho	10	17	16	69	76	83	R.I	73	94	125	136	141	143
Ill	494	474	560	640	658	751	S.C	204	157	175	714	772	814
Ind	812	785	835	293	278	287	S. Dak	19	14	13	80	86	94
Iowa	175	230	281	24	27	30	Tenn	359	342	710	201	210	211
Kans	504	307	363	358	363	359	Tex	2,024	2,095	2,778	2,351	2,436	2,237
Ky	167	188	221	626	642	671	Utah	141	145	227	337	349	405
La	477	303	391	414	360	350	Vt	123	129	119	8	9	12
Maine	55	284	323	82	87	89	Va	1,207	1,608	2,038	2,316	2,261	2,376
Md	802	982	1,092	1,123	1,127	1,139	Wash	1,637	1,289	1,738	751	806	812
Mass	1,770	1,956	2,395	276	283	298	W. Va	74	85	92	22	23	31
Mich	766	965	1,244	273	285	306	Wis	237	251	416	48	49	57
Minn	437	691	656	66	69	76	Wyo	29	21	19	53	58	61
Miss	973	935	493	314	324	352	Undist.[3]	6,036	5,730	7,212	(NA)	7	−

− Represents zero. NA Not available. [1] Military awards for supplies, services, and construction. Net value of contracts of over $10,000 for work in each State and D.C. (see also "Undistributed"). Figures reflect impact of prime-contracting on State distribution of defense work. Often the State in which a prime contractor is located is not the State in which the subcontracted work is done. See also headnote, table 595. [2] Result of cancelled Anti-Ballistic Missile site construction. [3] Includes contracts of less than $10,000; all contracts awarded for work in U.S. possessions, Puerto Rico, Trust Territories of the Pacific, and other areas subject to complete sovereignty of U.S.; contracts in a classified location; and any intragovernmental contracts entered into overseas.

Source: U.S. Dept. of Defense, Office of the Secretary, *Prime Contract Awards by State*, annual.

No. 598. DEFENSE-ORIENTED INDUSTRIES—SUMMARY: 1963 TO 1976

[For the most part, industries included are those shipping finished goods or components produced to military specifications; for details, see source]

SIC [1] code	YEAR AND INDUSTRY	Em- ployees (1,000)	VALUE ADDED BY MANUFACTURE		VALUE OF SHIPMENTS AND RECEIPTS (mil. dol.)		
			Total (mil. dol.)	Per- cent	Total	Govern- ment [2]	Non- govern- ment
(X)	1963	1,933	22,326	100.0	79,626	37,364	42,263
(X)	1965	3,859	54,577	100.0	105,987	28,785	77,202
(X)	1970	4,186	74,364	100.0	144,673	34,731	109,942
(X)	1971	3,846	73,683	100.0	146,053	30,342	115,711
(X)	1972	3,500	74,089	100.0	146,525	28,721	117,804
(X)	1973	3,920	91,275	100.0	180,582	30,079	150,503
(X)	1974	5,067	124,150	100.0	271,895	36,197	235,698
(X)	1975	4,643	129,502	100.0	287,220	39,726	247,494
(X)	1976, total	4,594	143,008	100.0	319,278	44,009	275,269
28	Chemicals and allied products	131	6,595	4.6	15,006	1,821	13,185
29	Petroleum and coal products	107	12,276	8.6	77,647	1,696	75,951
30	Rubber and misc. plastic products	114	2,774	1.9	5,159	187	4,972
3293	Gaskets, packing and sealing devices	32	512	.4	869	33	836
33	Primary metal industries	310	8,598	6.0	24,273	803	23,470
34	Fabricated metal products	523	14,000	9.8	27,091	3,098	23,993
35	Machinery, except electrical	968	29,042	20.3	54,393	2,731	51,662
36	Electrical equipment and supplies	1,202	31,915	22.3	53,392	9,249	44,143
37	Transportation equipment	760	22,836	16.0	39,638	22,418	17,220
38	Instruments and related products	418	13,319	9.3	20,640	1,633	19,007
(X)	Miscellaneous industries	29	1,141	.8	1,170	340	830

X Not applicable. [1] Standard industrial classification. [2] Comprises products shipped to, or receipts for work done for, Federal agencies, their contractors, subcontractors, and suppliers.

Source: U.S. Bureau of the Census, *U.S. Census of Manufactures, 1963*, and *Current Industrial Reports*, series MA 175.

No. 599. Employment—Defense-Related Agencies Compared with Total Federal and Total United States: 1960 to 1977

[In thousands, except percent. Annual averages]

EMPLOYMENT	1960	1965	1970	1972	1973	1974	1975	1976	1977
Total U.S. employment [1]	68,290	73,812	81,815	84,151	86,735	88,165	86,963	89,629	92,676
Federal	4,944	5,262	6,116	5,264	5,114	5,095	5,062	5,006	4,988
Armed Forces	2,514	2,723	3,188	2,449	2,326	2,229	2,180	2,144	2,133
Civilian personnel [2]	2,430	2,539	2,928	2,815	2,788	2,866	2,882	2,862	2,855
Federal defense-related agencies, excl. Armed Forces	1,057	1,053	1,211	1,105	1,061	1,061	1,036	1,008	994
Percent of Federal civilian personnel	43.5	41.5	41.4	39.3	38.1	37.0	36.0	35.2	34.8
Federal defense-related agencies [1]	3,571	3,776	4,399	3,554	3,387	3,289	3,216	3,152	3,127
As percent of:									
Total Federal [1]	72.2	71.8	71.9	67.5	66.2	64.6	63.5	63.0	62.7
Total U.S. [1]	5.2	5.1	5.4	4.2	3.9	3.7	3.7	3.5	3.4

[1] Includes Armed Forces.   [2] Includes all direct employment by U.S. Govt. abroad regardless of citizenship·

Source: U.S. Bureau of Labor Statistics, *Employment and Earnings*, monthly, and U.S. Civil Service Commission, *Monthly Release of Federal Civilian Work force Statistics.*

No. 600. Civil Defense—Federal Matching Funds Utilized, and State and Local Government Expenditures: 1952 to 1977

[In millions of dollars. As of June 30 except, beginning 1977, as of Sept. 30. States and outlying areas are required to match Federal funds on an equal basis]

FUNDS USED AND EXPENDITURES	1952-1977 total [1]	1952-1961	1962-1971	1972	1973	1974	1975	1976	1977
Federal matching funds utilized [2]	568	102	232	29.9	33.1	37.1	40.4	39.8	41.9
Emergency operating centers	83	5	40	5.2	6.3	6.9	6.7	5.5	4.0
Supporting materials/maintenance and service	156	93	33	3.3	3.4	4.3	5.7	4.7	6.8
Personnel and administrative expense	329	4	158	21.4	23.3	26.0	27.9	29.6	31.2
State and local expenditures [3]	1,533	200	682	83.5	91.6	102.6	110.0	115.8	122.2

[1] Includes transition quarter, July–Sept. 1976.   [2] Represents Federal matching fund payments made and outstanding obligations as of Sept. 30, 1977, for civil defense grant programs.   [3] Includes funds from U.S. Govt.

Source: U.S. Defense Civil Preparedness Agency, *Financial Digest, 1951–1977*, vol. 5.

No. 601. Armed Forces Personnel—Summary of Major Conflicts

[For Revolutionary War, number of personnel serving not known, but estimates range from 184,000 to 250,000; for War of 1812, 286,730 served; for Mexican War, 78,718 served. Dates of the major conflicts may differ from those specified in various laws providing benefits for veterans. See table 608 for data on Vietnam conflict. See also *Historical Statistics, Colonial Times to 1970*, series Y 856–903]

ITEM	Civil War [1]	Spanish-American War	World War I	World War II	Korean conflict	Vietnam conflict
Personnel serving 1,000	2,213	307	4,744	[2] 16,354	[3] 5,764	[4] 8,811
Army 1,000	2,129	[5] 281	4,057	11,260	2,834	4,368
Navy 1,000	} 84 {	23	599	4,183	1,177	1,842
Marines 1,000		3	79	669	424	794
Air Force [6] 1,000	(X)	(X)	[7]	[7]	1,285	1,740
Coast Guard [8] 1,000	(X)	(X)	9	241	44	67
Average duration of service months	20	8	12	33	19	23
Officers months	(NA)	8	14	39	24	(NA)
Enlisted months	(NA)	8	12	33	18	(NA)
Service abroad: Personnel serving percent	(NA)	[9] 29	53	73	[10] 56	(NA)
Average duration [11] months	(NA)	1.5	5.5	16.2	13.4	(NA)
Casualties: [12] Battle deaths 1,000	140	(Z)	53	292	34	[13] 46
Wounds not mortal 1,000	282	2	204	671	103	[13] 304
Draftees: Classified 1,000	777	(X)	24,234	36,677	9,123	[4] 75,717
Examined 1,000	522	(X)	3,764	17,955	3,685	[4] 8,611
Rejected 1,000	160	(X)	803	6,420	1,189	[4] 3,880
Inducted 1,000	46	(X)	2,820	10,022	1,560	[4] 1,759

NA Not available.   X Not applicable.   Z Fewer than 500.   [1] Union forces only. Estimates of the number serving in Confederate forces range from 600,000 to 1.5 million.   [2] Covers Dec. 1, 1941, to Dec. 31, 1946.   [3] Covers June 25, 1950, to July 27, 1953.   [4] Covers Aug. 4, 1964, to Jan. 27, 1973.   [5] Covers Apr. 21 to Aug. 13, 1898.   [6] Originally organized in 1907: Established as Air Force under Armed Services Unification Act of 1947. For World War I, known as Aviation Service and included in data for Army; for World War II, known as Army Air Forces and included in data for Army.   [7] Included in Army.   [8] Established Jan. 28, 1915.   [9] Based on Army and Marines only.   [10] Excludes Navy, Covers July 1950 through Jan. 1955. Represents Far East area only.   [11] During hostilities only.   [12] For periods covered, see footnotes 2, 3, 4, 5, and 9.   [13] Covers Jan. 1, 1961, to Jan. 27, 1973.

Source: The President's Commission on Veterans' Pensions, *Veterans' Benefits in the United States*, vol. I, 1956; and U.S. Dept. of Defense, Office of the Secretary, unpublished data.

No. 602. Department of Defense Personnel and Payroll: 1950 to 1977

[Except as noted, personnel as of June 30 and payroll for years ending June 30. Excludes "indirect hire" civilians, i.e. foreign nationals under special agreement by Defense Department with foreign country. See *Historical Statistics, Colonial Times to 1970*, series Y 904–916, for similar but not comparable personnel data:

YEAR	PERSONNEL (1,000)				PAYROLL (bil. dol.)			
	Total	Active duty military	Direct hire civilian	Military retirees	Total	Active duty military [1]	Direct hire civilian [2]	Military pensions payments [3]
1950	2,213	1,460	753	132	8.2	5.3	2.9	(NA)
1955	4,122	2,935	1,187	180	13.8	9.1	4.7	(NA)
1960	3,523	2,476	1,047	256	15.1	9.3	5.8	(NA)
1965	3,689	2,655	1,034	481	18.5	11.4	7.1	(NA)
1968	4,865	3,548	1,317	651	25.8	16.4	9.4	2.0
1969	4,802	3,460	1,342	714	28.2	17.9	10.3	2.2
1970	4,260	3,066	1,194	773	30.7	19.4	11.3	2.5
1971	3,842	2,715	1,127	831	30.8	19.2	11.6	3.1
1972	3,406	2,323	1,083	890	32.0	19.8	12.2	3.6
1973	3,284	2,253	1,031	948	32.6	20.3	12.3	4.1
1974	3,233	2,162	1,071	1,012	32.7	19.9	12.8	4.9
1975	3,170	2,128	1,042	1,073	34.0	20.2	13.8	6.1
1976	3,092	2,082	1,010	1,132	35.0	20.4	14.6	7.3
1977 [4]	3,057	2,075	982	1,200	36.8	21.0	15.8	8.2

NA Not available.   [1] Excludes troop subsistence, transportation, movement of personnel, etc.
[2] Excludes benefits, etc.   [3] For U.S. only.   [4] Personnel as of Sept. 30; payroll for year ending Sept. 30.

Source: Dept. of Defense, Office of the Secretary, *Selected Manpower Statistics*, annual, and unpublished data.

No. 603. Department of Defense Personnel, by Service: 1960 to 1977

[In thousands. As of Dec. 31. See headnote, table 602. See *Historical Statistics, Colonial Times to 1970*, series Y 904–916, for similar but not comparable data]

BRANCH OF SERVICE	1960	1965	1968	1969	1970	1971	1972	1973	1974	1975	1976	1977
Total [1]	3,526	3,915	4,681	4,561	4,026	3,642	3,428	3,228	3,183	3,112	3,067	3,044
Army	1,257	1,448	1,931	1,901	1,664	1,386	1,261	1,148	1,145	1,140	1,133	1,122
Military	877	1,075	1,463	1,432	1,234	966	862	782	773	767	775	771
Civilian	381	373	468	469	430	420	399	366	372	373	358	351
Air Force	1,117	1,134	1,198	1,164	1,056	1,047	981	942	898	860	827	816
Military	811	842	887	843	759	754	707	674	625	599	580	572
Civilian	307	292	311	322	297	293	274	268	273	261	247	244
Navy [2]	1,150	1,275	1,480	1,426	1,242	1,149	1,117	1,065	1,066	1,040	1,029	1,028
Military	806	940	1,058	1,024	882	799	777	746	742	718	717	717
Civilian	343	335	422	402	360	350	340	319	324	322	312	311

[1] Includes personnel assigned to Office of Secretary of Defense, Organization of Joint Chiefs of Staff, Army Corps of Engineers Civil Functions, and other defense activities, not shown separately.   [2] Includes Marine Corps.

Source: U.S. Dept. of Defense, Office of the Secretary, *Selected Manpower Statistics*, annual, and *Selected Defense Department Economic Indicators*, monthly.

No. 604. Blacks in the Armed Forces: 1965 to 1977

[As of Dec. 31, except as indicated. Includes women. Officers include warrant officers]

YEAR	TOTAL ARMED FORCES (1,000)			BLACK PERSONNEL (1,000)			PERCENT BLACK OF TOTAL		
	Total	Officers	Enlisted	Total	Officers	Enlisted	Total	Officers	Enlisted
1965	2,816	337	2,478	267	6	261	9.5	1.9	10.5
1968	3,394	417	2,977	313	9	304	9.2	2.1	10.2
1969	3,285	408	2,877	286	9	277	8.7	2.1	9.6
1970	2,861	389	2,472	279	8	271	9.8	2.2	11.0
1971	2,504	359	2,145	267	8	259	10.7	2.3	12.1
1972	2,335	329	2,006	278	8	271	11.9	2.4	13.5
1973	2,186	309	1,878	288	8	279	13.2	2.7	14.9
1974	2,123	293	1,830	306	9	297	14.4	3.0	16.2
1975	2,071	283	1,788	299	9	290	14.4	3.2	16.2
1976	2,059	279	1,780	314	10	303	15.2	3.6	17.1
1977 (June 30)	2,063	281	1,782	322	11	311	15.6	3.9	17.4

Source: U.S. Dept. of Defense, Office of Equal Opportunity, *The Black in the Armed Forces, Statistical Fact Book*, annual.

No. 605. MILITARY PERSONNEL ON ACTIVE DUTY, BY SERVICE: 1960 TO 1978

[In thousands. As of June 30 except, beginning 1977, as of Sept. 30. Includes National Guard, Reserve, and retired Regular personnel on extended or continuous active duty; excludes Coast Guard. Military cadets, Naval Academy midshipmen, Air Force Academy cadets, and other officer candidates are included under enlisted personnel. See also *Historical Statistics, Colonial Times to 1970*, series Y 904–916]

BRANCH OF SERVICE	1960	1965	1968	1969	1970	1971	1972	1973	1974	1975	1976	1977	1978, est.
Total	2,476	2,653	3,547	3,459	3,066	2,714	2,322	2,252	2,161	2,127	2,081	2,074	2,069
Female	32	31	38	40	41	43	45	55	75	97	109	119	131
Army	873	968	1,570	1,512	1,322	1,124	811	801	783	784	779	782	774
Officers	101	112	166	172	166	149	121	116	106	103	98	97	97
Enlisted	772	857	1,404	1,340	1,156	975	690	685	677	681	681	685	677
Navy	618	671	765	776	692	623	588	564	546	535	524	530	532
Officers	70	78	85	85	81	74	73	70	67	65	64	63	63
Enlisted	548	593	680	691	612	549	515	494	479	470	461	467	469
Marine Corps.	171	190	307	310	260	212	198	196	189	196	192	192	192
Officers	16	17	25	26	25	22	20	19	19	19	19	19	19
Enlisted	154	173	283	284	235	190	178	177	170	177	174	173	173
Air Force	815	824	905	862	791	755	726	691	644	612	585	570	571
Officers	130	131	140	135	130	126	121	115	110	105	100	96	95
Enlisted	685	692	765	727	662	629	604	576	534	507	486	474	476

Source: 1960, U.S. Dept. of Defense, Office of the Secretary, semiannual reports and unpublished data; beginning 1965, U.S. Office of Management and Budget, *The Budget of the United States Government*, annual.

No. 606. WOMEN IN THE ARMED FORCES: 1960 TO 1977

[As of June 30 except, beginning 1977, as of Sept. 30. See headnote, table 605]

ITEM	1960	1965	1969	1970	1971	1972	1973	1974	1975	1976	1977
Total military____1,000__	2,476	2,655	3,460	3,066	2,715	2,323	2,253	2,162	2,128	2,082	2,074
Women_____1,000__	32	31	40	42	43	45	55	75	97	109	119
Percent	1.3	1.2	1.1	1.4	1.6	1.9	2.5	3.5	4.6	5.2	5.7
Officers, total_____1,000__	317	339	419	402	371	336	321	303	292	281	276
Women_____1,000__	11	11	13	13	13	13	13	13	14	14	15
Percent	3.4	3.1	3.1	3.3	3.5	3.8	4.0	4.3	4.6	5.0	5.4
Enlisted personnel___1,000__	2,160	2,317	3,041	2,664	2,343	1,987	1,932	1,860	1,836	1,801	1,798
Women_____1,000__	21	20	26	28	30	32	43	62	83	95	104
Percent	1.0	.9	.9	1.1	1.3	1.6	2.2	3.3	4.5	5.3	5.8

No. 607. VIETNAM CONFLICT—U.S. MILITARY FORCES IN VIETNAM AND CASUALTIES INCURRED: 1961 TO 1975

[Military forces as of Dec. 31. All U.S. forces withdrawn by Jan. 27, 1973]

ITEM	1961–1975, total	1961–1964 [1]	1965	1966	1967	1968	1969	1970	1971	1972	1973–1975
Military forces, total	(X)	23,300	184,300	385,300	485,600	536,100	475,200	234,600	156,800	24,200	(²)
Battle deaths [3]	46,370	267	1,369	5,008	9,377	14,589	9,414	4,221	1,381	300	444
Killed	38,418	186	1,115	4,122	7,491	12,622	8,106	3,479	1,084	193	20
Died of wounds	5,168	10	103	576	978	1,594	1,166	552	157	26	6
Died while missing [4]	2,784	71	151	310	908	373	142	190	140	81	418
Wounded, nonfatal: [3]											
Hospital care	153,311	783	3,308	16,526	32,369	46,796	32,940	15,211	4,767	587	24
No hospital care	150,343	748	2,806	13,567	29,654	46,021	37,276	15,432	4,169	634	36

X Not applicable.   [1] Figures for military forces for 1964 only.   ² Fewer than 250.   [3] Casualties from enemy action. Deaths exclude servicemen who died in accidents or from disease.   [4] Includes died while captured.

Source of tables 606 and 607: U.S. Dept. of Defense, Office of the Secretary, *Selected Manpower Statistics*, annual, and unpublished data.

No. 608. COAST GUARD PERSONNEL ON ACTIVE DUTY: 1960 TO 1977

[As of June 30 except, beginning 1977, as of Sept. 30]

YEAR	Total	Officers	Cadets	Enlisted	YEAR	Total	Officers	Cadets	Enlisted
1960	30,616	4,020	405	26,191	1974	36,730	5,731	1,087	29,912
1965	31,776	4,476	440	26,860	1975	36,788	5,630	1,177	29,981
1970	37,689	5,512	653	31,524	1976	37,812	5,795	1,057	30,960
1973	36,645	5,798	1,119	29,728	1977	38,158	5,889	972	31,297

Source: 1960 and 1965, U.S. Dept. of the Treasury, *Annual Report of the Secretary of the Treasury on the State of the Finances;* thereafter, U.S. Dept. of Transportation, *Annual Report of the Secretary of Transportation.*

No. 609. MILITARY PERSONNEL ON ACTIVE DUTY, BY LOCATION: 1965 TO 1977

[In thousands. As of Dec. 31. Shore-based includes Navy personnel temporarily on shore]

YEAR	TOTAL			UNITED STATES [2]			FOREIGN COUNTRIES			
	Total	Shore-based	Naval afloat [1]	Total	Shore-based	Naval afloat [1]	Total	Percent of total	Shore-based	Naval afloat [1]
1965	2,857	2,517	340	2,004	1,789	215	853	29.9	728	125
1966	3,334	2,894	440	2,223	1,929	294	1,111	33.3	965	146
1967	3,398	2,984	414	2,218	1,950	268	1,180	34.7	1,034	146
1968	3,408	3,105	303	2,237	2,037	200	1,171	34.4	1,068	103
1969	3,298	3,008	290	2,209	2,012	197	1,088	33.0	996	92
1970	2,874	2,627	247	1,987	1,807	180	888	30.9	820	67
1971	2,519	2,290	229	1,846	1,677	169	673	26.7	613	60
1972	2,348	2,109	239	1,752	1,618	134	596	25.4	491	105
1973	2,202	1,982	220	1,709	1,544	165	493	22.4	438	55
1974	2,140	1,929	211	1,660	1,508	152	480	22.4	421	59
1975	2,084	1,884	200	1,630	1,480	150	454	21.8	405	50
1976	2,072	1,858	214	1,623	1,466	157	449	21.7	392	57
1977	2,060	1,842	218	1,600	1,435	165	460	22.3	407	53

[1] Navy and Marine Corps. [2] Includes outlying areas.

No. 610. U.S. MILITARY PERSONNEL ABROAD OR AFLOAT, BY COUNTRY: 1970 TO 1977

[In thousands. As of June 30 except, beginning 1977, as of Sept. 30. Data are unclassified approximations]

COUNTRY	1970	1973	1974	1975	1976	1977	COUNTRY	1970	1973	1974	1975	1976	1977
Troops outside U.S.[1]	1,071	585	519	517	464	483	Asia and Pacific	683	199	169	156	123	130
Europe [2]	304	319	297	314	297	313	Japan [5]	81	57	58	48	45	46
Germany, F.R [3]	214	229	208	220	209	224	Philippines	24	16	17	15	15	14
Greece	3	5	4	4	3	3	South Korea	54	42	38	42	40	40
Iceland	3	3	3	3	3	3	Taiwan	9	9	5	4	2	1
Italy	10	10	12	12	12	10	Thailand	41	42	31	20	1	(Z)
Spain	0	0	10	0	0	0	S. Vietnam	415	(Z)	(Z)	–	–	–
Turkey	7	7	6	7	4	5	Afloat	60	33	20	28	19	29
Un. Kingdom	21	21	21	21	20	21	U.S. outlying areas [6]	32	33	26	25	24	23
Other countries[4]	8	6	6	7	6	6	Troop dependents [7]	347	341	347	305	334	322
Afloat	28	28	26	30	29	32	Europe	206	222	225	239	225	215
							Western Pacific	91	75	79	82	72	63

– Represents zero. Z Fewer than 500. [1] Includes troops in countries not shown. [2] Western Europe and related areas. [3] Federal Republic. [4] Primarily Belgium, Morocco, Netherlands, and Portugal/Azores. [5] Includes Okinawa. [6] Primarily Guam, Panama Canal Zone, Puerto Rico, and Midway Islands. [7] Dependent data as of Sept. 30.

No. 611. MILITARY PERSONNEL—DESERTION AND ABSENT-WITHOUT-AUTHORITY RATES: 1951 TO 1977

[Rate per 1,000 average end-of-month strength. For years ending June 30 except as noted]

YEAR AND PERIOD	DESERTION RATE [1]					ABSENT-WITHOUT-AUTHORITY [2] RATE				
	Total	Army	Marine Corps	Navy	Air Force	Total	Army	Marine Corps	Navy	Air Force
Korean conflict: 1951	(NA)	14.3	10.1	3.1	(NA)	(NA)	(NA)	(NA)	28.4	(NA)
1952	(NA)	22.0	19.7	6.2	(NA)	(NA)	181.0	(NA)	31.9	62.0
1953	(NA)	22.3	29.6	8.7	(NA)	(NA)	158.0	(NA)	36.3	58.4
1954	(NA)	15.7	(NA)	6.9	(NA)	(NA)	115.3	(NA)	37.6	38.3
Vietnam: 1965	(NA)	15.7	18.8	6.7	.4	(NA)	60.1	(NA)	26.8	2.9
1966	(NA)	14.7	16.1	9.1	.4	(NA)	57.2	(NA)	29.2	3.3
1967	13.2	21.4	26.8	9.7	.4	46.8	78.0	(NA)	22.4	3.6
1968	15.7	29.1	30.7	8.5	.4	38.5	89.7	(NA)	14.4	3.6
1969	21.1	42.4	40.2	7.3	.6	46.9	112.3	(NA)	13.5	4.4
1970	25.8	52.3	59.6	9.9	.8	66.3	132.5	174.3	17.5	5.9
1971	33.9	73.5	56.2	11.1	1.5	84.0	176.9	166.6	19.0	9.4
1972	27.5	62.0	65.3	8.8	2.8	74.9	166.4	170.0	18.3	17.2
1973	24.6	52.1	63.2	13.6	2.2	77.0	159.2	234.3	21.7	16.1
1974	25.0	41.1	89.2	21.2	2.4	79.5	129.9	287.5	53.8	17.3
1975	22.4	26.0	105.0	22.4	1.9	73.7	95.4	300.9	73.0	13.0
Post Vietnam: 1976	20.0	17.7	69.2	24.8	1.2	67.8	70.3	201.8	77.5	7.8
1977	19.2	16.7	47.0	31.6	.6	48.6	47.0	103.5	76.9	3.8

NA Not available. [1] Absent without authority more than 30 days. [2] For 30 days or less.

Source of tables 609–611: U.S. Dept. of Defense, Office of the Secretary, *Selected Manpower Statistics*, annual, and unpublished data.

No. 612. Discharges of Enlisted Personnel, by Type: 1960 to 1977

[For years ending June 30 except, beginning 1977, ending Sept. 30]

YEAR	Total discharges	Honorable [1][2]	General [1][3]	Undesirable [1][4]	Bad conduct [5][6]	Dishonorable [5][7]	PERCENT OF TOTAL		
							Honorable	General	Other
1960	607,359	560,264	26,415	16,227	4,149	304	92.2	4.3	3.4
1965	718,898	678,100	25,477	13,178	2,088	55	94.3	3.5	2.1
1966	740,044	706,761	20,883	10,544	1,784	72	95.5	2.8	1.7
1967	689,617	657,684	19,562	9,741	2,565	65	95.4	2.8	1.8
1968	869,877	836,990	18,260	11,707	2,886	34	96.2	2.1	1.7
1969	1,016,470	980,376	19,853	12,392	3,662	187	96.4	2.0	1.6
1970	1,136,140	1,081,556	29,334	20,911	3,964	375	95.2	2.6	2.2
1971	1,018,822	944,365	40,256	29,139	4,737	325	92.7	4.0	3.4
1972	890,557	804,470	45,219	36,345	4,167	356	90.3	5.1	4.6
1973	719,789	646,720	40,680	29,049	2,906	434	89.8	5.7	4.5
1974	688,179	609,580	45,960	29,336	2,988	315	88.6	6.7	4.7
1975	682,952	603,058	48,999	27,015	3,587	293	88.3	7.2	4.4
1976	630,194	542,674	53,135	30,721	3,435	229	86.1	8.4	5.5
1977	611,749	523,416	48,815	36,740	2,463	315	85.6	8.0	6.5

[1] Administrative discharge.   [2] Based on proper military behavior and proficient performance of duty; honest and faithful service.   [3] Discharge under honorable conditions; satisfactory service; military record not sufficiently meritorious for honorable discharge.   [4] Unsatisfactory service (misconduct, security or resignation/request for discharge).   [5] Punitive, resulting from trial by court-martial.   [6] Usually punishment for repeated convictions of minor offenses.   [7] Granted after conviction of offenses usually recognized by civil law as felonies, or of military offenses requiring severe punishment.

Source: U.S. Dept. of Defense, Office of the Secretary, unpublished data.

No. 613. Classification of Selective Service Registrants: 1965 to 1975

[In thousands of registrants 18 to 26 years old. As of Dec. 31. Includes Puerto Rico and outlying areas. Inductions halted effective July 1, 1973. No classification actions taken since Jan. 1, 1976. See also *Historical Statistics, Colonial Times to 1970*, series Y 917-926]

CLASSIFICATION STATUS OF REGISTRANTS 18 TO 26 YEARS OLD	1965	1968	1969	1970	1971	1972	1973	1974	1975
Total registrants	17,967	20,829	21,785	22,705	16,098	15,012	14,840	9,511	4,064
Available for military service	1,485	1,446	1,468	2,596	3,601	514	784	916	849
Holding classification [1]	(X)	(X)	(X)	(X)	140	6,929	8,167	6,874	2,832
Completed service	2,399	2,946	3,308	3,801	2,825	2,010	1,082	125	17
Fulfilling military obligation	3,163	3,881	3,876	3,494	2,343	2,212	2,340	976	298
Conscientious objectors	13	20	25	38	50	20	13	8	5
Deferred	5,829	6,797	6,971	6,151	2,400	393	47	40	4
Exempted	104	126	129	130	97	36	35	27	7
Disqualified for military service	4,640	5,189	5,583	5,959	3,630	2,888	2,372	545	52
Unclassified	334	424	425	535	1,012	10	(Z)	–	–

– Represents zero.   X Not applicable.   Z Fewer than 500.
[1] Includes registrants not currently subject to processing for induction or alternate service.
Source: U.S. Selective Service System, National Headquarters, unpublished data.

No. 614. Selective Service Act Violations—Disposition of Defendants: 1960 to 1977

[For years ending June 30 except, beginning 1977, ending Sept. 30. Covers defendants charged in U.S. district courts with violations of Selective Training and Service Act of 1940 and Universal Military Training and Service Act of 1948. Excludes Canal Zone, Guam, and Virgin Islands all years, and District of Columbia through 1973. See also *Historical Statistics, Colonial Times to 1970*, series Y 927-942]

DISPOSITION	1960	1965	1968	1969	1970	1971	1972	1973	1974	1975	1976	1977 [1]
All defendants	239	341	1,192	1,744	2,833	2,973	4,906	3,495	2,094	1,376	696	2,175
Not convicted	73	99	408	844	1,806	1,937	3,264	2,518	1,295	1,147	573	2,146
Dismissed	65	88	353	747	1,570	1,701	2,937	2,338	1,196	1,133	562	2,142
Acquitted	8	11	55	97	236	236	327	180	99	14	11	4
Convicted	166	242	784	900	1,027	1,036	1,642	977	799	229	123	29
Percent of total	69.5	71.0	65.8	51.6	36.3	34.8	33.5	28.0	38.2	16.6	17.7	1.3
By plea of guilty or nolo	131	197	520	511	570	590	934	631	643	171	105	22
By court or jury	35	45	264	389	457	446	708	346	156	58	18	7
Imprisonment	126	189	580	544	450	377	458	260	155	20	12	4
Avg. sentence...mo.	21.5	21.0	37.3	36.3	33.5	29.1	22.0	17.5	14.5	(B)	(B)	(B)
Probation	37	52	202	350	572	650	1,178	707	637	203	108	22
Fine and other	3	1	2	6	5	9	6	10	7	6	3	3

B Base less than 25.
[1] Includes dismissal of violations (occurring between Aug. 4, 1964, and Mar. 28, 1973) under the Presidential Proclamation of Pardon for Violations of the Selective Service Act (Executive Order 11967) issued Jan. 21, 1977.
Source: Administrative Office of the U.S. Courts, *Annual Report of the Director*.

No. 615. Enlisted Military Personnel Procurement: 1960 to 1977

[In thousands. For years ending June 30 except, beginning 1977, ending Sept. 30]

BRANCH OF SERVICE	1960	1965	1967	1968	1969	1970	1971	1972	1973	1974	1975	1976	1977
Total	591	702	1,035	1,124	1,064	872	804	632	689	625	667	601	594
Inductions	90	103	299	340	265	207	156	27	36	(Z)	(Z)	(Z)	(Z)
First enlistments	324	318	483	513	554	423	396	396	428	391	415	397	381
Percent—													
Other than White [1]	6.8	10.8	8.8	10.2	11.4	11.6	13.7	15.8	18.5	20.9	18.1	17.3	20.6
High school graduates	60.8	66.7	79.1	73.8	72.2	71.2	66.8	65.8	64.1	65.7	71.7	72.3	68.9
Reenlistments	152	247	202	203	208	213	221	184	202	212	228	183	175
Reserves to active duty	25	34	50	69	37	28	31	25	23	22	24	21	38
Army [2]	260	294	576	637	539	472	414	239	279	264	283	250	258
First enlistments	102	102	190	199	201	177	158	160	179	185	191	186	173
Reenlistments	64	89	84	85	78	93	98	49	62	77	91	62	71
Navy [2]	148	170	188	195	212	164	146	153	171	156	166	144	143
First enlistments	91	94	101	123	147	100	79	89	99	84	90	85	90
Reenlistments	37	44	44	39	37	41	41	43	53	53	54	40	30
Marine Corps [2]	50	46	85	111	107	87	71	67	67	62	71	64	59
First enlistments	41	34	71	93	84	68	59	56	52	47	56	52	45
Reenlistments	9	11	9	9	10	8	10	11	14	15	15	12	11
Air Force [2]	133	192	186	182	206	148	173	173	172	143	147	143	134
First enlistments	90	88	121	98	122	78	101	91	98	75	78	74	73
Reenlistments	43	104	65	69	83	70	72	81	74	67	68	69	60

Z Fewer than 500.   [1] Black only, beginning 1974.
[2] For some years, totals include reserves to active duty and inductions, not shown separately.

No. 616. Reserve Officers Training Corps—Enrollment: 1960 to 1977

[In thousands. For May, or end of school year. Jr. ROTC refers to enrollment in high schools, academies, junior colleges, and National Defense Cadet Corps schools; after 1965, includes Jr. ROTC in all service branches]

ITEM	1960	1965	1968	1969	1970	1971	1972	1973	1974	1975	1976	1977
Senior ROTC	230	231	196	175	123	92	73	60	56	61	66	76
Junior ROTC	87	88	111	122	126	124	121	140	155	164	158	152

Source of tables 615 and 616: U.S. Dept. of Defense, Office of the Secretary, *Selected Manpower Statistics*, annual

No. 617. Average Annual Military Pay Rates: 1965 to 1978

[As of June 30 except, beginning 1977, as of Sept. 30. Covers all branches of the military service. Based on weighted averages. See also *Historical Statistics, Colonial Times to 1970*, series D 921–926 and Y 898–903]

ITEM	BASIC PAY ($1,000)							BASIC PAY PLUS ALLOWANCES [2] ($1,000)						
	1965	1970	1974	1975	1976	1977	1978 [1]	1965	1970	1974	1975	1976	1977	1978 [1]
Current dollars:														
All personnel	2.9	4.2	6.9	7.3	7.6	8.0	8.4	4.4	5.8	9.0	9.5	9.9	10.3	10.9
Officers	7.1	9.9	14.0	14.8	15.7	16.5	17.5	9.8	13.0	17.8	18.8	20.0	21.0	22.2
Enlisted	2.3	3.4	5.7	6.0	6.3	6.6	7.0	3.6	4.7	7.5	8.0	8.3	8.7	9.2
Constant dollars: [3]														
All personnel	5.5	5.3	6.1	5.7	5.7	5.6	5.5	8.4	7.3	7.5	7.5	7.4	7.3	7.2
Officers	13.6	12.5	12.3	11.6	11.7	11.6	11.5	18.7	16.4	14.8	14.8	14.9	14.8	14.7
Enlisted	4.4	4.3	5.0	4.7	4.7	4.6	4.6	6.9	5.9	6.2	6.2	6.2	6.1	6.1

[1] Estimate.   [2] Not strictly comparable, year to year, due to changes in allowances.   [3] Constant 1972 dollars.
Source: U.S. Office of Management and Budget, unpublished data.

No. 618. Monthly Rates of Military Basic Pay: 1970 to 1977

PAY GRADE AND YEARS OF SERVICE [1]	Jan. 1970	Oct. 1975	Oct. 1976	Oct. 1977	PAY GRADE AND YEARS OF SERVICE [1]	Jan. 1970	Oct. 1975	Oct. 1976	Oct. 1977
Recruit [2]—E-1 (0–2)	$125	$361	$374	$398	2d Lt.—O-1 (0–2)	418	666	690	733
Private—E-2 (0–2)	138	403	417	443	1st Lt.—O-2 (2–3)	577	838	869	922
Pvt. 1st class—E-3 (0–2)	168	418	433	460	Captain—O-3 (6–8)	840	1,219	1,263	1,341
Corporal—E-4 (2–3)	290	459	476	505	Major—O-4 (14–16)	1,063	1,544	1,599	1,698
Sergeant—E-5 (4–6)	371	539	558	593	Lt. Col.—O-5 (20–22)	1,317	1,913	1,982	2,104
Staff Sgt.—E-6 (14–16)	508	737	764	811	Colonel—O-6 (26–30)	1,671	2,426	2,514	2,669
Sgt. 1st class—E-7 (18–20)	597	867	899	954	Brig. Gen'l.—O-7 (26–30)	1,902	2,762	2,862	3,038
Master Sgt.—E-8 (20–22)	686	996	1,032	1,095	Maj. Gen'l.—O-8 (26–30)	2,188	[3]3,150	3,291	3,494
Warr. Offcr.—W-1 (10–12)	577	838	869	922	Lt. Gen'l.—O-9 (26–30)	2,427	[3]3,150	[3]3,300	3,877
Chief Warr.—W-4 (26–30)	1,055	1,531	1,586	1,684	General—O-10 (26–30)	2,750	[3]3,150	[3]3,300	[3]3,958

[1] Longevity pay step of typical military member.   [2] Under 4 months of service.   [3] Statutory limitation.
Source: U.S. Dept. of Defense, Office of the Comptroller, *The Economics of Defense Spending, A Look at the Realities*, July 1972; beginning 1973, White House Exec. Orders 11692, 11883, 11941, and 12010.

No. 619. MILITARY RESERVE PERSONNEL NOT ON ACTIVE DUTY: 1960 TO 1977

[In thousands. As of June 30 except, beginning 1977, as of Sept. 30. Reservists serve in one of three categories— ready, standby, or retired. The ready reserve includes selected reservists who are intended to assist active forces in a war and the individual ready reserve who, in a major war, would be used to fill out active and reserve units and later would be a source of combat replacements. The standby reserve cannot be called to active duty unless the Congress gives its explicit approval. The retired reserve represents a low potential for mobilization]

RESERVE STATUS AND BRANCH OF SERVICE	1960	1965	1970	1971	1972	1973	1974	1975	1976	1977
Total reserves	4,147	2,577	3,639	3,856	3,711	3,413	3,065	2,656	2,419	2,249
Ready reserve	2,418	1,802	2,574	2,571	2,495	2,148	1,856	1,529	1,308	1,183
Standby reserve	1,585	472	492	669	558	576	496	412	340	274
Retired reserve	144	303	573	616	658	689	713	715	771	792
Army	2,625	1,515	2,221	2,436	2,392	2,140	1,878	1,631	1,389	1,243
Army National Guard	408	386	410	403	388	387	412	403	377	365
Army Reserve	2,217	1,129	1,811	2,033	2,004	1,753	1,466	1,228	1,012	878
Navy	930	602	808	838	750	725	640	521	489	476
Naval Reserve	672	468	574	568	504	504	457	387	373	367
Marine Corps Reserve	258	134	234	270	246	221	183	134	116	109
Air Force	592	460	610	582	569	548	547	504	541	530
Air National Guard	71	76	90	86	89	90	94	96	91	92
Air Force Reserve	521	384	520	496	480	458	453	408	450	438

No. 620. MILITARY RESERVE COSTS: 1975 AND 1978

[In millions of dollars. 1975 as of June 30; 1978 as of Sept. 30]

TYPE OF COST	RESERVE COMPONENT COSTS, 1975					RESERVE COMPONENT COSTS, 1978				
	Total	Army [1]	Air Force [1]	Navy	Marine Corps	Total	Army [1]	Air Force [1]	Navy	Marine Corps
Total [2]	5,100	2,669	1,416	666	135	7,260	3,638	2,155	824	181
Personnel	1,760	1,140	344	211	65	2,036	1,315	422	217	82
Operations & maintenance	2,093	887	949	245	12	2,731	1,161	1,234	319	17
Construction	158	92	46	18	2	178	101	55	22	–
Procurement	546	478	49	6	13	1,491	985	422	49	35
Active-duty support	329	72	28	186	43	362	76	22	217	47

– Represents zero. 　[1] Includes National Guard. 　[2] Includes retirement costs.

Source of tables 619 and 620: U.S. Dept. of Defense, Office of the Secretary, *Selected Manpower Statistics*, annual, and unpublished data.

No. 621. NATIONAL GUARD—SUMMARY: 1950 TO 1977

[As of June 30 except, beginning 1977, as of Sept. 30. Includes Puerto Rico]

ITEM	1950	1955	1960	1965	1970	1973	1974	1975	1976	1977
Army National Guard: Units	4,863	5,205	4,386	3,999	3,052	3,261	3,303	3,245	3,299	3,297
Personnel [1] _____1,000_	353	378	408	386	410	387	412	403	376	364
Funds obligated [2]____mil. dol_	205	239	400	464	752	1,052	1,191	1,322	1,808	1,514
Value of equipment____mil. dol_	1,264	(NA)	1,500	1,478	1,600	3,100	3,100	4,100	4,600	4,100
Air National Guard: Units	516	572	546	728	958	1,041	1,046	1,106	1,018	1,020
Personnel [1] _____1,000_	45	61	71	76	90	90	95	96	91	91
Funds obligated [2]____mil. dol_	(NA)	164	233	321	467	636	751	890	1,223	1,044
Value of equipment____mil. dol_	(NA)	(NA)	(NA)	(NA)	(NA)	(NA)	3,300	3,100	4,000	3,970

NA Not available. 　[1] Officers and enlisted men; excludes Guardsmen on active duty except those undergoing basic training. 　[2] Federal funds; includes personnel, operations, maintenance, and military construction.

No. 622. NATIONAL GUARD—ARMY AND AIR, STATES AND OTHER AREAS: 1977

[Personnel in thousands; funds in millions of dollars. As of Sept. 30. Regarding personnel and funds, see footnotes 1 and 2, table 621]

STATE OR OTHER AREA	Personnel	Funds	STATE	Personnel	Funds	STATE	Personnel	Funds	STATE OR OTHER AREA	Personnel	Funds
Total	455.3	2,558.5	Ill	9.9	35.4	Nebr	4.1	15.8	S. Dak	4.1	17.3
Ala	19.5	53.4	Ind	13.0	37.6	Nev	1.9	11.3	Tenn	14.1	42.1
Alaska	2.7	18.1	Iowa	7.8	29.9	N.H	2.8	10.4	Tex	20.3	57.5
Ariz	5.7	28.7	Kans	6.8	30.6	N.J	13.9	47.3	Utah	5.3	17.6
Ark	10.5	33.8	Ky	6.0	21.2	N. Mex	4.1	17.2	Vt	3.5	13.2
Calif	23.7	88.5	La	9.3	27.0	N.Y	21.7	71.4	Va	7.1	25.0
Colo	3.9	18.0	Maine	3.9	15.6	N.C	11.9	30.0	Wash	6.8	27.8
Conn	6.9	21.6	Md	7.9	24.8	N. Dak	3.4	13.2	W. Va	4.5	17.8
Del	3.3	12.5	Mass	13.0	42.2	Ohio	17.4	58.9	Wis	9.7	30.8
D.C	3.6	15.1	Mich	10.9	53.1	Okla	10.0	30.2	Wyo	2.1	10.2
Fla	10.0	29.8	Minn	10.7	43.3	Oreg	7.3	26.5	Undistrib	–	980.4
Ga	13.3	40.0	Miss	12.6	47.5	Pa	18.0	55.4			
Hawaii	4.9	23.0	Mo	10.8	37.4	R.I	3.7	14.3	P.R	9.3	23.6
Idaho	3.5	19.1	Mont	2.9	15.9	S.C	10.8	28.7	V.I	.5	1.2

– Represents zero.

Source of tables 621 and 622: U.S. National Guard Bureau, *Annual Review of the Chief, National Guard Bureau,* and unpublished data.

No. 623. NUMBER OF LIVING VETERANS, BY PERIOD OF SERVICE: 1950 TO 1977

[Estimates in thousands. As of June 30 except, beginning 1977, as of Sept. 30. See also *Historical Statistics, Colonial Times to 1970*, series Y 957-970]

PERIOD OF SERVICE	1950	1955	1960	1965	1970	1974	1975	1976	1977
All veterans [1]	19,023	21,802	23,811	25,259	27,647	29,265	29,459	29,607	[2] 29,844
Percent of male population, 18 yr. and over [3]	37.0	35.2	42.1	42.1	42.7	42.3	41.8	41.3	40.9
War veterans [1]	19,023	21,798	22,431	22,107	24,522	26,166	26,367	26,522	26,497
Spanish-American War [4]	118	72	36	15	9	1	1	1	(Z)
World War I	3,518	3,150	2,673	2,121	1,536	1,075	963	867	748
World War II [5]	15,386	15,405	15,202	14,969	14,458	13,759	13,586	13,385	13,104
Korean conflict [6]	(X)	3,999	5,482	5,718	5,867	5,958	5,973	5,954	5,919
With service in World War II	(X)	828	962	1,150	1,262	1,255	1,250	1,238	1,218
No service in World War II	(X)	3,171	4,520	4,568	4,605	4,703	4,723	4,716	4,701
Vietnam [7]	(X)	(X)	(X)	456	4,173	7,088	7,597	8,070	8,474
With service in Korean conflict	(X)	(X)	(X)	22	255	460	503	503	530
In Korea and World War II	(X)	(X)	(X)	17	156	197	202	204	203
No service in Korean conflict	(X)	(X)	(X)	434	3,918	6,628	7,094	7,553	7,944
Between Korea and Vietnam only [8]	(X)	4	1,380	3,152	3,125	3,099	3,092	3,085	3,075

X Not applicable.   Z Fewer than 500.   [1] Detail indicates number of living veterans who served in each war; to avoid duplication, veterans counted once in total even though service in more than one war.
[2] Includes post-Vietnam era Veterans, not shown separately.   [3] Source: U.S. Bureau of the Census.   [4] Includes war with Spain, Philippine Insurrection, and Boxer Rebellion.   [5] Sept. 16, 1940, to July 25, 1947.
[6] June 27, 1950, to Jan. 31, 1955.   [7] Aug. 5, 1964, to May 7, 1975.   [8] Feb. 1, 1955, to Aug. 4, 1964.

No. 624. LIVING VETERANS, BY AGE AND PERIOD OF SERVICE: 1977

[In thousands, except percent. As of Sept. 30. Estimated. See *Historical Statistics, Colonial Times to 1970*, series Y 943-956, for all veterans]

AGE IN 1977	Total veterans	Percent [1]	World War I	World War II [2]	Korea, total [2][3]	Without service in WW II	Post-Korea peacetime [4]	Vietnam, total [3][5]	Without service in Korea	Post-Vietnam era [6]
18 years and over	29,844	40.9	748	13,104	5,919	4,701	3,075	8,474	7,944	272
18–19 years	96	2.2	–	–	–	–	–	7	7	89
20–24 years	1,078	10.7	–	–	–	–	–	919	919	159
25–29 years	2,822	31.9	–	–	–	–	–	2,802	2,802	20
30–34 years	3,491	45.7	–	–	–	–	285	3,202	3,202	4
35–39 years	2,499	41.4	–	–	10	10	1,611	881	878	(Z)
40–44 years	2,661	48.7	–	(Z)	1,478	1,478	1,076	221	107	–
45–49 years	3,625	64.6	–	648	3,036	2,866	92	208	19	–
50–59 years	8,914	81.1	–	8,562	1,149	332	11	193	9	–
60 years and over	4,658	33.5	748	3,894	246	15	–	41	–	–
Average age years	46.5	(X)	82.1	57.2	47.8	45.8	38.7	31.1	29.8	21.2

– Represents zero.   X Not applicable.   Z Fewer than 500.
[1] Of total males in each age group. Based on U.S. Bureau of the Census, *Current Population Reports*, series P-25, No. 704.   [2] Includes 1,218,000 veterans who served in both World War II and Korean conflict.   [3] Includes 530,000 veterans who served in both Korean conflict and Vietnam era; 203,000 of these also served in World War II.   [4] Feb. 1, 1955, to Aug. 4, 1964, only.   [5] Aug. 5, 1964, to May 7, 1975.   [6] Service after May 7, 1975, only.

No. 625. DISABLED VETERANS RECEIVING COMPENSATION: 1950 TO 1977

[In thousands. As of June 30 except, beginning 1977, as of Sept. 30. Totally disabled refers to veterans who have received a 100-percent disability rating]

MILITARY SERVICE	1950	1960	1965	1970	1973	1974	1975	1976	1977
Disabled, all wars [1]	1,990	2,027	1,993	2,092	2,204	2,211	2,220	2,232	2,247
Regular establishment	53	103	161	185	192	193	194	196	207
World War I	293	173	120	85	65	59	55	50	43
World War II	1,643	1,544	1,486	1,416	1,351	1,330	1,309	1,288	1,261
Korea	(X)	206	225	239	241	240	240	240	239
Vietnam	(X)	(X)	(X)	167	354	389	423	458	497
Totally disabled, all wars [1]	115	110	110	124	126	125	· 123	123	123
Regular establishment	9	11	16	16	16	16	16	16	17
World War I	31	23	16	11	8	7	6	6	5
World War II	74	61	63	63	61	60	58	57	56
Korea	(X)	15	15	16	17	16	16	16	16
Vietnam	(X)	(X)	(X)	18	24	25	26	28	29

X Not applicable.   [1] Includes Spanish-American War and Mexican Border service, not shown separately.
Source of tables 623-625: Except as noted, U.S. Veterans Administration, *Annual Report of Administrator of Veterans Affairs*, and unpublished data.

No. 626. Vietnam Era Veterans—Length of Service: 1965 to 1977

PERIOD OR YEAR	Service-men dis-charged (1,000)	VETERANS (1,000) WITH LENGTH OF SERVICE—				Median months of service	VETERANS WITH SERVICE IN VIETNAM	
		Less than 24 mo.	24–35 mo.	36–47 mo.	48 mo. or more		Number (1,000)	Percent of total
1965–1977, prel	8,982	2,341	2,354	1,853	2,434	34.0	2,894	32.2
1965–1966	1,046	181	271	256	338	39.3	56	5.4
1967	576	104	146	129	197	39.5	144	25.0
1968	788	143	324	114	207	33.3	321	40.7
1969	972	240	308	226	198	33.6	485	49.9
1970	1,043	314	270	256	203	33.2	560	53.6
1971	995	340	249	204	202	31.6	504	50.7
1972	870	346	213	131	180	29.0	300	34.5
1973	614	181	121	107	205	36.5	179	29.1
1974	567	154	103	109	201	38.9	135	23.8
1975	543	170	100	99	174	36.2	86	15.8
1976	432	104	103	93	132	36.1	78	18.1
1977, prel	536	64	146	129	197	40.4	46	8.5

No. 627. Vietnam Era Veterans—Educational Attainment at Time of Separation: 1965 to 1977

[In thousands of persons, except as indicated. As of June 30 except, beginning 1977, as of Sept. 30. Total of Vietnam era veterans separated from Armed Forces between Aug. 4, 1964, and Sept. 30, 1977, differs from total of veterans in civil life on Sept. 30, 1977, because 123,000 died after returning to civil life]

EDUCATIONAL ATTAINMENT	1965–1977, total	1965	1970	1971	1972	1973	1974	1975	1976	1977, prel.
Net separations	8,597.0	456.0	1,012.0	975.0	850.0	594.0	547.0	523.0	412.0	503.0
Years of school completed:										
8 years or less	256.4	28.3	34.8	29.5	23.0	13.4	11.9	10.3	5.5	4.4
Some high school	6,527.2	352.8	740.1	694.8	594.1	432.3	414.3	413.0	349.2	424.5
Percent	75.9	77.4	73.2	71.3	69.9	72.7	75.7	78.9	84.8	84.4
1–3 years	16.8	22.3	16.3	15.7	15.5	14.4	16.6	19.1	18.3	15.6
4 years	59.1	55.1	56.9	55.6	54.4	58.3	59.1	59.8	66.5	68.8
Some college	1,813.4	74.9	237.1	250.7	232.9	148.3	120.8	99.7	57.3	74.1
Percent	21.1	16.4	23.4	25.7	27.4	25.0	22.1	19.1	13.9	14.7
1–3 years	13.0	10.0	14.9	15.9	14.8	13.6	11.1	10.7	10.9	11.2
4 years or more	8.1	6.4	8.5	9.8	12.6	11.4	11.0	8.4	3.0	3.5
Median years completed	12.5	12.4	12.5	12.6	12.6	12.6	12.5	12.5	12.5	12.5

Source of tables 626 and 627: U.S. Veterans Administration, *Data on Vietnam Era Veterans*, annual.

No. 628. Unemployed Men, by Age, Veteran Status, and Race: 1973 to 1977

[Annual averages. Rate is percent of male civilian labor force in each category]

YEAR AND RACE	UNEMPLOYED MEN (1,000)					UNEMPLOYMENT RATE FOR MEN				
	Total, 16 yr. old and over	20–34 years old				Total, 16 yr. old and over	20–34 years old			
		Total, U.S.	Non-veter-ans	Post-Korea[1] veter-ans	Viet-nam[2] veter-ans		Total, U.S.	Non veter-ans	Post-Korea[1] veter-ans	Viet-nam[2] veter-ans
Total: 1973	2,240	938	632	40	266	4.1	4.7	4.9	2.5	5.0
1974	2,668	1,159	813	35	310	4.8	5.6	6.0	2.9	5.3
1975	4,385	2,022	1,405	52	565	7.9	9.5	9.8	5.7	9.3
1976	3,968	1,810	1,277	32	501	7.0	8.2	8.5	5.0	7.9
1977	3,588	1,684	1,193	19	472	6.2	7.4	7.5	4.9	7.3
White: 1973	1,818	749	488	36	224	3.7	4.2	4.3	2.4	4.6
1974	2,146	920	641	29	249	4.3	5.0	5.4	2.5	4.7
1975	3,597	1,643	1,124	47	474	7.2	8.7	9.0	5.5	8.6
1976	3,223	1,449	1,013	29	407	6.4	7.4	7.6	4.8	7.1
1977	2,843	1,308	919	17	372	5.5	6.5	6.6	4.6	6.4
Black and other: 1973	423	189	143	4	42	7.6	8.4	8.6	4.6	8.4
1974	521	239	172	7	61	9.1	10.3	10.1	9.4	11.3
1975	787	379	281	5	91	13.7	16.0	16.0	10.4	15.9
1976	745	361	264	3	94	12.7	14.6	14.5	8.3	15.1
1977	745	376	274	2	100	12.4	14.6	14.3	13.3	15.8

[1] Service during Feb. 1, 1955 to Aug. 4, 1964.　[2] Service during Aug. 5, 1964 to May 7, 1975.
Source: U.S. Bureau of Labor Statistics, unpublished data.

No. 629. Living Veterans—States and Other Areas: 1970 to 1977

[Estimates in thousands. As of June 30 except, beginning 1977, as of Sept. 30. These estimates were developed from benchmark veteran population statistics for the States as of June 30, 1970, based on 1970 Census of Population data on veterans place of residence, extended to Sept. 30, 1977, on the basis of (1) 1965-1970 veteran interstate migration statistics from the 1970 census; (2) Bureau of the Census provisional estimates of 1970-1971 net civilian migration of States, *Current Population Reports*, series P-25, No. 468, Oct. 5, 1971; and mobility of U.S. population, 1970-1971, *Current Population Reports*, series P-20, No. 235, April 1972. They are independent of, and not directly comparable with, estimates for June 30, 1970, through June 30, 1974, previously published by the VA]

STATE OR OTHER AREA	Total veterans, 1970	Total veterans, 1975 [1]	Total veterans, 1977 [1]	WAR VETERANS, 1977							
							Korean conflict		Vietnam [4]		
				Total [1]	World War I	World War II [2]	Total [2,3]	No service in World War II	Total [3]	No service in Korean conflict	Service between Korea and Vietnam only [5]	Post-Vietnam era [6]
Total	27,647	29,459	29,844	26,497	748	13,104	5,919	4,701	8,474	7,944	3,075	272
U.S	27,450	29,236	29,612	26,304	740	13,054	5,869	4,659	8,378	7,851	3,040	268
Ala	408	420	422	374	10	179	92	74	119	111	45	3
Alaska	30	41	41	35	(Z)	14	8	6	15	15	5	1
Ariz	234	290	308	274	9	132	64	47	91	86	31	3
Ark	216	258	264	237	9	123	48	37	72	68	25	2
Calif	2,992	3,238	3,315	2,949	71	1,456	743	530	961	892	335	31
Colo	290	351	362	318	8	144	75	55	118	111	40	4
Conn	436	461	465	414	10	208	97	79	125	117	47	4
Del	75	79	79	68	1	34	13	10	25	23	10	1
D.C	120	105	104	93	3	47	28	22	24	21	10	1
Fla	957	1,153	1,230	1,110	51	591	255	173	319	295	111	9
Ga	478	618	630	553	11	241	136	109	203	192	70	7
Hawaii	68	93	93	80	1	31	21	17	33	31	12	1
Idaho	97	100	102	91	3	44	19	16	3⌣	28	11	(Z)
Ill	1,576	1,559	1,560	1,387	38	694	312	268	413	387	159	14
Ind	703	721	727	640	18	301	135	114	219	207	79	8
Iowa	377	372	373	329	13	160	63	55	107	101	41	3
Kans	298	309	310	276	11	140	54	42	88	83	31	3
Ky	386	407	411	365	11	181	80	66	114	107	43	3
La	431	447	452	402	11	196	95	79	124	116	46	4
Maine	140	145	148	131	5	67	26	21	40	38	16	1
Md	523	610	623	552	11	263	138	104	185	174	65	6
Mass	824	868	870	773	23	385	170	137	244	228	89	8
Mich	1,175	1,190	1,191	1,050	27	500	221	191	351	332	129	12
Minn	522	547	553	486	16	223	92	77	179	170	61	6
Miss	218	244	244	218	7	113	50	41	61	57	24	2
Mo	646	693	703	626	21	310	137	113	195	182	71	6
Mont	97	101	101	89	3	44	17	14	30	28	11	1
Nebr	184	197	199	175	6	83	35	30	59	56	22	2
Nev	66	92	93	82	1	42	19	14	27	25	10	1
N.H	103	123	126	111	3	54	23	19	37	35	14	1
N.J	1,060	1,096	1,105	986	26	514	226	186	280	260	111	8
N. Mex	138	135	136	120	3	58	28	22	39	37	15	1
N.Y	2,553	2,519	2,514	2,258	64	1,201	510	438	596	555	236	20
N.C	537	614	619	546	13	257	119	99	187	177	68	5
N. Dak	72	64	62	54	2	28	9	8	18	16	7	1
Ohio	1,536	1,498	1,497	1,324	34	661	266	224	431	405	157	16
Okla	337	392	402	358	12	175	77	58	120	113	41	3
Oreg	312	361	373	332	11	167	66	48	112	106	37	4
Pa	1,785	1,756	1,754	1,566	43	827	317	259	467	437	173	15
R.I	131	151	152	135	3	70	29	22	42	40	16	1
S.C	263	322	328	290	6	130	66	54	106	100	35	3
S. Dak	86	79	77	68	3	35	15	13	19	17	9	(Z)
Tenn	484	529	537	476	13	224	107	90	158	149	56	5
Tex	1,370	1,594	1,628	1,445	36	713	320	245	480	451	168	15
Utah	132	143	146	127	3	55	26	19	53	50	17	2
Vt	57	63	64	55	2	26	10	8	20	19	8	1
Va	546	645	655	580	13	281	141	97	202	189	70	5
Wash	476	582	600	530	13	254	121	82	192	181	63	7
W. Va	262	235	234	211	8	112	41	35	60	56	22	1
Wis	590	577	583	514	19	245	101	86	175	164	63	6
Wyo	53	48	47	41	1	21	8	6	13	13	5	1
P.R	157	158	161	134	3	45	49	42	46	44	24	3
Other areas	40	65	71	59	5	5	1	(Z)	50	49	11	1

Z Less than 500.   [1] Includes living Spanish American War veterans, 421 in 1977.   [2] See footnote 2, table 624.
[3] See footnote 3, table 624.   [4] See footnote 7, table 623.   [5] See footnote 8, table 623.
[6] Service after May 7, 1975, only.

Source: U.S. Veterans Administration, *Annual Report of Administrator of Veterans Affairs*.

No. 630. Veterans Benefits—Expenditures From Appropriated Funds, by War: Total and 1940 to 1977

[In millions of dollars. For years ending **June 30** except, beginning **1977**, ending **Sept. 30**. Refers to expenditures of VA and predecessor agencies. See also *Historical Statistics, Colonial Times to 1970*, series Y 971–983]

PERIOD OR YEAR	Total, all wars	Mexican War and Indian Wars	Civil War	Span- ish– Amer- ican War	World War I	World War II	Korean con- flict	Post- Korean con- flict	Viet- nam [1]	Peace- time
Total __	[2] 277,929	191	8,574	5,728	59,407	129,895	23,499	8,017	34,355	8,144
To 1939_____	[2] 18,914	147	8,356	1,537	8,557	(X)	(X)	(X)	(X)	198
1940–1944_____	3,016	14	102	663	1,840	281	(X)	(X)	(X)	116
1945–1949_____	27,139	11	49	798	2,783	23,317	(X)	(X)	(X)	181
1950–1954_____	25,564	7	28	821	4,638	18,878	823	(X)	(X)	369
1955–1959_____	24,723	5	15	696	6,835	10,956	5,674	(X)	(X)	542
1960–1964_____	28,466	2	13	528	9,365	13,421	4,142	(X)	(X)	995
1965–1969_____	34,673	(Z)	6	334	9,646	16,732	3,656	1,569	1,331	1,399
1970–1974_____	57,154	3	5	229	9,584	23,474	4,707	3,496	13,676	1,980
1970_____	8,905	(Z)	1	54	1,944	3,881	898	481	1,328	318
1971_____	10,240	(Z)	1	51	1,917	4,317	865	648	2,083	358
1972_____	11,314	1	1	45	1,980	4,699	905	728	2,571	384
1973_____	12,817	1	1	40	1,908	5,138	988	791	3,535	415
1974_____	13,878	1	1	39	1,835	5,439	1,051	848	4,159	505
1975_____	16,419	1	(Z)	38	1,897	6,196	1,219	1,089	5,392	587
1976_____	18,798	1	(Z)	39	1,861	7,024	1,378	1,246	6,509	740
1976, TQ [3]___	4,197	(Z)	(Z)	9	458	1,811	354	113	1,260	192
1977_____	18,866	(Z)	(Z)	36	1,943	7,805	1,546	504	6,187	845

X Not applicable.   Z Less than $500,000.   [1] Service between Aug. 5, 1964, and May 7, 1975.
[2] Includes $70 million for the Revolutionary War and $49 million for the War of 1812.
[3] Transition quarter, July–Sept.

No. 631. Veterans Compensation and Pension Benefits—Number on Rolls and Average Payment, by Period of Service: 1960 to 1977

[As of **June 30** except, beginning **1977**, as of **Sept. 30**. Living refers to veterans receiving compensation for disability incurred or aggravated while on active duty and war veterans receiving pension and benefits for nonservice connected disabilities. Deceased refers to deceased veterans whose dependents were receiving pensions and compensation benefits. See also *Historical Statistics, Colonial Times to 1970*, series Y 998–999]

PERIOD OF SERVICE AND VETERAN STATUS	VETERANS ON ROLLS (1,000)						AVERAGE PAYMENT (annual basis) [1]				
	1960	1965	1970	1975	1976	1977	1965	1970	1975	1976	1977
Total_____	3,960	4,511	4,722	4,855	4,867	4,911	$909	$1,108	$1,496	$1,629	$1,768
Living veterans_____	3,009	3,217	3,181	3,227	3,236	3,279	925	1,159	1,631	1,787	1,958
Service connected_____	2,027	1,993	2,092	2,220	2,232	2,247	848	1,136	1,699	1,900	2,076
Nonservice connected____	982	1,224	1,089	1,006	1,003	1,031	1,050	1,204	1,481	1,535	1,702
Deceased veterans_____	951	1,294	1,541	1,628	1,631	1,633	869	1,000	1,227	1,316	1,387
Service connected_____	391	365	372	369	368	365	1,284	1,732	2,375	2,663	2,907
Nonservice connected____	560	929	1,169	1,259	1,263	1,268	706	768	890	924	950
Prior to World War I_____	116	78	48	27	24	21	868	1,012	1,139	1,170	1,212
Living_____	33	14	4	1	1	1	1,197	1,618	1,896	1,943	2,339
Deceased_____	83	64	43	26	23	20	796	950	1,098	1,135	1,133
World War I_____	1,491	1,673	1,405	1,046	974	904	937	1,030	1,159	1,192	1,324
Living_____	1,026	1,104	771	430	375	321	1,058	1,228	1,527	1,604	1,986
Deceased_____	465	568	634	616	599	583	703	789	902	934	960
World War II_____	1,964	2,243	2,463	2,612	2,639	2,679	867	1,080	1,478	1,606	1,719
Living_____	1,633	1,698	1,787	1,880	1,898	1,931	842	1,100	1,566	1,710	1,840
Deceased_____	331	545	676	732	741	748	943	1,024	1,252	1,339	1,407
Korean conflict [2]_____	253	309	366	428	441	457	1,008	1,266	1,722	1,882	2,014
Living_____	213	240	265	292	299	310	966	1,284	1,865	2,057	2,216
Deceased_____	40	69	101	136	142	147	1,157	1,218	1,414	1,514	1,587
Regular establishment_____	136	209	234	242	244	255	991	1,244	2,066	2,315	2,514
Living_____	103	161	185	194	196	207	783	1,022	1,886	2,119	2,310
Deceased_____	32	48	48	48	48	48	1,692	2,095	2,784	3,115	3,389
Vietnam era [3]_____	(X)	(X)	207	500	545	596	(X)	1,556	1,843	2,028	2,178
Living_____	(X)	(X)	169	430	467	509	(X)	1,411	1,749	1,933	2,090
Deceased_____	(X)	(X)	38	70	78	87	(X)	2,197	2,418	2,600	2,696

X Not applicable.   [1] Averages calculated by multiplying average monthly payment by 12.
[2] Service during period June 27, 1950, to Jan. 31, 1955.   [3] Service between Aug. 5, 1964, and May 7, 1975.

Source of tables 630 and 631: U.S. Veterans Administration, *Annual Report of Administrator of Veterans Affairs*, and unpublished data.

No. 632. Veterans Benefits—Expenditures, by Program: 1966 to 1977

[In millions of dollars. For years ending June 30 except, beginning 1977, ending Sept. 30. For 1966 and 1968 on a non-accrued expenditure basis; thereafter on an accrued expenditure basis. New data series begins with 1966 to reflect current programs and methods of presentation. See table 633 for earlier data]

PROGRAM	1966	1968	1970	1972	1973	1974	1975	1976	1977
Total [1]	7,417	8,495	10,201	12,723	13,974	15,282	18,003	20,168	20,285
Compensation and pensions [2]	4,380	4,596	5,330	6,126	6,519	6,735	7,551	8,242	9,038
Educational assistance and readjustment	54	477	1,047	1,978	2,745	3,269	4,529	5,543	3,891
Education and training [3]	[4] 31	[4] 444	991	1,889	2,613	3,121	4,328	5,214	3,769
Post-Korean veterans education [5]	(X)	407	939	1,812	2,513	3,006	4,165	5,029	3,567
Dependents education assistance	31	37	52	77	100	116	163	186	202
Vocational rehabilitation [3]	17	23	42	65	72	68	73	85	101
Automobiles, etc., for disabled veterans	1	3	6	11	7	5	17	19	13
Housing for paraplegics	5	4	8	7	13	11	14	14	14
Advanced payments [6]	(Z)	(Z)	1	6	40	63	97	210	−6
Medical services and administ. expenses [7]	1,407	1,621	2,009	2,651	2,966	3,290	3,919	3,997	5,073
Hospital and domiciliary construction [3] [8]	83	50	75	110	95	109	136	224	262
Insurance and indemnities [9]	876	1,090	1,181	1,234	965	1,128	1,345	1,249	1,028
Loan guaranty revolving fund [3]	378	328	249	322	373	449	423	484	521
Direct loans [3]	92	208	180	113	104	82	84	89	97
Miscellaneous expenditures [10]	146	124	131	189	206	221	17	340	374

X Not applicable. Z Less than $500,000.
[1] Excludes expenditures from personal funds of patients. Includes expenditures from VA Revolving Supply Fund and insurance trust funds. [2] Includes expenditures for statutory burial awards, special clothing allowance, mortgage life insurance, invalid lifts, headstones and markers, and other expenses; therefore, total for 1970–1974 differs from that shown in table 633 which excludes these items.
[3] Except as noted, comparable with data presented in table 633.
[4] Not comparable with 1965–1969 data in table 633. [5] Program initiated June 1966. Includes Post-Vietnam veterans. [6] Includes changes in receivables. [7] Not comparable with data in table 633. 1966–1970 includes National Cancer Institute expenditures (transfer to Veterans Administration).
[8] Includes construction grants for State extended care facilities. 1975 and later years include expenditures for health manpower training facilities. [9] Comparable with sum of insurance and servicemen's indemnities, and transfers to insurance trust funds in table 633. [10] Not comparable with data in table 633.
Source: U.S. Veterans Administration, *Annual Report of Administrator of Veterans Affairs.*

No. 633. Veterans Benefits—Expenditures: 1940 to 1974

[In millions of dollars, except as indicated. For years ending June 30. Refers to expenditures of Veterans Administration and includes trust, deposit, and working funds. This form of presentation discontinued by VA; for current data, see table 632. See also *Historical Statistics, Colonial Times to 1970*, series Y 984–997]

PROGRAM	1940–1944	1945–1949	1950–1954	1955–1959	1960–1964	1965–1969	1970–1974	1973	1974
Total [1]	3,236	21,864	31,045	28,204	33,063	39,746	63,046	13,906	14,977
Compensation and pensions	2,230	7,392	10,978	14,500	18,251	22,108	30,067	6,427	6,615
Percent of total	68.9	33.8	35.4	51.4	55.2	55.6	47.7	46.2	44.2
Readjustment benefits:									
Education and training [2]	−	7,680	7,076	3,481	910	1,463	10,206	2,613	3,121
Vocational rehabilitation [3]	1	943	646	158	61	103	306	72	68
Loan guaranty	−	185	338	330	1,182	1,722	1,661	373	449
Direct loans	−	−	359	791	1,335	842	626	104	82
Miscellaneous benefit payments [4]	93	165	272	310	506	700	876	207	200
Medical, hospital, and domiciliary services [5]	420	1,825	3,225	3,930	5,105	6,670	11,615	2,715	2,834
Hospital and domiciliary facilities [6]	30	345	508	174	296	318	474	95	109
Insurance and servicemen's indemnities [7]	356	1,023	6,433	3,664	4,540	4,841	5,635	954	1,124
Administration	107	1,406	1,210	869	880	977	1,580	346	375
Expenditures from appropriated funds	3,016	27,138	25,565	24,720	28,468	34,674	55,477	12,333	13,408
Transfers to insurance trust funds	149	3,587	882	158	45	43	52	11	4

− Represents zero.
[1] Excludes transfers from appropriations to insurance trust funds from which the actual payments are made, and expenditures from VA Revolving Supply Fund. Includes expenditures from personal funds of patients.
[2] Includes education and training allowances for veterans and servicemen, and educational assistance for wives, widows, sons, and daughters of deceased or totally disabled veterans.
[3] Includes subsistence allowances, tuition, supplies, and equipment for training of disabled veterans.
[4] Includes payments and allowances for various programs such as unemployment and self employment allowances, automobiles and other conveyances for disabled veterans, etc.
[5] Estimated; includes expenditures for hospital and domiciliary care, outpatient medical and dental treatment, medical research, and grants to Republic of Philippines for medical care and treatment of veterans.
[6] Comprises construction and related costs, and amounts transferred to Dept. of Army, Corps of Engineers, for construction of hospitals.
[7] Includes direct payments to beneficiaries from insurance appropriation, servicemen's indemnities, and benefits and dividends paid from insurance trust funds. Also includes some noncash transactions (e.g., interest credited to dividends left on deposit).
Source: U.S. Veterans Administration, *Annual Report of Administrator of Veterans Affairs.*

No. 634. VETERANS BENEFITS—SELECTED FEDERAL EXPENDITURES, STATES AND OTHER AREAS: 1976 AND 1977

[In millions of dollars. State data are estimates for years ending June 30 except, beginning 1977, ending Sept. 30]

STATE OR OTHER AREA	1976					1977				
	Total expenditures [1]	Compensation and pensions [2]	Education and training [3]	Medical services and administrative costs	Insurance and indemnities	Total expenditures [1]	Compensation and pensions [2]	Education and training [3]	Medical services and administrative costs	Insurance and indemnities
Total	19,032	8,074	5,214	4,491	865.1	19,144	8,875	3,769	5,075	985.0
U.S.	18,644	7,840	5,119	4,441	857.9	18,756	8,618	3,707	5,016	977.7
Ala.	383	159	124	84	10.9	384	175	97	94	12.4
Alaska	21	6	8	6	1.2	23	7	4	10	1.4
Ariz.	273	102	97	57	10.9	284	117	78	63	12.7
Ark.	260	135	48	65	6.3	286	151	50	72	7.2
Calif.	2,127	664	812	452	108.7	1,958	729	549	515	123.7
Colo.	265	92	97	56	13.0	255	102	71	62	14.8
Conn.	198	79	51	51	16.2	195	86	33	57	18.5
Del.	50	17	16	14	2.5	53	19	10	18	2.9
D.C.	381	35	49	257	6.6	379	38	11	292	7.3
Fla.	896	436	232	174	44.1	951	503	187	198	51.4
Ga.	472	216	136	97	17.2	493	242	112	107	19.6
Hawaii	75	20	42	7	5.2	60	22	22	8	6.1
Idaho	76	30	17	10	3.0	81	33	13	13	3.4
Ill.	732	251	205	227	43.7	715	266	136	252	49.4
Ind.	325	148	87	67	13.6	320	161	63	75	15.8
Iowa	213	90	47	61	10.9	223	96	41	69	12.4
Kans.	195	80	45	59	9.1	203	86	36	66	10.4
Ky.	303	157	73	59	8.6	314	172	57	65	9.8
La.	310	158	73	68	10.9	320	172	59	75	12.4
Maine	116	56	29	24	3.9	117	62	21	26	4.4
Md.	304	123	108	53	17.5	273	135	55	59	19.9
Mass.	569	270	127	140	26.5	580	294	86	158	30.0
Mich.	607	265	200	109	26.7	562	283	120	122	30.3
Minn.	341	143	80	90	18.8	353	151	67	100	21.3
Miss.	227	124	44	50	6.2	243	137	36	57	7.1
Mo.	449	182	134	111	17.0	439	196	88	127	19.4
Mont.	66	28	15	14	3.2	68	31	12	16	3.7
Nebr.	135	52	35	40	6.2	141	57	31	44	7.0
Nev.	59	22	19	14	2.7	59	26	14	15	3.2
N.H.	80	37	23	13	3.6	82	42	17	15	4.2
N.J.	428	209	99	81	34.9	427	225	63	93	39.7
N. Mex.	127	62	30	27	4.9	133	70	27	29	5.6
N.Y.	1,341	575	279	381	75.2	1,359	626	167	433	84.8
N.C.	503	223	164	95	14.3	511	252	133	105	16.4
N. Dak.	50	18	16	12	2.4	50	20	13	14	2.7
Ohio	729	342	176	162	37.6	729	367	125	182	42.6
Okla.	303	155	82	50	9.7	320	175	71	55	11.1
Oreg.	217	93	60	51	9.9	223	102	47	60	11.3
Pa.	854	419	161	217	47.5	859	452	100	244	53.9
R.I.	105	44	34	22	3.9	98	47	20	25	4.5
S.C.	262	113	92	44	8.5	270	124	80	49	9.8
S. Dak.	84	29	19	32	2.5	93	32	18	37	2.8
Tenn.	416	181	110	109	11.8	432	200	94	120	13.4
Tex.	1,203	549	336	256	45.3	1,260	623	268	293	52.1
Utah	101	31	35	28	4.4	100	34	27	31	5.0
Vt.	43	19	7	13	1.8	49	21	4	16	2.1
Va.	441	207	108	95	25.2	465	229	89	104	28.8
Wash.	363	147	113	80	18.2	374	161	91	90	20.9
W.Va.	188	93	35	51	5.0	204	101	32	61	5.7
Wis.	335	141	83	89	18.1	338	152	57	102	20.6
Wyo.	43	13	7	17	1.6	48	14	5	19	1.8
P.R.	226	115	60	48	1.2	223	130	34	57	1.6
Outlying areas	4	2	2	–	.3	4	3	1	–	.4
Foreign countries	158	117	33	2	5.7	161	124	27	2	5.3

 − Represents zero.   [1] Includes expenditures not shown separately. 1976 excludes $1,136 million and 1977 excludes $1,141 million shown in table 632 for expenditures not distributed by States.   [2] Excludes statutory burial awards and other expenses which are included in table 632.   [3] Educational assistance for wives and widows, sons and daughters of deceased or totally disabled veterans, and post-Korean conflict veterans. Excludes benefits paid to disabled veterans training under the Vocational Rehabilitation program.

Source: U.S. Veterans Administration, *Annual Report of Administrator of Veterans Affairs.*

No. 635. Veterans Administration Health Care Summary: 1970 to 1977

[For years ending June 30 except, beginning 1977, ending Sept. 30]

ITEM	1970	1975	1976	1977	ITEM	1970	1975	1976	1977
Facilities operating:					Inpatients treated____1,000__	879	1,220	1,287	1,323
Hospitals_____	166	171	171	171	VA facilities_____1,000__	821	1,143	1,208	1,239
Domiciliaries_____	16	18	18	16	Other facilities_____1,000__	58	77	79	84
Outpatient clinics_____	202	213	215	219	Avg. daily inpatients				
Nursing home units_____	63	85	88	89	1,000__	117	114	113	111
Restoration centers_____	6	–	–	–	VA facilities_____1,000__	102	96	94	91
Employment [1]_____1,000__	139	173	181	186	Other facilities_____1,000__	15	18	19	20
Operating costs____mil. dol__	1,775	3,461	3,975	4,525	Outpatient medical visits_____mil__	7.3	14.6	16.4	17.0
Medical care_____	1,694	3,328	3,839	4,376	VA staff_____mil__	6.1	12.6	14.2	14.6
Research in health care____	60	95	102	110	Fee-basis_____mil__	1.2	2.0	2.2	2.4
Other_____	21	37	35	39	Outpatient dental care:				
Prescriptions dispensed_____mil__	(NA)	28.0	32.0	32.0	VA staff exams_____1,000__	131.5	85.8	93.2	108.0
Laboratory procedures_mil__	(NA)	147	167	182	VA cases completed 1,000__	81.1	83.7	94.1	100.3
Radiology examinations_____mil__	(NA)	5.4	5.9	5.8	Fee-basis authorized 1,000__	54.7	130.9	122.0	107.2

– Represents zero.   NA Not available.   [1] Net full-time equivalent.

Source: U.S. Veterans Administration, *Annual Report of Administrator of Veterans Affairs.*

No. 636. Patients Receiving Health Care Authorized by Veterans Administration, and Operating Expenses of VA Hospitals: 1960 to 1977

[In thousands, except as indicated. For years ending June 30 except, beginning 1977, ending Sept. 30. See *Historical Statistics, Colonial Times to 1970,* series Y 1010–1027, for related data]

ITEM	1960	1965	1970	1972	1973	1974	1975	1976	1977
Patients admitted to hospitals [1]___	539.2	628.0	711.3	793.5	932.5	991.5	1,069.8	1,136.3	1,171.0
Psychiatric hospitals [2]_____	64.9	63.5	102.9	134.7	147.2	154.7	162.1	170.0	169.0
General hospitals [3]_____	474.3	564.5	608.4	658.9	785.3	836.8	907.7	966.3	1,002.0
VA hospitals_____	511.3	602.1	687.0	765.8	905.5	964.5	1,036.1	1,102.3	1,133.4
Non-VA and State hospitals_____	27.9	25.9	24.3	27.8	26.9	27.0	33.7	34.0	37.2
Patients receiving hospital care (average daily number) [1]_____	114.4	111.8	87.5	83.2	84.6	83.5	82.3	80.5	76.7
Psychiatric hospitals [2]_____	63.0	56.8	40.2	31.9	28.5	27.3	26.7	24.8	23.5
General hospitals [3]_____	51.4	55.0	47.2	51.3	56.1	56.2	55.6	55.7	53.2
VA hospitals_____	111.4	109.2	85.5	81.0	82.5	81.5	80.0	78.3	75.3
Veterans receiving care (average daily number):									
Domiciliary_____	26.3	23.6	18.7	17.3	16.3	15.6	15.0	14.7	14.3
Veterans Administration_____	16.9	14.4	12.0	11.4	10.3	9.7	9.2	9.1	9.0
State_____	9.4	9.1	6.7	6.0	6.0	5.9	5.8	5.6	5.3
Reimbursement by Federal Govt. per patient treated [4]_	(NA)	$451	$654	$664	$638	$768	$788	$794	$1,226
Nursing bed care_____	(NA)	.3	9.8	12.8	14.3	15.3	17.0	17.9	19.3
VA hospitals_____	(NA)	.2	3.8	5.4	6.1	6.4	6.7	7.0	7.2
State homes_____	(NA)	.2	2.4	3.3	3.7	4.0	4.1	4.2	4.6
Community nursing homes___	(NA)	(Z)	3.6	4.0	4.6	4.9	6.2	6.7	7.5
Reimbursement by Federal Govt. per patient treated: [4]									
State [4]_____	(NA)	$287	$1,024	$1,013	$996	$1,138	$1,151	$1,117	$2,569
Community [4]_____	(NA)	$258	$1,339	$1,627	$1,769	$1,794	$2,128	$2,413	$2,796
Visits by veterans for outpatient medical care_____	3,611	5,987	7,312	9,527	10,858	12,266	14,630	16,410	17,045
VA hospitals:									
Average operating beds_____	120	119	103	96	98	96	95	94	92
Psychiatric hospitals_____	55	56	42	28	28	26	22	21	19
General hospitals_____	65	63	61	68	70	70	73	73	73
Operating expenses____mil. dol__	763	946	1,279	1,569	1,745	1,937	2,212	2,519	2,840
Per diem cost_____	$18	$24	$38	$56	$58	$65	$76	$90	$104
Cost per patient treated_____	(NA)	(NA)	$1,524	$1,851	$1,769	$1,855	$1,984	$2,135	$2,346
Operating beds in VA nursing units and domiciliaries_____	17	17	18	19	18	18	17	17	18

NA Not available.   Z Fewer than 50.

[1] Includes VA beneficiaries cared for in Army, Navy, other Federal, and State and civil (contract) hospitals; includes nonveterans. Beginning 1970, includes data for State Home hospitals.   [2] 1960, neurological patients included in "Psychiatric"; thereafter, in "General."   [3] Includes tuberculosis patients.   [4] Excludes costs for VA nursing bed care and VA domiciliary care.

Source: U.S. Veterans Administration, *Annual Report of Administrator of Veterans Affairs,* and unpublished data.

No. 637. VA HOSPITALS—COMPENSATION AND PENSION STATUS OF PATIENTS REMAINING AND PATIENTS DISCHARGED: 1977

[In thousands. For year ending Sept. 30]

COMPENSATION AND PENSION STATUS	All patients [1]	General medical, surgical	Psychoses	Other psychiatric	COMPENSATION AND PENSION STATUS	All patients [1]	General medical, surgical	Psychoses	Other psychiatric
PATIENTS REMAINING					**PATIENTS DISCHARGED**				
Total	75.1	33.9	20.0	12.9	Total	942.1	656.7	75.1	139.9
With disability—					With disability—				
Service-connected	12.7	3.0	7.3	1.4	Service-connected	92.3	45.3	28.3	12.1
Non-service connected	62.1	30.8	12.6	11.5	Non-service connected	836.2	606.5	45.6	126.9
On VA pension rolls	19.9	9.5	5.1	2.9	On VA pension rolls	205.7	159.5	10.8	20.1
With service-connected compensable disability [2]	9.3	5.5	1.2	1.6	With service-connected compensable disability [2]	140.5	109.8	4.8	16.6
With no pension or compensation	32.9	15.8	6.3	7.0	With no pension or compensation	489.9	337.3	29.9	90.2
Non-veterans	.3	.1	.1	(Z)	Non-veterans	7.4	4.6	1.2	.9
					All Other	6.2	.3	(Z)	(Z)

Z Fewer than 50.   [1] Includes patients not shown separately.
[2] Compensable disability which does not require medical care.

No. 638. VETERANS ASSISTANCE TO PERSONS IN VOCATIONAL PROGRAMS: 1968 TO 1977

[In thousands. For years ending June 30 except, beginning 1977, ending Sept. 30. Represents persons in training during year]

PROGRAM	1968	1970	1971	1972	1973	1974	1975	1976	1977
Post-Korea Education Assistance [1]	687	1,211	1,585	1,864	2,126	2,359	2,692	2,822	1,938
Institutions of higher education	414	677	915	1,061	1,177	1,333	1,693	1,924	1,380
Resident schools other than college	} 255	} 417	231	359	333	383	420	450	314
Correspondence schools			293	282	427	431	387	302	132
On-the-job training	19	117	146	162	189	212	192	146	112
Children's Educational Assistance	40.5	45.4	50.7	55.0	57.7	63.0	71.4	80.7	88.2
Institutions of higher education	36.0	40.7	45.4	49.3	52.0	57.1	64.7	73.0	80.3
Schools other than college	4.4	4.6	5.3	5.7	5.6	5.5	6.3	7.2	7.4
Special restorative training	(Z)	.1	.1	.1	.1	.1	.1	.1	.1
On-the-job training	–	–	–	–	.1	.3	.4	.4	.5
Spouses, Widows/Widowers Educational Assistance Program [2]	(X)	7.1	8.8	9.6	10.5	13.0	16.5	19.1	19.5
Institutions of higher education	(X)	3.9	5.3	6.5	7.6	9.4	12.2	14.5	15.5
Schools other than college	(X)	3.2	3.5	3.1	2.9	3.5	4.3	4.5	4.0
On-the-job training [3]	(X)	(Z)	(Z)	(Z)	(Z)	.1	.1	.1	(Z)
Vocational Rehabilitation Program for Disabled Veterans	14.4	24.5	30.5	31.6	29.5	27.0	[4] 24.8	[5] 29.4	33.2
Institutions of higher education	6.5	14.9	20.1	22.1	21.0	19.5	18.5	21.0	25.0
Schools other than college	6.9	7.9	8.6	7.6	6.6	5.7	4.9	6.0	7.0
On-the-job training	1.1	1.4	1.6	1.7	1.7	1.6	1.3	1.0	1.0
Institutional on-farm	.1	.2	.2	.2	.2	.2	.2	.2	.2

– Represents zero.   X Not applicable.   Z Less than 50.   [1] Includes Post-Vietnam veterans.
[2] Program initiated December 1968.   [3] Includes special restorative training.
[4] Estimated.   [5] Total includes 1,200 with type of training unknown.

Source of tables 637 and 638: U.S. Veterans Administration, *Annual Report of Administrator of Veterans Affairs.*

No. 639. VETERANS LIFE INSURANCE: 1945 TO 1977

ITEM	1945	1950	1955	1960	1965	1970	1974	1975	1976	1977
Policies in force, number___mil__	13	7	6	6	6	5	5	5	5	5
Coverage_____bil. dol__	98.4	45.3	42.7	42.0	39.4	37.5	[1] 35.3	[1] 34.7	[1] 34.0	[1] 33.0
Benefit payments, total__mil. dol__	1,262	879	366	491	522	718	822	867	928	995
Death payments [2]_____mil. dol__	1,227	204	114	162	219	301	361	359	374	382
Dividends_____mil. dol__	8	625	196	262	222	274	335	376	403	444
Other_____mil. dol__	27	50	56	67	81	143	126	132	151	169
Suppl. payments [3]_____mil. dol__	240	325	319	307	238	216	188	183	184	178

[1] Excludes dividend additions.   [2] Face amounts of claims incurred during year, including amounts left to be paid under supplementary contracts.   [3] Total payments from accumulated insurance policy proceeds left to be paid in monthly installments, and withdrawals of dividend accumulations.

Source: U.S. Veterans Administration. Data in American Council of Life Insurance, New York, N.Y., *Life Insurance Fact Book*, annual.

No. 640. Veterans Life Insurance, by Type: 1960 to 1977

TYPE OF INSURANCE	1960	1965	1970	1973	1974	1975	1976	1977
NUMBER OF POLICIES IN FORCE (DEC. 31)								
National Service Life Insurance [1]____1,000__	5,244	4,833	4,388	4,136	4,060	3,981	3,893	3,808
Veterans Special Life Insurance [2]____1,000__	661	639	617	602	593	587	582	576
U.S. Government Life Insurance [3]___1,000__	315	247	191	161	150	141	132	123
Service-Disabled Vet. Insurance [4]___1,000__	45	62	105	150	158	164	171	177
Veterans Reopened Insurance [5]_____1,000__	(X)	74	193	187	184	181	179	176
INSURANCE IN FORCE (DEC. 31)								
National Service Life Insurance [1]__mil. dol__	34,380	31,614	28,959	27,266	26,746	26,195	25,564	24,953
Veterans Special Life Insurance [2]__mil. dol__	5,868	5,615	5,405	5,270	5,191	5,137	5,089	5,034
U.S. Govt. Life Insurance [3]_____mil. dol__	1,388	1,079	823	682	635	593	551	510
Service-Disabled Vet. Insurance [4]_mil. dol__	394	534	936	1,357	1,424	1,481	1,541	1,601
Veterans Reopened Insurance [5]___mil. dol__	(X)	528	1,350	1,302	1,283	1,264	1,245	1,225
INSURANCE DISBURSEMENTS								
National Service Life Insurance [1]_mil. dol__	[6] 661.6	645.8	793.1	819.1	849.7	891.8	946.9	992.7
Veterans Special Life Insurance [2]_mil. dol__	[6] 6.8	11.5	22.1	25.9	28.4	30.6	34.7	38.9
U.S. Govt. Life Insurance [3]_____mil. dol__	[6] 117.7	93.5	96.6	93.1	92.7	86.7	87.2	87.2
Service-Disabled Vet. Insurance [4]_mil. dol__	[6] 5.5	9.5	17.8	22.6	24.2	24.4	25.6	26.7
Veterans Reopened Insurance [5]___mil. dol__	(X)	6.9	11.1	14.5	16.8	16.8	18.6	20.0

X Not applicable. [1] Issued to veterans of World War II. [2] Issued to veterans of Korean conflict separated from service without a service-connected disability. Program initiated April 1951. [3] Issued to veterans of World War I. [4] Issued to World War II, Korea, and Vietnam veterans separated after April 24, 1951, with a service connected disability. Program initiated April 1951. [5] Issued to World War II and Korea conflict veterans with service-connected or serious nonservice-connected disabilities. Program initiated May 1965.
[6] For year ending June 30.

Source: U.S. Veterans Administration, *Government Life Insurance Programs for Veterans and Members of the Services*, annual.

No. 641. National Service Life Insurance Policies in Force, by Plan: 1950 to 1977

[As of **June 30** except, beginning **1977**, as of **Dec. 31.** Covers veterans of World War II and later conflicts]

PLAN	NUMBER (1,000)						COVERAGE (mil. dol.)					
	1950	1960	1965	1970	1975	1977	1950	1960	1965	1970	1975	1977
All plans_____	5,620	5,283	4,863	4,388	3,981	3,808	35,809	34,650	31,802	28,959	26,195	24,953
5-year term_____	3,782	3,092	2,681	2,000	1,516	1,383	27,592	23,759	20,606	15,441	11,782	10,754
Life: Modified [1]_____	(X)	(X)	3	264	411	421	(X)	(X)	21	2,097	3,194	3,224
Ordinary_____	310	463	506	612	642	638	1,659	2,814	3,169	3,925	4,138	4,110
20-payment____	909	970	948	901	856	836	3,761	4,287	4,277	4,139	3,966	3,883
30-payment____	319	410	408	395	377	366	1,592	2,218	2,243	2,183	2,088	2,033
Endowment:												
20-year_____	141	142	119	38	26	23	474	530	453	206	165	153
At age 60_____	68	93	89	80	66	58	349	509	493	445	376	335
At age 65_____	33	59	61	61	56	53	177	353	374	377	355	337
Extended_____	58	54	48	37	31	30	205	180	166	146	131	124

X Not applicable. [1] Modified life, a new form of NSLI, became available May 1, 1965.
Source: U.S. Veterans Administration; through 1965, *Annual Report of Administrator of Veterans Affairs;* thereafter, *Government Life Insurance Programs*, annual, and unpublished data.

No. 642. Veterans Guaranteed and Insured Loans: 1960 to 1977

[For years ending **June 30** except, beginning **1977**, ending **Sept. 30.** Total loans include types of loans not shown separately]

ITEM	1960	1965	1970	1973	1974	1975	1976	1977
Number of loans_____1,000__	178.8	176.3	186.2	365.1	311.3	290.2	326.7	382.6
Home_____1,000__	177.2	176.0	186.2	359.3	306.2	288.2	325.0	379.8
Amount of loans_____mil. dol__	2,376	2,765	3,683	8,358	7,710	8,091	9,951	13,136
Home_____mil. dol__	2,369	2,763	3,682	8,306	7,664	8,072	9,930	13,099
Guaranty and insurance_____mil. dol__	1,216	1,247	1,971	4,051	3,540	3,702	4,878	5,951
Home_____mil. dol__	1,215	1,246	1,971	4,036	3,526	3,696	4,872	5,933

Source: U.S. Veterans Administration, *Annual Report of Administrator of Veterans Affairs.*

Figure 13.1
Trends in the Labor Force: 1967 to 1978
(See table 645)

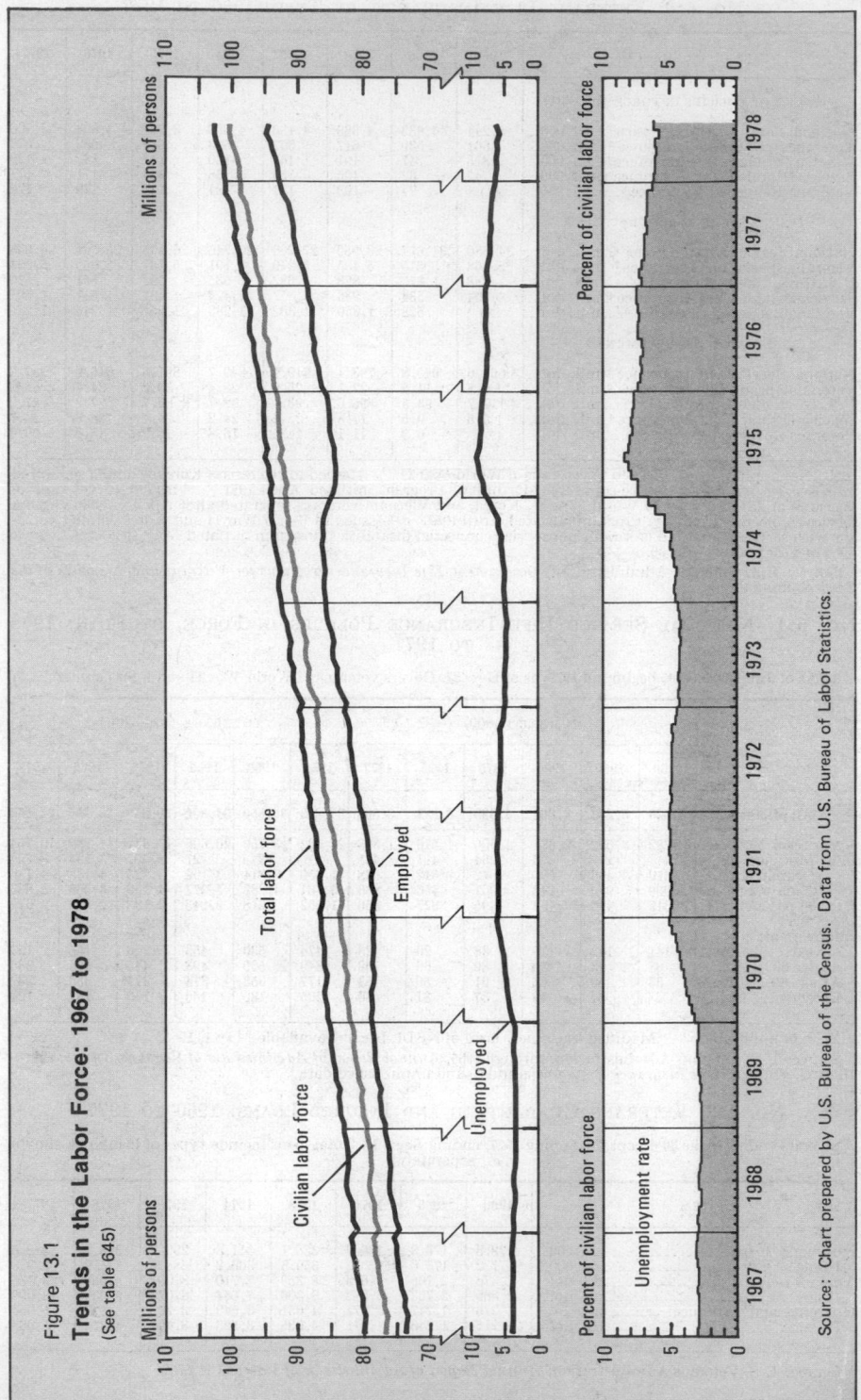

Source: Chart prepared by U.S. Bureau of the Census. Data from U.S. Bureau of Labor Statistics.

Section 13

Labor Force, Employment, and Earnings

This section presents statistics on the characteristics of the labor force; its distribution by occupation and industry affiliation; and the supply of, demand for, and conditions of labor.

The chief sources of these data are the census of population and the Current Population Survey conducted by the Bureau of the Census; and the monthly *Employment and Earnings*, the *Monthly Labor Review*, the annual *Handbook of Labor Statistics*, and the periodic *Special Labor Force Reports*, all published by the Bureau of Labor Statistics (BLS).

Types of data.—Most of the statistics in this section are obtained by two methods: household interviews or questionnaires and reports of establishment payroll records. Each method provides data which the other cannot suitably supply. Population characteristics, for example, are readily obtainable only from the household survey, while detailed industrial classification can be readily derived only from establishment records.

Data based on households are obtained from the decennial population census and from a monthly sample survey of the population. The decennial census provides detailed labor force information nationally and for each State, metropolitan area, county, and city, and for other areas. The data include characteristics (e.g. age, sex, race) of persons employed and unemployed. The Current Population Survey (CPS) is conducted during the week including the 12th of the month and provides current comprehensive data on the labor force (see text, p. 1). This household approach provides information on the work status of the population without duplication since each person is classified as employed, unemployed, or not in the labor force. Employed persons holding more than one job are counted only once, according to the job at which they work the most hours during the survey week.

Monthly data from CPS are published by the Bureau of Labor Statistics in *Employment and Earnings* and the related reports mentioned above. Data presented include national totals, by sex, race, and age, of the number of persons in the civilian labor force; the number employed, hours of work, and industry and occupational groups; the number unemployed, reasons for, and duration of, unemployment; and the number and work experience of nonparticipants in the labor force. Annual data shown in the tables in this section are monthly averages for each year, unless otherwise specified.

In addition to monthly national data, annual average estimates of employment and unemployment for each State and the 30 largest standard metropolitan statistical areas (SMSA's) are also produced from the Current Population Survey. They are published by the BLS in its annual *Geographic Profile of Employment and Unemployment*.

Current Population Survey figures may differ from decennial census data because of sampling variability as well as differences in the enumeration process and procedures. For further information, see *U.S. Census of Population: 1970*, vol. I.

Data based on establishment records are compiled by the BLS and cooperating State agencies as part of the ongoing Current Employment Statistics Program. Data are gathered from a sample of employers who voluntarily complete mail questionnaires monthly. These reports are supplemented by data from other government agencies and adjusted at intervals to data from government social insurance program reports. The estimates exclude proprietors of unincorporated businesses, self-employed persons, domestic servants, unpaid family workers, agricultural workers, and the Armed Forces. In March 1974, reporting establishments employed 12 million manufacturing workers (59 percent of the total manufacturing employment at the time), 11 million workers in nonmanufacturing industries (26 percent of the total in nonmanufacturing) and 9 million Federal, State, and local government employees (61 percent of total government).

The establishment survey counts workers each time they appear on a payroll during the survey week (as with CPS, the week including the 12th of the month). Thus, unlike CPS, a person with 2 jobs is counted twice.

The establishment survey is designed to provide detailed industry information on nonagricultural wage and salary employment, average weekly hours, average hourly and weekly earnings, and labor turnover of the Nation, States, and metropolitan areas.

Similar to CPS data, data from the establishment survey are published in *Employment and Earnings* and *Monthly Labor Review*. Historical data, in geographic detail, are shown in *BLS* Bulletin No. 1370–13, 1939–1977; *Employment and Earnings, States and Areas, 1939–75*; and in the *Handbook of Labor Statistics*.

Labor force.—According to CPS definitions, the *civilian labor force* comprises all civilians classified as employed or unemployed according to the criteria below; the "total labor force" also includes the Armed Forces. *Employed persons* comprise (a) all civilians who, during the survey week, did any work for pay or profit (minimum of an hour's work) or worked 15 hours or more as unpaid workers in a family enterprise, and (b) all persons who were not working but who had jobs or businesses from which they were temporarily absent for noneconomic reasons (illness, bad weather, vacation, labor-management dispute, etc). *Unemployed persons* comprise all civilians who had no employment during the survey week, who made specific efforts to find a job within the previous 4 weeks (such as applying directly to an employer, or to a public employment service, or checking with friends) and who were available for work during the survey week. Persons on layoff from a job or waiting to report to a new job within 30 days are also classified as unemployed. All other persons, 16 years old and over, are "not in the labor force."

Beginning in 1972, information from the 1970 Census of Population was introduced into estimation procedures, producing increases in the civilian noninstitutional population, labor force, and employment totals, but having essentially no effect on unemployment levels and rates. A subsequent population adjustment, introduced in March 1973, affected the statistics by race but had little effect on totals or rates. Further changes derived from a comprehensive revision in classification of occupations and industries for the 1970 census, and from inclusion of a question on major activities or duties in the December 1971 Current Population Survey. As a result, comparisons of occupational employment levels between 1971–1972 and prior periods and between those 2 years should be made with caution. For further explanation of the changes, see the February 1971 and 1972 issues of *Employment and Earnings*. The 1972 data are comparable with those for later years.

In order to produce more reliable State estimates, 9,000 additional occupied housing units in 24 States and the District of Columbia were added to the national sample beginning January 1978; adjustments were also made to incorporate this supplemental sample into the national sample. These changes added approximately one-quarter of a million people to the civilian labor force; unemployment levels and rates were unchanged. For more detail see the February 1978 issue of *Employment and Earnings*.

Hours and earnings.—Average hourly earnings, based on establishment data, are gross earnings (i.e. earnings before payroll deductions) and include overtime premiums; they exclude irregular bonuses and value of payments in kind. Hours are those for which pay was received. Persons who worked 35 hours or more are classified as working full time; those working less than 35 hours are considered part-time workers.

Industrial and occupational groups.—Establishments responding to the payroll survey are classified into industries on the basis of their principal product or activity (determined by annual sales volume) in accordance with the *Standard Industrial Classification (SIC) Manual*, Office of Management and Budget, 1972. The SIC is a classification structure for the entire national economy. The structure provides data on a division and industry code basis, according to the level of industrial detail. For example, manufacturing is a major industrial division; food and kindred products (code 20) is one of its major groups. One of the ways this group is further divided is into meat products (code 201) and meat packing plants (code 2011). Periodically, the SIC is revised to reflect changes in the industrial composition of the economy. The most recent revision was made in 1972.

The occupational and industrial groups used in classifying data from the CPS household interviews are defined as in the 1970 Census of Population. A comprehensive revision of the data and a change in the monthly questionnaire, as stated previously, resulted in a "break in series" of many groups in the CPS in 1971. As a result, comparisons must be made cautiously.

Productivity.—Measures of productivity reflect the relationship between production and output and labor input. Although the measures relate output to hours paid for, they do not measure the specific contribution of labor nor any other factor of production. Rather, they reflect the joint effect of a number of interrelated influences, such as changes in technology, capital investment per worker, and capacity utilization. Industry output per hour measures are limited to the extent that they do not account for quality change, and often do not reflect adequately changes in the degree of plant integration and specialization. In addition, there is not always strict comparability between output and labor input estimates. Finally, year-to-year changes in output per hour are irregular, and therefore not necessarily indicative of basic changes in long-term trends. Conversely, long-term trends are not necessarily applicable in any one year or period in the future.

Labor turnover.—Labor turnover is the gross movement of wage and salary workers into and out of employed status with respect to individual establishments. This movement, relating to a calendar month, is divided into two broad types: Accessions (new hires and rehires), and separations (quits, layoffs, and terminations). The data cover all workers, temporary or permanent, and full- or part-time.

Unions.—As defined here, unions include all affiliates of the AFL-CIO, all unaffiliated national unions, and all unaffiliated unions which are party to collective bargaining agreements with different employers in more than one State. The definition excludes unions whose activities are confined to a single locality or to a single employer. In addition, BLS accounts for all unions of Federal Government employees that have received exclusive recognition. Collective bargaining settlements data are available for unions of 1,000 members or more.

Work stoppages.—Work stoppages include all strikes and lockouts known to the Bureau of Labor Statistics and its cooperating agencies which last for at least one full day or shift and involve six or more workers. All stoppages, whether or not authorized by a union, legal or illegal, are counted. Excluded are work slowdowns and instances where employees report to work late, or leave early, to attend mass meetings or mass rallies.

Seasonal adjustment.—Many economic statistics reflect a regularly recurring seasonal movement which can be estimated on the basis of past experience. By eliminating that part of the change which can be ascribed to usual seasonal variation (e.g. climate or school openings and closings), it is possible to observe the cyclical and other nonseasonal movements in the series. However, in evaluating deviations from the seasonal pattern—that is, changes in a seasonally adjusted series—it is important to note that seasonal adjustment is merely an approximation based on past experience. Seasonally adjusted estimates have a broader margin of possible error than the original data on which they are based, since they are subject not only to sampling and other errors, but in addition, are affected by the uncertainties of the seasonal adjustment process itself.

Statistical reliability.—For discussion of statistical collection, estimation, and sampling procedures and measures of statistical reliability applicable to Census Bureau and BLS data, see Appendix III.

Historical statistics.—Tabular headnotes provide cross-references, where applicable, to *Historical Statistics of the United States, Colonial Times to 1970.* See Appendix I.

No. 643. LABOR FORCE AND EMPLOYMENT: 1947 TO 1978

[Persons 16 years old and over. Annual averages of monthly figures, except as indicated. See also *Historical Statistics, Colonial Times to 1970*, series D 11–19 and D 85–86]

YEAR	Total noninstitutional population [1] (mil.)	TOTAL LABOR FORCE [1]		CIVILIAN LABOR FORCE								NOT IN LABOR FORCE	
		Total (mil.)	Percent of noninstitutional population	Total (mil.)	Female		Employed		Unemployed			Total (mil.)	Percent of noninstitutional population
					Total (mil.)	Percent of civilian labor force	Total (mil.)	Percent of noninstitutional population	Total (mil.)	Percent of civilian labor force			
1947	103.4	60.9	58.9	59.4	16.7	28.1	57.0	55.2	2.3	3.9		42.5	41.1
1950	106.6	63.9	59.9	62.2	18.4	29.6	58.9	55.2	3.3	5.3		42.8	40.1
1955	112.7	68.1	60.4	65.0	20.5	31.6	62.2	55.2	2.9	4.4		44.7	39.6
1960	119.8	72.1	60.2	69.6	23.2	33.4	65.8	54.9	3.9	5.5		47.6	39.8
1965	129.2	77.2	59.7	74.5	26.2	35.2	71.1	55.0	3.4	4.5		52.1	40.3
1966	131.2	78.9	60.1	75.8	27.3	36.0	72.9	55.6	2.9	3.8		52.3	39.9
1967	133.3	80.8	60.6	77.3	28.4	36.7	74.4	55.8	3.0	3.9		52.5	39.4
1968	135.6	82.3	60.7	78.7	29.2	37.1	75.9	56.0	2.8	3.6		53.3	39.3
1969	137.8	84.2	61.1	80.7	30.5	37.8	77.9	56.5	2.8	3.5		53.6	38.9
1970	140.2	85.9	61.3	82.7	31.5	38.1	78.6	56.1	4.1	4.9		54.3	38.7
1971	142.6	86.9	61.0	84.1	32.1	38.2	79.1	55.5	5.0	5.9		55.7	39.0
1972	145.8	89.0	61.0	86.5	33.3	38.5	81.7	56.0	4.8	5.6		56.8	39.0
1973	148.3	91.0	61.4	88.7	34.5	38.9	84.4	56.9	4.3	4.9		57.2	38.6
1974	150.8	93.2	61.8	91.0	35.8	39.4	85.9	57.0	5.1	5.6		57.6	38.2
1975	153.4	94.8	61.8	92.6	37.0	39.9	84.8	55.3	7.8	8.5		58.7	38.2
1976	156.0	96.9	62.1	94.8	38.4	40.5	87.5	56.1	7.3	7.7		59.1	37.9
1977	158.6	99.5	62.8	97.4	40.0	41.0	90.5	57.1	6.9	7.0		59.0	37.2
1978, Jan.-Apr[2]	160.2	101.5	63.3	99.3	41.1	41.4	93.2	58.2	6.1	6.2		58.7	36.7

[1] Includes Armed Forces.   [2] Seasonally adjusted, except population figure.

Source: U.S. Bureau of Labor Statistics, *Employment and Earnings*, monthly.

No. 644. LABOR FORCE AND PARTICIPATION RATES, BY RACE, SEX, AND AGE: 1960 TO 1977

[Persons 16 years old and over. Labor force data are annual averages of monthly figures. Includes Armed Forces. Rates are based on total population as of July and represent proportion of each age in labor force. See also *Historical Statistics, Colonial Times to 1970*, series D 29–41]

RACE, SEX, AND AGE	TOTAL LABOR FORCE (millions)							PARTICIPATION RATES (percent)						
	1960	1965	1970	1974	1975	1976	1977	1960	1965	1970	1974	1975	1976	1977
Total	72.1	77.2	85.9	93.2	94.8	96.9	99.5	59.2	58.8	60.3	60.9	60.9	61.2	61.8
White	64.2	68.6	76.4	82.6	83.9	85.7	87.9	58.8	58.5	60.2	61.1	61.1	61.5	62.1
Male	44.1	45.9	48.8	51.3	51.6	52.2	53.1	82.6	80.4	79.7	78.9	78.1	77.9	78.0
Female	20.1	22.8	27.5	31.3	32.3	33.5	34.8	36.0	37.7	42.0	44.6	45.4	46.3	47.4
Black and other	7.9	8.6	9.5	10.6	10.9	11.3	11.7	63.0	62.1	61.1	59.5	58.8	59.1	59.5
Male	4.8	5.1	5.5	6.0	6.1	6.2	6.4	80.1	77.4	74.7	72.1	70.4	69.7	69.8
Female	3.1	3.5	4.0	4.6	4.8	5.1	5.3	47.2	48.1	48.9	48.6	48.7	49.7	50.5
Male	48.9	50.9	54.3	57.3	57.7	58.4	59.5	82.4	80.1	79.2	78.1	77.3	76.9	77.0
16–19 years	3.2	3.8	4.4	5.2	5.1	5.2	5.3	58.6	55.7	57.5	61.7	60.2	60.3	61.8
16–17	1.3	1.6	1.8	2.2	2.1	2.1	2.1	45.9	44.1	46.7	50.3	48.5	48.4	50.0
18–19	1.8	2.3	2.6	3.0	3.1	3.1	3.2	73.1	68.3	68.8	73.5	72.1	72.1	73.5
20–24 years	4.9	5.9	7.4	8.1	8.2	8.4	8.6	88.9	86.2	85.1	86.1	84.6	85.2	85.3
25–34 years	10.9	10.7	12.0	14.0	14.5	15.0	15.5	96.4	96.0	95.0	94.7	94.2	94.2	94.2
35–44 years	11.5	11.5	10.8	10.6	10.6	10.7	10.9	96.4	96.2	95.7	95.1	94.8	94.6	94.9
45–54 years	9.6	10.1	10.5	10.5	10.5	10.4	10.2	94.3	94.3	92.9	91.2	91.1	90.6	90.3
55–64 years	6.4	6.8	7.1	7.0	7.0	7.0	7.0	85.2	83.2	81.5	76.3	74.8	73.5	73.0
65 and over	2.4	2.1	2.2	1.9	1.9	1.8	1.8	32.2	26.9	25.8	21.5	20.8	19.4	19.3
Female	23.2	26.2	31.6	35.9	37.1	38.5	40.1	37.1	38.8	42.8	45.1	43.7	46.8	47.8
16–19 years	2.1	2.5	3.3	4.0	4.1	4.2	4.3	39.1	37.7	43.7	49.0	49.0	49.8	51.3
16–17	.8	1.0	1.3	1.7	1.7	1.7	1.7	28.6	27.5	34.6	40.1	40.0	40.6	41.9
18–19	1.3	1.6	1.9	2.3	2.4	2.5	2.6	51.0	48.6	53.4	58.1	58.1	58.9	60.4
20–24 years	2.6	3.4	4.9	5.9	6.1	6.3	6.6	46.1	49.7	57.5	63.0	63.9	65.0	66.4
25–34 years	4.2	4.3	5.7	7.8	8.5	9.2	9.9	35.8	38.5	44.8	52.2	54.3	56.9	59.2
35–44 years	5.3	5.7	6.0	6.3	6.5	6.8	7.2	43.1	45.9	50.9	54.5	55.6	57.6	59.4
45–54 years	5.2	5.7	6.5	6.7	6.7	6.7	6.7	49.3	50.5	54.0	54.3	54.3	54.6	55.5
55–64 years	3.0	3.6	4.2	4.2	4.2	4.3	4.4	36.7	40.6	42.5	40.4	40.6	40.7	40.6
65 and over	1.0	1.0	1.1	1.0	1.0	1.1	1.1	10.5	9.5	9.2	7.8	7.8	7.8	7.6

Source: U.S. Bureau of Labor Statistics, *Special Labor Force Reports*.

No. 645. EMPLOYMENT STATUS OF THE POPULATION, BY SEX AND RACE: 1960 TO 1978

[Persons 16 years old and over. Annual averages of monthly figures, except as indicated. See also *Historical Statistics, Colonial Times to 1970*, series D 11–19 and D 85–86]

YEAR OR MONTH, SEX, AND RACE	Total noninstitutional population [1] (1,000)	TOTAL LABOR FORCE [1]		CIVILIAN LABOR FORCE					NOT IN LABOR FORCE	
		Total (1,000)	Percent of population	Total (1,000)	Employed (1,000)	Employed/population ratio [2]	Unemployed		Total (1,000)	Percent of population
							Total (1,000)	Percent		
Total:										
1960	119,759	72,142	60.2	69,628	65,778	54.9	3,852	5.5	47,617	39.8
1965	129,236	77,178	59.7	74,455	71,088	55.0	3,366	4.5	52,058	40.3
1969	137,841	84,240	61.1	80,734	77,902	56.5	2,832	3.5	53,602	38.9
1970	140,182	85,903	61.3	82,715	78,627	56.1	4,088	4.9	54,280	38.7
1971	142,596	86,929	61.0	84,113	79,120	55.5	4,993	5.9	55,666	39.0
1972	145,775	88,991	61.0	86,542	81,702	56.0	4,840	5.6	56,785	39.0
1973	148,263	91,040	61.4	88,714	84,409	56.9	4,304	4.9	57,222	38.6
1974	150,827	93,240	61.8	91,011	85,936	57.0	5,076	5.6	57,587	38.2
1975	153,449	94,793	61.8	92,613	84,783	55.3	7,830	8.5	58,655	38.2
1976	156,048	96,917	62.1	94,773	87,485	56.1	7,288	7.7	59,130	37.9
1977	158,559	99,534	62.8	97,401	90,546	57.1	6,855	7.0	59,025	37.2
1978, Jan.–Apr.[3]	160,221	101,471	63.3	99,350	93,238	58.2	6,112	6.2	58,750	36.7
Male:										
1960	58,144	48,870	84.0	46,388	43,904	75.5	2,486	5.4	9,274	16.0
1965	62,473	50,946	81.5	48,255	46,340	74.2	1,914	4.0	11,527	18.5
1969	66,365	53,688	80.9	50,221	48,818	73.6	1,403	2.8	12,677	19.1
1970	67,409	54,343	80.6	51,195	48,960	72.6	2,235	4.4	13,066	19.4
1971	68,512	54,797	80.0	52,021	49,245	71.9	2,776	5.3	13,715	20.0
1972	69,864	55,671	79.7	53,265	50,630	72.5	2,635	4.9	14,193	20.3
1973	71,020	56,479	79.5	54,203	51,963	73.2	2,240	4.1	14,541	20.5
1974	72,253	57,349	79.4	55,186	52,519	72.7	2,668	4.8	14,904	20.6
1975	73,494	57,706	78.5	55,615	51,230	69.7	4,385	7.9	15,788	21.5
1976	74,739	58,397	78.1	56,359	52,391	70.1	3,968	7.0	16,341	21.9
1977	75,981	59,467	78.3	57,449	53,861	70.9	3,588	6.2	16,514	21.7
1978, Jan.–Apr.[3]	76,768	60,226	78.5	58,224	55,023	71.7	3,201	5.5	16,542	21.5
Black and other: [4]										
1960	5,595	(NA)	83.0	4,645	4,148	74.1	497	10.7	951	17.0
1965	6,330	5,084	80.3	4,855	4,496	71.0	359	7.4	1,246	19.7
1969	6,918	5,404	78.1	5,036	4,770	69.0	266	5.3	1,513	21.9
1970	7,098	5,507	77.6	5,182	4,803	67.7	379	7.3	1,591	22.4
1971	7,286	5,533	75.9	5,220	4,746	65.1	474	9.1	1,753	24.1
1972	7,533	5,630	74.7	5,335	4,861	64.5	475	8.9	1,902	25.2
1973	7,845	5,868	74.8	5,555	5,133	65.4	423	7.6	1,977	25.2
1974	8,107	6,028	74.4	5,700	5,179	63.9	521	9.1	2,079	25.6
1975	8,360	6,077	72.7	5,734	4,947	59.2	787	13.7	2,283	27.3
1976	8,622	6,196	71.9	5,853	5,108	59.2	745	12.7	2,425	28.1
1977	8,846	6,388	72.2	6,028	5,283	59.7	745	12.4	2,458	27.8
1978, Jan.–Apr.[3]	9,012	6,609	73.3	6,236	5,528	61.3	708	11.4	2,403	26.7
Female:										
1960	61,615	23,272	37.8	23,240	21,874	35.5	1,366	5.9	38,343	62.2
1965	66,763	26,232	39.3	26,200	24,748	37.1	1,452	5.5	40,531	60.7
1969	71,476	30,551	42.7	30,513	29,084	40.7	1,429	4.7	40,924	57.3
1970	72,774	31,560	43.4	31,520	29,667	40.8	1,853	5.9	41,214	56.6
1971	74,084	32,132	43.4	32,091	29,875	40.3	2,217	6.9	41,952	56.6
1972	75,911	33,320	43.9	33,277	31,072	40.9	2,205	6.6	42,591	56.1
1973	77,242	34,561	44.7	34,510	32,446	42.0	2,064	6.0	42,681	55.3
1974	78,575	35,892	45.7	35,825	33,417	42.5	2,408	6.7	42,683	54.3
1975	79,954	37,087	46.4	36,998	33,553	42.0	3,445	9.3	42,868	53.6
1976	81,309	38,520	47.4	38,414	35,095	43.2	3,320	8.6	42,789	52.6
1977	82,577	40,067	48.5	39,952	36,685	44.4	3,267	8.2	42,510	51.5
1978, Jan.–Apr.[3]	83,452	41,245	49.4	41,125	38,215	45.8	2,911	7.1	42,207	50.6
Black and other: [4]										
1960	6,369	(NA)	48.2	3,069	2,779	43.6	290	9.4	3,300	51.8
1965	7,133	3,467	48.6	3,464	3,147	44.1	317	9.2	3,666	51.4
1969	7,877	3,922	49.8	3,918	3,614	45.9	304	7.8	3,955	50.2
1970	8,114	4,019	49.5	4,015	3,642	44.9	373	9.3	4,095	50.5
1971	8,351	4,107	49.2	4,102	3,658	43.8	445	10.8	4,243	50.8
1972	8,736	4,254	48.7	4,249	3,767	43.1	482	11.3	4,481	51.3
1973	9,109	4,476	49.1	4,470	3,999	43.9	471	10.5	4,632	50.9
1974	9,455	4,643	49.1	4,633	4,136	43.7	497	10.7	4,812	50.9
1975	9,766	4,810	49.3	4,795	4,124	42.2	671	14.0	4,956	50.7
1976	10,075	5,062	50.2	5,044	4,356	43.2	688	13.6	5,013	49.8
1977	10,367	5,288	51.0	5,266	4,529	43.7	737	14.0	5,079	49.0
1978, Jan.–Apr.[3]	10,567	5,587	52.9	5,564	4,835	45.8	729	13.1	4,980	47.1

[1] Includes Armed Forces.   [2] Employed as percent of noninstitutional population.
[3] Seasonally adjusted, except population figure.   [4] Other than White.

Source: U.S. Bureau of Labor Statistics, *Employment and Earnings*, monthly.

No. 646. Labor Force—Percent Distribution, by Age and Sex: 1950 to 1977

[Prior to 1960, excludes Alaska and Hawaii. Includes Armed Forces at home and abroad. See headnote, table 644. See *Historical Statistics, Colonial Times to 1970*, series D 29–41, for similar but not exactly comparable data]

YEAR AND SEX	Total labor force (1,000)	PERCENT DISTRIBUTION						
		16–19 years	20–24 years	25–34 years	35–44 years	45–54 years	55–64 years	65 and over
Total: 1950	63,858	7.1	12.4	23.7	22.1	18.0	12.0	4.8
1960	72,142	7.3	10.6	20.9	23.1	20.7	13.0	4.4
1965	77,178	8.2	12.1	19.4	22.3	20.5	13.4	4.0
1970	85,903	8.9	14.3	20.6	19.5	19.8	13.1	3.7
1973	91,040	9.7	15.0	22.7	18.4	18.7	12.3	3.3
1974	93,240	9.9	15.0	23.4	18.2	18.4	12.0	3.1
1975	94,793	9.7	15.1	24.2	18.0	18.1	11.8	3.1
1976	96,917	9.6	15.2	24.9	18.0	17.6	11.6	3.0
1977	99,534	9.6	15.3	25.5	18.1	17.0	11.5	2.9
Male: 1950	45,446	6.2	11.5	24.3	21.9	17.9	12.8	5.4
1960	48,870	6.5	10.4	22.4	23.2	19.7	13.1	4.7
1965	50,946	7.5	11.6	20.9	22.6	19.9	13.3	4.2
1970	54,343	8.1	13.6	22.0	19.9	19.3	13.1	4.0
1973	56,479	8.9	14.2	23.8	18.7	18.5	12.4	3.4
1974	57,349	9.0	14.1	24.4	18.5	18.3	12.3	3.4
1975	57,706	8.9	14.2	25.1	18.3	18.1	12.1	3.3
1976	58,397	8.9	14.4	25.7	18.3	17.7	11.9	3.1
1977	59,467	8.9	14.5	26.1	18.3	17.2	11.8	3.1
Female: 1950	18,412	9.3	14.6	22.3	22.6	18.1	10.0	3.2
1960	23,272	8.9	11.1	17.8	22.8	22.7	12.8	3.9
1965	26,232	9.6	12.9	16.5	21.8	21.8	13.7	3.7
1970	31,560	10.3	15.5	18.1	18.9	20.7	13.2	3.3
1973	34,561	11.0	16.3	20.8	17.8	19.0	12.1	3.0
1974	35,892	11.2	16.3	21.8	17.7	18.6	11.6	2.8
1975	37,087	10.9	16.5	22.8	17.5	18.0	11.4	2.8
1976	38,520	10.8	16.5	23.8	17.7	17.3	11.2	2.7
1977	40,067	10.7	16.5	24.7	17.9	16.7	10.9	2.7

Source: U.S. Bureau of Labor Statistics, *Employment and Earnings*, monthly.

No. 647. Civilian Labor Force—Years of School Completed, by Sex and Race: 1977

[**Persons 16 years old and over**; noninstitutional population. As of **March**]

EMPLOYMENT STATUS, SEX, AND RACE	Population, 16 yr. old and over (1,000)	PERCENT DISTRIBUTION							
		Elementary school			High school		College		
		0–4 years [1]	5–7 years	8 years	1–3 years	4 years	1–3 years	4 years	5 years or more
Total	155,646	3.0	5.6	7.9	19.9	35.8	14.7	8.0	5.1
Civilian labor force	95,766	1.5	3.5	5.1	17.1	39.5	16.3	10.0	6.9
Employed	88,221	1.5	3.4	5.0	16.0	39.7	16.7	10.4	7.3
Unemployed	7,546	1.8	4.5	6.7	29.9	37.5	12.5	5.1	2.0
Not in labor force	59,880	5.5	9.0	12.3	24.3	29.9	12.0	4.8	2.1
Male, total	73,587	3.3	5.7	8.1	19.5	32.3	15.4	8.9	7.0
Civilian labor force	56,392	1.9	4.0	5.8	17.2	36.0	16.4	10.5	8.2
Employed	52,187	1.9	3.9	5.7	16.1	36.1	16.7	10.9	8.7
Unemployed	4,206	2.4	5.1	7.7	30.9	34.9	12.0	5.0	2.1
Not in labor force	17,195	7.7	11.2	15.4	27.0	20.0	12.1	3.7	2.9
Female, total	82,059	2.8	5.6	7.7	20.2	39.0	14.0	7.2	3.4
Civilian labor force	39,374	.9	2.8	4.1	17.0	44.6	16.3	9.4	5.0
Employed	36,034	.9	2.7	4.0	15.9	44.9	16.6	9.8	5.3
Unemployed	3,340	1.0	3.8	5.5	28.6	40.8	13.1	5.2	2.0
Not in labor force	42,685	4.6	8.2	11.1	23.2	33.9	12.0	5.2	1.8
White, total	136,970	2.4	5.1	8.0	18.9	36.8	15.1	8.4	5.4
Civilian labor force	84,769	1.2	3.0	5.1	16.3	40.1	16.7	10.4	7.2
Employed	78,679	1.2	2.9	4.9	15.4	40.3	17.0	10.8	7.6
Unemployed	6,090	1.4	4.3	6.7	29.0	37.9	12.7	5.6	2.3
Not in labor force	52,201	4.5	8.5	12.7	23.0	31.4	12.5	5.1	2.3
Black, total	16,106	7.3	10.4	7.5	28.7	28.8	11.3	4.0	2.1
Civilian labor force	9,408	3.8	8.1	5.9	24.4	35.5	13.4	5.8	3.1
Employed	8,068	3.9	8.5	5.8	22.8	35.5	13.7	6.3	3.5
Unemployed	1,339	3.3	5.5	6.3	34.2	35.8	11.8	2.5	.7
Not in labor force	6,698	12.1	13.7	9.7	34.8	19.4	8.2	1.5	.6

[1] Includes persons reporting no school.

Source: U.S. Bureau of Labor Statistics, *Special Labor Force Reports*, No. 209.

No. 648. CIVILIAN LABOR FORCE—EMPLOYMENT STATUS, BY SEX, RACE, AND AGE: 1977

[**Persons 16 years old and over**; noninstitutional population. Annual averages of monthly figures]

AGE AND RACE	Civilian labor force (1,000)	MALE					FEMALE				
		Total (1,000)	Employed		Unemployed		Total (1,000)	Employed		Unemployed	
			Total (1,000)	Percent of labor force	Total (1,000)	Percent of labor force		Total (1,000)	Percent of labor force	Total (1,000)	Percent of labor force
All workers	97,401	57,449	53,861	93.8	3,588	6.2	39,952	36,685	91.8	3,267	8.2
16–19 years	9,252	4,985	4,124	82.7	861	17.3	4,267	3,486	81.7	781	18.3
20–24 years	14,433	7,877	7,031	89.3	846	10.7	6,556	5,824	88.8	732	11.2
25–34 years	24,734	14,887	14,049	94.4	838	5.6	9,848	9,091	92.3	757	7.7
35–44 years	17,772	10,619	10,252	96.5	368	3.5	7,152	6,739	94.2	413	5.8
45–54 years	16,889	10,192	9,863	96.8	329	3.2	6,697	6,358	94.9	339	5.1
55–64 years	11,411	7,043	6,794	96.5	250	3.5	4,367	4,173	95.6	194	4.5
65 years and over	2,910	1,845	1,749	94.8	97	5.2	1,065	1,015	95.3	50	4.7
White	86,107	51,421	48,578	94.5	2,843	5.5	34,686	32,156	92.7	2,530	7.3
16–19 years	8,295	4,461	3,794	85.0	667	15.0	3,834	3,226	84.1	608	15.9
20–24 years	12,626	6,944	6,300	90.7	644	9.3	5,682	5,156	90.7	526	9.3
25–34 years	21,578	13,251	12,587	95.0	664	5.0	8,326	7,766	93.3	561	6.7
35–44 years	15,566	9,453	9,156	96.9	296	3.1	6,113	5,788	94.7	325	5.3
45–54 years	15,063	9,195	8,918	97.0	277	3.0	5,867	5,575	95.0	293	5.0
55–64 years	10,363	6,445	6,233	96.7	212	3.3	3,918	3,746	95.6	172	4.4
65 years and over	2,617	1,671	1,589	95.1	82	4.9	946	900	95.1	46	4.9
Black and other	11,294	6,028	5,283	87.6	745	12.4	5,266	4,529	86.0	737	14.0
16–19 years	957	524	330	63.0	194	37.0	433	261	60.3	173	39.9
20–24 years	1,807	934	731	78.3	202	21.7	874	667	76.3	207	23.6
25–34 years	3,157	1,635	1,462	89.4	173	10.6	1,521	1,325	87.1	196	12.9
35–44 years	2,206	1,167	1,095	93.8	71	6.1	1,039	951	91.5	88	8.5
45–54 years	1,826	996	945	94.9	52	5.2	830	783	94.3	47	5.6
55–64 years	1,047	598	560	93.6	38	6.4	449	427	95.1	22	4.9
65 years and over	293	174	160	92.0	14	8.3	119	115	96.6	4	3.6

Source: U.S. Bureau of Labor Statistics, *Employment and Earnings*, monthly.

No. 649. EMPLOYED PERSONS, BY SELECTED CHARACTERISTICS: 1970 TO 1977

[**In thousands of persons 16 years old and over**; noninstitutional population. Annual averages of monthly figures. Nonagricultural industries only]

AGE, SEX, AND MARITAL STATUS	1970	1971	1972	1973	1974	1975	1976	1977
Total employed	75,165	75,732	78,230	80,957	82,443	81,403	84,188	87,302
16–19 years	5,755	5,791	6,311	6,834	6,954	6,593	6,842	7,211
20–24 years	9,487	9,896	10,606	11,381	11,550	11,293	11,910	12,480
25 years and over	59,923	60,044	61,313	62,743	63,941	63,516	65,436	67,611
25–44 years	31,198	31,312	32,601	34,149	35,278	35,386	37,173	39,085
45–64 years	26,078	26,133	26,147	26,122	26,234	25,704	25,872	26,102
65 years and over	2,647	2,600	2,565	2,471	2,429	2,426	2,392	2,423
Male	46,099	46,455	47,791	49,130	49,618	48,429	49,675	51,222
16–19 years	3,073	3,126	3,412	3,685	3,697	3,425	3,547	3,793
20–24 years	5,035	5,351	5,828	6,302	6,319	6,047	6,435	6,717
25 years and over	37,992	37,977	38,551	39,144	39,603	38,958	39,692	40,712
25–44 years	20,338	20,366	20,986	21,696	22,102	21,866	22,617	23,491
45–64 years	15,986	15,990	15,997	15,956	15,999	15,609	15,657	15,779
65 years and over	1,668	1,622	1,568	1,491	1,502	1,482	1,419	1,442
Female	29,066	29,277	30,439	31,827	32,825	32,974	34,513	36,080
16–19 years	2,682	2,665	2,899	3,149	3,257	3,169	3,295	3,418
20–24 years	4,452	4,545	4,778	5,079	5,231	5,246	5,475	5,764
25 years and over	21,931	22,067	22,762	23,599	24,338	24,558	25,744	26,898
25–44 years	10,861	10,946	11,615	12,453	13,176	13,520	14,556	15,595
45–64 years	10,092	10,142	10,150	10,166	10,234	10,094	10,215	10,323
65 years and over	979	979	997	980	927	944	973	981
Males: Married, spouse present	35,955	35,991	36,467	36,970	36,989	35,993	36,251	36,624
Single (never married)	7,741	7,961	8,658	9,296	9,542	9,361	10,085	10,937
Widowed, divorced, separated	2,403	2,504	2,666	2,863	3,087	3,075	3,339	3,660
Females: Married, spouse present	17,108	17,198	17,757	18,644	19,155	19,146	19,869	20,544
Single (never married)	6,528	6,559	6,932	7,316	7,551	7,716	8,272	8,791
Widowed, divorced, separated	5,429	5,519	5,750	5,866	6,119	6,111	6,372	6,745

Source: U.S. Bureau of Labor Statistics, unpublished data.

No. 650. Persons of Hispanic Origin—Labor Force Participation: 1975 to 1977

[Persons 16 years old and over. As of March. Based on Current Population Survey; see text, p. 1]

ITEM	1975			1976			1977		
	Total [1]	Mexican	Puerto Rican	Total [1]	Mexican	Puerto Rican	Total [1]	Mexican	Puerto Rican
Total_____1,000__	6,724	3,921	972	6,681	3,906	1,015	6,953	3,958	1,004
Percent in labor force: Male_____	78.8	79.8	73.5	76.8	79.4	66.5	78.1	80.7	71.8
Female____	42.3	42.1	33.5	42.9	43.9	30.5	43.6	43.0	29.8
Percent unemployed: Male_____	13.1	12.2	19.3	10.7	10.5	14.3	10.5	9.5	15.6
Female____	12.2	11.9	14.7	12.5	14.0	14.0	12.9	13.3	12.0
Employed men_____1,000__	2,212	1,358	252	2,160	1,358	259	2,287	1,392	269
Percent: White-collar_____	26.2	21.4	28.7	23.8	18.2	22.1	23.4	16.8	28.1
Blue-collar_____	56.0	60.6	49.5	57.4	62.5	51.2	57.2	63.3	51.3
Farm_____	5.2	7.7	1.4	5.7	8.4	2.7	4.6	7.1	1.2
Service_____	12.6	10.4	20.5	13.1	10.9	24.0	14.8	12.9	19.4

[1] Includes persons of Cuban, Central or South American, and other Hispanic origin, not shown separately.
Source: U.S. Bureau of the Census, *Current Population Reports*, series P-20, Nos. 302 and 317.

No. 651. Full- and Part-Time Status of Civilian Labor Force: 1965 to 1977

[In thousands, except rate. Persons 16 years old and over. Annual averages of monthly figures. The part-time labor force consists of persons working part-time voluntarily and unemployed persons seeking part-time work]

ITEM	1965		1970		1975		1976		1977	
	Full-time	Part-time	Full-time	Part-time	Full-time	Part-time	Full-time	Part-time	Full-time	Part-time
Civilian labor force___	65,929	8,527	71,020	11,695	79,096	13,517	80,831	13,942	82,950	14,451
Employed_____	63,138	7,952	67,819	10,808	72,659	12,124	74,957	12,528	77,517	13,028
Unemployed_____	2,791	575	3,201	887	6,437	1,393	5,874	1,414	5,432	1,423
Unemployment rate[1]	4.2	6.7	4.5	7.6	8.1	10.3	7.3	10.1	6.5	9.8
Males, 20 yr. and over___	43,243	1,616	44,933	2,257	48,292	2,563	48,959	2,568	49,756	2,708
Employed_____	41,892	1,530	43,433	2,120	45,084	2,343	46,142	2,344	47,247	2,490
Unemployed_____	1,351	86	1,500	137	3,208	220	2,817	224	2,509	218
Unemployment rate[1]	3.1	5.3	3.3	6.1	6.6	8.6	5.8	8.7	5.0	8.1
Females, 20 yr. and over_	19,138	4,550	22,208	6,071	25,975	6,984	26,989	7,287	28,128	7,557
Employed_____	18,260	4,371	21,132	5,800	23,795	6,515	24,921	6,809	26,125	7,074
Unemployed_____	878	179	1,076	271	2,180	469	2,068	479	2,003	484
Unemployment rate[1]	4.6	3.9	4.8	4.5	8.4	6.7	7.7	6.6	7.1	6.4
Persons, 16–19 yr_____	3,549	2,361	3,878	3,368	4,829	3,969	4,883	4,087	5,066	4,186
Employed_____	2,986	2,050	3,253	2,888	3,780	3,266	3,894	3,376	4,146	3,465
Unemployed_____	563	311	625	480	1,049	703	989	712	921	721
Unemployment rate[1]	15.9	13.2	16.1	14.2	21.7	17.7	20.3	17.4	18.2	17.2

[1] Unemployed as percent of civilian labor force in specified group.
Source: U.S. Bureau of Labor Statistics, *Employment and Earnings*, monthly.

No. 652. Satisfied Workers as Percent of Total Workers: 1962 to 1977

[Survey questions asked were variants of "How satisfied are you with your job (or your work)?" Figures for "satisfied" combined responses such as "very satisfied," "somewhat satisfied," and "fairly satisfied"]

WORKER CHARACTERISTIC	1962	1964	1972	1973	1974	1975	1976	1977
Male_____	84	92	86	86	87	90	87	87
Female_____	81	(NA)	86	89	89	87	87	90
White_____	84	92	87	87	89	89	88	88
Black and other_____	[1] 76	[1] 88	78	85	83	85	79	85
21–29 years_____	74	[2] 87	76	80	81	82	84	83
30–39 years_____	82	[3] 93	88	87	84	88	91	88
40–49 years_____	84	92	89	88	91	92	89	86
50 years and over_____	88	94	92	93	94	93	93	95
Education: Grade school_____	83	94	86	86	86	87	83	88
High school_____	81	90	86	85	90	91	88	88
Some college_____	86	89	83	86	87	90	88	86
College degree_____	90	94	85	93	86	85	87	88
Graduate work_____	84	93	95	98	93	87	92	92

NA Not available. [1] Black only. [2] 21–30 years. [3] 31–40 years.
Source: National Opinion Research Center, Chicago, Ill., *Cumulative Codebook for the 1972–77 General Social Surveys*, and unpublished data.

No. 653. Persons Not in the Labor Force, by Reason, by Race, Age, and Sex: 1970 to 1977

[In thousands of persons 16 years old and over. Annual averages of monthly figures. – Represents zero]

AGE AND RACE	MALE					FEMALE				
	Home responsibilities	In school	Ill health, disability	Retirement, old age	All other	Home responsibilities	In school	Ill health, disability	Retirement, old age	All other
1970, total	221	3,618	2,253	5,216	1,755	32,867	3,508	2,105	703	2,027
White	185	3,108	1,876	4,848	1,457	30,134	2,948	1,663	643	1,731
Black and other	36	510	377	368	300	2,734	560	442	59	298
16–19 years old	14	2,559	40	–	522	777	2,749	35	–	568
20–24 years old	7	841	55	–	238	2,661	575	88	–	255
25–59 years old	42	217	992	62	580	18,591	174	1,002	7	1,036
60 and over	158	1	1,165	5,154	413	10,839	10	979	696	166
1976, total	244	3,929	2,868	6,816	2,484	31,713	3,897	2,494	1,780	2,901
White	211	3,173	2,301	6,231	2,000	28,748	3,086	1,932	1,601	2,409
Black and other	33	756	567	585	483	2,965	811	562	179	491
16–19 years old	16	2,669	40	–	583	684	2,784	30	–	649
20–24 years old	8	923	86	–	310	2,159	775	87	–	364
25–59 years old	63	333	1,457	148	993	16,955	326	1,284	22	1,612
60 and over	156	4	1,284	6,666	597	11,914	11	1,091	1,759	277
1977, total	297	3,845	2,842	7,076	2,453	31,219	3,892	2,459	1,891	3,041
White	253	3,059	2,326	6,452	1,967	28,262	3,069	1,926	1,712	2,461
Black and other	44	786	516	624	485	2,957	822	532	178	579
16–19 years old	20	2,570	31	–	562	676	2,727	31	–	602
20–24 years old	5	936	84	–	294	2,044	776	83	–	403
25–59 years old	73	337	1,476	176	995	16,474	371	1,244	21	1,740
60 and over	200	2	1,251	6,900	599	12,024	18	1,101	1,869	295

Source: U.S. Bureau of Labor Statistics, *Employment and Earnings*, quarterly issues.

No. 654. School Enrollment and Labor Force Status of Civilians 16 to 24 Years, by Selected Characteristics: 1976 and 1977

[In thousands, except percent. As of October. Based on survey conducted by Bureau of the Census. Data by race may include some duplication because persons of Hispanic origin may be of any race]

CHARACTERISTIC	NONINSTITUTIONAL POPULATION		CIVILIAN LABOR FORCE			EMPLOYED		UNEMPLOYED		
	1976	1977	1976, total	1977		1976	1977	1976, total	1977	
				Total	Percent [1]				Total	Rate [2]
Total, 16 to 24 yr	35,222	35,658	22,591	23,454	65.8	19,439	20,581	3,149	2,871	12.2
Enrolled in school	15,548	15,551	7,043	7,291	46.9	6,055	6,343	987	947	13.0
16 to 19 years	11,169	11,161	4,640	4,875	43.7	3,858	4,111	782	765	15.7
20 to 24 years	4,379	4,390	2,403	2,416	55.0	2,197	2,232	205	182	7.5
Male	8,065	8,110	3,796	3,920	48.3	3,232	3,433	566	487	12.4
Female	7,483	7,441	3,248	3,371	45.3	2,827	2,906	420	460	13.6
White	13,197	13,124	6,372	6,576	50.1	5,574	5,833	796	744	11.3
Black	2,047	2,069	547	567	27.5	381	380	166	187	33.0
Hispanic origin	846	815	323	331	40.6	251	273	70	57	17.2
Below college level	8,092	8,145	3,327	3,525	43.3	2,694	2,900	633	626	17.8
White	6,688	6,697	3,029	3,194	47.7	2,507	2,702	523	492	15.4
Black	1,266	1,311	255	289	22.0	159	164	99	125	43.3
Hispanic origin	522	524	149	176	33.6	109	131	41	47	26.7
College	7,456	7,406	3,718	3,765	50.8	3,365	3,443	352	322	8.6
Full-time	6,251	6,134	2,638	2,635	43.0	2,345	2,381	291	255	9.7
White	6,508	6,430	3,343	3,383	52.6	3,070	3,130	273	253	7.5
Black	781	758	291	278	36.7	223	219	70	62	22.3
Hispanic origin	323	290	174	155	53.4	147	140	30	12	7.7
Not enrolled in school	19,674	20,107	15,548	16,163	80.4	13,384	14,238	2,162	1,924	11.9
16 to 19 years	5,282	5,317	3,980	4,116	77.4	3,192	3,400	786	714	17.3
20 to 24 years	14,392	14,790	11,568	12,047	81.5	10,192	10,838	1,376	1,210	10.0
Male	9,145	9,321	8,423	8,693	93.3	7,327	7,773	1,095	919	10.6
Female	10,529	10,786	7,124	7,470	69.3	6,056	6,467	1,068	1,005	13.5
White	16,939	17,338	13,675	14,154	81.6	11,993	12,760	1,678	1,396	9.9
Black	2,420	2,480	1,635	1,804	72.7	1,191	1,299	444	506	28.0
Hispanic origin	1,213	1,309	837	915	69.9	703	826	132	115	12.6

[1] Percent of noninstitutional population. [2] Percent of labor force.
Source: U.S. Bureau of Labor Statistics, *Special Labor Force Reports*, Nos. 200 and 215.

No. 655. MARITAL STATUS OF WOMEN IN THE CIVILIAN LABOR FORCE: 1940 TO 1977

[Persons 14 years old and over through 1965; 16 years old and over thereafter. As of March, except as indicated. Prior to 1960, excludes Alaska and Hawaii. Figures for 1940 based on complete census revised for comparability with intercensal series. Later data based on Current Population Survey; see text, p. 1. Beginning 1955, figures not strictly comparable with previous years as a result of introduction into estimating procedure of 1950 census data through 1960, and of 1960 census data beginning 1965. See also *Historical Statistics, Colonial Times to 1970*, series D 49-62]

YEAR	FEMALE LABOR FORCE (1,000)					PERCENT DISTRIBUTION OF FEMALE LABOR FORCE			FEMALE LABOR FORCE AS PERCENT OF FEMALE POPULATION				
	Total	Single	Married, total	Married, husband present	Widowed or divorced	Single	Married	Widowed or divorced	Total	Single	Married, total	Married, husband present	Widowed or divorced
1940	13,840	6,710	5,040	¹4,200	2,090	48.5	36.4	15.1	27.4	48.1	16.7	14.7	32.0
1944, Apr	18,449	7,542	8,433	6,226	2,474	40.9	45.7	13.4	35.0	58.6	25.6	21.7	35.7
1947, Apr	16,323	6,181	7,545	6,676	2,597	37.9	46.2	15.9	29.8	51.2	21.4	20.0	34.6
1950	17,795	5,621	9,273	8,550	2,901	31.6	52.1	16.3	31.4	50.5	24.8	23.8	36.0
1955, Apr	20,154	5,087	11,839	10,423	3,227	25.2	58.7	16.0	33.5	46.4	29.4	27.7	36.0
1960	22,516	5,401	13,485	12,253	3,629	24.0	59.9	16.1	34.8	44.1	31.7	30.5	37.1
1965	25,952	5,912	16,154	14,708	3,886	22.8	62.2	15.0	36.7	40.5	35.7	34.7	35.7
1968	28,778	6,357	18,234	16,821	4,187	22.1	63.4	14.6	40.7	51.3	39.1	38.3	35.8
1969	29,898	6,501	19,100	17,595	4,297	21.7	63.9	14.4	41.6	51.2	40.4	39.6	35.8
1970	31,233	6,965	19,799	18,377	4,469	22.3	63.4	14.3	42.6	53.0	41.4	40.8	36.2
1971	31,681	7,187	19,986	18,530	4,508	22.7	63.1	14.2	42.5	52.7	41.4	40.8	35.7
1972	32,939	7,477	20,749	19,249	4,713	22.7	63.0	14.3	43.6	54.9	42.1	41.5	37.2
1973	33,904	7,739	21,343	19,821	4,822	22.8	63.0	14.2	44.1	55.8	42.8	42.2	36.7
1974	35,320	8,230	22,009	20,367	5,081	23.3	62.3	14.4	45.2	57.2	43.8	43.0	37.8
1975	36,496	8,433	22,796	21,143	5,266	23.1	62.5	14.4	45.9	56.8	45.0	44.4	37.7
1976	37,817	9,083	23,355	21,554	5,379	24.0	61.8	14.2	46.8	58.9	45.8	45.0	37.3
1977	39,374	9,470	24,092	22,377	5,812	24.1	61.3	14.8	48.0	58.9	47.1	46.6	39.0

¹ As of April.

Source: 1940-1955, U.S. Bureau of the Census, *Current Population Reports*, series P-50. Beginning 1960, U.S. Bureau of Labor Statistics, *Special Labor Force Reports*.

No. 656. CIVILIAN LABOR FORCE PARTICIPATION RATES, BY MARITAL STATUS, AGE, AND SEX: 1960 TO 1977

[Percent civilian labor force of civilian noninstitutional population]

YEAR AND MARITAL STATUS	MALE					FEMALE				
	16-19 years	20-24 years	25-44 years	45-64 years	65 and over	16-19 years	20-24 years	25-44 years	45-64 years	65 and over
1960: Married, spouse present	¹91.5	97.1	98.7	93.7	36.6	¹27.2	31.7	33.1	36.0	6.7
Single	¹42.6	80.3	90.5	80.1	31.2	¹30.2	77.2	83.2	79.8	24.3
Other²	¹68.8	96.9	94.7	83.2	22.7	¹43.8	58.0	67.2	60.0	11.4
1965: Married, spouse present	¹88.0	96.4	98.5	92.6	31.0	¹30.6	37.1	36.2	39.5	6.7
Single	¹40.9	75.7	89.0	78.1	23.2	¹28.8	72.9	82.4	76.1	22.4
Other²	¹77.8	96.6	93.8	80.8	18.7	¹42.1	59.2	67.2	61.6	10.5
1970: Married, spouse present	92.3	94.7	98.0	91.2	29.9	37.8	47.9	42.7	44.0	7.3
Single	54.6	73.8	87.4	75.7	25.2	44.7	73.0	80.5	73.0	19.7
Other²	68.8	90.4	92.3	78.5	18.3	48.5	60.3	67.2	61.9	10.0
1974: Married, spouse present	94.4	96.2	97.6	87.7	24.2	44.9	55.3	48.1	43.3	6.8
Single	59.4	78.7	86.0	70.8	20.2	49.9	73.1	80.2	69.2	13.3
Other²	72.0	93.6	92.7	74.4	16.1	46.2	65.6	69.0	59.9	8.5
1975: Married, spouse present	92.9	95.3	97.3	86.8	23.3	46.2	57.0	50.0	43.8	7.0
Single	57.9	77.9	86.0	69.9	21.0	49.6	72.5	80.3	68.3	15.8
Other²	70.6	88.8	91.1	73.4	15.4	47.6	65.3	68.9	59.0	8.3
1976: Married, spouse present	93.5	95.6	97.2	86.1	21.9	46.9	57.3	52.0	44.3	7.0
Single	58.2	79.1	86.5	68.8	20.7	50.3	73.8	81.4	69.6	15.6
Other²	79.2	92.3	91.2	71.5	13.6	49.6	64.4	71.2	58.2	8.3
1977: Married, spouse present	94.1	96.5	97.4	85.5	21.8	47.0	58.6	54.0	44.6	7.1
Single	60.0	79.7	87.0	67.8	19.6	51.9	74.6	81.0	67.6	14.4
Other²	77.8	93.0	92.7	71.5	13.1	50.8	66.0	73.2	58.5	8.2

¹ 14 to 19 years old.   ² Widowed, divorced, and married (spouse absent).

Source: U.S. Bureau of Labor Statistics, *Handbook of Labor Statistics*, annual.

No. 657. Married Women (Husband Present) in the Labor Force, by Presence and Age of Children: 1950 to 1977

[In thousands, except percent. As of March, except 1955, April. Prior to 1960, excludes Alaska and Hawaii. Beginning 1973, data not comparable with earlier years due to the use of 1970 census data in estimation procedure. Based on Current Population Survey conducted by the Bureau of the Census; see Appendix III. See also Historical Statistics, Colonial Times to 1970, series D 63–74]

PRESENCE AND AGE OF CHILDREN	1950	1955	1960	1965	1970	1973	1974	1975	1976	1977
Women, husband present	8,550	10,423	12,253	14,708	18,377	19,821	20,367	21,143	21,554	22,377
With no children under 18 yr	4,946	5,227	5,692	6,755	8,174	9,107	9,365	9,718	9,860	10,268
With children 6–17 yr. only	2,205	3,183	4,087	4,836	6,289	6,658	6,792	6,988	7,270	7,674
With children under 6 yr	1,399	2,012	2,474	3,117	3,914	4,056	4,210	4,438	4,424	4,435
Also with children 6–17 yr	651	1,086	1,351	1,709	2,040	1,786	1,867	1,925	2,003	1,989
PERCENT LABOR FORCE PARTICIPATION [1]										
Women, husband present	23.8	27.7	30.5	34.7	40.8	42.2	43.0	44.4	45.0	46.6
With no children under 18 yr	30.3	32.7	34.7	38.3	42.2	42.8	43.0	43.9	43.8	44.9
With children 6–17 yr. only	28.3	34.7	39.0	42.7	49.2	50.1	51.2	52.3	53.7	55.6
With children under 6 yr	11.9	16.2	18.6	23.3	30.3	32.7	34.4	36.6	37.4	39.3
Also with children 6–17 yr	12.6	17.3	18.9	22.8	30.5	30.9	32.9	34.2	36.2	38.1

[1] Married women in the labor force as percent of married women in the population.

No. 658. Employed Married Women, Husband Present, by Occupation: 1950 to 1977

[As of March, except as noted. Prior to 1960, excludes Alaska and Hawaii. See headnote, table 657]

OCCUPATION	1950	1955 [1]	1960	1965	1970	1973	1974	1975	1976	1977
Total, all groups millions	8.0	10.0	11.6	14.0	17.5	18.9	19.4	19.3	20.0	20.9
Percent distribution	100.0	100.0	100.0	100.0	100.0	100.0	100.0	100.0	100.0	100.0
Prof., tech., kindred workers	9.5	10.5	13.0	14.7	15.4	16.1	16.5	17.6	17.4	17.1
Farmers and farm managers	1.0	.7	.2	.2	.2	.3	.3	.3	.2	.2
Managers and administrators [2]	7.0	4.6	5.0	4.7	4.7	5.2	5.5	5.7	6.2	6.0
Clerical and kindred workers	} 32.4	{ 25.4	28.3	30.2	33.6	34.1	35.0	35.0	35.5	35.5
Salesworkers		9.4	8.4	8.1	7.1	7.2	6.8	6.8	6.4	6.5
Craft and kindred workers	1.2	1.3	1.0	1.3	1.3	1.5	1.8	1.6	1.5	1.6
Operatives and kindred workers	23.1	21.8	18.6	17.5	16.3	15.1	13.9	12.5	13.3	12.9
Private household workers	} 20.2	{ 6.3	6.2	5.1	3.5	2.6	2.4	2.2	1.9	1.9
Service workers, except priv. hshld		12.8	15.9	15.5	16.0	16.0	15.9	16.5	15.9	16.4
Farm laborers and supervisors	5.2	6.6	3.1	2.3	1.6	1.3	1.3	.9	.9	.9
Laborers, exc. farm and mine	.4	.6	.3	.5	.3	.7	.7	.8	.9	.9

[1] As of April. [2] Excludes farm.

Source of tables 657 and 658: 1950 and 1955, U.S. Bureau of the Census, Current Population Reports, series P–50, No. 62; thereafter, U.S. Bureau of Labor Statistics, Special Labor Force Reports.

No. 659. Divorced, Separated, and Married Women—Employment Status, by Presence and Age of Own Children: 1977

[In thousands of women 16 years old and over, except percent. As of March. See headnote, table 657]

MARITAL STATUS AND PRESENCE AND AGE OF CHILDREN	Total women	Total in labor force	Per-cent in labor force	Employed		Unemployed		Not in labor force
				Total	Per-cent full-time [1]	Total	Per-cent	
Divorced, total	4,863	3,561	73.2	3,258	86.1	303	8.5	1,303
With no children under 18 yr. old	2,609	1,822	69.8	1,684	85.5	138	7.6	787
Percent	53.7	51.2	(X)	51.7	(X)	45.5	(X)	60.4
With children 6–17 yr. old only	1,591	1,301	81.8	1,202	87.5	99	7.6	289
With children under 6 yr. old	664	437	65.9	372	83.9	66	15.0	226
Separated, total [2]	3,110	1,715	55.1	1,477	80.0	237	13.8	1,395
With no children under 18 yr. old	1,431	794	55.5	709	81.4	85	10.7	637
Percent	46.0	46.3	(X)	48.0	(X)	35.9	(X)	45.7
With children 6–17 yr. old only	895	555	62.0	488	79.5	67	12.1	340
With children under 6 yr. old	784	366	46.6	280	76.8	85	23.4	419
Married (husband present), total	47,984	22,377	46.6	20,854	71.0	1,523	6.8	25,607
With no children under 18 yr. old	22,886	10,268	44.9	9,647	76.4	621	6.1	12,618
Percent	47.7	45.9	(X)	46.3	(X)	40.8	(X)	49.3
With children 6–17 yr. old only	13,800	7,674	55.6	7,249	66.6	424	5.5	6,126
With children under 6 yr. old	11,298	4,435	39.3	3,958	65.8	478	10.8	6,863

X Not applicable. [1] Workers who, during the survey week, worked 35 hours or more and those who usually work full-time but worked 1 to 34 hours. [2] Married women who are either permanently or temporarily living apart from their husbands for specific reasons, excluding vacations, business meetings, and the like.

Source: U.S. Bureau of Labor Statistics, Monthly Labor Review, February 1978.

No. 660. Women Employees in Nonagricultural Industries: 1970 to 1977

[Annual averages of monthly figures]

INDUSTRY GROUP	1970			1976			1977		
	Number (1,000)	Percent of—		Number (1,000)	Percent of—		Number (1,000)	Percent of—	
		Industry group	Total employment		Industry group	Total employment		Industry group	Total employment
Total	26,060	37	37	31,498	40	40	32,994	40	40
Manufacturing	5,436	28	8	5,590	29	7	5,816	30	7
Durable goods	2,278	20	3	2,446	22	3	2,612	23	3
Nondurable goods	3,158	39	4	3,144	40	4	3,204	40	4
Mining	37	6	(Z)	58	7	(Z)	65	8	(Z)
Contract construction	177	5	(Z)	245	7	(Z)	268	7	(Z)
Transportation and public utilities	953	21	1	986	22	1	1,036	23	1
Wholesale trade	877	23	1	1,039	24	1	1,079	25	1
Retail trade	5,120	46	7	6,365	47	8	6,597	47	8
Finance, insurance, and real estate	1,907	52	3	2,377	55	3	2,523	56	3
Services	6,222	54	9	8,184	56	10	8,648	56	11
Government	5,331	42	8	6,656	45	8	6,961	46	8

Z Less than .5 percent.
Source: U.S. Bureau of Labor Statistics, *Employment and Earnings*, monthly.

No. 661. Persons With Two or More Jobs: 1970 to 1977

[In thousands of persons 16 years old and over, except percent. As of May]

YEAR AND INDUSTRY OF PRIMARY JOB	Persons with 2 or more jobs	Multiple job holding rate [1]	SECONDARY JOB IN—		YEAR AND INDUSTRY OF PRIMARY JOB	Persons with 2 or more jobs	Multiple job holding rate [1]	SECONDARY JOB IN—	
			Agriculture	Nonagriculture				Agriculture	Nonagriculture
1970, total	4,048	5.2	738	3,310	1976, total	3,948	4.5	674	3,273
Nonagriculture	3,772	5.1	667	3,105	Nonagriculture	3,749	4.5	620	3,129
1975, total	3,918	4.7	705	3,213	1977, total	4,558	5.0	755	3,803
Nonagriculture	3,665	4.6	637	3,028	Nonagriculture	4,333	5.0	697	3,637

[1] Percent of all employed in specified group.
Source: U.S. Bureau of Labor Statistics, *Special Labor Force Reports*, Nos. 139, 182, 194, and 211.

No. 662. Labor Turnover Rates in Manufacturing: 1960 to 1977

[Rate per 100 employees per month. Data refer to wage and salary workers. See *Historical Statistics, Colonial Times to 1970*, series D 1022–1028]

ITEM	1960	1965	1969	1970	1971	1972	1973	1974	1975	1976	1977
Accessions [1]	3.8	4.3	4.7	4.0	3.9	4.4	4.8	4.2	3.7	3.9	4.0
New hires	2.2	3.1	3.7	2.8	2.6	3.3	3.9	3.2	2.0	2.6	2.8
Separations [2]	4.3	4.1	4.9	4.8	4.2	4.2	4.6	4.8	4.2	3.8	3.8
Quits	1.3	1.9	2.7	2.1	1.8	2.2	2.7	2.3	1.4	1.7	1.8
Layoffs	2.4	1.4	1.2	1.8	1.6	1.1	.9	1.5	2.1	1.3	1.1

[1] Includes rehires.   [2] Includes discharges and military and miscellaneous separations.
Source: U.S. Bureau of Labor Statistics, *Employment and Earnings*, monthly.

No. 663. U.S. Employment Service Job Openings and Placements and Index of Help-Wanted Advertising: 1960 to 1977

[Openings and placements; 1960 and 1965, calendar years; thereafter, fiscal years; include Puerto Rico, Virgin Islands, and Guam, 1960 and 1965]

ITEM	1960	1965	1970	1971	1972	1973	1974	1975	1976	1977
Job openings: [1] Received____1,000	7,124	8,690	6,130	5,999	7,550	8,443	9,439	7,889	7,668	8,396
Avg. per mo____1,000	594	724	511	500	629	701	787	657	639	699
Nonagricultural placements [1]_1,000	5,818	6,473	4,604	3,311	3,610	4,517	4,913	4,374	5,234	5,544
Index of help wanted advertising in newspapers [2] (1967=100)	56	84	93	83	103	126	110	80	95	118

[1] As reported by State employment agencies.   [2] Source: The Conference Board, New York, N.Y. Further reproduction prohibited without permission. Limited to advertisements in classified sections of leading newspapers. Index based on number of advertisements rather than number of jobs advertised.
Source: Except as noted, U.S. Employment and Training Administration, unpublished data.

No. 664. Employment, by Industry: 1970 to 1977

[In thousands, except as indicated. Persons 16 years old and over. Annual averages of monthly figures. Based on household survey; see text, pp. 395 and 396]

INDUSTRY	1970	1972	1974	1975	1976	1977 Total	1977 Percent Female	1977 Percent Other than White
Total employed	78,627	81,702	85,936	84,783	87,485	90,546	40.5	10.8
Agriculture, forestry, fisheries	3,566	3,585	3,588	3,476	3,417	3,383	18.5	7.8
Mining	515	597	655	732	770	814	8.5	3.9
Construction	4,814	5,246	5,454	5,015	5,162	5,504	6.4	7.9
Manufacturing	20,737	19,866	20,879	19,275	20,044	20,637	29.8	11.0
Transportation, communication, and other public utilities	5,317	5,462	5,716	5,623	5,652	5,833	22.3	12.0
Wholesale and retail trade	14,996	16,470	17,253	17,470	18,025	18,706	44.3	7.6
Wholesale trade	2,670	3,060	3,323	3,333	3,462	3,597	23.6	7.2
Retail trade	12,327	13,410	13,930	14,137	14,563	15,109	49.2	7.7
Finance, insurance, and real estate	3,942	4,327	4,697	4,665	4,793	5,038	54.1	8.0
Banking and other finances	1,695	1,766	1,935	1,918	1,954	2,061	63.2	8.5
Insurance and real estate	2,246	2,561	2,763	2,747	2,840	2,977	47.8	7.7
Services [1]	20,266	21,749	23,041	23,759	24,829	25,658	60.5	13.8
Business services	1,402	1,456	1,656	1,668	1,763	1,924	43.0	10.1
Automobile services	599	664	659	697	746	794	11."	10.6
Personal services [1]	4,273	4,059	3,810	3,719	3,789	3,826	73.6	21.8
Private households	1,781	1,685	1,430	1,378	1,382	1,406	86.1	33.6
Hotels and lodging places	978	923	991	973	1,015	1,068	68.2	17.0
Entertainment and recreation	716	724	830	849	922	968	36.4	10.1
Professional and related services [1]	[2]12,894	14,454	15,636	16,373	17,158	17,644	64.5	13.1
Hospitals	2,841	3,026	3,269	3,394	3,568	3,645	76.0	18.9
Health services, exc. hospitals	1,626	2,017	2,285	2,471	2,554	2,683	72.9	11.4
Elementary, secondary schools	6,123 {	4,578	4,845	5,034	5,180	5,106	70.6	12.8
Colleges and universities	}	1,667	1,770	1,830	1,935	2,016	47.9	12.5
Welfare and religious agencies	827	1,049	1,147	1,231	1,321	1,429	57.5	16.4
Public administration [3]	[2]4,473	4,400	4,654	4,770	4,793	4,972	32.9	14.7

[1] Includes industries not shown separately.　[2] Not strictly comparable with later years due to reclassifications between "Professional and related services" and "Public administration."
[3] Includes workers involved in uniquely governmental activities, e.g., judicial and legislative.
Source: U.S. Bureau of Labor Statistics, *Employment and Earnings*, January 1978 and earlier issues.

No. 665. Civilians Employed, by Hours Worked: 1965 to 1977

[In thousands of persons 16 years old and over, except 1965, 14 and over. Annual averages of monthly figures, except 1965 for May]

HOURS WORKED	1965	1970	1972	1973	1974	1975	1976	1977
Nonagriculture employed [1]	67,278	75,165	78,230	80,957	82,443	81,403	84,188	87,302
Worked 1–14 hours	4,403	3,962	4,086	4,092	4,200	4,349	4,376	4,500
Worked 15–34 hours	7,563	14,260	12,463	13,381	14,075	14,189	15,239	15,756
Worked 35 or more hours	53,008	52,462	57,114	58,710	59,008	57,857	59,410	61,742
Percent of total	78.8	69.8	73.0	72.5	71.6	71.1	70.6	70.7
Agriculture, employed [1]	5,128	3,462	3,472	3,452	3,492	3,380	3,297	3,244
Worked 35 or more hours	3,475	2,255	2,282	2,265	2,301	2,227	2,186	2,149
Percent of total	67.8	65.1	65.7	65.6	65.9	65.9	66.3	66.2

[1] Includes persons who had a job or business, but did not work at all during survey week because of illness, bad weather, vacation, industrial dispute, or various personal reasons, not shown separately.

No. 666. Class of Worker of Employed Persons, by Sex: 1965 to 1977

[In thousands of persons 16 years old and over, except 1965, 14 and over. See headnote, table 679]

CLASS OF WORKER	1965 Male	1965 Female	1970 Male	1970 Female	1975 Male	1975 Female	1976 Male	1976 Female	1977 Male	1977 Female
Nonagriculture, employed	43,304	24,289	46,099	29,066	48,429	32,974	49,675	34,513	51,222	36,080
Wage and salary workers	38,434	22,331	42,116	27,330	44,205	31,093	45,456	32,585	46,819	33,986
Self-employed workers	4,794	1,419	3,929	1,288	4,171	1,456	4,168	1,520	4,348	1,658
Unpaid family workers	77	540	53	449	54	424	51	407	55	437
Agriculture, employed	3,729	856	2,861	601	2,801	579	2,716	582	2,639	605
Wage and salary workers	1,243	249	979	174	1,062	218	1,076	243	1,079	252
Self-employed workers	2,170	137	1,722	88	1,592	123	1,525	112	1,453	117
Unpaid family workers	316	470	160	339	147	239	115	227	107	236

Source of tables 665 and 666: U.S. Bureau of Labor Statistics, *Employment and Earnings*, monthly.

No. 667. Unemployed and Unemployment Insurance—Summary: 1965 to 1978

[Persons 16 years old and over. Annual averages of monthly figures, except as indicated. For other unemployment insurance data, see tables 556 and 557. See also *Historical Statistics, Colonial Times to 1970*, series D 87–101]

ITEM AND CHARACTERISTIC	1965	1970	1971	1972	1973	1974	1975	1976	1977	1978, Jan.-Apr.[1]
Total unemployed_____1,000__	3,365	4,088	4,994	4,840	4,304	5,076	7,830	7,288	6,855	6,112
Labor force time lost [2] percent__	5.0	5.4	6.4	6.0	5.2	6.1	9.1	8.4	7.6	6.6
Male_____1,000__	1,914	2,235	2,776	2,635	2,240	2,668	4,385	3,968	3,588	3,201
Female_____1,000__	1,452	1,853	2,217	2,205	2,064	2,408	3,445	3,320	3,267	2,911
White_____1,000__	2,691	3,337	4,074	3,884	3,411	4,057	6,371	5,855	5,373	4,662
Black and other_____1,000__	676	752	919	956	894	1,018	1,459	1,433	1,482	1,437
Full-time workers_____1,000__	2,791	3,201	3,949	3,769	3,291	3,941	6,437	5,874	5,432	4,740
Part-time workers_____1,000__	575	887	1,044	1,071	1,013	1,134	1,393	1,414	1,423	1,360
Percent of total unemployed_____	17.1	21.7	20.9	22.1	23.5	22.3	17.8	19.4	20.8	22.3
16–19 years old_____1,000__	874	1,105	1,257	1,302	1,225	1,410	1,752	1,701	1,642	1,581
Percent of total unemployed___	26.0	27.0	25.2	26.9	28.5	27.8	22.4	23.3	24.0	25.9
Male_____1,000__	479	599	691	707	647	749	957	928	861	827
Female_____1,000__	395	506	567	595	579	660	795	773	781	754
White_____1,000__	703	871	1,010	1,017	950	1,099	1,406	1,356	1,275	1,202
Black and other_____1,000__	169	235	248	284	275	311	347	345	367	384
20–24 years old_____1,000__	557	864	1,121	1,116	985	1,182	1,828	1,670	1,578	1,506
Percent of total unemployed___	16.5	21.1	22.5	23.1	22.9	23.3	23.3	22.9	23.0	24.6
Male_____1,000__	311	478	635	619	514	631	1,059	924	846	801
Female_____1,000__	246	386	486	497	471	552	769	746	732	705
White_____1,000__	437	678	884	879	746	910	1,455	1,303	1,169	(NA)
Black and other_____1,000__	119	185	237	237	239	272	373	367	409	(NA)
25–44 years old_____1,000__	1,076	1,230	1,553	1,436	1,289	1,568	2,684	2,507	2,375	2,008
Percent of total unemployed___	32.0	30.1	31.1	29.7	29.9	30.9	34.3	34.4	34.6	32.9
Male_____1,000__	577	643	827	738	633	791	1,465	1,315	1,206	983
Female_____1,000__	499	587	726	698	656	777	1,218	1,192	1,170	1,026
45–64 years old_____1,000__	758	784	953	876	717	816	1,410	1,264	1,112	877
Percent of total unemployed___	22.5	19.2	19.1	18.1	16.7	16.1	18.0	17.3	16.2	14.3
Male_____1,000__	474	444	552	499	389	434	801	708	579	476
Female_____1,000__	284	340	401	377	328	382	610	556	533	400
65 years and over_____1,000__	102	104	109	111	88	99	155	147	147	127
Unemployment rate (percent): [3]										
All workers_____	4.5	4.9	5.9	5.6	4.9	5.6	8.5	7.7	7.0	6.2
White_____	4.1	4.5	5.4	5.0	4.3	5.0	7.8	7.0	6.2	5.3
Male_____	3.6	4.0	4.9	4.5	3.7	4.3	7.2	6.4	5.5	4.7
Female_____	5.0	5.4	6.3	5.9	5.3	6.1	8.6	7.9	7.3	6.2
Black and other_____	8.1	8.2	9.9	10.0	8.9	9.9	13.9	13.1	13.1	12.2
Ratio to White_____	2.0	1.8	1.8	2.0	2.1	2.0	1.8	1.9	2.1	2.3
Male_____	7.4	7.3	9.1	8.9	7.6	9.1	13.7	12.7	12.4	11.4
Female_____	9.2	9.3	10.8	11.3	10.5	10.7	14.0	13.6	14.0	13.1
Men, 20 years old and over___	3.2	3.5	4.4	4.0	3.2	3.8	6.7	5.9	5.2	4.5
Women, 20 years old and over__	4.5	4.8	5.7	5.4	4.8	5.5	8.0	7.4	7.0	5.9
Household heads_____	2.7	2.9	3.6	3.3	2.9	3.3	5.7	5.1	4.5	3.7
Married men, wife present_____	2.4	2.6	3.2	2.8	2.3	2.7	5.1	4.2	3.6	2.9
White_____	2.2	2.4	3.0	2.6	2.1	2.5	4.8	4.0	3.4	(NA)
Black and other_____	4.4	3.9	5.0	4.5	3.8	4.3	8.3	7.0	6.2	(NA)
Teenagers (16–19 yr. old)_____	14.8	15.3	16.9	16.2	14.5	16.0	19.9	19.0	17.7	16.9
Male Vietnam-era veterans [4]___	(NA)	6.6	8.2	6.7	5.0	5.3	9.3	7.9	7.3	5.1
Blue-collar workers_____	5.3	6.2	7.4	6.5	5.3	6.7	11.7	9.4	8.1	7.0
White-collar workers_____	2.3	2.8	3.5	3.4	2.9	3.3	4.7	4.6	4.3	3.5
Experienced workers [5]_____	4.3	4.8	5.7	5.3	4.5	5.3	8.2	7.3	6.6	5.7
Percent without work for—										
4 weeks or less_____	48.4	52.3	44.7	45.9	51.0	50.6	37.0	38.3	41.7	44.6
5–10 weeks_____	21.0	23.4	22.9	22.5	22.4	22.7	22.2	21.0	22.0	(NA)
11–14 weeks_____	8.2	8.1	8.7	7.6	7.7	8.2	9.1	8.6	8.5	(NA)
15–26 weeks_____	12.0	10.4	13.3	12.3	11.0	11.1	16.5	13.8	13.1	13.3
Over 26 weeks_____	10.4	5.8	10.4	11.6	7.8	7.3	15.2	18.3	14.8	11.7
Unemployment duration, avg. wks.	11.8	8.8	11.4	12.1	10.0	9.7	14.1	15.8	14.3	12.6
Unemployment insurance: [6]										
Insured unemployed, avg.[7] 1,000__	1,328	1,805	2,150	1,848	1,632	2,262	3,986	2,991	2,647	(NA)
Percent of covered employm't__	3.0	3.4	4.1	3.5	2.7	3.5	6.0	4.6	3.9	(NA)
Initial claims, wkly. avg.[8] 1,000__	232	296	295	261	247	363	478	386	375	(NA)
Claimants exhausting benefits_____1,000__	1,086	1,295	2,007	1,809	1,495	1,926	4,195	3,270	2,850	(NA)
Percent of first payment claims_	21.5	24.4	30.1	29.2	27.7	31.0	37.8	37.8	33.4	(NA)
Avg. duration of benefits_____wk__	12.2	12.3	14.4	14.2	13.4	12.7	15.7	14.9	14.2	(NA)

NA Not available. [1] Seasonally adjusted average. Some detail will not add to total because of independent adjustments. [2] Aggregate lost by the unemployed and persons on part-time for economic reasons as a percent of potentially available labor force hours. [3] Percent of civilian labor force in specified group. [4] 20–24 years old. [5] Wage and salary workers. [6] Source: U.S. Employment and Training Administration. State programs only. See table 557. [7] Workers reporting completion of at least 1 week of unemployment. [8] Notices by workers to indicate they are starting periods of unemployment.

Source: Except as noted, U.S. Bureau of Labor Statistics, *Handbook of Labor Statistics*, annual, and *Employment and Earnings*, monthly.

No. 668. Total Unemployed and Insured Unemployed—States: 1974 to 1977

[In thousands of persons 16 years old and over, except percent. Annual averages of monthly figures. Unemployment estimates based on the Current Population Survey (CPS), except as noted in footnote 5; see text, p. 1]

| STATE | TOTAL UNEMPLOYED [1] | | | | | | | | INSURED UNEMPLOYED | | | | | |
| | Number (1,000) | | | | Percent [2] | | | | Number (1,000) | | | Percent [3] | | |
	1974	1975	1976	1977	1974	1975	1976	1977	1975	1976	1977 [4]	1975	1976	1977 [4]
Ala	78	111	100	114	5.5	7.7	6.8	7.4	58.3	41.3	38.5	6.3	4.6	4.0
Alaska [5]	9	10	13	16	7.7	6.7	8.0	9.4	7.0	9.7	13.3	8.0	8.1	10.3
Ariz.[5]	62	113	93	80	6.8	12.1	9.8	8.2	38.6	26.7	19.8	6.2	4.5	3.2
Ark.[5]	43	80	62	60	5.2	9.5	7.1	6.6	41.2	26.2	22.6	6.6	5.1	4.1
Calif	669	926	889	834	7.3	9.9	9.2	8.2	421.4	358.0	321.2	6.4	5.5	4.5
Colo.[5]	46	80	71	78	4.0	6.9	5.9	6.2	25.1	21.8	21.6	3.3	3.0	2.7
Conn	88	133	139	106	6.1	9.1	9.5	7.0	84.0	67.9	53.7	6.9	5.8	4.5
Del.[5]	17	25	23	23	6.7	9.8	8.9	8.4	11.7	8.4	7.6	5.5	4.1	3.6
D.C	20	26	30	32	6.0	7.6	9.1	9.7	13.5	12.0	11.5	3.7	3.4	3.3
Fla	208	366	314	289	6.2	10.7	9.0	8.2	129.6	98.4	78.1	3.7	3.7	3.0
Ga	109	185	179	156	5.2	8.6	8.1	6.9	84.2	48.8	42.0	5.7	3.5	2.9
Hawaii [5]	31	32	39	30	8.0	8.2	9.8	7.3	14.5	16.0	12.8	4.7	5.0	3.9
Idaho [5]	17	21	21	23	5.1	6.2	5.7	5.9	11.6	10.2	9.8	5.4	4.6	4.2
Ill	224	357	332	321	4.5	7.1	6.5	6.2	216.8	197.9	164.9	5.6	5.3	4.4
Ind	123	206	148	141	5.2	8.6	6.1	5.7	86.5	41.2	35.4	5.4	2.6	2.1
Iowa [5]	28	56	53	56	2.2	4.2	4.0	4.0	29.2	24.6	21.5	3.6	3.1	2.6
Kans.[5]	35	48	46	45	3.4	4.6	4.2	4.1	20.7	16.9	16.4	3.4	2.7	2.5
Ky	64	103	81	70	4.5	7.3	5.6	4.7	49.9	34.8	31.4	5.8	4.2	3.6
La	97	106	101	109	7.1	7.4	6.8	7.0	43.5	38.1	41.2	4.3	3.7	3.7
Maine [5]	29	47	42	39	6.4	10.3	8.9	8.4	23.2	17.9	17.7	8.0	6.3	5.9
Md	84	128	128	118	4.7	6.9	6.8	6.1	61.5	43.5	40.3	5.3	3.8	3.5
Mass	190	304	263	225	7.2	11.2	9.5	8.1	155.7	106.6	87.1	7.7	5.6	4.5
Mich	337	488	374	337	8.5	12.5	9.4	8.2	249.6	161.4	139.3	9.1	5.7	4.6
Minn	77	107	110	98	4.3	5.9	5.9	5.1	60.1	49.7	42.2	4.4	3.6	3.0
Miss.[5]	41	75	62	71	4.5	8.2	6.6	7.4	29.9	18.6	17.5	5.4	3.5	3.1
Mo	95	142	133	131	4.6	6.9	6.2	5.9	84.5	57.3	53.8	5.8	4.1	3.7
Mont.[5]	17	21	20	22	5.2	6.3	6.1	6.4	10.2	9.8	9.7	6.0	5.1	4.4
Nebr.[5]	18	28	24	28	2.6	3.9	3.3	3.7	16.4	10.9	9.5	3.7	2.5	2.1
Nev.[5]	21	28	27	23	7.6	9.7	9.0	7.0	14.0	11.9	9.9	6.5	5.5	4.3
N.H.[5]	20	34	25	24	5.4	9.1	6.4	5.9	16.8	8.9	6.2	6.5	3.6	2.2
N.J	203	333	345	316	6.3	10.2	10.4	9.4	178.8	141.0	125.6	7.7	6.5	5.6
N. Mex.[5]	34	44	43	39	8.0	10.0	9.1	7.8	14.7	11.9	10.5	5.7	4.6	3.7
N.Y	482	729	794	708	6.4	9.5	10.3	9.1	394.1	316.1	280.4	6.7	5.6	4.9
N.C	111	217	159	155	4.5	8.6	6.2	5.9	114.8	61.6	49.9	6.6	3.7	2.9
N. Dak.[5]	9	10	10	14	3.5	3.7	3.6	4.8	4.9	5.1	6.3	3.5	3.5	4.0
Ohio	225	429	369	311	4.8	9.1	7.8	6.5	189.3	114.6	102.2	4.9	3.1	2.7
Okla	49	83	65	61	4.4	7.2	5.6	5.0	29.1	24.3	18.7	4.0	3.5	2.5
Oreg	76	110	102	83	7.5	10.6	9.5	7.4	54.7	43.1	39.3	7.1	5.6	4.9
Pa	258	423	406	398	5.1	8.3	7.9	7.7	285.2	229.0	216.3	7.4	6.1	5.7
R.I.[5]	23	48	35	38	5.3	10.9	8.1	8.6	30.0	19.6	19.0	9.2	6.4	5.8
S.C.[5]	68	103	87	92	5.9	8.7	6.9	7.2	60.6	31.0	24.3	7.3	4.0	2.9
S. Dak.[5]	8	11	11	10	2.7	3.7	3.4	3.3	4.6	4.1	3.8	2.9	2.6	2.3
Tenn	92	151	110	120	5.1	8.3	6.0	6.3	85.7	52.2	44.7	6.7	4.3	3.5
Tex	220	294	318	310	4.3	5.6	5.7	5.3	81.4	62.6	57.6	2.3	1.7	1.5
Utah [5]	26	36	29	28	5.5	6.8	5.7	5.3	16.1	13.1	11.5	4.8	3.8	3.2
Vt.[5]	13	20	19	16	6.4	9.4	8.7	7.0	10.8	8.3	7.1	8.1	6.4	5.2
Va	98	145	136	127	4.5	6.4	5.9	5.3	47.8	29.7	28.5	3.5	2.1	2.0
Wash	108	147	137	144	7.2	9.5	8.7	8.8	83.8	73.8	64.5	8.6	7.4	6.1
W. Va.[5]	45	57	51	49	6.9	8.6	7.5	7.1	25.8	20.1	21.0	5.6	4.4	4.4
Wis	94	148	122	109	4.5	6.9	5.6	4.9	89.0	63.4	53.9	5.7	4.0	3.5
Wyo.[5]	5	7	7	7	3.4	4.2	4.1	3.6	2.3	2.2	2.0	2.2	2.0	1.7

[1] Data from U.S. Bureau of Labor Statistics.
[2] Total unemployment as percent of civilian labor force.
[3] Insured unemployment as percent of average covered employment.   [4] Preliminary.
[5] For 1974 and 1975, unemployment estimates were derived from data drawn from the CPS and the unemployment insurance program.

Source: U.S. Employment and Training Administration, *Manpower Report of the President*, annual, and U.S. Bureau of Labor Statistica, *Geographic Profile of Employment and Unemployment*, annual.

No. 669. Minority Race Unemployment, Selected States: 1975 to 1977

[Persons 16 years old and over. Minority refers to all races other than White. Annual averages based on information collected by Bureau of the Census as part of the Current Population Survey; see text, p. 1]

STATE	UNEMPLOYED (1,000)			RATE [1]			STATE	UNEMPLOYED (1,000)			RATE [1]		
	1975	1976	1977	1975	1976	1977		1975	1976	1977	1975	1976	1977
U.S.	1,458	1,433	1,482	13.9	13.1	13.1	Mass.	8	5	9	11.9	7.6	13.1
Ala.	31	37	49	10.0	11.0	14.5	Mich.	87	57	70	21.0	14.2	15.9
Ariz.	(NA)	5	4	(NA)	10.1	8.1	Miss.	(NA)	36	45	(NA)	11.8	13.8
Ark.	(NA)	17	21	(NA)	14.0	14.3	Mo.	17	33	29	14.5	16.1	13.5
Calif.	157	157	160	13.6	14.0	13.2	N.J.	58	56	60	15.7	16.2	16.3
Conn.	11	15	11	12.7	13.7	10.8	N.Y.	117	126	122	12.3	12.9	12.2
D.C.	(NA)	30	30	(NA)	9.1	12.2	N.C.	74	54	57	13.8	10.5	10.7
Fla.	106	97	83	17.0	14.9	13.0	Ohio.	69	59	57	16.2	14.0	13.6
Ga.	77	72	61	16.1	14.0	12.2	Okla.	17	12	15	20.3	15.2	14.2
Hawaii.	(NA)	25	21	(NA)	8.5	6.7	Pa.	54	61	72	15.8	17.0	19.4
Ill.	75	93	92	13.4	15.4	14.8	S.C.	38	33	34	13.2	11.3	11.3
Ind.	28	24	30	17.0	13.7	16.9	Tenn.	33	36	36	12.8	13.6	12.7
Kans.	(NA)	7	7	(NA)	12.5	12.3	Texas.	70	72	68	10.9	10.8	9.8
Ky.	13	10	10	12.7	9.9	10.0	Va.	43	42	45	10.9	10.3	11.2
La.	51	47	46	14.1	13.1	12.6	Wash.	13	15	13	14.8	17.5	18.6
Md.	42	39	41	12.1	11.2	11.1	Wis.	14	13	14	21.6	19.6	22.2

NA   Not available.   [1] Unemployed as percent of civilian labor force.

Source: U.S. Bureau of Labor Statistics, *Geographic Profile of Employment and Unemployment, 1975, 1976,* and *1977,* BLS reports 481, 539, and 560, respectively.

No. 670. Unemployed Persons, by Reason and Sex: 1968 to 1977

[In thousands of persons 16 years old and over, except percent. Annual averages of monthly figures]

UNEMPLOYED PERSONS	1968	1969	1970	1971	1972	1973	1974	1975	1976	1977
Total.	2,817	2,831	4,088	4,993	4,840	4,304	5,076	7,830	7,288	6,855
Job losers.	1,070	1,017	1,809	2,313	2,089	1,666	2,205	4,341	3,625	3,103
Percent.	38.0	35.9	44.3	46.3	43.2	38.7	43.4	55.4	49.7	45.3
Job leavers.	431	436	549	587	635	674	756	812	886	889
Reentrants.	909	965	1,227	1,466	1,444	1,323	1,441	1,865	1,895	1,926
New entrants.	407	413	503	627	672	642	672	812	882	938
Male.	1,419	1,403	2,235	2,776	2,635	2,240	2,668	4,385	3,968	3,588
Job losers.	683	639	1,197	1,542	1,376	1,080	1,436	2,877	2,389	1,977
Percent.	48.1	45.5	53.6	55.5	52.2	48.2	53.8	65.6	60.2	55.1
Job leavers.	218	219	282	304	318	333	364	367	393	402
Reentrants.	358	375	532	642	637	528	579	770	768	777
New entrants.	160	170	224	288	304	298	290	371	418	433
Female.	1,397	1,428	1,853	2,217	2,205	2,064	2,408	3,445	3,320	3,267
Job losers.	387	378	613	771	713	585	770	1,464	1,235	1,126
Percent.	27.7	26.5	33.1	34.8	32.3	28.3	32.0	42.5	37.2	34.5
Job leavers.	213	217	267	283	317	341	393	445	493	487
Reentrants.	551	589	695	824	807	794	863	1,095	1,128	1,149
New entrants.	247	243	279	338	368	343	383	441	464	505

No. 671. Persons With A Job But Not At Work: 1965 to 1978

[Persons 16 years old and over, except 1965, 14 years old and over. Annual averages of monthly figures, except as indicated. See *Historical Statistics, Colonial Times to 1970,* series D 116–126, for related but not comparable data]

REASON FOR NOT WORKING	1965	1970	1971	1972	1973	1974	1975	1976	1977	1978, Jan.– Apr.
All industries, number__1,000__	3,525	4,614	4,716	4,703	4,926	5,323	5,171	5,307	5,450	4,246
Percent of employed.	4.9	5.9	6.0	5.8	5.8	6.2	6.1	6.1	6.0	4.6
Nonagricultural industries__1,000__	3,368	4,481	4,586	4,568	4,775	5,162	5,007	5,164	5,303	4,067
Reason for not working:										
Vacation__1,000__	1,738	2,324	2,450	2,501	2,609	2,887	2,788	2,898	2,913	1,214
Percent.	49.3	50.4	52.0	53.2	53.0	54.2	53.9	54.6	53.4	28.6
Illness__1,000__	1,039	1,317	1,274	1,329	1,362	1,377	1,332	1,387	1,410	1,543
Bad weather__1,000__	79	127	123	141	191	143	138	99	236	526
Industrial dispute__1,000__	48	156	145	78	75	149	94	115	119	140
All other__1,000__	621	690	724	653	689	767	819	808	772	823

Source of tables 670 and 671: U.S. Bureau of Labor Statistics, *Employment and Earnings,* monthly.

No. 672. UNEMPLOYMENT RATE AND PERCENT DISTRIBUTION OF UNEMPLOYED: 1970 TO 1977

[Annual averages of monthly figures. Persons 16 years old and over. For number of unemployed, see table 667]

INDUSTRY AND OCCUPATION OF LAST JOB	1970	1971	1972	1973	1974	1975	1976	1977 Total	1977 Male	1977 Female
INDUSTRY GROUP				UNEMPLOYMENT RATE [1] (percent)						
All unemployed [2]	4.9	5.9	5.6	4.9	5.6	8.5	7.7	7.0	6.2	8.2
Experienced wage and salary workers	4.8	5.7	5.3	4.5	5.3	8.2	7.3	6.6	6.0	7.4
Agriculture	7.5	7.9	7.6	6.9	7.3	10.3	11.7	11.1	10.0	15.4
Mining	3.1	4.0	3.2	2.9	2.9	4.0	4.7	3.8	3.3	8.6
Construction	9.7	10.4	10.3	8.8	10.6	18.1	15.6	12.7	12.9	9.8
Manufacturing	5.6	6.8	5.6	4.3	5.7	10.9	7.9	6.7	5.3	9.7
Durable goods	5.7	7.0	5.4	3.9	5.4	11.3	7.7	6.2	5.3	8.9
Nondurable goods	5.4	6.5	5.7	4.9	6.2	10.4	8.1	7.4	5.3	10.4
Transportation and public utilities	3.2	3.8	3.5	3.0	3.2	5.6	5.0	4.7	4.6	5.0
Wholesale and retail trade	5.3	6.4	6.4	5.6	6.4	8.7	8.6	8.0	6.8	9.5
Finance, insurance, and real estate	2.8	3.3	3.4	2.7	3.1	4.9	4.4	3.9	3.0	4.5
Service industries	4.7	5.6	5.3	4.8	5.1	7.1	7.2	6.6	6.4	6.8
Government	2.2	2.9	2.9	2.7	3.0	4.0	4.4	4.2	3.5	4.8
PERCENT DISTRIBUTION OF UNEMPLOYED										
All unemployed [3]	100.0	100.0	100.0	100.0	100.0	100.0	100.0	100.0	100.0	100.0
Experienced wage and salary workers	86.2	85.7	84.4	83.5	85.1	87.9	86.3	84.6	85.5	83.5
Agriculture	2.3	2.0	2.1	2.2	2.1	1.9	2.4	2.4	3.3	1.4
Mining	.4	.5	.4	.4	.4	.5	.5	.5	.7	.2
Construction	9.3	8.5	9.2	9.3	9.4	10.2	9.4	8.5	15.4	.9
Manufacturing	29.2	28.0	23.7	21.5	24.4	29.5	23.0	21.1	22.1	20.0
Durable goods	17.6	16.8	13.4	11.5	13.7	18.1	13.4	11.5	14.3	8.5
Nondurable goods	11.6	11.2	10.3	10.1	10.8	11.4	9.7	9.6	7.8	11.5
Transportation and public utilities	3.7	3.5	3.5	3.3	3.1	3.5	3.3	3.5	5.0	1.8
Wholesale and retail trade	17.9	18.9	20.4	20.5	20.5	18.8	20.6	21.1	18.5	23.9
Finance, insurance, and real estate	2.5	2.6	2.8	2.7	2.7	2.7	2.7	2.7	1.7	3.7
Service industries	14.0	14.1	14.1	14.7	13.9	13.1	14.9	15.2	10.8	20.0
Government	6.9	7.7	8.3	8.8	8.6	7.8	9.4	9.7	8.0	11.5
No previous work experience	12.4	12.6	14.0	15.0	13.3	10.4	12.1	13.7	12.1	15.5
OCCUPATION GROUP				UNEMPLOYMENT RATE [1] (percent)						
Professional and technical	2.0	2.9	2.4	2.2	2.3	3.2	3.2	3.0	2.3	3.9
Managers and administrators, except farm	1.3	1.6	1.8	1.4	1.8	3.0	3.1	2.8	2.3	4.4
Sales workers	3.9	4.3	4.3	3.7	4.2	5.8	5.4	5.3	4.0	6.8
Clerical workers	4.1	4.8	4.7	4.2	4.6	6.6	6.4	5.9	5.0	6.1
Craft and kindred workers	3.8	4.7	4.3	3.7	4.4	8.3	6.9	5.6	5.5	7.4
Operatives, except transport	(NA)	(NA)	7.6	6.1	8.2	14.7	10.8	9.5	8.0	11.7
Transport equipment operatives	(NA)	(NA)	4.7	4.1	5.1	8.5	7.7	6.6	6.6	6.7
Nonfarm laborers	9.5	10.8	10.3	8.4	10.1	15.6	13.7	12.0	12.1	11.0
Service workers	5.3	6.3	6.3	5.7	6.3	8.6	8.7	8.2	7.5	8.6
Farm workers	2.6	2.6	2.6	2.5	2.5	3.5	4.5	4.6	4.0	7.6
PERCENT DISTRIBUTION OF UNEMPLOYED										
All unemployed	100.0	100.0	100.0	100.0	100.0	100.0	100.0	100.0	100.0	100.0
Experienced workers	87.6	87.4	86.0	85.0	86.7	89.6	87.9	86.3	87.9	84.5
Professional and technical	5.6	6.7	5.8	6.0	5.6	5.4	6.0	6.2	5.2	7.3
Managers and administrators, except farm	2.7	2.9	3.0	2.9	3.3	3.5	4.1	4.0	4.9	3.0
Sales workers	4.8	4.5	4.9	4.8	4.7	4.3	4.3	4.6	3.8	5.5
Clerical workers	14.2	13.7	14.5	14.6	14.6	13.6	14.6	14.6	5.0	25.3
Craft and kindred workers	9.7	10.2	10.0	10.1	10.3	12.7	11.4	10.3	18.4	1.5
Operatives, except transport	(NA)	(NA)	17.6	16.7	18.7	21.2	16.7	15.9	15.2	16.6
Transport equipment operatives	(NA)	(NA)	3.3	3.3	3.5	3.8	3.7	3.6	6.4	.5
Nonfarm laborers	9.6	9.8	10.0	9.2	9.7	9.8	9.4	9.0	15.7	1.6
Service workers	13.2	14.4	15.2	15.7	15.1	13.9	15.8	16.1	10.7	22.0
Farm workers	2.0	1.6	1.7	1.8	1.6	1.4	1.8	1.9	2.6	1.2
No previous work experience	12.4	12.6	14.0	15.0	13.3	10.4	12.1	13.7	12.1	15.5

NA Not available.
[1] Unemployed as a percent of labor force in each specified group.
[2] Includes the self-employed, unpaid family workers, and persons with no previous work experience, not shown separately.   [3] Includes the self-employed and unpaid family workers, not shown separately.

Source: U.S. Bureau of Labor Statistics, *Employment and Earnings*, monthly.

No. 673. NONAGRICULTURAL ESTABLISHMENTS—EMPLOYEES AND AVERAGE WEEKLY HOURS: 1960 TO 1978

[Excludes Alaska and Hawaii. Based on data from establishment reports. Includes all full- and part-time employees who worked during, or received pay for, any part of the pay period reported. Excludes proprietors, self-employed persons, farmworkers, unpaid family workers, domestic servants, and Armed Forces. Data are annual averages adjusted to March 1974 benchmark levels indicated by data from government social insurance programs. See also *Historical Statistics, Colonial Times to 1970*, series D 127–141 and D 803, 878, 881, 884, and 890]

ITEM AND YEAR	NONAGRICULTURAL ESTABLISHMENTS									GROUPED INDUSTRIES	
	Total	Manufacturing	Wholesale and retail trade	Government	Services	Transportation and public utilities	Finance, insurance, and real estate	Contract construction	Mining	Goods related [1]	Service related and all other
NUMBER (1,000)											
1960	54,234	16,796	11,391	8,353	7,423	4,004	2,669	2,885	712	20,393	33,840
1965	60,815	18,062	12,716	10,074	9,087	4,036	3,023	3,186	632	21,880	38,936
1970	70,920	19,349	15,040	12,561	11,621	4,504	3,687	3,536	623	23,507	47,412
1973	76,833	20,054	16,665	13,742	12,986	4,646	4,075	4,028	638	24,720	52,113
1974	78,413	20,046	17,017	14,177	13,617	4,696	4,208	3,957	694	24,697	53,715
1975	77,051	18,347	17,000	14,720	14,006	4,498	4,223	3,512	745	22,603	54,448
1976	79,443	18,956	17,694	14,948	14,644	4,509	4,316	3,594	783	23,332	56,111
1977	82,142	19,554	18,292	15,190	15,333	4,589	4,508	3,844	831	24,229	57,912
1978, Jan.–Apr.[2]	84,365	20,109	18,808	15,504	15,830	4,663	4,661	4,031	759	24,898	59,466
PERCENT DISTRIBUTION											
1960	100.0	31.0	21.0	15.4	13.7	7.4	4.9	5.3	1.3	37.6	62.4
1965	100.0	29.7	20.9	16.6	14.9	6.6	5.0	5.2	1.0	36.0	64.0
1970	100.0	27.2	21.2	17.7	16.4	6.4	5.2	5.0	.9	33.1	66.9
1973	100.0	26.1	21.7	17.9	16.9	6.1	5.3	5.2	.8	32.2	67.8
1974	100.0	25.6	21.7	18.1	17.4	6.0	5.4	5.0	.9	31.5	68.5
1975	100.0	23.8	22.1	19.1	18.2	5.8	5.5	4.6	1.0	29.3	70.7
1976	100.0	23.9	22.3	18.8	18.4	5.7	5.4	4.5	1.0	29.4	70.6
1977	100.0	23.8	22.3	18.5	18.7	5.6	5.5	4.7	1.0	29.5	70.5
1978, Jan.–Apr.[2]	100.0	23.8	22.3	18.4	18.8	5.5	5.5	4.8	.9	29.5	70.5
AVERAGE WEEKLY HOURS [3]											
1960	38.6	39.7	38.6	(NA)	(NA)	(NA)	37.2	36.7	40.4	(NA)	(NA)
1965	38.8	41.2	37.7	(NA)	35.9	41.3	37.2	37.4	42.3	(NA)	(NA)
1970	37.1	39.8	35.3	(NA)	34.4	40.5	36.8	37.3	42.7	(NA)	(NA)
1973	37.1	40.7	34.7	(NA)	34.0	40.7	36.9	37.0	42.5	(NA)	(NA)
1974	36.6	40.0	34.1	(NA)	33.9	40.2	36.7	36.9	42.4	(NA)	(NA)
1975	36.1	39.4	33.8	(NA)	33.8	39.6	36.5	36.6	42.3	(NA)	(NA)
1976	36.2	40.0	33.6	(NA)	33.5	39.9	36.6	37.1	42.8	(NA)	(NA)
1977	36.1	40.3	33.3	(NA)	33.4	40.1	36.6	36.9	44.1	(NA)	(NA)
1978, Jan.–Apr.[2]	35.9	40.1	32.9	(NA)	33.4	40.3	36.7	36.1	43.9	(NA)	(NA)

NA Not available.   [1] Mining, construction, and manufacturing.   [2] Seasonally adjusted. [3] See headnote, table 686.

Source: U.S. Bureau of Labor Statistics, *Employment and Earnings*, monthly.

No. 674. MINORITY RACES AS PERCENT OF NONAGRICULTURAL WAGE AND SALARY EMPLOYMENT, BY INDUSTRY: 1965 TO 1977

[Persons 16 years old and over except 1965, 14 years old and over. Annual averages of monthly figures. Covers all races other than White. Based on Current Population Survey; see text, p. 395. Excludes self-employed and unpaid family workers]

YEAR	Total	Manufacturing	Wholesale and retail trade	Government	Services (exc. pvt. households)	Transportation, public utilities	Finance, insurance, real estate	Construction	Mining	Goods related [1]	Service related and all other [2]
1965	11.0	8.3	8.9	12.4	13.3	7.7	5.0	11.5	5.5	8.7	10.4
1970	11.2	10.2	7.8	14.0	12.2	8.8	6.7	10.4	3.8	10.1	10.6
1972	11.0	10.0	7.5	14.6	11.9	9.0	6.8	9.9	4.6	9.8	10.6
1973	11.3	10.8	7.8	15.0	12.0	9.8	7.0	9.6	3.9	10.4	10.9
1974	11.3	11.1	7.9	14.7	11.8	10.3	7.7	9.4	4.1	10.7	10.9
1975	11.2	10.7	8.1	14.7	11.9	9.9	7.8	9.0	2.9	10.2	11.0
1976	11.3	11.1	7.8	15.1	12.0	10.3	8.1	8.0	3.5	10.4	11.1
1977	11.4	11.0	7.8	15.3	12.1	11.0	8.1	8.6	4.0	10.4	11.2

[1] Mining, construction, and manufacturing.   [2] Excludes private household.

Source: U.S. Bureau of Labor Statistics, unpublished data.

No. 675. EMPLOYEES IN NONAGRICULTURAL ESTABLISHMENTS—STATES: 1960 TO 1977

[In thousands. For coverage, see headnote, table 673. National totals differ from the sum of the State figures because of differing benchmarks among States and differing industrial and geographic stratification. Based on 1972 *Standard Industrial Classification Manual*, except as noted]

STATE	1960, total	1970, total	1975, total	1976, total	1977							
					Total[1]	Manu-facturing	Whole-sale and retail trade	Gov-ern-ment	Serv-ices	Trans-porta-tion, public utili-ties	Fi-nance, insur-ance, real estate	Con-struc-tion
U.S.	54,234	70,920	77,051	79,443	82,142	19,554	18,292	15,190	15,333	4,589	4,508	3,844
N. Eng.	3,699	4,544	4,656	4,772	4,926	1,391	1,077	769	1,016	218	284	170
Maine	278	332	357	375	388	106	84	77	67	18	15	21
N.H.	201	260	293	313	336	101	74	52	63	12	16	18
Vt.	108	148	162	168	176	43	37	32	40	8	7	8
Mass.	1,905	2,262	2,272	2,309	2,364	608	536	372	531	112	136	69
R.I.	292	344	349	367	379	128	77	58	72	13	19	12
Conn.	915	1,198	1,223	1,240	1,283	405	269	178	243	55	91	42
Mid. Atl.	11,912	14,111	13,963	14,049	14,222	3,570	2,989	2,474	2,863	864	938	467
N.Y.	6,182	7,155	6,827	6,779	6,827	1,459	1,426	1,260	1,483	425	577	190
N.J.	2,017	2,609	2,701	2,758	2,845	769	637	500	516	180	144	96
Pa.	3,713	4,347	4,435	4,512	4,550	1,342	926	714	864	259	217	181
E. No. Cent.	11,643	14,594	15,190	15,616	16,110	4,925	3,532	2,608	2,755	830	764	620
Ohio	3,147	3,881	4,016	4,095	4,216	1,341	918	637	728	219	184	161
Ind.	1,431	1,849	1,942	2,024	2,089	707	454	342	293	105	93	88
Ill.	3,522	4,329	4,419	4,509	4,608	1,238	1,056	728	844	274	268	173
Mich.	2,351	3,005	3,136	3,264	3,412	1,106	699	614	570	147	140	124
Wis.	1,192	1,530	1,677	1,724	1,785	533	405	287	320	85	79	74
W. No. Cent.	4,194	5,359	5,986	6,197	6,403	1,317	1,605	1,227	1,176	402	332	306
Minn.	960	1,317	1,474	1,521	1,596	338	405	285	312	93	83	70
Iowa	681	883	999	1,037	1,066	242	271	203	187	55	52	54
Mo.	1,345	1,662	1,741	1,798	1,844	437	442	321	336	128	96	77
N. Dak.	126	163	204	215	221	15	63	58	43	14	10	16
S. Dak.	142	175	209	219	226	23	61	56	47	12	10	12
Nebr.	381	482	558	572	586	91	154	127	101	42	38	32
Kans.	559	677	801	835	864	171	209	177	150	58	43	45
So. Atl.	7,215	10,620	12,095	12,482	12,829	2,866	2,803	2,746	2,232	714	661	697
Del.	154	213	230	236	236	68	52	41	39	12	11	14
Md. [2]	896	1,349	1,479	1,501	1,529	236	368	378	295	79	82	90
D.C. [2]	536	686	577	576	577	15	64	275	150	25	34	14
Va. [2]	1,018	1,520	1,779	1,848	1,912	400	399	455	325	107	90	114
W. Va.	460	517	575	596	605	124	122	111	86	40	20	36
N.C.	1,196	1,783	1,970	2,067	2,128	779	413	346	295	103	84	103
S.C.	583	842	983	1,038	1,079	380	199	212	134	45	41	66
Ga.	1,051	1,558	1,756	1,836	1,890	489	434	373	281	119	100	88
Fla.	1,321	2,152	2,746	2,784	2,873	375	752	555	627	184	199	172
E. So. Cent.	2,760	3,826	4,417	4,622	4,807	1,373	1,005	935	720	242	203	253
Ky.	654	910	1,064	1,112	1,157	283	248	223	185	64	47	60
Tenn.	926	1,328	1,506	1,575	1,629	507	350	290	251	77	70	76
Ala.	776	1,011	1,155	1,207	1,260	353	258	261	177	65	56	76
Miss.	404	577	692	728	761	230	149	161	107	36	30	41
W. So. Cent.	4,271	5,982	7,237	7,589	7,875	1,471	1,900	1,458	1,316	507	417	532
Ark.	367	534	624	660	693	209	149	128	97	38	29	37
La.	790	1,042	1,250	1,314	1,335	202	319	255	223	101	65	105
Okla.	582	770	900	931	975	163	232	215	159	59	49	49
Tex.	2,532	3,636	4,463	4,684	4,872	897	1,200	860	837	309	274	341
Mt.	1,872	2,663	3,406	3,566	3,733	464	888	845	760	228	192	234
Mont.	167	201	238	251	264	24	66	71	49	20	11	16
Idaho	155	208	273	291	306	54	76	67	52	18	16	19
Wyo.	97	109	146	157	168	9	37	37	24	13	6	17
Colo. [3]	515	743	947	975	992	144	241	214	195	63	61	52
N. Mex.	236	293	370	390	415	32	95	111	80	25	18	31
Ariz.	334	547	729	759	797	112	194	182	152	41	45	49
Utah	265	359	440	463	484	74	118	114	81	29	22	31
Nev.	103	203	263	280	307	15	61	49	127	19	13	19
Pac.	6,464	9,124	10,409	10,824	11,315	2,209	2,641	2,335	2,259	649	664	518
Wash.	813	1,080	1,219	1,271	1,343	261	328	278	247	78	75	75
Oreg.	509	709	837	879	930	205	224	186	162	54	57	42
Calif.	4,896	6,948	7,848	8,153	8,522	1,710	1,970	1,735	1,738	474	499	361
Alaska	57	93	162	172	163	10	28	50	27	15	8	20
Hawaii	189	294	343	349	357	23	91	86	85	28	25	20

[1] Includes mining, not shown separately. [2] Federal employment in the Maryland and Virginia sectors of the Washington, D.C., Standard Metropolitan Statistical Area is included only in data for the District of Columbia in 1960; in data for the District of Columbia, Maryland, and Virginia in 1970; and only in data for Maryland and Virginia beginning in 1975. [3] Based on 1967 *Standard Industrial Classification Manual*.

Source: U.S. Bureau of Labor Statistics, *Employment and Earnings*, monthly. Compiled from data supplied by cooperating State agencies.

No. 676. NONAGRICULTURAL INDUSTRIES—NUMBER OF EMPLOYEES, 1970 TO 1977, AND NUMBER AND EARNINGS OF PRODUCTION WORKERS, 1975 TO 1977

[Annual averages of monthly figures. Covers all full- and part-time employees who worked during, or received pay for, any part of the pay period including the 12th of the month. For mining and manufacturing, data refer to production and related workers; for contract construction industries, to employees engaged in actual construction work; and for other industries, to nonsupervisory employees and working supervisors. See also headnote, table 673. "N.e.c." means not elsewhere classified. See *Historical Statistics, Colonial Times to 1970*, series D 127–151, D 802–810, and D 877–892, for related data]

| INDUSTRY | ALL EMPLOYEES, NUMBER (1,000) | | | | PRODUCTION WORKERS | | | | | |
| | | | | | Number (1,000) | | | Average hourly earnings (dollars) | | |
	1970	1975	1976	1977	1975	1976	1977	1975	1976	1977
Total	70,920	77,051	79,443	82,142	(NA)	(NA)	(NA)	(NA)	(NA)	(NA)
Private sector [1]	58,359	62,330	64,496	66,952	51,149	53,054	54,936	4.54	4.87	5.25
Mining	623	745	783	831	565	593	623	5.90	6.42	6.88
Metal mining	94	92	93	90	71	72	68	6.13	6.75	7.27
Coal mining	145	202	214	218	172	183	179	[2]7.21	7.88	8.46
Oil and gas extraction	270	336	360	405	231	247	282	5.34	5.76	6.23
Nonmetallic minerals, except fuels	114	115	115	119	91	91	94	4.91	5.38	5.84
Contract construction	3,536	3,512	3,594	3,844	2,805	2,849	3,055	7.25	7.68	8.04
General building contractors	1,101	1,064	1,077	1,145	840	841	898	7.08	7.50	7.88
Heavy construction contractors	715	704	713	770	582	583	627	6.61	7.07	7.27
Special trade contractors	1,721	1,744	1,803	1,929	1,384	1,426	1,530	7.65	8.06	8.47
Manufacturing	19,349	18,347	18,956	19,554	13,070	13,625	14,066	4.81	5.19	5.63
Durable goods	11,195	10,679	11,026	11,480	7,543	7,866	8,220	5.14	5.55	6.02
Ordnance and accessories	242	171	158	155	80	72	71	5.23	5.72	6.25
Lumber and wood products, except furniture [3]	573	557	606	642	464	508	547	4.28	4.71	5.06
Logging camps and logging contr	72	73	75	74	(4)	(4)	(4)	(4)	(4)	(4)
Sawmills and planing mills	214	196	210	217	174	186	193	4.16	4.61	4.97
Millwork, plywood, and related products	168	178	203	227	145	168	190	4.42	4.86	5.24
Wooden containers	33	21	22	21	19	19	19	3.33	3.60	3.77
Furniture and fixtures [3]	460	451	490	510	364	402	419	3.75	3.98	4.30
Household furniture	320	321	354	369	268	300	312	3.55	3.76	4.06
Office furniture	38	36	38	42	27	30	34	4.15	4.51	4.86
Partitions and fixtures	51	49	52	54	36	39	41	4.55	4.82	5.20
Stone, clay, and glass products [3]	640	614	626	652	485	498	520	4.89	5.29	5.76
Flat glass	24	16	16	17	12	13	13	6.06	6.77	7.30
Glass and glassware, pressed or blown	132	126	132	136	108	114	118	4.98	5.40	5.99
Cement, hydraulic	34	30	30	30	24	23	24	6.33	7.26	7.92
Structural clay products	59	48	48	50	38	38	40	3.98	4.24	4.62
Pottery and related products	44	42	43	41	35	37	35	4.25	4.52	5.01
Concrete, gypsum, and plaster prod	187	188	188	201	145	146	156	4.91	5.29	5.67
Primary metal industries [3]	1,316	1,180	1,190	1,203	919	933	941	6.17	6.80	7.45
Blast furnace and basic steel prod	628	545	543	544	424	424	424	6.95	7.68	8.45
Iron and steel foundries	229	225	218	220	185	179	180	5.47	6.16	6.71
Nonferrous metals	90	82	84	85	62	64	64	5.96	6.60	7.33
Nonferrous rolling and drawing	213	181	194	198	130	144	146	5.50	6.01	6.60
Nonferrous foundries	83	75	79	83	61	66	69	4.86	5.22	5.67
Fabricated metal products [3]	1,380	1,336	1,387	1,451	996	1,046	1,100	5.04	5.43	5.84
Metal cans	75	64	63	61	55	54	52	6.44	7.01	7.48
Cutlery, hand tools, and hardware	150	155	167	177	117	129	138	4.76	5.13	5.63
Plumbing and heating, exc. electric	81	64	69	75	46	51	56	4.52	4.86	5.21
Fabricated structural metal prod	428	453	448	469	315	311	328	5.04	5.34	5.65
Screw machine products, bolts, etc.	104	95	98	106	73	76	83	4.82	5.24	5.64
Metal stampings	234	205	227	235	163	184	192	5.54	6.10	6.78
Metal services, n.e.c	86	83	90	96	67	74	78	4.20	4.43	4.72
Machinery, except electrical [3]	1,982	2,069	2,074	2,188	1,346	1,339	1,421	5.36	5.76	6.20
Engines and turbines	110	111	113	115	72	73	74	6.00	6.64	7.33
Farm machinery	129	152	146	147	108	102	102	5.70	6.08	6.56
Construction and related machinery	297	344	337	349	227	217	228	5.66	6.05	6.62
Metalworking machinery	319	310	309	329	225	225	242	5.51	5.94	6.44
Special industry machinery	198	182	176	179	116	112	114	4.92	5.36	5.81
General industrial machinery	285	289	286	298	190	187	196	5.36	5.73	6.17
Office and computing machines	283	284	292	322	116	117	134	5.00	5.29	5.43
Service industry machines	148	148	163	174	100	113	122	4.84	5.22	5.63
Electrical equipment and supplies [3]	1,917	1,761	1,832	1,935	1,140	1,210	1,286	4.58	4.91	5.34
Electric test and distributing equip.	204	192	193	205	127	129	139	4.70	5.10	5.47
Electrical industrial apparatus	217	202	212	224	140	151	160	4.58	4.97	5.40
Household appliances	184	154	165	178	116	129	140	4.56	4.87	5.27
Electric lighting and wiring equip	197	181	195	207	136	150	159	4.36	4.67	5.04

See footnotes at end of table.

No. 676. NONAGRICULTURAL INDUSTRIES—NUMBER OF EMPLOYEES, 1970 TO 1977, AND NUMBER AND EARNINGS OF PRODUCTION WORKERS, 1975 TO 1977—Continued

| INDUSTRY | ALL EMPLOYEES, NUMBER (1,000) | | | | PRODUCTION WORKERS | | | | | |
| | | | | | Number (1,000) | | | Average hourly earnings (dollars) | | |
	1970	1975	1976	1977	1975	1976	1977	1975	1976	1977
Private sector [1]—Continued										
Manufacturing—Continued										
Durable goods—Continued										
Electrical equip., supplies [3]—Con.										
Radio and TV receiving equipment.	133	121	129	134	87	94	97	4.26	4.51	4.90
Communication equipment	500	433	422	439	217	209	220	5.17	5.62	6.09
Electronic components and access	365	348	372	391	217	239	251	3.89	4.11	4.48
Transportation equipment [3]	1,799	1,649	1,733	1,798	1,148	1,226	1,274	6.02	6.54	7.18
Motor vehicles and equipment	797	774	851	891	593	662	693	6.47	7.10	7.90
Aircraft and parts	669	514	485	479	273	250	243	5.99	6.45	6.91
Ship and boat building and repairs	170	194	214	226	153	170	179	5.24	5.66	6.02
Railroad equipment	51	52	43	46	39	31	34	6.15	6.69	7.32
Instruments and related products	460	489	509	527	293	310	323	4.56	4.87	5.20
Engineering and scientific inst	71	61	59	59	31	29	28	4.81	5.13	5.51
Mech. measuring, control devices	110	109	117	123	67	75	80	4.42	4.73	5.10
Optical and ophthalmic goods	53	60	64	70	40	43	47	4.11	4.36	4.65
Medical instru. and supplies	83	103	109	116	68	73	78	4.05	4.32	4.59
Photographic equip. and supplies	112	126	130	130	62	66	67	5.69	6.14	6.58
Watches, clocks, and watchcases	31	30	31	30	24	24	23	3.71	3.92	4.20
Misc. manufacturing industries [3]	426	404	421	418	309	322	319	3.79	4.01	4.34
Jewelry, silverware, plated ware	51	50	54	55	37	40	41	4.07	4.27	4.54
Toys and sporting goods	118	115	120	117	90	93	90	3.50	3.71	4.02
Pens, pencils, office/art supplies	34	34	34	34	24	24	24	3.77	3.95	4.36
Costume jewelry and notions	41	52	54	51	42	44	41	3.36	3.55	3.83
Nondurable goods	8,154	7,668	7,930	8,074	5,528	5,759	5,846	4.35	4.68	5.07
Food and kindred products [3]	1,783	1,676	1,710	1,721	1,136	1,164	1,167	4.57	4.90	5.34
Meat products	343	339	351	362	277	289	298	4.74	5.09	5.41
Dairy products	241	197	194	193	101	101	101	4.56	4.92	5.25
Canned, cured, and frozen foods	288	293	299	289	245	250	238	3.95	4.27	4.63
Grain mill products	135	138	144	147	96	100	102	4.83	5.28	5.72
Bakery products	274	236	241	240	135	139	139	4.70	5.16	5.51
Sugar	36	35	35	30	27	27	23	4.94	5.39	5.99
Confectionery and related products	83	72	77	78	55	59	60	4.06	4.46	4.80
Beverages	237	223	223	233	108	106	111	5.38	5.87	6.38
Tobacco manufactures [3]	83	78	76	70	65	63	56	4.51	4.91	5.49
Cigarettes	44	45	46	44	37	37	35	5.52	5.94	6.62
Cigars	18	12	10	10	10	9	8	2.95	3.20	3.39
Textile mill products [3]	976	902	966	982	782	844	856	3.40	3.67	3.97
Weaving mills, cotton	216	164	175	172	148	159	155	3.43	3.77	4.14
Weaving mills, synthetic	100	114	123	121	101	110	108	3.50	3.83	4.17
Weaving and finishing mills, wool	37	21	23	23	17	19	19	3.51	3.76	4.06
Narrow fabric mills	30	23	26	26	20	23	23	3.25	3.46	3.69
Knitting mills	249	244	259	270	209	223	233	3.27	3.48	3.70
Textile finishing, except wool	82	77	82	81	65	69	69	3.69	3.97	4.25
Floor covering mills	57	58	60	64	46	47	51	3.52	3.77	4.12
Yarn and thread mills	130	139	154	157	126	141	144	3.19	3.44	3.73
Apparel and other textile products [3]	1,365	1,235	1,299	1,288	1,061	1,117	1,104	3.19	3.41	3.62
Men's and boys' suits and coats	119	87	89	88	76	78	78	3.92	4.18	4.47
Men's and boys' furnishings	375	355	383	383	304	328	328	2.86	3.08	3.27
Women's and misses' outerwear	424	384	389	373	336	341	325	3.27	3.51	3.70
Undergarments [5]	116	96	101	101	82	86	86	2.92	3.14	3.32
Hats, caps, and millinery	18	16	16	16	14	14	14	2.88	3.03	3.22
Children's outerwear	75	71	77	76	61	66	65	2.94	3.13	3.31
Fur goods and misc. apparel	75	63	67	68	54	58	58	3.26	3.45	3.65
Paper and allied products	706	643	676	698	483	512	525	4.99	5.43	5.92
Paper and pulp mills	219	192	199	202	146	153	155	5.55	6.11	6.72
Paperboard mills	72	67	70	71	52	56	56	5.68	6.28	6.87
Misc. converted paper products	190	190	197	208	135	141	146	4.52	4.88	5.28
Paperboard containers and boxes	225	195	209	217	149	163	168	4.55	4.91	5.34
Printing and publishing [3]	1,102	1,079	1,080	1,109	636	630	639	5.36	5.69	6.09
Newspapers	372	379	383	393	168	167	165	5.88	6.30	6.67
Periodicals	76	69	70	72	19	19	20	5.38	5.81	6.26
Books	101	92	88	90	49	47	47	4.59	4.95	5.30
Commercial printing	354	359	359	367	270	270	275	5.39	5.68	6.14
Blankbooks and bookbinding	57	50	50	52	41	41	42	4.07	4.39	4.71

See footnotes at end of table.

No. 676. NONAGRICULTURAL INDUSTRIES—NUMBER OF EMPLOYEES, 1970 TO 1977, AND NUMBER AND EARNINGS OF PRODUCTION WORKERS, 1975 TO 1977—Continued

| INDUSTRY | ALL EMPLOYEES, NUMBER (1,000) | | | | PRODUCTION WORKERS | | | | | |
| | | | | | Number (1,000) | | | Average hourly earnings (dollars) | | |
	1970	1975	1976	1977	1975	1976	1977	1975	1976	1977
Private sector [1]—Continued										
Manufacturing—Continued										
Nondurable goods—Continued										
Chemicals and allied products [3]	1,049	1,013	1,034	1,057	570	589	607	5.37	5.89	6.39
Industrial chemicals	323	324	336	347	171	180	187	5.93	6.57	7.16
Plastics materials and synthetics	218	203	205	204	133	136	137	5.25	5.76	6.27
Drugs	147	164	168	175	81	84	87	5.13	5.50	5.91
Soap, cleaners, and toilet goods	127	119	122	125	68	72	75	5.21	5.65	6.05
Paints and allied products	70	65	66	70	34	36	37	4.94	5.40	5.89
Agricultural chemicals	55	55	56	57	34	35	36	4.73	5.24	5.81
Petroleum and coal products	191	197	203	209	125	131	137	6.42	7.14	7.72
Petroleum refining	154	154	157	160	94	98	101	6.89	7.75	8.44
Other petroleum and coal products	37	43	46	49	31	34	36	5.03	5.40	5.75
Rubber and plastics prod., n.e.c. [3]	580	588	614	675	450	475	529	4.35	4.62	5.12
Tires and inner tubes	117	118	98	122	85	66	90	5.70	6.36	7.17
Leather and leather products [3]	320	257	272	264	219	234	226	3.23	3.44	3.64
Leather tanning and finishing	27	23	24	23	19	21	20	4.27	4.54	4.80
Footwear, except rubber	214	163	170	163	141	149	142	3.08	3.28	3.47
Handbags and pers. leather goods	34	33	36	35	27	30	29	3.11	3.28	3.52
Transp. and public utilities	4,504	4,498	4,509	4,589	3,857	3,862	3,901	5.92	6.46	6.94
Railroad transportation	627	538	528	534	(4)	(4)	(4)	(4)	(4)	(4)
Class I railroads [6]	559	491	490	497	(4)	(4)	(4)	6.05	6.88	(4)
Local and interurban pass. transit	279	270	268	261	(4)	(4)	(4)	(4)	(4)	(4)
Trucking and warehousing	1,083	1,086	1,096	1,131	969	977	1,001	6.05	6.43	6.92
Transportation by air	351	362	370	380	(4)	(4)	(4)	(4)	(4)	(4)
Pipeline transportation	18	17	17	17	13	12	12	6.92	7.47	8.20
Other transportation and services	330	329	343	357	(4)	(4)	(4)	(4)	(4)	(4)
Communication [3]	1,125	1,166	1,152	1,167	898	886	891	5.70	6.34	6.84
Telephone communication	939	962	943	951	735	717	716	5.76	6.46	6.94
Telegraph communication	31	19	17	(NA)	13	4	(NA)	5.85	6.36	(NA)
Radio and television broadcasting	137	153	157	162	122	126	129	5.50	5.91	6.44
Electric, gas, and sanitary services	691	733	736	745	611	612	615	5.99	6.56	7.05
Electric companies and systems	289	314	315	320	260	260	262	6.08	6.60	7.12
Gas companies and systems	161	160	160	158	132	131	130	5.53	6.08	6.64
Combination companies, systems	188	195	194	196	165	163	162	6.56	7.32	7.79
Water, steam, sanitary systems	52	64	67	71	55	57	61	4.91	5.31	5.68
Wholesale and retail trade	15,040	17,000	17,694	18,292	15,013	15,641	16,132	3.75	3.97	4.28
Wholesale trade	3,816	4,177	4,263	4,389	3,462	3,529	3,624	4.89	5.18	5.55
Retail trade [3]	11,225	12,824	13,431	13,903	11,552	12,113	12,508	3.34	3.55	3.83
Retail general merchandise	2,303	2,469	2,508	2,541	2,261	2,307	2,341	3.21	3.43	3.74
Food stores	1,731	1,968	2,061	2,116	1,825	1,907	1,955	3.95	4.31	4.69
Apparel and accessory stores	737	784	805	821	687	704	712	3.01	3.22	3.41
Furniture and home furn. stores	469	510	533	551	433	450	464	3.95	4.16	4.38
Eating and drinking places	2,572	3,332	3,624	3,854	3,112	3,380	3,586	2.50	2.64	2.90
Finance, insurance, real estate	3,687	4,223	4,316	4,508	3,221	3,293	3,433	4.13	4.36	4.60
Banking	1,044	1,275	1,299	1,342	1,007	1,024	1,047	3.55	3.69	3.88
Credit agencies other than banks	361	438	463	499	335	355	385	3.71	3.87	4.08
Security, commod. brokers, services	205	170	176	181	139	143	147	6.91	7.48	7.60
Insurance carriers	1,031	1,105	1,111	1,148	742	750	778	4.32	4.55	4.82
Insurance agents, brokers, services	274	331	342	365	(4)	(4)	(4)	(4)	(4)	(4)
Real estate	680	791	809	858	(4)	(4)	(4)	(4)	(4)	(4)
Other finance, insurance, real estate	91	114	116	116	(4)	(4)	(4)	(4)	(4)	(4)
Services [3]	11,621	14,006	14,644	15,333	12,617	13,191	13,727	4.06	4.36	4.71
Hotels and lodging places	771	990	1,058	1,079	(4)	(4)	(4)	(4)	(4)	(4)
Personal services	980	835	821	804	(4)	(4)	(4)	(4)	(4)	(4)
Miscellaneous business services	1,632	1,996	2,119	2,255	(4)	(4)	(4)	(4)	(4)	(4)
Motion pictures	204	202	203	206	(4)	(4)	(4)	(4)	(4)	(4)
Medical and other health services	3,057	4,194	4,441	4,731	(4)	(4)	(4)	(4)	(4)	(4)
Government	12,561	14,720	14,948	15,190	(NA)	(NA)	(NA)	(NA)	(NA)	(NA)
Federal Government	2,731	2,748	2,733	2,727	(NA)	(NA)	(NA)	(NA)	(NA)	(NA)
State and local government	9,830	11,973	12,215	12,463	(NA)	(NA)	(NA)	(NA)	(NA)	(NA)

NA Not available.   [1] Excludes government.   [2] 11-month average.
[3] Includes industries not shown separately.   [4] Included in "Private sector" total; not available separately.
[5] Women's and children's.   [6] Through 1975, for railroads with operating revenues of $5,000,000 or more. Beginning 1976, for line haul railroads with operating revenues of $10,000,000 or more.
Source: U.S. Bureau of Labor Statistics, *Employment and Earnings*, monthly.

No. 677. INDEXES AND ANNUAL PERCENT CHANGE OF PRODUCTIVITY AND RELATED MEASURES: 1960 TO 1977

[1977 preliminary. See also *Historical Statistics, Colonial Times to 1970*, series D 689–704 and W 22–25]

ITEM	1960	1965	1970	1971	1972	1973	1974	1975	1976	1977
INDEXES (1967=100)										
Output [1], private business	73.1	92.9	107.4	110.3	117.6	124.5	121.5	118.7	126.9	134.7
Nonfarm business	72.2	92.6	107.4	110.3	117.9	125.0	121.9	118.7	127.4	135.0
Manufacturing	67.7	92.6	102.6	104.0	113.7	123.2	114.9	107.6	120.0	127.1
Hours [2], private business	93.6	98.1	102.8	102.3	106.0	110.1	110.6	106.1	108.9	112.7
Nonfarm business	89.9	96.8	104.0	103.7	107.6	112.2	112.7	108.1	111.4	115.5
Manufacturing	85.9	94.3	98.2	94.2	98.0	103.2	101.8	92.5	96.6	100.1
Productivity [3], private business	78.1	94.7	104.5	107.8	111.0	113.1	109.9	111.8	116.5	119.5
Nonfarm business	80.3	95.7	103.3	106.3	109.5	111.4	108.1	109.9	114.3	116.9
Manufacturing	78.8	98.2	104.5	110.4	116.0	119.4	112.8	116.3	124.2	126.9
Compensation per hour [4], private business	71.4	88.4	123.3	131.5	138.9	150.3	164.3	180.2	196.5	214.0
Nonfarm business	73.7	89.1	121.9	129.9	137.4	148.1	162.0	177.6	193.1	210.0
Manufacturing	77.0	90.9	121.7	129.8	137.0	147.0	161.4	179.4	194.8	212.0
Unit labor cost [5], private business	91.4	93.4	118.1	121.9	125.2	132.9	149.5	161.1	168.7	179.0
Nonfarm business	91.7	93.2	118.1	122.2	125.5	133.0	149.8	161.7	168.9	179.7
Manufacturing	97.7	92.6	116.5	117.6	118.1	123.2	143.1	154.3	156.9	167.0
ANNUAL PERCENT CHANGE [6]										
Output [1], private business	1.8	7.0	−.9	2.8	6.6	5.9	−2.4	−2.4	7.0	6.1
Nonfarm business	1.6	7.1	−1.1	2.7	6.9	6.0	−2.5	−2.6	7.3	6.0
Hours [2], private business	.2	3.1	−1.6	−.4	3.6	3.9	.4	−4.1	2.7	3.4
Nonfarm business	.6	3.7	−1.2	−.3	3.7	4.3	.4	−4.1	3.1	3.7
Productivity [3], private business	1.6	3.7	.7	3.2	2.9	1.9	−2.8	1.8	4.2	2.6
Nonfarm business	1.0	3.3	.2	2.9	3.0	1.7	−2.9	1.6	4.1	2.2
Compensation per hour [4], private business	4.2	3.9	7.2	6.6	5.7	8.2	9.4	9.6	9.1	8.9
Nonfarm business	4.3	3.4	6.7	6.6	5.8	7.8	9.4	9.6	8.7	8.8
Unit labor cost [5], private business	2.6	.2	6.4	3.2	2.7	6.2	12.5	7.7	4.7	6.1
Nonfarm business	3.3	.1	6.5	3.5	2.7	6.0	12.7	7.9	4.5	6.4

[1] Refers to gross domestic product originating in the sector, in 1972 prices. [2] Hours of all persons engaged in the private business and nonfarm business sectors (employees, proprietors, and unpaid family workers); employees' and proprietors' hours in manufacturing; and employees' hours in nonfinancial corporations, where there are no self-employed. [3] Output per hour paid for. [4] Wages and salaries of employees plus employers' contributions for social insurance and private benefit plans. Also includes an estimate of same for self-employed. [5] Hourly compensation divided by productivity. [6] Changes for 1960, 1965, and 1970 are from immediately prior year. Minus sign (−) denotes decrease.

Source: U.S. Bureau of Labor Statistics, *Monthly Labor Review*.

No. 678. INDEXES OF OUTPUT PER HOUR—SELECTED INDUSTRIES: 1965 TO 1976

[1967=100. See also *Historical Statistics, Colonial Times to 1970*, series W 14, 17, and 19, W 30–54, and W 62–65]

INDUSTRY	ALL EMPLOYEES					PRODUCTION WORKERS				
	1965	1970	1974	1975	1976, prel.	1965	1970	1974	1975	1976, prel.
Manufacturing:										
Aluminum rolling and drawing	100.5	109.6	157.9	142.5	170.0	100.0	114.4	159.2	152.4	172.6
Bakery products	93.5	105.7	112.9	112.7	113.9	95.1	105.1	119.4	119.6	119.9
Bottled and canned soft drinks	100.2	105.2	120.9	129.5	142.6	102.4	113.0	135.0	147.2	161.4
Cement, hydraulic	95.2	110.3	119.0	111.0	118.1	94.7	111.3	118.4	111.6	118.0
Concrete products	90.5	104.4	116.3	113.2	(NA)	92.1	105.3	117.9	117.9	(NA)
Copper rolling and drawing	111.4	98.6	106.3	94.7	103.2	108.9	101.4	108.6	102.6	106.6
Corrugated, solid fiber boxes	92.8	111.8	137.7	142.2	146.6	92.7	112.8	143.2	151.8	153.9
Footwear	101.4	103.9	100.3	104.3	107.6	101.2	105.3	103.4	107.3	109.8
Gray iron foundries	104.9	105.8	128.0	124.2	131.2	103.9	107.4	129.7	128.5	135.5
Major household appliances	94.2	106.3	135.1	142.0	145.1	94.3	107.3	136.9	145.5	147.2
Malt beverages	89.0	119.6	157.2	165.6	181.3	88.7	119.4	151.7	160.0	167.8
Metal cans	94.1	105.4	113.3	116.0	117.9	95.6	106.7	116.0	121.0	122.3
Motor vehicles and equipment	99.0	102.0	121.1	129.3	141.1	96.0	103.3	121.5	129.0	138.7
Paints and allied products	99.6	101.7	123.3	128.7	133.7	98.8	100.8	126.0	136.9	140.0
Paper, paperboard, pulp mills	96.9	114.6	135.2	128.4	138.6	96.4	114.7	137.0	133.1	142.4
Petroleum refining	90.5	104.8	121.4	123.7	129.2	89.9	106.6	121.8	126.9	129.4
Pharmaceuticals	90.9	116.2	141.3	143.0	153.3	90.7	118.0	152.4	159.1	168.1
Primary aluminum	97.5	104.9	122.8	105.8	102.1	97.0	106.2	123.7	112.8	106.3
Primary copper, lead, and zinc	120.2	116.7	127.6	125.2	142.8	113.1	111.4	126.7	127.8	146.0
Radio and TV receiving sets	95.5	106.2	124.4	124.6	132.2	94.3	115.6	132.3	136.4	143.1
Steel	101.1	101.1	123.5	108.6	116.5	98.7	102.8	123.9	113.3	120.7
Steel foundries	100.5	96.2	118.5	113.0	118.7	98.4	97.9	119.9	115.4	123.7
Structural clay products	97.4	112.8	134.6	129.4	135.6	95.9	117.7	135.0	133.5	139.1
Sugar	95.3	111.6	110.0	108.1	119.2	94.4	110.3	112.1	111.0	123.9
Synthetic fibers	92.8	119.5	173.1	187.2	196.5	91.9	119.1	170.9	192.0	201.4
Tires and inner tubes	98.2	105.9	116.3	115.7	131.9	96.7	107.8	117.3	119.5	141.6
Tobacco products	100.2	104.3	111.9	114.2	119.4	99.5	104.4	114.7	119.0	124.2

See footnotes at end of table.

No. 678. Indexes of Output Per Hour—Selected Industries: 1965 to 1976—Con.

[1967=100. See also *Historical Statistics, Colonial Times to 1970*, series W 14, 17, and 19, W 30–54 and W 62–65]

INDUSTRY	ALL EMPLOYEES					PRODUCTION WORKERS				
	1965	1970	1974	1975	1976, prel.	1965	1970	1974	1975	1976, prel.
Mining: [1] Coal	91.4	97.5	76.9	71.9	69.4	91.0	97.6	78.4	73.1	70.5
Copper (crude ore)	109.3	129.3	121.4	123.7	149.0	99.4	122.6	117.3	122.9	149.2
Copper (recoverable metal)	113.8	118.0	91.9	92.5	110.0	103.5	111.8	88.8	91.9	110.2
Iron (crude ore)	93.3	113.8	120.8	117.3	113.9	92.6	115.6	122.4	119.5	116.5
Iron (usable ore)	91.0	110.5	111.2	107.2	104.9	90.3	112.3	112.7	109.3	107.3
Nonmetallic minerals	(NA)	(NA)	(NA)	(NA)	(NA)	93.7	116.1	124.8	122.5	120.0
Transportation, utilities, and trade:										
Air transportation [1]	83.5	109.6	133.0	134.6	146.7	(NA)	(NA)	(NA)	(NA)	(NA)
Gas and electric utilities [2]	89.2	117.3	128.8	132.3	137.2	88.5	117.9	132.3	136.9	142.8
Gasoline service stations [3]	93.7	122.5	139.0	135.6	148.8	(NA)	(NA)	(NA)	(NA)	(NA)
Intercity trucking [1]	98.6	106.8	120.5	121.2	(NA)	(NA)	(NA)	(NA)	(NA)	(NA)
Petroleum pipelines	79.4	121.3	156.5	154.5	154.9	79.2	127.7	167.2	168.7	174.0
Railroad transport (car miles) [4]	92.5	104.7	116.2	115.5	118.4	92.6	105.1	117.3	117.7	120.9
RR transport (revenue traffic) [4]	90.1	107.6	129.6	128.1	133.4	90.2	108.0	130.8	130.6	136.2
Telephone communications	89.1	109.6	139.3	152.6	168.6	(NA)	(NA)	(NA)	(NA)	(NA)

NA Not available.   [1] Refers to output per employee.   [2] Production workers refers to nonsupervisory workers.   [3] Data relate to all persons.   [4] Class I line-haul railroads and switching and terminal companies.

Source: U.S. Bureau of Labor Statistics, *Productivity Indexes for Selected Industries*, 1977 edition.

No. 679. Employed Persons, by Major Occupation Group and Sex: 1960 to 1978

[**In thousands of persons 16 years old and over.** Annual averages of monthly figures, except as indicated. Beginning 1973, not strictly comparable with prior years due to reclassification of census occupations. For details, see text, p. 396. See *Historical Statistics, Colonial Times to 1970*, series D 182–232, for related but not comparable data]

OCCUPATION GROUP AND SEX	1960	1965	1970	1973	1974	1975	1976	1977	1978, Jan.– Apr.
Total	65,778	71,088	78,627	84,409	85,936	84,783	87,485	90,546	91,846
White-collar workers	28,522	31,852	37,997	40,386	41,738	42,227	43,700	45,187	46,673
Percent of total	43.4	44.8	48.3	47.8	48.6	49.8	50.0	49.9	50.8
Professional and technical	7,469	8,872	11,140	11,777	12,338	12,748	13,329	13,692	14,252
Managers and administrators [1]	7,067	7,340	8,289	8,644	8,941	8,891	9,315	9,662	10,026
Salesworkers	4,224	4,499	4,854	5,415	5,417	5,460	5,497	5,728	5,795
Clerical workers	9,762	11,141	13,714	14,548	15,043	15,128	15,558	16,106	16,600
Blue-collar workers	24,057	26,247	27,791	29,869	29,776	27,962	28,958	30,211	30,095
Craft and kindred workers	8,554	9,216	10,158	11,288	11,477	10,972	11,278	11,881	11,853
Operatives, exc. transport	}11,950	13,345	13,909	{10,972	10,627	9,637	10,085	10,354	10,539
Transport equip. operatives				3,297	3,292	3,219	3,271	3,476	3,487
Nonfarm laborers	3,553	3,686	3,724	4,312	4,380	4,134	4,325	4,500	4,217
Service workers	8,923	8,936	9,712	11,128	11,373	11,657	12,005	12,392	12,608
Farmworkers	5,176	4,053	3,126	3,027	3,048	2,936	2,822	2,756	2,469
Male	43,904	46,340	48,960	51,963	52,519	51,230	52,391	53,861	53,904
White-collar workers	16,423	17,746	20,054	20,705	21,155	21,134	21,552	22,008	22,438
Percent of total	37.4	38.3	41.0	38.9	40.3	41.3	41.1	40.9	41.6
Professional and technical	4,766	5,596	6,842	7,066	7,346	7,481	7,726	7,856	8,114
Managers and administrators [1]	5,968	6,230	6,968	7,054	7,291	7,162	7,373	7,511	7,719
Salesworkers	2,544	2,641	2,763	3,175	3,152	3,137	3,140	3,250	3,191
Clerical workers	3,145	3,279	3,481	3,409	3,366	3,355	3,313	3,391	3,415
Blue-collar workers	20,420	22,107	23,020	24,625	24,581	23,220	23,852	24,856	24,625
Craft and kindred workers	8,332	8,947	9,826	10,826	10,966	10,472	10,733	11,282	11,209
Operatives, exc. transport	}8,617	9,581	9,605	{6,653	6,464	5,934	6,135	6,258	6,383
Transport equip. operatives				3,134	3,126	3,037	3,062	3,238	3,232
Nonfarm laborers	3,471	3,579	3,589	4,012	4,026	3,777	3,922	4,079	3,801
Service workers	2,844	3,194	3,285	4,120	4,218	4,400	4,622	4,715	4,758
Farmworkers	4,219	3,295	2,601	2,513	2,564	2,476	2,365	2,282	2,082
Female	21,874	24,748	29,667	32,446	33,417	33,553	35,095	36,685	37,942
White-collar workers	12,099	14,106	17,943	19,681	20,583	21,092	22,148	23,179	24,235
Percent of total	55.3	57.0	60.5	60.6	61.6	62.9	63.1	63.2	63.9
Professional and technical	2,703	3,276	4,298	4,711	4,992	5,267	5,603	5,836	6,138
Managers and administrators [1]	1,099	1,110	1,321	1,590	1,650	1,729	1,942	2,151	2,308
Salesworkers	1,680	1,858	2,091	2,240	2,265	2,324	2,357	2,478	2,605
Clerical workers	6,617	7,862	10,233	11,140	11,676	11,772	12,245	12,715	13,185
Blue-collar workers	3,637	4,140	4,771	5,244	5,195	4,742	5,106	5,355	5,470
Craft and kindred workers	222	269	332	463	511	500	545	599	644
Operatives, exc. transport	}3,333	3,764	4,303	{4,319	4,164	3,703	3,950	4,096	4,156
Transport equip. operatives				163	167	182	208	238	255
Nonfarm laborers	82	107	136	299	354	357	403	422	415
Service workers	5,179	5,742	6,427	7,008	7,156	7,258	7,383	7,677	7,850
Farmworkers	957	758	525	514	484	460	458	473	387

[1] Excludes farm.

Source: U.S. Bureau of Labor Statistics, *Employment and Earnings*, monthly.

No. 680. EMPLOYED PERSONS—PERCENT DISTRIBUTION, BY OCCUPATION AND RACE: 1960 TO 1977

[Covers persons 16 years old and over. Annual averages of monthly figures. 1974–1977 not strictly comparable with prior years due to reclassification of census occupations. "N.e.c." means not elsewhere classified]

OCCUPATION	WHITE					BLACK AND OTHER				
	1960	1970	1975	1976	1977	1960	1970	1975	1976	1977
Total employed_____1,000__	58,850	70,182	75,713	78,021	80,734	6,927	8,445	9,070	9,464	9.812
Percent_____	100.0	100.0	100.0	100.0	100.0	100.0	100.0	100.0	100.0	100.0
White-collar workers_____	46.6	50.8	51.7	51.8	51.7	16.1	27.9	34.7	34.7	35.3
Professional, technical, and kindred [1]__	12.1	14.8	15.5	15.7	15.5	4.8	9.1	11.4	11.7	11.8
Medical and other health_____	2.1	2.3	2.5	2.7	2.7	.8	1.6	2.7	2.5	2.6
Teachers, except college_____	2.6	3.2	3.6	3.6	3.4	1.7	2.9	3.1	3.2	3.0
Managers, administrators, exc. farm__	11.7	11.4	11.2	11.4	11.4	2.6	3.5	4.4	4.4	4.8
Salaried workers_____	5.9	8.4	9.0	9.2	9.2	.9	2.1	3.4	3.5	3.7
Self-employed_____	5.8	3.0	2.2	2.2	2.1	1.7	1.4	1.0	1.0	1.1
Salesworkers_____	7.0	6.7	6.9	6.7	6.8	1.5	2.1	2.7	2.5	2.6
Retail trade_____	4.1	4.0	3.8	3.7	3.7	1.0	1.6	2.0	1.6	1.7
Clerical workers_____	15.7	18.0	18.1	18.0	18.0	7.3	13.2	15.7	16.1	16.1
Stenographers, typists, and sec'ys___	3.9	4.7	5.4	5.3	5.2	1.4	2.3	3.4	3.6	3.5
Blue-collar workers_____	36.2	34.5	32.4	32.6	32.9	40.1	42.2	37.4	37.6	37.6
Craft and kindred workers [1]_____	13.8	13.5	13.4	13.4	13.6	6.0	8.2	8.8	8.7	9.0
Carpenters_____	1.4	1.1	1.2	1.2	1.4	.4	.7	.6	.5	.5
Constr. craftworkers, exc. carpenters	2.7	2.5	2.7	2.7	2.7	1.6	1.8	2.1	2.1	2.4
Mechanics and repairers_____	3.2	3.7	3.6	3.5	3.7	1.7	2.6	2.1	2.2	2.2
Metalcraft workers, except mechanics	1.8	1.6	1.4	1.4	1.4	.6	.8	.8	.9	.9
Blue-collar supervisors, n.e.c_____	1.9	2.0	1.7	1.7	1.8	.4	.9	1.0	1.0	1.2
Operatives_____	17.9	17.0	14.6	14.6	14.7	20.4	23.7	20.0	20.5	20.3
Operatives, except transport_____	(NA)	(NA)	10.9	11.0	11.0	(NA)	(NA)	15.0	15.6	15.1
Transport equipment operatives____	(NA)	(NA)	3.7	3.6	3.7	(NA)	(NA)	5.0	4.9	5.2
Drivers, motor vehicles_____	3.5	3.1	3.1	3.1	3.1	4.4	4.1	4.0	3.8	4.1
Nonfarm laborers_____	4.4·	4.1	4.4	4.5	4.6	13.7	10.3	8.7	8.3	8.3
Service workers_____	9.9	10.7	12.3	12.3	12.3	31.7	26.0	25.8	25.4	25.0
Private household workers_____	1.7	1.3	1.0	.9	.9	14.2	7.7	4.9	4.4	4.2
Service workers, exc. priv. household__	8.2	9.4	11.3	11.4	11.4	17.5	18.3	20.9	21.0	20.8
Protective service workers_____	1.2	1.3	1.5	1.5	1.4	.5	.9	1.7	1.5	1.6
Farmworkers_____	7.4	4.0	3.0	3.3	3.1	12.1	3.9	2.0	2.3	2.2
Farmers and farm managers_____	4.3	2.4	2.0	1.9	1.8	3.2	1.0	.6	.5	.4
Farm laborers and supervisors_____	3.0	1.6	1.5	1.5	1.4	9.0	2.9	2.0	1.8	1.8
Paid workers_____	1.7	1.0	1.1	1.1	1.0	6.6	2.6	1.8	1.7	1.7
Unpaid family workers_____	1.3	.7	.5	.4	.4	2.4	.3	.2	.2	.1

NA Not available.   [1] Includes occupations not shown separately.

Source: U.S. Bureau of Labor Statistics, Employment and Earnings, monthly.

No. 681. EMPLOYED PERSONS, BY RACE, SEX, AND OCCUPATION: 1972 AND 1977

[Covers civilians 16 years old and over. "Black and other" refers to races other than White. "N.e.c." means not elsewhere classified. See Historical Statistics, Colonial Times to 1970, series D 233–682, for similar data]

OCCUPATION	1972			1977		
	Total employed (1,000)	Percent		Total employed (1,000)	Percent	
		Female	Black and other		Female	Black and other
Total_____	81,702	38.0	10.6	90,546	40.5	10.8
Professional, technical, and kindred workers [1]_____	11,459	39.3	7.2	13,692	42.6	8.4
Accountants_____	714	21.7	4.3	868	27.5	6.8
Computer specialists_____	273	16.8	5.5	371	23.2	5.9
Engineers [1]_____	1,102	.8	3.4	1,267	2.7	5.5
Civil_____	154	.6	5.2	171	1.2	7.6
Electrical and electronic_____	287	.7	5.2	324	2.8	5.9
Industrial_____	170	2.4	2.4	214	7.0	4.2
Mechanical_____	191	–	3.1	215	.9	5.6
Lawyers and judges_____	320	3.8	1.9	462	9.5	3.2
Librarians, archivists, and curators_____	158	81.6	7.0	208	79.8	9.1
Life and physical scientists [1]_____	230	10.0	7.8	275	15.6	8.7
Chemists_____	119	10.1	8.4	124	13.7	10.5
Personnel and labor relations workers_____	310	31.0	9.0	370	43.5	11.9
Physicians, dentists, and related practitioners [1]___	624	9.3	6.3	724	10.6	6.9
Dentists_____	107	1.9	5.6	105	2.9	5.7
Pharmacists_____	126	12.7	3.2	138	17.4	4.3
Physicians, medical and osteopathic_____	328	10.1	8.2	403	11.2	9.2

See footnotes at end of table.

No. 681. EMPLOYED PERSONS, BY RACE, SEX, AND OCCUPATION: 1972 AND 1977—Con.

OCCUPATION	1972			1977		
	Total employed (1,000)	Percent		Total employed (1,000)	Percent	
		Female	Black and other		Female	Black and other
Professional, technical, and kindred workers—Con.						
Registered nurses, dietitians, and therapists [1]	949	92.6	8.1	1,285	92.8	11.5
Registered nurses	801	97.6	8.2	1,063	96.7	11.3
Therapists	115	59.1	4.3	178	68.5	9.6
Health technologists and technicians	315	69.5	11.1	462	71.4	12.1
Religious workers	292	11.0	10.6	347	13.0	8.6
Social scientists	141	21.3	5.7	224	28.6	3.1
Social and recreation workers	354	55.1	17.5	444	60.8	18.9
Teachers, college and university	461	28.0	7.2	562	31.7	7.5
Teachers, except college and university [1]	2,841	70.0	9.2	3,024	70.9	9.8
Elementary	1,251	85.1	10.0	1,313	84.2	11.4
Prekindergarten and kindergarten	188	96.8	13.3	231	98.7	15.2
Secondary	1,114	49.6	8.3	1,157	51.2	8.0
Engineering and science technicians [1]	828	9.1	5.2	892	14.9	7.0
Draftsmen	286	6.3	5.2	283	13.8	7.1
Electrical and electronic engineering technicians	164	5.5	6.1	194	10.3	9.8
Technicians, except health, engineering, and science	152	11.2	2.6	186	19.9	6.5
Vocational and educational counselors	134	50.0	11.9	175	49.1	14.3
Writers, artists, and entertainers [1]	897	31.7	4.8	1,141	35.5	5.4
Athletes and kindred workers	78	30.8	6.4	105	41.9	6.7
Editors and reporters	163	41.1	4.3	185	44.9	4.9
Research workers, not specified	86	27.9	7.0	111	40.5	12.6
Managers and administrators, except farm [1]	8,031	17.6	4.0	9,662	22.3	4.8
Bank officers and financial managers	427	19.0	2.6	543	27.3	4.4
Buyers, wholesale and retail trade	161	32.9	4.3	162	37.0	4.3
Health administrators	118	46.6	7.6	175	45.1	5.1
Managers and superintendents, building	136	42.6	8.8	151	49.0	5.3
Office managers, n.e.c	315	41.9	1.0	343	58.0	3.2
Officials and administrators, public administration, n.e.c	309	20.4	9.1	401	24.9	8.5
Purchasing agents and buyers, n.e.c	181	13.3	3.3	190	23.2	3.7
Restaurant, cafeteria, and bar managers	494	32.4	8.9	548	34.7	8.9
Sales managers	570	15.6	1.4	666	20.6	3.9
School administrators	304	26.0	8.2	391	34.0	10.2
Sales workers [1]	5,354	41.6	3.6	5,728	43.3	4.5
Hucksters and peddlers	230	73.0	6.1	198	79.8	7.1
Insurance agents, brokers, and underwriters	441	11.6	3.4	500	16.6	5.4
Real estate agents and brokers	349	36.7	2.6	502	43.8	2.0
Stock and bond sales agents	101	9.9	2.0	98	13.3	2.0
Sales representatives, manufacturing industries	400	6.8	1.5	336	13.1	3.6
Sales representatives, wholesale trade	696	4.7	1.4	850	7.6	2.6
Sales clerks, retail trade	2,348	68.9	5.0	2,316	70.4	5.8
Salesworkers, except clerks, retail trade	430	13.0	2.6	486	14.6	2.9
Salesworkers, services and construction	136	29.4	2.2	154	35.1	4.5
Clerical and kindred workers [1]	14,247	75.6	8.7	16,106	78.9	9.8
Bank tellers	288	87.5	4.9	408	90.0	7.6
Billing clerks	149	84.6	6.7	156	87.8	5.8
Bookkeepers	1,584	87.9	3.6	1,726	90.0	4.4
Cashiers	998	86.6	8.0	1,326	87.0	8.8
Clerical supervisors, n.e.c	199	57.8	10.1	226	65.9	9.7
Counter clerks, except food	329	73.9	6.4	343	77.8	9.6
Estimators and investigators, n.e.c	348	43.4	4.9	451	51.0	9.3
File clerks	272	84.9	18.0	274	84.7	20.4
Insurance adjusters, examiners, and investigators	108	34.3	6.5	168	50.6	10.1
Mail carriers, post office	270	6.7	14.1	242	9.5	10.3
Office machine operators [1]	674	71.4	13.1	759	73.8	14.9
Computer and peripheral equipment operators	196	37.8	10.2	302	54.6	11.6
Key punch operators	283	89.8	15.5	280	93.2	17.9
Postal clerks	281	26.7	19.6	267	31.8	26.2
Receptionists	436	97.0	7.6	531	96.8	8.1
Secretaries	2,949	99.1	5.2	3,421	99.1	5.4
Shipping and receiving clerks	451	14.9	13.7	467	19.5	13.7
Statistical clerks	299	70.9	8.4	357	75.6	11.2
Stenographers	125	90.4	8.0	83	91.6	12.0
Stock clerks and storekeepers	511	22.9	12.5	497	30.8	12.3
Telephone operators	392	96.7	12.8	342	95.3	14.0
Typists	1,021	96.1	12.0	1,006	96.3	14.5
Craftworkers and kindred workers	10,810	3.6	6.9	11,881	5.0	7.4
Carpenters	1,045	.5	5.9	1,171	.9	4.4
Other construction craftsworkers [1]	2,248	.6	8.9	2,404	1.0	9.7
Brickmasons and stonemasons	176	–	14.2	177	–	18.1
Electricians	494	.6	3.2	588	.2	4.8
Excavating, grading, and road machine operators	426	–	9.4	406	.2	9.6
Painters, construction and maintenance	428	1.9	10.1	461	3.3	10.2
Plumbers and pipe fitters	389	–	5.9	429	.5	8.2

See footnotes at end of table.

No. 681. Employed Persons by Race, Sex, and Occupation: 1972 and 1977—Con.

OCCUPATION	1972 Total employed (1,000)	1972 Percent Female	1972 Percent Black and other	1977 Total employed (1,000)	1977 Percent Female	1977 Percent Black and other
Craftworkers and kindred workers—Con.						
Blue collar worker supervisors, n.e.c.	1,413	6.9	6.0	1,554	9.0	7.4
Machinists and jobsetters	471	.6	6.2	576	2.6	8.0
Metalcraft workers, except mechanics, machinists, and jobsetters [1]	624	1.9	5.6	653	3.1	6.7
Sheet metal workers and tinsmiths	149	.7	4.2	154	1.9	7.1
Tool and die makers	184	.5	2.2	193	1.6	2.1
Mechanics, automobile	1,033	.5	8.5	1,161	.9	8.0
Mechanics, except automobile [1]	1,735	1.0	5.3	2,019	1.6	6.1
Air conditioning, heating, and refrigeration	174	–	6.3	194	.5	3.6
Aircraft	123	–	3.3	118	.8	9.3
Heavy equipment	714	.7	5.2	910	1.3	6.2
Radio and television	124	.8	6.5	134	3.7	6.0
Printing craftworkers [1]	397	14.9	5.5	389	22.4	8.0
Compositors and typesetters	177	16.4	6.8	166	27.1	6.0
Printing press operators	145	4.8	4.1	153	11.1	7.2
All other craftworkers [1]	1,845	9.3	7.3	1,954	13.3	7.4
Bakers	114	28.9	18.4	106	39.6	9.4
Crane, derrick, and hoist operators	150	1.3	16.0	169	.6	13.0
Electric power line and cable operators	102	–	3.9	107	–	3.7
Stationary engineers	190	1.1	5.8	183	.5	6.6
Telephone installers and repairers	310	1.9	4.2	279	5.0	6.5
Operatives, except transport [1]	10,340	38.6	13.2	10,354	39.6	14.3
Assemblers	1,017	46.7	13.2	1,136	50.3	15.7
Checkers, examiners, and inspectors, manufacturing	685	48.5	8.8	684	49.4	10.5
Cutting operatives, n.e.c.	238	27.7	16.0	252	31.7	12.3
Dressmakers and seamstresses, except factory	132	97.0	9.1	119	98.3	11.8
Garage workers and gas station attendants	502	4.6	8.4	427	5.2	8.9
Laundry and dry cleaning operatives, n.e.c.	165	69.7	28.5	165	64.8	27.9
Meat cutters and butchers, except manufacturing	201	3.5	7.5	187	7.0	9.1
Mine operatives	142	.7	6.3	200	1.5	4.0
Packers and wrappers, except meat and produce	647	61.1	14.7	610	63.6	17.4
Painters, manufactured articles	178	14.6	14.6	152	17.8	16.4
Precision machine operatives	389	10.0	6.9	372	10.2	8.3
Punch and stamping press operatives	157	27.4	10.8	152	36.2	15.1
Sewers and stitchers	936	95.8	13.7	820	95.2	18.8
Textile operatives	424	55.2	15.8	389	59.4	20.8
Welders and flame cutters	554	3.6	10.1	639	6.3	8.8
Machine operatives	1,567	27.0	14.4	1,647	30.3	14.3
Transport equipment operatives [1]	3,209	4.2	14.8	3,476	6.8	14.6
Bus drivers	252	34.1	17.1	339	42.2	15.9
Delivery and route workers	892	2.5	10.4	516	7.0	7.4
Fork lift and tow motor operatives	303	1.0	22.1	391	3.6	19.9
Taxicab drivers and chauffeurs	166	9.0	24.1	167	9.6	24.6
Truck drivers	1,441	.6	14.4	1,898	1.3	14.3
Laborers, except farm [1]	4,217	6.3	20.2	4,500	9.4	18.1
Construction laborers, including carpenters' helpers	943	.5	22.4	869	2.0	17.5
Freight and material handlers	761	5.9	22.1	783	7.9	19.4
Gardeners and groundskeepers, except farm	544	2.2	20.0	597	4.2	17.9
Stockhandlers	723	16.9	10.2	856	22.7	11.6
Farmers and farm managers	1,688	5.9	3.3	1,459	6.4	2.5
Farm laborers and supervisors [1]	1,381	32.1	15.1	1,296	29.4	13.5
Farm laborers, wage workers	886	15.3	21.9	936	17.0	17.2
Farm laborers, unpaid family workers	455	66.8	2.4	323	67.8	4.0
Service workers, except private household	9,529	57.0	18.5	11,234	58.3	18.1
Cleaning service workers	2,074	32.8	30.0	2,363	34.9	28.9
Food service workers [1]	3,263	69.8	13.9	4,095	68.5	13.8
Cooks, except private household	866	62.2	21.4	1,106	56.3	20.6
Waiters	1,124	91.8	6.9	1,310	90.4	7.6
Health service workers [1]	1,506	87.0	24.6	1,747	89.2	22.7
Health aides, except nursing, and trainees	157	79.6	21.0	245	84.5	18.0
Nursing aides, orderlies, and attendants	912	83.4	26.9	1,008	86.3	26.5
Practical nurses	343	96.5	25.7	371	96.8	21.6
Personal service workers [1]	1,542	71.5	13.1	1,705	74.0	13.6
Barbers	157	4.5	12.7	118	8.5	14.4
Child care workers, except private household	356	95.8	14.0	442	95.2	12.4
Hairdressers and cosmetologists	498	91.2	7.2	526	88.2	8.6
Protective service workers [1]	1,144	5.7	10.4	1,324	7.9	12.2
Firefighters	200	.5	4.0	225	.4	7.1
Guards	412	4.6	15.5	490	10.2	18.0
Police and detectives	416	2.6	8.4	498	3.8	9.2
Private household workers [1]	1,437	97.6	40.6	1,158	97.0	35.8
Child care workers	543	98.0	9.9	443	97.5	9.3
Maids and servants	713	97.2	64.2	574	96.5	55.4

– Represents zero or rounds to zero.   [1] Includes occupations not shown separately.

Source: U.S. Bureau of Labor Statistics, *Employment and Earnings*, October 1973, and U.S. Bureau of the Census, Current Population Survey, unpublished annual average tabulations.

No. 682. Average Weekly Earnings in Current and Constant (1967) Dollars, Private Nonagricultural and Manufacturing Industries: 1960 to 1978

[In dollars. Includes overtime. Based on reports from employing establishments and relate to full- and part-time wage and salary workers in nonagricultural establishments who worked during or received pay for, any part of the pay period which includes the 12th of the month. See headnote, table 686. See *Historical Statistics, Colonial Times to 1970*, series D 804, for average weekly earnings in manufacturing]

INDUSTRY AND ITEM	1960	1965	1970	1971	1972	1973	1974	1975	1976	1977	1978, Jan.- Apr.[1]
PRIVATE NONAGRICULTURAL											
Gross weekly earnings:											
Current dollars	80.7	95.1	119.5	127.3	136.2	145.4	154.5	163.9	176.3	189.5	197.4
Constant (1967) dollars [2]	91.0	100.6	102.7	104.9	108.7	109.3	104.6	101.7	103.4	104.4	104.3
Spendable weekly earnings: [3]											
Worker with no dependents:											
Current dollars	65.6	79.0	95.9	103.8	111.7	117.5	124.1	132.7	143.9	155.6	160.9
Constant (1967) dollars [2]	74.0	83.6	82.5	85.6	89.1	88.3	84.1	82.3	84.4	85.7	85.0
Worker with 3 dependents:											
Current dollars	73.0	86.3	104.6	112.4	121.1	127.4	134.4	145.9	156.5	170.3	176.0
Constant (1967) dollars [2]	82.3	91.3	90.0	92.7	96.6	95.7	91.0	90.5	91.8	93.9	93.0
MANUFACTURING INDUSTRIES											
Gross weekly earnings:											
Current dollars	89.7	107.5	133.7	142.4	154.7	165.7	176.4	189.5	207.6	226.9	237.5
Constant (1967) dollars [2]	101.2	113.8	115.0	117.4	123.5	124.5	119.4	117.6	121.8	125.0	125.5
Spendable weekly earnings: [3]											
Worker with no dependents:											
Current dollars	72.6	89.1	106.6	115.0	125.3	132.0	139.9	150.7	166.6	182.4	189.3
Constant (1967) dollars [2]	81.8	94.3	91.7	94.8	100.0	99.2	94.7	93.5	97.7	100.5	100.1
Worker with 3 dependents:											
Current dollars	80.1	96.8	115.9	124.2	135.6	142.9	151.3	165.3	180.0	198.6	206.0
Constant (1967) dollars [2]	90.3	102.4	99.7	102.4	108.2	107.4	102.4	102.6	105.6	109.4	108.9

[1] Preliminary.   [2] Earnings in current dollars divided by the consumer price index on a 1967 base.
[3] Average gross weekly earnings less social security and Federal income taxes.
Source: U.S. Bureau of Labor Statistics, *Employment and Earnings*, monthly. In U.S. Council of Economic Advisers, *Economic Report of the President*, January 1978.

No. 683. Annual Percent Changes in Earnings and Compensation: 1968 to 1977

ITEM	1968–1969	1969–1970	1970–1971	1971–1972	1972–1973	1973–1974	1974–1975	1975–1976	1976–1977
Current dollars:									
Hourly earnings, total [1][2]	6.6	6.6	7.1	6.5	6.4	8.2	8.8	7.3	7.3
Hourly earnings, manufacturing	6.0	5.3	6.3	6.7	7.1	8.1	9.1	7.9	8.5
Spendable weekly earnings [1][3]	4.9	4.6	7.5	7.7	5.1	5.6	8.6	7.2	8.8
Compensation per employee-hour [1]	6.5	6.7	6.6	5.8	7.8	9.4	9.6	8.7	8.8
Constant (1967) dollars:									
Hourly earnings, total [1]	1.2	.7	2.7	3.1	.2	−2.5	−.3	1.4	.8
Hourly earnings, manufacturing	.7	−.7	1.7	3.4	1.0	−2.6	−.3	2.0	2.0
Spendable weekly earnings [1][3]	−.4	−1.2	3.0	4.3	−1.1	−4.9	−.5	1.4	2.2
Compensation per employee-hour [1]	1.0	.7	2.2	2.4	1.4	−1.4	.5	2.8	2.2
Consumer price index	5.4	5.9	4.3	3.3	6.2	11.0	9.1	5.8	6.5

[1] Nonfarm business sector.   [2] Adjusted for overtime in manufacturing and interindustry employment shifts.
[3] Married worker with 3 dependents.
Source: U.S. Bureau of Labor Statistics, *Monthly Labor Review*.

No. 684. Hourly and Weekly Earnings (Including Overtime) in Current and Constant (1977) Dollars, Selected Industries: 1965 to 1977

INDUSTRY	HOURLY EARNINGS						WEEKLY EARNINGS					
	1965	1970	1974	1975	1976	1977	1965	1970	1974	1975	1976	1977
Current dollars:												
Private industry workers [1]	2.45	3.22	4.22	4.54	4.87	5.25	95	119	154	164	176	19
Manufacturing, prod. workers	2.61	3.36	4.41	4.81	5.19	5.63	108	134	176	190	208	22
Durable industries	2.79	3.55	4.69	5.14	5.55	6.02	117	143	191	205	225	24
Contract construction	3.70	5.24	6.75	7.25	7.68	8.04	138	195	249	265	285	29
Retail trade	1.82	2.44	3.09	3.34	3.55	3.83	67	82	101	108	114	12
Constant (1977) dollars: [2]												
Private industry workers [1]	4.70	5.02	5.18	5.11	5.19	5.25	182	186	190	185	188	19
Manufacturing, prod. workers	5.01	5.24	5.42	5.42	5.53	5.63	206	209	217	213	221	22
Durable industries	5.36	5.54	5.76	5.79	5.91	6.02	225	223	235	231	240	24
Contract construction	7.10	8.17	8.29	8.16	8.18	8.04	266	305	306	299	303	29
Retail trade	3.49	3.81	3.80	3.76	3.78	3.83	128	129	124	122	121	12

[1] Nonagricultural.   [2] Earnings in current dollars divided by consumer price index on base 1977=100.
Source: U.S. Council of Economic Advisers. Based on U.S. Dept. of Labor data.

No. 685. Full-Time Wage and Salary Workers—Weekly Earnings and Index of Earnings: 1970 to 1977

[Figures are for May and represent medians of usual weekly earnings. For definition of median, see p. xii]

CHARACTERISTIC	MEDIAN EARNINGS (current dollars)						INDEX (constant 1967 dollars=100)					
	1970	1973	1974	1975	1976	1977	1970	1973	1974	1975	1976	1977
All workers	$130	$159	$169	$185	$197	$212	102.8	110.1	105.5	105.5	106.4	107.3
Male	151	188	204	221	234	253	104.0	113.6	111.2	110.4	109.6	111.2
16–24 years old	112	136	146	149	159	168	99.0	106.2	103.1	95.9	95.9	94.8
25 years and over	160	203	219	235	251	273	104.6	116.8	113.7	112.2	112.2	114.5
Never married	113	134	144	153	161	173	102.1	106.3	103.2	100.0	100.0	100.0
Husbands	159	200	216	234	248	272	104.6	115.3	112.2	111.5	111.5	114.5
Other marital status	139	171	194	205	224	239	105.3	114.2	116.8	113.3	116.8	116.8
Female	94	116	124	137	145	156	103.8	112.8	109.0	109.0	109.0	110.3
16–24 years old	88	103	111	117	125	133	102.7	105.4	102.7	98.6	98.6	98.6
25 years and over	96	121	131	146	154	165	103.8	115.2	112.7	115.2	113.9	115.2
Never married	95	114	120	132	141	150	103.8	108.9	103.8	103.8	105.1	105.1
Wives	95	117	126	139	147	158	103.8	111.4	108.9	110.1	108.9	110.1
Other marital status	91	115	123	138	146	158	104.0	116.0	112.0	114.7	114.7	116.0
White	134	162	173	190	202	217	101.8	108.0	104.4	105.3	105.3	105.3
Male	157	193	209	225	239	259	103.8	112.3	110.0	107.7	107.7	110.0
Female	95	117	125	138	147	157	103.8	111.4	107.6	108.9	108.9	108.9
Black and other	99	129	140	156	162	171	107.6	124.1	121.5	122.8	120.3	119.0
Male	113	149	160	173	187	201	107.8	125.6	121.1	120.0	122.2	123.3
Female	81	107	117	130	138	147	111.1	128.6	127.0	128.6	128.6	128.6
Occupation:												
Professional and technical	181	212	228	246	256	277	106.9	110.3	107.6	105.5	103.4	104.8
Managers, administrators [1]	190	238	250	274	289	302	99.4	109.8	104.3	104.3	103.7	101.2
Salesworkers	133	163	172	189	198	225	100.9	108.8	103.5	104.4	102.7	109.7
Clerical workers	109	130	140	150	158	167	103.3	107.7	105.5	103.3	102.2	101.1
Craft and kindred workers	157	195	211	223	239	259	103.1	112.2	109.9	106.1	106.9	109.2
Operatives, except transport [2]	(NA)	132	141	157	162	171	(NA)	105.3	101.1	103.2	100.0	98.9
Transport equip. operatives	(NA)	169	180	198	214	231	(NA)	105.8	101.7	102.5	104.1	105.0
Nonfarm laborers	110	138	149	154	161	181	102.2	111.8	109.7	103.2	102.2	107.5
Private household workers	38	39	50	54	60	59	103.1	90.6	106.3	106.3	109.4	100.0
Other service workers	87	111	117	123	134	142	100.0	112.0	106.7	102.7	105.3	104.0
Farmworkers	71	96	107	111	120	127	105.2	125.9	125.9	119.0	122.4	120.7

NA Not available.   [1] Excludes farm.   [2] For index, May 1972=100.
Source: U.S. Bureau of Labor Statistics, News, Nov. 2, 1977.

No. 686. Hourly and Weekly Earnings, by Industry Group: 1965 to 1978

[For private industry only. Data are for production and related workers in mining and manufacturing, construction workers in contract construction, and nonsupervisory employees in other industries. Excludes agriculture. See also Historical Statistics, Colonial Times to 1970, series D 877–892]

INDUSTRY GROUP	1965	1970	1971	1972	1973	1974	1975	1976	1977	1978, Jan.–Apr.[1]
Total, gross hourly earnings	$2.45	$3.22	$3.44	$3.67	$3.92	$4.22	$4.54	$4.87	$5.25	$5.54
Manufacturing	2.61	3.36	3.57	3.81	4.07	4.41	4.81	5.19	5.63	5.96
Mining	2.92	3.85	4.06	4.41	4.72	5.21	5.90	6.42	6.88	6.98
Contract construction	3.70	5.24	5.69	6.03	6.38	6.75	7.25	7.68	8.04	8.32
Transportation and public utilities	3.03	3.85	4.21	4.64	5.03	5.43	5.92	6.46	6.94	7.34
Wholesale trade	2.61	3.44	3.67	3.88	4.12	4.49	4.89	5.18	5.55	5.87
Retail trade	1.82	2.44	2.57	2.70	2.87	3.09	3.34	3.55	3.83	4.09
Finance, insurance, and real estate	2.39	3.08	3.27	3.42	3.57	3.82	4.13	4.36	4.60	4.86
Services	2.05	2.81	3.02	3.23	3.46	3.76	4.06	4.36	4.71	5.02
Total, gross weekly earnings	$95	$119	$127	$136	$145	$154	$164	$176	$190	$197
Manufacturing	108	134	142	155	166	176	190	208	227	237
Mining	124	164	172	187	201	221	250	275	303	303
Contract construction	138	195	212	223	236	249	265	285	297	294
Transportation and public utilities	125	156	169	188	205	218	234	258	278	294
Wholesale trade	106	138	146	155	163	175	189	201	216	227
Retail trade	67	82	87	91	96	101	108	114	121	126
Finance, insurance, and real estate	89	113	121	127	132	140	151	160	168	178
Services	74	97	103	110	118	127	137	146	157	167

[1] Preliminary.
Source: U.S. Bureau of Labor Statistics, Employment and Earnings, monthly.

No. 687. PRODUCTION WORKERS, MANUFACTURING INDUSTRIES—HOURS AND GROSS EARNINGS, BY STATES: 1965 TO 1977

STATE	AVERAGE HOURLY EARNINGS (dollars)					AVERAGE WEEKLY EARNINGS (dollars)					AVERAGE WEEKLY HOURS				
	1965	1970	1975	1976	1977	1965	1970	1975	1976	1977	1965	1970	1975	1976	1977
U.S.	2.61	3.36	4.81	5.19	5.63	108	134	190	208	227	41.2	39.8	39.4	40.0	40.3
N. Eng.:															
Maine	2.06	2.71	3.81	4.16	4.52	85	109	152	166	180	41.3	40.1	39.9	39.9	39.8
N.H.	2.06	2.81	3.97	4.25	4.56	84	109	155	168	182	40.9	38.8	39.1	39.6	40.0
Vt.	2.17	2.93	4.07	4.40	4.70	92	120	164	180	192	42.4	41.0	40.4	41.0	40.8
Mass.	2.45	3.23	4.48	4.79	5.13	99	127	175	190	205	40.3	39.2	39.1	39.7	39.9
R.I.	2.18	2.85	3.84	4.15	4.39	89	112	149	164	172	40.6	39.2	38.9	39.5	39.1
Conn.	2.69	3.43	4.78	5.12	5.56	113	140	194	209	231	42.1	40.9	40.5	40.8	41.5
Mid. Atl.:															
N.Y.	2.68	3.46	4.91	5.27	5.67	106	135	191	208	225	39.7	38.9	38.9	39.4	39.6
N.J.	2.74	3.46	4.93	5.35	5.80	112	139	200	216	240	41.0	40.3	40.5	40.3	41.3
Pa.	2.66	3.36	4.98	5.36	1 5.85	108	132	193	210	1 231	40.5	39.2	38.8	39.2	1 39.5
E.No.Cent.:															
Ohio	3.01	3.81	5.57	6.10	6.74	127	155	224	253	283	42.2	40.6	40.3	41.4	42.0
Ind.	2.92	3.72	5.49	6.00	6.60	122	149	219	244	272	41.7	40.1	39.8	40.6	41.2
Ill.	2.83	3.65	5.53	5.85	6.28	117	147	219	236	255	41.4	40.3	39.7	40.4	40.6
Mich.	3.22	4.15	6.15	6.81	7.54	144	168	251	291	326	44.6	40.6	40.8	42.7	43.3
Wis.	2.75	3.61	5.26	5.69	6.16	115	146	212	231	250	41.7	40.4	40.4	40.6	40.6
W.No.Cent.:															
Minn.	2.72	3.54	5.10	5.53	5.97	112	141	200	220	239	41.2	40.0	39.2	39.8	40.0
Iowa	2.78	3.70	5.40	5.85	6.43	113	147	214	233	258	40.7	39.7	39.7	39.9	40.1
Mo.	2.62	3.39	4.75	5.20	5.75	106	133	185	207	231	40.3	39.3	39.0	39.8	40.2
N. Dak.	2.36	2.93	4.31	4.75	5.19	100	119	172	186	200	42.5	40.7	39.9	39.1	39.1
S. Dak.	2.37	2.98	4.20	4.51	4.84	104	133	172	180	190	43.8	44.6	41.0	39.9	39.3
Nebr.	2.40	3.21	4.51	4.93	(NA)	104	135	184	203	(NA)	43.1	42.0	40.7	41.1	(NA)
Kans.	2.69	3.25	4.62	4.95	5.33	114	135	189	203	219	42.3	41.6	40.9	41.0	41.1
So. Atl.:															
Del.	2.77	3.44	5.02	5.51	5.89	115	136	197	220	233	41.5	39.6	39.3	40.0	39.5
Md.	2.62	3.40	5.04	5.52	6.05	108	136	197	219	241	41.2	40.1	39.1	39.6	39.9
D.C. 2	2.82	3.81	5.52	5.44	5.50	114	148	213	210	211	40.2	38.8	38.5	38.6	38.4
Va.	2.11	2.73	3.99	4.30	4.69	88	109	156	172	187	41.5	40.0	39.2	39.9	39.9
W. Va.	2.74	3.42	4.93	5.42	6.06	111	136	192	212	239	40.4	39.8	39.0	39.2	39.5
N.C.	1.82	2.46	3.51	3.79	4.10	75	97	135	149	162	41.3	39.5	38.5	39.4	39.6
S.C.	1.88	2.51	3.59	3.91	4.28	79	101	141	158	174	41.9	40.2	39.4	40.4	40.6
Ga.	2.01	2.67	3.88	4.10	4.46	83	106	152	164	181	41.1	39.8	39.2	40.1	40.5
Fla.	2.16	2.89	4.11	4.36	4.63	91	119	164	176	188	42.3	41.1	40.0	40.4	40.7
E.So.Cent.:															
Ky.	2.51	3.27	4.65	5.14	5.69	103	129	180	203	225	41.0	39.4	38.8	39.4	39.5
Tenn.	2.09	2.73	3.93	4.24	4.68	85	109	156	171	188	40.8	39.9	39.8	40.3	40.2
Ala.	2.24	2.90	4.10	4.46	4.89	94	117	162	181	198	41.8	40.3	39.5	40.6	40.5
Miss.	1.82	2.43	3.58	3.83	4.15	75	98	141	153	166	41.2	40.2	39.3	40.0	40.1
W.So.Cent.:															
Ark.	1.83	2.48	3.59	3.91	4.30	75	99	139	155	171	41.0	39.8	38.8	39.6	39.7
La.	2.55	3.28	4.88	5.33	5.75	108	137	209	220	240	42.3	41.8	42.8	41.3	41.8
Okla.	2.41	3.09	4.45	4.83	5.31	101	126	178	195	215	42.0	40.0	40.1	40.3	40.4
Tex.	2.48	3.18	4.57	4.98	5.42	104	129	186	204	223	41.9	40.7	40.6	40.9	41.1
Mt.:															
Mont.	2.80	3.70	5.32	5.93	6.53	115	148	196	236	273	41.0	40.0	36.8	39.8	41.8
Idaho	2.65	3.29	4.77	5.29	5.82	106	128	185	205	229	40.0	38.8	38.8	38.7	39.3
Wyo.	2.86	3.36	5.11	5.43	5.72	108	130	205	218	228	37.9	38.7	40.2	40.2	39.8
Colo.	2.82	3.50	(NA)	(NA)	(NA)	116	141	(NA)	(NA)	(NA)	41.2	40.4	(NA)	(NA)	(NA)
N. Mex.	2.31	2.68	3.67	4.07	4.43	94	105	144	161	172	40.6	39.0	39.1	39.5	38.8
Ariz.	2.77	3.31	4.85	5.19	5.55	114	132	189	205	223	41.1	40.0	39.0	39.5	40.1
Utah	2.84	3 3.26	4.05	4.89	5.18	114	3 127	156	192	207	40.3	3 39.1	38.4	39.2	40.0
Nev.	3.18	4.09	5.26	5.61	6.10	127	161	201	218	237	39.9	39.3	38.2	38.9	38.8
Pac.:															
Wash.	3.09	4.06	5.79	6.36	6.83	122	159	224	249	268	39.5	39.1	38.7	39.1	39.2
Oreg.	2.94	3.82	5.54	6.07	6.67	117	148	213	236	257	39.8	38.8	38.4	38.9	38.6
Calif.	3.05	3.80	5.22	5.59	6.00	124	150	206	222	241	40.6	39.6	39.4	39.7	40.1
Alaska	3.70	4.66	8.09	7.82	9.12	159	192	296	317	395	43.1	41.2	36.6	40.5	43.3
Hawaii	2.28	3.17	4.68	5.14	5.51	90	127	183	200	209	39.3	40.0	39.1	39.0	38.0

NA Not available.   1 Data for 1977 not strictly comparable with prior years.
2 Represents Washington, D.C., Standard Metropolitan Statistical Area; data not comparable prior to 1975 due to change in area definition.
3 Data for 1970 not strictly comparable with 1965.

Source: U.S. Bureau of Labor Statistics, *Employment and Earnings*, monthly. Compiled from data supplied by cooperating State agencies.

No. 688. Major Collective Bargaining Settlements—Average Percent Change in Wages and Benefits Negotiated: 1969 to 1977

[In percent, except as indicated. Data represent private nonfarm industry settlements affecting production and related workers in manufacturing and nonsupervisory workers in nonmanufacturing industries. Data exclude possible adjustments in wages under cost-of-living escalator clauses, except increases guaranteed by the contract. Includes all settlements, whether wages and benefits were changed or not]

ITEM	1969	1970	1971	1972	1973	1974	1975	1976	1977
Wage-rate adjustments: [1]									
All industries:									
First year changes	9.2	11.9	11.6	7.3	5.8	9.8	10.2	8.4	7.8
Contracts with escalator clauses	(NA)	(NA)	12.9	7.9	5.7	9.5	12.2	8.4	8.0
Contracts without escalator clauses	(NA)	(NA)	10.3	7.2	5.8	10.2	9.1	8.3	7.6
Over life of contract [2]	7.6	8.9	8.1	6.4	5.1	7.3	7.8	6.4	5.8
Contracts with escalator clauses	(NA)	7.3	7.1	5.7	4.9	6.1	7.1	5.7	5.0
Contracts without escalator clauses	(NA)	10.1	9.2	6.5	5.3	9.1	8.3	7.3	6.9
Manufacturing:									
First year changes	7.9	8.1	10.9	6.6	5.9	8.7	9.8	8.9	8.4
Over life of contract [2]	6.0	6.0	7.3	5.6	4.9	6.1	8.0	6.0	5.5
Nonmanufacturing: [3]									
First year changes	10.8	15.2	12.2	7.8	5.7	10.5	10.4	7.7	7.4
Over life of contract [2]	9.3	11.5	8.9	6.9	5.3	8.0	7.8	6.8	6.0
Number of workers affected ____1,000_	2,836	4,675	3,978	2,424	5,320	5,139	2,890	4,050	4,010
Percent of civilian labor force	3	6	5	3	6	6	3	4	4
Manufacturing ____1,000_	1,459	2,184	1,913	913	2,403	1,854	778	2,075	1,638
Nonmanufacturing [3] ____1,000_	1,377	2,491	2,066	1,510	2,917	3,285	2,112	1,975	2,372
Wage and benefit adjustments: [4]									
First year changes	10.9	13.1	13.1	8.5	7.1	10.7	11.4	8.5	9.6
Over life of contract [2]	8.2	9.1	8.8	7.4	6.1	7.8	8.1	6.6	6.2

NA Not available.   [1] Covers only contracts in which each settlement involved 1,000 or more workers.
[2] Average annual rate of change.   [3] Includes construction.
[4] Covers only contracts in which each settlement involved 5,000 or more workers.
Source: U.S. Bureau of Labor Statistics, *Current Wage Developments*, monthly.

No. 689. Effective and Scheduled Federal Minimum Hourly Wage Rates, 1950 to 1981, and Coverage in 1977

[Employee estimates as of September 1977, except as indicated. The Fair Labor Standards Act of 1938 and subsequent amendments to 1977 provide for minimum wage coverage to be extended to specified nonsupervisory employment categories. Exempt from coverage are executives and administrators or professionals]

EFFECTIVE DATE	MINIMUM WAGE RATES				SEX, RACE, AND INDUSTRY	NONSUPERVISORY EMPLOYEES, 1977				
	Nonfarm workers			Farm workers [4]		Subject to minimum wage rates				
	Laws prior to 1966 [1]	Percent avg. earnings [2]	1966 and later [3]			Total (1,000)	Total (1,000)	Percent of total	Prior to 1966 [5] (1,000)	1966 and later Amendments [6] (1,000)
In effect:					Total	70,801	54,446	76.9	38,634	15,812
Jan. 25, 1950_	$ .75	54	(X)	(X)						
Mar. 1, 1956_	1.00	52	(X)	(X)	Male	41,070	31,969	77.8	24,614	7,355
Sept. 3, 1961_	1.15	50	(X)	(X)	Female	29,731	22,477	75.6	14,020	8,457
Sept. 3, 1963_	1.25	51	(X)	(X)	White	62,243	47,785	76.8	34,560	13,225
Feb. 1, 1967_	1.40	50	$1.00	$1.00	Black and other	8,558	6,661	77.8	4,074	2,587
Feb. 1, 1968_	1.60	54	1.15	1.15	Black only	7,821	6,111	78.1	3,738	2,373
Feb. 1, 1969_	(7)	(7)	1.30	1.30	**Private industry**	61,510	51,893	84.4	38,634	13,259
Feb. 1, 1970_	(7)	(7)	1.45	(7)	Agriculture	1,431	565	39.5	–	565
Feb. 1, 1971_	(7)	(7)	1.60	(7)	Mining	763	759	99.5	759	–
May 1, 1974_	2.00	46	1.90	1.60	Construction	3,740	3,720	99.5	3,039	681
Jan. 1, 1975_	2.10	45	2.00	1.80	Manufacturing	17,618	17,146	97.3	17,045	101
Jan. 1, 1976_	2.30	46	2.20	2.00	Transp., public util	4,124	4,052	98.3	3,956	96
Jan. 1, 1977_	(7)	(7)	2.30	2.20	Wholesale trade	3,799	3,039	80.0	2,926	113
Jan. 1, 1978_	2.65	[8] 45	2.65	2.65	Retail trade	12,645	9,871	78.1	4,756	5,115
Future rates:					Finance, ins., real estate	3,896	2,969	76.2	2,856	113
Jan. 1, 1979_	2.90	46	2.90	2.90	Service	11,600	8,557	73.8	3,297	5,260
Jan. 1, 1980_	3.10	46	3.10	3.10	Private households	1,894	1,215	64.1	–	1,215
Jan. 1, 1981_	3.35	46	3.35	3.35	Government [9]	9,291	2,553	27.5	–	2,553

– Represents zero.   X Not applicable.   [1] Applies to workers covered prior to 1961 Amendments and, after Sept. 1965, to workers covered by 1961 Amendments. Rates set by 1961 Amendments were: Sept. 1961, $1.00; Sept. 1964, $1.15; and Sept. 1965, $1.25.   [2] Percent of gross average hourly earnings of production workers in manufacturing.   [3] Applies to workers newly covered by Amendments of 1966, 1974, and 1977 and Title IX of Education Amendments of 1972.   [4] Included in coverage as of 1966, 1974, and 1977 Amendments.   [5] Currently employed workers subject to criteria in effect prior to 1966 Amendments.   [6] Currently employed workers subject to provisions.   [7] No change in rate.   [8] Preliminary.   [9] Federal, State, and local employees.

Source: U.S. Department of Labor, Employment Standards Administration, *Minimum Wage and Maximum Hours Standards Under the Fair Labor Standards Act*, 1978.

No. 690. Minimum Hourly Union Wage Rates—Indexes and Averages, Selected Trades: 1960 to 1976

[As of first working day in July. Data for 1960 exclude Alaska. Indexes of rates reflect changes in minimum hourly wage scales. Year-to-year changes in union scales are based on comparable quotations for each trade weighted by membership for current year. Average wage rates show current levels and should not be used for precise year-to-year comparisons because of fluctuations in membership in the classifications studied. See Historical Statistics, Colonial Times to 1970, series D 818–829]

TRADE	1960	1965	1969	1970	1971	1972	1973	1974	1975	1976
INDEXES (1967 = 100)										
Building trades	75.4	90.9	115.4	128.8	144.0	153.2	160.8	173.4	188.3	200.5
Journeymen	75.5	90.9	115.7	128.9	143.9	153.4	160.8	173.0	188.1	200.3
Helpers and laborers	74.0	90.8	113.9	128.1	144.4	152.2	160.8	175.4	189.4	201.9
Printing trades [1]	80.6	93.0	111.9	121.2	133.6	144.2	153.3	165.7	179.8	192.2
Book and job [2]	80.3	93.5	111.8	121.0	133.7	144.4	155.1	166.2	180.8	193.3
Newspaper	81.1	92.5	112.0	120.8	133.1	144.2	152.2	165.4	179.0	191.7
Motortruck drivers and helpers [3]	75.4	91.2	111.4	122.5	137.8	151.5	163.4	176.8	190.0	205.6
Local transit operators	73.9	89.8	115.0	125.2	135.8	144.9	155.4	173.3	192.9	205.2
AVERAGE WAGE RATES (dol.)										
Building trades	3.66	4.42	5.54	6.18	6.88	7.27	7.62	8.14	8.88	9.48
Journeymen	3.86	4.64	5.87	6.54	7.28	7.69	8.02	8.55	9.32	9.92
Helpers and laborers	2.88	3.54	4.33	4.86	5.43	5.68	6.06	6.53	7.06	7.54
Printing trades [1]	3.23	3.73	4.57	4.97	5.47	5.89	6.28	6.80	7.36	7.90
Book and job [2]	3.08	3.58	4.27	4.65	5.11	5.49	5.91	6.34	6.86	7.41
Newspaper	3.48	3.94	4.76	5.13	5.65	6.09	6.43	7.01	7.57	8.17
Motortruck drivers and helpers [3]	2.65	3.22	3.97	4.36	4.90	5.43	5.85	6.34	6.81	7.36
Local transit operators	2.37	2.88	3.71	4.03	4.38	4.68	5.04	5.62	6.25	6.63

[1] Beginning 1969, includes lithographers. [2] Includes semiskilled (bindery workers and press assistants and feeders). [3] Data based on all scales reported for these workers.

No. 691. Minimum Hourly Union Wage Rates—Selected Trades, Ten Largest Cities: 1970 to 1976

[In dollars. Represents rates agreed upon through collective bargaining between employers and trade unions]

TRADE	New York, N.Y.	Chicago, Ill.	Los Angeles, Calif.	Philadelphia, Pa.	Detroit, Mich.	Houston, Tex.	Atlanta, Ga.	Denver, Colo.	Washington, D.C.	Cleveland, Ohio
1970:										
Building trades	6.71	6.74	6.08	6.60	7.19	5.43	5.36	5.55	5.80	7.73
Journeymen	6.95	6.96	6.49	7.10	7.37	5.70	6.05	6.15	6.41	7.94
Helpers, laborers	5.75	5.44	4.71	5.02	5.76	4.18	3.19	4.02	4.38	6.53
Printing trades:										
Book and job [1]	5.39	5.29	4.92	4.21	5.01	4.12	4.04	3.93	4.36	4.16
Newspaper	6.10	5.29	5.07	4.74	5.04	4.62	4.51	5.11	5.46	5.61
Local trucking: [2]										
Drivers	4.23	4.36	4.35	4.26	4.79	4.26	4.25	4.02	3.63	4.42
Helpers	3.65	3.94	3.85	3.46	4.17	2.49	2.73	3.18	3.43	3.35
Local transit	4.45	4.57	4.00	3.81	4.30	3.25	3.40	3.57	4.37	3.74
1975:										
Building trades	9.63	9.54	9.51	9.76	9.46	8.07	7.67	8.32	8.97	9.67
Journeymen	10.01	10.14	9.69	10.27	9.70	8.46	8.27	9.07	9.58	9.96
Helpers, laborers	8.28	7.28	7.34	7.56	7.73	6.20	5.34	5.75	7.18	8.10
Printing trades [3]	8.65	8.27	7.43	6.72	7.61	6.52	6.51	7.24	8.51	6.96
Book and job [1]	8.73	7.69	6.81	6.09	7.22	6.41	6.30	5.86	7.84	6.27
Newspaper	9.04	8.02	7.75	7.04	7.87	6.56	6.65	8.03	9.14	7.33
Local trucking [2]	6.36	7.12	6.60	6.89	7.20	6.69	6.82	6.31	5.87	6.80
Drivers	6.53	7.15	6.64	7.00	7.24	6.70	6.83	6.33	6.01	6.89
Helpers	5.70	6.60	5.44	5.66	6.62	4.55	4.21	5.72	5.41	5.24
Local transit	6.72	7.12	6.25	5.88	6.41	5.05	5.74	5.78	6.90	5.75
1976:										
Building trades	10.13	10.03	10.25	9.80	9.95	9.11	8.25	8.97	9.62	10.34
Journeymen	10.65	10.43	10.45	10.61	10.15	9.58	8.75	9.70	10.12	10.68
Helpers, laborers	8.41	7.89	7.87	7.77	8.33	6.97	5.83	6.41	7.98	8.49
Printing trades [3]	9.30	8.83	8.00	7.14	8.13	6.93	7.04	7.60	8.93	7.52
Book and job [1]	9.33	8.41	7.26	6.53	7.50	6.97	6.80	6.33	8.41	6.77
Newspaper	9.83	8.70	8.25	7.56	8.38	6.88	7.16	8.31	9.51	7.83
Local trucking [2]	6.89	7.74	7.09	7.33	7.74	7.26	7.41	6.88	6.17	7.17
Drivers	7.10	7.80	7.13	7.39	7.78	7.27	7.47	6.91	6.28	7.26
Helpers	5.98	6.98	5.94	6.61	7.21	5.05	4.98	6.10	5.80	6.07
Local transit	6.95	7.55	6.46	6.38	6.91	5.60	6.24	6.35	7.27	6.38

[1] See footnote 2, table 690. This number of semiskilled workers organized in a city may have influence on the average for the city. [2] See footnote 3, table 690. Helpers were not reported for all truck classifications, and these averages do not reflect or indicate the scale differential between drivers and helpers in a particular city. [3] Includes lithographers, not shown separately.

Source of tables 690 and 691: U.S. Bureau of Labor Statistics, Union Wages and Hours, annual.

No. 692. PERCENT INCREASE IN AVERAGE SALARIES FOR SELECTED OCCUPATIONS IN PRIVATE INDUSTRY: 1969 TO 1977

[Based on sample and subject to sampling variability. Relates to metropolitan areas and nonmetropolitan counties in U.S. except Alaska and Hawaii. Minimum employment sizes of establishments studied were: 250 or more in mining, construction, retail trade, most manufacturing industries, and selected transportation industries; and 100 or more in selected manufacturing industries, most transportation, communication, electric, gas, and sanitary services, and in wholesale trade, finance, insurance, and real estate, and selected services. When changes made in survey coverage, year-to-year percent changes were based on data adjusted to represent same coverage in both years]

OCCUPATIONAL GROUP	1969-1970	1970-1971	1971-1972 [1]	1972-1973	1973-1974	1974-1975	1975-1976	1976-1977
Accountants	6.7	6.7	5.6	4.9	6.1	9.8	6.4	7.8
Auditors	7.0	7.0	5.5	5.2	5.2	6.8	5.5	6.8
Chief accountants	7.1	9.1	3.9	5.8	7.2	8.6	6.6	10.5
Attorneys	7.1	5.0	6.1	6.3	5.8	7.6	6.1	5.4
Buyers	6.1	7.0	6.3	5.0	6.0	9.2	6.7	7.0
Job analysts	4.1	7.7	6.8	5.2	6.1	7.5	6.0	6.5
Personnel directors	7.4	8.0	3.9	7.5	7.2	6.1	7.8	9.1
Chemists	5.9	5.5	5.1	3.7	7.1	10.1	6.6	7.0
Engineers	5.5	5.7	5.2	5.1	5.4	8.4	6.8	6.4
Engineering technicians	6.3	6.5	5.1	4.7	6.0	9.0	8.1	7.2
Drafting	4.9	5.6	7.2	6.2	6.7	8.0	7.4	6.0
Clerical	6.2	6.5	6.1	5.4	6.4	9.6	7.3	6.6

[1] Data for the 9-month period, June 1971-March 1972, have been prorated to represent a 12-month period.

Source: U.S. Bureau of Labor Statistics, *National Survey of Professional, Administrative, Technical, and Clerical Pay*, Bulletin No.1980.

No. 693. ANNUAL PERCENT INCREASE IN AVERAGE PAY FOR SELECTED OCCUPATIONS AND IN CONSUMER PRICES: 5-YEAR PERIODS, 1966 TO 1977

[5-year periods begin and end in **January** of years shown, except as noted]

OCCUPATION	1966-1971	1967-1972	1968-1973	1969-1974	1970-1975	1971-1976	1972-1977
Private industry:							
Prof., admin., tech., and clerical employees, avg. salaries: [1]							
Clerical and beginning technicians	5.5	5.8	5.9	6.1	6.7	6.9	7.1
Entry and development professional levels, advanced technical levels, supervisors of nonprofessional levels	5.9	6.1	5.7	5.6	6.1	6.1	6.3
Fully experienced professional working levels, supervisors of professional and program administration levels	5.5	5.8	6.0	6.0	6.5	6.6	7.0
Production and nonsupervisory workers, nonagric. industries:							
Average hourly earnings adjusted for overtime [2] (manufacturing only) and interindustry employment shifts	6.1	6.6	6.7	6.7	7.3	7.4	7.5
Police and firefighters: [3]							
Minimum annual salary scales	7.6	7.9	7.3	6.5	6.0	6.3	6.0
Maximum annual salary scales	7.7	7.7	8.1	7.4	7.1	7.3	6.9
Urban public classroom teachers, average annual salaries [4]	[5] 6.9	[5] 6.9	[6] 6.8	[6] 6.8	[7] 6.9	7.0	6.9
Federal general schedule employees: [8]							
Average annual salary rates	6.4	6.3	7.4	6.0	5.7	5.5	5.1
Average annual salaries	7.5	7.8	9.1	6.5	5.9	5.7	5.3
Consumer price index	4.5	4.6	4.6	5.5	6.6	6.9	7.3

[1] For further details, see *National Survey of Professional, Administrative, Technical, and Clerical Pay*, Bulletin No. 1980. [2] Data are subject to annual benchmark revision and are not seasonally adjusted. [3] For cities of 100,000 population or more in 1970. [4] For cities of 100,000 population or more in 1970, and counties of this size in standard metropolitan statistical areas with county-wide school systems. [5] 1967-71 data. [6] 1969-73 data. [7] 1971-75 data. [8] For 1966 and for 1968 to 1971, as of July 1; for 1967, as of October 1; and for 1972 to 1977, as of April 1. Rates show statutory changes and effect of changes in proportion of workers at each step within salary ranges for individual grades. Salaries measure effect of statutory changes in basic pay scales and in grade salary increases, and also changes in proportion of workers in various grades.

Source: U.S. Bureau of Labor Statistics, *Current Wage Developments*, February and March 1978.

No. 694. EMPLOYEE COMPENSATION PER HOUR, BY COMPENSATION ITEM: 1976

[Private nonfarm economy. Covers establishments employing 20 or more workers]

COMPENSATION ITEM	ALL EMPLOYEES			OFFICE EMPLOYEES			NONOFFICE EMPLOYEES		
	Percent of compensation	Compensation per hour		Percent of compensation	Compensation per hour		Percent of compensation	Compensation per hour	
		All paid hours	Work hours		All paid hours	Work hours		All paid hours	Work hours
Total compensation	100.0	$6.94	$7.53	100.0	$8.54	$9.43	100.0	$6.08	$6.54
Wages and salaries (gross payroll) [1]	84.7	5.87	6.37	85.6	7.31	8.07	84.0	5.11	5.49
Supplements to wages and salaries [2]	15.3	1.06	1.15	14.4	1.23	1.36	16.0	.97	1.05
Pay for time worked	76.7	5.32	5.77	75.7	6.47	7.14	77.4	4.71	5.06
Straight-time pay	74.7	5.18	5.63	74.9	6.40	7.06	74.6	4.54	4.88
Premium pay	1.9	.13	.15	.8	.07	.07	2.8	.17	.18
Paid leave (exc. sick leave)	6.1	.43	.46	6.7	.57	.63	5.7	.35	.38
Vacations	3.5	.24	.26	3.9	.33	.36	3.1	.19	.21
Holidays	2.3	.16	.17	2.5	.22	.24	2.1	.13	.14
Other	.4	.02	.03	.2	.02	.02	.4	.03	.03
Employer expenditures for—									
Social security retirement	4.3	.30	.32	4.0	.34	.37	4.6	.28	.30
Private retirement plans	4.3	.30	.32	5.1	.44	.48	3.7	.22	.24
Life, accident, health insurance	4.1	.28	.31	3.6	.31	.34	4.4	.27	.29
Sick leave	.9	.06	.06	1.2	.10	.11	.6	.04	.04
Workers' compensation	1.1	.07	.08	.4	.04	.04	1.5	.09	.10
Unemployment insurance	1.1	.08	.08	.8	.07	.08	1.3	.08	.08
Severance pay [3]	.2	.01	.01	.1	.01	.01	.2	.01	.01
Nonproduction bonuses	1.1	.08	.08	2.0	.17	.19	.4	.03	.03
Savings and thrift plans	.2	.01	.01	.4	.03	.04	.1	(Z)	(Z)

Z Less than $.005.   [1] Pay for time worked, vacations, holidays, sick leave, and civic and personal leave; severance pay; and nonproduction bonuses.
[2] Expenditures for retirement programs (including direct pay to pensioners under pay-as you-go private pension plans), life insurance and health benefit programs (except sick leave), unemployment benefit programs (except severance pay), and payments to vacation and holiday funds and to savings and thrift plans.
[3] Severance pay and severance pay funds and supplemental benefit funds.

Source: U.S. Bureau of Labor Statistics, Handbook of Labor Statistics, 1977—Reference edition.

No. 695. AVERAGE ANNUAL WAGES AND SALARIES AND WAGE SUPPLEMENTS PER FULL-TIME EQUIVALENT EMPLOYEE, BY INDUSTRY: 1965 TO 1976

[In dollars. Wage and salary payments include executives' compensation, bonuses, tips, and payments in kind; supplements to wages and salaries include employer contributions for social insurance, compensation for injuries, directors' fees, jury and witness fees, etc. See Historical Statistics, Colonial Times to 1970, series D 739-764 and D 893-904, for related but not comparable data]

INDUSTRY	ANNUAL WAGES AND SALARIES					ANNUAL SUPPLEMENTS				
	1965	1970	1974	1975	1976	1965	1970	1974	1975	1976
All domestic industries	5,812	7,711	9,989	10,843	11,620	554	885	1,461	1,677	1,882
Agriculture, forestry, fisheries	2,892	4,300	5,498	5,736	5,936	163	335	554	609	695
Mining	6,898	9,445	12,905	14,769	16,089	884	1,498	2,561	3,153	3,655
Construction	6,923	9,813	12,191	13,457	14,611	589	934	1,478	1,708	1,927
Manufacturing	6,566	8,381	10,847	11,905	12,888	785	1,195	1,928	2,250	2,516
Transportation	6,994	9,391	12,622	13,582	14,826	741	1,211	2,093	2,384	2,701
Communication	6,820	8,752	12,372	13,654	15,290	1,241	2,105	3,607	4,350	5,063
Electric, gas, sanitary services	7,476	10,023	13,088	14,310	15,790	1,075	1,681	2,621	3,108	3,561
Wholesale and retail trade	5,328	6,871	8,731	9,365	9,948	402	628	1,066	1,197	1,329
Finance, insurance, real estate	5,964	7,810	9,849	10,613	11,361	686	1,050	1,650	1,894	2,097
Services	4,557	6,244	8,164	9,097	9,762	280	517	914	1,071	1,193
Gov't and gov't enterprises	5,697	7,951	10,638	11,442	12,168	450	785	1,359	1,568	1,798

Source: U.S. Bureau of Economic Analysis, The National Income and Product Accounts of the United States, 1929-1974, and Survey of Current Business, July 1977.

No. 696. Percent of Workers in Establishments With Formal Provisions for Selected Supplementary Benefits in SMSA's: 1971–1974 and 1974–1976

[Relates to standard metropolitan statistical areas, as established by U.S. Office of Management and Budget. Based on sample of establishments with 50 or more employees, except in 13 largest SMSA's (100 or more for manufacturing, public utilities, and retail trade); see source. Excludes government, construction, and extractive industries. Excludes administrative, executive, and professional employees]

TYPE OF BENEFIT	PLANT WORKERS		OFFICE WORKERS		TYPE OF BENEFIT	PLANT WORKERS		OFFICE WORKERS	
	1971–1974 [1]	1974–1976 [2]	1971–1974 [1]	1974–1976 [2]		1971–1974 [1]	1974–1976 [2]	1971–1974 [1]	1974–1976 [2]
Retirement pension	78	79	85	86	Paid holidays [3]—Con.				
Insurance plans:					8 or more days	66	69	78	81
Life insurance	93	93	97	97	9 or more days	50	57	59	68
Hospitalization	95	95	97	98	10 or more days	26	37	35	46
Surgical	95	95	98	98	11 or more days	13	18	20	24
Medical	90	92	94	96	12 or more days	8	11	9	13
Major medical	74	79	93	95	Paid vacations: [4]				
Dental insurance	13	26	11	23	2 weeks or more:				
Sickness/accident insurance	63	61	46	45	After 1 year of service	32	36	80	82
Sick leave (full pay and no waiting period)	23	27	65	67	After 5 years of service	96	95	99	99
					3 weeks or more:				
Sick leave (partial pay and/or waiting period)	13	12	9	9	After 5 years of service	21	26	28	35
					After 10 years of service	74	78	87	90
Paid holidays: [3]					After 15 years of service	86	86	94	94
No paid holidays	4	5	(Z)	(Z)	4 weeks or more:				
6 or more days	89	89	97	98	After 15 years of service	29	37	29	39
7 or more days	78	79	88	89	After 20 years of service	61	64	71	77
					After 25 years of service	67	68	76	80

Z Less than .5 percent.   [1] Surveys conducted between July 1971 and June 1974 relate to 229 SMSA's.
[2] Surveys conducted between January 1974 and December 1976 relate to 262 SMSA's.
[3] Holidays provided annually. Represents half-day and full-day holidays combined.
[4] Such payments as percentages of annual earnings or flat-sum were converted to an equivalent time basis.
Source: U.S. Bureau of Labor Statistics, *Area Wage Surveys: Metropolitan Areas, United States and Regional Summaries, 1973–1974*, and *1976*, Bulletin Nos. 1795-29 and 1900-82.

No. 697. Membership in Large Unions: 1968 to 1976

[In thousands. AFL-CIO (except as noted) unions reporting 100,000 members or more in 1974 with headquarters in U.S. "Ind." = Independent or unaffiliated unions]

UNION	1968	1972	1974	1976	UNION	1968	1972	1974	1976
Teamsters (Ind.)	1,755	1,855	1,973	1,889	Plumbers	297	[9] 228	[9] 228	[9] 228
Automobile workers (Ind.)	1,473	1,394	1,545	1,358	Letter carriers	210	220	232	227
Steelworkers [1] [2]	1,352	1,400	1,300	1,300	Railway, steamship clerks [10]	280	238	235	211
Electrical (IBEW)	897	957	991	924	Rubber	204	183	191	211
Machinists	903	758	943	917	Retail, wholesale	175	198	180	200
Carpenters	793	820	820	820	Painters	200	208	211	195
State, county (AFSCME)	364	529	648	750	Iron workers	168	176	182	179
Retail clerks (RCIA)	552	633	651	699	Oil, chemical workers	173	172	177	177
Laborers (LIUNA)	553	600	650	627	Firefighters	133	160	172	174
Service employees (SEIU)	389	484	550	575	Electrical (UE) (Ind.)	167	165	163	165
Meat cutters [2] [3]	500	529	525	510	Sheet metal workers	140	153	161	153
Clothing and textile workers [2] [4]	569	539	517	502	Government (NAGE) (Ind.)	(NA)	100	(NA)	150
Communications workers	357	443	499	483	Transit union	134	130	140	150
Teachers (AFT)	165	249	444	446	Transport workers	98	150	150	150
Hotel and restaurant	459	458	452	432	Boilermakers	140	132	138	145
Engineers, operating	350	402	415	420	Bakery, confectionery [11]	(NA)	146	134	135
Garment, ladies' (ILGWU)	455	428	405	365	Bricklayers	160	149	148	135
Musicians	283	315	330	330	Maintenance of way	125	142	119	119
Paperworkers [2] [5]	328	389	301	300	Printing and graphic				
Mine workers (Ind.)	(NA)	213	220	277	(IPGCU)	(NA)	(NA)	129	109
United transportation [6]	(NA)	248	238	265	Woodworkers	96	106	108	109
Government (AFGE)	295	293	300	260	Typographical	123	115	111	100
Postal workers [7]	[8] 166	239	249	252	Graphic arts	(NA)	106	100	93
Electrical (IUE)	324	290	298	238	Federal Govt. (NFFE) (Ind.)	95	85	100	(NA)

NA Not available.   [1] Intl. Union of Mine, Mill, and Smelter Workers, and Intl. Union of District 50 merged with United Steelworkers of America in 1967 and 1972, respectively.   [2] Figures for all years represent the union as constituted after merger.   [3] In 1968 United Packinghouse, Food and Allied Workers merged with Amalgamated Meat Cutters and Butcher Workmen of North America.   [4] In 1976, Amalgamated Clothing Workers of America merged with Textile Workers Union of America to form Amalgamated Clothing and Textile Workers Union.   [5] United Papermakers and Paperworkers merged with Intl. Brotherhood of Pulp, Sulphite and Paper Mill Workers in 1972 to form United Paperworkers International Union.   [6] Merged with Brotherhood of Railroad Trainmen and three other railroad unions in 1969.   [7] American Postal Workers Union formed in 1971 by merger of the postal clerks union and 4 other unions.   [8] Postal clerks only.   [9] AFL-CIO per capita reports.   [10] Includes Transportation-Communication Employees Union.   [11] American Bakery and Confectionery Workers Intl. Union and Bakery and Confectionery Workers' Intl. Union of America merged in 1969.
Source: U.S. Bureau of Labor Statistics, *Directory of National Unions and Employee Associations, 1975*, and unpublished data.

No. 698. LABOR UNION AND EMPLOYEE ASSOCIATION MEMBERSHIP: 1950 TO 1976

[Estimates based on average number of dues-paying members of unions with headquarters in the U.S. Certain unions did not report as members persons not required to pay dues, such as apprentices and workers retired, unemployed, in Armed Forces, or involved in work stoppages. Excludes single-firm and local unaffiliated unions; includes local unions directly affiliated with the AFL-CIO, except as noted. Employee associations are similar to unions. See also *Historical Statistics, Colonial Times to 1970*, series D 933-934 and D 946-951]

ITEM	1950	1955	1960	1965	1970	1972	1974	1976, prel.
Union membership, total......1,000..	15,000	17,749	18,117	18,519	20,752	20,893	21,643	21,006
AFL-CIO......................1,000..	12,400	16,062	15,072	15,604	15,978	16,507	16,938	16,526
Independent or unaffiliated unions..1,000..	2,600	1,688	3,045	2,915	4,773	4,386	4,705	4,480
Male [1].....................1,000..	(NA)	(NA)	14,733	(NA)	16,408	16,315	16,985	16,805
Female [1]...................1,000..	(NA)	(NA)	3,304	(NA)	4,282	4,524	4,600	4,201
White-collar membership [1]........1,000..	(NA)	[2] 2,463	2,192	(NA)	3,353	3,434	3,762	3,857
Percent of total membership..........	(NA)	[2] 13.6	12.2	(NA)	16.2	16.5	17.4	18.4
U.S. members, excl. Canadians.....1,000..	14,267	16,802	17,049	17,299	19,381	19,435	20,199	19,432
Percent of total labor force............	22.0	24.4	23.6	22.4	22.6	21.8	21.7	20.1
Percent of nonagric. employment........	31.5	33.2	31.4	28.4	27.5	26.4	25.8	24.5
Canadian members of U.S. unions..1,000..	733	947	1,068	1,220	1,371	1,458	1,444	1,573
Number of unions, total..............	[3] 209	199	184	[4] 191	185	177	175	176
Unions affiliated with AFL-CIO..........	137	139	134	129	120	113	111	112
Association membership [5]....1,000..	(NA)	(NA)	(NA)	(NA)	1,868	2,221	2,610	3,031
Female membership................1,000..	(NA)	(NA)	(NA)	(NA)	1,116	1,212	1,438	1,790
White-collar membership............1,000..	(NA)	(NA)	(NA)	(NA)	1,564	1,768	2,119	2,603

NA Not available. [1] Excludes local unions directly affiliated with AFL-CIO.
[2] 1956 data. [3] 1949 data. [4] 1966 data. [5] Covers professional and State employee associations engaged in collective bargaining in more than one State or in one State in two or more cities.

Source: U.S. Bureau of Labor Statistics, *Handbook of Labor Statistics*, annual; and *Directory of National Unions and Employee Associations, 1975.*

No. 699. LABOR UNION MEMBERSHIP—TOTAL AND PERCENT OF NONAGRICULTURAL EMPLOYMENT, BY STATES: 1964 TO 1974

[Based on reports and estimates for national and local unions directly affiliated with AFL-CIO, and members in single firm and local unaffiliated unions. Excludes employee associations and membership outside U.S.]

STATE	TOTAL (1,000)			PERCENT OF EMPLOYMENT			STATE	TOTAL (1,000)			PERCENT OF EMPLOYMENT		
	1964	1970	1974	1964	1970	1974		1964	1970	1974	1964	1970	1974
U.S.......	17,188	19,757	20,566	29.5	28.0	26.2	Mont........	62	60	60	35.2	29.8	25.7
							Nebr.[1].......	78	86	83	19.2	17.8	15.1
Ala.[1]........	158	204	223	18.7	20.2	19.1	Nev.[1]........	49	66	71	32.8	32.5	27.4
Alaska.......	21	25	32	32.1	26.9	26.4	N.H........	42	45	46	20.1	17.3	15.1
Ariz........	71	96	118	18.5	17.5	16.0	N.J........	701	768	786	32.3	29.4	28.2
Ark.[1]........	73	95	108	17.0	17.8	16.8	N. Mex......	37	43	51	14.5	14.7	14.1
Calif........	1,857	2,137	2,212	33.3	30.8	28.2	N.Y........	2,453	2,555	2,693	38.5	35.7	38.0
Colo........	128	152	181	22.3	20.5	18.9	N.C.[1]........	100	137	140	7.4	7.7	6.9
Conn........	267	290	317	27.0	24.2	25.1	N. Dak.[1].....	21	28	29	14.8	17.2	15.1
Del........	41	48	47	24.0	22.5	20.1	Ohio........	1,180	1,413	1,389	36.7	36.4	33.2
Fla.[1]........	214	299	354	14.0	13.9	12.5	Okla........	94	124	132	15.1	16.1	15.0
Ga.[1]........	166	251	264	14.0	16.1	14.5	Oreg........	196	218	222	34.2	30.7	26.5
Hawaii.....	49	82	121	23.6	27.9	36.2							
Idaho.......	32	38	40	19.0	18.3	15.5	Pa........	1,462	1,617	1,695	38.7	37.2	37.5
							R.I........	86	89	101	28.3	25.9	27.3
Ill........	1,419	1,548	1,584	38.4	35.8	34.9	S.C.[1]........	48	81	82	7.4	9.6	8.0
Ind........	563	657	670	36.4	35.5	33.2	S. Dak.[1].....	15	21	23	10.0	11.9	11.0
Iowa [1]......	163	186	212	22.6	21.1	21.2	Tenn.[1]........	201	274	295	19.2	20.6	18.7
Kans.[1]......	109	112	110	18.6	16.5	14.1	Tex.[1]........	394	523	567	14.1	14.4	13.0
Ky........	195	250	269	27.0	27.5	25.1	Utah [1].......	53	75	65	18.0	20.9	14.9
La........	160	193	194	18.7	18.5	16.3	Vt........	21	24	28	18.7	16.2	17.7
Maine.....	59	61	59	20.8	18.4	16.2	Va.[1]........	184	245	247	15.8	16.7	13.8
Md. [2].......	369	463	462	22.9	23.4	21.6	Wash........	376	434	438	44.0	40.2	36.7
Mass........	549	573	579	28.0	25.1	24.4	W. Va........	206	221	218	44.7	42.8	38.2
Mich........	1,074	1,195	1,255	42.7	39.8	38.4	Wis........	424	482	490	33.4	31.5	28.7
Minn........	350	378	375	34.0	28.7	25.3	Wyo.[1]........	19	19	25	19.4	17.4	18.2
Miss.[1]......	62	76	84	13.5	13.2	12.0	Unallo-						
Mo........	537	594	575	37.9	35.7	32.3	cated......	-	108	146	(X)	(X)	(X)

- Represents zero. X Not applicable. [1] State has a right-to-work law. [2] Includes Dist. of Col.

Source: U.S. Bureau of Labor Statistics, *Directory of National and International Labor Unions in the United States, 1965*, and *Directory of National Unions and Employee Associations, 1975.*

No. 700. NATIONAL UNIONS—NUMBER AND MEMBERS, BY INDUSTRY AND AFFILIATION: 1970 AND 1974

[See headnote, table 698. Excludes employee associations and local unions directly affiliated with the AFL-CIO and members in single-firm and local unaffiliated unions]

INDUSTRY GROUP	ALL UNIONS, 1970			1974					
				All unions			AFL-CIO unions		
	Num-ber [1]	Members [2]		Num-ber [1]	Members [2]		Num-ber [1]	Mem-bers [2] (1,000)	Per-cent
		Number (1,000)	Per-cent		Number (1,000)	Per-cent			
All unions	185	20,689	100.0	175	21,585	100.0	111	16,879	100.0
Manufacturing [3]	100	9,173	44.3	98	9,144	42.4	70	6,746	40.0
Ordnance and accessories	16	157	.8	14	102	.5	7	91	.5
Food and kindred prod. (incl. beverages)	25	906	4.4	26	908	4.2	17	570	3.4
Tobacco manufactures	8	38	.2	6	43	.2	4	42	.2
Textile mill products	10	191	.9	11	169	.8	6	158	.9
Apparel and related products	16	852	4.1	14	750	3.5	11	734	4.3
Lumber and wood prod., exc. furniture	13	215	1.0	18	261	1.2	10	254	1.5
Furniture and fixtures	17	214	1.0	13	220	1.0	8	190	1.1
Paper and allied products	20	453	2.2	21	366	1.7	16	324	1.9
Printing, publishing, and allied industries	18	370	1.8	19	359	1.7	13	339	2.0
Chemicals and allied products	26	361	1.7	22	268	1.2	17	232	1.4
Petroleum refining and related industries	12	80	.4	10	82	.4	7	71	.4
Rubber and miscell. plastics products	19	272	1.3	24	275	1.3	17	248	1.5
Leather and leather products	13	140	.7	16	128	.6	13	125	.7
Stone, clay, glass, and concrete products	22	284	1.4	17	325	1.5	14	281	1.7
Primary metals industries	16	788	3.8	14	817	3.8	11	691	4.1
Fabricated metal products	33	918	4.4	28	726	3.4	19	516	3.1
Machinery, except electrical	23	550	2.7	16	726	3.4	11	425	2.5
Electrical machinery equip. and supplies	19	1,034	5.0	14	1,074	5.0	10	820	4.9
Transportation equipment	21	1,109	5.4	16	1,144	5.3	10	319	1.9
Nonmanufacturing [3]	104	9,198	44.5	101	9,520	44.1	73	7,687	45.5
Mining and quarrying (including crude petroleum and natural gas production)	15	369	1.8	17	372	1.7	10	141	.8
Contract constr. (bldg. and special trade)	28	2,576	12.5	28	2,738	12.7	21	2,634	15.6
Transportation	44	2,441	11.8	37	2,343	10.9	28	1,297	7.7
Telephone and telegraph	10	533	2.6	11	672	3.1	9	606	3.6
Electric, gas, sanitary serv. (incl. water)	17	312	1.5	11	243	1.1	9	234	1.4
Wholesale and retail trade	24	1,549	7.5	22	1,329	6.2	13	1,066	6.3
Service industries	48	1,287	6.2	45	1,665	7.7	27	1,571	9.3
Government	60	2,318	11.2	64	2,920	13.5	39	2,447	14.5
Federal	56	1,370	6.6	48	1,392	6.4	26	955	5.7
State and local	19	947	4.6	37	1,529	7.1	31	1,492	8.8

[1] Nonadditive; many unions have membership in more than one industry group.
[2] Membership computed by applying reported percentages to total membership, including that outside the U.S.
[3] Includes industries not shown separately.
Source: U.S. Bureau of Labor Statistics, *Directory of National Unions and Employee Associations, 1971* and *1975*.

No. 701. LABOR UNIONS—FINANCIAL SUMMARY, BY TYPE OF UNION: 1966 TO 1976

[For fiscal years ending during calendar year. Data from annual financial reports of labor organizations filed with Department of Labor under provisions of Labor-Management Reporting and Disclosure Act of 1959 (LMRDA) which covers substantially all labor unions in the United States, except those which are State or local central bodies. Classification by type is based mainly on union's self-classification in filed reports]

YEAR AND TYPE OF UNION	Total number of unions	NUMBER OF UNIONS BY SIZE OF RECEIPTS					Assets (mil. dol.)	Lia-bil-ities (mil. dol.)	Re-ceipts (mil. dol.)	Dis-burse-ments (mil. dol.)
		Under $10,000	$10,000–$49,999	$50,000–$99,999	$100,000–$999,999	$1,000,000 and over				
1966, total	52,272	32,617	13,151	3,074	3,239	191	2,157	143	(¹)	(¹)
National unions	207	21	22	16	62	86	995	47	728	695
Intermediate bodies	2,729	1,376	853	235	245	20	147	21	190	184
Local unions	49,336	31,220	12,276	2,823	2,932	85	1,015	75	1,298	1,250
1970, total	49,345	29,245	13,031	3,021	3,777	271	2,574	254	(¹)	(¹)
National unions	210	23	27	15	54	91	1,063	127	1,380	1,344
Intermediate bodies	2,596	1,200	728	275	351	42	199	23	260	252
Local unions	46,539	28,022	12,276	2,731	3,372	138	1,312	104	1,857	1,804
1976, total,[2] prel	52,293	30,147	12,744	3,647	5,259	496	3,941	321	(¹)	(¹)
National unions	205	14	20	11	54	106	1,851	113	2,129	2,132
Intermediate bodies	3,202	1,625	697	281	526	73	262	51	412	412
Local unions [3]	48,886	28,508	12,027	3,355	4,679	317	1,828	157	2,576	2,532

[1] Components not additive; contain duplication. [2] Includes Postal Employee Unions.
[3] Includes approximately 5,100 unions which have no receipts, disbursements, assets, and liabilities.
Source: U.S. Office of Labor-Management Standards Enforcement, *Union Financial Statistics, 1960–1970*, and unpublished data.

No. 702. Work Stoppages: 1950 to 1976

[Prior to 1960, excludes Alaska and Hawaii. Excludes work stoppages involving fewer than 6 workers or lasting less than 1 day. Information obtained directly from companies and unions involved as well as from various Government labor boards, conciliation services, and other neutral parties. See also *Historical Statistics, Colonial Times to 1970*, series D 970–976]

| YEAR | WORK STOPPAGES | | WORKERS INVOLVED | | WORKER-DAYS IDLE DURING YEAR | | |
	Number beginning in year	Average duration (calendar days)	Number [1] (1,000)	Percent of total employed [2]	Number (1,000)	Percent of estimated working time [3]	Per worker involved
1950	4,843	19.2	2,410	5.1	38,800	.33	16.1
1955	4,320	18.5	2,650	5.2	28,200	.22	10.7
1960	3,333	23.4	1,320	2.4	19,100	.14	14.5
1965	3,963	25.0	1,550	2.5	23,300	.15	15.1
1967	4,595	22.8	2,870	4.3	42,100	.25	14.7
1968	5,045	24.5	2,649	3.8	49,018	.28	18.5
1969	5,700	22.5	2,481	3.5	42,869	.24	17.3
1970	5,716	25.0	3,305	4.7	66,414	.37	20.1
1971	5,138	27.0	3,280	4.6	47,589	.26	14.5
1972	5,010	24.0	1,714	2.3	27,066	.15	15.8
1973	5,353	24.0	2,251	2.9	27,948	.14	12.4
1974	6,074	27.1	2,778	3.5	47,991	.24	17.3
1975	5,031	26.8	1,746	2.2	31,237	.16	17.9
1976	5,648	28.0	2,420	3.0	37,859	.19	15.6

[1] Workers counted more than once if involved in more than 1 stoppage during year. [2] In 1967, total employed workers were redefined to coincide with U.S. Bureau of Labor Statistics figures for nonagricultural employment, plus agricultural wage and salaried workers. Idleness computed on this basis is lower than the former series. [3] Estimated working time computed by multiplying average number of employed workers (see footnote 2) by number of days worked by most employees.

Source: U.S. Bureau of Labor Statistics, *Monthly Labor Review*, June or July issues, and *Analysis of Work Stoppages*, annual.

No. 703. Work Stoppages, by States: 1975 and 1976

[See headnote, table 702. Work stoppages affecting more than 1 State are counted as separate stoppages in each State affected, and workers involved and days idle are allocated among the appropriate States]

| STATE | WORK STOPPAGES | | WORKERS INVOLVED [1] (1,000) | | DAYS IDLE DURING YEAR (1,000) | | STATE | WORK STOPPAGES | | WORKERS INVOLVED [1] (1,000) | | DAYS IDLE DURING YEAR (1,000) | |
	1975	1976	1975	1976	1975	1976		1975	1976	1975	1976	1975	1976
U.S.	5,031	5,648	1,746	2,420	31,237	37,859	So. Atl.—Con.						
N. Eng.:							W. Va.	560	692	152	207	891	1,274
Maine	9	19	1	8	13	93	N.C.	13	36	3	15	173	431
N.H.	15	10	2	2	26	47	S.C.	7	12	2	2	52	43
Vt.	7	5	1	1	7	43	Ga.	46	52	21	20	256	328
Mass.	109	129	34	61	876	742	Fla.	54	55	22	17	638	269
R.I.	49	27	14	7	365	142	E. So. Cent.:						
Conn.	69	68	25	21	1,309	621	Ky.	171	211	57	111	666	1,339
Mid. Atl.:							Tenn.	73	110	15	51	407	1,077
N.Y.	338	345	170	167	2,228	1,927	Ala.	63	150	15	58	240	1,316
N.J.	191	248	65	69	1,040	1,397	Miss.	18	26	3	7	88	127
Pa.	654	721	245	243	2,852	2,840	W. So. Cent.:						
E. No. Cent.:							Ark.	13	23	3	8	86	271
Ohio	432	549	130	271	2,233	4,839	La.	49	46	18	9	536	160
Ind.	173	193	39	88	719	1,593	Okla.	29	32	4	11	165	395
Ill.	382	421	152	151	2,351	1,891	Tex.	113	115	74	34	3,705	816
Mich.	189	260	35	209	935	3,151	Mt.:						
Wis.	72	78	28	32	659	685	Mont.	30	23	6	3	85	15
W. No. Cent.:							Idaho	18	13	3	5	23	172
Minn.	91	115	42	23	672	465	Wyo.	8	7	2	2	44	36
Iowa	66	78	16	47	294	1,110	Colo.	47	38	15	8	205	91
Mo.	108	163	31	63	1,609	1,197	N. Mex.	13	19	2	9	47	63
N. Dak.	10	10	2	1	38	14	Ariz.	27	30	10	17	137	182
S. Dak.	11	5	1	4	68	16	Utah	24	14	10	4	109	32
Nebr.	17	14	7	7	101	176	Nev.	17	14	2	22	13	241
Kans.	28	31	3	15	115	505	Pac.:						
So. Atl.:							Wash.	94	93	26	38	393	1,387
Del.	33	8	13	3	141	22	Oreg.	46	62	13	15	166	312
Md.	58	52	23	21	591	391	Calif.	313	332	99	152	1,713	2,789
D.C.	31	16	33	5	808	111	Alaska	18	19	6	10	37	71
Va.	238	203	54	65	288	570	Hawaii	13	20	2	3	32	35

[1] Workers counted more than once if involved in more than 1 stoppage during year.

Source: U.S. Bureau of Labor Statistics, *Analysis of Work Stoppages*, annual.

No. 704. Work Stoppages—Major Issues, Duration, and Industry: 1974 to 1976

[Issues and industries data based on stoppages beginning in year; duration data on stoppages ending in year. See headnote, table 702. Stoppages affecting more than 1 industry are counted separately in each industry affected; workers involved and work-days idle are allocated among the appropriate industries. See *Historical Statistics, Colonial Times to 1970*, series D 977-1021, for related but not comparable data]

MAJOR ISSUES, DURATION, AND INDUSTRY GROUP	WORK STOPPAGES			WORKERS INVOLVED [1] (1,000)			WORK DAYS IDLE (1,000)		
	1974	1975	1976	1974	1975	1976	1974	1975	1976
MAJOR ISSUES									
All issues	6,074	5,031	5,648	2,778	1,746	2,420	47,991	31,237	37,859
General wage changes	3,638	2,619	2,857	1,952	810	1,211	38,924	22,222	23,779
Supplementary benefits	70	53	53	38	23	10	1,104	278	189
Wage adjustments	148	126	142	66	39	52	445	364	562
Hours of work	7	7	6	8	(Z)	2	444	10	57
Other contractual matters	97	75	142	85	24	19	819	406	338
Union organization and security	348	268	325	47	92	127	1,841	1,488	2,455
Job security	248	257	317	100	206	402	1,543	3,154	7,187
Plant administration	1,120	1,142	1,290	376	432	489	2,341	2,884	2,777
Other working conditions	91	137	185	27	40	50	256	198	178
Interunion or intraunion matters	240	317	285	74	78	55	188	201	288
Not reported	67	30	46	6	3	3	85	34	50
DURATION									
All stoppages	6,031	4,998	5,654	2,795	1,732	2,421	49,881	29,604	38,107
1 day	818	936	1,113	216	223	342	216	223	342
2-3 days	684	652	672	219	217	464	429	412	995
4-6 days	625	521	564	258	161	227	914	497	682
7-14 days	1,093	739	893	656	266	332	4,431	1,777	2,254
15-29 days	1,055	730	842	481	348	309	7,287	3,893	3,683
30-59 days	1,011	742	769	722	279	321	18,669	6,376	6,857
60-89 days	351	325	370	121	82	265	5,901	3,881	8,501
90 days and over	394	353	431	123	155	160	12,034	12,546	14,793
INDUSTRY GROUP									
All industries	6,074	5,031	5,648	2,778	1,746	2,420	47,991	31,237	37,859
Manufacturing	2,823	1,897	2,245	1,145	464	975	23,599	14,876	24,263
Ordnance and accessories	6	9	1	2	7	1	153	194	42
Food and kindred products	265	166	227	68	29	90	1,539	838	1,848
Tobacco manufactures	3	–	1	6	–	(Z)	68	–	3
Textile mill products	45	21	36	23	2	8	756	27	115
Apparel and other finished products, etc.	66	55	47	101	10	12	893	110	231
Lumber, wood products (exc. furniture)	87	61	69	20	17	11	332	283	429
Furniture and fixtures	88	57	73	20	12	10	209	354	267
Paper and allied products	136	68	95	36	12	23	685	622	479
Printing, publishing, and allied industries	69	47	54	34	14	13	545	238	225
Chemicals and allied products	156	109	129	42	18	29	1,600	747	1,117
Petroleum refining and related products	25	30	17	6	20	1	148	613	19
Rubber and misc. plastics products	126	57	120	38	10	93	971	238	6,082
Leather and leather products	15	9	12	6	1	3	123	9	55
Stone, clay, and glass products	167	140	146	35	18	28	1,004	484	613
Primary metal industries	225	161	197	73	43	55	1,586	1,169	1,304
Fabricated metal products [2]	423	309	309	88	49	64	2,102	1,779	1,632
Machinery (except electrical)	401	274	309	170	74	145	3,026	2,371	2,722
Electrical machinery equip. and supplies	220	120	204	183	34	135	3,643	851	2,236
Transportation equipment	197	137	130	181	78	238	3,739	3,405	4,323
Instruments and related products	41	32	29	14	11	5	165	288	128
Miscellaneous manufacturing industries	69	37	60	11	6	11	210	256	394
Nonmanufacturing	3,253	3,134	3,406	1,632	1,282	1,446	24,392	16,361	13,596
Agriculture, forestry, and fisheries	13	7	10	22	1	2	460	36	14
Mining	1,050	1,165	1,425	501	392	515	4,061	1,643	2,220
Contract construction	688	600	503	630	308	172	12,721	7,307	3,240
Transportation, communication, etc.	320	268	354	140	167	386	3,226	3,089	3,461
Wholesale and retail trade	549	371	467	137	63	56	1,758	1,426	1,311
Finance, insurance, real estate	29	18	27	3	3	25	63	169	273
Services—personal, business, etc.	220	228	243	39	30	107	700	487	1,384
Government	384	478	378	161	319	181	1,404	2,204	1,691

- Represents zero.   Z Less than 500 workers.   [1] See footnote 1, table 702.
[2] Except ordnance, machinery, and transport equipment.

Source: U.S. Bureau of Labor Statistics, *Monthly Labor Review*, June or July issues, and *Analysis of Work Stoppages*, annual.

No. 705. State and Local Governments—Full-Time Employment, Organized Employees, and Work Stoppages, by Function: 1975 and 1976

[For October, except as noted]

ITEM	1975, total	1976							
		Total [1]	Education			High-ways	Hospi-tals	Police and fire protec-tion	Public wel-fare
			Total	Instruc-tional	Other				
Full-time employees:									
Total_____1,000__	9,397	9,514	4,527	3,003	1,524	542	910	741	335
State_____1,000__	2,540	2,596	829	282	548	257	482	68	156
Local_____1,000__	6,857	6,919	3,698	2,721	976	285	428	673	178
Membership in employee organizations: [2]									
Total_____1,000__	4,702	4,737	2,637	2,060	577	240	360	439	138
Percent of full-time employees_____	49.9	49.8	58.3	68.6	37.9	44.3	39.5	59.2	41.3
State_____1,000__	1,005	992	237	97	140	138	230	35	61
Local_____1,000__	3,697	3,745	2,400	1,963	437	103	130	404	77
Work stoppages, number: [3][4]									
Total_____	490	377	184	146	98	65	17	48	17
State_____	36	27	6	2	4	4	4	–	1
Local_____	454	350	178	144	94	61	13	48	16
Employees involved in work stoppages: [3]									
Total_____1,000__	316	167	84	58	26	7	26	4	8
State_____1,000__	71	28	3	(Z)	2	2	8	–	4
Local_____1,000__	245	139	82	58	24	4	17	4	4
Days of idleness: [3]									
Total_____1,000__	2,421	1,654	916	595	321	62	123	10	88
State_____1,000__	290	124	13	1	12	6	29	–	12
Local_____1,000__	2,130	1,529	903	594	309	56	94	10	76

– Represents zero.   Z Less than 500.   [1] Includes other functions, not shown separately.   [2] Full-time employees only.   [3] Represents period from October 16 of previous year to October 15 of year stated.   [4] Contains duplication; each work stoppage is counted separately for each function affected, but only once in the total work stoppages.

Source: U.S. Bureau of the Census, *Labor-Management Relations in State and Local Governments: 1975* and *1976*, series GSS Nos. 81 and 88.

No. 706. Occupational Injury Rates in Private Industry, by Employee-Size Class and Industry Group: 1975 and 1976

[**Injuries per 100 full-time workers.** Based on a sample of approximately 210,000 employers in 1976, and subject to sampling variability. Based on the 1972 *Standard Industrial Classification Manual*]

INDUSTRY GROUP	All sizes	EMPLOYEE-SIZE CLASS							
		1–19	20–49	50–99	100–249	250–499	500–999	1,000–2,499	2,500 and over
1975									
Total private industry_____	8.8	4.3	8.4	11.1	12.2	11.4	10.1	8.8	7.3
Agriculture, forestry, fishing [1]____	9.7	6.1	9.2	11.2	11.9	13.8	10.5	28.6	(NA)
Mining_____	10.9	9.3	11.9	14.9	12.8	10.0	7.4	5.2	2.3
Construction_____	15.6	10.5	16.7	19.8	20.9	18.7	16.3	13.9	5.2
Manufacturing_____	12.5	9.0	13.9	16.1	16.6	14.2	11.8	9.5	7.7
Transportation, public utilities___	9.2	6.4	10.1	11.5	9.6	8.8	9.4	8.5	8.9
Wholesale and retail trade_____	7.2	3.6	7.4	9.9	10.6	10.9	10.7	10.7	6.8
Finance, insurance, real estate____	2.1	1.3	1.7	2.5	3.0	2.7	2.5	2.1	2.0
Services_____	5.2	2.0	3.8	6.0	7.5	7.4	8.1	7.3	5.6
1976									
Total private industry_____	8.9	3.9	8.7	11.2	12.6	12.0	10.3	8.8	7.3
Agriculture, forestry, fishing [1]____	10.2	6.0	9.7	12.8	14.2	16.3	15.7	21.8	(NA)
Mining_____	·10.9	7.0	11.8	15.3	12.5	12.3	8.6	4.3	.5
Construction_____	14.9	9.3	17.7	20.0	19.4	17.8	18.2	14.0	7.4
Manufacturing_____	12.6	8.9	14.0	17.2	17.3	14.5	11.5	9.2	7.2
Transportation, public utilities___	9.6	7.2	10.6	11.3	10.3	8.9	9.4	8.5	9.8
Wholesale and retail trade_____	7.3	3.1	7.8	9.8	11.4	11.2	10.7	11.6	9.1
Finance, insurance, real estate____	1.9	1.1	1.7	2.0	2.7	2.7	2.2	2.4	1.7
Services_____	5.1	1.7	3.7	5.5	6.7	8.2	8.4	8.2	5.6

NA Not available.   [1] Excludes farms with fewer than 11 employees.

Source: U.S. Bureau of Labor Statistics, *Occupational Injuries and Illnesses in the United States by Industry*, 1975, and *News*, Dec. 1, 1977.

No. 707. OCCUPATIONAL INJURY AND ILLNESS INCIDENCE RATES, SELECTED INDUSTRIES: 1974 TO 1976

[Rates per 100 full-time employees. For employment data, see table 676. Rates refer to any occupational injuries or illnesses resulting in (1) fatalities, (2) lost workday cases, or (3) nonfatal cases without lost workdays. Incidence rates were calculated as: Number of injuries and illnesses or lost workdays multiplied by 200,000 as base for 100 full-time equivalent workers (working 40 hours per week, 50 weeks a year) divided by total hours worked by all employees during year. 1974 based on the 1967 Standard Industrial Classification (SIC) Manual; beginning 1975, based on the 1972 SIC Manual]

INDUSTRY	TOTAL CASES [1]			LOST WORKDAY CASES			NONFATAL CASES, NO LOST WORKDAYS			LOST WORKDAYS		
	1974	1975	1976	1974	1975	1976	1974	1975	1976	1974	1975	1976
Private sector	10.4	9.1	9.2	3.5	3.3	3.5	6.9	5.8	5.7	54.6	56.2	60.5
Agriculture, forestry, fishing	9.9	10.5	11.0	4.5	4.4	4.7	5.3	6.0	6.3	73.8	70.9	83.3
Mining [2]	10.2	11.0	11.0	5.1	5.6	5.8	5.0	5.4	5.1	94.7	110.6	114.4
Metal mining	7.5	6.5	5.9	4.8	4.4	4.2	2.7	2.1	1.7	70.3	69.2	77.1
Anthracite mining	22.3	28.4	27.4	8.9	10.2	11.1	13.3	18.1	16.3	215.9	211.3	229.2
Bituminous coal and lignite	10.6	10.8	13.2	5.7	6.4	7.8	4.8	4.3	5.4	96.4	101.5	134.0
Oil and gas extraction	11.9	14.0	13.0	5.5	6.2	6.0	6.4	7.7	7.0	117.7	149.1	136.2
Nonmetallic minerals exc. fuels	6.8	6.0	5.0	3.7	3.5	3.3	3.0	2.4	1.7	50.8	45.6	49.8
Construction	18.3	15.9	15.3	5.9	5.5	5.5	12.4	10.4	9.8	99.8	100.2	105.0
Manufacturing	14.6	13.0	13.2	4.7	4.5	4.8	9.9	8.5	8.3	72.7	75.8	79.5
Durable goods	16.0	14.2	14.1	5.1	4.8	5.1	11.0	9.4	9.0	77.2	81.1	84.1
Ordnance and accessories	7.7	(NA)	(NA)	2.1	(NA)	(NA)	5.6	(NA)	(NA)	35.7	(NA)	(NA)
Lumber and wood products	22.2	21.0	22.1	9.0	8.5	9.7	13.2	12.5	12.3	156.5	156.7	167.3
Furniture and fixtures	17.8	15.9	16.9	5.3	5.1	6.0	12.6	10.8	10.9	78.6	80.8	94.5
Stone, clay, and glass prod	18.2	16.0	16.1	6.3	5.9	6.4	11.8	10.1	9.7	107.3	108.5	114.1
Primary metal industries	19.7	17.0	16.6	6.8	6.1	6.3	12.9	10.9	10.3	110.8	114.3	114.8
Fabricated metal products	21.2	19.1	18.9	6.8	6.6	6.8	14.4	12.5	12.0	99.0	104.3	109.8
Machinery, exc. electric	16.8	14.9	14.2	4.8	4.6	4.6	12.0	10.3	9.6	65.2	68.9	70.6
Electric and electronic equip	10.2	8.5	8.5	2.8	2.5	2.8	7.3	6.0	5.8	43.3	41.9	44.9
Transportation equipment	15.1	12.4	12.4	4.7	4.5	4.7	10.4	8.0	7.7	69.5	76.5	73.8
Instruments and related prod	8.0	6.9	7.2	2.2	2.1	2.4	5.8	4.8	4.8	31.6	36.7	36.7
Miscellaneous	12.6	11.3	11.7	3.8	3.6	4.0	8.8	7.7	7.7	58.9	58.0	59.4
Nondurable goods	12.6	11.4	11.8	4.1	4.1	4.4	8.4	8.8	7.4	65.9	66.7	72.8
Food and kindred products	19.6	18.3	19.3	7.4	7.3	8.0	12.2	11.0	11.3	107.7	113.6	123.8
Tobacco manufactures	8.5	10.3	10.0	2.8	3.9	4.1	5.6	6.4	5.9	39.9	56.4	62.5
Textile mill products	11.1	10.2	10.5	2.5	2.5	2.7	6.5	7.7	7.7	18.0	18.0	55.5
Apparel and other textile prod	7.1	6.0	6.7	1.8	1.6	1.9	5.3	4.3	4.8	26.6	27.5	31.0
Paper and allied products	15.1	13.3	13.7	4.4	4.1	4.7	10.7	9.1	9.0	85.8	85.6	94.8
Printing and publishing	7.5	6.7	6.8	2.4	2.4	2.6	5.0	4.3	4.2	33.5	38.7	40.3
Chemicals and allied prod	9.5	8.4	8.2	2.9	2.9	3.1	6.5	5.5	5.1	48.3	48.9	50.6
Petroleum and coal products	9.3	9.0	7.9	3.0	3.1	3.2	6.3	5.8	4.7	59.0	65.3	62.5
Rubber and miscellaneous plastics products	18.0	15.7	16.8	7.1	6.7	7.1	10.8	9.0	9.7	117.2	113.3	113.3
Leather and leather products	11.3	11.2	11.6	3.6	3.8	4.1	7.7	7.4	7.4	53.0	55.3	69.0
Transportation, public utilities	10.5	9.4	9.8	4.8	4.7	5.0	5.7	4.7	4.8	89.8	88.9	94.0
Railroad transportation	8.5	8.5	10.1	4.0	4.9	5.7	4.5	3.6	4.4	99.9	78.3	78.8
Local passenger transit [3]	8.2	8.4	9.7	4.2	4.2	4.8	3.9	4.1	4.8	74.4	80.8	101.9
Trucking and warehousing	18.0	14.8	15.1	8.4	7.5	7.9	9.5	7.2	7.1	152.2	144.9	157.0
Water transportation	15.5	15.8	15.2	7.9	8.2	7.8	7.6	7.6	7.4	266.9	294.1	283.5
Air transportation	14.4	14.9	14.2	6.9	7.4	7.4	7.5	7.5	6.7	77.6	84.7	89.6
Pipelines, except natural gas	5.1	4.7	3.9	1.6	1.6	1.3	3.5	3.0	2.6	27.9	79.3	24.6
Transportation services	6.4	6.2	5.6	2.6	2.9	2.4	3.7	3.3	3.2	33.1	53.9	37.2
Communication	3.1	3.0	2.7	1.4	1.5	1.4	1.7	1.5	1.3	25.8	31.9	29.1
Electric, gas, sanitary serv	10.1	9.3	9.8	3.5	3.7	4.2	6.6	5.6	5.6	56.8	68.5	76.2
Wholesale and retail trade	8.4	7.3	7.5	2.8	2.6	2.8	5.6	4.7	4.6	37.4	39.5	43.2
Wholesale trade	9.3	8.2	8.1	3.4	3.2	3.3	5.9	5.0	4.8	46.3	49.5	51.8
Retail trade	8.1	7.0	7.2	2.5	2.4	2.6	5.5	4.6	4.6	40.6	35.2	39.7
Finance, ins., real estate [2]	2.4	2.2	2.0	.8	.8	.7	1.6	1.4	1.2	10.2	10.8	11.6
Banking	1.6	1.8	1.5	.5	.6	.5	1.1	1.2	1.0	4.8	9.0	6.7
Security, commodity brokers	1.1	1.0	.8	.5	.4	.3	.6	.6	.5	4.7	5.5	4.1
Insurance carriers	1.8	1.7	1.7	.6	.6	.6	1.1	1.1	1.1	8.1	8.2	9.8
Real estate	6.6	5.0	4.6	2.1	1.9	1.8	4.5	3.1	2.7	28.9	28.7	31.7
Services [2]	5.8	5.5	5.3	1.9	2.0	2.0	3.9	3.5	3.3	28.3	32.6	38.4
Hotels and other lodging places	8.3	8.2	8.0	2.6	2.6	2.8	5.7	5.6	5.2	38.4	45.0	49.4
Personal services	3.6	3.3	3.2	1.4	1.3	1.3	2.2	2.0	1.9	21.2	20.8	26.1
Business services	5.4	5.0	4.7	1.8	2.0	1.9	3.5	3.0	2.9	29.8	32.9	36.4
Auto repair, serv., and garages	10.5	9.0	7.4	3.5	3.4	2.7	7.1	5.6	4.6	45.4	66.1	56.8
Amusement, recreation serv	8.3	8.6	8.3	2.8	2.8	2.8	5.5	5.7	5.5	57.9	40.0	43.8
Health services	7.2	6.8	6.9	2.3	2.5	2.6	4.9	4.3	4.3	34.8	40.3	56.6
Educational services	4.1	3.5	4.1	1.2	1.4	1.5	2.9	2.0	2.6	14.6	20.7	17.7
Membership organizations	(S)	3.0	2.4	(S)	1.1	.8	(S)	1.9	1.6	(S)	17.6	13.4
Miscellaneous services	2.3	2.3	2.1	.7	.7	.7	1.6	1.6	1.4	6.5	8.8	10.1

NA Not available. S Data do not meet publication guidelines. [1] "Cases" represents occurrences. Includes fatalities. [2] Includes categories not shown separately. [3] Includes interurban.

Source: U.S. Bureau of Labor Statistics, Occupational Injuries and Illnesses in the United States by Industry, 1975, and News, Dec. 1, 1977.

Figure 14.1

Gross National Product (GNP) in Current and Constant 1972 Dollars: 1960 to 1977

(See tables 710 and 712)

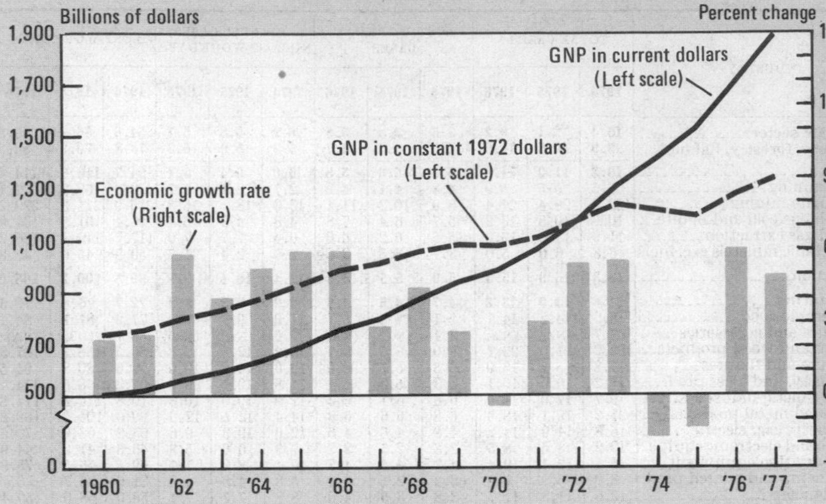

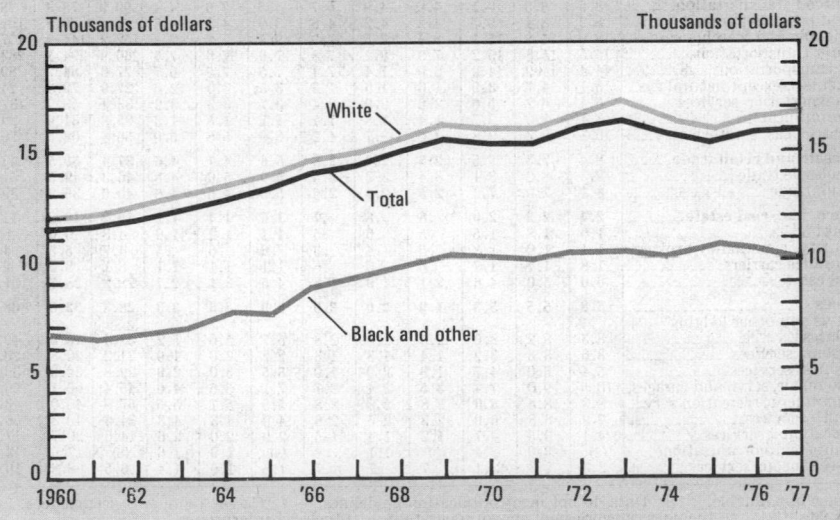

Billions of dollars   Percent change

GNP in current dollars (Left scale)

GNP in constant 1972 dollars (Left scale)

Economic growth rate (Right scale)

Source: Chart by U.S. Bureau of the Census. Data from U.S. Bureau of Economic Analysis.

Figure 14.2

Median Annual Money Income of Families, by Race, in Constant 1977 Dollars: 1960 to 1977

(See table 729)

Thousands of dollars   Thousands of dollars

White

Total

Black and other

Source: U.S. Bureau of the Census.

Section 14

Income, Expenditures, and Wealth

This section presents data on gross national product (GNP), rates of economic growth, per capita income, national and personal income, saving and investment, money income, poverty, national and personal wealth, and fixed business capital. The data on income and expenditure measure two aspects of the U.S. economy. One aspect relates to the national income and product accounts (NIPA), a summation reflecting the entire complex of the Nation's economic activities and the interaction of its major components; the other relates to the distribution of money income to families and individuals, or consumer income.

The primary source for data on GNP, national and personal income, gross savings and investment, and business capital is the *Survey of Current Business*, published monthly, with supplements, by the Department of Commerce, Bureau of Economic Analysis (BEA). Detailed historical data and a discussion of the conceptual framework of NIPA and of the statistical sources and methods used to derive the estimates appear in *The National Income and Product Accounts of the United States, 1929-74*, a Supplement to the *Survey of Current Business*, January 1976.

Sources of income distribution data are the decennial censuses of population and the Current Population Survey, both products of the Bureau of the Census (see text, page 1). Annual data on income of families, individuals, and households, by income class, are presented in *Current Population Reports—Consumer Income*, series P-60.

Data on individuals' saving and assets are published by the Board of Governors of the Federal Reserve System in the quarterly *Flow of Funds Accounts*; and detailed information on personal wealth is published periodically by the Internal Revenue Service in *Statistics of Income*, Supplemental Report, *Personal Wealth*.

National income and product.—*Gross national product* (GNP) is the total national output of goods and services valued at market prices. GNP can be viewed in terms of expenditure categories. These categories comprise purchases of goods and services by consumers and government, gross private domestic investment, and net exports of goods and services. The goods and services included are largely those bought for final use (excluding illegal transactions) in the market economy. There are a number of inclusions, however, which represent imputed values (estimates of "income in kind"), the most important of which is the rental value of owner-occupied dwellings. GNP, in this broad context, measures the output attributable to the factors of production—labor and property—supplied by U.S. residents. GNP differs from "national income" mainly in that GNP includes allowances for depreciation and for indirect taxes (such as sales and excise taxes); see table 716. *Gross domestic product* is GNP minus gross product originating outside the U.S.

National income is the aggregate of labor and property earnings which arise in the current production of goods and services by the Nation's economy. It is the sum of employee compensation, proprietors' income, rental income, net interest, and corporate profits. Thus, it measures the total factor costs of the goods and services produced by the economy. Earnings include direct taxes on earnings.

Capital consumption adjustment for corporations and nonfarm sole proprietorships and partnerships is the difference between capital consumption (i.e. depreciation charges and accidental damage to fixed business capital) claimed on income tax returns and capital consumption allowances that are measured at straightline depreciation, consistent service lives, and replacement cost. The tax return data are valued at historical costs and reflect changes over time in service lines and depreciation patterns as permitted by tax regulations. *Inventory valuation adjustment* represents the difference

437

between the book value of inventories used up in production and the cost of replacing them.

Personal income is the current income received by persons from all sources minus contributions for social insurance. Not only individuals (including owners of unincorporated enterprises), but nonprofit institutions, private trust funds, and private health and welfare funds are classed as "persons." Personal income includes transfers (payments not resulting from current production) from government and business such as social security benefits, military pensions, etc., but excludes transfers among persons. Although most of the income is in monetary form, there are important nonmonetary inclusions—chiefly, estimated net rental value to owner-occupants of their homes, the value of services furnished without payment by financial intermediaries, and the value of food consumed on farms.

Disposable personal income is personal income less personal tax and nontax payments. It is the income available to persons for spending and saving. Personal tax and nontax payments are tax payments (net of refunds) by persons (except personal contributions for social insurance) that are not chargeable to business expense, and certain personal payments to general government that are treated like taxes. Personal taxes include income, estate and gift, and personal property taxes. Nontax payments include passport fees, fines and penalties, donations, and tuitions and fees paid to schools and hospitals operated mainly by government.

Distribution of money income to families and individuals.—Money income statistics are based on data collected in various field surveys of income conducted since 1936. Since 1947, the Bureau of the Census has collected the data on an annual basis and published them in *Current Population Reports*, series P-60. In each of the surveys, enumerators interview representative samples of the population with respect to income received during the previous year. Money income as defined by the Bureau of the Census differs from the concept of "personal income" (see above) as defined and reported by the Bureau of Economic Analysis (BEA). Money income is income before the deduction of income taxes and social security taxes unless otherwise specified in the individual tables. *Nonmoney items of income*, such as wages received in kind, the value of food and fuel produced and consumed on farms, the net rental value of owner-occupied homes, the property income received by mutual life insurance companies, and the value of the services of banks and other financial intermediaries rendered to persons without the assessment of specific charges, *are not included*. None of the aggregate income concepts (gross national product, national income, or personal income) is exactly comparable with money income, although personal income is the closest.

In 1976, the method of collecting and processing the Current Population Survey money income data for 1975 and later years was revised. Data for 1974 were reprocessed using the revised method to provide a basis of comparison with the data for 1975. Revisions to the 1974 data resulted in an *overall* decrease in the estimated number of persons living in poverty by 3.7 percent (24.3 to 23.4 million) and an increase in the estimate of median family income by .5 percent ($12,836 to $12,902). Differences within most subgroups, however, are more pronounced. For example, family money income for Black and other races (excluding White) increased by 3.8 percent (see tables 729 and 756).

Poverty.—Unless otherwise specified, poverty level statistics represent measures of *money income* and are based on a "poverty index" first developed by the Social Security Administration (SSA) in 1964 and modified by a Federal Interagency Committee in 1969. At the core of this index is the 1961 Economy Food Plan designed by the Department of Agriculture. This index, based on food consumption requirements, provides a range of income cutoffs or "poverty income thresholds" adjusted by such factors as family size, sex and age of the family head, number of children under age 18, and farm-nonfarm residence. Until 1969, annual revisions of these levels were based on price changes of items in the economy food plan. In 1969, two changes were made: (1) SSA levels for nonfarm families were retained for the base year 1963, but annual adjustments in the levels were to be based on changes in the Consumer Price Index rather than on economy food plan costs, and (2) farm levels were raised from 70 to 85 percent of the corresponding nonfarm level.

Individuals' saving and assets.—The Board of Governors of the Federal Reserve System issues detailed estimates of individuals' saving as part of flow of funds accounts, showing the increase in financial assets, net investment in tangible assets, less increase in debt of individuals. Data back to 1946 are available upon request from the Federal Reserve.

Personal and national wealth.—Personal wealth estimates, issued by the Internal Revenue Service (IRS), are based on a sample of Federal estate tax returns which must be filed for deceased persons. Estimates are weighted to adjust for age, sex, and "social class" (as determined by IRS through insurance holdings). Gross estate is the gross value of all assets, including the full face value of life insurance (reduced by policy loans), before reduction by the amount of debts. Total assets are obtained by using the cash value of the insurance policy. Net worth is one's level of worth after all debts have been removed.

The national wealth data shown in table 777 are intended chiefly to indicate the order of magnitudes involved and to permit rough comparisons among types of wealth and of the growth over long periods. Definitions and analytical details are presented in the source publication.

Current and constant dollars.—Figures in a number of tables in this section are expressed in both current dollars and constant dollars. Current dollar figures reflect prices prevailing during the specified period. Constant dollar figures are computed values which eliminate the effect of price changes and are derived from prices of a specified base period. The constant dollar values are obtained by dividing current dollar values for a given period by the price indexes for the same period.

The national income and product account data are deflated to constant dollars by implicit price deflators for GNP and its components. The implicit price deflator for GNP is the ratio of GNP in current dollars to GNP in constant dollars after each of the components of GNP has been converted to base-year (i.e., 1972) prices. The money income statistics are deflated by means of the consumer price index prepared by the Bureau of Labor Statistics; see tables 792-793.

Statistical reliability.—For a discussion of statistical collection and estimation, sampling procedures, and measures of statistical reliability pertaining to Census Bureau data, see Appendix III.

Historical statistics.—Tabular headnotes provide cross-references, where applicable, to *Historical Statistics of the United States, Colonial Times to 1970.* See Appendix I.

No. 708. Gross National Product—Summary: 1929 to 1977

[In billions of dollars. Prior to 1960, excludes Alaska and Hawaii. See *Historical Statistics, Colonial Times to 1970*, series F 1 and F 32–70, for single-year figures prior to minor revisions issued in 1976]

ITEM	1929	1930	1933	1940	1945	1950	1955	1960	1965
Gross national product	103.4	90.7	55.8	100.0	212.3	286.2	399.3	506.0	688.1
Personal consumption expenditure	77.3	69.9	45.8	71.0	119.5	192.0	253.7	324.9	430.2
Gross private domestic investment	16.2	10.2	1.4	13.1	10.6	53.8	68.4	76.4	112.0
Net exports of goods and services	1.1	1.0	.4	1.7	−.6	1.9	2.2	4.4	7.6
Govt. purchases, goods and services	8.8	9.5	8.2	14.2	82.8	38.5	75.0	100.3	138.4
By major type of product: Goods	56.1	47.0	27.0	56.0	128.9	162.4	214.5	254.3	336.6
Services	35.9	34.5	25.9	35.7	76.9	88.2	135.3	193.2	272.7
Structures	11.4	9.2	2.9	8.3	6.5	35.6	49.5	58.4	78.8
By sector: Business	95.4	82.8	49.1	89.4	172.8	257.5	354.0	442.5	596.6
Households and institutions	2.9	2.7	1.7	2.4	4.1	6.4	9.1	13.8	19.2
Government	4.3	4.5	4.7	7.8	35.2	20.9	34.2	47.1	67.6
Rest of the world	.8	.7	.3	.4	.3	1.3	2.0	2.5	4.7

ITEM	1970	1971	1972	1973	1974	1975	1976	1977
Gross national product	982.4	1,063.4	1,171.1	1,306.6	1,412.9	1,528.8	1,706.5	1,889.6
Personal consumption expenditure	618.8	668.2	733.0	809.9	889.6	980.4	1,094.0	1,211.2
Gross private domestic investment	140.8	160.0	188.3	220.0	214.6	189.1	243.3	294.2
Net exports of goods and services	3.9	1.6	−3.3	7.1	6.0	20.4	7.8	−10.9
Govt. purchases, goods and services	218.9	233.7	253.1	269.5	302.7	338.9	361.4	395.0
By major type of product: Goods	456.2	479.8	526.0	598.8	638.6	686.2	764.2	834.7
Services	424.6	465.5	510.8	560.5	626.8	699.2	782.0	867.4
Structures	101.6	118.1	134.3	147.2	147.4	143.5	160.2	187.5
By sector: Business	831.5	896.9	989.5	1,108.0	1,193.7	1,289.6	1,444.3	1,603.6
Households and institutions	31.6	34.7	37.2	40.5	44.8	50.4	56.2	63.0
Government	114.7	125.2	137.4	149.1	161.4	178.2	191.6	205.8
Rest of the world	4.6	6.6	7.0	9.1	13.1	10.5	14.4	17.1

No. 709. Gross National Product, by Major Economic Groups: 1960 to 1977

[In billions of dollars. See *Historical Statistics, Colonial Times to 1970*, series F 1, 9, 20, 52, 63–66, and 162, for single year figures prior to minor revisions issued in 1976]

ITEM	1960	1965	1970	1972	1973	1974	1975	1976	1977
Gross national product	506.0	688.1	982.4	1,171.1	1,306.6	1,412.9	1,528.8	1,706.5	1.889,6
Persons:									
Disposable personal income [1]	342.0	460.4	669.4	782.4	880.2	961.3	1,060.6	1,159.9	1,278.5
Personal consumption expenditures	324.9	430.2	618.8	733.0	809.9	889.6	980.4	1,093.9	1,211.2
Personal saving	17.1	30.3	50.6	49.4	70.3	71.7	80.2	65.9	67.3
Business:									
Gross retained earnings [2]	58.7	84.6	101.4	131.0	140.2	137.9	179.2	206.6	226.5
Gross private domestic investment	76.4	112.0	140.8	188.3	220.0	214.6	189.1	243.3	294.2
Excess of investment (−)	−17.7	−27.4	−39.5	−57.3	−79.8	−76.7	−9.9	−36.8	−67.7
Government: [3]									
Receipts less transfer payments, etc.[4]	103.4	138.9	209.5	249.6	275.8	299.5	274.6	325.8	374.7
Purchases of goods and services	100.3	138.4	218.9	253.1	269.5	302.7	338.9	361.4	395.0
Surplus or deficit (−)	3.1	.5	−9.4	−3.5	6.3	−3.2	−64.3	−35.6	−20.3
Foreign:									
Transfer payments to foreigners (net) plus interest paid by Gov't to foreigners	2.6	3.3	4.3	6.5	7.7	8.5	8.5	8.7	10.0
Net exports of goods and services	4.4	7.6	3.9	−3.3	7.1	6.0	20.4	7.8	−10.9
Capital grants received by U.S. (net) [5]	−1.7	−4.3	.3	9.8	.6	2.5	−11.9	.9	20.9
Statistical discrepancy	−.7	.9	−2.1	1.7	2.6	5.8	5.9	5.5	−.2

[1] Less interest paid by consumers to business and personal transfers to foreigners (net).   [2] Undistributed corporate profits with inventory valuation and corporate capital consumption adjustments plus corporate and noncorporate capital consumption allowances with capital consumption adjustment, plus private wage accruals less disbursements.   [3] Federal, State, and local.   [4] Government receipts, less transfer payments to persons, transfer payments to foreigners (net), net interest paid, and subsidies less current surplus of government enterprises; plus wage accruals less disbursements.   [5] Less net foreign investment.

Source of tables 708 and 709: U.S. Bureau of Economic Analysis, *The National Income and Product Accounts of the United States, 1929–74; Survey of Current Business*, July 1977; and unpublished data.

No. 710. Gross National Product in Current and Constant (1972) Dollars: 1950 to 1977

[In billions of dollars, except as indicated. Prior to 1960, excludes Alaska and Hawaii. See *Historical Statistics, Colonial Times to 1970*, series F 1, F 5, and F 47–70 for single-year figures prior to minor revisions issued in 1976]

ITEM	1950	1955	1960	1965	1970	1972	1973	1974	1975	1976	1977
CURRENT DOLLARS											
Gross national product	286	399	506	688	982	1,171	1,307	1,413	1,529	1,707	1,890
avg. annual percent change[1]	10.9	6.9	4.9	6.3	7.4	9.2	11.6	8.1	8.2	11.6	10.7
Implicit price deflator[2]	53.6	61.0	68.7	74.3	91.4	100.0	105.8	116.0	127.2	133.9	141.3
Personal consumption expend	192	254	325	430	619	733	810	890	980	1,094	1,211
Durable goods	31	39	43	63	85	111	124	122	133	159	180
Nondurable goods	98	123	151	189	265	299	334	376	409	443	481
Services	63	92	131	179	269	322	352	391	438	492	551
Gross pvt. domestic investment	54	68	76	112	141	188	220	215	189	243	294
Fixed investment	47	62	73	102	137	179	202	206	201	230	276
Nonresidential	27	38	48	71	100	117	136	151	149	162	185
Residential	20	24	25	31	37	62	66	55	51	68	91
Business inventories change	7	6	4	10	4	9	18	9	−11	13	18
Net exports	2	2	4	8	4	−3	7	6	20	8	−11
Exports, goods and services	14	20	28	40	62	73	102	138	147	163	175
Imports, goods and services	12	18	23	32	59	76	94	132	127	155	186
Government purchases[3]	39	75	100	138	219	253	270	303	339	361	395
Federal	19	44	54	67	96	102	102	111	123	130	145
National defense	14	38	44	49	74	74	74	77	84	87	94
State and local	20	31	47	71	123	151	167	192	216	231	250
Final sales[4]	279	393	502	679	979	1,162	1,289	1,404	1,540	1,693	1,871
CONSTANT (1972) DOLLARS											
Gross national product	534	655	737	926	1,075	1,171	1,235	1,218	1,202	1,275	1,337
Annual percent change[1]	8.7	4.2	2.4	4.7	3.0	4.4	5.5	−1.4	−1.3	6.0	4.9
Potential GNP[5]	(NA)	651	772	925	1,106	1,186	1,228	1,272	1,317	1,364	1,412
Gap (potential less actual)[5]	(NA)	−3	35	−1	31	15	−7	54	115	89	75
Personal consumption expend	338	395	453	558	669	733	768	761	775	821	861
Durable goods	43	52	53	73	89	111	122	113	113	128	138
Nondurable goods	162	185	208	244	283	299	309	304	308	322	334
Services	133	158	192	241	297	322	337	344	355	372	389
Gross pvt. domestic investment	94	104	105	150	155	188	207	184	142	173	196
Fixed investment	83	96	101	139	150	179	191	176	152	165	184
Nonresidential	50	61	66	96	110	117	131	131	113	117	127
Residential	33	35	35	43	40	62	60	45	39	48	57
Business inventories change	11	8	4	11	4	9	17	8	−10	9	12
Net exports	4	5	6	8	1	−3	8	16	23	16	10
Exports, goods and services	22	28	36	49	67	73	87	93	90	96	98
Imports, goods and services	18	23	30	41	66	76	80	77	67	80	88
Government purchases[3]	98	151	173	210	250	253	253	258	263	264	271
Federal	47	87	91	101	111	102	97	96	97	97	101
State and local	51	64	82	109	140	151	156	162	166	168	170
Final sales[4]	523	647	732	915	1,071	1,162	1,219	1,210	1,212	1,266	1,326

NA Not available. [1] For 1950, change from 1949. [2] 1972=100. [3] Purchases of goods and services. [4] GNP minus inventory change. [5] Source: U.S. Council of Economic Advisers. Potential GNP is the output the economy could produce with the existing technology under assumed conditions of high, sustainable utilization of the factors of production. See *Economic Report of the President*, January 1978, for further explanation.

Source: Except as noted, U.S. Bureau of Economic Analysis, *The National Income and Product Accounts of the United States, 1929–74*, and *Survey of Current Business*, July 1977 and April 1978.

No. 711. Growth Rates of Gross Domestic Product—International Comparisons, Selected Periods: 1929 to 1976

[In percent. Rates represent average annual compounded changes in real output from initial to terminal year of period. See headnote, table 712. See also *Historical Statistics, Colonial Times to 1970*, series F 10–16]

PERIOD	U.S.		CANADA		FRANCE		GERMANY[1]		ITALY		U.K.		JAPAN	
	Total	Per capita	Total	Per capita	Total	Per capita	Total	Per capita	Total	Per capita	Total	Per capita	Total	Per capita
1929–1950	2.9	1.8	3.2	1.8	–	−.1	1.9	.7	1.0	.3	1.6	1.2	.6	(NA)
1950–1960	3.2	1.4	4.6	1.9	4.8	3.9	8.5	6.9	[2]5.5	[2]4.8	2.8	2.4	[3]8.0	[3]6.9
1950–1976	3.4	2.0	4.9	2.8	4.9	4.0	5.6	4.6	[2]4.9	[2]4.2	2.6	2.2	[3]8.5	[3]7.3
1960–1970	3.9	2.6	5.2	3.4	5.5	4.4	4.7	3.8	5.5	4.8	2.8	2.2	10.8	9.6
1960–1976	3.5	2.4	5.1	3.5	5.1	4.1	3.9	3.2	4.5	3.8	2.5	2.1	8.8	7.5
1970–1976	2.9	2.1	5.0	3.6	4.3	3.5	2.5	2.3	2.9	2.1	2.0	1.8	5.5	4.0
1973–1974	−1.3	−2.0	3.6	2.0	2.8	2.1	.5	.4	3.9	3.0	−.6	−.7	−1.0	−2.3
1974–1975	−1.0	−1.7	.9	−.6	.7	.2	−2.6	−2.2	−3.5	−4.2	−1.6	−1.6	2.4	1.1
1975–1976	5.8	5.1	5.2	3.8	5.4	5.0	5.6	6.1	5.6	5.0	2.6	2.7	6.0	4.9

– Represents zero. NA Not available. [1] Federal Republic of Germany. Beginning 1960, includes Saar and West Berlin. [2] Initial year 1951. [3] Initial year 1952.

Source: U.S. Bureau of Economic Analysis. Adapted from *Long Term Economic Growth, 1860–1970*, using data from the Organisation for Economic Co-operation and Development.

No. 712. Rates of Economic Growth: 1940 to 1977

[Percent. Figures represent average annual compounded rates of change in real gross national product, based on estimates by Department of Commerce of gross national product (expressed in constant 1972 dollars). Minus sign (−) denotes decline. To obtain annual rate of change between any 2 years shown, find column for initial year at top of table and read figure in that column opposite terminal year shown at left. See *Historical Statistics, Colonial Times to 1970*, series F 31, for single-year figures prior to minor revisions issued in 1976]

TERMINAL YEAR	INITIAL YEAR														
	1940	1945	1950	1955	1960	1965	1968	1969	1970	1971	1972	1973	1974	1975	1976
1941	15.4	(X)	(X)	(X)	(X)	(X)	(X)	(X)	(X)	(X)	(X)	(X)	(X)	(X)	(X)
1946	5.6	−14.7	(X)	(X)	(X)	(X)	(X)	(X)	(X)	(X)	(X)	(X)	(X)	(X)	(X)
1951	4.8	.5	8.1	(X)	(X)	(X)	(X)	(X)	(X)	(X)	(X)	(X)	(X)	(X)	(X)
1956	4.3	1.6	3.8	2.1	(X)	(X)	(X)	(X)	(X)	(X)	(X)	(X)	(X)	(X)	(X)
1961	3.8	1.9	3.2	2.4	2.5	(X)	(X)	(X)	(X)	(X)	(X)	(X)	(X)	(X)	(X)
1965	4.0	2.6	3.7	3.5	4.7	(X)	(X)	(X)	(X)	(X)	(X)	(X)	(X)	(X)	(X)
1968	4.1	2.8	3.8	3.7	4.5	4.3	(X)	(X)	(X)	(X)	(X)	(X)	(X)	(X)	(X)
1969	4.0	2.8	3.8	3.6	4.3	3.9	2.6	(X)	(X)	(X)	(X)	(X)	(X)	(X)	(X)
1970	3.9	2.7	3.6	3.4	3.9	3.0	1.1	−.3	(X)	(X)	(X)	(X)	(X)	(X)	(X)
1971	3.8	2.7	3.5	3.3	3.8	3.0	1.7	1.3	3.0	(X)	(X)	(X)	(X)	(X)	(X)
1972	3.9	2.8	3.6	3.5	3.9	3.4	2.7	2.8	4.4	5.7	(X)	(X)	(X)	(X)	(X)
1973	4.0	2.9	3.7	3.6	4.1	3.7	3.3	3.4	4.7	5.6	5.5	(X)	(X)	(X)	(X)
1974	3.8	2.7	3.5	3.3	3.7	3.1	2.5	2.5	3.2	3.2	2.0	−1.4	(X)	(X)	(X)
1975	3.6	2.6	3.3	3.1	3.7	2.6	1.9	1.8	2.3	2.1	.9	−1.3	−1.3	(X)	(X)
1976	3.7	2.7	3.4	3.2	3.5	2.9	2.4	2.4	2.9	2.9	2.1	1.1	2.3	6:0	(X)
1977	3.7	2.8	3.5	3.3	3.6	3.1	2.7	2.7	3.2	3.2	2.7	2.0	3.2	5.5	4.9

X Not applicable.

Source: U.S. Bureau of Economic Analysis. Adapted from *Long Term Economic Growth, 1860–1970*.

No. 713. Average 5-Year Real Growth Rates of Gross National Product (GNP) and Selected GNP Components: 1960 to 1977

[Percent. See headnote, table 712.

YEAR	GNP, total	Personal consumption expenditures	Gross private domestic investment	GOVT. PURCHASES			Imports	Exports
				Total	Federal	State and local		
1960–1964	3.5	3.1	4.6	3.2	2.1	4.5	4.0	6.0
1965–1969	3.1	3.3	2.3	4.1	3.9	4.3	9.1	4.8
1966–1970	1.9	2.7	−.8	1.8	−.3	3.6	6.8	5.4
1967–1971	1.9	2.8	1.8	.1	−3.7	3.4	6.2	4.6
1968–1972	2.2	3.0	3.4	−.5	−4.5	2.9	5.2	4.4
1969–1973	2.7	3.2	4.3	−.3	−4.5	2.9	4.7	7.0
1970–1974	2.4	2.6	3.1	.3	−3.0	2.7	4.3	7.8
1971–1975	1.7	2.3	−3.2	1.1	−1.4	2.7	−.3	5.8
1972–1976	1.7	2.3	−1.7	.9	−1.1	2.1	1.0	5.7
1973–1977	1.6	2.4	−1.2	1.4	1.1	1.7	2.2	1.8

No. 714. Per Capita Income and Product for Selected Items: 1950 to 1977

[Prior to 1960, excludes Alaska and Hawaii. Based on Bureau of the Census estimated population including Armed Forces abroad as of July 1, 1950–1973; thereafter, based on quarterly averages. See *Historical Statistics, Colonial Times to 1970*, series F 17–30, for single-year figures prior to minor revisions issued in 1976]

ITEM	1950	1955	1960	1965	1970	1972	1973	1974	1975	1976	1977
CURRENT DOLLARS											
Gross national product	1,887	2,416	2,801	3,541	4,795	5,608	6,210	6,666	7,159	7,930	8,713
Personal income	1,491	1,868	2,212	2,764	4,513	5,002	5,449	5,867	6,425	7,086
Disposable personal income	1,355	1,654	1,934	2,430	3,348	3,837	4,285	4,646	5,077	5,511	6,037
Personal consump. expend	1,266	1,535	1,798	2,214	3,020	3,510	3,849	4,197	4,591	5,084	5,585
Durable goods	203	234	239	323	415	533	588	576	622	738	829
Nondurable goods	648	744	836	971	1,292	1,433	1,587	1,775	1,917	2,057	2,217
Services	415	557	723	920	1,314	1,544	1,674	1,846	2,052	2,288	2,540
CONSTANT (1972) DOLLARS											
Gross national product	3,517	3,962	4,078	4,765	5,248	5,607	5,869	5,746	5,629	5,923	6,167
Disposable personal income	2,386	2,577	2,697	3,152	3,619	3,837	4,062	3,973	4,014	4,137	4,293
Personal consump. expend	2,229	2,391	2,507	2,872	3,265	3,510	3,648	3,589	3,629	3,817	3,971
Durable goods	286	316	291	378	434	533	579	531	528	592	637
Nondurable goods	1,067	1,122	1,153	1,256	1,380	1,433	1,470	1,434	1,440	1,494	1,539
Services	876	953	1,064	1,239	1,451	1,544	1,599	1,625	1,661	1,730	1,795

Source of tables 713 and 714: U.S. Bureau of Economic Analysis, *The National Income and Product Accounts of the United States 1929–74; Survey of Current Business*, July 1977 and April 1978; and unpublished data.

No. 715. Gross Product, by Industry, in Current and Constant (1972) Dollars: 1950 to 1976

[In billions of dollars. The current-dollar data differ from national income by industry (table 721) for two reasons: (1) Non-factor charges against gross product are included; and (2) profits have been shifted from a company to an establishment basis. See *Historical Statistics, Colonial Times to 1970*, series F 130–143, for single-year figures prior to minor revisions issued in 1976]

INDUSTRY	1950	1955	1960	1965	1970	1972	1973	1974	1975	1976
CURRENT DOLLARS										
All industries, total (GNP)	286.2	399.3	506.0	688.1	982.4	1,171.1	1,306.6	1,412.9	1,528.8	1,706.5
Agriculture, forestry, fisheries	20.8	19.9	21.5	23.8	28.7	35.3	53.9	52.2	53.4	52.7
Mining	9.2	12.3	12.6	13.5	17.4	18.9	21.4	31.9	38.4	41.4
Construction	13.0	18.5	23.2	32.7	48.2	58.0	64.7	67.6	67.6	74.2
Manufacturing	83.8	121.0	143.9	196.3	250.3	288.8	321.8	334.6	347.7	403.9
Transportation	16.0	19.9	22.5	28.8	38.9	46.2	51.3	55.5	55.9	62.9
Communication	4.5	7.1	10.5	15.2	23.6	29.4	32.7	35.5	39.8	44.5
Electric, gas, sanitary services	5.2	8.7	12.8	16.6	22.7	28.0	30.5	31.3	38.8	41.9
Wholesale and retail trade	51.3	66.2	84.6	112.8	167.3	201.2	223.8	243.4	270.9	302.2
Finance, insurance, real estate	31.2	48.9	70.1	95.5	140.2	167.3	177.9	194.6	214.4	238.3
Services	24.0	34.0	49.2	70.7	113.5	134.5	150.5	165.7	185.3	207.1
Govt. and govt. enterprises	23.8	38.5	53.4	76.7	129.1	154.9	166.5	181.7	200.4	217.4
Rest of world (incl. stat. discrep)	3.3	4.5	1.8	5.6	2.5	8.7	11.7	18.9	16.4	19.9
CONSTANT (1972) DOLLARS										
All industries, total (GNP)	533.5	654.8	736.8	925.9	1,075.3	1,171.1	1,235.0	1,217.8	1,202.1	1,274.7
Agriculture, forestry, fisheries	29.1	31.9	32.2	33.0	34.3	35.3	35.9	35.7	37.1	36.8
Mining	11.7	14.0	14.4	16.4	19.1	18.9	19.2	19.1	19.0	19.2
Construction	29.3	38.2	46.1	57.0	57.1	58.0	58.3	56.0	50.5	55.3
Manufacturing	131.3	165.8	172.0	235.1	260.6	288.8	313.0	291.9	273.3	304.9
Transportation	26.3	29.5	30.9	38.0	43.8	46.2	50.6	50.5	46.7	49.1
Communication	6.3	9.1	12.1	16.9	25.6	29.4	32.0	33.6	36.5	39.1
Electric, gas, sanitary services	7.0	10.8	15.0	19.4	25.7	28.0	30.0	28.3	29.6	28.7
Wholesale and retail trade	87.6	103.2	117.9	148.6	178.4	201.2	212.0	205.7	208.7	219.5
Finance, insurance, real estate	64.4	82.0	101.9	127.2	152.9	167.3	171.1	180.3	182.6	193.9
Services	59.4	67.5	82.2	101.2	124.7	134.5	143.1	144.7	145.0	152.3
Govt. and govt. enterprises	75.4	95.4	107.2	127.4	152.0	154.9	157.3	160.0	162.7	164.0
Rest of world (incl. residual)	5.8	7.3	5.0	5.7	1.3	8.7	12.5	12.1	10.5	11.9

No. 716. Relation of Gross National Product, National Income, and Personal Income: 1960 to 1977

[In billions of dollars. For definitions, see p. 437. See *Historical Statistics, Colonial Times to 1970*, series F 6–9 and F 144–162, for figures prior to minor revisions issued in 1976]

ITEM	1960	1965	1970	1972	1973	1974	1975	1976	1977
Gross national product	506.0	688.1	982.4	1,171.1	1,306.6	1,412.9	1,528.8	1,706.5	1,889.6
Less: Capital consumption allowances [1]	47.7	57.5	90.8	105.4	117.7	137.7	162.5	179.0	197.0
Equals: Net national product	458.3	630.6	891.6	1,065.8	1,188.9	1,275.2	1,366.3	1,527.4	1,692.6
Plus: Subsidies less current surplus of govt. enterprises	.4	1.6	2.7	3.6	3.9	1.0	2.3	.8	2.0
Less: Indirect business tax and nontax liability	45.4	62.6	94.0	111.0	120.2	128.6	138.7	150.5	165.2
Business transfers	2.0	2.8	4.0	4.7	5.4	5.9	7.0	8.1	9.0
Statistical discrepancy	−.7	.9	−2.1	1.7	2.6	5.8	5.9	5.5	−.2
Equals: National income	412.0	566.0	798.4	951.9	1,064.6	1,136.0	1,217.0	1,364.1	1,520.5
Less: Corporate profits [2]	46.6	77.1	67.9	92.1	99.1	83.6	99.3	128.1	139.9
Net interest	9.8	18.5	37.5	47.0	52.3	69.0	79.1	88.4	100.9
Contributions for social insurance	21.1	30.0	58.7	73.6	91.5	103.8	110.1	123.8	139.0
Wage accruals less disbursements	−	−	−	(Z)	−.1	−.5	−	−	−
Plus: Govt. transfer payments to persons	27.0	37.6	75.9	99.4	113.5	134.9	169.8	184.7	197.9
Personal interest income	23.3	37.2	64.3	74.6	84.1	103.0	115.6	130.3	147.8
Dividends	12.9	19.1	22.9	24.6	27.8	31.0	32.4	35.8	41.2
Business transfers	2.0	2.8	4.0	4.7	5.4	5.9	7.0	8.1	9.0
Equals: Personal income	399.7	537.0	801.3	942.5	1,052.4	1,154.9	1,253.4	1,382.7	1,536.7
Less: Personal tax and nontax payments	50.4	64.9	115.3	141.2	150.8	170.3	169.0	196.9	227.5
Equals: Disposable personal income	349.4	472.2	685.9	801.3	901.7	984.6	1,084.4	1,185.8	1,309.2
Less: Personal outlays	332.3	441.9	635.4	751.9	831.3	913.0	1,004.2	1,119.9	1,241.9
Equals: Personal saving	17.1	30.3	50.6	49.4	70.3	71.7	80.2	65.9	67.3

– Represents zero.   Z Less than $50 million.   [1] With capital consumption adjustment.
[2] With inventory valuation and capital consumption adjustments.

Source of tables 715 and 716: U.S. Bureau of Economic Analysis, *The National Income and Product Accounts of the United States, 1929–74*, and *Survey of Current Business*, July 1977 and April 1978.

No. 717. Personal Consumption Expenditures, by Product: 1950 to 1976

[In billions of dollars, except percent. Prior to 1960, excludes Alaska and Hawaii. Represents market value of goods and services purchased by individuals and nonprofit institutions, and value of food, clothing, housing, and financial services received by them as income in kind. See *Historical Statistics, Colonial Times to 1970*, series G 416–469, for single-year figures prior to minor revisions issued in 1976]

TYPE OF PRODUCT	1950	1955	1960	1965	1970	1972	1973	1974	1975	1976
Total consumption	**192.0**	**253.6**	**324.9**	**430.2**	**618.8**	**733.0**	**809.9**	**889.6**	**980.4**	**1,094.0**
Food, beverages,[1] and tobacco	58.1	72.2	88.0	107.0	147.1	162.6	181.2	203.7	224.2	241.6
Purchased meals	11.1	13.8	17.2	22.7	31.5	35.5	39.9	44.4	50.3	55.3
Food (excl. alcoholic beverages)	46.0	58.1	70.5	85.8	118.6	130.6	146.8	166.9	184.8	199.5
Alcoholic beverages	7.9	9.1	10.6	13.1	17.7	19.8	21.3	23.0	24.7	26.0
Tobacco	4.3	5.0	6.9	8.1	10.8	12.2	13.1	13.8	14.7	16.1
Clothing, accessories, jewelry[2]	23.7	28.0	32.2	40.3	55.6	64.8	71.8	76.3	82.0	89.3
Women's and children's[3]	10.0	12.4	14.4	18.4	25.1	29.9	33.3	35.8	38.7	42.2
Men's and boys'[3]	6.0	7.0	7.7	9.7	13.6	16.3	18.0	19.2	20.7	22.4
Jewelry and watches	1.3	1.7	1.9	2.6	4.1	4.7	5.4	5.8	6.3	7.1
Shoes, incl. cleaning, repair	3.5	3.8	4.7	5.6	8.0	9.2	10.2	10.4	11.0	11.9
Personal care	2.4	3.5	5.2	7.6	10.9	11.7	12.6	13.5	14.3	15.3
Housing	21.7	34.3	48.1	65.5	94.0	112.3	123.2	136.5	150.8	167.9
Household operations[2]	29.1	36.9	46.1	61.3	87.8	105.2	117.7	130.6	142.8	160.2
Furniture, equip., and supplies	16.2	19.1	22.2	30.6	44.1	53.0	59.8	64.9	68.5	75.2
Electricity	2.1	3.5	5.1	6.6	9.9	12.3	13.9	16.5	19.8	22.2
Gas	1.2	2.0	3.3	4.3	5.6	6.5	6.7	7.6	9.3	11.1
Telephone and telegraph	1.9	3.1	4.5	6.5	10.1	12.4	14.0	15.4	17.4	19.5
Domestic service	2.6	3.1	3.8	4.0	5.1	5.3	5.4	5.6	5.8	6.4
Medical care expenses	9.1	13.2	20.0	30.1	49.9	61.2	68.3	76.9	90.3	106.4
Personal business	6.6	9.5	14.2	19.7	31.3	37.4	40.6	45.5	51.8	55.6
Transportation	25.4	34.6	42.4	58.2	78.0	101.4	110.9	115.1	125.1	150.1
User-operated transportation	22.6	31.6	39.1	54.2	72.5	95.3	104.3	107.7	117.6	141.7
Purchased transportation	2.8	3.0	3.3	4.0	5.5	6.1	6.5	7.4	7.6	8.4
Recreation	11.1	14.1	17.9	25.9	41.0	49.1	55.2	60.9	66.2	72.6
Private education and research	1.7	2.4	3.7	5.7	9.9	11.6	12.6	13.8	15.4	16.9
Religious and welfare activities	2.3	3.3	4.9	6.1	8.5	10.1	10.6	11.6	12.5	13.8
Foreign travel and other, net	.7	1.6	2.1	2.9	4.7	5.6	5.2	5.3	5.0	4.2
Percent of total	**100.0**	**100.0**	**100.0**	**100.0**	**100.0**	**100.0**	**100.0**	**100.0**	**100.0**	**100.0**
Food, beverages,[1] and tobacco	30.3	28.5	27.1	24.9	23.8	22.2	22.4	23.0	22.8	22.2
Clothing, accessories, jewelry	12.3	11.0	9.9	9.4	9.0	8.8	8.9	8.6	8.4	8.2
Personal care	1.3	1.4	1.6	1.8	1.8	1.6	1.6	1.5	1.5	1.4
Housing	11.3	13.5	14.8	15.2	15.2	15.3	15.2	15.3	15.3	15.3
Household operations	15.2	14.6	14.2	14.2	14.2	14.4	14.5	14.7	14.5	14.6
Medical care expenses	4.7	5.2	6.2	7.0	8.1	8.3	8.4	8.6	9.2	9.7
Personal business	3.4	3.7	4.4	4.6	5.1	5.1	5.0	5.1	5.3	5.1
Transportation	13.2	13.6	13.1	13.5	12.6	13.8	13.7	12.9	12.8	13.7
Recreation	5.8	5.6	5.5	6.0	6.6	6.7	6.8	6.8	6.8	6.6
Other	2.4	2.9	3.3	3.4	3.7	3.7	3.5	3.5	3.4	3.2

[1] Includes alcoholic and nonalcoholic beverages. [2] Includes items not shown separately. [3] Except footwear.

Source: U.S. Bureau of Economic Analysis. *The National Income and Product Accounts of the United States, 1929–74*, and *Survey of Current Business*, July 1977.

No. 718. Percent Distribution and Average Annual Percent Change of Shares of National Income, by Type: 1950 to 1977

[See headnote, table 719]

TYPE OF INCOME	PERCENT DISTRIBUTION							ANNUAL PERCENT CHANGE			
	1950	1960	1965	1970	1975	1976	1977	1950–1960	1960–1970	1970–1975	1975–1977
National income, total	**100.0**	**100.0**	**100.0**	**100.0**	**100.0**	**100.0**	**100.0**	**5.7**	**6.8**	**8.8**	**11.8**
Compensation of employees	65.5	71.6	70.1	76.3	76.4	76.0	76.1	6.7	7.5	8.8	11.5
Wages and salaries	62.2	66.0	64.0	68.4	66.2	65.4	65.1	6.3	7.2	8.1	10.8
Supplements to wages and salaries	3.3	5.6	6.1	7.9	10.2	10.6	10.9	11.4	10.6	14.7	15.5
Proprietors' income[1]	16.3	11.4	10.0	8.2	7.1	6.5	6.5	2.0	3.3	5.7	6.9
Farm	5.7	2.8	2.2	1.7	1.9	1.4	1.3	−1.6	2.0	10.8	−7.9
Nonfarm	10.5	8.6	7.8	6.4	5.2	5.1	5.2	3.6	3.7	4.2	11.8
Rental income of persons[2]	3.0	3.3	3.0	2.3	1.8	1.7	1.7	6.9	3.0	3.7	6.5
Corporate profits[1]	14.3	11.3	13.6	8.5	8.2	9.4	9.2	3.3	3.8	7.9	18.7
Profits before tax	18.0	11.8	13.3	9.0	10.1	11.5	11.3	1.3	4.0	11.6	17.9
Profits after tax	10.5	6.3	7.8	4.6	6.0	6.8	6.7	.4	3.7	14.7	18.2
Inventory valuation adjust.	−2.1	.1	−.3	−.6	−1.0	−1.0	−1.0	(X)	(X)	(X)	(X)
Capital consumption adjust.	−1.7	−.6	.7	.2	−1.0	−1.1	−1.1	(X)	(X)	(X)	(X)
Net interest	1.0	2.4	3.3	4.7	6.5	6.5	6.6	15.7	14.4	16.1	12.9

X Not applicable.　[1] See footnote 2, table 716.　[2] See footnote 1, table 716.

Source: Compiled by U.S. Bureau of the Census; based on data from U.S. Bureau of Economic Analysis.

No. 719. National Income, by Type of Income: 1929 to 1977

[In billions of dollars. Prior to 1960, excludes Alaska and Hawaii. See *Historical Statistics, Colonial Times to 1970*, series F 163–185, for single-year figures prior to minor revisions issued in 1976]

TYPE OF INCOME	1929	1930	1933	1935	1940	1945	1947	1950	1955
National income	84.8	73.8	39.9	56.5	79.7	180.6	194.6	236.2	328.0
Compensation of employees	51.1	46.8	29.5	37.3	52.1	123.1	129.2	154.8	224.9
Proprietors' income [1]	14.9	11.7	5.8	10.7	12.9	31.7	35.8	38.4	42.5
Rental income of persons [2]	4.9	4.4	2.2	1.8	2.7	4.6	5.3	7.1	11.3
Corporate profits [1]	9.2	5.9	−1.7	2.6	8.7	19.0	22.2	33.7	44.6
Net interest	4.7	4.9	4.1	4.1	3.3	2.2	2.1	2.3	4.8

	1960	1965	1970	1971	1972	1973	1974	1975	1976	1977
National income	412.0	566.0	798.4	858.1	951.9	1,064.6	1,136.0	1,217.0	1,364.1	1,520.5
Compensation of employees	294.9	396.5	609.2	650.3	715.1	799.2	875.8	930.3	1,036.3	1,156.3
Wages and salaries	271.9	362.0	546.5	580.0	633.8	701.2	764.1	805.7	891.8	990.0
Private	222.8	292.1	430.5	454.2	496.2	552.6	604.1	630.3	704.6	790.1
Military	10.4	12.9	20.7	20.7	22.0	22.1	22.5	23.1	23.6	24.6
Government, civilian	38.7	56.9	95.3	105.1	115.6	126.5	137.5	152.3	163.6	175.3
Supplem'ts to wages, salaries	23.0	34.5	62.7	70.3	81.4	98.0	111.7	124.6	144.5	166.3
Employer contributions for social insurance	11.8	16.7	30.7	34.1	39.4	49.3	56.1	59.8	68.6	77.7
Other labor income	11.2	17.8	32.0	36.2	42.0	48.7	55.6	64.9	75.9	88.6
Proprietors' income [1]	47.0	56.7	65.1	67.7	76.1	92.4	86.2	86.0	88.0	98.2
Farm	11.4	12.6	13.9	14.3	18.0	32.0	25.4	23.2	18.6	19.7
Nonfarm	35.6	44.1	51.2	53.4	58.1	60.4	60.9	62.8	69.4	78.5
Rental income of persons with capital consumption adjust	13.8	17.1	18.6	20.1	21.5	21.6	21.4	22.3	23.3	25.3
Corporate profits [1]	46.6	77.1	67.9	77.2	92.1	99.1	83.6	99.3	128.1	139.9
Profits before tax	48.5	75.2	71.5	82.0	96.2	115.8	126.9	123.5	156.9	171.7
Profits tax liability	22.7	30.9	34.5	37.7	41.5	48.7	52.4	50.2	64.7	69.2
Profits after tax	25.8	44.3	37.0	44.3	54.6	67.1	74.5	73.4	92.1	102.5
Dividends	12.9	19.1	22.9	23.0	24.6	27.8	31.0	32.1	35.8	41.2
Undistributed profits	13.0	25.2	14.1	21.3	30.0	39.3	43.6	41.0	56.4	61.4
Inventory valuation adjust	.3	−1.9	−5.1	−5.0	−6.6	−18.6	−40.4	−12.0	−14.1	−14.6
Capital consump. adjustm't	−2.3	3.8	1.5	.3	2.5	1.9	−2.9	−12.2	−14.7	−17.2
Net interest	9.8	18.0	37.5	40.8	47.0	52.3	69.0	79.1	88.4	100.9

[1] See footnote 2, table 716.   [2] See footnote 1, table 716.

No. 720. National Income, by Sector: 1960 to 1977

[In billions of dollars. Minus sign (−) denotes loss. See *Historical Statistics, Colonial Times to 1970*, series F 192–209, for single-year figures prior to minor revisions issued in 1976]

SECTOR	1960	1965	1970	1972	1973	1974	1975	1976	1977
National income	412.0	566.0	798.4	951.9	1,064.6	1,136.0	1,217.0	1,364.1	1,520.5
Originating in business	348.6	474.5	647.4	770.3	866.0	916.7	977.8	1,102.0	1,234.6
Corporate business	233.6	332.3	470.9	564.3	630.6	671.4	717.6	821.8	920.8
Compensation of employees	190.8	259.7	399.3	470.6	533.3	585.9	612.9	690.4	777.3
Corporate profits [1]	44.7	73.8	64.1	87.2	92.2	74.0	93.1	119.9	130.6
Net interest	−1.9	−1.3	7.4	6.4	5.0	11.5	11.6	11.4	13.0
Sole proprietors, partnerships	84.0	98.9	118.0	134.5	157.3	157.9	162.9	172.8	(NA)
Compensation of employees	36.2	40.0	47.4	50.6	55.1	59.7	62.2	69.1	(NA)
Proprietors' income [1]	46.6	56.2	64.7	75.6	91.8	85.5	85.1	87.0	(NA)
Net interest	1.2	2.7	5.9	8.3	10.4	12.6	15.6	16.7	(NA)
Other private business [2]	25.4	35.5	45.8	56.3	61.4	68.4	76.0	84.2	(NA)
Compensation of employees	1.5	2.2	3.3	4.1	4.5	4.9	5.3	5.8	(NA)
Rental income of persons [3]	13.8	17.1	18.6	21.5	21.6	21.4	22.3	23.3	25.3
Proprietors' income [1]	.4	.5	.4	.6	.6	.7	.9	1.0	(NA)
Net interest	9.8	15.7	23.4	30.1	34.7	41.4	47.5	54.0	(NA)
Govt. enterprises [4]	5.6	7.8	12.7	15.1	16.7	19.1	21.3	23.2	25.3
Originating in—Government [4]	47.1	67.6	114.7	137.4	149.1	161.4	178.2	191.6	205.8
Households and institutions [5]	13.8	19.2	31.6	37.2	40.5	44.8	50.4	56.2	63.0
Rest of the world	2.5	4.7	4.6	7.0	9.1	13.1	10.5	14.4	17.1

NA Not available.   [1] See footnote 2, table 716.   [2] Consists of all business activities reported on the individual income tax return in Schedule E—Supplemental Income Schedule; tax-exempt cooperatives; and owner-occupied nonfarm dwellings and buildings and equipment owned and used by nonprofit institutions serving individuals, which are considered to be business activities selling their current services to their owners.
[3] See footnote 1, table 716.   [4] Compensation of employees.   [5] Compensation of employees in private households; social and athletic clubs; labor organizations; nonprofit schools and hospitals; religious, charitable, and welfare organizations; and all other nonprofit organizations serving individuals.

Source of tables 719 and 720: U.S. Bureau of Economic Analysis, *The National Income and Product Accounts of the United States, 1929–74*, and *Survey of Current Business*, July 1977 and April 1978.

No. 721. National Income Without Capital Consumption Adjustments, by Industrial Origin: 1960 to 1977

[In billions of dollars, except percent. Represents net value added to production by industry, measured at factor costs. See *Historical Statistics, Colonial Times to 1970*, series F 226–237, for single-year figures prior to minor revisions issued in 1976]

INDUSTRY	1960	1965	1970	1972	1973	1974	1975	1976	1977
National income	418.0	565.4	804.4	956.8	1,072.8	1,152.1	1,244.6	1,393.8	1,554.8
Agriculture, forestry, fisheries	17.5	20.4	24.5	30.6	47.0	42.2	42.8	40.5	44.6
Farms	16.5	18.8	22.2	27.9	43.8	38.7	39.4	36.2	39.8
Mining	5.6	6.0	7.8	8.7	10.1	15.5	18.1	20.3	23.2
Construction	21.4	30.4	44.6	53.6	59.7	62.2	61.8	67.7	77.2
Manufacturing	125.4	170.4	215.4	251.8	283.5	297.8	312.5	362.9	408.9
Food and kindred products	12.2	14.2	19.6	20.3	21.0	23.7	30.0	31.7	32.0
Tobacco manufactures	1.0	1.1	1.7	1.7	1.8	1.7	2.2	2.4	2.8
Textile mill products	4.5	5.9	7.5	8.4	8.7	9.9	8.8	10.5	11.8
Apparel and other textile products	4.9	6.5	8.7	9.6	10.3	10.4	10.8	12.3	13.2
Paper and allied products	4.7	6.0	8.0	9.4	10.9	11.9	11.8	14.2	15.5
Printing and publishing	6.7	8.7	11.9	13.5	14.9	15.2	16.7	18.5	20.8
Chemicals and allied products	8.9	12.1	15.7	18.0	19.9	21.3	23.8	28.1	30.7
Petroleum and coal products	4.4	4.8	6.6	7.1	8.5	14.0	12.9	17.3	19.4
Rubber and misc. plastics prod	2.9	4.2	6.2	7.8	8.8	8.8	8.7	10.2	12.7
Leather and leather products	1.6	1.8	2.2	2.1	2.4	2.4	2.4	2.8	2.9
Lumber and wood products	3.5	4.9	6.3	8.6	10.6	10.6	8.9	11.5	13.4
Furniture and fixtures	2.0	2.8	3.5	4.3	4.7	4.8	4.6	5.3	6.0
Stone, clay, and glass products	4.6	5.7	6.9	8.7	9.8	9.7	9.9	11.6	13.2
Primary metal products	10.6	13.9	15.1	17.8	21.1	26.6	24.2	26.1	29.2
Fabricated metal products	8.9	12.6	16.6	19.4	22.4	22.8	24.3	27.9	30.9
Machinery, except electrical	11.9	18.2	24.4	27.3	32.1	33.5	36.8	40.9	47.0
Electrical, electronic equipment	10.5	14.5	19.6	22.7	25.9	25.8	26.6	29.9	34.8
Transportation equipment [1]	7.5	10.4	12.6	13.1	13.8	14.1	15.7	16.8	19.0
Motor vehicles and equipment	8.4	14.5	12.1	20.2	23.1	17.7	19.0	28.4	34.8
Instruments, related products	3.3	4.6	6.4	7.2	8.0	8.2	9.0	10.4	12.4
Miscellaneous industries	2.3	2.9	3.7	4.6	5.0	4.9	5.4	6.1	6.4
Transportation [2]	18.1	23.1	30.3	36.5	41.1	44.2	44.5	51.6	58.4
Railroad transportation	6.7	7.0	7.6	8.4	9.7	10.1	10.0	11.8	12.6
Local and interurban passenger	1.6	1.9	2.3	2.5	2.5	2.8	2.9	3.2	3.4
Trucking and warehousing	5.9	8.4	11.8	15.5	17.5	18.7	18.4	21.0	24.1
Water transportation	1.6	2.0	2.5	2.5	2.8	3.3	3.3	3.7	4.2
Air transportation	1.4	2.6	4.4	5.7	6.4	6.9	7.1	8.6	10.1
Communications	8.2	11.5	17.6	20.3	22.6	24.5	27.1	31.4	35.0
Telephone and telegraph	7.3	10.3	15.9	18.2	20.4	22.2	24.4	27.9	31.1
Electric, gas, sanitary services	8.9	11.4	14.9	17.6	18.8	18.4	24.3	27.2	29.5
Wholesale and retail trade	64.7	84.7	122.2	144.6	161.6	175.0	194.2	215.3	237.0
Wholesale trade	24.7	31.9	46.9	56.8	65.7	76.6	80.6	89.6	96.5
Retail trade	40.1	52.8	75.3	87.8	95.8	98.3	113.7	125.7	140.5
Finance, insurance, real estate [2]	48.2	63.4	91.8	111.1	116.7	128.4	140.4	157.9	177.9
Banking	7.3	8.9	16.4	17.1	18.4	19.6	20.1	20.4	22.2
Insurance carriers	4.8	5.9	9.3	12.5	12.8	12.1	12.8	15.9	19.2
Insurance agents, brokers, etc	2.1	3.0	4.2	5.2	5.7	5.9	6.7	8.1	9.3
Real estate	33.5	45.2	61.0	75.0	83.0	93.2	100.1	111.8	125.8
Services [2]	44.6	64.1	103.3	122.3	136.8	150.2	168.5	188.9	213.1
Hotels, other lodging places	2.0	2.8	4.4	5.3	5.8	6.2	7.0	8.0	8.9
Personal services	4.6	5.9	7.4	7.5	7.7	8.1	8.3	9.1	9.8
Business services	5.4	8.9	15.0	17.4	20.3	22.0	23.9	27.6	31.7
Health services	10.6	15.8	29.4	36.5	40.9	46.3	54.1	61.1	69.4
Legal services	2.7	4.2	6.7	8.4	9.7	10.7	11.8	12.6	14.2
Educational services	2.2	3.7	5.9	7.1	7.8	8.7	10.0	11.0	11.9
Nonprofit membership organizations	4.5	6.4	10.0	12.0	13.1	14.2	16.0	17.5	19.6
Private households	3.8	4.0	5.1	5.3	5.4	5.6	5.8	6.5	7.1
Government and govt. enterprises	52.7	75.4	127.4	152.5	165.8	180.4	199.9	215.7	232.7
Federal	25.3	33.3	53.1	59.7	62.4	66.7	72.0	76.5	81.2
State and local	27.4	42.1	74.3	92.8	103.4	113.7	127.9	139.3	151.5
Rest of the world	2.5	4.7	4.6	7.0	9.1	13.1	10.5	14.4	17.3
Percent of national income	100.0	100.0	100.0	100.0	100.0	100.0	100.0	100.0	100.0
Agriculture, forestry, fisheries	4.2	3.6	3.0	3.2	4.4	3.7	3.4	2.9	2.9
Mining and construction	6.5	6.4	6.5	6.5	6.5	6.7	6.4	6.3	6.5
Manufacturing	30.0	30.1	26.8	26.3	26.4	25.9	25.1	26.0	26.3
Transportation	4.3	4.1	3.8	3.8	3.8	3.8	3.6	3.7	3.8
Communications and utilities	4.1	4.1	4.0	4.0	3.9	3.7	4.1	4.2	4.1
Wholesale and retail trade	15.5	15.0	15.2	15.1	15.1	15.2	15.6	15.4	15.2
Finance, insurance, real estate	11.5	11.2	11.4	11.6	10.9	11.1	11.3	11.3	11.4
Services	10.7	11.3	12.8	12.8	12.8	13.0	13.5	13.6	13.7
Govt. and govt. enterprises	12.6	13.3	15.8	15.9	15.5	15.7	16.1	15.5	15.0
Rest of the world	.6	.8	.6	.7	.8	1.1	.8	1.0	1.1

[1] Excludes motor vehicles and equipment.　[2] Includes items not shown separately.

Source: U.S. Bureau of Economic Analysis, *The National Income and Product Accounts of the United States, 1929–74*, and *Survey of Current Business*, July 1977 and July 1978.

No. 722. Personal Income and Its Disposition: 1950 to 1977

[In billions of dollars, except as noted. Prior to 1960, excludes Alaska and Hawaii. For definition of personal income, see text, pp. 437 and 438. See *Historical Statistics, Colonial Times to 1970*, series F 262–286, for single-year figures prior to minor revisions issued in 1976]

ITEM	1950	1955	1960	1965	1970	1972	1973	1974	1975	1976	1977
Personal income	226.1	308.8	399.7	537.0	801	943	1,052	1,155	1,253	1,383	1,537
Wage and salary disbursements	147.0	211.7	271.9	362.0	547	634	701	765	806	892	990
Commodity-producing industries [1]	64.8	93.1	113.1	146.0	203	227	254	275	275	309	346
Distributive industries [2]	39.8	53.4	68.2	87.2	130	152	168	184	195	217	243
Service industries [3]	19.8	28.6	41.4	58.9	98	118	130	145	160	179	201
Govt. and govt. enterprises	22.6	36.6	49.2	69.9	116	137	149	161	175	187	200
Other labor income	3.7	7.0	11.2	17.8	32	42	49	56	65	76	89
Proprietors' income [4]	38.4	42.5	47.0	56.7	65	76	92	86	86	88	98
Rental income of persons [4]	7.1	11.3	13.8	17.1	19	22	22	21	22	23	25
Dividends	8.8	10.3	12.9	19.1	23	25	28	31	32	36	41
Personal interest income	8.9	13.8	23.3	37.2	64	75	84	103	116	130	148
Transfer payments [5]	15.2	17.5	28.9	40.4	80	104	119	141	177	193	207
Old-age, survivors, disability, and health insurance	1.0	4.9	11.1	18.1	39	50	60	70	81	93	105
Unemployment insurance	1.5	1.5	3.0	2.3	4	6	4	7	17	16	13
Govt. employee retirement	1.0	1.7	3.1	5.2	10	14	16	19	23	26	29
Veterans' benefits	7.7	4.4	4.6	4.9	8	10	10	12	15	14	14
Other	4.0	4.9	7.1	10.0	20	26	28	33	41	44	47
Less: Personal contributions for social insurance	2.9	5.2	9.3	13.3	28	34	42	48	50	55	61
Less: Personal tax and nontax payments	20.6	35.4	50.4	64.9	115	141	151	170	169	197	228
Federal income tax, payments	17.4	30.4	41.8	51.1	88.4	103	109	126	121	142	(NA)
Equals: Disposable personal income	205.5	273.4	349.4	472.2	686	801	902	985	1,084	1,186	1,309
Less: Personal outlays	194.7	258.5	332.3	441.9	635	752	831	913	1,004	1,120	1,242
Personal consumption expend.	192.0	253.7	324.9	430.2	619	733	810	890	980	1,094	1,211
Interest paid by consumers	2.3	4.4	7.0	11.1	16	18	20	22	23	25	30
Transfer payments, net [6]	.4	.4	.4	.7	1	1	1	1	1	1	1
Equals: Personal saving	10.8	14.9	17.1	30.3	51	49	70	72	80	66	67
Percent of disposable personal income	5.3	5.4	4.9	6.4	7.4	6.2	7.8	7.3	7.4	5.6	5.1
Real (1972 prices) disposable personal income	361.9	425.9	487.3	612.4	742	801	855	842	857	890	931
Annual percent change [7]	7.7	3.3	2.7	4.7	3.9	4.2	6.7	−1.5	1.8	3.8	4.6

NA Not available.   [1] Includes agriculture, forestry, and fisheries; mining; construction; and manufacturing.
[2] Includes transportation; communication; electric, gas, and sanitary services; and trade.   [3] Includes finance, insurance, and real estate; services; and rest of the world.   [4] With capital consumption and inventory valuation adjustments.   [5] Government benefits.   [6] Payments to foreigners.   [7] Represents average for period of intervals shown here; for 1950, change from 1949.

Source: U.S. Bureau of Economic Analysis, *The National Income and Product Accounts of the United States, 1929–74*, and *Survey of Current Business*, July 1977 and April 1978.

No. 723. Sources of Personal Income—Percent Distribution: 1950 to 1977

[See headnote, table 722]

SOURCE OF INCOME	1950	1955	1960	1965	1970	1972	1973	1974	1975	1976	1977
Personal income	100.0	100.0	100.0	100.0	100.0	100.0	100.0	100.0	100.0	100.0	100.0
Wage and salary disbursements	65.0	68.6	68.0	67.4	68.2	67.2	66.6	66.2	64.3	64.5	64.4
Other labor income	1.6	2.3	2.8	3.3	4.0	4.4	4.6	4.8	5.2	5.5	5.8
Proprietors' income [1]	17.0	13.8	11.8	10.6	8.1	-8.1	8.8	7.5	6.9	6.4	6.4
Farm	6.0	3.7	2.9	2.3	1.7	1.9	3.0	2.2	1.8	1.3	1.3
Nonfarm	11.0	10.1	8.9	8.2	6.4	6.2	5.7	5.3	5.0	5.0	5.1
Rental income of persons [1]	3.1	3.7	3.5	3.2	2.3	2.3	2.0	1.8	1.8	1.7	1.6
Dividends	3.9	3.3	3.2	3.6	2.9	2.6	2.6	2.7	2.5	2.6	2.7
Personal interest income	3.9	4.5	5.8	6.9	8.0	7.9	8.0	8.9	9.2	9.4	9.6
Transfer payments	6.7	5.7	7.2	7.5	10.0	11.0	11.3	12.2	14.1	13.9	13.5
Personal contributions for social insurance	−1.3	−1.7	−2.3	−2.5	−3.5	−3.6	−4.0	−4.1	−4.0	−4.0	−4.0

[1] With capital consumption and inventory valuation adjustments.

Source: U.S. Bureau of Economic Analysis, unpublished data.

No. 724. Personal Income In Current and Constant (1972) Dollars—States: 1960 to 1977

[Represents a measure of income received from all sources during the calendar year by the residents of each State. Data exclude Federal employees overseas and totals may differ from those in tables 716 and 722. See text, pp. 437–438. See *Historical Statistics, Colonial Times to 1970*, series F 297–348, for single-year figures prior to minor revisions issued in 1976]

STATE	CURRENT DOLLARS (billions)				CONSTANT (1972) DOLLARS (billions)				PERCENT CHANGE		PERCENT OF U.S.		
	1960	1970	1975	1977	1960	1970	1975	1977	1960–1970	1970–1977	1960	1970	1977
U.S.	396.1	793.5	1,248.4	1,518.4	552.4	857.8	987.7	1,079.2	55.3	25.8	100.0	100.0	100.0
N.E.	25.5	50.4	73.5	87.9	35.5	54.5	58.1	62.5	53.5	14.7	6.4	6.4	5.8
Maine	1.8	3.2	5.0	6.2	2.5	3.5	4.0	4.4	40.0	25.7	.5	.4	.4
N.H.	1.3	2.8	4.4	5.5	1.8	3.0	3.5	3.9	66.7	30.0	.3	.3	.4
Vt.	.7	1.5	2.3	2.8	1.0	1.7	1.8	2.0	70.0	17.6	.2	.2	.2
Mass.	12.6	24.4	35.3	42.0	17.5	26.4	28.0	29.8	50.9	12.9	3.2	3.1	2.8
R.I.	1.9	3.7	5.3	6.3	2.6	4.0	4.2	4.5	53.8	12.5	.5	.5	.4
Conn.	7.2	14.8	21.1	25.1	10.1	16.0	16.7	17.8	58.4	11.3	1.8	1.9	1.7
M.A.	87.4	163.6	236.9	276.3	121.8	176.9	187.4	196.4	45.2	11.0	22.0	20.6	18.2
N.Y.	45.5	84.1	117.8	135.1	63.5	91.0	93.2	96.0	43.3	5.5	11.5	10.6	8.9
N.J.	16.5	33.7	49.8	58.6	23.0	36.4	39.4	41.6	58.3	14.3	4.2	4.2	3.9
Pa.	25.4	45.8	69.3	82.6	35.4	49.5	54.8	58.7	39.8	18.6	6.4	5.8	5.4
E.N.C.	85.9	163.3	247.6	301.6	119.8	176.5	195.9	214.4	47.3	21.5	21.7	20.6	19.9
Ohio	22.6	42.1	62.0	75.8	31.5	45.5	49.1	53.9	44.4	18.5	5.7	5.3	5.0
Ind.	10.0	19.3	29.8	36.9	14.0	20.9	23.6	26.2	49.3	25.4	2.5	2.4	2.4
Ill.	26.4	49.5	75.4	87.3	36.8	53.5	59.7	62.1	45.4	16.1	6.7	6.2	5.8
Mich.	18.2	36.0	54.6	69.6	25.4	38.9	43.2	49.4	53.1	27.0	4.6	4.5	4.6
Wis.	8.6	16.4	25.8	32.0	12.0	17.8	20.4	22.8	48.3	28.1	2.2	2.1	2.1
W.N.C.	31.2	59.8	95.5	115.3	43.5	64.6	75.5	82.0	48.5	26.9	7.9	7.5	7.6
Minn.	7.1	14.6	22.7	28.3	9.9	15.8	17.9	20.1	59.6	27.2	1.8	1.8	1.9
Iowa	5.4	10.3	16.9	19.8	7.5	11.1	13.3	14.1	48.0	27.0	1.4	1.3	1.3
Mo.	9.0	17.1	26.1	31.9	12.6	18.6	20.7	22.7	47.6	22.0	2.3	2.2	2.1
N. Dak.	1.1	1.9	3.8	4.0	1.5	2.1	3.0	2.9	40.0	38.1	.3	.2	.3
S. Dak.	1.2	2.1	3.4	4.1	1.7	2.2	2.7	2.9	29.4	31.8	.3	.3	.3
Nebr.	2.8	5.4	9.1	10.5	4.0	5.9	7.2	7.5	47.5	27.1	.7	.7	.7
Kans.	4.6	8.4	13.6	16.6	6.3	9.1	10.7	11.8	44.4	29.7	1.2	1.1	1.1
S.A.	47.9	109.7	184.5	224.2	66.9	118.6	145.9	159.4	77.3	34.4	12.1	13.8	14.8
Del.	1.2	2.5	3.8	4.5	1.7	2.7	3.0	3.2	58.8	18.5	.3	.3	.3
Md.	7.2	16.8	26.4	31.3	10.1	18.2	20.9	22.3	80.2	22.5	1.8	2.1	2.1
D.C.	2.2	3.5	5.2	6.2	3.0	3.8	4.1	4.4	26.7	15.8	.6	.4	.4
Va.	7.5	17.1	28.7	35.2	10.5	18.5	22.7	25.1	76.2	35.7	1.9	2.2	2.3
W. Va.	2.9	5.3	8.9	11.1	4.1	5.7	7.1	7.9	39.0	38.6	.7	.7	.7
N.C.	7.2	16.3	26.9	32.8	10.1	17.6	21.3	23.3	74.3	32.4	1.8	2.1	2.2
S.C.	3.3	7.7	13.1	16.2	4.7	8.3	10.4	11.5	76.6	38.6	.8	1.0	1.1
Ga.	6.5	15.2	24.8	30.4	9.1	16.4	19.6	21.6	80.2	31.7	1.6	1.9	2.0
Fla.	9.8	25.3	46.6	56.5	13.7	27.4	36.9	40.2	100.0	46.7	2.5	3.2	3.7
E.S.C.	18.0	37.7	62.8	78.2	25.1	40.7	49.7	55.6	62.2	36.6	4.5	4.7	5.1
Ky.	4.8	9.9	16.6	20.6	6.7	10.7	13.1	14.6	59.7	36.4	1.2	1.2	1.4
Tenn.	5.6	12.1	20.0	24.9	7.9	13.1	15.9	17.7	65.8	35.1	1.4	1.5	1.6
Ala.	4.9	10.0	16.8	20.7	6.9	10.8	13.3	14.7	56.5	36.1	1.2	1.3	1.4
Miss.	2.6	5.7	9.5	12.0	3.6	6.1	7.5	8.5	69.4	39.3	.7	.7	.8
W.S.C.	30.4	64.4	110.5	140.2	42.3	69.6	87.4	99.6	64.5	43.1	7.7	8.1	9.2
Ark.	2.4	5.4	9.5	11.9	3.4	5.8	7.5	8.4	70.6	44.8	.6	.7	.8
La.	5.4	11.0	18.3	23.2	7.5	11.9	14.5	16.5	58.7	38.7	1.4	1.4	1.5
Okla.	4.3	8.6	14.3	17.8	6.0	9.3	11.3	12.7	55.0	36.6	1.1	1.1	1.2
Tex.	18.2	39.4	68.3	87.3	25.4	42.6	54.1	62.0	67.7	45.5	4.6	5.0	5.8
Mt.	14.2	29.7	53.0	66.1	19.8	32.1	41.9	47.0	62.1	46.4	3.6	3.7	4.4
Mont.	1.3	2.4	4.0	4.7	1.9	2.6	3.2	3.3	36.8	26.9	.3	.3	.3
Idaho	1.2	2.3	4.2	5.1	1.7	2.5	3.3	3.6	47.1	44.0	.3	.3	.3
Wyo.	.7	1.2	2.3	3.1	1.0	1.3	1.8	2.2	30.0	69.2	.2	.2	.2
Colo.	4.0	8.5	15.2	18.8	5.5	9.2	12.0	13.3	67.3	44.6	1.0	1.1	1.2
N. Mex.	1.7	3.1	5.5	7.0	2.4	3.4	4.4	5.0	41.7	47.1	.4	.4	.5
Ariz.	2.6	6.5	11.9	14.9	3.7	7.0	9.4	10.6	89.2	51.4	.7	.8	1.0
Utah	1.8	3.4	5.9	7.5	2.5	3.7	4.7	5.3	48.0	43.2	.4	.4	.5
Nev.	.8	2.3	3.9	5.1	1.1	2.4	3.1	3.6	118.2	50.0	.2	.3	.3
Pac.	55.7	114.9	184.2	228.5	77.6	124.2	145.7	162.4	60.1	30.8	14.1	14.5	15.0
Wash.	6.7	13.7	22.4	27.5	9.4	14.8	17.7	19.6	57.4	32.4	1.7	1.7	1.8
Oreg.	3.9	7.7	13.2	16.7	5.4	8.3	10.4	11.8	53.7	42.2	1.0	1.0	1.1
Calif.	43.0	88.6	139.4	173.2	60.0	95.7	110.3	123.1	59.5	28.7	10.9	11.2	11.4
Alaska	.6	1.4	3.5	4.3	.9	1.5	2.8	3.1	66.7	106.7	.2	.2	.3
Hawaii	1.4	3.5	5.7	6.8	2.0	3.8	4.5	4.8	90.0	26.3	.4	.4	.4

Source: U.S. Bureau of Economic Analysis, *Survey of Current Business*, August 1978. Some data computed by Bureau of the Census.

No. 725. Personal Income Per Capita and Per Square Mile—States: 1960 to 1977

[Data exclude Federal employees overseas and totals may differ from those in tables 716 and 722. See headnote, table 724]

STATE AND REGION	PER CAPITA INCOME IN CURRENT DOLLARS												Income per sq. mi. of land area, 1977 ($1,000)
	Total (dol.)				Income rank				Percent of U.S.				
	1960	1970	1975	1977	1960	1970	1975	1977	1960	1970	1975	1977	
U.S.	2,201	3,893	5,861	7,019	(X)	(X)	(X)	(X)	100	100	100	100	429
N.E.	2,419	4,245	6,030	7,183	(X)	(X)	(X)	(X)	110	109	103	102	1,397
Maine	1,825	3,250	4,766	5,734	36	36	46	46	83	83	81	82	201
N.H.	2,172	3,720	5,417	6,536	21	20	31	30	99	96	92	93	61
Vt.	1,864	3,447	4,924	5,823	34	32	40	44	85	89	84	83	304
Mass.	2,436	4,276	6,077	7,258	9	10	13	14	111	110	104	103	5,362
R.I.	2,182	3,878	5,709	6,775	19	16	25	26	99	100	97	97	6,036
Conn.	2,839	4,871	6,799	8,061	1	1	2	2	129	125	116	115	5,153
M.A.	2,549	4,390	6,358	7,460	(X)	(X)	(X)	(X)	116	113	108	106	2,754
N.Y.	2,703	4,605	6,519	7,537	6	4	9	12	123	118	111	107	2,824
N.J.	2,699	4,684	6,794	7,994	7	2	3	3	123	120	116	114	7,790
Pa.	2,239	3,879	5,841	7,011	16	15	20	19	102	100	100	100	1,838
E.N.C.	2,367	4,050	6,047	7,347	(X)	(X)	(X)	(X)	108	104	103	105	1,236
Ohio	2,322	3,949	5,778	7,084	12	14	22	18	105	101	99	101	1,850
Ind.	2,149	3,709	5,609	6,921	22	22	28	21	98	95	96	99	1,022
Ill.	2,617	4,446	6,735	7,768	8	8	4	6	119	114	115	111	1,567
Mich.	2,327	4,041	5,991	7,619	11	12	14	9	106	104	102	109	1,224
Wis.	2,178	3,712	5,616	6,890	20	21	27	22	99	95	96	98	588
W.N.C.	2,022	3,657	5,719	6,830	(X)	(X)	(X)	(X)	92	94	98	97	227
Minn.	2,065	3,819	5,779	7,129	25	18	21	17	94	98	99	102	357
Iowa	1,960	3,643	5,894	6,878	30	29	17	23	89	94	101	98	354
Mo.	2,091	3,654	5,476	6,654	23	28	30	29	95	94	93	95	463
N. Dak.	1,681	3,077	5,888	6,190	40	42	18	33	76	79	100	88	58
S. Dak.	1,758	3,108	5,009	5,957	39	40	37	38	80	80	85	85	54
Nebr.	2,009	3,657	5,882	6,720	26	27	19	27	91	94	100	96	137
Kans.	2,085	3,725	5,958	7,134	24	19	16	16	95	96	102	102	203
S.A.	1,837	3,562	5,480	6,536	(X)	(X)	(X)	(X)	83	91	93	93	840
Del.	2,735	4,468	6,547	7,697	4	7	8	7	124	115	112	110	2,259
Md.	2,319	4,267	6,403	7,572	13	11	10	10	105	110	109	108	3,168
D.C.	2,829	4,644	7,262	8,999	(X)	(X)	(X)	(X)	129	119	124	128	101,803
Va.	1,882	3,677	5,772	6,865	33	[1] 24	23	24	86	94	98	98	886
W. Va.	1,592	3,038	4,962	5,986	3	45	38	36	72	78	85	85	462
N.C.	1,577	3,200	4,940	5,935	[2] 14	38	39	40	72	82	84	85	672
S.C.	1,396	2,951	4,665	5,628	48	47	47	47	63	76	80	80	536
Ga.	1,645	3,300	5,029	6,014	42	35	36	35	75	85	86	86	523
Fla.	1,962	3,698	5,631	6,684	29	23	26	28	89	95	96	95	1,044
E.S.C.	1,490	2,936	4,648	5,651	(X)	(X)	(X)	(X)	68	75	79	81	437
Ky.	1,576	3,076	4,887	5,945	46	43	42	39	72	79	83	85	519
Tenn.	1,577	3,079	4,804	5,785	[2] 44	41	44	45	72	79	82	82	602
Ala.	1,510	2,892	4,635	5,622	47	48	48	48	69	74	79	80	409
Miss.	1,196	2,547	4,047	5,030	50	50	50	50	54	65	69	72	254
W.S.C.	1,785	3,323	5,293	6,458	(X)	(X)	(X)	(X)	81	85	90	92	328
Ark.	1,358	2,791	4,510	5,540	49	49	49	49	62	72	77	79	229
La.	1,650	3,023	4,803	5,913	41	46	45	42	75	78	82	84	516
Okla.	1,850	3,341	5,280	6,346	35	34	34	32	84	86	90	90	259
Tex.	1,894	3,507	5,584	6,803	32	31	29	25	86	90	95	97	333
Mt.	2,054	3,557	5,508	6,589	(X)	(X)	(X)	(X)	93	91	94	94	77
Mont.	1,983	3,395	5,388	6,125	28	33	33	34	90	87	92	87	32
Idaho	1,812	3,243	5,179	5,980	38	37	35	37	82	83	88	85	62
Wyo.	2,210	3,672	6,123	7,562	17	26	12	11	100	94	104	108	32
Colo.	2,247	3,838	5,987	7,160	15	17	15	15	102	99	102	102	181
N. Mex.	1,815	3,045	4,843	5,857	37	44	43	43	82	78	83	83	57
Ariz.	1,994	3,614	5,391	6,509	27	30	32	31	91	93	92	93	132
Utah	1,954	3,169	4,900	5,923	31	39	41	41	89	81	84	84	91
Nev.	2,793	4,583	6,625	7,988	2	6	6	4	127	118	113	114	46
Pac.	2,608	4,317	6,518	7,820	(X)	(X)	(X)	(X)	118	111	111	111	255
Wash.	2,352	3,997	6,298	7,528	10	13	11	13	107	103	107	107	414
Oreg.	2,195	3,677	5,769	7,007	18	[1] 24	24	20	100	94	98	100	173
Calif.	2,710	4,423	6,575	7,911	5	9	7	5	123	114	112	113	1,108
Alaska	2,740	4,638	9,636	10,586	3	3	1	1	124	119	164	151	8
Hawaii	2,300	4,599	6,708	7,677	14	5	5	8	104	118	114	109	1,054

X Not applicable.   [1] In order to have the lowest rank equal to the number of States presented, the number 25 is omitted. Oreg. and Va. share the same rank, 24.   [2] In order to have the lowest rank equal to the number of States presented, the number 45 is omitted. N.C. and Tenn. share the same rank, 44.

Source: U.S. Bureau of Economic Analysis, *Survey of Current Business*, August 1978; and unpublished data.

No. 726. Ratio of Transfer Payments to Total Personal Income—Index, by State: 1965 to 1976

STATE AND REGION	TOTAL			INCOME MAINTENANCE [1]			UNEMPLOYMENT COMPENSATION [2]			RETIREMENT AND OTHER [3]		
	1965	1970	1976	1965	1970	1976	1965	1970	1976	1965	1970	1976
Ratio: U.S. transfer payments to total personal income, percent	7.6	10.1	14.0	.8	1.2	1.7	.4	.5	1.2	6.4	8.3	11.2
Index: U.S. ratio = 100	100	100	100	100	100	100	100	100	100	100	100	100
New England	98	100	107	85	98	112	118	149	142	99	97	103
Maine	127	127	126	105	106	119	77	117	122	133	131	127
New Hampshire	105	99	98	61	53	61	57	53	59	114	108	108
Vermont	120	113	116	94	101	122	114	106	140	124	115	112
Massachusetts	105	106	115	94	120	145	155	143	147	103	101	108
Rhode Island	115	117	124	108	104	111	114	200	176	116	114	120
Connecticut	74	79	86	65	67	66	84	172	147	75	75	83
Middle Atlantic	99	102	108	82	120	119	130	119	146	99	99	102
New York	100	105	111	95	143	142	148	119	135	97	98	104
New Jersey	84	85	93	54	77	89	130	142	164	85	83	86
Pennsylvania	107	111	114	78	109	104	98	100	152	112	112	111
East North Central	86	87	90	68	68	92	61	92	101	90	89	89
Ohio	95	88	93	80	64	86	66	66	80	99	93	96
Indiana	84	84	82	30	33	46	45	64	52	94	93	91
Illinois	81	82	87	76	76	99	66	75	112	83	84	83
Michigan	82	89	95	73	86	119	57	158	142	84	85	86
Wisconsin	93	95	93	49	56	82	77	104	86	100	100	95
West North Central	102	100	94	99	77	65	64	74	72	105	105	101
Minnesota	101	95	91	91	78	69	82	79	90	104	98	95
Iowa	96	100	90	72	79	58	32	60	72	104	106	97
Missouri	107	104	104	138	90	80	68	91	88	106	107	109
North Dakota	101	111	89	96	90	53	102	57	51	101	117	99
South Dakota	109	109	104	105	88	86	57	34	38	114	117	114
Nebraska	96	95	87	47	48	41	61	40	44	104	106	99
Kansas	100	99	88	92	63	51	68	87	44	103	105	98
South Atlantic	105	101	105	86	72	87	55	49	71	111	108	112
Delaware	69	72	83	53	56	67	73	87	113	70	74	82
Maryland	81	81	87	72	66	73	70	62	65	83	84	91
District of Columbia	135	139	154	80	142	174	100	96	117	144	142	155
Virginia	92	91	93	38	48	63	30	23	38	103	102	104
West Virginia	153	143	131	157	149	104	105	70	65	156	147	142
North Carolina	97	88	94	101	68	96	64	58	83	99	93	95
South Carolina	99	97	100	66	86	105	64	70	85	106	101	101
Georgia	97	92	97	128	103	107	48	45	83	97	94	97
Florida	130	123	127	85	50	77	39	30	70	142	139	141
East South Central	118	115	111	147	133	125	75	77	83	118	115	112
Kentucky	125	114	111	143	124	132	91	79	80	126	115	111
Tennessee	107	107	104	97	110	106	82	91	90	110	108	106
Alabama	118	117	115	186	133	114	64	72	94	113	117	117
Mississippi	130	130	121	190	196	169	57	51	53	128	125	120
West South Central	107	101	90	165	103	81	64	55	43	103	103	97
Arkansas	146	138	125	180	150	129	91	85	88	146	140	129
Louisiana	114	111	96	280	187	130	82	108	69	96	100	94
Oklahoma	132	118	108	282	130	92	64	53	58	118	120	116
Texas	93	89	80	101	67	59	52	36	28	95	96	89
Mountain	105	102	96	114	88	80	105	68	75	104	106	101
Montana	114	110	100	87	67	57	102	75	88	118	118	108
Idaho	104	106	93	80	63	57	102	94	77	108	113	100
Wyoming	97	92	71	72	46	29	92	43	32	101	102	81
Colorado	107	97	87	163	103	75	64	38	53	103	100	92
New Mexico	103	119	115	139	165	191	98	98	69	99	114	108
Arizona	119	108	110	108	76	79	120	57	90	120	116	116
Utah	96	98	90	85	78	61	141	96	73	94	101	96
Nevada	78	78	87	46	37	44	191	115	134	75	82	88
Pacific	107	109	101	143	148	121	195	166	113	96	99	97
Washington	114	115	103	99	107	85	139	270	117	114	107	105
Oregon	114	114	106	81	76	89	107	140	106	119	118	109
California	107	109	102	158	164	130	216	155	112	93	98	96
Alaska	55	62	50	100	134	106	180	181	118	41	43	34
Hawaii	68	72	93	57	76	130	95	102	144	67	70	82

[1] Federal, State, and local direct welfare payments (including supplemental security income payments), food stamp payments, and payments made through several other relief programs, such as refugee assistance.
[2] Payments to unemployed workers through State, Federal, and railroad unemployment insurance programs.
[3] Includes retirement and disability payments made through the social security programs and through railroad, military, and Federal civilian retirement programs; Medicare; educational assistance to veterans and others; and miscellaneous transfers, such as business transfer payments.

Source: U.S. Bureau of Economic Analysis, unpublished data.

No. 727. GROSS SAVING AND INVESTMENT: 1950 TO 1977

[In billions of dollars. See *Historical Statistics, Colonial Times to 1970*, series F 552-565, for single-year figures prior to minor revisions issued in 1976]

ITEM	1950	1955	1960	1965	1970	1972	1973	1974	1975	1976	1977
Gross saving	49.7	65.6	78.9	115.4	143.4	177.5	216.8	204.4	195.1	237.0	273.6
Gross private saving	41.6	62.4	75.8	114.9	151.9	180.4	210.5	209.5	259.4	272.5	293.9
Personal saving	10.8	14.9	17.1	30.3	50.6	49.4	70.3	71.7	80.2	65.9	67.3
Undistrib. corporate profits	6.9	12.2	11.0	27.1	10.5	25.9	22.6	.2	16.7	27.6	29.5
Undistributed profits	15.9	16.1	13.0	25.2	14.1	30.0	39.3	43.6	41.0	56.4	61.4
Inventory valuation adjust	−5.0	−1.7	.3	−1.9	−5.1	−6.6	−18.6	−40.4	−12.0	−14.1	−14.6
Capital consumption adjust	−4.0	−2.1	−2.3	3.8	1.5	2.5	1.9	−2.9	−12.2	−14.7	−17.2
Capital consump. allowances:											
Corporate [1]	12.8	19.5	27.5	33.7	55.1	65.4	71.9	84.6	101.7	111.8	121.9
Noncorporate [1]	11.1	15.8	20.2	23.8	35.7	40.0	45.8	53.1	60.8	67.2	75.1
Gov't surplus or deficit (−) [2]	8.0	3.1	3.1	.5	−9.4	−3.5	6.3	−3.2	−64.3	−35.6	−20.3
Federal	9.2	4.4	3.0	.5	−12.1	−17.3	−6.7	−10.7	−70.2	−54.0	−49.5
State and local	−1.2	−1.3	.1	(−z)	2.8	13.7	13.0	7.6	5.9	18.4	29.2
Capital grants received by U.S. (net)	–	–	–	–	.9	.7	–	−2.0	–	–	–
Gross investment	51.7	68.0	78.2	116.3	141.4	179.2	219.4	210.1	201.0	242.5	273.3
Gross pvt. domestic investment	53.8	68.4	76.4	112.0	140.8	188.3	220.0	214.6	189.1	243.3	294.2
Net foreign investment	−2.1	−.3	1.7	4.3	.5	−9.0	−.6	−4.5	11.8	−.9	−20.9
Statistical discrepancy	2.0	2.5	−.7	.9	−2.1	1.7	2.6	5.8	5.9	5.5	−.2

– Represents zero.   Z Less than $50 million.   [1] With capital consumption adjustment.
[2] National income and product accounts.

Source: U.S. Bureau of Economic Analysis, *The National Income and Product Accounts of the United States, 1929-74*, and *Survey of Current Business*, July 1977 and April 1978.

No. 728. COMPOSITION OF INDIVIDUALS' SAVING: 1960 TO 1977

[In billions of dollars. Individuals' saving represents combined statement for households, farm and nonfarm, noncorporate business, nonprofit organizations, and personal trusts. Minus sign (−) denotes decrease. See *Historical Statistics, Colonial Times to 1970*, series F 566-594, for similar but not exactly comparable data]

COMPOSITION OF SAVING	1960	1965	1970	1972	1973	1974	1975	1976	1977
Increase in financial assets	31.9	58.3	77.7	128.1	142.8	140.5	165.1	191.4	222.2
Demand deposits and currency	1.0	7.5	8.9	14.8	12.9	5.6	7.1	8.0	17.0
Savings accounts	12.1	28.0	43.6	71.0	67.8	57.2	84.9	108.8	108.9
Securities [1]	3.5	2.3	−4.4	1.7	20.6	33.2	20.1	2.9	9.5
U.S. savings bonds	−.3	.6	.3	3.3	2.7	3.0	4.0	4.7	4.7
Other U.S. Treasury securities	.5	.2	−13.3	−.1	12.8	6.8	12.9	−7.9	−4.8
State and local obligations	3.6	1.8	−.9	2.3	5.3	8.9	5.0	4.2	5.5
Corporate and foreign bonds	.7	.5	9.5	4.4	1.3	4.7	8.2	4.0	.2
Commercial paper	(z)	(z)	−3.2	−.2	3.4	8.1	−4.8	−.5	−1.3
Private life insurance reserves	3.2	4.7	5.1	6.5	7.2	6.4	5.3	6.7	7.7
Private pension reserves	5.3	7.5	10.4	11.2	14.0	17.1	22.5	28.4	37.1
Govt. insurance and pension reserves	3.2	4.7	8.9	11.6	11.8	12.6	15.0	18.5	20.2
Miscellaneous financial assets	3.8	3.6	5.3	11.3	8.6	8.5	10.2	18.1	21.8
Gross investment in tangible assets	80.8	111.5	142.4	195.3	218.6	201.8	214.8	257.4	301.2
Nonfarm homes	21.1	21.9	24.5	40.6	45.2	42.9	42.9	57.6	75.7
Noncorporate business plant and equip	15.5	24.6	32.6	41.6	45.0	40.9	38.3	41.3	43.5
Consumer durables	43.1	62.8	84.9	111.2	123.7	122.0	132.9	158.9	179.4
Inventories	1.1	2.2	.4	1.9	4.6	−4.0	.6	−.4	2.5
Capital consumption allowances	56.0	67.7	103.6	118.1	131.1	148.9	172.1	184.8	208.9
Nonfarm homes	6.8	8.5	12.8	14.7	17.1	19.8	22.2	24.8	27.2
Noncorporate business plant and equip	13.5	15.6	23.2	25.7	29.3	34.1	39.7	43.4	49.0
Consumer durables	35.7	43.7	67.5	77.6	84.8	95.0	110.3	116.6	132.7
Net investment in tangible assets	24.8	43.8	38.8	77.3	87.4	52.9	42.7	72.6	92.3
Nonfarm homes	14.3	13.4	11.7	25.9	28.2	23.1	20.8	32.8	48.5
Noncorporate business plant and equip	2.0	9.0	9.4	15.9	15.7	6.8	−1.4	−2.1	−5.5
Consumer durables	7.4	19.1	17.4	33.6	39.0	27.0	22.7	42.3	46.8
Inventories	1.1	2.2	.4	1.9	4.6	−4.0	.6	−.4	2.5
Net increase in debt [1]	21.8	40.0	34.0	92.6	98.3	65.8	64.8	114.4	162.0
Mortgage debt on nonfarm homes	11.7	17.0	14.1	41.6	47.1	35.4	38.0	61.2	86.8
Noncorporate business mortgage debt	2.5	6.5	8.5	16.8	15.9	12.7	7.5	10.8	18.1
Consumer credit	4.6	9.6	5.9	18.9	22.0	10.2	9.4	23.6	35.6
Individuals' saving	34.9	62.0	82.6	112.8	132.0	127.6	143.0	149.6	152.5
Less: Govt. insurance and pension reserves	3.2	4.7	8.9	11.6	11.8	12.6	15.0	18.5	20.2
Net investment in consumer durables	7.4	19.1	17.4	33.6	39.0	27.0	22.7	42.3	46.8
Capital gains dividends from investment companies	.4	.9	.9	1.4	.9	.5	.2	.5	.5
Net saving by farm corporations	(z)	(z)	−.1	.1	.4	−.1	.2	.2	.1
Equals: **Personal saving (flow of funds)** [2]	23.9	37.2	55.5	66.1	80.0	87.8	104.9	88.2	85.0

Z Less than $50 million.   [1] Includes items not shown separately.   [2] Personal saving on national income account basis measures personal saving as income less taxes and consumption; flow-of-funds basis measures the same concept from acquisitions of assets less borrowing.

Source: Board of Governors of the Federal Reserve System, *Flow of Funds Accounts*, quarterly.

No. 729. FAMILIES—PERCENT DISTRIBUTION BY MONEY INCOME LEVEL, BY RACE OF HEAD, IN CURRENT AND CONSTANT (1977) DOLLARS: 1950 TO 1977

[Families as of **March** of following year. Prior to 1960, excludes Alaska and Hawaii. Based on Current Population Survey; see text, pp. 1 and 437. Beginning 1974, data not strictly comparable with earlier years due to revised procedures; see text, p. 438. Excludes inmates of institutions and Armed Forces, except Armed Forces living off post or with their families on post. Includes a small number of families with no money income. For definition of race and family, see text, p. 3. For definition of median, see p. xii. See *Historical Statistics, Colonial Times to 1970*, series G 1–8, G 16–23, G 190–192, and, for data in 1967 dollars, series G 197–199]

RACE OF FAMILY HEAD AND YEAR	Total families (1,000)	PERCENT DISTRIBUTION OF FAMILIES, BY INCOME LEVEL (in dollars)—										MEDIAN	
		Under 3,000	3,000–4,999	5,000–5,999	6,000–6,999	7,000–9,999	10,000–11,999	12,000–14,999	15,000–19,999	20,000–24,999	25,000 and over	Income (dol.)	Index (1947= 100)
CURRENT DOLLARS													
All families:													
1950	39,929	42.5	34.3	9.0	5.2	5.8			3.2			3,319	110
1955	42,889	28.6	30.0	12.7	9.5	12.9	3.0	1.8	.9		.5	4,418	146
1960 [1]	45,539	21.7	20.3	12.9	10.8	20.0	6.5	4.1	2.8		.9	5,620	185
1965 [1]	48,509	16.1	15.6	9.3	9.5	24.2	10.1	7.6	6.2		1.4	6,957	230
1970 [1]	52,227	8.9	10.4	5.8	6.0	19.9	12.7	14.1	17.7		4.6	9,867	326
1974	55,698	5.0	7.7	4.4	4.4	13.8	10.1	14.1	18.1	10.5	11.9	12,902	426
1975	56,245	4.5	7.5	4.1	4.2	12.8	8.9	13.4	18.8	11.6	14.1	13,719	453
1976	56,710	3.9	6.5	3.9	3.9	11.8	8.1	12.1	19.1	12.9	17.8	14,958	494
1977	57,215	3.6	5.7	3.5	3.7	10.9	7.2	11.3	17.8	13.9	22.4	16,009	528
White:													
1950	(NA)	39.4	35.7	9.6	5.5	6.1			3.6			3,445	109
1955	38,982	25.7	30.3	13.4	9.9	13.9	3.3	1.9	1.0		.5	4,613	146
1960 [1]	41,123	19.1	19.9	13.3	11.2	21.3	6.9	4.4	3.1		1.0	5,835	185
1965 [1]	43,497	13.9	14.5	9.3	9.8	25.5	10.7	8.1	6.7		1.6	7,251	230
1970 [1]	46,535	7.5	9.5	5.5	5.8	20.1	13.1	14.8	18.7		5.0	10,236	324
1974	49,440	4.0	6.6	4.2	4.2	13.5	10.3	14.5	18.9	10.9	12.8	13,408	425
1975	49,873	3.7	6.5	3.9	4.0	12.6	8.9	13.8	19.5	12.2	15.1	14,268	452
1976	50,083	3.1	5.3	3.6	3.7	11.5	8.2	12.3	19.8	13.6	19.1	15,537	492
1977	50,530	2.8	4.8	3.2	3.4	10.5	7.1	11.5	18.4	14.6	23.9	16,740	530
Black and other races:													
1950	(NA)	76.9	17.8	1.9	1.5	1.7			.3			1,869	116
1955	3,907	57.3	28.3	5.8	4.8	3.1	.4	.2	–		–	2,544	158
1960 [1]	4,333	46.5	24.4	8.7	6.7	8.7	3.1	1.3	.6		–	3,230	200
1965 [1]	4,782	35.3	25.6	9.5	6.8	13.7	4.4	3.2	1.3		.1	3,993	247
1970 [1]	5,413	20.2	17.0	9.0	7.4	18.2	8.9	8.4	9.4		1.5	6,516	404
1974	6,258	12.9	15.7	6.4	6.5	15.8	8.4	11.2	11.7	6.9	4.6	8,578	531
1975	6,372	11.4	14.9	6.0	5.8	15.4	9.3	10.8	13.3	6.8	6.4	9,321	578
1976	6,627	9.6	14.9	6.0	5.8	14.4	7.7	11.5	13.9	7.9	8.3	9,821	608
1977	6,685	9.6	13.2	6.3	6.1	14.2	7.9	10.0	13.0	9.0	10.8	10,142	628
CONSTANT (1977) DOLLARS													
All families:													
1950	39,929	14.3	10.3	7.3	7.1	23.8	19.7	10.5	4.8	1.3	.8	8,356	102
1955	42,889	11.2	8.9	4.8	5.2	20.0	15.3	12.5	13.3	4.5	4.3	9,999	122
1960 [1]	45,539	8.6	8.5	4.1	4.7	15.0	14.8	13.2	17.2	6.4	7.4	11,500	140
1965 [1]	48,509	6.1	7.1	3.9	4.0	12.7	9.8	15.0	21.0	8.6	11.8	13,362	162
1970 [1]	52,227	4.3	5.7	3.2	3.5	11.0	7.9	13.0	22.8	10.5	18.2	15,399	187
1974	55,698	3.7	5.2	3.3	3.6	10.8	7.6	12.3	18.5	13.7	21.4	15,855	193
1975	56,245	3.9	6.0	3.6	3.6	11.5	7.7	12.1	18.4	13.8	19.4	15,447	188
1976	56,710	3.6	5.8	3.5	3.7	11.1	7.5	11.4	18.7	13.9	20.8	15,923	194
1977	57,215	3.6	5.7	3.5	3.7	10.9	7.2	11.3	17.8	13.9	22.4	16,009	195
White:													
1950	(NA)	12.5	9.5	7.0	7.0	24.4	21.0	11.3	5.2	1.4	.9	8,672	101
1955	38,982	9.5	8.0	4.5	5.0	20.0	16.0	13.1	14.3	4.8	4.7	10,439	122
1960 [1]	41,123	7.0	7.7	3.9	4.4	14.8	15.4	13.7	18.2	6.9	8.0	11,940	139
1965 [1]	43,497	5.1	6.2	3.5	3.6	12.1	9.9	15.5	22.2	9.2	12.8	13,927	163
1970 [1]	46,535	3.6	4.9	2.9	3.2	10.4	7.8	13.2	23.7	10.9	19.3	15,975	187
1974	49,440	3.0	4.3	3.0	3.4	10.3	7.5	12.5	19.1	14.3	22.7	16,476	192
1975	49,873	3.1	5.2	3.3	3.4	11.1	7.6	12.2	18.9	14.5	20.7	16,065	188
1976	50,083	2.9	4.7	3.2	3.4	10.7	7.5	11.5	19.3	14.6	22.2	16,539	193
1977	50,530	2.8	4.8	3.2	3.4	10.5	7.1	11.5	18.4	14.6	23.9	16,740	195
Black and other races:													
1950	(NA)	33.8	19.3	10.9	9.0	17.1	3.6	2.7	1.9	.8	1.0	4,704	107
1955	3,907	27.4	16.8	7.8	7.6	20.5	9.2	5.7	3.9	.7	.3	5,757	131
1960 [1]	4,333	23.1	15.9	6.7	7.3	16.9	10.3	7.9	7.9	2.3	1.7	6,610	151
1965 [1]	4,782	14.6	15.3	7.5	7.8	18.0	9.1	10.3	10.8	3.5	3.0	7,670	175
1970 [1]	5,413	10.5	11.8	5.6	5.5	16.1	9.1	11.3	15.4	6.3	8.4	10,169	232
1974	6,258	9.4	12.2	6.2	5.4	14.6	8.4	10.5	13.8	8.9	10.7	10,541	241
1975	6,372	9.5	12.8	6.1	5.2	14.2	8.8	11.0	14.2	8.7	9.4	10,495	240
1976	6,627	8.8	13.9	5.9	5.5	14.1	7.6	10.8	14.5	8.9	10.0	10,455	239
1977	6,685	9.6	13.2	6.3	6.1	14.2	7.9	10.0	13.0	9.0	10.8	10,142	232

– Represents zero or rounds to zero.   NA Not available.   [1] Data for "all families" revised using population controls based on the 1970 Census of Population. These controls were not available by race.

Source: U.S. Bureau of the Census, *Current Population Reports*, series P-60, forthcoming report, and unpublished data.

No. 730. Families—Percent Distribution, by Money Income Level in Constant (1977) Dollars, by Regions: 1960 to 1977

[Families as of March of following year. For composition of regions, see fig. I, inside front cover. Beginning 1975, data not strictly comparable with earlier years due to revised procedures. See also headnote, table 729. For definition of median, see p. xii]

REGION AND INCOME LEVEL	1960	1965	1970	1975	1977	REGION AND INCOME LEVEL	1960	1965	1970	1975	1977
Northeast:						**South:**					
Under $3,000	4.5	3.5	2.8	2.7	2.4	Under $3,000	15.3	10.9	6.7	5.5	5.1
$3,000–$4,999	6.3	5.4	4.5	5.2	5.6	$3,000–$4,999	11.9	10.5	7.6	7.6	6.9
$5,000–$6,999	7.3	6.4	5.7	6.7	6.9	$5,000–$6,999	11.7	10.3	7.8	8.5	8.1
$7,000–$9,999	15.4	11.6	9.6	10.5	10.4	$7,000–$9,999	16.8	14.6	13.3	13.0	12.2
$10,000–$11,999	16.2	10.0	7.5	7.8	6.6	$10,000–$11,999	13.2	10.1	8.8	8.4	7.8
$12,000–$14,999	14.6	15.9	12.6	12.3	11.1	$12,000–$14,999	10.9	13.7	13.1	12.2	11.5
$15,000–$24,999	26.8	33.3	36.1	33.2	33.3	$15,000–$24,999	15.6	22.1	28.4	28.9	29.7
$25,000 and over	8.8	13.9	21.1	21.6	23.8	$25,000 and over	4.7	7.7	14.4	15.9	18.8
Median income dol	12,394	14,562	16,692	16,305	16,804	Median income dol	8,971	10,773	13,346	13,777	14,567
No. Central:						**West:**					
Under $3,000	7.5	4.4	3.6	3.0	3.3	Under $3,000	4.7	3.7	3.4	3.5	2.8
$3,000–$4,999	8.5	6.3	4.8	5.2	4.7	$3,000–$4,999	5.7	5.0	5.2	5.4	5.4
$5,000–$6,999	8.5	6.9	6.2	6.1	6.5	$5,000–$6,999	6.6	7.2	6.6	7.3	7.3
$7,000–$9,999	14.1	12.0	10.1	10.4	9.9	$7,000–$9,999	13.0	11.9	10.0	11.6	10.8
$10,000–$11,999	15.7	10.0	7.4	7.6	7.0	$10,000–$11,999	14.6	8.7	7.6	6.7	7.0
$12,000–$14,999	13.9	15.9	13.2	12.2	11.2	$12,000–$14,999	13.8	14.6	13.0	11.1	11.2
$15,000–$24,999	25.1	32.7	35.8	35.1	33.3	$15,000–$24,999	30.4	32.7	34.4	32.8	30.9
$25,000 and over	6.6	11.9	18.9	20.4	24.0	$25,000 and over	11.2	16.1	19.8	21.6	24.7
Median income dol	11,841	14,025	16,117	16,372	16,845	Median income dol	13,393	14,794	16,032	16,119	16,512

Source: U.S. Bureau of the Census, *Current Population Reports*, series P-60, forthcoming report.

No. 731. Families—Percent Distribution by Money Income Level, by Race, Region, and Metro.—Nonmetro. Residence: 1977

[Families and residence as of March 1978. See headnote, table 729. For definitions, see text, p. 3. See *Historical Statistics, Colonial Times to 1970*, series G 1–8, for U.S. data for total, White, and Black and other races]

RACE, REGION, AND RESIDENCE	Number of families (1,000)	Under 3,000	3,000–4,999	5,000–6,999	7,000–8,999	9,000–11,999	12,000–14,999	15,000–19,999	20,000–24,999	25,000 and over	Median income [1] (dol.)
All families [2]	57,215	3.6	5.7	7.2	7.4	10.7	11.3	17.8	13.9	22.4	16,009
White	50,530	2.8	4.8	6.6	7.1	10.3	11.5	18.4	14.6	23.8	16,740
Black	5,806	10.0	14.0	13.0	10.2	13.0	9.9	12.8	8.2	9.0	9,563
REGION											
White:											
Northeast	11,797	2.1	4.8	6.3	6.7	9.9	11.2	18.7	15.4	24.9	17,302
North Central	14,045	2.9	4.0	6.0	6.7	10.0	11.3	19.2	15.0	25.1	17,231
South	15,521	3.4	5.4	7.2	7.7	11.4	11.8	18.2	13.5	21.3	15,721
West	9,167	2.4	4.9	6.8	6.8	10.4	11.4	17.1	14.7	25.4	16,985
Black:											
Northeast	1,035	4.0	15.0	13.8	12.3	9.5	10.3	13.9	10.2	11.0	10,285
North Central	1,152	8.4	13.7	12.5	7.6	12.4	10.7	11.9	10.9	12.0	10,690
South	3,067	13.2	14.4	12.5	10.1	14.0	9.9	12.7	6.9	6.2	8,962
West	552	6.5	10.5	15.6	12.7	15.0	7.2	12.7	5.6	14.3	9,917
RESIDENCE											
White:											
In metro. areas	32,824	2.1	3.9	5.8	6.3	9.4	10.5	18.1	15.6	28.3	18,211
In central cities	11,817	2.9	5.6	7.4	7.5	10.4	11.3	17.4	14.5	23.0	16,286
Outside central cities	21,007	1.7	3.0	5.0	5.5	8.9	10.0	18.5	16.2	31.2	19,210
Outside metro. areas	17,706	4.0	6.4	8.0	8.5	12.4	13.2	18.9	12.7	15.9	14,403
Black:											
In metro. areas	4,358	8.5	13.0	12.1	9.7	12.6	9.9	14.0	9.2	11.0	10,431
In central cities	3,188	8.5	14.9	13.4	10.5	12.5	10.0	12.5	8.2	9.6	9,610
Outside central cities	1,170	8.8	7.8	8.8	7.4	13.0	9.7	17.8	11.9	14.7	13,023
Outside metro. areas	1,448	14.2	17.0	15.8	11.8	14.0	9.8	9.1	5.2	3.0	7,512

[1] For definition of median, see p. xii.   [2] Includes other races not shown separately.

Source: U.S. Bureau of the Census, *Current Population Reports*, series P-60, forthcoming report.

No. 732. AGGREGATE MONEY INCOME—TOTAL AND PER CAPITA, IN COUNTIES WITHIN
50 MILES OF COASTAL SHORELINES: 1959 TO 1975

[1959 and 1969 based on census data; 1975 based on money income estimates developed for Federal revenue-sharing allocations; for details, see *Current Population Reports*, series P-25, No. 649. Excludes Alaska and Hawaii. Great Lakes includes St. Lawrence River region. Covers 611 counties and independent cities which are entirely or substantially within 50 miles of the U.S. coastal shorelines listed. For population and land area of those regions, see table 7]

REGION	AGGREGATE INCOME						PER CAPITA INCOME (dol.)			AGGREGATE INCOME PER SQUARE MILE ($1,000)		
	Total (bil. dol.)			Percent of U.S.								
	1959	1969	1975	1959	1969	1975	1959	1969	1975	1959	1969	1975
U.S. total_____	330.0	630.3	1,025.6	100.0	100.0	100.0	1,849	3,117	4,814	111	213	346
Coastal regions_	191.9	372.9	587.1	58.1	59.2	57.2	2,073	3,438	5,183	416	809	1,256
Atlantic_____	87.8	169.2	261.7	26.6	26.8	25.5	2,112	3,512	5,262	727	1,400	2,143
Pacific_____	37.3	78.6	126.6	11.3	12.5	12.3	2,221	3,657	5,521	317	667	1,076
Great Lakes_____	54.6	99.6	149.0	16.5	15.8	14.5	2,069	3,398	5,028	426	776	1,114
Gulf of Mexico_____	12.1	25.5	49.8	3.7	4.0	4.9	1,556	2,691	4,532	129	272	530
Balance of U.S__	138.1	257.4	438.4	41.8	40.8	42.8	1,608	2,745	4,396	55	103	176

Source: U.S. Bureau of the Census, compiled from unpublished data.

No. 733. MONEY INCOME OF FAMILIES—FAMILY CHARACTERISTICS, BY INCOME LEVEL:
1970 TO 1977

[See headnote, table 729. Minus sign denotes loss. For definition of mean and median, see p. xii]

YEAR AND CHARACTERISTIC	FAMILY INCOME LEVEL OF—										
	Under $2,000	$2,000-$2,999	$3,000-$3,999	$4,000-$4,999	$5,000-$5,999	$6,000-$6,999	$7,000-$9,999	$10,000-$14,999	$15,000-$24,999	$25,000-$49,999	$50,000 and over
1970											
Mean family income____	$937	$2,496	$3,480	$4,487	$5,455	$6,463	$8,470	$12,148	$18,431	$31,182	$66,580
Per capita family income_	$314	$856	$1,142	$1,417	$1,629	$1,890	$2,333	$3,217	$4,641	$7,838	$17,088
Average number of—											
Persons per family____	2.98	2.92	3.05	3.17	3.35	3.42	3.63	3.78	3.97	3.98	3.90
Children per family [1]_	1.17	1.01	1.09	1.13	1.27	1.30	1.45	1.48	1.36	1.22	1.30
Earners per family____	.71	.72	.95	1.14	1.34	1.46	1.61	1.90	2.33	2.33	1.97
Ratio of nonearners to earners [2]_____	3.21	3.03	2.21	1.77	1.51	1.34	1.25	.99	.71	.71	.98
Median school years completed by head [3]___	8.8	8.6	8.9	9.2	10.7	11.3	12.1	12.4	12.8	15.8	16.2
1975 [4]											
Mean family income____	$354	$2,526	$3,479	$4,481	$5,480	$6,459	$8,443	$12,404	$19,147	$31,752	$70,227
Per capita family income_	$113	$860	$1,222	$1,502	$1,871	$2,103	$2,664	$3,681	$5,360	$8,295	$18,793
Average number of—											
Persons per family____	3.14	2.94	2.85	2.98	2.93	3.07	3.17	3.37	3.57	3.83	3.74
Children per family [1]_	1.50	1.20	1.04	1.07	.96	1.06	1.09	1.20	1.20	1.09	1.09
Earners per family [5]__	.73	.62	.65	.77	.85	1.02	1.24	1.58	1.98	2.42	1.99
Ratio of nonearners to earners [6]_____	3.34	3.71	3.36	2.89	2.43	2.01	1.55	1.13	.81	.58	.88
Median school years completed by head [3]___	11.0	9.0	9.0	9.5	10.0	10.5	12.0	12.4	12.7	14.4	16.6
1977 [4]											
Mean family income____	−$153	$2,484	$3,492	$4,490	$5,458	$6,450	$8,442	$12,436	$19,480	$32,220	$69,491
Per capita family income_	−$51	$850	$1,269	$1,531	$1,855	$2,197	$2,790	$3,847	$5,653	$8,687	$18,286
Average number of—											
Persons per family____	3.01	2.92	2.75	2.93	2.94	2.94	3.03	3.23	3.45	3.71	3.80
Children per family [1]_	1.39	1.27	1.01	1.13	1.01	.97	.99	1.10	1.17	1.06	1.00
Earners per family [5]__	.75	.62	.53	.67	.79	.91	1.13	1.50	1.86	2.39	2.31
Ratio of nonearners to earners [6]_____	3.03	3.72	4.17	3.38	2.74	2.22	1.67	1.16	.85	.55	.64
Median school years completed by head [3]___	12.0	9.2	9.1	9.5	10.2	10.6	11.7	12.3	12.6	13.2	16.5

[1] Related children.   [2] The number of all persons without earnings in families divided by the number of persons 14 years old and over with earnings in families.   [3] Family head, 25 years old and over; for definition of median, see p. xii.   [4] Not strictly comparable with 1970 due to revised procedures.   [5] Civilian family members only.   [6] Civilian persons without earnings in families divided by total civilian persons 14 years old and over with earnings in families.

Source: U.S. Bureau of the Census, *Current Population Reports*, series P-60, forthcoming report.

No. 734. Money Income of Families—Percent of Aggregate Income Received by Each Fifth and Highest 5 Percent: 1950 to 1977

[See headnote, table 729, and *Historical Statistics, Colonial Times to 1970*, series G 85–102]

RACE AND INCOME RANK	1950	1955	1960	1965	1970	1973	1974 [1]	1975 [1]	1976 [1]	1977 [1]
All families	100.0	100.0	100.0	100.0	100.0	100.0	100.0	100.0	100.0	100.0
Lowest fifth	4.5	4.8	4.8	5.2	5.4	5.5	5.5	5.4	5.4	5.2
Second fifth	12.0	12.3	12.2	12.2	12.2	11.9	12.0	11.8	11.8	11.6
Middle fifth	17.4	17.8	17.8	17.8	17.6	17.5	17.5	17.6	17.6	17.5
Fourth fifth	23.4	23.7	24.0	23.9	23.8	24.0	24.0	24.1	24.1	24.2
Highest fifth	42.7	41.3	41.3	40.9	40.9	41.1	41.0	41.1	41.1	41.5
Highest 5 percent	17.3	16.4	15.9	15.5	15.6	15.5	15.5	15.5	15.6	15.7
White	100.0	100.0	100.0	100.0	100.0	100.0	100.0	100.0	100.0	100.0
Lowest fifth	4.8	5.2	5.2	5.6	5.8	5.8	5.8	5.7	5.8	5.6
Second fifth	12.4	12.7	12.7	12.6	12.5	12.3	12.3	12.1	12.1	12.0
Middle fifth	17.4	17.8	17.8	17.8	17.7	17.6	17.6	17.6	17.7	17.6
Fourth fifth	23.2	23.5	23.7	23.7	23.6	23.8	23.8	23.9	23.9	23.9
Highest fifth	42.2	40.8	40.7	40.3	40.5	40.5	40.6	40.7	40.6	40.9
Highest 5 percent	17.2	16.2	15.7	15.4	15.5	15.3	15.3	15.4	15.4	15.5
Black and other races	100.0	100.0	100.0	100.0	100.0	100.0	100.0	100.0	100.0	100.0
Lowest fifth	3.5	4.0	3.7	4.7	4.5	4.7	4.7	4.7	4.6	4.4
Second fifth	10.3	10.4	9.7	10.8	10.6	10.1	10.0	10.1	9.9	9.6
Middle fifth	17.6	17.8	16.5	16.6	16.8	16.3	16.4	16.7	16.5	15.9
Fourth fifth	25.2	25.6	25.2	24.7	24.8	24.8	25.0	25.1	25.3	25.2
Highest fifth	43.4	42.2	44.9	43.2	43.4	44.1	43.9	43.3	43.7	44.9
Highest 5 percent	16.5	14.3	16.2	15.1	15.4	16.0	15.9	15.4	15.6	16.1

[1] Beginning 1974, not strictly comparable with earlier years due to revised procedures.

No. 735. Money Income of Families—Income at Selected Positions, by Each Fifth and Highest 5 Percent, in Current and Constant (1977) Dollars: 1950 to 1977

[See headnote, table 729. See *Historical Statistics, Colonial Times to 1970*, series G 124–128, for data in current dollars]

INCOME RANK	1950	1955	1960	1965	1970	1973	1974 [1]	1975 [1]	1976 [1]	1977 [1]
CURRENT DOLLARS										
Median, all families	$3,319	$4,418	$5,620	$6,957	$9,867	$12,051	$12,902	$13,719	$14,958	$16,009
Upper limit of each fifth:										
Lowest fifth	1,661	2,221	2,784	3,500	5,100	6,081	6,628	6,914	7,441	7,903
Second fifth	2,856	3,780	4,800	5,863	8,320	10,034	10,894	11,465	12,400	13,273
Middle fifth	3,801	5,082	6,364	7,910	11,299	14,000	15,015	16,000	17,300	18,800
Fourth fifth	5,283	6,883	8,800	10,800	15,531	19,253	20,690	22,037	23,923	26,000
Highest 5 percent	8,615	10,605	13,536	16,695	24,250	30,015	32,199	34,144	37,047	40,493
CONSTANT (1977) DOLLARS										
Median, all families	$8,355	$9,998	$11,500	$13,362	$15,399	$16,433	$15,855	$15,447	$15,923	$16,009
Upper limit of each fifth:										
Lowest fifth	4,181	5,026	5,697	6,722	7,959	8,292	8,145	7,785	7,921	7,903
Second fifth	7,190	8,554	9,822	11,261	12,984	13,683	13,387	12,909	13,200	13,273
Middle fifth	9,568	11,501	13,022	15,192	17,633	19,091	18,451	18,015	18,416	18,800
Fourth fifth	13,299	15,577	18,007	20,743	24,238	26,254	25,425	24,812	25,466	26,000
Highest 5 percent	21,686	24,000	27,698	32,065	37,845	40,930	39,567	38,444	39,437	40,493

[1] Beginning 1974, not strictly comparable with earlier years due to revised procedures.

Source of tables 734 and 735: U.S. Bureau of the Census, *Current Population Reports*, series P–60, Nos. 114 and 116.

No. 736. Median Money Income of Families and Individuals: 1950 to 1977

[In dollars. See headnote, table 729. Beginning 1974, not strictly comparable with earlier years due to revised procedures. For definition of median, see p. xii. See also *Historical Statistics, Colonial Times to 1970*, series G 179–188]

FAMILY STATUS	1950	1955	1960	1965	1970	1974	1975	1976	1977
Families with male head	3,435	4,592	5,857	7,310	10,480	13,863	14,816	16,095	17,517
Married, wife present	3,446	4,599	5,873	7,330	10,516	13,923	14,867	16,203	17,616
Wife in paid labor force	(NA)	5,082	5,622	6,900	12,276	16,221	17,237	18,731	20,268
Wife not in paid labor force	(NA)	4,326	5,520	6,706	9,304	12,231	12,759	13,931	15,063
Other marital status	3,115	4,190	4,860	6,515	9,012	11,658	12,995	12,860	14,518
Families with female head	1,922	2,471	2,968	3,535	5,093	6,488	6,844	7,211	7,765
Unrelated individuals: Male	1,539	1,831	2,480	3,194	4,540	6,130	6,612	7,217	7,831
Female	846	1,054	1,377	1,767	2,483	3,656	3,978	4,318	4,840

NA Not available.

Source: U.S. Bureau of the Census, *Current Population Reports*, series P–60, No. 116, and earlier issues.

No. 737. Median Family Money Income and Per Capita Money Income—States: 1959 to 1975

[For 1959 and 1969 data, population and families as of April 1960 and April 1970, respectively. For 1975 data, families as of spring 1976 for median family income, population as of July 1976 for per capita income. Ranks for the 50 States based on descending order from highest to lowest income. For definition of median, see p. xii. See *Historical Statistics, Colonial Times to 1970*, series G 205–256, for median family income]

STATE RANKED BY 1975 MEDIAN INCOME	MEDIAN FAMILY INCOME						STATE RANKED BY 1975 PER CAPITA INCOME	PER CAPITA INCOME					
	1959 [1]		1969 [1]		1975 [2]			1959 [1]		1969 [1]		1975 [3]	
	Income	Rank	Income	Rank	Income	Rank		Income	Rank	Income	Rank	Income	Rank
U.S.	$5,660	(X)	$9,586	(X)	$14,094	(X)	U.S.	$1,850	(X)	$3,119	(X)	$4,838	(X)
HIGHEST FIFTH							**HIGHEST FIFTH**						
Alaska	7,305	1	12,441	1	22,432	1	Alaska	2,259	5	3,725	2	7,969	1
Hawaii	6,366	8	11,552	3	17,770	2	Md	2,003	11	3,512	7	5,626	2
Md	6,309	9	11,057	5	17,556	3	N.J	2,260	4	3,674	3	5,600	3
N.J.	6,786	3	11,403	4	16,432	4	Conn	2,352	2	3,885	1	5,571	4
Conn	6,887	2	11,808	2	16,244	5	Nev	2,356	1	3,554	6	5,493	5
Ill	6,566	6	10,957	7	16,062	6	Calif	2,308	3	3,614	4	5,464	6
Del	6,197	13	10,209	14	15,732	7	Wash	2,033	10	3,357	12	5,369	7
Mass	6,272	10	10,833	8	15,531	8	Ill	2,182	7	3,495	8	5,334	8
Mich	6,256	11	11,029	6	15,385	9	Hawaii	1,863	17	3,373	10	5,259	9
N.Y	6,371	7	10,609	11	15,288	10	Colo	1,889	15	3,106	17	5,193	10
FOURTH FIFTH							**FOURTH FIFTH**						
Calif	6,726	5	10,729	9	15,069	11	N.Y	2,236	6	3,608	5	5,166	11
Wis	5,926	15	10,065	15	15,064	12	Wyo	1,888	16	2,895	28	5,094	12
Colo	5,780	20	9,552	21	14,992	13	Del	2,086	8	3,265	13	5,013	13
Wash	6,225	12	10,404	12	14,962	14	Mass	2,050	9	3,408	9	4,964	14
Nev	6,736	4	10,687	10	14,961	15	Oreg	1,949	13	3,148	15	4,963	15
Ohio	6,171	14	10,309	13	14,822	16	Va	1,598	36	2,996	23	4,954	16
Wyo	5,877	18	8,944	27	14,784	17	Fla	1,728	27	3,058	20	4,908	17
Minn	5,573	24	9,928	17	14,740	18	Kans	1,775	23	2,929	27	4,905	18
Va	4,964	32	9,044	25	14,579	19	Mich	1,940	14	3,357	11	4,884	19
R.I	5,589	23	9,733	18	14,530	20	Minn	1,734	26	3,038	21	4,825	20
THIRD FIFTH							**THIRD FIFTH**						
Iowa	5,069	31	9,016	26	14,464	21	Pa	1,855	18	3,066	19	4,786	21
Ind	5,798	19	9,966	16	14,411	22	Ohio	1,957	12	3,199	14	4,772	22
Utah	5,899	16	9,320	23	14,329	23	R.I	1,818	21	3,121	16	4,769	23
N.H	5,636	22	9,682	19	14,258	24	Wis	1,844	19	3,032	22	4,722	4 24
Nebr	4,862	36	8,562	31	14,209	25	Nebr	1,629	31	2,797	30	4,722	4 24
Pa	5,719	21	9,554	20	14,153	26	Ind	1,832	20	3,070	18	4,673	26
Oreg	5,892	17	9,487	22	13,854	27	Ariz	1,764	24	2,937	26	4,670	27
N. Dak	4,530	40	7,836	39	13,626	28	Tex	1,626	32	2,792	31	4,641	28
Mont	5,403	26	8,509	32	13,608	29	Iowa	1,648	30	2,884	29	4,640	29
Ariz	5,568	25	9,185	24	13,569	30	Mo	1,751	25	2,952	25	4,571	30
SECOND FIFTH							**SECOND FIFTH**						
Kans	5,295	28	8,690	30	13,412	31	N. Dak	1,357	42	2,469	40	4,487	31
Mo	5,127	30	8,908	29	13,011	32	Okla	1,613	33	2,694	35	4,469	32
Idaho	5,259	29	8,380	34	12,844	33	Mont	1,679	29	2,696	34	4,463	33
Tex	4,884	34	8,486	33	12,672	34	N.H	1,794	22	2,985	24	4,460	34
La	4,272	41	7,527	43	12,576	35	Idaho	1,608	34	2,644	36	4,417	35
Ga	4,208	43	8,165	37	12,441	36	Utah	1,695	28	2,697	33	4,310	36
Vt	4,890	33	8,928	28	12,415	37	Ga	1,359	41	2,640	37	4,227	37
Fla	4,722	37	8,261	35	12,205	38	S. Dak	1,327	43	2,387	44	4,131	38
S.C	3,821	48	7,620	42	12,188	39	Vt	1,516	37	2,772	32	4,051	39
Okla	4,620	38	7,720	41	12,172	40	N.C	1,252	46	2,474	39	4,044	40
LOWEST FIFTH							**LOWEST FIFTH**						
S. Dak	4,251	42	7,490	44	12,051	41	N. Mex	1,599	35	2,437	42	4,019	41
W. Va	4,572	39	7,414	47	12,007	42	Tenn	1,318	45	2,464	41	4,015	42
Maine	4,873	35	8,205	36	11,839	43	W. Va	1,378	44	2,333	45	4,008	43
N.C	3,956	45	7,770	40	11,834	44	Ky	1,322	44	2,425	43	4,002	44
N. Mex	5,371	27	7,345	38	11,798	45	La	1,369	40	2,330	46	3,922	45
Ala	3,937	47	7,263	48	11,785	46	Ala	1,246	47	2,317	47	3,894	46
Tenn	3,949	46	7,446	45	11,341	47	Maine	1,514	38	2,548	38	3,879	47
Ky	4,051	44	7,439	46	11,019	48	S.C	1,142	48	2,303	48	3,819	48
Ark	3,184	49	6,271	49	10,106	49	Ark	1,125	49	2,142	49	3,648	49
Miss	2,884	50	6,068	50	9,999	50	Miss	967	50	1,925	50	3,323	50

X Not applicable. [1] From the 1960 and 1970 censuses of population. Based on sample; see Appendix III. [2] From the 1976 Survey of Income and Education (SIE), based on a sample of 151,000 households; subject to sampling variability; for details, see source. [3] Based on money income estimates developed for Federal revenue-sharing allocations; for details, see source. [4] Wisconsin and Nebraska share the same rank of 24. To make lowest rank equal to number of States shown, number 25 has been omitted.

Source: U.S. Bureau of the Census, *Census of Population: 1970*, vol. I; *Current Population Reports*, series P-60, Nos. 110–113; and unpublished data.

No. 738. Median Family Money Income, by Earners and Race: 1967 to 1977

[Beginning 1975, data not strictly comparable with earlier years due to revised procedures. See headnote, table 729. For definition of median, see p. xii]

YEAR AND NUMBER OF EARNERS	ALL FAMILIES, MEDIAN FAMILY INCOME (dollars)			FAMILIES WITH HEAD FULL-TIME WORKER [2]						BLACK–WHITE INCOME RATIO	
				Percent of all families			Median family income (dollars)			All families	Families with head full-time worker [2]
	All races [1]	White	Black	All races [1]	White	Black	All races [1]	White	Black		
All families, 1967___	7,933	8,234	4,875	67.6	68.8	55.2	9,263	9,495	6,331	.59	.67
No earners_____	2,447	2,534	1,991	.3	.3	.3	(B)	(B)	(B)	.79	(X)
1 earner_____	6,980	7,247	3,693	70.3	71.6	53.4	7,854	8,031	4,598	.51	.57
2 earners_____	8,931	9,214	6,275	75.2	76.1	67.3	9,693	9,931	7,043	.68	.71
3 earners_____	11,221	11,590	6,957	79.7	81.5	64.5	11,741	11,987	8,036	.60	.67
4 earners or more_	13,170	13,673	7,680	79.6	82.6	59.2	13,700	14,106	9,418	.56	.67
All families, 1970___	9,867	10,236	6,279	64.1	65.5	51.4	13,790	12,016	8,880	.61	.74
No earners_____	3,289	3,489	2,235	.1	.1	–	(B)	(B)	(B)	.64	(X)
1 earner_____	8,352	8,713	4,844	65.2	67.0	46.7	9,750	9,960	6,533	.56	.66
2 earners_____	11,190	11,450	8,430	72.6	73.4	66.2	12,263	12,507	9,776	.74	.78
3 earners_____	14,438	14,795	10,000	78.1	79.4	64.3	15,460	15,828	11,839	.68	.75
4 earners or more_	16,688	17,311	11,112	80.9	83.0	64.6	17,689	18,066	12,806	.64	.71
All families, 1975 [3]__	13,772	14,320	8,723	59.3	60.9	45.2	17,161	17,485	13,441	.61	.77
No earners_____	5,232	5,645	3,511	–	–	–	(B)	(B)	(B)	.62	(X)
1 earner_____	11,568	12,198	7,086	59.4	61.3	42.3	14,156	14,531	9,760	.58	.67
2 earners_____	16,058	16,360	12,914	71.3	72.1	64.1	17,606	17,842	14,902	.79	.84
3 earners_____	20,383	20,748	15,808	76.5	77.8	65.0	21,540	21,789	18,095	.75	.72
4 earners or more_	23,785	24,203	18,129	80.2	81.6	67.6	25,054	25,229	18,933	.75	.73
All families, 1977 [3]__	16,060	16,782	9,485	60.4	61.9	46.9	20,079	20,420	14,903	.57	.73
No earners_____	6,019	6,608	3,669	–	–	–	(B)	(B)	(B)	.56	(X)
1 earner_____	13,148	14,077	7,761	59.5	61.0	47.6	15,949	16,548	10,146	.55	.61
2 earners_____	18,704	19,019	14,984	73.5	74.3	65.7	20,368	20,567	17,415	.79	.85
3 earners_____	23,511	24,058	18,222	76.5	77.7	62.6	25,089	25,308	19,679	.76	.78
4 earners or more_	27,236	27,689	20,629	81.7	83.5	67.1	28,087	28,439	23,263	.75	.82

– Represents zero or rounds to zero. B Base less than 75,000. X Not applicable.
[1] Includes races not shown separately. [2] Employed year-round. [3] Civilian members 14 years old and over.
Source: U.S. Bureau of the Census, *Current Population Reports*, series P–60, No. 116, and earlier issues.

No. 739. Families—Percent Distribution by Money Income Level, by Race and Educational Attainment of Head: 1977

[Family heads, 25 years old and over. See headnote, table 729. For definition of median, see p. xii]

RACE AND EDUCATIONAL ATTAINMENT OF HEAD	Number of families (1,000)	PERCENT DISTRIBUTION—FAMILIES, BY INCOME LEVEL								Median income
		Under $3,000	$3,000–$4,999	$5,000–$6,999	$7,000–$9,999	$10,000–$11,999	$12,000–$14,999	$15,000–$24,999	$25,000 and over	
White families___	47,289	2.5	4.6	6.3	10.0	6.7	11.1	33.4	25.3	$17,285
Elementary school:										
Less than 8 years____	4,145	6.3	14.8	15.3	18.4	9.2	10.7	18.9	6.5	9,179
8 years_____	4,409	3.9	10.4	13.5	17.2	9.0	11.7	23.7	10.6	11,040
High school: 1–3 years__	6,460	3.0	6.1	9.2	14.2	8.9	13.5	31.2	13.8	13,904
4 years_____	16,347	2.1	3.1	4.8	9.1	7.1	12.3	38.1	23.4	17,592
College: 1–3 years_____	6,936	1.8	1.9	3.6	7.1	5.4	11.5	39.9	28.9	19,480
4 years or more_____	8,992	.8	.8	1.6	3.4	3.2	7.0	33.0	50.3	25,071
Black families___	5,238	7.9	13.3	12.9	15.0	8.6	10.2	22.1	9.9	10,174
Elementary school:										
Less than 8 years____	1,105	11.4	23.1	17.1	17.3	6.8	7.8	12.1	4.5	6,780
8 years_____	398	14.8	12.5	14.5	16.3	14.0	5.5	17.3	5.3	8,617
High school: 1–3 years__	1,205	10.3	14.6	15.4	16.5	9.4	8.5	18.6	6.7	8,834
4 years_____	1,570	5.5	9.6	11.5	14.6	8.2	13.6	27.6	9.4	12,109
College: 1–3 years_____	641	3.4	9.2	7.8	14.7	10.0	11.1	27.5	16.4	13,073
4 years or more_____	318	–	1.6	4.1	2.5	4.7	12.2	38.9	36.1	21,107

– Represents zero or rounds to zero.
Source: U.S. Bureau of the Census, *Current Population Reports*, series P–60, forthcoming report.

No. 740. MONEY INCOME OF FAMILIES—PERCENT OF FAMILIES BY TYPE OF INCOME RECEIVED, MEAN INCOME, AND PERCENT OF AGGREGATE INCOME, BY INCOME LEVEL: 1976

[Families as of **March 1977**. Based on Current Population Survey; see headnote, table 729. Minus sign (−) denotes loss. For limitations of these data, see source]

ITEM	FAMILIES WITH INCOME (in dollars) LEVEL OF—								
	Under 3,000	3,000–4,999	5,000–6,999	7,000–9,999	10,000–11,999	12,000–14,999	15,000–19,999	20,000–24,999	25,000 and over
Families with income, total_____1,000__	2,193	3,650	4,436	6,688	4,583	6,898	10,824	7,326	10,111
Percent of families by type of income received—									
Earnings:									
Wage or salary income_____	1.9	3.3	5.6	10.9	8.4	13.1	21.6	14.9	20.2
Self-employment income:									
Nonfarm_____	3.5	3.2	5.6	9.3	7.4	11.0	19.0	12.7	28.2
Farm_____	8.7	6.2	7.0	11.0	7.8	11.5	16.6	9.9	21.2
Income other than earnings:									
Social security and railroad retirement__	3.8	13.4	15.8	18.3	9.4	11.0	12.1	6.9	9.4
Veterans, unemployment, and workmen's compensation_____	1.9	4.9	8.2	13.7	9.1	14.4	20.8	13.0	14.0
Supplemental security income_____	10.1	26.3	19.6	16.4	5.4	5.5	7.2	5.4	4.2
Public assistance or welfare_____	20.3	31.4	18.6	12.1	5.6	4.5	4.1	2.2	1.3
Dividends, interest, rent, etc. [1]_____	1.3	2.4	4.9	9.0	6.7	11.2	21.5	16.5	26.5
Retirement income [2]_____	.7	3.0	10.0	19.2	9.9	12.8	16.7	10.9	16.7
Other income [3]_____	6.0	7.4	9.3	16.4	8.8	12.0	16.0	9.0	15.1
MEAN INCOME RECEIVED, BY TYPE (dollars)									
All families with income_____	1,368	3,998	5,955	8,448	10,921	13,410	17,300	22,223	35,956
Earnings:									
Wage or salary income_____	1,561	2,520	4,230	6,517	8,954	11,577	15,299	19,852	29,573
Self-employment income:									
Nonfarm_____	−2,537	1,488	2,310	3,735	4,487	5,331	5,837	7,748	18,372
Farm_____	−2,760	608	1,848	2,193	3,139	3,204	3,855	5,694	11,064
Income other than earnings:									
Social security and railroad retirement____	1,924	3,007	3,856	4,185	3,948	3,752	3,687	3,480	3,534
Veterans, unemployment, and workmen's compensation_____	979	1,425	1,477	1,775	1,884	1,705	1,650	1,512	1,701
Supplemental security income_____	1,169	1,355	1,769	1,592	1,458	1,484	1,468	1,443	(B)
Public assistance or welfare_____	1,582	2,719	2,941	2,285	1,884	1,960	1,620	2,032	(B)
Dividends, interest, rent, etc.[1]_____	447	451	661	813	873	931	861	925	2,842
Retirement income [2]_____	(B)	1,231	1,798	2,849	3,772	4,426	4,981	6,022	6,899
Other income [3]_____	876	1,406	1,529	1,738	2,085	1,940	1,961	2,283	3,086
PERCENT OF AGGREGATE INCOME									
All families with income_____	100.0	100.0	100.0	100.0	100.0	100.0	100.0	100.0	100.0
Earnings:									
Wage or salary income_____	48.7	27.3	42.9	59.2	71.1	77.9	83.7	86.0	77.8
Self-employment income:									
Nonfarm_____	−21.1	2.3	3.5	4.4	4.7	4.5	4.2	4.3	10.1
Farm_____	−21.1	.7	1.3	1.1	1.3	1.1	.9	.9	1.7
Income other than earnings:									
Social security and railroad retirement____	30.6	35.0	29.1	17.3	9.4	5.6	3.0	1.9	1.1
Veterans, unemployment, and workmen's compensation_____	6.1	4.8	4.6	4.3	3.4	2.7	1.8	1.2	.7
Supplemental security income _____	6.1	3.8	2.1	.7	.2	.1	.1	.1	−
Public assistance or welfare_____	36.0	19.7	7.0	1.6	.7	.3	.1	.1	−
Dividends, interest, rent, etc. [1]_____	5.9	2.3	3.7	3.9	3.6	3.4	3.0	2.8	6.3
Retirement income [2]_____	1.7	1.4	3.8	5.4	4.1	3.4	2.5	2.2	1.8
Other income [3]_____	6.9	2.8	2.1	2.0	1.4	1.0	.7	.5	.5

− Represents zero or rounds to zero.　　B　Base too small for statistical reliability.
[1] Includes income from estates, trusts, and net royalties.
[2] Includes private and government employee pensions and annuities.
[3] Includes alimony, child support, regular contributions from outside the household, etc.

Source: U.S. Bureau of the Census, *Current Population Reports*, series P-60, No. 114.

No. 741. Money Income of Families—Aggregate, Mean, and Per Capita, by Family Characteristics: 1977

[Families as of **March 1978**. Based on Current Population Survey; see headnote, table 729]

CHARACTERISTIC	ALL RACES [1]				WHITE				BLACK			
	All families (1,000)	Aggregate income (bil. dol.)	Mean income [2] (dol.)	Per capita income (dol.)	All families (1,000)	Aggregate income (bil. dol.)	Mean income [2] (dol.)	Per capita income (dol.)	All families (1,000)	Aggregate income (bil. dol.)	Mean income [2] (dol.)	Per capita income (dol.)
Total families_____	57,215	1,045.0	18,264	5,478	50,530	959.9	18,997	5,797	5,806	69.5	11,962	3,171
Age of head:												
14 to 24 years_____	3,851	42.2	10,970	4,068	3,241	38.0	11,727	4,447	569	3.8	6,673	2,201
25 to 34 years_____	13,432	223.8	16,661	4,864	11,668	202.0	17,311	5,080	1,501	17.7	11,815	3,288
35 to 44 years_____	11,528	237.8	20,631	4,883	10,033	215.4	21,466	5,139	1,264	17.7	14,021	3,065
45 to 54 years_____	10,888	251.0	23,049	6,227	9,720	232.6	23,927	6,554	1,012	15.2	14,983	3,662
55 to 64 years_____	9,304	187.7	20,170	7,202	8,404	175.8	20,918	7,701	783	9.4	11,976	3,354
65 years and over_____	8,212	102.5	12,482	5,312	7,463	96.2	12,889	5,644	679	5.7	8,363	2,739
Marital status of head:												
Male head, total_____	48,979	964.2	19,686	5,831	44,701	896.1	20,047	6,021	3,529	53.6	15,190	3,935
Married, wife present_____	47,385	938.1	19,798	5,825	43,423	873.9	20,125	6,008	3,260	50.4	15,449	3,926
Married, wife absent_____	273	4.3	15,585	5,359	192	3.4	17,441	6,032	75	.9	11,733	3,920
Separated_____	179	2.8	15,851	5,779	114	2.2	18,984	6,952	60	.7	(B)	(B)
Widowed_____	378	6.5	17,302	5,774	306	5.9	19,197	6,481	59	.6	(B)	(B)
Divorced_____	423	7.3	17,242	6,571	361	6.3	17,487	6,803	54	.8	(B)	(B)
Single_____	520	8.0	15,350	6,322	419	6.7	16,037	6,826	81	1.0	12,103	4,476
Female head, total____	8,236	80.8	9,811	3,181	5,828	63.8	10,947	3,809	2,277	15.8	6,959	1,913
Married, husband absent_____	1,781	12.9	7,255	2,072	1,088	8.5	7,818	2,445	667	4.2	6,294	1,570
Separated_____	1,485	10.7	7,182	2,033	870	6.7	7,732	2,419	599	3.8	6,281	1,556
Widowed_____	2,381	28.7	12,052	4,071	1,863	24.4	13,101	4,736	477	3.9	8,071	2,160
Divorced_____	2,787	28.7	10,311	3,382	2,252	24.1	10,719	3,646	486	4.2	8,668	2,420
Single_____	1,286	10.4	8,115	2,885	626	6.8	10,792	4,499	646	3.6	5,536	1,718
Size of family:												
Two persons_____	22,033	340.4	15,452	7,674	20,033	320.6	16,001	7,961	1,773	17.0	9,601	4,654
Three persons_____	12,629	231.1	18,300	6,064	11,078	211.6	19,097	6,337	1,343	16.2	12,079	3,942
Four persons_____	11,774	243.7	20,698	5,200	10,441	223.8	21,431	5,386	1,133	15.7	13,886	3,471
Five persons_____	6,269	133.8	21,343	4,292	5,431	121.6	22,398	4,507	700	9.0	12,933	2,578
Six persons_____	2,649	58.1	21,917	3,667	2,221	52.0	23,412	3,921	384	5.0	13,010	2,165
Seven or more_____	1,861	37.9	20,355	2,628	1,325	30.4	22,944	3,000	474	6.4	13,578	1,700
Occupation of head:												
White-collar workers__	19,611	488.7	24,919	7,320	18,197	462.4	25,408	7,484	1,069	18.0	16,889	4,830
Blue-collar workers___	17,787	323.9	18,210	5,040	15,816	293.0	18,525	5,213	1,764	27.3	15,468	3,785
Farm workers_____	1,459	18.8	12,889	3,664	1,366	18.0	13,179	3,816	75	.6	7,715	1,673
Service workers_____	3,420	48.8	14,263	4,166	2,570	39.0	15,187	4,577	761	8.4	11,072	2,964

B Base less than 75,000.   [1] Includes other races not shown separately.   [2] For definition of mean, see p. xii.
Source: U.S. Bureau of the Census, *Current Population Reports*, series P-60, No. 116.

No. 742. Wife's Contribution to Family Income—Families with Husband and Wife Working, by Race of Husband: 1970 and 1976

[Families as of **March 1971** and **March 1977**. See headnote, table 729. 1976 not strictly comparable with 1970 due to revised procedures. For definition of mean, see p. xii. For composition of regions, see fig. I, inside front cover]

RACE, REGION, AND WIFE'S CURRENT OCCUPATION GROUP	1970				1976			
	Husband-wife families, both working (1,000)	Average (mean) family income	Earnings of wife		Husband-wife families, both working (1,000)	Average (mean) family income	Earnings of wife	
			Average (mean)	Percent of family income			Average (mean)	Percent of family income
All White workers_____	18,401	$13,563	$3,490	25.7	20,834	$18,760	$5,295	28.2
North and West_____	12,969	14,022	3,537	25.2	14,241	19,241	5,336	27.7
South_____	5,432	12,467	3,376	27.1	6,593	17,720	5,207	29.4
Wife yr.-round, full-time worker___	(NA)	(NA)	(NA)	(NA)	11,349	20,128	7,321	36.4
Wife not yr.-round, full-time wrkr__	(NA)	(NA)	(NA)	(NA)	9,485	17,124	2,872	16.8
All Black workers_____	1,880	10,581	3,327	31.4	1,859	15,805	5,824	36.8
North and West_____	864	12,403	4,015	32.4	822	18,090	6,657	36.8
South_____	1,016	9,032	2,742	30.4	1,037	13,992	5,163	36.9
Wife yr.-round, full-time worker___	(NA)	(NA)	(NA)	(NA)	1,207	17,784	7,274	40.9
Wife not yr.-round, full-time wrkr__	(NA)	(NA)	(NA)	(NA)	652	12,143	3,141	25.9

NA Not available.
Source: U.S. Bureau of the Census, *Current Population Reports*, series P-23, No. 39, and unpublished data.

No. 743. Median Family Income of Husband-Wife Families—by Work Experience of Husband and Wife, Race, and Age of Head: 1970 and 1976

[Families and earners as of **March 1971** and **March 1977**. 1976 not strictly comparable with 1970 due to revised procedures. See headnote, table 729]

RACE AND AGE OF HEAD	1970						1976					
	All husband-wife families [1]		Only husband worked		Husband and wife worked		All husband-wife families [1]		Only husband worked		Husband and wife worked	
	Number (1,000)	Median income (dol.)	Number (1,000)	Median income (dol.)	Number (1,000)	Median income (dol.)	Number (1,000)	Median income (dol.)	Number (1,000)	Median income (dol.)	Number (1,000)	Median income (dol.)
Total, all races	(NA)	(NA)	(NA)	(NA)	(NA)	(NA)	47,497	16,203	13,276	14,257	23,058	18,897
Under 35 years	(NA)	(NA)	(NA)	(NA)	(NA)	(NA)	14,270	14,899	4,861	13,164	9,046	16,032
35–54 years	(NA)	(NA)	(NA)	(NA)	(NA)	(NA)	18,706	19,678	4,688	15,793	10,365	21,304
55 years and over	(NA)	(NA)	(NA)	(NA)	(NA)	(NA)	14,521	12,776	3,727	13,575	3,646	20,045
White, total	41,092	10,662	14,001	9,357	18,401	12,348	43,397	16,501	12,357	14,596	20,834	19,155
Under 35 years	11,516	9,796	4,905	9,065	6,387	10,396	12,994	15,073	4,544	13,427	8,147	16,181
35–54 years	17,357	25,543	5,319	20,807	8,579	27,925	16,962	20,141	4,284	16,261	9,336	21,652
55 years and over	12,220	16,094	3,778	14,892	3,435	23,127	13,442	13,034	3,529	13,912	3,351	20,320
Black, total	3,235	7,816	774	6,024	1,880	9,727	3,406	13,137	741	9,619	1,859	16,232
Under 35 years	965	8,032	296	5,965	651	9,267	1,056	13,299	242	8,993	768	14,563
35–54 years	1,381	18,499	291	13,425	892	21,208	1,419	15,028	320	10,800	839	17,861
55 years and over	890	10,492	188	9,683	338	8,889	931	8,687	180	7,269	252	15,564
Percent Black of White	7.9	73.3	5.5	64.4	10.2	78.8	7.8	79.6	6.0	65.9	8.9	84.7
Under 35 years	8.4	82.0	6.0	65.8	10.2	89.1	8.1	88.2	5.3	67.0	9.4	90.0
35–54 years	8.0	72.4	5.5	64.5	10.4	75.9	8.4	74.6	7.5	66.4	9.0	82.5
55 years and over	7.3	65.2	5.0	65.0	9.8	38.4	6.9	66.6	5.1	52.2	7.5	76.6

NA Not available.   [1] Includes other combinations, not shown separately.

Source: U.S. Bureau of the Census, *Current Population Reports*, series P–23, No. 39, and unpublished data.

No. 744. Unrelated Individuals—Percent Distribution by Money Income Level, by Race, in Current and Constant (1977) Dollars: 1950 to 1977

[See headnote, table 729. Unrelated individuals=persons not living with any relatives; see text, pp. 3 and 438. See also *Historical Statistics, Colonial Times to 1970*, series G 24–30, G 186–188, G 193–195, and G 200–202]

INCOME LEVEL	WHITE							BLACK AND OTHER RACES						
	1950	1955	1960	1965	1970	1975 [1]	1977 [1]	1950	1955	1960	1965	1970	1975 [1]	1977 [1]
CURRENT DOLLARS														
Under $1,500	57.7	52.4	44.6	36.7	21.4	7.9	8.4	70.5	66.5	60.8	47.6	35.1	15.0	15.4
$1,500–$2,999	25.1	21.7	20.1	21.9	25.6	19.5	11.9	22.2	24.7	19.5	21.9	24.1	29.4	18.8
$3,000–$4,999	14.3	19.0	20.4	17.8	17.7	21.8	21.3	6.4	7.6	13.6	16.7	17.5	18.1	17.9
$5,000–$6,999	1.6	4.8	10.0	12.4	12.4	13.4	13.7	.9	1.0	4.8	9.9	11.0	10.7	14.7
$7,000–$9,999	.7	1.1	3.6	7.5	12.7	15.3	15.2	–	.2	.7	3.2	9.6	11.7	12.2
$10,000–$14,999	.4	.4	1.0	2.5	6.9	13.5	16.2	–	.4	.5	2.2	10.8	13.0	
$15,000 and over		.4	.4	1.2	3.2	8.5	13.3		–	.1	.1	.5	4.3	8.1
Median income___dol.	1,115	1,400	1,860	2,245	3,283	5,099	6,131	817	935	1,068	1,637	2,243	3,392	4,639
CONSTANT (1977) DOLLARS														
Under $1,500	32.5	28.2	23.9	21.1	10.7	7.1	8.4	42.5	39.8	37.0	29.9	19.4	13.5	15.4
$1,500–$2,999	19.8	20.8	20.1	17.0	20.5	15.9	11.9	21.4	23.1	23.2	19.0	25.5	26.4	18.8
$3,000–$4,999	13.6	15.3	14.7	16.9	18.2	21.6	21.3	15.0	17.8	13.5	17.3	16.8	18.8	17.9
$5,000–$6,999	14.1	11.6	10.8	10.1	11.8	13.6	13.7	12.2	11.6	10.0	10.1	11.9	10.9	14.7
$7,000–$9,999	13.6	14.5	14.9	13.1	12.8	14.9	15.2	6.6	5.7	9.6	11.7	11.5	12.0	12.2
$10,000–$14,999	4.1	7.2	11.6	13.5	14.9	15.1	16.2	1.0	1.9	5.6	10.2	11.5	12.0	13.0
$15,000 and over	2.2	2.5	4.1	8.3	11.2	11.7	13.3	1.3	.2	1.1	1.8	3.4	6.4	8.1
Median income___dol.	2,806	3,169	3,805	4,313	5,124	5,741	6,131	2,056	2,116	2,185	3,144	3,501	3,819	4,639

– Represents zero or rounds to zero.
[1] Beginning 1975, not strictly comparable with earlier years due to revised procedures.

Source: U.S. Bureau of the Census, *Current Population Reports*, series P–60, forthcoming report.

No. 745. Money Income of Unrelated Individuals—Percent of Aggregate Income and Income at Selected Positions Received by Each Fifth and Highest 5 Percent: 1950 to 1977

[See headnote, table 729. Unrelated individuals=persons not living with any relatives; see text, pp. 3 and 438. For definition of median, see p. xii]

ITEM AND INCOME RANK	1950	1955	1960	1965	1970	1973	1974 [1]	1975 [1]	1976 [1]	1977 [1]
PERCENT DISTRIBUTION OF AGGREGATE INCOME										
All unrelated individuals	100.0	100.0	100.0	100.0	100.0	100.0	100.0	100.0	100.0	100.0
Lowest fifth	2.3	2.5	1.7	2.9	3.3	3.7	4.2	4.0	4.0	4.1
Second fifth	7.1	7.2	7.3	7.6	7.9	8.6	8.9	9.0	8.8	9.0
Middle fifth	13.8	13.3	13.7	13.6	13.8	14.4	14.6	14.7	14.8	14.7
Fourth fifth	26.5	24.7	26.0	25.0	24.4	23.9	24.1	24.3	24.1	24.0
Highest fifth	50.3	52.4	51.4	50.9	50.7	49.5	48.3	47.9	48.3	48.2
Highest 5 percent	19.3	22.5	20.2	20.0	20.8	20.0	19.5	18.7	19.3	19.6
INCOME AT SPECIFIED POSITIONS										
In current dollars:										
All unrelated individuals (median)	1,045	1,316	1,720	2,153	3,137	4,134	4,603	4,882	5,375	5,907
Upper limit of each fifth:										
Lowest fifth	360	496	650	900	1,368	1,872	2,175	2,320	2,464	2,800
Second fifth	787	952	1,200	1,560	2,320	3,095	3,417	3,760	4,032	4,542
Middle fifth	1,533	1,824	2,400	2,995	4,100	5,160	5,900	6,150	6,836	7,490
Fourth fifth	2,673	3,206	4,181	5,101	7,200	8,802	9,520	10,025	11,000	12,000
Highest 5 percent	4,139	5,298	6,611	8,727	12,270	15,000	16,000	17,100	18,675	20,055
In constant (1977) dollars:										
All unrelated individuals (median)	2,631	2,978	3,520	4,134	4,896	5,637	5,656	5,497	5,722	5,907
Upper limit of each fifth:										
Lowest fifth	906	1,122	1,330	1,729	2,135	2,553	2,673	2,612	2,623	2,800
Second fifth	1,981	2,154	2,455	2,996	5,181	4,220	4,199	4,233	4,292	4,542
Middle fifth	3,859	4,128	4,911	5,752	6,399	7,036	7,250	6,924	7,277	7,490
Fourth fifth	6,729	7,255	8,555	9,797	11,236	12,003	11,699	11,287	11,710	12,000
Highest 5 percent	10,419	11,990	13,528	16,761	19,149	20,455	19,661	19,253	19,880	20,055

[1] Beginning 1974, not strictly comparable with earlier years due to revised procedures.

Source: U.S. Bureau of the Census, *Current Population Reports*, series P-60, No. 116, and unpublished data.

No. 746. Households—Percent Distribution by Money Income Level, by Metro.-Nonmetro. Residence, Region, and Occupant Tenure: 1977

[Households as of **March 1978**. Based on Current Population Survey; see text, p. 1 and headnote, table 751. For definition of residence, see Appendix II. For definition of median, see p. xii. For composition of regions, see fig. 1, inside front cover]

RESIDENCE, REGION, AND TENURE	Total households (1,000)	PERCENT DISTRIBUTION, BY HOUSEHOLD MONEY INCOME								Median income (dol.)
		Under $3,000	$3,000-$4,999	$5,000-$6,999	$7,000-$9,999	$10,000-$14,999	$15,000-$19,999	$20,000-$24,999	$25,000 and over	
All households	76,030	7.3	9.2	8.6	11.7	17.9	15.6	11.5	18.1	13,572
Metropolitan areas	51,369	6.3	8.7	7.9	11.1	17.2	15.7	12.1	21.0	14,611
In central cities	22,914	8.4	11.5	9.6	12.8	18.1	14.1	10.2	15.3	12,059
Outside central cities	28,455	4.5	6.4	6.5	9.8	16.5	17.0	13.7	25.6	16,579
Nonmetropolitan areas	24,660	9.5	10.3	9.9	12.9	19.6	15.5	10.2	12.3	11,861
Region:										
Northeast	17,173	6.2	10.0	8.1	11.0	17.0	16.0	12.4	19.3	14,232
North Central	20,239	6.6	8.7	8.2	11.0	17.6	16.5	12.1	19.2	14,270
South	24,316	9.6	9.1	9.1	12.8	18.6	15.0	10.3	15.6	12,407
West	14,301	5.5	9.1	8.6	11.8	18.5	15.2	11.8	19.6	13,980
Tenure:										
Owner-occupied	49,398	5.1	6.6	6.8	9.6	16.4	17.1	14.0	24.4	16,404
Renter-occupied	25,013	11.0	13.7	11.8	15.7	20.9	13.1	6.9	6.6	9,522
Occupier paid no cash rent	1,619	17.9	15.0	11.6	13.2	17.5	11.8	7.2	5.8	8,108

Source: U.S. Bureau of the Census, *Current Population Reports*, series P-60, No. 117.

No. 747. HOUSEHOLDS—PERCENT DISTRIBUTION BY MONEY INCOME LEVEL IN CURRENT AND CONSTANT (1977) DOLLARS, BY RACE AND SPANISH ORIGIN OF HEAD: 1967 TO 1977

[Households as of **March** of following year. Based on Current Population Survey; see text, p. 1. Beginning 1974, data not strictly comparable with earlier years due to revised procedures. Persons of Spanish origin may be of any race. For definitions of household and race, see p. 3. For definition of median, see p. xii]

RACE OF HEAD AND YEAR	Number of households (1,000)	PERCENT DISTRIBUTION, BY INCOME LEVEL								Median income (dol.)
		Under $3,000	$3,000–$4,999	$5,000–$6,999	$7,000–$9,999	$10,000–$11,999	$12,000–$14,999	$15,000–$24,999	$25,000 and over	
CURRENT DOLLARS										
All households:										
1967	60,813	19.8	13.5	15.5	21.7	10.4	9.2	8.1	1.8	7,143
1970 [1]	64,778	15.8	11.6	11.8	18.5	11.0	12.2	15.1	4.0	8,734
1973	69,859	12.0	10.9	10.0	14.6	9.7	12.9	22.1	7.8	10,512
1974	71,163	10.5	10.1	9.7	13.9	9.5	12.5	24.0	9.9	11,197
1975	72,867	9.5	10.4	9.2	13.2	8.5	12.0	25.6	11.6	11,800
1976	74,142	8.4	9.5	9.0	12.4	7.9	11.2	27.2	14.6	12,686
1977	76,030	7.3	9.2	8.5	11.7	7.2	10.7	27.1	18.2	13,572
White:										
1967	54,188	18.2	12.7	15.4	22.5	10.9	9.8	8.6	2.0	7,449
1970	57,575	14.5	11.0	11.4	18.7	11.4	12.7	16.0	4.3	9,097
1973	61,965	10.8	10.2	9.6	14.4	9.9	13.4	23.3	8.4	11,017
1974	62,984	9.3	9.4	9.3	13.6	9.7	12.8	25.1	10.7	11,710
1975	64,392	8.3	9.8	9.0	13.0	8.5	12.3	26.6	12.6	12,340
1976	65,353	7.4	8.7	8.6	12.1	8.0	11.3	28.3	15.7	13,289
1977	66,934	6.3	8.5	8.0	11.4	7.2	10.9	28.3	19.4	14,272
Black:										
1967	5,728	35.7	20.8	17.1	14.1	5.6	4.1	2.4	.3	4,325
1970	6,180	28.2	17.2	15.6	16.2	7.6	7.0	7.3	.9	5,537
1973	7,040	22.5	17.3	13.3	16.3	8.3	8.9	11.1	2.3	6,485
1974	7,263	20.6	16.4	13.3	15.9	8.1	9.6	13.6	2.5	6,964
1975	7,489	19.6	16.9	11.4	14.6	8.7	9.4	15.2	4.0	7,408
1976	7,776	16.8	16.1	12.1	14.4	7.6	10.0	17.7	5.4	7,902
1977	7,977	15.3	14.8	13.0	14.7	7.6	9.4	18.1	7.2	8,422
Spanish origin:										
1974	2,897	11.5	13.9	13.4	17.5	10.4	12.4	16.7	4.2	8,906
1975	2,948	12.4	13.3	13.5	16.6	9.7	11.7	18.3	4.5	8,865
1976	3,081	11.1	13.0	12.2	16.0	9.3	11.2	21.2	6.0	9,569
1977	3,304	8.4	11.4	11.2	15.4	10.0	11.7	23.1	8.7	10,647
CONSTANT (1977) DOLLARS										
All households:										
1967	60,813	10.1	8.2	7.5	11.7	8.6	13.0	28.2	12.7	12,965
1970 [1]	64,778	9.2	7.9	7.5	11.2	7.7	11.9	28.9	15.6	13,630
1973	69,859	7.5	8.4	7.9	11.0	7.2	10.9	29.6	17.6	14,335
1974	71,163	7.6	8.4	8.0	11.5	7.5	11.6	28.9	17.7	13,759
1975	72,867	7.9	9.4	8.4	12.0	7.7	11.3	27.1	16.3	13,286
1976	74,142	7.6	9.0	8.4	11.8	7.6	10.8	27.6	17.2	13,504
1977	76,030	7.3	9.2	8.5	11.7	7.2	10.7	27.1	18.2	13,572
White:										
1967	54,188	9.3	7.5	7.0	11.2	8.5	13.4	29.5	13.6	13,520
1970	57,575	8.3	7.4	7.1	10.8	7.6	12.1	30.1	16.6	14,197
1973	61,965	6.6	7.7	7.4	10.6	7.1	11.0	30.8	18.8	15,023
1974	62,984	6.7	7.8	7.6	11.1	7.5	11.8	30.1	18.9	14,390
1975	64,392	6.9	8.7	8.1	11.8	7.6	11.4	28.0	17.5	13,894
1976	65,353	6.7	8.2	8.0	11.6	7.5	10.9	28.6	18.4	14,146
1977	66,934	6.3	8.5	8.0	11.4	7.2	10.9	28.3	19.4	14,272
Black:										
1967	5,728	18.5	14.7	12.5	16.2	9.1	9.7	15.4	3.9	7,850
1970	6,180	17.3	13.1	11.2	15.4	8.4	10.1	18.2	6.2	8,641
1973	7,040	14.9	14.2	11.8	14.5	8.6	10.1	19.3	6.7	8,843
1974	7,263	15.7	14.3	11.4	15.4	8.3	10.1	18.7	6.8	8,558
1975	7,489	16.5	15.6	11.6	13.5	8.4	10.1	18.2	6.0	8,341
1976	7,776	15.3	15.7	11.9	14.0	7.6	9.8	19.0	6.7	8,412
1977	7,977	15.3	14.8	13.0	14.7	7.6	9.4	18.1	7.2	8,422
Spanish origin:										
1974	2,897	8.4	10.4	11.8	15.2	9.3	12.8	23.4	8.7	10,944
1975	2,948	10.6	11.6	11.8	16.1	9.4	11.6	21.9	7.0	9,981
1976	3,081	10.1	12.4	11.4	15.4	9.3	11.5	22.2	7.7	10,186
1977	3,304	8.4	11.4	11.2	15.4	10.0	11.7	23.2	8.7	10,647

[1] Revised, using population controls based on the 1970 Census of Population; therefore, will not agree with data shown in table 748.

Source: U.S. Bureau of the Census, *Current Population Reports*, series P-60, No. 117.

No. 748. Money Income of Households—Aggregate, Mean, and Per Capita Income, by Selected Characteristics of Household Heads: 1970 and 1977

[Households as of **March 1971** and **March 1978**. Based on Current Population Survey; see text, pp. 1 and 438. Data for 1977 not strictly comparable with 1970 due to revised procedures. See headnote, table 747]

CHARACTERISTIC	1970						1977					
	Households		Household income				Households		Household income			
	Number (mil.)	Percent of total	Total (bil. dol.)	Percent of total	Mean income [1] (dol.)	Per capita (dol.)	Number (mil.)	Percent of total	Total (bil. dol.)	Percent of total	Mean income [1] (dol.)	Per capita (dol.)
Household heads___	**64.4**	**100.0**	**643.8**	**100.0**	**10,001**	**3,185**	**76.0**	**100.0**	**1,224.1**	**100.0**	**16,100**	**5,730**
Male_____	50.3	78.2	572.2	88.9	11,368	3,302	57.0	74.6	1,060.2	86.6	18,689	6,033
Female_____	14.0	21.8	71.6	11.1	5,100	2,485	19.2	25.4	163.8	13.4	8,489	4,326
White_____	57.6	89.4	596.0	92.6	10,351	3,364	67.0	88.2	1,119.7	91.5	16,729	6,043
Black_____	6.2	9.6	41.8	6.5	6,761	1,842	8.0	10.5	86.1	7.0	10,791	3,480
Spanish origin_____	(NA)	(NA)	(NA)	(NA)	(NA)	(NA)	3.3	4.3	41.5	3.4	12,565	3,614
Age of head:												
14–24 yr_____	4.7	7.3	33.5	5.2	7,115	2,743	6.2	8.2	65.3	5.3	10,494	4,708
25–34 yr_____	11.8	18.4	122.2	19.0	10,313	2,798	16.8	22.1	271.8	22.2	16,148	5,364
35–44 yr_____	11.7	18.2	143.1	22.2	12,193	2,736	13.0	17.1	260.7	21.3	20,101	5,142
45–54 yr_____	12.5	19.4	160.8	25.0	12,858	3,660	13.0	16.6	271.4	22.2	21,537	6,395
55–64 yr_____	11.0	17.0	115.8	18.0	10,573	4,305	12.2	16.0	213.2	17.4	17,498	7,286
65 yr. and over_____	12.6	19.6	68.4	10.6	5,418	2,960	15.2	20.0	141.7	11.6	9,309	5,309
Education of head:												
Less than 8 yr_____	9.0	14.0	51.9	8.1	5,747	1,935	8.0	10.5	70.1	5.7	8,774	3,315
8 yr_____	8.3	12.8	59.9	9.3	7,253	2,644	7.1	9.3	75.2	6.1	10,636	4,301
1–3 yr. high school____	10.6	16.4	92.7	14.4	8,757	2,676	11.1	14.6	137.3	11.2	12,358	4,259
4 yr. high school_____	20.1	31.3	209.9	32.6	10,422	3,167	25.3	33.3	407.3	33.3	16,079	5,517
1–3 yr. college_____	7.6	11.8	89.4	13.9	11,761	3,778	11.4	15.0	204.8	16.7	17,918	6,528
4 or more yr. college__	8.8	13.6	140.1	21.8	15,980	4,984	13.1	17.2	329.5	26.9	25,132	8,767

NA Not available.   [1] For definition of mean, see p. xii.

No. 749. Persons With Income—Percent Distribution by Money Income Level, and Median and Mean Money Income, by Sex and Race: 1950 to 1977

[Covers persons 14 years old and over as of **March** of following year. Based on Current Population Survey; see headnote, table 729. For definition of median and mean, see p. xii. See *Historical Statistics, Colonial Times to 1970*, series G 257–268, for percent distribution by income level, and median income]

YEAR AND RACE	All persons (1,000)	Total (1,000)	PERSONS WITH INCOME							Median income (dol.)	Mean income (dol.)
			Percent distribution by income level								
			Less than $2,000 or loss	$2,000–$3,999	$4,000–$6,999	$7,000–$9,999	$10,000–$14,999	$15,000 and over			
Male:											
1950_____	52,592	47,585	37.1	42.7	16.2	2.0	2.0			2,570	2,961
1960_____	60,359	55,172	27.5	21.4	33.6	11.3	4.1	2.0		4,080	4,617
1965_____	64,630	59,157	23.8	17.2	29.3	18.1	8.2	3.6		5,023	5,636
1970_____	70,592	65,008	18.7	13.7	19.9	20.9	17.7	9.1		6,670	7,537
1975 [1]_____	77,560	71,234	13.1	12.1	15.8	14.7	21.8	22.9		8,853	10,429
1976 [1]_____	78,782	72,775	12.3	11.3	15.2	13.7	20.6	27.0		9,426	11,165
1977 [1]_____	79,863	74,015	11.6	10.8	14.2	12.6	19.5	31.1		10,123	12,063
1970: White_____	63,002	58,447	17.8	12.9	19.1	21.4	18.8	9.9		7,011	7,840
Black_____	6,796	5,844	28.6	19.9	26.4	16.9	6.8	1.4		4,159	4,683
1977 [1]: White_____	70,407	65,974	11.0	10.3	13.5	12.5	19.8	33.0		10,603	12,537
Black_____	8,057	6,777	17.3	16.3	21.2	14.6	17.1	13.5		6,292	7,743
Female:											
1950_____	56,900	24,651	75.4	22.6	1.6	.2	.2			953	1,296
1960_____	65,282	36,526	62.8	25.1	11.0	.9	.2	–		1,261	1,861
1965_____	70,990	42,160	57.0	24.1	15.5	2.4	.6	.2		1,521	2,265
1970_____	77,649	51,647	46.8	22.1	20.6	7.5	2.4	.7		2,237	3,138
1975 [1]_____	84,982	60,807	31.9	23.9	21.5	12.4	7.8	2.4		3,385	4,513
1976 [1]_____	86,153	63,170	30.1	23.6	20.8	13.0	9.0	3.4		3,576	4,875
1977 [1]_____	87,399	65,407	27.6	23.0	20.8	13.5	10.7	4.4		3,941	5,291
1970: White_____	68,793	45,283	46.3	21.5	20.9	7.8	2.5	.6		2,266	3,185
Black_____	8,041	5,844	48.9	26.6	17.7	4.9	1.8	.1		2,063	2,743
1977 [1]: White_____	76,194	56,813	27.6	22.4	20.8	13.7	11.0	4.5		4,001	5,349
Black_____	9,684	7,562	26.7	28.2	21.1	12.2	8.7	3.3		3,455	4,803

– Represents zero or rounds to zero.
[1] Beginning 1975, not strictly comparable with earlier years due to revised procedures.
Source of tables 748 and 749: U.S. Bureau of the Census, *Current Population Reports*, series P–60, No. 116.

No. 750. Persons With Income Money, by Sex and Age: 1977

[Persons 14 years old and over. As of March of following year. See headnote, table 729]

SEX AND INCOME LEVEL	Total persons	14–19 years	20–24 years	25–34 years	35–44 years	45–54 years	55–64 years	65 and over
All males_____1,000	79,863	12,368	9,572	16,263	11,566	11,154	9,769	9,170
Males with income_____1,000	74,015	7,496	9,099	16,069	11,492	11,026	9,689	9,145
Percent distribution, by age: With income of—								
Under $2,000 or loss_____	100.0	57.1	16.1	7.3	4.3	4.8	4.5	5.8
$2,000–$3,999_____	100.0	18.6	18.3	9.1	5.0	6.8	11.1	31.1
$4,000–$6,999_____	100.0	6.6	21.3	17.0	7.8	8.5	12.1	26.6
$7,000–$9,999_____	100.0	2.9	18.4	26.5	11.5	11.7	14.2	14.6
$10,000–$14,999_____	100.0	.6	11.7	32.6	18.0	16.1	14.4	6.6
$15,000 and over_____	100.0	.1	2.5	24.8	27.0	24.8	16.3	4.5
All females_____1,000	87,399	12,313	9,989	16,857	12,285	11,917	10,740	13,298
Females with income_____1,000	65,407	6,825	8,354	12,667	8,981	8,384	7,875	12,322
Percent distribution, by age: With income of—								
Under $2,000 or loss_____	100.0	27.4	12.0	14.6	10.1	9.3	10.3	16.5
$2,000–$3,999_____	100.0	8.1	13.0	13.0	10.0	9.4	11.5	35.0
$4,000–$6,999_____	100.0	3.8	16.2	19.8	15.6	14.0	12.7	17.9
$7,000–$9,999_____	100.0	1.4	15.6	27.9	16.4	16.5	12.3	9.8
$10,000–$14,999_____	100.0	.4	8.4	32.4	19.3	18.6	13.5	7.3
$15,000 and over_____	100.0	.2	2.3	22.7	25.3	21.8	17.6	10.1

No. 751. Median Earnings of Workers, by Work Experience and Sex: 1977

[Covers civilians 14 years old and over as of March 1978 with earnings. For definition of median, see p. xii]

WEEKS WORKED	WORKED FULL-TIME Women Number (1,000)	WORKED FULL-TIME Women Median earnings	WORKED FULL-TIME Men Number (1,000)	WORKED FULL-TIME Men Median earnings	RATIO: WOMEN TO MEN Number	RATIO: WOMEN TO MEN Median earnings	WORKED PART-TIME Women Number (1,000)	WORKED PART-TIME Women Median earnings	WORKED PART-TIME Men Number (1,000)	WORKED PART-TIME Men Median earnings	RATIO: WOMEN TO MEN Number	RATIO: WOMEN TO MEN Median earnings
Total_____	30,734	$6,828	53,219	$12,465	.58	.55	15,461	$1,437	8,485	$1,404	1.82	1.02
13 weeks or less_____	2,800	823	2,822	1,176	.99	.70	3,752	557	2,268	571	1.65	.98
14–26 weeks_____	2,949	2,412	3,045	3,439	.97	.70	2,940	946	1,642	1,042	1.79	.91
27–39 weeks_____	2,656	4,290	3,356	6,662	.79	.64	2,032	1,925	969	2,158	2.10	.89
40–49 weeks_____	3,090	6,174	4,733	10,121	.65	.61	1,856	2,626	951	2,957	1.95	.89
50–52 weeks_____	19,238	8,618	39,263	14,626	.49	.59	4,881	3,149	2,655	2,813	1.84	1.12

No. 752. Median Money Income of Year–Round Full–Time Workers With Income, by Sex, Age, and Educational Attainment: 1970 to 1977

[Age as of March of following year. Refers to civilian workers. 1970 not strictly comparable with later years due to revised procedures. For definition of median, see p. xii]

AGE AND EDUCATIONAL ATTAINMENT	WOMEN 1970	WOMEN 1975	WOMEN 1977	MEN 1970	MEN 1975	MEN 1977	RATIO: WOMEN TO MEN 1970	RATIO: WOMEN TO MEN 1975	RATIO: WOMEN TO MEN 1977
Total with income_____	$5,440	$7,719	$8,814	$9,184	$13,144	$15,070	.59	.59	.58
14–19 years_____	3,783	4,568	5,632	3,950	5,657	6,042	.96	.81	.93
20–24 years_____	4,928	6,598	7,497	6,655	8,521	9,800	.74	.77	.77
25–34 years_____	5,923	8,401	9,543	9,126	12,777	14,129	.65	.66	.68
35–44 years_____	5,531	8,084	9,282	10,258	14,730	16,863	.54	.55	.55
45–54 years_____	5,588	7,980	9,142	9,931	14,808	17,029	.56	.54	.54
55–64 years_____	5,468	7,785	8,846	9,071	13,518	15,669	.60	.58	.56
65 years and over_____	4,884	7,273	7,829	6,754	11,485	13,963	.72	.63	.56
Total, 25 yr. old and over_____	5,616	8,117	9,257	9,521	13,821	15,726	.59	.59	.59
Elementary: Less than 8 years___	3,798	5,109	6,074	6,043	8,647	9,419	.63	.59	.64
8 years_____	4,181	5,691	6,564	7,535	10,600	12,083	.55	.54	.54
High school: 1 to 3 years_____	4,655	6,355	7,387	8,514	11,511	13,120	.55	.55	.56
4 years_____	5,580	7,777	8,894	9,567	13,542	15,434	.58	.57	.58
College: 1 to 3 years_____	6,604	9,126	10,157	11,183	14,989	16,235	.59	.61	.63
4 years or more_____	8,719	11,359	12,656	13,871	18,450	20,625	.63	.62	.61

Source of tables 750–752: U.S. Bureau of the Census, *Current Population Reports*, series P–60, No. 116, and earlier issues.

No. 753. Median Income of Women With Income and Median Earnings of Women With Earnings: 1967 to 1977

[In dollars. See headnote, table 749. Earnings consist of wages, salaries, and/or self-employment income; income includes earnings in addition to interest, dividends, unemployment compensation, and pensions]

ITEM	MEDIAN INCOME						MEDIAN EARNINGS					
	1967	1970	1974 [1]	1975 [1]	1976 [1]	1977 [1]	1967	1970	1974 [1]	1975 [1]	1976 [1]	1977 [1]
All women	1,801	2,237	3,082	3,385	3,576	3,941	2,340	2,730	3,563	3,953	4,265	4,641
White	1,855	2,266	3,117	3,420	3,606	4,001	2,449	2,800	3,599	3,952	4,225	4,611
Black	1,453	2,063	2,814	3,107	3,398	3,455	1,623	2,344	3,293	3,854	4,542	4,830
Full-time workers [2]	4,198	5,440	7,174	7,719	8,312	8,814	4,134	5,323	6,970	7,504	8,099	8,618
White	4,307	5,536	7,235	7,737	8,376	8,870	4,265	5,412	7,020	7,513	8,154	8,672
Black	3,185	4,536	6,677	7,392	7,831	8,290	3,178	4,447	6,563	7,237	7,650	8,097

[1] Beginning 1974, not strictly comparable with earlier years due to revised procedures.   [2] Year-round.

Source: U.S. Bureau of the Census, *Current Population Reports*, series P-60, Nos. 60, 80, 105, 114, and forthcoming report.

No. 754. Persons Below Poverty Level and Below 125 Percent of Poverty Level: 1959 to 1977

[For 1959–1968, data based on 1960 census of population controls; thereafter, on 1970 census controls. For definition of median, see p. xii. For explanation of poverty level, see table 735 and text, p. 438]

YEAR	PERSONS BELOW POVERTY LEVEL		PERSONS BELOW 125 PERCENT OF POVERTY LEVEL		AVERAGE INCOME CUTOFFS FOR NONFARM FAMILY OF 4		Percent poverty level of median income of 4-person [1] family	MEDIAN FAMILY INCOME OF ALL FAMILIES		Consumer price index (1972= 100)
	Number (mil.)	Percent of total population	Number (mil.)	Percent of total population	At poverty level	At 125 percent of poverty level		Total	Index (1972= 100)	
1959	39.5	22.4	54.9	31.1	$2,973	$3,716	(NA)	$5,417	48.7	69.5
1960	39.9	22.2	54.6	30.4	3,022	3,778	(NA)	5,620	50.6	70.7
1966	28.5	14.7	41.3	21.3	3,317	4,146	39.2	7,532	67.8	77.6
1000	25.4	12.8	35.9	18.2	3,553	4,441	35.7	8,632	77.7	83.1
1969	24.1	12.1	34.7	17.4	3,743	4,679	34.9	9,433	84.9	87.6
1970	25.4	12.6	35.6	17.6	3,968	4,960	35.2	9,867	88.8	92.8
1971	25.6	12.5	36.5	17.8	4,137	5,171	35.2	10,285	92.5	96.8
1972	24.5	11.9	34.7	16.8	4,275	5,344	33.1	11,116	100.0	100.0
1973	23.0	11.1	32.8	15.8	4,540	5,675	32.9	12,051	108.4	106.2
1974	24.3	11.6	34.6	16.5	5,038	6,298	34.0	12,836	115.5	117.8
1974 [2]	23.4	11.2	33.7	16.1	5,038	6,298	33.5	12,902	116.1	117.8
1975 [2]	25.9	12.3	37.2	17.6	5,500	6,875	34.5	13,719	123.4	128.7
1976 [2]	25.0	11.8	35.5	16.7	5,815	7,269	33.6	14,958	134.6	136.1
1977 [2]	24.7	11.6	35.7	16.7	6,191	7,739	33.1	16,009	144.0	144.9

NA Not available.   [1] For 1966–1974, base used is median income for nonfarm 4-person families. Beginning 1974 (revised), base used is median income for all 4-person families.

[2] Beginning 1974, not strictly comparable with earlier years due to revised procedures.

No. 755. Weighted Average Poverty Levels Based on Money Income for Nonfarm Families and Individuals, by Size of Family and Sex of Head: 1959 to 1977

[In dollars. Excludes inmates of institutions, members of Armed Forces living in barracks, and unrelated individuals under 14 years of age. Families and unrelated individuals are classified as being above or below the poverty level, using the poverty index adopted by a Federal Interagency Committee in 1969. For explanation of poverty level, see text, p. 438. 1977 not strictly comparable with earlier years due to revised procedures]

SIZE OF FAMILY UNIT	1959			1970			1977		
	Total, non-farm	Male head	Female head	Total, non-farm	Male head	Female head	Total, non-farm	Male head	Female head
1 person (unrelated individual)	1,467	1,529	1,428	1,954	2,044	1,898	3,075	3,214	2,969
Under 65 years	1,503	1,569	1,451	2,010	2,092	1,935	3,152	3,267	3,023
65 years and over	1,397	1,409	1,391	1,861	1,879	1,855	2,906	2,936	2,898
2 persons	1,894	1,904	1,843	2,525	2,534	2,471	3,951	3,961	3,907
Head under 65 years	1,952	1,964	1,883	2,604	2,619	2,522	4,072	4,095	3,981
Head 65 years and over	1,761	1,762	1,752	2,348	2,349	2,336	3,666	3,670	3,646
3 persons	2,324	2,335	2,235	3,099	3,113	3,003	4,833	4,860	4,708
4 persons	2,973	2,974	2,957	3,968	3,970	3,948	6,191	6,195	6,162
5 persons	3,506	3,507	3,483	4,680	4,684	4,639	7,320	7,329	7,238
6 persons	3,944	3,944	3,941	5,260	5,263	5,220	8,261	8,268	8,197
7 or more persons	4,849	4,856	4,763	6,468	6,486	6,317	10,216	10,249	9,995

Source of tables 754 and 755: U.S. Bureau of the Census, *Current Population Reports*, series P-23, No. 28, and P-60, Nos. 81, 115, and 116.

No. 756. Persons Below Poverty Level, by Family Status, Race, and Sex of Head: 1959 to 1977

[Persons as of **March** of following year. For explanation of poverty level, see table 755 and text, p. 438]

FAMILY STATUS, RACE, AND SEX OF HEAD	1959	1966	1970	1972	1973	1974	1974[1]	1975[1]	1976[1]	1977[1]
NUMBER BELOW POVERTY LEVEL (millions)										
All persons	39.5	28.5	25.4	24.5	23.0	24.3	23.4	25.9	25.0	24.7
In families	34.6	23.8	20.3	19.6	18.3	19.4	18.8	20.8	19.6	19.5
Head	8.3	5.8	5.3	5.1	4.8	5.1	4.9	5.5	5.3	5.3
Related children under 18 yr	17.2	12.1	10.2	10.1	9.5	10.2	10.0	10.9	10.1	10.0
Children 5–17 yr	(NA)	8.6	7.6	7.3	6.9	7.5	7.4	8.0	7.4	7.2
Other family members	9.0	5.9	4.8	4.4	4.0	4.1	3.9	4.5	4.2	4.2
Unrelated individuals	4.9	4.7	5.1	4.9	4.7	4.8	4.6	5.1	5.3	5.2
White	28.5	19.3	17.5	16.2	15.1	16.3	15.7	17.8	16.7	16.4
In families	24.4	15.4	13.3	12.3	11.4	12.5	12.2	13.8	12.5	12.4
Head	6.2	4.1	3.7	3.4	3.2	3.5	3.4	3.8	3.6	3.5
Related children under 18 yr	11.4	7.2	6.1	5.8	5.5	6.2	6.1	6.7	6.0	5.9
Other family members	6.9	4.1	3.5	3.0	2.7	2.9	2.8	3.2	2.9	2.9
Unrelated individuals	4.0	3.9	4.2	3.9	3.7	3.8	3.6	4.0	4.2	4.1
Black and other races	11.0	9.2	7.9	8.3	7.8	8.0	7.6	8.1	8.3	8.3
In families	10.1	8.4	7.0	7.3	6.9	6.9	6.6	7.0	7.1	7.1
Head	2.1	1.7	1.6	1.6	1.6	1.6	1.6	1.6	1.8	1.8
Related children under 18 yr	5.8	4.9	4.1	4.3	4.0	4.0	3.9	4.1	4.0	4.1
Other family members	2.2	1.8	1.4	1.4	1.3	1.3	1.2	1.2	1.3	1.3
Unrelated individuals	.9	.8	.9	.9	.9	1.0	1.0	1.1	1.1	1.2
Male head [2]	29.1	18.3	14.3	12.9	11.6	12.5	11.9	13.6	12.4	12.1
In families	27.5	16.9	12.8	11.5	10.1	10.9	10.4	11.9	10.6	10.3
Head	6.4	4.1	3.3	2.9	2.6	2.8	2.6	3.0	2.8	2.7
Related children under 18 yr	13.1	7.9	5.5	5.0	4.3	4.8	4.6	5.3	4.5	4.4
Other family members	8.1	5.0	4.0	3.6	3.2	3.3	3.2	3.6	3.3	3.2
Unrelated individuals	1.6	1.3	1.4	1.4	1.5	1.6	1.5	1.7	1.8	1.8
Female head [2]	10.4	10.3	11.2	11.6	11.4	11.8	11.5	12.3	12.6	12.6
In families	7.0	6.9	7.5	8.1	8.2	8.6	8.5	8.8	9.0	9.2
Head	1.9	1.7	2.0	2.2	2.2	2.4	2.3	2.4	2.5	2.6
Related children under 18 yr	4.1	4.3	4.7	5.1	5.2	5.4	5.4	5.6	5.6	5.7
Other family members	1.0	.9	.9	.9	.8	.8	.8	.8	.9	.9
Unrelated individuals	3.4	3.4	3.7	3.5	3.2	3.2	3.0	3.4	3.6	3.4
PERCENT OF POPULATION BELOW POVERTY LEVEL										
All persons	22.4	14.7	12.6	11.9	11.1	11.6	11.2	12.3	11.8	11.6
In families	20.8	13.1	10.9	10.3	9.7	10.2	9.9	10.9	10.3	10.2
Head	18.5	11.8	10.1	9.3	8.8	9.2	8.8	9.7	9.4	9.3
Related children under 18 yr	26.9	17.4	14.9	14.9	14.2	15.5	15.1	16.8	15.8	16.0
Children 5–17 yr	(NA)	17.1	14.5	14.5	13.7	15.1	14.8	16.3	15.2	15.2
Other family members	15.9	9.5	7.4	6.6	5.9	6.0	5.7	6.4	6.0	5.9
Unrelated individuals	46.1	38.3	32.9	29.0	25.6	25.5	24.1	25.1	24.9	22.6
White	18.1	11.3	9.9	9.0	8.4	8.9	8.6	9.7	9.1	8.9
In families	16.5	9.7	8.1	7.4	6.9	7.5	7.3	8.3	7.5	7.5
Head	15.2	9.3	8.0	7.1	6.6	7.0	6.8	7.7	7.1	7.0
Related children under 18 yr	20.6	12.1	10.5	10.1	9.7	11.2	11.0	12.5	11.3	11.4
Other family members	13.3	7.4	5.9	5.1	4.5	4.7	4.5	5.2	4.7	4.6
Unrelated individuals	44.1	36.1	30.8	27.1	23.7	23.2	21.8	22.7	22.7	20.4
Black and other races	56.2	39.8	32.0	31.9	29.6	29.5	28.3	29.3	29.4	29.0
In families	56.0	38.9	30.7	31.0	28.8	28.4	27.2	28.0	28.2	28.1
Head	50.4	33.9	28.1	27.7	26.2	26.0	25.1	25.3	26.4	26.5
Related children under 18 yr	66.7	48.2	39.6	41.3	38.3	38.4	37.1	38.9	38.3	38.8
Other family members	42.5	27.7	19.5	19.0	17.4	16.7	15.5	15.6	16.5	15.7
Unrelated individuals	57.4	53.1	46.7	40.9	37.8	40.0	38.0	40.9	39.5	35.9
Male head [2]	18.7	10.8	8.2	7.4	6.6	7.1	6.8	7.8	7.1	6.9
In families	18.2	10.3	7.7	6.8	6.0	6.5	6.2	7.1	6.4	6.2
Head	15.8	9.3	7.2	6.1	5.5	5.7	5.4	6.2	5.6	5.5
Related children under 18 yr	22.4	12.6	9.2	8.6	7.6	8.7	8.3	9.8	8.5	8.5
Other family members	15.3	8.7	6.5	5.7	5.1	5.2	5.0	5.7	5.2	5.0
Unrelated individuals	36.8	29.3	24.0	21.1	19.8	20.4	19.5	19.9	19.7	18.0
Female head [2]	50.2	41.0	38.2	36.9	34.9	34.4	33.6	34.6	34.4	32.8
In families	40.4	39.8	38.1	38.2	37.5	36.8	36.5	37.5	37.3	36.2
Head	42.6	33.1	32.5	32.7	32.2	32.5	32.1	32.5	33.0	31.7
Related children under 18 yr	72.2	58.2	53.0	53.1	52.1	51.5	51.5	52.7	52.0	50.3
Other family members	24.0	18.6	17.9	17.0	16.0	14.9	14.1	15.0	15.7	15.8
Unrelated individuals	52.1	43.5	38.4	34.3	29.7	29.3	27.3	28.9	28.7	26.1

NA Not available.   [1] Beginning 1974, not strictly comparable with prior years due to revised procedures.
[2] For persons in families, sex of family head; for unrelated individuals, sex of individual.

Source: U.S. Bureau of the Census, *Current Population Reports*, series P–60, Nos. 115 and 116.

No. 757. Persons Below 125 Percent of Poverty Level: 1959 to 1977

[Persons as of **March** of following year. For explanation of poverty level, see table 755, and text, p. 438]

FAMILY STATUS, RACE, AND SEX OF HEAD	1959	1966	1970	1972	1973	1974 [1]	1975 [1]	1976 [1]	1977 [1]
	NUMBER OF PERSONS (millions)								
All persons	54.9	41.3	35.6	34.7	32.8	33.7	37.2	35.5	35.7
In families	49.3	35.6	29.2	28.2	26.5	27.1	30.1	28.1	28.2
Head	11.8	8.6	7.5	7.3	7.0	7.2	8.0	7.6	7.7
Related children under 18 yr	24.3	17.7	14.3	14.1	13.1	13.6	15.0	13.7	13.8
Children 5–17 yr	(NA)	(NA)	10.6	10.2	9.6	10.0	11.0	10.0	10.2
Other family members	13.2	9.3	7.4	6.8	6.4	6.3	7.2	6.8	6.7
Unrelated individuals	5.6	5.7	6.4	6.4	6.3	6.6	7.1	7.4	7.5
White	41.8	29.5	25.4	24.2	22.6	23.5	26.6	24.7	24.6
In families	37.2	24.7	20.0	18.9	17.5	18.1	20.9	18.7	18.6
Head	9.2	6.5	5.5	5.2	4.9	5.1	5.8	5.4	5.3
Related children under 18 yr	17.5	11.5	9.1	8.7	8.0	8.6	9.8	8.5	8.5
Other family members	10.5	6.8	5.5	4.9	4.5	4.5	5.3	4.8	4.8
Unrelated individuals	4.7	4.7	5.3	5.3	5.2	5.3	5.7	6.0	6.0
Black and other races	13.1	11.8	10.3	10.5	10.2	10.2	10.6	10.8	11.0
In families	12.1	10.8	9.2	9.3	9.0	8.9	9.2	9.4	9.6
Head	2.6	2.2	2.0	2.1	2.1	2.1	2.2	2.3	2.4
Related children under 18 yr	6.8	6.2	5.2	5.3	5.1	5.0	5.2	5.2	5.2
Other family members	2.7	2.4	1.9	1.9	1.9	1.8	1.9	2.0	2.0
Unrelated individuals	1.0	1.0	1.1	1.1	1.1	1.3	1.4	1.4	1.4
In families with male head	43.1	28.9	21.9	20.0	18.4	18.7	21.4	19.5	19.3
In families	41.3	27.2	20.1	18.2	16.5	16.5	19.2	17.2	16.7
Head	9.6	6.5	5.1	4.6	4.3	4.3	4.9	4.5	4.4
Related children under 18 yr	19.7	12.7	8.7	7.9	6.9	7.1	8.3	7.2	7.0
Other family members	12.1	8.0	6.2	5.6	5.2	5.1	6.0	5.5	5.3
Unrelated individuals, males	1.8	1.6	1.8	1.9	1.9	2.1	2.2	2.4	2.5
In families with female head	11.8	12.4	13.7	14.6	14.4	15.0	15.7	16.0	16.4
In families	8.0	8.3	9.1	10.0	10.0	10.5	10.9	10.9	11.4
Head	2.2	2.1	2.4	2.7	2.7	2.9	3.1	3.1	3.3
Related children under 18 yr	4.6	4.9	5.6	6.1	6.1	6.5	6.7	6.5	6.8
Other family members	1.2	1.3	1.2	1.2	1.2	1.1	1.2	1.3	1.3
Unrelated individuals, females	3.8	4.1	4.6	4.6	4.4	4.4	4.8	5.0	4.9
	PERCENT OF POPULATION BELOW 125 PERCENT OF POVERTY LEVEL								
All persons	31.1	21.3	17.6	16.8	15.8	16.1	17.6	16.7	16.7
In families	29.7	19.6	15.7	14.9	14.0	14.2	15.8	14.7	14.8
Head	26.2	17.6	14.4	13.5	12.8	12.9	14.2	13.5	13.5
Related children under 18 yr	37.9	25.3	20.8	20.8	19.6	20.7	23.1	21.5	21.9
Children 5–17 yr	(NA)	(NA)	20.3	20.2	19.1	20.2	22.4	20.6	21.4
Other family members	23.3	14.9	11.3	10.1	9.4	9.1	10.3	9.6	9.4
Unrelated individuals	52.7	46.4	41.3	38.3	34.6	34.8	34.9	34.5	32.4
White	26.7	17.3	14.3	13.4	12.5	12.9	14.5	13.4	13.3
In families	25.2	15.5	12.2	11.4	10.6	10.9	12.6	11.3	11.2
Head	22.6	14.6	11.8	10.8	10.1	10.2	11.7	10.7	10.6
Related children under 18 yr	31.6	19.2	15.5	15.3	14.2	15.6	18.1	16.1	16.3
Other family members	20.4	12.2	9.3	8.1	7.5	7.3	8.6	7.7	7.7
Unrelated individuals	50.8	44.4	39.5	36.6	32.9	32.6	32.5	32.4	30.4
Black and other races	66.8	50.9	41.3	40.5	38.5	37.8	38.2	38.3	38.5
In families	67.0	50.3	40.2	39.7	37.8	36.7	37.0	37.3	37.8
Head	61.0	44.1	36.4	35.8	34.4	34.2	33.8	34.5	35.4
Related children under 18 yr	78.0	60.5	50.4	51.0	48.6	47.8	48.6	48.9	49.8
Other family members	53.4	38.6	28.0	26.4	25.4	23.6	24.0	24.3	24.3
Unrelated individuals	64.0	60.1	54.0	49.4	45.6	48.0	49.7	47.9	44.6
In families with male head	27.7	17.1	12.7	11.5	10.5	10.7	12.2	11.1	11.0
In families	27.3	16.6	12.0	10.8	9.8	9.9	11.5	10.3	10.1
Head	23.6	14.8	11.1	9.7	8.9	8.8	10.1	9.2	9.0
Related children under 18 yr	33.8	20.4	14.6	13.7	12.2	12.9	15.3	13.5	13.6
Other family members	22.8	13.9	10.2	9.1	8.4	8.1	9.3	8.5	8.3
Unrelated individuals, males	42.8	36.2	30.3	27.9	25.4	26.9	26.8	26.2	25.4
In families with female head	57.1	49.6	47.0	46.6	44.4	43.9	44.4	43.6	42.5
In families	56.2	48.3	46.4	47.2	46.0	45.5	46.3	45.2	45.0
Head	49.7	41.1	40.0	41.4	40.4	40.2	41.0	40.6	40.1
Related children under 18 yr	79.4	67.4	62.9	63.9	61.9	62.5	62.8	60.8	60.4
Other family members	29.8	26.6	24.1	23.0	22.7	20.4	21.8	22.3	22.5
Unrelated individuals, females	59.1	52.3	48.3	45.2	41.0	40.4	40.6	40.6	37.7

NA   Not available.   [1] Beginning 1974, not strictly comparable with earlier years due to revised procedures.
Source: U.S. Bureau of the Census, *Current Population Reports*, series P-60, Nos. 115 and 116, and unpublished data.

No. 758. FAMILIES BELOW POVERTY LEVEL UNDER ALTERNATIVE INCOME DEFINITIONS, BY RACE, AGE OF HEAD, AND REGION: 1976

[For year ending **June 30**. Data measure the incidence of poverty under different income concepts. Unrelated individuals are included in these data as "one-person families." Based on data from Current Population Survey, adjusted by source for underreporting of income and nonreporting of families residing in the outlying areas and institutions. Cash transfer income includes payments for social security and railroad retirement, government pensions, unemployment insurance, workmen's and veterans' compensation, veterans' pensions, supplemental security income, and aid to families with dependent children. In-kind transfers include food stamps, child nutrition, housing assistance, medicare, and medicaid. For composition of regions, see fig. I, inside front cover]

INCOME DEFINITION	Families, total	RACE		AGE OF HEAD		REGION			
		White	Black and other	Under 65	65 and over	North-east	North Cen-tral	South	West
		FAMILIES BELOW POVERTY LEVEL (1,000)							
Income before taxes and—									
Before receipt of cash transfers	21,436	17,330	4,106	11,789	9,647	4,765	4,881	7,873	3,918
After receipt of cash transfers [1]	10,716	8,006	2,709	8,029	2,686	2,072	2,268	4,552	1,824
After receipt of in-kind trans-fers [2]	6,441	4,948	1,492	5,463	977	1,005	1,194	3,041	1,200
Income after taxes and after re-ceipt of all types of transfers	6,597	5,091	1,506	5,615	982	1,032	1,240	3,092	1,233
		AS PERCENT OF ALL FAMILIES [3]							
Income before taxes and—									
Before receipt of cash transfers	27.0	24.7	43.8	18.6	59.9	26.4	23.3	30.8	26.2
After receipt of cash transfers [1]	13.5	11.4	28.9	12.7	16.7	11.5	10.8	17.8	12.2
After receipt of in-kind trans-fers [2]	8.1	7.1	15.9	8.6	6.1	5.6	5.7	11.9	8.0
Income after taxes and after re-ceipt of all types of transfers	8.3	7.3	16.1	8.9	6.1	5.7	5.9	12.1	8.2

[1] Corresponds to U.S. Bureau of the Census measure of income used to derive poverty status. See text, pp. 438 and 439, and table 755.   [2] Includes the additions to income of cash transfers.   [3] In the categories shown.

Source: Congress of the United States, Congressional Budget Office, Background Paper No. 17 (revised), *Poverty Status of Families Under Alternative Definitions of Income*, June 1977.

No. 759. FAMILIES AND UNRELATED INDIVIDUALS BELOW POVERTY LEVEL AND AGGREGATE INCOME DEFICIT (1976 DOLLARS), BY SEX AND RACE OF HEAD: 1959 TO 1976

[As of **March** of following year. Income deficit defined as the difference between the total income of families and unrelated individuals below poverty level and their respective poverty thresholds. In computing the income deficit, families reporting a net income loss are assigned zero dollars; for such cases, the deficit is equal to the poverty level. For explanation of poverty level, see table 755 and text, p. 438]

SEX AND RACE OF FAMILY HEADS AND UNRELATED INDIVIDUALS	BELOW POVERTY LEVEL					AGGREGATE INCOME DEFICIT (1976 DOLLARS)				
	1959	1967	1970	1975 [1]	1976 [1]	1959	1967	1970	1975 [1]	1976 [1]
	Millions					Bil. dol.				
Total	13.2	10.7	10.4	10.5	10.7	26.7	18.0	17.0	17.0	16.7
White	10.2	8.2	7.9	7.8	7.8	19.2	12.9	12.1	11.9	11.6
Black and other	3.0	2.5	2.5	2.7	2.9	7.5	5.1	4.9	5.1	5.1
	PERCENT					PERCENT				
Total	100.0	100.0	100.0	100.0	100.0	100.0	100.0	100.0	100.0	100.0
Families	62.8	53.1	50.8	51.7	49.8	71.8	64.8	64.6	66.0	63.2
Male head	48.3	36.5	32.0	28.7	26.0	52.3	41.1	37.5	34.9	32.4
Female head	14.5	16.6	18.9	23.1	23.9	19.4	23.8	27.1	31.0	30.9
Unrelated individuals	37.2	46.9	49.2	48.3	50.2	28.2	35.2	35.4	34.0	36.8
Male	11.7	12.2	13.9	15.8	16.8	8.7	9.5	11.4	12.7	13.8
Female	25.5	34.6	35.3	32.5	33.4	19.5	25.6	24.0	21.3	23.0
White	100.0	100.0	100.0	100.0	100.0	100.0	100.0	100.0	100.0	100.0
Families	60.5	49.5	47.1	49.1	45.8	68.1	60.1	60.3	62.7	59.0
Male head	48.4	36.9	33.1	31.3	28.1	51.5	42.1	40.6	39.3	36.5
Female head	12.1	12.7	14.0	17.8	17.7	16.7	18.0	19.7	23.3	22.4
Unrelated individuals	39.5	50.5	52.9	50.9	54.2	31.9	39.9	39.7	37.3	41.0
Male	11.3	12.0	13.9	15.7	17.0	9.0	9.8	11.9	13.1	14.4
Female	28.2	38.4	39.0	35.2	37.2	22.9	30.1	27.8	24.2	26.5
Black and other	100.0	100.0	100.0	100.0	100.0	100.0	100.0	100.0	100.0	100.0
Families	70.6	65.0	62.6	59.1	60.8	81.0	76.7	75.2	73.7	72.9
Male head	48.0	35.3	28.3	21.1	20.3	54.6	38.5	30.0	24.6	22.9
Female head	22.6	29.8	34.3	38.0	40.4	26.5	38.2	45.1	49.0	50.1
Unrelated individuals	29.4	35.0	37.4	40.9	39.2	19.0	23.3	24.8	26.3	27.1
Male	13.0	12.9	14.0	16.2	16.2	8.1	8.8	10.2	11.8	12.3
Female	16.3	22.0	23.4	24.7	23.1	10.7	14.5	14.7	14.5	14.9

[1] Beginning 1975, not strictly comparable with earlier years due to revised procedures.

Source: U.S. Bureau of the Census, *Current Population Reports*, series P–60, No. 115.

No. 760. Selected Characteristics of Families and Unrelated Individuals, by Type of Income and Poverty Status: 1977

[Families as of March 1978. Based on Current Population Survey; see text, p. 1. For explanation of poverty level, see table 755 and text, p. 438. For limitations of data, see source]

INCOME LEVEL AND TYPE OF INCOME	FAMILIES							UNRELATED INDIVIDUALS				
	Total			Female head		Head 65 yr. old and over		Total			65 yr. old and over	
	All races[1]	White	Black	White	Black	White	Black	All races[1]	White	Black	White	Black
ALL INCOME LEVELS												
Total..............mil..	57.2	50.5	5.8	5.8	2.3	7.5	.7	23.4	20.0	3.0	6.6	.7
Percent of total:[2]												
With income.............	99.8	99.8	99.4	98.9	98.8	99.9	100.0	97.1	98.0	92.1	99.7	99.9
With earnings[3]...........	87.6	88.2	81.9	78.1	67.9	47.1	59.4	63.1	63.4	59.9	17.3	18.6
With transfer income.....	39.1	37.7	51.9	58.4	69.2	94.1	95.6	45.2	45.9	43.6	95.4	96.6
Social security[4].........	22.6	22.8	21.7	34.0	22.8	92.9	87.9	34.9	36.5	25.9	93.3	86.7
Supplemental security[5]	2.8	2.1	8.3	5.6	10.3	6.5	28.7	5.8	4.9	12.2	10.4	32.6
Public assistance[5]......	6.0	4.0	22.6	19.6	46.5	1.3	12.7	2.4	1.7	7.3	1.3	5.0
Other transfer income[6]..	15.0	15.2	13.9	13.7	9.5	10.2	11.2	9.8	10.0	9.3	7.1	6.1
With all other income[7]...	59.1	63.0	25.5	57.0	19.2	78.6	31.8	50.5	55.2	19.2	67.0	28.2
BELOW POVERTY LEVEL												
Total..............mil..	5.3	3.5	1.6	1.4	1.2	.5	.2	5.5	4.2	1.2	1.6	.4
Percent of total:[2]												
With income.............	97.7	97.5	97.9	95.5	97.6	98.7	100.0	87.9	90.5	80.2	98.9	99.7
With earnings[3]...........	58.0	60.6	51.6	45.9	46.0	20.3	35.0	35.0	36.8	27.8	7.4	7.7
With transfer income.....	64.4	58.3	78.4	67.9	83.6	96.6	95.3	56.1	56.6	57.7	96.1	98.3
Social security[4].........	22.4	22.0	23.3	12.6	16.9	87.9	81.3	40.9	43.5	33.9	89.2	83.7
Supplemental security[5]	9.6	7.7	13.9	4.2	10.8	29.0	51.4	15.4	13.5	23.0	23.8	45.3
Public assistance[5]......	37.6	29.9	55.2	53.5	69.8	6.4	18.7	6.8	5.0	13.8	2.9	6.1
Other transfer income[6]..	10.4	11.3	8.5	5.2	5.1	4.7	4.7	6.8	7.5	5.0	5.7	6.1
With all other income[7]...	21.1	25.9	10.4	25.8	11.0	29.9	10.3	26.4	31.2	9.8	33.8	14.4

[1] Includes races not shown separately. [2] Some families and unrelated individuals may have more than one type of income. [3] Includes wages, salaries, and self-employment income. [4] Includes railroad retirement income. [5] See text, p. 325, for explanation of supplemental security income and public assistance. [6] Includes unemployment and workmen's compensation, and veterans' payments. [7] Includes income from private and government employee pensions, annuities, dividends, interest, rent, estates, trusts, alimony, child support, regular contributions from outside the household, etc.

Source: U.S. Bureau of the Census, *Current Population Reports*, series P–60, No. 119, and unpublished data.

No. 761. Percent Distribution of Persons Residing in Poverty Areas, by Poverty Status and Race: 1970 and 1978

[Persons' residence as of April 1970 and March 1978 respectively; poverty status based on income in 1969 and 1977, respectively. 1970 from Census of Population; 1978 from Current Population Survey. Poverty areas are those in which 20 percent or more of the population had income in 1969 below the poverty level. For definition of poverty level, see table 755 and text, p. 438. Metropolitan-nonmetropolitan status as of 1970. Metropolitan refers to 243 SMSA's as defined in 1970 census publications; see pp. 935–937, Appendix II. For further details, see source]

RESIDENCE	ALL PERSONS[1]			WHITE			BLACK		
	Total	Poor	Non-poor	Total	Poor	Non-poor	Total	Poor	Non-poor
1970 (April)									
Metropolitan areas[2].....................	100.0	100.0	100.0	100.0	100.0	100.0	100.0	100.0	100.0
Poverty areas.....................	15.4	39.5	12.3	9.9	25.8	8.4	54.8	69.5	48.7
Nonpoverty areas.................	84.6	60.5	87.7	90.1	74.2	91.6	45.2	30.5	51.3
Central cities...................	100.0	100.0	100.0	100.0	100.0	100.0	100.0	100.0	100.0
Poverty areas.....................	24.4	50.0	19.9	15.4	34.6	12.9	58.8	72.7	53.0
Nonpoverty areas.................	75.6	50.0	80.1	84.6	65.4	87.1	41.2	27.3	47.0
Nonmetropolitan areas[3]...............	100.0	100.0	100.0	100.0	100.0	100.0	100.0	100.0	100.0
Poverty areas.....................	35.1	56.5	30.0	30.9	47.5	27.9	74.3	81.6	66.0
Nonpoverty areas.................	64.9	43.5	70.0	69.1	52.5	72.1	25.7	18.4	34.0
1978 (March)									
Metropolitan areas[2].....................	100.0	100.0	100.0	100.0	100.0	100.0	100.0	100.0	100.0
Poverty areas.....................	11.1	34.3	8.4	6.6	19.7	5.5	41.2	60.6	33.4
Nonpoverty areas.................	88.9	65.7	91.6	93.4	80.3	94.5	58.8	39.4	66.6
Central cities...................	100.0	100.0	100.0	100.0	100.0	100.0	100.0	100.0	100.0
Poverty areas.....................	19.0	44.9	14.3	10.6	27.6	8.6	47.2	64.8	39.3
Nonpoverty areas.................	81.0	55.1	85.7	89.4	72.5	91.4	52.8	35.2	60.7
Nonmetropolitan areas[3]...............	100.0	100.0	100.0	100.0	100.0	100.0	100.0	100.0	100.0
Poverty areas.....................	34.4	53.1	31.4	30.6	43.6	29.0	70.4	78.1	65.4
Nonpoverty areas.................	65.6	46.9	68.6	69.4	56.4	71.0	29.6	21.8	34.7

[1] Includes races not shown separately. [2] Poverty areas defined in terms of census tracts. [3] Poverty areas defined in terms of minor civil divisions (townships, districts, etc.).

Source: U.S. Bureau of the Census, *Current Population Reports*, series P–23, No. 55, and P–60, No. 116.

No. 762. Persons and Families Below Poverty Level—States: 1959 to 1975

[Number in thousands. Persons and families as of April 1960 and 1970, and spring 1976. For explanation of poverty level, see text, p. 438. For 1959, excludes all persons in group quarters. For 1969, excludes unrelated individuals under 14 years of age and persons in specified types of group quarters, i.e., inmates of institutions, persons in Armed Forces living in barracks, and college students living in dormitories. For 1975, same as 1969, except college students living away from home are included at their family's home. Poverty criteria computed on a national basis only and not adjusted for regional, State, or other local variations in cost of living, 1975 data from the 1976 Survey of Income and Education (SIE), a special survey mandated by Congress as part of the Education Amendments of 1974 (Public Law 93–380); based on a sample of 151,000 interviewed households; subject to sampling variability. For details, see sources]

STATE	NUMBER BELOW POVERTY LEVEL						PERCENT BELOW POVERTY LEVEL					
	Persons			Families			Persons			Families		
	1959	1969	1975	1959	1969	1975	1959	1969	1975	1959	1969	1975
U.S.	38,682	27,125	23,991	8,315	5,462	5,051	22.1	13.7	11.4	18.4	10.7	9.0
No. East.	6,249	4,821	4,336	1,359	936	[1] 921	14.4	10.1	8.9	11.8	7.6	[1] 7.2
Maine	222	131	[1] 126	48	26	[1] 26	23.7	13.6	12.0	19.9	10.3	[1] 9.3
N.H.	87	65	[1] 65	19	12	[1] 13	14.9	9.1	7.9	12.2	6.7	5.9
Vt.	88	52	63	18	10	13	23.5	12.1	[1] 13.5	19.3	9.1	10.8
Mass.	608	473	408	130	87	[1] 90	12.2	8.6	7.1	10.1	6.2	[1] 6.1
R.I.	135	100	80	31	20	17	16.5	11.0	8.7	14.1	8.5	6.9
Conn.	236	212	[1] 204	52	41	[1] 46	9.6	7.2	[1] 6.7	8.0	5.3	[1] 5.6
N.Y.	2,319	1,986	1,671	497	391	[1] 357	14.2	11.1	9.4	11.5	8.5	7.6
N.J.	673	574	[1] 586	150	113	133	11.3	8.1	[1] 8.1	9.5	6.1	6.9
Pa.	1,881	1,228	[1] 1,133	414	237	[1] 227	17.0	10.6	[1] 9.7	14.3	7.9	[1] 7.4
No. Cen.	8,953	5,952	5,336	1,973	1,171	1,109	17.7	10.8	9.4	15.0	8.3	7.4
Ohio	1,508	1,041	[1] 997	325	205	[1] 208	15.9	10.0	[1] 9.4	13.2	7.6	[1] 7.3
Ind.	797	493	424	176	98	85	17.5	9.7	8.1	14.7	7.4	6.0
Ill.	1,446	1,112	[1] 1,150	316	214	[1] 238	14.7	10.2	[1] 10.5	12.2	7.7	[1] 8.3
Mich.	1,216	819	[1] 821	258	160	183	15.9	9.4	[1] 9.1	13.3	7.3	[1] 7.6
Wis.	607	421	352	132	80	69	15.7	9.8	7.7	13.4	7.4	5.8
Minn.	646	398	324	140	76	63	19.3	10.7	8.3	16.7	8.2	6.4
Iowa	583	319	225	135	64	44	21.5	11.6	7.9	18.9	8.9	5.8
Mo.	1,051	672	565	244	139	121	24.9	14.7	12.0	21.5	11.5	9.5
N. Dak.	169	93	66	35	18	13	27.1	15.7	10.6	23.5	12.4	8.0
S. Dak.	202	120	88	45	24	19	30.1	18.7	13.1	26.8	14.8	10.6
Nebr.	309	188	147	71	38	29	22.3	13.1	9.6	19.4	10.1	7.1
Kans.	419	275	178	96	56	38	19.7	12.7	8.0	16.9	9.7	6.1
South	19,104	12,388	10,406	4,072	2,581	2,202	35.6	20.3	15.3	30.0	16.2	12.1
Del.	73	58	47	16	11	[1] 10	16.8	10.9	8.2	13.9	8.2	6.6
Md.	523	387	313	107	75	[1] 66	17.4	10.1	7.7	14.0	7.7	6.2
D.C.	161	123	86	29	21	[1] 18	22.2	17.0	12.5	16.7	12.7	[1] 11.4
Va.	1,164	691	513	245	143	110	30.6	15.5	10.5	25.7	12.3	8.3
W. Va.	637	380	270	139	82	57	34.6	22.2	15.1	30.2	18.0	11.5
N.C.	1,796	996	788	373	211	182	40.6	20.3	14.7	34.1	16.3	12.1
S.C.	1,049	595	478	206	119	94	45.4	23.9	17.2	38.0	19.0	12.9
Ga.	1,505	924	[1] 883	314	192	[1] 188	39.0	20.7	18.0	33.1	16.7	14.6
Fla.	1,371	1,088	[1] 1,225	309	229	[1] 259	28.4	16.4	14.4	23.8	12.7	11.0
Ky.	1,137	718	596	253	159	136	38.3	22.9	17.7	33.6	19.2	14.9
Tenn.	1,374	836	660	306	186	146	39.3	21.8	15.8	34.2	18.2	12.6
Ala.	1,374	857	587	292	181	125	42.5	25.4	16.4	36.9	20.7	12.9
Miss.	1,173	767	607	240	154	122	54.5	35.4	26.1	47.9	28.9	20.4
Ark.	843	523	392	190	115	82	48.3	27.8	18.5	42.1	22.8	14.1
La.	1,274	933	720	262	188	141	39.5	26.3	19.3	34.0	21.5	15.0
Okla.	680	465	370	160	102	83	29.9	18.8	13.8	26.2	15.0	11.1
Tex.	2,970	2,047	1,870	631	413	[1] 381	31.7	18.8	15.2	26.4	14.6	11.7
West	4,376	3,965	[1] 3,912	913	774	[1] 818	16.1	11.7	10.4	13.0	8.9	8.2
Mont.	129	92	[1] 86	27	18	[1] 17	19.5	13.6	11.5	16.2	10.4	8.9
Idaho	124	92	[1] 85	27	20	[1] 18	18.7	13.2	10.3	16.4	10.9	8.2
Wyo.	51	38	33	11	8	[1] 7	15.6	11.7	8.7	13.1	9.3	7.0
Colo.	312	263	[1] 230	64	50	42	18.3	12.3	9.1	14.5	9.1	6.3
N. Mex.	278	227	[1] 223	55	45	[1] 46	29.9	22.8	19.3	24.7	18.5	15.5
Ariz.	314	264	314	62	50	64	24.9	15.3	[1] 13.8	20.0	11.5	[1] 10.8
Utah	135	118	103	28	23	[1] 21	15.4	11.4	8.5	13.3	9.1	7.0
Nev.	35	43	53	7	9	11	12.8	9.1	[1] 8.8	10.3	7.0	[1] 7.0
Wash.	397	336	[1] 299	86	65	[1] 61	14.3	10.2	8.5	11.9	7.6	6.6
Oreg.	262	235	204	59	46	[1] 41	15.1	11.5	8.9	12.9	8.6	6.7
Calif.	2,199	2,153	[1] 2,192	461	421	[1] 472	14.4	11.1	[1] 10.4	11.6	8.4	[1] 8.5
Alaska	38	35	23	7	6	4	19.0	12.6	6.7	14.7	9.3	5.2
Hawaii	102	69	[1] 67	19	13	[1] 13	17.1	9.3	7.9	14.7	7.6	6.4

[1] Change from the 1969 data is not statistically significant at the 95 percent confidence level (2 standard errors); for a discussion of confidence levels, see Appendix III.

Source: 1959, U.S. Office of Economic Opportunity, unpublished data. Thereafter, U.S. Bureau of the Census, *U.S. Census of Population: 1970*, vol. 1; and 1975, *Current Population Reports*, series P-60, Nos. 110–113.

No. 763. Persons Below the Poverty Level, by Residence, Race, and Family Status: 1975 and 1977

[Persons as of **March 1976** and **1978**. For explanation of poverty level, see table 755 and text, p. 438. Refers to 243 metropolitan areas as defined in 1970 census publications; see Appendix II]

FAMILY STATUS AND RESIDENCE	PERSONS BELOW POVERTY LEVEL (1,000)						PERCENT BELOW POVERTY LEVEL					
	All races		White		Black		All races		White		Black	
	1975	1977	1975	1977	1975	1977	1975	1977	1975	1977	1975	1977
Metropolitan areas	15,348	14,859	10,014	9,265	4,967	5,289	10.8	10.4	8.2	7.6	27.6	28.6
In families	12,125	11,477	7,593	6,752	4,247	4,492	9.5	9.1	7.0	6.3	26.4	27.9
Head	3,216	3,141	2,120	1,949	1,029	1,118	8.5	8.3	6.5	5.9	24.0	25.6
Related children [1]	6,646	6,208	3,909	3,412	2,591	2,681	15.4	15.1	11.1	10.2	37.4	39.1
Other family members [2]	2,263	2,128	1,564	1,390	627	694	4.8	4.5	3.8	3.4	12.9	14.2
Unrelated individuals	3,224	3,382	2,420	2,513	720	797	22.1	20.1	19.5	17.7	37.4	33.7
Inside central cities	9,090	9,203	4,874	4,762	4,033	4,254	15.0	15.4	10.8	10.7	29.1	31.2
In families	7,113	7,129	3,552	3,385	3,430	3,598	13.5	14.2	9.2	9.1	27.9	30.6
Head	1,863	1,925	1,003	986	830	892	11.8	12.5	8.2	8.3	25.4	28.0
Related children [1]	4,047	3,949	1,860	1,722	2,129	2,153	23.2	23.9	16.0	15.5	39.9	42.8
Other family members [2]	1,203	1,255	688	677	471	553	6.2	6.8	4.6	4.7	12.8	15.6
Unrelated individuals	1,977	2,074	1,323	1,377	603	656	24.2	22.2	20.5	18.9	38.5	35.1
Outside central cities	6,259	5,657	5,139	4,503	934	1,035	7.6	6.8	6.7	5.9	22.5	21.3
In families	5,012	4,348	4,042	3,367	817	894	6.6	5.7	5.7	4.8	21.6	20.5
Head	1,352	1,216	1,117	963	199	225	6.2	5.4	5.4	4.6	19.7	19.3
Related children [1]	2,599	2,259	2,049	1,691	462	528	10.1	9.2	8.7	7.6	28.9	28.8
Other family members [2]	1,060	873	875	712	156	141	3.8	3.1	3.3	2.7	13.2	10.4
Unrelated individuals	1,247	1,308	1,098	1,136	118	140	19.3	17.4	18.4	16.5	32.5	28.1
Nonmetro. areas	10,529	9,861	7,757	7,151	2,578	2,437	15.4	13.9	12.6	11.2	42.4	39.1
In families	8,664	8,027	6,205	5,613	2,287	2,174	13.8	12.4	11.0	9.7	40.8	37.9
Head	2,234	2,170	1,718	1,590	484	519	12.1	11.2	10.1	9.0	37.1	35.8
Related children [1]	4,236	3,820	2,838	2,531	1,293	1,168	19.6	17.6	15.0	13.4	52.9	48.8
Other family members [2]	2,194	2,038	1,649	1,492	510	487	9.8	8.6	8.1	6.9	27.4	25.8
Unrelated individuals	1,865	1,834	1,551	1,538	291	263	33.2	29.2	30.5	27.0	61.3	53.1

[1] Under 18 years.   [2] Includes spouses.

Source: U.S. Bureau of the Census, *Current Population Reports*, series P-60, No. 106, and forthcoming report.

No. 764. Mothers With Children Under 18 Years Old, by Work Experience, Poverty Status, and Race: 1976

[Based on Current Population Survey as of **March** of the following year; see headnote, table 729. For explanation of poverty level, see table 755 and text, p. 438]

WORK EXPERIENCE	ALL RACES			WHITE			BLACK		
	Total (1,000)	Below poverty level		Total (1,000)	Below poverty level		Total (1,000)	Below poverty level	
		Number (1,000)	Per-cent		Number (1,000)	Per-cent		Number (1,000)	Per-cent
All women with own children	30,510	3,840	12.6	26,157	2,458	9.4	3,790	1,274	33.6
Worked in 1976	17,647	1,434	8.1	14,979	939	6.3	2,333	458	19.6
50–52 weeks	8,509	356	4.2	7,052	226	3.2	1,286	123	9.5
27–49 weeks	4,103	335	8.2	3,513	213	6.1	522	116	22.2
1–26 weeks	5,034	743	14.8	4,413	501	11.4	525	220	41.9
Did not work in 1976	12,864	2,406	18.7	11,178	1,520	13.6	1,457	816	56.0
Main reason: Keeping house	11,630	1,912	16.4	10,386	1,293	12.4	1,038	556	53.6
Families and subfamilies headed by women with own children	5,403	2,279	42.2	3,548	1,245	35.1	1,783	997	55.9
Worked in 1976	3,458	864	25.0	2,417	484	20.0	999	370	37.0
50–52 weeks	1,894	185	9.8	1,336	82	6.1	540	100	18.6
27–49 weeks	764	225	29.5	558	127	22.8	197	98	49.7
1–26 weeks	800	454	56.8	524	275	52.5	263	171	65.0
Did not work in 1976	1,945	1,415	72.8	1,131	761	67.3	784	628	80.0
Main reason: Keeping house	1,400	1,020	72.9	895	604	67.4	482	396	82.3

Source: U.S. Bureau of the Census, *Current Population Reports*, series P-60, forthcoming report.

No. 765. WORK EXPERIENCE OF FAMILY HEADS BELOW THE POVERTY LEVEL, BY SEX AND RACE: 1975 AND 1977

[In thousands, except percent. Families as of March of the following year. Based on Current Population Survey; see headnote, table 729. For definition of poverty level, see headnote, table 755, and text, p. 438]

WORK EXPERIENCE	1975						1977					
	All races		White		Black		All races		White		Black	
	Male	Female	Male	Female	Male	Female	Male	Female	Male	Female	Male	Female
Total	3,020	2,430	2,444	1,394	509	1,004	2,701	2,610	2,140	1,400	475	1,162
Worked	1,857	887	1,533	518	272	362	1,631	937	1,329	506	243	410
Year-round, full-time...percent	39.4	15.2	40.3	14.5	34.9	16.6	48.0	13.8	48.8	11.1	47.3	17.3
Did not work	1,133	1,543	884	876	236	641	1,049	1,673	793	894	229	752
Ill or disabled	565	309	430	150	133	157	487	272	356	120	124	145
Keeping house	26	1,053	19	647	7	387	13	1,136	11	655	2	463
In school	30	43	13	13	12	30	30	84	23	38	5	45
Unable find work	117	99	92	41	22	55	76	131	66	51	10	80
Other	395	38	330	25	62	12	444	49	338	30	88	19
In Armed Forces	30	-	28	-	2	-	21	-	17	-	3	-

- Represents zero or rounds to zero.

No. 766. WOMEN 14 YEARS OLD AND OVER BELOW THE POVERTY LEVEL, BY AGE, FAMILY RELATIONSHIP, AND RACE: 1970 AND 1977

[Based on Current Population Survey as of March of following year; see headnote, table 729. 1977 not strictly comparable with 1970 due to revised procedures. For explanation of poverty level, see table 755 and text, p. 438]

AGE AND FAMILY RELATIONSHIP	NUMBER OF WOMEN (1,000)						PERCENT OF TOTAL			
	1970			1977			1970		1977	
	Total	White	Black	Total	White	Black	White	Black	White	Black
Total	10,500	7,695	2,694	10,516	7,211	3,110	100.0	100.0	100.0	100.0
14 to 21 years	1,959	1,254	677	2,414	1,483	889	16.3	25.1	20.6	28.6
22 to 44 years	2,994	2,022	923	3,694	2,444	1,152	26.3	34.3	33.9	37.0
45 to 54 years	1,043	691	341	1,005	685	300	9.0	12.7	9.5	9.6
55 to 64 years	1,347	1,017	324	1,187	860	312	13.2	12.0	11.9	10.0
65 years and over	3,157	2,711	430	2,216	1,739	457	35.2	16.0	24.1	14.7
Family relationship:										
Family heads	1,934	1,097	820	2,610	1,400	1,162	14.3	30.4	19.4	37.4
Spouses	3,133	2,517	570	2,524	2,033	419	32.7	21.2	28.2	13.5
Other family members	1,842	1,047	765	1,963	1,031	896	13.6	28.4	14.3	28.8
Unrelated individuals	3,592	3,033	539	3,419	2,747	636	39.4	20.0	38.1	20.5

No. 767. SELECTED CHARACTERISTICS OF PERSONS 60 AND 65 YEARS OLD AND OVER BELOW POVERTY LEVEL: 1959 TO 1977

[For 1959, persons as of April 1960; thereafter, persons as of March of following year. See headnote, table 765]

AGE, FAMILY STATUS, AND RACE	NUMBER BELOW POVERTY LEVEL (1,000)					PERCENT BELOW POVERTY LEVEL				
	1959	1970	1975[1]	1976[1]	1977[1]	1959	1970	1975[1]	1976[1]	1977[1]
Persons, 60 and over	(NA)	5,977	4,373	4,285	4,123	(NA)	21.3	14.2	13.7	12.9
Persons, 65 and over	5,481	4,793	3,317	3,313	3,177	35.2	24.6	15.3	15.0	14.1
White	4,744	4,011	2,634	2,633	2,426	33.1	22.6	13.4	13.2	11.9
Black	711	735	652	644	701	62.5	47.7	36.3	34.8	36.3
In families	3,187	2,013	1,191	1,185	1,176	26.9	14.8	8.0	7.9	7.8
Head	1,787	1,188	728	726	710	29.1	16.5	8.9	8.9	8.6
Male	1,507	980	585	561	551	29.1	15.9	8.3	8.0	7.8
Female	280	209	143	165	159	28.8	20.1	12.7	14.4	13.7
Other members	1,400	825	463	459	466	24.6	13.0	7.0	6.6	6.7
Unrelated individuals	2,294	2,779	2,125	2,129	2,001	61.9	47.2	31.0	30.3	27.3
Male	703	549	410	403	386	59.0	38.9	27.8	25.9	23.6
Female	1,591	2,230	1,716	1,726	1,615	63.3	49.8	31.9	31.5	28.4

NA Not available. [1] Beginning 1975, not strictly comparable with earlier years due to revised procedures.

Source of tables 765–767: U.S. Bureau of the Census, *Current Population Reports*, series P-60, Nos. 95, 106, 107, 115, 116, and forthcoming report.

No. 768. PERSONS OF SPANISH ORIGIN AND MEXICAN OR PUERTO RICAN ORIGIN, BY POVERTY STATUS, FAMILY STATUS, AND SEX OF HEAD: 1977

[In thousands, except as indicated. Families as of March 1978. For explanation of poverty level, see table 755 and text, p. 438]

CHARACTERISTIC	SPANISH ORIGIN [1]			MEXICAN			PUERTO RICAN		
	Total	Below poverty level		Total	Below poverty level		Total	Below poverty level	
		Number	Percent		Number	Percent		Number	Percent
ALL PERSONS									
Total	12,046	2,700	22.4	7,151	1,509	21.1	1,823	707	38.8
65 years and over	518	113	21.9	265	60	22.6	42	12	27.7
In families	11,249	2,463	21.9	6,765	1,386	20.5	1,690	667	39.5
Head	2,764	591	21.4	1,623	306	18.9	437	170	38.9
Wife of head	2,155	284	13.2	1,302	188	14.5	258	43	16.6
Related children under 18 years	5,000	1,402	28.0	3,053	785	25.7	835	415	49.7
Related children under 6 years	1,802	536	29.7	1,163	332	28.5	262	127	48.4
Other family members	1,330	185	13.9	787	107	13.6	159	39	24.7
Mean size of family	4.07	4.17	(X)	4.17	4.53	(X)	3.86	3.92	(X)
Mean family income___dollars	13,293	4,192	(X)	13,304	4,346	(X)	10,464	4,314	(X)
Unrelated individuals	797	237	29.8	386	123	31.8	133	40	29.9
Mean income_____dollars	6,496	1,692	(X)	6,055	1,604	(X)	5,980	1,841	(X)
PERSONS IN FAMILIES WITH FEMALE HEAD									
Total	2,259	1,204	53.3	1,068	519	48.6	671	473	70.4
65 years and over	136	46	34.0	69	25	36.3	19	6	30.9
Head	561	301	53.6	252	116	45.9	179	126	70.3
Related children under 18 years	1,001	686	68.6	465	291	62.6	367	303	82.6
Related children under 6 years	313	238	76.1	151	111	73.4	108	91	84.4
Other family members	338	89	26.5	191	45	23.3	63	25	39.9
Mean size of family	3.39	3.58	(X)	3.60	3.91	(X)	3.41	3.61	(X)
Mean family income___dollars	7,183	3,700	(X)	8,314	3,551	(X)	5,584	4,175	(X)

X Not applicable.   [1] Includes "other Spanish," not shown separately.

Source: U.S. Bureau of the Census, Current Population Reports, series P-60, forthcoming report.

No. 769. APPALACHIA—POPULATION AND UNEMPLOYMENT, 1970 AND 1977, AND PERSONS BELOW POVERTY AND NEAR-POVERTY LEVEL, 1969

["Appalachia" refers to a region delineated in The Appalachian Regional Development Act of 1965, as amended, containing 397 counties in 13 States. For definition of poverty level, see table 755, and text, p. 438]

AREA	POPULATION [1]			UNEMPLOYED			POVERTY LEVEL, 1969		NEAR-POVERTY [3] LEVEL, 1969	
	1970, April, total (1,000)	1977, July, total [2] (1,000)	Percent change, 1970–1977	1977, total (1,000)	Percent of labor force		Persons below (1,000)	Percent of 1970 population	Persons below (1,000)	Percent of 1970 population
					1970	1977				
United States	203,305	216,332	6.4	6,855	4.9	7.0	27,125	13.7	36,902	18.6
Appalachian States	76,090	78,829	3.6	2,489	4.6	7.1	11,406	15.4	15,270	20.6
Appalachian region	18,217	19,330	6.1	584	5.4	7.2	3,228	18.1	4,379	24.6
Appalachian portion of—										
Alabama	2,137	2,282	6.8	73	6.2	7.5	463	22.1	610	29.1
Georgia	814	1,001	23.0	27	3.8	6.3	136	17.0	190	23.6
Kentucky	877	1,001	14.2	22	7.5	5.6	334	38.8	408	47.4
Maryland	209	217	3.7	10	6.2	10.9	30	14.7	45	21.9
Mississippi	419	453	8.2	14	5.1	7.2	139	33.8	172	41.9
New York	1,057	1,086	2.8	40	5.1	8.5	117	11.5	172	16.9
North Carolina	1,039	1,133	9.0	31	4.5	5.6	190	18.7	261	25.7
Ohio	1,130	1,200	6.2	36	6.5	7.5	176	16.0	246	22.3
Pennsylvania	5,931	5,911	−.3	193	5.3	7.7	664	11.4	972	16.8
South Carolina	656	734	11.8	22	3.7	6.3	104	16.2	145	22.6
Tennessee	1,735	1,929	11.2	55	5.2	6.7	381	22.4	506	29.7
Virginia	470	524	11.4	14	[4] 5.4	6.4	113	24.4	152	32.7
West Virginia [5]	1,744	1,859	6.6	49	6.1	7.1	380	22.2	501	29.3
Non-Appalachian portions	57,873	59,499	2.8	1,904	4.4	7.1	8,178	14.5	10,891	19.3

[1] Revised 1970 census data from U.S. Bureau of the Census, Current Population Reports, series P-25, No. 615; current State estimates by county from series P-25 and P-26.
[2] W. Va. from U.S. Bureau of the Census State estimate; other areas estimated by source.
[3] 125 percent of poverty level.   [4] Estimated.   [5] Entire State lies within the Appalachian region.

Source: Appalachian Regional Commission. Based on population data from U.S. Bureau of the Census and on labor force data from U.S. Bureau of Labor Statistics and individual State reporting agencies.

No. 770. APPALACHIA—PER CAPITA AND FAMILY INCOME: 1965 TO 1975

[See headnote, table 769. See text, pp. 437 and 438, for explanation of differences between personal income and money income. For definition of median, see p. xii]

| AREA | PER CAPITA MONEY INCOME [1] | | | | PER CAPITA PERSONAL INCOME [2] | | | | FAMILY INCOME, 1969 [1] | |
| | Total | | Percent of U.S. | | Total | | Percent of U.S. | | Median money income | Percent of U.S. |
	1969	1974	1969	1974	1965	1975	1965	1975		
United States	$3,119	$4,572	100.0	100.0	$2,785	$5,903	100	100	$9,586	100.0
Appalachian States	3,000	4,375	96.2	95.7	2,664	5,675	96	96	9,206	96.0
Appalachian region	2,505	3,773	80.3	82.5	2,178	4,946	78	84	7,941	82.8
Appalachian portion of—										
Alabama	2,430	3,787	77.9	82.8	2,092	4,840	75	82	7,544	78.7
Georgia	2,419	3,711	77.6	81.2	1,944	4,546	70	77	7,777	81.1
Kentucky	1,732	2,834	55.5	62.0	1,378	3,901	49	66	5,055	52.7
Maryland	2,599	3,885	83.3	85.0	2,255	5,067	81	86	8,212	85.7
Mississippi	1,861	2,953	59.7	64.6	1,474	3,744	53	63	5,806	60.6
New York	2,845	3,912	91.2	85.6	2,505	5,235	90	89	9,310	97.1
North Carolina	2,437	3,808	78.1	83.3	2,090	4,830	75	82	7,466	77.9
Ohio	2,443	3,613	78.3	79.0	2,128	4,654	76	79	8,191	85.4
Pennsylvania	2,790	4,098	89.5	89.6	2,498	5,511	90	93	8,821	92.0
South Carolina	2,571	3,976	82.4	87.0	2,172	4,849	78	82	8,229	85.8
Tennessee	2,340	3,605	75.0	78.8	1,959	4,583	70	78	7,056	73.7
Virginia	2,064	3,344	66.2	73.1	1,543	4,318	55	73	6,536	68.2
West Virginia [3]	2,333	3,617	74.8	79.1	2,109	4,946	76	84	7,414	77.3
Non-Appalachian portions	3,156	4,569	101.2	99.9	2,823	5,909	101	100	9,703	101.2

[1] Data from U.S. Bureau of the Census, series P-60, Nos. 649–698.   [2] Data from U.S. Bureau of Economic Analysis.   [3] Entire State lies within the Appalachian region.

Source: Appalachian Regional Commission, unpublished data.

No. 771. PERCENT OF HOUSEHOLDS OWNING MOTOR VEHICLES AND TELEVISION SETS AND HAVING AVAILABLE SELECTED OTHER APPLIANCES: 1974

| CHARACTERISTIC | Total households (mil.) | PERCENT OWNING— | | | | | PERCENT WITH— | | | | |
| | | One or more motor vehicles [1] | One car | Two or more cars | TV set | Color TV set | Air-conditioning | | Refrigerator | Freezer | Washing machine |
							Central	Room			
All households	70.8	83.8	48.8	32.7	96.6	61.3	18.7	31.8	98.9	33.7	71.9
White	62.6	86.8	50.1	34.3	96.9	64.2	20.0	33.2	99.1	35.0	74.5
Black	7.3	58.5	39.2	18.2	93.7	37.8	8.5	21.9	97.5	24.1	51.4
Spanish origin	2.9	71.6	44.2	24.8	94.4	48.2	11.8	26.4	99.0	12.2	57.5
Region: [2]											
Northeast	16.6	75.6	44.4	30.5	97.3	59.2	6.3	36.2	99.3	22.7	68.4
North Central	18.9	86.2	49.5	34.9	96.9	64.1	18.6	32.7	98.5	39.0	76.5
South	22.5	85.5	50.1	32.5	96.4	58.1	29.9	37.5	99.1	38.6	71.9
West	12.8	87.9	51.4	32.7	95.5	65.7	15.2	14.8	98.8	31.5	69.8
Residence: [3]											
Central cities	22.3	72.4	44.9	26.4	95.6	56.1	17.3	33.1	98.4	20.3	60.0
Suburban rings	26.2	90.1	47.2	41.1	97.7	69.4	23.4	32.2	99.1	33.9	77.0
Outside metro. areas	22.3	87.8	54.7	29.1	96.3	57.0	14.5	30.1	99.2	47.0	77.9
Annual income:											
Under $3,000	8.0	46.2	37.0	6.2	89.7	31.6	7.9	21.7	96.6	19.7	50.7
$3,000 to $4,999	7.4	64.2	51.9	8.8	94.4	40.6	10.7	27.0	98.7	23.6	55.4
$5,000 to $7,499	8.9	79.4	60.4	15.6	96.1	50.4	13.0	30.5	98.7	26.6	62.6
$7,500 to $9,999	8.3	88.3	61.9	23.1	97.0	57.8	13.6	35.2	99.1	30.4	68.5
$10,000 to $14,999	15.9	93.9	54.9	36.8	97.9	67.4	18.2	35.5	99.4	37.0	77.2
$15,000 to $19,999	9.7	96.7	45.4	50.1	99.0	78.1	24.4	36.1	99.5	40.6	85.3
$20,000 to $24,999	5.2	97.4	36.8	60.1	99.0	80.2	28.7	34.3	99.7	44.2	86.0
$25,000 and over	7.1	97.2	29.4	67.2	98.7	84.4	38.6	30.4	99.7	48.4	89.2
Age of head:											
Under 25 years	6.1	85.6	56.9	25.0	93.0	41.5	17.4	28.9	98.5	8.9	44.1
25 to 29 years	7.5	89.3	57.0	29.8	95.9	53.3	19.9	34.9	99.3	20.3	62.7
30 to 34 years	6.9	90.3	53.8	34.0	97.8	69.8	22.9	33.2	99.3	32.1	75.9
35 to 44 years	12.3	90.3	45.5	43.2	97.9	71.0	21.6	30.2	99.2	45.9	83.3
45 to 54 years	12.6	89.4	39.5	48.1	97.3	68.4	21.0	33.2	98.8	44.0	81.7
55 to 64 years	11.6	85.7	48.5	34.7	97.2	63.8	16.2	33.6	98.9	39.5	77.1
65 years and over	13.7	64.2	50.1	11.7	95.7	49.8	13.9	29.5	98.7	27.6	63.8

[1] Includes pickup truck, camper, or other light truck.   [2] For composition of regions, see fig. I, inside front cover.   [3] Based on 243 SMSA's as defined for the 1970 census. See Appendix II.

Source: U.S. Bureau of the Census, "Selected Data From the 1973 and 1974 Surveys of Purchases and Ownership."

No. 772. PERSONAL WEALTH—TOP WEALTHHOLDERS, BY CHARACTERISTICS AND BY SIZE OF GROSS ESTATE, AND ASSET COMPOSITION: 1953 TO 1972

[Estimates based on Federal estate tax returns showing gross assets of $60,000 or more, filed with Internal Revenue Service. Comparability of data is affected by revisions in estimating techniques]

ITEM	TOTAL					PERCENT DISTRIBUTION				
	1953	1958	1962	1969	1972	1953	1958	1962	1969	1972
NUMBER	TOP WEALTHHOLDERS (1,000)					TOP WEALTHHOLDERS				
Total	1,979	3,009	4,132	9,013	12,815	100.0	100.0	100.0	100.0	100.0
Male [1]	1,330	1,936	2,539	5,643	7,810	67.2	64.3	61.4	62.6	60.9
Under 50 years	491	741	988	2,557	3,976	24.8	24.6	23.9	28.4	31.0
50–69 years	648	923	1,173	2,329	2,810	32.7	30.7	28.4	25.8	21.9
70 years and over	151	232	332	666	762	7.6	7.7	8.0	7.4	5.9
Female [1]	648	1,073	1,594	3,370	5,006	32.7	35.7	38.6	37.4	39.1
Under 50 years	197	299	471	932	1,951	10.0	9.9	11.4	10.3	15.2
50–69 years	306	530	758	1,630	2,001	15.5	17.6	18.3	18.1	15.6
70 years and over	120	209	324	726	875	6.1	6.9	7.8	8.1	6.8
SIZE OF GROSS ESTATE										
$60,000–$99,999	(NA)	1,193	1,593	3,341	4,938	(NA)	39.6	38.6	37.1	38.5
$100,000–$199,999	(NA)	1,179	1,627	} 5,214	{ 5,175	(NA)	39.2	39.4	} 57.8	{ 40.4
$200,000–$499,999	(NA)	488	692		2,059	(NA)	16.2	16.7		16.1
$500,000–$999,999	(NA)	102	149	311	425	(NA)	3.4	3.6	3.4	3.3
$1,000,000–$9,999,999	(NA)	45	69	143	} 218	(NA)	1.5	1.7	1.6	} 1.7
$10,000,000 or more	(NA)	2	2	4		(NA)	.1	(Z)	(Z)	
TYPE OF ASSET	ASSET COMPOSITION (bil. dol.)					ASSET COMPOSITION				
Total assets	356	542	752	1,581	2,152	100.0	100.0	100.0	100.0	100.0
Real estate	82	133	188	428	645	23.0	24.5	25.0	27.1	30.0
Bonds	36	36	48	85	124	9.9	6.6	6.4	5.4	5.8
Corporate stock	141	231	326	551	629	39.6	42.6	43.3	34.9	29.2
Cash [2]	34	46	71	190	278	9.5	8.5	9.4	12.0	12.9
Notes and mortgages	13	21	30	59	86	3.5	3.8	4.0	3.8	4.0
Insurance equity	7	11	16	31	42	2.0	2.0	2.1	2.0	2.0
Other	44	66	74	236	346	12.4	12.1	9.8	14.9	16.1
Debts	32	50	82	204	301	8.9	9.2	11.0	12.9	14.0
Net worth (less deficit)	324	492	669	1,377	1,852	91.1	90.8	89.0	87.1	86.1

NA Not available.   Z Less than .05 percent.   [1] Includes persons of unknown age.
[2] Includes checking and savings accounts, savings certificates, etc.
Source: U.S. Internal Revenue Service, *Statistics of Income, 1962, 1969,* and *1972,* Supplemental Report, *Personal Wealth.*

No. 773. PERSONAL WEALTH—NUMBER OF TOP WEALTHHOLDERS, BY SEX, MARITAL STATUS, AND AGE, AND BY SIZE OF NET WORTH: 1962 AND 1972

[In thousands. See headnote, table 772]

NET-WORTH CLASS	MALE					FEMALE				
	Married	Single [1]	Widowed	Under 50 years [2]	65 yr. and over	Married	Single [1]	Widowed	Under 50 years [2]	65 yr. and over
1962, total	2,121	258	159	1,034	576	761	283	550	512	509
Under $100,000 [3]	1,276	155	86	763	245	396	159	261	286	237
$100,000–$199,999	532	62	46	174	203	228	78	182	137	167
$200,000–$499,999	235	30	21	73	95	92	34	80	60	76
$500,000–$999,999	52	7	4	16	22	30	8	17	23	18
$1,000,000 or more	26	4	2	8	11	15	3	11	7	10
1972, total	6,303	986	521	4,238	1,258	2,269	946	1,791	2,129	1,300
Under $100,000 [3]	4,254	688	301	3,401	502	1,338	517	949	1,416	570
$100,000–$249,999	1,495	209	159	611	542	682	307	584	488	531
$250,000–$499,999	361	62	41	162	131	150	68	166	126	131
$500,000–$999,999	121	17	12	40	51	65	34	56	61	43
$1,000,000 or more	71	11	7	24	31	34	20	36	39	25

[1] Includes divorced persons.   [2] Includes persons of unknown age.
[3] Includes returns with negative net worth.
Source: U.S. Internal Revenue Service, *Statistics of Income, 1962* and *1972,* Supplemental Report, *Personal Wealth.*

No. 774. Personal Wealth—Share of Top One Percent: 1922 to 1972

[Persons 21 years old and over. Data differ from those in table 775 because the latter relate to all persons]

YEAR	Percent	YEAR	Percent	YEAR	Percent
1922	31.6	1949	20.8	1962	22.0
1929	36.3	1953	24.3	1965	23.4
1933	28.3	1954	24.0	1969	20.1
1939	30.6	1956	26.0	1972	20.7
1945	23.3	1958	23.8		

Source: 1922–1956, Robert J. Lampman, *The Share of Top Wealth-Holders in National Wealth*, National Bureau of Economic Research, 1962; 1958, James D. Smith and Staunton K. Calvert, "Estimating the Wealth of Top Wealth-Holders from Estate Tax Returns," *Proceedings of the American Statistical Association*, Philadelphia, Pa., 1965 (copyright); 1962–1972, James D. Smith, unpublished estimates, The Urban Institute, Washington, D.C., and The Pennsylvania State University (copyright).

No. 775. Personal Wealth—Value of Assets Held by All Persons, Top One-Half Percent, and Top One Percent: 1958 to 1972

[In billions of dollars, except as indicated. Wealth of all persons derived from national balance sheets. Wealth of top one-half percent and one percent of all persons estimated by estate multiplier technique. Detailed descriptions of methodology and attendant problems can be found in sources cited for table 774]

ASSET	1958					1962				
	Value of gross personal assets held by—			Percent held by—		Value of gross personal assets held by—			Percent held by—	
	All persons	Top ½ percent of all	Top 1 percent of all	Top ½ percent of all	Top 1 percent of all	All persons	Top ½ percent of all	Top 1 percent of all	Top ½ percent of all	Top 1 percent of all
Total assets	1,625.1	332.0	414.4	20.4	25.5	2,093.9	432.4	548.3	20.7	26.2
Real estate [1]	621.5	62.5	93.9	10.1	15.1	770.0	79.6	117.8	10.3	15.3
Corporate stock [2]	264.1	175.9	199.2	66.6	75.4	426.4	227.3	264.4	53.3	62.0
Bonds	87.0	31.3	36.0	36.0	41.4	94.5	33.2	38.4	35.1	40.6
Cash [3]	216.0	22.5	32.8	10.4	15.2	278.3	28.9	42.5	10.4	15.3
Debt instruments [4]	43.7	12.5	16.3	28.6	37.3	51.5	16.5	21.8	32.0	42.3
Life insurance [5]	79.9	7.5	11.3	9.4	14.1	93.8	7.1	10.7	7.6	11.4
Trusts [6]	30.3	25.8	27.9	85.1	92.1	46.1	(NA)	(NA)	(NA)	(NA)
Miscellaneous	312.9	19.8	24.9	6.3	7.9	379.4	39.8	52.7	10.5	13.9
Liabilities [7]	227.4	29.2	38.3	12.9	16.8	314.0	47.8	61.0	15.2	19.4
Net worth	1,396.7	302.8	376.1	21.7	26.9	1,779.9	384.6	487.3	12.6	27.4
Number of persons__mil__	(X)	.87	1.74	(X)	(X)	(X)	.93	1.87	(X)	(X)

ASSET	1969					1972				
	Value of gross personal assets held by—			Percent held by—		Value of gross personal assets held by—			Percent held by—	
	All persons	Top ½ percent of all	Top 1 percent of all	Top ½ percent of all	Top 1 percent of all	All persons	Top ½ percent of all	Top 1 percent of all	Top ½ percent of all	Top 1 percent of all
Total assets	3,484.1	672.4	848.8	19.3	24.4	4,344.4	822.4	1,046.9	18.9	24.1
Real estate [1]	1,188.8	117.0	170.7	9.8	14.4	1,492.6	150.9	225.0	10.1	15.1
Corporate stock [2]	832.1	366.3	423.3	44.0	50.8	870.9	429.3	491.7	49.3	56.5
Bonds	133.9	63.7	71.5	47.6	53.4	158.0	82.5	94.8	52.2	60.0
Cash [3]	496.9	48.1	71.2	9.7	14.3	748.8	63.6	101.2	8.5	13.5
Debt instruments [4]	72.4	21.9	29.6	30.2	40.9	77.5	30.3	40.8	39.1	52.7
Life insurance [5]	127.2	8.4	13.8	6.6	10.8	143.0	6.2	10.0	4.3	7.0
Trusts [6]	69.9	60.0	64.5	85.8	92.3	99.4	80.3	89.4	80.8	89.9
Miscellaneous	632.8	47.0	68.7	7.4	10.9	853.6	59.5	83.3	6.8	9.8
Liabilities [7]	557.5	75.8	100.5	13.6	18.0	808.5	100.7	131.0	12.5	16.2
Net worth	2,926.6	596.7	748.1	20.4	25.6	3,535.9	721.7	915.9	20.4	25.9
Number of persons__mil__	(X)	1.01	2.03	(X)	(X)	(X)	1.04	2.09	(X)	(X)

NA Not available.   X Not applicable.   [1] Market value without deduction of mortgages, liens, or other incumbrances. Beginning 1962, includes foreign real estate.   [2] Includes all common and preferred issues, shares in domestic or foreign firms, certificates and shares of building and loan and savings and loan associations, Federal land bank stock, accrued dividends, and other instruments representing equity interest in an enterprise. Stock held in trust is included, but value is understated.   [3] Includes checking and savings balances, currency on hand or in safe deposit boxes, cash balances with stock brokers, and postal savings accounts. Cash in trust is included, but understated.   [4] Includes notes and mortgages, security credit, and similar assets.   [5] Cash surrender value; i.e., the amount individuals could expect to receive were they to surrender their policies to the carriers. It takes account of policy loans, accrued dividends, and unearned premiums.   [6] Includes all assets owned in trust except real estate. Trust classification figures should not be used to arrive at total assets because these data are included in individual asset types.   [7] Includes all legal obligations except loans on life insurance policies.

Source: James D. Smith and Stephen D. Franklin, "The Concentration of Personal Wealth, 1922–1969," *The American Economic Review*, Volume LXIV, Number 2, May 1974 (copyright), and U.S. Congress, House Committee on the Budget, *Data on Distribution of Wealth in the United States*.

No. 776. Personal Wealth—Number and Assets of Top Wealthholders by States: 1962 and 1972

[See headnote, table 772. Totals derived from adding State data differ slightly from national totals shown here because of the sample weighting procedures used]

STATE	1962						1972					
	Number of top wealth-holders (1,000)			Total assets			Number of top wealth-holders (1,000)			Total assets		
					Percent						Percent	
	Total	Male	Female	Total (bil. dol.)	Corporate stock	Real estate	Total	Male	Female	Total (bil. dol.)	Corporate stock	Real estate
Total	4,132.2	2,538.6	1,593.6	752.0	43.3	25.0	12,815.2	7,809.6	5,005.7	2,151.9	29.2	30.0
Ala	31.5	21.3	10.1	5.0	26.7	36.6	123.5	75.4	48.1	21.3	27.2	34.4
Alaska	1.1	1.1	(1)	.2	20.4	53.3	8.8	7.7	1.1	1.5	22.4	47.4
Ariz	31.4	17.2	14.2	17.7	71.7	12.9	87.6	55.0	32.6	17.6	32.9	27.5
Ark	23.8	18.3	5.5	3.9	27.6	35.3	54.9	35.1	19.8	9.6	22.3	32.3
Calif	477.9	231.2	246.7	97.9	40.2	31.9	1,237.6	609.6	628.0	242.4	29.6	29.9
Colo	54.4	35.8	18.7	8.4	32.0	33.8	178.6	99.9	78.7	25.4	26.2	31.1
Conn	79.8	48.0	31.8	15.4	52.9	19.7	266.6	143.2	123.4	57.8	37.9	23.6
Del	14.0	9.0	5.0	3.3	51.9	26.1	42.5	21.3	21.1	7.3	17.8	31.8
D.C	21.2	9.9	11.2	4.4	46.1	18.0	(2)	(2)	(2)	(2)	(2)	(2)
Fla	153.1	95.6	57.5	28.0	40.3	29.2	572.4	334.5	237.9	131.0	34.6	26.1
Ga	66.1	38.0	28.1	13.4	37.8	26.9	219.1	161.2	57.9	44.1	24.4	36.8
Hawaii	11.3	7.7	3.6	1.9	36.6	42.0	53.7	37.5	16.3	7.9	23.6	40.4
Idaho	11.6	5.4	6.2	1.8	37.3	33.1	67.6	22.4	45.3	7.5	22.3	35.7
Ill	247.8	148.3	99.5	41.2	40.6	27.4	834.2	445.6	388.6	132.2	24.9	31.1
Ind	84.7	60.9	23.8	12.9	42.1	26.9	350.2	230.1	120.1	45.3	23.2	33.9
Iowa	97.4	72.2	25.2	10.6	17.0	43.2	328.8	204.0	124.9	38.7	14.8	42.7
Kans	62.5	43.4	19.1	8.8	24.6	38.8	183.1	125.4	57.7	31.3	25.4	35.4
Ky	40.5	25.3	15.2	6.1	35.5	28.7	135.7	86.2	49.6	24.6	26.5	27.2
La	42.8	24.4	18.4	7.0	25.1	36.9	125.9	68.1	57.0	23.0	33.?	32.8
Maine	17.3	9.6	7.7	3.7	49.6	12.3	76.7	55.8	20.9	12.0	31.1	25.0
Md	63.2	42.7	20.6	10.5	42.9	24.5	[2]200.7	[2]125.9	[2]74.8	[2]43.6	[2]33.0	[2]28.5
Mass	115.7	70.5	45.2	21.5	51.5	17.6	344.0	210.9	133.1	62.3	27.8	22.7
Mich	118.9	81.5	37.4	23.4	44.3	21.8	382.3	259.8	122.5	65.3	28.8	29.6
Minn	89.7	66.4	23.3	13.5	41.3	28.2	350.1	240.6	109.5	40.9	19.6	32.3
Miss	26.7	21.2	5.5	4.2	30.0	26.6	93.7	53.7	40.0	14.1	19.7	40.1
Mo	69.9	46.8	23.1	13.4	46.9	21.8	205.1	144.5	60.6	40.6	32.5	26.2
Mont	21.0	14.1	6.8	2.3	21.6	37.3	77.3	46.0	31.4	11.1	16.5	38.6
Nebr	45.1	32.6	12.6	6.0	19.2	43.0	184.5	131.4	53.2	24.3	10.0	43.5
Nev	10.3	6.0	4.3	2.5	36.0	32.2	17.2	8.5	8.7	4.5	26.7	38.9
N.H	11.8	7.9	3.9	2.8	45.1	12.6	40.7	15.3	25.4	7.7	32.0	24.5
N.J	184.0	115.5	68.5	28.9	45.9	20.8	597.9	379.5	218.4	100.6	34.5	27.9
N. Mex	14.9	7.4	7.5	1.9	30.4	36.3	50.7	43.5	7.3	7.6	36.4	30.6
N.Y	613.1	366.7	246.4	116.4	51.2	15.6	1,581.7	1,015.4	566.3	236.6	34.0	24.4
N.C	65.5	48.6	16.9	12.1	40.1	29.5	244.5	178.0	66.5	37.7	28.4	37.8
N. Dak	12.7	9.2	3.5	1.5	14.8	45.2	89.5	56.9	32.6	10.0	7.0	52.4
Ohio	186.1	110.4	75.7	33.9	43.9	21.1	667.1	417.2	249.9	115.1	35.5	24.0
Okla	50.2	36.9	13.3	8.1	28.2	33.3	147.6	98.7	49.0	20.4	20.9	41.2
Oreg	42.6	29.1	13.6	6.6	27.6	32.0	95.4	65.9	29.5	17.0	26.4	30.3
Pa	220.4	144.9	75.5	45.3	54.7	16.4	560.9	320.7	240.2	92.6	36.5	24.5
R.I	18.3	11.2	7.1	3.5	49.9	18.3	46.2	25.2	20.9	6.7	28.3	30.0
S.C	31.1	23.3	7.8	4.2	29.8	37.1	113.6	84.7	29.0	17.1	19.8	46.9
S. Dak	16.1	13.3	2.9	2.0	21.9	36.6	42.8	31.5	11.3	6.2	15.2	34.5
Tenn	42.4	30.0	12.4	8.7	40.6	24.6	205.3	137.9	67.4	29.4	27.4	32.2
Tex	194.1	95.6	98.5	40.8	39.5	32.2	563.2	310.1	253.1	119.4	24.8	38.8
Utah	10.1	7.0	3.1	1.7	33.0	25.5	28.4	20.0	8.4	4.7	21.3	35.0
Vt	8.0	5.4	2.7	1.0	49.1	20.5	26.7	21.0	5.6	3.0	30.3	27.0
Va	77.3	47.4	29.8	11.8	42.0	27.3	242.2	142.1	100.1	40.7	29.7	34.4
Wash	63.1	29.0	34.2	8.9	33.2	33.7	187.5	81.7	105.8	27.0	28.5	28.4
W. Va	22.8	16.1	6.7	5.4	52.3	24.1	52.2	23.8	28.3	7.9	33.8	25.0
Wis	97.7	66.6	31.1	12.3	36.9	26.1	392.0	280.3	111.8	49.2	27.8	27.4
Wyo	9.0	6.9	2.1	2.2	38.7	31.1	15.6	7.7	7.9	4.5	23.9	37.0
Other areas	10.2	6.0	4.1	2.7	58.9	44.3	20.7	13.1	7.6	3.7	28.3	21.1

[1] Estimate not shown separately because of high sampling variability.
[2] District of Columbia included with Maryland.

Source: U.S. Internal Revenue Service, Statistics of Income, 1962 and 1972, Supplemental Report, Personal Wealth.

No. 777. National Wealth, by Type of Asset: 1967 to 1975

[In billions of dollars. Consult source for methods and sources used to derive these estimates. See text, p. 439. See *Historical Statistics, Colonial Times to 1970*, series F 349–376 and F 422–469, for similar data]

TYPE OF ASSET	CURRENT DOLLARS				CONSTANT (1958) DOLLARS			
	1967	1970	1974	1975	1967	1970	1974	1975
Total tangible assets	2,679.5	3,485.1	5,205.4	5,587.6	2,152.6	2,373.9	2,737.5	2,772.1
Total reproducible assets	2,088.6	2,727.1	4,040.3	4,302.8	1,765.4	1,963.4	2,271.9	2,299.3
Structures [1]	1,215.9	1,614.4	2,381.5	2,555.3	958.1	1,040.5	1,173.5	1,187.3
Nonfarm	1,203.8	1,600.6	2,361.9	2,534.4	948.0	1,030.4	1,162.8	1,176.2
Residential [2]	425.7	536.9	863.8	952.9	337.9	366.9	436.0	440.1
Public nonresidential	356.2	495.1	715.8	745.4	281.1	300.8	315.2	318.7
Institutional	50.8	72.6	113.2	125.6	37.3	42.1	47.0	47.7
Other priv. nonresidential	371.1	496.0	669.1	710.5	291.7	320.6	364.6	369.7
Residential-rental	170.5	215.0	318.0	350.7	134.9	146.9	161.3	162.8
Farm structures	12.1	13.8	19.6	20.9	10.1	10.1	10.7	11.1
Equipment [1]	541.6	704.9	963.6	1,040.3	502.4	589.6	700.6	713.4
Priv. business and public equip.	315.9	403.3	510.7	543.7	277.4	317.9	352.5	358.6
Consumer durables	225.7	301.6	452.9	496.6	225.0	271.7	348.1	354.8
Inventories [3]	331.1	407.8	695.2	707.2	304.9	333.3	397.8	398.6
Private farm	27.7	32.9	43.8	43.9	26.4	26.6	31.6	31.4
Private nonfarm [4]	268.3	333.9	543.2	555.8	244.9	270.7	313.0	314.0
Public	35.1	41.0	108.2	107.5	33.6	36.0	53.2	53.2
Land [5]	590.9	758.0	1,165.1	1,284.8	387.2	410.5	465.6	472.8
Private farm	152.7	171.3	296.5	336.2	88.3	87.0	87.0	87.0
Private nonfarm	302.4	404.6	637.3	705.6	201.5	220.7	253.8	258.5
Public	135.8	182.1	231.3	243.0	97.4	102.8	124.8	127.3

[1] Estimates derived by "perpetual inventory" method which is intended to reflect reproduction cost of different types of assets. Estimates are obtained by: (*a*) reducing each year's gross capital expenditures in current prices to 1958 price level by means of the appropriate construction cost index; (*b*) depreciating gross capital expenditures in accordance with an assumed length of life for different types of assets, thus obtaining net capital expenditures for each year in 1958 prices; (*c*) cumulating net capital expenditures for as many years backwards as corresponds to the assured length of life of the type of asset involved.   [2] Owner occupied only.   [3] Current dollar estimates are based on book values; constant dollar estimates reflect book values reduced by means of wholesale price indexes.   [4] Includes business and household inventories.   [5] Private farm land estimates based on census or similar data. Private nonfarm land estimates are derived by application of rough ratios of land to structure values for different types of real estate. Excludes subsoil assets.

Source: Kendrick, John W., with Kyu Sik Lee and Jean Lomask, *The National Wealth of the United States, by Major Sector and Industry*, copyright by The Conference Board, New York, N.Y., 1976.

No. 778. Growth Rate of Fixed Business Capital Per Employed Person in Private Business: 1947 to 1977

[In percent. Rates based on capital valued in constant (1972) dollars. Excludes nonprofit institutions; see also headnote, table 780]

ITEM	1947–1977	1947–1957	1947–1967	1967–1977	1972–1973	1973–1974	1974–1975	1975–1976	1976–1977
Total gross	1.9	2.2	2.0	1.6	−.4	1.8	6.0	−.5	−.8
Plant	1.1	.7	1.7	.8	−1.3	.9	5.1	−1.0	−1.7
Equipment	3.6	5.4	2.7	2.7	1.0	3.1	7.2	.2	.4
Total net	2.3	2.7	2.5	1.6	–	1.7	5.0	−1.1	−1.2
Plant	1.6	1.6	2.4	.9	−.9	.9	4.4	−1.7	−2.2
Equipment	3.5	5.1	2.8	2.5	1.4	3.0	5.9	−.3	.3

– Represents zero.
Source: U.S. Bureau of Labor Statistics and U.S. Bureau of Economic Analysis, unpublished data.

No. 779. Fixed Nonresidential Business Capital—Average Age of Gross Stocks, Constant (1972) Cost Valuation: 1950 to 1977

[Age in years. As of Dec. 31. See headnote, table 780, and *Historical Statistics, Colonial Times to 1970*, series F 51–6527]

ITEM	1950	1955	1960	1965	1970	1972	1974	1975	1976	1977
All industries: Gross stocks	14.4	12.8	11.9	11.1	10.2	10.2	10.1	10.1	10.2	10.3
Equipment	6.3	6.6	7.1	7.0	6.5	6.5	6.4	6.4	6.5	6.4
Structures	19.7	17.6	15.7	14.4	13.4	13.4	13.4	13.5	13.7	13.8
Manufacturing: Gross stocks	11.5	11.0	10.9	10.9	10.0	10.1	9.9	10.0	9.9	9.8
Equipment	6.2	6.8	7.5	7.4	6.8	6.9	6.8	6.9	6.8	6.7
Structures	15.6	15.0	14.5	14.6	14.1	14.2	14.3	14.4	14.4	14.6
Nonfarm nonmfg.: Gross stocks	16.0	13.9	12.4	11.3	10.3	10.2	10.1	10.2	10.3	10.4
Equipment	6.7	6.6	6.9	6.8	6.3	6.3	6.2	6.2	6.3	6.3
Structures	21.1	18.6	16.1	14.2	13.1	13.0	13.0	13.1	13.3	13.4
Farm: Gross stocks	11.8	10.7	10.9	10.7	10.4	10.6	10.6	10.6	10.7	10.8
Equipment	5.0	5.9	7.0	7.1	6.6	6.6	6.6	6.6	6.6	6.6
Structures	20.2	17.5	16.1	15.4	15.4	15.7	15.8	16.0	16.2	16.4

Source: U.S. Bureau of Economic Analysis, *Fixed Nonresidential Business and Residential Capital in the United States, 1925–1975*, and unpublished data.

No. 780. Fixed Nonresidential Business Capital—Cost Valuation in Current and Constant (1972) Dollars: 1950 to 1977

[In billions of dollars. Stocks as of Dec. 31; depreciation over entire calendar year. Data refer to privately owned assets and are based on the fixed capital formation components of the gross national product. Excludes owner occupied nonfarm and farm residential capital and government enterprises; includes nonprofit institutions. Gross stocks allow for retirement, net stocks allow for retirement and depreciation. Estimates are based on straight-line depreciation and 85 percent of service lives given in *Bulletin F*, Internal Revenue Service. For single-year figures prior to minor revisions issued in 1976 and data in constant (1958) dollars, see *Historical Statistics of the United States, Colonial Times to 1970*, series F 480–527]

ITEM	1950	1955	1960	1965	1970	1972 [1]	1974	1975	1976	1977
					CURRENT DOLLARS					
All industries: [2]										
Gross stocks	376.5	525.1	680.6	837.7	1,339.0	1,582.7	2,135.3	2,392.4	2,603.5	2,849.4
Equipment	163.6	249.2	336.6	408.4	632.4	726.4	963.4	1,104.8	1,214.8	1,349.1
Structures	212.9	275.9	343.9	429.4	706.6	856.4	1,171.9	1,287.6	1,388.7	1,500.3
Net stocks	201.0	286.0	374.4	474.5	784.8	922.5	1,244.1	1,378.6	1,486.4	1,616.4
Equipment	96.9	138.6	179.0	220.6	354.0	401.1	532.8	605.2	660.2	731.0
Structures	104.1	147.4	195.4	253.8	430.7	521.5	711.3	773.4	826.2	885.4
Depreciation	17.8	26.9	36.7	44.2	71.2	83.6	107.3	127.9	139.4	151.7
Equipment	11.6	18.5	25.4	30.5	49.0	57.1	71.3	87.0	94.9	103.4
Structures	6.2	8.5	11.3	13.7	22.1	26.5	35.9	40.9	44.5	48.4
Manufacturing:										
Gross stocks	95.0	134.6	171.0	205.9	321.6	364.0	480.1	527.8	568.6	622.3
Equipment	42.0	69.8	97.7	118.2	181.7	203.4	269.8	307.0	341.1	383.9
Structures	53.0	64.8	73.4	87.8	139.9	160.6	210.3	220.8	227.5	238.4
Net stocks	52.6	73.3	90.7	108.6	176.1	195.6	257.6	280.4	301.9	330.7
Equipment	25.3	39.0	51.4	62.6	101.1	110.7	147.4	165.3	184.2	208.7
Structures	27.4	34.3	39.2	46.0	75.0	85.0	110.2	115.1	117.7	122.0
Depreciation	4.6	6.9	9.5	11.3	18.2	20.7	26.0	30.5	32.6	35.9
Equipment	2.9	4.8	7.0	8.3	13.3	15.2	18.8	22.5	24.6	27.4
Structures	1.7	2.1	2.5	3.0	4.8	5.5	7.2	8.0	8.0	8.5
Nonfarm nonmfg.:										
Gross stocks	245.7	342.2	453.6	565.8	919.8	1,106.7	1,508.9	1,700.5	1,854.1	2,029.7
Equipment	100.1	148.9	203.3	249.5	393.6	459.0	610.8	701.9	766.5	846.4
Structures	145.6	193.4	250.3	316.3	526.2	647.8	898.1	998.5	1,087.6	1,183.3
Net stocks	128.2	186.4	254.0	329.7	554.2	664.9	905.1	1,006.9	1,089.1	1,176.7
Equipment	58.8	83.6	110.0	137.3	222.9	256.9	341.4	388.6	418.2	458.5
Structures	69.4	102.8	144.0	192.4	331.3	408.1	563.6	618.3	665.9	718.2
Depreciation	11.2	16.9	23.7	28.9	47.3	56.6	73.6	88.4	96.8	104.7
Equipment	7.0	11.0	15.5	18.9	31.0	36.8	46.5	57.3	62.1	66.9
Structures	4.2	5.9	8.2	10.0	16.3	19.8	27.1	31.1	34.6	37.8
					CONSTANT (1972) DOLLARS					
All industries: [2]										
Gross stocks	693.6	830.2	963.9	1,135.2	1,421.6	1,527.6	1,656.6	1,701.7	1,746.2	1,800.1
Equipment	274.0	363.4	426.0	500.6	651.4	707.5	780.6	806.9	832.1	865.3
Structures	419.6	466.8	537.9	634.6	770.1	820.1	875.9	894.7	914.1	934.8
Net stocks	367.6	451.3	533.0	645.9	833.7	889.8	963.7	981.3	999.0	1,024.3
Equipment	162.1	201.7	225.9	269.7	364.4	390.4	431.8	442.3	452.8	470.2
Structures	205.4	249.6	307.1	376.2	469.3	499.4	532.0	539.0	546.2	554.1
Depreciation	33.4	42.7	49.8	58.5	77.0	83.6	91.9	96.6	98.9	101.3
Equipment	20.6	28.0	32.4	38.0	52.1	57.1	63.7	67.6	69.3	71.0
Structures	12.9	14.7	17.4	20.5	25.0	26.5	28.2	28.0	29.6	30.3
Manufacturing:										
Gross stocks	185.9	224.7	254.4	281.6	340.8	353.5	375.5	380.6	389.7	400.9
Equipment	80.3	110.5	130.5	147.9	188.9	200.1	218.6	223.0	231.9	242.9
Structures	105.7	114.2	123.9	133.7	151.9	153.4	156.9	157.6	157.7	157.9
Net stocks	102.6	121.9	134.7	148.3	186.5	190.0	201.6	202.2	206.8	212.8
Equipment	48.0	61.5	68.5	78.2	105.0	108.8	119.4	120.0	125.2	132.0
Structures	54.5	60.4	66.2	70.1	81.5	81.2	82.2	82.2	81.6	80.8
Depreciation	9.3	11.7	13.5	15.2	19.6	20.7	22.4	23.0	23.4	24.2
Equipment	5.7	7.8	9.2	10.5	14.1	15.2	16.7	17.3	17.7	18.5
Structures	3.6	3.9	4.3	4.7	5.4	5.5	5.6	5.7	5.7	5.7
Nonfarm nonmfg.:										
Gross stocks	444.5	529.3	629.9	766.2	979.0	1,068.0	1,168.8	1,205.6	1,239.8	1,277.4
Equipment	159.1	207.9	250.0	303.9	404.8	447.1	498.6	518.4	532.4	552.7
Structures	285.4	321.4	379.9	462.3	574.2	620.8	670.2	687.2	705.4	724.8
Net stocks	228.5	286.9	354.7	448.8	589.8	640.6	699.3	714.5	725.8	743.7
Equipment	92.4	115.8	134.4	166.2	228.5	249.6	278.3	286.9	290.8	300.4
Structures	136.1	171.1	220.3	282.6	361.3	391.0	420.9	427.6	435.0	443.3
Depreciation	20.3	26.0	31.5	38.2	51.2	56.6	63.0	66.9	68.5	69.9
Equipment	11.8	16.0	19.3	23.4	32.9	36.8	41.7	45.0	46.0	46.8
Structures	8.6	10.0	12.2	14.8	18.3	19.8	21.3	22.0	22.5	23.2

[1] For gross and net stocks, constant dollar data tend to be lower than current dollar data. Implicit price deflator is set equal to 1 at midpoint of year; due to inflation during last six months of 1972, implicit price deflator applied to stocks at year-end was greater than 1. Depreciation is considered to occur evenly throughout calendar year, and is deflated at midpoint of year. [2] Includes farm, not shown separately.

Source: U.S. Bureau of Economic Analysis, *Fixed Nonresidential Business and Residential Capital in the United States, 1925–1975; Survey of Current Business*, August 1976 and August 1977; and unpublished data.

Figure 15.1

**Producer Prices Indexes:
1965 to 1978**

(See table 787)

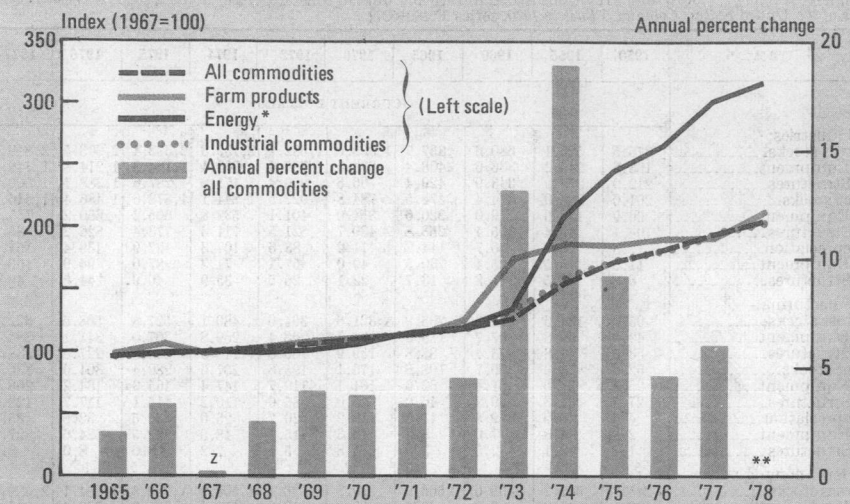

Index (1967=100)   Annual percent change

- All commodities
- Farm products
- Energy *
- Industrial commodities
- Annual percent change all commodities

(Left scale)

* Fuels, power, and related products.   ** Six-month average, Jan. to June.
Z Less than .5 percent.

Figure 15.2

**Consumer Price Indexes:
1965 to 1978**

(See table 793)

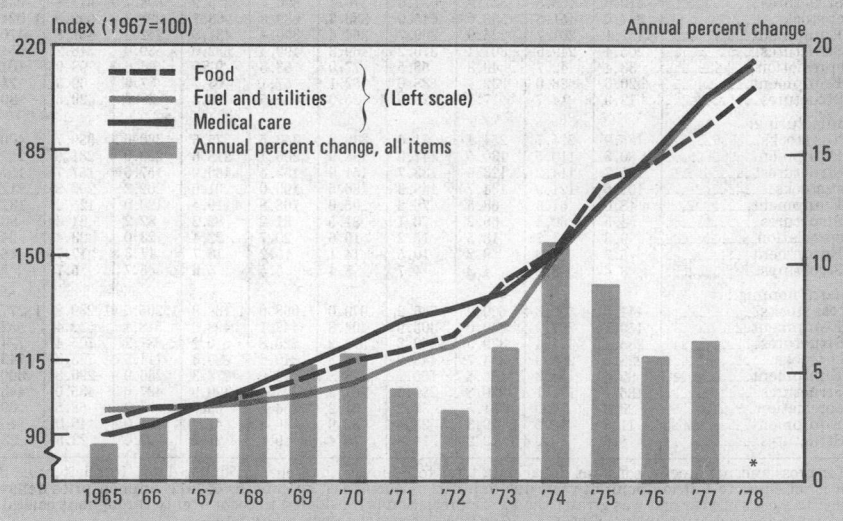

Index (1967=100)   Annual percent change

- Food
- Fuel and utilities
- Medical care

(Left scale)

Annual percent change, all items

*Six-month average, Jan. to June.
Source of Figs. 15.1 and 15.2: Charts prepared by U.S. Bureau of the Census.
                    Data from U.S. Bureau of Labor Statistics.

Section 15
Prices

This section presents indexes of producer and consumer prices, actual prices for selected commodities, and budgets for urban families and retired couples. The primary sources of these data are monthly publications of the Department of Labor, Bureau of Labor Statistics, which include: *Monthly Labor Review; Consumer Price Index; Estimated Retail Food Prices by Cities; Retail Prices and Indexes of Fuels and Utilities;* and *Producer* (formerly *Wholesale*) *Prices and Price Indexes.* The Bureau of Economic Analysis of the Department of Commerce is the source for the gross national product (GNP) implicit price deflator figures; see table 783. The Department of Agriculture's Economics, Statistics, and Cooperatives Service (ESCS) prepared indexes of prices received and prices paid by farmers; see section 24.

The Bureau of Labor Statistics prepares monthly indexes of producer prices for a large selection of commodities; monthly indexes of consumer prices for both commodities and services; and weekly indexes of spot market prices for 22 commodities. The single year 1967 is currently the standard reference base period for most general purpose index numbers prepared by Federal agencies.

Producer price index.—This index (formerly the wholesale price index), dating from 1890, is the oldest continuous statistical series published by the Bureau of Labor Statistics. It is designed to measure average changes in prices of all commodities, at all stages of processing, produced or imported for sale in primary markets in the United States.

The index has undergone several revisions (see *Monthly Labor Review*, February 1962). It is now based on approximately 2,800 commodity price series instead of the approximately 1,900 included in the 1947–60 period and the 900 included for the period prior to 1947. Prices used in constructing the index are collected from sellers, if possible, and generally apply to the first significant large-volume commercial transaction for each commodity—i.e., the manufacturer's or other producer's selling price, the importer's selling price, or the selling price on an organized exchange or at a central market.

The weights used in the index represent the total net selling value of commodities produced or processed in this country, or imported. The values are f.o.b. production point and are exclusive of excise taxes, interplant transfers, military products, and goods sold directly at retail from producing establishments. Effective January 1976, the weights are values of net shipments of commodities as derived from the industrial censuses of 1972 and other data. From January 1967 through 1975, weights were based on 1963 shipment values.

Consumer price index (CPI).—This index measures the average changes in the cost of a fixed, or constant, "market basket" of consumer goods and services purchased by urban wage earners and clerical workers (45 percent of the civilian noninstitutional population); see below, however, for change beginning 1978. Weights which reflect the relative importance of the components of the index (e.g. housing, food, entertainment) and which are used in calculating the index are based on studies of actual expenditures by consumers. Quantities and qualities of items in the "market basket" remain essentially the same between consecutive pricing periods (monthly for national data), so that the index measures the effect of *price change only* on the cost of living. It does not measure changes in the total amount families spend for living; geographic area indexes do not measure relative differences in prices or living costs between areas.

A study conducted during 1917–19 provided the composition of the "market basket" and the weights used until 1935. Since then, this index has undergone several major revisions which involved bringing the "market basket" of goods and services up to date, revising the weights, and improving the sample and methodology. The fourth revision, which is shown in this section and which was incorporated in a new series beginning in 1964, introduced expenditure weights relating to 1960–1961. The most recent revision, issued beginning January 1978, is based on an updated "market basket" of goods and services and revised expenditure weights relating to 1971–1972. This revision also establishes a second CPI index representing all urban consumers (80 percent of the civilian noninstitutional population). For a discussion of the history and concepts of the CPI, see *Consumer Price Index*, report number 517, published by the BLS.

The list of items priced for the index (prior to 1978) includes approximately 400 goods and services. The items priced are described by detailed specifications to insure that, as far as possible, the same quality is priced each time, and that differences in reported prices are measures of price change only. All taxes directly associated with the purchase or continued use of the items priced are included in the index.

The national index for the fourth revision of the CPI, which is shown in this section, is based on prices collected in 56 areas. These include the urban portions of 37 standard metropolitan statistical areas (SMSA's), the more extensive standard consolidated areas for Chicago and New York-Northeastern New Jersey; and 17 nonmetropolitan urban places. (See text, page 2, for explanation of the SMSA concept.) Area definitions are those established for the 1960 census and do not include any subsequent revisions. Foods, fuels, and a few other items are priced monthly in all areas. Prices of most other goods and services are obtained monthly in the 5 largest areas and every 3 months in other areas. Rents are surveyed bimonthly in the 5 largest areas and every 3 months in other areas. Between scheduled survey dates, prices are held at the level of their last pricing for all goods and services except new automobiles. Price data for the 56 areas are combined for the United States with weights based on 1960 population of the several areas represented by each sample area. Indexes are published for areas grouped by size of city and by region of the country, and for 23 separate metropolitan areas.

Food price indexes are computed as a subgroup of the consumer price index. The indexes have been computed from prices of 60 foods from 1950–52, 90 foods from 1953–63, and 96 foods beginning January 1964.

Statistical reliability.—For a discussion of statistical collection and estimation, sampling procedures, and measures of statistical reliability pertaining to the Producer Price Index and the CPI, see Appendix III.

Historical statistics.—Tabular headnotes provide cross-references, where applicable, to *Historical Statistics of the United States, Colonial Times to 1970.* See Appendix I.

No. 781. Purchasing Power of the Dollar: 1940 to 1978

[1967=$1.00. Producer prices prior to 1961, and consumer prices prior to 1964, exclude Alaska and Hawaii. Obtained by dividing the average price index for the 1967 base period (100.0) by the price index for a given period and expressing the result in dollars and cents]

YEAR	MONTHLY AVERAGE AS MEASURED BY—		YEAR	MONTHLY AVERAGE AS MEASURED BY—		YEAR	MONTHLY AVERAGE AS MEASURED BY—	
	Producer prices	Consumer prices		Producer prices	Consumer prices		Producer prices	Consumer prices
1940	$2.469	$2.381	1956	$1.103	$1.229	1968	$ .976	$ .960
1945	1.832	1.855	1957	1.072	1.186	1969	.939	.911
1946	1.605	1.709	1958	1.057	1.155	1970	.906	.860
1947	1.307	1.495	1959	1.055	1.145	1971	.877	.824
1948	1.208	1.387	1960	1.054	1.127	1972	.840	.798
1949	1.271	1.401	1961	1.058	1.116	1973	.742	.752
1950	1.222	1.387	1962	1.055	1.104	1974	.625	.678
1951	1.098	1.285	1963	1.058	1.091	1975	.572	.621
1952	1.129	1.258	1964	1.056	1.076	1976	.515	.587
1953	1.144	1.248	1965	1.035	1.058	1977	.515	.551
1954	1.142	1.242	1966	1.002	1.029	1978,		
1955	1.139	1.247	1967	1.000	1.000	May	.481	.518

Source: U.S. Bureau of Labor Statistics. Monthly data in U.S. Bureau of Economic Analysis, *Survey of Current Business.*

No. 782. PERCENT CHANGE PER YEAR IN SELECTED PRICE INDEXES: 1960 TO 1977

[Yearly averages. Minus sign (−) denotes decrease. GNP=Gross national product; see text, p. 437]

YEAR OR PERIOD	CONSUMER PRICES					PRODUCER PRICES					GNP DEFLATOR [2]		
	All items	Food	Fuel and utilities	Rent	Services	All commodities	Farm products	Processed foods and feeds	Industrial		Total	Domestic business	Business nonfarm
									Total	Energy [1]			
1960	1.6	1.0	2.2	1.4	3.3	.1	−.3	.1	−	.8	1.7	1.6	1.5
1965	1.7	2.2	−.1	1.0	2.2	2.0	4.3	3.5	1.3	1.9	2.2	1.9	1.6
1966	2.9	5.0	.5	1.3	3.9	3.3	7.3	6.0	2.2	2.4	3.3	3.1	2.7
1967	2.9	.9	1.2	1.8	4.4	.2	−5.6	−1.2	1.5	2.2	2.9	2.7	3.0
1968	4.2	3.6	1.3	2.4	5.2	2.5	2.5	2.2	2.5	−1.1	4.5	3.9	4.0
1969	5.4	5.1	2.3	3.2	6.9	3.9	6.4	5.0	3.4	2.0	5.0	4.7	4.6
1970	5.9	5.5	3.9	4.2	8.1	3.7	1.7	4.5	3.8	5.3	5.4	4.6	4.7
1971	4.3	3.0	6.9	4.6	5.6	3.3	1.7	2.1	3.7	8.5	5.1	4.4	4.5
1972	3.3	4.3	4.4	3.5	3.8	4.5	10.7	5.5	3.3	3.0	4.1	3.4	3.0
1973	6.2	14.5	5.7	4.3	4.4	13.1	41.0	22.6	6.8	13.2	5.8	5.5	4.1
1974	11.0	14.4	18.4	5.1	9.3	18.9	6.5	15.4	22.2	55.1	9.7	9.7	10.1
1975	9.1	8.5	11.7	5.1	9.5	9.2	−.5	6.8	11.5	17.7	9.6	9.9	10.5
1976	5.8	3.1	8.9	5.4	8.3	4.6	2.3	−2.5	6.4	8.4	5.3	4.9	5.2
1977	6.5	6.3	10.7	6.1	7.7	6.1	.8	4.6	7.0	13.8	5.5	5.3	5.5
1960–1965 [3]	1.3	1.4	.5	1.1	2.0	.4	.3	1.3	.2	−.1	1.6	1.6	1.0
1965–1970 [3]	4.2	4.0	1.8	2.6	5.7	2.7	2.4	3.3	2.7	2.1	4.2	4.2	3.8
1970–1975 [3]	6.7	8.8	9.3	4.5	6.5	9.6	11.0	10.3	9.3	18.2	6.9	6.8	6.4
1975–1977 [3]	6.1	4.7	9.8	5.7	8.0	5.4	1.5	1.0	6.7	11.0	5.4	5.1	5.3

− Represents zero. [1] Fuels, related products, and power. [2] See table 783. Source: U.S. Bureau of Economic Analysis, *Survey of Current Business*, monthly. [3] Average annual percent change.

Source: Except as noted, U.S. Bureau of Labor Statistics, *Monthly Labor Review*.

No. 783. GROSS NATIONAL PRODUCT, IMPLICIT PRICE DEFLATORS: 1960 TO 1977

[1972=100. See *Historical Statistics, Colonial Times to 1970*, series E 1–22, for data based on 1958=100]

ITEM	1960	1965	1969	1970	1971	1973	1974	1975	1976	1977
Gross national product	68.7	74.3	86.7	91.4	96.0	105.8	116.0	127.2	133.9	141.3
Business nonfarm	72.9	76.8	88.5	92.7	97.0	104.1	114.7	126.7	133.3	140.6
Farm	68.5	73.0	84.1	83.3	84.3	154.9	149.2	145.5	145.1	140.5
Government	49.7	60.2	76.8	84.8	92.1	107.3	113.7	123.2	131.5	139.6
Personal consumption expenditures	71.7	77.1	88.5	92.5	96.6	105.5	116.9	126.5	133.2	140.6
Durable	82.1	85.6	93.1	95.5	99.0	101.6	108.4	117.9	124.7	130.1
Nondurable	72.6	77.3	89.4	93.6	96.6	107.9	123.8	133.1	137.7	144.0
Services	68.0	74.3	86.1	90.5	95.8	104.7	113.6	123.5	132.3	141.5
Gross private fixed investment [1]	71.9	73.8	86.9	91.1	95.9	106.0	117.1	132.4	139.8	150.3
Nonresidential	72.2	74.5	86.6	91.3	96.4	103.8	115.3	132.3	138.7	146.0
Structures	63.1	65.9	81.1	88.0	94.4	107.8	128.1	145.8	150.7	160.3
Producers' durable equipment	79.3	80.6	90.0	93.4	97.6	101.7	109.2	125.9	133.1	139.8
Residential	71.4	72.3	87.7	90.6	94.9	110.8	122.3	132.8	142.5	159.9
Exports	77.1	80.5	87.9	93.1	96.6	116.2	148.3	163.8	170.0	179.2
Imports	76.7	78.0	83.3	89.1	93.5	118.2	171.0	188.2	194.3	211.0
Government purchases [2]	58.0	66.0	81.0	87.5	93.7	106.7	117.5	128.9	136.7	145.7
Federal	59.1	67.0	80.0	86.4	92.6	105.8	115.9	127.5	134.8	143.4
State and local	56.8	65.1	81.9	88.3	94.5	107.3	118.4	129.7	137.7	147.1

[1] Domestic investments only.   [2] Goods and services.

Source: U.S. Bureau of Economic Analysis, *The National Income and Product Accounts of the United States, 1929–74*, and *Survey of Current Business*, July 1977 and March 1978.

No. 784. INDEXES OF SPOT PRIMARY MARKET PRICES: 1960 TO 1978

[1967=100. Index computed daily through 1965; weekly beginning 1970. Represents unweighted geometric average of price quotations of 22 commodities, traded on organized exchanges. This index is much more sensitive to changes in market conditions than is a monthly producer price index]

ITEM AND NUMBER OF COMMODITIES	1960 (6–14)	1965 (6–15)	1970 (6–16)	1971 (6–15)	1972 (6–13)	1973 (6–12)	1974 (6–11)	1975 (6–24)	1976 (6–29)	1977 (6–28)	1978 (6–27)
All commodities 22	100.5	106.2	113.6	108.2	119.5	171.3	221.5	189.9	210.9	206.7	230.0
Food stuffs 9	97.8	94.4	112.2	111.2	113.3	172.7	211.5	215.3	213.7	210.6	238.1
Raw industrials 13	102.4	115.1	114.4	106.1	124.0	170.2	228.5	174.1	208.9	204.0	224.4
Livestock and products 5	105.3	121.4	123.6	116.6	143.9	222.6	190.1	240.8	224.4	234.6	278.0
Metals 5	80.9	114.2	125.2	103.1	114.9	145.6	261.4	166.8	215.4	203.0	220.6
Textiles and fibers 4	102.5	110.3	99.9	97.9	122.7	159.1	183.9	158.8	181.4	170.1	173.6
Fats and oils 4	100.3	114.8	128.6	126.1	114.9	187.9	224.3	213.6	208.3	235.7	253.5

Source: U.S. Bureau of Labor Statistics, *Tuesday Spot Market Price Indexes and Prices*, weekly and monthly.

No. 785. PRODUCER PRICE INDEXES—MAJOR COMMODITY GROUPS: 1950 TO 1978

[1967=100. Prior to 1961, excludes Alaska and Hawaii. See also *Historical Statistics, Colonial Times to 1970*, series E 23 and 24]

YEAR	All commodities	Farm products	Processed foods and feeds	INDUSTRIAL COMMODITIES		YEAR	All commodities	Farm products	Processed foods and feeds	INDUSTRIAL COMMODITIES	
				Total	Energy [1]					Total	Energy [1]
1950	81.8	106.7	83.4	78.0	87.1	1965	96.6	98.7	95.5	96.4	95.5
1951	91.1	124.2	92.7	86.1	90.3	1966	99.8	105.9	101.2	98.5	97.8
1952	88.6	117.2	91.6	84.1	90.1	1967	100.0	100.0	100.0	100.0	100.0
1953	87.4	106.2	87.4	84.8	92.6	1968	102.5	102.5	102.2	102.5	98.9
1954	87.6	104.7	88.9	85.0	91.3	1969	106.5	109.1	107.3	106.0	100.9
1955	87.8	98.2	85.0	86.9	91.2	1970	110.4	111.0	112.1	110.0	106.2
1956	90.7	96.9	84.9	90.8	94.0	1971	114.0	112.9	114.5	114.1	115.2
1957	93.3	99.5	87.4	93.3	99.1	1972	119.1	125.0	120.8	117.9	118.6
1958	94.6	103.9	91.8	93.6	95.3	1973	134.7	176.3	148.1	125.9	134.3
1959	94.8	97.5	89.4	95.3	95.3	1974	160.1	187.7	170.9	153.8	208.3
1960	94.9	97.2	89.5	95.3	96.1	1975	174.9	186.7	182.6	171.5	245.1
1961	94.5	96.3	91.0	94.8	97.2	1976	183.0	191.0	178.0	182.4	265.6
1962	94.8	98.0	91.9	94.8	96.7	1977	194.2	192.5	186.1	195.1	302.2
1963	94.5	96.0	92.5	94.7	96.3	1978,					
1964	94.7	94.6	92.3	95.2	93.7	May	207.9	215.7	202.5	207.3	319.7
						June	209.4	219.5	204.6	208.5	322.8

[1] Fuels, related products, and power.

No. 786. PRODUCER PRICE INDEXES, BY STAGE OF PROCESSING: 1960 TO 1978

[1967=100. 1960 excludes Alaska and Hawaii. See also *Historical Statistics, Colonial Times to 1970*, series E 73-86]

STAGE OF PROCESSING AND COMMODITY	1960	1965	1970	1971	1972	1973	1974	1975	1976	1977	1978, Jan.-Apr. avg.
All commodities	94.9	96.6	110.4	114.0	119.1	134.7	160.1	174.9	183.0	194.2	203.0
Crude materials for further processing	97.0	99.3	112.3	115.1	127.6	173.9	196.1	196.9	205.1	214.3	228.7
Foodstuffs and feedstuffs	95.1	97.1	112.0	114.2	127.5	179.9	189.4	191.8	190.1	190.9	204.8
Nonfoods, exc. fuel	101.4	104.5	109.8	110.7	121.9	161.5	205.4	188.3	210.2	217.3	225.7
For manufacturing	101.8	105.3	109.6	110.1	122.1	165.4	212.8	192.4	215.7	222.4	230.5
For construction	97.0	97.5	113.9	119.2	121.6	124.9	135.1	151.1	161.2	170.6	180.8
Fuel	92.8	93.5	122.6	139.0	148.7	164.5	219.4	271.5	314.7	400.4	439.5
Intermediate materials, supplies, components	95.6	96.8	109.9	114.1	118.7	131.6	162.9	180.0	189.3	201.7	209.8
Materials and components for manufacturing	96.5	97.4	110.0	112.8	117.0	127.7	162.2	178.7	185.6	195.5	202.7
Materials for—											
Food manufacturing	91.1	97.6	112.9	116.5	119.9	146.0	209.2	209.4	180.6	181.7	193.7
Nondurable mfg	102.1	100.0	103.8	105.3	109.4	121.2	155.2	174.7	180.6	189.2	191.9
Durable mfg	94.3	96.8	114.7	118.2	123.8	133.7	171.7	188.4	202.3	219.0	229.8
Components for mfg	93.1	93.8	111.1	114.8	117.6	121.4	139.9	158.3	165.6	176.0	184.1
Materials and components for construction	95.9	96.2	112.6	119.7	126.2	136.7	161.6	176.4	188.0	202.9	217.0
Processed fuels, lubricants	98.2	97.4	105.0	115.2	118.9	131.5	199.1	233.0	250.9	283.8	293.0
Containers	95.5	95.8	111.4	116.6	121.9	129.2	152.2	171.4	181.4	193.1	204.8
Supplies	90.7	95.2	108.0	111.0	115.6	140.6	154.5	168.1	179.2	188.0	191.4
For mfg. industries	96.2	95.9	110.0	112.9	115.1	121.1	141.7	157.9	166.2	174.2	178.6
For nonmfg. industries	88.5	95.0	107.2	110.0	115.9	150.7	161.1	173.4	186.1	209.5	198.2
Finished goods [1]	93.7	95.7	110.3	113.7	117.2	127.9	147.5	163.4	170.3	180.6	188.9
Consumer goods	94.5	96.1	109.9	112.9	116.6	129.2	149.3	163.6	169.0	178.9	186.7
Foods	92.1	95.4	113.5	115.3	121.7	146.4	166.9	181.0	180.2	189.2	199.6
Crude foods	100.6	98.6	116.3	115.8	121.2	160.2	180.8	181.2	194.8	201.8	209.2
Processed foods	90.7	94.9	113.1	115.1	121.7	143.9	164.6	181.3	177.4	186.4	197.1
Other nondurable goods	94.7	95.9	108.3	111.7	113.6	120.5	146.8	163.0	173.3	185.4	190.8
Durable goods	99.2	97.9	106.9	110.8	113.2	115.8	126.3	138.2	144.4	152.2	159.6
Producer finished goods	91.7	94.4	112.0	116.6	119.5	123.5	141.0	162.5	173.2	184.5	194.1
For mfg. industries	89.4	93.4	112.9	117.3	119.8	125.0	144.7	167.5	178.1	189.9	200.1
For nonmfg. industries	94.0	95.5	111.4	116.1	119.1	122.3	138.3	159.0	169.6	180.6	189.8

[1] Goods to users, including raw foods and fuels.

Source of tables 785 and 786: U.S. Bureau of Labor Statistics, *Producer* (formerly *Wholesale*) *Prices and Price Indexes*, monthly and annual.

No. 787. Producer Price Indexes, by Commodities: 1960 to 1978

[1967=100, except as indicated. 1960 excludes Alaska and Hawaii. See text, p. 481, and *Historical Statistics, Colonial Times to 1970*, series E 23–29]

COMMODITY GROUP	1960	1965	1970	1972	1973	1974	1975	1976	1977	1978, Jan.-Apr. avg.
All commodities	94.9	96.6	110.4	119.1	134.7	160.1	174.9	183.0	194.2	203.0
Farm products and processed foods and feeds	93.7	97.1	111.7	122.4	159.1	177.4	184.2	183.1	188.8	198.6
Farm products	97.2	98.7	111.0	125.0	176.3	187.7	186.7	191.0	192.5	202.5
Fresh and dried fruits, vegetables	99.0	100.2	111.6	127.6	168.1	192.3	183.7	178.4	192.2	207.6
Grains	102.2	97.2	98.8	102.9	183.6	257.9	223.9	205.9	165.0	179.4
Livestock	94.5	99.4	116.7	142.5	190.4	170.6	187.9	173.3	173.0	204.2
Live poultry	121.6	105.5	99.5	104.0	179.5	157.4	189.8	166.9	175.4	185.7
Plant and animal fibers	129.1	126.4	90.2	117.5	197.8	193.9	153.1	233.9	202.3	178.3
Fluid milk	84.7	84.9	115.3	122.2	145.0	172.8	180.2	201.2	202.8	212.5
Eggs	122.4	110.9	126.8	103.7	165.7	160.6	159.8	179.1	162.0	158.8
Hay, hayseeds, and oilseeds	82.5	97.8	99.4	118.1	220.1	228.6	200.2	210.4	234.2	204.0
Other farm products	92.7	98.0	117.3	125.0	147.4	164.4	169.7	223.4	325.9	275.9
Processed foods and feeds	89.5	95.5	112.1	120.8	148.1	170.9	182.6	178.0	186.1	195.7
Cereal and bakery products	88.1	93.1	107.7	114.7	134.4	171.2	178.0	172.1	173.4	185.7
Meats, poultry, and fish	93.1	96.2	115.8	130.0	167.5	163.5	191.0	181.6	182.0	203.7
Dairy products	86.1	89.0	111.2	118.6	131.1	146.4	155.8	168.5	173.4	180.4
Processed fruits and vegetables	92.8	95.2	110.6	119.7	129.6	154.6	169.8	170.2	187.4	195.3
Sugar and confectionery	90.1	96.5	115.8	121.6	132.3	258.9	254.3	190.9	177.4	192.4
Beverages and beverage materials	92.8	99.2	113.0	118.0	121.7	140.7	162.4	173.5	201.0	248.9
Animal fats and oils	103.8	136.0	140.4	127.4	230.4	327.7	341.8	210.2	267.0	277.0
Crude vegetable oils	91.9	112.5	121.0	107.5	174.6	291.1	208.1	162.5	197.5	203.5
Refined vegetable oils	94.0	105.1	119.2	114.5	154.5	265.8	213.2	187.5	198.9	224.7
Vegetable oil end products	88.7	99.2	111.9	121.2	143.6	224.8	211.5	174.2	198.1	203.0
Miscellaneous processed foods	94.3	100.9	113.1	114.8	123.3	158.6	178.4	174.7	190.0	195.7
Manufactured animal feeds	78.7	94.9	103.7	116.0	198.7	184.1	172.1	194.4	204.6	194.5
Industrial commodities	95.3	96.4	110.0	117.9	125.9	153.8	171.5	182.4	195.1	203.6
Textile products and apparel	99.5	99.8	107.1	113.6	123.8	139.1	137.9	148.2	154.0	157.1
Synthetic fibers								102.4	107.3	110.2
Processed yarns and threads	(NA)	(NA)	(NA)	(NA)	(NA)	(NA)	(NA)	99.5	100.9	110.0
Gray fabrics								106.1	104.7	111.3
Finished fabrics								101.1	103.7	103.3
Apparel	94.9	97.1	110.8	114.8	119.0	129.5	133.4	139.9	147.3	150.0
Textile housefurnishings	96.1	97.3	103.5	109.2	113.3	143.1	151.9	159.3	171.3	176.3
Hides, skins, leather, related products	90.8	94.3	110.3	131.3	143.1	145.1	148.5	167.8	179.3	188.5
Hides and skins	106.7	118.0	104.2	213.7	253.9	195.9	174.5	258.4	286.7	303.8
Leather	93.8	98.0	107.7	140.3	160.1	154.3	151.5	188.1	201.0	213.9
Footwear	87.6	90.7	113.3	124.5	130.5	140.0	147.8	158.9	168.7	176.7
Other leather and related products	92.0	93.6	106.4	117.8	129.8	136.5	141.0	152.9	163.4	171.1
Fuels, power, related products	96.1	95.5	106.2	118.6	134.3	208.3	245.1	265.6	302.2	314.6
Coal	95.6	93.4	150.3	193.8	218.1	332.4	385.8	368.7	389.4	410.8
Coke (foundry byproduct)	92.5	95.8	127.4	155.5	166.6	247.7	330.8	346.8	379.4	397.8
Gas fuels	87.2	92.8	103.6	114.1	126.7	162.2	216.7	286.8	387.8	422.7
Electric power	101.2	100.1	105.9	121.5	129.3	163.1	193.4	207.6	232.9	245.8
Crude petroleum	98.6	98.2	106.1	113.8	126.0	211.8	245.7	256.6	274.2	291.6
Petroleum products, refined	95.5	93.8	101.0	108.9	128.7	223.4	257.5	276.6	308.2	312.4
Chemicals and allied products	101.8	99.0	102.2	104.2	110.0	146.8	181.3	187.2	192.8	195.6
Industrial chemicals	103.2	97.5	100.9	101.2	103.4	151.7	206.9	219.3	223.9	224.3
Prepared paint	92.1	96.4	112.4	118.0	122.2	145.7	166.9	174.4	182.4	188.9
Paint materials	111.9	98.8	101.4	104.1	113.2	152.3	177.2	189.8	205.9	206.7
Drugs and pharmaceuticals	106.6	100.4	101.2	103.0	104.3	112.7	126.6	134.0	140.5	145.1
Fats and oils, inedible	100.2	138.6	132.8	115.8	228.3	338.2	255.2	249.9	279.0	285.2
Agricultural chemicals and prod	98.5	98.3	88.5	91.7	96.6	137.7	203.6	188.3	187.8	189.8
Plastic resins and materials	108.2	99.3	90.6	88.7	92.1	143.8	180.9	194.0	197.5	199.0
Other chemicals and allied prod	93.8	97.2	108.6	113.5	118.1	147.5	168.6	170.7	175.7	180.5
Rubber and plastic products	103.1	95.9	108.3	109.3	112.4	136.2	150.2	159.2	167.6	171.0
Crude rubber	128.3	105.6	101.6	99.2	111.9	139.4	145.6	161.0	171.7	180.4
Tires and tubes	96.9	93.8	109.0	109.2	111.4	133.4	148.5	161.5	169.9	172.5
Plastic construction products [1]	(NA)	(NA)	97.2	93.4	94.1	118.9	123.9	127.2	133.2	134.7
Miscellaneous rubber products	99.9	94.5	113.3	121.1	124.8	140.8	155.9	163.9	176.8	184.0
Laminated plastic sheets, high pressure [2]	(NA)	(NA)	(NA)	98.1	97.8	116.3	124.6	131.1	141.1	143.2

See footnotes at end of table.

No. 787. Producer Price Indexes, by Commodities: 1960 to 1978—Continued

[1967=100, except as indicated. See headnote, p. 485]

COMMODITY GROUP	1960	1965	1970	1972	1973	1974	1975	1976	1977	1978, Jan.– Apr. avg.
Industrial commodities—Con.										
Lumber and wood products	95.3	95.9	113.6	144.3	177.2	183.6	176.9	205.6	236.3	263.9
Lumber	92.1	94.0	113.7	159.4	205.2	207.1	192.5	233.0	276.5	309.5
Millwork	93.1	96.0	116.0	128.4	144.2	157.1	160.4	176.9	193.7	221.8
Plywood	109.6	103.5	108.4	130.7	155.2	161.1	161.2	187.0	212.2	227.8
Other wood products	(NA)	(NA)	117.3	124.6	149.7	166.6	161.9	166.2	184.3	200.1
Pulp, paper, and allied products	98.1	96.2	108.2	113.4	122.1	151.7	170.4	179.4	186.4	189.6
Pulp, paper, and products, exc. building paper and board	97.7	96.2	108.5	113.7	122.5	152.8	171.9	180.8	187.3	189.5
Woodpulp	102.2	100.1	109.6	111.5	128.3	217.8	283.4	286.0	281.1	263.3
Wastepaper	115.6	127.3	125.0	133.6	197.4	265.5	110.2	184.9	187.2	201.7
Paper	92.7	94.6	111.0	116.3	121.4	148.6	172.9	182.3	194.3	199.5
Paperboard	104.6	101.5	101.1	105.5	115.1	152.2	170.3	176.0	176.2	173.4
Converted paper and paperboard products	98.0	94.7	107.9	113.6	121.6	144.9	161.8	170.0	176.6	180.0
Building paper and board	110.3	100.9	101.0	106.4	112.8	123.5	127.1	138.7	157.0	182.6
Metals and metal products	92.4	96.4	116.6	123.5	132.8	171.9	185.6	195.9	209.0	219.8
Iron and steel	97.1	97.9	115.1	128.4	136.2	178.6	200.9	215.9	230.4	245.3
Steel mill products	96.4	97.5	114.2	130.4	134.1	170.0	197.2	209.8	229.9	246.3
Nonferrous metals	85.9	95.3	124.7	116.9	135.1	187.1	171.6	181.6	195.4	200.4
Metal containers	89.6	96.2	112.6	128.9	134.7	164.7	192.1	202.2	218.2	233.6
Hardware	90.3	93.1	111.5	120.2	124.7	140.7	163.0	173.1	185.4	194.2
Plumbing fixtures and brass fittings	93.3	93.3	111.2	119.7	125.8	149.1	162.3	174.1	186.6	195.2
Heating equipment	105.8	98.9	110.6	118.2	120.4	135.0	150.7	158.0	165.5	171.3
Fabricated structural metal prod	95.7	96.1	112.0	122.4	127.4	161.2	189.0	193.8	206.7	220.0
Miscellaneous metal products	88.3	96.0	114.3	124.2	129.5	157.3	181.1	186.9	196.2	205.3
Machinery and equipment	92.0	93.9	111.4	117.9	121.7	139.4	161.4	171.0	181.7	190.8
Agricultural	86.1	94.0	113.2	122.3	125.9	143.8	168.6	183.0	197.9	207.3
Construction	85.9	93.6	115.9	125.7	130.7	152.3	185.2	198.9	213.5	224.9
Metalworking	85.1	91.8	114.1	120.2	125.5	146.9	171.6	187.2	198.5	210.0
General purpose	91.2	92.5	113.7	122.4	127.0	151.2	178.5	189.8	201.8	210.4
Special industry	(NA)	92.5	115.7	123.7	130.1	151.0	175.0	188.4	202.7	215.8
Electrical	99.5	95.1	106.4	110.4	112.4	125.0	140.7	146.7	154.1	161.2
Miscellaneous machinery	93.1	96.2	112.8	120.2	124.0	139.5	162.3	171.9	180.7	190.0
Furniture and household durables	99.0	96.9	107.5	111.4	115.2	127.9	139.7	145.6	151.5	156.9
Household furniture	90.0	94.1	111.7	117.3	123.0	136.6	146.3	153.6	162.2	169.0
Commercial furniture	92.0	93.3	114.5	120.2	129.4	152.4	166.7	173.5	185.9	196.3
Floor coverings	107.5	104.5	99.4	98.6	102.2	115.4	124.9	131.4	136.4	140.4
Household appliances	107.5	98.9	105.3	107.6	108.5	117.9	132.3	139.2	145.1	150.4
Home electronic equipment	117.8	103.1	93.3	92.7	91.9	93.1	93.5	91.3	87.7	88.0
Other household durable goods	89.2	93.2	116.0	125.6	130.4	148.7	168.5	179.1	190.2	198.2
Nonmetallic mineral products	97.2	97.5	112.9	126.1	130.2	153.2	174.0	186.3	200.5	215.4
Flat glass	93.3	96.2	115.6	122.4	121.4	128.8	139.2	150.0	160.8	170.4
Concrete ingredients	97.0	97.5	112.6	126.9	131.2	148.7	172.3	186.7	199.0	211.2
Concrete products	97.2	96.3	112.2	125.6	131.7	151.7	170.5	180.1	191.8	205.4
Structural clay products	93.7	96.6	109.9	117.3	123.3	135.2	151.2	163.5	179.8	192.0
Refractories	97.6	98.1	120.9	129.0	136.3	143.5	166.0	184.0	199.5	210.7
Asphalt roofing	97.4	98.7	102.7	131.2	135.5	196.0	225.9	238.3	253.0	279.0
Gypsum products	99.1	101.2	99.7	114.7	120.9	137.6	144.0	154.4	183.5	216.0
Glass containers	98.0	97.0	120.4	135.1	138.9	155.5	179.7	195.4	214.2	236.6
Other nonmetallic minerals	100.8	99.3	112.2	127.0	128.4	188.7	220.3	232.5	250.5	266.4
Transportation equipment [2]	(NA)	(NA)	104.6	113.7	115.1	125.5	141.5	151.1	161.3	169.6
Motor vehicles and equipment	98.8	98.5	108.7	118.0	119.2	129.2	144.6	153.8	163.7	171.9
Motor vehicles	102.2	99.6	107.3	116.0	116.7	125.5	137.5	146.4	155.7	163.7
Railroad equipment	(NA)	97.4	115.1	128.7	134.7	163.8	201.2	216.7	233.5	245.8
Miscellaneous products	93.0	95.9	109.6	114.6	119.7	133.1	147.7	153.7	164.3	174.1
Toys, sporting goods, small arms, etc	94.7	97.1	109.3	114.4	117.9	132.3	146.0	150.0	155.2	161.3
Tobacco products	90.3	94.1	113.6	117.5	121.9	132.8	149.6	163.0	179.8	191.0
Notions	98.2	97.8	108.4	112.1	114.3	137.4	151.0	162.3	172.4	181.1
Photographic equipment and supplies	93.4	98.2	104.9	106.7	108.4	116.8	130.6	136.2	139.9	143.0
Other miscellaneous products	94.5	96.0	108.7	116.0	125.4	142.1	155.5	152.9	167.4	183.9

NA Not available.　¹ Dec. 1969=100.　² Dec. 1968=100.

Source: U.S. Bureau of Labor Statistics, *Producer* (formerly *Wholesale*) *Prices and Price Indexes*, monthly and annual.

No. 788. PRODUCER PRICES OF SELECTED COMMODITIES: 1965 TO 1978

[In dollars per unit. Annual averages of monthly figures. See *Historical Statistics, Colonial Times to 1970*, series E 123–134, for selected items]

COMMODITY	1965	1970	1973	1974	1975	1976	1977	1978, Jan.–Apr. avg.
Farm products:								
Wheat, hard winter, No. 1, Kansas City____bu__	1.56	1.48	3.58	4.68	3.81	3.34	2.53	3.04
Steers, choice_____100 lb__	25.72	30.04	44.90	42.24	44.36	39.27	40.28	47.51
Cotton, raw_____lb__	1 .30	.25	.56	.58	.45	.68	.61	.53
Wool, combing and staple_____lb__	1.25	1.03	2.50	1.78	1.49	2 1.82	1.83	1.80
Eggs, large_____doz__	.38	.43	.65	.63	.62	.70	.63	.62
Corn, No. 2 yellow, Chicago_____bu__	1.30	1.37	2.24	3.22	2.90	2.70	2.21	2.33
Sugar, raw cane_____100 lb__	6.75	8.09	10.24	29.04	23.00	13.49	10.69	13.46
Processed foods:								
Flour, Kansas City_____100 lb__	5.47	5.57	8.52	11.06	9.37	3 8.31	6.23	7.22
Sugar, granulated (excl. excise tax)_____5 lb__	(NA)	(NA)	.73	1.67	1.67	1.03	.92	1.07
Coffee, tin_____lb__	.80	.95	1.07	1.21	1.30	2.01	3.52	3.12
Lard, 1 and 2 lb. prints_____lb__	.18	.17	.25	.35	.36	.24	.34	.31
Beef, choice_____100 lb__	43.05	48.93	2 69.18	68.55	74.93	63.96	65.03	76.98
Lamb, choice_____100 lb__	(NA)	(NA)	73.13	82.56	84.45	102.15	107.29	129.08
Shrimp 4_____lb__	(NA)	(NA)	2.32	2.27	2.69	3.63	3.65	3.40
Salmon, No. 1, tall can_____case/48__	(NA)	(NA)	1.71	1.89	1.89	2.84	3.38	3.40
Haddock, unprocessed_____100 lb__	(NA)	(NA)	59.09	50.58	54.46	58.79	68.79	56.25
Textile products:								
Polyester/cotton twill_____yd__	(NA)	(NA)	(NA)	(NA)	(NA)	1.44	1.52	1.47
Polyester twill, textured_____yd__	(NA)	(NA)	(NA)	(NA)	(NA)	1.78	1.42	1.42
Hides, skins, leather, and leather products:								
Cattlehides, packer, heavy native, steer_____lb__	.14	.13	.34	.24	.23	.34	.37	.39
Lamb garment leather_____sq. ft__	(NA)	.39	.73	.72	.72	3 .76	.92	.97
Oxfords, men's, elk or kip side upper_____pair__	5.89	7.39	9.31	10.72	11.56	12.40	22.06	23.22
Fuel, power, and lighting materials:								
Bituminous coal_____sh. ton__	13.22	16.50	20.03	29.97	44.85	46.33	(NA)	(NA)
Elec. Power Indus., E. No. Cen___200,000 kWh__	(NA)	(NA)	3,137	4,361	5,281	5,675	6,276	6,815
Gasoline, unleaded_____gal__	(NA)	(NA)	(NA)	(NA)	(NA)	(NA)	(NA)	.45
Gasoline, regular, dealer tankwagon_____gal__	(NA)	(NA)	(NA)	(NA)	.35	.39	.42	.42
Gasoline, premium, dealer tankwagon_____gal__	(NA)	(NA)	(NA)	(NA)	(NA)	.42	.45	.46
Distillate fuel oil, No. 2, to resellers_____gal__	(NA)	(NA)	(NA)	(NA)	.29	.31	.36	.37
Chemicals and allied products:								
Aspirin_____lb__	.56	.58	.63	.82	1.00	1.08	1.14	1.20
Paint, outside_____gal__	(NA)	3 5.67	6.19	8.04	9.56	9.41	9.47	9.76
Paint, inside, latex_____gal__	(NA)	(NA)	5.40	5.93	6.57	6.82	7.19	7.52
Rubber and rubber products:								
Natural rubber, No. 1 ribbed, smoked sheets_lb__	.26	.21	.35	.40	.30	.40	.42	.44
Synthetic rubber, butyl, Grade I type_____lb__	(NA)	(NA)	.26	.32	.38	.41	.43	.47
Lumber and wood products:								
Softwood plywood, interior grade___1,000 sq. ft__	(NA)	(NA)	112	126	139	145	163	192
Redwood boards, clear, f.g. dry_____M. bd. ft__	(NA)	(NA)	382	494	506	505	603	743
Maple, No. 1, common_____M. bd. ft__	(NA)	(NA)	220	234	230	239	274	355
Southern pine, finish, C and better___M. bd. ft__	(NA)	(NA)	275	319	317	342	396	473
Pulp, paper, and allied products:								
Woodpulp, sulphate, bleached_____sh. ton__	148	162	188	285	364	331	363	341
Book paper, No. 3 uncoated_____100 lb__	5 16.78	21.57	23.21	23.59	24.25	25.28	26.68	27.40
Liner, 100 lb. test_____mil. sq. ft__	2.65	2.55	2.86	3.65	4.32	4.39	4.29	4.15
Toilet tissue_____case__	7.08	9.07	9.57	12.20	15.62	2 16.86	18.20	18.94
Paper towels_____case__	4.07	4.46	4.87	6.23	8.23	8.89	9.52	10.59
Metal and metal products:								
Iron ore, Mesabi_____long ton__	10.55	10.78	11.84	13.90	17.83	19.38	20.95	21.18
Iron and steel scrap, No. 1 heavy melting 6_____long ton__	35.17	42.04	57.20	104.17	70.92	79.13	66.96	76.25
Steel rails, standard 7_____100 lb__	5.83	6.80	8.35	10.53	12.72	14.17	15.17	16.39
Copper wirebar, domestic origin_____lb__	.35	(NA)	.59	.77	.64	.69	.66	.62
Red brass ingot_____lb__	.41	.56	.66	.84	.65	.70	.70	.70
Aluminum sheet_____lb__	(NA)	.46	.44	.57	.64	.73	.84	.92
Nails, wire, 8d, common 8_____50 lb__	4.65	(NA)	6.21	9.15	10.67	10.74	11.52	11.85
Nonmetallic mineral products:								
Brick, building_____1,000__	30.46	(NA)	45.57	49.94	56.09	62.76	72.32	80.65
Glass, window, single B_____50 sq. ft__	5.35	6.60	7.78	9.04	8.93	9.02	9.76	10.51
Shingles, asphalt roofing, strip_____square__	5.88	(NA)	8.30	11.56	13.24	14.04	14.95	16.69
Miscellaneous:								
Cigarettes, nonfilter tip (excl. excise tax)_1,000__	4.62	5.83	6.25	6.85	7.71	8.47	9.35	9.90
Soybean meal_____ton__	(NA)	79.08	234.00	142.42	123.65	161.54	190.58	169.75

NA Not available.   1 For 15 market average.   2 10-month average.   3 11-month average.   4 Fresh processed.   5 Book paper A grade.   6 Consumers' buying price, including brokerage, delivered, Pittsburgh district.   7 Standard, carbon steel, No. 1 open hearth, 115 lb. per linear yard, control cooled, base quantity, f.o.b. mill.   8 Price is for units of 50.

Source: U.S. Bureau of Labor Statistics, *Producer* (formerly *Wholesale*) *Prices and Price Indexes*, monthly and annual.

No. 789. AVERAGE PRICES (UNIT VALUES)—SELECTED COMMODITIES EXPORTED AND IMPORTED: 1965 TO 1977

[In dollars per unit. Includes trade of Puerto Rico with foreign countries. Unit values obtained by dividing annual values of domestic exports and of imports by annual quantities. Values of goods exported represent those at port of export. Values of goods imported, 1965 to 1973, represent market values in country from which imported; thereafter, transaction values f.a.s. (free alongside ship) at port of export. Unit values may show actual price movements only roughly for commodities subject to considerable price variations among different grades, methods of packing, etc., and to year-to-year variations in proportions of grades, etc. Unit values of agricultural exports also include effects of Commodity Credit Corporation sales for export]

COMMODITY	1965	1970	1972	1973	1974	1975	1976	1977
EXPORTS								
Wheat_____bu__	1.63	1.58	1.74	2.94	4.80	4.54	3.98	3.09
Milled rice, less than 75% broken kernels.lb__	.072	.079	.093	.161	.224	.189	.127	.140
Corn_____bu__	1.39	1.45	1.40	2.16	3.20	3.36	2.98	2.58
Grain sorghums_____bu__	1.21	1.32	1.46	2.12	3.07	3.05	2.82	2.51
Wheat flour_____100 lb__	4.04	3.85	4.21	6.52	10.91	10.34	9.97	8.24
Leaf tobacco, flue-cured, unstemmed___lb__	.777	.921	1.01	1.07	1.23	1.46	1.59	1.69
Cigarettes_____1,000__	4.57	5.45	5.83	6.02	6.41	7.38	8.30	9.20
Soybeans_____bu__	2.86	2.80	3.42	5.69	6.91	6.24	5.89	7.38
Synthetic rubber, "s" type [1]____lb__	.181	.177	.175	.190	.274	.283	.307	.364
Woodpulp, special alpha and dissolving grades_____sh. ton__	165.08	187.40	189.88	210.65	329.47	296.97	395.42	397.74
Cotton, upland, staple 1″ to 1⅛″_____lb__	.267	.259	.340	.352	.533	.542	.648	.704
Cotton, upland, staple, 1⅛″ and over.__lb__	.337	.308	.363	.392	.579	.601	.685	.757
Bituminous coal_____sh. ton__	9.27	13.40	17.38	18.96	40.39	49.23	48.59	48.64
Steel scrap, No. 1, heavy melting___sh. ton__	34.49	43.37	34.63	54.96	102.46	84.53	72.85	61.19
Tallow, inedible_____lb__	.090	.087	.079	.133	.199	.162	.169	.187
Soybean oil, crude_____lb__	.118	.122	.118	.142	.289	.332	.207	.253
Carbon steel sheets, cold rolled_____lb__	.077	.077	.071	.097	.139	.175	.138	.121
Polyethylene resin_____lb__	.189	.134	.121	.165	.342	.257	.269	.271
Styrene, polymer, and copolymer resins.lb__	.229	.193	.158	.234	.401	.343	.339	.372
Container board liners_____lb__	.058	.062	.063	.075	.116	.126	.120	.111
Nylon yarn, incl. monofilaments_____lb__	1.35	.953	.940	.933	1.14	1.15	1.17	1.19
Carbon black, furnace_____lb__	.078	.090	.094	.093	.139	.167	.218	.264
Copper, refined, crude forms_____lb__	.387	.671	.499	.671	.900	.654	.701	.685
Aluminum metal and alloys_____lb__	.227	.263	.240	.266	.375	.361	.389	.483
IMPORTS								
Canned beef_____lb__	.357	.425	.632	.772	1.07	.724	.744	.754
Cashew nuts_____lb__	.521	.599	.618	.697	.930	.846	.898	1.38
Raw sugar_____lb__	.057	.070	.079	.088	.195	.245	.126	.092
Coffee (Brazil)_____lb__	.399	.474	.438	.596	.655	.679	1.21	1.92
Coffee (Colombia)_____lb__	.455	.535	.496	.666	.684	.683	1.07	2.00
Cocoa (cacao beans, Africa)_____lb__	.156	.352	.244	.364	.562	.670	.617	.975
Tea (Sri Lanka)_____lb__	.468	.398	.426	.433	.504	.582	.534	1.06
Whisky, containers of 1 gal. or less (U.K.) proof gal__	6.53	7.48	6.85	7.07	7.94	8.22	8.37	8.31
Whisky, containers of 1 gal. or less (Canada)_____proof gal__	6.29	6.70	6.67	6.85	7.13	7.60	7.45	8.14
Cigarette leaf, unstemmed_____lb__	.732	.568	.503	.569	.796	1.03	1.31	1.20
Goat and kid skins, dry_____lb__	.766	1.06	1.06	1.44	1.23	1.26	2.04	1.22
Crude rubber, except milk_____lb__	.174	.189	.138	.239	.331	.238	.321	.360
Sawed lumber, fir_____mil. bd. ft__	63.07	71.13	110.44	144.92	138.19	137.64	170.17	194.93
Sawed lumber, spruce_____mil. bd. ft__	63.15	73.98	119.55	149.01	140.99	132.55	160.11	178.27
Woodpulp, sulphite, bleached, exc. rayon and special chemical grades_____sh. ton__	130.30	142.90	139.14	171.78	290.77	323.72	311.92	304.01
Woodpulp, sulphate, bleached____sh. ton__	135.60	143.68	138.20	170.03	286.17	353.41	350.47	332.81
Carpet wool, scoured [2]_____lb__	.668	.424	.567	.968	.957	.825	.835	.994
Apparel wool, 60's and finer [2]_____lb__	.993	.879	.926	1.92	2.40	1.59	1.51	1.56
Iron ore (Canada)_____ton__	11.13	12.42	13.64	14.42	17.51	22.15	25.12	27.46
Iron ore (Venezuela)_____ton__	7.98	8.33	9.15	9.75	12.30	15.64	16.87	19.27
Manganese ore, metallurgical grade [3]__lb__	.029	.020	.022	.027	.038	.050	.057	.062
Bauxite, crude_____ton__	11.26	10.91	11.08	11.33	11.79	20.67	24.16	25.73
Copper ores and concentrates [3]_____lb__	.381	.617	.457	.632	.718	.566	.646	.586
Crude petroleum [4] (Venezuela)_____bbl__	2.48	2.30	2.75	3.41	11.11	11.66	12.35	13.04
Newsprint_____sh. ton__	124.89	140.11	148.73	159.88	203.18	244.10	265.23	285.37
Jute burlap_____lb__	.225	.230	.297	.278	.304	.294	.241	.246
Concrete reinforcement bars_____lb__	.039	.051	.049	.077	.136	.092	.076	.080
Steel tubes and pipes, at least .065″ thick, ⅜″ diameter_____lb__	.063	.075	.080	.094	.168	.208	.134	.140
Copper, refined (Chile) [3]_____lb__	.348	.630	.480	.704	.880	.531	.583	.578
Nickel in pigs, ingots, shot, etc_____lb__	.736	1.30	1.33	1.44	1.61	1.88	2.07	2.15
Tin bars, blocks, pigs, etc. (Malaysia)__lb__	1.73	1.66	1.65	1.92	3.54	3.35	3.31	4.37

[1] Excludes latex (liquid).   [2] Clean content.
[3] Metal content.   [4] Testing 25⁰ API or more.
Source: U.S. Dept. of Commerce, Industry and Trade Administration, unpublished data.

No. 790. Import Price Indexes—Selected Commodities: 1970 to 1978

[Products classified and weighted by Tariff Schedule of the United States Annotated, a scheme for describing and reporting product composition and value of U.S. imports. Import prices are based on U.S. dollar prices paid by importer. Prices are f.o.b. (free on board) foreign port or c.i.f. (cost, insurance, and freight) U.S. port transaction prices, as indicated. Additional index series are available for the period after 1974]

COMMODITY	1970, June	1971, June	1972, June	1973, June	1974, June	1975, June	1976, June	1977, June	1978, June
Lumber, planed, tongued, grooved (c.i.f.)_____1969=100__	89.9	110.1	129.5	177.9	161.7	154.2	173.6	193.6	231.6
Rubber tires and tubes (c.i.f.)___1970=100__	100.0	106.7	121.2	125.1	145.5	154.0	159.8	171.4	183.4
Plywood [1] (c.i.f.)_____1973=100__	(NA)	(NA)	(NA)	100.0	101.4	85.5	102.5	112.5	116.3
Newsprint paper (c.i.f.)_____1967=100__	107.2	112.0	116.9	123.0	149.3	184.3	199.8	214.2	225.7
Tools, machine and hand (c.i.f.)_1973=100__	(NA)	(NA)	(NA)	100.0	120.9	124.7	116.4	125.3	140.8
Cutlery (f.o.b.)_____1972=100__	(NA)	(NA)	100.0	118.0	137.1	160.2	160.1	178.2	199.3
Iron or steel chain and pts. (c.i.f.)_1973=100__	(NA)	(NA)	(NA)	100.0	116.4	127.7	127.5	123.6	123.9
Machine tools for metal (f.o.b.)_1970=100__	100.0	106.4	118.7	137.6	156.6	206.0	200.8	210.4	243.1
Powered tools (f.o.b.)_____1974=100__	(NA)	(NA)	(NA)	(NA)	100.0	129.9	119.4	127.3	140.9
Sewing machines (f.o.b.)_____1974=100__	(NA)	(NA)	(NA)	(NA)	100.0	113.7	115.0	119.4	135.2
Electric apparatus [2] (f.o.b.)_____1969=100__	81.9	83.0	86.0	101.4	113.2	116.6	106.6	110.5	129.7
Radio broadcast receivers (f.o.b.)_1970=100__	100.0	95.1	100.7	109.1	113.7	111.1	109.6	111.5	116.2
Telephone and telegraph equip__1971=100__	(NA)	100.0	108.3	113.2	126.6	124.3	127.9	132.0	140.3
Bicycles and parts [3] (f.o.b.)_____1973=100__	(NA)	(NA)	(NA)	100.0	107.8	122.5	120.4	128.5	139.9
Clothing of textile fabric [4] (f.o.b.)_1973=100__	(NA)	(NA)	(NA)	100.0	117.3	95.3	114.0	120.5	125.9
Footwear (c.i.f.)_____1972=100__	(NA)	(NA)	100.0	115.5	145.6	159.0	171.0	180.3	201.4
Toys, indoor games (f.o.b.)_____1972=100__	(NA)	(NA)	100.0	110.0	117.0	120.4	123.3	130.6	141.3
Phonographs, tape recorders (f.o.b.)_____1971=100__	(NA)	100.0	105.6	117.1	114.6	108.7	107.5	110.1	123.9

NA Not available.   [1] Includes veneered panels.   [2] For making or breaking or for protecting electric circuits.   [3] Excludes motorized cycles.   [4] Excludes knitted or crocheted.

No. 791. Export Price Indexes—Selected Commodities: 1970 to 1978

[1967=100, except as indicated. Indexes are weighted by 1975 export values according to Schedule B classification system of U.S. Bureau of the Census. Prices used in these indexes were collected from a sample of U.S. manufacturers of exports and are f.o.b. (free on board) factory transaction prices, except as noted. Additional index series are available for the period after 1974]

COMMODITY	1970, June	1971, June	1972, June	1973, June	1974, June	1975, June	1976, June	1977, June	1978, June
Raw cotton_____1973=100__	(NA)	(NA)	(NA)	100.0	122.7	91.3	131.8	131.5	118.3
Organic coal tar, cyclic chemical intermediates_____1974=100__	(NA)	(NA)	(NA)	(NA)	100.0	86.4	87.4	93.4	90.1
Tools, machine and hand_____	108.5	112.1	117.8	123.5	159.0	178.2	186.3	217.6	234.5
Locksmiths' wares_____	111.7	116.9	123.3	126.5	137.4	138.9	142.9	150.4	169.6
Machinery and transportation equip. [1]_____1975=100__	(NA)	(NA)	(NA)	(NA)	(NA)	100.0	106.6	113.0	122.0
Engines, internal combustion [2]_____	106.3	112.0	115.3	118.6	135.2	159.8	173.1	181.2	195.4
Tractors [3]_____	112.9	119.9	130.0	136.9	156.8	188.5	201.5	218.1	243.3
Agricultural machinery [4]_____1971=100__	(NA)	100.0	102.5	108.2	124.9	158.2	170.5	181.1	193.5
Office machines [5]_____1969=100__	95.5	97.7	96.1	96.1	91.9	94.1	94.6	97.5	97.5
Machine tools_____	114.4	119.4	124.8	130.8	154.5	179.2	190.1	201.7	226.7
Textile machinery_____	109.7	119.9	125.9	138.6	149.3	159.6	174.6	187.3	206.8
Printing and bookbinding machinery and parts_____	110.8	113.0	115.3	116.6	122.8	131.8	145.5	163.1	176.7
Excavating, leveling, etc. machinery_____	122.4	125.5	130.9	134.7	151.7	183.3	197.7	218.7	238.9
Mineral crushing machinery_____	123.2	128.7	135.5	143.1	168.3	211.8	222.2	237.9	247.5
Heating and cooling equipment_____	110.3	114.9	118.5	121.6	132.4	155.4	162.0	171.1	180.4
Pumps and centrifuges_____	114.3	115.0	117.9	122.8	151.1	178.0	195.8	210.7	219.9
Forklift trucks_____1970=100__	100.0	103.2	108.5	111.9	137.0	161.5	174.0	184.0	198.3
Powered tools [6]_____	108.8	112.1	114.4	120.0	137.9	158.9	173.9	192.0	208.4
Non-electrical machines_____	111.8	111.8	113.4	119.8	133.6	148.4	162.1	172.3	187.9
Machinery and mechanical devices_____	106.7	108.5	112.6	114.4	131.5	149.7	158.3	165.4	177.9
Electric power machinery, excl. turbines____	108.1	113.2	116.1	121.6	134.4	155.5	162.5	174.8	183.1
Electrical apparatus [7]_____	103.6	110.7	113.9	116.7	126.1	131.8	140.7	150.5	163.6
Telecommunications equipment_____	109.5	113.3	117.0	123.5	133.9	154.5	160.2	153.5	159.9
Electric household appliances_____	105.6	110.6	110.2	109.7	120.0	138.8	142.9	149.7	156.8
Lorries and trucks_____	110.2	119.1	118.6	122.5	140.9	166.5	183.2	193.0	221.8
Motor vehicle parts, new [8]_____	102.4	115.0	118.2	118.7	128.3	155.9	163.1	168.2	189.2
Aircraft parts [9]_____	120.4	130.7	145.1	151.5	162.2	189.6	203.8	223.4	238.8
Aircraft, new [10] (f.a.f.)_____1973=100__	(NA)	(NA)	(NA)	100.0	106.4	116.2	126.6	137.5	149.8
Phonographs, tape recorders, etc_____	110.7	113.7	114.5	114.5	126.6	133.2	136.3	142.7	167.6

NA Not available.   [1] Excludes military and commercial aircraft.   [2] Excludes aircraft engines.   [3] Excludes road tractors for tractor-trailer combinations.   [4] Includes appliances for preparing and cultivating soil.   [5] Includes input, output, and storage devices for electronic computers and parts.   [6] Includes tools for working metals, wood, plastics, and hand carving materials.   [7] For making or breaking or for protecting electric circuits.   [8] Nonmilitary, excludes parts for assembly; prices are f.a.s. (free alongside ship). Excludes motorcycle parts.   [9] Excludes rubber tires, engines, and electrical parts.   [10] Excludes military, cargo, and passenger transport. Prices are f.a.f. (fly away factory).

Source of tables 790 and 791: U.S. Bureau of Labor Statistics, unpublished data.

No. 792. CONSUMER PRICE INDEXES, BY MAJOR GROUPS: 1950 TO 1978

[1967=100. Annual averages of monthly figures. Prior to 1965, excludes Alaska and Hawaii. Beginning 1965, except as indicated in text, p. 482, for 1978, indexes reflect buying patterns of urban wage earners and clerical workers in the 1960's, including single workers living alone as well as families of two or more persons; indexes for prior years apply only to families of two or more persons. See also *Historical Statistics, Colonial Times to 1970*, series E 135–173]

YEAR	All items	Food	Rent, residential	Home ownership	Household appliances [1]	Fuel oil and coal	Gas and electricity	Apparel and upkeep	TRANSPORTATION		Medical care	All commodities	All services
									Private	Public			
1950	72.1	74.5	70.4	(NA)	135.1	72.7	81.2	79.0	72.5	48.9	53.7	78.8	58.7
1951	77.8	82.8	73.2	(NA)	143.8	76.5	81.5	86.1	75.8	54.0	56.3	85.9	61.8
1952	79.5	84.3	76.2	(NA)	141.9	78.0	82.6	85.3	80.8	57.5	59.3	87.0	64.5
1953	80.1	83.0	80.3	75.0	140.4	81.5	84.2	84.6	82.4	61.3	61.4	86.7	67.3
1954	80.5	82.8	83.2	76.3	135.9	81.2	85.3	84.5	80.3	65.5	63.4	85.9	69.5
1955	80.2	81.6	84.3	77.0	129.3	82.3	87.5	84.1	78.9	67.4	64.8	85.1	70.9
1956	81.4	82.2	85.9	78.3	120.1	85.9	88.4	85.8	80.1	70.0	67.2	85.9	72.7
1957	84.3	84.9	87.5	81.7	117.7	90.3	89.3	87.3	84.7	72.7	69.9	88.6	75.6
1958	86.6	88.5	89.1	83.5	113.8	88.7	92.4	87.5	87.4	76.1	73.2	90.6	78.5
1959	87.3	87.1	90.4	84.4	113.6	89.8	94.7	88.2	91.1	78.3	76.4	90.7	80.8
1960	88.7	88.0	91.7	86.3	112.1	89.2	98.6	89.6	90.6	81.0	79.1	91.5	83.5
1961	89.6	89.1	92.9	86.9	109.8	91.0	99.4	90.4	91.3	84.6	81.4	92.0	85.2
1962	90.6	89.9	94.0	87.9	107.2	91.5	99.4	90.9	93.0	87.4	83.5	92.8	86.8
1963	91.7	91.2	95.0	89.0	105.2	93.2	99.4	91.9	93.4	88.5	85.6	93.6	88.5
1964	92.9	92.4	95.9	90.8	104.0	92.7	99.4	92.7	94.7	90.1	87.3	94.6	90.2
1965	94.5	94.4	96.9	92.7	101.6	94.6	99.4	93.7	96.3	91.9	89.5	95.7	92.2
1966	97.2	99.1	98.2	96.3	99.9	97.0	99.6	96.1	97.5	95.2	93.4	98.2	95.8
1967	100.0	100.0	100.0	100.0	100.0	100.0	100.0	100.0	100.0	100.0	100.0	100.0	100.0
1968	104.2	103.6	102.4	105.7	102.1	103.1	100.9	105.4	103.0	104.6	106.1	103.7	105.2
1969	109.8	108.9	105.7	116.0	104.3	105.6	102.8	111.5	106.5	112.7	113.4	108.4	112.5
1970	116.3	114.9	110.1	128.5	106.9	110.1	107.3	116.1	111.1	128.5	120.6	113.5	121.6
1971	121.3	118.4	115.2	133.7	109.1	117.5	114.7	119.8	116.6	137.7	128.4	117.4	128.4
1972	125.3	123.5	119.2	140.1	109.7	118.5	120.5	122.3	117.5	143.4	132.5	120.9	133.3
1973	133.1	141.4	124.3	146.7	109.8	136.0	126.4	126.8	121.5	144.8	137.7	129.9	139.1
1974	147.7	161.7	130.6	163.2	115.6	214.6	145.8	136.2	136.6	148.0	150.5	145.5	152.1
1975	161.2	175.4	137.3	181.7	128.1	235.3	169.6	142.3	149.8	158.6	168.6	158.4	166.6
1976	170.5	180.8	144.7	191.7	135.3	250.8	189.0	147.6	164.6	174.2	184.7	165.2	180.4
1977	181.5	192.2	153.5	204.9	140.1	283.4	213.4	154.2	176.6	182.4	202.4	174.7	194.3
1978, May	193.2	209.3	162.2	221.0	144.8	295.6	230.4	160.0	183.1	188.2	217.6	185.6	207.5

NA Not available.   [1] Excludes radio and television.

Source: U.S. Bureau of Labor Statistics, *Monthly Labor Review*. Also in *Handbook of Labor Statistics*, annual.

No. 793. CONSUMER PRICE INDEXES FOR SELECTED ITEMS AND GROUPS: 1960 TO 1978

[1967=100, except as noted. Annual averages of monthly figures. See headnote, table 792]

COMMODITY	1960	1965	1970	1972	1973	1974	1975	1976	1977	1978, May
All items	88.7	94.5	116.3	125.3	133.1	147.7	161.2	170.5	181.5	193.2
Food [1]	88.0	94.4	114.9	123.5	141.4	161.7	175.4	180.8	192.2	209.3
Food away from home	81.4	90.9	119.9	131.1	141.4	159.4	174.3	186.1	200.3	212.4
Restaurant meals	81.2	90.7	119.7	131.1	142.1	159.7	173.2	185.1	197.7	209.2
Total food at home	89.6	95.5	113.7	121.6	141.4	162.4	175.8	179.5	190.2	208.6
Cereal and bakery products	87.1	93.8	108.9	114.7	127.7	166.1	184.8	180.6	183.5	198.2
White bread	85.2	92.6	109.1	113.0	126.7	158.4	165.8	162.7	162.8	170.2
Meats, poultry, and fish	89.1	94.5	116.5	128.0	160.4	163.9	178.0	179.4	178.4	204.3
Meats	87.2	93.9	117.6	129.2	161.1	164.1	177.9	178.2	174.2	202.8
Poultry	106.9	101.2	108.4	110.4	154.8	146.9	162.4	155.7	156.7	171.4
Fish	85.0	90.8	118.0	141.9	162.8	187.7	203.3	227.3	251.6	268.4
Dairy products	88.4	90.0	111.8	117.1	127.9	151.9	156.6	169.3	173.9	182.8
Milk, fresh, grocery	91.1	90.3	111.6	116.3	127.3	152.5	152.7	160.7	162.3	169.3
Fruits and vegetables	88.3	98.0	113.4	125.0	142.5	165.8	171.0	175.4	191.6	222.8
Other food at home [2]	94.9	99.9	114.1	116.7	130.3	162.8	184.8	189.9	224.1	230.4
Eggs	113.2	105.0	125.6	107.7	160.2	160.8	157.8	172.4	166.9	152.1
Margarine	88.6	97.2	106.0	117.6	133.4	204.9	224.6	188.3	205.7	223.6
Sugar	92.2	96.1	107.4	115.0	124.9	267.8	308.8	201.2	180 9	206.6
Coffee, can and bag	94.0	107.2	119.0	119.4	135.0	160.5	172.9	243.6	451.2	420.7
Tea	100.9	100.2	105.0	108.7	111.1	121.1	145.6	150.7	180.0	205.4

See footnotes at end of table.

No. 793. CONSUMER PRICE INDEXES FOR SELECTED ITEMS AND GROUPS: 1960 TO 1978—Continued

[1967=100, except as noted. Annual averages of monthly figures. See headnote, table 792]

COMMODITY	1960	1965	1970	1972	1973	1974	1975	1976	1977	1978, May
Housing	90.2	94.9	118.9	129.2	135.0	150.6	166.8	177.2	189.6	202.4
Shelter	87.8	93.8	123.6	134.5	140.7	154.4	169.7	179.0	191.1	205.3
Rent, residential	91.7	96.9	110.1	119.2	124.3	130.6	137.3	144.7	153.5	162.2
Fuel and utilities [3]	95.9	98.3	107.6	120.1	126.9	150.2	167.8	182.7	202.2	214.3
Fuel oil and coal	89.2	94.6	110.1	118.5	136.0	214.6	235.3	250.8	283.4	295.6
Housefurnishings and operation [4]	93.8	95.3	113.4	121.0	124.9	140.5	158.1	168.5	177.0	186.7
Housefurnishings	99.3	97.1	111.4	116.2	119.0	130.8	144.4	150.7	156.5	162.8
Apparel and upkeep [5]	89.6	93.7	116.1	122.3	126.8	136.2	142.3	147.6	154.2	160.0
Apparel commodities	90.3	93.6	116.5	122.7	127.1	136.1	141.2	145.8	151.6	156.1
Apparel commodities [6]	91.5	94.5	116.3	122.3	126.5	135.7	140.6	144.9	150.6	154.6
Men's and boys'	88.9	94.0	117.1	121.9	126.4	136.4	142.2	147.2	154.0	159.5
Women's and girls'	91.6	93.8	116.0	123.0	127.3	134.9	138.1	141.9	146.4	149.0
Footwear	85.1	90.0	117.7	124.9	130.2	138.1	144.2	149.9	156.9	163.3
Transportation	89.6	95.9	112.7	119.9	123.8	137.7	150.6	165.5	177.2	183.7
Private	90.6	96.3	111.1	117.5	121.5	136.6	149.8	164.6	176.6	183.1
Automobiles, new	104.5	100.9	107.6	111.0	111.1	117.5	127.6	135.7	142.9	153.6
Automobiles, used	83.6	99.4	104.3	110.5	117.6	122.6	146.4	167.9	182.8	186.3
Gasoline	92.5	94.9	105.6	107.6	118.1	159.9	170.8	177.9	188.2	192.3
Auto insurance rates	77.5	90.8	126.7	140.5	138.0	138.1	145.9	187.9	210.5	214.4
Public	81.0	91.9	128.5	143.4	144.8	148.0	158.6	174.2	182.4	188.2
Local transit fares	77.1	89.4	134.5	150.1	150.1	148.0	155.5	173.3	178.5	181.3
Bus fares (intercity)	(NA)	93.7	118.4	140.1	145.7	161.0	186.0	196.9	223.5	244.7
Health and recreation	85.1	93.4	116.2	126.1	130.2	140.3	153.5	163.3	173.7	184.1
Medical care	79.1	89.5	120.6	132.5	137.7	150.5	168.6	184.7	202.4	217.6
Drugs and prescriptions	104.5	100.2	103.6	105.6	105.9	109.6	118.8	126.0	134.1	142.5
Physicians' fees [7]	77.0	88.3	121.4	133.8	138.2	150.9	169.4	188.5	206.0	221.8
Dentists' fees	82.1	92.2	119.4	132.3	136.4	146.8	161.9	172.2	185.1	198.5
Hospital daily services [8]	(NA)	(NA)	(NA)	102.0	105.6	115.1	132.3	148.7	164.1	177.9
Hospital, semiprivate rooms	57.8	75.9	145.4	173.9	182.1	201.5	236.1	268.6	299.5	326.0
Personal care	90.1	95.2	113.2	119.8	125.2	137.3	150.7	160.5	170.0	182.5
Toilet goods	98.9	99.4	110.4	116.9	120.0	133.3	150.0	158.5	167.5	178.6
Services	81.4	91.5	116.0	122.9	130.6	141.5	151.4	162.5	174.4	186.5
Reading and recreation	87.3	95.9	113.4	122.8	125.9	133.8	144.4	151.2	157.9	164.8
TV sets, incl. portable	127.1	107.3	99.8	99.5	98.0	98.9	101.6	102.9	101.7	100.7
Indoor movie admissions	65.0	86.5	130.0	141.5	147.3	157.2	170.8	177.5	185.0	193.2
Other goods and services [9]	87.8	94.2	116.0	125.5	129.0	137.2	147.4	153.3	159.2	167.2
All services	83.5	92.2	121.6	133.3	139.1	152.1	166.6	180.4	194.3	207.5
Services less rent	81.9	91.5	123.7	135.9	141.8	156.0	171.9	186.8	201.6	215.6
Household services less rent	85.0	92.1	126.8	139.2	146.8	166.0	184.7	198.4	213.8	230.7
Transportation services	83.3	92.9	123.1	136.0	136.9	141.9	152.7	174.3	188.4	195.6
Medical care services	74.9	87.3	124.2	138.2	144.3	159.1	179.1	197.1	216.7	233.3
Other services	80.8	92.6	116.7	125.8	131.6	141.6	152.1	161.1	171.1	181.7
Special groups:										
All items less shelter	88.9	94.6	114.4	122.9	131.1	146.1	159.1	168.3	179.1	190.1
All items less food	88.8	94.5	116.7	125.8	130.7	143.7	157.1	167.5	178.4	188.5
All items less medical care	89.4	94.9	116.1	124.9	132.9	147.7	160.9	169.7	180.3	191.8
All commodities	91.5	95.7	113.5	120.9	129.9	145.5	158.4	165.2	174.7	185.6
Durable	96.7	98.4	111.8	118.9	121.9	130.6	145.5	154.3	163.2	171.7
Nondurable	89.4	94.6	114.0	121.7	132.8	151.0	163.2	169.2	178.9	190.7
All commodities, less food	93.1	96.2	112.5	119.4	123.5	136.6	149.1	156.6	165.1	172.6
Household durables	101.9	98.7	110.2	115.0	118.8	128.9	140.3	146.0	151.5	158.0
Nondurables less food	90.7	94.8	113.1	119.8	124.8	140.9	151.7	158.3	166.5	173.3
Nondurables less food, apparel	90.9	95.5	111.2	118.2	123.4	143.8	157.9	165.7	175.3	183.5

NA Not available. [1] Includes snacks eaten away from home.
[2] Comprises fats and oils, sweets, nonalcoholic beverages, and miscellaneous foods. [3] Includes items not shown separately. [4] Includes housekeeping supplies and services. [5] Includes miscellaneous apparel and apparel services. [6] Less footwear. [7] Includes house and office visits. [8] January 1972=100. [9] Financial and miscellaneous personal expenses.

Source: U.S. Bureau of Labor Statistics, *Monthly Labor Review*.

No. 794. PERCENT INCREASES IN CONSUMER PRICES, UNITED STATES AND SELECTED COUNTRIES: 1965 TO 1977

[Covers member countries of Organisation for Economic Co-operation and Development (OECD). For consumer price indexes for OECD countries, see section 33]

COUNTRY	1965–1970, avg.	1970–1975, avg.	1975–1977, avg.	1970	1971	1972	1973	1974	1975	1976	1977
United States	4.2	6.7	6.1	5.9	4.3	3.3	6.2	11.0	9.1	5.8	6.5
OECD, total	4.2	8.4	8.9	5.6	5.3	4.7	7.7	13.2	11.4	8.7	9.2
OECD, Europe	3.9	9.8	12.1	5.0	6.6	6.5	8.7	13.6	13.9	11.7	12.5
Australia	3.1	10.2	12.9	3.9	6.1	5.8	9.5	15.1	15.1	13.5	12.3
Canada	3.8	7.3	7.8	3.3	2.9	4.8	7.6	10.8	10.8	7.5	8.0
Japan	5.5	11.5	8.7	7.7	6.1	4.5	11.7	24.5	11.8	9.3	8.1
New Zealand	1.9	10.2	15.6	6.5	10.4	6.9	8.2	11.1	14.7	16.9	14.3
Austria	3.3	7.3	6.4	4.4	4.7	6.3	7.6	9.5	8.4	7.3	5.5
Belgium	3.5	8.4	8.1	3.9	4.3	5.5	7.0	12.7	12.8	9.2	7.1
Denmark	6.4	9.3	10.1	5.8	5.8	6.6	9.3	15.3	9.6	9.0	11.1
Finland	4.7	11.7	13.5	2.8	6.5	7.1	10.7	16.9	17.9	14.4	12.6
France	4.3	8.8	9.7	5.2	5.3	6.1	7.3	13.7	11.7	9.6	9.8
W. Germany	2.6	6.1	4.2	3.4	5.3	5.5	6.9	• 7.0	6.0	4.5	3.9
Greece	2.5	12.3	12.7	3.2	3.0	4.3	15.5	27.0	13.4	13.3	12.1
Ireland	5.3	13.3	15.8	8.2	8.9	8.7	11.4	17.0	20.9	18.0	13.6
Italy	3.0	11.3	17.6	5.0	4.8	5.7	10.8	19.1	17.0	16.8	18.4
Luxembourg	3.0	7.2	8.2	4.6	4.7	5.2	6.1	9.5	10.7	9.8	6.7
Netherlands	4.8	8.6	7.7	3.6	7.5	7.8	8.0	9.6	10.2	8.8	6.7
Norway	4.9	8.4	9.1	10.6	6.2	7.2	7.5	9.4	11.7	9.1	9.1
Portugal	6.4	15.1	22.4	6.4	11.9	10.7	12.9	25.1	15.3	21.1	23.7
Spain	5.1	12.1	21.0	5.7	8.3	8.3	11.4	15.7	16.9	17.6	24.5
Sweden	4.5	8.0	10.8	7.0	7.4	6.0	6.7	9.9	9.8	10.3	11.4
Switzerland	3.5	7.7	1.5	3.6	6.6	6.7	8.7	9.8	6.7	1.7	1.3
Turkey	8.1	18.6	21.6	7.9	19.0	15.4	14.0	23.9	21.2	17.4	26.0
U. Kingdom	4.6	13.0	16.2	6.4	9.4	7.1	9.2	16.0	24.2	16.5	15.8

Source: Organisation for Economic Co-operation and Development, Paris, France, *Main Economic Indicators*, annual.

No. 795. CONSUMER PRICE INDEXES—U.S. REGIONS AND URBAN POPULATION SIZE GROUPS: 1968 TO 1977

[1967=100. See headnote, table 792. For composition of regions, see fig. I, inside front cover]

INDEX ITEM, REGION, AND SIZE GROUP	1968	1969	1970	1971	1972	1973	1974	1975	1976	1977
REGION										
All items:										
Northeast	104.2	110.3	117.6	123.8	128.5	136.7	151.8	164.0	173.3	183.0
No. Central	104.3	109.9	116.1	120.4	124.0	131.5	145.7	158.5	167.6	179.1
South	104.3	110.4	116.4	121.1	124.8	133.0	149.0	163.7	172.8	184.3
West	103.7	108.8	114.3	118.3	122.1	129.3	142.9	157.7	167.3	179.6
Food:										
Northeast	103.6	109.5	116.3	121.0	125.8	143.0	163.9	177.0	183.1	193.3
No. Central	103.6	109.2	114.7	117.6	122.8	141.2	161.8	173.3	179.9	191.4
South	103.8	109.7	115.3	118.3	123.6	142.9	160.9	178.7	183.1	195.1
West	102.8	107.2	112.0	115.2	120.4	136.7	156.1	169.9	173.7	187.0
Housing:										
Northeast	104.0	110.6	119.0	126.8	133.2	140.4	157.1	170.3	179.7	189.8
No. Central	104.3	110.3	118.2	122.0	126.0	130.4	143.9	160.0	169.9	182.4
South	104.5	112.0	120.1	125.1	129.4	135.6	153.4	171.8	183.2	196.1
West	103.9	110.9	118.8	122.7	127.1	133.0	147.1	165.5	177.7	192.8
POPULATION GROUP										
All items:										
3.5 million or more	104.3	110.2	117.4	122.9	127.5	135.6	150.2	162.5	171.6	181.8
1.4 to 3.5 million	104.4	110.4	116.6	121.7	125.5	133.0	147.0	160.4	169.8	181.5
250,000 to 1.4 mil	104.0	109.9	116.2	120.8	124.7	132.4	146.7	160.3	169.4	180.9
50,000 to 250,000	104.3	109.7	115.5	120.1	123.9	131.7	146.8	160.7	169.9	181.1
Food:										
3.5 million or more	103.8	109.5	116.2	120.2	125.6	143.1	163.6	176.4	181.7	192.4
1.4 to 3.5 million	103.7	109.4	115.3	118.5	123.2	141.1	161.4	175.1	181.1	192.7
250,000 to 1.4 mil	103.3	108.8	114.4	117.5	122.7	140.4	161.0	174.8	180.4	192.5
50,000 to 250,000	103.3	108.8	113.9	117.1	122.3	140.4	160.5	173.5	179.2	190.9
Housing:										
3.5 million or more	103.9	110.5	119.0	125.6	131.4	137.8	153.1	166.8	176.2	187.0
1.4 to 3.5 million	104.4	111.1	118.8	124.1	128.9	134.2	148.4	163.6	173.6	187.2
250,000 to 1.4 mil	104.3	111.6	120.0	124.5	128.9	134.6	149.1	165.7	176.2	189.0
50,000 to 250,000	104.3	110.5	118.0	122.9	127.7	133.9	150.5	167.9	178.9	191.7

Source: U.S. Bureau of Labor Statistics, *Monthly Labor Review*, February, 1978.

No. 796. CONSUMER PRICE INDEXES—SELECTED CITIES OR SMSA'S: 1960 TO 1977

[1967=100. Annual averages of monthly figures. For coverage details, see headnote, table 792, and text, p. 482. For definition of standard metropolitan statistical area (SMSA), see Appendix II]

CITY/SMSA	ALL ITEMS							1975		
	1960	1965	1970	1971	1972	1973	1974	All items	Food	Fuel oil and coal
City average [1][2]	88.7	94.5	116.3	121.3	125.3	133.1	147.7	161.2	175.4	235.3
Atlanta, Ga	89.3	94.0	116.5	121.7	125.5	133.7	148.5	161.7	181.8	(NA)
Baltimore, Md	89.1	94.4	117.0	123.4	126.3	134.9	152.4	165.2	178.2	229.4
Boston, Mass	86.5	94.5	116.7	122.7	127.1	134.7	148.7	162.1	175.2	230.7
Buffalo, N.Y	(NA)	94.2	116.1	121.8	126.6	134.8	149.5	161.8	173.6	235.3
Chicago, Ill.-Northwestern Ind	90.7	94.7	116.3	120.8	124.3	132.0	146.1	157.6	175.1	222.1
Cincinnati, Ohio-Ky	90.0	94.4	115.7	120.7	124.7	132.1	146.3	160.3	177.4	(NA)
Cleveland, Ohio	90.6	94.7	119.3	122.8	126.5	134.1	147.8	160.9	175.8	(NA)
Dallas, Tex	(NA)	93.8	117.8	121.3	124.9	132.0	145.3	158.2	172.5	(NA)
Detroit, Mich	88.2	92.6	117.4	121.7	126.2	134.5	149.0	160.1	171.6	226.7
Honolulu, Hawaii	(NA)	94.6	114.2	118.9	122.8	128.3	141.9	155.0	176.7	(NA)
Houston, Tex	89.2	94.8	116.8	120.9	125.2	132.3	147.8	164.9	181.2	(NA)
Kansas City, Mo.-Kans	86.9	95.5	115.8	120.5	124.0	130.3	144.2	157.9	177.8	(NA)
Los Angeles-Long Beach, Calif	88.5	95.7	114.3	118.5	122.3	129.2	142.5	157.6	170.1	(NA)
Milwaukee, Wis	90.2	95.8	115.8	120.1	123.7	131.5	144.1	157.0	171.9	237.7
Minneapolis-St. Paul, Minn	89.0	94.5	117.5	121.7	125.5	133.0	148.3	160.9	178.9	228.8
New York, N.Y.-Northeast. N.J	87.3	94.3	119.0	125.9	131.4	139.7	154.8	166.6	179.6	241.2
Philadelphia, Pa.-N.J	88.4	94.7	117.8	123.5	127.0	135.5	151.6	164.2	179.6	225.9
Pittsburgh, Pa	90.5	95.8	116.4	121.5	125.3	132.9	147.3	160.0	177.4	(NA)
Portland, Oreg. [3]	87.1	94.6	113.2	116.1	119.5	127.3	142.8	156.5	168.4	244.0
St. Louis, Mo.-Ill	87.7	94.1	115.2	119.6	122.3	129.3	142.2	156.1	174.3	247.5
San Diego, Calif	(NA)	95.2	115.3	119.8	124.4	132.5	147.2	160.8	173.7	(NA)
San Francisco-Oakland, Calif	87.8	94.7	115.8	120.1	124.3	131.5	144.4	159.1	171.2	(NA)
Scranton, Pa. [3]	86.9	94.1	116.3	121.4	125.9	134.7	151.1	164.7	172.9	347.6
Seattle, Wash	87.9	94.5	114.0	116.4	119.7	127.5	141.5	155.8	169.6	220.2
Washington, D.C.-Md.-Va	87.7	94.1	117.6	122.7	126.9	135.0	150.0	161.6	180.7	236.3

CITY/SMSA	1976			1977						
	All items	Food	Fuel oil and coal	All items	Food	Housing	Fuel oil and coal	Apparel and upkeep	Medical care	Transportation
City average [1][2]	170.5	180.8	250.8	181.5	192.2	189.6	283.4	154.2	202.4	177.2
Atlanta, Ga	169.2	185.8	(NA)	179.6	196.4	186.7	(NA)	153.9	214.0	162.6
Baltimore, Md	173.9	184.3	246.8	185.9	195.9	202.0	282.5	162.5	207.6	168.4
Boston, Mass	174.5	183.1	245.2	183.4	190.9	185.5	270.1	157.3	192.1	206.8
Buffalo, N.Y	170.6	178.6	249.9	181.7	189.2	191.5	293.4	174.3	182.1	171.3
Chicago, Ill.-Northwestern Ind	165.1	180.1	241.0	175.6	191.0	172.9	278.1	142.3	207.4	181.3
Cincinnati, Ohio-Ky	170.1	184.0	(NA)	182.2	197.8	185.7	(NA)	160.8	220.6	167.3
Cleveland, Ohio	169.0	185.9	(NA)	180.5	196.1	177.6	(NA)	156.9	225.5	170.3
Dallas, Tex	167.7	176.9	(NA)	180.2	191.3	183.4	(NA)	153.6	195.3	183.2
Detroit, Mich	168.8	175.6	248.6	180.4	186.4	184.6	285.7	146.7	234.8	174.7
Honolulu, Hawaii	162.8	183.0	(NA)	171.0	193.0	162.9	(NA)	152.2	203.0	159.7
Houston, Tex	177.3	187.6	(NA)	190.2	198.8	206.7	(NA)	170.6	217.7	167.8
Kansas City, Mo.-Kans	166.5	180.8	(NA)	178.3	193.0	183.3	(NA)	162.7	190.9	170.7
Los Angeles-Long Beach, Calif	168.0	173.5	(NA)	179.6	185.8	190.1	(NA)	144.8	204.2	179.9
Milwaukee, Wis	167.1	180.0	259.5	177.9	189.9	177.6	301.3	169.1	199.2	173.4
Minneapolis-St. Paul, Minn	170.9	186.6	246.8	183.0	196.7	196.7	288.1	147.3	185.9	167.5
New York, N.Y.-Northeast. N.J	176.3	185.4	258.9	185.5	195.4	191.8	291.2	149.3	217.1	194.1
Philadelphia, Pa.-N.J	172.4	186.2	241.3	183.5	198.4	190.8	275.2	143.0	220.6	181.7
Pittsburgh, Pa	168.3	181.1	(NA)	179.8	193.6	187.4	(NA)	146.8	198.5	178.2
Portland, Oreg. [3]	167.0	177.3	261.6	180.2	188.8	190.4	289.2	160.9	199.1	164.8
St. Louis, Mo.-Ill	165.1	180.5	262.9	176.5	192.8	178.3	287.8	151.2	186.7	168.8
San Diego, Calif	170.7	179.2	(NA)	182.0	190.5	200.1	(NA)	147.1	195.3	174.2
San Francisco-Oakland, Calif	168.0	173.9	(NA)	180.8	187.4	192.5	(NA)	150.8	199.7	176.5
Scranton, Pa. [3]	170.9	178.4	322.9	179.9	189.5	194.8	311.2	150.2	198.9	173.5
Seattle, Wash	164.5	175.0	235.7	177.6	187.9	189.7	258.1	153.9	192.3	161.2
Washington, D.C.-Md.-Va	171.2	186.5	254.9	183.5	199.7	187.8	293.9	152.6	215.9	175.1

NA Not available.   [1] Based on 46 cities for 1960, 50 urban areas for 1965, and 56 areas beginning 1970. Includes medium and small sized cities, not shown separately.   [2] Excludes Portland, Oreg., and Scranton, Pa. For 1965, excludes Cincinnati, Ohio-Ky.; Houston, Tex.; Kansas City, Mo.-Kans.; Milwaukee, Wis.; Minneapolis-St. Paul, Minn.; and San Diego, Calif.   [3] Old series (old market basket components).

Source: U.S. Bureau of Labor Statistics, *Monthly Labor Review*.

No. 797. URBAN BUDGETS FOR A 4-PERSON FAMILY AND FOR A RETIRED COUPLE: 1967 TO 1977

[In dollars. 4-person family refers to annual living costs for a family comprising a 38-year-old employed husband, a wife not employed outside the home, an 8-year-old girl, and a 13-year-old boy. Retired couple refers to a retired husband 65 years old or over and his wife. The 3 budget levels reflect costs of different specified types and amounts of goods and services. Each level provides for average inventories of clothing, housefurnishings, major durables, and other equipment. Metropolitan areas are as defined in May 1967]

ITEM	LOWER BUDGET [1]			INTERMEDIATE BUDGET			HIGHER BUDGET		
	Urban U.S.	Metro. areas [2]	Non-metro. areas [3]	Urban U.S.	Metro. areas [2]	Non-metro. areas [3]	Urban U.S.	Metro. areas [2]	Non-metro. areas [3]
4-PERSON FAMILY									
Total cost, spring 1967	5,915	5,994	5,564	9,076	9,243	8,332	13,050	13,367	11,640
Total cost, spring 1970	6,960	7,061	6,512	10,664	10,933	9,600	15,511	15,971	13,459
Total cost, autumn 1972	7,386	7,509	6,837	11,446	11,731	10,182	16,558	17,112	14,084
Total cost, autumn 1973	8,181	8,305	7,626	12,626	12,909	11,363	18,201	18,760	15,708
Total cost, autumn 1974	9,198	9,323	8,639	14,333	14,644	12,945	20,777	21,381	18,081
Total cost, autumn 1975	9,588	9,720	9,002	15,318	15,638	13,886	22,294	22,940	19,412
Total cost, autumn 1976	**10,041**	**10,189**	**9,382**	**16,236**	**16,596**	**14,625**	**23,759**	**24,492**	**20,486**
Cost of consumption, total	8,162	8,259	7,726	12,370	12,621	11,254	17,048	17,495	15,050
Food	3,003	3,046	2,814	3,859	3,917	3,598	4,856	4,966	4,369
Housing [4]	1,964	1,995	1,825	3,843	3,952	3,357	5,821	6,019	4,936
Transportation	767	729	933	1,403	1,411	1,369	1,824	1,859	1,670
Clothing and personal care	1,064	1,077	1,011	1,496	1,512	1,431	2,173	2,194	2,085
Medical care	896	925	766	900	929	771	939	968	805
Other family consumption	468	487	379	869	900	729	1,434	1,490	1,184
Other costs [5]	451	454	438	731	740	692	1,234	1,257	1,134
Social security and disability insurance payments	604	615	555	898	908	852	911	914	902
Personal income taxes	825	861	663	2,236	2,328	1,828	4,565	4,827	3,400
Total cost, autumn 1977	**10,481**	**10,636**	**9,790**	**17,106**	**17,498**	**15,353**	**25,202**	**25,983**	**21,712**
Cost of consumption, total	8,657	8,761	8,195	13,039	13,299	11,880	17,948	18,416	15,859
Food	3,190	3,235	2,989	4,098	4,160	3,823	5,159	5,275	4,642
Housing [4]	2,083	2,118	1,929	4,016	4,130	3,510	6,085	6,294	5,152
Transportation	804	765	978	1,472	1,480	1,434	1,913	1,950	1,750
Clothing and personal care	1,110	1,120	1,064	1,559	1,571	1,507	2,265	2,280	2,194
Medical care	980	1,012	837	985	1,017	842	1,027	1,060	880
Other family consumption	489	510	398	909	941	765	1,499	1,557	1,241
Other costs [5]	472	475	458	763	772	723	1,288	1,312	1,184
Social security and disability insurance payments	632	644	579	961	975	896	985	987	972
Personal income taxes	720	757	558	2,342	2,452	1,853	4,980	5,268	3,697
RETIRED COUPLE									
Total cost, spring 1967 [6]	2,671	2,730	2,492	3,857	3,997	3,440	6,039	6,342	5,137
Total cost, spring 1970 [6]	3,109	3,188	2,872	4,489	4,679	3,917	7,114	7,503	5,949
Total cost, autumn 1972 [6]	3,442	3,547	3,129	4,967	5,195	4,285	7,689	8,144	6,328
Total cost, autumn 1973 [6]	3,763	3,865	3,457	5,414	5,637	4,746	8,043	8,429	6,888
Total cost, autumn 1974 [6]	4,228	4,332	3,916	6,041	6,278	5,331	8,969	9,379	7,743
Total cost, autumn 1975 [6]	4,501	4,606	4,189	6,465	6,711	5,728	9,598	10,025	8,320
Total cost, autumn 1976 [6]	4,695	4,807	4,359	6,738	7,002	5,947	10,048	10,509	8,669
Total cost, autumn 1977	**5,031**	**5,151**	**4,671**	**7,198**	**7,479**	**6,358**	**10,711**	**11,203**	**9,237**
Cost of consumption, total	4,815	4,930	4,470	6,765	7,029	5,976	9,898	10,355	8,527
Food	1,535	1,554	1,479	2,035	2,071	1,928	2,554	2,604	2,405
Housing [4]	1,745	1,850	1,433	2,518	2,702	1,968	3,936	4,263	2,959
Transportation	337	305	433	658	667	631	1,215	1,244	1,128
Clothing and personal care	360	360	358	574	576	570	868	858	896
Medical care	628	635	608	632	639	613	637	643	618
Other family consumption	209	225	159	347	375	266	687	742	521
Other cost [6]	217	222	201	433	450	382	813	848	710

[1] Not intended to represent a minimum or subsistence level.
[2] For definition, see U.S. Office of Management and Budget, *Standard Metropolitan Statistical Areas*, 1967.
[3] Places with 2,500–50,000 population in 1960.   [4] Includes the weighted average cost of renter and homeowner shelter, housefurnishings, and household operations. Four-person families in the lower budget are assumed to be renters. A small allowance for lodging away from home city is included in the higher budget.   [5] Includes gifts, contributions, life insurance, and occupational expenses.   [6] Includes gifts and contributions and, at the higher level, an allowance for life insurance and, for 1967–1972, personal income taxes.

Source: U.S. Bureau of Labor Statistics, *3 Budgets for an Urban Family of Four Persons, 1969–70*; *Autumn Urban Family Budgets and Comparative Indexes for Selected Urban Areas*, annual (Supplements to Bulletin 1570–5); *3 Budgets for a Retired Couple in Urban Areas of the United States, 1969–70*; and *3 Budgets for a Retired Couple, Autumn*, annual. (Supplements to Bulletin 1570–6).

No. 798. Urban Intermediate Budget for a 4-Person Family and a Retired Couple—U.S. Cost, 1967 to 1977, and for Selected Metropolitan Areas, 1977

[In dollars, except percent. See headnote, table 797. Metropolitan areas are as defined in May 1967]

AREA	COST FOR 4-PERSON FAMILY					COST FOR RETIRED COUPLE				
	Total	Food	Housing[1]	Transportation	Other[2]	Total	Food	Housing[1]	Transportation	Other[2]
1967, urban U.S.	9,076	2,105	2,230	892	3,849	3,857	1,048	1,330	382	1,097
Percent	100.0	23.2	24.6	9.8	42.4	100.0	27.2	34.5	9.9	28.4
1970, urban U.S.	10,664	2,452	2,501	912	4,799	4,489	1,220	1,554	413	1,302
Percent	100.0	23.0	23.5	8.6	45.0	100.0	27.2	34.6	9.2	29.0
1974, urban U.S.	14,333	3,548	3,236	1,171	6,378	6,041	1,766	2,043	527	1,705
Percent	100.0	24.8	22.6	8.2	44.5	100.0	29.2	33.8	8.7	28.2
1975, urban U.S.	15,318	3,827	3,533	1,279	6,679	6,465	1,912	2,192	577	1,784
Percent	100.0	25.0	23.1	8.3	43.6	100.0	29.6	33.9	8.9	27.6
1976, urban U.S.	16,236	3,859	3,843	1,403	7,131	6,738	1,914	2,334	629	1,861
Percent	100.0	23.8	23.7	8.6	43.9	100.0	28.4	34.6	9.3	27.6
1977										
Urban U.S., total	17,106	4,098	4,016	1,472	7,519	7,198	2,035	2,518	658	1,987
Percent	100.0	24.0	23.5	8.6	44.0	100.0	28.3	35.0	9.1	27.6
Nonmetropolitan areas[3]	15,353	3,823	3,510	1,434	6,586	6,358	1,928	1,968	631	1,831
Metropolitan areas[4]	17,498	4,160	4,130	1,480	7,728	7,479	2,071	2,702	667	2,040
Atlanta, Ga	15,483	3,980	3,256	1,388	6,859	6,533	1,998	1,902	655	1,978
Austin, Tex	14,776	3,659	3,234	1,490	6,393	6,703	1,793	2,249	700	1,961
Bakersfield, Calif	15,686	3,790	3,406	1,569	6,921	6,727	1,870	2,212	730	1,915
Baltimore, Md	17,204	4,008	3,764	1,409	8,023	7,062	1,991	2,362	705	2,004
Baton Rouge, La	15,283	4,119	3,130	1,424	6,610	6,451	2,065	1,750	692	1,944
Boston, Mass	20,609	4,426	5,585	1,817	8,781	8,577	2,218	3,547	720	2,092
Buffalo, N.Y	18,298	4,229	4,239	1,583	8,247	7,903	2,109	2,920	770	2,104
Cedar Rapids, Iowa	16,681	3,664	3,880	1,489	7,648	7,014	1,818	2,474	684	2,038
Champaign-Urbana, Ill	17,223	3,944	4,166	1,500	7,613	7,415	1,975	2,623	706	2,111
Chicago, Ill.-Northwestern Ind	17,330	4,176	4,150	1,537	7,467	7,106	2,072	2,413	616	2,005
Cincinnati, Ohio-Ky.-Ind	16,547	4,125	3,740	1,469	7,213	6,946	2,063	2,250	663	1,970
Cleveland, Ohio	17,411	4,085	4,222	1,486	7,618	7,492	2,024	2,665	716	2,087
Dallas, Tex	15,313	3,777	3,420	1,517	6,599	6,731	1,852	2,175	734	1,970
Dayton, Ohio	15,695	3,970	3,465	1,402	6,858	6,859	1,976	2,234	676	1,973
Denver, Colo	16,711	3,937	3,666	1,457	7,651	6,978	1,968	2,277	694	2,039
Detroit, Mich	17,427	4,038	4,094	1,454	7,841	7,214	1,986	2,470	715	2,043
Durham, N.C	16,369	3,819	3,673	1,372	7,505	6,831	1,893	2,297	677	1,964
Green Bay, Wis	16,768	3,658	3,906	1,418	7,786	6,930	1,815	2,446	674	1,995
Hartford, Conn	17,796	4,413	4,438	1,625	7,320	7,974	2,204	2,897	769	2,104
Honolulu, Hawaii	20,883	4,932	4,939	1,541	9,471	8,107	2,506	2,665	817	2,119
Houston, Tex	15,488	3,953	3,364	1,482	6,689	6,875	1,962	2,231	701	1,981
Indianapolis, Ind	16,695	3,989	3,850	1,592	7,264	7,138	1,984	2,420	726	2,008
Kansas City, Mo.-Kans	16,486	4,041	3,577	1,523	7,345	7,092	1,999	2,312	708	2,073
Lancaster, Pa	16,322	4,222	3,655	1,466	6,979	7,097	2,085	2,402	710	1,900
Los Angeles-Long Beach, Calif	17,126	3,915	4,024	1,520	7,667	7,403	1,942	2,648	773	2,040
Milwaukee, Wis	18,230	3,819	4,363	1,448	8,600	7,355	1,904	2,667	706	2,078
Minneapolis-St. Paul, Minn	17,813	4,018	3,868	1,439	8,488	7,228	1,993	2,537	688	2,010
Nashville, Tenn	15,290	3,798	3,553	1,465	6,474	6,787	1,883	2,229	694	1,981
New York, N.Y.-Northeastern N.J	19,972	4,653	5,071	1,376	8,872	8,409	2,331	3,475	493	2,110
Orlando, Fla	14,910	3,721	3,386	1,414	6,389	6,665	1,828	2,206	699	1,932
Philadelphia, Pa.-N.J	17,792	4,572	3,914	1,420	7,886	7,521	2,287	2,687	582	1,965
Pittsburgh, Pa	16,516	4,266	3,563	1,450	7,237	7,287	2,128	2,469	721	1,969
Portland, Maine	17,578	4,448	4,155	1,509	7,466	7,643	2,219	2,672	716	2,036
St. Louis, Mo.-Ill	16,377	4,213	3,582	1,531	7,051	7,047	2,097	2,287	734	1,929
San Diego, Calif	16,721	3,809	3,936	1,514	7,462	7,089	1,892	2,499	727	1,971
San Francisco-Oakland, Calif	18,519	4,101	4,657	1,548	8,213	8,014	2,029	3,017	794	2,174
Seattle-Everett, Wash	17,211	4,229	4,125	1,492	7,365	7,802	2,118	2,836	720	2,128
Washington, D.C.-Md.-Va	18,026	4,193	4,314	1,486	8,033	7,634	2,079	2,750	736	2,069
Wichita, Kans	15,994	3,845	3,572	1,513	7,064	6,990	1,896	2,378	712	2,004

[1] Includes weighted average cost of renter and homeowner shelter, housefurnishings, and household operations.
[2] Includes medical care, clothing and personal care, other family consumption, gifts and contributions, personal income taxes (except for retired couple in 1974, 1975, 1976, and 1977), and, for 4-person families, also basic life insurance, occupational expenses, and social security. [3] Places with population of 2,500–50,000 in 1960.
[4] For components, see U.S. Office of Management and Budget, *Standard Metropolitan Statistical Areas, 1967*.

Source: U.S. Bureau of Labor Statistics, *Autumn Urban Family Budget and Comparative Indexes for Selected Urban Areas*, annual. (Suppl. to Bulletin 1570–5) and *3 Budgets for a Retired Couple, Autumn*, annual. (Suppl. to Bulletin 1570–6).

No. 799. ANNUAL BUDGET COSTS FOR A 4-PERSON FAMILY—PERCENT DISTRIBUTION, 1970 TO 1977, AND ANNUAL PERCENT CHANGE, 1967 TO 1977

[As of autumn. See headnote, table 797. Minus sign (−) denotes decrease]

ITEM	LOWER BUDGET			INTERMEDIATE BUDGET			HIGHER BUDGET		
	Percent distribution								
	1970	1975	1977	1970	1975	1977	1970	1975	1977
Total cost_____	100.0	100.0	100.0	100.0	100.0	100.0	100.0	100.0	100.0
Total consumption_____	79.8	81.3	82.6	76.9	76.5	76.2	73.2	72.4	71.2
Food_____	27.3	30.8	30.4	22.9	25.0	24.0	19.9	21.6	20.5
Housing_____	20.5	19.4	19.9	23.4	23.1	23.5	24.4	24.0	24.1
Transportation_____	7.3	7.3	7.7	8.6	8.3	8.6	7.6	7.4	7.6
Clothing, personal care_____	11.6	10.6	10.6	10.7	9.4	9.1	10.7	9.3	9.0
Medical care_____	8.1	8.5	9.4	5.3	5.4	5.8	3.8	3.8	4.1
Other_____	5.0	4.7	4.7	6.0	5.4	5.3	6.8	6.1	5.9
Other items_____	4.9	4.5	4.5	5.1	4.6	4.5	5.8	5.3	5.1
Social security_____	5.0	6.0	6.0	3.6	5.4	5.6	2.5	3.8	3.9
Personal income taxes_____	10.3	8.1	6.9	14.4	13.4	13.7	18.5	18.5	19.8
	Annual percent change								
	1967–1970	1970–1975	1975–1977	1967–1970	1970–1975	1975–1977	1967–1970	1970–1975	1975–1977
Total cost_____	5.6	6.6	4.6	.55	7.5	5.7	5.9	7.5	6.3
Total consumption_____	4.5	7.0	5.4	4.4	7.4	5.5	4.4	7.3	5.5
Food_____	5.0	9.2	4.0	5.2	9.3	3.5	6.1	9.3	3.5
Housing_____	3.1	5.4	5.9	3.9	7.2	6.6	4.1	7.3	6.6
Transportation_____	4.2	6.8	7.0	1.5	7.0	7.3	1.6	7.0	7.4
Clothing, personal care_____	4.9	4.8	4.4	4.9	4.7	4.3	4.6	4.7	4.3
Medical care_____	5.8	7.8	9.5	5.7	7.8	9.5	5.8	7.8	9.5
Other_____	5.4	5.3	4.6	5.0	5.4	4.6	3.0	5.4	4.6
Other items_____	2.9	4.9	4.1	3.2	5.4	4.3	3.5	5.5	4.4
Social security_____	9.2	10.8	4.7	8.5	16.6	7.3	8.5	16.8	8.2
Personal income taxes_____	15.0	1.7	−4.0	13.0	6.1	6.7	13.5	7.5	9.8

Source: U.S. Bureau of Labor Statistics, *3 Budgets for an Urban Family of Four Persons*, press releases, and Bulletin No. 1570–5.

No. 800. URBAN INTERMEDIATE BUDGET FOR SELECTED METROPOLITAN AREAS, BY SIZE AND TYPE OF UNIT: 1977

[See headnote, table 797, and text, p. 482. Includes only the cost of goods and services for family consumption]

STANDARD METROPOLITAN STATISTICAL AREA	Single person under 35 years	HUSBAND AND WIFE UNDER 35 YEARS OLD			HUSBAND AND WIFE 35–54 YEARS OLD		
		No children	1 child under 6 years	2 children under 6 years	1 child, 6–15 years	2 children, oldest 6–15 yr.	3 children, oldest 6–15 yr.
Urban U.S._____	$4,560	$6,390	$8,080	$9,390	$10,690	$13,039	$15,130
Atlanta, Ga._____	4,220	5,910	7,480	8,690	9,890	12,066	14,000
Baltimore, Md._____	4,450	6,230	7,880	9,150	10,420	12,705	14,740
Boston, Mass._____	5,360	7,500	9,490	11,020	12,550	15,302	17,750
Buffalo, N.Y._____	4,790	6,700	8,480	9,850	11,220	13,683	15,870
Chicago, Ill.-Northwestern Ind._____	4,680	6,560	8,290	9,630	10,970	13,378	15,520
Cincinnati, Ohio-Ky.-Ind._____	4,450	6,230	7,880	9,160	10,430	12,717	14,750
Cleveland, Ohio._____	4,720	6,610	8,360	9,710	11,060	13,485	15,640
Dallas, Tex._____	4,280	6,000	7,590	8,810	10,040	12,241	14,200
Detroit, Mich._____	4,620	6,470	8,190	9,510	10,830	13,212	15,330
Honolulu, Hawaii_____	5,290	7,400	9,360	10,870	12,380	15,103	17,520
Houston, Tex._____	4,320	6,050	7,660	8,900	10,130	12,356	14,330
Kansas City, Mo.-Kans._____	4,450	6,220	7,880	9,150	10,420	12,702	14,730
Los Angeles-Long Beach, Calif._____	4,590	6,420	8,120	9,430	10,740	13,103	15,200
Milwaukee, Wis._____	4,640	6,500	8,220	9,550	10,870	13,262	15,380
Minneapolis-St. Paul, Minn._____	4,460	6,250	7,910	9,180	10,460	12,754	14,790
New York, N.Y.-Northeastern N.J.___	5,150	7,200	9,120	10,590	12,060	14,702	17,050
Philadelphia, Pa.-N.J._____	4,640	6,500	8,230	9,550	10,880	13,268	15,390
Pittsburgh, Pa._____	4,390	6,150	7,780	9,040	10,290	12,553	14,560
St. Louis, Mo.-Ill._____	4,420	6,190	7,830	9,100	10,360	12,637	14,660
San Diego, Calif._____	4,490	6,280	7,950	9,230	10,510	12,816	14,870
San Francisco-Oakland, Calif._____	4,920	6,890	8,720	10,130	11,540	14,071	16,320
Seattle-Everett, Wash._____	4,760	6,670	8,430	9,790	11,150	13,603	15,780
Washington, D.C.-Md.-Va._____	4,690	6,570	8,310	9,650	11,000	13,409	15,550

Source: U.S. Bureau of Labor Statistics, *Revised Equivalence Scale: For Estimating Equivalent Incomes or Budget Costs, by Family Type*. (1570–2).

No. 801. Average Retail Prices of Selected Foods: 1965 to 1978

[In cents per pound, except as indicated. Represents averages of prices reported by retail dealers in cities included in the Retail Food Index. Data are estimated averages of prices reported by retail dealers. Number of cities varies according to the number of cities in which an item was priced and the availability of prices within the cities. Excludes sales taxes. Prices for individual cities combined on basis of population weights. See also *Historical Statistics, Colonial Times to 1970*, series E 187–202]

COMMODITY AND UNIT	1965	1970	1971	1972	1973	1974	1975	1976	1977	1978, Jan.–Apr. avg.
Cereals and bakery products:										
Flour, wheat	11.6	11.8	12.0	11.9	15.1	20.5	19.9	18.5	16.9	16.9
Rice	19.0	19.1	19.6	19.6	26.0	44.0	41.1	37.5	35.3	40.2
Corn flakes_____12 oz__	28.9	32.2	33.4	31.2	32.2	41.5	51.9	51.5	55.6	59.5
Bread, white	20.9	24.3	25.0	24.7	27.6	34.5	36.0	35.3	35.5	35.8
Meats, poultry, and fish:										
Steak, round	108.4	130.2	136.1	147.7	174.6	179.8	188.5	178.3	176.1	189.5
Steak, sirloin	113.7	134.9	142.3	153.2	174.9	180.0	198.7	193.0	191.8	204.8
Rump roast	108.0	128.9	134.8	146.3	170.3	175.5	183.6	174.6	170.1	181.9
Rib roast	89.7	111.7	118.0	129.5	152.2	158.5	179.6	177.4	182.1	200.2
Chuck roast	59.5	72.5	75.0	82.1	102.8	102.1	102.8	96.9	92.0	103.3
Hamburger	50.8	66.2	68.1	74.4	95.7	97.2	87.8	87.6	85.4	95.1
Beef liver	57.3	68.2	68.2	77.3	94.6	97.4	86.7	76.9	73.2	78.2
Pork chops, center cut	97.3	116.2	108.1	124.6	155.9	156.5	185.6	184.8	181.2	193.2
Pork roast, loin	68.7	82.6	76.4	88.2	116.4	116.6	141.3	142.8	135.7	148.9
Ham, whole [1]	66.6	78.6	71.0	78.2	106.2	105.4	123.9	136.9	129.8	140.2
Bacon, sliced	81.3	94.9	80.0	96.2	132.5	132.0	175.6	171.1	156.2	173.2
Frankfurters	66.2	82.7	81.9	88.8	115.9	114.5	119.3	119.1	116.2	129.7
Frying chickens	39.0	40.8	41.0	41.4	59.6	56.0	63.3	59.7	60.1	62.3
Chicken breast	67.9	74.1	75.0	77.5	101.8	98.5	109.9	110.0	111.8	115.6
Turkey	48.4	55.9	54.6	55.3	73.5	72.7	72.7	73.7	72.9	79.1
Ocean perch, fillet, frozen	52.7	64.1	72.5	76.8	98.8	108.1	112.6	140.8	167.9	177.4
Haddock, fillet, frozen	62.1	88.0	100.1	106.3	131.4	149.4	151.5	163.1	185.5	199.9
Tuna fish_____6½ oz__	32.0	39.8	44.0	45.5	49.2	57.7	60.3	64.0	72.3	78.4
Shrimp, frozen, breaded____10 oz__	73.1	101.8	104.3	116.9	135.6	149.4	160.8	204.0	224.8	220.0
Dairy products:										
Milk, fresh (grocery)_____½ gal__	47.3	57.4	58.9	59.8	65.4	78.4	78.5	82.7	83.9	85.6
Ice cream_____½ gal__	78.7	84.5	85.4	85.8	91.0	107.6	122.3	127.1	135.2	141.0
Butter	75.4	86.6	87.6	87.1	91.6	94.6	102.5	126.1	133.1	139.6
Cheese, American process	37.7	50.4	52.8	54.3	60.4	72.9	76.8	86.5	86.0	92.3
Fruits and vegetables:										
Fresh:										
Apples	17.8	21.9	23.5	24.6	30.2	34.3	34.0	33.2	39.0	42.9
Bananas	16.0	15.9	14.9	15.8	16.5	18.4	23.2	23.5	25.5	28.1
Oranges, size 200_____doz__	77.8	86.4	94.3	94.2	105.3	111.4	114.8	114.2	129.0	146.0
Potatoes	9.4	9.0	8.6	9.3	13.7	16.6	13.4	14.6	15.0	13.2
Onions	11.9	16.1	14.3	17.7	25.2	20.8	24.5	23.2	29.1	22.6
Lettuce, size 24_____head__	25.5	29.9	34.1	34.1	41.8	42.3	41.5	47.7	47.6	56.1
Tomatoes	34.3	42.0	46.6	46.8	48.2	54.8	57.8	57.8	67.8	65.7
Processed:										
Fruit cocktail, No. 303 can	26.1	28.3	30.7	31.6	33.8	40.8	46.2	46.0	47.8	48.8
Pears, No. 2½ can	47.0	49.5	52.9	53.5	56.6	65.2	74.9	71.4	71.7	73.9
Orange juice concentrate, frozen_____6 oz__	23.7	22.5	23.4	25.0	25.1	25.8	28.2	28.7	34.6	43.4
Peas, green, No. 303 can	23.7	25.3	26.3	26.4	27.0	32.2	39.2	38.6	38.3	37.7
Tomatoes, No. 303 can	16.1	21.3	22.6	22.8	24.7	29.8	35.3	35.1	37.6	38.0
Dried beans	17.5	19.2	22.2	24.8	31.2	69.1	42.1	49.2	42.2	51.8
Broccoli, frozen_____10 oz__	26.4	31.2	32.2	32.1	32.9	36.8	41.6	43.4	50.8	53.5
Chicken soup_____10½ oz__	18.2	18.4	18.4	18.2	18.6	22.3	23.2	23.6	25.7	27.3
Baby food_____4½ oz__	10.4	10.9	11.3	11.3	11.7	14.1	16.4	17.2	18.9	19.9
Other:										
Eggs, grade A, large_____doz__	52.7	61.4	52.9	52.4	78.1	78.3	77.0	84.1	82.3	81.5
Margarine	27.9	29.8	32.7	33.1	37.4	57.4	62.9	52.6	57.2	59.9
Salad or cooking oil [2]	34.9	56.6	63.3	64.5	70.6	106.8	115.9	95.4	107.0	110.4
Sugar	11.8	13.0	13.6	13.9	15.1	32.3	37.2	24.0	21.6	23.9
Grape jelly [3]	31.2	29.9	31.4	32.9	35.3	45.2	61.2	58.6	57.7	58.2
Coffee [4]	83.3	91.1	93.4	92.7	104.0	122.9	133.4	187.3	347.2	339.5
Coffee, instant_____6 oz__	95.2	104.7	109.3	109.3	116.0	138.5	160.3	205.0	312.3	342.3
Cola drink_____72 oz__	54.8	72.6	75.8	83.3	86.1	108.9	132.8	127.2	107.4	116.1
Tea (48-bag pk.)	61.2	63.1	64.5	64.9	66.1	72.0	87.5	90.3	107.9	123.5

[1] Includes ready-to-eat ham.   [2] 16 oz. for 1965, 24 oz. thereafter.   [3] 12 oz. for 1965, 10 oz. thereafter. [4] Vacuum pack can only.

Source: U.S. Bureau of Labor Statistics, *Retail Food Prices by Cities*, monthly, and *Estimated Retail Food Prices by Cities*, monthly.

No. 802. RETAIL PRICE INDEXES OF FOOD—SELECTED AREAS FOR URBAN WAGE EARNERS AND CLERICAL WORKERS: 1965 TO 1978

[1967=100. See text, p. 482. Indexes represent entire urban portion of standard metropolitan statistical area (SMSA) except that standard consolidated area is used for Chicago and New York]

SMSA	1965	1970	1971	1972	1973	1974	1975	1976	1977	1978, May
Total food [1]	[2] 94.4	114.9	118.4	123.5	141.4	161.7	175.4	180.8	192.2	209.3
Atlanta, Ga	94.0	114.8	118.1	124.4	144.0	165.6	181.8	185.8	196.4	215.3
Baltimore, Md	94.0	117.4	121.0	124.7	143.8	164.4	178.2	184.3	195.9	213.5
Boston, Mass	94.2	114.9	118.5	123.7	140.1	161.3	175.2	183.1	190.9	204.0
Buffalo, N.Y	94.6	116.2	119.7	123.5	141.0	160.1	173.6	178.6	189.2	205.4
Chicago, Ill.-Northwestern Ind	94.3	115.4	118.5	123.9	142.7	161.6	175.1	180.1	191.0	208.5
Cincinnati, Ohio-Ky	94.4	114.9	118.4	124.5	142.9	163.6	177.4	184.0	197.8	219.8
Cleveland, Ohio	94.1	117.5	118.9	123.3	142.1	161.1	175.8	185.9	196.1	213.6
Dallas, Tex	94.7	114.8	117.8	123.0	140.1	157.9	172.5	176.9	191.3	210.7
Detroit, Mich	92.0	115.2	117.3	122.9	143.6	164.1	171.6	175.6	186.4	206.3
Honolulu, Hawaii	94.9	114.1	118.1	123.2	135.2	158.7	176.7	183.0	193.0	208.7
Houston, Tex	94.3	115.5	118.8	125.0	143.3	164.9	181.2	187.6	198.8	216.8
Kansas City, Mo.-Kans	94.4	116.1	118.6	123.6	141.4	162.5	177.8	180.8	193.0	212.7
Los Angeles-Long Beach, Calif	97.0	112.2	114.9	120.4	136.5	156.3	170.1	173.5	185.8	203.7
Milwaukee, Wis	94.1	113.1	115.7	120.6	138.4	158.1	171.9	180.0	189.9	207.0
Minneapolis-St. Paul, Minn	95.0	116.5	119.2	124.4	142.0	163.6	178.9	186.6	196.7	216.4
New York, N.Y.-Northeast. N.J	94.9	117.9	123.1	128.6	145.4	166.1	179.6	185.4	195.4	209.0
Philadelphia, Pa.-N.J	93.6	115.8	120.1	124.4	142.7	165.2	179.6	186.2	198.4	214.5
Pittsburgh, Pa	96.7	115.6	118.9	122.8	141.7	164.2	177.4	181.1	193.6	211.0
Portland, Oreg	94.9	110.9	113.4	118.0	133.7	154.5	168.4	177.3	188.8	(NA)
St. Louis, Mo.-Ill	93.7	115.4	118.0	122.5	140.2	159.7	174.3	180.5	192.8	210.4
San Diego, Calif	95.4	113.6	117.3	123.3	139.6	159.6	173.7	179.2	190.5	210.0
San Francisco-Oakland, Calif	96.1	112.5	116.1	121.4	138.0	155.6	171.2	173.9	187.4	206.1
Scranton, Pa	94.8	115.7	120.1	123.4	141.9	161.7	172.9	178.4	189.5	208.4
Seattle, Wash	96.2	113.5	115.9	120.7	136.3	155.8	169.6	175.0	187.9	209.5
Washington, D.C.-Md.-Va	93.5	117.3	120.2	125.8	145.5	166.9	180.7	186.5	199.7	217.6

NA Not available.   [1] See footnote 1, table 796.   [2] See footnote 2, table 796.

Source: U.S. Bureau of Labor Statistics, *The Consumer Price Index, U.S. City Average and Selected Areas,* monthly.

No. 803. WEEKLY FOOD COST FOR FAMILIES, BY TYPE OF FAMILY: 1974 TO 1978

[In dollars. Based on moderate-cost food plan; assumes all meals are eaten at home or taken from home]

FAMILY TYPE	1974, Dec.	1975, Dec.	1976, Dec.	1977 March	1977 June	1977 Sept.	1977 Dec.	1978, March
Couple, 20–54 years old	34.50	37.10	36.60	38.20	39.20	39.30	39.70	40.50
Couple, 55 years and over	30.40	32.40	32.10	33.70	34.60	34.60	35.00	35.60
Couple with children:								
1 child, 1–5 years old	41.90	44.90	44.40	46.10	47.10	47.20	47.80	48.70
1 child, 15–19 years old	50.00	53.50	52.80	54.70	55.90	56.00	56.70	57.80
2 children, 1–5 years old	48.50	51.80	51.30	53.10	54.10	54.20	54.90	56.00
2 children, 6–11 years old	59.30	63.00	62.10	64.30	65.60	65.70	66.60	67.90
2 children, 12–19 years old	63.10	67.20	66.30	68.50	70.00	70.00	71.00	72.20

Source: U.S. Dept. of Agriculture, Science and Education Administration, *Food and Home Notes,* weekly.

No. 804. WEEKLY FOOD COST FOR FAMILIES, BY COST LEVEL AND REGION: 1977

[In dollars. Based on costs of food plans as estimated by using average price per pound of each food group paid by urban survey families at selected food cost levels in 1965–66. Prices adjusted to December 1977 level. For composition of regions, see fig. I, inside front cover]

REGION AND FAMILY TYPE	Low level	Moderate level	Liberal level	REGION AND FAMILY TYPE	Low level	Moderate level	Liberal level
Northeast:				**South:**			
Couple, 20–54 years	33.40	42.90	51.70	Couple, 20–54 years	31.80	39.40	45.60
Couple, 55 years and over	29.80	37.60	45.30	Couple, 55 years and over	28.30	34.50	39.90
4-person families:				4-person families:			
With preschool children [1]	46.40	59.10	71.20	With preschool children [1]	43.90	54.20	63.00
With school children [2]	55.80	71.60	86.30	With school children [2]	53.10	66.00	76.30
North Central:				**West:**			
Couple, 20–54 years	31.70	38.90	47.10	Couple, 20–54 years	31.80	40.30	48.50
Couple, 55 years and over	28.40	34.40	41.40	Couple, 55 years and over	28.40	35.40	42.60
4-person families:				4-person families:			
With preschool children [1]	44.20	54.10	65.20	With preschool children [1]	44.30	55.60	67.20
With school children [2]	53.20	65.60	79.20	With school children [2]	53.50	67.60	81.80

[1] Couple, 20–54 years; children, 1–2 and 3–5 years.   [2] Couple, 20–54 years; child, 6–8, and boy, 9–11 years.

Source: U.S. Dept. of Agriculture, Science and Education Administration, *Family Economics Review,* Summer 1978, ARS-NE-36, quarterly.

No. 805. Indexes of Residential Rents in Selected SMSA's: 1965 to 1978

[1967=100. Annual averages of monthly figures, except as indicated. See also headnote, table 802]

CITY/SMSA	1965	1970	1971	1972	1973	1974	1975	1976	1977	1978, May
Atlanta, Ga	96.9	109.9	113.8	117.0	120.3	125.1	129.0	131.2	135.3	[1]139.8
Baltimore, Md	97.6	106.9	110.2	112.6	116.1	121.3	127.4	135.5	143.9	[1]150.8
Boston, Mass	96.3	115.4	122.7	129.2	136.2	142.9	149.6	156.7	166.2	[2]171.3
Buffalo, N.Y	97.0	109.3	114.6	120.1	126.3	132.3	140.8	149.3	156.8	163.2
Chicago, Ill.-Northwestern Ind	97.5	107.6	110.4	113.2	121.6	127.6	132.8	137.7	142.7	150.5
Cincinnati, Ohio-Ky	99.0	105.7	108.1	109.6	111.6	115.4	120.1	124.0	133.4	[1]140.7
Cleveland, Ohio	98.2	107.5	111.4	113.0	115.0	118.6	123.7	130.8	139.8	149.4
Dallas, Tex	98.5	110.1	111.6	111.8	113.4	116.9	122.1	129.2	140.3	151.4
Detroit, Mich	94.5	111.5	116.4	120.2	124.2	129.8	135.9	141.5	150.4	[2]158.5
Honolulu, Hawaii	95.8	118.1	124.0	127.7	133.1	142.9	150.4	156.8	163.5	[1]168.5
Houston, Tex	97.7	106.9	109.8	110.9	112.3	116.1	125.3	140.1	155.8	[2]162.5
Kansas City, Mo.-Kans	98.8	106.3	109.0	110.7	112.6	115.3	119.2	124.0	131.3	[1]137.6
Los Angeles-Long Beach, Calif	97.8	111.9	116.3	118.5	121.9	128.0	134.8	144.3	157.2	172.7
Milwaukee, Wis	97.4	109.8	114.2	117.9	122.7	128.8	136.9	144.1	152.5	158.1
Minneapolis-St. Paul, Minn	97.9	114.2	118.6	121.1	122.8	126.9	132.8	141.5	150.6	[2]157.8
New York, N.Y.-Northeastern N.J	96.5	110.9	119.3	127.2	136.6	145.0	153.7	162.5	171.0	[2]178.8
Philadelphia, Pa.-N.J	96.9	112.5	119.1	124.4	129.6	136.7	146.4	155.7	166.1	174.0
Pittsburgh, Pa	97.5	109.0	114.2	117.0	119.7	123.6	129.0	137.0	149.2	[2]158.7
St. Louis, Mo.-Ill	98.1	105.6	107.6	108.6	110.2	112.7	116.1	120.4	127.0	[1]132.3
San Diego, Calif	97.8	123.6	130.5	133.6	136.9	141.8	148.7	158.3	170.2	185.2
San Francisco-Oakland, Calif	94.7	119.3	125.4	129.2	133.2	138.7	144.8	153.3	164.7	[1]173.3
Seattle, Wash	92.8	109.1	106.9	105.7	108.5	118.1	130.8	141.1	153.6	167.7
Washington, D.C.-Md.-Va	96.9	109.4	114.5	118.6	124.3	131.6	140.3	149.0	158.4	166.5

[1] March data. [2] April data.

Source: U.S. Bureau of Labor Statistics, *The Consumer Price Index, U.S. City Average and Selected Areas,* monthly.

No. 806. Retail Price Indexes of Fuels and Utilities: 1965 to 1978

[1967=100. A therm=100,000 Btu's. Annual averages for cities combined. See text, p. 482. See also *Historical Statistics, Colonial Times to 1970,* series E 203–211]

ITEM	1965	1970	1971	1972	1973	1974	1975	1976	1977	1978, May
Consumer price index: all items	94.5	116.3	121.3	125.3	133.1	147.7	161.2	170.5	181.5	193.2
Fuels and utilities	98.3	107.6	115.0	120.1	126.9	150.2	167.8	182.7	202.2	214.3
Gas and electricity	99.4	107.3	114.7	120.5	126.4	145.8	169.6	189.0	213.4	230.4
Gas, all types	99.6	108.5	116.2	122.3	127.9	143.9	172.5	201.2	239.3	264.1
Residential heating	99.9	107.4	115.2	122.1	127.8	147.4	182.1	218.5	267.7	300.2
Other than residential heating	99.3	109.4	117.3	122.5	128.0	140.6	163.5	184.9	212.7	230.3
10 therms	100.2	107.4	115.5	123.0	130.2	142.2	163.3	190.0	217.0	232.5
25 therms	99.7	108.4	116.4	121.5	125.8	137.1	157.6	179.7	206.7	223.6
40 therms	98.5	110.3	118.0	122.6	127.8	140.8	165.2	185.4	215.5	235.7
Gasoline, regular and premium	94.9	105.6	106.3	107.6	118.1	159.9	170.8	177.9	188.2	198.9
Electricity (composite)	99.1	106.2	113.2	118.9	124.9	147.5	167.0	177.6	189.3	295.6
Fuel oil and coal	94.6	110.1	117.5	118.5	136.0	214.6	235.3	250.8	283.4	292.1
Fuel oil #2	94.4	109.3	116.1	116.6	134.5	213.0	230.6	247.2	280.2	132.9
Telephone service, residential	100.8	102.5	107.5	113.5	116.5	121.4	125.3	129.8	131.3	192.3
Residential water and sewer services	94.4	120.4	133.4	138.5	146.1	154.8	169.9	188.7	209.1	222.7

No. 807. Average Price of Residential Heating Gas, Selected Metropolitan Areas: 1965 to 1978

[Dollars per 10 therms. One therm contains approximately 100 cubic feet of natural gas. As of January. Ranked from highest to lowest based on latest year]

SMSA	1965	1970	1975	1976	1977	1978	SMSA	1965	1970	1975	1976	1977	1978
U.S. average	.82	.87	1.38	1.67	2.09	2.36	Cincinnati	(NA)	.80	1.33	1.56	2.18	2.48
New York	1.36	1.32	2.29	3.02	3.65	4.05	Dallas	.73	.85	.91	1.51	2.08	2.47
Washington, D.C.	1.19	1.36	2.04	2.48	3.21	3.64	Minn.St. Paul	(NA)	.88	1.35	1.44	1.93	2.42
Baltimore	1.30	1.33	2.02	2.41	2.87	3.60	Pittsburgh	.76	.88	1.42	1.61	2.03	2.40
Boston	1.45	1.50	2.54	3.16	3.60	3.42	St. Louis	.82	.92	1.45	1.65	1.96	2.34
Philadelphia	1.37	1.38	2.01	2.38	2.55	3.05	Chicago	.91	.97	1.43	1.62	2.18	2.31
Seattle	.97	1.16	1.89	2.42	2.86	3.01	Cleveland	.74	.75	1.23	1.41	1.85	1.98
Houston	(NA)	.88	1.50	2.23	2.83	2.98	Atlanta	.82	.82	1.22	1.41	1.68	1.97
Buffalo	.90	.93	1.85	1.95	2.58	2.78	San Francisco-						
Milwaukee	(NA)	1.25	1.58	2.16	2.58	2.78	Oakland	.60	.62	1.29	1.53	1.69	1.71
Detroit	.86	.87	1.35	1.87	2.30	2.63	Kansas City	(NA)	.68	.93	1.05	1.51	1.63

NA Not available.

Source of tables 806 and 807: U.S. Bureau of Labor Statistics, *Retail Prices and Indexes of Fuels and Utilities,* monthly.

No. 808. Average Residential, Commercial, and Industrial Monthly Bills for Electricity: 1955 to 1977

[Residential, for cities of 2,500 or more population; commercial and industrial, for 452 large cities in United States and Puerto Rico with estimated total population of 76.9 million as of January 1, 1977. Composite average as of January 1, using latest available population weights. For 1955, excludes Alaska and Hawaii. kW=kilowatts; kWh=kilowatthours:

ITEM	1955	1960	1965	1970	1971	1972	1973	1974	1975	1976	1977
RESIDENTIAL											
Average bill, dollars:											
100 kWh	3.82	4.04	4.02	4.09	4.25	4.51	4.65	4.99	5.89	6.15	6.54
250 kWh	7.18	7.44	7.38	7.51	7.84	8.35	8.67	9.47	11.49	12.06	12.85
500 kWh	10.30	10.62	10.41	10.51	11.13	11.99	12.56	14.10	17.93	19.26	20.86
750 kWh	(NA)	(NA)	14.34	14.22	14.99	16.14	16.96	19.14	24.72	26.78	29.22
1,000 kWh	(NA)	(NA)	18.59	18.31	19.24	20.70	21.85	24.85	32.29	34.85	38.15
Average bill, cents per kWh:											
100 kWh	3.9	4.0	4.0	4.1	4.3	4.5	4.7	5.0	5.9	6.2	6.5
250 kWh	2.9	3.0	3.0	3.0	3.1	3.3	3.5	3.8	4.6	4.8	5.1
500 kWh	2.1	2.1	2.1	2.1	2.2	2.4	2.5	2.8	3.6	3.9	4.2
750 kWh	(NA)	(NA)	1.9	2.0	1.9	2.2	2.3	2.6	3.3	3.6	3.9
1,000 kWh	(NA)	(NA)	1.9	1.8	1.9	2.1	2.2	2.5	3.2	3.5	3.8
COMMERCIAL											
Average bill, dollars:											
6 kW, 750 kWh	27.20	28.15	26.99	27.09	28.45	30.40	31.80	34.25	41.30	44.05	47.09
12 kW, 1,500 kWh	51.63	53.51	50.98	51.64	55.88	59.65	62.53	68.57	83.49	87.61	94.68
30 kW, 6,000 kWh	159.16	165.12	161.01	162.91	171.92	184.76	193.67	215.35	268.71	285.86	309.99
40 kW, 10,000 kWh	(NA)	241.81	236.02	239.37	252.43	272.50	285.97	320.51	405.63	431.69	468.71
Average bill, cents per kWh:											
6 kW, 750 kWh	3.6	3.8	3.6	3.6	3.8	4.1	4.2	4.6	5.5	5.9	6.3
12 kW, 1,500 kWh	3.4	3.6	3.4	3.4	3.7	4.0	4.2	4.6	5.6	5.8	6.3
30 kW, 6,000 kWh	2.7	2.8	2.7	2.7	2.9	3.1	3.2	3.6	4.9	4.8	5.2
40 kW, 10,000 kWh	(NA)	2.4	2.4	2.4	2.5	2.7	2.9	3.2	4.1	4.3	4.7
INDUSTRIAL											
Average bill, dollars:											
150 kW, 30,000 kWh	606	627	634	648	692	749	790	899	1,157	1,231	1,354
300 kW, 60,000 kWh	1,091	1,134	1,160	1,183	1,269	1,377	1,457	1,685	2,199	2,348	2,595
1,000 kW, 200,000 kWh	3,168	3,309	3,423	3,492	3,774	4,137	4,402	5,196	6,888	7,395	8,224
Average bill, cents per kWh:											
150 kW, 30,000 kWh	2.0	2.1	2.1	2.2	2.3	2.5	2.6	3.0	3.9	4.1	4.5
300 kW, 60,000 kWh	1.8	1.9	1.9	2.0	2.1	2.3	2.4	2.8	3.7	3.9	4.3
1,000 kW, 200,000 kWh	1.6	1.7	1.7	1.8	1.9	2.1	2.2	2.6	3.4	3.7	4.1

NA Not available.

No. 809. Net Monthly Residential Electric Bills (Range of Lowest to Highest) for 250 Kilowatthours Use, 1970 to 1977, and by States, 1977

[In dollars. Based on rates as of January 1 for communities of 10,000 inhabitants or more]

YEAR AND STATE	COMMUNITIES WITH INHABITANTS OF—		STATE	COMMUNITIES WITH INHABITANTS OF—		STATE	COMMUNITIES WITH INHABITANTS OF—	
	10,000–49,999	50,000 or more		10,000–49,999	50,000 or more		10,000–49,999	50,000 or more
1970	3.00–15.00	3.00–12.78	Idaho	5.45– 9.67	[1] 9.67– 9.67	N.Y	3.23–22.47	12.01–22.76
1971	3.00–15.00	3.00–12.78	Ill	10.01–14.17	10.01–12.79	N.C	4.50–15.89	10.84–13.25
1972	3.00–15.90	3.40–12.78	Ind	6.68–14.39	9.59–14.39	N. Dak	10.98–11.57	[1] 11.20–11.20
1973	3.00–15.90	3.40–13.18	Iowa	7.87–13.04	12.33–14.04	Ohio	8.34–17.77	9.90–13.97
1974	3.00–15.90	3.59–15.62	Kans	6.15–14.91	8.59–11.93	Okla	10.28–14.43	10.51–11.84
1975	2.88–20.68	3.48–20.94	Ky	6.41–11.97	7.50–11.97	Oreg	3.48– 8.35	3.48– 8.35
1976	2.88–20.60	3.48–20.87	La	6.75–16.03	7.52–12.10	Pa	8.50–19.71	13.57–15.94
1977	2.88–23.24	3.48–22.76	Maine	11.96–14.10	[1] 11.96–11.96	R.I	14.04–15.87	14.04–15.87
			Md	11.26–16.30	13.71–14.39	S.C	9.47–14.27	10.73–14.27
Ala	6.40–13.35	6.66–10.77	Mass	11.78–18.49	11.21–17.38	S. Dak	6.20–18.35	7.75–11.69
Alaska	17.23–18.06	10.50–13.33	Mich	8.13–13.60	9.09–13.42	Tenn	6.65–11.63	7.13– 9.89
Ariz	13.63–15.83	9.78–14.94	Minn	5.90–15.11	9.73–12.91	Tex	7.22–15.53	9.67–15.97
Ark	6.25–14.53	10.78–11.66	Miss	6.66–16.67	[1] 14.62–14.62	Utah	8.26–12.11	6.93–12.60
Calif	4.90–19.01	4.90–14.44						
Colo	8.45–12.43	8.63–11.43	Mo	7.18–18.03	9.15–18.20	Vt	10.67–19.31	(2)
Conn	12.91–16.40	10.99–17.18	Mont	5.31– 8.84	[1] 8.84– 8.84	Va	7.60–15.28	11.23–15.28
			Nebr	9.88–13.74	10.85–12.14	Wash	2.88– 7.70	3.64– 7.55
Del	13.55–15.28	[1] 16.32–16.32	Nev	7.69–12.54	8.00–12.54	W. Va	10.82–14.06	[1] 11.25–11.25
D.C	(2)	[1] 10.21–10.21	N.H	14.45–15.95	[1] 14.45–14.45	Wis	8.05–13.48	10.58–13.48
Fla	11.26–16.47	11.26–13.70	N.J	9.98–18.46	[1] 17.35–17.35	Wyo	6.94– 8.57	(2)
Ga	8.21–16.93	10.32–14.38	N. Mex	10.34–12.60	[1] 10.61–10.61			
Hawaii	15.25–23.24	[1] 15.25–15.25						

[1] Only 1 community in this population group.   [2] No community in this population group.

Source of tables 808 and 809: U.S. Federal Power Commission, *Typical Electric Bills*, annual, and unpublished data.

Section 16
Elections

This section relates primarily to Presidential, congressional, and gubernatorial elections. Also presented are summary tables on congressional legislation, population of voting age, voter participation, and campaign expenditures.

Official statistics on Federal elections are collected by the Clerk of the House of Representatives and published biennially in *Statistics of the Presidential and Congressional Election* and *Statistics of the Congressional Election*. Federal and State election statistics appear also in *America Votes*, issued biennially by the Elections Research Center, Washington, D.C.; and data on Federal elections appear in the U.S. Congress, *Congressional Directory*, and in official State documents. Data on voter eligibility and participation are obtained by the U.S. Bureau of the Census as part of the Current Population Survey (CPS) and are published in *Current Population Reports*, series P-20 and P-25 (see text, p. 1).

Almost all Federal, State, and local governmental units in the United States conduct elections at various intervals for different offices and other purposes. The conduct of elections is regulated by State laws or, in some cities and counties, by local charter. An exception is that the U.S. Constitution prescribes the basis of representation in Congress and the manner of electing the President, and grants to Congress the right to regulate the times, places, and manner of electing Federal officers. Amendments to the Constitution have prescribed conditions for voting eligibility. The 15th Amendment, adopted in 1870, gave all citizens the right to vote regardless of race or previous condition of servitude. In 1920, women were given the right to vote by the 19th Amendment. The payment of poll taxes as a prerequisite to voting in Federal elections was banned by the 24th Amendment in 1964. In 1971, as a result of the 26th Amendment, eligibility to vote in national elections was extended to all citizens, age 18 and over.

Presidential election.—The Constitution specifies how the President and Vice President are selected. Each State elects, by popular vote, a group of electors equal in number to its total of Representatives and Senators. The electors meet in their respective States subsequent to the election to cast their ballots for President and Vice President. Usually, an elector votes for the candidate with the most popular votes. A majority vote of the entire number of electors is necessary to elect the President and Vice President. If no candidate receives a majority, the House of Representatives, with each State having one vote, is empowered to elect the President and Vice President, again, with a majority of votes required.

The 22d Amendment to the Constitution, adopted in 1951, limits presidential tenure to 2 elective terms of 4 years each, or to 1 elective term for any person who, upon succession to the Presidency, has held the office or acted as President for more than 2 years. The 23d Amendment, adopted in 1961, grants the District of Columbia 3 presidential electors, a number equal to that of the least populous State.

Congressional election.—The Constitution provides that Representatives be apportioned among the States according to their population; that a census of population be taken every 10 years as a basis for apportionment; and that each State have at least 1 Representative. At the time of each apportionment, Congress decides what the total number of Representatives will be. Since 1912, the total has been 435, except during 1960 to 1962 when it increased to 437 to accommodate granting 1 Representative each to Alaska and Hawaii. The total reverted to 435 after reapportionment following the 1960 census. Members are elected for 2-year terms, all terms covering the same period.

The Senate is composed of 100 members, 2 from each State, who are elected to serve for a term of 6 years. One-third of the Senate is elected every 2 years. Senators were originally chosen by the State legislatures. The 17th Amendment to the Constitution, adopted in 1913, prescribed that Senators be elected by popular vote.

Voter eligibility and participation.—The Census Bureau publishes estimates of the population of voting age and the percent casting votes in each State for Presidential and congressional election years. Voting-age population estimates include a number of persons who meet the age requirement but are not eligible to vote (e.g., aliens and institutionalized persons). It was estimated that, in November 1978, 4,000,000 aliens and 500,000 institutionalized persons were part of the voting-age population. Since 1964, voter participation and voter characteristics data based on the CPS (see above) conducted during November of election years have also been issued biennially.

Statistical reliability.—For a discussion of statistical collection and estimation, sampling procedures, and measures of statistical reliability applicable to Census Bureau data, see Appendix III.

Historical statistics.—Tabular headnotes provide cross-references, where applicable, to *Historical Statistics of the United States, Colonial Times to 1970.* See Appendix I.

No. 810. Vote Cast for President, by Political Parties: 1920 to 1976

[Prior to 1960, excludes Alaska and Hawaii. Vote cast for major party candidates includes the votes of minor parties cast for those candidates. See also *Historical Statistics, Colonial Times to 1970*, series Y 79–83 and Y 135]

YEAR	CANDIDATES FOR PRESIDENT		VOTE CAST FOR PRESIDENT					
	Democratic	Republican	Total popular vote [1]	Democratic			Republican	
				Popular vote		Electoral vote	Popular vote		Electoral vote
				Number	Percent		Number	Percent	
			1,000	1,000			1,000		
1920	Cox	Harding	26,748	9,130	34.1	127	16,143	60.4	404
1924	Davis	Coolidge	29,086	8,385	28.8	136	15,718	54.0	382
1928	Smith	Hoover	36,812	15,016	40.8	87	21,392	58.1	444
1932	F. D. Roosevelt	Hoover	39,732	22,810	57.4	472	15,759	39.7	59
1936	F. D. Roosevelt	Landon	45,643	27,753	60.8	523	16,675	36.5	8
1940	F. D. Roosevelt	Willkie	49,900	27,313	54.7	449	22,348	44.8	82
1944	F. D. Roosevelt	Dewey	47,977	25,613	53.4	432	22,018	45.9	99
1948	Truman	Dewey	48,794	24,179	49.6	303	21,991	45.1	189
1952	Stevenson	Eisenhower	61,551	27,315	44.4	89	33,936	55.1	442
1956	Stevenson	Eisenhower	62,027	26,023	42.0	73	35,590	57.4	457
1960	Kennedy	Nixon	68,838	34,227	49.7	303	34,108	49.5	219
1964 [2]	Johnson	Goldwater	70,645	43,130	61.1	486	27,178	38.5	52
1968 [2]	Humphrey	Nixon	73,212	31,275	42.7	191	31,785	43.4	301
1972 [2]	McGovern	Nixon	77,719	29,170	37.5	17	47,170	60.7	520
1976 [2]	Carter	Ford	81,556	40,831	50.1	297	39,148	48.0	240

YEAR	VOTE CAST FOR PRESIDENT—Con.				YEAR	VOTE CAST FOR PRESIDENT—Con.			
	Socialist and So. Labor	Misc. independent [3]	Prohibition	Communist		Socialist and So. Labor	Misc. independent [3]	Prohibition	Communist
	1,000	1,000	1,000	1,000		1,000	1,000	1,000	1,000
1920	952	334	189	–	1952	50	176	73	–
1024	[4] 36	[5] 4,853	58	[6] 36	1956	46	325	42	–
1928	289	74	20	[6] 21	1960	[4] 48	410	46	–
1932	915	63	82	103	1964 [2]	[4] 45	268	23	–
1936	200	897	38	80	1968 [2]	[4] 53	[7] 10,082	15	1
1940	131	3	59	46	1972 [2]	[4] 54	1,285	14	26
1944	124	147	75	–	1976 [2]	16	[8] 1,487	16	59
1948	169	2,351	104	–					

– Represents zero.   [1] Includes votes for minor party candidates, independents, unpledged electors, and scattered write-in votes.   [2] Includes District of Columbia.   [3] Mainly Progressive in 1924, States [Rights and Progressive in 1948, and American Independent in 1968 and 1972.   [4] Socialist Labor only.   [5] Includes 4,831,000 votes cast for LaFollette, candidate for the Progressive Party.   [6] Workers Party.   [7] Includes 9,906,000 votes cast for George Wallace, American Independent Party.   [8] Includes 756,691 votes cast for Eugene McCarthy, Independent; 173,011 for Roger MacBride, Libertarian Party; 170,531 for Lester Maddox, American Independent Party; and 160,773 for Thomas Anderson, American Party.

Source: 1920–1936, Edgar Eugene Robinson, *The Presidential Vote* and *They Voted for Roosevelt*, Stanford University Press, Stanford, 1934 and 1947, respectively. Thereafter, Elections Research Center, Washington, D.C., 1940–1964, *America at the Polls*; 1968–1976, *America Votes*, biennial. (Copyright.)

Figure 16.1

Popular Vote Cast for President, by Major Party: 1948 to 1976

(See table 810)

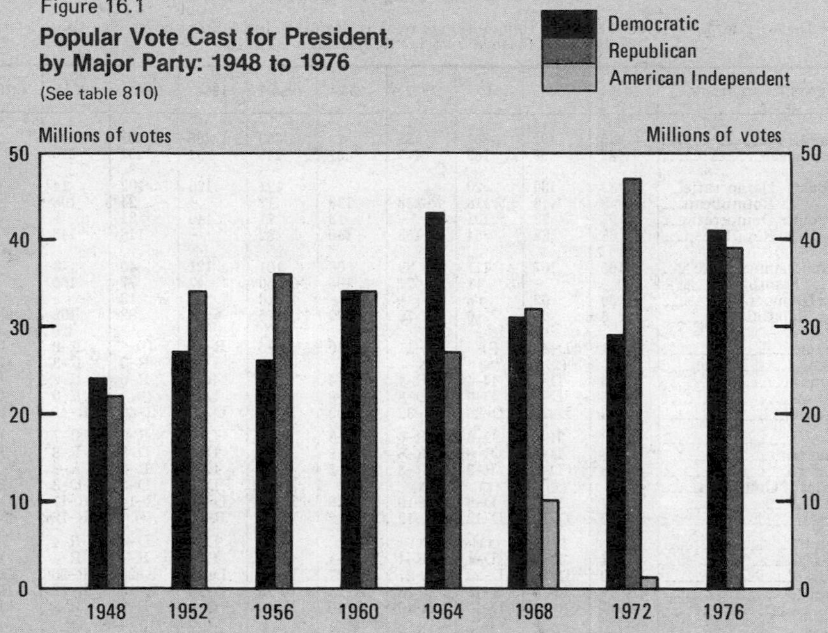
Democratic
Republican
American Independent
Millions of votes
Millions of votes
50
40
30
20
10
0
1948
1952
1956
1960
1964
1968
1972
1976

Source: Chart prepared by U.S. Bureau of the Census. Data from Elections Research Center.

Figure 16.2

Voter Participation in Presidential Elections: 1964 to 1976

(See table 836)

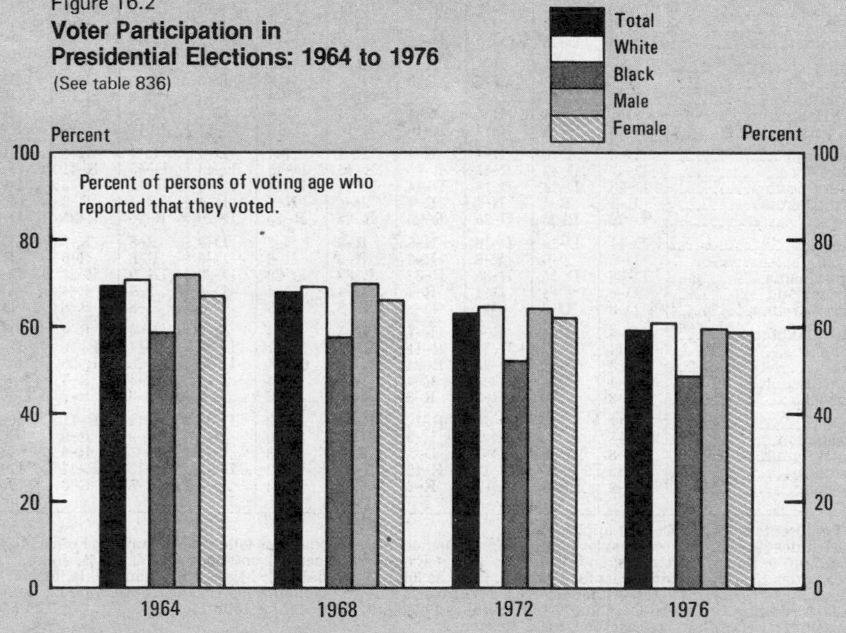
Total
White
Black
Male
Female
Percent
Percent
Percent of persons of voting age who reported that they voted.
100
80
60
40
20
0
1964
1968
1972
1976

Source: U.S. Bureau of the Census.

No. 811. Electoral Vote Cast for President, by Major Political Parties, by States: 1940 to 1976

[D = Democratic, R = Republican. For composition of regions, see fig. I, inside front cover. See also *Historical Statistics, Colonial Times to 1970*, series Y 84–134]

REGION AND STATE	1940	1944	1948[1]	1952	1956[2]	1960[3]	1964	1968[4]	1972[5]	1976[6]
Democratic	449	432	303	89	73	303	486	191	17	297
Republican	82	99	189	442	457	219	52	301	520	240
No. East: Democratic	132	130	20	–	–	121	126	102	14	86
Republican	8	8	118	133	133	12	–	24	108	36
No. Cent.: Democratic	93	73	101	–	13	71	149	31	–	58
Republican	68	82	54	153	140	82	–	118	145	87
South: Democratic	165	167	117	89	60	101	121	45	3	149
Republican	–	–	11	77	105	50	47	77	165	20
West: Democratic	59	62	65	–	–	10	90	13	–	4
Republican	6	9	6	79	79	75	5	82	102	97
Alabama	D-11	D-11	(1)	D-11	2 D-10	3 D-5	R-10	(4)	R-9	D-9
Alaska	(X)	(X)	(X)	(X)	(X)	R-3	D-3	R-3	R-3	R-3
Arizona	D-3	D-4	D-4	R-4	R-4	R-4	R-5	R-5	R-6	R-6
Arkansas	D-9	D-9	D-9	D-8	D-8	D-8	D-6	(4)	R-6	D-6
California	D-22	D-25	D-25	R-32	R-32	R-32	D-40	R-40	R-45	R-45
Colorado	R-6	R-6	D-6	R-6	R-6	R-6	D-6	R-6	R-7	R-7
Connecticut	D-8	D-8	R-8	R-8	R-8	D-8	D-8	D-8	R-8	R-8
Delaware	D-3	D-3	R-3	R-3	R-3	D-3	D-3	R-3	R-3	D-3
District of Columbia	(X)	(X)	(X)	(X)	(X)	(X)	D-3	D-3	D-3	D-3
Florida	D-7	D-8	D-8	R-10	R-10	R-10	R-10	R-14	R-17	D-17
Georgia	D-12	D-12	D-12	D-12	D-12	D-12	R-12	(4)	R-12	D-12
Hawaii	(X)	(X)	(X)	(X)	(X)	D-3	D-4	D-4	R-4	D-4
Idaho	D-4	D-4	D-4	R-4	R-4	R-4	D-4	R-4	R-4	R-4
Illinois	D-29	D-28	D-28	R-27	R-27	D-27	D-26	R-26	R-26	R-26
Indiana	R-14	R-13	R-13	R-13	R-13	R-13	D-13	R-13	R-13	R-13
Iowa	R-11	R-10	D-10	R-10	R-10	R-10	D-9	R-9	R-8	R-8
Kansas	R-9	R-8	R-8	R-8	R-8	R-8	D-7	R-7	R-7	R-7
Kentucky	D-11	D-11	D-11	D-10	R-10	R-10	D-9	R-9	R-9	D-9
Louisiana	D-10	D-10	(1)	D-10	R-10	D-10	R-10	(4)	R-10	D-10
Maine	R-5	R-5	R-5	R-5	R-5	R-5	D-4	D-4	R-4	R-4
Maryland	D-8	D-8	R-8	R-9	R-9	D-9	D-10	D-10	R-10	D-10
Massachusetts	D-17	D-16	D-16	R-16	R-16	D-16	D-14	D-14	D-14	D-14
Michigan	R-19	D-19	R-19	R-20	R-20	D-20	D-21	D-21	R-21	R-21
Minnesota	D-11	D-11	D-11	R-11	R-11	D-11	D-10	D-10	R-10	D-10
Mississippi	D-9	D-9	(1)	D-8	D-8	(3)	R-7	(4)	R-7	D-7
Missouri	D-15	D-15	D-15	R-13	D-13	D-13	D-12	R-12	R-12	D-12
Montana	D-4	D-4	D-4	R-4	R-4	R-4	D-4	R-4	R-4	R-4
Nebraska	R-7	R-6	R-6	R-6	R-6	R-6	D-5	R-5	R-5	R-5
Nevada	D-3	D-3	D-3	R-3	R-3	D-3	D-3	R-3	R-3	R-3
New Hampshire	D-4	D-4	R-4	R-4	R-4	R-4	D-4	R-4	R-4	R-4
New Jersey	D-16	D-16	R-16	R-16	R-16	D-16	D-17	R-17	R-17	R-17
New Mexico	D-3	D-4	D-4	R-4	R-4	D-4	D-4	R-4	R-4	R-4
New York	D-47	D-47	R-47	R-45	R-45	D-45	D-43	D-43	R-41	D-41
North Carolina	D-13	D-14	D-14	D-14	D-14	D-14	D-13	4 R-12	R-13	D-13
North Dakota	R-4	R-4	R-4	R-4	R-4	R-4	D-4	R-4	R-3	R-3
Ohio	D-26	R-25	D-25	R-25	R-25	R-25	D-26	R-26	R-25	D-25
Oklahoma	D-11	D-10	D-10	R-8	R-8	3 R-7*	D-8	R-8	R-8	R-8
Oregon	D-5	D-6	R-6	R-6	R-6	R-6	D-6	R-6	R-6	R-6
Pennsylvania	D-36	D-35	R-35	R-32	R-32	D-32	D-29	D-29	R-27	D-27
Rhode Island	D-4	D-4	D-4	R-4	R-4	D-4	D-4	D-4	R-4	D-4
South Carolina	D-8	D-8	(1)	D-8	D-8	D-8	R-8	R-8	R-8	D-8
South Dakota	R-4	R-4	R-4	R-4	R-4	R-4	D-4	R-4	R-4	R-4
Tennessee	D-11	D-12	1 D-11	R-11	R-11	R-11	D-11	R-11	R-10	D-10
Texas	D-23	D-23	D-23	R-24	R-24	D-24	D-25	D-25	R-26	D-26
Utah	D-4	D-4	D-4	R-4	R-4	R-4	D-4	R-4	R-4	R-4
Vermont	R-3	R-3	R-3	R-3	R 3	R-3	D-3	R-3	R-3	R-3
Virginia	D-11	D-11	D-11	R-12	R-12	R-12	D-12	R-12	5 R-11	R-12
Washington	D-8	D-8	D-8	R-9	R-9	R-9	D-9	D-9	R-9	6 R-8
West Virginia	D-8	D-8	D-8	D-8	R-8	D-8	D-7	D-7	R-6	D-6
Wisconsin	D-12	R-12	D-12	R-12	R-12	R-12	D-12	R-12	R-11	D-11
Wyoming	D-3	R-3	D-3	R-3	R-3	R-3	D-3	R-3	R-3	R-3

– Represents zero.   X Not applicable.
1 Excludes 39 electoral votes cast for States' Rights Democratic candidates as follows: Alabama 11; Louisiana 10; Mississippi 9; South Carolina 8; and Tennessee 1.   2 Excludes 1 electoral vote cast for Walter B. Jones.
3 Excludes 15 electoral votes cast for Harry F. Byrd as follows: Alabama 6; Mississippi 8; and Oklahoma 1.
4 Excludes 46 electoral votes cast for George C. Wallace as follows: Alabama 10; Arkansas 6; Georgia 12; Louisiana 10; Mississippi 7; North Carolina 1.   5 Excludes 1 electoral vote cast for John Hospers.
6 Excludes 1 electoral vote cast for Ronald Reagan.

Source: 1940–1972, U.S. Congress, Clerk of the House, *Statistics of the Presidential and Congressional Election*; 1976, Elections Research Center, Washington, D.C., *America Votes*, vol. 12 (copyright).

No. 812. Popular Vote Cast for President, and Percent of Vote for Majority Party, by Regions and States: 1948 to 1964

[In thousands, except percent. D=Democratic, R=Republican. Majority party vote refers to the party vote representing either a majority or a plurality for the victorious party. For composition of regions, see fig. I, inside front cover. See also tables 810 and 813, and *Historical Statistics, Colonial Times to 1970*, series Y 135–186]

REGION AND STATE	1948 Vote	1948 Percent for majority party	1952 Vote	1952 Percent for majority party	1956 Vote	1956 Percent for majority party	1960 Vote	1960 Percent for majority party	1964 Vote	1964 Percent for majority party
Total	48,794	D-49.6	61,551	R-55.1	62,027	R-57.4	68,838	D-49.7	70,645	D-61.1
Northeast	15,800	R-47.8	18,801	R-55.1	18,782	R-60.7	20,053	D-52.7	19,623	D-68.3
North Central	17,540	D-50.3	21,153	R-57.6	21,114	R-58.6	22,979	R-52.2	22,209	D-61.3
South	8,244	D-52.6	12,445	D-50.5	12,478	R-51.1	14,389	D-49.9	16,597	D-53.3
West	7,209	D-49.4	9,151	R-57.3	9,654	R-56.4	11,417	R-51.1	12,214	D-59.4
Alabama	215	(1)	426	D-64.6	497	D-56.5	570	D-56.8	690	R-69.5
Alaska	(X)	(X)	(X)	(X) .	(X)	(X)	61	R-50.9	67	D-65.9
Arizona	177	D-53.8	261	R-58.3	290	R-61.0	398	R-55.5	481	R-50.4
Arkansas	242	D-61.7	405	D-55.9	407	D-52.5	429	D-50.2	560	D-56.1
California	4,022	D-47.6	5,142	R-56.3	5,466	R-55.4	6,507	R-50.1	7,058	D-59.1
Colorado	515	D-51.9	630	R-60.3	657	R-60.0	736	R-54.6	777	D-61.3
Connecticut	884	R-49.5	1,097	R-55.7	1,117	R-63.7	1,223	D-53.7	1,219	D-67.8
Delaware	139	R-50.0	174	R-51.8	178	R-55.1	197	D-50.6	201	D-60.9
Dist. of Columbia	(X)	(X)	(X)	(X)	(X)	(X)	(X)	(X)	199	D-85.5
Florida	578	D-48.8	989	R-55.0	1,126	R-57.2	1,544	R-51.5	1,854	D-51.1
Georgia	419	D-60.8	656	D-69.7	670	D-66.4	733	D-62.5	1,139	R-54.1
Hawaii	(X)	(X)	(X)	(X)	(X)	(X)	185	(2)	207	D-78.8
Idaho	215	D-50.0	276	R-65.4	273	R-61.2	300	R-53.8	292	D-50.9
Illinois	3,984	D-50.1	4,481	R-54.8	4,407	R-59.5	4,757	D-50.0	4,703	D-59.5
Indiana	1,656	R-49.6	1,955	R-58.1	1,975	R-59.9	2,135	R-55.0	2,092	D-56.0
Iowa	1,038	D-50.3	1,269	R-63.8	1,235	R-59.1	1,274	R-56.7	1,185	D-61.9
Kansas	789	R-53.6	896	R-68.8	866	R-65.4	929	R-60.4	858	D-54.1
Kentucky	823	D-56.7	993	D-49.9	1,054	R-54.3	1,124	R-53.6	1,046	D-64.0
Louisiana	416	(1)	652	D-52.9	618	R-53.3	808	D-50.4	896	R-56.8
Maine	265	R-56.4	352	R-66.0	352	R-70.9	422	R-57.0	381	D 00.0
Maryland	597	R-49 4	902	R 55.4	933	R-60.0	1,055	D-53.6	1,116	D-65.5
Massachusetts	2,107	D-54.7	2,383	R-54.2	2,349	R-59.3	2,469	D-00.2	2,345	D-76.2
Michigan	2,110	R-49.2	2,799	R-55.4	3,080	R-55.6	3,318	D-50.9	3,203	D-66.7
Minnesota	1,212	D-57.2	1,379	R-55.3	1,340	R-53.7	1,542	D-50.6	1,554	D-63.8
Mississippi	192	(1)	286	D-60.4	248	D-58.2	298	(3)	409	R-87.1
Missouri	1,579	D-58.1	1,892	R-50.7	1,833	D-50.1	1,934	D-50.3	1,818	D-64.0
Montana	224	D-53.1	265	R-59.4	271	R-57.1	278	R-51.1	279	D-58.9
Nebraska	489	R-54.2	610	R-69.2	577	R-65.5	613	R-62.1	584	D-52.6
Nevada	62	D-50.4	82	R-61.4	97	R-58.0	107	D-51.2	135	D-58.6
New Hampshire	231	R-52.4	273	R-60.9	267	R-66.1	296	R-53.4	288	D-63.9
New Jersey	1,950	R-50.3	2,419	R-56.8	2,484	R-64.7	2,773	D-50.0	2,848	D-65.6
New Mexico	187	D-56.4	239	R-55.4	254	R-57.8	311	D-50.2	329	D-59.0
New York	6,177	R-46.0	7,128	R-55.5	7,096	R-61.2	7,291	D-52.5	7,166	D-68.6
North Carolina	791	D-58.0	1,211	D-53.9	1,166	D-50.7	1,369	D-52.1	1,425	D-56.2
North Dakota	221	R-52.2	270	R-71.0	254	R-61.7	278	R-55.4	258	D-58.0
Ohio	2,936	D-49.5	3,701	R-56.8	3,702	R-61.1	4,162	R-53.3	3,969	D-62.9
Oklahoma	722	D-62.7	949	R-54.6	859	R-55.1	903	R-59.0	932	D-55.7
Oregon	524	R-49.8	695	R-60.5	736	R-55.2	776	R-52.6	786	D-63.7
Pennsylvania	3,735	R-50.9	4,581	R-52.7	4,577	R-56.5	5,007	D-51.1	4,823	D-64.9
Rhode Island	328	D-57.6	414	R-50.9	388	D-58.3	406	D-63.6	390	D-80.9
South Carolina	143	(1)	341	D-50.7	301	D-45.4	387	D-51.2	525	R-58.9
South Dakota	250	R-51.8	294	R-69.3	294	R-58.4	306	R-58.2	293	D-55.6
Tennessee	550	D-49.1	893	R-50.0	939	R-49.2	1,052	R-52.9	1,144	D-55.5
Texas	1,250	D-66.0	2,076	R-53.1	1,955	R-55.3	2,311	D-50.5	2,627	D-63.3
Utah	276	D-54.0	330	R-58.9	334	R-64.6	375	R-54.8	401	D-54.7
Vermont	123	R-61.5	154	R-71.5	153	R-72.2	167	R-58.6	163	D-66.3
Virginia	419	D-47.9	620	R-56.3	698	R-55.4	771	R-52.4	1,042	D-53.5
Washington	905	D-52.6	1,103	R-54.3	1,151	R-53.9	1,242	R-50.7	1,259	D-62.0
West Virginia	749	D-57.3	874	D-51.9	831	R-54.1	838	D-52.7	792	D-67.9
Wisconsin	1,277	D-50.7	1,607	R-61.0	1,551	R-61.6	1,729	R-51.8	1,692	D-62.1
Wyoming	101	D-51.6	129	R-62.7	124	R-60.1	141	R-55.0	143	D-56.6

X Not applicable.
[1] Vote represented a victory for Thurmond (States' Rights Democratic Party) as follows: Alabama, 79.7 percent; Louisiana, 49.1 percent; Mississippi, 87.2 percent; and South Carolina, 72.0 percent.
[2] Percentages of 50.0 for both parties based on following vote: Democratic, 92,410; Republican, 92,295.
[3] Vote represented a victory for unpledged Democratic electors: 39.0 percent.

Source: 1948, Elections Research Center, Washington, D.C., *America at the Polls* (copyright); 1952–56, U.S. Bureau of the Census, *Congressional District Data Book* (*Districts of the 88th Congress*), 1963; and 1960 and 1964, U.S. Congress, Clerk of the House, *Statistics of the Presidential and Congressional Election.*

No. 813. Popular Vote Cast for President, by Political Parties, by Regions and States: 1968 to 1976

[In thousands, except percent. D = Democratic, R = Republican. See headnote, table 812. See also *Historical Statistics, Colonial Times to 1970,* series Y 135-186]

REGION AND STATE	1968				1972				1976			
	Total [1]	Democratic Party	Republican Party	Percent for majority party	Total [1]	Democratic Party	Republican Party	Percent for majority party	Total [1]	Democratic Party	Republican Party	Percent for majority party
Total	73,212	31,275	31,785	R-43.4	77,719	29,170	47,170	R-60.7	81,556	40,831	39,148	D-50.1
Northeast	19,239	9,657	8,278	D-50.2	19,953	8,277	11,483	R-57.6	19,520	9,929	9,272	D-50.9
No. Central	22,208	9,703	10,394	R-46.8	23,192	9,127	13,711	R-59.1	24,155	11,671	11,995	R-49.7
South	19,176	6,419	6,990	R-36.5	20,046	6,087	13,666	R-68.2	23,198	12,520	10,394	D-54.0
West	12,589	5,497	6,127	R-48.7	14,529	5,679	8,309	R-57.2	14,683	6,711	7,488	R-51.0
Ala	1,050	[2] 197	147	(³)	1,006	257	729	R-72.4	1,183	659	504	D-55.7
Alaska	83	35	38	R-45.3	95	33	55	R-58.1	124	44	72	R-57.9
Ariz	487	171	267	R-54.8	623	199	403	R-64.7	743	296	419	R-56.4
Ark	620	188	191	(³)	651	200	449	R-68.9	768	499	268	D-65.0
Calif	7,252	3,244	3,468	R-47.8	8,368	3,476	4,602	R-55.0	7,867	3,742	3,882	R-49.3
Colo	811	335	409	R-50.5	954	330	597	R-62.6	1,082	460	584	R-54.0
Conn	1,256	622	557	D-49.5	1,384	555	811	R-58.6	1,382	648	719	R-52.1
Del	214	89	97	R-45.1	236	92	140	R-59.6	236	123	110	D-52.0
D.C	171	140	31	D-81.8	163	128	35	D-78.1	169	138	28	D-81.6
Fla	2,188	677	887	R-40.5	2,583	718	1,858	R-71.9	3,151	1,636	1,470	D-51.9
Ga	1,250	334	380	(³)	1,175	290	881	R-75.0	1,467	979	484	D-66.7
Hawaii	236	141	91	D-59.8	270	101	169	R-62.5	291	147	140	D-50.6
Idaho	291	89	165	R-56.8	310	81	199	R-64.2	344	127	204	R-59.3
Ill	4,620	2,040	2,175	R-47.1	4,723	1,913	2,788	R-59.0	4,719	2,271	2,364	R-50.1
Ind	2,124	807	1,068	R-50.3	2,126	709	1,405	R-66.1	2,220	1,015	1,184	R-53.3
Iowa	1,168	477	619	R-53.0	1,226	496	706	R-57.6	1,279	620	633	R-49.5
Kans	873	303	479	R-54.8	916	270	620	R-67.7	958	430	503	R-52.5
Ky	1,056	398	462	R-43.8	1,067	371	676	R-63.4	1,167	616	532	D-52.8
La	1,097	310	258	(³)	1,051	298	687	R-65.3	1,278	661	587	D-51.7
Maine	393	217	169	D-55.3	417	161	256	R-61.5	483	232	236	R-48.9
Md	1,235	538	518	D-43.6	1,354	506	829	R-61.3	1,440	760	673	D-52.8
Mass	2,332	1,469	767	D-63.0	2,459	1,333	1,112	D-54.2	2,548	1,429	1,030	D-56.1
Mich	3,306	1,593	1,371	D-48.2	3,490	1,459	1,962	R-56.2	3,654	1,697	1,894	R-51.8
Minn	1,589	858	659	D-54.0	1,742	802	898	R-51.6	1,950	1,070	819	D-54.9
Miss	655	151	89	(³)	646	127	505	R-78.2	769	381	367	D-49.6
Mo	1,810	791	812	R-44.9	1,856	697	1,154	R-62.2	1,954	998	927	D-51.1
Mont	274	114	139	R-50.6	318	120	184	R-57.9	329	149	174	R-52.8
Nebr	537	171	321	R-59.8	576	170	406	R-70.5	608	234	360	R-59.2
Nev	154	61	73	R-47.5	182	66	116	R-63.7	202	92	101	R-50.2
N.H	297	131	155	R-52.1	334	116	214	R-64.0	340	148	186	R-54.7
N.J	2,875	1,264	1,325	R-46.1	2,997	1,102	1,846	R-61.6	3,014	1,445	1,510	R-50.1
N. Mex	327	130	170	R-51.8	386	141	236	R-61.0	418	201	211	R-50.5
N.Y	6,792	3,378	3,008	D-49.7	7,166	2,951	4,193	R-58.5	6,534	3,390	3,101	D-51.9
N.C	1,587	464	627	R-39.5	1,519	439	1,055	R-69.5	1,679	927	742	D-55.2
N. Dak	248	95	139	R-55.9	281	100	174	R-62.1	297	136	153	R-51.6
Ohio	3,960	1,701	1,791	R-45.2	4,095	1,559	2,442	R-59.6	4,112	2,012	2,001	D-48.9
Okla	943	302	450	R-47.7	1,030	247	759	R-73.7	1,092	532	546	R-50.0
Oreg	820	359	408	R-49.8	928	393	487	R-52.4	1,030	490	492	R-47.8
Pa	4,748	2,259	2,090	D-47.6	4,592	1,797	2,715	R-59.1	4,621	2,329	2,206	D-50.4
R.I	385	247	122	D-64.0	416	195	220	R-53.0	411	228	181	D-55.4
S.C	667	197	254	R-38.1	674	187	477	R-70.8	803	451	346	D-56.2
S. Dak	281	118	150	R-53.3	307	140	166	R-54.2	301	147	152	R-50.4
Tenn	1,249	351	473	R-37.8	1,201	357	813	R-67.7	1,476	826	634	D-55.9
Tex	3,079	1,267	1,228	D-41.1	3,471	1,154	2,299	R-66.2	4,072	2,082	1,953	D-51.1
Utah	423	157	239	R-56.5	478	126	324	R-67.6	541	182	338	R-62.4
Vt	161	70	85	R-52.8	187	68	117	R-62.7	188	81	102	R-54.4
Va	1,361	442	590	R-43.4	1,457	439	988	R-67.8	1,697	814	837	R-49.3
Wash	1,304	616	589	D-47.2	1,471	568	837	R-56.9	1,556	717	778	R-50.0
W. Va	754	374	308	D-49.6	762	277	485	R-63.6	751	436	315	D-58.0
Wis	1,692	749	810	R-47.9	1,853	810	989	R-53.4	2,104	1,040	1,005	D-49.4
Wyo	127	45	71	R-55.8	146	44	100	R-69.0	156	62	93	R-59.3

[1] Includes other parties.
[2] Excludes vote cast for George C. Wallace as a Democratic Party candidate.
[3] Vote represented a victory for Wallace (American Independent Party) as follows: Alabama, 65.8 percent; Arkansas, 38.9 percent; Georgia, 42.9 percent; Louisiana, 48.3 percent; and Mississippi, 63.4 percent.

Source: 1968 and 1972, U.S. Congress, Clerk of the House, *Statistics of the Presidential and Congressional Election of Nov. 5, 1968,* and *Statistics of the Presidential and Congressional Election of Nov. 7, 1972* (in some cases, figures have been revised by Elections Research Center, Washington, D. C.); 1976, Elections Research Center, Washington, D.C., *America Votes,* vol. 12 (copyright).

No. 814. POPULAR VOTE CAST FOR PRESIDENT, BY POLITICAL PARTIES, BY GEOGRAPHIC DIVISIONS: 1960 TO 1976

[For composition of divisions, see fig. I, inside front cover]

YEAR AND PARTY	Total	New England	Middle Atlantic	East North Central	West North Central	South Atlantic	East South Central	West South Central	Mountain	Pacific
1960, total_____1,000__	¹68,838	4,983	15,071	16,102	6,876	¹6,894	3,045	4,451	2,647	8,770
Democratic___percent__	49.7	56.0	51.6	48.4	45.8	52.0	47.2	48.5	46.3	49.2
Republican___percent__	49.5	43.9	48.1	51.4	54.1	47.9	48.3	46.5	53.5	50.4
Other_____percent__	.7	.1	.3	.2	.1	.1	4.5	5.0	.2	.4
1964, total_____1,000__	70,645	4,786	14,837	15,659	6,550	8,294	3,289	5,016	2,837	9,376
Democratic___percent__	61.1	72.8	66.8	61.6	60.6	55.5	41.3	57.5	56.4	60.4
Republican___percent__	38.5	27.0	32.9	38.2	39.1	44.4	52.2	42.3	43.3	39.4
Other_____percent__	.5	.2	.3	.1	.2	(z)	6.5	.2	.3	.2
1968, total_____1,000__	73,212	4,825	14,415	15,701	6,505	9,428	4,009	5,740	2,895	9,695
Democratic___percent__	42.7	57.1	47.9	43.9	43.2	34.5	27.3	36.0	38.1	45.3
Republican___percent__	43.4	38.5	44.6	45.9	48.9	39.2	29.2	37.0	52.9	47.4
Other_____percent__	13.9	4.4	7.6	10.2	7.9	26.3	43.5	27.0	9.0	7.3
1972, total_____1,000__	77,719	5,197	14,755	16,286	6,904	9,923	3,921	6,204	3,397	11,132
Democratic___percent__	37.5	46.7	39.6	39.6	38.8	31.0	28.4	30.6	32.6	41.1
Republican___percent__	60.7	52.5	59.3	58.9	59.8	68.0	69.5	67.6	63.6	55.2
Other_____percent__	1.8	.7	1.0	1.5	1.5	1.0	2.2	1.8	3.8	3.7
1976, total_____1,000__	81,556	5,351	14,169	16,809	7,346	11,392	4,596	7,210	3,815	10,867
Democratic___percent__	50.1	51.7	50.6	47.8	49.5	55.0	54.0	52.4	41.1	47.3
Republican___percent__	48.0	45.9	48.1	50.3	48.3	43.9	44.3	46.5	55.7	49.4
Other_____percent__	1.9	2.4	1.3	1.9	2.2	1.1	1.7	1.1	3.2	3.3

Z Less than .05 percent.   ¹ Excludes District of Columbia.
Source: Elections Research Center, Washington, D.C., *America Votes*, biennial. (Copyright.)

No. 815. PERCENT OF TOTAL AND VOTING-AGE POPULATION AND OF POPULAR AND ELECTORAL VOTE FOR PRESIDENT, BY REGIONS AND STATES: 1976

REGION ¹ AND STATE	Total population ²	Voting-age population ³	Popular vote for President	Electoral vote for President	STATE	Total population ²	Voting-age population ³	Popular vote for President	Electoral vote for President
U.S_____	100.0	100.0	100.0	100.0	Minnesota_____	1.8	1.8	2.4	1.9
					Mississippi_____	1.1	1.0	.9	1.3
Northeast_____	23.0	23.4	23.9	22.7	Missouri_____	2.2	2.3	2.4	2.2
North Central___	26.8	26.7	29.6	27.0	Montana_____	.4	.3	.4	.7
South_____	32.1	31.9	28.4	31.4	Nebraska_____	.7	.7	.7	.9
West_____	18.0	18.0	18.0	19.0					
					Nevada_____	.3	.3	.2	.6
Alabama_____	1.7	1.7	1.5	1.7	New Hampshire_	.4	.4	.4	.7
Alaska_____	.2	.2	.2	.6	New Jersey_____	3.4	3.5	3.4	3.2
Arizona_____	1.1	1.0	.9	1.1	New Mexico____	.5	.5	.5	.7
Arkansas_____	1.0	1.0	.9	1.1	New York_____	8.4	8.6	8.0	7.6
California_____	10.0	10.2	9.6	8.4					
					North Carolina_	2.5	2.5	2.1	2.4
Colorado_____	1.2	1.2	1.3	1.3	North Dakota__	.3	.3	.4	.6
Connecticut_____	1.5	1.5	1.7	1.5	Ohio_____	5.0	4.9	5.0	4.6
Delaware_____	.3	.3	.3	.6	Oklahoma_____	1.3	1.3	1.3	1.5
District of Col___	.3	.3	.2	.6	Oregon_____	1.1	1.1	1.3	1.1
Florida_____	3.9	4.1	3.9	3.2					
					Pennsylvania__	5.5	5.6	5.7	5.0
Georgia_____	2.3	2.3	1.8	2.2	Rhode Island___	.4	.4	.5	.7
Hawaii_____	.4	.4	.4	.7	South Carolina_	1.3	1.3	1.0	1.5
Idaho_____	.4	.4	.4	.7	South Dakota_	.3	.3	.4	.7
Illinois_____	5.2	5.2	5.8	4.8	Tennessee_____	2.0	2.0	1.8	1.9
Indiana_____	2.5	2.4	2.7	2.4					
					Texas_____	5.8	5.7	5.0	4.8
Iowa_____	1.3	1.3	1.6	1.5	Utah_____	.6	.5	.7	.7
Kansas_____	1.1	1.1	1.2	1.3	Vermont_____	.2	.2	.2	.6
Kentucky_____	1.6	1.6	1.4	1.7	Virginia_____	2.3	2.4	2.1	2.2
Louisiana_____	1.8	1.7	1.6	1.9	Washington____	1.7	1.7	1.9	1.7
Maine_____	.5	.5	.6	.7					
					West Virginia__	.8	.9	.9	1.1
Maryland_____	1.9	1.9	1.8	1.9	Wisconsin_____	2.1	2.1	2.6	2.0
Massachusetts___	2.7	2.8	3.1	2.6	Wyoming_____	.2	.2	.2	.6
Michigan_____	4.2	4.1	4.5	3.9					

¹ For composition of regions, see fig. I, inside front cover.   ² Estimated. As of Nov. 1. Includes Armed Forces stationed in area.   ³ Estimated. Resident population 18 years old and over.
Source: Compiled from U.S. Bureau of the Census, *Current Population Reports*, series P-25, No. 626; and Elections Research Center, Washington, D.C., *America Votes*, vol. 12 (copyright).

No. 816. Vote Cast for Major Political Offices, by Major Parties: 1960 to 1976

[D = Democratic Party. R = Republican Party]

YEAR AND OFFICE	Total votes cast (mil.)	DEMOCRATIC		REPUBLICAN		OTHER PARTIES		PLURALITY		
		Votes cast (mil.)	Per-cent	Votes cast (mil.)	Per-cent	Votes cast (mil.)	Per-cent	Party	Votes (mil.)	Per-cent
1960: President	68.8	34.2	49.7	34.1	49.5	.5	.7	D	.1	.2
U.S. House of Rep. (381 dist.)[1]	63.3	34.7	54.8	28.4	44.8	.3	.4	D	6.1	9.6
U.S. Senate (34 States)	33.5	18.3	54.6	15.0	44.8	.2	.6	D	3.3	9.8
State Governor (30 States)	35.5	18.7	52.9	16.6	46.8	.1	.3	D	2.1	6.0
1964: President	70.6	43.1	61.1	27.2	38.5	.3	.5	D	16.0	22.6
U.S. House of Rep. (403 dist.)[1]	65.9	37.7	57.2	27.9	42.3	.3	.5	D	9.8	14.9
U.S. Senate (34 States)	51.5	29.0	56.3	22.1	42.9	.5	.9	D	6.9	13.4
State Governor (25 States)	29.1	16.1	55.2	12.9	44.4	.1	.4	D	3.2	10.9
1968: President	73.2	31.3	42.7	31.8	43.4	10.2	13.9	R	.5	.7
U.S. House of Rep. (398 dist.)[1]	66.1	33.0	50.0	31.9	48.2	1.2	1.8	D	1.2	1.8
U.S. Senate (34 States)	50.8	25.0	49.2	24.2	47.5	1.7	3.3	D	.8	1.6
State Governor (22 States)	22.7	11.8	51.8	10.9	47.9	.1	.3	D	.9	3.9
1972: President	77.7	29.2	37.5	47.2	60.7	1.4	1.8	R	18.0	23.2
U.S. House of Rep. (401 dist.)[1]	71.2	36.8	51.7	33.1	46.5	1.3	1.9	D	3.7	5.2
U.S. Senate (34 States)	37.5	17.0	45.4	19.7	52.5	.8	2.1	R	2.7	7.2
State Governor (21 States)	23.9	12.1	50.5	11.1	46.6	.7	2.9	D	.9	3.9
1976: President	81.6	40.8	50.1	39.1	48.0	1.6	1.9	D	1.7	2.1
U.S. House of Rep. (423 dist.)[1]	74.3	41.7	56.2	31.2	42.1	1.3	1.7	D	10.5	14.1
U.S. Senate (33 States)	58.9	32.0	54.4	25.8	43.8	1.1	1.8	D	6.2	10.6
State Governor (14 States)	15.7	7.7	48.8	7.9	50.4	.1	.9	R	.3	1.6

[1] Number of districts in which votes were tabulated.

Source: Compiled by U.S. Bureau of the Census from Elections Research Center, Washington, D.C., *America Votes*, biennial. (Copyright.)

No. 817. Percent Popular Vote Cast for President and for U.S. Congress, by Party, and Party Composition of U.S. Congress, by Region: 1960 to 1976

[Dem.= Democratic Party, Rep.= Republican Party. Excludes minor parties and independents. For composition of regions, see fig. I, inside front cover]

YEAR AND REGION	PERCENT VOTE CAST FOR—						PARTY COMPOSITION (seats held) [1]			
	President		House of Representatives		Senate		House of Representatives		Senate	
	Dem.	Rep.	Dem.	Rep.	Dem.	Rep.	Dem.	Rep.	Dem.	Rep.
1960, U.S.	49.7	49.5	54.8	44.8	54.6	44.8	263	174	65	35
Northeast	52.7	47.1	52.3	46.8	44.5	54.9	56	59	7	11
North Central	47.6	52.2	49.5	50.4	52.1	47.6	51	78	12	12
South	49.9	47.6	71.0	28.2	64.9	33.7	123	11	26	6
West	48.5	51.1	52.2	47.8	51.5	48.2	33	26	20	6
1964, U.S.	61.1	38.5	57.2	42.3	56.3	42.9	295	140	68	32
Northeast	68.3	31.5	57.7	41.5	55.7	42.8	70	38	10	8
North Central	61.3	38.5	53.8	46.1	56.8	43.0	66	59	15	9
South	53.3	45.3	64.8	34.0	60.6	37.7	112	21	26	6
West	59.4	40.4	53.6	46.4	52.3	47.7	47	22	17	9
1968, U.S.	42.7	43.4	50.0	48.2	49.2	47.5	243	192	57	43
Northeast	50.2	43.0	48.4	46.7	39.2	50.9	64	44	8	10
North Central	43.7	46.8	45.8	54.1	49.5	50.2	46	79	13	11
South	33.5	36.5	60.9	37.9	57.2	40.4	97	36	22	10
West	43.7	48.7	45.7	53.2	52.5	46.4	36	33	14	12
1972, U.S.	37.5	60.7	51.7	46.5	45.4	52.5	239	192	56	42
Northeast	41.5	57.6	48.8	47.0	37.1	60.7	57	46	9	9
North Central	39.4	59.1	48.2	50.9	44.0	55.0	50	70	15	9
South	30.4	68.2	58.5	40.4	49.5	47.4	91	42	18	13
West	39.1	57.2	53.0	45.8	46.1	52.9	41	34	15	11
1976, U.S.	50.1	48.0	56.2	42.1	54.4	43.8	292	143	61	38
Northeast	50.9	47.5	56.3	41.8	54.2	44.7	73	31	10	8
North Central	48.3	49.7	52.3	46.7	53.3	44.5	68	53	16	8
South	54.0	44.8	61.9	36.2	59.0	39.5	100	34	22	9
West	45.7	51.0	54.7	43.0	51.2	45.9	51	25	13	13

[1] For beginning of the first session of Congress following the year shown. Excludes vacant seats.

Source: Compiled by U.S. Bureau of the Census from Elections Research Center, Washington, D.C., *America Votes*, biennial (copyright); and U.S. Congress, Joint Committee on Printing, *Congressional Directory*, annual.

No. 818. Vote Cast for United States Senators, by Major Political Parties, by States: 1972 to 1976

[In thousands, except percent. Excludes elections to fill vacancies for unexpired term]

STATE	1972 Total [1]	1972 Democratic	1972 Republican	1972 Percent for majority party	1974 Total [1]	1974 Democratic	1974 Republican	1974 Percent for majority party	1976 Total [1]	1976 Democratic	1976 Republican	1976 Percent for majority party
Alabama	1,051	654	348	62.3	523	502	–	95.8	(X)	(X)	(X)	(X)
Alaska	96	22	74	77.3	93	54	39	58.3	(X)	(X)	(X)	(X)
Arizona	(X)	(X)	(X)	(X)	550	230	320	58.3	741	400	321	54.0
Arkansas	635	386	248	60.9	543	461	82	84.9	(X)	(X)	(X)	(X)
California	(X)	(X)	(X)	(X)	6,102	3,693	2,210	60.5	7,472	3,503	3,749	50.2
Colorado	926	458	448	49.4	824	472	326	57.2	(X)	(X)	(X)	(X)
Connecticut	(X)	(X)	(X)	(X)	1,085	691	372	63.7	1,362	561	786	57.7
Delaware	230	116	113	50.5	(X)	(X)	(X)	(X)	225	98	126	55.8
Florida	(X)	(X)	(X)	(X)	1,801	781	737	43.4	2,858	1,800	1,058	63.0
Georgia	1,179	636	542	54.0	875	627	247	71.7	(X)	(X)	(X)	(X)
Hawaii	(X)	(X)	(X)	(X)	250	207	–	82.9	302	162	123	53.7
Idaho	310	141	162	53.5	259	145	109	56.1	(X)	(X)	(X)	(X)
Illinois	4,608	1,721	2,867	62.5	2,915	1,811	1,085	62.2	(X)	(X)	(X)	(X)
Indiana	(X)	(X)	(X)	(X)	1,753	889	814	50.7	2,171	879	1,276	58.8
Iowa	1,203	663	531	55.1	890	463	421	52.0	(X)	(X)	(X)	(X)
Kansas	872	201	623	75.6	794	390	404	50.9	(X)	(X)	(X)	(X)
Kentucky	1,038	529	494	50.9	746	399	329	53.5	(X)	(X)	(X)	(X)
Louisiana	1,085	599	207	55.2	435	435	–	100.0	(X)	(X)	(X)	(X)
Maine	421	224	197	53.2	(X)	(X)	(X)	(X)	486	293	193	60.2
Maryland	(X)	(X)	(X)	(X)	878	375	503	57.3	1,366	772	530	56.5
Massachusetts	2,371	823	1,506	64.7	(X)	(X)	(X)	(X)	2,491	1,727	723	69.3
Michigan	3,407	1,577	1,781	53.0	(X)	(X)	(X)	(X)	3,491	1,831	1,635	52.5
Minnesota	1,732	981	742	56.7	(X)	(X)	(X)	(X)	1,912	1,291	479	67.5
Mississippi	646	375	250	58.1	(X)	(X)	(X)	(X)	551	554		100.0
Missouri	(X)	(X)	(X)	(X)	1,224	735	481	60.1	1,915	814	1,090	56.9
Montana	315	164	151	52.0	(X)	(X)	(X)	(X)	321	206	115	64.2
Nebraska	569	266	302	53.1	(X)	(X)	(X)	(X)	598	314	284	52.4
Nevada	(X)	(X)	(X)	(X)	169	79	80	47.0	202	127	63	63.0
New Hampshire	324	184	140	56.9	2 263	2 141	2 113	2 53.6	(X)	(X)	(X)	(X)
New Jersey	2,792	964	1,744	62.5	(X)	(X)	(X)	(X)	2,771	1,681	1,055	60.7
New Mexico	378	174	204	54.0	(X)	(X)	(X)	(X)	413	176	235	56.8
New York	(X)	(X)	(X)	(X)	5,164	1,974	2,340	45.3	6,320	3,423	2,837	54.2
North Carolina	1,473	677	795	54.0	1,020	634	378	62.1	(X)	(X)	(X)	(X)
North Dakota	(X)	(X)	(X)	(X)	236	3 114	3 114	3 48.4	283	176	103	62.1
Ohio	(X)	(X)	(X)	(X)	2,988	1,931	918	64.6	3,921	1,941	1,824	49.5
Oklahoma	1,005	478	517	51.4	792	387	391	49.4	(X)	(X)	(X)	(X)
Oregon	921	425	495	53.7	766	339	421	54.9	(X)	(X)	(X)	(X)
Pennsylvania	(X)	(X)	(X)	(X)	3,478	1,596	1,843	53.0	4,546	2,127	2,382	52.4
Rhode Island	413	222	189	53.7	(X)	(X)	(X)	(X)	399	168	230	57.7
South Carolina	672	245	427	63.5	512	356	147	69.5	(X)	(X)	(X)	(X)
South Dakota	306	175	132	57.0	279	148	131	53.0	(X)	(X)	(X)	(X)
Tennessee	1,164	441	717	61.5	(X)	(X)	(X)	(X)	1,432	751	673	52.5
Texas	3,414	1,512	1,823	53.4	(X)	(X)	(X)	(X)	3,875	2,200	1,636	56.8
Utah	(X)	(X)	(X)	(X)	421	185	210	50.0	540	242	290	53.7
Vermont	(X)	(X)	(X)	(X)	143	71	66	49.5	189	86	94	50.0
Virginia	1,396	644	718	51.4	(X)	(X)	(X)	(X)	1,558	596	4 891	4 57.2
Washington	(X)	(X)	(X)	(X)	1,008	612	364	60.7	1,491	1,071	362	71.8
West Virginia	732	486	246	66.5	(X)	(X)	(X)	(X)	567	566	–	99.9
Wisconsin	(X)	(X)	(X)	(X)	1,199	741	429	61.8	1,935	1,397	522	72.2
Wyoming	142	41	101	71.3	(X)	(X)	(X)	(X)	155	71	85	54.6

– Represents zero.   X Not applicable.   [1] Includes vote cast for minor parties; excludes scattered votes.
[2] Special election, September 1975.
[3] Republican candidate was winner with 114,117 votes; Democratic candidate received 113,931 votes.
[4] Represents vote cast for Independent candidate.

Source: 1972 and 1974, U.S. Congress, Clerk of the House, *Statistics of the Presidential and Congressional Election* and *Statistics of the Congressional Election*; 1976, Elections Research Center, Washington, D.C., *America Votes*, vol. 12 (copyright).

No. 819. Apportionment of Membership in House of Representatives, by States: 1790 to 1970

[Total membership includes Representatives assigned to newly admitted States after the apportionment acts. Population figures used for apportionment purposes are those determined for States by each decennial census. No reapportionment based on 1920 population census. For method of calculating apportionment and a short history of apportionment, see House Report 91–1314, 91st Congress, 2d session, *The Decennial Population Census and Congressional Apportionment.* See also *Historical Statistics, Colonial Times to 1970,* series Y 220–271]

STATE	MEMBERSHIP BASED ON CENSUS OF—																	
	1790	1800	1810	1820	1830	1840	1850	1860	1870	1880	1890	1900	1910	1930	1940	1950	1960	1970
Total	106	142	186	213	242	232	237	243	293	332	357	391	435	435	435	437	435	435
Ala	(X)	(X)	[1]1	3	5	7	7	6	8	8	9	9	10	9	9	9	8	7
Alaska	(X)	(X)	(X)	(X)	(X)	(X)	(X)	(X)	(X)	(X)	(X)	(X)	(X)	(X)	(X)	[1]1	1	1
Ariz	(X)	(X)	(X)	(X)	(X)	(X)	(X)	(X)	(X)	(X)	(X)	(X)	[2]1	1	2	2	3	4
Ark	(X)	(X)	(X)	(X)	[1]1	1	2	3	4	5	6	7	7	7	7	6	4	4
Calif	(X)	(X)	(X)	(X)	(X)	[1]2	2	3	4	4	6	7	8	11	20	23	30	38	43
Colo	(X)	(X)	(X)	(X)	(X)	(X)	(X)	(X)	[1]1	1	2	3	4	4	4	4	4	5
Conn	7	7	7	6	6	4	4	4	4	4	4	5	5	6	6	6	6	6
Del	1	1	2	1	1	1	1	1	1	1	1	1	1	1	1	1	1	1
Fla	(X)	(X)	(X)	(X)	(X)	[1]1	1	1	2	2	2	3	4	5	6	8	12	15
Ga	2	4	6	7	9	8	8	7	9	10	11	11	12	10	10	10	10	10
Hawaii	(X)	(X)	(X)	(X)	(X)	(X)	(X)	(X)	(X)	(X)	(X)	(X)	(X)	(X)	(X)	[1]1	2	2
Idaho	(X)	(X)	(X)	(X)	(X)	(X)	(X)	(X)	(X)	[1]1	1	2	2	2	2	2	2	2
Ill	(X)	(X)	[1]1	1	3	7	9	14	19	20	22	25	27	27	26	25	24	24
Ind	(X)	(X)	[1]1	3	7	10	11	11	13	13	13	13	13	12	11	11	11	11
Iowa	(X)	(X)	(X)	(X)	(X)	[1]2	2	6	9	11	11	11	11	9	8	8	7	6
Kans	(X)	(X)	(X)	(X)	(X)	(X)	(X)	1	3	7	8	8	8	7	6	6	5	5
Ky	2	6	10	12	13	10	10	9	10	11	11	11	11	9	9	8	7	7
La	(X)	(X)	[1]1	3	3	4	4	5	6	6	6	7	8	8	8	8	8	8
Maine	(X)	(X)	7	7	8	7	6	5	5	4	4	4	4	3	3	3	2	2
Md	8	9	9	9	8	6	6	5	6	6	6	6	6	6	6	7	8	8
Mass	14	17	13	13	12	10	11	10	11	12	13	14	16	15	14	14	12	12
Mich	(X)	(X)	(X)	(X)	[1]1	3	4	6	9	11	12	12	13	17	17	18	19	19
Minn	(X)	(X)	(X)	(X)	(X)	(X)	[1]2	2	3	5	7	9	10	9	9	9	8	8
Miss	(X)	(X)	[1]1	1	2	4	5	5	6	7	7	8	8	7	7	6	5	5
Mo	(X)	(X)	(X)	1	2	5	7	9	13	14	15	16	16	13	13	11	10	10
Mont	(X)	(X)	(X)	(X)	(X)	(X)	(X)	(X)	(X)	[1]1	1	1	2	2	2	2	2	2
Nebr	(X)	(X)	(X)	(X)	(X)	(X)	(X)	[1]1	1	3	6	6	6	5	4	4	3	3
Nev	(X)	(X)	(X)	(X)	(X)	(X)	(X)	[1]1	1	1	1	1	1	1	1	1	1	1
N.H.	4	5	6	6	5	4	3	3	3	2	2	2	2	2	2	2	2	2
N.J.	5	6	6	6	6	5	5	5	7	7	8	10	12	14	14	14	15	15
N. Mex	(X)	(X)	(X)	(X)	(X)	(X)	(X)	(X)	(X)	(X)	(X)	(X)	[2]1	1	2	2	2	2
N.Y.	10	17	27	34	40	34	33	31	33	34	34	37	43	45	45	43	41	39
N.C.	10	12	13	13	13	9	8	7	8	9	9	10	10	11	12	12	11	11
N. Dak	(X)	(X)	(X)	(X)	(X)	(X)	(X)	(X)	(X)	[1]1	1	2	3	2	2	2	2	1
Ohio	(X)	[1]1	6	14	19	21	21	19	20	21	21	21	22	24	23	23	24	23
Okla	(X)	(X)	(X)	(X)	(X)	(X)	(X)	(X)	(X)	(X)	(X)	[1]5	8	9	8	6	6	6
Oreg	(X)	(X)	(X)	(X)	(X)	(X)	(X)	(X)	[1]1	1	2	2	3	3	4	4	4	4
Pa	13	18	23	26	28	24	25	24	27	28	30	32	36	34	33	30	27	25
R.I.	2	2	2	2	2	2	2	2	2	2	2	2	3	2	2	2	2	2
S.C.	6	8	9	9	9	7	6	4	5	7	7	7	7	6	6	6	6	6
S. Dak	(X)	(X)	(X)	(X)	(X)	(X)	(X)	(X)	(X)	[1]2	2	2	3	2	2	2	2	2
Tenn	[1]1	3	6	9	13	11	10	8	10	10	10	10	10	9	10	9	9	8
Tex	(X)	(X)	(X)	(X)	(X)	[1]2	2	4	6	11	13	16	18	21	21	22	23	24
Utah	(X)	(X)	(X)	(X)	(X)	(X)	(X)	(X)	(X)	(X)	[1]1	1	2	2	2	2	2	2
Vt	2	4	6	5	5	4	3	3	3	2	2	2	2	1	1	1	1	1
Va	19	22	23	22	21	15	13	11	9	10	10	10	10	9	9	10	10	10
Wash	(X)	(X)	(X)	(X)	(X)	(X)	(X)	(X)	(X)	[1]1	2	3	5	6	6	6	7	7
W. Va	(X)	(X)	(X)	(X)	(X)	(X)	(X)	(X)	3	4	4	4	5	6	6	6	5	4
Wis	(X)	(X)	(X)	(X)	(X)	[1]2	3	6	8	9	10	11	11	10	10	10	10	9
Wyo	(X)	(X)	(X)	(X)	(X)	(X)	(X)	(X)	(X)	[1]1	1	1	1	1	1	1	1	1

X Not applicable.
[1] Assigned after apportionment.   [2] Included in apportionment act in anticipation of statehood.

Source: U.S. Bureau of the Census, *Census of Population: 1970,* vol. I.

No. 820. POPULATION, 1960 AND 1970, OF CONGRESSIONAL DISTRICTS FOR THE 88TH AND 95TH CONGRESSES, BY DIFFERENCES IN SIZE—STATES

[As of April 1. Based on total resident population]

STATE	DISTRICTS OF 88TH CONGRESS, 1960 POPULATION					DISTRICTS OF 95TH CONGRESS, 1970 POPULATION					Year of last redistricting prior to 95th Congress
	Average (1,000)	Smallest district		Largest district		Average (1,000)	Smallest district		Largest district		
		Number (1,000)	Percent below average	Number (1,000)	Percent above average		Number (1,000)	Percent below average	Number (1,000)	Percent above average	
United States [1]	410	177	56.8	952	131.8	465	333	28.4	530	13.8	(X)
Alabama	[2] 3,267	(X)	(X)	(X)	(X)	492	490	.5	494	.3	1972
Alaska [3]	[4] 226	(X)	(X)	(X)	(X)	[4] 302	(X)	(X)	(X)	(X)	(X)
Arizona	434	198	54.3	664	52.9	443	443	.1	444	.1	1971
Arkansas	447	333	25.5	575	28.8	481	480	.2	481	.1	1971
California	414	302	27.0	589	42.4	464	463	.4	467	.5	1973
Colorado	438	196	55.4	654	49.1	441	439	.5	442	.2	1972
Connecticut	507	319	37.1	690	36.0	505	505	(z)	505	(z)	1972
Delaware [3]	[4] 446	(X)	(X)	(X)	(X)	[4] 548	(X)	(X)	(X)	(X)	(X)
Florida	413	237	42.5	660	60.0	453	452	.1	453	.1	1972
Georgia	394	272	31.0	824	108.9	459	456	.7	461	.4	1972
Hawaii	[5] 633	(X)	(X)	(X)	(X)	385	362	5.9	408	5.9	1969
Idaho	334	257	22.9	410	22.9	357	356	.1	357	.1	1971
Illinois	420	279	33.6	553	31.6	463	460	.7	466	.6	1971
Indiana	424	291	31.4	698	64.6	472	472	.1	473	.1	1972
Iowa	394	353	10.4	442	12.3	471	469	.4	472	.2	1971
Kansas	436	374	14.3	540	23.8	450	447	.6	454	.9	1971
Kentucky	434	351	19.2	611	40.8	460	459	.2	461	.2	1972
Louisiana	407	264	35.2	536	31.7	455	455	.1	456	.2	1972
Maine	485	464	4.3	505	4.3	497	496	.2	498	.2	1971
Maryland	443	244	45.0	711	00.5	490	483	1.6	495	1.0	1972
Massachusetts	429	376	12.3	479	11.6	474	469	1.0	477	.6	1971
Michigan	435	177	59.2	803	84.8	467	465	.4	468	.1	1972
Minnesota	427	375	12.0	483	13.2	476	473	.6	479	.8	1971
Mississippi	436	295	32.3	608	39.7	443	434	2.2	452	1.9	1972
Missouri	432	378	12.4	507	17.3	468	467	.2	470	.4	1972
Montana	337	274	18.7	401	18.7	347	347	.1	347	.1	1971
Nebraska	470	405	14.0	531	12.8	495	494	.1	495	.1	1968
Nevada [3]	[4] 285	(X)	(X)	(X)	(X)	[4] 489	(X)	(X)	(X)	(X)	(X)
New Hampshire	303	275	9.3	332	9.3	369	367	.5	371	.5	1972
New Jersey	404	255	36.9	586	44.8	478	475	.6	480	.4	1972
New Mexico	[5] 951	(X)	(X)	(X)	(X)	508	505	.6	511	.6	1968
New York	409	350	14.4	471	15.1	468	467	.2	469	.3	1974
North Carolina	414	278	32.9	491	18.7	462	454	1.7	472	2.1	1972
North Dakota	316	299	5.4	333	5.4	[6] 618	(X)	(X)	(X)	(X)	(X)
Ohio	422	236	44.0	726	72.1	463	462	.2	465	.3	1972
Oklahoma	388	228	41.3	553	42.5	427	426	.2	427	.2	1972
Oregon	442	265	40.0	523	18.2	523	522	.1	523	.1	1971
Pennsylvania	419	303	27.7	553	31.9	472	468	.8	478	1.4	1972
Rhode Island	430	400	7.0	460	7.0	475	474	.1	475	.1	1972
South Carolina	397	272	31.4	532	33.9	432	411	4.8	446	3.4	1971
South Dakota	340	183	46.3	498	46.3	333	333	(z)	333	(z)	1971
Tennessee	396	223	43.6	627	58.2	491	472	3.7	513	4.6	1972
Texas	435	216	50.3	952	118.5	467	466	.1	467	.1	1973
Utah	445	318	28.6	573	28.6	530	530	(z)	530	(z)	1971
Vermont [3]	[4] 390	(X)	(X)	(X)	(X)	[4] 445	(X)	(X)	(X)	(X)	(X)
Virginia	397	313	21.1	540	36.0	465	463	.4	466	.2	1972
Washington	408	343	16.0	511	25.2	487	478	1.8	523	7.3	1972
West Virginia	372	303	18.5	422	13.4	436	434	.4	438	.4	1971
Wisconsin	395	237	40.1	530	34.2	491	491	(z)	491	(z)	1971
Wyoming [3]	[4] 330	(X)	(X)	(X)	(X)	[4] 332	(X)	(X)	(X)	(X)	(X)

X Not applicable.   Z Less than .05 percent.   [1] Excludes District of Columbia.
[2] Total State population; 8 Representatives elected at large.   [3] 1 Representative elected at large.
[4] Total State population.
[5] Total State population; 2 Representatives elected at large.
[6] Total State population; 1 Representative elected at large.

Source: U.S. Bureau of the Census, *Congressional District Data Book, Districts of the 93d Congress*, and reports for *Districts of the 94th Congress* for California, New York, and Texas.

No. 821. Vote Cast for United States Representatives, by Major Political Parties, by States: 1972 to 1976

[In thousands, except percent. In each State, totals represent the sum of votes cast in each Congressional District, except as follows: In Alaska, Delaware, Nevada, Vermont, and Wyoming, only 1 Representative was elected for the State at large. In numerous States, one or other of the major parties had no candidate in some districts. In those cases where votes of a party as such are cast in endorsement of a candidate of another party, votes are counted as for the endorsing party. See also footnotes below. See also Historical Statistics, Colonial Times to 1970, series Y 211–214]

STATE	1972				1974				1976			
	Total [1]	Democratic	Republican	Percent for majority party	Total [1]	Democratic	Republican	Percent for majority party	Total [1]	Democratic	Republican	Percent for majority party
Total [2]	71,270	36,828	33,104	51.7	52,391	30,159	21,281	57.6	74,262	41,741	31,242	56.2
Ala	973	544	384	55.9	561	376	169	67.0	984	667	315	67.8
Alaska	95	54	42	56.2	96	44	52	53.8	118	34	84	70.8
Ariz	594	284	310	52.2	544	269	266	49.6	729	356	340	48.8
Ark.[3 4]	187	42	145	77.3	424	268	156	63.1	336	261	75	77.6
Calif	8,117	4,210	3,760	51.3	5,829	3,312	2,369	56.8	7,454	4,144	3,220	55.6
Colo	913	428	480	52.6	778	418	359	53.8	1,021	455	537	53.1
Conn	1,351	657	691	51.1	1,079	620	440	57.5	1,348	682	651	50.6
Del	226	83	141	62.5	160	63	94	58.5	215	102	111	51.5
D.C	160	95	39	59.4	104	66	9	63.8	160	123	22	77.3
Fla.[3 5]	1,932	1,031	901	53.4	1,062	477	581	54.7	2,083	1,126	937	54.1
Ga	892	639	253	71.6	822	589	234	71.6	1,253	931	322	74.3
Hawaii	275	154	121	55.9	259	158	101	61.1	294	184	78	62.7
Idaho	302	108	188	62.3	250	108	143	57.0	342	162	180	52.6
Ill	4,385	2,147	2,223	50.7	2,842	1,601	1,219	56.3	4,366	2,247	2,113	51.5
Ind	2,110	974	1,134	53.7	1,731	957	770	55.3	2,103	1,166	932	55.5
Iowa	1,196	616	577	51.5	904	488	413	54.0	1,242	709	527	57.1
Kans	878	281	582	66.2	776	325	418	53.9	909	349	545	60.0
Ky	986	494	488	50.1	679	425	239	62.6	989	606	374	61.2
La	678	574	87	84.6	546	397	140	72.6	1,014	624	365	61.5
Maine	413	219	195	52.9	353	141	212	60.1	473	151	315	66.5
Md	1,219	634	585	52.0	874	527	347	60.3	1,316	789	473	60.0
Mass	2,159	1,244	808	57.6	1,699	1,168	401	68.8	2,345	1,510	723	64.4
Mich	3,273	1,536	1,710	52.2	2,519	1,465	1,020	58.2	3,432	1,898	1,503	55.3
Minn	1,690	897	761	53.1	1,219	705	492	57.8	1,795	1,040	730	58.0
Miss	588	387	185	65.9	306	156	131	51.0	637	375	257	59.0
Mo	1,833	1,092	737	59.6	1,209	810	397	67.0	1,905	1,081	812	56.7
Mont	315	191	124	60.5	254	149	105	58.6	321	180	140	56.2
Nebr	569	194	375	66.0	448	211	236	52.7	602	211	386	64.1
Nev	180	86	94	52.2	168	94	61	55.8	200	154	24	77.1
N.H	315	93	222	70.4	220	97	123	55.9	325	174	149	53.4
N.J	2,832	1,391	1,416	50.0	2,084	1,241	795	59.6	2,811	1,539	1,218	54.7
N. Mex	374	210	163	56.3	316	162	149	51.2	401	185	215	53.5
N.Y.[6]	6,609	3,050	2,925	46.1	4,894	2,807	1,930	57.4	5,991	3,501	2,342	58.4
N.C	1,351	735	610	54.4	988	638	348	64.5	1,572	1,011	549	64.3
N. Dak	269	73	195	72.7	234	104	130	55.7	290	104	181	62.4
Ohio	3,836	1,684	2,071	54.0	2,945	1,397	1,458	49.5	3,842	1,818	1,917	49.9
Okla.[3 7]	817	497	310	60.8	506	295	208	58.2	1,068	683	372	64.0
Oreg	870	479	390	55.1	753	482	270	64.1	927	599	263	64.7
Pa	4,463	2,173	2,281	51.1	3,377	1,937	1,422	57.4	4,434	2,410	2,007	54.4
R.I	388	243	139	62.7	304	230	74	75.7	389	271	114	69.7
S.C	631	329	302	52.1	517	302	213	58.3	784	502	279	64.1
S. Dak	301	160	141	53.1	272	105	167	61.3	295	73	221	75.0
Tenn	1,102	505	589	53.5	902	533	364	59.1	1,251	775	453	61.9
Tex	2,886	2,032	835	70.4	1,489	1,075	407	72.2	3,663	2,369	1,277	64.7
Utah	473	260	203	55.0	413	231	163	55.8	544	267	251	49.0
Vt	186	65	121	65.0	141	56	75	52.9	185	60	124	67.4
Va	1,271	627	590	49.4	924	507	361	54.8	1,463	666	670	45.8
Wash	1,302	858	439	65.9	981	574	401	58.5	1,426	818	586	57.4
W. Va	721	477	244	66.2	416	290	125	69.8	663	447	157	67.3
Wis	1,801	1,013	767	56.2	1,197	704	475	58.8	1,962	1,190	761	60.7
Wyo	146	76	71	51.7	127	69	57	54.7	152	86	66	56.4

[1] Includes vote cast for minor parties. [2] Excludes District of Columbia. [3] State law does not require tabulation of votes for unopposed candidates. [4] 1972 data for 3d District only; 1974 data for 1st, 2d and 3d Districts; 1976 data for 1st and 2d Districts. [5] In 1972, Districts 1, 2, and 9 were unopposed; in 1974, Districts 1, 2, 3, 7, 11, and 13 were unopposed; in 1976, Districts 1, 2, 3, and 4 were unopposed. [6] Includes endorsing votes cast by other parties for Democratic and Republican candidates. [7] In 1972, District 3 was unopposed; in 1974, Districts 3 and 4 were unopposed.

Source: 1972 and 1974, U.S. Congress, Clerk of the House, Statistics of the Presidential and Congressional Election and Statistics of the Congressional Election (in some cases, revisions by Elections Research Center, Washington, D.C.); 1976, compiled by U.S. Bureau of the Census from Elections Research Center, Washington, D.C., America Votes, vol. 12 (copyright).

No. 822. Representatives Elected, by Percent of Vote Cast, by Major Party and by States: 1974 and 1976

[D = Democratic, R = Republican]

STATE	1974								1976							
	No opponent		30–54.9 percent of vote		55–64.9 percent of vote		65 percent and over of vote		No opponent		30–54.9 percent of vote		55–64.9 percent of vote		65 percent and over of vote	
	D	R	D	R	D	R	D	R	D	R	D	R	D	R	D	R
U.S.	40	1	46	56	63	59	142	28	22	4	51	25	60	56	159	58
Alabama	1	–	–	–	–	2	3	1	2	–	–	–	–	3	2	–
Alaska	–	–	–	1	–	–	–	–	–	–	–	–	–	–	–	1
Arizona	–	–	–	2	1	1	–	–	–	–	1	1	1	1	–	–
Arkansas	1	–	–	1	1	–	1	–	1	1	–	–	–	–	2	–
California	3	–	4	5	6	9	15	1	1	–	3	1	8	7	17	6
Colorado	–	–	1	1	1	1	1	–	–	–	3	1	–	–	–	1
Connecticut	–	–	–	2	3	–	1	–	–	–	–	–	3	1	1	1
Delaware	–	–	–	–	–	1	–	–	–	–	–	1	–	–	–	–
Florida	6	–	–	2	1	–	3	3	4	–	–	1	1	2	5	2
Georgia	2	–	2	–	1	–	5	–	–	–	2	–	–	–	8	–
Hawaii	–	–	–	–	2	–	–	–	–	–	1	–	–	–	1	–
Idaho	–	–	–	–	–	2	–	–	–	–	–	2	–	–	–	–
Illinois	1	–	3	5	2	3	7	3	–	–	1	1	2	4	9	7
Indiana	–	–	5	–	2	2	2	–	1	–	3	1	3	2	1	–
Iowa	–	–	4	1	1	–	–	–	–	–	1	1	1	1	2	–
Kansas	–	–	–	1	1	3	–	–	–	–	2	–	–	1	–	2
Kentucky	–	–	–	–	–	–	5	2	–	–	–	–	2	1	3	1
Louisiana	4	–	–	1	–	1	2	–	1	–	2	–	–	–	3	2
Maine	–	–	–	1	–	–	–	1	–	–	–	–	–	–	1	1
Maryland	1	–	1	1	–	1	3	1	–	–	–	2	1	1	4	–
Massachusetts	3	–	2	–	1	1	4	1	2	1	2	–	–	1	6	–
Michigan	–	–	3	5	2	2	7	–	–	–	2	4	2	2	7	2
Minnesota	–	–	–	1	2	2	3	–	1	–	–	–	1	1	3	2
Mississippi	1	–	–	–	–	–	2	2	1	–	–	–	1	–	1	2
Missouri	–	–	–	1	1	–	8	–	–	–	1	–	3	2	4	–
Montana	–	–	1	–	1	–	–	–	–	–	–	–	–	1	1	–
Nebraska	–	–	–	2	–	1	–	–	–	–	1	–	–	–	–	2
Nevada	–	–	–	–	1	–	–	–	–	–	–	–	–	–	1	–
New Hampshire	–	*–	1	–	–	1	–	–	–	–	–	–	–	1	1	–
New Jersey	–	–	1	2	4	–	7	1	–	–	2	1	4	1	5	2
New Mexico	–	–	–	–	1	1	1	–	–	–	–	–	–	–	1	1
New York	1	–	4	3	5	5	17	4	–	–	4	1	4	4	20	6
North Carolina	3	–	1	2	3	–	2	–	–	1	2	1	1	1	5	–
North Dakota	–	–	–	–	–	1	–	–	–	–	–	–	–	1	–	–
Ohio	–	1	2	5	–	6	6	3	–	–	3	1	1	4	6	8
Oklahoma	2	–	2	–	1	–	1	–	–	–	2	1	–	–	3	–
Oregon	–	–	1	–	1	–	2	–	–	–	1	–	1	–	2	–
Pennsylvania	1	–	–	4	4	6	9	1	–	1	3	1	3	5	11	1
Rhode Island	–	–	–	–	–	–	2	–	–	–	–	–	1	–	1	–
South Carolina	–	–	–	–	4	1	1	–	–	–	1	–	1	1	3	–
South Dakota	–	–	–	–	–	1	–	1	–	–	–	–	–	–	–	2
Tennessee	1	–	2	–	–	2	2	1	1	–	–	–	1	3	3	–
Texas	8	–	1	1	2	1	10	1	4	1	3	–	7	–	8	1
Utah	–	–	1	–	1	–	–	–	–	–	–	1	1	–	–	–
Vermont	–	–	–	1	–	–	–	–	–	–	–	–	–	–	–	1
Virginia	–	–	1	4	1	1	3	–	1	–	2	2	–	2	1	2
Washington	–	–	–	–	4	–	2	1	–	–	1	–	2	–	3	1
West Virginia	1	–	–	–	2	–	1	–	–	–	1	–	1	–	2	–
Wisconsin	–	–	2	1	1	1	4	–	1	–	1	–	2	1	3	1
Wyoming	–	–	1	–	–	–	–	–	–	–	–	–	1	–	–	–

– Represents zero.

Source: Compiled by U.S. Bureau of the Census from Congressional Quarterly, Inc., Washington, D.C., *Congressional Quarterly Almanac, 1974;* and *Congressional Quarterly Weekly Report,* No. 12, March 1977.

No. 823. Composition of Congress, by Political Party: 1933 to 1978

[D = Democratic, R = Republican. Data for beginning of first session of each Congress, except as noted; exclude vacancies at beginning of session. See also *Historical Statistics, Colonial Times to 1970*, series Y 204–210]

YEAR	Party and President	Congress	HOUSE			SENATE		
			Majority party	Minority party	Other	Majority party	Minority party	Other
1933	D (F. Roosevelt)	73d	D-310	R-117	5	D-60	R-35	1
1935	D (F. Roosevelt)	74th	D-319	R-103	10	D-69	R-25	2
1937	D (F. Roosevelt)	75th	D-331	R- 89	13	D-76	R-16	4
1939	D (F. Roosevelt)	76th	D-261	R-164	4	D-69	R-23	4
1941	D (F. Roosevelt)	77th	D-268	R-162	5	D-66	R-28	2
1943	D (F. Roosevelt)	78th	D-218	R-208	4	D-58	R-37	1
1945	{D (F. Roosevelt) {D (Truman)	}79th	D-242	R-190	2	D-56	R-38	1
1947	D (Truman)	80th	R-245	D-188	1	R-51	D-45	–
1949	D (Truman)	81st	D-263	R-171	1	D-54	R-42	–
1951	D (Truman)	82d	D-234	R-199	1	D-49	R-47	–
1953	R (Eisenhower)	83d	R-221	D-211	1	R-48	D-47	1
1955	R (Eisenhower)	84th	D-232	R-203	–	D-48	R-47	1
1957	R (Eisenhower)	85th	D-233	R-200	–	D-49	R-47	–
1959 [1]	R (Eisenhower)	86th	D-283	R-153	–	D-64	R-34	–
1961	D (Kennedy)	87th	D-263	R-174	–	D-65	R-35	–
1963	{D (Kennedy) {D (Johnson)	}88th	D-258	R-177	–	D-67	R-33	–
1965	D (Johnson)	89th	D-295	R-140	–	D-68	R-32	–
1967	D (Johnson)	90th	D-247	R-187	–	D-64	R-36	–
1969	R (Nixon)	91st	D-243	R-192	–	D-57	R-43	–
1971 [2]	R (Nixon)	92d	D-254	R-180	–	D-54	R-44	2
1973 [2][3]	R (Nixon)	93d	D-239	R-192	1	D-56	R-42	2
1975 [4]	R (Ford)	94th	D-291	R-144	–	D-60	R-37	2
1977 [5]	D (Carter)	95th	D-292	R-143	–	D-61	R-38	1
1978 [5][6]	D (Carter)	95th	D-287	R-146	–	D-59	R-38	1

– Represents zero. [1] Excludes Hawaii; 2 Senators (1-R, 1-D) and 1 Representative (D) seated August 1959.
[2] Senate had 1 Independent and 1 Conservative-Republican. [3] House had 1 Independent-Democrat.
[4] Senate had 1 Independent, 1 Conservative-Republican, and 1 undecided (New Hampshire).
[5] Senate had 1 Independent. [6] As of beginning of second session.
Source: U.S. Congress, Joint Committee on Printing, *Congressional Directory*, annual.

No. 824. Congressional Bills, Acts, and Resolutions: 1961 to 1977

[Excludes simple and concurrent resolutions. See also *Historical Statistics, Colonial Times to 1970*, series Y 189–198]

ITEM	87th Cong., 1961–62	88th Cong., 1963–64	89th Cong., 1965–66	90th Cong., 1967–68	91st Cong., 1969–70	92d Cong., 1971–72	93d Cong., 1973–74	94th Cong., 1975–76	95th Cong., 1977
Measures introduced	18,376	17,480	24,003	26,460	26,303	22,969	23,396	21,096	13,582
Bills	17,230	16,079	22,483	24,786	24,631	21,363	21,950	19,762	12,799
Joint resolutions	1,146	1,401	1,520	1,674	1,672	1,606	1,446	1,334	783
Measures enacted	1,569	1,026	1,283	1,002	941	768	772	729	250
Public	885	666	810	640	695	607	649	588	223
Private	684	360	473	362	246	161	123	141	27

Source: U.S. Congress, *Calendars of the U.S. House of Representatives and History of Legislation*, annual.

No. 825. Congressional Bills Vetoed: 1913 to 1977

[See also *Historical Statistics, Colonial Times to 1970*, series Y 199–203]

PERIOD	President	Total vetoes	Regular vetoes	Pocket vetoes	Vetoes sustained	Bills passed over veto
1913–1921	Wilson	44	33	11	38	6
1921–1923	Harding	6	5	1	6	–
1923–1929	Coolidge	50	20	30	46	4
1929–1933	Hoover	37	21	16	34	3
1933–1945	F. Roosevelt	635	372	263	626	9
1945–1953	Truman	250	180	70	238	12
1953–1961	Eisenhower	181	73	108	179	2
1961–1963	Kennedy	21	12	9	21	–
1963–1969	Johnson	30	16	14	30	–
1969–1974	Nixon [1]	42	24	18	36	6
1974–1977	Ford [1]	72	53	19	60	12
1977	Carter	2	2	–	2	–

– Represents zero. [1] Nixon resignation effective August 8, 1974.
Source: U.S. Congress, Senate Library, *Presidential Vetoes. . .1789–1968;* U.S. Congress, *Calendars of the U.S. House of Representatives and History of Legislation*, annual.

No. 826. Composition of Congress, by Political Party Affiliations, by States: 1973 to 1977

[Figures are for the beginning of the first session. Dem. = Democratic; Rep. = Republican]

STATE	REPRESENTATIVES						SENATORS					
	93d Congress, [1] 1973		94th Congress, 1975		95th Congress, [2] 1977		93d Congress, [3] 1973		94th Congress, [3][4] 1975		95th Congress, [5][6] 1977	
	Dem.	Rep.	Dem.	Rep.	Dem.	Rep.	Dem.	Rep.	Dem.	Rep.	Dem.	Rep.
Total	239	192	291	144	292	143	56	42	60	37	61	38
Alabama	4	3	4	3	4	3	2	–	2	–	2	–
Alaska	–	–	–	1	–	1	1	1	1	1	1	1
Arizona	1	3	1	3	2	2	–	2	–	2	1	1
Arkansas	3	1	3	1	3	1	2	–	2	–	2	–
California	23	20	28	15	29	14	2	–	2	–	1	1
Colorado	2	3	3	2	3	2	1	1	2	–	2	–
Connecticut	3	3	4	2	4	2	1	1	1	1	1	1
Delaware	–	1	–	1	–	1	1	1	1	1	1	1
Florida	11	4	10	5	10	5	1	1	2	–	2	–
Georgia	9	1	10	–	10	–	2	–	2	–	2	–
Hawaii	2	–	2	–	2	–	1	1	1	1	2	–
Idaho	–	2	–	2	–	2	1	1	1	1	1	1
Illinois	9	14	13	11	12	12	1	1	1	1	1	1
Indiana	4	7	9	2	8	3	2	–	2	–	1	1
Iowa	3	3	5	1	4	2	2	–	2	–	2	–
Kansas	1	4	1	4	2	3	–	2	–	2	–	2
Kentucky	5	2	5	2	5	2	1	1	2	–	2	–
Louisiana	6	1	6	2	6	2	2	–	2	–	2	–
Maine	1	1	–	2	–	2	2	–	2	–	2	–
Maryland	4	4	5	3	5	3	–	2	–	2	1	1
Massachusetts	8	3	10	2	10	2	1	1	1	1	1	1
Michigan	7	12	12	7	11	8	1	1	1	1	1	1
Minnesota	4	4	5	3	5	3	2	–	2	–	2	–
Mississippi	3	2	3	2	3	2	2	–	2	–	2	–
Missouri	9	1	9	1	8	2	2	–	2	–	1	1
Montana	1	1	2	–	1	1	2	–	2	–	2	–
Nebraska	–	3	–	3	1	2	–	2	–	2	1	1
Nevada	–	1	1	–	1	–	2	–	1	1	1	1
New Hampshire	–	2	1	1	1	1	1	1	1	–	2	–
New Jersey	8	7	12	3	11	4	1	1	1	1	1	1
New Mexico	1	1	1	1	1	1	1	1	1	1	–	2
New York	22	17	27	12	28	11	–	1	–	1	1	1
North Carolina	7	4	9	2	9	2	1	1	1	1	1	1
North Dakota	–	1	–	1	–	1	1	1	1	1	1	1
Ohio	7	16	8	15	10	13	–	2	1	1	2	–
Oklahoma	5	1	6	–	5	1	–	2	–	2	–	2
Oregon	2	2	4	–	4	–	–	2	–	2	–	2
Pennsylvania	13	12	14	11	17	8	–	2	–	2	–	2
Rhode Island	2	–	2	–	2	–	2	–	2	–	1	1
South Carolina	4	2	5	1	5	1	1	1	1	1	1	1
South Dakota	1	1	–	2	–	2	2	–	2	–	2	–
Tennessee	3	5	5	3	5	3	–	2	–	2	1	1
Texas	20	4	21	3	22	2	1	1	1	1	1	1
Utah	2	–	2	–	1	1	1	1	1	1	1	1
Vermont	–	1	–	1	–	1	–	2	1	1	1	1
Virginia	3	7	5	5	4	6	–	1	–	1	–	1
Washington	6	1	6	1	6	1	2	–	2	–	2	–
West Virginia	4	–	4	–	4	–	2	–	2	–	2	–
Wisconsin	5	4	7	2	7	2	2	–	2	–	2	–
Wyoming	1	–	1	–	1	–	1	1	1	1	–	2

– Represents zero. [1] Alaska, Ill., and La. each had 1 vacancy; Mass. had 1 Representative classified as Independent-Democrat. [2] Changes as of the beginning of the 2d session, 1978: Total, 287 Dem., 146 Rep., 2 vacancies; La., 5 Dem., 3 Rep.; Minn., 4 Dem., 4 Rep.; N.Y., 26 Dem., 11 Rep., 2 vacancies; Wash., 5 Dem., 2 Rep. [3] N.Y. had 1 Senator classified Conservative-Republican and Va. had 1 Senator classified Independent. [4] One Senate seat (N.H.) was undecided at beginning of session; subsequently became Democratic. [5] Changes as of the beginning of the 2d session, 1978: Total, 59 Dem., 38 Rep., 1 Independent, 2 vacancies; Minn. and Mont. each had 1 Dem. and 1 vacancy. [6] Va. had 1 Senator classified Independent.

Source: U.S. Congress, Joint Committee on Printing, Congressional Directory, annual.

No. 827. MEMBERS OF CONGRESS—INCUMBENTS RE-ELECTED: 1954 TO 1976

ITEM	MIDTERM ELECTIONS						PRESIDENTIAL-YEAR ELECTIONS					
	1954	1958	1962	1966	1970	1974	1956	1960	1964	1968	1972	1976
Representatives:												
Incumbent candidates	405	396	[1] 410	413	398	390	410	406	433	404	[2] 393	384
Re-elected	379	355	369	362	379	342	389	374	344	396	367	368
Percent of candidates	93.6	89.6	92.2	87.7	95.2	87.7	94.9	92.1	79.4	98.0	93.4	95.8
Defeated: In primaries	6	3	12	11	7	8	6	6	44	3	13	3
In general elections	20	38	29	40	12	40	15	26	45	5	13	13
Senators:												
Incumbent candidates	30	31	35	32	30	27	28	29	36	28	27	25
Re-elected	24	20	29	28	23	23	25	28	28	20	20	16
Percent of candidates	80.0	64.5	82.9	87.5	76.7	85.2	89.3	96.6	77.8	71.4	71.4	64.0
Defeated: In primaries	1	–	1	3	1	2	–	–	4	4	2	–
In general elections	5	11	5	1	6	2	3	1	4	4	5	9

– Represents zero.   [1] Includes 7 races, 2 incumbents each.   [2] Includes 3 races, 2 incumbents each.

Source: Congressional Quarterly Service, *Congressional Quarterly Weekly Report* (copyright); and Library of Congress, Congressional Research Service, unpublished data.

No. 828. MEMBERS OF CONGRESS—SELECTED CHARACTERISTICS: 1973 TO 1978
[As of first session, except 95th Cong., 1978, as of second session. Dem.= Democratic; Rep.= Republican]

CHARACTERISTIC	REPRESENTATIVES						SENATORS					
	93d Cong., 1973	94th Cong., 1975	95th Cong., 1977	95th Cong., 1978			93d Cong., 1973	94th Cong., 1975	95th Cong., 1977	95th Cong., 1978		
				Total	Dem.	Rep.				Total	Dem.	Rep.
Total	[1] 435	435	435	435	288	147	100	100	100	[2] 100	61	38
Male	419	416	417	417	275	142	100	100	100	[2] 99	60	38
Female	14	19	18	18	13	5	–	–	–	1	1	–
White	416	417	417	419	272	147	97	97	96	[2] 96	59	36
Black	15	15	16	14	14	–	1	1	1	1	–	1
Other	2	3	2	2	2	–	2	2	3	3	2	1
Married	399	381	379	379	249	130	96	94	91	[2] 90	54	35
Not married [3]	34	54	56	56	39	17	4	6	9	10	7	3
Seniority:												
Less than 2 years	72	96	71	74	51	23	13	11	18	21	13	8
2–9 years	183	162	207	201	132	69	38	41	41	39	24	15
10–19 years	120	125	116	117	68	49	36	34	24	[2] 24	14	9
20–29 years	48	42	33	35	29	6	10	10	12	11	6	5
30 years or more	10	10	8	8	8	–	3	4	5	5	4	1

– Represents zero.   [1] Includes 2 vacancies.   [2] Includes 1 Independent.   [3] Single, widowed, or divorced.

Source: Compiled by U.S. Bureau of the Census from Congressional Quarterly Inc., Wash., D.C., *Congressional Quarterly Almanac* (copyright); and U.S. Congress, Joint Committee on Printing, *Congressional Directory*, annual.

No. 829. MEMBERS OF CONGRESS, BY SEX AND AGE: 90TH TO 95TH CONGRESSES
[As of January 1 of the 1st year of each Congress. Figures for Representatives exclude vacancies]

MEMBERS OF CONGRESS AND YEAR	Male	Fe-male	AGE (in years)					
			Under 40	40–49	50–59	60–69	70–79	80 and over
REPRESENTATIVES								
90th Congress, 1967	424	10	56	150	135	73	15	
91st Congress, 1969	425	10	39	160	140	80	13	
92d Congress, 1971	421	12	40	133	152	86	19	
93d Congress, 1973	419	14	45	132	154	80	20	
94th Congress, 1975	416	19	69	138	137	75	14	
95th Congress, 1977	417	18	81	121	147	71	15	
SENATORS								
90th Congress, 1967	99	1	5	20	30	30	14	
91st Congress, 1969	99	1	5	25	28	29	13	
92d Congress, 1971	99	1	4	24	32	23	16	
93d Congress, 1973	100	–	3	25	37	23	11	
94th Congress, 1975 [1]	100	–	5	21	35	24	15	
95th Congress, 1977	100	–	6	26	35	21	10	

– Represents zero.   [1] Includes Sen. Durkin, N.H., seated Sept. 1975.

Source: Compiled by U.S. Bureau of the Census from U.S. Congress, Joint Committee on Printing, *Congressional Directory*, annual.

No. 830. Elected State and Local Government Officials, by Regions: 1967

[For composition of regions, see fig. I, inside front cover]

TYPE OF GOVERNMENT	Number of governments	Total elected officials	Average per government	ELECTED OFFICIALS IN—			
				Northeast	North Central	South	West
United States	81,298	521,758	6.4	112,627	246,958	101,632	60,541
State governments	50	13,038	260.8	2,583	3,517	4,338	2,600
Local governments [1]	81,248	508,720	6.3	110,044	243,441	97,294	57,941
Counties	3,049	74,199	24.3	3,574	30,724	32,196	7,705
Municipalities	18,048	143,927	8.0	25,089	68,186	37,281	13,371
Townships	17,105	129,603	7.6	54,925	74,346	–	332
School districts	21,782	107,663	4.9	18,245	53,911	19,496	16,011
Special districts	21,264	56,943	2.7	9,142	18,931	8,321	20,549

– Represents zero.   [1] Adjusted to exclude officials serving both county and township or city governments.
Source: U.S. Bureau of the Census, *Census of Governments: 1967*, vol. 6, No. 1, *Popularly Elected Officials of State and Local Governments.*

No. 831. Vote Cast for and Governor Elected, by States: 1970 to 1976

[In thousands, except percent. D = Democratic, R = Republican, I = Independent]

STATE	1970		1972		1974		1976		Candidate elected at most recent election
	Total vote [1]	Percent majority party	Total vote [1]	Percent majority party	Total vote [1]	Percent majority party	Total vote [1]	Percent majority party	
Ala	855	D-74.5	(X)	(X)	598	D-83.2	(X)	(X)	George C. Wallace.
Alaska	81	D-52.4	(X)	(X)	96	R-47.7	(X)	(X)	Jay S. Hammond.
Ariz	411	R-50.9	(X)	(X)	552	D-50.4	(X)	(X)	Raul H. Castro.
Ark	609	D-61.7	648	D-75.4	546	D-65.6	727	D-83.2	David H. Pryor.
Calif	6,510	R-52.8	(X)	(X)	6,248	D-50.1	(X)	(X)	Edmund Brown, Jr.
Colo	668	R-52.5	(X)	(X)	829	D-53.2	(X)	(X)	Richard D. Lamm.
Conn	1,083	R-53.8	(X)	(X)	1,103	D-58.4	(X)	(X)	Ella T. Grasso.
Del	(X)	(X)	229	D-51.3	(X)	(X)	230	R-56.9	Pierre du Pont.
Fla	1,731	D-56.9	(X)	(X)	1,828	D-61.2	(X)	(X)	Reubin Askew.
Ga	1,045	D-59.3	(X)	(X)	936	D-69.1	(X)	(X)	George Busbee.
Hawaii	239	D-57.6	(X)	(X)	250	D-54.6	(X)	(X)	George R. Ariyoshi.
Idaho	245	D-52.2	(X)	(X)	260	D-70.9	(X)	(X)	Cecil D. Andrus.
Ill	(X)	(X)	4,679	D-50.7	(X)	(X)	4,639	R-64.7	James R. Thompson.
Ind	(X)	(X)	2,121	R-56.8	(X)	(X)	2,175	R-56.8	Otis R. Bowen.
Iowa	791	R-51.0	1,210	R-58.4	920	D-58.1	(X)	(X)	Robert Ray.
Kans	745	D-54.3	922	D-62.0	784	R-49.5	(X)	(X)	Robert F. Bennett.
Ky.[2]	(X)	(X)	931	D-50.6	748	D-62.8	(X)	(X)	Julian Carroll.
La	(X)	(X)	1,122	D-57.2	[3]1,203	[3]62.4	(X)	(X)	Edwin W. Edwards.
Maine	325	D-50.1	(X)	(X)	364	I-39.1	(X)	(X)	James B. Langley.
Md	973	D-65.7	(X)	(X)	949	D-63.5	(X)	(X)	Marvin Mandel.
Mass	1,868	R-56.7	(X)	(X)	1,855	D-53.4	(X)	(X)	Michael S. Dukakis.
Mich	2,656	R-50.4	(X)	(X)	2,657	R-51.1	(X)	(X)	William Milliken.
Minn	1,365	D-54.0	(X)	(X)	1,253	D-62.8	(X)	(X)	Wendell Anderson.
Miss.[2]	(X)	(X)	781	D-77.0	708	D-52.2	(X)	(X)	Charles Finch.
Mo	(X)	(X)	1,866	R-55.2	(X)	(X)	1,934	D-50.2	Joseph P. Teasdale.
Mont	(X)	(X)	319	D-54.1	(X)	(X)	317	D-61.7	Thomas L. Judge.
Nebr	461	D-53.9	(X)	(X)	451	D-59.2	(X)	(X)	J. J. Exon.
Nev	147	D-48.1	(X)	(X)	169	D-67.4	(X)	(X)	Mike O'Callaghan.
N.H	222	R-46.0	323	R-41.4	227	R-51.1	343	R-57.7	Meldrim Thomson.
N.J.[4]	2,367	R-59.7	(X)	(X)	2,122	D-66.7	2,126	D-55.7	Brendan Byrne.
N. Mex	290	D-51.3	(X)	(X)	329	D-49.9	(X)	(X)	Jerry Apodaca.
N.Y	6,013	R-52.4	(X)	(X)	5,293	D-57.2	(X)	(X)	Hugh Carey.
N.C	(X)	(X)	1,505	R-51.0	(X)	(X)	1,664	D-65.0	James B. Hunt.
N. Dak	(X)	(X)	282	D-51.0	(X)	(X)	297	D-51.6	Arthur A. Link.
Ohio	3,184	D-54.2	(X)	(X)	3,072	R-48.6	(X)	(X)	James Rhodes.
Okla	699	D-48.4	(X)	(X)	805	D-63.9	(X)	(X)	David L. Boren.
Oreg	665	R-55.6	(X)	(X)	771	D-57.7	(X)	(X)	Robert Straub.
Pa	3,700	D-55.2	(X)	(X)	3,491	D-53.8	(X)	(X)	Milton Shapp.
R.I	346	D-50.1	413	D-52.5	322	D-78.5	399	D-54.8	J. Joseph Garrahy.
S.C	485	D-51.7	(X)	(X)	523	R-50.9	(X)	(X)	James Edwards.
S. Dak	240	D-54.8	308	D-60.0	278	D-53.6	(X)	(X)	Richard F. Kneip.
Tenn	1,108	R-52.0	(X)	(X)	1,041	D-55.4	(X)	(X)	Ray Blanton.
Tex	2,235	D-53.6	3,410	D-47.9	1,655	D-61.4	(X)	(X)	Dolph Briscoe.
Utah	(X)	(X)	476	D-69.7	(X)	(X)	540	D-52.0	Scott M. Matheson.
Vt	153	R-57.0	189	D-55.2	141	D-56.6	186	R-53.4	Richard A. Snelling.
Va.[4]	916	R-52.5	(X)	(X)	1,035	R-50.7	1,251	R-55.9	John Dalton.
Wash	(X)	(X)	1,473	R-50.8	(X)	(X)	1,546	D-53.1	Dixy Lee Ray.
W. Va	(X)	(X)	774	R-54.7	(X)	(X)	749	D-66.2	John D. Rockefeller.
Wis	1,343	D-54.2	(X)	(X)	1,182	D-53.2	(X)	(X)	Patrick J. Lucey.
Wyo	118	R-62.8	(X)	(X)	128	D-55.9	(X)	(X)	Ed Herschler.

X Not applicable.   [1] Includes minor party and scattered votes.   [2] Voting years, 1971 and 1975.
[3] Special election, Nov. 1975, held on a non-party basis.   [4] Voting years, 1969, 1973, and 1977.
Source: Elections Research Center, Washington, D.C., *America Votes*, biennial (copyright).

No. 832. COMPOSITION OF STATE LEGISLATURES, BY POLITICAL PARTY AFFILIATIONS: 1972 TO 1976

[Dates shown refer to election years in most States, to odd-year elections a year previously in a few; figures reflect immediate results of elections, including holdover members in partial renewal situations. Dem.=Democratic; Rep.=Republican. In general, Lower House refers to body consisting of State Representatives; Upper House, of State Senators]

STATE	LOWER HOUSE						UPPER HOUSE					
	1972 [1][2]		1974 [3][4]		1976 [5][6]		1972 [1][7]		1974 [3][8]		1976 [6][9]	
	Dem.	Rep.	Dem.	Rep.	Dem.	Rep.	Dem.	Rep.	Dem.	Rep.	Dem.	Rep.
U.S.	3,312	2,242	3,793	1,765	3,772	1,783	1,163	758	1,307	620	1,306	6
Ala.	104	2	105	–	103	2	35	–	35	–	34	–
Alaska [10]	20	19	30	9	25	15	9	11	13	7	12	8
Ariz.	22	38	27	33	22	38	12	18	18	12	16	14
Ark. [10]	99	1	98	2	95	5	34	1	34	1	34	1
Calif. [10]	49	31	55	25	57	23	20	19	25	15	26	14
Colo. [10]	28	37	39	26	30	35	13	22	16	19	17	18
Conn.	58	93	118	33	91	60	13	23	29	7	22	14
Del. [10]	20	21	25	16	26	15	10	11	13	8	13	8
Fla. [10]	78	42	86	34	93	27	25	14	27	12	30	9
Ga.	151	29	155	24	156	24	48	8	51	5	52	4
Hawaii	35	16	35	16	41	10	17	8	18	7	18	7
Idaho	19	51	27	43	22	48	12	23	13	22	15	20
Ill.	88	89	101	76	94	83	29	30	34	25	34	25
Ind. [10]	27	73	56	44	48	52	21	29	23	27	28	22
Iowa [10]	45	55	61	39	59	41	22	28	26	24	26	24
Kans.	45	80	53	72	65	60	13	27	14	26	19	21
Ky. [10]	80	20	78	22	78	22	29	9	30	8	29	9
La.	101	4	101	4	101	4	38	1	38	1	38	1
Maine	73	78	91	59	89	62	13	19	14	19	12	21
Md.	121	21	126	15	125	15	33	10	39	8	39	8
Mass.	184	51	190	45	192	44	32	8	33	7	34	6
Mich.	60	50	66	44	68	42	19	19	24	14	24	14
Minn.	78	56	103	31	100	34	38	28	38	28	48	19
Miss.	119	2	119	3	117	3	50	2	50	2	50	2
Mo. [10]	97	65	114	49	112	51	21	13	23	11	22	12
Mont. [10]	54	46	67	33	57	43	27	23	30	20	25	25
Nebr.	(11)	(11)	(11)	(11)	(11)	(11)	(11)	(11)	(11)	(11)	(11)	(11)
Nev. [10]	25	15	31	9	35	5	14	6	17	3	17	3
N.H.	137	263	167	233	175	219	10	14	12	12	12	12
N.J.	66	14	49	31	54	26	29	10	29	10	27	13
N. Mex.	50	20	51	19	48	22	30	12	29	13	33	9
N.Y.	69	79	88	62	87	58	21	37	26	34	21	36
N.C.	85	35	111	9	114	6	35	15	49	1	47	3
N. Dak. [10]	26	76	40	62	50	50	11	40	17	34	18	32
Ohio [10]	58	41	59	40	62	37	16	17	21	12	21	12
Okla. [10]	74	27	76	25	79	22	38	10	39	9	39	9
Oreg. [10]	33	27	38	22	37	23	18	12	22	7	24	6
Pa. [10]	94	107	114	89	118	84	26	24	29	20	28	20
R.I.	72	27	83	17	83	17	37	13	46	4	45	5
S.C. [10]	103	21	107	17	111	12	43	3	44	2	43	3
S. Dak.	35	35	33	37	22	48	18	17	19	16	12	23
Tenn.	51	48	63	35	66	32	19	13	20	12	23	9
Tex. [10]	132	17	134	16	131	19	28	3	28	3	27	4
Utah [10]	31	44	40	35	35	40	13	16	15	14	17	12
Vt.	58	91	65	75	75	74	7	23	12	18	9	21
Va.	65	20	78	17	76	21	34	6	35	5	35	5
Wash. [10]	57	41	62	36	62	36	31	18	30	19	29	20
W. Va. [10]	57	43	86	14	91	9	24	10	26	8	28	6
Wis. [10]	62	37	63	36	66	33	15	18	19	14	22	11
Wyo. [10]	17	44	29	32	29	32	13	17	15	15	12	18

– Represents zero.   [1] Status as of December 1973; includes elections held and vacancies filled in 1973.   [2] Excludes 1 Independent each for Alaska, Miss., R. I., Vt., and Wyo.; 2 Independents for Mass.; 15 Independents for Va.; 3 vacancies for Mass.; 2 vacancies each for N.Y. and Pa.; and 1 vacancy each for Mo. and Tex.   [3] Status as of late 1975; includes elections held and vacancies filled in 1975.   [4] Excludes 1 Independent each for Alaska, Maine, Tenn., and Wyo.; 3 Independents for Mass., 5 Independents for Va., and 10 Independents for Vt.; 1 vacancy for Ga. and 2 vacancies for Mass.   [5] Excludes 1 Independent each for Miss., N.Y., Tenn., Vt., and Wyo.; 3 Independents each for Mass. and Va.; 1 vacancy each for Md., Mass., Miss., Pa., and S.C.; 4 vacancies for N.Y., and 6 vacancies for N.H.   [6] Status as of January 1978; includes elections held and vacancies filled in 1977.   [7] Excludes 1 Independent each for Fla., Minn., N.J., and Tenn.; 2 vacancies for N.Y. and 1 vacancy for Calif.   [8] Excludes 1 Independent each for Fla., Minn., N.J., Oreg., and Tenn., and 1 vacancy for Pa.   [9] Excludes 1 Independent each for Ala., Fla., and Tenn.; 2 vacancies for Pa., and 3 vacancies for N.Y.   [10] Upper House members serve 4-year terms, some elected every 2 years.   [11] Single chamber (unicameral body) of 49 members, elected without party designation.

Source: The Council of State Governments, Lexington, Kentucky, *Book of the States*, and its *Supplement I*, both biennial.

No. 833. BLACK ELECTED OFFICIALS, BY OFFICE, 1970 TO 1978, AND BY REGIONS AND STATES, 1978

[As of April, except as indicated. As of July 1978, no Black elected officials had been identified in Idaho, Montana, North Dakota, South Dakota, Vermont, or Wyoming. For composition of regions, see fig. I, inside front cover]

YEAR, REGION, AND STATE	Total	U.S. and State legislatures[1]	City and county offices[2]	Law enforcement[3]	Education[4]	STATE	Total	U.S. and State legislatures[1]	City and county offices[2]	Law enforcement[3]	Education[4]
1970 (Feb.)	1,472	182	715	213	362	Ky	64	4	40	8	12
1972 (Mar.)	2,264	224	1,108	263	669	La	334	10	188	41	95
1973	2,621	256	1,264	334	767	Maine	3	1	2	-	-
1974	2,991	256	1,602	340	793	Md	86	[8]19	53	10	4
1975	3,503	299	1,878	387	939	Mass	22	[10]10	5	-	7
1976	3,979	299	2,274	412	994	Mich	256	[9][11]19	115	29	93
1977 (July)	4,311	316	2,497	447	1,051	Minn	8	2	-	3	3
						Miss	303	4	184	54	61
1978, July	4,503	316	2,595	454	1,138						
						Mo	137	[8]16	88	19	14
Northeast	529	57	188	72	212	Nebr	8	2	2	-	4
No. Central	966	91	541	99	235	Nev	6	3	-	1	2
South	2,733	141	1,784	223	585	N.H	1	1	-	-	-
West	275	27	82	60	106	N.J	146	5	74	-	67
						N. Mex	4	1	2	-	1
Ala	207	15	132	37	23	N.Y	183	[9]16	31	29	107
Alaska	2	-	1	-	1						
Ariz	13	2	4	2	5	N.C	237	6	161	6	64
Ark	223	4	135	1	83	Ohio	154	[8]13	93	18	30
Calif	213	[5][6]12	64	47	90	Okla	68	4	45	1	18
Colo	15	[6]4	4	4	3	Oreg	6	1	1	2	2
Conn	45	[7]7	26	3	9	Pa	123	[8]16	46	40	21
Del	14	3	9	-	2	R.I	6	1	4	-	1
						S.C	229	13	122	20	74
D.C	255	[8]1	247	-	7						
Fla	91	3	72	6	10	Tenn	117	[8]12	87	8	10
Ga	228	23	149	9	47	Tex	171	[8]14	65	17	75
Hawaii	1	1	-	-	-	Utah	1	1	-	-	-
Ill	279	[9]22	170	21	66	Va	90	5	81	4	-
Ind	67	6	49	6	6	Wash	14	2	6	4	2
Iowa	9	2	1	1	5	W. Va	16	1	14	1	-
Kans	34	6	16	1	11	Wis	14	3	7	1	3

- Represents zero.   [1] Includes elected State administrators and directors of State agencies.   [2] County commissioners and councilmen, mayors, vice mayors, aldermen, regional officials, and other.   [3] Judges, magistrates, constables, marshals, sheriffs, justices of the peace, and other.   [4] College boards, school boards, and other.   [5] Includes 3 U.S. Representatives and 1 State Superintendent of Public Instruction.   [6] Includes 1 Lieutenant Governor.   [7] Includes 1 State Treasurer.   [8] Includes 1 U.S. Representative.   [9] Includes 2 U.S. Representatives.   [10] Includes 1 U.S. Senator.   [11] Includes 1 Secretary of State.

Source: Joint Center for Political Studies, Washington, D.C., National Roster of Black Elected Officials, annual.

No. 834. VOTER REGISTRATION IN 11 SOUTHERN STATES, BY RACE: 1960 TO 1976

In thousands, except percent. For 1960 to 1970, population 21 yr. and over, except Ga., 18 yr. and over; beginning 1975, population 18 yr. and over for all Southern States. For voting age population, see table 840]

YEAR AND RACE	Total	Ala.	Ark.	Fla.	Ga.	La.	Miss.	N.C.	S.C.	Tenn.	Tex.	Va.
1960: White	12,276	860	518	1,819	1,020	993	478	1,861	481	1,300	2,079	867
Black	1,463	66	73	183	180	159	22	210	58	185	227	100
Percent White[1]	61.1	63.6	60.9	69.3	56.8	76.9	63.9	92.1	57.1	73.0	42.5	46.1
Percent Black[1 2]	29.1	13.7	38.0	39.4	29.3	31.1	5.2	39.1	13.7	59.1	35.5	23.1
1964: White	14,264	946	621	2,200	1,340	1,037	525	1,942	703	1,297	2,602	1,050
Black	2,164	111	95	300	270	165	29	258	144	218	375	200
1966: White	14,310	1,192	598	2,093	1,378	1,072	471	1,654	718	1,375	2,600	1,159
Black	2,689	250	115	303	300	243	175	282	191	225	400	205
1968: White	15,702	1,117	640	2,195	1,524	1,133	691	1,579	587	1,448	3,532	1,256
Black	3,112	273	130	292	344	305	251	305	189	228	540	255
1970: White	16,985	1,311	728	2,495	1,615	1,143	690	1,640	668	1,600	3,599	1,496
Black	3,357	315	153	302	395	319	286	305	221	242	550	269
1975: White	19,429	1,486	797	3,119	1,534	1,338	866	1,919	660	1,697	4,252	1,762
Black	[3]3,835	[3]307	[3]200	356	[3]556	393	[3]286	355	222	[3]262	[3]610	[3]289
1976: White	21,690	1,544	817	3,480	1,703	1,445	[4]866	2,137	828	1,886	5,191	1,794
Black	[3]4,149	[3]321	[3]204	410	[3]598	421	[3][4]286	396	285	[3]371	[3]640	[3]317
Percent White[1]	67.9	79.3	62.6	61.3	65.9	78.4	80.0	69.2	58.4	73.7	69.1	61.6
Percent Black[1]	63.1	58.4	94.0	61.1	74.8	63.0	60.7	54.8	56.5	66.4	65.0	54.7

[1] Of voting age population.   [2] Includes other minority races.   [3] Estimated.   [4] 1975 data.

Source: Voter Education Project, Inc., Atlanta, Ga., Voter Registration in the South, issued irregularly.

No. 835. Participation in Elections for President and U.S. Representatives: 1930 to 1976

[Population estimated, as of **November.** Resident population 21 years old and over, 1930–1970, except as noted, and 18 years old and over thereafter; includes Armed Forces. Prior to 1960, excludes Alaska and Hawaii; beginning 1964, vote cast for President includes D.C.]

YEAR	Resident population (incl. aliens) of voting age [1] 1,000	For President [2] (1,000)	Percent of voting age population	For U.S. Representatives [2] (1,000)	Percent of voting age population	YEAR	Resident population (incl. aliens) of voting age [1] 1,000	For President [2] (1,000)	Percent of voting age population	For U.S. Representatives [2] (1,000)	Percent of voting age population
1930	73,623	(X)	(X)	24,777	33.7	1954	102,075	(X)	(X)	42,580	41.7
1932	75,768	39,732	52.4	37,657	49.7	1956	104,515	62,027	59.3	58,426	55.9
1934	77,997	(X)	(X)	32,256	41.4	1958	106,447	(X)	(X)	45,818	43.0
1936	80,174	45,643	56.9	42,886	53.5	1960	109,672	68,838	62.8	64,133	58.5
1938	82,354	(X)	(X)	36,236	44.0	1962	112,852	(X)	(X)	51,267	45.4
1940	84,728	49,900	58.9	46,951	55.4	1964	114,090	70,645	61.9	65,895	57.8
1942	86,465	(X)	(X)	28,074	32.5	1966	116,638	(X)	(X)	52,908	45.4
1944	85,654	47,977	56.0	45,103	52.7	1968	120,285	73,212	60.9	66,288	55.1
1946	92,659	(X)	(X)	34,398	37.1	1970	124,498	(X)	(X)	54,173	43.5
1948	95,573	48,794	51.1	45,933	48.1	1972	140,068	77,719	55.5	71,270	51.1
1950	98,134	(X)	(X)	40,342	41.1	1974	145,035	(X)	(X)	52,391	36.3
1952	99,929	61,551	61.6	57,571	57.6	1976	150,041	81,556	54.3	74,262	49.6

X Not applicable.   [1] Population 18 and over in Georgia, 1944–1970, and in Kentucky, 1956–1970; 18 and over in Alaska and 20 and over in Hawaii, 1960–1970.   [2] Source, beginning 1960: Elections Research Center, Washington, D.C., *America Votes*, biennial (copyright).

Source: Except as noted, U.S. Bureau of the Census, *Current Population Reports*, series P-25, Nos. 311 and 626; and, through 1958, U.S. Congress, Clerk of the House, *Statistics of the Presidential and Congressional Election.*

No. 836. Participation in Presidential Elections, by Population Characteristics: 1968 to 1976

[As of **November.** Covers civilian noninstitutional population, 18 years old and over, except for 1968, 21 years old and over (see also footnote 1, table 835). Includes aliens. Figures are based on a population sample (see text, p. 1) and differ from those in tables 835 and 841 based on population estimates and official vote counts. Differences in percentages may also be due to overreporting of voting (reluctance of some persons in the sample who actually did not vote to so report)]

CHARACTERISTIC	1968 Persons of voting age (mil.)	1968 Persons reporting they voted Total (mil.)	1968 Persons reporting they voted Percent	1968 Percent reporting not voting [1]	1972 Persons of voting age (mil.)	1972 Persons reporting they voted Total (mil.)	1972 Persons reporting they voted Percent	1972 Percent reporting not voting [1]	1976 Persons of voting age (mil.)	1976 Persons reporting they voted Total (mil.)	1976 Persons reporting they voted Percent	1976 Percent reporting not voting [1]
Total	116.5	79.0	67.8	32.2	136.2	85.8	63.0	37.0	146.5	86.7	59.2	40.8
Male	54.5	38.0	69.8	30.2	63.8	40.9	64.1	35.9	69.0	41.1	59.6	40.4
Female	62.1	41.0	66.0	34.0	72.4	44.9	62.0	38.0	77.6	45.6	58.8	41.2
White	104.5	72.2	69.1	30.9	121.2	78.2	64.5	35.5	129.3	78.8	60.9	39.1
Black	10.9	6.3	57.6	42.4	13.5	7.0	52.1	47.9	14.9	7.3	48.7	51.3
Spanish origin [2]	(NA)	(NA)	(NA)	(NA)	5.6	2.1	37.4	62.6	6.6	2.1	31.8	68.2
18–20 years old	.4	.1	33.3	66.7	11.0	5.3	48.3	51.7	12.1	4.6	38.0	62.0
21–24 years old	11.2	5.7	51.1	48.9	13.6	6.9	50.7	49.3	14.8	6.8	45.6	54.4
25–34 years old	23.2	14.5	62.5	37.5	26.9	16.1	59.7	40.3	31.5	17.5	55.4	44.6
35–44 years old	22.9	16.2	70.8	29.2	22.2	14.7	66.3	33.7	22.8	14.4	63.3	36.7
45–64 years old	40.4	30.2	74.9	25.1	42.3	30.0	70.8	29.2	43.3	29.8	68.7	31.3
65 years and over	18.5	12.2	65.8	34.2	20.1	12.7	63.5	36.5	22.0	13.7	62.2	37.8
Median age [3] yr	45.2	46.7	(X)	(X)	42.4	44.9	(X)	(X)	41.5	45.1	(X)	(X)
Residence:												
Metropolitan	75.8	51.5	68.0	32.0	99.2	63.8	64.3	35.7	99.6	58.9	59.2	40.8
Nonmetropolitan	40.8	27.5	67.3	32.7	37.0	22.0	59.4	40.6	47.0	27.8	59.1	40.9
North and West [4]	81.6	58.0	71.0	29.0	93.7	62.2	66.4	33.6	99.4	60.8	61.2	38.8
South [4]	34.9	21.0	60.1	39.9	42.6	23.6	55.4	44.6	47.1	25.9	54.9	45.1
Sch'l yr. completed:												
8 yr. or less	30.4	16.6	54.5	45.5	28.1	13.3	47.4	52.6	24.9	11.0	44.1	55.9
9–11 yr	20.4	12.5	61.3	38.7	22.3	11.6	52.0	48.0	22.2	10.5	47.2	52.8
12 yr	39.7	28.8	72.5	27.5	50.7	33.2	65.4	34.6	55.7	33.1	59.4	40.6
More than 12 yr	26.0	21.1	81.2	18.8	35.1	27.7	78.8	21.2	43.7	32.2	73.5	26.5
Employed	70.0	49.8	71.1	28.9	80.2	52.9	66.0	34.0	86.0	53.3	62.0	38.0
Unemployed	1.9	1.0	52.1	47.9	3.7	1.9	49.9	50.1	6.4	2.8	43.7	56.3
Not in labor force	44.7	28.2	63.2	36.8	52.3	31.0	59.3	40.7	54.1	30.6	56.5	43.5

NA Not available.   X Not applicable.   [1] Includes do not know and not reported.   [2] Persons of Spanish origin may be of any race.   [3] For definition of median, see p. xii.   [4] See fig. I, inside front cover.

Source: U.S. Bureau of the Census, *Current Population Reports*, series P-20, Nos. 192, 253, and 322.

No. 837. Participation in National Elections, 1964 to 1976, and by Length of Residence, 1976

[As of November. See headnote, table 836]

YEAR AND LENGTH OF RESIDENCE	Persons of voting age[1] (mil.)	PERSONS REPORTING THEY REGISTERED		PERSONS REPORTING THEY VOTED		PERSONS REPORTING THEY DID NOT VOTE[1]			
		Total (mil.)	Percent	Total (mil.)	Percent	Total[2] (mil.)	Registered (mil.)	Not registered	
								Number (mil.)	Percent
1964	110.6	(NA)	(NA)	76.7	69.3	33.9	(NA)	(NA)	(NA)
1966	112.8	79.3	70.3	62.5	55.4	50.3	16.8	33.1	29.3
1968	116.5	86.6	74.3	79.0	67.8	37.6	7.6	30.0	25.7
1970	120.7	82.2	68.1	65.9	54.6	54.8	16.3	38.5	31.9
1972	136.2	98.5	72.3	85.8	63.0	50.4	12.7	37.7	27.7
1974	141.3	87.9	62.2	63.2	44.7	78.1	24.7	53.4	37.8
1976	146.5	97.8	66.7	86.7	59.2	59.9	11.1	48.8	33.3
1976, total citizens	142.2	97.8	68.8	86.7	61.0	55.5	11.1	44.4	31.2
Less than 1 year's residence	23.9	12.9	53.7	10.6	44.4	13.3	2.2	11.1	46.3
1–2 years	20.1	12.9	64.2	11.4	56.6	8.7	1.5	7.2	35.8
3–5 years	23.8	17.1	71.7	15.3	64.2	8.5	1.8	6.7	28.3
6 years or more	67.7	54.4	80.5	49.0	72.4	18.7	5.4	13.2	19.5
Not reported	6.6	.5	6.8	.4	5.8	6.2	.1	6.2	93.2

NA Not available. [1] Figures include aliens, except as specified.
[2] Includes "do not know" and not reported.

No. 838. Percent Nonvoters in National Elections, by Reasons for Non-Participation: 1976

[See headnote, table 836]

ITEM	Total[1]	White	Black	Spanish origin[2]	ITEM	Total[1]	White	Black	Spanish origin[2]
Total	100.0	100.0	100.0	100.0	Did not vote—Con.				
Voted	59.2	60.9	48.7	31.8	Not registered[4]	33.3	31.7	41.5	62.2
Did not vote[3]	40.8	39.1	51.3	68.2	Unable to register	3.0	2.5	1.5	25.3
Registered	7.5	7.4	9.7	6.0	Not a citizen	5.7	5.4	8.6	9.4
Unable to vote	4.0	3.9	5.1	2.8	Other reasons	17.4	17.0	20.6	19.8
Other reasons	3.0	3.0	3.3	2.6	Reason not reported	1.2	1.0	2.5	1.6
Reason not reported	.6	.5	1.4	.6					

[1] Includes other races, not shown separately.
[2] Persons of Spanish origin may be of any race.
[3] Includes persons who did not report on voting.
[4] Includes persons who did not report on registration, not shown separately.

No. 839. Reported Registration As Percent of Voting-Age Population, by Selected Characteristics: 1968 to 1976

[See headnote, table 836]

CHARACTERISTIC	PRESIDENTIAL ELECTIONS			CONGRESSIONAL ELECTIONS		CHARACTERISTIC	PRESIDENTIAL ELECTIONS			CONGRESSIONAL ELECTIONS	
	1968	1972	1976	1970	1974		1968	1972	1976	1970	1974
Total	74.3	72.3	66.7	68.1	62.2	18–20 years old	44.2	58.1	47.1	41.3	36.4
						21–24 years old	56.4	59.5	54.8	40.8	45.3
White	75.4	73.4	68.3	69.1	63.5	25–34 years old	68.4	68.4	62.3	59.4	54.7
Black	66.2	65.5	58.5	60.8	54.9	35–44 years old	76.5	74.8	69.8	71.2	66.7
Spanish origin[1]	(NA)	44.4	37.8	(NA)	34.9						
Male	76.0	73.1	67.1	69.6	62.8	45–54 years old	80.8	79.3	74.3	76.7	72.5
Female	72.8	71.6	66.4	66.8	61.7	55–64 years old	81.4	80.2	76.8	78.6	75.1
						65–74 years old	79.5	78.5	74.0	76.4	73.0
North and West[2]	76.5	73.9	67.7	70.0	63.3	75 years and over	69.2	70.7	66.9	69.2	65.2
South[2]	69.2	68.7	64.6	63.8	59.8						

NA Not available. [1] Persons of Spanish origin may be of any race. [2] See fig. I, inside front cover.

Source of tables 837–839: U.S. Bureau of the Census, *Current Population Reports*, series P-20, Nos. 143, 174, 192, 228, 253, 293, and 322.

No. 840. Estimated Population of Voting Age—States: 1960 to 1978

[In thousands. As of November. Includes Armed Forces stationed in each State, aliens, and institutional population]

STATE	1960 [1] Total	1960 [1] Black	1964 [1]	1968 [1]	1970 [1] Total	1970 [1] Black	1972 [2]	1976 [2] Total	1976 [2] Black	1978 [2] Total	1978 [2] Black
U.S.	109,674	10,098	114,085	120,285	124,498	11,935	140,068	150,127	15,398	155,492	16,198
Ala	1,850	480	1,919	1,993	2,042	452	2,314	2,506	550	2,604	576
Alaska	[3]139	[3]4	[3]153	[3]166	[3]178	[3]6	197	256	(s)	272	(s)
Ariz	760	23	878	975	1,056	26	1,295	1,527	33	1,642	44
Ark	1,049	191	1,108	1,143	1,180	174	1,354	1,471	217	1,535	209
Calif	9,895	420	10,789	11,771	12,376	760	13,969	15,326	1,079	16,052	1,141
Colo	1,056	23	1,142	1,251	1,328	36	1,586	1,792	54	1,900	63
Conn	1,608	61	1,724	1,826	1,886	94	2,089	2,213	115	2,279	120
Del	272	34	292	314	326	40	378	404	55	418	56
D.C	513	245	513	495	483	314	530	507	348	499	329
Fla	3,176	468	3,623	4,124	4,451	529	5,242	6,116	671	6,502	736
Ga	[2]2,507	[2]614	[2]2,634	[2]2,851	[2]2,985	[2]677	3,098	3,391	800	3,543	830
Hawaii	[4]371	[4]3	[4]404	[4]439	[4]473	[4]5	536	605	(s)	637	10
Idaho	377	1	379	397	418	1	491	559	(s)	597	(s)
Ill	6,298	584	6,422	6,667	6,795	747	7,532	7,791	953	7,975	998
Ind	2,799	149	2,845	3,003	3,104	185	3,496	3,653	242	3,752	256
Iowa	1,666	14	1,625	1,673	1,712	16	1,936	2,007	26	2,057	28
Kans	1,334	51	1,318	1,346	1,380	56	1,553	1,639	66	1,694	71
Ky	[2]1,950	[2]134	[2]1,964	[2]2,063	[2]2,136	[2]140	2,204	2,378	160	2,457	165
La	1,813	512	1,894	2,002	2,058	534	2,373	2,567	668	2,674	717
Maine	588	2	585	592	601	1	683	743	(s)	776	(s)
Md	1,867	284	2,065	2,271	2,372	372	2,690	2,885	523	2,991	589
Mass	3,266	66	3,349	3,459	3,538	92	3,968	4,133	146	4,230	147
Mich	4,598	402	4,719	5,032	5,200	530	5,868	6,220	709	6,405	736
Minn	2,017	12	2,050	2,154	2,248	18	2,546	2,730	24	2,828	28
Miss	1,177	418	1,207	1,229	1,253	379	1,435	1,554	471	1,612	494
Mo	2,706	220	2,709	2,813	2,913	254	3,228	3,386	311	3,471	366
Mont	395	1	402	403	410	1	469	516	(s)	538	(s)
Nebr	868	16	879	881	906	20	1,030	1,084	32	1,117	31
Nev	184	8	260	284	303	14	357	425	24	461	26
N.H	376	1	398	427	452	1	520	578	(s)	614	(s)
N.J	3,919	302	4,142	4,358	4,507	412	4,997	5,187	555	5,305	591
N. Mex	504	9	530	539	561	9	671	767	14	815	13
N.Y	10,965	890	11,324	11,450	11,543	1,229	12,663	12,863	1,622	12,967	1,622
N.C	2,585	537	2,723	2,921	3,043	569	3,496	3,805	722	3,964	763
N. Dak	357	1	362	354	360	1	413	442	(s)	461	(s)
Ohio	5,888	446	5,962	6,252	6,419	525	7,123	7,420	664	7,589	697
Okla	1,431	82	1,471	1,540	1,605	88	1,809	1,963	129	2,043	131
Oreg	1,079	10	1,141	1,231	1,308	14	1,503	1,658	18	1,750	23
Pa	7,122	496	7,100	7,273	7,412	567	8,193	8,455	688	8,611	707
R.I	540	10	545	573	596	13	671	669	18	678	19
S.C	1,272	371	1,333	1,427	1,487	377	1,748	1,923	504	2,011	547
S. Dak	395	1	395	384	389	1	447	471	(s)	484	(s)
Tenn	2,110	313	2,212	2,325	2,410	323	2,758	2,974	408	3,107	426
Tex	5,605	644	5,889	6,327	6,658	735	7,655	8,603	985	9,063	1,040
Utah	479	2	512	551	583	3	699	780	(s)	827	(s)
Vt	231	(z)	232	252	265	(z)	306	330	(s)	344	(s)
Va	2,349	434	2,539	2,717	2,823	458	3,202	3,556	580	3,736	638
Wash	1,727	27	1,754	1,975	2,078	38	2,306	2,546	47	2,651	58
W. Va	1,075	48	1,049	1,061	1,077	37	1,221	1,293	43	1,341	41
Wis	2,372	39	2,434	2,543	2,615	60	2,991	3,193	85	3,319	89
Wyo	192	1	192	190	198	1	229	269	(s)	290	(s)

S   Data not shown where fewer than 10,000 Black population (all ages) living in the State.
Z   Fewer than 500.
[1] Population age 21 and over, except as noted.
[2] Population age 18 and over.
[3] Population age 19 and over.
[4] Population age 20 and over.

Source: U.S. Bureau of the Census, *Current Population Reports*, series P-25, Nos. 626 and 732.

No. 841. Percent of Voting-Age Population Casting Votes—States: 1960 to 1976

[As of **November**. For total resident voting-age population, see table 840]

STATE	PERCENT CASTING VOTES FOR PRESIDENTIAL ELECTORS					PERCENT CASTING VOTES FOR U.S. REPRESENTATIVES						
	1960	1964	1968	1972	1976	1960	1964	1966	1968	1970	1972	1974	1976
U.S.[1]	62.8	61.9	60.9	55.5	54.3	58.5	57.8	45.4	55.1	43.5	51.1	36.3	49.6
Ala	30.8	35.9	52.7	43.4	47.2	23.7	32.2	35.8	46.1	36.3	42.0	23.4	39.3
Alaska	43.7	44.0	50.0	48.3	48.3	42.5	43.9	41.7	48.4	45.0	48.4	45.0	46.2
Ariz	52.4	54.8	49.9	48.1	48.6	49.6	52.5	39.7	47.6	38.1	45.9	37.7	47.7
Ark.[2]	40.9	50.6	54.2	48.1	52.2	6.6	11.7	26.1	26.1	14.7	13.8	29.8	22.9
Calif	65.8	63.9	61.0	59.9	51.3	62.6	61.8	54.8	58.9	51.1	58.1	39.9	48.6
Colo	69.2	68.0	64.8	60.1	60.4	67.7	66.3	54.7	62.4	48.0	57.6	45.5	57.0
Conn	76.1	70.7	68.8	66.3	62.4	75.8	70.1	56.6	66.1	56.8	64.7	50.2	60.9
Del	72.3	68.9	68.3	62.3	58.4	71.5	68.0	54.2	64.0	49.2	59.8	41.1	53.2
D.C	(X)	38.7	34.5	43.2	33.3	(X)	(X)	(X)	(X)	(X)	30.1	20.2	31.6
Fla.[2]	48.6	51.2	53.1	49.3	51.5	39.3	39.1	27.5	42.9	28.1	36.9	18.1	34.1
Ga	29.3	43.3	43.9	37.9	43.3	22.9	31.7	31.3	33.1	29.5	28.8	25.3	37.0
Hawaii	49.8	51.3	53.8	50.4	48.1	49.2	56.8	49.9	55.4	44.0	51.3	45.2	48.5
Idaho	79.7	77.2	73.4	63.2	61.6	77.0	75.1	64.6	69.7	56.1	61.4	47.4	61.2
Ill	75.5	73.2	69.3	62.7	60.6	73.1	71.2	57.1	66.3	51.4	58.2	37.3	56.0
Ind	76.3	73.5	70.7	60.8	60.8	75.9	72.9	57.6	67.9	55.7	60.4	48.4	57.6
Iowa	76.5	72.9	69.8	63.3	63.7	73.6	70.3	53.6	67.2	45.5	61.8	46.1	61.9
Kans	69.6	65.1	64.8	59.0	58.4	65.3	61.7	50.2	60.7	52.2	56.6	49.1	55.5
Ky	57.7	53.3	51.2	48.4	49.1	46.8	48.6	33.9	41.9	22.2	44.7	29.7	41.6
La	44.6	47.3	54.8	44.3	49.8	28.7	31.7	28.0	31.4	17.6	28.6	22.4	39.5
Maine	71.7	65.1	66.4	61.1	65.0	69.5	63.2	53.1	64.9	52.9	60.5	49.5	63.7
Md	56.5	54.1	54.4	50.3	49.9	52.5	49.0	35.2	44.9	37.3	45.3	34.1	45.6
Mass	75.0	70.0	67.4	62.0	61.6	69.2	63.0	53.4	59.5	50.9	54.4	41.9	56.7
Mich	72.2	67.9	65.7	59.5	58.7	69.8	64.8	48.5	60.5	49.3	55.8	41.5	55.2
Minn	76.4	75.8	73.8	68.4	71.4	75.1	74.2	58.6	71.2	59.6	66.4	46.3	65.7
Miss	25.3	33.9	53.3	45.0	49.5	21.9	29.9	31.5	36.5	24.9	41.0	20.3	41.0
Mo	71.5	67.1	64.3	57.5	57.7	68.1	65.4	38.0	61.6	41.1	56.8	36.6	56.3
Mont	70.2	69.3	68.1	67.7	63.7	68.9	68.8	64.3	65.4	60.3	67.2	51.5	62.2
Nebr	70.6	66.5	60.9	56.0	56.1	66.9	63.8	54.6	59.3	49.5	55.2	42.4	55.5
Nev	58.3	52.1	54.3	50.9	47.5	56.3	50.3	47.7	50.8	45.4	50.6	43.1	47.0
N.H	78.7	72.4	69.6	64.2	58.8	75.7	70.2	56.1	66.2	47.3	60.5	39.8	56.3
N.J	70.8	68.8	66.0	60.0	58.1	67.8	65.7	49.6	61.9	46.6	56.7	41.1	54.2
N. Mex	61.7	62.0	60.7	57.6	54.6	59.8	67.8	50.2	57.5	50.9	55.7	44.1	52.3
N.Y	66.5	64.8	59.9	56.6	50.8	64.4	61.1	49.3	54.0	47.2	52.2	38.5	46.6
N.C	52.9	52.3	54.4	43.4	44.1	50.4	47.9	32.8	47.9	30.6	38.6	26.9	41.3
N. Dak	78.0	71.4	70.0	67.9	67.2	71.8	68.8	55.2	67.3	58.4	65.1	55.0	65.6
Ohio	70.7	66.6	63.3	57.5	55.4	65.3	62.6	46.0	58.2	47.4	53.9	40.4	51.8
Okla.[2]	63.1	63.4	61.2	56.9	55.6	58.6	57.1	42.7	52.6	35.1	45.2	27.1	54.4
Oreg	72.0	68.9	66.6	61.7	62.1	70.6	67.3	56.1	63.9	49.9	57.9	47.6	55.9
Pa	70.3	67.9	65.3	56.1	54.7	69.6	63.7	55.5	62.9	48.8	54.5	40.6	52.4
R.I	75.1	71.6	65.2	62.0	61.5	72.6	68.5	58.1	63.7	54.6	57.8	46.5	58.1
S.C	30.4	39.4	46.7	38.6	41.7	25.8	32.9	26.5	44.0	28.7	36.1	28.1	40.7
S. Dak	77.6	74.2	73.3	68.8	63.8	76.2	72.8	58.5	70.7	60.4	67.3	59.4	62.6
Tenn	49.8	51.7	53.7	43.6	49.6	30.5	46.8	35.5	43.6	41.0	40.0	31.5	42.1
Tex	41.2	44.6	48.7	45.4	47.3	36.4	44.4	20.9	37.9	27.5	37.7	18.4	42.6
Utah	78.2	78.4	76.7	68.5	69.4	77.1	77.3	58.0	75.5	64.0	67.7	55.7	69.7
Vt	72.4	70.3	64.1	61.1	56.9	71.9	70.5	56.6	62.4	57.6	60.8	44.6	56.0
Va	32.8	41.1	50.1	45.5	47.7	27.2	36.6	26.2	46.7	32.1	39.7	27.4	41.1
Wash	71.9	71.8	66.0	63.8	61.1	65.1	68.3	51.3	61.0	49.2	56.5	40.6	56.0
W. Va	77.9	75.5	71.1	62.4	58.1	76.3	73.4	47.1	67.1	40.9	59.1	33.5	51.3
Wis	72.9	69.5	66.5	62.0	65.9	70.1	67.7	46.5	64.5	50.7	60.2	38.7	61.5
Wyo	73.3	74.3	67.0	63.6	58.1	70.0	72.5	64.9	64.9	58.7	63.9	51.8	56.5

X Not applicable.
[1] Excludes District of Columbia except for presidential elections of 1964, 1968, 1972, and 1976.
[2] State law does not require tabulation of votes for unopposed candidates.

Source: Compiled by U.S. Bureau of the Census. Population data from U.S. Bureau of the Census, *Current Population Reports*, series P-25, No. 626; and votes cast from Elections Research Center, Washington, D.C., *America Votes*, biennial (copyright).

No. 842. Voter Registration and Persons Voting, by States: 1972 and 1976

[Total persons voting restricted to number of ballots recorded by Secretaries of State as having been cast. For total resident voting-age population, see table 840]

STATE	1972					1976				
	Persons registered		Persons voting			Persons registered		Persons voting		
				Percent of—					Percent of—	
	Total (1,000)	Percent of voting age population	Total (1,000)	Persons registered	Voting age population	Total (1,000)	Percent of voting age population	Total (1,000)	Persons registered	Voting age population
U.S.	92,702	73.9	78,902	75.7	56.3	105,837	71.4	82,286	77.7	54.8
Ala	1,764	77.6	¹ 1,051	59.6	43.5	1,865	74.4	² 1,183	63.4	47.2
Alaska	149	74.5	99	66.2	48.2	207	80.9	128	61.8	50.0
Ariz	862	69.6	648	75.2	50.5	980	64.2	765	78.1	50.1
Ark	1,010	77.1	² 651	64.5	47.9	1,021	69.4	² 768	75.2	52.2
Calif	10,466	75.1	8,596	82.1	59.1	9,982	65.1	8,137	81.5	53.1
Colo	1,220	78.3	954	78.2	60.2	1,349	75.3	² 1,082	80.2	60.4
Conn	1,648	78.3	1,409	85.5	66.3	1,669	75.4	1,408	84.4	63.6
Del	293	78.9	² 236	80.5	62.4	301	74.5	² 236	78.4	58.4
D.C	305	58.9	166	54.3	30.8	268	52.9	171	63.8	33.7
Fla	3,487	68.3	² 2,583	74.1	49.3	4,094	66.9	² 3,151	77.0	51.5
Ga	2,043	65.8	¹ 1,179	57.7	37.9	2,302	67.9	² 1,467	63.7	43.3
Hawaii	338	63.6	287	84.8	50.4	363	60.0	309	85.1	51.1
Idaho	397	82.9	² 310	78.2	63.1	520	93.0	355	68.3	63.5
Ill	6,215	82.4	4,883	78.6	62.7	6,252	80.2	4,839	77.4	62.1
Ind	3,019	86.0	² 2,126	70.4	60.8	3,010	82.4	2,279	75.7	62.4
Iowa	(³)	(X)	² 1,226	(X)	63.3	1,407	70.1	² 1,279	90.9	63.7
Kans	(³)	(X)	⁴ 922	(X)	59.0	1,113	67.9	² 958	86.1	58.4
Ky	1,455	65.9	² 1,067	73.4	48.4	1,713	72.1	² 1,167	68.1	49.1
La	1,785	76.3	⁴ 1,122	62.8	44.3	1,866	72.7	² 1,278	68.5	49.8
Maine	616	92.4	¹ 421	68.4	61.1	696	93.7	¹ 486	69.8	65.4
Md	1,816	67.6	² 1,354	74.6	50.3	1,950	67.6	² 1,440	73.8	49.9
Mass	3,096	78.3	⁻ 2,508	81.0	62.0	2,912	70.5	2,594	89.1	62.8
Mich	4,763	81.1	² 3,490	73.3	59.5	5,202	83.6	3,722	71.5	59.8
Minn	(³)	(X)	1,774	(X)	68.4	2,566	94.0	1,979	77.5	72.5
Miss	(NA)	(X)	² 646	(X)	45.0	(³)	(X)	² 769	(X)	49.5
Mo	(³)	(X)	⁴ 1,866	(X)	57.3	2,553	75.4	² 1,954	76.5	57.7
Mont	387	84.1	327	84.6	67.8	455	88.2	339	74.5	65.7
Nebr	712	69.7	592	83.1	55.9	841	77.6	624	74.2	57.6
Nev	231	66.5	185	80.2	51.0	251	59.1	206	82.1	48.5
N.H	450	86.3	345	76.7	64.2	478	82.7	359	75.1	62.1
N.J	3,673	73.3	3,030	82.5	60.0	3,770	72.7	3,037	80.6	58.6
N. Mex	505	79.5	396	78.3	57.5	527	68.7	426	80.8	55.5
N.Y	9,207	72.1	7,323	79.5	56.6	8,199	63.7	6,668	81.3	51.8
N.C	2,358	68.1	² 1,519	64.4	43.4	2,554	67.1	² 1,679	65.7	44.1
N. Dak	(³)	(X)	289	(X)	68.0	(³)	(X)	309	(X)	69.9
Ohio	4,628	64.4	4,220	91.2	57.5	4,693	63.2	4,195	89.4	56.5
Okla	1,247	68.8	1,057	84.8	56.9	1,401	71.4	1,108	79.1	56.4
Oreg	1,198	79.8	953	79.6	61.7	1,420	85.6	1,049	73.9	63.3
Pa	5,872	72.0	² 4,592	78.2	56.0	5,750	68.0	² 4,621	80.4	54.7
R.I	532	79.0	² 416	78.2	62.0	545	81.5	² 411	75.4	61.5
S.C	1,034	60.6	² 674	65.5	38.6	1,113	57.9	² 803	72.1	41.7
S. Dak	392	90.4	⁴ 308	78.6	68.7	426	90.4	² 301	70.7	63.8
Tenn	1,990	73.4	² 1,201	60.4	43.6	1,912	64.3	² 1,476	77.2	49.6
Texas	⁵ 5,500	71.6	² 3,471	63.1	45.3	6,319	73.5	² 4,072	64.4	47.3
Utah	621	90.1	480	77.3	68.4	705	90.4	548	77.7	70.3
Vt	273	88.4	194	71.1	60.8	284	86.1	194	68.3	58.8
Va	2,107	65.9	² 1,457	69.1	45.5	2,124	59.7	1,716	80.8	48.3
Wash	1,975	83.3	1,520	77.0	63.8	2,065	81.1	1,585	76.8	62.3
W. Va	1,063	89.9	⁴ 774	72.9	62.4	1,084	83.8	² 751	69.3	58.1
Wis	(³)	(X)	² 1,853	(X)	62.0	2,566	80.4	² 2,104	82.0	65.9
Wyo	(NA)	(X)	152	(X)	63.8	195	72.5	160	82.1	59.5

NA Not available. X Not applicable. ¹ Total vote for largest race, Senator.
² Total vote for largest race, President. ³ No required statewide registration; excluded from totals for persons registered. ⁴ Total vote for largest race, Governor. ⁵ Estimated by Secretary of State.

Source: National Republican Congressional Committee, Washington, D.C., unpublished data.

No. 843. Estimated Population of Voting Age, by Age—States: 1978

[In thousands. As of November. See headnote, table 840]

STATE	Total, 18 years old and over	18-24 years	25-44 years	45-64 years	65 years and over	STATE	Total, 18 years old and over	18-24 years	25-44 years	45-64 years	65 years and over
U.S__	155,492	28,832	58,696	43,858	24,105	Miss_____	1,612	315	600	424	273
						Mo_____	3,471	631	1,265	943	632
Ala_____	2,604	486	981	727	410	Mont_____	538	101	199	157	81
Alaska___	272	78	124	60	10	Nebr_____	1,117	211	405	299	202
Ariz_____	1,642	310	614	451	266	Nev_____	461	87	182	139	54
Ark_____	1,535	258	560	424	293	N.H_____	614	106	244	167	96
Calif____	16,052	3,023	6,270	4,505	2,254	N.J_____	5,305	877	1,944	1,656	828
Colo_____	1,900	401	782	487	230	N. Mex__	815	175	313	224	103
						N.Y_____	12,967	2,178	4,802	3,885	2,102
Conn_____	2,279	400	852	679	349						
Del_____	418	86	161	116	55	N.C_____	3,964	757	1,560	1,096	551
D.C_____	499	99	200	129	71	N. Dak___	461	92	161	130	79
Fla_____	6,502	1,033	2,084	1,858	1,526	Ohio_____	7,589	1,436	2,866	2,157	1,129
Ga_____	3,543	701	1,441	929	472	Okla_____	2,043	367	755	564	358
Hawaii___	637	146	248	177	67	Oreg_____	1,750	308	670	489	283
						Pa_____	8,611	1,452	3,018	2,681	1,460
Idaho____	597	115	228	168	86	R.I_____	678	117	237	203	121
Ill_____	7,975	1,474	3,010	2,280	1,211	S.C_____	2,011	412	804	537	258
Ind_____	3,752	711	1,440	1,037	564	S. Dak___	484	94	162	140	89
Iowa_____	2,057	359	744	576	378	Tenn_____	3,107	549	1,210	870	479
Kans_____	1,694	323	607	465	298						
Ky_____	2,457	455	934	678	389	Tex_____	9,063	1,798	3,560	2,434	1,270
						Utah_____	827	197	323	205	102
La_____	2,674	542	1,040	719	373	Vt_____	344	65	137	88	55
Maine____	776	139	280	224	132	Va_____	3,736	767	1,468	1,032	469
Md_____	2,991	587	1,193	841	370	Wash_____	2,651	499	1,052	703	398
Mass_____	4,230	780	1,554	1,201	695	W. Va___	1,341	215	489	413	223
Mich_____	6,405	1,276	2,497	1,766	867	Wis_____	3,319	633	1,234	908	545
Minn_____	2,828	554	1,082	730	462	Wyo_____	290	58	109	87	36

Source: U.S. Bureau of the Census, *Current Population Reports*, series P-25, No. 732.

No. 844. Congressional Campaign Finances—Adjusted Receipts and Expenditures: 1975-1976

[Covers all campaign finance activity during Jan. 1, 1975,-Dec. 31, 1976 for primaries and general elections. Relates to 860 candidates for House of Representatives who received 5 percent or more of the votes in the General Election and to 64 candidates for the Senate. Data adjusted to exclude refunds, rebates, returned contributions, loan repayments, treasury notes, and certificates of deposits which were bought and redeemed]

ITEM	HOUSE		SENATE		ITEM	HOUSE		SENATE	
	Amount ($1,000)	Per-cent distri-bution	Amount ($1,000)	Per-cent distri-bution		Amount ($1,000)	Per-cent distri-bution	Amount ($1,000)	Per-cent distri-bution
Total receipts____	65,741	100.0	39,130	100.0	Incumbents_____	35,071	53.4	16,255	42.0
					Challengers_____	18,352	27.9	10,571	27.0
Contributions:					Open seat [2]_____	12,318	18.7	12,304	31.0
Less than $101_____	23,680	36.0	11,088	28.3					
$101-$499_____	7,538	11.5	5,229	13.4	Winners_____	42,491	64.6	21,053	53.8
$500 and over_____	7,271	11.1	10,593	27.1	Losers_____	23,250	35.4	18,077	46.2
Candidate_____	2,398	3.6	892	2.3					
Party committee__	5,126	7.8	1,399	3.6	Total ex-penditures__	60,908	100.0	[3] 38,105	100.0
Non-party comm__	14,745	22.4	5,798	14.8					
					Democrats_____	32,370	53.1	18,806	49.0
Loans outstanding: [1]					Republicans_____	28,059	46.1	18,495	49.0
Candidate_____	4,055	6.2	3,660	9.4	Other_____	479	.8	803	2.0
Other_____	617	.9	101	.2					
Other receipts_____	313	.5	364	.9	Incumbents_____	30,737	50.2	15,595	41.0
					Challengers_____	18,110	30.0	10,398	27.0
Democrats_____	35,058	53.3	19,480	50.0	Open seats [2]_____	12,061	19.8	12,111	32.0
Republicans_____	30,202	46.0	18,840	48.0					
Others_____	481	.7	809	2.0	Winners_____	38,054	62.4	20,131	52.8
					Losers_____	22,854	37.6	17,761	46.6

[1] As of December 31, 1976.   [2] Elections in which an incumbent was not a candidate.
[3] Includes $214,000 (.6%) spent for uncontested campaigns.

Source: U.S. Federal Election Commission, FEC Disclosure Series, No. 6: *1976 Senatorial Campaigns Receipts and Expenditures*, and No. 9: *1976 House of Representatives Campaigns Receipts and Expenditures*, 1977.

No. 845. PRESIDENTIAL CAMPAIGN FINANCES—PRIMARY AND GENERAL ELECTION RECEIPTS AND EXPENDITURES, BY POLITICAL PARTY: 1975–1976

[In millions of dollars. Covers the period Jan. 1, 1975, through Dec. 31, 1976. Based on disclosure documents submitted by candidates, their principal campaign committees, and other authorized committees. Figures adjusted to eliminate refunds and rebates, refunded contributions, loan repayments, and transfers to or from affiliated committees]

RECEIPTS AND EXPENDITURES	PRESIDENTIAL CAMPAIGN				PRIMARY CAMPAIGN			GENERAL ELECTION CAMPAIGN			
	Total	Demo-cratic	Re-pub-lican	Other[1]	Total	Demo-cratic	Re-pub-lican	Total	Demo-cratic	Re-pub-lican	Other[1]
Receipts, total	114.0	61.7	50.2	2.0	67.9	39.6	28.3	46.1	22.1	22.0	2.0
Private funds [2]	46.1	25.4	18.7	2.0	43.6	25.1	18.5	2.5	.3	.2	2.0
U.S. Treasury funds [3]	67.9	36.3	31.6	–	24.3	14.5	9.7	43.6	21.8	21.8	–
Expenditures, total	112.8	62.9	48.0	2.0	66.9	40.7	26.2	45.9	22.2	21.8	2.0

– Represents zero. [1] Covers candidates who were on the ballot in 10 or more States. Included under general election since a majority of their financial activity was directed toward that area. [2] Covers contributions, outstanding loans, interest, and miscellaneous income. [3] Represents matching funds given to qualified candidates in the primary campaign and grant funds to the Democratic and Republican party candidates in the general election.

Source: U.S. Federal Election Commission, *FEC Disclosure, No. 7: 1976 Presidential Campaign Receipts and Expenditures*, 1977.

No. 846. ELECTION CAMPAIGN COSTS FOR NATIONAL OFFICES: 1972

[Covers some prenomination expenditures. Data are provided by the U.S. General Accounting Office, Office of Federal Elections (O.F.E.), created to administer the Federal Elections Campaign Act of 1971, effective as of April 7, 1972. Previously, only committees operating in two or more States were required to report receipts and expenditures. In 1968 there were 222 such committees, not all of which contributed to a Presidential campaign. The new requirement of comprehensive disclosure resulted in 1,785 committees filing reports with the O.F.E. in 1972, all of which contributed in some way, but not exclusively to a Presidential candidate. Except for congressional spending, all other figures are from the O.F.E.]

ITEM	1972	ITEM	1972
Campaign costs mil. dol	225.2	Republican committees: [1]	
		Number reporting	418
National spending (includes Presidential and Party) mil. dol	137.3	Spending mil. dol	69.3
Congressional spending mil. dol	87.9	Percent of national spending	50.5
		Third party committees: [1]	
		Number reporting	57
Democratic committees: [1]		Spending mil. dol	1.2
Number reporting	1,048	Percent of national spending	.9
Spending mil. dol	66.8	Miscellaneous committees: [2]	
Percent of national spending	48.6	Number reporting	262
		Spending (direct disbursements) mil. dol	8.0

[1] Excluding congressional. [2] Includes labor, business, professional, and ideological committees.

Source: Citizens' Research Foundation, Princeton, N.J., unpublished data.

No. 847. EXPENDITURES FOR POLITICAL BROADCASTS FOR ELECTIONS, BY MEDIUM AND PARTY: 1960 TO 1972

[In thousands of dollars. Represents media charges before commissions and after discounts, except 1970 represents charges after both commissions and discounts]

MEDIUM AND PARTY	GENERAL ELECTION		ELECTIONS, 1968		ELECTIONS, 1970		ELECTIONS, 1972 [1]	
	1960	1964	General	Primary	General	Primary	General	Primary
Total	14,195	24,604	40,403	18,485	33,051	17,558	38,127	21,513
Republican	7,559	13,033	22,505	5,355	16,716	5,135	17,521	3,238
Democratic	6,205	11,013	15,448	12,418	14,385	11,709	17,506	16,908
Other	431	559	2,451	712	1,951	714	3,100	1,367
Television	10,052	17,496	27,087	10,891	21,633	10,254	24,567	12,641
Republican	5,431	9,431	15,183	3,521	11,143	3,219	11,619	1,824
Democratic	4,415	7,715	10,424	6,960	9,335	6,780	11,433	10,145
Other	206	350	1,480	409	1,154	255	1,515	672
Radio	4,143	7,108	13,316	7,594	11,419	7,304	13,510	8,849
Republican	2,128	3,601	7,322	1,834	5,573	1,916	5,879	1,411
Democratic	1,790	3,298	5,024	5,457	5,049	4,929	6,054	6,750
Other	225	209	970	303	797	459	1,577	688

[1] Includes cable television.

Source: U.S. Federal Communications Commission, *Report of Political Broadcasting*, April 1961, July 1965, August 1969, June 1971, and March 1973.

Section 17

Banking, Finance, and Insurance

This section presents data on the Nation's finances, various types of financial institutions, money and credit, securities, and insurance. The primary sources of these data are publications of several departments of the Federal Government, especially the Treasury Department, and independent agencies such as the Federal Deposit Insurance Corporation, the Federal Reserve System, and the Securities and Exchange Commission. National data on insurance are available primarily from private organizations, such as the American Council of Life Insurance.

Flow of funds.—The flow of funds accounts of the Federal Reserve System (see tables 848 to 854) bring together statistics on all of the major forms of financial transactions and financial claims to present an economy-wide view of asset and liability relationships. In flow form, the accounts relate borrowing and lending to one another and to the nonfinancial activities that generate income and production. Each claim outstanding is included simultaneously as an asset of the lender and as a liability of the debtor. The accounts also indicate the balance between asset totals and liability totals over the economy as a whole. Data included here present end-of-year asset and liability positions in financial claims rather than flows that occurred during the year. Three publications of the Board of Governors of the Federal Reserve System contain information on the flow of funds accounts: Summary data on flows, in the *Federal Reserve Bulletin* and in *Flow of Funds Accounts, 1946-1975*; and concepts and organization of the accounts, in *Introduction to Flow of Funds* (February 1975).

Banking system.—Banks in this country are organized under the laws of both the States and the Federal Government. State-chartered banks are supervised by officials of the respective States. "National" banks are supervised by the Comptroller of the Currency. *Reports of Condition* have been collected from national banks since 1863. Summaries of these reports are published in the Comptroller's *Annual Report*, which also presents data on the structure of the national banking system.

The Federal Reserve System was established in 1913 to exercise central banking functions, some of which are shared with the U.S. Treasury. It includes national banks and such State banks as voluntarily join the System. Statements of State bank members are consolidated by the Board of Governors of the Federal Reserve System with data for national banks collected by the Comptroller of the Currency into totals for all member banks of the System. Balance sheet data for member banks are published in condensed form in the *Federal Reserve Bulletin*.

The Federal Deposit Insurance Corporation (FDIC), established in 1933, insures each depositor up to $40,000 and also provides additional insurance coverage of up to $100,000 for certain time and savings deposits of official custodians of public funds in banks that are members of the Federal Reserve System and in such nonmember banks as join the insurance fund. A balance sheet for all banks in the country is published semiannually in *Assets, Liabilities, and Capital Accounts—Commercial and Mutual Savings Banks*, a joint publication of the FDIC, the Board of Governors of the Federal Reserve System, and the Comptroller of the Currency. Major item balance sheets for all commercial banks are published monthly in the *Federal Reserve Bulletin*.

Savings and loan and other credit agencies.—Savings and loan associations, insurance companies, finance companies dealing primarily in installment sales financing, credit unions, and personal loan companies represent important sources of funds for the credit market. Savings and loan associations which, unlike banks, are not engaged in deposit banking, are primarily involved in credit extension in the form of loans. Statistics on savings and loan associations are collected by the Federal Home Loan Bank Board. Statistics on loans, investments, cash, etc., of life insurance companies are published principally by the American Council of Life Insurance in its *Life Insurance Fact Book.* Consumer credit data are published currently in the *Federal Reserve Bulletin.*

Federally chartered credit unions are under the supervision of the National Credit Union Administration, established in 1970. State-chartered credit unions are supervised by the respective State supervisory authorities. The Administration publishes comprehensive program and statistical information on all Federal and federally-insured State credit unions in the *Annual Report of the National Credit Union Administration* and also publishes an *Annual Report* on the operations of all State-chartered credit unions.

Government corporations and credit agencies make available credit of specified types or to specified groups of private borrowers, either by lending directly or by insuring or guaranteeing loans made by private lending institutions. Data on operations of Government credit agencies, along with other Government corporations, are available in reports of individual agencies; data on their assets and liabilities are published in the *Treasury Bulletin.*

Currency.—Currency, including coin and paper money, represents almost one-fourth of all media of exchange in the United States, with most payments made by check. All currency is now issued by the Federal Reserve Banks and the Treasury.

"Currency and coin in circulation" (official *Statement of United States Currency and Coin*) refers to all coin and paper money outside the Federal Reserve Banks, except gold and silver coin known to have been exported and, beginning with 1934, all gold coin. It includes all coin and paper money held by the public in the United States. It also includes cash in vaults of commercial and savings banks, currency lost or destroyed, and currency carried abroad by travelers.

Securities.—The Securities and Exchange Commission (SEC) was established in 1934 to protect the interests of the public and investors against malpractices in the securities and financial markets and to provide the fullest possible disclosure of information regarding securities to the investing public. Since its inception, the SEC has compiled a comprehensive monthly data series on new corporate securities offerings which cover substantially all new issues offered for cash sale in the United States in amounts over $100,000 and with terms to maturity of more than one year. This series is published monthly in the Commission's *Statistical Bulletin.*

Insurance.—Insuring companies, which are regulated by the various States or the District of Columbia, are classified as either life or property. Companies which underwrite accident and health insurance only are included with life insurance; those which underwrite accident and health insurance in addition to one or more property lines are included with property insurance. Insuring companies, other than those classified as life, are permitted to underwrite one or more property lines provided they are so licensed and have the necessary capital and/or surplus.

There are a number of published sources for statistics on the various classes of insurance—life, health, fire, marine, and casualty. Individual States collect data on all insurers operating within their respective jurisdictions, and many of the States publish an annual insurance report giving individual company data and aggregates of certain items for the companies operating within the State. Organizations representing certain classes of insurers publish reports for these classes. Among them are the annual commercial publishers, such as The National Underwriter Company whose *Argus Chart* (annual) contains financial and operating data for individual health and accident insurance companies, including Blue Cross and Blue Shield Plans. The American Council of Life Insurance publishes statistics on life insurance purchases, ownership, benefit payments, and assets in its annual *Life Insurance Fact Book.*

Historical statistics.—Tabular headnotes provide cross-references, where applicable, to *Historical Statistics of the United States, Colonial Times to 1970.* See Appendix I.

Figure 17.1

Stock Prices: 1960 to 1978

(See table 895)

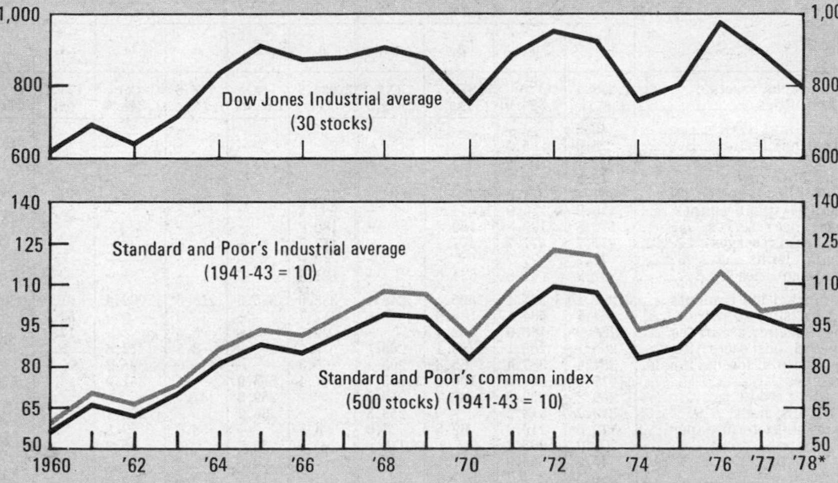

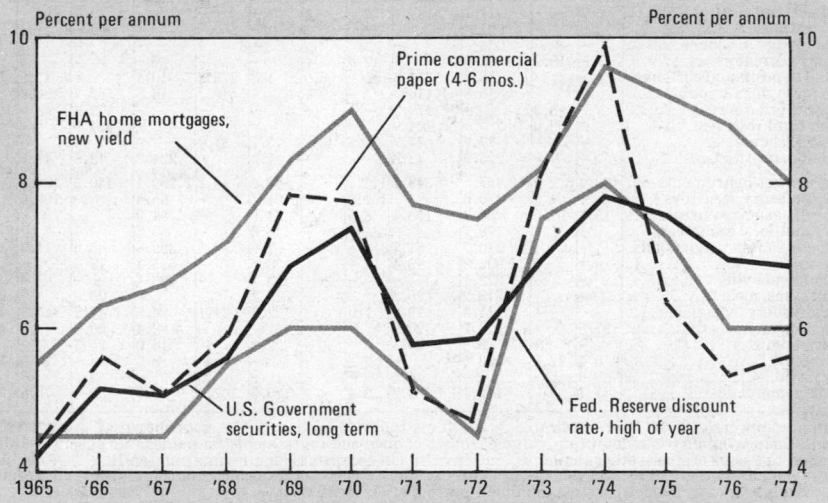

*Average, Jan. to June.

Source: Chart prepared by U.S. Bureau of the Census. Data from Board of Governors of the Federal Reserve System.

Figure 17.2

Money Market Rates: 1965 to 1977

(Annual averages; see table 890 and 893)

Source: Chart prepared by U.S. Bureau of the Census. Data from Board of Governors of the Federal Reserve System.

No. 848. Flow of Funds Accounts—Financial Assets and Liabilities of Financial and Nonfinancial Institutions, by Sector and Type of Instrument: 1977

[In billions of dollars. As of Dec. 31. Preliminary. A = Assets; L = Liabilities. SDR = special drawing rights. IMF = International Monetary Fund. "N.e.c." = not elsewhere classified]

TYPE OF INSTRUMENT	TOTAL A	TOTAL L	PRIVATE DOMESTIC NONFINANCIAL INSTITUTIONS — Total A	Total L	Households A	Households L	Business A	Business L	State and local govts. A	State and local govts. L
Financial assets	7,388.1	(x)	3,873.7	(x)	2,920.6	(x)	779.6	(x)	173.5	(x)
Liabilities	(x)	6,526.9	(x)	2,649.3	(x)	1,026.1	(x)	1,348.5	(x)	274.7
Gold stock and SDR's	60.5	–	–	–	–	–	–	–	–	–
IMF position	5.0	5.0	–	–	–	–	–	–	–	–
Official foreign exchange	(z)	(z)	–	–	–	–	–	–	–	–
Treasury currency	12.6	10.2	–	–	–	–	–	–	–	–
Demand deposits and currency	331.4	374.3	280.5	–	192.0	–	75.3	–	13.2	–
Time and savings accounts	1,116.9	1,116.9	1,079.0	–	992.4	–	28.1	–	58.5	–
Life insurance reserves	180.8	180.8	180.8	–	180.8	–	–	–	–	–
Pension fund reserves	477.7	477.7	477.7	–	477.7	–	–	–	–	–
Interbank claims	77.7	77.7	–	–	–	–	–	–	–	–
Corporate equities [1]	902.2	42.8	634.6	–	634.6	–	–	–	–	–
Credit market instruments	3,297.4	3,297.4	595.1	2,248.4	385.6	985.5	118.5	1,002.4	91.0	260.5
U.S. Treasury securities [2]	564.1	564.1	183.9	–	117.1	–	13.9	–	53.0	–
Federal agency securities [3]	165.9	165.9	52.4	–	29.8	–	5.5	–	17.2	–
State and local securities	265.1	265.1	86.4	265.1	77.2	–	3.5	–	5.7	252.5
Corporate and foreign bonds	387.4	387.4	65.3	295.2	65.3	–	–	295.2	–	–
Mortgages	1,019.0	1,019.0	106.6	1,005.7	91.4	–	–	351.9	15.1	–
Consumer credit	259.8	259.8	37.7	259.8	–	259.8	37.7	–	–	–
Bank loans, n.e.c	313.2	313.2	–	258.3	–	36.2	–	222.1	–	–
Private short-term paper	119.6	119.6	62.8	23.8	4.8	–	–	23.8	–	–
Other loans	203.2	203.2	–	140.5	–	35.7	–	96.9	–	8.0
Security credit	45.9	45.9	7.1	20.5	7.1	20.5	–	–	–	–
Trade credit [4]	386.5	354.7	355.4	322.7	–	11.8	355.4	296.8	–	14.2
Taxes payable	20.4	20.9	10.8	16.6	–	–	–	16.6	10.8	–
Miscellaneous claims	473.2	522.7	252.6	41.0	50.3	8.3	202.3	32.7	–	–

TYPE OF INSTRUMENT	U.S. GOVERNMENT A	U.S. GOVERNMENT L	FINANCIAL INSTITUTIONS — Total A	Total L	Monetary authority A	Monetary authority L	Commercial banks A	Commercial banks L	Nonbank finance A	Nonbank finance L	REST OF THE WORLD A	REST OF THE WORLD L
Financial assets	155.0	(x)	[5] 3,010.0	(x)	142.9	(x)	1,068.2	(x)	1,623.8	(x)	349.4	(x)
Liabilities	(x)	657.0	(x)	[5] 2,869.7	(x)	142.9	(x)	1,011.2	(x)	1,543.5	(x)	350.8
Gold stock and SDR's	2.7	–	11.7	–	11.7	–	–	–	–	–	46.1	–
IMF position	5.0	–	(z)	–	(z)	–	–	–	–	–	–	5.0
Official foreign exchange	–	–	(z)	–	(z)	–	–	–	–	–	–	(z)
Treasury currency	–	10.2	12.6	–	12.6	–	–	–	–	–	–	–
Demand deposits and currency	14.8	–	18.3	374.3	–	98.0	1.3	276.3	16.8	–	17.8	–
Time and savings accounts	.7	–	16.8	1,116.9	–	–	–	549.2	16.8	567.7	20.3	–
Life insurance reserves	–	8.5	–	172.3	–	–	–	–	–	172.3	–	–
Pension fund reserves	–	52.9	–	424.9	–	–	–	–	–	424.9	–	–
Interbank claims	–	–	77.7	77.7	3.9	40.7	73.7	37.0	–	–	41.7	–
Corporate equities [1]	–	–	225.9	42.8	–	–	1.2	–	224.7	42.8	41.7	–
Credit market instruments	108.2	572.5	[5] 2,457.5	[5] 348.1	112.2	–	883.2	40.2	1,289.1	149.5	136.5	128.3
U.S. Treasury securities [2]	–	564.1	[5] 270.6	–	–	102.8	101.4	–	65.4	–	109.6	–
Federal agency securities [3]	15.3	7.6	[5] 98.2	[5] 158.4	8.5	–	34.5	–	54.9	–	–	–
State and local securities	–	–	178.7	–	–	–	118.3	–	60.3	–	–	–
Corporate and foreign bonds	–	–	310.7	51.7	–	–	7.9	6.1	302.8	45.6	11.4	40.5
Mortgages	10.4	.9	[5] 902.0	12.4	–	–	176.7	–	595.3	12.4	–	–
Consumer credit	–	–	222.1	–	–	–	118.7	–	103.4	–	–	–
Bank loans, n.e.c	–	–	313.2	26.2	–	–	313.2	–	–	26.2	–	28.7
Private short-term paper	–	–	[5] 41.3	79.2	1.0	–	12.3	34.1	24.5	45.2	15.5	16.5
Other loans	82.6	–	[5] 120.7	20.2	–	–	–	–	82.4	20.2	–	42.5
Security credit	–	–	38.8	25.3	–	–	–	22.8	16.0	25.3	–	–
Trade credit [4]	6.4	12.9	8.5	–	–	–	–	–	–	8.5	16.3	19.1
Taxes payable	9.6	–	–	4.3	–	–	–	.6	–	3.7	–	–
Miscellaneous claims	7.7	(z)	[5] 142.1	[5] 283.2	2.4	4.2	86.0	107.8	51.9	157.4	70.8	198.5

– Represents zero. X Not applicable. Z Less than $50 million. [1] Assets shown at market value; nonbank finance liability is redemption value of shares of open-end investment companies. No specific liability attributed to issuers of stocks other than open-end investment companies for amounts outstanding. [2] Includes savings bonds and other nonmarketable debt held by public. [3] Issues by agencies in the budget and by sponsored credit agencies in financial sectors, and loan participation certificates.

[4] Asset is corporate only; noncorporate credit deducted in liability total to conform to quarterly flow tables. [5] Includes federally sponsored credit agencies and mortgage pools, not shown separately.

Source: Board of Governors of the Federal Reserve System, *Flow of Funds Accounts, 1946–1975; Annual Statistical Digest, 1972–1976;* and unpublished data

No. 849. FLOW OF FUNDS ACCOUNTS—FINANCIAL ASSETS OF FINANCIAL AND NONFINANCIAL INSTITUTIONS, BY HOLDER SECTOR: 1950 TO 1977

[In billions of dollars. As of December 31. See also *Historical Statistics, Colonial Times to 1970*, series X 192, X 229, X 821, and X 835]

SECTOR	1950	1960	1965	1970	1973	1974	1975	1976	1977
All sectors	1,006	1,998	2,981	4,102	5,269	5,345	5,979	6,771	7,388
Households	446	972	1,465	1,914	2,240	2,107	2,438	2,788	2,921
Nonfinancial business	126	210	291	409	535	574	618	688	780
Farm	8	8	9	11	13	14	15	16	17
Nonfarm noncorporate	15	21	24	29	33	35	37	40	43
Nonfinancial corporations	102	182	259	370	489	525	567	632	720
U.S. Government	41	54	71	89	100	106	123	147	155
State and local government	18	33	50	72	111	120	123	139	174
Monetary authorities	50	53	64	86	107	113	125	135	143
Commercial banking	150	230	344	519	763	851	884	966	1,068
U.S. Govt.-sponsored credit agencies and mortgage pools	3	12	20	51	88	112	127	148	175
Nonbank finance	143	370	588	827	1,114	1,128	1,282	1,461	1,624
Savings and loan associations	17	72	130	176	272	296	338	392	459
Mutual savings banks	22	41	59	79	107	109	121	135	147
Credit unions	1	6	11	18	28	31	37	43	52
Life insurance	63	116	154	201	245	255	280	311	338
Other insurance	12	26	37	50	70	68	77	89	100
Private pension funds	7	38	74	111	135	117	149	176	189
Govt retirement funds [1]	5	20	34	60	85	88	105	122	132
Finance companies	9	28	45	64	91	96	98	107	125
Real estate investment trusts	–	–	–	4	17	18	14	10	8
Investment companies	3	17	35	48	47	34	42	47	43
Money market funds	–	–	–	–	–	2	4	3	4
Security brokers and dealers	4	7	10	16	18	15	18	27	29
Rest of the world	30	64	88	134	213	235	258	301	349

– Represents zero.   [1] State and local government.

No. 850. FLOW OF FUNDS ACCOUNTS—ASSETS AND LIABILITIES OF HOUSEHOLDS, BY TYPE OF INSTRUMENT: 1960 TO 1977

[As of December 31. See also *Historical Statistics, Colonial Times to 1970*, series X 111 117]

TYPE OF INSTRUMENT	TOTAL (bil. dol.)					PERCENT DISTRIBUTION			
	1960	1965	1970	1976	1977	1965	1970	1976	1977
Total financial assets	972.1	1,465.3	1,914.4	2,788.1	2,920.6	100.0	100.0	100.0	100.0
Deposit and market instruments [1]	386.3	549.7	784.8	1,424.2	1,570.0	37.5	41.0	51.1	53.8
Demand deposits and currency	73.2	83.4	117.9	174.8	192.0	5.7	6.2	6.3	6.6
Time and savings accounts [2]	164.8	289.8	426.7	884.2	992.4	19.8	22.3	31.7	34.0
Credit market instruments [3]	148.3	176.4	240.1	365.1	385.6	12.0	12.5	13.1	13.2
U.S. Government securities	74.0	87.0	105.2	141.2	146.8	5.9	5.5	5.1	5.0
Treasury issues	71.5	81.0	82.9	116.8	117.1	5.5	4.3	4.2	4.0
Savings bonds	45.6	49.7	52.1	72.0	76.8	3.4	2.7	2.6	2.6
Other Treasury	25.9	31.3	30.8	44.7	40.3	2.1	1.6	1.6	1.4
Agency issues	2.5	6.0	22.3	24.4	29.8	.4	1.2	.9	1.0
State and local obligations	30.8	36.4	46.0	71.7	77.2	2.5	2.4	2.6	2.6
Corporate and foreign bonds	10.0	10.8	35.3	65.2	65.3	.7	1.8	2.3	2.2
Mortgages	33.4	42.2	52.9	79.8	91.4	2.9	2.8	2.9	3.1
Corporate equities	395.4	635.5	729.0	708.9	634.6	43.4	38.1	25.4	21.7
Investment company shares	17.0	35.2	47.6	47.0	42.8	2.4	2.5	1.7	1.5
Other corporate equities	378.4	600.2	681.4	661.9	591.9	41.0	35.6	23.7	20.3
Life insurance reserves	85.2	105.9	130.3	172.1	180.8	7.2	6.8	6.2	6.2
Pension fund reserves	90.8	154.8	239.6	431.8	477.7	10.6	12.5	15.5	16.4
Security credit	1.1	2.5	4.4	6.3	7.1	.2	.2	.2	.2
Miscellaneous assets	13.3	17.0	26.3	44.9	50.3	1.2	1.4	1.6	1.7
Total liabilities	225.9	356.2	497.6	890.4	1,026.1	100.0	100.0	100.0	100.0
Credit market instruments	216.0	340.8	476.8	854.5	985.5	95.7	95.8	96.0	96.0
Mortgages	145.8	227.9	309.7	566.1	653.9	64.0	62.2	63.6	63.7
Installment consumer credit	43.0	70.9	102.0	185.5	216.6	19.9	20.5	20.8	21.1
Other consumer credit	13.2	19.0	25.1	38.7	43.3	5.3	5.0	4.3	4.2
Bank loans, n.e.c. [4]	7.0	12.0	19.1	30.9	36.2	3.4	3.8	3.5	3.5
Other loans	7.0	11.0	20.9	33.4	35.7	3.1	4.2	3.8	3.5
Security credit	5.4	9.1	10.4	17.2	20.5	2.6	2.1	1.9	2.0
Trade credit	2.1	3.0	5.3	10.5	11.8	.8	1.1	1.2	1.1
Unpaid life insurance premiums [5]	2.4	3.3	5.1	8.2	8.3	.9	1.0	.9	.8

[1] Excludes corporate equities.   [2] Includes savings accounts at commercial banks and savings institutions. [3] Includes open-market paper and money-market fund shares, not shown separately. [4] "N.e.c." means not elsewhere classified.   [5] Includes deferred premiums.

Source of tables 849 and 850: Board of Governors of the Federal Reserve System, *Flow of Funds Accounts, 1946–1975; Annual Statistical Digest, 1972–1976;* and unpublished data.

No. 851. Flow of Funds Accounts—Assets and Liabilities of Private Non-Bank Financial Institutions, by Type of Transaction: 1977

[In billions of dollars. As of Dec. 31. Preliminary. A = Assets; L = Liabilities; "N.e.c." = Not elsewhere classified]

TYPE OF INSTRUMENT	TOTAL		MUTUAL SAVINGS BANKS		SAVINGS AND LOAN ASSO-CIATIONS		INSURANCE COM-PANIES		PENSION FUNDS [1]		FINANCE COM-PANIES		OTHER [2]	
	A	L	A	L	A	L	A	L	A	L	A	L	A	L
Financial assets	1,623.8	(X)	146.7	(X)	459.2	(X)	437.7	(X)	321.6	(X)	124.8	(X)	133.8	(X)
Liabilities	(X)	1,543.5	(X)	137.1	(X)	434.1	(X)	400.9	(X)	321.6	(X)	117.4	(X)	132.4
Demand deposits and currency	16.8	–	1.3	–	(Z)	–	4.4	–	3.8	–	4.3	–	3.0	–
Time and savings accounts	16.8	567.7	1.1	134.0	5.2	386.9	–	–	4.3	–	–	–	6.2	46.8
Reserves:														
Life insurance	–	172.3	–	–	–	–	–	172.3	–	–	–	–	–	–
Pension fund	–	424.9	–	–	–	–	–	103.3	–	321.6	–	–	–	–
Corporate equities	224.7	42.8	4.4	–	–	–	49.1	–	135.8	–	–	–	35.4	42.8
Credit market instruments	1,289.1	149.5	136.0	–	432.8	38.0	358.5	–	169.7	–	120.5	96.5	71.6	15.0
Securities:														
U.S. Treasury	65.4	–	6.1	–	11.9	–	15.2	–	24.3	–	–	–	7.9	–
Federal agency	54.9	–	11.3	–	20.6	–	6.1	–	12.5	–	–	–	4.4	–
State and local	60.3	–	2.8	–	1.1	–	52.9	–	2.4	–	–	–	1.1	–
Corporate and foreign bonds	302.8	45.6	21.4	–	–	–	152.8	–	119.5	–	–	43.7	9.1	1.9
Mortgages	595.3	12.4	88.0	–	381.2	10.0	96.0	–	10.9	–	10.5	–	8.7	2.4
Consumer credit	103.4	–	2.5	–	8.7	–	–	–	–	–	55.1	–	37.1	–
Bank loans, n.e.c.	–	26.2	–	–	–	7.8	–	–	–	–	–	11.7	–	6.7
Pvt. short-term paper	24.5	45.2	3.9	–	9.3	–	7.9	–	–	–	–	41.1	3.4	4.1
Other loans	82.4	20.2	–	–	–	20.2	27.5	–	–	–	54.9	–	–	–
Security credit	16.0	25.3	–	–	–	–	–	–	–	–	–	–	16.0	25.3
Taxes payable	8.5	–	–	–	–	–	8.5	–	–	–	–	–	–	–
Trade credit	–	3.7	–	–	–	.9	–	1.7	–	–	–	1.0	–	.1
Miscellaneous	51.9	157.4	3.9	3.1	21.3	8.3	17.2	123.6	8.0	–	–	19.9	1.5	2.5

– Represents zero or rounds to zero.   X Not applicable.   Z Less than $50 million.
[1] Retirement funds of State and local governments and private pension plans.   [2] Credit unions, money market funds, open-end investment companies, real estate investment trusts, and security brokers and dealers.

No. 852. Flow of Funds Accounts—Total Claims Related to Total Assets: 1950 to 1977

[In billions of dollars. As of December 31]

ITEM	1950	1960	1965	1970	1973	1974	1975	1976	1977 [1]
Total assets	1,006.4	1,998.2	2,980.9	4,101.7	5,268.9	5,345.0	5,978.8	6,771.4	7,388.1
Add—liabilities not allocated as assets	5.5	4.9	11.6	29.8	51.3	53.6	51.6	53.5	47.5
Add—floats not incl. assets	2.3	1.0	−1.5	−3.8	−8.3	−2.5	4.5	9.0	11.1
Demand deposits	6.7	9.1	12.1	18.6	26.3	32.6	34.8	39.7	42.9
Trade credit	−4.4	−8.1	−13.6	−22.4	−34.6	−35.1	−30.3	−30.7	−31.8
Deduct—financial assets not incl. in borrowing	178.1	474.5	756.9	904.1	918.5	628.3	817.7	1,003.1	919.9
Other corporate equities	142.7	434.0	713.7	859.4	857.4	567.3	756.7	942.6	859.4
Gold and special drawing rights (SDR)	35.4	40.5	43.2	44.7	61.1	61.0	61.0	60.5	60.5
Total liabilities	836.1	1,529.6	2,234.0	3,223.7	4,393.4	4,767.7	5,217.3	5,830.9	6,526.9
Credit market debt [2]	427.0	777.7	1,107.2	1,595.2	2,186.9	2,408.9	2,620.0	2,907.2	3,297.4
Other liabilities	409.1	752.0	1,126.9	1,628.7	2,206.5	2,359.0	2,597.3	2,923.7	3,229.3
Official foreign exchange	1.4	1.6	1.6	2.6	.6	1.9	2.3	4.8	5.0
Treasury currency and SDR certificates	2.4	2.7	3.1	6.0	7.4	7.7	8.7	9.9	10.2
Deposits at financial institutions	196.0	332.6	507.2	708.3	1,017.4	1,103.6	1,209.3	1,341.5	1,491.2
Insurance and pension reserves	79.3	176.0	260.7	369.9	462.3	460.5	532.3	603.9	658.5
Security credit	5.5	10.9	18.0	24.9	29.5	24.5	28.0	41.2	45.9
Trade debt	37.5	79.2	114.3	184.8	236.6	262.1	277.1	308.5	354.7
Profit taxes payable	18.1	16.0	22.0	14.0	18.2	19.4	16.0	23.5	20.9
Interbank claims	21.5	22.8	26.6	42.1	65.1	72.8	69.1	71.7	77.7
Miscellaneous	47.4	110.2	173.4	276.1	369.4	406.5	454.5	518.7	565.5

[1] Preliminary.   [2] See also table 853.

Source of tables 851 and 852: Board of Governors of the Federal Reserve System, *Flow of Funds Accounts, 1946–1975; Annual Statistical Digest, 1972–1976;* and unpublished data.

No. 853. FLOW OF FUNDS ACCOUNTS—SUMMARY OF CREDIT MARKET CLAIMS OUTSTANDING: 1950 TO 1977

[In billions of dollars. As of December 31. Excludes corporate equities. See also *Historical Statistics, Colonial Times to 1970*, series X 1-23]

TYPE OF CLAIM	1950	1960	1965	1970	1972	1973	1974	1975	1976	1977
Credit market debt	427	778	1,107	1,595	1,943	2,187	2,409	2,620	2,907	3,297
Owned by nonfinancial sectors	419	748	1,048	1,478	1,788	1,981	2,165	2,362	2,621	2,949
Federal	217	236	262	301	341	349	361	446	516	573
Foreign	13	23	39	52	62	68	82	95	116	128
Private domestic	190	488	746	1,125	1,385	1,564	1,722	1,821	1,989	2,248
Households	71	216	341	477	589	667	716	764	855	986
State and local governments	25	72	103	149	181	194	210	221	236	261
Corporate nonfinancial business	71	154	223	375	455	520	598	626	674	751
Other business	22	46	79	124	159	183	199	209	226	252
Owned by financial sectors	8	30	60	118	155	206	244	258	286	348

No. 854. FLOW OF FUNDS ACCOUNTS—STRUCTURE OF CREDIT SUPPLY: 1950 TO 1977

[In billions of dollars. As of December 31. Excludes corporate equities. See also *Historical Statistics, Colonial Times to 1970*, series X 64-105]

ITEM	1950	1960	1965	1970	1972	1973	1974	1975	1976	1977
Credit market debt claims against nonfinancial sectors	419	748	1,048	1,478	1,784	1,981	2,165	2,362	2,621	2,949
Public agency and foreign holdings	43	78	114	196	259	294	342	387	445	530
U.S. Government securities	24	39	56	85	127	137	149	171	198	238
Residential mortgages and FHLB advances [1]	2	10	14	39	50	66	87	99	110	135
Other loans and securities	17	28	44	72	82	92	106	117	137	158
Agency debt excluded from total [2]	2	8	15	44	58	78	101	115	133	158
Private domestic holdings [3]	377	678	949	1,325	1,582	1,765	1,924	2,090	2,309	2,578
U.S. Government securities	194	204	219	258	270	289	311	387	449	493
State and local securities	24	71	100	144	177	191	208	222	237	265
Corporate and foreign bonds	37	80	107	179	213	222	245	277	305	324
Residential mortgages	53	153	249	326	406	454	480	504	559	636
Other mortgages and loans	70	172	279	428	525	625	700	717	775	880
Less FHLB advances [1]	1	2	6	11	8	15	22	18	16	20
Private financial intermediation:										
Claims held by private financial institutions	248	497	752	1,070	1,331	1,495	1,621	1,742	1,929	2,172
Commercial banks	126	198	301	446	567	653	718	745	803	883
Savings institutions	38	109	183	254	341	379	405	457	529	614
Insurance and pension funds	75	160	219	292	325	347	377	418	466	528
Other finance	10	30	49	79	99	116	121	121	131	147
Sources of funds:										
Domestic deposits	155	280	438	618	808	895	964	1,055	1,178	1,313
Credit market debt	6	22	45	74	100	128	143	144	153	190
Insurance and pension reserves	63	133	182	242	261	282	313	341	375	429
Other	23	61	88	135	161	190	200	202	223	241
Private domestic nonfinancial investors:										
Credit market claims	136	203	241	329	352	398	447	491	533	595
U.S. Government securities	93	105	115	140	133	153	171	193	213	236
State and local obligations	12	36	43	51	53	60	70	76	81	86
Corporate and foreign bonds	5	10	11	35	48	49	56	64	65	65
Open market paper	(z)	3	7	21	23	35	40	43	47	63
Other	26	49	65	82	94	101	109	115	127	144
Deposits and currency	181	310	475	668	866	957	1,032	1,129	1,259	1,403
Time and savings accounts	70	172	311	455	618	694	761	846	959	1,079
Large negotiable CD's [4]	–	1	15	23	37	55	74	60	46	56
Other at commercial banks	35	69	126	201	265	295	322	361	419	459
At savings institutions	35	102	170	231	316	345	366	425	495	564
Demand deposits	86	108	127	163	190	200	203	209	-219	234
Currency	26	30	37	50	58	62	68	74	82	90

– Represents zero. Z Less than $500 million. [1] Federal Home Loan Bank advances to savings and loan associations. [2] Debt of sponsored agencies and mortgage pool securities are excluded from debt of nonfinancial sectors but included in holdings of debt claims below. [3] Claims held by private financial institutions, less sources of funds of credit market debt, plus private domestic nonfinancial investors credit market claims. [4] Certificates of deposit.

Source of tables 853 and 854: Board of Governors of the Federal Reserve System, *Flow of Funds Accounts, 1946-1975; Annual Statistical Digest, 1972-1976;* and unpublished data.

No. 855. FEDERAL RESERVE BANKS—ASSETS, LIABILITIES, AND CAPITAL ACCOUNTS: 1950 TO 1977

[In billions of dollars. As of December 31. See also *Historical Statistics, Colonial Times to 1970*, series X 796–805]

ITEM	1950	1960	1965	1970	1972	1973	1974	1975	1976	1977
Total assets or liabilities and capital accounts	47.2	53.0	62.7	85.9	94.8	103.1	110.8	120.4	52.3	137.8
Assets:										
U.S. Government securities [1]	20.8	27.4	40.8	62.1	71.2	80.5	[2] 85.7	[2] 94.1	[2] 104.1	[2] 111.3
Gold certificate reserves	21.5	17.5	13.4	10.5	10.3	11.5	11.7	11.6	11.6	11.7
Special drawing rights	(X)	(X)	(X)	.4	.4	.4	.4	.5	1.2	1.3
Cash and collection items	4.5	7.7	7.0	11.4	9.5	8.2	8.6	9.2	8.2	9.9
Loans and acceptances	.1	.1	.3	.4	2.1	1.3	1.3	1.4	1.0	1.2
Other assets	.3	.3	1.1	1.1	1.3	1.2	3.2	3.3	3.2	2.4
Liabilities and capital accounts:										
Federal Reserve notes	23.6	28.4	37.1	50.3	58.8	64.3	70.9	77.2	83.7	93.2
Deposits	19.8	18.3	19.6	26.7	28.7	31.3	30.6	34.8	37.3	35.6
Deferred availability cash items	2.9	4.9	4.7	6.9	5.2	4.9	6.3	5.5	5.2	5.8
Other, and accrued dividends	(Z)	(Z)	.2	.6	.6	1.0	1.1	1.1	1.1	1.2
Capital accounts	.9	1.2	1.1	1.4	1.6	1.7	1.8	1.9	2.0	2.0

X Not applicable.   Z Less than $50 million.   [1] Beginning 1970, includes securities loaned, fully secured by U.S. Government securities pledged with Federal Reserve banks.
[2] Excludes securities sold and scheduled to be bought back under matched sale-purchase transactions.

No. 856. FEDERAL RESERVE SYSTEM—MEMBER BANK RESERVES: 1950 TO 1977

[In billions of dollars. As of December; averages of daily figures]

ITEM	1950	1960	1965	1970	1972	1973	1974	1975	1976	1977
Factors supplying reserve funds:										
F. R. bank credit outstanding [1]	21.6	29.1	43.9	66.7	76.9	85.6	94.0	99.7	107.6	116.4
U.S. Government securities [2]	20.3	27.2	40.9	61.7	71.1	79.7	86.7	92.1	100.3	107.9
Float	1.1	1.7	2.3	3.6	3.5	3.4	2.7	3.0	3.6	5.3
Other F.R. assets	.1	.1	.5	1.4	2.2	2.4	3.8	3.7	3.2	3.1
Gold stock	22.9	18.0	13.8	11.1	10.4	11.6	11.6	11.6	11.6	11.7
Special drawing rights accounts	(X)	(X)	(X)	.4	.4	.4	.4	.5	1.2	1.2
Treasury currency outstanding	4.6	5.4	5.6	7.1	8.3	8.7	9.2	10.1	10.9	11.4
Factors absorbing reserve funds:										
Currency in circulation	27.8	33.0	42.2	57.0	66.1	71.6	79.0	85.8	93.7	102.9
Treasury cash holdings	1.3	.4	.8	.4	.4	.3	.2	.5	.5	.4
Deposits with F.R. banks [3]	1.9	1.3	1.1	1.7	2.4	3.0	3.0	5.1	7.4	6.6
Other F.R. accounts	.7	1.0	.4	2.3	2.4	2.9	3.3	3.2	3.2	3.7
Member bank reserves	17.4	19.3	22.7	29.3	[4] 31.4	[4] 35.1	36.9	[4] 35.0	[4] 35.1	[4] 36.5
With F.R. banks	17.4	16.7	18.7	23.9	24.8	28.4	29.8	27.2	26.4	27.1
Currency and coin [5]	–	2.6	4.0	5.3	6.1	6.6	7.2	7.8	8.5	9.4
Required reserves	16.4	18.5	22.3	29.0	31.1	34.8	36.6	34.7	35.0	36.3
Excess reserves	1.0	.8	.5	.3	[4] .2	[4] .3	.3	.3	.2	.2
Free reserves [6]	.9	.7	(−Z)	(−Z)	−.8	−1.0	−.4	.1	.1	−.4

– Represents zero.   X Not applicable.   Z Less than $50 million.   [1] Includes industrial loans and acceptances, when held.   [2] Includes Federal agency obligations.   [3] Other than member bank reserves.
[4] Includes $428 million for 1972 and $81 million for 1973 of reserve deficiencies of which Federal Reserve banks are allowed to waive penalties for a transition period. Transition period ended after second quarter, 1974. Beginning with week ending Nov. 19, 1975, adjusted to include waivers of penalties for reserve deficiencies.
[5] Beginning 1965, figures are estimates.   [6] Excess less borrowings.

No. 857. FEDERAL RESERVE BANKS—INCOME, EXPENSES, AND DIVIDENDS: 1950 TO 1977

[1950 excludes all member banks in Alaska and Hawaii; beginning 1960, includes one member bank in the Virgin Islands. Beginning 1970, data not comparable with prior years]

ITEM	1950	1960	1965	1970	1972	1973	1974	1975	1976	1977
Number of banks	6,873	6,174	6,221	5,767	5,704	5,735	5,780	5,787	5,758	5,668
Current revenue bil. dol.	3.3	8.9	13.8	27.9	31.3	41.7	53.8	51.4	63.6	70.5
Expenses bil. dol.	2.0	5.7	10.2	22.2	25.6	35.0	46.8	44.4	55.9	61.7
Net current earnings bil. dol.	1.2	3.3	3.6	5.7	5.7	6.7	7.0	7.0	7.7	8.8
Net income bil. dol.	.8	1.7	2.1	3.8	4.4	5.0	5.4	5.5	5.9	6.6
Cash dividends declared bil. dol.	.3	.7	1.1	1.8	1.8	2.0	2.3	2.5	2.5	2.6
Capital accounts [1] bil. dol.	9.5	16.7	24.1	33.1	39.3	43.0	46.6	50.2	53.0	59.1
Ratios to average capital accounts:										
Net current earnings percent	13.2	19.6	15.1	17.3	14.5	15.5	15.1	13.9	14.5	14.9
Net income percent	8.3	10.1	8.7	11.5	11.2	11.7	10.7	11.0	11.1	11.2
Cash dividends declared percent	3.7	4.4	4.4	5.3	4.7	4.7	4.9	4.9	4.7	4.4

[1] Averages of amounts reported for varying call dates; for details, see source.

Source of tables 855–857: Board of Governors of the Federal Reserve System, *Federal Reserve Bulletin*, monthly.

No. 858. Federal Reserve System—Member Bank Reserve Requirements: 1972 to 1978

[Under criteria effective **Nov. 9, 1972**, a reserve city is designated by the presence of a Federal Reserve Bank or branch or of the head office of a bank having net demand deposits of more than $400 million. Banks having net demand deposits of $400 million or less are considered to have character of business of banks outside reserve cities and may maintain reserves at ratios set for banks not in reserve cities. Reserves are required against net balances due from domestic offices of member banks to their foreign branches, against foreign branch loans to U.S. residents, and against borrowings from foreign banks by domestic offices of a member bank. Applicable reserve percentage in Nov. 1972 was 20, reduced to 8 effective June 21, 1973, and to 4 effective May 22, 1975. See also *Historical Statistics, Colonial Times to 1970*, series X 813–820]

EFFECTIVE DATE OF CHANGE	PERCENT OF NET DEMAND DEPOSITS [1]					PERCENT OF TIME DEPOSITS						
	$2 million or less	$2– $10 million	$10– $100 million	$100– $400 million	Over $400 million [2]	Savings [3]	$5 million and under,[4] maturing in—			Over $5 million,[4][5] maturing in—		
							30– 179 days	180 days– 4 yr.	4 yr. or more	30– 179 days	180 days– 4 yr.	4 yr. or more
1972—Nov. 9	8	10	12	[6] 16½	17½	[7] 3		[7] 3			[7] 5	
Nov. 16	8	10	12	13	17½	3		3			5	
1973—July 19	8	10½	12½	13½	18	3		3			5	
1974—Dec. 12	8	10½	12½	13½	17½	3		3		6		3
1975—Feb. 13	7½	10	12	13	16½	3		3		6		3
Oct. 30	7½	10	12	13	16½	3	3		[8] 1	6	3	[8] 1
1976—Jan. 8	7½	10	12	13	16½	3	3	[8] 2½	[8] 1	6	[8] 2½	[8] 1
Dec. 30	7	9½	11¾	12¾	16¼	3	3	[8] 2½	[8] 1	6	[8] 2½	[8] 1
In effect Apr. 30, 1978	7	9½	11¾	12¾	16¼	3	3	[8] 2½	[8] 1	6	[8] 2½	[8] 1

	Minimum	Maximum
Legal requirements as of Apr. 30, 1978:		
Net demand deposits, reserve city banks	10	22
Net demand deposits, other banks	7	14
Time deposits	3	10

[1] Demand deposits subject to reserve requirements are gross demand deposits minus cash items in process of collection and demand balances due from domestic banks. [2] Reserve city banks. [3] Christmas, vacation club, and like accounts are subject to same requirements as savings. [4] Other than savings. [5] Requirements on certain large time deposits increased by marginal reserve requirements of 3 to 5 percent during June 21, 1973, through Dec. 11, 1974. [6] Applied only to former reserve city banks for one week. Other banks continued requirement of 13 percent. [7] In effect prior to Nov. 9, 1972. [8] Average reserves on all time deposits must be at least 3 percent.

Source: Board of Governors of the Federal Reserve System, *Federal Reserve Bulletin*, monthly.

No. 859. Changes in Number of Operating Banking Offices: 1950 to 1977

[As of **December 31**. Includes Puerto Rico and outlying areas]

TYPE OF CHANGE	1950	1960	1965	1970	1973	1974	1975	1976	1977
Banking offices	19,851	25,105	30,958	37,166	42,886	45,308	47,239	48,654	50,692
Number of banks	14,693	13,999	14,324	14,199	14,676	14,961	15,130	15,170	15,207
Number of branches	5,158	11,106	16,634	22,967	28,210	30,347	32,109	33,484	35,485
Net change during year	257	863	1,231	1,584	2,224	2,422	1,931	1,415	2,038
Offices opened	384	1,060	1,454	1,864	2,424	2,730	2,224	1,819	2,521
Banks	68	132	202	186	345	408	277	193	206
Branches	316	928	1,252	1,678	2,079	2,322	1,947	1,626	2,315
Offices closed	127	197	223	280	200	308	293	404	483
Banks	105	137	159	165	105	123	108	153	169
Branches	22	60	64	115	95	185	185	251	314

No. 860. Banking Offices, by Deposit Insurance Status: 1960 to 1977

[See also *Historical Statistics, Colonial Times to 1970*, series X 716–724]

ITEM	1960	1965	1970	1972	1973	1974	1975	1976	1977
All banking offices	24,954	30,776	36,910	40,377	42,593	45,011	46,931	48,345	50,381
Commercial bank, total	23,954	29,556	35,330	38,538	40,620	42,890	44,610	45,792	47,600
Member, Federal Reserve Sys.	14,301	18,514	21,940	23,644	24,694	25,718	26,462	27,097	27,842
National banks	10,036	13,776	17,142	18,571	19,567	20,437	21,009	21,402	22,232
State banks	4,265	4,738	4,798	5,073	5,127	5,281	5,453	5,695	5,610
Nonmember banks	9,653	11,042	13,390	14,894	15,926	17,172	18,148	18,695	19,758
Insured	9,253	10,723	13,159	14,643	15,673	16,884	17,841	18,368	19,397
Noninsured	400	319	231	251	253	288	307	327	361
Mutual savings bank, total	1,000	1,220	1,580	1,839	1,973	2,121	2,321	2,553	2,781
Insured	706	911	1,222	1,437	1,562	1,706	1,896	2,125	2,302
Noninsured	294	309	358	402	411	415	425	428	479

Source of tables 859 and 860: U.S. Federal Deposit Insurance Corporation, *Annual Report*.

No. 861. BANK MERGERS RESULTING IN NATIONAL BANKS, BY ASSETS OF ACQUIRING AND ACQUIRED BANKS: 1970 TO 1976

[Includes all forms of acquisition involving two or more operating banks. The bank with the larger total assets in each transaction was considered to be the acquiring bank]

ASSETS OF ACQUIRING BANKS	ACQUIRING BANKS							ACQUIRED BANKS, 1970–1976					
	1970	1971	1972	1973	1974	1975	1976	Number	With assets (in millions of dollars)				
									Under $10	$10–$25	$25–$50	$50–$100	$100 or more
Total_____	82	58	57	56	70	40	75	[1] 438	175	140	79	15	29
Under $10 mil _____	2	2	2	3	5	4	3	21	21	–	–	–	–
$10–$25 mil_____	10	1	4	5	7	4	5	36	31	5	–	–	–
$25–$50 mil_____	9	16	5	5	8	2	10	55	29	18	8	–	–
$50–$100 mil_____	6	5	12	6	11	5	13	58	24	19	14	1	–
$100 mil or more___	55	34	34	37	39	25	44	268	70	98	57	14	29

– Represents zero.
[1] Comprises 411 transactions, 11 involving 3 banks, 3 involving 4, 1 involving 5, and 1 involving 9.

Source: U.S. Comptroller of the Currency, *Annual Report*.

No. 862. BANK SUSPENSIONS—NUMBER OF BANKS AND AMOUNT OF DEPOSITS: 1947 TO 1977

[Prior to 1959, excludes Alaska and Hawaii. Banks closed either permanently or temporarily, on account of financial difficulties, by order of supervisory authorities or by directors of banks. "Member" refers to membership in Federal Reserve System. All national banks are Federal Reserve System members; all members are insured. See *Historical Statistics, Colonial Times to 1970*, series X 741–755, for similar data]

PERIOD OR YEAR	NUMBER OF BANKS					DEPOSITS (mil. dol.)				
	Total	National banks	State member banks	Nonmembers		Total	National banks	State member banks	Nonmembers	
				Noninsured	Insured				Noninsured	Insured
1947–1950_____	6	–	–	6	–	3	–	–	3	–
1951–1955_____	17	2	1	7	7	58	5	19	5	29
1956–1960_____	19	3	1	8	7	41	18	1	5	16
1961–1965_____	28	5	1	11	11	99	48	2	6	43
1966–1970_____	10	4	2	–	4	35	24	5	–	6
1971–1977_____	11	1	–	2	8	90	1	–	37	52
1970_____	1	1	–	–	–	15	15	–	–	–
1971_____	4	1	–	1	2	6	1	–	1	4
1972_____	2	–	–	1	1	57	–	–	36	21
1973_____	3	–	–	–	3	20	–	–	–	20
1974–1977 [1]____	2	–	–	–	2	7	–	–	–	7

– Represents zero.   [1] There were no bank suspensions in 1974, 1976, and 1977.

No. 863. COMMERCIAL BANKS—SUMMARY, BY CLASS OF BANK: 1970 AND 1977

[Money figures in millions of dollars. As of December 31. See *Historical Statistics, Colonial Times to 1970*, series X 717–721, for related data on banking offices]

CLASS OF BANK	BANKS		BANKING OFFICES		ASSETS		DEMAND DEPOSITS		TIME DEPOSITS	
	1970	1977	1970	1977	1970	1977	1970	1977	1970	1977
All banks_____	13,686	14,707	35,531	47,461	577.0	1,166.1	247.9	383.0	233.9	556.5
National_____	4,621	4,654	17,157	22,153	340.8	651.4	145.1	211.6	138.6	308.5
State member_____	1,147	1,014	4,802	5,602	125.5	210.4	58.5	81.2	43.0	82.2
Insured nonmember_____	7,735	8,729	13,139	19,342	106.5	267.9	42.5	84.2	51.5	154.9
Noninsured_____	184	310	433	364	4.4	36.4	1.7	6.0	.9	10.9

Source of tables 862 and 863: Board of Governors of the Federal Reserve System, *Federal Reserve Bulletin*, monthly, and unpublished data.

No. 864. CHANGES IN COMMERCIAL BANKING STRUCTURE: 1953 TO 1977

[Minus sign (−) denotes decrease]

CHANGE	1953–1977	1963 and 1964	1965 and 1966	1967 and 1968	1969 and 1970	1971 and 1972	1973 and 1974	1975 and 1976	1977
All commercial banks:									
Number of banks, beginning of period	14,074	13,426	13,760	13,766	13,678	13,687	13,927	14,458	14,671
New banks organized	4,458	635	317	197	319	472	752	464	200
Mergers and absorptions	3,645	288	286	266	296	219	215	234	154
Voluntary liquidations and suspensions	177	13	25	19	14	13	6	17	7
Number of banks, end of period	14,710	13,760	13,766	13,678	13,687	13,927	14,458	14,671	14,710
Net change in banks	636	334	6	−88	9	240	531	213	39
Number of branches, end of period	32,890	14,610	16,907	19,013	21,644	24,611	28,432	31,119	32,890
Net change in branches	27,364	2,269	2,297	2,106	2,631	2,967	3,821	2,687	1,771
States with statewide branch banking: [1]									
Number of banks, beginning of period	[2]2,771	1,485	1,537	1,479	1,394	1,307	[3]1,548	[4]1,944	1,914
New banks organized	1,124	152	50	32	42	105	180	118	75
Mergers and absorptions	1,918	98	107	115	128	74	87	140	42
Voluntary liquidations and suspensions	33	2	1	2	1	1	2	8	3
Number of banks, end of period	1,944	1,537	1,479	1,394	1,307	1,337	1,639	1,914	1,944
Net change in banks	−827	52	−58	−85	−87	30	91	−30	30
Number of branches, end of period	17,149	6,243	7,085	7,910	8,923	9,997	12,529	16,720	17,149
Net change in branches	12,620	970	842	825	1,013	1,074	1,359	1,101	429
States with limited branch banking: [5]									
Number of banks, beginning of period	[6]6,146	5,184	5,123	5,058	4,995	4,940	[3]4,692	[4][6]5,373	[7]6,141
New banks organized	1,519	115	102	76	99	103	172	96	38
Mergers and absorptions	1,532	173	155	130	149	135	112	83	107
Voluntary liquidations and suspensions	63	3	12	9	5	5	1	2	2
Number of banks, end of period	6,070	5,123	5,058	4,995	4,940	4,903	4,751	5,384	6,070
Net change in banks	−76	−61	−65	−63	−55	−37	59	11	−71
Number of branches, end of period	14,002	7,750	9,098	10,210	11,654	13,283	14,028	12,797	14,002
Net change in branches	12,876	1,190	1,348	1,112	1,444	1,629	1,918	1,193	979
States with unit banking: [8]									
Number of banks, beginning of period	[2]5,157	6,757	7,100	7,229	7,289	7,440	7,687	[6]7,141	[7]6,616
New banks organized	1,815	368	165	89	178	264	400	250	87
Mergers and absorptions	195	17	24	21	19	10	16	11	5
Voluntary liquidations and suspensions	81	8	12	8	8	7	3	7	2
Number of banks, end of period	6,696	7,100	7,229	7,289	7,440	7,687	8,068	7,373	6,696
Net change in banks	1,539	343	129	60	151	247	381	232	80
Number of branches, end of period	1,739	617	724	893	1,067	1,331	1,875	1,602	1,739
Net change in branches	1,868	109	107	169	174	264	544	393	363

[1] Alaska, Ariz., Calif., Conn., Del., Hawaii, Idaho, Maine, Md., Nev., N.J., N.Y., N.C., Oreg., R.I., S.C., S. Dak., Utah, Vt., Va., Wash., and D.C.   [2] Adjusted for changes occurring in N.J., 1974; Ark., Iowa and N.Y., 1976; and Fla., 1977. See footnotes 3, 4, 6, and 8.   [3] Beginning 1974, adjusted for N.J. (from limited to statewide).   [4] Beginning 1976, adjusted for N.Y. (from limited to statewide).   [5] Limited usually to county where bank's head office is located or to contiguous counties: Ala., Ark., Fla., Ga., Ind., Iowa, Ky., La., Mass., Mich., Miss., N.H., N. Mex., Ohio, Pa., Tenn., and Wis.   [6] Beginning 1976, adjusted for Ark. and Iowa (from unit banking to limited).   [7] Beginning 1977, adjusted for Fla. (from unit banking to limited).   [8] Branch banking strictly limited or prohibited: Colo., Ill., Kans., Minn., Mo., Mont., Nebr., N. Dak., Okla., Tex., W. Va., and Wyo.

Source: Board of Governors of the Federal Reserve System, *Federal Reserve Bulletin*, monthly, and unpublished data.

No. 865. LARGEST COMMERCIAL BANKS—FINANCIAL DATA, BY RANK OF ASSETS: 1960 TO 1977

[In billions of dollars, except percent. As of December 31. See also table 866]

ASSET GROUP	1960		1965		1970		1975		1977	
	Assets	Deposits	Assets	Deposits	Assets	Deposits	Assets	Deposits	Assets	Deposits
50 largest	98.6	85.5	146.7	124.6	220.0	173.9	348.0	265.9	413.1	300.7
Percent of all commercial banks	39.1	38.5	39.4	38.4	34.3	32.2	35.7	33.5	35.2	31.9
Lowest ten	6.6	5.9	9.2	8.1	16.4	13.5	23.0	17.8	27.3	20.9
Second ten	8.1	7.2	12.1	10.6	19.5	16.4	28.7	22.1	34.1	24.5
Third ten	10.4	9.3	14.8	12.9	24.2	20.0	34.1	25.8	41.3	30.4
Fourth ten	19.3	16.8	28.9	24.8	42.4	33.6	67.2	51.7	82.1	62.5
Highest ten	54.3	46.4	81.7	68.1	117.4	90.5	195.0	148.5	228.2	162.3
Percent of total	100.0	100.0	100.0	100.0	100.0	100.0	100.0	100.0	100.0	100.0
Lowest ten	6.6	6.8	6.3	6.5	7.4	7.7	6.6	6.7	6.6	7.0
Second ten	8.2	8.4	8.2	8.5	8.9	9.4	8.2	8.3	8.3	8.1
Third ten	10.6	10.9	10.1	10.4	11.0	11.5	9.8	9.7	10.0	10.1
Fourth ten	19.5	19.6	19.7	19.9	19.3	19.3	19.3	19.4	19.9	20.8
Highest ten	55.0	54.3	55.7	54.7	53.4	52.0	56.1	55.9	55.2	54.0

Source: U.S. Federal Deposit Insurance Corporation, unpublished data.

No. 866. COMMERCIAL BANKS—ASSETS AND LIABILITIES: 1960 TO 1977

[In billions of dollars, except number of banks. As of December 31. Includes noninsured nondeposit trust companies. Includes outlying areas. Beginning 1965, includes asset and liability figures for American branches of foreign banks (tabulated as banks) licensed to do a deposit business. See *Historical Statistics, Colonial Times to 1970*, series X 588–609, for related data]

ITEM	1960	1965	1970	1973	1974	1975	1976	1977
Number of banks	13,484	13,818	13,705	14,194	14,488	14,657	14,698	14,738
Assets	260.7	382.9	581.5	842.9	927.5	974.7	1,040.1	1,176.6
Securities, total [1]	82.0	104.6	148.5	189.9	195.9	230.8	253.2	261.0
Investment securities [1][2]	82.0	104.6	142.7	181.2	187.9	225.5	243.7	252.9
U.S. Treasury	61.1	59.7	59.3	55.7	52.3	81.6	98.0	97.0
Obligations of States and subdivisions	17.6	38.7	67.9	91.8	97.6	101.6	103.3	113.7
Federal funds sold and sec. purchased [3]	–	2.1	16.3	35.4	40.1	39.3	48.5	54.2
Loans, gross	120.5	204.7	300.4	464.1	514.2	512.5	552.1	632.3
Commercial and industrial loans	43.4	71.9	113.4	160.8	188.6	181.0	185.1	207.3
Real estate loans	28.8	49.7	73.3	119.1	132.1	136.5	151.2	179.0
Construction and land development	(4)	(4)	(4)	(4)	(4)	(4)	17.3	21.4
Secured by farmland	1.6	2.9	4.4	5.4	6.0	6.4	6.7	7.8
Secured by residential properties	20.4	32.4	45.6	74.9	82.4	83.1	85.9	101.9
Secured by other properties	6.8	14.4	23.3	38.7	43.7	46.9	41.3	47.9
Loans to domestic commercial and foreign banks	1.0	2.2	2.7	10.3	12.4	12.8	15.5	16.7
Loans to other financial institutions	7.1	13.3	15.9	30.7	35.3	29.7	27.2	27.2
Securities loans (dealers and other)	5.1	8.5	9.8	12.0	9.2	11.1	15.4	17.4
Loans to farmers (excl. real estate)	5.7	8.2	11.2	17.3	18.2	20.2	23.2	25.7
Other loans to individuals	26.5	45.7	66.3	100.8	104.0	107.6	119.3	141.5
All other loans (incl. overdrafts)	2.9	5.3	7.7	13.3	14.3	13.6	15.1	17.5
Reserve for possible loan losses [5]	(X)	(X)	(X)	(X)	(X)	(X)	6.3	6.9
Unearned income on loans [6]	(X)	(X)	(X)	(X)	(X)	(X)	12.7	14.9
Net loans	(X)	(X)	(X)	(X)	(X)	(X)	533.2	610.5
Cash, balances with banks, etc [1]	52.2	61.0	94.0	119.2	128.8	134.5	136.8	170.1
Balances with banks, incl. reserve	30.6	33.6	47.1	63.7	69.6	74.7	76.1	89.3
Cash items in process of collection	18.3	22.5	39.8	44.8	47.5	47.4	48.5	66.6
Other	5.9	10.4	22.4	34.1	48.4	57.7	68.4	80.9
Liabilities and equity capital	260.7	382.9	581.5	842.9	927.5	974.7	1,040.1	1,176.6
Deposits	230.5	333.8	485.5	687.6	753.6	792.9	845.1	947.1
Demand	156.8	185.5	249.0	311.7	317.5	325.5	338.7	384.9
Time	73.7	148.5	236.5	375.9	436.1	467.4	506.4	562.2
Business and personal	189.0	276.8	397.3	558.7	608.9	652.9	704.8	788.3
Government	22.6	32.4	49.7	73.9	74.6	71.1	72.3	85.1
Domestic interbank	15.8	17.5	29.2	38.0	46.0	45.3	45.6	60.4
Foreign government and bank	3.1	7.0	9.3	16.9	24.2	23.5	22.4	13.3
Miscellaneous liabilities [5][6]	6.8	14.7	46.5	89.0	101.2	103.3	116.7	143.4
Reserves on loan and securities	2.4	4.0	6.3	7.8	8.7	9.1	(5)	(5)
Subordinated notes and debentures	.1	1.7	2.2	4.2	4.4	4.6	5.3	5.8
Equity capital	21.0	28.7	41.0	54.2	59.6	64.9	73.1	80.3
Stock	6.3	8.7	11.4	14.0	14.9	15.7	16.4	17.4
Surplus	10.0	13.6	18.2	23.7	25.5	26.9	29.3	31.7
Undivided profits and reserve [5]	4.7	6.5	11.4	16.5	19.1	22.3	27.4	31.2

- Represents zero. X Not applicable. [1] Includes other categories not shown separately.
[2] Prior to 1970, securities reported on net (after deduction of reserves) basis. [3] Under agreements to resell.
[4] Prior to 1976, included in other categories of real estate loans.
[5] Beginning 1976, reserves on loans and securities included under undivided profits and reserves and miscellaneous liabilities on the liability side and under reserve for possible loan losses on the asset side.
[6] Prior to 1976, unearned income on loans was reported under miscellaneous liabilities.

Source: U.S. Federal Deposit Insurance Corporation, *Assets and Liabilities: Commercial and Mutual Savings Banks*, semiannual.

No. 867. MUTUAL SAVINGS BANKS—ASSETS AND LIABILITIES: 1960 TO 1977

[In billions of dollars, except number of banks. As of Dec. 31. Includes Puerto Rico and Virgin Islands. See *Historical Statistics, Colonial Times to 1970*, series X 687–688 and X 821–833, for related data]

ITEM	1960	1965	1970	1972	1973	1974	1975	1976	1977
Number of banks	515	506	494	486	482	480	476	473	467
Assets	40.6	58.2	79.2	100.6	106.7	109.5	121.1	134.8	147.3
Loans and discounts, gross [1]	27.1	45.3	60.4	70.6	77.1	78.7	81.3	86.8	94.4
Real estate loans	26.9	44.6	57.9	67.6	73.2	74.9	77.2	81.6	88.2
Securities	12.0	11.0	16.2	26.3	25.2	26.0	34.2	42.0	46.6
U.S. Government	10.5	6.3	5.0	7.6	7.0	6.8	10.8	14.8	17.4
Other securities	1.5	4.7	11.2	18.7	18.2	19.1	23.4	27.2	29.1
Other assets	1.5	2.0	2.7	3.8	4.3	4.9	5.6	6.0	6.3
Liabilities and surplus accts	40.6	58.2	79.2	100.6	106.7	109.5	121.1	134.8	147.3
Deposits	36.4	52.8	72.1	92.2	97.2	99.4	110.6	123.7	134.9
Miscellaneous liabilities	.7	.8	1.2	1.4	1.9	2.2	2.1	2.1	2.4
Surplus accounts	3.6	4.7	5.9	7.0	7.6	8.0	8.4	9.1	10.0

[1] Prior to 1970, data net of valuation reserves and not comparable with later years. Includes other amounts not shown separately.

Source: U.S. Federal Deposit Insurance Corporation, *Annual Report*.

No. 868. Insured Commercial Banks—Assets and Liabilities, States and Other Areas: 1977

[In millions of dollars, except number of banks. As of December 31]

STATE OR OTHER AREA	Number of banks	Total assets	Loans and Federal funds sold	Investment and trading account securities	Loans Total	Loans Commercial and industrial	Real estate	Equity capital	Deposits Total	Deposits Demand	Deposits Time
Total	14,412	1,137,687	641,188	258,408	375,696	197,095	178,601	79,288	929,170	378,724	550,446
U.S.	14,397	1,129,712	636,322	257,271	372,370	195,459	176,911	79,084	922,665	377,034	545,631
Ala	310	13,579	7,933	3,585	4,347	2,168	2,179	1,020	11,701	4,490	7,211
Alaska	12	1,769	1,074	366	745	299	446	140	1,519	726	793
Ariz	17	8,730	5,546	1,496	3,152	1,475	1,677	418	7,601	2,981	4,620
Ark	259	8,552	5,120	2,175	2,938	1,218	1,720	628	7,447	2,926	4,521
Calif	220	124,780	73,804	21,106	45,281	21,633	23,648	7,100	101,010	37,516	63,494
Colo	288	11,231	6,956	2,185	3,635	2,085	1,550	772	9,635	4,344	5,292
Conn	71	10,383	6,062	2,048	3,693	1,674	2,019	669	8,987	4,193	4,795
Del	17	3,075	1,381	1,225	793	207	586	200	2,428	985	1,443
D.C	16	5,379	3,109	1,303	1,681	665	1,016	420	4,392	2,334	2,058
Fla	676	33,986	17,024	11,120	9,470	3,715	5,755	2,567	29,702	12,347	17,355
Ga	440	17,970	10,861	3,158	5,681	2,745	2,936	1,371	14,583	7,105	7,478
Hawaii	8	3,492	2,052	860	1,429	456	973	213	3,116	1,163	1,953
Idaho	24	3,777	2,341	849	1,260	604	656	230	3,288	1,181	2,108
Ill	1,235	87,225	49,214	23,767	29,094	17,755	11,339	6,115	68,837	24,503	44,333
Ind	407	25,556	14,361	7,351	8,727	2,962	5,765	1,791	21,804	7,493	14,312
Iowa	649	16,094	9,821	4,238	4,492	1,868	2,624	1,212	14,225	4,484	9,741
Kan	615	12,476	7,282	3,430	2,963	1,602	1,361	987	10,804	4,118	6,686
Ky	343	14,104	8,523	3,472	4,507	1,708	2,799	1,059	12,182	5,235	6,947
La	254	17,214	9,732	4,689	5,708	2,919	2,789	1,246	14,725	6,024	8,701
Maine	43	2,731	1,720	649	1,181	511	670	193	2,391	788	1,604
Md	108	12,478	7,675	2,515	4,778	1,614	3,164	896	10,618	4,198	6,420
Mass	145	20,704	10,963	4,463	6,989	4,615	2,374	1,477	16,334	8,044	8,290
Mich	361	41,776	24,661	10,323	15,635	5,664	9,971	2,835	36,094	11,109	24,984
Minn	752	21,742	12,555	5,773	7,396	3,594	3,802	1,470	18,028	6,223	11,805
Miss	184	8,341	4,701	2,295	2,440	1,035	1,405	607	7,351	2,780	4,572
Mo	712	26,049	14,816	6,731	7,595	3,513	4,082	1,857	21,286	9,273	12,013
Mont	157	4,006	2,437	1,036	1,261	596	665	277	3,600	1,225	2,375
Nebr	451	8,568	5,306	1,853	1,732	1,086	646	656	7,395	2,951	4,444
Nev	8	2,719	1,531	691	1,079	398	681	194	2,431	1,061	1,370
N.H	78	2,434	1,586	513	1,143	373	770	186	2,164	658	1,506
N.J	188	29,504	15,883	9,069	10,955	4,071	6,884	1,962	25,710	9,430	16,280
N. Mex	83	4,303	2,556	1,052	1,373	769	604	280	3,831	1,490	2,341
N.Y.[1]	231	193,942	95,924	29,731	57,422	43,774	13,648	14,721	139,990	77,633	62,358
N.C	89	17,324	9,937	3,865	5,205	3,169	2,036	1,172	14,419	6,160	8,259
N. Dak	170	3,476	2,125	964	1,008	497	511	266	3,144	1,049	2,095
Ohio	486	43,278	23,931	12,123	14,016	5,897	8,119	3,566	36,264	13,125	23,139
Okla	476	15,102	8,539	3,982	4,316	2,524	1,792	1,090	13,144	5,356	7,788
Oreg	53	9,715	5,783	1,912	3,424	1,790	1,634	548	7,766	3,050	4,716
Pa	381	64,866	37,328	16,850	23,457	11,553	11,904	4,451	51,830	17,570	34,260
R.I	14	4,733	2,961	1,034	2,351	882	1,469	295	3,772	991	2,780
S.C	88	5,779	3,312	1,481	1,581	841	740	445	4,967	2,680	2,287
S. Dak	157	3,822	2,443	1,014	1,065	487	578	281	3,443	1,009	2,434
Tenn	346	18,127	10,766	4,236	5,976	2,695	3,281	1,261	15,840	5,626	10,213
Tex	1,377	71,760	39,848	17,902	21,524	14,327	7,197	5,036	60,275	27,452	32,824
Utah	71	5,006	3,211	988	2,102	968	1,134	309	4,375	1,645	2,729
Vt	30	1,844	1,240	421	937	236	701	117	1,678	415	1,263
Va	279	18,882	11,459	4,487	6,984	2,645	4,339	1,358	16,418	5,849	10,568
Wash	86	15,054	9,714	2,185	5,765	3,379	2,386	847	12,203	4,926	7,277
W. Va	227	8,129	4,483	2,674	2,586	687	1,899	662	6,980	2,209	4,771
Wis	623	21,449	13,152	5,272	8,657	3,064	5,593	1,435	18,539	6,063	12,476
Wyo	82	2,425	1,393	663	784	400	384	181	2,156	792	1,364
P. Rico [2]	14	6,958	4,319	989	2,870	1,443	1,427	200	5,738	1,523	4,214
Guam [3] and Samoa	1	309	219	15	166	62	104	3	261	94	167
V.I.[4]	1	708	327	134	290	131	159	–	506	72	434

- Represents zero.
[1] Includes data for 19 insured branches operated by 3 State nonmember banks in Puerto Rico.
[2] Includes data for 23 insured branches operated by 2 national banks in New York.
[3] Consists of data for 11 insured branches located in Guam operated by 2 State nonmember banks in Hawaii, 2 State nonmember banks and a national bank in California, and 2 national banks in New York.
[4] Includes data for 24 insured branches operated by 2 national banks in New York, a national bank in California, and a national bank in Pennsylvania.

Source: U.S. Federal Deposit Insurance Corporation, *Assets and Liabilities: Commercial and Mutual Savings Banks*, semiannual.

No. 869. Savings and Loan Associations—Financial Items: 1950 to 1977

[In billions of dollars, except number of associations. As of December 31, except as indicated. Includes Puerto Rico and Guam. See headnote, table 870. Beginning 1965, excludes associations which have either liquidated or converted to banks; for details, see source. See also *Historical Statistics, Colonial Times to 1970*, series X 834–844]

ITEM	1950	1960	1965	1970	1972	1973	1974	1975	1976	1977, prel.
Number of associations_____1,000__	6.0	6.3	6.2	5.7	5.3	5.2	5.0	4.9	4.8	4.8
Number insured_____1,000__	2.9	4.1	4.5	4.4	4.2	4.2	4.1	4.1	4.0	4.1
Total assets_____	16.9	71.5	129.6	176.2	243.1	271.9	295.5	338.2	391.9	459.3
Cash and investment securities___	2.5	7.9	12.1	16.5	24.4	21.1	23.3	30.9	35.7	39.2
Mortgage loans outstanding ¹_____	13.7	60.1	110.3	150.3	206.2	231.7	249.3	278.6	323.0	381.2
FHA and VA_____	3.8	10.7	11.5	18.7	28.9	29.7	29.9	30.6	(NA)	(NA)
Conventional_____	9.8	49.3	98.8	131.7	177.3	202.0	219.4	248.0	(NA)	(NA)
Other assets_____	.8	3.5	7.2	9.3	12.6	19.1	22.9	28.7	33.2	38.9
Total liabilities_____	15.6	66.5	120.9	163.8	227.9	254.8	277.1	318.5	369.9	434.1
Savings capital_____	14.0	62.1	110.4	146.4	206.8	227.0	243.0	285.7	335.9	386.9
Other ²_____	1.6	4.4	10.5	17.4	21.1	27.9	34.1	32.7	34.0	47.2
Net worth_____	(NA)	(NA)	(NA)	12.4	15.2	17.1	18.4	19.8	22.0	25.2
Mortgage loans made during year ¹ ³ ⁴	5.2	14.3	24.2	21.4	51.4	49.4	39.0	55.0	78.8	107.4
Home construction ⁴_____	1.8	4.7	6.0	4.2	8.5	8.4	6.5	8.7	13.0	18.2
Home purchase ⁴_____	2.2	6.1	10.8	10.2	26.6	28.2	22.6	30.7	45.7	62.5
Net new savings ⁵_____	(NA)	(NA)	(NA)	5.3	23.9	10.5	4.7	29.3	34.4	32.0

NA Not available.
¹ Beginning 1970, real estate sold on contract included in mortgage lending data; prior years, in "Other assets."
² Prior to 1970, permanent stock included in "Other liabilities"; thereafter, in "Net worth."
³ Includes loans not shown separately. ⁴ Covers only 1–4 unit residential structures.
⁵ Insured associations only.

Source: U.S. Federal Home Loan Bank Board, *Savings and Home Financing Source Book*, annual.

No. 870. Savings and Loan Associations—Selected Financial Items, States and Other Areas: 1976

[In millions of dollars, except number of associations. As of December 31. Major balance sheet items for all operating and insured associations not identical with those shown in table 869, primarily because some State-chartered associations submit their reports on dates other than Dec. 31]

STATE OR OTHER AREA	Number of associations	Total assets	Mortgage loans outstanding	Savings capital	STATE OR OTHER AREA	Number of associations	Total assets	Mortgage loans outstanding	Savings capital
Total_____	4,821	390,407	321,961	334,390	Montana_____	16	695	593	600
					Nebraska_____	44	3,386	2,833	2,753
Alabama_____	60	3,165	2,587	2,829	Nevada_____	7	1,191	923	996
Alaska_____	4	240	204	188	New Hampshire_	17	769	662	665
Arizona_____	16	3,837	2,921	3,178	New Jersey_____	232	15,405	11,889	13,384
Arkansas_____	71	2,700	2,211	2,402	New Mexico_____	34	1,405	1,170	1,230
California_____	164	69,141	58,566	57,102					
					New York_____	138	21,047	15,967	18,257
Colorado_____	46	5,644	4,785	4,616	North Carolina___	181	7,816	6,746	6,967
Connecticut_____	36	3,153	2,564	2,719	North Dakota___	12	1,438	1,174	1,191
Delaware_____	20	222	196	189	Ohio_____	416	26,895	21,840	23,140
District of					Oklahoma_____	55	3,560	2,903	3,020
Columbia_____	16	3,991	3,509	3,338					
Florida_____	123	28,215	22,858	25,068	Oregon_____	28	4,304	3,529	3,591
					Pennsylvania____	428	17,029	14,293	14,457
Georgia_____	99	7,357	6,279	6,344	Rhode Island____	6	597	498	528
Hawaii_____	9	1,620	1,370	1,329	South Carolina__	73	4,121	3,523	3,596
Idaho_____	11	696	602	592	South Dakota____	19	687	558	596
Illinois_____	422	28,949	23,749	24,864					
Indiana_____	166	7,355	5,916	6,449	Tennessee_____	94	4,727	3,953	4,070
					Texas_____	318	19,999	16,184	16,972
Iowa_____	79	4,813	4,072	4,181	Utah_____	16	2,241	1,909	1,740
Kansas_____	86	4,840	4,218	4,058	Vermont_____	7	185	155	160
Kentucky_____	108	3,981	3,343	3,578	Virginia_____	80	5,594	4,830	4,890
Louisiana_____	113	5,162	4,275	4,552					
Maine_____	23	478	392	411	Washington_____	48	5,964	5,024	5,000
					West Virginia____	37	996	801	868
Maryland_____	206	7,259	6,176	6,288	Wisconsin_____	122	8,441	7,245	7,187
Massachusetts____	163	6,601	5,208	5,770	Wyoming_____	14	499	424	421
Michigan_____	66	11,365	9,379	10,181					
Minnesota_____	66	7,162	5,898	6,147	Puerto Rico_____	12	1,174	956	953
Mississippi_____	77	1,975	1,598	1,795	Guam_____	2	31	17	25
Missouri_____	115	10,291	8,487	8,965					

Source: U.S. Federal Home Loan Bank Board, *Asset and Liability Trends*, annual.

No. 871. Federal and State-Chartered Credit Unions—Summary: 1960 to 1977

[As of December 31. Includes District of Columbia, Puerto Rico, Canal Zone, Guam, and Virgin Islands, except as noted. See also *Historical Statistics, Colonial Times to 1970*, series X 864–878]

YEAR	CREDIT UNIONS REPORTING [1]		MEMBERS (1,000)		ASSETS (mil. dol.)		LOANS OUTSTANDING (mil. dol.)		SAVINGS (mil. dol.)	
	Federal	State [2]	Federal	State [2]	Federal	State [2]	Federal	State [2]	Federal	State [2][3]
1960	9,905	10,151	6,087	5,971	2,670	2,989	2,021	2,381	2,344	2,637
1965	11,543	10,521	8,641	8,115	5,166	5,385	3,865	4,233	4,538	4,682
1970	12,977	10,679	11,966	10,853	8,861	9,089	6,969	7,137	7,629	7,857
1972	12,708	10,354	13,572	12,118	12,514	12,275	9,424	9,239	10,956	10,670
1973	12,688	10,191	14,666	12,886	14,569	13,806	11,109	10,650	12,598	11,914
1974	12,748	10,105	15,870	13,581	16,715	15,233	12,730	11,702	14,371	13,148
1975	12,737	9,871	17,066	14,214	20,209	17,804	14,869	13,300	17,530	15,522
1976	12,757	9,776	18,624	15,246	24,396	20,829	18,311	16,073	21,130	18,043
1977, prel	12,752	9,696	20,229	16,283	29,574	24,510	22,717	19,338	25,849	20,983

[1] Does not represent number chartered; reports not received from all unions in operation, and some are inactive. However, number of Federal unions reporting is same as number in operation. [2] Alaska, Del., and, for 1960–1973, Hawaii, Nev., S. Dak., Wyo., C.Z., Guam, V.I., and, beginning 1965, Dist. of Col., have no State or local credit union law. [3] Includes members' deposits.

Source: 1960–1965, U.S. Social Security Administration, *Federal Credit Union Program*, annual. Beginning 1970, National Credit Union Administration, *Annual Report of the National Credit Union Administration* and *State-Chartered Credit Unions*.

No. 872. Selected Federal Credit Agencies—Major Balance Sheet Items: 1960 to 1977

[In millions of dollars. As of Dec. 31. Excludes capital accounts except for stock of home loan banks. Bonds, debentures, and notes valued at par; include only publicly offered securities and are not guaranteed by U.S. Government. Loans are gross of valuation reserves and represent cost for FNMA and unpaid principal for other agencies. See *Historical Statistics, Colonial Times to 1970*, series N 300, for FHLB advances]

AGENCY AND ITEM	1960	1965	1970	1973	1974	1975	1976	1977
Federal home loan banks (FHLB):								
Assets: Advances to members	1,981	5,997	10,614	15,147	21,804	17,845	15,862	20,173
Investments	1,222	1,640	3,861	3,507	0,094	4,370	0,079	5,749
Liabilities and capital: Bonds and notes	1,266	5,221	10,183	15,362	21,890	18,900	16,811	18,345
Deposits and borrowings	938	1,045	2,332	1,745	2,484	2,701	4,024	4,286
Capital stock	989	1,277	1,607	2,122	2,624	2,705	2,889	3,295
FNMA: [1]								
Assets: Mortgage loans	2,788	2,456	15,502	24,175	29,578	31,824	32,937	34,377
Liabilities: Debentures and notes	2,523	1,884	15,206	23,001	28,167	29,963	30,565	31,890
Banks for cooperatives:								
Assets: Loans to cooperatives	649	1,055	2,030	2,577	3,575	3,979	4,413	5,600
Liabilities: Debentures	407	797	1,755	2,695	3,589	3,655	4,330	4,434
Federal intermediate credit banks:								
Assets: Loans and discounts	1,501	2,516	4,974	7,198	8,848	9,994	11,312	12,758
Liabilities: Debentures	1,454	2,335	4,799	6,932	8,589	9,254	10,494	11,174
Federal land banks:								
Assets: Loans	2,564	4,281	7,186	11,071	13,643	16,564	19,127	22,813
Liabilities: Bonds	2,210	3,710	6,395	10,062	12,653	15,000	17,127	19,118

[1] Secondary market operations of Federal National Mortgage Association.

No. 873. Mortgage Debt Outstanding, by Type of Holder: 1960 to 1977

[In billions of dollars, except percent. As of Dec. 31. Includes Puerto Rico and Guam. 1977 data are preliminary. See also *Historical Statistics, Colonial Times to 1970*, series N 273 and N 276]

TYPE OF PROPERTY AND HOLDER	1960	1965	1970	1973	1974	1975	1976	1977	PERCENT			
									1965	1970	1975	1977
Total	207	333	474	682	743	802	889	1,020	100.0	100.0	100.0	100.0
Residential nonfarm	162	258	358	510	550	591	661	762	77.3	75.6	73.7	74.7
1- to 4-family homes	142	220	298	417	450	491	557	650	66.1	62.9	61.2	63.7
Savings and loan assns	55	94	125	188	202	224	261	308	28.3	26.4	27.9	30.2
Commercial banks	19	30	42	68	75	77	86	101	9.1	8.9	9.6	9.9
Mutual savings banks	21	34	42	49	49	50	53	58	10.1	8.9	6.2	5.7
Life insurance companies	25	30	27	20	19	18	16	15	8.9	5.6	2.2	1.5
Individuals and others	15	26	40	65	72	84	105	132	7.8	8.5	10.5	12.9
Federal agencies	7	6	22	27	33	38	36	36	1.9	4.6	4.7	3.5
5 or more units	20	37	60	93	100	101	105	111	11.2	12.7	12.6	10.9
Commercial	32	54	86	131	146	159	171	192	16.3	18.0	19.8	18.8
Farm	13	21	30	41	46	51	57	66	6.4	6.4	6.4	6.5

Source of tables 872 and 873: Board of Governors of the Federal Reserve System, *Federal Reserve Bulletin*, monthly.

No. 874. Mortgage Activity of Banks, Insurance Companies, and Savings and Loan Associations: 1950 to 1977

[In billions of dollars. Loans outstanding are as of end of year. Bank data include Puerto Rico; savings and loan data include Puerto Rico and Guam. See *Historical Statistics, Colonial Times to 1970*, series N 266-267, X 836-839, and X 911]

ITEM	1950	1960	1965	1970	1972	1973	1974	1975	1976	1977
Commercial banks:										
Loans outstanding [1]	13.7	28.8	49.7	73.3	99.3	119.1	132.1	136.2	151.3	176.7
Nonfarm residential	10.4	20.4	32.4	45.6	62.8	74.9	82.4	82.9	94.3	110.0
FHA-insured	(NA)	5.9	7.7	7.9	8.5	8.2	7.2	6.3	5.6	(NA)
VA-guaranteed	(NA)	2.9	2.7	2.6	3.2	3.3	3.2	3.1	3.0	(NA)
Conventional	(NA)	11.7	22.0	35.1	51.1	63.4	72.0	73.5	85.7	(NA)
Other nonfarm	2.3	6.8	14.4	23.3	31.8	38.7	43.7	46.9	50.3	58.7
Farm	1.0	1.6	2.9	4.4	4.8	5.4	6.0	6.4	6.7	8.0
Mutual savings banks:										
Loans acquired	2.5	4.4	8.7	5.9	12.9	13.3	8.7	9.4	11.9	(NA)
Loans outstanding [2]	8.3	26.9	44.6	57.9	67.6	73.2	74.9	77.2	81.6	88.0
Nonfarm residential	7.1	24.3	40.1	49.9	57.1	61.1	62.1	63.8	67.3	72.8
FHA-insured	1.6	7.1	13.8	16.1	16.0	15.5	14.8	14.4	14.6	(NA)
VA-guaranteed	1.5	9.0	11.4	12.0	12.6	12.9	12.7	12.4	12.3	(NA)
Conventional	4.0	8.2	14.9	21.8	28.5	32.7	34.6	37.0	40.4	(NA)
Other nonfarm	1.2	2.6	4.5	7.9	10.4	12.0	12.7	13.3	14.3	15.2
Life insurance companies:										
Loans acquired	4.9	6.1	11.1	7.2	8.7	11.5	11.4	9.6	9.7	13.6
Nonfarm	4.5	5.6	10.0	6.9	8.0	10.5	10.4	8.5	8.2	11.1
Farm	.4	.5	1.1	.3	.7	1.0	1.0	1.1	1.5	2.5
Loans outstanding	16.1	41.8	60.0	74.4	76.9	81.4	86.2	89.2	91.6	96.8
Nonfarm	14.8	38.8	55.2	68.7	71.3	75.4	79.9	82.4	84.1	87.9
FHA-insured	4.6	9.0	12.1	11.4	10.0	9.2	8.5	7.9	7.3	6.6
VA-guaranteed	2.0	6.9	6.3	5.4	4.7	4.4	4.2	3.9	3.6	3.3
Other	8.2	22.9	36.8	51.9	56.6	61.8	67.2	70.6	73.2	78.0
Farm	1.3	3.0	4.8	5.6	5.7	6.0	6.3	6.8	7.5	8.8
Savings and loan assns.:										
Loans made	5.2	14.3	24.2	21.4	51.4	49.5	39.0	55.0	78.8	(NA)
Loans outstanding [3]	13.7	60.1	110.3	150.3	206.2	231.7	249.3	278.6	323.0	381.2
FHA-insured	1.0	3.5	5.1	10.2	15.4	15.1	14.5	16.5	14.7	(NA)
VA-guaranteed	3.0	7.2	6.4	8.5	13.5	14.7	15.3	14.0	16.6	(NA)
Conventional	9.8	49.3	98.8	131.7	177.3	202.0	219.4	248.0	291.7	(NA)

NA Not available.   [1] Includes loans held by nondeposit trust companies; excludes holdings of trust departments of commercial banks.   [2] Includes a small amount of farm loans not shown separately.   [3] Beginning 1960, includes shares pledged against mortgage loans, and, beginning 1970, junior liens and real estate sold on contract. Beginning 1970, reflects minor downward adjustment for change in universe.

Source: Board of Governors of the Federal Reserve System. Current data in *Federal Reserve Bulletin*, monthly.

No. 875. Holdings of Construction, Long-Term Mortgage, and Land Loans, by Type of Loan, 1970 to 1976, and by Lender, 1976

[In billions of dollars. As of end of year]

					1976					
								Lender		
TYPE OF LOAN	1970	1973	1974	1975	Total [1]	Savings and loan assn.	Commercial banks	Mutual savings banks	Life insurance companies	Federal credit agencies
Mortgage credits, total	420.7	618.0	673.5	727.6	806.1	323.4	150.7	81.4	88.8	71.8
Construction loans	18.3	44.9	42.8	39.3	40.4	14.1	17.0	.9	.4	(Z)
1-4 unit family homes	5.4	14.7	13.1	14.1	15.8	8.9	4.8	.3	(Z)	-
Multifamily residential	6.2	16.0	14.6	11.0	9.8	2.3	3.5	.3	(Z)	(Z)
Nonresidential	6.5	14.1	15.0	14.1	14.8	2.9	8.7	.3	.4	-
Farm properties	.1	.1	.1	.1	.1	-	-	-	-	-
Long-term mortgage loans	398.2	561.2	616.9	675.6	754.6	306.7	129.5	80.2	88.1	71.8
1-4 unit family homes	265.6	363.1	394.0	431.8	489.9	253.5	77.5	52.4	15.5	36.6
FHA insured	61.2	66.6	65.6	67.8	71.3	13.0	5.1	11.9	5.9	14.7
VA guaranteed	36.6	48.1	52.6	55.1	61.3	16.2	3.0	12.2	3.6	10.4
Conventional	167.8	248.4	275.9	308.8	357.3	224.3	69.3	28.3	6.0	11.5
Multifamily	45.8	68.4	76.8	81.1	88.1	26.6	5.3	13.9	18.5	12.6
Nonresidential	66.4	103.0	115.8	128.9	138.7	26.2	39.9	13.9	46.8	3.9
Farm properties	20.3	26.7	30.3	33.8	37.8	.4	6.7	-	7.3	18.8
Land loans	4.2	12.0	13.8	12.6	11.1	2.6	4.2	.3	.3	-

- Represents zero.   Z Less than $50 million.   [1] Includes lenders, not shown separately.

Source: U.S. Dept. of Housing and Urban Development, *The Supply of Mortgage Credit, 1970-1974*, and press releases.

No. 876. CONSUMER CREDIT: 1950 TO 1978

[In billions of dollars, except percent. 1950 excludes Alaska and Hawaii. Estimated amounts of credit outstanding as of **end of year** or **month**; extended and repaid, for entire year or month. See also *Historical Statistics, Colonial Times to 1970*, series X 551–560]

TYPE OF CREDIT	1950	1960	1965	1970	1971	1972	1973	1974	1975	1976	1977	1978, May
Credit outstanding	21.5	56.1	89.9	127.1	139.4	157.3	181.1	191.3	200.7	224.2	260.8	271.2
Ratio to disposable income [1] _____percent	10.4	16.1	19.0	18.1	18.4	18.8	19.3	18.8	17.9	18.3	19.1	16.3
Installment	14.7	43.0	70.9	102.0	112.0	126.8	148.2	157.5	165.0	185.5	216.6	227.6
Automobile paper	6.1	17.7	28.4	35.2	39.4	46.6	52.4	52.9	55.9	66.1	79.4	86.0
Mobile home paper	(NA)	(NA)	(NA)	2.5	7.2	9.5	13.6	14.6	14.4	14.6	15.0	15.2
Home improvement loans	1.0	3.1	3.7	5.0	5.2	6.2	7.4	8.5	9.4	11.0	13.0	13.7
Bank credit card credit	(NA)	(NA)	(NA)	3.8	4.5	5.4	6.8	8.3	9.5	11.4	14.3	14.5
Bank check credit	(NA)	(NA)	(NA)	1.3	1.5	1.8	2.3	2.8	2.8	3.0	3.7	3.9
All other loans	(NA)	(NA)	(NA)	54.2	54.2	57.2	65.7	70.4	72.9	79.4	91.3	94.3
Noninstallment	6.8	13.2	19.0	25.1	27.4	30.5	32.9	33.8	35.7	38.7	44.2	43.6
Single-payment loans	1.8	4.5	7.7	9.7	10.9	12.6	13.7	13.4	13.7	14.4	15.9	15.9
Charge accounts	3.4	5.3	6.4	8.0	8.4	8.9	9.2	9.5	9.9	10.9	13.5	11.9
Service credit	1.6	3.3	4.9	7.5	8.2	9.0	10.0	10.9	12.0	13.4	14.8	15.8
Installment credit:												
Extended	21.6	49.8	78.7	112.3	123.8	137.1	157.9	157.2	164.2	193.3	225.6	24.0
Repaid	18.4	46.1	70.5	107.4	113.8	121.9	138.2	147.9	156.7	172.8	194.6	19.2
Net change	3.1	3.7	8.2	4.9	10.0	15.2	19.7	9.3	7.5	20.5	31.1	4.8
Life insurance policy loans [2]	2.4	5.2	7.7	16.1	17.1	18.0	20.2	22.9	24.5	25.8	27.6	28.0
Delinquency rate, 30 days and over, percent of installment debt [3]	2.20	1.93	1.81	2.14	1.93	2.19	2.53	3.13	2.77	2.57	2.62	2.77

NA Not available.   [1] See table 722.
[2] Source: American Council of Life Insurance, Washington, D.C. Year end figures are annual statement asset values; month end figures are book value of ledger assets. These loans are not included in "Credit outstanding."
[3] Source: American Bankers Association, Washington, D.C.

Source: Except as noted, Board of Governors of the Federal Reserve System, *Federal Reserve Bulletin*, monthly.

No. 877. CONSUMER INSTALLMENT CREDIT OUTSTANDING, BY HOLDER: 1950 TO 1978

[In billions of dollars. As of end of year or month. 1950 excludes Alaska and Hawaii. Estimated]

HOLDER	1950	1960	1965	1970	1971	1972	1973	1974	1975	1976	1977	1978, May
Total	14.7	43.0	70.9	102.0	112.0	126.8	148.2	157.5	165.0	185.5	216.6	227.6
Commercial banks	5.8	16.7	29.0	45.4	51.6	60.9	71.9	75.8	78.7	89.5	105.3	111.7
Finance companies	5.3	15.4	23.9	27.6	29.2	31.9	35.4	36.1	36.0	38.6	44.0	46.1
Credit unions	.6	3.9	7.3	13.0	14.8	17.0	19.6	21.9	25.7	30.5	37.0	40.0
Retailers [1]	2.9	6.3	9.8	13.7	13.9	14.8	16.4	17.9	18.0	19.1	21.1	20.1
Other [2]	.1	.6	1.0	2.3	2.5	2.3	4.9	5.7	6.6	7.7	9.1	9.7

[1] Excludes 30-day charge credit held by retailers, oil and gas companies, and travel and entertainment companies.
[2] Includes mutual savings banks, savings and loan associations, and auto dealers.

Source: Board of Governors of the Federal Reserve System, *Federal Reserve Bulletin*, monthly.

No. 878. CREDIT-CARD BANKING, BY CLASS OF BANK: 1967 TO 1977

[As of **Dec. 31**. Covers insured commercial banks offering credit-card plans]

CLASS OF BANK	1967	1970	1971	1972	1973	1974	1975	1976	1977
All banks _____number	390	1,432	1,535	1,631	1,765	1,912	2,027	2,155	2,317
Amount outstanding _____mil. dol	828	3,792	4,490	5,408	6,838	8,281	9,501	11,317	14,607
National banks _____number	187	704	766	801	840	861	927	963	1,020
Amount outstanding _____mil. dol	636	2,727	3,250	3,931	4,999	6,052	6,952	8,216	10,679
State member [1] banks _____number	50	175	187	182	191	212	214	226	234
Amount outstanding _____mil. dol	145	709	835	966	1,192	1,378	1,553	1,956	2,384
Nonmember [1] banks _____number	153	553	582	648	734	839	886	966	1,063
Amount outstanding _____mil. dol	47	356	405	511	647	851	996	1,145	1,544

[1] Refers to membership in Federal Reserve System; see headnote, table 862.

Source: Board of Governors of the Federal Reserve System, unpublished data.

No. 879. BANK RATES AND MATURITY FOR SHORT- AND LONG-TERM COMMERCIAL AND INDUSTRIAL LOANS AND FOR CONSTRUCTION AND LAND DEVELOPMENT LOANS, BY SIZE OF LOAN: 1977 AND 1978

[Represents loans made during the first full business week in the month designated. Based on a random sample of member banks of the Federal Reserve System and nonmember banks, totaling approximately 340 banks]

TYPE AND SIZE OF LOAN	AMOUNT (mil. dol.)			RATE (percent)			MATURITY (months)		
	May 1977	Nov. 1977	May 1978	May 1977	Nov. 1977	May 1978	May 1977	Nov. 1977	May 1978
Short-term commercial and industrial loans [1]	6,653	6,073	9,522	7.37	8.66	9.01	2.9	3.1	2.7
$1,000 to $24,999	807	851	1,181	9.04	9.53	9.82	3.2	2.8	2.7
$25,000 to $49,999	431	419	738	8.39	9.12	9.63	3.7	2.8	2.9
$50,000 to $99,999	504	666	929	8.04	9.02	9.37	3.8	3.6	2.3
$100,000 to $499,999	1,247	1,425	2,239	7.57	8.74	9.04	2.7	2.7	2.8
$500,000 to $999,999	606	452	768	7.11	8.47	8.90	2.7	3.3	3.0
$1 million and over	3,057	2,260	3,667	6.65	8.14	8.53	2.7	3.3	2.6
Long-term commercial and industrial loans [1]	1,651	1,036	1,897	8.24	8.71	9.67	35.0	44.7	47.6
$1,000 to $99,999	798	318	474	8.99	9.16	10.23	29.6	36.9	37.8
$100,000 to $499,999	189	154	421	8.03	9.03	10.29	49.1	35.6	40.5
$500,000 to $999,999	75	65	93	8.03	8.87	9.11	42.9	41.5	41.0
$1 million and over	589	498	909	7.18	8.30	9.15	41.5	52.9	56.7
Construction and land development loans	863	598	906	8.72	9.19	9.83	7.5	8.8	10.2
$1,000 to $24,999	167	183	170	9.28	9.36	9.53	8.0	8.3	5.7
$25,000 to $49,999	87	85	117	8.95	8.99	10.05	5.7	5.9	8.6
$50,000 to $99,999	332	82	164	8.79	9.68	10.08	4.8	8.2	13.6
$100,000 to $499,999	146	135	263	8.46	9.34	9.99	9.5	9.1	10.1
$500,000 and over	131	112	192	7.97	8.54	9.55	12.7	11.3	11.7

[1] Excludes construction and land development loans.

Source: Board of Governors of the Federal Reserve System, *Federal Reserve Bulletin*, monthly.

No. 880. FOREIGN LENDING BY LARGE U.S. BANKS, BY TYPE OF BORROWER, MATURITY, AND COUNTRY: 1977

[In millions of dollars. As of December. Covers 119 banks with assets of $1 billion or more which do nearly all of the foreign lending in the country. Data represent claims on foreign residents and institutions held at all domestic and foreign offices of covered banks]

COUNTRY	Total claims [1]	BORROWER		Maturity, under one year	COUNTRY	Total claims [1]	BORROWER		Maturity, under one year
		Banks	Public borrowers				Banks	Public borrowers	
Total [2]	194,575	96,168	38,336	129,968	Israel	667	451	181	526
					Italy	5,372	3,130	1,243	3,272
Algeria	1,541	383	928	321	Japan	12,268	4,945	246	8,383
Argentina	2,640	598	1,238	1,669	Korea, Rep. of	3,072	1,459	504	1,823
Australia	1,465	439	114	632	Kuwait	536	399	9	457
Austria	939	789	101	816	Liberia	1,835	6	68	360
Bahamas	9,700	9,616	17	9,630	Malaysia	511	106	259	217
Bolivia	446	51	194	234	Mexico	11,213	1,983	4,802	5,419
Brazil	11,993	3,364	2,993	4,063	Netherlands	2,827	2,304	9	2,481
British West Indies	2,751	2,693	6	2,708	New Zealand	595	54	328	268
Bulgaria	528	330	173	270	Nicaragua	563	175	204	361
Canada	5,933	3,664	626	4,823	Norway	2,068	133	268	603
Chile	821	257	359	521	Panama	2,445	1,166	278	1,646
China (Taiwan)	2,806	955	958	1,896	Peru	1,831	451	996	1,022
Costa Rica	425	55	148	227	Philippines	2,050	611	506	1,250
Czechoslovakia	193	160	28	131	Poland	1,314	744	501	542
Denmark	1,666	572	448	814	Portugal	585	369	144	504
Ecuador	1,040	157	480	633	Saudi Arabia	592	207	44	485
Egypt	428	205	170	344	Singapore	2,858	2,566	12	2,755
Finland	1,398	423	324	649	South Africa	2,278	425	924	1,187
France	8,916	6,380	790	6,959	Spain	3,560	1,051	1,093	1,456
German Dem. Rep	980	563	355	477	Sweden	2,151	925	439	1,119
Germany, Fed. Rep.	5,654	2,380	505	4,480	Switzerland	2,324	1,433	41	2,089
Greece	1,757	197	682	542	Thailand	857	391	109	715
Hong Kong	1,724	808	7	1,264	Turkey	1,465	794	479	1,121
Hungary	896	327	563	417	U.S.S.R.	1,552	824	709	727
India	188	29	66	74	United Kingdom	31,505	21,898	3,080	25,268
Indonesia	2,199	287	1,166	1,027	Venezuela	5,374	608	2,076	3,593
Iran	2,202	994	737	1,041	Yugoslavia	1,150	427	285	330
Ireland	557	111	221	291	Zaire	253	3	221	82

[1] Includes nonbank private borrowers and maturity over one year, not shown separately.
[2] Includes countries not shown separately.

Source: Board of Governors of the Federal Reserve System, press release.

No. 881. NET PUBLIC AND PRIVATE DEBT: 1950 TO 1976

[In billions of dollars. As of end of calendar year. See Historical Statistics, Colonial Times to 1970, series X 393–409]

TYPE OF DEBT	1950	1955	1960	1965	1970	1971	1972	1973	1974	1975	1976
Total debt	486	666	874	1,253	1,882	2,067	2,300	2,562	2,794	3,029	3,355
Public debt	240	274	308	374	485	528	561	601	648	748	833
Federal [1]	217	230	240	266	301	326	341	349	361	446	516
Federally sponsored credit agencies [2]	1	3	4	9	39	40	41	60	76	79	81
State and local	22	41	65	98	145	163	178	192	211	223	236
Private debt	246	392	566	879	1,397	1,539	1,739	1,961	2,145	2,281	2,521
Corporate	142	212	303	454	797	871	975	1,107	1,223	1,287	1,415
Individual and noncorporate	104	180	263	425	600	667	764	854	922	994	1,107
Farm [3]	12	19	25	39	58	63	68	79	89	98	108
Nonfarm	92	161	238	385	542	605	696	775	833	896	998
Mortgage	55	99	151	244	345	389	449	510	561	613	684
Commercial and financial [4]	16	24	31	51	70	77	90	86	83	86	96
Consumer	22	39	56	90	127	139	157	179	189	197	218

[1] Outstanding debt held by the public, as defined in The Budget of the United States Government, Fiscal Year 1978.
[2] Comprises debt of federally sponsored agencies in which there is no longer any Federal proprietary interest.
[3] Farm mortgages and farm production loans.   [4] Financial debt is debt owed to banks for purchasing or carrying securities, customers' debt to brokers, and debt owed to life insurance companies by policyholders.
Source: U.S. Bureau of Economic Analysis, Survey of Current Business, July 1977.

No. 882. USES AND SOURCES OF FUNDS—SUMMARY: 1960 TO 1977

[In billions of dollars, except as indicated. See tables 848–854 for related data on financial flows]

USE AND SOURCE	1960	1965	1970	1971	1972	1973	1974	1975	1976	1977
Uses, funds raised	40.3	66.8	97.2	144.5	188.1	188.2	184.7	199.5	261.6	329.6
Investment funds	28.6	46.1	72.5	104.3	123.0	120.5	116.5	120.1	147.8	190.9
Short-term funds	13.8	22.6	17.8	23.5	44.5	68.1	58.0	1.3	54.4	95.2
U.S. securities, privately held	−2.2	−1.9	6.9	16.7	20.5	−.4	10.2	78.1	59.4	43.5
Less: Financial intermediaries, funds raised	3.3	8.0	12.5	9.8	24.9	31.7	23.7	4.7	15.4	24.4
Sources, gross funds supplied	43.6	74.8	109.7	154.3	212.9	219.9	208.4	204.2	277.0	354.0
Commercial banks	9.5	28.6	36.5	49.7	74.6	78.3	59.3	29.7	64.7	80.7
Percent of total funds supplied	21.8	38.2	33.3	32.2	35.0	35.6	28.5	14.5	23.4	22.8
Insurance companies	6.5	9.7	13.0	18.1	20.2	21.7	19.6	25.0	39.2	45.5
Private noninsured pension funds	3.7	5.8	7.7	8.7	9.0	9.2	7.9	14.1	12.5	15.0
State and local govt. retirement funds	2.1	3.3	6.1	7.0	6.6	6.7	8.0	10.5	11.2	13.0
Savings and loan associations	7.3	9.6	12.5	28.1	35.8	26.4	19.5	36.3	51.9	64.5
Mutual savings banks	1.5	4.0	4.1	9.8	10.1	4.7	3.4	10.9	12.5	11.3
Credit unions	.6	1.1	1.6	2.5	3.0	3.7	3.1	5.1	6.9	7.5
Investment companies	1.1	1.9	1.9	.9	.7	.7	2.0	2.5	.3	2.3
Other financial intermediaries	3.2	5.0	3.9	6.9	13.0	16.3	4.3	−1.7	7.0	19.4
Business	−3.0	1.9	5.0	4.1	8.7	11.1	11.6	15.7	20.6	20.5
Government	2.5	4.1	10.8	1.1	10.3	11.5	20.5	21.3	16.3	22.6
Foreign investors	1.8	.3	11.0	27.1	10.6	3.3	11.3	9.1	17.1	37.0
Individuals and others	6.7	−.6	−4.4	−9.7	10.4	26.3	37.9	25.7	16.8	14.7
Total net sources	40.3	66.8	97.2	144.5	188.1	188.2	184.7	199.5	261.6	329.6

Source: Donald Woolley and Beverly Lowen, Credit and Capital Markets, 1978, Bankers Trust Company, New York, N.Y.

No. 883. FUNDS RAISED IN CREDIT MARKETS BY NONFINANCIAL SECTORS: 1970 TO 1977

[In billions of dollars]

ITEM	1970	1971	1972	1973	1974	1975	1976	1977
Funds raised, total	100.6	153.5	177.8	202.0	189.6	205.6	268.3	340.5
U.S. Government	11.9	24.9	15.1	8.3	11.8	85.4	69.0	56.8
Foreign	2.7	5.2	4.0	6.2	15.4	13.2	20.3	11.2
Private domestic nonfinancial sectors	86.0	123.5	158.7	187.5	162.4	107.0	179.0	272.5
Debt capital instruments	60.2	86.8	102.3	105.0	98.7	95.8	122.7	179.6
Other debt instruments	20.1	25.3	45.5	74.6	59.6	1.3	45.7	89.2
Corporate equities	5.7	11.4	10.9	7.9	4.1	9.9	10.5	3.7
Funds advanced	100.6	153.5	177.8	202.0	189.6	205.6	268.3	340.5
Private domestic nonfinancial sectors	63.4	85.9	119.6	133.3	120.2	138.1	166.9	202.7
Deposits	64.2	92.8	105.2	90.4	75.7	97.1	130.1	143.1
Credit market instruments, net	−.8	−6.9	14.4	42.9	44.5	41.0	36.8	59.6
Other sources	37.2	67.6	58.2	68.7	69.4	67.5	101.4	137.8

Source: Board of Governors of the Federal Reserve System, Federal Reserve Bulletin, monthly.

No. 884. MONEY STOCK AND DEPOSITS: 1960 TO 1977

[In billions of dollars, except as indicated. As of December, seasonally adjusted. Averages of daily figures. See *Historical Statistics, Colonial Times to 1970*, series X 410–417, for similar but not exactly comparable data]

ITEM	1960	1965	1970	1972	1973	1974	1975	1976	1977
Money stock	144	171	220	255	271	283	295	312	335
Currency	29	36	49	57	62	68	74	81	88
Demand deposits	115	135	171	198	209	215	221	232	247
Time and savings deposits	73	146	229	314	364	418	452	491	546
Large certificates of deposit	–	16	25	44	63	89	82	63	75
Other	73	130	204	270	301	329	370	428	471
Nonbank thrift deposits [1]	102	170	233	319	348	369	428	497	568
Money stock and time deposits [2]	217	301	424	525	571	612	664	740	807
Money stock and time [2] and non-bank [1] deposits	319	472	656	845	920	982	1,093	1,237	1,374
Average annual percent change: [3]									
Money stock	.6	3.8	5.7	9.0	6.3	4.4	4.2	5.8	7.4
Money stock and time deposits	2.9	7.7	8.2	11.2	8.8	7.2	8.5	11.4	9.1
Money stock and time and non-bank deposits	5.1	9.6	7.8	13.7	8.9	6.7	11.3	13.2	11.1

– Represents zero.   [1] Average of the beginning- and end-of-month figures for deposits of mutual savings banks, for savings capital at savings and loan associations, and for credit union shares.
[2] Deposits, other than large certificates, at commercial banks.
[3] From previous year shown. For 1960, change from 1959; for 1972, from 1971.
Source: Board of Governors of the Federal Reserve System, *Federal Reserve Bulletin*, monthly.

No. 885. PRIVATE LIQUID ASSET HOLDINGS, NONFINANCIAL INVESTORS: 1952 TO 1977

[Liquid assets in billions of dollars; ratios in percent. Averages of daily figures for December, except as noted. Includes holdings by households, nonfinancial business, State and local government, and personal trust funds]

TYPE OF ASSET	1952	1960	1965	1970	1973	1974	1975	1976	1977
Liquid assets, total	269	387	559	770	1,079	1,167	1,290	1,423	1,596
Currency and deposits	201	306	451	632	887	945	1,055	1,194	1,329
Currency	27	29	36	49	62	68	74	81	89
Demand deposits	92	105	119	152	183	187	192	199	214
Time deposits	82	172	296	432	643	690	789	915	1,027
Commercial banks	39	70	125	199	295	321	361	417	460
Nonbank thrift institutions	43	102	170	233	348	369	429	497	567
Other liquid assets	68	81	108	137	192	222	236	229	268
Certificates of deposit [1]	–	–	15	22	54	70	59	44	53
Other private money market instruments	1	3	8	21	35	41	43	47	62
U.S. Treasury securities:									
Short-term marketable	18	32	36	42	43	48	67	67	76
Savings bonds (E and H)	49	46	50	52	60	63	67	72	77
Ratios:									
Currency and demand deposits to liquid assets	44	35	28	26	23	22	21	20	19
Bank liability to liquid assets	49	45	46	48	49	50	47	46	46
Time deposits at thrift institutions to liquid assets	16	26	31	30	32	32	33	35	36
Liquid assets to GNP [2]	75	75	78	76	79	80	80	80	80
Currency and demand deposits to GNP [2]	34	26	22	20	18	18	17	16	16

– Represents zero.   [1] Negotiable c.d.'s over $100,000 at weekly reporting banks.
[2] GNP = Gross national product. Ratios based on 12-month averages of assets and annual GNP.
Source: U.S. Council of Economic Advisers, *Economic Indicators*, monthly. Data from Board of Governors of the Federal Reserve System.

No. 886. BANK DEBITS AND DEPOSIT TURNOVER: 1970 TO 1978

[Annual averages of monthly data, except as indicated]

ITEM	1970	1971	1972	1973	1974	1975	1976	1977	1978, Apr.[1]
DEBITS TO DEMAND DEPOSITS (bil. dol.)									
All commercial banks	11,308	13,124	15,043	18,856	22,938	25,029	29,180	34,327	39,131
Major New York City banks	4,044	4,871	5,464	6,755	8,435	9,671	11,467	13,861	15,232
Other banks	7,264	8,253	9,579	12,102	14,503	15,358	17,713	20,466	23,899
DEMAND DEPOSIT TURNOVER RATE [2]									
All commercial banks	63.4	68.9	73.3	84.8	99.0	105.3	116.8	129.1	137.0
Major New York City banks	170.0	204.7	230.2	274.1	321.6	356.9	411.6	503.3	551.7
Other banks	47.0	49.5	52.8	61.2	70.6	72.9	79.8	85.9	92.6

[1] Seasonally adjusted.   [2] Computed by dividing debits during a period (and converted to an annual rate) by average deposits against which debits are made, indicates number of times a deposit dollar is used during the period.
Source: Board of Governors of the Federal Reserve System, *Federal Reserve Bulletin*, monthly.

No. 887. Money Stock and Money in Circulation: 1950 to 1977

[In billions of dollars, except as indicated. Prior to 1970, as of June 30; thereafter, as of Dec. 31. See *Historical Statistics, Colonial Times to 1970,* series X 423, for money in circulation]

KIND OF MONEY	1950	1960	1965	1970	1972	1973	1974	1975	1976	1977
Total money stock	37.9	42.4	50.2	68.1	78.7	85.9	93.0	92.1	100.1	111.9
Percent gold	63.9	45.6	27.7	15.5	13.3	13.5	12.5	12.6	11.6	10.5
Bullion and coin, total	28.1	24.2	18.9	17.1	18.1	19.7	20.3	21.2	21.8	22.4
Held as security	25.5	21.6	14.7	10.5	10.3	11.5	11.7	11.6	11.6	11.7
Net	2.6	2.6	4.2	6.6	7.8	8.2	8.6	9.6	10.2	10.7
Gold [1]	24.2	19.3	13.9	10.6	10.4	11.6	11.7	11.6	11.6	11.7
Cupronickel-clad dollars	-	-	-	-	.3	.3	.3	.5	.6	.6
Subsidiary and minor coin	1.4	2.1	3.2	6.0	6.9	7.3	7.8	8.6	9.2	9.6
Other [2]	2.5	2.7	1.8	.5	.5	.5	.5	.5	.5	.5
Paper currency, net	35.3	39.8	46.0	61.5	70.8	77.7	84.3	82.5	89.9	101.1
Fed. Reserve notes and bank notes	23.9	28.5	37.4	53.8	62.6	68.2	75.2	81.9	89.4	100.6
Gold certificates, net [3][4]	8.7	8.5	7.4	7.1	7.7	8.9	8.6	(z)	(z)	(z)
Other	2.8	2.8	1.2	.5	.5	.5	.5	.5	.5	.5
Money in circulation	27.2	32.1	39.7	57.1	66.5	72.5	79.7	86.5	93.7	103.8
Per capita_____dol	179	177	204	276	317	343	375	403	433	477

- Represents zero.   Z Less than $50 million.   [1] Valued at $35 per fine ounce until May 7, 1972; valued at $38 per fine ounce until October 18, 1973; $42.22 thereafter. Excludes gold deposited with U.S. by International Monetary Fund from September 1965 to February 1972.   [2] Includes standard silver dollars.
[3] Includes gold certificates outside Treasury, credits payable in gold certificates, and redemption fund for Federal Reserve notes.   [4] Beginning 1975, not comparable with earlier years because of decision by Federal Reserve Banks to pledge substantially all gold certificates against Federal Reserve notes outstanding.

Source: U.S. Dept. of the Treasury, *Statistical Appendix to the Annual Report of the Secretary of the Treasury on the State of the Finances; Statement of United States Currency and Coin,* Form 1028, monthly; and unpublished data.

No. 888. Money in Circulation, by Denomination: 1960 to 1977

[In millions of dollars. As of December 31]

DENOMINATION	1960	1965	1970	1971	1972	1973	1974	1975	1976	1977
Total [1]	32,869	42,056	57,093	61,068	66,516	72,497	79,743	86,547	93,717	103,811
Coin and small dollar currency	23,521	29,842	39,639	41,831	45,105	48,288	51,606	54,865	57,645	62,543
Coin	2,427	4,027	6,281	6,775	7,797	7,759	8,330	9,059	9,480	10,071
$1 [2]	1,533	1,908	2,310	2,408	2,523	2,639	2,720	2,809	2,858	3,038
$2	88	127	136	135	135	135	135	135	637	650
$5	2,246	2,618	3,161	3,273	3,449	3,718	3,718	3,841	3,905	4,190
$10	6,691	7,794	9,170	9,348	9,827	10,226	10,503	10,777	10,775	11,361
$20	10,536	13,369	18,581	19,893	21,883	23,915	26,197	28,344	29,987	33,233
Large dollar currency	9,348	12,214	17,454	19,237	21,411	24,210	28,137	31,681	36,072	41,269
$50	2,815	3,540	4,896	5,377	5,868	6,514	7,444	8,157	9,026	10,079
$100	5,954	8,135	12,084	13,414	15,118	17,288	20,298	23,139	26,668	30,818
$500	249	245	215	203	193	185	179	175	172	169
$1,000	316	288	252	237	225	216	209	204	200	197
$5,000	3	3	3	2	2	2	2	2	2	2
$10,000	10	4	4	4	4	4	4	4	4	4

[1] Outside Treasury and Federal Reserve banks.   [2] Paper currency only; $1 silver coins reported under coin.

Source: 1960–1973, Board of Governors of the Federal Reserve System, *Federal Reserve Bulletin,* monthly; thereafter, U.S. Dept. of the Treasury, *Statement of United States Currency and Coin,* Form 1028, monthly.

No. 889. Production of U.S. Coins, by Denomination: 1960 to 1977

[In millions of pieces. Includes numismatic and uncirculated coins, as well as those produced for issue to the public. No gold coins have been minted since 1933; no standard silver dollars, since 1935. Public Law 93–127, Oct. 18, 1973, authorized the Secretary to mint and issue, after July 4, 1975, dollar, half-dollar, and quarter-dollar coins with designs emblematic of the Bicentennial, for general circulation; and production of 45 million numismatic silver-clad coins of same designs and denominations to be sold at premium prices]

YEAR	Total	Non-silver dollars [1]	Silver-clad dollars [1]	Half dollars	Quarter dollars	Dimes	5-cent pieces	1-cent pieces
1960	2,811	(X)	(X)	26	94	272	250	2,169
1965	7,920	(X)	(X)	186	1,339	1,315	2,016	3,064
1970	7,904	(X)	(X)	5	556	1,103	757	5,483
1973	9,766	7	3	151	583	773	649	7,600
1974	11,657	65	3	194	587	1,044	882	8,882
1975	13,499	175	2 [5]	2 [4]76	2 [1],394	902	587	9,960
1976	12,179	63	3 [2]	3 [1]50	3 [8]60	1,268	935	8,900
1977	11,541	49	4 (z)	4 [7]8	4 [7]29	1,177	886	8,622

X Not applicable.   Z Less than 500,000.   [1] Public Law 91–607, Dec. 31, 1970, authorized Secretary of Treasury to mint and issue dollar coins for general circulation and half dollars of same composition as 25-cent and 10-cent pieces; and production of not more than 150 million numismatic silver-clad dollars to be sold to public at premium prices.   [2] Includes 5 million silver-clad Bicentennial coins.
[3] Includes 2 million silver-clad Bicentennial coins.   [4] Includes 219,402 silver-clad Bicentennial coins.

Source: U.S. Bureau of the Mint, *Annual Report of the Director.*

No. 890. Money Market Interest Rates: 1960 to 1978

[**Percent per year.** Annual averages of monthly data, except as indicated. See also *Historical Statistics, Colonial Times to 1970*, series X 444–453]

TYPE	1960	1965	1970	1971	1972	1973	1974	1975	1976	1977	1978, Jan.–May avg.
Federal funds rate	3.22	4.07	7.17	4.67	4.44	8.74	10.51	5.82	5.05	5.54	6.91
Prime commercial paper [1]	3.85	4.38	7.72	5.11	4.69	8.15	9.87	6.33	5.35	5.60	6.87
Prime rate charged by banks	4.82	4.54	7.91	5.72	5.25	8.03	10.81	7.86	6.84	6.83	8.04
Euro-dollar deposits, 3-month	(NA)	(NA)	8.51	6.58	5.41	9.28	11.04	7.03	5.57	6.05	7.41
Finance company paper [2]	3.54	4.27	7.23	4.91	4.52	7.40	8.62	6.16	5.22	5.49	6.78
Prime bankers acceptances, 90-day [3]	3.51	4.22	7.31	4.85	4.47	8.08	9.92	6.30	5.19	5.59	6.94
Large negotiable certificates of deposit, 3-month, secondary market	(NA)	4.35	7.56	5.02	4.64	8.39	10.27	6.43	5.27	5.58	6.98
Federal Reserve discount rate [4]	3–4	4–4½	5½–6	4½–5¼	4½	4½–7½	7½–8	6–7¼	5¼–6	5¼–6	6–7
U.S. Govt. securities, taxable:											
3-month Treasury bills [5]	2.87	3.95	6.39	4.33	4.07	7.03	7.84	5.80	4.98	5.27	6.37
6-month Treasury bills [5]	3.20	4.06	6.51	4.52	4.49	7.20	7.95	6.11	5.26	5.53	6.77
9–12 month notes and bonds [6]	3.55	4.09	6.90	4.75	4.86	7.30	8.25	6.70	5.84	6.07	(NA)
1-year Treasury bill [5]	3.41	4.06	6.49	4.67	4.77	7.01	7.71	6.30	5.52	5.71	6.95
Prime 1-year municipals [7]	2.05	2.35	4.35	2.90	2.75	3.95	4.75	3.91	3.12	2.91	3.71

NA Not available. [1] 4 to 6 months; averages of daily offering rates of dealers. [2] Placed directly, 3 to 6 months; averages of daily offering rates, published by finance companies, for varying maturities within range shown. [3] Prior to Aug. 15, 1974, averages of daily offering rates of dealers; thereafter, averages of daily dealer closing rates. [4] Federal Reserve Bank of New York, low and high. [5] Averages based on daily closing bid yields in secondary market, bank discount basis. [6] Averages based on daily closing bid prices for maturity range shown. [7] Averages based on quotations for one day each month. Source: Salomon Brothers, New York, N.Y.

No. 891. Installment Credit—Finance Rates on Selected Types of Credit for Commercial Banks and Finance Companies: 1972 to 1978

[**Percent per year.** Annual averages, except as indicated. Commercial bank rates are "most common" rates for direct loans with specified maturities; finance company rates are weighted averages for purchased contracts, except personal loans]

TYPE	1972	1973	1974	1975	1976	1977	1978, May
COMMERCIAL BANKS							
New automobiles (36 months)	10.05	10.21	10.97	11.36	11.08	10.89	10.84
Mobile homes (84 months)	10.70	10.84	11.41	11.85	11.76	11.83	12.01
Other consumer goods (24 months)	12.45	12.60	13.02	13.11	13.02	12.98	13.11
Personal loans (12 months)	12.68	12.84	13.27	13.44	13.30	13.40	13.56
Credit-card plans	17.22	17.21	17.21	17.14	17.03	16.89	16.97
FINANCE COMPANIES							
New automobiles	11.90	12.08	12.61	13.12	13.17	13.14	13.11
Used automobiles	16.53	16.70	17.18	17.64	17.63	17.62	17.68
Mobile homes	12.42	12.78	13.29	13.63	13.44	13.58	13.50
Other consumer goods	19.35	18.87	19.09	19.78	19.51	19.21	18.90
Personal loans	21.09	20.61	20.74	20.97	21.04	20.54	20.29

No. 892. Federal Reserve Bank of New York—Discount Rates: 1968 to 1978

[**Percent per year.** See also *Historical Statistics, Colonial Times to 1970*, series X 454–455]

EFFECTIVE DATE	RATE	EFFECTIVE DATE	RATE	EFFECTIVE DATE	RATE	EFFECTIVE DATE	RATE
1968—Mar. 22	5	1971—Con.		1973—Con.		1976—Jan. 19	5½
Apr. 19	5½	Feb. 19	4¾	July 2	7	Nov. 22	5¼
Aug. 30	5¼	July 16	5	Aug. 14	7½		
Dec. 18	5½	Nov. 19	4¾	1974—Apr. 25	8	1977—Aug. 31	5¾
1969—Apr. 4	6	Dec. 17	4½	Dec. 9	7¾	Oct. 26	6
1970—Nov. 13	5¾	1973—Jan. 15	5	1975—Jan. 10	7¼	1978—Jan. 9	6½
Dec. 4	5½	Feb. 26	5½	Feb. 5	6¾	May 11	7
		May 4	5¾	Mar. 10	6¼		
1971—Jan. 8	5¼	May 11	6	May 16	6	In effect May 31, 1978	7
Jan. 22	5	June 11	6½				

Source of tables 890–892: Except as noted, Board of Governors of the Federal Reserve System, *Federal Reserve Bulletin*, monthly, and *Annual Statistical Digest, 1972–1976*.

No. 893. BOND YIELDS, STOCK YIELDS, AND MORTGAGE RATES: 1960 TO 1977

[Percent per year. Annual averages of monthly data, except as indicated. See also *Historical Statistics, Colonial Times to 1970*, series X 474–491]

TYPE	1960	1965	1970	1971	1972	1973	1974	1975	1976	1977
U.S. Treasury, constant maturities: [1]										
3–year	3.98	4.22	7.29	5.65	5.72	6.95	7.82	7.49	6.77	6.69
5–year	4.09	4.25	7.38	5.99	5.98	6.87	7.80	7.77	7.18	6.99
10–year	4.12	4.28	7.35	6.16	6.21	6.84	7.56	7.99	7.61	7.42
20–year	4.06	4.27	6.86	6.12	6.01	7.12	8.05	8.19	7.86	7.67
U.S. Govt., 3–5 year issues [2]	3.99	4.22	7.37	5.77	5.85	6.92	7.81	7.55	6.94	6.85
U.S. Govt., long–term bonds [2][3]	4.01	4.21	6.59	5.74	5.63	6.30	6.99	6.98	6.78	7.06
State and local govt. bonds, Aaa [4]	3.26	3.16	6.12	5.22	5.04	4.99	5.89	6.42	5.66	5.20
State and local govt. bonds, Baa [4]	4.22	3.57	6.75	5.89	5.60	5.47	6.53	7.62	7.49	6.12
High–graded municipal bonds (Standard & Poor's) [5]	3.73	3.27	6.51	5.70	5.27	5.18	6.09	6.89	6.49	5.56
Municipal (Bond Buyer, 20 bonds)	3.51	3.28	6.34	5.46	5.25	5.22	6.26	7.05	6.64	5.68
Corporate Aaa seasoned [4]	4.41	4.49	8.04	7.39	7.21	7.44	8.57	8.83	8.43	8.02
Corporate Baa seasoned [4]	5.19	4.87	9.11	8.56	8.16	8.24	9.50	10.61	9.75	8.97
Corporate Aaa utility bonds [6]	4.73	4.57	8.72	7.64	7.37	7.67	9.01	9.17	8.46	8.12
Corporate, by years to maturity: [7] 5 yr	4.73	4.29	8.10	5.85	6.50	6.85	7.47	7.70	7.96	7.25
10 yr	4.60	4.33	8.00	7.05	7.05	7.05	7.67	8.00	8.18	7.60
20 yr	4.55	4.35	7.60	7.12	7.05	7.20	7.80	8.35	8.30	7.75
30 yr	4.55	4.37	7.60	7.12	7.01	7.20	7.80	8.35	8.30	7.95
Corporate (Moody's)	4.73	4.64	8.51	7.94	7.63	7.80	9.03	9.57	9.01	8.43
Industrials (40 bonds [8])	4.59	4.61	8.26	7.57	7.35	7.60	8.78	9.25	8.84	8.28
Railroads (29 bonds)	4.92	4.72	8.77	8.38	7.99	8.12	8.98	9.39	8.85	8.13
Public utilities (40 bonds)	4.69	4.60	8.68	8.13	7.74	7.83	9.27	9.88	9.17	8.58
Stocks (Standard & Poor's): [5]										
Preferred (10 stocks [9])										
Common: Composite (500 stocks)	4.75	4.33	7.22	6.75	6.88	7.23	8.24	8.36	8.06	7.61
Industrials (400 stocks)	3.47	3.00	3.83	3.14	2.84	3.06	4.47	4.31	3.77	4.62
Home mortgages: [10]										
FHA insured, secondary market yield	6.16	5.47	9.03	7.70	7.53	8.19	9.55	9.19	8.82	8.68
Conventional, new–home [11]	(NA)	5.83	8.52	7.75	7.64	8.30	9.22	9.10	8.99	8.95
Conventional, existing–home [11]	(NA)	5.89	8.56	7.83	7.70	8.33	9.23	9.14	9.04	9.00

NA Not available.   [1] Yields on the more actively traded issues adjusted to constant maturities by the U.S. Treasury, based on daily closing bid prices.   [2] Unweighted averages for all outstanding notes and bonds in maturity ranges shown, based on daily closing bid prices.   [3] Includes all bonds neither due nor callable in less than 10 years.   [4] Source: Moody's Investors Service, New York, N.Y.   [5] Source: Standard & Poor's Corp., New York, N.Y., *Standard & Poor's Outlook*.   [6] Averages based on first trading day of each month, deferred call. Source: Salomon Brothers, New York, N.Y.   [7] Source: Scudder, Stevens & Clark, New York, N.Y.   [8] Number of issues as of Jan. 28, 1974; number varies for earlier years.   [9] Prior to Sept. 9, 1965, yields based on 14 stocks, 8 yields; thereafter, 10 stocks, 4 yields. Issues converted to a price equivalent to $100 par and a 7 percent annual dividend before averaging.   [10] Averages based on quotations for 1 day each month as compiled by FHA.   [11] Primary market.

Source: Except as noted, Board of Governors of the Federal Reserve System, *Federal Reserve Bulletin*, monthly.

No. 894. MAXIMUM INTEREST RATES PAYABLE ON TIME AND SAVINGS DEPOSITS AT FEDERALLY INSURED INSTITUTIONS: 1978

[Percent per year. Represents rates in effect on August 31, 1978]

TYPE AND MATURITY	COMMERCIAL BANKS		SAVINGS AND LOAN ASSNS.[1]		TYPE AND MATURITY	COMMERCIAL BANKS		SAVINGS AND LOAN ASSNS.[1]	
	Effective date	Rate	Effective date	Rate		Effective date	Rate	Effective date	Rate
Savings deposit	7/73	5	7/73	5¼	Time deposits—Con.				
Time deposits:					2½ to 4 years	7/73	6½	7/73	6¾
30 to 89 days:					4 to 6 years [3]	11/73	7¼	11/73	7½
Multiple-maturity	} 7/73	5	(X)	(X)	6 to 8 years [3]	12/74	7½	12/74	7¾
Single-maturity					8 years or more [3]	6/78	7¾	6/78	(4)
90 days to 1 year:					Government units				
Multiple-maturity	} 7/73	5½	7/73	2 5¾	(all maturities)	6/78	8	6/78	8
Single-maturity					Individual retirement				
1 to 2 years [2]	} 7/73	6	7/73	6½	accounts and Keogh				
2 to 2½ years [2]					(H.R. 10) plans [5]	6/78	8	6/78	8

X Not applicable.   [1] Includes mutual savings banks also.   [2] A minimum of $1,000 is required for savings and loan associations, except where mutual savings banks permit lower minimum denominations. This restriction was removed for deposits maturing in less than 1 year, effective Nov. 1, 1973.   [3] $1,000 minimum except for deposits representing funds contributed to an Individual Retirement Account (IRA) or a Keogh (H.R. 10) Plan. The $1,000 minimum requirement was removed for such accounts in December 1975 and November 1976, respectively.   [4] No separate account category.   [5] 3-year minimum maturity.

Source: Board of Governors of the Federal Reserve System, *Federal Reserve Bulletin*, monthly.

No. 895. SECURITY PRICES AND VOLUME OF TRADING: 1950 TO 1977

[Annual averages of monthly figures. See also *Historical Statistics, Colonial Times to 1970*, series X 492–498]

CLASS	1950	1960	1965	1970	1972	1973	1974	1975	1976	1977
Bond prices (dollars per $100 bond):										
U.S. Government, long term [1]	102.53	86.22	83.76	60.52	68.71	62.80	57.45	57.44	58.96	56.89
Standard & Poor's: Municipal [2]	133.4	103.9	110.6	72.3	84.4	85.4	76.3	68.9	72.5	81.3
Corporate AAA [2]	121.9	94.7	93.9	61.6	65.9	63.7	58.8	56.2	58.0	59.6
Stock prices:										
Standard & Poor's common index (500 stocks) (1941–43=10) [3]	18.40	55.85	88.17	83.22	109.20	107.43	82.84	87.17	102.01	98.18
Industrial	18.33	59.43	93.48	91.29	121.79	120.44	92.91	96.56	114.35	108.44
N.Y. Stock Exchange common stock index (Dec. 31, 1965=50), composite	10.87	30.01	47.39	45.72	60.29	57.42	43.84	45.73	54.45	53.69
Industrial	(NA)	(NA)	(NA)	48.03	65.73	63.08	48.08	50.52	60.44	57.86
Transportation	(NA)	(NA)	(NA)	32.14	50.17	37.74	31.89	31.10	39.57	41.09
Utility	(NA)	(NA)	(NA)	37.24	38.48	37.69	29.79	31.50	36.97	40.92
Finance	(NA)	(NA)	(NA)	54.64	78.35	70.12	49.67	47.14	52.94	51.56
American Stock Exchange market value index (Aug. 31, 1973=100)	(NA)	(NA)	(NA)	96.63	129.10	103.80	79.97	83.06	101.63	116.18
Dow-Jones and Co. Inc., total (65 stocks) [4]	77.69	204.57	318.50	243.92	319.36	286.73	237.33	247.25	303.91	301.70
Industrial (30 stocks)	216.31	618.04	910.88	753.19	950.71	923.88	759.37	802.49	974.92	894.62
Transportation (20 stocks)	60.72	138.93	216.41	152.36	241.44	180.55	164.05	163.39	214.03	225.16
Public utility (15 stocks)	41.29	91.39	157.88	108.75	112.83	103.39	75.84	79.81	92.28	110.96
Standard & Poor's:										
Dividend-price ratio____percent	(NA)	(NA)	(NA)	3.83	2.84	3.06	4.47	4.31	3.77	4.56
Earnings-price ratio____percent	(NA)	(NA)	(NA)	6.45	5.50	7.12	11.60	9.07	8.83	9.77
Volume of trading:										
Shares NYSE [5]____1,000	1,980	3,042	6,176	11,564	16,487	16,084	13,904	18,551	21,186	20,928
Value____bil. dol	(NA)	(NA)	(NA)	95.3	150.0	137.3	92.1	126.7	159.8	150.2
Shares Amex [6]____1,000	435	1,113	2,120	3,319	4,454	3,015	1,906	2,138	2,562	2,592

NA Not available.
[1] Derived from long-term yield on basis of assumed 3 percent, 20-year bond.
[2] Derived from average yields on basis of assumed 4 percent, 20-year bond; Wednesday closing prices.
[3] Effective July 1976, the index includes 400 industrial stocks (formerly 425), 20 transportation (formerly 15 rail), 40 public utility (formerly 60), and 40 financial stocks, not previously covered.
[4] Source: U.S. Bureau of Economic Analysis. Based on data from New York Stock Exchange.
[5] Daily average reported on New York Stock Exchange. Source: New York Stock Exchange, Inc., New York, N.Y., *Fact Book*, annual.
[6] Average daily volume. Source: American Stock Exchange, *Stock Trading Statistics*.

Source: Except as noted, Board of Governors of the Federal Reserve System, *Federal Reserve Bulletin*, monthly.

No. 896. SALES OF STOCKS AND BONDS ON REGISTERED EXCHANGES: 1950 TO 1977

[See also *Historical Statistics, Colonial Times to 1970*, series X 517–530]

EXCHANGE	1950	1960	1965	1970	1972	1973	1974	1975	1976	1977
ALL EXCHANGES										
Market value, all sales [1]____bil. dol	23	47	93	136	215	187	125	167	206	201
Stocks: [2] Market value___bil. dol	22	45	89	131	204	179	118	157	195	187
Shares____mil	857	1,389	2,587	4,539	6,310	5,723	4,846	6,231	7,036	7,023
Options: Market value__mil. dol	(NA)	(NA)	(NA)	(NA)	(NA)	(NA)	(NA)	(NA)	7,919	10,233
Contracts____mil	(NA)	(NA)	(NA)	(NA)	(NA)	(NA)	(NA)	(NA)	23	37
Option exercises: Market value____mil. dol	(NA)	(NA)	(NA)	(NA)	(NA)	(NA)	(NA)	(NA)	2,872	3,696
Shares____mil	(NA)	(NA)	(NA)	(NA)	(NA)	(NA)	(NA)	(NA)	1	1
Rights and warrants: Market value____mil. dol	25	75	305	576	1,529	984	394	295	256	190
Number of units____mil	35	51	82	295	208	176	104	150	89	112
NEW YORK STOCK EXCHANGE										
Market value, all sales [1]____bil. dol	20	40	77	108	169	155	106	143	165	157
Stocks: [2] Market value___bil. dol	19	38	73	103	160	146	99	134	165	157
Shares____mil	655	958	1,809	3,213	4,496	4,337	3,822	5,056	5,649	5,613
Rights and warrants: Market value____mil. dol	10	13	34	257	477	348	192	168	133	89
Number of units____mil	27	29	58	233	98	84	63	108	53	62
Sales by size: [3]										
At 100 shares____percent	(NA)	(NA)	(NA)	51.7	47.0	46.4	45.3	41.4	38.1	35.6
At 200–900 shares____percent	(NA)	(NA)	(NA)	40.7	44.0	44.5	45.7	47.8	49.2	49.7
At 1,000 shares and over____percent	(NA)	(NA)	(NA)	6.4	9.0	9.1	9.1	9.0	10.8	12.7	14.6

NA Not available.   [1] Includes bond sales through 1975, not shown separately.
[2] Includes voting trust certificates, American depositary receipts, and certificates of deposit for stocks.
[3] Sales printed on New York Stock Exchange. Source: New York Stock Exchange, Inc., New York, N.Y., *Fact Book*, annual.

Source: Except as noted, U.S. Securities and Exchange Commission. Monthly data in *Statistical Bulletin*.

No. 897. SECURITIES LISTED ON N. Y. STOCK EXCHANGE: 1950 TO 1977

[As of December 31]

ITEM	1950	1960	1965	1970	1972	1973	1974	1975	1976	1977
Bonds:										
Face value----bil. dol--	115	116	142	135	142	142	291	334	401	497
Market value-bil. dol--	116	108	132	113	128	121	255	315	402	480
Average price-----dol--	100.93	93.21	93.07	83.60	90.40	85.16	87.68	91.89	100.39	96.52
Stocks:										
Shares------------mil--	2,353	6,458	10,058	16,065	19,159	20,967	21,737	22,478	24,500	26,093
Market value-bil. dol--	94	307	537	636	872	721	511	685	858	797
Average price-----dol--	39.86	47.53	53.44	39.61	45.49	34.39	23.51	30.48	35.03	30.53
Cash dividends on common stock--mil. dol--	5,404	9,872	15,302	19,781	21,490	23,627	25,662	26,901	30,608	36,270
Industrial----mil. dol--	(NA)	(NA)	10,978	13,616	14,283	15,538	16,962	17,640	20,150	23,876
Transportation mil. dol--	(NA)	(NA)	564	543	502	521	598	616	639	752
Utilities------mil. dol--	(NA)	(NA)	3,309	4,483	5,066	5,481	6,027	6,726	7,673	9,000
Finance------mil. dol--	(NA)	(NA)	451	1,139	1,644	2,087	2,074	1,920	2,146	2,642

NA Not available.

Source: New York Stock Exchange, Inc., New York, N.Y., *Fact Book*, annual.

No. 898. STOCK OWNERSHIP—CHARACTERISTICS OF SHAREOWNERS: 1959 TO 1975

[In thousands. Includes outlying areas, most members of the Armed Forces, citizens living abroad, and minor children. Represents all publicly owned issues of common and preferred stocks. Based on national probability samples; see source for detailed explanation]

CHARACTERISTIC	1959	1965	1970	1975	CHARACTERISTIC	1959	1965	1970	1975
Total [1]	12,490	20,120	30,850	25,270	Income:				
					Under $5,000-----	3,575	3,183	2,577	841
Male---------------	5,740	9,060	15,689	12,698	$5,000–$7,999------	3,700	4,479	3,081	1,378
Female ------------	6,347	9,130	15,161	12,508	$8,000–$9,999------	2,221	3,113	3,152	1,462
Age:					$10,000–$14,999----	1,769	5,199	9,001	4,906
Under 21 years----	197	1,280	2,221	1,818	$15,000–$24,999----	700	2,649	8,272	9,461
21–34 years--------	2,444	2,626	4,500	2,838	$25,000 and over--	319	1,147	4,437	7,158
35–44 years--------	2,064	4,216	5,801	3,976					
45–54 years--------	2,800	4,752	7,556	5,675	Residence by				
55–64 years--------	2,666	3,549	6,084	5,099	SMSA size: [4]				
65 years and over--	2,113	3,347	4,330	5,800	Under 100,000----	(NA)	134	175	328
					100,000–249,000--	(NA)	1,254	2,245	2,059
Education:					250,000–499,999----	(NA)	1,897	2,686	2,691
High school: [2]									
3 years or less----	2,804	3,106	3,566	1,621	500,000–999,999----	(NA)	2,156	3,712	3,257
4 years-----------	3,130	5,344	8,697	6,580	1,000,000 and over-	(NA)	9,883	14,881	11,893
College: [2]									
1–3 years---------	2,587	4,012	5,867	5,301	Nonmetropolitan areas-------	(NA)	4,639	6,913	4,978
4 years or more--	3,566	6,028	9,999	9,886					
Minors [3]----------	197	1,280	2,221	1,818					

NA Not available.
[1] Includes small number of shareowners not distributed by breakdown.   [2] Persons 21 years old and over.
[3] Shareowners whose stockholdings are registered in accordance with the Gifts to Minors Statutes.
[4] SMSA = Standard metropolitan statistical area. For definition, see Appendix II.

Source: New York Stock Exchange, Inc., New York, N.Y., *Census of Shareowners*, 1959, 1965, 1970, and 1975.

No. 899. MUTUAL FUNDS—NET ASSETS, SALES, AND REDEMPTIONS: 1950 TO 1977

[See also *Historical Statistics, Colonial Times to 1970*, series X 536–539]

ITEM	1950	1960	1965	1970	1972	1973	1974	1975	1976	1977
Number of funds----------	98	161	170	361	410	421	431	426	452	477
Net assets------mil. dol--	2,531	17,026	35,220	47,618	59,831	46,519	35,777	45,823	51,268	48,937
Sales-----------mil. dol--	519	2,097	4,358	4,626	4,893	4,359	5,321	10,150	13,721	17,073
Redemptions----mil. dol--	281	842	1,962	2,988	6,563	5,651	3,937	9,653	16,410	16,686

Source: Investment Company Institute, Washington, D.C., *Mutual Fund Fact Book*, annual.

No. 900. New Corporate Securities Offered for Sale, by Type of Security and Issuer: 1950 to 1977

[In millions of dollars. Estimated gross proceeds derived by multiplying principal amounts or number of units by offering prices. Covers substantially all new securities offered for cash sale in U.S. in amounts over $100,000 and with terms of maturity of more than 1 year. Included in the new corporate sales data are some unregistered securities offered privately for sale mainly to insurance companies as well as securities registered with the Securities and Exchange Commission under the terms of the Securities Act of 1933. See table 488 for new issues of State and local government securities. See also *Historical Statistics, Colonial Times to 1970*, series X 499–500 and X 505–506]

SECURITY AND ISSUER	1950	1960	1965	1970	1972	1973	1974	1975	1976	1977
TYPE OF SECURITY										
Total	6,362	10,154	14,782	37,451	39,705	31,680	37,729	52,539	52,290	52,062
Publicly offered	3,681	6,657	6,486	32,524	29,661	22,903	31,028	41,759	35,910	32,373
Bonds and notes	2,360	4,806	4,688	24,365	16,921	12,899	25,335	31,492	25,263	22,042
Preferred stock	519	220	360	1,310	2,411	2,398	1,745	3,088	2,353	2,383
Common stock	802	1,631	1,438	6,849	10,328	7,606	3,947	7,179	8,296	7,945
Privately placed	2,680	3,497	8,296	4,926	10,045	8,781	6,701	10,779	16,384	19,691
Bonds and notes	2,560	3,275	7,897	4,658	8,706	7,798	6,160	10,172	15,927	18,007
Preferred stock	112	188	364	80	960	944	511	371	451	1,494
Common stock	8	33	35	188	381	37	28	235	9	188
ISSUER										
Manufacturing	1,200	2,152	5,414	10,647	6,398	4,832	10,408	18,651	15,493	13,776
Extractive	(1)	246	341	1,812	1,851	1,060	970	1,628	1,762	2,674
Electric, gas, water	2,649	2,851	2,934	11,009	11,314	10,269	12,837	15,894	14,415	13,711
	399	1,050	945	5,291	4,836	4,872	3,930	4,464	3,562	
Communication										4,442
Transportation	813	718	702	1,253	860	811	1,005	2,635	3,626	1,802
Financial and real estate	747	2,525	3,386	5,112	10,971	8,089	6,779	6,838	10,282	11,902
Commercial and other	1 553	612	1,060	2,328	3,476	1,748	1,802	2,429	3,148	3,757

1 "Extractive" included with "Commercial and other."

Source: U.S. Securities and Exchange Commission, *Statistical Bulletin*, various issues.

No. 901. Securities—Net Change in Corporate Securities Issued: 1950 to 1976

[In millions of dollars. Covers estimated cash transactions only. New issues exclude foreign companies, and include sales of securities held by affiliated companies, special offerings to employees, and also new stock issues and cash proceeds connected with conversions of bonds into stocks. Closed-end investment company issues are included from 1971 forward. Retirements include the same types of issues, and also securities retired with internal funds or with proceeds of issues for that purpose. See also *Historical Statistics, Colonial Times to 1970*, series X 507–509]

YEAR	ALL TYPES			BONDS AND NOTES			STOCKS		
	New issues	Retire-ments	Net change	New issues	Retire-ments	Net change	New issues	Retire-ments	Net change
1950	6,692	3,223	3,469	4,804	2,800	2,004	1,888	423	1,465
1955	11,190	5,108	6,081	7,571	3,383	4,188	3,619	1,725	1,893
1960	10,797	4,107	6,690	8,072	3,078	4,994	2,725	1,029	1,696
1965	15,952	7,891	8,061	12,747	4,649	8,098	3,205	3,242	−37
1969	28,841	10,813	18,027	19,523	5,767	13,755	9,318	5,045	4,272
1970	38,707	9,079	29,628	29,495	6,667	22,825	9,213	2,411	6,801
1971	46,687	9,507	37,180	31,917	8,190	23,728	14,769	1,318	13,452
1972	42,306	10,224	32,082	27,065	8,003	19,062	15,242	2,222	13,018
1973	33,558	11,804	21,754	21,501	8,810	12,691	12,057	2,993	9,064
1974	39,334	9,935	29,399	31,354	6,255	25,098	7,980	3,678	4,302
1975	53,254	10,991	42,263	40,468	8,583	31,886	12,786	2,408	10,377
1976	53,123	12,184	40,939	38,994	9,109	29,884	14,129	3,075	11,055

Source: U.S. Securities and Exchange Commission. Quarterly in *Statistical Bulletin*.

No. 902. Life Insurance in Force in the U.S.—Summary: 1950 to 1977

[As of **December 31** or **calendar years,** as applicable. Prior to 1960, excludes Alaska and Hawaii. Covers life insurance with life insurance companies only. Represents all life insurance in force on lives of U.S. residents whether issued by U.S. or foreign companies. "Families" includes families, subfamilies, and unrelated individuals; see definitions, p. 3. See also *Historical Statistics, Colonial Times to 1970,* series X 879–889]

YEAR	Policies [1] (mil.)	Coverage per family (dol.)	LIFE INSURANCE IN FORCE Value (bil. dol.)					Disposable personal income per family [3]	AVERAGE SIZE POLICY IN FORCE (dollars)		
			Total	Ordinary	Group	Industrial	Credit [2]		Ordinary	Group	Industrial
1950	202	4,600	234.2	149.1	47.8	33.4	3.9	4,100	2,320	2,480	310
1955	252	6,900	372.3	216.6	101.3	39.7	14.8	5,100	2,720	3,200	350
1960	282	10,200	586.4	340.3	175.4	39.6	31.2	6,100	3,360	4,030	390
1965	320	14,600	900.6	497.6	306.1	39.8	57.0	7,700	4,660	5,060	450
1969	351	19,400	1,284.5	678.9	483.2	38.6	83.8	9,600	5,770	6,470	490
1970	355	20,700	1,402.1	730.5	545.1	38.6	87.9	10,200	6,110	6,910	500
1971	357	21,700	1,503.3	787.7	581.4	39.2	95.0	10,800	6,440	7,170	520
1972	365	22,900	1,628.0	848.5	630.7	40.0	108.8	11,200	6,790	7,730	530
1973	369	24,400	1,778.3	928.2	708.3	40.6	101.2	12,400	7,230	8,010	540
1974	380	26,500	1,985.1	1,009.0	827.0	39.4	109.6	13,100	7,690	8,840	550
1975	380	28,100	2,139.6	1,083.4	904.7	39.4	112.0	14,200	8,090	9,360	570
1976	382	30,100	2,343.1	1,177.7	1,002.6	39.2	123.6	15,200	8,610	10,010	580
1977	390	32,400	2,582.8	1,289.3	1,115.0	39.0	139.4	16,400	9,530	10,550	590

[1] Total of ordinary, group, industrial, and credit.   [2] Insures borrower to cover loan in case of death.
[3] For total disposable personal income, see tables 716 and 722.

Source: American Council of Life Insurance, Washington, D.C., *Life Insurance Fact Book,* annual.

No. 903. U.S. Life Insurance Companies—Summary: 1950 to 1977

In billions of dollars, except number of companies and rate. As of December 31 or **calendar years** as applicable. 1950 excludes Alaska and Hawaii. Covers domestic and foreign business of U.S. companies. See also *Historical Statistics, Colonial Times to 1970,* series X 879 and X 890–907]

ITEM	1950	1960	1965	1970	1972	1973	1974	1975	1976	1977
Number of U.S. companies	649	1,441	1,629	1,780	1,753	1,766	1,757	1,746	1,742	1,750
Sales [1]	30.0	78.4	149.8	206.8	228.4	250.6	323.5	316.5	352.2	392.9
Ordinary	18.3	56.2	89.6	134.8	159.1	175.6	199.0	207.1	233.6	264.7
Group [1]	6.2	15.3	52.9	65.4	61.9	67.7	117.8	102.7	112.2	121.8
Industrial	5.5	6.9	7.3	6.6	7.4	7.2	6.7	6.7	6.4	6.4
Voluntary termination, ordinary policies (rate): [2]										
All policies in force in U.S.	(NA)	5.2	5.1	5.9	6.0	6.3	6.5	6.7	6.6	6.6
In force 2 years or more	(NA)	3.7	3.5	3.9	3.9	4.3	4.5	4.5	4.6	4.7
Income	11.3	23.0	33.2	49.1	58.8	64.8	70.0	78.0	88.6	98.0
Life insurance premiums	6.2	12.0	16.1	21.7	24.7	26.4	27.8	29.3	31.4	33.8
Annuity considerations	.9	1.3	2.2	3.7	5.5	6.8	7.7	10.2	14.0	15.0
Health insurance premiums	1.0	4.0	6.3	11.4	14.3	15.5	17.1	19.1	21.1	23.6
Investment and other	3.2	5.6	8.6	12.3	14.3	16.1	17.4	19.4	22.2	25.7
Disbursements	7.2	17.5	25.2	39.0	45.0	49.4	53.3	58.2	63.0	69.0
Payments to policyholders [3]	4.4	11.4	16.5	25.6	29.4	32.1	34.7	38.1	41.0	44.4
Death payments	[4] 1.6	3.4	4.9	7.2	8.1	8.6	8.9	9.3	9.7	10.2
Matured endowments	.5	.7	1.0	1.0	1.0	1.0	1.0	1.0	1.0	.9
Annuity payments	.3	.7	1.0	1.7	2.1	2.6	2.9	3.2	3.9	4.6
Policy dividends	.7	1.9	2.8	3.8	4.3	4.6	4.8	5.1	5.6	6.3
Surrender values	.7	1.7	2.0	2.9	3.0	3.4	3.7	3.8	4.2	4.3
Disability benefits	[4] .1	.1	.2	.2	.2	.3	.4	.4	.5	.5
Commissions, expenses, etc.	2.7	5.9	8.4	12.9	15.0	16.6	17.9	19.4	21.3	23.9
Dividends to stockholders	.1	.2	.2	.5	.6	.7	.7	.7	.7	.7

NA Not available.   [1] Includes servicemen's group life insurance of $27.4 billion in 1965, $16.8 billion in 1970, $28.8 billion in 1974, and $1.7 billion in 1975.   [2] The rate is the ratio of the number of policies lapsed or surrendered (for cash, extended term, or reduced paid up insurance), less reinstatements, to the mean number of policies in force. Includes policies issued by foreign companies, primarily Canadian.   [3] Total income and payments to policyholders include data on operations of accident and health departments of life insurance companies; since these data are not shown separately, components do not add to totals.   [4] Accidental death benefits included with disability benefits.

Source: American Council of Life Insurance, Washington, D.C. Based on data from *Life Insurance Fact Book* and from The Spectator, Philadelphia, Pa., *Insurance Yearbook.*

No. 904. Life Insurance in Force—States: 1976 and 1977

[See headnote, table 902]

STATE	1976 Number of policies [1] (1,000)	1976 Value (mil. dol.)	1977 [2] Total Number of policies [1] (1,000)	Total Value (mil. dol.)	Ordinary Number of policies (1,000)	Ordinary Value (mil. dol.)	Group Number of certificates (1,000)	Group Value (mil. dol.)	Industrial Number of policies (1,000)	Industrial Value (mil. dol.)	Credit Number of policies [1] (1,000)	Credit Value (mil. dol.)
U.S.	382,431	2,343,063	390,249	2,582,815	139,528	1,289,321	105,649	1,115,047	65,813	39,045	79,259	139,402
Ala.	11,766	37,236	11,981	41,538	1,859	20,064	1,571	15,550	6,819	2,674	1,732	3,250
Alaska.	541	4,393	622	5,443	122	2,128	358	2,966	10	3	132	346
Ariz.	4,308	24,546	4,709	28,024	1,670	15,978	1,400	9,692	150	88	1,489	2,266
Ark.	2,517	15,745	2,675	17,163	908	9,181	623	6,284	505	283	639	1,415
Calif.	29,167	225,579	30,051	250,191	10,410	124,641	12,022	113,610	2,011	1,388	5,608	10,552
Colo.	4,278	30,514	4,400	34,547	1,686	18,821	1,427	13,499	235	172	1,052	2,055
Conn.	5,443	41,195	5,634	44,903	2,348	21,682	1,824	21,339	302	212	1,160	1,670
Del.	1,421	9,252	1,430	10,224	500	4,106	384	5,417	236	153	310	548
D.C.	2,452	13,952	2,436	15,099	435	3,916	936	10,319	506	285	559	579
Fla.	15,101	80,263	15,387	88,277	4,945	49,096	3,423	31,363	3,735	2,540	3,284	5,278
Ga.	12,410	56,795	12,458	62,685	3,059	31,107	2,515	24,774	4,505	2,926	2,379	3,878
Hawaii.	1,557	13,197	1,636	14,449	568	7,764	696	5,948	5	2	367	735
Idaho.	1,255	7,644	1,321	9,046	510	4,923	475	3,418	26	12	310	693
Ill.	22,187	141,896	22,308	154,143	9,141	79,073	6,039	66,387	3,224	1,966	3,904	6,717
Ind.	9,998	58,774	10,179	65,033	3,977	33,037	2,626	27,238	1,664	996	1,912	3,762
Iowa.	4,828	32,616	4,846	36,078	2,496	20,710	1,310	13,124	243	126	797	2,118
Kans.	4,279	25,778	4,053	27,992	1,881	17,092	1,049	9,118	331	177	792	1,605
Ky.	6,371	29,911	6,426	33,256	2,058	16,017	1,317	13,795	1,700	959	1,351	2,485
La.	8,985	38,225	9,315	43,270	1,987	21,549	1,682	16,372	3,822	2,279	1,824	3,070
Maine.	1,784	9,391	1,938	10,589	708	5,571	695	4,248	78	50	457	720
Md.	7,899	46,497	8,073	50,902	2,793	25,956	1,782	21,359	1,817	1,037	1,681	2,550
Mass.	9,125	61,339	9,060	65,271	3,923	32,620	2,377	29,827	823	505	1,937	2,319
Mich.	16,233	111,844	16,089	121,976	5,482	46,995	5,520	67,763	1,957	1,187	3,130	6,031
Minn.	6,059	44,421	6,164	49,950	2,462	23,732	2,258	23,883	249	135	1,195	2,200
Miss.	3,480	17,482	3,831	19,926	874	9,917	823	7,507	760	507	1,374	1,995
Mo.	8,673	52,356	8,631	56,285	3,567	28,595	2,288	24,133	1,274	735	1,502	2,822
Mont.	1,013	6,642	1,090	7,417	421	4,452	335	2,334	25	10	309	621
Nebr.	2,727	18,203	2,665	20,016	1,355	12,196	698	6,753	126	67	486	1,000
Nev.	1,150	7,712	1,301	9,163	255	3,348	503	4,444	9	5	534	1,366
N.H.	1,290	8,289	1,405	9,700	647	5,514	339	3,567	95	61	324	558
N.J.	11,778	94,637	11,811	102,073	5,432	50,308	3,164	47,571	1,396	1,060	1,819	3,134
N. Mex.	1,707	10,472	1,823	11,698	566	5,790	665	4,974	76	43	516	891
N.Y.	26,938	201,092	27,063	216,972	11,332	102,024	7,613	103,974	1,980	1,359	6,138	9,615
N.C.	11,804	52,525	11,943	58,775	3,526	29,990	2,233	22,641	3,695	2,132	2,489	4,012
N. Dak.	884	6,417	942	7,158	428	4,235	283	2,308	4	2	227	613
Ohio.	19,906	124,026	20,423	136,906	8,054	68,500	5,132	58,474	3,371	2,105	3,866	7,827
Okla.	4,182	27,026	4,259	30,375	1,652	16,282	1,097	11,715	406	239	1,104	2,139
Oreg.	3,088	22,273	3,146	25,204	1,177	12,463	1,147	11,246	85	41	737	1,454
Pa.	24,143	132,071	24,521	142,783	9,807	71,916	5,486	59,906	4,589	2,703	4,639	8,258
R.I.	1,851	10,281	1,876	11,792	785	6,370	593	4,862	181	109	317	451
S.C.	7,372	26,842	7,507	30,025	2,269	15,187	1,345	11,194	2,588	1,557	1,305	2,087
S. Dak.	918	6,400	943	7,179	507	4,576	225	2,074	5	2	206	527
Tenn.	8,934	43,512	9,330	49,206	2,445	23,159	2,209	20,791	2,639	1,599	2,037	3,657
Tex.	21,686	135,069	23,135	153,478	7,819	79,871	6,392	62,168	3,634	2,301	5,290	9,138
Utah.	1,979	11,751	2,073	13,371	670	7,058	858	5,262	89	36	456	1,015
Vt.	784	4,600	764	5,046	339	2,823	194	1,892	36	23	195	308
Va.	10,301	58,626	10,440	63,541	3,220	29,970	2,375	28,746	2,542	1,465	2,303	3,360
Wash.	4,876	36,291	5,038	40,090	1,876	20,344	1,990	17,872	170	78	1,002	1,796
W. Va.	3,191	15,681	3,229	17,267	969	7,588	757	7,890	601	369	902	1,420
Wis.	7,267	47,887	7,299	52,843	3,364	28,599	2,414	21,766	480	279	1,041	2,199
Wyo.	545	3,897	570	4,477	244	2,487	182	1,690	4	3	140	297

[1] Includes group credit certificates.

[2] "Ordinary" and "Group" include credit life insurance on loans of more than 10 years duration; "Credit" is limited to 10 years or less and insures borrower to cover loans in case of death.

Source: American Council of Life Insurance, Washington, D.C., *Life Insurance Fact Book*, annual.

No. 905. U.S. LIFE INSURANCE COMPANIES—FINANCIAL ITEMS: 1950 TO 1977

[In billions of dollars, except percent. As of December 31. 1950 excludes Alaska and Hawaii. See also *Historical Statistics, Colonial Times to 1970*, series X 908–917]

ITEM	1950	1960	1965	1970	1972	1973	1974	1975	1976	1977
Assets	64.0	119.6	158.9	207.3	239.7	252.4	263.3	289.3	321.6	351.6
Government securities	16.1	11.8	11.9	11.1	11.4	11.4	12.0	15.2	20.3	23.6
Corporate securities	25.4	51.7	67.4	88.5	113.0	117.7	118.6	133.9	154.9	171.7
Bonds	23.2	46.7	58.2	73.1	86.1	91.8	96.7	105.8	120.7	137.9
Stocks	2.1	5.0	9.1	15.4	26.8	25.9	21.9	28.1	34.3	33.8
Mortgages	16.1	41.8	60.0	74.4	76.9	81.4	86.2	89.2	91.6	96.8
Real estate	1.4	3.8	4.7	6.3	7.3	7.7	8.3	9.6	10.5	11.1
Policy loans	2.4	5.2	7.7	16.1	18.0	20.2	22.9	24.5	25.8	27.6
Other	2.6	5.3	7.2	10.9	13.1	14.1	15.4	16.9	18.5	21.1
Interest earned on assets [1] _ percent	3.13	4.11	4.61	5.30	5.56	5.88	6.25	6.36	6.55	6.89
Liabilities [2]	59.4	109.9	145.0	189.9	220.8	232.5	244.7	268.7	299.5	328.1
Policy reserves [2]	54.9	98.5	127.6	167.6	192.1	203.7	215.4	235.1	259.2	281.0
Capital and surplus [2]	4.6	9.7	13.8	17.3	19.0	19.9	18.6	20.6	22.0	23.6

[1] Net rate.   [2] Includes business of accident and health departments of U.S. life insurance companies.

Source: American Council of Life Insurance, Washington, D.C., *Life Insurance Fact Book*, annual.

No. 906. LARGEST LIFE INSURANCE COMPANIES—ASSETS AND INSURANCE IN FORCE, BY RANK OF ASSETS: 1960 TO 1977

[In billions of dollars, except percent. As of December 31]

ASSET GROUP	1960 Assets	1960 Insurance in force [1]	1965 Assets	1965 Insurance in force [1]	1970 Assets	1970 Insurance in force [1]	1975 Assets	1975 Insurance in force [1]	1976 Assets	1976 Insurance in force [1]	1977 Assets	1977 Insurance in force [1]
50 largest companies	104.9	487	135.8	697	171.9	1,031	232.3	1,517	256.9	1,664	278.1	1,833
Lowest ten	2.9	21	4.1	36	5.6	55	7.9	86	8.9	86	10.1	93
Second ten	4.7	23	6.4	34	8.3	59	11.7	91	12.7	114	13.8	127
Third ten	7.7	38	10.4	64	13.2	93	17.7	127	19.4	142	20.7	188
Fourth ten	15.1	62	20.0	81	25.3	119	35.1	202	39.1	221	43.1	208
Highest ten	74.6	343	95.0	481	119.6	706	160.0	1,011	176.7	1,101	190.5	1,216
Percent of 50 largest	100.0	100.0	100.0	100.0	100.0	100.0	100.0	100.0	100.0	100.0	100.0	100.0
Lowest ten	2.7	4.3	3.0	5.2	3.2	5.3	3.4	5.7	3.5	5.2	3.6	5.1
Second ten	4.5	4.7	4.7	4.9	4.8	5.7	5.0	6.0	4.9	6.9	5.0	6.9
Third ten	7.3	7.9	7.6	9.2	7.7	9.0	7.6	8.4	7.6	8.5	7.4	10.3
Fourth ten	14.4	12.7	14.7	11.6	14.7	11.5	15.1	13.3	15.2	13.3	15.5	11.4
Highest ten	71.0	70.4	69.9	69.0	69.6	68.4	68.9	66.6	68.8	66.1	68.5	66.4
Percent of all cos.: [2]												
50 largest	87.7	83.1	85.5	77.4	82.9	73.5	80.3	70.9	79.9	71.0	79.1	71.0
10 largest	62.4	58.5	59.8	53.4	57.7	50.4	55.3	47.2	54.9	47.0	54.2	47.6

[1] Face value of all life policies outstanding.   [2] See tables 902 and 905 for all companies.

Source: Fortune, New York, N.Y., adapted from *The Fortune Directory*. (Copyright, by Time, Inc.)

No. 907. HEALTH INSURANCE—PREMIUM INCOME AND BENEFIT PAYMENTS: 1950 TO 1976

[In millions of dollars. Represents premium income and benefits paid by insurance companies only. Excludes Blue Cross-Blue Shield plans, medical-society sponsored plans, and all other independent plans]

ITEM	1950	1960	1965	1970	1972	1973	1974	1975	1976 [1]
Premiums [2]	1,266	4,671	7,352	11,546	14,771	16,104	17,915	21,233	24,265
Group policies [3]	629	2,895	4,683	8,149	10,946	11,807	13,193	16,356	19,129
Individual and family policies	637	1,776	2,669	3,397	3,825	4,297	4,722	4,877	5,136
Benefit payments [4]	755	3,069	5,160	9,089	10,622	11,863	13,636	15,149	18,213
Group policies	438	2,350	4,000	7,476	8,943	9,764	11,439	12,870	15,791
Individual and family policies	317	719	1,160	1,613	1,679	2,099	2,197	2,279	2,422
Type of coverage:									
Loss of income	(NA)	839	1,047	1,816	1,958	2,215	2,527	2,618	2,798
Medical expense	(NA)	2,230	4,114	7,133	8,463	9,386	10,777	12,005	14,464
Dental	(NA)	(NA)	(NA)	(NA)	140	201	262	332	951

NA Not available.   [1] Includes premium and benefit payments in Puerto Rico and other U.S. territories and possessions.   [2] Prior to 1972, refers to written premiums; for 1972–76 refers to earned income.   [3] Insurance company group premiums for 1975 and 1976 include Administrative Service Agreements and Minimum Premium Plans. Amounts for prior years contain only a portion of these data.   [4] Beginning 1972, excludes accidental death and dismemberment benefits and accident medical reimbursement benefits.

Source: Health Insurance Institute, Washington, D.C., *Source Book of Health Insurance Data*, annual. Data from Health Insurance Association of America, New York, N.Y.

No. 908. HEALTH INSURANCE COVERAGE, BY TYPE OF COVERAGE: 1950 TO 1976

[In millions. Duplication eliminated except as noted. "Hospital," "Surgical," and "Regular medical" represent coverage by insurance companies, Blue Cross-Blue Shield and medical society approved plans, and other plans. "Major medical" and "Dental" represent insurance company coverage only. "Disability income" represents coverage by insurance companies, paid sick leave plans, and employee organizations]

YEAR AND AGE GROUP	Hospital	Surgical	Regular medical	Major medical	DISABILITY INCOME [1]		Dental
					Short-term	Long-term	
1950	76.6	54.2	21.6	–	37.8	(2)	–
1955	101.4	85.7	53.0	5.2	39.5	(2)	–
1960	122.5	111.5	83.2	25.4	42.4	(2)	(NA)
1965	138.7	130.5	109.6	53.0	46.9	4.5	(NA)
1970	158.8	151.4	138.7	77.1	58.1	11.0	13.0
Under 65	148.7	142.8	130.4	75.0	58.1	11.0	13.0
65 and over	10.1	8.7	8.2	2.0	–	–	–
1974	173.1	166.4	158.2	91.0	65.3	17.8	33.3
Under 65	161.6	156.8	149.3	89.3	65.3	17.8	(NA)
65 and over	11.5	9.6	8.9	1.8	–	–	(NA)
1975 [3]	178.0	168.9	161.9	92.2	63.0	18.4	35.3
Under 65	165.4	158.5	152.2	90.1	63.0	18.4	(NA)
65 and over	12.6	10.4	9.7	2.0	–	–	(NA)
1976 [3]	176.6	167.4	163.1	93.2	60.8	17.8	43.9
Under 65	164.0	156.9	152.9	91.3	60.8	17.8	(NA)
65 and over	12.6	10.6	10.2	1.9	–	–	(NA)

– Represents zero.   NA Not available.   [1] Any duplication resulting from the combination of numbers for short-term and long-term protection has not been eliminated.   [2] Included in "short-term" with some possible duplication.   [3] Includes Puerto Rico and other U.S. territories and possessions.

Source: Health Insurance Institute, Washington, D.C., *Sourcebook of Health Insurance Data,* 1977–78. Data from Health Insurance Association of America, New York, N.Y.

No. 909. PRIVATE HEALTH INSURANCE ORGANIZATIONS—INCOME AND EXPENSES: 1960 TO 1976

[For types of plans covered, see table 910. See also *Historical Statistics, Colonial Times to 1970,* series X 957–959]

ITEM	1960	1965	1970	1971	1972	1973	1974	1975	1976
Total subscription or premium income mil. dol	5,841	10,001	17,185	19,659	22,685	25,196	28,282	33,599	39,422
Claims expense mil. dol	4,996	8,729	15,744	17,713	19,429	21,199	24,621	29,334	34,985
Percent of premium income	85.5	87.3	91.6	90.1	85.6	84.1	87.1	87.3	88.7
Operating expense mil. dol	[1] 845	1,418	2,402	2,738	3,225	3,525	3,979	4,390	5,048
Percent of premium income	[1] 14.5	14.2	14.0	13.9	14.2	14.0	14.1	13.1	12.8
Net underwriting gain mil. dol	(1)	−145	−961	−792	31	472	−318	−125	−611
Percent of premium income	(1)	−1.5	−5.6	−4.0	.1	1.9	−1.1	−.4	−1.5

[1] Data for net underwriting gain not available separately; included in operating expense.

No. 910. PRIVATE HEALTH INSURANCE ORGANIZATIONS—FINANCES, BY TYPE OF PLAN: 1976

[Minus sign (−) denotes loss. See also *Historical Statistics, Colonial Times to 1970,* series X 957–962]

ITEM	Total	BLUE CROSS-BLUE SHIELD			INSURANCE COMPANIES			Other plans
		Total	Blue Cross plans	Blue Shield plans	Total	Group policies	Individual policies	
Total income mil. dol	(NA)	17,560	12,243	5,317	(NA)	(NA)	(NA)	2,698
Total premium income mil. dol	39,422	17,268	12,037	5,231	19,504	16,222	3,282	2,650
Claims expense mil. dol	34,985	16,227	11,625	4,602	16,280	14,549	1,731	2,478
Percent of premium income	88.7	94.0	96.6	88.0	83.5	89.7	52.7	93.5
Operating expense mil. dol	5,048	1,193	623	570	3,689	2,154	1,535	166
Percent of premium income	12.8	6.9	5.2	10.9	18.9	13.3	46.8	6.3
Net underwriting gain mil. dol	−611	−151	−211	60	−465	−481	16	6
Percent of premium income	−1.5	−.9	−1.8	1.1	−2.4	−3.0	.5	.2
Net income mil. dol	(NA)	141	−5	146	(NA)	(NA)	(NA)	53
Percent of total income	(NA)	.8	(Z)	2.7	(NA)	(NA)	(NA)	2.0

NA Not available.   Z Less than .05 percent.

Source of tables 909 and 910: U.S. Social Security Administration, *Social Security Bulletin,* June 1978.

No. 911. PROPERTY AND LIABILITY INSURANCE: 1960 TO 1976

[In millions of dollars, except companies reporting. Premiums written represent total premiums on all insurance policies written by companies, with inception dates in years shown. See also *Historical Statistics, Colonial Times to 1970*, series X 918, 923, 928, 933, and 940]

ITEM	1960	1965	1970	1971	1972	1973	1974	1975	1976
Companies reporting	3,500	3,047	2,727	2,725	2,881	2,870	2,934	2,886	2,880
Premiums written [1]	**14,973**	**20,063**	**32,867**	**35,715**	**39,318**	**42,480**	**45,152**	**49,967**	**60,813**
Auto liability	3,883	5,424	8,958	9,977	10,367	10,757	10,937	12,110	14,546
Physical damage, auto	1,994	2,861	4,824	4,824	6,016	6,419	6,461	6,946	8,681
Liability, other than auto	963	1,137	2,140	2,381	2,555	2,701	2,936	3,824	5,225
Medical malpractice	(NA)	(NA)	(NA)	(NA)	(NA)	(NA)	(NA)	769	1,023
Fire [2]	2,406	2,215	3,147	3,172	3,406	3,417	3,456	3,590	3,982
Homeowners multiple peril	764	1,523	2,565	2,833	3,316	3,813	4,215	4,785	5,733
Commercial multiple peril	56	509	1,331	1,660	2,078	2,509	2,847	3,161	4,032
Workmen's compensation	1,419	2,042	3,492	3,660	4,014	4,761	5,413	6,114	7,435
Inland marine	381	489	812	884	968	1,058	1,127	1,221	1,386
Ocean marine	230	262	465	496	577	650	761	855	897
Surety and fidelity	(NA)	408	562	605	661	700	748	787	834
Burglary and theft	116	110	135	136	138	129	128	119	122
Crop-hail	103	117	125	124	132	192	260	312	325
Boiler and machinery	85	91	115	126	129	137	141	173	170
Glass	48	41	40	40	39	36	33	31	31
Assets and surplus:									
Assets	30,132	41,843	58,594	67,284	78,885	83,862	82,115	94,118	112,826
Policyholders' surplus	11,930	17,112	18,520	22,749	28,211	27,091	20,898	25,303	31,351

NA Not available.   [1] Includes all property, liability, and allied lines; other data are for principal lines only.
[2] Includes extended coverage and allied lines.

Source: Insurance Information Institute, New York, N.Y., *Insurance Facts*, annual.

No. 912. FIRE LOSSES—TOTAL AND PER CAPITA: 1940 TO 1977

[Prior to 1962, excludes Alaska and Hawaii. Includes allowance for uninsured and unreported losses but excludes losses to government property and forests. Based on paid losses through 1953, incurred losses thereafter]

YEARLY AVERAGE	Total (mil. dol.)	YEAR	Total (mil. dol.)	YEAR	Total (mil. dol.)	YEAR	Total (mil. dol.)	Per capita [1]
1946–50	643	1940	286	1966	1,497	1972	2,304	$11.07
1951–55	833	1950	649	1967	1,707	1973	2,639	12.57
1956–60	1,045	1955	885	1968	1,830	1974	3,190	15.09
1961–65	1,340	1960	1,108	1969	1,952	1975	3,560	16.71
1966–70	1,850	1964	1,367	1970	2,328	1976	3,558	16.59
1971–75	2,802	1965	1,456	1971	2,316	1977	3,751	17.34

[1] Based on Bureau of the Census estimated resident population as of July 1.

Source: 1940–1964, National Board of Fire Underwriters, New York, N.Y., *Report of the Committee on Statistics and Origin of Losses*. Thereafter, Insurance Information Institute, New York, N.Y., *Insurance Facts*, annual.

No. 913. FIRES—NUMBER AND LOSS, BY TYPE AND SELECTED PROPERTY USE: 1976

[Based on reports by public fire services. No adjustments were made for unreported fires and losses. Property loss includes direct property loss only]

TYPE AND PROPERTY USE	Number (1,000)	Property loss (mil. dol.)	PROPERTY USE	Number (1,000)	Property loss (mil. dol.)
TYPE OF FIRE			**PROPERTY USE—Con.**		
Total	2,939	3,360	Institutional	24	25
Building	964	2,656	Residential	665	1,433
Vehicle	493	215	1–2 family units	451	940
Brush and rubbish, outside bldgs.	1,128	20	Apartments	160	320
Other	354	469	Hotels and motels	16	63
			Mobile homes	17	59
PROPERTY USE			Other residential	22	51
			Stores and offices	76	508
Public assembly	38	189	Industry, utility, defense [1]	50	289
Educational	24	160	Storage [1]	42	235

[1] Data underreported as some incidents were handled by private fire brigades or fixed suppression systems which do not report.

Source: National Fire Protection Association, Boston, Mass., *Fire Journal*. (Copyright.)

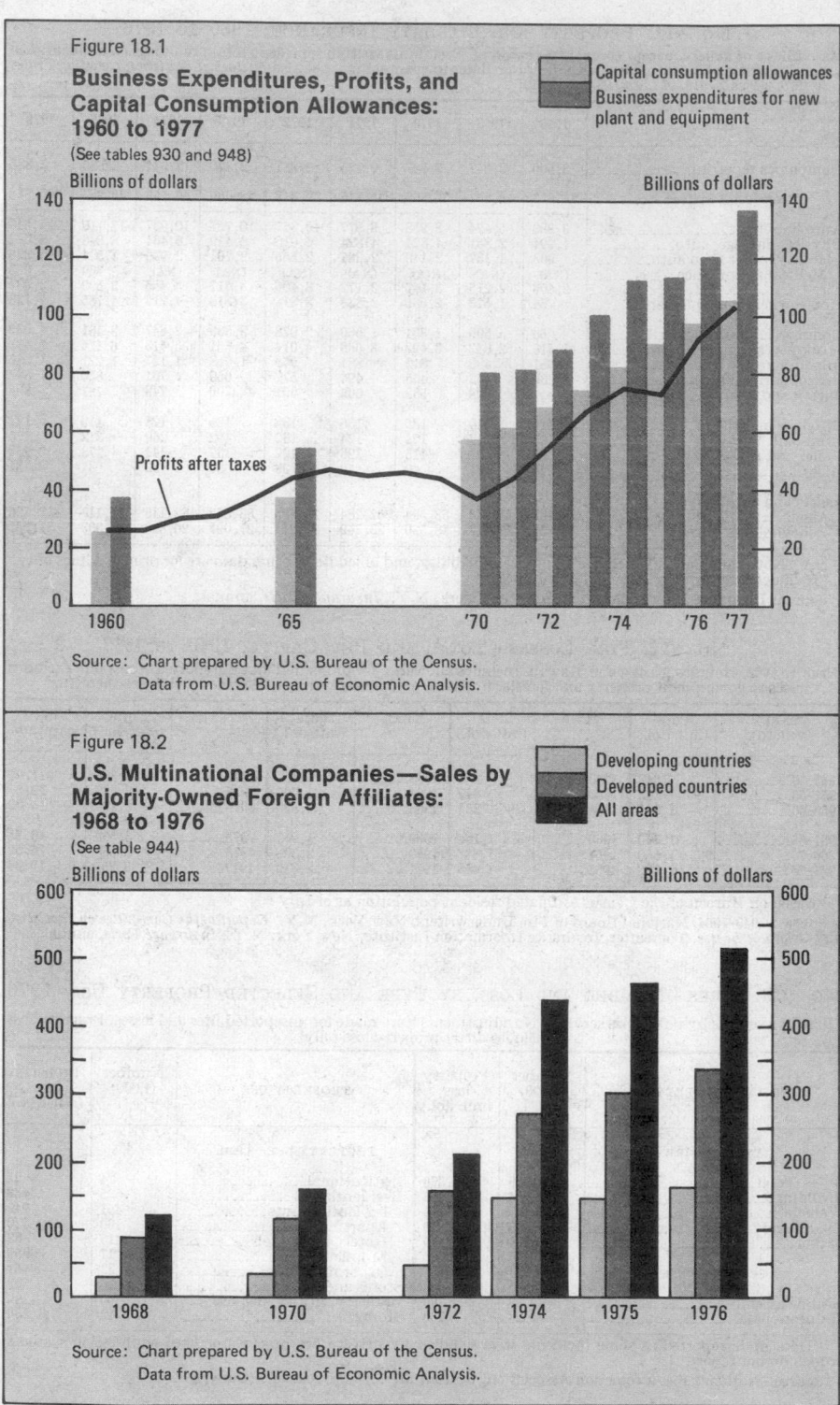

Figure 18.1

Business Expenditures, Profits, and Capital Consumption Allowances: 1960 to 1977

(See tables 930 and 948)

Capital consumption allowances

Business expenditures for new plant and equipment

Billions of dollars

Profits after taxes

Source: Chart prepared by U.S. Bureau of the Census.
Data from U.S. Bureau of Economic Analysis.

Figure 18.2

U.S. Multinational Companies—Sales by Majority-Owned Foreign Affiliates: 1968 to 1976

(See table 944)

Developing countries

Developed countries

All areas

Billions of dollars

Source: Chart prepared by U.S. Bureau of the Census.
Data from U.S. Bureau of Economic Analysis.

Section 18
Business Enterprise

This section relates to the place and behavior of the business firm and of business initiative in the American economy. It includes data on the number, types, and size of businesses; financial data of domestic and multinational corporations; business investment, expenditures, and profits; business sales and inventories; consumer cooperatives; minority-owned firms; mergers, acquisitions, and business failures.

The principal sources of these data are the *Survey of Current Business*, published by the Bureau of Economic Analysis (BEA); the *Federal Reserve Bulletin*, issued by the Board of Governors of the Federal Reserve System; the annual *Statistics of Income* reports of the Internal Revenue Service (IRS); *The Failure Record Through (Year)*, issued by Dun & Bradstreet, Inc., New York; and *Fortune* and *The Fortune Directory*, issued by Fortune, New York. Other sources are publications of the Securities and Exchange Commission (SEC), the Federal Trade Commission (FTC), and the Administrative Office of the United States Courts.

Business firms.—A business firm is generally defined as a business organization under a single management and may include one or more plants or outlets. The IRS concept of a business firm relates primarily to the legal entity used for tax reporting purposes. (See page 804 for explanation of the difference between "firm" or "company" and "establishment".) A firm doing business in more than one industry is classified by industry according to the major activity of the firm as a whole. The industrial classification is based on the *Standard Industrial Classification (SIC) Manual* (see text, page 396). The IRS *Statistics of Income* reports present data, based on a sample of tax returns before audit, separately for sole proprietorships, partnerships, and corporations. While many corporations file consolidated tax returns (i.e., one return for the parent firm and all its subsidiaries), most corporate tax returns represent individual corporations, some of which are affiliated through common ownership or control with other corporations filing separate returns.

Corporate assets and liabilities.—In its annual report, *Statistics of Income, Corporation Income Tax Returns*, the IRS presents balance sheet and income estimates for all active U.S. corporations. The FTC issues 2 current reports, the *Quarterly Financial Report for Manufacturing, Mining and Trade Corporations*, which presents quarterly income account and balance sheet data for manufacturing industries and the *Working Capital of U.S. Nonfinancial Corporations*, which presents data on components of current assets and liabilities of all nonfinancial U.S. corporations. Until 1978, the latter was issued by the SEC. Broker-dealer financial data are detailed in the *Annual Report* of the SEC.

Corporate income, profits, dividends, and taxes.—Several agencies, among them the IRS and the BEA, compile corporate income account data. These data, however, are not comparable because of differing methods of compilation.

The IRS publishes financial data for all business enterprises, based on a sample of income tax returns filed by sole proprietorships, partnerships, and corporations. These data appear in *Statistics of Income—Business Income Tax Returns* and *Corporation Income Tax Returns*. Supplemental reports published periodically present data on foreign income and taxes reported by U.S. corporations.

The corporate data issued by the BEA are a part of its national income and product accounts (see text, p. 437) and are defined as required for purposes of national income estimation. The primary sources for BEA estimates of profits, taxes, dividends, and undistributed profits are the original corporate tax returns submitted to the IRS. Var-

559

ious adjustments of the IRS data are required by the national income treatment, particularly with respect to profits which would be disclosed if all tax returns were audited, depletion, capital gain or loss, treatment of bad debts, measurement of income received from abroad, and intercorporate dividends to make the figures comparable with other entries in the national income accounts. BEA's corporate profits data also include net earnings of several federally sponsored credit agencies not included in *Statistics of Income*.

Sources and uses of corporate funds.—These data (table 927) show capital requirements of corporations and the manner in which they are financed. Sources of funds should be equal to their uses. Certain discrepancies, however, interfere with this equality due to omission of such factors as (1) money accruing to corporations from an excess of sales over purchases of used plant and equipment, (2) transactions in securities held as permanent investments except public offerings, and (3) net purchases of land. Also, the balance sheet data upon which many of the financial flow estimates are based are not fully comparable with the tax-return based estimates of internal sources, or the establishment series underlying the figures on inventory change.

Plant and equipment expenditures.—Estimates of actual and expected expenditures for new plant and equipment in the United States by most private, nonagricultural business firms are based on quarterly sample surveys conducted jointly by the Bureau of Economic Analysis and the Interstate Commerce Commission.

The sample was designed for complete coverage of all companies with gross assets of $50 million or more, and a random selection of companies with assets of less than $50 million. There are approximately 10,000 firms in the sample, with response rates varying from 70 to 75 percent. Published data are adjusted to reflect the expenditures of all companies. In 1972, the responding companies accounted for 68 percent of total capital expenditures in the United States.

For quarterly data, see current issues of the *Survey of Current Business*; for discussion of coverage, concepts, and methodology, see the January 1970 issue for actual expenditures and the February 1970 issue for expectations.

Business sales and inventories.—Business sales and inventories as defined by the BEA are the sum of data for manufacturing, merchant wholesalers, and retail trade. Sales are estimated aggregate values and inventories are book values at the end of the period. Sales signifies sales or shipments for retail and wholesale trade and billings or shipments for manufacturing. Trade inventories are valued at cost of merchandise on hand, while manufacturers' inventories are valued at approximate current costs or at book values, as reported by the manufacturer. Inventories data for manufacturing (see tables 932 and 933) are based on data from the *Census of Manufactures* and the *Annual Survey of Manufactures*. Data for manufacturing also appear in *Manufacturers' Shipments, Inventories, and Orders*, published by the Bureau of the Census in its Current Industrial Reports, series M3-1.

Industrial and commercial failures.—These data, published monthly in the *Failure Report* by Dun & Bradstreet, Inc., are available by years since 1857 and by months since 1900. The number of failures includes concerns involved in court proceedings or voluntary actions likely to end in loss to creditors; discontinuances with outside obligations paid in full are not included. Data cover manufacturers, wholesalers, retailers, building contractors, and certain types of commercial service, but exclude finance, insurance, and real estate companies; railroads and steamship lines; and amusement enterprises.

Statistical Reliability.—For a discussion of Statistical collection and estimation, sampling procedures and measures of statistical reliability applicable to Census Bureau data, see Appendix III.

Historical statistics.—Tabular headnotes provide cross-references, where applicable, to *Historical Statistics of the United States, Colonial Times to 1970*. See Appendix I.

No. 914. NEW BUSINESS CONCERNS AND BUSINESS FAILURES: 1950 TO 1977

[See also *Historical Statistics, Colonial Times to 1970*, series V 21-24]

FORMATIONS AND FAILURES	1950	1955	1960	1965	1970	1972	1973	1974	1975	1976	1977
Business formations:											
Index, net formations[1].. (1967=100)..	93.1	99.1	92.4	98.6	108.0	117.9	117.9	112.4	108.9	117.6	127.4
New incorporations [2]_____1,000..	93	140	183	204	264	317	329	319	326	376	436
Failures, number [3]_____1,000..	9.2	11.0	15.4	13.5	10.7	9.6	9.3	9.9	11.4	9.6	7.9
Rate per 10,000 concerns_____	34	42	57	53	44	38	36	38	43	35	28

[1] Source: U.S. Bureau of Economic Analysis.   [2] Prior to 1960, excludes Alaska.   [3] See footnote 2, table 958.
Source: Except as noted, Dun & Bradstreet, Inc., New York, N.Y., *Monthly New Business Incorporation Report*.

No. 915. PROPRIETORSHIPS, PARTNERSHIPS, AND CORPORATIONS—NUMBER, RECEIPTS, AND INCOME: 1950 TO 1975

[Figures are estimates based on samples for all years for proprietorships, beginning 1955 for corporations, and 1960 for partnerships. See also *Historical Statistics, Colonial Times to 1970*, series V 1-12]

ITEM	1950	1955	1960	1965	1970	1972	1973	1974	1975
Number_____1,000..	(NA)	(NA)	11,172	11,416	12,001	12,978	13,592	13,902	13,979
Receipts [1]_____bil. dol..	(NA)	(NA)	1.095	1,469	2,082	2,551	2,994	3,557	3,684
Net income (less deficit) [2].bil. dol..	(NA)	(NA)	73	111	109	145	176	201	196
Proprietorships, number [3]____1,000..	6,865	8,239	9,090	9,078	9,400	10,173	10,648	10,874	10,882
Business receipts [1]_____bil. dol..	(NA)	139	171	199	238	276	311	328	339
Net income (less deficit)__bil. dol..	15	18	21	28	33	39	47	46	45
Partnerships, number_____1,000..	(NA)	(NA)	941	914	936	992	1,039	1,062	1,073
Total receipts [4]_____bil. dol..	(NA)	(NA)	74	75	93	104	125	139	146
Net income (less deficit)__bil. dol..	(NA)	(NA)	8	10	10	9	9	9	8
Corporations, number_____1,000..	629	807	1,141	1,424	1,665	1,813	1,905	1,966	2,024
Total receipts [4]_____bil. dol..	458	642	849	1,195	1,751	2,171	2,558	3,090	3,199
Percent of all firms receipts_____	(NA)	(NA)	77.5	81.3	84.1	85.1	85.4	86.9	86.8
Net income (less deficit) [2][5].bil. dol..	43	47	44	74	66	97	120	146	143

NA Not available.   [1] See footnote 1, table 918.   [2] See footnote 3, table 916.   [3] Individually owned businesses and farms.   [4] Total taxable receipts before deduction of cost of goods sold, cost of operations, and net loss from sales of property other than capital assets. Excludes nontaxable income except nontaxable interest. See headnote, table 918.   [5] Beginning 1965, includes constructive taxable income from related foreign corporations.

No. 916. PROPRIETORSHIPS, PARTNERSHIPS, AND CORPORATIONS—NUMBER, RECEIPTS, AND NET INCOME, BY INDUSTRY: 1975

[Figures are estimates based on sample of unaudited tax returns filed for accounting periods ending between July 1 of year shown and June 30 of following year. Proprietorships are individually owned businesses and farms. See *Historical Statistics, Colonial Times to 1970*, series V 42-53, for number of active corporations]

INDUSTRY	NUMBER [1] (1,000)			BUSINESS RECEIPTS [1][2] (bil. dol.)			NET INCOME (less deficit) [1][3] (bil. dol.)		
	Propri-etor-ships	Active partner-ships	Active corpo-rations	Propri-etor-ships	Active partner-ships	Active corpo-rations	Propri-etor-ships	Active partner-ships	Active corpo-rations
Total_____	10,881	1,073	2,024	339.2	146.0	[4]3,120.4	44.6	7.7	142.6
Agric., forestry, and fishing_____	3,367	123	56	69.3	12.6	26.6	5.6	.9	.7
Mining_____	56	16	14	3.5	4.0	63.7	.3	−.5	23.6
Construction_____	892	61	191	31.0	12.3	143.4	4.4	.8	2.2
Manufacturing_____	222	29	217	8.7	6.8	1,258.3	1.0	.3	68.4
Transportation, public utilities [5]..	355	17	81	10.0	2.5	234.7	1.3	(Z)	10.1
Wholesale and retail trade_____	2,193	193	615	148.3	45.2	951.5	9.9	2.7	22.5
Wholesale_____	336	31	220	33.3	16.0	502.0	2.9	.8	13.9
Retail_____	1,765	162	395	112.5	29.1	449.3	6.7	1.8	8.6
Finance, insurance, real estate____	744	434	412	12.1	32.4	[4]315.8	3.8	−3.7	11.7
Services_____	3,034	199	436	56.0	30.2	125.7	18.4	7.2	3.4

Z Less than $50 million.   [1] Includes business not allocable to individual industries.
[2] See headnote and footnote 1, table 918.
[3] Net profit (or income) is defined differently by legal form of organization, basically as follows: (a) Proprietorships: Total taxable receipts less total deductions, including cost of sales and operations; investment and other income are excluded; (b) Partnerships: Total taxable receipts less total deductions, including cost of sales and operations; investment and other income, except capital gains, are included; (c) Corporations: Total taxable receipts less total deductions, including cost of sales and operations; investment and other income, such as capital gains and income from foreign corporations considered received for tax purposes only, are included; net profit is before income tax.   [4] Total receipts rather than business receipts are shown for finance industries.
[5] Includes sanitary services.
Source of tables 915 and 916: U.S. Internal Revenue Service, preliminary reports, *Statistics of Income, Business Income Tax Returns*, annual, and *Statistics of Income, Corporation Income Tax Returns*, annual.

No. 917. Proprietorships, Partnerships, and Corporations—Number and Business Receipts, by Size of Receipts: 1965 to 1974

[See headnote, tables 916 and 918, and *Historical Statistics, Colonial Times to 1970*, series V 1–12]

SIZE CLASS OF RECEIPTS	1965		1970		1974							
					Total		Number (1,000)			Receipts (bil. dol.)		
	Number (1,000)	Receipts (bil. dol.)	Number (1,000)	Receipts (bil. dol.)	Number (1,000)	Receipts (bil. dol.)	Proprietorships	Partnerships [1]	Corporations [1]	Proprietorships	Partnerships [1]	Corporations [1]
Total	11,417	1,393	12,001	2,036	13,902	3,320	10,874	1,062	1,966	328.3	137.2	2,854.8
Under $25,000 [2]	8,190	51	8,200	51	9,141	54	8,136	538	467	48.2	3.8	2.2
$25,000–$49,999	1,209	42	1,302	46	1,506	52	1,185	139	182	42.2	5.0	5.2
$50,000–$99,999	845	58	1,000	71	1,228	85	833	137	258	58.6	9.9	16.8
$100,000–$199,999	536	73	661	93	}1,512	315	454	117	} 639	{ 62.7	16.7	} 146.0
$200,000–$499,999	359	108	474	146			213	89		62.8	27.0	
$500,000–$999,999	138	94	181	126	241	163	37	25	179	25.0	17.3	120.4
$1,000,000 or more	139	969	182	1,503	273	2,651	14	17	242	28.8	57.5	2,564.2
	PERCENT DISTRIBUTION											
Under $25,000 [2]	71.7	3.7	68.3	2.5	65.8	1.6	74.8	50.7	23.8	14.7	2.8	.1
$25,000–$49,999	10.6	3.0	10.8	2.3	10.8	1.6	10.9	13.1	9.3	12.8	3.6	.2
$50,000–$99,999	7.4	4.1	8.3	3.5	8.8	2.6	7.7	12.9	13.1	17.9	7.2	.6
$100,000–$199,999	4.7	5.2	5.5	4.6	}10.9	9.5	4.2	11.0	} 32.5	{ 19.1	12.2	} 5.1
$200,000–$499,999	3.1	7.7	4.0	7.2			2.0	8.4		19.1	19.7	
$500,000–$999,999	1.2	6.7	1.5	6.2	1.7	4.9	.3	2.4	9.1	7.6	12.6	4.2
$1,000,000 or more	1.2	69.5	1.5	73.8	2.0	79.8	.1	1.6	12.3	8.8	41.9	89.8

[1] Active firms only. [2] Includes firms with no receipts.

Source: U.S. Internal Revenue Service, *Statistics of Income, Business Income Tax Returns*, annual, and *Statistics of Income, Corporation Income Tax Returns*, annual.

No. 918. Proprietorships and Partnerships—Number and Business Receipts, by States: 1975

[Because of minor variations in estimating techniques for deriving these data, totals differ slightly from those shown in other IRS tables in this section. See headnote, table 916]

STATE	PROPRIETORSHIPS		PARTNERSHIPS		STATE	PROPRIETORSHIPS		PARTNERSHIPS	
	Number (1,000)	Receipts [1] (mil. dol.)	Number (1,000)	Receipts [1] (mil. dol.)		Number (1,000)	Receipts [1] (mil. dol.)	Number (1,000)	Receipts [1] (mil. dol.)
U.S [2]	10,882	339,221	1,073	146,029	S.A.—Con.				
					W. Va	61	2,375	8	445
N.E.	452	13,441	43	4,719	N.C	296	7,742	22	2,156
Maine	59	1,864	3	272	S.C	119	3,682	10	1,300
N.H.	38	1,032	3	236	Ga	228	7,544	21	2,510
Vt	29	909	2	138	Fla	370	9,761	39	3,878
Mass	192	5,276	16	2,278					
R.I.	27	737	3	234	E.S.C.	802	22,972	61	8,172
Conn	107	3,623	16	1,561	Ky	284	6,402	17	2,032
					Tenn	253	7,510	22	3,012
M.A.	1,195	40,904	169	30,054	Ala	147	4,931	12	1,880
N.Y	565	16,681	84	18,475	Miss	118	4,129	10	1,248
N.J	214	7,223	36	4,104					
Pa	416	17,000	49	7,475	W.S.C.	1,299	42,486	121	17,547
					Ark	158	4,463	10	1,259
E.N.C.	1,991	59,537	180	23,437	La	149	5,340	13	2,223
Ohio	493	12,977	40	5,076	Okla	223	6,240	15	2,040
Ind	331	9,361	20	2,207	Tex	769	26,443	83	12,025
Ill	553	18,969	61	9,693					
Mich	355	11,281	38	4,537	Mt	598	18,455	62	6,610
Wis	259	6,949	21	1,924	Mont	69	2,142	5	489
					Idaho	70	2,504	6	886
W.N.C.	1,539	49,049	94	11,097	Wyo	31	1,052	3	321
Minn	288	8,157	20	2,025	Colo	173	4,975	19	1,830
Iowa	317	11,361	18	2,688	N. Mex	61	2,041	6	668
Mo	351	8,923	22	2,732	Ariz	100	3,009	11	1,147
N. Dak	85	2,897	5	421	Utah	63	1,758	8	819
S. Dak	89	3,174	5	449	Nev	31	974	4	450
Nebr	171	6,412	11	1,384					
Kans	238	8,125	13	1,398	Pac	1,532	49,184	204	28,320
					Wash	205	6,843	23	2,350
S.A.	1,467	43,080	142	15,946	Oreg	154	4,018	16	1,869
Del	21	728	2	385	Calif	1,106	36,640	157	22,972
Md	154	5,304	16	1,906	Alaska	25	848	3	377
D.C.	18	338	4	1,183	Hawaii	42	835	5	752
Va	200	5,606	20	2,183					

[1] Receipts from sales and services less allowances, rebates, and returns; excludes capital gains or losses, and investment income not associated with the taxpayer's business.
[2] U.S. totals include Puerto Rico and foreign returns.

Source: U.S. Internal Revenue Service, *Statistics of Income, Business Income Tax Returns*, annual.

No. 919. PROPRIETORSHIPS, PARTNERSHIPS, AND CORPORATIONS—NUMBER, RECEIPTS, AND NET INCOME, BY INDUSTRY AND SIZE OF BUSINESS RECEIPTS: 1974

[Number in thousands; receipts and profit in millions of dollars. See headnote, table 916. See *Historical Statistics, Colonial Times to 1970*, series V 42–53, for number of active corporations]

INDUSTRY	PROPRIETORSHIPS [1]			ACTIVE PARTNERSHIPS			ACTIVE CORPORATIONS		
	Under $50,000 [2]	$50,000–$99,999	$100,000 or more	Under $100,000 [2]	$100,000–$499,999	$500,000 or more	Under $500,000	$500,000–$999,999	$1,000,000 or more
All industrial divisions: [3]									
Number	9,321	833	719	814	206	42	1,545	179	242
Business receipts [4]	90,346	58,633	179,284	18,700	43,699	74,757	180,793	125,157	2,702,842
Net income [5]	17,241	12,328	16,286	−1,868	5,105	5,627	2,090	3,674	140,234
Agriculture, forestry, and fishing:									
Number	3,062	213	110	93	26	4	46	4	4
Business receipts [4]	28,410	14,643	23,813	2,399	5,290	4,833	5,511	2,624	16,048
Mining: Number	48	3	6	11	2	1	12	2	2
Business receipts [4]	400	237	2,354	152	457	2,983	1,137	1,042	60,686
Construction: Number	741	79	77	45	15	3	137	23	26
Business receipts [4]	8,665	5,509	18,569	1,452	3,063	6,921	20,255	16,149	97,272
Manufacturing:									
Number	170	22	21	21	8	2	128	30	53
Business receipts [4]	1,938	1,568	5,611	590	1,566	5,399	19,728	21,036	1,211,606
Transport and public utilities: [6]									
Number	322	22	15	11	3	1	65	7	8
Business receipts [4]	4,418	1,564	4,268	317	570	1,212	7,740	4,903	201,575
Wholesale and retail trade:									
Number	1,547	269	384	111	69	15	401	83	119
Business receipts [4]	18,091	19,311	104,893	4,047	15,253	24,277	67,180	58,230	781,497
Finance, insurance, and real estate:									
Number	697	27	15	383	38	9	397	11	17
Business receipts [4][7]	6,003	1,822	3,744	5,976	8,120	15,014	20,435	7,702	275,061
Services: Number	2,659	195	89	138	45	8	357	19	13
Business receipts [4]	21,941	13,754	15,646	3,760	9,369	14,101	38,597	13,325	58,576

[1] Individually owned businesses and farms.
[2] Includes businesses without receipts.   [3] Includes businesses not allocable to individual industries.
[4] See footnote 1, table 918.   [5] Less loss. See footnote 3, table 916.
[6] Includes sanitary services.
[7] For partnerships and corporations, total receipts rather than business receipts were used as the size classifier and for the amounts shown.

Source: U.S. Internal Revenue Service, *Statistics of Income, 1974, Business Income Tax Returns*, annual; and *Statistics of Income, 1974, Corporation Income Tax Returns*, annual.

No. 920. WOMEN-OWNED FIRMS—NUMBER AND RECEIPTS, BY INDUSTRY: 1972

INDUSTRY	FIRMS (1,000)			RECEIPTS (bil. dol.)		
	All firms [1]	Women-owned		All receipts [1]	Women-owned	
		Number of firms	Percent of all firms		Receipts	Percent of all firms
All industries, total	8,730	402	4.6	2,381.2	8.1	.3
Construction	1,020	15	1.5	146.2	.5	.3
Manufacturing	437	8	1.8	875.3	.3	(Z)
Transportation and public utilities	[2] 432	7	1.6	[2] 159.5	.1	.1
Wholesale trade	560	5	.9	349.4	.6	.2
Retail trade	2,381	133	5.6	474.9	4.2	.9
Finance, insurance, and real estate	1,318	37	2.8	252.8	.5	.2
Selected services	[3] 2,212	151	6.3	[3] 95.5	1.5	1.6
Other industries and industries not classified	[3] 370	45	12.2	[3] 27.6	.4	1.4

Z Less than .05 percent.   [1] Based on data from U.S. Internal Revenue Service, preliminary report, *Statistics of Income, Business Income Tax Returns, 1972*.
[2] Excludes railroads.   [3] Adjusted to exclude legal services and architectural and engineering services out-of-scope of women-owned businesses.

Source: U.S. Bureau of the Census, *Women-Owned Businesses, 1972*.

No. 921. MINORITY-OWNED FIRMS—NUMBER AND RECEIPTS, BY INDUSTRY: 1972

[Number and employment in thousands and receipts in billions of dollars, except percents. Based on a mail canvass, various published and unpublished source listings, and personal contacts with knowledgeable community and governmental representatives, and records of the Internal Revenue Service and the Social Security Administration. "Minority" identified to include the following groups: Black, Chinese, Japanese, Puerto Rican, Mexican or Latin American, American Indian, Filipino, Korean, Hawaiian, etc.]

INDUSTRY	BUSINESS FIRMS OWNED BY—						PERCENT CHANGE FROM 1969			
	All U.S. firms	All minorities	Percent minorities of all firms	Black	Spanish origin	Other	All minorities	Black	Spanish origin	Other
Number of firms, total [1]	8,730	382	4.4	195	120	67	19	20	20	14
With paid employees	(X)	76	(X)	32	29	15	-16	-17	-12	-22
With no paid employees	(X)	306	(X)	163	91	52	32	31	36	31
Construction	1,020	40	3.9	20	17	3	34	24	67	-11
Manufacturing	437	9	2.1	4	4	1	18	38	-	19
Transport and public util. [2]	432	30	6.9	22	6	2	28	30	29	3
Wholesale trade	560	7	1.3	2	3	2	31	26	41	20
Retail trade	2,381	121	5.1	57	42	22	25	25	26	22
Finance, insurance, real estate	1,318	19	1.4	8	6	5	-15	5	-22	-31
Selected services	2,212	120	5.4	68	32	20	19	22	11	21
Business receipts, total [1]	2,381.2	16.6	.7	7.2	5.3	4.1	56	60	58	46
Firms with paid employees	(X)	12.1	(X)	5.1	3.7	3.3	35	31	32	32
With no paid employees	(X)	4.5	(X)	2.1	1.6	.8	163	152	193	143
Construction	146.2	1.7	1.2	.8	.6	.3	84	77	125	38
Manufacturing	875.3	1.3	.1	.5	.5	.3	95	77	126	88
Transport and public util. [2]	159.5	.7	.4	.4	.2	.1	79	102	50	56
Wholesale trade	349.4	1.8	.5	.8	.5	.5	91	98	91	82
Retail trade	474.9	7.5	1.6	2.9	2.5	2.1	44	51	43	37
Finance, insurance, real estate	252.8	.9	.4	.5	.2	.2	59	59	64	54
Selected services	95.5	2.1	2.2	1.1	.6	.4	47	59	30	49
Employment, total [1]	56,466	456	.8	197	150	109	23	29	18	20
Construction	3,398	57	1.7	30	21	6	63	66	78	23
Manufacturing	18,696	54	.3	20	21	13	73	66	80	76
Transport and public util. [2]	3,895	19	.5	11	5	3	40	42	42	28
Wholesale trade	4,075	19	.5	8	6	5	44	37	39	63
Retail trade	11,648	173	1.5	58	59	56	3	6	-4	10
Finance, insurance, real estate	3,901	28	.7	18	4	6	91	99	74	85
Selected services	9,576	98	1.0	49	31	18	21	29	15	12

- Represents zero.　X Not applicable.　[1] Includes industries not shown separately.　[2] Excludes railroads.
Source: U.S. Bureau of the Census, *Minority-Owned Businesses: 1972.*

No. 922. CONSUMER COOPERATIVES, BY TYPE OF ASSOCIATION: 1965 TO 1976

[Members in thousands; business in millions of dollars]

TYPE OF ASSOCIATION	1965			1970			1976		
	Associations	Members	Business	Associations	Members	Business	Associations	Members	Business
Credit unions [1]	22,064	16,756	8,098	23,656	22,813	14,106	22,533	33,870	34,384
Electric power cooperatives [2]	885	4,964	781	875	5,789	1,195	913	7,531	3,285
Rural telephone cooperatives [3]	219	485	48	235	609	86	243	822	195
Nonprofit prepayment health plans [4]	569	8,684	582	[5] 457	10,532	1,016	383	11,462	2,398
Community	43	3,400	216	[5] 40	4,900	457	36	6,205	1,176
Employer-employee-union	507	5,068	366	[5] 418	5,500	559	308	5,095	1,177
Private group medical clinic	19	(NA)	(NA)	(NA)	(NA)	(NA)	(NA)	162	45
Farm supply cooperatives [6]	6,763	(NA)	2,910	6,209	(NA)	3,871	5,538	(NA)	9,412
Principally in farm supply	3,085	3,251	2,707	2,775	3,222	2,755	2,731	3,056	8,753
Producers' goods	4,400+	(NA)	1,851	4,200+	(NA)	2,399	3,900+	(NA)	6,146
Petroleum products	2,773	(NA)	643	2,774	(NA)	862	2,983	(NA)	2,098
Meats and groceries	775	(NA)	60	717	(NA)	83	486	(NA)	108
Miscellaneous	4,800+	(NA)	356	4,800+	(NA)	527	4,400+	(NA)	1,060

NA Not available.　[1] Source: 1965, U.S. Social Security Administration; 1970 and 1976, National Credit Union Administration, *Annual Report of the National Credit Union Administration.* "Business" refers to loans outstanding.　[2] Source: U.S. Rural Electrification Administration, *Annual Statistical Report—Rural Electric Borrowers.* Electric distribution cooperatives currently borrowing from REA, average number of consumers served, and total revenues.　[3] Source: U.S. Rural Electrification Administration, *Annual Statistical Report— Rural Telephone Borrowers.* Cooperatives currently borrowing from REA, number of subscribers at end of year, annual revenues.　[4] Source: U.S. Social Security Administration. Independent plans only. Estimated enrollees and annual income of plans. Enrollment is for most frequent type of benefit X-ray and lab exams.　[5] 1968 data.

[6] Data for fiscal years ending in year shown. 1976 is preliminary. Since many cooperatives do more than one type of business, totals are less than would be obtained by adding number of cooperatives handling individual items or performing individual services.

Source: Except as noted, U.S. Dept. of Agriculture, Economics, Statistics, and Cooperatives Service, unpublished data.

No. 923. SELECTED BUSINESS INDEXES: 1960 TO 1977

[1967=100]

TYPE OF INDEX	1960	1965	1970	1971	1972	1973	1974	1975	1976	1977, prel.
Industrial production	66.2	89.8	107.8	109.6	119.7	129.8	129.3	117.8	129.8	137.0
Manufacturing	65.4	89.7	106.4	108.2	118.9	129.8	129.4	116.3	129.5	137.1
Market groupings:										
Products, total	66.4	88.2	106.9	108.5	118.0	127.1	127.3	119.3	129.3	137.1
Final, total	65.3	87.6	105.3	106.3	115.7	124.4	125.1	118.2	127.2	134.9
Consumer goods	70.7	92.6	109.0	114.7	124.4	131.5	128.9	124.0	136.2	143.4
Equipment	58.1	80.7	100.1	94.7	103.8	114.5	120.0	110.2	114.6	123.2
Intermediate	70.0	90.6	112.9	116.7	126.5	137.2	135.3	123.1	137.2	145.1
Materials	66.1	92.4	109.2	111.3	122.3	133.9	132.4	115.5	130.6	136.9
Capacity utilization (percent)[1] in—										
Manufacturing	80.1	89.5	79.2	78.0	83.1	87.5	84.2	73.6	80.2	82.4
Industrial materials industries	(NA)	87.3	84.3	83.1	88.0	92.4	87.7	73.6	80.4	81.9
Construction contracts	68.6	93.2	123.1	145.4	166.1	183.3	173.9	162.3	190.2	253.2
Nonagricultural employment, total	82.4	92.3	107.7	108.1	111.9	116.7	119.1	117.0	120.6	124.7
Goods producing, total	87.6	94.7	101.0	98.0	101.2	106.3	106.2	97.1	100.3	104.1
Manufacturing, total	86.4	92.9	99.5	95.5	98.2	103.2	103.1	94.3	97.5	100.6
Production workers	88.0	93.9	98.0	94.1	97.5	103.2	102.1	91.3	95.2	98.3
Service-producing	79.5	91.4	111.3	113.6	177.8	122.5	126.1	127.8	131.7	136.0
Personal income, total [2]	63.8	85.7	127.9	137.1	150.4	168.0	184.3	200.0	220.7	245.2
Wages and salary disbursements	63.6	84.7	127.8	135.5	148.3	164.0	178.9	188.5	208.6	231.6
Manufacturing	66.9	86.1	118.0	119.5	130.8	146.3	157.6	157.3	177.6	199.3
Disposable personal income	64.2	86.7	126.0	136.4	147.2	165.9	180.8	199.2	217.8	240.4
Retail sales	70.2	90.2	117.9	130.2	142.6	159.7	170.1	184.6	203.5	224.4
Prices: Consumer	88.7	94.5	116.3	121.3	125.3	133.1	147.7	161.2	170.5	181.5
Wholesale	94.9	96.6	110.4	113.9	119.1	134.7	160.1	174.9	183.0	194.2

NA Not available.
[1] 1967 output=100. For explanation, see table 1404.   [2] For explanation, see text, p. 438.
Source: Board of Governors of the Federal Reserve System, *Federal Reserve Bulletin*, monthly.

No. 924. FEDERAL GOVERNMENT LOANS TO ALL SMALL BUSINESSES AND TO MINORITY-OPERATED SMALL BUSINESSES: 1968 TO 1977

[For years ending June 30 except, beginning 1977, ending Sept. 30. A small business must be independently owned and operated, must not be dominant in its particular industry, and must meet standards set by the Small Business Administration as to its annual receipts or number of employees]

LOANS APPROVED	1968–1977 [1] cum.	1968–1970 cum.	1971–1977 cum.	1970	1971	1972	1973	1974	1975	1976	1977
Number, all businesses 1,000	240.6	42.7	191.1	15.1	21.5	28.0	33.9	27.5	22.3	26.1	31.8
Minority-operated businesses 1,000	64.5	13.3	49.9	6.3	7.8	9.0	9.1	6.9	5.4	5.5	6.2
Percent of all businesses	27	31	26	41	36	32	27	25	24	21	19
Value of total loans mil. dol	16,176	2,033	13,560	710	1,128	1,574	2,196	1,948	1,594	2,071	3,049
Loans to minority-operated businesses mil. dol	2,312	306	1,938	160	214	258	334	289	229	262	352
Percent of all loans	14	15	14	23	19	16	15	15	14	13	12

[1] Includes transition quarter, July–Sept. 1976, not shown separately.
Source: U.S. Small Business Administration, unpublished data.

No. 925. NONFARM PROPRIETORS' INCOME, BY INDUSTRY: 1960 TO 1976

[In millions of dollars. Represents income without inventory valuation and capital consumption adjustments. Income equals business receipts (exclusive of capital gains) less business expenses (exclusive of capital losses and depletion allowances). See text, p. 396, for discussion of SIC. Minus sign (−) denotes loss. See *Historical Statistics, Colonial Times to 1970*, series V 66–67, for single-year figures prior to minor revisions issued in 1976]

FORM OF ORGANIZATION AND INDUSTRY	1960	1965	1970	1971	1972	1973	1974	1975	1976
Total	34,158	42,658	50,739	52,818	56,358	60,336	62,871	63,377	70,392
Proprietorships and partnerships	33,763	42,165	50,212	52,291	55,767	59,628	62,019	62,376	69,273
Services	12,748	17,402	24,132	24,643	25,412	27,318	27,862	30,455	32,237
Wholesale and retail trade	10,724	11,675	13,129	13,678	14,240	16,391	17,836	17,165	19,465
Contract construction	3,544	4,835	5,598	6,364	7,471	8,420	7,952	7,600	8,787
Finance, ins., and real estate	3,346	4,277	3,566	4,281	4,225	2,614	1,651	1,709	2,718
Manufacturing	1,831	1,869	1,633	1,598	1,989	2,246	2,423	1,966	2,392
Transportation	807	1,179	1,244	1,369	1,513	1,674	1,788	1,650	1,779
Agricultural services, forestry, and fisheries	418	568	685	746	754	882	945	862	820
Other	345	360	225	−388	163	83	1,562	969	1,075
Other private business	395	493	527	527	591	708	852	1,001	1,119

Source: U.S. Bureau of Economic Analysis, *The National Income and Product Accounts of the United States, 1929–74*, and *Survey of Current Business*, July 1977.

No. 926. GROSS DOMESTIC PRODUCT (GDP) OF CORPORATE BUSINESS: 1960 TO 1977

[In billions of dollars, except as indicated. Excludes gross product originating in the rest of the world. Capital consumption allowances and corporate profits include capital consumption adjustment. Minus sign (−) denotes decrease. See *Historical Statistics, Colonial Times to 1970*, series V 141–166, for single-year figures prior to minor revisions issued in 1976]

ITEM	1960	1965	1970	1971	1972	1973	1974	1975	1976	1977, prel.
Gross domestic product	291.0	409.8	592.4	637.6	708.9	789.5	848.6	919.2	1,041.9	1,161.4
GDP, financial corp. business [1]	13.7	17.7	31.8	35.2	37.9	37.5	39.8	44.0	51.0	56.2
GDP, nonfinancial corp. business	277.3	392.1	560.6	602.5	671.0	752.0	808.8	875.2	991.0	1,105.2
Capital consumption allowances	27.5	33.7	55.1	60.6	65.4	71.9	84.6	101.7	111.8	121.9
Indirect business taxes [2]	29.9	43.9	66.4	73.4	79.3	87.0	92.6	99.9	108.3	118.6
Domestic income	233.6	332.3	470.9	503.6	564.3	630.6	671.4	717.6	821.8	920.8

NONFINANCIAL CORPORATION BUSINESS

CURRENT DOLLARS										
GDP, total	277.3	392.1	560.6	602.5	671.0	752.0	808.8	875.2	991.0	1,105.2
Avg. annual percent change	[3] 4.4	7.2	7.4	7.5	11.4	12.1	7.6	8.2	13.2	11.5
Capital consumption allowances	27.0	32.8	53.1	58.2	62.6	68.7	80.8	97.3	107.0	116.6
Indirect business taxes [2]	28.3	41.1	61.8	68.2	73.5	80.5	85.7	92.1	99.4	108.6
Domestic income	222.0	318.2	445.7	476.0	534.8	602.8	642.3	685.8	784.6	880.1
Compensation of employees	181.1	246.1	377.1	399.4	443.8	503.8	552.9	576.6	650.3	733.1
Corporate profits [4]	37.4	66.1	51.6	58.7	72.0	76.0	59.5	78.3	101.9	110.2
Profits before tax	39.5	64.4	55.1	63.3	75.9	92.7	102.9	102.3	130.6	141.8
Profits tax liability	19.2	27.2	27.3	29.9	33.5	39.6	42.7	40.8	53.7	57.0
Profits after tax	20.3	37.2	27.9	33.3	42.4	53.1	60.2	61.6	76.9	84.9
Inventory valuation adjustm't	.3	−1.9	−5.1	−5.0	−6.6	−18.6	−40.4	−12.0	−14.1	−14.6
Capital consumption adjustm't.	−2.3	3.6	1.5	.5	2.7	1.8	−3.0	−12.0	−14.5	−17.0
Net interest	3.5	6.1	17.0	17.9	19.1	23.1	29.9	30.9	32.4	36.7
1972 DOLLARS										
GDP, total	358.9	494.6	600.6	619.3	671.0	720.4	695.0	678.9	731.0	774.4
Avg. annual percent change	[3] 3.3	6.6	4.0	3.1	8.3	7.4	−3.5	−2.3	7.7	6.0
Capital consumption allowances	36.4	43.4	57.4	60.0	62.6	65.8	69.4	72.9	74.9	76.9
Indirect business taxes [2]	41.8	54.3	65.7	69.2	73.6	78.7	77.9	78.3	82.9	86.7
Domestic income	280.7	397.0	477.5	490.1	534.8	575.9	547.7	527.7	573.2	610.8
GDP current dollar cost and profit per unit [5]	.773	.793	.933	.973	1.000	1.044	1.164	1.289	1.356	1.427
Capital consumption allowances	.075	.066	.088	.094	.093	.095	.116	.143	.146	.151
Indirect business taxes [2]	.079	.083	.103	.110	.110	.112	.123	.136	.136	.140
Compensation of employees	.505	.497	.628	.645	.661	.699	.796	.849	.890	.947
Profits tax liability [4]	.053	.055	.045	.048	.050	.055	.061	.060	.073	.074
Profits after tax [4]	.051	.079	.041	.046	.057	.050	.024	.055	.066	.069
Net interest	.010	.012	.028	.029	.028	.032	.043	.045	.044	.047

[1] Corporations comprising the finance, insurance, and real estate industry.   [2] Plus transfer payments less subsidies.   [3] Change from 1959.   [4] With inventory valuation adjustment.   [5] Per unit of constant dollar gross product. Equals the deflator for gross domestic product with the decimal point shifted two places to the left.

Source: U.S. Bureau of Economic Analysis, *The National Income and Product Accounts of the United States, 1929–74*, and *Survey of Current Business*, July 1977 and March 1978.

No. 927. SOURCES AND USES OF FUNDS: 1960 TO 1977

[In billions of dollars. Covers nonfarm nonfinancial corporate business]

SOURCE AND USE	1960	1965	1970	1971	1972	1973	1974	1975	1976	1977
Sources, total	47.6	90.9	104.3	127.1	152.9	180.7	180.7	148.4	213.5	257.5
Internal	34.7	56.1	58.9	68.6	80.8	83.8	75.7	107.8	125.8	136.4
Undistributed profits	9.8	21.7	9.6	15.3	22.5	32.5	39.1	35.5	48.4	52.5
Adjustments [1]	−2.0	1.7	−3.5	−4.5	−3.9	−16.7	−43.5	−23.9	−28.7	−31.5
Capital consumption allowances	26.8	32.6	52.7	57.9	62.2	68.1	80.0	96.3	106.0	115.4
External [2]	12.9	34.9	45.5	58.5	72.2	96.9	105.0	40.6	87.7	121.1
Percent of total	27.2	38.3	43.6	46.0	47.2	53.6	58.1	27.4	41.1	47.0
Credit market funds, net	11.9	20.5	40.7	44.5	57.7	72.7	81.8	36.6	58.3	85.3
Net new equity issues	1.4	−	5.7	11.4	10.9	7.9	4.1	9.9	10.5	8.1
Long-term debt [3]	7.2	13.4	28.5	29.8	34.2	41.2	47.3	33.7	37.5	50.2
Short-term debt [4]	3.3	7.1	6.5	3.3	12.6	23.6	30.4	−7.0	10.3	27.0
Other	1.0	14.4	4.8	14.1	14.5	24.2	23.2	4.1	29.4	35.9
Uses, total	40.6	82.2	95.9	114.6	136.5	162.6	163.5	132.3	197.2	247.9
Capital expenditures	38.0	62.0	80.3	86.0	100.3	123.3	134.7	98.6	140.3	168.4
Increase in financial assets	2.7	20.2	15.6	28.6	36.2	39.3	28.9	33.7	56.9	79.5
Discrepancy (sources less uses)	7.0	8.8	8.4	12.5	16.5	18.1	17.1	16.2	16.3	9.6

− Represents zero.   [1] Inventory valuation and capital consumption allowances adjustment. [2] Net increases in liability. [3] Corporate bonds, multi-family and commercial mortgages, and 40 percent of bank loans. [4] Sixty percent of bank loans, commercial paper, acceptances, finance company loans, and Government loans.

Source: Board of Governors of the Federal Reserve System, *Flow of Funds Accounts, 1946–1975*, and unpublished data.

No. 928. Gross Investment in the Domestic Economy, by Sector and by Type: 1950 to 1973

[Gross investment is defined to be all current outlays that augment income- and output-producing capacity (capital) for future periods plus outlays to offset capital consumption. For this table, gross investment consists of outlays for tangible durable goods (structures and equipment), and inventory accumulation of all sectors, tangible human investment, and intangible investments designed to enhance the efficiency of the tangible factors. Consult source for information on methodology and sources used to derive these estimates]

SECTOR AND TYPE	VOLUME (bil. dol.)						PERCENT DISTRIBUTION		
	1950	1955	1960	1965	1969	1973	1950	1960	1973
Gross investment, total	165.8	244.0	312.1	445.7	618.0	851.0	100.0	100.0	100.0
Personal	97.8	135.3	169.7	241.0	330.3	465.0	59.0	54.4	54.6
Business	46.3	58.6	70.7	107.9	147.3	208.8	27.9	22.7	24.5
Government	21.7	50.1	71.7	96.8	140.4	177.2	13.1	23.0	20.8
TYPE									
Intangible investment	49.6	76.2	114.8	175.1	267.8	369.6	29.9	36.8	43.4
Human intangible	46.9	69.2	100.8	154.1	241.6	339.5	28.3	32.3	39.9
Education and training [1]	33.6	50.9	75.3	118.4	192.4	262.6	20.3	24.1	30.9
Medical and health [2]	6.1	8.8	13.3	19.6	27.9	45.9	3.7	4.3	5.4
Mobility [3]	7.3	9.5	12.2	16.1	21.3	31.0	4.4	3.9	3.6
Nonhuman intangible	2.7	7.0	14.0	21.1	26.2	30.1	1.6	4.5	3.5
Basic research	.3	.7	1.5	3.1	3.7	(NA)	.2	.5	(NA)
Research and development	2.4	6.3	12.6	18.0	22.4	(NA)	1.4	4.0	(NA)
Tangible investment	116.2	167.8	197.2	270.6	350.2	481.4	70.1	63.2	56.6
Human [4]	19.9	30.0	40.7	51.3	64.0	(NA)	12.0	13.0	(NA)
Nonhuman	96.3	137.8	156.5	219.3	286.3	(NA)	58.1	50.1	(NA)
Structures	35.6	49.4	57.4	75.5	95.4	(NA)	21.5	18.4	(NA)
Equipment	53.4	78.7	92.8	129.1	179.0	(NA)	32.2	29.7	(NA)
Inventories	7.4	9.8	6.4	14.7	11.9	(NA)	4.5	2.1	(NA)

NA Not available. [1] Covers expenditures on formal, informal, and special education, and on employee training. [2] Expenditures which yield a return in decreased mortality, disability, and debility.
[3] Represents costs associated with transferring resources. Covers unemployment costs, job search and hiring costs, and migration costs.
[4] Covers personal consumption expenditures allocated to rearing children to working age (14 years old).

Source: Kendrick, John W., *The Formation and Stock of Total Capital*, National Bureau of Economic Research, New York, N.Y., 1976, and unpublished data.

No. 929. Capital Invested Per Employee: 1950 to 1976

[In thousands of 1972 dollars. Represents all persons working in industries indicated. Asset data based on National Technical Information Service analyses; for a detailed description of methodology, see *The National Wealth of the United States: By Major Sectors and Industries, 1976*, by the Conference Board]

INDUSTRY	1972 Industry code	1950	1955	1960	1965	1970	1972	1973	1974	1975	1976
Real estate	65	958.9	833.4	823.1	846.4	800.7	729.0	726.4	733.1	763.1	752.7
Public utilities	49	165.7	202.0	239.7	264.6	298.5	322.0	332.3	342.1	357.7	367.6
Petroleum	29	70.4	81.0	100.0	123.7	140.1	142.4	144.3	147.5	151.4	150.9
Communication	48	48.5	56.4	74.3	94.1	102.5	113.8	118.6	124.1	131.7	138.2
Transportation	41–47	86.9	96.1	104.2	105.6	101.7	102.8	99.2	98.2	104.1	102.8
Primary metals	33	28.7	34.9	45.6	46.9	55.2	59.1	55.2	55.4	64.8	65.6
Mining	10–14	43.3	47.5	61.0	59.7	70.1	71.2	70.4	65.8	61.6	59.1
Tobacco	21	34.1	42.5	46.3	49.7	49.1	58.0	52.8	55.9	55.3	58.7
Chemicals	28	34.7	39.5	43.9	45.4	48.6	51.8	51.3	52.3	54.9	55.1
Paper	26	31.4	32.4	33.8	35.8	39.3	41.0	41.1	42.6	47.2	46.3
Stone, clay, glass	32	18.2	21.1	26.5	28.0	31.5	31.7	31.2	32.4	36.3	36.4
Transportation equipment	37	13.7	12.8	16.5	18.1	23.1	24.7	24.2	25.9	27.9	27.2
Nonelectric machinery	35	14.8	16.5	18.3	19.2	22.7	24.6	24.1	24.0	25.7	26.5
Food	20	20.3	20.6	21.1	21.6	23.1	23.9	24.3	24.6	25.1	25.0
Services	70–89	19.0	17.3	18.3	20.6	22.5	23.0	22.8	22.7	23.0	22.8
Fabricated metals	34	9.9	12.8	15.3	16.5	18.6	19.0	18.8	19.4	21.8	21.6
Rubber and plastics	30	13.5	16.2	18.2	17.2	18.8	18.9	18.7	19.4	21.7	20.9
Finance and insurance	60–64	11.0	11.8	13.5	15.7	17.0	18.4	18.7	18.9	19.7	20.1
Lumber and wood	24	11.7	10.0	10.1	12.4	15.6	15.9	22.0	18.4	21.0	20.0
Instruments	38	12.3	12.3	13.8	14.6	16.8	17.4	18.0	18.5	19.5	19.4
Textiles	22	7.9	12.4	15.7	16.0	17.1	17.3	17.2	18.3	19.7	18.6
Electric machinery	36	9.8	9.7	9.8	11.8	14.9	16.0	15.9	16.5	18.4	18.1
Misc. manufacturing	39	9.4	8.4	8.8	10.1	14.7	14.6	14.4	15.0	16.0	15.7
Printing and publishing	27	12.1	10.4	9.9	11.0	12.8	13.6	13.9	14.3	14.9	15.3
Wholesale and retail trade	50–59	12.4	12.9	13.9	14.5	14.6	14.8	14.8	14.9	14.6	14.6
Construction	15–17	5.2	5.7	7.5	9.4	10.6	10.5	10.3	10.5	11.5	11.7
Furniture and fixtures	25	9.2	10.4	8.3	8.0	8.7	8.5	8.5	9.3	10.4	10.0
Leather	31	5.3	5.7	4.1	4.5	6.0	6.4	6.8	7.4	7.6	7.1
Apparel	3	3.3	3.1	2.8	3.7	4.8	5.2	5.3	5.8	6.3	6.1

Source: The Conference Board, New York, N.Y., *Road Maps of Industry*, monthly. (Copyright.)

No. 930. BUSINESS EXPENDITURES FOR NEW PLANT AND EQUIPMENT: 1960 TO 1978

[In billions of dollars. Excludes expenditures of agricultural business, professions, institutions, and real estate firms, and current account outlays. Based on sample and subject to sampling variability; see text, p. 560. Minus sign (−) denotes decrease. See also *Historical Statistics, Colonial Times to 1970*, series V 306–332]

INDUSTRY	1960	1965	1970	1972	1973	1974	1975	1976	1977	1978 [1]
All industries_____	36.75	54.42	79.71	88.44	99.74	112.40	112.78	120.49	135.80	151.05
Manufacturing_____	15.09	23.44	31.95	31.35	38.01	46.01	47.95	52.48	60.16	67.28
Durable goods_____	7.23	11.50	15.80	15.64	19.25	22.62	21.84	23.68	27.77	30.95
Primary metals_____	1.82	2.54	3.24	2.75	3.43	4.95	5.99	5.97	5.68	6.00
Blast furnaces, steel works_____	1.35	1.57	1.68	1.24	1.38	2.12	3.03	2.99	2.67	2.74
Nonferrous metals__	.32	.73	1.24	1.18	1.67	2.33	2.28	2.16	2.24	2.34
Electrical machinery [2]	.90	1.12	2.27	2.39	2.84	2.97	2.31	2.62	3.28	3.77
Machinery [3]_____	1.25	2.31	3.47	2.90	3.42	4.42	4.50	5.03	5.76	6.23
Transportation equip_	1.25	2.54	2.43	2.53	3.12	3.75	3.24	3.62	5.32	5.84
Motor vehicles_____	.79	1.89	1.59	1.83	2.28	2.70	2.06	2.45	4.06	4.44
Aircraft_____	.34	.46	.54	.43	.53	.80	.92	.94	1.02	1.12
Stone, clay, and glass_	.75	.92	.99	1.20	1.49	1.44	1.42	1.72	1.99	2.46
Other durables_____	1.26	2.07	3.41	3.87	4.96	5.10	4.38	4.73	5.73	6.65
Nondurable goods_____	7.85	11.94	16.15	15.72	18.76	23.39	26.11	28.81	32.39	36.34
Food and beverages___	1.34	1.83	2.84	2.55	3.11	3.25	3.26	3.75	4.18	4.96
Paper_____	.77	1.22	1.65	1.38	1.86	2.58	2.95	3.27	3.36	3.54
Chemicals_____	1.55	2.73	3.44	3.45	4.46	5.69	6.25	6.68	6.83	7.16
Petroleum_____	2.89	4.03	5.62	5.25	5.45	8.00	10.51	11.62	13.87	15.65
Rubber_____	.31	.56	.94	1.08	1.56	1.47	1.00	1.10	1.45	1.81
Other nondurables____	.99	1.58	1.66	2.00	2.33	2.39	2.14	2.40	2.70	3.21
Nonmanufacturing_____	21.66	30.98	47.76	57.09	61.73	66.39	64.82	68.01	75.64	83.76
Mining_____	1.30	1.46	1.89	2.42	2.74	3.18	3.79	4.00	4.50	4.76
Railroad_____	1.16	1.99	1.78	1.80	1.96	2.54	2.55	2.52	2.80	3.34
Air transportation_____	.66	1.22	3.03	2.46	2.41	2.00	1.84	1.30	1.62	2.20
Other transportation____	1.30	1.68	1.23	1.46	1.66	2.12	3.18	3.63	2.51	2.40
Public utilities_____	5.24	6.13	13.14	17.00	18.71	20.55	20.14	22.28	25.80	28.94
Electric_____	3.62	4.43	10.65	14.48	15.94	17.63	17.00	18.80	21.59	24.42
Communication_____	3.24	5.30	10.10	11.89	12.85	13.96	12.74	13.30	15.45	17.46
Commercial and other [4]	8.75	13.19	16.59	20.07	21.40	22.05	20.60	20.99	22.97	24.67
Average annual percent change: [5]										
All industries_____	[6]4.5	8.2	7.9	8.9	12.8	12.7	.3	6.8	12.7	11.2
Manufacturing_____	[6]4.9	9.2	6.4	4.5	21.2	21.1	4.2	9.5	14.6	11.8
Nonmanufacturing_____	[6]4.2	7.4	9.0	11.5	8.1	7.6	−2.4	4.9	11.2	10.7

[1] Estimates based on expected capital expenditures as reported by business in late Apr. and May 1978.
[2] Includes equipment.　[3] Excludes electrical.　[4] Trade, service, construction, finance, and insurance.
[5] Change from prior year shown here; e.g. 1965 from 1960, except as noted.　[6] Change from 1955.
Source: U.S. Bureau of Economic Analysis, *Survey of Current Business*, monthly.

No. 931. DETERMINANTS OF BUSINESS FIXED INVESTMENT: 1955 TO 1977

[Percent]

ITEM	1955	1960	1965	1970	1971	1972	1973	1974	1975	1976	1977, prel.
Ratio of real investment to real GNP [1]_	9.4	9.0	10.3	10.2	9.7	10.0	10.6	10.7	9.4	9.2	9.5
Capacity utilization rate in manufacturing [2]_____	87.0	80.1	89.6	79.2	78.1	83.1	87.6	84.2	73.6	80.2	82.3
Nonfinancial corporations:											
Cash flow as percent of GNP [1] [3]_____	9.3	8.9	10.4	7.9	8.2	8.6	8.0	6.9	8.8	9.1	9.0
Net rate of return on depreciable assets [4]_____	15.0	11.2	16.2	9.9	10.4	11.5	12.3	11.3	9.5	10.8	10.6
Rate of return on stockholders equity [5]_____	6.5	4.4	8.1	5.0	4.5	6.2	5.8	9.9	6.1	5.8	5.9
Ratio of market value to replacement cost of net assets [6]_____	.93	1.02	1.36	.91	1.01	1.09	1.03	.76	.75	.84	.79

[1] GNP=Gross national product.　[2] Federal Reserve Board index.　[3] Cash flow calculated as after-tax profits plus capital consumption allowances plus inventory valuation adjustment.　[4] Profits before taxes plus capital consumption adjustment plus net interest paid divided by the stock of depreciable assets valued at current replacement cost.　[5] After-tax profits corrected for inflation effects divided by net worth (physical capital component valued at current replacement cost).
[6] Equity plus interest-bearing debt divided by current replacement cost of net assets.

Source: U.S. Council of Economic Advisers, *Economic Report of the President*, annual. Data from U.S. Bureau of Economic Analysis and the Board of Governors of the Federal Reserve System.

No. 932. MANUFACTURING AND TRADE—SALES AND INVENTORIES: 1950 TO 1977

[In billions of dollars, except ratios. Prior to 1960, excludes Alaska and Hawaii. See *Historical Statistics, Colonial Times to 1970*, series V 78-107, for single year figures prior to minor revisions issued in 1976 and 1978]

ITEM	1950	1955	1960	1965	1970	1972	1973	1974	1975	1976	1977 [1]
Sales, total	463	620	730	963	1,292	1,561	1,820	2,102	2,155	2,409	2,686
Manufacturing	224	318	371	492	634	757	875	1,018	1,039	1,186	1,335
Durable goods	106	169	191	267	339	409	476	531	524	608	699
Nondurable goods	117	149	180	225	295	348	399	487	515	577	636
Retail trade	147	184	220	284	371	449	502	535	580	643	708
Durable goods	54	67	71	94	110	148	169	166	179	211	239
Nondurable goods	93	117	149	190	261	301	333	369	402	432	470
Merchant wholesalers	92	119	140	187	287	355	442	550	536	581	642
Durable goods	38	51	59	83	127	161	196	237	220	247	286
Nondurable goods	55	67	81	104	160	194	246	313	316	334	356
Inventories (book value), total [2]	60	80	95	121	178	203	234	285	284	309	335
Manufacturing	31	45	54	68	102	108	125	158	158	170	180
Durable goods	16	26	32	42	67	70	81	102	102	109	115
Nondurable goods	16	19	21	26	35	38	43	56	56	61	64
Retail trade	19	23	27	34	44	55	63	71	71	78	87
Durable goods	8	11	12	15	18	24	28	32	32	36	41
Nondurable goods	11	12	15	19	26	31	35	38	39	42	47
Merchant wholesalers	9	12	14	18	33	40	46	57	55	61	68
Durable goods	5	6	8	11	20	24	27	34	35	38	44
Nondurable goods	5	5	6	8	13	16	19	22	21	23	24
Inventory-sales ratio, total [3]	1.36	1.47	1.56	1.45	1.62	1.50	1.44	1.47	1.58	1.48	1.44
Manufacturing	1.48	1.62	1.76	1.60	1.90	1.67	1.58	1.65	1.83	1.66	1.58
Durable goods	1.55	1.75	2.08	1.82	2.33	2.00	1.89	2.05	2.36	2.07	1.93
Nondurable goods	1.41	1.47	1.42	1.34	1.39	1.28	1.21	1.22	1.28	1.23	1.19
Retail trade	1.38	1.43	1.45	1.39	1.40	1.40	1.41	1.48	1.43	1.39	1.40
Durable goods	1.52	1.79	2.02	1.86	1.98	1.83	1.88	2.12	2.10	1.94	1.93
Nondurable goods	1.29	1.22	1.18	1.16	1.15	1.18	1.18	1.20	1.14	1.12	1.13
Merchant wholesalers	1.07	1.13	1.22	1.15	1.29	1.27	1.17	1.12	1.24	1.21	1.21
Durable goods	1.29	1.36	1.69	1.49	1.77	1.72	1.56	1.53	1.88	1.78	1.73
Nondurable goods	.91	.95	.89	.87	.91	.90	.86	.82	.80	.79	.80

[1] Preliminary. [2] Seasonally adjusted, end-of-year data. [3] Average inventories to average monthly sales. Average inventories based on weighted averages of end-of-month figures.

Source: 1950 and 1955, U.S. Bureau of Economic Analysis, *Business Statistics, 1975;* thereafter, *Survey of Current Business,* January 1978, and subsequent monthly issues.

No. 933. NONFARM BUSINESS INVENTORIES IN CURRENT AND CONSTANT DOLLARS: 1950 TO 1977

[In billions of dollars. As of end of year. To ascertain net physical change in nonfarm inventories, book values of beginning and ending inventories of each year are expressed in terms of constant base year prices by means of selected Bureau of Labor Statistics producer (wholesale) price indexes appropriate to each industry. Net increment in deflated book value figures is then converted to a current price basis by index ratios or current prices to base year prices. See text, p. 396, for discussion of Standard Industrial Classification]

CLASS OF INVENTORY	1950	1955	1960	1965	1970	1971	1972	1973	1974	1975	1976	1977
CURRENT DOLLARS Total	74.6	94.6	111.3	143.0	212.5	225.1	243.9	289.6	363.7	363.4	401.7	443.3
Manufacturing	37.4	51.4	58.1	73.7	110.8	113.6	120.4	143.6	186.4	187.6	206.1	222.6
Wholesale trade	14.3	16.7	19.6	25.3	38.3	41.2	45.7	55.2	69.8	67.7	75.2	83.7
Retail trade	17.7	20.9	25.6	33.1	45.6	51.0	55.9	64.4	72.3	72.6	81.2	93.7
All other	5.2	5.6	8.1	10.9	17.7	19.2	21.8	26.4	35.2	35.5	39.1	43.4
CONSTANT (1972) DOLLARS Total	102.7	123.7	138.8	172.8	223.6	228.8	237.6	251.8	260.1	248.9	259.0	270.1
Manufacturing	51.8	66.7	72.4	89.1	117.1	115.4	117.5	123.6	128.6	124.0	128.1	131.2
Wholesale trade	18.3	21.4	24.3	30.5	40.4	42.0	44.4	47.4	50.6	47.1	49.7	52.8
Retail trade	23.9	27.2	31.5	39.4	47.3	51.9	54.4	58.2	56.5	54.5	57.7	62.3
All other	8.7	8.4	10.7	13.8	18.8	19.5	21.3	22.7	24.5	23.4	23.6	23.8

Source: U.S. Bureau of Economic Analysis, *The National Income and Product Accounts of the United States, 1929-74,* and *Survey of Current Business,* July 1977 and March 1978.

No. 934. Active Corporations—Assets and Liabilities: 1950 to 1975

[In billions of dollars. See headnote, table 447. For number of income tax returns, see table 936. See also *Historical Statistics, Colonial Times to 1970*, series V 108–127]

ASSETS AND LIABILITIES	1950	1955	1960	1965	1970	1971	1972	1973	1974	1975
Assets	598	889	1,207	1,724	2,635	2,889	3,257	3,649	4,016	4,287
Cash	71	87	97	117	177	196	228	259	281	290
Notes and accounts receivable [1]	109	192	242	392	595	650	762	891	998	1,021
Inventories	54	71	91	126	190	199	224	263	312	318
Investments, government obligations	110	132	135	157	197	223	240	250	256	316
Other current assets	([2])	([2])	10	32	73	83	100	119	129	145
Mortgage and real estate loans	([3])	([3])	129	([3])	328	366	418	463	508	548
Other investments	97	180	179	465	406	461	514	556	578	636
Capital assets [4]	145	206	293	395	600	634	685	750	831	892
Other assets	13	21	28	38	70	78	86	99	123	121
Liabilities	598	889	1,207	1,724	2,635	2,889	3,257	3,649	4,016	4,287
Notes and accounts payable [5]	47	76	112	174	320	334	386	461	539	536
Other current liabilities	([6])	([6])	365	583	892	1,005	1,163	1,316	1,459	1,577
Bonded debt and mortgages [7]	66	98	154	210	363	403	445	493	542	587
Other liabilities	262	409	167	220	308	339	376	421	460	490
Capital stock	94	113	140	161	201	210	221	228	240	252
Surplus and undivided profits (net) [8]	129	193	269	375	551	599	666	730	776	843

[1] Less allowance for bad debts. Includes loans and discounts of banks, except mortgage and real estate loans.
[2] Included partly in "Other investments" and partly in "Other assets."
[3] For 1950 and 1955, included partly in "Notes and accounts receivable" and partly in "Other investments"; for 1965, included in "Other investments."
[4] Less depreciation, amortization, and depletion reserves. Includes land and intangible assets.
[5] Includes bonds, notes, and mortgages payable with maturity of less than 1 year.
[6] Included in "Other liabilities."   [7] With maturity of 1 year or more.
[8] Beginning 1970, reduced by cost of treasury stock.
Source: U.S. Internal Revenue Service, *Statistics of Income, Corporation Income Tax Returns*, annual.

No. 935. Active Corporations, by Asset Size: 1950 to 1975

[Beginning 1955, figures are estimates based on samples of active corporations filing income tax returns. See *Historical Statistics, Colonial Times to 1970*, series V 42, for total active corporations]

ASSET SIZE-CLASS	NUMBER OF ACTIVE CORPORATIONS (1,000)						TOTAL ASSETS (bil. dol.)					
	1950	1955	1960	1965	1970	1975	1950	1955	1960	1965	1970	1975
Total	629.3	807.3	1,140.6	1,424.0	1,665.5	2,023.6	598	889	1,207	1,724	2,635	4,287
Under $100,000	[1] 397.9	[1] 491.5	684.6	846.2	961.0	}1,882.3	12	16	23	28	32	} 255
$100,000–$1 million	190.3	260.1	389.3	490.7	599.1		55	76	111	143	178	
$1 mil.–$10 million	35.6	47.6	56.3	73.5	87.0	116.4	100	136	159	206	240	310
$10 mil.–$25 million	} 4.2	4.7	5.8	7.4	9.8	12.2	} 85	72	89	115	153	193
$25 mil.–$50 million		1.6	2.1	2.9	3.9	5.6		55	73	99	135	195
$50 mil.–$100 million	.6	.8	1.1	1.5	2.1	3.1	42	56	80	104	145	213
$100 mil.–$250 mil	} .7	.6	.8	1.1	1.4	2.1	} 304	92	119	165	222	331
$250 mil. and over		.4	.6	.8	1.2	1.9		385	552	862	1,530	2,790

						PERCENT DISTRIBUTION						
Total	100.0	100.0	100.0	100.0	100.0	100.0	100.0	100.0	100.0	100.0	100.0	100.0
Under $100,000	[1] 63.2	[1] 60.9	60.0	59.4	57.7	} 93.0	2.1	1.8	1.9	1.6	1.2	} 5.9
$100,000–$1 million	30.2	32.2	34.1	34.5	36.0		9.3	8.5	9.2	8.3	6.8	
$1 mil.–$10 million	5.7	5.9	4.9	5.2	5.2	5.8	16.7	15.3	13.2	12.0	9.1	7.2
$10 mil.–$25 mil	} .7	.6	.5	.5	.6	.6	} 14.2	8.1	7.4	6.7	5.8	4.5
$25 mil.–$50 mil		.1	.2	.2	.2	.3		6.2	6.0	5.7	5.1	4.5
$50 mil.–$100 mil	.1	.1	.1	.1	.1	.2	6.9	6.5	6.6	6.1	5.5	5.0
$100 mil.–$250 mil	} .1	.1	.1	.1	.1	.1	} 50.8	10.3	9.9	9.6	8.4	7.7
$250 mil. and over		(Z)	.1	.1	.1	.1		43.4	45.8	50.0	58.1	65.1

Z Less than .05 percent.   [1] Includes returns of corporations not reporting balance sheet information.
Source: U.S. Internal Revenue Service, *Statistics of Income, Corporation Income Tax Returns*, annual.

No. 936. CORPORATION FEDERAL INCOME TAX RETURNS—SELECTED ITEMS: 1960 TO 1975

[In billions of dollars, except number of returns. Active corporations only. See headnote, table 447. See also *Historical Statistics, Colonial Times to 1970*, Series V 129–136]

ITEM	1960	1965	1970	1971	1972	1973	1974	1975, prel.
Number of returns------------1,000	1,140.6	1,424.0	1,665.5	1,733.3	1,812.8	1,904.7	1,965.9	2,023.6
With asse*s, end of year--------1,000	1,095.4	1,380.2	1,619.1	1,682.6	1,758.5	1,844.4	1,903.4	1,951.9
With net income-------------1,000	670.2	915.3	1,008.3	1,063.9	1,140.2	1,203.4	1,207.4	1,226.2
With income tax less credits [1]----1,000	(NA)	(NA)	734.8	750.7	771.7	751.7	803.1	732.9
Total receipts----------------------	849.1	1,194.6	1,750.8	1,906.0	2,171.2	2,557.7	3,089.7	3,198.6
Business receipts------------------	802.8	1,120.4	1,620.9	1,763.8	2,007.3	2,361.4	2,854.8	2,961.7
Interest [2]------------------------	23.6	37.2	71.6	76.1	86.3	113.3	143.0	143.3
Capital gain, net [3]---------------	3.1	5.3	5.5	6.7	9.1	9.1	8.2	8.4
Net gain, noncapital assets--------	1.9	2.9	5.3	7.6	8.5	7.7	7.0	7.8
Dividends received, domestic and foreign	4.2	6.7	8.7	9.7	11.1	14.8	21.2	14.3
Receipts not specified-------------	13.6	22.0	38.8	42.1	48.9	51.4	55.5	63.1
Total deductions-------------------	804.6	1,119.9	1,682.8	1,824.1	2,071.7	2,435.0	2,941.5	3,052.7
Cost of sales and operations-------	577.0	793.0	1,146.3	1,241.3	1,412.5	1,682.5	2,068.1	2,129.9
Interest paid----------------------	14.6	26.4	62.1	64.7	72.9	99.6	132.9	129.3
Depreciation, depletion [4]--------	26.9	39.2	59.3	64.3	71.6	80.6	98.4	92.4
Employee benefits, pension, stock bonus, etc-----------------------	7.2	11.4	19.6	23.0	27.3	31.9	36.6	42.2
Deductions not specified-----------	178.8	249.9	395.5	430.8	487.5	540.5	605.5	658.9
Receipts less deductions-----------	44.5	74.7	67.9	81.9	99.5	122.6	148.2	146.0
Net income less deficit------------	43.5	73.9	65.9	79.7	96.8	120.4	146.0	142.6
Income tax [5]---------------------	21.9	31.7	33.3	37.5	42.9	52.4	66.1	66.1
Income tax less credits [1]--------	20.6	27.3	27.9	30.2	33.5	39.1	41.1	39.7
Distributions to stockholders [6]--	17.2	26.0	32.0	32.6	36.0	41.8	49.3	45.2

NA Not available. [1] Credits includes foreign tax, investment, and work incentive (WIN) credits.
[2] Includes interest on Government obligations and other interest.
[3] Net long-term capital gain reduced by net short-term capital loss.
[4] Includes amortization.
[5] Income tax is before deductions for foreign tax credit, investment credit, and work incentive (WIN) credit. Beginning 1965, includes tax from recomputing prior year investment credit; 1970 and 1971, includes tax surcharge; 1970–1975 includes additional tax for tax preferences: beginning 1973, includes tax from recomputing prior year work incentive (WIN) credit. [6] Other than own stock.
Source: U.S. Internal Revenue Service, *Statistics of Income, Corporation Income Tax Returns*, annual.

No. 937. NONFINANCIAL CORPORATIONS—ASSETS AND LIABILITIES: 1960 TO 1976

[In billions of dollars, except ratio. As of December 31. Covers all nonfinancial U.S. corporations. 1960–1971 based on Internal Revenue Service, *Statistics of Income*, covering virtually all corporations in United States. *Statistics of Income* data may not be strictly comparable from year to year because of changes in the tax laws, etc. 1972–1976 estimated (subject to revision), based on data compiled from many different sources, including data on corporations registered with the Securities and Exchange Commission]

CURRENT ASSETS AND LIABILITIES	1960	1965	1970	1971	1972	1973	1974	1975	1976
Current assets----------------------	241.7	336.0	492.3	518.8	573.5	643.3	712.2	731.6	816.8
Cash on hand and in banks [1]-----	31.7	42.8	50.2	55.7	57.5	61.6	62.7	68.1	77.0
U.S. Government securities [2]-----	16.9	14.4	7.7	10.7	9.3	11.0	11.7	19.4	26.4
Receivables from U.S. Govt--------	3.1	3.9	4.2	3.5	3.4	3.5	3.5	3.6	4.3
Other notes, accounts receivable--	88.8	130.2	201.9	208.8	240.0	266.1	289.7	294.6	323.9
Inventories-----------------------	91.6	126.6	193.3	200.3	215.2	246.7	288.0	285.8	315.4
Other current assets--------------	9.6	18.1	35.0	39.7	48.1	54.4	56.6	60.0	69.8
Current liabilities-----------------	125.9	178.8	304.9	313.9	352.2	401.0	450.6	457.5	499.9
U.S. Govt. advances, prepayments--	1.8	3.1	6.6	4.9	4.0	4.3	5.2	6.4	7.0
Other notes and accounts payable--	78.6	118.4	204.7	207.3	230.4	261.6	287.5	281.6	295.9
Federal income tax liabilities-----	12.6	18.3	10.0	12.2	15.1	18.1	23.2	20.7	26.8
Other current liabilities-----------	32.9	39.0	83.6	89.5	102.6	117.0	134.8	148.8	170.2
Net working capital----------------	115.8	157.2	187.4	204.8	221.3	242.3	261.5	274.1	316.9
Ratio to current assets------------	47.9	46.8	38.1	39.5	38.6	37.7	36.7	37.5	38.8

[1] Includes time certificates of deposits. [2] Includes Federal agency issues.
Source: U.S. Securities and Exchange Commission, Statistical Series, *Net Working Capital of Nonfinancial U.S. Corporations*, quarterly.

No. 938. ACTIVE CORPORATIONS—INCOME TAX RETURNS, BY ASSET SIZE AND INDUSTRY: 1975

[In millions of dollars, except number of returns and percent. See headnote and footnotes, table 447. See also Historical Statistics, Colonial Times to 1970, series V 167–183 and V 193–196]

INDUSTRY AND ITEM	Total	ASSET SIZE-CLASS					
		Under 10 mil. dol.[1]	10–24.9 mil. dol.	25–49.9 mil. dol.	50–99.9 mil. dol.	100–249.9 mil. dol.	250 mil. dol. and over
All industrial divisions:[2]							
Number of returns	2,023,647	1,998,771	12,215	5,567	3,068	2,144	1,882
Total assets or liabilities	4,286,556	564,972	193,310	194,657	213,008	330,635	2,789,974
Total receipts	3,198,628	1,132,267	154,980	122,341	131,391	206,656	1,450,993
Total deductions [2]	3,052,675	1,104,352	148,166	116,911	125,785	197,748	1,359,713
Cost of sales and operations	2,129,928	793,159	108,600	82,847	88,143	137,902	919,277
Interest and taxes paid	210,838	43,766	9,228	9,387	10,409	15,284	122,764
Depreciation and amortization	87,013	21,687	3,189	2,504	2,756	4,742	52,135
Depletion	5,341	452	203	164	199	281	4,042
Net income less deficit [3]	142,637	27,629	6,331	4,943	5,195	8,519	90,020
Income tax [4]	66,144	11,716	3,041	2,401	2,439	4,154	42,393
Percent distribution:							
Number of returns [2]	100.0	98.7	.6	.3	.2	.1	.1
Total assets or liabilities	100.0	13.2	4.5	4.5	5.0	7.7	65.1
Total receipts	100.0	35.4	4.8	3.8	4.1	6.5	45.4
Total deductions	100.0	36.2	4.9	3.8	4.1	6.5	44.5
Cost of sales and operations	100.0	37.2	5.1	3.9	4.1	6.5	43.2
Interest and taxes paid	100.0	20.8	4.4	4.5	4.9	7.2	58.2
Depreciation and amortization	100.0	24.9	3.7	2.9	3.2	5.4	59.9
Depletion	100.0	8.4	3.8	3.1	3.7	5.3	75.7
Net income less deficit [3]	100.0	19.4	4.4	3.5	3.6	6.0	63.1
Income tax [4]	100.0	17.7	4.6	3.6	3.7	6.3	64.1
Agriculture, forestry, and fishing:							
Number of returns	56,280	56,168	82	11	9	9	1
Total assets or liabilities	21,178	16,530	1,196	394	633	1,537	888
Total receipts	28,119	21,514	1,707	541	549	1,766	2,042
Mining:							
Number of returns	14,242	13,844	204	74	50	38	32
Total assets or liabilities	64,505	7,590	3,134	2,615	3,475	5,683	42,008
Total receipts	65,910	9,873	2,788	1,927	2,505	3,289	45,528
Construction:							
Number of returns	191,219	190,551	454	125	45	27	17
Total assets or liabilities	76,692	49,846	6,844	4,246	3,153	4,041	8,562
Total receipts	146,955	113,379	10,024	5,038	2,798	6,065	9,651
Manufacturing:							
Number of returns	217,354	213,182	2,065	793	469	397	448
Total assets or liabilities	944,582	105,040	31,528	27,817	33,210	61,995	684,992
Total receipts	1,296,360	234,346	54,990	43,370	50,530	88,147	824,977
Transportation and public utilities:							
Number of returns	80,701	79,821	337	146	84	104	209
Total assets or liabilities	443,237	21,310	5,267	5,213	5,988	16,309	389,150
Total receipts	243,481	38,280	5,307	4,961	5,184	10,376	179,373
Wholesale and retail trade:							
Number of returns	614,632	612,310	1,394	456	247	141	84
Total assets or liabilities	323,497	172,767	21,183	15,960	16,824	21,659	75,104
Total receipts	969,939	576,220	60,445	46,434	48,276	66,003	172,561
Finance, insurance, real estate: [5]							
Number of returns	411,846	396,251	7,231	3,821	2,092	1,391	1,060
Total assets or liabilities	2,321,966	139,809	117,314	133,484	144,697	213,805	1,572,857
Total receipts	315,796	40,024	13,221	14,503	16,177	26,200	205,671
Services:							
Number of returns	435,672	434,946	446	140	72	37	31
Total assets or liabilities	90,534	51,776	6,814	4,897	5,027	5,606	16,414
Total receipts	131,377	97,993	6,459	5,556	5,371	4,809	11,189

[1] Includes returns of corporations with zero assets.
[2] Includes data not shown separately.   [3] Excludes wholly tax-exempt interest but includes income from related foreign corporations considered received for tax purposes only.   [4] Income tax before deductions for investment credit and work incentive (WIN) credit. Includes additional tax for tax preferences, taxes from recomputing prior year investment credit and prior year work incentive (WIN) credit.   [5] Includes lessors of real property.

Source: U.S. Internal Revenue Service, Statistics of Income, 1975, Corporation Income Tax Returns, annual.

No. 939. LARGEST INDUSTRIAL CORPORATIONS AND RETAILING COMPANIES—ASSETS, NET INCOME, AND EMPLOYEES, BY RANK OF SALES: 1965 TO 1977

[Assets and net income in billions of dollars, employees in thousands, except percent. Minus sign (−) denotes loss. See headnote, table 940]

RANK BY SALES GROUP	ASSETS [1]				NET INCOME [2]				EMPLOYEES [3]			
	1965	1970	1975	1977	1965	1970	1975	1977	1965	1970	1975	1977
INDUSTRIAL CORPS.												
First 500 largest	251.7	432.1	668.5	803.7	20.1	21.7	37.8	52.6	11,279	14,608	14,413	15,298
Lowest hundred	10.1	16.8	19.8	27.6	.7	.8	−.8	−.7	569	697	471	833
Second hundred	13.9	23.2	35.5	46.3	1.0	1.1	1.6	2.3	789	1,044	993	1,119
Third hundred	22.5	39.0	59.9	74.0	1.6	1.4	3.2	4.6	1,178	1,500	1,570	1,662
Fourth hundred	36.5	74.5	113.7	130.4	2.7	3.8	6.3	8.6	1,809	2,662	2,701	2,968
Highest hundred	169.0	278.6	439.5	525.4	14.1	14.5	27.5	37.8	6,934	8,706	8,679	8,716
Second 500 largest	(NA)	38.8	60.9	69.6	(NA)	1.5	3.3	4.6	(NA)	1,720	1,861	1,836
Percent of total, first 500	100.0	100.0	100.0	100.0	100.0	100.0	100.0	100.0	100.0	100.0	100.0	100.0
Lowest hundred	4.0	3.9	3.0	3.4	3.7	3.8	−2.1	−1.3	5.0	4.8	3.3	5.4
Second hundred	5.5	5.4	5.3	5.8	5.0	4.9	4.2	4.4	7.0	7.1	6.9	7.3
Third hundred	8.9	9.0	9.0	9.2	7.8	6.6	8.5	8.7	10.4	10.3	10.9	10.9
Fourth hundred	14.4	17.2	17.0	16.2	13.3	17.6	16.7	16.3	16.0	18.2	18.7	19.4
Highest hundred	67.1	64.5	65.7	65.4	70.2	67.1	72.8	71.9	61.5	60.0	60.2	57.0
RETAILING COS.												
50 largest	19.3	31.6	50.9	60.9	1.2	1.5	2.4	3.3	1,609	2,371	2,653	2,775
Lowest ten	1.5	1.5	5.2	3.8	.1	.1	.2	.1	120	151	197	131
Second ten	1.3	2.5	3.7	5.8	.1	.1	.1	.4	103	211	279	362
Third ten	2.3	4.5	4.7	5.7	.1	.1	.2	.3	180	294	277	319
Fourth ten	3.5	4.8	8.4	10.0	.2	.2	.4	.5	286	366	426	438
Highest ten	10.8	18.2	28.9	35.5	.7	1.0	1.5	2.1	920	1,348	1,474	1,524
Percent of total	100.0	100.0	100.0	100.0	100.0	100.0	100.0	100.0	100.0	100.0	100.0	100.0
Lowest ten	8.0	4.8	10.2	6.2	6.0	5.1	8.4	3.3	7.5	6.4	7.4	4.7
Second ten	6.5	7.9	7.3	9.6	5.7	5.9	6.0	10.6	6.4	8.9	10.5	13.1
Third ten	11.8	14.3	9.2	9.4	9.9	8.4	7.8	7.7	11.2	12.4	10.4	11.5
Fourth ten	18.0	15.3	16.5	16.5	17.9	13.5	15.2	15.3	17.7	15.4	16.1	15.8
Highest ten	55.7	57.7	56.8	58.3	60.5	67.1	62.6	63.0	57.2	56.9	55.6	54.9

NA Not available. [1] Total assets employed in business at end of fiscal year, less depreciation and depletion. [2] After taxes, special charges, and credits. [3] As of year end, or yearly average.

Source: Fortune, New York, N.Y., The Fortune Directory. (Copyright, by Time, Inc.)

No. 940. LARGEST INDUSTRIAL CORPORATIONS AND RETAILING COMPANIES—SALES, BY GROUP RANK: 1955 TO 1977

[Excludes large privately owned companies that do not publish sales. Includes sales of subsidiaries when they are consolidated. **Industrial corporations:** Includes service and rental revenues, but companies must derive more than 50 percent of revenues from manufacturing or mining for fiscal years ending not later than December 31 of year stated, except 1977, no later than **January;** excludes excise taxes collected by manufacturer. **Retailing companies:** Includes all operating revenues for fiscal years ending not later than March or April following year stated]

RANK BY SALES GROUP	VOLUME OF SALES (bil. dol.)						PERCENT DISTRIBUTION					
	1955	1960	1965	1970	1975	1977	1955	1960	1965	1970	1975	1977
INDUSTRIAL CORPORATIONS												
First 500 largest	161.4	204.7	298.1	463.9	865.2	1,086.6	100.0	100.0	100.0	100.0	100.0	100.0
Lowest hundred	6.3	8.5	12.5	19.9	34.8	41.4	3.9	4.1	4.2	4.3	4.0	3.8
Second hundred	8.6	11.7	17.7	28.8	49.0	58.8	5.3	5.7	5.9	6.2	5.7	5.4
Third hundred	13.7	18.5	27.7	43.6	78.5	96.7	8.5	9.0	9.3	9.4	9.1	8.9
Fourth hundred	24.5	32.6	47.2	82.7	141.8	173.3	15.2	15.9	15.8	17.8	16.4	15.9
Highest hundred	108.3	133.4	193.0	288.9	561.1	716.4	67.1	65.2	64.7	62.3	64.9	65.9
Second 500 largest	(NA)	15.7	(NA)	48.3	82.6	95.4	(X)	(X)	(X)	(X)	(X)	(X)
RETAILING COMPANIES												
50 largest	[1] 25.6	[1] 35.7	[1] 49.0	73.6	121.7	145.3	[1] 100.0	[1] 100.0	[1] 100.0	100.0	100.0	100.0
Lowest ten	1.2	2.2	3.3	4.4	7.5	9.0	4.6	6.2	6.7	5.9	6.2	6.2
Second ten	1.7	2.8	4.4	6.8	10.4	12.2	6.7	7.9	9.2	9.3	8.5	8.4
Third ten	2.7	4.1	6.1	9.0	14.1	16.2	10.6	11.5	12.4	12.3	11.6	11.2
Fourth ten	4.5	6.4	9.0	13.9	23.4	27.0	17.6	18.0	18.3	18.9	19.2	18.6
Highest ten	15.5	20.1	26.2	39.4	66.9	80.9	60.5	56.4	53.5	53.6	55.0	55.7

NA Not available. X Not applicable. [1] Includes wholesalers.

Source: Fortune, New York, N.Y., adapted from The Fortune Directory, May, June, and July issues. (Copyright, by Time Inc.)

No. 941. 500 LARGEST INDUSTRIAL CORPORATIONS—SELECTED FINANCIAL ITEMS, BY INDUSTRY: 1970 AND 1977

[Figures are medians based on sales in 1970 and 1977. See headnote, table 940. For definition of median, see p. xii]

INDUSTRY	Assets per employee ($1,000)		Sales per employee ($1,000)		Sales per dollar of stockholders' equity (dol.)		Return on stockholders' equity (percent)		Return on sales (percent)	
	1970	1977	1970	1977	1970	1977	1970	1977	1970	1977
Total	24.1	40.4	29.5	57.5	2.36	2.81	9.5	13.5	3.9	4.6
Petroleum refining	106.4	208.5	92.6	279.0	1.40	2.77	10.3	13.1	6.9	4.5
Mining, crude oil production	70.9	196.7	46.2	89.5	1.21	1.69	13.8	12.3	12.6	9.0
Broadcasting and motion picture	(NA)	81.7	(NA)	94.7	(NA)	3.32	(NA)	22.2	(NA)	7.9
Tobacco	63.7	76.4	35.9	72.6	1.66	2.28	12.4	15.3	7.5	5.5
Beverages	(1)	76.2	(1)	89.8	(1)	2.63	(1)	12.2	(1)	4.3
Chemicals	37.5	60.7	32.7	73.5	1.73	2.25	8.7	13.0	5.2	5.3
Metal manufacturing	35.6	59.5	32.8	66.7	1.58	2.46	5.7	6.4	3.2	2.5
Paper, fiber, and wood products	32.5	56.6	32.7	66.7	1.79	2.30	6.8	12.7	3.9	5.5
Pharmaceuticals	26.4	47.6	29.2	51.6	1.77	1.93	15.5	16.7	9.3	8.5
Glass, concrete, abrasives, gypsum	24.2	40.8	25.6	55.9	1.80	2.46	7.6	11.9	4.2	4.9
Publishing, printing	25.3	40.4	28.8	53.5	1.19	2.18	11.4	14.8	5.3	7.4
Soaps, cosmetics	25.6	40.2	38.5	66.2	2.77	2.65	15.7	16.5	7.1	6.4
Industrial and farm equipment	22.1	38.3	27.7	50.1	2.27	2.64	9.5	13.7	4.4	5.3
Food	1 25.0	38.2	1 52.6	89.9	1 3.91	4.89	1 12.2	13.2	1 2.7	2.5
Rubber, plastic products	21.6	36.4	24.7	50.3	2.38	2.95	8.4	11.4	2.1	2.9
Metal products	19.9	36.0	26.0	54.0	2.72	3.04	10.1	14.3	3.9	4.3
Shipbuilding, RR and transportation equipment	23.0	33.4	31.9	53.3	1.69	3.96	9.8	15.4	4.2	3.6
Office equipment (incl. computer)	18.4	33.2	18.7	38.4	1.96	2.46	7.9	12.7	3.3	5.7
Motor vehicles	20.7	33.1	27.6	57.1	2.82	3.91	6.0	14.8	2.3	4.0
Measuring, scientific, photo. equip.	19.1	30.1	25.2	37.8	1.93	2.05	13.1	14.9	7.9	7.8
Aerospace	17.8	28.5	27.5	50.9	3.61	3.82	8.5	14.4	2.3	3.8
Musical instr., toys, sporting goods	(NA)	28.2	(NA)	40.2	(NA)	3.11	(NA)	11.2	(NA)	3.8
Electronics, appliances	17.9	27.4	24.2	41.2	2.54	2.85	10.2	15.2	3.9	4.9
Textiles, vinyl flooring	16.3	22.0	20.5	34.9	2.46	3.04	7.0	8.8	2.8	3.6
Apparel	11.5	16.2	18.3	30.1	3.29	3.27	10.9	12.2	3.1	3.0

NA Not available.   1 Beverages included with foods.
Source: Fortune, New York, N.Y., *The Fortune Directory*. (Copyright, by Time, Inc.)

No. 942. PATENTS AND TRADEMARKS: 1956 TO 1977

[Covers patents issued to citizens of the United States and residents of foreign countries. For information on copyrights, see table 995. See also *Historical Statistics, Colonial Times to 1970*, series W 96–108]

ITEM	1956–1960	1961–1965	1966–1970	1971–1975	1972	1973	1974	1975	1976	1977
Patent applications filed	410,389	463,193	504,613	541,415	105,300	109,622	107,448	107,950	109,989	108,992
Inventions	384,782	436,082	476,239	510,409	98,928	103,695	102,206	101,014	102,344	100,931
Designs	23,865	25,251	26,260	28,575	5,867	5,425	4,780	6,292	7,061	7,258
Botanical plants	584	628	584	688	135	118	130	150	175	188
Reissues	1,158	1,232	1,530	1,743	370	384	332	494	409	615
Patents issued	251,872	275,443	342,889	396,668	78,183	78,618	81,274	76,804	75,400	69,781
Inventions	237,469	259,971	325,144	375,532	74,808	74,139	76,275	71,994	70,236	65,269
Individuals	76,589	69,945	73,379	87,032	17,729	16,929	18,083	17,192	14,084	14,027
Corporations:										
U.S	133,948	152,537	190,616	192,911	38,890	38,615	37,807	34,577	34,391	31,531
Foreign 1	21,043	30,992	52,771	86,005	16,414	16,513	18,686	18,344	19,934	18,220
U.S. Government	5,889	6,497	8,378	9,584	1,775	2,082	1,699	1,881	1,827	1,491
Designs	13,024	13,862	16,254	18,675	2,901	4,033	4,303	4,282	4,564	3,929
Botanical plants	567	576	426	813	199	132	261	150	176	173
Reissues	812	1,034	1,065	1,648	275	314	435	378	424	410
Published applications 2	–	–	586	807	201	143	135	121	133	105
Foreign country residents 3	36,513	48,322	75,986	119,282	23,293	22,638	25,632	25,391	26,074	23,886
Certificates of trademarks issued	108,246	106,635	128,465	158,305	28,889	31,509	33,612	37,063	33,080	31,918
Trademarks	90,727	91,946	104,181	129,413	23,252	26,112	28,099	30,931	26,326	25,858
Trademark renewals	17,519	14,689	24,284	28,892	5,637	5,397	5,513	6,132	6,754	6,060

– Represents zero.   1 Includes patents assigned to foreign governments.
2 Abstracts of the technical disclosure of patent applications published at request of applicant or owner. The current practice, called "Defensive Publications," began in November 1968.
3 Includes patent inventions and a small number of patents for designs and botanical plants.

Source: U.S. Patent and Trademark Office. Fiscal-year figures are published in the *Commissioner of Patents and Trademarks Annual Report*.

No. 943. U.S. MULTINATIONAL COMPANIES—SELECTED ITEMS: 1966 AND 1970

[In billions of dollars, except as noted. Based on sample survey for 1970 covering 298 U.S. enterprises and their 5,237 majority-owned foreign affiliates. Assets of the U.S. enterprises covered in the sample account for 39 percent of the assets of all U.S. multinational companies in 1966. Manufacturing enterprises account for 75 percent of the assets of all direct foreign investors]

| ITEM | 1966 | | | | 1970 | | | | | |
| | U.S. enterprises | | | Major-ity-owned foreign affili-ates | U.S. enterprises | | | Majority-owned foreign affiliates | | |
	Total	Man-ufac-turing	Pe-tro-leum		Total	Man-ufac-turing	Pe-tro-leum	Total	Man-ufac-turing	Pe-tro-leum
Assets, total [1]	247.4	140.1	50.8	66.2	350.5	200.7	68.3	102.4	42.9	35.0
Net property, plant and equip	115.3	50.5	26.3	27.8	167.7	75.7	36.2	41.3	16.5	17.4
Investment in foreign affiliates	19.7	9.9	8.7	(X)	29.7	15.1	12.8	(X)	(X)	(X)
Other foreign assets	2.7	1.7	.8	(X)	4.0	2.7	1.0	(X)	(X)	(X)
Liabilities	100.7	59.5	15.4	35.3	164.0	95.6	23.6	59.8	24.0	21.8
Net worth	146.7	80.6	35.4	30.8	186.5	105.1	44.7	42.6	18.9	13.2
Income, total [1]	243.4	167.2	37.4	72.6	319.3	213.5	51.2	117.5	52.9	43.7
Net sales of goods or services	236.8	164.0	34.8	71.2	309.2	208.0	47.7	114.7	52.2	42.5
Income from all foreign affiliates	3.7	1.7	1.7	(X)	5.9	2.9	2.6	(X)	(X)	(X)
Costs and expenses, total [1]	213.3	147.4	32.8	64.2	293.0	197.9	46.2	104.0	49.0	36.6
Depreciation, depletion, etc.[2]	11.0	6.2	2.3	3.0	15.4	8.7	3.2	4.4	2.2	1.5
Costs of goods or services sold	156.6	113.6	20.3	50.7	207.5	147.6	29.1	76.2	36.6	25.5
Selling and expenses	29.9	19.9	4.2	(NA)	46.2	29.7	6.0	11.7	6.0	2.9
Taxes other than income taxes	10.7	5.4	3.9	5.6	14.2	7.1	5.0	7.6	2.0	(NA)
Net income after income taxes	18.3	11.3	3.7	4.3	16.4	9.1	4.0	7.3	2.2	3.5
Before income taxes	30.1	19.8	4.5	8.4	26.3	15.6	4.9	13.5	3.9	7.1
Number of employees mil	8.0	5.9	.5	2.4	8.9	6.3	.5	3.0	2.2	.3
Payroll costs of employees	61.8	48.8	4.2	9.4	85.1	65.2	5.6	14.5	10.4	1.8

NA Not available. X Not applicable. [1] Includes items not shown. [2] Includes related charges.
Source: U.S. Bureau of Economic Analysis, *Special Survey of U.S. Multinational Companies, 1970.*

No. 944. U.S. MULTINATIONAL COMPANIES—SALES BY MAJORITY-OWNED FOREIGN AFFILIATES: 1966 TO 1976

[In billions of dollars, except percent. Universe estimates based on a sample survey covering foreign affiliates with U.S. ownership of at least 50 percent, directly or indirectly held]

| INDUSTRY AND AREA OR COUNTRY | 1966 | 1968 | 1970 | 1972 | 1974 | 1975 | 1976 | | | |
| | | | | | | | Total sales | Per-cent local sales [1] | Percent exports | |
									To U.S.	Else-where
Total [2]	97.8	120.8	155.9	212.3	437.7	463.1	514.7	65	7	28
Petroleum	27.5	34.0	42.4	59.2	184.9	183.5	205.5	53	8	39
Manufacturing [2]	47.4	59.6	78.3	107.6	175.7	192.3	212.8	76	7	18
Food products	5.6	6.2	7.5	10.4	17.0	18.3	20.4	90	2	8
Chemicals and allied products	7.4	9.8	12.6	17.8	36.2	37.6	43.1	78	1	20
Primary and fabricated metals	3.9	5.3	7.6	7.6	12.5	12.6	14.4	82	4	14
Machinery (except electrical)	6.5	8.6	12.3	17.0	27.4	32.1	34.2	66	5	29
Electrical machinery	4.4	5.1	7.7	10.8	17.4	18.8	18.4	80	5	15
Transportation equipment	11.2	14.2	16.8	24.4	32.7	38.1	44.8	68	16	16
Trade	14.1	16.2	21.6	30.1	46.1	52.2	58.0	60	6	34
Developed countries	71.6	88.0	116.2	158.2	272.2	302.8	337.3	75	6	19
Canada	23.9	29.8	35.1	45.0	71.4	78.5	89.0	77	17	5
Europe	40.5	49.1	68.4	95.9	165.8	186.5	206.7	71	2	27
Communities (9 countries)	34.3	41.2	57.6	80.7	138.5	155.8	171.5	74	2	25
France	5.3	6.5	8.3	13.1	22.1	26.1	26.7	82	1	16
Germany	7.7	8.8	14.6	20.5	34.6	38.1	44.3	81	1	18
United Kingdom	13.4	15.1	18.5	24.5	40.3	45.9	48.6	74	2	25
Other [3]	8.0	10.7	16.2	22.5	41.6	45.7	51.9	63	2	35
Other Europe	6.1	7.9	10.9	15.2	27.2	30.7	35.2	60	2	38
Japan	2.1	2.9	4.2	6.7	16.8	17.8	20.1	94	1	5
Australia, N. Zealand, So. Africa	5.1	6.2	8.5	10.6	18.2	20.1	21.5	88	1	11
Developing countries	23.5	29.2	35.1	48.3	148.3	146.6	163.9	43	10	47
Latin America	14.3	17.4	20.1	23.7	51.6	57.3	60.6	70	11	20
Africa (excl. So. Africa)	1.9	2.8	3.6	4.5	10.1	10.2	13.2	53	16	31
Middle East	4.0	4.7	5.8	11.1	64.1	57.4	66.5	13	7	80
Other Asia and Pacific	3.3	4.3	5.7	9.1	22.5	21.7	23.6	56	13	31
International and unallocated	2.7	3.6	4.6	5.8	17.2	13.7	13.5	70	8	22

[1] Local sales represents sales to customers in the country where the affiliate is located. [2] Includes industries not shown separately. [3] Includes Belgium, Denmark, Ireland, Italy, Luxembourg, and the Netherlands.
Source: U.S. Bureau of Economic Analysis, *Survey of Current Business,* March 1978.

No. 945. U.S. MULTINATIONAL COMPANIES—CAPITAL EXPENDITURES, BY MAJORITY-OWNED FOREIGN AFFILIATES: 1970 TO 1977

[Represents expenditures made to acquire, add to, or improve property, plant, and equipment. See headnote, table 944]

INDUSTRY AND AREA OR COUNTRY	EXPENDITURES (mil. dol.)							PERCENT OF TOTAL		
	1970	1972	1973	1974	1975	1976	1977[1]	1970	1975	1977[1]
Total	14.1	16.7	20.5	25.3	26.8	26.0	28.7	100.0	100.0	100.0
By industry of affiliate:										
Mining and smelting	1.2	1.1	1.1	1.1	1.2	.9	.7	8.5	4.5	2.3
Petroleum	4.0	5.2	6.4	7.8	8.9	8.9	10.4	28.4	33.2	36.3
Manufacturing	6.5	7.2	9.2	11.6	11.3	11.0	12.2	46.1	42.2	42.5
Food products	.4	.4	.6	.7	.7	.7	.8	2.8	2.6	2.8
Paper and allied products	.4	.5	.6	.9	.7	.6	.7	2.8	2.6	2.5
Chemicals and allied products	1.2	1.2	1.4	2.1	2.5	2.7	2.3	8.5	9.3	8.1
Rubber products	.2	.3	.3	.4	.4	.5	.4	1.4	1.5	1.6
Primary and fabricated metals	.7	.6	.8	.7	.7	.7	.6	5.0	2.6	2.1
Machinery (except electrical)	1.6	1.9	2.6	3.1	2.8	2.7	3.4	11.3	10.4	11.7
Electrical machinery	.6	.6	.9	1.1	.9	.8	1.0	4.3	3.4	3.3
Transportation equipment	1.0	.9	1.2	1.6	1.4	1.4	1.8	7.1	5.2	6.1
Other	.5	.7	.8	1.1	1.3	1.1	1.3	3.5	4.9	4.4
Trade	1.0	1.4	1.7	2.1	2.4	1.8	2.2	7.1	9.0	7.6
Other industries	1.4	1.8	2.0	2.6	3.1	3.4	3.2	9.9	11.6	11.3
By area of affiliate:										
Developed countries	10.1	11.8	14.2	17.8	18.8	18.8	21.2	71.6	70.1	73.9
Canada	3.0	3.5	4.2	5.5	5.0	5.6	5.9	21.3	18.7	20.6
Europe	5.7	6.8	8.3	10.2	11.7	11.5	13.2	40.4	43.7	46.0
European Communities (9 countries)	5.1	6.0	7.3	8.8	9.9	10.0	11.4	36.2	36.9	39.7
France	.8	1.1	1.3	1.5	1.9	1.2	1.5	5.7	7.1	5.2
Germany	1.2	1.6	1.9	2.3	2.1	2.0	2.0	8.5	7.8	7.0
United Kingdom	1.5	1.7	2.4	2.7	3.6	4.5	5.5	10.6	13.4	19.2
Other[2]	1.5	1.6	1.6	2.4	2.3	2.2	2.3	10.6	8.6	8.0
Other Europe	.6	.8	1.0	1.4	1.8	1.6	1.9	4.3	6.7	6.6
Japan	.5	.6	.6	.8	.8	.6	.8	3.5	3.0	2.8
Australia, New Zealand, South Africa	.9	.9	1.0	1.2	1.2	1.1	1.3	6.4	4.5	4.4
Developing countries	3.3	3.8	4.2	5.4	6.4	5.4	5.9	23.4	23.9	20.5
Latin America	2.0	2.0	2.3	2.9	3.1	2.9	2.7	14.2	11.6	9.4
Africa (excl. So. Africa)	.5	.4	.4	.6	.7	.6	.8	3.5	2.6	2.9
Middle East	.2	.7	.8	.8	1.3	1.1	1.4	1.4	4.9	5.0
Other Asia and Pacific	.6	.7	.7	1.1	1.3	.8	.9	4.3	4.9	3.2
International and unallocated	.7	1.1	2.1	2.0	1.7	1.8	1.6	5.0	6.3	5.6

[1] Projection based on survey of Dec. 1977.   [2] See footnote 3, table 944.

Source: U.S. Bureau of Economic Analysis, *Survey of Current Business*, March 1978.

No. 946. LARGEST MANUFACTURING CORPORATIONS—PERCENT SHARE OF ASSETS HELD: 1950 TO 1977

[Corporations ranked on value of assets in each year. Prior to 1969, excludes newspapers. Data prior to 1974 not strictly comparable with later years]

CORPORATION RANK GROUP	1950	1955	1960	1965	1969	1970	1971	1972	1973	1974	1975	1976	1977
100 largest	39.7	44.3	46.4	46.5	48.2	48.5	48.9	47.6	44.7	44.4	45.0	45.4	45.7
200 largest	47.7	53.1	56.3	56.7	60.1	60.4	61.0	60.0	56.9	56.7	57.5	58.0	58.4

Source: U.S. Federal Trade Commission, unpublished data.

No. 947. LARGEST MANUFACTURING COMPANIES—PERCENT SHARE OF TOTAL VALUE ADDED BY MANUFACTURE: 1947 TO 1972

[1962, 1966, and 1970 based on Annual Survey of Manufactures, other years on Census of Manufactures. "Largest companies" are those which were largest in each of the specified years in terms of value added. For details, see Appendix III. See also *Historical Statistics, Colonial Times to 1970*, series P 177-180]

COMPANY RANK	1947	1954	1958	1962	1963	1966	1967	1970	1972
Largest 50 companies	17	23	23	24	25	25	25	24	25
Largest 100 companies	23	30	30	32	33	33	33	33	33
Largest 150 companies	27	34	35	36	37	38	38	38	39
Largest 200 companies	30	37	38	40	41	42	42	43	43

Source: U.S. Bureau of the Census, *Concentration Ratios in Manufacturing Industry: 1972*, MC 72-SR-2.

No. 948. Corporate Profits, Taxes, and Dividends: 1950 to 1977

[In billions of dollars. Prior to 1960, excludes Alaska and Hawaii. Covers corporations organized for profit. Represents profits accruing to U.S. residents, without deduction of depletion charges and exclusive of capital gains and losses; intercorporate dividends from profits of domestic corporations are eliminated; net receipts of dividends and branch profits from abroad are added]

ITEM	1950	1955	1960	1965	1970	1972	1973	1974	1975	1976	1977, prel.
Profits before taxes	42.6	48.4	48.5	75.2	71.5	96.2	115.8	126.9	123.5	156.9	171.9
Less: Income tax liability (Fed., State)	17.9	22.0	22.7	30.9	34.5	41.5	48.7	52.4	50.2	64.7	69.1
Equals: Profits after taxes	24.7	26.4	25.8	44.3	37.0	54.6	67.1	74.5	73.4	92.1	102.5
Less: Net dividends [1]	8.8	10.3	12.9	19.1	22.9	24.6	27.8	31.0	32.4	35.8	41.2
Equals: Undistributed profits	15.9	16.1	13.0	25.2	14.1	30.0	39.3	43.6	41.0	56.4	61.3
Capital consumption allowances [2]	8.8	17.4	25.3	37.4	56.6	67.9	73.7	81.6	89.5	97.2	104.7
Profits after tax plus capital consumption allowances	33.5	43.8	51.1	81.7	93.6	122.5	140.8	156.1	162.9	189.3	207.2

[1] Represents amounts disbursed to U.S. residents, measured after eliminations of intercorporate dividends.
[2] Without capital consumption adjustment. Includes depreciation and accidental damages.

Source: U.S. Bureau of Economic Analysis, *The National Income and Product Accounts of the United States, 1929–74*, and *Survey of Current Business*, July 1977 and March 1978.

No. 949. Corporate Profits Before Taxes With Inventory Valuation Adjustment and Without Capital Consumption Adjustment: 1950 to 1977

[In billions of dollars. 1976 and 1977 data are preliminary]

ITEM	1950	1955	1960	1965	1970	1971	1972	1973	1974	1975	1976	1977
Total	37.6	46.7	48.9	73.3	66.4	76.9	89.6	97.2	86.5	111.5	142.7	157.1
Domestic industries	36.7	45.1	47.0	70.1	62.6	72.4	84.7	90.4	76.9	105.4	134.6	147.8
Financial	3.1	4.8	7.2	7.5	12.6	14.1	15.4	16.2	14.4	15.0	18.2	20.7
Nonfinancial	33.5	40.3	39.8	62.5	50.1	58.2	69.3	74.1	62.5	90.3	116.4	127.2
Manufacturing	20.9	26.0	23.9	38.3	27.1	32.4	40.6	44.1	36.6	47.9	66.3	75.4
Wholesale and retail trade	5.0	5.0	4.9	7.9	9.4	11.7	13.3	14.7	12.9	22.1	27.1	26.5
Other	7.6	9.2	10.9	16.3	13.5	14.1	15.4	15.3	13.0	20.3	23.0	25.3
Rest of the world	1.0	1.6	1.9	3.3	3.8	4.6	4.8	6.8	9.6	6.1	8.1	9.3

Source: U.S. Council of Economic Advisers, *Economic Report of the President*, annual. Data from U.S. Bureau of Economic Analysis.

No. 950. Large Manufacturing Corporations—Sales, Profits, and Dividends for Selected Industries: 1970 to 1977

[In billions of dollars. Includes all public manufacturing corporations with sales of $700 million or more for which a consistent set of data could be constructed. A few companies with sales of $500 million to $700 million are included to obtain increased representation in a particular industry]

INDUSTRY	1970	1974	1975	1976	1977	INDUSTRY	1970	1974	1975	1976	1977
Total (170 corp.): [1]						Primary metals and products (23):					
Sales, net	304.9	564.9	586.9	667.8	748.8	Sales, net	30.8	54.0	48.6	54.0	58.7
Profits before taxes	29.3	67.9	60.4	71.9	78.9	Profits before taxes	2.1	5.6	2.9	2.8	1.5
Profits after taxes	12.7	35.3	33.3	37.2	37.9	Profits after taxes	.8	2.4	1.1	1.2	1.6
Dividends	10.0	12.4	12.5	14.5	17.0	Dividends	.9	1.0	.9	.9	1.0
Food and kindred products (28):						Machinery (27):					
Sales, net	32.0	52.8	57.1	62.6	68.4	Sales, net	46.2	74.0	79.0	87.3	96.8
Profits before taxes	3.1	4.6	5.0	5.8	6.0	Profits before taxes	4.9	7.8	8.7	11.3	13.2
Profits after taxes	1.6	2.3	2.5	2.9	3.2	Profits after taxes	2.3	3.5	3.9	5.1	7.2
Dividends	.8	1.0	1.1	1.3	1.4	Dividends	1.3	2.0	2.0	2.4	2.9
Chemical and allied products (22):						Motor vehicles and equipment (9):					
Sales, net	31.1	55.1	57.7	64.1	70.3	Sales, net	48.9	80.4	85.9	107.6	127.0
Profits before taxes	3.9	8.3	7.1	8.2	8.5	Profits before taxes	2.2	2.9	3.1	8.9	10.7
Profits after taxes	1.8	3.4	3.2	3.7	4.6	Profits after taxes	.8	1.2	1.6	4.0	5.7
Dividends	1.3	1.6	1.7	1.9	2.2	Dividends	1.4	1.5	1.1	2.1	2.6
Petroleum refin. (15):											
Sales, net	61.4	165.2	172.6	196.2	221.7						
Profits before taxes	8.5	30.7	26.3	25.9	28.1						
Profits after taxes	3.4	18.9	17.8	16.3	10.1						
Dividends	2.9	3.6	3.8	4.1	4.6						

[1] Includes 46 companies in 6 industries not shown separately. Figures in parentheses represent number of corporations.

Source: Board of Governors of the Federal Reserve System, *Federal Reserve Bulletin*, monthly.

No. 951. CORPORATE MANUFACTURING ASSETS AND PROFITS, BY ASSET SIZE: 1970 TO 1977

[Corporations and assets as of **end of 4th quarter** profit for **entire year**. Corporations under $10 million based on sample; $10 million and over based on complete canvass. For further detail regarding methodology, see source for fourth quarter, 1977]

YEAR AND ITEM	Total	ASSET-SIZE CLASS						
		Under $10 mil.	$10–$25 mil.	$25–$50 mil.	$50–$100 mil.	$100–$250 mil.	$250 mil.– $1 bil.	$1 bil. and over
1970								
Corporations_____number__	197,807	[1] 195,000	1,202	533	366	289	218	102
Assets, total_____mil. dol__	578,234	69,101	20,471	20,138	25,946	47,783	112,475	282,320
Percent_____	100.0	12.0	3.5	3.5	4.5	8.3	19.5	48.8
Net profit, total [2]___mil. dol__	28,572	2,812	811	836	1,101	2,315	5,862	14,832
Percent_____	100.0	9.8	2.8	2.9	3.9	8.1	20.5	51.9
1975								
Corporations_____number__	(NA)	(NA)	1,750	705	450	392	276	151
Assets, total_____mil. dol__	810,910	98,147	31,307	24,720	31,395	62,524	139,113	423,705
Percent_____	100.0	12.1	3.9	3.0	3.9	7.7	17.2	52.3
Net profit, total [2]___mil. dol__	49,135	6,212	1,831	1,327	1,676	3,553	8,165	26,370
Percent_____	100.0	12.6	3.7	2.7	3.4	7.2	16.6	53.7
1976								
Corporations_____number__	(NA)	(NA)	(NA)	757	472	400	301	162
Assets, total_____mil. dol__	883,860	98,355	32,244	26,538	32,970	62,633	149,412	481,709
Percent_____	100.0	11.1	3.6	3.0	3.7	7.1	16.9	54.5
Net profit, total [2]___mil. dol__	64,519	7,799	2,238	1,714	2,070	3,945	10,422	36,330
Percent_____	100.0	12.1	3.5	2.7	3.2	6.1	16.2	56.3
1977								
Corporations_____number__	(NA)	(NA)	(NA)	809	501	409	327	174
Assets, total_____mil. dol__	965,522	102,111	35,603	28,595	35,032	63,418	161,655	539,108
Percent_____	100.0	10.6	3.7	3.0	3.6	6.6	16.7	55.8
Net profit, total [2]___mil. dol__	70,468	8,680	2,189	1,867	2,252	4,397	11,290	39,793
Percent_____	100.0	12.3	3.1	2.6	3.2	6.2	16.0	56.5

NA Not available.
[1] Data derived from U.S. Internal Revenue Service, *Statistics of Income*, annual.   [2] After taxes.

Source: U.S. Federal Trade Commission, *Quarterly Financial Report for Manufacturing, Mining and Trade Corporations*.

No. 952. CORPORATE PROFITS, BY INDUSTRY: 1960 TO 1977

[**In billions of dollars**. Profits are without inventory valuation and capital consumption adjustments. Minus sign (−) denotes loss. See headnote, table 948]

YEAR	All indus- tries	Manu- factur- ing	Whole- sale, retail trade	Finance, insurance, real estate [1]	Com- munica- tion [2]	Con- struc- tion [1]	Serv- ices	Trans- porta- tion	Min- ing	Agri- cul- ture [3]	Rest of the world
BEFORE TAXES											
1960_____	48.5	23.7	4.9	8.3	6.5	.6	.8	.9	.8	.1	1.9
1965_____	75.2	39.4	8.6	8.9	8.9	1.5	1.5	2.2	.9	.2	3.3
1970_____	71.5	29.7	11.3	13.7	8.5	1.9	1.6	.1	.9	.1	3.8
1972_____	96.2	43.9	16.0	16.5	7.7	2.2	2.3	1.5	.7	.5	4.8
1973_____	115.8	54.2	21.4	16.7	7.8	2.1	3.1	1.2	1.5	.8	6.8
1974_____	126.9	58.9	25.3	14.9	6.7	2.3	2.9	2.0	3.8	.4	9.6
1975_____	123.5	53.7	26.8	16.2	9.1	2.5	3.8	.8	3.7	.7	6.1
1976_____	156.9	73.0	31.6	19.6	11.0	2.8	4.6	2.0	3.4	.8	8.1
1977_____											
AFTER TAXES											
1960_____	25.8	12.4	2.5	4.2	3.2	.2	.4	.3	.7	(Z)	1.9
1965_____	44.3	22.5	5.3	4.5	4.9	1.0	.8	1.3	.6	.1	3.3
1970_____	37.0	14.8	6.5	5.7	4.4	1.1	.6	− .3	.6	(Z)	3.8
1972_____	54.6	24.0	10.1	7.3	4.6	1.2	1.2	.7	.4	.3	4.8
1973_____	67.1	30.2	13.9	6.6	4.6	1.1	1.9	.4	1.1	.5	6.8
1974_____	74.5	33.6	16.8	4.4	3.8	1.3	1.6	.9	2.6	(Z)	9.6
1975_____	73.4	29.4	18.4	6.0	6.7	1.4	2.4	−.1	2.6	.4	6.1
1976_____	92.1	40.2	21.1	7.2	8.2	1.4	2.6	.6	2.3	.4	8.1
1977_____											

Z Less than $50 million.   [1] Company basis, based on the 1972 Standard Industrial Classification (SIC); see text, p. 396.   [2] Includes public utilities.   [3] Includes forestry and fisheries.

Source: U.S. Bureau of Economic Analysis, *The National Income and Product Accounts of the United States 1929-74*, and *Survey of Current Business*, July 1977 and March 1978.

No. 953. MANUFACTURING CORPORATIONS—SALES, PROFITS, AND STOCKHOLDERS' EQUITY: 1960 TO 1977

[In billions of dollars. Prior to 1970, excludes newspapers. Data are not necessarily comparable from year to year due to changes in accounting procedures, industry classifications, sampling procedures, etc.; for detail see source. See also *Historical Statistics, Colonial Times to 1970,* series P 93–106]

YEAR	ALL MANUFACTURING CORPORATIONS				DURABLE GOODS INDUSTRIES				NONDURABLE GOODS INDUSTRIES			
	Sales (net)	Profits		Stock-holders' equity [1]	Sales (net)	Profits		Stock-holders' equity [1]	Sales (net)	Profits		Stock-holders' equity [1]
		Before taxes	After taxes			Before taxes	After taxes			Before taxes	After taxes	
1960____	345.7	27.5	15.2	165.4	173.9	14.0	7.0	82.3	171.8	13.5	8.2	83.1
1965____	492.2	46.5	27.5	211.7	257.0	26.2	14.5	105.4	235.2	20.3	13.0	106.3
1970____	708.8	48.1	28.6	306.8	363.1	23.0	12.9	155.1	345.7	25.2	15.7	151.7
1971____	751.4	53.2	31.3	320.9	382.5	26.5	14.5	160.6	368.9	26.7	16.7	160.3
1972____	849.5	63.2	36.5	343.4	435.8	33.6	18.4	171.4	413.7	29.6	18.0	172.0
1973____	1,017.2	81.4	48.1	374.1	527.3	43.6	24.8	188.7	489.9	37.8	23.3	185.4
1974____	1,060.6	92.1	58.7	395.0	529.0	41.1	24.7	196.0	531.6	51.0	34.1	199.0
1975____	1,065.2	79.9	49.1	423.4	521.1	35.3	21.4	208.1	544.1	44.6	27.7	215.3
1976____	1,203.2	104.9	64.5	462.7	589.5	50.7	30.8	224.3	613.7	54.3	33.7	238.4
1977____	1,331.2	115.3	70.5	497.2	663.4	58.3	35.1	241.8	667.8	57.0	35.4	255.4

[1] Annual data are average equity for the year (using four end-of-quarter figures).

No. 954. MANUFACTURING CORPORATIONS—RELATION OF PROFITS AFTER TAXES TO STOCKHOLDERS' EQUITY AND TO SALES: 1970 TO 1977

[Averages of quarterly figures at annual rates. Based on sample; see source for discussion of methodology]

INDUSTRY GROUP	RATIOS OF PROFITS TO STOCKHOLDERS' EQUITY (percent)							PROFITS PER DOLLAR OF SALES (cents)						
	1970	1972	1973	1974	1975	1976	1977	1970	1972	1973	1974	1975	1976	1977
All manufacturing corporations [1]____	9.3	10.6	12.8	14.9	11.6	14.0	14.2	4.0	4.3	4.7	5.5	4.6	5.4	5.3
Durable goods indus___	8.3	10.8	13.1	12.6	10.3	13.7	14.5	3.5	4.2	4.7	4.7	4.1	5.2	5.3
Stone, clay, and glass products_____	6.9	10.1	11.2	10.6	8.3	11.9	13.4	3.6	4.7	4.8	4.4	3.4	4.8	5.1
Primary metal indus__	7.0	6.0	10.1	16.5	8.6	8.5	4.9	4.1	3.3	4.6	6.6	4.4	4.0	2.1
Iron and steel_____	4.3	6.0	9.5	17.0	10.9	9.0	3.5	2.5	3.1	4.1	6.3	5.0	4.1	1.5
Nonferrous metals__	10.6	5.9	10.8	15.8	5.0	7.4	7.2	6.2	3.7	5.3	7.0	3.1	3.8	3.4
Fabricated metal prod__	8.5	10.9	13.8	16.0	13.2	15.4	15.8	3.0	3.5	4.0	4.6	4.2	4.8	4.8
Machinery, exc. elec__	9.8	10.6	13.4	13.4	13.7	15.4	16.7	4.6	4.9	5.6	6.0	6.4	7.4	7.6
Electrical and electronic equipment____	9.1	10.8	13.0	10.9	9.0	12.8	15.2	3.3	3.9	4.3	3.9	3.2	4.5	5.3
Transport equip_____	6.3	12.5	13.1	8.0	7.5	16.0	17.4	2.3	4.0	3.9	2.8	2.4	4.8	5.0
Motor vehicles and equip_____	6.1	14.7	15.1	7.1	6.2	17.2	18.7	2.6	4.8	4.5	2.7	2.2	5.5	5.5
Aircraft, guided missiles and parts__	6.8	7.9	10.3	10.4	11.0	12.8	15.0	2.0	2.5	2.9	2.9	2.9	3.4	4.2
Instruments and related products_____	14.3	14.9	15.9	16.3	13.5	14.7	16.9	7.3	8.2	8.4	9.3	7.6	7.9	9.0
Other durable goods__	(NA)	(NA)	(NA)	11.7	8.4	14.2	15.8	(NA)	(NA)	(NA)	3.5	2.7	4.2	4.4
Nondur. goods indus__	10.3	10.5	12.6	17.1	12.8	14.2	13.9	4.5	4.4	4.8	6.4	5.1	5.5	5.3
Food and kindred products_____	10.8	11.1	12.8	13.8	14.4	14.9	13.3	2.5	2.5	2.6	2.9	3.2	3.5	3.1
Tobacco manufctrs____	15.7	15.4	14.8	15.6	15.9	15.9	17.5	5.8	6.0	5.8	9.1	9.2	8.5	9.1
Textile mill products__	5.1	7.5	9.0	8.0	4.2	8.0	8.7	1.9	2.6	2.8	2.4	1.2	2.4	2.4
Paper and allied products_____	7.0	9.0	12.9	17.8	12.6	13.8	12.6	3.4	4.0	5.4	7.0	5.6	5.8	5.3
Printing and publishing_____	11.2	12.1	12.8	13.2	12.8	15.1	17.4	4.2	4.7	4.8	4.7	4.6	5.1	5.7
Chemicals and allied products_____	11.4	12.9	14.8	18.3	15.2	15.5	15.1	5.9	6.4	6.8	8.4	7.6	7.5	7.1
Industrial_____	8.5	10.0	13.0	17.6	13.2	14.3	13.4	5.0	5.5	6.5	8.4	6.9	6.9	6.4
Drugs_____	17.6	18.4	19.0	18.8	17.8	18.1	18.2	9.4	10.1	10.2	12.2	12.2	12.2	12.1
Petroleum and coal products_____	11.0	8.7	11.6	21.1	12.5	14.1	13.6	9.3	6.7	7.6	12.8	7.6	8.3	7.5
Rubber and misc. plastics products____	7.1	10.8	12.0	14.4	8.0	10.8	12.1	2.7	4.0	4.0	5.0	3.0	3.8	4.0
Other nondur. goods__	(NA)	(NA)	(NA)	11.7	11.2	13.2	13.2	(NA)	(NA)	(NA)	2.5	2.4	2.8	2.9

NA Not available.   [1] Beginning 1974, data not strictly comparable with earlier years.

Source of tables 953 and 954: U.S. Federal Trade Commission and U.S. Securities and Exchange Commission, *Quarterly Financial Report for Manufacturing, Mining and Trade Corporations.* In U.S. Council of Economic Advisers, *Economic Report of the President,* annual.

No. 955. Mergers and Acquisitions—Manufacturing and Mining Concerns Acquired: 1925 to 1977

[Prior to 1972, totals limited to actions reported by Moody's Investors Service, Inc., and Standard & Poor's Corporation. Included are partial acquisitions when they comprise whole divisions or subsidiaries of other companies. See also *Historical Statistics, Colonial Times to 1970*, series V 38]

PERIOD	Concerns acquired aggregate for period	Year	All concerns acquired total	Large concerns (assets of $10 million or more) acquired [1]					
				Number of mergers			Assets acquired (mil. dol.)		
				Total	Horizontal and vertical	Conglomerate	Total	Horizontal and vertical	Conglomerate
1925–1929	4,583	1960	844	51	14	37	1,535	453	1,082
1930–1934	1,687	1965	1,008	64	16	48	3,254	573	2,681
1935–1939	577	1969	2,307	138	24	114	11,043	2,915	8,128
1940–1944	906	1970	1,351	91	12	79	5,904	1,174	4,730
1945–1949	1,505	1971	1,011	59	8	51	2,460	578	1,882
1950–1954	1,424	1972	911	60	24	36	1,885	773	1,112
1955–1959	3,365	1973	874	64	25	39	3,149	1,093	2,056
1960–1964	4,366	1974	602	62	24	38	4,466	1,417	3,049
1965–1969	8,213	1975	439	59	7	52	4,950	267	4,683
1970–1974	4,749	1976	559	81	18	63	6,279	1,031	5,248
1975–1977		1977 [2]	590	99	30	69	8,670	1,937	6,733

[1] Concerns for which financial data are publicly available.   [2] Preliminary.

Source: U.S. Federal Trade Commission, *Report on Corporate Mergers and Acquisitions, 1955; Current Trends in Merger Activity, 1971;* and *Statistical Report on Mergers and Acquisitions*, annual.

No. 956. Mergers and Acquisitions—Manufacturing and Mining Concerns Acquired, by Industry Group of Acquiring Concern: 1960 to 1977

[See headnote, table 955]

INDUSTRY OF ACQUIRING CONCERN	1960–1964, total	1965–1969, total	1970–1974, total	1970	1971	1972	1973	1974	1975	1976	1977, prel.
Total concerns acquired	4,366	8,213	4,749	1,351	1,011	911	874	602	439	559	590
Mining	209	303	258	83	76	29	34	36	27	28	26
Manufacturing	3,694	6,642	3,428	1,045	760	627	578	418	288	375	393
Food and kindred products	326	538	384	109	85	73	77	40	27	42	43
Tobacco manufactures	24	37	18	9	3	1	3	2	4	1	5
Textiles and apparel	280	439	160	47	37	31	30	15	3	13	11
Lumber and furniture	109	250	175	48	33	36	31	27	7	14	12
Paper and allied products	133	175	120	31	16	22	21	30	8	10	18
Printing and publishing	158	224	158	42	44	26	28	18	21	29	24
Chemicals	443	615	334	108	59	55	65	47	44	39	46
Petroleum	78	73	34	6	9	6	6	7	3	7	2
Rubber and plastics products	74	139	71	26	17	9	12	7	2	10	16
Leather products	32	75	41	15	11	10	5	–	3	3	1
Stone, clay, and glass products	103	212	136	43	31	18	19	25	15	13	11
Primary metals	173	366	180	57	51	25	24	23	22	22	23
Fabricated metal products	225	471	214	54	46	44	45	25	24	43	29
Machinery, except electrical	397	817	413	153	87	69	59	45	48	44	51
Electrical machinery	573	1,160	478	145	112	109	67	45	35	47	47
Transportation equipment	272	483	218	71	44	33	39	31	10	12	20
Professional scientif. instruments	189	407	172	49	42	42	21	18	9	20	22
Misc. and ordnance	105	161	122	32	33	18	26	13	3	6	12
Nonmanufacturing [1]	463	1,268	1,063	223	175	255	262	148	124	156	171

– Represents zero.   [1] Includes unknown industries.

No. 957. Mergers and Acquisitions—Companies Acquired, by Asset Size of Acquiring and Acquired Companies and by Industry: 1976 and 1977

[Excludes pending mergers and acquisitions]

ASSET SIZE	Acquiring company 1976	1977	Acquired company 1976	1977	INDUSTRY	Acquiring company 1976	1977	Acquired company 1976	1977
Total	1,081	1,182	1,081	1,182	Total	1,081	1,182	1,081	1,182
Under $1 mil. [1]	181	152	776	840	Manufacturing	526	572	420	439
$1 mil. to $9.9 mil.	58	75	146	146	Mining	33	47	41	44
$10.0 mil. to $49.9 mil.	213	218	115	121	Wholesale, retail trade	110	109	162	127
$50.0 mil. to $99.9 mil.	114	156	21	37	Service and other [2]	293	321	125	143
$100.0 mil. and over	515	581	23	38	Unknown	119	133	333	429

[1] Includes companies of unknown asset size.   [2] Companies in insurance, construction, farming, finance, credit, real estate, transportation, communication; electric, gas, sanitary services; and holding companies.

Source of tables 956 and 957: U.S. Federal Trade Commission, *Statistical Report on Mergers and Acquisitions*, annual.

No. 958. INDUSTRIAL AND COMMERCIAL FAILURES—NUMBER AND LIABILITIES: 1946 TO 1977

[Excludes Hawaii prior to 1975, Alaska prior to 1976. Excludes all railroad failures. Excludes real estate and financial companies. Includes voluntary discontinuances with loss to creditors and small concerns forced out of business with insufficient assets to cover all claims. See also *Historical Statistics, Colonial Times to 1970*, series V 20–30]

YEARLY AVERAGE OR YEAR	Total concerns in business [1] (1,000)	FAILURES [2]				YEAR	Total concerns in business [1] (1,000)	FAILURES [2]			
		Number	Rate per 10,000 concerns	Current liabilities [3] (mil. dol.)	Average liability ($1,000)			Number	Rate per 10,000 concerns	Current liabilities [3] (mil. dol.)	Average liability ($1,000)
1946–1950	2,493	5,652	21	213	45	1965	2,527	13,514	53	1,322	98
1951–1955	2,635	9,317	35	370	39	1966	2,520	13,061	52	1,386	106
1956–1960	2,674	14,177	53	708	50	1967	2,519	12,364	49	1,265	102
1961–1965	2,565	14,849	57	1,261	86	1968	2,481	9,636	39	941	98
1966–1970	2,481	10,993	44	1,324	121	1969	2,444	9,154	37	1,142	125
1971–1975	2,559	10,117	40	2,730	270	1970	2,442	10,748	44	1,888	176
1950	2,687	9,162	34	248	27	1971	2,466	10,326	42	1,917	186
1955	2,633	10,969	42	449	41	1972	2,490	9,566	38	2,000	209
1960	2,708	15,445	57	939	61	1973	2,567	9,345	36	2,299	246
1961	2,641	17,075	64	1,090	64	1974	2,591	9,915	38	3,053	308
1962	2,589	15,782	61	1,214	77	1975	2,679	11,432	43	4,380	383
1963	2,544	14,37ı	56	1,353	94	1976	2,782	9,628	35	3,011	313
1964	2,524	13,501	53	1,329	98	1977	2,793	7,919	28	3,095	391

[1] Data represent number of names listed in July issue of *Dun & Bradstreet Reference Book*.
[2] Includes concerns discontinuing following assignment, voluntary or involuntary petition in bankruptcy, attachment, execution, foreclosure, etc.; voluntary withdrawals from business with known loss to creditors; also enterprises involved in court action, such as receivership and reorganization or arrangement which may or may not lead to discontinuance; and businesses making voluntary compromise with creditors out of court.
[3] Liabilities exclude long-term publicly held obligations; offsetting assets are not taken into account.

No. 959. INDUSTRIAL AND COMMERCIAL FAILURES—NUMBER AND LIABILITIES, BY STATES: 1976 AND 1977

STATE	NUMBER [1]		CURRENT LIABILITIES [1] (mil. dol.)		STATE	NUMBER [1]		CURRENT LIABILITIES [1] (mil. dol.)	
	1976	1977	1976	1977		1976	1977	1976	1977
U.S.	9,628	7,919	3,011.3	3,095.3	S.A.—Con.				
N.E.	578	482	192.6	301.1	Va.	172	139	42.1	25.6
Maine	26	39	4.8	4.5	W. Va.	19	34	3.9	3.0
N.H.	46	40	19.1	7.0	N.C.	69	21	15.7	37.9
Vt.	18	12	1.8	1.6	S.C.	32	26	22.8	6.9
Mass.	361	309	104.2	265.5	Ga.	224	107	67.5	20.7
R.I.	4	17	.3	3.3	Fla.	260	171	252.7	85.3
Conn.	123	65	62.2	19.2	E.S.C.	428	374	95.4	105.3
M.A.	2,208	1,800	800.0	1,293.6	Ky.	82	76	23.3	13.8
N.Y.	1,025	816	485.3	897.5	Tenn.	214	150	52.3	65.9
N.J.	660	535	174.5	195.0	Ala.	98	127	15.4	21.4
Pa.	523	449	140.2	201.1	Miss.	34	21	4.4	4.2
E.N.C.	1,810	1,395	327.8	273.9	W.S.C.	720	643	403.4	246.3
Ohio	424	203	64.1	28.7	Ark.	54	59	14.0	5.9
Ind.	131	178	17.5	39.4	La.	57	32	21.4	6.3
Ill.	507	444	127.3	110.5	Okla.	189	154	33.9	34.6
Mich.	575	485	90.1	83.9	Tex.	420	398	334.1	199.4
Wis.	173	85	28.7	11.4	Mt.	308	262	63.5	136.0
W.N.C.	566	572	183.9	116.7	Mont.	18	31	1.8	5.8
Minn.	247	206	51.2	22.5	Idaho	42	23	5.8	89.8
Iowa	67	66	14.0	19.7	Wyo.	-	2	-	.1
Mo.	120	107	92.7	42.0	Colo.	60	89	19.3	17.5
N. Dak.	23	36	2.3	3.8	N. Mex.	17	13	3.3	3.1
S. Dak.	14	42	1.0	4.8	Ariz.	119	77	17.2	14.4
Nebr.	47	46	8.2	12.4	Utah	20	5	4.0	3.0
Kans.	48	69	14.4	11.6	Nev.	32	22	12.0	2.2
S.A.	1,078	776	445.3	227.4	Pac.	1,932	1,615	499.5	395.1
Del.	6	9	.2	2.0	Wash.	393	276	52.0	56.1
Md.	276	265	38.7	45.6	Oreg.	238	192	92.6	21.1
D.C.	20	4	1.6	.4	Calif.	1,278	1,133	335.1	313.7
					Hawaii	22	9	19.7	1.8
					Alaska	1	5	1	2.4

- Represents zero.   [1] See headnote and footnotes 2 and 3, table 958.

Source of tables 958 and 959: Dun & Bradstreet, Inc., New York, N.Y., *The Failure Record Through 1977* and *Monthly Failure Report*.

No. 960. Industrial and Commercial Failures—Number and Liabilities, by Industry and Size of Liability: 1970 to 1977

[Excludes Hawaii prior to 1975, Alaska prior to 1976. See footnotes 2 and 3, table 958]

INDUSTRY AND SIZE OF LIABILITY	FAILURES						CURRENT LIABILITIES (mil. dol.)					
	1970	1973	1974	1975	1976	1977	1970	1973	1974	1975	1976	1977
Total	10,748	9,345	9,915	11,432	9,628	7,919	1,888	2,299	3,053	4,380	3,012	3,095
Mining and manufacturing	2,035	1,463	1,557	1,645	1,360	1,122	818	797	834	1,021	1,122	1,221
Under $100,000	1,069	697	750	789	614	479	43	29	32	35	27	23
$100,000 and over	966	766	807	856	746	643	775	769	802	986	1,094	1,198
Wholesale trade	984	940	964	1,089	1,028	887	179	274	275	407	414	613
Under $100,000	650	565	572	611	506	450	27	24	24	28	23	21
$100,000 and over	334	375	392	478	522	437	152	251	251	379	391	592
Retail trade	4,650	4,341	4,234	4,799	4,139	3,406	361	673	1,070	1,836	557	483
Under $100,000	3,984	3,570	3,302	3,520	3,050	2,368	124	120	120	136	126	98
$100,000 and over	666	771	932	1,279	1,089	1,038	236	553	950	1,700	430	384
Construction	1,687	1,419	1,840	2,262	1,770	1,463	232	309	527	641	429	420
Under $100,000	1,229	912	1,152	1,433	1,097	867	42	34	46	58	47	38
$100,000 and over	458	507	688	829	673	596	190	275	480	583	382	382
Commercial service	1,392	1,182	1,320	1,637	1,331	1,041	299	245	348	475	490	359
Under $100,000	1,087	883	957	1,151	909	697	33	29	34	42	34	28
$100,000 and over	305	299	363	486	422	344	265	216	314	433	456	331

Source: Dun & Bradstreet, Inc., New York, N.Y., *The Failure Record Through 1977* and *Monthly Failure Report.*

No. 961. Bankruptcy Cases Filed and Pending: 1905 to 1977

[In thousands. For years ending June 30 except, beginning 1977, ending Sept. 30. Covers all U.S. district courts. A bankruptcy case is a proceeding filed in a U.S. district court under the National Bankruptcy Act. "Filed" means the commencement of a proceeding through the presentation of a petition to the clerk of the court; "Pending" is a proceeding in which the administration has not been completed]

YEAR	Filed	Pending	YEAR	Filed	Pending	YEAR	Filed	Pending	YEAR	Filed	Pending
1905	17	28	1945	13	21	1964	172	157	1971	201	201
1910	18	25	1950	33	38	1965	180	162	1972	183	197
1915	28	44	1955	59	56	1966	192	169	1973	173	189
1920	14	30				1967	208	185	1974	190	201
1925	46	60	1960	110	95	1968	198	184	1975	254	262
1930	63	61	1961	147	124	1969	185	179	1976	247	271
1935	69	65	1962	148	134	1970	194	191	1977	214	254
1940	52	55	1963	155	148						

No. 962. Bankruptcy Cases Filed, by Type of Bankruptcy and Occupation of Debtor: 1965 to 1977

[For years ending June 30 except, beginning 1977, ending Sept. 30. See headnote, table 961]

ITEM	1965	1970	1971	1972	1973	1974	1975	1976	1977
Total	180,323	194,399	201,352	182,869	173,197	189,513	254,484	246,549	214,399
Straight bankruptcies	151,137	162,451	168,364	153,934	145,914	157,967	209,330	209,067	181,194
Voluntary	149,820	161,366	167,149	152,840	144,929	156,958	208,064	207,926	180,062
Involuntary	1,317	1,085	1,215	1,094	985	1,009	1,266	1,141	1,132
Corporate reorganization	88	115	179	105	101	163	189	141	96
Arrangements	1,071	1,320	1,902	1,453	1,550	2,343	3,786	3,760	3,686
Wage earners' plans	28,027	30,510	30,904	27,373	25,632	29,023	41,178	33,579	29,422
Other	–	3	3	4	–	17	1	2	1
OCCUPATION OF DEBTOR [1]									
Employees	148,965	156,343	156,077	139,437	131,122	141,877	184,078	166,394	144,754
Merchants	4,332	4,003	4,690	4,359	4,492	5,317	6,048	6,124	6,533
Manufacturers	688	731	992	688	649	710	756	681	779
Farmers	589	658	788	631	431	308	550	672	736
Members of professions	778	1,301	1,465	1,556	1,450	1,582	2,542	2,809	2,680
Other	23,628	30,264	36,106	35,081	34,056	38,699	59,224	68,703	57,775
In business	9,188	8,470	10,013	9,825	9,505	11,870	19,073	23,870	20,423
Not in business	14,440	21,794	26,093	25,256	24,551	26,829	40,151	44,833	37,352

– Represents zero.   [1] Excludes corporate and involuntary straight cases.

Source of tables 961 and 962: Administrative Office of the United States Courts, *Tables of Bankruptcy Statistics,* annual.

Section 19
Communications

This section presents statistics on usage, finances, and operations of the various communications media: Postal service, telephone, telegraph, radio, television, newspapers and periodicals, and books. Data on the U.S. Postal Service are included in the *Annual Report of the Postmaster General*. Statistics on revenues, volume of mail, and distribution of expenditures are presented in the U.S. Postal Service's annual report, *Revenue and Cost Analysis*. Principal sources of wire, radio, and television data are the U.S. Federal Communications Commission's *Annual Report*, its annual *Statistics of Communications Common Carriers*, and its annual releases of financial data reported by radio and television stations and networks. Statistics on number and circulation of newspapers and periodicals and on sales of books and pamphlets are issued by the Bureau of the Census in reports of the census of manufactures. Annual data on number and circulation of newspapers appear in *International Yearbook*, issued by Editor and Publisher Co., Inc., New York. Monthly data on new books and new editions are presented by R. R. Bowker Company, New York, in *Publishers Weekly*.

Postal Service.—The Postal Service provides mail processing and delivery services within the U.S. The Postal Reorganization Act of 1970 created the Postal Service, effective July 1971, as an independent establishment of the Federal Executive Branch; it also placed restrictions on the private delivery of mail.

"Revenue and cost analysis" is the term used by the Postal Service to describe its system of attributing revenues and costs to classes of mail and service. This system draws primarily upon probability sampling techniques to develop estimates of revenues, volumes, and weights, as well as costs by class of mail and special service. The costs attributed to classes of mail and special services are primarily incremental costs which vary in response to changes in volume; they account for roughly 65 percent of the total costs of the Postal Service. The balance represents "institutional costs" which includes funds for research and development, portions of personnel and of office supplies, etc.

Wire and other communication media.—The Federal Communications Commission (FCC) was established in 1934 to regulate wire and radio communications in the public interest; it also licenses radio and television stations. Only the largest carriers and controlling companies file annual or monthly financial reports. Regulatory jurisdiction of the FCC applies to domestic and overseas telegraph carriers and to the Communications Satellite Corporation, but not to a large number of telephone carriers which are engaged in intrastate or foreign service even if they rent the interstate facilities of another unaffiliated carrier. The gross operating revenues of the telephone carriers reporting annually to the FCC, however, are estimated to cover over 90 percent of the revenues of all U.S. telephone companies. Financial and other reports filed by the broadcasting industry cover substantially all commercial and educational radios and television units operating in the United States and its outlying areas. Total broadcasting revenues are defined as sales of time, talent, programs, and services of all networks and stations less commissions to agencies. Statistics covering the number of operating licenses issued are compiled from FCC records. Those covering the safety and special radio services represent the largest and most diverse group of licensees regulated by the FCC. These services primarily provide two-way radio communication for emergency and business purposes in the aviation, marine, land transportation, and other industries; police, fire, and other public safety programs; and amateur and personal operations.

Historical statistics.—Tabular headnotes provide cross-references, where applicable, to *Historical Statistics of the United States, Colonial Times to 1970*. See Appendix I.

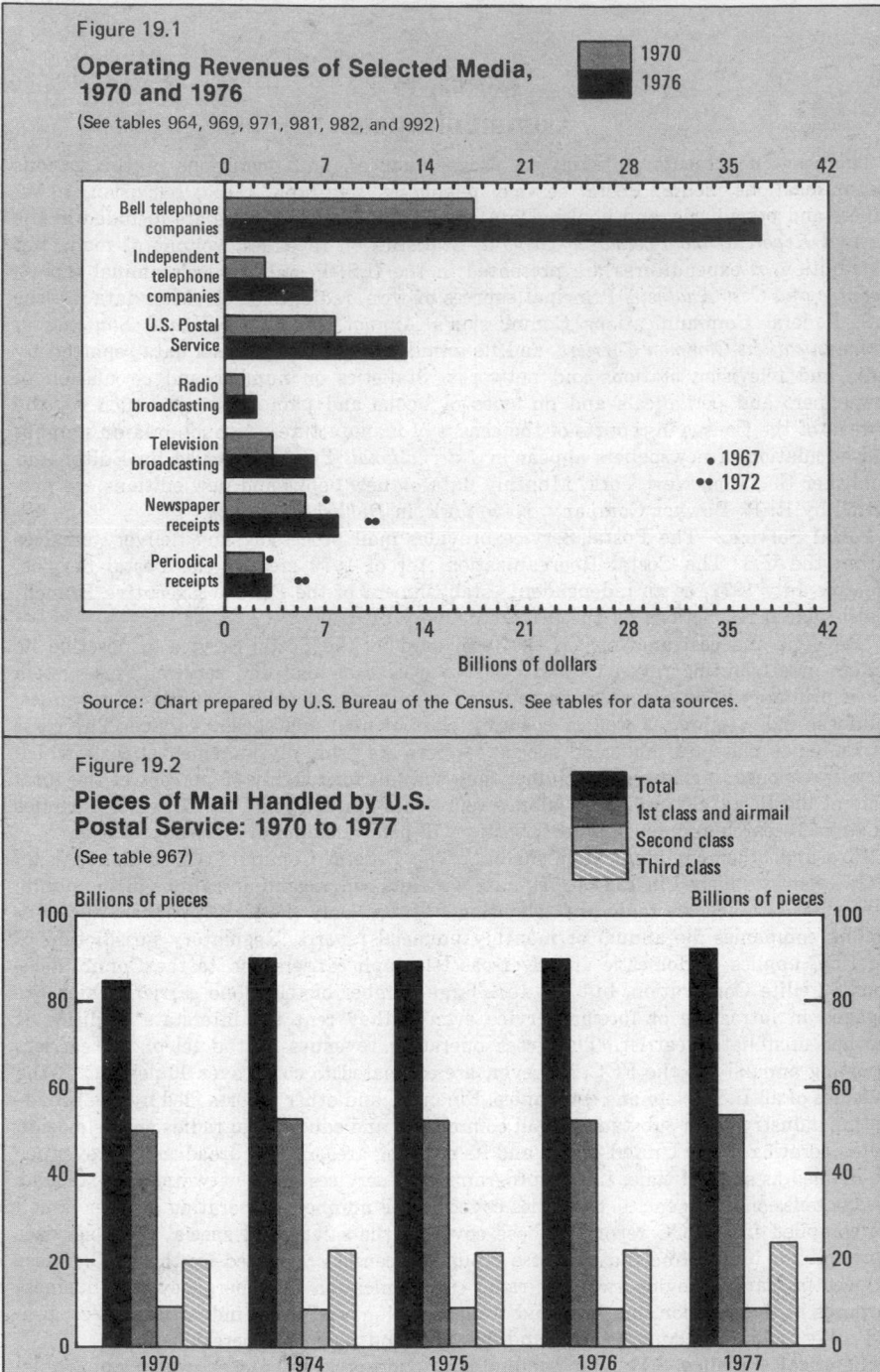

Figure 19.1

Operating Revenues of Selected Media, 1970 and 1976

(See tables 964, 969, 971, 981, 982, and 992)

1970
1976

Bell telephone companies
Independent telephone companies
U.S. Postal Service
Radio broadcasting
Television broadcasting
Newspaper receipts
Periodical receipts

• 1967
•• 1972

Billions of dollars

Source: Chart prepared by U.S. Bureau of the Census. See tables for data sources.

Figure 19.2

Pieces of Mail Handled by U.S. Postal Service: 1970 to 1977

(See table 967)

Total
1st class and airmail
Second class
Third class

Billions of pieces

1970   1974   1975   1976   1977

Source: Chart prepared by U.S. Bureau of the Census. Data from U.S. Postal Service.

No. 963. U.S. POSTAL SERVICE—SUMMARY: 1900 TO 1977

[For years ending **June 30**, except as noted. Includes Puerto Rico and all outlying areas except Canal Zone. See text, p. 583. See also *Historical Statistics, Colonial Times to 1970*, series R 163–171]

YEAR	Number of post offices	FINANCES [1]			Revenue per capita [3]	Money orders issued, total	Sales of stamps and stamped paper	Postage paid under permit and meter	PIECES OF MAIL HANDLED, est.		
		Revenues	Expenditures [2]	Deficit					Total [4]	First class [5]	Second class [5]
		Mil. dol.	*Mil. dol.*	*Mil. dol.*	*Dol.*	*Mil. dol.*	*Mil. dol.*	*Mil. dol.*	*Bil.*	*Bil.*	*Bil.*
1900	76,688	102	108	5	1.34	256	94	(6)	7.1	(NA)	(NA)
1910	59,580	224	230	6	2.43	638	202	4	14.9	(NA)	(NA)
1920	52,641	437	454	17	4.11	1,356	380	13	(NA)	(NA)	(NA)
1930	49,063	705	804	98	5.75	1,767	575	74	27.9	16.9	5.0
1940	44,024	767	808	41	5.84	2,108	522	177	27.7	15.2	4.6
1950	41,464	1,677	2,223	545	11.14	[7] 5,138	862	678	45.1	24.5	6.3
1955	38,316	2,349	2,712	363	14.33	5,883	999	1,136	55.2	28.7	6.7
1960	35,238	3,277	3,874	597	18.27	5,058	1,245	1,699	63.7	33.2	7.5
1965	33,624	4,483	5,276	793	23.17	4,540	1,528	2,529	71.9	38.1	8.6
1970	32,002	7,702	7,867	165	31.05	4,709	1,936	3,883	84.9	48.6	9.4
1971	31,947	8,751	8,955	204	32.24	4,728	1,999	4,126	87.0	50.0	9.6
1972	31,686	9,347	9,522	175	37.89	4,731	2,371	4,861	87.2	48.9	9.5
1973	31,385	9,913	9,926	13	39.77	4,700	2,399	5,141	89.7	51.0	9.0
1974	31,000	10,857	11,295	438	42.85	5,194	2,504	5,623	90.1	51.6	8.8
1975	30,754	11,590	12,578	988	47.08	5,856	2,819	6,241	89.3	51.4	9.1
1976	30,521	12,747	13,923	1,176	52.21	6,243	3,155	6,883	89.8	52.1	8.9
1976, TQ [8]	30,521	3,402	3,387	[9] 15	14.11	1,639	815	1,895	21.5	12.5	2.1
1977 [10]	30,521	14,622	15,310	688	60.18	5,636	3,658	7,951	92.2	53.7	8.7

NA Not available. [1] After allowance for reimbursements, embossed envelope purchases, indemnity claims, and miscellaneous revenue and expenditure offsets. Through 1950, includes some payments and receipts applicable to services in prior years; beginning 1955, expenditures are shown in year in which obligation was incurred, and revenues in year which gave rise to the earnings, whether collected or accrued. In 1954, the Postal Service began receiving reimbursement for penalty and franked mail, and discontinued payment of subsidies to airlines. Revenues for 1960 include $37.4 million reimbursement from the Treasury General Fund for statutory public services. These and other changes affect comparability of figures. See also footnote 5, table 964. [2] Includes capital expenditures for plant and equipment, and cost of materials and supplies, but no provision for depreciation. Also includes costs of certain services rendered to other agencies without reimbursement but excludes costs of certain services rendered to the Postal Service by other agencies. Beginning 1955, represents obligations incurred; beginning 1905, represents accrued expense including depreciation on fixed assets, reimbursable work for others, and expenses paid by certain other agencies without reimbursement by the Postal Service. [3] Operating revenue only; based on Bureau of the Census estimated total population as of Jan. 1, including Armed Forces abroad. [4] Includes other classes of mail not shown separately; see table 967. [5] For definition, see footnotes 9 and 12, table 965. [6] Service not inaugurated. [7] Includes postal notes issued under act of Congress. [8] Transition quarter, July–Sept. [9] Net income. [10] Year ending Sept. 30.

No. 964. U.S. POSTAL SERVICE REVENUES, BY SOURCE: 1960 TO 1977

[In millions of dollars. For years ending **June 30**, except as noted. Includes Puerto Rico and all outlying areas except Canal Zone. For basis of revenue analysis, see text, p. 583. Minus sign denotes loss]

REVENUE SOURCE	1960	1965	1970	1971	1972	1973	1974	1975	1976	1976, TQ [1]	1977 [2]
Total [3]	[4] 3,277	[4] 4,483	7,702	8,751	9,347	9,913	10,857	11,590	12,747	3,402	14,622
Operating postal revenue [5]	3,270	4,433	6,347	6,665	7,884	8,339	9,008	10,015	11,199	3,027	12,998
Stamps, postal cards, etc	1,245	1,528	1,936	1,999	2,371	2,399	2,504	2,819	3,155	815	3,658
Second-class postage paid in money (pound rates) [6]	86	131	192	191	214	224	259	284	319	94	427
Other postage paid under permit and meter	1,699	2,529	3,883	4,126	4,861	5,141	5,623	6,241	6,883	1,895	7,951
Box rents	29	34	44	49	58	61	63	67	103	25	109
Miscellaneous	[7] 147	154	236	245	325	460	507	556	675	175	748
Money-order revenues	64	57	56	55	55	54	52	53	63	23	105
Government appropriations	–	–	1,355	2,086	1,361	1,486	1,750	1,533	1,645	419	1,712
Percent of total revenue	–	–	17.6	23.8	14.6	15.0	16.1	13.2	12.9	12.3	11.7
Investment income, net	–	–	–	–	102	89	98	37	[8] −97	[8] −44	[8] −88

– Represents zero. [1] Transition quarter, July–Sept. [2] Year ending Sept. 30. [3] Net revenue after refunds of postage. Beginning 1965, includes operating reimbursements. [4] Includes small amounts for Postal Savings System, 1960 and 1965, and reimbursement by U.S. Congress in 1965. [5] The U.S. Postal Service was established July 1, 1971. Revenues prior to that date are those of the Post Office Department. Revenues for 1970 and 1971 have been restated to be consistent with subsequent years. See also footnote 1, table 963. [6] Includes controlled circulation publications [7] Includes $37.4 million appropriated to postal revenues for public services as provided by the Postal Policy Act of 1958. [8] Interest expense on loans exceeded interest income received from investments.

Source of tables 963 and 964: U.S. Postal Service, *Annual Report of the Postmaster General.*

No. 965. POSTAL REVENUES AND COSTS: 1970 TO 1977

[In millions of dollars, except as indicated. For years ending June 30, except as noted. Revenues exclude reimbursements from various sources which are included in revenue data shown in tables 963 and 964. See also *Historical Statistics, Colonial Times to 1970*, series R 172–182]

MAIL AND SERVICE	REVENUES		Per capita revenues [1] (dol.)	ATTRIBUTABLE COSTS [2]			
	Total	Percent of total		Total [3]	Direct labor	Transportation	Overhead
1970	6,477	(X)	31.69	4,143	3,072	572	399
1971	6,796	(X)	32.88	4,492	3,327	588	457
1972	9,358	(X)	44.97	4,761	3,579	533	526
1973	9,840	(X)	46.93	4,903	3,901	465	412
1974	10,857	(X)	51.65	5,420	4,297	495	491
1975	11,590	(X)	55.14	7,012	4,715	732	1,565
1976	12,747	(X)	59.43	10,322	8,651	547	1,124
1976, TQ [4]	3,402	(X)	15.86	(NA)	(NA)	(NA)	(NA)
1977,[5] total	14,622	100.00	67.70	[6] 10,322	[6][7] 8,651	[6] 547	[6][8] 1,124
First-class mail [9]	7,831	53.56	36.26	5,812	4,764	93	956
Airmail [10]	6	.04	.03	110	98	6	7
Priority mail [11]	468	3.20	2.16	184	114	65	5
Second-class publishers' mail [12]	363	2.48	1.68	648	561	30	57
Outside the county	341	2.33	1.45	575	501	29	45
Within the county and fees	22	.15	.10	73	60	1	12
Controlled circulation publications [13]	53	.36	.24	43	38	5	–
Third-class mail [14]	1,748	11.95	8.09	1,490	1,445	44	1
Bulk rate	1,508	10.31	6.98	1,279	1,239	40	–
Single piece rate and fees	240	1.64	1.11	211	206	4	1
Fourth-class mail [15]	769	5.26	3.56	854	694	133	27
Zone rate mail (parcels, catalogs, etc.)	600	4.11	2.78	567	458	92	17
Special fourth-class rate	152	1.04	.70	265	216	40	10
Library rate and fees	16	.11	.08	22	20	2	–
Government mail [16]	611	4.18	2.83	264	168	38	58
International mail [17]	493	3.37	2.28	315	168	133	14
Special services	553	3.78	2.56	587	587	–	–
Other [18]	1,729	11.82	8.00	15	14	1	–

– Represents zero.　NA Not available.　X Not applicable.　[1] Based on Bureau of the Census estimated population as of Jan. 1, including Armed Forces abroad.　[2] Costs which can be demonstrated to vary with changes in volume of a particular class or category of service, or even though fixed, to result from providing one specific class or category of service.　[3] Includes other direct and specific fixed costs not shown separately.　[4] Transition quarter, July–September.　[5] Year ending Sept. 30.　[6] 1976 data.　[7] Short- and longer-run direct and indirect costs. Does not include service-related costs.　[8] Service-related costs.　[9] Items mailed at 1st-class rates and weighing 12 ounces or less. Includes items wholly or partially in writing or typewriting, cards or bills and statements of account, items closed against postal inspection, etc.　[10] Letters and cards weighing 8 ounces or less mailed at airmail rates. Airmail service abolished as of May 1, 1977.　[11] Items otherwise qualified as 1st-class or airmail that exceed 12 ounces and 8 ounces, respectively.　[12] Includes mail paid at other than bulk rates. Publishers' mail includes printed publications periodically issued and mailed at a known post office to paid subscribers. These include regular rate newspapers and magazines, and classroom and nonprofit rate publications. Outside-the-county publications are those mailed to destinations outside the county of publication.　[13] Publications of at least 24 pages and containing at least 25 percent nonadvertising content issued quarterly or more frequently for mainly free distribution. Includes certain trade publications and "shopper" guides.　[14] Items less than 16 ounces in weight not mailed at either 1st- or 2d-class rates.　[15] Items not mailed at 1st-, 2d-, or 3d-class rates, except government and international mail. May include parcel post, catalogs weighing 16 ounces or more, books, films, and records.　[16] Penalty and franked mail.　[17] Mail from U.S. to foreign countries paid at international mail rates.　[18] For revenues, consists of unassignable services; for attributable costs, consists of free mail for blind and handicapped and nonpostal services for other agencies.

Source: U.S. Postal Service, *Revenue and Cost Analysis*, annual.

No. 966. U.S. POSTAL SERVICE RATES FOR LETTERS AND POST CARDS: 1949 TO 1978

[See also *Historical Statistics, Colonial Times to 1970*, series R 188–191]

DATE OF RATE CHANGE	SURFACE MAIL: LETTERS			Surface mail: Postal and post cards	DATE OF RATE CHANGE	DOMESTIC AIRMAIL: LETTERS			Domestic airmail: Postal and post cards
	Each ounce	First ounce	Each added ounce			Each ounce	First ounce	Each added ounce	
1952 (Jan. 1)	3¢	(X)	(X)	2¢	1949 (Jan. 1)	6¢	(X)	(X)	4¢
1958 (Aug. 1)	4¢	(X)	(X)	3¢	1958 (Aug. 1)	7¢	(X)	(X)	5¢
1963 (Jan. 7)	5¢	(X)	(X)	4¢	1963 (Jan. 7)	8¢	(X)	(X)	6¢
1968 (Jan. 7)	6¢	(X)	(X)	5¢					
1971 (May 16)	8¢	(X)	(X)	6¢	1968 (Jan. 7)	10¢	(X)	(X)	8¢
1974 (Mar. 2)	10¢	(X)	(X)	8¢	1971 (May 16)	11¢	(X)	(X)	9¢
1975 (Sept. 14)	(X)	10¢	9¢	7¢	1974 (Mar. 2)	13¢	(X)	(X)	11¢
1975 (Dec. 31) [1]	(X)	13¢	11¢	9¢	1975 (Dec. 31) [2]	(X)	17¢	15¢	14¢
1978 (May 29)	(X)	15¢	13¢	10¢					

X Not applicable.　[1] As of October 11, 1975, surface mail service upgraded to level of airmail.
[2] As of May 1, 1977, airmail service abolished.
Source: U.S. Postal Service, "United States Domestic Postage Rates: Recent History," and unpublished data.

No. 967. U.S. Postal Service—Volume of Mail, by Classes: 1970 to 1977

[For years ending **June 30**, except, beginning 1977, ending **Sept. 30**. Includes Puerto Rico and all outlying areas except Canal Zone. For definition of classes of mail, see footnotes, table 965. See also *Historical Statistics, Colonial Times to 1970*, series R 172–186]

CLASS OF MAIL	PIECES OF MAIL					WEIGHT OF MAIL (lb)				
	1970	1974	1975	1976	1977	1970	1974	1975	1976	1977
Total_____mil__	84,882	90,098	89,266	89,768	92,224	13,281	12,646	12,025	11,750	12,344
Domestic_____mil__	83,986	89,182	88,334	88,835	91,339	13,055	12,412	11,824	11,538	12,128
1st class and airmail_mil__	50,174	52,929	52,482	52,459	53,668	1,636	1,784	1,746	1,804	1,842
Priority mail_____mil__	185	222	207	192	202	371	452	440	435	499
2d class_____mil__	9,352	8,838	9,085	8,899	8,673	3,417	2,933	2,792	2,749	2,911
3d class_____mil__	19,974	22,537	21,867	22,514	24,050	2,032	2,365	2,283	2,334	2,474
4th class_____mil__	977	859	801	759	762	4,786	3,983	3,754	3,323	3,516
Controlled circulation publications_____mil__	562	620	628	612	690	224	242	232	228	267
Penalty_____mil__	2,544	2,844	2,928	2,959	2,962	540	608	527	617	565
Franked and free for blind_____mil__	218	333	336	440	332	49	45	50	49	54
Per capita: [1]										
1st class and airmail____	246	252	247	245	248	(X)	(X)	(X)	(X)	(X)
2d class_____	46	42	43	41	40	(X)	(X)	(X)	(X)	(X)
3d class_____	98	107	103	105	111	(X)	(X)	(X)	(X)	(X)
International__mil__	896	916	932	933	885	226	234	201	212	216

X Not applicable.   [1] Based on estimated total population as of Jan. 1, including Armed Forces abroad.

No. 968. U.S. Postal Service Employees, by Type: 1950 to 1977

[**In thousands**. As of **June 30** except 1977, ending **Sept. 30**. Includes Puerto Rico, and all outlying areas except Canal Zone. See *Historical Statistics, Colonial Times to 1970*, series R 187, for total employees]

ITEM	1950	1955	1960	1965	1970	1972	1973	1974	1975	1976	1977
Total employees_____	501	512	563	596	741	706	701	710	702	679	655
Regular_____	364	367	409	447	549	571	549	565	559	543	528
Postmasters_____	[1]45	[1]42	35	33	30	31	29	30	30	29	29
Office supvsr. and tech. personnel_____	169	175	27	30	37	38	34	37	37	39	36
Office clerks and mail handlers [2]_____			172	188	243	250	239	243	239	235	228
City carriers and vehicle drivers_____	90	91	110	133	165	175	172	171	167	161	157
Rural carriers_____	33	32	31	31	31	31	30	31	31	31	31
Other_____	27	26	34	32	42	45	45	51	55	48	47
Substitute (part-time)_____	137	145	154	148	193	136	152	146	143	136	127
Pieces of mail per employee, average___	90	108	113	121	115	123	128	127	127	132	141

[1] Includes assistant postmasters: 3,540 in 1950, and 3,917 in 1955.   [2] Includes mobile unit employees.
Source of tables 967 and 968: U.S. Postal Service, *Annual Report of the Postmaster General*.

No. 969. Bell Telephone Companies—Summary: 1950 to 1977

[As of **Dec. 31** or for **calendar year**, as applicable. Comprises American Telephone and Telegraph Company and its principal telephone subsidiaries, plus Southern New England and Cincinnati and Suburban Bell Telephone Companies. See also *Historical Statistics, Colonial Times to 1970*, series R 17–30]

ITEM	1950	1960	1965	1970	1973	1974	1975	1976	1977
Central offices, number [1]_____	8,656	11,212	13,425	15,135	16,483	16,872	17,232	17,512	17,763
Miles of—Wire_____mil__	144	308	423	602	752	800	832	871	910
Coaxial tube_____1,000__	63	97	169	287	326	331	333	338	337
Telephone grade carrier channel [2]_____mil__	14	76	167	414	569	608	645	672	720
Microwave radio relay [3]__1,000__	8	298	728	1,181	1,343	1,356	1,389	1,370	1,418
Book value of plant (cost)_mil. dol__	10,375	24,722	36,229	56,171	75,479	82,683	89,194	95,798	103,576
Depreciation reserves [4]___mil. dol__	2,905	5,402	7,794	12,610	15,791	16,582	17,578	18,673	19,894
Operating revenues [5]_____mil. dol__	3,342	8,111	11,320	17,369	24,072	26,761	29,591	33,518	37,260
Local exchange_____mil. dol__	1,997	4,665	6,114	8,685	11,712	13,131	14,368	15,977	17,482
Toll_____mil. dol__	1,208	3,058	4,706	8,042	11,524	12,729	14,224	16,399	18,468
Operating expenses [6]_____mil. dol__	2,653	5,586	7,857	12,867	17,805	19,814	22,155	24,802	27,674
Net income_____mil. dol__	370	1,279	1,887	2,303	3,125	3,306	3,292	3,999	4,749
Dividends declared [7]_____mil. dol__	263	770	1,144	1,508	1,861	2,131	2,158	2,562	2,872
Employees, number_____1,000__	535	595	627	793	818	812	789	778	785
Wages and salaries_____mil. dol__	1,742	3,283	4,169	6,641	9,282	10,209	11,121	12,163	13,428

[1] 1950 and 1960 not fully comparable with later years.   [2] Message circuits added to existing wire mileage, but not requiring additional wire. Also includes microwave radio.   [3] Broadband, 1-way channel.   [4] Includes amortization reserves.   [5] Includes miscellaneous and uncollectable, not shown separately.
[6] Includes operating taxes other than Federal income tax.   [7] Excludes intercompany dividends.
Source: American Telephone and Telegraph Company, New York, N.Y., compiled from reports of Bell System and Southern New England and Cincinnati and Suburban Bell Companies.

No. 970. Telephone and Telegraph Systems: 1950 to 1976

[Covers principal carriers filing annual reports with Federal Communications Commission. See *Historical Statistics, Colonial Times to 1970,* series R 46–70 and R 75–88, for data on telegraph systems]

ITEM	1950	1955	1960	1965	1970	1972	1973	1974	1975	1976
Domestic telephone: [1]										
Carriers_____number__	71	53	52	54	56	61	64	66	62	62
Telephones [2]_____mil__	39	50	66	82	105	116	121	126	130	135
Miles of wire_____mil__	147	205	316	436	628	728	788	838	872	913
Book cost of plant_____bil. dol__	10.7	16.2	25.7	38.0	59.9	73.3	81.0	88.6	95.5	103.1
Depreciation reserves [3]_____bil. dol__	3.0	4.1	5.6	8.1	13.2	15.6	16.8	17.7	18.8	20.2
Ratio to book cost_____percent__	27.8	25.3	21.7	21.4	22.1	21.2	20.7	20.0	19.7	19.6
Capital stock_____bil. dol__	3.2	6.0	8.4	10.0	10.8	11.3	11.5	11.7	12.4	12.7
Operating revenues_____bil. dol__	3.4	5.6	8.4	11.8	18.2	22.4	25.5	28.3	31.3	35.6
Operating expenses [4]_____bil. dol__	2.5	3.7	5.0	7.1	11.7	14.6	16.2	18.0	20.2	22.7
Net operating income [5]_____bil. dol__	.5	.8	1.4	2.1	3.1	3.9	4.6	5.2	5.6	6.5
Net income_____bil. dol__	.4	.7	1.3	1.9	2.3	2.7	3.2	3.5	3.6	4.3
Employees_____1,000__	565	649	627	655	839	849	874	865	840	832
Compensation of employees_____bil. dol__	1.8	2.7	3.4	4.3	7.0	8.8	9.8	10.7	11.7	12.4
Overseas telephone:										
Number of overseas calls_____mil__	.7	1.2	3.3	7.5	23.4	36.7	44.7	53.7	62.2	75.8
Revenue from overseas calls_____mil. dol__	9	16	42	101	252	364	368	496	562	664
Ocean cable systems_____number__	1	1	5	11	13	13	13	14	14	15
Communications satellites_____number__	–	–	–	1	4	4	5	5	5	5
Overseas TV transmission [6]_____hours__	–	–	–	33	445	724	801	692	789	(NA)
Domestic telegraph:										
Carriers_____number__	1	1	1	1	1	1	1	1	1	1
Revenue messages transmitted_____mil__	179	154	124	94	70	40	37	42	42	43
Message revenues [7]_____mil. dol__	152	189	190	192	234	181	184	192	197	202
Total operating revenues_____mil. dol__	178	229	262	306	402	432	455	484	505	528
Operating revenue deductions____mil. dol__	167	206	247	282	368	377	401	414	435	453
Operating income [8]_____mil. dol__	9	13	11	24	34	55	54	69	70	74
Teletypewriter messages_____mil__	15	23	33	47	46	47	57	52	54	53
Overseas telegraph: [9]										
Carriers_____number__	11	10	9	6	6	6	6	6	6	6
Revenue messages transmitted_____mil__	23	26	28	29	32	29	30	29	26	21
Message revenues [7]_____mil. dol__	42	50	71	78	124	141	172	213	217	238
Total operating revenues_____mil. dol__	50	68	87	107	194	228	263	299	316	344
Operating revenue deductions____mil. dol__	45	58	77	87	156	180	206	224	245	265
Operating income [7]_____mil. dol__	4	3	6	14	26	36	44	49	48	55

– Represents zero.　　NA Not available.　　[1] Includes Puerto Rico and, beginning 1965, Virgin Islands. Excludes intercompany duplications. Gross operating revenues of carriers reporting in 1972 estimated at 90 percent of all carriers.　　[2] Includes company, service, and private.　　[3] Includes amortization reserves.　　[4] Excludes taxes.　　[5] After tax deductions.　　[6] Includes overseas telegraph carriers. Service began July 1965.　　[7] Includes telex service; for domestic telegraph, excludes TWX.　　[8] After Federal income taxes.　　[9] Beginning 1965, excludes South American and most Caribbean operations of All America Cables and Radio, Inc.

Source: U.S. Federal Communications Commission, *Statistics of Communications Common Carriers,* annual, and unpublished data.

No. 971. Independent Telephone Companies—Summary: 1950 to 1976

[As of Dec. 31 or calendar year, as applicable. See also *Historical Statistics, Colonial Times to 1970,* series R 31–45]

ITEM	1950	1955	1960	1965	1970	1973	1974	1975	1976
All companies: [1]									
Number_____	5,541	4,713	3,299	2,421	1,841	1,695	1,641	1,618	1,590
Telephones_____1,000__	6,338	8,461	11,428	15,027	20,312	24,351	25,826	26,823	28,209
Total telephone plant____mil. dol__	1,096	2,043	4,019	6,826	12,390	17,419	19,600	21,200	23,000
Operating revenues_____mil. dol__	317	590	1,020	1,670	2,953	4,317	4,920	5,500	6,300
Reporting companies: [2]									
Number_____	379	406	550	669	684	701	698	731	763
Percent of all independent companies' telephones represented___	77.2	79.8	85.0	89.6	92.9	93.5	94.3	95.3	95.8
Telephones_____1,000__	4,922	6,750	9,718	13,648	19,182	23,167	24,355	25,548	27,029
Telephone plant in service.mil. dol__	878	1,656	3,396	6,056	11,175	15,912	17,676	19,520	21,323
Depreciation reserves_____mil. dol__	203	326	600	1,168	2,203	3,166	3,599	4,120	4,745
Operating revenues_____mil. dol__	270	503	1,040	1,530	2,791	4,188	4,714	5,294	6,072
Operating expenses [3]____mil. dol__	211	354	630	1,040	1,953	2,881	3,254	3,639	4,159
Net income_____mil. dol__	29	67	117	225	356	573	641	711	837
Employees_____1,000__	63	72	85	101	142	157	157	152	154
Wages and salaries_____mil. dol__	147	224	359	537	1,001	1,438	1,608	1,737	1,949

[1] All telephone companies independent of Bell System.　　[2] Comprises only companies submitting operating information to source cited below.　　[3] Excludes Federal income tax.

Source: United States Independent Telephone Association, Washington, D.C., *Statistics of the Independent Telephone Industry,* annual. (Copyright.)

No. 972. Telephones, Calls, and Rates: 1950 to 1977

[See also *Historical Statistics, Colonial Times to 1970*, series R 1-16]

ITEM	1950	1960	1965	1970	1972	1973	1974	1975	1976	1977
Telephones, Dec. 31 ____mil__	43	74	94	120	132	138	144	149	155	162
Total per 1,000 population____	281	408	478	584	628	655	677	695	718	744
Bell companies [1] ____mil__	37	63	79	100	109	114	118	122	127	132
Independent companies__mil__	6	11	15	20	23	24	26	27	28	30
Business_____mil__	[2] 13	21	26	33	36	37	39	39	41	42
Residence_____mil__	[2] 30	54	68	87	96	101	105	110	114	120
Households with telephone [3] percent__	[2] 62	79	85	91	92	94	94	95	95	96
Average daily conversations:										
Bell companies [1] [4] _____mil__	145	225	287	379	421	444	470	481	498	519
Local_____mil__	139	215	273	356	394	414	438	448	462	479
Long distance_____mil__	6	10	14	23	27	30	32	33	36	40
Independent companies [4]___mil__	31	60	80	107	125	132	143	146	146	160
Local_____mil__	30	58	77	103	119	125	136	137	137	150
Long distance_____mil__	1	2	3	4	6	7	7	9	9	10
Toll rates in effect, Dec. 31, from New York City to: [5]										
Philadelphia_____dol__	.45	.50	.50	.50	.55	.60	.60	.90	.99	1.29
Chicago_____dol__	1.55	1.45	1.40	1.05	1.05	1.15	1.15	1.20	1.50	1.50
Denver_____dol__	2.20	1.80	1.70	1.25	1.25	1.35	1.35	1.30	1.56	1.56
San Francisco_____dol__	2.50	2.25	2.00	1.35	1.35	1.45	1.45	1.36	1.62	1.62

[1] See headnote, table 969.   [2] Excludes Alaska and Hawaii.   [3] See footnote 2, table 975.   [4] Includes messages originating in independent company areas routed in part over Bell facilities.   [5] Source: Federal Communications Commission, tariff releases. Rates for dialing station-to-station, daytime, 3-minute call.

Source: Except as noted, American Telephone and Telegraph Company, New York, N.Y., unpublished data.

No. 973. Communication Rates Between Selected Cities: 1946 to 1978

[See also *Historical Statistics, Colonial Times to 1970*, series R 71-74 and R 89-92]

EFFECTIVE DATE	BETWEEN NEW YORK CITY AND—				EFFECTIVE DATE	BETWEEN NEW YORK CITY AND—			
	Philadelphia	Chicago	Denver	San Francisco		London	Cairo	Tokyo	Buenos Aires
TELEGRAPH RATES [1]					**CABLE AND RADIO TELEGRAPH RATES** [3]				
1960, Oct. 17_____	1.10	1.45	1.90	1.90					
1966, Jan. 1_____	1.27	1.70	2.23	2.23	1950, July 1_____	.19	.30	.30	.27
1968, Nov. 1_____	2.25	2.25	2.25	2.25	1958, Aug. 1_____	.21	.34	.34	.31
1970, Mar. 1_____	2.75	2.75	2.75	2.75	1966, Apr. 12_____	.23	.34	.34	.31
1971, July 4_____	3.75	3.75	3.75	3.75	In effect Jan. 1, 1978__	.23	.34	.34	.31
1974, Dec. 2-Jan. 1, 1978_	4.75	4.75	4.75	4.75					
TWX RATES [2]					**TELEPHONE RATES** [4]				
					1946_____	12.00	12.00	12.00	12.00
1960, Feb. 7_____	.45	1.15	1.65	1.75	1970, Mar. 1_____	9.60	12.00	12.00	12.00
1966, Sept. 1_____	.25	.45	.55	.60	In effect Jan. 1, 1978__	9.60	12.00	12.00	12.00
1970, Feb. 1-Jan. 1, 1978_	.25	.50	.65	.70					

[1] Beginning Sept. 1, 1951, minimum charge for 15 text words or less; prior to that, for 10 text words or less.
[2] Prior to September 1966, rates for 3 minutes or less, 2-way; thereafter, for each minute or fraction thereof.
[3] Per plain language telegraph-word including address and signature.   [4] For person-to-person, 3-minute call.
Source: U.S. Federal Communications Commission, tariff releases.

No. 974. REA and Rural Telephone Bank Program—Summary: 1950 to 1977

ITEM	1950	1960	1965	1970	1973	1974	1975	1976	1977
Loans and guarantees approved, Dec. 31: [1]									
Borrowers_____	61	727	845	862	892	905	921	939	930
REA amount_____mil. dol__	19	737	1,200	1,816	2,217	2,357	2,576	2,851	3,043
Guaranteed amount_____mil. dol__	–	–	–	–	–	33	237	394	394
Rural telephone bank amount__mil. dol__	–	–	–	–	319	474	618	768	979
Route miles of line,[2] Dec. 31_____1,000__	21	378	515	575	627	645	701	750	770
Subscribers, Dec. 31_____1,000__	75	1,467	2,066	2,506	2,935	3,100	3,561	3,907	4,119
Telephones in service_____1,000__	(NA)	1,280	2,046	2,989	3,714	4,084	4,355	4,796	[3] 5,399
Total operating revenues_____mil. dol__	(NA)	94	187	363	555	660	753	899	[3] 1,087
Total telephone plant_____mil. dol__	(NA)	635	1,168	2,085	2,964	3,422	3,850	4,374	[3] 5,074
Employees_____1,000__	(NA)	9.7	11.6	15.4	17.4	19.6	20.0	21.2	[3] 23.5

– Represents zero.   NA Not available.
[1] Cumulative net loans (recisions deducted).   [2] Line in service.   [3] Preliminary.
Source: U.S. Rural Electrification Administration, *Annual Statistical Report—Rural Telephone Borrowers*.

No. 975. Telephones in Use, by States: 1965 to 1976

[As of Dec. 31]

STATE	1965 Total (1,000)	1965 Percent owned by Bell companies¹	1965 Percent of households with telephones²	1970 Total (1,000)	1970 Percent owned by Bell companies¹	1970 Percent of households with telephones²	1976 Total (1,000)	1976 Percent owned by Bell companies¹	1976 Per 100 population	1976 Percent of households with telephones²	Residence (1,000)	Business (1,000)
U.S.	93,659	84	85	120,155	83	92	155,173	82	72	95	114,491	40,682
Ala.	1,197	86	70	1,563	84	80	2,183	84	59	86	1,666	518
Alaska	64	–	(NA)	85	–	(NA)	214	–	55	81	122	93
Ariz.	645	98	70	956	97	82	1,517	96	66	91	1,097	420
Ark.	620	74	63	859	73	77	1,257	71	60	87	951	306
Calif.	10,596	80	89	13,306	79	94	17,178	78	79	97	12,321	4,857
Colo.	1,023	98	86	1,374	98	93	1,923	98	74	95	1,357	565
Conn.	1,622	100	94	2,061	99	100	2,431	99	78	101	1,809	622
Del.	281	100	89	380	100	97	471	100	81	100	346	125
D.C.	757	100	91	878	100	100	1,024	100	147	97	503	521
Fla.	2,796	68	79	4,142	68	88	6,475	65	76	94	4,783	1,693
Ga.	1,688	86	73	2,413	86	83	3,533	86	71	91	2,642	892
Hawaii	323	–	(NA)	424	–	(NA)	597	–	67	102	394	203
Idaho	277	79	79	358	80	87	571	80	68	95	421	150
Ill.	5,823	84	89	7,110	83	94	8,999	83	80	97	6,674	2,325
Ind.	2,263	65	88	2,905	66	90	3,703	65	70	93	2,859	844
Iowa	1,328	69	95	1,625	70	95	2,065	69	72	97	1,577	488
Kans.	1,040	83	87	1,301	83	93	1,702	84	73	93	1,281	421
Ky.	1,078	74	70	1,435	73	80	2,020	72	59	88	1,533	487
La.	1,353	95	76	1,781	95	87	2,451	94	63	93	1,859	591
Maine	389	91	82	490	90	93	703	89	65	99	543	160
Md.	1,805	100	90	2,482	99	93	3,117	100	75	98	2,333	784
Mass.	2,871	100	95	3,523	99	98	4,145	100	71	97	3,012	1,133
Mich.	4,065	90	93	5,135	89	95	6,525	88	72	99	4,977	1,548
Minn.	1,730	81	94	2,248	82	97	2,870	80	72	99	2,139	731
Miss.	620	96	56	891	95	71	1,328	95	56	83	1,029	299
Mo.	2,178	83	85	2,753	83	91	3,404	80	71	94	2,541	863
Mont.	297	84	80	357	84	89	507	83	67	93	372	136
Nebr.	711	58	88	884	58	96	1,161	58	74	99	871	290
Nev.	224	41	69	333	35	84	564	32	91	96	375	189
N.H.	296	95	88	425	95	99	598	95	72	104	456	142
N.J.	3,750	98	91	4,786	98	99	5,888	98	80	102	4,391	1,497
N. Mex.	394	86	68	494	87	80	711	87	60	86	498	214
N.Y.	10,492	93	91	12,416	92	97	13,144	91	73	94	9,344	3,800
N.C.	1,625	54	69	2,385	52	82	3,442	53	63	91	2,629	813
N. Dak.	263	69	86	321	70	94	457	72	71	99	339	119
Ohio	5,005	78	90	6,201	77	94	7,442	75	70	97	5,626	1,816
Okla.	1,122	89	79	1,469	88	88	1,999	87	72	93	1,469	529
Oreg.	920	79	87	1,190	78	89	1,639	74	70	91	1,191	448
Pa.	6,033	84	90	7,476	83	95	9,003	82	76	97	6,846	2,156
R.I.	432	100	90	531	100	96	662	100	72	100	499	163
S.C.	796	75	68	1,168	74	80	1,773	73	62	88	1,331	442
S. Dak.	278	81	82	335	81	91	457	79	66	93	343	114
Tenn.	1,436	85	75	1,947	84	84	2,772	84	65	91	2,096	675
Texas	4,556	84	75	6,329	84	86	8,970	83	71	92	6,479	2,491
Utah	468	96	89	596	96	93	879	97	71	97	645	234
Vt.	169	88	89	236	87	97	314	87	66	102	227	86
Va.	1,788	80	77	2,476	80	86	3,372	78	67	95	2,496	875
Wash.	1,494	79	89	1,996	77	91	2,603	75	72	95	1,910	693
W. Va.	626	88	74	763	87	82	984	87	54	87	749	235
Wis.	1,890	74	91	2,370	72	95	3,131	71	68	98	2,331	800
Wyo.	162	94	79	196	94	89	295	94	74	91	209	86

– Represents zero.   NA   Not available.

¹ Includes 456,600 service telephones (non-company telephones for which switching service is provided) in 1965, 463,200 in 1970, and 392,926 in 1976.

² Households with service are sum of residence main, apartment house private branch exchange and residence service main telephones, and other residence private branch exchange systems. There tends to be a slight over-statement of the proportion of households with telephone service.

Source: U.S. Federal Communications Commission, *Statistics of Communications Common Carriers*, annual.

No. 976. Broadcast and Nonbroadcast Stations Authorized and Operators Licensed, by Class: 1975 to 1977

[1975 as of June 30; thereafter, as of Sept. 30. Includes Puerto Rico and Virgin Islands. See also *Historical Statistics, Colonial Times to 1970*, series R 140–148]

CLASS	1975	1976	1977	CLASS	1975	1976	1977
STATIONS AUTHORIZED (1,000)				STATIONS AUTHORIZED—Con. (Number)			
Safety and special radio services [1]	2,602.4	6,763.5	13,041.1	Broadcast services [3]	32,172	34,700	36,518
Amateur and disaster	276.8	292.8	340.9	Commercial AM	4,488	4,525	4,555
Citizens	1,530.8	5,613.6	11,653.4	Commercial TV	759	764	774
Aviation	184.4	188.5	207.8	Educational TV	256	268	265
Aircraft	154.7	158.2	176.9	TV translator	3,389	3,545	3,817
Aeronautical and fixed	7.4	7.5	7.7	Auxiliary TV	3,032	3,631	4,182
Civil air patrol	19.6	20.0	20.1	Experimental TV	3	3	2
Other	2.7	2.9	3.0	UHF signal booster	9	9	9
Industrial	244.6	277.1	357.9	Aural, studio-transmitter-			
Power	17.5	18.6	20.9	link, intercity relay	1,008	1,176	1,447
Business	155.2	179.2	248.4	Commercial FM	2,847	2,947	3,101
Petroleum	11.8	13.1	14.6	Educational FM	850	913	1,000
Forest products	4.3	4.5	5.0	International	4	4	4
Special industrial	40.7	45.4	57.6	Remote pickup	14,959	16,263	16,582
Other	15.1	16.2	11.1	Instructional TV, fixed	187	182	180
				Other	381	470	600
Land transportation	22.6	23.0	25.4	Common carrier services	27,304	36,317	43,035
Railroad	8.9	8.7	9.7	Point-to-point microwave	8,133	8,509	8,641
Taxicab	3.7	3.7	4.4	Multipoint distribution serv	69	95	158
Interurban property	2.2	2.2	2.8	Local TV transmission	64	67	66
Other	7.9	8.4	8.3	Rural radio	1,218	1,256	1,450
				Developmental	(NA)	(NA)	190
Marine	250.7	262.6	315.0	Public land mobile [1]	17,783	26,345	32,483
Ship	243.6	254.7	305.9	International control, fixed	25	25	8
Alaskan	2.1	2.1	2.2	Satellite earth stations	7	9	10
Coastal and other	5.0	5.8	6.9	Satellites in orbit	5	5	5
				Other	(NA)	6	24
Public safety	92.6	105.9	127.2				
Police	28.8	33.4	39.7	Experimental services	1,349	1,110	1,332
Fire	14.0	15.7	20.2	Cable television relay			
Forestry conservation	6.2	6.6	7.2	service [3]	877	943	1,094
Highway maintenance	7.7	8.4	9.5	RADIO OPERATORS			
Special emergency	12.4	14.3	20.9				
Other	23.5	27.5	29.5	Total _____ 1,000	4,222	4,386	4,649
				Commercial _____ 1,000	3,965	4,096	4,321
Operational fixed services [2]	(NA)	(NA)	13.6	Amateur _____ 1,000	257	290	329

NA Not available.
[1] Each license, construction permit, or combination construction permit and license is counted as one station; therefore, a station might include a transmitter and many mobile units. [2] Includes microwave operations. Prior to 1977, data not separable from other class categories. [3] Stations licensed or holding construction permits.
Source: U.S. Federal Communications Commission, *Annual Report.*

No. 977. Commercial Broadcast Stations, Number and Revenues: 1950 to 1976

[Covers only reporting stations. As of Dec. 31. Includes Puerto Rico and Virgin Islands. Total broadcast revenues are total time sales of all networks and stations, less commissions to agencies and plus incidental revenues (e.g., sale of talent and program material). See also *Historical Statistics, Colonial Times to 1970*, series R 111–112 and R 128–129]

STATION	1950	1955	1960	1965	1970	1971	1972	1973	1974	1975	1976
Stations	2,336	3,179	4,218	4,867	5,584	5,708	5,826	5,936	6,136	6,228	6,339
Revenues ____ mil. dol	550	1,198	1,866	2,757	3,945	4,008	4,586	4,967	5,384	5,819	7,218
AM and AM-FM:											
Stations	2,143	2,704	3,470	3,941	4,209	4,252	4,271	4,267	4,367	4,355	4,363
Revenues [1] ____ mil. dol	443	452	592	777	1,077	1,176	1,292	1,348	1,410	1,480	1,687
FM affiliates of AM stations:											
Stations	(NA)	(NA)	(NA)	(NA)	225	241	275	361	397	477	562
Revenues ____ mil. dol	(NA)	(NA)	(NA)	(NA)	19	26	38	58	65	102	152
FM independents:											
Stations	86	38	218	338	464	527	590	616	678	703	713
Revenues ____ mil. dol	1	1	6	16	41	55	77	96	128	143	180
TV:											
Stations	107	437	530	588	686	688	690	692	694	693	701
Revenues [2] ____ mil. dol	106	745	1,269	1,965	2,808	2,750	3,179	3,465	3,782	4,094	5,199

NA Not available.
[1] Prior to 1960, includes 4 national networks and 3 regional networks; 1960–1965, includes 4 national networks; thereafter, includes 7 national networks (CBS, MBS, NBC, and ABC's 3 AM and 1 FM). [2] Includes 4 networks through Sept. 15, 1955; 3 thereafter.
Source: U.S. Federal Communications Commission, *AM-FM Broadcast Financial Data*, annual, and *TV Broadcast Financial Data*, annual.

No. 978. COMMERCIAL BROADCAST STATIONS—STATES AND OTHER AREAS: 1970 AND 1977

[Represents licenses issued as of Jan. 1]

STATE	1970 AM	1970 FM	1970 TV	1977 AM	1977 FM	1977 TV	STATE	1970 AM	1970 FM	1970 TV	1977 AM	1977 FM	1977 TV
Total	4,256	2,044	683	4,474	3,007	725	Mont	41	7	10	45	21	12
U.S.	4,209	2,021	672	4,413	2,966	714	Nebr	47	15	14	48	31	14
Ala	134	51	15	138	75	17	Nev	20	8	7	22	12	7
Alaska	18	3	7	22	11	7	N.H.	25	10	3	28	17	1
Ariz	59	15	11	62	32	11	N.J.	32	26	4	38	35	5
Ark	84	35	7	86	56	8	N. Mex	55	19	7	56	29	9
Calif	231	145	50	231	198	56	N.Y.	157	91	27	160	121	30
Colo	67	26	11	71	50	11	N.C.	195	71	19	209	87	18
Conn	38	20	5	38	25	5	N. Dak	27	11	12	26	11	11
Del	10	4	–	10	8	–	Ohio	116	108	29	123	134	24
D.C.	6	6	6	7	10	5	Okla	64	35	9	67	52	10
Fla	191	88	24	202	114	31	Oreg	80	17	12	80	33	12
							Pa	169	109	23	177	125	25
Ga	169	57	15	180	90	18	R.I.	15	7	2	15	7	2
Hawaii	25	4	10	25	7	10	S.C.	101	37	11	108	56	11
Idaho	42	7	7	43	19	8	S. Dak	29	6	10	33	18	11
Ill	121	92	24	124	131	22	Tenn	139	61	16	155	75	18
Ind	83	72	17	86	100	20	Tex	285	122	55	288	183	55
Iowa	73	35	12	76	71	14	Utah	31	10	3	34	19	3
Kans	57	24	12	59	43	12	Vt	18	4	2	19	15	2
Ky	102	60	10	119	85	11							
La	90	41	15	95	63	15	Va	123	53	12	137	76	14
Maine	36	13	7	37	31	7	Wash	96	39	13	92	48	14
							W. Va	58	23	9	62	31	9
Md	52	31	5	50	36	6	Wis	97	74	17	100	95	17
Mass	62	38	11	65	44	12	Wyo	29	1	3	30	11	5
Mich	124	76	20	127	116	24	**Other areas**	47	23	11	61	41	11
Minn	83	39	12	91	67	13	P. Rico	43	21	8	53	35	8
Miss	99	34	9	106	69	10	Guam	1	1	1	3	2	1
Mo	104	41	21	111	73	22	Virgin Is	3	1	2	4	4	2

– Represents zero.

Source: U.S. Federal Communications Commission, *AM-FM Broadcast Financial Data*, annual; *TV Broadcast Financial Data*, annual; and unpublished data.

No. 979. PUBLIC TELEVISION STATIONS: 1961 TO 1976

[General programing is directed at the general community. Instructional programing is directed at students in the classroom or otherwise in the general context of formal education]

ITEM	1961	1964	1966	1968	1970	1972	1974	1976
Stations	56	88	115	[1] 153	[1] 190	220	[2] 238	[3] 253
Total weekly broadcast hours	2,186	3,715	5,688	8,534	12,217	15,587	18,321	22,096
General programs	1,431	1,992	3,248	4,671	7,697	7,904	10,868	14,329
Percent of total hours	65.5	54.0	57.5	54.7	63.0	50.7	59.3	64.8
Instructional programs	755	1,723	2,440	3,863	4,520	7,683	[4] 7,453	[5] 7,766
Percent of total hours	34.5	46.0	42.5	45.3	37.0	49.3	40.7	35.1
Average weekly broadcast hours per station	39.0	42.3	49.5	56.1	65.3	70.9	80.7	90.9
General programing	25.6	22.6	28.2	30.7	41.1	36.0	47.9	59.0
Instructional programing	13.8	19.6	21.2	25.4	24.2	34.9	[6] 32.8	[5] 31.9

[1] 152 stations reported in 1968 and 187 in 1970; details include data for reporting stations only. [2] Includes data for 227 stations only, representing 147 primary broadcasters; does not include secondary broadcasters. [3] Includes data for 243 stations only, representing 151 primary broadcasters. [4] Includes 3,766 hours of CTW (children's TV workshop) broadcasting, representing 20.6 percent of total weekly broadcasting hours. [5] Includes all material from CTW. [6] Includes 16.6 hours of CTW broadcasting.

Source: Through 1970, National Instructional Television Center, Bloomington, Ind., *One Week of Educational Television, 1970* (copyright); 1972, Corporation for Public Broadcasting, Washington, D.C., *One Week of Public TV, April 1972*; and unpublished data.

No. 980. CABLE TELEVISION—SYSTEMS AND SUBSCRIBERS: 1952 TO 1977

YEAR (As of Jan. 1)	Systems	Households subscribing (1,000)	YEAR (As of Jan. 1)	Systems	Households subscribing (1,000)	SUBSCRIBER SIZE-GROUP [1]	Systems, 1977 (Sept. 1)
1952	70	14	1971	2,639	5,300	20,000 and over	85
1955	400	150	1972	2,841	6,000	10,000–19,999	197
1960	640	650	1973	2,991	7,300	5,000–9,999	368
1965	1,325	1,275	1974	3,158	8,700	3,500–4,999	263
1967	1,770	2,100	1975	3,506	9,800	1,000–3,499	1,197
1968	2,000	2,800	1976	3,681	10,800	250–999	1,284
1969	2,260	3,600	1977	3,832	11,900	Less than 249	495
1970	2,490	4,500					

[1] Excludes 22 systems not available by size-group.

Source: Television Digest, Inc., Washington, D.C., *Television Factbook*, annual. (Copyright.)

No. 981. Television Broadcast Industry Finances: 1960 to 1976

[Includes Puerto Rico and Virgin Islands. See also headnote, table 977, and *Historical Statistics, Colonial Times to 1970*, series R 123–139]

ITEM	1960	1965	1970	1971	1972	1973	1974	1975	1976
Number of networks, Dec. 31	3	3	3	3	3	3	3	3	3
Stations reporting, Dec. 31	530	588	686	688	690	692	694	693	701
VHF	454	488	506	506	508	511	514	513	511
UHF	76	100	180	182	182	181	180	180	190
FINANCES (mil. dol.)									
Broadcast revenues, gross	1,504	2,328	3,337	3,264	3,770	4,107	4,479	4,860	6,191
Sales to advertisers	1,456	2,266	3,243	3,179	3,675	4,002	4,354	4,722	6,030
Network sales	747	1,142	1,551	1,490	1,688	1,840	2,005	2,157	2,675
National non-network sales	469	796	1,103	1,023	1,177	1,230	1,336	1,449	1,923
Local sales	240	328	589	666	810	932	1,012	1,116	1,432
Nonadvertising revenues	48	62	94	85	95	105	125	138	161
Broadcast revenues, net	1,269	1,965	2,808	2,750	3,179	3,465	3,776	4,094	5,198
3 networks	641	1,024	1,457	1,379	1,598	1,758	1,921	2,069	2,604
Other stations	628	941	1,351	1,371	1,581	1,707	1,855	2,025	2,594
Broadcast expenses of networks and stations	1,025	1,517	2,354	2,361	2,627	2,811	3,039	3,314	3,948
3 networks	546	862	1,290	1,234	1,385	1,470	1,590	1,755	2,150
Other stations	479	655	1,065	1,127	1,242	1,341	1,449	1,559	1,798
Broadcast income [1]	244	448	454	389	552	653	737	780	1,250
3 networks [2]	95	162	167	145	213	288	331	314	455
Other stations	149	286	286	244	339	365	406	466	796

[1] Before Federal income tax.   [2] Includes owned and operated stations.
Source: U.S. Federal Communications Commission, *TV Broadcast Financial Data*, annual.

No. 982. Radio Broadcast Industry Finances: 1960 to 1976

[Includes Puerto Rico and Virgin Islands. Minus sign (−) denotes loss. See also headnote, table 977, and *Historical Statistics, Colonial Times to 1970*, series R 106–122]

ITEM	1960	1965	1970	1971	1972	1973	1974	1975	1976
Number of networks, Dec. 31	4	4	7	7	7	7	7	7	7
Number of stations reporting, Dec. 31	3,688	4,279	4,898	5,020	5,136	5,244	5,436	5,535	5,638
AM and AM-FM	3,470	3,941	4,209	4,252	4,271	4,267	4,361	4,355	4,363
FM independents	218	338	464	527	590	616	678	703	713
FM affiliates of AM stations [1]	(NA)	(NA)	225	241	275	361	397	477	562
FINANCES (mil. dol.)									
Broadcast revenues, gross	665	880	1,272	1,403	1,564	1,664	1,774	1,911	2,247
Revenues from sales to advertisers	654	868	1,257	1,387	1,547	1,647	1,756	1,890	2,226
Network sales	45	54	49	55	65	59	60	73	92
National non-network sales	208	261	355	378	384	382	387	416	495
Local sales	401	553	853	954	1,098	1,205	1,309	1,401	1,639
Nonadvertising revenues	11	12	15	16	17	17	18	21	21
Broadcast revenues, net	598	793	1,137	1,258	1,407	1,502	1,603	1,725	2,019
AM and AM-FM	592	777	1,077	1,176	1,292	1,348	1,410	1,480	1,687
FM independents	6	16	41	55	77	96	128	143	180
FM affiliates of AM stations	(NA)	(NA)	19	26	38	58	65	102	152
Networks [2]	63	74	88	100	112	112	116	134	166
Other stations	535	719	1,049	1,158	1,295	1,398	1,487	1,591	1,853
Broadcast expenses of networks and stations	552	715	1,044	1,155	1,273	1,392	1,519	1,638	1,841
AM and AM-FM	544	696	973	1,059	1,145	1,227	1,315	1,384	1,529
FM independents	8	19	47	64	86	106	141	152	176
FM affiliates of AM stations	(NA)	(NA)	24	32	41	58	63	98	136
Networks [2]	66	71	90	97	103	109	116	128	157
Other stations	486	644	955	1,059	1,170	1,283	1,403	1,510	1,684
Broadcast income [3]	46	78	93	103	134	110	84	91	179
AM and AM-FM	48	81	104	118	147	121	95	95	158
FM independents	−2	−3	−6	−9	−9	−11	−13	−9	4
FM affiliates of AM stations	(NA)	(NA)	−5	−6	−4	−1	2	5	17
Networks [2]	−3	3	−1	3	9	3	−	6	9
Other stations	49	75	94	99	125	107	84	85	170

− Represents zero.   NA Not available.
[1] For 1960 and 1965, reports combined with AM stations; thereafter, separate reports filed when possible.
[2] Includes owned and operated stations.   [3] Before Federal income tax.
Source: U.S. Federal Communications Commission, *AM-FM Broadcast Financial Data*, annual.

No. 983. Broadcast Stations Sold—Number and Value of Transactions: 1965 to 1977

[Includes a very small number of stations exchanged or donated to nonprofit organizations. Value figures represent total considerations reported for all transactions, except minority interest transfers in which control of the station did not change hands. All sales approved by the U.S. Federal Communications Commission]

ITEM	1965	1968	1969	1970	1971	1972	1973	1974	1975	1976	1977
Number of stations sold:											
Radio	389	316	343	268	270	239	352	369	363	413	344
Combined radio-TV	15	9	5	3	1	–	2	5	–	1	–
TV	32	20	32	19	27	37	25	24	22	32	25
Value of sale transactions_____mil. dol__	135.1	152.5	231.7	174.8	393.5	271.3	230.3	307.8	259.5	290.9	289.9
Radio_____mil. dol__	55.9	71.3	108.9	86.3	125.5	114.4	160.9	169.0	131.1	180.7	161.2
Combined radio-TV_____mil. dol__	49.8	47.6	35.0	1.0	.8	–	2.8	19.8	–	1.8	–
TV_____mil. dol__	29.4	33.6	87.8	87.5	267.3	156.9	66.6	119.0	128.4	108.5	128.7

– Represents zero.

Source: Broadcasting Publications, Inc., Washington, D.C., *Broadcasting Magazine*, weekly. (Copyright.)

No. 984. Radio and Television Stations Owned by Newspapers and/or Magazines: 1961 to 1977

DATE	AM radio	FM radio	TV	DATE	AM radio	FM radio	TV
1961, Sept. 1	412	147	161	1971, Dec. 1	318	209	176
1965, Oct. 31	391	170	174	1972, Dec. 1	325	171	178
1966, Nov. 10	387	177	172	1973, Dec. 1	304	211	179
1967, Nov. 1	383	181	177	1974, Dec. 1	321	236	193
1968, Dec. 4	381	191	183	1975, Dec. 1	320	238	197
1969, Dec. 1	394	245	189	1976, Dec. 1	322	238	209
1971, Feb. 1	402	248	191	1977, Dec. 1	314	238	211

Source: Broadcasting Publications Inc., Washington, D.C., *Broadcasting Yearbook*. (Copyright.)

No. 985. Commercial Broadcast Stations, by Affiliation With Newspapers Within Same Community and by Extent of Ownership: 1967 to 1971

[As of **November**. Excludes noncommercial educational and religion stations. "Community" is the political jurisdiction (usually incorporated) to which a station is licensed. "In same community" indicates same city for radio stations, same television market (not necessarily the same city) for television stations]

TYPE OF STATION	1967			1970			1971		
	Radio only	TV only	Both radio and TV	Radio only	TV only	Both radio and TV	Radio only	TV only	Both radio and TV
Number of communities involved	155	16	77	142	16	73	132	15	74
Stations not affiliated with newspapers [1]	884	254	(x)	915	289	(x)	890	294	(x)
Stations affiliated with newspapers [1]	245	20	215	239	24	195	219	21	204
By extent of ownership:									
100% ownership, total	141	11	146	128	10	129	115	12	136
Only station in same community	53	1	5	42	1	7	34	1	7
Percent of total	37.6	9.1	3.4	32.8	10.0	5.4	29.6	8.3	5.1
Nonaffiliated stations in same community	646	190	(x)	640	200	(x)	628	211	(x)
Majority [2] ownership, total	89	4	55	87	6	48	79	4	47
Only station in same community	51	1	8	49	–	7	43	–	5
Percent of total	57.3	25.0	14.5	56.3	–	14.6	54.4	–	10.6
Nonaffiliated stations in same community	193	51	(x)	173	58	(x)	170	53	(x)
Minority [3] ownership, total	15	5	14	24	8	18	25	5	21
Only station in same community	7	1	3	8	1	4	9	1	4
Percent of total	46.7	20.0	21.4	33.3	12.5	22.2	36.0	20.0	19.0
Nonaffiliated stations in same community	45	13	(x)	102	31	(x)	92	30	(x)
Communities with only one daily newspaper only with ownership interest in:									
The only commercial radio station	76	(x)	(x)	65	(x)	(x)	53	(x)	(x)
Within metropolitan areas	8	(x)	(x)	9	(x)	(x)	9	(x)	(x)
Outside metropolitan areas	68	(x)	(x)	56	(x)	(x)	44	(x)	(x)
The only commercial TV station	(x)	29	(x)	(x)	12	(x)	(x)	10	(x)

– Represents zero.   X Not applicable.
[1] Within same community.   [2] 50 through 99 percent owned.   [3] Less than 50 percent owned.

Source: U.S. Federal Communications Commission, *Statistical Material on Newspaper-Broadcast Joint Interests as of November 1967*, and *Annual Report*. Data compiled by U.S. Bureau of the Census.

No. 986. PERCENT OF HOUSEHOLDS WITH TELEVISION SETS: 1955 TO 1974

[For definition of standard metropolitan statistical areas (SMSA's), see Appendix II. 1955 excludes Alaska and Hawaii. For 1955–1965, 212 SMSA's as defined at time of 1960 Census of Population; for 1970 and 1974, 243 SMSA's as defined Feb. 23, 1971. See *Historical Statistics, Colonial Times to 1970*, series R 105, for number of households with TV]

PERCENT OF ALL HOUSEHOLDS—	1955, June	1960, May	1965, Aug.	1970, Apr.	1974, Fall	PERCENT OF HOUSEHOLDS WITH—	1955, June	1960, May	1965, Aug.	1970, Apr.	1974, Fall
Total with TV	67	88	92	96	97	No set	33	12	8	4	3
						1 set	65	77	73	67	51
Inside SMSA's	78	91	94	96	97	2 sets or more	2	11	20	29	45
Outside SMSA's	50	82	89	94	96						
						Color	(NA)	(NA)	7	(NA)	43
						Black and white	(NA)	(NA)	93	(NA)	52

NA Not available.

Source: U.S. Bureau of the Census, *Current Housing Reports*, series H-121; *Census of Housing*, 1970, *Detailed Housing Characteristics*, HC(1)-B1; and "Selected Data From the 1973 and 1974 Surveys of Purchases and Ownership."

No. 987. HOUSEHOLDS WITH TELEVISION SETS—SELECTED CHARACTERISTICS: 1950 TO 1978

[Excludes Alaska and Hawaii. Through 1967, as of **January** of year shown; thereafter, as of **September** of prior year]

ITEM	1950	1955	1960	1965	1967	1970	1975	1976	1977	1978
Total households 1,000	43,000	47,620	52,500	56,900	58,900	61,410	70,520	71,460	73,100	74,700
Households with TV sets 1,000	3,880	30,700	45,750	52,700	55,130	58,500	68,500	69,600	71,200	72,900
Percent of total	9.0	64.5	87.1	92.6	93.6	95.3	97.1	97.4	97.4	97.6
Average number of sets	1.01	1.03	1.13	1.22	1.29	1.39	1.54	1.56	1.59	1.63
Multiset households 1,000	40	875	5,500	10,225	13,930	18,840	28,360	30,000	31,880	33,690
Color set households 1,000	–	5	340	2,810	9,000	20,910	46,850	51,230	54,870	56,850
Average viewing per day [1] hours	4.6	4.9	5.1	5.5	5.7	5.9	6.1	6.3	6.2	(NA)

– Represents zero.   NA Not available.   [1] Source: A. C. Nielsen Company, Northbrook, Ill. (copyright).

Source: Except as noted, 1950-1967, National Broadcasting Company, New York, N.Y.; thereafter, A. C. Nielsen Company, Northbrook, Ill. (copyright). In Television Bureau of Advertising, Inc., New York, "Trends in Television, 1950 To Date," April 1, 1978.

No. 988. RADIOS AND TELEVISION SETS—PRODUCTION AND IMPORTS, BY MODEL: 1956 TO 1977

[In thousands, except percent]

ITEM	1956	1960	1965	1970	1971	1972	1973	1974	1975	1976	1977
RADIOS [1]											
Total	14,008	24,463	41,726	44,427	47,610	55,311	50,198	43,992	34,515	44,101	52,926
Percent FM/AM-FM	(NA)	(NA)	15.2	48.0	47.9	49.2	47.9	59.4	65.0	59.6	65.9
Model:											
Table	3,360	4,511	4,370	5,714	4,760	4,926	3,023	2,764	2,253	2,876	1,990
Percent FM/AM-FM	7.0	16.8	32.0	72.8	73.9	77.0	83.6	81.7	80.6	66.4	54.5
Clock	2,475	3,780	5,448	4,874	6,460	7,474	10,425	9,174	6,641	7,353	11,447
Percent FM/AM-FM	(NA)	4.1	16.0	53.8	62.5	72.3	72.7	79.1	89.1	85.8	89.4
Portable	3,116	9,740	21,871	23,461	22,885	29,749	24,204	21,292	16,382	21,427	26,599
Percent FM/AM-FM	(NA)	1.4	15.7	55.9	55.2	50.1	42.9	61.9	68.4	55.4	61.4
Auto	5,057	6,432	10,037	10,378	13,505	13,162	12,546	10,762	9,239	12,445	12,890
Percent FM/AM-FM	(NA)	(NA)	6.3	13.8	19.4	23.7	28.3	31.8	37.7	49.7	56.0
TELEVISION SETS [2]											
Total	7,387	5,708	8,382	9,483	11,197	13,507	17,367	15,279	10,637	14,131	15,431
Monochrome sets	7,387	5,708	8,382	4,852	4,848	5,600	7,296	6,868	4,418	5,937	6,090
Table and portable	4,755	3,274	6,956	4,463	4,415	5,341	7,049	6,732	4,354	5,863	6,033
Console	2,526	2,211	1,318	389	433	259	247	136	64	74	57
Combinations	106	223	108	–	–	–	–	–	–	–	–
Color sets	[3]100	[3]120	[3]2,694	4,631	6,349	7,907	10,071	8,411	6,219	8,194	9,341
Table and portable	(NA)	(NA)	(NA)	2,495	3,570	4,721	6,700	5,698	4,186	5,785	6,722
Console	(NA)	(NA)	(NA)	2,018	2,673	3,106	3,313	2,674	2,008	2,377	2,591
Combinations	(NA)	(NA)	(NA)	118	106	80	58	39	25	32	28

– Represents zero.   NA Not available.   [1] Comprises products produced by U.S. manufacturers and imports by distributors or dealers for resale. Beginning 1971, also includes products purchased by U.S. manufacturers.   [2] Represents products produced or purchased by U.S. manufacturers for sale with their brand name. Beginning 1973, also includes products imported directly by distributors or dealers for resale.   [3] Estimated.

Source: Electronic Industries Association, Washington, D.C., *Electronic Market Data Book*, annual.

No. 989. Newspapers and Periodicals: 1950 to 1978

[Prior to 1960, excludes Alaska and Hawaii. Data refer to year of compilation of the Directory cited as the source, i.e., generally to year preceding year shown. See also *Historical Statistics, Colonial Times to 1970*, series R 232–243]

FREQUENCY OF PUBLICATION	1950	1955	1960	1965	1970	1973	1974	1975	1976	1977	1978
Newspapers	12,115	11,415	11,315	11,383	11,383	11,324	11,296	11,400	11,298	[1] 11,089	[1] 10,538
Semiweekly	337	324	324	357	423	459	523	506	511	550	569
Weekly	9,794	9,126	8,979	8,989	8,903	8,804	8,711	8,824	8,735	8,506	7,980
Daily	1,894	1,860	1,854	1,843	1,838	1,792	1,806	1,819	1,813	1,811	1,893
Other	90	105	158	194	219	269	256	251	239	225	206
Periodicals	6,960	7,648	8,422	8,990	9,573	9,630	9,755	9,657	9,872	9,732	9,582
Weekly	1,443	1,602	1,580	1,716	1,856	2,022	2,027	1,918	1,915	1,882	1,827
Semimonthly [2]	416	503	527	550	589	506	529	537	557	548	541
Monthly	3,694	3,782	4,113	4,195	4,314	4,107	4,123	4,087	4,144	4,019	3,846
Bimonthly	436	608	743	876	957	925	942	1,009	1,058	1,045	1,031
Quarterly	604	674	895	1,030	1,108	1,148	1,164	1,093	1,161	1,149	1,172
Other	367	479	564	623	749	922	970	1,013	1,037	1,089	1,165

[1] Due to processing errors, detail will not add exactly to total.　　[2] Includes fortnightly (every two weeks).

Source: Ayer Press, Philadelphia, Pa., *Ayer Directory of Publications*, annual. (Copyright.)

No. 990. Daily and Sunday Newspapers—Number and Circulation, by Circulation Size-Group: 1970 to 1977

[Circulation as of **Sept. 30** of year shown; number of newspapers as of **Feb. 1** of following year except, 1977, as of **Mar. 30, 1978**. Total number of newspapers and circulation figures have been adjusted to account for double listings]

CIRCULATION SIZE-GROUP	NUMBER OF NEWSPAPERS Daily Total [1]	Morn-ing	Even-ing	Sun-day	CIRCULATION (1,000) Daily Total [1]	Morn-ing	Even-ing	Sun-day	PERCENT OF ALL NEWSPAPERS Number Total daily	Sun-day	Circulation [2] Total daily	Sun-day
1970, total	1,748	334	1,429	586	62,108	25,934	36,174	49,217	100.0	100.0	100.0	100.0
500,001 and over	11	7	4	17	8,780	6,370	2,410	15,081	.6	2.9	14.1	30.6
250,001–500,000	27	11	16	34	9,532	4,167	5,365	11,652	1.5	5.8	15.3	23.7
100,001–250,000	92	45	47	62	14,687	7,612	7,075	9,799	5.3	10.6	23.6	19.9
50,001–100,000	127	57	70	82	8,394	3,736	4,658	5,661	7.3	14.0	13.5	11.5
25,001–50,000	243	69	179	104	8,597	2,398	6,199	3,791	13.9	17.7	13.8	7.7
10,001–25,000	489	76	422	146	7,850	1,247	6,603	2,385	28.0	24.9	12.6	4.8
10,000 or less	759	69	691	141	4,325	403	3,922	847	43.4	24.1	7.0	1.7
1975, total	1,756	339	1,436	639	60,655	25,490	35,165	51,096	100.0	100.0	100.0	100.0
500,001 and over	10	7	3	15	7,716	6,018	1,698	13,548	.6	2.3	12.7	26.5
250,001–500,000	26	14	13	34	9,135	4,795	4,340	11,674	1.5	5.3	15.1	22.8
100,001–250,000	81	40	41	65	12,832	6,476	6,356	10,575	4.6	10.2	21.2	20.7
50,001–100,000	135	62	75	89	9,065	3,999	5,066	6,212	7.7	13.9	14.9	12.2
25,001–50,000	259	70	196	132	9,197	2,460	6,737	5,465	14.7	20.7	15.2	10.7
10,001–25,000	511	77	441	167	8,345	1,330	7,015	2,759	29.1	26.1	13.8	5.4
10,000 or less	734	69	667	137	4,366	412	3,954	863	41.8	21.4	7.2	1.7
1976, total	1,762	346	1,435	650	60,976	25,857	35,118	51,565	100.0	100.0	100.0	100.0
500,001 and over	9	7	2	17	7,185	6,016	1,168	15,110	.5	2.6	11.8	29.3
250,001–500,000	27	14	14	31	9,877	4,886	4,991	10,698	1.6	4.8	16.2	20.8
100,001–250,000	83	40	43	67	12,958	6,495	6,463	10,861	4.7	10.3	21.3	21.1
50,001–100,000	131	65	68	87	8,848	4,276	4,572	6,046	7.4	13.4	14.5	11.7
25,001–50,000	266	71	202	138	9,446	2,481	6,965	5,073	15.1	21.2	15.5	9.8
10,001–25,000	518	76	449	175	8,337	1,266	7,071	2,943	29.4	26.9	13.7	5.7
10,000 or less	728	73	657	135	4,325	437	3,888	834	41.3	20.8	7.0	1.6
1977, total	1,753	352	1,435	668	61,495	26,742	34,753	52,429	100.0	100.0	100.0	100.0
500,001 and over	11	8	4	18	8,597	6,439	2,158	15,630	.6	2.7	14.0	29.8
250,001–500,000	26	15	11	30	8,560	5,083	3,477	10,324	1.5	4.5	13.9	19.7
100,001–250,000	85	42	45	69	13,246	6,610	6,636	11,168	4.9	10.3	21.5	21.3
50,001–100,000	137	73	74	89	9,139	4,515	4,624	6,227	7.8	13.3	14.9	11.9
25,001–50,000	274	77	207	146	9,559	2,566	6,993	5,269	15.6	21.9	15.5	10.0
10,001–25,000	515	65	457	182	8,171	1,080	7,091	2,956	29.4	27.2	13.3	5.6
10,000 or less	705	72	637	134	4,223	449	3,774	855	40.2	20.1	6.9	1.6

[1] All-day newspapers are included in circulation size-groups; adjustments for them are made in the total. Totals shown represent effects of downward adjustments to correct for duplications in the detail.
[2] Percents calculated on gross totals.

Source: Editor & Publisher Co., Inc., New York, N.Y., *Editor & Publisher International Year Book*, annual. (copyright).

No. 991. Daily and Sunday Newspapers—Number and Circulation, 1950 to 1977, and by States, 1977

[Prior to 1960, excludes Alaska and Hawaii. Number of newspapers as of the following dates: 1950–1960, Oct. 1; 1965, Jan. 1; 1970–1976, Feb. 1 of following years; and 1977 as of Mar. 30 of following year. Circulation figures as of Sept. 30, except 1950–1965 as of Oct. 1. For English language newspapers only. See also Historical Statistics, Colonial Times to 1970, series R 224–231]

| YEAR AND STATE | DAILY NEWSPAPERS | | | | | | SUNDAY NEWS-PAPERS | |
| | Total | | Morning | | Evening | | | |
	Number [1]	Net paid circulation (1,000)	Number	Net paid circulation (1,000)	Number	Net paid circulation (1,000)	Number	Net paid circulation (1,000)
1950	1,772	53,829	322	21,266	1,450	32,563	549	46,582
1955	1,760	56,147	316	22,183	1,454	33,964	541	46,448
1960	1,763	58,882	312	24,029	1,459	34,853	563	47,699
1965	1,751	60,358	320	24,107	1,444	36,251	562	48,600
1970	1,748	62,108	334	25,934	1,429	36,174	586	49,217
1972	1,761	62,510	337	26,078	1,441	36,432	603	49,339
1973	1,774	63,147	343	26,524	1,451	36,623	634	51,717
1974	1,768	61,877	340	26,145	1,449	35,732	641	51,679
1975	1,756	60,655	339	25,490	1,436	35,165	639	51,096
1976	1,762	60,977	346	25,858	1,435	35,119	650	51,565
1977, total, Mar. 30, 1978	[2] 1,753	61.495	352	26,742	1,435	34.753	668	52.429
Alabama	25	732	7	203	18	529	17	671
Alaska	7	89	1	14	6	75	1	49
Arizona	17	564	2	283	15	281	5	480
Arkansas	33	360	5	71	30	289	16	455
California	125	6,082	26	3,127	100	2,955	44	5,139
Colorado	27	836	4	345	24	491	9	838
Connecticut	26	890	6	352	20	538	7	651
Delaware	3	161	1	49	2	112	2	149
District of Columbia	2	890	1	541	1	349	2	1,099
Florida	51	2,412	18	1,562	34	850	34	2,398
Georgia	37	1,043	7	439	30	604	14	1,021
Hawaii	5	311	1	78	4	233	2	211
Idaho	15	201	4	88	11	113	6	166
Illinois	88	3,243	22	1,761	71	1,482	23	2,742
Indiana	79	1,665	7	444	72	1,221	18	1,173
Iowa	40	901	4	325	37	576	9	767
Kansas	51	647	5	227	47	420	14	447
Kentucky	27	781	5	321	22	460	13	616
Louisiana	26	860	5	407	21	453	14	776
Maine	9	278	5	209	4	69	1	113
Maryland	13	700	5	232	8	468	4	674
Massachusetts	46	2,016	5	900	41	1,116	8	1,457
Michigan	52	2,457	2	629	50	1,828	14	2,237
Minnesota	30	1,110	6	408	28	702	12	1,070
Mississippi	25	395	5	123	20	272	10	290
Missouri	54	1,683	9	726	45	957	16	1,140
Montana	11	195	4	150	7	45	7	191
Nebraska	19	492	3	172	16	320	4	370
Nevada	9	190	3	80	6	110	4	170
New Hampshire	9	178	1	33	9	145	2	70
New Jersey	27	1,722	7	649	21	1,073	13	1,350
New Mexico	21	256	1	77	20	179	12	228
New York	76	6,810	20	4,190	58	2,620	32	6,295
North Carolina	51	1,323	10	603	41	720	22	1,070
North Dakota	10	145	2	23	9	122	2	50
Ohio	96	3,405	8	860	89	2,545	23	2,414
Oklahoma	54	863	9	420	45	443	46	899
Oregon	22	665	3	285	19	380	5	569
Pennsylvania	106	3,887	31	1,273	80	2,614	14	3,058
Rhode Island	7	363	1	69	6	294	2	221
South Carolina	20	587	8	391	12	196	8	469
South Dakota	13	177	1	3	12	174	3	102
Tennessee	34	1,178	9	525	26	653	14	980
Texas	112	3,416	25	1,583	89	1,833	87	3,590
Utah	5	270	1	108	4	162	4	264
Vermont	8	125	2	69	8	56	4	73
Virginia	33	1,067	11	482	23	585	14	820
Washington	23	1,084	5	307	19	777	13	1,051
West Virginia	28	469	9	206	19	263	9	383
Wisconsin	36	1,228	4	256	32	972	6	851
Wyoming	10	93	6	64	4	29	3	62

[1] Beginning 1955, figures are adjusted to account for all-day papers listed in morning and evening figures (circulations divided between them). [2] Adjusted downward to allow for duplication of papers in individual State tabulations (circulations divided between States).

Source: Editor & Publisher Co., Inc., New York, N.Y., Editor & Publisher International Year Book, annual. (Copyright.)

No. 992. NEWSPAPERS AND PERIODICALS—CIRCULATION AND RECEIPTS: 1963 TO 1972

[Receipts in millions of dollars. See also *Historical Statistics, Colonial Times to 1970*, series R 244-257]

TYPE OF PUBLICATION	1963			1967			1972		
	Circulation per issue [1] (1,000)	Receipts		Circulation per issue [1] (1,000)	Receipts		Circulation per issue [1] (1,000)	Receipts	
		Total	Advertising		Total	Advertising		Total	Advertising
Newspapers, total [2]	(NA)	[3] 4,255	3,024	(NA)	[3] 5,550	3,896	(NA)	[3] 7,908	5,600
Daily and Sunday	(NA)	3,792	2,728	(NA)	[3] 4,962	[3] 3,653	(NA)	[3] 6,961	[3] 5,214
Morning [4]	2,602	124	81	3,442	206	135	3,770	280	184
Evening [4]	13,971	681	500	14,446	909	684	12,917	1,021	748
Morning and Sunday	31,663	891	628	31,623	1,301	951	31,726	1,806	1,341
Evening and Sunday	32,424	940	673	31,552	1,055	780	30,357	1,641	1,254
Morning and evening [4]	717	37	27	651	41	31	765	63	45
Morning, evening, and Sunday	34,002	1,119	819	36,942	1,443	1,065	37,406	2,138	1,634
Weekly and other	(NA)	379	296	(NA)	[5] 321	[5] 243	(NA)	[5] 493	[5] 386
Weekly [6]	(7)	288	219	(7)	248	182	(7)	377	291
Periodicals, total	(NA)	[3] 2,036	1,242	(NA)	[3] 2,668	1,547	(NA)	[3] 3,197	1,693
Farm	14,305	54	46	12,115	57	46	13,103	76	62
General	12,087	43	37	10,219	41	32	11,092	49	38
Specialized	2,218	11	9	1,896	16	14	2,011	27	23
Specialized	(NA)	[3] 535	[3] 413	(NA)	[3] 675	[3] 525	(NA)	[3] 910	[3] 648
Industrial, engineering, techn'l	12,113	247	217	[8] 12,952	353	308	17,609	359	280
Merchandising	(S)	127	106	(NA)	145	121	(S)	297	215
Profess'nal, instit'nal, service	(S)	121	65	[8] 8,303	159	87	11,924	250	152
General	(NA)	1,167	711	(NA)	1,473	880	(NA)	1,729	896
Comics	27,594	11	1	15,178	9	(Z)	(S)	(D)	(D)
Women and home services	72,573	316	204	74,541	362	245	(S)	488	295
General entertainment	102,501	659	380	136,567	847	457	(S)	855	374
General news	7,375	141	106	9,652	204	146	19,605	323	212
Business news	(S)	28	15	1,409	40	25	1,489	33	12
Not specified	(NA)	12	5	(NA)	11	6	(NA)	(D)	(D)
Other	141,943	230	73	[8] 127,215	284	97	(S)	282	88

D Withheld to avoid disclosing figures for individual companies.   NA Not available.   S Does not meet publication standards.   Z Less than $500,000.   [1] Includes paid, free bulk, etc. "Issue" defined as the sum of all editions published on a given day. Figures are totals of average circulation per issue.   [2] Includes foreign language newspapers.   [3] Includes types or amounts not specified by kind.   [4] No Sunday editions.   [5] Establishments with less than 10 employees were not required to file reports specifying source of receipts. Thus a substantial portion of "Not specified" is included in "Weekly and other."   [6] Includes those issued on Sunday only.   [7] Not shown because data not reported by many small newspapers.   [8] Partially estimated.

Source: U.S. Bureau of the Census, *Census of Manufactures: 1963*, vol. II, part 1; *Census of Manufactures: 1967*, vol. II, part 2; and *Census of Manufactures: 1972*, Industry series, Bulletin No. MC 72(2)-27A.

No. 993. NEWSPAPERS, PERIODICALS, BOOK PUBLISHING AND PRINTING—NUMBER OF COMPANIES, AND SHARE OF TOTAL SHIPMENTS BY LARGEST FIRMS: 1947 TO 1972

[Prior to 1967, excludes Alaska and Hawaii. Largest companies are ranked by value added by manufacture]

ITEM	NEWSPAPERS					PERIODICALS				
	1947	1958	1963	1967	1972	1947	1958	1963	1967	1972
Number of companies ___ 1,000	8.1	7.9	8.0	7.6	7.5	2.1	2.2	2.6	2.4	2.5
Value of shipments ___ bil. dol	1.9	3.6	4.5	5.8	8.3	1.1	1.7	2.3	3.1	3.5
Percent accounted for by:										
4 largest companies	21	17	15	16	17	34	31	28	24	26
8 largest companies	26	24	22	25	28	43	41	42	37	38
20 largest companies	36	35	36	40	43	58	55	59	56	54
50 largest companies	(NA)	51	52	56	60	(NA)	69	73	72	69

ITEM	BOOK PUBLISHING					BOOK PRINTING				
	1947	1958	1963	1967	1972	1947	1958	1963	1967	1972
Number of companies ___ 1,000	.6	.9	.9	1.0	1.1	(NA)	.8	.7	.7	.7
Value of shipments ___ bil. dol	.5	1.0	1.5	2.1	2.9	.1	.4	.5	.8	.9
Percent accounted for by:										
4 largest companies	18	16	20	20	19	(NA)	24	19	21	24
8 largest companies	29	29	33	32	31	(NA)	34	30	30	36
20 largest companies	48	48	56	57	56	(NA)	51	48	48	53
50 largest companies	(NA)	69	76	77	77	(NA)	68	66	64	68

.NA Not available.

Source: U.S. Bureau of the Census, *Census of Manufactures, 1972*, special report, *Concentration Ratios in Manufacturing*, MC72-SR-2.

No. 994. Newsprint Consumption and Newspaper Pages: 1960 to 1977

[Consumption data based on a 30-lb. weight. In 1974, a number of newsprint producers reduced the basic weight of newsprint from 32 pounds, for 500 sheets measuring 24″ by 36″, to 30 pounds. (A given area of printing surface of 30-pound paper weighs less than the same area of 32-pound paper.) Data prior to 1974 have been adjusted for comparability. See table 1277 for additional newsprint data. See also *Historical Statistics, Colonial Times to 1970*, series R 218–223]

ITEM	1960	1965	1970	1972	1973	1974	1975	1976	1977
Newsprint consumption,									
total [1]_____mil. sh. tons__	7.0	8.0	9.1	9.9	10.2	10.1	9.2	9.6	10.2
Per capita [2]_____lb__	77.4	82.8	89.5	95.5	97.2	95.6	86.1	89.3	94.6
By newspapers [3]_____mil. sh. tons__	6.9	8.0	9.0	9.8	10.0	9.5	9.0	9.3	9.5
Advertising content [4]_____percent__	59.4	60.5	61.5	64.4	65.5	65.6	63.7	63.5	[5] 63.1
Other content [4]_____percent__	40.6	39.5	38.5	35.6	34.5	34.4	36.3	36.5	[5] 36.9
Newspaper pages per issue [5]—									
Daily_____	43	50	47	56	59	60	57	55	54
Sunday_____	142	167	145	176	182	188	180	177	177

NA Not available.   [1] Estimated.   [2] Based on U.S. Bureau of the Census estimated resident population as of July 1.   [3] Estimated. Source: U.S. Industry and Trade Administration, unpublished data.   [4] Based on data from Media Records, Inc.   [5] Source: Editor and Publisher Co., Inc., New York, N.Y., *Editor and Publisher*, weekly (copyright).

Source: Except as noted, American Newspaper Publishers Association, Reston, Va., unpublished data.

No. 995. Registration of Copyrights, by Subject Matter: 1960 to 1977

[In thousands. For years ending **June 30** except 1977, ending **Sept. 30**. Comprises copyrights issued to citizens of the United States and residents of foreign countries. See also *Historical Statistics, Colonial Times to 1970*, series W 82–95]

SUBJECT MATTER OF COPYRIGHT	1960	1965	1970	1972	1973	1974	1975	1976	1977
Total_____	243.9	293.6	316.5	344.6	353.6	372.8	401.3	411.0	452.7
Books_____	60.0	76.1	88.4	103.2	104.5	104.8	111.9	113.2	122.1
Periodicals (issues)_____	64.2	78.3	83.0	84.7	88.6	92.2	95.1	96.0	106.5
Contrib. to newspapers, periodicals_____	3.3	2.1	1.9	2.0	2.1	2.2	2.6	3.1	3.4
Lectures, sermons, addresses_____	.8	.8	1.7	1.9	1.7	1.6	1.9	1.8	2.0
Dramatic or dramatico-musical comp_____	2.4	3.3	3.4	3.8	4.0	4.0	4.9	4.9	5.5
Musical compositions_____	65.6	80.9	88.9	97.5	95.3	104.5	114.8	118.5	131.2
Maps_____	1.8	3.3	1.9	1.6	1.9	1.5	1.8	1.6	1.8
Works of art, models, or designs_____	5.3	5.7	6.8	7.9	8.6	8.5	11.0	12.2	13.7
Reproductions of works of art_____	2.5	3.2	3.0	3.4	3.2	3.6	5.0	5.6	4.4
Scientific or technical drawings [1]_____	.8	1.2	.8	1.1	1.1	.8	.9	.9	1.4
Photographs, prints, and illustrations_____	4.2	3.8	4.5	5.7	5.8	6.1	6.6	7.6	8.9
Commercial prints and labels_____	8.1	7.5	5.3	4.1	4.2	5.0	4.7	4.5	5.0
Motion picture photoplays_____	2.8	2.5	1.2	1.8	1.4	1.3	1.0	1.9	2.6
Motion pictures not photoplays_____	.7	1.2	1.3	1.4	1.4	1.7	2.0	2.3	2.6
Sound recordings [2]_____	(X)	(X)	(X)	1.1	6.7	9.4	8.9	9.0	10.6
Renewals of all classes_____	21.4	23.5	23.3	23.2	23.1	25.5	28.2	27.7	31.0

X Not applicable.   [1] Includes plastic works.   [2] Registration began in 1972.

Source: The Library of Congress, *Annual Report*.

No. 996. Books—Imports and Translations into English: 1975 to 1977

[Imports cover all books printed abroad and distributed in U.S. on exclusive basis. See also headnote, table 997]

SUBJECT	IMPORTS			SUBJECT	IMPORTS			LANGUAGE	TRANSLATIONS		
	1975	1976 [1]	1977 [1]		1975	1976 [1]	1977 [1]		1975	1976 [1]	1977 [1]
Total_____	4,159	5,126	4,663	Law_____	52	80	68	**Total**_____	1,546	1,534	1,689
				Literature_____	210	221	185				
Agriculture_____	65	90	97	Medicine_____	421	531	462	French_____	352	354	397
Art_____	142	149	137	Music_____	17	37	24	German_____	357	247	312
Biography_____	96	139	133	Philosophy,				Italian_____	74	65	66
Business_____	66	84	88	psychology_____	122	152	140				
Education_____	123	156	131	Poetry, drama___	145	203	168	Oriental_____	70	89	76
								Russian_____	191	135	189
Fiction_____	37	79	77	Religion_____	83	110	85				
General works___	119	148	162	Science_____	817	865	835	Scandinavian___	62	70	49
History_____	188	295	225	Sociology,				Spanish_____	75	80	85
Home econom-				economics_____	909	1,093	971				
ics_____	27	38	37	Sports, recreation__	70	124	105	Other_____	365	494	515
Juvenile_____	13	36	35	Technical books___	211	272	331				
Language_____	125	127	104	Travel_____	101	97	63				

[1] Data on 18-month basis. See headnote, table 998.

Source: R. R. Bowker Co., New York, N.Y., *Publishers Weekly*. (Copyright by Xerox Corporation.)

No. 997. New Books and New Editions Published, by Subject: 1960 to 1977

[See headnote, table 998. Comprises new books (those published for the first time) and new editions (published with changes in text or format). Excludes government publications; subscription books, except encyclopedias; dissertations; periodicals and quarterlies; and pamphlets of under 49 pages. 1960 data not strictly comparable with later years due to changes in classifications. See also *Historical Statistics, Colonial Times to 1970,* series R 191–216]

SUBJECT	1960	1965	1970	1975	1976 (Jan.–Dec.)	1976 (Jan. 1976–June 1977)	1977 (Jan. 1977–June 1978) Total	1977 (Jan. 1977–June 1978) New books	1977 (Jan. 1977–June 1978) New editions
Total	15,012	28,595	36,071	39,372	35,141	41,698	42,780	33,292	9,488
Agriculture	156	270	265	456	477	600	594	455	139
Art	470	974	1,169	1,561	1,369	1,681	1,795	1,481	314
Biography	879	685	1,536	1,968	1,714	2,085	2,104	1,563	541
Business	305	537	797	820	843	983	1,077	839	238
Education	348	954	1,038	1,038	899	1,078	1,194	997	197
Fiction	2,440	3,241	3,137	3,805	3,458	3,836	3,681	2,317	1,364
General reference	282	634	846	1,113	1,034	1,261	1,448	1,151	297
History	865	1,682	1,995	1,823	1,934	2,295	2,022	1,427	595
Home economics	197	300	321	728	690	806	795	695	100
Juvenile	1,725	2,895	2,640	2,292	2,210	2,478	2,918	2,626	292
Language	228	527	472	438	409	523	556	407	149
Law	394	436	604	915	698	861	948	725	223
Literature	736	1,686	3,085	1,904	1,405	1,694	1,866	1,200	666
Medicine	520	1,218	1,476	2,282	2,128	2,587	2,833	2,233	600
Music	98	300	404	305	302	366	373	207	166
Philosophy, psychology	480	979	1,280	1,374	1,192	1,386	1,372	1,089	283
Poetry, drama	492	994	1,474	1,501	1,307	1,582	1,437	1,043	394
Religion	1,104	1,855	1,788	1,778	1,748	2,058	2,121	1,736	385
Science	1,089	2,562	2,358	2,942	2,342	2,852	3,015	2,474	541
Sociology, economics	754	3,242	5,912	6,590	5,960	6,993	6,814	5,602	1,212
Sports, recreation	286	591	799	1,225	1,034	1,224	1,119	907	212
Technology	698	1,153	1,141	1,720	1,489	1,888	2,218	1,784	434
Travel	466	883	1,394	794	499	581	480	334	146

No. 998. Books and Periodicals—Average Retail Prices: 1970 to 1977

[Prior to 1976, comprises all titles submitted for listing in Bowker's *Weekly Record* during calendar year. Beginning 1976, covers listings in year shown, plus titles issued in that year which were listed in following six months (i.e., 1976 titles which, due to delays in cataloguing, were not listed in the *Record* until June 1977)]

SUBJECT	AVERAGE PRICES OF BOOKS (per vol.) 1970	1975	1976	1977	SUBJECT	AVERAGE PRICES OF PERIODICALS [5] 1970	1975	1976	1977
Hard cover books [1]	$11.66	$16.19	$17.39	$19.22	Total	$10.41	$19.94	$22.50	$24.59
Agriculture	10.42	13.72	15.40	16.24	Agriculture	5.17	9.70	10.75	11.58
Art	16.16	17.90	20.29	21.24	Business and economics	9.03	15.26	16.98	18.62
Biography	11.49	14.09	15.05	15.34	Chemistry and physics	33.45	76.84	86.72	93.76
Business	12.45	16.54	17.28	18.00	Children's periodicals	2.65	4.69	5.32	5.82
Economics [2]	12.38	21.65	22.79	29.88	Education	7.09	14.72	16.00	17.54
Education	10.75	10.81	12.91	12.95	Engineering	12.07	26.64	31.87	35.77
Fiction	5.51	8.31	9.96	10.09	Fine and applied arts	7.50	11.09	12.42	13.72
Gen. reference	(NA)	21.60	26.61	30.99	History	6.90	11.14	11.94	12.64
History	14.75	15.85	16.74	17.12	Home economics	7.56	14.24	17.86	18.73
Home economics	7.30	10.27	11.18	11.16	Industrial arts	7.59	10.59	12.51	14.37
Juveniles	4.05	5.82	6.01	6.65	Journalism, communications	6.36	14.70	15.90	16.97
					Labor and industrial relations	3.59	7.40	10.33	11.24
Language	(NA)	15.80	16.62	14.96	Law	9.84	15.00	16.21	17.36
Law	16.41	23.22	20.65	25.04					
Literature	11.05	14.89	15.07	15.78	Library science	7.88	14.18	15.96	16.97
Poetry and drama	9.35	10.76	12.66	13.63	Literature and languages	6.15	10.41	11.60	11.82
Medicine	18.05	22.15	24.04	24.00	Mathematics, botany, geology, and general science	18.11	35.95	42.51	47.13
Music	11.44	14.83	16.38	20.13					
Religion	8.51	11.16	12.44	12.26	Medicine	23.44	42.38	47.47	51.31
Science	14.95	22.81	24.42	24.88	Philosophy and religion	5.84	9.05	9.94	10.89
Sports [3]	9.96	10.97	11.36	12.28	Physical ed. and recreation	5.34	7.80	9.27	10.00
Technology	14.91	19.66	21.19	23.61	Political science	6.72	12.79	13.09	14.83
Travel	(NA)	15.43	18.90	18.44	Psychology	17.12	27.51	29.39	31.74
					Sociology and anthropology	7.31	14.85	17.11	19.68
Paperbacks:					Zoology	16.86	27.37	31.34	33.69
Mass market [4]	.95	1.46	1.60	1.72	General interest periodicals	8.47	14.36	15.24	16.19
Trade or higher	4.81	5.24	5.63	5.93					

NA Not available.   [1] Excludes government documents, subscription books, and dissertations.   [2] Includes sociology.   [3] Includes recreation.   [4] "Pocket-sized" books sold through outlets other than book-stores (e.g. grocery or drug stores, etc.).   [5] Average annual subscription prices.

Source of tables 997 and 998: R. R. Bowker Co., New York, N.Y., book prices, *Publishers Weekly;* periodical prices, *Bowker Annual of Library and Book Trade Information.* (Copyright by Xerox Corporation.)

No. 999. Books and Pamphlets—Quantity Sold and Value of Receipts: 1963 to 1972

[Includes number of copies sold and dollar receipts reported by establishments classified in the "Books, publishing and printing" industry and by establishments reporting these receipts as "secondary" activities in other industries]

TYPE OF PUBLICATION	1963		1967		1972	
	Copies sold (mil.)	Receipts (mil. dol.)	Copies sold (mil.)	Receipts (mil. dol.)	Copies sold (mil.)	Receipts (mil. dol.)
Total	(NA)	1,547.8	(NA)	2,255.3	(NA)	2,915.4
All books	(NA)	1,484.3	(NA)	2,081.2	(NA)	2,711.2
Textbooks	(NA)	¹ 471.1	(NA)	¹ 733.6	(NA)	¹ 809.6
Elementary, grades 1–8:						
Hardbound	54.9	112.7	85.1	180.6	65.8	162.4
Paperbound	38.5	21.7	30.0	24.3	44.5	57.5
High school, grades 9–12:						
Hardbound	32.9	97.8	36.3	122.7	40.5	132.4
Paperbound	9.4	8.8	11.6	14.9	7.3	12.8
College, grades 13 and over: ²						
Hardbound	24.2	131.7	41.2	226.6	57.1	277.3
Paperbound	9.3	14.9	16.7	32.7	(S)	45.1
Workbooks, paperbound	106.3	61.1	124.3	88.6	97.1	88.7
Standardized tests, paperbound ³	137.3	19.3	188.0	28.5	24.1	14.2
General reference books	(NA)	(NA)	(NA)	(NA)	(NA)	¹ 235.3
Subscription ⁴	35.7	207.3	33.1	216.3	(S)	198.5
Other	(NA)	(NA)	(NA)	(NA)	(S)	33.4
Technical, scientific, and professional books	(NA)	¹ 156.3	(NA)	¹ 240.2	(NA)	¹ 403.0
Law, designed for the profession	6.5	57.4	8.4	74.0	28.2	146.9
Medical, designed for the profession ⁵	4.1	24.1	8.5	41.0	(S)	59.1
Business, nonfiction, for adults	1.2	5.6	3.7	20.1	5.3	42.0
Other	29.6	63.0	15.5	93.5	(S)	135.1
Religious books	(NA)	¹ 81.1	(NA)	¹ 110.4	(NA)	¹ 131.2
Hardbound and paperbound:						
Bibles, complete editions; testaments	15.3	26.4	10.5	36.7	29.3	52.6
Hymnals and devotionals ⁶	4.7	8.2	7.8	15.4	6.6	9.0
Other, fiction or nonfiction: ⁷						
Hardbound	16.9	31.3	14.7	29.7	18.3	30.0
Paperbound	22.5	12.6	24.1	15.7	39.7	28.3
General books, trade, etc	(NA)	¹ 458.2	(NA)	¹ 657.7	(NA)	¹ 1,006.7
Book club books, hardbound and paperbound	75.7	143.4	147.2	201.5	112.2	131.3
Wholesale paperbound books, digest size ⁸	241.4	60.5	201.1	67.7	159.8	90.3
Adult trade books, fiction or nonfiction: ⁹						
Hardbound	40.2	108.5	52.7	148.9	(S)	232.1
Paperbound	48.9	34.5	148.6	82.7	385.8	220.5
Juvenile, fiction and nonfiction: ⁹						
$1.00 and over retail	55.1	72.7	65.3	107.5	63.8	88.2
Under $1.00 retail	120.5	31.3	144.3	35.1	(D)	(D)
Other books, excluding pamphlets	(NA)	110.3	(NA)	(NA)	(NA)	¹ 125.4
Hardbound	(S)	84.4	29.5	108.1	(S)	71.0
Paperbound	41.4	25.9	(S)	(S)	25.6	29.2
Pamphlets	(NA)	(S)	(S)	(S)	(NA)	48.7
Religious	(S)	(S)	69.9	2.1	(NA)	(NA)
Other	(S)	32.9	(S)	(S)	(NA)	(NA)
Books and pamphlets, not specified by kind	(NA)	18.9	(NA)	97.0	(NA)	155.5

D Withheld to avoid disclosing figures for individual companies.   NA Not available.
S Does not meet publication standards.
¹ Includes receipts not specified by kind, as follows (in millions of dollars): Textbooks, 1963, 3.1; 1967, 14.7; and 1972, 19.2; general reference, 1972, 3.4; technical, scientific, and professional, 1963, 6.2; 1967, 11.6; and 1972, 19.9; religious, 1963, 2.6; 1967, 12.9; and 1972, 11.3; general, 1963, 7.3; 1967, 14.3; and 1972, withheld; other, excluding pamphlets, 1972, 25.2.
² Includes private business and secretarial school, post-high vocational schools, institutes, and training courses of college grade.   ³ Objective tests, manuals, etc.; includes answer sheets.
⁴ Represents books sold direct to the consumer through agents or distributors, usually on installment plan of payment. Includes multivolume encyclopedias, children's literature, biblical sets, etc. Copies sold represent number of volumes rather than sets.   ⁵ Includes nursing and dental subjects.
⁶ Includes missals and prayer books.
⁷ For adults and juveniles.
⁸ Digest size 4¼″ x 6½″; distributed 75 percent or more through magazine wholesalers in 1963, and 50 percent or more in 1967 and 1972.
⁹ Sold primarily through booksellers or book dealers (retail and wholesale) at trade discounts. Juvenile books represent hardbound and paperbound books, excluding toy books.
Source: U.S. Bureau of the Census, Census of Manufactures: 1963, vol. II, part 1; Census of Manufactures: 1967, vol. II, part 2; and Census of Manufactures: 1972, MC72(2)-27A.

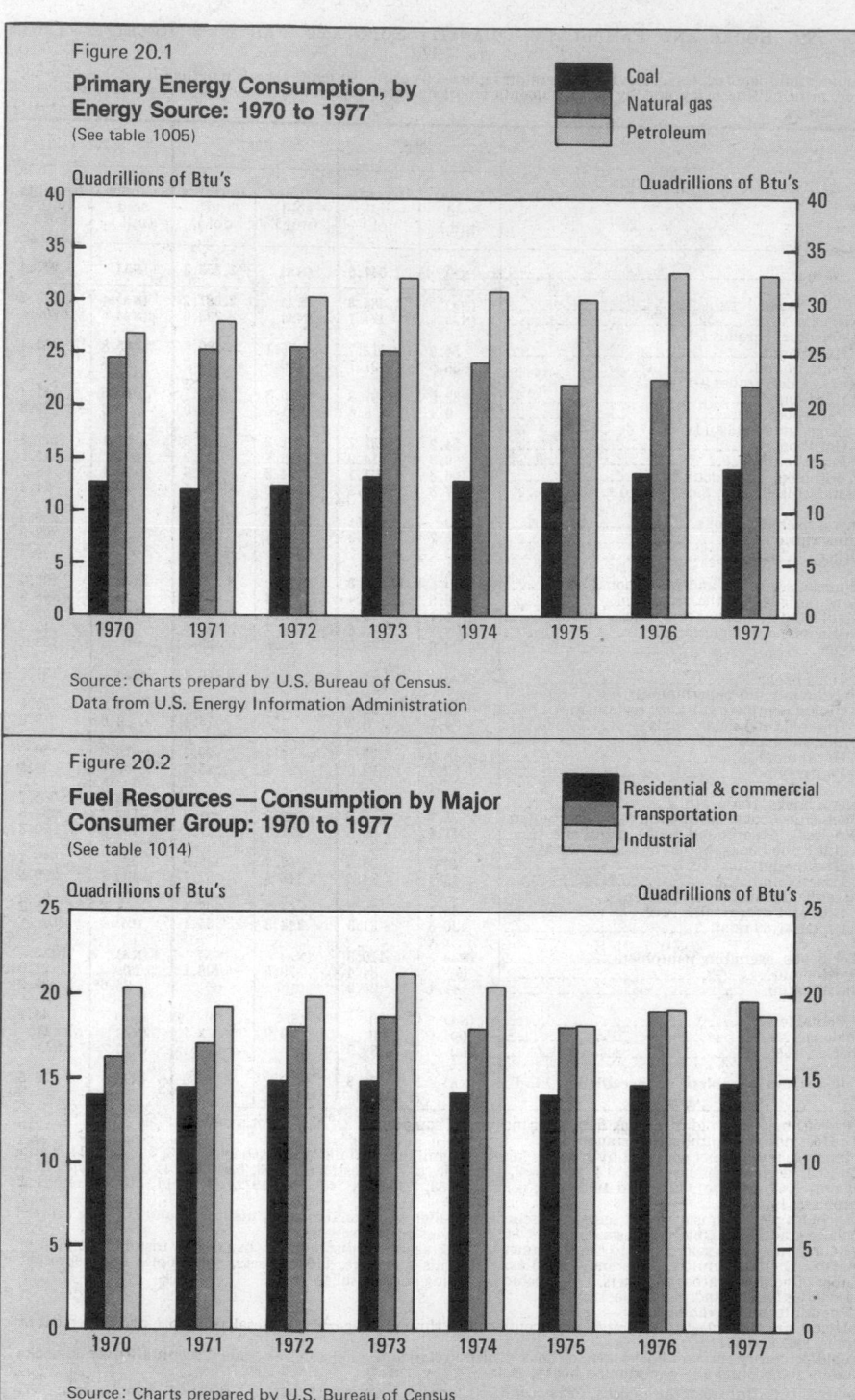

Figure 20.1

Primary Energy Consumption, by Energy Source: 1970 to 1977
(See table 1005)

Coal
Natural gas
Petroleum

Quadrillions of Btu's

Quadrillions of Btu's

Source: Charts prepard by U.S. Bureau of Census.
Data from U.S. Energy Information Administration

Figure 20.2

Fuel Resources — Consumption by Major Consumer Group: 1970 to 1977
(See table 1014)

Residential & commercial
Transportation
Industrial

Quadrillions of Btu's

Quadrillions of Btu's

Source: Charts prepared by U.S. Bureau of Census
Data from U.S. Energy Information Administration.

Section 20
Energy

This section presents statistics on fuel resources, energy production and consumption, electric energy, hydropower, nuclear power, and the electric and gas utility industries. The principal sources are the U.S. Department of Energy's Energy Information Administration (EIA), the Edison Electric Institute, New York, and the American Gas Association, Arlington, Va. The Department of Energy was created in September 1977 and assumed and centralized the responsibilities of all or part of several agencies including the Federal Power Commission (FPC), the U.S. Bureau of Mines, the Federal Energy Administration, and the U.S. Energy Research and Development Administration.

The EIA, in its *Annual Report to Congress*, provides statistics and trend data on energy supply, demand, and prices. Information is included on petroleum and natural gas, coal, electricity, nuclear power, and solar and geothermal energy. Among its annual reports (previously issued by the FPC) are *Statistics of Privately Owned Electric Utilities in the United States; Statistics of Publicly Owned Electric Utilities in the United States; Steam-Electric Plant Construction Cost and Annual Production Expenses; Hydroelectric Plant Construction Cost and Annual Production Expenses; Statistics for Interstate Natural Gas Pipeline Companies; Sales by Producers of Natural Gas to Natural Gas Pipeline Companies; All-Electric Homes*; and *Typical Electric Bills*. These various publications contain national and State data on production of electricity, capacity of generating plants, fuels used in energy production, energy sales and consumption, hydroelectric power, construction costs and production expenses of power plants, and depreciation practices. The EIA also issues the periodic *Energy Data Reports* series and the *Monthly Energy Review*.

In addition to the above, *United States Energy Through the Year 2000* and *Energy Perspectives 2*, prepared by the U.S. Bureau of Mines, present indicators of current and projected energy consumption; the Bureau of Mines' *Minerals Yearbook* and *Mineral Industry Surveys* contain data on coal, oil, and natural gas production and utilization; and *Energy Facts*, prepared for the Subcommittee on Energy of the House Committee on Science and Astronautics by the Library of Congress, has a comprehensive selection of U.S. and foreign energy statistics obtained from primary sources.

The Edison Electric Institute's monthly bulletin and annual *Statistical Year Book of the Electric Utility Industry for the Year* contain data on the distribution of electric energy by public utilities; information on the electric power supply, expansion of electric generating facilities, and the manufacture of heavy electric power equipment is presented in the annual *Year End Summary of the Electric Power Situation in the United States*. The American Gas Association, in its monthly and quarterly bulletins and its yearbook, *Gas Facts*, presents data on gas utilities, including sales, revenues, customers, prices, and other financial and operating statistics.

Other sources include the Rural Electrification Administration's *Annual Statistical Report—Rural Electric Borrowers* and the National Science Foundation, which publishes data annually on research and development funding in energy.

Historical statistics.—Tabular headnotes provide cross-references, where applicable, to *Historical Statistics of the United States, Colonial Times to 1970*. See Appendix I.

No. 1000. Total Horsepower of All Prime Movers: 1940 to 1977

[In millions. As of January, except as noted. Prior to 1960, excludes Alaska and Hawaii, except as noted. Prime movers are mechanical engines and turbines, and work animals, which originally convert fuels or force (as wind or falling water) into work and power. Electric motors, which obtain their power from prime movers, are excluded to avoid duplication. See also Historical Statistics, Colonial Times to 1970, series S 1–14]

ITEM	1940	1950	1955	1960	1965	1970	1973	1974	1975	1976, prel.	1977, prel.
Total horsepower	2,773	4,868	7,158	11,008	15,096	20,408	24,262	24,516	25,100	25,732	26,469
Automotive [1] [2]	2,511	4,404	6,632	10,367	14,306	19,325	23,029	23,224	23,752	24,339	25,025
Nonautomotive	262	464	526	641	790	1,083	1,233	1,292	1,348	1,393	1,444
Factories [3]	22	33	36	42	48	54	58	59	60	61	62
Mines [3]	7	22	31	35	40	45	46	46	47	47	47
Railroads [4]	92	111	60	47	44	54	57	61	62	64	62
Merchant ships and sailing vessels	[5] 9	[5] 23	[5] 24	24	24	22	20	21	22	22	23
Farms	70	165	212	240	272	290	308	315	318	324	[6] 328
Electric central stations [2]	54	88	138	217	307	435	562	605	654	692	728
Aircraft [4] [7]	[5] 7	[5] 22	[5] 26	37	55	183	182	185	185	184	194

[1] Includes passenger cars, trucks, buses, and motorcycles.   [2] As of July 1.   [3] Beginning 1965, data are estimates.   [4] Beginning 1965, not strictly comparable with earlier years.   [5] Includes Alaska and Hawaii.   [6] Includes estimates of about 1.5 million hp in work animals and 15,000 in windmills.   [7] Includes private planes and commercial airlines.

Source: 1940–1955, The Twentieth Century Fund, New York, N.Y., J. F. Dewhurst and Associates, *America's Needs and Resources, A New Survey*; and John A. Waring, *Transactions of Canadian Sectional Meeting, World Power Conference, 1958.* Beginning 1960, John A. Waring, Washington, D.C., unpublished estimates.

No. 1001. Mineral Fuel Resources and Electricity—Production and Consumption, by Major Source: 1940 to 1977

[A British thermal unit (Btu) is the quantity of heat required to raise the temperature of 1 pound of water 1°F at or near its point of maximum density. Prior to 1960, excludes Alaska and Hawaii, except data for bituminous coal include Alaska for all years. For Btu conversion factors, see source. See also Historical Statistics, Colonial Times to 1970, series M 76–92]

YEAR	Total production (tril. Btu)	PERCENT OF PRODUCTION				Total consumption (tril. Btu)	PERCENT OF CONSUMPTION			
		Coal	Crude petroleum [1]	Natural gas [2]	Electricity [3]		Coal	Crude petroleum [1]	Natural gas [2]	Electricity [3]
1940	25,088	53.3	31.3	11.9	3.5	23,908	52.4	31.4	11.4	3.8
1950	34,277	42.7	33.4	20.0	3.9	33,923	38.1	39.8	18.1	4.0
1955	38,956	32.6	37.0	27.0	3.4	39,666	29.1	44.2	23.3	3.9
1960	41,781	26.7	35.7	33.8	3.8	44,525	22.8	45.1	28.5	3.6
1961	42,285	25.4	36.0	34.7	3.9	45,280	21.9	45.2	29.2	3.7
1962	43,899	25.5	35.4	35.0	4.1	47,384	21.5	44.9	29.8	3.8
1963	46,186	26.4	34.6	35.2	3.8	49,271	21.7	44.5	30.1	3.6
1964	48,045	26.8	33.6	35.7	3.9	51,206	22.0	43.7	30.6	3.7
1965	49,637	27.0	33.3	35.6	4.2	53,313	22.3	43.6	30.2	3.9
1966	52,470	26.4	33.5	36.2	4.0	56,381	22.2	43.3	30.8	3.7
1967	55,348	25.7	33.7	36.3	4.3	58,234	21.0	43.5	31.3	4.1
1968	57,258	24.4	33.7	37.6	4.3	61,722	20.5	43.8	31.7	4.0
1969	59,381	24.0	32.9	38.5	4.7	64,947	19.6	43.8	32.4	4.3
1970	62,640	24.3	32.6	38.6	4.5	67,121	18.9	44.0	32.8	4.3
1971	61,650	22.1	32.5	40.2	5.2	68,326	17.6	44.7	32.9	4.7
1972	62,765	23.1	31.9	39.5	5.5	71,606	17.3	46.0	31.7	4.9
1973	62,386	23.1	31.2	39.7	6.0	74,563	17.8	46.7	30.2	5.2
1974	61,170	23.7	30.4	38.7	7.2	72,634	17.7	46.1	29.9	6.3
1975	60,173	25.6	29.5	36.6	8.4	70,598	18.2	46.4	28.3	7.2
1976	60,025	26.4	28.8	36.4	8.4	74,372	18.5	47.2	27.4	6.9
1977, prel	60,182	26.5	28.9	36.3	8.4	75,836	18.6	48.7	25.9	6.8

[1] Production includes lease condensate. Consumption includes domestically produced crude oil, natural gas liquids, and lease condensate, plus imported crude oil and products.   [2] Production includes natural gas liquids; consumption excludes natural gas liquids. Prior to 1971, consumption includes adjustments.   [3] Comprised of hydropower, nuclear power, and geothermal energy.

Source: 1940, U.S. Bureau of Mines, *Minerals Yearbook;* thereafter, U.S. Energy Information Administration, *Annual Report to Congress,* Vol. III.

No. 1002. Production of Energy Resources, by Major Sources: 1950 to 1977

[In trillions of British thermal units, except percent. See headnote, table 1001. Minus sign (−) denotes decrease]

YEAR	Total production [1]	FOSSIL FUELS				Hydro-power [1]	Nuclear power	Geo-thermal
		Total [1]	Petroleum [1]	Natural gas [1][2]	Coal			
PRODUCTION								
1950	34,277	32,937	11,449	6,841	14,647	1,340	–	–
1955	38,956	37,634	14,407	10,532	12,695	1,322	–	–
1960	41,781	40,210	14,935	14,135	11,140	1,566	5	–
1965	49,637	47,571	16,524	17,652	13,395	2,027	39	–
1967	55,348	52,955	18,653	20,087	14,215	2,311	82	–
1968	57,258	54,811	19,308	21,548	13,955	2,314	133	–
1969	59,381	56,619	19,558	22,838	14,223	2,614	148	–
1970	62,640	59,804	20,402	24,154	15,248	2,593	232	11
1971	61,650	58,443	20,031	24,805	13,607	2,790	406	11
1972	62,765	59,326	20,041	24,785	14,500	2,829	577	33
1973	62,386	58,629	19,493	24,754	14,382	2,829	885	43
1974	61,170	56,758	18,575	23,696	14,487	3,143	1,215	54
1975	60,173	55,143	17,730	22,019	15,394	3,122	1,839	69
1976	60,025	54,958	17,263	21,827	15,868	2,952	2,037	78
1977, prel	60,182	55,136	17,395	21,817	15,924	2,293	2,675	78
AVG. ANNUAL PERCENT CHANGE								
1950–1955	2.6	2.7	4.7	9.0	−2.8	−.3	(X)	(X)
1955–1960	1.4	1.3	.7	6.1	−2.6	3.5	(X)	(X)
1960–1965	3.5	3.4	2.0	4.5	3.8	5.3	50.8	(X)
1965–1967	5.6	5.5	6.3	6.7	3.0	6.8	45.0	(X)
1968	3.5	3.5	3.5	7.3	−1.8	.1	62.2	(X)
1969	3.7	3.3	1.3	6.0	1.9	13.0	11.3	(X)
1970	5.5	5.6	4.3	5.8	7.2	−.8	56.8	(X)
1971	−1.6	−2.3	−1.8	2.7	−10.8	7.6	75.0	–
1972	1.8	1.5	.1	−.1	6.6	1.4	42.1	200.0
1973	−.6	−1.2	−2.7	−.1	−.8	–	53.4	30.3
1974	−2.0	−3.2	−4.7	−4.3	.7	11.1	37.3	25.6
1975	−1.6	−2.9	−4.6	−7.1	6.3	−.7	51.4	27.8
1976	−.3	−.3	−2.6	−.9	3.1	−5.5	10.8	13.0
1977, prel	.3	.3	.8	−.1	.4	−22.4	31.3	–

– Represents zero.   X Not applicable.   [1] Prior to 1960, excludes Alaska and Hawaii.
[2] Includes natural gas liquids.

Source: U.S. Energy Information Administration, *Annual Report to Congress*, vol. III.

No. 1003. Energy Consumption Indicators: 1947 to 1976

[Btu=British thermal unit. For definition, see headnote, table 1001. Btu's were converted to coal equivalent on the basis of the 1972 average heat value of 24,050,000 Btu per ton]

YEAR	GROSS ENERGY INPUT (quadrillion Btu)			NET ENERGY INPUT (Btu)			NET ENERGY INPUT (coal equivalent)			Con-version effi-ciency [2] (percent)
	Total	Fuel uses	Nonfuel uses	Total (quad-rillion)	Per capita (mil.)	Per dollar GNP [1] (1,000)	Total (mil. tons)	Per capita (tons)	Per dollar GNP [1] (lb.)	
1947	33.0	31.6	1.4	29.2	202.8	62.4	1,214	8.4	5.19	88.5
1950	34.0	32.6	1.4	29.7	194.8	55.2	1,235	8.1	4.59	87.3
1955	39.7	38.0	1.7	34.3	206.7	52.4	1,426	8.6	4.36	86.4
1960	44.6	42.4	2.2	38.2	211.5	51.8	1,588	8.8	4.31	85.7
1965	53.3	50.7	2.6	45.3	232.1	48.9	1,884	9.7	4.07	85.0
1966	56.4	53.6	2.8	47.4	242.1	48.5	1,979	10.1	4.03	83.8
1967	58.3	55.2	3.1	49.4	248.6	49.0	2,054	10.3	4.07	86.4
1968	61.7	58.4	3.4	52.2	260.1	49.6	2,170	10.8	4.12	83.7
1969	65.0	61.2	3.8	54.4	268.5	50.4	2,262	11.2	4.19	83.7
1970	66.9	63.0	3.9	55.9	273.1	52.0	2,325	11.4	4.32	83.6
1971	68.3	64.4	3.9	56.6	273.7	51.1	2,355	11.4	4.25	82.9
1972	71.6	67.4	4.2	59.1	283.6	50.4	2,455	11.8	4.19	82.5
1973	74.6	70.1	4.5	61.1	292.0	49.6	2,541	12.1	4.12	82.0
1974	72.7	68.3	4.4	59.1	279.5	48.7	2,457	11.6	4.05	81.3
1975	70.6	66.8	3.8	56.9	267.0	47.8	2,366	11.1	3.97	80.6
1976	74.0	69.8	4.2	59.6	277.7	47.1	2,478	11.5	3.92	80.5

[1] In constant 1972 dollars.   [2] Difference between total gross energy inputs and net energy inputs, representing losses from conversion of primary fuels to electrical energy.

Source: U.S. Bureau of Mines, *United States Energy Through the Year 2000; Minerals Yearbook;* and *Mineral Industry Surveys.*

No. 1004. Energy Consumption—Total and Per Capita: 1920 to 1977

[Btu=British thermal units. See headnote, table 1001]

YEAR	ALL ENERGY [1]		NATURAL GAS [3]		COAL [4]		CRUDE PETROLEUM [5]	
	Total (tril. Btu)	Per capita [2] (mil. Btu)	Total (tril. Btu)	Per capita [2] (mil. Btu)	Total (tril. Btu)	Per capita [2] (mil. Btu)	Total (tril. Btu)	Per capita [2] (mil. Btu)
1920	19,782	186	827	8	15,504	146	2,634	25
1925	20,899	180	1,212	10	14,706	127	4,156	36
1930	22,288	181	1,969	16	13,639	111	5,652	46
1935	19,107	150	1,974	16	10,634	84	5,499	43
1940	23,908	180	2,726	21	12,535	95	7,487	57
1945	31,541	236	3,973	30	15,972	120	9,619	72
1950	33,923	223	6,150	40	12,913	85	13,489	89
1955	39,666	240	9,232	56	11,540	70	17,524	106
1960	44,525	247	12,699	71	10,140	56	20,067	111
1965	53,321	276	16,098	83	11,908	62	23,241	120
1970	67,121	329	22,029	108	12,698	62	29,537	145
1971	68,326	331	22,469	109	12,043	58	30,570	148
1972	71,606	344	22,698	109	12,423	60	32,966	158
1973	74,563	355	22,512	107	13,294	63	34,851	166
1974	72,634	344	21,733	103	12,889	61	33,468	158
1975	70,598	331	19,948	94	12,814	60	32,742	154
1976	74,372	346	20,344	95	13,748	64	35,086	163
1977, prel	75,836	351	19,613	91	14,117	65	36,956	171

[1] Includes hydropower, nuclear power, and geothermal energy, not shown separately.   [2] Based on estimated resident population as of July 1.   [3] Dry gas only. Marketed production minus shrinkage caused by liquids extraction (34 cubic feet per gallon produced).   [4] Includes bituminous coal, lignite, anthracite coal, and net imports of coke.   [5] Includes petroleum products and, beginning 1950, natural gas liquids.

Source: 1920–1945, U.S. Library of Congress, *Energy Facts*, November 1973; thereafter, U.S. Energy Information Administration, *Annual Report to Congress*, vol. III.

No. 1005. Primary Energy Consumption, 1970 to 1977, by Consuming Sector and Energy Source

[In quadrillions of British thermal units, except percent. For definition, see headnote, table 1001]

ITEM	1970	1971	1972	1973	1974	1975	1976	1977, est.
Total primary energy consumption	67.1	68.3	71.6	74.6	72.6	70.6	74.4	75.8
By consuming sector:								
Residential and commercial	14.0	14.5	14.9	14.9	14.2	14.1	14.7	14.8
Percent of total	21	21	21	20	20	20	20	20
Industrial and miscellaneous	20.4	19.3	19.9	21.3	20.5	18.2	19.2	18.8
Percent of total	30	30	28	28	28	28	26	25
Transportation	16.3	17.1	18.1	18.7	18.0	18.1	19.1	19.7
Percent of total	24	25	25	25	25	26	26	26
Electricity generation	16.2	17.2	18.5	19.7	19.9	20.2	21.4	22.5
Non-fuel uses [1]	3.9	3.9	4.2	4.5	4.4	3.8	4.2	(NA)
Percent of total	6	6	6	6	6	5	6	(NA)
By energy source:								
Petroleum	26.8	28.0	30.4	32.3	31.0	30.3	32.9	34.6
Domestic supply	20.4	20.0	20.0	19.5	18.6	17.7	17.3	17.4
Supplemental supply [2]	6.4	8.0	10.4	12.8	12.4	12.6	15.6	17.2
Percent of total	24	29	34	40	40	42	47	50
Natural gas	24.5	25.3	25.6	25.3	24.2	22.1	22.6	22.0
Domestic supply	24.1	24.8	24.8	24.8	23.7	22.0	21.8	21.8
Gas imports	.4	.5	.8	.5	.5	.1	.8	.2
Percent of total gas	2	2	3	2	2	(z)	4	1
Coal	12.7	12.0	12.4	13.3	12.9	12.8	13.7	14.1
Nuclear power	.2	.4	.6	.9	1.2	1.8	2.0	2.7
Hydropower	2.6	2.8	2.9	3.0	3.3	3.2	3.0	2.4
Geothermal	(z)	(z)	(z)	(z)	.1	.1	.1	.1

NA Not available.   Z Less than .05 quadrillion British thermal units or .5 percent.   [1] Primarily asphalt and road oil in the residential and commercial sectors, chemical feedstocks in the industrial sector, and lubes and greases in the transportation sector.   [2] From imports, shale oil, coal liquefaction, etc.

Source: U.S. Energy Information Administration, *Annual Report to Congress*, vol. III.

No. 1006. ENERGY CONSUMPTION, BY SECTOR AND PRIMARY SOURCE: 1974 TO 1977

[In trillions of Btu. See headnote, table 1001, for definition of Btu]

SECTOR	Total	Coal [1]	Natural gas, dry	Petro- leum [2]	Hydro- elec- tric [3]	Nuclear power	Geo- thermal	Elec- tricity distri- buted [4]	Elec- tric energy loss [5]
1974									
Final consuming sectors	72,728	4,427	18,220	30,181	36	–	–	5,821	14,045
Residential and commercial	25,895	297	7,427	6,484	–	–	–	3,424	8,263
Industrial	28,572	4,121	10,137	6,305	36	–	–	2,337	5,637
Transportation	18,261	9	656	17,392	–	–	–	60	145
Electric utilities	19,866	8,522	3,512	3,287	3,276	1,215	53	(X)	(X)
1975									
Final consuming sectors	70,648	4,066	16,715	29,645	35	–	–	5,902	14,285
Residential and commercial	26,177	253	7,688	6,135	–	–	–	3,538	8,562
Industrial	26,113	3,812	8,425	5,966	35	–	–	2,302	5,573
Transportation	18,359	1	602	17,544	–	–	–	62	150
Electric utilities	20,188	8,761	3,234	3,096	3,187	1,839	70	(X)	(X)
1976									
Final consuming sectors	74,409	4,018	17,184	31,723	33	–	–	6,265	15,187
Residential and commercial	27,260	243	7,706	6,726	–	–	–	3,676	8,909
Industrial	27,854	3,775	8,859	6,540	33	–	–	2,525	6,123
Transportation	19,295	–	619	18,457	–	–	–	64	155
Electric utilities	21,451	9,733	3,161	3,400	3,042	2,037	78	(X)	(X)
1977									
Final consuming sectors	75,934	3,838	16,338	33,131	17	–	–	6,586	16,024
Residential and commercial	28,157	246	7,462	7,117	–	–	–	3,884	9,448
Industrial	27,875	3,592	8,288	6,920	17	–	–	2,638	6,421
Transportation	19,901	–	588	19,094	–	–	–	64	155
Electric utilities	22,609	10,291	3,275	3,815	2,476	2,674	78	(X)	(X)

– Represents zero.   X Not applicable.   [1] Represents anthracite, bituminous, lignite, and net coke imports.   [2] Includes petroleum products, still gas, liquefied refinery gas, and natural gas liquids.   [3] Includes net imports of electricity.
[4] Electrical energy used by railroads and for street and highway lighting is included in transportation sector.
[5] Losses allocated by final end-use sector in proportion to their direct kilowatt-hour usage.
Source: U.S. Energy Information Administration, *Monthly Energy Review*.

No. 1007. FOSSIL FUEL PRICES IN CURRENT AND CONSTANT (1972) DOLLARS: 1960 TO 1977

[In cents per million British thermal units (Btu), except as indicated. All fuel prices taken as close to the point of production as possible. See headnote, table 1001, for explanation of Btu conversions from mineral fuels. Minus sign (−) denotes decrease]

FUEL	1960	1965	1970	1972	1973	1974	1975	1976	1977 [1]	PERCENT CHANGE—			
										1960– 1970	1970– 1973	1973– 1975	1973– 1977
CURRENT DOLLARS													
Composite [2]	29.8	28.6	30.4	36.5	41.9	75.7	85.4	94.6	108.0	2.0	37.8	109.8	157.8
Crude oil	49.7	49.3	54.8	58.4	67.0	116.2	130.4	140.3	146.6	10.3	22.3	105.8	118.8
Natural gas liquids	56.7	49.0	50.0	56.2	72.9	124.2	116.4	139.6	187.3	−11.8	45.8	113.7	156.9
Natural gas (dry)	13.6	15.1	16.6	18.0	21.0	29.5	43.6	56.6	76.4	22.1	26.5	101.9	263.8
Bituminous coal	17.9	16.9	23.9	31.9	35.5	65.6	81.8	84.1	92.1	33.5	48.5	120.0	159.4
Anthracite coal	30.8	33.5	42.6	47.2	52.0	36.1	127.2	136.6	142.0	38.3	22.1	89.2	173.1
CONSTANT DOLLARS													
Composite [2]	43.4	38.5	33.3	36.5	39.6	65.0	67.2	70.6	76.4	−23.3	18.9	75.8	92.9
Crude oil	72.4	66.3	60.0	58.4	63.3	100.0	102.5	104.8	103.8	−17.1	5.5	72.4	64.0
Natural gas liquids	82.6	65.9	54.7	56.2	68.9	106.9	91.5	104.3	132.6	−33.8	26.0	79.0	92.5
Natural gas (dry)	19.8	20.3	18.2	18.0	19.8	25.4	34.3	42.3	54.1	−8.1	8.8	69.7	173.2
Bituminous coal	26.1	22.7	26.2	31.9	33.5	56.5	64.3	62.8	65.2	.4	27.9	84.5	94.6
Anthracite coal	44.9	45.1	46.6	47.2	49.1	74.1	100.0	102.0	100.5	3.8	5.4	58.7	104.7
GNP price deflators 1972=100	68.7	74.3	91.4	100.0	105.8	116.0	127.2	133.9	141.3	33.0	15.9	19.4	33.6

[1] Preliminary.   [2] Weighted by relative importance of individual fuels in total mineral fuels production.
Source: 1960–1974, U.S. Department of the Interior, *Energy Perspectives 2*, June 1976; thereafter, U.S. Energy Information Administration, *Annual Report to Congress*, vol. III.

No. 1008. WORLD ENERGY CONSUMPTION, BY REGION AND ENERGY SOURCE: 1960 TO 1976

[In millions of metric tons, coal equivalent. Metric ton—1.1023 short tons. See text, p. 896, for general comments about the data]

REGION AND ENERGY SOURCE	CONSUMPTION							PERCENT DISTRIBUTION		
	1960	1965	1970	1973	1974	1975	1976	1960	1970	1976
World total	4,245.6	5,219.7	6,781.8	7,766.9	7,815.9	7,877.3	8,318.4	100.0	100.0	100.0
United States	1,475.1	1,774.3	2,258.8	2,469.8	2,401.3	2,352.9	2,485.5	34.7	33.3	29.9
Western Europe	831.2	1,057.0	1,368.2	1,546.9	1,519.9	1,470.9	1,573.0	19.6	20.2	18.9
Japan	109.1	178.5	345.1	425.8	421.5	403.7	414.9	2.6	5.1	5.0
Centrally planned economies	1,353.9	1,563.9	1,907.4	2,227.5	2,322.2	2,452.1	2,569.8	31.9	28.1	30.9
Rest of world	476.3	646.0	902.3	1,096.9	1,151.0	1,197.7	1,275.2	11.2	13.3	15.3
Energy source:										
Solid fuels	2,205.7	2,254.7	2,409.5	2,477.8	2,523.7	2,599.7	2,696.0	51.9	35.5	32.4
Liquid fuels	1,361.8	1,966.5	2,913.7	3,572.2	3,523.9	3,495.9	3,733.0	32.1	43.0	44.9
Natural gas	593.1	882.2	1,304.1	1,531.7	1,561.0	1,560.3	1,661.6	14.0	19.2	20.0
Hydropower and geothermal	84.7	113.3	144.8	161.7	177.1	179.2	178.9	2.0	2.1	2.1
Nuclear	.3	3.0	9.7	23.5	30.3	42.2	48.9	(z)	.2	.6

Z Less than .05 percent.
Source: Statistical Office of the United Nations, New York, N.Y., *World Energy Supplies*, Statistical Papers. series J, vol. 21; and unpublished data. (Copyright.)

No. 1009. CRUDE OIL, NATURAL GAS, AND COAL—WORLD PRODUCTION, BY REGION: 1960 TO 1976

FUEL AND REGION	PRODUCTION							PERCENT DISTRIBUTION		
	1960	1965	1970	1973	1974	1975	1976	1960	1970	1976
CRUDE OIL (mil. bbl.)										
World	7,674	11,063	16,711	20,368	20,539	19,502	21,192	100.0	100.0	100.0
United States	2,575	2,849	3,517	3,361	3,203	3,057	2,976	33.6	21.0	14.0
Other W. Hemisphere	1,555	1,979	2,377	2,542	2,405	2,123	2,113	20.3	14.2	10.0
Western Europe	99	131	116	114	116	200	312	1.3	.7	1.5
Africa	105	812	2,207	2,161	1,990	1,826	2,135	1.4	13.2	10.1
Middle East	1,923	3,054	5,096	7,745	7,987	7,161	8,116	25.1	30.5	38.3
Far East and Oceania	202	246	503	816	816	806	923	2.6	3.0	4.3
Sino-Soviet bloc [1]	1,215	1,993	2,896	3,629	4,022	4,329	4,617	15.8	17.2	21.8
NATURAL GAS (bil. cu. ft.)										
World	16,917	24,537	37,664	46,144	47,179	47,518	49,459	100.0	100.0	100.0
United States	12,771	16,040	21,921	22,648	21,601	20,109	19,952	75.5	58.2	40.4
Other W. Hemisphere	1,299	2,268	3,554	4,735	4,712	4,766	4,790	7.7	9.4	9.7
Western Europe	432	671	2,751	5,148	5,837	6,032	6,345	2.6	7.3	12.8
Africa	6	70	122	586	594	759	906	(z)	.3	1.8
Middle East	57	171	460	1,277	1,423	1,437	1,493	.3	1.2	3.0
Far East and Oceania	158	166	525	792	895	983	1,209	.9	1.4	2.4
Sino-Soviet bloc	2,194	5,152	8,331	10,958	12,117	13,432	14,764	13.0	22.1	29.9
COAL (mil. sh. tons)										
World	2,899	3,079	3,317	3,404	3,459	3,613	3,712	100.0	100.0	100.0
United States	434	527	613	599	607	655	685	15.0	18.5	18.5
Other W. Hemisphere	21	22	28	35	35	42	43	.7	.8	1.1
Western Europe	618	601	500	466	439	497	467	21.3	15.1	12.6
Africa	48	59	66	75	77	82	91	1.7	2.0	2.4
Middle East	11	10	10	12	19	21	22	.4	.3	.6
Far East and Oceania	189	237	240	233	250	278	288	6.5	7.2	7.8
Sino-Soviet Bloc	1,578	1,622	1,861	1,984	2,032	2,038	2,116	54.4	56.1	57.0

Z Less than .05 percent.   [1] Includes Cuba.
Source: 1960–1975, U.S. Dept. of Interior, *Energy Perspectives 2*, June 1976, and unpublished data; thereafter, U.S. Energy Information Administration, *International Petroleum Annual, World Natural Gas*, annual, and *Coal—Bituminous and Lignite*, annual.

No. 1010. U.S. Foreign Trade in Selected Mineral Fuels: 1950 to 1977

[Btu=British thermal units. See headnote, table 1001. Minus sign (−) denotes an excess of imports over exports. See also *Historical Statistics, Colonial Times to 1970*, series M 100, 101, 127, 128, 140, 141, 178, and 181]

YEAR	NATURAL GAS						CRUDE OIL					
	Imports		Exports		Net trade		Imports		Exports		Net trade	
	Bil. cu. ft.	Tril. Btu	Bil. cu. ft.	Tril. Btu	Bil. cu. ft.	Tril. Btu	Mil. bbl.	Tril. Btu	Mil. bbl.	Tril. Btu	Mil. bbl.	Tril. Btu
1950	–	–	25.7	27	25.7	27	178	1,029	35	201	−143	−828
1955	10.9	11	31.0	32	20.1	21	285	1,659	12	67	−273	−1,592
1960	155.6	161	11.3	12	−144.3	−149	372	2,116	3	18	−369	−2,098
1965	456.4	471	26.1	27	−430.3	−444	452	2,528	1	6	−451	−2,522
1970	820.8	846	69.8	72	−751.0	−774	483	2,716	5	28	−478	−2,688
1971	934.5	964	80.2	83	−854.3	−881	613	3,431	1	3	−612	−3,428
1972	1,019.5	1,051	78.0	80	−941.5	−971	811	4,541	(z)	1	−811	−4,540
1973	1,032.9	1,065	77.2	80	−955.7	−985	1,184	6,867	1	6	−1,183	−6,861
1974	959.0	982	76.8	79	−882.2	−903	1,269	7,360	1	6	−1,268	−7,354
1975	953.0	973	72.7	74	−880.3	−899	1,498	8,688	2	12	−1,496	−8,676
1976	963.8	983	64.7	66	−899.1	−917	1,935	11,223	3	17	−1,932	−11,206
1977	1,000.0	1,020	60.0	61	−940.0	−959	2,397	13,902	18	104	2,379	−13,798

YEAR	COAL						PETROLEUM PRODUCTS					
	Imports		Exports		Net trade		Imports		Exports		Net trade	
	1,000 sh. tons	Tril. Btu	1,000 sh. tons	Tril. Btu	1,000 sh. tons	Tril. Btu	Mil. bbl.	Tril. Btu	Mil. bbl.	Tril. Btu	Mil. bbl.	Tril. Btu
1950	365	10	29,360	766	28,995	756	133	833	77	438	−56	−395
1955	337	9	54,429	1,493	54,092	1,484	170	1,069	123	705	−47	−364
1960	262	7	37,981	1,044	37,719	1,037	293	1,839	71	393	−222	−1,446
1965	184	5	52,162	1,418	51,978	1,413	449	2,821	67	372	−382	−2,449
1970	36	1	72,411	1,991	72,375	1,990	765	4,672	90	519	−675	−4,153
1971	111	3	58,022	1,569	57,911	1,566	819	4,974	81	466	−738	−4,508
1972	47	1	57,151	1,546	57,104	1,545	924	5,571	81	463	−843	−5,108
1973	134	3	53,683	1,449	53,549	1,446	1,099	6,625	84	483	−1,015	−6,142
1974	2,080	48	59,926	1,618	57,846	1,570	962	5,747	79	476	−883	−5,323
1975	940	22	65,669	1,773	64,729	1,751	712	4,229	74	446	−638	−3,851
1976	1,203	27	60,021	1,621	58,818	1,594	741	4,430	79	448	−662	−3,982
1977	1,803	41	54,312	1,466	52,509	1,425	794	4,688	70	376	−724	−4,312

− Represents zero.   Z Less than 500,000.

Source: 1950–1972, U.S. Library of Congress, *Energy Facts*, November 1973; thereafter, U.S. Energy Information Administration, *Annual Report to Congress*, vol. III.

No. 1011. Crude Oil Imports into the U.S., by Country of Origin: 1970 to 1977
[In millions of 42-gallon barrels]

COUNTRY	1970	1971	1972	1973	1974	1975	1976	1977	PERCENT DISTRIBUTION					
									1970	1973	1974	1975	1976	1977
Total imports	483	613	811	1,184	1,269	1,498	1,935	2,397	100.0	100.0	100.0	100.0	100.0	100.0
Algeria	2	5	32	44	66	96	149	197	.4	3.7	5.2	6.4	7.7	8.2
Angola	–	1	6	18	18	26	2	6	–	1.5	1.4	1.8	.1	.3
Canada	245	263	312	365	289	219	136	101	50.7	30.8	22.8	14.6	7.0	4.2
Ecuador	–	–	5	17	15	21	19	20	–	1.4	1.2	1.4	1.0	.8
Egypt	8	7	3	5	3	2	6	13	1.7	.4	.2	.1	.3	.5
Indonesia	26	40	60	73	103	138	196	183	5.4	6.2	8.1	9.2	10.1	7.6
Iran	12	39	50	79	169	102	109	192	2.5	6.7	13.3	6.8	5.6	8.0
Iraq	–	1	1	2	–	(z)	10	28	–	.1	.2	(z)	.5	1.2
Kuwait	12	11	13	15	2	1	(z)	15	2.5	1.3	.2	.1	(z)	.6
Libya	17	19	40	49	1	81	162	254	3.5	4.1	.1	5.4	8.4	10.6
Mexico	–	–	–	(z)	1	26	32	65	–	(z)	.1	1.7	1.7	2.7
Nigeria	17	35	89	164	254	272	371	410	3.5	13.9	20.0	18.2	19.2	17.1
Norway	–	–	–	–	(z)	5	13	18	–	–	(z)	.3	.7	.8
Qatar	–	–	1	3	6	7	9	27	–	.1	.3	.5	.5	1.1
Saudi Arabia	15	42	64	169	160	256	447	500	3.1	14.3	12.6	17.1	23.1	20.9
Trinidad	(z)	–	9	22	23	42	38	48	(z)	1.9	1.8	2.8	2.0	2.0
United Arab Emirates [1]	23	29	27	26	25	43	93	121	4.8	2.2	2.0	2.9	4.8	5.0
Venezuela	98	111	93	126	116	144	88	91	20.3	10.6	9.1	9.6	4.5	3.8
Other	8	11	6	7	18	17	55	108	1.6	.6	1.4	1.1	2.8	4.5

− Represents zero.   Z Less than 500,000 or less than .05 percent.   [1] Abu Dhabi prior to 1972.

Source: 1970–1976, U.S. Bureau of Mines, *Minerals Yearbook* and *Mineral Industry Surveys*; thereafter, U.S. Energy Information Administration, *Energy Information Report*.

No. 1012. Petroleum and Coal Products—Sales, Net Profit, and Profit Per Dollar of Sales: 1960 to 1977

[Profit rates are averages of quarterly figures at annual rates]

ITEM	1960	1965	1970	1971	1972	1973	1974 [1]	1974 [2]	1975 [2]	1976 [2]	1977 [2]
Sales_____bil. dol__	30.0	41.4	64.1	71.6	78.1	97.8	180.4	113.5	121.8	141.3	161.7
Net profits before taxes [3]__bil. dol__	3.3	5.3	7.0	7.0	6.5	9.5	15.6	17.7	13.3	16.9	17.7
Net profits after taxes____bil. dol__	2.9	4.5	5.9	6.1	5.2	7.4	12.3	14.5	9.3	11.7	12.1
Depreciation [4]_____bil. dol__	2.3	2.9	4.5	4.7	5.0	5.7	(NA)	5.1	5.6	5.9	6.5
Profits per dollar of sales:											
Before taxes [3]_____cents__	11.0	12.7	11.0	9.8	8.4	9.8	8.6	15.6	10.9	12.0	10.9
After taxes_____cents__	9.7	10.9	9.2	8.5	6.7	7.6	6.8	12.8	7.6	8.3	7.5
Profits on stockholders' equity:											
Before taxes [3]_____percent__	11.4	13.9	13.0	12.4	11.0	14.9	(NA)	25.8	17.9	20.3	19.9
After taxes_____percent__	10.1	11.8	11.0	11.0	8.7	11.6	(NA)	21.1	12.5	14.1	13.6

NA Not available.   [1] Estimates based on FTC reporting requirements in use prior to 1974.
[2] Beginning 1974, based on new FTC reporting requirements.   [3] Federal income taxes.
[4] Includes depletion and accelerated amortization of emergency facilities.

Source: U.S. Federal Trade Commission, *Quarterly Financial Report for Manufacturing, Mining and Trade Corporations.*

No. 1013. Major Petroleum Companies—Financial Data Summary: 1968 to 1977

[Data represent a composite of approximately 40 major worldwide petroleum companies aggregated on a consolidated, total company basis]

ITEM	1968	1969	1970	1971	1972	1973	1974	1975	1976	1977
FINANCIAL DATA (bil. dol.)										
Net income_____	6.8	6.8	6.9	7.2	6.8	11.8	15.9	11.6	14.3	15.0
Depreciation, depletion, etc_____	5.2	5.7	7.4	8.0	9.1	10.5	13.0	11.3	14.8	16.8
Cash flow [1]_____	11.9	12.6	14.2	15.2	15.9	22.3	28.9	22.8	29.1	31.8
Dividends paid_____	3.3	3.7	3.8	3.8	3.8	4.0	4.5	4.7	5.4	6.1
Net internal funds available for investment or debt repayment [2]_____	8.6	8.9	10.5	11.4	12.1	18.3	24.5	18.1	23.7	25.7
Capital and exploratory expenditures_____	12.4	12.9	13.3	14.2	14.3	16.3	25.8	26.9	30.7	31.8
Long-term capitalization_____	73.4	78.7	84.5	90.5	93.7	102.9	112.9	121.1	137.8	155.6
Long-term debt_____	14.6	16.3	18.5	20.8	21.8	22.5	25.0	28.9	39.1	41.9
Preferred stock_____	.5	.5	1.3	.4	.4	.4	.4	.4	.3	.4
Common stock and retained earnings [3]_____	58.2	61.9	64.6	69.3	71.5	80.0	87.4	91.9	103.5	113.3
Excess of expenditures over cash income [4]_____	3.8	4.0	2.8	2.8	2.2	−2.0	1.3	8.9	6.9	6.1
RATIOS [5] (percent)										
Long-term debt to long-term capitalization_____	19.9	20.6	21.9	23.0	23.3	22.0	22.2	23.8	27.4	27.0
Net income to total average capital__	9.7	9.0	8.3	8.2	7.4	12.0	14.8	10.0	10.7	10.1
Net income to avg. common equity__	12.0	11.4	10.7	10.8	9.7	15.6	19.0	13.1	14.3	13.9

[1] Generally represents internally-generated funds from operations. Sum of net income and noncash charges such as depreciation, depletion, and amortization.   [2] Cash flow minus dividends paid.   [3] Includes common stock, capital surplus, and earned surplus accounts after adjustments.   [4] Capital and exploratory expenditures plus dividends paid minus cash flow.   [5] Represent approximate year-to-year comparisons because of changes in the makeup of the group due to mergers and other corporate changes.

Source: U.S. Dept. of Energy, *Summary of Aggregate Financial Data and Composite Annual Comparisons of 40 Major Petroleum Companies,* Nov. 1, 1977; and unpublished data. Data from C. H. Pforzheimer & Co., New York, N.Y.

No. 1014. Consumption of Fuel Resources, by Major Consumer Group: 1970 to 1977

[For definition of Btu, see headnote, table 1001. See also *Historical Statistics, Colonial Times to 1970,* series S 25-31]

CONSUMER GROUP	FUEL INPUTS (quadrillion Btu)						PERCENT DISTRIBUTION			
	1970	1973	1974	1975	1976	1977, est.	1970	1975	1976	1977, est.
Total_____	67.1	74.6	72.6	70.6	74.4	75.8	100.0	100.0	100.0	100.0
Residential and commercial_____	14.0	14.9	14.2	14.1	14.7	14.8	20.9	20.0	19.8	19.5
Industrial and miscellaneous_____	20.6	21.3	20.5	18.2	19.2	18.8	30.4	25.8	25.8	24.8
Transportation [1]_____	16.3	18.7	18.0	18.1	19.1	19.7	24.3	25.6	25.7	26.0
Electrical generation, utilities [2]_____	16.2	19.7	19.9	20.2	21.4	22.5	24.1	28.6	28.8	29.7

[1] Includes bunkers and military transportation.
[2] Includes outputs of hydropower and nuclear power converted to theoretical energy inputs calculated from national average heat rates for fossil-fueled steam-electric plants.

Source: U.S. Energy Information Administration, *Annual Report to Congress,* vol. III.

No. 1015. UTILITY ELECTRIC ENERGY USE, 1960 TO 1977, AND PROJECTED REQUIREMENTS, 1980 TO 1990

[Excludes generation by industrial facilities and railways having generating facilities of their own. Minus sign (−) denotes decrease]

ITEM	1960	1965	1970	1973	1974	1975	1976	1977 [1]	1980	1985	1990
Energy use_____bil. kWh__	764	1,060	1,534	1,873	1,867	1,918	2,037	2,124	2,505	3,238	4,142
Annual percent change [2]___	6.9	6.8	7.7	6.9	−.3	2.7	6.2	4.3	5.7	5.3	5.0
Kilowatthour per capita [3]__	4,229	5,457	7,487	8,902	8,811	8,984	9,470	9,797	11,274	13,903	17,010
Peak load_____mil. kW__	138	189	276	335	327	345	355	385	460	591	756
Annual percent change [2]___	7.1	6.5	7.9	6.7	−2.4	5.5	2.9	8.5	6.1	5.1	5.0

[1] Preliminary. [2] Average annual change from prior year shown; for 1960, change from 1955.
[3] Based on U.S. Bureau of the Census population data including Armed Forces abroad for July 1, except 1970. Projection figures used are for series II (see table 5, p. 8) based on 1976 estimates of the population.

Source: 1960–1975, U.S. Federal Power Commission, unpublished data; thereafter, U.S. Energy Information Administration, *Annual Summary of Capacity, Production, and Fuel Consumption*, and unpublished data.

No. 1016. ELECTRIC UTILITY INDUSTRY—CAPABILITY, PEAK LOAD, AND CAPABILITY MARGIN: 1970 TO 1977

[Excludes Alaska and Hawaii]

YEAR	CAPABILITY			PEAK LOAD		CAPABILITY MARGIN	
	Total (mil. kW)	Annual increase		Total (mil. kW)	Annual percent change [1]	Total (mil. kW)	Percent of capability
		Total (mil. kW)	Percent [1]				
1970: Summer_____	326.9	26.6	8.9	274.7	6.6	52.3	16.0
December_____	339.1	27.6	8.9	248.6	5.1	90.5	26.7
1973: Summer_____	415.5	33.8	8.9	343.9	7.8	71.6	17.2
December_____	432.5	38.5	9.8	289.4	5.2	143.1	33.1
1974: Summer_____	444.4	28.9	7.0	349.3	1.6	95.2	21.4
December_____	466.5	34.0	7.9	296.5	2.5	170.0	36.4
1975: Summer_____	479.3	34.9	7.9	356.8	2.2	122.5	25.6
December_____	494.8	28.3	6.1	324.6	9.5	170.2	34.4
1976: Summer_____	498.8	19.5	4.1	370.9	4.0	127.9	25.6
December_____	511.9	17.1	3.5	338.1	4.2	173.8	34.0
1977: Summer (prel.)___	516.0	17.2	3.5	396.4	6.9	119.6	23.2
December (prel.)_	531.1	19.2	3.8	351.3	3.9	179.8	33.9

[1] Percent change from previous year; e.g. 1970 from 1969 and 1973 from 1972.

Source: Edison Electric Institute, New York, N.Y., *1977 Year-End Summary of the Electric Power Situation in the United States* and *1978 Annual Electric Power Survey.*

No. 1017. FEDERAL ELECTRIC UTILITY PROJECTS—INSTALLED CAPACITY AND INVESTMENT ALLOCATED TO ELECTRIC PLANT: 1960 TO 1976

[As of June 30. Comprises only electricity-generating plant of these projects; excludes projects not primarily manufacturing electricity (e.g., West Point, Annapolis). Investments represent allocation to power projects for capital equipment and improvements. Reserves for depreciation not deducted]

PROJECT GROUP OR SYSTEM	INSTALLED CAPACITY (1,000 kW)					INVESTMENT ALLOCATED [1] (mil. dol.)				
	1960	1970	1974	1975	1976	1960	1970	1974	1975	1976
Total_____	22,616	36,650	42,910	47,394	50,343	5,398	10,121	13,440	15,043	17,246
Percent capacity of all electric utilities_____	13.5	10.7	9.0	9.7	9.8	(X)	(X)	(X)	(X)	(X)
Central Valley:										
Bureau of Reclamation_____	630	1,322	1,334	1,331	1,141	138	213	544	332	239
Columbia Basin:										
Bonneville Power Admin.[2]___	−	−	−	−	−	480	1,118	1,492	1,626	1,753
Bureau of Reclamation_____	2,282	2,464	2,599	2,733	3,848	277	359	562	621	693
Corps of Engineers_____	3,781	6,522	8,435	8,177	9,597	850	1,603	2,010	2,315	2,862
Hoover and Parker-Davis:										
Bureau of Reclamation_____	1,595	1,690	1,690	1,690	1,699	209	225	229	230	232
Missouri Basin:										
Bureau of Reclamation_____	397	693	691	691	663	304	508	535	552	578
Corps of Engineers_____	745	2,048	2,048	2,048	2,008	357	714	721	721	772
Southeastern Power Admin.:										
Corps of Engineers_____	1,271	1,910	2,010	2,083	2,401	410	644	699	746	912
Southwestern Power Admin.:										
S'western Power Admin.[2]___	−	−	−	−	−	27	56	61	61	62
Corps of Engineers_____	601	1,533	1,923	1,847	1,847	203	438	609	611	613
Tennessee Valley Authority___	11,032	17,256	20,836	25,450	25,795	2,054	3,703	5,430	6,671	7,722
Other projects_____	282	1,212	1,344	1,344	1,344	88	540	548	557	808

− Represents zero.   X Not applicable.   [1] Includes estimates.   [2] Transmission.

Source: 1960–1975, U.S. Federal Power Commission and, thereafter, U.S. Energy Information Administration, *Statistics of Publicly Owned Electric Utilities in the United States,* annual, and annual summaries.

612 Energy

No. 1018. ELECTRIC ENERGY PRODUCTION AND INSTALLED GENERATING CAPACITY, BY CLASS OF OWNERSHIP AND TYPE OF PRIME MOVER: 1960 TO 1977

[Production for calendar years; other data as of December 31. 1960 excludes Alaska and Hawaii. See also *Historical Statistics, Colonial Times to 1970*, series S 32–52, S 78–82, and S 86–94]

ITEM	1960	1965	1970	1972	1973	1974	1975	1976	1977
PRODUCTION									
Total_____bil. kWh__	842	1,158	1,636	1,855	1,965	1,968	2,003	2,124	2,211
Average annual percent change [1]___	6.0	6.6	7.2	6.5	5.9	.1	1.8	6.0	4.1
Production, kWh per kW of capacity_	4,529	4,548	4,438	4,448	4,262	3,960	3,801	3,862	3,839
Industrial plants [2]_____bil. kWh__	88	102	104	105	105	101	85	87	87
Electric utilities [3]_____bil. kWh__	753	1,055	1,532	1,750	1,860	1,867	1,918	2,037	2,124
Privately owned_____bil. kWh__	579	809	1,183	1,359	1,452	1,442	1,487	1,582	1,684
Percent of total utilities_____	76.8	76.7	77.2	77.7	78.1	77.2	77.5	77.7	79.0
Publicly owned_____bil. kWh__	175	246	349	391	408	425	431	455	440
Municipal_____bil. kWh__	37	50	71	79	81	79	82	78	83
Federal_____bil. kWh__	112	145	186	207	212	220	221	236	214
Cooperatives and other_____bil. kWh__	26	51	91	105	115	126	128	141	143
Source of energy (percent):									
Coal [4]_____	53.6	54.5	46.1	44.3	45.8	44.6	44.6	46.5	46.6
Nuclear_____			1.4	3.1	4.5	6.1	9.0	9.4	11.8
Oil_____	6.1	6.1	11.9	15.6	16.8	16.0	15.1	15.7	16.9
Gas_____	21.0	21.0	24.3	21.5	18.3	17.1	15.6	14.5	14.4
Hydro_____	19.3	18.4	16.2	15.8	14.8	16.3	15.8	14.1	10.5
INSTALLED CAPACITY									
Total_____mil. kW__	186	255	360	417	461	497	527	550	576
Average annual percent change [1]___	7.3	6.5	7.2	7.5	10.6	7.8	6.0	4.6	3.1
Industrial plants [2]_____mil. kW__	18	18	19	19	19	19	19	19	19
Electric utilities [3]_____mil. kW__	168	236	342	398	442	478	508	531	557
Privately owned_____mil. kW__	128	178	263	314	348	377	399	415	436
Percent of total utilities_____	76.5	75.2	76.9	78.9	78.7	78.9	78.5	78.2	78.3
Publicly owned_____mil. kW__	40	59	79	84	94	101	109	116	121
Municipal_____mil. kW__	11	15	21	23	25	27	29	31	32
Federal_____mil. kW__	22	32	39	40	45	46	50	52	53
Cooperatives and other_____mil. kW__	6	11	19	21	24	28	30	33	36
TYPE OF PRIME MOVER									
Electric utilities: [3]									
Number of plants, total [5]_____	3,435	3,290	3,533	3,614	3,681	3,691	3,674	3,662	3,622
Hydro_____	1,331	1,231	1,188	1,175	1,161	1,159	1,156	1,149	1,145
Steam conventional_____	1,055	1,059	998	996	992	994	984	976	951
Gas turbine_____			323	412	460	494	511	520	524
Steam nuclear_____	5	9	16	26	30	38	45	48	49
Internal combustion_____	1,044	991	1,008	1,005	1,038	1,006	978	969	953
Production_____bil. kWh__	753	1,055	1,492	1,750	1,861	1,867	1,918	2,038	2,124
Hydro_____bil. kWh__	146	194	249	273	272	301	300	284	220
Steam conventional_____bil. kWh__	602	852	1,201	1,387	1,469	1,414	1,417	1,534	1,619
Gas turbine_____bil. kWh__			15	29	30	32	22	24	29
Steam nuclear_____bil. kWh__	1	4	22	54	83	114	173	191	251
Internal combustion_____bil. kWh__	4	5	5	7	7	6	6	5	5
Installed capacity_____mil. kW__	168	236	340	398	442	479	508	531	557
Hydro_____mil. kW__	32	44	55	56	62	64	66	68	68
Steam conventional_____mil. kW__	133	188	260	294	321	338	353	368	386
Gas turbine_____mil. kW__			15	28	33	40	44	47	48
Steam nuclear_____mil. kW__	(z)	1	6	15	21	32	40	43	50
Internal combustion_____mil. kW__	3	3	4	5	5	5	5	5	5

Z Less than .5 million.   [1] Change from prior year shown; for 1960, change from 1955.
[2] Plants of 100 kilowatts and over, including stationary powerplants of railroads.   [3] For public use.
[4] Includes small percentage from wood and waste and geothermal sources.
[5] Each prime mover type in combination plants counted separately.

Source: 1960–1970, U.S. Federal Power Commission, *Electric Power Statistics*, and press releases; thereafter, U.S. Energy Information Administration, *Six-Year Summary of Power Production and Generating Capacity Data*.

No. 1019. ELECTRIC ENERGY—PRODUCTION AND INSTALLED GENERATING CAPACITY, 1970 TO 1977, AND PERCENT PRIVATELY OWNED, 1977, BY STATES

[Capacity as of **Dec. 31.** Covers utilities for public use and industrial plants. Minus sign (−) denotes decrease]

STATE	PRODUCTION (bil. kWh)				INSTALLED CAPACITY (mil. kW)				ANNUAL PERCENT CHANGE, 1970–1977		PERCENT PRIVATELY OWNED, 1977	
	1970	1975	1976	1977	1970	1975	1976	1977	Production	Capacity	Production	Capacity
U.S__	1,636.4	2,003.0	2,124.7	2,211.0	360.3	527.3	550.4	576.2	4.4	6.9	76.2	75.7
N.E_____	65.3	73.9	80.0	80.6	14.5	21.6	22.1	22.1	3.1	6.2	94.0	91.9
Maine____	7.1	10.5	11.8	10.8	1.4	2.3	2.3	2.3	6.2	7.4	72.9	73.4
N.H_____	5.4	5.0	5.2	5.6	1.2	1.6	1.6	1.6	.5	4.2	94.3	95.8
Vt_____	1.0	4.6	4.4	4.6	.3	.9	.9	1.0	24.4	18.8	95.9	90.9
Mass_____	30.2	31.3	33.7	34.1	6.6	9.8	10.3	10.4	1.8	6.7	96.7	92.0
R.I_____	1.6	.8	.5	.6	.4	.3	.3	.3	−13.1	−4.0	95.9	97.2
Conn_____	20.0	21.7	24.5	25.0	4.6	6.6	6.6	6.5	3.2	5.1	98.7	97.5
M.A_____	221.3	245.5	256.5	266.7	52.3	69.3	73.5	77.8	2.7	5.8	85.3	89.2
N.Y_____	97.7	109.5	111.4	115.0	22.7	28.9	30.9	31.8	2.4	4.9	70.0	77.8
N.J_____	38.2	24.0	26.0	31.2	8.9	11.6	11.6	12.8	−2.9	5.3	96.8	97.5
Pa_____	85.3	112.0	119.0	120.6	20.7	28.8	31.0	33.2	5.1	7.0	96.9	97.0
E.N.C____	312.2	373.3	390.6	394.9	67.8	95.6	97.7	102.0	3.4	6.0	92.3	91.6
Ohio_____	85.6	105.7	111.8	112.9	18.2	25.7	25.7	27.2	4.0	5.9	96.7	93.9
Ind_____	59.1	65.4	68.2	68.8	12.2	14.6	15.8	16.2	2.2	4.1	88.9	89.6
Ill_____	76.6	94.7	100.1	102.3	18.3	26.0	26.8	28.5	4.2	6.5	95.8	95.3
Mich_____	61.1	72.3	73.5	72.9	12.2	20.0	20.0	20.6	2.6	7.8	87.5	88.1
Wis_____	29.7	35.4	37.0	38.0	6.9	9.3	9.4	9.4	3.6	4.5	84.6	85.2
W.N.C____	102.8	136.6	145.9	154.4	24.7	37.7	39.3	43.1	6.0	8.3	67.5	64.5
Minn_____	20.4	28.3	31.4	35.1	4.5	7.3	7.9	8.7	8.1	9.9	90.7	83.0
Iowa_____	15.1	16.4	18.2	18.6	3.7	5.5	5.4	5.7	3.0	6.4	86.4	77.7
Mo_____	29.4	40.8	43.2	46.3	7.7	11.2	12.1	13.6	6.7	8.5	77.4	74.7
N. Dak___	6.7	8.4	10.4	10.4	1.4	1.7	1.7	2.2	6.5	6.7	6.4	7.3
S. Dak___	7.3	10.1	10.0	8.0	1.7	2.1	2.1	2.1	1.3	3.1	33.7	33.7
Nebr_____	8.0	13.3	13.3	14.9	2.0	3.8	3.9	3.9	9.3	10.0	−	−
Kans_____	15.9	19.2	19.4	21.0	3.7	6.0	6.1	6.9	4.1	9.3	80.9	74.7
S.A_____	263.3	355.5	383.3	401.7	56.6	95.2	99.9	104.6	6.2	9.2	90.8	89.3
Del_____	5.8	6.2	6.5	6.7	1.0	1.6	1.7	1.7	2.1	7.9	89.2	87.4
Md_____	29.9	28.1	32.4	34.7	5.3	7.8	8.4	9.3	4.9	8.4	96.8	96.9
D.C_____	3.1	1.2	1.3	1.8	1.1	1.3	1.3	1.3	−7.5	2.4	99.6	99.0
Va_____	31.0	37.3	39.2	40.3	6.8	10.2	10.2	10.2	3.8	6.0	93.7	92.4
W. Va____	39.1	63.5	68.9	68.4	7.2	12.5	12.4	12.4	8.3	8.1	96.9	95.6
N.C_____	53.1	54.6	62.5	65.2	10.0	15.2	15.2	16.1	3.0	7.0	95.4	95.5
S.C_____	19.0	40.3	39.7	41.2	4.6	11.1	11.2	11.5	11.7	14.0	81.1	80.8
Ga_____	29.4	44.2	49.3	54.2	6.7	13.4	14.4	14.6	9.1	11.8	90.9	89.0
Fla_____	57.8	80.1	83.5	89.1	13.9	22.1	25.3	27.6	6.4	10.3	83.4	82.3
E.S.C____	151.6	176.2	190.7	210.0	31.8	47.0	47.1	50.5	4.8	6.8	34.5	38.0
Ky_____	45.2	51.1	57.3	56.6	9.4	12.1	12.1	13.0	3.3	4.7	41.5	44.2
Tenn_____	45.0	55.9	62.0	61.1	9.8	14.6	14.6	14.6	4.5	5.9	1.3	1.2
Ala_____	49.9	57.1	56.6	75.2	10.2	15.6	15.6	17.6	6.0	8.1	43.8	48.1
Miss_____	11.6	12.1	14.8	17.2	2.5	4.7	4.7	5.3	5.8	11.3	89.1	91.3
W.S.C____	210.1	261.9	276.2	302.0	46.1	71.4	74.8	79.5	5.3	8.1	79.4	76.4
Ark_____	15.4	15.2	14.0	17.6	3.6	5.2	5.2	5.2	1.9	5.4	72.0	68.0
La_____	46.1	50.1	56.4	60.4	9.2	13.3	14.4	14.8	3.9	7.0	72.5	76.9
Okla_____	23.6	33.4	35.2	36.6	4.8	7.9	8.5	9.3	6.5	9.9	87.6	79.3
Tex_____	125.0	163.2	170.5	187.4	28.4	44.9	46.7	50.3	6.0	8.5	80.7	76.6
Mt_____	76.7	115.8	128.6	138.6	17.7	28.6	31.7	32.2	8.8	8.9	67.7	63.2
Mont_____	10.0	11.9	16.1	13.5	1.8	2.4	3.0	3.0	4.4	7.6	68.0	61.0
Idaho____	7.2	10.4	10.5	6.9	1.3	1.7	1.7	1.7	−.6	3.9	66.5	61.4
Wyo_____	6.6	12.2	16.1	20.0	1.2	2.8	3.4	3.4	17.2	16.0	94.7	91.2
Colo_____	12.2	16.8	18.3	20.7	2.9	4.4	4.6	4.6	7.9	6.8	68.7	64.4
N. Mex___	15.5	20.2	20.4	22.0	3.6	4.2	4.6	4.6	5.1	3.6	94.3	91.8
Ariz_____	14.4	23.0	27.3	31.1	4.3	7.9	9.1	9.1	11.6	11.3	18.6	28.7
Utah_____	4.7	7.4	5.7	8.5	1.0	1.5	1.5	1.9	8.8	9.6	72.5	78.0
Nev_____	5.9	13.8	14.2	15.9	1.6	3.6	3.7	3.7	15.2	12.7	89.3	79.9
Pac_____	233.1	264.4	273.1	262.1	48.8	61.1	63.9	64.5	1.7	4.1	53.9	48.8
Wash_____	73.0	93.5	103.4	80.0	13.0	17.1	18.5	18.6	1.3	5.3	14.7	13.5
Oreg_____	30.4	35.0	37.9	31.7	5.7	7.8	7.9	7.9	.6	4.8	38.3	43.5
Calif____	123.7	127.2	122.5	140.7	28.6	34.0	35.2	35.4	1.9	3.1	79.9	68.0
Alaska___	1.5	2.5	2.8	3.1	.4	.7	1.0	1.0	10.9	14.0	2.2	4.5
Hawaii___	4.4	6.2	6.4	6.6	1.1	1.4	1.4	1.6	6.0	5.5	91.3	89.4

− Represents zero.

Source: 1970, U.S. Federal Power Commission, *Electric Power Statistics*, monthly; thereafter, U.S. Energy Information Administration, *Six-Year Summary of Power Production and Generating Capacity Data*.

No. 1020. Consumption of Fuels by Electric Utilities: 1955 to 1977

[Prior to 1965, excludes Alaska and Hawaii. Includes use of fuels for stand-by purposes. See also *Historical Statistics, Colonial Times to 1970*, series S 95–107]

ITEM	1955	1960	1965	1970	1973	1974	1975	1976	1977
Net generation by fuel [1]_____bil. kWh__	434	607	861	1,244	1,588	1,566	1,618	1,755	1,903
Annual percent change [2]_____	13.3	6.9	7.2	7.6	8.5	−1.4	3.3	8.5	8.4
Coal_____bil. kWh__	301	403	571	675	849	830	853	945	985
Percent of total_____	69.4	66.4	66.3	54.3	53.5	53.0	52.7	53.8	51.8
Fuel oil_____bil. kWh__	37	46	65	179	313	299	289	320	358
Gas_____bil. kWh__	95	158	221	367	341	320	300	295	305
Nuclear_____bil. kWh__	(NA)	1	4	22	83	114	173	191	251
Fuel consumed:									
Total coal equivalent_____mil. sh. tons__	207	266	369	592	729	740	770	832	922
Coal, including lignite_____mil. sh. tons__	144	177	245	321	390	392	406	448	477
Oil_____mil. (42-gal.) bbl__	75	85	115	336	560	536	506	556	624
Gas_____bil. cu. ft__	1,153	1,724	2,321	3,932	3,659	3,443	3,158	3,081	3,189

NA Not available.　　[1] Beginning 1965, includes limited output of wood, waste, and geothermal power.
[2] Represents change from previous year shown; for 1955, change from 1950.

Source: 1955–1970, U.S. Federal Power Commission, *Electric Power Statistics*, and press releases; thereafter, U.S. Energy Information Administration, *Six-Year Summary of Power Production and Generating Capacity Data.*

No. 1021. Privately Owned Electric Utility Generating Plants—Number and Capacity, by Type and Size of Plant: 1970 to 1977

[Capacity as of **Dec. 31**]

TYPE AND SIZE OF PLANT	NUMBER						CAPACITY (mil. kilowatts)					
	1970	1973	1974	1975	1976	1977	1970	1973	1974	1975	1976	1977
Total_____	**2,037**	**2,101**	**2,137**	**2,123**	**2,123**	**2,102**	**262.8**	**348.5**	**377.3**	**398.9**	**415.4**	**436.1**
Steam conventional__	672	664	671	658	659	641	222.4	276.2	290.1	303.8	316.3	330.1
Under 100,000 kW__	220	195	182	164	159	148	8.2	7.5	7.2	6.8	6.6	6.0
100,000–500,000 kW_	299	274	276	267	257	244	77.1	71.5	72.4	70.0	67.3	63.8
Over 500,000 kW___	153	195	213	227	243	249	137.1	197.3	210.5	227.1	242.4	260.3
Steam, nuclear_____	15	27	31	35	37	41	5.7	19.7	28.2	33.5	35.4	41.7
Over 500,000 kW___	7	20	24	29	31	36	4.5	18.8	26.9	32.3	34.1	40.8
Hydro_____	754	731	734	730	732	730	18.9	21.8	22.8	23.1	23.1	23.1
Over 25,000 kW____	165	169	170	170	171	171	15.6	18.6	19.6	19.9	20.0	20.0
Gas turbine_____	265	360	387	397	394	397	14.4	29.3	34.8	37.0	38.8	39.6
Over 25,000 kW___	126	226	251	261	267	272	12.1	27.1	32.5	34.7	36.7	37.4
Internal combustion_	331	319	314	303	301	293	1.3	1.4	1.5	1.5	1.7	1.6
Under 5,000 kW___	238	216	208	199	189	184	.5	.4	.4	.4	.4	.4
Over 5,000 kW____	93	103	106	104	112	109	.9	1.0	1.1	1.1	1.3	1.2

No. 1022. Publicly Owned Electric Utility Plants—Number and Installed Generating Capacity, by Type and Size of Plant: 1970 to 1977

[Capacity as of **Dec. 31**]

TYPE AND SIZE OF PLANT	NUMBER						CAPACITY (mil. kilowatts)					
	1970	1973	1974	1975	1976	1977	1970	1973	1974	1975	1976	1977
Total_____	**1,496**	**1,580**	**1,554**	**1,551**	**1,539**	**1,520**	**78.8**	**94.0**	**100.3**	**109.3**	**115.6**	**120.9**
Steam, conventional____	326	328	323	326	317	310	37.7	44.8	47.6	49.6	52.1	55.6
Under 100,000 kW____	254	244	234	234	219	208	6.9	7.3	7.0	6.9	6.6	6.6
100,000–500,000 kW__	58	65	65	67	71	70	12.3	14.0	14.1	14.8	15.9	15.9
Over 500,000 kW_____	14	19	24	25	27	32	18.5	23.5	26.5	27.9	29.6	33.0
Steam, nuclear_____	1	3	7	10	11	8	.8	1.3	3.4	6.2	7.5	8.2
Over 500,000 kW_____	1	1	3	4	6	6	.8	.8	2.8	4.9	6.6	7.7
Hydro_____	434	430	425	426	417	415	36.3	40.2	40.9	42.8	44.6	45.2
Over 25,000 kW_____	164	178	179	184	184	184	35.1	39.1	39.7	41.7	43.5	44.0
Gas turbine_____	58	100	107	114	126	127	1.1	4.1	4.8	7.1	7.7	8.3
Over 25,000 kW_____	12	35	41	46	54	59	.4	3.1	3.8	6.0	6.6	7.2
Internal combustion____	677	719	692	675	668	660	3.0	3.6	3.6	3.6	3.6	3.7
Under 5,000 kW_____	471	457	435	416	411	395	1.0	.9	.9	.8	.8	.8
Over 5,000 kW_____	206	262	257	259	257	265	2.0	2.7	2.7	2.8	2.8	2.9

Source of tables 1021 and 1022: 1970, U.S. Federal Power Commission, *Electric Power Statistics*, annual, and press releases; thereafter, U.S. Energy Information Administration, *Six-Year Summary of Power Production and Generating Capacity Data.*

No. 1023. Electric Utilities—Balance Sheet and Income Account of Privately-Owned Companies: 1960 to 1976

[In millions of dollars. As of Dec. 31. On the basis of both assets and revenues, these classes (A and B utilities) comprise nearly 100 percent of the privately-owned sector of the electric light and power industry. See also *Historical Statistics, Colonial Times to 1970*, series S 133–146 and V 197–212]

ITEM	1960	1965	1970	1972	1973	1974	1975	1976
COMPOSITE BALANCE SHEET								
Assets and other debits	44,742	56,395	87,417	110,601	124,849	142,990	157,104	173,080
Electric utility plant [1]	45,456	59,703	93,303	116,644	130,840	146,007	160,711	177,566
Depreciation and amortization	*8,889*	*13,631*	*20,253*	*23,864*	*26,227*	*28,870*	*31,891*	*35,567*
Net electric utility plant	36,567	46,072	73,050	92,780	104,613	117,137	128,820	141,999
Other utility plant	4,852	6,613	8,974	10,234	10,799	11,281	11,673	12,097
Depreciation and amortization	*963*	*1,418*	*2,095*	*2,445*	*2,620*	*2,865*	*3,107*	*3,368*
Net other utility plant	3,889	5,195	6,879	7,789	8,179	8,416	8,566	8,729
Total utility plant	50,308	66,315	102,277	126,878	141,639	157,288	172,384	189,663
Depreciation and amortization	*9,852*	*15,048*	*22,348*	*26,309*	*28,847*	*31,735*	*34,998*	*38,935*
Net total utility plant	40,456	51,267	79,929	100,569	112,792	125,553	137,386	150,728
Other property and investments	1,004	1,247	1,742	2,507	3,412	4,014	4,498	4,822
Current and accrued assets	3,066	3,639	5,321	6,936	7,705	11,873	13,530	15,571
Deferred debits	216	242	425	589	940	1,550	1,691	1,959
Liabilities and other credits	44,742	56,395	87,417	110,601	124,849	142,990	157,104	173,080
Capital stock	13,322	15,668	20,782	27,463	30,836	33,984	37,773	41,613
Other paid-in capital	1,747	2,622	4,400	6,769	8,048	9,419	11,531	13,444
Retained earnings	3,736	5,712	9,363	11,295	12,396	13,299	14,668	16,233
Subsidiary earnings [2]	(X)	(X)	(X)	(X)	394	485	602	667
Long-term debt	21,035	25,502	41,937	51,553	56,673	64,499	70,820	76,210
Current and accrued liabilities	3,112	4,222	7,309	8,752	10,963	15,240	13,655	14,054
Deferred credits and operating reserves	277	546	945	1,349	1,540	1,855	2,689	4,046
Contributions in aid of construction	188	294	483	626	652	(X)	(X)	(X)
Accumulated deferred income taxes	1,325	1,829	2,198	2,794	3,347	4,209	5,368	6,813
COMPOSITE INCOME ACCOUNTS								
Electric operating revenues	10,116	13,400	19,791	25,354	29,104	37,225	44,598	50,552
Electric operating expenses	7,917	10,296	15,310	19,715	22,677	30,134	36,075	41,126
Net electric operating revenues	2,199	3,104	4,481	5,639	6,427	7,091	8,523	9,426
Electric utility operating income	2,201	3,107	4,481	5,639	6,427	7,091	8,523	9,426
Other utility operating income	198	304	404	400	433	495	522	634
Total utility operating income	2,397	3,409	4,885	6,099	6,860	7,586	9,045	10,060
Other income	178	191	774	1,303	1,571	1,992	2,208	2,489
Total income	2,575	3,600	5,659	7,403	8,431	9,578	11,253	12,549
Income deductions	792	1,019	2,251	2,987	3,500	4,454	5,091	5,355
Net income [3]	1,783	2,581	3,408	4,422	5,041	5,470	6,132	7,201

X Not applicable.   [1] Includes construction work in progress.
[2] Unappropriated undistributed.   [3] Beginning 1972, includes net extraordinary income.

Source: 1960–1975, U.S. Federal Power Commission and, thereafter, U.S. Energy Information Administration, *Statistics of Privately Owned Electric Utilities in the United States*, annual.

No. 1024. Largest Public Utility Companies—Assets, Revenues, Income, and Stockholders' Equity, by Rank of Assets: 1970 and 1977

[In millions of dollars, except percent. Excludes telephone and telegraph companies. As of **Dec. 31** or calendar year, as applicable]

ASSET GROUP	1970				1977			
	Assets [1]	Operating revenues [2]	Net income	Stock-holders' equity [3]	Assets [1]	Operating revenues [2]	Net income	Stock-holders' equity [3]
40 largest	73,787	21,349	2,640	26,244	150,791	56,894	5,975	56,368
Lowest ten	11,135	3,445	432	4,110	22,272	10,373	961	7,972
Second ten	13,944	4,489	505	4,911	26,993	11,576	1,145	9,922
Third ten	18,066	5,687	628	5,832	38,525	13,462	1,459	14,171
Highest ten	30,642	7,728	1,075	11,391	63,001	21,482	2,411	24,303
Percent of total	100.0	100.0	100.0	100.0	100.0	100.0	100.0	100.0
Lowest ten	15.1	16.1	16.4	15.7	14.8	18.2	16.1	14.1
Second ten	18.9	21.0	19.1	18.7	17.9	20.4	19.2	17.6
Third ten	24.5	26.6	23.8	22.2	25.6	23.7	24.4	25.1
Highest ten	41.5	36.2	40.7	43.4	41.8	37.8	40.4	43.1

[1] Total assets employed in business, net of depreciation; includes consolidated subsidiaries.   [2] Gross receipts from operations during year; includes nonutility revenues from manufacturing, transportation, etc.   [3] Capital stock, surplus, and retained earnings (i.e., net worth).

Source: Fortune, New York, N.Y., adapted from *The Fortune Directory*. (Copyright by Time, Inc.)

No. 1025. Electric Light and Power Industry—Energy Generated, Sales, Revenue, and Customers: 1950 to 1977

[Prior to 1960, excludes Alaska and Hawaii]

CLASS	1950	1955	1960	1965	1970	1973	1974	1975	1976	1977
Energy generated [1]_____bil. kWh__	329	547	753	1,055	1,532	1,860	1,867	1,918	2,037	2,124
Sales to ultimate customers [2]_____bil. kWh__	**281**	**481**	**683**	**953**	**1,391**	**1,703**	**1,701**	**1,733**	**1,850**	**1,951**
Residential or domestic_____bil. kWh__	70	125	196	281	448	554	555	586	613	652
Percent of total_____	25.0	26.1	28.7	29.5	32.2	32.5	32.6	33.8	33.2	33.4
Comm., small light and power__bil. kWh__	52	78	115	202	313	397	393	418	441	469
Indus., large light and power____bil. kWh__	142	258	345	433	573	687	689	662	725	757
Revenue from ultimate customers [2]_bil. dol__	**5.1**	**8.0**	**11.5**	**15.2**	**22.1**	**31.7**	**39.1**	**46.9**	**53.5**	**62.6**
Residential or domestic_____bil. dol__	2.0	3.3	4.9	6.3	9.4	13.2	15.7	18.8	21.1	24.7
Percent of total_____	39.7	41.4	42.2	41.8	42.7	41.6	40.1	40.1	39.6	39.4
Comm., small light and power____bil. dol__	1.4	1.9	2.8	4.3	6.3	9.1	11.2	13.5	15.2	18.0
Indus., large light and power_____bil. dol__	1.4	2.4	3.3	3.9	5.4	8.1	10.7	12.7	15.0	17.6
Ultimate customers, Dec. 31 [2]_____millions__	**45.0**	**52.6**	**58.9**	**65.6**	**72.5**	**78.5**	**80.1**	**81.8**	**83.6**	**85.6**
Residential or domestic_____millions__	38.9	45.8	51.4	57.6	64.0	69.4	71.0	72.6	74.2	75.9
Comm., small light and power__millions__	5.6	6.2	6.8	7.4	7.9	8.4	8.5	8.6	8.8	8.9
Indus., large light and power___millions__	.3	.4	.5	.3	.4	.4	.4	.4	.4	.4
Avg. kWh used per customer_____1,000__	**6.4**	**9.3**	**11.7**	**14.7**	**19.4**	**22.0**	**21.4**	**21.4**	**22.4**	**23.1**
Residential_____1,000__	1.8	2.8	3.9	4.9	7.1	8.1	7.9	8.2	8.4	8.7
Commercial, small light and power__1,000__	9.3	12.7	17.0	27.4	40.0	47.6	46.6	49.0	50.7	52.9
Avg. annual bill per customer_____dol__	**115**	**155**	**198**	**234**	**308**	**408**	**493**	**578**	**646**	**740**
Residential_____dol__	53	73	95	111	148	192	224	262	288	329
Commercial, small light and power____dol__	245	316	418	584	803	1,094	1,327	1,582	1,755	2,031
Avg. revenue per kWh sold_____cents__	**1.81**	**1.67**	**1.69**	**1.59**	**1.59**	**1.86**	**2.30**	**2.70**	**2.89**	**3.21**
Residential_____cents__	2.88	2.65	2.47	2.25	2.10	2.38	2.83	3.21	3.45	3.78
Comm., small light and power_____cents__	2.63	2.50	2.46	2.13	2.01	2.30	2.85	3.23	3.46	3.84
Indus., large light and power_____cents__	1.02	.94	.97	.90	.95	1.17	1.55	1.92	2.07	2.33

[1] Source: 1950–1975, U.S. Federal Power Commission; thereafter, U.S. Energy Information Administration, *Six-Year Summary of Power Production and Generating Capacity Data.*
[2] Includes other types not shown separately.

Source: Except as noted, Edison Electric Institute, New York, N.Y., *Statistical Year Book.*

No. 1026. Electric Energy Sales, by Class of Service, and by States: 1976

[In billions of kilowatthours]

STATE	Total [1]	Residential	Commercial	Industrial	STATE	Total [1]	Residential	Commercial	Industrial
Total_____	**1,836.0**	**602.9**	**423.6**	**740.0**	S.A.—Con.				
					W. Va_____	18.1	5.3	2.9	9.8
N.E._____	**71.1**	**27.5**	**21.8**	**20.1**	N.C._____	55.0	20.0	10.8	22.7
Maine_____	7.1	2.8	1.5	2.7	S.C._____	32.3	10.4	6.7	14.4
N.H._____	5.3	2.3	.9	2.0	Ga._____	44.3	16.9	11.8	15.1
Vt_____	3.2	1.5	.6	1.0	Fla_____	74.0	36.0	21.6	14.2
Mass_____	31.2	11.2	11.3	7.8	**E.S.C._____**	**170.0**	**52.4**	**20.4**	**93.7**
R.I._____	4.8	1.8	1.5	1.3	Ky_____	33.0	6.5	3.9	21.1
Conn_____	19.5	7.9	6.0	5.3	Tenn_____	72.7	23.6	6.9	41.4
M.A._____	**235.5**	**73.3**	**62.8**	**87.6**	Ala_____	44.3	14.1	5.9	23.7
N.Y._____	98.4	29.5	30.8	28.7	Miss_____	20.0	8.2	3.7	7.5
N.J._____	45.0	15.0	14.2	15.3	**W.S.C._____**	**221.4**	**70.7**	**47.2**	**94.0**
Pa._____	92.1	28.8	17.8	43.6	Ark_____	20.6	7.7	3.7	8.3
E.N.C._____	**358.9**	**105.2**	**71.2**	**169.7**	La_____	39.8	12.5	7.0	17.3
Ohio_____	112.3	28.7	17.4	62.6	Okla_____	24.5	9.3	5.5	8.1
Ind_____	56.3	16.7	8.9	30.1	Tex_____	136.5	41.2	31.0	60.3
Ill_____	88.1	26.3	23.3	32.2	**Mt_____**	**90.1**	**27.6**	**23.8**	**34.6**
Mich_____	69.7	21.3	13.8	33.2	Mont_____	9.9	2.3	1.5	5.9
Wis_____	32.5	12.2	7.8	11.6	Idaho_____	13.2	4.2	3.7	5.3
W.N.C._____	**121.5**	**46.9**	**29.1**	**41.5**	Wyo_____	4.9	.9	.7	3.1
Minn_____	27.9	10.5	4.4	12.3	Colo_____	16.7	5.3	5.1	5.6
Iowa_____	21.1	8.4	4.7	7.4	N. Mex_____	7.2	2.1	2.5	2.2
Mo_____	34.0	13.3	9.9	9.6	Ariz_____	22.1	7.3	6.0	7.2
N. Dak_____	4.0	2.1	.6	1.0	Utah_____	8.3	2.7	2.0	2.9
S. Dak_____	4.3	2.1	.7	1.2	Nev_____	7.8	2.8	2.3	2.4
Nebr_____	12.1	4.7	3.4	3.5	**Pac_____**	**259.8**	**80.8**	**71.3**	**96.2**
Kans_____	18.1	5.8	5.4	6.5	Wash_____	61.0	20.3	8.8	29.6
S.A._____	**307.7**	**118.5**	**76.0**	**102.6**	Oreg_____	35.0	12.1	8.2	14.1
Del_____	5.3	1.7	1.3	2.3	Calif_____	156.0	45.7	52.6	49.3
Md. [2]_____	36.0	11.0	10.7	13.6	Alaska_____	2.2	1.0	.6	.5
Va._____	42.7	17.2	10.2	10.5	Hawaii_____	5.6	1.7	1.1	2.7

[1] Includes "Other" service, not shown separately.   [2] Includes District of Columbia.

Source: U.S. Energy Information Administration, unpublished data.

No. 1027. RURAL ELECTRIFICATION ADMINISTRATION—ELECTRIC PROGRAM, SUMMARY OF OPERATIONS: 1960 TO 1977

[Includes Virgin Islands and Puerto Rico. See also *Historical Statistics, Colonial Times to 1970*, series S 147-159]

ITEM	1960	1965	1970	1973	1974	1975	1976	1977 [1]
Loans and guarantees approved, Dec. 31: [2]								
Borrowers [3]	1,087	1,103	1,096	1,091	1,094	1,095	1,093	1,097
REA amount_____mil. dol__	4,256	5,793	7,496	8,945	9,674	10,440	11,180	12,068
Guaranteed amount_____mil. dol__	–	–	–	–	1,075	2,450	6,124	8,573
Non-REA amount_____mil. dol__	–	–	–	660	917	1,086	1,290	1,566
Systems in operation, Dec. 31: [4]								
Systems [5]	1,038	1,052	1,050	1,046	1,047	1,050	1,048	1,051
Miles energized [6]_____1,000__	1,465	1,567	1,676	1,767	1,798	1,828	1,857	1,890
Consumers served_____1,000__	4,826	5,541	6,442	7,457	7,768	8,018	8,312	8,631
Borrowers' operations during year: [7]								
Energy generated_____mil. kWh__	4,922	8,834	23,814	32,045	32,795	33,463	38,660	46,015
Energy purchased_____mil. kWh__	26,057	39,104	60,478	79,235	84,520	91,875	100,140	102,627
Energy sold_____mil. kWh__	27,269	42,668	76,009	100,688	105,691	112,670	123,199	131,548
Revenue_____mil. dol__	615	847	1,309	1,913	2,316	2,972	3,556	4,212
Average monthly consumption per								
consumer, all consumers___kWh__	466	654	948	1,120	1,149	1,191	1,254	1,313
Residential consumers [8]_____kWh__	357	479	687	793	803	840	866	910
Total utility plant_____mil. dol__	3,697	4,979	7,715	9,043	10,109	11,845	14,031	17,266
Employees_____	(NA)	31,702	37,013	41,422	42,908	43,629	44,655	46,463

– Represents zero.   NA Not available.   [1] Preliminary, except loans approved.   [2] Cumulative net (excludes loans rescinded).   [3] Organizations, mainly cooperatives, to which loans for extending central station electric service in rural areas are made.   [4] Includes data at time of repayment of loan for borrowers whose loans have been repaid in full. As of Dec. 31, 1977, there were 110 such borrowers, with 25,498 miles energized and 144,266 consumers served.   [5] Rural electric distribution, generation, and transmission systems operated by REA borrowers.   [6] Pole miles of electric distribution and transmission line in service.   [7] Excludes energy sales and revenues of power sold by one REA borrower to another.   [8] Includes rural-nonfarm and farm consumers.

Source: U.S. Rural Electrification Administration, *Annual Statistical Report—Rural Electric Borrowers*.

No. 1028. PRIVATELY OWNED GAS UTILITY INDUSTRY—BALANCE SHEET AND INCOME ACCOUNT: 1960 TO 1977

[In millions of dollars. Excludes Alaska for 1960. The gas utility industry consists of pipeline and distribution companies. Excludes operations of companies distributing gas in bottles or tanks. See also *Historical Statistics, Colonial Times to 1970*, series S 205-218]

ITEM	1960	1965	1970	1973	1974	1975	1976	1977
COMPOSITE BALANCE SHEET								
Assets, total [1]	20,000	25,640	34,929	43,867	46,607	50,286	55,261	59,697
Total utility plant_____	20,835	28,205	38,541	45,616	47,484	49,384	52,066	55,020
Depreciation and amortization_____	4,570	7,205	10,696	13,883	15,358	16,779	18,693	20,586
Utility plant (net)_____	16,265	21,000	27,845	31,733	32,126	32,605	33,373	34,434
Investment and fund accounts [1]_____	1,380	1,885	3,024	6,696	7,539	9,198	10,876	12,513
Current and accrued assets_____	2,185	2,545	3,674	4,769	6,060	7,543	9,707	11,194
Deferred debits [2]_____	170	210	386	670	882	940	1,305	1,556
Liabilities, total [1]	20,000	25,640	34,929	43,867	46,607	50,286	55,261	59,697
Capitalization, total [1]_____	16,940	21,520	28,646	35,290	36,360	39,044	42,379	44,316
Capital stock [1]_____	7,810	10,005	12,965	17,123	17,942	19,500	21,593	23,840
Long-term debts_____	9,130	11,515	15,681	18,167	18,418	19,544	20,786	20,476
Current and accrued liabilities_____	2,420	3,035	4,832	6,162	7,765	8,158	9,063	10,636
Deferred income taxes [3]_____	350	660	788	1,392	1,665	2,052	2,525	2,794
Other liabilities and credits_____	290	425	663	1,023	817	1,032	1,294	1,951
COMPOSITE INCOME ACCOUNT								
Operating revenues, total_____	8,696	11,525	16,380	20,585	24,195	30,550	37,618	46,309
Operating expenses [4]_____	7,587	10,063	14,306	18,006	21,616	27,480	34,217	42,685
Operation and maintenance_____	5,951	7,973	11,636	14,582	17,450	22,957	28,949	36,958
Federal, State, and local taxes_____	1,058	1,292	1,569	2,043	2,291	2,763	3,363	3,719
Operating income_____	1,109	1,462	2,074	2,579	2,865	3,070	3,401	3,624
Utility operating income_____	1,137	1,503	2,159	2,708	3,012	3,221	3,542	3,723
Income before interest charges [1]_____	1,247	1,660	2,457	3,315	3,856	4,137	4,645	4,996
Net income [1]_____	830	1,107	1,427	1,977	2,303	2,502	2,877	3,193
Dividends_____	581	781	1,006	1,335	1,363	1,509	1,783	1,959

[1] Beginning 1973, not comparable with earlier years due to Federal Power Commission ruling requiring adoption of the equity method in reporting earnings of subsidiaries.   [2] Includes capital stock discount and expense and reacquired securities. Beginning 1960, reacquired securities are deducted from the appropriate capital account.   [3] Includes reserves for deferred income taxes and accumulated deferred income taxes.   [4] Includes expenses not shown separately.

Source: American Gas Association, Arlington, Va., *Gas Facts*, annual (copyright).

No. 1029. Gas Utility Industry—Summary: 1950 to 1977

[Excludes Hawaii through 1955 and Alaska through 1960. Covers natural, manufactured, mixed, and liquid petroleum gas. Based on questionnaire mailed to all privately owned gas utilities and municipally owned gas departments in the United States, except those with annual revenues less than $25,000, which, in the aggregate, account for only a negligible portion of the industry. See also *Historical Statistics, Colonial Times to 1970*, series S 190–204]

ITEM	1950	1955	1960	1965	1970	1973	1974	1975	1976	1977
Customers _____1,000..	24,001	28,479	33,054	37,338	41,482	43,711	44,267	44,555	44,942	45,274
Residential	22,146	26,283	30,418	34,341	38,097	40,116	40,628	40,950	41,338	41,682
Commercial	1,739	2,048	2,458	2,790	3,131	3,331	3,392	3,367	3,371	3,371
Industrial and other	116	149	178	207	254	264	249	237	233	220
Sales [2] _____trillion Btu [3] ..	4,209	6,659	9,288	11,980	16,044	16,480	16,000	14,863	14,814	14,341
Residential	1,384	2,239	3,188	3,999	4,923	4,994	4,865	4,991	5,014	4,946
Percent of total	32.9	33.6	34.3	33.4	30.7	30.3	30.4	33.6	33.9	34.5
Commercial	410	603	920	1,345	2,007	2,281	2,293	2,387	2,423	2,409
Industrial	2,289	3,535	4,710	6,146	8,439	8,371	8,153	6,837	7,107	6,711
Other	126	282	470	490	674	835	689	648	270	275
Revenues [2] _____mil. dol..	1,948	3,450	5,617	7,407	10,283	12,987	15,242	19,101	23,701	28,303
Residential	1,177	2,007	3,177	4,030	5,207	6,247	6,899	8,445	9,941	11,541
Percent of total	60.4	58.2	56.6	54.4	50.6	48.1	44.9	44.2	41.9	40.8
Commercial	266	424	723	1,054	1,620	2,172	2,539	3,302	4,075	4,980
Industrial	480	938	1,563	2,148	3,181	4,197	5,391	6,745	9,374	11,385
Other	26	81	153	176	274	371	413	608	311	397
Prices _____dol. per mil Btu [3]..	.46	.52	.60	.62	.64	.79	.95	1.29	1.60	1.97
Residential	.85	.90	1.00	1.01	1.06	1.25	1.42	1.69	1.98	2.33
Commercial	.65	.70	.79	.78	.81	.95	1.11	1.38	1.68	2.07
Industrial	.21	.27	.33	.35	.38	.50	.66	.99	1.32	1.70
Gas mains mileage _____1,000..	387	497	631	768	913	963	974	980	987	998
Field and gathering	33	46	56	62	66	66	66	68	70	71
Transmission	113	146	184	211	252	263	262	263	258	260
Distribution	242	305	391	495	595	634	646	649	659	667
Construction expenditure [4] mil. dol..	1,198	1,345	1,845	1,935	2,506	2,966	2,965	2,466	2,425	2,833
Transmission	716	593	848	770	1,019	746	632	590	530	670
Distribution	299	500	696	824	913	1,094	1,097	910	926	1,048
Production and storage	144	198	216	225	370	972	1,060	831	828	943

[1] Annual average.   [2] Excludes sales for resale.   [3] For definition, see headnote, table 1001.   [4] Includes general.

No. 1030. Gas Utility Industry—Prices, by Class of Service, and States: 1970 to 1977

[In dollars per million Btu. For definition of Btu, see headnote, table 1001. Excludes sales for resale]

REGION AND STATE	1970	1976	1977 Total	1977 Residential	1977 Commercial	1977 Industrial	REGION AND STATE	1970	1976	1977 Total	1977 Residential	1977 Commercial	1977 Industrial
U.S.	.64	1.60	1.97	2.33	2.07	1.70	So. Atl.—Con.						
N. Eng	1.60	3.31	3.67	4.11	3.52	2.76	W. Va	.64	1.49	1.91	2.11	1.92	1.70
Maine	2.23	3.34	3.92	5.13	3.85	3.02	N.C.	.70	1.92	2.60	2.83	2.89	2.25
N.H.	1.54	2.53	3.09	3.36	3.08	2.76	S.C.	.62	1.38	1.69	2.67	1.92	1.38
Vt	2.22	2.38	2.69	3.80	3.39	1.42	Ga	.57	1.40	1.78	2.26	1.67	1.38
Mass	1.64	3.32	3.68	4.08	3.52	2.71	Fla	.55	1.45	1.62	3.30	2.12	1.19
R.I.	1.36	3.34	3.68	4.04	3.75	2.76	E. So. Cent.	.51	1.26	1.64	1.96	1.78	1.41
Conn	1.60	3.40	3.78	4.30	3.53	2.98	Ky	.67	1.32	1.69	1.83	1.71	1.43
Mid. Atl.	1.06	2.30	2.72	3.03	2.68	2.15	Tenn	.53	1.23	1.60	1.78	1.85	1.43
N.Y	1.21	2.47	2.96	3.26	2.68	2.31	Ala	.52	1.25	1.65	2.21	1.76	1.37
N.J.	1.26	2.89	3.14	3.42	3.13	2.41	Miss	.38	1.24	1.63	2.05	1.76	1.46
Pa	.87	1.93	2.34	2.56	2.42	2.01	W. So. Cent.	.35	1.39	1.72	2.08	1.81	1.67
E. No. Cent..	.74	1.63	2.05	2.23	2.04	1.82	Ark	.37	.95	1.24	1.46	1.25	1.14
Ohio	.73	1.64	2.12	2.23	2.07	1.95	La	.30	1.13	1.46	1.93	1.60	1.37
Ind	.71	1.38	1.77	2.06	1.86	1.49	Okla	.46	1.09	1.45	1.73	1.48	1.39
Ill	.73	1.61	2.07	2.26	2.01	1.86	Tex	.35	1.57	1.89	2.36	2.10	1.85
Mich	.78	1.74	2.06	2.20	2.09	1.86	Mt	.49	1.21	1.56	1.90	1.67	1.34
Wis	.80	1.70	2.13	2.46	2.17	1.86	Mont	.54	1.34	1.57	1.69	1.48	1.53
W. No. Cent.	.56	1.21	1.57	1.93	1.65	1.27	Idaho	.67	1.88	2.29	3.20	2.60	1.93
Minn	.67	1.39	1.81	2.14	1.91	1.46	Wyo	.34	.96	1.28	1.66	1.47	1.07
Iowa	.62	1.26	1.61	1.93	1.67	1.34	Colo	.48	1.07	1.43	1.71	1.52	1.11
Mo	.54	1.37	1.81	2.08	1.83	1.33	N. Mex	.42	1.09	1.57	2.00	1.69	1.43
N. Dak	.82	1.53	1.81	2.03	1.59	1.86	Ariz	.57	1.33	1.68	2.59	1.85	1.25
S. Dak	.71	1.22	1.53	1.84	1.47	1.15	Utah	.46	1.11	1.32	1.55	1.43	1.10
Nebr	.51	1.13	1.40	1.74	1.47	1.12	Nev	.58	1.55	1.86	2.17	2.03	1.72
Kans	.39	.94	1.25	1.51	1.19	1.19	Pac	.58	1.63	1.99	1.93	2.08	2.00
So. Atl	.72	1.69	2.09	2.68	2.21	1.57	Wash	.65	1.99	2.37	3.02	2.56	2.03
Del	.93	2.08	2.60	3.16	2.79	2.03	Oreg	.74	2.21	2.48	3.29	2.90	2.06
Md	1.13	2.20	2.78	3.15	2.79	2.18	Calif	.56	1.57	1.93	1.81	1.99	2.00
D.C.	1.28	2.40	3.04	3.27	2.82	2.56	Alaska	.70	.94	1.05	1.70	1.31	.76
Va	.95	2.05	2.52	2.99	2.55	1.89	Hawaii	2.76	6.78	7.02	8.42	6.62	6.58

Source of tables 1029 and 1030: American Gas Association, Arlington, Va., *Gas Facts*, annual, (copyright).

No. 1031. Gas Utility Industry—Customers, Sales, and Revenues, by Class of Service, and States: 1977

[See headnote, table 1029]

REGION AND STATE	CUSTOMERS [1] (1,000)				SALES [3] (trillion Btu [4])				REVENUES [3] (mil. dol.)			
	Total [2]	Residential	Commercial	Industrial	Total [2]	Residential	Commercial	Industrial	Total [2]	Residential	Commercial	Industrial
U.S.	45,274	41,682	3,371	173	14,341	4,946	2,409	6,711	28,303	11,541	4,980	11,385
N. Eng	1,679	1,553	114	9	261	138	67	52	958	569	235	143
Maine	17	16	1	(Z)	2	1	1	1	8	3	2	2
N.H.	46	41	4	(Z)	8	4	2	2	25	14	6	5
Vt.	17	15	1	(Z)	4	1	1	1	10	5	2	2
Mass.	1,050	974	68	5	159	87	43	27	585	355	150	72
R.I.	160	149	10	2	24	14	4	6	88	56	16	16
Conn.	390	358	30	2	64	32	17	16	242	137	60	46
Mid. Atl.	8,090	7,504	550	24	1,480	800	273	377	4,031	2,419	730	810
N.Y.	3,955	3,706	227	12	579	351	110	98	1,714	1,143	296	227
N.J.	1,829	1,643	180	6	259	146	58	55	814	500	181	132
Pa.	2,307	2,156	143	6	642	303	104	224	1,503	776	253	450
E. No. Cent.	10,370	9,566	754	47	3,606	1,596	732	1,264	7,391	3,562	1,496	2,302
Ohio	2,737	2,534	194	6	872	430	161	275	1,844	960	333	535
Ind.	1,204	1,098	101	4	432	171	68	191	766	352	126	285
Ill.	3,190	2,945	226	19	1,134	518	246	370	2,349	1,168	494	686
Mich.	2,269	2,101	159	9	847	356	202	285	1,746	785	423	531
Wis.	970	888	73	9	321	121	55	143	686	298	120	265
W. No. Cent.	3,918	3,547	351	18	1,445	506	274	652	2,270	975	452	829
Minn.	741	674	60	7	249	100	44	102	450	214	85	148
Iowa	709	632	75	2	268	91	54	120	431	176	90	161
Mo.	1,182	1,096	85	1	334	157	82	93	603	326	150	124
N. Dak.	70	69	9	(Z)	23	10	11	2	41	21	17	4
S. Dak.	96	85	11	1	27	11	8	8	42	21	12	9
Nebr.	420	363	54	2	154	51	33	70	215	88	49	78
Kans.	691	629	57	5	390	86	42	258	489	129	50	305
So. Atl.	3,914	3,581	310	16	1,015	363	199	431	2,120	973	435	678
Del.	82	77	5	(Z)	18	8	3	6	46	24	9	13
Md.	771	717	49	5	137	71	22	43	382	224	61	94
D.C.	152	136	16	(Z)	26	14	10	2	78	44	29	4
Va.	523	478	42	2	115	49	27	34	289	147	68	64
W. Va.	395	362	33	(Z)	134	55	26	52	252	116	45	89
N.C.	344	301	38	2	79	30	18	30	206	84	51	68
S.C.	286	258	26	1	105	21	15	62	177	55	29	86
Ga.	945	870	70	4	261	100	50	109	464	226	83	150
Fla.	416	383	31	1	140	16	28	92	227	53	60	110
E. So. Cent.	2,161	1,954	190	7	702	220	112	355	1,153	431	199	502
Ky.	624	569	52	1	162	80	32	45	274	147	55	63
Tenn.	496	432	57	3	189	47	37	101	301	84	68	145
Ala.	655	606	45	2	216	61	26	128	357	135	47	175
Miss.	386	347	36	1	136	32	16	82	222	65	29	119
W. So. Cent.	5,226	4,761	432	28	3,088	444	246	2,251	5,298	923	445	3,761
Ark.	473	419	52	2	196	48	32	115	242	70	40	131
La.	955	888	64	2	488	78	29	365	714	151	47	499
Okla.	765	690	70	4	453	79	48	324	657	137	71	448
Tex.	3,033	2,763	246	20	1,952	239	137	1,448	3,686	565	288	2,682
Mt.	2,458	2,222	223	10	876	249	161	445	1,366	473	268	594
Mont.	180	160	19	1	66	23	16	24	104	39	23	37
Idaho	111	96	14	(Z)	50	9	10	31	114	29	25	60
Wyo.	109	96	13	(Z)	54	13	10	30	70	22	15	32
Colo.	746	664	80	2	236	84	63	89	338	143	96	98
N. Mex.	296	262	28	4	148	28	15	92	233	56	26	132
Ariz.	563	517	43	3	138	33	22	79	231	86	41	99
Utah	326	305	20	1	118	47	14	57	156	73	20	63
Nev.	128	123	6	(Z)	65	12	11	42	121	26	22	72
Pac.	7,458	6,994	449	15	1,870	630	347	884	3,716	1,216	720	1,767
Wash.	352	310	41	1	151	33	33	85	357	100	84	172
Oreg.	254	224	30	1	91	21	15	55	225	69	42	114
Calif.	6,785	6,402	370	12	1,596	569	292	732	3,078	1,030	579	1,462
Alaska	33	29	5	(Z)	29	6	7	11	31	10	9	8
Hawaii	34	30	2	2	4	1	1	2	25	7	6	12

Z Less than 500. [1] Averages for the year. [2] Includes "other" service, not shown separately. [3] Excludes sales for resale. [4] For definition, see headnote, table 1001.

Source: American Gas Association, Arlington, Va., *Gas Facts*, annual. (Copyright.)

No. 1032. WATER POWER—DEVELOPED AND ESTIMATED UNDEVELOPED, BY GEO-GRAPHIC DIVISION: 1950 TO 1976

[In millions of kilowatts. As of Dec. 31. Excludes Alaska and Hawaii for 1950 and all capacity of reversible equipment at pumped storage projects (9.8 million kilowatts at yearend 1976). Also excludes capacity precluded from development due to wild and scenic river legislation. For composition of divisions, see fig. I, inside front cover. See also *Historical Statistics, Colonial Times to 1970*, series S 160-175]

DIVISION	DEVELOPED [1]						UNDEVELOPED					
	1950	1960	1965	1970	1975	1976	1950	1960	1965	1970	1975	1976
United States____	18.7	33.2	44.5	52.0	57.0	58.6	87.6	114.2	124.1	128.0	113.7	109.9
New England_____	1.2	1.5	1.5	1.5	1.5	1.5	3.3	2.9	3.2	3.3	3.3	3.2
Middle Atlantic____	1.7	2.5	4.8	4.3	4.2	4.2	6.6	7.6	5.0	4.5	4.3	4.1
E. No. Central_____	.9	.9	.9	.9	.9	.9	2.3	3.0	1.4	1.6	1.4	1.4
W. No. Central_____	.6	1.6	3.0	2.7	2.8	2.8	5.8	6.4	4.1	4.4	2.1	2.1
South Atlantic_____	2.8	3.8	5.2	5.3	5.8	5.8	8.2	8.4	10.0	9.6	8.4	7.1
E. So. Central_____	2.7	3.8	4.5	5.2	5.5	5.5	4.7	4.6	4.3	3.8	3.1	3.1
W. So. Central_____	.5	.9	1.7	1.9	2.3	2.3	3.6	3.9	3.1	3.3	2.7	2.4
Mountain_____	2.3	4.6	5.6	6.2	6.9	7.1	23.4	23.6	26.5	26.7	19.6	19.0
Pacific_____	6.0	13.6	17.4	23.9	27.2	28.5	29.8	53.8	66.5	70.9	68.8	67.5

[1] Installed capacity as shown by nameplate ratings at existing plants of electric utilities and industrials.

Source: 1950-1975, U.S. Federal Power Commission, *Hydroelectric Power Resources of the United States, Developed and Undeveloped*, January 1, 1976; 1976, U.S. Federal Energy Regulatory Commission, unpublished data.

No. 1033. NUCLEAR POWER PLANTS—NUMBER, CAPACITY, AND GENERATION, 1965 TO 1977, AND PROJECTIONS, 1978 TO 1990

ITEM	1965	1970	1974	1975	1976	1977	1978	1985	1990
Operating reactors [1]_____	10	16	44	54	57	65	71	125	178
Capacity [1]_____megawatts__	933	5,150	29,690	38,568	41,129	47,023	53,400	111,000	172,000
Percent of total electric utility capacity_____	.4	1.9	6.6	7.7	8.1	9.0	(NA)	13.5	18.2
Electricity generated__bil. kWh__	3.7	21.8	114.0	172.5	191.1	250.9	269.6	565.6	935.8
Percent of total electric utility generation_____	.4	1.4	6.1	9.0	9.4	11.8	12.3	19.0	26.0

NA Not available.

[1] As of year end. Comprises only reactors in full or commercial operation (excludes 3 in startup phase in 1977).

Source: U.S. Energy Information Administration, *Annual Report to Congress*, vols. II and III, 1977.

No. 1034. COMMERCIAL NUCLEAR POWER GENERATION, BY COUNTRY: 1970 TO 1977

[Generation for **calendar years**; other data as of **December**. Excludes Communist countries]

COUNTRY	REACTORS			ELECTRICITY GENERATED [1] (bil. kWh)					GROSS CAPACITY (1,000 kW)				
	1970	1975	1977	1970	1974	1975	1976	1977	1970	1974	1975	1976	1977
Total_____	64	140	168	73.9	214.4	320.0	388.8	469.4	15,186	58,897	69,196	81,052	91,681
U. S_____	15	55	66	23.2	98.0	181.8	201.6	262.6	5,211	33,659	39,399	44,083	48,324
Argentina_____	–	1	1	–	1.0	2.5	2.6	1.6	–	340	340	340	340
Belgium_____	1	3	3	.3	.1	6.8	10.0	11.9	11	410	1,744	1,744	1,744
Canada_____	1	5	8	.9	15.4	13.2	18.0	26.8	220	2,380	2,380	3,130	4,787
Gr. Britain____	27	29	31	26.5	33.0	30.5	36.8	38.0	4,783	6,168	6,135	7,455	8,102
Finland_____	–	–	1	–	–	–	–	2.7	–	–	–	–	440
France_____	4	10	12	5.7	14.8	18.3	15.8	17.9	1,606	3,023	3,066	3,066	4,928
Germany, F.R. of_____	4	7	10	5.3	11.2	21.7	24.5	35.8	907	2,240	3,452	6,413	6,413
India_____	2	3	3	2.2	2.5	2.5	3.2	2.8	400	620	620	620	620
Italy_____	3	3	3	3.3	3.4	3.8	3.8	3.4	631	626	639	630	630
Japan_____	3	10	14	3.3	15.1	16.7	36.7	27.3	828	3,893	5,278	7,428	7,994
Netherlands___	1	2	2	.4	3.3	3.3	3.9	3.7	55	535	523	523	523
Pakistan_____	–	1	1	–	.6	.5	.5	.3	–	137	137	137	137
Spain_____	1	3	3	.9	6.9	7.5	7.5	6.5	160	1,100	1,117	1,117	1,117
Sweden_____	1	5	6	(z)	2.1	12.0	16.0	19.9	12	2,712	3,312	3,312	3,882
Switzerland____	1	3	3	1.9	7.0	7.7	7.9	8.1	364	1,054	1,054	1,054	1,064
Taiwan_____	–	–	1	–	–	–	–	.1	–	–	–	–	636

– Represents zero.   Z Less than 50,000,000 kWh.   [1] Gross.

Source: McGraw-Hill, Inc., New York, N.Y., *Nucleonics Week*, December issues. (Copyright.)

No. 1035. URANIUM SUPPLY, ENRICHMENT, AND RADIOACTIVE WASTES: 1965 TO 1977

[Years ending Dec. 31, except as noted. Metric ton=1.102 short tons or .984 long ton]

ITEM	1965	1970	1971	1972	1973	1974	1975	1976	1977
URANIUM (U₃O₈)									
Production_____sh. tons__	10,442	12,905	12,273	12,900	13,235	11,528	11,600	12,747	14,900
Exports_____sh. tons__	–	2,100	200	100	600	1,500	500	600	2,100
Imports_____sh. tons__	4,000	–	–	–	–	–	1,100	2,900	4,000
Delivered price_____dol./ton__	(NA)	(NA)	(NA)	(NA)	7.10	7.65	10.50	16.10	19.75
ENRICHMENT [1]									
Enriched product_____metric tons__	166	1,043	2,102	1,597	2,521	4,454	2,270	3,240	3,126
For domestic customers____metric tons__	68	779	1,469	1,123	1,030	1,151	1,005	1,430	1,827
For foreign customers_____metric tons__	98	264	633	474	1,491	3,303	1,265	1,810	1,299
Cost of services_____mil. dol__	(NA)	83.8	220.5	181.4	252.6	538.5	337.1	611.8	658.0
COMMERCIAL RADIOACTIVE WASTES [2]									
Annual discharge_____metric tons__	(NA)	67	110	241	149	454	547	730	949
Inventory, yearend_____metric tons__	(NA)	[3] 161	[3] 193	434	583	1,037	1,584	2,214	3,263

– Represents zero.   NA Not available.   [1] Through 1975, for years ending June 30; beginning 1976, years ending Sept. 30, 1976 includes transition quarter, July–Sept.   [2] Uranium content. Source: Nuclear Assurance Corporation, Atlanta, Ga.   [3] Allows for reprocessing.

Source: Except as noted, U.S. Dept. of Energy, Annual Report to Congress, vol. III, 1977; Statistical Data of the ranium Industry; and unpublished data.

No. 1036. FEDERAL RESEARCH AND DEVELOPMENT OBLIGATIONS FOR ENERGY DEVELOPMENT AND CONVERSION, BY FUNCTION: 1970 TO 1978

[In millions of dollars, except percent. Through 1976, for years ending June 30; thereafter, years ending Sept. 30. Excludes research and development plant. See table 1042 for Federal obligations for R and D]

FUNCTION	1970	1971	1972	1973	1974	1975	1976	1977	1978, est.
Total_____	317.3	323.6	382.7	441.6	605.1	1,109.7	1,387.6	2,390.4	2,797.7
Annual percent change_____	[1]—3.2	2.0	18.3	15.4	37.0	83.4	25.0	72.3	17.0
Nuclear [2]_____	295.9	285.8	334.9	376.5	469.7	674.3	825.2	1,316.4	1,516.9
Percent of total_____	93.3	88.3	87.5	85.3	77.6	60.8	59.5	55.1	54.2
Liquid metal fast breeder reactor_____	}194.3	195.6	234.0	256.7	289.6	399.0	{347.9	541.9	483.3
Nuclear research applications_____							103.9	137.4	156.9
Magnetic fusion_____	27.7	28.3	31.0	37.0	53.0	97.9	130.2	183.0	196.9
Fuel cycle R and D_____	}27.9	26.0	30.7	35.0	45.4{		34.0	50.6	168.5	342.5
Uranium enrichment-process_____							33.3	48.2	68.2	85.7
Reactor safety research_____	26.0	21.7	26.4	33.9	41.7	60.4	78.2	91.1	111.2
Laser fusion [3]_____	(NA)	(NA)	(NA)	(NA)	36.9	45.6	60.7	80.0	101.0
Fossil [2]_____	17.7	31.5	35.9	46.6	81.4	269.1	324.0	549.1	549.0
Coal utilization_____	12.6	25.6	29.7	40.1	70.2	229.7	284.6	464.9	437.5
Petroleum and natural gas_____	2.7	3.0	3.4	3.7	8.1	27.0	23.9	46.3	71.1
In situ technology [4]_____	2.4	2.8	2.9	2.9	3.0	10.8	14.5	35.7	39.0
Solar, geothermal, advance energy sys__	–	–	2.4	5.2	19.1	82.8	126.6	313.9	369.6
Solar energy development_____	–	–	1.7	4.0	12.0	54.7	95.9	260.6	284.1
Geothermal energy development_____	–	–	.7	1.1	7.1	28.0	30.7	53.3	85.5
Conservation_____	2.4	4.3	8.0	10.3	24.2	64.4	85.8	179.6	337.0
Other_____	1.3	2.0	1.4	3.0	10.8	19.1	26.0	31.3	25.2

– Represents zero.   NA Not available.   [1] Decrease from 1969.   [2] Includes other functions, not shown separately.   [3] Prior to 1974, included under national defense R and D and not shown separately.
[4] Covers oil shale technology and coal gasification.

Source: U.S. National Science Foundation, An Analysis of Federal R & D Funding by Function, 1969–1978.

No. 1037. INDUSTRIAL RESEARCH AND DEVELOPMENT EXPENDITURES FOR ENERGY, BY TYPE: 1975 TO 1977

[In millions of dollars. Covers research, applied research, and development. See also table 1044]

TYPE OF ENERGY	1975	1976	1977, est.	TYPE OF ENERGY	1975	1976	1977, est.
Total_____	1,374	1,611	1,862	Nuclear_____	700	800	916
Percent of total				Fission_____	659	743	843
industry R & D_	5.7	6.1	6.3	Fusion_____	41	57	73
				Geothermal_____	6	10	10
Fossil fuels_____	532	605	680				
Oil_____	321	374	409	Solar_____	19	44	51
Gas_____	66	75	82	Conservation and utilization____	52	78	102
Shale_____	14	14	15	Other_____	64	75	104
Coal_____	109	126	156				
Synthetic fuel_____	50	70	95				
Other_____	22	16	18				

Source: U.S. National Science Foundation, Research and Development in Industry, annual.

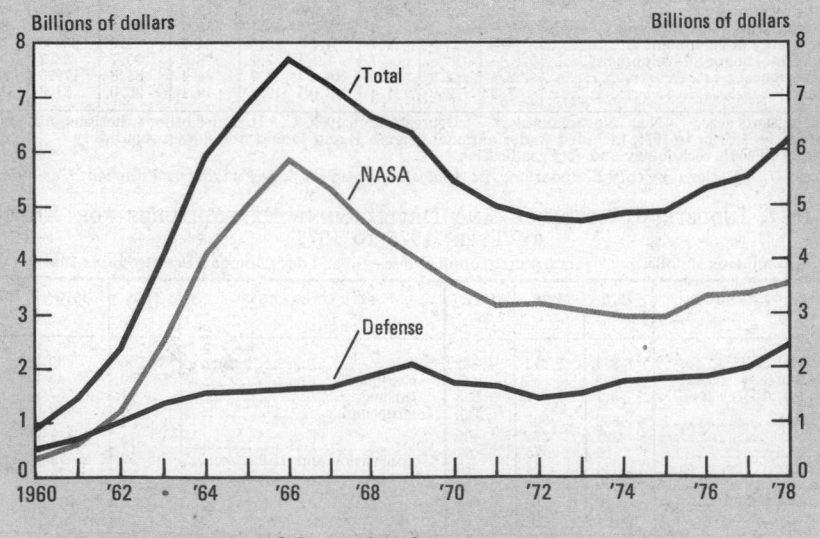

Figure 21.1

Research and Development Funds, By Performance Sector and Source: 1960 to 1978

(See table 1039)

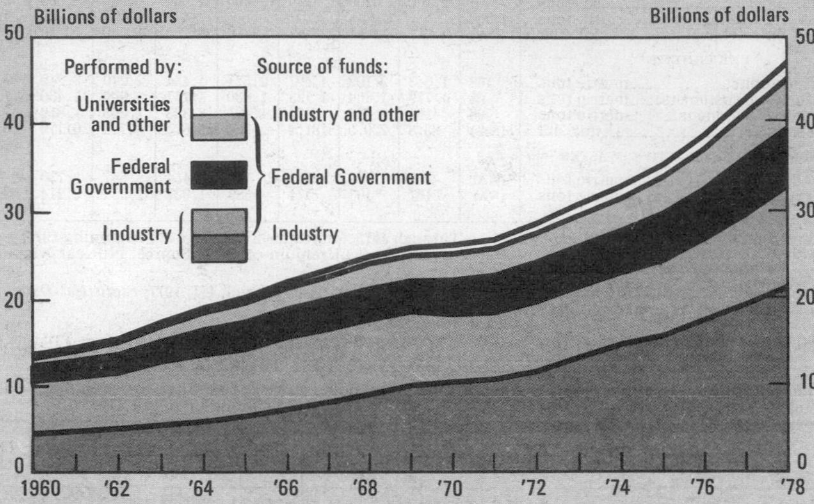

Source: Chart prepared by U.S. Bureau of the Census.
Data from the U.S. National Science Foundation.

Figure 21.2

Outlays for Federal Space Program: 1960 to 1978

(See table 1063)

Source: Chart prepared by U.S. Bureau of the Census.
Data from U.S. Office of Management and Budget.

Section 21

Science

This section presents statistics on scientific and technological resources, with emphasis on patterns of research and development funding and on scientific and technical manpower and education. Also included are statistics on space program outlays and accomplishments. Principal sources of these data are the National Science Foundation and the National Aeronautics and Space Administration.

The National Science Foundation (NSF) gathers data chiefly through recurring surveys. Some current NSF publications containing data on funds for research and development and on scientific and engineering personnel include the occasional bulletin series, *Reviews of Data on Science Resources* and *Science Resources Studies Highlights;* and annual, biennial, and periodic reports such as *Federal Funds for Research, Development, and Other Scientific Activities; Research and Development in Industry; National Patterns of R & D Resources; Manpower Resources for Scientific Activities at Universities and Colleges; Expenditures for Scientific Activities at Universities and Colleges; An Analysis of Federal R & D Funding by Function; Scientists, Engineers, and Physicians From Abroad; Federal Scientific, Technical, and Health Personnel; Graduate Science Education: Student Support and Postdoctorals; Federal Support to Universities, Colleges, and Selected Nonprofit Institutions; Characteristics of Doctoral Scientists and Engineers in the U.S.; Characteristics of Experienced Scientists and Engineers; Scientific and Technical Personnel in Private Industry;* and policy reports relating to national allocation of manpower and funds to science and technology. Statistical surveys in these areas pose particularly difficult problems of concept and definition and the data should, therefore, be regarded as broad estimates rather than precise quantitative statements. Detailed discussions of the scope and limitations of the data appear in the source publications.

The Budget of the United States Government, published by the U.S. Office of Management and Budget, contains summary financial data on Federal research and development programs. In addition, *Aerospace Facts and Figures,* published by Aerospace Industries Association of America, Inc., presents data on sales and orders of space vehicle systems and employment in NASA programs.

Research and development outlays.—The National Science Foundation defines research as a "systematic and intensive study directed toward a fuller knowledge of the subject studied" and development as "the systematic use of scientific knowledge directed toward the production of useful materials, devices, systems, methods, or processes." National data on outlays of funds are composed of four sectors: (*1*) *Government,* made up primarily of Federal executive agencies; (*2*) *industry,* consisting of manufacturing and nonmanufacturing firms and the federally funded research and development centers they administer; (*3*) *colleges and universities,* composed of colleges, universities and their affiliated institutions, agricultural experiment stations and associated schools of agriculture, and federally funded research and development centers administered by educational institutions; and (*4*) *other nonprofit institutions,* consisting of such organizations as private philanthropic foundations, nonprofit research institutes, voluntary health agencies, and federally funded research and development centers administered by nonprofit organizations. These centers are exclusively or substantially financed by the Federal government and, in most instances, were originally established to meet a particular research and development need of the Government. They are administered on a contractual basis, by companies, educational institutions, or other nonprofit organizations. The research and development funds reported consist of current operating costs, including those for planning and administration, except as otherwise noted. They

623

exclude funds for routine testing, mapping and surveying, collection of general-purpose data, dissemination of scientific information, and training of scientific manpower.

Scientists, engineers, and technicians.—Scientists and engineers are defined as persons engaged in scientific and engineering work at a level requiring a knowledge of sciences equivalent at least to that acquired through completion of a 4-year college course. They are generally classified according to the fields of their employment rather than the discipline in which they received their major training. Technicians are defined as persons engaged in technical work at a level requiring knowledge acquired through a technical institute, junior college, or other type of training less extensive than 4-year college training. Craftsmen and skilled workers are excluded.

Historical statistics.—Tabular headnotes provide cross-references, where applicable, to *Historical Statistics of the United States, Colonial Times to 1970.* See Appendix I.

No. 1038. RESEARCH AND DEVELOPMENT—DEFENSE, SPACE, AND OTHER OUTLAYS: 1955 TO 1978

[Includes basic research, applied research, and development. Defense-related outlays comprise all research and development spending by Dept. of Defense including space activities, and a portion of Department of Energy funds. Space related outlays are those of the National Aeronautics and Space Administration; they exclude space activities of other Federal agencies, estimated at less than 5 percent of all space research and development spending. Minus sign (−) denotes decrease]

YEAR	RESEARCH AND DEVELOPMENT OUTLAYS						PERCENT OF TOTAL RESEARCH AND DEVELOPMENT					
	Current dollars		Constant (1972) dollars		Defense-space related (bil. dol.)	Other (bil. dol.)	Federally funded defense-space related			Other outlays		
	Total 1 (bil. dol.)	Annual per-cent change	Total (bil. dol.)	Annual per-cent change			To-tal	De-fense	Space	To-tal	Non-fed-eral	Fed-eral
1955	6.2	2 9.4	10.1	2 7.0	3.0	3.1	49	48	1	51	43	8
1956	8.4	35.5	13.3	31.4	4.2	4.2	50	49	1	50	42	8
1957	9.8	16.9	15.0	13.1	5.3	4.5	54	53	1	47	38	9
1958	10.7	9.6	16.2	7.8	5.8	4.9	54	53	1	47	37	10
1959	12.4	15.4	18.3	12.9	7.0	5.3	57	54	3	43	35	8
1960	13.5	9.4	19.7	7.6	7.4	6.1	55	52	3	44	35	9
1961	14.3	5.9	20.7	4.9	8.0	6.3	56	50	6	44	35	9
1962	15.4	7.5	21.8	5.6	8.5	6.9	55	48	7	46	36	10
1963	17.1	10.8	23.8	9.2	9.4	7.7	55	41	14	44	34	10
1964	18.9	10.5	25.9	8.8	10.6	8.3	56	37	19	45	34	11
1965	20.0	6.3	27.0	4.0	10.8	9.2	54	33	21	46	35	11
1966	21.8	9.0	28.5	5.5	11.4	10.5	52	33	19	48	36	12
1967	23.1	6.0	29.3	2.9	11.3	11.8	49	35	14	51	38	13
1968	24.6	6.3	29.8	1.7	11.8	12.8	48	35	13	52	39	13
1969	25.6	4.2	29.6	−.8	11.5	14.1	45	34	11	55	42	13
1970	25.9	1.1	28.4	−4.0	11.1	14.8	43	33	10	57	43	14
1971	26.6	2.7	27.7	−2.3	10.9	15.7	41	32	9	59	44	15
1972	28.4	6.8	28.4	2.5	11.4	17.0	40	32	8	60	45	15
1973	30.6	7.7	28.9	1.8	11.6	19.0	38	31	7	62	47	15
1974	32.7	6.9	28.2	−2.6	11.4	21.2	35	28	7	65	49	16
1975	35.1	7.5	27.7	−1.7	12.3	22.8	35	27	8	65	48	17
1976	38.5	9.7	28.8	4.1	13.1	25.4	34	26	8	66	49	17
1977, est	42.7	10.9	30.3	5.1	14.1	28.6	33	25	8	67	49	18
1978, est	47.0	10.1	31.4	3.8	15.5	31.5	33	25	8	67	49	18

1 Includes revisions not shown in detail.   2 Change from 1954.

Source: U.S. National Science Foundation, *National Patterns of R & D Resources—Funds and Manpower in the United States, 1953–78;* and unpublished data.

No. 1039. FUNDS FOR PERFORMANCE OF RESEARCH AND DEVELOPMENT AND BASIC RESEARCH, BY SECTOR, DISTRIBUTED BY SOURCE: 1960 TO 1978

[In millions of dollars. Data primarily on calendar year basis—calendar year data for industry and other nonprofit institutions combined with Federal and university fiscal year data. Data refer, in general, to natural sciences including engineering and to social sciences in all but industry sector. Excludes capital expenditures data. Expenditures at associated federally funded research and development centers administered by industry and other nonprofit institutions included in totals of respective sectors. See also Historical Statistics, Colonial Times to 1970, series W 109–125]

PERFORMANCE SECTOR AND SOURCE OF FUNDS	1960	1965	1970	1972	1973	1974	1975	1976	1977, est.	1978, est.
Total research and development [1]	13,523	20,044	25,905	28,396	30,581	32,677	35,196	38,581	42,702	47,000
In 1972 dollars	19,693	26,970	28,355	28,396	28,904	28,165	27,674	28,818	30,285	31,439
Percent Federal as source	64.6	64.9	56.6	55.5	53.3	51.2	51.6	50.6	51.0	50.7
Federal Government	1,726	3,093	3,855	4,482	4,619	4,815	5,397	5,710	6,465	6,555
Industry	10,509	14,185	18,062	19,522	21,199	22,816	24,164	26,677	29,400	32,800
Federal funds	6,081	7,740	7,779	8,010	8,131	8,199	8,605	9,285	10,250	11,600
Industry funds	4,428	6,445	10,283	11,512	13,068	14,617	15,559	17,392	19,150	21,200
Universities and colleges	646	1,474	2,335	2,676	2,940	3,017	3,405	3,724	4,045	4,570
Federal funds	405	1,073	1,648	1,839	2,041	2,032	2,291	2,501	2,720	3,075
Industry funds	40	41	61	75	86	96	113	123	134	145
University and college funds [2]	149	267	461	576	613	671	743	815	886	1,000
Other nonprofit institutions funds [2]	52	93	165	186	200	218	258	285	305	350
Univ. and colleges, associated federally funded R and D centers	360	629	737	764	817	865	987	1,147	1,375	1,555
Other nonprofit institutions	282	663	916	952	1,006	1,164	1,243	1,323	1,417	1,520
Federal funds	166	477	649	653	690	822	875	925	987	1,050
Industry funds	48	62	95	101	105	111	115	120	124	130
Other [3]	68	124	172	198	211	231	253	278	306	340
Total research, basic and applied	4,217	6,891	9,226	9,781	10,527	11,512	12,543	13,955	15,346	16,820
In 1972 dollars	6,141	9,276	10,099	9,781	9,950	9,922	9,862	10,424	10,884	11,251
Percent Federal as source	57.0	62.9	59.9	58.5	58.1	56.8	58.1	57.7	58.0	57.8
Federal Government	755	1,354	1,862	1,943	2,096	2,309	2,499	2,868	3,160	3,300
Industry	2,405	3,250	4,028	4,086	4,426	4,948	5,287	5,925	6,435	7,055
Federal funds	912	1,224	1,207	1,079	1,122	1,177	1,297	1,395	1,585	1,755
Industry funds	1,493	2,026	2,821	3,007	3,304	3,771	3,990	4,536	4,850	5,300
Universities and colleges	612	1,417	2,223	2,566	2,772	2,884	3,257	3,556	3,865	4,370
Federal funds	387	1,036	1,564	1,759	1,918	1,961	2,213	2,407	2,618	2,960
Industry funds	37	39	56	72	81	90	106	115	125	135
University and college funds [2]	138	252	448	555	582	629	696	767	836	945
Other nonprofit institutions funds [2]	50	90	155	180	191	204	242	267	286	330
Univ. and colleges, associated federally funded R and D centers	219	412	485	476	523	567	654	686	900	1,035
Other nonprofit institutions	226	461	628	710	710	804	846	920	986	1,060
Federal funds	130	307	409	465	452	525	545	595	635	680
Industry funds	38	50	77	82	85	90	93	97	100	105
Other [3]	58	104	142	163	173	189	208	228	251	275
Total basic research	1,197	2,555	3,513	3,737	3,866	4,142	4,521	4,838	5,259	5,855
In 1972 dollars	1,743	3,438	3,845	3,737	3,654	3,570	3,555	3,614	3,730	3,916
Percent of total research and development	8.9	12.7	13.6	13.2	12.6	12.7	12.9	12.5	12.3	12.5
Percent Federal as source	59.7	70.8	69.8	68.2	68.2	68.5	68.3	70.0	69.2	69.3
Federal Government	160	364	541	538	537	611	682	719	790	850
Industry	376	592	602	582	620	688	719	790	835	905
Federal funds	79	186	158	127	129	160	151	176	185	205
Industry funds	297	406	444	455	491	528	570	612	650	700
Universities and colleges	433	1,138	1,796	2,022	2,055	2,147	2,406	2,531	2,745	3,120
Federal funds	299	879	1,296	1,421	1,456	1,522	1,697	1,819	1,965	2,230
Industry funds	24	26	40	53	57	61	72	72	75	80
University and college funds [2]	72	164	350	414	408	426	472	474	524	600
Other nonprofit institutions funds [2]	38	69	110	134	134	138	165	166	181	210
Univ. and colleges, associated federally funded R and D centers	97	208	269	250	297	300	307	359	410	460
Other nonprofit institutions	131	253	305	345	357	396	407	439	479	520
Federal funds	80	172	189	214	218	245	245	265	290	315
Industry funds	21	29	44	47	49	52	54	56	58	60
Other [3]	30	52	72	84	90	99	108	118	131	145

[1] Basic research, applied research, and development.
[2] Includes State and local government funds received by these institutions and used for research and development.
[3] Includes estimates for independent nonprofit hospitals and voluntary health agencies.

Source: U.S. National Science Foundation, National Patterns of R & D Resources—Funds and Manpower in the United States, 1953-78.

No. 1040. FEDERAL OBLIGATIONS FOR RESEARCH AND DEVELOPMENT BY AGENCY: 1965 TO 1978

[In millions of dollars. For years ending June 30 except, beginning 1977, ending Sept. 30. Includes social science research. See *Historical Statistics, Colonial Times to 1970*, series W 142, for total R & D expenditures]

AGENCY	1965	1970	1972	1973	1974	1975	1976	1977, est.	1978, est.
Total	13,811	15,340	16,498	16,800	17,415	19,013	20,759	24,465	26,317
Departments:									
Agriculture	200	281	350	367	379	420	462	525	574
Commerce	58	122	187	191	181	215	229	247	240
Defense ¹	6,628	7,360	8,318	8,404	8,420	9,012	9,655	11,172	12,108
Army	1,409	1,660	2,064	2,014	2,010	1,897	2,014	2,496	2,653
Navy	1,397	2,258	2,519	2,655	2,719	3,100	3,328	3,872	4,274
Air Force	3,360	2,990	3,254	3,274	3,216	3,513	3,727	4,091	4,403
Energy ²	1,241	1,346	1,298	1,363	1,489	2,072	2,499	3,610	4,143
Health, Education, and Welfare	681	1,221	1,751	1,838	2,290	2,363	2,546	2,960	3,009
National Institutes of Health	555	873	1,271	1,314	1,737	1,846	2,023	2,234	2,295
Interior	109	158	220	243	197	287	314	348	362
Transportation	–	328	311	311	370	312	295	407	398
Environmental Protection Agency	–	89	122	181	169	258	259	361	311
National Aero. and Space Admin	4,562	3,800	3,157	3,061	3,002	3,064	3,447	3,610	3,848
National Science Foundation	150	289	455	480	556	595	609	686	758
Veterans Administration	37	59	69	74	85	95	98	110	112
Other agencies	145	288	260	288	277	320	346	429	454

– Represents zero. ¹ Includes agencies not shown separately.
² Prior to 1978, represents Energy Research and Development Administration.

No. 1041. FEDERAL OBLIGATIONS FOR RESEARCH AND DEVELOPMENT: 1960 TO 1978

[In millions of dollars. For years ending June 30 except, beginning 1977, ending Sept. 30. Excludes research and development plant. For any given year, obligations differ from expenditures (see table 1040) because not all funds are expended during year obligated. See *Historical Statistics, Colonial Times to 1970*, series W 126, for total obligations]

ITEM	1960	1965	1970	1972	1973	1974	1975	1976	1977, est.	1978, est.
Total R and D	7,552	14,614	15,340	16,498	16,800	17,415	19,013	20,759	24,465	26,317
Basic research	610	1,690	1,762	1,974	2,001	2,039	2,279	2,425	2,755	3,012
Applied research	1,331	3,164	3,455	3,867	3,914	4,472	4,798	5,448	6,099	6,479
Development	5,611	9,760	10,123	10,657	10,885	10,904	11,936	12,885	15,612	16,826
Total research	1,941	4,854	5,217	5,841	5,915	6,510	7,077	7,873	8,853	9,490
Life sciences	511	1,167	1,507	1,904	1,958	2,283	2,450	2,646	2,983	3,105
Engineering sciences	690	1,576	1,847	1,726	1,712	1,883	2,051	2,378	2,602	2,811
Physical sciences	608 }	1,029	893	966	944	990	1,072	1,221	1,406	1,570
Environmental sciences	{	676	476	561	578	634	733	770	852	925
Social sciences	35	127	209	310	296	291	303	390	457	482
Math. and comp. sciences	25	105	101	136	124	127	136	153	166	184
Psychological sciences	38	103	112	121	112	143	145	140	164	178
Other sciences	33	70	72	116	190	160	187	175	224	235

Source of tables 1040 and 1041: U.S. National Science Foundation, *Federal Funds for Research, Development, and Other Scientific Activities,* annual.

No. 1042. FEDERAL OBLIGATIONS FOR RESEARCH AND DEVELOPMENT, BY FUNCTION: 1970 TO 1978

[In millions of dollars. For years ending June 30 except, beginning 1977, ending Sept. 30. Excludes research and development plant. See *Historical Statistics, Colonial Times to 1970*, series W 126, for total obligations]

FUNCTION	1970	1972	1973	1974	1975	1976	1977, est.	1978, est.
Total	15,340	16,512	16,800	17,415	19,013	20,759	24,465	26,317
National defense	7,976	8,898	8,998	8,975	9,621	10,346	11,917	12,907
Space	3,510	2,714	2,601	2,478	2,511	2,863	2,972	3,140
Health	1,126	1,564	1,624	2,096	2,177	2,366	2,622	2,683
Energy development and conversion	317	383	442	605	1,110	1,388	2,390	2,798
Science and technology base	525	606	605	695	782	839	953	1,060
Environment	354	547	652	693	837	899	1,101	1,098
Transportation and communications	590	617	630	703	641	636	769	805
Natural resources	238	625	341	341	445	489	547	610
Food, fiber, and other agricultural products	241	291	297	291	349	388	444	488
Education	147	208	214	174	149	142	284	269
Income security and social services	106	115	157	134	149	133	156	148
Area and community development, housing, and public services	91	102	97	96	102	104	111	99
Economic growth and productivity	80	78	75	72	67	84	98	97
Crime prevention and control	9	25	35	36	46	36	49	44
International cooperation and development	32	30	33	27	30	45	53	71

Source: U.S. National Science Foundation, *An Analysis of Federal R & D Funding by Function, 1969-78.*

No. 1043. INDUSTRIAL RESEARCH AND DEVELOPMENT FUNDS, BY GEOGRAPHIC DIVISION: 1970 TO 1976

[For composition of divisions, see fig. I, inside front cover]

GEOGRAPHIC DIVISION	1970 Total (mil. dol.)	1970 Percent	1973 Total (mil. dol.)	1973 Percent	1974 Total (mil. dol.)	1974 Percent	1975 Total (mil. dol.)	1975 Percent	1976 Total (mil. dol.)	1976 Percent	1976 Federal Govt. (mil. dol.)	1976 Private industry (mil. dol.)
United States [1]	18,062	100	20,921	100	22,399	100	24,164	100	26,677	100	9,285	17,392
New England	1,854	10	2,036	10	2,058	9	2,175	9	2,132	8	946	1,186
Mid. Atlantic	4,479	25	4,809	23	5,167	23	5,558	23	5,803	22	1,473	4,330
E. No. Central	3,622	20	4,587	22	4,695	21	4,833	20	5,496	21	513	4,983
W. No. Central	766	4	1,049	5	1,017	5	967	4	1,146	4	335	810
So. Atlantic	1,424	8	1,685	8	1,775	8	1,933	8	1,874	7	532	1,342
E. So. Central	346	2	373	2	388	2	483	2	437	2	242	195
W. So. Central	571	3	637	3	728	3	967	4	924	3	294	630
Mountain	687	4	633	3	662	3	725	3	919	3	515	404
Pacific	4,313	24	4,662	22	4,881	22	5,558	23	5,872	22	4,140	1,731

[1] Beginning 1973, includes undistributed funds, not shown separately.
Source: U.S. National Science Foundation, *Research and Development in Industry*, annual.

No. 1044. FUNDS FOR PERFORMANCE OF INDUSTRIAL RESEARCH AND DEVELOPMENT, BY INDUSTRY AND SOURCE OF FUNDS: 1965 TO 1976

[In millions of dollars. Covers basic research, applied research, and development. See also *Historical Statistics, Colonial Times to 1970*, series W 144–160]

INDUSTRY	1965	1970	1975 Total	1975 Federal Govt.	1975 Private industry	1976 Total	1976 Federal Govt.	1976 Private industry
Total [1]	14,185	18,062	24,164	8,605	15,559	26,677	9,285	17,392
Electrical equip. and communication	3,200	4,352	5,105	2,307	2,798	5,645	2,568	3,077
Aircraft and missiles	5,148	5,245	5,713	4,434	1,279	6,116	4,724	1,391
Machinery	1,065	1,649	3,196	509	2,687	3,487	537	2,950
Chemicals and allied products	1,356	1,766	2,727	236	2,490	3,021	267	2,754
Motor vehicles and other transp. equip.	1,230	1,582	2,430	365	2,065	2,873	375	2,498
Professional and scientific instruments	403	745	1,173	166	1,007	1,291	155	1,137
Petroleum refining and extraction	397	515	693	(NA)	(NA)	767	(NA)	(NA)
Primary metals	213	275	443	21	422	506	27	479
Food and kindred products	157	235	312	(NA)	(NA)	340	(NA)	(NA)
Fabricated metal products	145	200	324	27	297	354	36	318
Rubber products	162	220	467	(NA)	(NA)	499	(NA)	(NA)
Paper and allied products	94	178	249	(NA)	(NA)	279	(NA)	(NA)
Stone, clay, and glass products	112	157	233	(NA)	(NA)	268	(NA)	(NA)

NA Not available. [1] Includes industries not available separately.
Source: U.S. National Science Foundation, *Research and Development in Industry*, annual.

No. 1045. FEDERAL OBLIGATIONS TO UNIVERSITIES AND COLLEGES: 1965 TO 1977

[In millions of dollars, except percent. For years ending June 30 except, beginning 1977, ending Sept. 30. Minus sign (−) denotes decrease]

ITEM	1965	1970	1972	1973	1974	1975	1976	1977
Total Federal obligations	2,305	3,237	4,145	3,839	4,479	4,534	5,399	6,473
Annual percent change [1]	41.9	−6.5	18.5	−7.4	16.7	1.2	19.1	19.9
Academic science obligations	1,816	2,188	2,599	2,464	2,736	2,792	2,956	3,335
Percent of total	78.8	67.6	62.7	64.2	61.1	61.6	54.7	51.5
Research and development	1,095	1,447	1,853	1,871	2,085	2,225	2,419	2,772
Research and development plant	126	45	37	43	29	45	24	37
Other science activities	595	696	709	550	622	522	513	526
Non-science activities	489	1,049	1,545	1,375	1,743	1,741	2,443	3,138

[1] For 1965, change from 1964; for 1970, change from 1969; for 1972, change from 1971.
Source: U.S. National Science Foundation, *Federal Support to Universities, Colleges, and Selected Nonprofit Institutions*, annual.

No. 1046. Separately Budgeted Research and Development Expenditures in Science and Engineering in Universities and Colleges: 1964 to 1977

[In millions of dollars. Estimates for nonrespondents account for less than 7 percent of the total]

CHARACTERISTIC	1964	1966	1968	1970	1972	1974	1975	1976	1977 [1]
Total	1,275	1,715	2,149	2,335	2,677	3,017	3,405	3,724	4,054
In 1972 dollars [2]	1,733	2,230	2,611	2,569	2,677	2,682	2,732	2,792	2,853
Basic research	1,003	1,303	1,650	1,796	2,022	2,146	2,405	2,531	2,759
Applied research	232	328	404	427	544	737	851	1,025	1,083
Development	41	83	95	112	110	133	148	168	211
Source of funds:									
Federal Government	917	1,261	1,572	1,648	1,839	2,032	2,291	2,501	2,720
State and local governments	132	156	172	219	270	327	352	386	377
Institutions' own funds	103	147	218	243	306	344	390	430	509
Foundations and voluntary health agencies	61	77	95	110	128	142	168	183	198
Industry and other	61	74	91	116	134	172	204	225	250
Field of science:									
Engineering	162	259	309	319	347	346	381	432	496
Physical sciences [3]	217	287	320	307	330	333	350	384	424
Astronomy	16	23	24	19	22	24	27	26	28
Chemistry	70	88	105	102	110	116	121	140	163
Physics	120	159	173	162	162	169	173	188	199
Environmental sciences	55	68	120	125	192	235	255	286	319
Math. and computer sciences	33	42	58	72	71	77	85	86	103
Life sciences [3]	682	872	1,037	1,194	1,353	1,627	1,899	2,091	2,251
Biological and agricultural	315	422	491	547	682	856	987	1,120	1,232
Clinical medical	320	390	477	549	605	714	841	891	933
Psychology	32	40	59	59	70	74	80	77	83
Social sciences and other	96	146	245	258	313	324	355	367	378

[1] Preliminary.　　[2] Based on GNP implicit price deflator.　　[3] Includes sciences not shown separately.
Source: U.S. National Science Foundation, unpublished data.

No. 1047. Scientists and Engineers Employed in Research and Development, by Sector: 1954 to 1977

[In thousands of full-time equivalent employees. Yearly averages for industry sector only. Excludes those employed by State and local government agencies, except as noted]

SECTOR	1954	1958	1961	1965	1970	1973	1974	1975	1976	1977 [1]
Total	237.1	354.6	425.7	494.5	546.5	518.9	527.5	536.1	549.5	566.0
Industry (excl. social scientists) [2]	164.1	256.1	312.0	348.4	375.5	358.8	361.6	363.9	372.0	385.0
Universities and colleges, total	25.0	36.5	42.4	53.4	68.5	63.5	65.5	70.2	72.4	75.0
Scientists and engineers	20.3	29.2	33.6	40.4	50.3	46.9	48.0	51.6	53.5	54.9
Graduate students	4.7	7.3	8.8	13.0	18.2	16.6	17.5	18.6	18.9	20.1
Federal Government (incl. D.O.D.)	37.7	46.0	51.1	61.8	69.8	62.3	65.0	64.5	65.3	64.5
University-associated federally funded R & D centers (FFRDC's)	5.0	8.1	9.1	11.1	11.5	12.0	12.1	12.7	13.4	14.0
Other nonprofit institutions [2][3]	5.3	7.9	11.1	19.8	21.2	22.3	23.3	24.8	26.4	27.5

[1] Estimated.　　[2] Includes professional R & D personnel employed at FFRDC's administered by industry and other nonprofit institutions.
[3] Includes estimate for R & D scientists and engineers employed in State-affiliated institutions.
Source: U.S. National Science Foundation, *National Patterns of R & D Resources—Funds and Manpower in the United States, 1953-1978.*

No. 1048. Nobel Prize Laureates in Chemistry, Physics, and Physiology/Medicine—Selected Countries: 1901 to 1977

[Presented by location of award-winning research and by date of award]

COUNTRY	1901–1977, total	1901–1915	1916–1930	1931–1945	1946–1960	1961–1977	1901-1977 Physics	1901-1977 Chemistry	1901-1977 Physiology/Medicine
Total	320	52	41	49	74	104	109	90	121
United States	110	3	3	14	38	52	39	21	50
United Kingdom	61	7	8	11	14	21	21	21	19
West Germany [1]	50	15	12	11	4	8	14	24	12
France	20	10	3	2	–	5	8	6	6
U.S.S.R.	9	2	–	–	4	3	6	1	2
Other countries	76	15	15	11	14	15	21	17	32

– Represents zero.　　[1] Includes East Germany before 1946.
Source: U.S. National Science Foundation, *Science Indicators,* 1976, and unpublished data.

No. 1049. SCIENTISTS AND ENGINEERS BY FIELD, EMPLOYMENT STATUS, AND SEX: 1974 AND 1976

In thousands, except percent. Represents the total science and engineering population in the United States]

FIELD	1974			1976						
	Total		In labor force	Total	In labor force			Percent female		
	Number	Percent female			Total	Unemployed	Outside labor force [1]	Total	In labor force	Outside labor force
Total, all fields	1,973	9.4	1,678	2,706	2,452	75	254	9.2	8.6	15.1
Engineers	1,072	.7	1,009	1,375	1,268	27	107	.6	.5	1.2
Physical scientists	188	9.8	157	281	237	10	43	9.4	9.0	11.7
Chemists	138	11.3	115	186	157	7	29	11.2	10.7	13.6
Physicists/astronomers	42	5.9	35	70	61	2	9	3.8	3.3	6.3
Other physical scientists	8	3.8	8	20	19	1	5	12.3	12.9	9.8
Mathematical scientists	60	25.2	45	110	92	4	18	20.8	17.6	37.6
Mathematicians	44	25.1	33	98	82	3	16	20.8	17.6	37.6
Statisticians	17	24.9	13	13	11	(2)	2	20.8	17.6	37.5
Computer specialists	126	19.3	123	179	173	1	6	20.2	19.6	37.3
Environmental scientists	52	5.2	45	86	77	3	8	7.5	5.7	23.8
Earth scientists	46	5.7	39	80	72	3	8	7.9	6.0	25.0
Oceanographers	2	(2)	2	2	2	(2)	(2)	(2)	(2)	(2)
Atmospheric scientists	4	2.3	4	4	3	(2)	(2)	2.4	(2)	(2)
Life scientists	194	17.6	137	314	286	9	28	19.4	18.7	25.9
Biological scientists	118	22.5	69	140	124	5	16	29.3	28.9	32.0
Agricultural scientists	58	2.8	51	129	118	3	11	4.3	3.5	13.2
Medical scientists	18	32.6	17	46	45	(2)	1	31.3	30.4	78.7
Psychologists	95	28.6	62	123	106	8	17	24.6	24.3	28.7
Social scientists	187	29.9	101	237	211	13	26	24.4	23.3	33.6
Economists	55	9.2	39	60	52	(2)	8	6.9	4.9	18.1
Sociologists/anthropologists	50	46.8	22	51	42	7	8	37.9	35.5	50.0
Other social scientists	82	33.4	39	127	117	6	9	27.4	27.1	31.4

[1] Includes those not employed or not seeking employment as, for example, retirees.
[2] Too few cases to estimate.
Source: U.S. National Science Foundation, *U.S. Scientists and Engineers: 1974* (NSF 76-329) and *1976* (NSF forthcoming report).

No. 1050. CHARACTERISTICS OF SCIENTISTS AND ENGINEERS: 1976

[Represents the total science and engineering population in the United States]

CHARACTERISTIC	Total	Engineers	Physical scientists	Mathematical specialists	Computer specialists	Environmental scientists	Life scientists	Psychologists	Social scientists
Total 1,000	2,706	1,375	281	110	179	86	314	123	237
	PERCENT DISTRIBUTION								
Total	100.0	100.0	100.0	100.0	100.0	100.0	100.0	100.0	100.0
Male	90.8	90.4	90.6	79.2	79.8	92.5	80.6	75.4	75.6
Female	9.2	.6	9.4	20.8	20.2	7.5	19.4	24.6	24.4
Under 30 years	30.0	22.6	35.4	34.1	35.2	32.2	46.5	38.4	33.8
30–39 years	27.6	24.8	29.1	31.4	52.3	33.6	22.5	30.0	24.7
40–49 years	19.1	22.8	16.5	19.9	9.8	16.6	13.1	15.9	17.2
50–59 years	15.9	19.8	12.7	10.4	2.3	13.9	13.1	6.4	19.1
60 and over	7.5	10.0	6.3	4.1	.3	3.8	4.8	9.4	5.1
Highest degree	100.0	100.0	100.0	100.0	100.0	100.0	100.0	100.0	100.0
Doctorate	10.6	3.2	20.9	13.4	3.0	14.9	23.5	27.5	18.2
Master's	24.1	17.9	23.7	46.5	20.2	21.8	20.9	48.3	47.1
Bachelor's	62.4	74.8	54.6	37.6	76.7	63.2	51.5	24.1	34.6
Other	2.9	4.1	.7	2.5	.1	(B)	4.0	(B)	.1
Type of employer	100.0	100.0	100.0	100.0	100.0	100.0	100.0	100.0	100.0
Business, industry	60.3	77.4	47.8	38.1	73.1	54.0	36.8	19.1	22.2
Educational institutions	15.6	3.5	23.8	39.2	8.0	14.8	31.0	43.9	42.5
Nonprofit organizations	4.0	1.4	4.8	3.5	2.1	2.7	8.5	18.4	8.2
Federal Government	8.6	7.9	10.0	9.9	8.3	14.8	9.2	5.5	10.1
Military	.8	.8	.6	.9	.9	1.6	.6	.4	.6
Other government	6.7	5.0	6.2	6.8	3.8	7.8	10.4	7.4	14.5
Other	3.9	3.9	6.7	1.6	3.8	4.3	3.5	5.2	1.9

B Base too small to calculate percent.
Source: U.S. National Science Foundation, *U.S. Scientists and Engineers: 1976* (NSF forthcoming report).

No. 1051. Unemployment Rates for Scientists and Engineers: 1974 and 1976

[Percent]

FIELD	1974	1976 [1]	FIELD	1974	1976 [1]
Total, all fields	1.7	2.6–3.1	Life scientists	2.0	2.4–3.2
			Physical scientists	2.5	2.9–4.1
Computer specialists	.5	.6–.7	Environmental scientists	3.4	1.1–3.3
Engineers	1.3	2.1–2.2	Psychologists	4.7	7.0–7.5
Mathematical scientists	2.0	3.8–4.2	Social scientists	2.3	5.7–6.2

[1] The range of unemployment rates reflects different assumptions about the 1976 level of unemployment for members of the 1976 labor force who were not in the labor force in 1970. The higher unemployment rate for 1976 is consistent with the unemployment rate reported for 1974.

Source: U.S. National Science Foundation, unpublished data.

No. 1052. Research and Development Scientists and Engineers—Average Full-Time-Equivalent and Cost, by Industry and Source of Support: 1970 to 1976

[In thousands. Data for 1970 on man-years basis; thereafter, on average full-time-equivalent (FTE) basis. See *Historical Statistics, Colonial Times to 1970*, series W 167, for total cost per scientist or engineer]

INDUSTRY	1970			1975			1976		
	Total	Private industry	Federal Govt.	Total	Private industry	Federal Govt.	Total	Private industry	Federal Govt.
Average FTE of scientists and engineers	369.9	231.4	138.5	360.6	254.0	106.6	372.2	264.0	108.1
Chemicals and allied products	42.2	38.7	3.5	45.7	43.0	2.7	45.4	42.6	2.8
Machinery	43.1	36.0	7.2	43.2	38.2	5.0	56.1	48.3	7.8
Electrical equip. and communication	97.7	50.7	47.0	93.7	55.5	38.2	82.2	46.8	35.4
Motor vehicle and other transport equip.	24.2	19.5	4.7	(NA)	(NA)	(NA)	27.9	(NA)	(NA)
Aircraft and missiles	83.0	20.4	62.6	68.1	21.4	46.7	68.2	21.4	46.4
Other industries	79.7	66.1	13.5	83.2	73.3	10.2	92.2	(NA)	(NA)
Cost per scientist or engineer dol.	48.3	22.9	56.2	65.3	58.2	82.2	71.3	65.9	85.9
Chemicals and allied products	42.9	42.0	53.7	58.0	56.0	87.0	66.5	64.6	95.4
Machinery	40.1	40.1	39.2	61.6	59.8	73.8	60.1	61.1	68.8
Electrical equip. and communication	44.3	40.7	48.1	59.0	54.3	65.6	68.5	65.7	72.5
Motor vehicle and other transport equip.	61.0	63.2	51.7	(NA)	(NA)	(NA)	100.1	(NA)	(NA)
Aircraft and missiles	62.3	54.3	65.0	84.1	56.1	96.2	89.6	65.0	101.8
Other industries	42.0	39.4	55.0	55.3	52.4	75.5	50.8	(NA)	(NA)

NA Not available.

Source: U.S. National Science Foundation, *Research and Development in Industry*, annual.

No. 1053. Employment of Scientists and Engineers, by Occupation and Major Industrial Sector: 1975

[In thousands]

OCCUPATION	Total	Manu-facturing	Non-manu-facturing	OCCUPATION	Total	Manu-facturing	Non-manu-facturing
Total	1,184	670	514	Physical scientists	104	85	19
				Chemists	65	59	6
Engineers	853	507	346	Physicists	10	10	(Z)
Chemical	50	41	9	Other	28	16	13
Civil, sanitary	82	11	71	Metallurgists	9	9	(Z)
Electrical	292	143	149	Geologists	15	3	12
Industrial	67	57	9	Other	5	4	1
Materials, metals, ceramics	20	16	4	Life scientists	60	24	36
Mechanical, aeronautical	201	157	44	Mathematical scientists	14	7	7
Mining, petroleum, geological	18	3	15	Computer scientists	143	43	100
Nuclear	7	4	2	Social scientists (incl.			
Other	117	74	43	psychologists)	10	5	5

Z Fewer than 500.

Source: U.S. National Science Foundation, *Science Resource Studies Highlights*, NSF 77-312.

No. 1054. Scientists and Engineers—Employment in Institutions of Higher Education, by Field of Employment: 1965 to 1977

[In thousands. As of January. Includes full-time and part-time personnel. Excludes graduate students who receive stipends for part-time services as scientists or engineers. R and D = research and development]

FIELD OF EMPLOYMENT	1965	1971	1975	1976	1977	FIELD OF EMPLOYMENT	1965	1971	1975	1976	1977
Total	189.9	269.2	293.1	302.4	312.0	Life scientists	75.8	110.3	115.3	115.2	118.3
						Agricultural	13.5	18.0	14.6	13.7	14.0
Universities, colleges	178.9	257.9	280.6	289.1	298.1	Biological	24.3	31.8	38.2	40.0	42.8
Teaching staff	122.0	185.0	215.8	222.8	229.0	Medical	38.0	60.4	62.4	61.5	61.5
Engineers [1]	21.7	27.1	27.8	28.5	29.8	Psychologists	9.4	16.8	21.7	22.9	23.7
Aeronautical	1.1	1.5	1.1	1.2	1.2						
Chemical	1.6	1.8	1.9	1.9	1.9	Social scientists [1]	32.9	43.2	48.8	52.6	53.1
Civil	3.1	4.1	4.9	5.0	5.1	Economists	7.9	11.3	12.7	13.2	13.9
Electrical	5.5	6.9	6.8	6.9	6.9	Sociologists	6.3	11.3	14.2	15.2	15.5
Mechanical	4.1	5.4	5.3	5.3	5.5	Political science	5.9	8.9	10.6	11.3	11.3
Phy. and environmental science [1]	26.5	35.9	38.7	40.0	41.2	Federally funded R and D centers	11.0	11.3	12.5	13.3	13.9
Chemists	10.7	14.7	16.1	16.6	17.1	Engineers	5.0	5.1	5.9	6.0	6.4
Earth scientists	4.0	6.5	6.0	6.6	6.9	Phys. and environmental scientists	4.2	4.3	4.7	5.2	5.4
Physicists	9.1	12.2	12.3	12.2	12.5	Math. and computer scientists [2]	1.0	1.0	1.3	1.4	1.4
Math. and computer scientists	13.7	24.5	28.4	29.9	32.0	Other	.8	.7	.6	.8	.8

[1] Includes other engineers or scientists not shown separately. [2] Includes statisticians.

No. 1055. Full-Time Scientists and Engineers Employed in Universities and Colleges, by Field of Employment, and Sex: 1975 to 1977

[As of January. Excludes graduate students who receive stipends for part-time services as scientists or engineers. Excludes federally funded research and development centers]

FIELD OF EMPLOYMENT	TOTAL (1,000)			PERCENT MALE		FIELD OF EMPLOYMENT	TOTAL (1,000)			PERCENT MALE	
	1975	1976	1977	1976	1977		1975	1976	1977	1976	1977
Total	223.7	230.2	236.2	84.6	84.4	Social sciences	38.2	40.9	41.0	82.3	82.2
						Economics	10.2	10.4	10.7	90.9	91.1
Physical sciences	33.5	34.4	35.4	92.2	92.1	Sociology	10.7	11.4	11.6	74.4	74.0
Chemistry	13.8	14.2	14.4	89.3	89.3	Political science	8.7	9.1	9.1	88.6	88.4
Earth sciences [1]	6.8	7.3	7.9	94.6	93.9	Other	8.6	10.0	9.6	76.8	76.2
Physics	10.9	10.9	11.1	96.4	96.1						
Other	1.9	2.1	2.0	90.5	89.8	Engineers	22.6	22.9	23.9	98.0	97.9
						Aeronautical [2]	.9	1.0	1.0	97.0	97.7
Mathematicians	22.4	23.1	23.9	86.6	86.4	Chemical	1.6	1.6	1.7	97.7	97.8
Life sciences	91.1	92.0	94.8	80.2	80.1	Civil	3.8	4.0	4.1	98.0	97.8
Agricultural	13.2	12.5	12.7	91.6	92.1	Electrical	5.4	5.4	5.5	98.6	98.7
Biological	33.4	34.9	37.0	79.8	79.3	Mechanical	4.4	4.4	4.5	99.0	98.7
Medical	44.4	44.6	45.0	77.3	77.3	Other	6.5	6.5	7.2	97.2	97.0
Psychologist	16.0	16.8	17.3	76.2	75.5						

[1] Includes data for atmospheric scientists and oceanographers. [2] Includes astronautical.

Source of tables 1054 and 1055: U.S. National Science Foundation. Data derived from Survey of Scientific and Engineering Personnel Employed at Universities and Colleges.

No. 1056. Professional Scientific, Engineering, and Technical Personnel in the Federal Government, by Occupational Group: 1966 to 1976

[In thousands, except percent. 1966 data as of December, all other years as of October]

OCCUPATIONAL GROUP	1966	1970	1974	1975	1976	PERCENT FEMALE				
						1966	1970	1974	1975	1976
Total	192.7	206.2	209.7	221.9	226.4	16.6	16.4	19.3	19.7	20.3
Percent female	16.6	16.4	19.3	19.7	20.3	(X)	(X)	(X)	(X)	(X)
Scientific personnel	71.5	77.2	75.1	77.3	78.7	7.8	8.0	8.5	8.8	9.4
Physical sciences	27.3	29.8	26.3	27.1	27.1	6.4	6.4	6.4	6.6	6.7
Mathematics and statistics	7.3	8.6	9.4	10.0	10.4	20.0	17.4	16.2	15.9	16.8
Life sciences	26.0	26.9	26.2	26.4	27.0	3.7	4.1	4.8	5.1	5.8
Social sciences and community planning	5.8	6.6	7.3	8.0	8.3	14.5	16.2	17.3	17.6	22.6
Geography and cartography	3.2	3.3	2.9	2.9	3.0	8.6	8.5	7.9	7.9	8.4
Psychology	1.9	2.2	2.6	2.9	3.0	14.6	13.7	14.7	14.6	14.4
Engineering personnel	76.8	83.0	82.5	86.6	87.0	.5	.5	.6	.7	.8
Health professional personnel	44.3	46.0	52.1	58.0	60.7	58.8	59.2	64.5	62.7	62.3
Health officers	13.1	13.0	11.2	13.4	14.1	4.7	5.5	7.9	7.8	8.3

X Not applicable.

Source: U.S. National Science Foundation. Compiled from data supplied by U.S. Civil Service Commission.

No. 1057. SALARIES OF PROFESSIONAL, SCIENTIFIC, AND TECHNICAL PERSONNEL IN THE FEDERAL GOVERNMENT, BY OCCUPATIONAL FIELD, BY SEX: 1970 TO 1976

[In thousands of dollars. Mean annual salaries as of October; for definition of mean, see p. xii]

OCCUPATIONAL FIELD	ALL PERSONNEL				MALE			FEMALE		
	1970	1972	1975	1976	1970	1975	1976	1970	1975	1976
Engineering	17.8	19.4	24.2	25.8	17.8	24.2	25.8	15.5	19.2	20.4
Health officers	19.5	22.9	28.6	30.6	19.3	28.4	30.4	21.3	31.0	33.2
Nursing personnel	10.0	12.0	14.7	15.4	10.9	14.2	14.7	10.0	14.7	15.5
Scientific personnel	16.3	18.2	22.5	23.8	16.5	22.8	24.2	14.0	19.1	20.1
Physical sciences	17.8	19.7	24.4	25.9	18.1	24.8	26.3	13.6	19.2	20.3
General physical	20.5	23.9	28.1	29.8	20.7	28.3	30.0	15.0	21.7	23.0
Chemistry	16.0	17.6	22.5	23.7	16.5	23.1	24.4	13.4	18.9	19.8
Physics	17.8	20.2	25.5	27.3	17.9	25.6	27.5	15.7	21.0	22.5
Life sciences	14.3	16.2	20.0	21.2	14.3	20.1	21.4	13.0	17.5	18.1
General biological sciences	15.9	18.0	21.0	22.3	16.6	21.7	23.2	12.2	17.0	17.8
Agricultural sciences	13.2	14.9	18.6	19.6	13.2	18.6	19.7	14.9	16.2	15.2
Animal sciences	17.3	19.2	23.5	25.1	17.4	23.8	25.5	14.5	19.4	20.2
Microbiology	15.6	17.1	21.0	22.1	16.6	22.3	23.6	13.1	17.9	18.8
Plant sciences	14.5	16.6	20.8	21.7	14.5	21.0	22.0	12.5	17.5	16.9
Mathematics	15.5	17.6	22.0	23.5	15.8	22.5	24.2	14.1	19.4	20.6
Statistics	16.7	18.9	22.5	23.4	17.3	23.3	24.3	14.5	19.7	20.5
Social sciences	17.8	19.9	23.4	24.9	18.3	24.2	25.8	15.0	20.0	21.2
Economics	18.0	20.2	23.6	25.2	18.3	24.2	25.8	15.2	19.7	21.0
Geography and cartography	13.9	15.9	19.8	20.9	14.1	20.0	21.1	12.4	17.4	18.1
Psychology	18.2	19.8	23.9	25.5	18.5	24.5	26.1	15.9	20.5	22.4

Source: U.S. National Science Foundation, unpublished data. Data from U.S. Civil Service Commission.

No. 1058. SCIENTISTS, ENGINEERS, AND PHYSICIANS ADMITTED AS IMMIGRANTS, BY OCCUPATION: 1967 TO 1976

[For years ending June 30 except, beginning 1977, year ending Sept. 30. Includes professors and instructors]

OCCUPATION	1967–1970, total	1967	1970	1971	1972	1973	1974	1975	1976
Scientists and engineers	49,088	12,523	13,337	13,102	11,323	6,632	5,969	6,931	7,495
Engineers [1]	34,589	8,821	9,305	9,005	7,436	4,443	3,866	4,648	5,146
Chemical	2,974	668	908	860	791	438	333	438	446
Civil	4,305	840	1,509	1,666	1,461	700	575	694	697
Electrical	5,368	1,344	1,464	1,422	1,305	661	543	676	754
Mechanical	5,743	1,344	1,618	1,603	1,470	829	627	845	823
Natural scientists [1]	12,133	3,158	3,264	3,456	3,271	1,790	1,422	1,602	1,663
Agricultural scientists [2]	1,057	189	380	460	518	388	250	305	212
Biologists, medical scientists	1,389	377	388	495	527	309	222	238	268
Chemists	5,650	1,392	1,495	1,606	1,372	711	592	675	678
Physicists	1,726	540	401	296	325	118	113	137	152
Social scientists	2,366	544	768	631	616	399	681	681	686
Physicians and surgeons	12,896	3,325	3,155	5,748	7,143	7,119	4,537	5,361	6,184

[1] Includes occupations not shown separately.   [2] Includes foresters and conservationists.

Source: U.S. National Science Foundation, *Scientists, Engineers, and Physicians From Abroad*, annual. Based on data from U.S. Immigration and Naturalization Service.

No. 1059. GRADUATE STUDENTS, BY FIELD AND LEVEL OF STUDY: 1971 TO 1976

[In thousands. As of fall. Includes outlying areas]

FIELD OF SCIENCE	TOTAL STUDENTS						FULL-TIME STUDENTS					
	First-year			Beyond first-year			First-year			Beyond first-year		
	1971	1975	1976	1971	1975	1976	1971	1975	1976	1971	1975	1976
Total	124.8	132.2	127.6	121.3	129.3	130.7	69.4	72.5	69.7	81.6	81.8	82.1
Life sciences [1]	22.9	28.6	27.8	24.8	29.5	30.7	14.3	17.8	17.1	18.4	20.1	20.6
Physical sciences	16.7	14.9	15.3	22.3	20.6	20.9	10.7	9.9	10.0	17.0	15.1	15.4
Engineering [2]	30.7	32.4	30.7	28.6	26.9	26.6	14.9	15.9	15.5	16.5	14.9	15.0
Social sciences [3]	23.0	22.6	20.7	21.7	23.7	23.4	13.7	12.5	11.6	14.2	14.4	14.0
Psychology	14.8	18.5	17.6	12.0	16.8	17.8	8.4	10.0	9.2	8.3	10.7	10.8
Mathematics [4]	16.9	15.1	15.5	11.9	11.9	11.3	7.5	6.4	6.4	7.2	6.6	6.4

[1] Includes interdisciplinary majors in biological and physical sciences.   [2] Includes interdisciplinary majors; excludes engineering technologies.   [3] Includes agricultural economics, anthropology, archeology, demography, economics, geography, linguistics, political science and government, and sociology.
[4] Includes computer and information sciences.

Source: U.S. National Science Foundation. Data from U.S. National Center for Education Statistics. *Students Enrolled for Advanced Degrees*, annual.

No. 1060. DOCTORATES CONFERRED, 1970 TO 1977, AND SELECTED FIELDS, 1977, BY CHARACTERISTICS

CHARACTERISTIC	ALL FIELDS [1]			1977					
	1970	1975	1976	Total [1]	Physical sciences [2]	Engineering	Biological sciences [3]	Psychology	Social sciences [4]
Doctorates conferred	29,475	32,913	32,923	31,672	4,369	2,641	3,172	2,960	2,830
Percent distribution	100.0	100.0	100.0	100.0	100.0	100.0	100.0	100.0	100.0
Male	86.5	78.1	76.7	75.2	90.1	97.2	77.0	63.5	79.2
Female	13.5	21.9	23.3	24.8	9.9	2.8	23.0	36.5	20.8
White	(NA)	79.8	79.5	78.7	75.8	66.7			
Black and other	(NA)	12.1	12.4	14.1	16.0	24.5	} (NA)	(NA)	(NA)
Not reported	(NA)	8.1	8.1	7.3	8.2	8.9			
U.S. citizens	84.2	82.1	82.6	82.1	76.3	55.6	83.6	91.5	78.9
Foreign citizens	14.0	15.9	15.2	15.2	21.6	41.6	13.7	4.0	18.5
Citizenship unknown	1.6	2.0	2.2	2.7	2.1	2.8	2.7	4.5	2.6
Percent with master's degree	78.6	81.3	82.0	81.3	61.3	91.1	54.7	75.5	84.4
Median age at award_____years	30.7	31.5	31.6	31.6	29.2	30.0	29.5	29.9	31.9
Median time, baccalaureate to doctorate:									
Total time_____years	7.9	8.6	8.6	8.7	6.9	7.5	7.0	7.1	8.5
Registered time_____years	5.6	5.9	6.0	6.1	5.7	5.6	5.8	5.5	6.3

NA Not available. [1] Includes ars and humanities and other fields, not shown separately.
[2] Astronomy, physics, chemistry, earth sciences, and mathematics.
[3] Biochemistry, botany, microbiology, physiology, zoology, and related fields.
[4] Anthropology, sociology, economics, political science, public administration, and international relations.
Source: U.S. National Science Foundation. Data from National Research Council, *Summary Report, 1977: Doctorate Recipients from United States Universities*.

No. 1061. SCIENCE DOCTORATES CONFERRED AND ENROLLMENT FOR ADVANCED DEGREES: 1960 TO 1977

[Doctorates conferred, years ending June 30, except as noted; enrollment, as of fall term. See also *Historical Statistics, Colonial Times to 1970*, series H 767-771, 774, and 776-780]

FIELD OF SCIENCE	1960	1965	1970	1973	1974	1975	1976	1977 [1]
Science doctorates conferred	6,263	10,477	17,731	18,948	18,316	18,352	17,872	17,373
Life sciences	1,659	2,539	4,163	4,489	4,303	4,402	4,350	4,266
Biological sciences	1,245	1,963	3,360	3,636	3,473	3,498	3,562	3,484
Agricultural sciences [2]	414	576	803	853	830	904	788	782
Physical sciences	1,861	2,865	4,400	4,101	3,800	3,749	3,572	3,410
Chemistry	1,078	1,444	2,234	1,849	1,792	1,762	1,623	1,570
Physics and astronomy	530	1,046	1,655	1,590	1,334	1,293	1,235	1,149
Earth, environmental, and marine sciences	253	375	511	662	674	694	714	691
Social sciences	886	1,361	2,626	3,354	3,286	3,344	3,278	3,137
Economics	341	538	826	907	833	867	854	809
Sociology	162	239	504	599	645	680	734	725
Anthropology	69	82	217	324	381	385	428	386
Other social sciences [3]	314	502	1,079	1,524	1,427	1,412	1,262	1,217
Psychology	772	954	1,888	2,444	2,587	2,749	2,878	2,960
Engineering	794	2,073	3,432	3,338	3,144	2,959	2,791	2,641
Mathematics	291	685	1,222	1,222	1,196	1,149	1,003	959
Graduate enrollment, all fields_____1,000	314.3	535.3	816.2	908.1	965.0	1,053.8	1,030.0	
Science fields_____1,000	120.6	195.3	252.2	244.4	250.7	261.5	258.2	
Percent of total	38.4	36.5	30.9	26.9	26.0	24.8	25.1	
Engineering [4]_____1,000	36.6	57.5	64.8	54.6	56.0	59.3	57.3	
Social sciences [5]_____1,000	16.1	30.0	45.0	45.2	45.6	46.3	44.2	
Biological sciences [6]_____1,000	15.3	28.3	37.6	40.8	43.4	45.5	45.4	} (NA)
Physical sciences_____1,000	25.7	36.5	40.1	36.0	34.9	35.5	36.1	
Psychology_____1,000	10.7	15.6	25.3	30.9	32.8	35.3	35.4	
Mathematical subjects [7]_1,000	11.8	21.0	30.6	27.0	27.1	27.0	26.8	
Agriculture and forestry [2]_1,000	4.4	6.4	8.7	9.9	10.8	12.6	13.1	
Health fields_____1,000	5.8	8.9	14.2	27.3	30.4	35.5	38.1	
All other fields_____1,000	187.9	331.1	549.8	636.5	683.9	756.8	733.7	

NA Not available. [1] Year ending Sept. 30. [2] Excludes agricultural economics. [3] Includes econometrics, statistics, geography, political science and public administration, history and philosophy of science, archeology, linguistics, and agricultural economics. [4] Includes interdisciplinary studies; excludes engineering technologies. [5] Includes agricultural economics, anthropology, archeology, demography, economics, geography, linguistics, political science and government, and sociology. [6] Includes interdisciplinary studies in biological and physical sciences. Includes computer and information sciences. [7] Includes computer and information sciences.

Source: U.S. National Science Foundation. Data from National Research Council, Doctorate Record File; and U.S. National Center for Education Statistics, *Enrollment for Masters and Higher Degrees*, annual.

No. 1062. DOCTORAL SCIENTISTS AND ENGINEERS, BY STATES: 1977

[Includes doctoral scientists receiving their degrees between 1934 and June 1977]

STATE	Total	Natural scientists	Social scientists	Engi-neers	STATE	Total	Natural scientists	Social scientists	Engi-neers
Total	303,267	175,161	81,567	46,539	Mo	5,136	3,124	1,230	782
					Mont	981	687	206	88
Ala	3,013	1,714	830	469	Nebr	1,670	1,146	364	160
Alaska	510	363	108	39	Nev	556	260	227	69
Ariz	3,261	1,761	946	554	N.H	1,149	638	406	105
Ark	1,305	803	437	65	N.J	12,016	7,247	2,148	2,621
Calif	36,075	19,469	9,968	6,638	N. Mex	3,813	2,525	366	922
Colo	6,201	3,684	1,641	876	N.Y	29,563	16,457	9,513	3,593
Conn	5,260	2,898	1,575	787	N.C	6,003	3,795	1,623	585
Del	3,288	2,461	253	574	N. Dak	779	485	190	104
D.C	10,353	4,905	4,114	1,334	Ohio	12,608	7,111	3,065	2,432
Fla	6,812	3,723	2,090	999	Okla	2,690	1,620	580	490
Ga	4,351	2,703	1,224	424	Oreg	3,314	2,107	972	235
Hawaii	1,350	847	439	64	Pa	15,787	8,542	4,166	3,079
Idaho	1,199	714	241	244	R.I	1,370	797	444	129
Ill	14,264	7,966	4,166	2,132	S.C	2,489	1,512	644	333
Ind	5,969	3,529	1,591	849	S. Dak	679	448	181	50
Iowa	2,932	1,828	780	324	Tenn	4,775	3,026	1,026	723
Kans	2,705	1,414	1,037	254	Tex	14,592	8,768	3,112	2,712
Ky	2,695	1,557	919	219	Utah	2,581	1,415	623	543
La	3,368	2,271	584	513	Vt	830	482	257	91
Maine	1,252	651	439	162	Va	8,208	4,523	2,127	1,558
Md	10,696	7,310	2,088	1,298	Wash	5,792	3,152	1,692	948
Mass	13,062	7,369	3,633	2,060	W. Va	1,613	1,098	317	198
Mich	10,521	5,974	2,958	1,589	Wis	5,553	3,145	1,619	789
Minn	5,119	3,311	1,414	394	Wyo	694	388	244	62
Miss	1,777	1,029	526	222	Other areas	688	409	224	55

Source: U.S. National Science Foundation, *1977 Characteristics of Doctoral Scientists and Engineers in the United States*. Data derived from the Doctoral Roster of Scientists and Engineers.

No. 1063. FEDERAL SPACE PROGRAM—OUTLAYS, BY AGENCY: 1960 TO 1978

[Through 1976, for years ending June 30, except as noted; thereafter, years ending Sept. 30. NASA= National Aeronautics and Space Administration]

YEAR	Total [1] (mil. dol.)	NASA [2] Total (mil. dol.)	NASA [2] Per-cent of total	Dept. of De-fense (mil. dol.)	Dept. of Energy [3] (mil. dol.)	YEAR	Total [1] (mil. dol.)	NASA [2] Total (mil. dol.)	NASA [2] Per-cent of total	Dept. of De-fense (mil. dol.)	Dept. of Energy [3] (mil. dol.)
1960	888	329	37.0	518	41	1970	5,453	3,565	65.4	1,756	103
1961	1,468	604	47.3	710	64	1971	4,999	3,171	63.4	1,693	97
1962	2,387	1,226	51.4	1,029	130	1972	4,772	3,195	67.0	1,470	60
1963	4,079	2,517	61.7	1,368	181	1973	4,719	3,069	65.0	1,557	51
1964	5,900	4,101	69.5	1,564	220	1974	4,854	2,960	61.0	1,777	39
1965	6,856	5,005	73.0	1,592	232	1975	4,891	2,953	60.4	1,829	34
1966	7,689	5,828	75.8	1,637	188	1976	5,314	3,336	62.8	1,864	26
1967	7,208	5,307	73.6	1,673	184	1976, TQ [4]	1,361	869	63.9	458	8
1968	6,647	4,574	68.8	1,890	146	1977	5,532	3,373	61.0	2,292	23
1969	6,331	4,083	64.5	2,095	117	1978	6,209	3,596	57.9	2,770	35

[1] Includes agencies not shown separately.   [2] Excludes amounts for aircraft technology.
[3] Replaced Energy Research and Development Administration in 1978.   [4] Transition quarter, July–Sept.

Source: U.S. National Aeronautics and Space Administration, *Space Report of the President*, annual (Appendix by U.S. Office of Management and Budget).

No. 1064. EMPLOYMENT ON NASA PROGRAMS: 1960 TO 1978

[In thousands of employees. As of June 30. NASA = National Aeronautics and Space Administration]

YEAR	Total	NASA	Contrac-tors [1]	YEAR	Total	NASA	Contrac-tors [1]	YEAR	Total	NASA	Contrac-tors [1]
1960	46.8	10.3	36.5	1967	306.9	33.7	273.2	1973	134.9	26.9	108.0
1961	74.6	17.1	57.5	1968	267.9	32.5	235.4	1974	125.2	25.0	100.2
1962	137.7	22.2	115.5	1969	218.3	31.7	186.6	1975	127.7	24.3	103.4
1963	246.3	27.9	218.4								
				1970	160.9	31.4	129.5	1976	132.0	24.0	108.0
1964	379.1	32.0	347.1	1971	143.6	29.5	114.1	1977	124.1	23.6	100.5
1965	409.9	33.2	376.7	1972	138.8	27.5	111.3	1978, est.	126.0	23.2	102.8
1966	393.9	33.9	360.0								

[1] Employment by private firms with contracts to perform for NASA.

Source: Aerospace Industries Association of America, Inc., Washington, D.C., *Aerospace Facts and Figures*, 1978/79 (copyright).

No. **1065.** NATIONAL AERONAUTICS AND SPACE ADMINISTRATION—OUTLAYS FOR RESEARCH AND DEVELOPMENT: 1965 TO 1978

[In millions of dollars. Through 1976, years ending June 30, except as indicated; thereafter, years ending Sept. 30. Performance includes research and development, and research and program management]

YEAR	PERFORMANCE				FACILITIES			
	Total	Manned space flight	Space science, applica- tions, technology	Air transport and other	Total	Manned space flight	Space science, applica- tions, technology	Air transport and other
1965	4,562	3,138	1,126	298	531	401	78	52
1966	5,361	3,819	1,120	422	572	391	63	118
1967	5,137	3,477	1,160	500	289	172	47	70
1968	4,599	3,028	1,061	510	127	69	29	29
1969	4,187	2,754	893	540	65	27	21	17
1970	3,699	2,195	963	541	54	14	21	19
1971	3,338	1,877	926	535	44	8	6	30
1972	3,373	1,727	1,111	535	50	13	7	30
1973	3,271	1,532	1,220	519	45	5	11	29
1974	3,181	1,448	1,156	577	75	25	12	38
1975	3,181	1,500	1,076	606	85	35	9	42
1976	3,549	1,934	969	646	121	66	11	43
1976 (July–Sept.)	927	513	249	165	26	13	2	11
1977	3,840	2,195	1,002	643	105	56	4	45
1978, est	3,850	2,145	1,008	697	132	48	10	74

Source: U.S. Office of Management and Budget, *The Budget of the United States Government*, annual.

No. **1066.** SPACE VEHICLE SYSTEMS—SALES AND BACKLOG ORDERS: 1965 TO 1977

[In millions of dollars. Backlog orders as of Dec. 31. Based on data from approximately 55 companies engaged in manufacture of aerospace products. Excludes engines and propulsion units]

YEAR	NET SALES			BACKLOG ORDERS			YEAR	NET SALES			BACKLOG ORDERS		
	Total	Mili- tary	Non- mili- tary	Total	Mili- tary	Non- mili- tary		Total	Mili- tary	Non- mili- tary	Total	Mili- tary	Non- mili- tary
1965	2,449	602	1,847	2,203	503	1,700	1972	1,656	905	751	959	646	313
1966	2,710	734	1,976	1,494	428	1,066	1973	1,562	902	660	1,177	923	254
1967	2,199	789	1,410	1,974	1,096	878	1974	1,751	944	807	1,492	1,131	361
1968	2,357	899	1,458	1,329	834	495	1975	2,119	1,096	1,023	1,304	1,019	285
1969	2,282	1,187	1,095	1,330	869	461	1976	1,930	888	1,042	1,234	902	332
1970	1,956	1,025	931	1,184	786	398	1977	1,969	884	1,085	1,555	1,165	390
1971	1,725	860	865	916	603	313							

Source: Aerospace Industries Association of America, Inc., Washington, D.C., *Aerospace Facts and Figures*, 1978/79 (copyright).

No. **1067.** SPACECRAFT LAUNCHINGS: 1957 TO 1977

[Criterion of success is attainment of Earth orbit or Earth escape. A spacecraft is a vehicle which is intended to go beyond the Earth's atmosphere]

YEAR	UNITED STATES				U.S.S.R. successful launch- ings	YEAR	UNITED STATES				U.S.S.R. successful launch- ings
	Earth orbit		Earth escape				Earth orbit		Earth escape		
	Suc- cess	Fail- ure	Suc- cess	Fail- ure			Suc- cess	Fail- ure	Suc- cess	Fail- ure	
Total	798	110	54	13	1,443	1967	77	4	10	–	75
						1968	61	3	3	–	85
1957	–	1	–	–	2	1969	50	1	8	–	80
1958	5	8	–	4	1	1970	29	1	1	–	103
1959	9	9	1	2	3	1971	26	2	3	1	114
1960	16	12	1	2	3	1972	32	–	3	–	109
1961	35	12	–	1 2	8	1973	22	1	3	–	129
1962	54	12	4	1	26	1974	–	–	–	–	114
1963	60	11	–	–	20	1975	17	2	2	–	139
1964	69	8	4	–	39	1976	26	–	1	–	141
1965	94	8	3	–	75	1977	21	3	2	–	125
1966	95	12	5	1 1	52						

– Represents zero. 1 Attained Earth orbit and included in Earth orbit success totals.

Source: Report to the Congress from the President of the United States, *U.S. Aeronautical and Space Activities*, annual; U.S.S.R. data from Science Policy Research Division, Library of Congress.

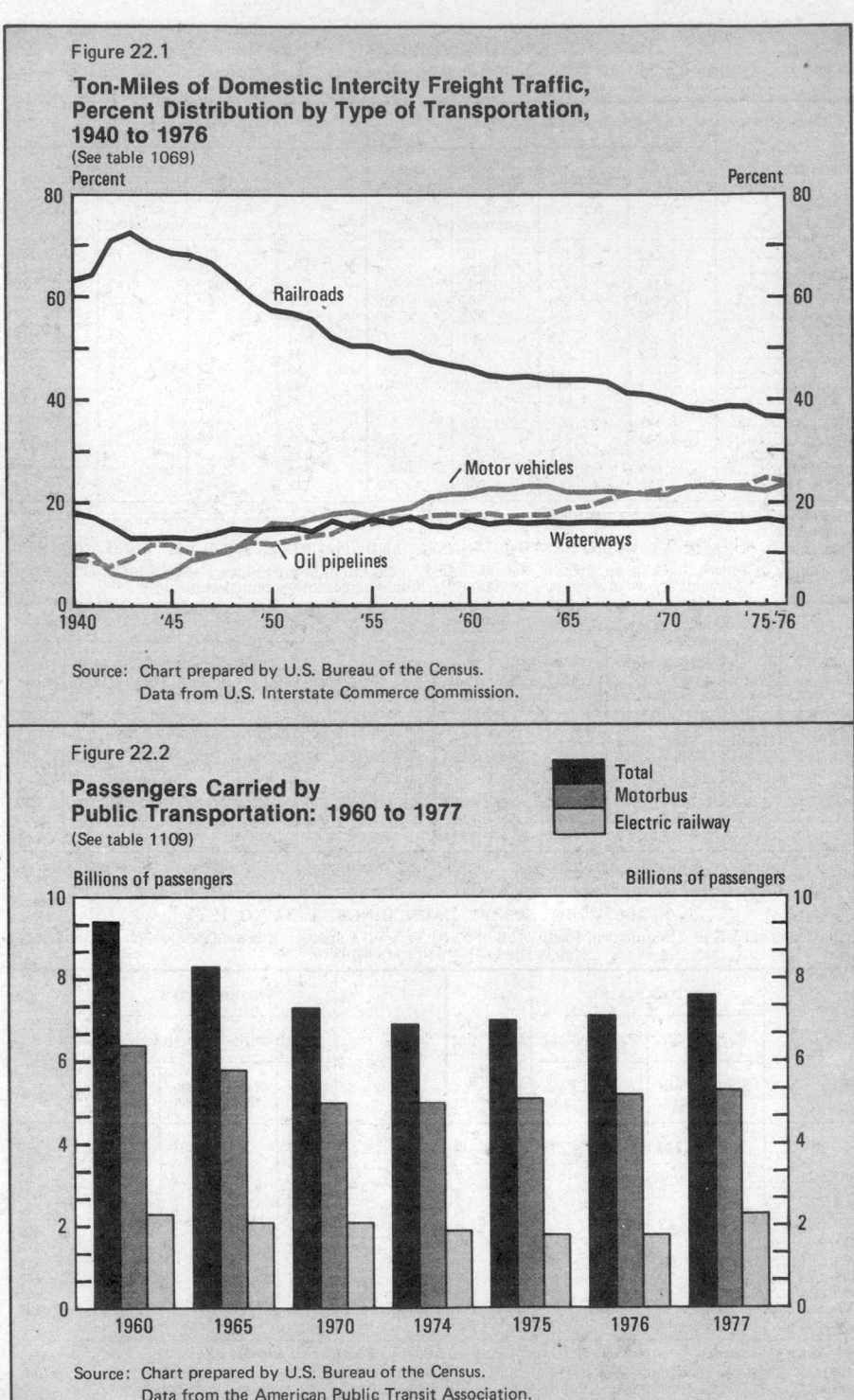

Figure 22.1

Ton-Miles of Domestic Intercity Freight Traffic, Percent Distribution by Type of Transportation, 1940 to 1976

(See table 1069)

Source: Chart prepared by U.S. Bureau of the Census.
Data from U.S. Interstate Commerce Commission.

Figure 22.2

Passengers Carried by Public Transportation: 1960 to 1977

(See table 1109)

Total
Motorbus
Electric railway

Source: Chart prepared by U.S. Bureau of the Census.
Data from the American Public Transit Association.

Section 22
Transportation—Land

This section presents statistics on operating revenues, passenger and freight traffic volume, and employment in various revenue-producing modes of the transportation industry, including commercial motor vehicles, trains, and pipelines. In addition, data are presented on commuting travel; highway mileage, construction, and cost; motor vehicle travel, accidents, sales, and registration; automobile operating costs; and characteristics of railroads.

The principal compiler of data on public roads and on operation of motor vehicles is the U.S. Department of Transportation's (DOT) Federal Highway Administration (FHWA). These data appear in FHWA's annual *Highway Statistics*. The U.S. National Highway Traffic Safety Administration issues data on traffic accident deaths and death rates in two annual reports: the *Fact Book* and the *Fatal Accident Reporting System Annual Report*. DOT's Federal Railroad Administration presents data on accidents involving railroads in its annual *Accident Bulletin*.

Another major source of data on interstate land transport is the U.S. Interstate Commerce Commission (ICC). Among its publications are the quarterly *Transport Economics* and the *Annual Report*, which contain data on domestic transport subject to ICC regulations, and the annual *Transport Statistics in the United States* volumes.

Various censuses and surveys conducted by the U.S. Bureau of the Census also provide data. Results of the censuses of transportation are presented in *Commodity Transportation Survey*, *National Travel Survey*, and *Truck Inventory and Use Survey*. The *Annual Survey of Manufactures* and reports of the Census of Manufactures and the Census of Business contain statistics on the motor-vehicle and equipment industry and on retail, wholesale, and services aspects of this industry. Data on persons commuting to work are contained in the 1970 Census of Population subject report, *Journey to Work*.

Data are also presented in many nongovernment publications. Among them are: The weekly and annual *Cars of Revenue Freight Loaded* and the annual *Yearbook of Railroad Facts*, both published by the Association of American Railroads, Washington, D.C.; *Bus Facts*, issued annually by the American Bus Association, Washington, D.C.; and the *Transit Fact Book*, containing electric railway and motorbus statistics, published annually by the American Public Transit Association, Washington, D.C. Useful annual handbooks in the field of motor-vehicle transport are *Motor Vehicle Facts and Figures*, issued by the Motor Vehicle Manufacturers Association of the United States, Inc., Detroit, Mich.; and *Accident Facts*, issued by the National Safety Council, Chicago, Ill.

Federal-aid highway systems.—Federal law provides that Federal funds be matched in varying proportions with State funds for the costs of planning, engineering, right-of-way acquisition, and construction of highways. Other costs, such as maintenance and policing, are borne entirely by the States and local agencies.

Effective July 1, 1976, a uniform road classification system was implemented which shortened the mileage of the highway system and redefined the three main systems of Federal-aid routes. The Federal-aid primary system is comprised of a network of main roads important to interstate, statewide, and regional travel. The system consists of main rural roads and their extensions into or through urban areas. The Federal-aid secondary system consists of rural roads of a more local nature, such as those which connect county seats and the larger population centers not served by the primary system.

The Federal-aid urban system is located in urban places of 5,000 or more persons and consists of major urban roads and streets, except those on the primary system.

Regulatory bodies.—The ICC, created by the U.S. Congress to regulate transportation in interstate commerce, has jurisdiction over railroads, trucking companies, bus lines, freight forwarders, water carriers, coal slurry pipelines, transportation brokers, and express agencies. The Federal Energy Regulatory Commission is responsible for setting rates and charges for transportation and sale of natural gas and for establishing rates or charges for transportation of oil by pipelines.

Motor carriers.—For 1960–1973, class I for-hire motor carriers were classified by the ICC as those with $1,000,000 or more of gross annual operating revenue. Beginning 1974, the gross revenue minimum for class I carriers was raised to $3,000,000.

Railroads.—The total railroad mileage of the United States comprises companies reporting to the ICC, grouped as follows: (1) Regular line-haul (intercity) railroads (and their nonoperating subsidiaries); (2) switching and terminal railroads; (3) private railroads prior to 1964 (identified by the Commission as "circular" because they reported on brief circulars); and (4) unofficial railroads, so designated when their reports are received too late for tabulation. For the most part, the last 3 groups are not included in the statistics.

Operating railroads are classified on the basis of operating revenues. Prior to 1956, the classification was: Class I, those having more than $1,000,000 gross annual operating revenue; class II, from $100,000 to $1,000,000; and class III, less than $100,000. From 1956 to 1964, class I railroads were those with $3,000,000 or more; from 1965 to 1975, $5,000,000 or more; beginning 1976, $10,000,000 or more.

Statistical reliability.—For a discussion of statistical collection and estimation, sampling procedures, and measures of statistical reliability applicable to Census Bureau data, see Appendix III.

Historical statistics.—Tabular headnotes provide cross-references, where applicable, to *Historical Statistics of the United States, Colonial Times to 1970*. See Appendix I.

No. 1068. Operating Revenues, by Type of Transport: 1950 to 1976

[Excludes Alaska and Hawaii, except as noted. Except for air carriers, data cover carriers regulated by U.S. Interstate Commerce Commission. See also *Historical Statistics, Colonial Times to 1970*, series Q 23–35]

TRANSPORT AGENCY	1950	1955	1960	1965	1970	1973	1974	1975	1976
REVENUES (mil. dol.)									
Railroads [1] [2] (class I, II)	9,924	10,590	9,955	10,738	12,511	15,620	17,889	17,400	19,900
Domestic scheduled air carriers [3]	558	1,215	2,129	3,609	7,131	9,605	11,448	12,020	13,901
International scheduled air carriers [3]	260	398	685	1,199	1,914	2,527	2,922	3,063	3,316
Supplemental air carriers [3]	42	77	83	141	337	374	429	433	417
Motor carriers of property [2] (class I, II, III)	3,737	5,535	7,214	10,068	14,585	20,800	22,700	22,000	26,000
Motor carriers of passengers [2] (class I, II, III)	539	552	667	885	1,062	1,172	1,347	1,360	1,387
Pipelines (oil) [4]	442	678	770	904	1,188	1,446	1,587	1,874	2,137
Waterlines [5]	330	452	427	426	502	618	879	946	1,035
REA Express [2] [6]	223	241	248	316	313	264	277	[7] 132	(X)
Electric railways	79	60	23	13	11	12	14	14	13
INDEX (1967=100)									
Railroads [1] [2]	91	98	92	99	115	144	164	160	183
Domestic scheduled air carriers [3]	11	25	44	74	146	197	234	246	284
International scheduled air carriers [3]	15	22	39	68	108	143	165	173	187
Supplemental air carriers [3]	16	30	32	55	130	145	166	167	161
Motor carriers of property [2]	33	49	64	89	129	184	201	195	230
Motor carriers of passengers [2]	57	58	71	94	112	124	143	144	147
Pipelines (oil) [4]	44	68	77	91	119	145	159	188	215

X   Not applicable.   [1] Includes Pullman (for 1950 to 1965), line-haul, and switching and terminal companies. [2] Beginning 1960, includes Alaska and Hawaii.   [3] Source: U.S. Federal Aviation Administration, *FAA Statistical Handbook of Aviation*, annual. Revenues for passenger/cargo operations. For scheduled air carriers, see also headnote, table 1134. Supplemental air carriers (see table 1136) cover domestic and international. [4] Beginning 1960, includes operations in Alaska.   [5] Domestic (inland and coastal) traffic only.   [6] Through 1965, data are after deducting payments to others for express privileges.   [7] Liquidated its assets in Nov. 1975.

Source: Except as noted, U.S. Interstate Commerce Commission, *Annual Report*; *Statistics of Class I, II, and III Motor Carriers, 1939–1956* (Statement No. 589); *Transport Economics*, issued monthly until April 1974, quarterly thereafter; and unpublished data.

No. 1069. VOLUME OF DOMESTIC INTERCITY FREIGHT TRAFFIC, BY TYPE OF TRANSPORT: 1950 TO 1976

[In billions of ton-miles, except percent. Prior to 1960, excludes Alaska and Hawaii, except as noted. A ton-mile is the movement of 1 ton (2,000 pounds) of freight for the distance of 1 mile. Comprises public and private traffic, both revenue and nonrevenue. See also *Historical Statistics, Colonial Times to 1970*, series Q 12–22]

YEAR	Total traffic, volume	RAILROADS [1] Volume	Percent of total	MOTOR VEHICLES Volume	Percent of total	INLAND WATERWAYS [2] Volume	Percent of total	OIL PIPELINES Volume	Percent of total	DOMESTIC AIRWAYS [3] Volume	Percent of total
1950	1,094	628	57.44	173	15.80	163	14.93	129	11.81	.3	.029
1955	1,298	655	50.43	223	17.20	217	16.68	203	15.66	.6	.037
1960	1,330	595	44.73	285	21.46	220	16.56	229	17.19	.8	.058
1961	1,326	586	44.17	296	22.36	210	15.82	233	17.59	.9	.068
1962	1,387	616	44.38	309	22.30	223	16.08	238	17.14	1.3	.093
1963	1,469	644	43.82	336	22.89	234	15.94	253	17.26	1.3	.088
1964	1,556	679	43.65	356	22.90	250	16.08	269	17.27	1.5	.096
1965	1,651	721	43.67	359	21.76	262	15.89	306	18.56	1.9	.116
1966	1,759	762	43.33	381	21.66	281	15.95	333	18.93	2.3	.128
1967	1,776	742	41.79	389	21.88	281	15.85	361	20.33	2.6	.145
1968	1,839	757	41.16	396	21.55	291	15.85	391	21.28	2.9	.157
1969	1,895	774	40.84	404	21.32	303	15.98	411	21.69	3.2	.168
1970	1,936	771	39.83	412	21.28	319	16.46	431	22.26	3.3	.170
1971	1,953	746	38.19	445	22.78	315	16.13	444	22.73	3.5	.170
1972	2,071	783	37.80	470	22.70	339	16.35	476	22.98	3.7	.179
1973	2,232	858	38.51	505	22.66	358	16.08	507	22.75	3.9	.175
1974	2,212	852	38.52	495	22.38	355	16.05	506	22.87	3.9	.180
1975	2,066	759	36.74	454	21.97	342	16.55	507	24.54	3.7	.193
1976	2,188	799	36.52	510	23.31	352	16.09	523	23.90	3.9	.182

[1] Includes electric railways. Beginning 1970, excludes mail and express.   [2] Includes Great Lakes and Alaska for all years, and Hawaii beginning 1960.
[3] Revenue service only for scheduled and supplemental carriers. Includes express, mail, and excess baggage.

Source: U.S. Interstate Commerce Commission, *Annual Report; Intercity Ton-Miles, 1939–1959*, (Statement No. 6103); and *Transport Economics*, quarterly.

No. 1070. VOLUME OF DOMESTIC INTERCITY PASSENGER TRAFFIC, BY TYPE OF TRANSPORT: 1950 TO 1976

[In billions of passenger-miles, except percent. Prior to 1960, excludes Alaska and Hawaii. A passenger-mile is the movement of 1 passenger for the distance of 1 mile. Comprises public and private traffic, both revenue and nonrevenue. See also *Historical Statistics, Colonial Times to 1970*, series Q 1–11]

YEAR	Total traffic, volume	PRIVATE AUTOMOBILES Volume	Percent of total	DOMESTIC AIRWAYS [1] Volume	Percent of total	BUS (excludes schoolbus) Volume	Percent of total	RAILROADS [2] Volume	Percent of total	INLAND WATERWAYS [3] Volume	Percent of total
1950	508	438	86.20	10	1.98	26	5.20	32	6.39	1.2	.23
1955	716	637	89.01	23	3.18	25	3.56	29	4.01	1.7	.24
1960	784	706	90.10	34	4.33	19	2.47	22	2.75	2.7	.34
1961	791	714	90.18	35	4.37	20	2.56	21	2.59	2.3	.30
1962	818	736	89.95	37	4.58	22	2.66	20	2.47	2.7	.33
1963	853	766	89.83	43	5.02	23	2.64	19	2.19	2.8	.32
1964	896	802	89.53	49	5.49	23	2.61	18	2.05	2.8	.32
1965	920	818	88.86	58	6.31	24	2.58	18	1.91	3.1	.34
1966	971	856	88.19	69	7.14	25	2.53	17	1.78	3.4	.35
1967	1,021	890	87.18	87	8.55	25	2.44	15	1.50	3.4	.33
1968	1,079	936	86.80	101	9.38	25	2.27	13	1.23	3.4	.32
1969	1,138	977	85.86	120	10.54	25	2.19	12	1.08	3.8	.33
1970	1,185	1,026	86.60	119	10.01	25	2.14	11	.92	4.0	.34
1971	1,230	1,071	87.11	120	9.76	26	2.07	9	.73	4.1	.33
1972	1,300	1,129	86.82	133	10.24	26	1.97	9	.66	4.0	.31
1973	1,356	1,174	86.58	143	10.55	26	1.92	9	.67	4.0	.29
1974	1,331	1,143	85.88	146	10.97	28	2.10	10	.75	4.1	.30
1975	1,352	1,164	86.09	148	10.95	26	1.92	10	.74	4.0	.30
1976	1,441	1,236	85.77	165	11.45	25	1.73	11	.76	4.0	.28

[1] Covers scheduled and supplemental commercial revenue service, and private pleasure and business flying.
[2] Includes electric railways.   [3] Includes Great Lakes.

Source: U.S. Interstate Commerce Commission, *Annual Report*, and *Transport Economics*, quarterly.

No. 1071. Largest Transportation Companies—Revenues and Assets, by Rank of Operating Revenues: 1960 to 1977

[Revenues include nontransportation activities; assets as of end of companies' fiscal years. Companies listed derive more than 50 percent of their operating revenues from the transport of passengers and/or freight (e.g., railroads, airlines, motor carriers, pipelines); excludes companies primarily engaged in freight forwarding, express shipping, or vehicle rental]

OPERATING REVENUE GROUP	1960		1970		1975		1976		1977	
	Reve-nues	Assets	Reve-nues	Assets	Reve-nues	Assets	Reve-nues	Assets	Reve-nues	Assets
	Bil. dol.		*Bil. dol.*		*Bil. dol.*		*Bil. dol.*		*Bil. dol.*	
50 largest, total	11.8	30.7	23.0	46.4	38.6	53.1	41.9	52.3	47.8	55.8
Lowest ten	.7	1.3	1.0	1.8	1.7	2.3	2.0	2.5	2.1	2.3
Second ten	1.1	1.9	1.4	1.7	3.0	3.0	3.0	3.3	3.4	3.2
Third ten	1.8	5.5	2.5	3.8	4.6	5.3	5.1	5.2	5.9	7.0
Fourth ten	2.7	7.6	5.6	12.7	10.5	18.1	11.2	17.4	12.6	17.4
Highest ten	5.5	14.4	12.6	26.4	18.8	24.5	20.5	23.9	23.8	26.0
	PERCENT		PERCENT		PERCENT		PERCENT		PERCENT	
Total	100.0	100.0	100.0	100.0	100.0	100.0	100.0	100.0	100.0	100.0
Lowest ten	6.1	4.2	4.4	3.8	4.4	4.3	4.8	4.8	4.4	4.2
Second ten	9.4	6.2	5.9	3.6	7.8	5.6	7.2	6.3	7.0	5.8
Third ten	15.1	18.1	10.8	8.3	11.9	10.0	12.2	9.9	12.4	12.5
Fourth ten	23.0	24.7	24.1	27.4	27.2	34.1	26.7	33.3	26.3	31.1
Highest ten	46.3	46.8	54.8	56.9	48.7	46.1	48.9	45.7	49.9	46.5

Source: Fortune, New York, N.Y.; adapted from *The Fortune Directory*. (Copyright, by Time, Inc.)

No. 1072. Intercity Carriers of Small Shipment Traffic—Volume and Revenues, by Type of Carrier: 1965 to 1976

[Volume in millions of net tons; revenues in millions of dollars, except as indicated. Covers shipments of less than 10,000 pounds by intercity carriers regulated by the U.S. Interstate Commerce Commission]

TYPE OF CARRIER	TOTAL								PERCENT		
	1965	1970	1971	1972	1973	1974	1975	1976 [1]	1965	1970	1976 [1]
Total volume	89.5	91.7	92.0	97.1	99.3	102.3	100.3	99.8	100	100	100
Motor carriers, cl. I and II [2]	76.9	78.1	78.5	82.8	83.8	86.1	85.0	85.0	86	85	85
Railroads, class I and II [3]	2.1	1.2	1.1	1.0	.7	.7	.5	.6	2	1	1
Bus express	.2	.2	.3	.3	.3	.3	.3	.3	(z)	(z)	(z)
Water and maritime carriers	.4	.2	.2	.2	.2	.2	.2	.3	(z)	(z)	(z)
Air freight	1.1	2.5	2.6	2.9	3.3	3.3	3.1	3.3	1	3	3
Airlines	.9	1.9	1.9	2.2	2.6	2.5	2.3	2.5	1	2	2
Forwarder	.2	.6	.6	.7	.8	.8	.8	.9	(z)	1	1
United Parcel Service [4]	.6	2.5	3.2	3.4	4.1	4.3	5.2	4.9	1	3	5
REA Express [5]	2.0	1.0	.8	.7	.8	.8	(x)	(x)	2	1	(x)
Freight forwarder	4.0	4.2	3.6	4.3	4.5	5.3	4.7	4.4	5	5	4
Parcel post	2.2	1.8	1.8	1.7	1.6	1.5	1.4	1.1	3	2	1
Surface	2.1	1.6	1.6	1.4	1.4	1.2	1.1	.9	2	2	1
Air [6]	(z)	.2	.2	.2	.2	.2	.2	.2	(z)	(z)	(z)
Total revenues	5,229	7,408	8,270	9,416	10,195	11,359	11,034	13,049	100	100	100
Motor carriers, cl. I and II [2]	3,100	4,193	4,833	5,528	5,799	6,569	6,030	7,300	59	57	56
Railroads, class I and II [3]	53	37	33	28	26	26	18	17	1	(z)	(z)
Bus express	61	102	104	110	115	122	131	152	1	1	1
Water and maritime carriers	14	11	7	8	11	7	8	16	(z)	(z)	(z)
Air freight	322	812	897	1,046	1,229	1,378	1,558	1,795	6	11	14
Airlines	209	462	496	564	658	728	767	919	4	6	7
Forwarder	113	349	400	482	571	650	790	876	2	5	7
United Parcel Service [4]	93	420	567	719	832	922	1,175	1,228	2	6	9
REA Express [5]	430	309	261	241	262	269	(x)	(x)	8	4	(x)
Freight forwarder	459	594	587	727	962	1,111	1,158	1,653	9	8	13
Parcel post	696	929	980	1,008	964	954	957	888	13	13	7
Surface	621	647	677	659	612	560	545	477	12	9	4
Air [6]	75	282	303	348	352	394	411	411	1	4	3

X Not applicable.   Z Less than 50,000 net tons or .5 percent.
[1] Preliminary.   [2] Less than truckload.   [3] Less than carload.
[4] Data are for intercity shipments only.   [5] Filed for reorganization under Bankruptcy Act in 1975.
[6] Beginning 1970, includes heavy-weighted pieces of first class mail.
Source: U.S. Interstate Commerce Commission, *Transport Economics*, vol. V, No. 1, 1978.

No. 1073. Employment in Transportation, by Type of Transport: 1960 to 1977

[Annual averages of monthly figures. See also *Historical Statistics, Colonial Times to 1970*, series Q 36–42]

TYPE OF TRANSPORT	NUMBER (1,000)							PERCENT				
	1960	1965	1970	1974	1975	1976	1977, prel.	1960	1965	1970	1975	1977, prel.
Total	2,549	2,532	2,689	2,765	2,601	2,623	2,772	100.0	100.0	100.0	100.0	100.0
Trucking [1]	771	882	998	1,094	996	1,009	1,131	30.2	34.8	37.1	38.3	40.8
Public warehousing	85	82	86	93	89	88	93	3.3	3.2	3.2	3.4	3.4
Railroads	885	735	627	583	538	528	534	34.7	29.0	23.3	20.7	19.3
Class I railroads [2]	781	640	559	527	491	490	497	30.6	25.3	20.8	18.9	17.9
Airlines [3]	191	229	351	368	362	370	380	7.5	9.0	13.1	13.9	13.7
Local and interurban passengers [4]	284	269	279	273	270	268	260	11.1	10.6	10.4	10.4	9.4
Local and suburban	101	83	77	68	69	69	68	4.0	3.3	2.9	2.7	2.5
Taxicabs	121	110	107	93	83	77	72	4.7	4.3	4.0	3.2	2.6
Intercity highway	41	42	43	42	39	40	39	1.6	1.7	1.6	1.5	1.4
Waterlines [3]	([5])	230	215	204	190	197	199	([5])	9.1	8.0	7.3	7.2
Pipeline [6]	23	20	18	16	17	17	17	.9	.8	.7	.7	.6
Transportation serv	[5] 310	85	115	134	139	146	158	[5] 12.2	3.4	4.3	5.3	5.7

[1] Includes terminals. [2] See text, p. 638. [3] Covers establishments engaged in domestic and/or international service. [4] Includes other transit services, not shown separately. [5] Figures for "Waterlines" included in "Transportation services." [6] Oil and other commodities except natural gas.

Source: U.S. Bureau of Labor Statistics, *Employment and Earnings*, monthly.

No. 1074. Rural and Municipal Highway Mileage, by Governmental Control: 1950 to 1976

[In thousands. As of Dec. 31. Prior to 1960, excludes Alaska and Hawaii. Municipal roads are those within incorporated places, densely populated New England towns, and certain of the more populous unincorporated areas. All other roads are classed as rural. See also *Historical Statistics, Colonial Times to 1970*, series Q 50, 51, and 55]

MILEAGE AND CONTROL	1950	1955	1960	1965	1970	1971	1972	1973	1974	1975	1976
Total mileage	3,313	3,418	3,546	3,690	3,730	3,759	3,787	3,807	3,816	3,838	3,857
Rural mileage	2,990	3,045	3,116	3,183	3,169	3,166	3,173	3,176	3,178	3,199	3,209
Under State control	581	619	659	687	707	713	712	711	706	711	711
Under local control	2,336	2,333	2,345	2,346	2,275	2,256	2,252	2,249	2,248	2,261	2,264
Under Federal control	73	93	112	150	187	197	209	216	224	227	234
Municipal mileage	323	373	430	507	561	593	614	631	638	639	648
Under State control	36	42	50	65	74	77	80	82	84	84	87
Under local control	287	331	380	442	487	516	534	549	554	555	561

No. 1075. Highway Mileage of Rural Roads: 1950 to 1976

[In thousands, except percent. As of Dec. 31. 1950 excludes Alaska and Hawaii. For definition of rural roads, see headnote, table 1074. For definition of surfaced roads, see footnote 2, table 1076. See also *Historical Statistics, Colonial Times to 1970*, series Q 51–54]

TYPE AND CONTROL	1950	1960	1965	1970	1971	1972	1973	1974	1975	1976
All rural roads	2,990	3,116	3,183	3,169	3,166	3,173	3,176	3,178	3,199	3,209
Primary State highways	363	403	414	408	408	408	410	410	412	411
Secondary roads under State control	209	241	249	273	275	276	273	267	268	268
County roads	1,719	1,742	1,740	1,733	1,727	1,736	1,728	1,731	1,739	1,737
Other roads under local control	617	603	607	542	529	516	521	517	522	527
National and State parks, forests, etc	81	127	173	213	227	237	244	253	258	266
Surfaced rural roads	1,679	2,165	2,302	2,411	2,416	2,433	2,436	2,452	2,483	2,509
Percent of all rural	53.8	69.5	72.3	76.1	76.3	76.7	76.7	77.2	77.6	78.2
Primary State highways	351	399	410	405	405	405	407	408	409	409
Secondary roads under State control	159	211	226	253	256	257	254	249	251	251
County roads	844	1,128	1,203	1,265	1,271	1,286	1,283	1,294	1,310	1,325
Other roads under local control	309	393	408	417	408	405	409	413	421	428
National and State parks, forests, etc	16	34	55	71	76	80	83	88	92	96

Source of tables 1074 and 1075: U.S. Federal Highway Administration, *Highway Statistics*, annual.

No. 1076. MUNICIPAL AND RURAL HIGHWAY MILEAGE—STATES: 1960 TO 1976

[As of Dec. 31. For definition of municipal and rural roads, see headnote, table 1074. Compiled for latest available year from reports of State authorities and planning survey data. Minus sign (−) denotes decrease]

STATE	1960, total (1,000)	1970, total (1,000)	1975, total (1,000)	1976 Total (1,000)	1976 Municipal (1,000)	Rural Total [1] (1,000)	Rural Percent surfaced [2]	Govt. control State [3] (1,000)	Govt. control Local (1,000)	Percent change in total mileage 1960–1970	Percent change in total mileage 1970–1976
U.S.	3,545.7	3,730.1	3,838.1	3,857.4	648.3	3,209.0	78.2	711	2,264	5.2	3.4
Ala	73.3	78.9	86.5	86.7	18.6	68.1	94.4	19	48	7.6	9.9
Alaska	4.6	7.3	9.9	9.9	1.7	8.3	59.8	5	2	58.7	35.6
Ariz	37.1	42.7	51.6	55.8	8.5	47.3	41.5	6	23	15.1	30.7
Ark	78.5	78.9	77.8	77.5	10.4	67.1	83.3	14	51	.5	−1.8
Calif	147.4	164.1	171.1	172.8	48.7	124.1	64.8	15	72	11.3	5.3
Colo	78.6	82.3	85.5	86.1	8.6	77.5	64.4	8	68	4.7	4.6
Conn	16.7	18.4	18.9	19.0	13.5	5.5	99.1	1	4	10.2	3.3
Del	4.6	4.9	5.2	5.2	1.0	4.2	99.8	4	-	6.5	6.1
D.C	1.3	1.1	1.1	1.1	1.1	(X)	(X)	(X)	(X)	−15.4	-
Fla	69.2	89.5	101.5	98.1	27.7	70.4	60.7	12	57	29.3	9.6
Ga	96.9	100.0	101.5	102.8	15.0	87.8	73.8	16	71	3.2	2.8
Hawaii	3.1	3.5	3.8	3.8	1.1	2.7	95.3	1	2	12.9	8.6
Idaho	42.2	56.0	57.5	57.8	3.4	54.4	52.7	5	25	32.7	3.2
Ill	123.4	129.9	131.5	133.6	30.9	102.6	94.3	13	89	5.3	2.8
Ind	102.2	91.0	91.2	91.7	16.4	75.3	97.0	9	66	−11.0	.8
Iowa	111.7	112.1	112.4	112.5	13.5	98.9	94.5	9	90	.4	.4
Kans	133.1	134.0	134.7	134.6	11.6	123.0	74.6	10	113	.7	.4
Ky	69.5	69.1	70.1	69.7	6.0	63.7	90.8	24	39	−.6	.9
La	48.4	52.8	54.7	54.8	12.0	42.8	93.9	14	28	9.1	3.8
Maine	20.8	21.4	21.6	21.7	2.7	19.0	93.4	11	8	2.9	1.4
Md	22.3	26.3	25.9	26.1	4.3	21.8	99.8	5	16	17.9	−.8
Mass	26.3	29.1	32.8	32.9	19.1	13.7	100.0	2	12	10.6	13.1
Mich	110.6	114.7	118.8	119.0	20.0	98.9	84.5	8	88	3.7	3.7
Minn	124.2	127.7	128.4	128.5	17.9	110.6	90.9	11	98	2.8	.6
Miss	63.8	66.8	67.5	67.7	7.5	60.2	97.7	10	50	4.7	1.3
Mo	112.7	115.3	117.0	117.2	18.1	99.1	94.2	30	69	2.3	1.6
Mont	75.1	78.3	78.2	77.9	2.6	75.3	59.5	6	59	4.3	−.5
Nebr	102.7	100.4	97.1	96.9	7.2	89.7	81.6	10	79	−2.2	−3.5
Nev	44.5	49.7	49.7	50.1	2.1	48.0	30.8	6	28	11.7	.8
N.H	14.0	14.8	15.3	15.3	5.3	10.1	80.3	3	7	5.7	3.4
N.J	31.1	32.1	33.0	33.1	19.5	13.6	95.5	2	12	3.2	3.1
N. Mex	62.5	67.3	70.6	70.9	5.4	65.4	27.2	12	46	7.7	5.3
N.Y	106.5	105.8	108.6	109.4	43.1	66.4	95.2	12	54	−.7	3.4
N.C	80.7	86.0	90.8	91.2	15.5	75.7	89.6	72	-	6.6	6.0
N. Dak	100.2	106.9	106.0	106.4	3.4	103.1	66.5	7	95	6.7	−.5
Ohio	104.5	108.9	110.6	110.6	24.3	86.4	98.4	17	69	4.2	1.6
Okla	103.4	107.9	109.4	109.6	15.8	93.8	74.8	12	82	4.4	1.6
Oreg	72.5	95.1	104.5	108.3	6.4	101.9	61.7	9	36	31.2	13.9
Pa	109.3	115.2	115.2	116.9	26.1	90.8	86.3	43	47	5.4	1.5
R.I	4.2	5.3	5.5	5.5	3.6	1.9	94.2	1	1	26.2	3.8
S.C	56.4	59.7	60.9	61.3	7.3	54.0	68.7	33	20	5.9	2.7
S. Dak	92.3	84.2	82.3	82.4	3.1	79.3	75.8	9	69	−8.8	−2.1
Tenn	75.2	78.7	81.3	81.6	12.6	69.0	97.6	8	60	4.7	3.7
Tex	230.8	245.5	255.9	257.7	59.3	198.3	70.4	62	136	6.4	5.0
Utah	34.5	40.4	48.9	48.5	4.8	43.7	42.2	5	22	17.1	20.0
Vt	13.7	14.5	13.9	13.9	1.0	12.9	92.7	3	10	5.8	−4.1
Va	56.6	61.1	62.8	63.4	10.1	53.4	97.9	50	1	8.0	3.8
Wash	60.5	75.1	84.3	84.3	10.4	73.9	79.6	17	40	24.1	12.3
W. Va	36.1	35.5	37.0	37.2	3.7	33.5	72.7	33	-	−1.7	4.8
Wis	97.9	103.2	105.2	105.5	15.0	90.5	94.2	11	80	5.4	2.2
Wyo	58.2	40.6	32.6	32.9	1.4	31.4	57.9	6	22	−30.2	−19.0

- Represents zero. X Not applicable. [1] Includes mileage under Federal control.
[2] Covers soil-surfaced roads and roads with slag, gravel, stone, bituminous, or concrete surfaces.
[3] Includes 32,087 miles of State park, forest, institutional, and other roads, and 2,412 miles of toll facilities that are not a part of the State or local highway system. Also includes mileage of local roads under State control in all counties of Delaware, North Carolina, and West Virginia; 10 counties in Alabama; rural boroughs in Alaska; all but 2 counties in Virginia; some county mileage in Kentucky; farm-to-market mileage in Louisiana; and the State-aid system in Maine.

Source: U.S. Federal Highway Administration, *Highway Statistics*, annual.

No. 1077. Mileage and Cost of Designated Federal-aid Highway Systems: 1960 to 1977

[Mileage as of **Dec. 31**, except as noted; cost for years ending **June 30** except, beginning **1977**, ending **Sept. 30**. Includes Puerto Rico. Beginning 1976, mileage data not comparable with earlier years due to reclassification of Federal-aid highway system; see text, pp. 637 and 638. See also *Historical Statistics, Colonial Times to 1970*, series Q 65–68]

ITEM	1960	1965	1970	1971	1972	1973	1974	1975	1976	1977
MILES OF HIGHWAY (1,000)										
Total	867	909	919	929	934	940	955	985	823	(NA)
Primary systems	265	269	272	272	270	268	268	275	307	(NA)
Interstate systems	41	41	43	43	43	43	43	43	43	43
Urban systems	(X)	(X)	(X)	8	13	17	37	65	124	(NA)
Secondary systems	601	640	647	649	651	655	651	645	392	(NA)
Completed during yr.[1]	29	19	11	11	12	10	8	7	8	9
Under construction [1]	26	26	20	19	18	16	14	16	17	19
COST (mil. dol.)										
Completed highway [2]	3,651	4,563	4,440	5,098	4,773	5,271	4,545	4,289	5,240	5,930
Federal funds	2,504	3,392	3,328	3,883	3,576	4,029	3,401	3,254	4,027	4,641
State funds	1,147	1,171	1,112	1,215	1,197	1,242	1,144	1,035	1,213	1,289
Projects under constrn: [2]										
Total cost	7,080	12,228	14,793	15,525	17,118	17,075	18,147	20,466	21,081	22,085
Federal funds	5,180	9,582	11,444	11,971	·13,292	13,167	14,122	16,187	16,922	17,782
State funds	1,900	2,646	3,349	3,554	3,826	3,908	4,025	4,279	4,159	4,303

NA   Not available.   X   Not applicable.   [1] Years ending June 30 except, beginning 1977, ending Sept. 30.
[2] Includes highway planning and research work.
Source: U.S. Federal Highway Administration, *Highway Statistics*, annual, and other releases.

No. 1078. Federal-aid Payments to State and Local Governments for Highway Construction—States and Puerto Rico: 1970 to 1977

[In millions of dollars. For years ending **June 30**, except as noted]

STATE	1970	1975	1976 [1]	1977 [2]	STATE	1970	1975	1976[1]	1977[2]	STATE OR OTHER AREA	1970	1975	1976[1]	1977[2]
Total	1,521	1,871	8,586	6,220	Iowa	63	88	150	106	Ohio	243	208	257	187
Highway					Kans	50	68	108	73	Okla	56	57	94	69
trust fund	4,336	4,583	8,200	6,005	Ky	96	98	221	98	Oreg	70	95	189	89
Other	188	291	386	216	La	110	113	211	184	Pa	238	267	472	254
					Maine	21	23	44	35	R.I	28	17	27	17
U.S.	4,520	4,860	8,553	6,199										
Ala	82	95	200	159	Md	66	122	218	141	S.C	35	47	99	59
Alaska	40	80	173	124	Mass	94	72	125	175	S. Dak	39	36	71	47
Ariz	68	89	134	111	Mich	160	174	321	225	Tenn	102	125	221	143
Ark	43	50	88	75	Minn	108	86	192	130	Tex	227	224	407	285
Calif	503	350	475	361	Miss	57	58	113	86	Utah	71	54	107	82
Colo	57	78	158	131	Mo	106	122	200	153	Vt	28	25	44	31
Conn	65	50	62	52	Mont	62	45	109	98	Va	112	179	241	211
Del	10	13	30	20	Nebr	38	58	92	61	Wash	93	113	173	148
D.C	32	13	46	26	Nev	35	26	57	56	W. Va	116	190	295	118
Fla	69	166	196	260	N.H	21	26	40	39	Wis	42	47	150	100
Ga	64	115	207	132	N.J	110	97	119	96	Wyo	38	33	79	52
Hawaii	33	43	73	58	N. Mex	55	60	76	50					
Idaho	37	42	77	71	N.Y	256	229	322	267	Undist	–	3	16	59
Ill	185	204	521	291	N.C	62	92	204	169	P. Rico	4	14	[3] 31	[3] 21
Ind	100	64	177	86	N. Dak	24	31	70	49					

– Represents zero.   [1] Figures are for 15-months ending Sept. 30.   [2] Year ending Sept. 30.
[3] For 1976, includes $3 million for V.I., Am. Samoa, Guam, and Trust Terr. of Pacific Is., for 1977, $7 million.
Source: U.S. Dept. of the Treasury, *Federal Aid to States*, annual.

No. 1079. Highway Construction—Contracts Awarded: 1960 to 1977

[In millions of dollars. Covers federally and State owned highways only; includes force-account construction authorized to start. See also *Historical Statistics, Colonial Times to 1970*, series Q 129–135]

OWNERSHIP AND SOURCE OF FUNDS	1960	1965	1970	1971	1972	1973	1974	1975	1976	1977, prel.
Total	4,030	4,935	6,520	6,327	6,505	6,516	7,304	7,242	6,333	7,355
Federally owned highways	129	135	52	171	206	116	158	176	168	164
State owned highways	3,901	4,800	6,468	6,156	6,299	6,400	7,146	7,066	6,165	7,191
Federally aided projects:										
Total value	3,097	3,896	4,877	4,595	4,876	4,554	5,266	5,846	5,153	5,858
Federal funds	2,218	2,976	3,619	3,422	3,598	3,342	4,229	4,726	4,102	4,707
Independent State projects:										
Total value	804	904	1,591	1,561	1,423	1,846	1,880	1,220	1,012	1,333
Toll facilities	165	49	49	159	99	147	14	11	10	21

Source: Data from U.S. Bureau of the Census. U.S. Bureau of Domestic Business Development, *Construction Review*, monthly.

No. 1080. Designated Federal-aid Highway Systems, 1976, and Projects, 1977—States and Puerto Rico

[Projects comprise those financed from the Federal-aid primary, secondary, urban, rural, TOPICS (urban traffic operations program to increase capacity and safety), and interstate funds. See text, pp. 637 and 638]

STATE OR OTHER AREA	MILEAGE OF SYSTEMS, 1976 (Dec. 31)					PROJECTS, 1977 (Sept. 30) [1]					
	Primary				Secondary	Completed during year			Under construction		
	Total	National system of interstate highways		Federal-aid, urban highway system		Miles	Total cost (mil. dol.)	Federal funds (mil. dol.)	Miles	Total cost (mil. dol.)	Federal funds (mil. dol.)
		Total	Open to traffic								
Total	307,052	42,500	38,182	123,633	392,070	9,358	5,818	4,570	19,411	21,742	17,542
U.S.	306,486	42,500	38,182	123,527	390,935	9,341	5,787	4,549	19,375	21,676	17,500
Ala.	7,814	900	723	2,311	11,198	192	174	136	314	634	527
Alaska	3,783	–	–	110	2,856	121	80	69	311	174	165
Ariz.	4,632	1,173	1,044	1,672	3,760	61	69	60	290	357	325
Ark.	5,840	526	515	857	5,965	154	71	50	176	167	130
Calif.	13,122	2,288	2,154	12,953	10,898	96	151	123	1,639	1,460	1,256
Colo.	5,229	976	853	2,198	3,459	285	106	90	135	301	259
Conn.	1,648	334	281	2,760	921	34	40	31	84	340	288
Del.	489	41	29	284	628	9	36	27	29	64	49
D.C.	76	24	12	318	–	9	18	15	12	175	136
Fla.	9,100	1,406	1,148	5,042	4,611	307	221	175	750	854	679
Ga.	10,588	1,155	983	2,987	14,211	438	120	85	2,139	719	570
Hawaii	581	51	24	202	461	10	82	56	15	251	200
Idaho	3,229	612	580	450	2,189	68	19	16	300	166	145
Ill.	12,856	1,729	1,609	6,089	12,816	585	474	376	657	590	479
Ind.	6,122	1,129	1,112	4,348	8,561	94	127	97	77	181	132
Iowa	10,056	789	728	2,195	13,378	481	107	79	692	221	173
Kans.	8,948	821	788	1,413	22,542	135	55	41	372	217	172
Ky.	4,619	737	648	1,731	7,340	70	134	108	156	404	309
La.	3,990	718	549	1,472	7,596	67	138	113	184	684	548
Maine	2,295	312	292	653	2,739	112	39	33	99	73	59
Md.	2,817	359	331	1,931	2,047	75	22	15	385	773	635
Mass.	2,814	450	419	5,581	2,106	58	120	91	84	629	490
Mich.	8,292	1,177	1,076	5,441	17,243	272	217	182	723	661	528
Minn.	10,123	920	777	1,945	16,232	394	177	140	783	464	379
Miss.	6,690	683	649	1,488	11,756	71	14	8	444	312	242
Mo.	6,906	1,147	1,054	2,086	18,097	210	173	127	275	417	327
Mont.	6,690	1,189	1,012	316	4,636	262	102	84	569	261	218
Nebr.	7,753	484	480	948	11,396	399	74	53	503	97	72
Nev.	2,416	540	464	369	2,481	27	17	15	147	173	160
N.H.	1,364	219	194	603	1,273	52	35	29	46	70	57
N.J.	1,968	388	306	5,168	1,921	33	152	116	112	590	451
N. Mex.	5,261	999	947	618	3,266	63	34	26	128	168	147
N.Y.	9,598	1,334	1,208	5,275	6,369	181	297	222	394	976	754
N.C.	5,399	839	679	1,613	10,606	132	153	114	388	553	436
N. Dak.	6,187	571	571	296	10,355	617	52	37	762	118	92
Ohio	8,065	1,538	1,452	7,400	11,788	131	250	191	572	865	672
Okla.	6,218	809	803	2,174	7,912	140	59	43	269	259	204
Oreg.	5,636	730	696	1,785	7,447	235	112	102	170	268	226
Pa.	11,591	1,567	1,462	6,688	8,031	122	223	170	611	2,109	1,600
R.I.	523	99	68	841	161	35	29	23	16	87	61
S.C.	6,532	763	693	972	8,889	262	61	45	536	198	160
S. Dak.	6,544	679	619	376	10,910	359	57	48	421	63	50
Tenn.	7,326	1,045	981	2,611	9,451	163	93	74	247	324	252
Tex.	20,204	3,163	2,860	5,370	32,915	557	289	215	725	903	724
Utah	3,529	939	708	751	2,697	274	98	90	247	251	230
Vt.	1,465	320	294	205	1,995	96	28	24	62	40	33
Va.	6,590	1,066	872	2,956	10,382	113	235	197	261	685	572
Wash.	6,008	762	630	4,039	7,211	254	132	111	285	389	342
W. Va.	3,402	513	450	730	6,373	20	86	69	80	642	554
Wis.	9,711	578	514	2,601	6,632	311	94	72	558	232	173
Wyo.	3,847	914	841	305	2,234	95	41	36	141	67	58
Pending	(X)	[2] –5	(X)	(X)	(X)	(X)	(X)	(X)	(X)	(X)	(X)
P. Rico	566	–	–	106	1,135	17	31	21	36	66	42

– Represents zero.   X Not applicable.   [1] Excludes highway planning and research work financed with 1½ percent Federal-aid highway funds available pursuant to 23 U.S.C. 307(c)(2). (Completed, $112 million total cost, $71 million Federal funds; underway, $343 million total cost, $240 million Federal funds.) [2] The minus mileage reserve, temporarily indicated, results from system measurements. The final mileage measurements will provide an adequate reserve in all designated routes on the system.

Source: U.S. Federal Highway Administration, *Federal Aid and Allied Highway Programs*, 1977.

No. 1081. Disbursements of State Highway Funds—Total, 1960 to 1976, and by Purpose, 1976, by States

[In millions of dollars. Comprises disbursements from current revenues or loans for construction, maintenance, interest and principal payments on highway bonds, transfers to local units, and miscellaneous. Includes transactions by State toll authorities. Beginning 1965, excludes amounts allocated for collection and nonhighway purposes, and bonds redeemed by refunding. See also *Historical Statistics, Colonial Times to 1970*, series Q 90–94]

STATE	1960	1965	1970	1973	1974	1975	Total	For State-administered highways			For county and local roads and streets [3]
								Capital outlay, roads and bridges [1]	Maintenance and traffic services [1]	Other [2]	
U.S.	8,957	11,465	16,535	18,775	19,702	21,131	21,391	10,580	3,165	4,477	3,169
Alabama	174	228	290	316	356	364	421	246	36	61	78
Alaska	19	71	99	155	183	254	234	127	49	56	2
Arizona	72	106	158	192	203	270	246	126	32	34	54
Arkansas	95	119	145	159	203	283	261	138	40	29	54
California	786	1,110	1,527	1,448	1,409	1,497	1,386	541	158	299	388
Colorado	91	129	177	195	228	239	288	158	39	31	60
Connecticut	161	216	293	332	369	351	277	89	42	128	18
Delaware	36	87	73	107	109	90	109	49	13	45	2
Dist. of Columbia	48	42	68	64	53	77	84	38	12	34	–
Florida	316	316	442	718	827	781	719	392	84	131	112
Georgia	167	208	278	348	438	487	459	303	56	91	9
Hawaii	23	35	74	85	93	105	112	71	10	18	13
Idaho	44	66	81	95	113	119	130	68	19	16	27
Illinois	475	471	889	878	943	1,189	1,302	765	122	181	234
Indiana	241	286	380	408	452	529	521	204	66	90	161
Iowa	169	193	291	315	366	409	404	205	40	43	116
Kansas	109	134	177	206	221	262	280	138	50	61	31
Kentucky	138	223	226	180	135	515	507	271	94	130	0
Louisiana	204	240	319	408	473	545	608	428	53	99	28
Maine	62	80	98	112	119	117	130	54	45	29	2
Maryland	166	217	388	561	492	443	521	259	50	141	71
Massachusetts	237	284	368	401	399	415	456	186	52	176	42
Michigan	418	427	570	731	780	794	809	311	70	135	293
Minnesota	167	230	297	356	336	358	420	209	61	58	92
Mississippi	110	160	205	246	286	339	358	235	17	60	46
Missouri	165	241	337	358	429	448	449	254	96	53	46
Montana	54	86	121	108	95	123	170	116	17	22	15
Nebraska	95	97	154	163	184	210	187	88	24	23	52
Nevada	22	58	59	71	75	85	84	37	19	22	6
New Hampshire	50	51	75	93	89	92	115	61	26	23	5
New Jersey	221	291	602	672	658	510	494	165	93	223	13
New Mexico	64	101	116	110	143	142	151	67	55	19	10
New York	652	752	1,237	1,341	1,219	1,129	1,108	404	216	377	111
North Carolina	179	219	396	445	471	541	607	331	122	123	31
North Dakota	50	51	75	76	83	97	110	67	14	10	19
Ohio	523	661	832	834	875	877	921	308	114	240	259
Oklahoma	134	179	237	269	297	290	297	122	43	52	80
Oregon	113	185	211	244	245	318	261	107	38	42	74
Pennsylvania	423	667	1,074	1,215	1,271	1,485	1,470	688	307	356	119
Rhode Island	42	62	54	61	74	52	72	37	12	23	–
South Carolina	109	114	157	208	244	255	224	116	48	43	17
South Dakota	57	68	81	98	103	98	110	62	19	15	14
Tennessee	187	238	304	344	381	467	457	280	36	55	86
Texas	493	513	730	706	817	984	791	456	149	143	43
Utah	49	89	114	126	114	125	147	83	17	30	17
Vermont	43	53	80	79	80	76	82	37	14	25	6
Virginia	211	353	447	593	688	574	634	373	117	106	38
Washington	171	235	372	421	394	417	412	170	77	92	73
West Virginia	110	169	317	428	401	417	527	308	117	102	–
Wisconsin	171	189	268	321	305	371	362	159	49	67	87
Wyoming	44	65	72	66	81	116	107	73	16	9	9

– Represents zero. [1] Includes some administration, engineering, and miscellaneous.
[2] Comprises, in millions of dollars: Administration and miscellaneous, 1,237; highway law enforcement, 1,424; bond interest, 917; and bond redemption, 899.
[3] Expenditures on county roads under State control in Ala. (10 counties), Del., N.C., Va. (except 2 counties), and W. Va. included with those for State-administered highways.

Source: U.S. Federal Highway Administration, *Highway Statistics*, annual.

No. 1082. Receipts and Disbursements for Highways, by Type: 1970 to 1976

[In millions of dollars. Data compiled from reports of State and local authorities. For Federal highway trust fund receipts, disbursements, and balances, see tables 425 and 426. State data include District of Columbia and cover State-administered highways]

TYPE	1970 Total [1]	1970 Federal	1970 State	1975 Total [1]	1975 Federal	1975 State	1976 Total [1]	1976 Federal	1976 State
Total receipts	21,747	6,124	11,720	28,648	7,741	15,061	31,211	8,072	16,169
Current income	19,861	6,124	10,415	26,455	7,741	13,649	28,897	8,072	14,710
Imposts on highway users [2]	15,311	5,295	9,688	18,624	5,699	12,387	19,819	5,995	13,302
Other taxes and fees	3,732	598	396	6,147	1,319	724	7,360	1,375	897
Investment income and other receipts	818	231	331	1,684	723	538	1,718	702	511
Bond issue proceeds (par value) [3]	1,886	–	1,305	2,193	–	1,412	2,314	–	1,459
Intergovernmental payments [4]	(X)	−4,750	+2,364	(X)	−6,655	+3,057	(X)	−7,154	+3,294
Funds drawn from (+) or placed in (−) reserves	−912	−943	+16	−495	−453	+72	−1,433	−185	−1,241
Total funds available	20,835	431	14,100	28,153	633	18,190	29,778	733	18,222
Total disbursements	20,835	431	14,100	28,153	633	18,190	29,778	733	18,222
Current disbursements	19,583	431	13,318	26,660	633	17,282	28,248	733	17,302
Capital outlay	11,575	262	9,327	14,261	332	11,011	14,295	375	10,580
Maint. and traffic services	4,720	46	1,967	7,070	89	2,987	7,883	98	3,165
Admin. and research	1,275	123	719	1,987	212	1,124	2,217	260	1,237
Highway law enforcement and safety	1,303	–	800	2,222	–	1,337	2,629	–	1,424
Interest on debt	710	–	505	1,120	–	823	1,224	–	896
Debt retirement (par value) [3]	1,252	–	782	1,493	–	908	1,530	–	920

– Represents zero.   X Not applicable.   [1] Includes other levels of government not shown separately. [2] Excludes amounts which were later allocated for nonhighway purposes.   [3] Excludes issue and redemption of short-term notes or refunding bonds. Premiums and discounts on sale of bonds and accrued interest are included with investment income and other receipts. Redemption premiums and discounts are included with interest on debt.   [4] Plus sign (+) indicates receipt of funds from other levels of government; minus sign (−) indicates disbursement of funds to other levels.

No. 1083. Public Highway Debt—State and Local Governments: 1960 to 1978

[In millions of dollars. Long-term obligations. State data are for calendar years; local data for varying fiscal years. Excludes duplicated and interunit obligations. Municipal debt includes other political subdivisions urban in character. See also Historical Statistics, Colonial Times to 1970, series Q 136–147]

ITEM	1960	1965	1970	1972	1973	1974	1975	1976	1977 [1]	1978 [2]
Total debt issued [3]	1,206	1,070	1,886	2,459	1,963	1,657	2,239	2,317	2,092	1,923
State	680	586	1,305	1,672	1,216	846	1,412	1,462	1,202	998
County and local rural	190	169	174	241	210	230	222	225	230	235
Municipal	336	315	407	546	537	581	605	630	660	690
Total debt redeemed [4]	616	855	1,252	1,270	1,405	1,445	1,492	1,532	1,614	1,656
State	300	459	782	783	883	887	908	920	979	996
County and local rural	96	123	152	148	158	163	166	170	175	180
Municipal	220	273	318	339	364	395	418	442	460	480
Total debt outstanding	13,166	15,316	19,107	22,264	22,881	23,016	23,801	24,586	25,064	25,331
State	9,384	10,905	13,903	16,626	16,959	16,918	17,422	17,964	18,187	18,189
County and local rural	1,280	1,363	1,685	1,770	1,810	1,775	1,822	1,877	1,932	1,987
Municipal	2,502	3,048	3,519	3,868	4,112	4,323	4,557	4,745	4,945	5,155

[1] Preliminary.   [2] Estimated.   [3] Excludes refunding issues.   [4] Excludes redemptions by refunding.

No. 1084. Speed of Motor Vehicles: 1960 to 1976

[Excludes Alaska and Delaware. Based on speed of each vehicle recorded on straight sections of rural interstate highways during off-peak hours. Excludes speed of vehicles during periods of bad weather and traffic congestion. Data based on 55 mile per hour Speed Limit Monitoring Program; for details, see source]

ITEM	1960	1965	1970	1971	1972	1973	1974	1975	1976 [1]
Number of vehicles recorded 1,000	(NA)	(NA)	200	178	160	181	203	102	515
Average speed, all vehicles m.p.h.	54.8	60.6	63.8	64.7	64.9	65.0	57.6	57.6	58.2
Vehicles exceeding—									
55 m.p.h. percent	47	72	87	88	89	89	65	68	69
60 m.p.h. percent	24	51	69	70	71	72	29	27	32
65 m.p.h. percent	(NA)	(NA)	44	47	49	50	9	7	10

NA Not available.   [1] For year ending September 30.

Source of tables 1082–1084: U.S. Federal Highway Administration, Highway Statistics, annual; releases; and unpublished data.

No. 1085. Motor-Vehicle Travel, by Type of Vehicle: 1960 to 1976

[In billions of vehicle-miles, except as indicated. Estimates based on automatic traffic recorder data. Urban travel includes all travel in municipalities and most travel in urbanized areas. All other travel is classed as rural. Minus sign (−) denotes decrease. See also *Historical Statistics, Colonial Times to 1970*, series Q 199–207]

ITEM	1960	1965	1970	1971	1972	1973	1974	1975	1976
Total travel	718.8	887.8	1,120.7	1,186.3	1,268.3	1,308.5	1,285.6	1,330.1	1,409.2
Avg. annual percent change	[1] 3.6	4.3	4.8	5.9	6.9	3.2	−1.8	3.5	5.9
Passenger cars [2]	588.1	711.6	901.0	954.2	1,003.5	1,036.5	1,013.1	1,050.5	1,096.5
Rural	303.3	333.4	406.4	428.9	436.0	444.3	427.3	440.9	464.6
Urban	284.8	378.2	494.5	525.2	567.5	592.2	585.8	609.6	631.9
Buses	4.4	4.8	5.0	5.1	5.1	5.0	5.1	5.1	5.8
Rural	2.3	2.6	2.8	2.9	3.0	2.9	3.0	3.0	3.2
Urban	2.1	2.2	2.2	2.2	2.1	2.1	2.1	2.2	2.6
Trucks and combinations	126.4	171.4	214.7	227.0	259.7	267.1	267.5	274.5	307.0
Rural	81.7	102.8	134.1	141.5	151.3	154.0	153.2	156.8	163.1
Urban	44.7	68.6	80.6	85.5	108.4	113.1	114.3	117.7	143.9
Average miles per vehicle:									
Passenger vehicles	9,474	9,310	9,798	9,938	9,980	9,774	9,233	9,413	9,517
Passenger cars [2]	9,446	9,286	9,783	9,926	9,969	9,767	9,225	9,406	9,506
Buses	16,004	15,215	13,306	12,819	12,553	11,662	11,320	11,140	12,045
Trucks and combinations	10,583	11,587	11,450	11,465	12,229	11,538	10,861	10,648	11,073

[1] Change from 1955. [2] Includes taxicabs and motorcycles.

Source: U.S. Federal Highway Administration, *Highway Statistics*, annual.

No. 1086. Motor Vehicle Accidents—Number and Deaths: 1960 to 1977

[See also *Historical Statistics, Colonial Times to 1970*, series Q 208 and Q 224–232]

ITEM	1960	1965	1970	1972	1973	1974	1975	1976	1977, prel.
Motor-vehicle accidents [1] mil	10.4	13.2	16.0	17.0	16.6	15.6	16.5	16.8	17.1
Vehicles involved by type:									
Cars mil	16.0	20.3	23.5	24.5	23.3	20.6	22.5	23.1	(NA)
Trucks mil	2.0	2.6	3.2	3.5	3.7	3.4	3.8	4.1	(NA)
Motorcycles 1,000	100	235	305	343	378	376	372	402	(NA)
Traffic deaths [2] 1,000	38.1	49.2	54.6	56.3	55.5	46.4	45.8	46.7	49.2
Noncollision accidents [3] 1,000	11.9	14.9	15.4	15.8	15.6	12.8	11.9	12.9	13.5
Collision accidents:									
With other vehicles 1,000	14.8	20.8	23.2	23.9	23.6	19.7	20.3	20.1	21.5
With pedestrians 1,000	7.9	8.9	9.9	10.3	10.2	8.5	8.6	8.3	8.5
With fixed objects [3] 1,000	1.7	2.2	3.8	3.9	3.8	3.1	3.1	3.2	3.5
Deaths occurring within 30 days									
of accident [4] 1,000	36.4	47.1	52.6	54.6	54.1	45.2	44.5	45.5	46.9
Vehicle occupants [5] 1,000	27.9	36.8	40.6	41.4	40.8	33.3	32.8	33.9	34.7
Pedestrians 1,000	7.2	8.0	8.9	9.2	8.9	7.5	7.5	7.4	7.5
Motorcyclists [6] 1,000	.8	1.6	2.3	3.0	3.2	3.4	3.2	3.3	4.1
Bicyclists 1,000	.5	.7	.8	1.0	1.1	1.0	1.0	.9	.9
Traffic death rates: [4][7]									
Per 100,000 resident population	20.2	24.3	25.8	26.2	25.8	21.4	20.9	21.2	21.7
Per 100,000 registered vehicles	48.9	51.3	47.3	44.5	41.6	33.5	32.3	31.7	31.5
Per 100 million vehicle miles	5.1	5.3	4.7	4.3	4.1	3.5	3.4	3.2	3.2
Per 100,000 licensed drivers	41.7	47.8	47.2	46.1	44.5	36.0	34.3	34.0	34.0
Motor vehicle accidents [8] mil	11.4	14.7	22.1	24.9	25.6	23.7	24.9	25.4	26.7
Injuries [8] 1,000	3,078	3,982	4,983	5,190	5,192	4,634	4,978	5,269	5,575
Economic loss [8][9] mil. dol	10,211	14,177	23,549	28,670	30,407	30,415	36,058	40,889	47,710

NA Not available. [1] Covers only accidents occurring on the road. [2] Deaths that occur within one year of the traffic accident. Includes collision categories not shown separately. Beginning 1970, excludes deaths to non-residents of U.S. [3] Beginning 1970, not comparable with previous years due to classification change. [4] Source: U.S. National Highway Traffic Safety Administration, *Fact Book*, 1976, and *Fatal Accident Reporting System Annual Report*. [5] Includes riders of animals and occupants of animal-drawn vehicles. [6] Includes riders of motor scooters and motorized bicyclists. [7] Based on 30-day definition of traffic deaths. [8] Estimates based on official reports from a representative cross-section of States. Includes all motor vehicle accidents on and off the road and all injuries regardless of length of disability. Source: Insurance Information Institute, New York, N.Y., *Traffic Accident Experience in the United States*, March 1973, and subsequent issues. [9] Wage loss; legal, medical, hospital, and funeral expenses; insurance administrative costs; and property damage.

Source: Except as noted, National Safety Council, Chicago, Ill., *Accident Facts*, annual. (Copyright.)

No. 1087. LICENSED DRIVERS AND DRIVERS INVOLVED IN FATAL ACCIDENTS, BY AGE-GROUP OF DRIVER: 1977

ITEM	Total	Under 20 years old	20–24 years old	25–34 years old	35–44 years old	45–54 years old	55–64 years old	65 years old and over
Licensed drivers_____mil__	138.1	11.8	18.7	33.2	22.9	20.7	17.1	13.7
Percent distribution_____	100.0	8.5	13.5	24.0	16.6	15.0	12.4	9.9
Drivers involved in fatal accidents_____1,000__	54.6	9.9	11.7	13.0	7.0	5.5	3.9	3.5
Percent distribution_____	100.0	18.1	21.4	23.9	12.8	10.0	7.1	6.4

Source: U.S. Federal Highway Administration, *Drivers Licenses,* annual, and U.S. National Highway Traffic Safety Administration, *Fatal Accident Reporting System Annual Report.*

No. 1088. DEATHS FROM MOTOR-VEHICLE ACCIDENTS—BY STATES: 1970 TO 1976

[Data differ from table 1086 because data are based on date of death, not date of accident, and on deaths occurring at any time after date of accident. By place of occurrence. Includes deaths to nonresidents of U.S.]

STATE	1970	1972	1973	1974	1975	1976	STATE	1970	1972	1973	1974	1975	1976
U.S._____	54,845	56,528	55,759	46,629	46,032	47,268	Mo_____	1,479	1,500	1,487	1,066	1,105	1,239
							Mont_____	340	408	334	301	294	307
Ala_____	1,297	1,356	1,376	1,118	1,087	1,139	Nebr_____	435	504	425	392	385	400
Alaska_____	107	64	68	74	120	133	Nev_____	278	290	292	235	236	240
Ariz_____	782	858	1,008	765	713	777	N.H_____	182	172	145	170	155	150
Ark_____	595	750	664	525	577	525	N.J_____	1,289	1,352	1,341	1,101	1,099	1,035
Calif_____	5,114	5,300	5,049	4,204	4,414	4,670	N. Mex_____	568	588	645	558	556	557
Colo_____	697	746	699	654	621	658	N.Y_____	3,117	3,140	2,929	2,483	2,277	2,233
Conn_____	448	444	516	400	404	413	N.C_____	1,801	2,026	1,942	1,605	1,560	1,582
Del_____	158	130	137	132	129	135							
D.C_____	140	100	103	91	91	81	N. Dak_____	194	206	230	168	183	208
Fla_____	2,181	2,570	2,704	2,280	2,067	2,021	Ohio_____	2,488	2,336	2,237	1,786	1,652	1,848
Ga_____	1,825	1,940	1,894	1,598	1,420	1,301	Okla_____	787	792	776	742	748	858
Hawaii_____	163	164	146	138	153	157	Oreg_____	739	774	658	693	582	664
							Pa_____	2,349	2,320	2,424	2,157	2,102	2,061
Idaho_____	320	324	342	326	291	290	R.I_____	143	144	141	120	140	136
Ill_____	2,267	2,216	2,293	1,700	1,816	2,027	S.C_____	1,070	1,148	995	895	837	834
Ind_____	1,587	1,578	1,629	1,253	1,139	1,273	S. Dak_____	240	312	299	249	216	238
Iowa_____	946	904	832	722	714	812	Tenn_____	1,525	1,526	1,599	1,383	1,280	1,280
Kansas_____	684	678	648	530	531	563							
Ky_____	1,081	1,114	1,155	812	885	900	Tex_____	3,570	3,714	3,699	3,127	3,472	3,240
La_____	1,194	1,136	1,176	855	993	1,007	Utah_____	354	354	377	263	285	282
Maine_____	288	252	252	225	235	234	Vt_____	116	126	137	110	124	95
Md_____	809	852	847	756	686	682	Va_____	1,251	1,256	1,264	1,095	1,069	1,062
Mass_____	918	1,042	1,029	978	895	827	Wash_____	902	836	826	808	804	862
Mich_____	2,172	2,236	2,186	1,863	1,811	1,955	W. Va_____	561	578	498	463	499	518
Minn_____	1,028	1,052	1,045	858	798	832	Wis_____	1,109	1,148	1,129	908	943	951
Miss_____	947	976	932	694	629	719	Wyo_____	210	196	200	200	210	257

Source: U.S. National Center for Health Statistics, *Vital Statistics of the United States,* annual.

No. 1089. AUTOMOBILE INSURANCE: 1960 TO 1977

[Money figures in millions of dollars. 1960 and 1965, direct premiums earned and direct losses incurred; 1970–1977 premiums earned basis. See also *Historical Statistics, Colonial Times to 1970,* series Q 163–174]

ITEM	1960	1965	1970	1973	1974	1975	1976 Private passenger	1976 Commercial	1977 Private passenger	1977 Commercial
Companies reporting_____	(NA)	(NA)	925	1,048	1,094	1,275	1,315		1,363	
Total insurance:										
Premiums earned_____	6,448	8,358	14,612	18,570	18,945	23,860	21,527	2,443	25,862	3,213
Losses paid [1]_____	3,645	5,221	11,198	13,428	14,206	19,657	16,733	1,808	18,015	2,249
Percent of premiums_____	56.5	62.5	76.6	72.3	75.0	82.4	77.7	74.0	69.7	70.0
Bodily injury liability: [2]										
Premiums earned_____	4,060	5,515	9,559	11,775	11,923	15,150	13,515	1,572	16,031	2,100
Losses paid [1]_____	2,372	3,484	7,547	8,814	9,089	12,277	10,392	1,207	11,506	1,557
Percent of premiums___	58.4	63.2	79.0	74.9	76.2	81.0	76.9	76.8	71.8	74.1
Physical damage: [3]										
Premiums earned_____	2,388	2,843	5,053	6,795	7,022	8,710	8,012	871	9,831	1,113
Losses paid [1]_____	1,273	1,737	3,651	4,614	5,117	7,380	6,341	600	6,509	692
Percent of premiums___	53.3	61.1	72.3	67.9	72.9	84.7	79.1	68.9	66.2	62.2

NA   Not available.   [1] Beginning 1970, includes adjusting expenses.
[2] Property damage included with bodily injury.   [3] Covers auto fire, theft, collision, and comprehensive.

Source: 1960 and 1965, The Spectator, Philadelphia, Pa., *Insurance by States;* thereafter, the National Underwriter Co., Cincinnati, Ohio, *Argus F. C. & S. Chart,* annual (copyright).

No. 1090. Motor Vehicles—Registrations and Factory Sales: 1950 to 1977

[Prior to 1960, registrations exclude Alaska and Hawaii. Minus sign (−) denotes decrease. See also *Historical Statistics, Colonial Times to 1970*, series Q 148–155]

| YEAR | REGISTRATIONS [1] (mil.) | | | Motor-cycle [1] registra-tions (1,000) | FACTORY SALES [2] | | | | | AVERAGE ANNUAL PERCENT CHANGE | |
| | Total cars, trucks, buses | Passen-ger cars and taxis | Trucks and buses | | Number (1,000) | | | Wholesale value [4] | | | |
					Total cars, trucks, buses	Pas-senger cars	Trucks and buses [3]	Pas-senger cars (mil. dol.)	Trucks and buses [3] (mil. dol.)	Regis-tra-tions [5]	Fac-tory sales [5]
1950	49.2	40.3	8.8	454	8,003	6,666	1,337	8,468	1,708	[6] 7.4	[6] 21.0
1955	62.7	52.1	10.5	412	9,169	7,920	1,249	12,453	2,021	5.0	2.8
1960	73.9	61.7	12.2	574	7,869	6,675	1,194	12,164	2,351	3.3	−3.0
1965	90.4	75.3	15.1	1,382	11,057	9,306	1,752	18,380	3,734	4.1	7.0
1966	94.0	78.1	15.8	1,753	10,329	8,598	1,731	17,554	3,953	4.0	−6.6
1967	96.9	80.4	16.5	1,953	8,976	7,437	1,539	16,653	3,592	3.2	−13.1
1968	100.9	83.6	17.3	2,089	10,718	8,822	1,896	19,352	4,670	4.1	19.4
1969	105.1	86.9	18.2	2,316	10,147	8,224	1,923	18,751	4,937	4.2	−5.3
1970	108.4	89.2	19.2	2,824	8,239	6,547	1,692	14,630	4,820	3.2	−18.8
1971	113.0	92.7	20.3	3,344	10,638	8,585	2,053	21,410	5,964	4.2	29.1
1972	118.8	97.1	21.7	3,760	11,271	8,824	2,447	23,133	7,654	5.1	6.0
1973	125.7	102.0	23.7	4,371	12,637	9,658	2,980	26,240	9,544	5.8	12.1
1974	129.9	104.9	25.1	4,966	10,059	7,331	2,727	21,653	10,163	3.4	−20.4
1975	133.0	106.7	26.2	4,964	8,985	6,713	2,272	23,400	9,900	2.3	−10.7
1976	138.5	110.4	28.2	4,989	11,477	8,498	2,979	(NA)	(NA)	4.2	27.7
1977	[7] 143.8	[7] 114.1	[7] 29.7	[7] 5,045	12,639	9,199	3,440	(NA)	(NA)	3.8	10.1

NA Not available. [1] Includes publicly owned vehicles. Excludes military services' vehicles. [2] Beginning 1965, excludes tactical vehicles. [3] A substantial part of trucks and buses reported comprises chassis without body; hence, excludes value of bodies for these chassis. [4] Includes standard equipment. [5] Excludes motorcycles. [6] Change from 1945. [7] Estimate.

Source: Sales—Motor Vehicle Manufacturers Assn. of the United States, Inc., Detroit, Mich., *Motor Vehicle Facts and Figures*, annual; registrations—U.S. Federal Highway Administration, *Highway Statistics*, annual.

No. 1091. Motor Vehicles—Establishments, Sales, Payroll, and Employment for Selected Kinds of Business: 1967 and 1972

| KIND OF BUSINESS | ESTABLISH-MENTS [1] (1,000) | | SALES OR RECEIPTS [2] (mil. dol.) | | ANNUAL PAYROLL [3] (mil. dol.) | | PAID EMPLOYEES [4] (1,000) | |
	1967	1972	1967	1972	1967	1972	1967	1972
RETAIL TRADE								
Automotive dealers	105.5	131.8	55,631	93,774	5,257	8,901	906.6	1,073.0
Motor vehicle dealers—new and used cars	} 62.0	64.2	48,636	77,833	{ 4,232	6,843	696.3	765.6
Motor vehicle dealers—used cars only					185	256	38.6	39.4
Tire, battery, and accessory dealers	29.2	37.5	4,236	7,543	604	1,103	129.6	167.7
Misc. automotive dealers	14.3	30.1	2,760	8,398	236	699	42.2	100.3
Gasoline service stations	213.1	226.5	22,709	33,655	1,898	2,974	575.2	747.7
WHOLESALE TRADE								
Motor vehicles and auto equipment	31.2	36.5	46,122	83,015	2,127	3,414	341.1	391.8
Automobiles and other motor vehicles	4.8	5.6	31,330	57,755	641	1,008	91.9	102.3
Automotive equipment	23.3	27.0	11,614	19,930	1,261	2,009	214.1	246.1
Tires and tubes	3.1	3.9	3,178	5,330	225	397	35.1	43.4
SERVICES								
Auto repairs, services, and garages	139.2	169.0	[5] 7,028	12,081	1,468	2,553	316.2	392.5
Automobile repair shops	109.9	127.2	4,086	7,045	943	1,699	187.9	237.9
Automobile parking	10.6	10.5	484	725	129	175	33.5	37.3
Car, truck rental and leasing; other services	18.7	31.3	2,489	4,311	396	679	95.0	117.3
MANUFACTURING								
Motor vehicles and equipment	2.7	3.4	13,666	22,036	5,930	9,448	739.4	806.6
Motor vehicles	.2	.2	7,354	11,783	2,700	4,300	321.2	339.2
Motor vehicle parts and accessories	1.7	2.1	5,712	9,145	2,891	4,587	364.9	399.9
Truck and bus bodies	.6	.8	332	659	192	355	30.4	42.8
Truck trailers	.2	.3	269	449	147	206	22.9	24.7

[1] As of Dec. 31; for wholesale trade and manufacturing, represents only establishments employing one or more workers at any time during year. [2] For manufacturing, data represent value added in manufacture. [3] Comprises salaries, wages, commissions, bonuses, vacation pay, and other remuneration. [4] Workweek including Mar. 12, except quarterly average for manufacturing. [5] Subtotals are corrected figures, total is uncorrected; therefore, breakdown will not add to total.

Source: U.S. Bureau of the Census, *Census of Business: 1967*, vols. II, III, and V; *Census of Retail Trade, 1972*, RC 72=L; *Census of Wholesale Trade, 1972*, vol. I; *Census of Selected Service Industries, 1972*, vol. I; *Census of Manufactures, 1967*, series MC 67(1)-1; and *Census of Manufactures: 1972*, series MC 72(2).

No. 1092. MOTOR-VEHICLE REGISTRATIONS, 1960 TO 1977, AND DRIVERS LICENSES, 1977, BY STATES

[In thousands, except as indicated. Motor-vehicle registrations include publicly, privately, and commercially owned vehicles; for uniformity, figures have been adjusted to a calendar-year basis as registration years in States differ; figures represent net numbers where possible, excluding re-registrations and nonresident registrations]

STATE	AUTOMOBILES, TRUCKS, AND BUSES [1]									Motor-cycles (incl. official) [1] 1977, est.	DRIVERS LICENSES, 1977		
						1977, est.		Percent change				Percent—	
	1960, total	1965, total	1970, total	1975, total	1976, total	Total	Auto-mo-biles (incl. cabs)	1960-1970	1970-1977		Total [2]	Male	Under 25 yr. old
U.S.	73,858	90,358	108,418	132,962	138,480	143,744	113,667	46.8	32.6	5,015	138,121	53.9	22.1
Ala	1,282	1,663	1,966	2,493	2,576	2,674	2,005	53.4	36.0	72	2,123	53.7	23.5
Alaska	81	109	139	226	250	257	162	71.6	84.9	13	226	58.9	25.5
Ariz	624	825	1,093	1,459	1,479	1,554	1,119	75.2	42.2	65	1,419	54.4	26.1
Ark	708	914	1,043	1,283	1,349	1,423	945	47.3	36.4	31	1,402	53.9	21.6
Calif	7,799	9,989	11,901	13,891	14,316	14,958	11,694	52.6	25.7	679	14,579	53.2	21.6
Colo	924	1,158	1,442	1,925	2,027	2,163	1,614	56.1	50.0	106	1,878	52.3	23.9
Conn	1,107	1,415	1,733	1,949	2,087	2,090	1,922	56.5	20.6	70	1,913	49.8	20.6
Del	192	244	312	351	362	374	308	62.5	19.9	8	384	51.8	23.7
D.C.	206	236	257	255	265	261	242	24.8	1.6	4	350	55.4	16.6
Fla	2,367	3,037	4,120	5,395	5,848	6,096	5,017	74.1	48.0	181	6,572	54.2	20.1
Ga	1,512	1,990	2,584	3,211	3,332	3,496	2,741	70.9	35.3	98	3,164	53.0	24.3
Hawaii	231	310	405	462	498	521	443	75.3	28.6	6	534	56.2	22.3
Idaho	375	434	488	647	682	718	444	30.1	47.1	45	595	53.3	27.1
Ill	3,776	4,437	5,238	6,344	6,677	6,861	5,713	38.7	31.0	239	6,741	53.8	23.0
Ind	2,046	2,427	2,818	3,315	3,451	3,586	2,740	37.7	27.3	153	3,474	52.5	22.8
Iowa	1,325	1,549	1,790	2,099	2,186	2,222	1,642	35.1	24.1	160	1,985	54.1	22.3
Kans	1,163	1,369	1,548	1,805	1,874	1,926	1,311	33.1	24.4	87	1,769	52.4	21.3
Ky	1,198	1,500	1,763	2,245	2,350	2,450	1,770	47.2	39.0	61	1,994	55.1	22.0
La	1,177	1,442	1,742	2,188	2,342	2,422	1,734	48.0	39.0	69	2,223	54.2	26.2
Maine	374	424	510	648	689	718	555	36.4	40.8	32	668	53.2	20.8
Md	1,155	1,481	1,872	2,423	2,505	2,587	2,192	62.1	38.2	69	2,530	52.8	21.7
Mass	1,803	2,104	2,575	3,107	3,201	3,520	3,122	42.8	36.7	86	3,652	51.1	20.8
Mich	3,306	3,991	4,569	5,545	5,701	5,986	4,954	38.2	31.0	261	6,150	52.7	25.5
Minn	1,592	1,890	2,207	2,525	2,768	2,813	2,107	38.6	27.5	149	2,598	53.7	24.4
Miss	723	921	1,117	1,377	1,446	1,494	1,064	54.5	33.8	28	1,573	55.5	25.2
Mo	1,720	2,085	2,408	2,866	2,941	3,053	2,302	40.1	26.8	95	3,100	53.0	20.7
Mont	373	429	485	611	639	672	407	30.0	38.6	40	516	55.7	22.3
Nebr	734	849	974	1,178	1,243	1,258	890	32.7	29.2	53	1,025	52.5	23.7
Nev	175	266	355	464	508	549	407	102.9	54.6	20	479	53.5	22.3
N.H.	256	331	390	485	527	593	503	52.3	52.1	34	584	53.1	21.6
N.J.	2,401	2,980	3,586	4,155	4,257	4,407	3,972	49.4	22.9	91	4,294	52.2	20.3
N. Mex.	426	525	637	827	884	907	593	49.5	42.4	39	774	51.5	28.5
N.Y.	5,067	5,939	6,718	7,591	7,651	7,730	6,799	32.6	15.1	132	8,970	56.0	18.5
N.C.	1,720	2,156	2,826	3,690	3,891	4,079	3,127	64.3	44.3	104	3,490	52.7	24.1
N. Dak.	345	396	428	551	563	580	344	24.1	35.5	26	395	53.4	26.4
Ohio	4,087	4,935	5,974	7,179	7,146	7,504	6,359	46.2	25.6	254	8,505	60.5	19.7
Okla	1,184	1,438	1,713	2,113	2,214	2,296	1,548	44.7	34.0	110	1,875	52.4	22.7
Oreg	919	1,119	1,369	1,628	1,734	1,776	1,378	49.0	29.7	85	1,754	54.2	21.9
Pa	4,287	4,968	5,818	7,659	8,127	8,102	6,891	35.7	39.3	232	7,026	55.9	20.1
R.I.	341	406	488	563	585	605	527	43.1	24.0	20	600	51.7	20.5
S.C.	879	1,094	1,360	1,772	1,770	1,858	1,462	54.7	36.6	41	1,741	53.5	23.1
S. Dak.	354	398	426	521	542	561	353	20.3	31.7	27	471	53.0	26.4
Tenn	1,307	1,655	2,050	2,727	2,805	2,996	2,308	56.8	46.1	87	2,597	52.9	22.2
Tex	4,457	5,610	6,693	8,396	8,970	9,489	6,971	50.2	41.8	286	8,192	52.8	23.1
Utah	417	525	664	845	877	908	623	59.2	36.7	53	771	51.9	27.4
Vt	152	175	229	287	305	320	255	50.7	39.7	17	332	53.2	21.1
Va	1,426	1,800	2,263	3,251	3,302	3,257	2,767	58.7	43.9	76	3,277	51.6	22.8
Wash	1,377	1,659	2,102	2,540	2,685	2,895	2,118	52.7	37.7	115	2,339	52.4	21.6
W. Va	601	696	801	966	1,042	1,136	777	33.3	41.8	56	1,367	57.4	23.6
Wis	1,600	1,839	2,182	2,591	2,649	2,667	2,206	36.4	22.2	133	2,841	53.2	23.8
Wyo	207	225	247	337	361	376	221	19.3	52.2	16	309	54.3	27.4

[1] Excludes vehicles owned by military services.   [2] Estimated from data reported by States for current and previous years; allowance has been made for deaths, emigration, or revocation by some States.

Source: U.S. Federal Highway Administration, *Highway Statistics*, annual, and *Drivers Licenses*, annual.

No. 1093. Motor Vehicles—Summary Statistics: 1965 to 1977

ITEM	1965	1970	1972	1973	1974	1975	1976	1977
SALES, EXPORTS, IMPORTS, AND SCRAPPAGE								
Passenger car factory sales_____1,000__	9,306	6,547	8,824	9,658	7,331	6,713	8,498	9,199
Passenger car (new), retail sales [1]___1,000__	9,332	8,405	10,950	11,439	8,867	8,640	10,110	11,185
Domestic [2]_____1,000__	8,763	7,119	9,327	9,676	7,454	7,053	8,611	9,109
Imports [3]_____1,000__	569	1,285	1,623	1,763	1,413	1,587	1,498	2,075
Passenger cars (new), exported [1] [4]___1,000__	205	359	471	579	610	640	680	697
Passenger cars (new), imported [1] [5]___1,000__	559	2,013	2,486	2,437	2,573	2,075	2,537	2,791
Canada_____1,000__	29	693	842	872	818	734	826	850
Germany, Federal Republic of____1,000__	377	675	677	677	620	370	350	424
Japan_____1,000__	26	381	698	625	792	696	1,129	1,342
Truck and bus factory sales_____1,000__	1,752	1,692	2,447	2,980	2,727	2,272	2,979	3,440
Truck and bus retail sales [6]_____1,000__	1,539	1,746	2,534	3,008	2,587	2,351	3,044	3,486
Light duty (Up to 14,000 GVW)[7]_1,000__	(NA)	(NA)	2,151	2,562	2,184	2,076	2,763	3,145
Med. duty (14,001–26,000 GVW) [7]_1,000__	(NA)	(NA)	221	254	224	169	162	172
Heavy duty (over 26,000 GVW) [7]__1,000__	101	126	162	192	179	106	119	169
Passenger car factory sales_____mil. dol__	18,380	14,630	23,133	26,240	21,653	23,400	(NA)	(NA)
Imports, new passenger cars [1]_____mil. dol__	640	3,719	5,704	6,479	7,544	7,483	9,399	11,080
Trucks and buses, new [1]_____mil. dol__	33	381	600	517	646	620	834	1,230
Exports [1]_____mil. dol__	2,198	3,871	5,296	6,561	8,604	10,658	12,046	12,544
Passenger cars (new)_____mil. dol__	393	822	1,303	1,764	2,303	2,852	3,228	3,568
Trucks and buses (new)_____mil. dol__	328	636	714	892	1,422	2,305	2,141	2,098
Parts and accessories [8]_____mil. dol__	1,476	2,413	3,279	3,904	4,879	5,501	6,678	6,877
Vehicles retired from use [9] [10]_____1,000__	6,440	8,298	8,106	9,195	8,241	6,576	7,926	9,902
Passenger cars_____1,000__	5,704	7,461	7,058	7,987	7,194	5,669	6,829	8,234
Trucks and buses_____1,000__	736	837	1,048	1,208	1,047	908	1,097	1,668
Average age of cars in use_____years__	5.90	5.55	5.66	5.74	5.72	5.99	6.16	6.23
Average age of trucks in use_____years__	7.98	7.33	7.15	6.95	6.97	6.94	6.97	6.93
Motorcycle registrations, new [10] [11]_1,000__	545	751	1,006	1,190	1,024	747	783	848
Motorcycle imports, total [12]_____1,000__	(NA)	1,091	1,690	1,206	1,556	981	738	1,053
Value [13]_____mil. dol__	(NA)	308	697	570	914	718	483	633
Vehicle drivers licenses_____mil__	99	112	118	122	125	130	134	138
Percent male_____	59.2	56.8	55.8	55.2	54.7	54.3	54.1	53.9
Percent under 25 yr. old_____	20.5	22.1	22.2	22.2	22.5	22.6	22.4	22.1
TIRES AND BATTERIES SHIPMENTS								
Tires, passenger car,[14] total_____mil__	148.5	168.6	194.9	202.0	174.4	167.6	177.2	190.2
Original equipment_____mil__	51.4	37.5	51.4	56.1	43.3	39.4	50.0	55.8
Replacement_____mil__	94.9	129.6	141.6	142.3	123.5	123.0	123.4	129.8
Tires, truck and bus,[14] total_____mil__	20.4	25.7	33.0	36.9	34.0	28.7	33.1	38.8
Original equipment_____mil__	6.9	8.6	12.6	13.5	11.8	8.1	10.1	11.9
Replacement_____mil__	12.8	16.7	20.1	22.9	21.1	19.8	22.4	26.1
Replacement automobile batteries [15]___mil__	29.5	37.9	43.2	43.5	43.8	39.3	49.2	54.6
SPECIAL MOTOR VEHICLE TAXES [16]								
Federal excise_____bil. dol__	5.7	6.8	5.1	5.9	5.8	5.6	6.0	6.9
State motor veh. carrier receipts___bil. dol__	2.5	3.8	4.4	4.8	5.0	5.1	6.1	6.1
State motor fuel, net_____bil. dol__	4.5	6.5	7.6	8.3	8.1	8.4	8.9	9.3
MOTOR VEHICLE REGISTRATIONS								
All vehicles,[17] world_____mil__	178.0	246.5	280.6	299.3	315.9	326.1	327.9	(NA)
United States_____mil__	90.4	108.4	118.6	124.5	130.0	132.9	133.0	(NA)
Other North and Central America_mil__	8.2	11.3	12.9	14.6	14.9	15.7	16.3	(NA)
South America_____mil__	5.1	8.1	9.9	11.2	12.2	13.0	13.0	(NA)
Europe, non-communist area_____mil__	50.1	74.3	86.1	91.5	95.8	96.6	97.5	(NA)
Europe, communist area_____mil__	6.4	10.4	11.9	12.4	14.3	16.6	16.6	(NA)
Africa_____mil__	3.4	4.5	4.7	5.4	6.2	6.6	6.5	(NA)
Asia, non-communist area_____mil__	9.5	22.9	28.8	32.1	34.4	36.2	37.0	(NA)
Asia, communist area_____mil__	.2	.5	.7	.7	.7	.7	.7	(NA)
Oceania_____mil__	4.7	6.0	6.9	7.0	7.4	7.8	7.7	(NA)

NA Not available. [1] Based on data from U.S. Dept. of Commerce. [2] Includes domestic models produced in Canada. [3] Excludes domestic models produced in Canada. [4] Includes export factory sales. [5] Includes other countries, not shown separately. [6] Excludes motorcoaches and imports from foreign manufacturers. Beginning 1973, includes imports by U.S. manufacturers. [7] Gross vehicle weight (fully loaded vehicle). [8] Includes rubber tires and tubes and used vehicles. [9] For years ending June 30. Represents vehicles failing to re-register. [10] Source: R. L. Polk & Company, Detroit, Mich. Reproduction prohibited without Polk permission. [11] *R. L. Polk & Co. New Motorcycle Registrations by States.* Excludes Oklahoma. [12] Source: Motorcycle Industry Council, Inc., Newport Beach, Calif. Data from U.S. Dept. of Commerce. Beginning 1974, includes motorized bicycles. [13] Dutiable value for customs purposes. [14] Includes exports, not shown separately. Source: The Rubber Manufacturers Association, Inc., Washington, D.C., *Rubber Industry Facts,* annual. Beginning 1965, figures for "Tires, passenger car" include motorcycle tires. Truck and bus tires include tires for mobile homes. [15] Source: Battery Council International, Chicago, Ill. [16] Special taxes on motor-vehicle users. Excludes income and property taxes on establishments engaged in the production, sale, and repairing of motor vehicles and their parts; and on truck operating companies. Source: U.S. Federal Highway Administration, *Highway Statistics,* annual, and *Estimates of State Highway-User Tax Receipts,* annual. [17] Cars, trucks, and buses. Source: 1965–1975, U.S. Bureau of Domestic Business Development, *World Motor Vehicle Production and Registration,* annual.

Source: Except as noted, Motor Vehicle Manufacturers Association of the United States, Inc., Detroit, Mich., *Motor Vehicle Facts and Figures,* annual, and *World Motor Vehicle Data,* annual.

No. 1094. Passenger Car Output and Imports: 1965 to 1977

ITEM	1965	1968	1969	1970	1971	1972	1973	1974	1975	1976	1977, prel.
Production and imports of new autos ___mil units__	9.9	10.3	10.0	8.6	10.9	11.3	12.3	9.6	9.0	10.8	12.1
Domestic output ___mil units__	9.3	8.8	8.2	6.5	8.6	8.8	9.7	7.3	6.7	8.5	9.2
Sales of imports ___mil units__	.6	1.5	1.8	2.0	2.3	2.5	2.6	2.2	2.3	2.3	2.9
Percent of total	6.0	14.4	17.6	23.7	21.0	21.8	21.4	23.4	25.6	21.5	24.0
VALUE IN CURRENT DOLLARS (bil.)											
Gross auto output	32	37	37	31	42	45	51	43	46	63	73
As percent of GNP [1]	4.6	4.2	3.3	3.1	4.0	3.9	3.9	3.0	3.0	3.7	3.9
Final sales	31	35	37	32	40	45	50	42	48	62	71
Personal consumption expenditures	25	30	31	28	35	39	43	36	41	55	64
New autos	21	25	25	22	29	32	35	28	30	39	46
Net purchases of used autos	4	5	5	6	7	7	8	9	11	16	18
Producers' durable equipment	5	6	6	5	7	8	9	8	8	9	10
New autos	7	8	9	8	10	10	12	12	13	16	19
Net purchases of used autos [2]	−2	−2	−2	−3	−3	−3	−3	−4	−5	−7	−9
Net exports	(z)	−1	−1	−1	−2	−2	−2	−3	−2	−3	−4
Exports	1	2	2	2	3	3	4	5	5	6	7
Imports	1	3	3	3	5	5	6	7	7	9	11
Govt. purchases of goods and services	(z)	(z)	1	1	1	1	1	1	1	1	1
Change in business inventories [3]	1	1	(z)	−1	2	(−z)	1	1	−1	1	1
Domestic output [4]	29	32	31	25	35	38	43	35	37	50	59
Sales of imports [5]	1	4	5	6	7	8	9	9	10	12	15
VALUE IN CONSTANT (1972) DOLLARS (billions)											
Gross auto output	37	41	40	33	42	45	51	40	40	50	56
As percent of GNP [1]	4.0	3.9	3.7	3.0	3.8	3.9	4.1	3.3	3.3	4.0	4.2
Final sales	37	39	40	34	40	45	50	39	41	49	54
Personal consumption expenditures	30	33	34	30	35	39	42	33	34	42	45
New autos	24	27	27	23	28	32	35	26	26	32	36
Net purchases of used autos	7	7	7	7	7	7	8	7	8	10	10
Producers' durable equipment	6	6	7	5	7	8	9	8	7	8	10
New autos	7	9	9	8	10	10	12	11	11	13	15
Net purchases of used autos [2]	−2	−2	−3	−3	−3	−3	−3	−3	−4	−5	−5
Net exports	(z)	−1	−1	−2	−2	−2	−2	−2	−1	−1	−1
Exports	1	2	3	2	3	3	4	4	5	5	5
Imports	1	3	4	4	5	5	6	6	5	6	7
Govt. purchases of goods and services	1	1	1	1	1	1	(z)	1	1	1	1
Change in business inventories [3]	1	1	(z)	−1	2	(−z)	1	1	−1	1	1
Domestic output [4]	32	34	33	26	35	38	43	33	32	41	46
Sales of imports [5]	1	4	6	6	7	8	9	8	9	9	12

Z Less than $500 million.   [1] For definition of gross national product (GNP), see text, p. 437.
[2] Minus sign (−) denotes greater sales than purchases of used autos.
[3] New and used autos. Minus sign (−) denotes decline in business inventories.
[4] Consists of final sales and change in business inventories of new autos produced in the United States.
[5] Consists of personal consumption expenditures, producers' durable equipment, and government purchases.
Source: U.S. Bureau of Economic Analysis, *The National Income and Product Accounts of the United States, 1929–74,* and *Survey of Current Business,* July 1976 and March 1977 and 1978.

No. 1095. Cars and Trucks in Use, by Age: 1965 to 1977

[As of July 1. Excludes vehicles for which age was not known]

AGE	NUMBER (mil.)						PERCENT					
	1965	1970	1974	1975	1976	1977	1965	1970	1974	1975	1976	1977
Total cars	68.9	80.4	92.6	95.2	97.8	99.9	100.0	100.0	100.0	100.0	100.0	100.0
Under 3 years	21.6	24.4	27.8	25.8	23.9	24.2	31.3	30.3	30.1	27.1	24.4	24.2
3–5 years	18.0	24.9	25.7	27.0	29.3	30.0	26.1	31.0	27.8	28.3	29.9	30.0
6–8 years	13.6	18.4	21.1	22.0	22.6	22.3	19.7	22.9	22.8	23.1	23.1	22.3
9–11 years	9.9	7.7	12.5	13.9	14.2	14.2	14.3	9.6	13.5	14.6	14.5	14.2
12 years and over	5.9	4.9	5.4	6.6	7.9	9.2	8.6	6.1	5.8	6.9	8.0	9.2
Total trucks	13.1	17.7	23.3	24.8	26.5	28.2	100.0	100.0	100.0	100.0	100.0	100.0
Under 3 years	3.2	4.7	7.1	6.9	6.8	7.0	24.6	26.5	30.3	27.9	25.5	24.9
3–5 years	2.5	4.3	5.2	5.8	6.8	7.7	18.9	24.1	22.5	23.3	25.8	27.4
6–8 years	2.0	3.0	4.0	4.4	4.7	4.9	14.9	16.7	17.3	17.9	17.7	17.2
9–11 years	1.8	1.9	2.8	3.2	3.4	3.5	14.1	10.5	12.2	13.0	12.9	12.4
12 years and over	3.6	3.9	4.1	4.4	4.8	5.1	27.6	22.2	17.7	17.8	18.0	18.0

Source: R. L. Polk & Co., Detroit, Mich. (Copyright; further reproduction prohibited without Polk permission.)

No. 1096. AUTOMOBILES—FACTORY-INSTALLED EQUIPMENT: 1965 TO 1977

[Refers to model-year production. For certain items, such as air conditioning, a significant number of units are installed on new vehicles after they leave the factory]

EQUIPMENT	UNITS INSTALLED (mil.)							PERCENT OF CARS PRODUCED						
	1965	1970	1973	1974	1975	1976	1977	1965	1970	1973	1974	1975	1976	1977
Transmission:														
Automatic	7.1	7.2	9.6	7.6	6.2	7.7	9.0	80.7	91.0	93.3	89.8	91.6	91.4	95.2
Manual	1.7	.7	.7	.9	.6	.7	.5	19.3	8.9	6.6	10.2	8.4	8.6	4.8
V-8 engine	6.5	6.7	8.4	5.7	4.9	5.8	7.2	73.4	84.2	81.5	67.9	71.4	68.6	76.0
6-cylinder engine	2.4	1.2	1.0	1.6	1.3	1.8	1.7	26.6	15.7	9.8	18.7	19.6	21.1	17.7
4-cylinder engine	(NA)	(NA)	.9	1.1	.6	.9	.6	(NA)	(NA)	8.6	13.3	9.0	10.3	6.3
Power brakes	2.9	4.4	7.8	5.6	5.2	6.8	8.5	32.3	56.0	75.5	66.2	75.8	80.6	90.0
Power steering	5.3	6.4	9.0	7.0	6.1	7.5	8.7	59.6	81.2	87.7	83.3	89.7	89.8	92.0
Power windows [1]	1.3	1.3	2.3	1.6	1.6	2.0	3.0	14.3	16.7	22.1	19.0	24.1	24.3	31.4
Air conditioning	2.1	4.8	7.5	5.6	4.9	6.3	7.8	23.3	60.9	73.2	67.0	73.1	75.5	81.8
Tinted glass [2]	4.6	5.5	8.1	6.3	5.5	6.8	8.2	51.7	69.5	78.6	75.0	80.6	80.9	86.9

NA Not available.   [1] Includes station wagon power rear windows.   [2] Covers windshield and other glass.

Source: Chilton Company, Radnor, Pa., *Annual Statistical Issue, Automotive Industries.* (Copyright.)

No. 1097. CARS IN OPERATION WITH EMISSION CONTROLS: 1965 TO 1977

[As of July 1. Figures show cars with emission controls whether or not the controls are in operation]

EMISSION CONTROLS	CARS (millions)								PERCENT	
	1965	1971	1972	1973	1974	1975	1976	1977	1971	1977
Total cars	68.9	83.1	86.4	89.8	92.6	95.2	97.8	99.9	100.0	100.0
Cars with one or more controls	22.9	70.3	76.9	83.0	87.6	91.2	94.5	97.2	84.6	97.3
Crankcase control [1]	22.9	35.8	32.8	29.0	24.8	21.4	17.7	13.9	43.1	13.9
Exhaust and crankcase controls [2]	–	27.7	27.2	26.4	25.5	24.6	22.9	20.5	33.3	20.5
Fuel evaporation and above controls [3]	–	6.8	16.2	18.7	18.6	18.5	17.9	17.2	8.2	17.3
Nitrogen oxide and above controls [4]	–	–	.7	9.0	18.7	22.0	21.8	21.1	–	21.4
Catalyst and above controls [5]	–	–	–	–	–	4.7	14.2	24.2	–	24.2
No emission controls	46.0	12.8	9.5	6.7	5.0	4.0	3.3	2.7	15.4	2.7

– Represents zero.

[1] Installed nationwide, starting with 1965 models, to reduce emissions of hydrocarbons.
[2] Exhaust controls introduced nationwide on 1968 models to accelerate the reduction of hydrocarbon emissions and emissions of carbon monoxide.
[3] Begun on 1971 models to eliminate losses from gasoline tanks and carburetors.
[4] Available on some 1971 and 1972 models and all 1973 and later models to lower emissions of oxides of nitrogen.
[5] Catalyst or equivalent control systems introduced on cars in 1975 to meet tougher emission levels for hydrocarbons and carbon monoxide.

Source: Motor Vehicle Manufacturers Association of the United States, Inc., Detroit, Mich., *Motor Vehicle Facts and Figures*, annual. Computed from R. L. Polk & Co. data.

No. 1098. MOTOR VEHICLE SAFETY DEFECT RECALLS, BY DOMESTIC AND FOREIGN MANUFACTURERS: 1970 TO 1977

[Covers manufacturers reporting to National Highway Traffic Safety Administration under section 151 of National Traffic and Motor Vehicle Safety Act of 1966, as amended]

MANUFACTURER	1970	1971	1972	1973	1974	1975	1976	1977
Motor vehicles:								
Total recall campaigns [1] ____number__	154	235	320	251	247	217	209	246
Domestic _____number__	100	182	277	208	208	190	169	195
Foreign _____number__	54	53	43	43	39	27	40	51
Total vehicles recalled _____1,000__	1,240	9,420	12,081	7,000	2,877	2,109	3,492	12,923
Domestic _____1,000__	738	8,790	7,813	6,667	2,345	1,829	3,019	10,693
Vehicles recalled by 4 leading auto manufacturers_____1,000__	563	8,483	7,653	6,477	2,194	1,602	2,854	10,331
Foreign _____1,000__	502	629	4,268	333	531	280	474	2,230
Motor vehicle tires:								
Recall campaigns [1] _____number__	11	16	4	20	26	22	28	35
Tires recalled _____1,000__	160	171	114	132	1,094	72	464	741

[1] A recall campaign is the notification to the Secretary of the U.S. Dept. of Transportation and to owners, purchasers, and dealers of a motor vehicle safety defect.

Source: U.S. National Highway Traffic Safety Administration, *Motor Vehicle Safety Defect Recall Campaigns*, annual.

No. 1099. Estimated Cost of Operating an Automobile: 1960 to 1976

[1976 estimates based on a 4-door sedan, operated from the Baltimore, Md. area, costing $4,900, with an assumed life-span of 10 years, 100,000 miles. Similar specifications used in 1960, 1970, and 1974]

ITEM	10-YEAR TOTAL COSTS ($1,000)				CENTS PER MILE COST, 1976 (January)					
	1960, Oct.	1970, Jan.	1974, Jan.	1976, Jan.	10-year average	1st year (14,500 miles)	3d year (11,500 miles)	5th year (9,900 miles)	7th year (9,500 miles)	10th year (5,700 miles)
Total	9.8	11.9	15.9	17.9	17.88	18.73	17.79	17.04	19.94	17.63
Costs excluding taxes	8.6	10.5	14.4	16.3	16.32	16.24	16.49	15.64	18.39	16.10
Depreciation	2.5	3.2	4.2	4.9	4.86	8.38	5.54	3.43	3.08	4.86
Repairs and maintenance [1]	1.7	1.5	2.9	3.7	3.67	1.08	3.61	4.11	7.42	.87
Replacement tires [2]	.2	.4	.4	.4	.45	.22	.21	.59	.59	.96
Accessories [3]	.1	(Z)	1	.1	.09	.06	.06	.07	.13	.15
Gasoline [4]	1.5	1.7	3.0	3.2	3.19	3.19	3.19	3.19	3.19	3.19
Oil [4]	.2	.2	.2	.2	.17	.10	.13	.19	.22	.24
Insurance [5]	1.3	1.7	1.6	1.7	1.68	1.48	1.74	1.84	1.47	2.46
Garaging, parking, etc. [6]	1.1	1.8	2.0	2.2	2.21	1.73	2.01	2.22	2.29	3.37
Taxes and fees [7]	1.2	1.4	1.5	1.6	1.56	2.49	1.30	1.40	1.55	1.53

Z Less than $50.   [1] For 1976, includes lubrications, repacking wheel bearings, flushing cooling system, aiming headlamps; replacement of minor parts such as spark plugs, fan belts, radiator hoses, distributor cap, fuel filter, and pollution control filters; minor repairs such as brake jobs, water pump, carburetor overhaul, and universal joints; and major repairs such as a complete "valve job."   [2] For 1976, covers 3 new regular tires and 4 new snow tires during life of car.   [3] For 1976, includes a set of vinyl floor mats, seat covers, and a pair of extra wheels.
[4] For 1976, gasoline use set at 15.0 miles per gallon; associated oil use at 1 gallon oil to 167 gallons gas.   [5] For 1976, includes $50,000 combined public liability ($15,000/$30,000 bodily injury, and $5,000 property damage), $2,500 personal injury protection, uninsured motorist coverage, and full comprehensive coverage for the 10-year period; $100 deductible collision insurance was assumed for the first 5 years.   [6] For 1976, includes monthly charges of $12 for garage rental or cost of owner's garaging facility, parking fee average of $70 per year, and toll average of $6.88 per year.   [7] For 1976, includes Federal excise taxes on tires of 10 cents per lb., lubricating oil of 6 cents per gallon, and gasoline of 4 cents per gallon; plus the Maryland tax on gasoline of 9 cents per gallon, titling tax of 4 percent of retail price, and registration fee of $20.00 for 3,700 lb. or less shipping weight, or $30.00 for vehicles over 3,700 lb. State sales tax of 4 percent included on certain items.

No. 1100. 10-Year Cost of Operating an Automobile, by Size of Car: 1976

[For basis of estimates for components of cost, see footnotes, table 1099. Estimates based on vehicle operated in Baltimore, Md. area with an assumed life-span of 10 years, 100,000 miles]

ITEM	Total [1]	Costs excl. taxes	Depreciation	Repairs	Tires	Gasoline	Insurance	Parking, etc.	Taxes and fees
Total costs:									
Standard [2]____$1,000__	17.9	16.3	4.9	3.7	.4	3.2	1.7	2.2	1.6
Compact [3]____$1,000__	14.6	13.4	3.8	3.0	.4	2.3	1.6	2.1	1.1
Subcompact [4]__$1,000__	12.6	11.7	3.2	2.7	.4	1.7	1.5	2.1	.9
Cents per mile cost:									
Standard [2]	17.88	16.32	4.86	3.67	.45	3.19	1.68	2.21	1.56
Compact [3]	14.56	13.42	3.83	2.96	.39	2.28	1.59	2.11	1.14
Subcompact [4]	12.64	11.71	3.19	2.66	.35	1.65	1.51	2.11	.93

[1] Includes accessories and oil.   [2] Fully equipped 4-door sedan, price $4,900.   [3] 2-door sedan, price $3,900.   [4] 2-door sedan, price $3,200.

No. 1101. Domestic Motor Fuel Consumption, by Use: 1950 to 1976

[Prior to 1960, excludes Alaska and Hawaii. Comprises all fuels (gas, diesel, or other fuels used for propulsion of vehicles) under State motor fuels laws. Excludes Federal purchases for military use. Minus sign (−) denotes decrease. See also Historical Statistics, Colonial Times to 1970, series Q 156–162]

ITEM	1950	1955	1960	1965	1970	1972	1973	1974	1975	1976
Total consumption____bil. gal__	35.6	47.6	57.9	71.1	92.3	105.1	110.5	106.3	109.0	115.7
Avg. annual change__percent__	[1] 13.3	6.0	4.0	4.2	5.4	6.7	5.2	−3.8	2.5	6.2
Passenger vehicles____bil. gal__	25.0	34.3	42.0	51.2	66.7	74.3	78.9	75.1	77.4	79.7
Cars [2]_____bil. gal__	24.3	33.5	41.2	50.3	65.8	73.5	78.0	74.2	76.5	78.7
Buses (incl. school)__bil. gal__	.7	.8	.8	.9	.9	.9	.8	.9	.9	1.0
Trucks [3]_____bil. gal__	10.6	13.3	15.8	19.9	25.6	30.7	31.6	31.2	31.6	36.0
Average gallons per vehicle	728	759	777	775	830	859	851	788	790	800
Cars [2]	603	644	661	656	722	730	736	676	685	680
Buses (incl. school)	3,752	3,021	3,040	2,844	2,491	2,165	1,991	1,919	1,937	2,015
Trucks [3]	1,257	1,278	1,330	1,347	1,365	1,446	1,361	1,268	1,227	1,299
Average mileage per gallon	12.87	12.67	12.42	12.49	12.14	12.07	11.85	12.09	12.20	12.18
Cars [2]	14.95	14.53	14.28	14.15	13.58	13.67	13.29	13.65	13.74	13.93
Buses (incl. school)	5.57	5.85	5.26	5.35	5.34	5.80	5.86	5.90	5.75	5.98
Trucks [3]	8.57	8.37	7.96	8.60	8.39	8.59	8.45	8.57	8.68	8.53

[1] Change from 1945.   [2] Includes taxicabs and motorcycles.   [3] Includes combinations.

Source of tables 1099–1101: U.S. Federal Highway Administration, Cost of Operating an Automobile, biennial, and Highway Statistics, annual.

No. 1102. GASOLINE—RETAIL PRICES, SELECTED COUNTRIES: 1973 TO 1978

[In U.S. cents per U.S. gallon. Price of gasoline includes tax. For most countries, taxes on regular gasoline are identical to those on premium. Based on exchange rates in effect on March 1, 1978. Minus sign (−) denotes decrease]

ITEM	1973, Oct.	1974, June	1975, June	1976, June	1977, June	1978, Feb.	Average annual per- cent change, 1973-1978
United States: Regular	40	55	57	59	63	[1] 62	10.6
Tax	12	12	12	12	12	[1] 12	−
Premium	44	59	61	64	69	[1] 68	10.6
Belgium: Regular	131	169	169	178	188	186	8.4
Tax	97	121	103	104	116	118	4.6
Premium	138	176	175	184	194	189	7.5
France: Regular	100	129	135	146	175	179	14.4
Tax	68	72	77	80	106	110	11.7
Premium	108	140	147	157	190	194	14.5
Germany, Fed. Rep. of: Regular	133	163	157	172	168	171	6.0
Tax	96	99	100	100	100	102	1.4
Premium	148	177	170	183	178	179	4.5
Italy: Regular	78	110	128	172	214	214	26.2
Tax	59	70	87	111	154	154	24.8
Premium	82	116	134	178	223	223	26.0
Japan: Regular	102	159	181	183	194	(NA)	[2] 19.2
Tax	46	55	55	55	68	(NA)	[2] 11.2
Premium	116	181	206	208	221	(NA)	[2] 19.2
Netherlands: Regular	136	167	174	182	186	182	7.0
Tax	94	114	104	107	114	112	4.1
Premium	141	172	178	188	190	186	6.6
Spain: Regular	54	82	82	99	120	145	25.6
Tax	27	27	27	27	35	35	6.2
Premium	68	99	99	122	145	188	26.5
Sweden: Regular	92	121	121	135	137	143	10.7
Tax	72	68	61	68	68	69	−1.0
Premium	95	124	124	140	142	148	10.8
United Kingdom: Regular	57	86	113	120	134	145	24.0
Tax	36	44	44	60	72	75	18.5
Premium	60	89	117	124	137	148	23.2

− Represents zero.   NA Not available.   [1] Source: U.S. Energy Information Administration, *Monthly Energy Review.*   [2] Avg. annual percent change, 1973-1977.

Source: Except as noted, U.S. Central Intelligence Agency, unpublished data.

No. 1103. FEDERAL AND STATE GASOLINE TAX—STATES: 1965 TO 1977

[Cents per gallon. In effect Dec. 31. See also *Historical Statistics, Colonial Times to 1970*, series Q 233-234]

STATE	1965	1970	1973	1974	1975	1976	1977	STATE	1965	1970	1973	1974	1975	1976	1977
Total	10.4	11.0	11.5	11.6	11.7	11.7	11.8	Miss	7	8	9	9	9	9	9
Federal	4.0	4.0	4.0	4.0	4.0	4.0	4.0	Mo	5	5	7	7	7	7	7
State avg.[1]	6.4	7.0	7.5	7.6	7.7	7.7	7.8	Mont	6	7	7	7	7.8	7.8	8
								Nebr.[4]	7.5	8.5	8.5	8.5	8.5	8.5	9.5
Ala	7	7	7	7	7	7	7	Nev	6	6	6	6	6	6	6
Alaska	8	8	8	8	8	8	8	N.H	7	7	9	9	9	9	10
Ariz	7	7	7	8	8	8	8	N.J	6	7	8	8	8	8	8
Ark	7.5	7.5	8.5	8.5	8.5	8.5	8.5								
Calif	7	7	7	7	7	7	7	N. Mex	6	7	7	7	7	7	7
Colo	7	7	7	7	7	7	7	N.Y	6	7	8	8	8	8	8
Conn	6	8	10	10	10	11	11	N.C	7	9	9	9	9	9	9
Del	7	7	9	9	9	9	11	N. Dak	6	7	7	7	7	7	8
D.C	6	7	8	8	10	10	10	Ohio	7	7	7	7	7	7	7
Fla	7	7	8	8	8	8	8	Okla	6.5	6.5	6.5	6.5	6.5	6.5	6.5
Ga	6.5	6.5	7.5	7.5	7.5	7.5	7.5	Oreg	6	7	7	7	7	7	7
Hawaii	[2]5	[2]5	5	5	8.5	8.5	8.5	Pa	7	8	8	9	9	9	9
Idaho	6	7	8.5	8.5	8.5	9.5	9.5	R.I	7	8	8	8	10	10	10
Ill	5	7.5	7.5	7.5	7.5	7.5	7.5	S.C	7	7	8	8	8	8	9
Ind	6	8	8	8	8	8	8	S. Dak	6	7	7	7	8	8	8
Iowa	7	7	7	7	7	7	7	Tenn	7	7	7	7	7	7	7
Kans	5	7	7	7	7	8	8	Tex	5	5	5	5	5	5	5
Ky.[3]	7	7	9	9	9	9	9	Utah	6	7	7	7	7	7	7
La	7	8	8	8	8	8	8	Vt	6.5	8	9	9	9	9	9
Maine	7	8	9	9	9	9	9	Va.[3]	7	7	9	9	9	9	9
Md	7	7	9	9	9	9	9	Wash	7.5	9	9	9	9	9	11
Mass	6.5	6.5	7.5	7.5	8.5	8.5	8.5	W. Va	7	8.5	8.5	8.5	8.5	8.5	8.5
Mich	6	7	9	9	9	9	9	Wis	6	7	7	7	7	7	7
Minn	6	7	7	7	9	9	9	Wyo	5	7	7	7	7	8	8

[1] Weighted average, based on net gallons taxed.   [2] 8 cents per gallon in Hawaii County; 5 cents elsewhere.
[3] Trucks or combinations with more than 2 axles pay motor-fuel tax of 2 cents per gallon higher than that shown.
[4] Beginning 1973, gasoline containing a grain alcohol additive in place of lead is taxed at 3 cents per gallon less.

Source: U.S. Federal Highway Administration, *Highway Statistics*, annual.

No. 1104. PERCENT OF HOUSEHOLDS OWNING AUTOMOBILES, BY SELECTED CHARACTERISTICS: 1960 TO 1974

[For composition of regions, see fig. 1, inside front cover]

CHARACTERISTIC	PERCENT OF HOUSEHOLDS OWNING—								PURCHASES PER 100 HOUSE-HOLDS, 1974		Miles driven per vehicle, 1974 (1,000)
	1960		1970			1974					
	One car	2 or more cars	One car	Two cars	3 or more cars	One car	Two cars	3 or more cars	New cars	Used cars	
U.S. total	58.6	16.4	50.3	24.6	4.7	48.8	26.8	5.9	12.0	19.4	11.8
Northeast	(NA)	(NA)	47.3	21.1	4.1	44.3	24.8	5.7	12.3	16.2	12.9
North Central	(NA)	(NA)	53.7	25.7	4.4	49.5	28.4	6.5	13.0	21.3	11.2
South	(NA)	(NA)	49.6	24.6	4.1	50.1	27.0	5.5	12.0	20.3	11.7
West	(NA)	(NA)	50.3	27.8	7.0	51.4	27.0	5.7	10.3	19.1	11.6
Metropolitan	55.3	13.6	47.3	25.5	5.0	47.4	27.6	6.0	12.5	18.4	11.8
In central cities	52.5	9.7	44.3	18.3	3.4	44.9	21.9	4.5	10.2	16.5	11.9
Nonmetropolitan	61.2	18.7	56.0	22.8	4.2	55.4	23.9	4.5	11.0	21.5	11.7
Owner-occupied	61.3	21.5	50.6	30.6	6.4	48.6	33.0	8.0	14.0	18.7	11.4
Renter-occupied	54.1	8.1	49.7	13.9	1.7	49.2	15.4	1.9	8.5	20.7	13.2
Income of household:											
Under $3,000	40.3	3.9	38.0	3.8	.7	37.0	5.5	.7	2.7	9.7	9.2
$3,000–$4,999	68.4	10.7	55.9	11.8	1.5	51.9	8.0	.8	4.7	15.4	8.9
$5,000–$7,499	72.0	19.7	64.3	19.5	2.6	60.4	13.6	2.0	6.3	20.1	10.9
$7,500–$9,999	63.7	31.4	56.9	29.9	4.8	61.9	20.9	2.2	9.2	22.0	12.4
$10,000–$14,999	52.7	42.7	47.5	40.2	8.2	54.9	32.4	4.4	12.5	23.2	11.5
$15,000 and over	35.4	58.8	33.1	50.4	12.7	39.3	44.1	12.9	20.9	20.4	12.6

NA Not available.

Source: U.S. Bureau of the Census, *Current Population Reports*, series P–65, No. 33, and "Selected Data from the 1973 and 1974 Surveys of Purchases and Ownership."

No. 1105. RECREATIONAL VEHICLES—SHIPMENTS, BY TYPE: 1961 TO 1977

TYPE	1961	1965	1970	1971	1972	1973	1974	1975	1976	1977
Total _____ 1,000	62.6	192.8	472.0	549.4	747.5	752.5	529.2	552.0	[1] 656.3	[1] 625.6
Pickup covers ___ 1,000	(NA)	(NA)	91.7	98.4	164.6	223.7	233.4	212.5	215.2	211.7
Travel trailers ___ 1,000	28.8	76.6	138.0	190.8	250.8	212.3	126.3	150.6	189.7	167.9
Motor homes ____ 1,000	(NA)	4.7	30.3	57.2	116.8	129.0	68.9	96.6	[1] 156.1	[1] 160.2
Camping trailers _ 1,000	18.0	67.2	116.1	95.8	110.2	97.7	55.2	48.1	53.3	53.9
Truck campers ___ 1,000	15.8	44.3	95.9	107.2	105.1	89.8	45.4	44.3	42.0	31.9

NA Not available. [1] Excludes vans with minimum life support systems (100,000 in 1976 and 120,000 in 1977).

Source: Motor Vehicle Manufacturers Association of the United States, Inc., Detroit, Mich., *Motor Vehicle Facts and Figures*, annual. Data from Recreation Vehicle Industry Association.

No. 1106. TRUCKS AND TRUCK MILES, BY CHARACTERISTICS: 1972

CHARACTERISTIC	TRUCKS		TRUCK-MILES		CHARACTERISTIC	TRUCKS		TRUCK-MILES	
	Total (1,000)	Excl. pick-ups, panels (1,000)	Total (bil.)	Excl. pick-ups, panels (bil.)		Total (1,000)	Excl. pick-ups, panels (1,000)	Total (bil.)	Excl. pick-ups, panels (bil.)
Total trucks	19,745	5,283	244.5	88.8	Year model:				
Light	14,598	1,084	154.5	10.2	1–2 years old	2,915	634	54.8	19.4
Medium	2,822	1,940	29.3	18.8	3–4 years old	3,722	866	62.9	24.0
Heavy	2,328	2,260	60.8	59.8	Over 4 years old	13,110	3,784	126.9	45.5
Major use:					Body type:				
Agriculture	4,258	1,433	37.1	10.2	Pickup, panel, etc.[1]	14,464	(X)	155.7	(X)
Forestry, lumbering	187	121	3.4	2.3	Platform, cattlerack	2,460	2,460	27.6	27.6
Construction	1,693	739	23.2	9.6	Van	1,134	1,134	35.1	35.1
Manufacturing	443	260	10.1	7.4	Utility truck	370	370	4.1	4.1
Wholesale, retail trade	1,875	928	32.0	18.6	Dump truck	468	468	6.5	6.5
For hire	770	678	29.6	28.3	Tank truck	316	316	8.0	8.0
Personal transportation	8,122	191	79.5	1.4	All other	536	536	7.5	7.5
Utilities and services	1,995	708	23.8	7.5	Range of operation:				
All other (incl. mining)	404	227	5.8	3.6	Local operation	16,057	4,037	163.2	40.1
					Other operation	3,690	1,247	81.3	48.7

X Not applicable. [1] Includes multistop.

Source: U.S. Bureau of the Census, *U.S. Census of Transportation: 1972*, vol. II.

No. 1107. Means of Transportation to Work, by Residence: 1975

[In thousands of workers 14 years old and over. Excludes workers living in group quarters. SMSA's refer to 243 standard metropolitan statistical areas as designated in 1970 census publications; for definitions, see text, Appendix II]

MEANS OF TRANSPORTATION	Total workers	INSIDE SMSA'S						OUTSIDE SMSA'S		
		Total	Inside central cities	Outside central cities				Total	Urban	Rural
				Total	Urban	Rural				
Total	80,125	55,418	22,760	32,658	24,840	7,818		24,707	9,648	15,059
Drive alone	52,294	36,378	13,622	22,756	17,233	5,523		15,916	6,491	9,425
Private automobile	44,830	32,522	12,414	20,109	15,591	4,518		12,308	5,453	6,855
Percent of total	56.0	58.7	54.5	61.6	62.8	57.8		49.8	56.5	45.5
Truck	7,464	3,856	1,208	2,647	1,642	1,005		3,608	1,038	2,570
Carpool	15,575	10,120	3,935	6,185	4,567	1,617		5,455	1,954	3,501
Private automobile	13,828	9,322	3,694	5,628	4,235	1,393		4,506	1,726	2,780
Truck	1,747	798	242	556	332	225		949	228	721
Public transportation	4,825	4,625	3,188	1,437	1,358	78		201	125	75
Bus or streetcar	3,100	2,953	2,028	924	874	50		147	85	62
Subway or elevated train	1,179	1,177	1,037	141	135	6		2	-	2
Railroad	405	395	52	343	320	22		11	6	5
Taxicab	141	100	72	29	29	-		41	34	6
Other means	1,067	734	289	446	352	95		332	170	162
Walked only	3,778	2,482	1,356	1,125	924	201		1,296	673	623
Worked at home	2,585	1,079	370	709	406	304		1,506	235	1,272

- Represents zero or rounds to zero.

Source: U.S. Bureau of the Census, unpublished data.

No. 1108. Places of Work and Residence, and Public Transportation Use, for Selected Cities: 1970

[Covers cities with 250,000 or more workers, 16 years old and over, working in them. Percent using public transportation refers to workers 14 years old and over]

CITY	WORKERS LIVING IN CITY				WORKERS WORKING IN CITY		PERCENT COMMUTING		Net worker movement (1,000)	Worker/ resident ratio [3]
	Total (1,000)	Place of work reported			Total (1,000)	Living outside city (1,000)	Out of city [1]	Into city [2]		
		Inside city (1,000)	Outside city (1,000)	Percent using public transp.						
New York, N.Y	3,094	2,524	153	61.8	3,100	576	5.7	18.6	423	1.16
Chicago, Ill	1,336	962	195	36.2	1,337	375	16.8	28.1	180	1.16
Los Angeles, Calif	1,113	699	292	9.3	1,127	429	29.5	38.0	137	1.14
Philadelphia, Pa	737	540	78	37.1	761	221	12.7	29.1	143	1.23
Detroit, Mich	533	311	153	18.4	535	223	32.9	41.8	70	1.15
Houston, Tex	504	395	43	7.8	520	125	9.8	24.1	82	1.19
Washington, D.C	334	215	51	37.8	505	290	19.1	57.5	240	1.90
Dallas, Tex	362	287	44	10.6	437	150	13.4	34.3	106	1.32
San Francisco, Calif	317	253	29	35.7	420	167	10.3	39.8	138	1.49
Boston, Mass	258	174	52	39.3	402	228	23.1	56.7	176	1.78
Cleveland, Ohio	277	180	61	22.1	398	218	25.2	54.7	157	1.65
Baltimore, Md	343	230	78	27.0	371	141	25.4	38.1	63	1.21
St. Louis, Mo	223	157	43	21.3	348	191	21.7	54.8	147	1.73
Atlanta, Ga	204	141	40	21.3	314	173	22.3	55.2	133	1.74
San Diego, Calif	283	221	44	5.5	305	84	16.6	27.5	40	1.15
Milwaukee, Wis	291	203	67	19.2	299	96	24.8	32.3	30	1.11
Indianapolis, Ind	293	220	55	7.9	289	69	20.1	23.9	14	1.05
Seattle, Wash	220	174	34	14.9	288	114	16.2	39.7	81	1.39
Pittsburgh, Pa	187	134	34	29.5	280	147	20.0	52.3	113	1.68
Denver, Colo	210	164	33	8.2	279	115	16.8	41.3	82	1.42
Kansas City, Mo	209	144	40	10.5	266	122	21.9	45.9	82	1.44
Minneapolis, Minn	188	127	48	19.0	260	132	27.5	51.0	84	1.48

[1] Percent of workers living in the city with place of work reported who commute to a place of work outside the city.
[2] Percent of workers working in the city who commute in from a residence outside the city.
[3] Number of persons reported as working in the city divided by the number of residents of the city whose place of work was reported.

Source: U.S. Bureau of the Census, *Census of Population: 1970*, vol. I, Part C, and Final Report, PC (2)-6D, *Journey to Work*.

No. 1109. Passenger Transit Industry—Summary: 1960 to 1977

[Beginning 1970, includes Puerto Rico. Comprises all privately and publicly owned organized local passenger transportation agencies except taxicabs, suburban railroads, and sightseeing and school buses. Covers (a) local motorbus lines, (b) light rail lines, (c) heavy rail lines, and (d) trolley coach lines. Based on financial and statistical reports received by American Public Transit Association from transit systems representing more than 85 percent of the industry. See also Historical Statistics, Colonial Times to 1970, series Q 238-250]

ITEM	1960	1965	1970	1972	1973	1974	1975	1976	1977, prel.
Operating systems	1,251	1,148	1,079	1,045	1,023	946	947	955	1,009
Motorbus systems [1]	1,236	1,145	1,075	1,042	1,020	941	941	950	1,004
Publicly owned systems [1]	54	78	144	160	185	308	333	375	455
Passenger vehicles owned	65,292	61,717	61.350	60.704	59,590	59,889	62,226	63,787	63,287
Motorbuses	49,600	49,600	49,700	49,075	48,286	48,700	50,811	52,382	51,968
Electric railway cars [2]	11,866	10,664	10,600	10,599	10,510	10,471	[3]10,712	[3]10,720	[3]10,674
Heavy rail	9,010	9,115	9,338	9,423	9,387	9,403	9,608	9,714	9,639
Trolley coaches	3,826	1,453	1,050	1,030	794	718	703	685	645
Operating revenue [4]____mil. dol	1,407	1,444	1,707	1,729	1,798	1,940	2,002	2,161	2,280
Motorbus____mil. dol	956	1,036	1,236	1,230	1,263	1,377	1,438	1,486	1,584
Electric railway [2]____mil. dol	369	366	440	466	510	542	[3]549	[3]660	[3]681
Heavy rail____mil. dol	282	310	384	417	461	506	517	631	653
Operating expenses____mil. dol	1,290	1,374	1,892	2,128	2,419	3,102	3,535	3,839	4,116
Net revenue____mil. dol	117	70	[5]184	[5]400	[5]622	[5]1,162	[5]1,533	[5]1,678	[5]1,836
Taxes (all)____mil. dol	87	81	104	113	116	137	171	182	189
Operating income____mil. dol	31	[5]11	[5]288	[5]513	[5]738	[5]1,300	[5]1,704	[5]1,860	[5]2,025
Operating assistance____mil. dol	(NA)	(NA)	(NA)	(NA)	(NA)	(NA)	1,408	1,647	1,904
Federal____mil. dol	(NA)	(NA)	(NA)	(NA)	(NA)	(NA)	302	423	585
State____mil. dol	(NA)	(NA)	(NA)	(NA)	(NA)	(NA)	407	367	478
Local____mil. dol	(NA)	(NA)	(NA)	(NA)	(NA)	(NA)	699	857	841
Revenue veh.-mi. operated [4] mil	2,143	2,008	1,883	1,756	1,835	1,907	1,990	2,026	2,021
Motorbus____mil	1,576	1,528	1,409	1,308	1,370	1,431	1,526	1,581	1,623
Electric railway [2]____mil	466	437	441	418	439	459	[3]448	[3]430	[3]383
Heavy rail____mil	391	395	407	386	407	432	423	407	361
Passengers carried [4]____mil	9,395	8,253	7,332	6,567	6,660	6,935	6,972	7,081	[6]7,616
Motorbus____mil	6,425	5,814	5,034	4,495	4,642	4,976	5,084	5,247	5,295
Electric railway [2]____mil	2,313	2,134	2,116	1,942	1,921	1,876	[3]1,810	[3]1,759	[3][6]2,251
Revenue passengers carried_mil	7,521	6,798	5,932	5,253	5,294	5,606	5,643	5,673	5,723
Motorbus____mil	5,069	4,730	4,058	3,561	3,653	3,998	4,095	4,168	4,246
Electric railway [2]____mil	2,005	1,882	1,746	1,593	1,567	1,549	[3]1,493	[3]1,450	[3]1,425
Heavy rail____mil	1,670	1,678	1,574	1,446	1,424	1,435	1,388	1,353	1,335
Trolley coach____mil	447	186	128	100	74	60	56	54	51
Average fares (in cents):									
Motorbus	17.96	20.55	29.41	33.07	32.40	31.76	31.99	32.77	34.90
Light rail	22.09	23.82	27.03	26.88	26.96	27.88	29.89	29.88	30.24
Heavy rail	16.14	16.63	23.42	27.80	30.74	33.91	36.34	45.56	47.51
Trolley coach	18.12	21.83	23.84	31.55	32.06	28.91	27.50	27.83	28.16
Employees, number (avg.)_1,000	156	145	138	138	138	141	153	160	163
Payroll, employee____mil. dol	857	964	1,274	1,455	1,624	1,967	2,236	2,404	2,419
Avg. earnings per employee_dol	5,481	6,645	9,230	10,515	11,544	12,849	13,993	14,751	14,885

NA Not available. [1] Comprises systems operating motorbuses exclusively and systems with combined services including motorbuses, heavy rail cars, light rail cars, trolley coaches, cable cars, and inclined plane cars. [2] Includes light rail. [3] Includes cable car and inclined plane. [4] Includes trolley coach, not shown separately. [5] Deficit. [6] Includes heavy rail transfer passengers.

Source: American Public Transit Association, Washington, D.C., Transit Fact Book, annual.

No. 1110. Bus and Truck Carriers, by Kind of Business: 1972

[Includes only establishments with payroll and not subject to regulation by the Interstate Commerce Commission; excludes bus carriers operated by municipalities or other governmental bodies]

CARRIERS BY KIND OF BUSINESS	Establishments	Operating revenue (mil. dol.)	Payroll (mil. dol.)	Paid employees [1] (1,000)	TYPE OF TRUCK CARRIER	Establishments [4]	OPERATING REVENUE [5] (mil. dol.)	
							Total [6]	Motor carrier [7]
Passenger transport. [2]	1,345	409	224.2	29.8	Total truck carriers	62,924	7,793	7,321
Local sched. carriers	693	293	174.5	21.7	General freight	10,947	1,692	1,637
Airport bus or limo	70	18	9.2	1.4	Household goods	7,891	987	707
Sightseeing bus	246	35	12.0	2.1	Sand and gravel	10,661	1,269	1,214
Intercity scheduled bus	130	26	14.0	2.0	Trash or garbage	8,292	945	939
Charter or special bus	206	37	14.5	2.7	Package delivery	1,410	155	153
Motor freight transport	62,924	7,793	2,686.0	327.8	Agricultural products	10,812	1,182	1,156
Local truck or draying	51,366	5,793	2,002.0	240.7	Mail, contract	2,685	200	198
Trucking, except local	6,871	1,177	345.3	41.7	Timber	1,878	192	189
Local trucking, storage [3]	4,687	824	338.7	45.4	Other commodities	8,348	1,171	1,126

[1] For week including March 12. [2] Excludes taxicabs, ambulance services, other nonscheduled carriers, school buses, and terminal and service facilities. [3] Includes household goods. [4] Establishments reporting represent between 50 and 59 percent of all establishments. [5] Revenue of establishments reporting its source represents 60–69 percent of total operating revenue of all establishments. Revenue of establishments reporting its source and type of carrier represents 50–59 percent of total operating revenue of all establishments. [6] Includes revenue from warehousing and storage and other sources. [7] Includes local trucking, moving, and storage.

Source: U.S. Bureau of the Census, Census of Selected Service Industries, 1972, subject report, SC 72-S-7.

No. 1111. INTERCITY BUS LINES—SUMMARY OF OPERATIONS: 1960 TO 1977

ITEM	1960	1965	1970	1972	1973	1974	1975	1976	1977, est.
Operating companies	1,150	1,100	1,000	1,000	1,000	950	950	1,000	1,050
Buses 1,000	21.0	19.8	22.0	21.4	20.8	21.0	20.5	20.1	20.1
Miles of highway served (Dec. 31) [1] 1,000	265	263	267	270	270	271	274	276	277
Employees (Dec. 31) [2] 1,000	45	45	50	49	48	49	47	46	44
Total bus miles billions	1.1	1.2	1.2	1.2	1.2	1.2	1.1	1.1	1.1
Revenue passengers millions	366	378	401	393	381	386	351	340	332
Revenue passenger-miles billions	19.3	23.8	25.3	25.6	26.4	27.7	25.4	25.1	25.7
Operating revenue, all services mil. dol	556	701	901	974	1,023	1,152	1,172	1,232	1,303
Operating expenses mil. dol	495	600	812	882	938	1,070	1,103	1,180	1,247
Net operating revenue [3] mil. dol	61	101	89	92	85	82	68	52	56

[1] Includes duplication between carriers. [2] Operating companies only. [3] Before income taxes.
Source: American Bus Association, Washington, D.C., Bus Facts, annual.

No. 1112. CLASS I INTERCITY MOTOR CARRIERS OF PASSENGERS: 1960 TO 1976
[Carriers subject to ICC regulations. See text, p. 638, for class limits. See also Historical Statistics, Colonial Times to 1970, series Q 69–75]

ITEM	1960	1965	1970	1972	1973	1974	1975	1976
Carriers reporting [1] number	143	156	71	74	75	81	77	78
Number of employees, average 1,000	35	35	34	34	34	36	34	32
Compensation of employees mil. dol	196	250	317	343	364	415	426	446
Operating revenue mil. dol	463	607	722	775	815	933	941	975
Passenger revenue [2] mil. dol	382	467	524	552	576	662	(NA)	(NA)
Special bus revenue and other mil. dol	81	141	198	223	239	271	(NA)	(NA)
Expenses mil. dol	405	514	639	690	738	859	880	937
Net operating revenue mil. dol	58	90	83	86	77	74	61	37
Ordinary income before income taxes mil. dol	55	90	88	93	87	93	(NA)	(NA)
Ordinary income after income taxes mil. dol	28	52	52	59	58	56	(NA)	(NA)
Passenger vehicles in service [2] 1,000	12.7	13.3	13.3	12.1	12.8	13.8	(NA)	(NA)
Owned end of year [2] 1,000	10.9	11.3	10.2	9.7	9.3	9.9	(NA)	(NA)
Intercity 1,000	11.1	10.1	9.2	8.9	8.8	8.6	(NA)	(NA)
Vehicle-miles, passenger mil	843	947	871	845	850	886	(NA)	(NA)
Number of revenue passengers carried 1,000	268	219	174	164	155	169	(NA)	(NA)
Miles per vehicle, average 1,000	65.6	67.7	60.4	58.6	55.1	52.6	(NA)	(NA)
Average fare per passenger, per carrier dol	2.12	2.73	3.81	4.24	4.73	5.13	(NA)	(NA)
Passenger revenue per vehicle-mile [3] dol	.49	.56	.69	.76	.80	.89	(NA)	(NA)
Expense per vehicle-mile dol	.48	.54	.73	.82	.87	.97	(NA)	(NA)

NA Not available. [1] Excludes carriers preponderantly in local or suburban service and carriers engaged in transportation of both property and passengers. [2] Regular route, intercity and local. [3] Regular route.
Source: U.S. Interstate Commerce Commission, Transport Statistics in the United States, 1960–1973, Part 7, and 1974, Part 2, annual; and, 1975 and 1976, Financial and Operating Statistics, Class I Motor Carriers of Passengers, statement No. 750, semiannual.

No. 1113. CLASS I INTERCITY MOTOR CARRIERS OF PROPERTY: 1960 TO 1976
[Carriers subject to ICC regulations. See text, p. 638, for class limits. See also Historical Statistics, Colonial Times to 1970, series Q 76–81]

ITEM	1960	1965	1970	1972	1973	1974	1975	1976 [1]
Carriers reporting number	935	1,114	1,376	1,525	1,442	757	770	852
Number of employees, average 1,000	327	375	500	542	580	500	409	445
Compensation of employees mil. dol	2,103	2,948	4,914	6,666	7,411	6,633	6,991	7,564
Operating revenue mil. dol	4,763	7,131	11,137	14,994	16,600	16,751	16,164	18,360
Expenses mil. dol	4,645	6,760	10,763	14,156	15,787	15,953	15,451	17,236
Net operating revenue mil. dol	119	371	375	838	813	797	713	1,124
Ordinary income, before taxes [2] mil. dol	81	329	275	763	691	744	(NA)	(NA)
Ordinary income, after taxes [2] mil. dol	37	209	150	460	427	438	264	332
Owned revenue vehicles 1,000	279	355	483	530	555	533	(NA)	(NA)
Trucks 1,000	31	36	54	56	58	53	(NA)	(NA)
Truck tractors 1,000	88	105	135	148	154	146	(NA)	(NA)
Trailers (semi and full) 1,000	161	214	294	327	343	334	(NA)	(NA)
Intercity vehicle-miles mil	7,203	9,154	11,498	14,177	14,900	13,160	(NA)	(NA)
Intercity revenue freight carried mil. ton	276	419	552	652	698	539	(NA)	(NA)
Intercity revenue per intercity vehicle-mile	$.64	$.74	$.91	$.99	$1.05	$1.14	(NA)	(NA)
Total expense per intercity vehicle-mile	$.65	$.72	$.94	$1.00	$1.06	$1.21	(NA)	(NA)

NA Not available. [1] Preliminary. [2] Income taxes.
Source: U.S. Interstate Commerce Commission, Transport Statistics in the United States, 1960–1973, Part 7, and 1974, Part 2, annual; 1975 and 1976, Financial and Operating Statistics, Class I Motor Carriers of Property, statement No. 800, semiannual.

No. 1114. RAILROADS—SUMMARY STATISTICS: 1950 TO 1975

[As of Dec. 31, or calendar year data, except as noted. Prior to 1960, excludes Alaska and Hawaii. Covers class I and II railroads, excluding switching and terminal companies, except as noted. Includes intercorporate duplications. See also *Historical Statistics, Colonial Times to 1970*, series Q 284–312, Q 330, Q 356–363, and Q 367–377]

ITEM	1950	1955	1960	1965	1970	1972	1973	1974	1975
Operating companies [1]___number__	471	441	407	372	351	332	331	341	340
Employees [2]_____1,000__	1,237	1,071	793	655	577	537	533	541	502
Compensation_____mil. dol__	4,645	5,045	4,957	4,887	5,646	6,531	7,294	7,671	7,674
Mileage:									
Road owned, first track [3]_1,000__	224	221	218	211	206	203	201	200	199
Track operated:									
Reporting railroads [4]____1,000__	396	391	382	371	360	356	354	354	348
First track [4]_____1,000__	237	234	230	226	220	218	216	217	215
Other main tracks____1,000__	40	39	35	31	29	28	28	28	28
Yardtrack and sidings_____1,000__	119	118	117	113	112	110	109	109	105
Operated by receivers [5]_1,000__	12	12	1	2	23	27	27	27	27
Equipment: [6]									
Locomotives in service____1,000__	43.0	33.5	31.2	30.1	29.1	29.3	29.9	30.2	30.2
Average tractive effort [7]_____1,000 lb__	57.1	65.0	61.3	63.1	[8] 1.9	[8] 2.0	[8] 2.1	[8] 2.1	[8] 2.1
Cars in service:									
Passenger-train_____1,000__	37.4	32.1	25.7	20.0	11.4	7.8	7.4	7.1	6.7
Freight train [9]_____1,000__	1,746	1,724	1,690	1,515	1,454	1,411	1,387	1,369	1,345
Average capacity [10]____tons__	52.6	53.7	55.4	59.8	67.1	69.6	70.5	71.4	73.0
Capital and property investment: [11]									
Road and equipment, book value [12]_____mil. dol__	30,174	33,035	35,513	35,489	37,918	37,359	37,897	38,937	40,196
Depreciation reserve [13]_mil. dol__	6,629	7,314	8,532	9,342	9,930	9,660	9,868	10,185	10,650
Capitalization outstanding [14]_____mil. dol__	18,274	(NA)	16,134	14,857	14,339	12,968	13,092	12,958	13,473
Capital surplus and retained income_____mil. dol__	7,037	(NA)	11,356	12,945	13,002	12,404	12,685	11,185	11,297
Stock paying dividends_____mil. dol__	6,769	7,300	5,617	4,845	3,595	3,472	3,359	3,297	3,402
Dividends declared_____mil. dol__	349	476	412	533	486	532	482	644	458
Interest accrued on funded debt_____mil. dol__	367	374	387	403	554	578	605	680	732
Income and expenses:									
Operating revenues____mil. dol__	9,587	10,230	9,642	10,425	12,209	13,822	15,244	17,458	16,929
Operating expenses____mil. dol__	7,135	7,724	7,657	8,003	9,806	11,016	12,068	13,758	13,967
Tax accruals_____mil. dol__	1,212	1,101	1,020	949	1,104	1,198	1,416	1,872	1,768
Net railway operating income_____mil. dol__	1,055	(NA)	595	980	506	705	725	539	36
Net income [11]_____mil. dol__	855	959	473	866	[15] 126	[15] 295	[15] 526	[15] 558	[15] 12
Passenger service:									
Passengers carried_____mil__	488	433	327	306	289	262	255	275	270
Passenger-miles_____mil__	31,790	28,548	21,284	17,454	10,786	8,572	9,308	10,349	9,948
Commutation [10]_____mil__	4,990	4,776	4,197	4,128	4,592	4,229	4,245	4,533	4,513
Coach [10]_____mil__	17,443	17,314	13,422	11,069	5,414	3,812	4,470	5,186	4,750
Parlor and sleeping car [10]_mil__	9,338	6,441	3,643	2,191	765	520	583	613	502
Passenger revenue_____mil. dol__	815	744	641	556	423	409	444	540	537
Revenue per passenger-mile_____cents__	2.56	2.61	3.01	3.19	3.92	4.77	4.77	5.21	5.40
Avg. journey per passenger_____miles__	65.14	65.88	65.05	57.07	37.26	32.71	36.44	37.68	36.88
Freight service:									
Freight revenue_____mil. dol__	7,934	8,665	8,152	9,037	11,124	12,790	14,003	15,993	15,623
Revenue-tons originated____mil__	1,421	1,459	1,301	1,479	1,572	1,531	1,616	1,619	1,470
Tons carried one mile_____bil__	592	627	575	706	771	783	858	852	759
Revenue ton-miles per mile of road_____1,000__	2,497	2,679	2,497	3,121	3,468	3,068	3,564	3,545	3,161
Revenue per ton-mile____cents__	1.341	1.382	1.417	1.281	1.443	1.634	1.632	1.876	2.060
Haul per ton, U.S. as a system_____miles__	416	430	442	477	490	511	531	527	516
Accidents: [16]									
Persons killed_____number__	3,398	2,667	2,248	2,399	2,225	1,945	1,916	1,908	1,560
Persons injured_____number__	33,255	27,832	19,577	25,789	21,327	17,930	18,245	20,818	54,300

NA Not available.   [1] Includes unofficial companies and, through 1960, circular companies; see text, p. 638.
[2] Average mid-month count.
[3] Includes lessors, proprietary, unofficial, and, through 1960, circular companies.
[4] Includes mileage in Canada.   [5] Includes track operated by trustees.
[6] Includes switching and terminal companies, except average tractive effort and average capacity.
[7] For 1950 and 1955, steam locomotives of class I railroads; beginning 1960, all locomotives of class I railroads.
[8] Represents horsepower. In thousands.   [9] Excludes caboose cars.   [10] Class I railroads only.   [11] Includes lessors.   [12] Increase in investment over a period of years cannot be obtained accurately by subtraction of 1 year's investment from that of another owing to reorganization, sale or abandonment, reclassification, etc. Also includes proprietary companies.   [13] Includes amortization applicable to proprietary companies.
[14] Comprises common stock, preferred stock, and funded debt unmatured.
[15] After extraordinary and prior period items.   [16] Includes highway grade crossing casualties. 1975 not comparable with previous years due to change in requirements for reporting injuries.

Source: U.S. Interstate Commerce Commission, *Transport Statistics in the United States*, Part 1, annual, and, 1950–1965, *Accident Bulletin*, annual. Beginning 1970, accident data from U.S. Federal Railroad Administration, *Accident Bulletin*, annual.

No. 1115. Railroad Companies, by Class: 1950 to 1975

[Prior to 1960, excludes Alaska and Hawaii. See text, p. 638, for explanation of class limits]

CLASS OF COMPANY	1950	1955	1960	1965	1970	1971	1972	1973	1974	1975
Total	[1] 1,038	[1] 935	[1] 842	763	708	700	683	676	677	663
Class I line-haul operating	127	126	106	76	70	70	69	70	74	74
Lessors to class I	179	155	128	116	114	112	113	111	115	107
Class II line-haul operating	171	155	304	302	273	269	262	260	258	245
Lessors to class II	6	8	8	15	14	14	14	14	9	8
Switching and terminal [2]	253	237	221	205	190	189	180	176	174	170
Proprietary [3]	100	67	53	45	39	38	38	38	38	38
Unofficial	9	6	1	4	7	8	7	7	9	21

[1] Includes class III railroads for 1950 and 1955, and circular railroads through 1960, not shown separately. [2] Includes operating, lessor, proprietary, and unofficial companies, and, through 1960, circular. [3] Excludes systems which file consolidated reports combining mileage, investment, and other items on a net system basis.

No. 1116. Railroads—Miles of Road Owned, by District: 1950 to 1975

[As of Dec. 31. Data are for actual length of line owned by line-haul companies in each State without duplication]

DISTRICT	1950	1960	1970	1971	1972	1973	1974	1975
Total	224,371	217,552	205,782	204,696	202,775	201,067	200,391	199,126
Eastern	51,350	56,295	52,266	51,533	51,247	50,695	50,412	50,073
Southern	47,009	38,581	37,441	37,547	37,430	37,354	37,259	37,045
Western	125,420	122,079	116,055	115,596	114,078	113,018	112,720	112,008
Unassigned	592	597	20		20	20	–	–

– Represents zero.

Source of tables 1115 and 1116: U.S. Interstate Commerce Commission, 1950, *Statistics of Railways in the United States*; thereafter, *Transport Statistics in the United States*, Part 1, annual.

No. 1117. Major Class I Railroads Controlled by Conglomerate Holding Companies: 1967 to 1974

ITEM	Operating revenues (mil. dol.)	Freight revenues (mil. dol.)	Ton miles (bil.)	ITEM	Operating revenues (mil. dol.)	Freight revenues (mil. dol.)	Ton miles (bil.)
1967: Class I railroads	10,366	9,130	719	1972: Class I railroads	13,586	12,572	778
Under direct conglomerate control	1,038	917	74	Under conglomerate control	7,827	7,384	461
Percent of total	10.0	10.0	10.2	Percent of total	57.6	58.7	59.2
				Directly controlled	6,825	6,407	396
				Percent of total	50.2	51.0	51.0
1970: Class I railroads	11,985	10,916	763				
Under direct conglomerate control	5,923	5,323	369	1974: Class I railroads	17,207	15,767	851
				Under conglomerate control	8,645	8,286	465
Percent of total	49.4	48.8	48.4	Percent of total	50.2	52.6	54.7

Source: 1967 to 1972, U.S. Congress, Senate Committee on Government Operations, *Disclosure of Corporate Ownership*, 1974; 1974, Interstate Commerce Commission, unpublished data.

No. 1118. Railroads—Employees, Hours, and Compensation: 1960 to 1977

[Excludes switching and terminal roads. See also *Historical Statistics, Colonial Times to 1970*, series Q 398–399]

ITEM	1960	1965	1970	1972	1973	1974	1975	1976	1977 [1]
Classes I and II line-haul railroads: [2]									
Employees, average _____1,000	793	655	577	537	533	541	502	(NA)	(NA)
Compensation of employees____mil. dol__	4,957	4,887	5,646	6,531	7,294	7,671	7,674	(NA)	(NA)
Class I line-haul railroads: [2]									
Employees, average_____1,000	780	640	566	527	524	533	494	496	501
Man-hours paid for_____mil	1,841	1,565	1,379	1,064	1,052	1,064	977	985	988
Average hours per employee	2,358	2,445	2,436	2,018	2,007	1,996	1,978	1,986	1,972
Compensation of employees:									
Total_____mil. dol	4,894	4,793	5,557	6,434	7,134	7,576	7,563	8,494	9,224
Average per hour_____dol	2.66	3.06	4.04	6.05	6.78	7.12	7.74	8.62	9.34
Average per year_____dol	6,270	7,490	9,841	12,209	13,615	14,214	15,310	17,125	18,411

NA Not available. [1] Preliminary. [2] See text, p. 638, for class limits.

Source: U.S. Interstate Commerce Commission, *Transport Statistics in the United States*, Part 1, annual, and Statement No. A-300, annual.

No. 1119. RAILROADS, CLASS I LINE-HAUL—REVENUES AND EXPENSES: 1950 TO 1976

[In millions of dollars. Minus sign (−) denotes deficit. See text, p. 638, for definition of class I. See also *Historical Statistics, Colonial Times to 1970,* series Q 364–366 and Q 378]

ITEM	1950	1955	1960	1965	1970	1972	1973	1974	1975	1976
Operating revenues	9,473	10,106	9,514	10,208	11,992	13,585	14,989	17,207	16,684	18,877
Amtrak	(X)	(X)	(X)	(X)	(X)	163	202	257	253	287
Freight	7,817	8,538	8,025	8,836	10,922	12,570	13,770	15,767	¹15,399	¹17,433
Passenger	813	743	640	553	420	406	442	538	536	592
Mail and express	455	405	431	388	183	101	91	103	(¹)	(¹)
Other	387	420	417	431	466	343	484	542	496	565
Operating expenses	7,059	7,668	7,565	7,850	9,660	10,854	11,899	13,592	13,792	15,624
Amtrak	(X)	(X)	(X)	(X)	(X)	286	327	463	531	651
Maintenance	2,995	3,175	2,952	3,011	3,778	4,386	4,640	5,278	5,429	6,130
Way and structures	1,287	1,387	1,192	1,236	1,613	1,927	2,041	2,365	2,433	2,719
Equipment	1,708	1,788	1,760	1,775	2,165	2,459	2,599	2,913	2,996	3,411
Transportation, rail line	3,491	3,770	3,833	4,020	4,873	5,341	6,061	6,979	6,987	7,621
Other	573	723	781	819	1,009	841	871	872	845	1,222
Tax accruals	1,195	1,081	999	916	1,069	1,159	1,371	1,823	1,640	1,928
Net operating income ²	1,040	1,128	584	962	486	681	698	514	21	−1
Ordinary income	(NA)	(NA)	(NA)	(NA)	227	344	401	459	−207	−196
Gross expenditures for capital improvements	1,065	908	919	1,631	1,351	1,241	1,436	1,804	1,987	2,026
Equipment	779	568	634	1,304	993	875	977	1,253	1,498	1,471
Roadway and structures	286	340	286	327	358	366	459	551	489	555

NA Not available.   X Not applicable.   ¹ Mail and express is included with freight.   ² Railway only.

No. 1120. RAILROADS, CLASS I LINE-HAUL—SELECTED PASSENGER STATISTICS: 1950 TO 1977

[See text, p. 638, for definition of class I. See also *Historical Statistics, Colonial Times to 1970,* series Q 313–315]

ITEM	1950	1955	1960	1965	1970	1972	1973	1974	1975	1976	1977
Avg miles of road operated ___1,000	146	120	94	77	50	29	28	31	32	33	32
Passenger revenue ___mil. dol	813	743	640	553	420	406	442	538	536	592	609
Revenue per passenger-mile:											
Incl. commutation passengers cents	2.56	2.60	3.01	3.18	3.90	4.76	4.76	5.22	5.50	5.59	5.91
Excl. commutation passengers cents	2.74	2.70	3.03	3.14	4.02	5.31	5.19	5.85	6.31	6.30	6.64
Revenue passengers carried ___mil	486	432	326	299	284	261	254	274	269	268	275
Amtrak ___mil	(X)	(X)	(X)	(X)	(X)	17	17	18	18	19	19
Revenue passenger-miles ___bil	31.8	28.5	21.3	17.4	10.8	8.6	9.3	10.3	9.9	10.6	10.3
Amtrak ___bil	(X)	(X)	(X)	(X)	(X)	3.0	3.8	4.3	3.9	4.3	4.2
Average distance ___miles	65.3	66.0	65.2	58.2	37.9	32.8	36.6	37.7	36.8	39.6	37.5
Revenue passenger-miles per train-mile	89	95	101	101	117	140	153	161	150	158	156
Revenue passenger-miles per car-mile	17.0	17.8	19.3	19.5	25.8	33.3	34.2	35.3	35.2	36.7	36.5
Passenger-train miles ___mil	358	299	209	172	92	61	61	64	66	67	66
Passenger-carrying car-miles ___mil	1,870	1,602	1,101	885	417	257	272	293	281	289	282
Train-miles per train-hour	37.4	39.8	40.7	41.3	40.1	38.3	37.6	38.2	39.2	32.7	33.0

X Not applicable.

No. 1121. RAILROADS, CLASS I LINE-HAUL—SELECTED FREIGHT STATISTICS: 1950 TO 1977

[Excludes switching and terminal roads. Tons of 2,000 pounds. See text, p. 638, for definition of class I. See *Historical Statistics, Colonial Times to 1970,* series Q 319, for train-miles per train-hour]

ITEM	1950	1955	1960	1965	1970	1972	1973	1974	1975	1976	1977
Avg. miles of road operated ___1,000	226	223	219	212	209	208	207	206	205	200	197
Freight revenue ___bil. dol	7.8	8.5	8.0	8.8	10.9	12.6	13.8	15.8	15.4	17.4	18.9
Per ton-mile ___cents	1.33	1.37	1.40	1.27	1.43	1.62	1.62	1.85	2.04	2.20	2.29
Per ton ___dol	3.04	3.25	3.51	3.48	4.18	4.94	5.10	5.91	6.32	7.42	8.00
Revenue freight:											
Tons originated ___mil	1,354	1,393	1,241	1,387	1,485	1,448	1,532	1,530	1,395	1,364	1,362
Tons carried ___mil	2,570	2,618	2,291	2,539	2,614	2,544	2,701	2,716	2,437	2,350	2,363
Net ton miles ___bil	589	624	572	698	765	777	852	851	755	795	826
Average distance ___miles	229	238	251	275	292	306	332	316	(NA)	(NA)	(NA)
Train miles ___mil	515	476	405	421	427	451	469	469	402	425	428
Freight car miles, loaded ¹ ___bil	19.6	20.1	17.3	17.9	17.3	17.1	18.0	17.6	15.1	15.8	16.3
Empty ___bil	10.1	11.1	10.9	11.4	12.6	13.2	13.2	13.1	12.5	12.7	12.4
Net ton-miles per train-mile ¹	1,224	1,374	1,466	1,683	1,820	1,774	1,844	1,875	1,938	2,232	2,029
Net ton-miles per loaded car-mile ¹	31.7	32.0	33.9	39.7	44.9	46.7	48.7	50.1	51.7	59.9	53.2
Train-miles per train-hour	16.8	18.6	19.5	20.1	20.1	20.0	19.8	19.9	20.0	20.1	19.8

NA Not available.   ¹ Revenue and nonrevenue freight.

Source of tables 1119–1121: U.S. Interstate Commerce Commission, *Annual Report; Transport Statistics in the United States,* Part 1, annual; related monthly and quarterly reports; *Financial and Operating Statistics, Class I Railroads,* Statement No. 100, semiannual; and unpublished data.

No. 1122. Railroads—Equipment in Service: 1950 to 1975

[Prior to 1960, excludes Alaska and Hawaii. See also *Historical Statistics, Colonial Times to 1970*, series Q 301-305]

ITEM	1950	1955	1960	1965	1970	1972	1973	1974	1975
Locomotives [1]	42,951	33,533	31,178	30,061	29,122	29,338	29,926	30,220	30,195
Steam	26,680	6,266	374	89	–	–	–	–	–
Electric	827	639	498	365	270	257	243	218	216
Diesel	15,396	26,563	30,240	29,552	28,773	28,983	29,419	29,709	29,688
New units installed [2]	3,215	1,097	389	1,387	271	962	597	649	588
Freight cars 1,000	1,746	1,724	1,690	1,515	1,454	1,411	1,387	1,369	1,345
Box 1,000	718	724	700	593	590	567	558	554	531
Gondola and hopper 1,000	875	846	831	754	724	712	697	684	685
Other 1,000	153	154	159	168	140	132	132	132	129
Aggregate capacity [2] 1,000 tons	90,465	91,229	91,948	88,323	95,556	96,079	95,644	95,666	95,886
Average capacity [2] tons	52.6	53.7	55.4	59.8	67.1	69.6	70.5	71.4	73.0
New units installed [2]	40,032	29,070	54,032	62,859	37,261	21,530	26,895	28,114	31,161
Passenger-train cars	37,359	32,118	25,746	20,022	11,378	7,763	7,363	7,080	6,658
Coaches	16,488	13,543	10,287	8,086	6,522	5,531	5,262	5,107	4,894
Average seating capacity [2]	75	75	76	76	88	94	96	96	(NA)
Nonpassenger (baggage, etc.)	13,817	13,388	10,077	8,411	3,227	1,022	899	776	597
Other	7,054	5,187	5,382	3,525	1,629	1,210	1,202	1,197	1,167
New units installed [2]	1,078	412	251	666	33	4	–	–	–

– Represents zero.   NA Not available.   [1] Includes other types not listed below.   [2] Class I railroads.

No. 1123. Railroads, Class I Line-Haul—Fuel and Power Consumed and Rails and Ties Laid: 1950 to 1975

[See text, p. 638, for definition of class I. See also *Historical Statistics, Colonial Times to 1970*, series Q 388-397]

ITEM	1950	1955	1960	1965	1970	1972	1973	1974	1975
Fuel and power consumed:									
Coal 1,000 short tons	55,452	11,427	39	4	1	1	1	1	1
Fuel oil mil. gal.	2,284	376	89	77	–	–	–	–	–
Diesel oil mil. gal.	1,827	3,393	3,472	3,742	3,808	4,074	4,223	4,199	3,806
Electricity mil. kWh	2,260	2,082	1,641	1,509	1,341	1,384	1,230	1,590	1,553
Rails and ties laid: [1]									
Rails 1,000 short tons	2,628	2,099	1,066	1,167	1,174	1,400	1,435	1,591	1,244
Crossties mil.	33.1	27.2	16.4	17.0	19.6	22.0	19.9	20.9	20.5
Switch and bridge ties mil. bd. ft.	118.1	99.9	63.4	61.7	60.0	59.9	58.1	64.5	60.1

– Represents zero.   [1] New and used rails laid for replacement, additional tracks, new lines, extensions.

Source of tables 1122 and 1123: U.S. Interstate Commerce Commission, *Transport Statistics in the United States*, Part 1, annual, and *Annual Report*.

No. 1124. Revenue Freight Originated, by Commodity Group—Class I Railroads, 1974 and 1975, and Motor Carriers of Property, 1973 and 1974

[See *Historical Statistics, Colonial Times to 1970*, series Q 332, for total carloads originated]

COMMODITY GROUP	RAILROADS						MOTOR CARRIERS					
	Carloads (1,000)		Tons (bil.)		Revenue [1] (mil. dol.)		Truckloads (1,000)		Tons (bil.)		Revenue [1] (mil. dol.)	
	1974	1975	1974	1975	1974	1975	1973	1974	1973	1974	1973	1974
Total	26,223	22,930	1,530.7	1,395.1	16,378	15,899	21,789	17,012	560.6	366.8	12,061	11,764
Coal	4,691	4,844	390.9	407.6	1,848	2,146	5	18	.3	.4	1	4
Food and kindred products	2,390	2,154	107.3	100.2	1,776	1,822	1,921	1,457	33.6	25.3	825	744
Nonmetallic minerals [2]	2,203	1,895	171.0	159.6	604	596	485	342	12.2	6.8	45	39
Farm products	2,124	1,873	142.2	134.4	1,511	1,472	395	228	8.1	4.4	131	109
Metallic ores	1,576	1,338	126.5	106.4	494	468	53	36	1.2	.7	9	9
Transportation equipment	1,263	1,135	29.8	27.3	1,271	1,283	2,229	2,018	27.2	23.9	676	696
Lumber and wood prod. [3]	1,970	1,615	105.3	88.6	1,132	1,066	356	214	7.0	4.1	88	74
Pulp, paper, allied products	1,221	1,015	48.2	40.6	1,058	977	843	638	13.1	9.9	277	251
Chemicals, allied products	1,521	1,313	101.4	91.4	1,739	1,681	2,553	2,244	46.2	40.4	820	860
Primary metal products	1,105	796	70.3	51.4	1,027	848	2,043	1,729	38.6	32.8	665	686
Basic textiles	66	57	1.3	1.1	46	42	395	277	5.4	3.7	152	130
Furniture and fixtures	231	162	2.1	1.4	131	103	62	43	.6	.4	28	24
Petroleum and coal prod.	954	787	53.0	45.8	600	573	5,607	3,965	139.5	97.0	573	465
Rubber, misc. plastics prod.	223	180	3.8	3.1	149	132	432	385	5.3	4.7	205	214
Stone, clay, and glass prod.	1,127	906	68.0	56.8	705	651	1,496	989	30.1	19.7	292	229
Fabricated metal prod. [4]	336	244	11.3	8.2	267	221	555	439	7.5	5.9	204	204
Machinery, exc. electrical	187	156	4.2	3.6	204	200	577	464	7.9	6.2	309	314
Electrical mchy., equip.	295	200	4.4	3.2	223	182	364	292	4.1	3.3	178	178
Waste and scrap materials	949	744	48.1	38.2	409	359	63	50	1.1	.9	19	19
Freight forwarder traffic	208	167	4.0	3.2	181	157	72	52	.9	.6	23	20
Other	1,583	1,344	37.5	[5] 31.8	1,001	[5] 920	1,281	1,130	170.7	75.8	6,539	[5] 6,495

[1] Gross.   [2] Except fuels.   [3] Except furniture.   [4] Except ordnance, machinery, and transport.
[5] Includes less than carload or truckload freight.

Source: U.S. Interstate Commerce Commission, *Freight Commodity Statistics—Class I Railroads in the United States*, annual; and *Class I Motor Carriers, Property Operating in Intercity Service*, annual.

No. 1125. Railroads, Class I—Cars of Revenue Freight Loaded, 1960 to 1977, and by Commodity Group: 1976 and 1977

[In thousands. Figures are 52-week totals. See text, p. 638, for definition of class I]

YEAR	CARLOADS Total	CARLOADS Piggy-back	COMMODITY GROUP	CARLOADS 1976	CARLOADS 1977	COMMODITY GROUP	CARLOADS 1976	CARLOADS 1977
1960___	30,441	554	Coal_____	4,709	4,713	Metals and products_____	972	923
1965___	29,248	1,034	Chemicals, allied products__	1,376	1,411	Nonmetallic minerals,		
1970___	27,160	1,257	Motor vehicles and equip.___	1,232	1,335	n.e.c.[1]_____	688	745
1971___	25,266	1,199	Metallic ores_____	1,513	1,312	Lumber, wood prod.,		
1972___	26,105	1,331	Grain_____	1,323	1,250	n.e.c.[1][2]_____	670	676
1973___	27,338	1,535	Primary forest products____	1,139	1,112	Waste and scrap materials__	693	673
1974___	26,184	1,512	Pulp, paper, allied prod____	1,101	1,103	Forwarder and shipper association traffic_____	417	476
1975___	23,217	1,221	Food and kindred prod.,			Petroleum products_____	370	383
1976___	23,457	1,506	n.e.c.[1]_____	1,062	1,028	Coke_____	364	348
1977___	23,298	1,689	Crushed stone, gravel, sand_	1,024	997	Farm products, exc. grain___	417	312
			Grain mill products_____	1,011	973	Less than carload_____	20	24
			Stone, clay, and glass prod__	947	947	All other carloads_____	2,409	2,556

[1] Not elsewhere classified.   [2] Except furniture.
Source: Association of American Railroads, Washington, D.C., *Cars of Revenue Freight Loaded*, annual.

No. 1126. Price Indexes for Total Railroad Freight and Selected Commodity Groups: 1970 to 1977

[1969=100. Reflects the railroads' prices for shipping a fixed set of commodities under specified and unchanging conditions]

COMMODITY	1970	1971	1972	1973	1974	1975	1976	1977
Total railroad freight_____	108.8	122.4	126.1	129.3	149.7	169.4	186.6	191.1
Farm products_____	108.3	120.8	123.4	125.2	145.3	165.0	182.7	191.3
Metallic ores_____	108.9	123.5	128.1	133.0	155.0	178.4	197.8	211.1
Coal_____	108.6	123.9	128.8	132.5	154.8	177.5	199.6	211.6
Nonmetallic minerals_____	108.0	120.7	125.6	130.0	150.5	172.4	191.7	205.5
Food products_____	108.9	122.4	126.2	128.8	148.9	168.5	185.1	195.3
Wood or lumber products_____	108.4	119.0	123.3	127.4	147.4	163.6	177.9	191.7
Pulp, paper, and allied products____	108.9	122.4	124.0	124.5	143.5	162.7	176.0	186.5
Chemical or allied products_____	108.6	121.8	124.8	127.7	147.9	168.4	183.8	197.1
Clay, concrete, glass, or stone products____	109.4	122.9	126.7	131.2	153.1	174.5	192.2	206.3
Primary metal products_____	109.5	124.3	128.4	132.1	153.3	174.8	191.6	204.7
Transportation equipment_____	109.4	123.7	127.3	131.9	153.5	173.5	190.2	204.3

Source: U.S. Bureau of Labor Statistics, *Wholesale Prices and Price Indexes*, monthly.

No. 1127. Railroad Accidents and Highway Grade Crossings—Persons Killed and Persons Injured, by Type of Accident: 1950 to 1976

[Prior to 1960, excludes Alaska and Hawaii. Covers all railroads, except as noted, and all reportable accidents, i.e., those resulting in personal casualty or in damage to railroad property exceeding amounts specified by Federal Railroad Administration. See also *Historical Statistics, Colonial Times to 1970*, series Q 385-387 and Q 400-401]

TYPE OF ACCIDENT	1950	1955	1960	1965	1970	1972	1973	1974	1975 [1]	1976 [1]
Persons killed, total_____	3,398	2,667	2,248	2,399	2,225	1,945	1,916	1,908	1,560	1,684
Train_____	336	259	156	191	210	171	149	139	82	158
Train incidents_____	2,921	2,316	2,042	2,136	1,936	1,704	1,704	1,692	1,241	1,299
Nontrain_____	141	92	50	72	79	70	63	77	237	227
Persons injured, total_____	33,255	27,832	19,577	25,789	21,327	17,930	18,245	20,818	54,300	65,387
Train_____	2,315	1,183	847	864	627	777	758	911	1,214	1,282
Train incidents_____	19,454	16,856	12,877	16,577	13,878	11,507	11,946	12,878	11,779	12,701
Nontrain_____	11,486	9,793	5,853	8,348	6,822	5,646	5,541	7,029	41,307	51,404
Highway grade crossings [2]___1,000__	227	226	225	216	211	210	208	209	(NA)	208
Specially protected [3]_____1,000__	36	39	42	44	47	48	49	49	(NA)	55
Accidents at crossings_____	4,000	3,846	3,195	3,820	3,559	3,379	3,379	3,268	[4]11,354	[4]12,114
Persons killed_____	1,576	1,446	1,364	1,534	1,440	1,260	1,185	1,220	[4]978	[4]1,160
Persons injured_____	4,368	4,014	3,424	3,801	3,336	3,285	3,283	3,249	[4]4,168	[4]4,887
Involving motor vehicles: [5]										
Persons killed_____	1,393	1,313	1,254	1,434	1,337	1,170	1,035	1,091	[4]765	[4]1,006
Persons injured_____	4,206	3,886	3,277	3,663	3,205	3,177	3,158	3,110	[4]3,568	[4]4,378

NA Not available.   [1] Not comparable with previous years due to change in requirements for reporting injuries.   [2] Class I railroads only.   [3] Includes crossings with operated gates or watchmen, or both, during at least part of day; and those with audible or visible signals, or both. Excludes those with fixed signs only.   [4] Includes nontrain accidents.   [5] Excludes motorcycles.

Source: U.S. Interstate Commerce Commission, *Accident Bulletin*, annual, and *Transport Statistics in the United States*, Part 1, annual. Beginning 1970, accident and, beginning 1973, highway grade crossings data from U.S. Federal Railroad Administration, *Accident/Incident Bulletin*, annual.

No. 1128. Petroleum Pipeline Companies—Summary: 1960 to 1976

[Refers to pipeline companies operating in interstate commerce and subject to jurisdiction of Interstate Commerce Commission. See also *Historical Statistics, Colonial Times to 1970*, series Q 251-263]

ITEM	1960	1965	1970	1972	1973	1974	1975	1976
Companies reporting_____number__	87	89	101	99	100	103	104	111
Employees, average_____1,000__	21	17	15	15	15	15	15	15
Compensation of employees_____mil. dol__	151	141	162	184	216	216	251	280
Miles of line operated_____1,000__	152	161	176	174	171	173	173	174
Gathering lines_____1,000__	49	47	47	43	42	41	43	39
Trunk lines_____1,000__	103	115	129	131	129	132	130	135
Investment in carrier property___mil. dol__	3,300	4,178	5,786	6,759	7,016	8,065	10,745	13,704
Investments and special funds___mil. dol__	114	59	250	327	331	444	328	298
Current assets_____mil. dol__	393	555	628	672	728	1,038	961	1,055
Current liabilities_____mil. dol__	187	301	480	549	691	887	1,078	1,571
Retained income_____mil. dol__	701	835	1,124	1,263	1,350	1,406	1,377	1,486
Capitalization_____mil. dol__	1,439	1,635	2,518	3,183	3,168	4,094	6,041	8,153
Capital stock_____mil. dol__	384	382	450	428	437	451	431	460
Long-term debt_____mil. dol__	1,056	1,253	2,068	2,755	2,731	3,643	5,610	7,693
Dividends declared_____mil. dol__	143	197	217	226	298	248	319	418
Operating revenues_____mil. dol__	770	904	1,188	1,338	1,446	1,587	1,874	2,137
Operating expenses [1]_____mil. dol__	418	515	672	780	844	943	1,038	1,155
Net carrier operating income____mil. dol__	(²)	389	516	558	602	644	836	982
Net income_____mil. dol__	169	218	312	332	375	352	457	599
Oil transported:								
Total received into system_____mil. bbl__	4,783	5,868	8,164	8,867	9,411	9,360	9,359	9,787
Total delivered out of system__mil. bbl__	4,783	5,864	8,147	8,889	9,415	9,333	9,341	9,757
To connecting carriers_____mil. bbl__	1,639	1,757	2,320	2,552	2,785	2,748	2,817	2,976
Crude oil_____mil. bbl__	1,400	1,361	1,767	1,914	2,054	2,055	2,126	2,256
Products_____mil. bbl__	240	396	553	638	731	692	691	720
Terminated_____mil. bbl__	3,144	4,107	5,827	6,336	6,630	6,585	6,523	6,781
Crude oil_____mil. bbl__	2,253	2,641	3,521	3,600	3,706	3,679	3,548	3,765
Products_____mil. bbl__	891	1,466	2,306	2,736	2,924	2,906	2,975	3,016
Trunk line movement:								
Crude oil_____mil. bbl__	3,091	3,505	4,756	5,112	5,423	5,391	5,369	5,824
Products_____mil. bbl__	1,124	1,872	2,864	3,358	3,633	3,589	3,645	3,813
Barrel-miles, trunk lines:								
Crude oil_____bil__	976	1,121	1,428	1,526	1,632	1,625	1,545	1,609
Products_____bil__	304	627	1,021	1,167	1,236	1,239	1,334	1,307

[1] Includes pipeline taxes; excludes Federal income taxes.
² 1960 based on a different system of accounts; therefore, comparable data not available.

Source: U.S. Interstate Commerce Commission, *Transport Statistics in the United States*, Part 6, annual.

No. 1129. Interstate Natural Gas Pipeline Companies—Summary: 1960 to 1976

[Excludes companies whose operations are limited to production of natural gas and sales of gas at or near the point of production. Covers classes A and B interstate natural gas pipeline companies with annual gas operating revenues of $1,000,000 or more]

ITEM	1960	1965	1970	1971	1972	1973	1974	1975	1976
Sales_____tril. cu. ft__	11.8	14.7	19.9	19.3	19.4	18.8	17.9	16.5	16.2
Residential_____tril. cu. ft__	.6	.6	.6	.6	.6	.6	.5	.5	.5
Commercial and industrial___tril. cu. ft__	2.4	2.5	2.9	2.8	2.7	2.5	2.3	1.9	1.8
For resale_____tril. cu. ft__	8.7	11.6	16.3	15.9	16.0	15.6	15.1	14.0	13.8
Operating revenues_____mil. dol__	4,571	5,584	7,955	8,578	9,404	9,870	11,637	14,278	17,317
From sales [1]_____mil. dol__	4,352	5,346	7,576	8,128	8,901	9,304	10,958	13,451	16,361
Residential_____mil. dol__	537	488	622	636	694	699	713	756	910
Commercial and industrial___mil. dol__	731	793	1,025	1,082	1,153	1,208	1,417	1,646	2,115
For resale_____mil. dol__	3,046	4,043	5,898	6,377	7,021	7,363	8,788	11,003	13,277
From transportation of gas to									
others_____mil. dol__	100	113	188	234	265	293	319	387	474
Other_____mil. dol__	119	126	191	215	238	272	359	440	482
Operation and maintenance									
expenses_____mil. dol__	3,091	3,873	5,602	5,868	6,410	6,706	7,995	10,374	12,796
Production_____mil. dol__	2,472	3,142	4,546	4,682	5,098	5,296	6,450	8,573	10,721
Storage_____mil. dol__	21	39	63	73	89	97	113	140	159
Transmission_____mil. dol__	306	379	534	615	670	718	788	912	1,065
Distribution_____mil. dol__	75	65	92	97	109	120	118	122	134
Administrative, general, and									
other_____mil. dol__	216	248	368	401	445	475	527	627	717
Pipeline mileage:									
Transmission lines_____1,000__	135.5	154.4	182.0	183.0	187.4	194.0	186.9	187.2	189.9
Field lines_____1,000__	42.5	47.7	51.6	53.0	54.7	55.0	55.2	57.1	58.6
Storage_____1,000__	2.9	3.1	3.5	3.6	3.9	4.0	3.6	4.2	4.3

[1] Includes other ultimate customers not shown separately.

Source: 1960-1975, U.S. Federal Power Commission and, thereafter, U.S. Energy Information Administration, *Statistics of Interstate Natural Gas Pipeline Companies*, annual.

Figure 23.1

Domestic Scheduled Air Carriers—Revenues, Miles Flown, and Passengers Carried: 1950 to 1977

(See tables 1130 and 1134)

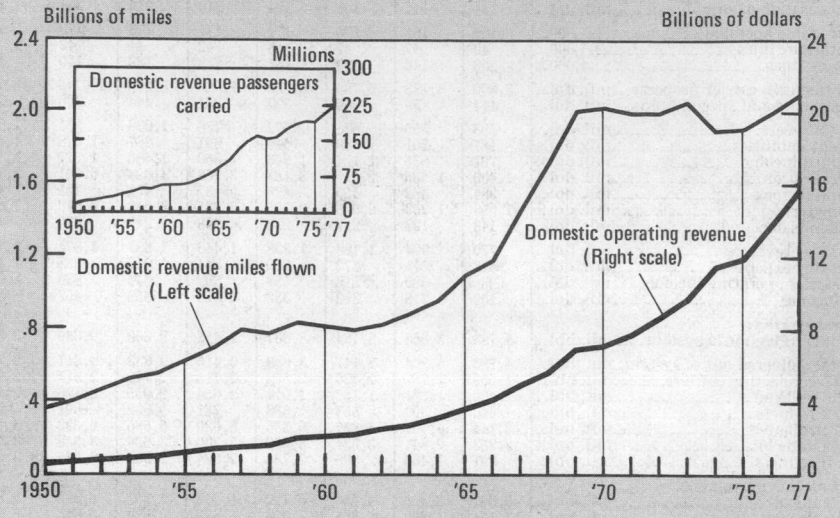

Source: Chart prepared by U.S. Bureau of the Census.
Data from U.S. Federal Aviation Administration.

Figure 23.2

Waterborne Commerce of the United States: 1950 to 1976

(See table 1145)

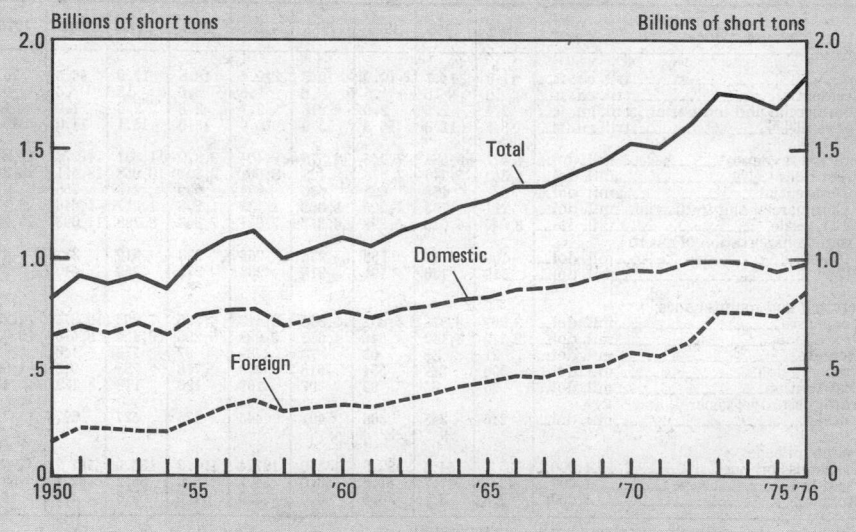

Source: Chart prepared by U.S. Bureau of the Census.
Data from U.S. Corps of Engineers.

Section 23

Transportation—Air and Water

This section presents statistics on civil air transportation, both passenger and cargo, and on water transportation, including inland waterways, oceanborne commerce, the merchant marine, cargo and vessel tonnages, and shipbuilding. The principal sources of these data are the annual *FAA Statistical Handbook of Aviation*, issued by the Federal Aviation Administration (FAA) and the annual *Waterborne Commerce of the United States* issued by the Corps of Engineers of the Department of the Army; the monthly and annual issues of *U.S. Waterborne Exports and General Imports*, and *U.S. Airborne Exports and General Imports*, the annual *Vessel Entrances and Clearances*, and the monthly *Highlights of U.S. Export and Import Trade*, issued by the Bureau of the Census.

Air transportation data are also presented annually by the Air Transport Association of America, Washington, D.C. in *Air Transport Facts and Figures*. Additional sources of data on water transportation include *A Statistical Analysis of the World's Merchant Fleets*, issued periodically by the U.S. Maritime Administration; *The Bulletin*, issued monthly by the American Bureau of Shipping, New York; and the *Annual Summary of Merchant Ships Launched in the World* and the *Register Book*, published by Lloyd's Register of Shipping, London, England.

Civil aviation.—Federal promotion and regulation of civil aviation are carried out by the FAA and the Civil Aeronautics Board (CAB). The CAB issues certificates permitting persons to engage in air transportation as a business, fixes air mail rates which they may charge, and may establish either maximum, minimum, or specific rates for transportation of passengers and goods. The responsibility for investigation of aviation accidents resides with the National Transportation Safety Board.

The principal activities of the FAA include: Controlling the use of navigable airspace; prescribing regulations dealing with the competency of airmen, airworthiness of aircraft, and air traffic control; operation of air route traffic control centers, airport traffic control towers, and flight service stations; the design, construction, maintenance, and inspection of navigation, traffic control, and communications equipment for the airways; development of general aviation; and promotion of air safety.

These agencies publish monthly and quarterly financial and traffic statistical data on the use of airway facilities; data related to the location of airmen, aircraft, and airports; the activity volume in the field of non-air carrier (general aviation) flying; and aircraft production and registration.

Air carriers and service.—The term *certificated route air carrier* refers to air carriers holding certificates of public convenience and necessity, issued by the CAB, authorizing the performance of scheduled service over specified routes and a limited amount of nonscheduled service. This general carrier grouping includes the so-called passenger/cargo carriers and the all-cargo carriers, and comprises all of the airlines certificated by the board, except the supplemental air carriers (see table 1136). Certificated route air carriers are often referred to as "scheduled airlines," although they may also perform nonscheduled service. *Nonscheduled service* comprises revenue flights that are not operated in regular scheduled service, such as charter flights, and all nonrevenue flights incident to such flights. *Scheduled service* is transport service operated over an air carrier's certificated routes, based on published flight schedules, including extra sections.

Vessel shipments, entrances, and clearances.—Shipments by dry cargo vessels

667

comprise shipments on all types of watercraft, except tanker vessels; shipments by tanker vessels comprise all types of cargo, liquid and dry, carried by tanker vessels.

A vessel is reported as entered only at the first port which it enters in the United States whether or not cargo is unloaded at that port. A vessel is reported as cleared only at the last port at which clearance is made to a foreign port, whether or not it takes on cargo. Army and Navy vessels entering or clearing without commercial cargo are not included in the figures.

Units of measurement.—Cargo tonnage and shipping weight both represent the gross weight of the cargo including the weight of containers, wrappings, crates, etc. However, shipping weight excludes lift and cargo vans and similar substantial outer containers. Other tonnage figures generally refer to stowing capacity of vessels, 100 cubic feet being called 1 ton. Gross tonnage comprises the space within the frames and the ceiling of the hull, together with those closed-in spaces above deck available for cargo, stores, passengers, or crew, with certain minor exceptions. Net or registered tonnage is the gross tonnage less the spaces occupied by the propelling machinery, fuel, crew quarters, master's cabin, and navigation spaces. Substantially, it represents space available for cargo and passengers. The net tonnage capacity of a ship may bear little relation to weight of cargo. Deadweight tonnage is the weight in long tons required to depress a vessel from light water line (that is, with only the machinery and equipment on board) to load line. It is, therefore, the weight of the cargo, fuel, etc., which a vessel is designed to carry with safety.

Historical statistics.—Tabular headnotes provide cross-references, where applicable, to *Historical Statistics of the United States, Colonial Times to 1970.* See Appendix I.

No. 1130. SCHEDULED PASSENGER/CARGO AIR CARRIERS—NUMBER, OPERATING REVENUES, AND EXPENSES: 1955 TO 1977

[In millions of dollars, except number of carriers. 1955 not strictly comparable with later years. Minus sign (−) denotes loss. See also headnote, table 1134, and *Historical Statistics, Colonial Times to 1970*, series Q 591–603]

ITEM	1955	1960	1965	1970	1972	1973	1974	1975	1976	1977 [1]
DOMESTIC										
Number of air carriers [2]	42	42	40	35	32	30	29	30	30	30
Revenues	1,215	2,129	3,609	7,131	8,588	9,605	11,448	11,911	13,774	15,667
Passenger	1,065	1,860	3,142	6,246	7,565	8,379	9,758	10,123	11,844	13,472
Mail (including subsidy)	61	113	158	205	228	258	259	247	288	333
Express and freight	62	103	220	461	541	615	673	715	830	960
Other	27	53	89	219	254	352	758	826	817	902
Expenses	1,091	2,091	3,165	7,128	8,097	9,117	10,649	11,781	13,197	15,013
Aircraft	559	1,043	1,811	3,970	4,338	4,838	5,662	6,347	7,115	8,162
Flying operations	328	601	855	2,098	2,325	2,606	3,297	3,869	4,398	5,223
Direct maintenance flight equip.	138	258	640	1,127	1,239	1,397	1,500	1,595	1,798	1,981
Depreciation and amortization of flight equipment and other	93	184	316	745	774	835	865	883	919	958
Ground and indirect	532	1,048	1,354	3,157	3,759	4,279	4,987	5,434	6,082	6,851
Net operating income	124	38	443	3	491	487	799	130	577	653
INTERNATIONAL										
Number of air carriers [2]	9	13	10	4	3	4	3	3	3	3
Revenues	398	685	1,199	1,914	2,284	2,527	2,922	3,064	3,316	3,774
Passenger	300	528	887	1,380	1,707	1,895	2,121	2,230	2,411	2,786
Mail (including subsidy)	30	48	82	103	77	71	84	90	78	80
Express and freight	33	59	131	197	242	268	336	356	382	425
Other	35	51	99	234	258	293	381	388	445	483
Expenses	380	639	1,001	1,894	2,234	2,460	2,995	3,060	3,182	3,552
Aircraft	181	304	509	944	1,108	1,212	1,608	1,627	1,650	1,793
Flying operations	115	180	263	515	596	681	1,038	1,050	1,089	1,170
Direct maintenance flight equip.	37	58	146	241	300	317	356	364	368	414
Depreciation and amortization of flight equipment and other	29	66	100	188	212	214	214	213	193	209
Ground and indirect	200	336	493	950	1,126	1,248	1,387	1,433	1,532	1,759
Net operating income	18	45	198	19	50	67	−73	4	134	222

[1] Preliminary.   [2] Each airline counted only in group in which greater portion of its operations prevailed.

Source: U.S. Federal Aviation Administration, *FAA Statistical Handbook of Aviation*, annual. Data from U.S. Civil Aeronautics Board.

No. 1131. CIVIL FLYING—SUMMARY: 1960 TO 1975

[As of Dec. 31 or for years ending Dec. 31. See also *Historical Statistics, Colonial Times to 1970*, series Q 604–623]

ITEM	1960	1965	1970	1972	1973	1974	1975	1976
Airports in operation [1]	6,881	9,566	11,261	12,405	12,700	13,062	13,251	13,770
Public	2,780	3,570	4,260	4,481	4,536	4,575	4,573	4,667
Private	4,101	5,996	7,001	7,924	8,164	8,487	8,678	9,103
Lighted airports	2,133	2,878	3,554	3,827	3,880	3,999	4,171	4,362
Airports with paved runways	1,893	2,747	3,805	4,390	4,527	4,716	4,865	5,106
Miles of Federal airways 1,000	(NA)	(NA)	324.7	402.1	415.4	405.7	403.9	413.5
Airport Development Aid Program: [2]								
Air carrier airports mil. dol	73.3	44.3	39.4	261.1	175.1	258.4	287.8	355.2
General aviation airports mil. dol	8.7	15.2	11.1	18.9	31.5	41.3	52.1	61.1
Total civil aircraft [3] 1,000	111.6	142.1	154.5	170.8	179.8	188.0	196.3	205.9
Active aircraft 1,000	78.8	97.7	134.5	147.7	156.2	164.2	171.2	180.9
Air carriers, total [4] 1,000	2.2	2.3	2.8	2.7	2.7	2.7	2.5	2.5
General aviation aircraft [5][6] 1,000	76.5	95.4	131.7	145.0	153.5	161.5	168.5	178.3
Fixed-wing: Multi-engine 1,000	7.2	12.0	18.4	19.8	21.9	23.4	24.6	25.7
Single-engine:								
4-place and over 1,000	34.8	49.8	64.6	71.0	74.8	78.9	82.6	88.2
3-place and less 1,000	33.5	31.4	44.9	49.4	51.4	53.0	54.4	56.7
Rotorcraft [6][7] 1,000	.6	1.5	2.2	2.8	3.1	3.6	4.1	4.5
Active airman certificates held [8] 1,000	549	719	1,060	1,104	1,056	1,091	1,097	1,125
Pilot [9] 1,000	348	480	733	751	715	734	728	744
Percent held by women	2.9	3.7	4.0	4.4	4.8	5.0	5.2	5.6
Airline transport 1,000	18	22	34	38	38	41	43	45
Commercial 1,000	90	117	187	196	182	192	189	188
Private 1,000	139	196	304	321	299	306	306	309
Student 1,000	99	139	196	181	182	181	177	189
Nonpilot [10] 1,000	170	204	290	315	305	314	324	335
Ground technicians [11] 1,000	151	175	241	263	253	262	271	291
Hours flown (general aviation [5]) [6] 1,000	13,121	16,733	26,031	26,974	30,048	32,475	34,165	36,128
Business [12] 1,000	5,699	5,857	7,204	7,239	8,558	9,140	9,545	10,095
Commercial [13] 1,000	2,365	3,348	6,849	4,831	5,608	6,294	6,480	7,029
Instructional 1,000	1,828	3,346	4,524	6,814	7,646	7,972	8,174	8,591
Personal 1,000	3,172	4,016	6,896	7,601	7,546	8,404	9,244	9,768
Miles flown (general aviation [5]) [6] mil	1,769	2,562	3,207	3,318	3,729	4,043	4,238	4,476
Business [12] mil	881	1,204	1,134	1,144	1,344	1,433	1,487	1,563
Commercial [13] mil	299	461	791	581	688	790	818	885
Instructional mil	194	359	450	692	778	815	829	873
Personal mil	387	512	753	834	825	920	1,008	1,068
Domestic air cargo, revenue ton-miles flown [14]	724	1,661	2,581	2,973	3,267	3,221	3,020	3,161
Scheduled carriers mil	476	1,112	2,215	2,567	2,922	2,888	2,718	2,888
Nonscheduled carriers [15] mil	135	330	80	147	54	52	39	36
Supplemental carriers [16] mil	112	220	285	259	292	280	263	237
Fuel consumed (general aviation [5]): [17]								
Gasoline mil. gal	(NA)	304	362	404	410	403	397	433
Jet fuel [18] mil. gal	(NA)	183	415	573	376	483	510	588
Aircraft accidents [19]	4,883	5,279	4,767	4,278	4,298	4,472	4,282	4,595
General aviation [5]	4,793	5,196	4,712	4,228	4,255	4,425	4,237	4,567
Fatal	429	538	641	695	723	729	675	636
Fatalities	787	1,029	1,310	1,426	1,412	1,438	1,345	1,188
Air carrier, exc. commercial operators	90	83	55	50	43	47	45	28
Fatal	17	9	8	8	9	9	3	4
Fatalities	499	261	146	190	227	467	124	45
Hijacking incidents, worldwide	–	5	83	62	22	26	25	18
U.S.-registered aircraft	–	4	27	31	2	7	12	4
Successful [20]	–	1	18	10	1	3	4	1
Foreign-registered aircraft	–	1	56	31	20	19	13	14
Successful [20]	–	–	37	13	10	5	3	6

– Represents zero.   NA Not available.
[1] Existing airports and airfields recorded with F.A.A. Includes military airports with joint civil and military use. Includes U.S. outlying areas. Airport-type definitions: Public—public use and public services, public control; Private—(a) public use and public services, private control, and (b) no public services, private control, military control, or Federal government control.   [2] Federal funds only. Includes U.S. outlying areas. Prior to July 1, 1970, data are for Federal-Aid Airport Program (FAAP).   [3] Includes gliders, dirigibles, balloons, and blimps.   [4] Registered, not necessarily in operation. Includes helicopters.   [5] See headnote, table 1132.   [6] Includes breakdown not shown separately.   [7] Includes autogyros; excludes air carrier helicopters.   [8] Includes flight instructors, not shown separately.   [9] Includes helicopter, glider, and lighter-than-air pilots, not shown separately.   [10] Includes control tower operators, flight navigators and engineers, and ground technicians.   [11] No medical examinations are required; therefore, data represent all certificates on record and include retired or otherwise inactive technicians.   [12] Corporation and individual business transportation, not for hire.   [13] Passenger and cargo transportation for hire, aerial application (crop dusting, spraying, seeding, etc.), patrol, survey, and other miscellaneous work use.   [14] Comprises express and freight ton-miles.   [15] Includes some military ton-miles and may include a small amount of international traffic.   [16] Civil and military.   [17] Source: 1965–1975, U.S. Department of the Interior; 1976, U.S. Department of Energy, *Crude Petroleum, Petroleum Products, and Natural Gas Liquids* (Final Summary).   [18] Includes kerosene-type and naphtha-type jet fuels.   [19] Beginning 1970, data not strictly comparable due to change of definition.   [20] Hijacker controls flight and reaches destination or objective.

Source: Except as noted, U.S. Federal Aviation Administration, *FAA Statistical Handbook of Aviation*, annual, and unpublished data. Includes data from U.S. Civil Aeronautics Board and U.S. National Transportation Safety Board.

No. 1132. General Aviation Aircraft, Airports, and Federal Airport Development Aid Program—States and Other Areas: 1976

[As of Dec. 31. General aviation comprises all civil flying (incluidng such commercial operations as commuter airlines, air taxis, agricultural application, powerline patrol, etc.), but excludes certificated route air carriers and supplemental operators]

STATE	General aviation aircraft	AIRPORTS [1] Public	AIRPORTS [1] Private	AIRPORT DEVELOPMENT AID PROGRAM [2] (mil. dol.) Total funds, 1970–1976	AIRPORT DEVELOPMENT AID PROGRAM [2] (mil. dol.) 1976 funds	STATE OR OTHER AREA	General aviation aircraft	AIRPORTS [1] Public	AIRPORTS [1] Private	AIRPORT DEVELOPMENT AID PROGRAM [2] (mil. dol.) Total funds, 1970–1976	AIRPORT DEVELOPMENT AID PROGRAM [2] (mil. dol.) 1976 funds
Total___	178,304	4,667	9,103	1,760.7	460.1	Mo_____	3,865	115	243	16.4	3.5
						Mont_____	1,986	115	57	16.6	6.1
Ala_____	2,425	92	39	17.4	3.7	Nebr_____	2,291	93	208	25.1	4.1
Alaska_____	4,687	545	217	96.9	21.5	Nev_____	1,409	59	59	18.8	3.2
Ariz_____	3,740	94	108	29.0	3.3	N.H_____	783	16	41	2.9	.8
Ark_____	2,295	77	89	12.1	4.4	N.J_____	3,593	31	208	41.4	8.2
Calif_____	22,317	292	512	114.0	27.4	N. Mex_____	1,764	63	76	12.8	4.9
Colo_____	3,244	80	175	56.7	25.8	N.Y_____	5,967	69	427	73.1	21.9
Conn_____	1,354	15	89	9.7	–						
Del_____	565	3	29	2.7	.1	N.C_____	3,490	72	179	41.2	7.1
						N. Dak_____	1,474	93	116	13.3	4.3
D.C_____	159	7	9	–	–	Ohio_____	7,299	121	437	36.1	8.1
Fla_____	8,677	121	270	84.3	30.2	Okla_____	3,709	127	158	31.1	10.0
Ga_____	3,525	114	148	73.6	14.4	Oreg_____	3,987	92	194	29.3	5.1
Hawaii_____	365	17	34	56.1	14.2	Pa_____	5,607	76	568	67.1	5.8
Idaho_____	1,801	128	59	11.8	2.5	R.I_____	294	8	14	2.7	–
Ill_____	7,309	97	770	79.6	21.7	S.C_____	1,552	63	60	14.1	8.3
Ind_____	3,985	67	226	46.1	22.1	S. Dak_____	1,235	74	57	16.7	5.9
Iowa_____	3,309	115	135	19.7	6.1						
Kans_____	3,848	123	211	11.5	3.0	Tenn_____	2,526	77	55	37.3	7.6
Ky_____	1,501	51	39	26.0	7.8	Tex_____	13,479	292	925	153.8	44.6
La_____	2,953	71	209	43.2	20.8	Utah_____	1,178	55	35	24.0	2.3
Maine_____	1,017	50	112	6.6	1.4	Vt_____	396	21	40	2.4	.9
Md_____	2,431	25	110	18.3	1.8	Va_____	2,416	55	185	26.2	9.9
Mass_____	2,541	30	111	19.9	6.1	Wash_____	5,157	116	218	32.6	9.8
Mich_____	6,444	132	289	62.5	10.7	W. Va_____	996	25	33	21.6	2.3
Minn_____	4,060	141	171	20.8	4.2	Wis_____	3,458	104	217	32.3	6.8
Miss_____	1,986	78	70	18.8	6.0	Wyo_____	930	42	48	10.6	3.5
						Other areas [3]_	925	28	14	23.4	5.9

– Represents zero.　[1] Includes military airports with joint civil and military use, heliports, seaplane bases, etc.　[2] Excludes contributions by State and local governments and by airport operators provided under various agreements. "Total" represents cumulative since enactment of Airport Development Aid Program, July 1, 1970, through Dec. 31, 1976.　[3] Puerto Rico, American Samoa, Guam, Virgin Islands, and Saipan.

Source: U.S. Federal Aviation Administration, *FAA Statistical Handbook of Aviation*, annual.

No. 1133. Scheduled Air Carriers—Service and Traffic: 1960 to 1977

[In millions, except as indicated]

ITEM	1960	1965	1970	1972	1973	1974	1975	1976	1977, prel.
Revenue ton-miles, all services_____	5,024	9,895	20,186	22,805	23,928	23,900	23,534	25,709	27,583
Revenue ton-miles, scheduled_____	4,729	8,985	18,166	20,746	22,242	22,425	22,186	24,121	25,909
Passenger [1]_____	3,777	6,672	13,171	15,241	16,196	16,292	16,281	17,899	19,322
U.S. mail_____	241	483	1,470	1,190	1,198	1,151	1,097	1,114	1,147
Foreign mail_____	9	10	10	11	11	12	12	12	13
Express_____	59	90	107	87	100	81	29	22	41
Freight_____	643	1,730	3,408	4,217	4,737	4,890	4,766	5,074	5,385
Revenue ton-miles, charter [2]_____	296	909	2,020	2,059	1,686	1,475	1,348	1,588	1,674
Available ton-miles, all services____	9,384	19,661	44,298	48,680	51,444	48,942	49,289	51,709	54,789
Ton-mile load factor_____percent__	53.5	50.3	45.6	46.8	46.5	48.8	47.7	49.7	50.3
Scheduled services total:									
Revenue passenger-miles____bil__	39	69	132	152	162	163	163	179	193
Available seat-miles_____bil__	66	124	265	287	311	297	303	323	346
Passenger load factor_percent__	59.3	55.2	49.7	53.0	52.1	54.9	53.7	55.4	55.9
Revenue passenger-miles per gallon of fuel_____number__	(NA)	(NA)	(NA)	17.2	17.5	19.5	19.5	20.7	21.2
Revenue plane-miles_____	₡98	1,354	2,418	2,376	2,448	2,258	2,241	2,320	2,419

NA Not available.　[1] A passenger ton-mile represents 1 ton of passenger weight, including free and excess baggage, transported 1 mile.　[2] Passenger and cargo.

Source: Air Transport Association of America, Washington, D.C., *Air Transport Facts and Figures*, annual. Data from Civil Aeronautics Board.

No. 1134. Scheduled Air Carriers—Summary of Operations: 1950 to 1977

[As of Dec. 31 or for calendar years, except as noted. Operations between conterminous U.S. and Hawaii (through 1965), Puerto Rico, and outlying areas included with international. Intra-Alaska included with domestic carriers and Mainland Alaska with international, as follows: Number of operators and traffic data, through 1965; fuel and financial data, 1955–1965; and personnel data, 1960 and 1965. Beginning 1970, Alaska and Hawaii included in domestic. See also *Historical Statistics, Colonial Times to 1970*, series Q 577–590 and Q 624–633]

ITEM	1950	1955	1960	1965	1970	1973	1974	1975	1976	1977
Domestic operators [1]	48	40	39	40	33	30	29	30	30	30
International operators [1]	6	7	10	9	3	3	2	2	2	2
Total personnel employed [2]__1,000	83	122	163	207	291	312	305	292	303	(NA)
Domestic__1,000	62	96	134	170	242	261	260	249	268	(NA)
International__1,000	21	27	29	37	49	51	45	43	35	(NA)
Route miles in operation [3]__1,000	184	196	250	248	377	395	373	371	371	(NA)
Domestic__1,000	77	79	101	105	172	176	169	172	175	(NA)
International [4]__1,000	106	117	148	143	206	219	204	199	196	(NA)
Aircraft in operation [5]	1,220	1,409	1,867	1,896	2,390	2,361	2,244	2,267	2,271	2,203
Fixed wing	1,209	1,390	1,842	1,875	2,374	2,348	2,234	2,260	2,266	2,200
Four-engine		679	1,160	1,055	908	735	612	578	556	465
Three-engine turbojet		(NA)	(NA)	168	627	844	893	961	992	1,040
Twin-engine	(NA)	709	677	615	825	754	717	714	708	695
Single-engine		2	5	37	14	15	12	7	10	–
Average available seats: [6]										
Domestic	37.5	51.2	65.5	89.2	110.4	123.8	127.7	130.4	134.1	136.9
International	41.0	56.4	89.9	129.1	154.9	201.9	213.7	224.8	230.0	236.7
Average speed (miles per hour):										
Domestic	180	208	235	314	350	404	402	403	406	408
International	218	244	307	451	482	481	481	482	484	487
Fuel consumed: [7]										
Gasoline__mil. gal	586	1,195	1,189	519	14	11	7	6	6	([8])
Jet fuel:										
Domestic__mil. gal	–	2	988	3,368	7,783	8,236	7,416	7,558	7,911	8,339
International__mil. gal	–	–	343	1,282	2,302	2,435	2,130	1,949	1,921	1,957
Revenue-miles flown (all scheduled services)__mil	464	780	998	1,354	2,418	2,448	2,258	2,241	2,320	2,419
Domestic__mil	370	640	829	1,099	2,027	2,058	1,900	1,909	2,001	2,104
International__mil	95	140	168	255	391	390	358	332	319	315
Revenue passengers carried__mil	19	42	62	103	169	202	208	205	223	240
Domestic__mil	17	38	56	92	153	183	190	189	206	222
International__mil	2	3	6	11	16	19	18	16	17	18
Revenue passenger-miles flown:										
Domestic__bil	8.0	19.9	30.6	51.9	104.1	126.3	129.7	131.7	145.3	156.6
International__bil	2.2	4.5	8.3	16.8	27.6	35.6	33.2	31.1	33.7	36.6
Average passenger-mile rate:										
Domestic__dollars	.055	.054	.061	.061	.060	.066	.075	.077	.078	.082
International__dollars	.073	.067	.064	.053	.050	.053	.064	.072	.060	.065
Express and freight, ton-miles flown [9]__mil	213	326	579	1,540	2,908	3,692	3,760	3,590	3,855	4,109
Domestic__mil	152	230	387	943	1,966	2,454	2,421	2,331	2,474	2,642
International__mil	61	96	192	597	942	1,238	1,339	1,259	1,381	1,467
Mail, ton-miles flown: [9]										
Domestic__mil	48	89	136	226	706	687	668	665	709	750
International__mil	26	61	103	254	549	361	348	312	292	298
Accidents (revenue operations): [10]										
Domestic, total	36	41	62	55	31	27	31	21	26	[11] 23
Fatal	4	8	[12] 10	6	1	4	3	2	3	[11] 4
Fatalities [13]	109	221	363	223	1	138	168	122	42	[11] 396
Passenger-fatalities per 100 million passenger-miles flown [14]	1.2	.8	.9	.4	–	.10	.12	.08	.029	.253
International, total	5	5	5	8	7	5	12	7	4	4
Fatal	2	1	2	1	1	2	4	–	1	–
Fatalities [13]	56	4	15	30	2	79	292	–	35	–
Passenger-fatalities per 100 million passenger-miles flown	2.1	(Z)	.1	.1	(Z)	.18	.51	–	.01	–

– Represents zero.   NA Not available.   Z Less than .05.   [1] Excludes all-cargo operators.
[2] For types of personnel, see table 1135. Beginning 1973, two small all-cargo carriers included in domestic rather than international. Therefore, data will not agree with table 1135.   [3] Not compiled for Intra-Alaska. Weighted average. Prior to 1970, refers to passenger/cargo carriers only; thereafter, includes all-cargo carriers. As of Dec. 31, based on fourth quarter.
[5] Represents aircraft of the certificated route air carriers; excludes those used for crew training and general utility purposes, or held for disposal. Beginning 1973, includes aircraft operated by the scheduled all-cargo carriers. Includes helicopters, not shown separately.
[6] Obtained by dividing passenger seat-miles by revenue-miles flown in passenger service.
[7] Includes air cargo.   [8] Included in "Jet fuel."   [9] Excludes freight flown by certificated all-cargo operators and irregular carriers.   [10] Beginning 1960, includes military contract operations.   [11] Preliminary.
[12] Includes mid-air collisions nonfatal to air carrier occupants (excluded in computation of fatal accidents).
[13] Includes crew members.
[14] Excludes passenger deaths occurring in dynamite accidents, as follows: Nov. 1, 1955, 39; Jan. 6, 1960, 29.

Source: U.S. Federal Aviation Administration, *FAA Statistical Handbook of Aviation*, annual. Includes data from U.S. Civil Aeronautics Board.

No. 1135. Scheduled Air Carriers—Personnel and Payroll: 1970 and 1976

[See headnote, table 1134. Average salary computed based on total payroll for calendar year divided by weighted quarterly average of full-time employees. Therefore, average salary overstated for categories with part-time employees. See *Historical Statistics, Colonial Times to 1970*, series Q 581, for number employed]

| ITEM | 1970 | | | | | | 1976 | | | | | |
| | Domestic | | | International | | | Domestic | | | International | | |
	Personnel (1,000)	Payroll (mil. dol.)	Avg. salary ($1,000)	Personnel (1,000)	Payroll (mil. dol.)	Avg. salary ($1,000)	Personnel (1,000)	Payroll (mil. dol.)	Avg. salary ($1,000)	Personnel (1,000)	Payroll (mil. dol.)	Avg. salary ($1,000)
Total [1]	242.2	3,085	12.7	48.5	495	10.2	262.6	5,646	21.5	40.3	692	17.9
Pilots, copilots	22.8	685	34.3	2.3	81	34.5	24.1	1,178	49.0	2.1	115	51.9
Flight attendants	28.7	210	7.3	4.9	43	8.7	38.1	473	12.4	4.2	57	12.9
Mechanics [2]	41.4	507	12.2	6.1	63	10.4	40.9	964	23.6	4.8	90	18.3
Aircraft and traffic servicing	66.4	714	10.7	14.9	117	7.9	74.7	1,420	19.0	12.1	159	13.9
Office employees	47.0	469	10.0	11.9	95	8.0	50.9	870	17.1	9.2	128	15.2

[1] Includes personnel not shown separately. [2] Includes other maintenance personnel.

No. 1136. Supplemental Air Carriers—Summary of Operations: 1960 to 1977

[Refers to carriers supplementing the scheduled service of certificated route air carriers, as authorized by the Civil Aeronautics Board. Includes international operations; see headnote, table 1134. Figures shown for military cover activities performed under charter or other contract with the Department of Defense]

ITEM	1960	1965	1970	1972	1973	1974	1975	1976	1977
Number of operators 1,000	30	13	14	13	9	8	8	7	7
Revenue passenger-miles mil	2,208	2,489	10,289	9,987	11,790	10,865	8,746	8,199	9,983
Commercial mil	671	1,069	6,044	7,783	10,161	9,016	6,885	6,647	8,352
Military mil	1,537	1,420	4,245	2,204	1,629	1,849	1,861	1,552	1,631
Revenue cargo ton-miles mil	120	298	391	457	403	366	362	384	329
Commercial mil	5	49	77	86	98	100	115	159	186
Military mil	115	249	314	371	305	266	247	225	143
Operating revenue mil. dol	83.4	141.0	337.2	331.1	374.2	428.8	433.2	417.5	516.2
Operating expenses mil. dol	85.3	116.9	330.7	326.8	380.9	431.9	404.8	418.1	500.8

Source of tables 1135 and 1136: U.S. Federal Aviation Administration, *FAA Statistical Handbook of Aviation* annual. Data from U.S. Civil Aeronautics Board.

No. 1137. Employment, Hours, and Earnings in Aircraft Industries—Annual Averages: 1960 to 1976

ITEM	1960	1965	1970	1972	1973	1974	1975	1976
Employment, total 1,000	674	619	690	501	514	532	514	485
Aircraft 1,000	371	330	388	272	275	289	275	262
Aircraft engines and parts 1,000	171	188	180	139	145	146	139	132
Other aircraft parts and equipment 1,000	132	101	122	91	95	97	100	91
Average weekly earnings:								
Aircraft industries dol	110	130	171	198	211	219	250	283
Aircraft engines and parts dol	112	133	166	193	211	224	250	281
Average hourly earnings:								
Aircraft industries dol	2.71	3.16	4.17	4.74	5.13	5.57	6.20	6.81
Aircraft engines and parts dol	2.73	3.17	4.10	4.70	5.05	5.43	6.03	6.86

Source: U.S. Federal Aviation Administration, *FAA Statistical Handbook of Aviation*, annual. Data from U.S. Bureau of Labor Statistics.

No. 1138. Civil Aircraft Shipments: 1960 to 1977

[Represents manufacturers' shipments of complete aircraft. Includes both domestic and export output]

ITEM	1960	1965	1970	1971	1972	1973	1974	1975	1976	1977
Total	8,181	12,646	8,190	8,143	10,523	14,748	15,117	15,196	16,446	17,605
Transports	238	221	313	230	230	295	263	314	238	180
General aviation	7,726	12,053	7,381	7,450	9,765	13,671	14,026	14,043	15,648	16,624
Single-engine:										
1- to 3-place	1,366	3,545	1,981	1,948	2,398	3,137	3,346	3,047	3,175	3,379
4-place and over	5,072	6,478	4,048	4,329	5,500	7,681	8,124	8,460	9,854	10,478
Multi-engine	1,288	2,030	1,352	1,173	1,867	2,853	2,556	2,536	2,619	2,767
Rotorcraft	217	372	496	463	528	782	828	839	560	801

Source: U.S. Federal Aviation Administration, *FAA Statistical Handbook of Aviation*, annual. Includes data from U.S. Bureau of the Census, *Current Industrial Reports*.

No. 1139. AIRCRAFT—SALES, NEW ORDERS, AND BACKLOG: 1970 TO 1976

[Reported by manufacturers of complete aircraft, aircraft engines, and propellers. See also *Historical Statistics, Colonial Times to 1970*, series Q 573]

ITEM	1970 Total (bil. dol.)	1970 Per-cent U.S. Govt.	1973 Total (bil. dol.)	1973 Per-cent U.S. Govt.	1974 Total (bil. dol.)	1974 Per-cent U.S. Govt.	1975 Total (bil. dol.)	1975 Per-cent U.S. Govt.	1976 Total (bil. dol.)	1976 Per-cent U.S. Govt.
Net sales	24.8	66.3	24.3	56.7	26.8	53.1	29.5	58.6	30.4	62.8
Aircraft and parts [1]	10.4	54.8	9.6	44.2	10.4	43.8	11.3	46.9	11.6	52.5
Aircraft engines and parts	3.1	61.5	2.7	48.0	3.1	45.3	3.4	47.0	3.6	52.8
Missiles and parts	5.4	96.9	5.6	87.2	5.9	86.3	6.3	93.7	5.6	94.6
Other products, services	5.9	(X)	6.4	(X)	7.4	(X)	8.5	(X)	9.4	(X)
Net new orders	21.2	71.4	27.0	56.2	32.7	55.6	29.0	64.1	36.0	58.6
Backlog, Dec. 31	24.7	52.1	29.7	55.2	35.5	57.2	35.0	63.2	39.6	58.7

X Not applicable.   [1] Includes propellers and propeller parts.

No. 1140. AIRCRAFT, AND AIRCRAFT PARTS AND ACCESSORIES—EXPORTS: 1970 TO 1976

[See *Historical Statistics, Colonial Times to 1970*, series Q 574–575, for number and value of aircraft exported]

ITEM	1970 Number of units	1970 Value (mil. dol.)	1974 Number of units	1974 Value (mil. dol.)	1975 Number of units	1975 Value (mil. dol.)	1976 Number of units	1976 Value (mil. dol.)
Aircraft, parts, and accessories	(X)	3,053	(X)	6,556	(X)	7,222	(X)	7,060
Commercial and civilian aircraft [1]	2,940	1,528	5,714	3,369	4,539	3,229	4,531	3,217
Cargo transports, new	7	32	7	109	6	44	11	108
Passenger transports, new	149	1,059	207	2,243	155	2,092	136	2,034
Passenger/cargo combinations, new	28	192	28	318	27	294	16	334
Personal and utility type:								
Single-engine, new	1,493	32	3,367	81	2,400	71	2,374	74
Multiple-engine, new	544	81	896	206	805	236	840	287
Rotary-wing, new	335	28	395	110	334	105	315	113
Used, rebuilt, modified, or converted [2]	358	104	690	299	581	387	591	264
Internal combustion engines, new	2,340	12	2,950	21	2,566	29	2,544	25
Aircraft engines, used	816	7	1,172	13	1,236	16	954	16
Aircraft components, parts, and access	(X)	1,506	(X)	3,154	(X)	3,948	(X)	3,802

X Not applicable.   [1] For number of units, includes new aircraft not elsewhere classified, not shown separately.   [2] Aircraft only; includes aircraft changed from military to nonmilitary type.

Source of tables 1139 and 1140: U.S. Bureau of the Census, *Current Industrial Reports*, series MQ-37D and M37G.

No. 1141. AIRBORNE IMPORTS AND EXPORTS—SHIPPING WEIGHT AND VALUE: 1970 TO 1976

[Weight in millions of pounds, value in millions of dollars, except as indicated. Includes trade of Puerto Rico]

CONTINENT	IMPORTS Weight 1970	1975	1976	IMPORTS Value 1970	1975	1976	EXPORTS Weight 1970	1975	1976	EXPORTS Value 1970	1975	1976
All carriers [1]	620.3	1,062.8	1,212.2	3,417	8,917	10,920	897.0	1,420.0	1,493.3	6,086	15,212	17,398
North America	85.8	141.2	149.0	316	775	840	224.5	292.6	332.1	795	1,552	1,836
South America	43.3	118.0	113.8	98	412	468	95.5	196.2	193.1	412	1,225	1,259
Europe	353.7	413.1	462.2	2,069	4,266	4,805	428.9	592.2	584.1	3,459	7,432	8,019
Asia	131.2	376.8	471.6	859	3,026	4,373	107.5	245.7	288.8	1,056	3,445	4,716
Other	6.6	12.5	14.8	76	436	433	34.9	78.8	82.3	260	5,200	1,077
U.S. carriers [1]	288.3	456.4	502.8	1,667	3,860	4,558	321.0	480.1	505.6	2,215	5,481	5,847
Percent of all	46.5	42.9	41.5	48.8	43.3	41.7	36.1	33.8	33.9	36.4	36.0	33.6
North America	39.1	50.6	51.1	140	329	357	91.9	109.6	136.5	367	711	872
South America	18.4	45.8	38.6	51	152	173	33.0	61.4	64.4	119	346	381
Europe	148.5	168.6	175.2	907	1,941	2,058	145.7	195.1	179.6	1,210	2,377	2,358
Asia	80.7	187.4	233.9	542	1,352	1,895	44.4	86.7	96.3	459	1,291	1,603
Other	1.6	4.0	4.0	28	86	76	6.7	20.0	23.5	59	246	346

[1] Includes shipments not shown separately by continent.

Source: U.S. Bureau of the Census, *United States Airborne Exports and General Imports*, FT 986, annual.

No. 1142. U. S. Receipts and Payments for International Transportation: 1960 to 1977

[In millions of dollars. Data are international transportation transactions recorded for balance of payment purposes (see table 1497). Receipts include freight on exports carried by U.S.-operated carriers and foreign carrier expenditures in U.S. ports. Payments include freight on imports carried by foreign carriers and U.S. carrier port expenditures abroad. Freight on exports carried by foreign carriers is excluded since such payments are directly or indirectly for foreign account. Similarly, freight on U.S. imports carried by U.S. carriers is a domestic rather than an international transaction. Minus sign (−) denotes excess of payments over receipts. See *Historical Statistics, Colonial Times to 1970*, series U 3 and U 10, for totals]

ITEM	1960	1965	1970	1971	1972	1973	1974	1975	1976	1977, prel.
Total receipts	1,782	2,446	3,657	3,892	4,254	5,409	6,756	6,824	7,754	8,249
Ocean transportation [1]	1,337	1,731	2,246	2,264	2,412	3,130	3,999	4,013	4,628	4,828
Export freight earnings	428	519	604	554	593	815	1,170	1,183	1,356	1,290
Freight earnings on shipments between foreign countries	136	153	209	195	203	221	307	328	353	376
Port expenditures	746	1,041	1,394	1,469	1,572	2,027	2,440	2,429	2,908	3,128
Charter hire	8	9	36	45	43	67	82	73	11	34
Air transportation	358	591	1,240	1,436	1,635	2,041	2,491	2,512	2,791	3,053
Export freight earnings	55	91	187	202	235	276	360	390	385	426
Passenger fares	156	262	541	614	698	975	1,104	1,039	1,225	1,352
Port expenditures	147	238	512	620	702	790	1,027	1,083	1,181	1,275
Other transportation	87	124	171	192	207	238	266	299	335	368
Total payments	1,915	2,668	4,031	4,368	5,057	6,381	7,912	7,798	8,849	10,107
Ocean transportation	1,333	1,803	2,353	2,468	2,798	3,822	4,679	4,352	4,952	5,655
Import freight payments	780	1,083	1,420	1,610	1,897	2,683	3,253	2,945	3,476	4,109
Passenger fares	212	207	245	236	264	285	259	278	270	261
Port expenditures	167	281	313	289	323	461	723	744	862	933
Charter hire	174	232	375	333	314	393	444	385	344	352
Air transportation	504	775	1,581	1,792	2,139	2,420	3,083	3,287	3,700	4,219
Import freight payments	22	40	115	158	185	192	219	273	359	421
Passenger fares	301	510	970	1,054	1,332	1,505	1,836	1,985	2,272	2,582
Port expenditures	181	225	496	580	622	723	1,028	1,029	1,069	1,216
Other transportation	78	90	97	108	120	138	150	159	197	233
Receipts balance	−133	−222	−374	−476	−803	−972	−1,156	−974	−1,095	−1,858

[1] Through 1973, includes small amount for passenger fares, not shown separately.

Source: U.S. Bureau of Economic Analysis, quarterly in *Survey of Current Business*.

No. 1143. Exports and Imports, by Method of Transport: 1960 to 1977

[Export data include both domestic and foreign; import data for general imports only. For details, see source]

ITEM	1960	1965	1970	1972	1973	1974	1975	1976	1977
Exports:									
All methods of transport [1] bil. dol	20.6	27.5	43.2	49.8	71.3	98.5	107.6	115.0	120.2
Vessel bil. dol	13.1	16.9	24.6	26.5	40.6	56.8	63.4	66.3	67.3
Percent of total	63.9	61.6	57.0	53.3	56.9	57.7	58.9	57.7	56.0
Air bil. dol	(NA)	2.3	6.0	7.6	10.4	14.0	15.2	17.4	20.3
Shipping weight: Vessel bil. lb	248.5	343.5	480.5	460.8	549.2	529.3	538.5	566.8	548.1
Air bil. lb	(NA)	.5	.9	1.1	1.4	1.6	1.4	1.5	1.8
Imports:									
All methods of transport [1] bil. dol	14.7	21.4	40.0	55.6	69.5	101.0	96.9	121.8	146.8
Vessel bil. dol	11.1	14.9	24.8	33.7	42.8	67.2	63.5	81.2	100.9
Percent of total	75.8	69.9	62.0	60.6	61.6	66.5	65.5	66.7	68.6
Air bil. dol	(NA)	1.3	3.4	5.2	7.0	8.9	8.9	10.9	12.5
Shipping weight: Vessel bil. lb	398.1	511.5	598.4	701.9	875.2	893.4	855.3	1,035.0	1,208.7
Air bil. lb	(NA)	.2	.6	.9	1.0	1.1	1.1	1.2	1.3

NA Not available.   [1] Includes types other than vessel and air.

Source: U.S. Bureau of the Census, *Highlights of U.S. Export and Import Trade*, FT 990, monthly.

No. 1144. Federal Expenditures for Civil Functions of the Corps of Engineers, United States Army: 1950 to 1977

[In millions of dollars. Through 1976, for years ending June 30; beginning 1977, ending Sept. 30. Includes Puerto Rico and other U.S. outlying areas. Represents funds expended for maintenance and improvement of rivers and harbors, flood control, etc. See also *Historical Statistics, Colonial Times to 1970*, series Q 558]

YEAR	Total	Rivers and harbors	YEAR	Total	Rivers and harbors	YEAR	Total	Rivers and harbors
1950	635	190	1970	1,186	1,051	1974	1,936	1,859
1955	512	456	1971	1,474	1,419	1975	2,199	2,121
1960	869	801	1972	1,535	1,522	1976	2,266	2,080
1965	1,211	1,093	1973	1,737	1,614	1977	2,560	2,244

Source: U.S. Corps of Engineers, *Performance Measurement Systems*, annual.

No. 1145. Waterborne Commerce, Foreign and Domestic—Cargo Tonnage: 1950 to 1976

[In millions of short tons. Includes Puerto Rico and outlying areas. Import and export figures differ slightly from those shown in tables 1151 and 1152 due to minor differences in basic concepts which are explained in the source. See also *Historical Statistics, Colonial Times to 1970,* series Q 530–541]

CLASS	1950	1955	1960	1965	1970	1972	1973	1974	1975	1976
Net total	821	1,016	1,100	1,273	1,532	1,617	1,762	1,747	1,695	1,835
Domestic commerce [1]	651	745	761	829	951	987	994	983	946	979
Coastwise, between ports	183	196	209	202	238	243	237	233	232	236
Great Lakes, between ports	170	185	155	154	157	145	157	146	129	132
Between— Seaports, Great Lakes ports, and inland waterways ports	107	113	104	103	81	90	93	88	78	84
Ports and river ports [1]	191	250	291	370	472	507	503	511	504	524
Ports of U.S. outlying areas	1	2	1	1	2	2	4	4	3	3
Foreign commerce	169	271	339	444	581	630	767	764	749	856
Imports, through seaports	96	144	198	245	313	372	462	474	455	540
Exports, through seaports	44	95	105	142	206	197	239	239	237	251
Imports, Great Lakes ports	6	9	13	25	26	25	28	23	21	31
Exports, Great Lakes ports	24	23	23	32	36	35	38	28	35	35

[1] Represents traffic among ports and communities utilizing mainly inland waterways.

No. 1146. Freight Carried on Inland Waterways, by System: 1950 to 1976

[In billions of ton-miles. Excludes Alaska and Hawaii, except as noted. Includes waterways, canals, and connecting channels]

SYSTEM	1950	1955	1960	1965	1970	1972	1973	1974	1975	1976
Total	163.3	216.5	220.3	262.4	318.6	338.7	358.2	354.9	342.2	372.9
Atlantic coast waterways	6.5	27.0	28.6	27.8	28.6	29.2	34.2	35.4	31.8	32.1
Gulf coast waterways	1.2	13.9	16.9	21.8	28.6	32.5	32.3	33.5	30.8	34.3
Pacific coast waterways [1]	1.7	4.7	6.0	6.6	8.4	9.5	10.5	10.3	9.7	11.3
Mississippi River system [2]	33.6	52.0	69.3	96.6	138.5	158.5	155.3	168.3	170.7	189.5
Great Lakes System [3]	120.3	118.9	99.5	109.6	114.5	108.9	125.9	107.5	99.2	105.6

[1] Beginning 1960, includes Alaskan waterways.   [2] Comprises main channels and all tributaries of the Mississippi, Illinois, Missouri, and Ohio Rivers.   [3] Does not include traffic between foreign ports.

Source of tables 1145 and 1146: U.S. Corps of Engineers, 1950, *Annual Report of the Chief of Engineers,* Part 2; thereafter, *Waterborne Commerce of the United States,* annual.

No. 1147. U.S. Freight Carried on Great Lakes System, 1970 to 1976, and by Area, 1976

[In millions of ton-miles]

YEAR AND AREA	Total	DOMESTIC				FOREIGN	
		Lake-wise	Coast-wise	In-ternal	Local	Cana-dian	Over-seas
1970	114,475	79,400	57	581	92	23,842	10,503
1972	108,939	73,126	41	576	108	19,849	15,238
1973	125,914	83,765	69	565	114	26,226	15,174
1974	107,451	78,880	35	625	112	19,371	8,429
1975	99,171	68,517	31	588	90	20,657	9,288
Total, 1976	105,648	70,684	45	488	83	23,689	10,659
Lake Superior	24,876	22,152	–	–	(z)	1,727	996
St. Marys River	4,632	4,139	–	–	(z)	330	164
Lake Michigan, including Port of Chicago [1]	19,359	14,490	1	461	66	3,076	1,266
Lake Huron	22,425	17,005	–	4	5	3,863	1,548
St. Clair River, incl. channels in Lake St. Clair	5,195	3,954	–	1	–	864	377
Detroit River	2,801	2,025	2	(z)	(z)	520	254
Lake Erie, including upper Niagara River	15,516	6,872	18	6	11	6,069	2,540
Welland Canal	1,194	6	2	1	–	867	317
Lake Ontario, including lower Niagara River	5,843	33	13	11	(z)	3,905	1,880
St. Lawrence River, between International Boundary Line and Lake Ontario	3,808	9	9	4	–	2,468	1,317

– Represents zero.   Z Less than 500,000.   [1] Comprises Chicago Harbor, North Branch, South Branch, Sanitary Ship Canal, Calumet-Sag Channel, Lake Calumet, and Calumet Harbor and River.

Source: U.S. Corps of Engineers, *Waterborne Commerce of the United States,* annual.

No. 1148. Freight Carried on Mississippi River System: 1950 to 1976

[Net traffic. Comprises main channels and all tributaries of the Mississippi, Illinois, Missouri, and Ohio Rivers]

ITEM	1950	1955	1960	1965	1970	1972	1973	1974	1975	1976
Total_____mil. short tons__	138	194	234	302	391	420	420	443	453	498
Inland_____mil. short tons__	115	164	188	238	297	327	318	330	330	346
Coastwise_____mil. short tons__	14	16	22	28	44	34	28	28	30	26
Foreign: Imports___mil. short tons__	4	6	11	13	17	19	27	37	46	67
Exports___mil. short tons__	5	8	13	23	34	40	47	47	48	60
Total_____bil. ton-miles__	33.6	52.0	69.3	96.6	138.5	158.5	155.3	168.2	170.7	189.5
Inland_____bil. ton-miles__	30.3	47.4	62.4	87.4	125.9	144.4	139.8	150.9	151.3	164.8
Coastwise_____bil. ton-miles__	2.1	2.5	3.2	3.6	4.9	4.9	4.2	4.2	4.5	4.1
Foreign: Imports____bil. ton-miles__	.6	1.0	1.8	2.3	2.8	3.3	4.7	6.5	8.0	11.7
Exports____bil. ton-miles__	.6	1.1	1.9	3.3	4.9	5.8	6.6	6.6	6.9	8.8

Source: U.S. Corps of Engineers, 1950, *Annual Report of the Chief of Engineers*, Part 2; thereafter, *Waterborne Commerce of the United States*, annual.

No. 1149. Vessels Entered and Cleared in Foreign Trade—Net Registered Tonnage, by Flag of Carrier Vessel: 1960 to 1976

[In millions of net tons, except as indicated. Includes Puerto Rico and Virgin Islands. Seaports comprise all ports except Great Lakes ports. See also *Historical Statistics, Colonial Times to 1970*, series Q 507–517]

YEARLY AVERAGE OR YEAR	ALL PORTS					SEAPORTS					
	Number of vessels	Tonnage, all vessels				Tonnage, all vessels			Tonnage, with cargo		
		Total	U.S.	Percent U.S.	Foreign	Total	U.S.	Foreign	Total	U.S.	Foreign
ENTERED											
1961–1965_____	49,670	188	33	17.9	155	166	30	136	128	19	109
1966–1970_____	53,459	232	29	12.5	203	206	27	180	157	18	139
1971–1975_____	53,760	319	30	9.5	290	292	28	264	220	24	196
1960_____	51,375	163	30	18.5	133	146	27	119	119	20	99
1965_____	51,357	209	34	16.3	175	184	31	153	139	18	121
1970_____	53,293	254	26	10.3	228	227	24	202	171	19	152
1974_____	54,565	346	36	10.4	311	322	32	289	244	29	214
1975_____	51,443	355	32	9.9	323	326	30	297	240	26	215
1976_____	54,021	401	33	9.0	368	370	31	339	279	26	253
CLEARED											
1961–1965_____	48,098	189	34	17.9	155	168	30	137	96	20	76
1966–1970_____	52,415	232	30	12.8	202	206	27	179	122	23	99
1971–1975_____	53,039	324	31	9.9	293	296	29	267	149	21	127
1960_____	49,809	167	31	18.8	135	150	28	122	84	19	66
1965_____	49,779	209	34	16.3	175	184	31	152	103	21	82
1970_____	52,195	253	27	10.6	226	226	25	201	132	20	112
1974_____	54,005	352	37	10.5	315	327	33	294	160	23	137
1975_____	51,017	363	34	10.3	329	334	31	303	168	23	144
1976_____	53,528	404	34	9.2	370	374	32	342	176	24	152

No. 1150. Vessels Entered and Cleared in Foreign Trade—Net Registered Tonnage, by Customs Districts: 1965 to 1976

[In millions of net tons. Excludes domestic trade. Beginning 1970, Puerto Rico included in South Atlantic Coast, Hawaii in South Pacific Coast, and Alaska in North Pacific Coast]

CUSTOMS DISTRICT	VESSELS ENTERED					VESSELS CLEARED				
	1965	1970	1974	1975	1976	1965	1970	1974	1975	1976
North Atlantic Coast_____	88.6	102.1	119.4	114.2	116.9	89.7	99.9	118.1	116.6	119.3
With cargo_____	76.5	85.4	99.4	92.3	95.1	37.8	43.7	45.6	50.6	50.6
South Atlantic Coast_____	10.9	27.3	38.1	33.8	36.7	11.2	25.5	38.6	33.2	36.3
With cargo_____	8.7	21.2	27.0	24.0	26.1	5.3	11.4	13.8	12.7	14.0
Gulf Coast_____	37.6	36.1	73.6	89.1	115.9	36.3	42.8	82.0	96.1	119.9
With cargo_____	18.5	23.0	52.1	60.8	85.3	29.0	36.8	51.3	54.2	59.4
South Pacific Coast_____	21.5	27.5	38.3	38.4	43.4	21.8	27.7	40.1	41.2	44.0
With cargo_____	17.7	21.8	32.6	32.4	37.5	16.1	20.9	23.2	24.0	23.7
North Pacific Coast_____	13.0	24.9	36.5	36.8	40.6	12.8	24.3	34.8	33.8	39.9
With cargo_____	7.9	13.6	20.3	21.1	23.8	9.8	19.0	25.4	24.5	27.4
Great Lakes_____	25.3	27.5	25.0	28.8	31.0	25.2	27.2	25.3	29.4	31.4
With cargo_____	14.5	15.2	14.2	14.0	17.9	18.6	20.2	16.7	21.2	20.5
Virgin Islands_____	12.2	8.8	15.9	14.2	16.3	11.7	5.8	13.1	12.8	13.8
With cargo_____	9.7	5.9	11.5	9.8	11.3	5.6	.5	1.0	1.6	1.3

Source of tables 1149 and 1150: U.S. Bureau of the Census, through 1965, *Foreign Commerce and Navigation of the United States*; thereafter, *Vessel Entrances and Clearances*, FT 975, annual.

No. 1151. WATERBORNE IMPORTS AND EXPORTS—CARGO TONNAGE, BY FLAG OF CARRIER VESSEL: 1950 TO 1976

[In millions of short tons, except percent. Excludes commodities classified for security reasons as "Special Category" and exports by Dept. of Defense (grant-aid shipments), and merchandise shipped in transit through the U.S. Beginning 1955, imports exclude shipments under 2,000 lb. shipping weight. See also *Historical Statistics, Colonial Times to 1970*, series Q 524–529]

YEAR	Total trade	Percent by U.S. flag	IMPORTS BY FLAG OF CARRIER VESSEL				EXPORTS BY FLAG OF CARRIER VESSEL			
			Total	U.S.	Foreign	Percent U.S.	Total	U.S.	Foreign	Percent U.S.
TOTAL										
1950	159	39.3	97	42.3	54	43.7	63	20.4	42	32.5
1955	254	23.5	141	37.4	104	26.5	113	22.1	91	19.6
1960	323	12.3	199	19.6	179	9.9	124	20.1	104	16.3
1965	427	8.1	256	15.6	240	6.1	172	19.0	153	11.1
1970	539	5.6	299	15.4	284	5.1	240	14.9	225	6.3
1972	581	5.0	351	15.7	335	4.5	230	13.2	217	5.8
1973	715	6.4	441	30.1	410	6.9	274	16.0	258	6.0
1974	711	6.9	447	33.9	413	7.6	264	15.4	249	5.8
1975	697	5.4	428	23.0	405	5.4	269	14.5	255	5.4
1976	795	5.2	517	24.3	493	4.7	278	16.8	261	6.0
DRY CARGO										
1950	100	31.2	47	14.8	32	31.8	54	16.4	37	30.7
1955	169	23.2	68	19.9	49	29.0	101	19.8	81	19.6
1960	202	15.2	95	13.8	81	14.6	108	17.0	91	15.8
1965	274	9.3	123	10.4	113	8.4	151	15.2	135	10.0
1970	358	6.4	138	9.9	128	7.2	220	12.9	207	5.8
1972	351	5.1	140	8.0	132	5.7	211	10.0	201	4.7
1973	401	5.4	149	10.0	139	6.7	252	12.0	240	4.7
1974	401	6.5	158	13.3	145	8.2	243	12.8	230	5.3
1975	387	5.5	137	10.0	127	7.3	250	11.4	238	4.6
1976	405	6.0	149	11.2	137	7.5	256	13.1	243	5.1
TANKER CARGO										
1950	59	53.0	50	27.4	23	54.8	9	1.0	5	43.4
1955	85	23.5	73	17.6	55	24.2	12	2.4	10	19.8
1960	120	7.5	104	5.8	98	5.6	16	3.2	13	19.3
1965	153	5.9	132	5.2	127	3.9	21	3.8	17	18.0
1970	181	4.2	161	5.5	156	3.4	20	2.0	18	10.3
1972	230	4.8	211	7.8	203	3.7	19	3.3	16	17.1
1973	314	7.6	292	20.1	271	7.2	22	4.0	18	18.3
1974	311	7.4	289	20.5	268	7.3	22	2.6	19	11.8
1975	311	5.2	291	13.1	278	4.5	20	3.1	16	15.6
1976	386	4.3	369	13.1	356	3.5	21	3.7	18	17.3

Source: U.S. Bureau of the Census, *Foreign Commerce and Navigation of the United States; U.S. Waterborne Exports and General Imports*, FT 985, annual; and unpublished data.

No. 1152. WATERBORNE IMPORTS AND EXPORTS—CARGO TONNAGE AND VALUE, BY COASTAL DISTRICT: 1960 TO 1976

[Includes commodities classified for security reasons as "Special Category" and exports by Dept. of Defense (grant-aid shipments), and merchandise shipped in transit through the U.S.]

DISTRICT	CARGO TONNAGE (mil. sh. tons)							VALUE (bil. dol.)						
	1960	1965	1970	1973	1974	1975	1976	1960	1965	1970	1973	1974	1975	1976
Imports:														
Atlantic	135	164	219	290	269	232	237	7.8	9.7	15.0	25.2	38.5	34.7	40.8
Gulf	27	37	47	86	116	134	194	1.3	1.8	2.9	5.5	12.3	14.3	20.0
Pacific	23	27	31	61	63	64	76	1.6	2.4	5.5	10.2	15.9	15.2	20.8
Great Lakes	13	25	26	28	23	22	31	.5	1.0	1.3	1.8	2.0	1.7	2.3
Exports:														
Atlantic	45	55	79	70	82	80	79	7.0	8.4	11.9	16.2	25.3	28.7	30.4
Gulf	37	59	78	113	104	106	117	3.7	5.0	13.7	19.5	21.4	21.8	21.8
Pacific	19	26	48	54	52	49	54	1.8	2.4	4.1	7.1	9.5	10.0	11.2
Great Lakes	23	32	36	39	28	35	35	.7	1.2	1.4	2.6	2.2	2.8	3.0

Source: U.S. Bureau of the Census, *Foreign Commerce and Navigation of the United States* and *U.S. Waterborne Exports and General Imports*, FT 985, annual.

No. 1153. Traffic Through the Panama Canal: 1950 to 1977

[Through 1976, for years ending June 30, except as noted; beginning 1977, ending Sept. 30. See also *Historical Statistics, Colonial Times to 1970*, series Q 553–555]

YEAR	ALL TRAFFIC Transits (1,000)	Cargo (mil. long tons)	COMMERCIAL OCEAN TRAFFIC [1] Transits (1,000)	Net tons [2] (mil.)	Tolls (mil. dol.)	Cargo (mil. long tons)	1977 Nationality of vessel	Transits	Net tons [2] (mil.)	Tolls (mil. dol.)	Cargo (mil. lg. tons)
1950	5.9	30.3	5.4	28.0	24.4	28.9	U.S.	1,022	10.9	13.3	8.7
1955	8.3	41.5	8.0	38.6	33.8	40.6	Percent	8.6	8.2	8.1	7.0
1960	12.1	60.4	10.8	58.3	50.9	59.3	Germany, F. R.	582	5.7	7.0	3.8
1965	12.9	78.9	11.8	74.7	65.4	76.6	Great Britain	1,106	12.2	15.0	10.0
1970	15.5	118.9	13.7	108.1	94.7	114.3	Greece	1,163	14.1	17.2	17.5
1971	15.3	121.0	14.0	111.0	97.4	118.6	Japan	893	12.1	14.9	9.2
1972	15.2	111.1	13.8	113.0	98.8	109.2	Liberia	1,852	27.7	33.8	29.7
1973	15.1	127.6	13.8	126.2	111.0	126.1	Netherlands	229	2.0	2.5	1.5
1974	15.3	149.7	14.0	135.7	119.4	147.9	Norway	553	8.8	10.9	8.3
1975	14.7	140.6	13.6	135.1	141.9	140.1	Panama	1,118	7.9	9.5	7.9
1976	13.2	117.4	12.2	127.8	134.2	117.2	Sweden	260	3.6	4.5	2.5
1976, TQ [3]	3.3	30.9	3.0	33.7	35.3	30.9	All others	3,118	28.4	35.2	23.9
1977	13.1	123.2	11.9	133.4	163.8	123.0					

[1] Comprises oceangoing toll-paying vessels and foreign naval vessels of 300 net tons and over (Panama Canal measurement) for vessels rated on net tonnage, or 500 tons displacement and over for vessels rated on displacement tonnage.   [2] Panama Canal net.   [3] Transition quarter, July–Sept.

Source: Panama Canal Company, Balboa Heights, Canal Zone, *Annual Report.*

No. 1154. U.S. Merchant Marine Vessels: 1950 to 1977

[Documented vessels of 5 net tons or more as of Jan. 1. Includes Puerto Rico, Guam, and Virgin Islands. Includes barges and non-self-propelled dredges. See also *Historical Statistics, Colonial Times to 1970*, series Q 417–418]

YEAR	Number	Gross tons (1,000)	YEAR	Number	Gross tons (1,000)	YEAR	Number	Gross tons (1,000)	YEAR	Number	Gross tons (1,000)
1950	36,083	31,215	1967	48,700	27,251	1971	50,750	27,400	1975	60,940	30,399
1955	39,242	29,958	1968	49,545	27,842	1972	52,355	27,057	1976	63,754	31,893
1960	43,088	28,581	1969	49,991	28,591	1973	54,436	27,406	1977	65,971	33,152
1965	45,579	26,516	1970	49,993	28,613	1974	57,928	29,375			

Source: U.S. Bureau of Customs and U.S. Coast Guard, unpublished data.

No. 1155. Merchant Vessels Completed by U.S. Shipyards: 1950 to 1977

[Vessels of 1,000 gross tons and over for domestic use, except 1950 and 1955, 2,000 gross tons and over. See also *Historical Statistics, Colonial Times to 1970*, series Q 438–448]

ITEM	1950	1955	1960	1965	1970	1972	1973	1974	1975	1976	1977
Merchant vessels, number	26	9	26	13	13	13	24	20	15	16	17
Gross tons 1,000	405	119	410	173	342	357	734	697	452	615	884
Cargo, number	3	7	15	11	6	7	18	11	3	4	2
Gross tons 1,000	27	84	134	121	120	151	419	314	65	57	25
Deadweight tons 1,000	44	95	163	154	134	187	450	402	71	76	37
Tanker, number	23	2	11	2	7	6	6	9	12	12	15
Gross tons 1,000	378	35	276	52	222	206	315	383	387	558	859
Deadweight tons 1,000	609	55	456	92	427	415	653	759	742	1,176	1,585

Source: Through 1960, American Bureau of Shipping, New York, N.Y., annually in *The Bulletin·* thereafter, U.S. Maritime Administration, *New Ship Construction*, annual.

No. 1156. Employees in Government and Private Shipyards: 1950 to 1977

[In thousands. Prior to 1960, excludes Alaska and Hawaii. Annual average employment in establishments primarily engaged in building and repairing all types of ships, barges, canal boats, and lighters of 5 gross tons and over, whether propelled by sail or motor power or towed by other craft]

YEAR	Total	Private yards [1]	Navy yards	YEAR	Total	Private yards [1]	Navy yards	YEAR	Total	Private yards [1]	Navy yards
1950	146	72	[2] 74	1970	216	133	83	1974	218	154	64
1955	208	101	[2] 107	1971	206	131	76	1975	218	153	65
1960	208	112	96	1972	208	138	70	1976	232	167	65
1965	213	129	84	1973	208	144	64	1977	244	176	68

[1] Includes all full- and part-time employees who worked during or received pay for any part of the pay period which includes the 12th of the month.   [2] Includes Curtis Bay (Md.) Coast Guard yard.

Source: U.S. Bureau of Labor Statistics, unpublished data. (Current data for private yards published monthly in *Employment and Earnings*.)

No. 1157. United States Flag Merchant Vessels, Steam and Motor: 1965 to 1977

[Deadweight tonnage in thousands. As of June 30 except, beginning 1977, as of Sept. 30. Covers oceangoing vessels of 1,000 gross tons and over engaged in foreign and domestic trade, and inactive vessels. Excludes special types such as tugs, barges, cable ships, fishing trawlers, and vessels employed on Great Lakes. Totals include combination passenger and cargo vessels, not shown separately. See also Historical Statistics, Colonial Times to 1970, series Q 487–502]

YEAR AND TYPE OF VESSEL	ALL VESSELS Number	ALL VESSELS Tons	ACTIVE: Total Number	ACTIVE: Total Tons	Foreign trade Number	Foreign trade Tons	Domestic trade Total Number	Domestic trade Total Tons	Coastwise Number	Coastwise Tons	Intercoastal Number	Intercoastal Tons	Noncontiguous Number	Noncontiguous Tons	Special service Number	Special service Tons	Temporarily inactive Number	Temporarily inactive Tons	Reserve fleet Number	Reserve fleet Tons
1965, total	2,425	28,755	779	11,821	512	6,877	217	3,953	118	2,667	27	417	72	869	50	993	200	3,104	1,446	13,830
Cargo	1,840	19,561	561	6,679	440	5,249	92	1,056	13	142	22	291	57	623	29	375	105	1,245	1,174	11,638
Tanker	349	7,636	199	4,985	54	1,475	124	2,892	105	2,525	5	126	14	242	21	618	82	1,735	68	916
1970, total	1,780	23,280	819	14,073	386	5,775	245	5,368	142	3,599	25	417	78	1,352	188	2,930	63	1,163	898	8,045
Cargo	1,302	14,298	557	7,173	344	4,605	68	837	10	116	17	252	41	482	145	1,731	33	399	712	6,726
Tanker	301	7,835	249	6,783	32	1,076	175	4,518	132	3,483	8	165	35	870	42	1,189	22	691	30	361
1973, total	1,051	17,297	595	12,847	312	6,618	196	4,725	113	3,026	17	281	66	1,418	87	1,504	49	916	407	3,534
Cargo	658	8,320	357	5,335	237	3,749	59	796	8	113	13	190	38	493	61	790	32	468	269	2,517
Tanker	273	8,220	232	7,462	71	2,832	135	3,916	105	2,913	4	91	26	912	26	714	13	409	28	349
1974, total	965	17,334	588	13,619	305	6,909	202	5,169	149	4,236	1	25	52	908	81	1,541	24	529	353	3,186
Cargo	594	7,981	345	5,553	241	4,082	53	800	20	341	–	–	33	459	51	671	11	137	238	2,291
Tanker	275	8,739	238	8,025	60	2,793	148	4,362	129	3,895	1	25	18	442	30	870	10	367	27	347
1975, total	891	17,608	532	13,105	267	6,204	205	5,687	153	4,653	11	271	41	763	60	1,214	69	1,714	290	2,789
Cargo	548	7,762	305	5,142	223	3,858	48	825	17	354	3	54	28	417	34	459	37	532	206	2,088
Tanker	279	9,433	221	7,913	39	2,303	156	4,855	136	4,299	8	217	12	339	26	755	31	1,173	27	347
1976, total	843	17,989	548	14,088	294	7,770	194	5,136	32	2,996	28	811	134	1,329	60	1,182	45	1,544	250	2,357
Cargo	521	7,519	316	5,357	230	4,140	50	731	10	147	4	61	36	523	36	486	17	254	188	1,908
Tanker	263	10,086	226	8,681	59	3,586	143	4,399	22	2,849	24	750	97	800	24	696	27	1,280	10	125
1977, total	841	19,468	564	15,542	281	6,817	214	7,442	125	3,931	15	401	74	3,110	69	1,283	36	1,568	241	2,358
Cargo	504	7,446	314	5,394	235	4,292	43	640	8	137	–	–	35	503	36	462	12	174	178	1,878
Tanker	275	11,618	239	10,060	41	2,481	170	6,796	117	3,794	15	401	38	2,601	28	783	24	1,394	12	164

– Represents zero.

Source: U.S. Maritime Administration, *Employment Report of the United States Flag Merchant Fleet Ocean-going Vessels 1,000 Gross Tons and Over*, annual.

No. 1158. SHIPBUILDING IN PRIVATE SHIPYARDS—SUMMARY: 1970 TO 1977

[Steel self-propelled vessels of 1,000 tons or over. See also *Historical Statistics, Colonial Times to 1970*, series Q 449–458]

TYPE OF VESSEL AND STATUS OF CONSTRUCTION	1970		1974		1975		1976		1977	
	Number	Tons (1,000)	Number	Tons (1,000)	Number	Tons (1,000)	Number	Tons (1,000)	Number	Tons (1,000)
Commercial (gross tons):										
Under construction, Jan. 1	49	1,388	97	4,010	96	5,064	79	4,674	72	4,238
Launched	11	322	27	680	18	759	25	1,142	19	988
Delivered	13	370	24	684	19	469	22	755	25	1,036
Under construction, Dec. 31	49	1,609	96	5,064	79	4,674	72	4,238	60	3,467
Naval (light displacement tons):										
Under construction, Jan. 1	108	621	56	526	63	663	76	690	88	712
Launched	23	117	10	79	8	110	9	48	12	91
Delivered	32	166	9	38	3	79	8	70	12	148
Under construction, Dec. 31	82	588	63	659	76	689	88	712	90	639

No. 1159. VESSELS REPAIRED OR CONVERTED IN PRIVATE SHIPYARDS: 1960 TO 1977

[See also *Historical Statistics, Colonial Times to 1970*, series Q 467–472]

ITEM	1960	1965	1970	1972	1973	1974	1975	1976	1977, prel.
All vessels: Volume _____mil. dol_	396	718	790	871	916	1,246	1,286	[1]1,430	[1]1,660
Commercial ships [2]_____mil. dol_	274	383	431	484	523	713	713	[1]740	[1]810
Naval ships_____mil. dol_	122	335	359	387	393	533	533	[1]690	[1]850
Over 1,000 gross tons: Yards reporting_	93	93	75	68	72	65	72	70	70
Commercial vessels_____1,000_	12.8	12.7	12.4	8.4	8.8	8.5	7.9	8.0	8.2

[1] Estimated.　[2] Includes Military Sealift Command work.

Source of tables 1158 and 1159: Shipbuilders Council of America, Washington, D.C., *Annual Report*, and unpublished data.

No. 1160. EMPLOYMENT ON U.S. FLAG MERCHANT VESSELS, 1950 TO 1977, AND BASIC MONTHLY WAGE SCALE FOR ABLEBODIED SEAMEN, 1970 TO 1978

[Employment in thousands; as of June 30, except as noted. See also *Historical Statistics, Colonial Times to 1970*, series Q 414–416]

YEAR	Employment [1]	YEAR	Employment [1]	YEAR AND MONTH	East coast wage rate [4]	West coast wage rate [4]	YEAR AND MONTH	East coast wage rate [4]	West coast wage rate [4]
1950___	56.6	1973__	25.2	1970, Jan__	$470	$652	1975, Jan__	$612	$900
1955___	57.5	1974__	24.8	1971, Jan__	499	704	1976, Jan__	688	1,001
1960___	49.2	1975__	20.5	1972, Jan__	528	756	1977, Jan__	737	1,072
1965___	[2]39.1	1976__	21.1	1973, Jan__	555	806	1978, Jan__	804	1,172
1970___	37.6	1977 [3]	20.9	1974, Jan__	583	856			

[1] Estimates of personnel employed on U.S. merchant ships, 1,000 gross tons and over. Excludes vessels on inland waterways, Great Lakes, and those owned by, or operated for, the U.S. Army and Navy, and special types such as cable ships, tugs, etc.　[2] Decrease due to seafaring strike.　[3] As of Sept. 30.　[4] Basic wage, over and above subsistence (board and room), paid to seamen having qualifying experience and employed on U.S. flag merchant vessels. Excludes overtime and fringe pay benefits. Seamen on both coasts receive extra pay for Saturdays and Sundays at sea; west coast incorporates this extra pay into base wages but east coast does not.

Source: U.S. Maritime Administration, 1950–1965, *Seafaring Wage Rates;* thereafter, unpublished data.

No. 1161. WORLDWIDE TANKER CASUALTIES, 1973 TO 1978, AND BY FLAG, 1977

[Covers tankers, ore/oil carriers, and bulk/oil vessels of 6,000 deadweight tons and over. Based on data from "Lloyd's List" published by Lloyd's of London. "Casualties" include weather damage, strandings, collisions and other contact, fires and explosions, machinery damage, and other mishaps]

YEAR	PROPERTY LOSS		PERSONNEL LOSS		OIL SPILLS		FLAG OF REGISTRY	VESSELS (Jan. 1, 1977)		CASUALTIES, 1977	
	Partial and total losses [1]	Total losses [1]	Deaths	Injuries	Number	Amount (1,000 tons)		Total	Percent of total	Total	Percent of total
1973_____	1,273	12	70	159	36	84.5	Total, 66 nations_	4,229	100.0	834	100.0
1974_____	1,168	14	94	62	48	67.1	American_____	294	7.0	73	8.8
1975_____	906	22	90	14	45	188.0	British_____	354	8.4	122	14.6
1976_____	819	20	226	87	29	204.2	Greek_____	326	7.7	130	15.6
1977_____	834	20	113	102	49	213.1	Japanese_____	288	6.8	16	1.9
1978, 1st qtr_____	161	6	9	3	7	240.7	Liberian_____	1,028	24.3	276	33.1
							Norwegian____	306	7.2	28	3.4
							Panamanian___	178	4.2	33	4.0
							Russian_____	226	5.3	7	.8
							Other nations_	1,229	29.1	149	17.9

[1] Includes actual and constructive (cost to repair damage exceeds value of vessel) total losses.

Source: Tanker Advisory Center, Inc., New York, N.Y., "Worldwide Tanker Casualty Returns."

No. 1162. Merchant Vessels—World and United States: 1960 to 1977

[Vessels of 100 gross tons and over. Excludes sailing ships, nonpropelled craft, and all ships built of wood. See also *Historical Statistics, Colonial Times to 1970*, series Q 473–480]

YEAR	WORLD: COMPLETED		WORLD: OWNED		U.S.: COMPLETED		U.S.: OWNED	
	Number	Gross tons (1,000)	Number	Gross tons (1,000)	Number	Gross tons (1,000)	Number	Gross tons (1,000)
1960	2,005	8,382	34,056	129,339	49	379	3,845	24,781
1965	2,202	11,763	39,628	159,979	116	218	3,224	21,478
1970	2,814	20,980	50,472	227,138	156	375	2,822	18,423
1972	2,776	26,749	55,251	267,965	292	482	3,305	14,951
1973	2,999	30,409	57,347	289,532	277	964	3,539	14,818
1974	2,949	33,541	58,957	310,934	233	733	3,566	14,337
1975	2,730	34,202	61,501	341,780	127	476	3,801	14,491
1976	2,723	33,922	63,611	371,612	143	815	4,035	14,810
1977	2,796	27,532	65,775	393,311	129	1,012	4,152	15,201

Source: Lloyd's Register of Shipping, London, England, *Statistical Tables*, annual; and *Annual Summary of Merchant Ships Completed in the World*.

No. 1163. Merchant Fleets of the World: 1970 to 1977

[Vessels of 1,000 gross tons and over. As of Dec. 31, except 1977 as of June 30. Specified countries have 100 or more ships]

YEAR AND COUNTRY OF REGISTRY, 1977	TOTAL		PASSENGER/ CARGO COMB.		FREIGHTERS		BULK CARRIERS [1]		TANKERS	
	Number	Average age (yr.)	Number	Average age (yr.)	Number	Average age (yr.)	Number	Average age (yr.)	Number	Average age (yr.)
1970, world total	19,980	13	895	21	11,899	13	2,954	8	4,232	11
United States	1,579	22	171	25	1,076	23	38	25	294	19
Foreign	18,401	12	724	20	10,823	13	2,916	8	3,938	10
1975, world total	22,872	12	714	21	12,575	13	4,272	9	5,311	11
United States	857	21	60	29	511	21	19	25	267	19
Foreign	22,015	12	654	21	12,064	13	4,253	9	5,044	11
1977, world total	23,902	13	696	22	13,040	14	4,752	9	5,414	11
United States	846	22	62	31	495	22	18	26	271	19
Privately-owned	577	17	6	17	296	16	18	26	257	18
Government-owned	269	32	56	32	199	32	–	–	14	34
Foreign	23,056	12	634	21	12,545	13	4,734	9	5,143	11
Argentina	162	21	7	25	92	18	15	17	48	26
Brazil	272	12	6	26	169	12	38	11	59	12
Bulgaria	110	14	4	11	59	14	28	12	19	14
China (People's Rep.)	381	17	24	30	249	16	44	16	64	14
China (Taiwan)	149	14	8	23	95	14	32	11	14	15
Cyprus	533	22	6	32	450	22	40	20	37	19
Denmark	374	7	8	13	249	8	45	6	72	7
Finland	195	11	7	16	105	11	31	8	52	12
France	461	10	6	15	239	11	60	9	156	9
German Dem. Rep.	161	13	4	25	128	12	18	16	11	16
Germany, Fed. Rep.	652	8	5	18	478	8	80	7	89	6
Greece	1,969	16	56	29	1,005	18	577	10	331	16
India	343	12	11	17	205	14	94	8	33	6
Indonesia	189	19	29	23	129	19	10	11	21	16
Italy	627	16	50	23	193	18	156	13	228	16
Japan	2,097	8	28	14	924	9	599	7	546	7
Korea (South)	197	13	–	–	128	14	34	9	35	13
Liberia	2,722	10	16	23	639	11	1,042	9	1,025	10
Netherlands	472	11	7	16	350	11	37	9	78	13
Norway	1,003	9	31	14	304	11	326	8	342	8
Panama	1,699	15	41	25	1,157	15	270	13	231	15
Philippines	158	18	22	16	97	20	10	6	29	20
Poland	303	10	4	13	205	11	79	8	15	4
Romania	121	7	2	20	84	8	28	5	7	7
Singapore	485	14	20	25	318	15	52	9	95	14
Somalia	221	19	2	28	182	20	24	15	13	17
Spain	481	11	29	24	262	11	64	7	126	10
Sweden	335	9	6	6	146	11	92	8	91	7
Turkey	128	17	15	31	71	17	14	7	28	13
United Kingdom	1,526	10	22	17	723	11	355	8	426	9
U.S.S.R.	2,439	12	91	19	1,717	12	163	14	468	13
Yugoslavia	245	14	10	17	175	15	45	8	15	13
All others	1,846	14	57	22	1,218	15	232	11	339	11

– Represents zero.   [1] Includes bulk/oil, ore/oil, and ore/bulk/oil carriers.

Source: U.S. Maritime Administration, *A Statistical Analysis of the World's Merchant Fleets*, annual.

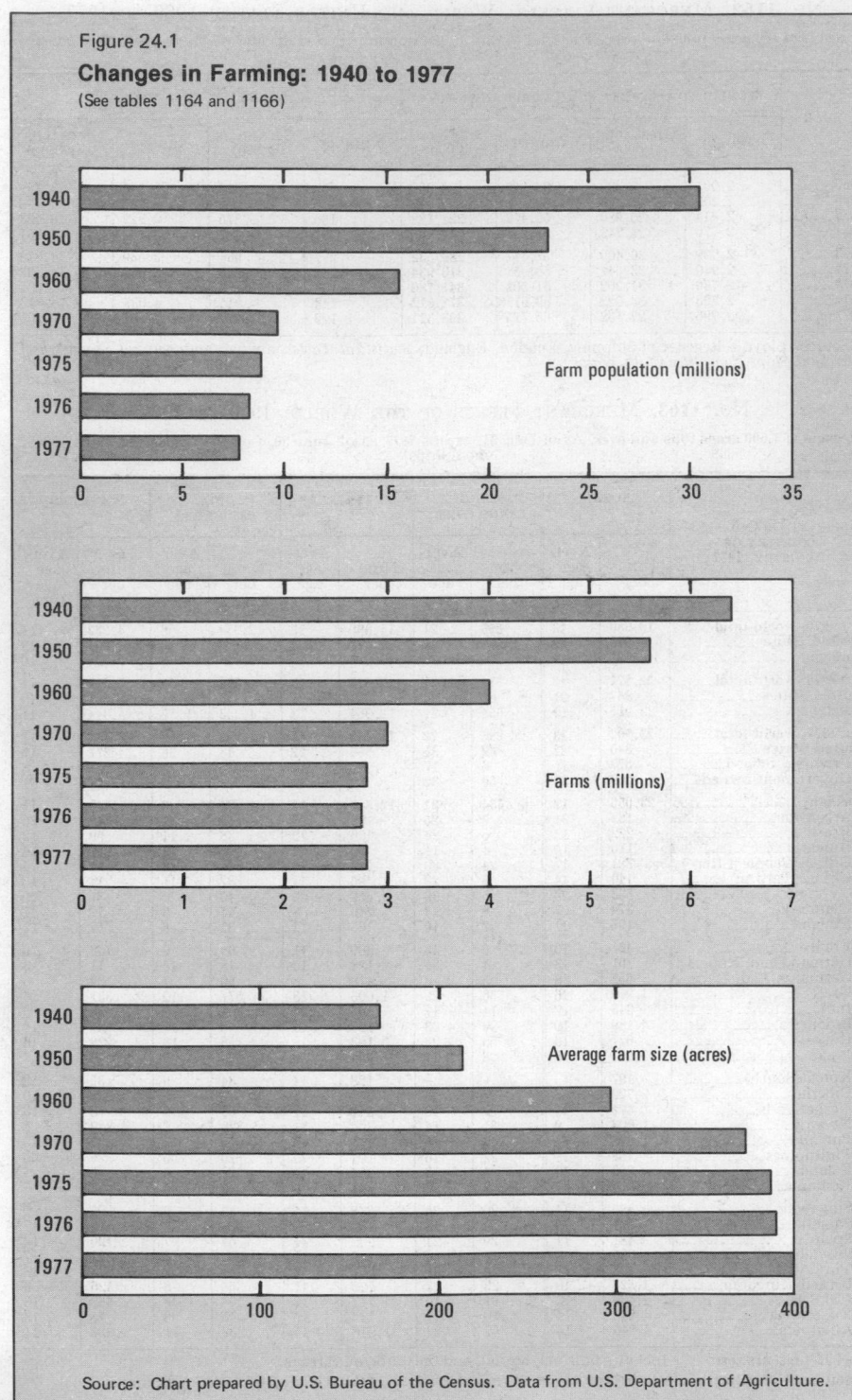

Figure 24.1

Changes in Farming: 1940 to 1977

(See tables 1164 and 1166)

Farm population (millions)

Farms (millions)

Average farm size (acres)

Source: Chart prepared by U.S. Bureau of the Census. Data from U.S. Department of Agriculture.

Section 24
Agriculture

This section presents statistics on farms and farm population; land use and conservation; farm income, expenditures, and debt; farmer cooperatives; farm output and marketings; foreign trade in agricultural products; specific crops; and livestock, poultry, and their products.

The principal sources of these data are the reports issued by the U.S. Bureau of the Census and the Economics, Statistics, and Cooperatives Service (ESCS) of the U.S. Department of Agriculture. The Bureau of the Census has taken a census of agriculture every 10 years from 1840 to 1920, and every 5 years from 1924 to 1974 (for years ending in 4 and 9). The 1974 Census of Agriculture is the most recent census for which reports are presently available; preliminary reports of the 1978 census are scheduled to become available in late 1979. Censuses of irrigation organizations and drainage augment the census of agriculture every 10 years (until 1978, for years ending in 9). The ESCS issues several annual reports including, *Agricultural Statistics, Crop Production, Crop Values, Balance Sheet of the Farming Sector, Changes in Farm Production and Efficiency,* and *Farm Income Statistics. Situation* reports issued periodically by the ESCS presents current data on a variety of crops. Sources of current data on agricultural exports and imports include *Foreign Agricultural Trade of the United States,* published by the ESCS, and the reports of the Bureau of the Census, particularly Report FT 135, *U.S. General Imports—Schedule A—Commodity by Country,* and Report FT 410, *U.S. Exports—Schedule B—Commodity by Country.* In addition, the ESCS provides agricultural employment estimates and wage rates in the monthly *Farm Labor* and the annual *The Hired Farm Working Force.* Also reported are days employed, earnings from farm and nonfarm work, personal characteristics of hired farm workers, and other pertinent information.

Annual agricultural statistics have been issued by the Department of Agriculture for over 100 years. The 44 field offices of the ESCS collect data on crops, livestock and livestock products, agricultural prices, farm employment, and other related subjects from over 1.1 million voluntary reporters, mostly farmers, who report for their own and nearby farms on some 150 crops and 50 livestock items, and scores of other items pertaining to agricultural production and farm family living. State estimates and other information are sent to the Crop Reporting Board of the ESCS, which issues reports containing State and national data.

Farms and farmland.—Over a period of time, the Bureau of the Census has used varying definitions of a farm. For the 1974 Census of Agriculture, a farm was newly defined to include all land on which agricultural operations were conducted under the day-to-day control of an individual management and from which $1,000 or more of agricultural products were, or potentially could be, sold during the census year. Control may have been exercised through ownership or management, or through a lease, rental, or cropping arrangement. The 1974 volume I census reports provide a more detailed explanation of the revised definition along with measures of the effect of the change in definition for each State and county. The effect of the change in farm definition must be taken into consideration when comparing coverage estimates for all farms in the 1974 census with those in previous censuses since a higher proportion of small farms is missed. In the 1959, 1964, and 1969 censuses, places of less than 10 acres were counted as farms if estimated sales of agricultural products for the year amounted to at least $250, and places of 10 or more acres if such sales amounted to at least $50. In the 1950 and 1954 censuses, places of 3 or more acres were counted as farms if the annual value of agricultural products, exclusive of home-garden products, amounted to $150 or more;

places of less than 3 acres were counted as farms only if the annual sales amounted to $150 or more. For definitions used in earlier censuses, see *U.S. Census of Agriculture*: *1964*, vol. II, Introduction.

In general, data for 1974 and earlier censuses are comparable only for farms with total value of sales of $2,500 or more. However, even for those farms, the difference in the timing of the censuses and a change in data collection procedures from personal interview to mail enumeration, beginning with the 1969 census, affect comparability.

Currently included as farms are such diverse agricultural enterprises as nurseries, greenhouses, sod farms, mushroom operations, cranberry bogs, feedlots, fish farms, and hatcheries; excluded are business enterprises exclusively engaged in forest production and in production of fish, oysters, fowl, etc. from the ocean, game preserves, parks, and the like, when not grown in captivity. In the case of landowners who had one or more tenants or renters, the land operated by each was counted as a separate farm.

Farmland refers to all land under the control of a farm operator and considered as part of his farm, including land not actually under cultivation or not used for pasture or grazing. Rent-free land was included as part of the farm only if the operator had sole use of it. Land used for pasture or grazing on a per head basis that was neither owned nor leased by the farm operator is not included except for grazing lands controlled by grazing associations leased on a per acre basis.

Preliminary estimates based on the coverage evaluation survey for the 1974 census indicate about 96 percent of the farms with a value of products sold of $2,500 or more were included in the census. Approximately 74 percent of the farms with value of sales less than $2,500 were included. The preliminary estimates for total farms indicate about 90 percent of all farms and 97 percent of the value of farm products sold were included in the census. The 1969 census was estimated to have included 97 percent of the farms with a value of products sold of $2,500 or more and 97 percent of the value of products sold from this group of farms.

Farm population.—Farm population consists of all persons living on farms in rural areas. Farm population data shown in this section, however, are based on the definition of a farm used for the 1969 Census of Agriculture (see p. 683).

Irrigation.—Irrigated land is defined by the Bureau of the Census as the acreage in farms to which water is artificially applied during the census year. Beginning with 1920, irrigated land has included cropland, pasture, and any other farm land irrigated. In addition to collecting information on irrigation from individual farms in the census of agriculture, the Bureau of the Census collects data on the operation of irrigation water supply organizations at 10-year intervals. In 1974, irrigation information was collected from farms.

Farm income.—Cash income comprises cash receipts from farm marketings and Federal payments made directly to farmers for farm related activities. Farm marketings represent agricultural products sold by farmers multiplied by prices received per unit of production at the local market. Gross farm income includes cash income, value of farm products consumed in farm homes, rental value of farm homes, and other farm related income.

Information on prices received for farm products is obtained by the Economics, Statistics, and Cooperatives Crop Reporting Board from over 4,200 voluntary reporters, including farmers, local merchants, and handlers of agricultural products. Season average prices received by farmers are calculated by weighting midmonth prices by monthly sales during the crop marketing season, beginning with the first month in which a particular crop harvest begins.

Crops.—Estimates of crop acreage and production by the ESCS are based on current sample survey data obtained from individual reporters and objective yield counts which are supplemented by State assessors' enumerations of agricultural information, reports of carlot shipments, warehouse receipts, personal field observations by field statisticians, and reports from other sources. Cotton acreage and production are based on sample survey data and on ginning information gathered by the Bureau of the Census. Following receipt of the U.S. census of agriculture information, the estimates made since the previous census are reviewed on the basis of historical and current data available from governmental or commercial sources. If necessary, revisions are made in the estimates based on this review.

Livestock.—Each census of agriculture from 1840 through 1900 was taken as of June 1. The various censuses since then have been taken as of January, April, or the fall, as specified in the published results. For the 1969 and 1974 censuses, inventories were as of December 31 and purchases, production, and sales data were for the calendar year. Comparison of livestock inventories from census to census is seriously affected by changes in date of enumeration. Volume II of *U.S. Census of Agriculture: 1964* gives a complete history of the enumeration of livestock and analyzes comparability from census to census.

Annual inventory numbers of livestock and estimates of livestock, dairy, and poultry production prepared by the Department of Agriculture are based on information from farmers and ranchers obtained by probability survey sampling methods.

Statistical Reliability.—For a discussion of statistical collection and estimation, sampling procedures, and measures of statistical reliability pertaining to Census Bureau and Department of Agriculture data, see Appendix III.

Historical statistics.—Tabular headnotes provide cross-references, where applicable, to *Historical Statistics of the United States, Colonial Times to 1970*. See Appendix I.

No. 1164. FARM POPULATION AND EMPLOYMENT. 1930 TO 1977

[In thousands, except percent. Prior to 1959, excludes Alaska and 1960, Hawaii. Minus sign (−) denotes decrease. For definition of farm population, see text, p. 684. See also *Historical Statistics, Colonial Times to 1970*, series C 76–78 and K 1–3 and K 174]

| YEAR | FARM POPULATION [1] | | NET CHANGE SINCE PRECEDING APRIL | | Farm employ-ment [4] | YEAR | FARM POPULATION [1] | | NET CHANGE SINCE PRECEDING APRIL | | Farm employ-ment [4] |
	Total	Percent of total popu-lation [2]	Births and deaths	Migra-tion [3]			Total	Percent of total popu-lation [2]	Births and deaths	Migra-tion [3]	
1930	30,529	24.9	426	−477	12,497	1962	14,313	7.7	156	−646	6,700
1935	32,161	25.3	383	−527	12,733	1963	13,367	7.1	140	−1,086	6,518
1940	30,547	23.2	410	−703	10,979	1964	12,954	6.8	121	−533	6,110
1945	24,420	17.5	353	−748	10,000	1965	12,363	6.4	112	−703	5,610
1950	23,048	15.3	392	−1,537	9,926	1966	11,595	5.9	90	−858	5,214
1951	21,890	14.2	373	−1,531	9,546	1967	10,875	5.5	73	−793	4,903
1952	21,748	13.9	341	−483	9,149	1968	10,454	5.3	60	−481	4,749
1953	19,874	12.5	328	−2,201	8,864	1969	10,307	5.1	51	−198	4,596
1954	19,019	11.8	296	−1,151	8,651	1970	9,712	4.8	47	−642	4,523
1955	19,078	11.6	268	−210	8,381	1971	9,425	4.6	43	−330	4,436
1956	18,712	11.2	261	−627	7,852	1972	9,610	4.6	29	156	4,373
1957	17,656	10.4	239	−1,295	7,600	1973	9,472	4.5	26	−164	4,337
1958	17,128	9.9	220	−748	7,503	1974	9,264	4.4	25	−233	4,389
1959	16,592	9.4	203	−740	7,342	1975	8,864	4.2	25	−425	4,342
1960	15,635	8.7	184	−1,142	7,057	1976	8,253	3.8	24	−635	4,374
1961	14,803	8.1	168	−1,000	6,919	1977	7,806	3.6	27	−474	4,152

[1] April, 1 except beginning 1960, April-centered annual averages. [2] Includes Armed Forces abroad. [3] Beginning 1940, includes inductions and enlistments into Armed Forces, and persons returning from Armed Forces. For all years, includes persons who did not move but who were in and out of the farm population because agricultural operations began or ceased, respectively, on the place where they were living. [4] Includes farm operators and family members doing farm work without wages.

Source: U.S. Dept. of Agriculture, Economics, Statistics, and Cooperatives Service, *Farm Population, Estimates for 1910–70, Farm Population Estimates*, annual, and *Farm Labor*, quarterly.

No. 1165. FARM POPULATION, BY CHARACTERISTICS: 1960 TO 1977

[1960, as of April; 1970 and 1977, April-centered annual averages. For definition of farm population, see text, p. 684]

| CHARACTERISTIC | FARM POPULATION (1,000) | | | | | PERCENT DISTRIBUTION | | | | |
| | 1960 | 1970 | 1977 | | | 1960 | 1970 | 1977 | | |
			Total	Male	Female			Total	Male	Female
Total	15,669	9,712	7,806	4,072	3,734	100.0	100.0	100.0	100.0	100.0
White	13,092	8,775	7,349	3,850	3,497	83.6	90.4	94.1	94.5	93.7
Black and other races	2,577	938	457	222	237	16.4	9.7	5.9	5.5	6.3
Under 14 years of age	4,995	2,490	1,555	808	747	31.9	25.6	19.9	19.8	20.0
14 years of age and over	10,674	7,222	6,251	3,264	2,987	68.1	74.4	80.1	80.2	80.0
14–19 years	1,868	1,316	1,076	590	486	11.9	13.6	13.8	14.5	13.0
20–24 years	763	502	517	297	220	4.9	5.2	6.6	7.3	5.9
25–34 years	1,461	770	730	374	355	9.3	7.9	9.4	9.2	9.5
35–44 years	1,803	1,061	891	446	445	11.5	10.9	11.4	11.0	11.9
45–64 years	3,453	2,452	2,086	1,074	1,012	22.0	25.2	26.7	26.4	27.1
65 years and over	1,326	1,122	950	483	467	8.5	11.6	12.2	11.9	12.5
In labor force [1]	6,266	4,293	3,838	2,606	1,232	58.7	59.4	61.4	79.8	41.2
Employed, agriculture	4,025	2,333	1,880	1,527	353	37.7	32.3	30.1	46.8	11.8
Percent of total	64.2	54.3	49.0	58.6	28.7	(X)	(X)	(X)	(X)	(X)
Self-employed	2,405	1,411	1,147	1,067	79	22.7	19.5	18.3	32.7	2.6
Wage and salary workers	782	395	377	321	55	7.3	5.5	6.0	9.8	1.8
Unpaid family workers	838	526	356	139	218	7.9	7.3	5.7	4.3	7.3
Employed, nonagriculture	2,064	1,878	1,856	1,035	821	19.3	26.0	29.7	31.7	27.5
Self-employed	(NA)	159	167	118	49	(NA)	2.2	2.7	3.6	1.6
Wage and salary workers	(NA)	1,698	1,672	915	757	(NA)	23.5	26.7	28.0	25.3
Unpaid family workers	(NA)	21	17	1	15	(NA)	.3	.3	–	.5
Unemployed	177	82	102	44	58	1.7	1.1	1.6	1.3	1.9
Not in labor force [1]	4,408	2,929	2,413	658	1,755	41.3	40.6	38.6	20.2	58.8

– Represents zero.   NA Not available.   X Not applicable.   [1] 14 years old and over.

Source: U.S. Bureau of the Census, *Current Population Reports*, series P-27, Nos. 42 and 51.

No. 1166. FARMS—NUMBER AND ACREAGE: 1930 TO 1978

[Estimated. Prior to 1959, excludes Alaska and Hawaii. For definition of farms and farmland, see text, pp. 683 and 684. Data for census years (indicated by italics) have been adjusted for underenumeration and for changes in definition of a farm; data for other years are based on trend and on indications of change in acreage and live-stock surveys. Minus sign (−) denotes decrease. See also *Historical Statistics, Colonial Times to 1970*, series K 4–7]

| YEAR | FARMS | | LAND IN FARMS | | YEAR | FARMS | | LAND IN FARMS | |
	Number (1,000)	Annual change [1] (1,000)	Total (mil. acres)	Average per farm (acres)		Number (1,000)	Annual change [1] (1,000)	Total (mil. acres)	Average per farm (acres)
1930	6,546	15	987	151	1962	3,692	−133	1,159	314
1935	6,814	54	1,055	155	1963	3,572	−120	1,152	322
1940	6,350	−93	1,061	167	*1964*	3,457	−115	1,146	332
1945	5,967	−77	1,142	191	1965	3,356	−101	1,140	340
1950	5,648	−64	1,202	213					
					1966	3,257	−99	1,132	348
1951	5,428	−220	1,204	222	1967	3,162	−95	1,123	355
1952	5,198	−230	1,205	232	1968	3,071	−91	1,115	363
1953	4,984	−214	1,206	242	*1969*	3,000	−71	1,108	369
1954	4,798	−186	1,206	251	1970	2,949	−51	1,102	374
1955	4,654	−144	1,202	258					
					1971	2,902	−47	1,097	378
1956	4,514	−140	1,197	265	1972	2,860	−42	1,092	382
1957	4,372	−142	1,191	273	1973	2,823	−37	1,088	385
1958	4,233	−139	1,185	280	*1974*	2,795	−28	1,084	388
1959	4,105	−128	1,183	288	1975	2,767	−28	1,081	391
1960	3,963	−142	1,176	297	1976	2,738	−29	1,078	394
1961	3,825	−138	1,168	305	1977	2,706	−32	1,075	397
					1978, prel	2,680	−26	1,072	400

[1] Average annual change from preceding year shown. For 1930, change from 1925.

Source: U.S. Dept. of Agriculture, Economics, Statistics, and Cooperatives Service, *Number of Farms, 1910–1959; Land in Farms 1950–1959, by States* (Statistical Bulletin No. 316); *Number of Farms and Land in Farms, 1959–70* (Statistical Bulletin No. 507); *Farms and Land in Farms, 1969–75* (Statistical Bulletin No. 594); and *Farm Numbers*, annual supplements.

No. 1167. Characteristics of Farm and Nonfarm Families, by Race: 1977

CHARACTERISTIC	ALL RACES			WHITE			BLACK		
	Total	Farm	Non-farm	Total	Farm	Non-farm	Total	Farm	Non-farm
Total families_____1,000__	56,710	2,184	54,526	50,083	2,072	48,011	5,804	97	5,707
Percent distribution:									
All types_____	100.0	100.0	100.0	100.0	100.0	100.0	100.0	100.0	100.0
Husband-wife_____	83.8	92.4	83.4	86.7	93.0	86.4	58.7	81.4	58.3
Male head, no wife present_____	2.6	3.8	2.6	2.4	3.8	2.4	4.2	4.1	4.2
Female head, no husband present_____	13.6	3.8	14.0	10.9	3.2	11.2	37.1	14.4	37.4
All sizes_____	100.0	100.0	100.0	100.0	100.0	100.0	100.0	100.0	100.0
2 persons_____	38.0	39.6	37.9	39.2	40.3	39.1	29.8	26.8	29.9
3 to 5 persons_____	53.2	49.0	53.4	53.0	49.6	53.2	53.5	40.2	53.7
6 or more persons_____	8.8	11.4	8.7	7.8	10.1	7.7	16.7	33.0	16.4
Mean size of family_____	3.37	3.47	3.36	3.31	3.41	3.30	3.78	4.60	3.77
All families with own children under 18_1,000__	30,145	1,029	29,116	26,014	971	25,043	3,589	47	3,542
Percent with—									
1 or 2 children_____	72.3	66.0	72.6	73.6	67.4	73.9	63.3	(B)	63.6
3 or 4 children_____	23.7	25.5	23.6	23.1	25.2	23.0	27.7	(B)	27.6
5 or more children_____	4.0	8.6	3.8	3.3	7.3	3.1	9.1	(B)	8.8
Mean number of own children_____	2.01	2.27	2.00	1.98	2.21	1.97	2.21	(B)	2.19

B Base figure too small to meet statistical standards for reliability of derived figure.
Source: U.S. Bureau of the Census, *Current Population Reports*, series P-20, No. 326.

No. 1168. Median Money Income of Farm and Nonfarm Families in Constant (1977) Dollars, by Race: 1970 to 1977

[Based on Current Population Survey, see headnote, table 729. For explanation of poverty level, see table 755 and text, p. 438]

YEAR AND ITEM	ALL RACES			WHITE			BLACK		
	Total	Farm	Non-farm	Total	Farm	Non-farm	Total	Farm	Non-farm
Total families, March 1978_1,000__	57,215	2,172	55,042	50,530	2,063	48,467	5,806	86	5,721
Percent distribution:									
Families by 1977 income_____	100.0	100.0	100.0	100.0	100.0	100.0	100.0	100.0	100.0
Under $4,999 _____	9.4	18.2	9.0	7.6	16.9	7.1	24.0	42.3	23.7
$5,000 to $9,999_____	18.1	20.8	18.1	17.0	20.3	16.8	28.1	30.5	27.0
$10,000 to $14,999_____	18.4	19.0	18.4	18.4	19.2	18.5	18.0	10.7	18.1
$15,000 to $19,999_____	17.7	15.7	17.9	18.5	16.3	18.6	12.8	5.9	12.9
$20,000 and over_____	36.3	26.3	36.7	38.5	27.4	38.9	17.2	4.7	17.4
Below poverty level_____	9.3	15.1	9.1	7.0	13.3	6.7	28.2	46.9	27.9
Above poverty level_____	90.7	84.9	90.9	93.0	86.7	93.3	71.8	53.1	72.1
Median family income (constant 1977 dollars):									
1970_____	15,399	10,570	15,616	15,974	10,949	16,212	9,799	4,724	9,979
1974 [1]_____	15,855	13,040	15,964	16,476	13,402	16,610	9,838	6,418	9,917
1975 [1]_____	15,447	12,211	15,570	16,065	12,652	16,203	9,885	5,564	9,988
1976 [1]_____	15,923	12,415	16,037	16,539	12,912	16,655	9,838	5,515	9,959
1977 [1]_____	16,009	12,637	16,140	16,740	13,082	16,892	9,563	5,561	9,649

[1] Beginning 1974, not strictly comparable with earlier years due to revised procedures.
Source: U.S. Bureau of the Census, *Current Population Reports*, series P-60, forthcoming report.

No. 1169. Farm Operators—Tenure and Characteristics: 1969 and 1974

[In thousands, except as indicated. See also *Historical Statistics, Colonial Times to 1970*, series K 82–113]

TENURE AND CHARACTERISTIC	ALL FARMS		FARMS WITH SALES OF $2,500 AND OVER		CHARACTERISTIC	ALL FARMS		FARMS WITH SALES OF $2,500 AND OVER	
	1969	1974 [1]	1969	1974 [1]		1969	1974 [1]	1969	1974 [1]
Total operators___	2,730	2,314	1,734	1,695	Principal occupation:				
					Farming_____	(NA)	1,427	(NA)	1,236
White_____	2,626	2,220	1,697	1,632	Other_____	(NA)	852	(NA)	427
Black and other_____	104	59	37	31	Place of residence:				
Under 25 years old_____	53	52	32	41	On farm operated_____	1,983	1,502	1,345	1,125
25–34 years old_____	274	240	180	176	On another farm_____		94		69
35–44 years old_____	523	400	350	291	In rural area, not on a	458		247	
45–54 years old_____	724	577	489	433	farm_____		67		45
55–64 years old_____	704	589	457	442	In urban area_____		210		146
65 years old and over___	453	421	225	280	Days worked off farm:				
Average age_____years__	51.2	51.7	50.3	51.4	None_____	(NA)	830	(NA)	691
Full owner_____	1,706	1,424	881	904	Less than 100_____	392	197	277	147
Part owner_____	672	628	581	566	100–199 days_____	220	157	112	102
Tenant_____	353	262	271	225	200 days or more_____	871	658	361	347

NA Not available. [1] Except for tenure, data apply only to individual or family operations and partnerships.
Source: U.S. Bureau of the Census, *Census of Agriculture: 1974*, vol. I.

No. 1170. Farm Population, by Regions, Divisions, and States: 1940 to 1970

[In thousands, except percent. See also *Historical Statistics, Colonial Times to 1970*, series K 17-81]

REGION AND STATE	FARM POPULATION				PERCENT DECREASE		REGION AND STATE	FARM POPULATION				PERCENT DECREASE	
	1940	1950	1960	1970	1950–1960	1960–1970		1940	1950	1960	1970	1950–1960	1960–1970
U.S.	30,547	23,048	15,635	9,712	32.2	37.9	S.A.—Con.						
							Md.	246	183	132	79	27.9	40.5
Region: [1]							Va.	986	732	467	238	36.2	49.0
No. East.	2,411	1,791	1,119	699	37.5	37.5	W. Va.	533	411	155	78	62.3	50.1
No. Cent.	9,349	7,433	5,836	4,305	21.5	26.2	N.C.	1,659	1,377	950	463	31.0	51.3
South.	16,400	11,896	7,160	3,754	39.8	47.6	S.C.	917	701	433	144	38.2	66.6
West.	2,387	1,929	1,520	954	21.2	37.2	Ga.	1,368	962	515	228	46.5	55.8
							Fla.	305	233	157	113	32.6	28.0
N.E.	623	403	232	128	42.4	44.7							
Maine.	176	122	61	30	50.0	50.2	E.S.C.	5,283	4,048	2,494	1,329	38.4	46.7
N.H.	71	47	22	11	53.2	48.9	Ky.	1,261	974	618	452	36.6	26.8
Vt.	107	81	56	32	30.9	43.2	Tenn.	1,276	1,016	677	384	33.4	43.3
Mass.	147	80	50	28	37.5	45.0	Ala.	1,343	960	519	216	45.9	58.4
R.I.	17	10	6	4	40.0	37.4	Miss.	1,403	1,097	680	277	38.0	59.3
Conn.	105	63	36	23	42.9	36.0							
							W.S.C.	5,057	3,215	1,828	1,069	43.1	41.6
M.A.	1,788	1,388	887	571	36.1	35.7	Ark.	1,113	802	415	228	48.3	45.0
N.Y.	730	578	387	239	33.0	38.4	La.	854	567	313	160	44.8	48.8
N.J.	143	105	71	47	32.4	33.7	Okla.	930	553	294	209	46.8	28.9
Pa.	915	705	428	284	39.3	33.6	Tex.	2,160	1,292	806	471	37.6	41.6
E.N.C.	4,638	3,703	2,821	2,053	23.8	27.2	Mt.	1,118	859	678	446	21.1	34.2
Ohio.	1,089	853	581	415	31.9	28.7	Mont.	176	136	115	90	15.4	21.7
Ind.	816	667	539	416	19.2	22.9	Idaho.	203	165	148	102	10.3	31.4
Ill.	979	763	621	473	18.6	23.9	Wyo.	73	57	47	33	17.5	29.4
Mich.	871	695	486	305	30.1	37.1	Colo.	253	198	143	94	27.8	34.5
Wis.	883	725	594	445	18.1	25.1	N. Mex.	178	132	72	45	45.5	37.5
							Ariz.	114	77	74	34	3.9	54.2
W.N.C.	4,711	3,729	3,015	2,252	19.1	25.3	Utah.	105	81	65	38	19.8	41.1
Minn.	915	740	624	482	15.7	22.7	Nev.	16	13	13	9	–	25.8
Iowa.	931	783	703	544	10.2	22.7							
Mo.	1,125	863	595	395	31.1	33.6	Pac.	1,270	1,070	842	508	21.3	39.7
N. Dak.	328	254	207	154	18.5	25.6	Wash.	340	274	199	133	27.4	33.4
S. Dak.	307	254	217	172	14.6	21.0	Oreg.	259	228	165	119	27.6	28.2
Nebr.	498	391	329	253	15.9	23.0	Calif.	670	568	463	249	18.5	46.2
Kans.	607	444	340	252	23.4	25.8	Alaska.	(NA)	(NA)	3	2	(NA)	50.2
							Hawaii.	(NA)	(NA)	12	6	(NA)	47.3
S.A.	6,060	4,633	2,838	1,357	38.7	52.2							
Del.	46	34	27	15	20.6	45.3							

- Represents zero.   NA Not available.   [1] For composition of regions, see fig. I, inside front cover.

Source: U.S. Dept. of Agriculture, Economics, Statistics, and Cooperatives Service, *Farm Population Estimates, 1910-70* (Statistical Bulletin No. 523).

No. 1171. Farms—Number, Acreage, and Value, by Type of Organization: 1969 and 1974

[Covers farms with sales of $2,500 and over]

TYPE OF ORGANIZATION	NUMBER OF FARMS (1,000)		LAND IN FARMS (mil. acres)		VALUE OF LAND AND BUILDINGS (mil. dol.)		VALUE OF FARM PRODUCTS SOLD (mil. dol.)	
	1969	1974	1969	1974	1969	1974	1969	1974
Total	1,734	1,695	918	906	179,448	308,890	44,476	80,598
Individual or family	1,481	1,518	665	678	134,892	241,236	30,179	54,516
Partnership	222	145	163	124	31,077	41,307	7,748	11,232
Corporation	22	29	81	97	11,824	24,556	6,295	14,426
Other	10	4	8	6	1,655	1,791	254	424
	PERCENT DISTRIBUTION							
Individual or family	85.4	89.5	72.4	74.9	75.2	78.1	67.8	67.6
Partnership	12.8	8.6	17.8	13.7	17.3	13.4	17.4	13.9
Corporation	1.3	1.7	8.8	10.7	6.6	8.0	14.1	17.9
Other	.6	.2	.9	.7	.9	.6	.6	.5

Source: U.S. Bureau of the Census, *Census of Agriculture: 1974*, vol. I.

No. 1172. Characteristics of Corporate Farms, by Type: 1974

ITEM	All corpo-rations [1]	TYPE OF CORPORATION			TYPE OF OWNERSHIP			
		Fam-ily [2]	Inde-pend-ent [3]	Par-ent [4]	Privately held			Publicly owned and other
					1–5 share-holders	6–10 share-holders	11 or more share-holders	
Farms_____number__	28,442	21,758	5,115	1,569	21,672	4,005	1,013	947
percent__	100.0	76.5	18.0	5.5	76.2	14.1	3.6	3.3
Land in farms_____mil. acres__	96.1	70.7	10.6	14.8	56.1	18.4	11.7	5.7
Average per farm_____acres__	3,380	3,250	2,067	9,460	2,589	4,596	11,527	6,060
Value of land and buildings bil. dol__	24.6	16.3	4.4	4.0	15.2	3.7	2.4	2.5
Average per farm_____$1,000__	866	747	855	2,551	701	936	2,348	2,602
Value of farm products sold bil. dol__	14.6	7.3	3.5	3.8	7.8	2.2	1.5	2.7
Average per farm_____$1,000__	515	337	691	2,405	360	557	1,526	2,885

[1] For type of ownership, includes shareholders not reported, not shown separately.   [2] Fifty-one percent or more of stock owned by persons related by blood or marriage.   [3] Not a family corporation, not owned or controlled by another corporation, and not owning or controlling any other corporations.   [4] Corporations which own or control one or more other corporations.

Source: U.S. Bureau of the Census, *Census of Agriculture: 1974*, vol. IV, part 5.

No. 1173. Farmer Cooperatives—Summary: 1950 to 1976

[For years ending **June 30**, with limited exceptions. 1950 excludes Alaska and Hawaii. Memberships and businesses are estimated. Comprises independent local associations, federations, large-scale centralized associations, and sales agencies. Data are for marketing season during which farm products are moved into channels of trade. Marketing seasons overlap. See also *Historical Statistics, Colonial Times to 1970*, series K 195–203]

YEAR	COOPERATIVES LISTED			MEMBERSHIPS [2] (1,000)			BUSINESSES [3] (mil. dol.)		
	Total	Mar-keting [1]	Farm supply	Total	Mar-keting [1]	Farm supply	Total	Mar-keting [1]	Farm supply
1950_____	10,035	6,922	3,113	6,584	4,075	2,509	8,726	7,083	1,643
1955_____	9,903	6,557	3,346	7,604	4,281	3,323	9,642	7,620	2,022
1960_____	9,345	6,048	3,297	7,273	3,673	3,000	12,036	9,628	2,408
1965_____	8,583	5,498	3,085	7,082	3,831	3,251	14,742	11,832	2,910
1970_____	7,770	5,015	2,775	6,355	3,133	3,222	19,080	15,208	3,872
1972_____	7,797	5,016	2,781	6,147	3,156	2,991	21,665	16,925	4,740
1973_____	7,854	5,053	2,801	6,128	3,140	2,988	26,171	20,256	5,915
1974_____	7,755	4,977	2,778	6,106	3,133	2,973	28,012	20,248	7,764
1975, prel_____	7,645	4,916	2,729	6,123	3,151	2,972	41,342	32,682	8,660
1976, prel_____	7,535	4,804	2,731	5,906	2,850	3,056	40,104	30,692	9,412

[1] Includes service associations.   [2] Excludes nonvoting patrons.
[3] Value of commodities sold or purchased for patrons and charges for rendering other services in marketing or purchasing. Beginning 1955, adjusted for duplication resulting from intercooperative business.

Source: U.S. Dept. of Agriculture, Economics, Statistics, and Cooperatives Service, *Statistics of Farmer Cooperatives*, annual.

No. 1174. Land Utilization, by Type: 1940 to 1974

[**In millions of acres, except percent.** For 1940 and 1950, excludes Alaska and Hawaii. See *Historical Statistics, Colonial Times to 1970*, series J 50–65, for similar data]

TYPE	1940		1950		1959		1969		1974	
	Land	Per-cent	Land	Per-cent	Land	Per-cent	Land	Per-cent	Land	Per-cent
Total land area_____	1,904	100.0	1,904	100.0	2,271	100.0	2,264	100.0	2,264	100.0
Cropland used for crops [1]_____	368	19.3	377	19.8	359	15.8	333	14.7	361	16.0
Idle cropland_____	31	1.6	32	1.7	33	1.5	51	2.3	21	.9
Cropland used only for pasture____	68	3.6	69	3.6	66	2.9	88	3.9	83	3.7
Grassland pasture [2]_____	650	34.1	631	33.1	633	27.9	604	26.7	598	26.4
Forest land [3]_____	608	31.9	601	31.6	728	32.1	723	31.9	718	31.7
Special uses [4]_____	} 179	9.4	} 194	10.2 {	148	6.5	174	7.7	182	8.0
Other land_____					304	13.4	291	12.9	301	13.3

[1] Cropland harvested, crop failure, and cultivated summer fallow.   [2] Grassland and other nonforest pasture and range.   [3] Excludes reserve forest land in parks and other specified uses of land. Includes forest grazing land.
[4] Includes urban and transportation areas, Federal and State areas used primarily for recreation and wildlife purposes, military areas, farmsteads, farm roads and lanes, and miscellaneous other uses.

Source: U.S. Dept. of Agriculture, Economics, Statistics, and Cooperatives Service, *Agricultural Statistics*, annual.

No. 1175. Farms—Number, Acreage, and Value, by Tenure of Operator: 1940 to 1974

[Number of farms in thousands; land in farms in millions of acres, except as indicated. Minority race figures for number of farms for 1959, and figures for average value of farms, land, and buildings, 1950 through 1964, based on sample. *Full owners* own all the land they operate. *Part owners* own a part, and rent from others the rest of the land they operate. See also *Historical Statistics, Colonial Times to 1970*, series K 109–153]

ITEM AND YEAR	All farms	Full owner	Part owner	Man-ager	Tenant	PERCENT OF ALL FARMS		
						Full owner	Part owner	Tenant
Number of farms:								
United States: 1940	6,102	3,085	616	37	2,365	50.6	10.1	38.8
1950	5,388	3,092	826	24	1,447	57.4	15.3	26.9
1959	3,711	2,119	811	21	760	57.1	21.9	20.5
1964	3,158	1,818	782	18	540	57.6	24.8	17.1
1969	2,730	1,706	672	(¹)	353	62.5	24.6	12.9
1974	2,314	1,424	628	(¹)	262	61.5	27.2	11.3
South, all races: 1940	3,007	1,328	217	14	1,449	44.2	7.2	48.2
1950	2,652	1,411	326	10	905	53.2	12.3	34.1
1959	1,646	942	314	9	381	57.2	19.1	23.1
1964	1,373	809	304	7	254	58.9	22.1	18.5
1969	1,161	780	245	(¹)	136	67.2	21.1	11.7
1974	930	623	214	(¹)	93	67.0	23.0	10.0
South, minority races: 1940	680	142	31	(Z)	507	20.9	4.6	74.6
1950	559	141	52	(Z)	366	25.2	9.3	65.5
1959	266	90	38	(Z)	138	33.8	14.3	51.9
1964	185	71	31	(Z)	82	38.4	16.8	44.3
1969	90	56	16	(¹)	18	62.2	17.8	20.0
1974	47	32	10	(¹)	6	66.9	20.6	12.5
Land in farms, U.S.: 1940	1,065	382	301	69	313	35.9	28.3	29.4
1950	1,161	419	423	107	212	36.1	36.4	18.3
1959	1,124	349	498	110	167	31.0	44.3	14.9
1964	1,110	319	533	113	145	28.7	48.0	13.1
1969	1,063	375	550	(¹)	138	35.2	51.8	13.0
1974	1,017	359	535	(¹)	122	35.4	52.6	12.0
Avg. value of land and buildings:								
United States: 1940	$5,532	$4,959	$9,936	$42,208	$4,566	(X)	(X)	(X)
1950	14,005	10,719	25,137	153,043	12,926	(X)	(X)	(X)
1959 ²	34,763	22,478	56,660	244,714	36,159	(X)	(X)	(X)
1964	50,646	30,297	83,251	(¹)	52,998	(X)	(X)	(X)
1969	75,725	47,578	137,606	(¹)	94,007	(X)	(X)	(X)
1974	147,838	90,736	263,539	(¹)	180,776	(X)	(X)	(X)

X Not applicable.   Z Less than 500.
[1] Data included under other tenure categories.   [2] Excludes Hawaii.

Source: U.S. Bureau of the Census, *Census of Agriculture: 1959, 1964,* and *1969*, vol. II; *1974*, vol. I.

No. 1176. Farms—Number, Acreage, and Value of Sales, by Type of Farm: 1969 and 1974

[Covers farms with sales of $2,500 or more. Farm was classified in a particular group if its sales for that product group amounted to 50 percent or more of the total value of farm products sold. The Standard Industrial Classification (SIC) code for each farm type is shown in parentheses]

ITEM AND YEAR	Total	Cash grain [1] (011)	Cotton (0131)	To-bacco (0132)	Live-stock [2] (021)	Dairy (024)	Poultry and eggs (025)	Fruit and nut (017)	Vege-table (016)	All other [3]
1969										
Number of farms ____1,000	1,734	369	41	90	648	261	58	54	20	194
Land in farms ____mil. acres	917.9	186.0	18.9	11.5	536.1	64.9	7.5	7.8	4.6	80.5
Products sold, value____mil. dol	44,476	6,631	814	941	17,783	6,580	3,936	1,682	1,175	4,933
Percent distribution:										
Number of farms	100.0	21.3	2.3	5.2	37.4	15.1	3.3	3.1	1.1	11.2
Land in farms	100.0	20.2	2.1	1.3	58.4	7.1	.8	.8	.5	8.8
Products sold, value	100.0	14.9	1.8	2.1	40.0	14.8	8.9	3.8	2.6	11.1
1974										
Number of farms ____1,000	1,695	580	31	95	494	196	43	51	20	185
Land in farms ____mil. acres	905.6	281.1	17.8	12.3	442.4	54.1	5.5	7.6	4.7	80.1
Products sold, value____mil. dol	80,598	23,673	1,850	1,652	22,125	9,592	6,357	2,858	2,144	10,347
Percent distribution:										
Number of farms	100.0	34.2	1.8	5.6	29.1	11.6	2.5	3.0	1.2	10.9
Land in farms	100.0	31.0	2.0	1.4	48.9	6.0	.6	.8	.5	8.8
Products sold, value	100.0	29.4	2.3	2.0	27.4	11.9	7.9	3.6	2.7	12.8

[1] Includes wheat, rice, corn for grain, soybeans, and other cash grains not elsewhere classified.
[2] Excludes dairy, poultry, and animal specialty farms.
[3] Includes SIC codes 0133, 0134, 0139, 018, 0191, 027, 0291, and not classified.

Source: U.S. Bureau of the Census, *Census of Agriculture: 1969*, vol. II and *1974*, vol. I.

No. 1177. Farms—Number, 1950 to 1974, and Acreage, 1969 and 1974, by Size

[1950 and 1959 excludes Alaska and Hawaii. See also *Historical Statistics, Colonial Times to 1970*, series K 162–173]

SIZE OF FARM	NUMBER OF FARMS (1,000)				LAND IN FARMS (mil. acres)		CROPLAND HARVESTED (mil. acres)		PERCENT DISTRIBUTION, 1974		
	1950	1959	1969	1974	1969	1974	1969	1974	Number of farms	All land in farms	Cropland harvested
Total	5,388	3,711	2,730	2,314	1,063.3	1,017.0	273.0	303.0	100.0	100.0	100.0
Under 10 acres	489	244	162	128	.6	.5	.2	.2	5.5	.1	.1
10–49 acres	1,480	813	473	380	13.3	10.8	4.3	4.3	16.4	1.0	1.4
50–99 acres	1,048	658	460	385	33.6	28.1	10.4	10.5	16.6	2.8	3.5
100–179 acres	1,103	773	542	443	74.0	60.5	26.5	25.1	19.2	5.9	8.3
180–259 acres	487	414	307	253	66.4	54.8	26.6	25.1	10.9	5.4	8.3
260–499 acres	478	472	419	363	149.3	129.8	65.0	65.9	15.7	12.7	21.7
500–999 acres	182	200	216	207	147.8	142.3	60.2	70.1	9.0	14.0	23.1
1,000–1,999 acres	121	79	91	93	123.6	125.7	40.9	51.7	4.0	12.4	17.1
2,000 acres and over	121	57	60	62	454.8	464.7	39.0	50.1	2.7	45.7	16.5

Source: U.S. Bureau of the Census, *Census of Agriculture: 1964* and *1969*, vol. II; *1974*, vol. I.

No. 1178. Farms—Number, Acreage, and Value of Sales, by Size of Sales: 1964 to 1974

[1964 is based on reports for a sample of farms. For definition of abnormal farm, see table 1181]

ECONOMIC CLASS OF FARM (value of farm products sold)	Farms (1,000)	ACREAGE		VALUE OF SALES		PERCENT DISTRIBUTION		
		Total (mil.)	Average per farm	Total (mil. dol.)	Average per farm ($1,000)	Farms	Acreage, total	Value of sales, total
1964: Farms with sales of—								
$2,500 or more	1,817	923	508	34,004	18.7	100.0	100.0	100.0
$2,500–$4,999	444	92	206	1,611	3.6	24.4	9.9	4.7
$5,000–$9,999	505	158	313	3,653	7.2	27.8	17.1	10.8
$10,000–$19,999	467	217	465	6,614	14.2	25.7	23.5	19.5
$20,000–$39,999	260	186	715	7,114	27.4	14.3	20.2	20.9
$40,000–$99,999	110	149	1,352	6,474	58.9	6.1	16.2	19.0
$100,000 and over	31	121	3,854	8,538	275.4	1.7	13.1	25.1
Less than $2,500	1,338	138	103	1,143	.9	100.0	100.0	100.0
$50–$2,499	348	42	122	364	1.0	26.0	30.9	31.9
Part-time	639	58	91	495	.8	47.8	42.4	43.3
Part-retirement	351	37	105	284	.8	26.2	26.7	24.8
Abnormal farms	2	50	22,777	146	67.0	100.0	100.0	100.0
1969: Farms with sales of—								
$2,500 or more	1,734	918	530	44,476	25.6	100.0	100.0	100.0
$2,500–$4,999	395	76	192	1,346	3.4	22.8	8.3	3.0
$5,000–$9,999	390	107	274	2,814	7.2	22.5	11.6	6.3
$10,000–$19,999	395	171	433	5,693	14.4	22.8	18.6	12.8
$20,000–$39,999	331	207	626	9,267	28.0	19.1	22.6	20.8
$40,000–$99,999	170	185	1,092	10,073	59.3	9.8	20.2	22.6
$100,000 and over	52	172	3,304	15,282	293.8	3.0	18.7	34.5
Less than $2,500	994	90	90	935	.9	100.0	100.0	100.0
$50–$2,499	193	19	96	188	1.0	19.4	20.6	20.1
Part-time	575	49	86	532	.9	57.8	54.9	56.9
Part-retirement	227	22	97	215	.9	22.8	24.5	23.0
Abnormal farms	2	55	26,174	153	72.3	100.0	100.0	100.0
1974: Farms with sales of—								
$2,500 or more	1,695	906	534	80,598	47.6	100.0	100.0	100.0
$2,500–$4,999	290	53	184	982	3.4	17.1	5.9	1.2
$5,000–$9,999	296	66	222	2,138	7.2	17.5	7.2	2.7
$10,000–$19,999	310	102	330	4,460	14.4	18.3	11.3	5.5
$20,000–$39,999	322	161	499	9,247	28.7	19.0	17.8	11.5
$40,000–$99,999	324	247	761	20,072	62.0	19.1	27.2	24.9
$100,000 and over	153	277	1,814	43,699	285.6	9.0	30.6	54.2
Less than $2,500	617	56	91	697	1.1	100.0	100.0	100.0
Occupation—Farming [1]	192	20	104	232	1.2	31.0	35.3	33.3
Occupation—Other than farming [1]	425	36	86	465	1.1	69.0	64.7	66.6
Abnormal farms	2	55	24,605	236	118.0	100.0	100.0	100.0

[1] Occupation determined by 50 percent or more of work time on farm or other occupation during 1974.
Source: U.S. Bureau of the Census, *Census of Agriculture: 1964* and *1969*, vol. II; *1974*, vol. I.

No. 1179. Farms—Number, Acreage, and Value, by States: 1964 and 1974

[For composition of regions, see fig. I, inside front cover. See also *Historical Statistics, Colonial Times to 1970*, series K 17–18]

REGION AND STATE	NUMBER OF FARMS (1,000)		ALL LAND IN FARMS (1,000 acres)		AVERAGE ACREAGE PER FARM		TOTAL VALUE [1] (mil. dol.)		AVERAGE VALUE PER FARM [1] ($1,000)		VALUE OF FARM PRODUCTS SOLD (mil. dol.)	
	1964	1974	1964	1974	1964	1974	1964	1974	1964	1974	1964	1974
U.S.	3,158	2,314	1,110,187	1,017,030	352	440	159,932	342,099	51	148	35,294	81,531
No. East.	202	128	31,979	23,359	158	183	6,901	15,460	34	121	2,575	4,291
No. Cen.	1,277	1,017	383,090	362,939	300	357	64,182	150,978	50	148	14,838	36,357
South.	1,373	930	346,228	305,670	252	329	52,068	110,362	38	119	10,586	23,364
West.	306	239	348,890	325,062	1,142	1,360	36,781	65,299	120	273	7,293	17,519
N.E.	42	23	7,744	4,801	185	206	1,459	2,915	35	125	716	1,028
Maine.	13	6	2,590	1,524	201	237	257	519	20	81	256	360
N.H.	5	2	903	506	194	210	118	286	25	118	49	72
Vt.	9	6	2,524	1,668	273	282	275	770	30	130	115	208
Mass.	8	4	902	602	113	134	349	578	43	129	139	180
R.I.	1	1	104	61	94	102	51	92	46	153	19	22
Conn.	6	3	721	440	119	129	409	671	67	196	139	187
M.A.	161	104	24,235	18,558	151	178	5,442	12,545	34	120	1,859	3,263
N.Y.	67	44	12,275	9,411	185	215	2,181	4,800	33	110	853	1,462
N.J.	11	7	1,156	961	109	130	782	1,737	73	244	216	297
Pa.	83	53	10,804	8,186	130	154	2,479	6,008	30	113	791	1,503
E.N.C.	574	445	99,486	90,005	173	202	27,909	61,406	49	138	6,105	13,385
Ohio.	120	92	17,619	15,668	146	170	5,221	11,056	43	120	1,013	2,263
Ind.	108	88	17,933	16,785	166	191	5,582	12,078	52	137	1,105	2,613
Ill.	133	111	29,958	29,095	226	262	10,744	24,628	81	222	2,123	4,665
Mich.	94	64	13,599	10,832	145	169	3,182	5,989	34	93	766	1,491
Wis.	119	89	20,378	17,625	172	197	3,180	7,656	27	86	1,097	2,353
W.N.C.	704	573	283,603	272,934	403	477	36,272	89,572	52	156	8,733	22,972
Minn.	131	99	30,805	27,605	235	280	5,125	11,855	39	120	1,376	3,470
Iowa.	154	126	33,758	33,045	219	262	9,181	23,754	60	188	2,597	6,320
Mo.	147	116	32,692	29,801	222	258	4,928	11,811	33	102	1,053	2,304
N. Dak.	49	43	42,717	42,387	875	992	2,854	8,268	58	194	570	1,803
S. Dak.	50	43	45,567	45,978	917	1,074	2,814	6,656	57	155	629	1,660
Nebr.	80	68	47,793	46,172	596	683	5,232	13,017	65	193	1,334	3,733
Kans.	92	79	50,271	47,946	544	605	6,138	14,211	66	179	1,175	3,682
S.A.	468	296	76,959	60,939	164	206	16,157	34,987	34	118	4,142	8,520
Del.	4	3	717	631	163	185	235	612	53	180	108	251
Md.	21	15	3,181	2,634	153	174	1,349	2,791	65	184	276	620
Va.	80	53	12,002	9,678	149	184	2,215	5,396	28	102	470	960
W. Va.	35	17	5,279	3,497	153	207	478	1,050	14	62	92	133
N.C.	148	91	14,382	11,244	97	123	3,622	6,634	24	73	1,068	2,121
S.C.	56	29	8,101	6,177	144	211	1,403	2,887	25	99	349	676
Ga.	83	55	17,887	13,878	215	253	2,431	6,576	29	120	826	1,860
Fla.	41	32	15,411	13,199	380	407	4,423	9,041	109	278	954	1,899
E.S.C.	468	306	64,509	53,688	138	175	10,251	22,006	22	72	2,382	4,537
Ky.	133	102	16,265	14,432	122	141	2,958	6,158	22	60	592	1,252
Tenn.	133	94	15,266	13,103	114	140	2,737	6,117	21	65	529	933
Ala.	93	57	15,226	11,853	165	209	1,902	4,310	21	76	537	1,122
Miss.	109	54	17,752	14,300	163	267	2,655	5,421	24	101	724	1,229
W.S.C.	436	328	204,760	191,043	469	582	25,660	53,369	59	163	4,063	10,308
Ark.	80	51	16,565	14,642	207	287	2,935	6,135	37	120	830	1,881
La.	62	33	10,411	9,133	167	275	2,413	4,679	39	141	407	1,194
Okla.	89	70	36,077	33,083	407	475	4,366	9,992	49	143	601	1,595
Tex.	205	174	141,706	134,185	691	771	15,945	32,563	78	187	2,225	5,638
Mt.	134	112	268,003	253,021	1,998	2,262	13,650	32,028	102	286	2,537	6,820
Mont.	27	23	65,834	62,158	2,437	2,665	2,791	6,952	103	298	390	1,033
Idaho.	30	24	15,302	14,274	516	603	2,022	4,833	68	204	478	1,381
Wyo.	9	8	37,053	34,272	4,100	4,274	1,043	2,751	115	343	151	361
Colo.	30	26	38,259	35,902	1,284	1,408	2,687	6,734	90	264	612	1,970
N. Mex.	14	11	47,647	47,046	3,354	4,170	1,663	3,649	117	323	227	522
Ariz.	6	6	40,559	37,944	6,262	6,539	2,141	4,197	331	723	469	1,081
Utah.	16	12	12,867	10,610	817	871	910	1,998	58	164	159	339
Nev.	2	2	10,483	10,814	4,862	5,209	393	915	182	441	51	133
Pac.	171	127	80,887	72,041	472	567	23,131	33,271	135	262	4,756	10,699
Wash.	46	29	19,053	16,662	418	567	2,931	5,828	64	198	637	1,658
Oreg.	40	27	20,509	18,241	516	682	2,349	4,552	59	170	428	1,025
Calif.	81	68	37,011	33,386	458	493	17,352	21,793	215	322	3,499	7,400
Alaska.	(Z)	(Z)	1,959	1,633	5,129	5,612	18	69	47	238	4	7
Hawaii.	5	3	2,354	2,119	484	702	481	1,029	99	341	188	610

Z Less than 500.   [1] Value of land and buildings. For 1964, based on reports for a sample of farms.

Source: U.S. Bureau of the Census, *Census of Agriculture: 1964*, vol. II; *1974*, vol. I.

No. 1180. Farms—Number and Acreage, by States: 1970 and 1978

[1978 data preliminary. See also *Historical Statistics, Colonial Times to 1970*, series K 4-7]

STATE	FARMS (1,000) 1970	1978	ACREAGE (mil.) 1970	1978	ACREAGE PER FARM 1970	1978	STATE	FARMS (1,000) 1970	1978	ACREAGE (mil.) 1970	1978	ACREAGE PER FARM 1970	1978
U.S.	2,949	2,680	1,102	1,072	374	400	Mo.	143	133	33	33	232	245
							Mont.	26	23	64	62	2,432	2,712
Ala.	82	76	15	14	180	189	Nebr.	73	68	48	48	659	706
Alaska	(Z)	(Z)	1 2	1 2	1 5,344	1 5,452	Nev.	2	2	9	9	4,286	4,286
Ariz.	6	7	41	41	6,556	6,167	N.H.	3	3	1	1	209	193
Ark.	72	68	18	17	244	254	N.J.	9	8	1	1	123	122
Calif.	64	75	37	34	572	453	N. Mex.	12	13	48	47	3,855	3,695
Colo.	30	29	40	39	1,302	1,345	N.Y.	58	57	11	11	193	195
Conn.	5	4	1	(Z)	120	118	N.C.	150	115	15	13	101	114
Del.	4	4	1	1	183	187	N. Dak.	46	42	42	42	921	1,005
Fla.	39	38	15	14	379	364	Ohio	118	108	18	17	149	156
Ga.	77	69	17	17	226	246	Okla.	90	85	37	37	412	432
Hawaii	4	4	2	2	511	561	Oreg.	34	34	20	19	583	565
Idaho	28	27	16	16	544	580	Pa.	74	72	10	10	138	139
Ill.	128	117	30	29	230	247	R.I.	1	1	(Z)	(Z)	93	92
Ind.	107	95	18	17	164	180	S.C.	52	45	8	8	160	171
Iowa	145	128	34	34	237	266	S. Dak.	47	43	46	46	968	1,058
Kans.	87	76	50	48	574	638	Tenn.	127	110	15	15	121	133
Ky.	127	117	16	16	128	132	Tex.	212	197	143	140	674	710
La.	51	43	12	11	231	258	Utah	14	13	13	13	936	963
Maine	9	8	2	2	222	222	Vt.	7	7	2	2	275	269
Md.	19	17	3	3	164	167	Va.	76	61	11	10	150	162
Mass.	6	5	1	1	121	126	Wash.	41	36	17	16	405	444
Mich.	84	72	13	11	151	158	W. Va.	29	26	5	5	176	177
Minn.	121	114	31	31	255	268	Wis.	110	99	20	19	183	192
Miss.	89	78	17	16	194	208	Wyo.	9	8	36	35	4,080	4,412

Z Less than 500 farms or 500,000 acres.

1 Alaska farmland totals about 70,000 acres, excluding grazing land leased from U.S. Government.

Source: U.S. Dept. of Agriculture, Economics, Statistics, and Cooperatives Service, *Farms and Land in Farms, 1969-1975* (Statistical Bulletin No. 594) and *Farm Numbers*, annual.

No. 1181. Farms—Number, by Value of Products Sold, by States: 1974

STATE	All farms [1]	WITH SALES OF— $2,500-$9,999	$40,000-$99,999	$100,000 plus	With sales less than $2,500	STATE	All farms [1]	WITH SALES OF— $2,500-$9,999	$40,000-$99,999	$100,000 plus	With sales less than $2,500
U.S.	2,314,013	586,356	324,310	152,599	616,728	S.A—Con.					
						W. Va.	16,909	3,982	463	210	10,786
N.E.	23,269	4,278	4,423	2,113	6,595	N.C.	91,280	25,753	9,003	4,131	28,753
Maine	6,436	1,112	1,182	834	1,869	S.C.	29,275	7,895	2,264	1,502	11,739
N.H.	2,412	484	317	141	941	Ga.	54,911	12,332	7,123	4,732	19,035
Vt.	5,906	821	1,596	355	1,363	Fla.	32,466	8,865	2,470	2,958	11,497
Mass.	4,497	1,001	678	344	1,295	E.S.C.	306,010	96,621	16,515	8,274	134,623
R.I.	597	133	85	46	175	Ky.	102,053	38,803	4,769	1,447	34,386
Conn.	3,421	727	565	393	952	Tenn.	93,659	31,002	3,470	1,341	45,335
M.A.	104,262	22,020	17,883	5,826	28,792	Ala.	56,678	13,924	4,774	2,460	27,370
N.Y.	43,682	7,938	8,761	2,647	11,446	Miss.	53,620	12,892	3,502	3,026	27,532
N.J.	7,409	1,844	1,099	741	1,878	W.S.C.	327,986	92,625	29,416	19,594	124,158
Pa.	53,171	12,238	8,023	2,438	15,468	Ark.	50,959	12,255	6,211	5,260	19,658
E.N.C.	444,695	114,579	72,343	26,037	84,069	La.	33,240	7,015	3,484	3,035	14,658
Ohio	92,158	27,024	11,658	4,071	21,818	Okla.	69,719	21,695	6,606	2,375	21,881
Ind.	87,915	25,559	13,098	5,508	16,929	Tex.	174,068	51,660	13,115	8,924	67,961
Ill.	111,049	22,463	26,213	11,275	13,311	Mt.	111,868	26,141	19,061	11,660	21,108
Mich.	64,094	19,769	6,848	2,809	17,423	Mont.	23,324	4,470	5,358	2,142	3,045
Wis.	89,479	19,764	14,526	2,374	14,588	Idaho	23,680	5,168	4,270	2,751	4,027
W.N.C.	572,672	120,961	120,514	43,262	74,864	Wyo.	8,018	1,884	1,434	776	1,079
Minn.	98,537	20,647	19,758	6,160	12,610	Colo.	25,501	5,882	4,646	3,057	4,373
Iowa	126,104	18,055	37,196	14,273	8,954	N. Mex.	11,282	3,175	1,168	857	3,482
Mo.	115,711	36,677	11,685	3,801	33,285	Ariz.	5,803	1,356	636	1,231	1,401
N. Dak.	42,710	6,169	11,226	3,335	2,019	Utah	12,184	3,722	1,250	590	3,277
S. Dak.	42,825	7,742	9,804	2,580	2,931	Nev.	2,076	484	299	256	424
Nebr.	67,597	12,076	16,546	7,042	4,998	Pac.	127,148	29,121	16,217	18,112	35,782
Kans.	79,188	19,595	14,299	6,071	10,067	Wash.	29,410	6,127	4,697	3,998	8,318
S.A.	296,103	80,010	27,938	17,721	106,737	Oreg.	26,753	6,549	2,838	2,414	9,681
Del.	3,400	711	734	679	409	Calif.	67,674	15,360	8,394	11,428	16,790
Md.	15,163	3,726	2,461	1,612	3,560	Alaska	291	117	18	18	84
Va.	52,699	16,746	3,423	1,897	20,958	Hawaii	3,020	968	270	254	909

1 Includes classes not shown separately.

Source: U.S. Bureau of the Census, *Census of Agriculture: 1974*, vol. I.

No. 1182. Farms—Number, by Type, by States: 1974

[Covers farms with sales of $2,500 or more. A farm was coded in a particular group if its sales for that product group amounted to 50 percent or more of the total value of farm products sold. The Standard Industrial Classification (SIC) for each product group is shown in parentheses. For composition of regions, see fig. 1, inside front cover]

REGION AND STATE	Total	Cash grain (011)	Cotton (0131)	To-bacco (0132)	Other field crops [1] (0133, 0134, 0139)	Vege-table (016)	Fruit and nut (017)	Live-stock [2] (021)	Dairy (024)	Poul-try and eggs (025)	All other and not classi-fied [3]
U.S	1,695,047	580,254	30,725	95,493	81,415	19,548	51,270	493,816	196,057	42,690	103,779
Percent	100.0	34.2	1.8	5.6	4.8	1.2	3.0	29.1	11.6	2.5	6.1
Northeast	91,943	9,912	–	363	7,121	3,673	4,753	11,613	40,694	3,786	10,028
North Central	857,929	411,126	522	3,205	20,383	5,256	4,775	250,456	116,548	6,731	38,927
South	563,977	123,246	26,887	91,925	31,471	5,807	11,192	175,812	27,391	29,966	40,280
West	181,198	35,970	3,316	–	22,440	4,812	30,550	55,935	11,424	2,207	14,544
N.E	16,606	85	–	130	2,671	813	1,084	1,295	7,047	1,351	2,130
Maine	4,553	50	–	–	1,539	103	298	282	1,217	663	401
N.H	1,458	3	–	–	179	66	63	162	626	112	247
Vt	4,531	9	–	–	421	31	78	295	3,378	52	267
Mass	3,185	13	–	37	256	378	485	283	914	187	632
R.I	419	2	–	–	58	56	27	38	118	33	87
Conn	2,460	8	–	93	218	179	133	235	794	304	496
M.A	75,337	9,827	–	233	4,450	2,860	3,669	10,318	33,647	2,435	7,898
N.Y	32,198	2,920	–	–	2,325	1,209	2,318	2,883	17,247	581	2,715
N.J	5,506	1,113	–	–	302	1,061	393	434	739	277	1,187
Pa	37,633	5,794	–	233	1,823	590	958	7,001	15,661	1,577	3,996
E.N.C	360,427	177,533	–	2,980	7,764	4,517	4,381	69,790	72,838	3,761	16,863
Ohio	70,283	38,348	–	1,457	1,228	620	631	13,621	8,877	1,152	4,349
Ind	70,942	43,821	–	1,007	657	372	207	16,891	4,098	1,112	2,777
Ill	97,703	67,516	–	–	485	367	190	21,781	4,382	506	2,476
Mich	46,647	20,091	–	–	2,578	1,275	2,875	7,279	8,530	525	3,494
Wis	74,852	7,757	–	516	2,816	1,883	478	10,218	46,951	466	3,767
W.N.C	497,502	233,593	522	225	12,619	739	394	180,666	43,710	2,970	22,064
Minn	85,905	36,036	–	2	3,507	455	97	16,997	22,966	931	4,914
Iowa	117,075	55,342	–	–	678	74	76	49,509	6,616	645	4,135
Mo	82,385	28,574	522	221	2,125	106	172	41,597	5,249	894	2,925
N. Dak	40,661	28,797	–	–	1,800	5	2	6,135	1,425	57	2,440
S. Dak	39,818	12,380	–	–	1,288	8	1	20,126	2,959	135	2,921
Nebr	62,570	30,039	–	–	1,995	30	8	25,891	2,121	131	2,355
Kans	69,088	42,425	–	2	1,226	61	38	20,411	2,374	177	2,374
S.A	189,119	35,953	1,656	51,223	11,774	2,853	9,069	37,617	9,203	13,943	15,828
Del	2,988	1,414	–	–	50	70	10	114	167	1,004	159
Md	11,586	3,358	–	1,742	217	265	107	1,428	2,071	1,405	993
Va	31,697	4,396	–	8,689	1,846	255	485	9,897	2,632	983	2,514
W. Va	6,099	265	–	208	433	33	184	3,473	782	297	424
N.C	62,473	11,366	264	32,057	2,882	529	590	6,261	1,773	3,637	3,114
S.C	17,513	5,835	561	4,880	523	246	325	2,968	415	542	1,218
Ga	35,836	7,466	802	3,015	4,741	337	416	8,849	926	5,194	4,090
Fla	20,927	1,853	29	632	1,082	1,118	6,952	4,627	437	881	3,316
E.S.C	171,245	30,980	9,410	40,681	7,528	1,173	381	48,146	11,424	7,711	13,811
Ky	67,628	9,525	1	31,459	2,268	108	75	13,592	5,217	236	5,147
Tenn	48,292	9,577	1,716	9,183	1,937	354	85	16,522	4,152	846	3,920
Ala	29,269	5,958	2,432	39	2,620	480	173	9,436	718	4,712	2,701
Miss	26,056	5,920	5,261	–	703	231	48	8,596	1,337	1,917	2,043
W.S.C	203,613	56,313	15,821	21	12,169	1,781	1,742	90,049	6,764	8,312	10,641
Ark	31,270	10,606	2,319	1	701	291	173	9,492	1,076	5,498	1,113
La	18,542	6,707	2,000	20	1,887	278	138	4,539	1,442	461	1,070
Okla	47,793	16,175	1,107	–	2,746	133	75	22,733	1,479	470	2,875
Tex	106,008	22,825	10,395	–	6,835	1,079	1,356	53,285	2,767	1,883	5,583
Mt	90,069	24,587	1,293	–	13,166	819	1,477	37,439	5,297	405	5,586
Mont	20,177	8,804	–	–	1,607	12	76	8,511	304	32	831
Idaho	19,530	5,426	–	–	4,112	173	182	5,458	2,470	44	1,665
Wyo	6,885	975	–	–	1,022	4	–	4,393	194	9	288
Colo	21,055	7,117	–	–	2,922	202	331	8,277	740	90	1,376
N. Mex	7,736	757	523	–	1,119	183	93	4,555	153	17	336
Ariz	4,321	305	763	–	491	110	480	1,634	155	22	361
Utah	8,745	1,153	–	–	1,405	128	311	3,710	1,212	189	637
Nev	1,620	50	7	–	488	7	4	901	69	2	92
Pac	91,129	11,383	2,023	–	9,274	3,993	29,073	18,496	6,127	1,802	8,958
Wash	21,056	5,294	–	–	2,538	838	4,319	4,038	1,896	248	1,885
Oreg	17,017	3,050	–	–	2,447	747	1,992	5,414	1,134	217	2,016
Calif	50,763	3,020	2,023	–	3,833	2,047	22,286	8,635	3,046	1,282	4,591
Alaska	201	7	–	–	77	4	–	34	20	6	53
Hawaii	2,092	12	–	–	379	357	476	375	31	49	413

– Represents zero. [1] Includes farms with sugar crops, Irish potatoes, hay, peanuts, and other field crops.
[2] Excludes dairy, poultry, and animal specialty farms.
[3] Includes SIC codes 018, 0191, 027, 0291, and not classified.
Source: U.S. Bureau of the Census, *Census of Agriculture: 1974*, vol. I.

No. 1183. FARM REAL ESTATE—VALUE OF LAND AND BUILDINGS, BY STATES: 1970 TO 1978

[Through 1975, as of **March 1**; beginning 1977, as of **Feb. 1**. Excludes Alaska and Hawaii. See also *Historical Statistics, Colonial Times to 1970*, series K 16]

STATE	VALUE OF LAND AND BUILDINGS (mil. dol.)				AVERAGE VALUE OF LAND AND BUILDINGS PER ACRE (dol.)				INDEXES OF AVERAGE VALUE PER ACRE (1967=100)			
	1970	1975	1977	1978	1970	1975	1977	1978	1970	1975	1977	1978
U.S.	215,042	367,157	482,148	523,952	196	341	450	490	117	213	283	308
Ala	2,960	5,351	6,264	6,509	200	364	432	452	121	233	275	288
Ariz	2,891	4,551	4,896	5,087	70	111	120	125	127	211	227	237
Ark	4,576	7,291	9,013	9,878	260	419	521	571	129	191	238	261
Calif	17,531	22,724	23,151	25,874	479	653	673	761	110	133	137	155
Colo	3,771	7,370	9,984	10,686	95	188	256	274	105	209	285	305
Conn	543	¹ 762	¹ 836	¹ 922	921	¹ 1,525	¹ 1,779	¹ 1,962	134	¹ 257	¹ 301	¹ 332
Del	357	655	891	982	499	971	1,340	1,500	116	242	334	374
Fla	5,254	² 9,727	² 10,956	² 11,732	355	² 685	² 777	² 838	121	² 224	² 253	² 273
Ga	4,072	8,058	8,653	9,588	234	474	509	564	138	298	322	357
Idaho	2,744	5,288	6,427	6,942	177	339	412	445	120	243	296	320
Ill	14,455	24,619	41,499	45,691	490	846	1,431	1,581	107	209	353	390
Ind	7,105	12,384	19,819	22,281	406	720	1,159	1,303	104	200	321	361
Iowa	13,485	24,590	41,690	43,239	392	719	1,219	1,268	114	234	397	413
Kans	7,934	14,474	18,311	18,430	159	296	376	380	107	211	267	270
Ky	4,124	6,661	9,223	10,400	253	427	595	671	116	203	281	317
La	3,788	5,939	6,507	7,426	321	512	581	669	116	191	218	251
Maine	308	¹ 576	¹ 676	¹ 745	161	¹ 341	¹ 400	¹ 441	128	¹ 257	¹ 301	¹ 332
Md	1,971	3,116	3,936	4,576	640	1,060	1,355	1,578	138	248	316	368
Mass	424	¹ 653	¹ 754	¹ 832	565	¹ 961	¹ 1,126	¹ 1,242	126	¹ 257	¹ 301	¹ 332
Mich	4,140	6,525	8,897	9,804	326	553	767	860	113	184	256	287
Minn	6,983	13,127	19,951	22,338	226	429	652	730	118	242	369	413
Miss	4,048	6,216	6,585	7,517	234	379	404	464	125	204	217	249
Mo	7,437	12,949	17,148	19,625	224	396	526	602	124	214	284	325
Mont	3,852	7,011	9,470	10,433	60	112	152	168	124	237	321	355
Nebr	7,407	13,536	19,248	18,480	154	282	401	385	115	215	307	275
Nev	477	765	783	873	53	86	87	97	155	299	307	341
N.H	160	¹ 327	¹ 383	¹ 423	239	¹ 564	¹ 661	¹ 729	149	¹ 257	¹ 301	¹ 332
N.J	1,158	1,852	2,034	2,078	1,092	1,807	2,004	2,057	144	340	377	387
N. Mex	2,008	3,697	4,210	4,399	42	78	89	93	120	197	227	236
N.Y	3,058	5,865	6,438	6,538	273	510	580	589	123	275	313	318
N.C	5,062	7,906	8,910	9,091	333	590	675	694	113	216	246	253
N. Dak	3,939	8,132	10,759	11,384	94	195	258	273	120	265	349	369
Ohio	7,022	12,073	18,945	21,218	399	706	1,121	1,263	115	208	331	373
Okla	6,418	11,114	13,432	14,753	173	302	365	402	115	212	258	284
Oreg	3,015	4,875	5,365	5,818	150	250	278	303	137	228	254	277
Pa	3,805	7,340	9,780	10,920	373	734	978	1,092	145	315	422	471
R.I	56	¹ 102	¹ 120	¹ 132	734	¹ 1,500	¹ 1,758	¹ 1,939	132	¹ 257	¹ 301	¹ 332
S.C	2,166	3,596	4,073	4,181	261	467	529	543	124	273	311	319
S. Dak	3,822	6,598	8,827	10,328	84	145	194	227	112	214	287	336
Tenn	4,127	6,958	8,012	8,877	268	467	545	608	123	236	275	307
Tex	21,134	34,312	40,040	44,177	148	243	286	316	119	193	228	252
Utah	1,214	2,425	3,032	3,199	92	188	235	248	137	232	289	305
Vt	450	¹ 832	¹ 974	¹ 1,075	224	¹ 462	¹ 541	¹ 597	155	¹ 257	¹ 301	¹ 332
Va	3,260	5,803	6,760	7,247	286	558	676	732	121	250	302	327
Wash	3,718	5,705	7,954	8,554	224	350	491	528	124	178	249	268
W. Va	694	1,440	1,832	1,854	136	300	394	403	137	317	417	426
Wis	4,663	8,463	11,135	13,110	232	434	583	690	124	240	322	381
Wyo	1,456	2,824	3,565	3,706	41	80	101	105	116	218	273	285

¹ Dollar values based on average rate of change for New England States. Index based on weighted average for New England States.
² Indexes based on percentage change in Georgia and Alabama. Dollar value based on the resulting index.

Source: U.S. Dept. of Agriculture, Economics, Statistics, and Cooperatives Service, *Farm Real Estate Market Developments*, annual.

No. 1184. Farm Real Estate—Summary: 1960 to 1978

[Through 1975, value data as of **March 1**; beginning 1976, as of **February 1**]

ITEM	1960	1965	1970	1972	1973	1974	1975	1976	1977	1978
Value of land and buildings_____bil. dol__	136.8	167.0	215.0	238.7	266.2	326.6	367.2	415.5	482.1	524.0
Land_____bil. dol__	104.5	131.6	175.5	196.5	219.3	269.8	303.6	344.1	399.2	434.4
Buildings_____bil. dol__	32.3	35.4	39.5	42.2	46.9	56.8	63.6	71.4	82.9	89.6
Avg. value per acre [1]_____dol__	117	147	196	219	246	302	341	387	450	490
Index_____1967=100__	68	86	117	132	150	187	213	242	283	308
Avg. value of operating unit_____$1,000__	34.6	49.8	73.0	83.6	94.5	117.0	132.9	152.0	178.4	195.8
Taxes on farm real estate__mil. dol__	1,243	1,536	2,169	2,463	2,514	2,652	2,855	3,035	(NA)	(NA)
Farm real estate sales [2]_____1,000__	(NA)	[3]113.6	89.0	105.9	125.0	125.0	99.1	85.4	84.6	80.7
Acres sold_____mil__	(NA)	[3]26.5	22.0	27.2	36.3	41.8	27.0	23.1	23.2	24.8
Value_____bil. dol__	(NA)	[3]5.3	5.4	7.2	10.6	14.2	11.8	12.2	15.1	14.7

NA Not available. [1] Land and buildings. [2] Represents only voluntary and estate sales of 10 acres or more. [3] 1966 data.

Source: U.S. Dept. of Agriculture, Economics, Statistics, and Cooperatives Service, *Farm Real Estate Market Developments* and *Farm Real Estate Taxes*, both annual.

No. 1185. Irrigation of Agricultural Land—Summary: 1930 to 1974

[See also *Historical Statistics, Colonial Times to 1970*, series J 85–91]

ITEM	17 WESTERN STATES AND LOUISIANA [1]						ALL STATES	
	1930	1940	1950	1959	1969	1974	1969	1974
Approximate land area_____mil. acres__	1,190	1,191	1,191	1,189	1,187	1,187	2,264	2,264
Farms, total_____1,000__	1,820	1,681	1,430	1,044	850	745	2,730	2,314
Irrigated_____1,000__	264	290	289	267	210	197	257	237
Percent irrigated of total farms_____	14.5	17.3	20.2	25.6	24.7	26.4	9.4	10.2
Land in farms, total_____mil. acres__	553	611	699	715	700	680	1,063	1,017
In irrigated farms_____mil. acres__	78	112	168	213	218	211	238	229
Land irrigated, total_____mil. acres__	14	18	25	31	35	37	39	41
Percent irrigated of total farms_____	2.5	2.9	3.6	4.3	5.0	5.4	3.7	4.0

[1] Excludes Alaska and Hawaii.

Source: U.S. Bureau of the Census, *Census of Agriculture: 1930, 1940, 1950, 1959, 1969*, and *1974, Irrigation of Agricultural Lands*.

No. 1186. Federal Irrigation Projects: 1950 to 1976

YEAR	ENTIRE AREA			FULL IRRIGATION SERVICE [1]			SUPPLEMENTAL AND TEMPORARY IRRIGATION SERVICE [2]		
	Irrigable acreage (1,000)	Irrigated acreage (1,000)	Gross crop value (mil. dol.)	Irrigable acreage (1,000)	Irrigated acreage (1,000)	Gross crop value (mil. dol.)	Irrigable acreage (1,000)	Irrigated acreage (1,000)	Gross crop value (mil. dol.)
1950_____	6,025	5,077	578	3,305	2,716	311	2,720	2,361	267
1955_____	7,368	6,262	828	3,826	3,163	429	3,542	3,099	399
1960_____	8,171	6,900	1,158	4,326	3,488	581	3,845	3,412	577
1965_____	9,612	8,012	1,557	4,540	3,731	675	5,072	4,281	882
1970_____	10,198	8,570	1,882	4,844	4,037	847	5,354	4,533	1,035
1971_____	10,560	8,834	2,124	4,853	4,050	943	5,707	4,784	1,182
1972_____	10,694	8,920	2,471	4,906	4,065	1,085	5,788	4,855	1,386
1973_____	10,884	9,202	3,902	4,906	4,160	1,593	5,978	5,042	2,309
1974_____	11,037	9,418	4,655	4,926	4,216	1,943	6,111	5,202	2,712
1975_____	10,930	9,309	4,419	4,925	4,213	1,858	6,005	5,096	2,561
1976_____	11,061	9,463	4,336	4,957	4,249	1,846	6,104	5,214	2,490

[1] Applies to irrigable land receiving its sole irrigation supply through Bureau of Reclamation-constructed facilities and to previously irrigated land in non-Federal projects where a substantial part of the facilities was constructed, rehabilitated, or replaced by the Bureau. [2] Applies to irrigable land receiving irrigation water through Bureau projects in addition to supply from non-project sources and to land for which water is delivered under temporary arrangements.

Source: U.S. Bureau of Reclamation, *Federal Reclamation Projects, Water and Land Resource Accomplishments*, annual.

No. 1187. Conservation Districts—Number and Area: 1950 to 1977

[For years ending June 30, except as noted. Soil conservation district legislation has been enacted in all 50 States, Puerto Rico, and the Virgin Islands. Soil conservation districts have broad authority for conservation and development of soil, water, and related resources and, in most cases, can accept Federal, State, county, and private assistance for their programs. Minus sign (−) denotes decrease]

ITEM	1950	1960	1965	1970	1972	1973	1974	1975	1976	1977 [1]
Number organized each year	121	6	18	9	−3	−62	−13	−5	−2	−3
Cumulative total	2,885	2,867	2,989	3,026	3,024	2,962	2,949	2,944	2,942	2,939
With supplemental memo: [2]										
Each year	133	23	13	−1	10	−87	−14	−17	29	−14
Cumulative	2,207	2,837	2,921	2,970	2,982	2,895	2,881	2,864	2,893	2,879
Area in districts:										
New and additions___mil. acres__	75	10	14	5	11	[3] 375	1	2	2	2
Cumulative_____mil. acres__	1,253	1,672	1,753	1,811	1,836	2,211	2,212	2,214	2,216	2,218

[1] Covers 15 month period, July 1976–Sept. 1977.   [2] Signed for assistance from Soil Conservation Service.
[3] Predominantly new area being included in Alaska.
Source: U.S. Soil Conservation Service, Report of Administrator of Soil Conservation Service, annual.

No. 1188. Agricultural Services—Summary: 1974

SIC code [1]	TYPE OF SERVICE	Establishments	Gross receipts (mil. dol.)	Paid employees (1,000)	Payroll (mil. dol.)
07	Agricultural services	61,347	3,555.0	501	1,206.4
071	Soil preparation services	730	40.5	3	10.8
072	Crop services	5,140	719.9	109	196.9
074	Veterinary services	10,452	867.9	52	258.0
0741	Cattle, hogs, sheep, goats, and poultry	3,081	205.5	10	47.4
0742	Other animals, bees, fish, and birds	7,371	662.4	42	210.6
075	Animal services, except veterinary	10,502	298.0	29	87.7
076	Farm labor and management services	905	286.5	161	165.5
078	Landscape and horticultural services	33,618	1,342.2	146	487.3

[1] Standard Industrial Classification Code.
Source: U.S. Bureau of the Census, Census of Agriculture: 1974, vol. III.

No. 1189. Commercial Fertilizers Consumed: 1960 to 1977

[For years ending June 30. Includes Puerto Rico. Includes fertilizers distributed by Government agencies. See Historical Statistics, Colonial Times to 1970, series K 193, for related but not comparable data]

ITEM	1960	1965	1970	1972	1973	1974	1975	1976	1977
All fertilizers_____mil. tons__	24.9	31.8	39.6	41.2	43.3	47.1	42.5	49.2	51.6
Percent: [1] Nitrogen	11.7	15.3	19.5	20.1	19.8	20.4	21.2	22.2	21.7
Phosphoric oxide	10.9	11.6	11.9	12.2	12.2	11.3	11.1	11.2	11.4
Potash	9.2	9.4	10.5	10.8	11.1	11.3	11.0	11.1	11.9
Mixed fertilizers_____mil. tons__	15.7	18.6	21.0	21.5	22.5	24.1	20.6	23.0	24.0
Percent: [1] Nitrogen	6.5	7.8	9.3	9.9	10.2	10.1	10.2	10.5	10.6
Phosphoric oxide	13.0	15.2	17.7	18.6	18.8	17.7	18.0	19.3	19.9
Potash	12.1	12.4	12.7	12.9	12.8	12.7	12.5	12.5	12.8
Primary nutrient materials_____mil. tons__	7.9	11.8	17.3	18.4	19.3	20.9	20.0	23.9	25.0
Secondary and micronutrients____mil. tons__	1.4	1.5	1.3	1.3	1.5	2.1	1.9	2.3	2.5

[1] Percent nutrient content based on fertilizer consumption excluding secondary and micronutrients.
Source: U.S. Dept. of Agriculture, Economics, Statistics, and Cooperatives Service, Agricultural Statistics, annual; and Commercial Fertilizers, Consumption in the United States, November 1978.

No. 1190. Agricultural Chemicals Used on Farms: 1969 and 1974

[Covers farms with sales of $2,500 or more]

TYPE OF CHEMICAL	1969			1974		
	Farms reporting (1,000)	Acres treated (1,000)	Cost (mil. dol.)	Farms reporting (1,000)	Acres treated (1,000)	Cost (mil. dol.)
Total	[1] 1,467	(X)	[2] 2,988	[1] 1,363	(X)	[2] 6,769
Commercial fertilizer	1,269	155,219	2,107	1,279	184,643	5,028
Lime	262	10,099	93	145	8,240	104
Chemicals for—						
Defoliation or growth control of crops	69	5,781	23	37	5,174	34
Insect control in livestock and poultry	352	(X)	26	132	(X)	19
Sprays, dusts, etc. for—						
Insects on hay and other crops	453	42,062	306	418	56,642	596
Nematodes in crops	34	1,267	17	27	1,754	29
Crop diseases	46	4,088	55	37	4,183	84
Weeds or grass in crops	645	84,914	346	549	110,793	784
Weeds or brush in pasture	78	4,967	10	44	4,003	13

X Not applicable.   [1] If more than 1 subentry was applicable, the farm was tabulated in each.
[2] Includes categories not shown separately.
Source: U.S. Bureau of the Census, Census of Agriculture: 1974, vol. I.

No. 1191. BALANCE SHEET OF THE FARMING SECTOR: 1950 TO 1978

[In billions of dollars, except percent. As of January 1. Prior to 1960, excludes Alaska and Hawaii. See also *Historical Statistics, Colonial Times to 1970*, series K 204–219, for data before revisions]

ITEM	1950	1955	1960	1965	1970	1973	1974	1975	1976	1977	1978, prel.
Assets	132.3	164.8	203.1	237.7	314.9	393.7	477.4	516.0	578.6	654.8	706.9
Annual percent increase [1]	7.1	4.5	4.3	3.2	5.8	7.7	21.3	8.1	12.1	13.2	8.0
Physical assets:											
Real estate	75.3	98.2	130.2	161.4	215.8	267.3	327.8	368.5	416.9	483.8	525.8
Non-real estate:											
Livestock [2]	12.9	11.2	15.2	14.5	23.5	34.1	42.4	24.6	29.5	29.1	32.0
Machinery, motor vehicles	12.2	18.6	22.7	24.8	32.3	39.3	44.3	55.7	65.0	72.3	75.4
Crops stored [3]	7.6	9.6	7.7	9.2	10.9	14.5	22.0	23.3	21.3	22.0	24.5
Household furnish., equipment	8.4	9.7	9.2	8.4	9.6	11.9	12.3	14.0	14.2	14.4	14.5
Financial assets:											
Deposits and currency	9.1	9.4	9.2	9.6	11.9	14.0	14.9	15.1	15.6	16.0	16.3
United States savings bonds	4.7	5.0	4.7	4.2	3.7	4.0	4.2	4.3	4.4	4.4	4.4
Investments in cooperatives	2.1	3.1	4.2	5.6	7.2	8.6	9.5	10.5	11.7	12.8	14.0
Claims	132.3	164.8	203.1	237.7	314.9	393.7	477.4	516.0	578.6	654.8	706.9
Liabilities	12.4	17.6	24.8	36.7	53.0	65.3	74.1	81.8	90.8	102.7	119.7
Real estate debt	5.6	8.2	12.1	18.9	29.2	35.7	41.3	46.3	51.1	56.6	64.2
Non-real estate debt to—											
Commodity Credit Corp.[4]	1.7	2.2	1.2	1.5	2.7	1.8	.7	.3	.3	1.0	4.5
Other reporting agencies [5]	2.8	4.0	6.7	10.0	15.8	22.0	26.2	29.2	33.1	37.8	42.7
Nonreporting creditors [6]	2.3	3.2	4.8	6.3	5.3	5.8	5.9	6.0	6.3	7.3	8.3
Proprietors' equities	119.9	147.3	178.3	201.0	261.9	328.4	403.3	434.2	487.8	552.1	587.2

[1] Average change from prior year shown; for 1950, change from 1945.　　[2] Beginning 1965, excludes horses and mules.　　[3] Includes all crops held on farms and crops held off farms by farmers as security for CCC loans. The latter totaled $1,827 million on Jan. 1, 1978.
[4] Nonrecourse CCC loans secured by crops owned by farmers are included as assets in this balance sheet.
[5] Loans of all operating banks, production credit associations, and Farmers Home Administration, and discounts of Federal intermediate credit banks for agricultural credit corporations and livestock loan companies.
[6] Loans and credits extended by dealers, merchants, finance companies, individuals, and others. Estimates based on fragmentary data.

Source: U.S. Dept. of Agriculture, Economics, Statistics, and Cooperatives Service, *Balance Sheet of the Farming Sector*, annual.

No. 1192. GROSS FARM PRODUCT—SUMMARY: 1950 TO 1977

[In billions of dollars. Prior to 1960, excludes Alaska and Hawaii. For definition of gross product and current and constant dollars, see text, pp. 437–439. Minus sign (−) denotes decrease. See *Historical Statistics, Colonial Times to 1970*, series K 220–239, for single-year figures prior to minor revisions issued in 1976]

ITEM	1950	1955	1960	1965	1970	1973	1974	1975	1976	1977
CURRENT DOLLARS										
Total value of farm output [1]	32.8	33.2	38.2	44.1	54.9	96.3	97.8	99.3	101.0	104.4
Farm marketings cash receipts [2]	28.5	29.2	34.4	39.4	50.4	87.2	92.7	87.9	94.0	94.2
Farm products consumed [3]	2.1	1.7	1.2	.8	.8	1.1	1.3	1.3	1.3	[4] 9.2
Change in farm inventories	.8	.5	.3	1.0	.1	3.2	−1.8	3.6	−1.6	1.0
Gross rental value of farm homes	1.5	1.7	2.1	2.5	3.0	3.9	4.7	5.3	5.9	[4]
Less: Intermediate products consumed	12.7	14.3	17.7	21.8	28.5	45.5	49.0	49.4	52.5	53.6
Plus: Other items	−.1	−.1	−.2	−.3	−.5	−.8	−.9	−.8	−.6	−.5
Equals: Gross farm product	20.0	18.8	20.2	22.0	25.9	50.1	48.0	49.2	47.9	50.3
Less: Capital consump. allowances [5]	2.5	3.5	4.1	4.8	6.4	8.4	9.9	11.9	13.1	14.5
Indirect business taxes	.8	1.0	1.3	1.5	2.0	2.1	2.3	2.5	2.6	[6] .4
Plus: Govt. payments to farm landlords	.2	.2	.6	2.1	3.3	2.3	.5	.7	.6	[6]
Equals: Income	16.9	14.5	15.5	17.9	20.8	41.8	36.2	35.5	32.7	35.4
CONSTANT (1972) DOLLARS										
Total value of farm output [1]	43.1	47.5	52.2	57.1	63.0	68.5	65.4	65.9	66.6	69.6
Farm marketings cash receipts [2]	35.3	40.5	45.7	50.4	57.5	61.3	60.6	59.6	63.3	63.8
Farm products consumed [3]	3.0	2.5	1.7	1.1	.9	.9	1.0	1.0	1.0	[4] 5.1
Change in farm inventories	1.4	.4	.3	1.1	.4	2.3	−.3	1.2	−1.6	.7
Gross rental value of farm homes	3.4	3.9	4.1	3.9	3.7	3.3	3.3	3.2	3.1	[4]
Less: Intermediate products consumed	16.1	18.1	22.3	26.7	31.3	35.8	32.6	31.6	33.2	33.4
Plus: Other items	−.2	−.2	−.3	−.4	−.6	−.4	−.4	−.5	−.4	−.4
Equals: Gross farm product	26.9	29.2	29.5	30.1	31.1	32.3	32.2	33.8	33.0	35.8

[1] Includes other farm income not shown separately.　　[2] Includes CCC loans.　　[3] In households where raised.
[4] Gross rental value of farm homes included with farm products consumed in farm households.
[5] With capital consumption adjustments.　　[6] Subsidies included with indirect business taxes.

Source: U.S. Bureau of Economic Analysis, *The National Income and Product Accounts of the United States, 1929–74*, and *Survey of Current Business*, July 1977 and March 1978.

No. 1193. Farm Income and Expenses: 1960 to 1977

[In millions of dollars, except as indicated. See also *Historical Statistics, Colonial Times to 1970*, series K 192, K 259–260, K 264–285, and K 326]

ITEM	1960	1965	1970	1972	1973	1974	1975	1976	1977
Gross income from farming, excl. inventory adjustment	38,497	45,507	58,569	70,119	95,505	99,951	96,938	104,087	108,100
Marketings, cash receipts	34,248	39,365	50,539	61,190	87,068	92,449	88,209	94,501	96,084
Crops	15,259	17,479	20,976	25,520	41,132	51,090	45,150	48,349	48,519
Livestock, livestock products	18,989	21,886	29,563	35,670	45,936	41,359	43,059	46,152	47,565
Government payments	702	2,463	3,717	3,961	2,607	531	807	734	1,819
Value of home consumption	1,205	811	751	831	1,104	1,295	1,269	1,334	1,324
Rental value of dwellings	2,098	2,481	3,019	3,474	3,913	4,687	5,420	6,166	7,326
Other farm income	244	387	543	663	813	989	1,233	1,352	1,547
Expenses of farm production	27,376	33,650	44,424	52,315	65,562	72,210	75,863	82,972	87,969
Operating expenses [1]	16,696	20,100	26,823	31,396	40,325	44,371	45,566	50,384	53,071
Feed purchased	4,552	5,674	8,028	8,397	13,224	14,513	12,647	14,291	13,840
Livestock purchased	2,506	2,912	4,324	6,668	8,065	5,131	4,950	5,871	6,736
Seed purchased [2]	519	720	927	1,115	1,617	2,082	2,293	2,537	2,856
Fertilizer and lime	1,344	1,994	2,390	2,690	3,354	5,808	6,383	6,032	6,089
Repairs and maintenance [3]	3,982	3,943	4,539	4,708	5,229	6,659	7,806	8,775	9,510
Miscellaneous [4]	3,793	4,857	6,615	7,818	8,836	10,178	11,487	12,878	14,040
Depreciation [5]	4,337	5,111	6,760	7,887	8,945	10,563	12,586	14,002	15,248
Taxes on farm property	1,529	1,874	2,596	2,815	2,888	3,096	3,333	3,607	3,809
Interest, farm mortgage debt	628	1,075	1,764	2,132	2,495	3,044	3,421	3,921	4,496
Wages paid hired farm labor	3,062	3,604	4,349	4,594	5,232	6,036	6,357	6,958	7,445
Net rent to nonoperator landlords	1,124	1,886	2,132	3,491	5,679	5,100	4,600	4,100	3,900
Net income of farm operators from farming, before inventory adjustment	11,121	11,857	14,145	17,804	29,943	27,741	21,075	21,115	20,131
Inventory change adjustment	397	1,042	6	861	3,406	−1,611	3,400	−2,365	412
Net income of farm operators from farming, after inventory adjustment	11,518	12,899	14,151	18,665	33,349	26,130	24,475	18,750	20,543
Average income per farm $1,000	2.9	3.8	4.8	6.5	11.8	9.3	8.8	6.8	7.6

[1] Excluding hired labor.   [2] Includes bulbs, plants, and trees.   [3] Includes expenditures for repairs and maintenance of farm buildings, petroleum fuel and oil, other motor-vehicle operations, and repairs on other machinery.   [4] Includes interest on non-real-estate debt, pesticides, ginning, electricity and telephone (business share), livestock marketing changes, containers, milk hauling, irrigation, grazing, binding materials, tolls for sirup, horses and mules, harness and saddlery, miscellaneous hardware (incl. blacksmithing), veterinary services and medicines, net insurance premiums (crop, fire, wind, and hail), machine hire and custom work, miscellaneous livestock and poultry, small hand tools, dairy supplies, nursery and greenhouse, apiary, and other miscellaneous.   [5] Includes other consumption of farm capital.

Source: U.S. Dept. of Agriculture, Economics, Statistics, and Cooperatives Service, *Farm Income Statistics*, July 1978.

No. 1194. Personal Income of the Farm Population: 1960 to 1977

[In millions of dollars, except as indicated. See *Historical Statistics, Colonial Times to 1970*, series K 256–258 and K 261–263, for data prior to revisions]

ITEM	1960	1965	1970	1972	1973	1974	1975	1976	1977
Net income of farm operators [1]	11,518	12,899	14,151	18,665	33,349	26,130	24,475	18,750	20,543
Less: Net income of nonresident operators	1,693	1,961	2,179	2,818	5,002	3,867	3,671	2,831	3,123
Plus: Wages, salaries, and other labor income of workers [2]	1,493	1,261	1,422	1,444	1,537	1,776	1,760	1,645	1,615
Less: Contributions of operators and workers to social insurance [2]	192	231	389	435	654	686	676	712	759
Equals: Personal income of farm population from farm sources	11,126	11,968	13,005	16,856	29,230	23,353	21,888	16,852	18,276
Plus: Personal income of farm population from nonfarm sources	7,236	10,627	14,473	17,751	19,690	21,798	22,660	24,364	24,684
Equals: Personal income of farm population	18,362	22,595	27,478	34,607	48,920	45,151	44,548	41,216	42,960
Per capita personal income:									
From all sources dol	1,174	1,828	2,829	3,601	5,165	4,874	5,026	4,994	5,503
From farm sources dol	711	968	1,339	1,754	3,086	2,521	2,469	2,042	2,341
From nonfarm sources dol	463	860	1,490	1,847	2,079	2,353	2,556	2,952	3,162
Per capita disposable personal income:									
Of farm population dol	1,083	1,692	2,520	3,244	4,700	4,355	4,520	4,427	4,946
Of nonfarm population dol	2,014	2,480	3,389	3,865	4,266	4,660	5,113	5,548	6,049
Percent farm of nonfarm	53.8	68.2	74.1	83.9	110.2	93.5	88.4	79.8	81.8

[1] Includes government payments.   [2] Farm residents only.

Source: U.S. Dept. of Agriculture, Economics, Statistics, and Cooperatives Service, *Farm Income Statistics*, July 1978.

No. 1195. INDEXES OF PRICES RECEIVED AND PAID BY FARMERS: 1950 TO 1977

[1967=100, except as noted. Prior to 1960, excludes Alaska and Hawaii. See also *Historical Statistics, Colonial Times to 1970*, series K 344–353]

ITEM	1950	1955	1960	1965	1970	1972	1973	1974	1975	1976	1977 [1]
Prices received, all products	103	93	95	98	110	125	179	192	185	186	183
Crops	103	103	99	103	100	114	175	224	201	197	193
Livestock and products	102	85	92	94	118	136	183	165	172	177	175
Prices paid, total	75	81	88	94	112	125	144	166	180	191	202
Living	76	84	90	95	114	123	133	151	166	176	170
Production	86	87	92	96	108	121	146	166	182	193	200
Interest payable per acre	18	28	45	79	134	160	188	229	271	287	331
Taxes payable per acre	36	47	69	87	129	142	145	154	166	178	195
Wage rates [2]	50	61	74	86	128	142	155	178	192	210	226
Parity ratio [3]	101	84	80	76	72	74	91	86	76	71	67

[1] Preliminary.   [2] Straight average of seasonally adjusted quarterly indexes.
[3] Ratio of prices received by farmers to prices paid, including interest, taxes, and wage rates; 1910–14=100.

Source: U.S. Dept. of Agriculture, Economics, Statistics, and Cooperatives Service, *Agricultural Prices: Annual Summary*.

No. 1196. PRODUCTION ASSETS USED IN AGRICULTURE: 1950 TO 1978

ITEM	1950	1955	1960	1965	1970	1972	1973	1974	1975	1976	1977	1978, prel.
Total [1] ____ bil. dol__	94.0	118.3	162.9	193.6	247.0	287.5	323.5	395.4	426.4	484.3	551.8	597.0
Average—												
Per farm____$1,000__	17.2	25.8	39.7	56.0	77.7	99.1	113.1	140.1	152.5	175.0	201.5	220.6
Per farm worker $1,000__	9.4	13.7	22.2	31.7	53.8	64.6	73.7	90.9	96.8	111.2	125.7	143.3

[1] Includes farm real estate less value of operators' dwellings; livestock; machinery; motor vehicles (40 percent of the value of automobiles and 78 percent of the value of trucks); one-half of the Jan. 1 inventory value of feed crops (excluding those under CCC loan), hay and forage stored on farms; and working capital needed to meet farm production expenses.

Source: U.S. Dept. of Agriculture, Economics, Statistics, and Cooperatives Service, *Balance Sheet of the Farming Sector*, annual.

No. 1197. GOVERNMENT PAYMENTS TO FARMS, BY PROGRAM, AND BY VALUE OF FARM SALES: 1960 TO 1977

[In millions of dollars, except average per farm. See also *Historical Statistics, Colonial Times to 1970*, series K 326–329]

ITEM	1960	1965	1970	1971	1972	1973	1974	1975	1976	1977
Total [1]	702	2,463	3,717	3,145	3,961	2,607	531	807	734	1,819
Program:										
Feed grain	–	1,391	1,504	1,054	1,845	1,142	101	279	196	187
Wheat	–	525	871	878	856	474	70	77	135	887
Cotton	–	70	919	822	813	718	42	138	108	89
Conservation	223	224	208	173	198	72	192	193	209	328
Soil Bank	370	160	2	–	–	–	–	–	–	–
Sugar Act	59	75	88	80	82	82	78	61	1	65
Wool	51	18	49	69	110	65	(Z)	13	39	5
Value of sales										
Less than $2,500	100	288	276	228	267	150	34	37	27	68
$2,500–$4,999	81	208	257	215	248	130	35	44	32	74
$5,000–$9,999	144	396	408	332	379	190	42	61	47	113
$10,000–$19,999	159	627	684	558	639	326	65	94	75	180
$20,000–$39,999	111	487	842	695	820	464	93	174	167	411
$40,000–$99,999	77	310	722	629	857	664	128	232	245	616
$100,000 to $199,999	} 30	} 147 {	269	247	366	323	56	90	91	230
$200,000 and over			259	241	385	360	78	75	50	127
Average value per farm____dol__	177	734	1,260	1,084	1,385	924	190	292	268	672
Farms with sales of—										
Less than $2,500	54	194	235	199	241	145	34	37	28	71
$2,500–$4,999	131	451	608	522	636	381	107	133	102	243
$5,000–$9,999	218	780	1,015	849	1,013	569	130	188	152	374
$10,000–$19,999	320	1,351	1,754	1,465	1,741	964	198	286	236	579
$20,000–$39,999	489	1,739	2,583	2,158	2,555	1,410	284	539	517	1,280
$40,000–$99,999	856	2,480	4,056	3,364	3,949	2,135	387	739	718	1,770
$100,000 to $199,999	} 1,304	} 4,083 {	6,897	5,744	6,655	3,549	560	968	875	2,150
$200,000 and over			14,389	12,050	14,259	7,826	1,560	1,596	943	2,309

– Represents zero.   Z Less than $500,000.   [1] Data by type of program include cropland adjustment beginning 1970, and miscellaneous programs beginning 1971, not shown separately.

Source: U.S. Dept. of Agriculture, Economics, Statistics, and Cooperatives Service, *Farm Income Statistics*, July 1978.

No. 1198. Farms, Farm Income, and Expenses, by Value of Sales: 1970 to 1977

[See table 1193 for components of income and expenses]

FARMS WITH VALUE OF SALES OF—	Number of farms (1,000)	Gross income (bil. dol.)	Cash receipts (bil. dol.)	Production expenses (bil. dol.)	Realized net income (bil. dol.)	PERCENT DISTRIBUTION				
						Number of farms	Gross income	Cash receipts	Production expenses	Realized net income
1970: Less than $2,500__	1,173	2.7	1.5	1.6	1.1	39.8	4.6	2.8	3.7	7.5
$2,500–$4,999_____	423	2.3	1.8	1.6	.7	14.3	4.0	3.4	3.6	5.1
$5,000–$9,999_____	402	4.1	3.6	2.8	1.3	13.6	6.9	6.5	6.2	9.2
$10,000–$19,999____	390	7.3	6.8	5.0	2.3	13.2	12.4	12.3	11.2	16.1
$20,000–$39,999____	326	11.3	10.7	7.9	3.4	11.1	19.2	19.5	17.7	24.0
$40,000–$99,999____	178	12.5	12.1	9.4	3.1	6.1	21.4	22.1	21.3	21.8
$100,000–$199,999__	39	6.0	5.9	5.0	1.0	1.3	10.2	10.8	11.2	7.2
$200,000 or more__	18	12.5	12.4	11.2	1.3	.6	21.3	22.6	25.1	9.1
1975: Less than $2,500__	1,007	3.3	1.1	2.0	1.4	36.4	3.5	1.2	2.6	6.4
$2,500–$4,999_____	330	2.1	1.4	1.6	.5	11.9	2.2	1.6	2.2	2.4
$5,000–$9,999_____	324	3.5	2.8	2.6	.9	11.7	3.6	3.1	3.5	4.2
$10,000–$19,999____	329	6.3	5.6	4.6	1.7	11.9	6.5	6.2	6.1	8.1
$20,000–$39,999____	323	11.7	10.9	8.4	3.3	11.7	12.0	12.1	11.0	15.7
$40,000–$99,999____	314	23.5	22.6	17.3	6.2	11.3	24.3	25.0	22.8	29.5
$100,000–$199,999__	93	14.9	14.5	11.4	3.5	3.4	15.3	16.1	15.0	16.6
$200,000 or more__	47	31.6	31.3	27.9	3.6	1.7	32.6	34.7	36.8	17.1
1977: Less than $2,500__	958	3.9	1.2	2.5	1.5	35.3	3.7	1.2	2.8	7.2
$2,500–$4,999_____	304	2.2	1.4	1.8	.5	11.2	2.0	1.4	2.0	2.3
$5,000–$9,999_____	302	3.6	2.7	2.8	.8	11.2	3.3	2.7	3.1	4.0
$10,000–$19,999____	311	6.3	5.4	4.8	1.6	11.5	5.8	5.4	5.4	7.7
$20,000–$39,999____	321	12.1	11.1	8.9	3.2	11.9	11.2	11.1	10.2	16.0
$40,000–$99,999____	348	26.8	25.5	20.4	6.4	12.9	24.8	25.6	23.2	32.0
$100,000–$199,999__	107	17.4	16.9	13.8	3.6	4.0	16.1	17.0	15.7	17.7
$200,000 or more__	55	35.7	35.4	33.1	2.6	2.0	33.1	35.6	37.6	13.1

No. 1199. Income Per Farm, by Value of Sales: 1970 to 1977

[In thousands of dollars]

VALUE OF SALES	1970			1975			1976			1977		
	Total	Off-farm	Net	Total	Off-farm	Net	Total	Off-farm	Net	Total	Off-farm	Net
Less than $2,500____	8.3	7.4	.9	14.2	12.8	1.3	15.8	14.4	1.4	16.6	15.1	1.5
$2,500–$4,999_____	7.9	6.2	1.7	13.7	12.2	1.5	15.3	13.8	1.5	16.1	14.6	1.5
$5,000–$9,999_____	8.7	5.5	3.2	12.9	10.2	2.7	14.2	11.6	2.6	14.9	12.2	2.7
$10,000 to $19,999____	10.0	4.2	5.9	13.1	7.9	5.2	14.0	9.0	5.0	14.5	9.5	5.0
$20,000 to $39,999____	13.8	3.4	10.4	16.1	5.8	10.3	16.5	6.6	9.9	16.9	7.0	10.0
$40,000 to $99,999____	21.3	3.9	17.3	24.9	5.1	19.8	24.8	5.7	19.1	24.5	6.0	18.5
$100,000 or more____	48.2	7.6	40.5	58.8	8.0	50.7	54.9	9.1	45.8	47.9	9.6	38.3

Source of tables 1198 and 1199: U.S. Dept. of Agriculture, Economics, Statistics, and Cooperatives Service, *Farm Income Statistics*, July 1978.

No. 1200. Farm Debt Outstanding, by Type of Lender: 1960 to 1978

[In billions of dollars, except percent. As of Jan. 1. See also *Historical Statistics, Colonial Times to 1970*, series K 361–367 and K 376–380]

LENDER	1960	1965	1970	1973	1974	1975	1976	1977	1978
Farm debt, total_____	24.8	36.8	53.1	65.4	74.2	81.8	90.8	102.7	119.7
Average annual percent change [1]_____	7.1	8.2	7.6	7.2	13.5	10.2	11.0	13.1	16.6
Real estate debt_____	12.1	18.9	29.2	35.8	41.3	46.3	51.1	56.6	64.2
Federal land banks_____	2.3	3.7	6.7	9.1	10.9	13.4	16.0	18.5	21.5
Life insurance companies_____	2.8	4.3	5.7	5.6	6.0	6.3	6.7	7.4	8.7
Commercial and savings banks_____	1.5	2.4	3.5	4.8	5.5	6.0	6.3	6.8	7.8
Farmers Home Administration [2]_____	.7	1.3	2.3	2.8	3.0	3.2	3.4	3.7	4.0
Individuals and others [3]_____	4.8	7.2	11.0	13.4	15.9	17.4	18.7	20.3	22.3
Non-real estate debt [4]_____	12.7	17.9	23.9	29.6	32.9	35.5	39.8	46.1	55.5
Commercial and savings banks_____	4.8	7.0	10.3	14.3	17.2	18.2	20.2	23.3	25.7
Production credit associations_____	1.4	2.3	4.5	6.6	7.8	9.5	10.8	12.2	13.5
Individuals and others [5]_____	4.9	6.3	5.3	5.8	5.9	6.1	6.4	7.3	8.2

[1] Change from prior year shown; for 1960, change from 1955.
[2] Includes direct and insured farm ownership, farm housing, soil and water related loans secured by farm real estate. [3] Includes seller and other individual financing of farm real estate sales and unclassified credit sources.
[4] Includes Federal intermediate credit banks, Farmers Home Admin., and CCC, not shown separately.
[5] Includes merchants and dealers, individuals, and all other unclassified credit sources.

Source: U.S. Dept. of Agriculture, Economics, Statistics, and Cooperatives Service, *Agricultural Outlook*, various issues.

No. 1201. Farm Income—Cash Receipts From Farm Marketings: 1960 to 1977

[See headnote, table 1202. See also *Historical Statistics, Colonial Times to 1970*, series K 286–302]

ITEM	TOTAL MARKET SALES (mil. dol.)								PERCENT		
	1960	1965	1970	1973	1974	1975	1976	1977	1960	1970	1977
Farm marketings	34,248	39,365	50,539	87,068	92,449	88,209	94,501	96,084	100.0	100.0	100.0
All crops	15,259	17,479	20,976	41,132	51,090	45,150	48,349	48,519	44.6	41.5	50.5
Percent of total	44.6	44.4	41.5	47.2	55.3	51.2	51.2	50.5	(X)	(X)	(X)
Cotton lint and seed	2,362	2,330	1,254	2,798	2,893	2,311	3,477	3,939	6.9	2.5	4.1
Tobacco	1,154	1,186	1,388	1,570	2,097	2,155	2,310	2,331	3.4	2.7	2.4
Food grains	2,450	2,042	2,542	7,194	8,511	7,760	6,898	6,139	7.1	5.0	6.4
Oilbearing crops	1,362	2,173	3,590	7,580	9,965	7,273	9,252	9,393	4.0	7.1	9.8
Feed crops	2,986	3,693	5,109	10,605	13,959	12,150	13,079	12,017	8.7	10.1	12.5
Vegetables [1]	1,980	2,618	2,814	4,351	5,329	5,350	5,245	5,661	5.8	5.6	5.9
Fruits and tree nuts [1]	1,529	1,650	2,070	3,444	3,435	3,525	3,617	4,262	4.5	4.1	4.4
Other [2]	1,436	1,787	2,209	3,590	4,901	4,626	4,471	4,777	4.2	4.4	5.0
All livestock and products	18,989	21,886	29,563	45,936	41,359	43,059	46,152	47,565	55.4	58.5	49.5
Percent of total	55.4	55.6	58.5	52.8	44.7	48.8	48.8	49.5	(X)	(X)	(X)
Hogs	2,869	3,607	4,508	7,604	6,975	7,883	7,261	7,327	8.4	8.9	7.6
Cattle and calves	7,380	8,942	13,633	22,410	17,819	17,524	19,302	20,230	21.5	27.0	21.1
Sheep and lambs	325	329	334	389	370	385	392	389	.9	.7	.4
Wool	108	95	57	120	79	54	73	77	.3	.1	.1
Dairy products	4,760	5,038	6,525	8,080	9,445	9,922	11,428	11,776	13.9	12.9	12.2
Eggs	1,738	1,785	2,110	2,975	2,881	2,814	3,136	2,917	5.1	4.2	3.0
Broilers and farm chickens	1,122	1,304	1,564	2,906	2,568	3,063	3,059	3,243	3.3	3.1	3.4
Turkeys, other poultry [3]	433	494	576	1,054	808	934	971	1,059	1.3	1.1	1.1
Other [4]	254	292	256	398	414	480	530	547	.7	.5	.6

X Not applicable.   [1] Melons included with vegetables.   [2] Sugar crops, greenhouse and nursery products, forest products, legume and grass seeds, hops, mint, broom-corn, popcorn, hemp fiber and seed, and flax fiber.   [3] Ducks, geese, guineas, pigeons, quail, pheasants, and turkey hatching eggs.   [4] Mohair, honey, beeswax, bees, goats, rabbits, and fur animals.

No. 1202. Farm Marketings, by Price Support Status: 1960 to 1977

[Farm marketings represent gross receipts from commercial market sales as well as net Commodity Credit Corporation loans. See also *Historical Statistics, Colonial Times to 1970*, series K 303–325]

CROP	TOTAL MARKET SALES (mil. dol.)						PERCENT DISTRIBUTION				
	1960	1965	1970	1975	1976	1977	1960	1965	1970	1975	1977
Total	34,248	39,365	50,539	88,209	94,501	96,084	100.0	100.0	100.0	100.0	100.0
Under price support	15,277	16,677	20,667	42,016	46,114	45,221	44.6	42.4	40.9	47.7	47.1
Mandatory support	13,729	14,382	17,072	35,082	37,153	36,290	40.1	36.6	33.8	39.8	37.8
Basic commodities	7,644	7,717	8,625	21,131	22,263	21,461	22.3	19.6	17.1	24.0	22.3
Cotton (lint)	2,137	2,065	1,037	2,006	3,095	3,580	6.2	5.2	2.1	2.3	3.7
Wheat	2,184	1,637	2,067	6,695	5,838	5,152	6.4	4.2	4.1	7.6	5.4
Corn	1,762	2,180	3,326	8,500	9,416	8,656	5.1	5.5	6.6	9.6	9.0
Tobacco	1,154	1,186	1,388	2,155	2,310	2,331	3.4	3.0	2.7	2.4	2.4
Rice	244	377	447	1,031	1,030	958	.7	1.0	.9	1.2	1.0
Peanuts	163	272	360	744	574	784	.5	.7	.7	.8	.8
Nonbasic [1]	6,085	6,665	8,447	13,951	14,890	14,829	17.8	17.0	16.7	15.8	15.5
Dairy products	4,760	5,038	6,525	9,923	11,428	11,776	13.9	12.8	12.9	11.3	12.3
Oats	206	195	230	342	339	293	.6	.5	.4	.4	.3
Barley	244	305	298	618	652	500	.7	.8	.6	.7	.5
Sorghum grain	369	496	641	1,298	1,163	1,113	1.1	1.3	1.3	1.5	1.2
Sugar beets	190	250	393	821	617	518	.6	.6	.8	.9	.5
Other [2]	316	381	360	949	691	629	.9	1.0	.7	1.1	.7
Nonmandatory [3]	1,548	2,295	3,595	6,934	8,961	8,931	4.5	5.8	7.1	7.9	9.3
Soybeans	1,126	1,812	3,164	6,432	8,617	8,541	3.3	4.6	6.3	7.3	8.9
Cottonseed	225	265	217	(4)	(4)	(4)	.6	.7	.4	(4)	(4)
Flaxseed	70	87	66	97	61	68	.2	.2	.1	.1	.1
Dry beans	127	131	148	405	283	322	.4	.3	.3	.5	.3
Not under price support	18,971	22,688	29,872	46,193	48,387	50,863	55.4	57.6	59.1	52.5	52.9

[1] Under legislation in effect in 1969.   [2] Includes wool, mohair, honey, tung nuts (1960–1970), rye, and sugarcane.   [3] Marketing not estimated for naval stores and castor beans.   [4] Not under price support.

Source of tables 1201 and 1202: U.S. Dept. of Agriculture, Economics, Statistics, and Cooperatives Service, *Farm Income Statistics*, July 1978.

No. **1203.** FARM INCOME—FARM MARKETINGS, 1974 TO 1977, AND PRINCIPAL COMMODITIES IN ORDER OF MARKETING RECEIPTS, 1977, BY STATES

[In millions of dollars. Cattle include calves; sheep include lambs; and greenhouse includes nursery. See table 1193]

STATE	1974	1975	1976	1977, prel. Total	Crops	Live-stock and products	Government payments	State rank for total farm marketing and principal commodities in order of marketing receipts, 1977
U.S.	92,449	88,209	94,501	96,084	48,519	47,565	1,818.9	Cattle, milk, corn, soybeans.
N.E.	1,139	1,105	1,255	1,238	429	809	5.7	
Maine	418	366	446	418	155	263	2.1	38- Potatoes, eggs, broilers, milk.
N.H.	71	73	78	79	24	55	.6	48- Milk, eggs, apples, greenhouse.
Vt.	221	226	262	267	22	245	2.0	42- Milk, cattle, eggs, apples.
Mass.	195	201	214	214	109	105	.6	45- Greenhouse, eggs, apples, cranberries.
R.I.	23	27	27	26	15	11	–	49- Greenhouse, milk, potatoes, eggs.
Conn.	211	212	228	234	104	130	.4	44- Milk, eggs, greenhouse, tobacco.
M.A.	3,393	3,490	3,868	3,979	1,377	2,602	17.2	
N.Y.	1,495	1,563	1,717	1,725	525	1,200	8.6	21- Milk, cattle, greenhouse, eggs.
N.J.	340	326	341	351	252	99	1.1	40- Milk, greenhouse, eggs, tomatoes.
Pa.	1,558	1,601	1,810	1,903	600	1,303	7.5	18- Milk, mushrooms, cattle, eggs.
E.N.C.	15,516	14,993	16,865	16,801	9,109	7,692	134.5	
Ohio	2,536	2,552	2,736	2,794	1,637	1,157	33.1	11- Soybeans, corn, milk, cattle.
Ind.	3,133	2,940	3,252	3,239	1,973	1,266	21.8	8- Corn, soybeans, hogs, cattle.
Ill.	5,731	5,193	6,137	5,792	3,920	1,872	32.1	4- Corn, soybeans, hogs, cattle.
Mich.	1,652	1,648	1,724	1,824	983	841	21.2	19- Milk, corn, cattle, dry beans.
Wis.	2,464	2,660	3,016	3,152	596	2,556	26.3	9- Milk, cattle, hogs, corn.
W.N.C.	27,110	23,734	24,599	25,236	10,940	14,296	710.0	
Minn.	4,430	3,810	3,892	4,323	2,084	2,239	82.8	5- Milk, cattle, soybeans, corn.
Iowa	7,456	6,487	7,091	7,065	2,765	4,300	28.9	2- Hogs, cattle, soybeans, corn.
Mo.	2,697	2,636	2,702	2,870	1,193	1,077	51.2	10- Cattle, soybeans, hogs, milk.
N. Dak.	2,426	1,831	1,676	1,539	1,056	483	122.6	25- Wheat, cattle, barley, milk.
S. Dak.	2,065	1,798	1,799	1,610	493	1,117	94.9	24- Cattle, hogs, wheat, milk.
Nebr.	4,070	3,859	3,827	3,980	1,724	2,256	92.9	6- Cattle, corn, hogs, wheat.
Kans.	3,966	3,313	3,612	3,849	1,625	2,224	236.7	7- Cattle, wheat, hogs, corn.
S.A.	9,661	10,149	10,440	10,296	5,698	4,598	134.8	
Del.	267	268	278	261	81	180	.4	43- Broilers, soybeans, corn, milk.
Md.	629	675	672	657	229	428	3.4	36- Broilers, milk, corn, soybeans.
Va.	949	989	1,024	1,004	444	560	17.1	32- Milk, tobacco, cattle, broilers.
W. Va.	143	138	141	148	43	105	4.5	46- Milk, cattle, apples, broilers.
N.C.	2,575	2,638	2,810	2,622	1,554	1,068	21.7	13- Tobacco, broilers, hogs, milk.
S.C.	861	807	833	784	507	277	15.7	35- Tobacco, soybeans, cattle, milk.
Ga.	2,087	2,143	2,179	2,194	960	1,234	51.2	15- Broilers, peanuts, eggs, cattle.
Fla.	2,150	2,491	2,503	2,626	1,880	746	20.8	12- Oranges, cattle, greenhouse, milk.
E.S.C.	5,231	5,216	6,227	6,386	3,246	3,140	73.2	
Ky.	1,483	1,441	1,646	1,806	1,065	741	7.2	20- Tobacco, cattle, milk, soybeans.
Tenn.	1,015	1,117	1,279	1,370	694	676	12.4	27- Soybeans, cattle, milk, tobacco.
Ala.	1,239	1,339	1,595	1,496	569	927	29.7	26- Broilers, cattle, eggs, soybeans.
Miss.	1,494	1,319	1,707	1,714	918	796	23.9	22- Soybeans, cotton, cattle, broilers.
W.S.C.	11,007	10,958	11,801	12,562	6,296	6,266	340.0	
Ark.	2,149	2,137	2,370	2,469	1,294	1,175	53.5	14- Soybeans, broilers, rice, cattle.
La.	1,296	1,115	1,326	1,257	851	406	44.4	28- Soybeans, cattle, rice, cotton.
Okla.	1,896	1,870	1,878	1,926	766	1,160	84.1	17- Cattle, wheat, milk, cotton.
Tex.	5,666	5,836	6,227	6,910	3,385	3,525	158.0	3- Cattle, cotton, sorghum grain, milk.
Mt.	7,311	6,812	7,128	7,138	2,823	4,315	221.2	
Mont.	1,154	1,009	1,039	957	443	514	61.4	33- Cattle, wheat, barley, hay.
Idaho	1,442	1,269	1,245	1,170	694	476	42.9	30- Cattle, potatoes, wheat, milk.
Wyo.	352	374	397	452	72	380	10.5	37- Cattle, sheep, sugar beets, wheat.
Colo.	2,103	1,919	1,994	2,060	561	1,499	65.4	16- Cattle, wheat, corn, milk.
N. Mex.	585	726	698	791	222	569	15.1	34- Cattle, cotton, milk, hay.
Ariz.	1,218	1,048	1,240	1,198	689	509	4.7	29- Cattle, cotton, milk, hay.
Utah	320	330	362	363	96	267	18.6	39- Cattle, milk, hay, turkeys.
Nev.	137	137	153	147	46	101	2.6	47- Cattle, milk, hay, potatoes.
Pac.	12,081	11,752	12,318	12,448	8,601	3,847	182.3	
Wash.	1,793	1,828	1,836	1,708	1,200	508	58.8	23- Wheat, milk, apples, cattle.
Oreg.	1,093	1,039	1,074	1,034	678	356	23.5	31- Cattle, wheat, milk, potatoes.
Calif.	8,613	8,497	9,070	9,370	6,456	2,914	75.2	1- Milk, cattle, cotton, grapes.
Alaska	7	10	10	11	7	4	.1	50- Greenhouse, milk, hay, potatoes.
Hawaii	575	378	328	325	260	65	24.7	41- Sugarcane for sugar, pineapple, milk, cattle.

- Represents zero.

Source: U.S. Dept. of Agriculture, Economics, Statistics, and Cooperatives Service, *Farm Income Statistics*, July bulletin and State supplement.

No. 1204. COMMODITY CREDIT CORPORATION—SUMMARY: 1960 TO 1977

[In millions of dollars. Through 1976, as of June 30 or for years ending June 30; beginning 1977, as of Sept. 30 or for years ending Sept. 30. The Commodity Credit Corporation (CCC) is a wholly government-owned corporation established by Congress in 1933. Its purpose is stabilizing, supporting, and protecting farm income and prices; assisting in maintenance of balanced adequate supplies of agricultural commodities; and facilitating orderly distribution of agricultural commodities. See also *Historical Statistics, Colonial Times to 1970*, series K 330-343]

ITEM	1960	1965	1970	1972	1973	1974	1975	1976	1977
Loans made	1,507	2,144	2,388	2,801	1,580	1,256	852	1,131	3,621
Loans outstanding [1]	1,347	2,534	2,952	2,474	1,418	720	334	637	3,245
Wheat	163	136	576	436	77	10	4	24	1,814
Corn	646	616	632	856	451	115	39	61	239
Cotton	9	775	170	23	26	34	143	24	13
Tobacco	418	826	845	671	481	249	118	353	652
Cost of acquisitions [1][2]	4,020	2,005	1,518	947	576	402	835	657	997
Wheat	371	169	217	81	56	130	4	14	72
Corn	361	140	49	89	43	6	2	5	2
Cotton	2,507	952	304	2	(Z)	(Z)	(Z)	(Z)	(Z)
Dairy products	223	325	253	385	160	55	480	115	721
Commodities owned [1][2]	6,021	3,892	1,858	1,090	479	114	416	659	985
Wheat	2,452	1,297	405	488	194	26	2	(Z)	23
Corn	1,700	595	293	172	99	11	(Z)	1	(Z)
Cotton	880	1,123	225	5	1	–	(Z)	–	(Z)
Dairy products	107	137	134	131	65	25	290	259	703
Sales and donations, cost [2]	3,234	2,458	902	1,065	1,190	766	530	457	640
Other expenses [2]	529	393	289	200	184	36	17	22	30

– Represents zero.   Z Less than $500,000.
[1] Includes amounts for commodities not shown separately.   [2] Data comparable for 1960–1970; price support commodities only. Thereafter, includes Commodity Export and Special Activities programs.

Source: U.S. Agricultural Stabilization and Conservation Service, *Commodity Credit Corporation Report of Financial Condition and Operations*, annual.

No. 1205. FARM EMPLOYMENT AND INDEX OF WAGE RATES: 1950 TO 1977

[Excludes Alaska and Hawaii. See also *Historical Statistics, Colonial Times to 1970*, series K 174-181]

ITEM	1950	1955	1960	1965	1970	1972	1973	1974	1975	1976	1977
Employment [1]_____1,000__	9,926	8,381	7,057	5,610	4,523	4,373	4,337	4,389	4,342	4,374	4,152
Family [2]_____1,000__	7,597	6,345	5,172	4,128	3,348	3,228	3,169	3,075	3,026	2,997	2,856
Hired [3]_____1,000__	2,329	2,036	1,885	1,482	1,175	1,146	1,168	1,314	1,317	1,377	1,296
Farm wage rates index 1967=100__	51	61	74	86	129	143	157	176	190	208	225

[1] 1950–1973, averages of monthly estimates of employed during last full calendar week ending at least one day before end of month; beginning 1974, annual quarterly averages.   [2] Includes farm operators doing 1 or more hours of farm work and unpaid family members doing 15 or more hours of farm work during survey week.
[3] Includes all persons doing 1 or more hours of farm work for pay during survey week. Members of operators' families doing any farm work for cash wages are counted as hired workers.

Source: U.S. Dept. of Agriculture, Economics, Statistics, and Cooperatives Service, *Farm Labor*, quarterly.

No. 1206. HIRED FARMWORKERS—CHARACTERISTICS AND EARNINGS: 1976 AND 1977

[Persons 14 years old and over; civilian noninstitutional population. As of December. Based on Current Population Survey; see text, p. 1. For composition of regions, see fig. I, inside front cover]

CHARACTERISTIC	WORKERS (1,000)		MEDIAN EARNINGS PER DAY		CHARACTERISTIC	WORKERS (1,000)		MEDIAN EARNINGS PER DAY	
	1976	1977	1976	1977		1976	1977	1976	1977
All workers	2,767	2,730	$15.85	$17.58	14–19 years	1,178	1,081	$13.30	$14.04
					Migratory	82	60	14.90	13.63
White	2,059	1,974	15.60	16.93	Nonmigratory	1,096	1,020	13.15	14.06
Hispanic	310	294	20.00	20.00					
Black and other	397	462	14.55	18.30	20 years and over	1,589	1,650	18.30	20.00
					Migratory	131	130	20.00	20.00
Male	2,086	2,092	16.50	18.37	Nonmigratory	1,458	1,519	17.95	20.00
Female	681	638	14.15	16.11	Hired farmwork:				
					Under 25 days	1,145	1,056	14.05	15.75
Region:					25–74 days	652	667	15.40	16.41
Northeast	223	214	14.50	15.23	75–149 days	347	322	18.05	19.46
North Central	748	730	15.10	16.65	150–249 days	290	295	19.80	20.00
South	1,150	1,150	14.95	16.96	250–299 days	155	170	20.00	20.00
West	645	636	20.00	20.00	300 days and over	179	221	20.00	19.98

Source: U.S. Dept. of Agriculture, Economics, Statistics, and Cooperatives Service, *The Hired Farm Working Force*, annual.

No. **1207.** Civilian Consumer Expenditures for Farm Foods—Farm Value and Marketing Bill: 1960 to 1977

[In billions of dollars, except percent. See *Historical Statistics, Colonial Times to 1970*, series K 358-360, for data before revisions]

ITEM	1960	1965	1970	1971	1972	1973	1974	1975	1976	1977, prel.
Consumer expenditures___	66.9	81.1	106.0	110.7	117.8	133.6	149.3	161.4	172.3	180.0
Farm value_____	22.3	27.1	34.8	35.3	39.3	51.1	56.0	54.9	56.3	56.5
Marketing bill [1]_____	44.6	54.0	71.2	75.4	78.4	82.5	93.3	106.5	116.0	123.5
Percent of total_____	66.6	66.6	67.2	68.1	66.6	61.8	62.5	66.0	67.3	68.6
Labor cost [2]_____	19.7	23.3	32.3	34.5	37.6	40.4	46.7	49.1	54.3	58.8
Railroad and truck transport [3]_____	4.1	4.2	5.2	6.0	6.1	6.1	7.3	8.3	9.5	10.4
Corporate profits: [4]										
Before taxes_____	2.1	3.0	3.6	3.9	3.5	4.6	5.3	8.2	8.3	8.1
After taxes_____	.9	1.6	1.6	2.0	2.1	2.6	3.0	4.4	4.6	4.5
Packaging materials___	5.4	6.2	8.5	9.0	9.4	9.9	11.6	13.4	15.0	16.0
Other [5]_____	13.3	17.3	21.6	22.0	21.8	21.6	22.4	27.5	28.9	30.2

[1] The difference between total civilian expenditures for domestic farm-originated food products and the farm value or payment farmers received for the equivalent farm products. Excludes food sold to the Armed Forces or exported. [2] Includes imputed earnings of proprietors, partners, and family workers not receiving stated remuneration, and supplements to wages and salaries such as social security and unemployment insurance taxes and health insurance premiums; excludes cost of for-hire transportation. [3] Includes charges for protective services, heating, and refrigeration; excludes local hauling. [4] Excludes profits of unincorporated firms or transportation firms. [5] Includes advertising, depreciation, fuel, electric power, containers, air and water transportation, interest on borrowed capital, taxes other than income, and noncorporate profits.

Source: U.S. Dept. of Agriculture, Economics, Statistics, and Cooperatives Service. In *Agricultural Statistics,* annual.

No. **1208.** Farm-Retail Spreads for A Basket of Farm-Originated Food Products Purchased Per Household, by Commodity Group: 1960 to 1977

[In dollars, except as indicated. These estimates are for a market basket of domestic farm-originated food products purchased annually per household in 1960-1961 by urban wage-earner and clerical-worker families and single workers living alone. Quantities of food valued do not change from year to year. See *Historical Statistics, Colonial Times to 1970*, series K 354-357, for earlier market basket totals]

COMMODITY GROUP AND VALUE	1960	1965	1970	1971	1972	1973	1974	1975	1976	1977, prel.
All farm food products,[1] retail cost_	996	1,037	1,228	1,250	1,311	1,537	1,750	1,876	1,895	1,937
Farm value_____	393	416	478	479	524	701	747	784	748	750
Percent of total retail cost____	39	40	39	38	40	46	43	42	39	39
Farm-retail spread_____	603	621	750	771	787	836	1,003	1,092	1,147	1,186
Meat products, retail cost_____	287	307	381	377	422	523	533	583	584	569
Farm value_____	163	181	210	207	246	331	299	348	314	313
Percent of total retail cost_____	57	59	55	55	58	63	56	60	54	55
Farm-retail spread_____	124	126	171	170	176	192	234	235	270	256
Dairy products, retail cost_____	177	178	219	225	229	249	297	303	331	341
Farm value_____	79	79	104	106	109	124	146	150	170	171
Percent of total retail cost_____	45	44	48	47	48	50	49	49	51	50
Farm-retail spread_____	98	99	115	119	120	125	151	153	161	170
Poultry and eggs, retail cost_____	91	85	94	88	89	129	125	131	134	133
Farm value_____	56	49	51	46	46	82	77	81	82	80
Percent of total retail cost_____	62	58	54	52	52	64	61	62	62	60
Farm-retail spread_____	35	36	43	42	43	47	48	50	51	53
Bakery and cereal products, retail cost_	153	161	186	193	192	214	277	304	299	305
Farm value_____	25	28	30	30	32	48	69	57	46	39
Percent of total retail cost_____	16	17	16	16	17	22	25	19	15	13
Farm-retail spread_____	128	133	156	163	160	166	208	247	253	266
Fruits and vegetables, retail cost_____	206	220	252	264	275	312	358	376	385	420
Farm value_____	54	61	63	67	70	86	98	102	99	106
Percent of total retail cost_____	26	28	25	25	25	28	27	27	26	25
Farm-retail spread_____	152	159	189	197	205	226	260	274	286	314
Fats and oils, retail cost_____	34	37	41	45	45	50	76	81	70	76
Farm value_____	10	12	12	14	12	19	35	28	23	29
Percent of total retail cost_____	28	31	30	31	27	38	47	34	33	38
Farm-retail spread_____	24	25	29	31	33	31	41	53	47	47

[1] Includes miscellaneous groups, not shown separately.

Source: U.S. Dept. of Agriculture, Economics, Statistics, and Cooperatives Service, *Farm-Retail Spreads for Food Products*, MP No. 741, Jan. 1972; *The Marketing and Transportation Situation*, Feb. 1975; and *Agricultural Outlook*, Jan.-Feb. issues.

No. 1209. Farm Food Prices—Distribution of Retail Price According to Farm Value and Marketing Function: 1976 and 1977

[In cents per unit indicated. The farm value is the gross return to farmers for the quantity of farm products equivalent to the unit sold at retail minus imputed value of byproducts]

FOOD ITEM	1976		1977						
	Farm value	Retail price	Farm value	Assembly and procurement	Processing	Intercity transportation	Wholesaling	Retailing [1]	Retail price
Beef, choice_____lb__	77.9	138.9	79.9	1.7	8.1	1.3	8.5	38.8	138.3
Pork_____lb__	78.4	134.3	73.4	1.9	11.0	1.4	8.0	29.7	125.4
Broilers_____lb__	32.6	59.7	33.0	1.1	8.0	1.4	3.7	12.9	60.1
Eggs, grade A or AA large___doz__	58.0	84.9	53.8	.9	10.3	1.5	3.5	12.3	82.3
Milk, sold in stores_____½ gal__	46.2	82.8	45.8	2.9	11.1	(NA)	(NA)	(NA)	83.9
Butter_____lb__	85.2	126.0	91.5	3.2	9.5	2.4	(NA)	(NA)	133.1
Bread, white_____lb__	5.5	35.3	4.5	[2] 1.4	12.5	[3] .4	13.6	3.1	35.5
Potatoes, fall_____10 lb__	51.5	167.3	44.3	(4)	16.9	24.1	13.2	66.6	165.1
Oranges, Calif._____doz__	30.7	127.5	36.2	2.3	20.6	14.5	11.2	55.5	140.3
Lettuce, Calif._____head__	10.7	51.0	5.1	.4	7.3	9.4	3.7	20.1	46.0
Orange juice, frozen_____6 oz__	10.4	28.7	9.0	.6	13.8	1.7	3.0	5.9	34.0
Tomatoes, Calif., whole.303 can__	4.0	35.1	3.9	.6	21.1	3.4	1.5	6.8	37.3
Margarine_____lb__	16.6	52.5	20.5	1.4	[5] 21.3	1.4	2.9	9.7	57.2
Salad and cooking oil____24 oz__	26.8	95.4	39.3	2.5	[5] 40.0	5.9	5.4	13.9	107.0
Vegetable shortening_____3 lb__	56.9	153.6	71.0	5.2	[5] 59.9	6.2	4.9	14.5	161.7

NA Not available.   [1] In store costs only. Headquarters and warehousing expenses are included in wholesaling.   [2] Assembly of wheat and milling.   [3] Flour only.   [4] Included in farm value.   [5] Includes oilseed crushing, crude oil refining, and manufacturing of finished product.

Source: U.S. Dept. of Agriculture, Economics, Statistics, and Cooperatives Service, *Developments in Marketing Spreads for Food Products in 1977.*

No. 1210. Supply and Utilization of Farm Commodities: 1950 to 1977

[In percent. Prior to 1960, excludes Alaska and Hawaii, except imports and exports include Alaska, Hawaii, and Puerto Rico for all years. "Net" means that commodities used for feed and seed are excluded to avoid double counting. See also *Historical Statistics, Colonial Times to 1970,* series K 384–391]

ITEM	1950	1955	1960	1965	1970	1971	1972	1973	1974	1975	1976	1977, prel.
Supply_____	100.0	100.0	100.0	100.0	100.0	100.0	100.0	100.0	100.0	100.0	100.0	100.0
Net production [1]_____	87.3	93.0	91.1	90.9	86.0	91.3	87.7	87.1	86.6	94.5	91.9	92.9
Net imports_____	12.4	11.0	11.1	10.5	10.9	11.0	11.6	11.1	10.1	10.7	10.8	10.6
Stock change [2]_____	+.3	−4.0	−2.2	−1.4	+3.1	−2.3	+.7	+1.8	+3.3	−5.2	−2.7	−3.5
Net utilization_	100.0	100.0	100.0	100.0	100.0	100.0	100.0	100.0	100.0	100.0	100.0	100.0
Domestic use_____	91.1	90.7	86.4	85.7	85.8	85.8	84.0	79.4	81.3	81.0	80.6	80.5
Food: Civilian_____	75.2	77.1	74.7	73.5	76.1	76.3	75.3	70.9	73.5	73.4	72.8	72.7
Military [3]___	1.7	1.7	1.2	1.6	1.1	1.0	.8	.6	.5	.6	.5	.5
Net nonfood [4]_____	14.2	11.9	10.5	10.6	8.6	8.5	7.9	7.9	7.3	7.0	7.3	7.3
Exports and shipments_____	8.9	9.3	13.6	14.3	14.2	14.2	16.0	20.6	18.7	19.0	19.4	19.5

[1] Meat production includes carcass weight of commercial and farm slaughter; excludes change in live animal inventory.   [2] Includes farm and commercial stocks and holdings under Government programs. Minus sign (−) indicates increase in stocks from beginning to end of year; plus sign (+) indicates withdrawals from stocks.   [3] Includes civilian feeding in areas occupied by our Armed Forces.   [4] Includes some waste and loss at farm level.

Source: U.S. Dept. of Agriculture, Economics, Statistics, and Cooperatives Service, *Agricultural Outlook.*

No. 1211. Selected Farm Indexes of Inputs: 1950 to 1977

[1967=100. Inputs based on physical quantities of resources used in production. See also *Historical Statistics, Colonial Times to 1970,* series K 486–495 for data before revisions]

INPUT	1950	1955	1960	1965	1970	1972	1973	1974	1975	1976	1977, prel.
Total_____	104	105	101	98	99	100	101	101	100	101	102
Farm labor_____	217	185	145	110	90	85	85	83	80	78	78
Farm real estate [1]_____	105	105	100	99	98	95	94	93	93	94	94
Mechanical power and machinery_____	84	97	97	94	100	101	105	109	112	113	114
Agricultural chemicals [2]_____	29	39	49	75	115	131	136	140	127	141	146
Feed, seed, and livestock purchases [3]____	63	72	84	93	104	113	116	107	100	107	109
Taxes and interest_____	82	88	94	100	100	100	100	101	101	100	101
Miscellaneous_____	87	94	105	109	109	115	111	110	104	116	113

[1] Includes service buildings, improvements.   [2] Includes fertilizer, lime, and pesticides.   [3] Nonfarm portion.

Source: U.S. Dept. of Agriculture, Economics, Statistics, and Cooperatives Service, *Changes in Farm Production and Efficiency,* annual. Also in U.S. Council of Economic Advisors, *Economic Report of the President,* January 1978.

No. 1212. Farm Machinery and Equipment: 1950 to 1977

[Prior to 1960, excludes Alaska and Hawaii. See also *Historical Statistics, Colonial Times to 1970*, series K 184–191]

ITEM	1950	1960	1965	1970	1971	1972	1973	1974	1975	1976	1977
Value of farm implements and machinery [1]_____bil. dol__	12.2	22.7	24.8	32.3	34.4	36.6	39.3	44.2	55.7	65.0	72.3
Number on farms, Jan. 1:											
Tractors [2]_____1,000__	3,394	4,688	4,787	4,619	4,584	4,549	4,518	4,493	4,469	4,434	4,402
Horsepower_____mil__	93	153	176	203	206	209	212	219	222	228	232
Motortrucks_____1,000__	2,207	2,834	3,030	2,984	2,994	3,003	3,013	3,023	3,032	3,043	3,052
Grain combines_____1,000__	714	1,042	910	790	760	725	701	698	524	527	535
Corn pickers [3]_____1,000__	456	792	690	635	630	625	621	618	615	610	605
Pickup balers_____1,000__	196	680	751	708	700	692	684	674	667	641	615
Field forage harvesters_____1,000__	81	291	316	304	300	298	292	295	255	263	270
Farmers' expenditures:											
Motor vehicles [4]_____mil. dol__	1,734	1,344	1,940	2,030	2,137	2,464	3,066	3,405	3,833	4,269	4,552
Machinery and equip____mil. dol__	1,418	1,458	2,239	2,888	2,736	3,231	4,581	4,790	4,820	4,930	4,880

[1] Inventory valuations at beginning of year. Includes family automobiles.   [2] Excludes garden tractors.
[3] Includes picker-shellers.   [4] For farm business use.

Source: U.S. Dept. of Agriculture, Economics, Statistics, and Cooperatives Service, *Balance Sheet of the Farming Sector*, annual, and *Farm Income Statistics*, July 1978. Also in *Agricultural Statistics*, annual.

No. 1213. Farm Productivity—Man-Hours and Indexes of Farm Output: 1950 to 1977

[Excludes Alaska and Hawaii. See also *Historical Statistics, Colonial Times to 1970*, series K 407–413, K 430–444, and W 67–81]

ITEM	1950	1955	1960	1965	1970	1971	1972	1973	1974	1975	1976	1977, prel.
Man-hours of labor required on farms [1]_____bil__	15.1	12.8	9.8	7.3	6.0	6.0	5.7	5.6	5.5	5.3	5.1	5.2
All productive livestock__bil__	5.5	4.9	3.8	3.0	2.3	2.2	2.1	2.0	1.8	1.7	1.6	1.6
All crops [2]_____bil__	6.9	6.0	4.6	3.4	2.9	2.9	2.8	2.9	2.9	2.9	2.8	2.9
Farm maintenance [3]____bil__	2.7	1.9	1.4	.9	.8	.8	.7	.7	.8	.7	.7	.7
INDEX, 1967=100												
Farm output per man-hour [4]____	34	44	65	89	112	126	129	133	129	144	152	149
All livestock and products____	37	46	62	86	121	130	138	144	156	160	175	180
Meat animals_____	54	61	70	89	116	126	131	137	147	150	166	166
Milk cows_____	35	42	60	87	127	136	148	153	168	178	202	202
Poultry_____	21	32	55	87	120	129	142	149	163	175	196	198
All crops_____	36	45	66	90	110	120	124	127	117	130	133	131
Feed grains_____	22	30	57	91	99	117	129	126	109	128	131	129
Hay and forage_____	40	46	61	85	106	108	113	116	113	120	116	111
Food grains_____	40	51	95	101	118	124	121	123	111	120	117	119
Vegetables_____	52	65	82	96	112	116	116	117	115	113	124	114
Fruits and nuts_____	69	78	79	98	109	112	108	115	121	126	147	138
Sugar crops_____	38	53	78	88	116	125	127	122	118	135	141	125
Cotton_____	26	39	57	102	129	132	150	158	134	142	146	162
Tobacco_____	57	65	74	82	129	134	149	147	158	157	164	147
Oil crops_____	52	69	94	104	114	120	125	126	112	131	123	128
Cropland used for crops [5]_____	111	111	104	99	98	100	98	104	106	108	109	110
Crop production per acre_____	69	74	89	100	104	112	115	115	103	112	111	117

[1] Man-equivalent hours; represents overhead, and time used by average adult males in performing farm operations on crops and livestock.
[2] Beginning 1965, excludes work on farm gardens.
[3] Beginning 1965, excludes work on horses and mules.
[4] Index of farm output (production) divided by index of man-hours used.
[5] Harvested acreages plus acreages of crop failure and summer fallow.

Source: U.S. Dept. of Agriculture, Economics, Statistics, and Cooperatives Service, *Changes in Farm Production and Efficiency*, annual. Also in *Agricultural Statistics*, annual.

No. 1214. Farm Output Indexes and Acreage of Principal Crops: 1950 to 1977

[Excludes Alaska and Hawaii. See also *Historical Statistics, Colonial Times to 1970*, series K 414-429]

ITEM	1950	1960	1965	1970	1971	1972	1973	1974	1975	1976	1977, prel.
INDEX, 1967=100											
Farm output [1]	74	91	98	101	111	110	112	106	114	117	121
Per unit of total input	71	90	100	102	111	110	111	105	115	116	119
Gross production:											
Livestock and products [2]	75	88	95	105	108	108	105	106	101	105	108
Meat animals	73	85	92	108	112	110	108	110	102	106	108
Dairy products	92	101	104	100	101	102	98	99	98	103	105
Poultry and eggs	57	76	90	106	107	109	106	106	103	110	111
Crops [3]	76	93	99	101	112	113	119	109	121	121	129
Feed grains	64	86	88	89	116	112	115	93	114	120	124
Hay and forage	78	90	98	99	105	104	109	104	108	102	108
Food grains	65	86	88	91	107	102	113	122	142	140	131
Vegetables	83	90	96	100	100	101	103	102	101	106	107
Fruits and nuts	96	93	100	109	116	104	124	125	135	130	136
Sugar crops	68	74	100	114	116	127	112	104	131	130	117
Cotton	138	170	205	139	145	187	175	158	112	142	195
Tobacco	103	99	94	97	86	88	88	101	110	109	98
Oil crops	46	68	95	117	121	131	155	127	153	132	171
ACREAGE, PRINCIPAL CROPS (millions acres)											
Planted or grown	353	324	297	293	306	295	319	326	332	336	343
Harvested	336	316	288	283	295	283	301	316	324	326	331

[1] Annual production available for eventual human use.   [2] Includes livestock products not shown separately, except horses and mules.   [3] Includes crops not shown separately.

Source: U.S. Dept. of Agriculture, Economics, Statistics, and Cooperatives Service, *Changes in Farm Production and Efficiency*, annual. Also in *Agricultural Statistics*, annual.

No. 1215. Farm Labor—Man-Hours Per Unit of Production, Selected Crops and Livestock: 1950-1954 to 1975-1976

[Excludes Alaska and Hawaii. Figures for each period are annual averages. See also *Historical Statistics, Colonial Times to 1970*, series K 445-485]

CROP, LIVESTOCK, AND ITEM	1950-1954	1955-1959	1960-1964	1965-1969	1970-1974	1975-1976 [1]
Corn for grain: Man-hours per acre [2]	13.3	9.9	7.0	5.8	5.2	3.7
Yield per acre bu.	39.4	48.7	62.2	78.5	83.9	87.1
Man-hours per 100 bu.	34	20	11	7	6	4
Wheat: Man-hours per acre [2]	4.6	3.8	3.0	2.9	2.9	2.9
Yield per acre bu.	17.3	22.3	25.2	27.5	31.1	30.4
Man-hours per 100 bu.	27	17	12	11	9	10
Hay: Man-hours per acre [2]	6.3	6.0	5.0	3.8	3.5	3.6
Yield per acre sh. tons	1.43	1.61	1.77	1.97	2.12	2.07
Man-hours per sh. ton	4.4	3.7	2.8	1.9	1.6	1.7
Potatoes: Man-hours per acre [2]	63.1	53.1	48.0	45.1	43.0	38.7
Yield per acre cwt.	151	178	195	213	234	258
Man-hours per sh. ton	8	6	5	4	4	3
Cotton: Man-hours per acre [2]	66	66	47	30	23	11
Yield per acre lb.	296	428	475	484	470	460
Man-hours per bale	107	74	47	30	23	12
Tobacco: Man-hours per acre [3]	464	475	493	427	298	262
Yield per acre 100 lb.	1.3	1.5	1.9	2.0	2.0	2.0
Man-hours per 100 lb	36	31	26	22	15	13
Milk cows:						
Man-hours per cow	121	109	93	78	62	50
Per cwt. of milk	2.2	1.7	1.2	.9	.6	.5
Milk per cow cwt.	5.4	6.3	7.5	8.8	10.1	10.6
Cattle, exc. milk cows:						
Man-hours per cwt. of beef produced [4]	3.6	3.2	2.6	2.1	1.7	1.4
Hogs: Man-hours per cwt. produced [4]	2.7	2.4	1.9	1.4	1.0	.7
Chickens (laying flocks and eggs):						
Man-hours per 100 layers	232	175	126	97	77	63
Per 100 eggs produced	1.3	.9	.6	.4	.3	.3
Rate of lay [5]	181	200	212	219	225	234
Chickens (farm raised):						
Man-hours per 100 birds	27	23	17	14	13	12
Per cwt. produced [4]	7.3	6.7	4.7	3.7	3.3	3.1
Chickens (broilers):						
Man-hours per 100 birds	8	4	3	2	1	1
Per cwt. produced [4]	2.4	1.3	.8	.5	.3	.2
Turkeys: Man-hours per cwt. produced [4]	6.8	4.4	2.4	1.3	.8	.6

[1] Preliminary.   [2] Man-hours per acre harvested, including preharvest work on acreages abandoned, grazed, and turned under.   [3] Per acre planted and harvested.   [4] Liveweight production.
[5] Eggs produced during year divided by average number of hens and pullets of layin6 age on hand during year.

Source: U.S. Dept. of Agriculture, Economics, Statistics. and Cooperatives Service. In *Agricultural Statistics*, annual.

No. 1216. Agricultural Exports and Imports—Value: 1960 to 1977

[In billions of dollars, except percent. Includes Puerto Rico. Excludes forest products and distilled liquors; includes crude rubber and similar gums (now mainly plantation products). See also *Historical Statistics, Colonial Times to 1970*, series K 251–255]

ITEM	1960–1964, avg.	1965–1969, avg.	1960	1965	1970	1971	1972	1973	1974	1975	1976	1977
Exports, domestic products___	5.4	6.3	4.8	6.2	7.3	7.7	9.4	17.7	22.0	21.9	23.0	23.7
Percent of all exports_____	24	20	24	23	17	18	19	23	23	21	20	20
Imports for consumption_____	3.9	4.6	3.8	4.1	5.8	5.8	6.5	8.4	10.2	9.3	11.0	13.5
Percent of all imports_____	24	16	25	19	15	13	12	12	10	10	9	9

Source: U.S. Dept. of Agriculture, Economics, Statistics, and Cooperatives Service, *U.S. Foreign Agricultural Trade Statistical Report*, Calendar Year 1977. Also in *Agricultural Statistics*, annual.

No. 1217. Principal Agricultural Exports—Value: 1961 to 1977

[In millions of dollars. Includes Puerto Rico. Excludes reexports of foreign products. Includes shipments under foreign aid programs]

COMMODITY	1961–1965, avg.	1966–1970, avg.	1971–1975, avg.	1970	1973	1974	1975	1976	1977
Agricultural exports_____	**5,644**	**6,480**	**15,735**	**7,358**	**17,682**	**21,996**	**21,886**	**22,996**	**23,671**
Meats and meat products_____	162	179	375	188	462	399	548	823	823
Eggs and dairy products_____	146	130	117	137	56	67	134	128	182
Animal fats and oils_____	195	179	348	244	330	580	355	439	588
Hides and skins_____	89	140	290	144	375	337	292	518	578
Bread grains and preparations____	1,268	1,197	3,391	1,144	4,278	4,678	5,382	4,113	2,964
Coarse grains and prepn., exc. rice_	841	1,082	2,359	1,099	3,598	4,727	5,327	6,082	4,976
Rice_____	178	311	579	314	539	853	858	629	730
Fodders and feeds_____	179	386	937	496	1,266	1,287	987	1,358	1,572
Vegetables and preparations_____	134	169	304	181	313	308	412	569	528
Fruits and preparations_____	285	311	493	330	424	585	687	607	679
Vegetable oils, fats and waxes, oilseeds, nuts and preparations__	774	1,182	3,187	1,642	3,417	4,805	5,941	4,810	5,888
Tobacco, unmanufactured_____	393	506	693	488	681	832	852	922	1,094
Cotton, unmanufactured_____	639	408	878	377	940	1,353	1,001	1,057	1,538
All other_____	362	299	1,783	571	1,003	1,035	1,107	942	1,530

Source: U.S. Bureau of the Census, *Foreign Commerce and Navigation of the United States; Quarterly Summary of Foreign Commerce of the United States; U.S. Exports—Schedule B—Commodity by Country*, FT 410, monthly.

No. 1218. Selected Farm Products—U.S. and World Production and Exports: 1975 and 1976

[Calendar year, except as indicated. Metric ton=1.102 short tons or .984 long ton]

ITEM	Wheat, grain only (mil. metric tons)	Corn for grain (mil. metric tons)	Soybeans (mil. metric tons)	Rice, rough [1] (mil. metric tons)	Oats (mil. metric tons)	Barley (mil. metric tons)	Lard (1,000 metric tons)	Tallow and greases (1,000 metric tons)	Tobacco, unmanufactured (1,000 metric tons)	Edible vegetable oils [2] (mil. metric tons)	Cotton [1] (1,000 bales) [3]
1975:											
Production:											
U.S._____	[4] 58	[5] 148	[6] 42	5	[4] 9	[4] 8	451	2,410	992	8.2	11,540
World_____	[7] 350	[7] 326	[6] 68	360	[7] 47	[7] 140	3,924	4,599	5,413	33.2	64,300
Percent U.S._	16.5	41.5	62.0	1.4	19.3	5.8	11.5	52.4	18.3	24.7	17.9
Exports:											
U.S._____	[4][8] 31.7	[5] 43.2	[9] 15.3	[10] 1.7	[4] .2	[4] .5	39.8	891	259	[11] 3.8	3,926
World_____	[7][8] 73.7	[7] 60.3	[9] 19.4	[10] 8.0	[7] 1.4	[7] 13.4	516.3	1,437	1,295	[12] 11.7	17,369
Percent U.S._	43.0	71.6	78.9	21.8	13.7	3.6	7.7	62.0	20.0	32.5	22.6
1976:											
Production:											
U.S._____	[4] 58	[5] 148	[6] 35	6	[4] 9	[4] 8	481	2,862	971	7	10,581
World_____	[7] 349	[7] 322	[6] 59	361	[7] 47	[7] 144	3,540	5,294	5,572	50	58,288
Percent U.S._	16.5	46.0	59.3	1.6	19.9	5.6	14.0	54.0	17.4	14.0	18.2
Exports:											
U.S._____	[4][8] 31.5	[5] 43.2	[13] 15.1	[10] 1.7	[4] .1	[4] .5	82	1,062	262	[11] 3.8	4,784
World_____	[7][8] 66.3	[7] 61.2	[13] 19.2	[10] 8.0	[7] 1.4	[7] 13.2	331	1,757	1,274	[12] 11.754	17,443
Percent U.S._	47.5	70.6	78.6	21.2	7.1	3.8	25.0	60.0	20.1	32.5	27.4

[1] Year beginning Aug. 1.   [2] Includes palm oils.   [3] Bales of 480 lb., net weight.   [4] Year beginning June 1.   [5] Year beginning Oct. 1.   [6] Year beginning Sept. 1.   [7] Year beginning July 1.   [8] Includes wheat flour in grain equivalent.   [9] Calendar year 1976.   [10] Includes milled rice.   [11] Includes oil equivalent of exported oilseeds.   [12] Exports from producing countries.   [13] Calendar year 1977.

Source: U.S. Foreign Agricultural Service, *Foreign Agriculture Circular*, periodic.

No. 1219. U.S. SALES AND DONATIONS UNDER FOOD FOR PEACE (PUBLIC LAW 480)
PROGRAMS: 1954 TO 1977

[In millions of dollars. For years ending June 30, except beginning 1977, ending Sept. 30]

TITLE AND PROGRAM	Total, 1954–1977 [1]	1969	1970	1971	1972	1973	1974	1975	1976	1977
Total	26,493	1,179	1,142	1,231	1,223	1,119	973	1,328	1,300	1,193
Title I sales (loans)	16,693	734	711	791	746	724	577	868	902	735
Repayable in dollars	6,862	507	485	546	683	724	577	868	902	735
Repayable in foreign currencies	9,831	227	226	245	63	–	–	–	–	–
Title II donations	9,800	445	432	440	477	394	396	460	398	458
Voluntary relief agencies	3,946	203	181	190	197	177	196	266	299	326
Emergency relief and other [2]	5,854	242	250	250	280	217	200	194	99	132

REGION AND COUNTRY	1972		1973		1974		1975		1976		1977	
	Sales	Dona-tions	Sales	Dona-tions	Sales	Dona-tions	Sales	Dona-tions	Sales	Dona-tions	Sales	Dona-tions
Total	682.5	540.2	724.3	394.3	577.1	396.2	867.5	460.6	902.0	397.9	735.3	458.2
Near East and South Asia [3]	125.1	336.8	156.4	204.9	104.2	135.7	582.4	149.3	622.5	125.7	398.4	156.0
Bangladesh	–	87.2	–	59.4	48.2	2.7	237.3	4.5	180.7	2.5	63.8	19.3
Egypt	–	–	–	.8	9.5	3.3	104.5	12.8	201.7	4.4	196.8	11.7
India	–	104.6	–	64.2	–	71.2	121.6	106.1	78.9	102.4	24.7	101.3
Israel	53.8	.4	59.4	.4	–	1.5	8.6	–	14.4	–	7.0	–
Jordan	1.7	2.1	5.9	4.2	8.2	3.1	6.4	5.2	11.6	3.9	9.8	3.8
Lebanon	7.1	10.0	–	1.2	–	5.7	–	2.9	–	.1	6.8	3.9
Pakistan	40.9	61.8	74.6	6.9	32.4	10.1	79.5	5.4	94.8	2.1	35.3	2.0
Sri Lanka	15.4	1.8	10.0	1.4	5.9	2.6	24.5	5.4	22.0	4.1	39.9	4.0
Turkey	–	7.9	–	6.1	–	3.7	–	3.6	–	–	–	.2
Yemen, Ppls. D.R.	–	.1	–	.1	–	1.6	–	(z)	–	–	–	–
Yemen Arab Rep	–	(z)	–	1.1	–	1.4	–	3.4	–	2.6	–	1.1
East Asia [3]	437.5	44.7	497.5	51.5	454.8	36.5	180.7	36.1	167.4	26.1	172.3	43.5
Dem. Kampuchea	19.9	.6	25.8	–	182.6	(z)	91.5	2.9	–	–	–	–
Indonesia	115.1	9.8	109.7	8.5	–	11.2	34.8	11.5	50.6	5.9	85.3	6.4
Korea	195.7	16.6	146.3	13.1	–	7.2	8.7	5.7	116.8	.3	75.1	–
Laos	–	3.3	–	3.0	–	4.3	–	1.3	–	–	–	–
Philippines	33.6	4.1	20.7	15.8	3.4	12.6	–	10.8	–	19.0	11.9	37.0
Vietnam	59.2	8.6	179.0	9.3	268.9	1.0	45.7	3.9	–	.8	–	–
Africa [3]	58.9	45.4	26.8	44.1	7.8	133.4	16.2	118.8	39.4	100.5	57.2	97.8
Botswana	–	9.8	–	.2	–	2.3	–	2.6	–	2.6	–	2.5
Chad	–	–	–	.3	–	6.2	–	.3	–	.5	–	5.3
Ethiopia	–	.8	–	1.0	–	13.9	–	5.2	3.4	3.8	–	4.6
Ghana	9.5	1.2	–	.9	–	2.1	–	2.8	–	3.9	–	6.5
Guinea	.4	.3	4.6	.2	5.0	.7	8.6	2.4	5.2	1.2	.7	.4
Lesotho	–	1.0	–	1.7	–	3.1	–	3.6	–	5.7	–	4.4
Mali, Rep. of	–	1.5	–	3.6	–	16.0	–	8.9	–	.2	–	–
Mauritania	–	1.4	–	1.4	–	8.5	–	2.4	–	2.3	–	1.7
Mauritius	–	.9	–	2.1	–	3.1	–	2.2	–	.8	–	.2
Morocco	27.9	7.8	8.0	8.7	–	17.0	–	12.7	11.8	17.2	8.0	15.1
Niger	–	.9	–	4.5	–	20.3	–	7.8	–	3.5	–	.4
Nigeria	–	.2	–	.4	–	3.0	–	2.3	–	.4	–	–
Senegal	–	1.1	–	1.6	–	7.9	–	2.1	–	2.3	–	2.9
Sudan	–	.1	2.1	2.2	2.8	2.2	–	8.2	–	1.5	4.6	1.8
Tanzania	–	1.2	–	1.6	–	2.6	7.6	16.0	4.3	19.6	7.6	10.3
Tunisia	17.4	6.1	9.4	4.3	–	6.9	–	10.1	2.3	5.6	6.9	5.1
Upper Volta	–	2.8	–	2.5	–	8.2	–	3.6	–	3.0	–	8.1
Latin America [3]	31.8	70.8	42.7	46.2	10.2	40.3	61.5	49.8	53.6	83.8	40.9	71.8
Bolivia	–	4.4	9.4	.9	6.4	1.9	–	5.1	–	6.2	–	6.7
Brazil	–	5.7	–	9.6	–	6.2	–	8.4	–	.7	–	1.3
Chile	–	5.9	–	2.5	–	3.2	57.8	4.6	46.6	10.2	14.3	17.2
Colombia	10.9	10.1	8.4	9.2	3.0	7.1	–	11.5	–	11.9	–	5.3
Dominican Rep	12.5	6.5	9.7	4.5	–	4.2	–	5.5	–	11.4	2.5	9.4
Ecuador	1.0	2.2	8.7	2.4	–	3.3	–	3.4	–	2.1	–	1.3
Haiti	–	1.7	–	1.2	–	2.0	2.3	3.3	4.9	9.0	10.7	8.6
Jamaica	–	3.9	–	1.4	.8	1.0	1.4	.2	–	.1	13.4	–
Nicaragua	–	1.7	–	3.0	–	2.4	–	1.4	–	.9	–	.4
Peru	–	11.1	–	4.2	–	3.7	–	6.4	–	8.7	–	5.3
All other [4]	29.2	42.5	2.7	47.6	–	50.3	26.7	106.5	19.1	61.8	66.5	89.1

– Represents zero.   Z Less than $50,000.   [1] Includes transition quarter, July–Sept., 1976.
[2] Includes economic development and world food programs.   [3] Includes countries not shown separately.
[4] Includes undistributed transportation cost.

Source: U.S. Agency for International Development, *U.S. Overseas Loans and Grants and Assistance From International Organizations*, annual.

No. 1220. AGRICULTURAL EXPORTS UNDER SPECIFIED GOVERNMENT-FINANCED PROGRAMS—VALUE, BY SELECTED COMMODITIES: 1960 TO 1977

[In millions of dollars, except percent. Includes Puerto Rico]

ITEM	1960	1965	1970	1971	1972	1973	1974	1975	1976	1977
Agricultural exports [1]	4,832	6,229	7,259	7,693	9,401	17,680	21,999	21,884	22,996	23,671
Outside Government programs [1][2]	3,371	4,880	6,226	6,624	8,248	16,812	21,140	20,456	21,597	22,257
Under Government programs [1]	1,461	1,349	1,033	1,069	1,153	868	859	1,428	1,399	1,414
Percent of total	30.2	21.7	14.2	13.9	12.3	4.9	3.9	6.5	6.1	6.0
Wheat	638.4	739.0	313.3	295.3	317.9	218.7	127.6	556.6	478.5	373.7
Wheat flour	118.5	87.5	86.2	77.3	65.4	41.8	78.5	68.1	91.7	103.0
Corn	65.5	56.0	26.5	29.5	58.5	47.6	21.4	14.8	108.1	212.2
Grain sorghums	22.2	20.4	26.2	36.4	34.4	46.1	46.2	4.0	10.6	4.2
Rice	86.5	72.1	171.3	133.6	259.7	210.8	292.0	311.6	224.4	141.7
Cotton	230.4	114.6	115.4	129.7	81.0	81.6	30.5	32.5	28.1	16.5
Soybean oil	72.2	109.6	92.2	112.8	111.9	60.8	84.8	36.3	59.5	99.1
Milk, nonfat, dried	40.7	58.8	91.4	91.2	70.9	3.1	–	60.3	39.3	72.2

– Represents zero. [1] Sources of values for Government-financed programs are different from those for total exports; therefore, not fully comparable in regard to valuation, shipping period, etc. Entries for "Outside Government programs" are the residuals of the other two series. [2] Exports outside specified Government-financed programs include, in addition to unassisted commercial transactions, shipments of some commodities with governmental assistance in the form of (a) barter for overseas procurement for other U.S. agencies, (b) short-term credits extended by the Commodity Credit Corporation and the Export-Import Bank, (c) sales of Government-owned commodities below domestic market prices, and (d) export payments in cash or in kind through 1974.

Source: U.S. Dept. of Agriculture, Economics, Statistics, and Cooperatives Service. In *Agricultural Statistics*, annual, and *Foreign Agricultural Trade of the United States*, monthly.

No. 1221. SELECTED FARM PRODUCTS—PRODUCTION AND EXPORTS: 1960 TO 1977

ITEM	1960	1965	1970	1971	1972	1973	1974	1975	1976	1977, prel.
Wheat: Production mil. bu	1,355	1,316	1,352	1,619	1,546	1,711	1,782	2,122	2,142	2,026
Exports [1] mil. bu	653	852	741	610	1,135	1,217	1,018	1,173	950	1,100
Percent of production	48.2	64.7	54.8	37.7	73.4	71.1	57.1	55.3	44.4	54.3
Corn for grain: Production mil. bu	3,907	4,103	4,152	5,646	5,580	5,671	4,701	5,829	6,200	6,357
Exports [1] mil. bu	292	687	517	796	1,258	1,243	1,149	1,711	1,684	1,750
Percent of production	7.5	16.7	12.5	14.1	22.5	21.9	24.4	29.4	26.9	27.5
Soybeans, for beans: Production mil. bu	555	846	1,127	1,176	1,271	1,548	1,216	1,547	1,288	1,716
Exports [1] mil. bu	135	251	434	417	479	539	421	555	564	595
Percent of production	24.3	29.7	38.5	35.5	37.7	34.8	34.6	35.9	43.8	34.7
Cotton: Production [2] mil. bales	14.2	14.9	10.2	10.5	13.7	13.0	11.5	8.3	10.6	14.4
Exports [1] mil. bales	6.9	3.0	3.9	3.4	5.3	6.1	3.9	3.3	4.8	5.5
Percent of production	48.6	20.1	38.2	32.4	38.7	46.9	33.9	39.8	45.3	38.5
Tobacco: Production [3] mil. lb	1,944	1,855	1,906	1,705	1,749	1,742	1,990	2,182	2,136	1,912
Exports [1] mil. lb	(NA)	538	639	571	639	732	653	654	678	623
Percent of production	(NA)	29.0	33.5	33.5	36.5	42.0	32.8	30.0	31.8	32.6
Fats and oils: Production [4] mil. lb	17,353	20,532	25,012	25,426	25,347	24,581	26,824	23,612	27,798	27,608
Exports [1] mil. lb	5,965	7,481	10,150	10,709	10,465	10,484	11,768	9,592	11,579	13,027
Percent of production	34.4	36.4	40.6	42.1	41.3	42.7	43.9	40.6	41.7	47.2

NA Not available. [1] Represents marketing year for each product. [2] 480 lb. net weight bales beginning 1965. Equivalent 500 lb. bales, gross weight, for 1960. [3] Farm sales weight. [4] Production from domestic materials.

Source: U.S. Dept. of Agriculture, Economics, Statistics, and Cooperatives Service. In *Agricultural Statistics*, annual.

No. 1222. ACREAGES OF CROPS HARVESTED FOR SPECIFIED PURPOSES: 1950 TO 1977

[See also *Historical Statistics, Colonial Times to 1970*, series K 496–499]

ITEM	1950	1960	1965	1970	1972	1973	1974	1975	1976	1977, prel.
Crops harvested [1] mil. acres	345	324	298	293	293	321	330	337	338	342
Domestic use [2] mil. acres	295	260	222	221	202	225	231	237	236	238
Per capita [3] acres	1.94	1.44	1.14	1.08	.97	1.07	1.10	1.10	1.10	1.10
Exports mil. acres	50	64	76	72	91	96	99	100	102	104
Percent of total	14.5	19.8	25.5	24.6	31.1	29.9	30.0	29.7	30.2	30.4
Crop failure mil. acres	12	6	6	5	6	5	6	5	7	10

[1] Area in principal crops harvested as reported by Economics, Statistics, and Cooperatives Service plus acreage in vegetables, fruits, tree nuts, and farm gardens. [2] Includes feed for horses and mules. [3] Based on Bureau of the Census estimated resident population as of July 1.

Source: U.S. Dept. of Agriculture, Economics, Statistics, and Cooperatives Service, *Changes in Farm Production and Efficiency*, annual.

No. 1223. Principal Crops—Production and Value, 1974 to 1977, and Principal Producing States, 1977

CROP AND PRODUCT	PRODUCTION (mil.)				VALUE [1] (mil. dol.)				States in order of production, 1977
	Unit	1974	1975	1976	1977	1974	1975	1976	1977	
Corn for grain___	Bu_____	4,701	5,829	6,266	6,357	14,232	14,789	13,472	12,887	Ill., Iowa, Ind., Nebr.
Wheat_____	Bu_____	1,782	2,122	2,142	2,026	7,287	7,535	5,851	4,677	Kans., N. Dak., Okla., Minn.
Soybeans for beans_____	Bu_____	1,216	1,547	1,288	1,716	8,071	7,618	8,769	9,945	Ill., Iowa, Mo., Ind.
Hay_____	Sh. tons_	126	132	120	131	5,791	6,449	6,811	6,801	Wis., Minn., Calif., Nebr.
Tobacco_____	Lb_____	1,990	2,182	2,136	1,912	2,160	2,238	2,404	2,236	N.C., Ky., S.C., Va.
Cotton [2]_____	Bales [3]__	12	8	11	14	2,374	2,044	3,255	3,569	Tex., Calif., Miss., Ariz.
Sorghums for grain_____	Bu_____	623	753	720	791	1,722	1,775	1,450	1,357	Kans., Tex., Nebr., Mo.
Irish potatoes___	Cwt_____	342	322	358	352	1,355	1,445	1,283	1,275	Idaho, Wash., Maine, Oreg.
Rice, rough_____	Cwt_____	112	128	116	99	1,261	1,072	811	936	Ark., Tex., Calif., La.
Oats_____	Bu_____	601	642	546	748	912	928	845	853	Minn., S. Dak., Iowa, Wis.
Sugar beets_____	Sh. tons_	22	30	29	25	1,036	821	617	662	Calif., Minn., N. Dak., Idaho

[1] Values are based on season average prices.   [2] Excludes linters. State production figures, which conform with U.S. Bureau of the Census annual ginning enumeration with allowances for cross-State ginnings, rounded to thousands and added for U.S. totals.   [3] Bales of 480 lb. net weight.

Source: U.S. Dept. of Agriculture, Economics, Statistics, and Cooperatives Service. In *Agricultural Statistics,* annual; *Crop Production,* annual; and *Crop Values,* annual.

No. 1224. Crops—Farms Reporting, Acreage, and Production: 1974

CROP	Farms (1,000)	Acreage (1,000)	PRODUCTION		CROP	Farms (1,000)	Acreage (1,000)	PRODUCTION	
			Unit	Number (millions)				Unit	Number (millions)
All farms:					Oats for grain_____	358	11,143	Bu____	526
Field corn:					Barley for grain_____	93	7,286	Bu____	273
For grain or seed___	883	61,654	Bu____	4,397	Rye for grain_____	19	637	Bu____	14
For other purposes_	307	10,677	(X)	(NA)	All hay_____	[4] 903	52,068	Tons [1]_	109
Sorghums:					Alfalfa and alfalfa				
For grain or seed___	120	12,929	Bu____	554	mixtures [5]_____	485	23,247	Tons [1]_	61
For other purposes_	55	1,862	(X)	(NA)	Clover, timothy,				
Soybeans for beans__	542	48,119	Bu____	1,146	and mixtures____	316	11,186	Tons [1]_	21
Peanuts for nuts_____	33	1,369	Lb____	3,169	Small grain hay____	52	1,590	Tons [1]_	2
Wheat_____	533	62,957	Bu____	1,692	Lespedeza for hay__	22	386	Tons [1]_	1
Other small grains____	478	24,174	(X)	(NA)	Wild hay_____	107	7,322	Tons [1]_	8
					Other hay_____	129	4,839	Tons [1]_	9
Cotton_____	90	12,224	Bales_	11	Grass silage_____	62	2,697	Tons__	16
Tobacco_____	198	877	Lb____	1,733	Hay crops cut and				
Irish potatoes_____	51	1,345	Cwt__	316	fed green_____	33	801	Tons__	5
Sweet potatoes_____	17	86	Bu____	17	Field seeds_____	41	1,759	(X)	(NA)
Hay crops_____	1,146	56,236	Tons [1]	115	Red clover seed___	17	271	Lb____	28
Vegetables, sweet					Alfalfa seed_____	9	400	Lb____	96
corn, or melons [2]__	79	3,124	(X)	(NA)	Soybeans for beans__	513	47,788	Bu____	1,140
Land in orchards_____	106	4,190	(X)	(NA)	Peanuts for nuts___	29	1,359	Lb____	3,157
Berries for sale_____	15	121	(X)	(NA)	Irish potatoes_____	33	1,334	Cwt__	315
Other crops_____	116	6,863	(X)	(NA)	Sweet potatoes_____	10	81	Bu____	17
					Tobacco_____	151	842	Lb____	1,674
Farms with sales of					Cotton_____	81	12,129	Bales__	11
$2,500 and over:					Vegetables [2]_____	[4] 59	3,070	(X)	(NA)
Field corn for:					Tomatoes_____	17	421	(X)	(NA)
Grain or seed_____	765	60,702	Bu____	4,355	Sweet corn_____	24	640	(X)	(NA)
Silage or green chop_	278	10,112	Tons__	108	Cucumbers and				
Other purposes_____	19	407	(X)	(NA)	pickles_____	10	101	(X)	(NA)
Sorghums for: [3]					Watermelons_____	9	136	(X)	(NA)
Grain or seed_____	114	12,828	Bu____	551	Snap beans, bush				
Silage or green chop_	27	843	Tons__	8	and pole_____	10	320	(X)	(NA)
Dry forage or hay___	17	584	Tons [1]_	1	Green peas_____	11	399	(X)	(NA)
Hogged or grazed___	8	342	(X)	(NA)	Berries for sale_____	10	114	(X)	(NA)
Wheat for grain_____	503	62,594	Bu____	1,683	Land in orchards___	71	4,048	(X)	(NA)

NA Not available.   X Not applicable.   [1] Dry.   [2] For sale.   [3] Except sirup.   [4] If more than 1 subentry was applicable, the farm was tabulated in each.   [5] Mixtures for hay or dehydrating.

Source: U.S. Bureau of the Census, *Census of Agriculture: 1974,* vol. I.

No. 1225. Principal Crops—Acreage, Production, and Value: 1961 to 1977

[Acreage, production, and yield of all crops revised on basis of census data. See *Historical Statistics, Colonial Times to 1970*, series K 506–563, for acreage harvested, production, and price data for all crops listed except sorghums]

ITEM	1961–1965, avg.	1965	1970	1971	1972	1973	1974	1975	1976	1977, prel.
Corn for grain:										
Acreage harvested___1,000 acres__	56,658	55,392	57,358	64,123	57,513	62,143	65,405	67,505	71,300	70,006
Production_____mil. bu__	3,758	4,103	4,152	5,646	5,580	5,671	4,701	5,829	6,266	6,357
Farm value [1]_____mil. dol__	4,243	4,754	5,515	6,101	8,743	14,463	14,232	14,789	13,472	12,887
Yield per acre_____bu__	66.3	74.1	72.4	88.1	97.0	91.3	71.9	86.3	87.9	90.8
Price [2]_____dol. per bu__	1.13	1.16	1.33	1.08	1.57	2.55	3.02	2.54	2.15	2.03
Wheat:										
Acreage harvested___1,000 acres__	48,017	49,560	43,564	47,685	47,303	54,148	65,368	69,391	70,771	66,216
Production_____mil. bu__	1,214	1,316	1,352	1,619	1,546	1,711	1,782	2,122	2,142	2,026
Farm value [1]_____mil. dol__	2,027	1,775	1,802	2,168	2,706	6,745	7,287	7,535	5,851	4,677
Yield per acre_____bu__	25.3	26.5	31.0	33.9	32.7	31.6	27.3	30.6	30.3	30.6
Price [2]_____dol. per bu__	1.69	1.35	1.33	1.34	1.76	3.95	4.09	3.56	2.73	2.31
Oats:										
Acreage harvested___1,000 acres__	21,162	18,522	18,594	15,705	13,410	13,770	12,608	13,092	11,946	13,447
Production_____mil. bu__	953	930	915	878	691	659	601	642	546	748
Farm value [1]_____mil. dol__	604	587	582	544	507	775	912	928	845	853
Yield per acre_____bu__	45.2	50.2	49.2	55.9	51.5	47.9	47.6	49.0	45.7	55.6
Price [2]_____dol. per bu__	.63	.62	.62	.60	.72	1.18	1.53	1.46	1.56	1.14
Sugar beets:										
Acreage harvested___1,000 acres__	1,212	1,249	1,413	1,342	1,329	1,218	1,213	1,517	1,479	1,218
Production_____mil. short tons__	20.7	20.9	26.4	27.1	28.4	24.5	22.1	29.7	29.4	25.1
Farm value [1]_____mil. dol__	248	250	392	416	456	726	1,036	821	617	662
Yield per acre_____short tons__	17.1	16.8	18.7	20.2	21.4	20.1	18.2	19.6	19.9	20.6
Price [2]_____dol. per ton__	11.98	11.90	14.80	15.40	16.00	29.60	46.80	27.60	21.00	26.50
Rice, rough:										
Acreage harvested___1,000 acres__	1,742	1,793	1,815	1,818	1,818	2,170	2,531	2,818	2,480	2,249
Production_____mil. cwt__	68	76	84	86	85	93	112	128	116	99
Farm value [1]_____mil. dol__	340	376	433	458	575	1,280	1,261	1,072	811	936
Yield per acre_____lb__	3,892	4,255	4,618	4,718	4,700	4,274	4,440	4,558	4,663	4,412
Price [2]_____dol. per cwt__	5.00	4.93	5.17	5.34	6.73	13.80	11.20	8.35	7.02	9.43
Sorghums for grain:										
Acreage harvested___1,000 acres__	12,131	13,029	13,568	16,142	13,212	15,700	13,809	15,355	14,723	14,065
Production_____mil. bu__	548	673	683	868	801	923	623	753	720	791
Farm value [1]_____mil. dol__	549	659	780	896	1,096	1,978	1,722	1,775	1,450	1,357
Yield per acre_____bu__	45.0	51.6	50.4	53.8	60.7	58.8	45.1	10.0	18.0	56.2
Price [2][3]_____dol. per bu__	1.01	.98	1.14	1.04	1.37	2.14	2.77	2.37	2.03	1.73
Cotton:										
Acreage harvested___1,000 acres__	14,617	13,613	11,155	11,471	12,984	11,970	12,547	8,796	10,914	13,279
Production [4]_____mil. bales [5]__	14.9	15.0	10.2	10.5	13.7	13.0	11.5	8.3	10.6	14.4
Farm value [1]_____mil. dol__	2,312	2,106	1,122	1,420	1,799	2,780	2,374	2,044	3,255	3,569
Yield per acre_____lb__	491	527	438	438	507	520	442	453	465	520
Price [2]_____cents per lb__	30.99	29.37	21.98	28.23	27.30	44.6	42.9	51.3	64.1	[6] 51.7
Hay:										
Acreage harvested___1,000 acres__	67,285	67,496	61,467	61,355	59,680	61,828	60,195	61,324	60,311	60,493
Production_____mil. short tons__	127	126	127	129	129	134	126	132	120	131
Farm value [1]_____mil. dol__	2,679	2,915	3,076	3,335	3,730	5,004	5,791	6,449	6,811	6,801
Yield per acre_____short tons__	1.78	1.86	2.07	2.10	2.15	2.17	2.10	2.16	1.99	2.17
Price [2][7]_____dol. per ton__	22.80	23.20	26.10	28.10	31.30	41.60	50.90	52.20	60.30	54.00
Soybeans for beans:										
Acreage harvested___1,000 acres__	29,694	34,449	42,249	42,705	45,683	55,667	51,341	53,579	49,358	57,911
Production_____mil. bu__	719	846	1,127	1,176	1,271	1,548	1,216	1,547	1,288	1,716
Farm value [1]_____mil. dol__	1,770	2,151	3,215	3,560	5,550	8,790	8,071	7,618	8,769	9,945
Yield per acre_____bu__	24.2	24.5	26.7	27.5	27.8	27.8	23.7	28.9	26.1	29.6
Price [2]_____dol. per bu__	2.46	2.54	2.85	3.03	4.37	5.68	6.64	4.92	6.81	5.79
Irish potatoes:										
Acreage harvested___1,000 acres__	1,361	1,383	1,421	1,391	1,256	1,307	1,392	1,264	1,375	1,349
Production_____mil. cwt__	272	291	326	319	296	300	342	322	358	352
Farm value [1]_____mil. dol__	580	731	715	603	896	1,472	1,355	1,445	1,283	1,275
Yield per acre_____cwt__	200	210	229	230	236	230	246	255	260	261
Price [2]_____dol. per cwt__	2.17	2.53	2.21	1.90	3.02	4.90	4.01	4.48	3.59	3.64
Tobacco:										
Acreage harvested___1,000 acres__	1,126	977	898	838	842	887	963	1,086	1,045	958
Production_____mil. lb__	2,160	1,855	1,906	1,705	1,749	1,742	1,990	2,182	2,136	1,912
Farm value [1]_____mil. dol__	1,311	1,207	1,389	1,340	1,451	1,569	2,160	2,238	2,404	2,236
Yield per acre_____lb__	1,921	1,898	2,122	2,035	2,076	1,965	2,067	2,008	2,045	1,997
Price [2]_____dol. per lb__	.61	.65	.73	.79	.83	.90	1.09	1.03	1.13	1.17

[1] Values are based on season average prices; see footnote 2.
[2] Season average price received by farmers. State prices weighted by sales to obtain U.S. price. For certain years, prices for wheat, rice, corn for grain, grain sorghums, oats, soybeans, and cotton include an allowance for un-redeemed loans and purchase agreement deliveries.
[3] Based on reported price of grain sorghums.
[4] State production figures, which conform with U.S. Bureau of the Census annual ginning enumeration with allowance for cross-State ginnings, rounded to thousands and added for U.S. totals.
[5] Bales of 500 pounds, gross weight. Beginning 1970, bales of 480 lb., net weight.
[6] Average price to April 1, 1978. [7] Prices are for hay sold baled.

Source: U.S. Dept. of Agriculture, Economics, Statistics, and Cooperatives Service. In *Agricultural Statistics*, annual; *Crop Production*, annual; and *Crop Values*, annual.

No. 1226. CROPS—ACREAGE AND VALUE, 1975 TO 1977, AND ORDER OF VALUE, 1976, BY STATES

STATE	ACREAGE HARVESTED (1,000)			FARM VALUE (mil. dol.)				Crops in order of value, 1976
	1975	1976	1977, prel.	1975	1976	1977, prel. Value	Rank	
U.S.[1]	324,202	325,517	331,338	56,778	55,655	54,634	(X)	Corn, soybeans, hay, wheat.
Ala	3,426	3,524	3,499	556	645	540	32	Soybeans, corn, cotton lint, peanuts.
Ariz	1,045	1,266	1,182	515	721	657	29	Cotton lint, wheat, hay, lettuce.
Ark	7,838	7,930	8,230	1,275	1,298	1,395	13	Soybeans, rice, cotton lint, wheat.
Calif	6,392	6,475	6,131	5,316	5,624	5,632	1	Cotton lint, hay, grapes, tomatoes.
Colo	5,904	5,830	5,837	721	625	588	31	Hay, corn, wheat, sugar beets.
Conn	148	146	141	59	52	46	46	Tobacco, hay, apples, potatoes.
Del	521	510	511	100	104	75	43	Corn, soybeans, potatoes, wheat.
Fla	1,340	1,436	1,358	1,454	1,547	1,285	14	Oranges, tomatoes, sugarcane for sugar and seed, grapefruit.
Ga	4,713	4,794	3,770	1,108	1,127	813	23	Peanuts, corn, tobacco, soybeans.
Hawaii	112	107	106	20	24	28	47	(NA)
Idaho	4,293	4,410	4,235	1,000	915	803	24	Potatoes, hay, wheat, barley.
Ill	22,958	23,030	23,361	5,231	4,919	4,632	2	Corn, soybeans, wheat, hay.
Ind	12,135	12,476	12,634	2,408	2,587	2,359	6	Corn, soybeans, wheat, hay.
Iowa	24,334	24,316	24,320	4,477	4,379	3,959	3	Corn, soybeans, hay, oats.
Kans	21,608	21,465	22,477	2,259	1,928	1,844	9	Wheat, corn, sorghum grain, hay.
Ky	4,564	4,774	5,071	1,023	1,268	1,227	16	Tobacco, corn, soybeans, hay.
La	3,725	4,265	4,563	752	913	777	25	Soybeans, cotton lint, rice, sugarcane for sugar and seed.
Maine	409	402	404	198	174	159	39	Potatoes, hay, apples, oats.
Md	1,541	1,563	1,533	295	322	255	35	Corn, soybeans, hay, tobacco.
Mass	162	164	160	70	67	62	44	Hay, apples, cranberries, tobacco.
Mich	6,412	6,490	6,500	1,143	1,004	1,108	17	Corn, hay, dry edible beans, wheat.
Minn	20,323	21,256	21,738	2,725	2,348	3,085	5	Corn, soybeans, hay, wheat.
Miss	5,450	5,985	6,198	793	989	1,033	19	Soybeans, cotton lint, hay, cottonseed.
Mo	13,162	13,600	14,063	1,566	1,558	1,805	10	Soybeans, corn, hay, wheat.
Mont	8,931	9,104	9,111	899	750	626	30	Wheat, hay, barley, sugar beets.
Nebr	17,659	17,758	18,111	2,424	2,082	2,305	7	Corn, hay, wheat, sorghum grain.
Nev	513	528	490	81	90	82	41	Hay, potatoes, wheat, alfalfa seed.
N.H	113	116	113	22	21	20	48	Hay, apples, maple sirup, potatoes.
N.J	442	509	531	159	176	178	37	Soybeans, corn, tomatoes, hay.
N. Mex	1,310	1,031	1,313	220	205	211	36	Hay, cotton lint, sorghum grain, corn.
N.Y	4,181	4,241	4,227	756	733	724	27	Hay, corn, potatoes, apples.
N.C	4,783	4,757	4,684	1,671	1,817	1,506	12	Tobacco, corn, soybeans, peanuts.
N. Dak	19,589	20,684	19,786	1,891	1,417	1,235	15	Wheat, barley, hay, sunflower seed.
Ohio	10,456	10,698	10,838	1,912	2,073	1,880	8	Corn, soybeans, hay, wheat.
Okla	10,004	9,705	10,323	903	806	888	21	Wheat, hay, peanuts, cotton lint.
Oreg	2,654	2,744	2,615	740	720	669	28	Wheat, hay, potatoes, peppermint oil.
Pa	4,356	4,334	4,383	746	797	853	22	Corn, hay, mushrooms, potatoes.
R.I	17	17	16	6	6	5	49	Potatoes, hay, apples.
S.C	2,682	2,661	2,675	581	606	506	34	Tobacco, soybeans, corn, cotton lint.
S. Dak	15,261	12,886	14,970	991	492	937	20	Hay, wheat, corn, oats.
Tenn	4,553	4,721	5,047	648	794	741	26	Soybeans, tobacco, corn, hay.
Tex	23,093	21,539	23,267	3,233	3,393	3,540	4	Cotton lint, sorghum grain, corn, wheat.
Utah	1,157	1,116	1,009	170	167	162	38	Hay, wheat, barley, sugar beets.
Vt	547	548	543	66	65	56	45	Hay, apples, maple sirup, potatoes.
Va	2,812	2,797	2,783	570	573	518	33	Tobacco, corn, hay, peanuts.
Wash	4,770	4,907	4,657	1,363	1,253	1,046	18	Wheat, apples, hay, potatoes.
W. Va	747	735	714	84	83	81	42	Hay, apples, corn, tobacco.
Wis	9,181	9,263	9,337	1,374	1,206	1,575	11	Hay, corn, oats, potatoes.
Wyo	1,876	1,904	1,773	204	192	123	40	Hay, sugar beets, barley, wheat.

NA   Not available.   X   Not applicable.   [1] Excludes Alaska.

Source: U.S. Dept. of Agriculture, Economics, Statistics, and Cooperatives Service, *Crop Production; Commercial Vegetables; Field Seeds;* and *Crop Values,* all annual.

No. 1227. Corn—Supply, Disappearance, and Price Support: 1960 to 1977

[In millions of bushels, except as noted. For years beginning October]

ITEM	1960	1965	1970	1971	1972	1973	1974	1975	1976	1977, prel.
Supply, total	5,695	5,251	5,161	6,314	6,708	6,380	5,187	6,192	6,668	7,242
Production	3,907	4,103	4,152	5,646	5,580	5,671	4,701	5,829	6,266	6,357
Imports [1]	1	1	4	1	1	1	2	2	3	1
Carryover stocks, Oct. 1	1,787	1,147	1,005	667	1,126	708	484	361	399	884
Disappearance, total	3,678	4,409	4,494	5,188	6,000	5,896	4,826	5,793	5,784	6,110
Domestic	3,387	3,722	3,978	4,392	4,742	4,653	3,677	4,082	4,100	4,360
Livestock feed	3,092	3,362	3,593	4,002	4,313	4,205	3,226	3,592	3,587	3,825
Food, industry, and seed	294	360	385	390	429	448	451	490	513	535
Exports [1]	292	687	517	796	1,258	1,243	1,149	1,711	1,684	1,750
Price support operations:										
National avg. loan rate dol. per bu	1.06	1.05	1.05	1.05	1.05	1.05	1.10	1.10	1.50	2.00
Quantity placed under loan	637	215	324	953	420	261	77	147	277	7,100
Percent of production	16	5	8	17	8	5	2	3	4	17
Support or target price dol. per bu.[2]	1.06	1.25	1.35	1.35	1.41	1.64	1.38	1.38	1.57	2.00

[1] Includes grain equivalent of corn products.
[2] Guaranteed on normal production from part or all of a participant's base or allotment acreage.

Source: U.S. Dept. of Agriculture, Economics, Statistics, and Cooperatives Service, *Feed Situation*, quarterly, and *Agricultural Supply and Demand Estimates*, annual. Also in *Agricultural Statistics*, annual.

No. 1228. Corn for Grain—Acreage, Production, and Value, by States: 1975 to 1977

[See *Historical Statistics, Colonial Times to 1970*, series K 502-505, for U.S. data on corn for all purposes]

STATE	ACREAGE HARVESTED (1,000 acres)			YIELD PER ACRE (bu.) [1]			PRODUCTION (mil. bu.) [1]			FARM VALUE (mil. dol.)			PRICE [2] (dol. per bu.)	
	1975	1970	1977, prel.	1975	1970	1977, prel.	1975	1970	1977, prel.	1975	1976	1977, prel.	1976	1977, prel.
Total	67,505	71,300	70,006	86	88	91	5,829	6,266	6,357	14,789	13,472	12,887	2.15	2.03
Ala	660	800	375	50	60	29	33	48	11	91	118	23	2.45	2.10
Calif	254	290	247	109	110	116	28	32	29	87	88	69	2.74	2.40
Colo	560	630	695	92	102	116	52	64	81	135	137	157	2.13	1.95
Del	170	195	185	92	88	56	16	17	10	41	43	21	2.50	2.00
Fla	375	480	299	45	60	35	17	29	10	46	75	17	2.60	1.60
Ga	1,880	2,160	1,000	55	62	24	103	134	24	278	309	46	2.31	1.90
Ill	10,810	11,590	10,980	116	107	105	1,254	1,240	1,153	3,210	2,654	2,479	2.14	2.15
Ind	5,630	6,300	6,210	98	110	102	552	693	633	1,368	1,455	1,267	2.10	2.00
Iowa	12,420	12,900	12,400	90	91	88	1,118	1,174	1,091	2,795	2,407	2,182	2.05	2.00
Kans	1,640	1,790	1,680	86	96	96	141	172	161	353	364	314	2.12	1.95
Ky	1,140	1,360	1,410	77	102	90	88	139	127	226	308	292	2.22	2.30
Md	550	630	600	92	92	72	51	58	43	133	144	86	2.49	2.00
Mich	2,090	2,230	2,250	80	69	85	167	154	191	393	314	373	2.04	1.95
Minn	5,820	5,600	6,000	70	59	100	407	330	600	1,019	671	1,140	2.03	1.90
Miss	145	172	160	41	47	36	6	8	6	17	21	11	2.59	2.00
Mo	2,700	2,850	2,700	63	61	76	170	174	205	441	395	410	2.27	2.00
Nebr	5,920	6,100	6,350	85	85	99	503	518	629	1,248	1,068	1,226	2.06	1.95
N.Y	545	573	640	83	76	80	45	44	51	116	105	113	2.42	2.20
N.C	1,590	1,880	1,690	67	80	51	106	150	86	287	358	190	2.38	2.20
Ohio	3,340	3,820	3,620	93	103	105	311	393	380	777	826	741	2.10	1.95
Pa	1,080	1,150	1,160	82	90	92	89	104	107	230	245	251	2.37	2.35
S.C	550	667	620	68	74	36	37	49	22	99	116	43	2.35	1.95
S. Dak	2,250	1,200	2,150	37	31	59	83	37	127	207	81	235	2.18	1.85
Tenn	615	715	730	60	79	65	37	56	47	101	147	100	2.60	2.10
Tex	1,150	1,550	1,650	103	120	90	118	186	149	315	433	327	2.33	2.20
Va	565	610	560	88	78	55	50	48	31	134	118	65	2.48	2.10
Wis	2,390	2,220	2,750	83	68	104	198	151	286	512	320	572	2.12	2.00
Other	666	838	895	74	76	74	49	64	67	133	152	137	(NA)	(NA)

NA Not available.   [1] 56 pounds per bushel.
[2] Season average price received by farmers. State prices weighted by sales to obtain U.S. prices. Includes an allowance for unredeemed loan and purchase agreement deliveries valued at average rate.

Source: U.S. Dept. of Agriculture, Economics, Statistics, and Cooperatives Service, *Crop Production*, annual, and *Crop Values*, annual.

No. 1229. Wheat—Supply, Disappearance, and Price Support: 1960 to 1977

[In millions of 60-pound bushels, except as noted. For years beginning **June 1**. Excludes Alaska, Hawaii, and Puerto Rico, except exports and imports. See *Historical Statistics, Colonial Times to 1970*, series K 507 and 509–510, for production and stocks]

ITEM	1960	1965	1970	1971	1972	1973	1974	1975	1976	1977, prel.
Supply	2,747	2,238	2,336	2,442	2,531	2,311	2,125	2,559	2,810	3,140
Production	1,355	1,316	1,352	1,619	1,546	1,711	1,782	2,122	2,142	2,026
Imports [1]	8	1	1	1	1	3	3	2	3	2
Stocks, June 1, total	1,384	921	983	823	983	597	340	435	665	1,112
Disappearance	1,245	1,577	1,513	1,459	1,934	1,970	1,690	1,894	1,698	1,930
Domestic use	591	725	772	849	799	754	672	721	748	830
Food [2]	496	518	517	524	527	530	521	559	553	550
Seed and feed [3]	95	207	255	325	272	223	151	162	195	280
Exports [1]	653	852	741	610	1,135	1,217	1,018	1,173	950	1,100
Price support operations:										
Support or target price per bu	$1.78	$1.72	$2.00	$1.79	$1.72	$1.46	$2.05	$2.05	$2.29	$2.90
Quantity under support	424	173	254	438	143	60	37	52	499	588
Percent of production	31.3	13.1	18.5	27.1	9.3	-3.5	2.1	2.4	23.2	29.0

[1] Imports and exports include flour and other products expressed in wheat equivalent. Compiled from reports of the U.S. Bureau of the Census.   [2] Used for food in the U.S., U.S. Territories, and by the military.
[3] Residual; approximates feed use and includes negligible quantities used for distilled spirits and beer.

Source: U.S. Dept. of Agriculture, Economics, Statistics, and Cooperatives Service. In *Agricultural Statistics*, annual, and *Wheat Situation*, quarterly.

No. 1230. Wheat—Acreage, Production, and Value, by States: 1975 to 1977

[See *Historical Statistics, Colonial Times to 1970*, series K 506–508, for U.S. acreage, production, and price]

STATE	ACREAGE HARVESTED (1,000 acres)			YIELD PER ACRE (bushels) [1]			PRODUCTION (mil. bushels) [1]			FARM VALUE (mil. dol.)			PRICE [2] (dol. per bu.)	
	1975	1976	1977, prel.	1975	1976	1977, prel.	1975	1976	1977, prel.	1975	1976	1977, prel.	1976	1977, prel.
Total	69,391	70,771	66,216	31	30	31	2,122	2,142	2,026	7,535	5,851	4,677	2.73	2.31
Ariz	260	431	140	70	75	72	18.2	32.3	10.1	57.7	126.5	26.2	3.91	2.60
Ark	450	630	660	30	39	39	13.5	24.6	25.7	38.7	77.1	52.8	3.14	2.05
Calif	1,001	940	678	61	64	65	61.2	59.7	43.7	204.3	210.5	118.8	3.53	2.72
Colo	2,495	2,440	2,575	23	22	22	56.3	53.2	57.1	182.3	125.7	120.3	2.36	2.11
Idaho	1,350	1,430	1,190	45	48	43	60.1	68.3	50.7	203.9	167.8	129.1	2.46	2.55
Ill	1,730	1,850	1,590	39	39	43	67.5	72.1	68.4	211.2	217.9	143.6	3.02	2.10
Ind	1,400	1,500	1,240	44	36	45	61.6	54.0	55.8	198.4	158.2	122.8	2.93	2.20
Kans	12,100	11,300	12,100	29	30	29	350.9	339.0	344.9	1,200.1	878.0	741.4	2.59	2.15
Ky	320	330	274	34	31	37	10.9	10.2	10.1	32.2	30.2	20.3	2.95	2.00
Md	156	138	118	34	38	37	5.3	5.2	4.4	15.3	16.4	9.2	3.12	2.10
Mich	900	870	825	38	38	40	34.2	33.1	33.0	110.1	83.6	66.0	2.53	2.00
Minn	2,867	4,056	3,327	31	32	40	88.4	130.5	131.9	352.6	357.7	330.3	2.74	2.50
Miss	122	120	105	24	29	34	2.9	3.5	3.6	8.4	10.8	7.1	3.10	2.00
Mo	1,470	1,760	1,550	33	33	39	48.5	58.1	60.5	148.4	170.7	126.9	2.94	2.10
Mont	4,975	5,415	5,060	31	31	26	155.9	167.3	130.9	559.7	406.8	311.5	2.43	2.38
Nebr	3,070	2,950	2,950	32	32	35	98.2	94.4	103.3	333.0	224.7	227.2	2.38	2.20
N. Mex	440	262	425	26	26	22	11.4	6.8	9.1	40.3	20.6	19.2	3.02	2.10
N.Y	205	175	175	40	38	39	8.2	6.7	6.8	24.3	17.8	13.3	2.67	1.95
N.C	275	240	200	31	29	30	8.5	7.0	6.0	23.8	20.9	13.2	3.00	2.20
N. Dak	10,213	11,655	9,254	26	25	25	264.4	287.8	229.9	1,132.0	748.9	560.5	2.60	2.44
Ohio	1,680	1,600	1,540	42	40	47	70.5	64.0	72.4	230.7	184.3	155.6	2.88	2.15
Okla	6,700	6,300	6,500	24	24	27	160.8	151.2	175.5	551.5	420.3	403.7	2.78	2.30
Oreg	1,255	1,333	1,200	46	45	38	58.0	60.3	45.3	219.4	168.2	120.1	2.79	2.65
Pa	317	300	270	32	30	33	10.1	9.0	8.9	30.3	27.0	21.4	3.00	2.40
S.C	130	125	95	27	26	29	3.5	3.3	2.8	9.7	9.9	5.9	3.05	2.15
S. Dak	2,965	2,990	3,016	21	13	24	62.6	39.5	72.0	256.8	108.6	180.6	2.75	2.51
Tenn	270	300	280	31	37	36	8.4	11.1	10.1	24.1	33.8	22.7	3.05	2.25
Tex	5,700	4,700	4,700	23	22	25	131.1	103.4	117.5	443.1	314.3	264.4	3.04	2.25
Utah	282	264	204	25	25	23	7.2	6.5	4.7	24.7	16.7	11.5	2.56	2.44
Va	292	240	205	31	32	31	9.1	7.7	6.4	26.3	23.3	13.7	3.03	2.15
Wash	3,060	3,200	2,985	48	45	34	147.9	144.0	101.3	553.1	394.7	268.4	2.74	2.65
Wyo	332	330	281	25	24	20	8.3	8.0	5.6	29.9	18.3	11.9	2.30	2.11
Other	609	597	504	31	35	35	18.8	20.6	17.6	58.6	61.2	37.8	2.97	2.15

[1] 60 pounds per bushel.   [2] See footnote 2, table 1228.

Source: U.S. Dept. of Agriculture, Economics, Statistics, and Cooperatives Service, *Crop Production*, annual, and *Crop Values*, annual.

No. **1231.** Sorghum Grain—Supply, Disappearance, and Price Support: 1960 to 1977

[In millions of bushels, except as noted. For years beginning October]

ITEM	1960	1965	1970	1971	1972	1973	1974	1975	1976	1977, prel.
Total supply	1,201	1,239	927	958	943	996	684	788	771	882
Production	620	673	683	868	801	923	623	753	720	791
Carryover stocks	581	566	244	90	142	73	61	35	51	91
Disappearance	499	848	837	816	870	935	649	737	680	681
Domestic, total	428	582	693	693	658	701	437	508	434	456
Livestock feed	415	569	684	684	652	694	431	502	428	450
Exports	71	266	144	123	212	234	212	229	246	225
Price support operations:										
Nat'l avg. loan rate dol. per cwt	1.52	1.65	1.61	1.73	1.79	1.79	1.88	1.88	2.55	3.39
Quantity placed under loan mil. cwt	113.6	59.4	17.1	86.5	16.7	10.4	2.2	4.9	11.8	113.1
Percent of production	33	16	4	18	4	2	1	1	3	26
Support or target price dol. per cwt.[1]	1.52	2.00	2.14	2.21	2.39	2.79	2.34	2.34	2.66	4.07

[1] Guaranteed on normal production from part or all of a participant's base or allotment acreage.

Source: U.S. Dept. of Agriculture, Economics, Statistics, and Cooperatives Service, *Feed Situation*, quarterly, and *Agricultural Supply and Demand Estimates*, periodic. Also in *Agricultural Statistics*, annual.

No. **1232.** Rice, Rough Equivalent—Supply, Disappearance, and Price Support: 1960 to 1977

[In millions of hundredweight, except as noted. For years beginning August. Milled rice converted to a rough rice basis. See *Historical Statistics, Colonial Times to 1970*, series K 539, for production]

ITEM	1960	1965	1970	1971	1972	1973	1974	1975	1976 [1]	1977 [1]
Supply, total	67.0	84.6	101.7	105.5	97.4	98.1	120.3	135.5	152.6	139.7
Farm production	54.6	76.3	83.8	85.8	85.4	92.8	112.4	128.4	115.6	99.2
Beginning stocks	12.1	7.7	16.4	18.6	11.4	5.1	7.8	7.1	36.9	40.5
Imports	.3	.7	1.4	1.1	.5	.2	(Z)	(Z)	.1	(NA)
Disappearance, total	56.4	74.2	80.9	92.3	89.8	87.5	110.5	96.8	108.3	111.8
Domestic	26.9	30.8	34.4	35.4	35.7	37.8	41.0	40.3	42.7	43.8
Food	19.9	23.4	25.1	25.5	25.1	26.1	28.6	27.7	29.2	30.0
Industry	4.9	4.7	6.8	7.4	7.7	8.1	8.4	9.1	10.3	10.0
Seed	2.1	2.7	2.5	2.5	3.0	3.6	4.0	3.5	3.2	3.8
Exports	20.5	43.3	46.5	56.0	54.0	49.7	69.5	50.5	65.6	68.0
Statistical discrepancy [3]	+.5	+2.2	+2.1	+1.8	+2.5	+2.7	+2.7	+1.8	+3.8	(NA)
Price support operations:										
Support price per cwt.[4] dol	4.42	4.50	4.86	5.07	5.27	6.07	7.54	8.52	8.25	8.25
Quantity under support	13.1	10.0	21.5	31.3	22.9	19.1	9.3	23.3	23.4	19.5
Percent of production	24.0	13.1	25.7	36.5	26.8	20.6	8.3	18.1	20.3	19.7

NA Not available. Z Less than 50,000. [1] Preliminary. [2] Adjusted on basis of bills of lading presented to U.S. Dept. of Agriculture. [3] Results from losses in storage and handling and errors in estimation. [4] Represents target price on allotted production.

Source: U.S. Dept. of Agriculture, Economics, Statistics, and Cooperatives Service, *Agricultural Statistics*, annual.

No. **1233.** Irish Potatoes—Acreage, Production, and Value, by States: 1975 to 1977

[Excludes Alaska and Hawaii. 1977 preliminary. See *Historical Statistics, Colonial Times to 1970*, series K 532–534, for U.S. acreage, production, and price]

STATE	ACREAGE HARVESTED (1,000 acres)			YIELD PER ACRE (cwt.)			PRODUCTION (mil. cwt.)			PRICE [1] (dol. per cwt.)			FARM VALUE (mil. dol.)		
	1975	1976	1977	1975	1976	1977	1975	1976	1977	1975	1976	1977	1975	1976	1977
Total	1,264	1,375	1,349	255	260	261	322	358	352	4.48	3.59	3.64	1,445	1,283	1,275
Calif	60	66	61	351	364	361	21	24	22	6.02	4.58	5.72	127	110	125
Fla	28	31	30	194	203	206	5	6	6	4.64	6.66	6.84	25	42	43
Idaho	322	363	360	244	244	245	78	89	88	3.75	2.95	2.85	294	261	251
Maine	122	112	118	220	245	240	27	27	28	6.05	4.95	4.50	162	136	127
Mich	36	42	40	222	231	257	8	10	11	5.56	4.17	4.44	45	40	46
Minn	65	75	79	181	174	189	12	13	15	4.32	3.23	2.75	51	42	41
N.Y	47	49	43	257	277	278	12	14	12	6.26	4.82	4.29	77	65	52
N. Dak	110	121	130	160	140	160	18	17	21	4.20	3.45	2.80	74	58	58
Oreg	55	65	58	440	441	441	24	29	26	3.19	2.71	2.72	78	78	70
Pa	29	28	26	235	255	250	7	7	6	5.75	5.00	4.90	39	36	31
Wash	105	124	107	460	450	455	48	56	49	3.15	2.50	2.85	152	140	139
Wis	50	53	56	300	290	325	15	15	18	5.40	3.95	3.90	80	61	70
Other	235	246	241	198	208	209	47	51	50	5.18	4.18	4.40	241	214	222

[1] Season average price received by farmers; State prices weighted by sales.

Source: U.S. Dept. of Agriculture, Economics, Statistics, and Cooperatives Service, *Crop Production*, annual, and *Crop Values*, annual.

No. 1234. Cotton—Summary: 1956 to 1977

[In thousands of bales, except as indicated. For years ending July 31, except as noted. Excludes linters. Excludes Alaska, Hawaii, and Puerto Rico, except for exports and imports. Production figures relate to crop of preceding calendar year and are compiled from reports of individual ginners. Price per pound is average price received by growers. For stocks, see *Historical Statistics, Colonial Times to 1970*, series K 554–556]

YEARLY AVERAGE OR YEAR	PRODUCTION		Consumption [1] (running bales)	Net exports of domestic cotton (running bales)	Net imports (equivalent 500-lb. bales)	Carry-over (running bales)	Average price per pound of upland cotton [2][3] (cents)	PRICE SUPPORT OPERATIONS [2][4]	
	Running bales (counting round as half bales)	Equivalent 480-lb. bales, net						Price per lb. (cents)	Quantity under support
									Total	Percent of production
1956–1960	12,905	[5] 13,013	8,708	5,100	137	10,207	31.8	29.8	6,498	50.9
1961–1965	14,779	[5] 14,795	8,688	4,924	142	10,589	31.0	32.2	6,764	45.7
1970	10,112	10,192	7,964	2,769	50	5,760	21.9	37.0	2,386	23.7
1971	10,229	10,477	8,068	3,740	36	4,252	28.1	35.0	1,210	11.9
1972	13,269	13,704	8,039	3,229	72	3,304	27.3	35.9	1,910	14.0
1973	12,611	12,974	9,568	4,500	34	3,929	44.4	41.5	1,736	13.5
1974	11,328	11,537	7,150	5,746	48	3,743	42.7	[6] 38.0	2,420	21.5
1975	8,151	[5] 8,296	5,604	3,746	34	5,481	49.9	[6] 38.0	691	8.4
1976	10,347	10,577	6,965	3,178	92	3,594	63.8	[6] 43.2	941	9.2
1977	10,300	10,506	6,478	4,565	38	2,920	51.4	[6] 47.8	[7] 4,519	[7] 32.5

[1] Adjusted to cotton season.   [2] Data from U.S. Dept. of Agriculture, Economics, Statistics, and Cooperatives Service.   [3] Data for 1956–1970 based on gross weight terms; beginning 1971, net weight terms.   [4] American upland.   [5] Equivalent 500-pound bales, gross weight.   [6] Represents target price. If the average market price is below the target price, the eligible producers will receive payment at a rate equal to the difference between the target price and the higher of the loan level or the average market price.   [7] Preliminary.

Source: U.S. Bureau of the Census, through 1964, *U.S. Cotton Production and Distribution*, annual; thereafter, *Current Industrial Reports*, series M22P, and *Cotton Ginnings*, series A10.

No. 1235. Cotton—Acreage, Production, and Value, by States: 1975 to 1977

[Cotton production excludes linters. Values shown are for marketing season or crop year and should not be confused with calendar-year income. See *Historical Statistics, Colonial Times to 1970*, series K 553–558 for U.S. totals]

STATE	ACRES HARVESTED (1,000)			YIELD PER ACRE (lb.)			BALES (480 lb. net wt.) (1,000)			FARM VALUE (mil. dol.)			FARM PRICE PER LB.[1] (cents)		
	1975	1976	1977	1975	1976	1977	1975	1976	1977	1975	1976	1977	1975	1976	1977
Total [2]	8,796	10,914	13,279	453	465	520	8,302	10,581	14,389	2,044	3,255	3,569	51.3	64.1	51.7
Ala	370	420	395	405	399	337	312	349	277	82	111	63	54.9	66.0	47.1
Ariz	298	370	557	985	1,147	978	611	884	1,135	161	281	318	54.7	66.4	58.3
Ark	680	950	930	485	392	534	687	776	1,035	172	229	260	52.2	61.6	52.4
Calif	875	1,120	1,390	1,072	1,064	963	1,954	2,482	2,790	511	809	733	54.5	67.9	54.7
Ga	160	240	170	443	398	232	148	199	82	39	64	20	55.5	66.7	49.8
La	310	560	540	535	474	583	346	553	656	88	169	159	52.8	63.7	50.6
Miss	1,100	1,470	1,360	454	376	581	1,040	1,151	1,645	262	340	411	52.5	61.5	52.0
Mo	210	260	262	449	305	431	196	165	235	48	47	60	50.8	59.2	53.0
N. Mex	98	71	137	360	520	605	73	76	173	20	27	46	56.4	72.8	55.6
N.C	53	71	83	412	489	305	46	72	53	12	26	13	54.5	74.0	50.5
Okla	295	335	520	277	251	402	170	175	436	39	51	96	47.2	61.1	46.1
S.C	103	159	153	454	438	342	98	145	109	25	46	28	53.9	66.4	53.1
Tenn	315	370	300	339	295	407	222	228	255	56	69	59	52.3	63.5	48.0
Tex	3,923	4,508	6,473	291	353	408	2,394	3,315	5,500	528	982	1,302	46.0	61.7	49.3

[1] Includes allowance for unredeemed loans in 1975 and 1976. For 1977, average price to Apr. 1, 1978, with no allowance for unredeemed loans.   [2] Includes States not shown separately.

Source: U.S. Dept. of Agriculture, Economics, Statistics, and Cooperatives Service, *Crop Production*, annual, and *Crop Values*, annual.

No. 1236. Tobacco—Production, Disappearance, and Stocks: 1956 to 1977

[In millions of pounds. Flue-cured and cigar wrapper, crop year, July–June; all other types, October–September. Excludes Alaska, Hawaii, and Puerto Rico, except for imports, farm-sales-weight basis. See *Historical Statistics, Colonial Times to 1970*, series K 562, for production]

ITEM	1956–1960, avg.	1961–1965, avg.	1965	1970	1972	1973	1974	1975	1976	1977
Production	1,864	2,161	1,855	1,906	1,749	1,746	1,994	2,182	2,136	1,912
Domestic disappearance [1]	1,408	1,468	1,462	1,278	1,309	1,353	1,288	1,290	1,229	[2] 1,255
Exports	538	563	538	639	639	732	653	654	678	660
Imports [3]	139	170	183	219	241	274	300	391	366	316
Stocks, end of year [4]	3,976	4,182	4,351	3,667	3,289	2,943	3,006	3,010	3,305	[2] 3,517

[1] U.S. tobacco only.   [2] Estimated.   [3] Source: U.S. Bureau of the Census. Calendar year, declared weight; includes stems, trimmings, and scrap.   [4] Marketing year.

Source: Except as noted, U.S. Dept. of Agriculture, Economics, Statistics, and Cooperatives Service, *The Tobacco Situation*, quarterly.

No. 1237. TOBACCO—ACREAGE, PRODUCTION, AND VALUE, BY STATES: 1975 TO 1977

[See *Historical Statistics, Colonial Times to 1970*, series K 561–563, for U.S. acreage, production, and price]

STATE	ACREAGE HARVESTED (1,000)			YIELD PER ACRE (pounds)			PRODUCTION (mil. lb.)			PRICE [1] (dol. per lb.)			FARM VALUE (mil. dol.)		
	1975	1976	1977	1975	1976	1977	1975	1976	1977	1975	1976	1977	1975	1976	1977
Total [2]	1,086	1,045	958	2,008	2,045	1,997	2,182	2,136	1,912	1.03	1.13	1.17	2,238	2,404	2,236
Conn	4	5	4	1,435	1,580	1,606	6	7	6	4.60	4.07	(D)	29	29	[3] 3
Fla	14	14	12	2,042	2,148	2,094	30	31	25	1.13	1.15	1.23	33	35	30
Ga	75	68	65	2,010	1,820	2,075	151	124	135	1.02	1.11	1.15	153	137	155
Ind	8	8	7	2,260	2,420	2,400	17	18	17	1.04	1.13	1.20	18	21	20
Ky	201	207	197	2,275	2,403	2,297	457	497	452	1.06	1.16	1.22	485	576	550
Md	23	23	23	950	1,300	1,300	22	30	30	1.09	1.10	1.19	24	33	35
N.C.	480	448	393	1,996	2,015	1,896	957	903	745	1.00	1.11	1.17	956	999	870
Ohio	11	11	10	2,097	2,103	2,143	24	23	22	1.01	1.07	1.12	24	25	25
Pa	12	14	14	1,650	1,750	1,940	20	24	26	.58	.60	.60	11	14	16
S.C	90	75	68	2,100	2,045	2,040	189	153	139	1.00	1.12	1.23	188	172	171
Tenn	66	68	68	2,038	2,040	1,997	134	140	137	1.03	1.17	1.18	139	164	161
Va	85	87	80	1,681	1,773	1,794	142	154	143	1.00	1.07	1.16	141	165	166
Wis	11	11	12	1,891	1,821	2,059	21	20	25	.75	.75	.86	16	15	21

D   Data withheld to avoid disclosure of individual operations.   [1] See footnote 2, table 1225.
[2] Includes States not shown separately.   [3] Excludes Connecticut Valley shade-grown tobacco.

Source: U.S. Dept. of Agriculture, Economics, Statistics, and Cooperatives Service, *Crop Production*, annual, and *Crop Values*, annual.

No. 1238. SUGAR, BEET AND CANE—SUPPLY AND DOMESTIC DISAPPEARANCE: 1960 TO 1977

[In thousands of short tons, raw value]

ITEM	1960	1965	1970	1972	1973	1974	1975	1976	1977, prel.
Total supply by supplying areas [1]	9,526	9,920	11,552	11,840	11,676	11,212	9,647	11,378	12,239
United States	3,629	5,261	6,375	6,402	6,343	5,442	5,764	6,720	6,103
Beet	2,165	3,025	3,569	3,511	3,512	3,024	3,283	3,822	3,513
Mainland cane [2]	619	1,099	1,308	1,630	1,613	1,272	1,430	1,710	1,509
Hawaii	845	1,137	1,146	1,113	1,142	989	955	985	979
Puerto Rico [3]	903	834	352	148	76	157	96	203	102
Foreign areas (imports)	4,994	3,825	5,177	5,438	5,333	5,770	3,883	4,658	6,136
Domestic production	3,076	4,152	4,712	4,896	4,931	4,620	5,192	5,748	5,053
Visible stocks, start of period	2,005	2,700	2,799	2,687	2,710	2,583	2,800	2,731	3,341
Receipts: Foreign sources	4,885	4,027	5,296	5,458	5,329	5,770	3,883	4,658	6,136
Offshore domestic areas	1,748	2,700	1,500	1,262	1,221	1,146	1,051	1,188	1,082
Domestic disappearance, total	9,336	10,151	11,459	11,528	11,538	11,273	10,127	10,924	11,245

[1] Sugar quotas governed through 1974 the supply of sugar from all sources, foreign and domestic, available to the conterminous United States. The formulas for allocating the quotas among the supplying areas were established by Congress through 1974; the size of the quotas is determined by the Secretary of Agriculture. For 1975–1977, a nonrestrictive quota of 7 million tons raw value was established by Presidential Proclamation 4334.
[2] Beginning 1973, includes Texas.
[3] Through 1965, includes Virgin Islands. Beginning 1970, Puerto Rico included in U.S. total.

Source: U.S. Agricultural Stabilization and Conservation Service, *Sugar and Sweetener Report*, monthly.

No. 1239. SUGAR, BEET AND CANE—U.S. AND WORLD PRODUCTION AND U.S. PRICES: 1960 TO 1977

[Production in thousands of short tons raw value, centrifugal only]

CROP YEAR	WORLD PRODUCTION		UNITED STATES PRODUCTION			CANE (cents per lb.)		
				Cane		Wholesale, N.Y.		Retail, granulated, U.S.
	Total	Percent U.S.	Beet	La. and Fla. [1]	Hawaii	Raw, 96° [2]	Refined	
1960	60,050	8.5	2,450	630	936	6.3	9.3	11.6
1965	69,283	8.8	2,894	1,104	1,218	6.8	10.0	11.8
1970	77,758	7.8	3,322	1,252	1,162	8.1	11.7	13.0
1971	77,547	8.1	3,552	1,206	1,230	8.5	12.2	13.6
1972	83,019	8.0	3,632	1,616	1,119	9.1	13.1	13.9
1973	88,799	6.8	3,200	1,420	1,129	10.3	14.1	15.1
1974	86,194	6.8	2,916	1,471	1,041	29.2	34.3	32.3
1975	90,346	8.0	4,019	1,827	1,107	22.5	31.4	37.2
1976	95,500	7.2	3,895	1,674	1,050	13.2	19.2	24.0
1977, prel.	99,508	6.3	3,367	1,584	1,033	10.8	17.3	21.6

[1] Includes Texas cane: 126,000 tons in 1975, 94,000 tons in 1976, and 95,000 tons in 1977.
[2] Centrifugal. Duty paid.

Source: U.S. Dept. of Agriculture, Economics, Statistics, and Cooperatives Service, in *Agricultural Statistics*, annual; and U.S. Agricultural Stabilization and Conservation Service, *Sugar and Sweetener Report*, monthly.

No. **1240.** Sugarcane, Beet and Cane Sugar, and Molasses—Acreage, Production, and Value: 1950 to 1977

[Prior to 1960 and as noted, excludes Hawaii. See also *Historical Statistics, Colonial Times to 1970*, series K 542–546]

ITEM	1950	1955	1960	1965	1970	1973	1974	1975	1976	1977 [1]
Sugarcane for sugar and seed:										
Acreage harvested____1,000 acres__	334	284	437	617	584	741	734	774	747	759
Yield per acre [2]_____tons__	20.8	25.5	37.7	38.4	41.1	34.9	34.2	36.6	37.6	35.3
Production_____mil. tons__	6.9	7.2	16.5	23.7	24.0	25.8	25.1	28.3	28.1	26.8
Price per ton [3][4]_____dollars__	7.80	6.50	7.41	7.90	10.50	20.91	48.50	19.60	13.70	18.60
Farm value [4]_____mil. dol__	54	47	57	110	140	333	756	366	257	328
Sugar produced:										
Beet, raw value [5]_____1,000 tons__	2,009	1,739	2,450	2,894	3,401	3,200	2,916	4,019	3,895	3,367
Cane, raw value [5]_____1,000 tons__	1,525	1,714	1,566	2,322	2,416	2,549	2,512	2,934	2,724	2,617
Per ton of cane [5]_____lb__	208	205	199	204	210	205	212	214	197	(NA)
Cane, refined basis [6]___1,000 tons__	1,425	1,602	1,464	2,170	2,258	2,383	2,347	2,743	2,546	2,445
Molasses made										
(excl. sirup)_____mil. gal__	49	53	101	146	141	181	156	183	183	164

NA Not available.   [1] Preliminary.   [2] Growth of 9 months in Louisiana and 12 months in Florida.
[3] Season average price received by farmers. Prices exclude Government payments under the Sugar Act.
[4] Excludes Hawaii.   [5] Raw value equals 96° sugar as defined in the Sugar Act of 1948.
[6] Calculated on basis of 100 pounds of raw sugar required to produce 93.46 pounds of refined sugar.

Source: U.S. Dept. of Agriculture, Economics, Statistics, and Cooperatives Service, *Crop Production*, annual, and *Crop Values*, annual.

No. **1241.** Fats and Oils—Supply, Disposition, and Utilization: 1960 to 1977

[In millions of pounds. Includes fat content of butter]

ITEM	1960	1965	1970	1972	1973	1974	1975	1976	1977
Total supply_____	**20,752**	**24,442**	**28,661**	**29,349**	**28,617**	**30,118**	**27,791**	**32,301**	**32,652**
Production from domestic									
materials [1]_____	17,353	20,532	25,012	25,347	24,586	26,824	23,612	27,798	27,608
Imports [2]_____	1,074	1,189	1,363	1,459	1,487	1,389	2,203	2,422	1,961
Stocks, Jan. 1 [3]_____	2,325	2,721	2,286	2,543	2,544	1,905	1,976	2,081	3,083
Disposition:									
Exports [1][4]_____	5,965	7,481	10,150	10,465	10,482	11,768	9,592	11,579	12,865
Domestic disappearance [5]_____	12,649	14,538	16,119	16,340	16,230	16,374	16,118	17,496	17,352
Food uses [6]_____	**8,241**	**9,517**	**10,808**	**11,288**	**11,337**	**11,241**	**11,324**	**11,965**	**11,698**
Butter (fat content)_____	1,112	1,040	890	837	812	776	821	762	766
Lard (direct)_____	1,361	1,226	940	787	705	681	632	585	502
Shortening_____	2,302	2,768	3,556	3,698	3,614	3,622	3,666	3,861	3,798
Margarine (fat content)_____	1,367	1,534	1,787	1,864	1,884	1,891	1,907	2,069	2,003
Other_____	2,094	2,949	3,635	4,102	4,322	4,271	4,298	4,688	4,629
Nonfood uses [6]_____	**4,419**	**5,002**	**5,141**	**5,305**	**5,158**	**5,451**	**5,015**	**5,711**	**5,610**

[1] Includes oil equivalent of cottonseed, soybeans, peanuts, and flaxseed exported for crushing abroad.   [2] Includes production from imports.   [3] Excludes Government strategic stockpiling of coconut, palm, castor, and sperm oils.   [4] Includes commercial exports, voluntary or civilian relief, reexports, shipments to Puerto Rico, American Samoa, Guam, and Virgin Islands.   [5] Includes Government stockpiling.   [6] Domestic. Not adjusted for trade and change in stocks of shortening, margarine, soap, and secondaries.

No. **1242.** Soybeans—Supply, Disappearance, and Price Support: 1960 to 1977

[For years beginning **September 1**, except as noted. See *Historical Statistics, Colonial Times to 1970*, series K 521, for production]

ITEM	1960	1965	1970	1971	1972	1973	1974	1975	1976	1977 [1]
Supply, total_____mil. bu__	607	875	1,357	1,275	1,343	1,607	1,387	1,736	1,533	1,819
Production_____mil. bu__	551	846	1,127	1,176	1,271	1,548	1,216	1,547	1,288	1,716
Stocks, Sept. 1_____mil. bu__	52	30	230	99	72	60	171	[1] 188	245	103
Disappearance, total_____mil. bu__	580	840	1,258	1,203	1,283	1,436	1,199	1,491	1,430	1,549
Crushed_____mil. bu__	406	538	760	721	722	821	701	865	790	860
Seed_____mil. bu__	33	43	48	51	61	56	57	54	65	70
Feed and residual_____mil. bu__	7	9	16	15	21	20	20	17	10	9
Net exports_____mil. bu__	135	251	434	417	479	539	421	555	564	610
Percent of total_____	23.2	29.8	34.5	34.6	37.4	37.6	35.1	37.2	39.5	39.4
Ending stocks_____mil. bu__	27	36	99	72	60	171	188	245	103	270
Price support:										
Support price per bu_____dol__	1.85	2.25	2.25	2.25	2.25	2.25	2.25	(2)	2.50	3.50
Quantity under support_mil. bu__	26	87	146	168	91	124	35	(2)	[3] 23	98
Percent of production_____	4.7	10.2	13.0	14.3	7.1	8.0	2.8	(X)	1.7	5.6

X Not applicable.   [1] Estimated.   [2] Price support not authorized for the 1975 crop.   [3] As of April.

Source of tables 1241 and 1242: U.S. Dept. of Agriculture, Economics, Statistics, and Cooperatives Service, *Fats and Oils Situation*, quarterly, and *Agricultural Statistics*, annual.

No. 1243. Soybeans for Beans—Acreage, Production, and Value, by States: 1975 to 1977

[See *Historical Statistics, Colonial Times to 1970*, series K 521, for U.S. totals]

STATE	ACREAGE HARVESTED (1,000 acres)			YIELD PER ACRE (bu.)			PRODUCTION (mil. bu.)			PRICE (dol. per bu.)			FARM VALUE (mil. dol.)		
	1975	1976	1977	1975	1976	1977	1975	1976	1977	1975	1976	1977	1975	1976	1977
Total [1]	53,579	49,358	57,911	28.9	26.1	29.6	1,547	1,288	1,716	4.92	6.81	5.79	7,618	8,769	9,945
Ala	1,260	1,170	1,600	24.5	24.0	21.0	31	28	34	4.88	6.44	5.75	151	181	193
Ark	4,700	4,320	4,600	25.0	19.0	22.0	118	82	101	4.69	6.50	6.30	551	534	638
Ga	1,160	870	1,090	25.5	23.5	20.0	30	20	22	4.65	6.44	5.95	138	132	130
Ill	8,320	7,560	8,850	36.0	33.0	37.0	300	249	327	5.11	7.05	5.90	1,531	1,759	1,932
Ind	3,630	3,280	3,870	33.5	34.0	36.0	122	112	139	4.98	6.70	5.50	606	747	766
Iowa	6,970	6,450	7,230	34.0	31.0	34.0	237	200	246	5.09	7.05	5.80	1,206	1,410	1,426
Kans	1,080	865	990	21.0	15.0	28.0	23	13	28	4.77	6.52	5.35	108	85	148
Ky	1,100	1,070	1,360	27.0	27.0	29.5	30	29	40	4.87	6.74	6.20	145	195	249
La	1,920	2,250	2,680	25.0	28.0	23.5	48	63	63	4.79	6.41	5.80	230	404	365
Mich	610	565	720	26.0	20.5	29.0	16	12	21	4.78	7.22	5.60	76	84	117
Minn	3,650	3,020	3,810	27.0	22.0	35.0	99	66	133	5.02	7.22	5.60	495	480	747
Miss	3,120	3,250	3,650	22.5	22.0	20.5	70	72	75	4.81	6.42	6.35	338	459	475
Mo	4,370	4,200	4,800	26.0	20.0	30.0	114	84	144	4.84	6.65	5.65	550	559	814
Nebr	1,200	980	1,180	27.0	20.0	34.0	32	20	40	4.81	6.48	5.50	156	127	221
N.C	1,420	1,120	1,320	23.5	22.0	22.0	.33	25	29	4.67	6.65	5.95	156	164	173
Ohio	3,100	2,880	3,380	33.0	33.0	34.5	102	95	117	5.00	6.99	5.65	512	664	659
S.C	1,380	1,190	1,300	22.0	18.0	20.0	30	21	26	4.71	6.82	5.90	143	146	153
Tenn	1,850	1,800	2,200	25.0	22.5	23.0	46	41	51	4.62	6.63	5.85	214	269	296
Tex	370	347	760	25.0	26.0	26.0	9	9	20	4.31	6.10	5.35	40	55	106
Va	433	398	430	25.0	20.5	18.5	11	8	8	4.74	7.00	5.80	51	57	46

[1] Includes States not shown separately.

Source: U.S. Dept. of Agriculture, Economics, Statistics, and Cooperatives Service, *Crop Production*, annual, and *Crop Values*, annual.

No. 1244. Peanuts—Acreage, Production, Value, and Price Support: 1960 to 1977

[Year beginning August]

ITEM	1960	1965	1970	1971	1972	1973	1974	1975	1976	1977 [1]
Acreage harvested ____ 1,000	1,395	1,438	1,469	1,455	1,486	1,496	1,472	1,504	1,522	1,514
Production for nuts ____ mil. lb	1,718	2,390	2,983	3,005	3,275	3,474	3,668	3,857	3,751	3,681
Farmers' stock ____ mil. lb	7.2	7.4	2.8	14.2	27.4	56.9	38.4	227.0	106.0	608.0
Yield per acre ____ lb	1,232	1,661	2,030	2,066	2,203	2,323	2,491	2,565	2,465	2,432
Average price per lb ____ cents	10.0	11.4	12.8	13.6	14.5	16.2	17.9	19.6	20.0	20.9
Value of production ____ mil. dol	172.0	272.4	383.0	408.4	475.4	562.5	657.6	756.5	750.3	770.9
Price support operations:										
Support price per lb ____ cents	10.1	11.2	12.8	13.4	14.3	16.4	18.3	19.7	20.7	21.5
Quantity under support ____ mil. lb	352	733	1,084	1,238	1,277	1,029	1,072	1,136	845	526
Percent of production	20.5	30.7	36.3	41.2	39.0	29.6	29.2	29.5	22.5	14.3

[1] Preliminary.

Source: U.S. Dept. of Agriculture, Economics, Statistics, and Cooperatives Service, *Fats and Oils Situation*, quarterly, and *Agricultural Statistics*, annual.

No. 1245. Peanuts Harvested for Nuts—Acreage, Production, and Value, by States: 1975 to 1977

[Year beginning August. See *Historical Statistics, Colonial Times to 1970*, series K 547-549, for U.S. acreage, production, and price]

STATE	ACREAGE HARVESTED (1,000 acres)			YIELD PER ACRE (lb.)			PRODUCTION (mil. lb.)			PRICE (cents per lb.)			FARM VALUE (mil. dol.)		
	1975	1976	1977	1975	1976	1977	1975	1976	1977	1975	1976	1977	1975	1976	1977
Total	1,504	1,522	1,514	2,565	2,465	2,432	3,857	3,751	3,681	19.6	20.0	20.9	757	750	771
Ala	206	214	212	2,600	2,400	2,780	536	513	589	19.6	20.6	22.2	105	106	131
Fla	55	55	55	3,230	3,000	3,100	178	165	171	19.9	20.4	20.7	35	34	35
Ga	524	526	519	3,295	2,955	2,865	1,726	1,554	1,487	19.8	20.0	20.9	342	311	311
Miss	9	9	7	1,550	1,450	1,500	13	12	11	18.7	20.5	22.0	3	3	2
N. Mex	9	10	10	2,290	2,280	2,520	20	22	24	22.0	24.5	25.0	4	5	6
N.C	165	166	166	2,265	2,655	2,600	374	441	432	20.0	19.6	20.6	75	86	89
Okla	115	120	125	2,020	2,050	2,140	232	246	267	19.2	20.9	21.4	45	51	57
S.C	15	15	15	1,900	1,590	1,880	29	25	28	19.5	19.8	20.7	6	5	6
Tex	304	304	303	1,525	1,525	1,275	464	464	386	18.6	19.1	19.4	86	89	75
Va	102	103	102	2,790	3,000	2,800	285	309	286	19.7	19.7	20.5	56	61	59

Source: U.S. Dept. of Agriculture, Economics, Statistics, and Cooperatives Service, *Crop Production*, annual, and *Crop Values*, annual.

No. 1246. Fruits—Production and Value, 1975 to 1977, and Leading States, 1977

FRUIT	Unit	PRODUCTION [1]			FARM VALUE (mil. dol.)			Leading States in order of production, 1977
		1975	1976	1977, prel.	1975	1976	1977, prel.	
Apples (34 States) [2]	Mil. lb	7,103	6,415	6,702	461	566	621	Wash., N.Y.
Peaches	Mil. lb	2,649	2,642	2,860	276	254	282	Calif., S.C.
Pears	1,000 tons	743	829	786	106	105	108	Calif., Wash., Oreg.
Grapes	1,000 tons	4,365	4,092	4,248	618	633	776	Calif., N.Y., Wash.
Cherries, sweet	1,000 tons	156	168	147	63	67	73	Wash., Oreg., Calif., Mich.
Cherries, tart	Mil. lb	246	147	214	25	37	63	Mich.
Plums and prunes (fresh)	1,000 tons	652	640	717	103	114	135	Calif.
Oranges and tangerines [3]	Mil. boxes [4]	243.1	248.1	250.0	677	705	678	Fla., Calif.
Grapefruit (4 States)	Mil. boxes [5]	61.6	70.1	74.5	154	155	168	Fla., Tex.
Lemons (2 States) [6]	Mil. boxes [7]	29.4	17.6	25.6	113	102	88	Calif., Ariz.

[1] Excludes quantities not harvested or not marketed because of economic conditions.
[2] Production in commercial orchards with 100 or more bearing age trees.   [3] Four States.
[4] Net content of box varies. In Calif. and Ariz., approximate average for oranges and tangerines is 75 lb.; Fla. oranges, 90 lb.; Tex. oranges, 85 lb., and Fla. tangerines, 95 lb.
[5] Approximate average, net weight, is 65 lb. in Ariz. and Calif., 85 in Fla., and 80 in Tex.
[6] Includes estimates for Ariz.   [7] About 76 lb. net.

Source: U.S. Dept. of Agriculture, Economics, Statistics, and Cooperatives Service, *Crop Production; Crop Values;* and *Noncitrus Fruits and Nuts.* Annual summaries.

No. 1247. Commercial Vegetable and Other Specified Crops—Area, Production, and Value, 1975 to 1977, and Leading States, 1977

[Relates to commercial production for fresh market and processing combined. Includes market garden areas but excludes minor producing acreage in minor producing States. Excludes production for home use in farm and nonfarm gardens. Value is for season or crop year and should not be confused with calendar-year income]

CROP	AREA [1] (1,000 acres)			PRODUCTION [2] (1,000 short tons)			VALUE [3] (mil. dol.)			States ranked by production, 1977
	1975	1976	1977	1975	1976	1977	1975	1976	1977	
Artichokes	10.2	10.6	10.8	36.7	40.3	35.7	11.8	11.6	13.8	Calif.
Asparagus	102.6	92.6	85.8	107.1	115.1	110.1	61.4	72.1	81.4	Calif., Wash.
Beans, lima	76.9	48.0	60.3	96.1	55.8	74.2	30.9	16.0	25.4	Calif., Wis.
Beans, snap	357.8	322.3	335.3	824.2	747.0	819.3	164.4	144.1	155.7	Wis., Oreg.
Beets	18.1	14.5	14.1	231.1	157.4	206.2	8.8	6.1	8.0	Wis., N.Y.
Broccoli	49.7	52.8	59.1	197.0	214.5	269.0	59.4	68.2	88.1	Calif., Oreg.
Brussels sprouts	5.8	4.9	5.4	34.8	29.4	32.4	12.2	10.9	12.8	Calif.
Cabbage	103.8	98.8	91.8	1,249.3	1,180.3	1,178.2	114.0	116.9	176.0	N.Y., Fla.
Cantaloups	75.1	75.0	79.5	488.7	500.3	539.1	102.2	109.7	114.0	Calif., Tex.
Carrots	70.2	73.4	72.7	953.7	962.4	1,000.6	132.2	114.6	151.7	Calif., Tex.
Cauliflower	32.0	33.6	34.4	149.9	154.1	162.1	45.5	51.9	64.2	Calif., N.Y.
Celery	31.8	33.7	33.6	791.3	845.2	830.4	118.1	133.3	148.2	Calif., Fla.
Corn, sweet	686.2	640.5	618.3	3,097.2	2,951.6	3,015.3	246.7	225.3	220.3	Minn., Wis.
Cucumbers	187.6	177.4	175.3	916.3	887.7	903.3	137.0	128.8	136.5	Fla., Mich.
Eggplant	3.4	3.5	3.1	35.1	35.1	31.8	7.3	7.3	7.2	Fla., N.J.
Escarole	7.6	7.7	7.8	54.6	55.5	50.4	13.2	15.5	15.9	Fla., N.J.
Garlic	10.8	8.8	10.4	70.2	46.2	57.2	18.4	12.0	16.3	Calif.
Honeydew melons	12.6	14.0	15.4	119.8	117.3	128.1	22.3	24.9	25.1	Calif., Tex.
Lettuce	228.8	225.0	228.7	2,682.9	2,697.8	2,771.2	366.2	468.4	438.4	Calif., Ariz.
Mint for oil	96.1	101.2	120.1	2.8	2.7	3.3	65.6	75.5	91.8	Oreg., Wash.
Onions	103.1	109.2	105.2	1,570.9	1,759.9	1,654.8	266.2	216.4	227.1	Calif., Tex.
Peas, green	437.7	393.0	352.2	570.8	513.2	491.6	124.6	102.0	100.8	Wis., Wash.
Peppers, green	50.5	53.8	55.6	255.3	262.8	269.7	84.9	88.2	90.3	Fla., Calif.
Spinach	32.3	31.1	30.3	190.7	195.4	192.8	20.6	22.8	24.0	Calif., Tex.
Strawberries	39.2	33.8	34.3	271.6	285.7	325.5	165.3	187.3	214.9	Calif., Oreg.
Tomatoes	508.6	436.8	471.2	9,551.0	7,558.3	8,756.0	927.8	793.6	914.1	Calif., Ohio
Watermelons	210.7	234.2	227.4	1,195.2	1,295.5	1,318.6	95.7	84.3	89.4	Fla., Tex.

[1] Area of crops for harvest for fresh market, including any partially harvested or not harvested because of low prices or other factors, plus area harvested for processing.   [2] Excludes some quantities not marketed.
[3] Fresh market vegetables valued at f.o.b. shipping point, except garlic, which is field run basis at packinghouse door. Processing vegetables are equivalent returns at packinghouse door.

Source: U.S. Dept. of Agriculture, Economics, Statistics, and Cooperatives Service, *Agricultural Statistics,* annual; and *Vegetables,* annual summary.

No. 1248. CANNED FOODS—PRODUCTION: 1960 TO 1977

[In millions of standard cases of 24 No. 303 cans, except as noted. Excludes Alaska and Hawaii, except as noted. See *Historical Statistics, Colonial Times to 1970*, series P 233–234, for corn and tomatoes in cases of 24 No. 2 cans]

PRODUCT	1960	1965	1968	1970	1971	1972	1973	1974	1975	1976	1977
Fruits [1]	97.9	103.9	111.4	100.6	97.7	88.4	96.3	103.5	92.2	88.5	92.8
Apples [2]	3.1	4.1	3.3	2.3	2.4	2.2	3.2	2.2	1.1	1.9	2.0
Applesauce [2]	11.8	15.9	14.1	14.1	15.1	11.9	15.2	16.6	9.6	8.9	10.7
Apricots	6.1	5.1	4.5	3.8	3.3	3.0	4.1	2.0	4.4	2.4	2.3
Berries	.8	.7	.5	.4	.4	.4	.4	.4	.5	.3	.1
Cherries, red, pitted	1.6	2.4	1.1	1.0	1.0	1.3	.6	1.2	1.3	.4	.6
Cherries, sweet	.6	.7	.5	.7	.5	.4	.5	.6	.4	.5	.5
Cranberry sauce [2]	2.2	3.4	3.8	3.9	3.5	3.5	4.7	4.3	3.4	3.5	3.4
Fruit cocktail [3]	12.8	14.5	16.6	13.1	13.3	11.9	13.4	14.9	13.7	13.6	13.0
Fruit salad [3]	.8	.7	.8	.7	.8	.7	.8	.9	.6	.5	.6
Grapefruit sections [2]	3.0	2.8	2.3	3.3	1.8	2.3	2.1	1.5	1.1	1.2	(NA)
Mixed fruits [3]	.4	.5	.5	.5	.7	.8	.7	1.0	.7	.7	1.6
Peaches	30.8	30.0	35.9	29.6	25.7	24.0	24.5	32.4	29.0	24.8	29.2
Pears	8.5	6.4	10.3	8.6	10.3	9.1	9.8	10.7	9.8	11.5	9.6
Pineapple [2][4]	15.0	15.0	16.5	17.8	17.7	16.5	15.0	13.9	14.9	17.3	18.4
Plums [5]	.4	1.7	.7	.8	1.2	.4	1.3	1.2	1.4	1.0	.8
Juices: [2][6]											
Apple	6.2	9.6	9.4	14.1	13.7	13.8	14.8	15.4	15.3	15.4	18.2
Grapefruit	11.0	13.8	20.5	26.0	26.8	28.3	29.0	21.6	25.8	27.7	(NA)
Orange	11.5	12.1	13.5	15.4	13.8	17.1	13.8	13.3	13.5	14.4	(NA)
Orange-grapefruit	3.2	2.9	2.6	2.5	1.9	2.1	2.0	1.7	2.8	1.6	(NA)
Pineapple [4]	14.4	15.4	14.0	13.7	15.7	12.3	11.3	8.5	8.7	10.2	12.0
Tomato [7]	33.0	32.8	32.9	29.5	31.5	25.5	27.8	29.6	29.0	26.5	22.9
Seasonal vegetables	175.3	204.1	250.4	208.8	223.0	221.8	235.2	241.9	248.9	217.5	236.1
Asparagus	8.0	7.2	6.9	6.0	5.5	5.9	5.8	5.6	3.6	3.6	3.7
Beans, green and wax	33.2	45.6	51.8	47.6	50.0	47.6	55.0	62.3	55.4	47.4	54.5
Beans, lima	3.8	3.0	3.8	2.8	3.1	2.1	3.1	2.5	3.7	2.8	2.7
Beets [2]	8.8	10.0	14.6	11.3	10.4	10.0	10.9	15.1	13.1	9.2	11.3
Carrots [2]	5.0	4.5	5.1	5.4	5.3	5.5	6.4	6.9	4.7	5.2	6.6
Corn, sweet	35.3	39.1	59.3	47.0	53.8	53.0	55.2	46.4	57.5	54.7	56.3
Greens, leafy	2.9	2.7	2.8	3.5	4.4	2.8	4.0	4.6	3.0	3.1	2.6
Peas, field	2.1	1.8	2.4	2.4	2.7	2.6	2.8	2.8	2.0	1.9	2.2
Peas, green	28.7	37.6	36.2	28.7	33.2	33.1	29.6	33.1	35.2	31.9	30.2
Pimentos	.9	.8	.8	.6	.7	.6	.3	.4	.6	.7	.4
Pumpkin and squash	5.0	3.9	4.8	4.0	4.6	4.1	4.6	4.2	5.8	5.5	3.0
Spinach [2]	7.8	6.4	8.0	7.3	7.7	8.3	8.9	10.8	8.3	6.3	7.1
Tomatoes	31.0	36.0	48.4	39.0	38.4	43.3	45.4	43.8	53.6	42.8	53.1
Other vegetable packs [8]	2.8	5.5	5.7	3.2	3.2	2.9	3.2	3.4	2.4	2.4	2.4
Nonseasonal vegetables:											
Sweet potatoes [2]	6.9	11.1	10.8	9.8	10.1	9.5	11.4	12.8	7.7	8.0	7.2
White potatoes [2]	4.2	5.0	5.7	6.6	7.8	5.0	5.7	8.1	6.8	6.2	7.1
Chili sauce	1.4	1.5	2.4	1.5	1.5	1.7	1.8	1.6	1.7	2.0	1.5
Tomato puree	5.4	6.5	13.8	5.9	7.8	9.7	9.9	10.3	13.8	8.4	9.8
Seafood, salmon [9]	(NA)	3.6	3.4	3.8	3.2	2.1	1.4	1.9	1.5	2.7	3.1

NA Not available.   [1] Basis: 24 No. 2½ cans.   [2] Pack beginning in year shown.   [3] California only.   [4] Represents U.S. pack and foreign operations.   [5] Beginning 1965, purple plums only.   [6] Basis: 24 No. 2 cans.   [7] Beginning 1968, excludes combination vegetable-tomato juices.   [8] Succotash, carrots and peas, okra, okra and tomatoes, and, for 1965 and 1968, mushrooms.   [9] Basis: 48–1 lb. cans. Includes Alaska.

Source: National Food Processors Association, Washington, D.C., *Canned Food Pack Statistics*, annual.

No. 1249. PRINCIPAL FROZEN FOODS—PRODUCTION: 1960 TO 1976

[In millions of pounds]

PRODUCT	1960	1965	1970	1971	1972	1973	1974	1975	1976
Total	10,868	14,144	17,415	18,594	19,363	21,862	23,101	23,452	(NA)
Vegetables:									
Total, excl. potatoes	1,407	1,800	1,912	2,009	2,281	2,467	2,488	2,212	2,156
Potato products	551	1,219	2,404	2,565	2,594	2,691	2,985	3,001	3,335
Fruits and berries	660	653	621	666	612	650	604	567	629
Juices and drinks [1]	4,556	5,514	5,360	5,480	5,051	6,345	6,237	6,287	(NA)
Meat	310	450	470	490	510	520	535	545	(NA)
Poultry	2,000	2,231	2,160	2,142	2,236	2,209	2,222	2,070	2,359
Prepared foods	1,100	1,875	4,100	4,880	5,710	6,570	7,690	8,470	(NA)
Seafoods	284	402	388	362	369	410	340	300	322

NA Not available.
[1] Includes single strength drinks, juices and concentrated juices, and drinks reconstituted.

Source: American Frozen Food Institute, Washington, D.C., *Frozen Food Pack Statistics*, annual. (Copyright.)

No. 1250. Livestock—Number on Farms and Value: 1950 to 1978

[Alaska and Hawaii excluded from census data prior to 1959 and from annual data prior to 1965. See also *Historical Statistics, Colonial Times to 1970*, series K 564–569]

YEAR	ALL CATTLE Number (mil. head)	ALL CATTLE Total value (bil. dol.)	ALL CATTLE Value per head (dol.)	HOGS AND PIGS Number (mil. head)	HOGS AND PIGS Total value (bil. dol.)	HOGS AND PIGS Value per head (dol.)	SHEEP AND LAMBS Number (mil. head)	SHEEP AND LAMBS Total value (bil. dol.)	SHEEP AND LAMBS Value per head (dol.)
CENSUS DATA									
1950 (Apr. 1)	76.9	9.1	118.77	55.8	1.1	19.70	31.4	.6	17.69
1954 (Oct.–Nov.)	95.0	8.2	86.64	57.1	1.9	33.13	[1] 31.6	.5	14.93
1959 (Oct. 1)	92.5	12.5	135.20	67.9	1.4	20.18	33.9	.6	16.38
1964 (Nov.–Dec.)	105.6	11.9	113.17	54.1	1.3	24.48	25.5	.4	16.06
1969 (Dec. 31)	106.4	19.0	178.73	55.5	2.2	38.85	21.6	.5	24.63
1974 (Dec. 31)	113.2	18.5	163.16	45.5	2.1	45.37	15.4	.5	30.79
ANNUAL DATA (JAN. 1) [2]									
1950	78.0	9.6	124.00	58.9	1.6	27.10	26.2	.5	17.80
1955	96.6	8.5	88.20	50.5	1.5	30.60	27.1	.4	14.90
1960	96.2	13.2	137.00	59.0	1.1	18.50	28.8	.5	16.50
1965	109.0	12.4	113.00	50.8	1.2	24.50	21.8	.3	15.80
1970	112.4	20.2	179.00	56.7	2.2	39.00	17.4	.4	24.80
1971	114.6	21.1	184.00	67.3	1.6	23.50	[3] 19.7	[3] .5	[3] 23.60
1972	117.9	24.5	208.00	62.4	1.8	28.50	18.7	.4	22.90
1973	121.5	30.6	252.00	59.0	2.5	42.00	17.6	.5	26.70
1974	127.8	37.5	293.00	60.6	3.7	60.40	16.3	.5	32.80
1975	132.0	21.0	159.00	54.7	2.5	44.90	14.5	.4	30.50
1976	128.0	24.3	190.00	49.3	4.0	80.40	13.3	.5	37.30
1977	122.8	25.3	206.00	54.9	2.6	47.00	12.8	.5	42.40
1978, prel	116.3	27.0	232.00	57.6	3.6	63.10	12.4	.6	51.50

[1] Not available for Florida, Georgia, and South Carolina.
[2] Beginning 1970, data for hogs and pigs as of Dec. 1, preceding year.   [3] Prior to 1971, data refer to stock sheep.

Source: Census data—U.S. Bureau of the Census, *Census of Agriculture: 1969*, vol. II and *1974*, vol. I. Annual data—U.S. Dept. of Agriculture, Economics, Statistics, and Cooperatives Service, *Agricultural Statistics*, annual, and annual livestock summaries.

No. 1251. Meats—Slaughtering, Production, and Trade: 1960 to 1977

[**Quantities represent carcass weight equivalent.** 1960–1970 exclude Alaska and Hawaii except for exports and imports. Covers inspected, noninspected, retail, and farm slaughter. Excludes edible byproducts. Excludes USDA exports, military civilian feeding, and voluntary relief feeding. See also *Historical Statistics, Colonial Times to 1970*, series K 583–594]

ITEM	1960	1965	1970	1972	1973	1974	1975	1976	1977
All meats:									
Animals slaughtered, total___mil. head__	135.0	130.7	137.3	135.7	124.0	132.6	124.8	130.5	133.1
Under Federal inspection____percent__	78	82	89	91	92	91	91	92	94
Production, total [1]_____mil. lb__	28,203	31,502	36,217	36,999	34,899	37,894	36,762	39,608	39,711
Federally inspected_____percent__	78	82	89	91	91	91	90	92	93
Exports of U.S. production_____mil. lb__	223	250	305	367	437	342	449	598	586
Imports for consumption_____mil. lb__	1,048	1,347	2,429	2,682	2,607	2,160	2,248	2,600	2,424
Beef:									
Animals slaughtered, total___mil. head__	26.0	33.2	35.4	36.1	34.0	37.3	41.5	43.2	42.4
Under Federal inspection____percent__	75	80	87	89	90	89	89	90	92
Production, total_____mil. lb__	14,728	18,699	21,651	22,381	21,277	23,138	23,976	25,969	25,279
Federally inspected_____percent__	78	82	88	90	91	90	90	91	92
Exports of U.S. production_____mil. lb__	55	91	101	113	144	115	110	158	167
Imports for consumption_____mil. lb__	760	923	1,792	1,960	1,990	1,615	1,758	2,079	1,939
Veal:									
Animals slaughtered, total___mil. head__	8.6	7.8	4.2	3.2	2.4	3.2	5.4	5.5	5.7
Under Federal inspection____percent__	61	65	72	76	76	74	72	80	85
Production, total_____mil. lb__	1,109	1,020	588	458	357	486	873	853	834
Federally inspected_____percent__	56	56	57	62	59	58	57	66	68
Lamb and mutton:									
Animals slaughtered, total___mil. head__	16.2	13.3	10.8	10.5	9.8	9.1	8.1	6.9	6.6
Under Federal inspection____percent__	86	88	93	94	94	94	94	94	96
Production, total_____mil. lb__	768	651	551	543	514	465	410	371	351
Federally inspected_____percent__	87	88	93	95	95	95	94	94	97
Pork:									
Animals slaughtered, total___mil. head__	84.2	76.4	87.0	85.9	77.8	83.1	69.8	74.9	78.4
Under Federal inspection____percent__	79	83	90	92	93	93	93	94	96
Production, total [1]_____mil. lb__	11,598	11,132	13,426	13,617	12,751	13,805	11,503	12,415	13,247
Federally inspected_____percent__	79	84	90	92	92	93	93	94	94

[1] Excludes lard.

Source: U.S. Dept. of Agriculture, Economics, Statistics, and Cooperatives Service, *Livestock and Meat Statistics*, annual.

No. 1252. LIVESTOCK ON FARMS, LIVEWEIGHT PRODUCTION, VALUE, AND ANNUAL AVERAGE PRICE RECEIVED BY FARMERS: 1960 TO 1977

[1960 excludes Alaska and Hawaii, except sheep excluded from Hawaii for all years. See also *Historical Statistics, Colonial Times to 1970*, series K 575–582]

PRODUCTION AND PRICE	1960	1965	1970	1971	1972	1973	1974	1975	1976	1977
All cattle: On farms_____mil__	96.2	109.0	112.4	114.6	117.9	121.5	127.7	131.8	128.0	122.8
Production [1]_____bil. lb__	28.8	34.0	39.3	39.4	41.2	44.2	42.8	40.9	41.4	40.9
Beef, price per 100 lb_____dol__	20.40	19.90	27.10	29.00	33.50	42.80	35.60	32.30	33.70	34.40
Calves, price per 100 lb_____dol__	22.90	22.00	34.50	36.40	44.70	56.60	35.20	27.20	34.20	36.90
Value of production_____bil. dol__	5.9	6.8	10.9	11.6	14.2	18.1	14.9	12.8	13.8	14.0
Hogs and pigs: On farms_____mil__	15.0	50.8	67.4	62.5	59.2	61.1	55.1	49.6	54.9	57.6
Production [1]_____bil. lb__	19.2	18.3	21.8	22.8	20.9	20.2	20.0	16.8	18.1	19.4
Price per 100 lb_____dol__	15.30	19.60	22.70	17.50	25.10	38.40	34.20	46.10	43.30	39.40
Value of production_____mil. dol__	2,946	3,573	4,955	3,991	5,245	7,738	6,838	7,751	7,844	7,634
Sheep: On farms_____mil__	33.2	25.1	20.4	19.7	18.7	17.7	16.4	14.5	13.4	12.7
Production [1]_____mil. lb__	1,628	1,217	1,099	1,071	1,004	896	807	781	733	698
Sheep, price per 100 lb_____dol__	5.60	6.34	7.52	6.56	7.26	12.90	11.20	11.30	13.20	13.40
Lambs, price per 100 lb_____dol__	17.90	22.80	26.40	25.90	29.10	35.10	37.00	42.10	46.90	51.30
Value of production_____mil. dol__	253	257	260	250	271	294	272	303	315	320

[1] Includes adjustment for livestock shipped in and inventory changes.

Source: U.S. Dept. of Agriculture, Economics, Statistics, and Cooperatives Service, *Agricultural Statistics*, annual, and *Meat Animals—Farm Production, Disposition, and Income, by States*, annual summary.

No. 1253. LIVESTOCK ON FARMS—NUMBER, SELECTED STATES: 1969 TO 1978

[In thousands. As of Jan. 1, except for hogs and pigs, Dec. 1]

STATE	ALL CATTLE			MILK COWS			SHEEP AND LAMBS			HOGS AND PIGS		
	1970	1975	1978	1970	1975 [1]	1978 [1]	1970	1975	1978	1969	1974	1977
U.S._____	112,369	131,826	116,265	12,091	11,211	10,930	20,423	14,512	12,387	57,046	55,062	57,587
Ala._____	1,953	2,700	2,130	122	92	85	6	4	4	949	950	650
Ariz._____	1,302	1,170	1,135	10	61	68	500	510	400	99	99	102
Ark._____	1,805	2,680	2,120	97	91	90	8	6	5	288	270	400
Calif._____	4,730	5,200	4,430	750	800	846	1,317	1,100	1,115	165	124	150
Colo._____	3,212	3,375	3,180	81	75	71	1,303	990	810	261	280	320
Fla._____	2,020	2,950	2,350	192	202	198	5	4	4	331	292	320
Ga._____	1,889	2,420	1,975	145	130	129	5	4	3	1,780	1,590	1,750
Idaho_____	1,780	2,150	1,870	142	149	138	840	595	536	124	110	60
Ill._____	3,325	3,200	2,950	308	257	233	386	229	184	6,842	6,500	6,100
Ind._____	1,918	2,125	2,025	243	218	208	274	196	176	4,499	4,300	4,100
Iowa_____	7,478	7,350	7,800	508	405	380	869	460	370	13,720	13,400	15,200
Kans._____	6,016	6,400	6,000	194	147	140	378	200	195	1,643	1,750	2,000
Ky._____	2,803	3,750	3,120	340	296	277	100	40	28	1,400	1,100	1,240
La._____	1,630	1,832	1,425	167	134	129	24	15	13	164	175	160
Mich._____	1,500	1,640	1,470	435	421	404	264	167	138	697	715	640
Minn._____	3,958	4,430	3,700	950	886	850	554	390	255	3,263	3,700	4,100
Miss._____	2,210	3,000	2,130	181	126	110	13	7	5	450	456	420
Mo._____	4,940	6,800	6,000	342	311	282	276	194	131	4,197	3,900	3,700
Mont._____	3,014	3,340	2,570	40	28	27	1,113	710	530	217	190	211
Nebr._____	6,330	6,900	6,500	175	156	128	377	280	237	3,000	3,050	3,200
Nev._____	626	657	570	14	14	15	227	151	114	9	10	9
N. Mex._____	1,572	1,720	1,550	33	31	31	773	578	571	65	66	60
N.Y._____	1,799	1,875	1,760	954	920	915	106	79	66	95	102	125
N.C._____	980	1,120	1,100	172	152	147	16	11	9	1,580	1,890	2,300
N. Dak._____	2,110	2,635	2,050	141	123	104	420	315	213	302	322	320
Ohio_____	2,031	2,350	2,025	448	405	398	728	517	370	2,557	1,950	1,750
Okla._____	4,985	6,500	5,900	144	122	114	138	89	81	348	310	330
Oreg._____	1,514	1,470	1,490	98	91	93	541	415	410	108	95	100
Pa._____	1,781	1,960	1,900	712	686	703	165	125	80	570	633	790
S.C._____	600	710	690	65	59	56	2	1	1	476	610	575
S. Dak._____	4,237	4,950	3,925	186	161	160	1,207	782	704	1,674	1,700	1,580
Tenn._____	2,308	3,300	2,700	296	217	205	50	19	15	1,163	780	1,180
Texas_____	12,830	16,600	14,500	354	345	314	3,708	2,688	2,460	1,005	940	890
Utah_____	808	900	864	76	79	76	1,053	697	491	43	41	42
Va._____	1,475	1,750	1,620	202	159	171	202	177	172	601	575	650
Wash._____	1,260	1,420	1,275	175	181	176	141	92	62	73	75	68
Wis._____	4,076	4,640	4,100	1,815	1,810	1,810	167	105	82	1,680	1,400	1,400
Wyo._____	1,476	1,690	1,280	17	13	12	1,883	1,350	1,115	41	39	32
Other_____	2,088	2,167	2,086	728	655	637	276	211	195	597	574	563

[1] Represents cows and heifers that have calved, kept for milk.

Source: U.S. Dept. of Agriculture, Economics, Statistics, and Cooperatives Service, annual livestock summaries.

No. 1254. Dairying—Cows and Dairy Products: 1960 to 1977

[In millions of pounds, except as indicated. See also *Historical Statistics, Colonial Times to 1970*, series K 595–608]

ITEM	1960	1965	1970	1972	1973	1974	1975	1976	1977, prel.
Cows and heifers, 2 years old and over, kept for milk, Jan. 1 [1]_____mil. head__	19.5	17.0	13.3	11.8	11.6	11.3	11.1	11.1	11.0
Milk produced on farms_____bil. lb__	123	124	117	120	115	116	115	120	123
Whole milk sold from farms [2]_____bil. lb__	106	115	113	116	112	112	112	117	120
Manufactured dairy products:									
Butter (incl. whey butter)_____	1,373	1,325	1,137	1,102	919	962	984	979	1,086
Cheese, total [3]_____	1,478	1,755	2,201	2,605	2,685	2,937	2,811	3,320	3,358
American (excl. full-skim American)____	1,003	1,167	1,428	1,652	1,678	1,862	1,655	2,049	2,042
Swiss (including block)_____	121	123	144	178	164	175	174	196	189
Munster, Brick, and Limburger_____	54	56	59	70	71	75	74	76	73
Cream and Neufchatel_____	106	123	126	133	140	150	160	168	176
All Italian varieties_____	158	244	394	512	565	606	672	747	793
All other varieties [3]_____	36	43	50	59	67	68	72	78	79
Cottage cheese:									
Curd, pot, and bakers'_____	594	630	726	784	763	690	701	711	704
Creamed [4]_____	799	865	1,038	1,115	1,086	978	991	1,010	1,017
Condensed bulk milk_____	1,205	1,346	1,237	1,214	1,115	964	1,041	1,044	1,091
Evaporated and condensed canned milk__	2,256	1,799	1,293	1,202	1,117	1,053	938	942	827
Dry whole milk_____	98	89	69	75	78	68	63	78	69
Nonfat dry milk solids [5]_____	1,844	2,013	1,456	1,236	927	1,026	1,009	932	1,114
Dry whey_____	277	404	621	762	772	851	596	662	625
Dry buttermilk_____	86	87	60	50	43	45	43	46	53
Ice cream of all kinds_____mil. gal__	700	757	762	770	774	782	837	818	804
Milk sherbet_____mil. gal__	41	45	49	50	53	50	49	50	50
Ice milk_____mil. gal__	145	231	287	289	292	296	299	286	293
Wholesale prices (cents per pound):									
Cheese, American:									
40-lb. blocks, Wis. assembly points_____	(NA)	38.4	55.0	59.8	73.0	79.9	86.6	96.3	96.8
Single daisies, Chicago_____	41.4	45.0	64.9	71.4	84.3	97.3	104.4	116.1	118.7
Butter, N.Y. (Grade A)_____	59.9	61.0	70.4	69.6	(NA)	67.4	81.8	94.4	101.5
Prices received by farmers:									
Milkfat in cream_____cents per lb__	60.5	61.1	70.0	67.8	67.2	63.5	70.3	83.4	91.4
Whole milk: Wholesale, per 100 lb___dol__	4.21	4.23	5.71	6.07	7.14	8.33	8.75	9.66	9.72
Retail_____cents per qt__	21.7	22.3	27.0	27.8	31.0	34.9	35.4	36.4	36.8

NA Not available.   [1] Beginning 1972, milk cows that have calved.   [2] Comprises sales to plants and dealers, and retail sales by farmers direct to consumers.   [3] Beginning 1974, includes full-skim.   [4] Includes partially creamed (low fat).   [5] Includes dry skim milk for animal feed.

Source: U.S. Dept. of Agriculture, Economics, Statistics, and Cooperatives Service, *Production of Manufactured Dairy Products*, annual; *Milk Production, Disposition, and Income*, annual; and *Agricultural Statistics*, annual.

No. 1255. Dairy Products and Whole Milk Sold, by Selected States: 1974 to 1977

STATE	1974, DAIRY PRODUCTS SOLD [1]		WHOLE MILK SOLD (mil. lb.)			STATE	1974, DAIRY PRODUCTS SOLD [1]		WHOLE MILK SOLD (mil. lb.)		
	Farms	Total (mil. dol.)	1975	1976	1977		Farms	Total (mil. dol.)	1975	1976	1977
U.S.___	246,973	8,194	110,385	115,558	118,418	Mo._____	7,425	161	2,725	2,818	2,880
						Nebr.____	5,038	81	1,330	1,325	1,265
Ala._____	946	57	635	630	635	N.H._____	671	29	320	319	322
Ariz._____	174	58	780	840	860	N.J._____	793	43	498	515	520
Ark._____	1,368	47	655	660	690	N.Y._____	17,755	756	9,645	9,875	9,920
Calif._____	3,288	780	10,405	11,145	11,530	N.C._____	2,156	117	1,390	1,495	1,570
Colo._____	1,129	58	765	750	760	N. Dak.__	4,613	55	805	860	865
Conn._____	819	51	575	585	595	Ohio_____	11,447	296	4,130	4,385	4,430
Fla._____	473	207	1,880	1,975	1,915	Okla.____	1,851	73	995	1,045	1,065
Ga._____	1,089	99	1,170	1,255	1,255	Oreg.____	1,526	73	910	940	975
Idaho_____	3,546	95	1,490	1,490	1,535	Pa._____	16,774	560	6,705	7,060	7,370
Ill._____	6,461	165	2,395	2,440	2,440	S.C._____	484	42	481	492	500
Ind._____	6,573	147	2,155	2,185	2,215	S. Dak.__	5,975	98	1,445	1,570	1,575
Iowa_____	14,243	244	3,700	3,780	4,070	Tenn.____	5,794	142	1,905	1,975	1,905
Kans._____	4,171	100	1,330	1,400	1,405	Tex._____	3,030	237	3,090	3,215	3,275
Ky._____	7,983	144	2,150	2,215	2,295	Utah_____	1,335	59	860	855	875
La._____	1,530	89	1,010	1,045	1,050	Vt._____	3,447	160	1,955	2,040	2,055
Maine_____	1,337	55	605	610	620	Va._____	3,441	141	1,695	1,825	1,860
Md._____	2,269	120	1,475	1,515	1,545	Wash.____	2,168	161	2,120	2,240	2,390
Mass._____	955	50	555	550	550	W. Va.____	962	28	311	320	298
Mich._____	9,861	315	4,280	4,490	4,625	Wis._____	49,102	1,261	18,340	19,740	20,500
Minn._____	29,504	571	8,705	9,010	9,270	Other____	1,903	103	1,175	1,249	1,313
Miss._____	1,564	66	840	830	830						

[1] For farms with sales of $2,500 and over. Source: U.S. Bureau of the Census, *Census of Agriculture: 1974*, vol. I.

Source: Except as noted, U.S. Dept. of Agriculture, Economics, Statistics, and Cooperatives Service, *Milk: Production, Disposition, and Income, 1975–77*.

No. 1256. Poultry—Number on Farms, Value, Eggs Produced, and Prices: 1960 to 1977

[Beginning 1970, data for chickens and eggs are for **Dec. 1** of previous year to **Nov. 30** of year stated. 1960 excludes Alaska and Hawaii. See also *Historical Statistics, Colonial Times to 1970,* series K 609–623]

ITEM	1960	1965	1970	1972	1973	1974	1975	1976	1977
Chickens [1]: Number, Dec. 1 [2]_____mil__	369	394	433	404	409	384	380	378	387
Value, total_____mil. dol__	391	462	525	516	663	653	660	644	652
Value per head_____dol__	1.06	1.17	1.21	1.28	1.62	1.70	1.74	1.70	1.69
Number produced_____mil__	260	240	264	233	251	242	233	229	247
Production value_____mil. dol__	139	101	107	100	176	115	105	145	146
Price per lb_____cents__	12.2	8.9	9.1	8.9	15.1	9.7	9.9	12.9	12.1
Eggs: Number produced_____mil. doz__	5,134	5,463	5,690	5,823	5,548	5,507	5,366	5,376	5,378
Price per dozen_____cents__	36.1	33.7	39.1	30.9	52.5	53.2	52.4	58.3	55.7
Gross income_____mil. dol__	1,848	1,841	2,221	1,781	2,886	2,910	2,819	3,133	2,994
Turkeys: Number, Jan. 1 [3]_____1,000__	5,633	6,100	3,389	3,303	3,553	2,943	3,098	3,064	3,045
Value, total [3]_____mil. dol__	28	27	20	21	34	29	33	34	34
Value per head [3]_____dol__	4.89	4.40	5.94	6.50	9.54	9.85	10.79	10.83	11.27
Number raised_____mil__	84	106	116	129	132	131	124	140	136
Gross income_____mil. dol__	377	424	499	539	936	679	794	825	905
Price per lb_____cents__	25.4	22.2	22.6	22.2	38.2	28.0	34.8	31.7	35.5

[1] Excludes commercial broilers.   [2] As of Jan. 1 for 1960 and 1965.   [3] Beginning 1970, data are for breeder hens only and cover the 26 major producing States; number of turkeys as of Dec. 1.

No. 1257. Poultry—Production, by Selected States: 1975 to 1977

[See *Historical Statistics, Colonial Times to 1970,* series K 611, 614, 617, and 621 for U.S. totals]

STATE	CHICKENS RAISED (mil.)			BROILERS PRODUCED (mil.)			CHICKS HATCHED COMMERCIALLY [1] (mil.)			TURKEYS RAISED (mil.)		
	1975	1976	1977	1975	1976	1977	1975	1976	1977	1975	1976	1977
U.S____	274.6	271.1	290.0	2,932.7	3,282.8	3,400.0	[3]3,622.9	[3]3,980.5	[3]4,138.6	[3]124.3	[3]140.0	[3]135.6
Ala____	14.3	15.6	15.2	395.8	430.2	428.1	432.4	465.0	479.3	(Z)	(D)	(D)
Ark____	20.1	18.8	22.5	481.9	540.4	569.6	561.8	618.8	667.1	7.1	10.1	10.3
Calif____	22.5	22.0	24.6	95.8	105.0	112.5	148.2	159.1	170.4	15.8	17.5	17.2
Colo____	2.2	2.2	2.0	–	–	–	(D)	(D)	(D)	3.6	3.7	3.5
Conn____	3.3	3.9	3.6	1.0	1.0	1.1	4.7	4.9	4.1	(Z)	(Z)	(Z)
Del____	.7	.7	.6	136.3	160.0	156.1	(D)	(D)	(D)	(D)	(D)	(D)
Fla____	11.3	11.4	12.5	64.3	74.3	75.7	116.6	129.6	131.1	(D)	(D)	(D)
Ga____	20.8	20.6	24.6	416.6	451.5	485.9	487.2	531.7	572.7	1.2	1.9	1.6
Ill____	5.5	5.2	5.5	–	–	–	(D)	(D)	(D)	.4	.4	.6
Ind____	12.5	12.7	14.4	12.3	13.9	13.6	51.1	53.9	55.9	5.1	5.2	4.2
Iowa____	10.6	9.8	8.5	3.3	3.8	3.5	(D)	(D)	(D)	6.3	6.5	6.0
Kans____	2.9	2.9	2.4	.6	–	–	5.8	5.2	5.4	.2	.1	.1
Ky____	3.0	3.8	3.8	5.9	6.7	3.6	(D)	(D)	(D)	(D)	(D)	(D)
La____	3.1	3.2	3.2	50.7	57.6	63.6	(D)	(D)	(D)	(Z)	(Z)	(Z)
Maine____	8.3	6.6	6.5	81.0	86.7	86.9	98.5	103.0	102.8	(Z)	(Z)	(Z)
Md____	1.5	1.7	1.8	179.8	199.0	198.5	(D)	(D)	(D)	(Z)	.1	.1
Mass____	1.7	1.7	2.0	–	–	–	(D)	(D)	(D)	.1	.1	.1
Mich____	6.0	5.6	5.4	.5	.8	.9	(D)	(D)	(D)	.7	1.2	1.2
Minn____	9.6	8.5	9.9	10.1	15.2	14.2	34.1	38.1	37.1	22.8	24.4	22.7
Miss____	10.3	10.0	10.0	231.3	257.4	255.8	248.4	263.8	265.5	–	–	–
Mo____	7.1	6.8	6.9	23.4	25.3	24.1	(D)	(D)	(D)	8.1	9.7	9.8
Nebr____	2.6	2.2	2.8	1.7	1.8	1.7	4.2	3.2	3.4	.5	.5	.5
N.J____	2.2	1.7	1.5	–	–	–	(D)	(D)	(D)	(Z)	.1	.1
N.Y____	8.5	8.4	8.5	1.5	.7	–	(D)	(D)	(D)	.1	.2	.1
N.C____	14.0	14.0	16.8	284.0	315.6	339.3	316.8	370.0	386.2	14.4	16.7	16.5
Ohio____	8.9	9.1	8.8	16.7	17.5	19.4	(D)	(D)	(D)	2.8	2.8	2.5
Okla____	2.1	2.0	2.1	28.8	31.4	29.3	(D)	(D)	(D)	1.4	1.8	1.3
Oreg____	1.6	1.6	1.9	14.0	15.2	15.6	28.5	28.8	30.1	1.0	1.3	1.4
Pa____	12.4	12.3	13.3	65.8	75.1	88.1	107.2	119.4	122.5	2.8	3.7	3.6
S.C____	6.0	5.1	5.5	27.4	33.4	34.5	32.6	38.4	45.8	2.6	2.6	2.4
S. Dak____	3.3	3.0	3.0	–	–	–	(D)	(D)	(D)	.9	1.0	1.1
Tenn____	2.3	3.8	3.9	18.0	38.3	48.9	(D)	(D)	(D)	(Z)	(Z)	(Z)
Tex____	11.0	12.0	12.5	162.8	190.7	185.3	201.9	230.8	229.6	8.8	9.3	8.6
Utah____	.9	.9	1.0	–	–	–	.9	.8	(D)	3.4	3.4	2.7
Va____	4.4	4.4	4.5	77.8	88.9	98.0	95.9	103.9	116.4	6.0	7.3	8.7
Wash____	4.7	4.7	5.3	15.2	15.9	16.8	18.8	21.4	21.7	.2	(D)	(D)
W. Va____	1.1	1.0	.9	15.8	15.1	16.3	(D)	(D)	(D)	1.5	1.8	2.1
Wis____	4.3	4.3	4.3	11.1	12.3	10.9	(D)	(D)	(D)	4.9	5.1	5.5
Other____	7.0	7.1	7.7	1.8	2.0	2.2	(D)	(D)	(D)	.9	1.0	.7

– Represents zero.   D Withheld to avoid disclosure.   Z Less than 50,000.   [1] By commercial hatcheries.   [2] Includes 627,176 for 1975; 690,552 for 1976; and 691,521 for 1977, not available separately by State.   [3] Includes 269,000 for 1975; 478,000 for 1976; and 300,000 for 1977, not available separately by State.

Source of tables 1256 and 1257: U.S. Dept. of Agriculture, Economics, Statistics, and Cooperatives Service, *Agricultural Statistics,* annual.

Figure 25.1

**Selected Timber Products—
Producer Price Indexes:
1960 to 1977**

(See table 1268)

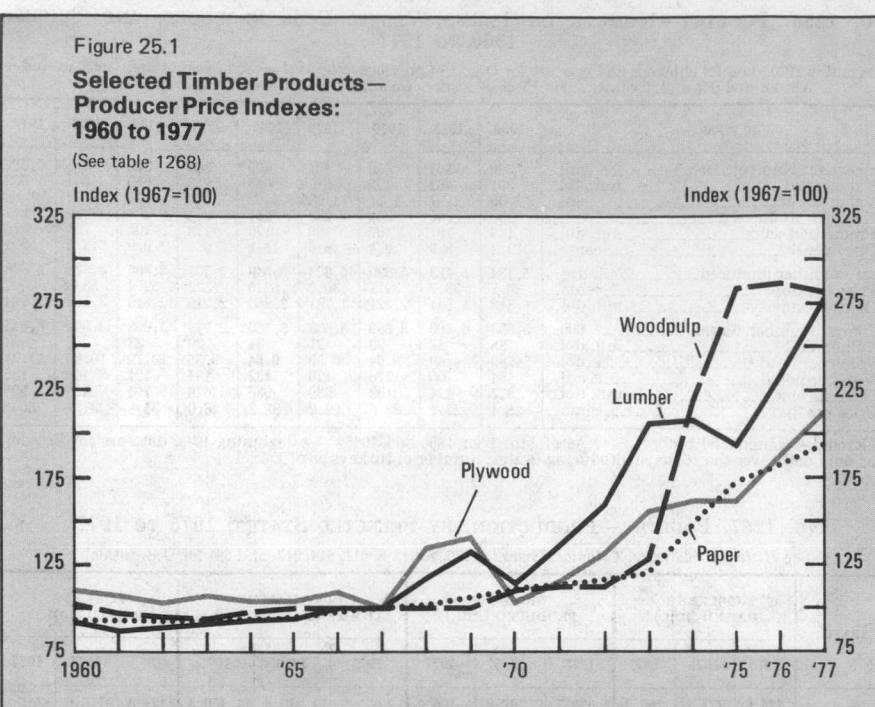

Source: Chart prepared by U.S. Bureau of the Census. Data from U.S. Bureau of Labor Statistics.

Figure 25.2

**Newsprint—Production, Stocks,
Consumption, and Imports: 1960 to 1977**

(See table 1277)

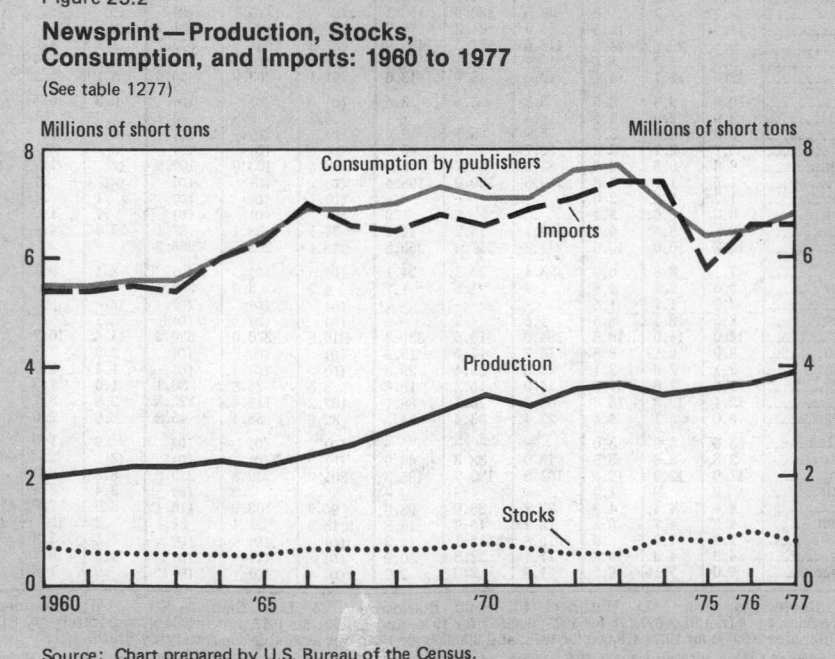

Source: Chart prepared by U.S. Bureau of the Census.
Data from U.S. Bureau of Economic Analysis.

Section 25
Forests and Forest Products

This section presents basic statistics on the area and ownership of commercial forest land, and on the growing stock and volume of timber on it; forestry statistics covering the National Forests and Forest Service cooperative programs; product statistics for lumber, pulpwood, woodpulp, paper and paperboard, turpentine, rosin, and veneer logs; and similar data.

The principal sources of these data are *The Outlook for Timber in the United States*, issued in 1973 by the Forest Service of the Department of Agriculture, and *The Demand and Price Situation for Forest Products, National Forest System*, and *Wildfire Statistics*, issued annually by the Forest Service; and reports of the census of manufactures (taken every five years) and the monthly and annual *Current Industrial Reports*, issued by the Bureau of the Census. Additional information is published in the *Annual Report* of the National Forest Reservation Commission; the monthly and annual *Naval Stores* of the Department of Agriculture's Economics, Statistics, and Cooperatives Service; the monthly *Survey of Current Business* of the Bureau of Economic Analysis; the monthly *Fingertip Facts and Figures* of the National Forest Products Association, Washington, D.C.; and the annual *Wood Pulp Statistics* and *The Statistics of Paper and Paperboard* of the American Paper Institute, New York, N.Y.

The Bureau of the Census also collects statistics on foreign trade of forest products. The Bureau of Labor Statistics publishes monthly and annual statistics of wholesale lumber prices. Information on the domestic movement of forest products is collected by the Interstate Commerce Commission and the Association of American Railroads, Washington, D.C.

The completeness and reliability of statistics on forests and forest products vary considerably. The data for forest land area and stand volumes are much more reliable for areas which have been recently surveyed than for those for which only estimates are available. Estimates of fire damage or causes of fires for Federal lands are considered much better than those for private lands. In general, much more data are available for lumber and other manufactured products such as veneer and plywood, pulp and paper, naval stores, etc., than for the primary forest products such as poles and piling, fuelwood, and fence posts.

Historical statistics.—Tabular headnotes provide cross-references, where applicable, to *Historical Statistics of the United States, Colonial Times to 1970*. See Appendix I.

No. 1258. FOREST LAND—TOTAL AND COMMERCIAL AREA, VOLUME OF SAWTIMBER, AND GROWING STOCK: 1953, 1963, AND 1970

[Area in millions of acres; sawtimber in billions of board feet. As of Jan. 1. For composition of regions, see table 1260]

YEAR AND REGION	Total forest land	COMMERCIAL TIMBERLAND, OWNERSHIP [1]					NET VOLUME OF SAWTIMBER [2]			Growing stock, net (bil. cu. ft.)
		All owner-ships	Fed-erally owned or managed	State, county, and munici-pal	Private Total	Private Percent of total	Total	Soft-wood	Hard-wood	
United States, 1953	748	495	111	28	356	71.9	2,412	1.979	433	517
North	178	170	13	19	138	81.2	246	59	187	111
South	214	192	14	3	175	91.1	391	186	205	114
West	356	133	84	6	43	32.3	1,774	1,734	40	292
United States, 1963	757	508	111	28	369	72.6	2,431	1,956	475	628
North	183	175	13	19	143	81.7	290	69	221	136
South	219	200	14	3	183	91.5	435	230	205	134
West	355	133	84	6	43	32.3	1,705	1,656	49	357
United States, 1970	754	500	107	29	364	72.8	2,420	1,905	515	649
North	186	178	12	20	146	82.0	332	80	252	156
South	212	193	14	3	175	90.7	484	276	208	160
West	355	129	81	6	42	32.6	1,605	1,549	56	334

[1] For definition of commercial timberland, see footnote 1, table 1260.   [2] See footnote 2, table 1260.

Source: U.S. Forest Service, *Timber Resources for America's Future*, 1958; *Timber Trends in the United States*, 1965; and *The Outlook for Timber in the United States*, 1973.

No. 1259. NATIONAL FOREST LANDS AND PURCHASES: 1950 TO 1976

[Area as of June 30, except 1976 as of Sept. 30; purchases for years ending June 30, except as noted. Includes Puerto Rico. Lands to be purchased must be approved by National Forest Reservation Commission, which also sets prices on such lands. Actual purchases are made by U.S. Department of Agriculture. See also *Historical Statistics, Colonial Times to 1970*, series L 10–14]

ITEM	1950	1955	1960	1965	1970	1973	1974	1975	1976 [1]
Gross area [2] _____mil. acres	229	236	227	226	226	226	226	226	226
National Forest System [3] ____mil. acres	181	188	186	187	187	187	187	188	188
Gross area approved for purchase _____1,000 acres	61	19	8	29	92	117	25	11	43
Average price per acre _____dollars	9	10	15	47	125	149	245	283	285
Total price _____mil. dol	.5	.2	.1	1.3	11.5	17.5	6.0	3.2	12.3
Purchases completed_____1,000 acres	97	12	8	33	113	104	31	34	39
Average price per acre _____dollars	7	12	31	39	96	150	207	268	282
Total price _____mil. dol	.7	.1	.2	1.3	10.9	15.6	6.4	9.0	10.9
Gross area of purchase units____mil. acres	53	62	56	56	56	56	56	56	56
Purchase completed, net area [4] _mil. acres	19	19	19	19	20	20	20	20	20
Average price per acre _____dollars	4	4	4	4	6	8	9	9	10
Total price _____mil. dol	71	73	75	79	125	163	170	179	190

[1] Purchase data for 15 months ending Sept. 30.   [2] Comprises all publicly and privately owned land within authorized boundaries of national forests, purchase units, experimental areas, and land utilization projects.
[3] Beginning 1970, excludes lands in process of acquisition.
[4] Cumulative total under the March 1, 1911, Act of Congress (Weeks Law), as amended, and related acts.

Source: U.S. Forest Service, *National Forest System*, annual; and U.S. National Forest Reservation Commission, *Annual Report*.

No. 1260. FOREST LAND AREA, COMMERCIAL AREA OWNERSHIP, AND VOLUME OF SAWTIMBER AND GROWING STOCK, BY STATES: JAN. 1, 1970

STATE	Total forest land (1,000 acres)	COMMERCIAL TIMBERLAND, OWNERSHIP [1] (1,000 acres)				SAWTIMBER, NET VOLUME [2]		GROWING STOCK, NET VOLUME [3]	
		Total	Federal, owned or managed	State, county, municipal	Private	Total (mil. bd. ft.)	Softwood (mil. bd. ft.)	Total (mil. cu. ft.)	Softwood (mil. cu. ft.)
U.S.	753,549	499,697	107,109	29,012	363,576	2,420,767	1,905,289	648,879	431,874
North	186,495	177,901	12,311	19,600	145,990	331,868	80,061	155,677	39,114
N.E.	33,411	32,367	912	1,081	30,374	57,270	34,813	35,211	20,191
Conn.	2,186	2,169	1	154	2,014	2,612	346	1,898	228
Maine	17,749	16,894	73	238	16,583	34,519	23,456	21,253	14,763
Mass.	3,520	3,491	29	370	3,092	3,128	1,324	2,717	770
N.H.	5,132	5,020	578	118	4,324	10,041	6,862	5,148	2,902
R.I.	433	429	–	26	403	193	25	267	20
Vt	4,391	4,364	231	175	3,958	6,779	2,800	3,928	1,508
M.A.	53,196	49,685	1,500	4,296	43,889	102,881	15,033	52,333	6,694
Del.	391	390	1	8	381	1,361	460	657	229
Md.	2,960	2,882	14	175	2,693	6,962	1,281	3,074	531
N.J.	2,463	2,354	17	237	2,100	4,276	749	1,729	385
N.Y.	17,378	14,489	57	835	13,597	24,980	7,273	12,518	3,292
Pa.	17,832	17,478	518	2,888	14,072	29,616	3,434	20,270	1,600
W. Va.	12,172	12,092	893	153	11,046	35,686	1,836	14,085	657
Lake	53,960	50,841	7,059	13,497	30,285	81,352	26,088	40,075	10,891
Mich.	19,274	18,800	2,494	3,947	12,359	38,088	11,026	16,559	4,313
Minn.	18,984	16,875	2,784	6,604	7,487	20,066	8,041	11,727	3,896
N. Dak.	422	406	115	10	281	563	–	276	–
S. Dak. (east)	335	223	74	3	146	339	58	102	19
Wis.	14,945	14,537	1,592	2,933	10,012	22,296	6,963	11,411	2,663
Central	45,928	45,008	2,840	726	41,442	90,365	4,127	28,058	1,338
Ill	3,790	3,680	256	11	3,413	7,834	25	2,327	19
Ind.	3,908	3,840	214	147	3,479	11,210	184	3,607	70
Iowa.	2,455	2,430	11	24	2,395	6,597	10	1,808	4
Kans.	1,344	1,187	27	10	1,150	1,904	1	534	–
Ky.	11,969	11,826	738	82	11,006	30,199	1,968	8,546	621
Mo.	14,919	14,600	1,373	213	13,014	16,050	1,072	6,496	385
Nebr.	1,045	1,023	83	12	928	1,991	489	507	115
Ohio.	6,498	6,422	138	227	6,057	14,580	378	4,233	124
South	211,885	192,542	14,277	3,002	175,263	483,851	275,876	159,517	78,405
S.A.	49,496	48,463	3,627	841	43,995	133,789	60,878	47,550	19,094
N.C.	20,613	20,193	1,350	373	18,470	58,127	28,611	19,680	8,509
S.C.	12,494	12,411	840	233	11,338	36,434	20,382	12,699	6,369
Va.	16,389	15,859	1,437	235	14,187	39,228	11,885	15,171	4,216
E. Gulf.	43,479	41,334	2,980	572	37,782	83,227	53,835	30,584	18,744
Fla.	17,933	16,231	1,653	492	14,086	30,464	19,966	10,888	6,904
Ga.	25,546	25,103	1,327	80	23,696	52,763	33,869	19,696	11,840
Ctr. Gulf.	51,820	51,454	3,035	1,019	47,400	123,841	67,652	40,284	18,221
Ala.	21,770	21,742	795	202	20,745	52,769	34,874	16,010	9,232
Miss.	16,914	16,892	1,300	471	15,121	44,732	28,079	13,878	7,189
Tenn.	13,136	12,820	940	346	11,534	26,340	4,699	10,396	1,800
W. Gulf.	67,090	51,291	4,635	570	46,086	142,994	93,511	41,099	22,346
Ark.	18,278	18,206	2,682	256	15,268	46,386	25,252	15,365	6,539
La.	15,380	15,342	692	168	14,482	53,997	35,011	13,603	7,596
Okla.	9,340	4,818	482	96	4,240	4,490	2,789	1,648	850
Tex.	24,092	12,925	779	50	12,096	38,121	30,459	10,483	7,361
West	355,169	129,254	80,521	6,410	42,323	1,605,048	1,549,352	333,685	314,355
Pac. NW.	172,553	49,713	27,070	3,576	19,067	962,233	922,575	186,975	175,487
Alaska.	119,051	5,639	5,256	353	30	179,375	178,102	34,767	34,469
Oreg.	30,404	25,673	14,581	938	10,154	457,735	434,671	87,093	81,061
Wash.	23,098	18,401	7,233	2,285	8,883	325,123	309,802	65,115	59,957
Pac. SW.	44,382	17,909	8,752	564	8,593	278,407	271,671	54,490	51,156
Calif.	42,408	16,828	8,743	77	8,008	277,554	271,653	54,251	51,152
Hawaii.	1,974	1,081	9	487	585	853	18	239	4
No. Rocky Mt.	55,854	36,669	26,360	1,587	8,722	253,493	251,387	63,828	63,106
Idaho.	21,591	15,193	11,292	880	3,021	131,666	130,986	29,498	29,258
Mont.	22,778	15,983	10,884	534	4,565	102,018	100,926	28,650	28,376
S. Dak. (west)	1,400	1,310	967	62	281	3,444	3,435	1,007	1,001
Wyo.	10,085	4,183	3,217	111	855	16,365	16,040	4,673	4,471
So. Rocky Mt.	82,380	24,963	18,339	683	5,941	110,915	103,719	28,392	24,606
Ariz.	18,583	3,690	3,490	34	166	21,582	20,903	4,810	4,584
Colo.	22,534	11,583	8,231	234	3,118	46,076	42,633	12,267	10,360
Nev.	7,661	129	55	5	69	1,344	1,320	250	237
N. Mex.	18,314	5,736	3,638	171	1,927	25,628	24,054	6,337	5,736
Utah.	15,288	3,825	2,925	239	661	16,285	14,809	4,728	3,689

– Represents zero. [1] All land producing, or capable of producing, usable crops of wood, economically available on date shown or prospectively, and not withdrawn from timber utilization. [2] International 1¼ inch rule. Commercial species which contain at least 1 saw log. Softwoods, must be at least 9 inches in diameter breast height, except in Calif., Oreg., Wash., and coastal Alaska where the minimum diameter is 11.0 inches. [3] All live trees, poletimber trees, saplings, and seedlings meeting specified standards of quality or vigor; excludes cull trees.

Source: U.S. Forest Service, The Outlook for Timber in the United States, 1973.

No. 1261. NATIONAL FOREST SYSTEM—SUMMARY: 1960 TO 1977

[Through 1976, for years ending June 30, except as noted; thereafter, ending Sept. 30. Includes Alaska and Puerto Rico, except as noted. See *Historical Statistics, Colonial Times to 1970*, series J 33–34, for similar but not comparable grazing data, and L 15–31]

ITEM	1960	1965	1970	1972	1973	1974	1975	1976	1977
Timber cut, total value____mil. dol__	157.1	161.9	308.6	382.9	480.1	509.9	368.4	495.4	735.9
Commercial and cost sales: [1]									
Volume_____mil. bd. ft__	9,367	11,244	11,527	11,700	12,357	10,958	9,174	9,575	10,482
Value_____mil. dol__	156.4	161.1	307.6	382.0	479.2	508.6	366.0	492.0	733.0
Free use: Volume_____mil. bd. ft__	123	191	179	179	190	449	618	[2]1,080	1,028
Value [3]_____mil. dol__	.2	.3	.3	.4	.4	.8	1.1	[2]2.1	2.1
Misc. forest products, value_____mil. dol__	.5	.5	.7	.5	.5	.5	1.4	1.2	1.0
Livestock grazing: [4]									
Cattle, horses, and swine [5]_1,000__	1,307	1,376	1,607	1,633	1,571	1,580	1,626	[2]1,690	1,534
Sheep and goats_____1,000__	2,574	2,112	2,105	2,049	1,598	1,470	1,549	[2]1,750	1,460
Roads and trails:									
Road construction [6]_____miles__	851	1,613	942	712	424	35	136	363	1,020
Trail construction [6]_____miles__	142	671	278	495	902	298	298	422	1,222
Expenditures_____mil. dol__	43.2	105.5	155.1	173.3	157.8	131	158	168	187
Receipts, total_____mil. dol__	148.2	149.2	299.7	350.0	469.7	485.7	373.1	454.7	691.6
Timber use_____mil. dol__	140.1	138.8	283.9	330.0	446.7	459.9	341.3	418.6	652.1
Grazing use_____mil. dol__	4.5	3.5	4.4	5.5	6.2	7.8	7.7	10.9	11.4
Special land use, etc____mil. dol__	3.6	6.9	11.4	14.5	16.8	18.0	24.1	25.2	28.1
Payments to States [7]_____mil. dol__	35.7	35.8	72.2	85.0	114.1	118.0	90.2	109.9	290.6
25-percent fund_____mil. dol__	35.2	35.3	70.8	84.5	113.7	117.5	89.8	109.5	224.1
Other_____mil. dol__	(Z)	(Z)	1.5	(Z)	(Z)	(Z)	(Z)	.4	(NA)
Allotments to Forest Service [8]_____mil. dol__	14.2	14.3	28.8	33.9	45.5	47.0	35.9	43.8	66.0

NA Not available. Z Less than $50,000. [1] Includes land exchanges.
[2] For 15 months ending Sept. 30. [3] Includes some free use timber not reducible to board feet.
[4] Number permitted to graze. 1973 represents number that actually grazed. Calendar-year data. Excludes Puerto Rico. [5] Excludes animals under 6 months of age. 1973 excludes swine.
[6] Includes reconstruction. Through 1965, excludes national grasslands.
[7] Payments made in following year. Includes Puerto Rico. [8] For use in following year.
Source: U.S. Forest Service. In *Agricultural Statistics*, annual, and unpublished data.

No. 1262. NATIONAL FOREST SYSTEM LANDS AND OTHER LANDS WITHIN UNIT BOUNDARIES—STATES AND OTHER AREAS: 1977

[In thousands of acres. As of Sept. 30. See also *Historical Statistics, Colonial Times to 1970*, series L 10–11]

STATE	Gross area within unit boundaries [1]	National forest system lands	Other lands within unit boundaries	STATE OR OTHER AREA	Gross area within unit boundaries [1]	National forest system lands	Other lands within unit boundaries
Total_____	226,165	187,709	38,456	Nevada_____	5,422	5,113	309
				New Hampshire_____	806	683	123
Alabama_____	1,275	641	634	New Mexico_____	10,272	9,246	1,026
Alaska_____	20,777	20,622	155	New York_____	13	13	
Arizona_____	11,937	11,271	666	North Carolina_____	3,166	1,154	2,012
Arkansas_____	3,495	2,467	1,028	North Dakota_____	1,106	1,106	(Z)
California_____	24,314	20,328	3,986	Ohio_____	833	168	665
Colorado_____	15,909	14,386	1,523				
Connecticut_____	(Z)	(Z)	–	Oklahoma_____	461	291	170
				Oregon_____	17,445	15,593	1,852
Florida_____	1,224	1,082	142	Pennsylvania_____	743	507	236
Georgia_____	1,912	857	1,055	South Carolina_____	1,380	607	773
Idaho_____	21,653	20,390	1,263	South Dakota_____	2,269	1,995	274
Illinois_____	840	257	583	Tennessee_____	1,212	621	591
Indiana_____	645	181	464	Texas_____	1,836	781	1,055
Kansas_____	108	108	–				
Kentucky_____	2,100	659	1,441	Utah_____	9,129	8,046	1,083
				Vermont_____	630	264	366
Louisiana_____	1,017	597	420	Virginia_____	3,228	1,608	1,620
Maine_____	94	52	42	Washington_____	10,026	9,070	956
Michigan_____	4,870	2,709	2,161	West Virginia_____	1,861	962	899
Minnesota_____	5,466	2,787	2,679	Wisconsin_____	2,023	1,493	530
Mississippi_____	2,311	1,139	1,172	Wyoming_____	9,691	9,252	439
Missouri_____	3,082	1,455	1,627				
Montana_____	19,087	16,768	2,319	Puerto Rico_____	56	28	28
Nebraska_____	441	352	89	Virgin Islands_____	(Z)	(Z)	–

– Represents zero. Z Less than 500 acres. [1] See footnote 2, table 1259.
Source: U.S. Forest Service, *National Forest System*, annual.

No. **1263.** Forest Tree Distribution and Forest Management: 1960 to 1977

[For years ending **June 30** except, beginning **1976**, ending **Sept. 30.** See also *Historical Statistics, Colonial Times to 1970*, series L 32-43]

ITEM	1960	1965	1970	1972	1973	1974	1975	1976	1977
Forest trees distributed [1]_____millions__	845	509	495	553	581	540	578	506	657
Costs, total_____$1,000__	6,573	6,865	8,544	5,810	6,200	6,890	5,537	(NA)	(NA)
Federal contributions [1]_____$1,000__	186	216	197	175	214	216	225	143	145
State expenditures_____$1,000__	6,387	6,649	8,347	5,636	5,986	6,674	5,312	(NA))	(NA)
Acreage planted [2]_____1,000__	2,137	1,325	1,600	1,680	1,750	1,604	1,931	1,892	1,976
Forest management program: [3]									
Woodland owners assisted_____1,000__	82	99	115	274	106	118	141	105	134
Woodland involved_____1,000 acres__	4,116	6,165	6,945	11,158	6,472	7,106	10,369	4,085	4,614
Products harvested_____mil. bd. ft__	596	717	1,226	956	1,579	907	678	597	921
Gross sale value_____mil. dol__	14	17	32	24	38	44	28	(NA)	(NA)
Expenditures, total_____mil. dol__	3.9	6.8	11.6	14.6	16.5	19.4	22.4	23.3	(NA)
Federal_____mil. dol__	1.4	2.7	3.7	4.3	4.1	4.3	4.7	4.7	5.5
State_____mil. dol__	2.5	4.1	8.0	10.3	12.4	15.2	17.8	18.6	(NA)

NA Not available. [1] Provided by Clarke-McNary program, Act of June 7, 1924, as amended.
[2] Includes areas planted by direct seeding; excludes areas satisfactorily reforested or established as wind barriers because some of the plantings or seedlings are not successful.
[3] Under the Cooperative Forest Management Act of August 25, 1950, and related legislation.
Source: U.S. Forest Service. In U.S. Dept. of Agriculture, *Agricultural Statistics*, annual.

No. **1264.** Wildfires—Summary: 1960 to 1977

[See also *Historical Statistics, Colonial Times to 1970*, series L 44-55]

ITEM	1960	1965	1970	1972	1973	1974	1975	1976	1977
ACREAGE (1,000)									
Protected area:									
Federal [1][2]_____	362,836	655,001	647,239	651,970	660,907	678,253	677,949	680,243	681,564
Area burned [1]_____	622	146	719	1,232	676	1,200	408	519	802
State and private [3][4]___	402,800	472,023	520,501	631,162	626,523	708,129	726,356	737,228	748,692
Area burned_____	1,909	1,206	1,541	1,050	1,086	1,511	1,119	2,119	2,096
Unprotected area:									
Federal_____	–	55	65,537	64,768	54,232	54,232	54,232	54,232	54,232
State and private_____	32,030	30,294	45,751	59,581	63,959	63,835	70,848	101,192	198,009
Area burned_____	1,947	1,300	1,019	(NA)	(NA)	(NA)	(NA)	2,472	(NA)
FIRES (1,000)									
Total_____	103.4	113.7	121.7	124.5	118.0	145.9	134.9	241.7	174.0
On protected areas [4]___	89.6	100.6	116.4	98.9	91.7	120.9	103.3	172.8	158.9
Percent of total_____	86.7	88.5	95.6	79.4	77.7	82.9	76.6	71.5	91.3
Federal area [5]_____	12.1	9.1	15.0	15.9	12.8	15.0	12.3	15.8	16.3
State and private_____	91.3	104.6	106.8	108.6	105.2	130.8	122.6	225.9	157.7
Protected_____	77.5	91.5	101.5	83.0	78.9	105.8	91.0	157.0	142.6
Unprotected_____	13.8	13.1	5.3	25.6	26.3	25.0	31.6	68.9	15.1
Cause of fires: [5]									
Incendiary (arson)_____	21.2	26.9	30.9	24.7	22.3	31.4	28.2	51.3	45.3
Debris burning_____	21.9	22.9	28.3	21.0	17.5	23.0	18.2	38.9	36.1
Smoking_____	16.0	16.5	14.5	10.0	10.4	13.4	10.5	17.7	15.4
Lightning_____	11.1	8.7	12.8	14.4	10.2	12.6	9.4	11.7	15.8
Caused by children____	(NA)	(NA)	7.7	7.1	8.4	11.1	10.8	14.4	13.1
Railroads_____	3.9	(7)	6.8	6.5	6.1	7.2	5.2	10.8	8.1
Equipment use_____	(NA)	(NA)	3.4	3.6	4.4	5.7	4.6	7.7	6.7
Campfires_____	3.6	3.4	3.8	3.5	3.5	4.3	4.0	5.1	4.6
Miscellaneous [8]_____	12.0	22.1	8.1	8.0	8.9	12.1	12.4	15.2	13.7
FIRE PROTECTION EXPENDITURES [3][9] (mil. dol.)									
Total_____	56.6	76.6	113.5	125.6	136.9	150.4	169.6	189.7	(NA)
Federal_____	9.4	12.8	16.4	20.0	20.0	20.1	25.2	22.6	30.0
State and county_____	45.1	62.6	95.3	104.7	116.0	} 130.3	144.4	167.0	(NA)
Private agencies_____	2.2	1.2	1.8	.8	.8				

– Represents zero.   NA Not available.   [1] Comprises land administered by U.S. Dept. of Agriculture, U.S. Dept. of Interior, and Tennessee Valley Authority, etc.   [2] Beginning 1965, includes nonforest watershed areas under U.S. Dept. of Interior protection.   [3] 1960 excludes Alaska; 1975 and 1977 include Guam.
[4] Includes nonforest watershed areas.   [5] For protected areas only.   [6] Excludes nonforested watershed lands under U.S. Dept. of Interior protection.   [7] Included in various other classifications.   [8] 1960, lumbering included in "Miscellaneous"; thereafter in various other classifications; no previous breakdown was shown for fires caused by children.   [9] For fire protection on State and private lands only; years ending June 30, through 1976; thereafter, ending Sept. 30.
Source: U.S. Forest Service, *Wildfire Statistics*, annual, and unpublished data.

No. **1265.** Timber Products—Industrial Roundwood Summary: 1950 to 1977

[In millions of cubic feet, roundwood equivalent. See also *Historical Statistics, Colonial Times to 1970*, series L 72-86]

YEAR	DOMESTIC PRODUCTION				APPARENT CONSUMPTION				
	Total [1]	Lumber	Plywood and veneer	Pulp products	Total [2]	Lumber	Plywood and veneer	Pulp products	Miscellaneous [3]
1950	8,525	[4] 5,905	345	[4] 1,500	9,910	6,360	350	2,385	770
1955	9,225	[4] 5,785	575	[4] 2,200	10,495	6,215	615	3,000	630
1960	8,920	[4] 5,080	705	2,575	10,145	5,560	765	3,290	510
1965	10,540	5,670	1,030	3,095	11,930	6,340	1,125	3,890	560
1970	11,120	5,355	1,070	3,835	12,130	6,110	1,225	4,395	425
1971	11,100	5,495	1,225	3,560	12,620	5,465	1,430	4,265	450
1972	11,370	5,605	1,360	3,485	13,060	6,795	1,600	4,225	430
1973	11,665	5,730	1,310	3,690	13,300	6,860	1,490	4,515	425
1974	11,200	5,145	1,140	4,125	12,380	5,965	1,240	4,780	380
1975	10,175	4,850	1,205	3,380	10,930	5,495	1,300	3,800	325
1976	11,385	5,475	1,380	3,635	12,555	6,430	1,515	4,220	380
1977	11,300	5,565	1,425	3,425	12,995	6,915	1,585	4,070	400

[1] Includes log exports and other products.   [2] Includes log imports and other products.   [3] Includes cooperage logs, poles and piling, fence posts, hewn ties, round mine timbers, box bolts, etc.   [4] Excludes Alaska and Hawaii.

No. **1266.** Timber Products—Production, Foreign Trade, and Consumption, by Type of Product: 1960 to 1977

[In millions of cubic feet, roundwood equivalent. See also *Historical Statistics, Colonial Times to 1970*, series L 72-86]

ITEM	1960	1965	1970	1972	1973	1974	1975	1976	1977, prel.
Industrial roundwood:									
Domestic production [1]	8,920	10,540	11,120	11,370	11,665	11,200	10,175	11,385	11,300
Softwoods	6,925	8,110	8,655	8,885	9,030	8,555	8,075	9,010	9,020
Hardwoods	1,995	2,430	2,470	2,490	2,640	2,650	2,700	2,375	2,280
Imports	1,675	2,100	2,425	3,045	3,105	2,695	2,145	2,735	3,175
Exports	455	715	1,370	1,360	1,475	1,520	1,390	1,560	1,480
Apparent consumption [2]	10,145	11,930	12,180	13,060	13,300	12,380	10,930	12,555	12,995
Softwoods	8,065	9,385	9,615	10,365	10,490	9,680	8,800	10,120	10,650
Hardwoods	2,080	2,545	2,565	2,695	2,815	2,700	2,130	2,440	2,350
Lumber:									
Domestic production	[3] 5,080	5,670	5,355	5,605	5,730	5,145	4,850	5,475	5,565
Imports	610	815	955	1,405	1,425	1,085	885	1,230	1,600
Exports	135	145	200	215	295	265	240	275	255
Apparent consumption	5,560	6,340	6,110	6,795	6,860	5,965	5,495	6,430	6,915
Plywood and veneer:									
Domestic production	705	1,030	1,070	1,360	1,310	1,140	1,205	1,380	1,425
Imports	60	100	170	265	220	150	160	195	195
Exports	(z)	5	15	25	40	45	65	60	30
Apparent consumption	765	1,125	1,225	1,600	1,490	1,240	1,300	1,515	1,585
Pulp products:									
Domestic production	2,575	3,095	3,835	3,485	3,690	4,125	3,380	3,635	3,425
Imports	985	1,175	1,280	1,365	1,455	1,450	1,090	1,295	1,360
Exports	275	380	720	625	630	795	665	715	710
Apparent consumption	3,290	3,890	4,395	4,225	4,515	4,780	3,800	4,220	4,070
Logs: Imports	20	10	25	5	5	15	15	15	25
Exports	45	190	430	495	505	415	420	510	485
Miscellaneous, apparent consumption [4]	510	560	425	430	425	380	325	380	400
Fuelwood, apparent consumption	**1,300**	**915**	**540**	**475**	**500**	**535**	**575**	**600**	**635**

Z Less than 500,000 cubic feet.   [1] Includes log exports and other products.   [2] Includes log imports and other products.   [3] Excludes Alaska and Hawaii.   [4] Includes cooperage logs, poles and piling, fence posts, hewn ties, round mine timbers, box bolts, etc.

No. **1267.** Timber Products—Per Capita Consumption: 1950 to 1977

[Based on total population estimated as of **July 1**. See also *Historical Statistics, Colonial Times to 1970*, series L 87-97]

PRODUCT		1950	1955	1960	1965	1970	1972	1973	1974	1975	1976	1977, prel.
All products	cu. ft	80.0	73.8	63.3	66.1	62.1	64.8	65.6	60.9	53.9	61.2	62.9
Industrial roundwood	cu. ft	65.1	63.3	56.1	61.4	59.4	62.5	63.2	58.4	51.2	58.4	59.9
Lumber	cu. ft	41.8	37.5	30.8	32.7	29.8	32.5	32.6	28.2	25.7	29.9	31.9
Plywood and veneer	cu. ft	2.3	3.7	4.2	5.8	6.0	7.7	7.1	5.9	6.1	7.1	7.3
Pulp products	cu. ft	15.6	18.1	18.2	20.0	21.5	20.2	21.5	22.6	17.8	19.6	18.8
Miscellaneous products	cu. ft	5.1	3.8	2.8	2.9	2.1	2.1	2.0	1.8	1.5	1.8	1.8
Fuelwood	cu. ft	14.9	10.5	7.2	4.7	2.6	2.3	2.4	2.5	2.7	2.8	2.9
Lumber	bd. ft	269	242	199	212	193	219	219	189	173	201	213
Plywood and veneer	bd. ft	13.5	21.9	25.4	34.9	36.1	46.1	42.7	35.6	37.1	42.9	44.5
Pulp products	cords (128 cu. ft.)	.2	.2	.2	.3	.3	.3	.3	.3	.2	.3	.2

Source of tables 1265-1267: U.S. Forest Service, *The Demand and Price Situation for Forest Products*, annual.

No. 1268. SELECTED TIMBER PRODUCTS—WHOLESALE PRICE INDEXES: 1960 TO 1977

[1967=100. 1960 excludes Alaska and Hawaii. See also *Historical Statistics, Colonial Times to 1970*, series L 206-210]

PRODUCT	1960	1965	1970	1971	1972	1973	1974	1975	1976	1977
Lumber products_____	92	94	114	136	159	205	207	193	233	277
Softwood lumber_____	93	93	113	142	168	214	211	201	248	297
Douglas fir_____	89	92	109	140	161	210	214	212	251	291
Southern pine_____	94	91	115	134	152	188	185	175	217	263
Ponderosa pine, #3 boards_____	104	94	116	141	192	264	246	211	271	340
Hardwood lumber_____	91	97	115	113	126	169	190	160	176	200
Oak, red, flooring, select_____	99	108	113	114	128	202	203	159	(NA)	227
Gum #1, common_____	68	82	93	97	109	142	159	115	125	127
Poplar #1, common_____	80	86	105	105	108	150	173	121	131	137
Birch #1, common_____	89	96	91	88	96	123	140	122	127	179
Plywood_____	110	104	108	115	131	155	161	161	187	212
Softwood_____	113	106	114	127	155	194	187	201	248	296
Hardwood_____	105	101	103	101	104	113	130	120	123	128
Insulation board_____	114	98	111	115	119	122	134	144	161	183
Woodpulp_____	102	100	110	112	112	128	218	283	286	281
Paper_____	93	95	111	114	116	121	149	173	182	194
Paperboard_____	105	102	101	102	106	115	152	170	176	176
Containerboard_____	106	104	99	100	104	113	146	172	176	172
Hardboard and particleboard_____	104	104	93	94	96	106	115	114	124	141

NA Not available.
Source: U.S. Bureau of Labor Statistics. Current data in *Monthly Labor Review*.

No. 1269. SELECTED SPECIES—STUMPAGE AND LOG PRICES: 1960 TO 1977

[In dollars per 1,000 board feet. Based on sales from National Forests. See also *Historical Statistics, Colonial Times to 1970*, series L 199-205]

SPECIES	1960	1965	1969	1970	1971	1972	1973	1974	1975	1976	1977
Softwoods:											
Douglas fir_____	32.00	42.60	82.20	41.90	49.10	71.70	138.10	202.40	169.50	176.20	225.90
Southern pine_____	34.50	31.70	51.70	44.10	52.20	65.60	93.40	76.20	57.00	87.00	100.30
Sugar pine_____	29.00	23.30	75.20	38.50	47.90	66.20	89.20	104.00	99.20	187.20	169.60
Ponderosa pine [1]_____	19.10	19.80	71.00	32.10	37.60	65.80	92.30	100.60	71.20	103.20	131.40
Western hemlock_____	10.50	19.10	45.10	20.50	20.60	49.00	99.20	110.80	68.80	79.70	89.30
Hardwoods:											
All eastern hardwoods____	22.80	25.00	30.20	26.90	24.60	34.30	46.00	44.40	34.00	34.90	37.90
Oak, white, red, and black_	23.40	21.30	28.20	26.60	21.20	26.60	43.60	54.70	29.70	43.40	60.00
Maple_____	35.00	31.90	41.10	34.40	37.80	59.40	71.40	79.50	39.60	36.60	42.10
Douglas fir log prices: [2]											
Saw logs [3]_____	58.40	63.00	98.70	89.30	90.20	95.10	172.30	180.50	168.70	202.90	(NA)
Peeler logs [4]_____	100.10	93.90	137.70	136.60	132.60	148.90	320.40	299.30	274.40	377.70	(NA)

NA Not available. [1] Includes Jeffrey pine. [2] (Scribner log scale.) Prices are for western Washington and northwest Oregon and represent average transactions which may take place at a variety of points in the distribution process, e.g., at a river dump, reloading or truck scaling station, or on delivery to a mill. [3] Includes mixed grades, ungraded, and, beginning 1972, grade 4 logs. [4] Includes special fir peeler or special mill grade.

No. 1270. AVERAGE HOURLY EARNINGS IN TIMBER-BASED INDUSTRIES: 1970 TO 1977

[Earnings for production or nonsupervisory workers. See also *Historical Statistics, Colonial Times to 1970*, series L 212-223]

ITEM	EARNINGS (dollars)						INDEX (1967=100)					
	1970	1973	1974	1975	1976	1977	1970	1973	1974	1975	1976	1977
Lumber and wood prod [1]_____	2.96	3.58	3.91	4.28	4.71	5.06	125	151	165	181	199	214
Logging camps and contractors [2]	4.72	5.63	6.12	6.72	7.56	8.19	128	152	165	182	204	221
Sawmills and planing mills_____	2.84	3.48	3.79	4.16	4.61	4.97	126	155	168	185	205	221
Millwork, veneer, and plywood [3]_____	3.12	3.73	4.03	4.42	4.86	5.24	123	147	159	174	191	206
Paper and allied products_____	3.44	4.19	4.50	4.99	5.43	5.92	120	146	157	174	189	206
Furniture and fixtures_____	2.77	3.26	3.49	3.75	3.98	4.30	119	140	150	161	171	185

[1] Excludes furniture. [2] Data for State of Washington. [3] Includes fabricated structural wood products.
Source of tables 1269 and 1270: U.S. Forest Service, *The Demand and Price Situation for Forest Products*, annual.

No. 1271. Lumber Production and Consumption, by Kind of Wood: 1960 to 1976

[In millions of board feet, except as indicated. 1960 excludes Alaska and Hawaii. Based on sample survey; see source for sampling variability. See also *Historical Statistics, Colonial Times to 1970*, series L 98–112 and L 122–137]

ITEM	1960	1965	1970	1971	1972	1973	1974	1975	1976 [1]
Total production	32,926	36,762	34,668	36,988	37,745	38,595	34,608	29,630	33,386
Softwoods [2]	26,672	29,295	27,530	30,039	30,975	31,586	27,704	24,694	27,940
Cedar	(S)	633	633	714	756	785	811	821	940
Douglas fir	8,832	8,783	7,727	8,211	8,459	8,686	7,901	7,329	8,328
Hemlock	2,032	2,576	1,980	2,367	2,692	2,711	2,105	2,020	2,470
Ponderosa pine	3,169	3,776	3,429	3,780	4,001	4,030	3,580	3,544	4,145
Redwood	1,000	1,087	1,078	1,141	1,242	1,277	1,170	1,054	1,226
Southern yellow pine	5,660	6,628	7,063	7,736	7,884	7,895	6,921	6,967	7,575
White fir	2,224	2,422	2,063	2,283	2,307	2,438	2,071	2,012	2,204
White pine	675	693	898	978	1,056	1,069	925	947	1,052
Hardwoods [2]	6,254	7,467	7,138	6,949	6,770	7,009	6,904	4,936	5,446
Ash	125	141	159	151	148	140	143	124	140
Beech	195	182	188	188	182	176	167	136	140
Cottonwood	206	198	229	218	268	326	312	253	309
Elm	195	206	155	154	141	145	155	117	125
Maple	602	786	742	735	624	623	574	531	604
Oak	2,789	3,356	3,250	3,177	3,121	3,227	3,160	2,724	2,970
Sweet (red and sap) gum	331	387	376	340	332	342	294	245	283
Tupelo and black gum	292	385	335	329	319	309	331	251	279
Yellow poplar	592	681	606	600	628	701	710	555	596
Domestic consumption [3]	35,225	40,782	38,368	44,292	47,166	45,919	39,343	36,584	42,923
Percent net imports [4]	8.7	10.6	12.6	14.7	16.9	16.5	14.1	11.8	14.9
Softwoods	28,974	32,701	31,880	36,633	39,773	38,452	32,559	30,793	36,448
Per capita bd. ft.	164	172	156	177	190	183	154	144	169
Mill stocks, yearend	5,285	4,539	4,859	4,289	3,571	3,998	4,332	4,092	4,211
Exports	688	777	1,152	927	1,196	1,773	1,506	1,373	1,583
Imports	3,631	4,895	5,769	7,246	8,977	9,002	6,807	5,711	7,950
Canada [5]	3,576	4,856	5,723	7,189	8,878	8,841	6,736	[1] 5,677	[6] 7,913
Mexico [5]	37	8	6	5	19	18	5	[1] 1	[6] 1
Hardwoods	6,252	8,081	6,488	7,659	7,393	7,467	6,784	5,791	6,475
Per capita bd. ft.	35	39	32	37	35	35	32	27	30
Mill stocks, yearend	2,067	1,066	1,506	999	581	460	802	875	882
Exports	173	145	138	170	252	222	235	245	262
Imports	291	338	347	373	457	558	464	237	297
Canada [5]	118	161	145	143	151	155	116	[1] 62	[6] 83
Mexico [5]	5	2	2	2	2	3	4	(Z)	(Z)

S Figure does not meet publication standards.   Z Less than 500,000.   [1] Preliminary.   [2] Includes kinds of wood not shown separately.   [3] Source: Mackay-Shields Economics, Inc., New York, N.Y.   [4] Imports minus exports.   [5] Source: See source for table 1270.   [6] Estimate.

Source: Except as noted, U.S. Bureau of the Census, reports of census of manufactures and *Current Industrial Reports*, series MA-24T, annual.

No. 1272. Lumber Production, by Geographic Divisions: 1970 to 1976

[Production in billions of board feet, lumber tally. Data based in part on a sample of sawmills and are estimates which may vary from figures obtained from a complete census; subject to sampling variability, see source. For composition of divisions, see fig. I, inside front cover. See *Historical Statistics, Colonial Times to 1970*, series L 113–121, for data by regions]

GEOGRAPHIC DIVISION	PRODUCTION					PERCENT		
	1970	1973	1974	1975	1976, prel.	1970	1975	1976, prel.
United States	34.7	38.6	34.6	32.6	36.9	100.0	100.0	100.0
North [1]	4.4	4.6	4.4	4.2	5.0	12.7	12.9	13.6
Hardwood	3.4	3.5	3.3	3.0	3.6	9.8	9.2	9.8
Softwood	1.0	1.1	1.1	1.2	1.5	2.9	3.7	4.1
South [1]	10.8	11.4	10.4	9.7	11.2	31.1	29.8	30.4
Hardwood	3.6	3.4	3.4	2.8	3.1	10.4	8.6	8.4
Softwood	7.2	8.0	7.0	7.0	8.1	20.8	21.5	22.0
West [1][2]	19.4	22.6	19.7	18.7	21.4	55.9	57.4	58.0
New England	.7	.8	.8	.8	.9	2.2	2.5	2.5
Middle Atlantic	.8	.8	.9	.7	.8	2.3	2.2	2.2
East North Centra	1.2	1.3	1.2	1.1	1.2	3.5	3.4	3.3
West North Central	.6	.6	.6	.5	.6	1.8	1.7	1.6
South Atlantic	5.2	5.5	5.1	4.7	4.9	15.1	14.6	13.3
East South Central	3.4	3.6	3.4	3.0	3.4	9.8	9.1	9.1
West South Central	3.2	3.3	2.9	3.0	3.2	9.3	9.1	8.6
Mountain	4.2	4.6	3.9	3.9	4.6	12.0	12.1	12.4
Pacific	15.3	18.0	15.8	14.8	17.4	44.0	45.4	47.1

[1] Source: U.S. Forest Service, *The Demand and Price Situation for Forest Products*, annual.
[2] Includes small volumes of western hardwoods—about .2 billion board feet in recent years.

Source: Except as noted, U.S. Bureau of the Census, *Current Industrial Reports*, series MA-24T, annual.

No. 1273. Plywood—Production, Imports, Exports, Consumption, and Value
of Shipments: 1960 to 1977

[In millions of square feet, ⅜″ basis, except as indicated. See also *Historical Statistics, Colonial Times to 1970*, series
L 151–165]

ITEM	1960	1965	1970	1971	1972	1973	1974	1975	1976	1977 [1]
Total production	8,861	14,477	15,945	18,277	19,940	19,861	16,857	16,913	19,221	19,910
Softwood	7,759	12,428	14,149	16,353	17,843	17,929	15,306	15,706	17,841	18,500
Hardwood	1,102	2,049	1,796	1,924	2,096	1,932	1,550	1,207	1,380	1,410
Imports	725	1,052	2,049	2,548	3,162	2,531	1,670	1,949	2,382	2,280
Exports	15	37	172	114	247	503	610	859	797	357
Apparent consumption	9,571	15,492	17,822	20,711	22,855	21,889	17,917	18,002	20,806	21,834
Per capita consum.[2] sq. ft	53	80	87	100	109	104	85	84	97	101
Shipments, total[3] mil. dol	(NA)	1,124	1,268	1,571	2,038	2,337	2,020	2,073	2,986	(NA)
Softwood [4] mil. dol	(NA)	775	959	1,244	1,666	1,928	1,626	1,726	2,542	(NA)
Hardwood mil. dol	(NA)	349	310	327	372	409	394	347	444	(NA)

NA Not available.   [1] Preliminary.   [2] Based on total population estimated as of July 1.
[3] Source: U.S. Bureau of the Census, *Current Industrial Reports*, series MA–24F and MA–24H, both annual.
[4] Includes interplant transfers.

No. 1274. Pulpwood—Production, Consumption, and Prices: 1950 to 1977

[In millions of standard cords of 128 cubic feet, except as indicated. Excludes Alaska in 1950 and Hawaii prior to
1965. See *Historical Statistics, Colonial Times to 1970*, series L 166 and L 168, for similar data]

ITEM	1950	1955	1960	1965	1970	1971	1972	1973	1974	1975	1976	1977 [1]
Production, total	20.7	30.9	40.0	52.3	70.5	68.3	71.2	77.1	81.7	68.9	77.1	77.1
Softwood	17.8	25.6	31.5	39.8	53.4	51.6	53.2	56.7	59.5	52.2	57.8	58.2
Hardwood	2.9	5.3	8.5	12.5	17.1	16.8	18.0	20.4	22.2	16.6	19.3	18.9
North [2]	5.0	6.5	7.9	9.0	11.4	10.8	10.8	12.9	13.9	10.8	12.2	12.4
South	12.4	18.4	23.6	30.8	42.2	41.9	44.3	47.1	49.1	42.3	47.4	45.5
West [2]	3.3	6.0	8.5	12.5	17.0	15.6	16.2	17.1	18.7	15.8	17.5	19.2
Consumption [3]	23.6	33.4	40.5	52.0	67.6	67.2	71.5	73.6	74.3	65.4	73.2	(NA)
Softwood	20.4	27.7	32.1	39.7	51.3	50.6	53.6	54.8	54.6	48.9	54.8	(NA)
Hardwood	3.2	5.6	8.4	12.3	16.3	16.6	17.9	18.8	19.8	16.5	18.4	(NA)
Prices: (dol. per standard cord)												
Southern pine:												
Midsouth	12.15	14.60	16.05	16.30	18.80	19.10	20.80	23.85	28.25	28.70	29.75	31.40
Southeast	11.90	14.40	16.45	17.65	21.10	21.15	22.85	28.20	32.80	33.20	33.60	34.65
Louisiana	(NA)	14.10	14.85	15.70	17.70	17.95	19.25	22.50	28.30	29.25	30.45	31.65
Hardwoods:												
Midsouth	10.65	12.90	13.10	13.80	16.95	17.35	18.55	21.30	25.30	25.70	26.50	28.10
Southeast	(NA)	(NA)	13.60	14.35	17.15	17.15	18.95	21.15	24.10	24.55	24.55	26.55
Louisiana	(NA)	12.25	12.15	13.65	17.45	17.85	19.00	22.00	25.00	26.20	26.10	27.20
New Hampshire	14.50	(NA)	18.50	16.10	20.00	23.50	26.50	26.50	28.50	31.65	33.00	35.00

NA Not available.   [1] Preliminary.   [2] 1950–1960, domestic receipts at pulp mills.
[3] Source: U.S. Bureau of the Census, *Current Industrial Reports*, series M26A, monthly and annual.

Source of tables 1273 and 1274: Except as noted, U.S. Forest Service, *The Demand and Price Situation for Forest
Products*, annual.

No. 1275. Woodpulp—Production, Imports, Exports, and Consumption: 1950
to 1977

[In millions of short tons. Prior to 1965, excludes Hawaii. See also *Historical Statistics, Colonial Times to 1970*,
series L 169–170]

ITEM	1950	1955	1960	1965	1970	1972	1973	1974	1975	1976	1977 [1]
Total new supply	17.1	22.3	26.6	35.7	44.0	48.1	50.0	49.7	43.6	50.0	51.0
Production, total [2]	14.8	20.7	25.3	34.0	43.5	46.8	48.3	48.3	43.1	48.8	49.8
Sulphate	7.5	11.3	14.6	21.5	29.5	31.8	33.0	33.0	29.2	33.6	34.9
Unbleached	5.7	7.7	8.7	12.7	16.2	17.8	18.2	17.6	15.4	18.1	18.4
Bleached and semi-bleached	1.8	3.6	5.9	8.8	13.3	14.0	14.9	15.4	13.8	15.5	16.5
Groundwood	2.2	2.7	3.3	3.6	4.4	4.6	4.7	4.7	4.4	4.8	4.5
Other	5.1	6.7	7.4	8.9	9.7	10.3	10.6	10.6	9.5	10.4	10.4
Imports	2.4	2.2	2.4	3.1	3.5	3.7	4.0	4.1	3.1	3.7	3.9
Exports	.1	.6	1.1	1.4	3.1	2.3	2.3	2.8	2.6	2.5	2.6
Consumption in paper and board	16.5	21.5	25.7	34.0	43.2	47.3	48.8	48.3	42.4	48.7	50.1

[1] Preliminary.   [2] Source: U.S. Bureau of the Census, *Current Industrial Reports*, through 1976.

Source: Except as noted, American Paper Institute, Inc., New York, N.Y., *Wood Pulp Statistics*, annual. Data
compiled from reports of U.S. Bureau of the Census.

No. 1276. PAPER AND PAPERBOARD—PRODUCTION AND CONSUMPTION: 1965 TO 1977

[In millions of short tons. See also *Historical Statistics, Colonial Times to 1970*, series L 172, L 174, and L 178–191]

ITEM	PRODUCTION						CONSUMPTION					
	1965	1970	1974	1975	1976	1977 [1]	1965	1970	1974	1975	1976	1977 [1]
Paper and paperboard, a.l grades [2]	44.1	53.5	61.1	52.8	60.5	61.9	49.1	57.9	65.5	56.0	64.3	66.3
Paper [2]	19.2	23.6	26.9	23.3	26.5	27.4	25.2	30.1	33.8	28.3	32.5	33.7
Newsprint	2.1	3.3	3.6	3.7	3.7	3.9	8.4	9.8	10.8	9.4	10.2	10.3
Coated printing, converting	2.8	3.3	3.8	3.2	4.0	4.3	2.8	3.2	3.7	3.1	3.9	4.2
Book paper, uncoated	2.1	2.6	2.8	2.3	2.8	3.0	2.1	2.7	3.0	2.4	2.9	3.2
Other printing, writing, etc.	4.2	5.1	6.8	5.5	6.4	6.6	4.3	5.3	6.8	5.3	6.2	6.6
Packaging and industrial converting	5.0	5.4	5.8	4.6	5.5	5.4	4.8	5.3	5.6	4.3	5.2	5.2
Tissue and other mach. creped.	2.9	3.8	4.1	4.0	4.2	4.3	2.9	3.8	4.1	3.9	4.2	4.3
Paperboard [2]	20.8	25.5	28.9	24.8	28.4	29.0	19.7	23.4	26.3	22.8	26.2	26.7
Unbleached kraft	7.8	11.6	13.3	11.5	13.3	13.7	6.9	9.9	11.8	10.5	12.1	12.4
Bleached kraft	2.3	3.4	3.8	3.3	3.8	3.7	2.2	3.3	3.5	3.1	3.5	3.3
Semichemical	2.7	3.4	4.2	3.7	4.1	4.3	2.6	3.4	4.0	3.6	4.0	4.1
Recycled furnish	8.1	7.0	7.6	6.2	7.2	7.3	8.0	6.9	7.6	6.2	7.1	7.3
Wet machine board	.1	.1	.1	.1	.1	.1	.2	.1	.1	.1	.1	.1
Construction paper and board	3.9	4.3	5.1	4.6	5.4	5.5	4.1	4.4	5.3	4.7	5.6	5.7

[1] Preliminary.   [2] Consumption data adjusted for net exports of converted products.

Source: American Paper Institute, New York, N.Y., *The Statistics of Paper and Paperboard*, annual (title varies). 1965 and 1970 production data compiled from reports of U.S. Bureau of the Census.

No. 1277. NEWSPRINT—PRODUCTION, STOCKS, CONSUMPTION, IMPORTS, AND PRICE: 1960 TO 1977

[In thousands of short tons, except price. See also *Historical Statistics, Colonial Times to 1970*, series L 192–198]

COUNTRY AND ITEM	1960	1965	1970	1972	1973	1974	1975	1976	1977
Canada, including Newfoundland:									
Production	6,739	7,720	8,607	8,820	9,140	9,548	7,679	8,915	8,988
Shipments from mills	6,752	7,747	8,592	8,901	9,199	9,597	7,727	8,712	9,005
Stocks at mills, end of year	140	150	236	251	193	143	95	299	282
United States: [1]									
Consumption by publishers [2][3]	5,532	6,387	7,130	7,569	7,658	7,022	6,363	6,534	6,772
Production [3]	2,038	2,245	3,464	3,636	3,678	3,481	3,614	3,686	3,870
Shipments from mills [3]	2,031	2,248	3,457	3,651	3,682	3,480	3,613	3,678	3,866
Stocks, end of year:									
At mills [3]	26	19	33	27	23	25	21	29	34
At and in transit to publishers	628	573	749	544	603	827	734	921	796
Imports [4]	5,412	6,323	6,635	7,101	7,410	7,399	5,847	6,569	6,559
Wholesale price index (1967=100)	96.1	94.6	107.6	116.7	122.2	151.2	184.0	198.2	215.4

[1] Excludes Alaska and Hawaii, except as noted.
[2] As reported by publishers accounting for about two-thirds of total newsprint consumption in recent years. For total and per capita consumption, see table 994.   [3] Beginning 1965, includes Alaska and Hawaii.
[4] Source: Reports of U.S. Bureau of the Census. Includes Alaska, Hawaii, and Puerto Rico.

Source: Except as noted, U.S. Bureau of Economic Analysis. Data from the American Newspapers Publishers Association, Reston, Va., and Newsprint Division, American Paper Institute, Inc., New York, N.Y. In *Survey of Current Business*.

No. 1278. WASTEPAPER UTILIZATION, AND RECOVERY AND SALVAGE RATES—UNITED STATES AND WESTERN EUROPE: 1960 TO 1977

[In millions of short tons, except percent. Salvage rate is ratio of consumption to new supply. See *Historical Statistics, Colonial Times to 1970*, series L 175, for U.S. wastepaper consumption]

ITEM	1960	1965	1970	1972	1973	1974	1975	1976	1977
United States:									
Paper and board, new supply	39.1	49.1	57.9	64.4	66.7	64.4	56.0	64.3	66.3
Wastepaper consumption	9.0	10.2	11.8	12.9	14.1	14.0	11.7	13.6	14.0
Recovery rate, total (percent) [1]	23.3	21.2	21.3	21.3	22.6	23.9	23.3	24.0	24.7
Western Europe: [2]									
Paper and board, new supply	21.0	27.9	36.8	39.2	42.8	43.2	34.0	39.3	(NA)
Wastepaper consumption	5.4	7.2	10.1	11.3	12.2	13.3	10.8	10.7	(NA)
Salvage rate (percent)	25.6	26.0	27.6	28.9	28.6	30.7	31.9	27.3	(NA)

NA Not available.   [1] Includes wastepaper collected for exports and other usage.
[2] 1975–1977 data compiled by American Paper Institute from Food and Agriculture Organization of the United Nations, *Waste Paper Data 1975–1976*.

Source: Except as noted, American Paper Institute, Inc., New York, N.Y., *Wood Pulp Statistics*, annual.

No. 1279. Logs—Exports and Imports, by Major Species: 1960 to 1977

[In millions of board feet, log scale. See also *Historical Statistics, Colonial Times to 1970*, series L 138–150]

ITEM	1960	1965	1970	1972	1973	1974	1975	1976	1977
Exports_____	266.3	1,192.8	2,753.0	3,143.3	3,221.6	2,642.4	2,666.9	3,249.9	3,080.1
Softwoods_____	210.3	1,111.4	2,684.1	3,049.4	3,107.2	2,523.7	2,600.6	3,155.7	2,980.0
Douglas fir_____	27.5	111.3	487.7	662.2	899.2	752.7	820.4	1,022.4	1,007.2
Port Orford cedar_____	37.2	39.1	54.1	45.1	29.7	35.6	38.7	38.4	20.7
Other_____	145.6	961.0	2,142.3	2,342.0	2,178.3	1,735.4	1,741.5	2,094.9	1,952.1
Hardwoods_____	56.0	81.4	68.9	93.9	114.4	118.7	66.3	94.3	100.1
Walnut_____	10.2	23.6	17.4	15.2	16.1	7.8	8.5	7.4	18.1
Other_____	45.9	57.9	51.5	78.7	98.2	110.8	57.9	86.9	82.0
Imports_____	112.5	68.1	144.4	39.3	33.5	76.6	85.5	81.6	155.4
Softwoods_____	32.3	13.5	106.5	11.3	8.5	45.6	68.5	67.4	140.3
Hardwoods_____	80.2	54.6	37.9	28.0	25.0	31.0	17.0	14.2	15.1
Mahogany_____	25.2	12.8	6.8	3.6	2.1	3.4	1.6	1.2	2.4
Other_____	55.1	41.8	31.1	24.5	22.9	27.6	15.3	13.0	12.7

Source: U.S. Forest Service, *The Demand and Price Situation for Forest Products*, annual.

No. 1280. Wood Products—Production: 1960 to 1977

ITEM	1960	1965	1970	1973	1974	1975	1976	1977, prel.
Hardwood flooring_____mil. bd. ft__	915	808	333	300	205	155	190	205
Softwood plywood____mil. sq. ft., ⅜″ basis__	7,759	12,428	14,149	17,929	15,596	15,265	17,841	18,500
Insulation boards_____1,000 short tons__	1,098	1,258	1,219	1,547	1,295	1,240	1,441	1,297
Hardboard_____1,000 short tons__	686	1,093	1,443	2,000	1,978	1,784	2,145	1,915
Particleboard_____mil. sq. ft., ¾″ basis__	268	780	1,764	3,494	3,094	2,367	3,000	3,320

Source: U.S. Bureau of Domestic Business Development, *Construction Review*, monthly. Based on reports of U.S. Bureau of the Census and National Particleboard Association, Silver Spring, Md.

No. 1281. Turpentine—Production, Imports, Exports, and Consumption: 1960 to 1977

[In thousands of 50-gallon barrels, except as indicated. For years beginning **April 1**. See *Historical Statistics, Colonial Times to 1970*, series L 176, for total production]

ITEM	1960	1965	1970	1972	1973	1974	1975	1976	1977, prel.
Production_____	604.8	700.7	575.8	566.1	530.6	487.0	447.6	482.2	477.6
Gum_____	119.0	111.4	25.8	26.6	21.4	15.6	20.7	17.4	14.5
Wood_____	485.8	589.3	550.0	539.5	509.2	471.4	426.9	464.8	463.0
Value of production_____$1,000__	2,849	3,091	1,550	1,389	863	1,084	1,640	1,278	1,035
Price per gallon_____dol__	.479	.555	1.200	1.046	.806	1.389	1.585	1.427	1.425
Imports_____	15.6	18.0	24.1	42.3	33.6	29.7	58.6	16.3	7.9
Exports_____	81.8	45.1	39.7	89.2	30.7	16.3	4.2	20.3	19.4
Gum_____	23.2	21.5	6.1	.8	3.2	2.1	1.5	2.1	.9
Wood_____	58.6	23.6	33.5	88.4	27.5	14.2	2.7	18.2	18.5
Industrial consumption_____	376.8	535.6	536.2	467.5	443.4	439.7	423.5	480.6	472.9
Gum_____	3.5	8.2	3.1	2.5	1.9	2.0	2.2	1.8	1.6
Wood_____	373.2	527.4	533.1	465.1	441.4	437.7	421.2	478.8	471.4

No. 1282. Rosin—Production, Imports, Exports, and Consumption: 1960 to 1977

[In thousands of drums (520 pounds net weight for wood; 517 pounds for gum), except as indicated. For years beginning **April 1**. See *Historical Statistics, Colonial Times to 1970*, series L 177, for total production]

ITEM	1960	1965	1970	1972	1973	1974	1975	1976	1977, prel.
Production_____	2,010	2,067	1,656	1,629	1,584	1,306	1,088	1,357	1,301
Gum_____	370	361	88	89	74	54	72	61	51
Wood_____	1,640	1,706	1,568	1,540	1,510	1,252	1,016	1,296	1,250
Value of production_____$1,000__	27,787	19,352	6,818	8,694	8,737	10,106	9,338	7,971	6,702
Price per 100 lb. net_____dol__	14.52	10.36	15.03	18.89	22.72	35.92	25.15	24.46	25.35
Imports_____	(z)	1	(z)	24	106	162	21	25	31
Exports_____	628	541	570	467	424	268	174	280	203
Gum_____	157	81	124	72	26	18	13	15	14
Wood_____	471	460	446	395	398	250	161	265	189
Industrial consumption_____	1,409	1,536	1,462	1,382	1,271	1,103	1,046	1,203	1,068
Gum_____	258	136	121	76	100	110	104	56	70
Wood_____	1,151	1,400	1,341	1,306	1,171	993	942	1,146	998

Z Less than 500.

Source of tables 1281 and 1282: U.S. Dept. of Agriculture, Economics, Statistics, and Cooperatives Service, *Agricultural Statistics*, annual, and *Naval Stores*, annual summary, 1977.

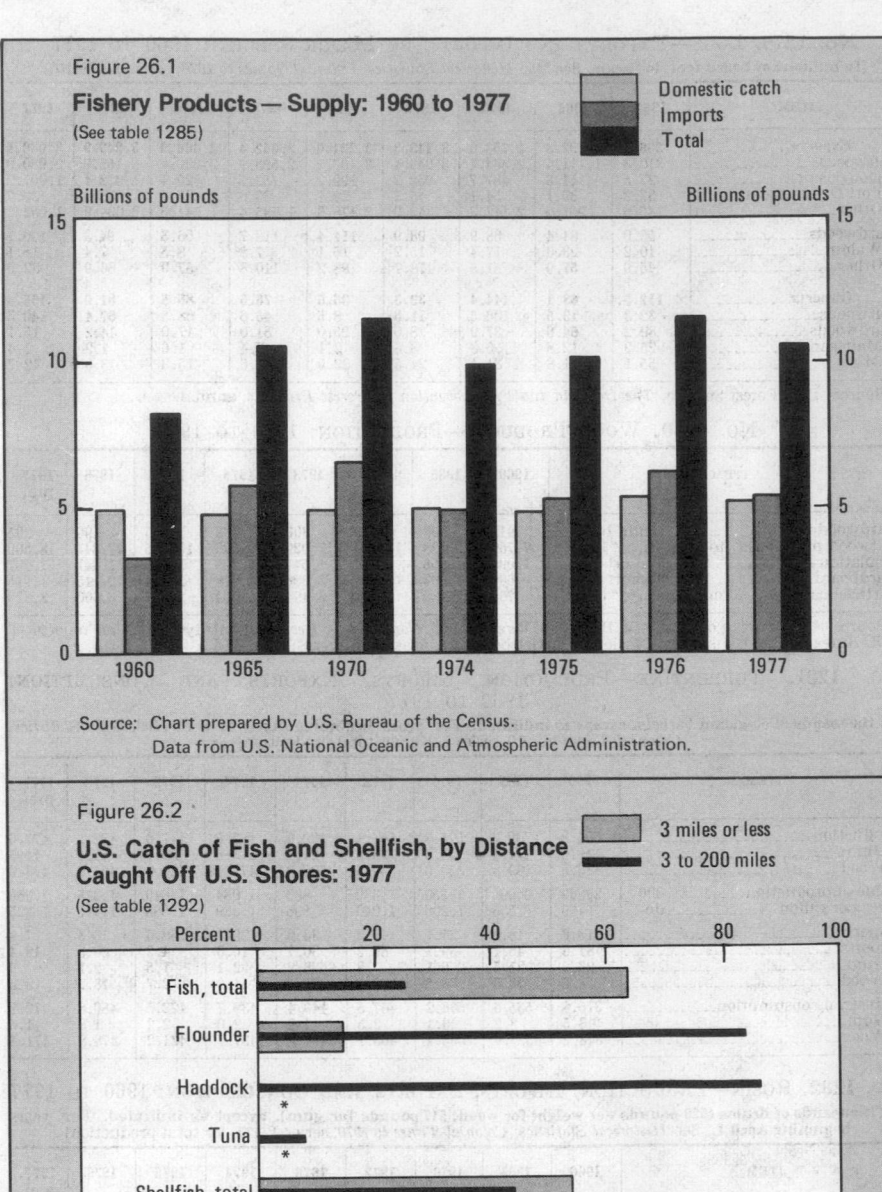

Figure 26.1
Fishery Products — Supply: 1960 to 1977
(See table 1285)

Domestic catch
Imports
Total

Billions of pounds

Source: Chart prepared by U.S. Bureau of the Census.
Data from U.S. National Oceanic and Atmospheric Administration.

Figure 26.2
U.S. Catch of Fish and Shellfish, by Distance Caught Off U.S. Shores: 1977
(See table 1292)

3 miles or less
3 to 200 miles

*Negligible catch within three miles or less.

Source: Chart prepared by U.S. Bureau of the Census.
Data from U.S. National Oceanic and Atmospheric Administration.

Section 26
Fisheries

This section presents statistics relating to commercial fishing and the fish processing industry. The principal sources of these data are *Fishery Statistics of the United States* and *Fisheries of the United States*, both issued annually by the National Marine Fisheries Service (NMFS), National Oceanic and Atmospheric Administration (NOAA).

The NMFS publishes monthly data on commercial landings of fish and shellfish, freezings, and holdings of fishery products, fish meal and oil production, and foreign trade in fishery products. Quarterly data are published on U.S. output of fish sticks, fish portions, and breaded shrimp. Annual reports for fisheries include data on quantity and value of commercial landings, of fish and shellfish (by species, region, State, and type of fishing gear), disposition of landings, number of fishermen, and number and kinds of fishing vessels and fishing gear. Reports for the fish-processing industry include annual data on output of canned, packaged, and industrial products and, for wholesaling and fish processing establishments, annual and seasonal employment, and number of firms, by product and State. Annual data are published on foreign trade in fishery products and per capita consumption of edible fishery products.

The first comprehensive survey of U.S. fisheries and fishery industries, made for the year 1880, did not include the Mississippi River and its tributaries. A complete survey was conducted in 1908 by the Bureau of the Census and in 1931 by the Bureau of Fisheries. A complete survey including manufacturing and wholesaling operations was made for 1950. Beginning in 1954, complete data have been collected annually. For 1963 and 1967, the Bureau of the Census, in cooperation with the Bureau of Commercial Fisheries, conducted a Census of Commercial Fisheries.

The Fishery Conservation and Management Act of 1976 established a Fisheries Conservation Zone (FCZ) which gave the Federal Government exclusive authority over domestic and foreign fisheries within 200 nautical miles of U.S. shores and over certain living marine resources beyond the FCZ. Within the FCZ, the total allowable level of foreign fishing, if any, is that portion of the "optimum yield" not harvested by U.S. vessels. Adjustments in the "optimum yield" level may occur periodically. For details, see *Fisheries of the United States, 1977*, cited above.

The value of catch as presented in various tables is in "ex-vessel" terms. It represents the price received by fishermen for fish, shellfish, etc. landed at the dock.

Historical statistics.—Tabular headnotes provide cross-references, where applicable, to *Historical Statistics of the United States, Colonial Times to 1970*. See Appendix I.

No. 1283. FISHERIES—QUANTITY AND VALUE OF DOMESTIC CATCH: 1940 TO 1977

[Prior to 1950, excludes Hawaii. See also *Historical Statistics, Colonial Times to 1970*, series L 224–226, L 229, and L 310]

YEAR	QUANTITY (mil. lb.[1])			Ex-vessel value (mil. dol.)	Average price per lb. (cents)	YEAR	QUANTITY (mil. lb.[1])			Ex-vessel value (mil. dol.)	Average price per lb. (cents)
	Total	For human food	For industrial products [2]				Total	For human food	For industrial products [2]		
1940	4,060	2,675	1,385	99	2.4	1971	5,018	2,441	2,577	651	13.0
1945	4,598	3,167	1,431	270	5.9	1972	4,806	2,435	2,371	748	15.6
1950	4,901	3,307	1,594	347	7.1	1973	4,858	2,398	2,460	937	19.3
1955	4,809	2,579	2,230	339	7.1	1974	4,967	2,496	2,471	932	18.7
1960	4,942	2,498	2,444	354	7.2	1975, prel	4,842	2,430	2,412	971	20.0
1965	4,777	2,587	2,190	446	9.3	1976, prel	5,350	2,760	2,590	1,353	25.2
1970	4,917	2,537	2,380	613	12.5	1977, prel	5,198	2,900	2,298	1,515	29.1

[1] Live weight.   [2] Meal, oil, fish solubles, homogenized condensed fish, shell products, bait, and animal food.
Source: U.S. National Oceanic and Atmospheric Administration, *Fishery Statistics of the United States*, annual.

No. 1284. FISHERIES—DISPOSITION OF DOMESTIC CATCH: 1950 TO 1977

[Live weight of catch in millions of pounds. Prior to 1960, excludes Hawaii. 1975–1977 preliminary. In addition to whole fish, a large portion of waste (400–500 million lb.) derived from canning, filleting, and dressing fish and shellfish is utilized in production of fish meal and oil in each year shown. See *Historical Statistics, Colonial Times to 1970*, series L 305–310, for similar but not entirely comparable data]

DISPOSITION	1950	1955	1960	1965	1970	1971	1972	1973	1974	1975	1976	1977
Total	4,884	4,794	4,942	4,777	4,917	5,018	4,806	4,858	4,967	4,842	5,350	5,198
Fresh and frozen	1,692	1,568	1,631	1,751	1,595	1,580	1,612	1,685	1,660	1,666	1,855	2,025
Canned	1,720	1,039	1,043	1,042	1,150	1,019	976	882	1,005	935	1,094	1,078
Cured	100	86	82	76	71	76	70	91	69	69	53	55
Reduced to meal, oil, etc	1,372	2,101	2,186	1,908	2,101	2,343	2,148	2,200	2,233	2,172	2,348	2,040

No. 1285. FISHERY PRODUCTS—SUPPLY: 1960 TO 1977

[Live weight, in millions of pounds, except percent. 1975–1977 preliminary. See *Historical Statistics, Colonial Times to 1970*, series L 224–226, for domestic catch]

ITEM	1960	1965	1970	1971	1972	1973	1974	1975	1976	1977
Total	8,223	10,535	11,474	11,804	13,849	10,378	9,875	10,129	11,555	10,579
For human food	4,264	5,163	6,213	6,023	6,889	7,109	6,638	6,359	7,389	7,414
Finfish	(NA)	(NA)	(NA)	(NA)	(NA)	(NA)	4,971	4,837	5,655	5,589
Shellfish [1]	(NA)	(NA)	(NA)	(NA)	(NA)	(NA)	1,667	1,522	1,734	1,825
For industrial use	3,959	5,372	5,261	5,781	6,960	3,269	3,237	3,770	4,166	3,165
Domestic catch	4,942	4,777	4,917	5,018	4,806	4,858	4,967	4,842	5,350	5,198
Percent of total	60.1	45.3	42.8	42.5	34.7	46.8	50.2	47.8	46.3	49.1
For human food	2,498	2,587	2,537	2,441	2,435	2,398	2,496	2,430	2,760	2,900
Finfish	(NA)	(NA)	(NA)	(NA)	(NA)	(NA)	1,522	1,537	1,774	1,781
Shellfish [1]	(NA)	(NA)	(NA)	(NA)	(NA)	(NA)	974	893	986	1,119
For industrial use	2,444	2,190	2,380	2,577	2,371	2,460	2,471	2,412	2,590	2,298
Imports [2]	3,281	5,758	6,557	6,786	9,043	5,520	4,908	5,287	6,205	5,381
Percent of total	39.9	54.7	57.2	57.7	65.3	53.2	49.8	52.2	53.7	50.9
For human food	1,766	2,576	3,676	3,582	4,454	4,709	4,142	3,929	4,629	4,514
Finfish	(NA)	(NA)	(NA)	(NA)	(NA)	(NA)	3,449	3,300	3,881	3,808
Shellfish	(NA)	(NA)	(NA)	(NA)	(NA)	(NA)	693	629	748	706
For industrial use [3]	1,515	3,182	2,881	3,204	4,589	811	766	1,358	1,576	867

NA Not available. [1] For univalve and bivalve mollusks (conchs, clams, oysters, scallops, etc.), the weight of meats, excluding the shell, is reported. [2] Excludes imports of edible fishery products into Puerto Rico; includes landings of tuna caught by foreign vessels in American Samoa. [3] Fish meal and sea herring.

No. 1286. FISHERIES—FISHERMEN AND CRAFT, 1975, AND CATCH, 1976, BY AREAS

[See *Historical Statistics, Colonial Times to 1970*, series L 236–253, for data on quantity and ex-vessel value of catch]

AREA	1975 [1]			1976					
	Fisher-men	Fish-ing vessels	Fish-ing boats [2]	Catch (mil. lb.)			Value of catch (mil. dol.)		
				Total	Fin-fish	Shell-fish	Total	Fin-fish	Shell-fish
United States	166,235	16,211	85,805	5,350	4,350	1,000	1,353	656	697
New England States	31,685	769	15,768	544	469	75	175	80	95
Middle Atlantic States	16,119	492	11,396	266	205	61	69	17	52
Chesapeake Bay States	24,274	1,911	16,424	588	491	97	74	20	54
South Atlantic States	10,242	1,546	5,656	315	257	58	72	27	45
Gulf States	26,560	4,670	10,203	1,753	1,473	280	389	80	309
Pacific Coast States	44,840	7,031	13,336	1,743	1,316	427	543	401	142
Great Lakes States	1,201	226	554	67	67	–	11	11	–
Mississippi River States	12,993	–	12,491	62	59	3	13	12	1
Hawaii	2,197	109	1,278	12	12	(Z)	7	7	(Z)

– Represents zero. Z Less than 500,000 pounds or $500,000. [1] As of Dec. 31. [2] Refers to craft having capacity of less than 5 net tons.

Source of tables 1284–1286: U.S. National Oceanic and Atmospheric Administration, *Fishery Statistics of the United States*, annual, and *Fisheries of the United States*, annual.

No. **1287.** Fisheries—Employment, Fishing Craft, and Establishments: 1950 to 1976

[In thousands. As of Dec. 31. See also *Historical Statistics, Colonial Times to 1970*, series L 254–261]

ITEM	1950	1955	1960	1965	1970	1971	1972	1973	1974	1975	1976, prel.
Persons employed in U.S.	263	242	224	215	227	231	230	243	253	258	(NA)
Fishermen	161	144	130	129	141	140	139	149	161	166	(NA)
Shore workers [1]	102	98	94	87	87	91	91	94	92	92	92
Craft used	92	83	77	80	87	86	86	90	101	102	(NA)
Vessels, 5 net tons and over	11	12	12	12	14	14	15	15	16	16	(NA)
Motorboats	46	58	57	64	72	71	70	72	83	84	(NA)
Other boats	35	13	8	3	2	2	2	2	2	2	(NA)
Fishery shore establishments	3.9	4.1	4.2	4.2	3.7	3.7	3.7	3.6	3.5	3.6	3.7

NA Not available.   [1] Seasonal average.

No. **1288.** Commercial Fishery Products—Per Capita Consumption: 1950 to 1977

[**Pounds of edible meat.** Based on U.S. Bureau of the Census estimates of the civilian resident population as of July 1. See also *Historical Statistics, Colonial Times to 1970*, series L 294–304]

PRODUCT	1950	1955	1960	1965	1970	1971	1972	1973	1974	1975	1976, prel.	1977, prel.
Total	11.8	10.5	10.3	10.8	11.8	11.5	12.4	12.9	12.2	12.1	13.0	12.8
Fresh and frozen	6.3	5.9	5.7	6.0	6.9	6.7	7.1	7.4	7.0	7.4	8.2	7.8
Fish [1]	4.7	4.2	3.8	3.8	4.5	4.3	4.8	5.2	4.5	4.9	5.6	5.2
Shellfish	1.6	1.7	1.9	2.2	2.4	2.4	2.3	2.2	2.5	2.5	2.6	2.6
Canned	4.9	3.9	4.0	4.3	4.5	4.3	4.9	5.1	4.8	4.3	4.3	4.6
Salmon	1.4	1.0	.7	.9	.7	.7	.7	.4	.3	.4	.4	.4
Sardines	1.4	.6	.4	.3	.4	.4	.4	.5	.4	.2	.3	.3
Tuna	1.1	1.1	2.0	2.0	2.3	2.4	2.9	3.1	3.1	2.9	2.9	2.9
Shellfish	.4	.4	.4	.5	.5	.5	.5	.6	.6	.4	.4	.6
Other	.6	.5	.5	.3	.4	.3	.4	.5	.4	.4	.3	.4
Cured	.6	.7	.6	.5	.4	.5	.4	.4	.4	.4	.5	.4

[1] Beginning 1973, includes consumption of artificially cultivated catfish.

No. **1289.** Fisheries—Catch and Value of Principal Species: 1965 to 1977

[Catch in live weight, except as indicated. Data exclude landings by U.S. flag vessels at Puerto Rico and other ports outside the 50 States, and production of artificially cultivated fish and shellfish. 1975–1977 preliminary]

SPECIES	CATCH (mil. lb.)						VALUE (mil. dol.)					
	1965	1970	1974	1975	1976	1977	1965	1970	1974	1975	1976	1977
Fish:												
Cod, Atlantic	36	53	59	56	56	76	3	6	11	13	14	17
Flounder	180	169	162	156	165	170	18	23	36	43	52	59
Haddock	134	27	8	16	13	28	14	6	3	5	6	9
Halibut	40	35	18	22	21	18	9	9	12	15	19	17
Herring, sea	110	79	128	119	151	156	2	2	6	6	11	12
Jack mackerel	67	47	25	30	39	110	2	2	1	1	2	6
Menhaden	1,726	1,837	2,001	1,803	2,039	1,796	27	34	67	49	67	68
Ocean perch, Atlantic	84	55	41	32	32	35	3	3	3	3	4	5
Salmon, Pacific	327	410	201	202	309	336	65	99	120	116	196	222
Tuna	319	393	392	391	486	345	42	75	119	108	150	136
Whiting	83	45	30	42	48	45	2	4	3	4	4	4
Shellfish:												
Clams (meats)	71	99	122	112	81	96	17	29	41	41	63	74
Crabs	335	277	332	301	345	399	31	39	85	84	137	203
Lobsters, American	30	34	29	30	32	32	22	33	43	49	53	58
Oysters (meats)	55	54	50	53	54	46	28	29	41	43	53	53
Scallops (meats)	23	11	9	13	24	28	15	12	13	22	41	46
Shrimp	244	367	372	344	404	477	82	130	180	226	331	355

Source of tables 1287–1289: U.S. National Oceanic and Atmospheric Administration, *Fishery Statistics of the United States*, annual, and *Fisheries of the United States*, annual.

No. 1290. FISHERIES—COMMERCIAL CATCH, WORLD AND SELECTED COUNTRIES: 1970 TO 1976

[In billions of pounds, live weight. Includes catch of fish, crustaceans, mollusks (including weight of shells), and other aquatic plants and animals, except whales and seals. Data from Food and Agriculture Organization of the United Nations. World total includes countries not shown separately]

COUNTRY	1970	1973	1974	1975	1976	COUNTRY	1970	1973	1974	1975	1976
World total	153.4	145.7	155.4	154.1	162.0	Indonesia	2.8	2.9	2.9	3.0	3.2
						Philippines	2.2	2.7	2.8	3.0	3.2
United States	6.1	5.9	6.1	6.0	6.6	Chile	2.6	1.5	2.5	2.0	2.8
Japan	20.5	23.7	23.8	23.2	23.4	Canada	3.1	2.6	2.3	2.3	2.5
U.S.S.R	16.0	19.0	20.4	21.9	22.3	Iceland	1.2	2.0	2.1	2.2	2.2
Peru	27.8	5.2	9.1	7.6	9.6	S. Vietnam (est.)	1.1	1.6	2.2	2.2	2.2
Norway	6.6	6.6	5.8	5.6	7.6						
						Brazil (est.)	1.1	1.3	1.5	1.8	2.1
India	3.8	4.3	5.0	5.1	5.3	France	1.7	1.8	1.8	1.8	1.8
Korea, Rep. of	2.1	3.7	4.5	4.7	5.3	North Korea (est.)	1.8	1.8	1.8	1.8	1.8
Denmark	2.7	3.2	4.0	3.9	4.2	Poland	1.0	1.3	1.5	1.8	1.6
Thailand	3.2	3.7	3.3	3.4	3.6	S. Africa, Rep. of	3.4	2.9	3.1	1.4	1.4
Spain	3.3	3.5	3.3	3.4	3.3	Great Britain	2.4	2.5	1.2	1.1	1.1

No. 1291. CATCH, CATCH LIMITS, AND PRINCIPAL SPECIES CAUGHT BY FOREIGN COUNTRIES IN THE U.S. FISHERY CONSERVATION ZONE (FCZ), BY COUNTRY: 1977

[In millions of pounds live weight. Preliminary. Excludes tunas. (In 1977, U.S. domestic catch of tunas in FCZ was 345 mil. lb.) Allocations (catch limits) set by species for countries fishing within 200 miles of U.S. shores. For details, see text, p. 741, and source]

COUNTRY	Actual catch	Allo- cation	Principal species caught	COUNTRY	Actual catch	Allo- cation	Principal species caught
Total catch in FCZ	8,599.4	(X)	(X)	Foreign—Con. Spain	32.2	50.4	Squid
U.S	4,852.9	(X)	(X)	Germany Dem. Rep	17.8	44.6	Mackerel (Atl.)
Foreign	3,746.6	(X)	(X)	Italy	11.8	15.2	Squid
Japan	2,487.4	2,648.7	Pollock; flounder	Bulgaria	10.5	17.8	Mackerel (Atl.)
U.S.S.R	843.9	1,432.9	Hake; pollock				
Korea, Rep. of	176.7	179.0	Pollock	Cuba	3.5	39.1	Mackerel (Atl.)
Poland	88.9	148.2	Hake; herring	China (Taiwan)	3.3	12.1	Pollock
Canada [1]	68.7	48.9	Scallops	Romania	2.0	3.1	Mackerel (Atl.)

X Not applicable.   [1] Excess over catch limit covered by reciprocal fishery privileges.

No. 1292. U.S. CATCH AND VALUE OF FISH AND SHELLFISH, BY DISTANCE CAUGHT OFF U.S. SHORES—SELECTED SPECIES: 1977

[Preliminary. Catch is shown in live weight, except as indicated. Includes landings by U.S. flag vessels at Puerto Rico and other ports outside the 50 States]

SPECIES	Total U.S. catch [1] (mil. lb.)	BY DISTANCE FROM U.S. SHORES						Value of U.S. catch [1] (mil. dol.)	PERCENT OF TOTAL VALUE, BY DISTANCE CAUGHT OFF U.S. SHORES		
		Catch (mil. lb.)			Percent of U.S. catch				3 miles or less [2]	3 to 200 miles	Over 200 mi.
		3 miles or less [2]	3 to 200 miles	Over 200 mi.	3 miles or less [2]	3 to 200 miles	Over 200 mi.				
Fish, total [3]	4,185.9	2,661.8	1,047.7	476.3	63.6	25.0	11.4	752.4	48.3	29.0	22.7
Cod, Atlantic	75.5	4.4	69.5	1.6	5.8	92.1	2.1	17.1	6.7	90.6	2.7
Flounder	169.6	24.4	142.0	3.2	14.4	83.7	1.9	59.5	14.0	85.2	.8
Haddock	28.4	.2	24.5	3.7	.7	86.3	13.0	9.3	.8	86.3	12.9
Halibut	17.7	2.2	15.5	(Z)	12.4	87.6	(Z)	17.3	12.6	87.3	.1
Herring, sea	155.9	144.0	11.9	–	92.4	7.6	–	11.6	95.7	4.3	–
Jack mackerel	110.2	12.2	98.0	–	11.1	88.9	–	5.5	11.1	88.9	–
Ocean perch	40.7	.1	32.6	8.0	(Z)	80.3	19.7	6.1	(Z)	80.0	20.0
Salmon, Pacific	335.6	318.9	16.6	.1	95.0	5.0	(Z)	221.9	87.5	12.5	(Z)
Tuna	468.9	.4	36.5	432.0	.1	7.8	92.1	181.6	.1	11.0	88.9
Whiting	45.3	4.0	41.3	(Z)	8.8	91.2	(Z)	4.2	10.3	89.6	(Z)
Shellfish, total [3]	1,151.4	622.1	507.9	21.4	54.0	44.1	1.9	835.5	45.1	50.7	4.2
Clams (meats)	96.2	37.1	59.1	–	38.6	61.4	–	74.3	61.8	38.2	–
Crabs	398.5	223.9	174.6	–	56.2	43.8	–	202.5	40.2	59.8	–
Lobsters	37.2	26.3	9.8	1.1	70.7	26.3	3.0	67.3	69.8	27.3	2.9
Scallops (meats)	27.8	2.2	25.6	–	7.9	92.1	–	46.0	11.6	88.4	–
Shrimp [4]	492.0	237.8	234.0	20.2	48.3	47.6	4.1	382.0	35.4	55.9	8.7

– Represents zero.   Z Less than 50,000 pounds or .05 percent.   [1] Includes catch from international waters or off foreign shores.   [2] Includes all landings in Great Lakes and other inland waters.   [3] Includes other shellfish and squid, not shown separately.   [4] Includes landings at Gulf Coast and foreign ports.

Source of tables 1290–1292: U.S. National Oceanic and Atmospheric Administration, *Fisheries of the United States,* annual.

No. 1293. Fisheries—Quantity and Value of Catch, by States, and Catch of Principal Species, by Areas: 1960 to 1976

[Catch in millions of pounds, live weight, except as indicated; ex-vessel value in millions of dollars. See also *Historical Statistics, Colonial Times to 1970*, series L 262–293]

STATE, CATCH, AND VALUE	1960	1965	1970	1972	1973	1974	1975, prel.	1976, prel.
New England:								
Catch	852	702	531	489	518	523	498	544
Value	61	75	91	107	117	124	155	175
Maine: Catch	295	205	159	149	143	148	138	178
Value	20	22	31	35	43	41	49	54
New Hampshire: Catch	1	1	1	2	2	3	3	3
Value	(Z)	1	1	1	1	1	1	1
Massachusetts: Catch	480	442	287	252	269	270	274	288
Value	36	46	47	57	56	62	83	97
Rhode Island: Catch	69	49	79	82	97	97	79	72
Value	4	5	11	13	15	17	19	20
Connecticut: Catch	6	5	5	4	7	5	4	3
Value	1	2	2	2	2	3	3	3
Catch for certain species:								
Cod	35	35	53	46	50	58	55	55
Flounder	62	112	104	94	88	81	77	79
Haddock	119	134	27	12	8	8	16	13
Herring, sea	155	75	66	88	57	71	79	110
Lobster, American	29	29	30	29	26	26	29	30
Ocean perch, Atlantic	141	84	55	59	54	41	32	32
Whiting	104	75	40	18	34	20	33	37
Middle Atlantic:								
Catch	784	356	140	240	257	211	188	266
Value	22	25	30	39	42	44	50	69
New York: Catch	126	147	32	37	36	35	37	34
Value	9	12	16	22	22	25	28	32
New Jersey: Catch	374	160	98	191	210	167	144	227
Value	10	11	13	14	18	17	20	35
Delaware: Catch	284	48	10	13	11	9	7	5
Value	3	1	1	2	2	2	2	2
Catch for certain species:								
Clams (meats)	32	52	63	44	41	42	53	43
Menhaden	671	151	31	140	156	108	67	151
Oysters (meats)	1	1	1	3	3	3	3	4
Scup	27	17	4	5	6	10	10	9
Chesapeake Bay:								
Catch	436	592	630	736	701	597	509	588
Value	35	40	41	46	62	58	56	74
Maryland: Catch	69	87	80	70	70	70	64	60
Value	14	13	19	19	21	22	23	31
Virginia: Catch	367	505	551	666	631	530	445	528
Value	21	27	22	27	41	36	33	43
Catch for certain species:								
Alewives	19	38	21	12	11	15	12	4
Clams (meats)	8	11	23	34	53	67	47	24
Crabs	71	86	70	75	59	68	62	47
Menhaden	249	360	450	557	506	385	322	447
Oysters (meats)	27	21	25	24	25	25	23	22
South Atlantic:								
Catch	379	357	280	286	240	305	333	315
Value	20	27	30	45	57	51	64	72
North Carolina: Catch	265	234	173	176	138	207	238	226
Value	7	9	9	12	16	18	20	28
South Carolina: Catch	24	27	16	22	21	19	20	21
Value	4	5	4	8	11	7	13	14
Georgia: Catch	28	20	14	18	17	18	18	15
Value	3	4	4	7	11	7	12	12
Florida (east coast): Catch	61	76	76	71	64	61	57	53
Value	6	8	12	18	19	19	19	18
Catch for certain species:								
Crabs	45	46	43	36	32	38	31	27
Menhaden	215	192	136	106	85	134	167	145
Shrimp	31	26	21	25	25	27	25	26

See footnotes at end of table.

No. 1293. FISHERIES—QUANTITY AND VALUE OF CATCH, BY STATES, AND CATCH OF PRINCIPAL SPECIES, BY AREAS: 1960 TO 1976—Continued

[Catch in millions of pounds, live weight, except as indicated; ex-vessel value in millions of dollars. See also *Historical Statistics, Colonial Times to 1970*, series L 262–293]

STATE, CATCH, AND VALUE	1960	1965	1970	1972	1973	1974	1975, prel.	1976, prel.
Gulf States:								
Catch	1,266	1,463	1,698	1,588	1,544	1,776	1,654	1,753
Value	85	114	167	224	267	242	271	389
Florida (west coast): Catch	136	136	116	108	112	123	116	112
Value	21	27	31	39	46	52	57	70
Alabama: Catch	12	18	30	36	37	34	31	32
Value	3	5	10	18	18	17	21	34
Mississippi: Catch	314	368	298	257	268	301	306	288
Value	8	9	11	11	17	16	14	21
Louisiana: Catch	566	787	1,107	1,072	1,029	1,223	1,115	1,228
Value	26	37	61	72	95	86	86	137
Texas: Catch	238	154	147	115	98	94	86	93
Value	28	36	53	85	91	72	93	127
Catch for certain species:								
Crabs	36	38	36	37	46	43	41	38
Menhaden	841	1,023	1,209	1,107	1,074	1,296	1,197	1,238
Mullet	33	34	27	29	31	28	26	22
Oysters (meats)	16	19	18	18	15	15	19	21
Shrimp	206	195	230	229	182	186	170	210
Great Lakes: [1]								
Catch	68	56	72	60	68	78	60	67
Value	7	6	6	7	9	11	10	11
Superior: Catch	14	9	5	4	5	6	5	6
Value	1	1	1	1	1	2	2	2
Michigan: Catch	24	27	53	44	51	60	45	48
Value	2	2	4	4	5	6	5	5
Huron: Catch	6	5	2	2	2	2	2	2
Value	1	1	(Z)	(Z)	(Z)	(Z)	1	1
Erie: Catch	21	14	10	8	8	10	8	9
Value	2	1	1	1	1	2	2	3
Pacific Coast:								
Catch	1,061	1,147	1,480	1,322	1,433	1,391	1,526	1,743
Value	112	148	235	264	363	381	345	543
Washington: Catch	113	127	134	124	144	147	145	131
Value	16	18	30	39	69	59	61	81
Oregon: Catch	49	69	98	93	92	96	89	99
Value	6	9	23	24	30	37	26	49
California: Catch	541	458	703	649	731	685	850	897
Value	50	51	86	99	112	140	129	186
Alaska: Catch	358	492	545	456	466	463	442	616
Value	41	70	96	102	152	145	129	227
Catch for certain species:								
Anchovies	5	6	193	150	278	177	331	257
Crabs	65	161	126	169	154	174	163	224
Flounder	48	46	46	53	55	54	50	58
Halibut	51	40	34	26	26	18	21	20
Herring, sea	84	35	22	19	45	56	40	40
Salmon	235	327	410	232	222	201	202	309
Sardines	58	2	(Z)	(Z)	(Z)	(Z)	(Z)	(Z)
Shrimp	12	20	93	109	152	141	137	165
Tuna	288	296	378	370	331	381	379	472
Mississippi River and tributaries:								
Catch	86	85	75	70	83	68	72	62
Value	8	8	10	10	13	14	15	13
Hawaii:								
Catch	11	20	11	14	14	11	9	12
Tuna	9	17	9	12	12	9	7	9
Value	3	4	4	6	6	6	6	7

Z Less than 500,000 pounds or $500,000.

[1] Collected largely by State fishery agencies, and compiled by National Marine Fisheries Service. Includes, in addition to lakes shown, small amounts for Lake Ontario, Lake St. Clair, Lake of the Woods, Namakan Lake, and Rainy Lake.

Source: U.S. National Oceanic and Atmospheric Administration, *Fishery Statistics of the United States*, annual.

No. 1294. Prices Received by Fishermen: 1960 to 1977

[Cents per pound. Based on prices received by fishermen from processors. See also *Historical Statistics, Colonial Times to 1970*, series L 321–337]

SPECIES	Point of pricing	1960	1965	1970	1972	1973	1974	1975 [1]	1976 [1]	1977 [1]
Clams, soft	Maine	39.7	49.1	47.5	60.4	78.5	76.4	86.9	101.6	118.3
Cod	Massachusetts	6.5	8.0	11.2	17.7	18.5	19.6	24.2	26.2	21.5
Crabs, blue	Maryland, Virginia	5.5	7.6	6.6	8.7	12.1	12.7	15.7	21.4	20.1
Flounder	Massachusetts	12.2	9.5	15.3	21.4	23.7	26.5	34.9	37.5	36.9
Haddock	Massachusetts	7.9	8.9	22.7	36.8	38.1	36.9	32.8	33.5	28.4
Lobsters, American	Maine	45.7	75.2	94.7	114.3	136.5	141.0	161.5	153.9	173.6
Menhaden	(No specific point)	1.0	1.6	1.9	1.6	3.9	3.4	2.7	3.3	3.8
Ocean perch	Maine, Mass	4.0	4.1	4.9	5.6	7.7	8.1	10.3	13.7	15.3
Oysters, eastern	Maryland, Virginia	68.2	78.6	61.1	63.2	66.0	70.1	80.1	103.7	109.9
Salmon, chinook [2]	(No specific point)	50.8	48.3	86.0	79.6	108.0	102.9	99.3	147.4	190.7
Salmon, coho [2]	(No specific point)	40.8	30.1	58.8	67.8	83.1	85.2	87.7	117.2	134.8
Sea scallops	New Bedford, Mass	34.9	67.5	135.6	200.3	177.6	154.2	188.8	184.0	165.8
Shrimp	So. Atlantic, Gulf	44.4	58.0	75.4	114.0	151.9	116.1	169.5	208.4	180.5
Tuna, albacore	(No specific point)	15.7	15.7	26.2	32.8	41.5	41.0	33.8	49.4	54.1

[1] Preliminary.   [2] Troll-caught.

Source: U.S. National Oceanic and Atmospheric Administration, *Prices Received by Fishermen*, H.S. No. 12 (C.F.S. No. 4657 Revised) and *Fishery Statistics of the United States*, annual.

No. 1295. Supply of Tuna, Salmon, and Sardines: 1965 to 1977

[In millions of pounds]

ITEM	1965	1970	1972	1973	1974	1975	1976	1977
Tuna:								
Domestic landings, live weight	373	478	535	519	557	568	660	469
Imports, fresh and frozen, live weight [1]	379	465	765	817	839	517	641	670
Canned tuna, total supply	409	510	676	674	713	581	658	594
From domestic landings	162	204	234	224	250	261	285	211
From imported fresh and frozen [1]	197	234	386	412	410	268	314	349
Imported canned	51	70	57	30	53	52	59	34
Canned salmon, total for U.S. consumption	150	169	83	63	88	59	111	118
Domestic pack	174	183	93	72	88	78	128	139
Imports	(z)	2	12	8	9	3	3	1
Exports	25	17	21	17	8	22	20	21
Canned sardines, total supply	75	66	107	91	94	57	79	74
Maine sardines	30	19	37	23	25	26	25	24
Imports	45	47	70	67	69	31	54	50

Z Less than 500,000 pounds.
[1] Includes foreign-caught fish landed or packed in Puerto Rico and American Samoa.

Source: U.S. National Oceanic and Atmospheric Administration, *Fishery Statistics of the United States*, annual.

No. 1296. Fishery Products—Imports and Exports: 1950 to 1977

[Quantity in millions of pounds; value in millions of dollars. Includes Puerto Rico; beginning 1955, imports also include landings of tuna by foreign vessels in American Samoa. See also *Historical Statistics, Colonial Times to 1970*, series L 227–235]

YEAR	IMPORTS				EXPORTS			
	Total value	Edible products		Non-edible, value	Total value	Edible products		Non-edible, value
		Quantity	Value			Quantity	Value	
1950	198	640	158	40	27	122	19	9
1955	259	780	209	50	40	110	25	15
1960	363	1,095	311	53	44	61	26	19
1965	601	1,399	479	121	69	96	49	20
1970	1,037	1,873	813	225	117	140	94	24
1973	1,583	2,416	1,398	185	299	239	242	57
1974	1,711	2,267	1,495	215	262	178	195	67
1975, prel	1,637	1,913	1,367	270	305	218	267	37
1976, prel	2,332	2,228	1,917	415	385	241	330	55
1977, prel	2,621	2,176	2,078	543	520	331	473	47

Source: U.S. National Oceanic and Atmospheric Administration, *Fishery Statistics of the United States*, annual, and *Fisheries of the United States*, annual. Compiled from data furnished by U.S. Bureau of the Census.

No. 1297. SELECTED FISHERY PRODUCTS—IMPORTS AND EXPORTS: 1970 TO 1977

[Includes Puerto Rico. See *Historical Statistics, Colonial Times to 1970*, series L 312–318, for selected imports]

PRODUCT	QUANTITY (mil. lb.)						VALUE (mil. dol.)					
	1970	1973	1974	1975	1976	1977, prel.	1970	1973	1974	1975	1976	1977, prel.
IMPORTS												
Edible:												
Fresh or frozen:												
Whitefish [1]	8.4	7.7	7.2	8.4	8.2	9.0	4.8	4.6	4.7	5.6	6.1	7.0
Halibut [1]	18.2	12.6	5.4	8.0	7.4	6.5	8.1	10.1	5.2	8.0	9.9	9.1
Salmon [1]	7.4	18.2	12.5	9.2	7.7	5.7	6.7	16.5	14.0	11.5	13.6	10.8
Sea herring	103.9	97.6	86.9	99.2	76.5	70.7	1.9	5.1	4.7	5.1	5.5	8.9
Smelt	8.5	11.3	8.8	8.8	10.5	9.0	1.6	3.1	2.8	3.2	3.8	3.6
Tuna	442.8	773.5	789.4	478.6	607.4	633.3	100.5	216.8	216.1	121.2	249.4	255.3
Groundfish fillets, blocks [2]	458.8	578.8	431.4	513.8	607.0	602.6	134.6	313.5	250.5	278.4	398.6	502.2
Other fillets and steaks	136.1	199.3	149.9	167.6	185.0	180.7	63.6	122.2	100.8	117.3	149.4	161.0
Scallops (meats)	16.8	19.8	18.1	19.7	25.3	29.8	19.7	33.6	28.1	37.2	53.0	53.0
Lobster, American and spiny	54.9	54.3	55.3	58.1	64.4	60.0	93.8	147.9	178.2	188.6	240.7	250.3
Shrimp and prawn	214.8	199.6	222.8	201.5	227.5	225.2	196.8	278.4	379.8	346.2	460.7	488.3
Canned:												
Anchovies, in oil	5.5	6.2	4.8	3.6	4.8	5.4	6.3	9.5	8.2	5.6	8.3	11.2
Salmon	2.4	7.9	8.6	3.3	2.5	.6	1.6	6.2	11.9	3.9	3.0	1.2
Sardines, in oil	34.1	36.1	29.4	18.5	26.9	25.7	15.8	23.4	22.0	16.3	23.7	25.0
Sardines, herring, not in oil	25.3	46.5	55.7	24.9	39.1	35.1	8.3	18.7	23.7	15.9	21.3	20.8
Tuna	72.3	38.4	52.7	51.7	58.9	34.6	44.3	34.3	51.1	46.0	67.5	44.7
Bonito and yellowtail	1.2	1.4	.3	.1	.1	1.4	.5	.8	.2	.1	.1	1.0
Crab meat	2.8	2.0	2.4	1.4	2.1	3.5	5.3	3.2	5.2	2.9	4.6	8.0
Oysters	15.0	19.8	16.0	12.4	14.4	19.2	8.1	11.6	10.1	8.4	10.7	17.9
Lobster, American and spiny	2.5	1.8	1.7	2.1	2.9	2.9	8.0	8.0	8.6	10.9	13.9	15.6
Pickled or salted:												
Cod, haddock, hake, pollock, cusk	41.2	38.7	37.8	33.6	36.5	35.7	13.6	24.0	29.8	26.8	31.4	33.4
Herring	30.6	21.7	18.6	20.6	30.9	19.5	5.4	6.0	6.0	6.6	10.0	7.0
Nonedible (scrap and meal)	502.0	136.0	136.0	236.7	280.8	163.0	37.7	14.3	15.7	23.6	32.9	26.5
EXPORTS												
Canned salmon	16.8	16.9	8.3	22.5	19.6	21.3	13.1	26.8	13.3	34.6	33.9	34.0
Canned sardines	1.5	1.7	1.7	2.2	1.8	1.2	.7	1.1	1.1	1.8	1.6	.1
Fish oil, nonedible	158.8	247.8	199.1	191.8	179.2	90.6	15.7	33.9	39.6	27.8	29.9	18.1

[1] Excludes fillets. [2] Includes cod, cusk, haddock, hake, pollock, and Atlantic ocean perch.

Source: U.S. National Oceanic and Atmospheric Administration, *Fishery Statistics of the United States*, annual. Compiled from data furnished by U.S. Bureau of the Census.

No. 1298. FRESH AND FROZEN FISHERY PRODUCTS: 1970 TO 1977

[Excludes Alaska and Hawaii, except frozen fishery products includes Alaska]

PRODUCT	PRODUCTION (mil. lb.)						VALUE (mil. dol.)					
	1970	1973	1974	1975	1976	1977, prel.	1970	1973	1974	1975	1976	1977, prel.
Fresh and frozen fish fillets and steaks	133.5	133.4	135.5	131.9	142.6	150.0	74.8	111.4	119.8	137.9	167.1	180.4
Cod	13.6	17.1	19.1	15.2	16.7	22.0	7.4	13.8	16.4	14.6	19.1	25.6
Flounder	46.7	40.3	40.9	41.9	48.2	43.2	28.7	40.5	44.6	53.1	72.4	67.6
Haddock	8.9	6.4	8.9	8.2	4.7	8.3	6.9	9.1	12.1	12.3	14.7	21.4
Ocean perch, Atlantic	16.0	15.6	12.1	8.4	9.4	10.4	4.9	8.2	6.2	5.7	8.1	10.1
Whiting	.8	2.8	2.0	.1	1.0	1.0	.3	1.1	.6	.1	.6	.5
Other	47.6	51.2	52.5	58.1	62.6	65.1	26.6	38.7	39.9	52.1	52.2	55.2
Frozen fishery products	388.3	410.4	339.9	299.7	321.7	345.7	(NA)	(NA)	(NA)	(NA)	(NA)	(NA)

NA Not available.

Source: U.S. National Oceanic and Atmospheric Administration, *Fishery Statistics of the United States*, annual.

No. 1299. CANNED FISHERY PRODUCTS—PRODUCTION AND VALUE, BY SPECIES: 1970 TO 1977

[See also *Historical Statistics, Colonial Times to 1970*, series L 338–357 (production data in cases) and L 358]

PRODUCT	PRODUCTION (mil. lb.)						VALUE (mil. dol.)					
	1970	1973	1974	1975	1976	1977, prel.	1970	1973	1974	1975	1976	1977, prel.
Total	1,346	1,647	1,554	1,386	1,568	1,433	742	1,167	1,306	1,071	1,430	1,558
Salmon	183	71	88	78	128	139	139	111	137	115	205	202
Sardines, Maine	19	23	25	26	25	23	11	16	22	25	24	27
Tuna	438	636	660	529	599	560	381	705	824	653	853	931
Jack mackerel	1 8	3	4	10	7	33	2 2	1	1	3	2	17
Shrimp	25	25	22	12	20	24	37	55	44	28	49	70
Clam products	65	91	88	76	64	74	26	38	43	42	39	63
Oysters	2	2	2	2	1	1	2	3	3	4	3	3
Other	606	796	665	653	724	579	144	238	232	201	255	245

1 Includes a small amount of Pacific mackerel.
Source: U.S. National and Atmospheric Administration, *Fishery Statistics of the United States*, annual.

No. 1300. PROCESSED FISHERY PRODUCTS—SUMMARY: 1970 TO 1977

[Includes Puerto Rico and American Samoa. See *Historical Statistics, Colonial Times to 1970*, series L 362–365, for meal, scrap, and oil]

PRODUCT	PRODUCTION (mil. lb.) 1						VALUE (mil. dol.)					
	1970	1973	1974	1975	1976	1977	1970	1973	1974	1975	1976	1977
Total	(X)	(X)	(X)	(X)	(X)	(X)	1,727	2,754	2,756	2,655	3,473	(NA)
Packaged fresh and frozen	1,158	1,214	1,121	1,113	1,248	(NA)	800	1,276	1,129	1,309	1,739	(NA)
Fish not breaded:												
Fillets and steaks, raw	131	132	136	132	143	150	75	111	120	138	167	180
Dressed	32	34	46	55	38	(NA)	9	19	21	43	24	(NA)
Other 2	10	18	19	26	29	31	5	13	14	22	29	37
Fish breaded, raw and cooked:												
Sticks	116	127	103	91	94	87	58	80	65	62	73	69
Fillets, portions, and steaks	296	316	283	286	335	(NA)	137	217	204	211	277	(NA)
Shellfish:												
Not breaded	328	325	327	315	389	(NA)	343	533	443	534	798	(NA)
Breaded, raw and cooked	119	137	115	128	127	(NA)	129	209	172	220	257	(NA)
Specialties, fish and shellfish	124	123	92	79	92	(NA)	45	94	91	79	112	(NA)
Canned products 3	1,346	1,647	1,554	1,386	1,568	1,433	742	1,167	1,306	1,072	1,430	1,558
Fish and shellfish	805	951	963	802	907	922	633	996	1,127	920	1,232	1,393
Animal food	540	696	590	583	660	511	105	167	175	148	196	161
Cured fish 4	71	60	70	55	55	(NA)	77	91	114	102	112	116
Salted 5	37	29	39	29	32	(NA)	30	35	49	43	50	(NA)
Smoked	31	28	29	24	22	(NA)	43	54	62	56	59	(NA)
Dried (cod) lutefisk	2	1	1	2	1	(NA)	1	1	1	1	1	(NA)
Industrial products	(X)	(X)	(X)	(X)	(X)	(X)	108	221	208	173	193	207
Meal and scrap tons	(Z)	(Z)	(Z)	(Z)	(Z)	(Z)	46	120	84	66	97	98
Oil (body and liver)	206	225	238	246	205	134	18	26	49	33	31	28
Fish solubles tons	(Z)	(Z)	(Z)	(Z)	(Z)	(Z)	5	15	12	9	14	24
Other 6	(X)	(X)	(X)	(X)	(X)	(X)	38	60	63	67	51	58

NA Not available.   X Not applicable.   Z Less than 500,000 tons.   1 Except as indicated.
2 Includes unbreaded portions and, for 1970, whale meat for animal feeding.   3 Includes salmon eggs for bait.
4 Includes sun dried and freeze dried.   5 Includes spiced and pickled.
6 Includes buttons from fresh water mussel and marine shell, sealskins processed in South Carolina, fish meal further processed from imported fish meal, and oyster shell grit and lime.

Source: U.S. National Oceanic and Atmospheric Administration, *Fishery Statistics of the United States*, annual.

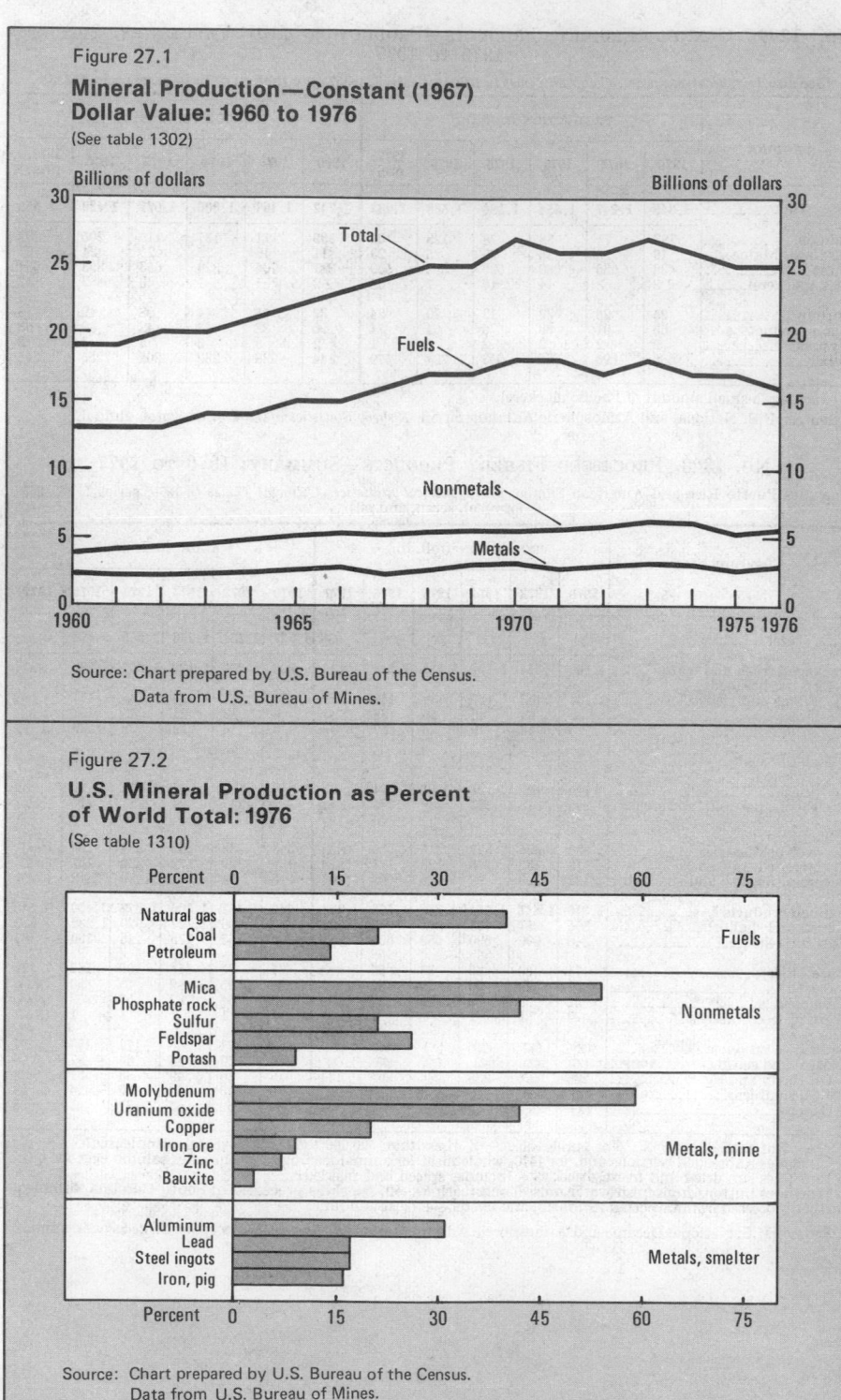

Figure 27.1

Mineral Production—Constant (1967) Dollar Value: 1960 to 1976

(See table 1302)

Billions of dollars

Billions of dollars

Total

Fuels

Nonmetals

Metals

Source: Chart prepared by U.S. Bureau of the Census.
        Data from U.S. Bureau of Mines.

Figure 27.2

U.S. Mineral Production as Percent of World Total: 1976

(See table 1310)

Percent

Natural gas
Coal
Petroleum
Fuels

Mica
Phosphate rock
Sulfur
Feldspar
Potash
Nonmetals

Molybdenum
Uranium oxide
Copper
Iron ore
Zinc
Bauxite
Metals, mine

Aluminum
Lead
Steel ingots
Iron, pig
Metals, smelter

Percent

Source: Chart prepared by U.S. Bureau of the Census.
        Data from U.S. Bureau of Mines.

Mining and Mineral Products

This section presents data relating to mineral industries and their products, general summary measures of production and employment, and more detailed data on production, prices, imports and exports, consumption, and distribution for specific industries and products. Data on mining and mineral products may also be found in sections 29 and 33 of this *Abstract*.

"Mining" comprises the extraction of minerals occurring naturally (coal, ores, crude petroleum, natural gas) and quarrying, well operation, milling, and other preparation customarily done at the mine site or as a part of mining activity. (Mineral preparation plants are usually operated together with mines or quarries.) Exploration for minerals is included as is the development of mineral properties.

The principal governmental sources of these data are the three-volume *Minerals Yearbook*, published by the Bureau of Mines, Department of the Interior, and various monthly and annual publications of the Energy Information Administration, Department of Energy. In addition, the Bureau of the Census conducts a census of mineral industries every 5 years. Non-government sources include the *Annual Statistical Report* of the American Iron and Steel Institute, Washington, D.C.; *Metals Week* and the monthly *Engineering and Mining Journal*, issued by the McGraw-Hill Publishing Co., New York; *The Iron Age*, issued weekly by the Chilton Co., Philadelphia; and the *Joint Association Survey of the U.S. Oil and Gas Industry*, conducted by the American Petroleum Institute, Independent Petroleum Association of America, and Mid-Continent Oil and Gas Association.

Mineral statistics, with principal emphasis on commodity detail, have been collected by the Geological Survey or by the Bureau of Mines since 1880. Current data in Bureau of Mines publications include quantity and value of nonfuel minerals produced, sold or used by producers, or shipped; quantity of minerals stocked; crude materials treated and prepared minerals recovered; and consumption of mineral raw materials. The U.S. Mining Enforcement and Safety Administration also collects and publishes data on man-hours, employment, and accidents and injuries in the mineral industries. In October 1977, fuel data collection activities of the Bureau of Mines were transferred to the Energy Information Administration.

Censuses of mineral industries have been conducted by the Bureau of the Census at various intervals since 1840. Beginning with the 1967 census, legislation provides for a census to be conducted every fifth year for years ending in "2" and "7." The censuses provide, for the various types of mineral establishments, information on operating costs, capital expenditures, labor, equipment, and energy requirements in relation to their value of shipments and other receipts. Commodity statistics on many manufactured mineral products are also collected by the Bureau at monthly, quarterly, or annual intervals and issued in its *Current Industrial Reports* series. Included in this series, beginning in 1973, is the *Annual Survey of Oil and Gas*.

In general, figures shown in the individual commodity tables include data for outlying areas, and may therefore not agree with summary table 1308. Except for crude petroleum, the export and import figures include foreign trade passing through the customs districts of Alaska, Hawaii, and Puerto Rico, but exclude shipments between conterminous United States and outlying areas.

Historical statistics.—Tabular headnotes provide cross-references, where applicable, to *Historical Statistics of the United States, Colonial Times to 1970*. See Appendix I.

No. 1301. National Income Originating in Mining: 1950 to 1977

[In millions of dollars. 1950 excludes Alaska and Hawaii. Data are without capital consumption adjustment. For definition of national income, see text, p. 437. See *Historical Statistics, Colonial Times to 1970*, series F 228, for single-year figures prior to minor revisions issued in 1976]

TYPE OF MINING	1950	1960	1965	1970	1972	1973	1974	1975	1976	1977
Total mining	5,259	5,613	6,013	7,810	8,700	10,149	15,539	18,149	20,267	23,179
Metal mining	658	807	856	1,179	1,073	1,489	1,596	1,635	1,900	2,067
Coal mining	2,006	1,286	1,372	2,231	2,493	2,869	5,208	6,228	5,874	6,289
Oil and gas extraction	2,053	2,606	2,670	3,099	3,563	3,908	6,661	8,075	10,232	12,483
Nonmetallic minerals, exc. fuels	542	914	1,115	1,301	1,571	1,883	2,074	2,211	2,261	2,340

Source: U.S. Bureau of Economic Analysis, *The National Income and Product Accounts of the United States, 1929–74*, and *Survey of Current Business*, July 1978.

No. 1302. Value of Mineral Production, Imports, and Exports: 1950 to 1976

[In billions of dollars. Includes Puerto Rico and U.S. outlying areas. For products covered, see table 1308. See also *Historical Statistics, Colonial Times to 1970*, series M 13–14, M 20, M 30, and M 38–53]

MINERAL [1]	1950	1955	1960	1965	1970	1971	1972	1973	1974	1975	1976, est.
CURRENT DOLLARS											
Production, total	[2] 11.9	15.9	18.0	21.5	29.8	30.7	32.2	36.8	55.1	62.3	69.2
Fuels	8.7	10.8	12.1	14.0	20.2	21.2	22.1	25.0	40.9	47.6	52.5
Metals	1.4	2.1	2.0	2.5	3.9	3.4	3.6	4.4	5.5	5.2	6.1
Nonmetals	1.8	3.1	3.9	4.9	5.7	6.1	6.5	7.4	8.6	9.5	10.6
Imports, total	(NA)	3.0	3.3	2.6	3.4	3.7	4.5	6.7	19.5	22.7	30.5
Fuels	(NA)	1.0	1.5	1.3	1.6	2.1	2.9	4.8	16.5	19.9	27.7
Metals	1.0	1.6	1.5	1.0	1.2	1.0	1.0	1.1	1.8	1.6	1.7
Nonmetals	.3	.3	.3	.4	.6	.6	.6	.8	1.2	1.2	1.2
Exports, total	(NA)	1.7	1.9	.8	1.6	1.4	1.5	1.7	3.5	4.7	4.3
Fuels	(NA)	1.1	.8	.5	1.1	1.0	1.1	1.2	2.7	3.6	3.3
Metals	.2	.5	.9	.2	.3	.2	.2	.3	.3	.4	.4
Nonmetals	.1	.1	.1	.2	.2	.2	.2	.3	.5	.7	.6
CONSTANT (1967) DOLLARS [3]											
Production, total	[2] 13.5	17.7	18.7	22.2	26.7	26.1	25.7	27.0	26.1	24.6	24.8
Fuels	10.0	12.1	12.5	14.5	18.1	17.7	17.1	17.7	17.0	16.6	16.4
Metals	1.8	2.4	2.3	2.6	3.1	2.7	2.9	3.1	3.0	2.6	2.9
Nonmetals	1.8	3.3	3.8	5.1	5.5	5.6	5.8	6.2	6.1	5.3	5.6

NA Not available.   [1] Through 1965, uranium included with metals; thereafter, with fuels.
[2] Excludes Alaska and Hawaii.   [3] Values deflated by the index of implicit unit value.

Source: U.S. Bureau of Mines, *Minerals Yearbook*.

No. 1303. Bureau of Mines Index of Physical Volume of Mineral Production: 1950 to 1976

[1967 = 100. Excludes Puerto Rico and outlying areas. See also *Historical Statistics, Colonial Times to 1970*, series M 54–67]

MINERAL	1950	1955	1960	1965	1970	1971	1972	1973	1974	1975	1976
Minerals, total	65.3	75.4	79.1	93.5	112.1	109.9	112.7	114.1	110.4	103.8	105.5
Fuels	66.4	74.8	77.5	89.2	111.7	109.7	111.2	109.3	105.4	102.3	101.4
Coal	103.9	89.3	78.4	93.7	108.3	98.9	105.9	105.1	107.1	114.9	120.2
Crude oil and natural gas	57.2	72.6	78.3	88.5	112.0	111.3	111.4	109.3	104.1	98.7	96.6
Metals	105.3	109.8	104.4	114.5	135.8	122.3	127.5	136.8	130.4	117.5	127.4
Ferrous	106.5	124.0	100.0	100.9	109.3	96.9	98.4	116.0	108.3	96.2	99.8
Nonferrous	100.1	95.0	108.9	125.6	157.4	143.0	151.1	153.6	148.4	134.8	149.8
Base	106.8	103.9	104.9	132.7	167.3	151.0	162.8	166.5	159.3	142.7	158.0
Monetary	145.3	117.8	102.0	115.0	123.9	110.6	102.7	94.5	86.9	86.2	85.1
Other	59.3	64.7	123.1	89.8	119.5	115.5	112.6	114.8	122.8	119.2	142.8
Nonmetals	46.1	65.6	76.1	97.6	103.4	105.2	111.0	119.0	117.2	102.8	108.6
Construction	44.8	67.2	79.6	100.6	103.1	106.2	111.7	120.8	115.2	99.5	104.9
Chemical	43.6	56.4	62.3	87.8	103.1	101.9	108.7	112.2	121.3	112.2	117.2
Other	70.2	79.4	81.7	97.2	109.1	105.5	112.2	122.7	128.6	109.4	124.1

Source: U.S. Bureau of Mines, *Minerals Yearbook*.

No. 1304. FEDERAL RESERVE BOARD PRODUCTION INDEXES—MINING AND METALS: 1960 TO 1977

[1967=100. See also *Historical Statistics, Colonial Times to 1970*, series M 68–71]

MINING AND METALS	1960	1965	1970	1971	1972	1973	1974	1975	1976	1977
Mining	80	93	112	110	113	115	115	113	114	118
Coal	79	94	108	99	106	105	106	113	117	118
Oil and gas extraction	78	91	112	111	114	114	114	113	112	118
Metal mining	112	115	132	121	119	130	126	116	123	105
Stone and earth minerals	75	95	106	105	113	119	122	107	118	125
Primary metals	72	102	107	100	112	127	123	96	109	110
Iron and steel	78	105	105	96	107	122	120	96	105	103
Nonferrous metals	62	95	110	108	121	135	129	98	116	122

Source: Board of Governors of the Federal Reserve System, *Federal Reserve Bulletin*, monthly.

No. 1305. SUMMARY OF MINERAL OPERATIONS: 1954 TO 1972

[Includes mines operated in conjunction with manufacturing establishments. Beginning 1967, excludes single unit establishments without paid employees. See also *Historical Statistics, Colonial Times to 1970*, series M 1–11]

ITEM	1954	1958	1963	1967	1972
Number of establishments	38,858	37,966	40,532	29,688	26,178
Employees, total mil. 1,000	807	755	637	583	610
Production and development 1,000	668	585	502	448	456
All other 1,000	140	170	135	136	154
Man-hours, production and development workers mil.	1,292	1,120	1,014	922	935
Principal expenses:					
Wages, production and development workers mil. dol.	2,647	2,702	2,773	2,969	4,353
Salaries, all other employees mil. dol.	819	1,133	1,070	1,306	1,981
Cost of supplies, etc., and purchased machinery installed mil. dol.	6,148	7,585	9,066	10,647	14,979
Value added in mining mil. dol.	11,752	13,685	16,231	19,621	26,870
Value of shipments and receipts: [1] Gross mil. dol.	15,160	18,463	22,030	26,208	36,811
Net mil. dol.	14,465	16,729	19,210	22,784	(NA)
Capital expenditures mil. dol.	2,728	2,807	3,268	4,062	5,038

NA Not available. [1] Includes estimated value of minerals produced and used in the same establishment in making manufactured products.

Source: U.S. Bureau of the Census, *Census of Mineral Industries, 1963, 1967*, and *1972*.

No. 1306. SELECTED MINERAL PRODUCTS—AVERAGE PRICES: 1951 TO 1977

[Excludes Alaska and Hawaii, except as noted. See *Historical Statistics, Colonial Times to 1970*, series M 96, M 139, M 209, M 248, and M 262, for bituminous coal, crude petroleum, iron ore, lead, and aluminum, respectively]

YEARLY AVERAGE OR YEAR	Iron ore pellets [1]	Copper, electro-lytic [2]	Lead (New York)	Tin (New York) [3]	Zinc [4]	Alumi-num, de-livered [5]	Sulfur, crude (f.o.b. works)	Bitumi-nous coal [6]	Crude petro-leum [7]
	Cents per long ton unit, iron	Cents per lb.	Cents per lb.	Cents per lb.	Cents per lb.	Cents per lb.	Dol. per long ton	Dol. per short ton	Dol. per barrel
1951–1955	(NA)	29.3	15.3	106.0	13.6	21.0	29.66	4.75	2.66
1956–1960	(NA)	32.5	13.4	99.3	11.9	25.0	24.29	4.84	2.93
1961–1965	(NA)	32.0	12.2	136.1	12.6	24.0	21.52	4.47	2.88
1966–1970	25.5	44.3	14.6	160.9	14.4	26.2	29.73	5.01	3.00
1960	(NA)	32.5	11.9	101.4	12.9	26.0	23.13	4.69	2.88
1965	25.2	35.4	16.0	178.2	14.5	24.5	22.47	4.44	2.86
1970	26.6	58.2	15.6	174.2	15.3	28.7	23.14	6.26	3.18
1971	28.0	52.0	13.9	167.3	16.1	29.0	17.47	7.07	3.39
1972	28.0	51.2	15.0	177.5	17.8	26.3	17.03	7.66	3.39
1973	29.4	59.5	16.3	227.6	20.7	25.3	17.84	8.53	3.89
1974	40.6	77.3	22.5	396.3	35.9	34.1	28.88	15.75	6.74
1975	47.2	64.2	21.5	339.8	39.0	39.8	45.63	19.23	7.56
1976	53.1	69.6	23.1	379.8	37.0	44.6	46.45	19.43	8.14
1977, prel	55.5	66.7	30.6	529.0	34.4	51.6	44.75	21.00	8.50

NA Not available. [1] Lower Great Lakes ports. Price as of end of year per long ton unit of contained iron, natural, delivered rail or vessel. Lake Superior ore. [2] Domestic market. [3] Straits tin. [4] Prime western. Beginning 1971, delivered price. [5] Prices 1951–1955, for 99+ percent virgin ingot aluminum; beginning 1956, for 99+ percent unalloyed ingot. [6] Average value at mine. Includes Alaska. [7] Average value at well. Beginning 1958, includes Alaska, and 1959, Hawaii.

Source: 1951–1974 compiled from *Metals Week* (copyright); *Producer (Wholesale) Prices and Price Indexes* (U.S. Bureau of Labor Statistics); *Minerals Yearbook* and *Commodity Data Summaries* (U.S. Bureau of Mines); thereafter, *Minerals Yearbook*.

No. 1307. MINERAL INDUSTRIES—

[Excludes establishments for which both value of shipments and expenditures amounted to less than $500.

Times to 1970,

MINERAL INDUSTRY	1963 [1]			1967			
	Estab-lish-ments	Pay-roll [2]	Value added in min-ing [3]	Estab-lish-ments	All employees		Value added in min-ing [3]
					Number [4]	Pay-roll [2]	
		Mil. dol.	Mil. dol.		1,000	Mil. dol.	Mil. dol.
1 All industries	38,651	3,742	15,920	28,579	567	4,187	19,330
2 Metal mining	1,614	515	1,418	1,155	71	552	1,557
3 Iron ores	208	162	549	146	23	186	662
4 Copper ores	160	187	417	156	21	171	437
5 Lead and zinc ores	205	49	84	167	9	61	103
6 Gold and silver ores	466	25	49	183	4	26	51
7 Gold ores and placers	359	16	27	125	2	17	35
8 Silver ores	107	9	22	58	1	8	16
9 Bauxite	17	3	18	17	1	4	23
10 Ferroalloy ores, except vanadium	58	20	66	43	4	32	73
11 Metal mining services	83	14	25	148	3	19	34
12 Miscellaneous metal ores	417	54	210	295	7	54	175
13 Uranium-radium-vanadium ores	335	45	191	188	5	41	142
14 Mercury ores and misc. metal ores	82	9	19	107	2	13	32
15 Anthracite mining	1,069	59	121	403	7	41	82
16 Anthracite	1,026	53	111	371	6	37	75
17 Anthracite mining services	43	6	10	32	1	5	7
18 Bituminous coal and lignite mining	6,305	762	1,607	4,081	124	926	2,009
19 Bituminous coal and lignite	6,174	755	1,590	3,966	123	916	1,987
20 Coal mining services, n.e.c	131	7	17	115	1	10	22
21 Oil and gas extraction	21,242	1,745	11,020	16,358	245	1,855	13,394
22 Crude petroleum and natural gas	14,378	1,016	9,016	8,796	126	1,049	10,965
23 Natural gas liquids	652	97	762	684	12	100	905
24 Oil and gas field services	6,212	632	1,241	6,878	106	707	1,524
25 Drilling oil and gas wells	2,836	318	653	2,347	43	295	627
26 Oil and gas exploration services	373	48	90	636	8	53	126
27 Oil and gas field services, n.e.c	3,003	266	498	3,895	55	359	770
28 Nonmetallic minerals mining	8,421	661	1,755	6,582	120	812	2,288
29 Dimension stone [8]	319	8	15	244	2	9	18
30 Crushed and broken stone [9]	2,256	229	582	2,033	43	281	705
31 Sand and gravel [9]	4,616	212	514	3,232	35	229	548
32 Clay and related minerals [9]	423	42	114	356	9	58	155
33 Chemical and fertilizer minerals	235	137	443	233	24	188	741
34 Barite	54	7	11	30	1	5	15
35 Fluorspar	30	4	9	32	1	5	11
36 Potash, soda, and borate minerals	23	52	156	33	8	68	188
37 Phosphate rock	66	32	105	69	8	60	199
38 Rock salt	25	16	50	26	3	19	71
39 Sulfur	17	21	100	31	3	31	253
40 Chemical and fertilizer mining, n.e.c	20	6	12	12	(Z)	2	3
41 Nonmetallic minerals, services	119	5	9	106	1	6	11
42 Miscellaneous nonmetallic minerals [9]	453	28	78	378	7	41	111

- Represents zero.   Z Less than 500 or 500,000.
[1] Includes single-unit establishments without paid employees.
[2] Gross earnings paid to all employees on payroll.
[3] Computed by subtracting cost of supplies, minerals received for preparation, purchased fuel and electric energy, contract work, and purchased machinery from the value of shipments and capital expenditures.
[4] Excludes proprietors and firm members of unincorporated concerns.
[5] Represents employees up through the working foreman level engaged in manual work. Includes development and exploration workers.

SUMMARY: 1963, 1967, AND 1972

"N.e.c." means not elsewhere classified. Minus sign (−) denotes decrease. See also *Historical Statistics, Colonial* series M 1-12]

	1972										
Estab-lish-ments	All employees		Production workers [5]			Value added in min-ing [3]	Value of ship-ments and re-ceipts [7]	Capi-tal expend-itures	Percent change, 1967-1972		
	Num-ber [4]	Pay-roll [2]	Num-ber	Man-hours [6]	Wages				Employ-ees	Value added	
	1,000	*Mil. dol.*	*1,000*	*Millions*	*Mil. dol.*	*Mil. dol.*	*Mil. dol.*	*Mil. dol.*			
25,269	595	6,226	443	909	4,250	26,471	36,319	5,036	5	37	1
1,014	81	853	63	127	622	2,382	3,515	402	14	53	2
111	20	218	15	30	156	702	1,065	60	−13	6	3
181	36	387	28	56	279	1,025	1,589	209	71	135	4
101	8	72	6	12	55	200	251	26	−15	95	5
132	3	30	2	5	23	61	75	5	−24	17	6
81	2	20	2	3	15	47	56	4	−31	32	7
51	1	10	1	2	7	14	19	2	−17	−15	8
10	1	4	(z)	1	3	24	28	4	−17	7	9
44	4	40	3	5	29	137	164	36	−5	86	10
172	3	31	2	5	26	54	72	4	8	61	11
263	7	71	6	12	52	180	272	57	−3	3	12
144	6	58	5	10	43	149	227	43	9	5	13
119	1	13	1	2	9	31	45	15	−35	−6	14
230	5	35	4	8	30	68	130	7	−37	−17	15
213	4	32	3	7	27	63	123	6	−37	−16	16
17	1	3	(z)	1	3	6	7	1	−37	−26	17
3,365	155	1,742	133	261	1,437	3,685	5,395	697	25	83	18
3,191	152	1,714	130	257	1,412	3,626	5,313	688	24	82	19
174	3	29	3	5	24	60	82	9	107	175	20
14,498	241	2,525	154	319	1,393	17,612	23,627	3,456	−2	31	21
7,609	117	1,375	52	102	499	14,422	15,688	2,954	−8	32	22
680	11	117	9	18	96	1,019	5,058	106	−14	13	23
6,209	113	1,033	93	199	799	2,172	2,881	395	7	43	24
1,907	45	422	40	84	361	881	1,244	225	5	40	25
715	10	89	8	18	65	212	254	30	17	67	26
3,587	58	522	46	96	373	1,079	1,383	141	6	40	27
6,162	114	1,070	89	195	769	2,723	3,652	475	−5	19	28
198	2	13	2	3	11	26	31	2	5	44	29
1,937	42	388	34	76	291	982	1,319	186	−3	39	30
2,929	34	322	27	57	233	776	1,004	138	−2	42	31
309	9	78	7	16	57	198	293	30	−3	28	32
204	20	203	14	29	127	583	784	89	−16	−21	33
27	1	5	1	1	5	20	22	2	−11	28	34
38	1	8	1	2	6	16	29	3	14	48	35
31	7	77	5	10	49	211	262	59	−13	12	36
47	6	53	4	9	33	154	251	16	−27	−23	37
30	3	26	2	4	18	74	87	7	4	5	38
24	3	32	1	3	15	104	128	7	−19	−59	39
7	(z)	1	(z)	(z)	1	4	6	1	−33	6	40
126	1	11	1	2	9	20	29	2	25	82	41
459	7	55	5	11	41	138	190	28	−	24	42

[6] Excludes paid vacations, holidays, and sick leave; includes actual overtime hours (not straight-time equivalent).
[7] Represents value of shipments of primary and secondary products of the industry and amount received for services performed for other establishments on a contract, fee, or other basis.
[8] Excludes data for dimension stone quarries operated in conjunction with dressing plants.
[9] Excludes data for mining included in establishments classified in manufacturing industries.

Source: U.S. Bureau of the Census, *Census of Mineral Industries: 1963, 1967,* and *1972,* final industry series reports.

No. 1308. Mineral Production, 1965 to 1976, and Principal Producing States, 1976

[Data represent production as measured by mine shipments, mine sales, or marketable production (including consumption by producers). See Historical Statistics, Colonial Times to 1970, series M 13–37, for selected values]

MINERAL	Unit	PRODUCTION QUANTITY					PRODUCTION VALUE (mil. dol.)					Principal producing States ranked by quantity, 1976
		1965	1970	1974	1975	1976	1965	1970	1974	1975	1976	
Total mineral production	(X)	(X)	(X)	(X)	(X)	(X)	21,524.0	29,791.0	55,077.0	62,266.0	69,178.0	(X)
Mineral fuels	(X)	(X)	(X)	(X)	(X)	(X)	14,047.0	20,152.0	40,937.0	47,559.0	52,545.0	(X)
Asphalt and related bitumens (native)[1]	1,000 sh. tons	1,912	1,981	2,021	1,902	2,012	9.5	8.9	16.7	17.8	17.6	Tex., Utah, Ala., Mo.
Carbon dioxide, natural (est.)	mil. cu. ft	1,174	1,110	966	1,070	1,357	.2	.2	.2	.3	.2	N. Mex., Colo., Calif., Utah.
Coal: Bituminous and lignite	mil. sh. tons	512	603	603	648	679	2,276.0	3,772.7	9,502.3	12,472.5	13,189.5	Ky., W. Va., Pa., Ill.
Pennsylvania anthracite	mil. sh. tons	15	10	7	6	6	122.0	105.3	144.7	198.5	209.2	Pa.
Helium[2]	mil. cu. ft	4,386	4,600	883	1,079	1,339	68.7	64.2	20.3	23.9	25.9	Kans., Okla., Tex.
Natural gas	bil. cu. ft	16,040	21,921	21,601	20,109	19,952	2,494.5	3,745.7	6,573.4	8,945.1	11,571.8	Tex., La., Okla., N. Mex.
Natural gas liquids:												
Natural gasoline and cycle products	mil. bbl.[3]	174	206	168	152	150	494.4	603.0	1,107.2	878.7	985.4	} Tex., La., Okla., N. Mex.
LP-gases	mil. bbl.[3]	288	400	448	444	437	417.2	672.1	1,980.8	1,893.9	2,298.6	
Peat	1,000 sh. tons	604	526	706	746	947	6.1	6.0	11.0	12.3	17.1	Mich., Ind., Pa., Ill.
Petroleum (crude)	mil. bbl.[3]	2,849	3,517	3,203	3,057	2,976	8,158.3	11,173.7	21,580.5	23,116.1	24,229.5	Tex., La., Calif., Okla.
Nonmetallic minerals[4]	(X)	(X)	(X)	(X)	(X)	(X)	4,933.0	5,712.0	8,639.0	9,516.0	10,547.0	(NA)
Abrasive stone[4]	sh. tons	3,603	3,055	3,134	2,953	2,696	.7	.6	.7	1.1	1.4	Calif., Vt., Ariz., N.C.
Asbestos	1,000 sh. tons	118	125	109	99	115	10.2	10.7	13.4	14.2	23.7	
Barite	1,000 sh. tons	852	854	1,106	1,318	1,234	10.2	12.8	16.8	21.2	28.7	Nev., Mo., Ark., Ga.
Boron minerals	1,000 sh. tons	807	1,041	1,185	1,172	1,246	64.2	86.8	128.3	158.8	184.9	Calif.
Bromine	mil. lb.	328	350	432	407	440	77.3	60.6	117.7	113.1	107.7	Ark. and Mich.
Calcium chloride	sh. tons	(D)	633	739	594	649	(D)	15.2	24.6	29.0	32.9	Mich. and Calif.
Cement: Portland	mil. sh. tons	69.0	71.6	76.0	65.2	69.2	1,154.4	1,268.7	1,992.7	2,015.6	2,330.4	Calif., Tex., Pa., Mich.
Masonry	mil. sh. tons	3.3	3.0	3.4	2.9	3.3	66.0	67.5	111.1	111.8	139.6	Ind., Pa., Ala., Mich.
Clays	mil. sh. tons	55.1	54.9	60.8	49.0	52.4	204.9	267.9	422.5	424.6	528.7	Ga., Ohio, Tex., N.C.
Diatomite	1,000 sh. tons	(D)	598	664	573	631	(D)	32.6	50.7	45.8	55.0	Calif., Nev., Wash.
Emery	1,000 sh. tons	10.7	(D)	(D)	3.5	(D)	.2	(D)	(D)	(5)	(D)	N.Y.
Feldspar	1,000 sh. tons	699	726	763	670	740	6.3	9.6	11.4	11.7	17.5	N.Y., Conn., Calif., Ga.
Fluorspar	1,000 sh. tons	240	269	201	140	188	10.9	13.9	14.3	10.9	17.9	Ill., Ky., Tex., Nev.
Garnet (abrasive)	1,000 sh. tons	19.3	18.8	24.7	17.2	24.6	1.7	1.9	2.6	1.7	2.7	Idaho and N.Y.
Gem stones (estimate)	(X)	(NA)	(NA)	(NA)	(NA)	(NA)	2.2	2.4	4.6	13.9	8.9	Ariz., Nev., Maine, Oreg.
Gypsum	mil. sh. tons	10.0	9.4	12.0	9.8	12.0	37.4	35.1	52.9	44.7	59.9	Mich., Calif., Iowa, Tex.
Lime	mil. sh. tons	16.8	19.7	21.6	19.1	20.2	232.9	286.2	473.7	523.8	609.0	Ohio, Pa., Mich., Mo.
Magnesium compounds[6]	1,000 sh. tons	638	708	908	(D)	(D)	47.2	62.4	96.7	(5)	(D)	Mich., Calif., N.J., Fla.
Mica: Scrap	1,000 sh. tons	120	119	137	135	127	3.5	2.5	5.5	5.2	5.7	N.C., Ala., N. Mex., Ga.
Sheet	1,000 lb.	716	-	20.0	5.0	5.0	(2)	-	(Z)	(Z)	(Z)	N.C.
Perlite	1,000 sh. tons	392	456	555	512	553	3.4	4.9	7.0	7.3	9.4	N. Mex., Ariz., Calif., Idaho
Phosphate rock	mil. sh. tons	29.5	38.7	45.7	48.8	49.2	193.3	203.2	501.4	1,122.7	949.4	Fla., Idaho, N.C., Tenn.
Potassium salts[7]	1,000 sh. tons	3,140	2,729	2,552	2,501	2,500	129.8	98.1	159.1	223.1	202.6	N. Mex., Utah, Calif.
Pumice	1,000 sh. tons	3,371	3,036	3,937	3,892	4,134	6.6	4.7	4.2	11.2	10.5	Oreg., Ariz., Calif., N. Mex.
Pyrites	1,000 lg. tons	875	(D)	424	625	750	5.3	(D)	4.2	4.8	8.2	Tenn., Colo., Ariz.

Mineral	Unit	Quantity					Value					Principal producing States
Salt (common)	mil. sh. tons	34.7	45.9	46.5	41.0	44.2	215.7	304.8	360.8	308.1	431.0	La., Tex., N.Y., Ohio
Sand and gravel	mil. sh. tons	908	944	905	789	585	957.4	1,115.7	1,421.2	1,416.3	1,774.0	Calif., Alaska, Mich., Tex.
Sodium carbonate (natural)	1,000 sh. tons	1,494	2,688	4,059	4,328	5,216	34.7	56.3	137.5	182.6	259.3	Wyo., and Calif.
Sodium sulfate (natural)	1,000 sh. tons	620	602	684	667	663	11.0	10.9	16.4	27.7	32.7	Calif., Tex., Utah.
Stone [8]	mil. sh. tons	780	875	1,044	901	902	1,203.8	1,474.9	2,186.2	2,120.3	2,221.0	Ill., Pa., Tex., Mo.
Sulfur: Frasch-process mines	1,000 lg. tons	7,251	6,419	7,898	6,077	5,860	164.7	151.8	241.1	304.8	300.0	Tex. and La.
Other mines	1,000 lg. tons	3	3				(2)					(X)
Talc, soapstone, pyrophyllite	1,000 sh. tons	863	1,028	1,289	965	1,092	6.3	7.8	9.6	8.9	9.9	Vt., Mont., N.Y., Tex.
Tripoli	1,000 sh. tons	71	68	85	81	124	.4	.5	.6	.6	.8	Ill., Okla., Ark., Pa.
Vermiculite	1,000 sh. tons	249	285	341	330	304	4.5	6.5	10.1	13.8	14.0	Mont. and S.C.
Nonmetallic minerals, undistributed [9]	(X)	(X)	(X)	(X)	(X)	(X)	66.0	34.4	34.1	157.2	169.5	(X)
Metals.		(X)	(X)	(X)	(X)	(X)	2,544.0	3,928.0	5,501.0	5,191.0	6,086.0	(X)
Antimony ore and concentrate	sh. tons [10]	845	1,130	661	886	283	(11)	(11)	2.0	2.1	(11)	Mont. and Idaho.
Bauxite	1,000 lg. tons [12]	1,654	2,082	1,949	1,772	1,958	18.6	30.1	25.7	25.1	26.6	Ark., Ala., Ga.
Copper [13]	1,000 sh. tons [13]	1,352	1,720	1,597	1,413	1,606	957.0	1,984.5	2,469.0	1,814.8	2,235.0	Ariz., Utah, N. Mex., Mont.
Gold [13]	1,000 troy oz.	1,705	1,743	1,127	1,052	1,048	59.7	63.4	180.0	169.9	131.3	Nev., S. Dak., Utah, Ariz.
Iron ore, usable [14]	mil. lg. tons [15]	84.1	87.2	85.0	75.7	76.7	801.4	941.7	1,388.4	1,620.6	1,860.1	Minn., Mich., Calif., Wyo.
Lead [13]	1,000 sh. tons	301	572	664	621	610	94.0	178.6	298.7	267.2	281.6	Mo., Idaho, Colo., Utah.
Manganese ore [16]	1,000 sh. tons [16]	29.3	4.7	-	-	-	(11)	(11)	-	-	-	Minn., N. Mex., S.C.
Manganiferous ore [17]	1,000 sh. tons [16]	333	368	273	159	257	(11)	(11)	2.3	1.4	2.3	Nev. and Calif.
Mercury	76 lb. flasks	19,582	27,296	2,189	7,366	23,133	11.2	11.1	.6	1.2	2.8	Calif.
Molybdenum [18]	mil. lb.	77	110	118	105	115	120.8	190.1	234.7	259.3	333.5	Colo., Ariz., N. Mex., Utah
Nickel [19]	1,000 sh. tons	16.2	15.9	16.6	17.0	16.5	(11)	(11)	(11)	(11)	(11)	Oreg.
Silver [13]	mil. troy oz.	39.8	45.0	33.8	34.9	34.3	51.5	79.7	159.0	154.4	149.3	Idaho, Ariz., Colo., Mont.
Tin content of concentrate	lg. tons	47	(D)	139	(D)	(D)	(11)	(11)	(11)	(11)	(11)	Colo. and N. Mex.
Titanium concentrate: Ilmenite [13]	1,000 sh. tons [15]	949	921	755	702	618	18.1	18.6	22.7	26.9	27.6	Fla., N.J., N.Y.
Tungsten ore and concentrate	1,000 lb. [20]	7,566	9,312	7,836	5,490	5,869	13.0	23.8	29.1	37.4	37.3	Calif., Colo., Nev.
Uranium [13]	mil. lb.	19.7	24.7	23.2	22.9	25.1	157.8	149.5	276.1	192.6	404.8	N. Mex., Wyo., Utah, Colo.
Vanadium [13]	sh. tons [13]	5,226	5,226	4,870	4,743	7,376	18.3	34.9	49.3	38.3	81.3	Ark., Colo., Idaho, Utah.
Zinc [13]	1,000 sh. tons	611	534	500	469	485	178.3	163.7	366.1	358.9	358.5	Mo., Tenn., N.Y., Colo.
Metals, undistributed [9]	(X)	(X)	(X)	(X)	(X)	(X)	44.3	58.4	127.5	89.7	153.5	(X)

- Represents zero.   N.A. Not available.   Z Less than $50,000.   X Not applicable.   D Withheld to avoid disclosing individual company data.   [1] Contains bituminous limestone and sandstone, and gilsonite.   [2] Crude and refined.   [3] 42 gal. bbl.   [4] Grindstones, pulpstones, millstones, grinding pebbles, sharpening stones, and tube-mill liners.   [5] Value included in "Nonmetallic minerals, undistributed."   [6] From sea water and brines, except for metals (MgO equiv.).   [7] K_2O equivalent.   [8] Excludes abrasive stone, bituminous limestone and sandstone, and ground soapstone, all included elsewhere in table. Includes calcareous marl and slate.

[9] Comprises value of items that cannot be disclosed.   [10] Antimony content.   [11] Included with "Metals, undistributed."   [12] Dried equivalent.   [13] Recoverable content of ores, etc.   [14] Excluding byproduct iron sinter.   [15] Gross weight.   [16] 35 percent or more Mn.   [17] 5 to 35 percent Mn.   [18] Content of concentrate.   [19] Content of ore and concentrate.   [20] Tungsten content.

Source: U.S. Bureau of Mines, *Minerals Yearbook*.

No. 1309. MINERAL PRODUCTION—VALUE, 1965 TO 1976, AND RANK AND PRINCIPAL MINERALS IN ORDER OF VALUE, 1976, BY STATES

[In millions of dollars]

REGION AND STATE	1965	1970	1974	1975	1976 Value	1976 Rank	1976 Principal minerals in order of value
U.S___	21,524	29,791	55,077	62,266	69,178	(X)	**Petroleum, coal, natural gas, natural gas liquids.**
N.E_____	113	143	187	181	203	(X)	(X)
Maine__	18	24	36	37	40	45	Sand and gravel, cement, zinc, stone.
N.H___	8	9	14	17	18	48	Sand and gravel, clays, gemstones.
Vt_____	27	28	34	29	35	46	Stone, asbestos, sand and gravel, talc.
Mass____	36	50	62	59	70	43	Stone, sand and gravel, lime, clays.
R.I.____	3	4	6	6	6	49	Sand and gravel, stone, gemstones.
Conn___	21	28	35	33	34	47	Stone, sand and gravel, feldspar, lime.
M.A_____	1,284	1,485	2,956	3,430	3,589	(X)	(X)
N.Y____	290	300	441	398	428	29	Cement, stone, salt, sand and gravel.
N.J_____	80	89	141	124	120	40	Sand & gravel, stone, zinc, titanium concentrate.
Pa_____	914	1,096	2,374	2,908	3,041	6	Coal, cement, stone, lime.
E.N.C_____	1,915	2,316	3,846	4,813	5,300	(X)	(X)
Ohio___	464	612	1,108	1,356	1,436	14	Coal, petroleum, lime, stone.
Ind_____	219	256	441	542	607	24	Coal, cement, stone, petroleum.
Ill_____	593	689	1,148	1,491	1,581	12	Coal, petroleum, stone, sand and gravel.
Mich___	566	671	1,035	1,292	1,544	13	Iron ore, petroleum, cement, natural gas.
Wis_____	73	88	115	132	132	37	Sand and gravel, stone, iron ore, cement.
W.N.C____	1,629	1,962	3,144	3,403	3,902	(X)	(X)
Minn____	508	633	1,026	1,097	1,218	15	Iron ore, sand and gravel, stone, lime.
Iowa____	113	121	177	196	216	32	Cement, stone, sand and gravel, coal.
Mo_____	226	393	691	723	785	21	Lead, cement, stone, iron ore.
N. Dak_	94	96	159	202	244	30	Petroleum, coal, natural gas, natural gas liquids.
S. Dak_	51	62	103	102	102	42	Gold, cement, stone, sand and gravel.
Nebr____	84	73	99	112	123	39	Petroleum, cement, sand and gravel, stone.
Kans___	553	584	889	971	1,214	16	Petroleum, natural gas, natural gas liquids, sulfur.
S.A_____	1,693	2,406	5,304	7,191	7,254	(X)	(X)
Del_____	2	2	4	2	2	50	Sand and gravel, magnesium compounds, clays, gemstones.
Md_____	78	88	173	165	185	36	Coal, stone, cement, sand and gravel.
Va_____	268	374	1,057	1,262	1,161	17	Coal, stone, cement, lime.
W.Va__	860	1,285	2,403	3,390	3,498	3	Coal, natural gas, petroleum, natural gas liquids.
N.C____	60	98	156	153	203	34	Stone, phosphate rock, sand and gravel, lithium minerals.
S.C_____	41	56	105	115	125	38	Cement, stone, clays, sand and gravel.
Ga_____	135	203	363	333	428	28	Clays, stone, cement, sand and gravel.
Fla_____	249	300	1,044	1,771	1,652	11	Phosphate rock, petroleum, cement, stone.
E.S.C_____	1,105	1,640	4,115	4,541	5,035	(X)	(X)
Ky_____	466	847	2,563	2,739	3,115	5	Coal, petroleum, stone, natural gas.
Tenn___	183	220	396	423	440	27	Coal, stone, zinc, cement.
Ala_____	246	323	765	969	1,030	20	Coal, petroleum, cement, stone.
Miss____	210	250	391	410	450	26	Petroleum, natural gas, cement, sand & gravel.
W.S.C____	8,795	12,868	24,384	26,741	30,120	(X)	(X)
Ark_____	179	226	406	436	535	25	Petroleum, bromine, natural gas, cement.
La_____	2,988	5,102	8,147	8,513	8,652	2	Petroleum, natural gas, natural gas liquids, sulfur.
Okla___	909	1,138	2,123	2,267	2,790	7	Petroleum, natural gas, natural gas liquids, coal.
Tex_____	4,719	6,402	13,708	15,525	18,143	1	Petroleum, natural gas, natural gas liquids, cement.
Mt_____	3,117	4,545	7,639	8,014	9,323	(X)	(X)
Mont___	228	313	575	573	636	22	Petroleum, coal, copper, cement.
Idaho__	105	120	209	234	210	33	Silver, phosphate rock, zinc, lead.
Wyo____	515	706	1,421	1,644	1,852	9	Petroleum, sodium compounds, coal, natural gas.
Colo____	340	390	746	958	1,110	18	Petroleum, molybdenum, coal, natural gas.
N. Mex.	807	1,060	1,920	2,092	2,510	8	Petroleum, natural gas, copper, natural gas liquids.
Ariz____	583	1,167	1,562	1,288	1,727	10	Copper, molybdenum, sand and gravel, cement.
Utah___	439	603	948	966	1,044	19	Petroleum, copper, coal, uranium.
Nev_____	100	186	258	259	234	31	Copper, gold, sand and gravel, barite.
Pac_____	1,873	2,426	3,505	3,949	4,450	(X)	(X)
Wash___	88	91	143	159	187	35	Cement, coal, sand and gravel, stone.
Oreg___	83	68	104	106	113	41	Stone, sand and gravel, cement, nickel.
Calif___	1,597	1,900	2,797	3,153	3,483	4	Petroleum, natural gas, cement, sand and gravel.
Alaska_	84	338	419	481	625	23	Petroleum, sand and gravel, natural gas, stone.
Hawaii_	21	29	42	50	42	44	Stone, cement, sand and gravel, pumice.

X   Not applicable.

Source: U.S. Bureau of Mines, *Minerals Yearbook.*

No. 1310. Principal Fuels, Nonmetals, and Metals—U.S. Production as Percent of World Production: 1965 to 1976

MINERAL	Unit	WORLD PRODUCTION					PERCENT U.S. OF WORLD				
		1965	1970	1974	1975	1976, prel.	1965	1970	1974	1975	1976, prel.
Fuels: [1]											
Coal	bil. sh. tons	3.1	3.3	3.5	3.6	3.7	17	18	18	18	18
Petroleum (crude)	bil. bbl	11.1	16.7	20.5	19.5	21.2	26	21	16	16	14
Natural gas (marketable)	tril. cu. ft	(NA)	37.9	47.2	47.5	49.5	(NA)	58	46	42	40
Nonmetals:											
Asbestos	1,000 sh. tons	3,140	3,851	4,589	4,564	5,566	4	3	2	2	2
Barite	1,000 sh. tons	3,860	4,338	4,944	5,358	5,457	22	20	22	25	23
Feldspar	1,000 sh. tons	2,162	2,786	3,310	2,893	2,850	32	26	23	23	26
Fluorspar	1,000 sh. tons	3,110	4,620	5,337	5,015	4,889	8	4	4	3	4
Gypsum	mil. sh. tons	53.0	56.9	64.6	62.9	66.2	19	17	19	16	18
Mica (incl. scrap)	1,000 sh. tons	218	180	208	250	236	55	66	53	54	54
Nitrogen, agricultural [2]	mil. sh. tons	18.5	33.4	44.6	46.7	48.4	27	25	23	20	21
Phosphate rock	mil. sh. tons	70.3	93.6	122.1	118.3	117.9	34	41	37	41	42
Potash (K₂O equiv.)	mil. sh. tons	15.1	20.0	26.4	27.4	26.9	21	14	10	9	9
Sulphur, elemental	mil. lg. tons	15.3	22.2	49.4	50.2	50.1	48	39	23	22	21
Metals, mine basis:											
Bauxite	mil. lg. tons	36.8	56.9	76.8	74.5	76.3	4	4	3	2	3
Copper [3]	1,000 sh. tons	5,590	6,638	8,063	7,672	8,213	24	26	20	18	20
Gold	mil. troy oz	46.2	47.5	39.9	38.7	39.9	4	4	3	3	3
Iron ore	mil. lg. tons	611	754	899	887	881	14	12	9	9	9
Lead [3]	1,000 sh. tons	2,990	3,742	3,832	3,750	3,701	10	15	17	17	16
Mercury	1,000 flasks [4]	276	284	261	252	244	7	10	1	3	9
Molybdenum [3]	mil. lb	115	181	189	177	191	67	61	59	60	59
Nickel [3]	1,000 sh. tons	468	692	871	868	886	3	2	2	2	2
Silver	mil. troy oz	257	301	295	298	305	16	15	11	12	11
Titanium concentrates:											
Ilmenite [5]	1,000 sh. tons	2,723	3,962	3,099	3,218	3,512	36	23	24	22	19
Tungsten	mil. lb	59.8	71.4	81.5	84.3	91.8	13	13	9	7	6
Uranium oxide (U₃O₈) [5]	1,000 sh. tons	21	24	25	27	30	49	53	47	43	42
Vanadium [3]	1,000 sh. tons	9.1	20.2	21.1	23.2	25.9	58	26	23	20	28
Zinc [3]	1,000 sh. tons	4,695	6,023	6,281	6,428	6,490	13	9	8	7	7
Metals, smelter basis:											
Aluminum	mil. sh. tons	7.0	10.6	14.5	13.4	13.8	37	37	34	29	31
Cadmium	mil. lb	26.1	36.5	38.1	33.9	37.8	27	26	18	13	12
Copper	1,000 sh. tons	6,105	6,752	8,111	7,793	8,164	24	24	19	19	19
Iron, pig (incl. ferroalloys)	mil. sh. tons	369	474	565	529	549	25	19	17	15	16
Lead	1,000 sh. tons	2,911	3,628	3,858	3,656	3,788	14	18	17	17	17
Magnesium	1,000 sh. tons	178	242	145	138	148	46	46	(NA)	(NA)	(NA)
Steel ingots and castings	mil. sh. tons	507	655	780	713	748	26	20	19	16	17
Tin	1,000 m. tons [6]	200	227	236	231	229	2	(NA)	3	3	2
Zinc	1,000 sh. tons	4,353	5,321	6,022	5,592	5,978	23	16	9	8	8

NA Not available.   [1] Source: U.S. Dept. of Energy, *Annual Report to the President.*   [2] For years ending June 30. U.S. production includes Puerto Rico.   [3] Content of ore and concentrate.   [4] 76-lb. flasks.   [5] Excludes U.S.S.R.   [6] Metric tons.

Source: Except as noted, U.S. Bureau of Mines, *Minerals Yearbook,* annual.

No. 1311. Federal Strategic and Critical Materials Inventory: 1965 to 1977

[In millions of dollars. As of Dec. 31. Covers strategic and critical materials essential to military and industrial requirements in time of national emergency. Market values are estimated current trade values of similar materials and not necessarily amount that would be realized at time of sale]

INVENTORY	1965	1970	1972	1973	1974	1975	1976	1977
Acquisition cost:								
Total in storage	8,033	6,373	5,957	5,220	4,136	3,960	3,852	3,721
National stockpile	5,285	4,248	3,948	3,421	2,661	2,555	2,479	2,501
Supplemental stockpile	1,403	1,420	1,360	1,289	1,130	1,095	1,076	1,059
Defense Production Act	1,341	705	649	510	346	310	297	161
Market value:								
Total in storage	7,804	7,105	6,694	7,400	8,037	7,433	8,160	9,153
National stockpile	5,642	5,081	4,894	5,612	5,742	5,259	6,014	7,122
Supplemental stockpile	1,317	1,587	1,438	1,502	2,080	1,948	1,900	1,393
Defense Production Act	841	437	362	286	215	226	246	138

Source: U.S. General Services Administration, *Statistical Supplement, Stockpile Report to the Congress* (OP-4).

No. 1312. U.S. Direct Investment Abroad in Mining and Smelting and in Petroleum—Value, 1966 to 1977, and Earnings, 1977, by Country

[Minus sign (−) denotes loss. See also *Historical Statistics, Colonial Times to 1970*, series U 41–46]

COUNTRY	DIRECT INVESTMENT POSITION [1] (mil. dol.)								EARNINGS, 1977 [2] (mil. dol.)	
	Mining and smelting				Petroleum				Mining, smelting	Petroleum
	1966	1970	1975	1977 [2]	1966	1970	1975	1977 [2]		
All areas	3,983	5,405	6,548	7,066	13,893	19,754	25,972	30,887	750	5,470
Developed countries	2,328	3,286	4,398	4,802	7,661	11,205	20,129	24,854	541	2,001
Canada	1,976	2,574	3,053	3,212	3,171	4,337	6,220	7,722	219	1,002
Europe	19	36	41	40	3,627	5,481	11,165	13,926	−3	727
Japan	−	−	−	−	287	525	1,313	1,549	−	79
Australia, New Zealand, and South Africa	333	675	1,305	1,549	576	863	1,430	1,657	325	193
Developing countries	1,655	2,119	2,150	2,265	5,051	6,644	2,519	3,014	209	3,451
Latin America	1,340	1,712	1,476	1,579	2,456	2,703	3,324	3,378	178	601
Africa [3]	(D)	340	488	544	791	1,750	1,336	1,520	31	456
Middle East [4]	(Z)	(Z)	5	9	1,277	1,265	−4,888	−4,378	2	1,606
Other Asia and Pacific	(D)	67	181	132	527	926	2,746	2,493	−2	788
Internat'l and unallocated	(X)	(X)	(X)	(X)	1,180	1,905	3,323	3,019	(X)	18

− Represents zero.   D Withheld to avoid disclosure of individual company data.   X Not applicable.
Z Less than $500,000.   [1] Value at yearend.   [2] Preliminary.   [3] Excludes South Africa.   [4] Includes Bahrain, Iran, Israel, Jordan, Kuwait, Lebanon, Qatar, Saudi Arabia, South Yemen, Syria, Trucial States, Oman, and Yemen. Negative direct investment position occurs when U.S. parent company's liabilities to the foreign affiliate are greater than its investment in the foreign affiliate. For further explanation, see the June 1977 issue of source.

Source: U.S. Bureau of Economic Analysis, *Survey of Current Business*, Aug., Sept., and Oct. issues.

No. 1313. Net U.S. Imports of Selected Minerals and Metals as Percent of Apparent Consumption, 1960 to 1977, and by Major Foreign Sources, 1973–1976

[In percent. Figures based on net imports which equal the difference between imports and exports plus or minus Government stockpile and industry stock changes]

MINERAL	1960	1965	1970	1972	1973	1974	1975	1976	1977	Rank of major foreign sources, 1973–1976
Columbium	100	100	100	100	100	100	100	100	100	Brazil, Thailand, Nigeria, Malaysia.
Mica (sheet)	94	94	100	100	100	100	100	100	100	India, Brazil, Malagasy Republic.
Strontium	100	100	100	100	100	100	100	100	100	Mexico, Spain.
Manganese	89	94	95	98	98	98	98	98	98	Brazil, Gabon, South Africa.
Cobalt	66	92	98	98	98	99	98	98	97	Zaire, Belg.-Lux., Norway, Finland.
Tantalum	94	95	96	96	87	87	81	96	97	Thailand, Canada, Australia, Brazil.
Platinum group	82	87	78	82	87	87	83	90	92	South Africa, U.S.S.R., U.K.
Bauxite [1]	74	85	88	90	92	92	91	91	91	Jamaica, Australia, Surinam, Guinea.
Chromium	85	92	89	91	91	90	91	89	89	South Africa, U.S.S.R., Turkey.
Tin	82	80	81	83	84	84	84	85	86	Malaysia, Thailand, Bolivia, Indonesia.
Asbestos	94	85	83	84	82	87	82	85	85	Canada, South Africa.
Fluorine	48	77	80	77	79	81	85	79	80	Mexico, Spain, Italy, South Africa.
Nickel	72	73	71	65	69	72	72	70	70	Canada, Norway, New Caledonia, Dom. Rep.
Potassium	(2)	7	42	45	53	58	51	61	66	Canada, Israel.
Gold	56	72	59	71	48	63	52	76	60	Canada, Switzerland, U.S.S.R.
Zinc	46	53	54	61	64	59	61	59	58	Canada, Mexico, Australia, Peru.
Antimony	43	36	40	50	50	44	49	54	52	South Africa, Peo. Rep. of China, Bolivia.
Cadmium	13	20	7	38	41	46	41	64	51	Canada, Australia, Belg.-Lux.
Selenium	25	44	11	24	57	59	66	59	47	Canada, Japan, Mexico, Yugoslavia.
Petroleum [3]	16	19	21	29	35	37	35	41	46	Saudi Arabia, Nigeria, Libya, Venezuela.
Mercury	25	49	41	61	78	86	69	62	46	Spain, Algeria, Mexico, Yugoslavia.
Silver	43	16	26	50	66	55	30	50	42	Canada, Mexico, Peru, U.K.
Barium	45	46	45	39	37	38	32	42	40	Peru, Ireland, Mexico.
Titanium [4]	22	9	24	28	28	33	25	29	38	Canada, Australia.
Tungsten	32	57	50	43	66	68	55	54	38	Canada, Bolivia, Peru, Thailand.
Vanadium	(2)	15	21	27	43	36	38	37	37	South Africa, Chile, U.S.S.R.
Gypsum	35	37	39	38	35	37	34	35	35	Canada, Mexico, Jamaica, Dom. Rep.
Iron ore	18	32	30	37	35	37	30	29	33	Canada, Venezuela, Brazil, Liberia.
Iron and steel	(2)	7	4	17	10	7	9	7	13	Japan, Europe, Canada.
Aluminum	(2)	4	(2)	12	18	4	(2)	9	8	Canada.

[1] Includes alumina.   [2] Net exports.   [3] Includes natural gas liquids. Source: Beginning 1977, Energy Information Administration, *P.A.D. Supply and Demand*, annual.   [4] Ilmenite.

Source: Except as noted, U.S. Bureau of Mines, *Minerals Yearbook*; import and export data from U.S. Bureau of the Census.

No. 1314. SELECTED MINERAL AND METAL PRODUCTS—IMPORTS AND EXPORTS: 1965 TO 1977

[Includes trade of Puerto Rico with foreign countries]

PRODUCT	Unit	QUANTITY					VALUE (mil. dol.)				
		1965	1970	1975	1976	1977	1965	1970	1975	1976	1977
IMPORTS [1]											
Petroleum, crude	Mil. bbl	502	535	1,581	2,051	2,508	1,120	1,260	18,290	25,456	33,398
Nonmetallic minerals:											
Asbestos	1,000 sh. tons	684	639	525	619	587	66	74	108	134	141
Diamonds: Gem	Mil. carats	3.2	4.3	4.6	5.6	6.4	307	425	722	1,012	1,445
Industrial	Mil. carats	12.2	11.2	10.9	12.2	15.5	54	44	45	51	65
Ores and concentrates:											
Bauxite	Mil. lg. tons	12.5	14.3	11.6	12.6	13.2	143	156	235	304	339
Chromite	1,000 sh. tons	1,518	1,406	1,253	1,261	1,293	25	32	61	70	66
Copper	1,000 sh. tons [2]	11	66	29	35	18	6	79	36	50	21
Iron ore	Mil. lg. tons	45.1	44.9	46.7	44.4	37.9	444	479	860	980	957
Lead	1,000 sh. tons [2]	129	43	45	89	98	27	8	12	29	40
Manganese ore	1,000 sh. tons	3,892	1,735	1,574	1,325	937	110	34	77	74	57
Nickel [3]	1,000 sh. tons [2]	31	33	23	26	23	41	96	78	120	96
Tin	1,000 lg. tons [2]	4	5	6	6	7	13	14	44	39	61
Tungsten	Sh. tons [2]	1,802	642	3,235	2,650	3,597	4	3	32	28	56
Metals (incl. scrap): [4]											
Aluminum	1,000 sh. tons	555	387	489	661	388	227	177	344	485	101
Copper	1,000 sh. tons	137	137	164	449	468	94	154	188	490	512
Lead [5]	1,000 sh. tons	232	253	105	149	270	70	80	53	66	162
Nickel	1,000 sh. tons	136	137	176	179	198	208	327	520	581	620
Platinum group	1,000 troy oz	1,220	1,411	1,719	2,657	2,519	73	105	255	290	272
Tin [6]	1,000 lg. tons	41	51	52	47	48	160	188	315	329	462
Zinc	1,000 sh. tons	159	262	380	702	571	44	74	275	484	363
EXPORTS [7]											
Fuels:											
Bituminous coal	Mil. sh. tons	50.3	71.0	65.8	59.5	35.4	466	955	3,242	2,897	1,724
Petroleum, crude	1,000 bbl	1,004	4,991	19	2,242	16,459	3	17	(z)	27	209
Nonmetallic minerals:											
Cement, hydraulic	1,000 bbl	748	847	988	932	478	4	5	28	27	24
Phosphate rock	1,000 sh. tons	862	815	1,285	1,084	1,187	11	10	37	27	28
Potash material	1,000 sh. tons	1,099	1,046	1,524	1,730	1,690	43	37	112	111	109
Sulfur [8]	1,000 lg. tons	2,635	1,433	1,288	1,183	1,059	66	34	70	60	48
Metals (incl. scrap): [4]											
Aluminum [9]	1,000 sh. tons	242	466	253	261	199	105	236	163	182	159
Copper [9]	1,000 sh. tons	424	348	145	115	241	312	403	126	103	103
Iron and steel, scrap [10]	1,000 sh. tons	6,170	10,112	9,442	7,879	5,854	197	432	763	602	381
Molybdenum [9]	Sh. tons	55	336	159	112	166	(z)	1	1	(z)	1

Z Less than $500,000.   [1] Imports for consumption.   [2] Of metal.   [3] Includes matte and oxide.
[4] Excludes semifabricated forms, except as noted.   [5] Includes alloys in chief value of lead.
[6] Includes alloys in chief value of tin.   [7] Includes shipments under foreign aid programs.
[8] Includes crude (containing 85 percent or more sulfur), crushed, ground, refined, sublimed, and flowers.
[9] Includes alloys.   [10] Includes tin plated and terne plated scrap.

Source: U.S. Bureau of the Census, *U.S. Imports for Consumption and General Imports, TSUSA Commodity and Country*, FT 246, annual; *U.S. Exports, Schedule B Commodity and Country*, FT 410, monthly; and unpublished data.

No. 1315. SELECTED MINERAL INDUSTRIES—AVERAGE WEEKLY AND HOURLY EARNINGS AND WEEKLY HOURS: 1960 TO 1976

ITEM	1960	1965	1968	1969	1970	1971	1972	1973	1974	1975	1976
All mining:											
Weekly earnings dol	104	122	141	153	160	168	181	196	213	229	256
Hourly earnings dol	2.45	2.77	3.20	3.43	3.66	3.87	4.17	4.47	4.91	5.42	5.99
Weekly hours	42.5	44.0	44.3	44.6	43.8	43.5	43.4	44.0	43.5	42.4	42.9
Crude petroleum and natural gas:											
Weekly earnings dol	103	116	138	147	156	160	170	192	224	249	273
Hourly earnings dol	2.46	2.74	3.39	3.59	3.83	3.75	3.97	4.69	5.33	6.05	6.59
Weekly hours	42.0	42.4	40.7	41.0	40.7	42.6	42.8	40.9	42.0	40.8	41.4
Coal mining:											
Weekly earnings dol	110	138	153	167	184	194	216	227	237	283	312
Hourly earnings dol	3.11	3.46	3.83	4.20	4.52	4.79	5.30	5.69	6.20	7.21	7.88
Weekly hours	35.5	39.9	40.0	39.7	40.6	40.6	41.0	39.9	38.2	39.3	39.5
Metal mining:											
Weekly earnings dol	111	127	148	157	166	171	186	200	227	251	281
Hourly earnings dol	2.68	3.06	3.42	3.65	3.88	4.12	4.47	4.76	5.43	6.13	6.75
Weekly hours	41.6	41.6	43.3	43.1	42.7	41.6	41.5	42.1	41.8	40.9	41.6
Nonmetal mining incl. quarrying:											
Weekly earnings dol	98	117	137	149	156	165	177	197	209	211	237
Hourly earnings dol	2.27	2.57	3.04	3.27	3.48	3.68	3.95	4.18	4.52	4.85	5.38
Weekly hours	43.3	45.7	44.9	45.6	44.7	44.9	44.8	47.1	46.3	43.5	44.0

Source: U.S. Bureau of Mines, *Minerals Yearbook*.

No. 1316. Selected Mineral Industries—Employment: 1950 to 1976

[Prior to 1972, excludes Alaska and Hawaii, except as noted. Beginning 1972, no estimates of persons or man-hours were made to cover nonrespondent establishments and, beginning 1973, data for all industries except coal mines include office workers. See also *Historical Statistics, Colonial Times to 1970*, series M 287–306]

INDUSTRY	1950	1955	1960	1965	1970	1972	1973	1974	1975	1976
PERSONS WORKING DAILY [1] (1,000)										
Coal mines	[2] 483	[2] 260	[2] 190	[2] 149	[2] 144	162	147	177	218	215
Metal mines	[2] 68	[2] 65	[2] 61	[2] 51	[2] 46	40	56	59	61	60
Nonmetal mines [3]	[2] 12	[2] 15	[2] 19	[2] 17	[2] 15	[4] 12	[4] 20	[4] 22	[4] 25	[4] 21
Sand and gravel operations	(NA)	(NA)	52	54	51	31	39	47	50	45
Stone quarries [5]	86	78	95	90	82	64	81	88	86	93
Metal mills	15	18	23	19	22	18	27	30	33	33
Nonmetal mills	(NA)	9	40	31	27	[4] 20	23	25	24	26
MAN-HOURS WORKED (mil.)										
Coal mines	[2] 711	[2] 419	[2] 282	[2] 249	[2] 260	268	278	297	368	383
Metal mines	[2] 148	[2] 137	[2] 120	[2] 112	[2] 108	95	108	115	113	114
Nonmetal mines [3]	[2] 28	[2] 31	[2] 37	[2] 38	[2] 32	[4] 25	[4] 35	[4] 38	[4] 43	[4] 38
Sand and gravel operations	(NA)	(NA)	96	100	95	57	58	62	65	65
Stone quarries [5]	190	176	202	194	184	144	145	152	146	170
Metal mills	35	40	54	49	57	45	52	55	59	67
Nonmetal mills	(NA)	20	86	71	62	[4] 47	44	47	46	52

NA Not available.   [1] Average number of persons at work each day mines were active.   [2] Includes Alaska.   [3] Includes clay mines. Beginning 1960, includes Hawaii.   [4] Excludes extraction of Frasch process sulfur.   [5] Includes manufacture of cement and lime, except, beginning 1972, excludes cement manufacturing. Beginning 1960, includes Alaska and Hawaii.

Source: 1950–1970, U.S. Bureau of Mines, *Minerals Yearbook*, and unpublished data; thereafter, U.S. Mining Enforcement and Safety Administration, Denver, Colorado, unpublished data.

No. 1317. Mineral Industries—Injuries and Fatalities: 1950 to 1976

[Prior to 1972, data for coal mining and metal and nonmetal mining exclude Hawaii, except as noted. Excludes data on iron smelting and steel industries. See also *Historical Statistics, Colonial Times to 1970*, series M 271–286]

ITEM	1950	1955	1960	1965	1970	1972	1973	1974	1975	1976
Coal mining:										
Injuries, total	37,907	19,305	12,227	11,397	11,812	12,485	11,352	8,678	11,262	14,530
Fatal	643	420	325	259	260	156	132	133	155	141
Nonfatal	37,264	18,885	11,902	11,138	11,552	12,329	11,220	8,545	11,107	14,389
Rate per million man-hours:										
Fatal	.9	1.0	1.2	1.0	1.0	.6	.5	.5	.4	.4
Nonfatal	52	45	42	45	44	46	40	29	30	38
Fatalities per 1,000 employed [1]	1.33	1.61	1.71	1.74	1.81	.96	.90	.75	.71	.66
Quarrying and related industries: [2] [3]										
Injuries, total	4,816	3,864	4,707	3,353	3,709	3,038	2,501	2,664	2,566	2,926
Fatal	54	53	39	48	43	46	60	48	36	33
Nonfatal	4,762	3,811	4,668	3,305	3,666	2,992	2,441	2,616	2,530	2,893
Rate per million man-hours:										
Fatal	.3	.3	.2	.3	.2	.3	.4	.3	.2	.2
Nonfatal	25	22	23	17	20	21	17	17	17	17
Metal and nonmetal mining: [2] [4]										
Injuries, total	8,744	8,343	7,253	6,328	6,730	5,392	5,037	5,460	5,169	4,923
Fatal	110	104	121	92	93	152	75	71	66	56
Nonfatal	8,634	8,239	7,132	6,236	6,637	5,240	4,962	5,389	5,103	4,867
Rate per million man-hours:										
Fatal	.6	.6	.8	.6	.7	.7	.3	.3	.3	.2
Nonfatal	49	49	45	42	47	25	21	21	20	18
Rate per 1,000 workers: [1]										
Fatal	1.4	1.3	1.5	1.4	1.5	1.7	.6	.5	.5	.4
Nonfatal	108	103	89	92	109	58	39	40	36	35

[1] See footnote 1, table 1316.   [2] Includes office workers.   [3] Includes manufacture of cement and lime, except, beginning 1972, excludes cement manufacturing.   [4] Beginning 1960, nonmetal mines include clay mines and also Hawaii. Beginning 1972, nonmetal mines exclude extraction of Frasch process sulfur.

Source: 1950–1970, U.S. Bureau of Mines, *Minerals Yearbook*, and unpublished data; thereafter, U.S. Mining Enforcement and Safety Administration, Denver, Colorado, unpublished data.

No. 1318. COAL AND COKE—SUMMARY: 1960 TO 1977

[Includes coal consumed at mines. Demonstrated coal reserve base for United States on Jan. 1, 1974, was 437 billion tons. Recoverability varies between 40 and 90 percent for individual deposits; 50 percent or more of overall U.S. coal reserve base is recoverable. See also *Historical Statistics, Colonial Times to 1970*, series M 93–126]

ITEM	1960	1965	1970	1972	1973	1974	1975	1976	1977 [1]
Total production...mil. sh. tons..	434	527	613	602	599	610	655	685	678
Value................mil. dol..	2,098	2,398	3,878	4,647	5,140	9,631	12,671	13,398	14,330
World production..mil. sh. tons..	2,899	3,079	3,295	3,339	3,399	3,457	3,612	3,727	(NA)
COAL [2]									
Bituminous:									
Production........mil. sh. tons..	416	512	603	595	592	603	648	679	672
Value, total.........mil. dol..	1,950	2,276	3,773	4,562	5,050	9,486	12,472	13,189	14,112
Average per ton....dollars..	4.69	4.44	6.26	7.66	8.53	15.75	19.23	19.43	21.00
Method of mining:									
Underground..mil. sh. tons..	285	333	339	304	299	277	292	295	272
Cut by machine...percent..	67.8	53.9	46.1	37.4	35.8	33.0	32.0	(NA)	(NA)
Surface.........mil. sh. tons..	131	179	264	291	292	326	356	384	400
As percent of total prod....	31.4	35.1	43.8	48.9	49.5	54.0	54.8	56.6	59.5
Exports..........mil. sh. tons..	37	50	71	56	53	60	66	59	54
Value..............mil. dol..	332	465	951	973	1,002	2,420	3,233	2,886	2,628
Imports [3]........1,000 sh. tons..	260	184	36	47	127	2,080	940	1,203	1,803
Value [3]............mil. dol..	2	2	(Z)	1	2	58	22	18	40
Consumption [4]...mil. sh. tons..	380	459	516	517	556	553	556	599	620
Electric power utilities.......	174	243	319	349	387	390	403	447	475
Manufacturing, mining ind...	173	197	184	159	161	154	146	145	138
Number of mines...............	7,865	7,228	5,601	4,879	4,744	5,247	6,168	6,161	6,200
Average men employed [5].1,000..	169	134	140	149	148	167	190	202	215
Average days worked...........	191	219	228	225	227	206	232	232	220
Average tons per man: Per day..	12.83	17.52	18.84	17.74	17.58	17.58	14.74	14.46	14.30
Per year..	2,453	3,829	4,296	3,992	3,991	3,848	3,420	3,355	3,146
Production, by State:									
Alabama........mil. sh. tons..	13.0	14.8	20.6	20.8	19.2	19.8	22.6	21.5	22.0
Illinois.........mil. sh. tons..	46.0	58.5	65.1	65.5	61.6	58.2	59.5	58.2	56.0
Indiana.........mil. sh. tons..	15.5	15.6	22.3	25.9	25.3	23.7	25.1	25.4	24.0
Kentucky.......mil. sh. tons..	66.8	85.8	125.3	121.2	127.6	137.2	143.6	144.0	142.0
Ohio............mil. sh. tons..	34.0	39.4	55.4	51.0	45.8	45.4	46.8	46.6	45.0
Pennsylvania mil. sh. tons..	65.4	80.3	80.5	75.9	70.4	80.5	84.1	83.8	83.0
Virginia........mil. sh. tons..	27.8	34.1	35.0	34.0	34.0	34.3	35.5	40.0	43.0
West Virginia..mil. sh. tons..	118.9	149.2	144.1	123.7	115.4	102.5	109.3	108.8	96.0
Wyoming.......mil. sh. tons..	2.0	3.3	7.2	10.9	14.9	20.7	23.8	30.8	43.0
Other States...mil. sh. tons..	26.0	31.3	47.4	66.4	71.5	81.1	98.1	117.6	116.0
Anthracite (Pa.):									
Production........mil. sh. tons..	19	15	10	7	7	7	6	6	6
Value, total.........mil. dol..	147	122	105	85	90	145	198	209	216
Average per ton....dollars..	7.82	8.21	10.83	12.00	13.65	22.19	31.99	34.14	36.00
COKE									
Production [6]......mil. sh. tons..	57.2	66.9	66.5	60.5	64.3	61.6	57.2	58.3	53.5
Oven coke [7].......mil. sh. tons..	56.2	65.2	65.7	59.9	63.5	60.7	56.5	57.7	53.1
Value of prod. at plant..mil. dol..	1,382	1,429	2,193	2,376	2,931	5,262	5,261	5,941	(NA)
Coke and breeze.......mil. dol..	1,075	1,118	1,899	2,080	2,575	4,609	4,607	5,021	(NA)
Avg. market value per ton...dol..	18.31	16.84	27.71	33.21	37.97	73.24	84.34	86.06	(NA)
Coal charged.......mil. sh. tons..	81.4	95.3	96.5	87.7	94.1	90.2	83.6	84.7	77.7
Average value per ton.dollars..	9.82	9.40	12.47	15.66	18.24	36.49	44.27	44.16	(NA)
Yield of coke from coal..percent..	70.3	70.4	69.1	69.0	68.4	69.3	68.4	68.9	(NA)

NA Not available.   Z Less than $500,000.   [1] Preliminary.   [2] Relates to mines having an output of 1,000 tons a year or more, including lignite and small output of anthracite produced outside Pennsylvania.   [3] Except for 1960, includes anthracite.   [4] Includes some categories not shown separately.   [5] Average number of men working daily.   [6] Includes beehive coke.   [7] Excludes screenings or breeze.

Source: 1960 to 1976, U.S. Bureau of Mines, *Minerals Yearbook;* thereafter, U.S. Energy Information Administration, *Annual Report to Congress*, vol. III.

No. 1319. PETROLEUM INDUSTRY—EXPENDITURES FOR NEW PLANT AND EQUIPMENT, BY FUNCTION: 1960 TO 1977

EXPENDITURE FUNCTION	1960	1965	1970	1971	1972	1973	1974	1975	1976	1977, est.
Total...............bil. dol..	3.0	3.6	5.6	5.9	5.3	5.5	8.0	10.5	11.6	13.0
Production.............bil. dol..	1.6	2.1	2.2	2.2	2.2	2.6	3.9	5.1	5.6	6.6
Refining...............bil. dol..	.6	.9	1.4	1.5	1.2	1.1	2.2	2.9	3.4	3.4
Marketing.............bil. dol..	.5	.7	1.1	1.0	1.0	.6	.5	.5	.6	.7
Transportation........bil. dol..	.2	.2	.4	.5	.3	.4	.5	.8	1.1	1.0
Other.................bil. dol..	.1	.2	.6	.6	.6	.7	.9	1.2	1.1	1.4

Source: U.S. Bureau of Economic Analysis, *Survey of Current Business*, March issues.

No. 1320. PETROLEUM INDUSTRY—SUMMARY: 1940 TO 1977

YEAR	PRODUCING OIL WELLS		COMPLETED WELLS DRILLED (1,000)				DOMESTIC OIL PRODUCTION			Imports, crude petroleum (mil. bbl.)	Refinery capacity (mil. bbl.)
	Total (1,000)	Daily output per well (bbl.)	Total	Oil	Gas	Dry	Total (mil. bbl.)	Value at wells (bil. dol.)	Avg. price per bbl. (dol.)		
1940	389	9.6	30	19	2	7	1,353	1.4	1.02	43	1,694
1945	416	11.3	27	14	3	7	1,714	2.1	1.22	74	1,935
1950	466	11.8	43	24	3	15	1,974	5.0	2.51	178	2,444
1955	524	13.2	57	32	4	21	2,484	6.9	2.77	285	3,074
1960	591	12.0	44	21	5	18	2,575	7.4	2.88	372	3,624
1965	589	13.3	40	19	5	16	2,849	8.2	2.86	452	3,933
1970	531	18.0	27	13	4	11	3,517	11.2	3.18	483	4,407
1971	517	18.1	25	11	4	10	3,454	11.7	3.39	613	4,752
1972	508	18.4	26	11	5	11	3,455	11.7	3.39	811	4,918
1973	497	18.3	26	10	6	10	3,361	13.1	3.89	1,184	5,038
1974	498	17.6	31	13	7	12	3,203	21.6	6.74	1,269	5,289
1975	500	16.8	37	16	8	13	3,057	23.4	7.67	1,498	5,537
1976	499	16.3	41	17	9	15	2,976	24.4	8.19	1,935	5,646
1977, prel.	507	16.3	45	19	11	15	2,985	25.6	8.57	2,397	6,063

Source: 1940–1955, American Petroleum Institute, Washington, D.C., *Petroleum Facts and Figures*, biennial; beginning 1960, U.S. Bureau of Mines, *Minerals Yearbook*.

No. 1321. FUEL CONSUMPTION, BY TYPE OF USE: 1960 TO 1976

FUEL AND USE	CONSUMPTION								PERCENT USE		
	1960	1965	1970	1972	1973	1974	1975	1976 [1]	1965	1970	1976 [1]
Petroleum [2] **mil. bbl.**	3,611	4,202	5,365	5,990	6,317	6,078	5,958	6,391	100	100	100
Fuel use mil. bbl.	3,301	3,802	4,787	5,326	5,606	5,390	5,299	5,676	90	89	89
Nonfuel use mil. bbl.	310	400	578	664	711	688	659	715	10	11	11
Residential and commercial mil. bbl.	853	978	1,129	1,169	1,166	1,058	1,007	1,095	23	21	17
Industrial mil. bbl.	644	740	961	1,105	1,166	1,141	1,046	1,175	18	18	18
Transportation mil. bbl.	1,934	2,272	2,903	3,187	3,349	3,268	3,336	3,503	54	54	55
Electrical generation mil. bbl.	90	119	334	504	587	560	518	553	3	6	9
Miscellaneous mil. bbl.	90	93	38	25	49	51	51	65	2	1	1
Natural gas bil. cu. ft.	12,269	15,598	21,367	22,429	22,245	21,223	19,537	19,947	100	100	100
Fuel use bil. cu. ft.	11,949	15,216	20,815	21,870	21,691	20,664	19,008	19,390	97	97	97
Nonfuel use bil. cu. ft.	320	382	552	559	554	559	529	557	3	3	3
Residential and commercial bil. cu. ft.	4,123	5,347	6,894	7,413	7,167	7,049	7,192	7,434	34	32	37
Industrial bil. cu. ft.	4,535	5,958	7,889	8,167	8,744	8,306	6,979	6,967	37	37	35
Pipeline fuel bil. cu. ft.	347	501	722	766	728	669	583	548	3	3	3
Electrical generation bil. cu. ft.	1,725	2,318	3,894	3,979	3,605	3,429	3,147	3,078	14	18	15
Lease and plant fuel bil. cu. ft.	1,237	1,156	1,399	1,456	1,496	1,477	1,396	1,634	10	7	8
Miscellaneous bil. cu. ft.	302	318	569	648	505	293	240	286	2	3	1
Coal [3] **mil. sh. tons.**	[4] 407	[4] 473	524	523	562	558	562	604	100	100	100
Fuel use mil. sh. tons.	393	467	518	518	558	554	562	604	99	99	100
Nonfuel use mil. sh. tons.	5	5	6	5	4	4	(Z)	(Z)	1	1	(Z)
Residential and commercial mil. sh. tons.	37	26	16	12	11	11	10	10	6	3	2
Industrial mil. sh. tons.	175	201	187	161	162	155	146	139	43	36	22
Electrical generation mil. sh. tons.	177	245	321	350	388	392	448	476	52	61	76

Z   Less than 500,000 short tons or .5 percent.
[1] Preliminary.
[2] Products refined and processed from crude oil, including still gas, liquefied refinery gas, and natural gas liquids.
[3] Includes anthracite, bituminous, and lignite coals.
[4] Includes transportation and miscellaneous, not shown separately.

Source: Through 1975, U.S. Bureau of Mines, *United States Energy Through the Year 2000*, December 1972; and *Minerals Yearbook* (in some cases data have been revised by EIA); thereafter, U.S. Energy Information Administration, *Annual Report to Congress*, vol. III.

No. 1322. Crude Petroleum and Refined Products: 1960 to 1977

[Barrels of 42 gallons. See also *Historical Statistics, Colonial Times to 1970*, series M 138-142, M 178, and M 181]

ITEM	1960	1965	1970	1972	1973	1974	1975	1976	1977 [1]
Crude petroleum:									
Domestic production_____mil. bbl__	2,575	2,849	3,517	3,455	3,361	3,203	3,057	2,976	2,985
Value at wells_____bil. dol__	7.4	8.2	11.2	11.7	13.1	21.6	23.1	24.2	25.6
Average price per barrel at wells____dol__	2.88	2.86	3.18	3.39	3.89	6.74	7.67	8.19	8.57
Wholesale price index (1967=100) [2]_____	98.6	98.2	106.1	113.8	126.0	211.8	245.7	253.6	274.2
World production_____mil. bbl__	7,689	11,058	16,719	18,601	20,561	20,537	19,475	21,192	21,826
U.S. proportion of world total_percent__	33	26	21	19	17	16	16	14	14
Imports_____mil. bbl__	372	452	483	811	1,184	1,269	1,498	1,935	2,397
From OPEC [3] countries_____mil. bbl__	340	316	214	462	765	927	1,172	1,664	2,047
Exports_____mil. bbl__	3	1	5	–	1	1	2	3	18
Stocks, Dec. 31_____mil. bbl__	240	220	276	246	242	265	271	285	348
Producing oil wells, Dec. 31_____1,000__	591	589	531	508	497	498	500	499	507
Proved reserves, Dec. 31_____mil. bbl__	31,613	31,352	39,001	36,339	35,300	34,250	32,682	30,942	29,486
Refinery capacity:									
Total_____mil. bbl__	3,624	3,933	4,407	4,918	5,038	5,289	5,537	5,646	6,113
Receipts at refineries_____mil. bbl__	2,951	3,297	3,973	4,279	4,546	4,436	4,546	4,920	5,347
By pipeline: Domestic_____mil. bbl__	2,149	2,363	2,840	2,964	2,905	2,754	2,662	2,643	2,536
Foreign_____mil. bbl__	41	107	237	318	409	370	398	443	561
By water: Domestic_____mil. bbl__	387	444	610	454	399	342	305	271	319
Foreign_____mil. bbl__	330	344	244	490	775	896	1,101	1,487	1,834
By tank cars and trucks_____mil. bbl__	44	38	43	53	58	74	80	76	97
Refined products:									
Completed refineries, Dec. 31__number__	311	286	279	277	284	290	287	291	302
Daily crude oil capacity_____mil. bbl__	10.0	10.5	13.0	13.8	14.5	15.2	15.4	16.6	17.2
Average dealer's net price (excl. tax) of gasoline (55 cities) [4]_____cents per gal__	16.08	15.38	17.68	17.72	19.48	30.54	35.78	38.99	42.51
Yield of gasoline_____percent__	45.1	44.0	45.3	46.2	45.6	45.9	46.5	45.5	43.1
Imports_____mil. bbl__	293	449	765	924	1,099	962	712	741	794
Exports_____mil. bbl__	71	67	89	81	84	79	74	79	70
Stocks, Dec. 31_____mil. bbl__	516	580	741	713	766	809	862	826	963

– Represents zero.   [1] Preliminary.   [2] Source: U.S. Bureau of Labor Statistics.   [3] Organization of Petroleum Exporting Countries. Comprises Algeria, Ecuador, Gabon, Indonesia, Iran, Iraq, Kuwait, Libya, Nigeria, Qatar, Saudi Arabia, United Arab Emirates, and Venezuela.   [4] Source: Platt's Oilgram Price Service.

No. 1323. Petroleum—Runs to Stills and Refinery Products, by Class: 1960 to 1977

[In millions of barrels, except percent. Barrels of 42 gallons, except as indicated. 1960 excludes Alaska and Hawaii. See also *Historical Statistics, Colonial Times to 1970*, series M 162-177]

PRODUCT	1960	1970	1972	1973	1974	1975	1976	1977, prel.	PERCENT			
									1970	1975	1976	1977, prel.
Input_____	3,119	4,252	4,593	4,845	4,714	4,814	5,189	5,576	100.0	100.0	100.0	100.0
Crude petroleum_____	2,952	3,967	4,281	4,537	4,429	4,541	4,910	5,331	93.3	94.3	94.6	95.6
Domestic_____	2,581	3,485	3,474	3,360	3,169	3,047	2,990	2,941	82.0	63.3	57.6	52.7
Foreign_____	371	482	807	1,177	1,260	1,494	1,920	2,390	11.3	31.0	37.0	42.9
Natural-gas liquids [1]_____	167	285	312	308	285	273	279	245	6.7	5.7	5.4	4.4
Output_____	3,119	4,252	4,593	4,845	4,714	4,814	5,189	5,576	100.0	100.0	100.0	100.0
Gasoline_____	1,510	2,100	2,316	2,399	2,336	2,393	2,516	2,568	49.4	49.7	48.5	46.1
Kerosene_____	136	95	79	79	56	55	62	62	2.2	1.2	1.1	1.1
Distillate fuel oil_____	667	896	962	1,029	974	968	1,070	1,197	21.1	20.1	20.6	21.5
Residual fuel oil_____	332	258	293	354	390	451	504	639	6.1	9.4	9.7	11.5
Jet fuel_____	88	302	310	344	305	318	336	356	7.1	6.6	6.5	6.4
Lubricants_____	59	66	65	69	71	56	62	65	1.6	1.2	1.2	1.2
Wax (1 bbl.=280 lb.)_____	6	6	6	7	7	6	7	7	.1	.1	.1	.1
Coke (5 bbl.=1 sh. ton)_____	60	108	120	132	124	129	130	134	2.5	2.7	2.5	2.4
Asphalt (5.5 bbl.=1 sh. ton)___	99	147	155	168	164	144	140	154	3.5	3.0	2.7	2.8
Still gas (1 bbl.=3,600 cu. ft.)___	129	164	171	177	176	175	180	193	3.9	3.6	3.5	3.5
Liquefied gases_____	78	116	121	128	117	109	119	122	2.7	2.3	2.3	2.2
Petrochemical feedstocks_____	(NA)	100	124	132	135	122	164	191	2.3	2.5	3.2	3.4
Other finished products_____	30	63	65	68	71	68	89	87	1.5	1.4	1.7	1.6
Other unfinished oils (net) [2]_____	*22*	*38*	*52*	*46*	*37*	*13*	*8*	*9*	*.9*	*.3*	*.2*	*.1*
Shortage [2]_____	*53*	*131*	*142*	*165*	*175*	*168*	*175*	*190*	*3.1*	*3.5*	*3.4*	*3.4*

NA Not available.   [1] Includes other liquid hydrocarbons.   [2] Negative quantities.

Source of tables 1322 and 1323: Through 1976, U.S. Bureau of Mines, *Minerals Yearbook*; thereafter, U.S. Energy Information Administration, *Petroleum Statement, Annual Energy Data Report, 1977*.

No. 1324. Crude Petroleum and Natural Gas—Wells Drilled, Footage, and Drilling Cost, by Type of Well: 1960 to 1976

[Includes all costs incurred for drilling and equipping wells to point of completion as productive wells or abandonment after drilling becomes unproductive. Based on sample of operators of different size drilling establishments]

ITEM AND YEAR	WELLS DRILLED		Footage drilled (mil. ft.)	DRILLING COST (mil. dol.)		Average depth per well (ft.)	AVERAGE COST PER WELL ($1,000)		Average cost per ft. (dol.)
	Total	Offshore		Total	Offshore		Total	Offshore	
All wells____1960__	44,133	538	186.4	2,424	208	4,223	55	386	13.01
1965__	39,596	1,037	178.7	2,401	428	4,513	61	413	13.44
1970__	27,177	1,058	136.9	2,579	599	5,037	95	566	18.84
1973__	26,244	888	136.7	3,075	578	5,207	117	651	22.50
1974__	31,481	830	150.9	4,367	680	4,795	139	819	28.93
1975__	36,960	1,028	177.6	6,571	1,174	4,806	178	1,142	36.99
1976__	38,941	1,028	184.4	7,462	1,475	4,736	192	1,435	40.46
Oil wells____1960__	21,294	301	84.0	1,111	98	3,946	52	326	13.22
1965__	18,857	487	76.5	1,067	193	4,059	57	396	13.94
1970__	12,547	533	56.4	1,088	282	4,496	87	528	19.29
1973__	9,705	296	44.7	1,007	182	4,602	104	615	22.54
1974__	13,073	253	51.8	1,440	170	3,960	110	670	27.82
1975__	16,276	283	66.1	2,257	253	4,059	139	892	34.15
1976__	16,878	275	68.3	2,550	322	4,044	151	1,172	37.35
Gas wells____1960__	5,262	87	29.1	540	53	5,526	103	606	18.58
1965__	4,772	118	26.5	486	67	5,552	102	571	18.35
1970__	3,844	193	23.1	618	139	6,007	161	720	26.75
1973__	6,427	193	36.3	998	154	5,654	155	798	27.46
1974__	6,695	155	37.1	1,267	152	5,546	189	978	34.11
1975__	7,654	271	43.4	2,005	338	5,667	262	1,247	46.23
1976__	8,904	273	48.4	2,407	396	5,432	270	1,450	49.78
Dry holes____1960__	17,577	150	73.3	774	57	4,168	44	377	10.56
1965__	15,967	432	75.7	849	167	4,739	53	387	11.21
1970__	10,786	332	57.4	873	178	5,320	81	536	15.21
1973__	10,112	399	55.7	1,070	242	5,504	106	608	19.22
1974__	11,713	422	62.0	1,660	359	5,297	142	850	26.76
1975__	13,030	474	68.2	2,309	584	5,234	177	1,232	33.86
1976__	13,159	480	67.8	2,505	757	5,152	190	1,577	36.94

Source: American Petroleum Institute, Independent Petroleum Association of America, and Mid-Continent Oil and Gas Association, Joint Association Survey of the U.S. Oil and Gas Producing Industry, annual.

No. 1325. Crude Petroleum—Producing Oil Wells, 1970 and 1977, Production, 1961 to 1977, and Proved Reserves, 1970 and 1977, by States

[Barrels of 42 gallons. See also Historical Statistics, Colonial Times to 1970, series M 138 and M 142]

STATE	PRODUCING OIL WELLS, DEC. 31 (1,000)		PRODUCTION (million barrels)									PROVED RESERVES [1] (million barrels)	
	1970	1977	1961–1965, avg.	1966–1970, avg.	1971–1975, avg.	1970	1973	1974	1975	1976	1977, prel.	1970	1977
Total_	531.0	507.0	2,737	3,292	3,306	3,517	3,361	3,203	3,057	2,976	2,985	39,001	29,486
Ala_____	.6	.6	8	8	11	7	12	13	13	14	18	65	44
Alaska___	.2	.3	10	53	73	84	72	71	70	63	169	10,149	9,616
Ark_____	7.1	7.8	27	21	17	18	18	17	16	18	20	130	86
Calif_____	40.4	43.5	303	365	337	372	336	323	322	326	350	3,984	3,632
Colo_____	1.8	3.0	39	30	34	25	36	37	38	39	39	389	242
Ill_____	26.1	23.8	73	54	32	44	31	27	26	26	26	229	150
Ind_____	4.0	5.1	19	9	6	7	5	5	5	5	5	37	26
Kans_____	43.5	42.4	109	94	68	85	66	62	59	59	57	539	359
Ky_____	11.7	14.0	12	14	9	12	9	8	8	7	7	61	35
La_____	27.9	23.9	512	804	809	907	832	737	651	607	563	5,710	3,113
Mich_____	4.3	3.9	17	13	16	12	15	18	24	30	33	46	133
Miss_____	3.1	2.8	56	60	56	65	56	51	47	46	43	355	203
Mont_____	3.2	3.3	31	40	34	38	35	35	33	33	33	242	152
Nebr_____	1.2	1.4	22	13	8	11	7	7	6	6	6	41	31
N. Mex__	17.3	14.3	113	127	105	128	101	99	95	92	87	761	491
N. Dak__	1.5	1.6	25	24	21	22	20	20	20	22	23	192	150
Ohio_____	15.9	17.3	9	11	9	10	9	9	10	10	12	128	129
Okla_____	78.0	73.8	201	225	190	224	191	178	163	161	156	1,351	1,121
Texas____	177.2	163.7	970	1,142	1,261	1,250	1,295	1,262	1,222	1,190	1,138	13,195	8,467
Utah_____	.9	1.4	30	24	33	23	33	39	42	34	33	182	182
Wyo_____	9.3	11.1	140	146	141	160	142	140	136	134	112	1,017	816
Other____	55.9	48.0	11	15	36	13	40	45	50	54	55	198	308

[1] December 31. From reports of Committee on Petroleum Reserves, American Petroleum Institute. Figures for California, Louisiana, and Texas include offshore reserves.

Source: Through 1976, U.S. Bureau of Mines, Minerals Yearbook; thereafter, U.S. Energy Information Administration, Petroleum Statement, Annual Energy Data Report, 1977.

No. 1326. CRUDE PETROLEUM AND NATURAL GAS—SALES VOLUME AND LEASE REVENUES, 1967 TO 1976, AND DRILLING EXPENDITURES AND EMPLOYMENT, 1973 TO 1976

[Figures on a gross operator basis, under which individual companies responsible for management and operation of oil and gas field leases reported on all properties operated for their own account and account of others. Lease revenues represent revenues generated from sales of either crude petroleum or natural gas, comparable to sales volume reported and including production payment, royalty, and nonoperating working interest shares]

ITEM AND YEAR	All companies, total	COMPANIES RANKED BY LEASE REVENUES					PERCENT OF TOTAL		
		Top 8	Next 8	Next 16	Top 50	Top 100	Top 8	Top 16	Top 32
Sales volume of—									
Crude petroleum (mil. bbl.): [1] 1967	3,044	1,647	517	263	2,552	2,659	54	71	80
1972	3,373	1,818	613	317	2,852	2,977	54	72	81
1973	3,348	1,802	619	299	2,840	2,964	54	72	81
1974	3,159	1,708	581	291	2,693	2,811	54	72	82
1975	3,086	1,654	553	282	2,626	2,753	54	72	81
1976	2,905	1,482	588	270	2,436	2,585	51	71	81
Natural gas (bil. cu. ft.): 1967	17,126	7,904	3,105	2,551	14,377	15,560	46	64	79
1972	21,902	10,607	3,546	2,800	18,170	19,446	48	65	77
1973	22,315	11,322	3,578	2,703	18,505	19,851	51	67	79
1974	21,878	9,861	4,065	2,529	17,539	19,098	45	64	75
1975	20,455	8,898	3,864	2,391	16,207	17,661	44	62	74
1976	19,902	8,727	3,515	2,598	15,906	17,273	44	62	75
Lease revenues for—									
Crude petroleum (mil. dol.): [1] 1967	8,800	4,899	1,475	730	7,456	7,763	56	72	81
1972	11,332	6,194	2,024	1,053	9,608	10,018	55	73	82
1973	13,040	7,036	2,448	1,136	11,103	11,601	54	73	81
1974	20,938	11,205	3,708	1,812	17,495	18,345	54	71	80
1975	22,852	11,961	3,948	1,915	18,900	19,978	52	70	78
1976	22,936	11,537	4,279	2,004	18,673	19,951	50	69	78
Natural gas (mil. dol.): 1967	2,888	1,341	501	419	2,438	2,640	46	64	78
1972	4,317	2,062	687	591	3,596	3,843	48	64	77
1973	5,064	2,493	794	634	4,160	4,494	49	65	77
1974	6,726	3,036	1,238	777	5,400	5,894	45	64	75
1975	8,929	3,859	1,618	1,048	7,018	7,755	43	61	73
1976	11,784	4,813	1,939	1,558	9,251	10,168	41	57	71
Drilling expenditures (mil. dol.): [2] 1973	3,194	1,095	367	344	2,202	2,529	36	48	58
1974	4,607	1,388	585	529	2,711	3,388	29	42	53
1975	6,507	1,866	815	838	3,932	4,719	29	41	54
1976	8,071	2,706	958	1,036	5,475	6,184	34	45	58
Employment (1,000): 1973	124	38	18	13	74	81	31	45	55
1974	125	38	16	16	75	83	30	43	56
1975	137	40	18	15	79	88	29	42	53
1976	136	43	18	15	81	90	31	44	55

[1] Includes condensate. [2] Represents expenditures incurred during the year for drilling and equipping wells.
Source: U.S. Bureau of the Census, *Annual Survey of Oil and Gas.*

No. 1327. OIL AND GAS LEASES AND PRODUCTION ON THE OUTER CONTINENTAL SHELF, BY STATES: 1975 AND 1976

[Barrels of 42 gallons. Covers leases made in ocean waters belonging to the U.S. and subject to its jurisdiction and control under provisions of the Outer Continental Shelf Lands Act. See also table 389]

STATE	1975					1976				
	Number of leases	Acres (1,000)	Production			Number of leases	Acres (1,000)	Production		
			Oil (1,000 bbl.)	Gas (mil. cu. ft.)	LP gas [1] (mil. gal.)			Oil (1,000 bbl.)	Gas (mil. cu. ft.)	LP gas [1] (mil. gal.)
Total	1,675	7,761	339,333	3,383	2,040	1,878	8,823	322,810	3,493	1,944
Alabama	13	74	–	–	–	11	63	–	–	–
Alaska	–	–	–	–	–	76	409	–	–	–
California	68	347	16,129	5	–	124	657	14,705	4	–
Florida	62	357	–	–	–	50	288	–	–	–
Louisiana	1,171	5,047	322,023	3,246	1,982	1,217	5,254	306,896	3,386	1,921
Mississippi	6	35	–	–	–	6	35	–	–	–
Texas	355	1,901	1,181	132	58	394	2,117	1,209	103	23

– Represents zero. [1] Liquid petroleum gas. Includes gasoline production.
Source: U.S. Bureau of Land Management, *Public Land Statistics*, annual.

No. **1328.** Natural Gas—Supply, Production, Consumption, Reserves, and Marketed Production, by States: 1950 to 1977

[Prior to 1960, excludes Alaska. See also *Historical Statistics, Colonial Times to 1970,* series M 147–161]

ITEM	1950	1955	1960	1965	1970	1972	1973	1974	1975	1976	1977
Producing wells_____1,000__	65	71	91	112	117	121	124	128	132	137	(NA)
Production value											
at wells,[1]_____mil. dol__	409	978	1,790	2,495	3,746	4,186	4,894	6,573	8,945	11,572	15,000
Avg. per 1,000 cu. ft.cents__	6.5	10.4	14.0	15.6	17.1	18.6	21.6	30.4	44.5	58.0	77.9
Proved reserves[2]tril. cu. ft__	185	224	264	286	291	266	250	237	228	216	209
SUPPLY											
(bil. cu. ft.)											
Total supply_____	6,457	9,853	13,640	17,456	24,200	25,308	25,213	24,261	22,822	22,837	(NA)
Marketed production[1]_____	6,282	9,405	12,771	16,040	21,921	22,532	22,647	21,601	20,109	19,952	19,942
Drawn from storage_____	175	437	713	960	1,459	1,757	1,533	1,701	1,760	1,921	(NA)
Imports[3]_____	–	11	156	456	821	1,019	1,033	959	953	964	1,011
Consumption, total_____	6,026	9,070	12,509	16,033	22,046	23,009	22,966	22,111	20,409	20,801	(NA)
Residential_____	1,198	2,124	3,103	3,903	4,837	5,126	4,879	4,786	4,924	5,051	(NA)
Commercial_____	388	629	1,020	1,443	2,057	2,287	2,288	2,263	2,268	2,383	(NA)
Industrial[4]_____	4,440	6,317	8,386	10,687	15,152	15,596	15,799	15,062	13,218	13,366	(NA)
Utilities_____	629	1,153	1,725	2,318	3,894	3,979	3,605	3,429	3,147	3,078	(NA)
Field_____	1,187	1,508	1,780	1,910	2,305	2,364	2,412	2,365	2,269	2,488	(NA)
Refineries_____	455	625	775	860	1,029	1,071	1,074	1,040	946	919	(NA)
Pipeline fuel_____	126	245	347	501	722	766	728	669	583	548	(NA)
Exports[3]_____	26	31	11	26	70	78	77	77	73	65	56
Stored_____	230	505	844	1,078	1,857	1,893	1,974	1,784	2,104	1,756	(NA)
Transmission loss_____	175	247	274	319	228	328	196	289	235	216	(NA)
PRODUCTION											
(bil. cu. ft.)											
Marketed production:[1]											
Alaska_____	(NA)	(NA)	(Z)	7	112	126	131	129	160	166	173
Ark_____	48	32	55	83	181	167	158	124	116	110	106
Calif_____	559	538	518	660	649	487	449	365	318	354	345
Colo_____	11	49	107	126	106	117	138	145	172	184	192
Kans_____	364	471	634	793	900	889	893	887	844	829	781
La_____	832	1,680	2,988	4,467	7,788	7,973	8,242	7,754	7,091	7,007	7,218
N. Mex_____	213	541	799	937	1,139	1,216	1,219	1,245	1,217	1,231	1,196
Okla_____	482	615	824	1,321	1,595	1,807	1,771	1,639	1,605	1,727	1,769
Tex_____	3,127	4,731	5,893	6,637	8,358	8,658	8,514	8,171	7,486	7,192	7,051
W. Va_____	190	213	209	207	242	215	209	202	155	153	153
Wyo_____	62	78	182	236	339	375	358	327	316	329	264
Other_____	394	457	562	566	512	502	566	613	629	670	694
World production_____	(NA)	(NA)	(NA)	(NA)	37,542	43,525	46,144	47,179	47,518	49,459	50,900
Percent U.S. of world_____	(NA)	(NA)	(NA)	(NA)	58.4	51.8	49.1	45.8	42.3	40.4	39.2

– Represents zero.   NA Not available.   Z Less than 500 million cubic feet.
[1] Comprises gas sold or consumed by producers, including loss due to natural gas liquids recovery, losses in transmission, amounts added to storage, and increases in gas in pipelines. Beginning 1965, data on pressure base of 14.73 pounds per square inch absolute; prior years, 14.65.   [2] Estimated, end of year. Source: American Gas Association, Arlington, Va. (Copyright.)   [3] Beginning 1970, includes imports of liquefied natural gas.
[4] Includes other use, not shown separately.

Source: Except as noted, through 1975, U.S. Bureau of Mines, *Minerals Yearbook* (in some cases data have been revised by EIA); thereafter, U.S. Energy Information Administration, *Natural Gas Production and Consumption*, annual.

No. **1329.** Natural Gas Liquids—Production and Value: 1960 to 1977

[Barrels of 42 gallons. Prior to 1960, excludes Alaska. See also *Historical Statistics, Colonial Times to 1970,* series M 143–146]

ITEM	1960	1965	1970	1972	1973	1974	1975	1976	1977
Total produced_____mil. bbl__	340	442	606	638	634	616	596	587	590
Natural gasoline and mixtures[1]____mil. bbl__	107	130	165	164	161	148	134	133	133
Liquefied petroleum gases[2]_____mil. bbl__	201	268	400	445	447	448	444	437	443
Cycle products_____mil. bbl__	32	44	41	29	26	20	18	17	14
Value at plants:									
Natural gasoline[1]_____mil. dol__	313	361	469	500	568	975	778	882	900
Liquefied petroleum gases[2]_____mil. dol__	392	417	672	848	1,188	1,981	1,894	2,299	2,500
Cycle products_____mil. dol__	104	134	134	104	101	132	101	103	90
Avg. value, all light products____dol. per bbl__	2.39	2.06	2.10	2.28	2.93	5.01	4.65	5.59	5.92
Natural gas processed_____tril. cu. ft__	10	14	19	20	20	19	18	18	18
Average yield, all light									
products_____gal. per 1,000 cu. ft__	1.46	1.35	1.37	1.34	1.35	1.38	1.42	1.39	1.42

[1] Beginning 1955, includes isopentane; included in LP-gases for 1950.   [2] Includes ethane.
Source: Through 1976, U.S. Bureau of Mines, *Minerals Yearbook*; thereafter, U.S. Energy Information Administration.

No. 1330. CEMENT—SUMMARY: 1960 TO 1976

[In thousands of short tons, except as indicated. Includes Puerto Rico. Excludes Alaska except for imports and exports. See *Historical Statistics, Colonial Times to 1970*, series M 188–189, for related data]

ITEM	1960	1965	1970	1971	1972	1973	1974	1975	1976
Production of finished cement [1]	62,816	73,103	76,116	80,317	84,556	87,573	82,888	69,721	74,495
Portland	59,974	69,827	73,168	77,097	80,744	83,551	79,486	66,796	71,227
Prepared masonry	2,736	3,223	2,948	3,309	3,812	4,022	3,402	2,925	3,268
Active plants, number:									
Portland	176	181	181	176	174	172	176	174	169
Natural, slag, hydraulic lime	4	4	2	2	1	–	–	–	–
Shipments	61,492	73,637	76,385	82,397	85,280	90,727	82,914	70,684	75,226
Value_____mil. dol.	1,104	1,245	1,366	1,566	1,756	2,017	2,221	2,220	2,576
Average per ton_____dollars	17.95	16.91	17.88	19.01	21.56	22.23	26.79	31.41	34.24
Portland	58,711	70,328	73,406	79,005	81,432	86,597	79,482	67,776	71,922
Prepared masonry	2,678	3,256	2,978	3,392	3,848	4,130	3,432	2,908	3,304
Natural, slag, hydraulic lime	103	52	(D)	(D)	(D)	–	–	–	–
Stock at mills, Dec. 31 (Portland)	6,700	6,207	7,228	6,114	6,709	5,230	7,156	6,575	6,790
Imports	772	1,035	2,473	3,057	4,851	6,647	5,702	3,702	3,107
Exports	35	141	123	84	83	268	199	494	466
World prod., est_____mil. sh. tons	349	478	630	680	729	773	776	774	808

– Represents zero. D Withheld to avoid disclosing individual company data.
[1] Includes natural, slag, and hydraulic lime plants, not shown separately, except 1970 excludes slag cement.

No. 1331. GYPSUM—SUMMARY: 1950 TO 1977

[Quantities in thousands of short tons; values in millions of dollars. Excludes Alaska, Hawaii, and Puerto Rico, except for imports and exports. See *Historical Statistics, Colonial Times to 1970*, series M 190, gypsum mined]

ITEM	1950	1960	1965	1970	1972	1973	1974	1975	1976	1977, prel.
Active establishments [1]_____number	87	96	113	108	108	112	116	110	117	118
Crude gypsum: [2]										
Mined	8,193	9,825	10,033	9,436	12,328	13,558	11,999	9,751	11,980	13,410
Imports for consumption	3,219	5,301	5,911	6,128	7,718	7,661	7,424	5,448	6,231	7,074
Exports	24	17	28	41	51	63	132	75	284	17
Apparent supply [3]	11,388	15,109	15,916	15,523	19,995	21,156	19,291	15,124	17,927	20,467
Calcined gypsum produced	7,341	8,591	9,320	8,449	12,005	12,592	10,993	9,181	11,036	12,090
Value	60	121	133	132	196	205	206	186	237	286
Gypsum products sold, value [4]	205	361	420	353	561	633	623	514	655	1,074
Uncalcined uses, quantity	2,218	3,716	4,577	4,258	5,195	5,719	5,852	4,904	5,375	5,759
Value	8	15	20	21	27	31	39	33	41	48
Industrial uses, quantity	266	284	319	284	299	353	326	294	306	326
Value	5	6	8	9	11	14	15	15	17	20
Building uses, value	193	339	391	323	523	588	570	466	598	1,006

[1] Each mine, plant, or combination mine and plant is counted as 1 establishment.
[2] Excludes byproduct gypsum. [3] Amount mined, plus imports minus exports.
[4] Made from domestic, imported, and byproduct gypsum.

No. 1332. SAND AND GRAVEL—QUANTITY SOLD AND VALUE: 1960 TO 1976

[Quantities in millions of short tons. See also *Historical Statistics, Colonial Times to 1970*, series M 193]

ITEM	1960	1965	1970	1971	1972	1973	1974	1975	1976
Total sold or used by producers [1]	710	908	944	920	914	984	905	789	885
Processed sand	227	284	321	328	330	347	323	265	(NA)
Processed gravel	415	481	517	484	462	510	404	354	(NA)
Unprocessed sand and gravel	50	118	77	82	92	98	149	143	(NA)
Total value_____mil. dol.	720	957	1,116	1,149	1,201	1,359	1,417	1,340	1,774
Average per ton_____dollars	1.01	1.05	1.18	1.25	1.31	1.38	1.57	1.79	2.00
Use:									
Construction	692	883	915	894	884	955	876	762	855
Industrial sand and gravel	18	25	29	26	30	29	29	27	30
Type of project:									
Commercial	523	656	732	773	786	847	679	556	(NA)
Publicly funded	187	252	212	147	128	137	226	233	(NA)
Number of operations	(NA)	(NA)	5,918	5,738	5,384	5,681	6,967	7,014	7,599
Employment_____1,000	52.0	53.0	45.5	44.0	43.0	49.0	39.0	[2] 40.0	[2] 40.0

NA Not available. [1] Includes industrial sand and gravel shown below. [2] Estimate.
Source of tables 1330–1332: U.S. Bureau of Mines, *Minerals Yearbook*.

No. 1333. STONE—QUANTITY SOLD OR USED BY PRODUCERS, AND VALUE: 1965 TO 1977

[See *Historical Statistics, Colonial Times to 1970*, series M 194, for total quantity]

KIND OF STONE	QUANTITY SOLD OR USED [1] (mil. short tons)							VALUE (mil. dol.)						
	1965	1970	1973	1974	1975	1976	1977	1965	1970	1973	1974	1975	1976	1977
Total [2]	780	869	1,060	1,044	901	902	955	1,204	1,470	1,990	2,186	2,120	2,221	2,457
Granite	60	87	121	119	95	99	109	121	183	263	290	271	296	331
Basalt [3]	76	77	84	97	78	75	77	121	147	178	218	193	193	208
Sandstone	29	24	31	31	27	27	30	62	59	78	87	85	89	100
Marble	2	2	2	2	2	2	2	39	34	34	42	32	31	36
Limestone	555	626	775	752	665	663	707	766	961	1,334	1,446	1,437	1,516	1,679
Other stone	34	29	26	23	18	18	13	46	40	51	43	37	42	31
Shell	22	22	20	18	15	14	13	34	31	38	44	53	37	33
Slate	1	1	2	1	1	1	1	14	13	16	17	12	13	16

[1] Quantities of stone not sold by short tons are expressed in approximate short ton equivalents.
[2] Includes calcareous marl, not shown separately.   [3] Includes related rocks.

No. 1334. LIME—QUANTITY SOLD OR USED BY PRODUCERS: 1960 TO 1977

[Quantities in thousands of short tons. Excludes Puerto Rico. See also *Historical Statistics, Colonial Times to 1970*, series M 191-192]

ITEM	1960	1965	1970	1972	1973	1974	1975	1976	1977, prel.
Active plants number	157	212	194	185	175	172	171	163	161
Quantity sold [1]	12,935	16,794	19,747	20,229	21,090	21,606	19,133	20,229	19,813
Value mil. dol.	173	233	286	339	366	474	524	609	696
Per ton dollars	13.35	13.87	14.49	16.72	17.35	21.92	27.38	30.11	35.12
Open-market lime	8,189	10,449	12,718	13,353	14,394	14,640	12,840	14,024	14,181
Captive tonnage lime	[2] 4,746	6,345	7,029	6,937	6,696	6,966	6,292	6,205	5,727
Quicklime	8,271	12,009	15,248	16,611	17,230	17,795	15,875	16,924	16,282
Hydrated	2,715	2,609	3,126	2,604	2,610	2,533	2,344	2,298	2,470
Dead-burned dolomite	1,949	2,176	1,373	1,075	1,250	1,278	914	1,007	1,061
By use:									
Agricultural	187	217	142	137	140	109	97	136	79
Building	1,209	1,477	(D)	1,586	1,611	1,463	1,276	1,280	1,204
Chemical and industrial	9,591	12,924	(D)	17,492	18,131	18,089	16,846	17,806	17,469
Refractory [3]	1,949	2,176	1,373	1,075	1,250	1,278	914	1,007	1,061

D   Withheld to avoid disclosing individual company data.   [1] Includes quantity used by producers.
[2] Incomplete; only partial coverage of captive plants.   [3] Dead-burned dolomite.

No. 1335. PHOSPHATE ROCK—SUMMARY: 1960 TO 1977

[Quantities in thousands of short tons. See also *Historical Statistics, Colonial Times to 1970*, series M 203-204]

ITEM	1960	1965	1970	1972	1973	1974	1975	1976	1977
Mine production	60,858	84,305	125,514	126,651	139,713	155,847	187,516	170,097	166,893
P2O5 content	9,276	14,320	18,634	18,557	19,013	20,753	23,483	20,060	20,328
Marketable production	19,618	29,482	38,739	40,831	42,137	45,686	48,816	49,241	47,256
P2O5 content	6,096	9,132	11,998	12,839	13,106	14,053	15,028	15,118	14,561
Value mil. dol.	117.0	193.3	203.2	207.9	238.7	501.4	1,122.2	949.4	821.7
Per ton dollars	5.97	6.55	5.25	5.09	5.66	10.98	22.99	19.28	17.39
Sold or used by producers	19,266	29,039	38,765	43,755	45,043	48,435	46,439	44,677	47,437
P2O5 content	5,994	9,015	12,066	13,753	13,972	14,946	14,270	13,677	14,660
Value mil. dol.	115.4	188.6	203.8	223.0	254.8	529.1	1,053.0	857.2	829.1
Per ton dollars	5.99	6.49	5.26	5.10	5.66	10.92	22.67	19.19	17.48
Imports for consumption [1]	144	148	136	55	65	182	36	51	158
Value mil. dol.	3.8	3.0	3.8	1.4	1.3	9.0	1.6	2.2	6.1
Per ton dollars	26.07	20.14	27.87	25.75	19.82	49.45	43.83	43.59	38.61
Exports	4,473	7,323	11,738	14,275	13,875	13,897	12,272	10,400	13,230
P2O5 content	1,445	2,313	3,796	4,673	4,502	4,468	3,955	3,332	4,251
Value mil. dol.	26.6	51.1	60.0	75.4	83.0	194.0	429.2	272.8	288.6
Per ton dollars	5.95	6.98	5.11	5.28	5.98	13.96	34.98	26.23	21.81
Consumption, apparent [2]	14,937	21,864	27,163	29,535	31,233	34,720	34,203	34,328	34,365
World production	46,110	70,298	93,635	98,981	108,858	119,898	118,586	117,748	[3] 108,024

[1] Data on P2O5 content not available.   [2] Amount sold or used plus imports minus exports.   [3] Preliminary.
Source of tables 1333-1335: U.S. Bureau of Mines, *Minerals Yearbook*.

No. 1336. POTASH—SUMMARY: 1960 TO 1977

[Quantities in thousands of short tons. See also *Historical Statistics, Colonial Times to 1970*, series M 201–202]

ITEM	1960	1965	1970	1972	1973	1974	1975	1976	1977
Production of potassium salts (marketable)	4,472	5,401	4,853	4,738	4,684	4,716	4,576	4,427	4,675
Approximate equivalent K_2O	2,638	3,140	2,729	2,659	2,603	2,552	2,501	2,400	2,457
Value[1] _____ mil. dol	89.7	129.8	98.1	106.7	112.6	159.1	223.1	202.4	206.3
Sales of potassium salts by producers	4,412	5,027	4,703	4,653	5,174	4,708	3,819	4,612	4,688
Approximate equivalent K_2O	2,602	2,931	2,669	2,618	2,865	2,545	2,094	2,500	2,469
Value at plant _____ mil. dol	88.4	121.2	92.4	104.7	123.7	158.6	187.9	210.8	206.9
Per ton _____ dollars	20.04	24.10	19.64	22.50	23.92	33.69	49.19	45.70	44.13
Imports for consumption of potash materials	415	1,867	4,403	4,979	6,046	7,245	6,271	7,575	8,381
Approximate equivalent K_2O	226	1,108	2,605	2,961	3,587	4,326	3,797	4,594	5,076
Value _____ mil. dol	15.4	52.7	94.7	119.7	145.7	236.7	267.2	344.0	373.8
Exports of potash materials	833	1,099	966	1,353	1,579	1,415	1,419	1,670	1,650
Approximate equivalent K_2O	491	648	544	764	889	787	779	945	932
Value _____ mil. dol	25.9	42.5	28.5	45.9	58.0	66.2	92.7	91.9	90.2
Apparent consumption of potassium salts[2]	3,994	5,795	8,140	8,279	9,641	10,538	8,671	10,517	11,419
Approximate equivalent K_2O	2,337	3,391	4,730	4,815	5,563	6,084	5,112	6,149	6,613
World production (marketable), approximate equivalent K_2O	10,000	15,100	20,553	20,841	23,585	26,228	27,352	26,876	28,800

[1] Derived from reported value of amount sold or used.   [2] Amount sold or used plus imports minus exports.

No. 1337. SULFUR—SUMMARY: 1960 TO 1977

[Quantities in thousands of long tons. Excludes Alaska, Hawaii, and Puerto Rico, except for imports and exports. See also *Historical Statistics, Colonial Times to 1970*, series M 195–199]

ITEM	1960	1965	1970	1972	1973	1974	1975	1976	1977
Production, sulfur, all forms[1]	6,661	8,196	9,557	10,218	10,921	11,419	11,259	10,707	10,558
Sulfur from Frasch mines	5,037	6,116	7,082	7,290	7,605	7,901	7,211	6,264	5,822
Recovered elemental sulfur	707	1,215	1,457	1,950	2,416	2,600	2,600	3,138	3,567
Pyrites, sulfur content only	416	354	339	283	212	162	237	286	166
Gross weight of total pyrites	1,016	875	845	741	559	424	625	750	435
Byproduct sulfuric acid[2]	345	388	537	546	600	654	767	942	945
Shipments, Frasch mines	5,130	6,938	6,504	7,613	7,438	7,898	6,077	5,860	5,935
Approximate value _____ mil. dol	118	158	154	132	139	241	305	300	295
Avg. value per long ton _____ dol	23.08	22.71	23.65	17.39	18.63	30.52	50.16	51.19	49.66
Imports for consumption:									
Crude sulfur	741	1,486	1,537	1,138	1,222	2,150	1,897	1,727	1,977
Pyrites, sulfur content[3]	146	160	130	50	–	–	–	–	–
Exports, sulfur	1,787	2,635	1,433	1,852	1,776	2,663	1,352	1,270	1,178

– Represents zero.   [1] Includes other byproduct sulfur compounds, not shown separately.
[2] Represents sulfur content. Produced at copper, lead, and zinc plants.   [3] Estimate.

No. 1338. SALT—SUMMARY: 1960 TO 1976

[In thousands of short tons, except value. Prior to 1970, production includes Puerto Rico. See *Historical Statistics, Colonial Times to 1970*, series M 28 and M 200, for value and production]

ITEM AND STATE	1960	1965	1970	1971	1972	1973	1974	1975	1976
Production[1]	25,479	34,687	45,896	44,077	45,022	43,910	46,536	41,030	44,191
Louisiana	4,792	8,126	13,584	13,352	13,514	13,152	13,543	12,166	13,491
Michigan	4,088	4,171	4,899	4,458	4,358	4,818	4,445	4,020	4,219
New York	4,008	5,002	5,990	5,303	5,604	5,202	6,464	5,978	6,495
Ohio	3,108	5,026	5,329	5,709	6,147	4,657	5,029	5,083	5,052
Texas	4,756	6,964	10,184	9,217	9,744	10,354	11,379	8,560	9,718
Other States	4,727	5,398	5,910	6,037	5,655	5,727	5,676	5,223	5,216
Evaporated (manufactured)	4,104	4,925	5,498	5,928	5,850	5,884	5,922	5,345	5,607
In brine	14,911	19,952	26,228	24,449	24,737	25,680	25,779	21,401	22,917
Rock salt	6,466	9,810	14,170	13,700	14,434	12,347	14,835	14,283	15,668
Total value[2] _____ mil. dol	161	216	305	304	297	306	361	368	431
Exports	420	688	423	670	869	609	521	1,332	1,007
Imports for consumption	1,057	2,410	3,536	3,855	3,463	3,207	3,358	3,215	4,352

[1] Represents sales plus quantities used by producers.
[2] F.o.b. mine or refinery; excludes cost of cooperage or containers.
Source of tables 1336–1338: U.S. Bureau of Mines, *Minerals Yearbook*.

No. 1339. IRON ORE—SUMMARY: 1960 TO 1977

[In thousands of long tons, except as indicated. Excludes Alaska, Hawaii, and Puerto Rico, except for imports and exports. See also Historical Statistics, Colonial Times to 1970, series M 205–211]

ITEM	1960	1965	1970	1972	1973	1974	1975	1976	1977
Production [1]	88,784	87,439	89,760	75,434	87,669	84,355	78,866	79,993	55,750
Lake Superior	71,792	66,432	69,636	61,550	72,416	70,723	66,735	67,413	43,952
Northeastern	4,125	5,173	3,491	2,612	2,608	2,358	1,860	2,438	2,020
Western	4,583	[2]13,065	14,314	10,528	12,035	10,496	9,643	10,142	9,779
Hematite [3]	[2][4]68,147	47,043	33,584	21,595	28,224	24,052	19,244	19,348	11,479
Magnetite [3]	18,205	36,927	53,792	52,344	58,089	58,813	58,395	59,295	43,134
Other	2,432	3,469	2,381	1,494	1,356	1,490	1,226	1,350	1,137
Number of mines	247	183	74	58	58	66	67	65	54
Shipments [5]	82,963	84,073	87,176	77,885	90,863	85,112	75,695	77,076	54,053
Value [5] mil. dol	724	801	942	950	1,166	1,391	1,621	1,871	[6]1,423
Avg. per ton at mine dol	8.73	9.53	10.80	12.20	12.84	16.34	21.41	24.28	[6]26.32
Stocks, Dec. 31 [7]	12,337	12,667	15,316	14,679	10,876	9,405	12,299	13,993	14,811
Imports [8]	34,578	45,103	44,891	35,761	43,296	48,029	46,743	44,390	37,905
Value mil. dol	322	444	480	416	533	696	860	980	957
Exports	5,273	7,085	5,492	2,095	2,747	2,323	2,537	2,913	2,143
Value mil. dol	58	80	68	27	38	35	60	82	63
World prod. [6] mil. lg. tons	514	611	754	757	851	879	888	886	[9]844

[1] Includes Southeastern district and byproduct ore, not shown separately. Beginning 1976, Western includes byproduct ore and Northeastern includes Southeastern. [2] Includes undistributed. [3] Predominant mineral. [4] Includes brown ore from Tenn., Mo., and Tex.; also magnetite from Calif., Utah, and Wyo. [5] Beginning 1976, includes byproduct ore. [6] Estimated. [7] At mines. [8] For consumption. [9] Preliminary.

Source: U.S. Bureau of Mines, Minerals Yearbook.

No. 1340. PIG IRON AND FERROALLOYS—SUMMARY: 1960 TO 1977

[In thousands of short tons, except furnaces]

ITEM	1960	1965	1970	1972	1973	1974	1975	1976	1977
Blast furnaces, number, Jan. 1	263	239	228	216	216	206	199	196	193
Number in blast, Jan. 1	229	191	169	126	141	163	136	119	107
Blast furnace production	67,320	88,859	91,816	89,400	101,208	95,909	79,923	86,870	81,328
Total production	68,566	90,918	93,470	91,338	103,089	97,778	81,200	88,355	82,657
Basic	58,261	80,431	86,438	83,961	96,202	91,193	75,911	82,894	78,198
Bessemer and low-phosphorus	3,791	2,936	1,593	1,441	1,343	1,206	1,227	1,262	376
Foundry (incl. ferrosilicon) [1]	2,152	2,303	2,257	1,977	1,581	1,528	1,321	1,489	1,610
All other [1]	4,362	5,248	3,182	3,959	3,963	3,851	2,741	2,710	2,473
Production of pig iron: [2]									
Alabama	3,541	4,290	4,654	4,086	3,817	3,872	3,638	3,297	3,005
Illinois	5,307	6,294	7,401	7,201	7,902	7,170	5,228	6,432	6,203
Indiana	8,404	11,020	13,348	15,330	17,128	16,998	15,656	17,439	16,492
New York	4,205	6,100	5,569	3,997	5,397	4,671	3,299	4,362	3,541
Ohio	11,788	15,407	15,554	16,359	18,391	17,439	14,115	15,754	14,677
Pennsylvania	16,533	21,789	20,768	20,357	22,646	22,168	17,593	18,025	16,636
Other	16,703	23,285	24,141	21,612	25,556	23,591	20,394	21,561	20,774

[1] For 1960, silvery pig iron included in "Foundry"; thereafter, in "All other."
[2] Beginning 1974, includes blast furnace ferroalloys.
Source: American Iron and Steel Institute, Washington, D.C., Annual Statistical Report. (Copyright.)

No. 1341. MOLYBDENUM CONCENTRATES—SUMMARY: 1960 TO 1977

[In millions of pounds of contained molybdenum, except as indicated. See Historical Statistics, Colonial Times to 1970, series M 227–228, for production and exports of ores and concentrates]

ITEM	1960	1965	1970	1972	1973	1974	1975	1976	1977 [1]
Production	68.2	77.4	111.4	112.1	115.9	112.0	106.0	113.2	122.4
Shipments from mines	69.9	77.3	110.4	102.2	135.1	118.2	105.2	114.5	125.0
Average price per pound [2] dol	1.25	1.55	1.72	1.72	1.72	2.02	2.48	2.94	3.68
Exports [3][4]	30.2	24.1	55.7	45.4	74.0	78.7	62.6	62.5	65.7
Imports for consumption [4]	–	.1	(z)	.4	.5	.2	2.6	2.1	2.0
Consumption	44.8	68.1	76.1	62.6	82.5	91.7	90.0	85.0	91.0
Stocks (industry), Dec. 31 [5]	3.5	4.2	9.7	45.2	22.0	18.7	10.7	9.4	9.2
World production, estimate [6]	89.1	98.5	161.1	156.7	161.4	166.2	156.7	170.7	184.5

– Represents zero. Z Less than 50,000 pounds. [1] Preliminary.
[2] Of molybdenum included in concentrate, f.o.b., Climax, Colorado. [3] Includes roasted concentrates.
[4] Includes Alaska, Hawaii, and Puerto Rico. [5] At mines and at plants making molybdenum products.
[6] Beginning 1965, free world.
Source: U.S. Bureau of Mines, Minerals Yearbook.

No. 1342. Copper—Summary: 1960 to 1977

[In thousands of short tons, except as indicated. Excludes Hawaii and Puerto Rico, except for imports and exports. See also *Historical Statistics, Colonial Times to 1970*, series M 235–241]

ITEM	1960	1965	1970	1972	1973	1974	1975	1976	1977, prel.
New (primary) copper produced—									
Mines (from domestic ores)	1,080	1,352	1,720	1,665	1,718	1,597	1,413	1,606	1,504
Copper ore produced [1]__mil. sh. tons	135	173	258	267	290	293	263	284	(NA)
Average yield of copper__percent	.73	.70	.59	.55	.53	.49	.47	.51	(NA)
Smelters (from domestic ores)	1,143	1,403	1,605	1,649	1,705	1,532	1,374	1,461	1,394
Percent of world total	23	23	24	22	22	19	18	18	(NA)
Refineries (from domestic ores)	1,121	1,336	1,521	1,680	1,698	1,421	1,286	1,423	1,411
From foreign ores, matte, etc., refinery reports	398	376	244	193	170	234	157	117	85
Total new refined, domestic and foreign	1,519	1,712	1,765	1,873	1,868	1,655	1,443	1,539	1,496
Secondary copper produced	871	1,253	1,248	1,301	1,377	1,344	972	1,145	1,150
Recovered from old scrap only	429	513	504	458	486	483	369	419	425
Imports (unmanufactured) [2][3]	524	523	392	416	421	609	324	535	517
Refined	143	137	132	192	203	314	147	382	391
Exports (unmanufactured) [3]	506	372	307	236	278	191	234	172	125
Exports of metallic copper [4]	510	379	274	242	285	244	303	218	192
Refined	434	325	221	183	189	127	172	112	52
Stocks (producers), Dec. 31	359	281	470	338	302	425	519	511	580
Mine production of primary copper	1,080	1,352	1,720	1,665	1,718	1,597	1,413	1,606	1,504
Arizona	539	703	918	909	927	859	813	1,024	924
Montana	92	115	120	123	132	131	88	91	86
New Mexico	67	99	166	168	205	197	146	172	165
Utah	218	259	296	260	257	231	177	185	194
Other States	163	176	220	205	197	180	189	134	135
Avg. price, domestic prod__cents per lb	32.1	35.4	58.2	51.2	59.5	77.3	64.2	69.6	66.8
World smelter production, new copper	5,040	6,105	6,752	7,405	7,878	8,068	7,793	8,164	(NA)

NA Not available. [1] Includes old tailings, smelted or retreated. Not comparable with mine production figures which include recoverable copper content of ores not classified as "copper."
[2] Includes copper imported for immediate consumption plus material entering country under bond.
[3] Comprises copper in ores and concentrates, matte, refined, blister, and scrap.
[4] Comprises refined, semimanufactures, scrap and (1976 and 1977) blister.

No. 1343. Gold and Silver—Summary: 1950 to 1977

[See *Historical Statistics, Colonial Times to 1970*, series M 268–269, for mine production]

ITEM	1950	1955	1960	1965	1970	1972	1973	1974	1975	1976	1977
GOLD											
Ore produced [1]__1,000 sh. tons	3,584	2,234	2,267	3,113	3,687	3,316	4,715	4,598	5,722	3,063	(NA)
Production, U.S.__mil. fine oz	2.4	1.9	1.7	1.7	1.7	1.4	1.2	1.1	1.1	1.0	1.1
Value__mil. dol	84	66	58	60	63	85	115	180	170	131	163
Production, world__mil. fine oz	28.3	30.4	37.8	46.2	47.4	44.8	43.3	40.1	38.7	39.9	38.5
Industrial consumption, U.S., net__mil. troy oz	2.8	1.3	3.0	5.3	6.0	7.3	6.7	4.7	4.0	4.6	4.9
Imports__mil. dol	163	104	335	102	237	358	356	397	457	331	674
Exports__mil. dol	514	7	2	1,285	38	63	146	228	493	375	1,113
Price per fine oz [2]__dol	35.0	35.0	35.0	35.0	36.4	58.6	97.8	159.7	161.5	125.3	148.3
Production: [3]											
Nevada__1,000 fine oz	170	77	66	[4] 205	480	420	260	299	333	288	324
South Dakota__1,000 fine oz	572	527	551	[4] 656	579	407	358	344	305	319	305
Utah__1,000 fine oz	392	442	314	[4] 389	408	362	307	255	190	187	211
SILVER											
Ore produced [1][5]__1,000 sh. tons	1,060	690	988	958	934	737	717	758	919	1,821	(NA)
Production, U.S.__mil. fine oz	42	37	31	40	45	37	37	34	35	34	38
Value__mil. dol	38	34	28	51	80	63	96	159	154	149	176
Production, world__mil. fine oz	203	224	241	257	301	302	308	292	298	305	318
Industrial consumption, U.S., net [6]__mil. fine oz	110	101	102	137	128	152	196	176	158	171	154
Imports__mil. dol	79	71	54	63	104	102	330	624	395	378	407
Exports__mil. dol	4	4	27	51	49	49	28	82	148	61	96
Price per fine oz [2]__dol	.91	.91	.91	1.29	1.77	1.69	2.56	4.71	4.42	4.35	4.62
Production: [3]											
Idaho__mil. fine oz	16.0	14.0	17.8	[4] 18.1	19.1	14.3	13.6	12.4	13.9	11.6	15.3
Arizona__mil. fine oz	5.1	4.6	5.3	[4] 6.1	7.3	6.7	7.2	6.4	6.3	7.6	6.8
Utah__mil. fine oz	6.8	6.3	5.1	[4] 5.2	6.0	4.3	3.6	3.2	2.8	3.1	3.3
Colorado__mil. fine oz	3.3	2.5	2.1	[4] 2.0	2.9	3.7	3.6	2.8	3.4	4.1	4.7

NA Not available. [1] Gold and silver are also produced from base-metal ores and placers. In 1975, those sources accounted for 38 percent of gold produced and 65 percent of silver. [2] Selling price, except New York price for silver, beginning 1965. [3] Source: 1950–1965, U.S. Bureau of the Mint, *Annual Report of the Director*. [4] Refinery production. [5] Includes gold-silver ore. [6] Excludes coinage.

Source of tables 1342 and 1343: U.S. Bureau of Mines, *Minerals Yearbook*.

Mining and Mineral Products

No. 1344. LEAD—SUMMARY: 1960 TO 1977

[In thousands of short tons, except as indicated. Excludes Alaska, Hawaii, and Puerto Rico, except for imports and exports and as noted. See also *Historical Statistics, Colonial Times to 1970*, series M 242–248]

ITEM	1960	1965	1970	1972	1973	1974	1975	1976	1977, prel.
Smelter production of refined primary lead	382	418	667	680	674	673	636	653	605
Domestic ores and base bullion [1]	229	305	528	577	567	580	530	569	507
Foreign ores and base bullion	154	113	139	103	107	93	106	84	98
Recovery of secondary lead	470	576	597	617	654	699	658	727	732
Imports, general:									
Lead in pigs, bars, and old	214	227	251	246	181	120	106	150	268
Lead in ores and matte	146	123	112	101	110	94	88	76	81
Exports of refined pig lead [2]	2	8	8	8	67	62	21	6	10
Consumption of metal, primary and secondary	1,021	1,241	1,361	1,485	1,541	1,599	1,297	1,490	1,491
Average price, common lead:									
New York____cents per lb	11.95	16.00	15.69	15.03	16.29	22.53	21.53	23.10	30.70
London____cents per lb	9.04	14.37	13.76	13.68	19.47	26.83	18.73	20.46	28.00
Mine production of recoverable lead [3]	247	301	572	619	603	664	621	610	589
Value [3]____mil. dol	58	94	179	186	196	299	267	282	360
World smelter production, est	2,550	2,911	3,628	3,723	3,838	3,829	3,656	3,788	3,750

[1] Excludes lead content of antimonial lead.   [2] Pigs, bars, and anodes.   [3] Includes Alaska.

No. 1345. NICKEL—SUMMARY: 1960 TO 1977

[Quantities in thousands of short tons. Excludes Alaska, Hawaii, and Puerto Rico, except for imports and exports. See also *Historical Statistics, Colonial Times to 1970*, series M 231–234]

ITEM	1960	1965	1970	1972	1973	1974	1975	1976	1977, prel.
Mine production	14	16	16	17	18	17	17	16	17
Plant production: Primary	14	14	16	16	14	14	14	14	13
Secondary [1]	27	51	49	67	66	65	42	47	50
Imports for consumption (est. nickel content)	103	163	156	174	190	221	161	188	185
Exports (gross weight)	54	21	31	22	22	30	30	48	31
Consumption	108	172	156	159	198	208	146	163	160
Stocks (consumer), Dec. 31	11	14	25	26	29	45	35	32	15
Price per pound [2]____dollars	.74	.79	1.33	1.53	1.53	2.01	2.20	2.41	2.20
World production, est	353	468	693	674	757	849	868	886	800

[1] Includes nickel recovered from iron and steel scrap.   [2] Peak price quoted U.S. buyers by International Nickel Co., Inc., for electrolytic nickel, U.S. duty included, f.o.b. Port Colborne, Ontario.

No. 1346. TIN—SUMMARY: 1960 TO 1977

[Excludes Alaska, Hawaii, and Puerto Rico, except for imports and exports]

ITEM	1960	1965	1970	1972	1973	1974	1975	1976	1977, prel.
Production:									
Domestic smelters_metric tons	(D)	3,138	(D)	4,369	4,877	6,096	6,500	5,700	6,70(
Secondary sources_metric tons	22,404	25,478	20,322	20,504	20,806	19,200	15,869	16,446	15,38(
Imports for consumption:									
Metal_____metric tons	40,173	41,471	51,365	53,293	46,581	40,238	44,366	45,055	48,33(
Ore (tin content)_metric tons	14,271	4,304	4,742	4,284	4,875	5,971	6,415	5,733	6,72(
Exports_____metric tons	871	2,874	4,523	1,152	3,461	8,550	3,596	2,338	5,48'
Monthly price of Straits tin at New York, average cents per pound	101	178	174	177	228	396	340	380	61
Consumption_____1,000 m. tons	82	85	75	70	76	66	56	63	6
World mine production, est. 1,000 m. tons	183	204	232	244	238	233	221	226	22

D Withheld to avoid disclosure of individual company data.

Source of tables 1344–1346: U.S. Bureau of Mines, *Minerals Yearbook*.

No. 1347. Tungsten Concentrate—Summary: 1960 to 1977

[Excludes Alaska and Hawaii. See *Historical Statistics, Colonial Times to 1970*, series M 225–226, for related data]

ITEM	1960	1965	1970	1972	1973	1974	1975	1976	1977, prel.
Production:									
Concentrates [1]_____1,000 sh. tons__	7.0	(D)	10.1	8.6	8.0	7.8	5.9	6.1	6.0
Tungsten content_____mil. lb__	6.7	(D)	9.6	8.2	7.6	7.4	5.6	5.8	5.7
Shipments from mines:									
Reported value f.o.b. mines_____mil. dol__	9.8	13.0	23.8	18.1	19.2	37.4	29.1	37.3	69.4
Average value per lb. of tungsten_____dollars__	1.40	1.72	2.55	2.56	2.71	4.77	5.30	6.35	9.91
Tungsten content:	5.2	3.5	1.3	5.9	11.0	11.8	6.9	5.8	6.3
Imports, general_____mil. lb__									
Consumption_____mil. lb__	11.6	13.9	16.7	14.1	15.4	16.3	14.0	16.1	15.1
Stocks [2]_____mil. lb__	5.5	1.8	2.2	4.2	1.7	2.1	2.5	1.2	1.7
World production_____mil. lb__	68.7	59.6	71.4	85.0	83.6	81.5	82.6	89.8	94.6

D Withheld to avoid disclosure of individual company data.
[1] 60% WO₃ basis. A short ton of 60% tungsten trioxide (WO₃) contains 951.72 pounds of tungsten.
[2] Producers and consumers, end of year.

No. 1348. Uranium—Summary: 1960 to 1977

[See also *Historical Statistics, Colonial Times to 1970*, series M 266–267]

ITEM	1960	1965	1970	1972	1973	1974	1975	1976	1977, prel.
Mine ore shipments [1]_____1,000 sh. tons__	7,970	4,386	6,324	6,418	6,537	7,116	7,400	9,198	10,100
Value_____mil. dol__	152	84	94	104	[2] 106	[2] 113	[2] 123	(NA)	(NA)
Recoverable content [3]_____mil. lb__	34.5	19.7	24.4	25.8	25.8	23.2	22.9	25.1	29.0
Value [4]_____mil. dol__	297	158	148	162	[2] 168	193	241	405	580
Production, concentrate [3]___1,000 sh. tons__	17.8	10.3	12.9	12.9	13.2	11.5	11.6	12.7	14.9
Imports, concentrate [3][5]____1,000 sh. tons__	15.8	3.0	.7	2.3	5.6	1.8	1.2	5.5	3.9
Value_____mil. dol__	(NA)	58	8	30	61	30	24	204	88
World production [3][6]_____1,000 sh. tons__	41.1	20.6	24.2	25.6	25.5	23.8	25.0	30.1	33.8

NA Not available. [1] Receipts at mills. [2] Estimated. [3] U₃O₈.
[4] Based on estimated average market price for delivery during the year.
[5] Mainly for enrichment and export of enriched uranium product, 1965–77. [6] Excludes Communist countries.

No. 1349. Zinc—Production and Prices: 1960 to 1977

[Quantities in thousands of short tons. Excludes Alaska and Hawaii. See *Historical Statistics, Colonial Times to 1970*, series M 249–250, for production]

ITEM AND STATE	1960	1965	1970	1972	1973	1974	1975	1976	1977, prel.
Smelter production of primary slab zinc_____	800	994	878	633	583	555	438	499	454
From domestic ores_____	334	551	404	401	399	347	308	382	331
From foreign ores_____	465	443	474	232	184	208	130	117	123
Value_____mil. dol__	205	291	236	225	241	399	341	369	312
Production of redistilled secondary slab zinc_	69	84	77	74	83	79	58	64	52
Avg. price of common zinc____cents per lb__	13.0	14.5	15.3	17.8	20.7	36.0	39.0	37.0	34.4
Mine production, recoverable zinc_____	435	611	534	478	479	500	469	485	458
Colorado_____	31	54	57	64	58	49	48	51	43
Idaho_____	37	58	41	39	46	39	41	47	32
Missouri_____	3	4	51	62	82	92	75	84	83
New Jersey_____	–	38	29	38	33	33	31	34	33
New York_____	66	70	59	61	81	93	77	74	72
Pennsylvania_____	14	28	30	18	19	20	21	22	23
Tennessee_____	91	122	118	102	64	86	83	83	92
Utah_____	35	28	35	22	17	13	20	22	18
Other States_____	158	209	114	72	79	75	73	68	62
World smelter production, est_____	3,335	4,353	5,321	5,656	5,877	6,183	5,592	5,978	6,020

– Represents zero.
Source of tables 1347–1349: U.S. Bureau of Mines, *Minerals Yearbook.*

No. 1350. Bauxite—Summary: 1960 to 1977

[In thousands of long tons, except as indicated. See also *Historical Statistics, Colonial Times to 1970*, series M 256–257]

ITEM	1960	1965	1970	1972	1973	1974	1975	1976	1977, prel.
Production:									
Crude ore	2,409	1,990	2,522	2,200	2,287	2,370	2,164	2,382	2,372
Dried-bauxite equivalent	1,998	1,654	2,082	1,812	1,879	1,949	1,772	1,958	1,958
Value _____mil. dol__	21.1	18.6	30.1	23.2	26.6	25.7	25.1	26.6	27.5
Shipments: [1]									
Gross weight (as shipped)	1,925	2,065	2,343	2,258	2,246	2,284	2,058	2,171	2,170
Dried-bauxite equivalent	1,654	1,785	2,078	2,017	2,005	2,021	1,836	1,941	1,940
Value _____mil. dol__	19.6	21.1	32.3	29.6	32.4	32.9	31.1	36.4	37.7
Imports for consumption [2]	8,739	11,199	12,620	11,976	12,778	14,308	10,782	11,646	12,092
Value _____mil. dol__	78.0	143.0	156.4	151.0	(NA)	(NA)	(NA)	(NA)	(NA)
Exports (as shipped)	29	147	3	29	12	16	19	15	25
Value _____mil. dol__	2.6	10.7	.2	1.3	.3	1.2	1.7	1.3	2.3
World production, est	27,205	36,849	56,873	63,921	69,244	78,362	74,503	76,337	81,000

NA Not available. [1] Shipments from mines and processing plants to consumers.
[2] Crude and dried. Figures for Jamaica, Haiti, and Dominican Republic adjusted to dry equivalent; other imports on "as shipped" basis.

No. 1351. Aluminum—Summary: 1960 to 1977

[In thousands of short tons, except as indicated. Imports and exports include Puerto Rico. See also *Historical Statistics, Colonial Times to 1970*, series M 258–262]

ITEM	1960	1965	1970	1972	1973	1974	1975	1976	1977, prel.
Total production	2,344	3,395	4,757	5,067	5,567	5,896	4,859	5,406	5,699
Primary aluminum	2,014	2,754	3,976	4,122	4,529	4,903	3,879	4,251	4,539
Secondary aluminum [1]	329	641	781	946	1,040	993	980	1,155	1,160
From old scrap	63	160	146	189	197	212	283	341	367
From new scrap	267	481	635	757	843	780	697	814	793
Value [2] _____mil. dol__	1,201	1,651	2,644	2,585	2,731	3,683	3,728	4,815	5,881
Primary aluminum	1,030	1,338	2,191	2,085	2,206	3,006	2,976	3,785	4,684
Price _____cents per lb.[3]	26.0	24.5	28.7	26.3	25.3	34.1	39.8	44.6	51.6
Secondary aluminum	171	313	453	501	525	677	752	1,030	1,197
Imports for consumption [4]	196	620	468	794	614	629	550	749	836
Value _____mil. dol__	103	266	231	375	285	403	410	582	799
Exports [4]	384	315	612	329	561	524	440	484	407
Value _____mil. dol__	174	170	360	209	370	482	436	496	499
Net domestic shipments [5]	2,366	3,788	4,476	5,743	6,873	6,394	4,555	5,952	6,300
World production, est	4,950	6,951	10,641	12,133	13,364	14,516	13,352	13,774	15,515

[1] Recoverable aluminum content. [2] Based on published producers' prices for primary metal.
[3] Average of prices for 99+ percent primary aluminum, quoted by *American Metal Market*.
[4] Crude and semicrude (including metal and alloys, plates, bars, etc., and scrap).
[5] Compiled by Aluminum Association from data on net shipments of aluminum ingot and mill products. In cludes changes in aluminum industry and government inventories and net trade.

No. 1352. Magnesium—Summary: 1960 to 1977

[In thousands of short tons, except as indicated. Imports and exports include Puerto Rico. See *Historical Statis tics, Colonial Times to 1970*, series M 263–265, for production]

ITEM	1960	1965	1970	1972	1973	1974	1975	1976	1977, prel.
Production (ingot equivalent):									
Primary magnesium	40.1	81.4	112.0	120.8	122.4	(D)	(D)	(D)	(D)
Secondary magnesium	10.3	13.6	12.0	15.7	17.6	14.9	27.3	31.0	33.0
Average price per lb., primary (quoted) _____cents	35.25	35.25	35.25	37.25	38.25	}41.25–75.00	{ 82.00 }	87.00–92.00	96.00–99.00
Exports	4.5	17.8	35.7	17.6	39.6	46.4	32.6	13.4	28.0
Imports, metallic and scrap [1]	.4	2.6	3.3	4.5	3.3	5.3	7.9	14.9	6.0
Domestic consumption [2]	37.1	69.6	93.5	103.7	115.8	130.0	94.1	104.5	110.0
World primary production [3]	102.5	178.3	242.3	257.5	266.4	[4]142.7	[4]138.3	[4]148.1	[4]153.4

D Withheld to avoid disclosing individual company data. [1] Represents imports for consumption.
[2] Primary only. [3] Estimated. [4] Excludes U.S. production.

Source of tables 1350–1352: U.S. Bureau of Mines, *Minerals Yearbook*.

Section 28
Construction and Housing

This section presents data on the construction industry and on various indicators of its activity and costs; on housing units and their characteristics, occupants, and financing; and on low-rent public housing.

The principal source of these data is the U.S. Bureau of the Census, which issues a variety of publications. Current construction statistics compiled by the Bureau appear in its monthly *Construction Reports* series with various quarterly or annual supplements; *Housing Starts* and *Housing Completions* present data by type of unit and by 4 major census regions; *New One-Family Homes Sold and For Sale* provides statistics annually on physical and financial characteristics for all new one-family homes by the 4 major census regions; *Value of New Construction Put in Place* includes monthly composite construction cost indexes, and a special supplement which contains historical data, 1947 to 1974, as well as several tables showing data for 1915–1946; *Price Index of New One-Family Houses Sold* presents quarterly figures and annual regional data; and *Housing Authorized by Building Permits and Public Contracts* covers approximately 14,000 permit-issuing jurisdictions in the United States. Statistics on expenditures by owners of residential properties are issued quarterly and annually in *Residential Alterations and Repairs*.

Other Census Bureau publications include the *Current Housing Reports* series, which comprises the quarterly *Housing Vacancies*, the quarterly *Market Absorption of Apartments*, the *Annual Housing Survey*, and various reports of the censuses of housing and of construction industries. *Construction Review*, published monthly by the Bureau of Domestic Business Development, U.S. Department of Commerce, contains many of the census series and other construction statistics series from the Federal Government and private agencies.

Other sources include the monthly *Dodge Construction Potentials* of F. W. Dodge Division, McGraw-Hill Information Systems Company, New York, N.Y., which presents State data on construction contracts; the Bureau of Economic Analysis, which presents data on residential capital; and the Federal Home Loan Bank Board, the Department of Housing and Urban Development (HUD), and the Veterans Administration, which publish financial data. Data on home mortgages are provided by the Federal Home Loan Bank Board. The Department of Housing and Urban Development provides data on the gross flow of long-term mortgage loans in its study, *The Supply of Mortgage Credit, 1970–1974*. Data on mortgages insured by the Federal Housing Administration (FHA) and on VA-guaranteed loans are also presented in this section. In addition, the *Statistical Yearbook*, published by HUD, also contains housing data.

Data bases.—Censuses of the construction industry were first conducted by the Bureau of the Census for 1929, 1935, and 1939; beginning in 1967, a census has been taken every five years (for years ending in "2" and "7"). The latest reports are for 1972.

The 1972 Census of Construction Industries, in accordance with the 1972 *Standard Industrial Classification Manual* (see text, page 396), defines a construction establishment as a relatively permanent place of business where the usual business activities related to construction are conducted.

From 1850 through 1930, the Bureau of the Census collected some housing data as part of its censuses of population and agriculture. Beginning in 1940, separate censuses of housing have been taken at 10-year intervals. For the 1970 census, data on year-round housing units were collected and issued on occupancy and structural characteristics, plumbing facilities, value, and rent.

777

Evaluation studies of the 1950, 1960, and 1970 censuses estimated the underenumeration of occupied housing units at 2.9 percent, 2.4 percent, and 1.7 percent, respectively. The net undercount in the 1970 census is estimated at approximately 1.5 million housing units. The estimates for the various censuses are not strictly comparable due to differences in timing, procedures, and other factors. The census figures have not been adjusted to reflect the estimated undercounts.

The Annual Housing Survey (*Current Housing Reports*, Series H-150 and H-170), which began in 1973, provides a current and ongoing series of data on selected housing and demographic characteristics. It is based on a national sample and on separate samples for 60 SMSA's selected to represent a cross section of the housing stock in these areas. Annual Housing Survey estimates are subject to both sampling and nonsampling errors; caution should, therefore, be used in making comparisons with 1970 census data.

Data on residential mortgages were collected continuously from 1890 to 1970, except 1930, as part of the decennial census by the Bureau of the Census. Since 1973, mortgage status data, which are limited to single family homes on less than ten acres with no business on the property, have been presented in the Annual Housing Survey.

Housing units.—In general, a housing unit is a group of rooms or a single room occupied or intended for occupancy as separate living quarters, that is, the occupants do not live and eat with any other persons in the structure, and there is either (1) direct access from the outside or through a common hall, or (2) complete kitchen facilities for the exclusive use of the occupants. Transient accommodations, barracks for workers, and institutional-type quarters are not counted as housing units.

Statistical Reliability.—For a discussion of statistical collection and estimation, sampling procedures, and measures of statistical reliability applicable to Census Bureau data, see Appendix III.

Historical statistics.—Tabular headnotes provide cross-references, where applicable, to *Historical Statistics of the United States, Colonial Times to 1970*. See Appendix I.

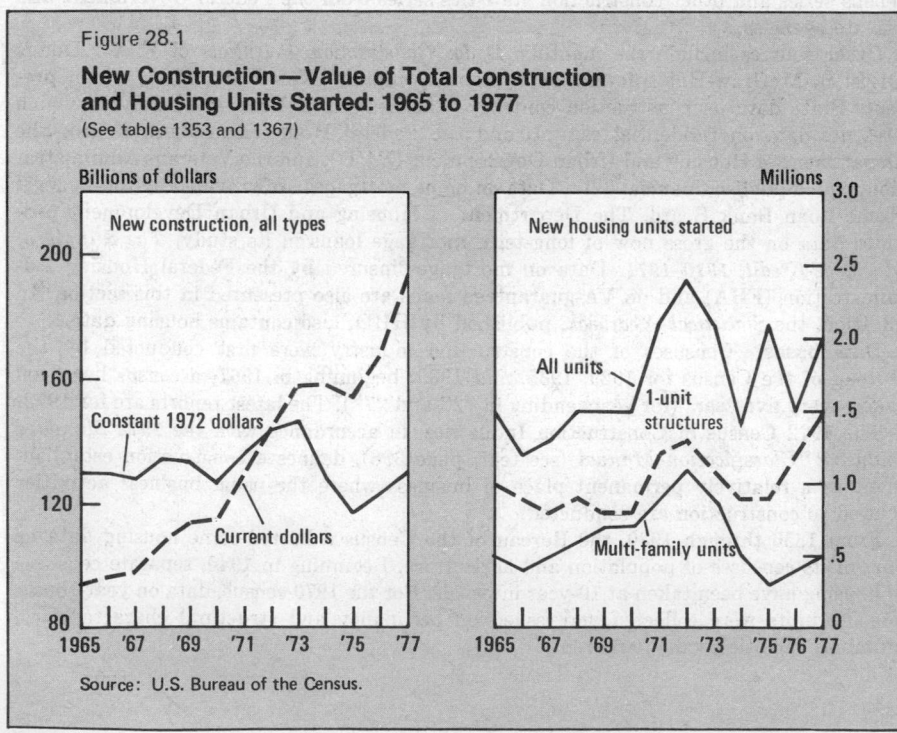

Figure 28.1

New Construction—Value of Total Construction and Housing Units Started: 1965 to 1977
(See tables 1353 and 1367)

Source: U.S. Bureau of the Census.

No. 1353. VALUE OF NEW CONSTRUCTION PUT IN PLACE: 1965 TO 1977

[In millions of dollars, except percent. Represents value of construction put in place during year; differs from building permit and construction contract data in timing and coverage. Includes installed cost of normal building service equipment and selected types of industrial production equipment (largely site fabricated). Excludes cost of shipbuilding, land, and most types of machinery and equipment. See also *Historical Statistics, Colonial Times to 1970*, series N 1-29 and N 66-69]

ITEM	1965	1970	1971	1972	1973	1974	1975	1976	1977
Total	73,747	94,855	109,950	124,085	137,917	138,501	134,535	148,778	172,552
Average annual percent change [1]	6.1	5.2	15.9	12.9	11.1	.4	−2.9	10.6	15.7
Private	51,685	66,759	80,079	93,901	105,412	100,166	93,651	110,467	134,724
Percent of total	70.1	70.4	72.8	75.7	76.4	72.3	69.6	74.2	78.1
Residential buildings (incl. farm)	27,934	31,864	43,267	54,288	59,727	50,376	46,472	60,520	80,956
New housing units	21,712	24,272	35,066	44,879	50,087	40,644	34,408	47,277	65,749
Structures with—									
1 unit	15,705	14,754	22,202	27,632	30,649	26,293	27,423	40,049	55,271
2 or more units	6,007	9,518	12,864	17,247	19,438	14,351	6,986	7,228	10,478
Additions, alterations	4,736	6,234	6,807	7,420	7,274	8,045	10,925	12,308	14,209
Nonhousekeeping	1,486	1,358	1,394	1,989	2,366	1,687	1,139	935	998
Nonresidential buildings	16,509	21,417	22,479	24,038	27,584	29,637	26,407	26,091	28,695
Industrial	(NA)	6,538	5,423	4,676	6,243	7,902	8,018	7,183	7,712
Commercial	(NA)	9,754	11,619	13,464	15,453	15,944	12,806	12,756	14,783
Religious	(NA)	931	813	844	814	918	867	956	1,046
Educational	(NA)	865	943	968	837	655	567	660	660
Hospital and institutional	(NA)	2,529	2,864	3,172	3,152	3,201	3,209	3,396	3,290
Other nonresidential	(NA)	800	817	914	1,085	1,017	939	1,140	1,203
Farm (nonresidential)	1,038	1,512	1,557	1,432	2,003	2,529	2,325	2,502	2,700
Public utilities	5,788	11,020	11,783	13,202	15,185	16,624	17,379	20,276	21,072
Telephone, telegraph	1,463	2,968	3,005	3,302	3,967	4,279	3,683	3,777	4,345
Other public utilities	4,325	8,052	8,778	9,900	11,218	12,345	13,696	16,499	16,727
Railroads	310	306	291	359	422	575	514	555	722
Electric light, power	2,589	5,808	6,725	7,582	8,778	9,246	9,888	11,777	12,831
Gas	1,304	1,653	1,334	1,675	1,709	1,739	1,350	1,270	1,952
Petroleum pipelines	122	285	428	284	309	785	1,944	2,887	1,222
All other private	416	946	993	941	913	1,000	1,068	1,077	1,301
Public	22,062	28,096	29,871	30,184	32,505	38,334	40,884	38,311	37,827
Percent of total	29.9	29.6	27.2	24.3	23.6	27.7	30.4	25.8	21.9
Buildings	7,893	10,657	11,397	11,500	12,995	14,990	15,474	13,480	12,751
Housing, redevelopment	603	1,107	1,136	875	941	1,006	754	736	959
Industrial	368	499	572	534	606	766	918	973	1,146
Educational	4,284	5,619	5,564	5,720	6,647	7,310	7,760	6,265	5,433
Hospital	520	837	981	1,008	1,002	1,238	1,745	1,786	1,679
Other public	2,118	2,595	3,144	3,363	3,799	4,670	4,296	3,720	3,534
Highways and streets	7,550	9,981	10,658	10,429	10,505	12,065	10,854	9,777	9,372
Military facilities	830	718	901	1,087	1,166	1,185	1,389	1,520	1,517
Conservation, development	2,019	1,908	2,095	2,172	2,313	2,741	3,257	3,751	3,879
Other public construction	3,770	4,832	4,820	4,996	5,526	7,352	9,911	9,782	10,308
Sewer systems	1,195	1,544	1,829	1,702	1,954	2,681	4,801	5,286	5,386
Water supply facilities	1,266	1,094	996	1,076	1,068	1,381	1,765	1,595	1,822
Misc. construction	1,309	2,194	1,995	2,218	2,504	3,290	3,345	2,901	3,100
Public ownership:									
Federal Government	4,014	3,290	3,983	4,392	4,851	5,293	6,318	6,752	7,388
Buildings	1,460	902	1,077	1,130	1,330	1,504	1,894	1,955	2,250
Military facilities	830	718	901	1,087	1,166	1,185	1,389	1,520	1,517
Conservation and develop	1,506	1,367	1,645	1,762	1,955	2,246	2,638	2,857	3,104
Misc. (incl. highways and streets)	218	303	360	413	400	357	397	420	517
State and local government	18,048	24,806	25,888	25,792	27,654	33,042	34,566	31,560	30,440
Buildings	6,433	9,755	10,320	10,370	11,665	13,487	13,580	11,526	10,501
Highways and streets	7,381	9,728	10,370	10,130	10,237	11,808	10,547	9,438	8,964
Conservation, development	513	541	450	410	358	495	618	894	775
Other	3,721	4,782	4,748	4,882	5,394	7,252	9,821	9,701	10,200

NA Not available.
[1] Change from prior year shown; for 1965, change from 1960. Minus sign (−) denotes decrease.

Source: U.S. Bureau of the Census, *Construction Reports*, series C30.

No. 1354. Value in Constant (1972) Dollars of New Construction Put in Place: 1965 to 1977

[In millions of dollars, except percent. For details on derivation of constant values and description of revised series, see source. For description of nature of revisions and deflators used, see *Construction Reports*, series C30-74S. See also *Historical Statistics, Colonial Times to 1970*, series N 30-60, for value in 1957-59 dollars]

ITEM	1965	1970	1971	1972	1973	1974	1975	1976	1977
New construction	109,678	107,009	116,037	123,920	126,924	109,132	97,229	103,467	110,192
Private	75,948	75,113	84,530	93,764	96,659	80,078	68,628	77,029	85,579
Percent of total	69.2	70.2	72.8	75.7	76.2	73.4	70.6	74.4	77.7
Residential buildings [1]	39,684	35,707	45,836	54,192	54,308	41,489	35,256	42,656	50,629
New housing units	30,840	27,206	37,143	44,791	45,541	33,492	26,096	33,302	41,082
1 unit structures	22,308	16,532	23,507	27,567	27,851	21,619	20,780	28,210	34,521
2 or more unit structures	8,532	10,674	13,636	17,224	17,690	11,873	5,317	5,092	6,561
Additions and alterations	6,733	6,979	7,217	7,419	6,614	6,602	8,293	8,693	8,920
Nonhousekeeping	2,111	1,522	1,476	1,983	2,153	1,395	866	661	627
Nonresidential buildings [2]	25,770	24,143	23,502	24,023	25,409	22,699	19,073	18,792	19,430
Industrial	7,948	7,369	5,680	4,673	5,739	6,038	5,791	5,175	5,223
Office	}10,466	10,995	12,137	{ 5,266	5,517	4,695	3,591	3,430	3,571
Other commercial				8,189	8,719	7,521	5,658	5,757	6,435
Religious	1,873	1,049	851	844	751	703	627	689	708
Educational	1,141	975	986	967	771	504	409	475	447
Hospital and institutional	2,179	2,852	2,995	3,172	2,907	2,459	2,318	2,445	2,232
Other nonresidential	2,163	903	853	912	1,005	779	678	821	814
Farm (nonresidential)	1,617	1,702	1,626	1,430	1,838	1,935	1,679	1,802	1,833
Public utilities	8,252	12,497	12,519	13,182	14,258	13,195	11,888	13,053	12,856
Telephone and telegraph	2,231	3,355	3,225	3,293	3,770	3,529	2,795	2,650	2,910
Other public utilities	6,024	9,142	9,294	9,889	10,488	9,667	9,093	10,402	9,946
Railroad	466	345	309	355	394	433	352	374	462
Electric light and power [3]	3,766	6,638	7,145	7,580	8,200	7,257	6,635	7,478	7,628
Gas	1,638	1,843	1,395	1,669	1,604	1,368	870	782	1,136
Petroleum pipelines	154	316	445	285	290	609	1,236	1,768	720
All other private	625	1,067	1,049	940	851	759	733	726	831
Public	33,730	31,896	31,507	30,156	30,265	29,054	28,601	26,438	24,613
Percent of total	30.8	29.8	27.2	24.3	23.8	26.6	29.4	25.6	22.3
Buildings	12,245	12,008	11,941	11,488	11,986	11,556	11,207	9,705	8,595
Housing and redevelopment	856	1,239	1,210	873	855	827	572	520	602
Industrial	576	561	597	532	559	588	663	701	777
Educational	6,693	6,336	5,820	5,713	6,139	5,618	5,607	4,516	3,682
Hospital	813	947	1,029	1,009	923	950	1,261	1,287	1,140
Other public buildings	3,307	2,925	3,285	3,361	3,510	3,573	3,104	2,681	2,393
Highways and streets	11,651	11,282	11,232	10,418	9,884	8,682	7,269	6,686	6,126
Military facilities	1,272	817	951	1,086	1,086	905	992	1,074	1,011
Conservation and development	2,956	2,160	2,212	2,169	2,139	2,183	2,286	2,490	2,427
Other public construction	5,606	5,629	5,171	4,995	5,170	5,729	6,847	6,484	6,454
Sewer systems	1,871	1,872	1,999	1,702	1,825	2,136	3,369	3,513	3,367
Water supply facilities	1,767	1,270	1,064	1,079	1,002	1,096	1,187	1,017	1,098
Miscellaneous	1,968	2,487	2,108	2,214	2,343	2,496	2,292	1,954	1,989

[1] Including farm.   [2] Excludes building by privately owned public utilities.
[3] Includes construction with Rural Electrification Administration (REA) funds.

Source: U.S. Bureau of the Census, *Construction Reports*, series C30.

No. 1355. Value of Privately Owned Nonresidential Building Projects, by Construction Status, 1973 to 1977, and by Type of Project, 1977

[In billions of dollars]

CONSTRUCTION STATUS	1973	1974	1975	1976	1977				
					Total	Industrial	Office building	Other commercial	Hospital and institutional	Other [1]
Value of projects—									
Started	28.4	27.7	20.1	23.8	28.4	6.7	5.1	10.3	3.1	3.1
Completed	24.6	26.9	27.9	25.9	27.2	6.8	5.2	9.3	3.3	2.7
Under construction at yearend	42.8	46.1	41.9	41.4	44.8	16.8	8.6	8.3	7.8	3.4

[1] Privately owned religious, educational, and miscellaneous nonresidential building projects.
Source: U.S. Bureau of the Census, *Construction Reports*, series C30.

No. 1356. VALUATION OF PRIVATE CONSTRUCTION AUTHORIZED BY BUILDING PERMITS: 1970 TO 1977

[In millions of dollars. "13,000 and 14,000 place" series are based on U.S. total of approximately 13,000 and 14,000 places identified in 1967 and 1972, respectively, with local building permit systems]

TYPE OF CONSTRUCTION	13,000 PLACE SERIES			14,000 PLACE SERIES					
	1970	1971	1972	1972	1973	1974	1975	1976	1977, prel.
Total	37,472	48,198	58,382	59,445	61,835	50,827	47,330	63,144	85,473
New housing units	19,169	28,306	35,204	35,857	33,669	23,479	23,855	35,528	49,872
In structures with—									
1 unit	11,486	17,284	20,860	21,430	20,691	16,774	19,761	28,998	39,934
2–4 units	968	1,541	1,886	1,910	1,706	1,025	1,119	1,796	2,562
5 units or more	6,716	9,481	12,457	12,517	11,272	5,680	2,974	4,734	7,376
New nonhousekeep. resid. bldgs.	789	872	1,290	1,414	1,689	876	705	770	1,181
New nonresidential buildings	13,224	15,005	17,042	17,289	20,903	20,483	16,200	19,182	25,877
Industrial buildings	2,435	2,308	2,826	2,899	4,525	4,505	3,041	3,923	6,893
Office buildings	2,806	3,718	3,740	3,758	4,058	3,872	2,965	3,091	4,415
Stores and other mercantile	2,601	2,998	4,128	4,159	4,807	4,308	3,446	4,326	5,750
Hospitals and other institutional	1,735	1,774	1,886	1,898	1,875	2,024	1,963	2,442	2,009
All other nonresidential	3,644	4,207	4,462	4,575	5,637	5,774	4,786	5,400	6,810
Additions and alterations	4,290	4,015	4,846	4,885	5,574	5,990	6,570	7,664	8,543

No. 1357. PRICE, WAGE SCALE, AND COST INDEXES FOR CONSTRUCTION: 1965 TO 1977

[1967=100. Excludes Alaska and Hawaii, except as noted. Indexes of certain of these firms are published on bases different from those shown here. See Historical Statistics, Colonial Times to 1970, series N 118–137, for construction cost indexes on a 1947–49 base]

ITEM	1965	1970	1971	1972	1973	1974	1975	1976	1977
Price index for new one-family houses sold [1]	93.2	117.4	123.2	131.0	144.8	158.1	174.3	191.4	215.5
Union hourly wage scales, building trades [2]	90.9	128.8	144.0	153.2	160.8	173.4	188.3	200.5	212.3
Bricklayers	91.8	127.7	144.9	153.4	159.5	172.3	184.0	194.1	204.2
Carpenters	90.7	128.9	141.5	150.9	160.1	172.1	187.0	198.2	208.7
Electricians	91.5	130.4	148.4	158.8	164.9	175.1	193.8	206.8	220.4
Painters	90.9	126.6	139.5	152.1	160.6	172.8	187.9	202.0	214.5
Plasterers	92.1	126.0	140.9	150.0	157.5	170.5	182.7	195.9	207.5
Plumbers	91.4	130.5	145.8	152.8	158.8	172.7	186.7	199.6	211.8
Building laborers	90.5	129.3	144.4	152.2	160.5	176.1	190.7	203.3	216.3
Construction cost indexes:									
Dept. of Commerce composite [3]	93	122	131	139	152	173	189	198	216
Fed. Highway Admin.: Highways [4]	90.3	125.6	131.7	138.2	152.4	201.8	203.8	199.3	216.4
Environmental Protection Agency:									
Sewers	93.7	120.4	134.3	149.1	160.4	183.5	208.0	221.0	234.9
Sewage treatment plant	93.8	120.3	133.8	144.0	152.9	180.6	209.4	219.7	233.1
ICC: Pipeline	97	109	117	122	130	154	190	200	(NA)
American Appraisal Co.: Building const. [5]	91	124	138	151	167	177	189	206	220
E. H. Boeckh, building cost index: [6]									
Small residential structures	90.4	122.4	132.8	145.8	159.2	172.0	183.5	198.6	216.5
Apartments, hotels, and office buildings	90.7	124.4	135.0	145.4	154.5	168.4	185.0	199.6	216.1
Commercial and factory buildings	90.0	123.1	133.9	144.8	154.4	172.0	188.8	204.9	221.3
Engineering News-Record: [7]									
Building construction	93.3	124.4	140.5	155.2	168.4	178.3	193.3	210.9	228.6
General construction	90.8	128.9	146.8	163.0	176.5	188.2	205.7	223.4	239.9
Turner Construction Co.: Building const. [8]	94	129	143	154	162	188	198	202	209
Handy-Whitman public utility: [9] Building	93	121	133	144	158	190	213	217	228
Electric light and power [10]	94	119	128	135	144	171	201	214	228

NA Not available.   [1] Includes value of site.   [2] Based on minimum wage rates agreed upon through collective bargaining; excludes overtime. As of July 1. Includes Honolulu, Hawaii, beginning in 1976. Source: U.S. Bureau of Labor Statistics, Union Wages and Hours: Building Trades, annual.   [3] Covers both building and nonbuilding construction, excluding maintenance and repair. Represents a weighted average of various indexes used for different types of construction.   [4] Based on average contract unit bid prices for composite mile (involving specific average amounts of excavation, paving, reinforcing steel, structural steel, and structural concrete).   [5] Average for 30 cities of 4 types of buildings: Wood-frame, brick-wood frame, brick-steel frame, and reinforced concrete. Covers materials and labor costs in structural portion of buildings but excludes those for plumbing, heating, lighting, sprinklers, and elevators. Reflects employee-benefit costs, and allows for contractors' overhead and profit.   [6] Average of 20 cities for types shown. Weights based on surveys of building costs. Wage rates used for both common and skilled labor. Reflects payment of sales taxes and social security payroll taxes.   [7] Building construction index computed on basis of hypothetical unit of construction requiring 6 bbl. of portland cement, 1,088 M bd. ft. of 2" x 4" lumber, 2,500 lb. of structural steel, and 68.38 hours of skilled labor. General construction index based on same materials components combined with 200 hours of common labor.   [8] Eastern cities. Based on firm's cost experience with respect to labor rates, materials prices, competitive conditions, efficiency of plant and management, and productivity. Reflects payment of sales taxes and employee-benefit costs.   [9] Based on data covering public utility construction costs for 95 items in 6 geographic regions. Covers skilled and common labor; does not reflect tax payments nor employee-benefit costs.   [10] As derived by U.S. Bureau of the Census. Covers steam production plants only; excludes hydraulic plants.

Source of tables 1356 and 1357: Except as noted, U.S. Bureau of the Census. In U.S. Bureau of Domestic Business Development, Construction Review.

No. 1358. Construction Materials—Indexes of Producer Prices: 1970 to 1977

[1967=100. For discussion of producer price index, see text, p. 481. Covers materials incorporated as integral part of a building or normally installed during construction and not readily removable. Excludes consumer durables such as kitchen ranges, refrigerators, etc. See also *Historical Statistics, Colonial Times to 1970,* series N 140-155]

COMMODITY	1970	1972	1973	1974	1975	1976	1977
All materials	**112.5**	**126.6**	**138.5**	**160.9**	**174.0**	**187.7**	**204.9**
Softwood lumber: Douglas fir	108.7	161.1	209.6	213.7	212.0	250.7	291.4
Southern pine	114.7	151.5	187.9	184.5	175.3	217.4	262.5
Other	115.0	177.0	226.6	220.8	205.3	257.8	312.6
Hardwood lumber	114.6	126.2	169.0	189.5	160.3	176.0	200.3
Millwork	116.0	128.4	144.2	157.1	160.4	176.9	193.7
Plywood	108.4	130.7	155.2	161.1	161.2	187.0	212.2
Softwood	113.6	154.9	194.0	186.8	200.6	247.6	295.8
Hardwood	102.5	104.3	112.7	130.2	119.5	122.5	127.7
Building paper and board	101.0	106.4	112.8	123.5	127.1	138.8	157.0
Prepared paint	112.4	118.0	122.2	145.7	166.9	174.4	182.4
Finished steel products:							
Structural shapes	115.3	134.6	140.7	179.0	216.3	227.1	229.0
Reinforcing bars	110.3	114.7	124.1	201.5	199.2	182.5	185.8
Black pipe, carbon	113.3	132.5	137.8	178.7	204.6	219.1	247.9
Wire nails, 8d common	114.8	133.5	140.4	207.1	241.4	243.6	261.3
Nonferrous metal products	124.7	116.9	135.0	187.1	171.6	181.6	195.4
Copper water tubing	122.9	116.4	133.3	174.7	134.2	147.7	165.6
Building wire	123.2	92.9	108.2	169.7	125.8	118.4	126.7
Plumbing fixtures	111.2	119.7	125.8	149.1	162.3	174.1	186.6
Enameled iron	107.2	121.2	129.6	158.1	188.4	201.2	214.6
Vitreous china	106.3	115.6	120.8	134.2	146.6	159.0	174.2
Brass fittings	115.7	122.2	128.8	155.7	162.2	174.1	186.5
Heating equipment	110.6	118.2	120.4	135.0	150.7	158.0	165.5
Steam and hot water	110.8	119.7	122.7	139.0	153.9	162.4	173.2
Metal doors, sash, trim	113.0	120.5	124.5	147.3	162.5	171.3	188.7
Plate glass	(NA)	115.0	115.0	115.0	120.4	126.4	160.8
Concrete ingredients	112.6	126.9	131.2	148.7	172.3	186.7	199.0
Concrete products	112.2	125.6	131.7	151.7	170.5	180.1	191.8
Pipe	103.8	116.0	118.6	143.6	169.4	169.1	175.4
Structural clay products [1]	109.9	117.3	123.3	135.2	151.2	163.5	179.8
Gypsum products	99.7	114.7	120.9	137.6	144.0	154.4	183.5
Asphalt roofing	102.7	131.2	135.5	196.0	225.9	238.3	253.0
Insulation materials	123.2	136.9	137.4	156.5	196.2	212.6	235.9
Vinyl covering	96.3	102.5	103.2	117.9	135.4	144.5	153.0

NA Not available.   [1] Excludes refractories.

Source: U.S. Bureau of Labor Statistics, *Producer* (formerly Wholesale) *Prices and Price Indexes,* monthly and annual.

No. 1359. Construction Contracts—Value of Construction and Floor Space of Buildings, by Class of Construction: 1965 to 1977

[**Value in billions of dollars; space in million square feet.** 1965 excludes Alaska and Hawaii. Includes new structures and additions to existing structures (both value and floor area), and major alterations to existing structures which affect only valuation, since no additional floor area is created by "alteration". See also *Historical Statistics, Colonial Times to 1970,* series N 78-100]

CLASS OF CONSTRUCTION	AMOUNT							PERCENT DISTRIBUTION			
	1965	1970	1973	1974	1975	1976	1977	1965	1970	1975	1977
Value of construction, total	**49.3**	**68.3**	**99.3**	**93.7**	**92.7**	**110.1**	**139.2**	**100.0**	**100.0**	**100.0**	**100.0**
Residential buildings	21.2	24.8	45.7	33.6	31.3	44.2	61.4	43.0	36.3	33.8	44.1
Nonres. buildings, total	17.3	24.6	31.4	33.2	31.6	30.0	35.3	35.1	36.0	34.1	25.4
Commercial [1]	5.5	9.1	12.8	11.8	9.2	10.2	13.6	11.2	13.3	9.9	9.8
Manufacturing	3.1	3.7	4.8	5.6	6.8	4.5	5.2	6.3	5.4	7.3	3.7
Educational and science	4.2	5.3	5.1	6.3	5.9	4.9	5.2	8.5	7.8	6.4	3.7
Hospital	1.5	2.8	3.3	3.8	3.7	4.5	4.5	3.0	4.1	4.0	3.2
Public buildings	.8	1.0	2.0	2.1	2.1	2.1	2.3	1.6	1.5	2.3	1.7
Religious	.8	.6	.7	.8	.8	.9	1.0	1.6	.9	.9	.7
Social and recreational [2]	1.4	2.1	2.7	2.8	3.1	3.0	3.5	2.8	3.1	3.3	2.5
Nonbuilding construction	10.8	19.0	22.1	27.0	29.8	35.9	42.5	21.9	27.8	32.2	30.5
Floor space, total	**2,843**	**2,938**	**4,013**	**2,938**	**2,390**	**2,819**	**3,519**	**100.0**	**100.0**	**100.0**	**100.0**
Residential buildings	1,711	1,781	2,574	1,657	1,441	1,867	2,418	60.2	60.6	60.3	68.7
Nonres. buildings, total	1,131	1,157	1,439	1,282	949	953	1,101	39.8	39.4	39.7	31.3
Commercial [1]	415	530	717	594	409	440	567	14.6	18.0	17.1	16.1
Manufacturing	265	212	293	246	146	152	171	9.3	7.2	6.1	4.9
Educational and science	225	195	156	176	152	118	112	7.9	6.6	6.4	3.2
Hospital	60	75	76	75	63	71	67	2.1	2.6	2.6	1.9
Public buildings	36	29	49	47	46	42	43	1.3	1.0	1.9	1.2
Religious	45	27	28	27	28	31	33	1.6	.9	1.2	.9
Social and recreational [2]	85	89	120	117	105	99	107	3.0	3.0	4.4	3.0

[1] Includes nonindustrial warehouses.   [2] Includes miscellaneous.

Source: F.W. Dodge Division, McGraw-Hill Information Systems Company, New York, N.Y. In *Dodge Construction Potentials.*

No. 1360. CONSTRUCTION CONTRACTS—VALUE, BY STATES: 1970 TO 1977

[In millions of dollars. See headnote, table 1359. Represents value of construction in States in which work was actually done]

STATE	1970	1975	1976	Total¹ (1977)	Residential (1977)	Nonresidential (1977)	STATE	1970	1975	1976	Total¹ (1977)	Residential (1977)	Nonresidential (1977)
Total	68,294	92,659	110,061	139,213	61,433	35,299	Mo	1,171	1,645	2,669	2,451	1,082	622
							Mont	184	393	388	443	198	138
Ala	1,036	3,084	1,937	1,968	1,016	585	Nebr	334	747	962	1,197	418	261
Alaska	238	4,826	881	837	308	187	Nev	364	479	680	926	595	207
Ariz	1,063	1,704	2,431	3,834	1,179	546	N.H	188	313	346	1,651	200	117
Ark	506	1,301	1,150	1,237	731	260							
Calif	6,739	8,663	11,405	14,447	9,135	3,825	N.J	2,741	1,950	2,064	4,773	1,103	918
							N.Mex	394	660	632	952	492	233
Colo	834	1,380	1,871	2,027	1,151	539	N.Y	5,589	3,955	4,593	4,329	1,377	1,312
Conn	1,154	804	1,788	1,169	546	402	N.C	1,722	2,240	2,329	2,995	1,667	860
Del	208	228	376	283	123	110	N. Dak	296	865	394	727	264	160
D.C	313	542	445	432	95	218							
Fla	3,537	3,607	4,038	6,946	3,514	1,604	Ohio	3,046	3,924	4,165	7,267	2,561	1,667
							Okla	754	1,166	1,410	2,425	1,051	594
Ga	1,555	1,825	3,332	5,209	1,490	846	Oreg	634	1,036	1,234	1,929	1,060	448
Hawaii	601	979	694	610	249	189	Pa	3,192	3,009	3,869	3,797	1,634	1,300
Idaho	197	399	397	701	340	215	R.I	194	244	261	308	162	92
Ill	3,596	3,907	8,459	5,802	3,148	1,698							
Ind	1,460	2,211	2,536	4,280	1,563	962	S.C	883	2,143	1,342	1,556	818	468
							S. Dak	160	275	370	467	216	113
Iowa	701	1,252	1,405	1,509	763	392	Tenn	1,562	1,678	1,782	6,233	1,298	737
Kans	530	1,324	1,489	3,100	717	304	Tex	4,119	6,372	7,880	10,414	5,044	3,639
Ky	1,185	1,444	1,827	2,265	997	641	Utah	334	735	845	1,048	641	267
La	1,359	1,847	3,708	3,593	1,252	690							
Maine	216	398	481	399	220	86	Vt	148	144	158	236	117	61
							Va	1,891	2,932	2,677	3,503	1,740	820
Md	1,270	1,886	2,097	2,203	974	795	Wash	1,478	2,019	3,480	2,916	1,661	759
Mass	1,791	1,415	1,473	1,831	728	634	W. Va	846	926	1,038	653	137	234
Mich	2,950	3,187	3,176	4,292	2,159	1,527	Wis	1,206	1,667	2,548	2,620	1,409	825
Minn	1,094	1,667	1,977	2,568	1,348	668	Wyo	161	229	1,609	438	139	152
Miss	570	1,030	961	1,415	604	373							

¹ Includes nonbuilding construction.

Source: F. W. Dodge Division, McGraw-Hill Information Systems Company, New York, N.Y. Figures reported currently in *Dodge Construction Potentials*.

No. 1361. CONSTRUCTION ESTABLISHMENTS, BY SIZE OF RECEIPTS: 1967 AND 1972

[Receipt figures contain considerable duplication. Work of one firm may be subcontracted out to other firms causing receipts to be included under both firms. Figures for establishments with payroll based on sample and subject to sampling variability; see source]

ITEM	Total	BY RECEIPT SIZE						
		$1–$24,999	$25,000–$49,999	$50,000–$99,999	$100,000–$249,999	$250,000–$499,999	$500,000–$999,999	$1,000,000 or more
1967								
All establishments:								
Number 1,000	794.8	482.3	97.6	80.4	70.7	30.1	17.5	16.1
Proprietors¹ 1,000	696.8	470.6	91.3	68.0	47.4	12.3	4.5	2.7
Total receipts bil. dol	101.7	3.3	3.4	5.7	11.3	10.8	12.4	54.8
Establishments with payroll:								
Number 1,000	368.8	101.8	73.5	68.5	63.3	28.6	17.0	16.0
Proprietors¹ 1,000	270.5	88.2	66.4	56.6	41.1	11.3	4.3	2.6
Employees 1,000	3,436	146	188	276	472	406	421	1,528
Total receipts bil. dol	95.9	1.3	2.6	4.9	10.1	10.3	12.1	54.6
1972								
All establishments:								
Number 1,000	920.8	499.5	115.6	105.6	100.8	45.7	26.7	26.9
Proprietors¹ 1,000	748.3	(NA)	(NA)	(NA)	(NA)	(NA)	(NA)	(NA)
Total receipts bil. dol	164.5	3.7	4.1	7.5	15.8	16.0	18.6	98.7
Establishments with payroll:								
Number 1,000	437.9	83.8	78.3	88.7	90.8	43.6	26.1	26.6
Proprietors¹ 1,000	274.4	(NA)	(NA)	(NA)	(NA)	(NA)	(NA)	(NA)
Employees 1,000	4,146	96	166	292	554	501	523	2,014
Total receipts bil. dol	155.9	1.1	2.8	6.3	14.3	15.3	18.2	97.8

NA Not available.   ¹ Includes working partners.

Source: U.S. Bureau of the Census, *Census of Construction Industries, 1967*, series CC 67-I-1B and *Census of Construction Industries, 1972*, series CC72-I.

No. 1362. SELECTED CONSTRUCTION INDUSTRIES—SUMMARY, BY INDUSTRY: 1972

[Based on a probability sample of about 167,000 construction establishments with payroll]

INDUSTRY	Establishments with payroll (number)	EMPLOYEES (1,000)		PAYROLL (mil. dol.)		RECEIPTS (mil. dol.)		Value added [2] (mil. dol.)
		Total	Construction workers	Total	Construction workers	Total	Net construction [1]	
Total	437,941	4,146	3,487	40,005	32,187	155,850	111,232	68,197
Contract construction	430,027	4,083	3,464	39,528	32,036	152,722	110,716	67,810
General building contractors	133,054	1,150	938	10,159	7,740	64,350	33,245	17,884
Heavy construction contractors	27,991	827	709	9,255	7,537	31,461	25,357	16,200
Highway and street construction	9,232	278	244	2,846	2,365	11,326	8,986	5,838
Special trade contractors [3]	268,982	2,107	1,817	20,114	16,759	56,911	52,114	33,726
Plumbing, heating, air conditioning	53,301	456	371	4,788	3,810	15,615	13,594	7,795
Painting, paperhanging, decorating	29,011	137	126	1,081	961	2,406	2,290	1,839
Electrical work	32,455	324	271	3,793	3,151	9,608	9,229	5,797
Masonry and other stonework	23,896	166	156	1,311	1,199	3,105	2,978	2,057
Plastering, drywall, insulation	13,415	170	152	1,685	1,446	4,195	3,839	2,585
Terrazzo, tile, marble, mosaic work	4,270	31	27	260	213	717	685	419
Carpentering	23,524	124	115	925	842	2,356	2,128	1,505
Floor laying and floor work, n.e.c [4]	9,052	44	36	367	291	1,210	1,132	649
Roofing and sheet metal work	18,535	158	134	1,406	1,137	4,000	3,752	2,348
Concrete work	17,772	148	135	1,197	1,045	3,699	3,452	2,141
Water well drilling	4,159	17	15	125	102	557	523	326
Structural steel erection	2,760	58	50	638	534	1,496	1,386	1,013
Glass and glazing work	2,459	20	14	190	133	657	585	341
Excavating and foundation work	15,981	105	93	923	787	3,054	2,723	2,188
Wrecking and demolition work	1,027	9	8	80	64	237	203	195
Subdividers and developers, n.e.c [4]	7,914	62	22	477	151	3,128	516	[4] 387

[1] Construction receipts less payments for construction work subcontracted to others, not shown separately.
[2] Total receipts less (a) payments for materials, components, and supplies, (b) payments for construction work subcontracted to others, not shown separately.   [3] Includes other, not shown separately.
[4] N.e.c.—not elsewhere classified.   [5] Excludes land receipts.
Source: U.S. Bureau of the Census, *Census of Construction Industries, 1972*, series CC 72-I.

No. 1363. CONSTRUCTION ESTABLISHMENTS—SUMMARY, BY STATES: 1972

[See headnote, table 1361]

STATE	ALL ESTABLISHMENTS		ESTABLISHMENTS WITH PAYROLL			STATE	ALL ESTABLISHMENTS		ESTABLISHMENTS WITH PAYROLL		
	Number (1,000)	Receipts (mil. dol.)	Number (1,000)	Employees (1,000)	Receipts (mil. dol.)		Number (1,000)	Receipts (mil. dol.)	Number (1,000)	Employees (1,000)	Receipts (mil. dol.)
U.S.	920.8	164,458	437.9	4,146	155,850	S.A.—Con.					
						W. Va.	5.7	665	2.8	23	640
N.E.	62.0	9,620	31.3	243	9,136	N.C.	25.5	3,770	13.6	131	3,610
Maine	6.5	586	3.1	20	554	S.C.	12.6	2,189	6.7	74	2,093
N.H.	5.8	643	2.9	19	603	Ga.	26.8	4,072	12.8	113	3,780
Vt.	3.7	296	1.8	9	276	Fla.	43.2	9,075	22.3	243	8,670
Mass.	26.5	4,765	13.1	114	4,539	E.S.C.	60.2	8,053	25.7	238	7,602
R.I.	4.4	809	2.5	20	783	Ky.	15.9	1,739	6.3	51	1,631
Conn.	15.2	2,521	8.0	62	2,381	Tenn.	19.9	2,995	8.6	86	2,848
M.A.	133.4	26,650	68.6	657	25,109	Ala.	14.5	2,197	6.5	66	2,074
N.Y.	59.2	12,319	30.4	291	11,799	Miss.	9.8	1,122	4.2	36	1,049
N.J.	28.1	5,350	15.5	130	5,108	W.S.C.	114.7	17,065	45.6	482	15,884
Pa.	46.1	8,982	22.7	237	8,202	Ark.	13.5	1,244	4.6	35	1,120
E.N.C.	162.8	28,929	75.1	676	27,474	La.	14.2	2,746	6.8	85	2,605
Ohio	45.7	7,578	19.8	181	7,186	Okla.	18.4	1,858	6.3	52	1,651
Ind.	22.3	3,429	10.1	91	3,220	Tex.	68.6	11,218	27.9	310	10,507
Ill.	39.1	8,932	19.2	204	8,566	Mt.	48.8	9,637	23.9	233	9,216
Mich.	35.1	6,306	16.4	131	5,961	Mont.	4.1	398	1.6	10	370
Wis.	20.6	2,684	9.7	70	2,542	Idaho	5.3	670	2.0	17	614
W.N.C.	86.5	11,163	35.4	285	10,504	Wyo.	2.3	274	1.0	7	251
Minn.	18.4	3,064	8.0	75	2,926	Colo.	15.9	2,998	7.5	76	2,852
Iowa	15.4	1,553	6.4	42	1,449	N. Mex.	4.0	777	2.3	24	752
Mo.	24.6	3,248	9.5	81	3,043	Ariz.	8.7	2,747	4.8	56	2,668
N. Dak.	3.1	382	1.5	10	368	Utah	6.0	1,008	3.2	25	962
S. Dak.	3.7	299	1.5	9	280	Nev.	2.5	765	1.5	18	748
Nebr.	8.9	1,101	3.9	29	1,043	Pac.	98.3	24,242	51.8	494	23,268
Kans.	12.4	1,516	4.7	38	1,395	Wash.	16.2	2,665	8.2	62	2,534
S.A.	154.1	29,100	80.5	837	27,655	Oreg.	12.9	1,635	6.0	39	1,517
Del.	2.5	898	1.5	19	863	Calif.	64.9	18,390	35.1	362	17,717
Md.	16.1	4,237	8.7	106	3,944	Alaska	2.0	442	1.1	7	414
D.C.	1.1	561	.6	14	549	Hawaii	2.3	1,109	1.6	25	1,086
Va.	20.7	3,634	11.4	114	3,505						

Source: U.S. Bureau of the Census, *Census of Construction Industries, 1972*, area series CC 72-A.

No. 1364. Gross Housing Product—Summary: 1960 to 1977

[In billions of dollars. For definition of current and constant dollars, see text, p. 439]

ITEM	1960	1965	1970	1971	1972	1973	1974	1975	1976	1977
CURRENT DOLLARS										
Total value of housing output [1]	46.7	63.3	90.3	99.2	108.2	118.6	131.6	144.7	160.1	177.7
Nonfarm housing	44.4	60.8	87.3	95.9	104.8	114.7	126.9	139.2	153.9	170.4
Owner-occupied	31.3	42.7	61.3	67.5	74.0	81.3	90.5	100.1	110.9	123.6
Tenant-occupied	13.3	18.2	26.0	28.4	30.8	33.4	36.3	39.1	43.0	46.8
Farm housing	2.1	2.5	3.0	3.2	3.5	3.9	4.7	5.4	6.2	7.3
Less: Intermediate goods and services consumed	7.8	8.8	12.2	14.5	16.0	17.8	19.6	21.3	24.0	25.0
Equals: Gross housing product	38.9	54.5	78.1	84.7	92.2	100.9	112.0	123.4	136.1	152.7
CONSTANT (1972) DOLLARS										
Total value of housing output [1]	61.9	78.7	98.1	102.8	108.2	113.3	119.1	124.0	129.8	135.3
Nonfarm housing	57.9	74.8	94.5	99.2	104.8	110.0	115.8	120.8	126.7	132.4
Owner-occupied	40.6	52.5	66.3	69.8	74.0	78.0	82.6	86.9	91.3	96.0
Tenant-occupied	17.2	22.3	28.1	29.4	30.8	32.0	33.2	33.9	35.4	36.4
Farm housing	4.1	3.9	3.7	3.6	3.5	3.3	3.3	3.2	3.0	2.9
Less: Intermediate goods and services consumed	10.3	11.0	13.3	15.0	16.0	17.0	17.8	18.3	19.6	19.1
Equals: Gross housing product	51.7	67.7	84.9	87.8	92.2	96.3	101.3	105.8	110.2	116.2

[1] Equals personal consumption expenditures for housing less expenditures for transient hotels, motels, clubs, schools, and institutions.

Source: U.S. Bureau of Economic Analysis, *The National Income and Product Accounts of the United States, 1929-74,* and *Survey of Current Business,* July 1978.

No. 1365. Residential Capital—Stocks and Average Age: 1960 to 1977

[As of **Dec. 31.** Data based on fixed residential capital formation components of the gross national product; see text, p. 437. For nonresidential business capital, see table 780. See *Historical Statistics, Colonial Times to 1970,* series F 528-534 and N 200-223 for related data]

ITEM	1960	1965	1970	1972	1973	1974	1975	1976	1977
Capital in current dollars (bil. dol.):									
Gross stocks [1]	716.6	846.9	1,233	1,442	1,655	1,862	2,044	2,295	2,646
Private nonfarm: 1-4 units	587.9	681.9	971	1,119	1,274	1,425	1,566	1,763	2,040
5 or more units	48.5	72.4	127	165	201	232	254	284	327
Public: Federal, State and local	12.5	16.8	27	32	37	42	45	51	58
Farm (1-4 units)	43.8	43.5	54	58	64	70	75	82	91
Private nonhousekeeping	14.3	19.5	30	36	42	47	52	57	64
Mobile homes	4.9	7.5	17	23	29	36	40	45	52
Net stocks [1][2]	450.3	545.5	797	942	1,085	1,217	1,328	1,487	1,714
Private nonfarm: 1-4 units	380.0	445.2	629	727	827	922	1,009	1,137	1,319
5 or more units	27.5	48.4	91	122	150	174	189	209	238
Public: Federal, State and local	10.1	13.2	20	24	27	30	33	36	40
Farm (1-4 units)	19.6	18.8	23	24	26	29	30	33	37
Private nonhousekeeping	7.3	12.3	20	24	28	32	34	37	41
Mobile homes	3.2	4.7	11	16	20	24	26	28	31
Capital in constant (1972) dollar (bil. dol.):s									
Gross stocks [1]	956.4	1,119.6	1,277	1,371	1,419	1,451	1,477	1,510	1,551
Private nonfarm: 1-4 units	787.1	903.7	1,007	1,063	1,090	1,109	1,129	1,157	1,191
5 or more units	64.9	95.9	132	157	172	180	183	186	191
Public: Federal, State and local	16.8	22.3	28	39	31	32	33	33	34
Farm (1-4 units)	58.7	57.6	56	55	55	54	54	54	53
Private nonhousekeeping	19.2	25.8	31	34	36	37	37	37	38
Mobile homes	5.3	8.4	16	23	26	29	30	32	34
Net stocks [1][2]	601.2	721.4	826	895	930	948	959	978	1,005
Private nonfarm: 1-4 units	508.7	590.0	652	690	708	717	728	746	770
5 or more units	36.9	64.1	94	116	129	135	136	137	139
Public: Federal, State and local	13.6	17.5	21	22	23	24	24	24	24
Farm (1-4 units)	26.2	25.0	24	23	23	22	22	22	22
Private nonhousekeeping	9.8	16.3	21	23	24	25	25	24	24
Mobile homes	3.5	5.2	11	16	18	20	20	20	21
Average age [3] (years):									
Gross stocks	27.9	26.4	25.8	25.1	24.8	24.9	25.0	25.1	25.0
Private nonfarm: 1-4 units	27.5	26.7	26.8	26.5	26.4	26.6	26.7	26.6	26.4
5 or more units	27.9	21.4	18.4	16.7	16.0	16.0	16.4	16.9	17.2
Federal	14.7	16.0	19.7	20.1	20.1	20.4	21.1	21.8	22.5
State and local	9.8	11.7	13.1	13.9	14.4	15.0	15.7	16.5	17.1
Farm (1-4 units)	45.0	45.5	45.9	46.0	46.2	46.4	46.4	46.4	46.4
Private nonhousekeeping	21.2	16.0	13.4	13.9	13.6	13.6	13.9	14.3	14.8
Mobile homes	5.4	6.1	5.4	5.1	5.0	5.1	5.4	5.9	6.2

[1] Includes other, not shown separately. [2] Using straight-line depreciation. [3] Constant-dollar stocks.

Source: U.S. Bureau of Economic Analysis, *Fixed Nonresidential Business and Residential Capital in the United States, 1925-75,* and unpublished data.

No. 1366. New Housing Units Started: 1960 to 1978

[In thousands. Minus sign (−) denotes decrease. See also *Historical Statistics, Colonial Times to 1970*, series N 156–159]

YEAR	Total	Percent change	PRIVATELY-OWNED Total	PRIVATELY-OWNED 1-unit structures	Publicly-owned	YEAR AND MONTH	Total	Percent change	PRIVATELY-OWNED Total	PRIVATELY-OWNED 1-unit structures	Publicly-owned
1960	1,296	[1] −16.6	1,252	995	44	1973	2,057	−13.5	2,045	1,132	12
1961	1,365	5.3	1,313	974	52	1974	1,352	−34.3	1,338	888	15
1962	1,492	9.3	1,463	991	30	1975	1,171	−13.4	1,160	892	11
1963	1,635	9.6	1,603	1,012	32	1976	1,548	32.2	1,538	1,162	10
1964	1,561	−4.5	1,529	970	32	1977	1,990	28.6	1,987	1,451	3
1965	1,510	−3.3	1,473	964	37						
						1978:[2] Jan	(NA)	(NA)	1,548	1,156	(NA)
1966	1,196	−20.8	1,165	779	31	Feb	(NA)	(NA)	1,569	1,103	(NA)
1967	1,322	10.5	1,292	844	30	Mar	(NA)	(NA)	2,047	1,429	(NA)
1968	1,545	16.9	1,508	899	38	Apr	(NA)	(NA)	2,165	1,492	(NA)
1969	1,500	−2.9	1,467	811	33	May	(NA)	(NA)	2,054	1,478	(NA)
1970	1,469	−2.1	1,434	813	35	June	(NA)	(NA)	2,124	1,441	(NA)
1971	2,085	41.9	2,052	1,151	32	July	(NA)	(NA)	2,128	1,453	(NA)
1972	2,379	14.1	2,357	1,309	22	Aug.[3]	(NA)	(NA)	2,029	1,442	(NA)

NA Not available.   [1] Change from 1959.   [2] Seasonally adjusted annual rate.   [3] Preliminary.

No. 1367. New Housing Units Started—Selected Characteristics: 1960 to 1977

[In thousands. For composition of regions, see fig. I, inside front cover. See also *Historical Statistics, Colonial Times to 1970*, series N 156–163]

CHARACTERISTIC	1960	1965	1970	1971	1972	1973	1974	1975	1976	1977
Total	1,296	1,510	1,469	2,085	2,379	2,057	1,352	1,171	1,548	1,990
Northeast	237	281	224	271	334	278	183	150	170	202
North Central	304	369	301	440	445	442	320	295	401	465
South	441	589	629	884	1,068	906	561	448	575	784
West	315	271	315	490	532	431	288	278	402	539
Units inside SMSA's [1]	889	1,035	1,034	1,519	1,733	1,502	932	767	1,048	1,378
Units outside SMSA's [1]	407	475	435	566	646	556	420	405	499	612
Publicly owned	44	37	35	32	22	12	15	11	10	3
Privately owned	1,252	1,473	1,434	2,052	2,357	2,045	1,338	1,160	1,538	1,987
With FHA aid	261	197	421	528	[2] 371	[2] 161	[2] 94	[2] 104	[2] 151	[2] 178
With VA aid	75	49	61	94	[2] 104	[2] 86	[2] 73	[2] 77	[2] 100	[2] 131
In structures with:										
1 unit	1,009	965	815	1,153	1,311	1,133	889	896	1,166	1,452
2–4 units	} 288	{ 101	96	133	151	124	77	68	89	122
5 units or more		444	558	799	917	800	387	208	292	415

[1] For definition of standard metropolitan statistical area (SMSA), see text, Appendix II. 1960 based on 1959 definitions; 1965–1975, on 1967 definitions as amended through 1974; thereafter, on 1974 definitions as amended through 1975.

[2] Source: U.S. Dept. of Housing and Urban Development, *HUD Statistical Yearbook*.

Source of tables 1366 and 1367: Except as noted, U.S. Bureau of the Census, *Construction Reports*, series C20. Includes data from U.S. Federal Housing Administration and U.S. Veterans Administration.

No. 1368. Price Index—New One-Family Houses Sold, by Region: 1965 to 1978

[1972=100. Based on fixed proportions of ten characteristics of new houses sold in 1974. For composition of regions, see fig. I, inside front cover]

YEAR	U.S.	Northeast	North Central	South	West	YEAR AND QUARTER	U.S.	Northeast	North Central	South	West
1965	71.2	62.2	70.6	71.1	75.9	1973	108.9	108.4	107.7	106.9	112.7
1966	74.2	66.8	74.7	74.3	78.2	1974	119.1	118.3	115.8	115.2	126.3
1967	76.4	69.1	77.7	75.8	79.4	1975	131.0	128.3	126.8	125.7	141.7
1968	80.3	75.8	82.4	79.0	81.7						
						1976	142.0	133.5	138.1	134.6	157.3
1969	86.5	82.7	90.5	84.5	88.9	1977	159.3	142.1	153.3	147.3	186.4
1970	89.1	88.2	90.7	87.5	90.3	1978,					
1971	93.9	93.8	94.1	94.2	93.3	1st qtr	172.2	(NA)	(NA)	(NA)	(NA)

NA Not available.

Source: U.S. Bureau of the Census, *Current Construction Reports*, series C27, quarterly.

No. 1369. New Housing Units Authorized by States: 1975 to 1977

[Includes public housing contract awards. Based on about 14,000 places in U.S. having building permit systems]

AND STATE	HOUSING UNITS 1975 Total (1,000)	1975 Percent— Single unit structures[1]	1975 Percent— Multi-unit structures[1]	1976 Total (1,000)	1976 Percent— unit structures[1]	1976 Percent— unit structures[1]	1977[2] Total (1,000)	1977[2] Percent— Single unit structures[1]	1977[2] Percent— Multi-unit structures[1]	VALUATION (mil. dol.) 1975	1976	1977[2]
U.S.	949.2	72	21	1,302.7	69	24	1,687.5	67	26	24,107	35,714	49,945
N. Eng	43.0	69	25	49.0	73	22	58.6	72	24	1,024	1,294	1,634
Maine	4.1	84	11	4.2	75	21	4.7	69	25	96	107	122
N.H	3.6	86	8	6.0	79	17	6.2	77	19	97	171	191
Vt	1.8	84	11	2.2	71	24	2.3	65	30	44	54	63
Mass	18.0	60	33	18.2	75	21	24.7	75	22	420	472	660
R.I	3.4	70	26	4.6	63	33	5.4	57	40	68	97	125
Conn	12.1	70	23	13.9	71	22	15.2	72	23	299	393	474
Mid. Atl	87.2	73	20	103.3	73	21	124.5	70	24	2,073	2,658	3,472
N.Y	30.8	73	18	30.5	78	13	38.5	65	28	699	766	1,005
N.J	23.4	69	24	30.7	67	25	34.5	71	23	583	800	1,017
Pa	33.0	75	20	42.1	73	23	51.5	73	23	791	1,093	1,450
E. No. Cent	164.5	70	24	220.0	67	27	270.0	66	28	4,341	6,187	8,479
Ohio	39.1	70	22	48.7	66	27	60.7	66	27	1,069	1,397	1,928
Ind	23.1	74	21	30.7	72	24	35.4	66	29	607	848	1,067
Ill	39.3	66	28	59.5	64	30	76.2	65	29	1,085	1,757	2,529
Mich	37.0	73	24	45.9	72	24	59.2	69	27	945	1,264	1,808
Wis	26.0	68	23	35.3	65	26	38.4	65	26	636	922	1,146
W. No. Cent	78.3	70	22	106.3	67	24	125.1	67	25	1,955	2,844	3,735
Minn	19.2	78	19	27.0	73	22	37.5	67	29	548	827	1,258
Iowa	14.7	60	31	19.4	55	34	21.1	64	24	332	478	608
Mo	16.1	76	16	22.7	74	17	29.0	72	18	402	579	773
N. Dak	5.1	45	44	6.1	48	43	6.0	48	43	119	163	174
S. Dak	3.1	60	32	4.8	48	44	5.8	16	45	66	104	134
Nebr	7.9	83	11	10.5	78	15	10.1	81	14	164	226	257
Kans	12.1	67	21	15.7	68	19	15.6	70	18	324	467	531
So. Atl	163.7	80	16	210.0	81	14	300.2	73	22	4,010	5,596	8,442
Del	3.0	71	26	2.6	96	3	3.4	81	18	65	71	92
Md	19.7	77	22	27.0	82	17	30.1	78	21	473	717	870
D.C	.4	50	46	2.2	21	71	2.1	35	63	7	46	51
Va	33.2	81	17	39.9	84	13	60.6	74	24	818	1,112	1,714
W. Va	2.1	60	31	2.6	67	26	2.5	65	30	46	61	66
N.C	20.9	86	9	26.0	86	10	31.6	78	19	515	676	851
S.C	15.4	82	14	18.4	88	8	19.5	83	14	343	491	521
Ga	21.0	91	6	24.5	89	8	31.3	78	19	517	619	824
Fla	48.0	73	18	66.7	73	18	119.1	68	24	1,227	1,803	3,454
E. So. Cent	43.2	77	16	56.7	74	21	75.7	62	33	957	1,303	1,745
Ky	10.7	73	21	13.4	72	20	16.3	58	34	266	338	402
Tenn	14.5	76	16	19.1	76	19	26.2	66	29	319	450	652
Ala	12.8	78	17	17.2	70	27	25.1	57	39	258	361	498
Miss	5.2	89	8	6.9	83	13	8.2	72	21	114	154	194
W. So. Cent	91.5	69	26	139.0	60	34	194.2	56	38	2,110	3,242	5,018
Ark	6.9	80	10	8.8	71	19	10.6	65	24	161	215	276
La	11.7	85	10	17.1	76	15	24.7	62	26	306	432	646
Okla	10.2	85	9	15.8	79	16	20.1	79	17	281	433	663
Tex	62.7	63	33	97.3	54	42	138.8	51	44	1,361	2,163	3,433
Mt	76.2	79	14	107.4	71	20	157.3	72	20	1,807	2,798	4,460
Mont	3.1	63	22	4.8	51	27	6.2	52	25	67	101	147
Idaho	8.2	79	11	9.5	69	15	11.7	66	17	179	241	322
Wyo	2.6	66	24	4.1	62	31	5.2	66	25	58	100	141
Colo	16.8	85	8	25.0	79	16	36.6	83	13	434	685	1,118
N. Mex	6.9	79	15	8.3	68	23	13.8	63	29	187	228	379
Ariz	18.5	84	12	24.0	79	17	42.7	80	17	384	547	1,110
Utah	13.0	79	9	18.1	71	15	21.4	74	11	308	491	646
Nev	7.2	61	35	13.6	57	39	19.8	54	41	189	405	596
Pac	201.7	66	25	310.9	63	26	382.0	64	25	5,830	9,792	12,960
Wash	35.2	64	27	47.9	62	28	59.6	65	24	855	1,275	1,775
Oreg	20.1	71	15	29.5	65	21	37.9	65	18	500	775	1,093
Calif	131.2	69	22	220.1	64	26	269.8	64	25	3,984	7,310	9,577
Alaska	2.9	45	38	5.2	41	46	6.9	37	47	90	165	241
Hawaii	12.2	28	65	8.2	48	48	7.9	59	37	401	266	274

[1] Privately owned. Multiunit refers to 5-or-more unit structures. [2] Preliminary. The relative standard error of the preliminary estimate of total private housing units authorized in permit places is less than 10 percent for all States except as follows (in percent): Del. (above 50); Mont. (15); Wyo. (12); R.I. (11).

Source: U.S. Bureau of the Census, *Construction Reports,* series C40, annual, and December issues.

No. 1370. PRIVATE HOUSING STARTS, BY REGION, AND MOBILE HOMES: 1965 TO 1977

[In thousands of units, except percent. For composition of regions, see fig. I, inside front cover. See also *Historical Statistics, Colonial Times to 1970,* series N 157 and N 170]

ITEM	1965	1970	1971	1972	1973	1974	1975	1976	1977
Private housing starts [1]	1,473	1,434	2,052	2,357	2,045	1,338	1,160	1,538	1,987
Single family	964	813	1,151	1,309	1,132	888	892	1,162	1,451
Condominiums [2]	(NA)	(NA)	(NA)	(NA)	69	46	20	30	41
Northeast	163	113	145	170	155	119	112	127	156
North Central	226	166	238	256	269	225	222	294	337
South	416	377	526	612	478	367	366	464	588
West	159	157	242	272	230	176	192	277	370
Multifamily	509	621	901	1,047	913	450	268	375	536
Percent of total	34.6	43.3	43.9	44.4	44.6	33.6	33.0	24.4	27.0
Condominiums [2]	(NA)	(NA)	(NA)	(NA)	172	130	45	64	91
Northeast	107	105	119	159	122	64	37	43	46
North Central	136	128	196	187	171	92	72	106	128
South	159	235	343	445	421	186	76	104	195
West	107	154	244	255	199	108	83	122	168
MOBILE HOMES [3]									
Shipments to dealers	216	401	497	576	567	329	213	246	277
Percent of total private starts and mobile homes	12.8	21.9	19.5	19.6	21.7	19.7	15.5	13.8	12.2
Percent of single-family private starts and mobile homes	18.3	33.0	30.1	30.5	33.4	27.0	19.3	17.5	16.0

NA Not available.　　[1] Includes farm housing.　　[2] Type of ownership under which the owners of the individ‾ual housing units are also joint owners of the common areas of the building or community. Includes a small number of cooperatively owned units.
[3] A mobile home is a vehicular portable structure built on a chassis and designed to be used without a permanent foundation as a year-round dwelling when connected to utilities. The homes are defined as units more than 8 feet wide or 32 feet in length.

Source: U.S. Bureau of the Census, *Construction Reports,* series C20. Mobile home shipments data provided by Manufactured Housing Institute, Arlington, Va.

No. 1371. PERCENT OF NEW PRIVATELY OWNED COMPLETED ONE-FAMILY HOUSES WITH VARIOUS CHARACTERISTICS: 1970 TO 1977

[Percent distribution, except total houses. Data beginning 1974 show percent distribution of characteristics for all houses completed (includes new houses completed, houses built for sale completed, contractor-built and owner-built houses completed, and houses completed for rent). Data for 1970 cover contractor-built, owner-built, and houses for rent for year construction started and houses sold for year of sale. Percents exclude houses for which characteristics specified were not reported. See also headnote, table 1392]

CHARACTERISTIC	1970	1974	1975	1976	1977	CHARACTERISTIC	1970	1974	1975	1976	1977
Total houses 1,000	793	940	875	1,034	1,258	Bathrooms	100	100	100	100	100
						1 or less	32	22	24	20	17
Financing	100	100	100	100	100	1½	20	18	17	13	13
Mortgage	84	83	82	85	86	2	32	40	40	45	47
FHA-insured	30	7	9	6	7	2½ or more	16	21	20	22	23
VA-guaranteed	7	8	8	8	8						
Conventional	} 47	69	{ 58	67	70	Foundation	100	100	100	100	100
Farmers Home Admin			7	5	4	Full or partial basement	37	45	45	45	44
Cash or equivalent	16	17	18	15	14	Slab	36	36	35	36	38
						Crawl space	27	19	20	19	18
Floor area (sq. ft.)	100	100	100	100	100						
Under 1,200	36	24	25	22	20	Heating fuel	100	100	100	100	100
1,200–1,597	28	29	30	29	30	Electricity	28	49	49	48	50
1,600–1,999	16					Gas	62	41	40	39	38
2,000–2,399	} 21	{} 34	34	37	38	Oil	8	9	9	11	9
2,400 and over		{ 13	11	12	13	Other	1	1	2	2	2
Number of stories	100	100	100	100	100	Central air condition	100	100	100	100	100
1	74	65	65	63	63	With	34	48	46	49	54
2 or more	17	25	23	25	26	Without	66	52	54	51	46
Split level	10	10	12	12	11						
						Parking facilities	100	100	100	100	100
Bedrooms	100	100	100	100	100	Garage	58	68	67	72	73
2 or less	13	13	14	12	11	Carport	17	10	9	8	7
3	63	64	65	65	66	No garage or carport	25	22	24	20	19
4 or more	24	23	21	23	23						

Source: U.S. Bureau of the Census and U.S. Dept. of Housing and Urban Development, *Construction Reports,* series C25, *Characteristics of New One Family Homes* (a joint publication).

No. 1372. Estimates of the Housing Inventory: 1970 to 1976

TENURE, RACE, AND VACANCY STATUS	TOTAL UNITS, 1970		TOTAL UNITS, 1976		Percent average annual change, 1970-1976	NEW UNITS CONSTRUCTED, 1970-1976 [1]		UNITS REMOVED, 1973-1976 [2]	
	Number (1,000)	Percent	Number (1,000)	Percent		Number (1,000)	Percent	Number (1,000)	Percent
All housing units	68,672	100.0	80,881	100.0	2.8	12,622	100.0	2,272	100.0
All year-round units	67,699	98.6	79,316	98.1	2.7	12,493	99.0	2,247	98.9
Occupied units	63,445	92.4	74,005	91.5	2.6	11,520	91.3	1,758	77.4
Owner occupied [3]	39,886	58.1	47,904	59.2	3.1	7,786	61.7	704	31.0
White	37,005	53.9	44,024	54.4	2.9	7,262	57.5	623	27.4
Black	2,568	3.7	3,371	4.2	4.6	414	3.3	74	3.3
Renter occupied [3]	23,560	34.3	26,101	32.3	1.7	3,734	29.6	1,054	46.4
White	19,601	28.5	21,090	26.1	1.2	3,251	25.8	760	33.5
Black	3,607	5.3	4,340	5.4	3.1	411	3.3	271	11.9
Vacant year-round	4,254	6.2	5,311	6.6	3.8	973	7.7	489	21.5
For sale only	501	.7	617	.8	3.5	227	1.8	28	1.2
For rent	1,666	2.4	1,544	1.9	-1.3	275	2.2	139	6.1
Other vacant	2,087	3.0	3,151	3.9	7.1	471	3.7	322	14.2
Vacant or seasonal [4]	973	1.4	1,565	1.9	8.2	128	1.0	25	1.1

[1] Apr. 1, 1970, to Oct. 31, 1976.   [2] Removed between Oct. 1973 and Oct. 31, 1976, by demolition, disaster, or other means.   [3] Includes races not shown separately.   [4] Includes migratory.

Source: U.S. Bureau of the Census, *Current Housing Reports*, series H-150-76, Annual Housing Survey: 1976, part A, *General Housing Characteristics for the United States and Regions.*

No. 1373. Housing Units—Summary of Characteristics: 1960 to 1976

[In thousands, except as indicated. Refers to 243 standard metropolitan statistical areas (SMSA's) as defined in 1970 census reports. For definition of SMSA, see text, Appendix II. For definition of median, see p. xii]

CHARACTERISTIC	1960	1970				1976			
		Total	Inside SMSA's		Outside SMSA's	Total	Inside SMSA's		Outside SMSA's
			Total	In central cities			Total	In central cities	
All housing units	58,326	68,672	46,289	22,608	22,383	80,881	53,934	24,576	26,947
All year-round units	56,584	67,699	46,083	22,584	21,616	79,316	53,606	24,547	25,710
Occupied units	53,024	63,445	43,859	21,395	19,586	74,005	50,452	22,930	23,553
Owner occupied	32,797	39,886	26,090	10,300	13,796	47,904	30,895	11,349	17,009
Percent of all occupied	61.9	62.9	59.5	48.1	70.4	64.7	61.2	49.5	72.2
Renter occupied	20,227	23,560	17,769	11,095	5,790	26,101	19,557	11,581	6,544
Vacant year-round	3,560	4,254	2,224	1,189	2,030	5,311	3,154	1,617	2,157
For sale only	522	501	298	130	203	617	404	183	213
Homeowner vacancy rate	1.6	1.2	1.1	1.2	1.5	1.3	1.3	1.6	1.2
For rent	1,453	1,666	1,142	745	524	1,544	1,168	749	376
Rental vacancy rate	6.7	6.6	6.0	6.3	8.3	5.5	5.6	6.0	5.4
Other vacant	1,084	2,087	784	314	1,303	3,151	1,583	684	1,567
Vacant, seasonal and migratory	1,742	973	206	24	766	1,565	328	28	1,237
Urban	40,764	50,145	(NA)	(NA)	(NA)	56,651	46,547	24,576	10,104
Rural	17,562	18,527	(NA)	(NA)	(NA)	24,230	7,388	(X)	16,842
Cooperatives and condominiums:									
Owner occupied	(NA)	(NA)	(NA)	(NA)	(NA)	1,039	952	399	87
Cooperatives	(NA)	(NA)	(NA)	(NA)	(NA)	405	365	239	39
Condominiums	(NA)	(NA)	(NA)	(NA)	(NA)	634	586	160	48
Vacant for sale only	(NA)	(NA)	(NA)	(NA)	(NA)	80	71	35	9
Units in structure [1]—									
1-unit	43,758	46,791	29,033	11,430	17,758	53,611	33,162	12,218	20,449
Percent of total units	77.3	69.1	63.0	50.6	82.2	67.6	61.9	49.8	79.5
2-4 units	7,552	9,007	7,184	4,753	1,823	10,189	8,134	5,210	2,055
5 or more units	6,238	9,829	8,934	6,225	895	11,888	10,753	6,878	1,135
Mobile home or trailer	767	2,073	933	176	1,140	3,627	1,556	241	2,071
Year structure built: [1]									
April 1970 or later	(X)	(X)	(X)	(X)	(X)	12,493	8,262	2,599	4,231
1960-March 1970	(X)	16,956	11,849	4,172	5,106	17,674	12,330	4,410	5,344
1950-1959	16,046	14,499	10,708	4,304	3,791	13,840	10,037	3,978	3,803
1940-1949	8,640	8,786	6,147	}14,108	2,639	8,103	5,483	2,724	2,620
1939 or earlier	33,632	27,458	17,378		10,080	27,206	17,494	10,835	9,712
Percent built prior to 1940	57.7	40.6	37.7	(NA)	46.6	34.3	32.6	44.1	37.8

See footnotes at end of table.

No. 1373. Housing Units—Summary of Characteristics: 1960 to 1976—Continued

[See headnote, p. 789]

CHARACTERISTIC	1960	1970 Total	1970 Inside SMSA's Total	1970 Inside SMSA's In central cities	1970 Outside SMSA's	1976 Total	1976 Inside SMSA's Total	1976 Inside SMSA's In central cities	1976 Outside SMSA's
Units with [1]—									
1-3 rooms	11,400	11,028	8,305	5,461	2,725	11,864	8,987	5,668	2,877
4 rooms	12,435	14,113	9,230	4,904	4,883	16,169	10,738	5,262	5,431
5 rooms	14,323	16,998	11,233	5,286	5,765	19,262	12,462	5,505	6,800
6 rooms	11,141	13,609	9,271	4,078	4,338	16,091	10,783	4,623	5,309
7 or more rooms	9,020	11,950	8,044	2,856	3,906	15,929	10,635	3,490	5,294
Median number of rooms	4.9	5.0	5.0	4.7	5.1	5.1	5.1	4.7	5.2
Persons per unit (median):									
Owner occupied	3.1	3.0	3.1	2.8	2.7	2.8	2.9	2.6	2.6
Renter occupied	2.6	2.3	2.2	2.1	2.6	2.1	2.0	1.9	2.2
Units lacking some or all plumbing facilities [1]	7,699	4,398	1,494	716	2,904	2,661	921	492	1,739
Percent	13.2	6.5	3.2	3.2	13.4	3.4	1.7	2.0	6.8
Percent of units with—									
Telephone [2]	78.5	87.0	89.1	86.5	82.2	90.3	91.6	88.8	87.6
Air conditioning [1]	12.4	36.7	39.7	38.2	30.0	51.0	53.5	50.1	45.9
Central system [1]	1.9	10.7	12.3	11.0	7.5	21.5	23.4	19.5	17.4
One or more automobiles [2]	78.4	82.5	81.4	71.6	85.0	83.8	82.9	73.3	85.7
Public sewer [1]	(NA)	70.2	82.1	96.2	47.9	72.9	84.3	97.3	49.2
Public or prvt. co. water [1]	(NA)	81.7	91.0	99.0	61.7	83.2	91.9	99.2	64.9
Basement [1]	54.0	50.9	55.5	58.3	41.1	47.6	51.7	55.4	39.2
Second home owner [2]	(NA)	4.6	4.5	4.2	4.7	3.9	4.0	3.3	3.8
Percent of units with [3]—									
Storm windows or other protective covering [4]	(NA)	(NA)	(NA)	(NA)	(NA)	56.8	55.8	49.8	58.3
Storm doors [4]	(NA)	(NA)	(NA)	(NA)	(NA)	60.0	59.1	55.0	61.5
Attic or roof insulation	(NA)	(NA)	(NA)	(NA)	(NA)	75.7	77.4	71.2	73.0

NA Not available. X Not applicable. [1] For 1960, all housing units, based on a complete count, but tabulated on a 20-percent sample basis. For 1970 and 1976, all year-round units. [2] Occupied housing units. [3] Covers only occupied 1-family homes and mobile homes and trailers. [4] Some or all covered.

Source: U.S. Bureau of the Census, *U.S. Census of Housing: 1960*, vol. 1, and *Current Housing Reports*, series H–150–76, Annual Housing Survey, part A, *General Housing Characteristics for the United States and Regions*.

No. 1374. Housing Units, by Geographic Regions: 1960 to 1976

[In thousands, except percent. Covers 243 SMSA's as defined in 1970 census publications. For definition of standard metropolitan statistical areas, see text, Appendix II. For composition of regions, see fig. I, inside front cover:]

YEAR AND LOCATION	TOTAL U.S.	TOTAL North-east	TOTAL North Central	TOTAL South	TOTAL West	PERCENT DISTRIBUTION U.S.	PERCENT DISTRIBUTION North-east	PERCENT DISTRIBUTION North Central	PERCENT DISTRIBUTION South	PERCENT DISTRIBUTION West
1960, total	58,326	14,798	16,798	17,173	9,558	100.0	100.0	100.0	100.0	100.0
Inside SMSA's	38,633	11,834	10,514	9,052	7,233	66.2	80.0	62.6	52.7	75.7
Central cities	20,440	6,005	5,695	5,208	3,531	35.0	40.6	33.9	30.3	36.9
Not in central cities	18,193	5,829	4,818	3,844	3,701	31.2	39.4	28.7	22.4	38.7
Outside SMSA's	19,693	2,964	6,284	8,121	2,325	33.8	20.0	37.4	47.3	24.3
1970, total	68,672	16,642	18,971	21,030	12,029	100.0	100.0	100.0	100.0	100.0
Inside SMSA's	46,289	13,036	12,206	11,651	9,395	67.4	78.3	64.3	55.4	78.1
Central cities	22,608	6,212	5,978	6,166	4,252	32.9	37.3	31.5	29.3	35.3
Not in central cities	23,681	6,824	6,228	5,486	5,143	34.5	41.0	32.8	26.1	42.8
Outside SMSA's	22,383	3,606	6,765	9,379	2,634	32.6	21.7	35.7	44.6	21.9
1975, total	79,087	18,053	21,035	25,364	14,635	100.0	100.0	100.0	100.0	100.0
Inside SMSA's	53,031	13,873	13,503	14,221	11,434	67.1	76.8	64.2	56.1	78.1
Central cities	24,245	6,226	6,107	6,975	4,937	30.7	34.5	29.0	27.5	33.7
Not in central cities	28,785	7,647	7,395	7,247	6,497	36.4	42.4	35.2	28.6	44.4
Outside SMSA's	26,057	4,180	7,532	11,143	3,201	32.9	23.2	35.8	43.9	21.9
1976, total	80,881	18,283	21,381	26,115	15,102	100.0	100.0	100.0	100.0	100.0
Inside SMSA's	53,934	13,972	13,673	14,553	11,736	66.7	76.4	63.9	55.7	77.7
Central cities	24,576	6,300	6,153	7,122	5,001	30.4	34.5	28.8	27.3	33.1
Not in central cities	29,359	7,672	7,521	7,432	6,734	36.3	42.0	35.2	28.5	44.6
Outside SMSA's	26,947	4,311	7,708	11,562	3,366	33.3	23.6	36.1	44.3	22.3

Source: U.S. Bureau of the Census, *Census of Housing, 1960*, vol. I; and *Current Housing Reports*, series H–150, Annual Housing Survey, part A, *General Housing Characteristics for the United States and Regions*.

No. 1375. YEAR-ROUND HOUSING UNITS—TENURE AND RACE, INSIDE AND OUTSIDE SMSA'S: 1960 TO 1976

[In thousands. Refers to 243 standard metropolitan statistical areas (SMSA's) as defined in 1970 census publications. For definition of SMSA, see text, Appendix II]

ITEM	Total	OWNER OCCUPIED			RENTER OCCUPIED			VACANT YEAR ROUND	
		Total	Black	White and other	Total	Black	White and other	Total	For rent
1960, total	56,551	32,795	1,811	30,984	20,226	2,979	17,246	3,531	1,592
Lacking some or all plumbing	8,992	3,470	644	2,826	4,315	1,363	2,952	1,208	469
Inside SMSA's	37,939	21,311	1,186	20,125	14,556	2,182	12,374	2,072	1,088
In central cities	20,147	9,141	852	8,289	9,942	1,862	8,080	1,064	720
Outside central cities	17,792	12,170	334	11,836	4,614	320	4,295	1,008	368
Outside SMSA's	18,612	11,484	625	10,858	5,670	797	4,872	1,459	504
1970, total	67,699	39,886	2,568	37,319	23,560	3,607	19,953	4,254	1,666
Lacking some or all plumbing	4,672	1,809	386	1,423	1,963	656	1,308	900	236
Inside SMSA's	46,083	26,090	1,825	24,265	17,769	2,913	14,856	2,224	1,142
In central cities	22,584	10,300	1,335	8,965	11,095	2,498	8,597	1,189	745
Outside central cities	23,499	15,790	490	15,300	6,674	416	6,259	1,035	397
Outside SMSA's	21,616	13,796	742	13,054	5,790	693	5,097	2,030	524
1976, total	79,316	47,904	3,371	44,533	26,101	4,340	21,761	5,311	1,544
Lacking some or all plumbing	2,661	740	195	545	1,204	423	781	717	162
Inside SMSA's	53,606	30,895	2,420	28,475	19,557	3,572	15,985	3,154	1,168
In central cities	24,547	11,349	1,740	9,609	11,581	2,899	8,682	1,617	749
Outside central cities	29,059	19,546	680	18,866	7,976	673	7,303	1,537	418
Outside SMSA's	25,710	17,009	951	16,058	6,544	768	5,776	2,157	376

Source: U.S. Bureau of the Census, *Census of Housing, 1970*, vol. VI and *Current Housing Reports*, series H–150 Annual Housing Survey: 1976, part A, *General Housing Characteristics for the United States and Regions*.

No. 1376. HOUSING UNITS—SELECTED CHARACTERISTICS, BY STATES: 1970

REGION AND STATE	All year-round units (1,000)	Occupied units (1,000)	PERCENT—			REGION AND STATE	All year-round units (1,000)	Occupied units (1,000)	PERCENT—		
			Owner occupied	With all plumbing[1]	With 1.01 or more persons per room[2]				Owner occupied	With all plumbing[1]	With 1.01 or more persons per room[2]
U.S.	67,657	63,450	62.9	94.0	7.0	S.A.—Con.					
						Va.	1,484	1,391	62.0	87.9	5.2
N.E.	3,844	3,645	60.9	96.0	5.8	W. Va.	592	547	68.9	83.7	5.6
Maine	337	303	70.1	87.7	5.7	N.C.	1,618	1,510	65.4	85.6	6.5
N.H.	247	225	68.2	94.6	6.0	S.C.	805	734	66.1	82.6	7.1
Vt.	149	132	69.1	94.1	5.7	Ga.	1,466	1,369	61.1	87.7	7.3
Mass.	1,836	1,760	57.5	96.7	5.8	Fla.	2,489	2,285	68.6	95.1	7.9
R.I.	306	292	57.9	97.2	5.8	E.S.C.	4,169	3,868	66.7	83.0	6.9
Conn.	968	933	62.5	97.5	6.0	Ky.	1,060	984	66.9	81.1	6.5
M.A.	12,331	11,837	56.6	96.8	6.3	Tenn.	1,297	1,213	66.7	86.4	6.7
N.Y.	6,152	5,914	47.3	97.2	7.3	Ala.	1,115	1,034	66.7	84.3	6.7
N.J.	2,303	2,218	60.9	97.7	5.9	Miss.	697	637	66.3	77.3	7.9
Pa.	3,876	3,705	68.8	95.6	5.1	W.S.C.	6,565	5,952	65.3	91.8	9.0
E.N.C.	13,108	12,383	67.5	95.7	6.9	Ark.	673	615	66.7	83.2	6.8
Ohio	3,447	3,289	67.7	95.5	6.0	La.	1,146	1,052	63.1	89.4	11.3
Ind.	1,712	1,609	71.7	94.5	7.3	Okla.	938	851	69.2	94.0	6.2
Ill.	3,693	3,502	59.4	95.9	7.4	Tex.	3,808	3,432	64.7	93.5	9.4
Mich.	2,842	2,653	74.4	96.8	7.3	Mt.	2,718	2,518	65.5	95.5	8.8
Wis.	1,414	1,329	69.1	94.5	6.7	Mont.	240	217	65.7	93.4	8.5
W.N.C.	5,559	5,154	69.3	93.5	6.4	Idaho	238	219	70.1	96.2	8.6
Minn.	1,219	1,154	71.5	93.5	6.8	Wyo.	114	105	66.4	95.8	8.1
Iowa	955	896	71.7	93.9	5.4	Colo.	742	691	63.4	96.4	6.4
Mo.	1,664	1,521	67.2	92.3	7.0	N. Mex.	322	289	66.4	91.1	11.3
N. Dak.	200	182	68.4	89.9	7.9	Ariz.	578	539	65.3	95.3	10.4
S. Dak.	222	201	69.6	90.0	7.2	Utah	312	298	69.3	97.9	10.2
Nebr.	512	474	66.4	95.6	5.9	Nev.	172	160	58.5	97.3	8.4
Kans.	787	727	69.1	95.8	5.6	Pac.	9,220	8,653	57.1	97.9	7.5
S.A.	10,142	9,438	63.5	90.0	6.8	Wash.	1,204	1,106	66.8	97.4	5.2
Del.	175	165	68.0	95.5	4.8	Oreg.	735	692	66.1	97.0	5.3
Md.	1,235	1,175	58.8	95.9	5.9	Calif.	6,977	6,574	54.9	98.3	7.7
D.C.	278	263	28.2	97.9	11.9	Alaska	88	79	50.3	86.2	12.2
						Hawaii	216	203	46.9	94.7	18.6

[1] Includes hot and cold piped water, as well as a flush toilet and bathtub or shower inside the structure for exclusive use of the people in the unit. [2] For units with all plumbing facilities.

Source: U.S. Bureau of the Census, *Census of Housing, 1970*, vol. I.

No. 1377. Occupied Housing Units—Tenure, and Population Per Occupied Unit, by Race of Household Head and by Residence: 1920 to 1976

[In thousands, except as indicated. Prior to 1960, excludes Alaska and Hawaii. Tenure allocated for housing units which did not report. Minus sign (−) denotes decrease. See also *Historical Statistics, Colonial Times to 1970*, series N 238–245]

YEAR, RACE, AND RESIDENCE	OCCUPIED UNITS [1]					AVERAGE ANNUAL PERCENT CHANGE [2]		Population per occupied unit [4]
	Total	Owner occupied		Renter occupied		Total occupied units	Total population [3]	
		Number	Percent	Number	Percent			
TOTAL								
1920	24,352	11,114	45.6	13,238	54.4	1.9	1.4	4.3
1930	29,905	14,280	47.8	15,624	52.2	2.1	1.5	4.1
1940	34,855	15,196	43.6	19,659	56.4	1.5	.7	3.8
1950	42,826	23,560	55.0	19,266	45.0	2.1	1.4	3.4
1960	53,024	32,797	61.9	20,227	38.1	2.2	1.7	3.3
1970	63,445	39,886	62.9	23,560	37.1	1.8	1.2	3.1
1975	72,523	46,867	64.6	25,656	35.4	2.7	.9	(NA)
1976	74,005	47,904	64.7	26,101	35.3	2.0	.8	(NA)
RACE								
White:								
1920	21,826	10,511	48.2	11,315	51.8	(NA)	1.5	4.3
1930	26,983	13,544	50.2	13,439	49.8	2.1	1.5	4.1
1940	31,561	14,418	45.7	17,143	54.3	1.6	.7	3.7
1950	39,044	22,241	57.0	16,803	43.0	2.2	1.3	3.3
1960	47,880	30,823	64.4	17,057	35.6	2.1	1.6	3.2
1970	56,529	36,979	65.4	19,551	34.6	1.7	1.2	3.1
1975	63,860	43,072	67.4	20,788	32.6	2.5	.8	(NA)
1976	65,114	44,024	67.6	21,090	32.4	2.0	.6	(NA)
Black and other:								
1920	2,526	603	23.9	1,923	76.1	(NA)	.6	4.3
1930	2,922	737	25.2	2,185	74.8	1.5	1.4	4.3
1940	3,293	778	23.6	2,516	76.4	1.2	.7	4.1
1950	3,783	1,319	34.9	2,464	65.1	1.4	1.6	3.9
1960	5,144	1,974	38.4	3,171	61.6	3.1	2.4	3.9
1970	6,920	2,907	42.0	4,014	58.0	3.0	2.3	3.5
1975	8,663	3,795	43.8	4,868	56.2	4.6	2.1	(NA)
1976	8,891	3,880	43.6	5,011	56.4	2.6	2.0	(NA)
RESIDENCE								
Nonfarm:								
1920	17,600	7,189	40.8	10,411	59.2	2.2	(NA)	4.2
1930	23,300	10,721	46.0	12,579	54.0	2.8	2.3	4.0
1940	27,748	11,413	41.1	16,335	58.9	1.8	.9	3.7
1950	37,105	19,802	53.4	17,304	46.6	2.9	2.4	3.3
1960 [5]	49,458	30,164	61.0	19,294	39.1	2.9	2.5	3.3
1970 [5]	60,351	37,393	62.0	22,957	38.0	2.0	1.7	3.1
1975 [5]	69,880	44,714	64.0	25,166	36.0	3.0	(NA)	(NA)
1976 [5]	71,335	45,711	64.1	25,624	35.9	2.1	(NA)	(NA)
Farm:								
1920 [6]	6,751	3,925	58.1	2,827	41.9	1.0	(NA)	4.7
1930	6,605	3,560	53.9	3,045	46.1	−.2	−.5	4.6
1940	7,107	3,783	53.2	3,324	46.8	.7	(Z)	4.3
1950	5,721	3,758	65.7	1,963	34.3	−2.1	−2.8	4.0
1960 [5]	3,566	2,633	73.8	933	26.2	−4.6	−3.8	3.8
1970 [5]	3,095	2,492	80.5	603	19.5	−1.4	−4.7	3.4
1975 [5]	2,644	2,154	81.5	490	18.5	−3.1	(NA)	(NA)
1976 [5]	2,670	2,193	82.1	477	17.9	1.0	(NA)	(NA)

NA   Not available.   Z   Less than .05 percent.
[1] Statistics on the number of occupied units are essentially comparable although identified by various terms— the term "family" applies to figures for 1910 and 1930; "occupied dwelling unit," 1940 and 1950; and "occupied housing unit," 1960, 1970, 1975, and 1976. For 1920, includes the small number of quasi-families; for 1930, represents private families only.
[2] For 1920, change from 1910.   [3] Total resident population; see tables 1 and 27.
[4] From 1950 to 1970, population in occupied housing units was determined by dividing population in housing units by number of occupied housing units. Population data exclude persons in institutions and other group quarters (see table 72).
[5] Not comparable with data for earlier censuses because of a basic change in definition of farm residence. For definitions used in 1960 and 1970, see text, p. 684.
[6] Includes a small proportion of urban-farm families in addition to rural-farm.

Source: U.S. Bureau of the Census, *Census of Population and Housing: 1960* and *1970;* and *Current Housing Reports,* series H–150–76, Annual Housing Survey: 1976, part A, *General Characteristics for the United States and Regions.*

No. 1378. OCCUPIED HOUSING UNITS—FINANCIAL SUMMARY 1970 AND 1976

[In thousands, except as indicated. For definition of standard metropolitan statistical area (SMSA), see Appendix II. For definition of median, see p. xii]

CHARACTERISTIC	1970					1976				
	Total	Inside SMSA's			Outside SMSA's	Total	Inside SMSA's			Outside SMSA's
		Total	In central cities	Not in central cities			Total	In central cities	Not in central cities	
Occupied units, total_	63,445	43,859	21,395	22,464	19,586	74,005	50,452	22,930	27,522	23,553
Median income (dol.):										
Owner occupied units____	9,700	11,000	10,100	11,600	7,500	14,400	16,200	14,200	17,300	11,700
Renter occupied units____	6,300	6,700	6,100	7,700	5,300	8,100	8,500	7,500	10,100	7,100
Specified owner occupied ¹__	31,726	22,059	8,543	13,516	9,667	37,934	25,884	9,453	16,431	12,050
With value of—										
Less than $20,000_____	19,556	11,963	5,608	6,356	7,594	8,537	4,334	2,517	1,818	4,202
$20,000–$24,999_____	4,680	3,740	1,214	2,526	940	3,907	2,407	1,076	1,331	1,500
$25,000–$34,999_____	4,444	3,709	1,044	2,665	736	8,915	6,144	2,389	3,755	2,771
$35,000–$49,999_____	2,050	1,760	444	1,316	289	9,178	6,868	1,983	4,886	2,311
$50,000 and over_____	997	887	234	653	110	7,396	6,130	1,488	4,642	1,266
Median—										
Value_____dol__	17,100	19,000	16,400	20,800	12,200	32,300	35,100	29,400	38,300	26,100
Real estate taxes ²_dol__	(NA)	(NA)	(NA)	(NA)	(NA)	408	517	424	579	212
Monthly housing costs for units ³—										
With mortgages.dol__	(NA)	(NA)	(NA)	(NA)	(NA)	251	264	237	281	218
Owned clear____dol__	(NA)	(NA)	(NA)	(NA)	(NA)	88	99	92	106	74
Specified renter occupied ⁴__	22,334	17,433	11,033	6,401	4,900	25,420	19,439	11,581	7,858	5,981
With gross rent of—										
Less than $80_____	5,466	3,499	2,619	879	1,968	2,456	1,478	1,126	353	979
$80–$99_____	3,701	2,879	2,099	779	822	1,647	1,047	759	289	600
$100–$119_____	3,332	2,739	1,845	894	592	2,055	1,380	1,002	378	675
$120–$149_____	3,772	3,283	1,967	1,316	485	3,587	2,609	1,788	821	978
$150–$199_____	3,304	2,986	1,525	1,461	318	6,553	5,334	3,235	2,100	1,219
$200–$299_____	1,194	1,110	547	563	84	6,166	5,451	2,697	2,755	715
$300 and over_____	265	254	145	108	12	1,678	1,515	693	821	163
No cash rent_____	1,300	685	284	400	615	1,277	624	202	849	653
Median rent_____dol__	108	114	107	130	84	167	178	165	195	132

NA Not available. ¹ Includes only 1-family homes on less than 10 acres and no business on the property. ² Taxes paid previous year. ³ Covers real estate taxes, property insurance, utilities, fuel, water, garbage and trash collection, and mortgage. ⁴ Excludes 1-family homes on 10 acres or more.

Source: U.S. Bureau of the Census, *Current Housing Reports*, H-150-76, Annual Housing Survey: 1976, part A, *General Housing Characteristics for the nited States and Regions*.

No. 1379. OCCUPIED HOUSING UNITS—PERCENT OF HOME OWNERSHIP, BY RACE OF HOUSEHOLD HEAD, INSIDE AND OUTSIDE SMSA's, BY REGION: 1960 TO 1976

[Refers to 243 standard metropolitan statistical areas (SMSA's) as defined in 1970 census publications. For definition of SMSA's, see text, Appendix II. For composition of regions, see fig. I, inside front cover]

YEAR AND REGION	TOTAL		INSIDE SMSA'S						OUTSIDE SMSA'S	
			Total		In central cities		SMSA remainder			
	White	Black ¹	White	Black ¹	White	Black ¹	White	Black ¹	White	Black ¹
1960: United States____	64.4	38.4	62.1	35.7	51.1	31.7	73.4	51.6	69.0	44.8
Northeast_____	58.1	27.0	55.5	26.4	37.5	22.3	72.6	46.7	70.0	42.0
North Central__	69.1	35.8	67.3	34.2	56.0	31.4	79.2	56.5	72.0	54.3
South_____	66.4	41.6	65.9	39.7	60.5	35.9	72.3	51.3	67.1	43.6
West_____	62.5	44.6	61.6	42.5	55.0	38.4	67.7	54.0	65.5	54.6
1970: United States____	65.4	41.6	62.3	38.5	51.3	34.8	71.1	54.1	72.1	51.7
Northeast_____	60.4	28.6	57.4	28.1	38.8	24.2	71.7	47.3	72.1	42.6
North Central__	70.2	42.0	67.8	41.3	56.5	38.9	76.5	58.8	74.4	56.3
South_____	68.2	46.9	65.3	43.4	59.5	39.1	70.7	57.3	71.9	52.0
West_____	60.2	40.1	58.6	40.0	52.0	36.6	63.6	49.6	66.1	42.1
1976: United States____	67.6	43.7	64.6	40.4	53.3	37.5	72.3	50.3	73.7	55.3
Northeast_____	63.1	30.0	60.3	29.6	41.5	26.5	72.7	43.1	72.5	37.2
North Central__	71.6	50.0	69.6	44.0	58.6	42.0	76.8	55.0	75.0	60.6
South_____	70.2	48.6	65.9	43.8	57.9	40.0	72.2	54.4	75.4	56.3
West_____	63.3	41.9	62.2	42.0	55.5	42.1	66.6	41.7	66.9	42.1

¹ For 1960, represents Black and other races.

Source: U.S. Bureau of the Census, Census of Population and Housing: 1970, PHC(2), *General Demographic Trends for Metropolitan Areas, 1960 to 1970;* and *Current Housing Reports,* series H-150-76, part A.

No. 1380. Occupied Units—Selected Characteristics of Owner Occupied and Renter Occupied Units: 1960 to 1977

[Percent distribution, except as indicated. Annual averages, except as noted]

CHARACTERISTIC	1960 [1]			1970			1977		
	Total occupied	Owner occupied	Renter occupied	Total occupied	Owner occupied	Renter occupied	Total occupied	Owner occupied	Renter occupied
Percent of total	100.0	61.9	38.1	100.0	64.2	35.8	100.0	64.8	35.2
Median [2] rooms number	4.9	5.5	3.9	5.2	5.7	4.1	5.2	5.8	4.1
Percent distribution	100	100	100	100	100	100	100	100	100
Rooms in unit:									
1 room	2		5	1		3	1		3
2 rooms	4	6	9	3	3	7	2	2	7
3 rooms	11		23	9		21	9		21
4 rooms	21	17	28	19	14	30	20	12	34
5 rooms	26	29	19	26	28	21	25	28	19
6 rooms	20	26	10	22	27	11	21	27	10
7 rooms or more	16	22	6	20	28	7	22	31	6
Units in structure:									
1 unit	76	94	48	74	94	38	73	95	34
2 units	8	4	13	9	4	18	7	3	14
3 and 4 units	5		12	5		11	5		12
5–9 units	11	2	9	4	2	11	5	2	13
10 units or more			18	8		22	10		27
Plumbing facilities:									
With all facilities	84	89	77	95	97	91	97	98	95
Lacking facilities	16	11	23	5	3	9	3	2	5
Year structure built:									
1965 or later	(X)	(X)	(X)	12	13	9	27	28	26
1960–1964	(X)	(X)	(X)	12	13	10	9	10	7
1950–1959	27	34	16	19	24	12	19	22	14
1940–1949	15	16	13	14	14	13	11	10	11
1939 or earlier	58	50	71	43	36	56	34	30	42

X Not applicable.   [1] As of April 1.   [2] For definition of median, see p. xii.

Source: U.S. Bureau of the Census, *Current Housing Reports*, series H–111.

No. 1381. Selected Household and Housing Characteristics of Homeowners and Renters, by Income: 1976

[Income data refer to the 12 months prior to interviews, which were conducted between October and December]

CHARACTERISTIC	OWNER OCCUPIED UNITS—INCOME				RENTER OCCUPIED UNITS—INCOME			
	Under $10,000	$10,000 to $14,999	$15,000 to $24,999	$25,000 and over	Under $10,000	$10,000 to $14,999	$15,000 to $24,999	$25,000 and over
Occupied units, total 1,000	15,332	9,573	14,046	8,953	15,567	5,318	3,949	1,268
Percent with:								
Male head, wife present, no relatives	52.0	78.4	88.3	91.9	30.2	55.4	68.3	74.1
Female head (2 or more persons)	14.2	9.1	4.5	2.4	23.1	11.4	6.8	4.3
One-person household	30.6	8.6	3.8	2.6	40.1	26.1	18.6	15.2
Household head 65 years and over	48.2	17.0	6.8	5.7	24.2	5.8	4.8	8.0
Own children under 18 years	23.3	48.7	57.9	54.0	31.9	39.9	38.4	36.3
Percent:								
Lacking some or all plumbing facilities	3.8	.9	.4	.2	6.8	1.8	1.2	.5
With 1.01 persons or more per room	3.5	4.8	4.0	2.7	6.7	6.4	5.0	3.7
Built 1960 or later	29.5	38.3	45.0	51.6	29.6	38.5	45.6	53.2
With units inside SMSA's [1]	53.9	61.0	70.0	77.7	72.1	76.9	80.3	84.1
In central cities	23.9	24.5	23.4	22.9	46.9	41.3	39.2	42.3
Owned second home	2.8	3.7	4.8	9.8	1.2	2.5	3.8	8.7
With air conditioning [2]	46.3	56.4	61.9	67.2	35.6	52.4	60.1	67.1
Reporting failures in:								
Water supply [3]	2.3	2.0	2.1	1.6	2.6	2.7	2.5	3.4
Heating equipment [4]	5.6	6.2	5.7	6.0	8.5	9.7	9.2	12.0

[1] For definition, see text, Appendix II.   [2] Covers room units and central systems.   [3] For units with piped water inside structure, occupied 3 months or longer.   [4] For units with heating equipment, occupied previous winter.

Source: U.S. Bureau of the Census, *Current Housing Reports*, series H–150–76. Annual Housing Survey: 1976, part C, *Financial Characteristics of the Housing Inventory for the United States and Regions.*

No. 1382. HEATING EQUIPMENT AND FUELS FOR OCCUPIED UNITS: 1950 TO 1976

[In thousands, except percent]

ITEM	1950	1960	1970	1975	1976	PERCENT DISTRIBUTION				
						1950	1960	1970	1975	1976
Occupied units, total	42,826	53,024	63,445	72,523	74,005	100.0	100.0	100.0	100.0	100.0
Warm air furnace	[1]11,508	17,378	27,515	36,999	38,787	[1]26.9	32.8	43.4	51.0	52.4
Steam or hot water	10,071	11,990	13,211	13,792	13,598	23.5	22.6	20.8	19.0	18.4
Built-in electric units	-	664	3,236	4,625	4,794	-	1.3	5.1	6.4	6.5
Floor, wall, or pipeless furnace	([1])	6,088	5,552	6,580	6,417	([1])	11.5	8.8	9.1	8.7
Room heaters with flue	[2]15,399	[2]11,183	7,209	4,747	4,585	[2]36.0	[2]21.1	11.4	6.5	6.2
Room heaters without flue	5,268	5,218	3,558	3,330	3,338	12.3	9.8	5.6	4.6	4.5
Fireplaces, stoves, or portable heaters	([2])	([2])	2,766	1,982	2,023	([2])	([2])	4.4	2.7	2.7
None	581	503	398	468	463	1.4	.9	.6	.6	.6
House heating fuel:										
Utility gas	11,387	22,851	35,014	40,933	41,219	26.6	43.1	55.2	56.4	55.7
Fuel oil, kerosene, etc	9,686	17,158	16,473	16,299	16,451	22.6	32.4	26.0	22.5	22.2
Electricity	283	933	4,876	9,173	10,151	.7	1.8	7.7	12.6	13.7
Bottled, tank, or LP gas	787	2,686	3,807	4,146	4,239	1.8	5.1	6.0	5.7	5.7
Coal or coke	14,828	6,456	1,821	573	484	34.6	12.2	2.9	.8	.7
Wood and other fuel	4,855	2,460	1,060	930	998	11.3	4.6	1.7	1.3	1.3
None	999	478	395	468	463	2.3	.9	.6	.6	.6
Cooking fuel:										
Utility gas	22,084	27,296	31,244	32,493	32,299	51.6	51.5	49.2	44.8	43.6
Electricity	6,403	16,351	25,768	33,944	35,669	15.0	30.8	40.6	46.8	48.2
Bottled, tank, or LP gas	3,417	6,491	5,314	5,440	5,473	8.0	12.2	8.4	7.5	7.4
Other fuel	10,796	2,603	908	332	275	25.2	4.9	1.4	.5	.4
None	124	280	213	315	287	.3	.5	.3	.4	.4

- Represents zero. [1] "Floor, wall, or pipeless furnace" included in "Warm air furnace."
[2] "Fireplaces, stoves, or portable heaters" included in "Room heaters with flue."
Source: U.S. Bureau of the Census, Census of Heating, 1960, vol. I, No. 1; Census of Housing, 1970, vol. I; and Current Housing Reports, series H-150, Annual Housing Survey, part A, General Housing Characteristics for the United States and Regions.

No. 1383. SELECTED ELECTRICAL APPLIANCES—NUMBER AND PERCENT OF HOMES WITH APPLIANCES: 1960 TO 1977

[As of December 31. Percentages based on total number of homes wired for electricity]

ITEM	HOMES WITH APPLIANCES (mil.)						PERCENT WITH APPLIANCES					
	1960	1965	1970	1975	1976	1977	1960	1965	1970	1975	1976	1977
Number of wired homes	51.7	57.6	64.0	72.7	74.1	75.8	(X)	(X)	(X)	(X)	(X)	(X)
Air-conditioners, room	7.8	13.9	26.0	38.4	40.3	41.9	15.1	24.2	40.6	52.8	54.4	55.3
Bed coverings	12.2	20.0	31.7	41.4	43.4	45.4	23.6	34.7	49.5	57.0	58.6	59.9
Blenders	4.2	7.5	23.4	32.9	35.3	37.9	8.0	13.0	36.5	45.2	47.6	50.0
Can openers	2.5	14.2	29.1	39.7	41.8	43.9	4.8	24.7	45.5	54.6	56.4	57.9
Coffeemakers	30.2	41.3	56.7	71.0	73.6	75.6	58.3	71.7	88.6	97.7	99.4	99.7
Dishwashers	3.7	7.8	17.0	27.9	29.4	31.0	7.1	13.5	26.5	38.3	39.6	40.9
Disposers, food waste	5.4	7.8	16.3	28.2	30.2	32.4	10.5	13.6	25.5	38.8	40.7	42.8
Dryers, clothes (incl. gas)	10.1	15.2	28.6	42.0	43.4	44.9	19.6	26.4	44.6	57.7	58.6	59.3
Freezers, home	12.1	15.7	20.0	31.6	32.9	33.9	23.4	27.2	31.2	43.5	44.4	44.8
Frypans	22.5	28.3	36.0	45.8	47.1	48.8	43.4	49.2	56.2	63.0	63.6	64.4
Hotplates and buffet ranges	12.5	13.1	15.7	19.1	19.7	20.2	24.2	22.7	24.5	26.2	26.6	26.7
Irons, total	45.7	57.1	63.8	72.6	74.0	75.8	88.4	99.1	99.7	99.9	99.9	99.9
Steam and steam/spray	30.6	43.5	56.5	70.7	72.4	74.8	59.2	75.5	88.2	97.2	97.7	98.6
Microwave ovens	(NA)	(NA)	(NA)	2.3	3.4	5.0	(NA)	(NA)	(NA)	3.2	5.1	6.7
Mixers	29.0	41.9	52.8	65.6	67.5	70.1	56.0	72.8	82.4	90.2	91.1	92.4
Radios	50.3	57.3	63.9	72.6	74.0	75.8	[1]94.3	[1]99.5	99.8	99.9	99.9	99.9
Ranges: Free-standing	16.0	18.5	25.9	35.8	37.4	39.2	30.9	32.1	40.5	49.2	50.4	51.8
Built-in	3.3	5.9	9.6	14.0	14.6	15.2	6.4	10.3	15.0	19.3	19.7	20.1
Refrigerators	50.8	57.3	68.9	72.6	73.9	75.8	98.2	99.5	99.8	99.9	99.8	99.9
Television: Black and white	46.2	55.9	63.2	72.6	74.0	75.8	89.4	97.1	98.7	99.9	99.9	99.9
Color	(NA)	5.5	27.2	54.1	57.5	61.7	(NA)	9.5	42.5	74.4	77.7	81.3
Toasters	37.2	48.1	59.3	71.7	73.6	75.8	72.0	83.6	92.6	98.6	99.4	99.9
Vacuum cleaners	38.4	48.1	58.9	72.1	73.7	75.8	74.3	83.5	92.0	99.2	99.5	99.9
Washers, clothes	28.6	33.1	39.8	50.8	53.7	55.6	55.4	57.4	62.1	69.9	72.5	73.3
Water heaters	9.8	13.5	20.2	29.4	30.9	(NA)	18.9	23.4	31.6	40.4	41.7	(NA)

NA Not available.   X Not applicable.   [1] Based on 53,300,000 homes in 1960, and 58,566,000 in 1965.
Source: Billboard Publications, Inc., New York, N.Y., Merchandising, annual statistical issues. (Copyright.)

No. 1384. Occupied Units—Selected Neighborhood Characteristics of Home-owners and Renters, Inside and Outside SMSA's: 1975 and 1976

[In thousands of units. Data based on respondent's opinion of his/her neighborhood. Refers to 243 standard metropolitan statistical areas (SMSA's) as defined in 1970 census publications; see text, Appendix II:

CHARACTERISTIC	1975, total	1976								
		Total	Owner occupied units				Renter occupied units			
			Total	Inside SMSA's		Outside SMSA's	Total	Inside SMSA's		Outside SMSA's
				Total	Central cities			Total	Central cities	
Occupied units, total [1]	72,523	74,005	47,904	30,895	11,349	17,009	26,101	19,557	11,581	6,544
NEIGHBORHOOD CONDITIONS										
No undesirable conditions	16,609	16,844	11,483	7,192	2,551	4,291	5,361	3,759	2,057	1,602
Undesirable conditions [2]	55,634	56,945	36,304	23,622	8,764	12,682	20,650	15,722	9,476	4,928
Percent	76.7	77.0	75.8	76.5	77.2	74.6	79.1	80.4	81.8	75.3
Airplane noise	11,864	13,140	8,595	6,830	2,579	1,766	4,545	3,904	2,232	641
Street noise	25,069	25,754	15,483	10,343	4,214	5,140	10,271	7,893	4,927	2,379
Heavy traffic	21,883	22,476	13,230	8,370	3,499	4,859	9,246	7,160	4,613	2,086
Streets need repair	12,378	12,960	8,846	4,912	1,800	3,934	4,114	2,902	1,806	1,213
Roads impassable	7,725	7,880	5,325	3,276	1,377	2,049	2,555	1,860	1,168	694
Inadequate street lighting	18,106	18,023	12,988	7,734	1,789	5,254	5,035	3,427	1,673	1,608
Crime	13,330	13,152	7,425	5,998	2,721	1,427	5,727	5,097	3,620	630
Litter	10,413	11,343	6,898	4,500	2,013	2,398	4,445	3,577	2,525	868
Abandoned buildings	4,962	5,237	2,784	1,761	969	1,023	2,453	2,006	1,545	447
Rundown housing	6,864	7,411	4,212	2,858	1,349	1,354	3,199	2,498	1,832	701
Commercial or industrial	12,366	15,060	7,063	4,718	2,196	2,345	7,997	6,471	4,192	1,527
Odors	6,412	7,000	4,398	3,039	1,245	1,359	2,602	2,106	1,363	496
NEIGHBORHOOD SERVICES										
Adequate services	36,649	38,118	22,570	16,655	7,473	5,915	15,548	12,793	8,074	2,756
Inadequate services [2]	35,562	35,634	25,186	14,138	3,834	11,048	10,448	6,678	3,458	3,770
Percent	49.0	48.2	52.6	45.8	33.8	65.0	40.0	34.1	29.9	57.6
Public transportation	26,140	25,539	19,163	10,241	1,833	8,922	6,376	3,384	1,048	2,992
Schools	2,592	2,931	2,002	1,249	521	753	929	679	414	250
Shopping	9,618	9,760	6,748	3,642	1,251	3,106	3,012	2,053	1,255	958
Police protection	6,117	6,833	4,433	2,403	962	2,030	2,400	1,774	1,244	626
Fire protection	3,092	3,562	2,621	866	193	1,756	941	472	268	469
Hospitals or health clinics	8,570	9,188	6,448	3,498	860	2,949	2,740	1,727	884	1,013

[1] Includes respondents who did not report conditions or services.
[2] Figures will not add to total because more than one condition or service may be reported for the same unit.

Source: U.S. Bureau of the Census, *Current Housing Reports*, series H-150, Annual Housing Survey, part B, *Indicators of Housing and Neighborhood Quality for the United States and Regions.*

No. 1385. Expenditures by Residential Property Owners for Improvements and Maintenance and Repairs: 1970 to 1977

[In millions of dollars, except averages]

YEAR AND TYPE OF EXPENDITURE	All properties	1-unit properties with owner occupant	Other properties	Additions and alterations			Major construction replacements	Maintenance and repairs
				Total	Residential	Other property		
1970: All properties [1]	14,770	9,469	5,301	6,246	4,950	1,296	2,629	5,895
Average per property	$297	$265	(NA)	(NA)	(NA)	(NA)	(NA)	(NA)
Heating and air conditioning [2]	1,365	1,027	338	532	532	(NA)	548	286
Plumbing	1,376	704	672	337	337	(NA)	495	544
Roofing	1,019	691	328	(NA)	(NA)	(NA)	614	405
Painting	2,547	1,373	1,174	(NA)	(NA)	(NA)	(NA)	2,547
1975: All properties [1]	25,239	15,684	9,556	10,997	8,815	2,182	4,484	9,758
Average per property	$459	$382	$685	$200	$160	$40	$82	$178
Heating and air conditioning [2]	1,631	1,097	534	457	457	(NA)	689	484
Plumbing	2,287	1,174	1,113	532	532	(NA)	859	896
Roofing	2,325	1,493	832	(NA)	(NA)	(NA)	1,471	854
Painting	3,895	2,088	1,807	(NA)	(NA)	(NA)	(NA)	3,895
1977: All properties [1]	31,280	21,761	9,519	14,237	11,160	3,077	5,699	11,344
Average per property	$549	$517	$639	$250	$196	$54	$100	$199
Heating and air conditioning [2]	1,934	1,289	645	484	484	(NA)	821	630
Plumbing	2,975	1,558	1,417	552	552	(NA)	1,002	1,421
Roofing	2,407	1,582	825	(NA)	(NA)	(NA)	1,483	925
Painting	4,007	2,371	1,637	(NA)	(NA)	(NA)	(NA)	4,007

NA Not available.   [1] Includes types of expenditures not separately specified.   [2] Central air conditioning.
Source: U.S. Bureau of the Census, *Construction Reports*, series C 50.

No. 1386. Low Rent Public Housing—Families Moving In: 1974 to 1977

[For years ending Sept. 30. See headnote, table 1387]

CHARACTERISTIC	All families [1]	White (non-minority)	Negro	American Indian	Spanish American	Oriental	Percent elderly	Percent receiving aid [2]	Percent with no workers
Number moving in during—									
1974	163,235	73,824	69,764	1,197	16,216	539	32	67	63
1975	137,036	64,090	57,777	1,105	11,863	548	36	72	68
1976	74,175	29,758	32,849	739	9,941	416	34	74	70
1977	139,667	61,376	61,674	1,416	13,279	1,124	33	73	68
Median: [3]									
Age of family head___yr__	34	48	30	33	33	38	(X)	(X)	(X)
Annual income____dol__	3,651	3,625	3,544	4,445	4,168	4,172	(X)	(X)	(X)
Monthly gross rent__dol__	62	63	59	69	71	71	(X)	(X)	(X)
Avg. number of minors_____	1.49	1.07	1.79	2.07	1.98	1.94	(X)	(X)	(X)

X Not applicable. [1] Includes data for families not available by minority group.
[2] Includes families receiving benefits. [3] For definition of median, see p. xii.
Source: U.S. Dept. of Housing and Urban Development, *HUD Statistical Yearbook.*

No. 1387. Low-Rent Public Housing Units, by Progress Stage: 1960 to 1977

[In thousands. As of Dec. 31. Includes Puerto Rico and Virgin Islands. Covers units subsidized by HUD under annual contributions contracts. See also *Historical Statistics, Colonial Times to 1970,* series N 186–191]

YEAR AND PROGRAM	Total	Occupied units [1]	Under construction	Other [2]	YEAR AND PROGRAM	Total	Occupied units [1]	Under construction	Other [2]
1960	593.3	478.2	36.4	78.8	1976	1,305.4	1,181.5	63.4	60.5
Elderly [3]	18.9	1.1	4.1	13.7	Elderly [3]	321.3	293.0	14.9	13.4
1965	735.7	604.9	42.4	88.4	New construction	1,094.8	1,031.2	39.2	24.4
Elderly [3]	97.7	36.2	21.6	40.0	Conventional [4]	861.2	832.2	15.6	13.4
1970	1,155.3	893.5	126.8	135.0	Turnkey [5]	233.0	199.0	20.0	11.0
Elderly [3]	249.4	143.4	65.7	40.3	Acquisition [6]	47.3	32.9	9.7	4.7
					Leased housing [7]	163.3	117.4	14.5	31.4
1972	1,260.2	1,055.0	105.9	99.3	1977	1,308.8	1,187.7	63.6	57.5
Elderly [3]	316.7	232.0	49.1	35.6	Elderly [3]	322.3	295.0	15.3	12.0
1973	1,323.6	1,109.1	96.7	117.8	New construction	1,100.0	1,036.7	41.3	22.0
Elderly [3]	333.9	261.8	35.8	36.3	Conventional [4]	862.5	835.5	15.8	11.2
1974	1,314.0	1,151.0	64.8	98.2	Turnkey [5]	237.5	201.2	25.5	10.8
Elderly [3]	327.3	265.1	32.3	29.9	Acquisition [6]	45.5	33.4	7.8	4.3
1975	1,316.7	1,180.4	52.9	83.4	Leased housing [7]	163.3	117.6	14.5	31.2
Elderly [3]	336.3	288.3	24.3	23.7	New	72.5	44.8	12.3	15.4

[1] Under management or available for occupancy.
[2] To be constructed or to go directly "under management" because no rehabilitation needed.
[3] Designed for persons 62 years old or over, disabled, or handicapped.
[4] New housing constructed on the Local Housing Authority (LHA) site pursuant to a contract let by the LHA.
[5] New housing purchased by the LHA from a private developer upon completion of construction pursuant to an earlier agreement. [6] Existing housing acquired by the LHA.
[7] Existing housing leased by LHA from an owner under a contract permitting LHA to sub-lease the units.
Source: U.S. Dept. of Housing and Urban Development, *HUD Statistical Yearbook,* and unpublished data.

No. 1388. Vacant Housing Units—Percent, by Status: 1974 to 1977

[Annual averages. See headnote, table 1389. See also *Historical Statistics, Colonial Times to 1970,* series N 247–248]

STATUS	TOTAL				INSIDE SMSA'S				OUTSIDE SMSA'S			
	1974	1975	1976	1977	1974	1975	1976	1977	1974	1975	1976	1977
All units	100.0	100.0	100.0	100.0	100.0	100.0	100.0	100.0	100.0	100.0	100.0	100.0
Occupied	91.1	91.3	91.6	91.6	92.7	92.8	93.0	93.2	87.7	88.1	88.5	88.3
Vacant, seasonal	2.3	2.1	2.0	2.0	1.0	.9	.9	.8	4.8	4.6	4.2	4.5
Vacant, year-round	6.6	6.6	6.4	6.4	6.3	6.3	6.1	6.0	7.5	7.3	7.3	7.2
For rent	2.1	2.1	1.9	1.8	2.4	2.4	2.2	2.1	1.6	1.5	1.3	1.3
For sale only	.7	.7	.7	.7	.7	.8	.7	.6	.7	.7	.8	.9
Rented or sold [1]	.7	.7	.7	.8	.8	.7	.8	.9	.6	.5	.6	.6
Held off market [2]	3.1	3.1	3.1	3.1	2.4	2.4	2.4	2.4	4.6	4.6	4.6	4.4
Occasional use	.8	.8	.9	.9	.4	.5	.5	.5	1.6	1.6	1.7	1.6

[1] Awaiting occupancy. [2] Includes "other," not shown separately.
Source: U.S. Bureau of the Census, *Current Housing Reports,* series H-111.

No. 1389. VACANCY RATES FOR HOUSING UNITS—CHARACTERISTICS: 1974 TO 1977

[In percent. Annual averages. Based on Current Population Survey and Quarterly Household Survey. Rate is relationship between vacant housing for rent or for sale and the total supply, which comprises occupied units, units rented or sold and awaiting occupancy, and vacant units available for rent. For composition of regions, see fig. I, inside front cover. SMSA refers to 243 standard metropolitan statistical areas as defined in 1970 census publications; see Appendix II. See also *Historical Statistics, Colonial Times to 1970*, series N 249–258]

RENTAL UNITS	1974	1975	1976	1977	HOMEOWNER UNITS	1974	1975	1976	1977
Total rental units	**6.2**	**6.0**	**5.6**	**5.2**	**Total homeowner units**	**1.2**	**1.2**	**1.2**	**1.2**
Inside SMSA's	6.2	6.1	5.7	5.3	Inside SMSA's	1.2	1.3	1.2	1.0
Outside SMSA's	6.2	5.7	5.1	5.2	Outside SMSA's	1.1	1.1	1.2	1.4
Northeast	4.2	4.1	4.7	5.1	Northeast	.8	1.0	1.0	.9
North Central	6.1	5.7	5.6	5.1	North Central	1.0	1.0	1.0	.9
South	8.0	7.7	6.4	5.7	South	1.5	1.5	1.6	1.7
West	6.2	6.2	5.4	5.0	West	1.5	1.5	1.2	.9
Units in structure: 1 unit	3.8	3.6	3.2	3.1	Units in structure: 1 unit	1.0	1.0	1.0	.9
2 or more	7.5	7.3	6.8	6.4	2 or more	4.7	5.4	5.3	5.4
5 or more	8.8	8.3	7.8	7.1	5 or more	12.6	14.4	14.4	16.3
Units with: 3 rooms or less	9.0	8.4	8.1	7.7	Units with: 3 rooms or less	3.6	3.5	5.1	5.1
4 rooms	6.0	5.8	4.9	4.7	4 rooms	2.1	2.1	1.8	2.2
5 rooms	4.8	4.6	4.8	4.6	5 rooms	1.2	1.1	1.1	1.0
6 rooms or more	3.2	3.3	2.9	2.8	6 rooms or more	.9	1.0	1.0	.9
Monthly rent: Less than $60	5.6	5.5	4.8	4.4	Value: Less than $10,000	1.1	1.4	1.8	1.2
$60–$79	5.8	5.7	6.2	5.5	$10,000–$19,999	1.0	1.0	1.1	.9
$80–$99	6.4	4.6	5.0	5.3	$20,000–$24,999	1.0	.9	.9	.6
$100 or more	6.8	6.7	5.9	5.4	$25,000 or more	1.3	1.4	1.3	.9
Year built: 1960 or later	8.6	8.3	6.5	5.6	Year built: 1960 or later	1.9	2.2	1.9	1.6
1965 or later	9.8	9.0	7.3	5.8	1965 or later	2.4	2.7	2.4	2.0
1940–1959	5.3	4.8	4.8	4.2	1940–1959	.6	.5	.6	.7
1939 or earlier	5.5	5.4	5.5	5.7	1939 or earlier	1.1	1.1	1.2	1.2
Plumbing: With all facilities	6.1	5.9	5.4	5.0	Plumbing: With all facilities	2.2	1.3	1.2	1.1
Lacking facilities	10.0	11.2	10.7	12.4	Lacking facilities	1.4	2.0	3.1	3.4

Source: U.S. Bureau of the Census, *Current Housing Reports*, series H–111.

No. 1390. NEW APARTMENTS COMPLETED AND RENTED IN 3 MONTHS: 1973 TO 1977

[Structures with 5 or more units, privately financed, nonsubsidized, unfurnished apartments. Based on sample and subject to sampling variability. For definition of median, see p. xii]

YEAR AND ITEM	Total	Rent under $150	Rent, $150–$174	Rent, $175–$199	Rent, $200–$249	Rent, $250 or more	Less than 2 bedrooms	2 bedrooms	3 or more bedrooms	Median monthly rent
1973: Number 1,000	490	66.0	100.8	121.8	127.9	73.5	225.9	236.2	27.8	$191
Percent rented in 3 mo	70	81	73	71	66	59	74	66	62	(X)
1974: Number 1,000	390	32.3	78.6	97.8	107.2	74.5	177.5	189.6	23.3	$197
Percent rented in 3 mo	68	83	75	70	65	56	73	65	57	(X)
1975: Number 1,000	217	14.3	33.7	46.2	61.9	60.3	98.3	105.8	12.4	$211
Percent rented in 3 mo	70	80	77	74	73	58	73	68	63	(X)
1976: Number 1,000	157	6.8	14.4	35.0	56.9	43.9	75.1	74.5	7.4	$220
Percent rented in 3 mo	80	84	82	82	80	79	86	77	59	(X)
1977:[1] Number 1,000	195	6.6	14.4	30.4	72.7	71.2	87.4	100.6	7.3	$232
Percent rented in 3 mo	80	85	75	83	83	77	83	78	78	(X)

X Not applicable.   [1] Preliminary.

Source: U.S. Bureau of the Census, *Current Housing Reports*, series H–130, and unpublished data.

No. 1391. EXISTING ONE-FAMILY HOUSES SOLD AND PRICE, BY REGION: 1968 TO 1977

[Based on data (adjusted and aggregated to regional and national totals) reported by participating real estate multiple listing services. For definition of median, see p. xii. For composition of regions, see fig. I, inside front cover]

REGION	1968	1969	1970	1971	1972	1973	1974	1975	1976	1977
Houses sold, U.S. 1,000	**1,569**	**1,594**	**1,612**	**2,018**	**2,252**	**2,334**	**2,272**	**2,452**	**3,002**	**3,572**
Northeast 1,000	243	240	251	311	361	367	354	377	458	549
North Central 1,000	490	508	501	583	630	674	645	685	843	1,035
South 1,000	529	538	568	735	788	847	839	899	1,110	1,372
West 1,000	308	308	292	389	473	446	434	491	591	615
Median sales price, U.S. $1,000	**20.1**	**21.8**	**23.0**	**24.8**	**26.7**	**28.9**	**32.0**	**35.3**	**38.1**	**42.9**
Northeast $1,000	21.4	23.7	25.2	27.1	29.8	32.8	35.8	39.3	41.8	44.4
North Central $1,000	18.2	19.0	20.1	22.1	23.9	25.3	27.7	30.1	32.9	36.7
South $1,000	19.0	20.3	22.2	24.3	26.4	29.0	32.3	34.8	36.5	39.8
West $1,000	22.9	23.9	24.3	26.5	28.4	31.0	34.8	39.6	46.1	57.3

Source: National Association of Realtors, Washington, D.C., *Existing Home Sales*, monthly. (Copyright.)

No. 1392. New Private One-Family Houses Sold, by Region, Type of Financing, and Sales Price: 1970 to 1977

[In thousands. Based on a national probability sample of monthly interviews with builders or owners of 1-family houses for which building permits have been issued or, for nonpermit areas, on which construction has started. For details, see source. For composition of regions, see fig. I, inside front cover]

YEAR AND SALES PRICE	NUMBER SOLD					PERCENT SOLD					FINANCING TYPE	
	Total [1]	N.E.	N.C.	So.	West	Total	N.E.	N.C.	So.	West	Conventional [2]	FHA and VA
1970 [1]	485	61	100	203	121	100	100	100	100	100	202	232
Under $35,000	394	38	77	178	100	81	62	77	88	83	127	224
Under $20,000	169	10	20	99	38	35	16	20	49	31	31	122
$20,000–$29,999	178	20	47	62	49	37	33	47	31	40	65	92
$30,000–$34,999	47	8	9	17	13	10	13	9	8	11	31	10
$35,000 and over	92	23	22	26	21	19	38	22	13	17	75	7
$35,000–$39,999	35	7	8	10	9	7	11	8	5	7	(NA)	(NA)
$40,000–$49,999	37	10	9	10	7	8	16	9	5	6	(NA)	(NA)
$50,000 and over	20	5	5	5	5	4	8	5	2	4	(NA)	(NA)
1974	519	69	103	207	139	100	100	100	100	100	378	112
Under $35,000	248	24	49	109	66	48	35	48	53	47	155	80
Under $30,000	149	12	26	74	37	29	17	25	36	27	90	53
$30,000–$34,999	99	12	23	35	29	19	17	22	17	21	65	27
$35,000 and over	271	45	54	98	73	52	65	52	47	53	223	32
$35,000–$39,999	84	11	18	31	24	16	16	17	15	17	63	17
$40,000–$49,999	98	16	18	38	26	19	23	17	18	19	80	13
$50,000 and over	89	19	18	28	23	17	28	17	14	17	80	(S)
1975	549	71	106	222	150	100	100	100	100	100	363	122
Under $35,000	190	18	35	93	45	35	25	33	42	30	72	67
Under $30,000	110	9	17	60	24	20	13	16	27	16	29	37
$30,000–$34,999	80	9	18	33	21	15	13	17	15	14	42	30
$35,000 and over	359	52	72	128	106	65	73	68	58	71	291	54
$35,000–$39,999	98	10	20	40	28	18	14	19	18	19	67	28
$40,000–$49,999	127	18	25	47	37	23	25	24	21	25	101	22
$50,000–$59,999	65	12	13	20	20	12	17	12	9	13	59	[3] 3
$60,000 and over	69	12	14	21	21	13	17	13	9	14	64	(S)
1976	646	72	128	247	199	100	100	100	100	100	458	134
Under $35,000	149	14	27	77	31	23	19	21	31	16	60	58
Under $30,000	79	6	13	44	16	12	8	10	18	8	22	31
$30,000–$34,999	70	8	14	33	15	11	11	11	13	8	38	27
$35,000 and over	496	56	101	170	167	77	78	79	69	84	398	76
$35,000–$39,999	101	8	21	43	28	16	11	16	17	14	66	30
$40,000–$49,999	168	18	33	64	53	26	25	26	26	27	128	34
$50,000–$59,999	100	16	20	28	35	15	22	16	11	18	87	9
$60,000–$74,999	76	9	17	22	29	12	13	13	9	15	70	[3] 3
$75,000 and over	51	6	10	13	22	8	8	8	5	11	47	(S)
1977	819	86	162	317	255	100	100	100	100	100	592	166
Under $35,000	130	13	18	72	28	16	15	11	23	11	51	50
$35,000 and over	689	73	143	244	228	84	85	88	77	89	542	117
$35,000–$39,999	102	8	17	50	27	12	9	10	16	11	61	36
$40,000–$49,999	200	19	40	84	57	24	22	25	26	22	140	51
$50,000–$59,999	149	18	34	50	47	18	21	21	16	18	123	19
$60,000–$74,999	123	16	31	35	40	15	19	19	11	16	109	9
$75,000 and over	115	12	21	25	57	14	14	13	8	22	108	[3] 2

NA Not available.   S Estimate does not meet publication standards.   [1] Includes types of financing not shown separately.   [2] 1970 and 1974 include houses financed by Farmers Home Administration.   [3] VA only.

Source: U.S. Bureau of the Census, *Construction Reports*, series C 25, *Characteristics of New Housing*, annual, and *New One-Family Houses Sold and For Sale*, monthly.

No. 1393. MEDIAN SALES PRICE OF NEW PRIVATE ONE-FAMILY HOUSES SOLD, BY REGION: 1965 TO 1977

[In dollars. See headnote, table 1392. For definition of median, see p. xii]

YEAR	U.S.	North-east	North Central	South	West	YEAR AND QUARTER	U.S.	North-east	North Central	South	West
1965	20,000	21,500	21,600	17,500	21,600	1971	25,200	30,600	27,200	22,500	25,500
1966	21,400	23,500	23,200	18,200	23,200	1972	27,600	31,400	29,300	25,800	27,500
1967	22,700	25,400	25,100	19,400	24,100	1973	32,500	37,100	32,900	30,900	32,400
1968	24,700	27,700	27,400	21,500	25,100	1974	35,900	40,100	36,100	34,500	35,800
1969	25,600	31,600	27,600	22,800	25,300	1975	39,300	44,000	39,600	37,300	40,600
1970	23,400	30,300	24,400	20,300	24,000	1976	44,200	47,300	44,800	40,500	47,200
						1977 [1]	48,800	51,600	51,500	44,100	53,500

[1] 1978, U.S. total: 1st qtr., $53,000, 2d qtr., $55,200.

Source: U.S. Bureau of the Census, *Construction Reports*, series C25, *Characteristics of New Housing*, annual, and *New One-Family Houses Sold and For Sale*, Monthly.

No. 1394. MORTGAGE STATUS OF NONFARM DWELLING UNITS: 1920 TO 1976

[In thousands, except percent. Prior to 1960, excludes Alaska and Hawaii. For 1920, mortgage data are for owner-occupied units in all types of structures; for 1940 and 1950, for owner-occupied dwelling units in 1- to 4-dwelling unit structures without business; for 1960, for properties with 1- to 4-dwelling units, and for 1971–1976, for properties with 1 housing unit. See also *Historical Statistics, Colonial Times to 1970*, series N 302–307]

ITEM	1920	1940	1950	1960	1971	1974	1975	1976
Owner occupied units	7,041	11,413	19,802	27,862	33,206	36,151	37,203	37,934
Reporting mortgage status	6,868	10,611	17,796	27,862	33,206	36,151	37,203	37,934
Mortgaged	2,736	4,805	7,825	15,816	20,110	22,960	23,438	24,089
Percent	39.8	45.3	44.0	56.8	60.6	63.5	63.0	63.5
Not mortgaged	4,132	5,806	9,971	12,046	13,096	13,191	13,764	13,845

Source: U.S. Bureau of the Census, *Census of Housing: 1950*, vol. I; *1960* and *1970*, vol. V; and *Current Housing Reports*, series H–150, Annual Housing Survey, part C, *Financial Characteristics of the Housing Inventory for the United States and Regions.*

No. 1395. VOLUME OF LONG-TERM MORTGAGE LOANS ORIGINATED, BY TYPE OF PROPERTY, 1970 TO 1976, AND BY LENDER, 1976

[In billions of dollars. Covers credit extended in primary mortgage markets for financing real estate acquisitions]

TYPE OF PROPERTY	1970	1972	1973	1974	1975	1976, BY LENDER						
						Total [1]	Savings and loan	Commercial banks	Mortgage cos.	Life insurance cos.	Fed'l credit agencies	Mutual savings
Loans, total	59.8	121.6	127.7	111.4	120.7	157.4	72.6	36.9	17.1	8.6	9.1	9.5
1–4 unit family home	35.6	75.9	79.1	67.5	77.9	110.1	61.9	22.1	15.4	.4	2.7	6.4
New units	12.6	25.8	28.0	24.1	24.7	31.4	17.7	5.6	4.9	.1	1.5	1.3
Existing units	23.0	50.0	51.2	43.4	53.3	78.7	44.2	16.5	10.5	.3	1.2	5.2
Multifamily residential	8.8	15.4	14.0	12.3	10.7	12.5	5.1	2.1	.7	.8	1.1	1.4
New units	7.0	9.2	8.7	8.4	5.8	4.6	1.2	.7	.5	.4	1.0	.4
Existing units	1.8	6.2	5.3	3.9	4.9	7.9	3.9	1.5	.1	.3	.1	1.0
Non-residential	12.5	24.5	27.4	24.0	24.2	25.0	5.0	10.3	1.0	6.0	.2	1.7
Farm properties	3.0	5.8	7.1	7.7	7.9	9.8	.6	2.4	–	1.4	5.2	(Z)

– Represents zero.   Z Less than $50 million.   [1] Includes lenders not shown separately.

Source: U.S. Dept. of Housing and Urban Development, *The Suppl_ of Mortgage Credit, 1970–1974*, and press releases.

No. 1396. RESIDENTIAL LOANS UNDERWRITTEN BY FHA: 1960 TO 1977

[In millions of dollars. Federal Housing Administration (FHA) insured loans represent gross amount of insurance written. Figures do not take account of principal repayments on previously insured or guaranteed loans. See also *Historical Statistics, Colonial Times to 1970*, series N 291–297]

LOAN	1960	1965	1970	1972	1973	1974	1975	1976	1977
FHA-insured loans	6,293	8,689	11,982	12,319	7,592	5,903	7,941	9,746	12,998
Home mortgages: New properties	2,197	1,705	2,667	3,459	1,675	752	1,149	1,087	1,664
Existing properties	2,403	5,760	5,447	4,608	2,798	3,182	5,017	5,275	7,177
Project type mortgages	711	591	3,251	3,448	2,286	1,213	976	2,315	2,816
Property improvement loans [1]	982	634	[2] 617	[2] 805	[2] 832	[2] 756	[2] 799	[2] 1,071	[2] 1,341

[1] Not ordinarily secured by mortgages.   [2] Includes mobile home loans.

Source· U.S. Dept. of Housing and Urban Development, *HUD Statistical Yearbook.*

No. 1397. Characteristics of Conventional First Mortgage Loans for Purchase of Single-Family Homes: April 1973 to April 1978

[Percent, except as indicated. April averages. Refers to loans originated directly (rather than through correspondents) by savings and loan associations, mortgage companies, commercial banks, and mutual savings banks]

LOAN CHARACTERISTIC	NEW HOMES						EXISTING HOMES					
	1973	1974	1975	1976	1977	1978	1973	1974	1975	1976	1977	1978
Contract interest rate	7.53	8.47	8.71	8.67	8.73	9.07	7.55	8.43	8.92	8.85	8.74	9.14
Initial fees and charges [1]	1.11	1.21	1.53	1.52	1.30	1.44	.96	.99	1.16	1.21	1.23	1.26
Term to maturity yr	26.6	26.1	26.5	27.3	27.3	28.4	23.9	22.9	23.9	24.5	25.8	26.6
Loan to price ratio	78.2	77.3	76.4	75.3	75.5	76.1	77.3	73.2	73.5	73.2	76.1	76.1
Purchase price $1,000	36.9	38.5	44.5	48.5	53.4	61.6	30.1	32.7	37.5	40.1	45.7	52.1

[1] Rate applies to any general or specific charges paid by borrower or seller, in order to obtain a loan, except those for mortgage, credit, life, or property insurance; for property transfer; and for title search and insurance.

Source: U.S. Federal Home Loan Bank Board, monthly news releases.

No. 1398. One-Family Homes, FHA-Insured Mortgages: 1972 to 1977

[Data are for sec. 203(b) of the National Housing Act only. For definition of median, see p. xii]

CHARACTERISTIC	NEW HOMES						EXISTING HOMES					
	1972	1973	1974	1975	1976	1977	1972	1973	1974	1975	1976	1977
Avg. mo., occupant expenses:												
Real estate taxes dol	40	35	40	49	54	56	36	34	35	40	40	41
Maintenance and repair dol	15	18	19	22	24	24	14	15	16	20	21	22
Heating and utilities dol	31	32	36	42	46	54	33	33	36	43	48	53
Avg. purchase transactions:												
Total acq. cost [1] $1,000	25.3	25.2	27.4	33.0	35.3	37.2	20.3	19.5	22.2	26.9	27.4	29.2
Closing costs dol	548	562	584	672	706	701	483	482	538	606	614	660
Market price of site [2] $1,000	5.4	5.3	5.5	6.4	7.0	7.3	4.3	4.0	4.5	5.5	5.6	5.8
Median value and cost:												
Amount of mortgage $1,000	22.8	22.8	24.1	29.7	32.2	34.0	18.4	17.6	20.2	24.6	25.4	27.1
Estimated value $1,000	24.7	24.6	26.8	32.5	35.2	37.2	19.7	18.7	22.0	26.2	26.8	28.9
Loan/value ratio percent	92.9	93.0	91.5	92.8	92.9	92.0	94.4	94.6	93.7	94.9	95.1	94.8
Income of occupant [3] $1,000	12.8	12.8	13.9	17.1	18.2	18.8	11.6	11.6	13.2	15.5	15.9	16.6
Mo. mortgage payment dol	208	201	236	284	318	329	170	162	202	245	255	260
Term of mortgage years	30.0	30.0	30.0	30.0	30.0	29.9	29.0	28.8	29.0	29.3	29.4	29.4

[1] Sales price plus closing costs. [2] Includes street improvements or utilities, rough grading, terracing and retaining walls, if any, for site. [3] Annual.

Source: U.S. Dept. of Housing and Urban Development, *HUD Statistical Yearbook*.

No. 1399. Home Loans Guaranteed and Insured by VA: 1972 to 1977

[Based on complete count of primary loans closed for conventionally built homes. See also table 642]

LOAN CHARACTERISTICS	NEW HOMES						EXISTING HOMES					
	1972	1973	1974	1975	1976	1977	1972	1973	1974	1975	1976	1977
Average loan $1,000	25.4	26.6	29.4	32.9	35.7	39.6	22.2	22.9	25.7	28.6	30.6	34.6
	PERCENT OF HOME LOANS											
Loan amount:												
Less than $15,000	1.0	.7	.5	.3	.3	.2	15.7	13.7	9.7	6.7	4.9	2.8
$15,000–$19,999	19.7	12.9	5.3	2.0	1.4	.7	25.9	24.4	18.7	14.5	11.8	7.9
$20,000–$24,999	33.2	31.1	21.1	9.9	5.8	2.8	26.9	27.3	23.7	19.3	16.8	12.5
$25,000–$29,999	25.5	29.8	31.2	23.8	17.6	11.0	17.7	19.1	21.0	20.5	20.2	16.8
$30,000–$34,999	12.2	15.1	24.2	31.2	24.6	19.5	7.8	8.9	12.8	15.7	16.2	16.6
$35,000–$39,999	5.3	6.4	10.6	19.5	25.4	23.1	3.2	3.6	6.8	10.2	12.3	15.0
$40,000 and over	3.1	4.0	7.1	13.3	24.9	42.7	2.8	3.0	7.3	13.1	17.8	28.4
Mortgage maturity:												
Less than 25 years	.3	.3	.4	.3	.3	.3	3.6	3.5	3.0	2.9	2.7	2.1
25 years	.6	.7	.5	.5	.6	.5	7.9	7.6	6.7	6.1	5.8	4.5
26–29 years	4.7	5.1	5.6	4.9	2.9	1.8	3.5	3.3	3.2	1.2	.5	.5
30 years	94.4	93.9	93.5	94.3	96.2	97.4	85.0	85.6	87.1	89.8	91.0	92.9
Downpayment status:												
With downpayment	36.9	37.3	39.0	42.9	27.6	44.5	25.8	23.4	26.3	26.5	24.3	26.4
With no downpayment	63.1	62.7	61.0	57.1	72.4	55.5	74.2	76.6	73.7	73.5	75.7	73.6

Source: U.S. Veterans Administration, unpublished data.

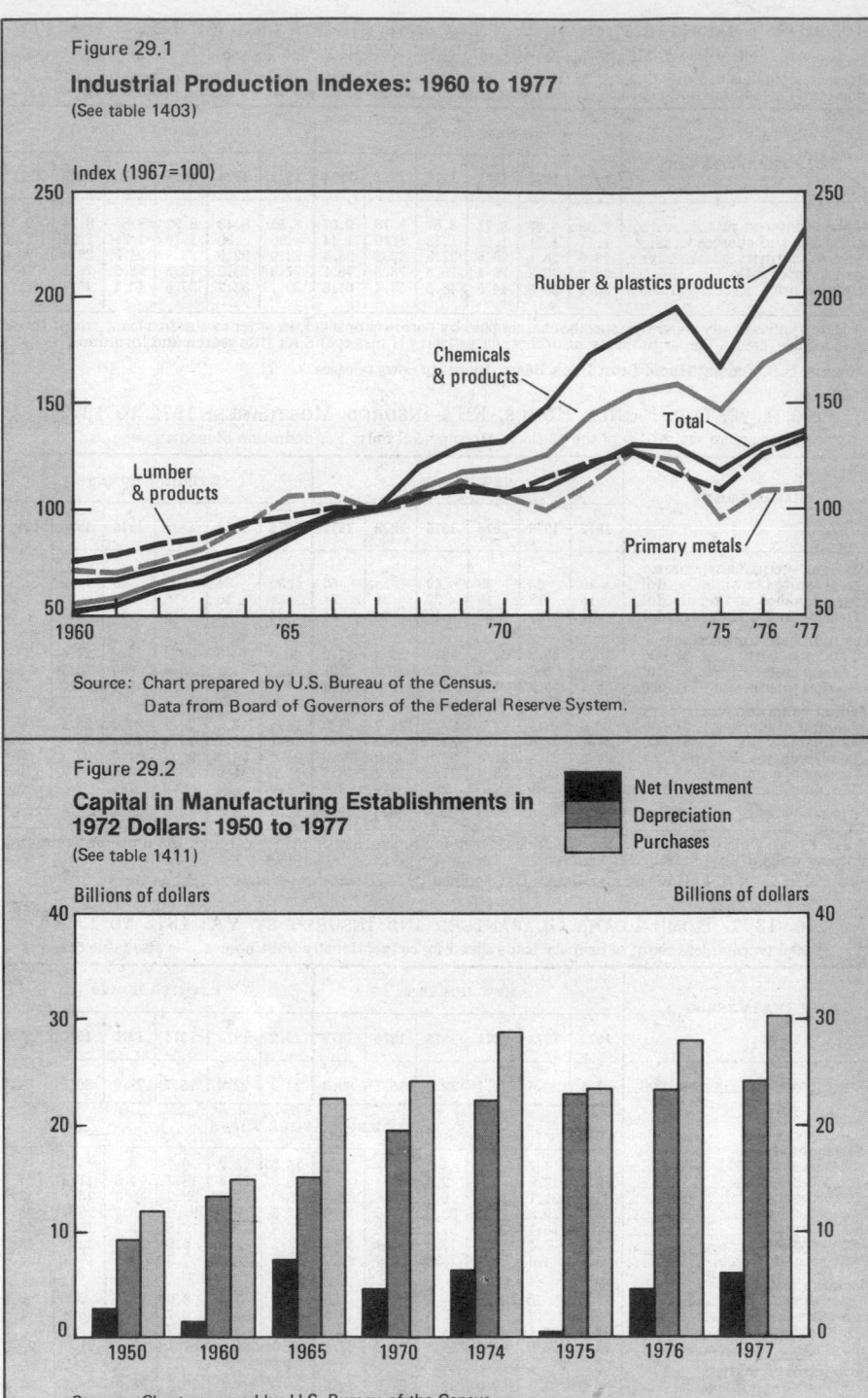

Figure 29.1

Industrial Production Indexes: 1960 to 1977

(See table 1403)

Index (1967=100)

Source: Chart prepared by U.S. Bureau of the Census.
Data from Board of Governors of the Federal Reserve System.

Figure 29.2

Capital in Manufacturing Establishments in 1972 Dollars: 1950 to 1977

(See table 1411)

Net Investment
Depreciation
Purchases

Billions of dollars

Source: Chart prepared by U.S. Bureau of the Census.
Data from U.S. Bureau of Economic Analysis.

Section 29

Manufactures

This section presents summary data for manufacturing as a whole and more detailed information for major industry groups and selected specific products. The types of measures shown at the different levels include data for establishments; employment and wages; raw materials, fuels, and electricity consumed; plant and equipment expenditures; value and quantity of production and shipments; value added by manufacture; inventories; and various indicators of financial status.

The principal sources of these data are Bureau of the Census reports of the census of manufactures conducted every five years; the *Annual Survey of Manufactures;* and the *Current Industrial Reports* series, which presents monthly, quarterly, or annual data on production, shipments, and stocks for particular commodities. Indexes of industrial production are presented monthly in the Federal Reserve Board's *Federal Reserve Bulletin.* Reports on current activities of industries, or current movements of individual commodities, are also compiled by such government agencies as the Bureau of Labor Statistics, the Economics, Statistics, and Cooperatives Service of the Department of Agriculture, and the Bureau of Domestic Business Development; and by private research or trade associations such as The Conference Board, Inc., New York; and the American Iron and Steel Institute and the National Canners Association, both in Washington, D.C.

Data on financial aspects of manufacturing industries are collected from time to time by the Securities and Exchange Commission (SEC), the Bureau of Economic Analysis (BEA), and the Federal Trade Commission (FTC). Industry aggregates in the form of balance sheets, profit and loss statements, analyses of sales and expenses, lists of subsidiaries, and types and amounts of security issues are published for leading manufacturing corporations registered with the SEC. The BEA issues data on capital in manufacturing industries and capacity utilization rates in manufacturing. The FTC has made several comprehensive studies of individual industries.

Censuses and annual surveys.—The first census of manufactures covered the year 1809. Between 1809 and 1963, a census was conducted at periodic intervals. Since 1967 it has been taken every 5 years (for years ending in "2" and "7"). Census data, either direct reports or estimates from administrative records, are obtained for every manufacturing plant with one employee or more.

The Annual Survey of Manufactures, conducted for the first time in 1949, collects data for the years between censuses for the more general measures of manufacturing activity covered in detail by the censuses. The annual survey data are estimates derived from a scientifically selected sample of companies. The most recent annual survey is based on a sample of about 70,000 of an approximate total of 312,000 establishments. It comprises all large plants, which account for approximately two-thirds of total U.S. manufacturing employment, and a representative selection of the more numerous small plants. Government-owned and -operated establishments are excluded.

The basic statistical measures of manufacturing activity, such as employment, payrolls, value added, etc., are defined in essentially the same way for both the annual surveys and the census of manufactures. However, the bases for computing average employment vary for different years. For example, beginning with 1949, average employment was calculated from the figures reported for the pay periods ending nearest the fifteenth of March, May, August, and November, whereas for 1947 such averages were based on 12 monthly employment figures. In 1967 and 1972, the average employment calculation was revised to the pay periods which include the 12th of March, May, August, and November to provide data more comparable with other statistical series.

Establishments and classification.—The censuses of manufactures for 1947 through 1972 covered operating manufacturing establishments as defined in the *Standard Industrial Classification Manual*, issued by the U.S. Office of Management and Budget (see text, page 396). The comparability of manufactures data over time is affected by changes in the official definitions of industries as presented in the *Manual*. It is important to note therefore that the 1972 edition of the *Manual* was used for the 1972 census while the 1967 *Manual* was used for the 1967 census. For the censuses from 1947 to 1963, reports were required from all establishments employing one or more persons at any time during the census year. For the 1967 and 1972 censuses, reports were required only from establishments with 10 or more employees and establishments operated by multi-establishment companies. Data for single unit companies with less than 10 employees were estimated on the basis of Government administrative records and industry averages. Each of the establishments tabulated was classified in one of the more than 450 manufacturing industries as defined by the Standard Industrial Classification system in 1972, as compared to 400 industries in the 1967 census. This system defines an industry as a number of establishments producing a single product or a closely related group of products. In the main, an establishment is classified in a particular industry if its production of this product or product group exceeds in value its production of any other product group. While some establishments produce only the products of the industry in which they are classified, few within an industry specialize to that extent. The statistics on employment, payrolls, value added, inventories, and expenditures, therefore, reflect both the primary and secondary activities of the establishments in that industry. For this reason care should be exercised in relating such statistics to the total shipments figures of products primary to the industry.

The censuses for 1947 through 1972 were conducted on an establishment basis. The term "establishment" signifies a single physical plant site or factory. It is not necessarily identical with the business unit or company, which may consist of one or more establishments. A company operating establishments at more than one location is required to submit a separate report for each location. An establishment engaged in distinctly different lines of activity and maintaining separate payroll and inventory records is also required to submit separate reports.

Statistical reliability.—For a discussion of statistical collection and estimation, sampling procedures and measures of statistical reliability applicable to Census Bureau data, see Appendix III.

Historical statistics.—Tabular headnotes provide cross-references, where applicable, to *Historical Statistics of the United States, Colonial Times to 1970*. See Appendix I.

No. 1400. National Income Originating in Manufacturing: 1947 to 1977

[In billions of dollars, except percent. Prior to 1963, excludes Alaska and Hawaii. For definition of national income, see text, p. 437. Refers to national income without capital consumption adjustment. Data represent net value added at factor costs. See *Historical Statistics, Colonial Times to 1970*, series F 230, for single-year figures prior to minor revisions issued in 1976]

ITEM	1947	1954	1958	1963	1965	1967	1970	1972	1973	1974	1975	1976	1977
Total manufacturing__	60	95	108	143	170	193	215	252	284	298	312	365	412
Percent of national income_____	30	31	29	30	30	29	27	26	26	26	25	26	26
Durable goods_____	32	55	62	86	105	119	127	154	176	179	184	218	251
Percent of total_____	53	58	58	60	62	61	59	61	62	60	59	60	61
Nondurable goods_____	28	40	46	57	65	75	88	98	107	119	127	147	161

Source: U.S. Bureau of Economic Analysis, *The National Income and Product Accounts of the United States, 1929-74*, and *Survey of Current Business*, July 1977 and March 1978.

No. 1401. MANUFACTURES—SUMMARY: 1947 TO 1976

[Prior to 1958, excludes Alaska and Hawaii. Census data, except as noted. Covers all establishments employing 1 or more persons at any time during year. See also *Historical Statistics, Colonial Times to 1970*, series P 1-12]

ITEM	1947	1954	1958	1963	1967	1970 1	1972	1975 1	1976 1
Number of establishments 2 ....1,000..	3 241	3 287	303	312	311	(NA)	321	(NA)	(NA)
With 20 or more employees........1,000..	(NA)	3 90	95	102	107	(NA)	114	(NA)	(NA)
All employees,4 annual average 5 ......mil..	3 14.3	16.1	16.0	17.0	19.3	19.2	19.0	18.3	18.8
Payroll, all employees...........bil. dol..	3 40	66	78	100	132	153	174	210	233
Payroll per employee............$1,000..	3 2.8	4.1	4.9	5.9	6.8	8.0	9.2	11.5	12.4
Production workers, annual average...mil..	11.9	12.4	11.7	12.2	14.0	13.5	13.5	12.6	13.1
Man-hours, production workers........bil..	24.3	24.3	22.7	24.5	27.8	26.7	26.7	24.1	25.4
Man-hours per worker............1,000..	2.0	2.0	1.9	2.0	2.0	2.0	2.0	1.9	1.9
Wages, production workers........bil. dol..	30	45	50	62	81	92	106	121	138
Wages per worker.................$1,000..	2.5	3.6	4.3	5.1	5.8	6.8	7.8	9.6	10.5
Wages per worker man-hour..........dol..	1.24	1.83	2.19	2.53	2.92	3.44	3.95	5.02	5.43
Value added by manufacture 6 .....bil. dol..	74	117	142	192	262	300	354	442	511
Per production worker...........$1,000..	6.2	9.5	12.1	15.7	18.8	22.2	26.2	35.1	39.0
Per production worker man-hour....dol..	3.04	4.81	6.25	7.83	9.42	11.23	13.25	18.34	20.12
Per dollar of workers' wages........dol..	2.47	2.60	2.84	2.90	3.23	3.26	3.34	3.65	3.70
Cost of materials................bil. dol..	(NA)	(NA)	(NA)	230	299	337	407	597	681
Value of shipments 7 ....bil. dol..	(NA)	(NA)	(NA)	421	557	634	757	1,039	1,186
Per production worker...........$1,000..	(NA)	(NA)	(NA)	34.4	39.9	46.9	55.9	82.5	90.5
End-of-year inventories...........bil. dol..	26	40	49	60	84	101	108	158	170
Capital expenditures, new 8 ....bil. dol..	6.0	8.2	9.5	11.4	21.5	22.2	24.1	37.3	40.7
Indexes: (1967=100):									
Employment..................................	74	83	83	88	100	99	98	95	97
Value added..................................	29	45	54	73	100	115	135	169	195
Shipments....................................	(NA)	(NA)	(NA)	76	100	114	136	187	213
Ratios:									
Value added to shipments..................	(NA)	(NA)	(NA)	45.6	47.0	47.3	46.7	42.5	43.1
Inventories to shipments..................	(NA)	(NA)	(NA)	14.2	15.0	15.9	14.2	15.2	14.3
Payroll to value added....................	54.0	50.4	54.9	50.0	50.3	51.0	10.1	47.5	45.6
Gross book value of depreciable assets..................bil. dol..	(NA)	(NA)	(NA)	158	218	267	301	369	395
Machinery and equipment......bil. dol..	(NA)	(NA)	(NA)	(NA)	157	193	218	271	292
Assets per employee...............$1,000..	(NA)	(NA)	(NA)	9.3	11.3	13.9	16.4	20.2	21.0

NA Not available.   1 Estimated data based on *Annual Survey of Manufactures;* see text, p. 803.
2 Includes administrative and auxiliary units, except as noted.
3 Excludes administrative offices and auxiliary units.
4 Includes data for employees of manufacturing establishments engaged in distribution and construction work.
5 Data for most industries in 1954 and for all industries since 1954 are based on pay periods ending nearest 15th of March, May, August, and November. For 1947, and industries of a seasonal type in 1954, data represent average of 12 monthly figures.
6 Unadjusted for 1947; thereafter, adjusted. Unadjusted value added is obtained by subtracting cost of materials, supplies, containers, fuel, purchased electric energy, and contract work from value of shipments for products manufactured plus receipts for services rendered. Adjusted value added also takes into account (a) value added by merchandising operations (that is, difference between the sales value and cost of merchandise sold without further manufacture, processing, or assembly), plus (b) net change in finished goods and work-in-process inventories between beginning and end of year.   7 Includes extensive and unmeasurable duplication from shipments between establishments in the same industry classification.
8 Beginning 1954, includes plants under construction and not yet in operation.

Source: U.S. Bureau of the Census, *Census of Manufactures, 1947, 1954, 1958, 1963, 1967,* and *1972,* final reports; and *Annual Survey of Manufactures.*

No. 1402. FINANCES OF MANUFACTURING CORPORATIONS: 1960 TO 1977

[In billions of dollars. Annual data are averages of four end-of-quarter figures]

ITEM	1960	1965	1967	1969	1970	1971	1972	1973	1974	1975	1976	1977
Net sales.......................	346	492	575	695	709	751	850	1,017	1,061	1,065	1,203	1,331
Net operating profit.............	26	46	48	58	50	55	66	86	84	77	97	107
Net profit:												
Before Federal taxes 1	28	47	48	58	48	53	63	81	97	80	105	115
After Federal and State taxes.	15	28	29	-33	29	31	36	48	59	49	65	71
Cash dividends.................	8	12	13	15	15	15	16	18	19	20	23	27
Retained earnings..............	7	16	16	18	14	16	20	30	39	29	42	44

1 Beginning 1974, data include State as well as Federal taxes.
Source: U.S. Federal Trade Commission, *Quarterly Financial Report for Manufacturing Corporations,* fourth quarter reports.

No. 1403. INDUSTRIAL PRODUCTION—INDEXES, BY INDUSTRY: 1950 TO 1978

[1967=100. Quarterly data adjusted for seasonal variation. Based on 1967 *Standard Industrial Classification Manual* (see text, p. 804). See also *Historical Statistics, Colonial Times to 1970*, series P 13 and P 18–39]

MAJOR INDUSTRY GROUP	1950	1955	1960	1965	1970	1971	1972	1973	1974	1975	1976	1977	1978, Jan.- June
Industrial production	45	59	66	90	108	110	120	130	129	118	130	137	142
Manufacturing	45	58	65	90	106	108	119	130	129	116	130	137	142
Durable manufactures	44	59	63	89	102	102	114	127	126	109	122	130	135
Primary metals	70	83	72	102	107	100	112	127	123	96	109	110	111
Fabricated metal products	56	68	71	91	102	104	112	125	124	110	123	131	139
Electrical machinery	30	40	52	82	108	108	122	143	144	117	132	142	150
Nonelectrical machinery	38	51	57	85	104	100	116	134	140	125	135	145	152
Transportation equipment	42	68	65	95	90	98	108	118	109	97	111	121	125
Instruments	26	44	58	83	112	110	120	138	144	132	148	159	168
Clay, glass, and stone products	57	70	79	98	106	111	121	134	133	118	137	146	155
Lumber and products	66	76	75	96	106	114	121	126	116	108	125	133	137
Furniture and fixtures	53	67	72	95	108	116	131	144	138	118	133	141	151
Miscellaneous manufactures	51	68	71	94	111	112	127	138	138	128	144	149	153
Nondurable manufactures	47	57	69	91	112	117	127	134	135	126	141	148	152
Textile mill products	60	65	69	93	112	117	133	143	133	122	136	137	138
Apparel products	64	73	82	97	101	105	109	117	114	108	122	124	124
Leather and products	84	91	90	98	90	87	88	83	78	77	81	75	74
Paper and products	46	57	68	92	115	120	129	137	135	116	133	137	145
Printing and publishing	49	60	71	88	107	107	113	118	118	113	121	125	129
Chemicals and products	26	40	56	88	120	126	144	155	159	147	169	181	186
Petroleum products	48	66	77	92	113	117	122	129	125	124	133	141	141
Rubber and plastics products	29	41	52	86	132	148	172	184	195	167	200	232	247
Foods	58	66	79	92	109	113	117	121	124	123	132	138	141
Tobacco products	69	74	91	100	102	101	106	112	110	112	118	114	118
Mining	64	78	80	93	112	110	113	115	115	113	114	118	122
Utilities	27	44	63	89	125	131	139	145	144	146	151	157	159
Energy	(NA)	59	70	89	117	120	125	128	126	126	129	133	132

NA Not available.
Source: Board of Governors of the Federal Reserve System, *Federal Reserve Bulletin*, monthly.

No. 1404. CAPACITY UTILIZATION RATES IN MANUFACTURING: 1965 TO 1977

[In percent. Annual figures are averages of quarterly data, except yearend 1965 and midyear and yearend 1967. Capacity represents maximum practical amount of output that can be produced with current stock of plant and equipment]

INDUSTRY	1965	1967	1968	1969	1970	1971	1972	1973	1974	1975	1976	1977
All manufacturers	86	84	85	85	81	80	83	86	83	77	81	83
Firms with assets of—												
$100 million and over	89	86	88	87	83	83	86	88	85	78	84	85
$10 million–$99.9 million	85	83	83	83	79	78	81	83	81	75	78	80
Under $10 million	80	78	78	77	73	73	77	79	77	72	76	78
Durable goods [1]	88	83	84	84	78	78	82	85	82	76	81	84
Electrical and electronic equip.	83	78	80	80	76	76	81	82	83	73	80	82
Machinery, except electrical	95	91	90	92	86	81	84	87	88	83	86	89
Transportation equipment [1]	89	84	87	84	75	81	85	87	78	76	82	86
Motor vehicles	96	87	93	90	81	92	97	100	83	83	93	99
Aircraft	79	82	82	77	68	65	69	69	71	65	65	68
Primary metals	(NA)	84	84	87	82	75	86	88	88	73	78	80
Nondurable goods [1]	85	85	86	86	83	83	85	86	84	79	82	82
Food, including beverages	75	80	82	82	82	81	81	81	80	77	77	78
Textiles	93	87	87	84	82	84	89	90	81	78	85	86
Paper	95	90	91	93	88	88	90	94	91	79	87	86
Chemicals	86	81	83	84	82	81	84	88	85	74	80	78
Petroleum	95	98	98	98	95	94	94	97	89	89	93	92
Rubber	93	96	92	89	82	86	89	89	85	74	80	85

NA Not available.   [1] Includes items not shown separately.
Source: U.S. Bureau of Economic Analysis, *Survey of Current Business*, monthly. (These data appear quarterly.)

No. 1405. INDEX OF MANUFACTURING CAPACITY AND RELATION OF OUTPUT TO CAPACITY: 1950 TO 1978

[1967 output= 100. Annual figures are averages of quarterly data. Capacity represents estimated quantity of output, relative to output in 1967, which the current stock of plant and equipment in manufacturing industries was capable of producing. Primary processing industries comprise textiles, lumber, paper and pulp, petroleum, rubber, stone, clay, glass, primary metals, fabricted metals, and a portion of chemicals. Advanced processing industries comprise chemical products, food, beverages, tobacco, apparel, furniture, printing and publishing, leather, machinery, transportation equipment, instruments, ordnance, and miscellaneous industry groups]

YEAR	Index of capacity	RELATION OF OUTPUT TO CAPACITY (percent)			YEAR	Index of capacity	RELATION OF OUTPUT TO CAPACITY (percent)		
		All manufacturing	Primary processing	Advanced processing			All manufacturing	Primary processing	Advanced processing
1950	54	83	89	80	1972	143	83	88	81
1955	67	87	92	84	1973	148	88	92	85
1960	82	80	80	81	1974	154	84	88	82
1965	100	90	91	89	1975	158	74	74	74
1967	115	87	86	88	1976	162	80	82	79
1968	122	87	88	87	1977	166	82	84	82
1969	129	86	89	85	1978:				
					1st qtr	170	82	84	81
1970	134	79	83	77	2d qtr	172	84	86	83
1971	139	78	82	76	3d qtr., prel	174	85	88	83

Source: Board of Governors of the Federal Reserve System, *Federal Reserve Bulletin*, November 1976, and *Capacity Utilization in Manufacturing and Materials*, G.3., monthly. (Based on data from Federal Reserve Board, U.S. Dept. of Commerce, U.S. Bureau of Labor Statistics, and McGraw-Hill Information Systems Company, New York, N.Y.)

No. 1406. OPERATING MANUFACTURING ESTABLISHMENTS—SELECTED DATA, BY LEGAL FORM OF ORGANIZATION: 1947 TO 1972

[Prior to 1958, excludes Alaska and Hawaii. Covers all establishments employing 1 or more persons at any time during year, except as noted. See also *Historical Statistics, Colonial Times to 1970*, series P 205–211]

FORM OF ORGANIZATION AND YEAR	Establishments [1] (1,000)	ALL EMPLOYEES		PRODUCTION WORKERS		Value added by manufacture [3] (mil. dol.)	Capital expenditures, new (mil. dol.)
		Total [2] (1,000)	Payroll (mil. dol.)	Total [2] (1,000)	Wages (mil. dol.)		
Corporate:							
1947	118.1	12,856	36,580	10,649	27,637	68,294	(NA)
1954	148.5	14,273	59,051	11,206	41,480	109,669	7,752
1958	162.7	14,215	69,885	10,398	45,455	135,644	8,926
1963	176.2	15,245	89,356	11,426	59,064	184,100	10,791
1967 [4]	153.9	17,697	*119,530	13,260	78,429	253,261	20,988
1972	233.2	18,545	171,143	13,118	103,254	347,086	23,620
Noncorporate, total: [5]							
1947	122.7	1,438	3,115	1,269	2,607	5,996	(NA)
1954	138.4	1,372	3,912	1,166	3,111	7,363	449
1958	135.4	1,165	3,787	969	3,016	7,515	605
1963	130.4	990	3,932	806	3,030	8,002	580
1967 [4]	33.2	530	2,709	433	2,008	5,636	370
1972	87.5	482	3,043	408	2,237	6,908	453
Individual proprietorship:							
1947	69.5	586	1,184	522	1,001	2,162	(NA)
1954	88.2	593	1,527	507	1,237	2,735	176
1958	91.3	542	1,637	461	1,349	3,115	317
1963	99.2	536	2,033	440	1,595	3,916	315
1967 [4]	24.9	243	1,187	210	933	2,361	141
1972	42.5	213	1,303	183	963	2,885	186
Partnership:							
1947	50.8	757	1,687	673	1,432	3,347	(NA)
1954	47.9	703	2,108	602	1,684	4,054	216
1958	42.0	543	1,836	452	1,458	3,663	223
1963	27.7	334	1,034	277	1,062	2,726	141
1967 [4]	6.7	193	971	157	730	1,895	114
1972	17.7	167	1,067	139	792	2,413	150

NA Not available. [1] Beginning 1958, includes administrative offices and auxiliary units. [2] For method of calculation, see text, p. 803. [3] For definition, see footnote 6, table 1401. [4] Excludes establishments with fewer than 10 employees. [5] Includes forms of organization not shown separately.

Source: U.S. Bureau of the Census, *Census of Manufactures, 1967*, vol. I, and special report, *Type of Organization*, MC 72(SR)–3.

No. 1407. Manufactures—Summary, by Type of Operation: 1947 to 1972

[A multiunit company operates establishments at more than one location. See headnote, table 1406]

ITEM	1947	1954	1958	1963	1967	1972
Multiunit companies:						
Establishments	35,202	31,769	41,871	45,862	51,707	70,198
Employees 1,000	8,007	9,480	10,064	11,015	13,310	14,264
Production workers 1,000	6,686	7,402	7,174	8,110	9,790	9,792
Payroll, all employees mil. dol	22,788	40,623	51,785	68,202	93,756	138,758
Wages, production workers mil. dol	17,787	28,987	33,469	44,721	60,875	81,941
Value added by manufacture mil. dol	43,947	79,604	105,306	146,605	206,437	286,126
Capital expenditures, new mil. dol	(NA)	6,485	7,525	8,934	18,596	20,040
Single unit companies:						
Establishments	205,605	255,045	256,311	260,755	[1] 253,974	[1] 250,512
Employees 1,000	6,287	6,165	5,317	5,220	[1] 5,188	[1] 4,765
Payroll, all employees mil. dol	16,907	22,340	21,887	25,087	[1] 30,155	[1] 35,447
Value added by manufacture mil. dol	30,343	37,428	37,853	45,497	[1] 55,546	[1] 67,868

NA Not available. [1] Includes data obtained from Federal administrative records.

Source: U.S. Bureau of the Census, *Census of Manufactures, 1967*, vol. I, and special report, *Type of Organization*, MC72(SR)-3.

No. 1408. Manufacturers Shipments, Inventories, and Orders: 1960 to 1977

[In billions of dollars, except ratios. See also *Historical Statistics, Colonial Times to 1970*, series P 74-92]

ITEM	1960	1965	1969	1970	1971	1972	1973	1974	1975	1976	1977
Shipments	370.5	491.9	642.5	634.0	671.1	756.5	875.4	1,017.9	1,039.4	1,185.7	1,335.1
Durable goods	190.6	266.7	353.7	338.6	359.7	408.5	476.4	531.0	524.1	608.4	699.2
Nondurable goods	179.9	225.3	288.8	295.4	311.4	348.0	399.0	486.8	515.3	577.4	635.9
Inventories (Dec. 31)	53.6	68.0	97.8	101.3	102.3	108.0	124.4	157.8	158.2	170.4	180.1
Durable goods	32.0	42.0	64.3	66.3	65.8	69.8	80.8	101.1	101.1	108.5	114.9
Nondurable goods	21.5	26.0	33.5	35.0	36.5	38.2	43.6	56.7	57.1	61.9	65.3
Ratio of inventories to sales	1.79	1.58	1.81	1.91	1.76	1.58	1.63	1.86	1.74	1.62	1.52
Durable goods	2.13	1.78	2.18	2.35	2.11	1.90	2.01	2.32	2.24	1.99	1.86
Nondurable goods	1.44	1.34	1.36	1.40	1.34	1.21	1.20	1.37	1.24	1.22	1.15
New orders	362.8	505.2	648.1	624.9	672.2	770.4	914.7	1,046.4	1,020.7	1,189.6	1,354.1
Durable goods	183.6	279.3	359.1	329.1	360.4	421.2	514.7	561.4	503.2	612.0	717.5
Nondurable goods	179.2	225.9	289.0	295.8	311.8	349.2	400.0	485.0	517.5	577.6	636.6
Unfilled orders (Dec. 31)	44.9	79.2	115.1	106.0	107.1	121.0	160.3	188.8	170.1	174.0	193.0
Durable goods	42.4	75.4	110.9	101.5	102.2	114.8	153.1	183.5	162.5	166.1	184.5
Nondurable goods	2.5	3.8	4.2	4.6	5.0	6.2	7.2	5.3	7.6	7.9	8.5

Source: U.S. Bureau of the Census, *Manufacturers' Shipments, Inventories, and Orders: 1958-1977* (Revised), and *Current Industrial Reports*, series M3-1.7.

No. 1409. Manufacturing Employment and Value Added—Percent Distribution, by Geographic Divisions: 1950 to 1976

[For composition of divisions, see fig. I, inside front cover. For definition of "value added," see table 1401]

GEOGRAPHIC DIVISION	1950	1954	1958	1963	1965	1967	1970	1972	1974	1975	1976
EMPLOYMENT											
New England	9.8	9.0	8.7	8.4	8.2	8.1	7.6	7.2	7.2	7.1	7.1
Middle Atlantic	26.9	26.6	25.7	24.0	23.4	22.6	21.8	20.7	19.7	19.5	18.7
East North Central	30.0	28.6	26.6	26.4	27.2	26.7	26.0	25.9	26.1	25.5	25.5
West North Central	5.6	6.0	6.0	6.0	6.0	6.2	6.3	6.6	6.6	6.8	6.7
South Atlantic	11.1	11.0	11.8	12.5	12.7	12.9	13.6	14.4	14.3	14.3	14.6
East South Central	4.4	4.5	4.9	5.2	5.6	5.7	6.1	6.6	6.7	6.7	6.9
West South Central	4.0	4.5	5.0	5.14	5.3	5.6	6.1	6.5	6.7	7.0	7.2
Mountain	1.1	1.1	1.4	1.7	1.6	1.6	1.8	2.0	2.2	2.2	2.3
Pacific	7.0	8.8	10.0	10.6	10.0	10.6	10.3	10.4	10.7	10.9	11.0
VALUE ADDED											
New England	8.3	7.8	7.4	7.1	7.1	7.2	6.8	6.4	6.1	6.2	6.2
Middle Atlantic	26.2	26.0	24.6	22.7	22.5	21.9	21.4	19.9	18.6	18.5	17.8
East North Central	33.2	31.2	28.9	29.3	30.2	28.6	27.5	28.2	28.3	26.9	27.5
West North Central	5.7	6.1	6.3	6.1	6.2	6.4	6.9	6.7	6.7	7.0	7.0
South Atlantic	9.4	9.1	10.1	11.0	11.1	11.2	11.8	12.5	12.2	12.1	12.8
East South Central	3.8	4.0	4.5	4.8	5.1	5.2	5.7	6.0	6.1	6.1	6.1
West South Central	4.3	4.9	5.5	5.7	5.8	6.3	6.7	7.0	8.1	8.9	8.6
Mountain	1.2	1.2	1.6	1.8	1.6	1.7	1.9	2.1	2.3	2.4	2.3
Pacific	7.9	9.7	11.1	11.5	10.7	11.3	11.1	11.3	11.6	11.9	11.7

Source: U.S. Bureau of the Census, *Census of Manufactures: 1963; 1967; 1972: General Summary*, MC72(1)-1; and *Annual Survey of Manufactures*.

No. 1410. Manufactures—Summary, by Employee Size-Class: 1954 to 1972

ITEM AND YEAR	All establishments	ESTABLISHMENTS WITH TOTAL EMPLOYEES—					PERCENT DISTRIBUTION				
		Under 20	20–99	100–249	250–999	1,000 and over	Under 20	20–99	100–249	250–999	1,000 and over
Establishments (1,000): [1]											
1954	287	196	64	16	9	2	68.4	22.3	5.5	3.1	.7
1963	307	207	70	18	10	2	67.6	22.9	5.7	3.2	.6
1967	306	199	74	20	11	2	65.0	24.2	6.5	3.6	.7
1972	313	203	76	21	12	2	64.9	24.3	6.7	3.8	.6
Employees (1,000): [1]											
1954	15,646	1,196	2,835	2,430	4,082	5,103	7.7	18.1	15.5	26.0	32.6
1963	16,235	1,175	3,072	2,727	4,312	4,951	7.3	18.9	16.8	26.5	30.5
1967	18,492	1,042	3,276	3,069	5,042	6,062	5.6	17.7	16.6	27.3	32.8
1972	18,032	1,114	3,356	3,232	5,155	5,175	6.2	18.6	17.9	28.6	28.7
Payroll (mil. dol.): [1]											
1954	62,963	3,765	10,246	9,171	16,264	23,516	6.0	16.3	14.6	25.9	37.3
1963 [2]	93,289	5,502	15,191	13,926	23,740	34,772	6.0	16.3	15.0	25.5	37.3
1967	123,481	6,080	19,205	18,172	31,688	48,335	4.9	15.6	14.7	25.7	39.1
1972	160,414	8,645	25,787	25,348	43,348	57,286	5.4	16.1	15.8	27.0	35.7
Value added by manufacture (mil. dol.): [3]											
1954	116,848	7,207	18,013	17,143	31,286	43,199	6.1	15.4	14.7	26.8	37.0
1963 [2]	192,102	11,310	30,073	28,826	51,054	71,056	5.9	15.6	15.0	26.5	36.9
1967	261,984	13,271	39,138	38,922	71,036	99,617	5.1	14.9	14.9	27.1	38.0
1972	353,973	19,127	54,870	56,467	99,923	123,586	5.4	15.5	16.0	28.2	34.9
Capital expenditures, new (mil. dol.):											
1954	8,201	[4] 870	1,023	1,111	2,052	3,144	10.6	12.5	13.5	25.0	38.3
1963 [2]	11,371	[4] 1,215	1,783	1,603	2,675	4,133	10.7	15.7	14.1	23.4	36.3
1967	21,503	[4] 1,860	2,730	2,996	5,713	8,204	8.6	12.7	13.9	26.6	38.2
1972	24,073	1,412	3,866	3,853	6,551	8,391	5.9	16.1	16.0	27.2	34.9

[1] Excludes administrative offices and auxiliary units. [2] Individual size-class data do not add to total because they were derived from separate tabulations. [3] For definition, see footnote 6, table 1401. [4] Includes expenditures for plants under construction and not yet in operation.

Source: U.S. Bureau of the Census, *Census of Manufactures, 1967, Size of Establishments*, MC67(1)-2, and *Census of Manufactures, 1972, General Summary*, MC72(1)-1.

No. 1411. Capital in Manufacturing Establishments: 1950 to 1977

[In billions of dollars. Minus sign (−) denotes loss. 1950 excludes Alaska and Hawaii. Data refer to privately owned manufacturing establishments and are based on the capital expenditures data from the census of manufactures, the Annual Survey of Manufactures, and the inventory investment component of GNP. For details, see source. See *Historical Statistics, Colonial Times to 1970*, series P 107–122, for single-year figures prior to minor revisions issued in 1976:

ITEM	1950	1960	1965	1970	1972	1973	1974	1975	1976	1977
Purchases:										
In current dollars	5.7	10.3	16.8	22.4	22.8	27.9	32.8	31.3	39.2	44.8
Equipment	4.0	7.4	12.5	16.5	17.7	21.7	25.0	23.4	32.0	37.6
Structures	1.8	2.9	4.3	5.9	5.1	6.2	7.7	7.9	7.2	7.3
In 1972 dollars	12.0	15.0	22.6	24.2	22.9	26.9	28.8	23.5	28.0	30.3
Equipment	7.8	9.8	15.8	17.5	17.8	21.1	22.3	17.9	22.9	25.4
Structures	4.1	5.1	6.8	6.7	5.1	5.7	6.5	5.6	5.1	4.9
Depreciation (straight-line): [1]										
In current dollars	4.6	9.5	11.3	18.2	20.7	22.4	26.0	30.5	32.6	35.9
Equipment	2.9	7.0	8.3	13.3	15.2	16.3	18.8	22.5	24.6	27.4
Structures	1.7	2.5	3.0	4.8	5.5	6.1	7.2	8.0	8.0	8.5
In 1972 dollars	9.3	13.5	15.2	19.6	20.7	21.5	22.4	23.0	23.4	24.2
Equipment	5.7	9.2	10.5	14.1	15.2	15.9	16.7	17.3	17.7	18.5
Structures	3.6	4.3	4.7	5.4	5.5	5.6	5.6	5.7	5.7	5.7
Net investment: [2]										
In current dollars	1.1	.8	5.5	4.2	2.1	5.5	6.8	.8	6.6	8.9
Equipment	1.1	.4	4.2	3.2	2.5	5.4	6.2	.9	7.4	10.2
Structures	.1	.4	1.3	1.1	− .4	.1	.5	− .1	− .8	−1.2
In 1972 dollars	2.7	1.5	7.4	4.6	2.2	5.4	6.4	.5	4.6	6.1
Equipment	2.1	.6	5.3	3.4	2.6	5.2	5.6	.6	5.2	6.9
Structures	.5	.8	2.1	1.3	− .4	.1	.9	− .1	− .6	− .8
Real net value of equip., structures, and inventories in 1972 dollars [3]	154.4	207.1	237.4	303.6	307.5	318.9	330.2	326.2	334.9	344.0
Equipment and structures [4]	102.6	134.7	148.3	186.5	190.0	195.3	201.6	202.2	206.8	212.8
Equipment	48.0	68.5	78.2	105.0	108.8	113.9	119.4	120.0	125.2	132.0
Structures	54.5	66.2	70.1	81.5	81.2	81.4	82.2	82.2	81.6	80.8
Inventories	51.8	72.4	89.1	117.1	117.5	123.6	128.6	124.0	128.1	131.2

[1] Estimates derived by using perpetual inventory method and assuming, in general, service lives of 85 percent of those shown in Internal Revenue Service's Bulletin F. [2] Represents the difference between purchases and depreciation. [3] End of year. [4] Represents real net value of equipment and structures at preceding year end plus net investment based on straight-line depreciation for year shown.

Source: U.S. Bureau of Economic Analysis, *Fixed Nonresidential Business and Residential Capital in the United States, 1925–1975; Surve_ of Current Business*, July issues; and unpublished data.

No. 1412. Large Manufacturing Companies—Adequacy of Capital Facilities to Meet Current Demand: 1965 to 1977

[**Percent distribution.** As of **July.** Number of companies weighted by company assets. Based on replies to The Conference Board's *Quarterly Survey of Capital Investment and Supply Conditions,* conducted among the 1,000 largest manufacturing companies as listed by total assets]

YEAR	Inadequate	Sufficient	More than adequate	YEAR	Inadequate	Sufficient	More than adequate
1965	30.9	67.5	1.6	1973	45.3	52.7	2.0
1968	26.1	71.8	2.1	1974	57.1	40.1	2.8
1969	37.3	58.7	4.0				
1970	28.4	59.5	12.1	1975	19.1	43.1	37.8
1971	18.5	58.6	22.9	1976	17.5	65.0	17.5
1972	16.3	70.4	13.3	1977	20.1	66.1	13.8

Source: The Conference Board, New York, N.Y., *Quarterly Survey of Capital Investment and Supply Conditions in Manufacturing.* (Copyright.)

No. 1413. Large Manufacturing Companies—Capital Appropriations and Expenditures, by Industry: 1970 to 1976

[**In millions of dollars, except percent.** Based on reports submitted by companies responding to The Conference Board's *Quarterly Survey of Capital Appropriations.* This survey is conducted among the 1,000 largest manufacturing companies as listed by total assets. **Appropriations:** Authorizations by management to spend funds for new plant and equipment; **Expenditures:** Cost of new plant and equipment]

YEAR AND ITEM	Total	Food and bev- erages	Paper and allied prod- ucts	Chem- icals and allied prod- ucts	Petro- leum and coal prod- ucts	Pri- mary iron and steel	Elec- trical machin- ery and equip.	Machin- ery, except elec- trical	Motor vehicles and equip- ment	Other manu- factur- ing
1970: Appropriations	25,337	1,587	1,034	3,036	5,704	1,534	2,584	3,098	1,276	5,484
Expenditures	26,321	1,598	1,046	3,143	5,559	1,746	2,408	3,093	1,689	6,039
Percent of appropriations	103.9	100.7	101.2	103.5	97.5	113.8	93.2	99.8	132.4	110.1
1973: Appropriations	44,510	3,214	1,930	5,730	8,485	1,998	3,056	4,269	3,926	11,902
Expenditures	29,086	2,073	1,227	3,648	4,963	1,423	2,378	3,420	2,105	7,849
Percent of appropriations	65.3	64.5	63.6	63.7	58.5	71.2	77.8	80.1	53.6	65.9
1974: Appropriations	56,908	3,240	3,157	7,503	14,642	5,423	2,652	5,919	1,690	12,682
Expenditures	41,066	2,764	1,908	5,675	7,745	2,141	2,671	4,652	2,513	10,997
Percent of appropriations	72.2	85.3	60.4	75.6	52.9	39.5	100.7	78.6	148.7	86.7
1975: Appropriations	45,423	3,623	1,899	7,454	14,270	3,199	1,952	3,764	1,014	8,248
Expenditures	45,568	3,083	1,901	7,172	11,785	3,538	2,256	4,054	1,829	9,950
Percent of appropriations	100.3	85.1	100.1	96.2	82.6	110.6	115.6	107.7	180.4	120.6
1976: Appropriations	49,787	3,838	1,542	7,854	11,021	2,889	2,861	5,001	3,538	11,243
Expenditures	46,937	3,658	2,061	7,473	12,587	3,545	2,410	4,413	1,675	9,115
Percent of appropriations	94.3	95.3	133.7	95.1	114.2	122.7	84.2	88.2	47.3	81.1

Source: The Conference Board, New York, N.Y., *Quarterly Survey of Capital Appropriations.* (Copyright.)

No. 1414. Manufactures—Capital Expenditures: 1970 to 1976

[**In millions of dollars.** Represents expenditures for new plant and equipment]

MAJOR INDUSTRY GROUP	1970	1974	1975	1976	MAJOR INDUSTRY GROUP	1970	1974	1975	1976
All industries	22,143	35,699	37,262	40,545	Petroleum, coal prod	1,218	1,845	2,418	2,712
					Rubber, misc. plastics products [1]	828	1,457	1,140	1,317
Food, kindred prod	2,144	3,018	3,434	3,817	Leather, leather prod	39	76	78	89
Tobacco manufactures	56	185	145	130	Stone, clay, glass prod	920	1,588	1,581	1,504
Textile mill products	811	1,172	997	1,087	Primary metal indus.[1]	2,737	3,752	4,165	4,179
Apparel, other textile mill products	300	391	381	423	Fabr. metal prod.[1][2]	1,140	1,981	2,074	2,223
Lumber, wood prod.[1]	535	1,357	1,264	1,232	Machinery exc. elec	1,855	3,312	3,355	3,428
Furniture, fixtures	231	351	252	295	Elec., electronic equip.[1]	1,520	2,426	1,877	2,241
Paper, allied products	1,397	2,214	2,718	3,010	Trans. equip.[1][2]	1,612	3,176	2,762	3,131
Printing, publishing	873	1,141	1,175	1,261	Instr., related prod.[1]	436	822	794	783
Chemicals, allied prod	3,111	5,072	6,353	7,122	Misc. mfg. industries	253	362	302	561
					Ordnance, accessories [3]	127	(2)	(2)	(2)

[1] Data for 1970 not directly comparable with following years because of revision of Standard Industrial Classification (SIC) system in 1972. [2] "Ordnance, accessories" combined with "Fabricated metal products" and "Transportation equipment" in 1972 revision of SIC system. [3] Excludes government owned and operated.

Source: U.S. Bureau of the Census, *Annual Survey of Manufactures.*

No. 1415. U.S. SHARE OF WORLD EXPORTS OF MANUFACTURES: 1960 TO 1977

[World exports=exports from 15 major trading countries: U.S., Austria, Belgium-Luxembourg, Canada, Denmark, France, Fed. Rep. of Germany, Italy, Japan, Netherlands, Norway, Sweden, Switzerland, and U.K. Percents are calculated from the values of exports of the six commodity groups from each of the 15 countries. Incorporated in the calculations are the changing relationships between each supplier's currency and the currencies of its trading partners. For this purpose, export-weighted exchange rate indices are calculated for each supplier, using official rates of exchange in 67 principal markets]

ITEM	1960	1965	1970	1971	1972	1973	1974	1975	1976	1977, prel.
U.S. exports:										
Manufactures, total [1] ___bil. dol__	12.7	17.6	29.7	30.8	34.3	45.6	64.6	72.1	78.5	82.0
Nonelectric machinery___bil. dol__	3.3	5.1	8.4	8.6	9.6	12.2	16.8	21.1	22.2	22.5
Transport equipment___bil. dol__	2.7	3.5	6.5	7.9	8.3	10.8	14.6	17.3	18.3	18.7
Chemicals___bil. dol__	1.8	2.4	3.8	3.9	4.2	5.8	8.9	8.7	10.0	10.9
Electric machinery___bil. dol__	1.1	1.7	3.0	3.1	3.7	5.1	7.2	7.8	9.5	10.5
Basic manufactures [2]___bil. dol__	([3])	([3])	([3])	4.5	5.1	7.4	11.5	11.2	11.5	11.7
Misc. articles [4]___bil. dol__	[3] 3.9	[3] 5.0	[3] 7.9	2.8	3.3	4.2	5.6	6.0	6.9	7.7
Percent of world exports:										
Manufactures, total [1]	25.3	22.8	21.3	20.1	19.1	19.5	20.2	21.2	20.5	19.8
Nonelectric machinery	32.7	30.9	28.1	25.6	25.1	25.2	26.3	27.8	26.8	25.1
Transport equipment	33.2	28.4	29.0	29.7	26.4	27.0	29.0	27.8	25.1	23.8
Chemicals	29.6	24.7	21.9	20.0	18.6	19.1	18.6	20.1	20.6	21.1
Electric machinery	28.2	24.0	22.7	21.1	20.9	21.6	23.0	22.3	23.3	23.2
Basic manufactures [2]	([3])	([3])	([3])	10.8	10.5	11.4	12.3	12.5	11.9	11.4
Misc. articles [4]	[3] 17.6	[3] 15.8	[3] 14.0	16.1	15.5	16.2	17.3	17.3	17.1	16.8

[1] Excludes mineral fuel products, processed food, fats, oils, firearms of war, and ammunition.
[2] Includes semimanufactures of various materials, such as metals, fibers, wood, glass, leather, rubber, and certain finished products of metal. [3] Basic manufactures included with miscellaneous articles.
[4] Includes mainly nondurable consumer goods and professional and scientific instruments.

Source: U.S. Dept. of Commerce, Industry and Trade Administration, *Commerce America*, biweekly.

No. 1416. EXPORTS AND EXPORT-RELATED EMPLOYMENT OF MANUFACTURING ESTABLISHMENTS: 1960 TO 1976

[Includes only direct exports and products shipped to exporters or others for export. Excludes output of the supplying establishments that furnish parts or materials to the manufacturer producing the product exported. Therefore, estimates tend to understate the importance of the export trade for the domestic economy when compared to the total value of shipments of all manufacturers]

ITEM	1960	1963	1966	1069	1071	1072	1976
Value of shipments, total___mil. dol__	(NA)	420,528	538,737	642,636	670,971	756,467	1,185,695
For export___mil. dol__	14,546	16,473	21,299	29,210	33,132	36,608	83,098
Percent of total	(NA)	3.9	4.0	4.5	4.9	4.8	7.0
Manufacturing employment, total [1] 1,000__	16,763	16,958	19,024	20,036	18,363	19,027	18,753
Export related___1,000__	(NA)	(NA)	(NA)	779	746	770	1,173
Percent of total	(NA)	(NA)	(NA)	3.9	4.1	4.0	6.3

NA Not available. [1] Includes employees of central administrative and auxiliary offices.

No. 1417. EXPORTS AND EXPORT-RELATED EMPLOYMENT OF MANUFACTURING ESTABLISHMENTS, BY INDUSTRY: 1976

[See headnote, table 1416]

INDUSTRY GROUP	VALUE OF SHIPMENTS (mil. dol.)		MANUFACTURING EMPLOYMENT [1] (1,000)		INDUSTRY GROUP	VALUE OF SHIPMENTS (mil. dol.)		MANUFACTURING EMPLOYMENT [1] (1,000)	
	Total	For exports	Total	Export related		Total	For exports	Total	Export related
Manufacturing, total	1,185,695	83,098	18,753	1,173	Rubber, misc. plastics products	31,765	1,270	627	23
Food & kindred prod__	180,930	5,883	1,536	37	Leather, leather prod__	7,176	280	247	6
Tobacco manufactures_	8,786	1,020	65	10	Stone, clay, glass prod_	30,635	902	599	17
Textile mill products__	36,389	1,225	876	28	Primary metal indus__	93,002	2,936	1,106	30
Apparel, other textile products	34,758	729	1,271	16	Fabricated metal prod_	77,507	3,703	1,471	70
Lumber & wood prod__	31,239	1,892	629	23	Machinery, exc. elec__	105,525	19,037	1,960	295
Furniture, fixtures___	14,232	185	426	5	Elec., electronic equip_	73,867	9,170	1,579	196
Paper and allied prod_	48,218	2,261	615	21	Transportation equip__	141,026	16,518	1,668	203
Printing, publishing__	42,838	574	1,086	12	Instruments and related products	25,030	3,758	518	80
Chemicals, allied prod_	104,139	9,271	851	75	Misc. manufacturing__	16,286	1,336	410	25
Petroleum, coal prod__	82,347	1,152	145	3					

[1] Includes employees of central administrative and auxiliary offices, not shown separately.

Source of tables 1416 and 1417: U.S. Bureau of the Census, *Annual Survey of Manufactures*, 1976, M76(AS)-8.

No. 1418. MANUFACTURES SUMMARY,

[Sum of State totals may not add to U.S. total

	STATE	1967					1972				
		Establishments [1]		All employees [2]		Value added by manufacture [4]	Establishments [1]		All employees [2]		Value added by manufacture [4]
		Total	With 20 or more employees	Number [3]	Payroll		Total	With 20 or more employees	Number [3]	Payroll	
				1,000	*Mil. dol.*	*Mil. dol.*			*1,000*	*Mil. dol.*	*Mil. dol.*
1	U.S.	311,140	110,256	19,323	132,209	261,984	320,701	114,195	19,027	174,187	353,973
2	N.E.	24,286	9,164	1,562	10,190	18,972	23,731	8,718	1,362	11,905	22,501
3	Maine	2,385	615	111	577	1,070	2,075	590	100	696	1,376
4	N.H.	1,481	566	95	513	932	1,434	566	90	663	1,279
5	Vt.	925	281	43	259	515	860	274	37	311	576
6	Mass.	10,963	4,471	714	4,646	8,715	10,770	4,153	619	5,486	10,678
7	R.I.	2,703	922	122	700	1,351	2,756	904	118	888	1,764
8	Conn.	5,829	2,309	478	3,494	6,390	5,836	2,231	399	3,860	6,828
9	M.A.	76,422	29,002	4,360	30,527	57,262	71,808	26,983	3,933	37,120	70,330
10	N.Y.	42,911	14,730	1,929	13,852	25,247	38,341	12,995	1,679	16,219	30,402
11	N.J.	14,740	5,903	881	6,325	12,738	15,069	5,918	836	8,107	16,409
12	Pa.	18,771	8,369	1,550	10,350	19,277	18,398	8,070	1,418	12,794	23,519
13	E.N.C.	63,062	24,563	5,151	38,495	75,016	64,673	24,761	4,933	50,958	99,949
14	Ohio	15,428	6,285	1,397	10,523	20,435	16,390	6,487	1,346	13,810	27,171
15	Ind.	6,920	2,917	710	5,023	10,308	7,354	3,049	704	6,882	14,112
16	Ill.	18,536	7,477	1,397	10,014	20,017	18,617	7,345	1,306	12,800	25,847
17	Mich.	14,340	5,157	1,134	9,357	17,242	14,467	5,019	1,076	12,745	23,376
18	Wis.	7,838	2,727	512	3,578	7,014	7,845	2,861	501	4,722	9,443
19	W.N.C.	20,623	6,893	1,206	8,165	16,773	21,467	7,393	1,202	10,923	23,585
20	Minn.	5,409	1,778	300	2,107	4,080	5,698	1,930	302	2,889	5,524
21	Iowa	3,388	1,092	210	1,435	3,251	3,387	1,170	216	2,039	4,758
22	Mo.	6,545	2,457	452	3,049	5,895	6,732	2,470	434	3,897	8,169
23	N. Dak.	454	92	8	42	113	482	117	10	79	201
24	S. Dak.	604	137	16	93	171	606	151	17	135	285
25	Nebr.	1,672	525	77	476	1,150	1,723	598	85	704	1,733
26	Kans.	2,551	812	144	965	2,112	2,839	957	137	1,181	2,915
27	S.A.	37,961	13,138	2,502	14,014	29,313	41,534	14,981	2,739	20,638	44,349
28	Del.	528	253	71	588	958	567	243	69	755	1,292
29	Md.	3,401	1,463	288	1,956	3,781	3,579	1,437	256	2,386	4,707
30	D.C.	593	155	23	179	333	564	135	19	220	389
31	Va.	4,938	1,620	340	1,905	4,068	4,837	1,768	375	2,826	6,178
32	W. Va.	1,844	563	124	832	2,170	1,734	607	121	1,098	2,647
33	N.C.	8,266	3,379	643	3,066	6,607	8,632	3,794	744	4,929	11,015
34	S.C.	3,465	1,251	304	1,502	3,030	3,719	1,441	345	2,345	4,966
35	Ga.	6,976	2,268	423	2,231	4,684	7,627	2,663	467	3,330	7,370
36	Fla.	7,950	2,186	285	1,755	3,683	10,275	2,893	343	2,750	5,787
37	E.S.C.	15,746	5,528	1,092	5,909	13,718	16,525	6,246	1,249	9,211	21,234
38	Ky.	2,994	1,135	225	1,352	3,636	3,167	1,259	259	2,160	5,682
39	Tenn.	5,040	2,022	418	2,190	4,921	5,647	2,291	467	3,352	7,662
40	Ala.	4,951	1,446	289	1,603	3,526	4,984	1,630	323	2,397	5,065
41	Miss.	2,761	925	160	764	1,635	2,727	1,066	200	1,302	2,825
42	W.S.C.	21,883	6,727	1,083	6,855	16,617	24,018	7,873	1,239	10,281	24,596
43	Ark.	2,911	927	144	666	1,558	2,897	1,053	181	1,152	2,800
44	La.	3,639	1,016	165	1,084	2,790	3,657	1,133	179	1,601	4,273
45	Okla.	2,611	745	118	764	1,346	3,042	897	143	1,188	2,270
46	Tex.	12,722	4,039	658	4,340	10,922	14,422	4,790	736	6,340	15,253
47	Mt.	8,679	2,243	315	2,123	4,522	10,119	2,831	388	3,469	7,446
48	Mont.	923	191	20	130	312	943	206	21	185	463
49	Idaho	1,131	303	37	220	503	1,190	350	43	340	821
50	Wyo.	331	65	6	37	86	377	78	7	57	144
51	Colo.	2,461	664	104	731	1,509	2,841	834	133	1,298	2,504
52	N. Mex.	749	169	17	99	205	926	227	24	157	358
53	Ariz.	1,630	424	77	543	995	2,037	597	94	855	1,880
54	Utah	1,124	353	47	315	778	1,358	430	57	486	1,069
55	Nev.	330	74	7	50	134	447	109	10	92	208
56	Pac.	42,433	12,972	2,050	15,911	29,675	46,826	14,400	1,982	19,682	39,968
57	Wash.	5,014	1,375	271	2,119	3,764	5,345	1,463	226	2,308	4,721
58	Oreg.	4,437	1,275	163	1,083	2,061	4,670	1,461	179	1,627	3,490
59	Calif.	31,962	10,012	1,584	12,515	23,394	35,699	11,149	1,545	15,478	31,175
60	Alaska	323	95	8	56	130	342	91	8	77	171
61	Hawaii	697	215	25	140	326	770	236	25	191	410

[1] Includes central administrative offices and auxiliary units.
[2] Includes employment and payroll at administrative offices and auxiliary units.
[3] "Production workers" represents the average of the employment for the payroll periods ended nearest the 12th of March, May, August, and November. "All employees" represents the average of "production workers" plus all other employees for the payroll period ended nearest the 12th of March.

BY STATES: 1967 TO 1976
because figures were independently derived]

All employees		Production workers		Value added by manufacture [4]	Value of shipments [5]	Capital expenditures, new [6]	Leading major industry groups in value added by manufacture	
Number	Payroll	Number	Wages					
1,000	Mil. dol.	1,000	Mil. dol.	Mil. dol.	Mil. dol.	Mil. dol.		
18,753	233,389	13,052	137,565	511,471	1,185,695	40,770	Trans. equip.; machinery, exc. electrical; food.	1
1,336	15,635	899	8,451	31,475	59,654	2,138	Mach. exc. elect.;elect. equip.; fabricated metal.	2
99	930	81	676	2,041	4,423	507	Paper; leather; food.	3
88	883	66	540	1,832	3,495	138	Mach., exc. electrical; electrical equip.; leather.	4
41	450	29	248	952	2,056	96	Mach., exc. elec.; paper; print. and publishing.	5
591	6,943	388	3,661	14,421	26,918	782	Mach., exc. elec.; elec. equip.; instruments.	6
115	1,150	89	720	2,295	4,533	143	Misc. mfg. (jewelry); textiles; primary metal.	7
402	5,279	246	2,606	9,934	18,229	472	Trans. equip.;mach. exc. elec.; fabricated metal.	8
3,501	44,983	2,281	23,968	91,359	193,717	5,521	Chemicals; elec. equip.; mach., exc. electrical.	9
1,455	18,787	907	9,243	38,849	76,087	2,304	Print. and publishing; instruments; elec. equip.	10
736	9,704	458	4,851	20,288	45,711	1,216	Chemicals; electrical equipment; food.	11
1,310	16,492	916	9,874	32,222	71,919	2,001	Primary metal; mach., exc. elec.; elec. equip.	12
4,786	67,564	3,324	41,917	140,972	326,886	9,495	Trans. equip.;mach.,exc.elec.;fabricatedmetal.	13
1,283	17,855	889	11,235	37,608	83,600	2,141	Mach., exc. elec.; trans. equip.; primary metal.	14
677	9,160	498	6,108	19,983	45,181	1,475	Elec. equip.; primary metal; trans. equip.	15
1,256	16,831	825	9,557	36,085	82,351	2,335	Mach., exc. electrical; food; electrical equip.	16
1,050	17,107	741	10,793	32,390	80,327	2,631	Trans. equip.;mach. exc. elec.; fabricated metal.	17
520	6,611	371	4,224	14,906	35,427	913	Mach., exc. electrical; food; fabricated metal.	18
1,268	15,490	861	9,121	35,825	94,957	2,403	Food; mach., exc. electrical; trans. equipment.	19
321	4,142	198	2,128	8,473	20,440	495	Mach., exc. electrical; food; fabricated metal.	20
231	2,995	164	1,910	7,799	20,772	710	Mach., exc. electrical; food; electrical equip.	21
424	5,060	290	2,961	11,121	27,469	598	Transportation equipment; food; chemicals.	22
14	139	9	79	387	1,236	55	Food; mach. exc. elec.; stone, clay, glass prod.	23
22	217	16	150	494	1,609	49	Food; machinery, exc. electrical; lumber.	24
88	987	63	635	2,692	8,773	168	Food; machinery, exc. elec.; electrical equip.	25
168	1,950	121	1,258	4,859	14,658	328	Trans. equip.; food; mach., exc. electrical.	26
2,732	27,923	2,060	17,685	64,101	148,057	5,680	Textiles; chemicals; apparel.	27
66	1,064	32	383	1,581	5,043	160	Chemicals; food; rubber.	28
243	3,126	164	1,810	6,682	14,762	421	Food; primary metal; electrical equipment.	29
18	278	9	122	553	932	20	Printing and publishing; food; electrical equip.	30
375	3,851	287	2,548	9,368	20,471	907	Chemicals; food; electrical equipment.	31
120	1,521	89	1,024	3,558	7,938	289	Chemicals; prim. metal; stone, clay, glass prod.	32
739	6,655	592	4,505	15,822	35,819	1,295	Textiles; tobacco; chemicals.	33
371	3,406	299	2,383	7,164	16,610	868	Textiles; chemicals; machinery, exc. electrical.	34
469	4,506	362	2,950	11,093	28,391	853	Textiles; food; transportation equipment.	35
331	3,516	226	1,960	8,280	18,091	867	Food; transportation equipment; elec. equip.	36
1,296	12,912	1,006	8,774	31,478	73,881	2,792	Chemicals; food; machinery, exc. electrical.	37
277	3,058	210	2,039	8,645	20,269	522	Electrical equip.; food; mach., exc. electrical.	38
479	4,686	360	3,040	10,724	24,756	781	Chemicals; electrical equipment; food.	39
330	3,351	266	2,388	7,716	17,988	1,152	Primary metal; paper; textiles.	40
210	1,817	170	1,307	4,393	10,868	337	Lumber; apparel; transportation equipment.	41
1,353	15,640	953	9,391	43,909	123,076	7,213	Chemicals; electrical equipment; food.	42
188	1,650	153	1,201	4,278	10,605	473	Food; electrical equipment; lumber.	43
190	2,395	140	1,576	8,423	25,225	1,561	Chemicals; food; petroleum.	44
150	1,743	100	953	3,608	10,126	411	Mach., exc. electrical; food; fabricated metal.	45
825	9,852	560	5,661	27,600	77,120	4,768	Chemicals; food; machinery, exc. electrical.	46
439	5,271	295	3,048	12,145	29,475	1,160	Food; primary metal; machinery exc., electrical.	47
22	270	17	203	771	2,525	86	Lumber; primary metal; food.	48
53	614	39	396	1,525	3,448	160	Lumber; food; chemicals.	49
7	83	5	55	279	833	31	Petroleum; stone, clay, glass products; food.	50
143	1,871	92	1,016	3,990	9,536	385	Food; machinery, exc. electrical; trans. equip.	51
30	273	23	175	635	1,534	120	Food; electrical equip.; stone, clay, glass prod.	52
99	1,237	63	652	2,882	6,233	183	Elec. equip.; prim. metal; machinery, exc. elec.	53
71	779	48	464	1,709	4,641	142	Trans. equip.; food; mach., exc. electrical.	54
14	144	8	87	354	725	53	Stone, clay, glass products; chemicals; food.	55
2,064	27,567	1,372	15,208	70,049	135,960	4,134	Transportation equipment; food; lumber.	56
244	3,594	163	2,087	7,297	18,843	662	Transportation equipment; lumber; food.	57
188	2,371	145	1,675	5,392	12,229	378	Lumber; food; paper.	58
1,600	21,215	1,041	11,202	56,156	102,041	2,867	Transportation equip.; food; electrical equip.	59
8	121	6	90	504	992	171	Food; paper; lumber.	60
24	266	17	154	700	1,855	56	Food; printing and publ.; stone, clay, glass prod.	61

[4] For definition, see footnote 6, table 1401.   [5] See footnote 5, table 1419.
[6] See footnote 8, table 1419.

Source: U.S. Bureau of the Census, Census of Manufactures, 1967, General Summary, MC 67(1)-1; Census of Manufactures, 1972, General Summary, MC 72(1)-1; and Annual Survey of Manufactures, 1976, M 76(AS)-6.

No. 1419. MANUFACTURES SUMMARY

[Data based on various editions of the *Standard Industrial Classification Manual*, published by the Office of

Industry code [1]	INDUSTRY GROUP	1967				1972			
		Establishments	All employees		Value added by manufacture [3]	Establishments	All employees		Value added by manufacture [3]
			Number [2]	Payroll			Number [2]	Payroll	
		Number	*1,000*	*Mil. dol.*	*Mil. dol.*	*Number*	*1,000*	*Mil. dol.*	*Mil. dol.*
(X)	All manufacturing establishments, incl. central administrative offices	311,140	19,323	132,208	261,984	320,701	19,027	174,187	353,973
20	Food and kindred products	[6]32,518	1,650	10,077	26,621	28,183	1,569	12,920	35,615
201	Meat products	4,914	310	1,954	3,551	4,437	308	2,544	4,961
202	Dairy products	6,188	232	1,449	3,466	4,590	189	1,596	4,054
203	Preserved fruits and vegetables	3,528	223	1,084	[7]3,238	2,557	233	1,534	4,514
204	Grain mill products	3,202	112	758	2,882	3,080	111	1,013	3,699
205	Bakery products	4,390	264	1,665	3,495	3,633	235	2,029	4,537
206	Sugar and confectionery products	182	114	644	1,900	1,249	107	832	2,473
207	Fats and oils	(NA)	44	297	919	860	40	366	1,291
208	Beverages	4,376	221	1,525	4,790	3,624	212	2,033	6,689
209	Misc. foods and kindred products	4,498	130	700	2,375	4,153	134	974	3,397
21	Tobacco products	329	75	377	[7]2,032	272	66	502	2,637
211	Cigarettes	16	37	221	[7]1,640	20	38	345	2,188
212	Cigars	148	19	71	[7]196	124	14	68	192
213	Chewing and smoking tobacco	46	4	18	[7]64	37	3	23	103
214	Tobacco stemming and redrying	119	16	66	[7]133	91	11	66	154
22	Textile mill products	7,080	929	4,391	8,153	7,201	953	6,051	11,716
221	Weaving mills, cotton	393	203	938	1,624	307	121	745	1,256
222	Weaving mills, manmade fiber	396	109	529	922	412	150	979	1,832
223	Weaving, finishing mills, wool	310	42	216	429	198	19	132	239
224	Narrow fabric mills	384	26	121	214	376	27	162	289
225	Knitting mills	2,698	241	1,036	1,914	2,723	277	1,647	3,181
226	Textile finishing, except wool	641	74	416	710	655	80	564	1,114
227	Floor covering mills	385	44	228	599	527	60	415	1,076
228	Yarn and thread mills	768	119	505	946	807	148	866	1,580
229	Misc. textile goods	1,105	72	401	795	1,196	72	540	1,149
23	Apparel, other textile products	26,393	1,357	5,582	10,064	24,438	1,368	7,212	13,488
231	Men's and boys' suits and coats	1,003	136	642	1,048	856	125	770	1,342
232	Men's and boys' furnishings	2,853	345	1,212	2,181	2,787	363	1,692	3,242
233	Women's and misses' outerwear	9,416	409	1,756	3,183	9,526	433	2,270	4,102
234	Women's, children's undergarments	1,213	114	444	867	1,002	105	525	1,049
235	Hats, caps, and millinery	843	24	102	164	496	15	73	133
236	Children's outerwear	1,334	78	298	538	1,061	75	368	709
237	Fur goods	1,304	9	59	117	797	5	41	86
238	Misc. apparel and accessories	1,397	71	285	510	1,302	62	335	636
239	Misc. fabricated textile products	7,030	173	785	1,457	6,611	186	1,139	2,188
24	Lumber and wood products [8]	36,795	554	2,799	4,973	33,949	691	4,986	10,310
241	Logging camps, log contractors	16,334	71	339	695	13,238	80	524	1,163
242	Sawmills and planing mills	11,461	216	1,028	1,784	9,452	204	1,488	3,259
243	Millwork, plywood, and structural members [8]	4,558	154	896	1,505	5,506	191	1,474	2,908
244	Wood containers [8]	905	31	135	239	1,160	37	204	359
245	Wood buildings and mobile homes	(NA)	(NA)	(NA)	(NA)	993	97	745	1,491
249	Misc. wood products [8]	3,537	83	401	750	3,600	82	550	1,129
25	Furniture and fixtures	10,008	425	2,258	4,170	9,233	462	3,205	6,097
251	Household furniture [8]	6,306	298	1,456	2,650	5,369	317	2,024	3,861
252	Office furniture	365	35	225	478	433	39	330	660
253	Public bldg., related furniture	438	23	132	234	422	21	158	296
254	Partitions and fixtures	1,970	48	324	587	2,010	57	484	871
259	Misc. furniture and fixtures	929	22	121	221	999	27	210	410
26	Paper and allied products	5,890	639	4,436	9,756	6,038	633	5,992	13,064
261	Pulpmills	61	15	126	334	60	11	126	307
262	Papermills, except building paper	354	140	1,121	2,356	349	130	1,440	2,909
263	Paperboard mills	283	67	534	1,509	273	69	778	1,994
264	Misc. converted paper products	2,492	187	1,187	2,833	2,525	189	1,630	4,008
265	Paperboard containers and boxes	2,606	219	1,387	2,541	2,739	224	1,907	3,599
266	Building paper and board mills	94	12	83	184	92	12	112	247

For footnotes, see pp. 818 and 819.

FOR INDUSTRY GROUPS: 1967 TO 1976

Management and Budget; see text, p. 804. See also *Historical Statistics, Colonial Times to 1970*, series P 58-67]

1975				1976						
All employees		Value added by manufacture³	Capital expenditures, new⁴	All employees		Production workers		Value added by manufacture³	Value of shipments⁵	Capital expenditures, new⁴
Number²	Pay-roll			Number²	Pay-roll	Number²	Wages			
1,000	Mil. dol.	Mil. dol.	Mil. dol.	1,000	Mil. dol.	1,000	Mil. dol.	Mil. dol.	Mil. dol.	Mil. dol.
18,302	209,519	442,485	37,262	18,753	233,389	13,052	137,565	511,471	1,185,695	40,670
1,525	15,856	48,095	3,434	1,536	17,289	1,067	10,806	52,760	180,930	3,817
308	3,161	7,169	423	311	3,474	253	2,621	7,531	45,827	424
170	1,823	4,942	294	164	1,908	88	968	5,261	24,830	336
223	1,918	6,041	430	222	2,032	190	1,551	6,799	17,722	433
114	1,329	5,644	452	115	1,453	80	955	6,083	21,189	475
237	2,584	6,288	270	242	2,837	145	1,511	6,909	12,230	335
103	988	3,677	283	106	1,137	84	822	3,658	10,405	348
41	472	1,649	232	41	502	30	331	2,034	12,801	191
204	2,417	8,110	755	204	2,629	100	1,222	8,833	21,069	977
126	1,165	4,576	296	131	1,317	97	825	5,653	14,857	298
66	655	3,722	145	65	704	55	544	4,128	8,786	130
40	477	43,203	102	41	521	35	412	3,592	6,030	98
10	58	166	3	8	56	8	45	148	268	5
3	27	143	3	3	29	2	20	161	297	3
13	92	210	37	13	98	10	67	228	2,192	24
835	6,397	12,044	997	876	7,368	765	5,769	14,495	36,389	1,087
107	769	1,337	133	110	917	101	786	1,687	3,718	124
152	1,150	1,965	192	161	1,398	144	1,161	2,600	5,869	246
14	112	198	11	16	134	13	99	265	572	42
19	140	259	12	20	160	17	120	322	647	11
231	1,686	3,301	228	232	1,788	202	1,356	3,452	8,626	204
68	612	1,151	92	72	688	60	518	1,315	3,542	117
49	416	1,040	53	49	456	40	311	1,211	3,795	60
131	915	1,567	161	145	1,136	132	940	2,118	5,844	167
64	596	1,227	115	71	692	57	481	1,526	3,777	117
1,214	7,700	14,749	381	1,271	8,563	1,109	6,460	16,860	34,758	423
98	738	1,250	16	98	787	85	615	1,370	2,406	25
333	1,842	3,654	76	358	2,148	320	1,712	4,426	9,108	100
402	2,511	4,786	127	427	2,758	372	2,042	5,274	10,749	128
87	514	973	24	91	566	78	413	1,145	2,192	21
15	99	158	3	15	98	13	76	149	346	4
64	364	708	13	64	386	55	290	774	1,514	14
4	38	86	3	3	35	3	26	75	246	1
55	363	683	16	56	381	48	270	744	1,528	27
156	1,232	2,451	103	160	1,404	135	1,016	2,905	6,669	103
588	5,231	10,356	1,264	629	6,143	543	4,817	13,454	31,239	1,232
67	664	1,713	378	72	798	65	677	2,173	4,461	308
194	1,642	3,041	472	208	1,947	185	1,624	4,225	9,752	490
159	1,526	2,836	187	173	1,792	146	1,381	3,756	8,995	213
31	233	472	37	33	251	29	196	512	1,040	23
58	540	1,050	36	62	625	50	418	1,291	3,693	40
78	626	1,243	155	82	731	69	521	1,497	3,298	159
396	3,310	6,290	252	426	3,772	352	2,690	7,370	14,232	295
266	2,036	3,801	149	290	2,341	247	1,740	4,544	9,041	180
37	370	756	30	39	414	30	283	860	1,451	40
20	174	331	16	21	196	16	126	373	744	16
48	492	940	36	51	558	39	372	1,061	1,952	38
25	239	462	21	26	262	20	170	533	1,044	22
589	6,990	17,944	2,718	615	8,047	478	5,692	20,604	48,218	3,010
13	191	821	294	16	261	12	195	975	2,055	375
121	1,668	3,973	832	128	1,977	101	1,483	4,878	11,768	1,944
65	911	2,832	807	65	1,018	51	770	3,128	6,724	844
193	2,075	5,729	412	200	2,356	154	1,595	6,448	14,920	394
188	2,040	4,351	347	197	2,322	152	1,559	4,935	12,234	335
9	106	238	26	9	113	8	90	240	516	19

No. 1419. MANUFACTURES SUMMARY

[See headnote,

In-dus-try code [1]	INDUSTRY GROUP	1967				1972			
		Estab-lish-ments	All employees		Value added by manu-facture [3]	Estab-lish-ments	All employees		Value added by manu-facture [3]
			Num-ber [2]	Pay-roll			Num-ber [2]	Pay-roll	
		Num-ber	1,000	Mil. dol.	Mil. dol.	Num-ber	1,000	Mil. dol.	Mil. dol.
27	**Printing and publishing**	37,989	1,031	7,152	14,355	42,103	1,057	9,831	20,210
271	Newspapers	8,094	336	2,224	4,185	8,116	349	3,168	6,220
272	Periodicals	2,510	79	634	1,869	2,534	67	709	2,110
273	Books	1,766	97	688	1,967	1,905	98	919	2,540
274	Misc. publishing	1,493	31	197	418	2,041	39	331	776
275	Commercial printing [8]	19,497	331	2,358	3,944	22,282	344	3,277	5,695
276	Manifold business forms	542	34	240	551	667	39	344	824
277	Greeting card publishing [8]	222	28	151	372	199	24	192	527
278	Blankbooks and bookbinding	1,462	54	294	506	1,465	52	372	687
279	Printing trades services [8]	2,403	42	366	544	2,894	47	521	831
28	**Chemicals and allied products** [8]	[6]11,799	[6]841	[6]6,443	[6]23,550	11,425	837	8,731	32,414
281	Industrial inorganic chemicals [8]	2,032	248	2,090	7,737	1,049	100	1,079	3,343
282	Plastics materials, synthetics [8]	771	172	1,292	3,799	461	162	1,666	4,935
283	Drugs	1,129	118	942	4,073	1,078	130	1,413	6,131
284	Soap, cleaners, toilet goods [8]	2,508	97	684	3,930	2,573	112	1,058	6,201
285	Paints and allied products	1,701	66	492	1,319	1,599	66	647	1,792
286	Industrial organic chemicals	(NA)	131	1,130	4,406	827	137	1,614	6,073
287	Agricultural chemicals [8]	1,278	46	281	1,006	1,233	48	438	1,737
289	Misc. chemical products [8]	2,196	88	628	1,587	2,605	83	814	2,203
29	**Petroleum and coal products**	1,880	142	1,216	5,426	2,016	140	1,638	5,793
291	Petroleum refining	437	107	965	4,745	323	101	1,247	4,595
295	Paving and roofing materials	1,098	27	186	456	1,199	30	297	846
299	Misc. petroleum and coal products	345	8	65	225	494	9	94	352
30	**Rubber and miscellaneous plas-tics products** [8]	6,456	517	3,287	6,800	9,237	618	5,165	11,653
301	Tires and inner tubes	182	93	775	1,823	206	108	1,214	3,071
302	Rubber, plastics footwear [8]	65	29	141	245	107	32	183	370
303	Reclaimed rubber	24	2	12	23	20	1	9	16
304	Rubber, plastics hose, belting	(NA)	(NA)	(NA)	(NA)	90	32	309	619
306	Fabricated rubber products, n.e.c. [8]	1,189	142	923	1,741	1,116	99	809	1,573
307	Misc. plastics products [8]	4,996	252	1,436	2,968	7,698	347	2,642	6,005
31	**Leather and leather products**	[6]3,685	[6]329	[6]1,459	[6]2,627	3,201	273	1,589	2,917
311	Leather tanning and finishing	519	31	186	319	517	26	200	368
313	Boot, shoe cut stock, findings	379	14	60	109	248	9	50	86
314	Footwear, except rubber	1,083	211	889	1,620	917	176	973	1,796
315	Leather gloves and mittens	147	6	22	36	106	5	22	43
316	Luggage	333	21	97	186	277	17	107	194
317	Women's handbags and purses	792	37	163	279	688	34	195	345
319	Leather goods, n.e.c. [8]	365	6	26	46	448	7	43	84
32	**Stone, clay, and glass products**	15,580	590	3,826	8,333	16,015	623	5,547	12,587
321	Flat glass	64	24	197	423	32	21	242	662
322	Glass, pressed or blown	305	109	688	1,501	369	119	1,058	2,341
323	Products of purchased glass	887	29	182	394	913	34	296	669
324	Cement, hydraulic	197	33	248	812	198	30	349	1,154
325	Structural clay products	851	60	344	612	775	52	391	771
326	Pottery and related products	619	43	247	419	620	45	335	601
327	Concrete, gypsum, plaster products	10,004	169	1,103	2,478	10,115	193	1,741	3,840
328	Cut stone and stone products	811	17	91	148	908	15	109	191
329	Misc. nonmetallic mineral prod. [8]	1,842	106	726	1,547	2,085	115	1,025	2,359
33	**Primary metal industries** [8]	6,837	1,281	9,851	19,978	6,792	1,143	12,167	23,258
331	Blast furnace and basic steel prod.	861	617	5,022	10,170	970	553	6,389	12,116
332	Iron and steel foundries	1,438	233	1,641	2,631	1,400	219	2,155	3,481
333	Primary nonferrous metals	144	53	405	1,382	177	59	627	1,706
334	Secondary nonferrous metals	403	17	123	271	381	18	170	411
335	Nonferrous rolling and drawing	833	195	1,438	3,325	903	188	1,871	3,800
336	Nonferrous foundries	1,886	90	609	1,068	1,841	81	722	1,269
339	Misc. primary metal products [8]	1,272	76	613	1,132	1,120	25	233	476

For footnotes, see pp. 818 and 819.

FOR INDUSTRY GROUPS: 1967 TO 1976—Continued

pp. 814 and 815]

	1975				1976					
All employees		Value added by manufacture [3]	Capital expenditures, new [4]	All employees		Production workers		Value added by manufacture [3]	Value of shipments [5]	Capital expenditures, new [4]
Number [2]	Payroll			Number [2]	Payroll	Number [2]	Wages			
1,000	Mil. dol.	Mil. dol.	Mil. dol.	1,000	Mil. dol.	1,000	Mil. dol.	Mil. dol.	Mil. dol.	Mil. dol.
1,070	11,655	24,641	1,175	1,086	12,680	629	6,737	27,647	42,838	1,261
360	3,770	7,578	363	364	4,068	162	1,785	8,482	11,659	377
73	880	2,652	62	73	951	14	129	3,084	5,044	65
99	1,131	3,187	138	101	1,212	49	500	3,521	5,295	129
34	362	862	38	35	388	14	124	946	1,333	40
355	3,900	6,890	413	367	4,326	279	3,025	7,870	13,646	470
40	440	1,156	75	39	468	29	317	1,202	2,328	59
19	195	559	16	18	214	10	98	607	907	16
47	417	856	33	47	446	39	326	920	1,343	36
43	560	901	37	43	608	33	434	1,016	1,283	70
842	11,227	44,976	6,353	851	12,365	520	6,518	51,408	104,139	7,122
109	1,538	5,213	721	109	1,684	66	921	6,165	11,611	813
150	1,985	5,525	1,439	153	2,187	107	1,347	6,648	17,156	1,369
150	2,039	8,030	475	151	2,223	77	894	9,333	13,016	471
108	1,278	7,248	255	110	1,415	69	739	8,469	14,741	288
60	737	2,126	122	60	810	32	353	2,562	5,931	123
137	2,079	9,511	2,120	142	2,348	90	1,357	11,349	25,685	2,684
52	653	4,546	960	52	722	33	413	3,763	9,195	1,054
75	919	2,777	261	74	976	45	496	3,119	6,803	321
141	2,147	10,500	2,418	145	2,437	100	1,578	13,169	82,347	2,837
101	1,666	8,927	2,275	102	1,887	71	1,246	11,410	77,507	2,656
30	345	1,065	85	32	397	23	263	1,184	3,145	114
11	137	507	57	11	153	6	69	575	1,695	66
585	5,923	13,599	1,140	627	6,742	489	4,518	15,950	31,765	1,317
106	1,332	3,463	272	104	1,364	79	955	3,534	7,714	244
25	176	320	10	25	176	21	129	310	539	14
1	9	16	1	1	7	1	5	15	23	(Z)
27	307	695	80	30	357	21	211	804	1,412	54
90	884	1,748	86	93	1,010	72	677	2,081	3,888	146
335	3,214	7,357	691	375	3,829	296	2,541	9,207	18,193	859
240	1,651	3,187	78	247	1,805	216	1,379	3,559	7,176	89
23	220	444	23	23	244	19	181	521	1,326	33
8	53	74	3	8	61	7	47	94	252	5
146	934	1,826	35	150	1,012	133	811	1,982	3,747	35
6	32	55	1	6	34	5	26	62	148	1
17	125	245	4	18	144	14	95	289	565	5
34	231	427	6	35	250	31	177	482	857	10
7	57	117	5	7	60	6	42	129	282	2
589	6,390	14,849	1,581	599	7,086	474	5,145	16,773	30,635	1,504
21	298	654	57	22	353	18	287	838	1,336	40
111	1,219	2,931	278	115	1,403	100	1,154	3,267	5,155	344
33	341	665	49	35	398	27	272	829	1,651	47
29	411	1,333	355	28	445	22	343	1,461	2,604	201
47	411	834	64	47	446	38	325	930	1,595	54
44	389	733	44	45	427	37	320	801	1,165	63
178	1,958	4,419	433	174	2,062	128	1,361	4,660	10,020	466
15	121	234	8	15	137	13	102	274	433	20
113	1,241	3,047	294	118	1,415	91	980	3,712	6,677	270
1,089	14,994	30,367	4,165	1,106	16,975	875	12,639	34,182	93,002	4,179
532	8,106	15,783	2,288	532	9,166	418	6,884	17,274	46,687	2,373
221	2,713	4,976	520	216	2,996	179	2,310	5,497	9,787	643
58	844	2,411	599	59	963	46	710	2,980	9,970	431
17	208	576	62	18	237	13	147	633	3,179	120
162	2,008	4,590	473	171	2,339	131	1,666	5,360	18,753	439
76	816	1,435	165	85	951	70	711	1,738	3,389	114
24	299	596	59	25	324	18	211	702	1,236	59

No. 1419. MANUFACTURES SUMMARY

[See headnote,

Industry code [1]	INDUSTRY GROUP	1967				1972			
		Establishments	All employees		Value added by manufacture [3]	Establishments	All employees		Value added by manufacture [3]
			Number [2]	Payroll			Number [2]	Payroll	
		Number	1,000	Mil. dol.	Mil. dol.	Number	1,000	Mil. dol.	Mil. dol.
34	**Fabricated metal products** [8]	[6] 27,418	[6] 1,342	[6] 9,320	[6] 18,043	29,525	1,493	13,821	26,946
341	Metal cans, shipping containers [8]	299	60	474	1,142	553	79	840	2,005
342	Cutlery, handtools, hardware	1,939	156	1,043	2,318	1,904	159	1,405	3,253
343	Plumbing and heating, ex. electric [8]	838	65	428	872	757	61	524	1,132
344	Fabricated structural metal prod	10,151	388	2,687	4,934	10,351	395	3,532	6,743
345	Screw machine products, bolts, etc	2,536	116	847	1,621	2,482	101	948	1,845
346	Metal forgings, stampings [8]	2,710	226	1,686	3,031	3,188	264	2,791	5,057
347	Metal services, n.e.c.	4,684	81	481	864	4,761	82	624	1,120
348	Ordnance and accessories, n.e.c. [8]	(NA)	(NA)	(NA)	(NA)	315	110	1,015	1,507
349	Misc. fabricated metal products [8]	2,711	189	1,309	2,591	5,214	244	2,142	4,283
35	**Machinery, exc. electrical**	37,892	1,865	14,226	27,836	40,792	1,828	18,523	37,563
351	Engines and turbines	182	100	820	1,598	253	116	1,320	2,900
352	Farm and garden machinery	1,618	136	947	2,042	1,658	125	1,211	2,701
353	Construction and related machinery	2,305	273	2,041	4,130	2,517	275	2,856	5,962
354	Metalworking machinery	9,439	337	2,860	5,091	9,652	268	2,859	4,902
355	Special industry machinery	3,312	207	1,570	2,880	3,685	190	1,854	3,732
356	General industrial machinery	3,760	279	2,137	4,107	3,863	262	2,585	5,020
357	Office and computing machines	594	190	1,462	3,332	995	208	2,277	4,905
358	Refrigeration, service machinery	1,573	140	947	2,125	1,769	198	1,864	4,427
359	Misc. machinery, except electrical [8]	15,109	203	1,443	2,531	16,400	184	1,697	3,016
36	**Electric and electronic equip.** [8]	10,706	1,875	12,968	24,487	12,270	1,662	15,189	30,558
361	Electric distributing equipment [8]	1,218	176	1,230	2,509	784	116	1,040	2,060
362	Electrical industrial apparatus	1,316	207	1,420	2,792	1,510	188	1,665	3,218
363	Household appliances	637	169	1,101	2,540	645	163	1,369	3,563
364	Electric lighting and wiring equip	1,868	157	950	2,214	1,897	177	1,414	3,277
365	Radio and TV receiving equipment	661	130	720	1,587	939	107	798	2,183
366	Communication equipment	1,402	525	4,397	6,993	1,976	454	4,912	8,453
367	Electronic components, accessories	2,439	403	2,435	4,359	2,867	336	2,869	5,306
369	Misc. electrical equipment, supplies	1,165	107	715	1,494	1,652	120	1,121	2,498
37	**Transportation equipment** [8]	7,483	1,834	15,174	28,174	8,802	1,719	19,880	39,799
371	Motor vehicles and equipment [8]	2,675	739	5,930	13,666	3,391	808	9,461	22,056
372	Aircraft and parts [8]	1,273	802	7,209	11,327	1,094	439	5,282	9,124
373	Ship and boat building and repairing	2,011	169	1,239	1,705	2,232	185	1,704	2,398
374	Railroad equipment	123	57	427	788	163	51	529	1,113
375	Motorcycles, bicycles, parts	91	12	70	136	222	18	140	315
376	Guided missiles, space vehicles	(NA)	(NA)	(NA)	(NA)	147	160	2,317	3,969
379	Misc. transportation equipment [8]	1,310	55	298	551	1,553	59	448	824
38	**Instruments and related prod.** [8]	4,453	394	2,822	6,418	5,983	453	4,286	10,580
381	Engineering, scientific instruments	677	46	327	617	743	37	365	681
382	Measuring and control devices [8]	766	104	732	1,392	1,611	153	1,437	2,724
383	Optical instruments and lenses [8]	303	21	163	284	494	19	193	384
384	Medical instruments and supplies	1,466	67	427	966	1,807	91	758	1,821
385	Ophthalmic goods	461	26	143	284	499	27	183	416
386	Photographic equip. and supplies	557	95	820	2,481	627	96	1,120	4,088
387	Watches, clocks, and watchcases	223	35	209	393	202	31	230	466
39	**Misc. manufacturing** [8] [9]	14,489	824	5,819	10,189	15,187	446	3,180	6,769
391	Jewelry, silverware, and plated ware	2,212	52	320	641	2,296	53	425	851
393	Musical instruments	343	25	144	238	344	25	173	339
394	Toys and sporting goods	2,435	116	559	1,205	2,460	133	881	1,999
395	Pens, office and art goods	959	35	200	412	966	32	244	557
396	Costume jewelry and notions	1,608	52	252	528	1,482	50	323	720
399	Misc. manufactures [8] [9]	6,932	544	4,345	7,163	7,639	153	1,134	2,303
60	**Administrative and auxiliary** [10]	5,460	831	8,728	(X)	8,039	994	13,772	(X)

- Represents zero.   NA Not available.   X Not applicable.   Z Less than $500,000.
[1] Standard Industrial Classification code; see text, p. 804.
[2] "All employees" represents the average of "production workers" plus all other employees for the payroll period ended nearest the 15th of March.   [3] See footnote 6, table 1401.
[4] Includes expenditures for plants in operation and plants under construction but not yet in operation.
[5] Includes extensive duplication arising from shipments between establishments in the same industry classification. Comprises for all manufacturing establishments classified in an industry value of (a) products primary to the industry, (b) secondary products which are primary to other industries, (c) miscellaneous receipts such as those for contract and commission work on materials owned by others, scrap, salable refuse, repair, etc., and (d) resales, i.e., products resold in the same condition as bought.
[6] Includes industries not shown separately.

FOR INDUSTRY GROUPS: 1967 TO 1976—Continued

pp. 814 and 815]

1975				1976						
All employees		Value added by manufacture³	Capital expenditures, new⁴	All employees		Production workers		Value added by manufacture³	Value of shipments⁵	Capital expenditures, new⁴
Number²	Pay-roll			Number²	Pay-roll	Number²	Wages			
1,000	Mil. dol.	Mil. dol.	Mil. dol.	1,000	Mil. dol.	1,000	Mil. dol.	Mil. dol.	Mil. dol.	Mil. dol.
1,417	16,334	34,203	2,074	1,471	18,382	1,123	12,596	39,145	77,507	2,223
74	1,040	2,826	249	72	1,131	60	904	3,085	7,984	150
147	1,619	3,602	205	158	1,900	123	1,327	4,486	7,393	243
53	551	1,162	75	51	579	37	372	1,336	2,608	60
397	4,488	9,257	483	401	4,802	293	3,100	10,048	21,584	638
97	1,085	2,255	122	100	1,220	77	835	2,515	4,396	122
241	3,077	6,039	415	265	3,788	217	2,846	7,554	15,250	430
81	774	1,431	104	90	889	74	635	1,788	2,877	109
82	994	1,635	63	75	976	48	541	1,664	2,804	62
246	2,705	5,997	359	259	3,097	193	2,036	6,669	12,612	409
1,967	24,555	51,044	3,355	1,960	26,480	1,332	15,831	57,357	105,525	3,428
121	1,677	3,434	339	125	1,939	85	1,187	4,200	9,009	298
150	1,872	4,365	347	146	1,949	108	1,313	4,783	10,534	288
318	4,178	9,473	804	312	4,378	210	2,708	9,646	19,741	831
290	3,671	6,862	295	290	3,954	214	2,632	7,459	11,278	363
199	2,394	4,871	200	196	2,557	126	1,411	5,175	9,454	215
290	3,565	7,428	458	281	3,746	190	2,301	8,043	14,197	469
225	3,033	6,441	390	229	3,277	107	1,071	8,102	13,723	480
158	1,791	3,893	187	173	2,152	125	1,383	5,214	10,660	183
215	2,375	4,277	336	209	2,530	168	1,825	4,735	6,931	302
1,524	17,401	34,845	1,877	1,579	19,253	1,080	10,891	41,746	73,867	2,240
105	1,154	2,492	69	104	1,193	75	747	2,702	4,688	85
185	2,030	4,209	233	195	2,284	141	1,441	4,916	8,453	289
145	1,486	3,601	176	157	1,699	122	1,170	4,454	9,161	210
145	1,450	3,392	163	159	1,700	123	1,137	4,204	7,342	162
86	853	1,934	90	90	956	68	619	2,544	5,823	107
434	5,714	10,324	422	422	6,050	233	2,708	11,656	19,138	513
302	3,358	5,984	536	323	3,763	219	1,964	7,568	12,433	651
121	1,358	2,909	188	130	1,607	99	1,105	3,704	6,829	224
1,605	22,772	45,337	2,762	1,668	26,442	1,206	17,296	55,657	141,026	3,131
699	9,856	21,466	1,831	797	13,019	662	10,270	30,949	95,381	2,055
438	6,601	12,801	369	408	6,665	237	3,285	12,735	23,463	431
202	2,305	3,552	329	207	2,605	165	1,915	4,032	7,517	387
60	798	1,566	73	51	740	38	510	1,455	3,616	68
14	148	254	16	14	151	11	111	284	791	17
148	2,624	4,764	109	142	2,723	53	828	5,027	7,142	126
44	440	933	35	50	539	40	376	1,176	3,117	48
500	5,829	14,158	794	518	6,598	322	3,214	16,386	25,030	783
46	561	1,112	40	44	576	25	263	1,224	1,847	44
163	1,898	3,618	142	169	2,100	102	985	4,102	6,180	160
23	283	572	24	26	349	15	150	695	1,029	25
109	1,110	2,621	170	111	1,248	75	662	2,957	4,766	153
27	248	478	15	28	276	21	169	588	852	28
100	1,441	5,177	388	107	1,732	58	780	6,077	8,845	347
32	287	580	16	33	318	26	205	743	1,513	26
393	3,487	7,580	302	410	3,868	317	2,446	8,822	16,286	561
50	481	998	29	56	572	41	336	1,181	2,691	69
25	219	392	16	26	242	21	169	538	925	16
113	917	2,161	106	119	1,033	95	670	2,660	4,746	182
31	281	624	34	32	296	23	178	726	1,293	47
44	347	835	21	47	386	38	256	881	1,531	43
131	1,241	2,571	97	130	1,339	99	837	2,837	5,100	205
1,128	19,015	-	-	1,070	20,391	-	-	-	-	-

[7] Value of production. The formula for computing value added by manufacture was modified to exclude any change in finished products inventories between beginning and end of year.
[8] Due to changes in industry classification, 1967 data not comparable with later data.
[9] For 1967, includes ordnance from privately owned and/or operated establishments classified in "Ordnance and accessories." Excludes government-owned and-operated equipment.
[10] Manufacturing concerns often reported separately for central offices or auxiliaries which serve the manufacturing establishments of a company, rather than the general public. Separate reports were obtained from such units if at a different location or if they serviced more than one establishment.

Source: U.S. Bureau of the Census, *Census of Manufactures, 1967* and *1972, General Summary_,* MC67(1)- and MC72(1)-1; and *Annual Surve_ of Manufactures, 1976,* M76(AS)-1.

No. 1420. EXPORTS AND EXPORT-RELATED EMPLOYMENT OF MANUFACTURING ESTABLISHMENTS, BY STATES: 1976

[See headnote, table 1416]

STATE	VALUE OF SHIPMENTS (mil. dol.)		MANUFACTURING EMPLOYMENT[1] (1,000)		STATE	VALUE OF SHIPMENTS (mil. dol.)		MANUFACTURING EMPLOYMENT[1] (1,000)	
	Total	For exports	Total	Export related		Total	For exports	Total	Export related
U.S.	1,185,695	83,098	18,753	1,173	Mo	27,469	1,622	424	23
					Mont	2,525	44	22	(Z)
Ala	17,988	832	330	13	Nebr	8,773	309	88	4
Alaska	992	233	8	2	Nev	725	27	14	(Z)
Ariz	6,233	639	99	12	N.H	3,495	291	88	7
Ark	10,605	651	188	7	N.J	45,711	2,660	736	35
Calif	102,041	8,072	1,600	124	N. Mex	1,534	69	30	1
Colo	9,536	616	143	9	N.Y	76,087	5,320	1,455	84
Conn	18,229	1,958	405	37	N.C	35,819	2,202	739	32
Del	5,043	188	66	2	N. Dak	1,236	85	14	1
D.C	932	7	18	(Z)	Ohio	83,600	5,794	1,283	84
Fla	18,091	1,363	331	20	Okla	10,126	579	150	9
Ga	28,391	1,364	469	21	Oreg	12,299	824	188	13
Hawaii	1,855	183	24	3	Pa	71,919	4,706	1,310	82
Idaho	3,448	169	53	2	R.I	4,533	269	115	6
Ill	82,351	6,660	1,256	87	S.C	16,610	935	371	16
Ind	45,181	2,828	677	40	S. Dak	1,609	68	22	1
Iowa	20,772	1,500	231	20	Tenn	24,756	1,253	479	19
Kans	14,658	635	168	10	Tex	77,120	5,201	825	59
Ky	20,269	1,137	277	12	Utah	4,641	224	71	4
La	25,225	1,383	190	9	Vt	2,056	200	41	4
Maine	4,423	255	99	4	Va	20,471	1,545	375	21
Md	14,762	641	243	11	Wash	18,843	3,235	244	30
Mass	26,918	2,502	591	48	W. Va	7,938	447	120	5
Mich	80,327	6,888	1,050	74	Wis	35,427	2,209	520	32
Minn	20,440	1,567	321	23	Wyo	833	10	7	(S)
Miss	10,868	698	210	10					

S Withheld, estimate did not meet publication standards.   Z Fewer than 500.
[1] Includes employees of central administrative and auxiliary offices. Total State data do not add to U.S. total; figures were independently derived.

No. 1421. FUELS AND ELECTRIC ENERGY USED IN MANUFACTURING: 1950 TO 1976

[For 1950, excludes Alaska and Hawaii. Refers to use for heat and power only]

ITEM	1950	1954	1960	1963	1967	1970	1972	1974	1975	1976
Cost of purchased fuels and electric energy___mil. dol__	4,185	4,932	5,765	6,370	7,692	9,425	11,772	19,433	23,237	27,587
Cost of fuels[1]_____mil. dol__	2,924	3,204	3,193	3,409	3,975	4,846	6,056	10,984	12,951	15,505
Cost of electric energy__mil. dol__	1,260	1,728	2,572	2,961	3,717	4,579	5,716	8,449	10,286	12,082
Electric energy purchased_____bil. kWh__	131	187	292	334	428	501	557	611	591	635
Generated less sold[2]__bil. kWh__	(NA)	61	70	73	78	83	87	81	63	65

NA Not available.   [1] Interplant transfer value excluded after 1954.   [2] Represents net consumption.

No. 1422. FUELS AND ELECTRIC ENERGY USED FOR HEAT AND POWER IN MANUFACTURING: 1958 TO 1976

[See also Historical Statistics, Colonial Times to 1970, series P 216–226]

FUEL	QUANTITY PURCHASED (tril. Btu[1])						COST (mil. dol.)					
	1958	1962	1967	1971	1975	1976	1958	1962	1967	1971	1975	1976
Coal	2,143	2,342	1,967	1,608	1,169	1,253	638	640	552	658	1,310	1,342
Coke and breeze	354	460	353	357	342	407	271	305	249	318	881	1,141
Fuel oil, related products	967	1,142	1,092	1,496	1,726	1,990	523	623	536	989	3,519	4,011
Gas	3,267	4,523	5,492	6,679	5,942	6,042	901	1,456	1,749	2,560	5,653	7,536
Other fuels	120	275	135	219	406	433	148	337	220	378	850	907
Fuels not classified	534	(2)	1,312	1,011	443	335	356	(2)	669	458	739	569
Purchased electric energy	863	1,071	1,458	1,756	2,018	2,166	2,231	2,823	3,717	5,071	10,286	12,082

[1] For definition of Btu, see headnote, table 1001.
[2] Fuels not classified by kind were prorated into specified fuels.

Source of tables 1420–1422: U.S. Bureau of the Census, Census of Manufactures, 1972, and Annual Survey of Manufactures, 1976, M76(AS)–4.1.

No. 1423. PERCENT SHARE OF VALUE ADDED BY MANUFACTURE FOR LARGEST COMPANIES IN MANUFACTURING, 1947 TO 1972, AND OF SHIPMENTS AND EMPLOYEES, 1972

[Companies ranked on value added by manufacture; companies in each group are not identical for all years. See also *Historical Statistics, Colonial Times to 1970*, series P 177–180]

ITEM	1947	1954	1963	1967	1970	1972		
						Value added	Shipments, value [1]	Employ- ment [2]
Largest 50 companies____	17	23	25	25	24	25	24	17
Largest 100 companies___	23	30	33	33	33	33	32	23
Largest 150 companies___	27	34	37	38	38	39	38	28
Largest 200 companies___	30	37	41	42	43	43	43	31

[1] Includes central administrative offices and auxiliaries.   [2] See footnote 5, table 1419.

Source: U.S. Bureau of the Census, *Annual Surve_ of Manufactures, 1970, Value of Shipment Concentration Ratios*, M70(AS)-9, and *Census of Manufactures, 1972, Concentration Ratios in Manufacturing*, MC72(SR)-20.

No. 1424. PERCENT OF SHIPMENTS ACCOUNTED FOR BY LARGE MANUFACTURING COMPANIES, SELECTED INDUSTRIES: 1963 TO 1972

[Prior to 1967, excludes Alaska and Hawaii. First 32 industries (excluding those classified as "Miscellaneous" or "Not elsewhere classified") as determined by value added by manufacture in 1972 of $2 billion or more. Industry codes and descriptions are based on the 1972 *Standard Industrial Classification Manual* (SIC), see text, p. 804. Determination of company affiliation of establishment is based on census reports and publicly available records. "Largest" companies are determined by each company's value added by manufacture *in the specified industry*. Industries in the "not elsewhere classified" category are omitted, regardless of their value added]

Indus- try code [1]	INDUSTRY AND YEAR	Num- ber of com- panies	Value added by man- ufac- ture [2] (mil. dol.)	Total value of ship- ments [3] (mil. dol.)	PERCENT OF SHIPMENTS, RANKED BY COMPANY SIZE			
					4 larg- est	8 larg- est	20 larg- est	50 larg- est
3711	Motor vehicles and car bodies_____1967__	107	7,354	27,296	92	98	99+	99+
	1972__	165	11,783	42,906	93	99	99+	99+
3312	Blast furnaces and steel mills_____1963__	161	7,506	16,418	51	70	86	97
	1967__	200	8,910	19,621	48	66	83	96
	1972__	245	10,305	23,947	45	65	84	96
3714	Motor vehicle parts and accessories_____1967__	1,424	5,712	11,624	60	68	78	87
	1972__	1,748	9,165	18,334	61	69	78	86
2711	Newspapers_____1963__	7,982	3,202	4,484	15	22	36	52
	1967__	7,589	4,184	5,757	16	25	40	56
	1972__	7,461	6,220	8,263	17	28	43	60
3662	Radio and TV communications equip_____1963__	1,001	4,328	7,146	29	45	69	84
	1967__	1,111	5,456	8,556	22	37	61	81
	1972__	1,524	5,803	9,140	19	33	58	77
2834	Pharmaceutical preparations_____1963__	944	2,596	3,314	22	38	72	89
	1967__	791	3,720	4,696	24	40	73	90
	1972__	680	5,640	7,150	26	44	75	91
3721	Aircraft_____1963__	82	[4] 3,543	[4] 6,317	59	83	99	99+
	1967__	91	[4] 5,448	[4] 11,080	69	89	99	99+
	1972__	141	5,083	8,779	66	86	99	99+
2911	Petroleum refining_____1963__	266	3,137	16,497	34	56	82	95
	1967__	276	4,745	20,294	33	57	84	96
	1972__	152	4,595	25,921	31	56	84	95
3861	Photographic equipment and supplies_____1963__	499	1,270	1,851	63	76	86	93
	1967__	505	2,481	3,665	69	81	89	95
	1972__	555	4,088	5,624	74	85	92	95
2051	Bread, cake, and related products_____1963__	4,339	2,404	4,506	23	35	45	56
	1967__	3,445	2,753	5,103	26	38	47	58
	1972__	2,800	3,518	6,132	29	39	50	62
3585	Refrigeration and heating equipment_____1963__	655	893	(NA)	25	39	58	77
	1967__	624	1,480	(NA)	31	45	62	78
	1972__	655	3,517	7,084	40	53	70	85
3573	Electronic computing equipment_____1967__	134	1,926	3,771	66	83	92	98
	1972__	518	3,419	6,471	51	63	78	90
2752	Commercial printing, lithographic_____1963__	6,738	1,392	2,150	6	10	16	25
	1967__	6,718	1,898	3,139	5	8	15	25
	1972__	8,160	3,155	5,125	4	8	15	24

See footnotes at end of table.

No. 1424. PERCENT OF SHIPMENTS ACCOUNTED FOR BY LARGE MANUFACTURING COMPANIES, SELECTED INDUSTRIES: 1963 TO 1972—Continued

[See headnote, p. 821]

Industry code [1]	INDUSTRY AND YEAR	Number of companies	Value added by manufacture [2] (mil. dol.)	Total value of shipments [3] (mil. dol.)	PERCENT OF SHIPMENTS, RANKED BY COMPANY SIZE			
					4 largest	8 largest	20 largest	50 largest
3531	Construction machinery_____1963__	561	1,301	2,696	42	53	70	84
	1967__	578	2,506	4,138	41	53	72	85
	1972__	644	3,131	6,091	43	54	72	86
3011	Tires and inner tubes_____1963__	105	1,322	2,950	70	89	97	99+
	1967__	119	1,823	3,734	70	88	97	100
	1972__	136	3,071	5,747	73	90	98	99+
2011	Meatpacking plants_____1963__	2,833	1,908	12,435	31	40	49	60
	1967__	2,529	2,221	15,576	26	39	49	61
	1972__	2,293	2,968	23,003	22	37	51	66
3761	Guided missiles and space vehicles_____1967__	(NA)	3,339	4,641	(NA)	(NA)	(NA)	(NA)
	1972__	23	2,949	4,124	62	88	(D)	100
2621	Papermills, exc. building paper_____1963__	186	1,857	3,825	26	42	63	85
	1967__	203	2,356	4,844	26	43	65	86
	1972__	194	2,909	6,385	24	40	66	88
2421	Sawmills and planing mills, general_____1963__	11,931	1,376	3,156	11	14	20	29
	1967__	10,016	1,556	3,506	11	15	22	31
	1972__	7,664	2,907	6,421	18	23	33	45
2844	Toilet preparations_____1963__	673	1,233	1,793	38	52	75	90
	1967__	628	1,731	2,516	38	52	74	90
	1972__	593	2,834	4,053	38	53	74	91
3465	Automotive stampings_____1972__	388	2,664	5,286	69	72	79	87
3661	Telephone, telegraph apparatus_____1963__	65	1,014	1,736	92	96	99	99+
	1967__	82	1,537	2,591	92	96	99	99+
	1972__	157	2,650	4,525	(D)	(D)	98	99+
2026	Fluid milk_____1963__	4,030	2,203	7,026	23	30	40	48
	1967__	2,988	2,351	7,826	22	30	42	51
	1972__	2,024	2,552	9,396	18	26	42	56
2086	Bottled and canned soft drinks_____1963__	3,569	1,233	2,211	12	17	24	34
	1967__	3,057	1,679	3,173	13	20	28	38
	1972__	2,271	2,337	5,454	14	21	32	44
3321	Gray iron foundries [5]_____1963__	1,062	1,169	1,985	28	37	51	65
	1967__	969	1,543	2,638	27	36	50	64
	1972__	893	2,257	3,877	34	45	59	71
3523	Farm machinery and equipment_____1963__	1,481	(NA)	2,842	43	55	67	77
	1967__	1,526	2,042	4,300	44	56	68	77
	1972__	1,465	2,248	4,530	47	61	69	78
2111	Cigarettes_____1963__	7	[6] 1,310	[6] 2,655	80	100	(X)	(X)
	1967__	8	[6] 1,640	[6] 3,045	81	100	(X)	(X)
	1972__	13	[6] 2,188	[6] 3,745	84	(D)	100	(X)
2821	Plastics materials and resins_____1972__	193	2,161	4,478	27	41	65	90
2721	Periodicals_____1963__	2,562	1,349	2,296	28	42	59	73
	1967__	2,430	1,869	3,096	24	37	56	72
	1972__	2,451	2,110	3,511	26	38	54	69
2824	Organic fibers, noncellulosic_____1963__	14	922	1,403	94	99	100	(X)
	1967__	22	1,252	2,033	84	94	(D)	100
	1972__	36	2,040	3,639	74	91	99+	100
2841	Soap and other detergents_____1963__	641	1,137	2,128	72	80	88	93
	1967__	599	1,404	2,593	70	78	86	92
	1972__	577	2,039	3,394	62	74	85	92
2751	Commercial printing, letterpress_____1963__	11,979	(NA)	2,645	13	19	28	38
	1967__	11,955	(NA)	3,256	14	21	29	39
	1972__	13,040	2,015	3,292	14	19	26	35

D Withheld to avoid disclosure.   NA Not available.   X Not applicable.   [1] See headnote. [2] See footnote 6, table 1401.   [3] See footnote 5, table 1419.   [4] Value of work done reported instead of value of shipments; therefore, value added not adjusted for inventory change.   [5] Includes foundries producing gray-iron castings for other plants of the same company. Accordingly, percentages do not reflect market shares in industry as such.   [6] Value of production reported instead of value of shipments; therefore, formula for computing adjusted value added modified to include only changes in work-in-process inventories between beginning and end of year.

Source: U.S. Bureau of the Census, *Census of Manufactures, 1972, Concentration Ratios in Manufacturing,* MC72 (SR)-2.

No. 1425. Beverage Industry—Summary: 1965 to 1976

YEAR AND ITEM	Total	Malt bev- erages	Malt	Wines, brandy, brandy spirits	Dis- tilled liquor, exc. brandy	Soft drinks (bot- tled, canned)	Flavor- ing, ex- tracts, sirups
1965: Employees----------------------1,000--	211	61	2	6	19	114	9
Payroll-------------------------mil. dol--	1,348	488	16	42	126	614	63
Value added by manufacture----------mil. dol--	4,151	1,360	51	167	713	1,373	487
Value of shipments-----------------mil. dol--	7,728	2,497	204	396	1,288	2,505	837
1970: Employees----------------------1,000--	228	57	2	9	21	129	11
Payroll-------------------------mil. dol--	1,884	616	19	71	171	916	91
Value added by manufacture----------mil. dol--	6,144	2,028	58	258	887	2,121	792
Value of shipments-----------------mil. dol--	12,373	3,822	210	591	1,758	4,631	1,361
1975: Employees----------------------1,000--	204	47	2	11	16	117	11
Payroll-------------------------mil. dol--	2,417	726	24	131	198	1,209	129
Value added by manufacture----------mil. dol--	8,109	2,008	121	500	1,056	3,321	1,103
Value of shipments-----------------mil. dol--	20,395	5,641	591	1,197	2,003	8,602	2,361
1976: Employees----------------------1,000--	204	42	2	10	16	122	12
Payroll-------------------------mil. dol--	2,629	750	24	133	211	1,364	147
Value added by manufacture----------mil. dol--	8,833	2,266	87	540	1,101	3,556	1,283
Value of shipments-----------------mil. dol--	21,069	6,025	515	1,213	2,115	8,780	2,421

Source: U.S. Bureau of the Census, *Annual Survey of Manufactures.*

No. 1426. Alcoholic Beverages—Summary: 1960 to 1977

[For years ending **June 30** except, beginning 1977, ending Sept. 30. Includes Puerto Rico. Excludes imports. See *Historical Statistics, Colonial Times to 1970*, series P 235 for beer production, and P 236a for distilled spirits]

ITEM	Unit	1960	1965	1970	1973	1974	1975	1976	1977
Beer:									
Breweries operated-------------	Number--------	229	197	154	129	118	117	96	(NA)
Production--------------------	Mil. bbl.[1]-------	95	108	135	143	153	158	161	170
Tax-paid withdrawals----------	Mil. bbl.[1]-------	89	100	123	134	142	147	149	156
Stocks on hand, June 30-------	Mil. bbl.[1]-------	11	13	15	14	14	14	14	14
Per capita consumption [2]------	Gallons--------	24.02	25.46	28.55	29.68	31.02	32.77	31.15	32.07
Of domestic output----------	Gallons--------	23.91	25.29	28.35	29.45	30.75	32.43	30.75	31.54
Distilled spirits:									
Production facilities operated--	Number--------	178	153	140	115	120	115	107	(NA)
Warehouses operated ---------	Number--------	241	268	274	262	255	241	233	(NA)
Production, total [3]------------	Mil. tax gal.[4][5]--	273	276	355	282	258	278	234	226
Whisky--------------------	Mil. tax gal.[4][5]--	150	118	160	112	93	50	79	82
Tax-paid withdrawals, total [6]--	Mil. tax gal.[4][5]--	178	205	256	283	292	295	304	296
Whisky--------------------	Mil. tax gal.[4][5]--	84	90	112	136	138	137	135	126
Stocks on hand, June 30, total [3]-	Mil. tax gal.[4][5]--	932	990	1,091	985	933	836	782	726
Whisky--------------------	Mil. tax gal.[4][5]--	814	841	960	926	876	780	723	668
Bottled for consumption, total-	Mil. wine gal.[7]--	204	244	312	337	349	357	369	361
Whisky--------------------	Mil. wine gal.[7]--	147	161	192	188	184	182	179	166
Per capita consumption [2]------	Wine gal.[7]------	1.87	2.13	2.61	2.81	2.89	2.49	2.11	2.03
Of domestic output----------	Wine gal.[7]------	1.54	1.66	1.91	2.00	2.03	1.75	2.00	1.89
Still wines:									
Production[8]-------------------	Mil. wine gal.[7]--	511	565	713	599	848	782	768	771
Tax-paid withdrawals [9]--------	Mil. wine gal.[7]--	148	163	204	275	274	287	303	304
Stocks on hand, June 30 [9][10]------	Mil. wine gal.[7]--	143	157	207	237	307	325	325	392
Per capita consumption [2]------	Wine gal.[7]------	1.36	1.44	1.70	2.31	2.26	2.20	2.40	2.36
Of domestic output----------	Wine gal.[7]------	1.28	1.32	1.52	1.95	1.91	1.96	1.95	2.11
Effervescent wines: [11]									
Production--------------------	Mil. wine gal.[7]--	4.1	6.4	20.0	20.4	20.3	18.0	20.2	21.2
Tax-paid withdrawals---------	Mil. wine gal.[7]--	3.3	5.7	17.1	19.7	18.7	17.6	18.8	21.2
Stocks on hand, June 30-------	Mil. wine gal.[7]--	2.7	3.6	8.1	9.2	9.5	9.0	9.4	10.4
Per capita consumption [2]------	Wine gal.[7]------	.04	.06	.15	.15	.14	.13	.14	.15
Of domestic output----------	Wine gal.[7]------	.03	.05	.13	.14	.13	.12	.12	.13

NA   Not available.   [1] Barrels of 31 wine gallons (see footnote 7).
[2] Source: U.S. Bureau of Domestic Business Development. Based on U.S. Bureau of the Census estimated population 18 years old and over, as of Jan. 1, including Armed Forces abroad.   [3] Excludes alcohol produced for industrial use.   [4] A tax gallon for spirits of 100 proof or over is equivalent to the proof gallon; for spirits of less than 100 proof to the wine gallon. (See footnotes 5 and 7).   [5] A proof gallon is the alcoholic equivalent of a U.S. gallon at 60° F, containing 50 percent of ethyl alcohol by volume.   [6] Includes ethyl alcohol.
[7] A wine gallon is the U.S. gallon equivalent to the volume of 231 cubic inches.
[8] Production represents total amount removed from fermenters, including distilling material, and, beginning 1970, includes increase after fermentation (by amelioration, sweetening, and addition of wine spirits). In 1972, 407 million gallons of distilling materials were produced; 1973, 258 million gal.; 1974, 389 million gal.; 1975, 359 mil. gal; 1976, 343 million gal. and 1977, 347 million gal.   [9] Includes special natural wines.   [10] Excludes distilling materials.   [11] Includes champagne, other effervescent wines, and artificially carbonated wines.

Source: Except as noted, U.S. Bureau of Alcohol, Tobacco, and Firearms, *Alcohol and Tobacco Summary Statistics*, annual.

No. 1427. Tobacco Products—Production and Consumption: 1950 to 1977

[Beginning 1960, production data are for years ending June 30. Excludes cigars produced in customs bonded manufacturing warehouses. See also *Historical Statistics, Colonial Times to 1970*, series P 239–241]

ITEM	1950	1955	1960	1965	1970	1972	1973	1974	1975	1976	1977
Production:											
Cigarettes [1] ____ billions __	392	412	506	562	562	593	616	652	627	688	673
Cigars [1] _____ billions __	5.5	5.8	6.9	8.9	8.0	8.0	11.4	8.7	8.3	6.7	5.8
Tobacco [2] _____ mil. lb __	235	198	176	169	164	157	149	152	155	153	155
Per capita consumption: [3]											
All products _____ lb. [4] __	12.29	11.99	11.82	11.51	9.63	9.65	9.53	9.40	9.14	8.61	8.33
Cigarettes ____ number __	3,522	3,597	4,171	4,258	3,985	4,043	4,148	4,141	4,123	4,092	4,064
Weight _____ lb. [4] __	9.54	9.49	9.64	9.37	7.78	7.95	7.92	7.90	7.73	7.27	7.07
Cigars [4][5] _____ number __	53	55	61	70	60	52	49	44	39	36	32
Weight _____ lb. [4] __	1.25	1.28	1.18	1.24	1.00	.83	.77	.70	.63	.57	.52
Tobacco [2] _____ lb. [4] __	1.50	1.22	.99	.88	.83	.79	.75	.75	.72	.73	.70

[1] Large and small. Source: U.S. Bureau of Alcohol, Tobacco, and Firearms, *Alcohol and Tobacco Summary Statistics*, annual. [2] Smoking and chewing tobaccos and snuff. Source: U.S. Dept. of Agriculture, Agricultural Marketing Service, *Manufacture and Sales of Snuff, Smoking, and Chewing Tobacco*, quarterly. [3] Based on U.S. Bureau of the Census estimated population 18 years old and over, as of July 1, including Armed Forces abroad. 1977 data preliminary. [4] Unstemmed processing weight equivalent. [5] Weighing over 3 pounds per 1,000.

Source: Except as noted, U.S. Dept. of Agriculture, Economics, Statistics, and Cooperatives Service, *Tobacco Situation*, quarterly.

No. 1428. Mill Consumption of Natural and Manmade Fibers: 1950 to 1977

[Totals in millions of pounds; per capita in pounds. Prior to 1960, excludes Alaska and Hawaii. Per capita figures based on U.S. Bureau of the Census population estimates as of July 1, including Armed Forces abroad. See *Historical Statistics, Colonial Times to 1970*, series P 229 and P 230, for wool and silk]

| YEAR | COTTON [1] | | WOOL (scoured basis) [2] | | MANMADE FIBERS | | | | FLAX | | SILK | |
| | | | | | Rayon and acetate [3] | | Non-cellulosic [3] | | | | | |
	Total	Per capita	Total	Per capita	Total	Per capita	Total	Per capita	Total	Per capita	Total	Per capita
1950	4,683	30.9	635	4.2	1,350	8.9	141	.9	11	.07	11	.07
1955	4,382	26.5	414	2.5	1,419	8.6	432	2.6	8	.05	11	.07
1960	4,234	23.4	411	2.3	1,055	5.8	762	4.2	5	.03	7	.04
1965	4,522	23.2	387	2.0	1,550	8.0	1,962	10.1	8	.04	6	.03
1970	3,854	18.8	240	1.2	1,414	6.9	4,086	19.9	6	.03	2	.01
1971	3,986	19.3	191	.9	1,486	7.2	5,044	24.4	6	.03	2	.01
1972	3,864	18.5	219	1.0	1,413	6.8	6,153	29.5	6	.03	2	.01
1973	3,658	17.4	151	.7	1,390	6.6	7,275	34.6	7	.03	3	.01
1974	3,309	15.6	93	.4	1,111	5.2	6,589	31.1	7	.02	3	.01
1975	3,027	14.2	110	.5	801	3.8	6,615	31.0	3	.01	1	.01
1976	3,414	15.9	122	.6	862	4.0	7,220	33.6	4	.02	3	.01
1977, prel	3,179	14.7	108	.5	872	4.0	8,021	37.0	3	.02	2	.01

[1] Reported by U.S. Bureau of the Census. For American cotton, tare as reported by Crop Reporting Board is deducted. For foreign cotton, 15 pounds deducted, 1950–1965; 20 pounds thereafter. [2] Reported by U.S. Bureau of the Census. Excludes consumption in cotton and other spinning systems and consumption in batting and felt manufacture. [3] From *Textile Organon*. Represents domestic shipments plus imports for consumption. Includes textile glass-fiber and producers waste consumed at mills.

Source: U.S. Dept. of Agriculture, Economics, Statistics, and Cooperatives Service, *Cotton and Wool Situation*, April 1978. (1950 data in U.S. Bureau of Domestic Business Development, *Wool and Manmade Fibers in the United States*.)

No. 1429. Finished Bleached, Dyed, or Printed Broadwoven Goods—Production, by Type: 1960 to 1977

[In millions of linear yards. Excludes Alaska and Hawaii. Fabrics are classified by chief fiber content]

PRODUCT	1960	1965	1970	1971	1972	1973	1974	1975	1976	1977
Total broadwoven goods _____	9,559	10,988	9,718	9,748	10,157	9,728	8,351	8,041	8,326	8,212
Cotton _____	7,440	7,710	5,229	5,233	5,116	4,479	3,614	3,474	3,491	3,337
Manmade fiber fabrics and silk [1]	2,119	3,278	4,489	4,515	5,041	5,249	4,738	4,565	4,835	4,875
Bleached and white finished [2] ____	4,975	6,354	6,095	5,817	6,057	5,773	5,197	4,728	5,110	5,122
Cotton _____	3,158	3,514	2,436	2,317	2,292	2,008	1,778	1,627	1,632	1,575
Manmade fiber fabrics and silk [1][2]	1,817	2,840	3,659	3,500	3,765	3,765	3,419	3,100	3,478	3,547
Plain dyed and finished goods, cotton _____	2,516	2,722	1,760	1,773	1,808	1,578	1,205	1,193	1,260	1,185
Printed and finished goods [3] _____	2,068	1,912	1,862	2,157	2,292	2,377	1,949	2,120	1,956	1,905
Cotton _____	1,766	1,474	1,032	1,142	1,016	893	630	654	599	577
Manmade fiber fabrics and silk [1]	302	438	830	1,015	1,276	1,484	1,319	1,465	1,357	1,328

[1] Fabrics made of polyester, rayon, acetate, nylon, silk, glass, acrylic fibers, etc. [2] Includes plain dyed manmade fibers. [3] Includes roller, screen, and block printed; excludes printed towels, tablecloths, flock, plisse, moire, or embossed. Source: U.S. Bureau of the Census, *Current Industrial Reports*, series MA–22S.

No. 1430. RAW COTTON—SPINDLES, CONSUMPTION, AND STOCKS: 1950 TO 1977

[For years ending **July 31.** Excludes Alaska and Hawaii. Consumption and stocks are expressed in running bales, counting round as half bales, except foreign cotton which is in equivalent 500-pound bales. See *Historical Statistics, Colonial Times to 1970,* series P 228, for total cotton consumed including linters]

YEAR	COTTON-SYSTEM SPINDLES (1,000)				Spindle hours consuming 100% cotton (bil.)	COTTON CONSUMED [3] (1,000 bales)				COTTON STOCKS AT END OF YEAR (1,000 bales)			
	Total in place [1]	Total active [2]	Cotton-growing States	Other States		Total	Cotton-growing States	Other States		Total [4]	Do-mestic [4]	For-eign [4]	Lint-ers [5]
1950	22,995	21,790	17,673	4,117	109	8,851	8,030	821		6,496	6,399	97	208
1955	22,273	20,716	18,230	2,486	113	8,841	8,358	484		10,985	10,920	65	148
1960	19,956	19,221	17,801	1,420	113	9,017	8,670	346		7,344	7,307	37	305
1965	19,332	18,757	18,114	643	102	9,171	8,968	203		14,061	13,994	67	463
1970	19,860	19,056	18,653	403	74	7,965	7,840	125		5,400	5,373	27	342
1971	19,231	18,452	18,133	319	70	8,068	7,980	88		3,852	3,837	15	413
1972	19,104	18,301	18,003	298	70	8,039	7,958	81		3,154	3,130	24	362
1973	19,172	17,833	17,564	269	66	7,568	7,488	80		3,929	3,916	13	289
1974	18,765	17,942	17,706	236	61	7,150	7,078	72		3,743	3,730	11	294
1975	18,274	16,812	16,685	127	44	5,604	5,546	58		5,205	5,188	17	486
1976	18,021	17,029	16,904	125	51	6,965	6,916	49		3,444	3,396	48	444
1977	17,815	16,752	16,621	131	40	6,478	6,443	35		2,845	2,834	11	278

[1] All spindles in place regardless of fiber spun.
[2] Active last day of year, regardless of type of fiber spun. On July 30, 1977, there were 7,008,000 spindles active on cotton, 9,744,000 on manmade and other fibers and blends, and 992,000 idle.
[3] Excludes linters. Includes foreign and domestic cotton. [4] Excludes linters. Includes stocks at public storage and compresses. [5] Stocks held by consuming establishments.

Source: U.S. Bureau of the Census, *Cotton Production and Distribution,* annual, and *Current Industrial Reports,* series M22P.

No. 1431. BROADWOVEN FABRICS—PRODUCTION, BY TYPE: 1960 TO 1977

[In millions of linear yards; in terms of gray goods except woolen and worsted, which are in terms of finished yardage. Excludes Alaska and Hawaii. Fabrics classified according to primary fiber content.]

PRODUCT	1960	1965	1970	1972	1973	1974	1975	1976	1977 [1]
Total goods	12,056	13,432	11,453	11,299	11,301	10,718	9,452	10,904	10,420
Cotton woven goods over 12 in. in width [2]	9,366	9,238	6,246	5,666	5,086	4,714	4,095	4,719	4,098
Sheeting, allied coarse, medium yarn fabrics	2,482	2,635	1,804	1,501	1,253	1,116	880	905	711
Print cloth yarn fabrics	3,320	3,120	2,392	2,136	1,968	1,868	1,451	1,836	1,691
Carded colored yarn fabrics	449	479	389	473	482	511	681	792	618
Other	3,114	3,005	1,662	1,556	1,384	1,219	1,082	1,186	1,078
Manmade fiber fabrics	(NA)	3,926	5,028	5,531	6,109	5,923	5,278	6,088	6,220
100 percent filament yarn fabrics	(NA)	1,641	1,461	1,723	1,895	1,963	1,688	1,952	2,024
100 percent spun yarn fabrics [3]	(NA)	1,535	2,872	3,062	3,527	3,309	3,036	3,522	3,569
Polyester blends with cotton	(NA)	714	1,963	2,190	2,514	2,381	2,360	2,713	2,664
Other	(NA)	751	695	746	687	652	554	614	627
Woolen and worsted [4]	286	267	179	102	106	81	79	97	102

NA Not available. [1] Preliminary. [2] Excludes tire fabrics.
[3] Except blanketing. [4] Except woven felts.
Source: U.S. Bureau of the Census, *Current Industrial Reports,* series MQ–22T.

No. 1432. WOMEN'S, MISSES', AND JUNIORS' OUTERWEAR—SELECTED GARMENTS CUT: 1960 TO 1977

[See also *Historical Statistics, Colonial Times to 1970,* series P 243]

TYPE OF GARMENT	1960	1965	1970	1971	1972	1973	1974	1975	1976	1977 [1]
Blouses_____mil. doz__	15.6	19.0	13.3	12.6	15.9	17.0	17.2	18.3	19.7	19.5
Unit-priced dresses_____mil. units__	155	178	159	147	156	147	129	115	117	114
Dozen-priced dresses_____mil. doz__	8.2	8.6	7.7	7.2	7.4	6.7	5.1	4.9	4.5	4.4
Suits_____mil. units__	9.4	11.9	8.8	6.8	7.3	8.0	7.8	9.0	11.7	(NA)
Skirts_____mil. doz__	8.3	8.9	6.9	5.9	5.2	5.0	4.4	4.3	4.9	5.4
Untrimmed coats_____mil. units__	21.0	19.1	17.0	15.8	}23.7	22.9	20.5	18.4	20.7	17.6
Fur-trimmed coats_____mil. units__	2.5	6.1	4.7	4.9						
Knit outerwear:										
Sweaters, jackets, jerseys_____mil. doz__	12.9	14.7	10.6	11.0	12.5	13.7	13.2	10.8	11.1	(NA)
Sport shirts_____mil. doz__	22.1	22.8	22.4	30.8	40.8	42.8	47.8	42.5	32.0	(NA)

NA Not available. [1] Preliminary.
Source: U.S. Bureau of the Census, *Current Industrial Reports,* series MA–23A and M23H.

No. 1433. Wool—Production, Price, and Supply: 1960 to 1977

[In millions of pounds, except as indicated. For 1960 and as noted, excludes Alaska and Hawaii. See *Historical Statistics, Colonial Times to 1970*, series K 559–560, for shorn wool production and price, and series P 229, for wool consumed in manufacturing]

ITEM	1960	1965	1970	1972	1973	1974	1975	1976	1977[1]
Stocks of apparel wool, Jan. 1 [2]___	101	73	75	69	57	41	(NA)	39	31
Sheep and lambs shorn___mil__	31	24	19	19	17	16	14	14	13
Weight per fleece___lb__	8.5	8.5	8.4	8.4	8.3	8.2	8.3	8.1	8.1
Shorn wool production (grease basis)___	265	201	162	159	144	131	120	111	107
Price per pound [3]___cents__	42.0	47.1	35.4	35.0	82.7	59.2	44.7	65.7	72.0
Pulled wool production (actual)___	34	23	15	10	8	6	5	4	2
Total wool production (grease basis)___	299	225	177	168	152	137	125	115	109
Wool, clean basis:									
Total production___	145	113	88	82	75	68	61	56	55
Imports of dutiable wool [4]___	74	163	80	25	18	12	17	38	34
Imports of duty free wool [4]___	154	109	73	72	40	15	17	19	19
Exports of apparel wool [5]___1,000 lb__	60	617	200	11,224	3,726	4,271	7,664	1,130	385
Total new supply [6]___	320	349	243	176	150	121	(NA)	133	120
Consumed in manufacturing, total [7][8]___	411	387	240	219	151	94	110	122	108
Apparel class [9]___	246	275	164	142	110	75	94	107	95
Carpet class___	165	112	77	76	41	19	16	15	13
Woolen and worsted looms in place [8]___	16,058	12,784	7,257	3,611	3,619	3,422	3,089	(NA)	(NA)

NA Not available.   [1] Preliminary.   [2] Scoured basis.   [3] Weighted season average price received by farmers. 1960, April–March marketing season; thereafter, calendar year.   [4] Imports for consumption. Dutiable imports include all apparel wool and duty-free imports include all carpet wool.   [5] Beginning 1965, includes carpet wool.   [6] Production, imports, and stock of apparel wool Jan. 1.   [7] Scoured wool, plus greasy wool reduced to scoured basis. Wool regarded as suitable for apparel purposes; formerly "Combing and Clothing."   [8] Excludes Alaska and Hawaii.   [9] Includes raw wool consumed on woolen and worsted systems only.

Source: U.S. Dept. of Agriculture, Economics, Statistics, and Cooperatives Service, *Agricultural Statistics*, annual. Exports and imports from U.S. Bureau of the Census.

No. 1434. Men's and Boys' Clothing—Selected Garments Cut: 1960 to 1977

[See *Historical Statistics, Colonial Times to 1970*, series P 242, for suits and separate coats combined]

TYPE OF GARMENTS	1960	1965	1970	1971	1972	1973	1974	1975	1976	1977
Men's suits___mil. units__	21.3	21.9	17.7	16.5	18.7	16.7	16.8	[1]13.7	[1]16.2	[1]16.1
Boys' suits [2]___mil. units__	5.1	6.6	4.7	3.8	3.5	3.0	2.9	[1]2.5	[1]2.5	(NA)
Separate trousers (men's)___mil. units__	100.3	142.3	173.6	183.7	166.6	171.1	156.6	118.9	132.2	125.8
Separate coats___mil. units__	14.2	16.3	16.1	18.5	24.3	25.3	21.1	[3]13.1	[3]13.8	(NA)
Men's and youths'___mil. units__	10.2	12.3	11.8	14.4	21.3	21.3	18.6	11.5	12.9	13.7
Boys'___mil. units__	4.0	4.0	4.3	4.1	3.0	4.0	2.5	1.6	.9	(NA)
Woven shirts, men's [4]___mil. doz__	23.2	28.2	20.8	20.8	22.0	20.1	20.4	17.4	19.5	15.1
Overalls [5]___mil. doz__	7.5	10.6	17.9	19.6	22.9	23.1	22.0	22.7	25.1	(NA)
Men's___mil. doz__	3.0	4.9	11.8	12.9	15.4	16.2	15.1	16.5	18.2	18.7
Boys'___mil. doz__	4.6	5.7	6.1	6.7	7.5	6.9	6.9	6.2	6.9	(NA)
Work shirts (incl. flannels)___mil. doz__	3.8	4.0	4.1	4.1	4.5	4.1	3.4	2.9	3.7	(NA)

NA Not available.   [1] Excludes leisure suits.   [2] Beginning 1970, includes uniform suits and coats.   [3] Excludes leisure coats.   [4] Includes dress and sport.   [5] Includes jean-cut casual slacks.

Source: U.S. Bureau of the Census, *Current Industrial Reports*, series MA–23A and M23B.

No. 1435. Hosiery—Production, by Type: 1960 to 1977

[In millions of dozens of pairs. Excludes Alaska and Hawaii.. Excludes slipper socks]

TYPE	1960	1965	1970	1972	1973	1974	1975	1976	1977
All types___	154.9	198.2	244.1	227.9	227.4	216.4	224.8	253.9	257.4
Women's___	65.0	92.7	125.7	102.7	99.9	88.7	97.7	113.8	110.6
Pantyhose___	(NA)	(NA)	88.4	80.9	75.0	60.0	61.3	70.4	68.7
Stockings___	64.9	92.3	36.3	17.2	15.6	13.2	8.9	7.6	6.6
Knee-highs and anklets (sheer)___	.2	.4	1.0	4.6	9.3	15.5	27.6	35.9	35.3
Infants' and children's [1][2]___	17.8	18.8	20.6	21.7	22.7	22.1	22.0	27.7	28.4
Anklets___	17.1	17.4	15.3	17.3	17.8	17.3	17.3	21.3	21.3
Knee-highs___	.7	1.4	4.2	3.6	4.1	4.2	4.1	5.5	6.1
Girls', boys', and women's [3]___	20.8	35.2	33.6	40.0	41.2	41.4	41.9	46.4	49.0
Foot socks___	(NA)	.9	2.8	4.5	4.1	4.7	4.4	5.7	6.8
Anklets___	19.4	28.9	20.4	21.3	22.2	20.7	20.7	21.3	20.2
Knee-highs___	1.5	5.5	10.4	14.2	15.0	16.1	16.8	19.4	21.9
Men's (sizes 10 and up) [2]___	51.2	51.6	64.2	63.5	63.7	64.2	63.2	66.0	69.3
Anklets___	39.0	43.5	54.0	52.8	52.8	53.8	51.1	51.3	50.5
Mid-calf and knee-highs___	(NA)	8.1	10.0	10.5	10.8	10.3	11.9	14.5	18.6

NA Not available.   [1] Sizes 3–8½.   [2] Beginning 1970, includes types not shown separately.   [3] Sizes 8–11.

Source: National Association of Hosiery Manufacturers, Charlotte, N.C., *Hosiery Statistics*, annual. (Copyright.)

No. 1436. LEATHER—PRODUCTION, BY PRINCIPAL TYPES OF RAW STOCK: 1955 TO 1975

[In thousands. Excludes Alaska and Hawaii]

ITEM	1955	1960	1965	1970	1971	1972	1973	1974	1975
Cattle hides and side kips	25,832	21,969	23,436	20,353	20,477	20,084	17,768	17,084	18,830
Calf and whole kip skins	10,393	6,332	6,263	2,717	1,621	1,603	1,262	(NA)	(NA)
Goat and kid skins	26,109	18,835	14,557	3,979	3,148	3,522	(NA)	(NA)	(NA)
Sheep and lamb skins [1]	26,434	30,478	30,316	23,598	21,385	20,191	14,504	13,069	11,675

NA Not available.   [1] Includes flesh side-leather of split sheepskins (fleshers); excludes grain leather (skivers).
Source: Tanner's Council of America, Inc., New York, N.Y., unpublished data.

No. 1437. SHOES AND SLIPPERS—PRODUCTION, BY CLASS: 1960 TO 1977

[In millions of pairs. Excludes Alaska and Hawaii, except as noted. Excludes rubber and plastic footwear. 1977 preliminary. See *Historical Statistics, Colonial Times to 1970*, series P 260-261, for men's and women's shoes]

CLASS	1960	1965	1970	1971	1972	1973	1974	1975	1976	1977
Footwear, except slippers [1]	[2] 526.6	536.0	466.1	437.6	428.4	398.9	367.6	342.5	357.7	320.7
Shoes, sandals, playshoes	514.1	526.2	451.8	425.9	417.6	386.7	355.3	331.1	345.5	308.0
Men's, youths', boys'	124.7	143.8	143.5	139.8	149.9	140.9	128.0	121.2	128.1	118.6
Women's	279.8	280.0	230.2	207.1	193.2	179.3	167.1	154.1	155.9	140.0
Misses'	40.2	36.5	23.2	25.4	25.2	17.5	15.8	13.1	15.6	12.5
Children's	32.7	33.5	25.9	25.4	23.0	23.8	20.6	18.5	21.0	16.4
Infants' and babies'	36.6	32.5	29.0	28.2	26.3	25.2	23.8	24.2	24.9	20.5
Athletic shoes	7.0	7.0	9.0	8.4	8.7	9.7	9.9	7.9	10.1	10.1
Slippers for housewear	73.5	90.2	96.2	98.1	98.3	91.2	85.5	70.5	64.9	63.7

[1] Includes other footwear, not shown separately.   [2] Includes Hawaii, not distributed by class.
Source: U.S. Bureau of the Census, *Current Industrial Reports*, series M31A.

No. 1438. CHEMICALS AND ALLIED PRODUCTS—VALUE OF SHIPMENTS: 1965 TO 1976

[In millions of dollars. "N.e.c." means not elsewhere classified]

PRODUCT	1965	1970	1971	1972	1973	1974	1975	1976
Alkalies and chlorine	575	666	701	806	876	1,232	1,673	1,866
Industrial gases	495	664	667	659	721	793	906	1,047
Cyclic crudes and intermediates	1,452	2,014	2,078	2,332	2,764	4,141	4,202	5,230
Inorganic pigments	549	683	689	756	893	1,196	964	1,266
Industrial organic chemicals, n.e.c. [1]	5,023	6,470	6,815	7,466	8,548	12,743	14,098	16,794
Miscellaneous cyclic chemical products	233	371	393	465	559	801	936	1,242
Miscellaneous cyclic chemicals, except urea	3,773	4,526	4,697	5,435	6,023	9,027	9,964	11,735
Synthetic organic chemicals, n.e.c., exc. bulk	514	719	786	723	880	1,234	1,166	1,528
Industrial inorganic chemicals, n.e.c.	3,339	4,109	3,882	[2] 3,003	[2] 3,514	[2] 4,609	[2] 4,675	[2] 5,751
Potassium and sodium compounds	547	543	525	503	583	900	910	1,074
Plastics materials and resins	3,471	4,502	4,820	4,486	5,678	8,444	7,747	10,455
Synthetic rubber (vulcanizable elastomers)	959	1,114	1,153	1,289	1,397	1,862	1,820	2,204
Cellulosic manmade fibers	741	665	680	685	744	898	781	814
Organic fibers, noncellulosic	1,833	2,468	2,821	2,949	3,954	3,867	4,035	4,414
Polyamide fibers, nylon, exc. nontextile monofilaments	1,079	1,097	1,173	1,252	1,527	1,567	1,469	1,614
Biological products	172	351	415	495	559	684	788	874
Medicinals and botanicals	464	747	761	794	986	1,467	1,489	1,774
Pharmaceutical preparations	3,621	5,264	5,611	6,295	6,841	7,463	8,247	9,217
Soap and detergents	1,956	2,509	2,522	2,852	3,033	3,500	3,963	4,490
Polishes and sanitation goods	890	1,306	1,355	1,736	1,844	1,980	2,196	2,431
Specialty cleaning and sanitation products	448	755	802	899	937	1,071	1,197	1,316
Toilet preparations [1]	2,286	3,770	3,920	4,247	4,573	4,797	5,178	5,882
Hair preparations (incl. shampoos)	706	1,034	1,094	1,065	1,100	1,129	1,306	1,408
Perfumes, toilet water, colognes	264	536	571	677	716	755	918	1,007
Dentifrices, mouthwashes, gargles, etc	259	468	462	485	(S)	535	536	627
Paints and allied products	2,566	3,019	3,141	3,520	3,914	4,578	4,672	5,415
Fertilizers	1,434	1,394	1,423	[2] 2,642	[2] 3,033	[2] 5,203	[2] 6,588	[2] 6,026
Agricultural chemicals, n.e.c.	582	908	935	1,196	1,327	1,843	2,298	2,559
Adhesives and sealants	446	580	631	[3] 954	[3] 1,152	[3] 1,404	[3] 1,464	[3] 1,656
Explosives	200	213	189	238	247	359	450	425
Printing ink	324	389	408	498	528	623	698	764

S Does not meet publication standards.   [1] Includes data for products not shown separately.
[2] Synthetic ammonia, nitric acid, and ammonium compounds included in fertilizers.   [3] Excludes gelatin.
Source: U.S. Bureau of the Census, *Census of Manufactures, 1972*, and *Annual Survey of Manufactures*.

No. 1439. CHEMICALS—PRODUCTION, BY KIND: 1965 TO 1976

[In thousands of short tons, except as indicated. Data for chemicals shown are restricted to a selected group composed for the most part of inorganic chemicals and related products which are sufficiently important economically to justify publication. Includes data for chemicals produced by Tennessee Valley Authority, and by Government-owned privately operated plants. See *Historical Statistics, Colonial Times to 1970*, series P 248, 249, and 251, for sodium hydroxide, ammonia (anhydrous), and sulfuric acid, respectively]

CHEMICAL	1965	1970	1973	1974	1975	1976
Acetylene [1]_____mil. cu. ft__	16,659	14,834	8,278	7,807	6,704	7,111
Aluminum chloride:						
Anhydrous (100% AlCl₃)_____	33	31	37	37	27	35
Liquid and crystal (32° Bé)_____	26	23	(D)	(D)	(D)	(D)
Aluminum sulfate (17% Al₂O₃): [2]_____	1,063	1,191	1,252	1,278	1,163	1,230
Commercial Iron free_____	59	71	230	232	252	174
Ammonia, synthetic anhydrous_____	8,869	13,824	15,093	15,732	16,419	16,716
Ammonium nitrate, original solution (100% NH₄NO₃)_____	4,663	6,456	7,157	7,542	7,088	7,186
Ammonium sulfate, synthetic (technical) [3]____	1,947	1,894	2,054	2,060	2,106	2,010
Argon (refined)_____mil. cu. ft__	1,286	2,742	4,382	4,688	4,457	5,107
Calcium carbide (commercial)_____	1,098	791	290	324	253	244
Calcium phosphate dibasic (100% CaHPO₄)____	263	594	540	611	522	668
Carbon, activated [4]_____	85	80	84	75	74	72
Carbon dioxide (liquid, gas, and solid) [5]_____	1,086	1,135	1,568	1,804	1,850	1,967
Chlorine, gas [6]_____	6,517	9,764	10,402	10,753	9,167	10,378
Chrome, yellow and orange (C.P.)_____	29	32	37	38	26	35
Chrome orange, molybdate (C.P.)_____	9	11	14	15	10	16
Hydrochloric acid (100% HCl)_____	1,370	2,014	2,516	2,451	2,009	2,496
Hydrofluoric acid, anhydrous and aqueous (100% HF)_____	150	240	269	282	213	182
Hydrogen, high purity (99.5–100%) [7]_____bil. cu. ft__	30	} 60	65	82	74	82
Hydrogen, lower purity (less than 99.5%) [7]____bil. cu. ft__	92					
Hydrogen peroxide (100% by weight)_____	53	61	80	94	80	94
Nitric acid (100% HNO₃)_____	4,893	6,679	8,441	8,120	7,527	7,892
Nitrogen, high purity (99.5–100%)_____bil. cu. ft__	72	151	[8] 228	[8] 243	[8] 252	[8] 290
Nitrogen solutions (100% N)_____	1,112	1,721	1,947	2,102	2,068	2,068
Oxygen, high purity (99.5–100% O)_____bil. cu. ft__	182	284	} 392	390	353	383
Oxygen, lower purity (less than 99.5%)____bil. cu. ft__	2,170	1,899				
Phosphoric acid (100% P₂O₅)_____	3,905	5,683	6,848	7,213	7,677	7,955
Phosphorus (white and red)_____	555	597	526	524	450	437
Potassium hydroxide (88–92% KOH)_____	181	175	220	208	236	252
Potassium pyrophosphate (100% K₄P₂O₇)_____	55	40	42	40	41	40
Sodium bichromate and chromate_____	141	154	159	179	125	157
Sodium carbonate: Synthetic (58% Na₂O): [9]						
Total crude bicarbonate equivalent [10]_____	4,926	4,393	3,813	3,507	2,802	2,344
Finished light [11]_____	2,272	1,771	1,768	1,711	1,284	1,016
Finished dense_____	2,399	2,483	1,920	1,643	1,396	1,033
Natural [12]_____	1,494	2,678	3,707	4,048	4,353	5,216
Sodium chlorate (100% NaClO₃)_____	134	198	174	203	173	199
Sodium hydroxide (caustic soda):						
Liquid (100% NaOH)_____	6,842	10,141	9,307	11,189	9,299	9,987
Sodium phosphate:						
Tribasic (100% Na₃PO₄)_____	55	53	54	52	57	60
Meta (100% NaPO₃)_____	81	87	74	80	54	63
Tetra (100% Na₄P₂O₇)_____	107	56	46	46	34	37
Tripoly (100% Na₅P₃O₁₀)_____	923	1,208	961	903	770	724
Sodium silicate (soluble silicate glass, liquid and solid) (anhydrous) [13]_____	588	628	723	770	724	747
Sodium sulfate:						
High purity (more than 99% Na₂SO₄)_____	428	812	754	783	796	766
Glauber's salt (100% Na₂SO₄·10H₂O)_____	} [14] 976	561	551	565	431	466
Lower purity (99% or less Na₂SO₄)_____						
Sulfuric acid gross (100% H₂SO₄) [15]_____mil. sh. tons__	25	30	32	34	32	34
Titanium dioxide (composite and pure) (100% TiO₂)_____	577	655	785	787	603	713

D   Withheld to avoid disclosing figures for individual companies.
[1] Excludes quantities of acetylene produced and consumed by railroad shops, shipyards, and small establishments using portable generators.   [2] Excludes quantities produced and consumed by municipalities.
[3] Excludes byproduct coke-oven production.
[4] Includes data for decolorizing and water purification grades only.
[5] Excludes quantities produced and consumed in plants manufacturing soda ash or urea.
[6] Total production, including quantities liquefied for use, storage, or shipment.
[7] Excludes quantities produced and consumed in manufacture of methanol and ammonia, produced by ammonia dissociation process, or disposed of as waste, e.g., vented, used as fuel, etc. Beginning 1970, excludes amounts of hydrogen produced in petroleum refineries for captive use.   [8] Combined with low purity.
[9] Includes quantities used to manufacture caustic soda, sodium bicarbonate, finished light and dense soda ash.
[10] Ammonia soda and caustic carbonation processes.
[11] Excludes quantities converted to finished dense soda ash.
[12] Collected by or in cooperation with U.S. Bureau of Mines.
[13] Excludes amounts produced and consumed in making meta-, ortho-, and sesquisilicates.
[14] Includes Glauber's salt converted to 100% Na₂SO₄.   [15] Includes sulfuric acid of oleum grades.

Source: U.S. Bureau of the Census, compiled from manufacturers, reports and published in *Current Industrial Reports*, series M28A, M28B, and M28C.

No. 1440. RUBBER—NEW SUPPLY, DISTRIBUTION, AND STOCKS: 1950 TO 1976

[In thousands of long tons. Prior to 1965, excludes Alaska and Hawaii, except for imports and exports, which also include Puerto Rico. Natural rubber refers to dry weights of all types, including liquid latex, guayule, etc. Synthetic comprises SBR (including weight of oil content, beginning 1960), neoprene, butyl, and butadiene-acrylonitrile, all years; beginning 1965, also includes polyisobutylene, chlorosulfonated polyethylene, and polysulfide, silicone, acrylic, stereo, and fluorocarbon rubbers. Reclaimed comprises both natural and synthetic]

ITEM	1950	1955	1960	1965	1970	1971	1972	1973	1974	1975	1976
New supply	1,618	1,946	2,150	2,581	3,042	3,177	3,340	3,547	3,285	2,826	3,272
Domestic production [1]	789	1,296	1,729	2,094	2,398	2,440	2,611	2,768	2,492	2,077	2,436
Synthetic	476	970	1,436	1,813	2,197	2,241	2,417	2,566	2,358	1,958	2,331
Imports [2]	829	649	420	487	644	737	729	779	793	749	836
Natural	802	638	411	445	550	613	618	643	682	658	714
Distribution	1,590	1,961	2,203	2,657	3,001	3,183	3,140	3,584	3,344	2,956	3,157
Domestic consumption	1,562	1,842	1,835	2,326	2,677	2,871	2,851	3,268	3,039	2,706	2,854
Natural	720	635	479	515	559	578	641	701	727	655	661
Reclaimed	304	313	277	270	200	200	188	165	137	118	100
Synthetic	538	895	1,079	1,540	1,918	2,093	2,292	2,402	2,175	1,933	2,093
Exports [3]	28	118	368	331	324	312	289	316	305	250	303
Synthetic	8	94	342	282	299	282	265	295	284	226	281
Stocks, end of year [3]	178	279	359	442	645	643	632	629	644	528	646
Synthetic	53	138	249	312	515	487	496	499	510	400	478

[1] Includes reclaimed.   [2] Reclaimed and synthetic.   [3] Natural and reclaimed.
Source: U.S. Bureau of the Census, *Current Industrial Reports*, series MA–30A.

No. 1441. PETROLEUM AND COAL PRODUCTS—VALUE OF SHIPMENTS AND INVENTORIES: 1963 TO 1976

[In millions of dollars. See also table 1323]

ITEM AND PRODUCT	1963	1967	1970	1971	1972	1973	1974	1975	1976
Shipments, total	16,916	20,821	23,676	25,260	[1] 27,349	[1] 33,367	[1] 55,959	[1] 66,459	[1] 78,844
Petroleum refining	15,984	19,692	22,260	23,541	[1] 25,415	31,190	[1] 53,230	[1] 63,540	[1] 75,564
Gasoline	7,978	9,844	11,704	12,308	13,030	15,729	24,946	31,502	36,840
Jet fuel	633	1,100	1,221	1,302	1,372	1,638	2,935	3,702	4,229
Kerosene	375	431	390	401	372	450	706	701	698
Distillate fuel oil	2,896	3,306	3,835	4,014	4,408	5,476	9,761	11,298	13,554
Residual fuel oil	622	566	663	907	1,107	1,660	3,643	4,626	5,243
Liquefied refinery gases	703	1,136	1,300	1,252	1,153	1,430	3,026	2,910	3,604
Lubricating oils and greases	[1] 1,210	[1] 1,327	881	899	[1] 1,537	[1] 1,779	[1] 2,507	[1] 2,502	[1] 2,855
Unfinished oils and lubricating oils base stock	526	613	637	635	734	891	1,420	1,612	2,195
Asphalt	361	424	541	651	672	808	1,489	1,541	1,564
Other finished petroleum prod	681	945	1,089	1,173	1,031	1,323	2,767	3,056	4,652
Paving and roofing materials	862	1,049	1,298	1,573	1,795	2,020	2,525	2,665	2,929
Paving mixtures and blocks	403	530	672	748	893	962	1,167	1,203	1,229
Asphalt felts and coatings	460	519	626	826	902	1,058	1,358	1,463	1,700
Products, not elsewhere classified	69	80	118	146	139	157	204	253	351
Inventories, total [2]	1,818	2,030	2,291	2,408	2,224	2,572	4,101	4,751	5,213
Petroleum refining	1,696	1,904	2,131	2,229	2,083	2,449	3,914	4,545	4,802
Other petroleum and coal prod [3]	122	126	160	179	141	123	187	206	411

[1] Includes lubricating oils and greases from purchased materials.   [2] Inventories as of end of reporting year.
[3] Includes paving and roofing materials and other petroleum products, not elsewhere classified.
Source: U.S. Bureau of the Census, *Census of Manufactures, 1963*, vol. I; *1967*, vols. I and II; *1972*, vols. I and II; and *Annual Surve_ of Manufactures*.

No. 1442. PHARMACEUTICAL PREPARATIONS—VALUE OF SHIPMENTS: 1962 TO 1976

[In millions of dollars. Excludes biologicals]

PRODUCT	1962	1965	1970	1971	1972	1973	1974	1975	1976
Total shipments [1]	2,796	3,583	5,280	5,707	6,066	6,463	7,090	7,899	8,733
Drugs acting on—									
Central nervous system and sense organs	698	960	1,442	1,532	1,636	1,700	1,795	2,036	2,192
Cardiovascular systems	127	175	305	356	400	461	542	634	733
Respiratory systems	278	329	489	500	561	611	646	749	858
Digestive or genitourinary system	392	491	688	706	746	755	867	945	1,052
Skin	136	209	299	354	344	375	432	457	529
Drugs affecting—									
Neoplasms and endocrine system [2]	254	351	523	577	615	650	743	819	862
Parasitic and infective diseases	483	621	859	934	948	1,033	1,116	1,164	1,255
Vitamin, nutrient, and hematinic drugs	310	326	492	555	587	626	697	828	885
Preparations for veterinary use	101	120	182	193	227	250	250	268	365

[1] Includes products not shown separately.   [2] Includes metabolic diseases.
Source: U.S. Bureau of the Census, *Current Industrial Reports*, series MA–28G.

No. 1443. IRON AND STEEL INDUSTRY—SUMMARY: 1950 TO 1977

[Reporting companies in 1977 represented 89 percent of raw steel production of entire industry]

ITEM	1950	1955	1960	1965	1970	1973	1974	1975	1976	1977
Steel mill products, apparent supply_____mil. sh. tons__	70.6	81.6	71.5	100.6	97.1	122.5	119.6	89.0	101.1	108.4
Net shipments____mil. sh. tons__	72.2	84.7	71.1	92.7	90.8	111.4	109.5	80.0	89.4	91.1
Exports_____mil. sh. tons__	2.6	4.1	3.0	2.5	7.1	4.1	5.8	3.0	42.7	2.0
Imports_____mil. sh. tons__	1.0	1.0	3.4	10.4	13.4	15.2	16.0	12.0	14.3	19.3
Percent of total supply_____	1.4	1.2	4.7	10.3	13.8	12.4	13.4	13.5	14.1	17.8
Scrap consumed_____mil. sh. tons__	53.7	63.9	52.1	69.8	69.3	82.5	81.1	62.8	68.4	69.0
Scrap produced_____mil. sh. tons__	31.0	37.4	33.3	46.7	46.4	50.4	47.4	40.1	43.5	42.4
Scrap inventory_____mil. sh. tons__	3.8	5.7	7.7	6.0	6.5	6.0	6.9	7.6	8.6	8.0
All iron and steel products:										
Exports_____mil. sh. tons__	3.1	4.6	4.1	3.1	8.1	5.1	7.1	4.1	3.9	3.2
Imports_____mil. sh. tons__	2.0	1.5	4.1	12.0	14.6	17.0	18.0	13.9	16.3	21.7
Revenues_____bil. dol__	9.5	14.0	14.2	18.0	19.3	28.9	38.2	33.7	36.5	39.8
Net income_____bil. dol__	.8	1.1	.8	1.1	.5	1.3	2.5	1.6	1.3	(Z)
Stockholders' equity [1]____bil. dol__	5.5	7.9	10.5	12.0	13.0	14.5	14.5	16.2	17.2	18.0
Total assets_____bil. dol__	8.3	12.1	15.9	18.8	23.6	26.1	29.5	30.4	33.6	35.4
Net fixed assets_____bil. dol__	3.7	5.6	8.8	10.0	14.1	14.5	15.0	16.9	18.7	19.7
Capital expenditures_____bil. dol__	.5	.7	1.5	1.8	1.7	1.4	2.1	3.2	3.3	2.9
Working capital ratio_____	2.2	2.5	2.6	2.4	1.9	1.9	1.8	2.0	1.9	1.8
Inventories_____bil. dol__	1.4	2.1	3.0	3.2	1.1	3.7	4.4	5.4	6.4	6.0
Average employment_____1,000__	592	625	572	584	531	509	512	457	454	452
Man-hours worked_____mil__	1,214	1,285	1,087	1,421	1,220	1,320	1,313	855	877	876
Index of output per man-hour [2]____	(NA)	(NA)	82.3	101.1	101.1	123.8	123.4	108.6	116.5	[3]118.2

NA Not available. Z Less than $50 million.
[1] Prior to 1974, as of December 31; thereafter, as of January 1. [2] 1967—100. [3] Preliminary.
Source: American Iron and Steel Institute, Washington, D.C., *Annual Statistical Report*. (Copyright.)

No. 1444. WORLD STEEL TRADE—SELECTED DATA: 1960 TO 1976

[In millions of net tons, raw steel equivalent. A net ton equals 1.10 metric tons]

ITEM	1960	1965	1969	1970	1971	1972	1973	1974	1975	1976
Raw steel production, total_____	381.6	503.1	632.0	654.2	639.9	694.5	768.8	782.8	712.0	753.1
United States_____	99.3	131.5	141.3	131.5	120.4	133.2	150.8	145.7	116.6	128.0
Apparent consumption _____	71.5	100.6	102.7	97.1	102.5	106.6	122.5	119.6	89.0	101.2
Net shipments_____	71.1	92.7	93.9	90.8	87.0	91.8	111.4	109.5	80.0	89.6
Imports_____	3.4	10.4	14.0	13.4	18.3	17.7	15.2	16.0	12.0	14.3
From Japan_____	.6	4.4	6.3	5.9	6.9	6.4	5.6	6.2	5.8	8.0
From EEC(9) [1]_____	2.1	4.9	6.1	5.4	8.5	7.8	6.5	6.4	4.1	3.2
From all others_____	.7	1.1	1.7	2.0	2.9	2.7	3.0	3.4	2.0	3.1
Exports_____	3.0	2.5	5.2	7.1	2.8	2.9	4.1	5.8	3.0	2.7
Japan_____	24.4	45.4	90.5	102.9	97.6	106.8	131.5	129.1	112.8	118.4
Apparent consumption _____	21.2	31.3	67.4	76.8	63.4	75.6	94.8	81.8	71.0	66.0
Exports_____	3.5	14.0	23.1	26.0	34.1	31.1	36.8	47.3	41.7	52.4
EEC(9) [1]_____	107.9	125.5	148.5	151.7	141.3	153.4	165.5	171.5	138.1	148.1
Red Bloc_____	115.9	146.0	182.1	192.9	204.9	215.8	227.3	237.3	244.7	253.5
Rest of free world_____	34.1	54.7	69.6	76.2	75.7	85.3	93.7	99.2	99.8	105.1

[1] European Economic Community, comprising nine countries; see text, p. 895.
Source: Putnam, Hayes & Bartlett, Inc., Newton, Mass., *Economics of International Steel Trade*, May 1977.

No. 1445. IRON AND STEEL—WHOLESALE PRICE INDEXES: 1960 TO 1977

[1967=100. 1960 excludes Alaska and Hawaii:

YEAR	Iron and steel, total	STEEL MILL PRODUCTS			Pig iron and ferro-alloys	Iron ore	Scrap, iron and steel	Foundry and forge shop products
		Total	Finished	Semi-finished				
1960_____	97.1	96.4	96.3	97.1	120.4	108.0	110.2	92.0
1965_____	97.9	97.5	97.5	98.3	100.3	100.7	112.6	94.6
1970_____	115.1	114.2	114.2	112.2	114.8	100.1	138.8	112.1
1971_____	121.8	122.9	122.9	122.8	126.3	103.0	114.5	119.6
1972_____	128.4	130.4	130.4	130.9	125.4	103.0	121.8	124.3
1973_____	136.2	134.1	134.1	133.9	129.4	106.7	188.0	131.5
1974_____	178.6	170.0	170.0	169.0	188.1	123.3	353.2	161.4
1975_____	200.9	197.2	196.6	206.7	264.7	154.3	245.6	194.3
1976_____	215.9	209.8	209.0	223.1	261.6	171.0	259.0	218.6
1977_____	230.4	229.9	229.0	243.6	257.1	186.1	231.2	230.5
1978, June_____	252.1	253.6	252.4	272.8	256.7	196.3	258.7	247.4

Source: U.S. Bureau of Labor Statistics, *Wholesale Prices and Price Indexes*, monthly and annual.

No. 1446. Raw Steel Production and Aggregate Exports: 1950 to 1977

[In millions of net tons, except as indicated. See also *Historical Statistics, Colonial Times to 1970*, series P 265-269]

ITEM	1950	1955	1960	1965	1970	1972	1973	1974	1975	1976	1977
World production	207.9	297.5	379.7	503.1	654.2	694.5	768.6	782.8	712.0	745.6	[1] 742.5
U.S. production	96.8	117.0	99.3	131.5	131.5	133.2	150.8	145.7	116.6	128.0	125.3
Percent of world	46.6	39.4	26.0	26.2	20.1	19.2	19.6	18.6	16.4	17.2	[1] 16.9
Index (1967=100)	76.1	92.0	78.0	103.3	103.4	104.7	118.5	114.5	(NA)	(NA)	(NA)
Open hearth [2]	90.8	108.7	87.6	94.8	48.0	34.9	39.8	35.5	22.2	23.5	20.0
Electric	6.0	8.1	8.4	13.8	20.2	23.7	27.8	28.7	22.7	24.6	27.9
Basic oxygen process	–	.3	3.3	22.9	63.3	74.6	83.3	81.6	71.8	79.9	77.4
Carbon	88.3	106.4	90.9	116.7	117.4	117.7	132.7	126.6	100.4	112.0	108.1
Alloy and stainless	8.6	10.7	8.4	14.8	14.1	15.5	18.1	19.1	16.3	16.0	17.2
Exports: [3] Tonnage	3.2	9.7	11.5	8.9	15.4	11.0	16.5	14.8	12.9	11.0	8.9
Value mil. dol	465	979	1,187	1,202	1,968	2,642	2,618	4,353	4,348	3,766	3,466

– Represents zero. NA Not available. [1] Preliminary. [2] Includes bessemer. [3] Source: U.S. Bureau of the Census, *Foreign Commerce and Navigation of the United States; U.S. Exports, Schedule B Commodity and Countr_, FT410, monthly; Quarterl_ Summar_ of Foreign Commerce of the United States.* Includes exports of Puerto Rico to foreign countries. Includes ferromanganese. Excludes steam and hot water heating boilers and radiators. Includes shipments under foreign aid programs and civilian supply shipments. Beginning 1955, quantity figures exclude, but value figures include, data for wire cloth and other items for which quantities were not reported.

No. 1447. Steel Products—Net Shipments, by Market Classes: 1960 to 1977

[In thousands of short tons. Comprises carbon, alloy, and stainless steel. "N.e.c." means not elsewhere classified]

MARKET CLASS	1960	1965	1970	1972	1973	1974	1975	1976	1977
Total [1]	71,149	92,666	90,798	91,805	111,430	109,472	79,957	89,447	91,147
Steel for converting and processing	2,928	3,932	3,443	4,199	4,714	4,486	3,255	4,036	3,679
Independent forgers, n.e.c	841	1,250	1,048	1,007	1,213	1,339	1,098	952	998
Industrial fasteners [2]	1,071	1,234	1,005	1,030	1,278	1,331	675	912	848
Steel service centers, distributors	11,125	14,813	16,025	16,797	20,383	20,400	12,700	14,615	15,346
Construction, incl. maintenance	9,664	11,836	8,913	8,589	10,731	11,360	8,119	7,508	7,553
Contractors' products	3,602	5,018	4,440	5,055	6,459	6,249	3,927	4,502	4,500
Automotive	14,610	20,123	14,475	18,217	23,217	18,928	15,214	21,351	21,490
Rail transportation	2,525	3,805	3,098	2,730	3,228	3,417	3,152	3,056	3,238
Freight cars, passenger cars, locomotives	1,763	2,875	2,005	1,511	1,997	2,097	1,794	1,428	1,709
Rails and all other [3]	762	930	1,093	1,219	1,231	1,320	1,358	1,628	1,529
Shipbuilding and marine equip	622	1,051	859	872	1,019	1,339	1,413	969	869
Aircraft and aerospace	78	94	56	63	69	79	69	59	63
Oil and gas industries	1,759	1,936	3,550	2,789	3,405	4,210	4,171	2,653	3,650
Mining, quarrying, and lumbering	288	392	497	502	534	644	596	536	486
Agricultural, incl. machinery	1,003	1,483	1,126	1,439	1,772	1,859	1,429	1,784	1,648
Machinery, industrial equip., tools	3,958	5,873	5,169	5,396	6,351	6,440	5,173	5,180	5,566
Electrical equipment	2,078	2,985	2,694	2,824	3,348	3,242	2,173	2,671	2,639
Appliances, utensils, and cutlery	1,760	2,179	2,160	2,362	2,747	2,412	1,653	1,950	2,129
Other domestic commercial equip	1,959	2,179	1,778	1,816	1,990	1,941	1,390	1,813	1,846
Containers, packaging, shipping	6,429	7,331	7,775	6,616	7,811	8,218	6,053	6,914	6,714
Cans and closures	4,976	5,867	6,239	5,128	6,070	6,349	4,859	5,290	5,173
Ordnance and other military	165	289	1,222	899	918	654	405	219	193
Exports (reporting companies only)	2,563	2,078	5,985	2,555	3,138	3,961	1,755	1,839	1,076

[1] Total includes nonclassified shipments, and, beginning 1970, data include estimates for a relatively small number of companies which report raw steel production but not shipments. [2] Bolts, nuts, rivets, and screws. [3] Includes railways, rapid transit systems, railroad rails, trackwork, and equipment.

Source of tables 1446 and 1447: Except as noted, American Iron and Steel Institute, Washington, D.C., *Annual Statistical Report.* (Copyright.)

No. 1448. Aluminum and Magnesium Mill Products—Net Shipments: 1960 to 1977

[In millions of pounds. 1960 excludes Alaska and Hawaii. Producers' net shipments consist of total shipments less shipments to other metal mills for further fabrication into other forms of mill products]

PRODUCT	1960	1965	1970	1972	1973	1974	1975	1976	1977 [1]
Aluminum mill products	3,049	5,692	7,358	9,246	10,900	10,461	7,427	9,716	10,420
Plate, sheet, and foil	1,637	3,019	4,247	5,441	6,516	6,374	4,664	6,356	6,846
Rolled structural shapes, rod, bar, and wire	392	800	963	1,113	1,349	1,387	924	985	935
Extruded shapes and tubing	937	1,719	1,823	2,343	2,636	2,384	1,643	2,141	2,396
Powder, flake and paste	33	59	205	226	257	177	99	132	121
Forgings and impacts	50	95	120	123	142	138	97	100	121
Magnesium mill products	21	32	31	31	32	29	22	(NA)	(NA)

NA Not available. [1] Preliminary.
Source: U.S. Bureau of the Census, *Current Industrial Reports*, series M33-2 and MA33G.

No. 1449. Ferrous Castings—Shipments: 1960 to 1976

[In thousands of short tons. 1960 excludes Alaska and Hawaii. Gray iron castings are based on a sample of foundries; all other data on a complete count]

ITEM	1960	1965	1970	1971	1972	1973	1974	1975	1976
Gray iron castings [1][2]	11,594	15,713	13,945	13,839	15,302	17,047	15,661	12,407	14,168
Pressure pipe and fittings	1,336	1,876	1,691	1,749	1,996	2,105	1,957	1,253	1,332
Soil pipe and fittings	782	958	953	1,006	1,044	956	771	595	657
All other gray iron castings	9,476	12,879	11,301	11,085	12,262	13,986	12,933	10,559	12,179
Malleable iron castings	821	1,136	852	882	961	1,031	912	729	848
For sale	467	648	521	506	579	616	553	431	491
For own use	354	488	331	376	382	415	359	298	357
Standard malleable	632	827	628	635	682	734	669	509	569
Pearlitic malleable	189	309	224	247	279	297	243	220	279
Steel castings [1]	1,392	1,961	1,724	1,579	1,584	1,894	2,091	1,974	1,804
Carbon	1,016	1,378	1,147	1,068	1,066	1,277	1,394	1,336	1,188
Alloy	376	583	577	511	518	617	697	638	616

[1] Includes shipments "for own use."　　[2] Includes ductile (nodular) iron castings.
Source: U.S. Bureau of the Census. Monthly data in *Current Industrial Reports*, series M33A.

No. 1450. Nonferrous Castings—Shipments: 1960 to 1977

[In millions of pounds. Shipments include "for own use." Data based on sample and subject to sampling variation; see text, p. 803:

ITEM	1960	1965	1970	1972	1973	1974	1975	1976	1977 [1]
Shipments, all types	2,201	3,437	3,033	3,506	3,800	3,211	2,534	3,157	3,331
Copper and copper-base alloy	760	889	751	763	780	671	519	549	579
Aluminum and aluminum-base alloy	775	1,409	1,506	1,856	2,026	1,759	1,375	1,845	2,011
Zinc and zinc-base alloy	623	1,065	695	799	908	693	572	691	661
Magnesium and magnesium-base alloy	24	32	34	43	45	49	32	39	49
Lead and lead-base alloy die [1]	21	42	45	46	41	39	36	32	31

[1] Preliminary.　　[2] Excludes lead die casting for battery plates and parts.
Source: U.S. Bureau of the Census, *Current Industrial Reports*, series M33E.

No. 1451. Copper-Base Mill and Foundry Products—Shipments: 1960 to 1976

[In millions of pounds, metal weight. Excludes Alaska and Hawaii]

PRODUCT	1960	1965	1970	1971	1972	1973	1974	1975	1976 [1]
Total	4,298	6,288	5,640	5,822	6,477	7,195	6,196	4,639	5,512
Brass mill products	1,878	2,974	2,513	2,711	3,015	3,319	2,813	2,025	2,517
Alloyed [2]	1,128	1,711	1,542	1,632	1,895	2,060	1,816	1,324	1,643
Unalloyed	750	1,263	971	1,079	1,120	1,259	997	701	873
Copper wire mill products [3]	1,521	2,177	2,329	2,354	2,641	3,032	2,647	2,056	2,383
Brass and bronze foundry products	862	1,075	751	705	767	780	667	512	547
Copper-base powder mill products	39	62	47	52	54	64	69	46	65

[1] Preliminary.　　[2] Excludes webbing scrap (military ammunition cups and discs).　　[3] Copper content.
Source: U.S. Bureau of the Census and U.S. Bureau of Domestic Commerce, *Current Industrial Reports*, series DIB-917, annual.

No. 1452. Air-Conditioning and Refrigeration—Shipments: 1965 to 1976

[See *Historical Statistics, Colonial Times to 1970*, series P 280, for room air-conditioners]

PRODUCT	NUMBER (1,000)					VALUE (mil. dol.)				
	1965	1970	1974	1975	1976	1965	1970	1974	1975	1976
Condensing units [1]	599	485	475	335	417	69	72	109	92	113
Air-cooled	563	461	417	321	403	55	56	90	75	90
Compressors and comp. units [1]	8,526	14,653	19,140	15,034	19,518	333	628	1,007	840	1,247
Centrifugal-refrig. systems	3	4	4	5	3	63	106	125	161	116
Heat-transfer equipment	(NA)	(NA)	(NA)	657	684	217	360	476	254	289
Room air-conditioners	2,868	5,365	4,495	2,648	2,743	383	776	673	464	527
Unitary air-conditioners	837	1,459	2,393	1,561	2,248	425	755	1,246	923	1,258
Ice-making machines	87	103	142	128	158	43	58	93	88	111

NA Not available.　　[1] Excludes units for ammonia refrigerants.
Source: U.S. Bureau of the Census, *Current Industrial Reports*, series MA-35M.

No. 1453. MACHINERY (EXCEPT ELECTRICAL)—VALUE OF SHIPMENTS: 1960 TO 1976

[In millions of dollars. Based on sample; see Appendix III. "N.e.c." means not elsewhere classified]

PRODUCT	1960	1965	1970	1972	1973	1974	1975	1976 [1]
Addressing, dictating, duplicating, and other office machines, n.e.c	247	312	402	467	500	581	547	652
Automatic vending machines	185	240	266	306	309	329	225	306
Ball and roller bearings and components	836	1,224	1,295	1,419	1,696	1,961	2,046	2,195
Blowers and fans	269	386	647	682	905	1,034	1,247	1,400
Commercial laundry, dry-cleaning, and pressing machines [2][3]	120	178	204	185	227	203	184	202
Electronic computing equipment [2]	(NA)	2,964	5,671	6,108	7,085	8,668	8,443	10,134
Calculating and accounting machines [2]			525	694	990	1,207	837	790
Carburetors, pistons, piston rings, valves	(NA)	(NA)	530	794	922	890	898	1,120
Construction machinery, except tractors	1,451	2,444	2,630	3,972	4,739	5,748	6,350	6,681
Mining machinery	338	444	715	730	841	1,148	1,657	1,835
Conveyors and conveying equipment	367	532	814	826	1,004	1,285	1,333	1,385
Elevators and moving stairways [2]	205	261	326	412	447	462	388	396
Farm machinery (except tractors) [4]	1,449	2,060	3,065	2,928	3,724	4,793	5,316	5,907
Food products machinery	462	617	823	867	1,112	1,313	1,411	1,394
Hoists, cranes, and monorails	201	292	487	446	531	603	756	809
Industrial furnaces and ovens	215	309	377	341	450	515	532	585
Indus. trucks, tractors, trailers, stackers [3][5]	389	637	890	1,005	1,231	1,526	1,302	1,340
Internal combustion engines [6]	1,215	1,762	2,762	3,353	4,106	5,095	5,191	6,138
Mechanical power-transmission equipment	711	1,095	1,412	1,568	1,984	2,316	2,516	2,537
Metal-cutting machine tools [2]	747	1,386	1,544	1,259	1,719	2,136	2,406	2,146
Metal forming machine tools	379	569	735	670	877	1,053	1,026	1,051
Presses, including forging	105	214	242	183	259	327	283	268
Office machines and typewriters [2]	456	638	978	1,047	1,139	1,431	1,334	1,563
Oil and gas field mach. and tools [7]	507	685	934	980	1,211	1,714	2,412	2,637
Paper industries machinery [2]	348	424	455	381	458	685	761	773
Printing trades machinery and equipment [2]	350	482	657	737	842	913	940	1,006
Pumps and compressors	1,107	1,614	2,203	2,356	2,917	3,496	4,067	4,593
Refrigeration machinery [8]	1,809	2,956	5,053	6,232	6,917	6,871	6,151	7,563
Scales and balances [2]	66	108	153	182	200	235	268	299
Small cutting tools for machine tools and metal working machinery	401	625	700	738	928	1,129	1,185	1,277
Special dies, tools, jigs, and fixtures	1,751	2,139	2,775	2,714	3,169	3,549	3,068	3,620
Steam engines and turbines	623	623	1,640	2,080	2,285	2,482	2,585	1,803
Textile machinery [2]	494	664	712	738	821	987	861	918
Tractors, except tractor-shovel loaders [2]	1,142	2,028	2,227	2,896	3,568	4,576	5,710	5,561
Woodworking machinery	176	270	341	442	523	684	637	756

NA Not available. [1] Preliminary. [2] Includes parts and attachments. [3] Beginning 1972, excludes coin-operated washers and dryers with less than 10 lb. capacity. [4] Beginning 1972, excludes lawn and garden equipment. [5] Excludes parts and attachments for garden tractors except for 1965, 1972, and 1973. [6] Excludes automotive and aircraft. [7] Includes drilling equipment. [8] Includes non-electric warm-air furnaces.

Source: U.S. Bureau of the Census, Annual Survey of Manufactures, Census of Manufactures, 1972, and Current Industrial Reports.

No. 1454. TRANSPORTATION EQUIPMENT—VALUE OF SHIPMENTS: 1960 TO 1976

[In millions of dollars. "N.e.c." means not elsewhere classified]

TYPE OF EQUIPMENT	1960	1965	1970	1971	1972	1973	1974	1975	1976, prel.
Motor vehicles and car bodies [1]	16,739	26,310	26,811	38,206	41,046	48,009	41,950	43,394	59,753
Passenger cars and chassis	14,009	21,852	19,391	28,554	29,246	33,358	27,154	28,883	39,746
Truck tractors, chassis, trucks	2,573	4,289	5,734	7,519	9,566	12,167	12,846	11,872	16,597
Motor vehicle parts and accessories	2,273	[2]18,875	13,189	16,297	19,417	22,856	22,670	23,023	30,385
Truck trailers, truck and bus bodies	341	1,164	1,548	1,661	1,703	2,052	2,432	1,748	2,262
Aircraft [1]	[3]4,653	5,277	8,722	8,019	7,538	9,486	10,364	10,881	11,723
Complete aircraft, military	[3]2,395	2,657	3,833	3,855	2,803	2,884	3,186	4,017	4,671
Complete aircraft, personal [4]		337	2,835		474	870	811	1,003	1,204
Commercial transport (complete)	1,270	1,275			2,787	3,873	4,207	3,653	3,355
Aircraft engines and parts	2,779	3,871	4,594	3,759	3,070	3,687	4,026	4,488	4,928
Aircraft equipment, n.e.c	3,966	3,883	5,273	4,767	3,437	4,074	4,458	4,842	5,102
Shipbuilding and repairing [1][3]	1,216	1,918	2,594	2,661	3,201	3,888	4,712	5,513	5,833
Self-propelled ships, military [5]	406	742	1,086	1,047	1,100	1,333	1,714	1,768	1,957
Self-propelled ships, nonmilitary [5]	351	282	514	578	816	1,202	1,290	1,806	1,825
Boat building and repairing	331	423	644	691	1,031	1,159	1,121	1,290	1,571
Railroad equipment	1,087	2,027	(D)	(D)	2,284	2,512	3,308	3,885	3,336
Motorcycles, bicycles, and parts	123	226	395	443	541	721	880	705	688
Travel trailers and campers	(NA)	(NA)	(NA)	(NA)	1,277	1,134	781	1,083	1,356

D Withheld to avoid disclosure. NA Not available. [1] Includes data for industries not shown separately. [2] Includes combat vehicles. [3] Value of work done. [4] Includes utility. [5] U.S., new.

Source: U.S. Bureau of the Census, Census of Manufactures, 1972, and Annual Survey of Manufactures, 1976, M76(AS)-2.

No. 1455. ELECTRICAL MACHINERY AND PRODUCTS SHIPMENTS: 1960 TO 1976

[In millions of dollars. All figures based on sample and subject to sampling variability. "N.e.c." means not elsewhere classified]

PRODUCT	1960	1965	1970	1972	1973	1974	1975	1976, prel.
Cathode ray picture tubes	213	432	458	634	697	600	514	605
Communications equipment, exc. telephone [1]	597	1,145	1,869	1,555	1,989	(NA)	(NA)	(NA)
Current carrying wiring devices	622	644	983	1,207	1,417	1,524	1,240	1,641
Electric housewares and fans	598	1,002	1,261	1,448	1,704	1,643	1,687	1,979
Electric lamps (bulbs only)	490	643	885	1,069	1,166	1,199	1,225	1,477
Electrical welding apparatus	283	433	470	570	663	897	908	870
Electron tubes, receiving types	307	263	220	190	177	150	130	113
Electron tubes, transmitting types (exc. X-ray)	256	270	336	366	428	415	417	446
Capacitors for electronic application	271	358	413	454	619	686	535	655
Resistors for electronic application	212	370	348	438	557	518	466	618
Electronic coils, transformers, reactors, chokes	215	367	389	385	461	528	489	539
Electronic connectors	(NA)	2,276	3,134	524	658	793	839	838
Electronic components, n.e.c.				3,210	3,725	3,569	3,445	4,262
Electronic navigational aids	361	1,080	1,131	1,074	1,007	(NA)	(NA)	(NA)
Electronic search and detection apparatus [2]	1,301	1,257	2,303	2,264	2,226	(NA)	(NA)	(NA)
Engine electrical equipment	772	1,059	1,437	1,781	2,052	2,049	2,050	2,649
General industry power circuit devices and controls	567	825	1,154	1,246	1,542	1,870	1,874	2,013
Household cooking equipment	469	624	811	1,027	1,201	1,211	1,101	1,514
Household laundry equipment [3]	695	871	1,024	1,290	1,370	1,317	1,255	1,445
Household refrigerators and freezers	805	960	1,220	1,419	1,634	1,750	1,611	1,579
Household vacuum cleaners	[4] 161	221	328	439	501	516	544	654
Lighting fixtures [5]	928	1,359	1,795	2,294	2,534	2,513	2,366	2,741
Residential lighting fixtures	(NA)	(NA)	(NA)	746	800	686	640	782
Commercial lighting fixtures	(NA)	(NA)	(NA)	702	766	873	796	901
Missile-borne and space vehicle-borne equipment	(NA)	880	915	903	945	(NA)	(NA)	(NA)
Motors and generators	1,508	1,936	2,478	2,636	3,137	3,628	3,677	4,129
Noncurrent-carrying wiring devices	360	536	700	834	959	1,252	1,074	1,171
Phonograph records and prerecorded tapes [6]	149	198	402	537	561	569	649	742
Primary batteries, dry and wet	153	221	290	317	346	394	456	606
Radio and TV receiving sets [5]	1,641	2,984	2,966	3,610	4,158	3,892	3,545	4,143
Radios and radio-phono-combinations [7]	415	698	618	775	908	736	676	824
Household TV receivers	775	1,687	1,756	2,149	2,432	2,229	1,924	2,225
Sewing machines, household and industrial	130	114	126	152	182	203	204	258
Solid state semiconductor devices	(S)	839	1,582	2,361	3,178	3,575	3,038	4,079
Storage batteries	405	610	766	953	1,059	1,222	1,291	1,504
Switchgear and switchboard apparatus	899	1,269	1,849	2,059	2,350	2,520	2,509	2,662
Telephone, telegraph apparatus	1,431	1,953	3,575	3,974	4,427	4,883	4,734	5,132
Transformers	725	891	1,378	1,436	1,675	2,001	1,769	1,821
X-ray equipment	88	121	235	383	423	593	740	820

NA Not available.   S Withheld because data did not meet publication standards.   [1] Commercial, industrial, and military.   [2] Includes radar, infrared, and sonar.   [3] Beginning 1972, includes coin-operated washers and dryers with less than 10-lb. capacity.   [4] Includes commercial and industrial vacuum cleaners.   [5] Includes items not shown separately.   [6] Includes record blanks.   [7] Household and auto radios.

Source: U.S. Bureau of the Census, *Annual Survey of Manufactures, Census of Manufactures, 1972,* and *Current Industrial Reports.*

No. 1456. SELECTED FARM MACHINES AND EQUIPMENT—SHIPMENTS: 1960 TO 1976

[In millions of dollars. Excludes tractors and irrigation systems]

PRODUCT	1960	1965	1970	1972	1973	1974	1975	1976
Total	1,001	1,432	1,553	1,981	2,625	3,637	4,179	4,481
Farm machines and equip. (complete units)	798	1,169	1,271	1,616	2,187	3,042	3,485	3,726
Attachments and parts	203	263	282	365	438	595	693	755
Complete units, attachments, and parts:								
Plows	61	96	76	99	131	182	250	267
Harrows, rollers, pulverizers, stalk cutters	86	133	153	189	249	395	476	478
Planting, seeding, and fertilizing mach	98	140	161	197	245	354	480	517
Cultivators, weeders, sprayers, dusters	96	122	115	138	204	302	383	383
Harvesting and haying machinery	464	651	631	834	1,089	1,501	1,735	1,944
Machinery for preparing crops for market or use	38	59	85	111	172	255	262	234
Farm poultry equipment	29	45	73	63	72	76	70	100
Farm dairy machines and equipment	20	31	42	61	67	80	68	77
Hog and other barn equipment	44	67	114	135	182	213	175	220
Farm elevators and blowers	28	37	35	52	69	92	100	88
Farm wagons and other transport equip	37	51	69	104	145	186	179	173

Source: U.S. Bureau of the Census, *Current Industrial Reports,* series MA-35A.

No. 1457. HOME APPLIANCES—SALES AND RETAIL VALUE: 1965 TO 1977

[Compiled from reports of associations and manufacturers. Sales include exports, except that data for consumer electronics cover domestic production only. Except as indicated, covers electric appliances only]

PRODUCT	MANUFACTURERS SALES (1,000 units)						RETAIL VALUE (mil. dol.)					
	1965	1970	1974	1975	1976	1977	1965	1970	1974	1975	1976	1977
Home laundry	6,567	7,075	8,532	7,098	7,666	8,486	1,399	1,482	1,944	2,062	2,402	2,782
Dryers, clothes	2,098	2,981	3,584	2,870	3,174	3,553	367	525	670	717	836	988
Electric	1,388	2,129	2,845	2,198	2,466	2,817	236	360	515	539	639	775
Gas	710	852	739	672	708	736	131	165	155	178	198	213
Washing machines	4,430	4,094	4,948	4,228	4,492	4,933	1,014	957	1,274	1,346	1,566	1,794
Automatic and semi-automatic	3,810	3,869	4,713	4,032	4,288	4,739	934	925	1,235	1,310	1,527	1,754
Other appliances	16,873	19,961	25,955	21,416	23,948	[1]20,816	3,103	3,796	5,381	4,691	5,735	[1]6,739
Dishwashers	1,260	2,116	3,320	2,702	3,140	3,356	276	466	759	697	855	994
Food waste disposers	1,360	1,977	2,553	2,080	2,515	2,941	82	129	194	187	252	324
Freezers	1,160	1,359	3,219	2,457	1,548	1,598	271	302	754	600	422	490
Microwave ovens	(X)	30	635	840	1,661	2,175	(X)	15	217	337	696	982
Ranges, electric	2,065	2,362	2,925	2,082	2,463	3,009	446	540	702	496	665	919
Ranges, gas	2,266	2,362	1,950	1,613	1,825	1,753	435	510	447	382	490	537
Refrigerators, electric	4,930	5,286	5,982	4,582	4,817	5,707	1,282	1,448	1,765	1,425	1,686	2,426
Trash compactors	(X)	(X)	315	233	249	277	(X)	(X)	66	52	57	67
Water heaters, electric	1,095	1,684	2,487	2,195	2,616	(NA)	92	152	241	241	288	(NA)
Water heaters, gas	2,737	2,785	2,569	2,632	3,114	(NA)	219	234	236	274	324	(NA)
Electric housewares	65,693	73,268	80,447	71,708	85,777	[2]82,245	1,379	1,737	2,455	2,302	2,586	[2]2,684
Bed coverings	4,610	4,050	4,410	4,032	4,370	4,490	78	81	97	89	101	112
Blenders	1,800	5,100	4,300	4,000	4,490	5,250	45	128	90	92	99	121
Broilers	1,890	2,605	2,475	2,006	2,156	2,150	43	71	75	66	74	75
Can openers [3]	4,300	5,000	5,435	5,120	5,475	5,550	60	65	87	87	82	87
Coffee makers, auto	6,600	8,100	10,422	9,566	13,693	9,970	104	130	244	245	316	239
Corn poppers	1,105	2,300	3,000	2,430	2,468	3,071	7	23	45	29	35	43
Floor polishers	1,181	1,156	640	530	566	530	47	46	31	27	21	21
Frypan skillets	2,650	3,200	3,547	2,611	2,613	2,500	56	93	117	89	94	87
Griddles, automatic	390	500	725	640	715	(NA)	8	13	22	18	21	(NA)
Hair dryers (all types)	4,325	4,100	6,200	6,852	12,555	11,400	78	98	118	145	277	267
Heating pads	3,000	3,900	4,225	3,500	3,780	3,800	15	23	43	32	34	30
Irons	9,860	9,275	9,700	7,883	8,003	8,736	140	159	220	187	214	236
Steam and steam spray	7,950	7,985	8,750	7,086	7,311	8,150	123	144	210	177	205	228
Mixers, food	3,925	4,675	4,970	4,477	5,105	5,095	59	90	114	106	129	123
Stand	950	875	1,080	900	1,305	1,250	29	33	48	41	64	65
Portable	2,975	3,800	3,890	3,577	3,800	3,845	30	57	66	64	65	58
Oral hygiene devices [4]	3,300	2,850	1,935	1,602	824	840	45	46	28	23	12	13
Slicing knives	5,900	2,075	2,075	1,577	1,700	1,700	97	42	44	30	29	24
Toasters, automatic	4,750	5,975	7,177	6,204	7,397	7,400	74	108	144	138	177	190
Vacuum cleaners	5,107	7,382	8,251	7,650	8,767	8,705	398	502	922	879	852	997
Waffle, sandwich grills	1,000	1,025	960	1,028	1,100	1,058	22	19	15	20	19	19
Air treatment	13,216	20,195	20,062	16,332	17,452	18,696	935	1,679	1,426	1,099	1,228	1,463
Air-conditioners, room	2,945	5,887	4,564	2,683	2,962	3,270	624	1,207	931	644	741	912
Dehumidifiers	210	598	586	392	440	314	16	47	53	37	52	47
Fans	7,703	9,875	10,187	9,236	10,056	10,515	236	283	263	246	259	285
Heaters	1,808	2,835	3,625	2,990	2,748	3,133	29	70	94	90	69	87
Humidifiers	550	1,000	1,100	1,031	1,246	1,464	30	72	85	82	106	132
Consumer electronics	34,800	30,063	63,717	50,277	[5]48,407	[5]61,196	[6]3,916	[5]3,660	[5]6,079	[5]4,572	[5]5,886	[5]7,096
Phonographs, production	6,245	3,860	4,807	3,164	3,855	4,625	796	505	590	400	564	839
Table and portable	4,436	2,856	3,942	2,641	3,201	3,900	271	174	355	251	349	585
Console and comb.[7]	1,809	1,004	865	523	654	725	525	331	235	149	215	254
Radios, production	14,082	8,261	33,231	25,277	31,656	41,800	302	173	686	593	822	1,168
Table and clock	8,051	3,676	11,938	8,895	10,229	13,800	187	95	281	216	393	552
Portable radios	6,031	4,585	21,292	16,382	21,427	28,000	115	78	405	377	429	616
TV production:												
Black and white	8,382	4,851	6,868	4,418	5,196	5,664	1,336	643	881	584	567	651
Table and portable	6,956	4,463	6,732	4,354	5,134	5,617	974	558	855	571	554	640
Console and comb.[7]	1,426	388	136	64	62	47	362	85	26	13	13	11
Color	2,646	4,632	8,411	6,219	7,700	9,107	1,482	2,339	3,922	2,996	3,933	4,438
Table and portable	316	2,495	5,699	4,187	5,428	6,600	(NA)	973	2,279	1,716	2,415	2,779
Console and comb.[7]	2,330	2,137	2,713	2,032	2,272	2,507	(NA)	1,366	1,642	1,279	1,518	1,659
Tape recorders [7]	3,445	8,459	10,400	11,200	(NA)	(NA)	(NA)	(NA)	(NA)	(NA)	(NA)	(NA)
Power lawn mowers	4,500	5,650	7,645	5,670	6,000	6,085	421	791	1,238	992	(NA)	1,026

NA Not available.   X Not applicable.
[1] Excludes water heaters.   [2] Excludes griddles.   [3] Includes combination can openers/knife sharpeners/ice crushers.   [4] Includes imports; for 1965, toothbrushes only; thereafter, includes water-pulsating units.
[5] Excludes tape recorders.   [6] Excludes tape recorders and color TV.
[7] Includes phonograph and/or radio combinations.

Source: Billboard Publications, Inc., New York, N.Y., *Merchandising*, annual statistical issues.

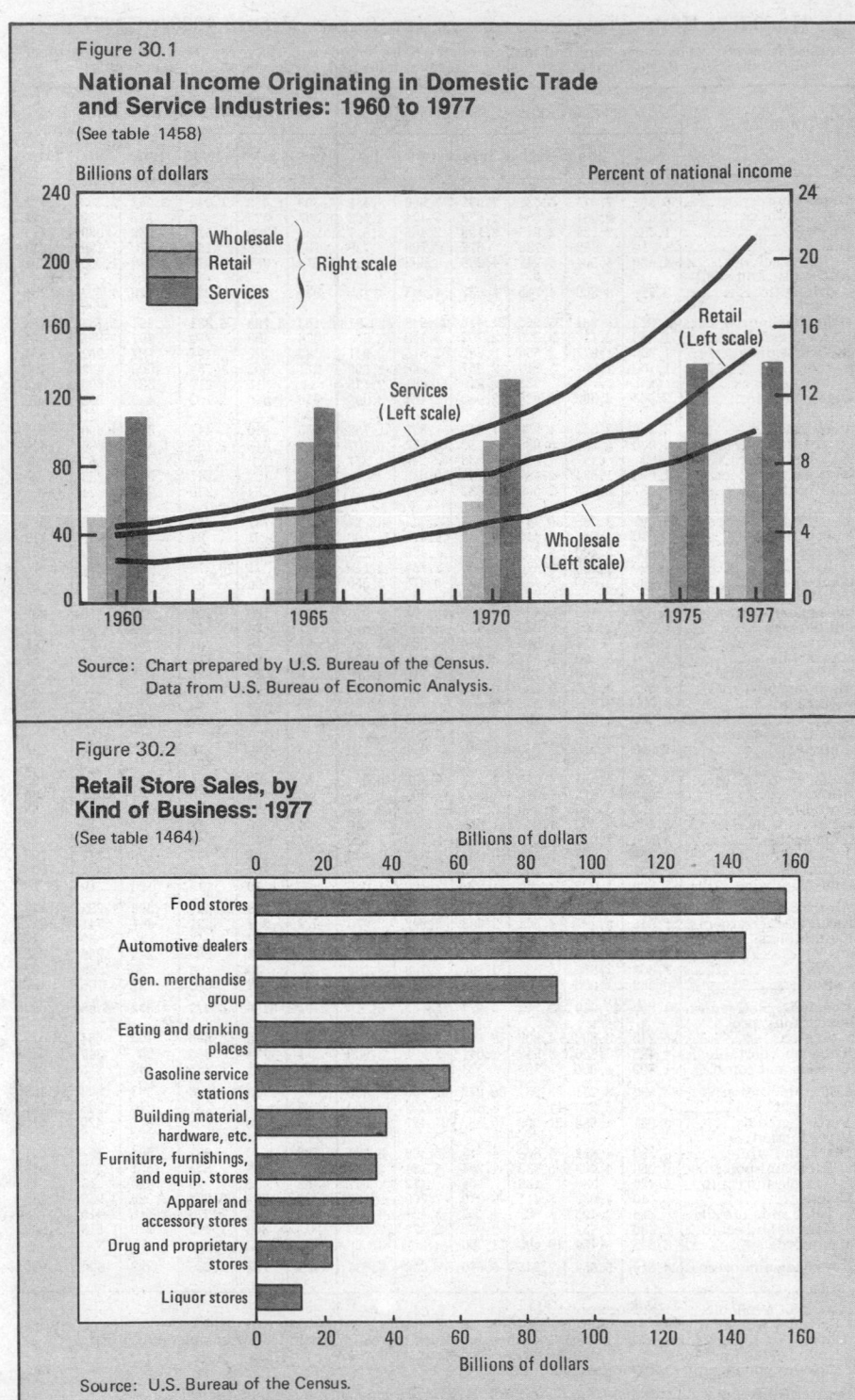

Figure 30.1

National Income Originating in Domestic Trade and Service Industries: 1960 to 1977

(See table 1458)

Billions of dollars   Percent of national income

Legend:
- Wholesale
- Retail
- Services
Right scale

Retail (Left scale)

Services (Left scale)

Wholesale (Left scale)

1960   1965   1970   1975   1977

Source: Chart prepared by U.S. Bureau of the Census.
Data from U.S. Bureau of Economic Analysis.

Figure 30.2

Retail Store Sales, by Kind of Business: 1977

(See table 1464)

Billions of dollars

- Food stores
- Automotive dealers
- Gen. merchandise group
- Eating and drinking places
- Gasoline service stations
- Building material, hardware, etc.
- Furniture, furnishings, and equip. stores
- Apparel and accessory stores
- Drug and proprietary stores
- Liquor stores

Billions of dollars

Source: U.S. Bureau of the Census.

Section 30

Domestic Trade and Services

This section presents statistics relating to retail and wholesale trades and selected service industries. Data shown for the trades, classified by kind of business, and for the various categories of services (e.g. personal, business, repair, hotel) cover sales or receipts, establishments, employees, payrolls, and other items. Also included are data for franchised businesses, public warehousing facilities, and advertising expenditures.

The principal sources of these data are census reports and annual and monthly survey reports of the Bureau of the Census. Data on national income originating in trade and services appear in the monthly *Survey of Current Business*, issued by the Bureau of Economic Analysis. Financial data for firms engaged in retail, wholesale, or service activities appear in the annual *Statistics of Income*, published by the Internal Revenue Service.

Censuses and current surveys.—Censuses of business have been taken at various intervals since 1929. Beginning with the 1967 census, legislation provides for a census to be conducted every 5 years (for years ending in "2" and "7").

Current sample surveys conducted by the Bureau of the Census cover various aspects of the retail and wholesale trades and selected service industries. National estimates of weekly sales in retail stores are shown, by kind of business, in the Bureau's *Weekly Retail Sales Report*. Its *Monthly Retail Trade Report* contains monthly estimates of sales and end-of-month accounts-receivable balances of all retail stores, and of retail organizations operating 11 or more stores, for the United States, by kind of business. In addition, monthly retail sales data for census regions and divisions, 19 large States, and 28 large standard metropolitan statistical areas are included, as well as data on the number of department stores and the monthly sales of these stores in 243 selected areas; these data are subsequently republished in *Monthly Department Store Sales in Selected Areas*. Annual figures on sales, sales-stock ratios, merchandise purchases, and year-end inventories and accounts-receivable balances, by kind of business, appear in the *Annual Retail Trade Report*.

Statistics from the Bureau's monthly wholesale trade survey include national estimates of merchant wholesalers' sales, inventories, and stock-sales ratios by kind of business, as well as sales and inventory trends by kind of business and by geographic divisions. Monthly sales estimates are also shown by geographic divisions for the summary groups—durable and nondurable goods wholesalers and all wholesalers combined. These data, based on reports submitted by a sample of firms, appear in the *Monthly Wholesale Trade Report*. The monthly *Selected Services Receipts Report* provides monthly estimates of receipts for six major kind-of-business groups and seven kind-of-business categories for the United States as a whole; these estimates appear also in the *Survey of Current Business*, cited above.

Estimates obtained from annual and monthly surveys are based on sample data and are not expected to agree exactly with results that would be obtained from a complete census of all establishments. Data include estimates for establishments not reporting.

Establishments and coverage.—The establishments covered in the censuses of business are classified into 3 groups as defined in the *Standard Industrial Classification Manual* (see text, page 396). *Retail trade* refers to places of business primarily engaged in selling merchandise for personal or household consumption; *Wholesale trade*, to establishments primarily engaged in selling goods to dealers and distributors for resale or to purchasers who buy for business and farm uses; and *Selected services*, to establishments engaged primarily in the sale of services as contrasted with the sale of merchandise. Figures for establishments refer to those in business at the end of the year.

The censuses exclude the activities of doctors, dentists, and others performing a professional or scientific service. In 1967 and 1972, however, dental laboratories, law firms, architects, and engineers were covered (see table 314 for legal services, 1972). Also excluded are educational institutions; religious or charitable institutions; hospitals and infirmaries; public utilities; and Government-operated enterprises, except wholesale and retail liquor operations. Most of these last groups will be covered in the 1977 census reports.

Data from the 1958 census exclude retail and service nonemployer establishments which had receipts of less than $2,500 and $1,000, respectively. In the 1963, 1967, and 1972 censuses, nonemployer establishments which did not operate the entire year were included if, during the period they operated, their receipts were at a rate which would have reached the annual totals specified had they operated the entire year. Wholesale trade establishments with no paid employment are excluded.

For the current sample survey programs, retail trade coverage is the same as for the census; wholesale trade coverage is limited to merchant wholesalers; and selected services coverage is less inclusive than the census.

Advertising.—The statistics on advertising expenditures are compiled primarily by private organizations. McCann-Erickson, Inc., which compiles certain of the data shown, defines national advertising as the advertising done for companies whose products are distributed nationally, and for which national media rates are paid; and local advertising as the advertising done for companies which market their products locally and which may pay special "local" media rates. Monthly figures are published regularly in *Advertising Age* and in the *Survey of Current Business*. Total corporate expenditures for advertising, by industry, appear in *Statistics of Income*, cited above.

Statistical reliability.—For a discussion of statistical collection and estimation, sampling procedures, and measures of statistical reliability applicable to Census Bureau data, see Appendix III.

Historical statistics.—Tabular headnotes provide cross-references, where applicable, to *Historical Statistics of the United States, Colonial Times to 1970*. See Appendix I.

No. 1458. NATIONAL INCOME ORIGINATING IN DOMESTIC TRADE AND SERVICE INDUSTRIES: 1950 TO 1977

[In billions of dollars. Prior to 1960, excludes Alaska and Hawaii. Data unadjusted for capital consumption and represent net value added at factor costs. Data based on 1972 Standard Industrial Classification. See *Historical Statistics, Colonial Times to 1970*, series T 1–14, for single-year data prior to minor revisions issued in 1977]

INDUSTRY	1950	1955	1960	1965	1970	1972	1973	1974	1975	1976	1977
Wholesale and retail trade	41.0	52.3	64.7	84.7	122.2	144.6	161.6	175.0	194.2	215.3	237.0
Wholesale trade	14.2	18.9	24.7	31.9	46.9	56.8	65.7	76.6	80.6	89.6	96.5
Retail trade	26.8	33.4	40.1	52.8	75.3	87.8	95.8	98.3	113.7	125.7	140.5
Services	21.7	31.1	44.6	64.1	103.3	122.3	136.8	150.2	168.5	188.9	213.1
Hotels and other lodging places	1.4	1.7	2.0	2.8	4.4	5.3	5.8	6.2	7.0	8.0	8.9
Personal services	3.0	3.7	4.6	5.9	7.4	7.5	7.7	8.1	8.3	9.1	9.8
Miscellaneous business serv	1.8	3.1	5.4	8.9	15.0	17.4	20.3	22.0	23.9	27.6	31.7
Auto repair, serv., and garages	.9	1.2	1.7	2.4	3.6	4.5	5.1	5.4	5.9	6.8	7.9
Miscellaneous repair services	.7	.9	1.1	1.5	2.1	2.5	2.8	3.3	3.5	3.8	4.4
Motion pictures	.9	1.0	.9	1.2	1.6	1.6	1.7	1.7	1.8	2.4	2.9
Amusement and recreation serv	.8	1.1	1.7	2.2	3.3	3.7	4.3	4.6	5.3	5.9	6.6
Medical and other health serv	4.4	7.1	10.6	15.8	29.4	36.5	40.9	46.3	54.1	61.1	69.4
Legal services	1.3	1.9	2.7	4.2	6.7	8.4	9.7	10.7	11.8	12.6	14.2
Educational services	1.0	1.3	2.2	3.7	5.9	7.1	7.8	8.7	10.0	11.0	11.9
Nonprofit membership organiz.[1]	1.9	2.8	4.5	6.4	10.0	12.0	13.1	14.2	16.0	17.5	19.6
Misc. professional services	1.2	2.2	3.4	5.2	8.7	10.6	12.2	13.5	15.0	16.6	18.8
Private households	2.6	3.1	3.8	4.0	5.1	5.3	5.4	5.6	5.8	6.5	7.1

[1] Includes social services.

Source: U.S. Bureau of Economic Analysis, *The National Income and Product Accounts of the United States, 1929–74*, and *Survey of Current Business*, July 1977 and July 1978.

No. 1459. Domestic Trade and Services—Summary: 1948 to 1972

[Prior to 1958 and as noted, excludes Alaska and Hawaii. 1972 not strictly comparable with prior years due to changes in Standard Industrial Classification; for details, see source. See also *Historical Statistics, Colonial Times to 1970*, series T 43-47, T 79-91, T 274-279, and T 391-401]

INDUSTRY AND ITEM	1948	1954	1958	1963	1967	1972
RETAIL TRADE						
Firms, total_____1,000__	(NA)	(NA)	(NA)	1,532	1,577	1,665
Multiunit establishments [1]_____1,000__	163	167	[2] 183	220	220	291
Establishments, total_____1,000__	1,770	1,722	1,795	1,708	1,763	1,913
With payroll_____1,000__	1,119	1,124	1,185	1,206	1,192	1,265
With sales of $1,000,000 or more_____1,000__	(NA)	(NA)	(NA)	(NA)	(NA)	74
Consumer price index, 1967=100, all items_____	72.1	80.5	86.6	91.7	100.0	125.3
Consumer price index, 1967=100, all commodities_____	80.4	85.9	90.6	93.6	100.0	120.9
Sales_____bil. dol__	130.5	170.0	200.4	244.2	310.2	449.1
By establishments with payroll_____bil. dol__	118.4	157.9	187.8	233.1	295.2	440.2
By multiunit establishments [1]_____bil. dol__	38.7	51.2	[2] 67.2	89.5	123.5	201.8
Percent of total sales_____	29.6	30.1	33.5	36.6	39.8	44.0
Percent of multiunit sales by 101-or-more establishment multiunits_____	41.6	41.8	[1] 42.4	43.1	46.7	55.8
In 1967 dollars_____bil. dol__	166.4	197.0	221.3	263.2	313.9	379.1
Percent of sales by corporations_____	46.9	48.4	53.0	61.9	67.4	76.4
Per capita sales: [3]						
Current dollars_____	890	1,043	[1] 1,146	1,290	1,561	2,198
Constant (1967) dollars_____	1,107	1,214	1,265	1,378	1,561	1,818
Sales as percent of personal income_____	62.1	58.6	[1] 55.5	52.5	49.3	48.9
Sales, inside SMSA's [4]_____bil. dol__	80.9	(NA)	[1] 133.0	169.8	221.4	(NA)
Percent of total sales_____	62.0	(NA)	66.4	69.5	71.4	(NA)
Percent of SMSA sales in central cities_____	71.4	(NA)	64.0	57.2	55.0	(NA)
Payroll entire year_____bil. dol__	13.6	18.2	21.7	27.6	36.2	55.4
Percent of sales_____	10.4	11.5	[1] 11.5	11.3	11.7	12.1
Average weekly wage_____dol__	(NA)	50	52	66	74	95
Paid employees, Nov. 15 workweek [5]_____1,000__	6,918	7,124	7,942	8,410	9,381	11,211
Active proprietors of unincorporated businesses_____1,000__	1,742	1,766	1,825	1,546	1,624	(NA)
WHOLESALE TRADE						
Firms, total_____1,000__	(NA)	(NA)	(NA)	232	233	276
Establishments, total_____1,000__	216	250	287	308	311	370
With sales of $1,000,000 or more_____1,000__	21	(NA)	(NA)	62	75	103
Sales, all establishments_____bil. dol__	180.6	234.0	285.7	358.4	459.5	695.2
Merchant wholesalers_____bil. dol__	76.5	100.1	122.1	157.4	206.1	353.9
Inventories, end of year_____bil. dol__	10.0	13.0	15.0	20.1	28.1	45.7
Payroll, entire year_____bil. dol__	7.7	10.9	13.2	18.1	23.9	36.9
Paid employees, Nov. 15 workweek [5]_____1,000__	2,305	2,555	2,808	3,089	3,519	4,026
Active proprietors of unincorporated businesses_____1,000__	131	150	158	133	122	(NA)
SELECTED SERVICE INDUSTRIES						
Firms, total_____1,000__	(NA)	(NA)	(NA)	1,017	1,136	[6] 1,525
Single unit establishments_____1,000__	(NA)	751	928	1,001	1,130	[5] 1,505
Multiunit establishments [1]_____1,000__	(NA)	35	51	61	58	[6] 85
Establishments, total_____1,000__	665	786	979	1,062	1,188	[6] 1,590
With payroll_____1,000__	370	375	444	504	521	684
With receipts of $1,000,000 or more_____1,000__	(NA)	(NA)	(NA)	(NA)	6	13
Receipts, total_____bil. dol__	13.3	23.5	32.5	44.6	60.5	[6] 113.0
For establishments with payroll_____bil. dol__	12.2	21.3	29.1	41.0	55.5	103.2
Average receipts per establishment_____$1,000__	32.9	50.7	65.5	81.3	106.5	151.0
For establishments without payroll_____bil. dol__	1.1	2.2	3.4	3.6	5.0	9.7
Average receipts per establishment_____$1,000__	3.8	5.5	6.3	6.4	7.5	10.7
By multiunit establishments [1]_____bil. dol__	(NA)	5.7	9.2	13.9	22.0	37.8
Percent of total receipts_____	(NA)	24.3	28.3	31.1	36.4	33.5
Payroll entire year_____bil. dol__	4.2	6.5	9.0	12.2	17.5	[6] 33.4
Paid employees, Nov. 15 workweek [5]_____1,000__	2,100	2,362	2,904	3,262	3,841	[6] 5,305
Active proprietors of unincorporated businesses_____1,000__	667	781	996	1,017	1,082	(NA)
PUBLIC WAREHOUSING [7]						
Establishments, total_____	(NA)	7,565	8,447	8,838	9,433	10,026
Revenue_____mil. dol__	(NA)	757	936	1,119	1,625	2,124
Payroll, entire year_____mil. dol__	(NA)	304	358	454	634	823
Payroll, Nov. 15 workweek_____mil. dol__	(NA)	6	7	9	(NA)	(NA)
Paid employees, Nov. 15 workweek [5]_____1,000__	(NA)	94	97	102	115	112

NA Not available.   [1] Establishments operated by firms which operate at two or more locations.   [2] Excludes Alaska and Hawaii.   [3] Based on estimated population as of July 1.   [4] Based on 263 standard metropolitan statistical areas (SMSA's) as of Aug. 15, 1973. For definition of SMSA, see Appendix II.   [5] 1967 and 1972 data for week including March 12.   [6] Includes architectural, engineering, land surveying, legal services, and dental laboratories.   [7] Includes establishments furnishing local trucking and storage services.

Source: U.S. Bureau of the Census, *U.S. Census of Business: 1948*, vols. I, IV, and VI; *1954*, vols. I, III, and V; *1958*, vols. I, III, and V; *1963*, vols. I, IV, and VI; *1967*, vols. I, III, and V, Part 1; and *1972 Census of Retail Trade* (RC 72-S-1), *Wholesale Trade* (WC 72-S-1), and *Selected Service Industries* (SC 72-S-1, SC 72-S-7).

No. 1460. Persons in Domestic Trade and Service Industries: 1950 to 1976

[In thousands. Prior to 1960, excludes Alaska and Hawaii. Data represent man-years of full-time equivalent employment by persons working for wages or salaries and by active partners and proprietors of unincorporated businesses. Based on 1972 Standard Industrial Classification. See *Historical Statistics, Colonial Times to 1970*, series T 15–28, for single year data prior to minor revisions issued in 1977]

INDUSTRY	1950	1955	1960	1965	1970	1972	1973	1974	1975	1976
Wholesale and retail	10,764	11,714	12,429	13,109	14,757	15,333	15,972	16,314	16,226	16,865
Wholesale trade	2,773	3,116	3,370	3,600	4,076	4,200	4,428	4,579	4,482	4,640
Retail trade	7,991	8,598	9,059	9,509	10,681	11,133	11,544	11,735	11,744	12,225
Services	7,893	8,352	9,767	11,248	13,439	14,280	14,862	15,243	15,204	15,888
Hotels and other lodging	605	632	688	829	993	1,009	1,052	1,098	1,108	1,090
Personal services	1,207	1,165	1,221	1,341	1,349	1,251	1,238	1,197	1,163	1,194
Misc. business services	394	540	815	1,155	1,655	1,782	1,954	2,067	2,039	2,143
Auto repair, serv., garages	310	308	385	440	494	554	575	583	596	636
Misc. repair services	248	252	262	292	312	334	344	383	387	390
Motion pictures	224	192	162	159	180	192	207	206	211	213
Amusement, recreat. serv	282	272	308	340	397	455	486	509	507	541
Medical, other health serv	1,217	1,448	1,763	2,101	2,870	3,318	3,558	3,767	3,843	4,121
Legal services	234	248	297	330	385	399	422	448	462	488
Educational services	473	504	621	792	907	954	952	971	996	1,014
Nonprofit member org.[1]	728	876	1,206	1,465	1,750	1,889	1,908	1,961	1,958	2,073
Misc. professional serv	261	367	442	528	735	800	874	926	897	911
Private households	1,710	1,548	1,597	1,476	1,412	1,343	1,292	1,127	1,037	1,074

[1] Includes social services.

Source: U.S. Bureau of Economic Analysis, *The National Income and Product Accounts of the United States, 1929–74; Survey of Current Business*, July 1977; and unpublished data.

No. 1461. Retail Trade—Sales of all Retail Stores: 1960 to 1978

[Beginning 1964, data reflect use of sample based on definition and classifications according to the 1963 Census of Business. 1960 data adjusted for sample revision effective with Oct. 1963 data. 1963 through 1966 data adjusted for sample revision effective with Aug. 1968 data. Beginning 1967, data reflect use of a sample based on definition and classifications according to the 1972 Census of Business; adjusted for sample revision effective with August 1977 data. Quarterly data adjusted for seasonal variation and trading day differences. See also *Historical Statistics, Colonial Times to 1970*, series T 197, 245, 246, and 255]

YEAR	Total current dol. (bil. dol.)	Total 1972 dol. (bil. dol.)	Per capita sales [1] (dol.)	Index of sales (1972= 100)	Durable goods (bil. dol.)	Nondurable goods (bil. dol.)	YEAR AND QUARTER	Total current dol. (bil. dol.)	Total 1972 dol. (bil. dol.)	Per capita sales [1] (dol.)	Index of sales (1972= 100)	Durable goods (bil. dol.)	Nondurable goods (bil. dol.)
1960	219.5	287.3	1,232	49.0	70.6	149.0	1970	371.1	400.0	1,840	82.6	109.9	261.2
1963	246.7	314.4	1,323	55.0	79.9	166.7	1971	410.0	420.4	2,007	91.3	129.9	280.1
1964	261.9	330.3	1,375	58.4	84.6	177.3	1972	449.1	449.1	2,175	100.0	148.4	300.7
1965	284.1	354.4	1,483	63.4	94.2	189.9	1973	502.5	471.3	2,415	111.9	169.1	333.4
1966	304.0	371.1	1,572	67.8	98.3	205.7	1974	534.5	448.1	2,549	119.0	165.8	368.7
1967 [2]	313.8	375.4	1,608	70.0	100.2	213.6	1975	580.4	449.6	2,746	129.2	178.9	401.5
1967 [3]	293.0	(NA)	1,501	65.2	88.7	204.3	1976	642.5	478.6	3,016	143.1	210.5	432.0
1968	325.1	393.7	1,649	72.4	101.9	223.2	1977	708.3	500.4	3,299	157.7	238.8	469.5
1969	348.5	395.7	1,750	77.6	109.1	239.4	1978, 1st qtr.	184.2	126.1	853	41.0	61.3	122.9

NA Not available. [1] Based on Bureau of the Census estimates of civilian resident population as of July 1, except 1976, as of March 1. [2] Old sample. [3] New sample.

Source: U.S. Bureau of the Census, *Monthly Retail Trade Report*. Monthly data in U.S. Bureau of Economic Analysis, *Survey of Current Business* and *Business Conditions Digest*, both monthly.

No. 1462. Department Stores—Sales, Inventories, and Accounts Receivable: 1975 to 1977

[In millions of dollars, except as indicated. Covers stores normally employing 25 or more persons and carrying a general line of apparel, homefurnishings, and housewares, with no one of the 3 categories accounting for as much as 80 percent of total sales]

ITEM	1975	1976	1977	ITEM	1975	1976	1977
Sales, total	57,442	62,900	71,583	Sales-inventory ratio, stores only [2]	(NA)	7.6	(NA)
Per capita [1] dol	272	295	334				
Percent dept. of all retail	9.9	9.8	10.1				
Merchandise inventories (Dec. 31):				Accounts receivable (Dec. 31)	(NA)	(NA)	16,001
Warehouse and stores	8,996	10,061	(NA)	Charge accounts [3]	(NA)	(NA)	1,019
Stores only	(NA)	8,249	(NA)	Installment accounts [4]	(NA)	(NA)	14,982

NA Not available. [1] Based on Bureau of the Census estimates of civilian population as of July 1. [2] Ratio of annual sales to year-end inventories. [3] Receivables for which full payment is scheduled to be made at end of customary billing period. [4] Receivables scheduled to be paid in 2 or more payments.

Source: U.S. Bureau of the Census, *Annual Retail Trade Report*.

No. 1463. RETAIL TRADE—TOTAL AND PER CAPITA SALES, BY GEOGRAPHIC REGION AND DIVISION, AND FOR SELECTED STATES: 1976 AND 1977

[For composition of regions and divisions, see fig. I, inside front cover. Data reflect sample revision effective Aug. 1977; see Appendix III]

GEOGRAPHIC REGIONS AND DIVISIONS	1976		1977		STATE	1976		1977	
	Total sales (bil. dol.)	Per capita sales [1] ($1,000)	Total sales (bil. dol.)	Per capita sales [1] ($1,000)		Total sales (bil. dol.)	Per capita sales [1] ($1,000)	Total sales [1] (bil. dol.)	Per capita sales [1] ($1,000)
Total	642.5	3.0	708.3	3.3	California	68.0	3.2	76.6	3.5
					Florida	26.9	3.2	31.1	3.7
Northeast	139.8	2.8	151.5	3.1	Illinois	35.6	3.2	39.3	3.5
North Central	178.2	3.1	195.6	3.4	Indiana	16.8	3.2	18.2	3.4
South	201.7	3.0	223.8	3.2	Massachusetts	16.8	2.9	18.1	3.1
West	122.8	3.2	137.4	3.5	Michigan	25.2	2.8	29.5	3.2
					Minnesota	11.6	2.9	13.4	3.4
New England	36.2	3.0	39.2	3.2	Missouri	14.7	3.1	16.0	3.4
Mid-Atlantic	103.6	2.8	112.4	3.0					
E. No. Central	123.4	3.0	137.4	3.4	New Jersey	21.8	3.0	24.1	3.3
W. No. Central	54.8	3.3	58.3	3.5	New York	47.2	2.6	50.6	2.8
So. Atlantic	99.6	3.0	110.8	3.3	North Carolina	14.8	2.8	16.2	3.0
E. So. Central	37.4	2.8	41.5	3.0	Ohio	32.1	3.0	35.2	3.3
W. So. Central	64.7	3.1	71.5	3.3	Pennsylvania	34.6	2.9	37.7	3.2
Mountain	30.7	3.2	34.6	3.5	Texas	40.5	3.3	45.1	3.6
Pacific	92.1	3.3	102.8	3.6	Wisconsin	13.7	3.0	15.1	3.3

[1] Based on civilian population estimates as of July 1.

Source: U.S. Bureau of the Census, *Annual Retail Trade Report*.

No. 1464. RETAIL TRADE—SALES, BY KINDS OF BUSINESS: 1967 TO 1978

[In billions of dollars. Based on 1972 Standard Industrial Classification. Data reflect sample revision effective Aug. 1977; see Appendix III. See also *Historical Statistics, Colonial Times to 1970*, series T 245–271]

KIND OF BUSINESS	1967	1970	1971	1972	1973	1974	1975	1976	1977	1978, 1st. qtr.[1]
Retail trade, total	293.0	371.1	410.0	449.1	502.5	534.5	580.4	642.5	708.3	167.9
Durable goods stores, total [2]	88.7	109.9	129.9	148.4	169.1	165.8	178.9	210.5	238.8	55.4
Automotive dealers	53.8	63.1	78.3	88.5	101.6	95.3	105.3	125.7	143.7	34.7
Motor vehicle, misc. automotive dealers	49.7	57.5	71.9	81.1	93.5	86.7	95.9	115.6	131.4	31.9
Auto and home supply stores	4.2	5.6	6.4	7.4	8.1	8.6	9.4	10.1	12.3	2.8
Furniture, home furnishings, equip. stores [2]	14.2	17.8	19.0	22.0	25.0	27.1	28.1	31.4	34.5	7.9
Furniture and home furnishings stores	8.3	10.6	11.6	13.7	15.7	16.8	16.7	18.7	20.8	4.8
Household appliance, radio, and TV stores	5.0	6.1	6.2	6.8	7.6	8.2	8.9	9.8	10.7	2.3
Building materials, hardware, garden supply, and mobile home dealers [2]	13.3	17.6	20.3	23.3	26.3	26.0	26.3	32.2	38.0	7.8
Building materials and supply stores	9.0	11.2	12.9	15.0	17.1	17.7	17.8	22.2	26.7	5.4
Hardware stores	2.8	3.2	3.5	3.9	4.2	4.2	4.9	5.7	6.4	1.3
Nondurable goods stores, total [2]	204.2	261.2	280.1	300.7	333.4	368.7	401.5	432.0	469.5	112.5
Apparel and accessory stores [2]	16.3	20.7	22.8	24.1	27.3	29.2	31.7	33.2	33.5	7.1
Men's, boys' clothing, furnishings stores	3.4	4.6	5.0	5.5	6.1	6.3	6.8	6.7	6.7	1.4
Women's clothing, specialty stores, furriers.	6.4	7.7	8.7	9.2	10.1	10.7	11.8	12.7	12.8	2.8
Shoe stores	2.9	3.9	4.0	4.0	4.9	5.3	5.6	5.6	5.8	1.3
Drug stores and proprietary stores	10.8	13.8	14.3	15.3	16.8	18.2	19.4	20.7	22.4	5.6
Eating and drinking places	23.5	31.5	33.5	36.2	40.3	45.2	51.4	58.0	63.8	15.2
Food stores	69.4	89.8	94.2	99.0	110.3	124.5	138.0	145.9	156.3	39.8
Grocery stores	64.2	82.5	86.7	91.7	102.5	115.8	128.9	136.1	145.9	37.2
Gasoline service stations	22.6	29.3	31.1	33.4	37.7	43.8	47.4	51.3	56.5	13.7
General merchandise group stores [2]	41.0	50.0	55.1	60.9	66.2	69.8	73.8	79.3	89.2	18.2
Department stores	31.1	38.4	42.9	47.3	51.5	54.1	57.4	62.9	71.6	14.6
Variety stores	5.3	6.5	6.4	7.2	7.7	8.0	8.3	7.6	8.0	1.6
Liquor stores	6.6	8.3	9.2	9.7	10.3	11.2	12.2	12.7	13.1	2.9
Mail-order houses (department store mdse.) [3]	2.7	3.5	3.9	4.3	5.0	5.4	5.5	6.1	6.8	1.5

[1] Unadjusted for seasonal variation.   [2] Includes kinds of business not shown separately.
[3] Includes sales made by mail-order catalog desks in department stores of mail-order firms.

Source: U.S. Bureau of the Census, *Monthly Retail Trade Report*.

No. 1465. RETAIL TRADE—SALES OF MULTIUNIT ORGANIZATIONS: 1970 TO 1976

[In billions of dollars. Data based on sales of organizations operating 11 or more retail stores as of the 1967 Census of Business. See also *Historical Statistics, Colonial Times to 1970,* series T 197–219]

KIND OF BUSINESS	1970	1972	1973	1974	1975	1976	PERCENT OF ALL RETAIL SALES				
							1970	1973	1974	1975	1976
Total sales_____	117.2	¹137.7	154.5	169.4	183.1	199.6	31.2	30.7	31.5	31.3	30.6
Durable goods stores ²_____	8.6	9.1	9.6	9.9	10.3	11.6	7.5	5.6	5.9	5.7	5.4
Tire, battery, accessory dealers___	1.8	2.1	2.2	2.2	2.3	2.3	32.8	27.8	26.5	25.3	23.0
Furniture, homefurnishings ³_____	1.5	1.9	2.1	(S)	(S)	(S)	8.5	8.8	(S)	(S)	(S)
Nondurable goods stores ²____	108.6	128.6	144.9	159.5	172.8	188.0	41.6	43.5	43.0	42.8	43.0
Apparel and accessory stores ²____	5.5	6.1	6.6	6.4	6.8	7.0	27.6	27.4	25.7	25.5	24.5
Men's, boys' wear stores_____	.8	.8	.7	(S)	(S)	(S)	17.7	12.5	(S)	(S)	(S)
Women's apparel, accessory stores_____	1.9	2.2	2.4	2.4	2.6	2.6	24.7	26.4	25.0	25.0	23.4
Shoe stores_____	1.5	1.7	1.9	1.7	1.8	1.7	42.1	45.2	42.5	43.9	38.6
Drug and proprietary stores_____	4.4	5.2	5.9	6.5	7.1	8.2	32.5	38.1	38.7	39.2	41.6
Eating and drinking places_____	2.9	2.9	3.2	(S)	(S)	(S)	9.6	8.4	(S)	(S)	(S)
Food stores_____	44.1	49.8	55.9	63.4	69.3	74.4	51.2	52.9	52.9	52.6	52.8
Grocery stores_____	43.2	49.2	55.2	62.6	68.4	73.5	54.1	56.1	56.2	55.7	56.1
General merchandise group ²_____	46.1	58.1	65.6	70.6	75.6	83.0	75.2	78.8	79.1	79.2	79.7
Department stores ⁴_____	31.9	41.1	46.4	49.8	54.2	60.7	85.5	88.7	89.1	89.3	89.3
Variety stores_____	5.4	5.9	6.6	7.0	7.4	6.6	77.8	80.5	80.5	81.3	79.5

S Does not meet statistical standards for publication. ¹ Based on comparable 1967 Standard Industrial Classification definitions, retail sales as reported in 1972 Census of Retail Trade were 4.8 percent higher than earlier estimates from monthly survey of retail trade. ² Includes kinds of business not shown separately. ³ Includes equipment stores. ⁴ Includes sales made by mail-order catalog desks in department stores of mail order firms.

Source: U.S. Bureau of the Census, *Monthly Retail Trade Report.*

No. 1466. RETAIL TRADE—MERCHANDISE INVENTORIES AND SALES-INVENTORY RATIOS: 1975 AND 1976

[As of Dec. 31. Data reflect sample revision effective Aug. 1977; see Appendix III]

KIND OF BUSINESS	INVENTORIES AT COST ¹ (mil. dol.)			SALES-INVENTORY RATIOS ²			MERCHANDISE PURCHASED, RETAIL STORES (mil. dol.)	
	All retail stores and warehouses		Retail stores, 1976	All retail stores and warehouses		Retail stores, 1976	1975	1976
	1975	1976		1975	1976			
Total ³_____	68,931	76,115	69,129	8.4	8.4	9.3	414,967	465,733
Durable goods stores ³_____	31,643	35,895	34,488	5.7	5.9	6.1	132,460	162,389
Furniture, home furnishings, and equipment stores ³_____	5,669	6,070	5,521	5.0	5.2	5.7	18,382	20,451
Furniture, homefurnishings_____	3,135	3,488	3,189	5.3	5.4	5.9	9,661	11,659
Furniture stores_____	2,397	2,661	2,409	4.8	4.7	5.2	6,799	7,845
Household appliances, TV, radio_____	1,890	1,886	1,660	4.7	5.2	5.9	6,412	6,779
Bldg. materials, hardware, garden supply, and mobile home dealers_____	5,128	6,083	5,773	5.1	5.3	5.6	18,909	23,655
Bldg. materials, supply, hardware_____	4,528	5,153	4,866	5.0	5.4	5.7	16,624	20,252
Bldg. materials and supply stores_____	3,194	3,613	3,373	5.6	6.1	6.6	13,129	16,336
Hardware stores_____	1,334	1,540	1,493	3.7	3.7	3.8	3,495	3,916
Automotive dealers ³_____	15,952	18,031	17,661	6.6	7.0	7.1	82,918	104,848
Motor vehicle dealers_____	12,682	14,389	14,213	7.0	7.5	7.6	71,925	92,070
Auto and home supply stores_____	1,867	2,105	1,985	5.0	4.8	5.1	5,927	6,830
Nondurable goods stores ³_____	37,288	40,220	34,641	10.8	10.7	12.5	282,507	303,344
Food stores_____	8,227	8,880	6,963	16.8	16.4	21.0	110,543	115,686
Grocery stores_____	7,893	8,540	6,647	16.3	15.9	20.5	104,543	109,134
Eating and drinking places_____	1,221	1,471	1,371	42.1	39.4	42.3	23,694	27,074
General merchandise group stores_____	12,457	13,660	11,443	5.9	5.8	6.9	50,520	53,574
Dept. stores, misc. general mdse. stores__	10,715	11,954	9,947	6.1	6.0	7.2	44,316	48,402
Department stores_____	8,996	10,061	8,249	6.4	6.3	7.6	38,631	42,080
Variety stores_____	1,742	1,706	1,496	4.8	4.5	5.1	6,204	5,172
Apparel and accessory stores ³_____	6,187	6,693	6,415	5.1	5.0	5.2	18,384	20,433
Men's, boys' clothing, furnishings_____	1,319	1,545	1,509	5.2	4.3	4.4	3,450	4,083
Women's ready-to-wear stores_____	1,792	1,776	1,743	5.4	6.4	6.5	6,750	6,994
Shoe stores_____	1,297	1,351	1,224	4.3	4.1	4.6	3,218	3,385
Gasoline service stations_____	1,868	1,840	1,676	25.4	27.9	30.6	38,277	41,702
Drug and proprietary stores_____	3,275	3,561	3,193	5.9	5.8	6.5	13,578	14,612
Liquor stores_____	1,341	1,351	1,155	9.1	9.4	11.0	8,766	9,699
Mail-order houses (dept. store merchandise)	858	957	909	6.5	6.4	6.7	4,266	4,914

¹ Excludes supplies and equipment used in store and warehouse operations that are not for resale. ² Relates annual sales to yearend inventories. ³ Includes kinds of business not shown separately.

Source: U.S. Bureau of the Census, *Annual Retail Trade Report.*

No. 1467. RETAIL TRADE—ESTABLISHMENTS AND SALES, 1963 TO 1972, AND PAID EMPLOYEES AND PAYROLL, BY STATES: 1972

[Data for 1972 based on 1967 Standard Industrial Classification for comparability with prior years shown]

STATE	ALL ESTABLISHMENTS, NUMBER (1,000)			SALES, ALL ESTABLISHMENTS (bil. dol.)			ESTABLISHMENTS WITH PAYROLL, 1972				PERCENT—	
	1963	1967	1972	1963	1967	1972	Number (1,000)	Sales (bil. dol.)	Paid employees[1] (1,000)	Payroll, entire year (bil. dol.)	Change in sales, 1967–1972	Of total U.S. sales, 1972
U.S __	1,707.9	1,763.3	1,934.5	244.2	310.2	470.8	1,286.5	452.0	11,359.6	56.4	51.8	100.0
N.E_____	102.7	102.6	111.4	15.1	19.0	28.2	77.5	27.2	726.3	3.5	48.8	6.0
Maine__	10.1	10.3	11.0	1.2	1.5	2.3	7.4	2.2	53.3	.3	55.7	.5
N.H____	7.0	7.2	8.3	.9	1.2	2.1	5.6	2.0	46.1	.2	75.5	.4
Vt_____	4.6	4.6	5.3	.5	.7	1.1	3.7	1.1	25.7	.1	61.8	.2
Mass____	47.2	46.9	50.0	7.4	9.2	13.4	35.3	12.9	368.7	1.8	46.0	2.8
R.I_____	8.8	8.3	8.8	1.1	1.4	2.0	6.0	1.9	53.1	.3	46.6	.4
Conn____	25.0	25.3	27.9	3.9	5.0	7.3	19.5	7.0	179.3	.9	44.2	1.5
M.A_____	336.7	329.9	331.4	46.9	58.0	82.5	216.3	78.4	1,965.0	10.3	42.4	17.5
N.Y_____	164.5	162.2	159.2	24.0	29.1	40.0	108.3	38.3	953.5	5.3	37.4	8.5
N.J_____	62.6	61.3	58.7	9.1	11.4	16.9	40.1	16.3	394.9	2.1	49.0	3.6
Pa_____	109.6	106.4	113.5	13.9	17.5	25.6	67.9	23.8	616.6	3.0	46.5	5.4
E.N.C____	333.7	321.4	352.9	50.6	64.6	92.4	237.1	89.5	2,268.6	11.2	43.0	19.6
Ohio____	84.3	81.2	91.5	12.9	16.3	23.3	61.4	22.6	593.4	2.9	42.8	4.9
Ind_____	43.3	42.4	46.6	6.5	8.3	11.9	31.8	11.5	296.1	1.4	42.5	2.5
Ill_____	92.1	89.2	95.4	15.2	19.3	26.6	63.1	25.7	654.2	3.3	38.2	5.6
Mich___	69.8	63.6	72.4	10.9	14.1	20.9	49.7	20.3	465.5	2.4	48.3	4.4
Wis___	44.3	45.1	47.2	5.2	6.6	9.7	31.0	9.3	259.4	1.2	46.9	2.1
W.N.C____	158.3	167.0	176.4	21.1	26.6	37.8	119.6	36.3	942.0	4.3	42.1	8.0
Minn___	32.5	32.9	37.0	4.5	6.0	8.7	25.1	8.4	229.4	1.0	46.2	1.9
Iowa___	30.9	31.3	32.8	3.9	5.0	6.8	22.8	6.6	164.7	.7	35.6	1.4
Mo_____	42.3	45.6	46.9	5.9	7.6	10.7	31.2	10.3	266.1	1.3	41.6	2.3
N. Dak_	6.7	7.1	7.2	.9	1.0	1.4	5.2	1.4	32.9	.2	42.7	.3
S. Dak_	7.7	8.1	8.5	.9	1.0	1.4	5.9	1.4	35.1	.1	40.0	.3
Nebr___	16.1	16.9	17.6	2.1	2.6	3.6	12.1	3.5	90.8	.4	40.5	.8
Kans___	22.2	25.0	26.4	2.8	3.4	5.1	17.4	4.8	122.8	.5	47.1	1.1
S.A_____	239.2	248.5	292.8	32.4	42.8	73.3	192.9	70.5	1,744.1	8.6	71.2	15.6
Del ____	4.5	4.1	5.4	.7	.9	1.5	3.7	1.4	35.8	.2	63.4	.3
Md_____	23.9	25.0	31.6	4.2	5.8	9.6	19.7	9.2	230.0	1.2	65.7	2.0
D.C____	5.4	4.9	4.6	1.4	1.6	1.8	3.8	1.8	53.7	.3	12.2	.4
Va_____	32.2	32.3	35.6	4.8	6.2	10.2	24.9	10.0	253.0	1.2	66.5	2.2
W. Va__	16.9	15.6	15.8	1.8	2.1	3.3	10.4	3.2	75.9	.4	59.0	.7
N.C____	43.9	45.4	50.2	5.0	6.6	11.0	32.6	10.4	250.3	1.2	65.0	2.3
S.C____	22.2	23.5	26.6	2.3	3.1	5.3	16.1	5.0	118.7	.6	70.8	1.1
Ga_____	37.0	39.0	46.4	4.6	6.2	10.7	30.4	10.3	247.8	1.2	73.9	2.3
Fla_____	53.3	58.7	76.6	7.6	10.3	19.8	51.4	19.2	478.9	2.3	92.2	4.2
E.S.C____	111.6	112.5	124.2	12.4	15.9	26.0	79.6	24.7	590.4	2.7	63.6	5.5
Ky_____	30.1	28.9	30.1	3.2	4.0	6.4	18.7	6.0	148.3	.7	59.9	1.4
Tenn___	33.2	34.3	38.8	4.0	5.3	8.7	25.1	8.3	202.0	.9	65.1	1.9
Ala____	29.1	28.8	32.7	3.3	4.1	6.7	21.2	6.4	151.5	.7	63.5	1.4
Miss___	19.2	20.5	22.6	1.9	2.5	4.2	14.6	3.9	88.5	.4	66.3	.9
W.S.C____	162.3	191.3	209.3	21.0	27.4	43.7	133.5	41.3	1,051.7	4.8	59.6	9.3
Ark____	18.3	21.1	22.5	2.0	2.5	4.1	13.9	3.8	87.7	.4	63.2	.9
La_____	24.6	30.6	32.9	3.4	4.8	7.4	21.1	7.0	176.5	.8	55.9	1.6
Okla___	23.0	28.7	29.7	2.9	3.6	5.7	18.7	5.3	135.9	.6	55.8	1.2
Tex____	96.4	110.8	124.3	12.7	16.4	26.5	79.7	25.2	651.6	3.0	61.0	5.6
Mt_____	69.3	74.6	92.7	10.1	12.2	21.5	62.4	20.8	526.7	2.5	76.4	4.6
Mont___	7.8	7.5	9.0	1.0	1.1	1.7	6.3	1.6	39.7	.2	49.2	.4
Idaho__	7.3	7.6	8.9	.9	1.1	1.8	6.0	1.7	41.2	.2	56.8	.4
Wyo___	4.0	4.1	4.6	.5	.5	.8	3.2	.8	20.4	.1	63.6	.2
Colo___	17.3	19.8	24.6	2.6	3.3	6.0	16.0	5.8	147.9	.7	82.5	1.3
N. Mex_	9.0	9.4	11.3	1.2	1.4	2.3	7.5	2.2	58.0	.3	72.4	.5
Ariz___	12.9	14.3	18.6	2.0	2.5	4.8	12.6	4.7	120.3	.6	95.7	1.0
Utah___	7.4	7.8	10.0	1.2	1.4	2.4	6.8	2.3	63.2	.3	72.8	.5
Nev____	3.6	4.1	5.7	.7	.9	1.6	4.0	1.6	36.1	.2	80.1	.3
Pac_____	194.3	215.5	243.3	34.6	43.8	65.3	167.6	63.4	1,544.8	8.5	49.1	13.9
Wash__	26.4	27.1	31.9	4.0	5.5	7.7	21.9	7.5	182.9	1.0	40.7	1.6
Oreg___	17.3	18.8	22.8	2.7	3.3	5.3	15.3	5.1	126.5	.7	59.1	1.1
Calif___	144.4	162.4	179.2	26.9	33.5	49.6	123.9	48.2	1,160.5	6.5	48.2	10.5
Alaska_	1.6	2.0	3.0	.3	.4	.8	1.9	.7	14.8	.1	91.8	.2
Hawaii_	4.6	5.2	6.4	.8	1.1	1.9	4.5	1.8	60.2	.3	74.6	.4

[1] Week including Mar. 12.

Source: U.S. Bureau of the Census, *U.S. Census of Business: 1963*, and *1967*, vol. II; and *Census of Retail Trade: 1972*, Area Series, RC 72-A-1 to 52.

No. 1468. RETAIL TRADE—ESTABLISHMENTS AND SALES, BY KIND OF BUSINESS, BY STATES: 1972

[Based on 1967 Standard Industrial Classification, except as noted]

STATE	TOTAL [1]		FOOD STORES		AUTOMOTIVE DEALERS		GENERAL MERCHANDISE GROUP STORES		EATING AND DRINKING PLACES		GASOLINE SERVICE STATIONS	
	Establishments	Sales	Establishments	Sales	Establishments	Sales	Establishments	Sales	Establishments	Sales	Establishments	Sales
		Mil. dol.		Mil. dol.		Mil. dol.		Mil. dol.		Mil. dol.		Mil. dol.
U.S.[2]	1,912,871	459,040	267,352	100,719	121,369	90,030	56,245	65,091	359,524	36,868	226,459	33,655
U.S.	1,934,466	470,806	267,352	100,719	131,825	93,774	76,030	66,676	359,524	36,868	226,459	33,655
N.E.	111,364	28,192	14,762	6,285	6,841	4,780	5,072	3,874	20,066	2,268	11,105	1,814
Maine	10,996	2,290	1,877	546	968	467	624	280	1,604	140	1,224	163
N.H.	8,325	2,071	1,158	497	655	406	443	253	1,260	125	888	137
Vt.	5,298	1,146	794	262	373	219	295	117	779	72	596	87
Mass.	50,024	13,385	6,202	2,905	2,786	2,125	2,339	1,899	9,683	1,227	4,698	795
R.I.	8,813	2,026	1,201	434	518	334	392	309	1,892	171	901	127
Conn.	27,908	7,274	3,530	1,640	1,541	1,229	979	1,016	4,848	533	2,798	505
M.A.	331,357	82,535	52,184	19,139	16,893	13,130	11,033	12,224	69,155	7,140	28,383	4,902
N.Y.	159,155	39,975	26,362	9,526	7,028	5,562	5,378	5,943	34,620	3,813	11,359	2,022
N.J.	58,709	16,934	9,152	3,948	2,809	2,778	1,983	2,539	12,170	1,424	5,768	1,100
Pa.	113,493	25,627	16,670	5,665	7,056	4,791	3,672	3,742	22,365	1,903	11,256	1,780
E.N.C.	352,941	92,421	42,548	19,384	22,288	18,529	11,650	13,873	75,627	7,615	42,270	6,730
Ohio	91,452	23,272	12,121	5,073	5,904	4,693	2,953	4,082	18,698	1,906	11,723	1,762
Ind.	46,559	11,870	4,806	2,401	3,422	2,508	1,720	1,720	8,342	904	6,235	988
Ill.	95,365	26,597	10,897	5,207	5,203	4,958	3,163	3,737	21,388	2,255	10,211	1,795
Mich.	72,413	20,938	9,817	4,710	5,013	4,550	2,307	2,985	13,988	1,610	8,919	1,482
Wis.	47,152	9,744	4,907	1,993	2,746	1,821	1,507	1,349	13,211	940	5,182	703
W.N.C.	176,386	37,790	18,070	7,018	12,564	7,481	6,906	5,023	32,269	2,687	23,304	3,235
Minn.	37,031	8,742	4,116	1,583	2,468	1,567	1,301	1,271	6,558	659	4,585	711
Iowa	32,764	6,804	2,996	1,235	2,128	1,269	1,263	769	6,277	451	4,484	593
Mo.	46,943	10,706	5,442	2,125	3,588	2,249	2,058	1,574	8,478	773	6,280	887
N. Dak.	7,190	1,429	784	231	484	311	264	146	1,546	101	910	123
S. Dak.	8,495	1,448	828	260	561	292	346	142	1,624	107	1,171	142
Nebr.	17,570	3,589	1,536	615	1,225	660	634	460	3,347	279	2,265	322
Kans.	26,393	5,072	2,368	971	2,110	1,134	1,040	661	4,439	317	3,609	456
S.A.	292,799	73,275	48,153	15,281	22,348	15,939	14,028	10,346	43,519	5,071	37,286	5,396
Del.	5,394	1,499	657	320	343	263	219	257	841	105	557	100
Md.	31,559	9,619	4,361	2,077	1,780	1,804	1,067	1,514	5,342	731	3,012	687
D.C.	4,638	1,799	583	297	132	180	125	229	1,134	257	318	96
Va.	35,645	10,239	6,219	2,213	2,735	2,193	2,047	1,553	5,202	637	4,648	806
W. Va.	15,773	3,350	3,034	794	1,148	730	957	486	2,942	192	2,156	265
N.C.	50,174	10,972	9,362	2,307	4,256	2,549	2,900	1,352	6,097	601	6,946	797
S.C.	26,642	5,302	5,438	1,199	2,259	1,193	1,397	661	3,465	292	3,720	427
Ga.	46,402	10,735	8,089	2,062	3,925	2,452	2,326	1,462	5,895	680	6,730	866
Fla.	76,572	19,761	10,410	4,011	5,770	4,575	2,990	2,832	12,601	1,575	9,199	1,352
E.S.C.	124,242	26,027	24,599	5,686	10,460	5,992	7,164	3,491	16,338	1,441	16,313	1,990
Ky.	30,136	6,369	5,818	1,434	2,474	1,335	1,617	836	4,063	394	3,921	544
Tenn.	38,767	8,725	7,018	1,826	3,104	2,028	2,064	1,251	5,468	510	5,157	663
Ala.	32,720	6,736	6,586	1,471	2,975	1,616	2,018	922	3,844	349	4,510	476
Miss.	22,619	4,197	5,177	955	1,907	1,013	1,465	482	2,963	189	2,725	307
W.S.C.	209,348	43,716	31,455	9,431	17,662	10,017	8,657	5,926	35,486	2,869	28,336	3,285
Ark.	22,467	4,135	4,068	880	2,040	991	1,179	451	3,081	198	3,144	336
La.	32,947	7,418	6,500	1,820	2,168	1,552	1,483	1,013	6,502	518	3,921	511
Okla.	29,670	5,682	3,517	1,198	2,657	1,355	1,278	707	5,054	371	4,153	439
Tex.	124,264	26,480	17,369	5,533	10,797	6,119	4,717	3,754	20,849	1,782	17,118	1,999
Mt	92,714	21,542	9,045	4,307	6,821	4,856	3,370	2,756	17,710	1,728	12,815	1,730
Mont.	8,975	1,696	952	358	660	388	301	145	2,111	153	1,190	150
Idaho	8,938	1,801	925	347	748	428	344	161	1,833	132	1,193	140
Wyo.	4,602	850	351	155	365	187	199	85	841	72	772	101
Colo.	24,582	5,988	1,964	1,151	1,638	1,323	789	836	4,384	492	3,170	417
N. Mex.	11,345	2,343	1,253	471	845	552	533	292	1,961	172	1,831	227
Ariz.	18,577	4,839	2,157	1,028	1,381	1,069	663	733	3,573	395	2,357	357
Utah	9,967	2,417	1,004	471	760	559	366	292	1,746	168	1,504	190
Nev.	5,728	1,610	439	326	424	350	175	213	1,261	144	798	149
Pac.	243,312	65,308	26,536	14,188	15,948	13,049	8,150	9,166	49,354	6,049	26,647	4,572
Wash.	31,928	7,687	3,591	1,740	2,452	1,498	930	1,031	6,063	674	3,945	576
Oreg.	22,806	5,323	2,635	1,207	1,725	1,218	711	579	4,298	439	2,828	392
Calif.	179,186	49,633	19,238	10,652	11,330	9,951	5,932	7,097	36,913	4,588	19,153	3,445
Alaska	2,976	772	298	175	194	(D)	208	116	662	87	241	53
Hawaii	6,416	1,892	774	415	247	(D)	369	344	1,418	261	480	107

D Withheld to avoid disclosure of individual data.
[1] Includes kinds of business not shown separately.   [2] Based on 1972 Standard Industrial Classification.

Source: U.S. Bureau of the Census, *Census of Retail Trade, 1972*, Area Series, RC 72-A-1 to 52.

No. 1469. RETAIL TRADE—ESTABLISHMENTS WITH PAYROLL, 1967, AND ESTABLISHMENTS, SALES, AND PERSONNEL, 1972, BY KIND OF BUSINESS

[Data for 1972 based on 1967 Standard Industrial Classification (SIC) for comparability with 1967, except as noted. See also *Historical Statistics, Colonial Times to 1970*, series T 79–196]

KIND OF BUSINESS	1967 Establishments with payroll		1972 All establishments, number	1972 Establishments with payroll, number	1972 Sales		1972 Payroll, entire year	1972 Paid employees [1]
	Number	Sales			All establishments	Establishments with payroll		
	1,000	*Mil. dol.*	*1,000*	*1,000*	*Mil. dol.*	*Mil. dol.*	*Mil. dol.*	*1,000*
Retail trade, total	1,191.5	295,170	1,934.5	1,286.5	470,806	451,987	56,385	11,360
Building materials, hardware, farm equipment dealers	69.0	16,644	76.8	62.0	25,575	24,966	2,891	434
Building materials, supply stores	36.3	9,381	40.9	33.8	16,049	15,762	1,883	263
Lumber, other bldg. materials [2]	24.3	7,864	(NA)	23.1	(NA)	13,527	1,551	216
Heating, plumbing equipment	2.4	340	(NA)	(NA)	(NA)	(NA)	(NA)	(NA)
Paint, glass, wallpaper stores [2]	8.8	1,019	(NA)	8.8	(NA)	1,501	233	35
Electrical supply stores	.8	158	(NA)	(NA)	(NA)	(NA)	(NA)	(NA)
Hardware stores	19.3	2,556	26.4	18.5	3,957	3,634	490	95
Farm equipment dealers	13.3	4,708	9.6	9.6	5,569	5,569	518	75
General merchandise group stores	51.8	43,127	76.0	55.8	66,676	66,135	9,232	1,948
Department stores	5.8	32,344	7.7	7.7	51,084	51,084	7,226	1,437
Variety stores	19.0	5,348	21.9	18.4	7,344	7,220	1,113	290
Miscellaneous general merchandise	27.0	5,435	46.4	29.7	8,249	7,831	893	221
Food stores [3]	171.7	66,041	267.4	173.1	100,719	96,375	8,820	1,722
Grocery stores, incl. delicatessens	128.7	61,771	194.3	128.1	93,328	90,048	7,846	1,472
Meat markets	9.2	1,383	} 16.6	10.7	2,810	2,506	254	48
Fish (seafood) markets	1.8	178	}					
Fruit stores, vegetable markets	3.2	324	8.4	3.1	695	518	50	11
Candy, nut, confectionery stores	6.3	369	12.9	6.8	691	494	76	25
Retail bakeries	15.7	1,249	19.2	15.1	1,664	1,547	426	119
Automotive dealers	76.9	54,597	131.8	92.9	93,774	92,092	8,901	1,073
Motor vehicle dealers	44.4	47,913	64.2	44.3	77,833	76,817	7,099	805
New and used cars	32.9	45,480	(NA)	31.6	(NA)	73,254	6,843	766
Used cars only	11.5	2,433	(NA)	12.8	(NA)	3,563	256	39
Tire, battery, accessory dealers [4]	22.5	4,044	37.5	29.1	7,543	7,271	1,103	168
Miscellaneous automotive dealers	10.0	2,640	30.1	19.4	8,398	8,004	699	100
Gasoline service stations	165.2	20,589	226.5	183.4	33,655	31,440	2,974	748
Apparel and accessory stores [3]	91.4	16,223	129.2	105.7	21,741	21,115	3,602	800
Women's ready-to-wear stores	27.8	5,288	38.8	33.4	8,451	8,308	1,222	300
Women's accessory, specialty stores	7.6	868	8.9	6.2	746	686	108	28
Furriers and fur shops	1.3	204	2.0	1.0	199	179	33	5
Men's, boys' clothing, furnishings stores [5]	16.7	3,385	(NA)	21.0	(NA)	5,497	860	149
Other apparel and accessory stores	54.7	9,862	79.6	65.1	15,344	14,942	2,240	468
Furniture, homefurnishings, equipment [3]	71.3	13,824	116.9	82.5	22,533	21,505	3,113	475
Furniture, homefurnishings stores	39.9	8,116	66.7	47.7	14,064	13,512	2,060	302
Household appliance stores	15.7	2,877	20.3	14.6	3,824	3,627	473	73
Radio, television stores	9.7	1,919	} 29.9	12.7	} 4,645	2,919	374	62
Music stores	6.0	913	}	7.5	}	1,446	206	37
Eating and drinking places	271.2	22,219	359.5	287.3	36,868	35,048	8,735	2,634
Eating places	189.4	17,955	253.1	208.9	30,385	29,313	7,620	2,317
Drinking places (alcoholic beverages)	81.8	4,263	106.4	78.4	6,482	5,735	1,114	317
Drug and proprietary stores	49.1	10,713	51.5	47.6	15,599	15,420	2,202	454
Drug stores	46.2	10,288	(NA)	45.0	(NA)	14,901	2,149	440
Proprietary stores	2.8	425	(NA)	2.6	(NA)	519	54	14
Miscellaneous retail stores	158.1	24,507	336.7	176.7	39,097	35,186	4,239	794
Liquor stores	31.0	6,209	42.0	33.7	9,874	9,342	632	127
Antique stores, secondhand stores	11.5	778	33.4	11.9	1,495	1,180	207	44
Sporting goods, bicycle shops	8.3	1,009	22.5	12.4	2,538	2,284	278	51
Jewelry stores	14.6	2,018	25.3	16.0	3,118	2,904	473	86
Fuel, ice dealers	16.6	3,447	19.9	15.3	4,793	4,601	731	103
Florists	14.6	972	24.5	16.5	1,605	1,450	295	71
Cigar stores, stands	2.9	282	4.5	2.6	422	358	41	9
Other miscellaneous retail stores [3]	58.6	9,793	164.7	68.4	15,253	13,068	1,581	302
Book, stationery stores [2]	6.9	822	14.3	10.1	1,661	1,567	232	55
Hay, grain, feed stores	11.6	3,845	(NA)	(NA)	(NA)	(NA)	(NA)	(NA)
Other farm, garden supply stores	6.9	2,074	(NA)	(NA)	(NA)	(NA)	(NA)	(NA)
News dealers, newsstands [2]	2.8	260	(NA)	2.7	(NA)	347	40	11
Camera, photographic supply [2]	2.8	462	4.7	3.3	767	736	92	16
Nonstore retailers	15.9	6,687	162.1	19.7	11,568	9,705	1,675	277
Mail-order houses	4.4	3,061	8.0	5.4	4,574	4,528	737	122
Merchandising machine operators	4.5	1,097	12.8	5.4	3,011	2,829	455	70
Direct selling establishments	7.0	1,719	141.3	8.9	3,984	2,349	484	85

NA Not available. [1] Week including Mar. 12. [2] Data for 1972 based on 1972 SIC and not comparable with 1967. [3] Includes kinds of business not shown separately. [4] For 1967, includes home and auto supply stores. [5] Excludes custom tailors.

Source: U.S. Bureau of the Census, *Census of Business: 1967*, vol. II; and *Census of Retail Trade, 1972, U.S. Summary*, SC 72–A–52.

No. 1470. RETAIL TRADE—SIZE OF ESTABLISHMENT AND LEGAL FORM OF ORGANIZATION: 1967 AND 1972

[Establishments and paid employees in thousands; money figures in millions of dollars. 1972 not strictly comparable with 1967 due to changes in Standard Industrial Classification; for details, see source. See also *Historical Statistics, Colonial Times to 1970*, series T 43–57]

ITEM	1967					1972				
	Estab-lish-ments	Sales	Payroll		Paid employ-ees [1]	Estab-lish-ments	Sales	Payroll		Paid employ-ees [1]
			Entire year	1st qtr.				Entire year	1st qtr.	
All establishments	1,763	310,214	36,175	8,812	9,381	1,913	459,040	55,372	13,033	11,211
Operated entire year	1,671	299,430	34,986	8,525	9,022	1,710	427,640	51,828	12,305	10,459
With annual sales of—										
Less than $30,000	583	8,033	754	267	316	516	6,673	378	119	165
$30,000–$49,999	227	8,769	889	263	348	188	7,354	746	182	263
$50,000–$99,999	323	22,888	2,503	648	883	304	21,972	2,573	608	788
$100,000–$299,999	359	60,290	7,500	1,781	2,193	450	77,724	10,217	2,407	2,542
$300,000–$499,999	74	28,110	3,749	882	969	106	40,497	5,832	1,380	1,261
$500,000–$999,999	55	38,464	4,697	1,120	1,109	71	48,823	6,667	1,585	1,304
$1,000,000 or more	50	132,876	14,895	3,565	3,204	74	224,597	25,415	6,025	4,136
With paid employment of [1]—										
Less than 4 employees [2]	1,151	56,458	4,162	1,012	984	1,104	63,665	4,300	961	892
4–7 employees	247	37,390	4,342	1,063	1,283	282	53,110	6,529	1,555	1,463
8–19 employees	182	61,167	7,861	1,921	2,138	212	84,667	11,562	2,755	2,486
20 or more employees	90	144,414	18,621	4,529	4,618	112	226,197	29,436	7,033	5,617
Not operated entire year	93	10,785	1,188	287	358	203	31,401	3,545	728	752
Single units operated	1,543	186,709	20,513	5,190	5,532	1,621	[3]245,168	[3]27,834	[3]6,464	[3]5,606
Multiunits	220	123,505	15,662	3,622	3,848	291	[3]201,838	[3]26,264	[3]6,200	[3]5,206
Corporations	451	209,153	27,068	6,462	6,377	566	343,094	44,999	10,600	8,319
All other legal forms	1,312	101,062	9,107	2,350	3,004	1,346	115,946	10,373	2,433	2,892

[1] Week including Mar. 12.   [2] Includes no paid employees.   [3] Establishments in business at end of year.

Source: U.S. Bureau of the Census, *Census of Business: 1967*, vol. I, and *Census of Retail Trade, 1972*, RC 72–S–1.

No. 1471. RETAIL TRADE—CAPITAL EXPENDITURES, FIXED ASSETS, RENTAL PAYMENTS, AND SUPPLEMENTAL LABOR COSTS, BY SELECTED KINDS OF BUSINESS: 1972

[In millions of dollars. Data derived from the annual retail trade survey based on the probability sample used to produce national monthly estimates of retail sales; see text, p. 837]

KIND OF BUSINESS	CAPITAL EXPENDITURES				FIXED ASSETS [2] (end of year)		RENTAL PAYMENTS		SUPPLEMEN-TARY LABOR COSTS	
	All establish-ments		Cor-por-ate estab-lish-ments, total	Multi-unit organi-zations [1]	All estab-lish-ments	Cor-por-ate estab-lish-ments	All estab-lish-ments	Cor-por-ate estab-lish-ments	All estab-lish-ments	Cor-por-ate estab-lish-ments
	Total	New struc-tures and facili-ties								
Total	7,955	7,251	6,064	3,112	61,252	45,706	9,354	7,222	6,267	5,349
Durable goods stores [3]	1,761	1,606	1,310	234	12,400	8,783	2,352	1,901	1,619	1,377
Automotive group	665	608	539	(NA)	4,874	3,828	833	717	791	707
Furniture and appliance group	350	317	(NA)	(NA)	2,311	1,501	576	457	304	252
Building materials, hardware, farm equipment group	502	456	370	(NA)	3,237	2,304	470	419	339	273
Nondurable goods stores [3]	6,194	5,645	4,754	2,878	48,852	36,923	7,002	5,321	4,648	3,972
Food group	1,454	1,338	1,224	917	10,680	8,372	1,416	1,174	1,254	1,138
Grocery stores	1,316	1,220	1,149	891	9,523	7,734	1,254	1,088	1,153	1,073
Eating and drinking places	1,464	1,226	879	(NA)	10,967	6,846	1,410	925	791	561
Eating places	1,119	938	725	(NA)	8,225	5,528	1,136	815	668	494
GAF,[4] total	2,464	2,371	2,216	(NA)	19,081	17,301	3,284	2,937	2,149	2,039
General merchandise group with nonstores [3][5]	1,670	1,635	1,603	1,342	14,014	13,502	1,775	1,692	1,499	1,477
Department stores and dry goods	1,247	1,233	1,220	1,043	10,526	10,229	1,343	1,281	1,090	1,072
Department stores	1,076	1,065	1,074	955	9,247	9,233	1,052	1,051	948	947
Variety stores	143	141	128	126	1,348	1,242	299	281	135	130
Gasoline service stations	407	360	177	(NA)	3,548	1,361	705	169	254	106

NA Not available.   [1] Organizations operating 11 or more retail stores.   [2] Gross value.   [3] Includes kinds not shown separately.   [4] General merchandise, apparel, and furniture and appliance groups.
[5] Nonstore establishments primarily selling merchandise through coin-operated vending machines, house-to-house canvass, and mail order.

Source: U.S. Bureau of the Census, *Census of Retail Trade, 1972*, series RC72–S–2.

No. 1472. Franchising—Summary: 1969 to 1977

[Franchising is a form of marketing or distribution in which a parent company customarily grants an individual or a company the right, or privilege, to do business in a prescribed manner over a certain period of time in a specified place. The parent company is termed the franchisor; the receiver of the privilege the franchisee; and the right, or privilege, the franchise]

ITEM	1969	1970	1971	1972	1973	1974	1975	1976	1977 [1]
Number of franchised establishments___1,000__	384	396	431	445	454	441	435	443	451
Company-owned [2]_____1,000__	69	72	75	78	79	79	81	83	85
Franchisee-owned_____1,000__	315	324	356	368	375	362	354	360	366
Sales of products and services_____bil. dol__	120	111	129	144	162	166	182	217	248
Company-owned [2]_____bil. dol__	25	25	19	21	24	26	29	33	37
Franchisee-owned_____bil. dol__	95	86	110	123	138	139	154	185	211
Average sales per establishment_____1,000 dol__	311	281	299	323	357	376	420	490	550
Employment_____1,000__	(NA)	(NA)	(NA)	2,904	3,287	3,447	3,511	3,792	(NA)

NA Not available.   [1] Estimated by respondents.
[2] Represents franchised establishments owned by the parent company.

No. 1473. Franchising—Number of Establishments and Sales, by Kinds of Franchised Business: 1970 to 1977

[See headnote, table 1472, for definition of franchising]

KIND OF FRANCHISED BUSINESS	NUMBER OF ESTABLISHMENTS (1,000)					SALES (mil. dol.)				
	1970	1974	1975	1976	1977 [1]	1970	1974	1975	1976	1977 [1]
All franchising, total_	396.3	440.7	434.5	443.3	450.6	111,245	165,621	182,313	217,377	247,575
Auto and truck dealers [2]__	37.2	32.4	31.8	31.9	31.7	53,139	82,126	90,538	113,034	132,171
Percent_____	9.4	7.4	7.3	7.2	7.0	47.8	49.6	49.7	52.0	53.4
Gasoline service stations [2]__	222.0	196.1	189.5	186.8	176.5	26,500	39,910	43,895	47,731	52,409
Percent_____	56.0	44.5	43.6	42.2	39.1	23.8	24.1	24.1	22.0	21.2
Fast food restaurants_	32.6	39.8	43.0	46.9	52.2	4,602	10,351	12,262	14,606	17,074
Percent_____	8.2	9.0	9.9	10.6	11.6	4.1	6.2	6.7	6.7	6.9
Retailing (nonfood)_____	30.7	41.4	37.2	39.2	42.9	13,133	8,672	9,031	10,067	10,882
Soft drink bottlers [2][3]_____	2.7	2.5	2.4	2.2	2.1	4,102	6,720	8,165	10,009	11,044
Automotive products and services [4]_____	20.4	47.8	47.5	48.0	49.8	1,936	4,685	5,006	5,643	6,202
Hotels and motels_____	3.4	5.4	5.4	5.3	5.5	3,540	4,511	4,540	4,769	5,069
Convenience stores_____	8.8	12.7	13.5	13.6	14.4	1,727	3,464	3,906	3,719	4,040
Business aids and services_	10.5	19.5	22.2	25.1	29.2	723	1,304	1,397	1,812	2,185
Employment services___	2.9	2.6	2.7	3.1	3.3	516	496	553	747	847
Tax preparation services_	4.7	7.3	7.5	8.0	8.5	85	146	161	182	222
Accounting, credit, collection, and general__	1.1	2.8	3.5	3.6	4.0	20	138	165	178	188
Other_____	1.7	6.8	8.3	10.4	13.3	101	524	518	706	927
Food retailing [5]_____	(NA)	11.9	11.8	12.7	13.6	(NA)	1,268	1,445	2,306	2,529
Auto, truck rental services_	[6] 10.7	6.1	6.5	6.5	6.8	[6] 1,177	1,233	1,475	1,650	1,753
Construction, home improvement, maintenance, and cleaning_____	.7	12.5	10.8	12.1	13.2	63	675	639	783	868
Laundry, dry cleaning services_____	4.1	3.7	3.2	2.9	2.7	144	237	214	179	191
Recreation, entertainment, travel_____	2.7	2.9	3.4	3.8	4.1	77	135	162	187	223
Equipment rental services_	(6)	1.4	1.4	1.5	1.6	(6)	126	157	168	190
Educational products and services_____	4.9	1.1	1.3	1.2	1.3	86	154	173	170	188
Miscellaneous_____	4.8	3.6	3.7	3.4	3.0	295	466	475	542	556

NA Not available.   [1] Estimated by respondents.   [2] Estimated by source on basis of Bureau of the Census and trade association data.   [3] Includes soft drinks, fruit drinks and ades, syrups, flavoring agents and bases. Excludes independent private label and contract-filler bottling companies which accounted for 24 percent of value of shipments of the total industry in 1975.   [4] Includes some establishments with significant sales of nonautomotive products such as household appliances, garden supplies, etc.   [5] Excludes convenience stores.
[6] Equipment rental services included with auto, truck rental services.

Source of tables 1472 and 1473: U.S. Bureau of Domestic Business Development, *Franchising in the Economy, 1976–78.*

No. 1474. WHOLESALE TRADE—MERCHANT WHOLESALERS SALES, STOCKS, AND STOCK-SALES RATIOS: 1950 TO 1977

[In billions of dollars, except ratios. Beginning 1968, based on revised sample effective August 1977; see Appendix III. See *Historical Statistics, Colonial Times to 1970*, series T 375–383, for sales]

YEAR	ALL ESTABLISHMENTS			DURABLE GOODS			NONDURABLE GOODS		
	Sales [1]	Stocks, end of year [2]	Stock-sales ratios [3]	Sales [1]	Stocks, end of year [2]	Stock-sales ratios [3]	Sales [1]	Stocks, end of year [2]	Stock-sales ratios [3]
1950 [4]	92.3	9.3	1.07	37.7	4.7	1.29	54.6	4.6	.91
1955 [4]	118.7	11.7	1.13	51.4	6.3	1.36	67.3	5.4	.95
1960 [4]	139.9	14.1	1.22	58.6	8.1	1.69	81.3	6.0	.89
1965	187.3	18.3	1.15	82.9	10.6	1.49	104.5	7.7	.87
1968	250.1	26.6	1.25	110.9	16.3	1.71	139.3	10.3	.89
1969	271.3	29.1	1.23	122.2	17.9	1.68	149.1	11.2	.87
1970	287.3	32.8	1.29	127.2	19.7	1.77	160.1	13.1	.91
1971	315.1	35.8	1.30	140.9	22.0	1.77	174.1	13.8	.92
1972	355.0	39.8	1.27	161.1	24.3	1.72	193.9	15.5	.90
1973	441.9	46.3	1.17	195.9	27.0	1.56	246.0	19.3	.86
1974	550.0	56.5	1.12	237.0	34.1	1.53	313.0	22.5	.82
1975	535.6	55.1	1.24	220.1	34.6	1.88	315.5	20.5	.80
1976	580.9	61.3	1.21	246.7	38.2	1.78	334.2	23.1	.79
1977	642.1	68.0	1.21	285.6	44.4	1.73	356.5	23.6	.80

[1] Annual totals.   [2] Seasonally adjusted.   [3] Ratio of average stocks to average monthly sales. Average stocks based on weighted averages of end-of-month figures.   [4] Excludes Alaska and Hawaii.

Source: U.S. Bureau of Economic Analysis and U.S. Bureau of the Census. In *Survey of Current Business*, monthly, and *Monthly Wholesale Trade Report*.

No. 1475. WHOLESALE TRADE—TYPES OF OPERATION AND KINDS OF BUSINESS: 1967 AND 1972

[Data for 1972 based on 1967 Standard Industrial Classification (SIC) for comparability, except as noted. "N.e.c." means not elsewhere classified. See also *Historical Statistics, Colonial Times to 1970*, series T 274–287 and T 352–369]

TYPE OF OPERATION AND KIND OF BUSINESS	1967				1972			
	Estab-lish-ments (1,000)	Sales (mil. dol.)	Pay-roll, entire year (mil. dol.)	Paid employ-ees [1] (1,000)	Estab-lish-ments (1,000)	Sales (mil. dol.)	Pay-roll, entire year (mil. dol.)	Paid employ-ees [1] (1,000)
Wholesale trade, total	311.5	[2]459,476	23,922	3,519	348.2	683,659	35,887	3,878
Merchant wholesalers	213.0	206,055	15,368	2,417				
Manufacturers sales branches, offices	30.7	157,097	5,877	685				
Petroleum bulk stations, terminals	30.2	24,822	905	150	[3]	[3]	[3]	[3]
Merchandise agents, brokers	26.5	61,347	1,377	182				
Farm products assemblers	11.1	10,156	395	84				
KIND OF BUSINESS								
Motor vehicles, automotive equipment	31.2	46,122	2,127	341	36.5	83,016	3,415	392
Drugs, chemicals, allied products	11.5	27,795	1,353	182	13.2	39,288	1,881	187
Piece goods, notions, apparel	11.4	21,280	977	132	12.4	27,933	1,389	134
Groceries and related products	40.1	74,458	3,327	535	39.1	109,781	4,885	585
Farm products—raw materials	15.0	38,148	539	107	14.8	52,401	709	118
Electrical goods	16.7	32,115	1,694	227	20.6	49,101	2,574	253
Hardware, plumbing, heating equipment, supplies	13.5	12,055	1,123	163	16.2	18,310	1,667	175
Machinery, equipment, supplies	52.4	50,432	4,920	650	64.2	75,128	7,482	725
Metals and minerals, n.e.c.	7.9	33,704	1,005	128	8.0	43,488	1,358	127
Petroleum, petroleum products	34.5	33,373	1,157	187	31.3	46,284	1,547	194
Scrap, waste materials	7.9	4,626	411	79	7.5	6,035	544	75
Tobacco, tobacco products	2.6	6,048	207	37	2.4	7,741	288	38
Beer, wine, distilled alcoholic beverages	7.3	14,164	757	101	7.0	19,885	1,185	111
Paper, paper prod., excl. wallpaper	9.6	12,783	900	129	10.7	17,280	1,291	130
Furniture, homefurnishings	8.0	7,723	593	84	9.5	12,359	926	97
Lumber, construction materials	13.6	16,390	1,045	153	15.8	27,943	1,709	179
Other miscellaneous products	28.2	28,737	1,794	285	39.0	47,687	3,039	359

[1] Week including Mar. 12.   [2] Data corrected only at level significantly affected; hence, detail will not add to total.   [3] 1972 data not comparable with 1967 due to change in SIC classification.

Source: U.S. Bureau of the Census, *Census of Business: 1967*, vol. III, and *Census of Wholesale Trade, 1972*, U.S. Summary, WC72–A–52.

No. 1476. WHOLESALE TRADE—SUMMARY, BY STATES: 1963 TO 1972

[Data for 1972 based on 1967 Standard Industrial Classification for comparability with prior years shown]

STATE	1963 Establishments	1963 Sales (bil. dol.)	1967 Establishments	1967 Sales (bil. dol.)	1972 Establishments	1972 Sales (bil. dol.)	1972 Payroll, entire year (mil. dol.)	1972 Paid employees [1] (1,000)	Merchant wholesalers Establishments	Merchant wholesalers Sales (bil. dol.)
U.S.	308,177	358.4	311,464	459.5	348,168	683.7	35,887	3,878.2	249,390	321.6
N.E.	16,685	16.8	16,830	21.6	17,998	33.6	2,024	214.6	13,993	16.5
Maine	1,495	1.0	1,440	1.2	1,521	1.8	120	15.8	1,164	1.1
N.H.	794	.5	822	.7	1,025	1.1	83	9.7	822	.8
Vt.	482	.3	513	.4	635	.6	47	5.7	485	.4
Mass.	8,730	10.4	8,715	13.2	9,059	19.2	1,110	114.8	6,955	9.0
R.I.	1,436	1.2	1,465	1.5	1,454	2.1	141	15.8	1,198	1.2
Conn.	3,748	3.5	3,875	4.7	4,304	8.8	524	52.8	3,369	4.0
M.A.	66,576	97.0	65,673	119.4	67,292	163.2	8,104	791.8	52,997	81.6
N.Y.	40,160	66.2	39,205	78.0	38,977	99.6	4,619	430.4	31,154	51.9
N.J.	9,626	12.8	10,098	17.9	11,509	31.7	1,650	161.6	9,005	15.1
Pa.	16,790	18.0	16,370	23.5	16,806	31.9	1,835	199.8	12,838	14.6
E.N.C.	58,621	73.4	58,410	97.7	63,380	135.0	7,204	731.8	43,470	57.0
Ohio	14,299	18.2	14,497	23.7	15,853	33.3	1,822	189.4	11,087	13.6
Ind.	7,257	6.5	7,162	8.3	8,033	13.0	764	87.8	5,394	5.7
Ill.	18,691	29.3	18,689	39.5	20,085	52.1	2,623	251.7	13,563	21.3
Mich.	11,635	14.0	11,436	18.8	12,208	26.2	1,369	133.4	8,453	11.1
Wis.	6,740	5.5	6,626	7.3	7,201	10.4	626	69.5	4,973	5.3
W.N.C.	33,236	34.4	32,626	43.1	36,281	62.0	2,910	338.8	21,589	26.5
Minn.	6,953	8.4	6,901	10.6	7,861	14.7	755	81.3	4,868	6.6
Iowa	6,025	4.7	5,823	6.0	6,753	9.2	433	53.5	3,834	3.9
Mo.	8,642	12.3	8,600	15.0	9,293	20.3	965	104.9	6,127	8.8
N. Dak.	2,035	1.2	1,995	1.5	2,140	2.1	94	13.0	929	.8
S. Dak.	1,740	1.0	1,688	1.3	1,835	1.8	79	11.7	887	.6
Nebr.	3,199	3.4	3,158	4.4	3,610	6.0	254	33.0	2,183	2.5
Kans.	4,642	3.4	4,461	4.4	4,789	7.9	329	41.4	2,761	3.3
S.A.	36,531	38.0	38,617	51.7	47,075	86.2	4,675	551.0	34,273	37.3
Del.	565	1.1	588	1.4	684	2.5	130	10.9	516	.6
Md.	3,658	4.5	3,943	6.0	4,511	10.0	568	61.1	3,344	4.2
D.C.	1,184	2.1	988	2.4	734	1.7	135	13.1	550	1.0
Va.	4,317	4.4	4,577	6.2	5,338	10.1	567	67.7	3,785	4.3
W. Va.	2,028	1.4	2,001	1.7	2,125	2.4	177	22.6	1,665	1.5
N.C.	6,615	7.0	7,011	9.5	8,269	15.6	775	94.5	5,719	6.5
S.C.	2,738	2.0	2,918	2.7	3,594	4.6	273	35.6	2,643	2.7
Ga.	6,530	8.1	6,941	11.5	8,814	19.5	921	103.2	6,050	6.6
Fla.	8,896	7.5	9,650	10.3	13,006	19.7	1,128	142.3	10,001	9.9
E.S.C.	15,211	15.1	15,972	19.4	19,039	32.5	1,632	205.2	13,821	16.8
Ky.	3,632	3.2	3,715	4.0	4,241	6.8	354	44.5	3,088	3.4
Tenn.	5,100	6.7	5,381	8.6	6,552	14.6	663	78.4	4,764	7.3
Ala.	3,935	3.4	4,253	4.4	5,115	7.4	410	53.6	3,708	3.9
Miss.	2,544	1.8	2,623	2.3	3,131	3.7	203	28.7	2,261	2.2
W.S.C.	29,888	27.9	31,213	36.7	37,181	61.2	3,117	387.4	26,073	30.7
Ark	2,566	1.5	2,659	2.0	3,230	3.2	186	26.7	2,240	1.9
La.	4,852	4.6	5,243	6.6	6,106	9.6	526	65.7	4,427	5.2
Okla.	4,175	3.5	4,175	4.3	4,880	6.7	339	43.0	3,326	3.1
Tex.	18,295	18.3	19,136	23.9	22,965	41.5	2,066	252.0	16,080	20.5
Mt.	13,238	9.9	13,265	11.8	16,048	21.3	1,228	149.8	10,915	10.9
Mont.	1,590	.8	1,509	1.1	1,645	1.5	85	11.5	962	.8
Idaho	1,473	.8	1,467	.9	1,736	1.6	93	15.1	1,048	.9
Wyo.	672	.2	626	.3	742	.7	30	4.2	470	.5
Colo.	3,720	3.6	3,713	4.4	4,508	7.9	425	47.7	3,050	3.4
N. Mex.	1,406	.8	1,425	.9	1,664	1.5	98	12.8	1,156	.8
Ariz.	2,199	1.8	2,281	2.1	2,967	4.3	262	30.8	2,184	2.3
Utah	1,628	1.5	1,635	1.7	1,992	2.9	170	20.6	1,422	1.5
Nev.	550	.4	609	.5	794	.9	66	7.1	623	.7
Pac.	38,191	45.9	38,858	58.1	43,876	88.9	4,990	507.8	32,265	44.2
Wash.	5,593	5.2	5,512	6.7	6,211	9.8	587	62.8	4,286	4.8
Oreg.	3,768	4.4	3,855	5.9	4,377	9.2	451	46.8	3,117	5.4
Calif.	27,565	35.4	28,096	44.2	31,476	67.8	3,787	380.4	23,515	32.6
Alaska	291	.2	365	.3	500	.6	44	3.4	339	.4
Hawaii	974	.7	1,030	1.0	1,312	1.5	121	14.4	1,008	1.0

[1] Week including Mar. 12.

Source: U.S. Bureau of the Census, *Census of Business: 1967*, vol. IV, and *Census of Wholesale Trade, 1972, U.S. Summary*, WC72-A-52.

No. 1477. Merchant Wholesalers—Estimated Sales, by Kinds of Business: 1967 to 1978

[In billions of dollars. Based on a revised sample effective August 1977. See *Historical Statistics, Colonial Times to 1970*, series T 280–371, for related data]

KIND OF BUSINESS	1967	1970	1974	1975	1976	1977	1978, 1st qtr.
Merchant wholesalers	233.3	287.3	550.0	535.6	580.9	642.1	[1] 167.6
Durable goods, total [2]	99.7	127.2	237.0	220.1	246.7	285.6	75.8
Motor vehicles and automotive equipment	14.1	21.4	38.3	39.0	44.9	54.0	16.0
Furniture and homefurnishings	4.3	5.5	8.3	8.1	9.6	11.0	2.9
Lumber and construction materials	9.2	11.6	18.8	16.6	20.9	26.2	6.0
Electrical goods	12.4	15.0	25.4	23.5	27.9	31.7	8.3
Hardware, plumbing, and heating equipment	8.7	10.5	18.1	16.8	19.2	22.4	5.5
Machinery, equipment, and supplies	28.7	33.8	63.0	65.9	71.4	82.0	21.2
Nondurable goods, total [2]	133.6	160.1	313.0	315.5	334.2	356.5	91.8
Paper and paper products	6.4	7.4	12.3	11.5	13.4	15.5	4.1
Drugs, proprietaries, and sundries	4.7	5.6	8.6	9.3	10.1	10.9	2.7
Apparel, piece goods, and notions	8.9	10.2	15.3	15.7	17.6	19.6	5.2
Groceries and related products	42.5	54.4	88.8	95.0	99.8	110.8	28.7
Farm-product raw materials	24.0	24.8	79.2	74.2	72.7	70.1	18.4
Beer, wine, and distilled beverages	10.4	13.1	18.1	20.1	21.6	23.4	5.7
Miscellaneous nondurable goods	22.4	25.9	47.3	44.2	45.5	48.8	11.8

[1] Estimate includes March preliminary.   [2] Includes kinds of business not shown separately.
Source: U.S. Bureau of the Census, *Monthly Wholesale Trade Reports.*

No. 1478. Merchant Wholesalers—Inventories and Stock-Sales Ratios, by Kinds of Business: 1967 to 1978

[Based on a revised sample effective August 1977]

KIND OF BUSINESS	INVENTORIES [1] (bil. dol.)						STOCK-SALES RATIOS [2] (percent)					
	1967	1970	1975	1976	1977	1978,[3] Mar.	1967	1970	1975	1976	1977	1978,[3] Mar.
Merchant wholesalers	25.3	32.8	55.1	61.3	68.0	71.8	125	133	121	120	119	122
Durable goods, total [4]	15.2	19.7	34.6	38.2	44.4	46.2	171	184	181	176	168	168
Motor vehicles, automotive equip	2.1	2.9	6.1	6.6	7.4	8.0	164	153	167	163	142	139
Furniture and home furnishings	.5	.7	1.1	1.3	1.5	1.6	133	148	152	159	142	148
Lumber, construction materials	.9	1.2	1.9	2.1	2.7	2.7	110	124	122	110	110	122
Electrical goods	1.7	2.3	3.5	4.0	4.7	4.8	153	184	163	165	161	155
Hardware, plumbing, heating equip	1.4	1.8	2.9	3.2	3.7	3.9	184	197	196	187	183	196
Machinery, equipment, and supplies	5.6	6.8	12.0	13.0	16.0	16.0	229	243	215	211	212	207
Nondurable goods, total [4]	10.1	13.1	20.5	23.1	23.6	25.6	89	94	78	79	77	82
Paper and paper products	.6	.7	1.1	1.2	1.3	1.4	109	111	104	102	91	95
Drugs, proprietaries, and sundries	.6	.7	1.1	1.2	1.3	1.3	144	136	135	142	141	139
Groceries and related products	2.0	2.4	4.3	5.1	5.5	5.5	53	54	54	59	55	55
Beer, wine, and distilled beverages	1.0	1.2	1.8	2.0	1.9	2.0	106	105	108	113	93	90

[1] As of end of year, except 1978. Adjusted for seasonal variations.   [2] Based on December adjusted sales and inventory estimates.   [3] Preliminary estimate.   [4] Includes kinds of business not shown separately.
Source: U.S. Bureau of the Census, *Monthly Wholesale Trade Report.*

No. 1479. Merchant Wholesalers—Establishments, Sales, and Payroll, by Sales Size of Establishments: 1972

SALES SIZE	Establishments (1,000)	Total sales (mil. dol.)	Percent sales	Payroll (mil. dol.)	SALES SIZE	Establishments (1,000)	Total sales (mil. dol.)	Percent sales	Payroll (mil. dol.)
All establishments	290.0	353,919	100.0	25,916	With annual sales of—Con.				
Operated all year	277.2	337,588	95.4	24,728	$1,000,000–$1,999,999	34.5	48,051	13.6	4,560
With annual sales of—					$2,000,000–$4,999,999	23.3	67,626	19.1	5,474
Less than $100,000	48.6	2,486	.7	371	$5,000,000–$9,999,999	6.4	43,713	12.4	2,912
$100,000–$199,999	41.8	6,107	1.7	809	$10,000,000–$19,999,999	2.5	33,886	9.6	1,826
$200,000–$299,999	30.5	7,487	2.1	947	$20,000,000 and over	1.5	78,489	22.2	2,229
$300,000–$499,999	39.7	15,463	4.4	1,852					
$500,000–$999,999	48.4	34,281	9.7	3,747	Not operated all year	13.8	16,331	4.6	1,189

Source: U.S. Bureau of the Census, *Census of Wholesale Trade, 1972*, Size Report, WC72-S-1.

No. 1480. Selected Services, by Kind of Business: 1967 and 1972

[Data for 1972 based on 1967 Standard Industrial Classification for comparability with 1967. See also *Historical Statistics, Colonial Times to 1970*, series T 391–443]

KIND OF BUSINESS	ESTABLISHMENTS WITH PAYROLL, 1967		ALL ESTABLISHMENTS, 1972		ESTABLISHMENTS WITH PAYROLL, 1972			
	Receipts (mil. dol.)	Paid employees[1] (1,000)	Number (1,000)	Receipts (mil. dol.)	Number (1,000)	Receipts (mil. dol.)	Payroll entire year (mil. dol.)	Paid employees[1] (1,000)
Selected services	55,527	3,841.2	1,370.6	92,815	569.9	84,754	27,002	4,671.3
Hotels, motels, tourist courts, camps	6,738	616.8	79.7	10,638	46.5	10,197	2,971	726.6
Hotels	3,766	378.0	14.0	4,794	10.8	4,745	1,602	347.0
Motels, tourist courts	1,557	128.8	(NA)	(NA)	27.7	3,854	933	273.1
Motor hotels	1,017	93.8	(NA)	(NA)	2.3	1,234	343	91.0
Trailer parks	194	8.8	13.8	284	2.5	139	26	5.0
Sporting, recreational camps	204	7.5	7.2	266	3.2	225	67	10.5
Personal services	10,003	1,029.8	506.4	14,361	199.7	11,994	4,428	(NA)
Laundry, cleaning, other garment services	5,002	572.5	94.1	5,562	58.7	5,103	2,017	(NA)
Beauty shops	1,947	255.0	189.1	3,025	79.6	2,418	1,165	279.3
Barber shops	603	67.2	91.8	885	19.8	394	179	38.2
Photographic studios	597	35.8	33.0	1,079	8.5	845	239	(NA)
Shoe repair, shoeshine, etc	134	11.5	12.9	210	4.0	126	38	8.6
Funeral service, crematories	[2]1,395	63.1	20.9	2,218	15.4	[2]2,071	464	70.2
Misc. personal services	325	24.6	64.6	1,382	13.7	1,038	327	(NA)
Misc. business services	21,427	1,212.4	320.7	36,355	120.5	34,058	11,578	(NA)
Advertising	8,201	109.1	28.4	10,605	10.0	10,342	1,288	111.5
Services to dwellings and other buildings	1,290	223.2	51.3	2,529	21.3	2,307	1,312	333.5
Business and consulting serv	2,852	163.0	92.3	7,470	25.2	6,724	2,837	(NA)
Other misc. business services[3]	9,084	717.1	148.7	15,751	64.0	14,685	6,141	(NA)
Credit bureaus, collection agencies	677	61.0	(NA)	(NA)	6.2	803	385	63.1
Duplicating, mailing, steno. serv	772	64.4	(NA)	(NA)	5.5	969	357	57.1
Commercial research development laboratories	1,068	57.0	(NA)	(NA)	1.6	980	485	(NA)
Detective agencies and protective services	522	101.8	(NA)	(NA)	3.5	912	669	176.3
Equip. rental, leasing services	1,320	41.1	(NA)	(NA)	9.6	2,596	610	(NA)
Photofinishing laboratories	686	31.6	(NA)	(NA)	2.0	1,165	301	44.4
Auto rpr., auto serv., garages	[4]6,368	316.2	169.0	12,081	90.5	10,929	2,553	392.5
Auto repair shops	3,505	187.9	127.2	7,045	65.5	6,134	1,699	237.9
General auto repair	1,531	82.1	71.9	3,176	30.7	2,569	653	98.2
Top and body repair	717	41.3	31.8	1,776	18.3	1,578	486	65.7
Other auto repair	1,257	64.5	23.5	2,093	16.6	1,988	560	74.0
Auto parking	473	33.5	10.5	725	9.4	711	175	37.3
Car, truck rental, leasing, n.e.c.[5]	2,421	95.0	31.3	4,311	15.6	4,083	679	117.3
Misc. repair services	3,089	179.1	149.0	5,941	46.8	4,922	1,628	(NA)
Electrical repair shops	1,050	59.3	53.5	2,228	16.7	1,815	615	(NA)
Reupholstery, furniture repair	257	18.4	24.5	491	6.8	334	106	19.1
Other repair shops, related serv	1,782	101.4	71.1	3,222	23.3	2,772	906	113.3
Motion pictures	3,452	176.7	21.5	4,804	16.6	4,723	1,193	(NA)
Motion picture prod., distr., serv	2,169	64.6	8.8	2,971	4.9	2,907	812	(NA)
Motion picture theaters	1,283	112.1	12.7	1,833	11.7	1,816	381	127.4
Amusement, recreation services, except motion pictures	4,448	310.2	124.3	8,635	49.3	7,931	2,651	(NA)
Producers, orchestras, entertainers	759	59.1	47.7	1,436	7.6	1,111	474	58.3
Bowling alleys, billiards, pool	973	95.5	14.3	1,204	9.0	1,142	324	94.9
Other amusement, recreation serv[3]	2,716	155.5	62.3	5,995	32.6	5,679	1,853	(NA)
Commercial sports	927	39.3	(NA)	(NA)	2.7	1,520	433	48.3

NA Not available.   [1] Week including Mar. 12.
[2] About 7 percent in 1967 and 12 percent in 1972 represent repayment of cash advances which are not part of cost of complete funeral service.   [3] Includes other services not shown separately.
[4] Data corrected only at level significantly affected; hence, detail will not add to total.
[5] N.e.c. = Not elsewhere classified.

Source: U.S. Bureau of the Census, *Census of Business: 1967*, vol. V, and *Census of Selected Service Industries, 1972, U.S. Summary*, SC 72–A–52.

No. 1481. SELECTED SERVICE INDUSTRIES—SUMMARY, BY STATES: 1972

[Data based on 1967 Standard Industrial Classification. Discrepancies in figures identified after tabulation process was completed have been corrected only at level significantly affected; hence, detail may not add to total]

STATE	ALL ESTABLISHMENTS		ESTABLISHMENTS WITH PAYROLL				HOTELS, MOTELS, TOURIST COURTS, CAMPS		PERSONAL SERVICES		AUTO REPAIR, AUTO SERVICES, GARAGES	
	Number (1,000)	Receipts (mil. dol.)	Number (1,000)	Receipts (mil. dol.)	Payroll, entire year (mil. dol.)	Paid employees[1] (1,000)	Establishments	Receipts (mil. dol.)	Establishments	Receipts (mil. dol.)	Establishments	Receipts (mil. dol.)
U.S.	1,370.6	92,815	569.9	84,754	27,002	4,671.3	79,685	10,638	506,444	14,361	168,959	12,081
N.E.	78.3	4,735	33.1	4,258	1,434	252.4	5,069	542	27,112	801	8,480	678
Maine	7.2	262	3.0	229	64	13.4	1,325	72	2,352	49	958	49
N.H.	6.0	287	2.4	253	78	15.6	1,038	70	1,881	45	667	44
Vt.	3.6	166	1.5	147	46	11.2	760	59	1,029	20	438	18
Mass.	37.4	2,564	15.3	2,327	805	133.2	1,308	237	13,163	402	3,892	350
R.I.	5.5	293	2.5	260	86	16.8	172	23	2,306	67	701	44
Conn.	18.5	1,163	8.3	1,043	355	62.2	466	81	6,381	218	1,824	174
M.A.	235.7	22,490	98.3	20,913	6,213	916.5	9,230	1,638	90,148	2,758	26,590	2,298
N.Y.	120.8	15,090	53.2	14,313	3,971	534.3	4,628	903	43,001	1,491	11,015	1,150
N.J.	40.9	3,242	18.7	2,981	1,077	167.8	1,844	278	14,806	505	4,663	448
Pa.	74.0	4,158	26.4	3,619	1,165	214.4	2,758	457	32,341	763	10,912	700
E.N.C.	244.1	16,104	98.3	14,712	4,532	795.9	11,826	1,333	97,542	2,893	28,840	2,134
Ohio	63.7	3,803	26.1	3,466	1,137	209.5	2,210	291	25,510	754	8,382	567
Ind	31.3	1,416	12.3	1,255	399	80.8	1,325	145	13,730	352	4,127	248
Ill.	73.8	6,071	28.0	5,608	1,690	267.4	2,057	447	31,119	910	7,455	659
Mich.	48.7	3,504	20.8	3,223	939	162.2	3,376	278	18,416	610	5,745	474
Wis.	26.5	1,310	11.1	1,160	366	76.0	2,858	172	8,765	268	3,131	186
W.N.C.	120.0	5,630	46.6	4,961	1,514	310.9	8,344	687	46,556	1,076	16,769	907
Minn	25.9	1,422	9.7	1,266	388	77.3	2,511	189	8,780	245	3,263	186
Iowa	21.4	775	8.1	660	190	43.7	1,134	87	8,922	173	3,146	149
Mo.	33.9	2,037	13.6	1,847	591	110.9	1,961	221	13,867	354	4,714	314
N. Dak.	4.1	134	1.7	112	32	7.9	419	27	1,446	31	546	25
S. Dak.	5.2	162	2.1	135	34	8.4	685	34	1,781	33	728	33
Nebr.	11.9	492	4.7	427	124	28.0	728	61	4,438	94	1,769	85
Kans.	17.6	610	6.7	515	156	34.7	906	68	7,322	145	2,603	115
S.A.	200.3	13,019	89.4	11,908	3,982	765.7	15,363	2,174	73,426	2,222	25,048	1,857
Del.	3.5	228	1.5	203	66	12.6	176	19	1,316	39	442	36
Md.	23.1	1,745	9.1	1,590	618	99.5	635	122	8,382	282	2,269	227
D.C.	6.2	827	3.0	791	304	44.7	113	123	2,181	98	525	77
Va.	23.5	1,582	11.4	1,474	516	98.2	1,494	249	9,143	303	2,955	225
W. Va.	8.6	401	4.0	364	117	23.4	576	58	3,784	95	1,199	49
N.C.	31.0	1,474	14.4	1,327	415	86.9	2,084	181	13,366	376	4,832	266
S.C.	15.3	666	6.6	588	175	39.9	1,251	121	6,446	149	2,163	116
Ga.	28.7	1,779	12.6	1,627	505	101.9	1,595	257	11,334	310	4,355	321
Fla.	60.4	4,316	26.7	3,945	1,265	258.6	7,439	1,042	17,474	570	6,308	541
E.S.C.	71.0	3,539	30.8	3,186	1,015	203.1	3,823	446	30,517	762	10,559	583
Ky.	17.3	793	7.0	700	215	46.2	929	112	7,459	202	2,582	121
Tenn.	23.8	1,430	10.9	1,318	435	79.2	1,345	168	10,025	268	3,392	219
Ala.	18.2	878	8.2	790	252	50.8	956	94	7,810	181	2,769	160
Miss.	11.7	438	4.8	378	112	26.9	593	71	5,223	111	1,816	83
W.S.C.	141.9	7,120	56.7	6,363	2,034	409.9	6,993	819	56,993	1,309	20,342	1,099
Ark.	13.5	498	5.2	429	125	28.3	1,028	77	5,879	113	2,103	96
La.	21.3	1,179	8.6	1,068	354	69.7	910	157	9,258	189	2,752	152
Okla.	21.7	795	7.5	672	206	43.9	1,047	86	9,351	169	3,141	152
Tex.	85.4	4,648	35.4	4,194	1,350	268.0	4,008	499	32,505	837	12,346	699
Mt.	71.1	4,957	30.6	4,561	1,491	268.5	8,369	1,387	21,035	571	8,721	568
Mont.	6.0	194	2.4	162	49	11.5	1,013	51	1,790	36	798	31
Idaho	6.1	226	2.3	191	59	13.3	760	49	1,943	39	790	37
Wyo.	3.5	143	1.5	124	33	7.6	767	63	898	18	404	18
Colo.	20.6	1,121	8.5	1,003	324	65.9	1,999	188	6,107	168	2,491	172
N. Mex.	7.3	573	3.4	540	206	30.3	953	76	2,388	56	943	51
Ariz.	14.2	898	6.5	814	251	53.7	1,480	166	3,878	132	1,760	141
Utah	7.8	394	3.2	355	104	22.8	571	54	2,683	61	1,002	69
Nev.	5.7	1,406	2.8	1,372	464	63.4	826	738	1,348	61	533	48
Pac.	208.2	15,220	86.2	13,891	4,786	748.4	10,668	1,612	63,115	1,968	23,610	1,957
Wash.	24.6	1,160	10.1	1,027	344	64.2	1,650	144	7,983	209	3,171	192
Oreg.	16.5	808	6.8	710	223	44.8	1,533	126	5,006	142	2,149	142
Calif.	159.2	12,539	65.8	11,488	4,001	596.6	7,023	1,065	47,819	1,543	17,416	1,531
Alaska	2.4	130	.9	112	37	6.4	238	36	614	20	241	14
Hawaii	5.6	583	2.6	554	180	36.4	224	242	1,693	55	633	78

[1] Week including Mar. 12.

Source: U.S. Bureau of the Census, *Census of Selected Service Industries, 1972, U.S. Summary,* SC 72–A–52.

No. 1482. Selected Services—Receipts, by Kinds of Business: 1972 to 1978

[In millions of dollars. Based on revised sample effective August 1977. Jan.-June data adjusted for seasonal variation and trading day differences]

KIND OF BUSINESS	1972	1973	1974	1975	1976	1977 Total	1977 Jan.-June	1978, Jan.-June, prel.
Selected services, total	93,439	103,272	114,667	123,438	141,766	160,179	78,408	89,002
Hotels, motels, tourist courts, camps, and trailering parks	10,574	11,593	12,396	13,689	15,818	17,188	8,649	9,988
Hotels, motels, and tourist courts	10,027	10,955	11,757	13,002	15,129	16,413	8,224	9,672
Personal services [1]	13,908	14,527	14,843	15,661	16,788	18,374	9,076	10,099
Laundry, cleaning, and garment services	5,719	5,682	5,791	6,004	6,231	6,771	3,294	3,695
Beauty shops	3,007	3,143	3,313	3,376	3,529	4,176	2,004	2,351
Barber shops	885	925	.885	947	988	1,104	504	557
Business services	37,754	42,110	47,494	50,551	59,295	67,691	32,776	37,477
Advertising	10,584	11,437	12,422	12,771	15,584	17,233	8,452	9,445
Automotive repair, services, and garages	12,040	13,721	15,142	16,582	18,816	21,415	10,441	12,039
Automotive repair shops	7,024	7,963	9,310	10,565	12,071	13,386	6,544	7,322
Miscellaneous repair services	5,785	7,201	8,097	8,908	10,301	12,708	6,113	7,183
Amusement and recreation services, incl. motion pictures	13,378	14,120	16,695	18,047	20,748	22,803	11,353	12,216

[1] Includes services not shown separately.
Source: U.S. Bureau of the Census, *Monthly Selected Services Receipts*, series BS.

No. 1483. Selected Service Establishments—Capital Expenditures, Gross Value of Fixed Assets, and Lease and Rental Payments: 1968 and 1972

[In billions of dollars]

LEGAL FORM OF ORGANIZATION	CAPITAL EXPENDITURES				FIXED ASSETS, GROSS VALUE, 1972		LEASE AND RENTAL PAYMENTS	
	Total [1]		New facilities [2]					
	1968	1972	1968	1972	Jan. 1	Dec. 31	1968	1972
All	4.9	7.8	4.5	7.0	49.6	53.6	2.1	3.7
Corporations only	3.7	5.8	3.5	5.4	36.1	38.8	1.5	2.8

[1] Expenditures for improvements and for new and used structures, machinery, and equipment.
[2] Expenditures for improvements and new structures, machinery, and equipment.
Source: U.S. Bureau of the Census, *Census of Selected Service Industries, 1972*, SC 72-S-8.

No. 1484. Warehouse and Storage Space, by Selected Kinds of Business: 1972

[Covers only establishments with payroll. Based on 1972 Standard Industrial Classification. See also table 1459]

KIND OF BUSINESS	Number of establishments	Revenue (mil. dol.)	PUBLIC STORAGE SPACE (mil. sq. ft.)			REFRIGERATED SPACE (mil. cu. ft.)		Frozen food lockers (1,000)
			Total [1]	General merchandise	Household goods	Total	Freezer	
Total	10,026	2,124.3	589.0	319.2	67.3	1,243.3	1,082.9	137.6
Local trucking and storage [2]	4,687	824.0	63.8	9.8	52.4	.4	.2	–
Household goods warehousing and storage	423	46.7	(B)	(B)	(B)	(B)	(B)	(B)
General	2,170	610.6	301.2	296.1	1.0	5.7	2.1	–
Refrigerated, incl. food lockers	1,534	351.7	28.4	8.9	.4	1,236.8	1,080.7	137.6
Farm products	744	154.5	(B)	(B)	(B)	(B)	(B)	(B)
Special	468	136.9	(B)	(B)	(B)	(B)	(B)	(B)

– Represents zero.   B Base too small to be reliable.   [1] Includes other categories not shown separately.
[2] Includes household goods; covers only establishments not regulated by Interstate Commerce Commission.
Source: U.S. Bureau of the Census, *Census of Selected Service Industries, 1972*, SC 72-S-7.

No. 1485. Hotel and Motor Hotel Operations—Occupancy Ratio, Sales Indexes, and Room Rate Index: 1960 to 1977

[Excludes Alaska and Hawaii. Based on reports from approximately 500 lodging establishments]

ITEM	1960	1965	1969	1970	1971	1972	1973	1974	1975	1976	1977
Occupancy ratio....percent..	65	62	59	55	54	62	66	65	62	66	68
Sales indexes (1967=100):											
Total sales_____	94	94	109	107	107	113	121	128	132	147	163
Room sales_____	90	91	113	112	113	121	129	137	145	164	185
Restaurant sales_____	97	97	104	100	100	106	112	118	119	129	139
Room rate index (1967=100)_	86	91	117	125	128	132	139	150	165	178	194

Source: Laventhol & Horwath, Philadelphia, Pa., *Trend of Business in the Lodging Industry*, monthly. (Copyright, 1978, by Laventhol & Horwath.)

No. 1486. Hotels, Motels, and Motor Hotels—Summary: 1958 to 1972

[1958 excludes Alaska and Hawaii. Covers commercial establishments primarily engaged in providing lodging, or lodging and meals, to the general public. Includes establishments with payroll only]

ITEM	HOTELS				MOTELS				MOTOR HOTELS		
	1958 [1]	1963 [1]	1967 [1]	1972	1958 [2]	1963 [2]	1967	1972	1963 [2]	1967	1972
Number_____	16,741	15,372	13,947	10,750	21,310	23,159	22,697	27,739	2,642	3,516	2,348
Guest rooms_____1,000_	[3] 1,097	[3] 957	[3] 887	755	(NA)	(NA)	(NA)	1,034	(NA)	(NA)	206
Receipts_____mil. dol_	2,482	2,710	3,392	4,745	702	1,063	1,557	3,854	484	1,017	1,234
Payroll_____mil. dol_	883	961	1,165	1,602	140	209	346	933	129	277	343
Paid employees [4]_1,000_	381	350	353	347	76	96	129	273	54	94	91
Establishments with:											
Less than 25 rooms____	5,600	5,138	4,372	3,368		15,529	15,200	15,000	904	1,052	519
25–49 rooms_____	4,903	4,602	4,950	3,817	19,362	4,314	4,791	7,307	608	736	521
50–99 rooms_____	3,376	3,077	2,444	1,783		1,255	1,823	3,186	651	876	478
100–299 rooms_____	2,308	2,048	1,724	1,335	1,084	350	864	2,147	448	800	754
300 rooms or more_____	554	507	457	447		9	19	99	26	52	76

NA Not available. [1] Year-round hotels only. [2] Not all establishments reported number of rooms; therefore, size-class breakdown will not add to total. [3] Hotels with 25 guest rooms or more. [4] 1958 and 1963, employees for workweek ended nearest Nov. 15; 1967 and 1972, employees for workweek including Mar. 12.

Source: U.S. Bureau of the Census, *Census of Business, 1958*, vol. V; *1963*, vol. VI; and *Census of Selected Service Industries, 1972*, SC 72–S–2.

No. 1487. Advertising—Estimated Expenditures: 1950 to 1977

[In millions of dollars. 1977 preliminary. See also *Historical Statistics, Colonial Times to 1970*, series T 444–446]

YEAR	Total	National	Local	YEAR	Total	National	Local	YEAR	Total	National	Local
1950_____	5,700	3,260	2,440	1968_____	18,090	10,800	7,290	1973_____	25,120	13,775	11,345
1955_____	9,150	5,380	3,770	1969_____	19,420	11,400	8,020	1974_____	26,780	14,760	12,020
1960_____	11,960	7,305	4,655	1970_____	19,550	11,350	8,200	1975_____	28,230	15,410	12,820
1965_____	15,250	9,340	5,910	1971_____	20,740	11,775	8,965	1976_____	33,720	18,585	15,135
1966_____	16,630	10,150	6,480	1972_____	23,300	13,030	10,270	1977_____	38,100	21,090	17,010
1967_____	16,870	10,210	6,660								

No. 1488. Advertising—Indexes of National Advertising Expenditures, by Medium: 1950 to 1977

[1967=100. Based on the average monthly expenditure for those major media which give national coverage. See also *Historical Statistics, Colonial Times to 1970*, series T 472–484]

MEDIUM	1950	1955	1960	1965	1970	1971	1972	1973	1974	1975	1976	1977
General index_____	25	49	67	90	112	112	125	130	140	146	183	211
Network television_	6	38	56	85	114	109	124	135	147	158	196	237
Spot television_____	3	26	53	90	125	116	133	139	151	164	218	229
Magazines_____	38	56	73	93	104	110	116	116	121	118	144	174
Weeklies_____	40	61	81	94	95	96	94	90	97	94	115	137
Women's_____	46	57	65	95	107	121	130	128	132	130	162	206
Monthly_____	28	43	64	90	120	129	148	161	161	155	187	223
Newspapers_____	61	84	92	93	105	117	130	131	141	144	178	198

Source of tables 1487 and 1488: McCann-Erickson Advertising Agency, Inc., New York, N.Y. Compiled for Crain Communications, Inc. In *Advertising Age* (copyright).

No. 1489. ADVERTISING—ESTIMATED EXPENDITURES, BY MEDIUM: 1965 TO 1977

[In millions of dollars, except percent. See also *Historical Statistics, Colonial Times to 1970*, series R 106–109, R 123–126, and T 444–471]

MEDIUM	1965 Expenditures	1965 Percent of total	1970 Expenditures	1970 Percent of total	1975 Expenditures	1975 Percent of total	1976 Expenditures	1976 Percent of total	1977, prel. Expenditures	1977, prel. Percent of total
Total	15,250	100.0	19,550	100.0	28,230	100.0	33,720	100.0	38,100	100.0
National	9,340	61.2	11,350	58.1	15,410	54.6	18,585	55.1	21,090	55.4
Local	5,910	38.8	8,200	41.9	12,820	45.4	15,135	44.9	17,010	44.6
Newspapers	4,426	29.0	5,704	29.2	8,442	29.9	9,910	29.4	11,132	29.2
National	784	5.1	891	4.6	1,221	4.3	1,502	4.5	1,677	4.4
Local	3,642	23.9	4,813	24.6	7,221	25.6	8,408	24.9	9,455	24.8
Magazines	1,161	7.6	1,292	6.6	1,465	5.2	1,789	5.3	2,165	5.6
Weeklies	610	4.0	617	3.2	612	2.2	748	2.2	890	2.3
Women's	269	1.8	301	1.5	368	1.3	457	1.4	580	1.5
Monthlies	282	1.8	374	1.9	485	1.7	584	1.7	695	1.8
Farm publications	71	.5	62	.3	74	.3	86	.3	100	.3
Television	2,515	16.5	3,596	18.4	5,263	18.6	6,721	19.9	7,637	20.1
Network	1,237	8.1	1,658	8.5	2,306	8.2	2,857	8.5	3,455	9.1
Spot	892	5.9	1,234	6.3	1,623	5.7	2,154	6.4	2,234	5.9
Local	386	2.5	704	3.6	1,334	4.7	1,710	5.0	1,948	5.1
Radio	917	6.0	1,308	6.7	1,980	7.0	2,330	6.9	2,595	6.8
Network	60	.4	56	.3	83	.3	105	.3	120	.3
Spot	275	1.8	371	1.9	436	1.5	518	1.5	580	1.5
Local	582	3.8	881	4.5	1,461	5.2	1,707	5.1	1,895	5.0
Direct mail	2,324	15.2	2,766	14.1	4,181	14.8	4,813	14.3	5,340	14.0
Business papers	671	4.4	740	3.8	919	3.3	1,035	3.1	1,200	3.2
Outdoor	180	1.2	234	1.2	335	1.2	383	1.1	419	1.1
National	120	.8	154	.8	220	.8	252	.7	275	.7
Local	60	.4	80	.4	115	.4	131	.4	144	.4
Miscellaneous	2,985	19.6	3,848	19.7	5,571	19.7	6,653	19.7	7,512	19.7
National	1,745	11.5	2,126	10.9	2,882	10.2	3,474	10.3	3,944	10.3
Local	1,240	8.1	1,722	8.8	2,689	9.5	3,179	9.4	3,568	9.4

Source: McCann-Erickson Advertising Agency, Inc., New York, N.Y. Compiled for Crain Communications, Inc. In *Advertising Age* (copyright). Percentages derived by U.S. Bureau of the Census.

No. 1490. NEWSPAPER ADVERTISING—EXPENDITURES FOR NATIONAL ADVERTISING, BY TYPE OF PRODUCT: 1974 TO 1977

[In millions of dollars. Data are compiled on basis of actual space measurements of bulk of national advertising carried by weekday and Sunday newspapers. Excludes production costs. "N.e.c." means not elsewhere classified]

TYPE OF PRODUCT	1974	1975	1976	1977	TYPE OF PRODUCT	1974	1975	1976	1977
Total	1,116.9	1,142.1	1,405.0	1,568.8	Insurance	21.4	20.2	23.1	26.2
					Jewelry, watches [1]	2.8	3.2	3.5	4.3
Alcoholic beverages	77.7	72.2	78.5	71.2	Mail order	37.0	41.9	41.8	42.8
Liquors	70.5	64.2	70.3	58.9	Medical prod., drugs	13.8	12.9	17.4	22.7
Amusements	6.0	6.2	7.6	8.4	Pets and pet supplies	8.6	8.4	11.5	9.9
Automotive	195.1	175.7	215.2	250.5	Political	11.3	5.2	22.6	6.5
New passenger cars	148.3	129.6	163.5	188.6	Professional and services	5.4	5.6	4.9	5.9
Cameras, photo supplies and services	11.3	10.0	14.1	12.5	Public service utilities and communications	19.6	19.2	23.9	27.3
Educational	8.2	10.0	12.3	15.2					
Farm and garden	18.0	18.5	21.2	23.7	Publishing [2]	79.9	83.4	104.3	125.1
Foods	114.6	131.1	147.8	162.0	Books	21.1	21.9	25.8	27.2
Beverages	19.9	26.1	31.8	34.8	Radio and TV	47.0	48.4	65.2	81.9
Franchise offers	3.4	3.0	3.6	4.4	Real estate	11.2	8.8	8.8	8.2
Help wanted	15.5	10.3	16.4	28.3	Sporting equipment [3]	6.2	6.9	8.2	8.1
Home heat. and equip	3.3	2.9	3.7	5.2	Tobacco	125.4	148.1	200.8	234.2
Hotels and resorts	39.7	44.1	49.2	50.9	Cigarettes	121.8	145.5	197.6	229.9
Household furniture and furnishings	8.0	7.4	8.0	8.2	Toiletries, toilet goods	16.1	16.1	19.2	19.4
Household supplies	20.7	24.8	29.2	31.0	Transportation	143.0	154.7	191.6	202.1
Household equipment and appliances	32.6	30.4	38.9	50.3	Airways	93.0	97.8	110.4	116.3
					Wearing apparel	20.5	20.2	24.2	30.4
Industrial	14.9	13.9	18.0	20.5	General, n.e.c.	25.8	26.9	35.7	53.0

[1] Includes silverware. [2] Includes magazines, newspapers, and other media.
[3] Includes leisure time equipment.

Source: Media Records, Inc., New York, N.Y., *Media Decisions*, August 1978.

No. 1491. Newspaper Advertising—Expenditures for 64 Cities: 1957 to 1977

[In millions of dollars. Based on stratified random sample of 64 cities of different size, including suburban as well as central city newspapers]

TYPE OF ADVERTISING	1957	1970	1972	1973	1974	1975	1976	1977
Total	1,611	3,120	3,497	3,668	3,845	4,117	5,352	5,997
Automotive	63	93	98	96	109	93	127	155
Classified	313	724	881	985	967	982	1,342	1,570
Financial	42	117	115	135	135	131	148	161
General	326	426	478	471	514	547	731	804
Retail	866	1,759	1,925	1,980	2,120	2,364	3,005	3,308

Source: Compiled by Media Records, Inc. Current data in U.S. Bureau of Economic Analysis, *Survey of Current Business*, monthly.

No. 1492. Magazine Advertising—Revenue, by Product, 1960 to 1977 and Percent Distribution, 1970 to 1977

[In millions of dollars. 1960–1970 represents advertising revenue of general magazines and national farm magazines; 1975–1977 represents general magazines only. Space cost based on one-time rate; special rates used where applicable. Year-to-year data not strictly comparable, as a few minor publications are added or deleted]

TYPE OF PRODUCTION	1960	1965	1970	1975	1976	1977	PERCENT DISTRIBUTION		
							1970	1975	1977
Revenue	853	1,083	1,181	1,329	1,627	1,965	100.0	100.0	100.0
Apparel, footwear, and accessories [1]	57	65	51	46	58	70	4.3	3.5	3.6
Automotive, incl. accessories and equip.[1]	94	112	95	101	142	177	8.0	7.6	9.0
Beer, wine, and liquor	51	70	98	101	111	132	8.3	7.6	6.7
Building materials, equip., and fixtures	36	32	21	21	28	36	1.8	1.6	1.8
Consumer services [1]	40	58	74	103	104	119	6.3	7.8	6.1
Drugs and remedies [1]	29	41	38	33	40	51	3.2	2.5	2.6
Food and food products	104	113	86	86	113	140	7.3	6.5	7.1
Household equipment and supplies [1]	37	39	33	25	37	47	2.8	1.9	2.4
Household furnishings [1]	30	36	38	30	47	66	3.2	2.3	3.4
Industrial materials [1]	55	47	44	34	47	49	3.7	2.6	2.5
Insurance	26	32	26	22	28	39	2.2	1.7	2.0
Radios, TV sets, phonographs, musical instruments, and accessories	20	32	38	35	51	58	3.2	2.6	3.0
Smoking materials	26	42	65	143	162	194	5.5	10.8	9.9
Toiletries and toilet goods [1]	51	77	119	105	125	151	10.1	7.9	7.7
Travel, hotels, and resorts	29	46	50	65	69	83	4.2	4.9	4.2
All other (incl. retail and direct-mail) [1]	168	243	305	379	462	552	25.8	28.5	28.1

[1] Due to classification changes, data not comparable with earlier years beginning 1970 for drugs and remedies, and beginning 1975 for other products.

Source: Magazine Publishers Association, Inc., New York, N.Y., from data compiled by Publishers Information Bureau, Inc.

No. 1493. Television Advertising—Estimated Time Charges for Spot Advertising: 1974 to 1977

[In millions of dollars. Spot television advertising, as distinguished from network advertising in table 1494, is defined as any television activity sponsored by a national or regional advertiser, and selected and bought on a station-by-station basis. Includes announcements between both network and nonnetwork programs as well as complete programs. Excludes activity designated as "retail/local." Each commercial is locally originated, whereas network programs and commercials are centrally originated. Data represent activity in the 75 markets monitored by Broadcast Advertisers Reports, Inc. (BAR), covering approximately 263 stations]

TYPE OF PRODUCT	1974	1975	1976	1977	TYPE OF PRODUCT	1974	1975	1976	1977
Estimated time charges	1,572	1,706	2,229	2,312	Insurance	25	24	23	26
					Jewelry, optical goods, and cameras	12	15	22	26
Apparel, footwear, and accessories	50	46	51	47	Laundry soaps, cleansers, polishers	99	96	124	108
Automotive	128	136	190	210	Pet products	49	49	66	64
Beer and wine	79	69	78	91	Proprietary medicines	91	97	97	90
Building material, equipment, and fixtures	16	23	36	39	Publishing and media	41	33	42	75
Confectionery, soft drinks	97	135	187	190	Records, tapes, radios, and TV sets	82	81	104	143
Consumer services	42	50	56	65	Toiletries and toilet goods	150	158	213	192
Food and food products	344	388	482	469	Toys and sporting goods	59	84	128	126
Gasoline, lubricants, etc.	21	27	44	46	Travel, hotels, and resorts	58	46	66	66
Household equipment and supplies, furnishings	100	104	140	158	All other	29	41	80	81

Source: Television Bureau of Advertising, Inc., New York, N.Y., from data compiled by Broadcast Advertisers Reports, Inc., New York, N.Y.

No. 1494. Television Advertising—Net Time and Program Costs for National Network Advertising: 1965 to 1977

[In millions of dollars. Excludes spot advertising (see table 1493). Basically, net time and program costs are estimates of the sale of time plus program production and talent costs incurred by the advertisers]

CATEGORY	1965	1970	1971	1972	1973	1974	1975	1976	1977
Net time and program costs	1,260	1,733	1,628	1,834	2,044	2,257	2,431	2,992	3,619
Apparel, footwear, and accessories	18	34	29	32	45	68	55	72	99
Automotive	99	130	142	179	217	245	235	289	344
Beer and wine	20	30	26	35	32	41	70	94	135
Building materials, equip., and fixtures	16	13	10	13	21	24	24	34	42
Confectionery and soft drinks	30	49	59	61	66	69	85	102	125
Consumer services	13	28	39	38	42	47	51	65	84
Department and discount stores	(1)	(1)	(1)	(1)	(1)	(1)	56	64	89
Entertainment and amusements	3	12	17	20	34	51	66	85	114
Food and food products	205	282	285	306	332	359	403	520	626
Gasoline, lubricants, and other fuel	23	35	52	53	36	32	44	48	64
Household equip., supplies, and furnishings	52	69	65	92	107	125	134	154	182
Insurance	15	29	29	39	46	47	40	47	50
Jewelry, optical goods, and cameras	20	35	32	30	37	41	42	56	80
Laundry soaps, cleansers, and polishes	112	161	148	163	192	209	204	248	279
Office equipment, stationery, and supplies	10	12	13	18	25	22	22	24	27
Pet products	21	27	41	43	45	70	67	100	104
Proprietary medicines	144	211	204	223	245	264	273	308	334
Records, tapes, radios, and TV sets	14	15	18	20	28	27	17	20	35
Tobacco products and supplies	145	160	14	15	16	18	20	21	12
Toiletries and toilet goods	265	304	299	329	371	372	415	468	576
Toys and sporting goods	18	36	39	39	49	52	49	64	89
Travel, hotels, and resorts	5	20	12	10	18	16	21	20	32
All other	12	41	55	76	40	58	38	89	97

1 Costs categorized by items advertised; separate data not available.

Source: Television Bureau of Advertising, Inc., New York, N.Y.; 1965, from data compiled by Leading National Advertisers, Inc., New York, N.Y.; thereafter, from Broadcast Advertisers Reports, Inc., New York, N.Y.

No. 1495. Active Corporation Expenditures for Advertising, Compared With Receipts, by Industry: 1974

[Compiled from income tax returns; see headnote and footnotes, table 447]

INDUSTRY	Total receipts (bil. dol.)	ADVERTISING EXPENDITURES		INDUSTRY	Total receipts (bil. dol.)	ADVERTISING EXPENDITURES	
		Total (mil. dol.)	Percent of receipts			Total (mil. dol.)	Percent of receipts
Total	3,089.7	24,640	.8	Transportation and public utilities [6]	222.1	799	.4
				Transportation	97.1	459	.5
Agriculture, forestry [1]	25.5	67	.3				
Mining	64.8	33	.1	Wholesale and retail trade	923.4	8,040	.9
Construction	137.0	292	.2	Wholesale trade	499.3	1,643	.3
Manufacturing [2]	1,297.3	11,649	.9	Retail trade [2]	423.9	6,396	1.5
Food and kindred prod	158.1	2,909	1.8	Food stores	97.8	853	.9
Tobacco manufactures	13.5	495	3.7	General merchandise stores	83.1	2,112	2.5
Textile mill products	31.1	212	.7	Apparel and accessory stores	20.8	444	2.1
Apparel, textile products	30.6	212	.7	Auto dealers [7]	96.9	776	.8
Lumber and wood prod	31.4	113	.4				
Furniture and fixtures	10.3	94	.9	Finance, insurance, and real estate [2]	303.2	2,242	.7
Paper and allied products	35.7	200	.6	Banking	90.5	728	.8
Printing, publishing	37.4	302	.8	Insurance	120.8	397	.3
Chemicals, allied products	96.7	2,802	2.9	Real estate	25.7	454	1.8
Petroleum, coal products	274.6	274	.1				
Rubber, plastics products	25.1	255	1.0	Services [2]	115.6	1,496	1.3
Leather, leather products	7.7	83	1.1	Hotels, other lodging	9.1	186	2.0
Stone, clay, glass prod	27.1	147	.5	Personal services	8.3	124	1.5
Primary metal industries	92.5	168	.2	Business services	35.1	429	1.2
Fabricated metal prod. [3]	60.2	354	.6	Auto., other repair serv	12.2	111	.9
Machinery, exc. electric	94.7	632	.7	Motion pictures	7.8	261	3.3
Electric, electronic equip	83.6	848	1.0	Amusement and recreation services [8]	7.7	157	2.0
Motor veh. and equip	105.7	627	.6				
Transportation equip. [4]	41.8	132	.3	Not allocable	1.0	21	2.3
Instruments and prod. [5]	21.1	420	2.0				

1 Includes fishing.   2 Includes other industries, not shown separately.   3 Includes ordnance; excludes machinery and transportation equipment.   4 Excludes motor vehicles.   5 Includes watches and clocks.
6 Comprises transportation, communications, and electric, gas, and sanitary services.
7 Includes gasoline service stations.   8 Excludes motion pictures.

Source: U.S. Internal Revenue Service, Statistics of Income, 1974, Corporation Income Tax Returns.

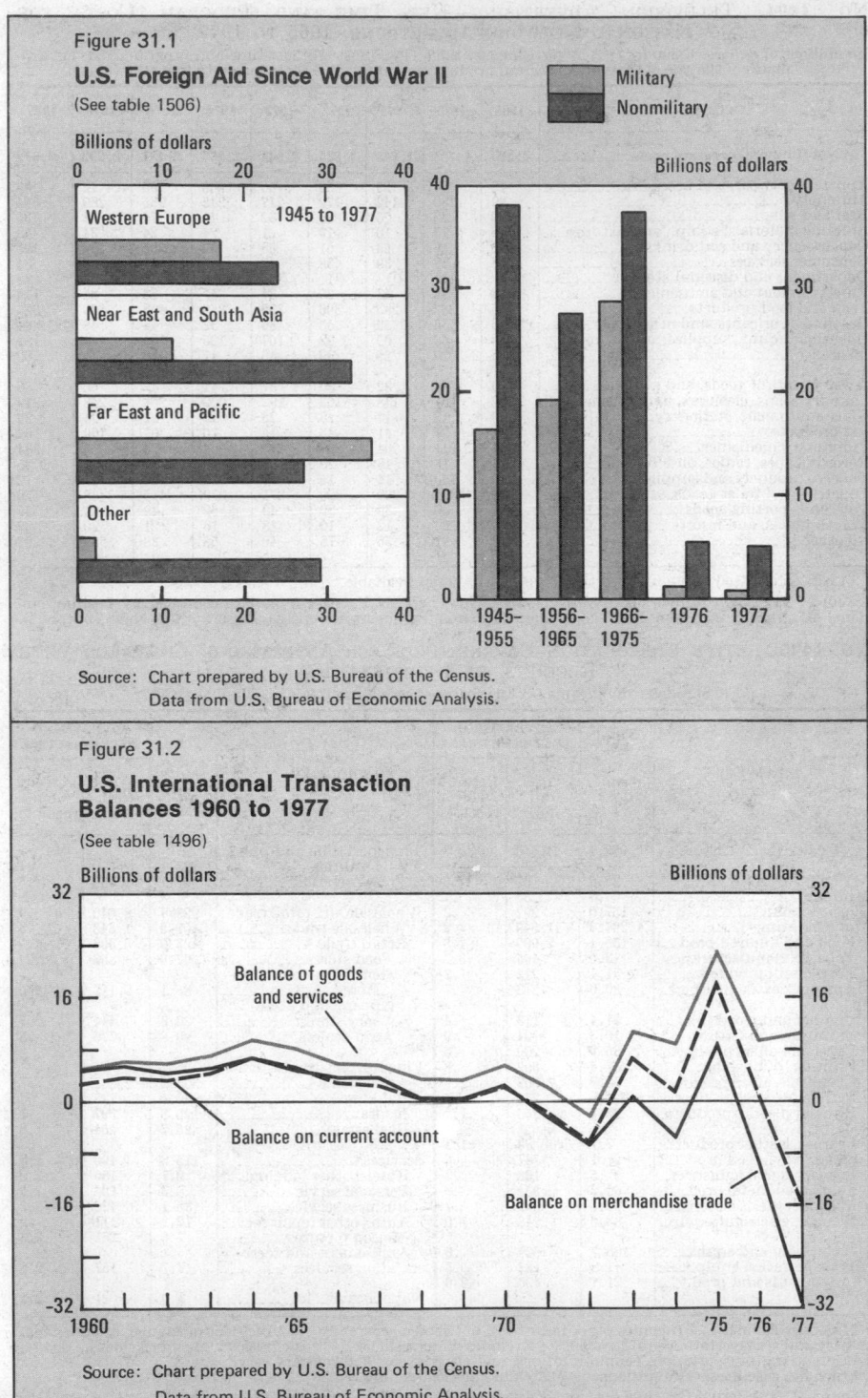

Figure 31.1

U.S. Foreign Aid Since World War II

(See table 1506)

Military
Nonmilitary

Billions of dollars

1945 to 1977

Western Europe

Near East and South Asia

Far East and Pacific

Other

Billions of dollars

1945–1955　1956–1965　1966–1975　1976　1977

Source: Chart prepared by U.S. Bureau of the Census.
Data from U.S. Bureau of Economic Analysis.

Figure 31.2

U.S. International Transaction Balances 1960 to 1977

(See table 1496)

Billions of dollars

Balance of goods and services

Balance on current account

Balance on merchandise trade

1960　'65　'70　'75　'76　'77

Source: Chart prepared by U.S. Bureau of the Census.
Data from U.S. Bureau of Economic Analysis.

Section 31

Foreign Commerce and Aid

This section presents data on the flow of goods, services, and capital between the United States and other countries; changes in official gold reserves of the United States; international investments; foreign assistance programs; and import duties.

The Bureau of Economic Analysis publishes current figures on U.S. international transactions and international investment position in its monthly *Survey of Current Business*. Figures for earlier periods are presented in *Balance of Payments—Statistical Supplement*, 1963 revised edition, in the periodic *Foreign Grants and Credits by the United States Government*, and in the June issues of the *Survey of Current Business*. Statistics for the foreign aid programs are presented by the Agency for International Development in its annual *Operations Report* and its annual *U.S. Overseas Loans and Grants and Assistance from International Organizations*; and by the Department of Agriculture in its *Foreign Agricultural Trade of the United States*.

The principal source of merchandise import and export data is the Bureau of the Census. Current data are presented monthly in Report FT 135, *U.S. General Imports, Schedule A Commodity by Country*; Report FT 410, *U.S. Exports, Schedule B Commodity by Country*; and Report FT 990, *Highlights of U.S. Export and Import Trade*. For a complete list of the Bureau's monthly and annual reports in this field, consult the *Bureau of the Census Catalog* and the *Guide to Foreign Trade Statistics*. In addition, the Industry and Trade Administration and the Bureau of Economic Analysis present summary and selected commodity and country data for U.S. foreign trade in the *Overseas Business Reports* and the *Survey of Current Business*, respectively. The Treasury Department's *Annual Report of the Secretary* contains information on import duties.

International accounts.—The international transactions tables (Nos. 1496 and 1497) show, for given time periods, the transfer of goods, services, grants, and financial assets and liabilities between the United States and the rest of the world.

The international investment position table (No. 1501) presents, for specific dates, the value of U.S. investments abroad and of foreign investments in the United States. The movement of foreign and U.S. capital as presented in the balance of payments is not the only factor affecting the total value of foreign investments. Among the other factors are: Changes in the valuation of assets or liabilities, including securities; defaults; expropriations; write-offs; and reinvested earnings of subsidiaries operating abroad and of foreign subsidiaries operating in the United States.

Foreign aid.—Foreign assistance is divided into three major categories—grants (military supplies and services, and other grants), credits, and other assistance (through net accumulation of foreign currency claims from the sale of agricultural commodities). The U.S. Government's capital investments in the international financial institutions constitute an additional measure taken by the Government to promote foreign economic recovery and development.

Grants are transfers for which no payment is expected (other than a limited percentage of the foreign currency "counterpart" funds generated by the grant), or which at most involve an obligation on the part of the receiver to extend aid to the United States or other countries to achieve a common objective. *Credits* are loan disbursements or transfers under other agreements which give rise to specific obligations to repay, over a period of years, usually with interest. All known returns to the U.S. Government stemming from grants and credits (reverse grants, returns of grants, and payments of principal) are taken into account in net grants and net credits, but no allowance is made for interest or commissions. *Other assistance* represents the transfer of U.S. farm

859

products in exchange for foreign currencies (plus, since enactment of Public Law 87–128, currency claims from principal and interest collected on credits extended under the farm products program), *less* the Government's disbursements of the currencies as grants, credits, or for purchases. The net acquisition of currencies represents net transfers of resources to foreign countries under the agricultural programs, in addition to those classified as grants or credits.

Figures as published in the *Foreign Grants and Credits* series are not identical with figures shown for Government unilateral transfers and capital in the balance of payments, mainly because of differences in treatment of particular items by the two sets of accounts. Such items include: Contributions to the multilateral construction program of the North Atlantic Treaty Organization; Government investments in certain productive enterprises abroad; Government receipts on funded claims; and net changes in foreign currency holdings resulting from transactions other than those under the farm products program, such as by collection of principal and interest and by purchase for dollars.

The basic instrument for extending military aid to friendly nations has been the Mutual Defense Assistance Program authorized by the Congress in 1949. Prior to 1952, economic and technical aid was authorized in the Foreign Assistance Act of 1948, the 1950 Act for International Development, and other legislation which set up programs for specific countries. In 1952, these economic, technical, and military aid programs were combined under the Mutual Security Act, which in turn was followed by the Foreign Assistance Act passed in 1961. Appropriations to provide military assistance to certain countries in Southeast Asia were made in the Department of Defense Appropriation Act (rather than the Foreign Assistance Appropriation Act) beginning in 1966 and in other legislation concerning programs for specific countries (such as Israel). Figures on activity under the Foreign Assistance Act as reported in the *Foreign Grants and Credits* series differ from data published by the Agency for International Development or its immediate predecessors due largely to differences in reporting, timing, and treatment of particular items.

Exports.—The Bureau of the Census compiles export data primarily from Shipper's Export Declarations required to be filed with customs officials for shipments leaving the United States. They include U.S. exports under mutual security programs and exclude shipments to U.S. Armed Forces for their own use.

The value reported in the export statistics is generally equivalent to a free alongside ship (f.a.s.) value at the U.S. port of export, based on the transaction price, including inland freight, insurance, and other charges incurred in placing the merchandise alongside the carrier at the U.S. port of exportation. This value, as defined, should exclude transportation and other costs beyond the U.S. port of exportation. The country of destination is defined as the country of ultimate destination or country where the merchandise is to be consumed, further processed, or manufactured, as known to the shipper at the time of exportation. When ultimate destination is not known, the shipment is statistically credited to the last country to which the shipper knows the merchandise will be shipped in the same form as exported.

For certain low-valued shipments, the export statistics include estimates based upon selected samples of such shipments. In general, shipments valued $100–$499 were estimated for July 1953 through September 1969. For Canada, the upper value limit of the sampled shipments was increased from $499 to $1,999, effective January 1963. Effective October 1969, data are estimated for shipments valued $251–$1,999 to Canada and $251–$499 to other countries. The statistics also include estimates for shipments under $100 prior to October 1969 and for those under $251 effective October 1969, not classified by commodity. The over-$251 sampled shipments represent about 3 percent of the total value of exports, and the under-$251 shipments about 1.0 percent.

Imports.—The Bureau of the Census compiles import data from various customs forms required to be filed with customs officials. Effective 1974, import values published by the Bureau of the Census are presented on three bases: The transaction values f.a.s. (free alongside ship) at the foreign port of export, the c.i.f. (cost, insurance, and freight), and the previously reported customs import value (the value as appraised by the U.S, Customs Service in accordance with the legal requirements of Sections 402 and 402a of the Tariff Act of 1930, as amended). This latter valuation is primarily used for collection of import duties and frequently does not reflect the actual transaction value. The country of origin is defined as the country where the merchandise was grown, mined, or manufactured. If the country of origin is unknown, the country of shipment is reported.

Imports are classified either as "General Imports" or "Imports for Consumption." General imports are a combination of entries for immediate consumption and entries into customs bonded warehouses, and thus generally reflect total arrivals of merchandise. Imports for consumption are a combination of entries for immediate consumption and withdrawals from warehouses for consumption, and thus generally reflect the total of the commodities entered into U.S. consumption channels.

The import statistics include estimates, not classified by commodity, for certain low-valued shipments. From July 1953 through June 1965, data for informal entries (generally items valued under $251) and various types of formal entries valued under $100, in general, were estimated, while data for formal and informal entries valued under $251 have been estimated since July 1965. The estimates are included in country and continent figures and in total import figures. The estimated low-valued shipments generally amount to about 1 percent of the import total.

Area coverage.—Except as noted, the geographic area covered by the export and import trade statistics is the United States customs area, which includes the 50 States, the District of Columbia, and Puerto Rico.

Statistical reliability.—For a discussion of statistical collection and estimation, sampling procedures, and measures of statistical reliability applicable to Census Bureau data, see Appendix III.

Historical statistics.—Tabular headnotes provide cross-references, where applicable, to *Historical Statistics of the United States, Colonial Times to 1970*. See Appendix I.

No. 1496. U.S. International Transactions—Summary: 1960 to 1978

[In billions of dollars. Minus sign (−) denotes debit. See headnote, table 1497]

YEAR	Merchandise trade balance	Military transactions balance	Net investment income	Net travel and transportation receipts	All goods and services balance	Current account balance	Foreign assets in U.S., net	U.S. assets abroad, net	U.S. official reserve assets, net (end of period)
1960	4.9	−2.8	3.4	−1.0	5.1	2.8	2.3	−4.1	19.4
1965	5.0	−2.1	5.4	−1.3	8.3	5.4	.7	−5.7	15.5
1966	3.8	−2.9	3.6	−1.3	4.5	1.6	3.3	−5.5	14.9
1967	3.8	−3.2	4.0	−1.8	4.4	1.3	6.9	−8.0	14.8
1968	.6	−3.1	6.0	−1.5	3.6	.6	9.9	−11.0	15.7
1969	.6	−3.3	6.1	−1.8	3.4	.4	12.7	−11.6	17.0
1970	2.6	−3.4	6.2	−2.0	5.7	2.4	6.4	−9.3	14.5
1971	−2.3	−2.9	7.3	−2.3	2.3	−1.4	23.0	−12.5	12.2
1972	−6.4	−3.6	8.2	−3.0	−2.1	−6.0	21.7	−14.5	13.2
1973	.9	−2.3	12.0	−3.1	10.8	6.9	18.7	−22.8	14.4
1974	−5.3	−2.1	15.5	−3.1	8.9	1.7	34.7	−34.7	15.9
1975	9.0	−.9	12.8	−2.5	23.1	18.4	15.6	−39.4	16.2
1976	−9.4	.3	15.9	−2.2	9.4	4.3	37.0	−50.6	18.7
1977	−31.1	1.3	17.5	−3.0	−10.5	−15.2	50.9	−34.7	19.3
1978, 1st qtr	−11.2	.3	4.8	−.8	−5.7	−7.0	17.8	−14.3	19.2

Source: U.S. Council of Economic Advisers, *Economic Indicators*, monthly. Data from U.S. Bureau of Economic Analysis and U.S. Dept. of the Treasury.

No. 1497. U.S. International Transactions: 1965 to 1977

[In millions of dollars. Minus sign (−) denotes debits. The account definition has been changed to include reinvested earnings on foreign investments and historical data have been revised accordingly. See also *Historical Statistics, Colonial Times to 1970*, series U 1–25]

TYPE OF TRANSACTION	1965	1970	1972	1973	1974	1975	1976	1977
Exports of goods and services [1]	41,090	65,659	77,197	109,853	146,086	155,655	171,274	183,214
Merchandise, excl. military [2]	26,461	42,469	49,381	71,410	98,306	107,088	114,694	120,585
Transfers under U.S. military agency sales contracts	830	1,501	1,163	2,342	2,952	3,919	5,213	7,079
Travel and transportation	3,826	5,988	7,071	8,821	10,788	11,666	13,740	14,513
Miscellaneous services	2,533	3,950	4,888	5,584	6,499	7,623	8,384	8,938
Income on U.S. investments abroad [3][4]	7,441	11,751	14,694	21,697	27,541	25,359	29,244	32,100
Transfers of goods and services under U.S. military grants, net	1,636	2,713	4,492	2,810	1,818	2,207	373	194
Imports of goods and services	−32,801	−60,005	−79,321	−99,087	−137,182	−132,595	−161,913	−193,727
Merchandise, excl. military [2]	−21,510	−39,866	−55,797	−70,499	−103,649	−98,041	−124,047	−151,644
Direct defense expenditures	−2,952	−4,855	−4,784	−4,629	−5,032	−4,795	−4,901	−5,745
Travel and transportation	−5,106	−8,011	−10,099	−11,907	−13,893	−14,188	−15,985	−17,557
Miscellaneous services	−1,146	−1,760	−2,099	−2,399	−2,524	−3,006	−3,670	−4,189
Income on foreign investments in U.S. [3][4]	−2,088	−5,516	−6,544	−9,655	−12,084	−12,564	−13,311	−14,593
U.S. military grants of goods and services, net	−1,636	−2,713	−4,492	−2,810	−1,818	−2,207	−373	−194
Unilateral transfers (excl. military grants), net	−2,854	−3,294	−3,854	−3,881	−7,186	−4,615	−5,022	−4,708
U.S. Government grants	−1,808	−1,736	−2,173	−1,938	−5,475	−2,894	−3,145	−2,776
U.S. Govt. pensions, private remittances, other transfers	−1,046	−1,558	−1,681	−1,943	−1,711	−1,721	−1,878	−1,932
U.S. assets abroad, net (increase/capital outflow (−))	−5,718	−9,340	−14,461	−22,823	−34,712	−39,444	−50,608	−34,650
U.S. official reserve assets, net	1,222	2,477	32	209	−1,434	−607	−2,530	−231
U.S. Govt. assets, other than official reserve assets, net	−1,605	−1,589	−1,568	−2,644	366	−3,470	−4,213	−3,679
U.S. loans and other long-term assets	−2,463	−3,293	−3,819	−4,638	−5,001	−5,936	−6,943	−6,445
Repayments on U.S. loans [5]	874	1,721	2,086	2,596	4,826	2,475	2,597	2,720
U.S. foreign currency holdings and U.S. short-term assets, net	−16	−16	165	−602	541	−9	133	47
U.S. private assets, net	−5,335	−10,228	−12,925	−20,388	−33,643	−35,368	−43,865	−30,740
Direct investments abroad [4]	−5,010	−7,589	−7,747	−11,353	−9,052	−14,244	−11,614	−12,215
Foreign securities	−759	−1,076	−618	−671	−1,854	−6,235	−8,852	−5,398
U.S. claims on unaffiliated foreigners reported by U.S. nonbanking concerns	341	−596	−1,054	−2,383	−3,221	−1,357	−2,030	−1,700
U.S. claims reported by U.S. banks, n.i.e. [6]	93	−967	−3,506	−5,980	−19,516	−13,532	−21,368	−11,427
Long-term	−232	155	−1,307	−933	−1,183	−2,357	−2,362	−751
Short-term	325	−1,122	−2,199	−5,047	−18,333	−11,175	−19,006	−10,676
Foreign assets in the U.S., net (increase/capital inflow (+))	740	6,357	21,696	18,663	34,677	15,550	36,969	50,869
Foreign official assets in the U.S., net	132	6,907	10,705	6,299	10,981	6,907	18,073	37,124
Other foreign assets in the U.S., net	607	−550	10,991	12,364	23,696	8,643	18,897	13,746
Direct investments in U.S. [4]	415	1,464	949	2,800	4,760	2,603	4,347	3,338
U.S. Treasury securities	−131	81	−34	−214	697	2,590	2,783	563
U.S. securities other than U.S. Treasury securities	−358	2,189	4,507	4,041	378	2,503	1,284	2,869
U.S. liabilities to unaffiliated foreigners reported by U.S. nonbanking concerns	178	2,014	815	1,035	1,844	319	−507	257
U.S. liabilities reported by U.S. banks, n.i.e. [6]	503	−6,298	4,754	4,702	16,017	628	10,990	6,719
Long-term	241	23	149	227	9	−280	231	373
Short-term	262	−6,321	4,605	4,475	16,008	908	10,759	6,346
Allocations of special drawing rights	-	867	710	-	-	-	-	-
Statistical discrepancy (sum of above items with sign reversed)	−457	−244	−1,966	−2,725	−1,684	5,449	9,300	−998

- Represents zero.   [1] Excludes transfers of goods and services under U.S. military grant programs.   [2] Excludes exports of goods under U.S. military agency sales contracts identified in Bureau of the Census export documents, excludes imports of goods under direct defense expenditures identified in Census import documents, and reflects various other adjustments (for valuation, coverage, and timing) of census statistics to a balance of payments basis.   [3] Consists of interest, dividends, and branch earnings.   [4] Includes reinvested earnings of foreign incorporated affiliates of U.S. firms, or of U.S. incorporated affiliates of foreign firms.   [5] Includes sales of foreign obligations to foreigners.   [6] Not included elsewhere.

Source: U.S. Bureau of Economic Analysis, *Survey of Current Business*, June 1978.

No. 1498. U.S. Balances on International Transactions, by Areas and Selected Countries: 1975 to 1977

[In millions of dollars. Balances by area have some shortcomings due to statistical discrepancies including errors, omissions, and incorrect area attributions. Minus sign (−) denotes debits]

AREA OR COUNTRY	1975, BALANCE ON—			1976, BALANCE ON—			1977, BALANCE ON—		
	Merchandise trade [1]	Goods and services	Current account	Merchandise trade [1]	Goods and services	Current account	Merchandise trade [1]	Goods and services	Current account
All areas	9,047	23,060	18,445	−9,353	9,361	4,339	−31,059	−10,514	−15,221
Euro. Econ. Community [2]	6,341	3,700	3,823	7,195	5,393	5,443	4,414	2,734	2,853
United Kingdom	1,144	254	258	947	23	−21	901	604	545
Belgium-Luxembourg	1,280	1,299	1,291	1,889	1,883	1,875	1,697	1,841	1,832
France	962	1,204	1,164	1,005	1,118	1,072	530	726	680
Germany	−306	−2,014	−1,684	−192	−949	−616	−1,412	−2,904	−2,471
Italy	464	290	170	533	490	350	−250	−421	−570
Netherlands	2,727	2,519	2,509	3,134	2,893	2,881	2,736	2,628	2,615
Other Western Europe	2,779	2,161	1,867	1,689	1,521	1,165	1,490	1,241	827
Eastern Europe	2,515	2,662	2,596	3,226	3,423	3,351	1,786	1,998	1,936
Canada	1,827	6,809	6,673	−139	5,931	5,794	−1,371	4,896	4,752
Latin Amer., other W. Hem.	931	5,276	4,604	−361	4,789	4,032	−3,252	2,604	1,842
Japan [3]	−1,690	−1,178	−1,220	−5,335	−5,359	−5,402	−7,984	−8,091	−8,134
Australia and South Africa [4]	1,266	2,518	2,494	1,441	3,132	3,104	988	2,542	2,510
Other Asia and Africa	−4,922	1,441	−1,721	−16,760	−8,937	−12,311	−26,476	−17,334	−20,414
International and unallocated	-	−329	−671	−309	−532	−838	−654	−1,104	−1,394

- Represents zero. [1] Adjusted to balance of payments basis; excludes exports under U.S. military sales contracts and imports under direct defense expenditures. [2] Includes Denmark, Ireland, European Atomic Energy Community, European Coal and Steel Community, and European Investment Bank, not shown separately. [3] Includes Ryukyu Islands. [4] Includes New Zealand.

Source: U.S. Bureau of Economic Analysis, *Survey of Current Business*, June 1978.

No. 1499. U.S. Reserve Assets: 1960 to 1978

[In millions of dollars. As of end of year or month]

TYPE	1960	1965	1970	1972	1973	1974	1975	1976	1977	1978, June
Total	19,359	15,450	14,487	13,151	14,378	15,883	16,226	18,747	19,312	18,864
Gold stock [1]	17,804	13,806	11,072	10,487	11,652	11,652	11,599	11,598	11,719	11,706
Special drawing rights	-	-	851	1,958	2,166	2,374	2,335	2,395	2,629	2,804
Convertible foreign currencies	-	781	629	241	8	5	80	320	18	84
Reserve position in IMF [2]	1,555	863	1,935	465	552	1,852	2,212	4,434	4,946	4,270

- Represents zero.
[1] Includes gold in Exchange Stabilization Fund; excludes gold held under earmark at Federal Reserve banks for foreign and international accounts. [2] International Monetary Fund.

No. 1500. U.S. Liabilities to Foreigners, by Areas and Countries: 1975 to 1978

[In millions of dollars. As of end of year or month. Represents liabilities as reported by banks in the U.S. "Foreigners" refers to international and regional organizations, foreign governments, central banks, and other official institutions, as well as banks, organizations, and individuals domiciled abroad and foreign subsidiaries and offices of U.S. banks and commercial firms]

AREA OR COUNTRY	1975	1976	1977	1978, May	AREA OR COUNTRY	1975	1976	1977	1978, May
Total	95,590	110,659	126,168	137,028	Latin American and Caribbean [1]	15,028	19,132	23,670	24,894
Europe [1]	44,072	47,076	60,295	62,932	Bahamas	1,874	2,770	3,596	3,324
France	7,726	4,876	5,269	6,275	British West Indies	1,311	1,877	3,998	3,961
Germany, F. R.	4,543	6,241	7,239	9,537	Venezuela	3,309	3,118	2,929	3,299
Italy	1,059	3,182	6,857	6,364	Asia [1]	22,384	29,766	30,488	35,495
Netherlands	3,407	3,003	2,869	2,993	Japan	10,207	14,363	14,616	19,999
Switzerland	8,476	9,460	12,343	12,515	Middle East oil-exporting countries [2]	7,355	9,360	8,979	7,842
United Kingdom	6,867	10,018	14,125	11,606	Other	5,488	4,310	3,832	3,908
Canada	2,919	4,659	4,607	6,620	Int'l and regional [3]	5,699	5,714	3,274	3,179

[1] Includes countries not shown separately. [2] Bahrain, Iran, Iraq, Kuwait, Oman, Qatar, Saudi Arabia, and United Arab Emirates. [3] Excludes Bank for International Settlements, which is included in Europe.

Source of tables 1499 and 1500: Board of Governors of the Federal Reserve System, *Federal Reserve Bulletin*, monthly.

No. 1501. INTERNATIONAL INVESTMENT POSITION, 1970 TO 1976, AND BY SELECTED AREAS, 1976

[In billions of dollars. Estimates for end of year; subject to considerable error due to nature of basic data. Direct investments at book value; other types at market or face values. See *Historical Statistics, Colonial Times to 1970*, series U 26–39, for similar data]

TYPE OF INVESTMENT	1970	1972	1973	1974	1975	1976			
						Total [1]	Western Europe	Canada	Latin American Republics [2]
U.S. net international investment position_	58.6	37.1	47.9	58.8	74.6	82.5	−45.9	48.0	52.5
U.S. assets abroad_____	165.5	199.0	222.8	256.2	295.6	347.4	90.8	68.7	79.5
U.S. official reserve assets_____	14.5	13.2	14.4	15.9	16.2	18.7	(Z)	(Z)	.3
Gold_____	11.1	10.5	11.7	11.7	11.6	11.6	–	–	–
Special drawing rights_____	.9	2.0	2.2	2.4	2.3	2.4	–	–	–
Reserve position in the International Monetary Fund_____	1.9	.5	.6	1.9	2.2	4.4	–	–	–
Foreign currencies_____	.6	.2	(Z)	(Z)	.1	.3	(Z)	(Z)	.3
U.S. Government assets, other than official reserve assets_____	32.1	36.1	38.8	38.4	41.8	46.0	9.1	.3	9.6
U.S. loans and other long-term assets__	29.7	34.1	36.2	36.3	39.8	44.1	9.0	.3	9.6
Repayable in dollars [3]_____	23.5	28.4	30.6	33.1	36.8	41.3	8.3	.3	9.0
Other [4]_____	6.2	5.7	5.6	3.2	3.0	2.8	.7	–	.6
U.S. foreign currency holdings and short-term assets_____	2.5	2.0	2.6	2.1	2.0	1.9	.1	(Z)	(Z)
U.S. private assets_____	118.8	149.7	169.6	202.0	237.6	282.6	81.7	68.4	69.5
Direct investments abroad_____	75.5	89.9	101.3	110.2	124.2	137.2	55.9	33.9	23.5
Foreign securities_____	21.0	27.6	27.8	28.6	35.2	44.6	4.9	26.6	2.0
Bonds_____	14.4	17.1	17.8	19.6	25.6	35.1	2.3	20.8	1.9
Corporate stocks_____	6.6	10.5	10.0	9.0	9.6	9.5	2.7	5.9	.1
U.S. claims on unaffiliated foreigners [5]__	8.5	11.4	13.8	17.0	18.4	20.1	6.6	4.1	5.2
Long-term_____	4.2	4.7	5.1	5.5	6.0	6.0	1.6	1.7	1.6
Short-term_____	4.4	6.8	8.7	11.5	12.5	14.2	5.0	2.5	3.6
U.S. claims reported by U.S. banks [6]____	13.8	20.7	26.7	46.2	59.8	80.7	14.2	3.7	38.8
Long-term_____	3.0	5.1	6.0	7.2	9.5	11.7	2.4	.6	4.8
Short-term_____	10.8	15.7	20.7	39.1	50.2	69.0	11.8	3.1	34.0
Foreign assets in the U.S_____	106.8	161.8	174.9	197.4	221.0	264.8	136.7	20.6	26.9
Foreign official assets in the U.S_____	26.1	63.2	69.6	80.3	87.5	106.3	[7] 47.7	[7] 3.5	[7] 5.1
U.S. Government securities_____	17.7	52.9	53.8	57.7	63.3	73.6	(7)	(7)	(7)
U.S. Treasury securities_____	17.7	52.6	52.9	56.2	60.8	70.2	(7)	(7)	(7)
Other_____	(Z)	.3	.9	1.6	2.4	3.4	(7)	(7)	(7)
Other U.S. Government liabilities____	1.7	1.6	2.8	3.5	5.2	10.1	1.9	.1	.3
U.S. liabilities reported by U.S. banks [6]_	6.7	8.5	12.6	18.4	16.3	17.2	(7)	(7)	(7)
Other foreign official assets_____	–	.2	.5	.6	2.7	5.5	(7)	(7)	(7)
Other foreign assets in the U.S_____	80.7	98.7	105.3	117.1	133.6	158.5	[8] 89.0	[8] 17.1	[8] 21.8
Direct investments_____	13.3	14.9	20.6	25.1	27.7	30.2	19.9	5.9	3.1
U.S. securities [9]_____	34.7	50.7	46.1	34.9	45.3	54.8	38.5	7.3	2.1
Corporate and other bonds_____	7.5	11.6	12.6	10.7	10.0	11.9	10.4	1.1	.3
Corporate stocks_____	27.2	39.1	33.5	24.2	35.3	42.9	28.1	6.3	1.8
U.S. liabilities to unaffiliated foreigners [5]_	8.8	10.7	11.7	13.6	13.8	13.0	7.3	.6	1.5
Long-term_____	4.9	6.2	6.5	6.4	6.8	5.8	4.4	.2	.5
Short-term_____	3.9	4.5	5.2	7.2	7.1	7.2	3.0	.4	1.0
U.S. long-term liabilities reported by U.S. banks_____	1.0	.9	1.2	1.2	.9	1.1	(8)	(8)	(8)
U.S. Treasury securities and other short-term liabilities reported by U.S. banks_____	22.9	21.5	25.7	42.3	45.8	59.4	(8)	(8)	(8)
U.S. Treasury securities_____	1.2	1.2	1.0	1.7	4.2	7.0	(8)	(8)	(8)
Bills and certificates_____	.4	.4	.4	1.0	3.2	3.0	(8)	(8)	(8)
Bonds and notes_____	.8	.8	.6	.6	1.0	4.0	(8)	(8)	(8)
U.S. short-term liabilities reported by U.S. banks [6]_____	21.7	20.3	24.8	40.7	41.6	52.4	(8)	(8)	(8)

– Represents zero.   Z Less than $50 million.
[1] Includes other countries, international organizations, and unallocated, not shown separately.
[2] Includes other Western Hemisphere.
[3] Includes paid-in capital subscription to international financial institutions and outstanding amounts of miscellaneous claims. Excludes World War I debts that are not being serviced.
[4] Includes indebtedness that the borrower may contractually, or at its option, repay with its currency, with a third country's currency, or by delivery of materials or transfer of services.
[5] Reported by U.S. nonbanking concerns.
[6] Not included elsewhere.
[7] Data included in "Foreign official assets in the U.S."
[8] Data included in "Other foreign assets in the U.S."
[9] Excludes U.S. Treasury securities.

Source: U.S. Bureau of Economic Analysis, *Survey of Current Business*, various monthly issues.

No. 1502. U.S. Direct Investment Abroad—Direct Investment Position and Income, by Country, 1970 to 1977, and by Selected Industries, 1977

[In millions of dollars. For definition of "direct," see headnote, table 1503. Minus sign (−) denotes decrease. See also Historical Statistics, Colonial Times to 1970, series U 41–46]

COUNTRY	DIRECT INVESTMENT POSITION (at yearend)									INCOME [2]								
	1970	1973	1974	1975	1976	1977, prel. Total [1]	1977 Manufacturing	1977 Petroleum	1977 Finance, insurance	1970	1973	1974	1975	1976	1977, prel. Total [1]	1977 Manufacturing	1977 Petroleum	1977 Finance, insurance
All areas	75,480	101,313	110,078	124,050	136,396	148,782	65,604	30,887	19,972	8,169	16,542	19,156	16,615	18,999	19,851	7,326	5,481	3,095
Developed countries	51,819	72,214	82,895	90,695	100,398	108,047	53,364	24,854	9,668	4,577	10,052	10,418	9,509	11,461	11,889	6,018	2,086	1,280
Canada	21,015	25,541	28,404	31,038	33,932	35,398	16,658	7,722	3,700	1,618	2,844	3,394	3,412	3,837	3,341	1,344	992	307
Europe [3]	25,255	38,255	44,652	49,305	55,139	60,591	31,390	13,926	5,491	2,401	5,751	5,713	4,989	6,169	7,125	4,155	822	848
Euro. Econ. Commun. (EEC) [4]	20,104	30,919	35,323	38,773	43,215	47,539	27,502	11,267	3,620	1,919	4,473	4,042	3,620	4,755	5,617	3,755	582	607
Belgium and Luxembourg	1,546	2,512	2,945	3,306	3,558	4,155	2,498	452	435	158	426	375	270	263	360	308	−119	95
Denmark and Ireland	571	858	1,160	1,295	1,632	1,888	1,025	514	32	45	131	165	170	267	259	222	−45	8
France	2,643	4,295	4,902	5,743	5,947	6,093	4,138	913	204	237	585	383	657	484	378	312	−7	14
Germany	4,313	7,650	7,971	8,726	10,497	11,003	6,993	606	993	588	1,415	1,079	956	1,945	1,609	1,388	16	102
Italy	1,464	2,212	2,680	3,097	2,934	2,969	1,964	606	99	85	225	205	90	290	301	267	−42	41
Netherlands	1,550	2,352	3,127	3,509	3,797	4,010	2,011	1,233	192	180	413	753	540	664	909	290	454	52
United Kingdom	8,016	11,040	12,537	15,137	17,420	17,420	8,872	5,311	1,525	626	1,278	1,671	1,081	842	1,802	967	325	297
Other Western Europe [3]	5,151	7,336	9,329	10,532	11,924	13,052	3,889	364	2,010	483	1,277	1,277	1,369	1,414	1,508	410	239	241
Japan (incl. Okinawa)	[5]1,482	2,671	3,319	3,339	3,797	4,082	1,889	1,549	148	228	514	393	233	417	512	299	76	67
Australia, N. Zealand, So. Africa	4,067	5,746	6,520	7,013	7,530	7,976	3,428	1,657	329	430	943	919	875	1,038	911	210	196	58
Developing countries [6]	19,192	22,904	19,848	26,288	28,884	33,706	12,239	3,014	8,759	2,941	5,840	7,927	6,703	7,047	7,756	1,308	3,362	1,787
Latin American Republics [7]	11,104	13,527	14,597	16,394	17,125	17,729	9,331	1,708	2,295	1,206	2,000	2,297	2,155	1,906	2,241	904	369	350
Mexico, Panama, and other Central America	3,644	4,506	5,141	5,811	5,617	6,124	2,733	190	1,052	264	609	820	926	370	647	221	35	121
Argentina	1,022	1,144	1,138	1,154	1,306	1,505	930	223	91	109	91	71	103	246	273	70	139	26
Brazil	1,526	2,885	3,760	4,579	5,416	5,956	3,935	364	564	208	426	464	657	731	681	362	60	115
Chile	758	643	287	174	179	187	52	(D)	1	81	46	6	(Z)	22	15	5	(D)	9
Colombia	584	608	617	648	654	706	436	71	93	43	90	90	53	79	92	68	9	(Z)
Peru	744	859	900	1,221	1,506	1,409	157	328	8	74	623	573	344	262	76	−4	31	12
Venezuela	2,241	2,051	1,804	1,872	2,775	1,779	623	223	151	395	512	848	534	310	310	157	61	12
Other Western Hemisphere	1,858	2,957	4,931	5,773	6,809	9,009	917	1,611	5,783	215	668	848	1,067	1,573	1,672	108	220	1,146
Other Africa [8]	2,477	2,376	2,233	2,414	2,783	3,085	266	1,520	76	522	931	1,029	1,610	1,610	586	29	461	12
Middle East [9]	1,545	226	−6,432	−4,040	−3,730	−3,085	193	−4,378	153	711	1,730	2,092	1,941	1,941	1,891	10	1,607	85
Other Asia and Pacific	2,260	3,318	4,519	5,904	5,904	5,904	1,826	2,493	453	287	650	1,660	1,017	1,017	1,367	257	706	195
International and unallocated [6]	4,469	6,196	7,335	7,067	7,114	7,029	(X)	3,019	1,546	650	623	811	492	492	205	(X)	34	28

D Withheld to avoid disclosure of data of individual companies. X Not applicable. Z Less than $500,000. [1] Includes industries not shown separately. [2] Equals sum of interest, dividends, and reinvested earnings. [3] Includes Mediterranean possessions and countries. Excludes Eastern Europe. [4] As of Jan. 1, 1973, United Kingdom, Denmark, and Ireland became members of EEC. For consistency, data for all years are shown on same basis. [5] Excludes Okinawa. [6] Shipping companies operating under flags of convenience, primarily Panama and Liberia, included in "International and unallocated." [7] Includes countries not shown below. [8] Includes Egypt and all other in Africa except South Africa. [9] Includes Bahrain, Iran, Israel, Jordan, Kuwait, Lebanon, Qatar, Saudi Arabia, South Yemen, Syria, Trucial States, Oman, and Yemen. Negative position occurs when U.S. parent company's liabilities to the foreign affiliate are greater than its investment in the foreign affiliate.

Source: U.S. Bureau of Economic Analysis, Survey of Current Business, August 1978, and supplement titled Revised Data Series on U.S. Direct Investment Abroad, 1966–76.

No. 1503. U.S. INTERNATIONAL INVESTMENTS—INCOME, BY FOREIGN AREAS: 1966 TO 1977

[In millions of dollars. Figures abstracted from the general pattern of balance of payments. "Direct" investments represent private enterprises in one country controlled by investors in another country or in the management of which foreign investors have an important voice. "Other private" investments represent long-term miscellaneous holdings such as government or corporate bonds, interests in trusts, and estates, or bank loans]

AREA AND TYPE OF INVESTMENT	1966		1970		1975		1976		1977	
	Receipts	Payments	Receipts	Payments	Receipts	Payments	Receipts	Payments	Receipts	Payments
Total, all areas	7,532	2,480	11,752	5,516	25,359	12,564	29,244	13,311	32,100	14,593
Direct	5,259	710	8,169	875	16,595	2,234	18,999	3,110	19,851	2,829
Other private	1,669	1,221	2,671	3,617	7,644	5,788	8,955	5,681	10,881	6,224
U.S. Government	604	549	912	1,024	1,120	4,542	1,290	4,520	1,368	5,540
Canada	1,859	390	2,424	618	5,127	1,076	5,904	1,105	5,856	958
Direct	1,294	157	1,518	71	3,412	430	3,837	479	3,341	374
Other private	565	159	905	373	1,700	394	2,050	402	2,497	421
U.S. Government	(Z)	74	1	174	15	252	17	224	18	163
Western Hemisphere [1]	1,769	196	2,137	480	5,730	1,163	6,739	1,339	7,967	1,546
Direct	1,326	8	1,421	18	3,201	242	3,479	387	3,913	354
Other private	321	175	556	448	2,282	862	2,983	898	3,756	1,105
U.S. Government	122	13	160	14	247	59	277	54	298	87
Europe [2]	1,628	1,462	3,263	3,443	6,606	7,626	7,957	7,561	9,183	8,011
Direct	1,050	529	2,401	702	4,989	1,670	6,169	2,102	7,125	1,805
Other private	346	616	501	2,193	1,303	3,413	1,525	3,170	1,922	3,360
U.S. Government	232	317	361	548	314	2,543	263	2,289	136	2,846
Other countries [3]	2,276	433	3,929	975	7,895	2,699	8,644	3,306	9,094	4,078
Direct	1,589	16	2,829	84	4,993	−108	5,514	142	5,472	296
Other private	438	272	710	603	2,358	1,119	2,397	1,211	2,706	1,338
U.S. Government	249	145	390	288	544	1,688	733	1,953	916	2,444

Z Less than $500,000.   [1] Except Canada.   [2] Includes Finland, Spain, and Yugoslavia.   [3] Includes international institutions and shipping companies operating under flags of the Bahamas, Honduras, and Panama.

Source: U.S. Bureau of Economic Analysis, *Survey of Current Business*, June 1978.

No. 1504. FOREIGN DIRECT INVESTMENT IN THE UNITED STATES—VALUE, BY AREA AND INDUSTRY: 1950 TO 1977

[In millions of dollars. Book value at yearend. Prior to 1973, covers U.S. firms, including real estate investments in which foreign interest or ownership was 25 percent or more; thereafter, ownership of 10 percent or more. See also *Historical Statistics, Colonial Times to 1970*, series U 47–74]

AREA AND INDUSTRY	1950	1955	1960	1965	1970	1972	1973	1974	1975	1976	1977, prel.
All areas [1]	3,391	5,076	6,910	8,797	13,270	14,868	20,556	25,144	27,662	30,770	34,071
Petroleum	405	853	1,238	1,710	2,992	3,272	4,792	5,614	6,213	5,921	6,566
Manufacturing	1,138	1,759	2,611	3,478	6,140	7,262	8,231	10,387	11,386	12,619	13,706
Finance and insurance	1,065	1,499	1,810	2,169	2,256	2,911	3,414	2,723	3,152	2,943	4,429
Trade, wholesale and retail	(NA)	(NA)	634	748	994	550	3,117	4,387	4,844	6,123	7,208
Canada	1,029	1,542	1,934	2,388	3,117	3,466	4,203	5,136	5,352	5,907	5,999
Petroleum	56	196	203	208	190	243	426	547	596	676	710
Manufacturing	468	711	932	1,219	1,836	2,201	2,319	2,905	3,061	3,386	3,436
Finance and insurance	153	179	246	370	324	353	293	311	341	422	345
Europe	2,228	3,369	4,707	6,076	9,554	11,087	13,937	16,756	18,584	20,162	22,666
Petroleum	349	657	1,028	1,478	2,777	3,011	4,079	4,714	5,478	4,999	5,520
Manufacturing	669	1,040	1,611	2,167	4,091	4,836	4,790	6,109	6,673	7,426	8,405
Finance and insurance	870	1,272	1,504	1,724	1,805	2,335	2,086	1,829	2,088	2,637	3,042
United Kingdom	1,168	1,749	2,248	2,852	4,127	4,987	5,403	5,744	6,331	5,802	6,337
Petroleum	95	204	339	511	1,220	1,297	1,212	1,502	(D)	602	485
Manufacturing	337	510	722	839	1,391	1,719	1,551	1,792	1,833	1,964	2,246
Finance and insurance	554	836	953	1,176	1,141	1,567	1,198	854	932	1,211	1,425
Netherlands	334	613	947	1,304	2,151	2,357	4,017	4,698	5,347	6,255	7,091
Petroleum	226	411	639	887	1,311	1,407	(D)	(D)	(D)	(D)	(D)
Manufacturing	44	127	213	328	652	769	997	1,213	1,345	1,500	1,677
Switzerland	348	522	773	940	1,545	1,675	1,420	1,949	2,138	2,295	2,400
Manufacturing	204	282	427	590	1,147	1,194	922	1,222	1,308	1,357	1,513
Finance and insurance	147	223	300	303	351	416	313	263	365	(D)	481
Other Europe	377	485	739	980	1,731	2,068	3,097	4,366	4,768	5,810	[2] 6,838
Petroleum	28	42	50	80	246	308	(D)	(D)	494	(D)	(D)
Manufacturing	84	121	249	410	901	1,154	1,319	1,882	2,187	2,605	2,969
Finance and insurance	135	176	209	209	255	307	426	442	445	(D)	572
Japan	} 134	165	269	{ 118	229	[3] −154	152	345	591	1,178	1,741
Other areas				214	370	468	2,264	2,907	3,135	3,523	3,666

D Withheld to avoid disclosure of data of individual companies.   NA Not available.   [1] Area totals include industries not shown separately.   [2] Direct investments (in millions of dollars): Belgium and Luxembourg, 1,190; France, 1,793; Germany, 2,494; Italy, 281; and Sweden, 695.   [3] At yearend, Japanese firms' net debt to their U.S. affiliates exceeded their equity position in those affiliates.

Source: U.S. Bureau of Economic Analysis, *Foreign Business Investments in the United States*, 1962; and *Survey of Current Business*, August 1978.

No. 1505. U.S. Government Foreign Grants and Credits: 1945 to 1977

[In millions of dollars. "P.L." means Public Law. For explanation of minus sign (−), see headnote, table 1506. See also text, pp. 859–861, and *Historical Statistics, Colonial Times to 1970*, series U 75–101]

PROGRAM	Post WW II period,1 total	1945–1955, total	1956–1965, total	1966–1972, total	1973	1974	1975	1976	1977, prel.
Total, net	185,949	55,132	47,317	46,049	6,804	7,323	8,671	7,930	6,723
Investments in 6 international financial institutions 2	5,982	635	655	1,155	373	537	654	1,102	870
Under assistance programs, net	179,967	54,497	46,662	44,894	6,431	6,785	8,017	6,828	5,853
Net new military grants	66,421	16,445	19,159	20,134	2,853	2,842	2,891	1,339	757
Gross new grants	66,946	16,679	19,400	20,158	2,862	2,850	2,895	1,342	760
Foreign Assistance Act 3	65,293	15,062	19,364	20,158	2,862	2,850	2,895	1,342	760
Military supplies and services	41,032	13,917	18,256	5,659	838	975	814	375	196
Military assistance, service funded 4	18,169	–	8	13,934	1,981	849	1,396	–	–
Financing of military purchases 5	2,963	–	–	–	–	937	647	878	501
Other special programs	3,130	1,145	1,100	566	43	88	38	88	62
Other	1,653	1,617	36	–	–	–	–	–	–
Less: Reverse grants and returns	525	234	241	24	10	7	4	3	3
Net new economic and technical aid grants 6	72,833	28,869	17,675	13,024	1,938	4,538	2,247	2,266	2,275
Developed countries 7	20,892	20,291	780	−61	−119	−1	−1	(Z)	2
Developing countries 7	51,941	8,578	16,896	13,085	2,057	4,539	2,248	2,266	2,273
Gross new grants	74,765	30,222	17,993	13,155	2,059	4,540	2,249	2,272	2,275
Foreign Assistance Act 3	45,264	17,711	12,189	7,740	1,335	1,562	1,554	1,623	1,551
Farm products disposals:									
Foreign currencies, P.L. 83–480 8	6,337	–	2,048	1,702	197	2,316	20	39	16
Famine and other urgent relief	6,752	530	2,704	1,991	247	316	309	304	353
Payment of transportation	1,630	–	494	624	81	121	120	94	95
Supplies to military or trusteeship administration areas	6,717	5,872	132	326	62	71	77	88	89
Peace Corps	1,289	–	232	672	80	88	72	74	71
Other	6,775	6,110	194	100	57	66	97	51	99
Less: Reverse grants and returns	1,932	1,353	318	131	120	2	2	6	–
Net new credits 9	38,752	8,642	7,025	12,759	1,689	−348	2,849	3,275	2,860
Developed countries 7	3,773	6,646	−3,207	−22	181	13	138	181	−157
Developing countries 7	34,979	1,996	10,232	12,782	1,508	−360	2,711	3,093	3,017
New credits	76,270	12,039	15,429	23,406	4,251	4,468	5,293	5,838	5,546
Export-Import Bank Act	28,519	4,271	5,257	8,758	1,680	2,578	2,490	2,004	1,482
Foreign Assistance Act 3	25,245	1,919	6,196	8,202	1,133	1,186	1,533	2,409	2,668
Country program loans	17,638	1,765	5,722	6,546	613	583	620	913	877
Financing of military purchases	6,472	9	247	1,237	479	550	823	1,448	1,679
Social Progress Trust Fund	784	–	226	407	34	24	21	34	38
Other	351	145	2	11	7	29	69	14	75
P.L. 83–480 8	12,484	48	3,839	5,057	587	560	952	747	694
Loans of foreign currency:									
To foreign governments	5,182	48	3,285	1,823	8	9	2	6	(Z)
To private enterprises	424	–	202	205	7	4	1	4	1
Long-term credit sales	6,878	–	352	3,028	572	547	949	737	693
P.L. 80–806 10	3,813	–	–	1,169	799	147	318	678	702
Other	6,210	5,801	137	221	52	−2	(Z)	(Z)	1
Less: Principal collections	37,518	3,397	8,404	10,647	2,562	4,816	2,444	2,563	2,686
Export-Import Bank Act	17,701	1,803	4,458	6,090	1,089	1,111	992	1,029	1,129
Foreign Assistance Act 3	6,409	38	1,263	1,880	403	748	526	776	776
Country program loans	4,264	1	944	1,419	229	529	304	477	361
Financing of military purchases	1,693	2	222	342	145	185	180	255	362
Social Progress Trust Fund	272	–	9	113	26	29	31	32	33
Other	180	35	88	6	3	6	11	12	19
P.L. 83–480 8	4,405	–	180	836	416	2,265	235	222	250
Loans of foreign currency:									
To foreign governments	2,630	–	111	254	117	1,874	108	82	83
To private enterprises	248	–	43	123	18	18	16	16	14
Long-term credit sales	1,527	–	27	459	280	373	111	124	154
Lend-lease, surplus property, and grant settlements	4,269	677	2,001	957	248	103	130	99	54
P.L. 80–806 10	2,578	–	–	453	321	510	478	425	391
Other	2,156	880	501	431	84	79	83	12	86

See footnotes at end of table.

No. 1505. U.S. GOVERNMENT FOREIGN GRANTS AND CREDITS: 1945 TO 1977—Con.

[In millions of dollars. See headnote, p. 867]

PROGRAM	Post WW II period,[1] total	1945– 1955, total	1956– 1965, total	1966– 1972, total	1973	1974	1975	1976	1977, prel.
Other assistance (net accumulation of foreign currency claims) [11] ___	1,962	541	2,802	−1,023	−49	−247	30	−53	−39
Developed countries [7] _____	261	190	330	−136	−17	−21	−28	−23	−33
Developing countries [7] _____	1,701	351	2,472	−887	−32	−226	58	−30	−6
Currency claims acquired _____	19,503	813	11,498	4,124	361	2,214	189	129	175
Sales of farm products_____	14,996	813	11,170	3,002	5	1	5	(Z)	(Z)
Second-stage operations [12]_____	4,507	–	329	1,122	356	2,213	184	129	175
Less: Currencies disbursed_____	17,542	272	8,696	5,147	410	2,461	159	182	214
Economic grants and credits to purchasing country_____	13,340	182	6,863	3,691	207	2,318	21	42	16
Other uses_____	4,201	90	1,833	1,456	203	143	138	140	198

– Represents zero. Z Less than $500,000. [1] July 1, 1945, through Dec. 31, 1977. All lend-lease and conversions of prior grants to credits are from V-J Day (Sept. 2, 1945). [2] For details, see table 1506.
[3] Foreign Assistance Act of 1961 (P.L. 87–195), as amended. Also includes predecessor and related programs.
[4] Includes military assistance under Dept. of Defense Appropriation Act, 1966 (P.L. 89–394) and later acts.
[5] Includes funds made available under Public Law 93–199 and subsequent legislation to release Israel from its contractual liability to pay for defense articles and services purchased under other legislation. [6] Net new grants are not adjusted for settlements for postwar relief and other grants under agreements, and net new credits exclude prior grants converted into credits, which were as follows: July 1945–December 1955, $2,198 million; 1956–66, $491 million; 1972, $994 million. Repayments on these settlements are included in net new credits.
[7] Developed countries include Australia, Canada, Japan, New Zealand, Republic of South Africa, all countries listed under "Western Europe" in table 1506, except Portugal, Spain, Yugoslavia, and Malta, and all countries listed under "Eastern Europe" in table 1506. Developing countries include all other countries listed in table 1506.
[8] Agricultural Trade Development and Assistance Act. [9] Outstanding credits on Dec. 31, 1977, totaled $41,610 million representing net credits extended since organization of Export-Import Bank, Feb. 12, 1934, less chargeoffs, and net adjustments due to exchange rates ($1,537 million), and excluding World War I debts. The amount repayable in dollars at U.S. Government option was $39,018 million; the remainder was repayable in foreign currencies, commodities, or services, at the option of the borrowers.
[10] Commodity Credit Corporation Charter Act.
[11] Equivalent value of currencies still available to be used, including some funds advanced from foreign governments and after loss by exchange rate fluctuations ($1,962 million), was $555 million on Dec. 31, 1977.
[12] Includes foreign currencies acquired from triangular trade operations and principal and interest collections on credits, originally extended under P.L. 83–480, which—since enactment of P.L. 87–128—are available for the same purposes as P.L. 83–480 currencies.

Source: U.S. Bureau of Economic Analysis, *Foreign Grants and Credits by the United States Government*, periodic.

No. 1506. U.S. GOVERNMENT FOREIGN GRANTS AND CREDITS, BY COUNTRIES: 1945 TO 1977

[In millions of dollars. See text, pp. 859–860. Negative figures (−) occur when the total of grant returns, principal repayments, and/or foreign currencies disbursed by the Government exceeds new grants and new credits utilized and/or acquisitions of foreign currencies through new sales of farm products. See also *Historical Statistics, Colonial Times to 1970*, series U 75–186]

TYPE AND COUNTRY	Post WW II period,[1] total	1945– 1955, total	1956– 1965, total	1966– 1972, total	1973	1974	1975	1976	1977, prel.
Total, net_____	185,949	55,132	47,317	46,049	6,804	7,323	8,671	7,930	6,723
Investment in int'l financial instit'ns___	5,982	635	655	1,155	373	537	654	1,102	870
African Development Fund_____	25	–	–	–	–	–	–	15	10
Asian Development Bank_____	216	–	–	67	12	2	30	75	31
Inter-American Development Bank___	2,183	–	300	665	197	192	268	255	307
Int'l Bank for Reconst. and Develop.	648	635	–	1	12	–	–	–	–
International Development Assn_____	2,874	–	320	422	152	344	357	757	521
International Finance Corporation____	35	–	35	–	–	–	–	–	–
Under assistance programs_____	179,967	54,497	46,662	44,894	6,431	6,785	8,017	6,828	5,853
Military grants [2]_____	66,421	16,445	19,159	20,134	2,853	2,842	2,891	1,339	757
Western Europe (excl. Greece and Turkey)_____	17,190	9,580	6,554	663	73	108	48	93	71
Near East [2] (incl. Greece, Turkey, Egypt) and South Asia_____	11,389	2,061	3,873	1,847	250	1,152	759	927	522
Africa (excl. Egypt)_____	424	7	166	174	11	19	21	17	10
Far East and Pacific_____	35,604	4,403	7,618	17,107	2,491	1,534	2,033	280	137
Western Hemisphere_____	1,361	236	712	310	25	24	25	16	13
Unspecified areas_____	454	159	237	32	3	6	6	6	5
Other grants, credits, and other assistance (through net accumulation of foreign currency claims)___	113,546	38,052	27,503	24,760	3,579	3,943	5,126	5,488	5,096
Developed countries [3]_____	24,925	27,127	−2,097	−220	45	−9	109	159	−188
Developing countries [3]_____	88,621	10,925	29,600	24,979	3,533	3,952	5,017	5,330	5,284

See footnotes at end of table.

No. 1506. U.S. GOVERNMENT FOREIGN GRANTS AND CREDITS, BY COUNTRIES: 1945 TO 1977—Continued

[In millions of dollars. See headnote, p. 868. See also *Historical Statistics, Colonial Times to 1970*, series U 75-186]

TYPE AND COUNTRY	Post WW II period,[1] total	1945–1955, total	1956–1965, total	1966–1972, total	1973	1974	1975	1976	1977, prel.
Western Europe	24,087	24,767	−951	−243	−20	131	271	182	−51
Austria	1,085	1,019	87	−13	−2	−3	−2	−2	−4
Belgium and Luxembourg	662	726	−70	−20	3	15	18	−2	−8
Denmark	299	284	−19	−11	24	10	15	−4	(z)
Finland	50	86	−26	−21	−6	(z)	7	10	−2
France	4,080	5,477	−1,238	−77	12	−11	−15	−41	−27
Germany, Federal Republic of	2,907	3,907	−852	−198	8	46	33	−22	−14
Iceland	53	34	33	−6	−3	−3	3	−3	−3
Ireland	58	146	−16	−8	−10	−15	−18	−6	−13
Italy	2,984	2,795	120	91	11	−8	−13	−13	1
Netherlands	946	1,051	−224	−27	52	34	56	14	−10
Norway	497	309	−71	39	38	95	92	30	−36
Portugal	453	67	93	−19	11	7	15	113	166
Spain	1,348	195	685	126	106	91	94	18	33
Sweden	119	108	−20	8	−1	6	4	11	4
United Kingdom	5,671	6,920	−532	−163	−132	−162	−89	−18	−152
Yugoslavia	2,089	860	1,042	117	−44	−27	39	78	23
Euro. Atomic Energy Community	34	–	51	5	−1	−5	−6	−5	−5
Euro. Coal and Steel Community	13	100	−27	−32	−5	−5	−6	−6	−6
European Payments Union	6	238	–	−114	−118	–	–	–	–
Other [4] and unspecified	734	444	33	79	38	67	44	26	3
Eastern Europe	2,203	1,097	501	17	369	−102	−58	166	214
Albania	20	20	–	–	–	–	–	–	–
Czechoslovakia	191	191	–	–	–	–	–	–	–
Eastern Germany	17	17	(z)	–	–	–	–	–	–
Hungary	17	18	5	−4	1	−1	−1	(z)	–
Poland	1,182	425	555	−70	11	−24	9	142	135
Romania	94	–	–	46	−1	27	20	22	−21
U.S.S.R.	682	425	−59	45	359	−104	−86	2	99
Near East and South Asia	33,099	3,163	12,338	8,944	1,027	623	1,936	2,407	2,661
Afghanistan	471	31	224	125	30	9	18	20	13
Bangladesh	876	–	–	79	137	105	380	78	97
Cyprus	107	–	19	6	−1	1	14	21	47
Egypt	1,968	41	1,009	177	−20	27	87	231	417
Greece	2,168	1,324	330	1	43	65	112	121	172
India	9,153	399	4,796	3,662	67	−182	243	120	46
Iran	1,180	211	477	551	221	37	−103	−109	−105
Iraq	35	7	37	(z)	−2	−2	−2	−2	−2
Israel	5,931	390	483	937	238	199	803	1,405	1,476
Jordan	1,175	26	455	271	64	57	63	100	139
Kuwait	–	–	–	25	−10	−10	−5	–	–
Lebanon	207	15	70	21	4	22	37	7	32
Nepal	220	3	86	74	12	10	8	16	12
Pakistan	4,975	178	2,416	1,654	134	122	134	253	84
Saudi Arabia	18	13	3	66	−17	−21	−11	−12	−4
Sri Lanka (Ceylon)	298	(z)	89	104	24	2	20	21	38
Syria	144	1	57	−3	(z)	(z)	18	23	48
Turkey	2,969	385	1,418	767	65	121	73	57	83
Yemen (Sana)	78	–	40	8	2	8	6	8	7
UNRWA [5]	795	131	274	215	20	33	28	39	55
Other and unspecified	332	7	57	204	17	21	12	8	6
Africa	6,681	143	2,096	2,186	298	465	409	509	576
Algeria	506	1	135	56	50	115	41	67	40
Benin	34	–	7	7	(z)	3	2	7	9
Cameroon	80	–	16	41	3	1	5	5	9
Chad	42	(z)	5	7	1	8	5	6	11
Ethiopia	341	9	109	102	18	26	30	34	14
Ghana	301	(z)	64	189	6	1	6	16	19
Guinea	144	–	58	44	8	6	9	9	9
Ivory Coast	80	–	14	38	16	3	1	(z)	8
Kenya	186	(z)	34	52	6	9	9	18	58
Lesotho	39	–	(z)	16	3	5	4	6	6
Liberia	255	25	135	86	−3	−2	(z)	15	−1
Libya	206	25	183	−2	(z)	–	–	–	–
Madagascar	22	(z)	7	10	(z)	1	2	1	3
Malawi	46	–	5	20	1	4	5	5	5
Mali	78	–	10	16	8	22	11	5	6
Morocco	975	7	443	331	13	30	8	105	37
Niger	86	–	5	14	10	29	11	9	8
Nigeria	366	(z)	87	241	24	10	8	3	−7
Senegal	85	–	15	24	8	7	8	8	14
Sierra Leone	76	(z)	22	27	2	3	4	7	10

See footnotes at end of table.

No. 1506. U.S. GOVERNMENT FOREIGN GRANTS AND CREDITS, BY COUNTRIES: 1945 TO 1977—Continued

[In millions of dollars. See headnote, p. 868. See also *Historical Statistics, Colonial Times to 1970*, series U 75–186]

TYPE AND COUNTRY	Post WW II period,[1] total	1945–1955, total	1956–1965, total	1966–1972, total	1973	1974	1975	1976	1977, prel.
Africa—Continued									
Somalia	95	(z)	42	40	1	(z)	6	3	3
South Africa	-92	20	-101	-11	-	-	(z)	(z)	(z)
Sudan	142	-	86	16	16	7	13	-4	9
Tanzania	227	2	34	67	8	11	37	37	30
Togo	34	-	9	10	2	3	3	3	4
Tunisia	784	2	392	302	12	17	12	13	33
Uganda	45	-	12	30	2	1	(z)	(z)	(z)
Upper Volta	69	-	5	16	7	11	6	8	15
Zaire	721	(z)	248	150	11	63	97	37	116
Zambia	75	-	1	13	8	9	5	8	31
Other and unspecified	635	51	13	236	57	58	65	76	81
Far East and Pacific	27,156	6,754	7,785	7,336	948	1,370	1,161	1,081	720
Australia	181	1	(z)	419	-59	-62	-23	-46	-50
Brunei	(z)	-	-	15	4	(z)	-	-20	-
Burma	120	22	76	16	1	(z)	-1	-1	8
Cambodia	847	28	228	97	128	288	78	-	-
China (Taiwan)	2,849	1,257	862	166	39	119	191	145	69
Hong Kong	81	3	35	9	(z)	13	19	6	-4
Indonesia	2,468	246	437	840	160	125	165	333	163
Japan	2,087	2,302	238	-245	-230	2	10	58	-48
Korea, Republic of	6,485	1,358	2,517	1,426	214	63	314	344	250
Laos	908	37	398	366	54	36	16	-	-
Malaysia	153	1	30	67	-5	19	3	15	24
New Zealand	115	5	-2	41	8	16	30	13	3
Papua New Guinea	(z)	-	(z)	27	3	(z)	(z)	-12	-18
Philippines	1,888	833	297	307	71	43	77	109	151
Ryukyu Islands	391	221	90	81	-	-	-	-	-
Thailand	723	39	324	229	21	19	11	7	72
Trust Territory of the Pacific Islands	788	30	89	272	64	73	79	90	91
Vietnam	6,689	245	2,088	3,170	437	585	164	-	-
Other and unspecified	381	126	78	34	37	29	29	42	8
Western Hemisphere	12,940	1,151	4,469	4,213	529	799	826	518	434
Argentina	402	86	294	14	-11	-4	-4	20	6
Bahamas	7	(z)	(z)	11	-2	-1	21	-1	-21
Bermuda	4	-	-	13	11	-2	-5	-8	-6
Bolivia	654	77	275	191	10	26	12	30	32
Brazil	3,313	470	1,200	922	78	263	193	145	41
Canada	259	-1	-5	75	65	87	45	13	-19
Cayman Islands	12	-	-	-	-	10	2	-1	1
Chile	1,367	85	651	450	28	84	128	-71	12
Colombia	1,234	31	386	620	95	45	36	21	1
Costa Rica	212	16	81	74	10	9	10	7	5
Cuba	41	18	23	-	-	-	-	-	-
Dominican Republic	543	-1	173	276	19	10	36	29	1
Ecuador	269	27	96	101	11	7	7	15	5
El Salvador	166	4	52	68	9	4	7	9	14
Guatemala	368	23	136	89	15	17	21	43	24
Guyana	91	(z)	7	47	4	5	16	7	6
Haiti	185	27	70	24	4	3	11	18	28
Honduras	197	6	50	58	10	13	24	18	18
Jamaica	152	16	2	54	18	22	25	8	7
Mexico	816	226	177	143	-4	95	70	34	75
Nicaragua	242	8	60	86	20	18	13	17	21
Panama	362	10	102	109	42	29	24	36	10
Paraguay	142	4	63	48	5	7	7	3	4
Peru	634	42	212	166	43	-19	50	43	96
Trinidad and Tobago	50	-	35	14	1	6	(z)	-4	-1
Uruguay	153	6	54	83	5	1	(z)	5	(z)
Venezuela	219	6	146	155	-16	-13	-19	-22	-19
Other[6] and unspecified	845	-38	129	323	63	78	95	103	93
Other international organizations and unspecified areas	7,379	976	1,265	2,306	427	657	581	626	541

- Represents zero.   Z Less than $500,000 or net minus (-) of less than $500,000.
[1] July 1, 1945, through Dec. 31, 1977. All lend-lease and conversions of prior grants to credits from V-J Day (Sept. 2, 1945). For additional details on immediate postwar period, see prior editions of the *Statistical Abstract*.   [2] See table 1505, footnote 5.   [3] See table 1505, footnote 7.   [4] Includes European Productivity Agency, North Atlantic Treaty Organization, and former Organization for European Economic Cooperation.   [5] United Nations Relief and Works Agency for Palestine refugees.   [6] Includes Caribbean Development Bank, Central American Bank for Economic Integration, Inter-American Institute of Agricultural Sciences, Organization of American States, and Pan American Health Organization.

Source: U.S. Bureau of Economic Analysis, *Foreign Grants and Credits by the United States Government*, periodic.

No. 1507. U.S. FOREIGN ECONOMIC AND MILITARY AID PROGRAMS: 1946 TO 1977

[In millions of dollars. For years ending June 30 except, beginning 1977, ending Sept. 30. Economic aid shown here represents total U.S. economic aid—not just aid under Foreign Assistance Act. Major components in recent years include AID, Food for Peace, Peace Corps, and paid-in subscriptions to international financial institutions, such as IBRD, and IDB. Cumulative totals for 1946–1977 are true totals net of deobligation; annual figures, however, are gross unadjusted program figures. Military aid includes Military Assistance Program (MAP) grants, foreign military credit sales, service-funded programs, and excess defense articles]

PERIOD OR YEAR	Total economic and military aid	ECONOMIC AID			MILITARY AID		
		Total	Loans	Grants	Total	Loans	Grants
1946–1977, total	199,609	120,891	41,257	79,634	78,718	9,137	69,581
1946–1952	34,988	31,186	8,518	22,668	3,801	–	3,801
1953–1961	48,296	24,053	5,850	18,203	24,243	164	24,079
1962–1965	25,602	17,039	8,346	8,693	8,564	436	8,127
1966–1969	27,114	16,353	7,075	9,279	10,761	1,184	9,577
1970	6,787	3,676	1,389	2,288	3,111	70	3,041
1971	8,078	3,442	1,299	2,143	4,635	743	3,892
1972	9,243	3,940	1,639	2,301	5,303	550	4,753
1973	9,875	4,117	1,391	2,726	5,758	550	5,208
1974	8,978	3,906	1,150	2,756	5,073	1,396	3,677
1975	7,239	4,908	1,679	3,229	2,331	750	1,581
1976	6,605	3,878	1,759	2,119	2,727	1,442	1,285
1976, TQ [1]	2,642	1,931	840	1,091	711	494	217
1977	7,946	5,591	2,083	3,508	2,355	1,411	944

– Represents zero.   [1] Transition quarter, July–Sept.

Source: U.S. Agency for International Development, *U.S. Overseas Loans and Grants and Assistance From International Organizations*, annual; *Operations Report*, annual; and unpublished data.

No. 1508. U.S. FOREIGN MILITARY AID, BY SELECTED COUNTRIES: 1970 TO 1977

[In millions of dollars, except percent. For years ending June 30 except, beginning 1976, ending Sept. 30. Military aid data include Military Assistance Program (MAP) grants, foreign military credit sales, service programs, and excess defense articles]

REGION AND COUNTRY	1970–1977		1975, total	1976, total [1]	1977, total	REGION AND COUNTRY	1970–1977		1975, total	1976, total [1]	1977, total
	Total	Percent grants					Total	Percent grants			
Total	32,004	76.9	2,331	2,727	2,355						
Near East and So. Asia [2]	9,625.9	48.2	600.5	1,795.8	1,438.7	East Asia [2]	18,591.1	92.9	1,233.6	422.4	352.9
Greece	861.7	35.9	86.0	156.6	156.0	Cambodia	1,260.1	100.0	256.0	–	–
Iran	18.7	100.0	–	–	–	China,					
Israel	6,665.2	44.3	300.0	1,500.0	1,000.0	Rep. of	986.6	55.4	82.7	81.1	35.5
Jordan	591.1	61.5	104.6	138.3	131.5	Indonesia	234.3	76.7	21.0	46.0	40.8
Lebanon	51.5	12.6	.1	.1	25.0	Korea	2,952.4	80.2	144.7	188.6	155.0
Saudi Arabia	15.2	13.2	(z)	–	–	Laos	1,119.5	100.0	19.9	–	–
Turkey	1,414.2	69.2	109.1	–	125.0	Malaysia	101.1	3.8	5.0	17.3	36.3
						Philippines	264.5	77.3	36.3	24.0	38.1
Latin America [2]	816.8	24.0	157.2	140.1	49.4	Thailand	627.2	88.1	42.5	65.4	47.2
Argentina	137.9	6.5	30.1	34.3	.7	Vietnam	11,041.9	100.0	625.1	–	–
Bolivia	47.4	64.1	7.4	3.4	3.1						
Brazil	214.2	6.6	65.4	44.6	.1	Africa [2]	488.8	25.0	70.5	92.9	115.4
Chile	50.4	15.9	.7	–	–	Ethiopia	122.4	70.6	37.6	7.4	2.7
Colombia	56.1	25.5	.7	20.3	.7	Kenya	51.2	2.3	5.0	15.9	15.2
Dominican						Liberia	8.2	26.8	1.9	1.8	.6
Republic	13.5	81.5	1.6	.8	1.5	Morocco	122.7	4.8	14.9	30.8	30.8
Ecuador	29.0	13.8	.4	10.4	15.4	Tunisia	78.4	23.9	7.2	15.6	25.4
El Salvador	10.4	66.3	5.5	1.0	.6	Zaire	92.0	7.2	3.8	19.3	30.4
Guatemala	22.2	53.2	2.9	2.1	.5						
Honduras	13.9	42.4	4.2	3.4	3.1	Europe [2]	435.8	72.5	3.0	3.2	170.5
Mexico	6.9	100.0	.1	.1	.1	Italy	11.6	100.0	–	–	–
Nicaragua	20.1	60.2	4.3	3.6	3.1	Portugal	48.6	100.0	.4	2.4	33.5
Panama	10.1	70.3	.6	1.2	3.1	Spain	374.6	68.0	2.6	.8	137.0
Paraguay	17.8	94.4	1.6	2.4	.7						
Peru	72.1	9.2	21.4	.8	10.9	Oceania	2.8	100.0	–	–	–
Uruguay	38.5	53.2	9.2	1.0	(z)	Interregional	2,042.3	100.0	266.3	273.3	228.0
Venezuela	49.0	18.4	.7	10.6	.1						

– Represents zero.   Z Less than $50,000.   [1] Includes transition quarter, July–Sept.
[2] Includes amounts not shown separately. Regional totals include aid to entire regions or sub-regions.

Source: U.S. Agency for International Development, *U.S. Overseas Loans and Grants and Assistance from International Organizations*, annual.

No. 1509. U.S. FOREIGN AID—COMMITMENTS FOR ECONOMIC ASSISTANCE, BY REGIONS AND COUNTRIES: 1948-1977 AND 1962-1977

[In millions of dollars, except percent. For periods ending Sept. 30. Falls under economic portion of the Foreign Assistance Act. Data cover commitments for economic and technical assistance by AID and predecessor agencies. The 1948-1977 totals are on a net basis, representing total new obligations entered into during the entire period, adjusted for any deobligations. Data for 1962-1977, are on a gross basis, i.e., representing total new obligations entered into, not adjusted for deobligations of prior years' funds. See text, pp. 859 and 860]

REGION AND COUNTRY	NET CUMULATIVE TOTAL,[1] 1948-1977		GROSS CUMULATIVE TOTAL, 1962-1977		REGION AND COUNTRY	NET CUMULATIVE TOTAL,[1] 1948-1977		GROSS CUMULATIVE TOTAL, 1962-1977	
	Total	Loan portion	Total	Loan portion		Total	Loan portion	Total	Loan portion
Economic assistance	66,149	20,248	37,442	16,748	Africa	3,523	1,560	3,046	1,412
					Algeria	4	–	4	–
Near East and S. Asia	17,627	9,823	12,466	8,493	Benin (Dahomey)	8	1	6	1
Afghanistan	333	85	252	74	Cameroon	28	13	28	13
Bangladesh	484	131	490	131	Central African Emp	6	–	6	–
Cyprus	74	–	77	2	Chad	21	–	18	–
Egypt	2,015	1,564	1,854	1,461	Ethiopia	261	135	224	137
Greece	1,126	164	135	114	Ghana	208	168	205	166
India	3,789	3,325	2,991	2,860	Guinea	46	8	52	10
Iran	600	219	96	45	Ivory Coast	14	7	13	7
Iraq	19	–	2	–					
Israel	2,567	729	2,150	641	Kenya	113	63	112	64
Jordan	966	110	730	94	Liberia	205	97	188	98
Lebanon	77	5	20	–	Libya	137	7	34	–
Nepal	72	(z)	62	9	Madagascar	10	5	10	5
Pakistan	2,755	2,022	2,012	1,833	Malawi	20	9	21	10
Saudi Arabia	27	–	–	–	Mali, Republic of	45	3	41	4
Sri Lanka (Ceylon)	73	56	61	58	Morocco	378	342	179	154
Syria	263	249	283	269	Niger	27	3	24	3
Turkey	2,115	1,128	1,080	880	Nigeria	310	83	349	120
Yemen Arab Rep	62	1	56	1	Senegal	30	–	27	1
Central Treaty Org	55	16	34	18					
Regional	153	18	80	–	Sierra Leone	13	–	14	–
					Somalia	62	16	57	17
Latin America	7,001	4,911	6,750	5,136	Southern Rhodesia	7	5	2	–
Argentina	137	120	143	126	Sudan	86	24	61	34
Bolivia	535	283	399	284	Tanzania	79	29	81	28
Brazil	1,392	1,187	1,480	1,311	Togo	7	–	7	–
Chile	664	585	644	607	Tunisia	347	201	235	168
Colombia	920	843	990	925	Uganda	36	10	44	17
Costa Rica	127	93	113	87	Upper Volta	19	–	15	–
Dominican Republic	352	205	375	225	Zaire	334	122	274	124
Ecuador	169	99	153	97	Zambia	11	5	6	–
El Salvador	103	60	96	61					
Guatemala	262	124	178	114	Regional:				
Guyana	80	60	83	64	Central and W. Africa	143	64	180	74
Haiti	132	28	92	27	East Africa	24	4	36	4
Honduras	171	113	153	107	Southern Africa	109	64	111	65
Jamaica	75	59	76	60	Africa	326	68	336	82
Mexico	78	66	70	67	Other	49	4	49	6
Nicaragua	206	165	194	159					
Panama	250	185	238	182	Europe	15,472	1,974	266	99
Paraguay	109	57	82	44	Austria	726	–	–	–
Peru	253	158	229	154	Belgium-Luxembourg	560	68	–	–
Trinidad and Tobago	39	–	31	–	Denmark	281	33	–	–
Uruguay	80	61	82	62	France	3,190	226	–	–
Venezuela	72	55	57	40	Germany:				
ROCAP [2]	274	224	274	222	Berlin (West)	119	–	1	–
East Caribbean Reg	64	61	65	63	Federal Rep. of	1,472	217	–	–
Regional	450	19	448	49	Iceland	60	25	(z)	–
Other	8	1	3	1	Ireland	147	128	–	–
					Italy	1,673	96	23	–
East Asia	14,744	1,897	8,534	1,546	Malta	67	5	67	5
Burma	60	34	22	8	Netherlands	992	153	–	–
Cambodia	550	–	379	–	Norway	277	39	–	–
China, Republic of	1,366	212	70	62	Poland	61	61	–	–
Indochina, undistrib	826	–	–	–	Portugal	186	129	135	93
Indonesia	985	686	799	659	Spain	596	99	38	–
Japan	22	–	1	–	Sweden	107	20	–	–
Korea	3,042	482	1,080	502	United Kingdom	3,835	385	–	–
Laos	875	–	643	–	Yugoslavia	574	188	3	(z)
Malaysia	20	20	–	–	Regional	551	103	–	–
Philippines	627	249	378	204					
Thailand	615	77	411	56	Non-Regional	7,781	83	6,379	61
Vietnam	5,467	128	4,490	50					
East Asia Regional	289	10	262	5					

See footnotes at end of table.

No. 1509. U.S. FOREIGN AID—COMMITMENTS FOR ECONOMIC ASSISTANCE, BY REGIONS AND COUNTRIES (continued): 1975 TO 1977

[In millions of dollars, except percent. See text, pp. 859 and 860, and headnote, p. 872]

REGION AND COUNTRY	GROSS CUMULATIVE TOTAL, 1975–1977 [1]		1975, total	1976, total	1977, total	REGION AND COUNTRY	GROSS CUMULATIVE TOTAL, 1975–1977 [1]		1975, total	1976, total	1977, total
	Total	Percent loan					Total	Percent loan			
Ec. assistance	9,345	40.1	2,519	2,333	3,178	East Asia	775	34.4	507	134	105
						Cambodia	55	–	55	–	–
Near East and						Indonesia	152	76.8	43	50	42
S. Asia	[2]4,947	[2]54.1	1,012	1,189	[2]1,838	Korea	26	90.0	20	6	(Z)
Afghanistan	44	22.7	16	6	20	Laos	24	–	24	–	–
Bangladesh	160	66.2	62	27	62	Philippines	152	74.0	55	54	35
Cyprus	1,747	78.6	25	10	18	Thailand	31	45.0	4	13	13
Egypt	73	–	253	258	699	Vietnam	193	–	191	2	–
Greece	65	100.0	–	–	–	East Asia Reg	142	–	113	10	15
India	20	100.0	20	–	–						
Israel	1,855	26.7	345	700	735	Africa [2]	589	34.3	171	134	232
Jordan	290	22.4	88	46	70	Cameroon	4	–	–	1	3
Nepal	13	–	3	3	7	Central African					
Pakistan	305	83.9	96	106	71	Empire	2	–	–	1	1
Sri Lanka						Chad	13	–	4	(Z)	7
(Ceylon)	39	98.0	9	10	21	Ethiopia	24	30.4	17	6	1
Syria	258	95.2	83	17	80	Ghana	22	44.8	3	12	5
Turkey	1	–	1	–	–	Guinea	2	–	1	(Z)	1
Yemen Arab Rep.	25	5.7	3	4	16	Kenya	51	73.5	16	4	30
Central Treaty						Liberia	34	60.5	12	3	19
Organization	2	–	1	1	1	Mali	27	–	13	3	10
Regional	31	–	9	2	19	Morocco	26	80.2	9	14	2
Latin America	734	67.9	239	238	187	Niger	15	–	(Z)	7	7
Bolivia	80	86.9	20	22	36	Nigeria	7	–	7	–	–
Brazil	5	(Z)	3	1	1	Senegal	17	–	6	1	9
Chile	53	94.9	31	21	1	Sierra Leone	1	–	1	(Z)	1
Colombia	36	85.0	14	14	1	Somali Rep	1	–	1	–	–
Costa Rica	14	82.1	1	7	6	Tanzania	32	38.1	16	7	7
Dominican Rep.	23	87.6	6	16	1	Tunisia	16	38.8	2	3	11
Ecuador	2	–	2	–	–	Upper Volta	10	–	5	1	3
El Salvador	3	–	1	2	–	Zaire	41	74.8	2	13	20
Guatemala	56	64.9	9	29	14	Regional:					
Guyana	9	98.9	1	2	6	Central and					
Haiti	45	28.9	4	9	21	West Africa	59	46.5	28	16	9
Honduras	50	76.2	25	15	8	East Africa	3	–	1	1	1
Jamaica	19	79.5	1	1	18	South. Africa	54	38.6	5	5	43
Nicaragua	59	91.2	40	17	1	Africa	94	5.1	12	33	35
Panama	49	89.1	8	23	14	Europe	204	45.7	28	45	88
Paraguay	14	51.8	7	4	2	Italy	23	–	–	1	3
Peru	40	82.7	9	13	17	Malta	33	–	10	10	10
Uruguay	14	83.7	13	1	1	Portugal	135	69.1	15	35	65
ROCAP [3]	28	71.9	6	2	3	Spain	13	–	3	–	10
East Caribbean											
Regional	33	95.4	9	17	7						
Regional	103	3.9	29	24	30	Non-Regional	2,097	.5	563	592	728

– Represents zero.   Z Less than $500,000 or .05 percent.   [1] Includes transition quarter, July 1 to Sept. 30, 1976.   [2] Includes countries not shown separately.
[3] Regional programs covering Costa Rica, El Salvador, Guatemala, Honduras, Nicaragua, and Panama.

Source: U.S. Agency for International Development, *U.S. Overseas Loans and Grants and Assistance from International Organizations*, annual; *Operations Report*, annual; and unpublished data.

No. 1510. EXPORTS FINANCED BY FOREIGN AND AGRICULTURAL AID: 1960 TO 1977

[In millions of dollars, except percent. Beginning 1970, includes silver ore and bullion. Excludes insurance and freight. See headnote, table 1507]

ITEM	1960	1965	1970	1972	1973	1974	1975	1976	1977
Total exports	20,575	27,478	43,224	49,759	71,339	98,507	107,592	114,992	120,163
Exports financed under F.A.A. and P.L. 480 [1]	2,685	3,242	2,543	2,283	1,923	1,929	2,307	1,897	1,859
Percent of total	13.0	11.8	5.9	4.6	2.7	2.0	2.1	1.6	1.5
Loans and grants (AID)	432	1,140	957	658	657	570	665	671	802
Military grant-aid	949	779	565	560	516	599	461	190	62
Agricultural aid (P.L. 480)	1,304	1,323	1,021	1,065	750	760	1,181	1,036	995
Sales for foreign currencies	1,014	899	276	70	4	–	–	–	–
Donations	173	253	255	377	209	272	257	265	292
Barter for strategic materials	117	19	–	–	–	–	–	–	–
Long-term dollar and convertible foreign currency credit sales	–	152	490	618	537	488	924	771	703

– Represents zero.   [1] Foreign Assistance Act and Public Law 480; see table 1219.
Source: U.S. Industry and Trade Administration, *Overseas Business Reports, U.S. Foreign Trade*, annual.

No. 1511. Exports and Imports of Merchandise: 1960 to 1977

[In millions of dollars, except per capita and percent. Beginning 1970, includes silver ore and bullion. For basis of dollar values, see text, pp. 860 and 861. See also *Historical Statistics, Colonial Times to 1970,* series U 190–195 and U 207–212]

ITEM	1960	1965	1970	1972	1973	1974	1975	1976	1977
Domestic and foreign exports [1]	20,575	27,478	43,224	49,778	71,339	98,507	107,592	114,992	120,163
Domestic	20,375	27,135	42,590	48,979	70,246	97,144	106,102	113,319	117,963
Per capita [2] _____dol__	111	138	206	235	334	458	497	527	544
Annual percent change [3] _____	16.8	3.7	13.7	12.6	43.4	38.3	9.2	6.8	4.1
Foreign (initially imports)_____	200	343	634	800	1,093	1,363	1,489	1,673	2,200
Total, excl. Special Category____	19,735	26,240	41,862	48,579	69,754	96,371	104,554	112,381	116,955
Special Category_____	840	1,238	1,362	1,200	1,585	2,136	3,037	2,611	3,208
Total, excl. M.A.P.[4] Grant-Aid shipments_____	19,626	26,699	42,659	49,219	70,823	97,908	107,130	114,802	120,101
M.A.P.[4] Grant-Aid shipments [5]_	949	779	565	560	516	599	461	190	62
General imports [6] _____	14,654	21,366	39,952	55,563	69,476	100,997	96,902	120,678	146,817
Per capita [2] _____dol__	80	108	193	266	328	477	454	566	677
Annual percent change [3] _____	−3.6	14.4	10.8	21.9	25.0	45.4	−4.1	25.7	20.5
Entered for immediate consump	13,282	19,661	38,064	53,080	66,513	97,364	93,145	117,080	(NA)
Entered for warehouse_____	1,372	1,705	1,888	2,483	2,963	3,633	3,758	3,597	(NA)
Merchandise trade balance_____	4,972	5,333	2,707	−6,344	1,347	−3,089	10,228	−5,876	−26,716
Imports for consumption_____	14,650	21,283	39,756	55,290	69,024	100,140	96,516	121,121	147,075
Per capita [2] _____dol__	80	108	192	265	326	473	452	563	678
Withdrawn from warehouse____	1,368	1,623	1,692	2,210	2,511	2,776	3,332	2,937	(NA)
Free_____	5,780	7,434	13,870	18,915	28,258	52,052	31,030	37,190	43,633
Percent of total_____	39	35	35	34	41	52	32	31	30
Dutiable_____	8,870	13,849	25,886	36,375	40,766	48,088	65,486	83,931	103,442
Duties calculated_____	1,084	1,643	2,584	3,124	3,620	3,771	3,780	4,675	5,485
Percent of imports_____	7.4	7.7	6.5	5.7	5.2	3.8	3.9	3.9	3.7

NA Not available.
[1] Includes "Special Category" items; certain commodities are grouped into special categories for security reasons.
[2] Based on estimated population including Armed Forces abroad as of July 1, except 1970 as of April 1.
[3] From previous year. (For 1960, from 1959, 1965 from 1964, etc.)
[4] M.A.P. = Military Assistance Program.
[5] Data represent shipments only from United States and differ from U.S. Dept. of Defense figures because of differences in statistical definitions.   [6] Prior to 1976, customs value basis; thereafter, f.a.s. value basis.
Source: U.S. Bureau of the Census. For 1960, *Foreign Commerce and Navigation of the United States;* thereafter, *Highlights of U.S. Export and Import Trade,* FT 990, monthly; *U.S. Imports, General and Consumption, Schedule A Commodity and Country,* FT 135, monthly; *U.S. Exports, Schedule B Commodity and Country,* FT 410, monthly; and unpublished data.

No. 1512. Merchandise Trade—Balance of Payments Basis: 1960 to 1977

[In billions of dollars. Adjusted to balance of payments basis, from basic data of U.S. Bureau of the Census]

ITEM	1960	1965	1968	1969	1970	1971	1972	1973	1974	1975	1976	1977, prel.
Exports_____	19.7	26.5	33.6	36.4	42.5	43.3	49.4	71.4	98.3	107.1	114.7	120.5
Imports_____	−14.8	−21.5	−33.0	−35.8	−39.9	−45.6	−55.8	−70.5	−103.7	−98.0	−124.0	−151.7
Balance_____	4.9	5.0	.6	.6	2.6	−2.3	−6.4	.9	5.4	9.0	−9.4	−31.1

Source: U.S. Bureau of Economic Analysis, *Survey of Current Business,* June 1978.

No. 1513. Export and Import Unit Value Indexes—Selected Countries: 1960 to 1977

[Indexes in U.S. dollars, 1975=100. A unit value is an implicit price derived from value and quantity data]

COUNTRY AND ITEM	1960	1965	1967	1968	1969	1970	1971	1972	1973	1974	1976	1977
United States: Export_____	46	49	51	52	54	57	59	60	70	89	104	105
Import_____	40	40	42	42	43	46	49	52	62	93	103	112
Japan: Export_____	57	48	50	50	52	55	57	64	78	100	98	112
Import_____	38	38	38	38	38	40	42	45	56	93	101	108
France: Export_____	43	46	47	47	48	49	52	58	72	84	98	105
Import_____	46	46	47	46	46	48	50	55	67	91	99	108
Germany: Export_____	40	44	44	44	46	51	54	60	75	88	100	110
Import_____	45	47	48	47	48	52	54	58	74	95	101	110
Italy: Export_____	48	48	47	47	49	51	54	60	70	88	94	[1] 106
Import_____	37	38	39	39	40	41	43	48	61	95	98	[1] 108
United Kingdom: Export_____	47	51	53	50	51	55	59	63	70	86	98	112
Import_____	42	43	44	43	44	46	49	52	65	94	100	112
Canada: Export_____	49	47	50	51	52	56	58	61	69	94	106	104
Import_____	53	54	55	56	58	60	64	67	71	90	104	108

[1] Average for first three quarters.
Source: International Monetary Fund, *International Financial Statistics,* monthly.

No. 1514. Exports and Imports—Indexes of Total Value, Unit Value (Average Price), and Quantity: 1966 to 1977

[1967 average=100. See headnote, table 1513. See also *Historical Statistics, Colonial Times to 1970*, series U 225–248]

INDEX AND ECONOMIC CLASS	EXPORTS OF U.S. MERCHANDISE [1]						GENERAL IMPORTS					
	1966–1970, avg.	1971–1973, avg.	1974	1975	1976	1977 [2]	1966–1970, avg.	1971–1973, avg.	1974	1975	1976	1977 [2]
Total value	112.3	175.2	315.0	344.7	369.1	384.7	120.3	211.5	375.6	360.4	452.9	549.8
Foods: Crude	99.9	195.4	400.2	454.8	440.0	363.6	112.2	152.1	187.8	183.8	263.7	356.6
Manufactured	107.2	164.4	262.9	264.5	298.5	335.6	113.4	179.1	245.8	236.4	249.2	268.2
Materials, crude	108.5	178.5	338.5	330.5	358.5	424.4	107.0	157.9	539.5	633.5	863.6	1099.1
Manufactures:												
Semi	118.6	156.6	316.2	285.5	310.7	314.2	115.9	190.5	394.8	309.8	366.5	447.9
Finished	113.7	177.3	303.2	353.0	381.3	401.8	128.5	250.9	369.5	354.5	441.3	521.2
Unit value	103.0	123.1	174.5	195.1	202.1	211.8	103.2	130.7	223.3	241.2	248.8	269.2
Foods: Crude	98.0	123.2	242.7	242.5	219.0	189.5	106.3	131.3	173.0	168.0	230.0	371.1
Manufactured	101.8	136.6	209.4	200.5	184.1	201.4	103.6	132.2	204.5	216.2	187.4	178.5
Materials, crude	101.5	135.6	227.5	250.7	256.2	284.3	102.8	118.4	349.1	364.8	393.7	424.5
Manufactures:												
Semi	99.2	109.2	195.6	198.7	188.0	196.3	103.2	128.0	275.4	280.0	275.8	302.9
Finished	105.1	123.3	149.3	176.4	192.0	204.1	102.8	133.8	186.1	211.4	215.7	226.2
Quantity	108.7	140.9	180.5	176.7	182.7	181.7	116.0	160.8	168.2	149.4	182.1	204.2
Foods: Crude	101.7	149.2	164.9	187.5	200.9	191.9	105.5	115.8	108.6	109.4	114.7	96.1
Manufactured	105.2	120.1	125.6	131.9	162.2	166.6	108.9	134.7	132.2	109.2	133.0	150.3
Materials, crude	106.7	129.9	148.6	131.8	139.9	149.3	104.1	131.4	154.5	174.3	219.4	258.9
Manufactures:												
Semi	119.6	141.8	161.6	143.7	165.3	160.1	112.1	147.9	143.4	110.7	132.9	147.9
Finished	107.6	143.2	203.0	200.3	198.5	169.9	124.1	186.3	198.6	167.7	204.6	230.4

[1] Excludes military grant-aid. [2] Preliminary.

Source: U.S. Bureau of the Census, *Indexes of U.S. Exports and Imports by Economic Class, 1919–1971*, and unpublished data.

No. 1515. Exports of Leading Commodities—Value, by Areas: 1976 and 1977

[In millions of dollars, except percent. Includes silver ore and bullion]

COMMODITY	1976					1977				
	Total [1]	Canada	American Republics	Western Europe [2]	Far East [3]	Total [1]	Canada	American Republics	Western Europe [2]	Far East [3]
Total	114,992	24,106	15,487	32,396	20,495	120,163	25,749	16,346	33,752	21,391
Percent	100.0	21.0	13.5	28.2	17.8	100.0	21.4	13.6	28.1	17.8
Agricultural commodities:										
Grains and preparations [4]	10,911	135	916	2,997	3,213	8,755	110	880	2,416	2,426
Fruits, nuts, vegetables [4]	1,535	505	82	545	284	1,597	549	94	510	293
Tobacco, unmanufactured	922	3	25	437	343	1,094	4	30	485	415
Soybeans	3,315	87	76	1,901	882	4,393	97	127	2,508	1,240
Cotton, excl. linters and waste	1,049	47	4	103	865	1,530	68	4	219	1,160
Nonagricultural: [5]										
Ores and scrap, metal	1,285	171	81	636	387	1,197	169	71	531	406
Coal, coke, and briquettes	2,988	760	192	941	1,059	2,730	792	212	709	938
Petroleum products	998	146	158	383	165	1,276	348	157	418	178
Chemicals	9,959	1,433	2,165	3,527	1,715	10,827	1,539	2,350	3,737	1,952
Machinery [5][6]	32,031	6,792	5,460	8,460	4,571	33,343	6,927	5,588	9,213	4,562
Agricultural machines, tractors, parts [6]	2,930	1,085	525	510	122	2,780	1,012	562	527	133
Other nonelectrical [5]	19,823	4,152	3,320	5,453	2,478	20,278	4,300	3,295	5 907	2,308
Electrical apparatus	9,278	1,555	1,615	2,497	1,971	10,285	1,615	1,731	2 779	2,121
Road motor vehicles [5][7]	9,950	6,413	1,230	571	273	10,690	7,143	1,326	630	286
Automotive parts, non-military	4,213	3,094	484	254	93	4,673	3,461	535	291	95
Aircraft, civilian, and parts for all aircraft	5,134	165	496	1,488	859	4,680	201	392	1,408	980
Pulp, paper, and manufactures	2,621	499	460	927	386	2,564	430	489	871	429
Metals and manufactures	5,181	1,524	916	1,184	582	5,149	1,627	918	1,069	447
Iron and steelmill products [8]	1,833	571	427	296	189	1,608	605	354	201	122
Textile yarn, fabrics, and made-up articles	1,971	520	257	702	142	1,959	518	296	649	137
Other (incl. Special Category)	25,142	4,906	2,969	7,594	4,769	28,379	5,227	3,412	8,379	5,542

[1] Includes areas not shown separately. [2] Includes Greece and Turkey. [3] Asia, excluding Near East.
[4] Includes shipments for relief by individuals and private agencies. [5] Excludes "Special Category."
[6] Includes parts for tractors. [7] Excludes parts for tractors. [8] Excludes pig iron.

Source: U.S. Dept. of Commerce, Industry and Trade Administration, *Overseas Business Reports, U.S. Trade with Major World Areas*, periodic.

No. 1516. Exports and Imports of Merchandise, by Continents, Areas, and Countries: 1960 to 1977

[In millions of dollars, except percent. Beginning 1965, includes uranium, thorium, and related products; beginning 1970, includes silver ore and bullion. See Historical Statistics, Colonial Times to 1970, series U 317–352, for selected countries]

CONTINENT, AREA, AND COUNTRY	EXPORTS, DOMESTIC AND FOREIGN [1]								GENERAL IMPORTS [2]							
	1960	1965	1970	1973	1974	1975	1976	1977	1960	1965	1970	1973	1974	1975	1976	1977
Total [3]	20,576	27,478	43,224	[4]71,339	[4]98,507	[4]107,592	[4]114,992	[4]120,163	14,654	21,366	39,952	[4]69,476	[4]100,997	[4]96,902	[4]120,678	[4]146,817
Developed countries [5]	13,250	18,315	29,877	47,209	63,020	64,780	70,595	73,837	8,605	14,067	29,259	48,530	60,475	56,700	66,996	78,206
Percent of total	64.4	66.7	69.1	66.2	64.0	60.2	61.4	61.4	58.7	65.8	73.2	69.9	59.9	58.5	55.5	53.3
Developing countries [5]	7,131	9,023	12,993	20,963	32,695	39,215	40,364	43,282	5,965	7,142	10,442	20,312	39,500	39,311	52,628	67,480
Communist areas, total	194	140	354	2,491	2,240	3,092	3,640	2,716	84	142	227	593	1,007	891	1,059	1,119
Africa	793	1,229	1,580	2,306	3,659	4,949	5,206	5,546	534	878	1,113	2,583	6,621	8,299	12,644	17,024
Asia	4,186	6,012	10,027	18,419	25,785	28,223	29,729	31,429	2,721	4,528	9,621	18,157	27,522	27,252	39,367	49,422
Australia and Oceania	514	956	1,189	1,744	2,697	2,340	2,690	2,877	266	463	871	1,562	1,505	1,508	1,171	1,720
Europe	7,399	9,364	14,817	23,161	30,070	32,732	35,901	36,296	4,268	6,292	11,395	19,812	24,625	21,623	23,640	28,331
North America	5,506	7,742	12,367	20,175	27,889	30,040	35,479	34,412	4,429	6,579	13,970	22,810	31,735	30,976	35,594	40,823
South America	2,177	2,175	3,244	7,856	7,856	8,803	8,595	9,276	2,435	2,624	2,958	4,512	8,975	7,232	7,761	9,343
West. Hemisphere	7,684	9,917	15,612	25,033	35,745	38,843	41,074	43,687	6,864	9,203	16,928	27,322	40,710	38,209	43,356	50,309
Canada	3,810	5,643	9,079	15,104	19,936	21,744	24,106	25,749	2,901	4,832	11,092	17,715	22,286	22,151	26,237	29,356
20 Latin American countries	3,577	3,788	5,695	8,921	14,501	15,655	15,487	16,347	3,528	3,675	4,779	7,827	13,679	11,847	13,228	16,335
Other Western Hemisphere	297	487	837	1,008	1,309	1,444	1,481	1,592	436	696	1,057	1,780	4,745	4,210	3,891	4,618
Central American Common Market	216	341	425	621	1,032	968	1,153	1,478	180	279	416	686	788	810	1,208	1,529
Costa Rica	45	61	95	150	232	212	255	323	35	57	117	142	170	179	233	285
El Salvador	43	61	64	111	202	194	232	314	32	48	48	119	161	182	287	427
Guatemala	64	96	100	148	240	255	334	377	59	67	87	168	211	173	293	334
Honduras	35	54	89	103	159	151	162	240	34	72	103	150	150	145	216	253
Nicaragua	30	69	77	109	199	156	169	223	21	36	61	109	97	131	181	181
Latin American Free Trade Association	2,978	3,224	4,885	7,708	12,569	13,773	13,395	13,895	2,838	3,205	4,071	6,703	12,200	10,100	11,208	13,848
Argentina	359	268	441	451	597	628	544	731	98	122	172	278	381	215	308	383
Bolivia	25	42	46	105	105	138	133	214	9	31	25	38	102	89	114	161
Brazil	494	348	840	1,916	3,088	3,056	2,809	2,482	570	512	670	1,189	1,705	1,467	1,737	2,246
Chile	203	237	300	248	452	533	508	520	193	209	157	102	311	138	222	261
Colombia	253	198	395	437	659	643	703	782	299	277	269	409	517	596	655	822
Ecuador	57	80	127	173	326	410	415	565	65	106	109	185	473	463	539	609
Mexico	831	1,106	1,704	2,937	4,855	5,141	4,990	4,806	443	638	1,219	2,306	3,386	3,066	3,598	4,685
Paraguay	9	16	18	25	30	33	38	51	8	13	11	21	21	21	20	23
Peru	147	282	214	415	647	896	573	500	183	241	341	375	609	397	379	499
Uruguay	63	20	41	29	42	51	54	74	21	36	19	16	16	24	62	88
Venezuela	567	626	759	1,033	1,768	2,243	2,628	3,171	948	1,018	1,082	1,787	4,679	3,625	3,574	4,072
Other Latin America	383	222	385	592	900	914	940	973	510	191	292	438	691	937	812	959
Cuba	225	(Z)	(Z)	(Z)	(Z)	(Z)	(Z)	1	357	(Z)	(Z)	(Z)	(Z)	(Z)	(Z)	(Z)
Dominican Republic	42	76	143	229	410	453	432	424	110	111	184	308	471	634	523	631
Haiti	25	21	34	77	125	144	150	203	18	20	32	64	112	107	148	169

Other Western Hemisphere	4,618	3,891	4,210	4,745	1,780	1,057	696	436	1,592	1,481	1,444	1,309	1,008	837	487	297
Bahamas	1,050	670	880	961	290	82	24	8	224	199	208	253	206	173	107	49
Barbados	32	30	34	32	12	9	5	1	59	49	36	38	34	22	9	6
Bermuda	6	4	3	2	2	1	1	2	87	79	63	63	52	92	44	32
British Honduras (Belize, 1973)	18	13	34	30	14	7	7	2	31	23	26	19	12	11	8	5
French West Indies	4	5	1	1	1	9	7	(Z)	34	32	26	33	19	15	11	4
Greenland	18	8	7	4	8	2	4	1	3	4	8	6	2	1	(Z)	1
Guyana	55	62	87	83	45	43	21	11	62	95	89	66	41	25	20	12
Jamaica	347	312	307	233	176	187	125	54	271	285	381	337	268	218	87	48
Leeward & Windward Is.	9	19	15	27	10	6	2	2	65	38	41	34	31	32	13	6
Netherlands Antilles	1,236	1,174	1,559	2,018	738	416	319	265	304	248	228	193	159	126	75	65
Surinam	120	87	108	73	64	56	33	30	119	93	79	73	44	35	36	18
Trinidad and Tobago	1,658	1,500	1,171	1,273	410	232	142	55	306	309	256	192	133	84	75	36
Other	15	8	8	8	9	8	5	3	27	24	3	4	7	4	1	18
Western Europe	27,417	22,789	20,892	23,734	19,286	11,169	6,155	4,187	33,752	32,396	29,945	28,637	21,360	14,463	9,224	7,204
Organis. for Econ. Coop. and Develop. (OECD)	27,070	22,398	20,627	23,460	19,114	11,070	6,091	4,091	33,338	32,048	29,575	28,267	21,095	14,279	9,066	6,983
European Econ. Com.[6][7]	22,087	17,844	16,733	19,206	15,607	9,222	4,982	3,382	26,476	25,409	22,865	22,069	16,747	11,298	7,145	5,650
Belgium and Luxembourg	1,441	1,119	1,199	1,683	1,273	696	494	364	3,171	2,993	2,417	2,294	1,623	1,195	650	467
Denmark[6]	584	560	464	477	460	284	147	98	532	444	445	360	404	227	209	146
France[6]	3,031	2,509	2,164	2,305	1,732	942	615	396	3,503	3,446	3,031	2,942	2,263	1,483	971	699
Germany, West	7,215	5,592	5,410	6,429	5,345	3,127	1,341	897	5,982	5,731	5,194	4,985	3,756	2,741	1,650	1,272
Ireland[7]	234	201	178	247	204	135	58	28	378	280	193	193	159	112	69	43
Italy	3,038	2,530	2,457	2,593	2,002	1,316	620	393	2,788	3,071	2,867	2,752	2,119	1,353	891	715
Netherlands	1,477	1,080	1,089	1,449	934	528	251	213	4,796	4,643	4,193	3,979	2,859	1,661	1,088	817
Trieste, Free Territory of.	(X)	(X)	(X)	(X)	(X)	1				(X)	(X)	(X)	2	(X)	2	4
United Kingdom[6]	5,068	4,254	3,773	4,023	3,657	2,194	1,405	963	5,380	4,801	4,527	4,574	3,564	2,536	1,615	1,487
Other OECD	4,983	4,553	3,894	4,255	3,507	1,848	1,159	709	6,862	6,639	6,710	6,199	4,348	2,981	1,921	1,334
Austria[8]	281	237	243	457	230	120	66	49	245	197	181	148	118	74	58	80
Finland[7][8]	276	189	149	212	179	114	84	(7)	195	243	261	201	133	99	76	(7)
Greece	176	146	110	158	93	52	44	33	539	591	450	488	375	203	172	103
Iceland	159	124	85	75	78	47	20	10	36	35	32	38	26	13	18	12
Norway	754	651	403	311	263	142	124	66	541	500	510	498	296	196	140	108
Portugal	146	128	157	241	195	92	56	35	551	400	427	407	232	126	75	45
Spain[8]	970	914	836	899	762	353	133	88	1,875	2,020	2,164	1,899	1,319	712	472	208
Sweden[8]	990	918	887	858	757	399	243	170	1,099	1,029	925	908	542	543	336	332
Switzerland[8]	1,085	1,025	879	902	817	459	306	198	1,359	1,173	1,153	1,150	960	700	369	263
Turkey	145	222	145	142	133	70	83	60	424	451	608	463	347	315	205	178
Special category[9]	(X)	(X)	(X)	(X)	(X)	(X)	(X)	(X)	(X)	(X)	-	-	-	(X)	(X)	5

- Represents zero.   X Not applicable.   Z Less than $500,000.
[1] For 1960 and 1965, reflects declassification of Special Category commodities as authorized January 5, 1968; area and country totals reflect relaxation of security restrictions as authorized July 17, 1969.
[2] 1960–1975, customs value basis; thereafter, f.a.s. value basis.
[3] Includes estimates for low-valued shipments from countries which could not be identified because of illegible reporting on import entries.
[4] Includes unidentified countries, not shown separately.
[5] Developed countries include Canada, Western Europe, Japan, Australia, New Zealand, and Republic of South Africa; developing countries include rest of the world excluding Communist areas in Europe and Asia. Assignment of countries generally follows that made by United Nations. (See table 1549.)
[6] As of January 1, 1973, United Kingdom, Denmark, and Ireland became members of EEC. For consistency, data for all years are shown on same basis.
[7] Finland included in other Western Europe for 1960, and in OECD thereafter.
[8] Excludes special category exports, if any, for 1960; thereafter includes special category exports, if any.
[9] Prior to 1973, security regulations required that information on exports of Special Category commodities be excluded from the totals for certain countries.

No. 1516. EXPORTS AND IMPORTS OF MERCHANDISE, BY CONTINENTS, AREAS, AND COUNTRIES: 1960 TO 1977—Continued

[In millions of dollars, except percent. Beginning 1965, includes uranium, thorium, and related products; beginning 1970, includes silver ore and bullion. See *Historical Statistics, Colonial Times to 1970*, series U 317–352, for selected countries]

CONTINENT, AREA, AND COUNTRY	EXPORTS, DOMESTIC AND FOREIGN [1]								GENERAL IMPORTS [2]							
	1960	1965	1970	1973	1974	1975	1976	1977	1960	1965	1970	1973	1974	1975	1976	1977
West. Europe—Con.																
Other West. Europe [7]	221	158	183	267	370	369	348	414	95	65	99	176	274	265	392	347
Finland [7][8]	57	(7)	(7)	(7)	(7)	(7)	(7)	(7)	52	(7)	(7)	(7)	(7)	(7)	(7)	(7)
Yugoslavia	88	149	168	236	310	328	298	357	41	61	96	170	268	261	385	335
Other & Spec. Category [9]	76	9	15	31	60	41	51	61	2	3	3	6	6	4	6	8
Communist areas in Europe	194	140	354	1,801	1,433	2,787	3,504	2,544	81	137	226	526	891	731	856	914
Bulgaria	(Z)	4	15	6	22	30	43	24	1	2	2	5	8	20	27	18
Czechoslovakia	5	28	23	72	49	53	149	75	12	17	24	35	46	31	37	37
Germany, East	4	12	33	28	22	17	65	36	1	7	9	11	75	11	14	17
Hungary	2	9	28	33	56	76	63	81	2	2	6	17	75	35	48	47
Poland	143	35	70	350	396	583	623	439	39	66	98	183	266	243	310	325
Romania	1	6	66	117	278	191	250	260	1	2	13	56	131	133	197	233
Union of Soviet Socialist Republics	39	45	119	1,194	608	1,835	2,310	1,628	23	43	72	220	350	255	220	234
Other	1	(Z)	(Z)	1	1	2	1	2	(Z)	(Z)	1	1	1	3	3	3
Asia	4,186	6,012	10,027	18,419	25,785	28,223	29,729	31,429	2,721	4,528	9,621	18,157	27,522	27,252	39,367	49,422
Japan	1,447	2,080	4,652	8,313	10,679	9,563	10,145	10,522	1,149	2,414	5,875	9,676	12,456	11,425	15,504	18,623
Communist areas in Asia	–	(Z)	(Z)	690	807	305	136	172	3	4	1	67	116	160	203	205
Other Asia	2,739	3,932	5,375	9,416	14,300	18,356	19,448	20,735	1,570	2,110	3,745	8,414	14,950	15,667	23,660	30,593
Near East Asia	532	831	1,346	2,815	5,102	8,263	9,234	10,038	312	376	348	1,371	4,671	5,401	9,011	12,811
Bahrain	8	10	12	41	80	90	280	203	3	3	3	17	61	100	30	74
Iran	156	195	326	772	1,734	3,244	2,772	2,731	51	88	67	343	2,136	1,398	1,480	2,789
Iraq	37	49	22	56	285	310	382	211	27	20	3	16	1	19	110	382
Israel	130	224	592	962	1,206	1,551	1,409	1,447	27	62	150	269	280	314	423	570
Jordan	20	27	63	79	105	195	234	302	(Z)	(Z)	(Z)	(Z)	(Z)	1	(Z)	3
Kuwait	41	66	62	120	209	366	472	548	124	47	25	65	13	111	38	215
Lebanon	45	75	64	162	287	368	49	124	3	6	13	33	30	33	5	43
Saudi Arabia	46	137	141	442	835	1,502	2,774	3,575	65	106	20	515	1,670	2,623	5,213	6,359
Syrian Arab Republic	38	13	11	21	40	128	273	134	7	2	2	6	7	7	10	16
Other	11	35	52	160	322	508	590	764	4	41	61	109	478	796	1,702	2,361
East and South Asia	2,207	3,100	4,030	6,601	9,198	10,095	10,213	10,698	1,258	1,735	3,397	7,048	10,279	10,267	14,649	17,782
Afghanistan [10]	10	14	11	3	10	19	13	8	20	12	1	3	4	8	12	1
Burma [11]	10	14	11	4	5	10	13		20	1	1	2	2	2	2	15
China (Taiwan)	277	234	527	1,170	1,427	1,659	1,635	1,798	139	93	549	1,784	2,107	1,946	2,989	3,681
Hong Kong	125	191	406	740	882	808	1,117	1,292	228	343	944	1,450	1,637	1,573	2,413	2,916
India [11]	650	928	572	527	760	1,290	1,136	779	216	348	298	437	561	549	708	781
Indonesia	100	42	266	442	531	810	1,035	763	7	165	182	505	1,693	2,222	3,004	3,491
Khmer Rep. (Cambodia)	9	2	2	144	180	66	(Z)	(Z)	5	54	370	974	1,460	1,442	2,404	2,895

Country	1	2	3	4	5	6	7	8	9	10	11	12	13	14	15	16
Laos [10]	7	9	8	10	19	4	(Z)	–	(X)	(z)	(z)	(Z)	1	(Z)	1	1
Malaysia [11]	(X)	91	67	157	377	393	336	561	36	270	212	440	775	772	940	1,322
Pakistan [11]	182	336	325	239	396	372	394	293	307	80	45	40	61	49	70	57
Philippines	307	349	373	495	747	832	318	876	(X)	472	369	670	1,091	756	883	1,103
Singapore	(X)	(X)	240	684	988	994	965	1,172	39	26	33	467	553	534	695	875
Sri Lanka [11] (Ceylon)	14	10	12	23	23	38	37	53	56	100	41	30	41	40	43	67
Thailand [10]	71	107	150	256	369	357	347	510	(X)	1	(X)	141	186	217	276	350
Vietnam, South	(X)	(X)	352	314	675	213	(X)	(X)	184	16	14	3	8	6	(X)	(X)
Other & Spec. Category	214	501	64	145	263	468	151	204	(X)	(X)	(X)	101	98	149	207	225
Australia and Oceania	514	956	1,189	1,744	2,697	2,340	2,690	2,877	266	453	871	1,562	1,505	1,508	1,671	1,720
Australia	423	797	986	1,439	2,157	1,815	2,185	2,356	142	311	611	1,067	1,044	1,147	1,211	1,185
New Zealand & W. Samoa	78	133	135	248	454	411	417	406	119	130	222	410	348	245	330	358
Other	14	25	68	56	86	114	88	115	6	12	38	85	113	116	130	178
Africa	793	1,229	1,580	2,306	3,659	4,949	5,206	5,546	534	878	1,113	2,583	6,621	8,299	12,644	17,024
Algeria	28	21	62	161	315	632	487	527	1	8	10	215	1,091	1,359	2,209	3,065
Angola	11	13	38	38	62	53	35	38	26	48	68	167	378	425	264	310
Cameroon, Fed. Rep. of	(X)	7	19	15	20	30	40	54	(X)	13	25	30	27	18	24	37
Central African Republic	(X)	1	1	3	1	1	1	1	(X)	10	6	8	7	5	2	4
Egypt	151	158	77	225	455	683	810	982	32	16	23	26	70	28	93	170
Ethiopia	12	22	26	25	33	70	78	58	27	64	67	79	64	49	94	90
Gabon	(X)	5	7	19	33	59	46	30	(X)	11	9	12	162	197	190	225
Ghana	17	36	59	63	77	100	133	146	52	59	91	90	126	151	155	214
Ivory Coast	(X)	11	36	69	49	78	64	89	(X)	46	92	108	95	157	248	318
Kenya	(X)	24	34	39	49	49	43	77	(X)	13	23	26	39	36	60	92
Liberia	36	39	46	46	70	90	85	91	39	51	51	72	96	99	99	107
Libya	43	65	34	104	139	232	277	314	(Z)	30	39	216	72	1,045	2,243	3,796
Malagasy Republic	3	4	108	15	7	7	6	7	13	29	32	40	96	46	60	79
Mauritania	(X)	4	7	9	11	14	19	18	(X)	1	1	1	60	(Z)	(Z)	(Z)
Morocco	36	56	89	113	184	200	297	372	10	10	10	14	20	10	17	21
Mozambique	10	9	22	32	32	18	13	13	5	18	18	34	45	36	41	66
Nigeria	26	74	129	161	286	536	770	988	40	60	71	652	3,289	3,281	4,938	6,096
South Africa, Republic of	288	438	563	746	1,160	1,302	1,348	1,054	108	226	290	377	609	840	925	1,269
Sudan	7	15	7	39	64	103	106	87	5	11	12	9	27	24	24	19
Tanzania	(X)	7	12	11	51	66	36	39	(Z)	24	7	8	8	29	47	78
Tunisia	22	44	49	60	87	90	82	111	(Z)	3	33	27	21	26	56	11
Uganda	(X)	2	4	2	8	15	6	14	(X)	43	48	33	26	61	107	248
Zaire	(X)	71	62	110	145	188	99	114	(X)	38	41	57	61	67	193	173
Zambia	(X)	(X)	31	39	68	86	48	49	(X)	(X)	2	71	68	68	161	105
Other	103	103	89	163	252	251	277	302	174	77	59	213	227	331	396	431

– Represents zero. X Not applicable. Z Less than $500,000.

[1] For 1960 and 1965, reflects declassification of Special Category commodities as authorized Jan. 5, 1968; area and country totals reflect relaxation of security restrictions as authorized July 17, 1969.

[2] 1960–1975, customs value basis; thereafter, f.a.s. value basis.

[7] Finland included in Other Western Europe for 1960 and in OECD thereafter.

[8] Excludes Special Category exports, if any, for 1960; thereafter, includes Special Category exports, if any.

[9] Prior to 1973, security regulations required that information on exports of Special Category commodities be excluded from the totals for certain countries.

[10] Includes Special Category exports, if any, for 1960; excludes Special Category exports, if any, thereafter, except for 1973.

[11] Excludes Special Category exports, if any, for all years except 1973.

Source: U.S. Bureau of the Census, Foreign Commerce and Navigation of the United States; Highlights of U.S. Export and Import Trade, FT 990, monthly; and unpublished data.

No. 1517. EXPORTS AND IMPORTS—VALUE, BY BROAD END-USE CLASS: 1967 TO 1977

[Data are adjusted to balance of payments basis, excluding military; for details, see source. Exports include re-exports. See also *Historical Statistics, Colonial Times to 1970*, series U 249–263]

END-USE CLASS	TOTAL (bil. dol.)								PERCENT			
	1967	1970	1972	1973	1974	1975	1976	1977	1967	1970	1975	1977
Exports, total_____	30.7	42.5	49.4	71.4	98.3	107.1	114.7	120.6	100	100	100	100
Foods, feeds, and beverages_____	5.0	5.9	7.5	15.2	18.6	19.2	19.8	19.8	16	14	18	16
Industrial supplies and materials_	10.0	13.9	14.1	20.0	30.6	30.8	32.5	34.5	33	33	29	29
Capital goods, except automotive_	9.9	14.6	16.8	21.8	30.4	35.8	38.7	39.8	32	34	33	33
Automotive vehicles, parts, and engines_____	2.8	3.9	5.5	6.9	8.6	10.6	12.1	13.0	9	9	10	11
Consumer goods (nonfood), exc. automotive_____	2.1	2.8	3.6	4.8	6.4	6.5	8.0	8.9	7	7	6	7
All other_____	.8	1.5	1.9	2.7	3.6	4.1	3.6	4.5	3	3	4	4
General imports, total_____	26.9	39.9	55.8	70.5	103.7	98.0	124.0	151.7	100	100	100	100
Foods, feeds, and beverages_____	4.6	6.2	7.3	9.1	10.6	9.7	11.6	14.0	17	15	10	9
Industrial supplies and materials_	12.0	15.4	21.1	28.2	54.7	51.4	64.7	81.0	45	39	52	53
Capital goods, except automotive_	2.5	4.0	5.8	8.1	9.5	9.7	11.1	13.5	9	10	10	9
Automotive vehicles, parts, and engines_____	2.4	5.6	8.8	10.3	12.1	11.8	16.4	18.9	9	14	12	13
Consumer goods (nonfood), exc. automotive_____	4.2	7.6	11.4	13.2	14.8	13.7	18.4	22.4	16	19	14	15
All other_____	1.1	1.1	1.5	1.5	2.0	1.7	1.8	1.9	4	3	2	1

Source: U.S. Bureau of Economic Analysis, *Surve_ of Current Business*, June 1978.

No. 1518. IMPORTS OF LEADING COMMODITIES, BY AREAS (F.A.S. TRANSACTION VALUE BASIS): 1976 AND 1977

[In millions of dollars, except percent. Includes silver ore and bullion. "F.a.s." means free alongside ship]

ITEM	1976					1977				
	Total [1]	Canada	American Republics	Western Europe [2]	Far East [3]	Total [1]	Canada	American Republics	Western Europe [2]	Far East [3]
General imports, total____	120,677	26,237	13,227	22,784	30,152	146,817	29,356	16,335	27,417	36,405
Percent_____	100.0	21.7	11.0	18.9	25.0	100.0	20.0	11.1	18.7	24.8
Imports for consumption___	120,014	26,144	13,140	22,587	29,925	146,047	29,156	16,226	27,324	36,217
Meat and preparations_____	1,447	82	327	295	9	1,273	74	276	261	5
Fruits, nuts, and vegetables___	1,186	39	604	180	262	1,551	61	839	185	332
Coffee_____	2,632	–	1,784	6	136	3,861	(z)	2,646	6	269
Sugar_____	1,154	10	604	5	322	1,079	29	533	11	292
Alcoholic beverages_____	1,174	245	30	878	7	1,282	298	33	930	7
Pulp, paper, and manufactures_	3,367	3,110	41	139	50	3,634	3,312	49	175	64
Ores and scrap metal_____	2,251	991	477	73	50	2,234	995	444	77	55
Petroleum, crude and partly refined_____	26,384	2,275	2,197	371	2,568	33,714	1,612	2,705	752	2,885
Petroleum products_____	5,411	278	1,888	350	240	7,812	343	2,343	904	428
Chemicals_____	4,772	1,287	183	2,205	462	5,432	1,451	212	2,465	554
Machinery [4]_____	15,446	2,647	1,111	4,803	6,729	17,937	3,014	1,218	5,519	8,015
Transport equipment [4]_____	14,378	6,574	146	3,284	4,326	17,556	7,697	207	3,928	5,668
Automobiles, new_____	8,928	3,477	(z)	2,548	2,904	10,626	3,795	(z)	2,940	3,890
Iron and steelmill products [5]____	3,809	406	72	1,057	2,232	5,281	584	99	1,959	2,468
Nonferrous base metals_____	2,941	1,090	297	679	446	3,368	1,227	416	712	576
Textile yarn, fabrics, and made-up articles_____	1,635	32	144	464	884	1,772	49	162	541	922
Fish, including shellfish_____	1,855	376	473	339	416	2,056	418	506	416	426
Other imports_____	30,835	6,796	2,849	7,656	11,013	36,975	8,192	3,647	8,576	13,439

– Represents zero.   Z   Less than $500,000.   [1] Includes areas not shown separately. [2] Includes Greece and Turkey.   [3] Asia, excluding Near East and Communist areas. [4] Machinery includes, and transport equipment excludes, parts for tractors. The Bureau of the Census reports tractor parts with transport equipment.   [5] Excludes pig iron.

Source: U.S. Dept. of Commerce, Industry and Trade Administration, *Overseas Business Reports, U.S. Trade with Major World Areas*, periodic.

No. 1519. PERCENT DISTRIBUTION OF DOMESTIC EXPORTS AND GENERAL IMPORTS, BY BROAD COMMODITY GROUPS: 1960 TO 1977

COMMODITY GROUP	1960	1965	1970	1972	1973	1974	1975	1976	1977
Exports:									
Food and live animals	13.2	14.7	10.2	11.6	17.0	14.4	14.6	13.9	12.0
Beverages and tobacco	2.4	1.9	1.6	1.9	1.4	1.3	1.2	1.3	1.6
Crude materials, inedible, exc. fuels	13.7	10.5	10.8	10.3	11.9	11.3	9.2	9.6	10.9
Mineral fuels and related materials	4.1	3.5	3.7	3.2	2.4	3.5	4.2	3.7	3.5
Chemicals	8.7	8.8	9.0	8.4	8.2	9.1	8.2	8.8	9.2
Machinery and transport equipment	34.3	37.3	42.0	44.0	39.7	39.3	43.0	43.7	43.3
Other manufactured goods	18.7	18.0	17.9	16.5	15.8	17.0	15.6	15.7	15.8
Imports:									
Food and live animals	19.9	16.1	13.5	11.5	11.5	9.4	8.8	8.5	8.5
Beverages and tobacco	2.6	2.6	2.1	1.8	1.8	1.3	1.5	1.3	1.1
Crude materials, exc. fuels	18.3	14.5	8.3	6.9	7.2	6.0	5.8	5.8	5.4
Mineral fuels and related materials	10.5	10.4	7.7	8.6	11.8	25.4	27.5	28.2	30.2
Chemicals	5.3	3.6	3.6	3.6	3.5	4.0	3.8	4.0	3.7
Machinery and transport equipment	9.7	13.8	28.0	31.3	30.3	24.0	24.4	24.7	24.2
Other manufactured goods	30.3	35.1	33.3	33.0	30.9	27.1	24.9	25.0	24.7

Source: U.S. Dept. of Commerce, Industry and Trade Administration, *Overseas Business Reports, U.S. Foreign Trade*, periodic. Also in U.S. Bureau of the Census, *Highlights of U.S. Export and Import Trade*, Report FT 990, monthly.

No. 1520. DOMESTIC EXPORTS, BY SELECTED COMMODITY GROUPS: 1960 TO 1977

[In millions of dollars. Totals and subtotals include data for commodities not shown separately. Total exports of silver ore and bullion included through 1965, domestic merchandise shipments thereafter. Beginning 1965, data not comparable with 1960 due to change in U.S. export classification effective January 1, 1965; however, to achieve best comparability possible with 1965, 1960 data have been retabulated on the basis of major content of commodity items. "N.e.c." means not elsewhere classified. See also *Historical Statistics, Colonial Times to 1970*, series U 274–294]

COMMODITY GROUP	1960	1965	1970	1972	1973	1974	1975	1976	1977
U.S. merchandise	20,408	27,178	42,590	48,959	70,246	97,144	106,100	110,018	117,062
Food and live animals	2,684	4,002	4,356	5,661	11,930	13,986	15,484	15,710	14,103
Meat and preparations	115	162	175	252	444	371	528	798	797
Meat, fresh, chilled, or frozen	84	136	147	222	405	336	491	759	750
Dairy products and eggs	123	191	137	143	56	67	134	128	182
Grains and preparations	1,761	2,637	2,596	3,501	8,496	10,331	11,642	10,911	8,755
Wheat, including wheat flour	1,029	1,184	1,112	1,452	4,154	4,589	5,293	4,040	2,883
Rice	151	244	314	389	539	852	858	629	730
Coarse grains	518	1,135	1,072	1,532	3,558	4,673	5,272	6,023	4,913
Corn	285	833	824	1,241	2,836	3,772	4,448	5,223	4,139
Grain sorghums	108	209	196	220	468	689	699	642	604
Fruits and nuts	265	339	406	526	662	757	871	976	1,080
Fruit, fresh	119	145	164	235	284	326	404	434	458
Vegetables	133	148	178	209	307	391	406	559	517
Feed for animals	87	278	497	596	1,266	1,287	987	1,358	1,572
Beverages and tobacco	483	517	702	908	1,008	1,247	1,308	1,524	1,847
Tobacco and manufactures	477	506	679	879	970	1,193	1,253	1,457	1,732
Leaf tobacco	379	378	481	639	681	832	852	922	1,094
Cigarettes	87	105	159	202	250	301	368	510	615
Crude mater'ls, inedible, exc. fuels	2,805	2,855	4,605	5,030	8,380	10,934	9,784	10,891	12,815
Hides and skins, except fur skins	76	109	145	293	377	339	295	522	583
Soybeans	336	650	1,216	1,508	2,762	3,537	2,865	3,315	4,393
Synthetic rubber	201	161	176	161	196	290	261	329	327
Wood in the rough	38	124	366	444	823	744	751	945	1,000
Wood shaped or simply worked	104	119	193	285	473	468	413	563	551
Lumber, softwood	78	94	162	209	422	399	342	471	444
Woodpulp	154	190	464	358	420	820	875	844	875
Textile fibers and wastes	1,111	617	543	751	1,313	1,782	1,345	1,426	1,902
Raw cotton, excluding linters	980	486	372	503	929	1,335	991	1,049	1,530
Ores and metal scrap	493	435	940	508	1,081	1,475	1,355	1,284	1,197
Iron and steel scrap	242	197	447	244	598	849	780	634	413
Ores and scrap, nonferrous base	183	154	397	226	427	522	461	499	600
Mineral fuels and related materials	842	947	1,595	1,552	1,671	3,444	4,470	4,226	4,179
Coal	354	477	962	984	1,014	2,437	3,259	2,910	2,655
Petroleum and products	468	418	488	444	518	792	908	998	1,276
Lubricating oils	196	185	175	169	174	298	275	292	335
Animal and vegetable oils and fats	295	472	493	508	684	1,423	944	978	1,341
Tallow, inedible	99	179	176	173	287	483	299	377	504
Soybean oil	110	162	192	175	150	519	266	238	440

See footnotes at end of table.

No. 1520. DOMESTIC EXPORTS, BY SELECTED COMMODITY GROUPS: 1960 TO 1977—Continued

[In millions of dollars. See headnote, p. 881. See also *Historical Statistics, Colonial Times to 1970*, series U 274–294]

COMMODITY GROUP	1960	1965	1970	1972	1973	1974	1975	1976	1977
Chemicals	1,776	2,403	3,826	4,133	5,749	8,819	8,691	9,959	10,827
Chemical elements and comp'ds	612	970	1,642	1,697	2,338	3,613	3,623	4,408	4,811
Dyeing, tanning, color'g mater'ls	73	93	137	157	216	304	244	310	352
Medicinal, pharmaceutical prod	238	256	420	474	626	800	866	997	1,081
Fertilizers, manufactured	72	153	178	298	407	815	1,083	613	701
Plastic materials and resins	315	425	653	696	1,028	1,618	1,166	1,672	1,733
Machinery and transport equip	6,992	10,139	17,882	21,513	27,869	38,189	45,668	49,501	51,036
Machinery [1]	4,476	6,935	11,685	13,562	17,588	24,318	29,215	32,113	33,426
Machinery, nonelectrical [1]	3,386	5,275	8,686	9,864	12,556	17,298	21,633	22,835	23,140
Power generating machinery	490	841	1,405	1,842	2,218	2,882	3,551	3,662	3,619
Agricultural machinery	147	219	182	249	346	544	704	707	717
Tractors and parts	418	646	750	827	1,098	1,484	2,126	2,223	2,064
Electronic computers, parts and accessories	100	256	1,236	1,341	1,717	2,198	2,228	2,588	3,270
Other office machines	108	215	311	282	368	501	411	349	375
Metalworking machinery	293	332	396	410	489	639	922	953	730
Metalcutting machines	117	159	213	148	206	264	344	290	258
Textile, leather machinery	180	207	273	272	375	528	486	457	423
Other machines	1,650	2,559	4,133	5,139	5,945	8,522	11,205	11,896	11,942
Construction, excavating, and maintenance equip	270	324	434	467	568	868	1,277	1,381	1,352
Materials handling equip	193	397	607	648	880	1,230	1,846	1,859	1,664
Air-conditioning and refrigerating equip	135	210	397	461	580	858	928	1,055	1,245
Pump. equip., incl. parts	81	143	241	262	327	433	543	606	630
Pipe valves and parts	64	111	196	213	250	335	458	518	548
Electrical apparatus	1,090	1,660	2,999	3,698	5,032	7,019	7,582	9,278	10,285
Power mach., switchgear	250	472	611	787	1,066	1,492	1,709	2,139	2,301
Generators, generating sets	85	149	117	167	286	421	548	800	889
Transforming, converting, transmission apparatus	83	120	156	192	232	343	417	487	518
Telecommunications app'tus	228	345	660	836	1,040	1,361	1,574	1,997	2,125
Radio, television app'tus	180	304	576	741	895	1,157	1,339	1,729	1,827
Domestic electrical equip	112	116	119	158	223	378	359	463	521
Transport equipment [2]	2,517	3,204	6,197	7,951	10,281	13,871	16,452	17,388	17,611
Railway vehicles	133	138	91	212	219	282	462	392	305
Road motor vehicles, parts [2]	1,270	1,744	3,245	4,473	5,573	7,248	9,290	10,132	10,887
Automobiles, nonmilit., new	237	393	822	1,304	1,790	2,303	2,852	3,228	3,568
Trucks and tractor trucks, commercial, new	339	279	452	563	715	1,140	1,712	1,509	1,513
Parts, accessories, comm'c'l	524	875	1,603	2,211	2,616	3,193	3,620	4,213	4,673
Aircraft, parts, and accessories	1,024	1,130	2,656	2,995	4,119	5,766	6,136	6,100	5,866
Civilian aircraft	537	478	1,528	1,707	2,315	3,366	3,169	3,204	2,747
Other manufactured goods	3,815	4,890	7,636	8,094	11,112	16,515	16,592	17,781	18,590
Rubber manufactures	152	166	186	231	308	544	544	491	588
Paper and manufactures	255	389	622	726	919	1,522	1,447	1,624	1,517
Paper and paperboard	185	325	526	606	738	1,232	1,131	1,291	1,162
Nonmetallic mineral mfrs., n.e.c.	198	302	475	565	810	994	964	1,166	1,275
Metals and manufactures	1,632	1,787	2,978	2,314	3,468	5,725	5,661	5,180	5,149
Iron and steelmill products [3]	635	607	1,188	800	1,258	2,500	2,382	1,833	1,608
Plates and sheets	381	184	335	184	382	687	327	338	272
Tubes, pipes, and fittings	102	160	226	247	345	852	1,412	778	677
Silver bullion, refined	24	51	31	44	20	28	104	33	39
Nonferrous base metals	517	539	893	567	950	1,301	1,090	1,088	1,058
Copper	291	293	358	248	384	415	333	282	196
Aluminum	154	159	358	196	346	478	433	469	480
Metal manufactures, n.e.c	427	553	744	828	1,111	1,665	1,891	2,089	2,339
Tools for hand or machine	110	141	204	223	288	406	480	498	555
Textiles, other than clothing	478	528	603	779	1,225	1,795	1,624	1,971	1,959
Textile yarn and thread	114	131	145	138	271	407	298	374	414
Cotton broad-woven fabrics, exc. remnants	142	98	103	204	263	384	376	499	438
Textile fab., woven, exc. cotton	102	135	151	171	283	413	386	423	399
Clothing	140	143	198	240	278	400	403	510	608
Professional, scientific, and controlling instruments	241	480	857	980	1,214	1,662	1,792	1,951	2,238
Photographic supplies	63	130	250	334	417	548	606	703	813
Printed matter	137	226	327	346	393	486	548	607	668
Other transactions	718	954	1,496	1,560	1,842	2,587	3,161	2,749	3,224
Firearms of war and ammunition	485	644	682	617	633	852	1,361	1,261	1,612
Shipments of $100 or less, est.[4]	174	245	692	834	1,091	1,563	1,572	1,190	1,244

[1] Includes parts for tractors. [2] Excludes parts for tractors. [3] Excludes pig iron.
[4] Beginning 1970, data are estimates for shipments of $250 or less.

Source: U.S. Dept. of Commerce, Industry and Trade Administration, *Overseas Business Reports, U.S. Foreign Trade*, periodic. Also in U.S. Bureau of the Census, *Highlights of U.S. Export and Import Trade*, Report FT 990, monthly.

No. 1521. GENERAL IMPORTS, BY SELECTED COMMODITY GROUPS (F.A.S. TRANSACTION VALUE BASIS): 1960 TO 1977

[In millions of dollars. Prior to 1974, imports are on the customs value basis. Totals and subtotals include commodities not shown separately. "F.a.s." means free alongside ship. "N.e.c." means not elsewhere classified. See also *Historical Statistics, Colonial Times to 1970*, series U 295–316]

COMMODITY	1960	1965	1970	1972	1973	1974	1975	1976	1977
General imports	15,073	21,427	39,952	55,583	69,476	100,251	96,116	120,677	146,817
C.i.f. values [1]	(NA)	(NA)	42,429	58,862	76,199	107,996	103,389	129,565	156,695
Food and live animals	2,996	3,460	5,375	6,370	8,014	9,386	8,503	10,267	12,490
Cattle, except for breeding	62	98	111	152	193	108	77	159	187
Meat and preparations	314	426	1,014	1,223	1,671	1,353	1,141	1,447	1,273
Meat, fresh or frozen	176	231	647	827	1,124	808	640	840	739
Ham, shoulders, and bacon [2]	86	132	241	264	389	350	397	434	378
Fish	308	469	794	1,205	1,392	1,500	1,356	1,855	2,056
Fruits and nuts	218	339	447	496	578	627	638	760	959
Bananas	79	162	188	186	193	197	220	277	304
Vegetables	96	139	289	350	410	388	355	426	592
Sugar	507	443	725	832	925	2,247	1,865	1,154	1,079
Coffee, green	1,003	1,058	1,160	1,182	1,570	1,505	1,561	2,632	3,861
Cocoa or cacao beans	143	120	201	151	212	317	321	358	486
Tea	56	57	53	63	70	80	88	96	176
Beverages and tobacco	396	553	855	1,009	1,221	1,322	1,419	1,624	1,663
Alcoholic beverages	273	426	725	824	1,000	1,029	1,033	1,174	1,282
Tobacco, unmanufactured	117	121	111	157	191	254	343	392	319
Crude materials, inedible, except fuels	2,752	3,102	3,307	3,860	5,014	6,066	5,566	7,014	7,944
Hides and skins, except fur skins	70	80	51	65	85	78	78	89	97
Fur skins, undressed	96	113	59	52	78	79	79	101	122
Rubber, including latex	322	182	231	190	340	507	353	513	645
Lumber, softwood	260	318	439	1,063	1,372	1,007	797	1,355	1,974
Lumber, hardwood	49	57	61	89	122	134	69	97	124
Woodpulp	305	399	480	490	657	1,126	1,032	1,237	1,215
Textile fibers and wastes	395	435	202	196	237	225	174	249	225
Wool and other animal hair	235	282	116	95	123	74	73	123	120
Industrial diamonds	52	56	39	39	62	48	42	46	61
Asbestos, unmanufactured	65	70	75	88	99	131	117	149	152
Ores and metal scrap	761	971	1,149	1,022	1,304	1,855	1,078	2,251	2,234
Iron ore and concentrates	322	444	480	416	534	700	864	982	957
Silver ore and base bullion	38	56	40	56	102	164	98	75	83
Nonferrous base metals [3]	365	421	522	459	518	696	783	895	872
Bauxite, crude	78	143	165	163	159	183	267	330	362
Mineral fuels and related materials	1,587	2,221	3,075	4,799	8,174	25,454	26,476	33,996	44,287
Petroleum and products	1,550	2,092	2,764	4,300	7,614	24,293	24,814	31,794	41,526
Petroleum, crude and partly refined	957	1,215	1,448	2,607	4,593	16,546	19,293	26,384	33,714
Petroleum products	593	877	1,316	1,693	3,021	7,748	5,521	5,411	7,812
Natural gas	33	105	258	403	346	505	1,081	1,619	1,945
Animal and vegetable oils and fats	95	116	160	180	259	544	554	464	538
Chemicals	807	768	1,450	2,015	2,463	4,018	3,696	4,772	5,432
Organic chemicals	61	160	355	509	639	1,363	1,027	1,193	1,427
Inorganic chemicals	133	158	371	427	529	740	835	937	1,176
Medicinal and pharmaceutical products	47	58	87	149	167	211	235	269	318
Fertilizers, manufactured	77	112	192	232	280	631	626	683	829
Machinery and transport equipment	1,466	2,948	11,172	17,420	21,076	24,060	23,457	29,824	35,494
Machinery	724	1,800	5,375	7,916	10,150	11,809	11,970	15,446	17,937
Machinery, nonelectrical	438	1,160	3,103	4,539	5,652	6,470	7,059	8,021	9,505
Engines and parts	24	195	782	1,242	1,478	1,501	1,615	1,934	2,217
Agricultural machinery	89	156	173	237	313	394	474	496	504
Tractors and parts	46	93	175	260	359	498	571	554	630
Office machines	68	136	505	700	915	1,007	1,052	1,341	1,584
Metalworking machinery	37	63	164	140	189	300	361	362	434
Textile and leather machinery	70	157	361	638	630	606	518	636	638
Other nonelectrical machines	103	360	943	1,322	1,768	2,164	2,468	2,698	3,498
Electrical apparatus	286	640	2,271	3,377	4,499	5,339	4,911	7,424	8,432
Power machinery and switchgear	23	67	247	356	461	567	550	758	967
Telecommunications apparatus	127	314	1,102	1,672	2,070	2,281	2,077	3,655	3,719
Electron tubes, transistors, semiconductor devices, and parts	13	63	224	396	704	1,033	899	1,223	1,492
Transport equipment	742	1,148	5,798	9,504	10,926	12,251	11,487	14,378	17,557
Automobiles and parts	627	810	5,068	7,965	9,252	10,264	9,921	13,104	15,842
Automobiles, new	514	658	3,722	5,724	6,517	7,298	7,124	8,928	10,626
Motorcycles	13	134	307	697	571	914	707	485	630
Aircraft and parts	54	140	274	415	563	508	519	434	601
Other manufactured goods	4,572	7,528	13,285	18,332	21,462	27,145	23,927	30,179	36,278
Leather manufactures and dressed furs	52	87	118	182	191	188	132	247	238
Rubber tires and tubes	21	45	205	386	546	491	475	738	855
Wood manufactures (excl. furniture)	163	270	409	648	771	685	573	827	1,028
Paper and manufactures	756	870	1,087	1,261	1,458	1,852	1,673	2,103	2,392
Newsprint	688	790	930	1,054	1,186	1,503	1,427	1,742	1,872

See footnotes at end of table.

No. 1521. General Imports, by Selected Commodity Groups (F.A.S. Transaction Value Basis): 1960 to 1977—Continued

[In millions of dollars. See headnote, p. 883]

COMMODITY	1960	1965	1970	1972	1973	1974	1975	1976	1977
Other manufactured goods—Con.									
Construction materials [4]	45	71	106	173	230	245	186	203	290
Glass, glassware, and pottery	142	168	338	452	522	535	531	653	784
Diamonds, excluding industrial	166	308	433	637	827	775	730	1,018	1,453
Metals and manufactures	1,529	2,874	4,508	6,004	6,913	11,111	8,944	9,898	12,246
Pig iron and ferroalloys	55	94	78	183	242	394	558	538	524
Iron and steelmill products	431	1,140	1,952	2,743	2,775	4,756	4,037	3,809	5,281
Bars, rods, shapes, and pilings	188	377	486	705	764	1,507	930	848	1,126
Plates and sheets	86	475	906	1,395	1,330	2,059	1,680	1,795	2,693
Steel wire	39	79	119	141	165	299	225	211	283
Tubes, pipes, and fittings	83	144	349	380	396	736	1,008	792	963
Nonferrous base metals	762	1,198	1,502	1,754	2,002	3,038	2,063	2,941	3,368
Copper	353	425	532	516	678	1,189	419	777	841
Nickel	89	189	317	349	376	483	456	524	540
Aluminum	107	264	238	369	287	386	415	554	762
Lead	61	61	74	64	53	60	49	64	163
Tin	88	167	190	200	199	295	315	329	465
Silver, refined bullion	16	7	53	42	216	431	274	289	315
Platinum group metals	13	69	98	137	246	453	244	271	255
Metal manufactures, n.e.c	251	367	825	1,144	1,431	2,039	1,769	2,051	2,503
Textiles, other than clothing	562	800	1,135	1,527	1,580	1,615	1,219	1,635	1,772
Textile yarn and thread	36	66	223	305	262	190	128	192	228
Cotton fabrics, woven	97	134	173	260	310	356	219	390	351
Textile fabrics, woven, exc. cotton [5]	275	423	499	631	608	528	433	521	583
Twine and cordage	34	48	35	46	62	185	123	82	79
Floor coverings	57	45	53	76	103	98	88	120	148
Clothing	304	541	1,269	1,883	2,168	2,331	2,562	3,634	4,154
Footwear	148	160	629	915	1,082	1,134	1,275	1,686	1,848
Professional, scientific, photographic, and controlling instruments	82	178	356	513	674	750	726	969	1,303
Clocks and watches	70	100	184	246	335	389	426	627	716
Musical instruments, sound recorders and reproducers, and parts	47	157	505	812	946	943	781	1,216	1,538
Printed matter	46	77	160	216	230	270	284	322	340
Articles of plastic and rubber, n.e.c	6	71	236	287	352	425	429	602	602
Toys, games, and sporting goods	84	155	427	568	657	724	633	903	1,159
Artworks and antiques	73	141	162	277	352	948	677	580	720
Other transactions	401	730	1,274	1,598	1,794	2,256	2,518	2,538	2,692

NA Not available.   [1] Value on a cost, insurance, and freight basis: cost (to the U.S. importer) of commodities at port of exportation plus insurance and freight to U.S. customs port of entry. 1970 to 1973 are estimated. [2] Canned, cooked, and boned.   [3] Includes concentrates. [4] Materials of lime, cement, and clay.   [5] Excludes narrow or special fabrics.

Source: U.S. Dept. of Commerce, Industry and Trade Administration, *Overseas Business Reports, U.S. Foreign Trade*, periodic. Also in U.S. Bureau of the Census, *Highlights of U.S. Export and Import Trade*, Report FT 990, monthly.

No. 1522. Imports—Coffee, Tea, and Cocoa and Chocolate: 1950 to 1977

[All coffee on green coffee basis; exports and reexports include roasted and soluble coffee. See also *Historical Statistics, Colonial Times to 1970*, series P 227 and U 296–299]

ITEM	1950	1955	1960	1965	1970	1972	1973	1974	1975	1976	1977
Coffee imports_____mil. lb__	2,442	2,602	2,943	2,844	2,609	2,746	2,891	2,546	2,684	2,617	1,959
Value_____mil. dol__	1,092	1,357	1,003	1,058	1,160	1,182	1,570	1,504	1,562	2,633	3,861
Net per capita [1]_____lb__	16.48	15.41	15.92	14.95	13.72	13.87	13.67	12.84	12.37	12.30	9.4
Avg. price___cents per lb__	44.6	52.6	34.4	37.6	44.4	43.0	54.4	59.1	58.2	100.6	197.1
Tea, net imports____mil. lb__	113	104	114	130	137	151	175	178	159	181	203
Value_____mil. dol__	53	64	55	57	53	63	70	79	88	95	175
Cocoa and chocolate: [2]											
Imports_____mil. lb__	712	605	677	934	847	889	799	728	743	816	678
Value_____mil. dol__	176	224	172	146	265	222	295	446	447	572	798

[1] Source: U.S. Bureau of Domestic Business Development. Based on total population including Armed Forces abroad as estimated by Bureau of the Census.   [2] Includes prepared, except confectionery.

Source: Except as noted, U.S. Bureau of the Census, *Foreign Commerce and Navigation of the United States, Quarterly Summary of Foreign Commerce of the United States; U.S. Imports for Consumption and General Imports*, Report FT 246; and unpublished data.

No. 1523. EXPORTS AND IMPORTS OF MERCHANDISE FOR CONSUMPTION, BY CUSTOMS REGIONS: 1967 TO 1977

In millions of dollars. Exports include reexports; imports are on customs value basis. See *Historical Statistics, Colonial Times to 1970*, series U 264–273, for related data]

CUSTOMS REGIONS	1967	1968	1969	1970	1971	1972	1973	1974	1975	1976	1977
EXPORTS											
U.S. total [1]	31,534	34,413	38,006	43,226	44,137	49,676	71,339	98,507	107,592	114,992	120,163
Boston	2,762	2,939	3,379	3,297	3,964	4,478	5,713	7,713	7,809	8,667	9,613
New York	8,087	8,574	8,743	10,037	8,871	9,839	12,738	17,476	18,733	19,372	19,920
Baltimore	2,267	2,479	2,864	3,912	3,836	4,397	6,310	10,347	12,525	13,074	12,335
Miami	1,343	1,538	1,664	1,983	2,005	2,658	3,518	5,442	6,232	7,298	8,692
New Orleans	2,989	2,977	3,032	3,946	3,783	4,560	7,452	10,725	11,314	12,202	12,787
Houston	3,325	3,640	3,251	4,028	4,209	4,634	7,932	11,278	12,877	12,455	12,180
Los Angeles	1,373	1,765	2,107	2,508	2,206	2,408	4,059	5,878	6,446	7,136	7,274
San Francisco	3,237	3,557	4,401	4,936	5,114	5,622	8,782	11,666	11,465	13,088	13,375
Chicago	4,572	5,281	6,208	6,241	7,637	8,665	11,480	13,484	15,328	17,130	18,817
IMPORTS											
U.S. total [1]	26,816	33,114	36,043	39,963	45,602	55,555	69,024	100,140	96,516	121,121	147,075
Boston	3,588	4,662	5,427	5,678	6,529	7,491	8,997	11,037	9,946	12,376	14,671
New York	7,844	9,353	9,250	10,050	10,362	12,568	15,557	20,417	18,053	21,995	26,160
Baltimore	2,727	3,242	3,359	3,936	4,542	5,640	7,257	12,719	11,888	13,232	15,266
Miami	1,647	2,008	2,085	2,412	2,940	4,051	4,811	7,118	6,444	7,920	9,241
New Orleans	1,184	1,467	1,476	1,630	1,894	2,145	2,873	5,724	6,790	9,307	12,945
Houston	1,117	1,408	1,462	1,754	2,206	2,666	3,825	7,873	8,789	12,604	17,273
Los Angeles	1,624	2,155	2,830	3,268	3,652	4,916	6,531	9,049	8,569	11,078	13,782
San Francisco	2,120	2,589	3,191	3,569	4,052	5,074	6,394	10,497	10,599	13,333	15,978
Chicago	4,682	5,908	6,659	7,341	9,026	10,621	12,407	15,327	15,061	18,921	21,368

[1] Includes data on low-value shipments for exports and shipments valued under $251 for imports, not shown separately.

Source: U.S. Bureau of the Census, *Highlights of U.S. Export and Import Trade,* FT 990, monthly.

No. 1524. IMPORTS FOR CONSUMPTION—VALUES AND DUTIES: 1946 TO 1977

[Imports are on customs value basis. Beginning 1965, includes uranium, thorium, and related products; beginning 1970, includes silver ores and bullion. For basis of dollar values and for area coverage, see text, p. 861. See also *Historical Statistics, Colonial Times to 1970*, series U 207–212]

YEARLY AVERAGE OR YEAR	VALUES				Duties calculated [1]	RATIO OF DUTIES TO VALUES		Duties per capita [2]
	Total	Free	Dutiable	Percent free		Total imports	Dutiable imports	
	Mil. dol.	*Mil. dol.*	*Mil. dol.*		*Mil. dol.*	*Percent*	*Percent*	*Dollars*
1946–1950 avg	6,584	3,843	2,741	58	439	7	16	2.94
1951–1955 avg	10,784	5,975	4,809	55	582	5	12	3.58
1956–1960 avg	13,570	5,843	7,727	43	882	7	11	4.98
1961–1965 avg	17,557	6,571	10,986	37	1,300	7	12	6.78
1966–1970 avg	32,141	11,755	20,386	37	2,282	7	11	11.23
1971–1975 avg	73,374	29,190	44,184	39	3,412	5	8	16.22
1950	8,743	4,767	3,976	55	522	6	13	3.38
1955	11,337	6,037	5,300	53	633	6	12	3.76
1960	14,650	5,780	8,870	39	1,084	7	12	5.92
1965	21,283	7,434	13,849	35	1,643	8	12	8.35
1970	39,756	13,870	25,886	35	2,584	6	10	12.48
1971	45,516	15,286	30,230	34	2,767	6	9	13.36
1972	55,290	18,915	36,375	34	3,124	6	9	14.96
1973	69,024	28,258	40,766	41	3,620	5	8	17.20
1974	100,140	52,052	48,088	52	3,771	4	8	17.80
1975	96,516	31,030	65,486	32	3,780	4	6	17.70
1976	121,121	37,190	83,931	31	4,675	4	6	21.73
1977	147,075	43,633	103,442	30	5,485	4	5	25.30

[1] 1947–1959 data from U.S. Bureau of Customs. Customs duties (including import excise taxes) calculated on the basis of reports of quantity and value of imports of merchandise entered directly for consumption or withdrawn from bonded customs warehouses.

[2] Based on estimated population including Armed Forces abroad as of July 1, except 1970 as of April 1.

Source: Except as noted, U.S. Bureau of the Census, *Foreign Commerce and Navigation of the United States, Quarterly Summary of Foreign Commerce of the United States; Highlights of U.S. Export and Import Trade,* FT 990, monthly; and unpublished data.

No. 1525. DUTIABLE IMPORTS FOR CONSUMPTION, AND PERCENT FREE OF TOTAL IMPORTS FROM SELECTED AREAS AND COUNTRIES—VALUE: 1970 TO 1977

[Includes imports of silver ore and bullion. For total value of general imports, see table 1517]

AREA AND COUNTRY OF ORIGIN	VALUE OF DUTIABLE IMPORTS (mil. dol.)					PERCENT OF TOTAL IMPORTS FREE FROM DUTY				
	1970	1974	1975	1976	1977	1970	1974	1975	1976	1977
Total imports [1]	25,890	48,100	65,486	83,931	103,442	35	52	32	31	30
Developed countries [2]	19,503	34,998	35,826	42,161	50,141	33	42	36	38	36
Developing countries [2]	6,202	12,602	29,049	41,003	52,448	40	68	26	22	22
Communist areas in Europe and Asia	162	488	600	761	842	25	50	31	27	24
Western Hemisphere [3]	6,659	9,122	17,190	18,331	20,630	61	77	55	58	59
Canada	3,513	4,115	6,747	7,182	7,396	68	81	69	73	75
20 Latin American Republics [3]	2,567	4,782	7,492	7,921	9,356	45	65	37	40	42
Central American Common Market [4]	129	321	373	371	391	68	58	55	69	74
Latin American Free Trade Assn. [3]	2,281	4,049	6,413	7,104	8,557	43	67	36	36	38
Argentina	136	319	170	189	234	21	14	19	39	39
Brazil	206	982	620	458	578	69	41	57	73	74
Chile	9	12	52	118	128	94	10	62	41	44
Colombia	67	139	214	176	174	75	73	64	73	79
Mexico	899	2,266	2,197	2,446	3,163	25	33	27	31	32
Peru	109	226	161	185	179	68	61	58	52	63
Venezuela	813	18	2,667	3,190	3,720	25	100	28	11	8
Dominican Republic	123	309	511	294	251	34	34	19	43	63
Jamaica	26	66	56	35	23	86	71	82	89	93
Trinidad and Tobago	153	22	987	1,433	1,604	34	98	17	5	3
Netherlands Antilles	305	10	1,110	1,068	1,204	26	100	30	10	7
Europe	9,835	18,668	17,686	19,507	24,000	13	22	18	18	16
Western Europe	9,673	18,253	17,178	18,876	23,303	13	22	17	17	16
OECD countries [5]	9,581	18,032	16,954	18,663	23,107	13	22	17	17	15
European Economic Community	7,965	14,867	13,715	14,856	18,873	13	22	18	17	15
Belgium and Luxembourg	601	1,368	956	909	1,216	14	18	20	19	16
Denmark [6]	266	408	391	455	473	6	14	15	19	19
France	786	1,797	1,722	1,940	2,532	15	20	19	22	17
Ireland [6]	106	210	148	174	197	21	14	17	16	17
Italy	1,235	1,866	2,208	2,335	2,824	6	27	9	8	8
Netherlands	433	788	781	822	1,130	17	45	28	25	24
West Germany	2,936	5,711	4,770	5,152	6,721	6	11	11	10	9
United Kingdom [6]	1,601	2,720	2,738	3,068	3,781	27	31	27	28	26
Other OECD countries [3]	1,616	3,165	3,239	3,807	4,234	15	24	16	15	16
Austria	117	231	193	219	273	2	49	21	9	5
Spain	324	740	753	822	868	8	17	10	9	10
Sweden	375	804	815	832	920	6	8	8	10	8
Switzerland	399	704	743	910	951	12	19	14	12	13
Other Western Europe [3]	93	221	224	213	195	3	18	11	45	44
Yugoslavia	91	216	221	210	190	2	18	11	45	44
Communist areas in Europe [7]	162	415	508	631	697	25	52	28	25	23
Asia	8,517	18,979	23,825	34,896	43,730	11	31	12	11	12
Japan	5,646	11,562	10,848	15,045	18,239	4	7	5	3	3
Near East Asia [3]	270	315	4,458	8,705	12,364	22	93	17	3	3
Iran	41	53	1,146	1,423	2,711	39	98	18	4	3
Israel	128	236	257	263	366	14	16	17	38	36
Saudi Arabia	14	(Z)	2,159	5,166	6,285	30	100	18	1	8
South Asia [3]	274	318	358	428	427	33	56	49	52	56
India	202	265	309	368	363	32	52	43	48	53
Pakistan	67	45	38	51	41	16	21	24	26	28
Asia, not elsewhere classified [3]	2,326	6,711	8,070	10,590	12,555	22	29	15	23	25
China (Taiwan)	535	2,039	1,888	2,201	2,695	2	2	3	26	27
Indonesia	57	22	1,705	2,538	2,773	69	99	23	23	20
Malaysia	19	224	271	392	684	93	71	65	58	48
Philippines	379	992	683	747	889	23	11	8	14	16
Thailand	11	74	125	131	133	89	59	43	51	61
Communist areas in Asia [8]	1	73	91	130	145	14	32	42	34	28
Australia and Oceania [3]	601	948	884	882	880	30	36	40	47	45
Australia	433	667	694	655	647	28	35	38	46	45
New Zealand and Western Samoa	158	266	170	222	228	29	25	30	32	36
Africa [3]	255	372	5,890	10,309	14,192	77	94	29	18	16
Congo (Brazzaville)	8	1	15	51	31	82	64	21	7	3
Ghana	4	37	69	85	124	91	71	51	47	42
Nigeria	42	14	2,785	4,865	6,016	42	100	15	1	12
South Africa, Republic of	78	136	191	182	329	73	77	77	80	73
Egypt	22	12	23	87	159	6	83	15	6	6

Z   Less than $500,000.   [1] Includes unidentified countries.   [2] Developed countries include Australia, Canada, Japan, New Zealand, Republic of South Africa, and Western Europe; developing countries include rest of the world, excluding Communist areas in Asia and Europe.   [3] Includes countries not shown separately.   [4] Guatemala, El Salvador, Honduras, Nicaragua, and Costa Rica.   [5] Organization for Economic Cooperation and Development.   [6] As of Jan. 1, 1973, United Kingdom, Denmark and Ireland became members of EEC. For consistency, data for all years are shown on same basis.   [7] East Germany, Czechoslovakia, Hungary, Estonia, Latvia, Lithuania, Poland, U.S.S.R., Albania, Romania, and Bulgaria.
[8] Vietnam, China (mainland), Outer Mongolia, and North Korea.

Source: U.S. Bureau of the Census, *Highlights of U.S. Export and Import Trade*, FT 990, monthly.

Section 32

Outlying Areas Under the Jurisdiction of the United States

This section presents summary economic and social statistics for the Commonwealth of Puerto Rico, the principal possessions of the United States (Virgin Islands, Guam, and American Samoa), the Canal Zone, and, wherever possible, the Trust Territory of the Pacific Islands.

Primary sources are the decennial censuses of population, housing, and agriculture, and the censuses of business and manufactures (taken every five years) conducted by the Bureau of the Census; the annual *Vital Statistics of the United States*, issued by the National Center for Health Statistics; and the annual *Statistics of Public Elementary and Secondary Day Schools* of the National Center for Education Statistics.

Jurisdiction.—The United States gained jurisdiction over these areas as follows: The islands of *Puerto Rico* and *Guam*, surrendered by Spain to the United States in October 1898, were ceded to the United States by the Treaty of Paris, ratified in 1899. Puerto Rico became a commonwealth on July 25, 1952, thereby achieving a high degree of local autonomy under its own constitution. the *Virgin Islands*, comprising 50 islands and cays, were purchased by the United States from Denmark in 1917. *American Samoa*, a group of 7 islands, was acquired by the United States in accordance with a convention among the United States, Great Britain, and Germany, ratified in February 1900. The use, occupation, and control of the Canal Zone were granted to the United States under the terms of a treaty with the Republic of Panama, ratified in 1904. The *Trust Territory of the Pacific Islands* comprises 2,141 atolls and islands, about 96 of which are inhabited. This territory, formerly under Japanese mandate, was placed under the United Nations trusteeship system by an agreement approved by the Security Council and the United States in 1947.

For a brief summary of U.S. territorial development, see tables 3 and 339.

Censuses.—Because characteristics of the outlying areas differ, the presentation of census data for them is not uniform. The 1960 Census of Population covered all of the places listed above except the Trust Territory of the Pacific Islands (the census of which was conducted in April 1958 by the Office of the High Commissioner), whereas the 1960 Census of Housing also excluded the Canal Zone and American Samoa. The 1970 Census of Population and Housing covered all six areas. The 1959 and 1969 censuses of agriculture covered Puerto Rico, American Samoa, Guam, and the Virgin Islands; the 1964 census covered the same areas except American Samoa. Beginning in 1967, Congress authorized the economic censuses, covering business, manufactures, and, for Guam and the Virgin Islands, mineral industries, to be taken at 5-year intervals, for years ending in 2 and 7. Prior economic censuses were conducted in Puerto Rico for 1954, 1958, and 1963, and in Guam and the Virgin Islands for 1958 and 1963. In 1972, the census of construction industries was added for the first time for these three areas.

Information in other sections.—In addition to the specialized statistics presented in this section, other data are included as integral parts of many tables showing distribution by States in various sections of the *Abstract*. See "Outlying areas of United States" in the index.

For definition and explanation of terms used, see section 1, Population; section 5, Education; section 24, Agriculture; section 28, Construction and Housing; section 29, Manufactures; and section 30, Domestic Trade and Services.

Statistical reliability.—For a discussion of statistical collection and estimation, sampling procedures, and measures of statistical reliability applicable to Census Bureau data, see Appendix III.

No. 1526. Estimated Population, by Area: 1950 to 1976

[In thousands. As of July 1. Includes estimates of Armed Forces stationed in area]

AREA	1950	1955	1960	1965	1970	1971	1972	1973	1974	1975	1976
Puerto Rico	2,218	2,250	2,358	2,594	2,724	2,771	2,861	2,943	3,018	3,105	3,205
American Samoa	19	20	20	25	27	28	28	29	29	30	30
Canal Zone	53	55	(NA)	(NA)	44	42	42	41	41	41	40
Guam	60	69	67	74	86	91	94	102	97	96	96
Virgin Islands	27	28	32	43	64	68	74	82	86	91	95
Trust Territory of the Pacific Islands [1]	57	66	75	86	102	107	111	114	118	122	126
Northern Mariana Isls.[1]	(NA)	(NA)	(NA)	(NA)	12	13	13	14	15	15	16

NA Not available.   [1] Data consistent with apportionment census of September 1973 which showed a total population of 14,333 for the Marianas and 114,982 for the Trust Territory. (Excludes 4,462 for Kwajalein Missile Range Facility and 269 with residence not specified.) The Federal census of 1970 showed a population of 90,940, with 3,960 for Kwajalein Island and 9,640 for the Marianas.

Source: U.S. Bureau of the Census, *Current Population Reports*, series P-25, Nos. 80, 336, and 603.

No. 1527. Estimates of Components of Population Change, by Area: 1960 to 1970 and 1970 to 1976

[In thousands, except percent. Resident population, including Armed Forces stationed in area. Minus sign (−) denotes decrease. For explanation of methodology, see source]

AREA	APRIL 1, 1960, TO APRIL 1, 1970					APRIL 1, 1970, TO JULY 1, 1976				
	Net increase		Births	Deaths	Net migration	Net change		Births	Deaths	Net migration
	Number	Percent				Number	Percent			
Puerto Rico	362.0	15.4	734.0	172.0	−200.0	493.0	18.2	436.0	118.0	176.0
American Samoa	7.1	35.4	10.1	1.3	−1.7	2.9	10.8	6.6	.9	−2.8
Canal Zone	2.1	4.9	7.0	1.4	−3.6	−4.2	−9.6	4.0	.6	−7.6
Guam	18.0	26.8	25.6	3.4	−4.2	10.9	12.8	19.3	2.5	(NA)
Virgin Islands	30.4	94.6	18.6	3.9	15.7	32.5	52.0	17.2	3.2	18.4
Trust Territory of the Pacific Islands [1]	[2] 20.3	27.2	30.9	4.8	−5.7	24.9	24.7	23.9	3.5	(NA)
N. Mariana Islands [1]	(NA)	(NA)	(NA)	(NA)	(NA)	3.5	29.2	3.2	.5	(NA)

NA Not available.   [1] See footnote 1, table 1526.   [2] Census taken in 1958, not 1960.

Source: U.S. Bureau of the Census, *Current Population Reports*, series P-25, No. 603, and unpublished estimates.

No. 1528. Population, by Age and Areas, 1960 and 1970, and by Sex, 1970

[In thousands, except median age. For definition of median, see p. xii]

AREA, YEAR, AND SEX	Under 5 yr.	5–13 yr.	14–17 yr.	18–20 yr.	21–24 yr.	25–34 yr.	35–44 yr.	45–54 yr.	55–64 yr.	65 yr. and over	18 yr. and over	Median age (years)
Puerto Rico:												
1960	354.4	588.7	220.8	123.6	134.1	262.9	238.0	180.8	123.9	122.2	1,185.6	18.5
1970, total	318.1	605.5	251.0	158.7	182.8	339.3	274.0	227.5	178.0	177.1	1,537.4	21.6
Male	161.3	307.0	126.0	75.1	84.6	158.2	129.7	112.5	89.8	85.7	735.7	20.9
Female	156.8	298.5	125.0	83.6	98.2	181.1	144.3	115.0	88.2	91.4	801.7	22.2
American Samoa:												
1960	3.7	5.7	2.1	1.0	1.1	2.3	1.8	1.2	.7	.5	8.6	15.2
1970, total	4.7	7.5	2.6	1.6	1.6	3.2	2.4	1.8	1.0	.7	12.3	16.1
Male	2.4	3.8	4 1.4	.8	.8	1.6	1.2	.9	.5	.3	6.2	16.1
Female	2.3	3.7	1.3	.8	.9	1.6	1.2	.9	.5	.4	6.1	16˙1
Canal Zone:												
1960	4.7	8.9	3.2	2.6	3.1	5.9	6.7	4.4	1.8	.9	25.4	23.3
1970, total	3.8	9.3	3.7	3.2	4.3	6.8	5.5	4.7	2.1	.7	27.4	23.0
Male	1.9	4.7	1.9	2.2	3.0	3.5	3.0	2.5	1.3	.3	15.7	23.1
Female	1.9	4.5	1.9	1.0	1.3	3.3	2.5	2.2	.8	.5	11.6	22.9
Guam:												
1960	10.8	15.2	3.6	4.3	5.0	12.2	8.6	4.4	1.9	1.1	37.4	20.8
1970, total	11.6	20.1	6.8	5.4	8.0	12.6	10.3	5.8	2.8	1.5	46.4	20.4
Male	6.0	10.4	3.4	3.2	5.1	7.1	6.3	3.5	1.6	.7	27.5	21.6
Female	5.7	9.7	3.4	2.2	2.9	5.5	4.0	2.3	1.2	.8	18.9	18.2
Virgin Islands:												
1960	4.9	7.1	2.7	1.4	1.7	3.9	3.5	2.8	1.9	2.2	17.3	20.7
1970, total	8.3	12.8	4.4	3.2	4.9	11.4	7.1	5.0	3.0	2.4	37.0	23.0
Male	4.2	6.4	2.2	1.6	2.4	5.8	3.6	2.6	1.5	1.0	18.4	23.1
Female	4.1	6.4	2.3	1.6	2.5	5.6	3.5	2.4	1.5	1.4	18.5	23.0
Trust Territory of the Pacific Islands:												
1970, total	15.6	23.6	9.0	5.3	5.3	9.3	8.4	6.8	4.3	3.3	42.7	16.9
Male	7.8	12.0	4.5	2.7	2.7	4.8	4.4	3.6	2.4	1.7	22.2	17.2
Female	7.8	11.6	4.5	2.6	2.5	4.5	4.0	3.3	2.0	1.6	20.6	16.6

Source: U.S. Bureau of the Census, *Census of Population: 1960*, vol. I; and *1970*, vol. I, *Characteristics of the Population*, parts 53–58.

No. 1529. LAND AREA AND POPULATION CHARACTERISTICS, BY AREA: 1970

[For definition of median, see p. xii]

ITEM	Puerto Rico	American Samoa	Canal Zone	Guam	Virgin Islands	Trust Territory of the Pacific Islands
Land area_____sq. miles..	3,421	76	362	209	132	717
Total population_____	2,712,033	27,159	44,198	84,996	62,468	90,940
Per square mile_____	793	357	122	407	473	127
Percent increase, 1960–1970_____	15.4	35.4	4.2	26.8	94.6	28.6
Urban_____	1,575,491	(X)	2,569	21,671	15,240	(X)
Rural_____	1,136,542	(X)	41,629	63,325	47,228	(X)
Male_____	1,329,949	13,682	24,254	47,362	31,157	46,482
Female_____	1,382,084	13,477	19,944	37,634	31,311	44,458
Males per 100 females_____	96.2	101.5	121.6	125.8	100.5	104.6
Median age_____years..	21.6	16.1	23.0	20.4	23.0	16.9
Male_____years..	20.9	16.1	23.1	21.6	23.1	17.2
Female_____years..	22.2	16.1	22.9	18.2	23.0	16.6
School years completed, persons 25 years old and over____	1,196,692	9,022	19,855	32,976	28,896	32,155
No school years completed_____	172,653	631	205	1,006	456	10,969
Elementary: 1–8 years_____	569,597	4,387	4,069	10,288	13,382	14,796
High school: 1–3 years_____	130,900	2,233	1,761	5,364	3,788	2,183
4 years or more_____	323,542	1,771	13,820	16,318	11,270	4,207
Median school years completed_____	6.9	8.4	12.5	11.9	9.5	4.1
Marital status, persons 14 years old and over_____	1,788,392	14,925	31,110	53,219	41,372	51,688
Single_____	591,765	5,855	10,847	17,152	14,752	17,705
Married [1]_____	1,037,901	8,216	18,974	33,611	23,780	30,077
Widowed or divorced_____	158,726	854	1,289	2,456	2,840	3,906
Households and families:						
Population in households_____	2,676,270	26,796	39,119	75,233	60,749	87,148
Number of households_____	632,348	3,858	10,054	15,569	17,761	15,214
Population per household_____	4.23	6.95	3.89	4.83	3.42	5.73
Families_____	563,448	3,666	8,803	14,315	13,135	12,980
Husband-wife families _____	443,907	2,870	8,297	12,012	9,750	10,167
Married couples [1]_____	(NA)	3,322	8,321	12,798	9,964	11,705

NA Not available. X Not applicable. [1] Includes consensually married couples and separated couples.
Source: U.S. Bureau of the Census, *Census of Population: 1970*, vol. I, *Characteristics of the Population*, parts 53–58.

No. 1530. POPULATION, BY PLACE OF BIRTH, PERIOD OF IMMIGRATION OF FOREIGN BORN, AND CITIZENSHIP STATUS—BY AREA: 1970

ITEM	American Samoa	Canal Zone	Guam	Virgin Islands	Trust Territory of the Pacific Islands
Total population_____	27,159	44,198	84,996	62,468	90,940
Native born, total_____	21,286	33,813	71,512	41,140	89,891
Percent of total_____	78.4	76.5	84.1	65.9	98.8
Born in U.S._____	1,211	23,559	23,934	8,058	3,504
Born in a U.S. territory_____	20,067	9,076	47,472	29,068	86,385
Born in Puerto Rico_____	8	1,178	106	4,014	2
Foreign born, total [1]_____	5,873	10,385	13,484	21,328	1,049
Percent of total_____	21.6	23.5	15.9	34.1	1.2
Europe_____	43	1,459	821	847	88
Asia_____	4,593	440	11,391	225	428
Americas, other than U.S.____	20	7,849	228	18,984	37
Other_____	1,021	97	120	94	79
By period of immigration:					
Before 1950_____	700	2,959	879	1,047	72
1950–1959_____	788	1,419	1,255	1,554	277
1960–1970_____	4,385	6,007	11,350	18,727	700
By citizenship status:					
Naturalized_____	149	1,338	3,491	2,165	412
Permanent alien_____	4,331	3,066	5,027	7,619	295
Temporary alien_____	1,336	3,944	4,045	11,309	243
Born abroad of American parents___	57	2,037	921	235	99

[1] Includes foreign born persons for whom country was not reported.
Source: U.S. Bureau of the Census, *Census of Population: 1970*, vol. I, *Characteristics of the Population*, parts 54–58.

No. 1531. Vital Statistics—Specified Areas: 1950 to 1976

[Births, deaths, and infant deaths by place of residence; marriages and divorces by place of occurrence. Rates for 1950, 1960, and 1970 based on population enumerated as of April 1; for all other years, on population estimated as of July 1]

AREA AND YEAR	BIRTHS		DEATHS		DEATHS UNDER 1 YEAR		MARRIAGES		DIVORCES [3]	
	Number	Rate [1]	Number	Rate [1]	Number	Rate [2]	Number	Rate [1]	Number	Rate [1]
Puerto Rico:										
1950	86,038	38.9	21,895	9.9	5,807	67.5	20,532	9.3	3,591	1.6
1955	77,830	34.6	16,221	7.2	4,343	55.8	18,912	8.4	4,738	2.1
1960	76,314	32.5	15,791	6.7	3,307	43.3	20,212	8.6	5,386	2.3
1965	79,608	30.2	17,686	6.7	3,406	42.8	25,184	9.6	8,035	3.1
1970	67,628	24.8	18,080	6.7	1,930	28.6	29,740	11.1	9,713	3.6
1972	68,914	24.0	19,011	6.6	1,866	27.1	33,555	11.7	13,269	4.6
1973	71,132	24.1	19,479	6.6	1,716	24.1	34,025	11.5	12,593	4.3
1974	69,886	23.1	18,948	6.3	1,511	21.6	32,760	10.8	(NA)	(NA)
1975	69,702	22.5	17,805	5.8	1,335	19.2	32,760	10.6	(NA)	(NA)
1976	71,888	22.4	19,286	6.0	1,437	20.0	(NA)	(NA)	(NA)	(NA)
Guam:										
1965	2,523	32.8	336	4.4	82	32.5	471	6.1	60	.8
1970	2,842	28.8	355	5.8	62	21.6	874	9.9	84	1.0
1973	3,219	32.2	416	4.2	73	22.6	2,510	27.0	100	1.1
1974	3,164	33.0	423	4.4	74	23.4	(NA)	(NA)	(NA)	(NA)
1975	3,156	32.0	427	4.3	65	20.6	(NA)	(NA)	(NA)	(NA)
1976	3,038	32.5	446	4.8	55	18.1	(NA)	(NA)	(NA)	(NA)
Virgin Islands:										
1950	894	33.5	374	14.0	51	57.0	138	5.2	271	10.2
1955	913	33.1	311	11.3	41	44.9	221	8.0	103	3.7
1960	1,180	36.8	332	10.3	42	35.6	360	10.8	135	4.2
1965	1,998	46.2	416	9.6	60	30.0	595	12.0	249	5.7
1970	2,898	46.8	469	7.9	72	24.6	1,089	17.4	270	4.6
1972	2,360	31.5	454	6.1	58	24.5	1,463	19.5	239	3.2
1973	2,375	28.8	459	5.6	71	29.8	1,299	15.7	271	3.3
1974	2,449	27.7	462	5.2	61	24.9	1,254	14.2	460	5.2
1975	2,372	24.9	477	5.0	62	26.1	1,056	11.1	337	3.5
1976	2,343	24.8	447	4.7	68	29.0	(NA)	(NA)	(NA)	(NA)

NA   Not available.   [1] Per 1,000 population.   [2] Per 1,000 live births.   [3] Includes reported annulments.
Source: U.S. National Center for Health Statistics, *Vital Statistics of the United States*, annual, and *Monthly Vital Statistics Report*.

No. 1532. Public Elementary and Secondary Schools, by Areas: 1977

ITEM	Puerto Rico	American Samoa	Canal Zone	Guam	Virgin Islands
Enrollment [1]	688,592	9,950	10,019	28,570	25,026
Elementary [2]	475,979	7,746	5,557	16,943	15,506
Secondary [3]	212,613	2,204	4,462	11,625	9,520
High-school graduates [4]	29,579	420	693	1,366	930
Average daily attendance	646,150	(NA)	9,588	26,318	23,340
Percent of enrollment	93.8	(NA)	95.7	92.1	93.3
Average length of term in days [5]	(NA)	(NA)	175.0	180.0	180.0
Average number of days attended per enrollee [5]	(NA)	(NA)	166.5	148.5	168.2
Instructional staff	27,424	577	585	1,469	1,713
Supervisors or consultants (excl. supt. and assist.)	168	8	15	14	95
Principals and assistants	1,121	38	21	41	69
Teachers	24,761	378	372	1,294	1,361
Male	(NA)	203	126	279	(NA)
Female	(NA)	175	246	1,015	(NA)
Other professional and educational personnel	1,374	153	177	120	188
Average salary for classroom teachers_____dol__	7,696	5,100	(NA)	12,488	10,738
Average salary for other professional educ. staff_____dol__	9,007	(NA)	21,070	14,724	12,917
Total expenditures_____$1,000__	407,091	3,746	22,061	36,292	41,261
Current expenditures [6]_____$1,000__	398,266	3,746	19,023	36,004	35,823
Per pupil [7]_____dollars__	616	(NA)	1,984	1,368	1,535
Other current expenditures [8]_____$1,000__	5,549	(NA)	2,659	288	938
Capital outlay_____$1,000__	3,276	–	379	–	4,500
Per pupil [7]_____dollars__	5	–	40	–	19

–   Represents zero.   NA   Not available.   [1] Fall 1976 estimates for 1976–77 school year.   [2] Kindergarten through grade 8.   [3] Grades 9 through 12 and postgraduates.   [4] For 1975–76.   [5] For 1974.   [6] Public elementary and secondary day schools.   [7] Annual expenditures per pupil in average daily attendance.
[8] Community services, summer schools, adult education, and community colleges.

Source: U.S. National Center for Education Statistics, *Statistics of Public Elementary and Secondary Day Schools, Fall 1976*.

No. 1533. SCHOOL ENROLLMENT AND EMPLOYMENT STATUS, 1970, AND PERCENT DISTRIBUTION OF FAMILY INCOME, 1969, BY AREA

ITEM	Puerto Rico	American Samoa	Canal Zone	Guam	Virgin Islands	Trust Territory of the Pacific Islands
SCHOOL ENROLLMENT, 1970						
Total enrolled, 3–34 years old	821,046	10,246	14,012	27,065	17,638	29,425
Elementary, total [1]	589,670	8,079	9,757	19,886	13,799	24,713
Public	541,106	7,181	9,154	16,323	10,514	22,164
Private, total	48,564	898	603	3,563	3,285	2,549
Parochial	20,789	401	213	2,553	1,735	1,562
High school (4 years), total	168,047	2,089	3,242	5,741	3,258	4,276
Public	154,264	1,912	3,172	5,025	2,519	3,279
Private, total	13,783	177	70	716	739	997
Parochial	5,086	81	17	507	412	508
College, total	63,329	78	1,013	1,438	581	436
Public	44,500	72	498	1,346	360	390
EMPLOYMENT STATUS, 1970						
Total persons, 16 years old and over	1,654,712	13,587	29,184	49,548	39,034	46,970
In labor force	679,745	5,395	18,900	32,493	25,724	14,263
Percent of total	41.1	39.7	64.8	65.6	65.9	30.4
Armed Forces	7,330	10	8,569	9,997	32	128
Civilian labor force	672,415	5,385	10,331	22,496	25,692	14,135
Employed	634,961	5,094	9,776	22,112	24,501	13,377
Unemployed	37,454	291	555	384	1,191	758
Percent of civilian labor force	5.6	5.4	5.4	1.7	4.6	5.4
Not in labor force	974,967	8,192	10,284	17,055	13,310	32,707
FAMILY INCOME, 1969						
Families, 1970	564,751	3,666	8,803	14,315	13,135	12,980
Percent distribution, by income class	100.0	100.0	100.0	100.0	100.0	100.0
Less than $1,000	21.4	23.7	1.3	4.5	6.4	53.5
$1,000–$1,999	10.8	13.0	.6	2.2	4.6	16.9
$2,000–$3,999	25.5	27.3	5.2	8.5	16.9	14.9
$4,000–$5,999	14.5	15.3	15.7	17.8	17.9	6.4
$6,000–$7,999	9.1	7.2	17.8	18.2	13.8	2.8
$8,000–$9,999	5.4	4.1	11.2	13.7	9.3	1.6
$10,000–$14,999	6.3	5.8	23.5	20.5	14.9	2.4
$15,000–$24,999	3.1	3.0	19.6	12.2	11.3	1.2
$25,000 or more	.9	.7	5.1	2.6	4.9	.4
Median income [2] ___ dol	3,063	2,840	9,684	7,886	6,612	773

[1] Includes nursery, kindergarten, and grades 1–8.   [2] For definition of median, see p. xii.

Source: U.S. Bureau of the Census, *Census of Population: 1970*, vol. I, *Characteristics of the Population*, parts 53–58.

No. 1534. PUERTO RICO—NET INCOME, BY INDUSTRIAL ORIGIN: 1960 TO 1977
[In millions of dollars. For years ending June 30]

INDUSTRY	1960	1965	1970	1971	1972	1973	1974	1975	1976	1977
All industries	1,349	2,230	3,668	4,135	4,554	5,068	5,580	5,920	6,206	6,581
Agriculture	180	190	178	198	209	218	325	310	322	325
Manufacturing	289	553	958	1,074	1,283	1,543	1,869	1,941	2,383	2,845
Food and related products	67	125	161	175	196	209	244	274	303	307
Apparel and related products	51	89	172	165	186	200	216	205	245	262
Metal products and machinery	55	82	192	223	302	365	446	478	598	780
Other manufacturing	116	257	433	510	599	769	963	983	1,237	1,497
Mining	2	5	7	8	8	8	6	6	6	5
Contract construction	87	175	338	438	436	436	456	409	347	287
Transp. and other public utilities [1]	127	213	342	375	412	484	538	621	648	739
Trade	237	402	631	694	782	841	869	945	1,030	1,105
Finance, insurance, and real estate	141	253	504	550	627	683	722	700	727	765
Services [1]	127	250	448	489	527	586	666	727	791	868
Commonwealth Government [2]	175	307	610	736	877	1,029	1,091	1,334	1,390	1,444
Rest of the world	−16	−118	−347	−425	−607	−760	−961	−1,072	−1,438	−1,803

[1] Estimates for radio and television, formerly included in services, are now included under transportation and other public utilities.   [2] Includes public enterprises, not elsewhere classified.

Source: Puerto Rico Planning Board, San Juan, P.R., *Ingreso y Producto*, annual.

No. 1535. PUERTO RICO—GROSS PRODUCT AND IMPORTS: 1960 TO 1977

[In millions of dollars. For years ending June 30]

ITEM	1960	1965	1970	1972	1973	1974	1975	1976	1977
Gross Commonwealth product	1,676	2,764	4,688	5,727	6,270	6,798	[1]7,136	[1]7,439	[1]7,914
Average annual percent change	[2]8.0	10.5	12.5	9.0	9.5	8.4	5.0	4.2	6.4
Sales of domestic production and imports	2,897	4,872	8,440	10,447	11,707	13,268	14,551	15,825	17,412
Goods and services to P.R. users	2,012	3,479	5,964	7,646	8,244	8,842	10,118	11,038	11,420
Consumers	1,397	2,251	3,747	4,743	5,222	5,690	6,390	7,361	8,106
Commonwealth and municipal govts	218	380	765	1,041	1,231	1,326	1,612	1,616	1,713
Construction	227	501	989	1,285	1,117	1,282	1,487	1,207	904
Producers durable equipment	128	219	413	476	486	396	426	489	550
Changes in inventories	42	128	50	101	188	148	203	365	147
Goods and services to rest of world	885	1,393	2,476	2,801	3,463	4,426	4,433	4,787	5,992
Less: Imports of goods and services	1,221	2,108	3,752	4,720	5,438	6,470	7,549	8,406	9,520

[1] Includes other investments by Puerto Rico Maritime Shipping Authority of $133 million in 1975, $21 million in 1976, and $22 million in 1977, not included in breakdown. [2] Change from 1955.

Source: Puerto Rico Planning Board, San Juan, P.R., *Ingreso y Producto*, annual, and unpublished data.

No. 1536. PUERTO RICO—RECEIPTS AND EXPENDITURES OF THE CENTRAL GOVERNMENT, BY MAJOR ITEM: 1960 TO 1977

[In millions of dollars. For years ending June 30. 1977, preliminary]

ITEM	1960	1965	1970	1972	1973	1974	1975	1976	1977
Receipts	351	672	1,275	1,777	1,949	2,029	2,402	2,929	3,075
Taxes	237	408	735	997	1,085	1,102	1,294	1,605	1,712
Personal	40	88	188	261	296	330	397	462	528
Corporate	26	54	92	149	157	169	167	171	176
Indirect business	172	265	456	587	632	603	730	972	1,008
Contributions to social insurance	45	81	162	221	250	270	335	362	381
Profits from governm't business enterprises	6	11	6	−8	−38	−14	−63	−78	−113
Interest and dividends	10	17	49	59	67	75	73	79	90
Sales of goods and services	9	37	67	94	93	97	112	138	160
Transfers from Federal Government	44	118	257	413	492	500	651	823	845
Transfers from private enterprises	–	–	–	1	1	(Z)	(Z)	(Z)	(Z)
Expenditures	287	548	1,105	1,549	1,797	1,957	2,416	2,617	2,797
Purchases of goods and services	227	417	831	1,134	1,325	1,422	1,725	1,754	1,873
Compensation of employees	174	307	610	877	1,029	1,091	1,334	1,390	1,444
Other purchases	103	197	390	516	561	585	671	616	668
Less: Capital expenditures	50	87	169	259	265	253	279	252	239
Interest	7	19	38	61	73	89	116	140	149
Subsidies	9	11	33	51	72	91	98	99	114
Transfer payments to persons	44	82	173	266	284	307	405	545	572
Transfer payments to Federal Government	(Z)	19	30	37	44	47	71	80	89
Savings [1]	64	124	170	228	152	72	−13	311	278

– Represents zero. Z Less than $500,000.
[1] Includes disbursements for land acquisition, equipment purchases, and other capital investments.

Source: Puerto Rico Dept. of the Treasury, San Juan, P.R., unpublished data.

No. 1537. PUERTO RICO—CONSTRUCTION SUMMARY: 1967 AND 1972

[Money figures in millions of dollars. Based on 1972 Standard Industrial Classification, except as noted]

INDUSTRY	1967 Establishments	1967 Total receipts	1972 Establishments	1972 Total receipts	1972 Payroll, entire year	1972 Employees	1972 Value added
Construction [1]	1,230	774	1,516	1,129	268	60,470	497
General building contractors and operative builders	[2]571	[2]498	684	693	136	32,759	260
General contractors, residential buildings	(NA)	(NA)	441	425	91	21,809	169
Single-family houses	(NA)	(NA)	384	289	58	14,035	119
Operative builders	85	141	82	157	19	4,287	54
General contractors, nonresidential buildings	(NA)	(NA)	161	111	26	6,663	38
Heavy construction, general contractors	128	132	150	[3]207	65	12,183	[3]112
Special trade contractors [3]	496	132	648	216	64	15,026	118
Plumbing, heating, air conditioning	77	28	103	47	12	2,286	22
Painting, paperhanging, decorating	33	3	49	(D)	2	456	(D)
Electrical work	83	29	125	47	15	2,856	23
Masonry, plastering, and tile setting	77	10	85	13	11	3,005	9
Carpentering and flooring	35	[4]1	43	[4]1	1	393	[4]1
Concrete work	19	(D)	48	(D)	9	2,935	(D)

D Withheld to avoid disclosure. NA Not available. [1] Includes data for subdividers and developers, not shown separately. [2] Based on 1967 classification and not comparable with 1972.
[3] Includes data not shown separately. [4] Flooring only.

Source: U.S. Bureau of the Census, *Census of Construction Industries, 1967: Puerto Rico*, series CC67–PR; and *Censuses of Outlying Areas, 1972, Construction Industries: Puerto Rico*, series OAC72–3.

No. 1538. Puerto Rico—Manufactures, by Industry: 1967 and 1972

[Money figures in millions of dollars. Based on 1972 Standard Industrial Classification]

INDUSTRY	1967			1972						
	Establishments	All employees [1]	Value added by manufacture [2]	Establishments	All employees		Production workers		Value of shipments [3]	Value added by manufacture [2]
					Number [1]	Salaries and wages	Number [1]	Wages		
All industries [4]	2,367	121,537	1,002.8	2,340	149,748	616.8	130,566	475.5	4,143.6	1,915.4
Food and kindred products	443	21,187	259.8	321	27,739	121.2	20,351	79.7	970.6	343.4
Tobacco products	44	6,899	41.0	28	4,508	16.0	4,274	15.0	111.4	46.4
Textile mill products	66	5,753	35.0	81	7,819	27.9	7,379	24.2	168.8	67.1
Apparel and other textile prod.	405	34,474	144.7	473	39,624	124.1	37,523	110.6	466.0	252.5
Lumber and wood products	140	1,711	9.0	100	1,194	4.5	1,115	3.9	18.1	8.2
Furniture and fixtures	153	2,794	16.4	140	3,213	13.0	2,874	9.6	53.9	29.3
Paper and allied products	27	1,287	12.2	37	1,567	8.2	1,399	6.7	42.6	17.9
Printing and publishing	129	2,482	19.8	129	2,968	16.7	1,785	9.6	64.0	41.8
Chemicals and allied prod.	(NA)	(NA)	(NA)	125	8,979	58.8	7,185	38.1	768.6	451.2
Petroleum and coal products.	10	1,709	(D)	16	2,181	20.7	1,728	12.6	469.1	91.7
Rubber and misc. plastic prod.	(NA)	(NA)	(NA)	56	3,494	14.0	3,240	11.9	48.0	27.4
Leather and leather products.	78	10,312	46.6	57	6,611	20.4	6,337	18.2	78.6	39.3
Stone, clay, and glass prod.	235	6,211	58.6	189	6,250	29.0	5,018	21.5	130.5	73.1
Primary metal industries	17	838	9.1	16	956	5.3	784	3.7	33.1	14.3
Fabricated metal products	(NA)	(NA)	(NA)	219	5,247	27.6	4,547	21.0	156.8	78.2
Machinery, exc. electrical	35	1,006	12.2	64	2,229	12.8	1,767	10.0	56.1	37.6
Electric and electronic equip.	91	8,432	82.5	105	14,671	50.4	13,617	40.7	287.5	169.6
Instruments and related prod.	36	3,836	33.4	25	712	3.1	624	2.5	12.6	6.8
Transportation equipment	17	517	(D)	44	6,066	29.0	5,497	23.8	130.5	84.2

D Withheld to avoid disclosure. NA Not available. [1] Average for year. [2] Value of shipments less cost of materials, supplies, fuels, electric energy, and contract work plus net change in finished goods and work-in-process inventory and value added in merchandising activities. [3] Represents net selling value, f.o.b. plant. Excludes freight charges and excise taxes. Includes extensive duplication arising from shipments between establishments in the same industry. [4] Includes data for industries not shown separately.

Source: U.S. Bureau of the Census, Censuses of Outlying Areas, Manufactures, Puerto Rico, series OAC72-4.

No. 1539. Puerto Rico—Business Summary: 1967 and 1972

[Money figures in millions of dollars. Based on 1967 Standard Industrial Classification. For discussion of coverage, see text, pp. 837–838]

KIND OF BUSINESS	1967		1972			
	Establishments	Total receipts	Establishments	Total receipts	Payroll, entire year	Employees [1]
Wholesale trade [2]	1,675	1,540	2,074	2,510	166	26,609
Motor vehicles, automotive equipment	70	56	141	163	13	2,101
Drugs, chemicals, allied products	155	130	176	224	20	2,983
Dry goods, apparel	165	70	168	116	6	1,083
Groceries and related products	489	515	500	780	31	5,957
Electrical goods	102	101	107	131	13	1,878
Machinery, equipment, supplies	259	153	290	254	31	4,437
Petroleum bulk stations	39	127	34	207	4	560
Retail trade [2]	32,201	1,689	29,980	2,967	275	69,669
Building materials, hardware, farm equip. dealers [2]	795	123	982	263	27	5,784
Hardware stores	383	38	575	105	11	2,510
General merchandise group stores [2]	997	187	1,544	359	42	10,073
Department stores	38	110	47	217	26	6,167
Food stores, eating and drinking places [2]	23,327	613	18,839	905	77	22,842
Grocery stores, eating and drinking places	21,084	577	16,319	839	70	20,942
Automotive dealers, gasoline service stations [2]	1,576	342	2,231	(D)	(D)	(D)
Motor vehicle dealers—new and used cars	152	188	308	456	26	4,421
Gasoline service stations	1,029	100	1,317	172	11	3,625
Apparel, accessory stores [2]	2,189	163	2,288	294	34	9,327
Men's, boys' apparel and access. stores, custom-tailors	522	39	614	(D)	(D)	(D)
Women's clothing, specialty stores	914	57	949	(D)	(D)	(D)
Family clothing stores	429	21	312	33	4	1,014
Furniture, homefurnishings, equipment stores	1,161	122	1,418	(D)	(D)	(D)
Selected services [2]	10,429	348	14,150	512	148	31,955
Hotels, tourist courts, motels	218	99	263	130	53	9,518
Personal services	3,212	34	3,008	52	12	3,519
Auto repair, auto services, garages	1,181	30	1,438	63	12	2,900
Amusement, recreation services, and motion pictures	4,589	127	7,824	87	14	3,743

D Withheld to avoid disclosure. [1] For week including Mar. 12. [2] Includes data not shown separately.

Source: U.S. Bureau of the Census, Census of Outlying Areas, Wholesale Trade, Retail Trade, and Selected Service Industries, 1972: Puerto Rico, series OAC72-1.

No. 1540. Puerto Rico—Employment Status, by Sex: 1960 to 1977

[In thousands of persons 14 years old and over except, beginning 1977, 16 years old and over. Annual averages of the civilian noninstitutional population]

EMPLOYMENT STATUS	1960, total	1965, total	1970, total	1975			1976			1977		
				Total	Male	Female	Total	Male	Female	Total	Male	Female
Total	1,369	1,555	1,743	2,099	1,003	1,096	2,173	1,038	1,135	2,093	993	1,100
In the labor force	635	698	778	875	599	276	912	616	296	937	628	308
Employed	558	617	694	715	480	235	734	481	253	750	489	261
Working	525	585	658	667	451	216	678	448	230	693	458	235
30 hours or more [1]	406	470	570	487	341	145	446	307	139	521	353	168
Less than 30 hours [2]	119	115	88	181	110	71	232	141	91	172	105	67
Not working	33	31	35	48	29	19	56	33	23	56	31	25
Unemployed	77	81	84	159	119	40	179	136	43	187	139	48
Percent	12.1	11.6	10.7	18.2	19.9	14.5	19.6	22.1	14.5	20.0	22.1	15.6
Not in the labor force	734	856	965	1,224	404	820	1,261	422	839	1,156	365	792

[1] Beginning 1976, 35 hours or more.　　[2] Beginning 1976, less than 35 hours.

Source: Puerto Rico Dept. of Labor, Bureau of Labor Statistics, San Juan, P.R., unpublished data.

No. 1541. Puerto Rico—Imports and Exports: 1960 to 1977

[In millions of dollars]

ITEM	1961–1965, avg.	1966–1970, avg.	1971–1975, avg.	1960	1965	1970	1973	1974	1975	1976	1977
Merchandise imports	1,274	2,144	3,929	924	1,543	2,681	3,593	4,961	4,885	5,928	6,200
From United States	1,054	1,700	2,641	771	1,275	2,070	2,623	2,945	3,029	3,677	3,552
From other countries	220	444	1,288	153	263	611	970	2,016	1,856	2,251	2,649
Merchandise exports	863	1,426	2,596	604	1,006	1,680	2,727	3,275	3,000	3,735	4,516
To United States	837	1,337	2,330	588	969	1,563	2,479	2,871	2,633	3,298	4,009
To other countries	27	89	266	16	37	117	248	404	367	437	507

Source: U.S. Bureau of the Census, *Foreign Commerce and Navigation of the United States*, annual; *U.S. Trade with Puerto Rico and U.S. Possessions*, FT 800; and unpublished data.

No. 1542. Puerto Rico—Agriculture: 1969 and 1974

[1 cuerda = .97 acre]

CROP	LAND HARVESTED (1,000 cuerdas)		PRODUCTION (millions)			Sales, 1974 (mil. dol.)	CROP	LAND HARVESTED (1,000 cuerdas)		PRODUCTION (millions)			Sales, 1974 (mil. dol.)
	1969	1974	Unit	1969	1974			1969	1974	Unit	1969	1974	
Sugarcane	180.4	128.3	Sh. tons	5.9	3.9	98.1	Tobacco	3.7	2.4	Lb	4.8	3.5	1.9
Coffee	125.5	114.8	Lb	17.5	23.1	15.1	Bananas	14.1	32.3	Number	332	1,040	(NA)
Vegetables							Oranges	16.2	16.7	Number	134	112	(NA)
for sale	4.6	5.1	(X)	(X)	(X)	5.7	Taniers	5.2	5.6	Lb	13.8	16.8	(NA)
Pineapples	3.5	2.7	Sh. tons	.05	.04	2.9	Pigeon peas	6.2	7.9	Lb	4.0	5.7	(NA)
Plantains	8.3	13.2	Number	95	166	(NA)							

NA Not available.　　X Not applicable.

Source: U.S. Bureau of the Census, *Census of Agriculture: 1974*, vol. I.

No. 1543. Guam and Virgin Islands—Business Summary: 1972

[Based on 1972 Standard Industrial Classification. For discussion of coverage, see text, pp. 837–838]

KIND OF BUSINESS	GUAM				VIRGIN ISLANDS			
	Establishments	Sales or receipts ($1,000)	Payroll ($1,000)	Paid employees [1]	Establishments	Sales or receipts ($1,000)	Payroll ($1,000)	Paid employees [1]
Total	710	(X)	54,296	11,128	1,861	(X)	104,357	18,812
Manufacturing	29	62,635	6,751	1,201	97	626,686	25,981	3,375
Wholesale trade	60	60,737	5,742	945	106	70,407	5,373	833
Retail trade	416	137,573	16,768	3,867	883	223,162	27,693	5,681
Selected services	135	29,297	8,525	2,141	590	60,574	19,507	4,709
Construction	70	50,154	16,510	2,974	185	77,624	25,803	4,214

X Not applicable.　　[1] Week including Mar. 12.

Source: U.S. Bureau of the Census, *Censuses of Outlying Areas, 1972: Virgin Islands and Guam*, series OAC 72–5 and 72–6, respectively.

Section 33

Comparative International Statistics

This section presents statistics for the world as a whole and for many countries on a comparative basis with the United States. Selected data are shown for area and population, births and deaths, social and industrial indicators, finances, agriculture, transportation and communication, and military affairs.

The principal sources for the data presented in this section are the United Nations *Statistical Yearbook* and the U.S. Bureau of the Census publication *World Population*. Statistics of the individual nations may be found primarily in official national publications, generally in the form of yearbooks, issued by most of the nations at various intervals in their own national languages, expressed in their own or customary units of measure. For handier reference, especially for international comparisons, the Statistical Office of the United Nations compiles and issues a number of international summary publications, generally in English and French. Among these are the *Statistical Yearbook*; the *Demographic Yearbook*; the *Yearbook of International Trade Statistics*; the *Yearbook of National Accounts Statistics*: Vol. II, *International Tables*; *Population and Vital Statistics Reports* (quarterly); the *Monthly Bulletin of Statistics*; and *World Energy Supplies*.

The Bureau of the Census, in *Country Demographic Profiles*, series ISP-30, presents data on individual countries for both a recent census year and the current period; and in *World Population*: *1977*, estimates of basic demographic measures for countries and regions of the world. The *International Population Statistics Reports*, series P-90 and P-91, issued by the Bureau of the Census, also present population figures for many foreign countries. Other sources for foreign agricultural, labor, and education statistics are publications of specialized agencies of the United Nations, such as the *Production Yearbook* issued by the Food and Agriculture Organization, the *Yearbook of Labour Statistics* issued by the International Labour Office, and the *Statistical Yearbook* issued by the Educational, Scientific, and Cultural Organization.

Statistical coverage, country names, and classifications.—Problems of space and availability of data limit the number of countries and the extent of statistical coverage shown. The list of countries included is based almost entirely on a U.S. Department of State list of sovereign nations, dependencies, and areas of special sovereignty published annually by the U.S. Department of State in *Status of the World's Nations*. Country names are shown here as specified in that publication. In the few cases where a lack of comparability exists between State Department and United Nations' terminology, the State Department's preferences are used.

The countries and regions in tables 1546, 1549, and 1550 are classified as either "more developed" or "less developed", according to the United Nations *regional* classification system. The system is based on the assumption that, within regions, levels of such factors as industrial development, literacy rate, gross reproduction rate, per capita income, etc., are somewhat constant. According to the scheme, countries in Northern America, Europe, Japan, Australia, New Zealand, and the U.S.S.R. are "more developed"; all others are "less developed" (Cyprus, Israel, and Turkey are included in Southern Europe).

Economic associations.—The Organisation for European Economic Co-operation (OEEC), a regional grouping of Western European countries established in 1948 for the purpose of harmonizing national economic policies and conditions, was succeeded on September 30, 1961, by the Organisation for Economic Co-operation and Development

895

(OECD). The member nations of the OECD are Austria, Greece, Iceland, Norway, Portugal, Spain, Sweden, Switzerland, Turkey, the "Common Market" countries (see below)—and also Finland, Canada, the United States, Japan, Australia, and New Zealand, plus Yugoslavia in special status category.

The European Economic Community (EEC), or "Common Market," consists of Belgium, France, Germany (Federal Republic), Italy, Luxembourg, the Netherlands, and, beginning 1973, Denmark, Ireland, and the United Kingdom. The EEC was formed in 1958 as the European Economic Community for the purpose of promoting European economic integration. It is based on agreement among the member nations to stimulate their economic growth, primarily through the gradual elimination of trade barriers among themselves, the establishment of a common external tariff, the coordination of monetary, fiscal, and agricultural policies, and the removal of restrictions on movement of services, labor, capital, and business enterprises within the community. The European Free Trade Association (EFTA), established in 1959, consists of Austria, Finland, Iceland, Norway, Portugal, Sweden, Switzerland, and, prior to 1973, included Denmark and the United Kingdom. It represents an agreement among the member nations to promote free trade and economic cooperation in Europe through gradual elimination of tariffs and quotas among themselves but without establishment of a common external tariff. Other regional economic groupings are the Central American Common Market (Costa Rica, El Salvador, Guatemala, Honduras, and Nicaragua) and the Latin American Free Trade Association (Argentina, Bolivia, Brazil, Chile, Colombia, Ecuador, Mexico, Paraguay, Peru, Uruguay, and Venezuela).

Quality and comparability of the data.—The quality and comparability of the data presented here are affected by a number of factors:

(1) The year for which data are presented may not be the same for all subjects for a particular country, or for a given subject for different countries, though the data shown are the most recent available. All such variations have been noted. The data shown are for calendar years except as otherwise specified.

(2) The bases, methods of estimating, methods of data collection, extent of coverage, precision of definition, scope of territory, and margins of error may vary for different items within a particular country, and for like items for different countries. Footnotes and headnotes to the tables give a few of the major time-period and coverage qualifications attached to the figures; considerably more detail is presented in the source publications. Many of the measures shown are, at best, merely rough indicators of magnitude.

(3) Figures shown in this section for the United States may not always agree with figures shown in the preceding sections. Disagreements may be attributable to the use of differing original sources, a difference in the definition of geographic limits (the 50 States, conterminous United States only, or the United States including certain outlying areas and possessions), or to possible adjustments made in the United States figures by the United Nations or other sources in order to make them more comparable with figures from other countries.

Conversion factors.—To facilitate comparison in terms of familiar units, some items shown in metric units in the source have been converted to U.S. equivalents by means of the abbreviated conversion factors shown below. Additional conversion factors appear on p. x.

CONVERSION FACTORS

Metric units	U.S. equivalents
1 square kilometer	0.3861 sq. mile
1 metric ton (1,000 kilograms)	1.1023 short tons
1 hectolitre	26.4172 U.S. gallons
1 cubic meter	35.3147 cubic feet

No. 1544. WORLD SUMMARY: 1960 TO 1976

[See text, p. 896, for general comments concerning quality of the data]

ITEM	Unit	1960	1965	1970	1972	1973	1974	1975	1976
Population	Millions	2,986	3,288	3,610	3,782	3,818	3,890	3,967	4,044
Farm products, wood, fish:									
Barley	Mil. sh. tons	100	117	154	168	186	189	173	203
Coffee	Mil. sh. tons	4.7	5.6	4.2	5.0	4.7	5.4	4.9	4.0
Corn	Mil. sh. tons	226	250	289	337	344	325	358	368
Cotton (lint)	Mil. sh. tons	11	13	13	15	15	15	14	14
Peanuts (groundnuts)	Mil. sh. tons	15	18	20	18	19	19	21	20
Potatoes	Mil. sh. tons	314	314	344	309	348	323	316	321
Rice	Mil. sh. tons	261	282	348	337	366	367	397	386
Soybeans	Mil. sh. tons	30	40	51	57	69	63	76	68
Tobacco	Mil. sh. tons	4.2	5.0	5.1	5.4	5.3	5.8	6.0	6.2
Wheat	Mil. sh. tons	269	295	351	383	415	397	391	461
Wool, greasy	Mil. sh. tons	2.8	2.9	3.1	2.8	2.7	2.9	2.9	2.8
Roundwood	Bil. cu. ft	67	73	85	87	88	89	85	88
Fish catches	Mil. sh. tons	44	59	78	73	74	77	77	81
Industrial production:									
Electric energy	Bil. kWh	2,304	3,380	4,923	5,664	6,087	6,265	6,462	6,917
Energy (coal equivalent)	Mil. sh. tons	4,737	5,870	7,704	8,853	9,312	9,410	9,350	9,867
Coal	Mil. sh. tons	2,170	2,218	2,362	2,388	2,439	2,479	2,608	2,668
Lignite	Mil. sh. tons	700	816	874	888	910	928	951	984
Coke oven coke	Mil. sh. tons	274	346	385	379	401	411	407	409
Crude petroleum	Bil. bbl	8	11	17	19	21	21	20	21
Iron ore	Mil. sh. tons	283	359	466	472	516	566	559	565
Nickel ore	1,000 sh. tons	371	483	727	718	763	827	821	883
Tin concentrate [1]	1,000 sh. tons	153	171	204	215	204	199	194	191
Meat	Mil. sh. tons	68	77	93	97	97	103	104	106
Wheat flour [1]	Mil. sh. tons	109	118	134	137	137	136	137	143
Sugar	Mil. sh. tons	58	72	80	83	86	87	90	95
Wine	Bil. gal	6	8	8	8	8	10	9	8
Beer	Bil. gal	11	13	17	18	19	20	21	21
Cigarettes [1]	Billions	1,899	2,296	2,688	2,873	2,944	3,111	3,112	3,252
Noncellulosic fibers	1,000 sh. tons	772	2,260	5,368	7,220	8,631	8,477	8,223	9,529
Sawnwood	Bil. cu. ft	12	13	14	15	15	15	14	15
Woodpulp	Mil. sh. tons	65	87	115	117	128	132	114	123
Newsprint	Mil. sh. tons	15	19	24	24	24	25	23	24
Cement	Mil. sh. tons	349	477	626	713	766	766	762	804
Pig iron and ferroalloys	Mil. sh. tons	286	369	484	512	564	581	538	557
Crude steel	Mil. sh. tons	382	506	655	690	764	776	710	744
Magnesium	1,000 sh. tons	100	173	250	262	269	272	291	256
Tin [1]	1,000 sh. tons	163	166	202	209	204	197	193	198
Merchant vessels, launched [1]	Mil. gr. tons	8.4	12.2	21.7	26.7	31.5	34.6	35.9	31.0
Motor vehicles	Millions	16.5	24.3	29.3	35.5	38.6	34.3	33.0	38.2
External trade:									
Imports, c.i.f	Bil. U.S. dol	136	197	329	430	591	853	903	1,021
Exports, f.o.b	Bil. U.S. dol	128	186	313	416	577	836	871	989
Transport:									
Railway freight	Bil. sh. ton-mi	2,286	2,873	3,438	3,696	3,948	4,097	4,104	4,179
Merchant shipping, freight [2]	Mil. sh. tons	1,224	1,849	2,833	3,153	3,516	3,624	3,500	3,695
Civil aviation, miles flown [3]	Millions	1,926	2,548	4,356	4,480	4,673	4,580	4,673	4,878

[1] Excludes People's Republic of China. Tin, tin concentrate, and merchant vessels exclude U.S.S.R. For other exclusions, see source. [2] Freight loaded. [3] Scheduled services of members of Int'l Civil Aviation Organization.

Source: Statistical Office of the United Nations, New York, N.Y., *Statistical Yearbook*. (Copyright.)

No. 1545. WORLD POPULATION AND AREA, BY SIZE OF COUNTRY: 1970 AND 1977

[Covers only countries listed in table 1549. See headnote, table 1549]

POPULATION CLASS	1970						1977					
	Countries		Population		Area		Countries		Population		Area	
	Total number	Percent of total	Total (mil.)	Percent of total	Total (1,000 sq. mi.)	Percent of total	Total number	Percent of total	Total (mil.)	Percent of total	Total (1,000 sq. mi.)	Percent of total
Total	169	100.0	3,720	100.0	51,335	100.0	169	100.0	4,256	100.0	51,562	100.0
Under 1 million	45	26.6	15	.4	1,171	2.3	44	26.0	16	.4	1,159	2.2
1–5 million	47	27.8	133	3.6	5,737	11.2	42	24.9	126	3.0	5,321	10.3
5–10 million	26	15.4	189	5.1	4,291	8.4	28	16.6	202	4.8	4,135	8.0
10–25 million	25	14.8	387	10.4	14,057	27.4	25	14.8	388	9.1	11,807	22.9
25–50 million	11	6.5	368	9.9	2,854	5.6	15	8.9	533	12.5	5,742	11.1
Over 50 million	15	8.9	2,628	70.6	23,224	45.2	15	8.9	2,990	70.3	23,400	45.4

Source: Compiled from data in U.S. Bureau of the Census, *World Population: 1977—Recent Demographic Estimates for the Countries and Regions of the World*, forthcoming report.

No. 1546. World Population and Growth, by Continent and Region: 1950 to 1977

[For explanation of "more developed" and "less developed" categories, see text, p. 895]

CONTINENT AND REGION	MIDYEAR POPULATION (millions)							ANNUAL RATE OF GROWTH (percent)				
	1950	1955	1960	1965	1970	1975	1977	1950–1960	1960–1965	1965–1970	1970–1975	1975–1977
World total	2,526	2,770	3,058	3,371	3,722	4,100	4,258	1.9	2.0	2.0	1.9	1.9
More developed regions	855	913	975	1,037	1,087	1,137	1,154	1.3	1.2	1.0	.9	.7
Less developed regions	1,671	1,856	2,082	2,335	2,634	2,963	3,103	2.2	2.3	2.4	2.4	2.3
Percent of world	66.1	67.0	68.1	69.3	70.8	72.3	72.9	(X)	(X)	(X)	(X)	(X)
Africa [1]	222	247	277	313	356	407	431	2.2	2.5	2.6	2.7	2.8
Asia	1,387	1,534	1,710	1,903	2,133	2,382	2,486	2.1	2.1	2.3	2.2	2.1
More developed regions	106	116	124	133	143	156	160	1.6	1.4	1.5	1.6	1.4
Less developed regions	1,281	1,418	1,586	1,769	1,990	2,227	2,326	2.1	2.2	2.3	2.3	2.2
East Asia [2]	673	744	828	912	1,018	1,130	1,175	2.1	1.9	2.2	2.1	2.0
South Asia [2]	714	790	882	990	1,115	1,252	1,311	2.1	2.3	2.4	2.3	2.3
Latin America [1]	166	189	216	249	284	324	342	2.7	2.8	2.7	2.6	2.6
Middle America [1] [2]	36	42	49	57	67	79	84	3.0	3.2	3.2	3.2	3.2
Caribbean [1] [2]	17	18	20	23	25	28	29	1.9	2.2	1.9	2.0	1.8
South America [1] [2]	113	129	147	168	192	218	229	2.7	2.7	2.6	2.5	2.5
Northern America [2] [3]	166	182	199	214	226	236	240	1.8	1.5	1.1	.9	.8
Europe [3]	393	408	425	444	459	474	478	.8	.9	.7	.6	.4
U.S.S.R.[3]	180	196	214	231	243	254	259	1.7	1.5	1.0	.9	.9
Oceania	13	14	16	18	19	21	22	2.3	2.2	1.9	1.9	1.3
Australia and New Zealand [3]	10	11	13	14	15	17	17	2.3	2.1	1.8	1.7	1.0
Less developed regions	2	3	3	3	4	4	5	2.6	2.7	2.6	2.5	2.4

X   Not applicable.   [1] Less developed region.
[2] For component countries, see table 1550.   [3] More developed region.

No. 1547. World Population Characteristics, 1975 and 1977, and Projections to 2000

[Source of data presents 3 levels or series of projections: Medium, high, and low. Figures shown here are for *medium series*]

ITEM	1975	1977	1980	1985	1990	1995	2000
World total_____mil__	4,100	4,258	4,500	4,918	5,365	5,849	6,353
Population per sq. mi	78	81	86	94	102	112	121
Males_____mil__	2,050	2,130	2,253	2,465	2,691	2,936	3,191
Females_____mil__	2,051	2,128	2,247	2,453	2,673	2,912	3,162
Under 5 years old_____percent__	13.6	13.4	13.0	12.5	12.1	11.9	11.6
5 to 14 years old_____percent__	23.3	23.1	22.9	22.3	21.5	20.9	20.6
65 years old and over_____percent__	5.3	5.3	5.4	5.4	5.6	5.9	6.1
Median age_____years__	21.7	21.9	22.3	22.9	23.6	24.3	25.0
More developed regions [1]_____mil__	1,137	1,154	1,179	1,224	1,268	1,309	1,345
Less developed regions [1]_____mil__	2,963	3,103	3,321	3,694	4,097	4,540	5,008

[1] See headnote, table 1546.

No. 1548. World Vital Statistics and Life Expectancy, 1976, and Projections to 2000

[1976, for calendar year. Projections, for year ending June 30]

ITEM	1976	1980	1985	1990	1995	2000
World growth rate_____percent__	1.9	1.9	1.8	1.8	1.7	1.6
Crude birth rate [1]_____per 1,000 population__	31.0	30.1	28.5	27.7	26.9	25.6
Crude death rate [1]_____per 1,000 population__	12.4	11.5	10.6	10.1	9.5	9.0
Total fertility rate [2]_____	[3] 4.3	4.0	3.7	3.5	3.4	3.3
Life expectancy at birth, both sexes_____years__	[3] 58.7	60.3	61.8	63.2	64.4	65.6
Male_____years__	[3] 56.7	58.4	59.9	61.2	62.5	63.6
Female_____years__	[3] 60.6	62.1	63.7	65.1	66.4	67.6

[1] See headnote, table 1551.   [2] Total fertility rate: Average number of children that would be born per woman if all women lived to the end of their childbearing years and, at each year of age, they experienced the birth rates occurring in the specified year.   [3] 1975 data.

Source of tables 1546–1548: U.S. Bureau of the Census, *World Population: 1977—Recent Demographic Estimates for the Countries and Regions of the World*, forthcoming; and unpublished data.

No. 1549. POPULATION AND AREA, BY REGION AND COUNTRY

[Population data generally are de facto figures for the present territory. See table 1550 for country components of regions. See text, p. 896, for general comments concerning the data. For details of methodology, coverage, and reliability, see source. Minus sign (−) denotes decrease]

REGION, COUNTRY, AND STATUS OF DEVELOPMENT ● = More developed ★ = Less developed	LATEST POPULATION CENSUS [1] Year	LATEST POPULATION CENSUS [1] Number (1,000)	MIDYEAR POPULATION ESTIMATES 1970, number (1,000)	MIDYEAR POPULATION ESTIMATES 1977 Number (1,000)	MIDYEAR POPULATION ESTIMATES 1977 Rank	Average annual percent change, 1970–77	Population per sq. mile, 1977	AREA [2] Square miles	AREA [2] Rank
World total	(X)	(X)	3,721,518	4,257,655	(X)	1.9	81	52,443,963	(X)
Africa	(X)	(X)	356,384	430,757	(X)	2.7	37	11,706,166	(X)
Northern America [3]	(X)	(X)	226,308	240,258	(X)	.9	29	8,306,942	(X)
Latin America	(X)	(X)	284,295	341,599	(X)	2.6	43	7,940,533	(X)
Middle America	(X)	(X)	67,270	84,269	(X)	3.2	87	963,706	(X)
Caribbean	(X)	(X)	24,986	28,615	(X)	1.9	311	91,892	(X)
South America [4]	(X)	(X)	192,039	228,715	(X)	2.5	33	6,884,935	(X)
East Asia	(X)	(X)	1,018,139	1,175,280	(X)	2.1	259	4,538,992	(X)
South Asia	(X)	(X)	1,114,733	1,310,765	(X)	2.3	215	6,110,033	(X)
Europe	(X)	(X)	459,460	478,196	(X)	.6	251	1,906,176	(X)
U.S.S.R	(X)	(X)	242,757	258,900	(X)	.9	30	8,649,412	(X)
Oceania	(X)	(X)	19,442	21,900	(X)	1.7	7	3,285,711	(X)
COUNTRIES									
● United States	1970	204,335	204,878	216,817	4	.8	60	3,628,150	4
★ Afghanistan	s 1972	10,020	12,059	14,067	45	2.2	56	251,000	39
★ Albania	1960	1,626	2,136	2,513	110	2.3	226	11,100	125
★ Algeria	1966	11,822	13,465	17,049	37	3.4	19	919,951	10
★ Angola	1970	5,646	5,575	6,295	74	1.7	13	481,351	21
★ Argentina	1970	23,362	23,758	26,150	29	1.4	24	1,072,067	8
● Australia	1976	13,548	12,670	14,062	46	1.5	5	2,967,909	6
● Austria	1971	7,456	7,426	7,522	68	.2	232	32,374	107
★ Bahamas, The	1970	169	171	220	154	3.6	50	4,404	140
★ Bahrain	1971	216	212	257	151	2.7	1,113	231	162
★ Bangladesh	1974	71,479	69,727	83,511	8	2.6	1,515	55,126	89
★ Barbados	1970	238	239	269	150	1.7	1,620	166	164
● Belgium	1970	9,651	9,656	9,827	56	.3	834	11,779	122
★ Benin	s 1961	2,106	2,653	3,198	100	2.7	74	43,483	96
★ Bhutan	1969	1,035	1,048	1,235	124	2.3	64	19,305	115
★ Bolivia	1976	4,648	4,140	4,950	85	2.6	12	424,162	26
★ Botswana	1971	609	630	727	132	2.0	3	222,000	44
★ Brazil	1970	93,139	96,822	117,685	6	2.8	36	3,286,470	5
● Bulgaria	1975	8,728	8,490	8,805	61	.5	206	42,829	99
★ Burma	1973	28,886	27,078	31,958	25	2.4	122	261,789	38
★ Burundi	s 1970	3,250	3,589	4,113	93	1.9	383	10,739	127
★ Cameroon	1976	7,663	6,886	7,851	66	1.9	43	183,568	48
● Canada	1976	22,993	21,324	23,323	31	1.3	6	3,851,809	2
★ Cape Verde	1970	272	269	315	146	2.3	202	1,557	148
★ Central African Empire	s 1959	1,203	1,612	1,870	116	2.1	8	241,313	41
★ Chad	s 1963	3,254	3,707	4,324	91	2.2	9	495,752	19
★ Chile	1970	8,885	9,369	10,531	55	1.7	37	286,396	37
★ China, People's Rep. of	1953	582,603	846,580	982,531	1	2.1	266	3,691,502	3
★ China, Rep. of	1975	16,206	14,598	16,793	38	2.0	1,236	13,592	121
★ Colombia	1973	21,176	21,373	25,014	30	2.2	55	455,355	25
★ Comoros	1966	244	266	310	148	2.2	447	693	154
★ Congo	1974	1,300	1,184	1,425	122	2.6	11	132,046	56
★ Costa Rica	1973	1,872	1,736	2,071	115	2.5	105	19,653	114
★ Cuba	1970	8,569	8,551	9,604	59	1.7	217	44,218	95
● Cyprus	1973	632	615	640	133	.6	179	3,572	144
● Czechoslovakia	1970	14,345	14,319	15,030	42	.7	304	49,371	92
● Denmark	1970	4,938	4,929	5,089	83	.5	306	16,615	117
★ Djibouti	1960	81	95	111	167	2.2	12	8,996	130
★ Dominican Republic	1970	4,009	4,343	5,250	80	2.7	281	18,704	116
★ Ecuador	1974	6,522	5,958	7,323	69	2.9	69	105,685	67
★ Egypt	1976	38,228	33,020	38,831	20	2.3	100	386,872	28
★ El Salvador	1971	3,555	3,582	4,387	90	2.9	531	8,260	133
★ Equatorial Guinea	1960	246	285	322	145	1.7	30	10,832	126
★ Ethiopia	(NA)	(NA)	25,934	31,108	26	2.6	68	457,142	24
★ Fiji	1976	588	526	600	135	1.9	85	7,055	136
● Finland	1970	4,598	4,606	4,740	88	.4	36	130,119	57
● France	1975	52,658	50,784	53,103	15	.6	249	212,973	45
★ Gabon	1960	449	493	531	137	1.1	5	102,317	70

See footnotes at end of table.

No. 1549. Population and Area, by Country—Continued

[See headnote, p. 899]

COUNTRY AND STATUS OF DEVELOPMENT ● = More developed ★ = Less developed	LATEST POPULATION CENSUS [1]		MIDYEAR POPULATION ESTIMATES				Population per sq. mile, 1977	AREA [2]	
	Year	Number (1,000)	1970, number (1,000)	1977 Number (1,000)	1977 Rank	Average annual percent change, 1970-77		Square miles	Rank
★Gambia, The	1973	493	458	553	136	2.7	138	4,003	142
● German Dem. Rep	1971	17,068	17,070	16,768	39	−.3	413	40,646	101
● Germany, Fed. Rep. of	1970	60,651	60,714	61,392	12	.2	641	95,815	72
★Ghana	1970	8,559	8,789	11,002	53	3.2	119	92,100	75
● Greece	1971	8,769	8,793	9,252	60	.7	183	50,547	91
★Guatemala	1973	5,160	5,262	6,437	72	2.9	153	42,042	100
★Guinea	(X)	(NA)	4,069	4,988	84	2.9	53	94,925	73
★Guinea-Bissau	1970	487	487	611	134	3.2	44	13,948	120
★Guyana	1970	702	715	802	130	1.6	10	83,000	79
★Haiti	1971	4,330	4,605	5,405	78	2.3	504	10,714	128
★Honduras	1974	2,657	2,683	3,399	97	3.4	79	43,277	97
● Hungary	1970	10,322	10,338	10,648	54	.4	296	35,919	105
● Iceland	R 1970	205	204	222	153	1.2	6	39,702	102
★India [5]	1971	548,160	553,619	643,040	2	2.1	523	1,229,737	7
★Indonesia	1971	119,232	121,717	141,462	5	2.1	192	735,268	14
★Iran	1976	33,592	30,129	37,121	22	3.0	58	636,363	16
★Iraq	1977	12,171	9,466	12,048	52	3.4	70	172,000	51
● Ireland	1971	2,978	2,950	3,196	101	1.1	120	26,600	111
● Israel	1972	3,148	2,974	·3,611	95	2.8	452	7,992	134
● Italy	1971	54,137	53,661	56,436	13	.7	485	116,303	63
★Ivory Coast	1975	6,671	5,867	7,073	70	2.7	57	124,503	61
★Jamaica	1970	1,849	1,944	2,170	114	1.6	492	4,411	139
● Japan	1975	111,940	104,345	113,860	7	1.2	793	143,574	55
★Jordan	1961	(NA)	2,228	2,848	107	3.5	76	37,297	104
★Kampuchea, Democratic	1962	5,729	7,060	7,895	64	1.6	113	70,000	84
★Kenya	1969	(NA)	11,252	14,311	43	3.4	64	224,960	43
★Korea, Dem. Peo. Rep. of	(X)	(NA)	14,185	17,571	36	3.1	376	46,768	93
★Korea, Republic of	1975	34,709	32,976	38,195	21	2.1	1,004	38,031	103
★Kuwait	1975	995	748	1,134	125	5.9	146	7,780	135
★Laos	(X)	(NA)	2,962	3,462	96	2.2	38	91,428	77
★Lebanon	s 1970	2,126	2,330	2,796	108	2.6	696	4,015	141
★Lesotho	1976	1,214	1,066	1,248	123	2.3	107	11,716	123
★Liberia	1974	(NA)	1,335	1,678	119	3.3	39	43,000	98
★Libya	1973	2,257	1,991	2,648	109	4.1	4	679,536	15
● Luxembourg	1970	340	339	357	142	.7	357	999	151
★Madagascar	1974	7,520	6,759	7,962	63	2.3	35	230,035	42
★Malawi	1977	5,572	4,441	5,309	79	2.6	116	45,747	94
★Malaysia	1970	10,439	10,835	13,004	50	2.6	101	128,328	58
★Maldives	1974	129	115	138	162	2.6	1,200	115	167
★Mali	1976	6,035	5,186	6,101	76	2.3	13	464,873	23
● Malta	1967	316	326	332	143	.3	2,721	122	166
★Mauritania	1976	1,481	1,307	1,496	121	1.9	4	419,229	27
★Mauritius	1972	851	830	910	128	1.3	1,156	787	153
★Mexico	1970	48,225	50,480	63,687	11	3.3	84	761,601	13
★Mongolia	1969	1,198	1,248	1,537	120	3.0	3	604,247	17
★Morocco	1971	15,379	15,126	18,592	35	2.9	108	171,953	52
★Mozambique	1970	8,169	8,133	9,629	58	2.4	32	303,073	34
★Nepal	1971	11,556	11,311	13,341	49	2.4	245	54,362	90
● Netherlands	1971	13,046	13,032	13,853	47	.9	992	13,967	119
● New Zealand	1976	3,129	2,828	3,153	103	1.6	30	103,736	68
★Nicaragua	1971	1,878	1,908	2,336	112	2.9	41	57,143	88
★Niger	s 1959	2,876	4,016	4,850	87	2.7	10	489,206	20
★Nigeria	(X)	(NA)	55,073	66,628	10	2.7	187	356,699	30
● Norway	1970	3,874	3,877	4,044	94	.6	32	125,181	60
★Oman	(X)	(NA)	657	817	129	3.1	10	82,000	80
★Pakistan [6]	1972	65,309	61,091	75,472	9	3.0	220	342,750	32
★Panama	1970	1,428	1,453	1,764	117	2.8	61	28,753	109
★Papua New Guinea	1971	2,490	2,418	2,908	105	2.6	16	183,540	49
★Paraguay	1972	2,358	2,446	2,982	104	2.8	19	157,047	53
★Peru	1972	13,538	13,504	16,362	40	2.7	33	496,222	18
★Philippines	1975	41,831	37,537	44,863	17	2.5	388	115,707	64
● Poland	1970	32,642	32,526	34,698	24	.9	288	120,359	62
● Portugal	1970	8,663	8,723	9,725	57	1.6	275	35,340	106
★Qatar	(X)	(NA)	126	157	157	3.1	39	4,000	143
● Romania	1977	21,559	20,253	21,664	33	1.0	236	91,699	76
★Rwanda	s 1970	3,573	3,560	4,318	92	2.8	425	10,169	·129

See footnotes at end of table.

No. 1549. POPULATION AND AREA, BY COUNTRY—Continued

[See headnote, p. 899]

COUNTRY AND STATUS OF DEVELOPMENT ●=More developed ★=Less developed	LATEST POPULATION CENSUS [1] Year	Number (1,000)	MIDYEAR POPULATION ESTIMATES 1970, number (1,000)	1977 Number (1,000)	Rank	Average annual percent change, 1970-77	Population per sq. mile, 1977	AREA [2] Square miles	Rank
★Saudi Arabia	1974	7,013	6,200	7,626	67	3.0	9	873,000	12
★Senegal	1976	5,085	4,385	5,245	81	2.6	69	76,124	81
★Sierra Leone	1974	2,729	2,701	3,193	102	2.4	114	27,925	110
★Singapore	1970	2,075	2,075	2,308	113	1.5	10,258	225	163
★Somalia	(X)	(NA)	2,806	3,309	98	2.4	13	246,155	40
★South Africa	1970	21,794	22,465	26,764	27	2.5	57	471,819	22
●Spain	1970	33,956	33,779	36,351	23	1.0	187	194,883	47
★Sri Lanka	1971	12,690	12,532	14,068	44	1.7	556	25,322	112
★Sudan	1973	14,902	15,720	19,638	34	3.2	20	967,491	9
★Surinam	1971	380	373	382	141	.3	6	63,251	87
★Swaziland	1976	499	420	511	138	2.8	76	6,705	137
●Sweden	1975	8,209	8,043	8,255	62	.4	48	173,665	50
●Switzerland	1970	6,270	6,267	6,289	75	.1	395	15,941	118
★Syria	1970	6,305	6,258	7,863	65	3.3	110	71,498	83
★Tanzania	1967	12,313	13,286	16,334	41	3.0	45	362,820	29
★Thailand	1970	34,397	37,091	44,287	18	2.5	223	198,455	46
★Togo	1970	1,951	1,964	2,390	111	2.8	109	21,853	113
★Trinidad and Tobago	1970	941	940	921	127	−.3	465	1,980	147
★Tunisia	1975	5,588	5,118	6,077	77	2.5	96	63,378	86
●Turkey	1975	40,198	35,322	41,759	19	2.4	139	301,380	35
●Uganda	1969	9,549	9,806	12,353	51	3.3	136	91,134	78
●U.S.S.R	1970	241,720	242,757	258,900	3	.9	30	8,649,490	1
★United Arab Emirates	1975	656	323	781	131	12.6	24	32,000	108
●United Kingdom	1971	55,515	55,522	55,956	14	.1	594	94,214	74
★Upper Volta	1975	6,144	5,465	6,364	73	2.2	60	105,869	66
★Uruguay	1975	2,782	2,824	2,876	106	.3	42	68,548	85
★Venezuela	1971	10,722	10,709	13,598	48	3.4	39	352,143	31
★Vietnam	1974	23,787	42,984	49,948	16	2.1	395	126,436	59
★Western Samoa	1076	151	142	153	158	1.1	135	1,133	150
★Yemen, Peo. Dem. Rep. of	1973	1,590	1,508	1,717	118	1.9	15	111,000	65
★Yemen Arab Republic	1975	4,526	4,335	4,938	86	1.9	66	75,290	82
●Yugoslavia	1971	20,523	20,371	21,768	32	.9	220	98,766	71
★Zaire	1970	21,638	21,638	26,313	28	2.8	29	905,063	11
★Zambia	1974	4,695	4,241	5,224	82	3.0	18	290,724	36
AREAS OF SPECIAL SOVEREIGNTY AND DEPENDENCIES									
★Belize	1970	120	122	149	159	2.9	17	8,866	131
★Brunei	1971	136	128	182	156	5.0	82	2,226	146
★Channel Islands	1971	123	122	127	165	.6	1,693	75	168
★French Polynesia	1977	137	110	138	161	3.2	89	1,544	149
★Gaza Strip	1967	356	333	411	140	3.0	2,815	146	165
★Guadeloupe	1974	325	328	328	144	−	478	686	156
★Hong Kong	1976	4,420	3,959	4,514	89	1.9	11,342	398	158
★Macao	1970	249	248	279	149	1.7	46,500	6	169
★Martinique	1974	235	333	311	147	−1.0	722	431	157
★Namibia	1970	762	766	936	126	2.9	3	318,261	33
★Netherlands Antilles	1971	218	218	236	152	1.1	744	317	159
★New Caledonia	1976	133	110	137	163	3.1	16	8,548	132
★New Hebrides	1967	78	83	100	169	2.7	18	5,700	138
★Pacific Is., Tr. Terr. of	1973	115	101	129	164	3.5	188	687	155
★Puerto Rico	1970	2,712	2,724	3,215	99	2.4	936	3,435	145
★Reunion	1974	477	445	478	139	1.0	493	970	152
★Saint Lucia	1970	101	103	117	166	1.8	492	238	161
★Saint Vincent	1970	87	88	106	168	2.7	424	250	160
★Solomon Islands	1976	197	163	206	155	3.3	18	11,500	124
★Southern Rhodesia	1969	5,099	5,546	7,054	71	3.4	47	150,333	54
★Western Sahara	1970	76	72	139	160	9.4	1	102,703	69

− Represents zero. NA Not available. X Not applicable. [1] For countries in which no recent census has been taken, survey or national registry data (identified respectively as "S" and "R") are shown.
[2] Includes inland waters. Source: U.S. Department of State, *Status of the World's Nations*, annual. [3] Includes Bermuda, Canada, Greenland, St. Pierre and Miquelon, and United States. [4] Includes both temperate and tropical South American countries. [5] Includes the Indian-held part of Jammu and Kashmir. [6] Excludes the Pakistani-held part of Jammu and Kashmir.

Source: Except as noted, U.S. Bureau of the Census, *World Population: 1977—Recent Demographic Estimates for the Countries and Regions of the World*, forthcoming.

No. 1550. Population Projections, by Region and for Selected Countries: 1975 to 2000

[In millions. Source of data presents 3 series of projections. Figures shown here are for *medium series*]

REGION AND COUNTRY	1975	1980	1990	2000	REGION AND COUNTRY	1975	1980	1990	2000
World, total	3,967	4,373	5,279	6,253	East Asia—Con.				
More developed¹	1,132	1,181	1,278	1,361	Japan	111.1	117.5	126.2	132.9
Less developed¹	2,835	3,192	4,002	4,893	Other East Asia²	55.7	61.9	75.4	88.2
					Hong Kong	4.2	4.5	5.1	5.6
Africa	401.1	460.7	613.7	813.1	Korea, Dem. Peo.				
Eastern Africa²	114.5	132.0	177.6	239.9	Rep. of	15.9	17.9	22.6	27.5
Burundi	3.8	4.3	5.6	7.3	Korea, Republic of	33.9	37.4	45.1	52.0
Ethiopia	28.0	31.5	40.7	53.7					
Kenya	13.3	15.7	22.1	31.0	South Asia	1,249.8	1,426.8	1,836.3	2,267.3
Madagascar	8.0	9.3	12.8	17.8	Eastern South Asia²	323.8	370.9	478.7	591.6
Malawi	4.9	5.6	7.3	9.5	Burma	31.2	35.2	44.6	54.9
Mozambique	9.2	10.4	13.4	17.6	Cambodia	8.1	9.4	12.5	15.8
Rwanda	4.2	4.9	6.6	8.7	Indonesia³	136.0	154.9	196.6	237.5
Somalia	3.2	3.7	4.9	6.5	Laos	3.3	3.7	4.7	5.7
Southern Rhodesia	6.3	7.5	10.8	15.1	Malaysia	12.1	14.0	18.3	22.1
Uganda	11.4	13.2	18.0	24.2	Philippines	44.4	52.2	70.1	89.7
Tanzania	15.4	18.1	24.8	34.0	Singapore	2.2	2.4	2.8	3.1
Zambia	5.0	5.9	8.2	11.6	Thailand	42.1	49.5	66.8	85.6
					Vietnam	43.5	48.6	61.3	75.8
Middle Africa²	45.3	51.2	66.7	87.7					
Angola	6.4	7.2	9.4	12.5	Middle South Asia²	837.8	954.0	1,221.7	1,501.2
Cameroon	6.4	7.1	9.0	11.6	Afghanistan	19.3	22.0	28.7	36.7
Chad	4.0	4.5	5.5	6.9	Bangladesh	73.7	84.8	112.7	144.3
Zaire	24.5	28.0	37.1	49.5	India	613.2	694.3	876.1	1,059.4
					Iran	32.9	38.5	51.9	66.6
Northern Africa²	98.2	113.1	149.7	191.8	Nepal	12.6	14.2	18.3	23.2
Algeria	16.8	19.8	27.7	36.7	Pakistan	70.6	83.0	113.2	146.9
Egypt	37.5	42.1	52.6	64.6	Sri Lanka	14.0	15.5	18.5	21.3
Libya	2.3	2.6	3.6	4.7					
Morocco	17.5	20.4	27.6	35.9	Western South Asia²	88.2	102.0	135.9	174.4
Sudan	18.3	21.4	29.4	39.0	Iraq	11.1	13.1	18.3	24.4
Tunisia	5.7	6.6	8.6	10.9	Israel⁴	3.4	3.9	4.8	5.6
					Jordan	2.7	3.2	4.4	5.9
Southern Africa²	27.7	32.0	42.3	55.7	Lebanon	2.9	3.4	4.6	6.1
South Africa	24.7	28.5	37.9	50.0	Saudi Arabia	9.0	10.4	14.1	18.6
					Syria	7.3	8.5	11.8	15.8
Western Africa²	115.5	132.5	177.3	238.0	Turkey	39.9	45.4	58.7	72.6
Benin	3.1	3.5	4.7	5.9	Yemen⁵	6.7	7.7	10.4	13.8
Ghana	9.9	11.4	15.7	21.2					
Guinea	4.4	5.0	6.5	8.5	Europe (excl. U.S.S.R.)	473.1	486.6	513.8	539.8
Ivory Coast	4.9	5.6	7.4	9.6	Eastern Europe	106.3	109.7	115.8	121.7
Mali	5.7	6.5	8.5	11.3	Bulgaria	8.8	9.1	9.6	10.0
Niger	4.6	5.3	7.0	9.6	Czechoslovakia	14.8	15.2	15.9	16.8
Nigeria	62.9	72.6	98.5	134.9	German Dem. Rep.	17.2	17.4	17.8	18.2
Senegal	4.4	5.0	6.4	8.2	Hungary	10.5	10.7	10.9	11.1
Togo	2.2	2.6	3.5	4.6	Poland	33.9	35.3	37.8	39.8
Upper Volta	6.0	6.8	8.7	11.0	Romania	21.2	22.1	23.8	25.8
Latin America	324.1	371.6	485.6	619.9	Northern Europe²	82.0	83.7	87.4	91.3
Caribbean²	27.1	30.0	36.8	44.5	Denmark	5.0	5.1	5.2	5.4
Cuba	9.5	10.5	12.9	15.3	Finland	4.7	4.7	4.7	4.7
Dominican Rep	5.1	6.1	8.5	11.8	Ireland	3.1	3.3	3.7	4.0
Haiti	4.6	5.0	6.0	7.0	Norway	4.0	4.1	4.3	4.5
Jamaica	2.0	2.2	2.5	2.7	Sweden	8.3	8.5	9.0	9.4
					United Kingdom	56.4	57.5	60.0	62.8
Middle America²	78.7	92.6	128.2	172.7					
El Salvador	4.1	4.8	6.6	8.8	Southern Europe²	132.4	137.1	146.7	155.7
Guatemala	6.1	7.1	9.5	12.4	Albania	2.5	2.8	3.6	4.3
Honduras	3.0	3.6	5.0	6.9	Greece	8.9	9.1	9.4	9.6
Mexico	59.2	70.0	97.6	132.2	Italy	55.0	56.3	58.7	60.9
Nicaragua	2.3	2.7	3.8	5.2	Portugal	8.8	9.0	9.5	9.9
					Spain	35.4	37.2	41.0	44.9
Temperate South America	38.7	41.6	47.2	52.1	Yugoslavia	21.3	22.3	24.1	25.7
Argentina	25.4	27.1	30.2	32.9					
Chile	10.3	11.2	13.4	15.4	Western Europe²	152.5	156.0	163.9	171.1
Uruguay	3.1	3.3	3.6	3.9	Austria	7.5	7.6	7.9	8.1
					Belgium	9.8	10.1	10.5	10.8
Tropical South America²	179.6	207.4	273.4	350.7	France	52.9	55.1	58.8	62.1
Bolivia	5.4	6.2	8.0	10.3	Germany, Fed. Rep.	61.7	62.0	64.2	66.2
Brazil	109.7	126.4	165.8	212.5	Netherlands	13.6	14.1	15.1	16.0
Colombia	25.9	30.2	40.3	51.5	Switzerland	6.5	6.7	7.1	7.4
Ecuador	7.1	8.3	11.3	14.8					
Paraguay	2.6	3.1	4.1	5.3	U.S.S.R.	255.0	268.1	293.7	315.0
Peru	15.3	17.7	23.5	30.6					
Venezuela	12.2	14.1	18.7	23.6	Oceania²	21.3	23.5	28.1	32.7
					Australia	13.8	15.1	17.8	20.2
Northern America	236.8	248.8	275.1	296.2	New Zealand	3.0	3.3	3.8	4.3
Canada	22.8	24.6	28.4	31.6	Papua New Guinea	2.7	3.1	4.0	5.0
United States	214.0	224.1	246.6	264.4					
East Asia	1,005.7	1,087.0	1,232.7	1,369.1					
China	838.8	907.6	1,031.1	1,148.0					

¹ Regions.   ² Includes countries not shown separately.   ³ Including West Irian.   ⁴ Includes Jerusalem and Israeli residents in Gaza Strip and West Bank.   ⁵ Covers Peo. Dem. Rep. of Yemen and Yemen Arab Rep.

Source: Population Division of the United Nations, New York, N.Y., *Selected World Demographic Indicators, by Countries, 1950-2000.*

No. 1551. POPULATION UNDER AGE 15, GROWTH, BIRTH, DEATH, AND INFANT MORTALITY RATES, AND LIFE EXPECTANCY, FOR THE 75 MOST POPULOUS COUNTRIES

[Growth rate: Annual increase (or decrease) to the population resulting from a surplus or deficit of births over deaths and a surplus or deficit of migrants into or out of the country, expressed as a percentage of the base population. Crude birth rate: Number of births during 1 year per 1,000 persons (based on midyear population). Crude death rate: Number of deaths during 1 year per 1,000 persons (based on midyear population). Infant mortality rate: Number of deaths of children under 1 year of age per 1,000 live births in a calendar year. Life expectancy at birth: Number of years to be lived by persons born in a certain year if mortality rates for each age group remain constant in the future. Minus sign (−) denotes decrease]

COUNTRY	POPULATION UNDER 15 YEARS OLD		Growth rate of population, 1976 (percent)	Crude birth rate, 1976	Crude death rate, 1976	INFANT MORTALITY		EXPECTATION OF LIFE AT BIRTH	
	Year or period	Percent of total population				Year or period	Rate	Year or period	Both sexes (yr.)
United States	1970	28	.7	15	9	1976	15	1975	72
Afghanistan	1972–73	45	1.8–2.5	50–53	28–32	1972–73	217–235	1972–73	35–39
Algeria	1966	47	3.3–3.5	50	15–17	1969–71	142	1969–71	53
Angola	1960	42	2.4	47	23	(X)	(NA)	(X)	(NA)
Argentina	1970	29	1.3	22–23	9–10	1970	59	1969–70	66
Australia	1971	29	1.0	16	8	1975	14	1971–73	71
Austria	1975	23	−	12	13	1976	18	1976	76
Bangladesh	1974	46	2.6–3.0	46–48	18–20	1969–74	153	1969–74	42
Belgium	1976	22	.1	12	12	1976	14	1968–72	71
Brazil	1970	44	2.5–2.9	35–39	10	1960–70	102	1960–70	54
Bulgaria	1976	22	.6	17	10	1976	23	1969–71	71
Burma	1973	40	2.3–2.4	38–39	15	(X)	(NA)	(X)	(NA)
Cameroon	1960–65	41–42	1.8–2.2	41–43	21–23	1960–65	137–167	1960–65	38
Canada	1975	26	1.3	16	7	1974	15	1971	73
Chile	1970	38	1.5–1.6	22–23	7	1975	61	1969–70	62
China, People's Rep. of	1953	36	1.6–2.2	26–36	9–13	(X)	(NA)	(X)	(NA)
China, Republic of	1975	36	2.1	26	5	1975	25	1975	70
Colombia	1973	45	2.1–2.3	33–34	10	1973	98	1973	59
Cuba	1975	37	1.4	20	6–7	1976	23	1970	70
Czechoslovakia	1976	24	.8	19	11	1976	21	1976	70
Ecuador	1974	44	2.9–3.1	41–43	11	1970–75	100	1970–75	57
Egypt	(X)	(NA)	2.6	39	13	1974	100	1065–67	53
Ethiopia	1971	45	2.2–2.6	43–52	20–26	1964–70	155–200	1964–70	36–44
France	1977	23	.3	14	11	1976	13	1974	73
German Dem. Rep	1976	19	−.2	12	14	1976	14	1975	71
Germany, Fed. Rep. of	1976	21	−.3	10	12	1976	17	1973–75	71
Ghana	1970	46	3.1–3.3	45–48	14–15	1970	115	1970	49
Greece	1975	24	1.3	16	9	1976	22	1970	72
Guatemala	1973	44	2.5–2.6	39–40	14	1974	75	1970–72	53
Hungary	1977	21	.5	18	12	1976	30	1974	70
India	1971	41	2.1	36–37	15	1969	134	1969	47
Indonesia	1971	43	1.8–2.3	35–40	16–17	1971	126	1971	42
Iran	1973–76	46	3.0	41–42	11–12	1973–76	104	1973–76	57
Iraq	1965	48	3.4	48	14	(X)	(NA)	(X)	(NA)
Italy	1976	24	.5	14	10	1976	19	1970–72	72
Ivory Coast	1955–58	43	2.0–3.1	45–52	21–25	(X)	(NA)	(X)	(NA)
Japan	1976	24	1.0	16	6	1975	10	1975	74
Kampuchea, Dem	1962	46	(NA)	(NA)	(NA)	(X)	(NA)	(X)	(NA)
Kenya	1969	48	3.4–3.7	48–51	14–15	1969	119	1969	49
Korea, Dem. Peo. Rep. of	(X)	(NA)	3.1	43	12	(X)	(NA)	(X)	(NA)
Korea, Republic of	1975	39	1.8–1.9	25–26	6	1970	47	1970	64
Madagascar	1966	46	2.4–2.6	46–48	22	(X)	(NA)	1965–66	38
Malaysia	1970	45	2.4–2.5	30–31	6	1975	32	1975	68
Mexico	1970	48	2.9–3.5	37–44	7	1969–71	71	1969–71	61
Morocco	1971	46	2.9–3.0	46–48	16–17	1962–72	153	1962–72	48
Mozambique	1970	45	2.4–3.1	42–48	18–19	1970	148	(X)	(NA)
Nepal	1971	40	2.4–2.5	45–47	19–22	1974–76	132–133	1974–76	42–44
Netherlands	1976	25	.6	13	8	1976	11	1975	75
Nigeria	1953	44	2.4–3.0	48–50	20–24	1965–66	178	1965–66	37
Pakistan	1972	44	3.0–3.1	44–45	13–15	1962–65	139	1962–65	46
Peru	1972	44	2.7–2.9	39–42	13	1970–75	122	1970–75	55
Philippines	1970	46	2.2–2.6	32–37	10	1970	80	1970	58
Poland	1977	24	1.0	20	9	1976	24	1975	71
Portugal	1975	28	.6	19	10	1975	39	1974	69
Romania	1976	25	1.0	19	10	1976	31	1974–76	70
Saudi Arabia	(X)	(NA)	3.0	49	19	(X)	(NA)	(X)	(NA)
South Africa	1970	42	2.3–2.5	36–37	12–13	1970	88–95	1965–70	57
Southern Rhodesia	1969	46	3.5	47–50	14–15	(X)	(NA)	(X)	(NA)
Spain	1970	28	1.1	18	8	1976	16	1970	72
Sri Lanka	1971	39	1.5–1.6	26–27	9	1973	47	1970–72	64
Sudan	1973	47	3.2	49	17	(X)	(NA)	(X)	(NA)
Sweden	1977	21	.3	12	11	1976	8	1975	75
Switzerland	1977	22	−.6	12	9	1976	11	1968–73	73

See footnotes at end of table.

No. 1551. Population Under Age 15, Growth, Birth, Death, and Infant Mortality Rates, and Life Expectancy, for the 75 Most Populous Countries—Con.

[See headnote, p. 903]

COUNTRY	POPULATION UNDER 15 YEARS OLD		Growth rate of popu- lation, 1976 (per- cent)	Crude birth rate, 1976	Crude death rate, 1976	INFANT MORTALITY		EXPECTATION OF LIFE AT BIRTH	
	Year or period	Percent of total popu- lation				Year or period	Rate	Year or period	Both sexes (yr.)
Syria	1970	49	3.2-3.3	47	14-15	1970	114	(X)	(NA)
Tanzania	1967	44	2.7-3.3	45-49	16-18	1973	120-130	1973	45-49
Thailand	1970	44	2.2-2.5	32-35	10	1970	90	1970	58
Turkey	1975	40	2.2-2.3	34	11-12	1967	153	1966	54
U.S.S.R.	1975	26	.9	18	9	1975	30	1971-72	70
Uganda	1969	46	2.8-3.4	46-50	16-18	(X)	(NA)	(X)	(NA)
United Kingdom	1976	23	-	12	12	1976	14	1973-75	72
Upper Volta	1960-61	42	2.2	50	28	1960-61	190-243	1960-61	32
Venezuela	1971	45	3.3	36	6	1965-70	45	1965-70	63
Vietnam	(X)	(NA)	2.1-3.0	40-44	15-19	(X)	(NA)	(X)	(NA)
Yugoslavia	1976	25	1.0	18	8	1976	37	1972-73	68
Zaire	1955-58	39-42	2.2-3.0	43-47	17-20	1955-58	165-177	1955-58	37-40

- Represents zero.   NA Not available.   X Not applicable.

Source: U.S. Bureau of the Census, *World Population: 1977—Recent Demographic Estimates for the Countries and Regions of the World*, forthcoming.

No. 1552. Life Expectancy at Birth, by Sex, for 30 Most Populous Countries

[Selection of countries based on 1977 population as shown in table 1549]

COUNTRY	Year or period	Male (yr.)	Female (yr.)	COUNTRY	Year or period	Male (yr.)	Female (yr.)
United States	1975	68.7	76.5	Japan	1976	72.2	77.4
Argentina	1970-1975	65.2	71.4	Korea, Rep. of	1970	63.0	67.0
Bangladesh [1]	1970-1975	35.8	35.8	Mexico	1975	62.8	66.6
Brazil	1960-1970	57.6	61.0	Nigeria	1965-1966	37.2	36.7
Burma [1]	1970-1975	48.6	51.5	Pakistan [1]	1962	[3] 53.7	[3] 48.8
China, Peo. Rep. of [1] [2]	1970-1975	59.9	63.3	Philippines [1]	1970-1975	56.9	60.0
Colombia [1]	1970-1975	59.2	62.7	Poland	1976	66.9	74.6
Egypt	1960	51.6	53.8	South Africa [1]	1970-1975	49.8	53.3
Ethiopia [1]	1970-1975	36.5	39.6	Spain	1970	69.7	75.0
France	1974	69.0	76.9	Thailand	1960	53.6	58.7
Germany, Fed. Rep. of	1973-1975	68.0	74.5	Turkey [1]	1966	53.7	
India	1951-1960	41.9	40.6	U.S.S.R.	1971-1972	64	74
Indonesia	1960	47.5	47.5	United Kingdom	1968-1970	67.8	73.8
Iran [1]	1970-1975	50.7	51.3	Vietnam [1]	1970-1975	43.2	46.0
Italy	1970-1972	69.0	74.9	Zaire [1]	1970-1975	41.9	45.1

[1] Estimated.   [2] Includes Taiwan.   [3] Includes Bangladesh.

Source: Statistical Office of the United Nations, New York, N.Y., *Statistical Yearbook*. (Copyright.)

No. 1553. Literacy of Population, 15 Years Old and Over, by Region: 1960 and 1970

[In millions, except percent. Literacy is defined as the ability to both read and write. See text, p. 896, for general comments concerning the data]

REGION	1960				1970			
	Total adults	Literate adults	Illiterate adults		Total adults	Literate adults	Illiterate adults	
			Number	Percent			Number	Percent
World [1]	1,869	1,134	735	39.3	2,287	1,504	783	34.2
Africa	153	29	124	81.0	194	51	143	73.7
North America	137	133	3	2.4	161	158	2	1.5
Latin America	123	83	40	32.5	163	125	39	23.6
Asia [1]	982	440	542	55.2	1,237	658	579	46.8
Europe and U.S.S.R.	464	439	24	5.3	521	502	19	3.6
Oceania	11	9	1	11.5	13	12	1	10.3

[1] Excludes People's Republic of China, Democratic People's Republic of Korea, and former Democratic Republic of Vietnam.

Source: Statistical Office of the United Nations, New York, N.Y., *World Statistics in Brief*, 1977. (Copyright.)

No. 1554. Education and Illiteracy, by Country

[Teachers and students: Data cover both public and private schools for school year beginning in year stated and exclude adult education and correspondence schools. Expenditures: Include both capital and current expenditures on public education and subsidized private education converted to U.S. dollars at par values of exchange rates then in effect. Illiteracy: Defined as inability both to read and write in any, or a specified, language. See text, p. 896, for general comments concerning the data. For additional qualifications for individual countries, see source]

COUNTRY	Year	1ST LEVEL [1] Teachers (1,000)	1ST LEVEL [1] Students enrolled (1,000)	2D LEVEL [2] Teachers (1,000)	2D LEVEL [2] Students enrolled (1,000)	PUBLIC EXPENDITURE Year	Total (mil. dol.)	Percent of— Total public expenditure	Percent of— Gross national product	ILLITERATE Year	Percent of population, 15 years old and over
United States	1975	1,354	26,846	1,109	20,546	1975	100,700	18.1	6.2	1969	[3] 1.0
Afghanistan	1975	22	843	[4] 9	106	1974	28	12.7	1.3	1965	93.6
Albania	1971	21	518	3	48	1971	129	11.6	(NA)	1947	3.3
Algeria	1975	65	2,663	20	512	1976	[5] 673	[5] 11.0	(NA)	1971	73.6
Angola	1972	13	516	5	79	1972	[6] 48	[6] 11.9	[6] 2.2	1950	[7] 97.0
Argentina	1976	[8] 196	[8] 3,579	170	1,283	1974	[9] 1,489	[9] 18.8	[9] 4.0	1971	[10] 8.4
Australia	1975	78	1,790	74	1,096	1975	5,735	14.4	6.3	(X)	(NA)
Austria	1975	[11][12] 62	502	([12])	756	1975	2,153	8.5	5.7	(X)	(NA)
Bangladesh	1975	[13] 155	8,192	[13] 94	2,443	1975	106	11.7	1.2	1961	78.4
Belgium	1975	49	941	[11] 789	1973	[6][9] 2,332	[6][9] 18.4	[6][9] 5.1	(X)	(NA)
Bolivia	1975	39	881	[14][15] 8	[16] 127	1974	60	(NA)	(NA)	1960	61.2
Brazil	1974	887	19,287	156	1,682	1974	3,522	21.1	(NA)	1970	33.8
Bulgaria	1975	48	980	27	344	1975	812	8.5	[17] 5.5	1965	9.4
Burma	1974	[14] 74	[18] 3,476	[16] 23	[16] 890	1971	73	19.4	3.4	1962	40.3
Canada	1975	(NA)	2,555	(NA)	2,640	1975	12,480	(NA)	7.9	(X)	(NA)
Chile	1976	[8] 66	2,243	[8] 30	466	1974	[9] 745	[9] 12.5	[9] 3.8	1970	11.9
China, People's Rep. of	1959	(NA)	90,000	(NA)	[19] 9,990	1960	3,200	(NA)	(NA)	(X)	(NA)
Colombia	1974	115	3,792	66	1,284	1973	327	21.2	3.3	1973	19.2
Congo	1975	5	319	[15] 2	[15] 95	1975	[20] 60	[20] 18.2	(NA)	1961	84.4
Costa Rica	1976	11	366	5	116	1973	[20] 78	[20] 31.3	[20] 5.7	1973	11.6
Cuba	1975	77	1,796	42	554	1974	735	(NA)	(NA)	1953	22.1
Cyprus	1975	[21] 2	[21] 57	[21] 2	[21] 49	1975	[22] 31	[22] 14.3	[22] 4.3	1960	24.1
Czechoslovakia	1975	96	1,881	25	321	1975	3,200	7.0	[17] 4.7	(X)	(NA)
Denmark	1975	[12] 58	568	([12])	291	1975	2,931	15.2	8.3	(X)	(NA)
Dominican Rep	1972	15	833	[23] 6	[13] 151	1973	61	16.4	2.6	1970	32.8
Ecuador	1975	[24] 32	[24] 1,266	23	380	1971	[20] 52	[20] 19.8	[20] 3.2	1962	32.5
Egypt	1975	118	4,121	79	2,108	1975	670	(NA)	5.8	1960	[25] 74.2
El Salvador	1976	[24][26] 15	796	[14] 2	59	1973	46	28.4	3.6	1971	42.9
Ethiopia	1973	19	[11] 959	7	191	1974	[9] 68	(NA)	[9] 2.5	1965	94.0
Finland	1974	23	406	[4] 36	[4] 507	1975	1,766	16.7	6.7	(X)	(NA)
France [27]	1975	257	4,602	[13] 264	[4] 5,026	1974	12,881	[20] 17.3	4.7	1946	3.6
German Dem. Rep.	1975	159	2,579	(NA)	461	1974	[6] 4,254	[6] 7.6	[6][17] 5.6	(X)	(NA)
Germany, Fed. Rep. of	1975	[13] 269	6,425	[13] 314	3,815	1974	17,386	14.4	4.5	(X)	(NA)
Ghana	1975	[26] 38	[26] 1,157	22	549	1974	[20] 198	[20] 19.7	(NA)	1970	[28] 56.8
Greece	1973	30	925	[15] 17	665	1974	[26] 343	[26] 8.0	[26] 1.7	1971	15.6
Guatemala	1973	16	571	6	104	1973	[20] 44	[20] 16.7	[20] 1.7	1973	53.9
Guyana	1973	4	132	3	68	1974	25	13.5	6.3	1960	12.9
Haiti	1971	7	337	[16][29] 1	[16][29] 27	1974	[9] 5	[9] 11.2	[9][30] .7	1971	76.7
Honduras	1975	13	[18] 483	3	52	1974	32	21.7	3.3	1961	55.0
Hong Kong	1975	21	659	15	369	1975	252	20.7	[30] 3.3	1971	[31] 22.7
Hungary	1975	67	1,051	23	372	1975	2,280	6.1	[17] 4.8	1970	2.0
Iceland	1974	1	27	2	25	1975	51	13.3	4.2	(X)	(NA)
India	1975	1,559	64,708	[16] 1,180	[15] 24,793	1975	[32] 2,160	[32] 26.1	(NA)	1971	66.6
Indonesia	1975	603	18,233	219	3,361	1975	878	12.5	3.1	1971	43.4
Iran	1975	152	4,468	82	2,183	1974	1,344	12.2	(NA)	1971	[28] 63.1
Iraq	1975	69	1,765	[4] 20	[4] 523	1975	[20] 365	[20] 7.3	(NA)	1965	75.8
Ireland	1975	13	405	19	271	1975	[20] 512	[20] 10.8	[20] 6.5	(X)	(NA)
Israel	1975	[13] 37	535	[13] 16	[4] 170	1974	901	8.3	7.3	1961	[3] 15.8
Italy	1975	253	4,835	(NA)	4,480	1975	8,684	11.7	5.0	1971	6.1
Jamaica	1975	12	370	6	214	1974	162	20.2	7.1	1960	18.1
Japan	1975	417	10,365	512	9,125	1975	27,488	22.6	5.5	1960	[31] 2.2
Jordan	1975	[33] 11	[33] 386	[33] 8	[33] 164	1975	[33] 55	(NA)	[33] 4.4	1961	67.6

See footnotes at end of table.

No. 1554. EDUCATION AND ILLITERACY, BY COUNTRY—Continued

[See headnote, p. 905]

COUNTRY	Year	1ST LEVEL [1] Teachers (1,000)	1ST LEVEL Students enrolled (1,000)	2D LEVEL [2] Teachers (1,000)	2D LEVEL Students enrolled (1,000)	PUBLIC EXPENDITURE FOR EDUCATION Year	Total (mil. dol.)	Percent of— Total public expenditure	Percent of— Gross national product	ILLITERATE POPULATION Year	Percent of population, 15 years old and over
Korea, Rep. of	1976	110	5,504	88	3,397	1973	34 507	34 22.8	34 4.1	1970	12.4
Lebanon	1972	(NA)	498	(NA)	175	1973	85	20.5	3.0	(X)	(NA)
Liberia	1975	4	158	35 (Z)	34	1975	15	13.4	2.2	1962	91.1
Libya	1975	24	556	12	166	1975	635	(NA)	(NA)	1964	78.3
Luxembourg	1973	2	36	1	15	1973	94	13.9	5.2	(X)	(NA)
Malawi	1975	11	642	1	17	1974	15	13.4	2.4	1966	77.9
Malaysia	1976	36 50	36 1,608	16 36 30	36 37 851	1974	36 427	(NA)	(NA)	1962	47.2
Mali	1975	9	253	11 15 1	4 51	1975	27	26.9	4.7	1962	97.5
Mauritius	1975	6	151	2	67	1974	20 17	20 9.9	20 3.1	1962	38 39.2
Mexico	1975	256	11,461	170	2,939	1974	2,129	13.1	(NA)	1970	25.8
Morocco	1975	26 37	1,548	39 20	476	1973	282	10.4	(NA)	1971	78.6
Netherlands	1975	53	1,453	16 48	1,284	1973	5,223	20 25.1	7.9	(X)	(NA)
New Zealand	1975	40 21	393	40 12	352	1974	9 742	9 17.0	9 5.6	(X)	(NA)
Nicaragua	1972	8	11 329	2	13 63	1974	20 36	20 15.6	(NA)	1971	42.5
Niger	1975	4	142	1	14	1974	9 14	9 19.5	(NA)	1962	98.6
Nigeria	1973	(NA)	4,890	(NA)	568	1974	956	(NA)	(NA)	1962	84.6
Norway	1974	12 45	387	12 10	331	1975	2,006	14.7	7.1	(X)	(NA)
Pakistan	1975	131	5,294	109	2,032	1975	251	5.2	2.3	1961	84.6
Panama	1976	13	343	6	128	1974	20 100	20 21.7	20 5.9	1970	21.7
Paraguay	1974	23 41 16	455	7	72	1974	19	17.2	1.4	1972	19.9
Peru	1976	74	2,961	35	890	1974	464	21.7	4.2	1972	27.6
Philippines	1975	262	8,365	73	2,255	1975	20 246	20 9.4	20 1.6	1970	17.4
Poland	1975	208	4,310	16 34	1,441	1975	6 15,185	6 8.5	6 17 3.4	1970	2.2
Portugal	1974	35	933	49	668	1974	347	(NA)	2.4	1970	29.0
Romania	1975	145	24 3,020	11 43	11 802	1975	3,054	(NA)	(NA)	1956	11.4
Senegal	1975	26 6	312	13 26 42(Z)	43 64	1974	5 65	5 26.0	5 3.3	1961	44 94.4
Singapore	1975	11	328	8	183	1975	165	8.6	2.9	1970	31.1
South Africa	1972	45 120	45 4,653	(45)	(45)	1968	6 103	6 5.1	(NA)	1960	43.0
Spain	1974	(NA)	18 3,624	46 30	2,918	1974	20 1,440	20 11.0	20 1.7	1970	9.8
Sri Lanka	1976	(NA)	26 1,385	42 1	1,088	1974	9 27 87	9 27 10.0	9 27 2.7	1971	22.4
Sudan	1975	32	1,169	13	282	1974	34 196	34 14.8	34 8.0	1966	85.3
Sweden	1975	34	699	11 55	11 532	1974	4,162	13.9	7.5	(X)	(NA)
Switzerland	1975	(NA)	557	(NA)	372	1975	2,867	19.4	5.1	(X)	(NA)
Syria	1975	38	1,274	35 1	15 455	1975	213	7.5	(NA)	1970	60.0
Thailand	1975	(NA)	6,686	15 31	15 1,003	1975	520	20.7	(NA)	1970	21.4
Turkey	1974	159	5,355	13 57	13 1,517	1972	891	20.6	5.6	1970	48.7
U.S.S.R.	1975	12 2,399	35,961	12 218	10,738	1975	37,181	12.9	17 7.6	1970	47 .3
United Kingdom 48	1973	242	5,386	312	4,230	1972	8,513	(NA)	(NA)	(X)	(NA)
Uruguay	1974	14	331	13 4	194	1970	20 88	20 26.1	20 3.6	1963	9.6
Venezuela	1974	63	1,990	36	631	1973	883	21.8	5.3	1971	23.5
Vietnam	1975	205	7,404	16 108	16 2,916	(X)	(NA)	(NA)	(NA)	(X)	(NA)
Yugoslavia	1974	128	2,867	23	828	1975	1,664	(NA)	5.0	1971	16.5
Zambia	1975	18	872	16 3	16 73	1975	9 152	9 11.9	(NA)	1969	52.7

NA Not available.   X Not applicable.   Z Less than 500.
[1] Schools providing basic instruction in the tools of learning; length of this education may vary from 4 to 9 years among countries. Excludes nursery school and kindergarten.   [2] Middle, secondary, or high schools providing general or specialized instruction more advanced than primary level.   [3] Population age 14 and over.   [4] Covers general and vocational education only.   [5] Ministry of Education expenditure for first and second level.   [6] Current expenditure only.   [7] Population all ages.   [8] For 1975.   [9] Ministry of Education expenditure only.   [10] Population age 18 and over.   [11] For 1974.   [12] Data on general education at 2d level are included with 1st level.   [13] For 1973.   [14] For 1972.   [15] Covers general and teacher-training education only.   [16] Covers general education only.   [17] Percent of net material product.   [18] For 1976.   [19] For 1958.   [20] Central or Federal Government expenditure only.   [21] Excludes data for Turkish schools.   [22] Expenditure by Office of Greek Education only.   [23] For 1971.   [24] Includes evening schools.   [25] Excludes nomad population.   [26] Covers public education only.   [27] Expenditure data exclude universities and, for France, include overseas departments.   [28] Population age 6 and over.   [29] Urban education only.   [30] Percent of gross domestic product.   [31] Persons with no schooling are defined as illiterates.   [32] Expenditure of departments of education for States and territories of the union only.   [33] Data refer to East Bank only.   [34] Includes private expenditure.   [35] Covers teacher-training education only.   [36] West Malaysia only.   [37] Covers general, teacher-training, and public vocational education only.   [38] Population age 3 and over.   [39] Covers teacher-training and public general education only.   [40] Some data for 2d level are included with 1st level.   [41] Includes preprimary education.   [42] Covers vocational education only.   [43] Covers general and public vocational education only.   [44] Illiteracy defined as inability to read and write French.   [45] Data on 2d level are included with first level.   [46] Covers teacher-training and vocational education only.   [47] Population ages 9 through 49.   [48] Education and expenditure data cover England and Wales only.

Source: Statistical Office of the United Nations, New York, N.Y., *Statistical Yearbook* (copyright); and United Nations Educational, Scientific, and Cultural Organization, Paris, France, *UNESCO Yearbook* (copyright).

No. 1555. HOUSING AND HEALTH, BY COUNTRY

[Housing: Data generally intended to refer to conventional (permanent) dwellings only. For some countries, however, data include nonpermanent structures, improvised shelters, and mobile trailers, or, as noted, refer to housing units and to household accommodation (the space occupied by a private household) rather than to dwellings. Health: Hospital data refer to hospitals and other medical establishments with beds but exclude old people's homes and establishments for custodial or preventive care only; personnel data refer to persons fully qualified from medical or dental schools and working within the country. See text, p. 896, for general comments concerning the data. For additional qualifications of data for individual countries, see source]

	DWELLINGS				HEALTH						
COUNTRY			Percent with [1]—			Hospitals			Physicians, number	Persons per physician (1,000)	Dentists, number
	Year	Occupied (1,000)	Piped water [2]	Electric lighting	Year	Number	Beds (1,000)	Population per bed			
United States [3]	1970	63,450	97.5	(NA)	1975	7,336	1,401.6	152	[4] 378,572	[4] .6	[5] 107,320
Algeria [6]	1966	1,792	[7] 22.7	33.7	1969	149	39.1	356	1,698	8.2	222
Australia [3]	1971	3,671	(NA)	98.4	1972	2,297	160.6	81	17,972	.7	(NA)
Austria	1972	2,460	[7] 87.8	(NA)	1975	(NA)	85.5	88	[8] 15,702	.5	[8][9] 1,464
Belgium	1970	3,228	86.6	(NA)	1974 [10]	479	87.2	112	[8] 18,506	.5	[8][9] 2,273
Brazil [3]	1972	18,029	[7] 33.0	53.3	1973 [11]	4,431	383.0	266	48,726	2.0	27,553
Canada	1971	5,970	[12] 98.5	(NA)	1974 [10]	1,368	206.8	109	39,104	.6	8,922
Chile	1970	(NA)	[7][13] 59.6	(NA)	1975	304	38.3	362	[14] 4,414	(NA)	1,345
China, Rep. of [3][15]	1975	2,671	(NA)	(NA)	1976	8,736	32	503	[16] 11,361	1.4	[17] 1,532
Costa Rica	1973	[18] 315	81.0	68.8	1975	43	7.5	261	1,293	1.5	360
Czechoslovakia	1970	4,239	[7] 75.4	99.7	1975	422	150.0	99	[8] 35,383	.4	[8][9] 6,440
Denmark	1970	1,801	98.7	(NA)	1970 [11]	296	47.7	103	8,000	.6	3,800
Finland	1970	1,419	72.1	95.6	1975	379	71.1	66	[16] 6,701	.7	[18] 3,254
France	1975	[3] 17,786	[3][19] 96.6	[20] 98.8	1973 [10]	(NA)	534.0	98	77,882	.7	25,272
German Dem. Rep.	1971	[21] 5,933	[7] 82.1	100.0	1974 [10]	584	184.2	92	31,300	.5	7,720
Germany, F. R.	1972	20,966	99.2	99.7	1975 [22]	3,481	729.8	85	120,260	.5	31,613
Greece	1971	2,483	[7][23] 65.0	[23] 88.3	1975	722	58.5	155	18,421	.5	5,930
Guatemala [24]	1973	935	25.4	28.5	1973 [25]	159	12.1	457	1,208	4.3	244
Hungary	1973	3,209	[7] 44.0	94.3	1974 [10]	(NA)	90.1	116	21,127	.5	2,461
India [26]	1971	92,494	(NA)	(NA)	1969 [10]	14,286	331.6	1,590	146,000	4.1	9,100
Indonesia [27]	1971	[24] 22,471	[7][24] 2.2	63.5	1975 [22]	1,115	83.7	1,625	7,027	18.9	1,900
Iran	1966	(NA)	[7][21] 13.1	[21] 25.4	1974 [5]	535	49.2	650	11,373	2.8	1,846
Israel	1974	817	[7] 86.1	(NA)	1975	86	19.5	174	[16] 9,143	.4	[16] 1,789
Italy	1971	15,301	[7] 86.1	99.0	1972 [5]	2,189	575.2	95	[8][16] 109,166	.5	(NA)
Jamaica	1970	420	[7] 21.6	(NA)	1974	34	7.8	257	570	3.5	107
Japan	1968	24,198	94.9	(NA)	1975 [22]	[28] 8,294	[29] 1,163.7	(NA)	[16] 15,722	2.2	[16] 2,422
Korea, Rep. of	1970	4,334	35.2	49.9	1974	175	22.1	1,515			
Mexico [3]	1970	8,286	[7] 38.7	58.9	1974	1,575	67.4	863	[29] 31,571	(NA)	[29] 1,879
Morocco	1971	[30] 880	[30] 64.8	[30] 81.5	1975	133	23.1	748	1,238	14.0	128
Netherlands	1971	3,660	[3] 96.9	(NA)	1973 [10]	600	136.2	99	21,825	.6	4,350
New Zealand	1976	939	(NA)	(NA)	1973 [10]	(NA)	32.0	93	4,110	.7	1,046
Nicaragua [3]	1971	305	[7] 27.9	40.9	1975	65	4.7	462	1,400	1.5	350
Norway [3]	1970	1,297	[7] 94.4	(NA)	1975	866	56.6	71	6,886	.6	(NA)
Panama	1970	277	[7] 26.1	52.4	1975	61	5.9	284	1,251	1.3	222
Philippines	1967	(NA)	[13] 34.4	[13] 22.9	1973 [10]	813	62.9	639	13,480	3.2	4,241
Poland	1970	8,081	[7] 47.3	96.2	1975	1,265	264.1	129	58,226	.5	15,949
Romania	1966	5,250	[7] 12.3	48.6	1974 [5]	(NA)	191.9	110	25,870	.8	5,289
Spain	1970	9,542	[7] 77.6	(NA)	1974	1,261	185.2	190	[8][16] 55,000	.4	[8][16] 3,446
Sri Lanka [3]	1971	2,217	[7] 4.4	9.0	1973 [11]	456	39.7	333	3,251	4.0	280
Sweden	1975	3,320	[7] 98.7	(NA)	1974	725	124.4	66	13,260	.6	7,180
Switzerland	1970	2,012	(NA)	(NA)	1971 [10]	440	72.3	86	11,466	.6	2,582
Turkey	1970	(NA)	35.9	41.1	1975	807	85.9	456	21,714	1.8	5,046
U.S.S.R.	1965	[30] 31,000	(NA)	(NA)	1975	(NA)	3,009.2	85	733,700	.3	101,500
United Kingdom [31]	1971	16,455	(NA)	(NA)	1974	(NA)	[32] 420.9	117	64,600	.8	[14] 14,200
Venezuela	1971	[21] 1,844	[33] 72.4	(NA)	1974	380	35.9	334	13,108	.9	3,497
Yugoslavia	1971	4,935	[7] 34.0	87.9	1975 [22]	490	127.6	167	24,920	.8	[9] 4,793

NA Not available. [1] Computed on basis of occupied dwellings where available; otherwise on total dwellings. [2] Either inside or outside. [3] Housing data refer to housing units. [4] 1976 data. Excludes osteopaths. [5] Personnel data are for 1973. [6] Housing data exclude semi-permanent dwellings. [7] Inside only. [8] Stomatologists and odontologists included with physicians. [9] Includes non-university level dentists. [10] Personnel data are for 1975. [11] Personnel data are for 1972. [12] 1975 data. [13] Data refer to households. [14] Personnel in government service. [15] Source: U.S. Bureau of the Census. Data from Republic of China publications. [16] Registered personnel. [17] Includes assistants. [18] Excludes semi-permanent dwellings. [19] 1973 data. [20] 1968 data. [21] Data refer to living quarters. [22] Personnel data are for 1974. [23] Households in dwellings. [24] Housing data refer to households in housing units. [25] Personnel data are for 1971. [26] Housing data include Indian-held part of Jammu and Kashmir. [27] Housing data exclude rural populations of Western Irian. [28] Incomplete data. [29] Personnel in hospitals only. [30] Urban areas only. [31] England and Wales. [32] Government establishments only. [33] Housing units, excluding units not intended for habitation but in use for that purpose.

Source: Except as noted, Statistical Office of the United Nations, New York, N.Y., Statistical Yearbook. (Copyright.)

No. 1556. Suicide Rates for Selected Countries, by Sex and Age Group: 1975

[Rate per 100,000 population. Includes deaths resulting indirectly from self-inflicted injuries]

COUNTRY	MALES					FEMALES				
	Total	15–24 yr.	25–44 yr.	45–64 yr.	65 and over	Total	15–24 yr.	25–44 yr.	45–64 yr.	65 and over
U.S.	25.5	18.9	24.0	28.9	36.8	8.9	4.8	9.9	11.9	8.0
Austria	47.4	23.6	38.6	58.1	81.3	17.6	7.3	12.3	19.9	29.5
Belgium [1]	28.1	10.9	20.0	30.4	66.5	13.0	3.7	9.2	17.9	20.3
Denmark	38.8	13.8	34.5	52.3	56.4	23.6	4.7	18.6	38.4	28.0
France [1]	29.9	11.5	21.5	39.0	62.6	11.3	4.8	7.6	14.3	19.2
Germany, Fed. Rep.[1]	36.2	20.4	31.4	44.3	56.0	18.5	7.4	12.8	24.8	26.7
Ireland [1]	8.7	5.3	10.5	10.6	7.2	2.4	1.2	3.4	3.0	1.6
Japan	28.5	19.7	25.6	29.2	57.4	18.9	12.2	13.8	17.5	51.8
Netherlands	14.5	7.8	10.6	18.6	30.2	9.3	2.8	8.3	14.2	12.1
Norway [1]	21.6	14.1	19.3	29.9	19.9	5.9	4.4	4.3	8.9	5.2
Portugal	18.9	5.2	12.9	27.9	41.5	5.5	3.4	3.4	6.8	10.6
Sweden	35.2	22.0	30.9	43.1	43.3	13.9	9.5	12.9	18.0	12.7
Switzerland	42.3	31.4	35.5	54.9	52.5	16.4	9.9	14.2	18.7	23.7
United Kingdom [1][2]	12.6	5.8	11.0	15.7	19.1	8.2	2.9	6.1	11.2	11.5

[1] 1974 data.   [2] England and Wales only. Excludes Northern Ireland and Scotland.

Source: World Health Organization, Geneva, Switzerland, *World Health Statistics*, annual.

No. 1557. Gross Domestic Product of Selected Countries as Percent of United States: 1950 to 1976

[Comparisons are based on constant (1970) dollar data converted to U.S. dollars using 1970 exchange rates. See text, p. 437]

COUNTRY	GROSS DOMESTIC PRODUCT						PER CAPITA GROSS DOMESTIC PRODUCT					
	1950	1960	1965	1970	1975	1976	1950	1960	1965	1970	1975	1976
United States	100	100	100	100	100	100	100	100	100	100	100	100
Canada	6	7	8	8	10	10	72	75	77	81	90	89
France	11	12	13	14	16	16	38	49	52	58	63	63
Germany, Fed. Rep. of	11	17	18	19	19	19	34	57	59	64	64	65
Italy	[1]6	8	8	9	9	9	[1]21	29	31	36	36	36
Japan	[2]7	11	14	20	23	23	[2]13	20	27	40	45	45
United Kingdom	14	14	13	12	12	12	43	47	46	46	46	45

[1] Based on 1951 data.   [2] Based on 1952 data.

Source: U.S. Bureau of Economic Analysis. Adapted from *Long Term Economic Growth, 1860–1970*, using data from the Organization for Economic Cooperation and Development.

No. 1558. Tax Revenues—Selected Countries: 1970 to 1975

[Covers national and local taxes and social security contributions. GDP = Gross domestic product; see text, p. 437]

COUNTRY	TAX REVENUE (bil. dol.)			AS PERCENT OF GDP			TAX REVENUE PER CAPITA (dol.)		
	1970	1974	1975	1970	1974	1975	1970	1974	1975
United States	287.7	407.9	436.6	30.1	30.2	30.3	1,404	1,925	2,044
Australia	9.5	25.3	27.7	26.0	29.3	30.1	763	1,893	2,051
Austria	5.2	12.6	14.8	36.1	38.5	39.3	698	1,676	1,959
Belgium	9.1	20.6	25.8	35.3	38.6	41.4	965	2,107	2,631
Canada	27.1	53.8	56.6	32.1	35.0	34.0	1,269	2,394	2,481
Denmark	6.4	14.1	15.3	41.0	46.8	43.1	1,296	2,800	3,016
Finland	3.4	7.9	10.0	33.1	35.3	37.6	744	1,685	2,122
France	50.1	95.0	123.9	35.4	35.8	36.9	988	1,809	2,348
Germany, F.R.	61.1	138.1	149.7	32.4	35.8	35.2	1,006	2,225	2,420
Greece	2.4	4.4	5.0	24.0	23.3	24.0	272	493	554
Italy	28.0	48.2	55.7	30.3	31.6	32.3	521	871	997
Japan	39.8	104.2	102.0	19.5	22.2	20.2	384	949	919
Netherlands	12.6	31.4	38.1	39.8	45.2	46.9	968	2,321	2,789
New Zealand	1.7	4.4	4.3	27.8	33.1	32.2	615	1,447	1,374
Norway	4.4	10.4	12.7	39.0	44.6	44.7	1,124	2,605	3,157
Portugal	1.4	3.0	3.7	23.3	22.6	25.0	165	338	386
Spain	6.4	16.1	20.5	17.2	18.8	20.3	188	462	583
Sweden	13.3	24.8	31.9	40.5	44.1	46.0	1,657	3,036	3,890
Switzerland	5.0	12.9	16.0	23.8	27.3	29.5	799	2,008	2,494
United Kingdom	46.0	68.8	83.8	37.9	36.0	36.8	828	1,227	1,495

Source: Organisation for Economic Co-operation and Development, Paris, France, *Revenue Statistics of OECD Member Countries*, annual.

No. 1559. Average Annual Rates of Change of Gross Domestic Product, by Kind of Economic Activity

[In percent. Based on gross domestic product at constant prices. Methods used to obtain estimates of gross domestic product at constant prices and the years to which these prices relate vary widely among countries. In general, "Agriculture" includes forestry, hunting, and fishing; "Industrial activity" covers mining, manufacturing, electricity, gas, and water; and "Other" comprises financing, insurance, real estate, and business services; community, social, and personal services; and public administration and defense. Unless otherwise stated, data are calculated on the former System of National Accounts (see *Yearbook of National Accounts Statistics*, 1969). Minus sign (−) denotes decrease]

COUNTRY	Period	GROSS DOMESTIC PRODUCT		Agriculture	INDUSTRIAL ACTIVITY		Construction	Transport and communication	Wholesale and retail trade	Other
		Total	Per capita		Total	Manufacturing				
United States [1]	1970-76	2.6	1.8	.9	1.9	2.0	−1.0	4.3	3.0	3.1
Argentina	1970-76	3.2	1.7	2.3	3.7	3.7	−1.6	2.2	3.0	4.2
Australia [1]	1970-72	[2] 4.8	[2] 3.1	[2] .2	4.9	4.0	1.8	4.5	2.6	5.3
Austria	1970-76	4.0	3.8	2.5	3.8	(NA)	4.7	5.1	[2] 5.5	[2] 4.4
Bangladesh	1972-76	7.6	4.6	4.5	22.1	22.6	6.3	11.3	20.3	2.2
Belgium	1970-75	4.0	3.7	−.2	4.5	4.3	3.0	2.6	4.4	4.5
Bolivia	1970-74	5.7	3.0	3.0	4.3	5.5	3.0	6.2	4.9	9.2
Brazil	1970-73	11.0	7.9	6.2	(NA)	13.8	12.3	9.9	12.3	(NA)
Burma	1970-76	2.2	(Z)	1.5	1.1	.9	−1.3	−.3	2.1	5.6
Canada [1]	1970-76	4.9	3.4	.2	4.1	4.0	4.0	5.6	6.0	4.9
Chile	1970-76	−.5	−2.3	.8	−1.4	−4.7	−7.7	−.9	−1.6	2.1
Colombia	1970-75	6.5	3.6	5.4	6.3	7.3	4.6	8.5	6.1	7.5
Denmark [1]	1970-76	2.1	1.7	.4	2.3	2.3	−1.6	3.2	2.5	3.1
Dominican Republic	1970-76	9.1	5.9	3.5	14.1	9.4	12.5	8.2	9.2	8.8
Egypt	1970-71	3.9	1.6	4.0	2.8	(NA)	1.8	2.4	6.6	5.4
Ethiopia	1970-75	2.8	.2	.9	3.2	3.1	1.7	5.6	4.0	6.6
Finland	1970-76	4.0	3.5	−1.9	4.3	4.2	2.5	3.8	5.5	5.5
France	1970-71	5.1	4.1	1.1	5.5	(NA)	2.8	4.1	6.2	5.4
Germany, Fed. Rep. of [1]	1970-76	2.3	2.0	1.3	2.0	1.8	−.9	2.2	−.6	4.7
Greece	1970-76	4.8	4.1	3.1	7.7	7.5	−1.6	7.4	6.6	5.5
Guatemala	1970-76	5.9	2.9	5.9	5.6	5.3	16.1	9.4	5.2	4.8
India [1]	1970-74	1.4	−.7	−.7	3.2	3.1	−.6	2.2	2.3	4.5
Indonesia	1970-75	8.2	5.4	4.2	13.8	14.8	20.9	11.8	[3] 2.6	8.5
Iran	1970-76	10.2	7.4	5.0	7.3	16.7	15.3	18.4	14.4	17.4
Ireland	1970-73	4.4	3.2	4.1	[4] 6.7	(NA)	[4]	[5]	[5] 4.3	5.4
Italy [1]	1970-75	2.9	2.1	.9	3.4	(NA)	−.5	4.3	3.1	3.4
Kenya [1]	1970-76	4.4	.8	3.5	8.2	8.5	2.6	3.0	1.0	−8.0
Korea, Republic of	1970-76	10.9	8.9	4.9	19.3	20.0	7.4	13.8	10.7	4.4
Libya	1962-70	23.8	19.0	2.3	33.0	10.4	19.4	19.0	13.3	14.1
Mexico [1]	1970-76	5.5	1.9	1.1	6.3	5.8	8.1	9.7	5.0	6.2
Morocco	1970-75	4.6	1.5	−.1	6.7	5.7	11.1	[6] 5.0	5.8	[6]
Netherlands [1]	1970-76	3.6	2.7	4.0	(NA)	3.7	−1.4	4.0	4.4	[7] 2.6
Nicaragua [1]	1970-76	5.8	2.4	5.6	6.2	6.3	14.6	5.6	5.6	4.1
Nigeria	1970-75	5.1	2.3	−1.8	14.1	17.6	18.8	17.4	7.5	13.5
Norway [1]	1970-76	4.7	4.0	3.9	5.5	2.9	3.9	3.2	4.9	4.3
Pakistan	1970-76	3.6	.7	2.1	2.7	2.3	9.7	4.9	4.6	6.4
Panama	1970-76	4.1	.9	2.1	3.1	1.6	1.8	8.9	3.3	5.4
Peru [1]	1970-76	5.1	2.0	−.4	5.9	7.0	13.4	8.6	6.8	4.6
Philippines	1970-76	6.3	3.3	4.6	6.8	7.0	19.5	9.9	4.7	5.4
Portugal	1970-75	5.0	3.5	−.1	7.0	6.6	4.5	7.4	2.0	8.8
Saudi Arabia [1]	1970-76	13.1	9.8	3.7	13.1	4.1	21.7	17.8	15.7	8.8
Spain [1]	1970-75	6.1	5.0	3.0	8.2	(NA)	4.4	[5]	[5] 7 6.2	[7] 8 5.1
Sri Lanka	1970-76	4.7	3.0	1.7	9.1	8.3	−1.3	3.9	4.5	2.8
Sweden [1]	1970-76	2.5	2.1	(Z)	2.4	2.2	.1	3.4	2.5	−4.7
Syria	1970-76	10.4	6.9	8.1	11.4	9.5	15.2	6.0	11.7	11.5
Tanzania [1] [9]	[1] 1970-76	4.2	1.4	2.5	3.6	4.4	.7	5.5	1.7	9.0
Thailand	1970-76	6.7	3.8	4.4	10.6	10.3	1.2	7.3	5.9	7.8
Tunisia	1970-76	9.4	6.8	9.7	9.5	12.7	12.4	9.4	[10] 23.2	−7.4
Turkey [1]	1970-75	7.1	4.6	2.5	9.7	9.9	5.5	9.4	11.4	[10] 6.2
Uganda [1]	1970-76	−.1	−3.3	1.3	−5.4	−4.5	−6.4	1.5	−7.6	2.6
United Kingdom [1]	1970-76	2.0	1.8	.6	(NA)	.8	−2.2	2.8	1.9	[7] 1.2
Uruguay	1970-75	.2	−.9	−1.5	1.3	1.1	(Z)	1.2	−.1	.1
Venezuela [1]	1970-76	5.3	2.2	3.2	.6	6.1	14.2	8.4	6.9	7.2
Zaire [1]	1970-76	2.8	(Z)	1.7	2.2	3.1	5.6	.2	4.2	6.3

NA Not available.   Z Less than .05 percent.   [1] Relates to present system of national accounts.
[2] 1970-73.   [3] 1960-68.   [4] Construction included in industrial activity.   [5] Transport and communications included in wholesale and retail trade.   [6] All services included in transport and communications.
[7] Public administration and defense.   [8] All services included in wholesale and retail trade.
[9] Former Tanganyika only.   [10] 1970-72.

Source: Statistical Office of the United Nations, New York, N.Y., *Statistical Yearbook*. (Copyright.)

No. 1560. ORGANIZATION FOR ECONOMIC COOPERATION AND DEVELOPMENT (OECD)—
GROSS NATIONAL PRODUCT, 1975 TO 1977, AND CHANGE, 1972–1977 AND 1976–1977

COUNTRY	GROSS NATIONAL PRODUCT (GNP)					GNP PER CAPITA					Inflation rate,[2] 1976–1977 (per cent)
	Total in constant (1977) dollars (bil.) [1]			Annual per cent change [2]		In constant (1977) dollars [1]			Annual per cent change [2]		
	1975	1976	1977	1972–1977	1976–1977	1975	1976	1977	1972–1977	1976–1977	
United States____	1,699	1,801	1,890	2.7	4.9	7,958	8,374	8,715	1.9	4.1	5.3
OECD Europe [4]__	1,909	1,990	2,032	2.5	2.1	4,987	5,172	5,253	1.8	1.6	10.5
Belgium_____	75.4	77.2	79.1	2.6	2.5	7,697	7,859	7,982	2.2	1.6	7.0
Luxembourg___	2.5	2.5	2.6	1.5	2.0	6,861	7,056	7,194	1.0	2.0	[5] 7.0
Denmark_____	40.1	42.1	41.9	1.2	−.5	7,925	8,306	8,232	.6	−.9	9.5
France_____	351.6	369.9	381.0	3.0	3.0	6,661	6,990	7,176	2.5	2.7	9.3
Germany, F.R.	474.9	502.0	514.0	2.3	2.4	7,680	8,161	8,371	2.3	2.6	3.3
Ireland_____	8.6	8.8	9.3	2.5	5.3	2,738	2,798	2,919	1.2	4.3	13.0
Italy_____	176.9	186.8	190.6	2.8	2.0	3,169	3,326	3,376	2.0	1.5	18.5
Netherlands___	98.6	103.2	105.8	2.8	2.5	7,226	7,493	7,636	2.0	1.9	7.0
U. Kingdom___	240.6	245.7	246.4	1.4	.3	4.300	4,392	4,410	1.4	.4	14.3
Austria_____	44.4	46.7	48.4	3.3	3.5	5,907	6,222	6,432	3.2	3.4	6.0
Finland_____	29.7	29.8	29.6	2.1	−.8	6,302	6,300	6,236	1.6	−1.0	12.0
Greece_____	24.0	25.5	26.6	4.0	4.3	2,655	2,778	2,860	3.1	3.0	13.0
Iceland_____	1.7	1.7	1.8	2.9	3.9	7,727	7,864	8,182	1.9	4.0	[5] 34.4
Norway_____	32.3	34.2	35.7	4.6	4.3	8,042	8,484	8,805	3.9	3.8	8.0
Portugal_____	14.9	15.7	16.7	4.1	6.0	1,573	1,622	1,709	1.6	5.4	[5] 27.3
Spain_____	111.5	113.7	116.3	3.7	2.3	3,131	3,161	3,199	2.6	1.2	24.0
Sweden_____	78.7	79.9	77.9	1.4	−2.5	9,608	9,717	9,433	1.1	−2.9	11.0
Switzerland___	62.2	61.4	63.1	−.2	2.8	9,704	9,669	10,035	.1	3.8	1.3
Turkey_____	40.3	43.2	45.5	6.9	5.2	1,030	1,077	1,105	4.2	2.6	[5] 36.0
Australia_____	89.4	93.3	93.8	2.7	.5	6,495	6,702	6,664	1.0	−.6	10.3
Canada_____	181.7	190.6	195.0	3.7	2.3	7,960	8,238	8,312	2.2	.9	6.8
Japan_____	608.0	646.3	685.1	4.6	6.0	5,450	5,732	6,017	3.4	5.0	5.5
New Zealand___	12.8	12.6	12.5	1.9	−.5	4,160	4,065	4,006	.5	−1.4	14.8

[1] National currency values converted into dollars by the average 1977 Par Rate/Market Rate, as published by the International Monetary Fund, Washington, D.C. [2] Minus sign (−) denotes decrease. [3] GNP or GDP (Gross Domestic Product) implicit price deflators; totals weighted by 1976 (base year) GNP data, in 1976 prices. [4] See text, p. 895. [5] Estimate.

Source: U.S. Department of State, Bureau of Intelligence and Research, *Economic Growth of OECD Countries, 1967–1977*, Report No. 928, 1978.

No. 1561. ORGANISATION FOR ECONOMIC CO-OPERATION AND DEVELOPMENT (OECD)—
SELECTED DATA: 1974 TO 1977

[Base for indexes, 1970=100. Imports c.i.f., except as noted; exports f.o.b. See text, pp. 895–896]

COUNTRY	INDUSTRIAL PRODUCTION INDEX				AVERAGE MONTHLY IMPORTS (mil. dol.)				AVERAGE MONTHLY EXPORTS (mil. dol.)			
	1974	1975	1976	1977	1974	1975	1976	1977	1974	1975	1976	1977
United States____	120	109	120	127	[1] 8,414	[1] 8,078	[1] 10,149	[1] 12,321	8,209	8,971	9,583	10,014
OECD_____	120	110	120	125	48,590	48,948	56,359	(NA)	44,411	47,317	52,541	(NA)
Australia_____	119	110	116	114	[1] 929	[1] 832	[1] 932	[1] 1,020	923	992	1,093	1,105
Austria_____	126	118	126	130	752	783	960	1,184	597	627	709	816
Belgium_____	120	108	118	118	[3] 2,475	[3] 2,559	[3] 2,946	[3] 3,354	[2] 2,355	[2] 2,401	[2] 2,737	[2] 3,124
Canada_____	127	121	127	132	[1] 2,691	[1] 2,830	[1] 3,163	[1] 3,295	2,732	2,692	3,219	3,463
Denmark_____	(NA)	(NA)	(NA)	(NA)	821	861	1,035	1,105	643	726	759	839
Finland_____	128	123	125	122	568	635	616	635	458	459	528	640
France_____	123	114	124	124	4,402	4,520	5,366	5,874	3,825	4,351	4,651	5,293
Germ'y, F.R.[3]_	111	105	113	116	5,748	6,184	7,315	8,389	7,430	7,502	8,503	9,825
Greece_____	144	151	167	170	365	443	501	(NA)	169	191	212	(NA)
Iceland_____	(NA)	(NA)	(NA)	(NA)	43	41	39	51	28	26	33	43
Ireland_____	122	114	125	(NA)	318	317	350	449	210	268	276	366
Italy_____	119	108	121	121	3,414	3,197	3,614	(NA)	2,524	2,902	3,077	(NA)
Japan_____	123	110	122	127	5,176	4,822	5,400	5,901	4,628	4,646	5,602	6,712
Luxembourg___	119	93	99	99	[2]	[2]	[2]	[2]	[2]	[2]	[2]	[2]
Netherlands___	125	119	126	127	2,767	2,929	3,329	3,800	2,703	2,870	3,229	3,660
New Zealand__	(NA)	(NA)	(NA)	(NA)	305	264	(NA)	(NA)	202	182	(NA)	(NA)
Norway_____	120	128	137	138	703	806	926	(NA)	524	600	660	(NA)
Portugal_____	139	129	(NA)	(NA)	370	319	351	(NA)	188	162	151	(NA)
Spain_____	150	140	149	167	1,286	1,355	1,455	1,481	591	640	727	850
Sweden_____	[4] 117	[4] 115	[4] 114	[4] 111	1,312	1,504	1,597	1,676	1,319	1,451	1,537	1,590
Switzerland___	111	97	98	103	1,204	1,109	1,231	1,492	995	1,080	1,237	1,462
Turkey_____	(NA)	(NA)	(NA)	(NA)	311	387	419	477	128	117	162	145
U. Kingdom__	109	103	104	106	4,519	4,438	4,664	5,308	3,225	3,646	3,855	4,793
Yugoslavia____	140	147	152	(NA)	637	641	614	(NA)	339	339	405	(NA)

NA Not available. [1] Imports f.o.b. [2] Luxembourg included with Belgium. [3] Federal Republic of Germany. [4] Mining and manufacturing.

Source: Organisation for Economic Co-operation and Development, Paris, France, *Main Economic Indicators*, monthly, and *Statistics of Foreign Trade* (series A), April 1978.

No. 1562. INDEXES OF PRODUCTION, EMPLOYMENT, PRICES, AND RETAIL TRADE, BY COUNTRY: 1976

[1970=100, except as noted. See text, p. 896, for general comments concerning the data. For additional qualifications of the data for individual countries, see source]

COUNTRY	PRODUCTION Agriculture[1] All commodities	Food	Mining[2]	Manufacturing industries[2]	Employment in manufacturing[3]	PRICES[4] Consumer prices Total	Food	Wholesale prices[5]	Retail trade sales[4]
United States	133	141	104	123	98	147	157	166	179
Argentina	135	139	101	122	(NA)	6,539	6,632	7,770	5,184
Australia	136	153	(NA)	[6]112	[9]100	185	173	[7]196	[8]218
Austria	121	121	126	126	[9]100	153	144	143	184
Belgium	[10]123	[10]125	68	122	[11]91	163	160	147	188
Bolivia	175	173	(NA)	[12]297	(NA)	267	292	(NA)	(NA)
Brazil	160	184	[12]109	183	(NA)	[13]254	[13]267	372	(NA)
Burma	124	123	(NA)	(NA)	(NA)	285	300	(NA)	(NA)
Canada	135	138	115	127	104	153	168	179	204
Chile	123	125	126	82	[11]91	86,565	112,040	258,663	(NA)
China, Rep. of[14]	108	97	[15]110	[15]149	[16,17]121	(NA)	(NA)	(NA)	(NA)
Colombia	143	147	[12]90	[12]139	[18]121	281	329	354	567
Costa Rica	189	197	(NA)	[19]132	(NA)	196	192	242	(NA)
Cuba	120	122	(NA)	(NA)	[9,15,17,20]106	(NA)	(NA)	(NA)	(NA)
Cyprus	124	127	65	104	[12]83	148	164	(NA)	(NA)
Czechoslovakia	137	138	121	148	109	102	101	(NA)	135
Denmark	97	97	(NA)	114	90	170	181	175	190
Dominican Republic	146	148	(NA)	[17]143	[17]126	[15]173	[15]169	165	(NA)
Ecuador	145	144	(NA)	191	[17]114	208	245	(NA)	(NA)
Egypt	131	138	[12]196	[12]139	[11,17]112	147	174	[21]142	(NA)
El Salvador	(NA)	(NA)	(NA)	[12]128	[17,22]118	162	165	208	(NA)
Finland	136	135	100	123	[9,20]106	202	209	210	250
France	122	122	83	124	100	168	174	[23]160	156
German Dem. Rep.	131	132	108	146	[9]108	97	100	(NA)	134
Germany, Fed. Rep. of	118	118	87	112	87	141	137	141	160
Ghana	(NA)	(NA)	[24]108	[24]129	[11,24]96	352	414	[25]278	(NA)
Greece	165	171	143	166	126	202	215	220	229
Guatemala	175	177	(NA)	[19]122	[12,15]87	[26]111	[26]110	176	(NA)
Honduras	161	163	(NA)	[12]122	(NA)	142	154	(NA)	(NA)
Hungary	146	144	112	142	[27]101	120	121	[28]127	171
India	133	132	137	129	[29]113	161	156	177	(NA)
Indonesia	160	154	(NA)	(NA)	(NA)	292	338	[15]286	(NA)
Iran	177	182	[24,30]143	[24,30]137	(NA)	175	172	[25,30]167	(NA)
Iraq	138	139	(NA)	(NA)	(NA)	150	153	148	(NA)
Ireland	136	137	96	129	[11,29]96	220	227	231	235
Israel	203	199	99	146	[9]118	388	402	405	799
Italy	125	125	99	120	108	200	202	236	224
Japan	128	130	73	125	99	188	196	165	197
Korea, Republic of	169	163	143	385	234	235	274	267	278
Lebanon	(NA)	(NA)	(NA)	(NA)	(NA)	[12,25]130	[12,25]148	(NA)	(NA)
Libya	200	203	(NA)	(NA)	(NA)	130	96	(NA)	(NA)
Luxembourg	[10]	[10]	56	102	[17]113	156	161	(NA)	(NA)
Malaysia	[31]208	[31]217	73	198	(NA)	146	162	(NA)	(NA)
Mexico	137	152	113	139	(NA)	204	208	205	265
Morocco	154	154	120	143	(NA)	[32]117	[32]119	168	(NA)
Netherlands	159	159	213	115	86	165	152	[33]173	[34]177
New Zealand	130	141	[35]135	[35]137	[15]108	190	186	200	219
Nicaragua	(NA)	(NA)	(NA)	[17]154	(NA)	[32]111	[32]109	(NA)	(NA)
Norway	105	105	652	116	[13]111	163	167	163	197
Pakistan	159	166	[6]115	[6,12]120	(NA)	[15]212	[15]222	[21]243	(NA)
Panama	166	168	(NA)	126	[11,12]120	145	156	202	(NA)
Paraguay	154	144	(NA)	122	(NA)	180	200	(NA)	(NA)
Peru	125	137	(NA)	[12]145	[24]113	242	263	[7,12]138	(NA)
Philippines	184	187	134	141	[12]117	182	178	[25]270	(NA)
Poland	132	131	137	184	[9,36]115	118	118	(NA)	204
Portugal	98	99	[38]83	[38]140	[12]169	244	264	208	(NA)
Romania	180	181	[17]119	[17]167	[9,20,36]141	103	106	(NA)	[12]151
South Africa	139	145	99	124	119	174	184	204	223
Spain	150	153	107	153	116	208	210	191	(NA)
Sri Lanka	116	142	[39]103	[19]108	[11,12,15]94	145	148	(NA)	(NA)
Sweden	119	119	106	114	[12,40]101	162	169	[41]174	181
Switzerland	124	124	(NA)	97	[40]80	147	139	132	129
Syria	153	166	345	168	[11,12,13]106	195	198	191	(NA)

See footnotes at end of table.

No. 1562. Indexes of Production, Employment, Prices, and Retail Trade, by Country: 1976—Continued

[1970=100, except as noted. See text, p. 896, for general comments concerning the data. For additional qualifications of the data for individual countries, see source]

	PRODUCTION					PRICES [4]			
	Agriculture [1]		Min-ing [2]	Manu-factur-ing indus-tries [2]	Employ-ment in manu-factur-ing [3]	Consumer prices		Whole-sale prices [5]	Retail trade sales [4]
COUNTRY	All com-modi-ties	Food				Total	Food		
Thailand	169	172	(NA)	(NA)	(NA)	160	173	185	(NA)
Tunisia	172	172	99	142	(NA)	136	142	154	(NA)
Turkey	170	167	[12] 136	[12] 158	[11] [12] 136	252	277	272	(NA)
U.S.S.R	140	140	132	152	[12] [36] [42] 109	100	101	[41] 97	141
United Kingdom	118	118	89	103	[11] 88	215	247	[43] 299	218
Uruguay	115	128	(NA)	112	(NA)	2,086	2,128	2,281	(NA)
Venezuela	168	172	61	139	[44] 134	142	164	163	[25] 277
Yugoslavia	154	156	134	154	[9] [36] 131	271	278	[41] 242	393
Zambia	(NA)	(NA)	103	125	[11] [17] [25] 109	168	177	[12] 127	(NA)

NA Not available.   [1] Refers to calendar year in which all or most of the harvest took place, generally 1976. All commodities index relates to food, fibers, tobacco, industrial oilseeds, and rubber; food index relates to crops and livestock products for human consumption. Deductions made for feed and seed used in production process. 1961=100.   [2] Components of these indexes vary considerably among countries; for details, see source. [3] Refers, in general, to salaried employees and wage earners in manufacturing. Includes workers on holiday or vacation; excludes employers, self-employed, and workers on strike, on temporary military leave, or temporarily laid off.   [4] In many instances, represents index only for principal city (or cities) of particular country. [5] General wholesale price index numbers usually weighted by gross value of sales on wholesale markets. [6] Year beginning July 1.   [7] Building materials.   [8] Year ending June 30.   [9] Includes mining and quarrying.   [10] Data for Luxembourg included in Belgium.   [11] Data for 1 month.   [12] For 1975.   [13] 1972=100. [14] Source: U.S. Bureau of the Census. Data from Republic of China publications.   [15] 1971=100.   [16] 1965=100. [17] For 1974.   [18] July 1970–June 1971=100.   [19] For 1973.   [20] Including electricity, gas, and water. [21] July 1969–June 1970=100.   [22] Area of San Salvador.   [23] Industrial products.   [24] For 1972.   [25] Averages of less than 12 months.   [26] 1975=100.   [27] State industry.   [28] Producers' prices of industrial products. [29] Includes working proprietors.   [30] Year beginning March 21.   [31] Data refer to West Malaysia only. [32] 1974=100.   [33] Raw materials, including semi-manufactured goods.   [34] Groceries.   [35] Year beginning April 1.   [36] Socialized sector.   [37] Includes sea fishing.   [38] Annual figures are monthly averages. [39] For 1971.   [40] Wage earners only.   [41] Producers' goods.   [42] Excluding publishing.   [43] Basic materials. [44] Establishments with 10 or more workers.

Source: Except as noted, Statistical Office of the United Nations, New York, N.Y., *Statistical Yearbook.* (Copyright.)

No. 1563. Consumer Price Indexes—Selected Countries: 1970 to 1977

COUNTRY	TOTAL INDEXES (1967=100)						Average annual percent change, 1970–1977	INDEXES FOR SELECTED ITEMS, 1977 (1967=100)			
	1970	1973	1974	1975	1976	1977		Food [1]	Cloth-ing	Hous-ing [2]	Trans-portation
United States	116.3	133.1	147.7	161.2	170.5	181.5	6.6	192.2	154.2	189.6	177.2
Australia	109.8	134.9	155.3	178.7	202.9	227.9	11.0	207.6	243.2	258.3	(NA)
Austria	110.6	132.4	145.0	157.2	168.7	178.0	7.0	[3] 170.0	[3] 155.5	[3] 200.6	[3] 184.8
Belgium	110.7	130.3	146.8	165.6	180.7	193.6	8.3	189.1	(NA)	(NA)	(NA)
Canada	112.4	130.3	144.5	160.1	172.1	185.9	7.5	200.3	154.3	195.3	178.0
Denmark	119.1	146.8	169.2	185.5	202.2	224.7	9.5	251.2	[3] 162.3	(NA)	(NA)
Finland	114.6	146.1	171.6	202.0	231.1	260.4	12.4	288.0	[3] 193.4	(NA)	(NA)
France	117.1	140.7	160.0	178.9	196.1	214.5	9.0	228.1	195.7	216.2	234.6
Germany, F.R	107.0	127.1	136.0	144.1	150.6	156.5	5.6	149.1	154.7	165.8	161.1
Greece	105.8	131.3	166.7	189.0	214.2	240.1	12.4	262.0	[3] 189.5	(NA)	(NA)
Iceland	159.7	229.2	327.8	488.2	645.2	[3] 829.3	[4] 26.5	(NA)	(NA)	(NA)	(NA)
Ireland	121.7	160.4	187.7	226.8	267.6	304.2	14.0	318.7	[3] 244.4	(NA)	(NA)
Italy	109.2	134.2	159.8	186.9	218.3	[3] 257.6	[4] 13.0	[3] 257.2	[3] 274.9	[3] 231.4	[3] 308.7
Japan	119.3	148.5	183.0	204.5	223.7	241.9	10.6	257.1	248.0	195.9	261.1
Luxembourg	109.9	128.4	140.7	155.7	171.0	182.4	7.5	184.6	[3] 157.6	(NA)	(NA)
Netherlands	115.5	145.2	159.4	175.3	190.9	203.8	8.5	183.3	218.0	201.4	192.6
New Zealand	116.6	148.9	165.3	189.6	221.8	253.7	11.8	250.9	[3] 217.5	(NA)	(NA)
Norway	118.0	144.4	158.0	176.5	192.6	210.1	8.6	219.4	[3] 177.8	(NA)	(NA)
Portugal	122.7	171.8	214.8	247.6	299.6	371.2	17.1	408.3	[3] 219.4	(NA)	(NA)
Spain	113.3	148.0	171.2	200.3	235.5	293.2	14.6	[3] 278.4	[3] 246.5	(NA)	(NA)
Sweden	112.0	136.2	149.6	164.3	181.1	201.8	8.8	219.3	164.1	217.3	(NA)
Switzerland	108.8	134.5	147.6	157.5	160.2	162.3	5.9	147.2	[3] 153.0	(NA)	(NA)
Turkey	120.1	188.1	233.0	282.5	331.6	418.1	19.5	(NA)	(NA)	(NA)	(NA)
United Kingdom	117.4	150.3	174.3	216.5	252.4	292.4	13.9	348.0	236.1	270.9	296.8
Yugoslavia	125.5	202.4	245.0	309.2	340.0	[3] 397.5	[4] 17.9	[3] 431.2	[3] 330.2	(NA)	(NA)

NA Not available.   [1] Restaurant meals, alcohol, and tobacco are included for some countries, excluded for others.   [2] Includes shelter, utilities, and household furnishings and operations. However, actual coverage and measurement methods vary significantly from country to country.   [3] June 1977.   [4] 1970 to June 1977.

Source: U.S. Bureau of Labor Statistics, *Handbook of Labor Statistics,* annual, and unpublished data.

No. 1564. COST-OF-LIVING OF UNITED NATIONS PERSONNEL IN SELECTED CITIES AS REFLECTED BY INDEX OF RETAIL PRICES: 1970 AND 1977

[New York City=100. As of December. Price comparisons weighted according to expenditures in New York City and selected cities]

CITY	1970	1977	CITY	1970	1977
Addis Ababa, Ethiopia	86	92	La Paz, Bolivia	78	99
Amman, Jordan	78	113	Lima, Peru	76	87
Ankara, Turkey	76	91	London, England	78	97
Athens, Greece	82	117	Manila, Philippines	89	86
Baghdad, Iraq	76	86	Mexico City, Mexico	85	73
Bangkok, Thailand	81	78	Montevideo, Uruguay	75	84
Belgrade, Yugoslavia	76	94	Montreal, Canada	84	84
Bogota, Colombia	69	77	Nairobi, Kenya	78	91
Bonn, Germany, F.R. of	83	134	New Delhi, India	76	75
Buenos Aires, Argentina	75	90	Paris, France	89	121
Bujumbura, Burundi	[1] 92	100	Quito, Ecuador	70	81
Cairo, Egypt	71	77	Rabat, Morocco	78	103
Caracas, Venezuela	90	105	Rio de Janeiro, Brazil	90	99
Colombo, Sri Lanka	71	50	Rome, Italy	81	86
Copenhagen, Denmark	86	123	San Jose, Costa Rica	78	83
Damascus, Syria	66	104	San Salvador, El Salvador	82	90
Geneva, Switzerland	80	141	Santiago, Chile	73	92
Guatemala City, Guatemala	82	90	Seoul, Korea, Rep. of	86	99
The Hague, Netherlands	79	128	Sydney, Australia	[1] 81	96
Havana, Cuba	86	82	Teheran, Iran	75	111
Jakarta, Indonesia	94	115	Tokyo, Japan	(NA)	156
Kabul, Afghanistan	74	82	Tunis, Tunisia	78	114
Islamabad, Pakistan	87	78	Vienna, Austria	77	122
Kathmandu, Nepal	74	76	Vientiane, Laos	83	95
Kingston, Jamaica	77	83	Washington, D.C., U.S.A	91	95

NA Not available.   [1] For 1971.

Source: Statistical Office of the United Nations, New York, N.Y., *Monthly Bulletin of Statistics*, December 1970 and March 1978. (Copyright.)

No. 1565. PRIMARY ENERGY PRODUCTION BY SOURCE OF ENERGY AND REGION: 1960 TO 1975

[In millions of metric tons of coal equivalent. See text, p. 896, for general comments concerning the data]

SOURCE OF ENERGY AND YEAR	World total	Africa	Northern America	Latin America	Asia	Europe	U.S.S.R.	Oceania
Total primary energy: 1960	4,478	65	1,512	316	1,004	872	679	31
1965	5,582	215	1,841	403	1,170	943	969	42
1970	7,386	498	2,368	464	1,748	980	1,254	72
1975	8,555	456	2,305	420	2,476	1,132	1,650	116
Coal and lignite: 1960	2,191	43	401	7	551	766	393	29
1965	2,269	54	485	9	459	792	430	39
1970	2,397	60	565	10	529	730	450	55
1975	2,640	75	597	13	662	713	507	73
Crude petroleum and natural gas liquids: 1960	1,605	20	603	289	431	44	217	–
1965	2,304	157	700	358	675	55	357	–
1970	3,467	431	895	403	1,150	56	519	13
1975	4,035	358	817	338	1,694	73	722	32
Natural gas: 1960	597	–	477	16	10	34	62	–
1965	893	3	616	31	17	54	172	–
1970	1,367	5	856	41	48	146	269	2
1975	1,658	18	806	51	91	280	405	7
Hydro and nuclear electricity: 1960	85	1	31	4	11	30	6	1
1965	116	2	39	6	16	40	10	2
1970	154	3	53	11	22	48	16	3
1975	221	5	85	17	30	65	17	4

– Represents zero.

Source: Statistical Office of the United Nations, New York, N.Y., *World Statistics in Brief*, 1977. (Copyright.)

No. 1566. Labor Force, Manufacturing, Steel, Iron Ore, Cement, Cotton Yarn, and Fish, by Country: 1976

[See text, p. 896, for general comments about the data. For additional data qualifications for countries, see source]

COUNTRY	Economically active population [1] (1,000)	Persons engaged in manufacturing [2] (1,000)	STEEL Production [3] (mil. metric tons)	STEEL Consumption [4] Total (mil. metric tons)	STEEL Consumption [4] Per capita (kilograms)	PRODUCTION Iron ore [5] (iron content) (mil. metric tons)	PRODUCTION Cement [6] (mil. metric tons)	PRODUCTION Cotton yarn [7] (1,000 metric tons)	Fish catches [8] (1,000 metric tons)
World, total	(NA)	(NA)	675.0	(NA)	(NA)	512.7	729.0	(NA)	73,500
United States	[9] 82,897	(NA)	[10] 116.1	130.0	604	[11] 50.2	68.3	1,230	3,004
Algeria	2,565	(NA)	.2	1.2	71	1.5	1.3	[12] 9	35
Argentina	9,011	(NA)	2.2	3.3	129	[13] .2	5.7	[14] 92	282
Australia	5,330	[15][16] 1,197	[15] 7.9	4.7	346	[15] 58.3	5.0	[15][17] 26	[15] 114
Austria	3,098	[12][18][19] 677	4.4	2.7	359	1.2	5.9	21	2
Belgium	3,638	[18][20] 1,215	12.1	[21] 4.6	[21] 467	(Z)	7.5	54	44
Brazil	29,557	[18][22][23] 3,638	9.1	10.7	98	[13] 60.6	19.1	[24] 70	[25] 950
Bulgaria	4,268	[26] 1,297	2.5	2.1	236	.7	4.4	79	167
Canada	[27] 8,162	[12] 1,744	13.1	12.6	543	[28] 35.0	9.9	[12] 62	1,136
Chile	2,607	[22][29] 254	[30] .5	.5	48	6.2	1.0	[14][31] 23	1,264
China, People's Rep	(NA)	(NA)	[13] 27.0	27.0	32	[13] 32.5	[13] 35.0	[14][32] 1,450	[25] 6,880
China, Rep. of [33]	5,748	1,607	.6	2.8	170	(NA)	9.0	267	811
Colombia	5,134	[12][18][34] 455	.3	7	30	.5	3.6	[22] 28	75
Cuba	2,633	(NA)	.3	1.0	107	(NA)	2.5	[14] 22	[25] 204
Czechoslovakia	6,996	[26] 2,471	14.7	11.4	767	.5	9.6	125	17
Denmark	2,313	[12][35] 377	.7	2.3	448	(Z)	2.4	2	1,912
Dominican Rep	856	(NA)	(NA)	.1	26	(NA)	.6	[12][36] 1	7
Ecuador	1,443	[18][22][37] 66	(NA)	.2	29	(NA)	.6	[12] 1	[25] 223
Egypt	7,782	[15][20][38] 651	[13] .5	1.3	34	.6	3.3	[14] 193	[25] 107
El Salvador	1,315	[18][22][39] 50	(NA)	.1	13	(NA)	.3	[14] 5	9
Finland	2,129	[23] 495	1.6	1.8	390	.8	1.8	12	121
France	20,439	[40] 5,767	23.2	22.6	426	13.8	29.5	[17] 253	806
German Dem. Rep	8,214	[41] 3,092	6.7	9.9	590	(Z)	11.3	[17][42] 138	279
Germany, F.R. of	26,494	[34] 7,155	42.4	36.8	593	.8	34.2	[17] 208	454
Ghana	3,332	[20][43][44] 61	(NA)	.1	8	(NA)	.7	(NA)	[45] 238
Greece	[46] 3,388	[22] 557	[13] .8	1.6	171	.9	8.8	[12][14] 79	[25] 71
Guatemala	1,364	[18][22][23] 64	(NA)	.2	26	(NA)	[12] .3	(NA)	4
Hong Kong	1,655	774	(NA)	1.2	264	(Z)	.8	222	158
Hungary	4,989	[26] 1,446	3.7	3.4	324	.1	4.3	[47] 59	32
India	180,373	[12][48][49] 5,518	9.3	8.2	13	27.2	18.7	[50] 1,006	2,400
Indonesia	40,100	[12][51] 734	(NA)	1.4	10	(NA)	1.8	[31] 54	1,448
Iran	7,584	[12][34][52] 396	(NA)	4.9	147	[13][53] .7	5.5	[20][36] 42	[25] 2
Iraq	(NA)	[22][54] 125	(NA)	1.1	94	(NA)	[13] 2.4	[12][14] 1	[25] 22
Ireland	1,120	[31][55] 203	[13] .1	.5	150	(NA)	1.6	5	94
Israel	956	[56] 273	[13] .1	.7	195	(NA)	2.0	24	26
Italy	18,750	[12][57] 3,624	23.4	21.9	389	.2	36.3	234	420
Japan	53,321	[18][22][58] 12,024	107.4	60.2	534	[59] .5	68.7	498	10,620
Korea, Dem. Peo. Rep	(NA)	(NA)	[13] 3.0	3.0	186	[13] 3.8	[13] 6.0	(NA)	[25] 800
Korea, Rep. of	10,378	[12][23][44] 1,420	[30] 2.7	5.4	151	.3	11.9	175	2,407
Lebanon	(NA)	(NA)	(NA)	.1	30	(NA)	[13] 1.7	[14][27] 5	[25] 3
Liberia	412	(NA)	(NA)	(Z)	17	14.0	[13] .1	(NA)	[25] 17
Luxembourg	131	[12][57] 45	4.6	[21]	[21]	.6	.3	(NA)	(NA)
Malaysia	3,430	[18][31] 298	(NA)	.8	68	.2	[60] 1.7	[14] 18	517
Mexico	12,910	(NA)	5.2	6.0	96	3.6	12.7	[12][14] 158	572
Morocco	3,981	(NA)	[12][61] (Z)	.7	41	.2	2.1	[22] 14	281
Netherlands	4,169	[62][63] 1,049	5.2	5.1	368	(NA)	3.5	33	284
New Zealand	[9] 1,026	[22][48][64] 248	(NA)	2.1	677	−	1.0	(NA)	70
Nigeria	18,036	[18][31][53] 170	(NA)	1.3	20	(NA)	1.3	[12][14] 5	495
Norway	1,469	[12][23] 367	.9	1.8	444	2.5	2.7	2	3,435
Pakistan	39,591	[23][31] 258	[13] .3	.5	7	(NA)	[15] 3.2	[14][15][50] 350	206
Peru	3,872	[23][23] 258	[13] .3	.5	34	3.1	[13] 2.0	[15] 20	4,343
Philippines	11,355	[22][23] 532	(NA)	1.2	27	.4	4.2	[14][47] 33	1,430
Poland	16,944	[26] 4,230	15.2	18.3	533	[66] .2	19.8	[17] 219	750
Portugal	3,424	[12][18][67] 617	.4	1.1	118	(Z)	3.7	[17] 121	339
Romania	10,362	[68] 2,909	10.7	[12] 9.8	[12] 464	.7	13.1	[17][47] 165	127
South Africa	7,986	[58][69] 1,132	[70] 6.9	[71] 6.1	[71] 212	9.8	7.0	72	[25] 638
So. Rhodesia	110	−	[13] .3	.5	77	[13] .4	.5	(NA)	[25] 2
Spain	11,865	[12][18][72] 2,266	11.1	11.0	305	4.0	25.3	73	[25] 1,483
Sri Lanka	3,459	(NA)	(NA)	.1	5	(NA)	.4	[14] 6	136
Sweden	3,413	[12][23] 927	5.2	6.0	725	19.1	2.8	6	209
Switzerland	3,005	[18][73] 677	[74] .5	2.0	314	−	3.5	44	4
Syria	1,525	168	(NA)	.9	117	(NA)	1.1	[14] 32	[25] 2
Thailand	16,850	[18][34][75] 211	[13] .2	1.4	32	(Z)	4.4	[12][14][47] 67	1,640
Tunisia	1,094	[12][18][76] 78	[61] .1	.3	51	.3	.5	[12][14] 7	[25] 43
Turkey	15,829	[12][34] 706	1.5	3.4	85	1.9	13.2	[50] 167	[25] 155
U.S.S.R	115,204	30,046	144.8	145.6	567	130.9	124.2	1,583	10,134

See footnotes at end of table.

No. 1566. LABOR FORCE, MANUFACTURING, STEEL, IRON ORE, CEMENT, COTTON YARN, AND FISH, BY COUNTRY: 1976—Continued

[See headnote, page 914]

COUNTRY	Economically active population [1] (1,000)	Persons engaged in manufacturing [2] (1,000)	STEEL Production [3] (mil. metric tons)	Consumption [4] Total (mil. metric tons)	Consumption [4] Per capita (kilograms)	PRODUCTION Iron ore [5] (iron content) (mil. metric tons)	Cement [6] (mil. metric tons)	Cotton yarn [7] (1,000 metric tons)	Fish catches [8] (1,000 metric tons)
United Kingdom	[77] 22,754	[12] 7,504	22.3	22.8	407	1.1	15.8	133	1,063
Uruguay _____ *	1,012	(NA)	(Z)	(Z)	14	–	[13] .7	(NA)	34
Venezuela	3,015	[12] 324	.8	2.8	229	11.6	3.8	[20] 16	146
Vietnam	[78] 5,742	(NA)	(NA)	.3	6	(NA)	[13] .7	[14] [31] [78] 10	[25] [78] 1,014
Yugoslavia	8,890	[12] [79] 1,640	2.8	4.1	182	1.4	7.6	117	59

– Represents zero. NA Not available. Z Less than 50,000 metric tons. [1] Comprises all persons engaged in or actively seeking productive work in some branch of the economy during a specified period of time. Generally, data are for a specific date in the 1960's and 1970's. [2] Comprises average number of employees, working proprietors, and unpaid family workers engaged in production of manufactured goods, including assembly of component parts and, except in the case of consumer goods, repair services. Except as noted, excludes gas manufacture and electricity. [3] Total production of crude steel, both ingots and steel for castings. Excludes wrought (puddled) iron. [4] Data represent apparent consumption (i.e., production plus imports minus exports) and do not take into account changes in stocks. [5] Refers generally to iron content of marketable ores mined, including manganiferous iron ores but excluding pyrites. Some data are rough estimates obtained by applying a fixed percentage to figures for crude production. [6] Covers, as far as possible, all hydraulic cements used for construction (portland, metallurgic, aluminous, natural, etc.). [7] Covers pure and mixed yarn, including yarn spun from cotton waste, and excludes tire cord yarn, except as noted. [8] Covers both sea and inland fisheries, in terms of live weight. Includes shellfish; excludes whales, dolphins, etc. [9] Excludes Armed Forces abroad. [10] Excludes steel for castings made in foundries operated by companies not producing ingots. [11] Excludes manganiferous iron ores containing 5 percent or more of manganese. [12] For 1975. [13] Data from U.S. Bureau of Mines. [14] Pure cotton yarn only. [15] Year ending June 30. [16] All establishments except single-establishment enterprises with fewer than 4 employees. [17] Includes tire cord yarn. [18] For one period of the year indicated. [19] Establishments with 20 or more employees. [20] For 1972. [21] Luxembourg included with Belgium. [22] For 1974. [23] Establishments with 5 or more engaged. [24] Production in the State of São Paulo only. [25] FAO estimate. [26] All enterprises in socialist sector except publishing. [27] Excludes armed services. [28] Shipments from mines. [29] Establishments with 50 or more engaged. [30] Ingots only. [31] For 1970. [32] For 1969. [33] Source: U.S. Bureau of the Census. Data from Republic of China publications. [34] Establishments with 10 or more engaged. [35] Establishments with 6 or more employees. [36] Mixed yarn only. [37] Establishments with 7 or more engaged. [38] Private establishments with 10 or more engaged and all public establishments. [39] Establishments with 5 or more employees. [40] Total mining and manufacturing. [41] All enterprises. [42] Includes thread. [43] Establishments with 30 or more engaged. [44] Includes homeworkers. [45] Excludes catches by chartered foreign vessels. [46] Includes Armed Forces abroad. [47] Excludes yarn made from waste. [48] Year ending March 31. [49] Establishments with 10 or more engaged using power, or with 20 or more engaged not using power. [50] Factory production only. [51] Establishments with 20 or more workers. [52] Year ending March 20. [53] Year beginning March 21. [54] Establishments with 10 or more employees. [55] Establishments with 3 or more engaged. [56] Establishments with at least 1 employee. [57] Enterprises with 20 or more engaged. [58] All private establishments. [59] Includes iron content of iron sand and pyrites. [60] West Malaysia only. [61] Crude steel for casting only. [62] Person-years. [63] All kind-of-activity units in mining and manufacturing. [64] Establishments with 2 or more engaged. [65] For 1967. [66] Includes iron content of iron pyrites. [67] Establishments in selected industries. [68] State enterprises under direction of central government. [69] For one period in year ending June 30, 1972. [70] Includes concast steel billets. [71] Includes data for Botswana, Lesotho, Namibia, and Swaziland. [72] All establishments, but certain industries not covered. [73] Establishments subject to labor laws. [74] Data from UN Economic Commission for Europe. [75] For 1971. [76] All units with 5 or more employees. [77] For England and Wales only. [78] Data for former Republic of South Vietnam only. [79] All enterprises in the socialist sector, except licensed handicrafts.

Source: Except as noted, Statistical Office of the United Nations, New York, N.Y., Statistical Yearbook and Demographic Yearbook. (Copyright.)

No. 1567. LABOR FORCE AND UNEMPLOYMENT—INTERNATIONAL COMPARISONS: 1970 TO 1977

[Data on basis of U.S. labor force definitions adopted in 1967 (see text, p. 396) except that minimum age for population base varies as follows: United States, France, Sweden, and, beginning in 1973, Great Britain, 16 years; Australia, Canada, Japan, Germany, and, prior to 1973, Great Britain, 15 years; Italy, 14 years]

COUNTRY	CIVILIAN LABOR FORCE (millions)						PERCENT UNEMPLOYED					
	1970	1973	1974	1975	1976	1977	1970	1973	1974	1975	1976	1977
United States	82.7	88.7	91.0	92.6	94.8	97.4	4.9	4.9	5.6	8.5	7.7	7.0
Australia	5.4	5.7	5.9	6.0	6.1	6.2	1.4	1.9	2.3	4.4	4.4	5.2
Canada	8.4	9.3	9.7	10.1	10.3	10.6	5.7	5.6	5.4	6.9	7.1	8.1
France	21.0	21.6	22.0	22.0	22.2	[1] 22.3	2.6	2.7	3.0	4.2	4.6	[1] 5.2
Germany, Fed. Rep. of [2]	26.3	26.4	26.1	25.7	25.4	[1] 25.3	.8	.8	1.7	3.6	3.6	[1] 3.6
Great Britain	24.3	24.5	24.5	[1] 24.8	[1] 25.1	[1] 25.4	3.1	3.2	2.8	[1] 4.7	[1] 6.4	[1] 6.9
Italy	20.1	19.8	20.1	20.3	20.5	21.4	3.1	3.4	2.8	3.2	3.6	3.3
Japan	50.7	52.6	52.4	52.5	53.1	53.8	1.2	1.3	1.4	1.9	2.0	2.0
Sweden	3.9	4.0	4.0	4.1	4.1	4.2	1.5	2.5	2.0	1.6	1.6	1.8

[1] Preliminary estimates based on incomplete data. [2] Includes West Berlin.

Source: U.S. Bureau of Labor Statistics, Handbook of Labor Statistics, annual.

No. 1568. INDEXES OF OUTPUT AND COMPENSATION PER HOUR, AND OF UNIT LABOR COSTS IN MANUFACTURING—SELECTED COUNTRIES: 1970 TO 1977

[1967=100]

ITEM	United States	Can-ada	Bel-gium	Den-mark	France	Ger-many, F.R.[1]	Italy	Japan	Neth-er-lands	Swe-den	United King-dom
Output per hour: 1970	104.5	114.7	129.5	129.3	121.2	116.1	117.8	146.5	134.0	124.5	108.6
1973	119.4	133.4	166.7	159.8	143.7	136.6	147.8	179.0	170.2	147.4	126.3
1974	112.8	135.6	174.1	165.1	147.8	145.0	155.9	180.3	184.3	152.1	127.6
1975	116.3	133.4	183.7	175.7	151.1	150.4	150.2	172.4	181.0	150.4	124.4
1976	124.2	137.8	204.0	187.9	165.3	162.8	161.5	194.8	198.9	152.9	128.7
1977 [2]	126.9	143.3	(NA)	185.1	171.6	169.6	162.3	206.6	(NA)	156.6	126.6
Compensation per hour, national currency: [3] 1970	121.7	124.0	131.2	145.0	134.7	133.5	141.1	164.3	146.2	131.4	132.1
1973	147.0	158.2	200.0	203.4	191.7	192.2	237.6	264.2	228.4	184.7	188.2
1974	161.4	182.9	245.5	244.9	229.1	221.9	297.4	345.2	272.2	215.7	240.4
1975	179.4	209.4	302.3	291.2	271.4	250.2	386.7	403.3	313.8	261.6	306.8
1976	194.8	236.0	337.0	323.7	312.9	265.2	457.9	438.7	350.3	311.3	362.4
1977 [2]	212.0	259.8	(NA)	350.4	352.4	289.7	561.3	480.8	(NA)	350.2	398.6
Real hourly compensa-tion: [3][4] 1970	104.7	110.4	118.5	121.8	119.4	125.1	129.0	137.7	126.6	116.2	111.8
1973	110.5	121.4	153.5	138.5	141.4	152.4	177.3	177.9	158.1	131.0	123.9
1974	109.3	126.5	167.2	144.7	148.6	164.7	185.7	188.6	171.8	139.2	136.3
1975	111.3	130.8	182.6	157.0	157.5	175.0	206.1	197.2	179.7	153.8	140.5
1976	114.3	137.1	186.5	160.1	165.6	177.3	209.4	196.1	184.4	166.0	142.2
1977 [2]	116.8	139.8	(NA)	156.0	170.6	186.9	215.1	198.8	(NA)	167.7	133.7
Unit labor costs, national currency: 1970	116.5	108.1	101.3	112.2	111.1	115.0	119.8	112.2	109.1	105.6	121.7
1973	123.2	118.6	120.0	127.3	133.4	140.7	160.8	147.6	134.2	125.2	149.1
1974	143.1	134.8	141.0	148.3	155.0	153.1	190.8	191.5	147.7	141.8	188.4
1975	154.3	157.0	164.6	165.8	179.6	166.3	257.4	233.9	173.3	173.9	246.6
1976	156.9	171.3	165.2	172.2	189.2	162.9	283.6	225.2	176.1	203.6	281.5
1977 [2]	167.0	181.3	(NA)	189.3	205.4	170.8	345.9	232.7	(NA)	223.7	314.8
Unit labor costs, U.S. dollar basis: [5] 1970	116.5	111.8	101.4	104.4	98.9	125.7	119.2	113.4	108.7	105.1	106.0
1973	123.2	127.9	153.6	147.6	147.9	211.7	172.5	197.3	174.0	148.5	132.8
1974	143.1	148.7	180.2	170.2	158.7	236.3	183.1	237.9	198.3	165.2	160.3
1975	154.3	166.5	222.9	201.8	206.4	270.0	246.2	285.6	247.5	216.7	199.2
1976	156.9	187.4	212.8	198.9	195.0	258.1	213.2	275.2	240.1	241.3	184.7
1977 [2]	167.0	184.1	(NA)	220.2	205.6	293.4	244.6	314.7	(NA)	258.5	199.7

NA Not available. [1] Federal Republic of Germany. Includes West Berlin. [2] Preliminary. Estimates for Italy based on partial year data. [3] Compensation includes, but real hourly compensation excludes, adjustments for payroll and employment taxes that are not compensation to employees, but are labor costs to employers. [4] Index of hourly compensation divided by the index of consumer prices to adjust for changes in purchasing power. [5] Indexes in national currency adjusted for changes in prevailing exchange rates.

No. 1569. ENERGY, PETROLEUM, AND COAL, BY COUNTRY: 1970 AND 1976

[See text, p. 896, for general comments about the data. For additional data qualifications for countries, see source]

COUNTRY	ENERGY CONSUMED [1] (coal equiv.) Total (mil. metric tons) 1970	1976	Per capita (kilograms) 1970	1976	ELECTRIC ENERGY PRODUCTION [2] (bil. kWh) 1970	1976	CRUDE PETROLEUM PRODUCTION [3] (mil. metric tons) 1970	1976	COAL PRODUCTION [4] (mil. metric tons) 1970	1976
World, total	6,820.1	8,318.4	1,892	2,069	4,923	6,917	2,277	2,864	2,143	2,420
United States	2,269.5	2,485.5	11,077	11,554	[5] 1,640	[5] 2,123	475.3	401.2	550.4	585.7
Algeria	6.6	12.6	460	729	2.0	4.6	49.0	50.4	(Z)	
Argentina	39.2	46.4	1,691	1,804	21.7	30.3	20.0	20.8	.6	.6
Australia	67.2	90.8	5,375	6,657	[6] 53.9	[6] 76.6	[7] 8.5	[7] 20.5	45.2	67.8
Austria	25.3	30.2	3,424	4,013	30.0	35.3	2.8	1.9	–	–
Bahrain	1.0	3.2	4,720	11,998	[8] .2	[8] .7	3.8	2.9	(NA)	(NA)
Belgium	59.3	59.8	5,923	6,049	30.5	47.3	(NA)	(NA)	11.4	[9] 7.7
Brazil	44.6	79.8	478	731	[5] 45.5	[5] 88.4	8.0	8.1	2.4	3.3
Bulgaria	33.4	41.3	3,937	4,710	19.5	27.7	.3	.1	.4	.3
Canada	201.1	230.3	9,393	9,950	[5] 204.7	[5] 293.4	60.4	62.2	11.6	20.8
Chile	12.5	10.3	1,287	987	7.6	9.3	1.5	.9	1.4	1.2
China, People's Rep.	391.2	590.1	515	706	(NA)	(NA)	23.9	85.0	[10][11] 360.0	[10][11] 480.0
China, Rep. of [12]	15.3	29.4	1,055	1,778	13.2	26.9	.1	.2	4.5	3.2

See footnotes at end of table.

No. 1569. ENERGY, PETROLEUM, AND COAL, BY COUNTRY: 1970 AND 1976—Continued

[Metric ton=1.1023 short tons. See text, p. 896, for general comments about the data. For additional data qualifications for countries, see source]

COUNTRY	ENERGY CONSUMED [1] (coal equiv.)				ELECTRIC ENERGY PRODUCTION [2] (bil. kWh)		CRUDE PETROLEUM PRODUCTION [3] (mil. metric tons)		COAL PRODUCTION [4] (mil. metric tons)	
	Total (mil. metric tons)		Per capita (kilograms)							
	1970	1976	1970	1976	1970	1976	1970	1976	1970	1976
Colombia	12.7	16.7	601	685	8.8	15.3	11.3	7.6	2.3	3.6
Cuba	9.4	11.6	1,109	1,225	4.9	7.2	.2	.1	(NA)	(NA)
Czechoslovakia	93.3	110.3	6,510	7,397	45.2	62.7	.2	.1	28.2	[9] 28.6
Denmark	28.8	27.0	5,838	5,320	[5] 18.9	[5] 19.6	−	.2	(NA)	(NA)
Ecuador	1.8	3.3	293	455	.9	1.9	.2	9.5	(NA)	(NA)
Egypt	8.8	18.0	265	473	7.6	11.0	16.4	16.8	−	−
Finland	19.2	[13] 24.5	4,159	[135] 5,177	[5] 21.2	[5] 27.8	(NA)	(NA)	(NA)	(NA)
France	192.8	231.9	3,794	4,380	[5] 140.7	[5] 194.6	2.3	1.1	[9] 37.8	[9] 23.3
German Dem. Rep	102.1	114.0	5,984	6,789	67.7	89.2	.1	.1	1.0	.5
Germany, Fed. Rep	317.8	364.3	5,239	5,922	242.6	333.7	7.5	5.5	[14] 116.3	[14] 95.9
Greece	11.2	20.6	1,274	2,250	9.4	16.7	−	−	(NA)	(NA)
Hong Kong	4.0	5.8	1,010	1,313	[8] 5.1	[8] 8.3	(NA)	(NA)	(NA)	(NA)
Hungary	32.9	37.7	3,185	3,553	14.5	22.1	1.9	2.1	[9] 4.2	[9] 2.9
India	96.8	132.9	179	218	[16] 61.2	[15] 95.3	6.8	8.7	73.7	100.9
Indonesia	13.3	30.4	112	218	[8] 2.1	[8] 3.8	42.6	74.2	.2	.2
Iran	27.1	49.8	945	1,490	7.0	[16] 17.3	191.3	295.1	[10] [16] .5	[16] .9
Iraq	5.8	8.4	617	725	[8] 1.9	[8] 4.6	76.5	112.3	(NA)	(NA)
Ireland	[13] 9.0	[13] 10.0	[13] 3,064	[13] 3,170	[15] 6.1	[15] 8.6	(NA)	(NA)	.2	(Z)
Israel	7.4	9.0	2,524	2,541	6.8	10.4	[17] 5.0	(Z)	(NA)	(NA)
Italy	144.1	184.5	2,689	3,284	117.4	163.6	1.4	1.1	.3	(Z)
Jamaica	2.6	4.0	1,377	1,937	1.5	2.4	(NA)	(NA)	(NA)	(NA)
Japan	332.4	414.9	3,215	3,679	[15] 359.5	[15] 511.8	.8	.6	[18] 39.7	[18] 18.4
Korea, Dem. Peo. Rep	28.2	49.9	2,027	3,072	(NA)	(NA)	(NA)	(NA)	[10] 21.8	[10] 40.0
Korea, Republic of	25.4	36.6	819	1,020	9.6	24.4	(NA)	(NA)	12.4	16.4
Kuwait	10.0	[19] 9.5	13,352	[199] 9,198	[8] 2.2	[8] 5.2	[19] 150.6	[19] 108.0	(NA)	(NA)
Libya	1.1	4.0	577	1,589	[8] .4	[8] 1.5	159.8	93.5	(NA)	(NA)
Malaysia	[20] 4.3	[20] 6.0	[20] 468	[20] 578	[20] 3.3	[20] 6.0	.9	8.0	(NA)	(NA)
Mexico	60.7	76.4	1,241	1,227	[5] 28.7	[5] 46.6	21.5	41.3	3.0	5.7
Netherlands	66.0	85.7	5,066	6,224	40.9	58.1	1.9	1.4	4.3	−
New Zealand	8.0	11.4	2,835	3,617	[8 15] 13.7	[8 15] 20.9	[7] .1	[7] .5	2.2	2.3
Nigeria	2.5	6.1	45	94	1.6	3.4	54.2	103.5	.1	.0
Norway	18.7	21.2	4,822	5,263	[5] 57.6	[5] 82.2	−	13.8	.5	.5
Pakistan	[21] 12.2	13.1	[21] 93	181	[6 21] 8.7	[6] 10.9	.5	.3	[6 11] 1.3	[6 11] 1.3
Peru	8.6	10.3	633	642	5.5	8.7	3.6	3.8	.2	−
Philippines	10.8	14.4	292	329	8.7	14.7	(NA)	(NA)	(Z)	.2
Poland	138.9	180.5	4,270	5,253	64.5	104.1	.4	.5	140.1	179.3
Portugal	6.1	10.1	702	1,050	7.5	10.1	(NA)	(NA)	.3	.2
Romania	58.4	86.6	2,883	4,036	35.1	58.3	13.4	14.7	[9] 6.4	[9] 7.1
Saudi Arabia	6.3	[19] 17.6	808	[191] 1,901	[8] .7	[8] 2.3	[19] 188.4	[19] 425.8	(NA)	(NA)
Singapore	1.7	5.2	808	2,262	[8] 2.2	[8] 4.6	(NA)	(NA)	(NA)	(NA)
South Africa	[22] 63.2	[22] 87.4	[222] 2,618	[222] 2,985	50.8	79.1	(NA)	(NA)	54.6	75.7
Spain	[23] 50.2	86.3	[231] 1,485	[231] 2,399	56.5	90.8	.2	1.8	[9] 10.8	[9] 10.7
Sweden	49.7	49.7	6,183	6,046	60.6	86.4	(NA)	(NA)	(Z)	(NA)
Switzerland	21.6	21.3	3,475	3,340	[5 24] 33.2	[5 24] 36.2	(NA)	(NA)	(NA)	(NA)
Syria	2.9	5.7	457	744	.9	1.8	4.2	10.0	(NA)	(NA)
Thailand	8.8	13.2	256	308	4.5	10.3	[10] (Z)	(Z)	(NA)	(NA)
Trinidad and Tobago	4.7	4.7	4,542	4,272	1.2	1.4	7.2	11.0	(NA)	(NA)
Tunisia	1.3	2.6	257	456	.8	1.5	4.2	3.7	(NA)	(NA)
Turkey	16.9	29.8	480	743	8.6	18.2	3.5	2.6	4.6	4.6
U.S.S.R.	[131] 1,054.7	[131] 1,349.9	[144] 4,345	[135] 5,259	740.9	1,111.4	[7] 353.0	[7] 519.7	432.7	494.4
United Arab Emirates	1.3	3.1	7,446	13,322	[25] .1	[25] .6	37.7	95.3	(NA)	(NA)
United Kingdom	300.2	295.3	5,377	5,268	249.0	277.0	.1	11.6	[9] 147.1	[9] 123.8
Uruguay	2.6	3.1	913	1,000	2.2	2.8	(NA)	(NA)	(NA)	(NA)
Venezuela	25.6	35.1	2,457	2,838	12.7	23.3	194.3	120.2	(Z)	.1
Vietnam	[26] 5.5	5.8	[26] 302	124	[26] 1.2	[26 27] 1.3	(NA)	(NA)	[10 28] 3.0	[10 28] 5.4
Yugoslavia	29.3	43.5	1,438	2,016	26.0	43.6	2.9	3.9	.6	.6
Zaire	1.8	1.6	81	62	3.2	3.5	−	1.3	.1	.1
Zambia	2.1	2.8	494	548	[5] .9	[5] 7.0	(NA)	(NA)	.6	.8

− Represents zero. NA Not available. Z Less than 50,000 metric tons. [1] Based on apparent consumption of coal, lignite, petroleum products, natural gas, and hydro and nuclear electricity. [2] Comprises production by utilities generating primarily for public use, and production by industrial establishments generating primarily for own use. Relates to production at generating centers, including station use and transmission losses. [3] Includes shale oil, but excludes natural gasoline. [4] Excludes lignite and brown coal, except as noted. [5] Net production, i.e., excluding station use. [6] Year ending June 30. [7] Includes gas condensates. [8] Excludes production by industrial establishments for own use. [9] Includes slurries. [10] Data from U.S. Bureau of Mines. [11] Includes lignite and brown coal. [12] Source: U.S. Bureau of the Census. Data from Republic of China publications. [13] Includes peat. [14] Includes low grade coal at its hard-coal equivalent. [15] Year beginning April. [16] Year beginning March 21. [17] Includes estimated production in the occupied Sinai Peninsula (1970, 4.9 million metric tons). [18] Includes brown coal. [19] Includes share of production and consumption in the Neutral Zone. [20] West Malaysia only. [21] Includes Bangladesh. [22] Includes data for Botswana, Lesotho, Namibia, and Swaziland. [23] Includes Canary Islands and Ceuta. [24] Year ending Sept. 30. [25] Abu Dhabi only. [26] Data for former Republic of South Vietnam only. [27] For 1975. [28] Data for former Democratic Republic of Vietnam only.

Source: Except as noted, Statistical Office of the United Nations, New York, N.Y., Statistical Yearbook. (Copyright.)

No. 1570. Wheat and Rice—Production, by Country: 1961 to 1976

[In thousands of metric tons. Rice data cover rough and paddy, except as noted. Data for each country pertain to the calendar year in which all or most of the crop was harvested. See text, p. 896, for general comments concerning quality of the data]

COUNTRY	WHEAT					RICE				
	1961–65 average	1966–70 average	1974	1975	1976	1961–65 average	1966–70 average	1974	1975	1976
World, total	254,427	314,826	359,866	354,626	418,383	255,324	288,629	332,793	359,782	350,260
United States	33,040	38,992	48,497	57,765	58,307	3,084	4,121	5,098	5,826	5,246
Afghanistan	2,207	2,240	2,500	2,850	2,930	343	382	420	435	448
Argentina	7,541	6,249	5,970	8,570	11,200	193	283	316	351	309
Australia	8,222	10,697	11,357	11,982	11,713	136	224	409	388	417
Austria	704	949	1,102	945	1,234	(1)	(1)	(1)	(1)	(1)
Bangladesh	37	70	111	117	218	15,048	16,560	16,930	19,143	17,627
Belgium	826	763	2 1,078	2 716	2 932	(1)	(1)	(1)	(1)	(1)
Brazil	574	1,064	2,859	1,788	3,226	6,123	6,639	6,483	7,538	9,560
Bulgaria	2,213	2,920	2,911	2,771	3,152	37	54	58	68	41
Burma	38	55	25	64	60	7,786	7,715	8,583	9,145	9,307
Canada	15,364	16,727	13,295	17,078	23,587	(1)	(1)	(1)	(1)	(1)
Chile	1,082	1,258	939	1,002	866	85	73	34	76	95
China, People's Rep.[3]	22,230	28,157	37,001	41,003	43,001	88,138	100,769	127,213	128,667	129,054
China, Rep. of [4]	30	17	1	3	1	2,167	2,419	5 2,452	5 2,494	5 2,713
Colombia	118	87	63	62	59	576	708	1,540	1,614	1,560
Cuba	(1)	(1)	(1)	(1)	(1)	151	165	437	447	420
Czechoslovakia	1,779	2,869	5,059	4,202	4,807	(1)	(1)	(1)	(1)	(1)
Denmark	535	445	592	520	592	(1)	(1)	(1)	(1)	(1)
Ecuador	70	79	55	65	39	164	171	266	378	368
Egypt	1,459	1,417	1,884	2,033	1,960	1,845	2,343	2,242	2,423	2,300
Ethiopia	663	762	576	734	694	(1)	(1)	(1)	(1)	(1)
Finland	448	456	593	622	654	(1)	(1)	(1)	(1)	(1)
France	12,495	13,590	19,100	15,013	16,150	120	98	49	48	35
German Dem. Rep	1,357	2,006	3,154	2,736	2,715	(1)	(1)	(1)	(1)	(1)
Germany, Fed. Rep	4,607	5,642	7,761	7,014	6,702	(1)	(1)	(1)	(1)	(1)
Greece	1,765	1,836	2,153	2,140	2,351	88	91	105	104	82
Hungary	2,020	3,008	4,971	4,007	5,148	36	42	56	69	32
India	11,191	15,414	21,778	24,104	28,846	52,733	57,140	59,650	73,352	64,363
Indonesia	(1)	(1)	(1)	(1)	(1)	12,396	16,277	22,732	22,330	23,300
Iran	2,873	4,245	4,700	5,570	6,044	851	1,038	1,313	1,430	1,566
Iraq	849	1,128	1,339	845	1,312	142	268	69	61	163
Ireland	343	325	245	195	200	(1)	(1)	(1)	(1)	(1)
Israel	90	156	274	243	206	(1)	(1)	(1)	(1)	(1)
Italy	8,857	9,585	9,695	9,610	9,516	612	739	1,047	1,009	907
Japan	1,332	853	232	241	222	16,444	17,764	15,967	17,101	15,292
Kampuchea, Democratic	(1)	(1)	(1)	(1)	(1)	2,461	2,880	635	3 1,500	3 1,800
Korea, Dem. Peo. Rep	85	3 96	3 140	3 150	3 145	2,498	3 2,780	3 3,500	3 3,700	3 3,800
Korea, Republic of	170	256	74	97	82	4,809	5,212	6,178	6,485	7,243
Laos	(1)	(1)	(1)	(1)	(1)	609	827	905	910	3 850
Madagascar	(1)	(1)	(1)	(1)	(1)	1,563	1,836	1,844	1,840	1,814
Malaysia	(1)	(1)	(1)	(1)	(1)	1,139	1,422	2,093	1,998	1,853
Mexico	1,672	2,009	2,789	2,798	3,363	314	385	469	711	460
Nepal	135	202	308	332	387	2,147	2,170	2,452	2,605	2,385
Netherlands	606	667	746	528	710	(1)	(1)	(1)	(1)	(1)
New Zealand	248	365	248	203	427	(1)	(1)	(1)	(1)	(1)
Pakistan	4,153	5,716	7,629	7,673	8,691	1,824	2,848	3,470	3,926	4,106
Panama	(1)	(1)	(1)	(1)	(1)	122	150	178	185	144
Peru	150	128	127	143	148	324	430	494	537	570
Philippines	(1)	(1)	(1)	(1)	(1)	3,957	4,735	5,660	6,160	6,455
Poland	2,988	4,260	6,408	5,207	5,745	(1)	(1)	(1)	(1)	(1)
Portugal	562	552	546	611	694	167	164	130	133	97
Romania	4,321	4,688	5,007	4,862	6,724	40	63	53	69	37
South Africa	834	1,125	1,596	1,792	2,239	2	(NA)	3	3	3
Spain	4,365	4,921	4,535	4,302	4,436	386	379	367	379	406
Sri Lanka	(1)	(1)	(1)	(1)	(1)	967	1,298	1,602	1,154	1,253
Sweden	909	932	1,826	1,455	1,763	(1)	(1)	(1)	(1)	(1)
Switzerland	355	383	411	356	408	(1)	(1)	(1)	(1)	(1)
Syria	1,093	767	1,630	1,550	1,790	1	(NA)	2	5	1
Thailand	(1)	(1)	(1)	(1)	(1)	11,267	12,774	13,386	15,300	15,800
Turkey	8,585	10,020	11,080	14,830	16,578	222	233	250	240	251
U.S.S.R	64,207	90,192	83,913	66,224	96,900	390	1,011	1,913	2,009	2,001
United Kingdom	3,520	3,690	6,132	4,488	4,740	(1)	(1)	(1)	(1)	(1)
Uruguay	465	356	526	456	505	67	115	158	193	213
Venezuela	1	(NA)	1	1	1	136	227	297	363	277
Vietnam	(1)	(1)	(1)	(1)	(1)	9,629	9,130	11,023	12,000	3 10,800
Yugoslavia	3,599	4,493	6,283	4,408	5,979	23	24	31	37	23

NA Not available.   1 None or negligible.   2 Includes Luxembourg.   3 FAO estimate.
4 Source: U.S. Bureau of the Census. Data from Republic of China publications.   5 Paddy only.
Source: Except as noted, Statistical Office of the United Nations, New York, N.Y., *Statistical Yearbook*. (Copyright.)

No. 1571. CORN, MEAT, AND SUGAR—PRODUCTION, BY COUNTRY: 1970 TO 1976

[In thousands of metric tons. Data for each country pertain to the calendar year in which all or most of the crop was harvested. See text, p. 896, for general comments concerning the data]

COUNTRY	CORN			MEAT [1]			SUGAR [2]		
	1970–1974 average	1975	1976	1970–1974 average	1975	1976	1970–1974 average	1975	1976
World, total	296,213	324,922	334,276	88,343	94,361	95,820	75,879	81,643	86,513
United States	130,817	148,062	159,173	16,680	16,675	17,965	5,347	5,680	6,163
Argentina	8,950	7,700	5,855	2,618	2,805	3,184	1,285	1,367	1,551
Australia	173	133	131	[3] 2,139	[3] 2,249	[3] 2,592	2,726	2,930	3,395
Austria	776	981	936	440	482	492	358	523	426
Belgium [4]	20	37	30	828	892	870	682	800	721
Brazil	14,726	16,354	17,845	2,802	2,953	3,035	6,067	6,299	7,236
Bulgaria	2,412	2,822	3,031	340	427	486	228	215	230
Canada	2,698	3,645	3,771	1,542	1,578	1,659	120	120	156
Chile	288	329	248	229	300	244	154	219	240
China, People's Rep. of	[5] 29,875	[5] 32,138	[5] 33,114	[5] 11,795	[5] 12,424	[5] 12,882	3,260	4,000	4,000
China, Rep. of [6]	75	138	114	449	401	534	(NA)	(NA)	(NA)
Colombia	850	800	810	[5] 496	[5] 511	[5] 625	790	970	935
Cuba	123	125	[5] 125	[5] 226	[5] 227	[5] 237	5,901	6,427	6,151
Czechoslovakia	574	843	514	[7] 1,004	[7] 1,112	[7] 1,088	743	780	620
Denmark	(NA)	(NA)	(NA)	950	971	959	356	410	432
Dominican Republic	48	53	35	51	56	63	1,145	1,170	1,287
Egypt	2,462	2,781	3,047	269	[5] 286	[5] 294	545	537	576
El Salvador	347	439	342	[8] 38	44	49	[9] 184	[9] 244	[9] 261
Ethiopia	916	1,470	[5] 1,200	354	321	336	124	135	136
France	8,874	8,194	5,544	3,213	3,524	3,587	2,779	2,981	2,721
German Dem. Rep	13	2	–	1,289	1,563	1,531	[10] 504	[10] 683	[10] 609
Germany, Fed. Rep. of	552	531	480	3,586	3,738	3,856	2,341	2,571	2,844
Ghana	430	343	300	[5] 35	[5] 35	[5] 41	8	8	12
Greece	542	468	501	273	317	[5] 317	163	308	386
Guatemala	743	683	686	76	75	82	259	384	517
Hungary	5,314	7,172	5,141	770	995	861	301	335	395
India	6,068	7,256	6,257	[5] 612	[5] 630	[5] 634	4,155	5,048	5,033
Indonesia	2,923	2,903	2,572	295	305	320	848	1,000	1,380
Iran	34	65	80	[5] 316	[5] 341	[5] 351	605	606	650
Ireland	(NA)	(NA)	(NA)	431	565	459	168	(NA)	(NA)
Italy	4,841	5,326	5,321	1,783	1,801	1,846	1,150	1,429	1,758
Japan	22	11	11	1,194	1,392	1,255	637	459	506
Kenya	1,501	1,600	[5] 1,550	[5] 146	[5] 133	[5] 145	142	175	182
Malaysia	[5] [11] 14	[5] [11] 24	[5] [11] 26	[11] 71	[11] 55	[5] [11] 57	7	59	50
Mexico	8,856	8,308	8,393	903	963	[5] 988	2,625	2,724	2,710
Morocco	337	371	493	164	[5] 164	[5] 166	223	268	250
Netherlands	9	6	5	1,149	1,302	1,345	780	923	947
Nigeria	[5] 885	[5] 1,000	[5] 1,050	[5] 319	[5] 302	[5] 330	31	40	30
Pakistan	729	802	764	[5] 255	[5] 277	[5] 282	[12] 562	490	677
Peru	613	625	670	191	188	181	888	[13] 964	930
Philippines	2,141	2,697	2,767	455	518	502	2,200	2,672	2,984
Poland	13	79	231	2,107	2,420	2,342	1,713	1,847	1,774
Portugal	561	506	429	214	242	222	[13] [14] 10	[14] 13	[14] 12
Romania	7,808	9,241	11,583	885	[5] 1,055	[5] 1,104	542	583	561
South Africa	7,936	9,140	7,312	697	676	663	1,881	1,968	2,113
Southern Rhodesia	1,148	1,400	1,400	[5] 137	[5] 160	[5] 163	203	257	220
Spain	1,972	1,794	1,545	1,032	1,226	1,213	864	800	1,162
Sweden	(NA)	(NA)	(NA)	404	431	448	269	278	301
Switzerland	96	141	114	360	381	399	70	65	83
Thailand	2,089	2,863	2,675	[5] 369	[5] 320	[5] 360	[13] 732	1,216	1,757
Turkey	1,101	1,200	1,310	514	604	[5] 615	787	758	1,090
Uganda	439	571	629	79	88	92	111	27	20
U.S.S.R	10,635	7,328	10,138	[7] 11,926	[7] 13,197	[7] 11,658	9,010	8,200	8,500
United Kingdom	(NA)	(NA)	(NA)	2,150	2,301	2,130	970	724	657
Uruguay	190	157	210	386	413	476	76	95	120
Venezuela	587	653	532	283	341	390	507	535	510
Vietnam	[5] 285	[5] 320	[5] 320	[5] [8] 473	[5] 494	[5] 505	(NA)	(NA)	(NA)
Yugoslavia	7,718	9,389	9,106	658	766	761	425	500	580
Zaire	400	420	410	[5] [8] 46	[5] 50	[5] 54	51	63	65

- Represents zero.   NA Not available.
[1] Beef and veal (incl. buffalo meat), pork (incl. bacon and ham), and mutton and lamb (incl. goat meat). Refers to meat from animals slaughtered within the national boundaries irrespective of origin of animals, and relates to commercial and farm slaughter. In terms of carcass weight. Excludes lard, tallow, and edible offals, except as noted.   [2] Beet and cane. Data generally in terms of raw sugar.   [3] Year ending June 30.   [4] Includes Luxembourg for corn and meat.   [5] FAO estimate.   [6] Source: U.S. Bureau of the Census. Data from Republic of China publications.   [7] Includes slaughter fats and edible offals.   [8] Excludes data for 1971.   [9] Crop year.   [10] Total refinery output less imports of raw sugar.   [11] For corn, data refer to West Malaysia and Sabah only; for meat, West Malaysia only.   [12] Prior to 1972, data for Bangladesh included with Pakistan.   [13] Polarization or grade unknown.   [14] Azores and Madeira only.

Source: Except as noted, Statistical Office of the United Nations, New York, N.Y., *Statistical Yearbook*. (Copyright.)

No. 1572. FOREIGN TRADE AND TRANSPORTATION—SHIPPING, RAILWAYS, AVIATION, AND MOTOR VEHICLES, BY COUNTRY: 1976

[See text, p. 896, for general comments about the data. Statistical coverage of all these items varies considerably among countries; for details, see source]

COUNTRY	FOREIGN TRADE [1]		SHIPPING			RAIL TRAFFIC [4]		Civil aviation, kilometers flown [5] (mil.)	Motor vehicles in use [6] (1,000)
	Imports (mil. dol.)	Exports (mil. dol.)	Merchant shipping fleets [2] (1,000 gross tons)	Freight [3] (mil. metric tons) Loaded	Un-loaded	Passenger-kilometers (mil.)	Freight, net-ton kilometers (mil.)		
World, total	[7][8]1,021,100	[7][8]988,700	372,000	(NA)	(NA)	(NA)	(NA)	7,850	340,880
United States	128,872	113,323	[9]14,908	[10][11]258.2	[10][11]488.2	[12]15,688	[12]1,146,492	3,731.7	135,155
Algeria	5,312	5,163	463	46.3	9.7	1,369	1,727	24.7	[13]441
Angola	[14]625	[14]1,227	(NA)	[14]10.0	[14]4.0	[14]418	[14]5,461	(NA)	[15]163
Argentina	3,033	3,916	1,470	[16]15.3	[16]9.2	14,480	11,038	68.4	[14]2,907
Australia	[17]11,084	12,868	1,247	[13][18]166.8	[13][18]27.2	(NA)	[18]30,816	187.4	6,329
Austria	11,523	8,507	(NA)	(NA)	(NA)	6,712	10,685	16.8	2,287
Belgium	[19]35,368	[19]32,847	1,499	33.8	60.1	8,191	6,637	47.8	3,032
Brazil	13,622	10,128	3,096	[16]89.7	[16]61.5	11,638	63,246	173.3	[13]5,984
Bulgaria	[17]5,626	5,382	933	3.0	23.2	7,499	17,055	10.3	(NA)
Canada	[17]37,910	38,128	[9]2,639	[11]114.8	[11]56.5	3,090	195,642	297.6	[13]11,028
Chile	1,684	2,083	410	[15][16]9.9	[16][20]6.2	2,464	2,165	20.6	[13]424
China, People's Rep. of	(NA)	(NA)	3,589	(NA)	(NA)	(NA)	[21]301,000	(NA)	(NA)
China, Rep. of [22]	7,599	8,166	1,297	19.9	41.0	8,412	2,700	(NA)	315
Colombia	1,572	1,694	212	[16]2.3	[16]2.2	511	1,157	49.9	[23]495
Cuba	4,066	3,573	604	6.1	13.1	767	1,848	10.1	112
Czechoslovakia	[17]9,706	9,035	149	(NA)	(NA)	17,910	70,748	30.7	1,953
Denmark	12,419	9,113	5,143	7.2	30.9	[13][24]3,415	[13][24]1,805	37.8	1,606
Dominican Republic	[17]764	716	(NA)	2.4	3.1	(NA)	(NA)	(NA)	117
Ecuador	993	1,127	181	[13][16]9.6	[13][16]3.1	[13]65	[13]46	11.5	[14]112
Egypt	[25]3,808	1,522	376	[13]4.1	[13]13.1	[13]8,831	[13]2,260	20.9	303
Finland	7,393	6,342	2,115	12.0	23.3	2,985	6,547	30.0	1,174
France	64,404	55,817	11,278	[14]30.5	[14]190.7	51,168	68,508	265.6	18,310
German Dem. Rep.	[8][17]13,196	[8]11,361	1,437	3.2	11.6	21,955	58,181	(NA)	2,600
Germany, Fed. Rep. of	87,782	102,032	9,265	29.0	110.9	36,451	59,219	180.3	20,274
Ghana	[13]805	[13]760	183	[15]2.3	[15]2.7	431	305	3.5	110
Greece	6,013	2,543	25,035	13.2	25.9	1,583	[26]844	43.5	747
Hong Kong	8,882	8,526	423	6.0	17.4	251	47	(NA)	167
Hungary	5,529	4,934	(NA)	(NA)	(NA)	13,365	22,552	10.7	866
India	5,515	5,424	5,094	[13][24]31.6	[13][24]30.6	[13][24]148,916	[13][24]134,874	83.0	1,397
Indonesia	5,673	8,547	1,046	[16]83.7	[16]12.0	3,258	717	65.5	684
Iran	12,894	23,480	683	[14][27]279.1	[27]13.6	[14]2,126	[14]4,917	37.1	[14]700
Iraq	3,470	8,841	749	36.0	[15]1.5	[13][24]704	[13][24]2,252	11.5	[13]160
Ireland	4,192	3,313	202	(NA)	(NA)	788	585	19.4	615
Israel	4,052	2,310	482	[28]3.7	[28]5.1	280	449	31.8	401
Italy	43,428	36,969	11,078	31.1	217.9	39,118	16,376	134.6	17,607
Ivory Coast	1,296	1,620	114	[13]3.2	[13]3.5	[14]918	[14]529	2.7	[20]148
Jamaica	913	633		[29]7.6	[29]2.6	69	159	16.8	[15]138
Japan	64,799	67,225	41,663	76.5	575.6	322,911	47,550	276.4	29,486
Korea, Rep. of	8,774	7,715	1,796	14.3	41.4	14,305	9,728	38.6	214
Kuwait	3,321	[30]9,842	1,107	[13][30]107.2	[13][30]2.5	(NA)	(NA)	12.3	321
Lebanon	[15]1,224	[13]497	214	[14]25.8	[14]4.4	[14]2	[14]42	48.5	[14]244
Liberia	399	476	73,477	20.5	1.3	(NA)	(NA)	(NA)	[14]22
Libya	3,950	8,438	459	[13]73.0	[13]9.6	(NA)	(NA)	9.4	[13]394
Malaysia	[31][22]3,355	[31][32]3,955	443	[29][31]7.2	[29][31]10.1	[31]1,139	[31]1,648	29.9	[31]599
Mexico	6,030	3,298	594	14.3	7.2	4,058	34,821	101.8	3,568
Morocco	2,618	1,262	137	17.3	7.9	828	3,143	19.5	493
Netherlands	39,574	40,167	5,920	82.5	255.8	8,218	2,700	95.2	4,118
New Zealand	3,254	2,795	164	[33]8.2	[33]10.0	[34]589	[34]3,649	48.7	1,427
Nigeria	8,199	10,565	182	[20]87.6	[20]4.7	[14][24]785	[14][24]972	10.2	[15]232

See footnotes at end of table.

No. 1572. FOREIGN TRADE AND TRANSPORTATION—SHIPPING, RAILWAYS, AVIATION, AND MOTOR VEHICLES, BY COUNTRY: 1976—Continued

[See text, p. 896, for general comments about the data. Statistical coverage of all these items varies considerably among countries; for details, see source]

COUNTRY	FOREIGN TRADE [1]		SHIPPING			RAIL TRAFFIC [4]		Civil aviation, kilometers flown [5] (mil.)	Motor vehicles in use [6] (1,000)
	Imports (mil. dol.)	Exports (mil. dol.)	Merchant shipping fleets [2] (1,000 gross tons)	Freight [3] (mil. metric tons)		Passenger kilometers (mil.)	Freight, net-ton kilometers (mil.)		
				Loaded	Unloaded				
Norway	11,109	7,917	27,944	[16] 34.2	[16] 22.0	1,997	2,709	52.3	1,170
Pakistan	2,134	1,144	483	[18] 2.4	[18] 7.7	[35] 12,957	[35] 8,677	35.3	[13] 288
Panama	838	227	15,631	1.1	[13] 4.8	(NA)	(NA)	(NA)	[13] 86
Peru	2,183	1,365	525	[16] 9.1	[16] 7.1	[13] 455	[13] 707	24.1	[14] 407
Philippines	3,953	2,574	1,018	11.2	16.4	780	40	41.5	667
Poland	[17] 13,867	11,017	3,263	35.8	23.6	42,799	130,857	26.0	1,757
Portugal	4,317	1,820	1,174	4.3	14.6	5,235	854	34.9	1,322
Romania	[17] 6,095	6,138	994	[28] 36 4.3	[28] 36 4.9	[13] 26 22,380	67,560	17.2	[36] [37] 45
Saudi Arabia	11,759	[30] 38,286	589	[14] 30 390.1	[15] 30 2.2	[14] 72	[14] 66	38.9	[14] 112
Singapore	9,070	6,585	5,482	20.3	37.7	(NA)	(NA)	40.8	193
South Africa	[17] 6,751	4,776	477	23.9	[28] 9.5	(NA)	[24] 38 69,336	58.3	2,990
Spain	17,463	8,727	6,028	23.8	84.2	16,686	9,842	135.8	6,443
Sri Lanka	548	527	91	1.6	4.3	[13] 39 2,898	[39] 282	4.4	143
Sweden	19,334	18,440	7,971	32.4	55.1	5,548	16,283	63.5	3,043
Switzerland	14,774	14,845	213	(NA)	(NA)	8,124	5,652	86.0	[14] 1,900
Syria	1,986	1,065	(NA)	24.7	7.4	166	305	9.8	119
Thailand	3,572	2,980	195	12.7	13.1	[13] 5,640	[13] 2,353	36.5	[13] 533
Trinidad and Tobago	1,976	2,213	(NA)	20.3	13.0	(NA)	(NA)	12.5	[13] 127
Tunisia	1,529	789	(NA)	5.0	4.7	[26] 641	1,277	11.5	[13] 170
Turkey	4,993	1,960	1,079	[13] 3.8	[13] 17.7	4,615	7,278	21.9	[14] 484
U.S.S.R.	[17] 38,108	37,169	20,668	[16] 134.6	[16] 41.2	315,061	3,295,399	(NA)	(NA)
United Kingdom	55,986	46,271	32,923	55.6	181.5	[13] 40 36,840	[40] 20,400	330.0	16,460
Uruguay	599	536	151	.6	2.5	372	372	3.6	[14] 237
Venezuela	[17] 6,023	9,149	543	[15] [16] 189.9	[13] [16] 6.7	[21] 42	[21] 15	40.4	[13] 1,325
Yugoslavia	7,367	4,878	1,944	4.0	16.2	9,941	21,017	30.6	1,923
Zaire	824	930	107	.5	.7	[15] 447	[15] 3,017	14.9	[14] 161
Zambia	[17] 780	1,046	(NA)	(NA)	(NA)	(NA)	(NA)	14.9	[14] 148

NA Not available. [1] Covers merchandise, including silver (except current coin); excludes gold and issued paper currency. Imports generally valued c.i.f. (cost, insurance, and freight); exports, f.o.b. (free on board). Generally includes government trade (including foreign aid, war reparations, and military goods), trade of foreign concessionaires, and postal trade. See source for "general trade" or "special trade" distinctions. Roughly half the countries shown fall into each category, thus affecting comparability. [2] As of June 30. Represents gross registered tons (see text, p. 668). Excludes vessels without mechanical means of propulsion; includes sailing vessels with auxiliary power. [3] Represents weight of all goods (including their packing) in external trade loaded to and unloaded from sea-going vessels of all flags at ports of country specified. For most countries, excludes bunkers, ships' stores, ballast, and transshipment (goods transshipped from an importing vessel to an exporting vessel). [4] Relates to domestic and international traffic on all railway lines within each country shown, excluding railways entirely within an urban unit and plantation, industrial mining, funicular, and cable railways. In general, passenger-kilometers include all passengers except military, government, and railway personnel when carried without revenue; ton-kilometers relate to freight net ton-kilometers and include all goods whether carried by fast or ordinary trains except service traffic, mail, baggage, and nonrevenue governmental stores. [5] Covers both domestic and international scheduled services operated by companies registered in each country. Includes supplementary services occasioned by overflow traffic on regularly scheduled trips and preparatory flights for new scheduled services. [6] Represents officially estimated number of vehicles in use. Includes passenger cars and commercial vehicles. For most countries shown, excludes 2- and 3-wheeled cycles and motorcycles, trams, trolley buses, ambulances, hearses, military vehicles, police and special purpose or government security vehicles, trailers, and farm tractors. [7] Excludes trade among each of the following countries: People's Republic of China, Mongolia, and Dem. People's Rep. of Korea. [8] Includes trade between the Federal Republic of Germany and German Democratic Republic. [9] Includes the Great Lakes. [10] Excludes traffic with U.S. Virgin Islands. [11] Includes Great Lakes and St. Lawrence River international traffic. [12] Class 1 railways only. [13] For 1975. [14] For 1974. [15] For 1973. [16] Excludes transit traffic and packing. [17] Imports f.o.b. [18] Year ending June 30. [19] Includes Luxembourg. [20] For 1972. [21] For 1971. [22] Source: U.S. Bureau of the Census. Data from Republic of China publications. [23] Includes vehicles no longer in circulation. [24] Year beginning Apr. 1. [25] Excludes crude petroleum imported without stated value. [26] Includes military traffic. [27] Year beginning Mar. 21. [28] Excludes petroleum. [29] Includes coastwise traffic. [30] Includes petroleum from Neutral Zone. [31] West Malaysia only. [32] Includes inter-trade between Malaysian states. [33] Million manifest tons. [34] Year ending Mar. 31. [35] Year beginning July 1. [36] For 1970. [37] Commercial vehicles only. [38] Includes Namibia. [39] Year ending Sept. 30. [40] Excludes Northern Ireland.

Source: Except as noted, Statistical Office of the United Nations, New York, N.Y., *Statistical Yearbook*. (Copyright.)

No. 1573.   Communications — Telephones, Mail, Newspapers, Radio, and Television, by Country

[See text, p. 896, for general comments about the data. For additional data qualifications for countries, see source]

COUNTRY	Telephones in use,[1] 1976 (1,000)	Telephones per 100 population, 1976	Pieces of mail sent, domestic,[2] 1976 (millions)	DAILY NEWSPAPERS,[3] 1975			RECEIVING SETS, 1975	
				Number	Circulation		Radios per 1,000 population [4]	Television sets per 1,000 population [5]
					Total (1,000)	Copies per 1,000 population		
World, total	398,182	9.8	(NA)	(NA)	(NA)	(NA)	(NA)	(NA)
United States	155,173	72.1	[6][7] 87,661	1,812	61,222	287	1,882	[8] 571
Algeria	273	1.5	211	4	285	17	[8] 198	30
Argentina	2,302	9.0	619	164	[9] 2,773	(NA)	[7] 838	[8] 180
Australia	[10] 5,502	[10] 39.5	[11][12] 2,044	70	5,320	394	[13][14] 211	[14] 274
Austria	2,281	30.4	[7] 1,394	30	2,405	320	[14] 342	[8][14] 247
Bangladesh	[11] 80	[11] .1	238	30	[15] 356	(NA)	(NA)	(NA)
Belgium	2,949	30.0	2,292	30	2,340	239	[8][14] 384	[14] 255
Bolivia	[7] 49	[7] .9	1	14	199	35	76	–
Brazil	4,036	3.5	1,683	[7] 280	[7] 4,050	[7] 39	158	100
Bulgaria	853	9.7	(NA)	13	2,023	232	[8][14] 262	[8][14] 168
Burma	32	.1	[11] 75	7	319	10	[8][14] 22	–
Canada	13,885	59.6	[16][17] 5,594	121	[18] 4,872	(NA)	959	411
Chile	451	4.6	[19] 143	47	(NA)	(NA)	[8] 298	[8] 72
China, People's Rep. of	(NA)	(NA)	(NA)	(NA)	(NA)	(NA)	[13] 16	[7] 1
China, Rep. of [20]	986	6.0	[21] 732	31	(NA)	(NA)	92	57
Colombia	1,769	7.0	[8] 119	40	[22] 1,248	(NA)	119	51
Costa Rica	127	6.2	[11][19] 28	6	174	88	74	79
Cuba	[8] 289	[8] 3.2	[11] 42	15	[23] 53	(NA)	224	64
Cyprus	77	12.0	18	12	[24] 78	(NA)	[14] 322	[8][14] 133
Czechoslovakia	2,743	18.3	[7][25] 2,216	29	4,436	300	[14] 265	[8][14] 245
Denmark	[26] 2,505	[26] 49.4	[16] 1,220	49	1,723	341	[14] 331	[14] 308
Dominican Republic	127	2.6	[11] 6	10	197	42	40	34
Ecuador	202	2.9	[11] 7	29	331	49	[13] 279	37
Egypt	[8] 503	[8] 1.4	[11] 133	[8] 14	[8] 773	[8] 21	138	17
El Salvador	60	1.4	21	12	[27] 234	(NA)	349	34
Ethiopia	73	.3	[7] 21	8	70	3	7	1
Finland	1,936	40.9	621	60	(NA)	(NA)	[14] 431	[14] 306
France	15,554	29.3	11,382	98	11,341	214	[14] 346	[14] 268
German Dem. Rep.	2,751	16.4	936	40	7,946	472	[8][14] 356	[14] 307
Germany, Fed. Rep. of	21,162	34.4	11,908	334	19,298	312	[14] 338	[14] 306
Ghana	62	.7	[16] 55	4	500	51	107	6
Greece	2,180	23.8	264	106	(NA)	(NA)	[8] 279	126
Guatemala	[7] 53	[7] 1.0	27	11	[28] 165	(NA)	45	19
Honduras	19	.7	[11] 15	8	[29] 99	(NA)	53	15
Hong Kong	1,132	25.3	[16][17] 149	82	(NA)	(NA)	574	[8][14] 185
Hungary	1,076	10.1	1,533	27	2,454	233	[8][14] 243	[14] 223
Iceland	91	41.1	[19] 17	5	94	431	[14] 294	234
India	[30] 2,096	[30] .3	[16] 7,109	835	9,383	16	[14] 24	[8][14] 1
Indonesia	314	.2	172	172	[31] 2,171	(NA)	[14] 37	2
Iran	782	2.3	[33] 858	20	484	15	[8] 249	51
Iraq	320	2.8	33	7	[33] 192	(NA)	113	[13] 37
Ireland	480	15.0	[8][16] 308	7	693	222	[8][14] 287	[14] 192
Israel	888	24.7	[16] 309	23	[34] 1,337	(NA)	[13][14] 222	[8][14] 180
Italy	15,246	27.1	[11] 5,781	78	6,296	113	[8][14] 228	[8][14] 213
Jamaica	109	5.4	77	3	[23] 131	(NA)	(NA)	54
Japan	[30] 48,431	[30] 42.6	[16] 12,186	[8] 108	[8] 57,820	[8] 526	465	235
Kampuchea, Dem.	[11] 71	[11] 11.2	[7] 1	16	(NA)	(NA)	14	[8] 3
Kenya	132	1.0	[11] 821	3	134	10	[14] 38	3
Korea, Republic of	1,643	4.6	643	36	6,010	173	[8] 144	[8][14] 48
Kuwait	140	13.6	[16] 5	[8] 6	[8] 80	[8] 86	[8] 231	[8] 196
Lebanon	[13] 192	[13] 6.8	[35] 26	33	[36] 283	(NA)	460	143
Luxembourg	158	44.2	46	7	[37] 161	(NA)	[14] 493	[8][14] 257
Madagascar	32	.4	[11] 22	[8] 9	[8] 59	[8] 9	[8] 112	1
Malaysia	330	2.7	[38] 315	31	1,038	87	[14] 38	[8][14] 33
Mexico	3,309	5.4	1,068	256	(NA)	(NA)	[8] 301	[8] 84
Morocco	204	1.5	79	9	360	21	[14] 92	[14] 27
Netherlands	5,412	39.1	3,602	[13] 95	[13] 4,100	[13] 315	[8][14] 284	[8][14] 259
New Zealand	1,610	51.5	[16] 629	39	(NA)	(NA)	876	[14] 259
Nigeria	121	.2	858	12	[24] 613	(NA)	79	[8] 2

See footnotes at end of table.

No. 1573. COMMUNICATIONS—TELEPHONES, MAIL, NEWSPAPERS, RADIO, AND TELEVISION, BY COUNTRY—Continued

[See text, p. 896, for general comments about the data. For additional data qualifications for countries, see source]

COUNTRY	Telephones in use,[1] 1976 (1,000)	Telephones per 100 population, 1976	Pieces of mail sent, domestic,[2] 1976 (millions)	DAILY NEWSPAPERS,[3] 1975 Number	Circulation Total (1,000)	Copies per 1,000 population	RECEIVING SETS, 1975 Radios per 1,000 population [4]	Television sets per 1,000 population [5]
Norway	1,476	36.6	[12] 914	80	1,657	412	[14] 319	[14] 255
Pakistan	[11] 240	[11] .3	502	102	[39] 358	(NA)	[14] 16	[8] 2
Panama	155	9.0	[8] 7	6	131	79	159	111
Paraguay	40	1.4	(NA)	8	[29] 73	(NA)	68	20
Peru	389	2.4	(NA)	35	(NA)	(NA)	131	32
Philippines	542	1.2	[35] 630	15	[40] 686	(NA)	44	[8] 17
Poland	2,753	8.0	[19] 1,730	44	8,429	248	[8] [14] 237	[14] 179
Portugal	1,119	11.9	388	30	612	70	[14] 173	[14] 65
Puerto Rico	515	14.4	(NA)	[8] 5	[8] 405	[8] 132	570	204
Romania	[8] 1,076	[8] 5.1	[11] 686	[8] 20	[8] 2,716	[8] 129	[14] 146	[14] 120
Saudi Arabia	160	2.1	[35] 31	[8] 11	[8] 96	[8] 11	28	14
Singapore	329	14.4	116	[8] 10	(NA)	(NA)	[14] 158	[14] 120
South Africa	2,064	8.1	1,355	24	1,776	70	92	–
Southern Rhodesia	190	2.9	103	3	116	18	40	11
Spain	8,605	23.9	3,882	115	3,491	98	228	184
Sri Lanka	[11] 72	[11] .5	[11] [16] 847	18	(NA)	(NA)	38	–
Sudan	60	.3	[19] 40	4	(NA)	(NA)	[8] [14] 77	6
Sweden	5,673	68.9	[19] 2,545	135	4,678	572	[14] 380	[14] 352
Switzerland	4,016	63.4	2,729	95	2,573	402	[14] 322	[14] 273
Syria	177	2.3	[7] 23	6	(NA)	(NA)	[13] 224	30
Thailand	334	.8	151	56	(NA)	(NA)	131	[8] 17
Trinidad and Tobago	70	6.5	[41] 21	3	[33] 100	(NA)	[8] [14] 235	[8] 94
Tunisia	135	2.4	68	4	190	33	49	[13] 10
Turkey	1,131	2.8	[11] 471	[13] 437	(NA)	(NA)	[14] 105	[8] 12
U.S.S.R	18,000	7.0	[42] 7,923	691	100,928	397	[8] 461	[8] 208
United Kingdom	22,012	39.4	[16] [42] 8,795	111	21,700	388	[8] 750	[14] 320
Uruguay	258	9.2	(NA)	30	[35] 637	(NA)	490	115
Venezuela	742	6.0	[8] 202	49	[43] 1,067	(NA)	171	107
Vietnam [44]	[7] 47	[7] .3	[7] 59	(NA)	(NA)	(NA)	(NA)	(NA)
Yugoslavia	1,431	6.5	[7] 1,096	26	1,896	89	[8] [14] 193	[8] [14] 132

– Represents zero. NA Not available. [1] Comprises public and private telephones installed which can be connected to a central exchange. [2] Items mailed for distribution within national territories. Comprises letters, postcards, printed matter, merchandise samples, small packets, and phonopost packets. Includes mail carried without charge, but excludes ordinary packages, and insured letters and boxes. [3] Publications containing general news and appearing at least 4 times a week; may range in size from a single sheet to 50 or more pages. Circulation data refer to average circulation per issue or number of printed copies per issue and include copies sold outside the country. [4] Data cover estimated number of receivers in use, except as noted, and apply to all types of receivers for radio broadcasts to the public, including receivers connected to a radio "redistribution system" but excluding television sets. [5] Estimated number of sets in use, except as noted. [6] Includes ordinary packages as well as insured letters and boxes. [7] For 1973. [8] For 1974. [9] 147 dailies. [10] Year ending June 30. [11] For 1975. [12] Year beginning July 1. [13] For 1970. [14] Number of licenses issued. [15] 27 dailies. [16] Year beginning April 1. [17] Excludes postcards. [18] 117 dailies. [19] Excluding small packets. [20] Source: U.S. Bureau of the Census. Data from Republic of China publications. [21] Refers to "mail delivered." [22] 34 dailies. [23] 2 dailies. [24] 10 or more dailies. [25] Domestic and foreign. [26] Includes Faeroe Islands and Greenland. [27] 8 dailies. [28] 7 dailies. [29] 4 dailies. [30] As of March 31 of the following year. [31] 55 dailies. [32] For 1971. [33] 5 dailies. [34] 19 dailies. [35] For 1969. [36] 17 dailies. [37] 6 dailies. [38] Data refer to West Malaysia only. [39] 18 dailies. [40] 12 dailies. [41] For 1972. [42] Excludes printed matter. [43] 30 dailies. [44] Data are for former Rep. of South Vietnam.

Source: Except as noted, Statistical Office of the United Nations, New York, N.Y., Statistical Yearbook. (Copyright.)

924 Comparative International Statistics

No. 1574. MILITARY EXPENDITURES, IN CURRENT AND CONSTANT (1975) DOLLARS: 1967 TO 1976

[In millions of dollars, except as indicated. See also tables 588. Data for expenditures and for GNP were based on local currencies which were deflated to constant 1975 local currency values before conversion to U.S. dollar equivalents. In general the rates used for conversion are the 1975 average par/market exchange rates as supplied by IBRD (International Bank for Reconstruction and Development). Data by country exclude countries with 1976 military expenditures less than 375 million dollars]

COUNTRY	CURRENT DOLLARS					CONSTANT (1975) DOLLARS			Per capita (dollars)		Percent of GNP [1]	
	1967	1970	1974	1975	1976	1967	1970	1976	1970	1976	1970	1976
World total [2]	201.1	241.6	332.7	370.8	398.9	318.7	331.9	380.4	88	90	6.3	5.8
Europe [2]	92.8	116.9	177.1	196.7	214.5	146.9	160.7	204.5	218	261	6.5	6.8
North America [2][3]	77.7	80.1	88.5	94.0	94.4	123.2	110.0	89.9	486	374	7.4	5.1
Latin America [2]	2.2	3.0	5.1	6.1	5.7	3.5	4.2	5.4	15	15	2.0	1.8
Near East [2][4]	4.1	6.6	14.4	18.8	25.2	6.5	9.1	24.0	90	197	9.0	13.8
East Asia [2]	19.8	28.6	38.7	44.0	46.3	31.4	39.3	44.3	30	29	5.7	4.6
South Asia [2]	1.5	2.0	2.8	3.7	4.1	2.3	2.7	3.9	3	5	2.9	3.4
Africa [2][4]	1.4	2.4	4.0	4.9	5.9	2.2	3.3	5.7	11	14	2.7	3.4
Oceania [2]	1.7	1.9	2.1	2.7	2.9	2.7	2.6	2.7	165	135	3.5	3.0
United States	75,700	77,900	85,600	90,900	91,000	120,000	107,000	86,700	522	400	7.8	5.4
Argentina	372	444	581	862	904	590	610	861	25	33	1.8	2.4
Australia	1,550	1,740	1,900	2,430	2,640	2,460	2,390	2,510	191	182	3.7	3.2
Austria	212	251	360	434	440	336	345	419	46	55	1.1	1.1
Belgium	866	1,100	1,610	1,900	2,100	1,370	1,520	2,000	157	204	2.9	3.1
Brazil	746	1,160	1,970	2,380	1,640	1,180	1,600	1,560	17	14	2.3	1.3
Bulgaria	745	934	1,580	1,700	1,810	1,180	1,284	1,724	151	196	8.4	8.7
Canada	2,010	2,160	2,860	3,070	3,370	3,190	2,970	3,210	139	139	2.4	2.0
China, People's Rep.	15,700	22,400	29,300	32,700	34,400	24,900	30,800	32,800	37	34	14.0	10.7
China, Rep. of	526	783	929	1,310	(NA)	833	1,080	(NA)	74	[5] 81	10.6	[5] 8.9
Cuba	170	229	339	389	(NA)	270	314	(NA)	37	[5] 42	4.9	[5] 6.2
Czechoslovakia	1,850	1,980	2,990	3,200	3,230	2,931	2,721	3,077	190	207	5.9	5.6
Denmark	470	552	799	919	955	745	759	909	154	178	2.4	2.5
Egypt	292	742	1,260	1,060	1,100	462	1,020	1,050	31	28	12.8	10.5
Finland	185	235	358	438	439	293	323	419	70	89	1.5	1.6
France	7,720	8,450	11,700	13,100	14,200	12,200	11,600	13,600	228	256	4.2	3.8
German Dem. Rep.	1,510	2,390	3,450	3,950	4,290	2,392	3,285	4,087	192	242	6.3	6.5
Germany, Fed. Rep.	8,650	9,340	14,500	15,300	16,000	13,700	12,800	15,300	211	245	3.3	3.4
Greece	355	568	770	1,360	1,200	563	780	1,140	89	126	4.7	5.1
Hungary	673	969	1,310	1,420	1,450	1,066	1,332	1,381	129	130	6.3	5.4
India	1,165	1,557	2,175	2,857	3,149	1,845	2,140	3,000	4	5	3.0	3.4
Indonesia	267	497	704	1,110	1,110	423	683	1,060	5	7	3.3	3.6
Iran	837	1,480	5,250	7,770	7,830	1,330	2,040	7,460	68	207	7.8	12.2
Iraq	421	746	1,530	1,390	1,610	666	1,030	1,530	110	134	12.9	10.6
Israel	644	1,640	3,260	4,010	4,320	1,020	2,250	4,120	755	1,141	25.0	32.2
Italy	2,540	2,990	4,750	4,750	4,980	4,030	4,110	4,740	77	84	2.7	2.7
Japan	1,500	2,280	4,090	4,670	5,070	2,380	3,140	4,830	30	43	.8	.9
Korea, Dem. Peo. Rep.	472	701	698	720	1,000	747	963	953	68	56	15.8	9.6
Korea, Rep. of	207	332	703	958	1,380	328	456	1,320	14	36	3.9	6.1
Kuwait	192	255	565	410	502	304	351	478	468	451	3.1	3.1
Malaysia	120	146	353	421	424	191	201	404	19	31	3.2	4.0
Mexico	167	226	378	527	505	265	311	482	6	8	.7	.8
Netherlands	1,440	1,772	2,555	2,887	3,178	2,281	2,435	3,028	187	219	3.4	3.3
Nigeria	252	732	840	1,170	1,537	400	1,006	1,464	18	23	5.9	5.3
Norway	452	587	777	913	997	716	807	950	208	235	3.5	3.2
Oman	(NA)	148	299	698	844	(NA)	204	804	311	1,020	15.2	40.1
Pakistan	274	389	552	696	688	434	534	655	4	9	5.8	5.7
Peru	181	222	399	566	700	287	306	667	23	42	3.3	5.2
Philippines	67	94	245	361	397	106	130	378	3	8	1.1	2.3
Poland	2,220	2,830	4,490	5,010	5,450	3,520	3,890	5,190	120	151	6.5	5.9
Portugal	448	592	1,030	779	658	709	814	627	93	74	6.5	3.9
Romania	1,070	1,460	1,950	2,240	2,330	1,695	2,007	2,220	99	103	5.9	4.4
Saudi Arabia	1,270	1,050	1,270	1,940	7,460	2,000	1,450	7,110	269	932	6.3	19.4
South Africa	388	478	1,070	1,450	1,950	615	657	1,860	31	69	2.4	5.4
Spain	1,260	1,720	2,560	3,010	3,090	2,000	2,360	2,950	70	82	3.1	2.9
Sweden	1,290	1,560	2,060	2,220	2,350	2,040	2,140	2,240	266	271	3.5	3.2
Switzerland	710	834	1,070	1,090	1,180	1,120	1,150	1,120	183	171	2.1	2.0
Syria	313	340	506	886	873	496	467	832	75	109	11.8	14.7
Thailand	119	232	336	373	422	188	319	402	9	9	3.1	2.7
Turkey	604	775	1,180	1,640	2,340	957	1,070	2,230	30	53	4.3	5.6
U.S.S.R.	50,000	67,000	103,000	115,000	127,000	79,200	92,100	121,000	379	471	12.1	12.6
United Kingdom	6,940	7,270	10,900	11,500	12,600	11,000	10,000	12,000	180	213	4.8	5.2
Venezuela	257	288	466	545	535	408	396	510	36	39	1.9	1.8
Yugoslavia	562	768	1,370	1,650	(NA)	890	1,060	(NA)	52	[5] 77	4.5	[5] 5.0

NA Not available.   [1] Military expenditure as percent of gross national product.
[2] In billions of dollars, except per capita and percent. World and regional totals include countries not listed.   [3] U.S. and Canada only.   [4] Egypt assigned to Near East rather than to Africa.   [5] 1975 data.

Source: U.S. Arms Control and Disarmament Agency, World Military Expenditures and Arms Transfers, annual.

No. 1575. Armed Forces Personnel—Total and per 1,000 Persons, by Country: 1967 to 1976

[Personnel data as of July. Armed Forces refer to active-duty military personnel, including paramilitary forces where those forces resemble regular units in their organization, equipment, training, or mission. Reserve forces are not included]

COUNTRY	ARMED FORCES PERSONNEL (1,000)						ARMED FORCES PER 1,000 POPULATION					
	1967	1970	1973	1974	1975	1976	1967	1970	1973	1974	1975	1976
World total	23,600	24,900	26,100	27,300	26,500	26,200	6.67	6.63	6.66	6.84	6.51	6.26
Europe	9,270	9,600	9,690	9,960	9,920	9,710	12.90	13.00	13.10	13.10	12.90	12.50
North America	3,490	3,170	2,340	2,250	2,210	2,080	15.90	14.00	10.10	9.59	9.32	8.65
Latin America	1,050	1,120	1,210	1,250	1,300	1,330	4.10	4.03	4.02	4.04	4.08	4.07
Near East	844	988	1,280	1,410	1,680	1,750	9.04	9.73	11.60	12.40	14.40	14.40
East Asia	6,420	7,130	8,030	8,990	7,850	7,840	5.30	5.50	5.79	6.35	5.44	5.27
South Asia	1,900	2,080	2,320	2,410	2,460	2,360	2.57	2.61	3.00	3.04	3.03	2.79
Africa	564	764	936	965	1,000	1,090	1.94	2.43	2.75	2.76	2.79	2.93
Oceania	85	100	84	81	83	84	5.66	6.32	5.06	4.79	4.83	4.15
United States	3,380	3,070	2,250	2,170	2,130	2,000	17.00	15.00	10.70	10.20	9.95	9.22
Argentina	160	140	160	150	160	155	6.93	5.79	6.35	5.86	6.18	5.92
Australia	72	86	71	68	70	71	6.10	6.88	5.42	5.11	5.19	5.14
Austria	60	55	60	60	50	40	8.20	7.40	7.98	7.95	6.63	5.28
Belgium	115	110	105	100	87	87	12.00	11.40	10.80	10.20	8.89	8.86
Brazil	330	375	420	435	455	450	3.86	4.04	4.16	4.18	4.25	4.09
Bulgaria	176	175	177	174	175	177	21.20	20.60	20.53	20.05	20.02	20.14
Canada	105	95	85	80	77	78	5.15	4.46	3.85	3.56	3.38	3.34
China, People's Rep. of	2,710	2,850	3,250	4,300	4,300	4,300	3.46	3.39	3.62	4.69	4.60	4.45
China, Rep. of	547	522	503	493	504	475	39.90	35.80	32.45	31.20	31.30	28.27
Cuba	110	140	140	140	120	125	13.70	16.50	15.70	15.40	12.97	13.27
Czechoslovakia	259	222	223	218	210	210	18.10	15.50	15.30	14.80	14.20	14.10
Denmark	50	45	45	35	35	35	10.30	9.13	8.95	6.93	6.90	6.85
Egypt	220	255	390	410	400	400	7.12	7.68	11.02	11.33	10.78	10.53
Finland	40	40	40	40	40	36	8.68	8.68	8.58	8.55	8.51	7.63
France	595	570	560	580	575	585	12.00	11.20	10.70	11.00	11.00	11.00
German Dem. Rep.	201	202	202	215	220	220	11.80	11.80	11.90	12.70	13.00	13.00
Germany, Fed. Rep	490	510	505	505	495	495	8.25	8.40	8.15	8.15	7.99	7.93
Greece	170	180	180	180	191	200	19.50	20.50	20.16	20.09	21.20	22.10
Hungary	156	146	140	125	118	118	15.30	14.20	13.50	11.90	11.20	11.10
India	1,420	1,550	1,620	1,620	1,670	1,440	2.76	2.82	2.76	2.70	2.72	2.23
Indonesia	347	358	310	270	260	257	2.99	2.86	2.33	1.99	1.87	1.80
Iran	210	245	285	310	385	420	7.61	8.14	8.66	9.14	11.03	11.67
Iraq	90	95	105	110	155	190	10.60	10.10	10.10	10.28	13.96	16.67
Israel	75	105	130	160	190	190	27.70	35.20	39.63	47.48	55.23	52.63
Italy	430	435	520	500	500	432	8.16	8.10	9.47	9.03	8.96	7.69
Japan	231	236	233	237	237	236	2.29	2.27	2.16	2.15	2.14	2.11
Korea, Dem. People's Rep. of	383	438	470	470	470	500	29.50	30.80	30.32	29.38	28.48	29.41
Korea, Rep. of	612	645	634	634	630	610	20.30	19.90	18.27	17.91	17.40	16.53
Kuwait	8	10	14	15	25	25	14.00	13.30	15.64	15.81	24.75	23.58
Malaysia	40	58	70	75	76	80	4.00	5.37	5.98	6.25	6.13	6.15
Mexico	80	80	80	85	95	100	1.77	1.60	1.45	1.49	1.60	1.63
Netherlands	120	115	115	105	112	112	9.52	8.85	8.58	7.78	8.18	8.12
Nigeria	35	200	305	300	270	270	.68	3.63	5.12	4.89	4.29	4.18
Norway	35	35	35	35	35	39	9.23	9.02	8.84	8.77	8.73	9.65
Oman	3	4	8	10	12	18	5.00	6.09	11.10	13.46	15.67	22.84
Pakistan	351	390	466	500	502	604	2.90	2.98	7.13	7.43	7.24	8.00
Peru	70	80	75	90	95	100	5.74	6.02	5.14	6.00	6.13	6.29
Philippines	45	59	63	90	120	140	1.31	1.57	1.54	2.13	2.76	3.12
Poland	305	314	328	366	435	435	9.62	9.66	9.82	10.90	12.80	12.70
Portugal	195	230	260	310	217	60	21.80	26.40	30.40	36.30	25.50	7.07
Romania	190	211	192	218	220	220	9.84	10.40	9.23	10.40	10.40	10.20
Saudi Arabia	50	65	75	80	95	95	10.10	12.10	12.76	13.22	15.25	12.45
South Africa	50	40	40	45	50	59	2.54	1.86	1.69	1.85	1.99	2.20
Spain	370	365	365	375	375	368	11.30	10.80	10.46	10.65	10.53	10.22
Sweden	70	75	75	75	75	66	8.89	9.32	9.21	9.19	9.16	7.99
Switzerland	25	25	25	25	25	25	4.13	3.99	3.89	3.87	3.85	3.81
Syria	80	75	115	130	230	230	14.10	12.00	16.67	18.23	31.21	30.22
Thailand	151	175	233	221	227	228	4.52	4.79	5.84	5.39	5.38	5.10
Turkey	530	540	545	535	453	460	16.20	15.30	14.27	13.61	11.24	11.00
U.S.S.R.	3,900	4,300	4,500	4,500	4,600	4,600	16.50	17.70	18.00	17.90	18.10	17.90
United Kingdom	425	375	370	350	345	344	7.74	6.76	6.61	6.24	6.15	6.11
Venezuela	40	45	50	50	55	55	4.45	4.13	4.17	4.03	4.17	4.17
Vietnam	418	452	630	665	643	637	20.20	20.50	26.92	27.82	26.46	13.76
Yugoslavia	297	257	258	262	270	275	15.00	12.60	12.29	12.36	12.68	12.79

Source: U.S. Arms Control and Disarmament Agency, World Military Expenditures and Arms Transfers, annual.

No. 1576. MILITARY SHIPS OF SELECTED COUNTRIES, BY TYPE: 1978

[Includes vessels in reserve and ships under construction. Figures for miscellaneous craft and therefore total craft are based on different criteria from country to country]

COUNTRY	Total	Aircraft carriers	Submarines	Cruisers	Destroyers and frigates	Corvettes, fast attack, and patrol craft	Mine-warfare forces	Amphibious forces	Oilers and supply ships	Miscellaneous
United States	1,854	23	155	37	202	13	25	169	137	1,093
Argentina	121	1	6	2	18	21	6	33	13	21
Australia	84	1	6	-	13	27	3	7	9	18
Belgium	71	-	-	-,	4	6	43	-	4	14
Brazil	134	1	10	-	16	38	6	22	19	22
Bulgaria	87	-	2	-	2	17	18	20	6	22
Burma	89	-	-	-	2	75	-	-	2	10
Canada	1 203	-	3	-	20	13	-	-	12	72
Chile	64	-	3	2	11	12	-	11	8	17
China, People's Rep. of	2,131	-	80	-	27	946	23	511	99	445
China, Rep. of	191	-	2	-	33	28	22	51	13	42
Colombia	55	-	6	-	8	23	-	-	4	14
Cuba	89	-	-	-	1	67	-	7	6	8
Denmark	102	-	6	-	10	65	15	-	2	4
Dominican Republic	43	-	-	-	3	22	2	3	4	9
Ecuador	35	-	2	-	3	15	-	2	3	10
Egypt	156	-	14	-	10	87	14	19	-	12
Finland	140	-	-	-	4	31	18	13	-	74
France	441	3	34	2	54	34	55	58	33	168
German Dem. Republic	237	-	-	-	1	102	52	20	12	50
Germany, Fed. Rep. of	319	-	24	-	32	46	58	41	38	80
Greece	206	-	11	-	16	54	16	68	14	27
India	107	1	8	2	27	30	8	7	10	14
Indonesia	107	-	5	-	14	49	7	11	16	5
Iran	75	-	3	-	11	23	5	4	8	21
Iraq	65	-	-	-	-	59	-	3	-	3
Israel	94	-	3	-	-	68	-	12	-	11
Italy	339	-	12	4	27	18	59	61	14	144
Japan	208	-	15	-	51	31	38	6	15	52
Korea, Dem. People's Rep. of	573	-	17	-	2	379	-	70	-	105
Korea, Rep. of	117	-	-	-	17	52	9	21	16	2
Malaysia	83	-	-	-	3	40	6	3	2	29
Mexico	119	-	-	-	8	80	17	3	4	8
Netherlands	137	-	6	-	30	11	46	11	9	24
New Zealand	18	-	-	-	4	4	-	-	4	6
Norway	109	-	15	-	5	62	14	7	3	3
Pakistan	54	-	10	1	7	19	7	-	3	7
Peru	68	-	10	4	7	16	-	4	13	14
Philippines	236	-	-	-	8	66	2	110	7	43
Poland	235	-	4	-	1	62	44	38	7	79
Portugal	62	-	3	-	13	18	4	14	6	4
Romania	100	-	-	-	-	80	20	-	-	-
South Africa	36	-	3	-	4	10	8	-	3	8
Spain	324	2	12	-	36	34	24	93	23	100
Sweden	396	-	20	-	12	80	86	147	8	43
Thailand	144	-	-	-	6	54	16	49	8	11
Turkey	263	-	14	-	14	84	41	57	17	36
U.S.S.R.	2,827	3	471	40	229	575	417	290	299	503
United Kingdom	499	3	34	12	73	23	41	70	46	197
Venezuela	74	-	6	-	14	27	-	6	3	18
Yugoslavia	182	-	7	-	1	76	31	26	11	30

- Represents zero.　　¹ Includes Coast Guard.

Source: Franklin Watts, Inc., New York, N.Y., *Jane's Fighting Ships*, annual. Edited by John E. Moore. (Copyright by Macdonald and Jane's Publishers Ltd., London, England.)

No. 1577. MILITARY SHIPS, BY TYPE GROUPS—SELECTED COUNTRIES: 1970 TO 1978

[Includes vessels in reserve and ships under construction]

YEAR AND ITEM	United States	China, People's Rep. of	France	Germany, Fed. Rep. of	Italy	Japan	U.S.S.R.	United Kingdom
1970: Aircraft carriers	33	–	2	–	–	–	–	4
Submarines	157	33	20	12	8	10	395	35
Cruisers	32	–	2	–	4	–	27	3
Destroyers, frigates	329	23	46	21	21	40	206	81
Corvettes, fast attack and patrol craft	40	440	28	46	36	30	700	8
Minewarfare forces	168	27	94	77	61	37	300	56
Amphibious forces	163	70	19	24	26	4	230	71
1976: Aircraft carriers	25	–	3	–	–	–	3	3
Submarines	155	75	31	24	11	18	406	36
Cruisers	39	–	2	–	3	–	39	12
Destroyers, frigates	202	35	62	29	23	33	208	76
Corvettes, fast attack and patrol craft	34	926	33	46	23	36	722	21
Minewarfare forces	37	22	50	58	45	46	506	45
Amphibious forces	169	517	36	50	62	6	160	70
1977: Aircraft carriers	23	–	3	–	–	–	3	2
Submarines	150	73	41	24	14	17	432	35
Cruisers	34	–	2	–	4	–	40	12
Destroyers, frigates	191	25	61	29	32	51	272	71
Corvettes, fast attack and patrol craft	14	942	45	46	23	26	574	19
Minewarfare forces	33	18	49	58	55	40	406	46
Amphibious forces	205	503	38	41	61	6	286	70
1978: Aircraft carriers	23	–	3	–	–	–	3	3
Submarines	155	80	34	24	12	15	471	34
Cruisers	37	–	2	–	4	–	40	12
Destroyers, frigates	202	27	54	32	27	51	229	73
Corvettes, fast attack and patrol craft	13	946	34	46	18	31	575	23
Minewarfare forces	25	23	55	58	59	38	417	41
Amphibious forces	169	511	58	41	61	6	290	70

– Represents zero.

Source: Franklin Watts, Inc., New York, N.Y., *Jane's Fighting Ships,* annual; edited by John E. Moore. (Copyright by Macdonald and Jane's Publishers Ltd., London, England.)

No. 1578. FOREIGN EXCHANGE RATES: 1965 TO 1977

[In U.S. cents per unit of foreign currency]

COUNTRY	Currency unit	1965	1970	1971	1972	1973	1974	1975	1976	1977
Australia	Dollar	222.78	111.36	113.61	119.23	141.94	143.89	130.77	122.15	110.82
Austria	Schilling	3.87	3.87	4.00	4.32	5.16	5.36	5.75	5.57	6.05
Belgium	Franc	2.01	2.01	2.06	2.27	2.58	2.57	2.73	2.59	2.79
Canada	Dollar	92.74	95.80	99.02	100.94	99.98	102.26	98.30	101.41	94.11
Denmark	Krone	14.46	13.33	13.51	14.38	16.60	16.44	17.44	16.55	16.66
France	Franc	20.40	18.09	18.15	19.83	22.54	20.80	23.35	20.94	20.34
Germany	Deutsche mark	25.04	27.42	28.77	31.36	37.76	38.72	40.73	39.74	43.09
India	Rupee	20.94	13.23	13.34	13.25	12.07	12.46	11.93	11.15	11.41
Ireland	Pound	279.59	239.59	244.42	250.08	245.10	234.03	222.16	180.48	174.49
Italy	Lira	.16	.16	.16	.17	.17	.15	.15	.12	.11
Japan	Yen	.28	.28	.29	.33	.37	.34	.34	.34	.37
Mexico	Peso	8.01	8.01	8.01	8.00	8.00	8.00	8.00	6.92	4.42
Netherlands	Guilder	27.77	27.65	28.65	31.15	35.98	37.37	39.63	37.85	40.75
Norway	Krone	13.98	13.99	14.21	15.18	17.41	18.12	19.18	18.33	18.79
Portugal	Escudo	3.48	3.50	3.55	3.70	4.11	3.95	3.93	3.32	2.62
South Africa	Rand	139.27	139.24	140.29	129.43	143.88	146.98	136.47	114.85	114.99
Spain	Peseta	1.67	1.43	1.44	1.56	1.72	1.73	1.74	1.50	1.33
Sweden	Krona	19.39	19.28	19.59	21.02	22.97	22.56	24.14	22.96	22.38
Switzerland	Franc	23.11	23.20	24.33	26.19	31.70	33.69	38.74	40.01	41.71
United Kingdom	Pound	279.59	239.59	244.42	250.08	245.10	234.03	222.16	180.48	174.49

Source: Board of Governors of the Federal Reserve System, *Federal Reserve Bulletin,* monthly.

No. 1579. Foreign Exchange Rates, by Country: 1975 to 1977

[National currency units per U.S. dollar. As of December 31. Represents mid-point market quotations to extent available. For countries with fixed relationships to a third currency, represents exchange rates of the third currency times the fixed relationships. For currencies not quoted in exchange markets, represents official rates. For countries with multiple exchange rate systems, represents rate applicable to principal trade transactions]

COUNTRY	Currency unit	Exchange Rate 1975	1976	1977
Afghanistan	Afghani	45.0	45.0	45.0
Algeria	Dinar	4.13	4.36	4.04
Argentina	Peso	60.9	274.5	597.5
Australia	Dollar	.795	.920	.876
Austria	Schilling	18.5	16.8	15.1
Barbados	Dollar	2.00	2.00	2.01
Belgium	Franc	39.5	36.0	32.9
Benin	CFA Franc	224	248	235
Bolivia	Peso	20.0	20.0	20.0
Botswana	Pula	.870	.870	.828
Brazil[1]	Cruzeiro	9.07	12.3	16.1
Burma	Kyat	6.68	6.73	7.09
Burundi	Franc	78.8	90.0	90.0
Cameroon	CFA Franc	224	248	235
Canada	Dollar	1.02	1.01	1.09
Central African Rep.	CFA Franc	224	248	235
Chad	CFA Franc	224	248	235
Chile	Peso	8.50	17.4	28.0
Colombia[1]	Peso	33.1	36.5	38.1
Congo	CFA Franc	224	248	235
Costa Rica	Colon	8.57	8.57	8.57
Cyprus	Pound	.393	.412	.382
Denmark	Krone	6.18	5.79	5.78
Dominican Rep.	Peso	1.00	1.00	1.00
Ecuador	Sucre	25.0	25.0	25.0
Egypt: Official rate	Pound	.391	.391	.391
El Salvador	Colon	2.50	2.50	2.50
Ethiopia	Birr	2.09	2.09	2.09
Finland	Markka	3.85	3.77	4.02
France	Franc	4.49	4.97	4.71
Gabon	CFA Franc	224	248	235
Gambia	Dalasi	1.98	2.35	2.10
Germany, Fed. Rep. of	D. Mark	2.62	2.36	2.11
Ghana	New Cedi	1.15	1.15	1.15
Greece	Drachma	35.7	37.0	35.5
Guatemala	Quetzal	1.00	1.00	1.00
Guinea	Syli	21.1	21.2	20.3
Guyana	Dollar	2.55	2.55	2.55
Haiti	Gourde	5.00	5.00	5.00
Honduras	Lempira	2.00	2.00	2.00
Iceland	Krona	171	190	213
India: Central rate	Rupee	8.94	8.88	8.21
Indonesia	Rupiah	415	415	415
Iran	Rial	69.3	70.6	70.5
Iraq	Dinar	.295	.295	.295
Ireland	Pound	.494	.587	.523
Israel	Pound	7.10	8.75	15.39
Italy	Lira	684	875	872
Ivory Coast	CFA Franc	224	248	235
Jamaica	Dollar	.909	.909	.909
Japan	Yen	305	293	240
Jordan	Dinar	.330	.331	.315
Kenya	Shilling	8.25	8.31	7.95
Korea, Rep. of	Won	484	484	484
Kuwait	Dinar	.294	.287	.280
Lebanon	Pound	2.43	2.93	3.06
Lesotho	Rand	.870	.870	.870
Liberia	Dollar	1.00	1.00	1.00
Libya	Dinar	.296	.296	.296
Luxembourg	Franc	39.5	36.0	32.9
Malawi	Kwacha	.900	.907	.868
Malaysia	Ringgit	2.59	2.54	2.37
Maldives	Rupee	7.71	8.83	(NA)
Mali	Franc	449	497	471
Malta	Pound	.404	.427	.395
Mauritania	Ouguiya	45.2	43.6	46.1
Mauritius	Rupee	6.59	6.64	6.35
Mexico	Peso	12.5	20.0	22.7
Morocco	Dirham	4.18	4.48	4.33
Nepal	Rupee	12.5	12.5	12.5
Netherlands	Guilder	2.69	2.46	2.28
New Zealand	NZ Dollar	.958	1.05	.981
Nicaragua	Cordoba	7.03	7.03	7.03
Niger	CFA Franc	224	248	235
Nigeria	Naira	.627	.631	.651
Norway	Krone	5.59	5.19	5.14
Pakistan	Rupee	9.93	9.93	9.93
Panama	Balboa	1.00	1.00	1.00
Paraguay[1]	Guarani	126	126	126
Peru	Sol	45.0	69.4	130.4
Philippines	Peso	7.51	7.44	7.38
Portugal	Escudo	27.5	31.5	39.9
Rwanda	Franc	92.8	92.8	92.8
Saudi Arabia	Riyal	3.53	3.53	3.51
Senegal	CFA Franc	224	248	235
Sierra Leone	Leone	.988	1.17	1.05
Singapore	Dollar	2.49	2.46	2.34
Somalia	S. Shilling	6.30	6.30	6.30
South Africa	Rand	.870	.870	.870
Spain	Peseta	59.8	68.3	80.9
Sri Lanka	Rupee	7.71	8.83	15.56
Sudan	Pound	.348	.348	.348
Swaziland	Lilangeni	.870	.870	.870
Sweden	Krona	4.39	4.13	4.67
Switzerland[2]	Franc	2.62	2.45	2.01
Syria[1]	Pound	3.70	3.95	3.95
Tanzania	Shilling	8.26	8.32	7.96
Thailand	Baht	20.4	20.4	20.4
Togo	CFA Franc	224	248	235
Trinidad and Tobago	Dollar	2.37	2.40	2.40
Tunisia	Dinar	.425	.431	.412
Turkey	Lira	15.2	16.7	19.4
Uganda	Shilling	8.26	8.31	7.95
United Kingdom	Pound	.494	.587	.525
Upper Volta	CFA Franc	224	248	235
Uruguay[1]	New Peso	2.73	4.00	5.41
Venezuela[1]	Bolivar	4.29	4.29	4.29
Yemen Arab Rep.	Rial	4.56	4.56	4.56
Yemen, People's Dem. Rep. of	Dinar	.345	.345	.345
Yugoslavia	Dinar	18.0	18.2	18.4
Zaire	Zaire	.500	.861	.831
Zambia	Kwacha	.643	.793	.760

NA Not available. [1] Selling. [2] Buying.

Source: International Monetary Fund, *International Financial Statistics*, monthly.

No. 1580. TOTAL RESERVE ASSETS, 1965 TO 1977, AND BY TYPE OF ASSETS, 1977

[In millions of U.S. dollars. Assets include gold stock, holdings of convertible foreign currencies, special drawing rights, and reserve position in International Monetary Fund]

COUNTRY	1965	1970	1973	1974	1975	1976	1977 Total assets	1977 Gold stock	1977 Currency holdings[1]
All countries [2]	70,865	93,250	185,682	220,593	227,655	258,296	318,534	43,162	243,512
United States	15,450	14,487	14,378	16,058	15,883	18,320	19,392	11,800	18
Algeria	184	339	1,143	1,689	1,353	1,987	1,917	234	1,588
Argentina	236	673	1,318	1,315	452	1,608	3,331	177	3,064
Australia	1,317	1,693	5,697	4,269	3,256	3,170	2,384	326	1,829
Austria	1,305	1,751	2,874	3,430	4,439	4,410	4,244	893	2,839
Bahrain	23	71	74	142	296	442	510	6	498
Belgium	2,334	2,847	5,100	5,345	5,797	5,206	5,761	1,805	2,515
Brazil	484	1,187	6,415	5,272	4,034	6,541	7,256	64	6,787
Canada	3,037	4,679	5,768	5,825	5,326	5,843	4,608	936	2,315
Chile	138	389	180	102	109	460	484	58	360
China, Rep. of	300	622	1,124	1,191	1,169	1,607	1,447	102	1,345
Colombia	96	206	534	449	521	1,158	1,821	74	1,623
Denmark	587	484	1,324	935	877	915	1,671	82	1,383
Ecuador	46	83	241	350	286	515	671	17	644
Egypt	193	167	363	356	294	339	534	103	402
Ethiopia	77	71	177	275	288	306	225	12	204
Finland	289	460	619	634	470	498	570	39	480
France	6,343	4,960	8,529	8,852	12,593	9,728	10,194	4,322	4,694
Germany, F.R. of	7,430	13,610	33,171	32,398	31,034	34,801	39,737	5,029	30,625
Greece	250	310	1,047	936	931	925	1,020	159	845
Guatemala	68	78	212	202	304	511	690	22	640
India	600	1,006	1,142	1,325	1,373	3,074	5,184	312	4,691
Indonesia	21	160	807	1,492	586	1,499	2,492	7	2,376
Iran	251	208	1,236	8,383	8,897	8,833	12,266	160	10,824
Iraq	234	462	1,553	3,273	2,727	4,601	6,996	176	6,745
Ireland	409	697	1,025	1,267	1,532	1,837	2,372	21	2,216
Israel	643	449	1,815	1,901	1,109	1,070	1,571	49	1,495
Italy	4,800	5,352	6,436	6,941	4,774	6,654	11,608	3,525	7,939
Japan	2,152	4,840	12,246	13,519	12,815	16,605	23,261	920	20,126
Jordan	140	256	304	347	492	491	678	35	627
Korea, Rep. of	146	610	1,094	1,056	1,550	2,961	4,307	6	4,288
Kuwait	124	203	501	1,399	1,655	1,929	2,990	107	2,006
Lebanon	251	386	862	1,674	1,579	1,677	1,961	392	1,566
Libya	246	1,590	2,127	3,616	2,198	3,209	4,890	103	4,779
Malaysia	470	664	1,345	1,618	1,524	2,472	2,866	74	2,688
Malta	79	158	325	402	500	622	735	15	698
Mexico	538	744	1,355	1,395	1,533	1,253	1,723	74	1,592
Morocco	99	140	266	417	377	491	532	27	495
Netherlands	2,413	3,241	6,547	6,957	7,109	7,387	8,065	2,323	3,899
New Zealand	173	258	893	640	428	492	445	2	401
Nigeria	239	222	583	5,626	5,609	5,203	4,262	27	3,742
Norway	476	813	1,575	1,929	2,237	2,229	2,200	46	1,757
Oman	(NA)	129	107	194	239	309	401	4	372
Pakistan	229	190	480	461	406	532	518	69	414
Peru	175	336	568	968	467	330	(NA)	(NA)	(NA)
Philippines	193	251	1,038	1,504	1,358	1,640	1,524	45	1,456
Portugal	938	1,504	2,839	2,354	1,534	1,302	1,377	1,177	195
Saudi Arabia	726	662	3,877	14,285	23,319	27,025	30,034	131	27,212
Singapore	430	1,012	2,286	2,812	3,007	3,364	3,858	–	3,846
South Africa	600	1,012	1,234	1,159	1,216	940	829	413	368
Spain	1,422	1,817	6,772	6,485	6,090	5,284	6,590	613	5,918
Sweden	972	761	2,529	1,736	3,077	2,491	3,668	253	3,011
Switzerland	3,444	5,132	8,520	9,011	10,428	12,993	13,830	3,541	9,814
Syria	45	55	413	500	735	361	(NA)	(NA)	(NA)
Thailand	739	906	1,306	1,858	1,775	1,893	1,915	102	1,735
Trinidad and Tobago	29	43	47	390	751	1,014	1,483	1	1,433
Tunisia	36	60	307	418	385	371	358	6	325
Turkey	141	431	2,120	1,861	1,064	1,123	774	154	620
United Arab Emirates	(NA)	(NA)	92	453	989	1,929	824	24	683
United Kingdom	3,004	2,827	6,476	6,939	5,459	4,230	21,057	945	19,504
Uruguay	179	175	240	232	218	315	459	152	296
Venezuela	819	1,021	2,412	6,513	8,861	8,578	8,214	479	6,558
Yemen Arab Rep	(NA)	(NA)	127	199	338	720	1,240	(Z)	1,231
Yugoslavia	103	140	1,338	1,147	871	2,049	2,104	64	2,027

- Represents zero.   NA Not available.   Z Less than $500,000.
[1] Holdings of convertible foreign currencies.   [2] Includes countries not shown separately.
Source: International Monetary Fund, *International Financial Statistics*, monthly with annual supplements.

No. 1581. NET FLOW OF FINANCIAL RESOURCES TO DEVELOPING COUNTRIES, BY ORIGIN AND TYPE OF RESOURCE: 1965 TO 1976

[In billions of U.S. dollars, Net flow covers loans, grants, and grant-like flows minus amortization on loans. Developing countries cover countries designated by U.N. as developing (see table 1549), Greece, Malta, Portugal, Spain, and Yugoslavia. Official development assistance covers all flows to developing countries and multilateral institutions provided by official agencies, including State and local governments, or by their executive agencies, which are administered with the promotion of economic development and welfare of developing countries as their main objective and whose financial terms are intended to be concessional in character with grant element of at least 25 percent. Other official flows cover export credits and portfolio investment from the official sector]

ORIGIN AND TYPE OF RESOURCE	1965	1970	1972	1973	1974	1975	1976
Development Assistance Committee countries [1]	[2] 10.3	15.8	19.5	22.6	22.1	40.4	40.5
Official development assistance	5.9	6.8	8.5	9.4	11.3	13.6	13.7
Bilateral grants [3]	3.7	3.3	4.4	4.5	5.3	6.3	6.5
Bilateral loans	1.8	2.4	2.3	2.6	2.9	3.5	3.0
Multilateral contributions	.3	1.1	1.9	2.3	3.0	3.8	4.2
Other official flows	.3	1.1	1.6	2.5	2.2	3.0	3.3
Private flows	4.1	7.0	8.3	9.4	7.4	22.4	22.2
Direct investment	2.5	3.7	4.2	4.7	1.1	10.5	7.6
Private export credits	.8	2.2	1.4	1.2	2.5	4.1	5.4
Portfolio investment	.9	1.2	2.7	3.5	3.7	7.8	9.2
Private voluntary agencies	(NA)	.9	1.0	1.4	1.2	1.3	1.4
Organization of Petroleum Exporting Countries [4]	(NA)	(NA)	.5	1.7	6.0	8.2	8.0
Official development assistance	(NA)	(NA)	.4	1.3	3.4	5.5	5.2
Other official flows	(NA)	(NA)	.1	.4	2.5	2.7	2.8
Centrally-planned economies [5]	(NA)	(NA)	.9	1.0	.9	.6	.6
Official development assistance	(NA)	(NA)	.8	.9	.8	.6	.5
Other official flows	(NA)	(NA)	.1	.1	.1	.1	.1
Euro-lending [6]	(NA)	.6	1.4	8.5	8.0	9.5	[7] 22.7
Total net flow to developing countries, by DAC [1] Country	10.3	15.8	19.5	22.6	22.1	40.4	40.5
United States	5.4	6.3	7.4	6.3	4.3	17.5	12.3
Australia	.1	.4	.4	.4	.5	.6	.5
Austria	(Z)	.1	.1	.1	.2	.2	.4
Belgium	.2	.3	.4	.5	.6	.9	1.2
Canada	.2	.6	1.0	1.1	1.7	2.0	2.5
Denmark	(Z)	.1	.1	.2	.2	.3	.5
Finland	(X)	(Z)	(Z)	(Z)	.1	.1	.1
France	1.3	1.8	2.1	2.8	3.4	3.9	5.3
Germany, Fed. Rep. of	.7	1.5	1.8	1.8	3.2	5.0	5.3
Italy	.3	.7	.7	.6	.4	1.6	1.5
Japan	.5	1.8	2.7	5.8	3.0	2.9	4.0
Netherlands	.2	.4	.7	.6	.9	1.3	1.7
New Zealand	(X)	(Z)	(Z)	(Z)	.1	.1	.1
Norway	(Z)	.1	.1	.1	.2	.3	.5
Sweden	.1	.2	.3	.4	.6	.8	1.1
Switzerland	.2	.1	.2	.3	.4	.7	1.3
United Kingdom	1.0	1.2	1.5	1.5	2.4	2.4	2.2

NA Not available. X Not applicable. Z Less than $50 million.
[1] Includes flows to OPEC countries (see footnote 4). Comprises as donors Australia, Austria, Belgium, Canada, Denmark, Finland, France, Federal Republic of Germany, Italy, Japan, Netherlands, New Zealand, Norway, Sweden, Switzerland, United Kingdom, and United States.   [2] Excludes Finland and New Zealand.
[3] Includes "grant-like" flows denominated in recipients' currencies.   [4] Algeria, Iran, Iraq, Kuwait, Libya, Nigeria, Qatar, Saudi Arabia, United Arab Emirates, and Venezuela.   [5] Bulgaria, Czechoslovakia, German Democratic Republic, Hungary, Poland, Romania, and U.S.S.R.   [6] Loans by private banks in a currency other than that of their country of origin. Through 1975 estimate based on published syndicated bank loans.
[7] Net change in outstanding foreign currency assets of banking sector; includes short-term transactions of some 50 percent.

Source: Organisation for Economic Co-operation and Development, OECD Observer, July 1977, and unpublished data.

No. 1582. UN AND WORLD HEALTH ORGANIZATION—MEMBER ASSESSMENTS: 1978

[In thousands of U.S. dollars, except as indicated]

COUNTRY	UNITED NATIONS (UN)		WHO [1]		COUNTRY	UNITED NATIONS (UN)		WHO [1]	
	Percent	Amount	Percent	Amount		Percent	Amount	Percent	Amount
Gross budget	(X)	498,513	(X)	187,215	Kuwait	.15	732	.16	291
Other income [2]	(X)	−10,741	(X)	−5,600	Laos	.01	49	.02	36
Total assessments	100.0	487,771	100.0	181,615	Lebanon	.03	146	.03	54
					Lesotho	.01	49	.02	36
United States	25.00	121,943	25.00	45,404	Liberia	.01	49	.02	36
Afghanistan	.01	49	.02	36	Libya	.16	780	.17	309
Albania	.01	49	.02	36	Luxembourg	.04	195	.04	73
Algeria	.10	488	.10	182	Madagascar	.01	49	.02	36
Angola	.02	98	.02	36	Malawi	.01	49	.02	36
Argentina	.84	4,097	.81	1,471	Malaysia	.09	439	.09	163
Australia	1.54	7,512	1.48	2,688	Maldive Islands	.01	49	.02	36
Austria	.64	3,122	.61	1,108	Mali	.01	49	.02	36
Bahamas	.01	49	.02	36	Malta	.01	49	.02	36
Bahrain	.01	49	.02	36	Mauritania	.01	49	.02	36
Bangladesh	.04	195	.04	73	Mauritius	.01	49	.02	36
Barbados	.01	49	.02	36	Mexico	.79	3,853	.76	1,380
Belgium	1.08	5,268	1.03	1,871	Monaco	(3)	(3)	.02	36
Benin	.01	49	.02	36	Mongolia	.01	49	.02	36
Bhutan	.01	49	(3)	(3)	Morocco	.05	244	.05	91
Bolivia	.01	49	.02	36	Mozambique	.02	98	.02	36
Botswana	.01	49	.02	36	Namibia	(3)	(3)	.01	18
Brazil	1.04	5,073	1.02	1,852	Nepal	.01	49	.02	36
Bulgaria	.14	683	.13	236	Netherlands	1.42	6,926	1.33	2,415
Burma	.01	49	.02	36	New Zealand	.26	1,268	.28	509
Burundi	.01	49	.02	36	Nicaragua	.01	49	.02	36
Byelorussian S.S.R	.41	2,000	.40	726	Niger	.01	49	.02	36
Cameroon	.01	49	.02	36	Nigeria	.13	634	.13	236
Canada	3.04	14,828	2.87	5,212	Norway	.45	2,195	.42	763
Cape Verde	.01	49	.02	36	Oman	.01	49	.02	36
Central African Rep	.01	49	.02	36	Pakistan	.07	341	.06	109
Chad	.01	49	.02	36	Panama	.02	98	.02	36
Chile	.09	439	.09	163	Papua New Guinea	.01	49	.02	36
China, People's Rep	5.50	26,827	5.37	9,753	Paraguay	.01	49	.02	36
Colombia	.11	537	.11	200	Peru	.06	293	.06	109
Comoros	.01	49	.02	36	Philippines	.10	488	.10	182
Congo	.01	49	.02	36	Poland	1.30	6,780	1.40	2,543
Costa Rica	.02	98	.02	36	Portugal	.19	927	.20	363
Cuba	.11	537	.13	236	Qatar	.02	98	.02	36
Cyprus	.01	49	.02	36	Romania	.24	1,171	.26	472
Czechoslovakia	.84	4,097	.85	1,544	Rwanda	.01	49	.02	36
Denmark	.64	3,122	.61	1,108	Sao Tome	.01	49	.02	36
Dominican Republic	.02	98	.02	36	Saudi Arabia	.23	1,122	.24	437
Ecuador	.02	98	.02	36	Seychelles	.01	49	(3)	(3)
Egypt	.08	390	.08	145	Senegal	.01	49	.02	36
El Salvador	.01	49	.02	36	Sierra Leone	.01	49	.02	36
Equatorial Guinea	.01	49	(3)	(3)	Singapore	.08	390	.08	145
Ethiopia	.01	49	.02	36	Socialist Rep. of				
Fiji	.01	49	.02	36	Vietnam	(3)	(3)	.03	54
Finland	.44	2,146	.41	745	Somalia	.01	49	.02	36
France	5.82	28,388	5.53	10,043	South Africa	.42	2,049	.40	726
Gabon	.01	49	.02	36	Southern Rhodesia	(3)	(3)	.01	18
Gambia	.01	49	.02	36	Spain	1.53	7,463	1.52	2,761
German Dem. Rep	1.33	6,487	1.31	2,379	Sri Lanka	.02	98	.02	36
Germany, Fed. Rep. of	7.70	37,558	7.52	13,657	Sudan	.01	49	.02	36
Ghana	.02	98	.02	36	Surinam	.01	49	.02	36
Greece	.35	1,707	.38	690	Swaziland	.01	49	.02	36
Grenada	.01	49	.02	36	Sweden	1.24	6,048	1.16	2,107
Guatemala	.02	98	.02	36	Switzerland	(3)	(3)	.94	1,707
Guinea	.01	49	.02	36	Syria	.02	98	.02	36
Guinea-Bissau	.01	49	.02	36	Tanzania	.01	49	.02	36
Guyana	.01	49	.02	36	Thailand	.10	488	.10	182
Haiti	.01	49	.02	36	Togo	.01	49	.02	36
Honduras	.01	49	.02	36	Tonga	(3)	(3)	.02	36
Hungary	.33	1,610	.34	617	Trinidad and Tobago	.03	146	.02	36
Iceland	.02	98	.02	36	Tunisia	.02	98	.02	36
India	.68	3,317	.70	1,271	Turkey	.30	1,463	.30	545
Indonesia	.14	683	.14	254	Uganda	.01	49	.02	36
Iran	.40	1,951	.43	781	Ukrainian S.S.R	1.53	7,463	1.50	2,724
Iraq	.08	390	.10	182	U.S.S.R	11.60	56,581	11.33	20,577
Ireland	.15	732	.14	254	United Arab Emir	.07	341	.08	145
Israel	.23	1,122	.23	418	United Kingdom	4.52	22,047	4.44	8,064
Italy	3.38	16,487	3.21	5,830	Upper Volta	.01	49	.02	36
Ivory Coast	.02	98	.02	36	Uruguay	.04	195	.04	73
Jamaica	.02	98	.02	36	Venezuela	.39	1,902	.40	726
Japan	8.64	42,143	8.49	15,419	Western Samoa	.01	49	.02	36
Jordan	.01	49	.02	36	Yemen (Peo. Dem.				
Kampuchea, Dem	.01	49	.02	36	Rep.)	.01	49	.02	36
Kenya	.01	49	.02	36	Yemen (Arab Rep.)	.01	49	.02	36
Korea, Dem. Peo. Rep	(3)	(3)	.05	91	Yugoslavia	.39	1,902	.38	690
Korea, Republic of	(3)	(3)	.13	236	Zaire	.02	98	.02	36
					Zambia	.02	98	.02	36

X Not applicable. [1] World Health Organization.
[2] Miscellaneous income and adjustments to prior year budgets. [3] Nonmember.
Source: U.S. Dept. of State, Bureau of International Organizational Affairs, unpublished data.

APPENDIX I

Historical Series—Index to Tables in Which *Historical Statistics* Series Appear

[The most recent historical supplement to the *Statistical Abstract* is the bicentennial edition, *Historical Statistics of the United States, Colonial Times to 1970* (see inside back cover). Listed below are statistical time series (identified by number) appearing in this edition, for which tables in the *Statistical Abstract* present comparable figures. Historical series are listed only where related or comparable data are available for one or more years later than 1970. In a few instances, it may be necessary to combine figures shown in the *Abstract* to obtain totals comparable to the series shown in *Historical Statistics*]

Historical Statistics series	1978 Abstract table number	Historical Statistics series	1978 Abstract table number	Historical Statistics series	1978 Abstract table number	Historical Statistics series	1978 Abstract table number
A		**C**		**F**		**H—Con.**	
A 6–8	2			F 1	709	H 421–429	210
A 9–22	3			F 5	710	H 442–476	219
A 23–25	5	C 1–10	44	F 9	709	H 487–507	236
A 29–41	5	C 25–75	12	F 10–16	711	H 513–519	211
A 43–72	22	C 76–78	1164	F 17–30	714	H 520–530	236
A 73–90	21	C 89	120	F 31	712	H 531–534	249
A 91–104	38	C 89–119	123	F 32–70	708	H 535–544	242
A 105–118	40	C 120–142	121	F 130–143	715	H 572–581	283
A 119–134	29	C 143–157	122	F 144–162	716	H 587–597	258
A 135–142	40	C 144	130	F 163–185	719	H 598–601	257
A 143–149	27	C 149–157	134	F 192–209	720	H 602–617	226
A 158–159	114	C 158–160	130	F 226–237	721	H 648–661	229
A 160–171	51	C 162–167	138	F 262–286	722	H 669–688	230
A 172	10	C 168	137	F 297–348	724	H 689	208
A 195–196	10	C 169–179	139	F 349–376	777	H 690–692	262
A 197–198	36	C 180	137	F 422–469	777	H 699–705	261
A 199–201	35	C 195–295	43	F 480–527	780	H 705	262
A 204–209	30	C 296–331	413	F 528–534	1365	H 710	261
A 210–263	340			F 552–565	727	H 716–738	273
A 264–275	15			F 566–594	728	H 747–749	273
A 276–287	16	**D**				H 752–756	257
A 288–319	56			**G**		H 767–771	1061
A 320–334	60	D 11–19	645	G 1–8	729	H 774	1061
A 335–349	58	D 29–41	644	G 16–23	729	H 776–780	1061
A 353–358	61	D 49–62	655	G 24–30	744	H 793–799	75
A 359–371	72	D 63–74	657	G 85–102	734	H 806–828	393
B		D 85–86	645	G 124–128	735	H 829–835	396
B 1–5	78	D 87–101	667	G 179–188	736	H 836–848	397
B 5–7	79	D 116–126	671	G 193–195	744	H 849–861	399
B 8–10	81	D 127–141	673	G 197–199	729	H 862–864	401
B 11	80	D 142–151	676	G 205–256	737	H 865–870	402
B 12–19	81	D 182–232	679	G 257–268	749	H 871	401
B 20–27	82	D 233–682	681	G 416–469	717	H 872	402
B 28–35	91	D 689–704	677	G 851–856	197	H 874	401
B 49–66	89	D 739–764	695	G 881–915	200	H 875–876	403
B 107–115	98	D 802–810	676	**H**		H 877	401
B 116–125	99	D 818–829	690	H 1–47	517	H 878–893	400
B 136–147	106	D 877–892	676	H 51–56	523	H 899–920	414
B 142	78	D 893–904	695	H 57–69	525	H 921–940	412
B 149–166	108	D 913	270	H 70–114	542	H 946–951	415
B 163–165	112	D 918–919	162	H 115–124	545	H 952–961	286
B 167–173	102	D 921–926	617	H 125–171	524	H 971–986	295
B 181–192	102	D 933–934	698	H 172–185	526	H 987–998	301
B 214–220	114	D 946–951	698	H 186–196	523	H 999–1011	305
B 221–235	142	D 970–976	702	H 197–229	532	H 1012–1027	309
B 222–232	143	D 977–1021	704	H 238–242	528	H 1028–1062	315
B 248–261	140	D 1022–1028	662	H 245–259	534	H 1063–1078	319
B 262–272	141			H 262–270	536	H 1079–1096	320
B 275–290	151			H 271–286	541	H 1097–1111	321
B 291–303	189			H 287–304	539	H 1112–1118	323
B 305–318	165	**E**		H 305–317	557	H 1119–1124	327
B 331–344	165			H 318–331	555	H 1125–1140	328
B 359–362	169	E 1–22	783	H 332–345	559	H 1155–1167	337
B 381–388	168	E 23–24	785	H 346–354	563		
B 389–400	166	E 23–29	787	H 355–367	562	**J**	
B 401–412	147	E 73–86	786	H 392	554	J 1–2	339
B 413–422	167	E 123–134	788	H 393–397	553	J 3–6	378
B 428–443	177	E 135–173	792	H 398–411	579	J 8	386
B 444–447	196	E 187–202	801	H 413–417	208	J 10–15	385
B 448–450	198	E 203–211	806	H 420	236	J 16–19	388
						J 26–32	385

Historical Series—Index to Tables in Which *Historical Statistics* Series Appear—Continued

[See headnote, p. 932]

Appendix I

Historical Series—Index to Tables in Which *Historical Statistics* Series Appear—Continued

[See headnote, p. 932]

Historical Statistics series	1978 Abstract table number	Historical Statistics series	1978 Abstract table number	Historical Statistics series	1978 Abstract table number	Historical Statistics series	1978 Abstract table number
S—Con.		**V**		**X—Con.**		**Y**	
S 133–146....	1023	V 1–12......	915	X 61–105.....	854	Y 79–83......	810
S 147–159....	1027	V 20–30......	958	X 64–105.....	854	Y 84–134....	811
S 160–175....	1032	V 21–24......	914	X 114–147....	850	Y 135–186....	812
S 190–204....	1029	V 38.........	955	X 192........	849	Y 189–198....	824
S 205–218....	1028	V 42–53......	916	X 229........	849	Y 199–203....	825
		V 66–67......	925	X 393–409....	881	Y 204–210....	823
T		V 78–107....	932	X 410–417....	884	Y 211–214....	821
		V 108–127....	934	X 423........	887	Y 220–271....	819
T 1–14.......	1458	V 129–136....	936	X 444–453....	890	Y 272–307....	504
T 15–28......	1460	V 137........	448	X 454–455....	892	Y 308–317....	458
T 43–47......	1459	V 141–166....	926	X 474–491....	893	Y 318–331....	460
T 43–57......	1470	V 167–183....	938	X 492–498....	895	Y 335–338....	424
T 79–196.....	1469	V 182–196....	448	X 499–500....	900	Y 339–342....	416
T 197–219....	1465	V 197–212....	1023	X 505–506....	900	Y 343–351....	420
T 245–271....	1464	V 306–332....	930	X 507–509....	901	Y 358–373....	434
T 274–287....	1475			X 517–530....	896	Y 381–392....	447
T 280–371....	1477	**W**		X 536–539....	899	Y 393–411....	437
T 375–383....	1474			X 551–560....	876	Y 412–439....	442
T 391–443....	1480	W 14.........	678	X 588–609....	866	Y 458–460....	586
T 444–471....	1489	W 17.........	678	X 687–688....	867	Y 461........	449
T 472–484....	1488	W 19.........	678	X 716–724....	860	Y 466–487....	422
		W 22–25.....	677	X 717–721....	863	Y 493–494....	449
U		W 30–54.....	678	X 741–755....	862	Y 497........	450
		W 62–65.....	678	X 796–805....	855	Y 500–504....	450
U 1–25......	1497	W 67–81.....	1213	X 813–820....	858	Y 505–637....	477
U 26–39......	1501	W 82–95.....	995	X 821–833....	867	Y 638–651....	478
U 41–46......	1502	W 96–108....	942	X 834–844....	869	Y 652–848....	477
U 47–74......	1504	W 109–125...	1039	X 864–878....	871	Y 856–903....	601
U 75–186....	1506	W 126.......	1042	X 879–889....	902	Y 904–916....	603
U 190–195....	1511	W 142.......	1040	X 890–907....	903	Y 917–926....	613
U 207–212....	1524	W 144–160...	1044	X 908–917....	905	Y 927–942....	614
U 225–248....	1514	W 167.......	1052	X 918........	911	Y 943–956....	624
U 249–263....	1517			X 923........	911	Y 957–970....	623
U 264–273....	1523			X 928........	911	Y 971–983....	630
U 274–294....	1520	**X**		X 933........	911	Y 984–997....	633
U 295–316....	1521			X 940........	911	Y 998–999....	631
U 317–352....	1516	X 1–23.......	853	X 957–962....	910	Y 1010–1027..	636

APPENDIX II
Metropolitan Area Concepts and Components

Statistics for metropolitan areas shown in the *Statistical Abstract* represent areas designated by the U.S. Office of Federal Statistical Policy and Standards (OFSPS) as standard metropolitan statistical areas (SMSA's). Definitions of the SMSA's in terms of their geographic components are presented in Office of Management and Budget (OMB), *Standard Metropolitan Statistical Areas*, 1975, Revised Edition. (OFSPS) issues amendments to update this publication when changes in SMSA definitions are made. See also U.S. National Bureau of Standards, *Metropolitan Statistical Areas*, Federal Information Processing Standards Publication (FIPS Pub. 8–4, June 30, 1974).

The complete list of areas, their components, and population totals, which follows tables A, B, and C below (see p. 938) is based on the SMSA definitions in effect on Dec. 31, 1977. On that date, there were 281 SMSA's (including 4 in Puerto Rico).

The general concept of a metropolitan area is one of an integrated economic and social unit with a large population nucleus. Standard definitions of metropolitan statistical areas were first issued by the then Bureau of the Budget (predecessor of OMB) in 1949, under the designation "Standard Metropolitan Areas"; the present designation was adopted in 1959. In October 1977 the Office of Federal Statistical Policy and Standards was transferred to the U.S. Department of Commerce.

The criteria for the establishment and definition of SMSA's have undergone several modifications since 1949. The current criteria were adopted in March 1976; they provide that each SMSA must include at least:

(a) One city with 50,000 or more inhabitants, or
(b) A city with at least 25,000 inhabitants, which, together with contiguous places (incorporated or unincorporated) having population densities of at least 1,000 persons per square mile, has a combined population of 50,000 and constitutes for general economic and social purposes a single community, provided that the county or counties in which the city and contiguous places are located has a total population of at least 75,000. (In New England, the cities and towns qualifying for inclusion in an SMSA must have a total population of at least 75,000.)

In addition to the central city or cities, the criteria provide that the SMSA include the county in which the central city is located, and adjacent counties that are determined to be metropolitan in character and economically and socially integrated with the county of the central city, according to specific rules. (In New England, as noted below, the units comprising the area are cities and towns rather than counties.) The largest city in each SMSA is designated a "central city"; in addition, there may be up to two additional central cities if certain criteria are met. With two exceptions (Nassau-Suffolk, N.Y. and Northeast Pennsylvania), the title of each SMSA includes the names of its central city or cities. An SMSA may include other cities of 50,000 or more besides its central cities, and may include territory in more than one State.

Recent previous editions (1967–1975) of the *Statistical Abstract* have included a section entitled "Metropolitan Area Statistics," which presented numerous items of statistical information for SMSA's. That section was omitted beginning with the 1976 edition. In its place, a much more comprehensive *State and Metropolitan Area Data Book* will be issued on a biennial basis; the first issue is scheduled for release in 1979.

New England SMSA's and NECMA's. Because SMSA's in New England are defined in terms of cities and towns, rather than counties, some statistical data that are available only for counties cannot be compiled for individual New England SMSA's. Therefore, for New England areas data are shown for both New England County Metropolitan Areas (NECMA's) and SMSA's wherever possible. The NECMA's provide a county version of the New England areas defined following criteria adopted by OMB in March 1976 which are identical to those used to define SMSA's in the other States. NECMA's do not replace New England SMSA's as the standard areas.

Standard Consolidated Statistical Areas.—Standard consolidated statistical areas (SCSA's), defined under criteria adopted by OMB in August 1975, include two or more contiguous SMSA's which meet certain criteria of size, urban character, integration, and contiguity of urbanized areas.

Effect of changes in SMSA definitions.—Changes in the definitions of SMSA's since 1949 have included the recognition of new areas as, for example, cities reached 50,000 population, and large counties (or towns in New England) were added to existing SMSA's. Also, several formerly separate SMSA's have been merged, and occasionally territory has been transferred from one SMSA to another or (in rare instances) from an SMSA to nonmetropolitan territory. Comparisons of SMSA figures over time may be affected in cases where the SMSA definitions were changed. To maintain comparability, data for an earlier period have been revised in this volume, where possible, to reflect the SMSA boundaries of the more recent period. However, this could not always be done. For data based on a sample survey, in particular, it is usually not possible to reflect changes in SMSA definitions that occurred after the survey was made.

In the three tables that follow, data are given for SMSA's as defined for specified dates, thereby indicating the extent of change in population and land area resulting from revisions in definitions.

TABLE A. NUMBER, POPULATION, AND LAND AREA OF SMSA'S AS DEFINED AT SPECIFIED DATES: 1940 TO 1976

[The differences in population shown here for each year in the successive columns of the table result entirely from net expansion of metropolitan territory through changes in the SMSA definitions. The differences in population shown for each SMSA definition (on the successive lines of the table) result entirely from population changes within that territory, unaffected by changes in SMSA definitions. The changes in 1970 land area result entirely from net expansion of SMSA territory. All data include Alaska and Hawaii and exclude Puerto Rico. Subtraction of any line of the table from the line below will show the net effect of change in population and land area undergone by the SMSA's as the result of changes in definitions between the specified dates. Such changes typically occurred throughout the period, not on any single date, and may have included subtractions from, as well as additions to, SMSA territory. Census population data do not include corrections made since publication; therefore, data will not strictly agree with those shown in other tables of this *Abstract*. The area data for the 1950 and 1960 census definitions of SMSA's differ from the data published in those censuses because they are based on a remeasurement of land areas made during the 1960's, and also reflect changes in inland water area occurring up to 1970]

SMSA DEFINITION AS OF—	Number of SMSA's	POPULATION (1,000)						Land area, 1970 (1,000 sq. mi.)
		1940, Apr. 1	1950, Apr. 1	1960, Apr. 1	1970, Apr. 1	1975, July 1	1976, July 1	
1950 census (Mar. 1952)_____	169	[1] 69,535	[2] 84,854	106,345	122,132	124,644	125,204	207
1960 census (Nov. 1960)_____	212	[3] 72,845	89,317	[4] 112,885	130,925	134,839	135,586	310
1964 (Aug. 31) [5]_____	217	74,869	91,644	115,876	134,639	139,005	139,826	350
1968 (Jan. 31) [6]_____	230	76,408	93,630	118,414	137,915	142,728	143,623	378
1970 census (Feb. 28, 1971)__	243	77,155	94,579	[7] 119,593	[8] 139,419	144,373	145,291	[9] 388
1974 (Apr. 30) [10]_____	265	[11] 82,038	[12] 100,220	[13] 126,614	148,132	154,214	155,295	491
1977 (Dec. 31)_____	277	82,805	101,109	127,675	149,414	155,651	156,754	510

[1] Corresponds to total 1940 population for 1950 SMSA's published in 1950 census (69,279,675), with addition of Honolulu SMSA, and corrected by subtracting population (3,194) of Colonial Heights town erroneously included in Richmond SMSA.
[2] Corresponds to total SMSA population for 1950 published in 1950 census (84,500,680), plus Honolulu SMSA.
[3] Corresponds to total 1940 population for 1960 SMSA's published in 1960 census (72,834,468), corrected by adding population (13,277) erroneously omitted from Stamford SMSA (remainder of Stamford town), and subtracting population (3,194) of Colonial Heights town erroneously included in Richmond SMSA.
[4] Corresponds to total SMSA population for 1960 published in 1960 census (112,885,178), corrected by subtracting population (39) erroneously included in Franklin County, Ohio (Columbus SMSA).
[5] SMSA's as defined for the 1963 economic censuses.   [6] SMSA's as defined for the 1967 economic censuses.
[7] Corresponds to total 1960 population for 1970 SMSA's published in 1970 census (119,594,754), corrected by subtracting 1,256 population from Lawrence-Haverhill SMSA; this represented an addition to the 1960 population of Andover town made subsequent to the original census tabulations, and therefore not reflected in State or national totals.   [8] Corresponds to total SMSA population for 1970 published in 1970 census.
[9] Corresponds to total SMSA land area published in 1970 census (387,616 square miles), corrected by subtracting 15 square miles erroneously included in Roanoke SMSA and 3 square miles included due to erroneous addition of area data.   [10] SMSA's as defined for the 1972 economic censuses.
[11] Includes estimated 1939 population (4,429) of Anchorage Census Division, as defined in 1970.
[12] Includes estimated 1950 population (32,060) of Anchorage Census Division, as defined in 1970.
[13] Includes 1960 population (82,833) of Anchorage Census Division, as defined in 1970.

Source: U.S. Bureau of the Census, 1940–1970, *U.S. Census of Population*, vol. I; thereafter, *Current Population Reports*, series P-25, forthcoming report.

TABLE B. NONMETROPOLITAN POPULATION AND LAND AREA AT SPECIFIED DATES: 1940 TO 1976

[See headnote for table A, p. 936. Nonmetropolitan population and land area are equivalent to that portion of the total national population and land area not included within SMSA's at the dates specified]

NONMETROPOLITAN POPULATION AS OF—	POPULATION (1,000)						Land area, 1970 (1,000 sq. mi.)
	1940, Apr. 1	1950, Apr. 1	1960, Apr. 1	1970, Apr. 1	1975, July 1	1976, July 1	
1950 census (Mar. 1952)	62,630	66,472	72,979	81,080	88,530	89,665	3,329
1960 census (Nov. 1960)	59,320	62,009	66,438	72,287	78,336	79,283	3,227
1964 (Aug. 31)	57,295	59,682	63,447	68,573	74,169	75,042	3,187
1968 (Jan. 31)	55,756	57,696	60,910	65,297	70,446	71,246	3,159
1970 census (Feb. 28, 1971)	55,010	56,747	59,730	63,793	68,801	69,577	3,149
1974 (Apr. 30)	50,127	51,106	52,709	55,080	58,961	59,574	3,046
1977 (Dec. 31)	49,360	50,217	51,648	53,798	57,523	58,114	3,026

Source: U.S. Bureau of the Census, 1940–1970, *U.S. Census of Population*, vol. I; thereafter, *Current Population Reports*, series P-25, forthcoming report.

TABLE C. PERCENT OF TOTAL U.S. POPULATION AND PERCENT OF LAND AREA INSIDE SMSA's AS DEFINED AT SPECIFIED DATES: 1940 TO 1976

[See headnote for table A, p. 936]

PERCENT AS OF—	POPULATION						Land area, 1970
	1940, Apr. 1	1950, Apr. 1	1960, Apr. 1	1970, Apr. 1	1975, July 1	1976, July 1	
1950 census (Mar. 1952)	52.6	56.1	59.3	60.1	58.5	58.3	5.9
1960 census (Nov. 1960)	55.1	59.0	63.0	64.4	63.3	63.1	8.8
1964 (Aug. 31)	56.6	60.6	64.6	66.3	65.2	65.1	9.9
1968 (Jan. 31)	57.8	61.9	66.0	67.9	67.0	66.8	10.7
1970 census (Feb. 28, 1971)	58.4	62.5	66.7	68.6	67.7	67.6	11.0
1974 (Apr. 30)	62.1	66.2	70.6	72.9	72.3	72.3	13.9
1977 (Dec. 31)	62.7	66.8	71.2	73.5	73.0	73.0	14.4

Source: U.S. Bureau of the Census, 1940–1970, *U.S. Census of Population*, vol. I; thereafter, *Current Population Reports*, series P-25, forthcoming report.

APPENDIX II

Standard Metropolitan Statistical Areas as of December 31, 1977

Area	1976 Population (1,000)
Abilene, Tex	132.2
Callahan County	9.5
Jones County	16.4
Taylor County	106.3
Akron, Ohio	669.6
Portage County	133.0
Summit County	536.5
Albany, Ga	102.5
Dougherty County	92.8
Lee County	9.7
Albany-Schenectady-Troy, N.Y	796.8
Albany County	287.3
Montgomery County	55.1
Rensselaer County	151.7
Saratoga County	146.6
Schenectady County	156.2
Albuquerque, N. Mex	392.8
Bernalillo County	369.1
Sandoval County	23.8
Alexandria, La	138.5
Grant Parish	14.8
Rapides Parish	123.7
Allentown-Bethlehem-Easton, Pa.-N.J	623.3
Carbon County, Pa	52.2
Lehigh County, Pa	264.7
Northampton County, Pa	224.5
Warren County, N.J	81.9
Altoona, Pa	133.9
Blair County	133.9
Amarillo, Tex	155.4
Potter County	92.3
Randall County	63.1
Anaheim-Santa Ana-Garden Grove, Calif	1,755.6
Orange County	1,755.6
Anchorage, Alaska	179.5
Anchorage Census Div	179.5
Anderson, Ind	138.4
Madison County	138.4
Ann Arbor, Mich	248.3
Washtenaw County	248.3
Anniston, Ala	112.6
Calhoun County	112.6
Appleton-Oshkosh, Wis	285.9
Calumet County	28.7
Outagamie County	125.8
Winnebago County	131.4
Asheville, N.C	167.6
Buncombe County	150.6
Madison County	16.9

Area	1976 Population (1,000)
Atlanta, Ga	1,804.8
Butts County	12.4
Cherokee County	40.2
Clayton County	133.9
Cobb County	244.7
De Kalb County	453.7
Douglas County	45.7
Fayette County	19.0
Forsyth County	22.3
Fulton County	571.0
Gwinnett County	120.6
Henry County	29.0
Newton County	32.2
Paulding County	22.0
Rockdale County	29.0
Walton County	29.2
Atlantic City, N.J	189.0
Atlantic County	189.0
Augusta, Ga.-S.C	285.0
Columbia County, Ga	30.7
Richmond County, Ga	158.6
Aiken County, S.C	95.7
Austin, Tex	461.1
Hays County	34.8
Travis County	375.4
Williamson County	50.9
Bakersfield, Calif	355.7
Kern County	355.7
Baltimore, Md	2,144.5
Baltimore city	827.4
Anne Arundel County	346.9
Baltimore County	642.4
Carroll County	84.1
Harford County	139.9
Howard County	103.6
Baton Rouge, La	425.9
Ascension Parish	41.7
East Baton Rouge Parish	320.7
Livingston Parish	45.5
West Baton Rouge Parish	18.1
Battle Creek, Mich	183.0
Barry County	41.8
Calhoun County	141.2
Bay City, Mich	119.6
Bay County	119.6
Beaumont-Port Arthur-Orange, Tex	357.4
Hardin County	35.6
Jefferson County	244.7
Orange County	77.1
Billings, Mont	99.6
Yellowstone County	99.6
Biloxi-Gulfport, Miss	173.5
Hancock County	19.1
Harrison County	145.9
Stone County	8.4

Area	1976 Population (1,000)
Binghamton, N.Y.-Pa	306.1
Broome County, N.Y	219.6
Tioga County, N.Y	49.1
Susquehanna County, Pa	37.4
Birmingham, Ala	799.7
Jefferson County	650.1
St. Clair County	34.2
Shelby County	50.9
Walker County	64.5
Bloomington, Ind	91.2
Monroe County	91.2
Bloomington-Normal, Ill	117.5
McLean County	117.5
Boise City, Idaho	139.8
Ada County	139.8
Boston, Mass	2,861.8
Essex County (pt.)	330.1
Middlesex County (pt.)	1,064.4
Norfolk County (pt.)	605.6
Plymouth County (pt.)	157.7
Suffolk County	703.9
(See also Boston NECMA, p. 944.)	
Bradenton, Fla	124.3
Manatee County	124.3
Bridgeport, Conn	395.2
Fairfield County (pt.)	331.1
New Haven County (pt.)	64.1
(See also Bridgeport NECMA, p. 944.)	
Bristol, Conn	73.3
Hartford County (pt.)	62.7
Litchfield County (pt.)	10.6
(See also Hartford NECMA, p. 944.)	
Brockton, Mass	164.7
Bristol County (pt.)	14.6
Norfolk County (pt.)	5.3
Plymouth County (pt.)	144.9
(See also Boston NECMA, p. 944.)	
Brownsville-Harlingen-San Benito, Tex	177.8
Cameron County	177.8
Bryan-College Station, Tex	75.8
Brazos County	75.8
Buffalo, N.Y	1,328.0
Erie County	1,089.4
Niagara County	238.6
Burlington, N.C	98.7
Alamance County	98.7
Canton, Ohio	403.1
Carroll County	26.0
Stark County	377.1

[1] Estimates. Source: U.S. Bureau of the Census, *Current Population Reports*, series P-25, forthcoming report.

	1976 Population [1] (1,000)
Cedar Rapids, Iowa	167.3
Linn County	167.3
Champaign-Urbana-Rantoul, Ill	164.4
Champaign County	164.4
Charleston-North Charleston, S.C.	378.4
Berkeley County	69.3
Charleston County	261.7
Dorchester County	47.4
Charleston, W. Va	257.5
Kanawha County	225.7
Putnam County	31.8
Charlotte-Gastonia, N.C.	593.0
Gaston County	154.9
Mecklenburg County	375.5
Union County	62.6
Chattanooga, Tenn.-Ga	393.4
Hamilton County, Tenn.	265.5
Marion County, Tenn.	22.4
Sequatchie County, Tenn.	7.3
Catoosa County, Ga.	32.7
Dade County, Ga.	11.5
Walker County, Ga.	54.0
Chicago, Ill	6,993.1
Cook County	5,332.3
Du Page County	558.3
Kane County	268.8
Lake County	406.2
McHenry County	128.8
Will County	298.6
Cincinnati, Ohio-Ky.-Ind	1,364.3
Clermont County, Ohio	110.8
Hamilton County, Ohio	881.0
Warren County, Ohio	87.2
Boone County, Ky.	38.5
Campbell County, Ky.	84.8
Kenton County, Ky.	130.6
Dearborn County, Ind.	31.4
Clarksville-Hopkinsville, Tenn.-Ky	142.0
Montgomery County, Tenn.	75.7
Christian County, Ky.	66.4
Cleveland, Ohio	1,967.2
Cuyahoga County	1,586.3
Geauga County	68.7
Lake County	210.4
Medina County	101.9
Colorado Springs, Colo	283.9
El Paso County	277.9
Teller County	6.0
Columbia, Mo	85.8
Boone County	85.8
Columbia, S.C.	372.2
Lexington County	121.3
Richland County	250.9
Columbus, Ga.-Ala	229.8
Columbus (consolidated govt.), Ga.	163.4
Chattahoochee County, Ga.	19.8
Russell County, Ala.	46.6

	1976 Population [1] (1,000)
Columbus, Ohio	1,072.0
Delaware County	50.3
Fairfield County	85.6
Franklin County	859.1
Madison County	32.8
Pickaway County	44.2
Corpus Christi, Tex	302.6
Nueces County	251.1
San Patricio County	51.5
Dallas-Fort Worth, Tex	2,610.8
Collin County	97.7
Dallas County	1,435.4
Denton County	97.6
Ellis County	52.0
Hood County	10.6
Johnson County	56.1
Kaufman County	35.1
Parker County	34.5
Rockwall County	9.4
Tarrant County	760.6
Wise County	21.8
Danbury, Conn	132.2
Fairfield County (pt.)	114.8
Litchfield County (pt.)	17.4
(See also Bridgeport NECMA, p. 944.)	
Davenport-Rock Island-Moline, Iowa-Ill	372.6
Scott County, Iowa	152.3
Henry County, Ill.	55.6
Rock Island County, Ill.	164.7
Dayton, Ohio	836.9
Greene County	129.1
Miami County	87.3
Montgomery County	584.7
Preble County	35.8
Daytona Beach, Fla	209.7
Volusia County	209.7
Decatur, Ill	125.7
Macon County	125.7
Denver-Boulder, Colo	1,438.4
Adams County	220.9
Arapahoe County	226.1
Boulder County	167.8
Denver County	479.5
Douglas County	18.4
Gilpin County	1.9
Jefferson County	323.8
Des Moines, Iowa	333.4
Polk County	301.3
Warren County	32.2
Detroit, Mich	4,405.9
Lapeer County	64.7
Livingston County	81.0
Macomb County	674.2
Oakland County	971.6
St. Clair County	130.4
Wayne County	2,483.9
Dubuque, Iowa	95.2
Dubuque County	95.2
Duluth-Superior, Minn.-Wis	264.7
St. Louis County, Minn.	219.8
Douglas County, Wis.	44.9
Durham, N.C.	
(See Raleigh-Durham SMSA.)	

	1976 Population [1] (1,000)
Eau Claire, Wis	123.1
Chippewa County	49.3
Eau Claire County	73.8
El Paso, Tex	430.9
El Paso County	430.9
Elmira, N.Y	99.8
Chemung County	99.8
Erie, Pa	276.2
Erie County	276.2
Eugene-Springfield, Oreg	245.5
Lane County	245.5
Evansville, Ind.-Ky	287.3
Gibson County, Ind.	31.2
Posey County, Ind.	22.8
Vanderburgh County, Ind.	161.6
Warrick County, Ind.	34.7
Henderson County, Ky.	37.0
Fall River, Mass.-R.I	182.9
Bristol County, Mass. (pt.)	151.5
Newport County, R.I. (pt.)	31.3
(See also New Bedford NECMA, p. 944.)	
Fargo-Moorhead, N. Dak.-Minn	128.6
Cass County, N. Dak.	46.9
Clay County, Minn.	81.6
Fayetteville, N.C	229.9
Cumberland County	229.9
Fayetteville-Springdale, Ark	150.7
Benton County	60.3
Washington County	90.4
Fitchburg-Leominster, Mass	97.2
Middlesex County (pt.)	10.0
Worcester County (pt.)	87.2
(See also Worcester NECMA, p. 944.)	
Flint, Mich	523.5
Genesee County	454.7
Shiawassee County	68.9
Florence, Ala	123.8
Colbert County	49.5
Lauderdale County	74.3
Fort Collins, Colo	120.4
Larimer County	120.4
Fort Lauderdale-Hollywood, Fla	846.6
Broward County	846.6
Fort Myers, Fla	159.6
Lee County	159.6
Fort Smith, Ark.-Okla	181.5
Crawford County, Ark.	31.0
Sebastian County, Ark.	87.3
Le Flore County, Okla.	36.2
Sequoyah County, Okla.	27.1
Fort Wayne, Ind	371.2
Adams County	27.3
Allen County	287.4
De Kalb County	31.8
Wells County	24.7

[1] Estimates. Source: U.S. Bureau of the Census, *Current Population Reports*, series P-25, forthcoming report.

940 Appendix II

	1976 Population[1] (1,000)
Fort Worth, Tex.	
(See Dallas-Fort Worth SMSA.)	
Fresno, Calif.	463.6
Fresno County	463.6
Gadsden, Ala.	96.0
Etowah County	96.0
Gainesville, Fla.	125.9
Alachua County	125.9
Galveston-Texas City, Tex.	188.5
Galveston County	188.5
Gary-Hammond-East Chicago, Ind.	643.8
Lake County	545.1
Porter County	98.7
Gastonia, N.C.	
(See Charlotte-Gastonia SMSA.)	
Grand Forks, N.D.-Minn.	100.3
Grand Forks County, N.D.	64.7
Polk County, Minn.	35.6
Grand Rapids, Mich.	569.0
Kent County	425.8
Ottawa County	143.2
Great Falls, Mont.	84.4
Cascade County	84.4
Greeley, Colo.	108.4
Weld County	108.4
Green Bay, Wis.	172.5
Brown County	172.5
Greensboro-Winston-Salem-High Point, N.C.	766.0
Davidson County	100.7
Forsyth County	226.7
Guilford County	300.5
Randolph County	82.6
Stokes County	28.6
Yadkin County	26.9
Greenville-Spartanburg, S.C.	527.6
Greenville County	265.7
Pickens County	69.6
Spartanburg County	192.3
Hamilton-Middletown, Ohio	246.7
Butler County	246.7
Harrisburg, Pa.	425.9
Cumberland County	170.6
Dauphin County	222.9
Perry County	32.5
Hartford, Conn.	729.6
Hartford County (pt.)	608.5
Litchfield County (pt.)	4.7
Middlesex County (pt.)	26.2
New London County (pt.)	7.5
Tolland County (pt.)	82.7
(See also Hartford NECMA, p. 944.)	
Honolulu, Hawaii	714.6
Honolulu County	714.6
Houston, Tex.	2,422.8
Brazoria County	129.9
Fort Bend County	82.4
Harris County	2,066.2
Liberty County	39.1
Montgomery County	89.4
Waller County	15.9

	1976 Population[1] (1,000)
Huntington-Ashland, W. Va.-Ky.-Ohio	292.6
Cabell County, W. Va.	105.4
Wayne County, W. Va.	39.9
Boyd County, Ky.	52.7
Greenup County, Ky.	35.2
Lawrence County, Ohio	59.4
Huntsville, Ala.	287.5
Limestone County	43.5
Madison County	184.6
Marshall County	59.4
Indianapolis, Ind.	1,140.8
Boone County	32.9
Hamilton County	70.9
Hancock County	41.0
Hendricks County	62.2
Johnson County	70.6
Marion County	775.8
Morgan County	48.7
Shelby County	38.7
Jackson, Mich.	148.7
Jackson County	148.7
Jackson, Miss.	291.6
Hinds County	232.6
Rankin County	59.0
Jacksonville, Fla.	695.3
Baker County	12.8
Clay County	52.8
Duval County	560.1
Nassau County	29.7
St. Johns County	39.9
Jersey City, N.J.	572.7
Hudson County	572.7
Johnson City-Kingsport-Bristol, Tenn.-Va.	403.0
Carter, Tenn.	46.3
Hawkins, Tenn.	37.5
Sullivan, Tenn.	135.5
Unicoi, Tenn.	15.9
Washington, Tenn.	81.8
Bristol City, Va.	20.5
Scott, Va.	24.8
Washington, Va.	40.7
Johnstown, Pa.	267.2
Cambria County	188.4
Somerset County	78.8
Kalamazoo-Portage, Mich.	264.9
Kalamazoo County	202.8
Van Buren County	62.2
Kankakee, Ill.	95.8
Kankakee County	95.8
Kansas City, Mo.-Kans.	1,281.3
Cass County, Mo.	48.6
Clay County, Mo.	132.5
Jackson County, Mo.	620.9
Platte County, Mo.	39.8
Ray County, Mo.	19.3
Johnson County, Kans.	242.5
Wyandotte County, Kans.	177.6
Kenosha, Wis.	123.8
Kenosha County	123.8
Killeen-Temple, Tex.	207.1
Bell County	160.1
Coryell County	47.0
Knoxville, Tenn.	442.6
Anderson County	63.1
Blount County	70.8
Knox County	298.2
Union County	10.5

	1976 Population[1] (1,000)
Kokomo, Ind.	103.2
Howard County	87.2
Tipton County	16.0
La Crosse, Wis.	86.4
La Crosse County	86.4
Lafayette, La.	129.0
Lafayette Parish	129.0
Lafayette-West Lafayette, Ind.	114.1
Tippecanoe County	114.1
Lake Charles, La.	154.2
Calcasieu Parish	154.2
Lakeland-Winter Haven, Fla.	276.9
Polk County	276.9
Lancaster, Pa.	344.0
Lancaster County	344.0
Lansing-East Lansing, Mich.	448.7
Clinton County	52.5
Eaton County	78.4
Ingham County	269.5
Ionia County	48.3
Laredo, Tex.	83.0
Webb County	83.0
Las Vegas, Nev.	345.6
Clark County	345.6
Lawrence, Kans.	64.4
Douglas County	64.4
Lawrence-Haverhill, Mass.-N.H.	269.4
Essex County, Mass. (pt.)	224.2
Rockingham County, N.H. (pt.)	45.3
(See also Boston NECMA, p. 944.)	
Lawton, Okla.	113.6
Comanche County	113.6
Lewiston-Auburn, Maine	71.9
Androscoggin County (pt.)	71.9
(See also Lewiston NECMA, p. 944.)	
Lexington-Fayette, Ky.	291.3
Bourbon County	18.6
Clark County	26.1
Fayette County	188.7
Jessamine County	22.1
Scott County	19.0
Woodford County	16.8
Lima, Ohio	212.1
Allen County	108.3
Auglaize County	42.3
Putnam County	32.2
Van Wert County	29.2
Lincoln, Nebr.	183.1
Lancaster County	183.1
Little Rock-North Little Rock, Ark.	363.8
Pulaski County	320.4
Saline County	43.4
Long Branch-Asbury Park, N.J.	494.3
Monmouth County	494.3

[1] Estimates. Source: U.S. Bureau of the Census, *Current Population Reports*, series P-25, forthcoming report.

	1976 Popula- tion [1] (1,000)
Longview, Tex	129.6
Gregg County	83.8
Harrison County	45.8
Lorain-Elyria, Ohio	**266.1**
Lorain County	266.1
Los Angeles-Long Beach, Calif.	**6,997.4**
Los Angeles County	6,997.4
Louisville, Ky.-Ind	**887.0**
Bullitt County, Ky	35.4
Jefferson County, Ky	690.7
Oldham County, Ky	19.4
Clark County, Ind	84.8
Floyd County, Ind	56.7
Lowell, Mass.-N.H	**229.1**
Middlesex County, Mass	221.6
Hillsborough County, N.H	7.4
(See also Boston NECMA, p. 944.)	
Lubbock, Tex	**200.2**
Lubbock County	200.2
Lynchburg, Va	**146.9**
Lynchburg city	65.3
Amherst County	27.8
Appomattox County	11.3
Campbell County	42.5
Macon, Ga	**240.1**
Bibb County	144.2
Houston County	72.8
Jones County	15.2
Twiggs County	7.9
Madison, Wis	**309.5**
Dane County	309.5
Manchester, N.H	**142.8**
Hillsborough County (pt.)	100.9
Merrimack County (pt.)	15.1
Rockingham County (pt.)	26.9
(See also Manchester NECMA, p. 944.)	
Mansfield, Ohio	**129.9**
Richland County	129.9
McAllen-Pharr-Edinburg, Tex.	**232.0**
Hidalgo County	232.0
Melbourne-Titusville- Cocoa, Fla.	**226.4**
Brevard County	226.4
Memphis, Tenn.-Ark.- Miss.	**876.6**
Shelby County, Tenn	744.8
Tipton County, Tenn	31.0
Crittenden County, Ark	50.0
De Soto County, Miss	50.8
Meriden, Conn	**57.3**
New Haven County (pt.)	57.3
(See also New Haven NECMA, p. 944.)	
Miami, Fla	**1,449.8**
Dade County	1,449.8
Midland, Tex	**71.8**
Midland County	71.8
Milwaukee, Wis	**1,415.0**
Milwaukee County	1,012.5
Ozaukee County	65.0
Washington County	76.8
Waukesha County	260.7

	1976 Popula- tion [1] (1,000)
Minneapolis-St. Paul, Minn.-Wis	**2,048.2**
Anoka County, Minn	193.5
Carver County, Minn	33.8
Chisago County, Minn	22.7
Dakota County, Minn	179.5
Hennepin County, Minn	918.9
Ramsey County, Minn	460.8
Scott County, Minn	40.8
Washington County, Minn	108.2
Wright County, Minn	50.4
St. Croix County, Wis	39.5
Mobile, Ala	**415.7**
Baldwin County	70.8
Mobile County	344.9
Modesto, Calif	**224.6**
Stanislaus County	224.6
Monroe, La	**129.6**
Ouachita Parish	129.6
Montgomery, Ala	**252.2**
Autauga County	28.6
Elmore County	39.9
Montgomery County	183.7
Muncie, Ind	**129.0**
Delaware County	129.0
Muskegon-Norton Shores-Muskegon Heights, Mich	**178.7**
Muskegon County	158.0
Oceana County	20.8
Nashua, N.H	**104.8**
Hillsborough County (pt.)	104.8
(See also Manchester NECMA, p. 944.)	
Nashville-Davidson, Tenn	**763.5**
Cheatham County	17.1
Davidson County	454.9
Dickson County	26.5
Robertson County	31.8
Rutherford County	69.3
Sumner County	71.6
Williamson County	46.7
Wilson County	45.6
Nassau-Suffolk, N.Y	**2,677.2**
Nassau County	1,399.3
Suffolk County	1,277.9
New Bedford, Mass	**166.9**
Bristol County	152.2
Plymouth County	14.7
(See also New Bedford NECMA, p. 944.)	
New Britain, Conn	**144.7**
Hartford County (pt.)	144.7
(See also Hartford NECMA, p. 932.)	
New Brunswick-Perth Amboy-Sayreville, N.J.	**592.6**
Middlesex County	592.6
New Haven-West Haven, Conn	**413.0**
Middlesex County (pt.)	11.1
New Haven County (pt.)	401.9
(See also New Haven NECMA, p. 944.)	

	1976 Popula- tion [1] (1,000)
New London-Norwich, Conn	**252.8**
Middlesex County, Conn. (pt.)	8.9
New London County, Conn. (pt.)	219.9
Washington County, R.I. (pt.)	24.0
(See also New London NECMA, p. 944.)	
New Orleans, La	**1,136.8**
Jefferson Parish	413.7
Orleans Parish	581.0
St. Bernard Parish	60.0
St. Tammany Parish	82.3
New York, N.Y.-N.J	**9,508.6**
New York City, N.Y	7,422.8
Bronx County, N.Y	1,331.0
Kings County, N.Y	2,386.5
New York County, N.Y	1,409.2
Queens County, N.Y	1,968.5
Richmond County, N.Y	327.5
Putnam County, N.Y	70.6
Rockland County, N.Y	254.5
Westchester County, N.Y	887.0
Bergen County, N.J	873.7
Newark, N.J	**1,992.8**
Essex County	872.4
Morris County	395.2
Somerset County	208.0
Union County	517.1
Newport News-Hampton, Va	**358.5**
Hampton city	128.5
Newport News city	141.3
Poquoson city [2]	7.6
Williamsburg city	11.4
Gloucester County	17.1
James City County	20.8
York County [2]	31.8
Norfolk-Virginia Beach- Portsmouth, Va.-N.C	**782.4**
Chesapeake city, Va	107.9
Norfolk city, Va	284.0
Portsmouth city, Va	109.1
Suffolk city, Va	46.4
Virginia Beach city, Va	224.6
Currituck County, N.C	10.3
Northeast Pennsylvania	**632.4**
Lackawanna County	234.8
Luzerne County	342.0
Monroe County	55.7
Norwalk, Conn	**127.8**
Fairfield County (pt.)	127.8
(See also Bridgeport NECMA, p. 944.)	
Odessa, Tex	**101.1**
Ector County	101.1
Ogden, Utah (See Salt Lake City SMSA.)	
Oklahoma City, Okla	**761.9**
Canadian County	45.3
Cleveland County	103.3
McClain County	18.8
Oklahoma County	543.8
Pottawatomie County	50.7

[1] Estimates. Source: U.S. Bureau of the Census, *Current Population Reports*, series P-25, forthcoming report.
[2] Poquoson city became independent of York County in 1975.

	1976 Population [1] (1,000)
Omaha, Nebr.-Iowa	581.4
Douglas County, Nebr	412.3
Sarpy County, Nebr	82.7
Pottawattamie County, Iowa	86.4
Orlando, Fla	582.8
Orange County	406.7
Osceola County	37.9
Seminole County	138.2
Owensboro, Ky	80.9
Daviess County	80.9
Oxnard-Simi Valley-Ventura, Calif	448.1
Ventura County	448.1
Panama City, Fla	89.5
Bay County	89.5
Parkersburg-Marietta, W. Va.-Ohio	152.8
Wirt County, W. Va	4.9
Wood County, W. Va	88.0
Washington County, Ohio	59.9
Pascagoula-Moss Point, Miss	110.1
Jackson County	110.1
Paterson-Clifton-Passaic, N.J	469.6
Passaic County	469.6
Pensacola, Fla	274.5
Escambia County	225.6
Santa Rosa County	48.8
Peoria, Ill	357.6
Peoria County	200.0
Tazewell County	127.3
Woodford County	30.3
Petersburg-Colonial Heights-Hopewell, Va	128.6
Colonial Heights city	17.4
Hopewell city	23.9
Petersburg city	46.8
Dinwiddie County	19.7
Prince George County	20.8
Philadelphia, Pa.-N.J	4,803.0
Bucks County, Pa	465.4
Chester County, Pa	296.4
Delaware County, Pa	585.9
Montgomery County, Pa	631.9
Philadelphia County, Pa	1,797.4
Burlington County, N.J	355.2
Camden County, N.J	474.0
Gloucester County, N.J	196.7
Phoenix, Ariz	1,224.1
Maricopa County	1,224.1
Pine Bluff, Ark	84.2
Jefferson County	84.2
Pittsburgh, Pa	2,303.5
Allegheny County	1,500.2
Beaver County	208.9
Washington County	213.5
Westmoreland County	380.9
Pittsfield, Mass	93.5
Berkshire County (pt.)	93.5
(See also Pittsfield NECMA, p. 944.)	
Portland, Maine	177.7
Cumberland County (pt.)	159.3
York County (pt.)	18.4
(See also Portland NECMA, p. 944.)	

	1976 Population [1] (1,000)
Portland, Ore.-Wash	1,096.4
Clackamas County, Oreg	211.5
Multnomah County, Oreg	525.6
Washington County, Oreg	200.5
Clark County, Wash	158.9
Poughkeepsie, N.Y	233.7
Dutchess County	233.7
Providence-Warwick-Pawtucket, R.I.-Mass	905.4
Bristol County, R.I	45.7
Kent County, R.I. (pt.)	147.5
Newport County, R.I. (pt.)	3.7
Providence County, R.I. (pt.)	564.8
Washington County, R.I. (pt.)	49.6
Bristol County, Mass. (pt.)	80.3
Norfolk County, Mass. (pt.)	5.5
Worcester County, Mass. (pt.)	8.3
(See also Providence NECMA, p. 944.)	
Provo-Orem, Utah	170.7
Utah County	170.7
Pueblo, Colo	124.5
Pueblo County	124.5
Racine, Wis	175.9
Racine County	175.9
Raleigh-Durham, N.C	478.4
Durham County	141.3
Orange County	68.5
Wake County	268.6
Reading, Pa	304.7
Berks County	304.7
Reno, Nev	149.7
Washoe County	149.7
Richland-Kennewick, Wash	112.3
Benton County	83.5
Franklin County	28.8
Richmond, Va	594.2
Richmond city	226.6
Charles City County	6.4
Chesterfield County	108.3
Goochland County	11.2
Hanover County	48.8
Henrico County	174.2
New Kent County	7.3
Powhatan County	11.3
Riverside-San Bernardino-Ontario, Calif	1,264.7
Riverside County	544.3
San Bernardino County	720.4
Roanoke, Va	214.0
Roanoke city	102.0
Salem city	24.2
Botetourt County	21.1
Craig County	3.9
Roanoke County	62.8
Rochester, Minn	89.9
Olmsted County	89.9

	1976 Population [1] (1,000)
Rochester, N.Y	978.0
Livingston County	57.2
Monroe County	713.9
Ontario County	86.2
Orleans County	38.7
Wayne County	82.1
Rockford, Ill	268.6
Boone County	26.3
Winnebago County	242.3
Sacramento, Calif	907.9
Placer County	96.3
Sacramento County	702.4
Yolo County	109.2
Saginaw, Mich	228.6
Saginaw County	228.6
St. Cloud, Minn	153.8
Benton County	22.5
Sherburne County	27.0
Stearns County	104.3
St. Joseph, Mo	99.6
Andrew County	13.7
Buchanan County	85.8
St. Louis, Mo.-Ill	2,383.5
St. Louis city, Mo	519.3
Franklin County, Mo	64.5
Jefferson County, Mo	124.6
St. Charles County, Mo	115.0
St. Louis County, Mo	982.4
Clinton County, Ill	30.2
Madison County, Ill	247.8
Monroe County, Ill	18.9
St. Clair County, Ill	280.7
Salem, Oreg	209.3
Marion County	170.0
Polk County	39.4
Salinas-Seaside-Monterey, Calif	271.5
Monterey County	271.5
Salt Lake City-Ogden, Utah	799.8
Davis County	117.1
Salt Lake County	525.2
Tooele County	22.8
Weber County	134.7
San Angelo, Tex	77.6
Tom Green County	77.6
San Antonio, Tex	996.1
Bexar County	926.9
Comal County	29.7
Guadalupe County	39.4
San Diego, Calif	1,624.2
San Diego County	1,624.2
San Francisco-Oakland, Calif	3,157.9
Alameda County	1,095.9
Contra Costa County	594.1
Marin County	220.4
San Francisco County	663.5
San Mateo County	584.1
San Jose, Calif	1,205.4
Santa Clara County	1,205.4
Santa Barbara-Santa Maria-Lompoc, Calif	289.7
Santa Barbara County	289.7
Santa Cruz, Calif	162.9
Santa Cruz County	162.9

[1] Estimates. Source: U.S. Bureau of the Census, *Current Population Reports*, series P-25, forthcoming report.

	1976 Population [1] (1,000)		1976 Population [1] (1,000)		1976 Population [1] (1,000)
Santa Rosa, Calif.	250.3	Stockton, Calif.	304.0	Washington, D.C.-Md.-Va.	3,037.4
Sonoma County	250.3	San Joaquin County	304.0	District of Columbia	700.1
				Charles County, Md.	62.1
Sarasota, Fla.	160.3	Syracuse, N.Y.	651.5	Montgomery County, Md.	573.8
Sarasota County	160.3	Madison County	65.7	Prince Georges County, Md.	674.1
		Onondaga County	475.2	Alexandria city, Va.	108.1
Savannah, Ga.	211.8	Oswego County	110.6	Fairfax city, Va.	21.6
Bryan County	8.3			Falls Church city, Va.	9.6
Chatham County	187.4	Tacoma, Wash.	420.2	Manassas city, Va.[2]	12.8
Effingham County	16.0	Pierce County	420.2	Manassas Park city, Va.[2]	9.6
				Arlington County, Va.	154.1
Scranton, Pa. (See Northeast Pennsylvania SMSA.)		Tallahassee, Fla.	136.1	Fairfax County, Va.	530.8
		Leon County	127.3	Loudoun County, Va.	52.7
		Wakulla County	8.9	Prince William County, Va.[2]	128.0
Seattle-Everett, Wash.	1,418.7	Tampa-St. Petersburg, Fla.	1,366.7		
King County	1,150.2	Hillsborough County	585.9	Waterbury, Conn.	227.5
Snohomish County	268.5	Pasco County	138.4	Litchfield County (pt.)	32.4
		Pinellas County	642.5	New Haven County (pt.)	195.2
Sherman-Denison, Tex.	82.7				
Grayson County	82.7	Terre Haute, Ind.	171.7	(See also New Haven NECMA, p. 944.)	
		Clay County	24.5		
Shreveport, La.	353.3	Sullivan County	19.7		
Bossier Parish	70.9	Vermillion County	16.9	Waterloo-Cedar Falls, Iowa.	135.6
Caddo Parish	241.5	Vigo County	110.6	Black Hawk County	135.6
Webster Parish	40.9				
		Texarkana, Tex., Texarkana, Ark.	118.3	West Palm Beach-Boca Raton, Fla.	464.6
Sioux City, Iowa-Nebr.	119.9	Bowie County, Tex.	72.5	Palm Beach County	464.6
Woodbury County, Iowa	103.7	Little River County, Ark.	11.7		
Dakota County, Nebr.	16.2	Miller County, Ark.	34.1	Wheeling, W. Va.-Ohio	181.8
				Marshall County, W. Va.	39.4
Sioux Falls, S. Dak.	100.7	Toledo, Ohio-Mich.	780.2	Ohio County, W. Va.	60.1
Minnehaha County	100.7	Fulton County, Ohio	35.6	Belmont County, Ohio	82.2
		Lucas County, Ohio	476.5		
South Bend, Ind.	276.5	Ottawa County, Ohio	39.1	Wichita, Kans.	390.5
Marshall County	38.0	Wood County, Ohio	101.3	Butler County	40.6
St. Joseph County	238.5	Monroe County, Mich.	127.7	Sedgwick County	349.9
Spokane, Wash.	309.4	Topeka, Kans.	180.4	Wichita Falls, Tex.	130.9
Spokane County	309.4	Jefferson County	13.4	Clay County	8.6
		Osage County	13.9	Wichita County	122.3
Springfield, Ill.	183.8	Shawnee County	153.1		
Menard County	10.9			Wilkes-Barre-Hazelton, Pa. (See Northeast Pennsylvania SMSA.)	
Sangamon County	172.9	Trenton, N.J.	318.1		
		Mercer County	318.1		
Springfield-Chicopee-Holyoke, Mass.-Conn.	546.0	Tucson, Ariz.	451.0	Williamsport, Pa.	115.1
Hampshire County, Mass. (pt.)	85.6	Pima County	451.0	Lycoming County	115.1
Hampden County, Mass. (pt.)	449.4	Tulsa, Okla.	598.3	Wilmington, Del.-N.J.-Md.	517.9
Worcester County, Mass. (pt.)	3.4	Creek County	50.7	New Castle County, Del.	400.9
Tolland County, Conn. (pt.)	7.5	Mayes County	28.0	Salem County, N.J.	62.5
		Osage County	32.3	Cecil County, Md.	54.4
		Rogers County	34.6		
(See also Springfield NECMA, p. 944.)		Tulsa County	424.8	Wilmington, N.C.	129.0
		Wagoner County	27.9	Brunswick County	33.0
				New Hanover County	96.0
Springfield, Mo.	186.9	Tuscaloosa, Ala.	124.5		
Christian County	19.9	Tuscaloosa County	124.5	Worcester, Mass.	377.0
Greene County	167.0			Worcester County (pt.)	377.0
		Tyler, Tex.	109.8		
Springfield, Ohio	183.6	Smith County	109.8	(See also Worcester NECMA, p. 944.)	
Champaign County	31.7				
Clark County	151.9	Utica-Rome, N.Y.	332.6		
		Herkimer County	67.9	Yakima, Wash.	156.9
Stamford, Conn.	202.6	Oneida County	264.8	Yakima County	156.9
Fairfield County (pt.)	202.6				
		Vallejo-Fairfield-Napa, Calif.	284.5	York, Pa.	351.0
(See also Bridgeport NECMA, p. 944.)		Napa County	89.7	Adams County	62.5
		Solano County	194.7	York County	288.5
Steubenville-Weirton, Ohio-W. Va.	164.9	Vineland-Millville-Bridgeton, N.J.	133.5	Youngstown-Warren, Ohio	544.1
Jefferson County, Ohio	94.2	Cumberland County	133.5	Mahoning County	300.3
Brooke County, W. Va.	30.7			Trumbull County	243.8
Hancock County, W. Va.	40.0	Waco, Tex.	158.2		
		McLennan County	158.2		

[1] Estimates. Source: U.S. Bureau of the Census, *Current Population Reports*, series P-25, forthcoming report.
[2] Manassas and Manassas Park cities became independent of Prince William County in 1975.

NEW ENGLAND COUNTY METROPOLITAN AREAS (NECMA's)

	1976 Population [1] (1,000)		1976 Population [1] (1,000)		1976 Population [1] (1,000)
Boston-Lowell-Brockton-Lawrence-Haverhill, Mass.-N.H	3,893.1	Lewiston-Auburn, Maine Androscoggin County	94.6 94.6	Pittsfield, Mass Berkshire County	147.9 147.9
Essex County, Mass	625.9				
Middlesex County, Mass	1,394.1	Manchester-Nashua, N.H	246.8	Portland, Maine	231.5
Norfolk County, Mass	616.4	Hillsborough County	246.8	Cumberland County	205.1
Plymouth County, Mass	385.5			Sagadahoc County	26.4
Suffolk County, Mass	703.9				
Rockingham, N.H	167.3	New Bedford-Fall River, Mass	463.7	Providence-Warwick-Pawtucket, R.I	855.5
		Bristol County	463.7	Bristol County	45.7
Bridgeport-Stamford-Norwalk-Danbury, Conn	799.1			Kent County	149.5
				Providence County	574.8
Fairfield County	799.1	New Haven-West Haven-Waterbury-Meriden, Conn	759.1	Washington County	85.4
		New Haven County	759.1	Springfield-Chicopee-Holyoke, Mass	596.9
Hartford-New Britain-Bristol, Conn	1,056.1			Hampden County	459.7
Hartford County	817.4	New London-Norwich, Conn	243.3	Hampshire County	137.1
Middlesex County	125.7	New London County	243.3	Worcester-Fitchburg-Leominster, Mass	646.3
Tolland County	113.0			Worcester County	646.3

[1] Estimates.

Source: U.S. Bureau of the Census, *Current Population Reports*, series P-25, forthcoming report.

STANDARD CONSOLIDATED STATISTICAL AREAS (SCSA's)

	1976 Population [1] (1,000)		1976 Population [1] (1,000)
Boston-Lawrence-Lowell, Mass.-N.H	3,525.0	Miami-Fort Lauderdale, Fla	2,296.4
Boston, Mass	2,861.8	Miami, Fla	1,449.8
Lawrence-Haverhill, Mass.-N.H	269.4	Fort Lauderdale-Hollywood, Fla	846.6
Lowell, Mass.-N.H	229.1		
Brockton, Mass	164.7	Milwaukee-Racine, Wis	1,590.9
		Milwaukee, Wis	1,415.0
Chicago-Gary, Ill.-Ind	7,636.8	Racine, Wis	175.9
Chicago, Ill	6,993.1		
Gary-Hammond-East Chicago, Ind	643.8	New York-Newark-Jersey City, N.Y.-N.J.-Conn	16,638.2
		New York, N.Y.-N.J	9,508.6
Cincinnati-Hamilton, Ohio-Ky.-Ind	1,611.0	Nassau-Suffolk, N.Y	2,677.2
Cincinnati, Ohio-Ky.-Ind	1,364.3	Newark, N.J	1,992.8
Hamilton-Middleton, Ohio	246.7	Jersey City, N.J	572.7
		New Brunswick-Perth Amboy-Sayreville	
Cleveland-Akron-Lorain, Ohio	2,903.0	N.J	592.6
Cleveland, Ohio	1,967.2	Paterson-Clifton-Passaic, N.J	469.6
Akron, Ohio	669.6	Long Branch-Asbury Park, N.J	494.3
Lorain-Elyria, Ohio	266.1	Stamford, Conn	202.6
		Norwalk, Conn	127.8
Detroit-Ann Arbor, Mich	4,654.2		
Detroit, Mich	4,405.9	Philadelphia-Wilmington-Trenton, Pa.-Del.-N.J.-Md	5,639.0
Ann Arbor, Mich	248.3	Philadelphia, Pa.-N.J	4,803.0
		Wilmington, Del.-N.J.-Md	517.9
Houston-Galveston, Tex	2,611.3	Trenton, N.J	318.1
Houston, Tex	2,422.8		
Galveston-Texas City, Tex	188.5	San Francisco-Oakland-San Jose, Calif	4,647.7
		San Francisco-Oakland, Calif	3,157.9
Los Angeles-Long Beach-Anaheim, Calif	10,465.8	San Jose, Calif	1,205.4
Los Angeles-Long Beach, Calif	6,997.4	Vallejo-Fairfield-Napa, Calif	284.5
Anaheim-Santa Ana-Garden Grove, Calif	1,755.6		
Riverside-San Bernardino-Ontario, Calif	1,264.7	Seattle-Tacoma, Wash	1,839.0
Oxnard-Simi Valley-Ventura, Calif	448.1	Seattle-Everett, Wash	1,418.7
		Tacoma, Wash	420.2

[1] Estimates.

Source: U.S. Bureau of the Census, *Current Population Reports*, series P-25, forthcoming report.

APPENDIX III
Statistical Methodology and Reliability

Introduction.—The data presented in this *Statistical Abstract* came from many sources. The sources include not only Federal statistical bureaus and other organizations that collect and issue statistics as their principal activity, but also governmental administrative and regulatory agencies, private research bodies, trade associations, insurance companies, health associations, and private organizations such as the American Red Cross and philanthropic foundations. Consequently, the data vary considerably as to reference periods, definitions of terms, and, for ongoing series, the number and frequency of time periods for which data are available.

The data also vary as to how they were obtained. Some are based on complete enumeration (every person or item is counted); some on records kept for administrative or regulatory purposes (school enrollment, hospital records, securities registration, financial accounts, etc.); some on sample survey results (see below); and some on estimation procedures which range from highly sophisticated techniques to crude "informed guesses." In virtually all data collection operations, various types of errors will be present in the data. The types and sources of errors are discussed later.

Prior to carrying out a census or sample survey, the group of people or items of interest, referred to as the *universe* or *population*, must be clearly defined. For example, if data are collected for the universe of farms in the United States, it is necessary to define a "farm" before data are collected.

A large portion of the data appearing in the tables was obtained from sample surveys. A *sample survey* is a data collection operation in which data are obtained for only a part (i.e., a *sample*) of the entire population being surveyed. In many other cases the data came from a complete *census*—a data collection operation in which an attempt is made to enumerate each member of the universe. For most censuses and sample surveys, the data were obtained from completed questionnaires. However, in some cases, data were obtained from other sources as noted above.

In cases in which a sample survey is used to obtain data about a universe, the sample selected for the survey is usually a *probability sample*. It is a sample obtained from a universe by using a chance device in such a way that every possible sample of universe members has a known probability (or chance) of selection as the survey sample. When probability sampling is used, the probability of selection of each population unit can be determined. The *probability* of selection of a unit from the universe is a number, between zero and one, which represents the likelihood that the unit will be chosen for the sample.

For large-scale sample surveys, the probability sample of units is often selected as a *multistage sample*. The first stage of a multistage sample is the selection of a probability sample of large groups of population members, referred to as *primary sampling units* (PSU's). For example, in a national multistage household sample, PSU's are often counties or groups of counties. The second stage of a multistage sample is the selection, within each PSU selected at the first stage, of smaller groups of population units, referred to as secondary sampling units. In subsequent stages of selection, smaller and smaller nested groups are chosen until the ultimate sample of population units is obtained. To qualify a multistage sample as a probability sample, all stages of sampling must be carried out using probability sampling methods.

Prior to selection at each stage of a multistage (or a single-stage) sample, a list of the sampling units for that stage, referred to as a *sampling frame*, must be obtained. For example, for the first stage of selection of a national household sample, a list of the counties and county groups that form the PSU's must be obtained. For the final stage of selection, lists of households, and sometimes persons within households, have to be

945

compiled in the field. If a single-stage sample of the Nation's hospitals is to be selected, a list of hospitals must be obtained to use as the sampling frame. Unfortunately, it is virtually impossible to obtain a complete, up-to-date frame for a hospital survey. This is a problem incurred for most surveys of institutions and for many other types of surveys as well.

Whenever the quantities in a table refer to an entire universe, but are constructed from data collected in a sample survey, the table quantities are referred to as *sample estimates*. In constructing a sample estimate, an attempt is made to come as close as is feasible to the corresponding universe quantity that would be obtained from a complete census of the universe. The errors that can be present in a sample estimate of a universe quantity are classified as either *sampling errors* or *nonsampling errors*.

The *sampling error* is that part of the difference between the estimate and the corresponding population quantity that arises because only a portion (i.e., a sample) of the universe was used to estimate the universe quantity. The measure of sampling error that is often used is the *standard error* (S.E.) of the estimate. Valid estimates of the standard errors of survey estimates can usually be calculated from the data collected in a probability sample survey. Under most circumstances, the estimated standard error of an estimate can be used as follows in measuring the sampling error: The chances are about two out of three (68 percent) that a sample estimate will be within one standard error of the corresponding universe quantity that would be obtained from a complete census, using the same data collection procedures. Also, the chances are about 19 out of 20 (95 percent) that a sample estimate will be within two standard errors of the corresponding population value.

As a measure of sampling error, some statisticians prefer to use the relative standard error, or *coefficient of variation*, of an estimate, rather than the standard error. The coefficient of variation (CV) of an estimate is the standard error of the estimate expressed as a percent of the estimate. That is, the CV of an estimate is the standard error of the estimate divided by the *expected value* of the estimate (i.e., divided by the average value of the estimate taken over repeated samples). It can be used as a measure of sampling error in a way similar to the use of the standard error. For example, if the estimated CV of an estimate is 2.3 percent, the chances are about 19 out of 20 that the estimate will not differ from the population quantity by more than 4.6 percent of the estimate (i.e. two times 2.3 percent).

Any error in a sample estimate that arises from sources other than sampling is classified as a *nonsampling error*. Nonsampling errors arise from such sources as varying interpretation of questions by interviewers, unwillingness or inability of respondents to give correct answers, nonresponse, improper coverage, and processing errors in coding, editing, and tabulating data.

Nonsampling errors are of two kinds—random and nonrandom. *Random errors* arise because of the varying interpretation of questions by respondents, interviewers, coders, or other processors. To the extent that people do not ask questions, record answers, code responses, or process data in other ways in a uniform manner, random errors result. The impact of random errors is usually an overstatement of the precision of the survey estimates. Since special experiments are necessary to measure the magnitude of these random errors, their magnitudes are generally unknown.

Nonrandom errors in survey estimates result from nonresponse, from incorrect responses, from undercoverage of certain population groups, and other such sources. Estimates of the magnitude of nonrandom errors also require special experiments or access to independent data and, consequently, are seldom available.

To compensate for suspected nonrandom errors, adjustments of the sample estimates are often made. For example, adjustments are frequently made for nonresponse, both total and partial. *Total nonresponse* refers to a case in which no usable survey responses were obtained from a sample person. *Partial* or *item nonresponse* refers to a case in which only a portion of the survey items was not obtained.

Adjustments made for either type of nonresponse are often referred to as *imputations*. Imputation for total nonresponse is usually made essentially by substituting for the questionnaire responses of the nonrespondents the "average" questionnaire responses of the respondents. These imputations are usually made separately within various groups of sample members, formed by attempting to place respondents and nonrespondents together that have "similar" survey characteristics. Imputation for item nonresponse is usually made by substituting for a missing item the response to that item of a respondent having characteristics that are "similar" to those of the nonrespondent.

For an estimate calculated from a sample survey, the *total error* in the estimate is composed of the sampling error, which can usually be estimated from the sample, and the nonsampling error, which usually cannot be estimated from the sample. The total error present in a population quantity obtained from a complete census is composed of only nonsampling errors. Ideally, estimates of the total error associated with data given in the *Statistical Abstract* tables should be given. However, due to the unavailability of estimates of nonsampling errors, only estimates of the levels of sampling errors, in terms of estimated standard errors or coefficients of variation, are available.

Principal data bases.—Beginning on page 948 are brief descriptions of 39 of the sample surveys and censuses that provide a substantial portion of the data contained in this *Abstract*.

SUBJECT, SOURCE, TITLE, TABLES	UNIVERSE, FREQUENCY, TYPES OF DATA	TYPE OF DATA COLLECTION OPERATION
SECTION 1. POPULATION		
Bureau of the Census *Census of Population* See tables citing *Census of Population* in section 1 and also in sections 2, 5, 7, 13, 14, 16, 22, 28, and 32.	Complete count of U.S. population conducted every 10 years since 1790; every 5 years beginning 1985. Data obtained on number and characteristics of inhabitants.	In 1970, complete census for some items—age, sex, race, marital status, and relationship to household head. Other items collected from a 5% and a 15% probability sample of the population.
Current Population Survey (CPS) See tables citing *Current Population Reports* primarily in section 1, but also in sections 2, 4, 5, 11, 13, 14, 16, 24, and 32. Many Bureau of Labor Statistics' (BLS) tables in section 13 are CPS based.	Monthly survey of civilian noninstitutional population, 14 years old or over, to obtain data on employment, unemployment, and a number of other characteristics.	Multistage probability sample of about 55,000 households in 376 PSU's. A continual sample rotation system is used. Households are in sample 4 months, out for 8 months, and in for 4 more. Month-to-month overlap is 75%; year-to-year overlap is 50%.
SECTION 2. VITAL STATISTICS		
National Center for Health Statistics *Vital Registration System* See tables 78–86, 91, and 102–112.	Annual data on births and deaths in the United States.	Mortality data based on complete file of death records, except 1972, based on 50% sample. Natality statistics for most years, 1951–1971, based on 50% sample of birth records received by NCHS. Beginning 1972, data from some States received through Cooperative Health Statistics System and complete file used; data from other States based on 50% sample.

(See section 1 above for information pertaining to tables 87–90, 92, 115, and 116.)

SECTION 4. HEALTH AND NUTRITION		
National Center for Health Statistics *Health Interview Survey (HIS)* See tables 157, 179, 181–184, 186, 187, 195, and, in section 5, table 250.	Continuous data collection covering the civilian noninstitutional population to obtain information on personal and demographic characteristics, illnesses, injuries, impairments, chronic conditions, and other health topics.	Multistage probability sample of 41,000 households (in 376 PSU's) selected in groups of about four geographically adjacent households.
Master Facility Inventory (MFI) See tables 164, 173, and 175.	Annual survey of hospitals with 6 or more beds and biennial surveys of nursing and related care homes with 3 or more beds and other custodial or remedial care facilities to update file. Information obtained on names, locations, and types of facilities, and number of beds and residents or patients.	Complete census of eligible institutions. Comprehensive file periodically updated to include names and addresses of newly established inpatient facilities from State licensing agencies.
National Nursing Home Survey (NNHS) See tables 173 and 174.	Survey of 23,105 nursing homes, classified in 1973 Master Facility Inventory or open for business in 1976, conducted in the summer and winter of 1977. Data collected on expenditures, staff, and residents of nursing homes, and discharges from nursing homes.	Probability sample of 1,698 nursing homes. In each home, probability samples of about 5 residents, 4 discharges, and 10 employees chosen.

DATA COLLECTION AND IMPUTATION PROCEDURES	INFORMATION ON ERRORS IN THE DATA		SOURCES OF ADDITIONAL MATERIAL
	Estimates of sampling error	Other (nonsampling) errors	
In 1970, extensive use of mail questionnaires in urban areas; personal interviews in most rural areas. Extensive telephone and personal followup for nonrespondents. Imputations made for missing characteristics.	The CV's for national and State estimates are generally very small. For example, the estimated CV for the estimated number of persons in poverty is less than 1% at the State and national level.	Based on the 1970 census evaluation, an estimate of the net undercount is 2.5%.	Bureau of the Census, *Estimates of Coverage of the Population by Sex, Race, and Age: Demographic Analysis*, PHC(E)-4; and *Census of Population: 1970*, PC(1)-C, Appendix C.
For first and fifth months that a household is in sample, personal interviews; other months, data collected by phone.	Estimated CV for labor force, total employment, and nonagricultural employment, .3 percent; for total unemployment and agricultural employment, 1.5 to 3.0 percent.	Unemployment underestimated by about .5 percent. Other statistics less biased. Four to 6 percent of sample households unavailable for interviews.	Bureau of the Census and Bureau of Labor Statistics, *Concepts and Methods Used in Labor Force Statistics from Current Population Survey* (Census series P-23, No. 62; BLS report No. 463) and Bureau of the Census, *The Current Population Survey* (Tech. Paper 40).
Reports based on records from registration offices of all States, District of Columbia, Puerto Rico, Virgin Islands, Guam, and certain cities.	For births, CV's are small due to large portion of total file in sample (except for very small estimated totals).	In 1964–1968, underregistration of births estimated to be .7%. Data on deaths believed to be as complete.	U.S. National Center for Health Statistics, *Vital Statistics of the United States, 1976*, vol. 1 and vol. II, part A and part B, forthcoming.
Personal household interviews. Extensive followup of nonrespondents. Data adjusted for nonresponse by imputation procedure based on "average" characteristics of persons in interviewed households in same geographic area.	Estimated CV's: For physician visits by males, 1.5%; for workdays lost by males, 3.5%; for persons injured at home, 4.7%	Response rate was 96% in 1976.	U.S. National Center for Health Statistics, *Vital Statistics of the United States*, series 10–No. 119, DHEW No. (PHS) 78–1547, Nov. 1977.
Mail questionnaires to facilities. Missing questionnaire items imputed by using either previously reported information or by using current data from similar responding facilities.	Not applicable.	The response rate in the 1976 survey of hospitals was about 92%. In 1976, coverage was 95% complete for nursing care and related homes and other custodial or remedial care facilities.	U.S. National Center for Health Statistics, "Design and Methodology of the 1967 Master Facility Inventory Survey", *Vital and Health Statistics*, PHS Pub. No. 1000, Series 1–No. 9, Jan. 1971.
Data on facilities through personal interviews with administrators; patient data through medical records; personal interviews with nurses and expenditure data by questionnaires to accountants; staff data by self-administered questionnaires. Data adjusted for nonparticipation of a home and for item nonresponse.	The provisional 1977 CV for estimated number of beds in proprietary homes was 4.7%; for residents in homes with less than 50 beds, 10%. In 1976, CV for days of care to residents in homes in Northeast was 4.7%.	Response rates were 94% for facilities, 99% for residents, 85% for expenditures, 81% for staff, and 97% for discharges.	U.S. National Center for Health Statistics, "A Comparison of Nursing Home Residents and Discharges from the 1977 NNHS: United States," *Advance Data from Vital and Health Statistics*, No. 29, May 17, 1978; "An Overview of Nursing Home Characteristics: 1977 NNHS—Provisional Data," *Advance Data from Vital and Health Statistics*, forthcoming.

SUBJECT, SOURCE, TITLE, TABLES	UNIVERSE, FREQUENCY, TYPES OF DATA	TYPE OF DATA COLLECTION OPERATION
SECTION 4. HEALTH AND NUTRITION— CON. **Health Care Financing Administration** *Survey of Independent Health Insurance Plans* See tables 147 and 148 and, in section 17, tables 909 and 910.	Annual survey of health insurance plans not underwritten by insurance companies or Blue Cross– Blue Shield (465 for 1972 census) to obtain operating characteristics, coverages, and financial data.	Complete census every 4 to 5 years; certainty sample of 32 large plans and random sample of remaining plans in other years.
SECTION 5. EDUCATION **National Center For Education Statistics (NCES)** *Revenue and Expenditures for Public Elementary and Secondary Schools* See tables 211, 212, 253–255, and, in section 32, table 1532.	Annual survey of U.S. public elementary and secondary schools, including U.S. outlying areas, to obtain data on school revenues and expenditures.	Complete census.
Statistics of Public Elementary and Secondary Schools See tables in section 5 which present data from NCES pertaining to State public school systems.	Annual survey of U.S. public elementary and secondary schools, including U.S. outlying areas, to obtain data on pupils, staff, estimated expenditures, and teachers salaries.	Complete census.
Higher Education General Information Survey (HEGIS) See tables 261–264, 267, 271, 273, 274, and 276.	Annual survey of all public and private two- and four-year colleges listed in the *Education Directory: Colleges and Universities* to obtain data on enrollment by sex, attendance status, grade level, financial status, and student charges.	Complete census.
Earned Degrees Conferred See tables 257 and 277–279.	Annual survey of institutions listed in the *Education Directory, 1973–1974, Higher Education*, granting bachelor's, master's, and doctorate degrees (1,857 in 1975–76) in the U.S. and outlying areas to obtain information on the number and level of degrees conferred per university, by field of degree and sex of student.	Complete census.

(See section 1 above for information pertaining to the Bureau of the Census; and section 2 above for National Center for Health Statistics data.)

SECTION 6. LAW ENFORCEMENT, FEDERAL COURTS, AND PRISONS **Law Enforcement Assistance Administration (LEAA)** *National Crime Survey* See tables 291–294.	Monthly survey of individuals, households, and commercial establishments in the U.S. to obtain data on criminal victimization of those units for compilation of annual estimates.	National probability sample survey of about 72,000 households in 376 PSU's selected from a list of addresses from the 1970 census, supplemented by new construction permits. Also, an establishment sample of about 15,000 establishments selected from 34 PSU's increased in 1976 to about 50,000 establishments from 58 PSU's.

(See section 2 above for details pertaining to tables 295, 296, and 298; section 10 for details on tables 309 and 311; and section 30 for table 314.)

| DATA COLLECTION AND IMPUTATION PROCEDURES | INFORMATION ON ERRORS IN THE DATA | | SOURCES OF ADDITIONAL MATERIAL |
	Estimates of sampling error	Other (nonsampling) errors	
Mail questionnaire with telephone followup.	Not applicable.	Item nonresponse rate was about 25% for enrollment data and 30% for financial data in 1972 census. In 1972, 383 plans out of 465 provided usable responses.	U.S. Health Care Financing Administration, *HCFA Health Notes*, "Independent Health Insurance Plans," published annually.
Mail survey with followup for nonresponse through direct contact or other records.	Not applicable.	Some distortion in expenditures by function due to variations in State accounting systems.	U.S. National Center for Education Statistics, *Revenues and Expenditures for Public Elementary and Secondary Education, 1975–76.*
Mail survey. Imputations for missing data included in national totals; imputations are derived based on data reported over previous 5 years.	Not applicable.	Arise from differences in interpretation of questions, definitions, and instructions.	U.S. National Center for Education Statistics, *Statistics of Public Elementary and Secondary Day Schools,* published annually.
Survey package mailed in spring; followup procedures for nonrespondents. Missing data imputed by using data for an earlier year, adjusted for trends observed in earlier HEGIS surveys, or data of similar institutions.	Not applicable.	For 1976, 100% response rate for enrollment data; 94% response rate for financial statistics of institutions. Imputed expenditures amounted to about 3% of total expenditures in 1976.	U.S. National Center for Education Statistics, *Financial Statistics of Institutions of Higher Education: Fiscal Year 1976,* State Data.
Conducted by mail, with mail and phone followup. Missing data imputed by using previous year's reports.	Not applicable.	Due to nature of institutional record keeping, number of specialized undergraduate degrees understated; not all types of degrees identified on survey form.	U.S. National Center for Education Statistics, *Earned Degrees Conferred, 1975–76,* Summary Data.
Personal interviews conducted every 6 months for 3 years for each household in sample; for indefinite period for establishments in sample. 12,000 households and 2,500 establishments (8,300 in 1976) enumerated monthly.	CV in 1976: 4% for estimate of personal robbery counts; 1.6% for household burglary count.	For establishments, nonresponse rate about 1%. For household survey, 4% of eligible households were not interviewed and 2% of persons within responding households did not participate.	U.S. Law Enforcement Assistance Administration, *Criminal Victimization in the United States, A Comparison of 1975 and 1976 Findings,* Report No. SD-NCS-N-8, Nov. 1977.

SUBJECT, SOURCE, TITLE, TABLES	UNIVERSE, FREQUENCY, TYPES OF DATA	TYPE OF DATA COLLECTION OPERATION
SECTION 8. PUBLIC LANDS, PARKS, RECREATION, AND TRAVEL **Bureau of the Census** *Census of Transportation National Travel Survey* See tables 410 and 411.	Survey of all persons in the U.S. conducted every 5 years to obtain information on number and characteristics of long-distance trips and all other trips in a designated 24-hour period.	Probability sample of about 24,000 households in which residents were asked about trips they had taken.
SECTION 10. STATE AND LOCAL GOVERNMENT FINANCES AND EMPLOYMENT **Bureau of the Census** *Census of Governments* See tables in section 10 citing *Census of Governments*; in section 11, tables 537 and 538; and in section 16, table 830.	Survey of all governmental units in the U.S. conducted every 5 years to obtain data on government revenue, expenditures, debt, employment and employee-retirement systems, property values, public school systems, and number, size, and structure of governments.	Complete census. List of units derived through classification of government units recently authorized in each State and identification, counting, and classification of existing local governments and public school systems.
Annual Survey of State and Local Government. See tables citing *Public Employment* and *Governmental Finances*.	Sample survey conducted annually to obtain data on revenue, expenditure, debt, and employment of State and local governments. Universe is all governmental units in the U.S. (about 80,000).	Sample of about 16,000 units includes all State governments, county governments with 50,000+ population, municipalities with 25,000+ population, and other governments meeting certain financial criteria; probability sample for remaining units.
SECTION 11. SOCIAL INSURANCE AND WELFARE SERVICES **Social Security Administration** *Aid to Families with Dependent Children (AFDC)* See tables 549, 562–564, 566, 567, and 569.	Survey conducted periodically of all families receiving financial assistance under the AFDC program.	Probability sample survey of .5% of each State's caseload. Sample size was 33,809 families in 1973 and 31,063 families in 1975.
Benefit Data See tables 532–534 and 571.	All persons receiving monthly benefits under Title II of Social Security Act. Data on types of benefits paid, State monthly benefits, benefits withheld and terminated, and value of benefits awarded.	Data based on administrative records.
Supplemental Security Income Program (SSI) See tables 522, 562–565, 568, and 570.	All eligible aged, blind, or disabled persons receiving SSI benefit payments under SSI program. Data include number of persons receiving federally administered SSI, amounts paid, and State administered supplementation.	Data based on administrative records.

(See section 1 above for information pertaining to the Current Population Survey and section 10 for information pertaining to Census of Government.)

| DATA COLLECTION AND IMPUTATION PROCEDURES | INFORMATION ON ERRORS IN THE DATA | | SOURCES OF ADDITIONAL MATERIAL |
	Estimates of sampling error	Other (nonsampling) errors	
Quarterly personal interviews in census year, supplemented by telephone followups.	S.E. for estimate of total household trips (79,926,000) in the first quarter of 1977 is approximately 3,106,000.	Areas of possible nonsampling errors include memory loss on the part of the respondents in reporting trips and in the methods used to estimate trip mileage. Problems in the representation of new construction and mobile homes, and in undercoverage of persons in households also create nonsampling errors. The nonresponse rate was about 10%.	Bureau of the Census, *Census of Transportation: 1977, National Travel Survey*, Report No. TC77-N-1.
Field compilation of financial data from official records and reports for States and large local governments; mail canvas of other units, with mail and telephone followups.	Not applicable.	Some response errors may arise due to respondents interpretation of definitions and instructions.	Bureau of the Census, *Census of Governments, 1977*, various reports.
Field compilation of financial data from official records and reports for States and large local governments; mail canvas of other units with mail and telephone followups of nonrespondents. Data for nonresponses imputed from previous year.	CV for estimates of major employment and financial items are generally less than 2% for most States and less than 1% for the majority of States.	Nonresponse rate about 15% for number of units (about 5% for value items). Other possible errors may result from undetected inaccuracies in classification, response, and processing.	Bureau of the Census, *Public Employment in 1976*, GE 76, No. 1, and *Governmental Finances in 1975–76*, GF 76, No. 5.
Data obtained through administrative records.	S.E. for estimated recipient rates, .5% or less for States.	Processing errors, which are believed to be small.	Social Security Administration, *Findings of the 1975 Study*, September 1977.
Records used consist of actions pursuant to applications for benefits, updated by subsequent post-entitlement actions.	Not applicable.	See above.	Social Security Administration, *Annual Statistical Supplement* to the *Social Security Bulletin*.
Data adjusted to reflect returned checks and overpayment refunds. For federally administered, actual adjusted amounts used; for State administered, payments deflated for average rate across all States.	Not applicable.	See above.	See above.

SUBJECT, SOURCE, TITLE, TABLES	UNIVERSE, FREQUENCY, TYPES OF DATA	TYPE OF DATA COLLECTION OPERATION
SECTION 13. LABOR FORCE, EMPLOYMENT, AND EARNINGS **Bureau of Labor Statistics (BLS)** *Current Employment Statistics Program (CES)* See tables 660, 673–676, 682, 683, 686, and 687.	Monthly survey covering about 4 million nonagricultural establishments to obtain data on employment, hours, and earnings, by industry.	Probability sample survey of about 160,000 establishments.

(See section 1 above for information pertaining to the Current Population Survey.)

SECTION 14. INCOME, EXPENDITURES, AND WEALTH
(See section 1 above for information pertaining to the Current Population Survey.)

SECTION 15. PRICES **Bureau of Labor Statistics** *Consumer Price Index (CPI)* See tables 141, 781, 782, 792–796, and 802.	Monthly survey of price changes of all types of consumer goods and services purchased by urban wage earners and clerical workers (prior to revisions introduced in 1978).	Sample of various consumer items in 56 urban areas.
Producer Price Index See tables 781, 782, and 785–788; in section 25, table 1268; in section 28, table 1358; and, in section 29, table 1445.	Monthly survey of producing companies to determine price change of all commodities produced or imported for sale in commercial transactions in primary markets in the U.S. Data on agriculture, forestry, fishing, manufacturing, mining, gas, electricity, and public utilities.	Nonprobability sample of 2,800 commodities and about 10,000 respondents.

SECTION 16. ELECTIONS

See sections 1 and 10 above for information pertaining to tables 815, 830, 835–841, and 843.

SECTION 17. BANKING, FINANCE, AND INSURANCE

See section 4 above for information pertaining to tables 909 and 910.

SECTION 18. BUSINESS ENTERPRISE

See section 29 below for information pertaining to table 947.

SECTION 19. COMMUNICATIONS

See section 28 below for information pertaining to table 986 and section 29 for tables 992, 993, and 999.

DATA COLLECTION AND IMPUTATION PROCEDURES	INFORMATION ON ERRORS IN THE DATA		SOURCES OF ADDITIONAL MATERIAL
	Estimates of sampling error	Other (nonsampling) errors	
Cooperating State agencies mail questionnaires to sample establishments to develop State and local estimates; information forwarded to BLS where national estimates prepared.	Estimated CV for average weekly hours paid, .1%; for average hourly earnings, .2%.	Incorrect responses believed to be somewhat offsetting. Estimates of employment adjusted annually to reflect complete universe. Average adjustment of .2%.	U.S. Bureau of Labor Statistics, *Employment and Earnings, Explanatory Data*, tables I–O.
Prices of 400 items obtained from about 1,800 food outlets, 30,000 tenants, and 16,000 other reporters in 56 areas. Prices of most goods and services obtained monthly in the 5 largest areas and every 3 months in others.	Estimates of standard errors for monthly, quarterly, and annual percent changes respectively are: All items (.04, .05, .10); food at home (.10, .11, .22); food away from home (.08, .14, .31); housing (.06, .10, .18); apparel and upkeep (.15, .27, .25); transportation (.07, .12, .20); medical care (.14, .19, .27); personal care (.16, .26, .64); reading and recreation (.09, .16, .33); and other goods and services (.11, .12, .18).	Errors result from inaccurate reporting, difficulties in defining concepts and their operational implementation, lack of systematic method for incorporating new outlets in the sample, and introduction of product quality changes and new products.	See text, pp. 481–482.
Data collected by mail. If transaction prices not supplied, list prices used. Some prices obtained from trade publications, organized exchanges, and government agencies. To calculate index, price changes multiplied by their relative weights based on total net selling value of all commodities in 1972.	Not applicable.	Transaction prices at time of shipment not always available, so list and order prices sometimes used. Only about half of the total value of the mining and manufacturing sectors covered by current program. Double counting bias present because gross shipment values are used as weights.	U.S. Bureau of Labor Statistics, *Handbook of Methods*, Bulletin 1910 (1976).

SUBJECT, SOURCE, TITLE, TABLES	UNIVERSE, FREQUENCY, TYPES OF DATA	TYPE OF DATA COLLECTION OPERATION
SECTION 22. TRANSPORTATION—LAND **Bureau of the Census** *1972 Truck Inventory and Use Survey* See table 1106.	Survey of truck owners conducted every five years to obtain data on truck resources, excluding government owned vehicles.	Probability sample of 114,000 trucks (private and commercial) from 20 million registrations on file in motor vehicle departments in the States and District of Columbia.

(See section 1 above for information pertaining to tables 1107 and 1108 and section 2 for information pertaining to table 1088.)

SUBJECT, SOURCE, TITLE, TABLES	UNIVERSE, FREQUENCY, TYPES OF DATA	TYPE OF DATA COLLECTION OPERATION
SECTION 23. TRANSPORTATION—AIR AND WATER **Bureau of the Census** *Foreign Trade—Export Statistics* See Bureau of the Census citations for export statistics in source notes in sections 23 and 31 and also tables 1217, 1314, and 1541.	The export declarations collected by Customs are processed each month to obtain data on the movement of U.S. merchandise exports to foreign countries. Data obtained include value, quantity, and shipping weight of exports by commodity, by country of destination, by Customs district of exportation, and by mode of transportation.	Shipper's Export Declarations are required to be filed for the exportation of merchandise valued over $250. Customs officials collect and transmit the documents on a flow basis for data compilation. Probability sampling is used in the compilation process for low-value shipments (which account for 3% of total value), i.e., shipments to Canada valued $251–$1,999 and to other countries valued $251–$999.
Foreign Trade—Import Statistics See Bureau of the Census citations for import statistics in source notes in sections 23 and 31 and also tables 1314 and 1541.	The import entry documents collected by Customs are processed each month to obtain data on the movement of merchandise imported into the United States. Data obtained include value, quantity, and shipping weight by commodity, by country of origin, by Customs district of entry, and by mode of transportation.	Import entry documents are required to be filed for the importation of goods into the United States. Customs officials collect and transmit statistical copies of the documents on a flow basis for data compilation. A 1% sample of entries is processed for shipments valued $250 or less, which account for less than .5% of the total import value.
SECTION 24. AGRICULTURE **Bureau of the Census** *1974 Census of Agriculture* See tables citing Census of Agriculture in section 24 and, in section 32, table 1542.	Census of all farm operators in the U.S. every five years, to obtain data on farm acreage, crops and livestock, equipment, farm sales, income, expenses, and other items, by State and county.	Complete census of most farms; sample of other farms. Self enumeration by mail using lists of persons and organizations in agriculture maintained by Internal Revenue Service, Social Security, and Agricultural Stabilization and Conservation Service (ASCS).
U.S. Department of Agriculture, Economics, Statistics, and Cooperatives Service (ESCS) *Basic Area Frame Sample* See tables citing ESCS in source notes in section 24 and tables 1281, 1282, and 1433 which pertain to this or the following two surveys.	Two annual surveys of all U.S. farm operators in the U.S. June survey collects data on planted acreage and livestock inventories; December survey collects data on livestock inventories and fall-seeded crop acreage.	Stratified probability sample of about 16,000 land area units of about 1 sq. mile (range from .1 sq. mile in cities to several sq. miles in open grazing areas). Sample includes 60,000 parcels of agricultural land. About 20% of the sample replaced annually.

DATA COLLECTION AND IMPUTATION PROCEDURES	INFORMATION ON ERRORS IN THE DATA		SOURCES OF ADDITIONAL MATERIAL
	Estimates of sampling error	Other (nonsampling) errors	
Questionnaire mailed to owner of each truck. Two mail followups for non-respondents.	Estimated CV's for major characteristics at State level, 1% to 2%; much larger CV's for detailed characteristics.	Response rate of 90%. Sample verification of coding and punching allowed maximum of 3% error in average quality.	U.S. Bureau of the Census, *Census of Transportation: 1972*, vol. II, *Truck Inventory and Use Survey*.
Statistical copies of Shipper's Export Declarations received on a daily basis from Customs ports throughout the country are subjected to a monthly processing cycle. They are fully processed to the extent they reflect items valued $1,000 and over, and in the case of exports to Canada, $2,000 and over. Estimates for shipments valued at $250 or less are made, based on established percentages of individual country totals.	Estimated CV's for total value of exports about .1% and, for major commodity groupings, about 1%. CV's less than 1% for total value over $10 million, less than 2% for totals between $3 million and $10 million, and less than possible errors due to rounding for values less than $3 million.	Clerical and complex computer checks intercept most processing errors and minimize otherwise significant reporting errors; other nonsampling errors are caused by undercounting of exports to Canada due to the non-receipt of some Shipper's Export Declarations.	U.S. Bureau of the Census, *U.S. Exports, Schedule E, Commodity by Country*, FT 410.
Statistical copies of import entry documents, received on a daily basis from Customs ports of entry throughout the country, are subjected to a monthly processing cycle. They are fully processed to the extent they reflect items valued $251 and over.	Estimated CV for world area and country totals less than .1% for totals over $20 million; less than .5% for totals between $1 million and $20 million and less than possible errors due to rounding for values less than $1 million.	Verification of statistical data reporting by Customs officials prior to transmittal and a subsequent program of clerical and computer checks hold nonsampling errors arising from reporting and/or processing errors to a minimum.	U.S. Bureau of the Census, *U.S. General Imports, Schedule A, Commodity by Country*, FT 135.
Questionnaire to all farms with $2,500+ sales; shorter questionnaire to other (only a sample from ASCS list if not also on other lists). Nonrespondent followup by letters and phone calls. Published data adjusted for nonresponse, but not for underenumeration.	Standard errors by county and State for farm acreage, value of land and buildings, various crop and livestock values given in Appendix A tables of each 1974 State volume. The estimated CV for U.S. land in farms and value of crops sold is .04%.	Undercoverage of farms (chiefly small farms) was about 11% nationally; amount of land missed 7%; and value of farm products sold underestimated by 3%. Estimates of undercoverage in each State in 1969 and 1974 given in State volumes. Adjustment for farm nonresponse as a percent of the U.S. total represented 12.3% for number of farms, 5.9% for land in farms, and 4.1% for value of products sold.	U.S. Bureau of the Census, *Census of Agriculture, 1974*, State and county volumes and vol. IV, part 3, *Coverage Evaluation*.
Data collection by personal enumeration. Imputation based on enumerator observation or data reported by respondents having similar agricultural characteristics.	CV's range from 1% to 2% for national estimates of major crop acreage and livestock inventories and from 3% to 8% for corresponding State estimates.	Minimized through rigid quality controls on the collection process and careful review of all reported data.	U.S. Department of Agriculture, SRS, *Scope and Methods of the Statistical Reporting Service*, Miscellaneous Publication No. 1308, July 1975.

SUBJECT, SOURCE, TITLE, TABLES	UNIVERSE, FREQUENCY, TYPES OF DATA	TYPE OF DATA COLLECTION OPERATION
SECTION 24. AGRICULTURE, —CON.		
Multiple Frame Surveys	Surveys of all U.S. farm operators to obtain data on major livestock inventories, selected crop acreages and production, and farm labor characteristics; and to obtain farm economic data for price indexing.	Primary frame from general or special purpose lists, supplemented by a probability sample of land areas.
Objective Yield Surveys	Surveys for data on corn, cotton, potatoes, soybeans, and wheat to forecast and estimate yields.	Random location of plots in probability sample of fields. Fields selected in June or December from Basic Area Frame Sample (see above).

(See section 1 above for information pertaining to the Current Population Survey, and section 23 for information pertaining to table 1217.)

SECTION 28. CONSTRUCTION AND HOUSING		
Bureau of the Census *Census of Construction Industries* See tables 1361–1363 and, in section 32, table 1537.	Census every five years. In 1972 it covered all establishments primarily engaged in contract construction, in construction for sale on their own account (operative builders), or in subdividing real property into lots (438,000 firms with paid employees, 483,000 without paid employees).	Probability sample of 145,000 firms, which comprised all medium and large size employers in the universe and a probability sample of small employers. Also all 483,000 firms without paid employees are included in the sample coverage.
Monthly Survey of New Construction See tables 1366–1368, 1370, 1371, 1392, and 1393.	Survey conducted monthly of newly constructed housing units (excluding mobile homes, and nonhousekeeping residential buildings such as motels, hotels, courts, and cabins). Data collected on the start, completion, and sale of housing. (Annual figures are aggregates of monthly estimates.)	Probability sample of housing units obtained from building permits selected from 14,000 permit-issuing places. (Estimates for those places adjusted to account for buildings not requiring permits.) For nonpermit places, multistage probability sample of new housing units selected in 137 PSU's. In those areas, "knowledgable" persons provide list of housing starts verified by phone or visit; areas also canvassed.
Value of New Construction Put in Place See tables 1353 and 1354.	Survey conducted monthly on total value of all construction put in place in the current month, both public and private projects. Construction values include costs of materials and labor, contractors' profits, overhead costs, cost of architectural and engineering work, and miscellaneous project costs. (Annual figures are aggregates of monthly estimates.)	Varies by type of activity: Total cost of private one-family houses started each month is distributed into value in place using fixed patterns of monthly construction progress; using a multistage probability sample, data for private multifamily housing are obtained by mail from owners of multiunit projects. Data for residential additions and alterations are obtained in a quarterly survey measuring expenditures; monthly estimates are interpolated from quarterly data. Estimates of private nonhousekeeping, nonresidential buildings and State and local government construction are obtained by mail from owners (or agents) for a probability sample of

projects; estimates of farm nonresidential construction expenditures are based on U.S. Department of Agriculture annual estimates of construction; public utility estimates are obtained from reports submitted to Federal regulatory agencies and from private utility companies; estimates for all other private construction (nonbuilding) are obtained by phasing F. W. Dodge contract award data; government estimates of Federal construction are based on monthly data supplied by Federal agencies.

DATA COLLECTION AND IMPUTATION PROCEDURES	INFORMATION ON ERRORS IN THE DATA		SOURCES OF ADDITIONAL MATERIAL
	Estimates of sampling error	Other (nonsampling) errors	
Mail or personal interviews used for initial data collection. Mail nonrespondent followup by phone, mail, and personal interviews.	Estimated CV for number of hired farm workers is about 3%. See above for CV's of other national and State estimates.	Nonresponse rates vary from 5% to 15%.	See above.
Enumerators and analysts count and measure plant characteristics in sample fields.	CV's for national estimates of production are about 2% to 3%.	See above.	See above.
Survey data for employers collected by questionnaire. IRS business tax forms used for establishments without paid employees. Followup on problems with questionnaire responses. Within industry, by State cross-classifications, missing data imputed based on relationships of known responses to administrative data	Estimated CV of about 1% at national level for estimated totals of all construction and about .5% for construction subindustries.	Response rate 85% to 90% for most items. Computer scan used to indentify incomplete questionnaires for review.	U.S. Bureau of the Census, *Census of Construction Industries, 1972*, vol. 1, *Industry and Special Statistics.*
Data obtained by telephone inquiry and field visit.	Estimated CV of 3% to 4% for estimates of national totals; as high as 20% for estimated totals of more detailed characteristics, such as residential multi-unit structures.	Response rate over 90% for most items. Nonsampling errors attributed to definitional problems, differences in interpretation of questions, incorrect reporting, inability to obtain information about all cases in the sample, and processing errors.	U.S. Bureau of the Census, *Construction Reports,* Series C20, *Housing Starts,* C22; *Housing Completions,* C25; *Housing Sales*; and C27, *Price Index of New One-Family Houses Sold.*
See "Type of Data Collection Operation". Imputation accounts for approximately 20% of estimated value of construction each month.	CV estimates for private nonresidential building construction range from 1% for estimated number of office buildings to 6% for religious institutions. CV approximately 1% for total new private nonresidential buildings.	For directly measured data series based on samples, some nonsampling errors may arise from processing errors, imputations, and misunderstanding of questions. Indirect data series are dependent on the validity of the underlying assumptions and procedures.	U.S. Bureau of the Census, *Construction Reports,* Series C30, *Value of New Construction Put in Place.*

SUBJECT, SOURCE, TITLE, TABLES	UNIVERSE, FREQUENCY, TYPES OF DATA	TYPE OF DATA COLLECTION OPERATION
SECTION 28. CONSTRUCTION AND HOUSING—CON.		
Census of Housing See tables 986, 1373–1377, 1379, 1382, and 1394.	Census of all occupied and vacant housing, excluding group quarters, conducted every 10 years as part of the decennial census (see section 1 above) to determine adequacy and quality of U.S. housing.	For 1970, a complete count of 12 housing items. Other items collected from 5% and 15% probability samples selected for two sets of detailed questions on housing (these two sets having some common items). Mailing lists compiled from several sources and checked by the Post Office were supplemented with listings of possible housing units observed by enumerators.
Annual Housing Survey See tables citing Annual Housing Survey in source notes in section 28 and, in section 19, table 986.	Conducted nationally in the fall of each year to obtain data on the approximately 80 million occupied or vacant housing units in the U.S. (group quarters are excluded). Data include characteristics of occupied housing units, housing inventory changes, vacant units, new housing and mobile home units, recently relocated households, and housing and neighborhood quality indicators.	The national sample is a multistage probability sample with about 75,500 units eligible for interview. Sample units, selected within 461 PSU's, are surveyed over a 3-month period.
Housing Vacancy Survey See tables 1388 and 1389.	Survey to obtain data on vacancy rates, characteristics of vacant units, tenure of occupied units from 1 sample; and characteristics of occupied units from a second.	Consists of 2 samples: First one from CPS (see section 1 above); second sample, the Quarterly Household Survey (QHS), is a probability sample of 6,000 households in 103 PSU's.

(See section 1 above for information pertaining to the Census of Population.)

SECTION 29. MANUFACTURES		
Bureau of the Census *Census of Manufactures* See tables citing *Census of Manufactures* in source notes in section 29 and also tables 598, 947, 992, 993, 999, 1091, 1271, and 1538.	Conducted every five years to obtain information on labor materials, capital input and output characteristics, plant location, and legal form of organization for all plants in the U.S. with one or more employees.	Complete enumeration of survey frame, which contained about 312,000 firms, obtained from IRS and Social Security Administration records. In 1972, about 120,000 firms were small single-unit firms; about 104,000 firms with no employees were excluded.
Annual Survey of Manufactures See tables citing *Annual Survey of Manufactures* in source notes in section 29.	Conducted annually to provide basic measures of manufacturing activity for intercensal years for all manufacturing establishments having one or more paid employees.	Sampling frame is 312,000 firms in the 1972 Census of Manufactures (see above), supplemented by Social Security Administration lists of new manufacturers, from which a probability sample of 70,000 establishments is selected. All companies having at least one establishment with 250+ employees included in the sample along with a sample of other companies. All establishments within selected companies are included.

(See section 24 above for information pertaining to table 1433 and section 15 for information pertaining to table 1445.)

DATA COLLECTION AND IMPUTATION PROCEDURES	INFORMATION ON ERRORS IN THE DATA		SOURCES OF ADDITIONAL MATERIAL
	Estimates of sampling error	Other (nonsampling) errors	
In 1970, a self-enumeration census using a mail-out/mail-back procedure used in most areas (previously, enumerators visited households). Followup for nonrespondents and identification of vacant units done by phone and personal visit.	Estimated CV's of the estimates at the national level are very small. Most of the CV's are less than .6%. As an example, the estimated CV for the estimated number of housing units with warm air furnaces is less than .03%.	In 1970, undercount of housing units estimated at 1.4%; 1950 undercount, 2.3%, and 1960 undercount, 2%. Estimates of various censuses not strictly comparable due to differences in timing, procedures, etc.	U.S. Bureau of the Census, *U.S. Census of Population and Housing: Procedural History, 1960 and 1970.*
Survey conducted by personal interview with subsequent followup by telephone or personal visit.	For the national sample, illustrations of the S.E. of the estimates are provided in the appendix of each report. As an example, the estimated CV is about .3% for the estimate of the number of owner occupied housing units.	Errors result from incorrect or incomplete responses, errors in coding and recording, and processing errors. For the 1976 national sample, about 700,000 units were not included in the sample coverage. A multistage estimation procedure corrected coverage deficiencies for the total, but subtotal biases still remain. A reinterview study also indicates some inconsistencies in the data.	U.S. Bureau of the Census, *Current Housing Reports,* Series H-150 and H-170, Annual Housing Survey.
First contact with a household is personal interview; subsequent interviews often conducted by phone.	As an example, S.E. for estimated annual average vacancy rate for rental units with six units or more is .2%. Other S.E.'s shown in census publication.	Due to interviews and respondent errors. Response rate for QHS is 95%. (See section 1 above for CPS.)	U.S. Bureau of the Census, *Current Housing Reports,* Series H-111, *Housing Vacancies.*
Data on single-unit firms estimated from administrative records; data on others from questionnaires. Five mail followups and phone calls to large companies held imputation from administrative records to a minimum. Approximately 4.1% of total value of shipments were unreported and required imputation.	Not applicable.	Based on evaluation studies, estimates of nonsampling errors are about 1.3% for estimated total payroll; 2% for total employment; and 1% for value of shipments.	U.S. Bureau of the Census, *Census of Manufactures, 1972,* vol. 1, *Subject and Special Statistics.*
Survey conducted by mail with phone and mail followups of nonrespondents.	Estimated S.E. for number of employees and for value added totals given in annual publications. For State totals, estimated CV's are 2% or less, but vary considerably for detailed characteristics.	Response rate about 85%. Nonsampling errors include response, collection, reporting, and transcription errors, many of which are corrected through computer and clerical checks.	U.S. Bureau of the Census, *Annual Survey of Manufactures,* and Technical Paper 24.

SUBJECT, SOURCE, TITLE, TABLES	UNIVERSE, FREQUENCY, TYPES OF DATA	TYPE OF DATA COLLECTION OPERATION

SECTION 30. DOMESTIC TRADE AND SERVICES

Bureau of the Census
Census of Wholesale Trade, Census of Retail Trade, Census of Selected Service Industries

See tables citing the above censuses or the *Census of Business* in source notes in section 30.

Conducted every five years to obtain data on number of establishments, number of employees, total payroll size, and total sales. In 1972, universe was all employer establishments primarily engaged in wholesale trade, and employer and nonemployer establishments primarily engaged in retail trade or selected service industries.

All wholesale firms with paid employees surveyed; all retail and selected service industries with 4+ paid employees surveyed plus a sample of smaller firms. Firms with no employees not required to file a census return.

Annual Retail Trade Survey

See tables 1462, 1463, and 1466.

Annual survey to obtain estimates of retail sales and inventories in the U.S. for all employers and nonemployer retail establishments operating at the end of the calendar year.

Probability sample from firms in the sample of the Current Business Survey (CBS); see below. Sample consists of all firms in the CBS sample with 11+ establishments according to the most recent update of census files, and a probability sample of other organizations.

Current Business Surveys

See tables 1461, 1464, 1465, 1474, 1477, 1478, and 1482.

Provides monthly estimates of services receipts in the U.S. by kind of industry, merchandise exchanges between wholesalers and other businesses, retail sales by kind of business and geographic area, and accounts-receivable balances of retail stores. Universe consists of all retail and selected service establishments and employer establishments primarily engaged in wholesale trade.

Probability sample of establishments from a list frame and an area frame. List frame is the Bureau's Standard Statistical Establishment List (SSEL) updated quarterly for recent "births" from the Social Security Administration list of establishments having an employer identification number. The largest firms are included monthly; a sample of others is included every three months on a rotating basis. The area frame covers business not subjected to sampling on the list frame. The area sample consists of selected land segments in which all inscope businesses are canvassed and those businesses determined not to be subjected to sampling on the list frame are tabulated.

SECTION 31. FOREIGN COMMERCE AND AID

See section 23 above for information pertaining to tables citing import and export statistics in source notes in this section.

DATA COLLECTION AND IMPUTATION PROCEDURES	INFORMATION ON ERRORS IN THE DATA		SOURCES OF ADDITIONAL MATERIAL
	Estimates of sampling error	Other (nonsampling) errors	
Mail and telephone followups for nonrespondents. Data for nonrespondents and "nonselected" firms in retail trade and selected services from administrative records of IRS and the Social Security Administration. Imputation from related responses or administrative records from IRS or SSA.	Not applicable.	Response rate 84.4% for single establishment firms; 92% for multi-establishment firms. Item response ranged from 60% to 90% with higher rates for less detailed questions.	U.S. Bureau of the Census, Appendix A of Census of Retail Trade, vol. 1; Census of Selected Services, vol. 1; Census of Wholesale Trade, vol. 1; and Economic Censuses, Procedural History, January 1976.
Survey questionnaire mailed early in year and followed by mail and phone followups. Imputation based on previous reports of the firm in current monthly surveys or latest business census, supplemented by administrative records.	CV for national estimates of total sales and inventories is about 3.5%. For more detailed estimates by kind of business, or geographic areas, estimated CV's range from 0 to 7%, occasionally as high as 10.5%.	Nonresponse rate, 5% or less. Incomplete response ranges from 5% for inventories to 9% for sales.	U.S. Bureau of the Census, Retail Trade, 1975, BR-75-13; and Census of Retail Trade, 1972, vol. 1, Chapter 2.
Imputation made for each nonresponse item and each item failing edit checks.	CV's about .6% for estimated total retail sales, 1.4% for wholesale sales, 1.2% for wholesale inventories, and 3.5% for selected service receipts. Sampling errors shown in monthly publications.	Nonresponse rate, 5% or refusals, about 10% monthly. Incomplete response for wholesale inventories and retail accounts receivable range between 20% and 25% monthly. Response error from area sample cases about .1%. Special studies indicate a tendency to underreport current month sales and exclude sales tax in sales reports.	U.S. Bureau of the Census, Monthly Retail Trade Reports, Monthly Wholesale Trade Reports, and Monthly Selected Services Receipts Reports.

APPENDIX IV

Guide to Sources of Statistics

Alphabetically arranged by subject, this guide contains references to the important primary sources of statistical information for the United States. Secondary sources have been included if the information contained in them is presented in a particularly convenient form or if primary sources are not readily available. Nonrecurrent publications presenting compilations or estimates for years later than 1968 or types of data not available in regular series are also included.

Much valuable information may also be found in State reports (see pp. 1008-1011) and in reports for particular commodities, industries, or similar segments of our economic and social structure, many of which are not included here.

Publications listed under each subject are divided into two main groups: "U.S. Government" and "Other." The location of the publisher of each report is given except for Federal agencies located in Washington, D.C. Most Federal publications may be purchased from the Superintendent of Documents, U.S. Government Printing Office, Washington, D.C. 20402, tel. (202) 783-3238, or from Government Printing Office bookstores in certain major cities. In some cases, Federal publications may be obtained from the issuing agency.

Major reports, such as the Census of Population, which consist of many volumes, are listed by their general, all-inclusive titles.

Abortions—*see* Vital Statistics.

Accidents—*see also* Health; Insurance; *and* Vital Statistics

U.S. Government

Bureau of Labor Statistics
Occupational Injuries and Illness in the United States, by Industry. Annual.

Civil Aeronautics Board
Supplement to the Handbook of Airline Statistics. Biennial.

Department of Transportation
Transportation Safety Information Report. Quarterly.

Federal Aviation Administration
FAA Statistical Handbook of Aviation. Annual.

Federal Railroad Administration
Accident Bulletin. Summary and Analysis of Accidents on Railroads in United States. Annual with monthly summary.
Rail-Highway Grade-Crossing Accidents. Annual.
Summary of Accidents/Incidents Reported by All Line Haul and Switching and Terminal Railroad Companies. Monthly with quarterly summary.

Accidents—Con.

U.S. Government—Con.

Mining Enforcement and Safety Administration
Safety Reviews:
Coal-Mine Fatalities. Monthly.
Coal-Mine Injuries and Worktime. Monthly.
Metal and Nonmetal Mine Injuries. Quarterly.

National Center for Health Statistics
Current Estimates from the Health Interview Survey. Annual.
Vital Statistics of the United States. Annual.

Other

Metropolitan Life Insurance Company, New York
Statistical Bulletin. Quarterly.

National Safety Council, Chicago
Accident Facts. Annual.

The Travelers Insurance Companies, Hartford
Annual Accident Series.

964

Agriculture—*see also* Construction; Food; Irrigation; Labor; Money and Banking; *and* Population

U.S. Government

Bureau of the Census

Census of Agriculture. Quinquennial. (1974, most recent.)

U.S. Commodity Exports and Imports as Related to Output. Annual. (Series ES2.)

Bureau of the Census and Bureau of Mines

Raw Materials in the United States Economy: 1900–1969. (Issued 1972. Working Paper No. 35.)

Commodity Exchange Authority

Commodity Futures Statistics. Annual. (Statistical Bulletin No. 516.)

Department of Agriculture, Agricultural Stabilization and Conservation Service

Commodity Credit Corporation Report of Financial Condition and Operations. Quarterly.

Department of Agriculture, Economics, Statistics, and Cooperatives Service

Agricultural Finance Statistics. Annual.

Agricultural Outlook. Monthly.

Agricultural Statistics. Annual.

Balance Sheet of the Farming Sector. Annual. (Agricultural Information Bulletin No. 411.)

Changes in Farm Production and Efficiency; Summary Report. Annual. (Statistical Bulletin No. 581.)

Citrus Fruits: Production, Use, and Value.

Crop Production. (Acreage, yield, and production, by States.) Monthly with annual summary.

Crop Values. Annual.

Dairy Products. Monthly and annual.

Economic Tables. Annual.

Farm Income Statistics. Annual. (Statistical Bulletin No. 576.)

Farm-Retail Spreads for Food Products. (Miscellaneous Publication No. 741.) 1972.

Feed Statistics. (Statistical Bulletin No. 410.) Supplemented annually.

Agriculture—Con.

U.S. Government—Con.

Department of Agriculture, Economics, Statistics, and Cooperatives Service—Con.

Field Crops: Production, Disposition, and Value of Principal Crops. Annual.

Food and Fiber System and How It Works, March 1975. (Agricultural Information Bulletin 383.)

Food Consumption, Prices, and Expenditures. (Agricultural Economics Report No. 138.) Supplemented annually.

Foreign Agricultural Trade of the United States. Monthly with annual supplements on calendar year and fiscal year trade data.

Handbook of Agricultural Charts. (Agricultural Handbook No. 524.) Annual.

The Hired Farm Working Force. Annual.

Livestock and Meat Statistics. July 1976. (Statistical Bulletin No. 522.) Supplemented annually.

Livestock, Poultry, and Dairy Reports: Inventory Numbers, Production, Disposition, and Income. (Meat animals, chickens, eggs, turkeys, and milk.) Annual.

Livestock-Feed Relationships. (Statistical Bulletin No. 530.) Supplemented annually.

Major Uses of Land in the United States. Summary for 1969. December 1973. (Agricultural Economics Report No. 247.)

Milk Production, Disposition, and Income. Annual.

Noncitrus Fruits and Nuts. Annual with mid-year supplements.

Number of Farms and Land in Farms by States. Annual.

Potatoes and Sweetpotatoes, Disposition and Value. Annual.

Poultry and Egg Statistics, 1972–75. (Statistical Bulletin No. 525.) Supplemented periodically.

Seed Crops: Production, Disposition, Value, Supply, and Disappearance. Preliminary issued in January, final in May.

Situation Reports. Issued for cotton and wool, dairy products, fats and oils, feed, fertilizer, fruit, livestock and meat, poultry and eggs, rice, sugar and sweeteners, tobacco, vegetables, wheat, and world agriculture. Monthly, quarterly, annual.

Business—Con.

U.S. Government—Con.

Internal Revenue Service
Statistics of Income. (Annual reports on Corporation and Business Income Tax Returns. Periodic reports on Foreign Income and Tax Reported on U.S. Corporation Tax Returns.)

Patent and Trademark Office
Commissioner of Patents and Trademarks Annual Report.

Securities and Exchange Commission
Statistical Bulletin. Monthly.
Working Capital of Nonfinancial U.S. Corporations. Quarterly. Published in the Statistical Bulletin of the SEC until Jan. 1978 when published by the Federal Reserve Board.

Senate, Committee on Government Operations
Disclosure of Corporate Ownership. 1973. (93d Congress, 1st Session.)

Small Business Administration
Annual Report.

Other

The Conference Board, New York
Road Maps of Industry. Monthly.

Dun & Bradstreet, Inc., New York
The Failure Record. Annual.
Monthly Failure Report.
Monthly New Business Incorporation Report.
Quarterly Businessmen's Expectations Report.

Fortune (Time, Inc.), New York
The Fortune Directory of the 500 Largest Industrial Corporations. (Annual supplement to Fortune.)

National Bureau of Economic Research, New York
The Behavior of Industrial Prices, by George J. Stigler and James K. Kindahl. 1970. (General Series 90.)
The Business Cycle Today, by Victor Zarnowitz. 1972. (General Series 96, Vol. I.)
The Channels of Monetary Effects on Interest Rates, by Phillip Cagan. 1972. (General Series 97.)
Conference on Research in Taxation, Michael Boskin, editor. Published as Supplement to Journal of Political Economy, April 1978.

Business—Con.

Other—Con.

National Bureau of Economic Research—Con.
Conference on Secular Inflation, Karl Brunner, editor. 1973. (Universities—National Bureau Conference 25.)
Economic Growth, by William D. Nordhaus and James Tobin. 1972. (General Series 96, Vol. V.)
Forecasts with Macroeconometric Models, by Yoel Haitovsky, George Treyz, and Vincent Su. 1974. (Studies in Business Cycles 23.)
The Formation and Stocks of Total Capital, by John W. Kendrick. 1976. (General Series 100.)
Institutional Investors and Corporate Stock—A Background Report, Raymond Goldsmith, editor, 1973. (Studies in Capital Formation and Financing 13.)
Measures of Credit Risk and Experience, by Edgar R. Fiedler. 1971. (General Series 95.)
Monetary Statistics of the United States: Estimates, Sources, Methods, by Milton Friedman and Anna Jacobson Schwartz. 1970. (Studies in Business Cycles 20.)
Orders, Production, and Investment—A Cyclical and Structural Analysis, by Victor Zarnowitz. 1973. (Business Cycles 22.)
Postwar Productivity Trends in the United States, by John W. Kendrick. 1973. (General Series 98.)
Substituting a Value-Added Tax for the Corporate Income Tax, by S. P. Dresch, An-loh Linn, and D. K. Stout. (Ballinger Publishing Co., Cambridge, Mass.)

Urban Land Institute, Washington, D.C.
The Dollars and Cents of Shopping Centers. Triennial.

Canal Zone—*see* Outlying Areas.

Child Welfare—*see* Education; *and* Social Insurance.

City Government—*see* State and Local Government.

Civil Service—*see* Federal Government; *and* State and Local Government.

Climate—*see also* Health

U.S. Government

National Oceanic and Atmospheric Administration
Climatological Data. National Summary; also issued in sections for States and outlying areas. Monthly with annual summary.
Comparative Climatic Data Through 1977.
Daily River Stages. Annual.
General Summary of Tornadoes. Annual.
Hourly Precipitation Data. Monthly with annual summary; for each State.
Local Climatological Data. Monthly with annual summary; for major cities.
Storm Data. Monthly.
Weekly Weather and Crop Bulletin. National summary.

Commerce—*see* Foreign Commerce; Retail and Wholesale Trade; *and* Transportation.

Commodity Prices—*see also* Economic Indexes

U.S. Government

Board of Governors of the Federal Reserve System
Federal Reserve Bulletin. Monthly.
Bureau of Labor Statistics
Announcement to Users of the Consumer Price Index. 1978.
City Worker's Family Budget, Pricing Procedures, Specifications, and Average Prices, (Bulletin No. 1570-3.) Updated in annual press releases; titles vary.
Consumer Expenditure Survey Series: Daily Data, 1972. 1975. (Report Series 448.)
Consumer Price index. Monthly.
Consumer Price Index, U.S. City Average and Selected Items, Groups, and Areas. Monthly.
Facts About the Revised Consumer Price Index. 1978.
Handbook of Labor Statistics. Annual.
Monthly Labor Review.
Producer Prices and Price Indexes. Monthly and annual.
Productivity and Costs. Quarterly.
Productivity and Costs in Non-financial Corporations. Quarterly.

Commodity Prices—Con.

U.S. Government—Con.

Bureau of Labor Statistics—Con.
Relative Importance of Items in the Consumer Price Index. Annual.
Retail Food Prices by Cities. Monthly and annual averages.
Retail Prices and Indexes of Fuels and Utilities. Monthly.
Three Budgets for a Retired Couple in Urban Areas of the United States. (Bulletin No. 1570-6 and supplements.) Updated in annual press releases; titles vary.
Three Standards of Living for an Urban Family of Four Persons. (Bulletin No. 1570-5 and supplements.) Updated in annual press releases; titles vary.
Tuesday Spot Market Price Indexes and Prices. Weekly and monthly summary.
Department of Agriculture, Economics, Statistics, and Cooperatives Service.
Agricultural Prices. Monthly and annual.
Agricultural Statistics. Annual.

Other

Commodity Research Bureau, New York
Commodity Yearbook. Annual.
Morgan Guaranty Trust Company of New York
The Morgan Guaranty Survey. Monthly. (Wholesale price index.)
Wall Street Journal. (Dow Jones & Co., New York.) Daily except Saturdays, Sundays, and holidays.

Communications—*see also* Newspapers

U.S. Government

Bureau of the Census
Households With Television Sets in the United States. Irregular. (Current Housing Reports, H-121, Housing Characteristics.)
Federal Communications Commission
AM-FM Broadcast Financial Data. Annual.
Annual Report.
Statistics of Communications Common Carriers. Annual.
TV Broadcast Financial Data. Annual.

Communications—Con.

U.S. Government—Con.

Rural Electrification Administration
Annual Statistical Report—Rural Telephone Borrowers.

U.S. Postal Service
Annual Report of the Postmaster General.
Revenue and Cost Analysis. Annual.

Other

American Telephone and Telegraph Company, New York
The World's Telephones. Annual.

John Blair & Company, New York
Statistical Trends in Broadcasting. Annual.

Broadcasting Publications, Inc., Washington, D.C.
Broadcasting Yearbook.

Corporation for Public Broadcasting, Washington, D.C.
One Week of Public TV, April 1972; May 1973.

Editor and Publisher Co., Inc.
International Year Book. Annual.

Electronic Industries Association, Washington, D.C.
Electronic Market Data Book. Annual.

National Instructional Television Center, Bloomington, Ind.
One Week of Educational Television. Number Six. March 9–15, 1970. 1971.

Television Digest, Inc., Washington, D.C.
Television Factbook. Annual.

United States Independent Telephone Association, Washington, D.C.
Statistics of the Independent Telephone Industry. Annual.

Construction, Housing, and Real Estate— *see also* Money *and* Roads

U.S. Government

Board of Governors of the Federal Reserve System
Federal Reserve Bulletin. Monthly.

Bureau of the Census
Census of Construction Industries. Quinquennial. (1977, most recent.)

Construction, Housing, and Real Estate— Con.

U.S. Government—Con.

Bureau of the Census—Con.
Census of Housing. Decennial. (1970, most recent.)
Current Construction Reports: Housing Starts, C20 (monthly); New Residential Construction in Selected Standard Metropolitan Statistical Areas, C21 (quarterly); Housing Completions C22 (monthly); New One-Family Houses Sold and for Sale, C25 (monthly and annual); Price Index of New One-Family Houses Sold, C27 (quarterly); Value of New Construction Put in Place, C30 (monthly with occasional historical supplement); Housing Authorized by Building Permits and Public Contracts, C40 (monthly and annual); Housing Units Authorized for Demolition in Permit-Issuing Places, C45 (annual); Residential Alterations and Repairs, C50 (quarterly and annual).
Current Housing Reports: Housing Vacancies, H-111 (quarterly and annual); Market Absorption of Apartments, H-130 (quarterly and annual); Characteristics of Apartments Completed, H-131 (annual); Annual Housing Survey, H-150 (series of six annual reports); Annual Housing Survey—Housing Characteristics for Selected Metropolitan Areas, H-170.
Housing Starts, 1959 to 1971. 1972.
Social Indicators, 1973; 1976.

Bureau of Domestic Business Development.
Construction Review. Monthly.

Bureau of Economic Analysis
Fixed Nonresidential Business and Residential Capital in the United States, 1925–75. 1976.
National Income and Product Accounts of the United States, 1929–74; Statistical Tables. 1976.
Survey of Current Business. Monthly. Supplemented by Business Statistics, weekly and biennial.

Bureau of Labor Statistics
Consumer Price Index. Monthly. (Housing, rent, and home ownership indexes.)
Employment and Earnings. Monthly.

Construction, Housing, and Real Estate—Con.

U.S. Government—Con.

Bureau of Labor Statistics—Con.

Employment and Earnings, States and Areas. Annual.

Employment and Earnings, United States. Annual.

Labor and Material Requirements for (selected types of) Construction. (Bulletins issued at irregular intervals.)

Monthly Labor Review.

Rent or Buy? Evaluating Alternatives in the Shelter Market. 1974. (Bulletin 1823.)

Union Wages and Hours: Building Trades. Annual with quarterly releases.

Department of Agriculture, Economics, Statistics, and Cooperatives Service

Farm Real Estate Historical Series Data: 1850–1970. June 1973.

Farm Real Estate Market Developments. Annual with supplements.

Farm Real Estate Taxes. Annual.

Department of Housing and Urban Development

Annual Report.

Housing and Urban Development Trends. Monthly and annual.

Statistical Yearbook.

Supply of Mortgage Credit, 1970–1974.

Federal Home Loan Bank Board

Annual Report.

Savings and Home Financing Source Book. Annual.

Veterans Administration

Loan Guaranty Highlights. Monthly.

Other

Dodge, F. W., Division, McGraw-Hill Information Systems Co., New York

Dodge Construction Potentials. Monthly.

National Association of Realtors, Washington, D.C.

Existing Home Sales. Monthly.

National Bureau of Economic Research, New York

Long Swings in Urban Development, by Manuel Gottlieb. 1976. (Urban and Regional Studies 4.)

Construction, Housing, and Real Estate—Con.

Other—Con.

National Bureau of Economic Research—Con.

Residential Location and Urban Housing Markets, by Gregory K. Ingram, editor. (Ballinger Publishing Company, Cambridge, Mass.)

Whitman, Requardt and Associates, Baltimore

The Handy-Whitman Index of Public Utility Construction Costs. Semiannual.

Consumer Income and Expenditures— *see also* Agriculture; Economic Indexes; Investments; *and* National Income

U.S. Government

Board of Governors of the Federal Reserve System

Volume and Composition of Individuals' Savings. Quarterly.

Bureau of the Census

Census of Population. Decennial. (1970, most recent.)

Current Population Reports. (Series on Consumer Income, P-60.)

Family (Money) Income 1947–1971: Summarizing Twenty-Five Years of a Summary Statistic. (Technical Paper No. 35.)

Social Indicators, 1973; 1976.

Bureau of Economic Analysis

Local Area Personal Income, 1970–75. Annual personal income by type of income and by major industries, and population and per capita income, for States, counties, BEA economic areas, and standard metropolitan statistical areas. Nine volumes published by the National Technical Information Service, Springfield, Va.

Personal Income by States Since 1929. (Supplement to Survey of Current Business.) 1956. Updated and published twice annually—preliminary in the April Survey and final in the August Survey.

Personal Income by States Since 1948. Updated and published quarterly in January, April, July, and October issues of Survey of Current Business.

Consumer Income and Expenditures—Con.

U.S. Government—Con.

Bureau of Economic Analysis—Con.
Survey of Current Business.
Monthly. Supplemented by Business Statistics, weekly and biennial.

Bureau of Labor Statistics
Consumer Expenditure Survey:
Diary Survey, July 1972–June 1974. 1977. (Bulletin No. 1959.)
Consumer Expenditure Survey Series:
Diary Survey, July 1973–June 1974. 1976. (Report 448–3.)
Interview Survey, 1972–73. 1977. (Report 455–4.)
Digest of Selected Pension Plans, 1976–78 edition. 1977.
Handbook of Labor Statistics. Annual.
Monthly Labor Review.
Three Budgets for a Retired Couple in Urban Areas of the United States. (Bulletin No. 1570–6 and supplements.) Updated in annual press releases; titles vary.
Three Standards of Living for an Urban Family of Four Persons. (Bulletin No. 1570–5 and supplements.) Updated in annual press releases; titles vary.

Internal Revenue Service
Statistics of Income. (Annual report on Individual Income Tax Returns. Supplemental. Report on Personal Wealth.)

Office of Economic Opportunity
Poverty Program Information. Fiscal Year 1970.

Securities and Exchange Commission
Statistical Bulletin. Monthly.

Other

Michigan, The University of, Survey Research Center, Ann Arbor
Survey of Consumer Finances. Annual. (Discontinued in 1972.)

Miller, Herman P. (Thomas Y. Crowell, New York)
Rich Man, Poor Man. 1971.

National Bureau of Economic Research, New York
The Business Cycle Today, by Victor Zarnowitz. 1972. (General Series 96, Vol. I.)

Consumer Income and Expenditures—Con.

Other—Con.

National Bureau of Economic Research—Con.
Household Production and Consumption, Nestor E. Terleckyj, editor. 1976. (Studies in Income and Wealth, Vol. 40.)
The Measurement of Economic and Social Performance, Milton Moss, editor. 1974. (Studies in Income and Wealth, Vol. 38.)
Measures of Credit Risk and Experience, by Edgar R. Fiedler. 1971. (General Series 95.)

National Consumer Finance Association, Washington, D.C.
Finance Facts Yearbook. Annual.

Resources for the Future, Inc., Washington, D.C. (Johns Hopkins Press, Baltimore)
Resources in America's Future: Patterns of Requirements and Availabilities, 1960–2000, by Hans H. Landsberg and others. 1963.

Consumer Prices—*see* Commodity Prices.

Corporations—*see* Business; *and* Manufactures.

Correctional Institutions—*see* Law Enforcement.

Cost of Living—*see* Commodity Prices.

Courts—*see* Law Enforcement.

Crime—*see* Law Enforcement.

Crops—*see* Agriculture.

Deaths—*see* Vital Statistics.

Defense—*see* National Defense.

Divorce—*see* Vital Statistics.

Domestic Trade—*see* Retail and Wholesale Trade.

Drainage—*see* Irrigation.

Economic Indexes—*see also* Agriculture; Business; Commodity Prices; *and* Manufactures

U.S. Government

Board of Governors of the Federal Reserve System
Annual Statistical Digest: 1971–1975; 1972–1976.

Economic Indexes—Con.

U.S. Government—Con.

Board of Governors of the Federal Reserve System—Con.

Federal Reserve Bulletin. Monthly. (Also monthly releases on business and industrial production indexes.)

Federal Reserve Monthly Chart Book. With annual historical supplement.

Industrial Production: 1976.

Bureau of Economic Analysis

Business Conditions Digest. Monthly.

Long-term Economic Growth, 1860–1970. 1973.

Survey of Current Business. Monthly. Supplemented by Business Statistics, weekly and biennial.

Bureau of Labor Statistics

Chartbook on Prices, Wages, and Productivity. Monthly.

Monthly Labor Review

Patterns of U.S. Economic Growth. 1970. (Bulletin No. 1672.)

Productivity and the Economy. 1977. (Bulletin No. 1926.)

The U.S. Economy in 1985. 1974. (Bulletin No. 1809.)

Council of Economic Advisers

Economic Indicators. Monthly.

Economic Report of the President. Annual.

Other

Business Week. (Billboard Publications, Inc., New York.) (Index of Business Activity.)

The Conference Board, New York

The Conference Board Record. Monthly.

Federal Reserve Banks

Monthly review published by each bank with special reference to its own Federal Reserve district.

Michigan, The University of, Survey Research Center, Ann Arbor

Survey of Consumer Finances. Annual. (Discontinued in 1972.)

National Bureau of Economic Research, New York

The Business Cycle Today, by Victor Zarnowitz. 1972. (General Series 96, Vol. I.)

Economic Indexes—Con.

Other—Con.

National Bureau of Economic Research—Con.

Conference on Secular Inflation, Karl Brunner, editor. 1973. (Universities-National Bureau Conference 25.)

Dating U.S. Growth Cycles, by Ilse Mintz, Exploration in Economic Research, Vol. I, No. 1. Summer 1974.

The Measurement of Economic and Social Performance, Milton Moss, editor. 1974. (Studies in Income and Wealth, Vol. 38.)

Orders, Production and Investment, by Victor Zarnowitz. 1973. (Business Cycles 22.)

Postwar Productivity Trends in the United States, by John W. Kendrick. 1973. (General Series 98.)

Education—*see also* Scientific Resources; *and* Vocational Rehabilitation

U.S. Government

Bureau of the Census

Census of Population. Decennial. (1970, most recent.)

Current Population Reports. (Series on Population Characteristics, P-20; Technical Studies, P-23; and Population Estimates, P-25.)

Social Indicators, 1973; 1976.

Bureau of Indian Affairs

Statistics Concerning Indian Education. Annual.

Bureau of Labor Statistics

Handbook of Labor Statistics. Annual.

Monthly Labor Review.

Occupational Manpower and Training Needs. 1974. (Bulletin 1824.)

Special Labor Force Reports. Irregular.

Department of Health, Education, and Welfare

Annual Report.

Higher Education Prices and Price Indexes. 1976. Supplemented annually.

Vocational and Technical Education. Annual.

Employment and Training Administration

Manpower Report of the President. Annual.

Education—Con.

U.S. Government—Con.

Equal Employment Opportunity Commission

Employment Opportunity in the Schools. Job patterns of minorities and women in public elementary and secondary schools. 1975.

National Center for Education Statistics

Associate Degrees and Other Formal Awards Below the Baccalaureate. Annual.

Bond Sales for Public School Purposes. Annual

College and University Library Survey. Latest, 1977.

The Condition of Education. Annual.

Course Offerings and Enrollments in Secondary Schools. Latest, 1972–73.

Digest of Education Statistics. Annual.

Earned Degrees Conferred. Annual.

Employees in Institutions of Higher Education. Latest, 1977.

Fall Enrollment in Higher Education. Annual.

Financial Statistics of Institutions of Higher Education: Current Funds, Revenues, and Expenditures. Annual.

Financial Statistics of Institutions of Higher Education: Property. Annual.

National Longitudinal Study. Reports issued 1972–78 on high school seniors from class of 1972 and their transition to higher education and the labor force.

Participation in Adult Education. Latest, 1975.

Preprimary Enrollment. Latest, 1975.

Projections of Education Statistics. Annual.

Residence and Migration of College Students. Latest, 1975.

Revenues and Expenditures for Public Elementary and Secondary Education. Annual.

Statistics of Local Public School Systems. Annual.

Education—Con.

U.S. Government—Con.

National Center for Education Statistics—Con.

Statistics of Nonpublic Elementary and Secondary Schools. Latest, 1976–77.

Statistics of Public Elementary and Secondary Day Schools. Fall. Annual.

Statistics of State School Systems. Biennial.

Students Enrolled for Advanced Degrees. Annual.

Survey of Public Libraries. Latest, 1974.

National Science Foundation

Federal Support to Universities, Colleges, and Selected Nonprofit Institutions. Annual.

Graduate Science Education: Student Support and Postdoctorals. Annual.

Projections of Degrees and Enrollment in Science and Engineering Fields to 1985. (NSF 76–301.)

Projections of Science and Engineering Doctorate Supply and Utilization, 1980 and 1985. (NSF 76 301.)

Young and Senior Science and Engineering Faculty, 1974. Support, Research Participation, and Tenure. (NSF 75–302.)

Office for Civil Rights

Directory of Public Elementary and Secondary Schools in Selected Districts—Enrollment and Staff by Racial-Ethnic Group, Fall 1972.

Racial and Ethnic Enrollment Data From Institutions of Higher Education. Fall 1974.

Other

American Council on Education, Washington, D.C.

A Fact Book on Higher Education. Quarterly.

National Norms for Entering College Freshmen. Annual.

Bowker (R.R.) Company, New York

American Library Directory. Biennial.

The Bowker Annual of Library and Book Trade Information.

Educational Media Yearbook. Annual.

Education—Con.

Other—Con.

Bureau of Social Science Research, Washington, D.C.

Education and Employment—The Early Careers of College Graduates, by Laure M. Sharp. (Johns Hopkins Press, Baltimore, 1970.)

Ferriss, Abbott L. (Russell Sage Foundation, New York)

Indicators of Trends in American Education, 1969.

National Bureau of Economic Research, New York

Education as an Industry, by Joseph N. Froomkin, Dean T. Jamison, and Roy Radner, editors. (Ballinger Publishing Co., Cambridge, Mass.)

Education, Income, and Human Behavior, by F. Thomas Juster. 1974. (Other Conference 9.)

Education, Income, and Human Capital, by W. Lee Hansen. 1970. (Studies in Income and Wealth, No. 35.)

The Effect of Education on the Efficiency in Consumption, by Robert Michael. 1972. (Occasional Paper 116.)

Schooling, Experience, and Earnings, by Jacob Mincer. 1974. (Human Behavior and Social Institutions 2.)

National Catholic Educational Association, Washington, D.C.

Catholic Schools in America. Annual (beginning in 1975).

A Statistical Report on Catholic Elementary and Secondary Schools for the years 1967–68 to 1969–70.

U.S. Catholic Schools. 1973–74, latest.

National Education Association, Washington, D.C.

Estimates of School Statistics. Annual.

Status of the American Public School Teacher, 1975–76.

Summary of Salaries Paid in Higher Education. Biennial.

Teacher Supply and Demand in Public Schools, 1974, 1975, 1976, with Population Trends and Their Implications for Schools, 1976–1977.

Elections

U.S. Government

Bureau of the Census

Congressional District Computer Profiles for the 93d Congress. 1972. A series of separate State reports.

Congressional District Data:

Districts of the 93d Congress. 1973.

Districts of the 94th Congress. Reports for California, New York, and Texas. 1974.

Current Population Reports. (Series on Population Characteristics, P-20, and Population Estimates, P-25.)

Commission on Civil Rights

The Voting Rights Act: Ten Years After. 1975.

Congress. Clerk of the House

Statistics of the Congressional Elections. Biennial. (Titled Statistics of the Presidential and Congressional Election Years.)

Congress. Joint Committee on Printing

Congressional Directory. Annual.

Other

Council of State Governments, Lexington, Ky.

The Book of the States and its Supplement I. Biennial.

David, Paul T. (University Press of Virginia, Charlottesville, Va.)

Party Strength in the United States, 1872–1970.

Elections Research Center, Washington, D.C.

America Votes. A Handbook of Contemporary American Election Statistics, compiled and edited by Richard M. Scammon. Biennial.

Joint Center for Political Studies, Washington, D.C.

National Roster of Black Elected Officials. Annual.

Michigan, The University of, Center for Political Studies, Institute for Social Research, Ann Arbor

Who Voted and for Whom. Biennial.

National Republican Congressional Committee, Washington, D.C.

1970 Congressional Vote Statistics. 1971.

Elections—Con.

Other—Con.

Newspaper Enterprise Association, Inc., New York
The World Almanac. Annual.

Voter Education Project, Inc., Atlanta, Ga.
Voter Registration in the South. Issued irregularly.

Electrical Industries—see Energy.

Emigration—see Immigration.

Employment—see Federal Government; Labor; and State and Local Government.

Energy—see also Communications; Manufactures; Minerals; and Transportation

U.S. Government

Bureau of the Census
Current Industrial Reports. Monthly, quarterly, and annual series on various industries.

Bureau of the Census and Bureau of Mines
Raw Materials in the United States Economy· 1900–1969. (Issued 1972. Working Paper No. 35.)

Bureau of Labor Statistics
Retail Prices and Indexes of Fuels and Utilities. Monthly.

Bureau of Mines
United States Energy Through the Year 2000 (revised). December 1975.

Congress. Committee on Government Operations
Investigation of the Petroleum Industry. 1973. (93d Congress, 1st Session.)

Congress. Committee on Science and Astronautics
Energy Facts. 1973. (93d Congress, 1st Session.)
Energy Facts II. 1975. (94th Congress.)

Congress. Joint Committee on Atomic Energy
Understanding the National Energy Dilemma. 1973. (93d Congress, 1st Session.)

Congress. Joint Economic Committee
Energy Conservation. 1973. (93d Congress, 1st Session.)

Energy—Con.

U.S. Government—Con.

Congress. Joint Economic Committee—Con.
The Energy Outlook for the 1980's. 1973. (93d Congress, 1st Session.)

Department of the Interior
Energy Perspectives. February 1975. June 1976.

Energy Information Administration
All-Electric Homes: Annual Bills. Annual.
Annual Report.
Annual Report of Cost and Quality of Fuels of Steam-Electric Plant.
Annual Summary of Capacity, Production, and Fuel Consumption.
Electric Power Disturbances. Quarterly.
Electric Power Statistics. Production of energy and capacity of plants, fuel consumption of electric power plants, electric utility system loads, sales of electric energy, financial statistics of private utilities. Monthly.
Gas Turbine Electric Plant Construction Costs and Annual Production Expenses. Annual.
Hydroelectric Plant Construction Cost and Annual Production Expenses. Annual.
International Petroleum. Annual.
Monthly Comparison of Peak Demand and Energy for Load. Annual.
Monthly Energy Review.
Monthly Report on Electric Energy and Peak Load Data.
Power Production, Fuel Consumption, and Installed Capacity. Monthly.
Residential Electric Bills in Major Cities—500 kWh. Quarterly.
Six-Year Summary of Power Production and Generating Capacity Data. Annual.
Statistics for Interstate Natural Gas Pipeline Companies. Annual.
Statistics of Major Interstate Companies. Composite report of average prices paid and received for natural gas, imports, purchases, production, storage, sales, and major revenue, expense, and balance sheet items, by major pipelines carrying about 90 percent of gas subject to Commission jurisdiction. Monthly press release.

Environment—Con.

U.S. Government—Con.

Environmental Protection Agency—Con.

National Air Quality and Emissions Trends Report. Annual. 1975.

National Emissions Report. 1972.

Nationwide Air Pollutant Emission Trends, 1940–1970 (AP–115.) 1973.

Pesticides Monitoring Journal. Quarterly.

Radiation Data and Reports. Monthly.

Sewage Facility Construction. Annual.

Statistical Summary (Year) Inventory of Municipal Waste Facilities. Quinquennial.

Summary of Water Enforcement Actions Pursued by EPA since December 3, 1970. (Updated continuously.)

Federal Water Quality Administration

Clean Waters for the 1970's. June 1970.

Geological Survey

Estimated Use of Water in the United States in 1975. (Geological Survey Circular 765.)

Executions—see Law Enforcement.

Exports—see Foreign Commerce.

Family Characteristics—see Population.

Farms and Farm Characteristics—see Agriculture.

Federal Government Finances and Employment—see also Elections; Scientific Resources; and State and Local Government

U.S. Government

Army Corps of Engineers

Statements of Costs. Annual.

Board of Governors of the Federal Reserve System

Annual Statistical Digest: 1971–1975; 1972–1976.

Federal Reserve Bulletin. Monthly.

Federal Reserve Monthly Chart Book. With annual historical supplement.

Federal Government Finances and Employment—Con.

U.S. Government—Con.

Bureau of Economic Analysis

Survey of Current Business. Monthly. Supplemented by Business Statistics, weekly and biennial.

Civil Service Commission

Annual Report.

Civil Service Journal. Quarterly.

Equal Employment Opportunity Statistics. Annual.

Federal Civilian Employment in the United States by Geographic Area. Annual.

Monthly Release of Federal Civilian Workforce Statistics.

Occupations of Federal Blue-Collar Workers. Annual.

Occupations of Federal White-Collar Workers. Annual.

Pay Structure of the Federal Civil Service. Annual.

Report on Civil Service Retirement, Federal Employees Group Life Insurance, Federal Employees Health Benefits, Retired Federal Employees Health Benefits. Annual.

Congress. House Committee on Government Operations

Federal Real and Personal Property Inventory Report. Biennial.

Congress. Joint Economic Committee

The Economics of Federal Subsidy Programs, January 11, 1972. (92d Congress, 1st Session.)

The Military Budget and National Economic Priorities, 1969. (91st Congress, 1st Session.)

Council of Economic Advisers

Economic Report of the President. Annual.

Council on Environmental Quality

Environmental Quality. Annual.

Department of Labor

Annual Report of the Secretary.

Department of the Treasury

Combined Statement of Receipts, Expenditures, and Balances of the United States Government. Annual.

Federal Government Finances and Employment—Con.

U.S. Government—Con.

Department of the Treasury—Con.

Daily Statement of the U.S. Treasury.

Federal Aid to States. Annual.

Monthly Statement of the Public Debt of the United States.

Monthly Treasury Statement of Receipts and Outlays of the United States Government.

Statistical Appendix to Annual Report of the Secretary of the Treasury on the State of the Finances.

Treasury Bulletin. Monthly.

Internal Revenue Service

Annual Report of the Commissioner.

Small Area Data from Individual Income Tax Returns. Biennial.

Statistics of Income (Annual reports on Individual, Corporation, and Business Income Tax Returns. Periodic reports on Fiduciary Income, Estate, and Gift Tax Returns, and on Foreign Income and Tax Reported on U.S. Corporation Tax Returns).

ZIP Code Area Data, Individual Income Tax Returns. 1969.

National Science Foundation

An Analysis of Federal R&D Funding by Function. Annual.

Energy and Energy-Related R&D Activities of Federal Installations and Federally Funded Research and Development Centers: Estimated Funds, FY 1973–75 and Manpower, Jan. 1973–75. (NSF 76–304.)

Federal Funds for Research, Development, and Other Scientific Activities. (Includes geographic distribution.) Annual.

Federal Scientific, Technical, and Health Personnel. Periodic.

Federal Support to Universities, Colleges and Selected Nonprofit Institutions. A report to the President and Congress. Annual.

Office of Economic Opportunity

Poverty Program Information. Fiscal year 1970.

Federal Government Finances and Employment—Con.

U.S. Government—Con.

Office of Management and Budget

The Budget of the United States Government. Published annually in a group of five documents:

The Budget of the United States Government.

The Budget of the United States Government, Appendix.

The Budget of the United States Government, District of Columbia.

Special Analyses, Budget of the United States Government.

The U.S. Budget in Brief.

President

Report to the Congress from the President of the United States: United States Aeronautical and Space Activities, 1970.

Other

Moody's Investors Service, New York

Moody's Municipal and Government Manual; American and Foreign. Annual with semiweekly supplements.

National Bureau of Economic Research, New York

Conference on Research in Taxation, Michael Boskin, editor. Published as Supplement to Journal of Political Economy, April 1978.

Substituting a Value-Added Tax for the Corporate Income Tax, by S.P. Dresch, An-loh Linn, and D.K. Stout. (Ballinger Publishing Co., Cambridge, Mass.)

Finance—*see* Federal Government; Investments; Money; *and* State and Local Government.

Fisheries

U.S. Government

Environmental Protection Agency, Water Quality Office

Pollution-Caused Fish Kills. Annual.

National Oceanic and Atmospheric Administration

Fisheries of the United States. Annual.

Fishery Statistics of the United States. (Statistical Digest.) Annual.

Fisheries—Con.

U.S. Government—Con.

National Oceanic and Atmospheric Administration—Con.
Prices Received by Fishermen, H.S. No. 12 (C.F.S. No. 4657 Revised.) 1970.
1970 Salt-Water Angling Survey. 1973.

Food—see also Agriculture

U.S. Government

Bureau of the Census
Canned Food Report. (Issued 5 times a year.)

Bureau of Labor Statistics
Retail Food Prices by Cities. Monthly and annual averages.

Department of Agriculture, Economics, Statistics, and Cooperatives Service
Agricultural Outlook. Monthly.
Developments in Marketing Spreads for Agricultural Products in 1976. (Agricultural Economics Report No. 367.) Revised annually.
Food and Fiber System and How It Works. March 1975. (Agricultural Information Bulletin 383.)
Food Consumption, Prices, and Expenditures. (Agricultural Economics Report No. 138.) Supplemented annually.
National Food Review. Quarterly.
Price Spreads for Farm Foods. Monthly.

Department of Agriculture, Food and Nutrition Service
National School Lunch Program. Annual.

Department of Agriculture, Science and Education Administration
Family Economics Review. Quarterly.

Other

American Frozen Food Institute, Washington, D.C.
Frozen Food Pack Statistics. Annual.

National Food Processors Association, Washington, D.C.
Canned Food Pack Statistics. Annual.

Foreign Commerce—see also Economic Indexes; and International Accounts and Aid

U.S. Government

Army, Corp of Engineers
Waterborne Commerce of the United States (in 5 parts). Annual.

Bureau of the Census
Highlights of U.S. Export and Import Trade. Monthly and cumulative. (FT 990.)
Survey of the Origin of Exports of Manufacturing Establishments. Triennial. (Current Industrial Reports MA-161 (69)–2.)
U.S. Airborne Exports and General Imports. (Summary Report.) Monthly and annual. (FT 986.)
U.S. Commodity Exports and Imports as Related to Output. Annual. (Series ES 2.)
U.S. Exports, Commodity Groupings by World Area. Annual. (FT 450.)
U.S. Exports of Domestic Merchandise, SIC-Based Products by World Area. Annual. (FT 610.)
U.S. Exports, Schedule B Commodity by Country. Monthly, cumulative. (FT 410.)
U.S. Exports, World Area by Commodity Groupings. Annual. (FT 455.)
U.S. General Imports, Schedule A Commodity by Country. Monthly, cumulative. (FT 135.)
U.S. General Imports, Schedule A Commodity Groupings by World Area. Annual. (FT 150.)
U.S. General Imports, World Area by Commodity Groupings. Annual. (FT 155.)
U.S. Gold Movements. Monthly and cumulative, beginning July 1969. (FT 2402. Discontinued after December 1974; data published in Report FT 990 beginning January 1975.)
U.S. Gold and Silver Movements. Monthly and annual, through June 1969. (FT 2402.)
U.S. Imports for Consumption and General Imports, SIC-Based Products by World Area. Annual. (FT 210.)
U.S. Imports for Consumption and General Imports, TSUSA Commodity by Country of Origin. Annual. (FT 246.)

Foreign Commerce—Con.

U.S. Government—Con.

Bureau of the Census—Con.
U.S. Trade with Puerto Rico and U.S. Possessions. Monthly and annual. (FT 800.)
U.S. Waterborne Exports and General Imports. Monthly and annual. (FT 985.)

Bureau of Economic Analysis
Survey of Current Business. Monthly. Supplemented by Business Statistics, weekly and biennial. (June issues contain data on balance of payments.)

Bureau of International Commerce
Overseas Business Reports. Irregular.

Department of Agriculture, Economics, Statistics, and Cooperatives Service
Foreign Agricultural Trade of the United States. Monthly with annual supplements on calendar year and fiscal year trade statistics.

Department of Commerce
Commerce America. Biweekly. (Issues in March, June, September, and December contain quarterly data on U.S. share of world exports of manufactures.)
Export Administration Report, East-West Trade: Quarterly Report to the President, Senate, and House of Representatives.

Department of the Treasury
Statistical Appendix to Annual Report of the Secretary of the Treasury on the State of the Finances.

Foreign Agricultural Service
World Agricultural Production and Trade, Statistical Report. Monthly.

Industry and Trade Administration
International Economic Indicators. Quarterly.
Market Share Reports. Annual.
Overseas Business Reports. Irregular.

International Trade Commission
Annual Report.

Maritime Administration
Annual Report.

Foreign Commerce—Con.

Other

Commodity Research Bureau, New York
Commodity Yearbook. Annual.

National Bureau of Economic Research, New York
Foreign Dollar Balances and the International Role of the Dollar, by Raymond F. Mikesell and J. Herbert Furth. 1974. (Studies in International Economic Relations 8.)
Foreign Trade Regimes and Economic Development: Liberalization Attempts and Consequences, by Anne O. Krueger. (Ballinger Publishing Co., Cambridge, Mass.)
International Mobility and Movement of Capital, by Fritz Machlup. 1972. (Universities-National Bureau Conference Series, No. 24.)
The Technology Factor in International Trade. Raymond Vernon, editor. 1970. (Universities-National Bureau Conference Series 22.)

Forests and Lumber—*see also* Economic Indexes

U.S. Government

Bureau of the Census
Census of Manufactures. Quinquennial. (1977, most recent.)
Current Industrial Reports. Monthly, quarterly, and annual series on various industries.

Bureau of Domestic Business Development
Construction Review. Monthly.

Bureau of Labor Statistics
Monthly Labor Review.

Department of Agriculture, Economics, Statistics, and Cooperatives Service
Agricultural Statistics. Annual.
Naval Stores. Monthly and annual.

Forest Service
The Demand and Price Situation for Forest Products. Annual.
National Forest System. Annual.
The Outlook for Timber in the United States. 1973.
Wildfire Statistics. Annual.

Forests and Lumber—Con.

U.S. Government—Con.

National Forest Reservation Commission

Annual Report. (Issued in the Senate Documents Series.)

Other

American Paper Institute, New York

Statistics of Paper and Paperboard. Annual; title varies.

Wood Pulp Statistics. Annual.

National Forest Products Association, Washington, D.C.

Fingertip Facts and Figures. Monthly.

Gas Utilities—*see* Energy.

Geography—*see also* Environment *and* Public Lands

U.S. Government

Bureau of the Census

Boundary and Annexation Survey, 1970–1975. GE 30–2: Statistics on boundary change information for incorporated municipalities of 2,500 or more population. Information also on new incorporations, disincorporations, and other important status changes.

Census of Population. Decennial. (1970, most recent.)

United States Maps, Series GE–50 and GE–70—Statistical maps in color showing standard metropolitan statistical areas, congressional districts, and the geographic distribution of population, housing, income, age, race, and other demographic characteristics.

Geological Survey

Elevations and Distances in the United States. 1973.

The National Atlas of the United States of America, 1970.

Principal Lakes of the United States. Latest, 1973. (Geological Survey Circular 476.)

Government—*see* Federal Government; *and* State and Local Government.

Guam—*see* Outlying Areas.

Health Insurance—*see* Insurance.

Health and Medical Care—*see also* Accidents; Environment; Food; Insurance; Social Insurance; *and* Vital Statistics

U.S. Government

Bureau of the Census

Social Indicators, 1973; 1976.

Bureau of Domestic Business Development

Water Use in the United States, 1900–1980. 1960.

Bureau of Labor Statistics

Consumer Price Index. U.S. City Average and Selected Areas. Monthly.

Industry Wage Survey Bulletin. Separate bulletins published annually for selected industries.

Monthly Labor Review.

Three Budgets for a Retired Couple in Urban Areas of the United States. (Bulletin No. 1570–6 and supplements.) Updated in annual press releases; titles vary.

Three Standards of Living for an Urban Family of Four Persons. (Bulletin No. 1570–5 and supplements.) Updated in annual press releases; titles vary.

Center for Disease Control

Morbidity and Mortality Weekly Report. (DHEW Pub. Nos. CDC 76–8017, 77–8017.)

Reported Morbidity and Mortality in the United States. Morbidity and Mortality Weekly Report (annual supplement), 1976. (DHEW Pub. No. CDC 77–8241.)

Department of Agriculture, Food and Nutrition Service

National School Lunch Program. Annual.

Department of Health, Education, and Welfare

Annual Report.

Fluoridation Census. 1971, 1972, 1975.

Hill-Burton Program; Progress Report. Annual. (Hospital and medical facilities series reports. Analyses.)

Mental Health Statistics. Current facility reports and reference tables on patients in mental health facilities, by age, sex, and diagnoses, U.S., 1969.

Outpatient Psychiatric Clinics. Special statistical reports. Annual.

Health and Medical Care—Con.

U.S. Government—Con.

Department of Health, Education, and Welfare—Con.

Reported Tuberculosis Data. Biennial.

Statistical Note 23. April 1970.

Tuberculosis Beds in Hospitals and Sanatoria, Index of Beds Available. Biennial.

Drug Enforcement Administration

Drug Abuse and Law Enforcement Statistics. Irregular.

National Center for Health Statistics

Current Estimates from the Health Interview Survey. Annual.

Decennial Census Data for Selected Health Occupations: United States, 1970. (DHEW Publication No. HRA 76–1231.)

Facts at Your Fingertips—Almost. A guide to sources of statistical information on major health topics. 1977.

Health Resources Statistics. Annual. (DHEW Pub. No. HRA 74–1509.)

Health: United States. Annual. (DHEW Pub. No. HRA 76–1232.)

Hospitals: A County and Metropolitan Area Data Book. 1972. (DHEW Pub. No. HRA 75–1223.)

Nursing Homes: A County and Metropolitan Area Data Book, 1971. (DHEW Pub. No. HRA 74–1224.)

Preliminary Findings of the First Health and Nutrition Examination Survey, United States, 1971–1972: Dietary Intake and Biochemical Findings (DHEW Pub. No. HRA 76–1219–1) and Anthropometric and Clinical Findings (DHEW Pub. No. HRA 75–1229).

Vital and Health Statistics. A series of statistical reports covering health-related topics.

Series 10: Health Interview Survey Statistics. Irregular.

Series 11: Health and Nutrition Examination Surveys Statistics. Irregular.

Series 12: Health Records Survey Statistics. Irregular.

Health and Medical Care—Con.

U.S. Government—Con.

National Center for Health Statistics—Con.

Series 13: Health Resources Utilization Statistics. Irregular.

Series 14: Health Resources: Manpower and Facilities Statistics. Irregular.

National Institute on Drug Abuse

Nonmedical Use of Psychoactive Substances. 1976.

Office of Human Development Services

Residents in Public Institutions for the Mentally Retarded. Annual.

Social Security Administration

The Benefit Structure of Private Health Insurance. 1970. (Research Report No. 32.)

Compendium of National Health Expenditures Data. 1976.

Financing Mental Health Care Under Medicare and Medicaid. 1971. (Research Report No. 37.)

Health Insurance Administrative Costs, 1975. (Staff Paper No. 21.)

Health Insurance Statistics. A series of statistical notes covering Medicare data.

Income of Physicians, Osteopaths, and Dentists from Professional Practice, 1965–69. (Staff Paper No. 12.)

Medical Care Expenditures, Prices, and Costs: Background Book. 1975.

Medicare Statistical Reports. Annual data on enrollment, participating providers, and summary for persons served.

National Health Expenditures, Calendar Year 1974. (Research and Statistics Note No. 5, 1976.)

National Health Systems in Eight Countries, 1975.

The Net Income of Hospitals, 1961–69. (Staff Paper No. 6.)

Personal Health Care Expenditures by States, 1966 and 1969; Public Funds (Vol. I); Public and Private Funds (Vol. II).

Prescription Drug Data Summary. 1975.

The Size and Shape of the Medical Care Dollar. (Chart Book/1975.)

Health and Medical Care—Con.

U.S. Government—Con.

Social Security Administration—Con.

Social Security Bulletin. Monthly with annual statistical supplement. Data on the health insurance benefits program and on medical care of public assistance recipients.

Social Security Survey of Disabled and Nondisabled Adults: 1972.

Social Security Survey of Recently Disabled Adults: 1971.

Source of Increase in Selected Medical Care Expenditures, 1929-69. (Staff Paper No. 4.)

Veterans Administration

Annual Report of Administrator of Veterans Affairs.

Other

American Dental Association, Chicago

Dental Students' Register. Annual.

Distribution of Dentists in the United States by State, Region, District, and County. Triennial.

Survey of Dental Practice. Biennial.

American Hospital Association, Chicago

Hospital Statistics. Annual.

American Medical Association, Chicago

Foreign Medical Graduates in the United States, 1970.

Physician Distribution and Medical Licensure in the U.S. Annual.

Reference Data on the Profile of Medical Practice. Annual.

American Nurses Association, Kansas City, Missouri

Facts About Nursing: A Statistical Summary. Annual.

The Nation's Nurses: 1972 Inventory of Registered Nurses.

American Osteopathic Association, Chicago

Statistical Study of the Osteopathic Profession. Annual.

The Carnegie Foundation for the Advancement of Teaching, Sacramento, California

Trends and Projections of Physicians in the United States 1967-2002, by Mark S. Blumberg. 1971.

Health and Medical Care—Con.

Other—Con.

Medical Economics, Oradell, New Jersey

Physicians Earnings and Expenses. Published annually in Medical Economics magazine.

Metropolitan Life Insurance Company, New York

Statistical Bulletin. Quarterly.

National Bureau of Economic Research, New York

The Demand for Health: A Theoretical and Empirical Study, by Michael Grossman. 1972. (Occasional Paper 119.)

Essays on the Economics of Health and Medical Care, by Victor R. Fuchs. 1972. (Human Resources and Social Institutions 1.)

The Role of Health Insurance in the Health Services Sector, Richard N. Rosett, editor. 1976. (Universities-National Bureau Conference Series, No. 27.)

Rutgers Center of Alcohol Studies, Journal of Studies on Alcohol, Inc., New Brunswick, New Jersey.

Statistics on Consumption of Alcohol and on Alcoholism, by M. Keller and C. Gurioli, 1976.

Hospitals—*see* Health.

Hotels—*see* Service Establishments.

Household Appliances—*see* Consumer Income and Expenditures.

Housing—*see* Construction.

Immigration and Naturalization

U.S. Government

Bureau of Security and Consular Affairs

Report of the Visa Office, annual. (Dept. of State Pub. 8810.)

Department of Transportation

Report of Passenger Travel Between the United States and Foreign Countries. Annual, semiannual, quarterly, monthly.

Immigration and Naturalization Service

Annual Indicator of the Immigration into the United States of Aliens in Professional and Related Occupations. (Fiscal years 1967-1970.)

Immigration and Naturalization—Con.

U.S. Government—Con.

Immigration and Naturalization Service—Con.

Annual Report.

I & N Reporter. Quarterly.

National Science Foundation

Scientists, Engineers, and Physicians From Abroad. Periodic.

Imports—*see* Foreign Commerce.

Income—*see* Consumer Income *and* National Income.

Industry—*see* Business; Economic Indexes; *and* Manufactures.

Institutions—*see* Education; Health; *and* Law Enforcement.

Insurance—*see also* Social Insurance

U.S. Government

Bureau of Economic Analysis

Survey of Current Business. Monthly. Supplemented by Business Statistics, weekly and biennial.

Social Security Administration

Coverage and Vesting of Full-time Employees Under Private Retirement Plans in the U.S. 1973.

Health Insurance Plans Other Than Blue Cross, Blue Shield Plans, or Insurance Companies, 1969 Survey. (Research Report No. 35.)

Health Insurance Statistics. A series of statistical notes covering Medicare data.

Historical Statistics for Five Temporary Disability Insurance Programs, 1942–1969. (Research and Statistics Note No. 17. 1971.)

Independent Health Insurance Plans in 1974. (Research and Statistics Note No. 21, 1976.)

Private Health Insurance Organizations as Intermediaries or Fiscal Agents Under Government Health Programs. 1971. (Staff Paper No. 7.)

Selected State Data, Medicare, Fiscal Years 1968–1973.

Veterans Administration

Annual Report of Administrator of Veterans Affairs.

Government Life Insurance Programs. Annual.

Insurance—Con.

Other

American Council of Life Insurance, New York

Life Insurance Fact Book. Annual.

American Medical Association, Chicago

Charts and Graphs: Statistical Data on Voluntary Prepayment Medical Benefit Plans. Supplement to Voluntary Prepayment Medical Benefit Plans. Annual.

Best (Alfred M.) Co., New York

Best's insurance publications. Monthly and annual publications on life, fire, and casualty companies.

Health Insurance Institute, Washington, D.C.

Source Book of Health Insurance Data. Annual.

Insurance Information Institute, New York

Insurance Facts. Yearbook.

National Bureau of Economic Research, New York

The Role of Health Insurance in the Health Services Sector, Richard N. Rosett, editor. 1976. (Universities-National Bureau Conference Series, No. 27.)

National Fire Protection Association, Boston

Fire Journal. Monthly.

The National Underwriter Co., Cincinnati

Argus Chart. Health insurance company financial data. Annual.

Argus F.C. & S. Chart. Property and liability insurance company financial data. Annual.

Life Rates and Data. Premiums, values, dividends, and contract analysis by company. Annual.

Life Reports. Life company financial data. Annual.

Timesaver. Health insurance costs and contract analysis by company. Annual.

The Spectator, Philadelphia

Health Insurance Review. Annual.

Life Insurance Review. Annual.

Property Liability Insurance Review. Annual.

The Spectator Magazine. Monthly.

International Accounts and Aid

U.S. Government

Agency for International Development
Operations Report. Annual.
U.S. Overseas Loans and Grants and Assistance From International Organizations. Annual.

Board of Governors of the Federal Reserve System
Annual Statistical Digest: 1971–1975; 1972–1976.
Banking and Monetary Statistics, 1941–1970.
Federal Reserve Bulletin. Monthly.

Bureau of Economic Analysis
Survey of Current Business. Monthly. Supplemented by Business Statistics, weekly and biennial. (March, June, September, and December issues contain data on U.S. international transactions. Articles on the net U.S. investment position abroad, direct investments, travel, and other topics appear periodically in other issues.)

Council on International Economic Policy
International Economic Report of the President.

Department of Defense
Foreign Military Sales and Military Assistance Facts. Annual.

Department of State
United States Contribution to International Organizations. Issued in the House Documents series. Annual.

Department of the Treasury
Foreign Credits by the United States Government. Semiannual.
Treasury Bulletin. Monthly.

Export-Import Bank of the United States
Report to Congress. Semiannual.

National Advisory Council on International Monetary and Financial Policies
Annual Report to the President and to the Congress.

Office of Management and Budget
The Budget of The United States Government. Published annually in a group of five documents; see listing under "Federal Government Finances and Employment."

International Accounts and Aid—Con.

Other

International Bank for Reconstruction and Development, Washington, D.C.
Annual Report.

International Monetary Fund, Washington, D.C.
Annual Report.
Balance of Payments Yearbook. (Looseleaf.)
International Financial Statistics. Monthly with annual supplement.

International Statistics—see also International Accounts

U.S. Government

Bureau of the Census
Country Demographic Profiles. (Series ISP–30.)
Demographic Reports for Foreign Countries. Irregular. (Series P–96.)
The Geographical Mobility of Americans—An International Comparison, by Larry H. Long and Celia G. Duertlein. Current Population Reports, Special Studies, Series P–23, No. 64.
International Population Reports. Irregular. (Series P–91.)
Social Indicators, 1973; 1976.
World Population: 1975; 1978.

Bureau of Labor Statistics
Handbook of Labor Statistics. Annual.
Labor Developments Abroad. (Contains international comparative labor statistics and U.S. Dept. of State indexes of living costs abroad and living quarters allowances.) Monthly.

Other

Food and Agriculture Organization of the United Nations, Rome, Italy
Production Yearbook.
Trade Yearbook.
Yearbook of Fishery Statistics.
Yearbook of Forest Products.

Inter-American Development Bank, Washington, D.C.
Annual Report.

International Statistics—Con.

Other—Con.

The International Institute for Strategic Studies, London, England

The Military Balance. Annual.

International Labour Office, Geneva, Switzerland

Yearbook of Labour Statistics.

International Monetary Fund, Washington, D.C.

International Financial Statistics. Monthly with annual supplement.

Jane's Fighting Ships Publishing Co., Ltd., London, England

Jane's All the World's Aircraft. Annual.

Jane's Fighting Ships. Annual.

Motor Vehicle Manufacturers Association of the United States, Inc., Detroit

World Motor Vehicle Data. Annual.

National Bureau of Economic Research, New York

International Mobility and Movement of Capital, by Fritz Machlup. 1972. (Universities-National Bureau Conference Series, No. 24.)

Organisation for Economic Co-operation and Development, Paris, France

Energy Statistics, 1973–1975. February 1977.

Foreign Trade Statistics. Monthly.

General Statistics Bulletin. Bimonthly.

Industrial Production, 1960–1975. November 1976.

Labour Force Statistics. Quarterly.

Main Economic Indicators. Monthly. Historical Statistics, 1960–1975. November 1976.

National Accounts Bulletin. Quarterly.

OECD Financial Statistics. Annual with supplements.

Revenue Statistics of OECD Member Countries, 1965–1974. November 1976. (Revised annually.)

Study of Trends in World Supply and Demand of Major Agricultural Commodities. September 1976.

International Statistics—Con.

Other—Con.

United Nations Educational, Scientific, and Cultural Organization, Paris, France

Statistical Yearbook.

United Nations Population Division, New York

Selected World Demographic Indicators, by Countries, 1950–2000.

United Nations Statistical Office, New York

Demographic Yearbook.

Monthly Bulletin of Statistics.

1972 Supplement to the Statistical Yearbook and the Monthly Bulletin of Statistics, Methodology and Definitions.

Population and Vital Statistics Report. (Statistical Papers, Series A.) Quarterly.

Statistical Yearbook.

World Energy Supplies, 1950–74. 1976. Supplement, 1971–75. 1977.

Yearbook of Construction Statistics.

Yearbook of International Trade Statistics.

Yearbook of National Accounts Statistics.

World Health Organization, Geneva, Switzerland

Annual Epidemiological and Vital Statistics.

Epidemiological and Vital Statistics Report. Monthly.

World Health Statistics. Annual.

International Trade—*see* Foreign Commerce; *and* International Statistics.

Investments and Securities—*see also* Business; Construction; Insurance; International Accounts; *and* Money

U.S. Government

Board of Governors of the Federal Reserve System

Annual Statistical Digest: 1971–1975; 1972–1976.

Banking and Monetary Statistics, 1941–1970.

Federal Reserve Bulletin. Monthly.

Commodity Exchange Authority

Commodity Futures Statistics. Annual. (Statistical Bulletin No. 516.)

Investments and Securities—Con.

U.S. Government—Con.

Securities and Exchange Commission
An Economic Analysis of the 1971
New Issues Market. Craig A.
Simmons. 1973.

Analysis of the Impact of Competitive Commission Rates on Aggregate Price Volatility of NYSE
Stocks, by Raymond H. Marcotte, Jr. 1975.

Analysis of the Impact of Competitive Rates on the Liquidity of
NYSE Stocks, by Peter G.
Martin. 1975.

Annual Report.

The Broker-Dealer Community,
Historic Trends and Current
Financial Structure by Terry
M. Chuppe and Jeffry L. Davis.
1973.

Condominiums Registered Under
the Securities Act of 1933, 1967–
1974, by Peter Straub.

Cost of Flotation of Registered
Issues, 1971–1972, by Craig Simmons and Stephen Muller. 1974.

The Financial Condition of Broker-Dealers: A Question of the Adequacy of Capital and Regulatory
Safeguards, by Le Manh Tri and
Terry M. Chuppe. 1971.

The Market Value of Outstanding
Corporate Stock in the U.S.
(1964–1970), by Le Manh Tri.
1971.

Official Summary of Security Transactions and Holdings. Monthly.

Real Estate Investment Trusts:
A Background Analysis and
Recent Industry Developments,
1961–1974, by Peter Straub. 1975.

Report to Congress on the Effects
of the Absence of Fixed Rates on
Commission. December 1975.
Second, Third, Fourth, and Fifth
Reports dated March 1976,
August 1976, January 1977, and
May 1977, respectively.

Securities Traded on Exchanges
Under the Securities Exchange
Act. Annual with quarterly
supplements.

Statistical Bulletin. Monthly.

Stock Trading Statistics. Monthly.

Stock Transactions of Financial
Institutions. Quarterly.

Other

Bankers Trust Company, New York
The Investment Outlook. Annual.

Investments and Securities—Con.

Other—Con.

Commercial and Financial Chronicle.
(William B. Dana Co., New York.)
Semi-weekly.

Michigan, The University of, Survey
Research Center, Ann Arbor
Survey of Consumer Finances.
Annual. (Discontinued in 1972.)

Moody's Investors Service, New York
Moody's Manuals. (Volumes on
Industrials, Banks and Finance,
Municipals and Governments,
Transportation, and Public
Utilities.) Annual with semi-weekly supplements.

National Bureau of Economic Research, New York
The Behavior of Industrial Prices,
by George J. Stigler and James
K. Kindahl. 1970. (General Series
90.)

The Channels of Monetary Effects
on Interest Rates, by Phillip
Cagan. 1972. (General Series 97.)

Conference on Secular Inflation,
Karl Brunner, editor. 1973. (Universities-National Bureau Conference 25.)

Institutional Investors and Corporate Stock—A Background Report, Raymond Goldsmith,
editor. 1973. (Studies in Capital
Formation and Financing 13.)

New York Stock Exchange, Inc., New
York
Fact Book, Annual.

Shareownership, 1970 and 1975.

Securities Industry Association, New
York
Municipal Market Developments.
Monthly.

Standard and Poor's Corporation,
New York

Analyst's Handbook. Annual with
monthly cumulative supplements.

Corporation Records. 6 basic
volumes; News Supplements,
daily; and Dividend Record,
daily, and cumulative monthly
and annual.

Security Owner's Stock Guide.
Monthly.

Statistical Section. (Basic business,
industry, and financial statistics
with monthly supplement.)

Wall Street Journal. (Dow Jones &
Co., New York.) Daily except
Saturdays, Sundays, and holidays.

Labor—Con.

U.S. Government—Con.

Bureau of Labor Statistics—Con.

Industry—Occupational Wage Survey. (Separate bulletins for selected manufacturing and non-manufacturing industries; studies made on a 3- to 5-year cycle.)

Labor and Material Requirements for Selected Types of Construction. (Bulletin issued at irregular intervals.)

Monthly Labor Review.

National Survey of Professional, Administrative, Technical, and Clerical Pay. Annual.

Occupational Employment Statistics, 1960–70. (Bulletin No. 1738.)

Occupational Injuries and Illnesses by Industry. Annual.

Productivity and the Economy. 1973. (Bulletin No. 1779.)

Productivity Indexes for Selected Industries. Annual.

Quarterly Review of Productivity and Costs.

Special Labor Force Reports. Irregular.

The Structure of the U.S. Economy in 1980 and 1985. (Bulletin 1831.)

Tomorrow's Manpower Needs, Vol. IV. The National Industry—Occupational Matrix and Other Manpower Data, 1971. (Bulletin No. 1737.)

Union Wages and Hours. (Annual bulletins on Local-Transit Operating Employees, Motortruck Drivers and Helpers, Printing Industry; annual and quarterly supplements on Building Trades.)

The U.S. Economy in 1985. 1974. (Bulletin No. 1809.)

U.S. Workers and Their Jobs: The Changing Picture. 1976. (Bulletin No. 1919.)

U.S. Working Women: A Chartbook. 1975. (Bulletin No. 1880.)

U.S. Working Women: A Databook. 1977. (Bulletin No. 1977.)

Who Are the Unemployed? A chartbook. 1977. (Bulletin No. 1965.)

Civil Service Commission

Occupations of Federal Blue-Collar Workers. Annual.

Occupations of Federal White-Collar Workers. Annual.

Labor—Con.

U.S. Government—Con.

Civil Service Commission—Con.

Study of Employment of Women in the Federal Government. Annual.

Study of Minority Group Employment in the Federal Government. Annual.

Department of Agriculture, Economics, Statistics, and Cooperatives Service

Farm Labor. Quarterly and annual data. (Included in February quarterly report.)

The Hired Farm Working Force. Annual.

Department of Labor

Annual Report of the Secretary.

Employment and Training Administration

Area Trends in Employment and Unemployment. Monthly.

Employment and Wages of Workers. Quarterly.

Employment and Wages of Workers Covered by Unemployment Insurance Programs. Quarterly.

Employment Service Statistics. Monthly.

Farm Labor Developments. Employment and Wage Supplement. Monthly.

Manpower Report of the President. Annual.

Unemployment Insurance Claims. Weekly.

Equal Employment Opportunity Commission.

Employment Opportunity in the Schools. Job patterns of minorities and women in public elementary and secondary schools. 1975.

Interstate Commerce Commission

Wage Statistics of Class I Railroads in the United States. (Statement No. 300.) Monthly with calendar year issue.

Law Enforcement Assistance Administration and Bureau of the Census

Expenditure and Employment Data for the Criminal Justice System. Annual.

Labor—Con.

U.S. Government—Con.

Maritime Administration

Employment Report of United
States Flag Merchant Fleet
Ocean-going Vessels 1,000 Gross
Tons and Over. Annual.
(Monthly and quarterly data
maintained in office, but not
published.)

Seafaring Wage Rates. Biennial.

Office of Labor-Management Standards Enforcement

Union Financial Statistics, 1960–
1970.

Social Security Administration

Average Earnings of Workers in
Large Metropolitan Areas, 1969.
(Research and Statistics Note No.
14, 1976.)

Earnings Distributions in the
United States, 1969.

Economic Value of a Housewife.
(Research and Statistics Note
No. 9, 1975.)

Household Employment Under
OASDHI, 1971. (Research and
Statistics Note No. 17, 1975.)

Income of the Population Aged 60
and Older, 1971. (Staff Paper No.
26, 1977.)

1972 Lifetime Earnings by Age,
Sex, Race, and Education
Level. (Research and Statistics
Note No. 12, 1976.)

Self-Employment of Black Men,
1960 and 1970. (Research and
Statistics Note No. 4, 1976.)

Social Security Farmworker Sta-
tistics, 1972 with Preliminary
Data for 1973. (Research and
Statistics Note No. 16, 1976.)

State and Local Government Employment Under OASDHI.
Annual.

Studies in Income Distribution.
(A series of studies presenting
information on the distribution
of income, taxes, and transfer
payments.)

Wife's Earnings as a Source of
Family Income. (Research and
Statistics Note No. 10, 1974.)

Women's Bureau

Handbook on Women Workers.
Periodic.

Labor—Con.

Other

National Academy of Sciences,
Washington, D.C.

Mineral Resources and the Environment. 1975.

National Bureau of Economic Research, New York

Education, Income, and Human
Behavior, F. Thomas Juster.
1974. (Other Conference 9.)

Education, Income, and Human
Capital, by W. Lee Hansen. 1970.
(Studies in Income and Wealth,
No. 35.)

The Measurement of Economic
and Social Performance, Milton
Moss, editor. 1974. (Studies in
Income and Wealth, Vol. 38.)

Schooling, Experience, and Earn-
ings, by Jacob Mincer. 1974.
(Human Behavior and Social
Institutions 2.)

Law Enforcement, Federal Courts, and
Prisons

U.S. Government

Administrative Office of the United
States Courts

Annual Report of the Director
. . . with, as issued, Reports of
the Proceedings of the Judicial
Conference of the United States.

Census of Persons Under Supervision of the Federal Probation
System. 1973.

Court Management Statistics.
Annual.

Federal Offenders in the United
States District Courts. Annual.

Juror Utilization in United States
Courts. Annual.

Bureau of the Census

Census of Population. Decennial.
(1970, most recent.)

Historical Statistics on Expenditure
and Employment for the Criminal Justice System, 1971–73. GSS
No. 73.

Social Indicators, 1973; 1976.

Trends in Expenditure and Employ-
ment Data for the Criminal
Justice System, 1971–74. GSS
No. 79.

Bureau of Prisons

Statistical Report. Annual through
1975.

Law Enforcement, Federal Courts, and Prisons—Con.

U.S. Government—Con.

Drug Enforcement Administration
Drug Abuse and Law Enforcement Statistics. Irregular.

Federal Bureau of Investigation
Uniform Crime Reports for the United States. Annual. Supplemented by Uniform Crime Reporting. Quarterly with annual summary. (Releases of preliminary crime data for the United States.)

Law Enforcement Assistance Administration
Capital Punishment. Annual.
Children In Custody: A Report on the Juvenile Detention and Correctional Facility Census of 1971.
Children In Custody: Advance Report on the Juvenile Detention and Correctional Facility Census of 1972–73, 1974, and 1975.
Crime in Eight American Cities. 1974.
Crime in the Nation's Five Largest Cities 1974. Advance Report.
Criminal Justice Agencies in the United States: 1975.
Criminal Victimization Surveys in Chicago, Detroit, Los Angeles, New York, Philadelphia: 1972 vs. 1974.
Criminal Victimization Surveys in Eight American Cities: 1971–72 vs. 1974–75.
Criminal Victimization in the United States. Annual.
Criminal Victimization Surveys in 13 American Cities. June 1975.
Expenditure and Employment Data for the Criminal Justice System. Annual.
1970 National Jail Census. 1971.
National Prisoner Statistics. Periodic bulletins and reports.
National Survey of Court Organization, 1973; and 1977 Supplement to State Judicial Systems.
The Nation's Jails. A report on the Census of Jails From the 1972 Survey of Inmates of Local Jails. May 1975.
Prisoners in State and Federal Institutions on December 31, 1971, 1972, and 1973.
Sourcebook of Criminal Justice Statistics. 1974.

Law Enforcement, Federal Courts, and Prisons—Con.

U.S. Government—Con.

Law Enforcement Assistance Administration—Con.
Survey of Inmates of Local Jails: Advance Report: 1973.

National Center for Juvenile Justice
Juvenile Court Statistics. Annual.
Statistical Series. Annual. (A series of reports including juvenile court statistics.)
Statistics on Public Institutions for Delinquent Children. Irregular.

Other

American Bar Foundation, Chicago
The 1971 Lawyer Statistical Report. 1971.

National Bureau of Economic Research, New York.
Essays on the Economics of Crime and Punishment, by Gary S. Becker and William Landes, 1974. (Human Behavior and Social Institutions 3.)

National Governors' Conference Center for Policy Research and Analysis, Washington, D.C.
Marijuana: A Study of State Policies and Penalties.
Vol. I—Executive Summary.
Vol. II—Findings and Analysis.
Vol. III—Research and Case Studies.

Libraries—*see* Education.

Livestock—*see* Agriculture.

Lumber—*see* Forests and Lumber.

Manufactures—*see also* Agriculture; Business; Economic Indexes; Forests; Investments; Labor; *and* Minerals

U.S. Government

Board of Governors of the Federal Reserve System
Annual Statistical Digest: 1971–1975; 1972–1976.
Capacity Utilization: Manufacturing and Materials. (402.) Monthly.
Federal Reserve Bulletin. Monthly.
Federal Reserve Measures of Capacity and Capacity Utilization. February 1978.
Industrial Production: 1976.
Industrial Production (414.) Monthly.

Manufactures—Con.

U.S. Government—Con.

Bureau of Alcohol, Tobacco, and Firearms
Alcohol and Tobacco Summary Statistics. Annual.

Bureau of the Census
Annual Survey of Manufactures.
Canned Food Report. (Issued 5 times a year.)
Census of Manufactures. Quinquennial. (1977, most recent.)
Concentration Ratios in Manufacturing Industry. (1972, most recent.)
Cotton Production and Distribution. Annual.
Current Industrial Reports. Monthly, quarterly, and annual series on various industries.
Indexes of Production, 1972. (1972 Census of Manufactures and Mineral Industries.)
Industry Profiles, 1958–1971.
Manufacturers' Export Sales and Orders of Durable Goods. Monthly. (Current Industrial Reports M4-A.)
Manufacturers' Shipments, Inventories, and Orders: 1958–1976 (Revised). Monthly, with annual summary. (Current Industrial Reports M3–16.)
Shipments of Defense-Oriented Industries, 1973. (Current Industrial Reports MA 175 (73)–1.)
Survey of the Origin of Exports by Manufacturing Establishments. Triennial. (Current Industrial Reports MA–161 (72)–2.)
Survey of Plant Capacity, 1973. (Current Industrial Reports MQ–C1(73)–1.)
U.S. Commodity Exports and Imports as Related to Output. Annual. (Series ES2.)

Bureau of Domestic Business Development
The U.S. Industrial Outlook. Annual.

Bureau of Economic Analysis
Survey of Current Business. Monthly. Supplemented by Business Statistics, weekly and biennial.

Federal Trade Commission
Quarterly Financial Report for Manufacturing Corporations. Fourth quarter reports.

Manufactures—Con.

U.S. Government—Con.

International Trade Commission
Synthetic Organic Chemicals, U.S. Production and Sales. Annual.

Other

American Frozen Food Institute, Washington, D.C.
Frozen Food Pack Statistics. Annual.

American Iron and Steel Institute, Washington, D.C.
Annual Statistical Report.

American Paper Institute, New York
1970 Paperboard Industry Statistics. August 1971.

Billboard Publications, Inc., New York.
Merchandising. Monthly.

Commodity Research Bureau, New York
Commodity Yearbook. Annual.

The Conference Board, New York
Quarterly Survey of Capital Appropriations.
Quarterly Survey of Capital Investment and Supply Conditions in Manufacturing.

Electronic Industries Association, Washington, D.C.
Electronic Market Data Book. Annual.

National Bureau of Economic Research, New York
Postwar Productivity Trends in the United States, by John W. Kendrick. 1973. (General Series 98.)

National Food Processors Association, Washington, D.C.
Canned Food Pack Statistics. Annual.

Marine Corps—*see* National Defense.

Marriage—*see* Vital Statistics.

Medical Care; Mental Diseases—*see* Health.

Merchant Vessels—*see* Transportation.

Military Services—*see* National Defense.

Minerals—*see also* Economic Indexes; Energy; Foreign Commerce; *and* Manufactures

U.S. Government

Bureau of the Census
Annual Survey of Oil and Gas. (Current Industrial Reports MA–13K.)
Census of Mineral Industries. Quinquennial. (1972, most recent.)

Bureau of the Census and Bureau of Mines
Raw Materials in the United States Economy: 1900–1969. (Issued 1972. Working Paper No. 35.)

Bureau of Mines
Apparent Consumption of Industrial Explosives and Blasting Agents in the United States. Annual.
International Coal Trade. Monthly.
Mineral Commodity Summaries. Annual.
Mineral Industry Surveys. (Weekly, monthly, quarterly, or annual reports.)
Minerals and Materials. (Monthly survey.)
Minerals in the U.S. Economy. Annual.
Minerals Yearbook. Annual. (Issued in 3 volumes.)
Vol. I—Metals and Minerals.
Vol. II—Area Reports: Domestic.
Vol. III—Area Reports: International.

Bureau of the Mint
Annual Report of the Director.

Department of the Treasury
Treasury Bulletin. Monthly.

Energy Information Administration
Annual Report to Congress.

Other

American Bureau of Metal Statistics, New York
Year Book.

American Gas Association, Washington, D.C.
Gas Facts. Annual.
Year Book.

American Gas Association, American Petroleum Institute, and Canadian Petroleum Association
Reserves of Crude Oil, Natural Gas Liquid, and Natural Gas in the United States and Canada and United States Productive Capacity. Annual.

Minerals—Con.

Other—Con.

American Metal Market, New York
Metal Statistics. Annual.

American Petroleum Institute, Washington, D.C.
Petroleum Facts and Figures. Biennial.
Quarterly Review of Drilling Statistics for the United States.

Commodity Research Bureau, New York
Commodity Yearbook. Annual.

The Independent Petroleum Association of America, Tulsa, Okla.
The Oil Producing Industry in Your State. Annual.

McGraw-Hill, Inc., New York
Engineering and Mining Journal. Monthly.

National Bureau of Economic Research
Alternative for Growth: The Engineering and Economics of Natural Resource Development, Harvey McMains and Lyle Wilcox, editors. (Ballinger Publishing Co., Cambridge, Mass.)

National Coal Association, Washington, D.C.
Bituminous Coal Facts. Biennial.

Petroleum Publishing Co., Tulsa, Okla.
The Oil and Gas Journal. Weekly.

Money and Banking—*see also* Construction; Insurance; International Accounts; *and* Investments

U.S. Government

Administrator of National Banks
Annual Report.

Board of Governors of the Federal Reserve System
Annual Report.
Annual Statistical Digest: 1971–1975; 1972–1976.
Assets and Liabilities of all Commercial Banks, by Class of Bank. (113.) Semiannual.
Banking and Monetary Statistics: 1941–1970, 1976.
Federal Reserve Bulletin. Monthly.
Federal Reserve Monthly Chart Book. With annual historical supplement.
Flow of Funds Accounts, 1946–1975.
Money Stock Measures. (508.) Weekly.

Money and Banking—Con.

U.S. Government—Con.

Board of Governors of the Federal Reserve System, Comptroller of the Currency, and Federal Deposit Insurance Corporation

Assets and Liabilities: Commercial and Mutual Savings Banks. Semiannual.

Bureau of the Mint

Annual Report of the Director.

Comptroller of the Currency

Annual Report.

Department of the Treasury

Daily Treasury Statement.

Federal Aid to States. Annual.

Monthly Treasury Statement of Receipts and Outlays of the United States Government.

Statement of United States Currency and Coin. Monthly.

Statistical Appendix to Annual Report of the Secretary of the Treasury on the State of the Finances.

Treasury Bulletin. Monthly.

Farm Credit Administration

Annual Report on the Work of the Cooperative Farm Credit System.

Production Credit Association: Summary of Operations. Annual.

Report to the Federal Land Bank Associations. Annual.

Federal Deposit Insurance Corporation

Annual Report.

Bank Operating Statistics. Annual.

Summary of Accounts and Deposits in All Banks. Annual.

Trust Assets of Insured Commercial Banks. Annual.

Federal Home Loan Bank Board

Annual Report.

Asset and Liability Trends. Annual.

Savings and Home Financing Source Book. Annual.

National Credit Union Administration

Annual Report.

Federal Credit Union Program. Annual.

Money and Banking—Con.

Other

Bank and Quotation Record. (William B. Dana Co., New York.) Monthly.

Bankers Trust Company, New York

The Investment Outlook. Annual.

Credit Union National Association, Madison, Wisconsin

The Credit Union Yearbook.

Federal National Mortgage Association

Semiannual Report.

Investment Company Institute, Washington, D.C.

Mutual Fund Fact Book. Annual.

National Association of Mutual Savings Banks

National Fact Book: Mutual Savings Banking. Annual.

National Bureau of Economic Research, New York

Analysis of Inflation: 1965–1974, Joel Popkin, editor. (Ballinger Publishing Co., Cambridge, Mass.)

The Channels of Monetary Effects on Interest Rates, by Phillip Cagan. 1972. (General Series 97.)

Conference on Secular Inflation, Karl Brunner, editor. 1973. (Universities-National Bureau Conference 25.)

Foreign Dollar Balances and the International Role of the Dollar, by Raymond F. Mikesell and J. Herbert Furth. 1974. (Studies in International Economic Relations 8.)

Institutional Investors and Corporate Stock—A Background Study, Raymond F. Goldsmith, editor. 1973. (Studies in Capital Formation and Financing 13.)

International Mobility and Movement of Capital, by Fritz Machlup. 1972. (Universities-National Bureau Series, No. 24.)

Monetary Statistics of the United States: Estimates, Sources, Methods, by Milton Friedman and Anna Jacobson Schwartz. 1970. (Studies in Business Cycles 20.)

Mortgages—see Construction; and Money.

Motor Carriers and Vehicles—see Roads and Transportation.

National Defense—*see also* Federal Government

U.S. Government

Bureau of the Census
Defense Indicators. Monthly.

Department of Defense
Annual Fact Sheet of Department of Defense.
Annual Report of Secretary of Defense.
The Black in the Armed Forces, Statistical Fact Book. Annual.
Foreign Military Sales and Military Assistance Facts. Annual.
Military Posture Report. Annual.
Military Prime Contract Awards. Annual.
Prime Contract Awards by State. Annual.
Real and Personal Property of the Department of Defense. Annual.
Selected Defense Department Economic Indicators. Monthly.
Selected Manpower Statistics. Annual.

National Guard Bureau
Annual Report of the Chief.

Office of Civil Defense
Annual Statistical Report.

Office of Management and Budget
The Budget of the United States Government. Published annually in a group of five documents; see listing under "Federal Government Finances and Employment."

Selective Service System, National Headquarters
Annual Report of the Director of Selective Service.

U.S. Arms Control and Disarmament Agency
World Military Expenditures and Arms Transfers. Annual.

Veterans Administration
Annual Report of Administrator of Veterans Affairs.
Data on Vietnam Era Veterans, 1976.

Other

Army Times Publishing Company, Washington, D.C.
Military Market Facts. Annual.

National Defense—Con.

Other—Con.

National Bureau of Economic Research, New York
Economic Growth, by William D. Nordhaus and James Tobin. 1972. (General Series 96, Volume V.)

Udis, Bernard et al
Adjustments of the U.S. Economy to Reductions in Military Spending. 1970.

National Income and Wealth—*see also* Consumer Income; *and* Money and Banking

U.S. Government

Bureau of Economic Analysis
Business Conditions Digest. Monthly.
Fixed Nonresidential Business and Residential Capital in the United States, 1925–75. 1976.
Handbook of Cyclical Indicators. May 1977.
National Income and Product Accounts of the United States, 1929–74; Statistical Tables. 1976.
Readings in Concepts and Methods of National Income Statistics, available from National Technical Information Service, Springfield, Va.
Survey of Current Business. Monthly. Supplemented by Business Statistics, weekly and biennial.

Council of Economic Advisers
Economic Indicators. Monthly.
Economic Report of the President. Annual.

Internal Revenue Service
Statistics of Income, 1972, Supplemental Report, Personal Wealth. Irregular.

Other

American Economic Review, vol. LXIV, No. 2, May 1974, "The Concentration of Personal Wealth, 1922–1969," by James D. Smith and Stephen Franklin.

Kendrick, John W., with Kyu Sik Lee and Jean Lomask, The National Wealth of the United States, by Major Sector and Industry.

Population and Population Character-istics—*see also* Vital Statistics

U.S. Government

Bureau of the Census

Census of Agriculture. Quin-quennial. (1974, most recent.)

Census of Population. Decennial. (1970, most recent.)

Current Population Reports. (Series on Population Characteristics, P-20; Special Studies, P-23; Population Estimates and Pro-jections, P-25; Federal-State Co-operative Program for Population Estimates, P-26; Farm Popula-tion, P-27; Special Censuses, P-28; and Consumer Income, P-60.)

The Geographical Mobility of Americans—An International Comparison, by Larry H. Long and Celia G. Boertlein. Current Population Reports, Special Studies, Series P-23, No. 64.

Social Indicators, 1973; 1976.

Bureau of the Census and Department of Agriculture, Economics, Sta-tistics, and Cooperatives Service

Farm Population. Irregular. (Series Census-ERS, P-27.)

Bureau of Labor Statistics

Black Americans: A Decade of Occupational Change. (Revised 1972.) (Bulletin No. 1760.)

The Social and Economic Status of Negroes in the United States, 1970. (BLS Report No. 394.)

U.S. Workers and Their Jobs: The Changing Picture. 1976. (Bulletin No. 1919.)

U.S. Working Women: A Chart-book. 1975. (Bulletin 1880.)

Department of Agriculture, Econom-ics, Statistics, and Cooperatives Service

Farm Population Estimates, 1910–70. 1973. (Statistical Bulletin No. 523.) Supplemented annually.

Farm Population, Estimates for 1976. (Agricultural Economics Report No. 383.)

Office of Economic Opportunity

Poverty Facts and Figures. Tech-nical Note No. 1, Jan. 31, 1971.

Poverty Program Information. Fiscal Year 1970.

Veterans Administration

Annual Report of Administrator of Veterans Affairs.

County Veteran Population, March 1977. (Research Monograph 12.)

Population and Population Character-istics—Con.

Other

Population Association of America, Chicago

Demography. Quarterly.

Population Index. (Princeton Uni-versity, Princeton, N.J., Woodrow Wilson School of Public and Inter-national Affairs for the Population Association of America, Inc.) Quarterly.

Postal Service—*see* Communications.

Power—*see* Energy.

Prices—*see* Commodity Prices; *and* Eco-nomic Indexes.

Prisons and Prisoners—*see* Law Enforce-ment.

Public Assistance—*see* Social Insurance.

Public Lands and Park Systems—*see also* Federal Government; *and* Recreation

U.S. Government

Bureau of Land Management

Public Land Statistics. Annual.

Bureau of Outdoor Recreation

Outdoor Recreation: A Legacy for America. December 1973.

Selected Outdoor Recreation Sta-tistics. August 1971.

Congress. House Committee on Gov-ernment Operations

Federal Real and Personal Property Inventory Report (Civilian and Military) of the United States Government Covering Its Prop-erties Located in the United States, in the Territories, and Overseas. Annual. (Committee Print.)

General Services Administration

Inventory Report on Real Property Leased to the United States Throughout the World. Annual.

Inventory Report on Real Property Owned by the United States Throughout the World. Annual.

National Park Service

Areas Administered by the Na-tional Park Service. Semiannual.

Camper Days in Areas Adminis-tered by the National Park Service. Annual, 1960–1970; dis-continued in 1971.

Campground Use in the National Park Service. Irregular.

Public Lands and Park Systems—Con.

U.S. Government—Con.

National Park Service—Con.

Overnight Stays. Annual.

Overnight Visits in Commercial Accommodations in the National Park System. Annual, 1960–1970; discontinued in 1971.

Public Use of the National Parks. Monthly through December 1972.

Statistical Abstract. Annual.

Public Utilities—see Communications; Energy; and Transportation.

Puerto Rico—see Outlying Areas.

Radio—see Communications.

Railways—see Transportation.

Real Estate—see Agriculture; and Construction.

Reclamation Projects—see Irrigation.

Recreation—see also Public Lands and Park Systems

U.S. Government

Bureau of the Census

Census of Transportation. Quinquennial. (1977, most recent.)

Social Indicators, 1973; 1976.

Bureau of Economic Analysis

Survey of Current Business. Monthly. Supplemented by Business Statistics, weekly and biennial.

Coast Guard

Boating Statistics. Annual.

Department of Transportation

U.S. International Air Travel Statistics. Annual.

Fish and Wildlife Service

Federal Aid in Fish and Wildlife Restoration. Annual.

National Survey of Fishing and Hunting. Quinquennial.

Heritage Conservation and Recreation Service

The 1970 Survey of Outdoor Recreation Activities. October 1972.

National Park Service

Camper Days in Areas Administered by the National Park Service. Annual, 1960–1970; discontinued in 1971.

Public Use of the National Parks. Monthly through December 1972.

Recreation—Con.

Other

American Association of Museums, Washington, D.C.

1971 Financial and Salary Survey.

Marex, Inc., Chicago

Annual Market Research Notebook: The Marine Market. Annual.

Boating. (A Statistical Report on America's Top Family Sport.) Annual.

Outboard Motor Sales by County. Annual.

State Boat Registration. Annual.

National Association of State Racing Commissioners, Lexington, Ky.

Statistical Reports on Greyhound Racing in the United States. Annual.

Statistical Reports on Horse Racing in the United States. Annual.

National Golf Foundation, Inc., North Palm Beach, Fla.

Golf Facilities in the United States. Annual. (Information Sheet ST1.)

National Recreation and Park Association, Washington, D.C.

Parks & Recreation. August 1971.

Recreation and Park Yearbook. Quinquennial. (1971, most recent.)

Religious Bodies

Other

National Council of the Churches of Christ in the U.S.A., New York

Yearbook of American and Canadian Churches. Annual.

Research and Development—see Scientific Resources.

Retail and Wholesale Trade—see also Commodity Prices; Economic Indexes; and Service Establishments

U.S. Government

Board of Governors of the Federal Reserve System

Federal Reserve Bulletin. Monthly.

Bureau of the Census

Annual Retail Trade Report.

Canned Food: Stocks, Pack, Shipments. Issued 5 times per year.

Census of Retail Trade, Wholesale Trade and Selected Service Industries. Quinquennial. (1972, most recent.)

Retail and Wholesale Trade—Con.

U.S. Government—Con.

Bureau of the Census—Con.

County Business Patterns. Annual.

Department Store Sales in Selected Areas.

Green Coffee: Inventories, Imports, and Roastings. Quarterly.

Monthly Retail Trade Report.

Monthly Wholesale Trade Report. Sales and Inventories.

Value Produced, Capital Expenditures, Fixed Assets, Rental Payments and Supplemental Labor Costs of Merchant Wholesalers, 1972.

Weekly Retail Trade Report.

Bureau of Economic Analysis

Survey of Current Business. Monthly. Supplemented by Business Statistics, weekly and biennial.

Bureau of Labor Statistics

Employment and Earnings. Monthly.

Employment and Earnings, States and Areas. Annual.

Employment and Earnings, United States. Annual.

Handbook of Labor Statistics. Annual.

Monthly Labor Review.

Wholesale Prices and Price Indexes. Monthly.

Other

Chain Store Age. (Lebhar-Friedman Publications, New York.) Monthly.

Merchandising. (Billboard Publications, Inc., New York.) Monthly.

Roads—see Transportation.

Sales—see Retail and Wholesale Trade.

Savings—see Consumer Income; and Money.

Savings and Loan Associations—see Money.

Scientific Resources

U.S. Government

Bureau of the Census

Characteristics of Persons in Engineering and Scientific Occupations. 1972. (Technical Paper 33.)

Scientific Resources—Con.

U.S. Government—Con.

Bureau of Labor Statistics

Employment of Scientists and Engineers, 1950–70. 1973. (Bulletin 1781.)

Energy Research and Development Administration

The Nuclear Industry. Annual.

National Aeronautics and Space Administration

Satellite Situation Report. Semimonthly.

National Center for Education Statistics

Engineering Enrollments and Degrees. Annual.

Enrollment for Masters and Higher Degrees. Annual.

National Science Foundation

An Analysis of Federal R&D Funding by Function. Annual.

Characteristics of Doctoral Scientists and Engineers in the U.S. A report based on the NSF Manpower Characteristics System. Biennial.

Characteristics of Experienced Scientists and Engineers. Biennial.

Expenditures for Scientific Activities at Universities and Colleges. Annual.

Federal Funds for Research, Development, and Other Scientific Activities. (Includes geographic distribution.) Annual through 1975.

Federal Scientific, Technical, and Health Personnel. Periodic.

Federal Support to Universities, Colleges, and Selected Nonprofit Institutions. A report to the President and Congress. Annual.

Graduate Science Education: Student Support and Postdoctorals. Annual.

Manpower Resources for Scientific Activities at Colleges and Universities. Annual.

National Patterns of R&D Resources, Funds, and Manpower in the United States. Annual.

1985 R&D Funding Projections (NSF 76–314.)

Projections of Degrees and Enrollment in Science and Engineering Fields to 1985. (NSF 76–301.)

Scientific Resources—Con.

U.S. Government—Con.

National Science Foundation—Con.

Projections of Science and Engineering Doctorate Supply and Utilization, 1980 and 1985. (NSF 75–301.)

R&D Activities of Independent Nonprofit Institutions, 1973. (NSF 75–308.)

Research and Development in Industry. Annual.

Research and Development in State Government Agencies. Biennial.

Reviews of Data on Science Resources. Occasional.

No. 26: Energy and Energy-Related R&D Activities of Federal Installations and Federally Funded Research and Development Centers: Funds and Manpower, 1973–75. (NSF 76–304.)

No. 29: Current and Future Utilization of Scientific and Technical Personnel in Energy-Related Activities. (NSF 77–315.)

Science Indicators, 1976. (NSB 77–1.)

Scientific and Technical Personnel, by Private Industry. Biennial.

Scientists, Engineers, and Physicians From Abroad. Periodic.

U.S. Scientists and Engineers: 1976. Biennial.

Women and Minorities in Science and Engineering. (NSF 77–304.)

Young and Senior Science and Engineering Faculty, 1974. Support, Research Participation, and Tenure. (NSF 75–302.)

Patent and Trademark Office

Commissioner of Patents and Trademarks Annual Report.

Other

American Institute of Physics, New York

Physics Manpower, 1969. Education and Employment Statistics.

Engineering Manpower Commission, Engineers Joint Council, New York

Engineers' Salaries, Special Industry Report, 1970.

Professional Income of Engineers, 1970.

Salaries of Engineers in Education. Special Report, 1970.

Salaries of Engineers in Government. Special Report, 1970.

Scientific Resources—Con.

Other—Con.

National Academy of Sciences, Washington, D.C.

Summary Report. Doctorate Recipients from United States Universities. Annual.

Securities—*see* Investments; *and* Money.

Service Establishments—*see also* Retail and Wholesale Trade

U.S. Government

Bureau of the Census

Census of Retail Trade, Wholesale Trade, and Selected Service Industries. Quinquennial. (1977, most recent.)

Monthly Selected Services Receipts. (Series BS.)

Internal Revenue Service

Statistics of Income. (Annual reports on Corporation and Business Income Tax Returns. Periodic reports on Foreign Income and Tax Reported on U.S. Corporation Tax Returns.)

Other

Decker Communications, Inc., New York

Marketing Communications. (Advertising.) Monthly.

Harris, Kerr, Forster & Company, New York

Trends in the Hotel-Motel Business. Annual.

Laventhol & Horwath, New York

The Accountant. Monthly.

Lodging Industry. (A report on hotel and motor hotel operations.) Annual.

Social Insurance and Welfare Services—*see also* Insurance; *and* Labor

U.S. Government

Bureau of the Census

Census of Governments. Quinquennial. (1977, most recent.)

Finances of Employee-Retirement Systems of State and Local Governments. Annual.

Finances of Selected Public Employee Retirement Systems. Quarterly.

Social Indicators, 1973; 1976.

Bureau of Labor Statistics

Monthly Labor Review.

Social Insurance and Welfare Services—
Con.

U.S. Government—Con.

Civil Service Commission
Annual Report.
Monthly Release of Federal Civilian
Workforce Statistics.
Report on Civil Service Retirement,
Federal Employees Group Life
Insurance, Federal Employees
Health Benefits, Retired Fed-
eral Employees Health Benefits.
Annual.

Department of Health, Education,
and Welfare
Annual Report.

Department of Labor
Annual report of the Secretary.

Employment and Training Ad-
ministration
Unemployment Insurance Claims.
Weekly.
Unemployment Insurance Sta-
tistics. Monthly.

Office of Human Development Serv-
ices
Caseload Statistics of State Vo-
cational Rehabilitation Agencies
in Fiscal Year. Annual.
Characteristics of Clients Rehabil-
itated in Fiscal Year. Annual.
Social Services, USA. Quarterly.
State Vocational Rehabilitation
Agency Program Data in Fiscal
Years. Annual.

Railroad Retirement Board, Chicago
Annual Report.
RRB Quarterly Review.

Securities and Exchange Commission
Annual Report.
Statistical Bulletin. Monthly.

Social Security Administration
Almost 65: Baseline Data From
the Retirement History Study,
1976. (Research Report No. 49.)
American Indian SSI Beneficiaries:
Estimates for Selected Areas.
(Research and Statistics Note
No. 6. 1977.)
Beneficiaries Residing Abroad
Under the Retirement, Sur-
vivors, and Disability Insur-
ance Program, 1974 Selected
Data, 1975.
Benefits and Beneficiaries Under
Public Employee Retirement
Systems. Calendar year 1975.

Social Insurance and Welfare Services—
Con.

U.S. Government—Con.

Social Security Administration—Con.
(Research and Statistics Note
No. 17. 1976.)

Denials Under the SSI Program,
January 1974–July 1975. (Research and Statistics Note No.
26. 1976.)

Distribution of Beneficiaries Under
the SSI Program, by Race, June
1975. (Research and Statistics
Note No. 25. 1976.)

The Early Retirement Decision:
Evidence From the 1969 Retire-
ment History Study. 1978. (Staff
Paper No. 29.)

Earnings Replacement From Social
Security Benefits: Newly Entitled
Beneficiaries, 1974. (Research
and Statistics Note No. 13. 1976.)

The Effects of Vocational Rehabilitation on the Earnings of Disabled Persons. 1977. (Staff Paper
No. 27.)

Employment and Earnings of SSI
Beneficiaries, December 1975.
(Research and Statistics Note
No. 4. 1977.)

Employment of SSI Beneficiaries
(Research and Statistics Note
No. 16. 1975.)

Financial Assets of New SSI Beneficiaries. (Research and Statistics
Note No. 17. 1977.)

Financing Mental Health Care
Under Medicare and Medicaid.
1971. (Research Report No. 37.)

Findings of the 1973 AFDC
Study, Aid to Families With
Dependent Children. (Part I,
Demographic and Program
Characteristics, June 1974.)
(Part II, Financial Circum-
stances, September 1974 and
September 1975.) (Part III,
Services to Families, October
1974.) (Part IV, Discontinuances
for AFDC money payments dur-
ing 1973, January 1975.)

Findings of the 1970 OAA Study,
Old-age Assistance. (Part I,
Demographic and Program
Characteristics, September 1972.)
(Part II, Financial Circum-
stances, December 1972.)

Social Insurance and Welfare Services—Con.

*U.S. Government—*Con.

Social Security Administration—Con.

Findings of the 1970 APTD Study, Aid to the Permanently and Totally Disabled. (Part I, Demographic and Program Characteristics, September 1972.) (Part II, Financial Circumstances, December 1972.)

Findings of the 1970 AB Study, Aid to the Blind. (Part I, Demographic and Program Characteristics, September 1972.) (Part II, Financial Circumstances, December 1972.)

Health Insurance for the Aged: Amounts Reimbursed, by State and County. Annual.

Health Insurance Statistics. (A series of statistical notes covering Medicare data.)

Household Employment Under OASDHI, 1971. (Research and Statistics Note No. 17. 1975.)

Initial Awards to Widowed Father Beneficiaries. (Research and Statistics Note No. 20. 1976.)

Medicare Statistical Reports. (Annual data on enrollment, participating providers, and summary for persons served.)

Mortality Experience of Alcoholics and Drug Addicts Under SSI, January 1974–April 1975. (Research and Statistics Note No. 1. 1977.)

National Expenditures on Social Security in Selected Countries, 1968 and 1971. (Research and Statistics Note No. 29. 1974.)

1975 Recipient Characteristic Study. (HEW Pub. No. SSA 111777.)

OASDHI Cash Benefits by State and County, Dec. 31, 1975. 1976.

Older Worker Earnings and the 1965 Amendments. 1971. (Research Report No. 38.)

The Pensionable Age in Selected Industrialized Countries. (Research and Statistics Note No. 15. 1977.)

A Precise Formula for Primary Insurance Amounts, 1976. (Staff Paper No. 22.)

Reaching Retirement Age: Findings From a Survey of Newly Entitled Workers, 1968–70. (Research Report No. 47.)

Selected State Data, Medicare, Fiscal Years 1968–1973.

Social Insurance and Welfare Services—Con.

*U.S. Government—*Con.

Social Security Administration—Con.

Self-employed Doctors of Medicine Under OASDHI, 1967–70. (Research and Statistics Note No. 31. 1974.)

Self-Employment and Retirement Age. (Research and Statistics Note No. 15. 1976.)

Social Security Beneficiaries in Metropolitan Areas, 1975.

Social Security Beneficiaries Under Representative Payment, 1970, 1972, 1973.

Social Security Benefits by Zip Code Area. Annual.

Social Security Benefits and Earnings of Minority Groups in Covered Employment. (Research and Statistics Note No. 5. 1971.)

Social Security Bulletin. Monthly with annual statistical supplement. (Data on OASDHI, supplemental security income, and black lung programs.)

Social Security Disability Applicant Statistics. 1970.

Social Security Programs in the United States. 1973.

Social Security Programs Throughout the World, 1977. (Research Report No. 50.)

SSI Beneficiaries Medically Determined to be Alcoholics or Drug Addicts. (Research and Statistics Note No. 8. 1977.)

SSI Beneficiaries Residing in Urban Areas. (Research and Statistics Note No. 8. 1976.)

State and Local Government Employment Under OASDHI. Annual.

Supplemental Security Income for the Aged: A Comparison of Five Countries. (Staff Paper No. 15.)

Supplemental Security Income, State and County Data. Biannually, June and December.

Survey of the Low-Income Aged and the Disabled: 1974.

Survey of Student Beneficiaries: 1973. (Research and Statistics Note No. 24. 1976.)

Women and Social Security: Law and Policy in Five Countries. 1973. (Research Report No. 42.)

Work Disability in the United States; a Chartbook. 1977.

Social Insurance and Welfare Services—Con.

U.S. Government—Con.

Veterans Administration
Annual Report of Administrator of Veterans Affairs.
Government Life Insurance Programs. Annual.

Other

American Association of Fund-Raising Counsel, Inc., New York
Giving USA. Annual.

The American National Red Cross, Washington, D.C.
Annual Report.

Boy Scouts of America, National Council, North Brunswick, N.J.
Annual Report.

The Foundation Center, New York
The Foundation Directory, Edition 6. 1977.
The Foundation Grants Index. Annual.

Girl Scouts of the U.S.A., New York
Annual Report.

National Bureau of Economic Research, New York
The Measurement of Economic and Social Performance, Milton Moss, editor. 1974. (Studies in Income and Wealth, Vol. 38.)

United Way of America, Alexandria, Va.
Annual Directory.

Soil Conservation—*see* Irrigation.

Sports—*see* Recreation.

State and Local Government—*see also* Federal Government

U.S. Government

Advisory Commission on Intergovernmental Relations
Changing Public Attitudes on Governments and Taxes. 1974.
City Financial Emergencies: The Intergovernmental Dimension. 1973.
Financing Schools and Property Tax Relief—A State Responsibility. 1973.
Measuring the Fiscal Capacity and Effort of State and Local Areas. 1971.
The Property Tax in a Changing Environment. 1974.

State and Local Government—Con.

U.S. Government—Con.

Advisory Commission on Intergovernmental Relations—Con.
State Aid to Local Governments. 1969. State-Local Finances and Suggested Legislation, 1970. 1971.
The Value-Added Tax and Alternative Sources of Federal Revenue. 1973.

Bureau of the Census
Census of Governments. Quinquennial. (1977, most recent.)
City Employment. Annual. (GE No. 2.)
City Government Finances. Annual. (GF No. 4.)
County Government Employment. Annual. (GE No. 4.)
County Government Finances. Annual. (GF No. 8.)
Environmental Quality Control. Governmental Finances: Fiscal Year 1975–76. (GSS No. 8.)
Finances of Employee-Retirement Systems of State and Local Governments. Annual. (GF No. 2.)
Finances of Selected Public Employee Retirement Systems. Quarterly. (GR No. 3.)
Governing Boards of County Governments: 1973. (GSS No. 68.)
Governmental Finances and Employment: 1971–72 and 1972–73. (GSS No. 71.)
Governmental Finances. Annual. Covers Federal, State, and local governments. (GF No. 5.)
Governmental Fiscal Years in 1972. (GSS No. 65.)
Labor-Management Relations in State and Local Governments: 1974. (GSS No. 75.)
Land Title Recording in the United States: A Statistical Summary. 1974. (GSS No. 67.)
Local Government Employment in Selected Metropolitan Areas and Large Counties. Annual. (GE No. 3.)
Local Government Finances in Selected Metropolitan Areas and Large Counties. Annual. (GF No. 6.)
National Data Needs, Fire Service Statistics. 1971.
Property Values Subject to Local General Property Taxation in the United States. 1975. (GSS No. 80.)

State and Local Government—Con.

U.S. Government—Con.

Bureau of the Census—Con.
Public Employment. Annual. (GE No. 1.)
Quarterly Summary of State and Local Tax Revenue. (GT No. 4.)
State and Local Government Expenditure for Election Administration. 1970–1973. (GSS No. 74.)
State and Local Ratio Studies and Property Assessment. (GSS No. 72.)
State Government Finances. Annual. (GF No. 3.)
State Government Tax Collections. Annual. (GF No. 1.)
Taxes and Intergovernmental Revenue of Counties, Municipalities, and Townships. Annual. (GF No. 9.)

Federal Highway Administration Highway Statistics. Annual.

Law Enforcement Assistance Administration and Bureau of the Census
Expenditure and Employment Data for the Criminal Justice System. Annual.

National Science Foundation
Research and Development in Local Governments. Periodic.
Research and Development in State Government Agencies. Periodic.

Office of Management and Budget
The Budget of the United States Government. Published annually in a group of five documents; see listing under "Federal Government Finances and Employment."

Social Security Administration
State and Local Government Employment Under OASDHI. Annual.

Other

The Council of State Governments, Lexington, Ky.
The Book of the States. Biennial.
The Projection of Federal Aid to State and Local Governments by State and by Function. February 1971.
Salaries and Compensation of Legislators and State Administrative Officials: Annual Salaries.

State and Local Government—Con.

Other—Con.

International City Management Association, Washington, D.C.
Municipal Year Book. Annual.

Stocks and Bonds—see Investments.

Stores—see Retail and Wholesale Trade and Service Establishments.

Tax Collections—see Federal Government; and State and Local Government.

Telephone and Telegraph Systems—see Communications.

Television—see Communications.

Trade—see Foreign Commerce; Retail and Wholesale Trade; and Service Establishments.

Transportation—see also Foreign Commerce; and Roads

U.S. Government

Bureau of the Census
Census of Transportation. Quinquennial. (1977, most recent.)
U.S. Waterborne Foreign Commerce. Irregular.
U.S. Waterborne Exports and General Imports. Monthly and annual. (FT 985.)
Vessel Entrances and Clearances: Annual Report. (FT 975.)

Bureau of Economic Analysis
Survey of Current Business. Monthly. Supplemented by Business Statistics, weekly and biennial.

Civil Aeronautics Board
Air Carrier Financial Statistics. Quarterly.
Air Carrier Traffic Statistics. Monthly.
Handbook of Airline Statistics. Annual, with biennial supplements.

Civil Aeronautics Board and Federal Aviation Administration
Airport Activity Statistics of Certificated Route Air Carriers. Semiannual.

Coast Guard
Merchant Vessels of the United States. Annual.

Corps of Engineers
Waterborne Commerce of the United States (in 5 parts). Annual.

Transportation—Con.

U.S. Government—Con.

Department of Transportation
U.S. International Air Travel Statistics. Annual.

Federal Aviation Administration
Census of U.S. Civil Aircraft. Annual.
FAA Air Traffic Activity. Annual, for calendar and fiscal years.
FAA Statistical Handbook of Aviation. Annual.

Federal Highway Administration
Cost of Operating an Automobile. Biennial.
Drivers Licenses. Annual.
Federal Aid and Allied Highway Programs. Annual.
Highway Statistics. Annual.
Traffic Speed Trends. Annual.

Interstate Commerce Commission
Annual Report.
Financial and Operating Statistics, Class I Motor Carriers of Passengers. Semiannual.
Financial and Operating Statistics, Class I Motor Carriers of Property. Semiannual.
Financial and Operating Statistics, Class I Railroads. Semiannual.
Freight Commodity Statistics, Class I Motor Carriers of Property Operating in Intercity Service. Annual.
Freight Commodity Statistics, Class I Railroads in the United States. Annual.
Revenue and Traffic of Carriers by Water. Quarterly, with summary for calendar year.
Transport Economics. Monthly until April 1974; quarterly thereafter.
Transport Statistics in the United States. Issued annually in 6 separate parts:
Part 1—Railroads, Their Lessors and Proprietary Companies, and Electric Railways.
Part 2—Motor Carriers.
Part 3—Freight Forwarders.
Part 4—Private Car Lines.
Part 5—Carriers by Water.
Part 6—Oil Pipe Lines.

Transportation—Con.

U.S. Government—Con.

Maritime Administration
Annual Report.
Employment Report of United States Flag Merchant Fleet Ocean-going Vessels 1,000 Gross Tons and Over. Annual. (Monthly and quarterly data available from source.)
Maritime Manpower Report. Monthly.
New Ship Construction. Annual.
A Statistical Analysis of the World's Merchant Fleets. Annual.

Panama Canal Company
Annual Report.

Passport Office
Summary of Passport Statistics. Annual.

Senate, Committee on Government Operations
Disclosure of Corporate Ownership. 1973. (93d Congress, 1st Session.)

Other

Aerospace Industries Association of America, Washington, D.C.
Aerospace Facts and Figures. Annual.

Air Transport Association of America, Washington, D.C.
Air Transport Facts and Figures. Annual. Quarterly Review.

American Bureau of Shipping, New York
The Bulletin. Monthly.

American Bus Association, Washington, D.C.
Bus Facts. Annual.

American Public Transit Association, Washington, D.C.
Passenger Transport. Weekly.
Transit Fact Book. Annual.

Association of American Railroads, Washington, D.C.
Cars of Revenue Freight Loaded. Weekly with annual summary.
Yearbook of Railroad Facts.

Automotive News Almanac. (Slocum Publishing Company, Detroit.) Annual.

Transportation—Con.

Other—Con.

Aviation Week. (Billboard Publications, Inc., New York.) Weekly.

Chilton Company, Radnor, Pa.

Annual Statistical Issue, Automotive Industries.

General Aviation Manufacturers Association, Washington, D.C.

1977 Statistical Data. Report issued periodically.

Lake Carriers' Association, Detroit

Annual Report.

Lloyd's Register of Shipping, London, England

Annual Summary of Merchant Ships Completed in the World.

Annual Summary of Merchant Ships Totally Lost, Broken Up, etc., in the World. Also quarterly.

Quarterly Shipbuilding Returns (Merchant Ships Under Construction, and Ships Not Commenced in the World).

Statistical Tables. Annual. Analysis of world merchant fleet.

Michigan, The University of, Survey Research Center, Ann Arbor

Survey of Consumer Finances. Annual. (Discontinued in 1972.)

Motor Vehicle Manufacturers Association of the United States, Inc., Detroit

Motor Vehicle Facts and Figures. Annual.

World Motor Vehicle Data. Annual.

Railway Age. (Simmons-Boardman Publishing Corp., New York.) Weekly. (Annual review and outlook issue.)

Shipbuilders Council of America, Washington, D.C.

Annual Report.

Tanker Advisory Center, Inc., New York

Worldwide Tanker Casualty Returns. Quarterly newsletter.

Transportation Association of America, Washington, D.C.

Transportation Facts and Trends.

Travel—*see* Recreation *and* Transportation.

Unemployment Insurance—*see* Labor; *and* Social Insurance.

Utilities, Public—*see* Communications; Energy; *and* Transportation.

Veterans—*see* National Defense; *and* Population.

Virgin Islands of the United States—*see* Outlying Areas.

Vital Statistics—*see also* Accidents; *and* Health

U.S. Government

Center for Disease Control

Abortion Surveillance Report—Legal Abortions. Annual.

Department of Health, Education, and Welfare

Morbidity and Mortality Weekly Report. Annual summary also.

National Center for Health Statistics

Monthly Vital Statistics Report, Provisional Statistics. Annual summary also.

United States Life Tables: 1969–71. Decennial.

Vital and Health Statistics. (A series of statistical reports covering health-related topics.)

Series 20: Mortality Data. Irregular.

Series 21: Natality, Marriage, and Divorce Data. Irregular.

Vital Statistics of the United States. Annual.

Other

National Bureau of Economic Research, New York

Economic Growth, by William D. Nordhaus and James Tobin. 1972. (General Series 96, Volume V.)

Marriage, Family Human Capital, and Fertility, by T. W. Schultz. 1974. (Other Conference 7.)

The Measurement of Economic and Social Performance, Milton Moss, editor. 1974. (Studies in Income and Wealth, Vol. 38.)

New Economic Approaches to Fertility, by T. W. Schultz. 1973. (Other Conference 6.)

Sullivan, E., C. Tietze, and J. G. Dryfoos, Abortion in the United States, 1975–1976. In Alan Guttmacher Institute, New York, Family Planning Perspectives, Vol. 9, No. 3.

Vital Statistics—Con.

Other—Con.

Tietze, C., New York, Legal Abortions in the United States: Rates and Ratios by Race and Age, 1972–1974. In Alan Guttmacher Institute, New York, Family Planning Perspectives, Vol. 9, No. 1.

Tietze, C., F. Jaffe, E. Weinstock, and J. G. Dryfoos, Abortion 1974–1975: Need & Services in the United States, Each State & Metropolitan Area. 1976. The Alan Guttmacher Institute, New York.

United Nations Statistical Office, New York

Demographic Yearbook.

1972 Supplement to the Statistical Yearbook and the Monthly Bulletin of Statistics, Methodology and Definitions.

Population and Vital Statistics Report. (Statistical Papers, Series A.) Quarterly.

Statistical Yearbook.

World Health Organization, Geneva, Switzerland

Annual Epidemiological and Vital Statistics.

Epidemiological and Vital Statistics Report. Monthly.

World Health Statistics. Annual.

Vocational Rehabilitation and Education

U.S. Government

Bureau of the Census
Social Indicators, 1973; 1976.

Department of Health, Education, and Welfare
Annual Report.

National Center for Education Statistics
Digest of Annual Reports of State Boards for Vocational Education.
Vocational and Technical Education. Annual.

Vocational Rehabilitation and Education —Con.

U.S. Government—Con.

Office of Human Development Services
Caseload Statistics of State Vocational Rehabilitation Agencies in Fiscal Year. Annual.

Characteristics of Clients Rehabilitated in Fiscal Years. Annual.

State Vocational Rehabilitation Agency Program Data in Fiscal Years. Annual.

Office of Management and Budget
The Budget of the United States Government. Published annually in a group of five documents; see listing under "Federal Government Finances and Employment."

Social Security Administration
Social Security Bulletin. Monthly, with annual statistical supplement. See listing under Health and Medical Care.

Veterans Administration
Annual Report of Administrator of Veterans Affairs.

Information Bulletins—Veterans Benefits under Current Educational Programs—April, June, November.

Wages and Wage Rates—*see* Labor; *and* Social Insurance.

Wealth—*see* National Income.

Weather—*see* Climate.

Welfare Services—*see* Health; *and* Social Insurance.

Wholesale and Retail Trade—*see* Retail and Wholesale Trade.

Wholesale Prices—*see* Commodity Prices.

Work Relief—*see* Social Insurance.

Work Stoppages—*see* Labor.

Bureau of the Census Publications

In most cases, separate reports of the most recent censuses are available for each State, subject, industry, etc. Complete information on publications of all the censuses and current surveys conducted by the Bureau of the Census appears in the *Bureau of the Census Catalog*, which is published quarterly and cumulated to the annual issue, with monthly supplements. A list of data files (computer tapes and punchcards) and unpublished materials is also included, beginning with the 1964 issues. A sample copy of the *Catalog* is available from the Bureau of the Census on request. The annual subscription price is $19.00 for 4 quarterly issues and 12 monthly supplements ($4.75 additional for foreign mailing).

Guide to State Statistical Abstracts

This bibliography includes the most recent statistical abstracts for States and Puerto Rico published since 1969 plus those that will be issued in late 1978 or early 1979. For some States, a near equivalent has been listed in substitution for, or in addition to, a statistical abstract. All sources contain statistical tables on a variety of subjects for the State as a whole, its component parts, or both. The page counts given for publications cited as "In process" are approximate.

Alabama

University of Alabama, University, Center for Business and Economic Research
Economic Abstract of Alabama. 1977. 300 pp.

Alaska

Department of Commerce and Economic Development, Juneau, Division of Economic Enterprise
The Alaska Economy. 96 pp. (Issued annually.)
The Alaska Economic Information and Reporting Service Quarterly Report. 20 pp.

Arizona

Valley National Bank, Phoenix
Arizona Statistical Review, 34th ed. 1978.
University of Arizona, Tucson, Division of Economic and Business Research, College of Business and Public Administration
Statistical Abstract of Arizona, 1976. 519 pp.

Arkansas

Arkansas Almanac, Incorporated, Little Rock
Arkansas Almanac, 1976. 14th ed. 1976. 250 pp. (No longer published.)

California

Department of Finance, Sacramento
California Statistical Abstract, 1978. 170 pp. (To be released in Dec. 1978.)

Colorado

Transrep/bibliographics, Denver
Statistical Abstract of Colorado, 1976–1977, Thomas G. Tyler, compiler-editor. 1977. 515 pp. (1978–1979 edition in process.)

Connecticut

Connecticut Department of Commerce, Hartford, Business Office
Connecticut Market Data. 1976. 108 pp.

Delaware

Delaware Office of Management, Budget and Planning, Dover
Dimensions on Delaware, 1977.

District of Columbia

D.C. Municipal Planning Office, District of Columbia
District of Columbia Data. 1976. 102 pp.
District of Columbia Advisory Neighborhood Commission Census Report. 1977. (Selected 1970 census data.) 106 pp.

Florida

University of Florida, Gainesville, Bureau of Economic and Business Research
Florida Statistical Abstract, 1978. 12th ed. 1978.

Georgia

University of Georgia, Athens, Division of Research, College of Business Administration
Georgia Statistical Abstract, 1978. 1978. 412 pp.

Hawaii

Department of Planning and Economic Development, Honolulu
The State of Hawaii Data Book 1978: A Statistical Abstract. 12th ed. 1978. 370 pp. (Available late 1978.)
University of Hawaii Press, Honolulu.
Historical Statistics of Hawaii. 1977. 711 pp.

Idaho

University of Idaho, Moscow, Center for Business Development and Research
Idaho Statistical Abstract. 1971. 298 pp.
Centerpoint: Focus on Business and Economics. 4 pp. (Issued quarterly.)

Illinois

Department of Business and Economic Development, Springfield
Illinois State and Regional Economic Data Book—1976. 1976. 245 pp.

Indiana

Indiana State Planning Services Agency, Indianapolis
Indiana Fact Book, 1979. (To be available in late 1978.)

Iowa

Iowa Development Commission, Des Moines, Resource and Support Division
1979 Statistical Profile of Iowa. 121 pp.

Kansas

University of Kansas, Lawrence, Institute for Social and Environmental Studies
Kansas Statistical Abstract, 1977. 13th ed. 1978. 290 pp.

Kentucky

Department of Commerce, Frankfort
Kentucky Deskbook of Economic Statistics. 15th ed. 1978.

Louisiana

University of New Orleans, New Orleans, Division of Business and Economic Research
Statistical Abstract of Louisiana. 6th ed. 1977.

Maine

Maine State Development Office, Augusta
Facts About Industrial Maine. (Updated continuously.)

Maryland

Department of Economic and Community Development, Annapolis
Maryland Statistical Abstract. 1977.
An Economic and Social Atlas of Maryland. 1974.
Supplement to an Economic and Social Atlas of Maryland. 1974.

Massachusetts

Department of Commerce and Development, Boston
Massachusetts Fact Book. 1978

Michigan

Michigan State University, East Lansing, Graduate School of Business Administration, Division of Research
Michigan Statistical Abstract. 13th ed. 1978. 1,200 pp. (In process.)

Minnesota

Minnesota Department of Economic Development, Saint Paul, Research Division
Minnesota Statistical Profile. 1978.

Mississippi

Mississippi State University, Mississippi State, College of Business and Industry, Division of Research
Mississippi Statistical Abstract. 1977.

Missouri

University of Missouri, Columbia, Extension Division
Data for Missouri Counties. 1970. (Loose leaf; updated periodically.)

Montana

Montana State Division of Research
and Information Systems, Helena
Montana Data Book. 1970. 262 pp.
(Loose leaf; updated periodically.)
Montana County Profiles. 1978. (Separate county reports and regional
summaries; updated periodically.)

Nebraska

Department of Economic Development, Lincoln, Division of
Research
Nebraska Statistical Handbook. 1978–
1979. 300 pp.

Nevada

State Planning Coordinator's Office,
Carson City
Nevada Statistical Abstract. 1977.
218 pp.

Department of Economic Development, Carson City
County Datafiles. (Separate leaflets
updated irregularly.)

New Hampshire

Department of Resources and Economic Development, Concord
New Hampshire Economic Indicators.
1974.

New Jersey

Office of Demographic and Economic
Analysis, Trenton
County Data Summary, 1977.

New Mexico

University of New Mexico, Albuquerque, Bureau of Business and
Economic Research
New Mexico Statistical Abstract. Vol.
4. 1977. 221 pp. (1979 edition in
process.)

New York

Division of Budget, Albany, Technical
Service Unit
New York State Statistical Yearbook.
8th ed. 1977. 268 pp.

North Carolina

Department of Administration, Raleigh, Division of State Budget and
Management, Research and Planning Services Section
*North Carolina State Government
Statistical Abstract* and supplement,
North Carolina Statistical Guide,
1978.
Profile—North Carolina Counties. 4th
ed. 1977. 269 pp.

North Dakota

Business and Industrial Development
Department, Bismarck
North Dakota Growth Indicators.
17th ed. 1978. 74 pp.

Ohio

Department of Economic and Community Development, Columbus,
Office of Research
Statistical Abstract of Ohio: 1978.

Oklahoma

University of Oklahoma, Norman,
Center for Economic and Management Research
Statistical Abstract of Oklahoma, 1978.
1978. 450 pp.

Oregon

University of Oregon, Eugene, Bureau
of Business Research
Oregon Economic Statistics, 1977.
1977. 100 pp. (No longer published.)

Pennsylvania

Department of Commerce, Harrisburg,
Bureau of Statistics, Research
and Planning
*Pennsylvania Statistical Abstract,
1978.* 20th ed. 1978. 400 pp.

Rhode Island

Department of Economic Development, Providence
Rhode Island Basic Economic Statistics. 1977–1978. 200 pp.

South Carolina

Budget and Control Board, Columbia, Division of Research and Statistical Services
South Carolina Statistical Abstract: 1977. 1977. 164 pp.
Economic Report for South Carolina: 1977. 1977. 140 pp.
Inventory of Statistical Series of South Carolina: 1977. 1977. 50 pp.

South Dakota

University of South Dakota, Vermillion, Business Research Bureau
South Dakota Economic and Business Abstract, 1972. 1972. 280 pp.
South Dakota State Planning Bureau, Pierre
South Dakota Facts. 1976. 328 pp.

Tennessee

University of Tennessee, Knoxville, Center for Business and Economic Research
Tennessee Statistical Abstract, 1977. 4th ed. 1977. 740 pp. (Triennial.)
Tennessee Pocket Data Book, 1975. 3d ed. 1975. 183 pp.

Texas

Dallas Morning News, Dallas
Texas Almanac, 1978-1979. 1977. 704 pp.

Utah

University of Utah, Salt Lake City, Bureau of Economic and Business Research
1979 Statistical Abstract of Utah. 1979. (Available early 1979.)
Utah Foundation, Salt Lake City
Statistical Review of Government in Utah. 1978. 99 pp. (1979 edition to be issued in Mar. 1979.)

Vermont

Department of Budget and Management, Montpelier
Vermont Facts and Figures, 1975. 3d ed. 1975. 461 pp.

Virginia

Department of Planning and Budget, Richmond
Data Summary (Separate reports for individual counties and cities— each updated triennially.)
Projections and Economic Base Analysis. (Separate reports on economic regions of the State—updated periodically).

Washington

Washington State Office of Financial Management, Olympia
State of Washington Pocket Data Book, 1977. 288 pp.
Washington State Research Council, Olympia
The Research Council's Handbook. 4th ed. 1973. 675 pp. (With annual supplements.)
The Book of Numbers. 1978. 59 pp.

West Virginia

West Virginia Research League, Inc., Charleston
The 1977 Statistical Handbook. 1977. 68 pp.
West Virginia University, Morgantown, Bureau of Business Research
West Virginia Statistical Handbook. 1974 edition. Business and Economics Studies, Vol. 12, No. 1. 1974. 268 pp.

Wisconsin

Department of Administration, Madison, Bureau of Program Management, Information Systems Unit
Wisconsin Statistical Abstract. 4th ed. 1977. 215 pp.
Legislative Reference Bureau, Madison
1977 Wisconsin Blue Book. 1,000 pp. (Biennial.)
Wisconsin Department of Business Development, Madison
Economic Profiles of Wisconsin Counties. 1976.

Wyoming

University of Wyoming, Laramie, Institute for Policy Research
Wyoming Data Book. 1972.

Puerto Rico

Planning Board, Santurce, Bureau of Statistics
Statistical Yearbook, 1976. 215 pp.

Index